Still The Most Extraordinary Bible Ever Published!

TEN YEARS AFTER it was first published, *The Holy Bible In Its Original Order* is *still* the most unique Bible to ever be produced. *Here's why...*

First, it is the **only** *complete*, **single-volume Bible ever published** *in the world* **that follows the original, God-inspired manuscript order**. Scholars recognize this inspired order but overlook its importance. This Bible gives proof of the original order, tracing how it was altered in the 4th century. Once the original order of the 66 biblical books has been restored, the Seven Divisions of the Bible are also reestablished: The *Old Testament* contains: 1) The Law; 2) The Prophets; and 3) The Writings. The *New Testament* contains: 4) The Gospels and Acts; 5) The General Epistles; 6) The Epistles of Paul; and 7) The Book of Revelation. With this restoration, God's purposeful design of the Scriptures begins to unfold, revealing His divine inspiration.

Second, this *new* translation is easy to understand and reflects the meaning of the original Hebrew and Greek with fidelity and accuracy. It also combines current scholarship with the latest in archeological findings.

Third, *The Holy Bible In Its Original Order* recaptures the original, inspired teachings of the Scriptures through its translation and numerous commentaries. Over the centuries, doctrinal errors have developed from inaccurate translations and the adherence to religious tradition. Setting aside such traditions, this Bible restores more than the canonical order—it restores the very truth of God!

What's Inside

Included are **Commentaries** detailing the writing and canonization of the Bible. **Appendices** cover topics such as: When was Jesus born? How did Christ fulfill the Law and the Prophets? When was Jesus crucified? When was He resurrected? What does it mean to be "born again"? What are "works of law"? What are the true teachings of the early church? How do we understand Paul's difficult writings? **Chronologies** show an accurate timeline from creation to the present, and detailed **Footnotes** explain difficult passages. Includes center column references; word definitions and alternate renderings; artwork of the Temple in Jesus' time; maps; and 280 pages of **Commentary**.

At 1.5 inches thick, *The Holy Bible In Its Original Order* features a genuine handcrafted lambskin or calfskin cover with gold stamped lettering, premium paper with gold gilded edges, wide margins for note-taking, and is triple bound for extra long life.

On Sale Now! To order, visit
www.theoriginalbiblerestored.com

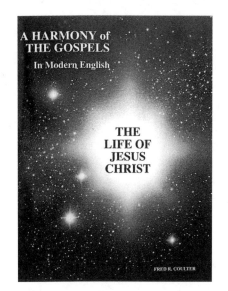

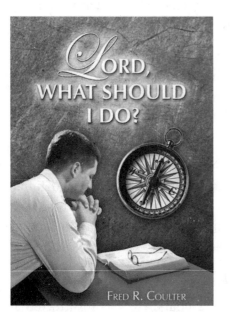

GOD'S PLAN
FOR MANKIND REVEALED
BY HIS SABBATH AND
HOLY DAYS

FRED R. COULTER

York Publishing Company
Post Office Box 1038
Hollister, California 95024-1038

Unless otherwise noted,
all Scriptures used in
this book are quoted from
*The Holy Bible In Its
Original Order—A Faithful
Version With Commentary.*
ISBN 978-0-9675479-7-2

ISBN: 978-0-9961757-2-2
Copyright 2007, 2021 ©
York Publishing Company
Post Office Box 1038
Hollister, California 95024-1038

Table of Contents

God's Plan For Mankind Revealed
By His Sabbath And Holy Days

Personal

From the Desk of
Fred R. Coulter

The contemporary world in which we live encourages *individual* opinions, insisting that everyone's opinion is of *equal* validity. On the one hand, a person may consider something to be true simply because he or she *believes* it to be so—even when the facts do not support such a belief. A second person, however, may hold to an opinion exactly opposite the first—likewise accepted as fact because he or she *believes* it to be true. A dichotomy results in which truth becomes *relative.* Carrying this process one step further, when a conglomeration of divergent opinions on a subject is accepted as true, because people believe them to be true, we end up with a cacophony of opinions—which is confusion! Everyone believes and does what is right in their *own* eyes. Consequently, the majority of people today do not believe that there is *absolute truth* to the exclusion of all other opinions.

When viewing all the religions of the world—including Orthodox Christianity—we see precisely the same thing. We find a panorama of complex opinions and beliefs about God, and a confusing array of speculative schemes of men who are eager to promote their ideas about the purpose of life and the plan of God. Because learned teachers of philosophy and religion use some parts of the Word of God, their theories have a smattering of truth that sounds persuasive. Still others follow the inspiration of demons, unknowingly venerating Satan the devil himself, who appears as an "angel of light."

The result—billions of people have been deceived and wholly embrace religious falsehoods as foundational truth. Sincerely believing what they have been taught, they have dedicated their lives to false gods and false saviors through their devotion to idols, religious works, vows of poverty, life-long celibacy and virginity—all for the purpose of achieving a greater reward in heaven. Fully convinced that what they have been taught is the direct will of God—and with great sacrifice of worldly gain and even life itself—the obedient and dedicated have traveled the world over preaching their version of the Gospel, as they genuinely try to save others. Ordinary people have resolutely adhered to religious fallacies for fear of death and being forever delivered into the torments of hell. Horrifying many as well is the nightmare of being reincarnated into insects or animals because of an unworthy life. And increasingly, the world today is confronted by Islamic fanatics driven by hatred, who irrationally believe that the road to heaven is through holy jihad.

The Bible tells us: "God is not the author of confusion" (I Cor. 14:33). Therefore, we can conclude that the mainstay of all these religions, philosophies and teachings—conjoined with their opinions about the purpose of life for mankind—*cannot* be correct!

But where is the truth? Is it possible to find and understand it?

The answer is, *Yes!* It is found in the Bible—the true Word of God. Isaiah gives us the starting point: "And when they shall say unto you, 'Seek unto them that have familiar spirits, and unto wizards that peep, and that mutter'—but should not a people [rather] seek unto their God? Should the dead be sought on behalf of the living? To the Law [the Old Testament] and to the testimony [the New Testament]! If they do not speak according to this word, it is because there is no light in them" (Isa. 8:19-20). In other words, if we truly believe God the Father and Jesus Christ and prove that the entire Word of God is true, then we can find the truth—the absolute truth of God. We can then begin to comprehend God's plan for mankind as revealed by His Sabbath and holy days.

The Old and New Testaments combined comprise one complete book—the Word of God—the Holy Bible. To begin with, we need to understand certain fundamental truths about God as revealed in the Old Testament, which is the foundation of truth—the absolute truth of God. Here are a few scriptures that *define* the true God:

- The Lord God of the Bible is the *true* God (II Chron. 15:3; Jer. 10:10); the everlasting God (Isa. 40:28); the most high God (Gen. 14:20); the holy God (Psa. 99:9); the God of heaven (Psa. 136:26); and there is none other (Isa. 45:5).
- God is love (Deut. 4:37; 6:4-5; 7:6-9); God is merciful and gracious (Psa. 57:10; 130:8); God is forgiving (Psa. 51:1-4; 86:5; 103:3).
- The Law of God is truth (Psa. 119:142); all His commandments are truth (Psa. 119:151); His word is true from the beginning (Psa. 119:160); the Law of God is perfect (Psa. 19:7); the way of the Lord is perfect (Psa. 18:30).

From the New Testament we learn more of the truth of God:

- It is impossible for God to lie (Heb. 6:18; Titus 1:2); God is love (I John 4:8, 16). God loves the world (John 3:16); God is merciful (Luke 7:46-47; 18:13; I Pet. 1:3); God is forgiving (Luke 23:34; Eph. 1:7; 4:32; Col. 2:14; I John 1:7-10).
- Jesus Christ was God manifested in the flesh (I Tim. 3:16; John 1:1-3, 14); Jesus came to reveal God the Father (Matt. 11:27; John 14:28); Jesus is the Lamb of God, sent to take away the sin of the world (John 1:29, 36; Rev. 13:8); Jesus is Savior (Luke 1:47; 2:11; John 4:42; Eph. 5:23; Phil. 3:20; I Tim. 1:1; 2:3; I John 4:14); Jesus is full of grace and truth (John 1:14); Jesus is the First and the Last, the Beginning and the Ending (Isa. 41:4; Rev. 1:8, 11, 17; 21:6; 22:13).
- The Word of God is truth—Old and New Testaments (John 17:17; Col. 1:5; II Tim. 2:15; I Pet. 1:22); Paul and the apostles completed the Word of God—the commandments of the Lord (I Cor. 14:37; Col. 1:25; II Pet. 1:16-21; Rev. 1:11, 19; 2:1, 8, 12, 18; 3:1, 7, 14; 21:5; 22:18-19).

Once we have an overview of the entire Bible, we can see **the unity of the truth contained in both the Old and New Testaments**—how they are intricately woven together through Jesus Christ and God the Father, thus forming the complete Word of God to the exclusion of all other so-called "sacred books."

In fact, the truth is personalized by and in Jesus Christ Himself Who said, "I am the way, and the truth, and the life; no one comes to the Father except through Me" (John 14:6). Also, Jesus emphasizes, "No one can come to Me unless the Father, Who sent Me, draws him" (John 6:44).

While some may consider this to be "spiritual snobbery," it is not. In the Bible and the Bible *alone* lies the complete revelation of God's plan.

Because God is love, He does indeed have an awesome plan and purpose for all mankind—a fantastic destiny of eternal life. Yet, **because of the sins of man**, God has concealed this vital knowledge in the writings of the Bible. But in these last days, through the inspiration of the Holy Spirit, God has unveiled the secrets of His plan as contained in His Word—by His

Sabbath and holy days. This knowledge is now available to those who truly love and obey God the Father and Jesus Christ.

May God the Father and Jesus Christ bless you with the spirit of understanding, that with confidence in Christ you may comprehend and take hold of the meaning and purpose of your life—"according to *the* faith of God's elect and *the* knowledge of *the* truth that *is* according to godliness; **in *the* hope of eternal life, which God Who cannot lie promised before the ages of time**" (Titus 1:1-2).

About This Book

Everyone wants to know, *What is God doing?* What is His purpose, His plan? Does He even *have* a plan? Is man's struggle through this human existence merely a prelude to spending eternity in heaven? Is heaven even for real? How can we know? How can we know God's *true* plan for humanity—and know with certainty and confidence?

Make no mistake, God's plan *is* revealed in His Word—the Old and New Testaments. But very *few* have understood that plan. Why? The number one reason is *tradition*. Men have created numerous religious traditions—and today's "Christianity" is full of such traditions—that present a completely different perspective on God's purpose and plan. While these traditions may sound good and right, and while they may even appear to be based on Scripture, they are in fact gross error. And they have led to nothing but confusion!

Thus, the key to understanding God's plan is to completely lay aside all past religious teachings—yes, even "Christian" *teachings*! You need a fresh start—a new perspective. Man's destiny is far greater than even today's "Christian" has dared to imagine. **And the book you hold in your hands—truly a one-of-a-kind book—reveals that awesome destiny using a methodical, step-by-step approach that will make the truth understandable for everyone.**

God's Plan for Mankind Revealed by His Sabbath and Holy Days is unique in four major ways. **First**, it is intended for the advanced, serious-minded Bible student who has a sound, basic knowledge of the Bible, as well as an understanding of God's weekly Sabbath and holy days. This book contains what the apostle Paul calls "strong meat" or "solid food"—as opposed to the "milk of the Word," which is for beginners. "For everyone who is partaking of milk *is* unskilled in *the* word of righteousness because he is an infant. But solid food [strong meat] is for those who are fully grown [spiritually mature and grounded in the Word of God through years of study], who **through repeated practice have had their senses trained to discern between good and evil**" (Heb. 5:13-14).

While this book is generally not for "novices" who have newly come to the faith of Jesus Christ—or for those who are simply curious—it is possible for anyone to understand what is presented here. However, such individuals will need to apply themselves more diligently in order to fully grasp the deeper spiritual meaning of the Scriptures. Consequently, it is strongly recommended that those who are "new in the faith" first read the book *Occult Holidays or God's Holy Days—Which?* This book details the basic meaning of God's Sabbath and holy days as contrasted with the holidays of the pagan "Christianity" of the orthodox religious establishments of this world. After first reading *Occult Holidays or God's Holy Days—Which?*, the meatier material contained in *God's Plan for Mankind Revealed by His Sabbath and Holy Days* will be much easier to comprehend.

Second, this book is a compilation of message transcripts. As such, it is not written in customary book-style composition. Rather, the transcriptions are a literal, word-for-word rendering of some of the best in-depth messages by the author about God's Sabbath and holy days. The message transcripts have a more flexible style and cadence in comparison to the more rigid style and structure of formal composition.

Third, it is not designed for passive reading. Rather, this book is to be used for active, in-depth Bible study in combination with the eighty messages that have been recorded on the accompanying set of two CDs (MP3 format). When you listen to the messages and actively study along with the transcripts, you will absorb and retain the information longer because you are using *both* the sense of sight and sound in a concentrated manner at the same time.

Fourth, the bibliography for this book includes *only* the Holy Bible. No other sources have been used, with the exception of a few short quotes from historical sources that substantiate a few specific scriptures. As such, this book follows God's direct charge for ministers to preach and teach the Holy Scriptures—and not the mythological religious traditions of men. Notice Paul's charge to Timothy: "I charge you, therefore, in the sight of God, even the Lord Jesus Christ, Who is ready to judge *the* living and *the* dead at His appearing and His kingdom: **Preach the Word! Be urgent in season and out of season; convict, rebuke, encourage, with all patience and doctrine**. For there shall come a time when they will not tolerate sound doctrine; but according to their own lusts they shall accumulate to themselves *a great number of* teachers, having ears itching *to hear what satisfies their cravings*; **but they shall turn away their own ears from the truth; and they shall be turned aside unto myths** [the religious traditions of men]" (II Tim. 4:1-4).

Finally, this book lays out the critically important scriptural meaning of God's weekly Sabbath and annual holy days, which are the major keys to understanding prophecy and that reveal God's master plan for mankind. This knowledge has been concealed from the majority of people because they refuse to believe God—refuse to hear His Word, to obey His laws and commandments, and do not live their lives by *every* word of God. Consequently, the established Orthodox Christianity of this world disparages, rejects and refuses to keep God's Sabbath and holy days.

For those who already have a basic knowledge of the Bible, this book can systematically cement your understanding of the deeper spiritual meaning of God's Word. The reader is encouraged to start at the beginning and go step-by step through the book to the end, while simultaneously listening to the messages. May God the Father and Jesus Christ bless you with understanding so that you may learn the inspired, deeper spiritual truths of God as you read this book and listen to the messages.

Fred R. Coulter
Summer 2021

Introduction

Astonishingly, God has not openly revealed His plan even in the pages of the Holy Scriptures—choosing instead to deliberately *conceal* this vital knowledge. Indeed, the prophets of old—when writing the Old Testament under the inspiration of God—understood *few* aspects of His plan.

The prophet Daniel, for example, was inspired to write a major prophetic outline of events spanning from the 600s BC to the establishment of the Kingdom of God at Jesus Christ's return. Naturally, Daniel wanted to know what the prophecies meant. But God's final message to Daniel was that it was not for him to know: "And he said, 'Go your way, Daniel: **for the words are closed up and sealed till the time of the end**. Many shall be purified, and made white, and tried; but the wicked shall do wickedly: and none of the wicked shall understand; **but the wise shall understand**' " (Dan. 12:9-10).

During His ministry Jesus told the apostles that they would come to understand things that even the prophets had never understood: "**[It] has been given to you to know the mysteries of the kingdom of heaven**, but to them [the people and religions of the world] it has not been given. For whoever has *understanding*, to him more shall be given, and he shall have an abundance; but whoever does not have *understanding*, even what he has shall be taken away from him…. And in them is fulfilled the prophecy of Isaiah, which says, 'In hearing you shall hear, and in no way understand; and *in* seeing you shall see, and in no way perceive, for the heart of this people has grown fat, and their ears are dull of hearing, and their eyes they have closed….'

"**But blessed *are* your eyes, because they see; and your ears, because they hear. For truly I say to you, many prophets and righteous *men* have desired to see what you see, and have not seen; and to hear what you hear, and have not heard**" (Matt. 13:11-12, 14-17).

The apostle Peter reaffirms what Jesus said. "Concerning which salvation the prophets who prophesied of the grace *that would come* to you have diligently searched out and intently inquired, searching into what *way* and what manner of time the Spirit of Christ *which was* in them was indicating, testifying beforehand of the sufferings of Christ, and these glories that would follow; **to whom it was revealed that, not for themselves, but to us they were ministering these things**, which now have been announced to you by those who have preached the gospel to you by *the* Holy Spirit, sent from heaven—**into which things the angels desire to look**" (I Peter 1:10-12).

Jesus Christ provided substantially more knowledge of God's plan—the "Mystery of God"—to the apostles than any of the prophets and writers of the Old Testament. Yet, He did not reveal the *fullness* of God's plan to all of the apostles. Most of them—with the exception of John, Philip and Andrew—died without a complete knowledge of God's plan. Jesus revealed the *final* missing pieces of the puzzle to the apostle John, who then wrote the book of Revelation and canonized the entire New Testament, with the help of Philip, Andrew and Mark.

Indeed, the apostles received more knowledge and understanding of God's plan than any of God's servants had up to that time. It was not until the New Testament was completed and canonized, however, that God's *entire* plan for mankind was recorded. And although the complete Word of God was subsequently preserved and made widely available, the *knowledge* of God's plan remained, for the most part, *hidden*—and would continue to be a "mystery" until the time of the end, just as the Lord had told Daniel (Dan. 12:10). As we will see, the next vital step in God's plan was to raise up His true Church through Jesus Christ, His only begotten Son—God manifested in the flesh.

God Revealed His Plan to His Church—the True Church of God: Jesus Christ personally proclaimed that He would build His Church and that the gates of the grave would not prevail against it (Matt. 16:18)—and that He would always be with His Church even to the end of the age (Matt. 28:20). Jesus Christ Himself established the Church of God on the day of Pentecost in AD 30 (Acts 2). Under the inspiration and power of the Holy Spirit, Jesus Christ used the apostles to preach the true Gospel of salvation and to raise up the many congregations that would comprise the Church of God. The true Church of God is not a building, cathedral, or corporation. Rather, it consists of all the men and women whom God the Father and Jesus Christ have chosen and called out of this world. It is a "little flock" (Luke 12:32) that has been set apart and sanctified by the blood of Jesus Christ and by the Holy Spirit.

In New Testament Greek the word for "church" is *ekklesia*, which means "the assembly of called-out ones." Jesus Christ is the living Head of the Church—also called the "body of Christ" (I Cor. 12:27)—for God the Father "has given Him [Jesus Christ] *to be* head over all things to the church, which is His body" (Eph. 1:22-23). Throughout the New Testament we find that the body of Christ—which is the *true* Church of God—consists of many churches, or assemblies, of called-out believers. It was through the preaching of the Gospel from the prophetic Scriptures of the Old Testament—the Law, the Prophets, and the Psalms—and later the inspired writings of the apostles that the New Testament churches were raised up. We find the early history of the Church of God in the book of Acts, the epistles of James, Peter and John, and especially in the writings of Paul.

Jesus Christ revealed God's plan and purpose for mankind to His apostles and New Testament prophets, and they in turn taught the congregations of the Church of God. The apostle Paul, for example, wrote: "For this cause I, Paul, *am* the prisoner of Christ Jesus for you Gentiles, if indeed you have heard of the ministry of the grace of God that was given to me for you; **how He made known to me by revelation the mystery** (even as I wrote briefly before, so that when you read *this*, **you will be able to comprehend my understanding in the mystery of Christ**), which **in other generations was not made known to the sons of men, as it has now been revealed to His holy apostles and prophets by *the* Spirit**; that the Gentiles might be joint heirs, and a joint body, and joint partakers of His promise in Christ through the gospel, of which I became a servant according to the gift of the grace of God, *which was* given to me through the inner working of His power.

"To me, who am less than the least of all the saints, was this grace given, that I might preach the gospel among the Gentiles—*even* the unsearchable riches of Christ; and **that I might enlighten all *as to* what *is* the fellowship of the mystery that has been hidden from the ages in God**, Who created all things by Jesus Christ; so that the manifold wisdom of God might now be made known through the church to the principalities and the powers in the heavenly *places*, **according to *His* eternal purpose, which He has wrought in Christ Jesus our Lord**, in Whom we have boldness and *direct* access with confidence through His *very* own faith" (Eph. 3:1-12).

Paul explains that the purpose of the ministry is to teach the brethren, grounding them firmly into the perfection of Jesus Christ: "And He gave some *as* apostles, and some prophets, and some evangelists; and some, pastors and teachers for the perfecting of the saints, for *the* work of *the* ministry, for *the* edifying of the body of Christ; until we all come into the unity of the faith and of the knowledge of the Son of God, unto a perfect man, unto *the* measure of *the* stature of the fullness of Christ; so that we no longer be children, tossed and carried about with every wind of doctrine by the sleight of men in *cunning* craftiness, with a view to the systematizing of the error; but holding the truth in love, may in all things grow up into Him Who is the Head, *even* Christ from Whom all the body, fitly framed and compacted together by *that which* every joint supplies, according to *its* inner working in *the* measure of each individual part, is making the increase of the body unto *the* edifying of itself in love" (Eph. 4:11-16).

Remember Jesus' instruction to His disciples: "[It] has been given to you [the true disciples and the true Church of God] to know the mysteries of the kingdom of heaven, but to them [the world with its counterfeit religions] it has not been given" (Matt. 13:11). Thus, the true scriptural knowledge and understanding of God's plan for mankind—as revealed by His Sabbath and holy days—will not be found in the churches of Orthodox Christianity. God only imparts this knowledge to those who love Him and keep His commandments—including His commanded seventh-day Sabbath and annual holy days. On the other hand, all who reject God's Sabbath and holy days—and instead observe Sunday and various pagan holidays—are excluded from this vital, *revealed* knowledge. As Jesus said, in "seeing, they see not; and hearing, they hear not; neither do they understand. And in them is fulfilled the prophecy of Isaiah, which says, 'In hearing you shall hear, and in no way understand; and *in* seeing you shall see, and in no way perceive; for the heart of this people has grown fat, and their ears are dull of hearing, and their eyes they have closed...' " (verses 13-15).

Consequently, very little of the knowledge of God's plan for mankind that you will read in this book and hear from the CD messages will be found in the Orthodox Christianity of this world. It is *only* found in the Word of God and revealed to those ministers and congregations of the *true* Church of God who observe the Sabbath and annual holy days. As Jesus said to His disciples, "**Blessed *are* your eyes, because they see; and your ears, because they hear. For truly I say to you, many prophets and righteous *men* have desired to see what you see, and have not seen; and to hear what you hear, and have not heard**" (verses 16-17).

May Jesus' blessing be upon you as you read and study this book and listen to the messages—so that you may be able to truly understand the biblical truth about God's plan for mankind as revealed by His Sabbath and holy days.

Prologue

As incredible as it may seem, God has deliberately hidden His plan for mankind from the wise and intelligent of this world—from the leaders in government, religion and education—as well as from philosophers, ancient and modern. In fact, God has blinded men to His true purpose throughout all ages!

Why has He done this? Surely God would want us to have an understanding of His plan, to know *why* mankind was created, *why* we are here—would He not? The answer is simple: Beginning with Adam and Eve, all humans have **sinned and rebelled** against God (Rom. 3:9, 23). Sin is the transgression of the Law (I John 3:4). Rebellion is the refusal to walk and live God's way. Consequently, the human mind has been spiritually blinded, and God has hidden His plan from mankind.

This sin and rebellion began with Adam and Eve, who had direct personal access to their Creator God in the Garden of Eden. They walked with God and talked with God. They had personal, face-to-face fellowship with Him daily—and especially on the holy Sabbath. After putting Adam in the garden to dress and keep (or guard) it, "God commanded the man saying, 'You may freely eat of every tree in the garden. But you shall not eat of the Tree of the Knowledge of Good and Evil. For in the day you eat of it, in dying you shall surely die' " (Gen. 2:16-17).

However, instead of loving and obeying their Creator, Adam and Eve chose to believe the serpent, Satan the devil. He lied to them and assured them that if they ate of the fruit of the Tree of the Knowledge of Good and Evil, that "in dying you shall not surely die." (Gen. 3:4)

As a result, true to God's word, they received in their very being a sinful nature that is enmity against God and His laws—and came under the penalty of death. Likewise, all of their descendants received by inheritance this sinful nature, which is the inner "law of sin and death" (Rom. 8:2). After Cain murdered his brother Abel, sin and rebellion against God multiplied and intensified until the whole civilization of man became so corrupt and wicked that God had to destroy all flesh with the universal flood of Noah's time, saving only Noah and his family and the animals in the ark.

The apostle Paul describes this rebellion of men and their rejection of God—as well as God's punishment against them: "Indeed, *the* wrath of God is revealed from heaven upon all ungodliness and unrighteousness of men who suppress the truth in unrighteousness; because that which may be known of God is manifest among them, for God has manifested *it* to them; for the invisible things of Him are perceived from *the* creation of *the* world, being understood by the things that were made—both His eternal power and Godhead—so that they are without excuse; because when they knew God [before and after the flood], they glorified *Him* not as God, neither were thankful; but **they became vain in their own reasonings, and their foolish hearts were darkened. While professing themselves to be *the* wise ones, they became fools and changed the glory of the incorruptible God into *the* likeness of an image of corruptible man, and of birds, and four-footed creatures, and creeping things**.

"For this cause, God also abandoned them to uncleanness through the lusts of their hearts, to disgrace their own bodies between themselves, **who exchanged the truth of God for the lie** [Satan the devil's lie that he was god]; **and they worshiped and served the created thing more than the one Who is Creator, Who is blessed into the ages**. Amen" (Rom. 1:18-25).

As a result of mankind's sin and rebellion, both before and after the flood, God blinded their hearts and minds to His spiritual truths and abandoned them to their own devices and religions. In fact, because of their sin and worship of Satan, God deliberately hid the true knowledge of His plan and purpose for mankind.

Where then did God hide this precious knowledge? Must we go up into the heavens to find it? Or, shall we go to the bottom of the ocean to locate it? Is it written in some long-lost book, or inscribed on golden tablets buried deep in the earth that are yet to be discovered? Where is the knowledge of God's plan for mankind and how do we find it?

The truth is that today the plan of God, also called the mystery of God, is hidden in plain sight—right in front of everyone's eyes. It's in the Bible. Incredibly, however, the vast majority of the billions of people who possess Bibles do not understand God's true plan and purpose as revealed in the Scriptures. Yet, God put it there in plain sight! But people do not recognize the truth—because the truth must be revealed spiritually by God through the proper handling of the Word of God. While some people who read the Bible may know a *few* details about God's plan, the fullness of that plan has been hidden.

Why is it possible for people to have the Word of God, read it, and yet not comprehend God's plan for mankind?

First, most people do not keep the commandments of God, because they believe God's laws have been "done away": "[All] His commandments are sure. They stand fast for ever and ever, and are done in truth and uprightness…. The fear of the LORD is the beginning of wisdom: **a good understanding have all they who do his commandments**…. Blessed is the man who fears the LORD, who delights greatly in His commandments" (Psa. 111:7-8, 10; 112:1). **Without** *first* **keeping the commandments of God, it is impossible for anyone to truly understand the Word of God and truly come to the knowledge of His plan**.

Second, the majority of people who have the Bible have closed their eyes to God's Sabbath and holy days—which are also holy Sabbaths—and refuse to keep them. They have instead substituted their own traditions—Sunday-keeping and the holidays of this world. God's message to them is: Repent, obey My voice, and keep My laws, My commandments, My Sabbath and My holy days. As the prophet Isaiah admonished the children of Israel, and the Gentiles as well: "Thus says the LORD, 'Keep you judgment, and do justice: for My salvation is near to come, and My righteousness to be revealed [together with His purpose and plan for mankind]. Blessed is the man who does this, and the son of man who lays hold on it; that keeps the Sabbath from polluting it, and keeps his hand from doing any evil' " (Isa. 56:1-2). And again, "If you turn away your foot from the Sabbath, from doing your pleasure on **My holy day; and call the Sabbath a delight, the holy of the LORD**, honorable; and shall honor Him, not doing your own ways, nor finding your own pleasure, nor speaking your own words: then shall you delight yourself in the LORD…" (Isa. 58:13-14).

Jesus Himself reminds us that He is Lord of the *Sabbath Day* (Mark 2:27-28)—not Sunday. Later in the New Testament, in Paul's epistle to the Hebrews, he makes it abundantly clear that Sabbath-keeping is for New Testament Christians: "There remains, therefore, Sabbath-keeping for the people of God [Jews and Gentiles]" (Heb. 4:9).

Third, most do not have the Holy Spirit of God to lead them to understand the spiritual meaning of the Word of God. Jesus said, "It is the Spirit that gives life; the flesh profits nothing. The words that I speak to you, *they* are spirit and *they* are life" (John 6:63). Furthermore, God does not give His Holy Spirit unless one has repented of sin and has been baptized, and is living a life of love and obedience to God (Acts 2:38; 5:32).

Thus, we find that although people may read the Bible, they cannot understand God's plan contained in its pages. To them it is a great, unfathomable mystery!

God's Plan for Mankind is Hidden Throughout the Bible

God's plan actually begins in the book of Genesis, the first book of the Bible. That plan, however, was not fully unveiled until the apostle John wrote the Book of Revelation, the last book of the Bible, in AD 95-98.

Few people realize that the Lord God of the Old Testament was the One Who became Jesus Christ of the New Testament. He was the One Who created Adam and Eve and all things. He was the One Who dealt directly with the godly men of old—Abel, Enoch and Noah. He was the One Who called the patriarchs—Abraham, Isaac and Jacob—and personally dealt with them. He was the One Who called Moses to bring Israel out of their slavery in Egypt. He was the One Who gave them the Law at Mount Sinai.

He was the Word of God Who spoke to the prophets of old, such as Samuel, Isaiah, Jeremiah, Ezekiel and Daniel and all the other prophets. He inspired the Psalms of David, the Proverbs of Solomon and the other writings of the Old Testament. In every one of these inspired writings, various aspects of God's plan and purpose for mankind are concealed—hence, God's plan is a mystery. Though these great men of God were inspired to write the words of God, they did not fully grasp His plan or timetable for working out that plan. God intentionally did not divulge it to them. Even Daniel—to whom God revealed many prophecies that stretched from his time, in the fifth century BC, to the end of the age and the beginning of the Kingdom of God on earth—did not understand them. After receiving his final vision, he asked the Lord: "And I heard, but I did not understand. Then I said, 'O my lord, what shall be the end of these things?' And he said, '**Go your way, Daniel, for the words *are* closed up and sealed until the time of the end. Many shall be purified, and made white, and refined. But the wicked shall do wickedly; and none of the wicked shall understand, but the wise** [those who love and obey God] **shall understand'** " (Dan. 12:8-10).

The Teachings of Jesus Christ in the New Testament Reveal More of God's Plan—the Mysteries of the Kingdom of God

God's plan for man predates Adam and Eve—predates even the founding of the world. As Paul wrote to Timothy, God's purpose was ordained "**in Christ Jesus before the ages of time**" (II Tim. 1:9). That plan and purpose ultimately began with **God**; then came the creation of the **heavens** and the **earth**, then the creation of the **angels**. But eventually one-third of the angels were led by Satan, a fallen archangel, in a **rebellion** against God—leading to earth-wide destruction and the first Flood; thus, the Spirit of God "hovered" over a **flooded earth** (Gen. 1:2). A long interlude ensued, perhaps millions of years in duration (science verifies that the earth is millions of years in age). Finally, some 6,000 years ago, the final stage of creation took place—the *recreation* of the earth's surface in preparation for the **creation of man**. But as Peter also shows, Jesus' all-important role in God's plan was predetermined and ordained long beforehand—as Jesus was "**foreknown before *the* foundation of *the* world**" (I Pet. 1:20).

It was more than 4,000 years after God created Adam and Eve that He began to more fully reveal His plan for mankind through Jesus Christ, the Son of God the Father. Jesus was God manifested in the flesh, born of the virgin Mary. He came to magnify the Law and make it honorable, as Isaiah prophesied: "The LORD is well pleased for His righteousness' sake; He will magnify the Law, and make it honorable" (Isa. 42:21). In magnifying the Law, Jesus brought the

Law to its fullest measure, making clear its spiritual meaning and intent. The Hebrew word for "magnify" is *gadal*, which means: to advance, boast, exceed; to become, do, give, make greater, increase and magnify. The Hebrew word "honorable" is *adar*, which means: to expand, to be great or magnificent.

Contrary to what many religious leaders teach, Jesus did not do away with the Law. Beginning with the Sermon on the Mount (Matt. 5-7), Jesus magnified the Law by teaching the spiritual meaning of the Law and the Prophets: "**Do not think that I have come to abolish the Law or the Prophets; I did not come to abolish, but to fulfill** [to *complete* the Word of God]. For truly I say to you, until the heaven and the earth shall pass away, one jot or one tittle shall in no way pass from the Law until everything has been fulfilled" (Matt. 5:17-18). Moreover, He also said, "It is written, 'Man shall not live by bread alone, but by every word that proceeds out of *the* mouth of God' " (Matt. 4:4). (To understand how Jesus fulfilled the Law and the Prophets, see *A Harmony of the Gospels—the Life of Jesus Christ*, Coulter, pp. 73-96.)

Jesus Christ's first coming fulfilled hundreds of prophecies as recorded in the Law, the Prophets and the Psalms. In addition to magnifying the Law and the Prophets, Jesus revealed a great deal more about the meaning of God's Sabbath and holy days.

Luke writes this account of Jesus' teaching on the Sabbath day in Nazareth: "And He came to Nazareth, where He had been brought up; and according to His custom, He went into the synagogue on the Sabbath day and stood up to read. And there was given Him *the* book of the prophet Isaiah; and when He had unrolled the scroll, He found the place where it was written, '*The* Spirit of *the* Lord *is* upon Me; for this reason, He has anointed Me to preach the gospel to *the* poor; He has sent Me to heal those who are brokenhearted, to proclaim pardon to *the* captives and recovery of sight to *the* blind, to send forth in deliverance those who have been crushed, to proclaim *the* acceptable year of *the* Lord' " (Luke 4:16-19). In fact, recorded in the Gospels of Matthew, Mark, Luke and John are the direct teachings of Jesus Christ. Furthermore, the Gospel of Jesus Christ is God's message of the good news of personal salvation and the coming Kingdom of God, which is also revealed by the Sabbath and holy days.

When Jesus began His three and one-half-year ministry, He preached repentance and forgiveness of sin: "Jesus came into Galilee, proclaiming the gospel of the kingdom of God, and saying, 'The time has been fulfilled, and the kingdom of God has drawn near; repent, and believe in the gospel' " (Mark 1:14-15).

Another primary purpose of Jesus coming in the flesh was to reveal God the Father to those whom He would call: "At that time Jesus answered and said, '**I praise You, O Father, Lord of heaven and earth, that You have hidden these things from the wise and intelligent, and have revealed them to babes**. Yes, Father, for it was well pleasing in Your sight *to do* this. **All things were delivered to Me by My Father; and no one knows the Son except the Father; neither does anyone know the Father except the Son, and the one to whom the Son personally chooses to reveal** *Him*' " (Matt. 11:25-27). Jesus did not reveal God the Father to the world in general, but only to His called and chosen disciples—those truly converted believers who love Him and keep His commandments (I John 5:2-3).

For this reason Jesus spoke to the people in parables. His disciples, however, did not understand His use of parables and questioned Him: "And He answered *and* said to them, 'Because **it has been given to you to know the mysteries of the kingdom of heaven, but to them it has not been given**. For whoever has *understanding*, to him more shall be given, and he shall have an abundance; but whoever does not have *understanding*, even what he has shall be taken away from him. For this *reason* I speak to them in parables, because seeing, they see not;

and hearing, they hear not; neither do they understand. And in them is fulfilled the prophecy of Isaiah, which says, "In hearing you shall hear, and in no way understand; and *in* seeing you shall see, and in no way perceive; for the heart of this people has grown fat, and their ears are dull of hearing, and their eyes they have closed; lest they should see with their eyes, and should hear with their ears, and should understand with their hearts, and should be converted, and I should heal them." **But blessed *are* your eyes, because they see; and your ears, because they hear. For truly I say to you, many prophets and righteous *men* have desired to see what you see, and have not seen; and to hear what you hear, and have not heard'** " (Matt. 13:11-17).

The apostle Peter later confirmed Jesus' words, stating that even the prophets of old—though they had some partial knowledge and even wrote of the coming grace of God—did not understand God's plan of salvation: "Concerning which salvation the prophets who prophesied of the grace *that would come* to you have diligently searched out and intently inquired, searching into what *way* and what manner of time the Spirit of Christ *which was* in them was indicating, testifying beforehand of the sufferings of Christ, and these glories that would follow; to whom it was revealed that, not for themselves, but to us they were ministering these things, which now have been announced to you by those who have preached the gospel to you by *the* Holy Spirit, sent from heaven—into which things the angels desire to look" (I Pet. 1:10-12).

Before Jesus' death and resurrection, He revealed to His apostles and disciples additional knowledge of the mysteries of the kingdom of God—the secret plan of God. Then, on the night of Jesus' last Passover, before His arrest and subsequent crucifixion, Jesus informed them that God the Father would send the power of the Holy Spirit upon them which would give them additional insight and revelation: "But *when* the Comforter *comes, even* the Holy Spirit, which the Father will send in My name, that one **shall teach you all things, and shall bring to your remembrance everything that I have told you**…. [When] that one has come, *even* the Spirit of the truth, it will lead you into all truth because it shall not speak from itself, but whatever it shall hear, it shall speak. And it **shall disclose to you the things to come** [in prophecy and more of God's plan]. That one shall glorify Me because it shall disclose to you *the things that* it receives from Me" (John 14:26; 16:13-14). Indeed, when they received the Holy Spirit they began to comprehend the spiritual meaning of Jesus' teachings—just as He had said.

Jesus Revealed More of God's Plan to the Apostles After He was Raised From the Dead

After God the Father raised Jesus from the dead, Jesus personally appeared to His apostles and disciples and began to explain God's plan as contained in the Old Testament. In fact, the apostles and disciples themselves did not fully fathom the meaning of the Scriptures until Jesus opened their minds: "And He said to them, 'These *are* the words that I spoke to you when I was yet with you, that all *the* things which were written concerning Me in the Law of Moses and *in the* Prophets and *in the* Psalms must be fulfilled.' **Then He opened their minds to understand the Scriptures**, and said to them, 'According as it is written, it was necessary for the Christ to suffer, and to rise from *the* dead the third day. And in His name repentance and remission of sins should be preached to all nations, beginning at Jerusalem. For you are witnesses of these things. And behold, I send the promise of My Father upon you; but remain in the city of Jerusalem until you have been clothed with power from on high' " (Luke 24:44-49).

With the exception of the apostle John, Paul wrote more about the mystery of God than any other New Testament writer. When Paul wrote to the Corinthians, he made it clear that in order to understand the mystery of God, one must have the Holy Spirit—for that mystery is spiritually revealed. All the human wisdom, philosophies and religions of the world cannot expound God's plan. Notice: "Rather, **we speak *the* wisdom of God in a mystery, *even* the hidden *wisdom* that God foreordained before the ages unto our glory** which not one of the rulers of this world has known (for if they had known, they would not have crucified the Lord of glory); but according as it is written, '**The eye has not seen, nor *the* ear heard, neither have entered into *the* heart of man, *the* things which God has prepared for those who love Him.**'

"**But God has revealed *them* to us by His Spirit, for the Spirit searches all things— even the deep things of God**. For who among men understands the things of man except *by* the spirit of man which *is* in him? In the same way also, the things of God no one understands except *by* the Spirit of God. Now we have not received the spirit of the world, but **the Spirit that *is* of God, so that we might know the things graciously given to us by God**; which things we also speak, not in words taught by human wisdom, but in *words* taught by *the* Holy Spirit *in order to* communicate spiritual things by spiritual *means*. **But *the* natural man does not receive the things of the Spirit of God; for they are foolishness to him, and he cannot understand *them* because they are spiritually discerned**" (I Cor. 2:7-14).

When Paul wrote to the Ephesians, he again emphasized that the knowledge of the mystery of God and of Christ **must be revealed** by God Himself through His Spirit and the Word of God: "For this cause [the preaching of the Gospel] I, Paul, *am* the prisoner of Christ Jesus for you Gentiles, if indeed you have heard of the ministry of the grace of God that was given to me for you; **how He made known to me by revelation the mystery** (even as I wrote briefly before, so that when you read *this*, **you will be able to comprehend my understanding in the mystery of Christ** [God's secret plan for mankind], **which in other generations was not made known to the sons of men, as it has now been revealed to His holy apostles and prophets by *the* Spirit**; that the Gentiles might be joint heirs, and a joint body, and joint partakers of His promise in Christ through the gospel" (Eph. 3:1-6).

In writing to the Colossians, Paul revealed that part of the mystery of Christ is Christ *dwelling in* every converted believer through the power of the Holy Spirit. He also made it clear that what he was writing to them was to become part of the New Testament, thus completing the Word of God. God has preserved His Word so that those whom He would call in future generations would have the knowledge of this great mystery: "Now, I am rejoicing in my sufferings for you, and I am filling up in my flesh that which is behind of the tribulations of Christ, for the sake of His body, which is the church; of which I became a servant, according to the administration of God that *was* given *to* me for you *in order* **to complete the Word of God**; *even* **the mystery that has been HIDDEN FROM AGES AND FROM GENERATIONS, but has now been revealed to His saints; to whom God did will to make known what *is* the riches of the glory of this mystery among the Gentiles; which is Christ in you**, **the hope of glory**; Whom we preach, admonishing every man and teaching every man in all wisdom, so that we may present every one perfect in Christ Jesus" (Col. 1:24-28).

In the early AD 60s, God revealed additional knowledge of His plan to His apostles and prophets. In some of the most eloquent and spiritually inspiring words of the Bible, Paul wrote of God's new fantastic revelation of His purpose for those whom He had called and described their personal participation in that plan: "Blessed *be* the God and Father of our Lord Jesus Christ, Who has **blessed us with every spiritual blessing in the heavenly *things* with Christ**; according as **He has personally chosen us for Himself** before *the* foundation of *the* world in order that we might be holy and blameless before Him in love; **having predestinated us for**

sonship to Himself through Jesus Christ, according to the good pleasure of His own will, to *the* praise of *the* glory of His grace, wherein He has made us objects of *His* grace in the Beloved *Son*.

"In Whom we have redemption through His blood, *even* the remission of sins, according to the riches of His grace, which He has made to abound toward us in all wisdom and intelligence; **having made known to us THE MYSTERY OF HIS OWN WILL, according to His good pleasure, which He purposed in Himself; that in** *the divine* **plan for the fulfilling of** *the* **times**, He might bring all things together in Christ, both the things in the heavens and the things upon the earth; *yes*, in Him, in Whom we also have obtained an inheritance, **having been predestinated according to His purpose, Who is working out all things according to the counsel of His own will**; that we might be to *the* praise of His glory, who first trusted in the Christ; in Whom you also trusted after hearing the Word of the truth, the gospel of your salvation; in Whom also, after believing, you were sealed with the Holy Spirit of promise, which is *the* earnest of our inheritance until *the* redemption of the purchased possession, to *the* praise of His glory" (Eph. 1:3-14).

Paul warned the Gentile brethren in Colosse and Laodicea to hold fast to the teachings and knowledge of God's plan because there were false teachers who were trying to drag them back into the vanities of pagan religious philosophy and angel worship: "Now I want you to understand what great concern I have for you, and *for* those in Laodicea, and as many as have not seen my face in *the* flesh; **that their hearts may be encouraged, being knit together in love unto all riches of the full assurance of understanding, unto** *the* **knowledge of the mystery of God, and of** *the* **Father, and of Christ; in Whom are hid all the treasures of wisdom and knowledge**.

"Now I say this so **that no one may deceive you by persuasive speech**. For though I am indeed absent in the flesh, yet I am with you in spirit, rejoicing and beholding your order, and the steadfastness of your faith in Christ. **Therefore, as you have received Christ Jesus the Lord, be walking in Him; being rooted and built up in Him, and being confirmed in the faith, exactly as you were taught**, abounding in it with thanksgiving.

"Beware lest anyone takes you captive through **philosophy and vain deceit**, according to the **traditions of men**, according to the elements of the world, and not according to Christ. **For in Him dwells all the fullness of the Godhead bodily; and you are complete in Him**, Who is the Head of all principality and power. In Whom you have also been circumcised with *the* circumcision not made by hands, in putting off the body of the sins of the flesh by the circumcision of Christ; having been buried with Him in baptism, by which you have also been raised with *Him* through the inner working of God, Who raised Him from the dead.

"For you, who were *once* dead in *your* sins and in the uncircumcision of your flesh, He has *now* made alive with Him, having forgiven all your trespasses. He has blotted out the note of debt against us *with* the decrees *of our sins*, which was contrary to us; and He has taken it away, having nailed it to the cross. After stripping the principalities and the powers, He made a public spectacle of them, *and* has triumphed over them in it [the crucifixion and resurrection]" (Col. 2:1-15).

Paul admonished the Colossian brethren to realize that they were complete in Christ Jesus. They had true forgiveness of sin and true conversion through the baptism of Jesus Christ and the receiving of the Holy Spirit. Although as Gentiles they were not physically circumcised, they did have the spiritual circumcision of the heart in Christ Jesus (also see Rom. 2:28-29). Since they were now living a life of love and obedience to God the Father and Jesus Christ, they were keeping the Sabbath and holy days of God instead of being involved in pagan sun worship and the heathen religious holidays of the past. As a result, false teachers from outside the church at Colosse were trying to deceive them. With persuasive words they tried to convince the brethren to forsake the true way of the Lord and to once again embrace their former beliefs, which they had forsaken.

In verses 13-14, Paul was not abrogating the laws and commandments of God or His Sabbaths and festivals. Rather, he makes it clear to these Gentile Christians that it is absolutely essential that they obey God and keep the Sabbath and holy days of God.

Therefore, he admonished them to not unduly worry about what other people thought, nor let anyone judge or condemn them because they were now obeying God and observing His commanded Sabbaths and festivals: "Therefore, **do not allow anyone to judge you** in eating or in drinking, or with regard to a **festival**, or new moon, or *the* Sabbaths, **which are a foreshadow of the things that are coming**, but the body of Christ.

"Do not allow anyone to defraud you of the prize *by* doing *his* will in self-abasement and *the* worship of angels, intruding into things that he has not seen, vainly puffed up by his own carnal mind" (verses 16-18).

Upon further examination of his epistles, it is evident that God's revelations to Paul progressively built a clearer picture of the mystery of God. Thus, we understand *why* God had blinded the children of Israel—so that the Gentiles might receive salvation as well. While he did not fully understand the timing, Paul also knew that at a future time all Israel would be saved: "For I do not wish you to be ignorant of **this mystery**, brethren, in order that you may not be wise in your own conceits: that a partial hardening *of the heart* has happened to Israel until the fullness of the Gentiles be come in; and **so all Israel shall be saved**, according as it is written: 'Out of Sion shall come the Deliverer, and He shall turn away ungodliness from Jacob. For this *is* My covenant, which I will make with them when I have taken away their sins.' On the one hand, concerning the gospel, *they are* enemies for your sakes; but on the other hand, concerning the election, *they are* beloved for the fathers' sakes; because the gifts and the calling of God *are* never revoked. For just as you once did not believe God, but have now been shown mercy through their unbelief, in the same way also, **they have not believed at this time** in order that through the mercy shown to you, they also may have mercy shown *to them*. For God has given them all over to unbelief in order that He might show mercy to all" (Rom. 11:25-32).

Realizing that in the future God would most certainly save all Israel, he glorified God for the greatness of His plan: "O *the* depth of *the* riches of both *the* wisdom and *the* knowledge of God! How unfathomable *are* His judgments and unsearchable *are* His ways! For who did know *the* mind of *the* Lord, or who became His counselor? Or who first gave to Him, and it shall be recompensed to him again? For from Him, and through Him, and unto Him *are* all things; to Him *be* the glory into the ages of eternity. Amen" (verses 33-36).

At the end of his epistle to the Romans, Paul again states that in past ages the knowledge of God's mystery had been kept secret. "Now to Him who has the power to establish you, according to my gospel and the proclamation of Jesus Christ, according to *the* **revelation of *the* mystery that in past ages has been kept secret**; but now *is* made manifest, and by *the* prophetic scriptures [NT], according to *the* commandment of the eternal God, **has been made known** to all the nations unto *the* obedience of faith; to the only wise God, through Jesus Christ, *be* the glory into the ages *of eternity*. Amen" (Rom. 16:25-27). Again, we see that Paul recognized that God's revelation was not yet complete.

Later, when Paul writes to the Ephesians, he mentions that he had received additional revelations from Jesus Christ about the mystery of God—that the resurrected saints would form **a great spiritual family of God the Father**: "If indeed you have heard of the ministry of the grace of God that was given to me for you; how **He made known to me by revelation the mystery** (even as I wrote briefly before, so that when you read *this*, you will be able to comprehend **my understanding in the mystery of Christ**), which **in other generations was not made known to the sons of men, as it has now been revealed to His holy apostles and prophets by** *the* **Spirit**; that the Gentiles might be joint heirs, and a joint body, and joint partakers of His promise in Christ through the gospel, of which I became a servant according to the gift of the grace of God, *which was* given to me through the inner working of His power.

"To me, who am less than the least of all the saints, was this grace given, that I might preach the gospel among the Gentiles—*even* **the unsearchable riches of Christ**; and that **I might enlighten all** *as to* **what** *is* **the fellowship of the mystery that has been hidden from the ages in God**, Who created all things by Jesus Christ; so that the manifold wisdom of God might now **be made known through the church** to the principalities and the powers in the heavenly *places*, **according to** *His* **eternal purpose**, which He has wrought in Christ Jesus our Lord, in Whom we have boldness and *direct* access with confidence through His *very* own faith. So then, I beseech *you* not to faint at my tribulations for you, which are *working for* your glory.

"For this cause I bow my knees to the Father of our Lord Jesus Christ, of Whom **the whole family in heaven and earth is named**, that He may grant you, according to the riches of His glory, to be strengthened with power by His Spirit in the inner man; that Christ may dwell in your hearts by faith; *and* that being rooted and grounded in love, **you may be fully able to comprehend with all the saints what** *is* **the breadth and length and depth and height** [of God's purpose], and to know the love of Christ, which surpasses *human* knowledge; so **that you may be filled with all the fullness of God**. Now to Him Who is able to do exceeding abundantly above all that we ask or think, according to the power that is working in us, to Him *be* glory in the church by Christ Jesus throughout all generations, *even* into the ages of eternity. Amen" (Eph. 3:2-21).

The Keys to Understanding the Mysteries of God: Jesus Christ promised that His true, converted, spirit-led disciples would be given the knowledge of the mysteries of the Kingdom of God. Here are the *keys* to understanding the plan of God for mankind, as revealed by His Sabbath and holy days:

- We must fully understand and absolutely believe that *all* Scripture is "God-breathed" (II Tim. 3:16) and "that no prophecy of Scripture [OT or NT] originated as anyone's own *private* interpretation; because prophecy was not brought at any time by human will, but the holy men of God spoke as they were moved by *the* Holy Spirit" (II Pet. 1:20-21).
- In order to understand the Bible and the meaning of the Sabbath and holy days, we must *rightly divide* the Word of God—which is given precept upon precept, line upon line, here a little and there a little (II Tim. 2:15; Isa. 28:9-10).
- God reveals His mysteries only to those who have the Spirit of God, truly love Him, keep His commandments and His Sabbath and holy days, and worship God the Father in spirit and truth (Mark 12:28-30; Col. 2:16; Heb. 4:9; John 4:23-24).

A Prayer of Encouragement: When Paul first informed the brethren of Ephesus about the purpose of God the Father and Jesus Christ, he ended with this prayer for them. It is fitting that we also end this Prologue with his prayer. May God answer this prayer for all those who read and study about the mystery of God and of Christ in *God's Plan for Mankind Revealed by*

His Sabbath and Holy Days: "I do not cease to give thanks for you, making mention of you in my prayers; **that the God of our Lord Jesus Christ, the Father of glory, may give you *the* spirit of wisdom and revelation in *the* knowledge of Him. *And* may the eyes of your mind be enlightened in order that you may comprehend what is the hope of His calling, and what *is* the riches of the glory of His inheritance in the saints, and what is the exceeding greatness of His power toward us who believe, according to the inner working of His mighty power**, which He wrought in Christ, when He raised Him from *the* dead, and set *Him* at His right hand in the heavenly *places*, far above every principality and authority and power and lordship, and every name that is named—not only in this age, but also in the *age* to come; for He has subordinated all things under His feet, and has given Him *to be* head over all things to the church, which is His body—the fullness of Him Who fills all things in all" (Eph. 1:16-23).

Thus, the prophecy of Moses is fulfilled through the New Covenant with Jesus Christ and God the Father: "**The secret things belong unto the LORD our God: but those things which are revealed** [in both the Old and New Testaments] **belong unto us and to our children for ever** [the Church of God, which is spiritual Israel, the children of God] that we may do all the words of this Law [which now includes the entire Bible]" (Deut. 29:29).

Even with all the knowledge that God the Father and Jesus Christ have revealed by the Holy Spirit through the Word of God and His Sabbath and holy days, we also realize that comprehending the absolute reality of God's spiritual plan for mankind is still like looking through a glass darkly. However, at the first resurrection we will understand the fullness of God's plan for mankind: "For we know in part, and we prophesy in part; but when that which is perfect has come, then that which is in part shall be set aside. When I was a child, I spoke as a child, I understood as a child, I reasoned as a child; but when I became a man, I set aside the things of a child. **For now we see through a glass darkly, but then *we shall see* face to face; now I know in part, but then I shall know exactly as I have been known**. And now, these three remain: faith, hope *and* love; but the greatest of these *is* love" (I Cor. 13:9-13).

"The secret of the Lord is with them who fear Him;
and He will show them His covenant."
(Psa. 25:14)

"It is the glory of God to conceal a thing;
but the honor of kings is to search out a matter."
(Prov. 25:2)

"Open my eyes to behold
wondrous things out of your Law!"
(Psa. 119:18)

"Prove all things;
hold fast to that which is good."
(I Thess. 5:21)

Fourteen Rules for Bible Study

Please see Appendix A for an expanded version of these rules.

1) Begin with passages that are easy to understand, where there is little or no dispute as to the meaning—then move on to more difficult ones.

2) Let the Bible interpret and prove the Bible. Don't look for what you want to prove; look for what the Bible *actually* proves. Do this by looking at *all* of the passages relevant to the study.

3) Understand the context—the verses before and after, the chapters before and after. Does your understanding of a particular verse harmonize with the rest of the Bible?

4) Understand the original language, Hebrew or Greek. Never try to establish dogmatic doctrine or teachings by using *Strong's Concordance*. It can be helpful at times, but it is quite limited.

5) Ask, "What does the passage clearly say?"

6) Ask, "What does the passage not say?"

7) Ask, "To whom was the book written?"

8) Ask, "Who wrote it?"

9) Ask, "Who said it?"

10) Understand the historical time frame and cultural setting of when the book was written.

11) Don't bring your *personal* assumptions and preconceived notions into your understanding or conclusions.

12) Base your study on the biblical understanding you already have. What do you *know* up to this point in time?

13) Do not form conclusions based on partial facts or insufficient information, or the opinions and speculations of others.

14) Personal opinions or convictions, regardless of how sincere, don't count. Scripture alone must be your standard and guide.

These guidelines represent a thorough and careful approach to study. When undertaking a study of the Bible, we should always use this approach, coupled with prayer, trusting God to lead us with His Holy Spirit. We know that He will fulfill His promise to **lead us into all truth**—*if* we arc diligently seeking to understand the Word of God.

The Beginning and the Ending

Welcome to *God's Plan for Mankind Revealed by His Sabbath and Holy Days*. You are about to embark on the most exciting journey of discovery of your life! Through this book you will discover the truth about *what* God is doing on this earth—*how* He is doing it and *why*. Indeed, you will come to understand the very *purpose* of God for mankind.

We are commanded to keep God's holy days. But why are His holy days so important? The simple, yet profound, answer is this: God's holy days form a roadmap that tells us where we have been and where we are going. Each of God's seven annual high days marks a specific stage of His divine plan. Sometimes a holy day points *back* at key events that have already occurred, that have moved God's plan along its path. Similarly, other holy days look *forward* to major prophetic events yet to occur. But note this well: you cannot understand God's plan—what God is actually *doing* on this earth—without the understanding of His Sabbath and holy days.

This will be an intensive study. If you are not familiar with the Bible, you may need to learn some basic study skills. Please carefully read the following section, *Fourteen Rules for Bible Study*. It will help you greatly as you go through this in-depth study. And by the way, don't let the size of this book intimidate you! You will find that reading along with a CD is actually quite easy—and helps you to understand and retain what you read.

What you are about to discover is and has been a *mystery*. Notice what Jesus said: "And His disciples came to Him and asked, 'Why do You speak to them in parables?' And He answered *and* said to them, 'Because **it has been given to you to know the mysteries of the Kingdom of Heaven**…' " (Matt. 13:10-11).

Mystery means *secret—God's secret!* And that secret is *opened* only to those individuals God calls (John 6:44)—those who are striving to obey and serve God. But His plan remains a secret to those whose minds are closed because of disobedience. Jesus continues: "But to them it has not been given. For whoever has *understanding*, to him more shall be given, and he shall have an abundance; but whoever does not have *understanding*, even what he has shall be taken away from him. For this *reason* I speak to them in parables, because seeing, they see not; and hearing, they hear not; neither do they understand" (vv. 11-13).

That's what this book does—it gives understanding to those who God calls. God grants understanding. But those who are steeped in this world's ways are actually void of understanding. Because they refuse to give up worldly practices, refuse to get serious about sin, refuse to put Scripture above human tradition—*they remain blind*. Yes, they have the Bible. They can go to church on Sunday. They can keep the traditional Christian holidays—Easter, Christmas, etc. But they will never understand God's plan. And what little understanding they might have will be taken from them—replaced by more fables and heresies. (If you are new to the biblical Sabbath and holy days, please request *Occult Holidays or God's Holy Days—Which?* We'll be happy to send you a copy—it goes hand-in-hand with this book.)

So Jesus adds: "And in them is fulfilled the prophecy of Isaiah, which says, 'In hearing you shall hear, and in no way understand; and *in* seeing you shall see, and in no way perceive; for the heart of this people has grown fat [through sin], and their ears are dull of hearing [because they want to do their own thing], and their eyes they have closed, lest they should see with their eyes, and should hear with their ears, and should understand with their hearts, and should be converted, and I should [spiritually] heal them" (vv. 14-15).

The result is that they are cut off from salvation—for now, as they will have their calling *later*, in another age.

Isaiah 29 is another prophecy concerning *why* people don't understand the Bible. Start in verse 9: "Be stunned and amazed! Blind your eyes and be blind! They are drunk [with the wine of the spiritual fornication of Babylon the Great (Rev. 17:2)], but not with wine [not physical wine, but *false doctrine*]; they stagger, but not *with* strong drink, for the LORD has poured out upon you the spirit of deep sleep, and has closed your eyes; He has covered [the spiritual eyes of] the prophets and your rulers, *and* the seers. And the vision of all has become to you like the words of a book that is sealed, which they give to one who is learned saying, 'Please read this,' and he says, 'I cannot, for it is sealed.' And the book is delivered to him who is not learned, saying, 'Please read this,' and he says, 'I am not learned' " (vv. 9-12).

The Bible to them is a "sealed book"—or it is like they simply cannot read.

As we continue in Isaiah 29, note this vital key: You must not approach this study as a mere curiosity. ***You must be absolutely serious in your commitment to God!***

Isaiah continues, showing why people cannot understand the Bible: "Because this people draws near *Me* with their mouth, and with their lips [they] honor Me [they *say* all the right Christian-sounding things], but their worship of Me is made up of the traditions of men learned by rote, and their fear toward Me is *taught* by the commandments of men [traditions of men that water down God's standards]; therefore, behold, I will proceed to do again a marvelous work among this people, *even* a marvelous work and a wonder, for the wisdom of their wise ones shall perish, and the wisdom of their intelligent ones shall vanish" (vv. 13-14).

Verse 15: "Woe *to* those who go deep to hide *their* purpose from the LORD! And their works are in the dark, and they say, 'Who sees us? And who knows us?' Surely, you have turned things upside down!"

That's what the pagan "Christianity" of this world has done—*turned God's way upside down.* The very thing they ought to keep—the Sabbath and holy days—*they don't keep.* So they don't understand God's plan. And the very things God says you shall *not* keep—pagan days like Sunday, Easter, Christmas—*that's what they keep.*

Indeed, they have everything upside down! It's like the *clay* trying to tell the potter what to do (verse 16). The result: spiritual blindness.

You need to understand something very important: The Bible is the *truth of God!* Jesus said, "*Your Word is the truth.*" In Psalm 119, David says, "*All Your commandments are true. Your Law is true! All your precepts are true from the beginning.*" You need to understand that unless you are willing to be honest with yourself and honest with the Word of God—and apply yourself to the Bible the way God wants you to—*you will never understand.* You'll be just like those of Isaiah 29 who say, of the Bible, "It is sealed."

The apostle Paul wrote about the coming world ruler, the *beast* of Revelation 13, who is going to proclaim himself to be "God on earth." There is also going to be a *false prophet* who is going to endorse the "beast" as a manifestation of God in the flesh. Paul writes: "*Even* the one whose coming is according to *the* inner working of Satan, with all power and signs and lying wonders [if you don't know the Bible, you'll never know what is happening] and with all deceivableness of unrighteousness in those who are perishing **because they did not receive the love of the Truth**, so that they might be saved" (II Thess. 2:9-10).

So you must love the truth! God is true, and God cannot lie. But most preachers and ministers and theologians have never received a genuine "love of the truth."

Verses 11-12: "And for this cause God will send upon them **a powerful deception that will cause them to believe *the* lie**, so that all may be judged **who did not believe the Truth**, but who took pleasure in unrighteousness."

So where do you start? If God has "given to you" (Matt. 13:11) the understanding of His mysteries, then you start by "rightly dividing the Word of truth" (II Tim. 2:15). And you have to move beyond the "milk of the Word." Notice: "Whom shall He teach knowledge? And whom shall He make to understand doctrine? *Those* who are weaned from the milk…" (Isa. 28:9). Paul says we need to go beyond mere milk—we need the *meat* of God's Word (Heb. 5:12-13). This book is going to be *meat*—even *strong meat*. So you will have to apply yourself to understand it.

How do you "rightly divide" Gods Word? Back to Isaiah 28: "For precept *must be* upon precept, precept upon precept; line upon line, line upon line; here a little, there a little" (v. 10). That's how you "rightly divide" the Bible: compare verse with verse, compare truth to truth. Get all the verses together on any given subject so you can see the whole picture. Only then can you understand.

Everything God wants us to know about Him and His plan is in the Scriptures. But it is spiritually understood. That's why Jesus said, "But **blessed *are* your eyes, because they see; and your ears, because they hear.** For truly I say to you, many prophets and righteous *men* have desired to see what you see, and have not seen; and to hear what you hear, and have not heard" (Matt. 13:16-17). To be given understanding is a *great blessing!*

In preparing the apostles for their work, Jesus promised that the Holy Spirit would lead them into all truth. "I have yet many things to tell you, but you are not able to bear them now. However, when that one has come, even the Spirit of the Truth, it will lead you into **all Truth**…" (John 16:12-13).

The Spirit of God is the power of God, the Spirit of truth from God—who cannot lie, who will not lie. ***God's Word is the truth!*** *That's a promise we can claim!* Not because we're anything, but because God wants His Word revealed—and ***woe to those who understand His Word but don't preach it, but teach false ideas of men instead!***

Jesus added that the Holy Spirit "shall not speak from itself, but whatever it shall hear, it shall speak. And it shall <u>disclose to you the things to come</u>" (v. 13).

Now let's see an astounding verse, Psalm 119:18: "**Open my eyes so that I may behold wondrous things out of Your Law**." The Hebrew for "open" means *reveal*. **God has to <u>reveal</u> His truth to us!**

What is contained in the Law? Where are the Sabbath and holy days listed? ***In the Law!*** God's Sabbaths and holy days are filled with His presence. They are also vehicles He uses to give us understanding as we study God's Word.

So we need godly wisdom—the wisdom of God, not man. Concerning Christ, Paul writes that "we have redemption through His blood, *even* the remission of sins, according to the riches of His grace, which He has made to abound toward us <u>in all wisdom and intelligence</u>" (Eph. 1:7-8). God wants us to be wise, intelligent—to educate ourselves *biblically*—with His Word!

The Bible, coupled with the Holy Spirit, provides ***a lifelong education program to prepare for eternal life!*** God wants us to have ***wisdom*** and ***intelligence***—to be able to think, to be able to make wise choices, to be able to make righteous judgments.

Notice verse 9: "<u>Having made known to us the mystery</u>…" ***God's mystery—His plan for mankind—is revealed through His Sabbath and holy days!*** Remember, this *mystery* is the *secret* of God, which the world cannot know.

God does this "of His own will, according to His good pleasure, which He purposed in Himself; that **in *the Divine* plan** for the fulfilling of *the* times [revealed in the Sabbath and holy days] He might bring all things together in Christ, both the things in the heavens and the things upon the earth; *yes,* in Him, in Whom we also have obtained an inheritance, having been predestinated according to His purpose, Who is working out all things according to the counsel of His own will" (vv. 9-11).

That's why this book focuses on: the plan of God, the purpose of God, the love of God, the Law of God, the truth of God, the prophecies of God, and the meaning of the holy days of God. All of this shows *what* God is doing and *how* He is working out His great plan.

Paul then says that his earnest prayer is that we might be given of God the "spirit of wisdom and revelation in *the* knowledge of Him" (v. 17). Thus it is of God that we grow in grace and knowledge, grow in spiritual understanding, and grow overall in the Word of God. Now notice especially what Paul writes next:

"And **may the eyes of your mind be enlightened**"—*That is the spiritual understanding that comes from God because of the working of God's Holy Spirit in your mind!* —"in order that you may comprehend [He wants us to *know*] what is the hope of His calling, and what *are* the riches of the glory of His inheritance in the saints, and what is the exceeding greatness of His power toward us who believe, according to the inner working of His mighty power, which He wrought in Christ, when He raised Him from *the* dead, and set *Him* at His right hand in the heavenly *places*, far above every principality and authority and power and lordship, and every name that is named—not only in this age, but also in the *age* to come; for He has subordinated all things under His feet, and **has given Him *to be* head over all things to the *Church***, which is His body—the fullness of Him Who fills all things in all" (vv. 18-23).

Let's understand something: ***no man*** is the head of the Church. ***Christ is!*** All teachers, ministers, pastors, evangelists, apostles are on the sidelines to teach the brethren. *Jesus is the great Teacher!* John 6:45: "It is written in the prophets, 'And **they shall all be taught by God**.'…" *That happens by the power of the Holy Spirit!* Jesus is the great Teacher.

So with God's guidance through the Holy Spirit, this book is designed to help you to understand the Scriptures—to understand the plan of God for mankind. Only at this time in history do we have such an opportunity—where there is peace and the freedom of thought, expression, and assembly. And God expects us to be zealously doing, learning, growing, and overcoming for greatest goal possible: to be spirit beings in the Kingdom of God.

Now let's see another principle, this one from I Corinthians 2. The church at Corinth was the most carnal of all the churches, filled with sin, filled with a spirit of competition. In effect, Paul had told them, "I wanted to bring you strong meat, but you weren't able to take it, so I had to give you milk—and you were hardly able to endure that!"

Remember, Paul tells us that now is the time to pursue *strong meat* rather than milk. That is what this book is designed to do—bring you strong meat. So again, if you find it difficult to follow, take your time and be thorough—and periodically come back to this introduction as you are going through the chapters. I'm calling this introduction *The Beginning and the Ending* because I want you to come back here again and again—and at the end!

Notice I Corinthians 2: "And my message and my preaching *was* not in persuasive words of human wisdom; rather, *it was* in demonstration of *the* Spirit and of power; **so that your faith might not be in *the* wisdom of men, but in *the* power of God**. Now we speak wisdom among the ***spiritually* mature**…" (vv. 4-6). The *King James* says "perfect" instead of *mature*. But the

Greek means *mature*. We are to *become* (a process) perfect (KJV) or mature just as God is perfect (Matt. 5:48). This requires a level of understanding.

Paul continues, saying that this wisdom "*is not the* wisdom of this world"—That is why the Bible is the only *source* used for this book!—"nor of the rulers [experts and scholars] of this world, who are coming to nothing. Rather, we speak ***the* wisdom of God in a mystery** [but it is only a mystery to the world—not to us], ***even*** **the hidden *wisdom*** that God foreordained before the ages unto our glory" (vv. 6-7).

Think about the knowledge and understanding God has given to us, what God has opened our minds to—how tremendous that is! We are being given knowledge and understanding that has *never* in the history of man been known! That is amazing!

Verses 8-9: "Which not [even] one of the [secular or religious] rulers of this world has [ever] known; (for if they had known, they would not have crucified the Lord of glory); but according as it is written: '*The* eye has not seen, nor *the* ear heard, neither have entered into *the* heart of man, *the* things which God has prepared **for those who love Him.**' "

What is the love of God? Jesus answers: "This is the love of God, that we keep His commandments; and His commandments are not burdensome" (I John 5:3). He adds: "If you love Me you will keep My commandments" (John 14:15).

Continuing in I Corinthians 2: "But God has revealed *them* to us [the apostles, now written for us in the Word of God] by His Spirit [which reveals all truth—John 16:13]; **for the Spirit searches all things—even the deep things of God**" (v. 10).

This book covers some of the *deeper things* of God. "For who among men understands the things of man except *by* the spirit of man, which *is* in him? In the same way also, **the things of God no one understands except *by* the Spirit of God**. Now we have not received the spirit of the world, but the Spirit that *is* of God, **so that we might know the things graciously given to us by God**" (vv. 11-12).

The "spirit of the world" leads to keeping Sunday, Christmas, Easter, Halloween—occult holidays. But God's Spirit gives us the true, deeper things of God! Indeed, any understanding we might have is through the grace of God. He wants us to have it! But He is not going to give it to those who are not going to *use it*. That's why Jesus said, "Don't cast your pearls before swine"—*because they'll just trample on it!* Don't give the truth to those who don't care to live it!

Verse 13: "Which things we also speak, not in words taught by human wisdom, but in *words* taught by *the* Holy Spirit ***in order to* communicate spiritual things by spiritual *means***."

Combine this with what Jesus said in John 6:63: "It is the Spirit that gives life; the flesh profits nothing. The words that I speak to you, **they are Spirit and *they* are Life**."

Do you see how "comparing spiritual things with spiritual things" and "rightly dividing the Word of God" and "precept upon precept" all tie together? **This is how you understand the Word of God!**

But again, it will be *given* only to those whose eyes are not closed due to unbelief and disobedience! The carnal mind *cannot* understand these things. Verse 14: "But *the* natural man [the carnal mind, one who doesn't have the Spirit of God] does not receive the things of the Spirit of God; for they are foolishness to him, and **he cannot understand *them* because they are spiritually discerned**."

You must have the Spirit of God *in* you if you are to receive the things of God—because they are spirit and they are life! If you have not yet been baptized and received the Holy Spirit, you can still understand—*but not fully*. However, as long as you are yielded to God, His Spirit is *with* you. But to fully receive the spiritual things of God, you must have the Holy Spirit living inside you.

It is my sincere hope that this book will illuminate your understanding of God's divine plan for mankind as revealed through His weekly Sabbath and annual holy days!

Recommend books/booklets related to this study:

• *Occult Holidays or God's Holy Days—Which?*
• *A Harmony of the Gospels*
• *Which is the True Calendar of God?*
• *The Holy Bible In Its Original Order—A Faithful Version*

Section I

The Sabbath

CHAPTER ONE

The Background in Genesis I
Creation Week—Genesis 1
Fred R. Coulter

Let's go to the Gospel of John and read a promise that is given to us here. Let's apply that to today, because we're going to go back and look at some very basic things, beginning in the book of Genesis, and we are going to see that there is an awful lot there.

I remember making the comment sometime ago, 'I wonder what it would have been like to hear a message by the Apostle Paul,' going into the Old Testament to tell us and show this, that and the other thing that is there. Here's a promise that is given that the Holy Spirit will do for us:

John 14:26: "But *when* the Comforter *comes*, *even* the Holy Spirit, which the Father will send in My name, that one **shall teach you all things**…" *That's quite a promise!*

- *IF* we have the Holy Spirit of God, which we do
- *IF* we're yielding to God and trying to live by every Word of God

Will the Holy Spirit teach us all things? *That is what we need to know for salvation!* It's not going to teach us all information in the world, obviously. It doesn't mean that.

"…and shall bring to your remembrance everything that I have told you" (v 26). *That can't happen to us because we didn't hear the words of Jesus Christ!*

Here's another promise concerning the Holy Spirit, John 16:13: "However, when that one has come, *even* the Spirit of the Truth, **it will lead you into all Truth**…"

There is this special blessing that comes when we really take God at His Word, study His Word, and add precept upon precept. Here's tremendous promise given to us, *IF* we follow the Word of God and we do put 'line upon line, here a little there a little,' and put it together *correctly*, *here's a promise*:

"…**it will lead you into all Truth**… [the Greek means: all *the* Truth] …because it shall not speak from itself, but whatever it shall hear, it shall speak. And it shall disclose to you the things to come" (v 13)

This is the thing necessary for us to understand concerning how we're going to understand the Truth. I think we're going to understand this even more in relationship to the very beginning parts of the Bible.

Luke 24—here's something else that we add to the knowledge of the Scriptures. I think this is very, very profound; I think it's also most comforting and understanding when Jesus gave this promise here:

Luke 24:44: "And He said to them, 'These *are* the words that I spoke to you when I was yet with you… [Jesus' promise that the Holy Spirit would bring to remembrance *all things* that He said] …that all *the* things, which were written concerning Me, in the Law of Moses and *in the* Prophets and *in the* Psalms must be fulfilled.' Then He opened their minds to understand the Scriptures" (vs 44-45).

We've seen and we've experienced this from time-to-time a little bit as we're going along step-by-step. I've been working on the publication: *The Grace of God in the Bible,* and there's one thing I've learned with writing: you have to get in it, and you have to really have your mind concentrating on it and be able to know the things that are there. What I've been doing, I've been writing concerning the Grace of God *in the Old Testament.* It's brought out some very interesting things and helped me clarify and understand even the first part of the Bible even more. I guess, when we get down to it, we will have to say that you never know anything the way that you really ought to truly know it.

What I did, since we have—thanks to Carl Franklin making copies of it for us—the *Interlinear Hebrew-English Old Testament (Genesis-Exodus)* by George Ricker Berry. We checked out and, unfortunately, he did not do the whole Bible. He just did Genesis and Exodus. However, I think in there there's quite a bit that we can learn. This is going to help us also understand more about how important the Sabbath is right at a time when people are *throwing away* the Sabbath. It's almost a dichotomy that is unreal.

Let's take the literal translation of the Hebrew and let's begin in Gen. 1:1. There's something that is going to make it just a little difficult in following along, and that is the English must be read from the right to the left, rather than from the left to the right. With the literal translation in linear form it must be done that way, because Hebrew is read from the right to left.

We're going to see something just little different *but profound* translations of different words that really mean more to us. We're going to go into other sections of the Bible as we're going along, but let's read the English from the *Interlinear*. You will also see that the verb in Hebrew is put before the subject.

If the Interlinear is too hard for you to follow along, then you can follow along with your own Bible. The purpose of this is because there are several sections, which are important for us to know and understand.

Genesis 1:1 (*Int*): "In the beginning [when] created God the heavens and the earth…"

Let's understand something that's important: *God had to be **before** the beginning!* If God were not *before* the beginning, then God would *be the beginning.* As you will notice, when we're going through here, there may be some changes in your notes in the margin of your Bible.

There is only one real ***the*** beginning in relationship to us, and what the Bible reveals to us. That is ***the beginning!*** Some people have put down there *a* beginning trying to indicate that there was *a* beginning before ***the*** beginning. But you cannot have *a* beginning before ***the*** beginning, otherwise ***the*** beginning is not ***the*** beginning. You have **one beginning** and:

- you may have subsequent *renewals*
- you may have subsequent *changes*
- you may have subsequent *additions*

*But there is only **one the** beginning!*

The reason it is justified in the minds of some by saying, 'a beginning,' because some people have in mind that there was '*a* beginning' before '***the*** beginning' of the heaven and earth *as we know it!* However, in this particular case it is not talking about this.

Let's look at some other Scriptures concerning *the beginning.* John is the one who does this. I'm going to go in a little more detail on this later on when I go through a very thorough word-by-word analysis of the Gospel of John, the first chapter. There are only three places in all of the Scriptures—Old Testament and New Testament—that talks about 'in ***the*** beginning.'

In the Gospel of John we find it is not *a* beginning, but ***the*** beginning. This is very important

for us to understand concerning the nature of God. I will give a little detail here and, at a later time, I will amplify it even more.

John 1:1 "In *the* beginning was **the Word,** and the Word was **with God,** and the Word **was** God."

The important thing that we need to understand is this: "**In *the* beginning…**"—*and it can actually read*: **before** the beginning. I don't want to get in too much detail with the Greek.

"…**was the Word**…" (v 1). Why did He have to be in existence before the beginning? *Because He's the Creator!*

"…**and the Word was with God**…" (v 1). This is very important from the point of view of a paper written concerning 'the thinker and the thought.' What they're trying to do is eliminate two beings Who are God *and say there's only one Being* who is God by saying that the Word was 'the thought' of God. Since He was 'the thought' in 'the thinker' He was with God. *But that's not what this means at all,* because when we get to the detailed study of it, we will see it is *with*—and the Greek is 'pros'—which means *with or toward face-to-face!*

"…**and the Word was God**" (v 1). *So that we understand **Who the One is**, it was **the One Who became Jesus Christ!*** All of this is, is to counteract and go against all the philosophical doctrines of the nature of God. When we get there it's going to open your mind like you have never understood this before.

I want to get it all prepared and laid out word for word so that you can see it clearly. I'm currently reading a book by John Goodenough, which is called *Light by Light.* Of course, it says a lot about light here in the John 1. What he's essentially showing is the pagan's concept of the nature of God. Going through that, I can see how (in this and other papers) that they were going *absolutely contrary* to those religions at that time, which are philosophies that are being resurrected and being dumped upon us today.

Verse 2: "He was in the beginning with God…. [which means He had to be there] …All things came into being **through Him,** and **not even one *thing* that was created came into being without Him**" (vs 2-3).

- no such thing as creation by sub-gods
- no such thing as creation by angels
- no such thing as evolution

All was made by Him!

1-John 1—we want to have it in here; we're talking about something just a little bit ***different*** in relationship to it. We're talking about the One Who was _**from**_ the beginning. That is _**after**_ everything was created, the One Who became Jesus Christ as the Lord God of the Old Testament continually existed from the time of the creation. He existed _**before**_ the creation; He existed _**after**_ the creation. John is giving us a very, very personal account of their relationship with Jesus Christ.

1-John 1:1: "That which was from _the_ beginning, that which we have heard, that which we have seen with our own eyes, that which we observed for ourselves and our own hands handled, concerning the Word of life; (and the life was manifested, and we have seen, and are bearing witness, and are reporting to you the eternal life, which was with the Father, and was manifested [revealed] to us); that which we have seen and have heard we are reporting to you in order that you also may have fellowship with us; for the fellowship—indeed, our fellowship—_is_ with the Father and with His own Son Jesus Christ" (vs 1-3).

In Heb. 1 we find something that adds to this:

- concerning the beginning
- concerning God
- concerning what He did
- concerning what Christ was

We know that _in the beginning was God._ We know that the word for God is 'Elohim,' a word that means _more than one._ So, there was a time when there were the two of 'Elohim' and then there was a time when one of Them became the Father and the other became the Son.

Hebrews 1:1: "God Who spoke to the fathers at different times in the past and in many ways by the prophets, has spoken to us in these last days by _His_ Son, Whom He has appointed **heir of all things**…" (vs 1-2).

When it says that we're going to be 'co-heirs with Christ,' I don't even think that our mind can _grasp the magnitude of what that is going to be!_ He's the heir of all things.

"…by Whom also He made the worlds; Who, being _the_ brightness of _His_ glory and _the_ exact image of His person…" (v 2-3).

We're dealing with the fact that God is a person as revealed throughout the Scriptures. That is why God wants us to have a personal relationship with Him and with Christ.

"…and upholding all things **by the Word of His own power**…" (v 3), _or by the power of His Word,_ because when God created, when He _spoke_ it came into existence.

"…when he had **by Himself** purged our sins, sat down at _the_ right hand of the Majesty on high; having been made so much greater than _any of_ the angels, inasmuch as He has inherited a name exceedingly superior to them. For to which of the angels did He ever say, 'You are My Son; this day I have begotten You'?…." (vs 3-5).

That's when the Elohim who became the Father, _**became**_ the Father. That's when the Elohim who became the Son, _**became**_ the Son.

Verse 5: "For to which of the angels did He ever say, 'You are My Son; this day I have begotten You'? And again, 'I will be a Father to Him, and He will be a Son to Me'? And again, when He brought the Firstborn into the world, He said, 'Let all _the_ angels of God worship Him'" (vs 5-6).

This is telling us about the person and the power and the work and the activity of Jesus Christ. When we are talking about _the beginning_ it is _the_ beginning—not '_a_.' Anything subsequent of _the_ beginning is _an addition or renewal_ or whatever, but it is not _a_ beginning.

Genesis 1:1 (_Int_): "In the [when] beginning created God the heavens and the earth…" _As I mentioned, the verb comes before the subject._ God here being 'Elohim' means _more than one._ That's why He said, "Let Us…" (v 26).

Verse 2: "(and) the earth being a desolation and a waste…"

How did the earth become "…**a desolation and a waste**…"? _When He got done creating the earth He said,_ 'Behold, it was _**very good**_.' Let's see how this came to be. Let's first understand that these two words mean—coming from the Hebrew—'tohu' and 'bohu'—_chaos_ and _confusion!_ Is God the author of confusion? _NO!_

1-Corinthians 14:33[transcriber's correction]: "For **God is not the author of confusion**…"

How did it become this way? _There was something before human beings, which was on this earth, that's what happened!_ Let's look at the Scriptures that help us with this, to give us understanding. Let's see what Isaiah tells us concerning God and His creation. You will also note that the _King James_ translation says, "The earth was without form and void" (Gen. 1:2).

Isaiah 45:18: "For thus says the LORD the Creator of the heavens… [we're talking about 'in the beginning God created the heavens and the earth'] …He Himself _is_ God, Who formed the earth and made it; He has established it. He created it not in vain…"—'tohu'—_it's not in vain!_

How could it become 'in vain' right at the beginning after God created it, if He didn't make it 'in vain' or in chaos and confusion?

"...*but* formed it to be inhabited. 'I *am* the LORD, and *there is* no other'" (v 18).

Jer. 4—we will see another place where the expression, 'tohu' and 'bohu' is used. This will give us an understanding as to how the earth **became** that way. This is talking about the punishment coming to Jerusalem and Judah. It's talking about the things that are happening in punishment.

Jeremiah 4:19: "My bowels, my bowels! I writhe in pain. O walls of my heart! My heart is beating wildly within me; I cannot be silent because you have heard, O my soul, the sound of the ram's horn, the alarm of war."

This is going to tell us how the earth became that way, and why the earth is so literally upside down.

Verse 20: "Destruction upon destruction is cried; for the whole land is laid waste. Suddenly my tents are laid waste, my curtains in a moment. How long shall I see the banner of war *and* hear the sound of the ram's horn? 'For My people *are* foolish; they have not known Me; they are stupid children, and they have no understanding. They are wise to do evil, but to do good they have no knowledge.' I looked on the earth, and, lo, *it was* **without form, and void**…" (vs 20-23)—*a condition subsequent to the creation!*

In this case, a condition subsequent to what we find of the completed creation (Gen. 1), and this is 'tohu' and 'bohu' or being *a desolation and a waste*. That's what war does!

Was there war in heaven *before* the creation of man? That becomes very important. In all the accounts that we have concerning Adam and Eve and the garden and so forth, we have four beings who are noted in the Scriptures besides all the animals in the creation. Who are those four beings?

1. God
2. Adam
3. Eve
4. the serpent: Satan the devil

Revelation 12:9: "And the great dragon was cast out, the ancient serpent who is called the Devil and Satan, **who is deceiving the whole world**…"

Was Satan *already evil* by the time he met Adam and Eve? *Yes!* That means he had to *become* evil and Satan, **before** Adam and Eve were created.

* When was that?
* How did that happen?

Ezek. 28 is a very interesting chapter because it talks about:

* the 'prince of Tyre'
* it talks about Tyre
* it talks about the king of Tyre or Tyrus

But we want to focus in on something that is very important because this tells us some very important facts. This is very basic, fundamental. I think it's important that we go through it because there are some people who are denying that Satan is even a being, today, even within the Church of God.

Ezekiel 28:11: "And the Word of the LORD came to me, saying, 'Son of man, lift up a lamentation over the king of Tyre…" (vs 11-12).

Verse 2: "Son of man, say to the prince of Tyre. 'Thus says the Lord GOD, "Because your heart *is* lifted up, and you have said, 'I *am* a god, I sit *in* the seat of God…'"'"

You can't get any higher than that, can you? *No! Why does he address the king of Tyre? Because, in this case, the king of Tyre is the spirit power behind the prince,* who **says** he's God. We're going to see that this is **the same spirit power** that in the book of Revelation inspires the final Beast Power to say, 'I am God.' *All the world is going to worship him and worship the devil!*

Notice what it says about this king of Tyre, which has to be the one who became Satan the devil as we will see by what the Scriptures tell us here.

"…and say to him, 'Thus says the Lord GOD, "You seal up the measure of perfection, full of wisdom and perfect in beauty. **You have been in Eden, the Garden of God**…"'" (v 12-13).

We have the four identified who were in the garden: *God, Adam, Eve and the serpent!* What happened after Adam and Eve sinned? *They were put out of the Garden of Eden, and no one could enter into it!*

If he was in Eden, the Garden of God, this could only be talking about the one who became Satan the devil, because no one else went into the Garden of Eden after the sin of Adam and Eve. They were cast out and cherubim were put there with flaming swords to keep the way so they couldn't go back in there.

"…You have been in Eden, the Garden of God…" (v 13)—and then it talks about all of his beauty, all of the tremendous coverings and the stones, which is a sign of *regalness, royalty* and *exalted position!*

"…The workmanship of your settings and of your sockets was prepared in you in the day that you were created" (v 13).

We saw that everything was created by Jesus Christ. **Nothing** *came into existence that He did not make!* So, we have a created being. Now let's find out a little bit more about him:

Verse 14: "You *were* the anointed cherub that covers…" *We know that over the Ark of the Covenant were two cherubs guarding it!* Here we find an additional cherub that has nothing to do with the two cherubs that are over the Ark of the Covenant, nor having anything to do with the two cherubs placed at the gate going into the Garden of Eden.

"…and I set you so; you were upon the Holy mountain of God…" (v 14). *The Garden of Eden was **not** the Holy Mount!* This is talking about a time prior to when the earth became desolate and without form or void, or 'tohu' and 'bohu.'

"…you have walked up and down in the midst of the stones of fire" (v 14)—*showing that he was right there with God!* This is talking about the way you could visualize things composed of spirit.

Verse 15: "You *were* perfect in your ways from the day that you were created, until iniquity was found in you."

We don't know how long it was, the Bible doesn't tell us. But something happened, and it happened over a period of time.

I was given this little saying, so I entitled it *An Old Proverb,* and this is true:

You don't go bad in a single day,
You just sort of shuffle along.
Then lighten the load of your moral code
Till you don't know right from wrong.

I thought that was a very nice little proverb!

But it's the same way with Satan the devil, same way with the one who was the 'covering cherub'—right over the Throne of God. "…until iniquity was found in him…" shows us that there had to be a period of time. There had to be an activity by the angels. Angels do not exist just to pluck on harps. Angels are greater in power and ability than human beings. What kind of civilization did the angels have before they fell? *We don't know!* But it had to be **greater** than ours, because they had greater abilities.

Verse 16: "By the multitude of your merchandise…" *I don't know what it was that they were doing,* but what is it that Satan is inspiring the whole world to do today? *To buy, sell, trade and* merchandise! Is that what he did with the angels also, and then do it illegally, do it improperly? *Could very well be!*

"…they have filled your midst *with* violence, and you have sinned…." (v 16). *Sin is the transgression of the laws and commandment of God!*

- Do you not suppose that there are commandments for angels that they have to obey?
- *If* you have righteous angels, are they not obedient angels?
- *If* you have disobedient angels who have become demons

then you have also apply the principle:

- *If* you don't believe that there are laws and commandments for angels to follow:
- What is that principle? *Where there is no Law there is no sin!*

So, he could not have sinned unless there was some Law or commandment that he broke.

"…Therefore, I will cast you as profane from the mountain of God, and I will destroy you, O covering cherub, from among the stones of fire. Your heart was lifted up because of your beauty; you have corrupted your wisdom by reason of your brightness…. [got totally sold on himself] …I will cast you to the ground; I will lay you before kings, that they may behold you. By the multitude of your iniquities, by the unrighteousness of your trade, you have profaned your sanctuaries…" (vs. 16-18).

There must have been some form of angelic worship with sanctuaries, what we might call *assemblies* or *churches.* We have to deduce that from here, because you cannot have a sanctuary unless there is some place that's set aside to be Holy!

Verse 18: "By the multitude of your iniquities, by the unrighteousness of your trade, you have profaned your sanctuaries; therefore I brought forth a fire from your midst; it shall devour you, and I will bring you to ashes upon the earth, before the eyes of all who see you."

It carries forth right from there to the final, final punishment of Satan the devil. Rev. 12 tells us what occurred, and then we'll go from there to the book of Jude and then to the book of Isaiah.

Let's understand something concerning fallen angels, which are called *demons.* There's going to be a future war, and that future war is going to result in again, the casting down of Satan the devil to the earth, which is just somewhere in the very near future ahead of us.

Revelation 12:9: "And the great dragon was cast out, the ancient serpent…"

What happened when he was cast out the first time? This is the second casting out; the first one was a 'fall.'

"…who is called the Devil and Satan, who is deceiving the whole world; he was cast down to the earth, and his angels were cast down with him" (v 9).

Those angels are called in the Gospels: *demons* or *unclean spirits.* Now, we've seen in the past that sin causes uncleanness: *spiritual and physical!*

Verse 1: "Then there appeared a great wonder in heaven: a woman clothed with the sun…" *This is symbolic of the whole completed work of God* with the Bride of Christ. This is depicting the woman: the Bride of Christ.

"…and *having* the moon under her feet, and on her head a crown of twelve stars. And being with child, she cried in travail, and was in pain to deliver. And another sign was seen in heaven: and behold, a great red dragon… [Satan the devil] …having seven heads and ten horns… [so, we have the powers and principalities] …and seven crowns on his heads; and his tail swept away a third of the stars of heaven, and cast them to the earth…." (vs 1-4).

When did that happen? This first fall? *Let's see what Jesus said concerning Satan and the demons,* because this is also a very revealing Scripture.

Luke 10:17: "Then the seventy returned with joy, saying, 'Lord, even the demons are subject to us through Your name.' And He said to them, **'I beheld Satan fall as lightning from heaven'**" (vs 17-18).

Revelation 12:4: "…his tail swept away a third of the stars of heaven…" We know that in Rev. 1, that *a star* is an angel. So, this is saying— combined together—that when Satan 'fell as lightning from heaven' **he drew a third of the angels with him!**

Let's confirm that by this Scripture in the little book of Jude, what Jude wrote concerning the angels and see what he says about them.

Jude 6: "And the angels who did not keep their own original domain… [they rebelled against God] …but deserted their habitation, He is holding in eternal bonds under darkness unto the judgment of *the* great day."

We also know that Satan had to fall before man was created, otherwise he would not show up in the Garden of Eden as Satan. So, let's put this all together and let's see what happened. Let's understand that Satan is called *the god of this world!*

2-Corinthians 4:3: "But if our Gospel is hidden, it is hidden to those who are perishing; in whom **the god of this world**…" (vs 3-4).

Jesus called him the 'prince' of this world or the 'ruler' of this world. He's also called *'the prince of the power of the air; that spirit that now works within the children of disobedience'* (Eph. 2). *The "god of this world!"*

Isa. 14—we will put this all together and we will see *when* Satan was cast down; *when* the war took place. When there is war, what happens? We saw in Jer. 4, when there's war there's desolation and destruction, *wasting!*

Isaiah 14:12: "How you are fallen from the heavens, **O shining star, son of the morning!**…."

Isn't that what Jesus said? *That He saw Satan 'fall from heaven as lightning'!* Lucifer means *light-bringer.* He was to be the 'light-bringer' in God's plan, but he rebelled.

In all of the *secret religions* of the philosophies and also in Masonry, *they worship Lucifer as the 'light-bringer'!* Lucifer is declared unequivocally by Albert Pike as 'God.' They know what they're worshipping. That's why they have to have degrees, to kind of let you in on the secret step-by-step. If they told a new initiate first out what they were doing, they would undoubtedly reject it. You have to be brainwashed and brought along, degree-by-degree. When you get to be the 33rd degree, then they know that they are coming to the stream of light from Lucifer.

"…*How* you are cut down to the ground, you who weakened the nations! For you have said in your heart, 'I will ascend *into* the heavens… [this had to happen before the creation of man] …I will exalt my throne above **the stars** of God… [angels, 'above the *angels* of God,' get the advantage] …I will also sit upon the mount of the congregation, in the sides of the north'" (vs 12-13)—*which is the Mt. of God where the central Government of God the Father and Jesus Christ is located, wherever that is in the universe!* I'm convinced that it's a whole lot closer to the earth than maybe we have imagined.

Verse 14: "I will ascend above the heights of the clouds…"

- Where are clouds? *Clouds are on the earth!*
- What do you need to make clouds? *You need water!*
- Where's the only place that they truly have found any amount of water where

there can be clouds, in as far as our whole solar system is concerned? *That's the earth!*

They think that on Mars they can detect some things where there used to be water—*possible!* So, I just throw this in the mix as just a thought, it makes you wonder (speculation): Was there something on Mars before it was desolated in its present condition? *Could be!* Everyone is anxious to find out what is on Mars. Some people have said that there are some temple-looking buildings or something on Mars, but the United States government is holding back the information on that. I do not know. You can read that in the *Enquire* or *Star,* whichever you prefer.

"…'I will ascend *into* the heavens, I will exalt my throne above the stars of God…'" (v 13). **Could that refer to literal stars?** *Yes!* It could refer to angels; It could refer to both and still have the same meaning.

"…I will also sit upon the mount of the congregation, in the sides of the north. I will ascend above the heights of the clouds; **I will be like the Most High**" (vs 13-14). *That's an impossibility!*

Why? *Well, we have a lesson from Paul,* 'Shall the thing created—which it was—be greater than the Creator?' *No! or* 'Shall the thing created say to the Creator, *What are you making?*' That's what he's doing by this statement: "…I will be like the Most High."

Verse 15: "Yet, you shall be brought down to the grave, to the sides of the pit." *That's what's going to happen!*

What we are dealing with in Gen. 1 is that after God created the heavens and the earth, in the beginning **something happened,** and the word **was** can be translated *became,* or it's state of being *became* a desolation and a waste (Gen. 1:2). So then, what we are dealing with here, which is true, when we are looking at the earth in this condition, what does God do from that time forward? *He renews the surface of the earth,* or recreates it.

When Christ returns, is He going to make a new heaven and a new earth? *Yes, He is!* Because all the stars are, again, be out of whack! The earth is going to be all suffering from the wars and desolation and plagues.

He's going to have to make a new heaven and new earth. How? *By renewing the one that is here!* It talks about that during the Millennium one of the things we will be doing is helping the people rebuild the waste places, which is the result of war.

Genesis 1:2: "And the earth was without form and void, and darkness *was* upon the face of the deep [abyss]…"

Who is the prince of darkness? *Satan the devil!* So, we have dual meaning here.

1. The light of God was not shinning, because Christ is the Light (John 1)
2. Satan is the prince of darkness

So we have:

- *symbolic*: the spiritual quality of the absence of light and darkness
- *literal darkness*: that it was dark, maybe a thick darkness like it was in Egypt during the plagues

"…and darkness *was* upon the face of the deep, and the Spirit of God moved upon the face of the waters" (v 2).

What is one way to get rid of radiation? *You bury it in water,* and you keep it there a long time. We do not know how old the earth literally is. It could be many hundreds of millions of years old as we reckon time; could even be billions of years old. When you look at the geographical strata what do you see? *You see two floods!* You see the killing of the warm-blooded animals in the Flood of Noah; and you see the killing of the dinosaurs in a *different* strata in a *different* time; and that is always buried way down low with the so-called 'primitive rocks.'

I will have to say that most of the things that they test, they don't test the literal thing. I found out this concerning the testing. They go to Africa like Professor Leeky and he's walking along the ground and sees part of a skull there. He picks up this part of the skull and he says, 'I wonder how old this is? Well, we'll take it in and do a scientific testing.' So, what they do, they go and get some of the dirt and they test the dirt for the age, not the skull.

If you understand the *error* in that, then you'll understand why most of these things are wrong with the carbon dating and even the argon carbon dating, though the dating is correct. The age of the soil maybe totally different than the age of the bone which is found in the soil.

We have a member who used to live in Utah where the Dinosaur National Park where the dinosaur bones are right in the limestone. So, when you test the stone…

Let's look at it this way: You could take a calf, it died, you bury it, it's left there—say, maybe 50 years. Someone comes back and does an archeological excavation. They find these bones, they want to know how old the bones are, how long has it been there? Well, if they take the bones and test the bones, they will get an accurate test. But if they take the soil in which the calf was buried and test the soil, they're not going to get an accurate result because the soil was there long before the calf was buried in it. That's why you find this great divergence.

How long it was that the angels were here in peace and harmony before sin, we don't know. But God had to renew the face of the earth, which is what He did here. We have the spiritual darkness and we have the physical darkness and now God is going to do something about it.

Verse 3: "And God said…" *We note that 'by His Word, He commands'!* This is going to be so **profound** when we come to the creation of Adam and Eve. This also tells us our relationship and our destiny with God that God intended from the very beginning of the creation of Adam and Eve. So, He commanded:

"…'Let there be light.' And there was light…. [light came into being] …And God saw the light that *it was* good; and God divided between the light and the darkness. And God called the light day… [or assigned to it the name 'day'] …and He called the darkness night. And the evening and the morning were day one" (vs 3-5)—*in the re-creation of the earth for human existence!*

He already began with an earth that was in 'chaos and confusion'—a wasteland and desolation—as a result of the war with Satan and his angels, who fell and became demons.

Let's also notice something here that's important: when there was night and when there was day, what do we literally have? *We have on half of the earth it is night, half of the earth it is day continuously at all times!*

But when it says "…the evening and the morning were day one" *the evening ended the darkness where God was when He created and called into existence the light and separated it!*

The evening ended the darkness. Just like when we go through—and that follows the pattern all the way through the Bible—when you come to evening or sunset, it ends that day. This first evening ended the darkness because it was light just enough where God was so that it was evening; and then morning was day one.

Verse 6: "And God said, 'Let there be a firmament in the midst of the waters, and let it divide the waters *from* the waters.' And God made the firmament, and divided the waters, which *were* under the firmament from the waters, which *were* above the firmament; and it was so. And God called the firmament heavens. And the evening and the morning were day two" (vs 6-8).

Some people think that the waters above had to do with perhaps an envelope of water or some sort of water-covering above the earth. I do not know whether that speculation has any validity or not. Some people have said well maybe there was a ring of water around the earth. If there was a ring of water around the earth, it had to then end up being frozen, because once you get out of the temperature it's going to freeze. *Possible!* This doesn't tell us exactly

Verse 6: "And God said, 'Let there be a firmament in the midst of the waters, and let it divide the waters *from* the waters.' And God made the firmament, and divided the waters, which *were* under the firmament from the waters, which *were* above the firmament; and it was so" (vs 6-7).

- Could this also refer to clouds?
- Are clouds full of water? *Yes! They are when it rains!*
- Do they contain lots and lots of water? *Yes, they do!*

Especially when you get caught in some horrendous rain you wonder when it's going to stop.

I would have to surmise from what is here that what He was doing was separating the waters from the oceans, which became the oceans, from the water, which He wanted to have in the clouds. Now, whether there was a ring of water or a disc of frozen water around the earth, I do not know. It doesn't tell us. We have to leave that in the realm of speculation.

Verse 8: "…And the evening and the morning were day two. And God said, 'Let the waters under the heavens be gathered together to one place, and let the dry land appear.'"…." (vs 8-9).

There is some evidence geologically speaking that there was **one major continent** on the earth at one time and the seas all around it. Could be! This seems to lend some credence to that. Then they say that the earth was moved around and formed the continents as we have them now.

When you look at some of these continents, you can see that it makes sense. Some of them, which are close by, you can see the difference. Like in the English Channel, you have the white cliffs of Dover on one side and then you have the white cliffs, but not as much, on the other side, and you can tell that it was ripped apart and separated. However, I do not believe any of these things were gradual. I think they happened suddenly and it happened, not a gradual thing.

When you look at the mountains— especially those that go straight up—that didn't happen just a little at a time—it happened all at once. So, there was the dry land.

"…and He called the gathering together of the waters seas; and God saw that *it was* good. And God said, 'Let the earth bring forth vegetation—*the* herb yielding seed *and* the fruit tree producing fruit **after its kind**…'" (v 10-11).

We're beginning to get a lesson here, as he's teaching us, that it's **after its kind.** I think that if we ever do get to the point of Noah's Flood, I think it's telling us that the whole earth was corrupted. I think the animals were, the vegetables were, everything that man set his hand to do was corrupted. Just like today. Everything is becoming hybrid and cross-genetics.

Men have thought of and conceived quite a few things. If you have potatoes now that you cut open and they never turn black, you know that they have inserted a gene from a moth into that potato to keep it from turning black. They have done that, yes! They've done that with genetics. I know some may not believe it. That's what they say. What else they can do I don't know. It's *'after its kind.'*

"…and the tree producing fruit after its kind, whose seed *is* in itself. And God saw that *it was* good. And the evening and the morning were day three" (vs 12-13).

Each one of these things in their sequence. I want you to understand that God is **speaking** or **commanding** all of these things into existence. If you want to know the power of the Word of God, and if you want to know what God can do, here's part of it. He can **command** and it exists!

Verse 14: "And God said, 'Let there be lights in the firmament of the heavens to divide between the day and the night, and let them be for signs, and for appointed seasons, and for days and years.'"

This also let's us know that since there was light and day, and we're up to the third day, the question becomes: Did God wait until the fourth day to create the moon and the sun? *No!* I think He set them back in the proper orbit that they needed to be, because I believe (speculation) that they were knocked out of orbit when there was a war. The war between Satan and his demons and God and the angels.

What does God use? *God uses the things that He has made!* When you look at the moon, look at it very carefully. I think you will see that the majority of those things are not really volcanoes, but craters from different elements—rocks or parts of the universe—hitting it.

We have an unusual thing in our solar system. There is an asteroid belt between Mars and Jupiter. They know, from what they've been able to see, looking out into the heavens, that these are really just chunks of junk rock. That's all they are. In cleaning up the universe around us, God just took all of those and put them into that orbit.

When *stars fall from heaven* as we look at stars from heaven, is that going to be God sending a lot of those meteoroids back down to the earth and when they hit our atmosphere they're burning up. I do not know, could very well be. But everywhere you look in our solar system, there are signs of chaos, confusion and war. In the earth, though it's re-created for man's habitation, and Mars in particular, and with the asteroid belt that is there.

Some of the other planets, we would have to say we don't know if there was any habitation on them. I would have to doubt that there would be just looking at the way that they are now. Then He set them for times, for seasons, for years.

Verse 15: "And let them be for lights in the firmament of the heavens to give light upon the earth.' And it was so. And God *had* made two great lights, the greater light to rule the day and the lesser light to rule the night; and *God had made* the stars *also.* And God set them in the firmament of the heavens to give light upon the earth, and to rule over the day and over the night, and to divide between the light and the darkness. And God saw that *it was* good" (vs 15-18).

Here's another reason why the Holy Days are to be kept: they are part of the creation of God based upon seasons.

Verse 19: "And the evening and the morning were day four. And God said, 'Let the waters abound *with* **swarms of living creatures**…'" (vs 18-20).

Verse 20 (*KJV*): "…'Let the waters bring forth abundantly the **moving** creature'…."

Swarming is a good way—when you see some of these pictures of the schools of fish and so forth—a good word.

"…and let fowl fly over the earth on the face of the firmament of heaven.' And God created great sea-animals, and every living creature that moves *with* which the waters swarmed after their kind, and every winged fowl after its kind. And God saw that *it was* good. And God blessed them, saying, 'Be fruitful and multiply, and fill the waters of the seas, and let the fowl multiply in the earth.' And the evening and the morning we day five" (vs 20-23).

Again, God is commanding this creation by the Word of His power. They're coming into existence. So therefore, let's understand that when God told, for example: Moses or anyone who was to write the Scriptures, 'Write this and put it in a book.' You know, it has power to it. That's why the Word of God is, is a *living Word!*

Verse 24: "And God said, 'Let the earth bring forth living creatures after their kind—livestock, creeping things, and beasts of the earth—each after its kind.'…. [you find a breakdown of the animals as God would see it] …And it was so. And God made the beasts of the earth after their kind, and the livestock after their kind, and every creeping thing upon the earth after their kind. And God saw that it was good" (vs 24-25). *Again, God did it by speaking!*

Let's see what happened here beginning with man. Then we'll go to Gen. 2 because there's some very interesting things concerning man.

Verse 26: "And said God, 'Let Us [now this phrase "Let Us…"

Carl Franklin wrote in his paper *The Two Jehovahs of the Pentateuch,* he's showing that grammatically in the syntax in the Hebrew—which means *the way that it's written* and *the meaning behind the words*—this is not God talking to angels. This is not God talking to a council in heaven. This is one of Elohim saying to the other of Elohim:

"…'Let **Us** make man in **Our** image, after **Our** likeness…" (v 26). He didn't say any of the cattle or any of the birds or any other thing was after the likeness of God; they were after their *own created kind!*

What is true concerning an image is very important. An image is made in the likeness of something that is other than the image. In other words, in this case, being God. God is the reality from which the image was patterned. After His image, after His likeness. Supreme creation as far as the physical things are concerned.

So supreme that He said: "'…after Our likeness; and let them have dominion over the fish of the sea and over the fowl of heaven and over the livestock and over all the earth and over every creeping thing that crawls upon the earth.' And God created man…" (vs 26-27).

Notice that He didn't *speak! God created!* In the other cases, God made and created *by speaking.*

"…And **God created** man in His *own* image, in the image of God He created him. He created them male and female. And God blessed them.…" (vs 27-28). *We will see that it was a special creation!* That's why it's recorded this way for us.

"…And God said to them, 'Be fruitful and multiply, and replenish the earth, and subdue it; and have dominion over the fish of the sea and over the fowl of heaven and over every living thing that moves upon the earth.' And God said, 'Behold, I have given you every herb bearing seed which *is* upon the face of all the earth, and every tree upon which *is the* fruit of a tree bearing seed… [in other words, *the seed in itself*] …to you shall they shall be for food" (vs 28-29).

There are those who say that, at this time they did not eat any meat. We don't know whether that is exactly so. He didn't say they couldn't eat of any of the animals here at this point, but He was describing what kind of vegetation or fruits that they could eat, and that was with its seed within itself.

Today we have oranges with no seeds. They can't quite get away with it, because it pops up with a seed every once in a while. I'm sure, in the scheme of things, God intended that there be certain things that man could do with plants and animals that are lawful and legal and proper. But, I'm also sure that we're entering a time where there are a lot of things that human beings are doing to plants and animals that are not lawful. I think we are reducing the seed reservoir, in particularly for wheat, because everyone is trying to have great abundance of wheat and rice, and they are getting into the hybridized production of those that I heard of in one, one show that I saw, that they are down to just maybe a dozen genesis seeds of wheat. I don't know what it is for rice, but I do remember the wheat.

Now, what they're doing in the potato, they're going to South America to try and get new genetic strains from the potatoes down there—because we've pretty well destroyed the genetic strains that we have up here. They're subject to all kinds of weakness and sickness and disease. You can't outdo God's way! When God made this, this was tremendous, this was great!

"…to you they shall be for food. And to every animal of the earth and to every fowl of heaven and to all the living creatures that crawl upon the earth, every green plant *is given* for food.' And it was so. And God saw everything that He had made…" (vs 29-31)—*or the soul of them, which is a living soul, as it were, the soul of life*. It's true!

Let's understand something absolutely profoundly true concerning all flesh, concerning human beings.

Isaiah 40:6: "A voice says, 'Cry!' And he

said, 'What shall I cry? "All flesh *is* grass, and all the beauty of it *is* as the flower of the field. The grass withers, the flower fades because the breath of the LORD blows upon it; surely the people *are* grass. The grass withers, the flower fades; but the Word of our God shall stand forever"'" (vs 6-8).

It is actually literally true. **We are all grass!** Even if you eat a steak, guess where that came from? *Grass!* Some kind of vegetation. You eat a chicken, where did that come from? *Grass,* and worms and a few other things.

People even smoke it. *Yes!* There are various kinds of grass: you have tobacco and then you have marijuana and you have other things. It's amazing what people do. Sometimes all you can do is just shake your head as how great that our creation is, of our bodies and everything. Because what mankind does to itself, and still survives is really just something else.

Genesis 1:31: "And God saw everything that He had made, and indeed, *it was exceedingly* good...."

The Hebrew there for *good* means *gracious or beautiful.* In a sense, the whole creation of God was an *act of grace* by giving and providing all of these things rightly.

"...*it was exceedingly* good. And the evening and the morning were the sixth day" (v 31).

Genesis 2:1: "Thus the heavens and the earth were finished, and all the host of them. And by *the beginning of* the seventh day God finished His work which He had made...." (vs 1-2).

If you look at the way the Hebrew *seventh* is spelled. Just look at the letters and compare that with *sixth.* You see the only difference between the two is a middle letter. Letters are the same, but there's a different letter in the middle.

God ended His work on the sixth day and rested the seventh. He didn't end His work on the seventh day.

What have we always had to say of that verse. That means He ended His work just before the seventh day began, which may or may not be exactly true. But if it is, God ended His work on the sixth day; He's following His own laws! **"Six days shall you labor and do all your work."**

So, I thought this was really a very meaningful understanding of what was going on here. God finished His work in the sixth day, #6.

"...His work, which He had made. And He rested... [both cases *in*] ...on the seventh day from all His work, which He had made" (v 2). *That helps clarify a lot!*

One day I was in busy doing some things and all of a sudden the fax went, and here was this page faxed to me from Carl, noting these things. I had the *Interlinear* and hadn't had a chance to get in and study it, yet, and here is a very profound, meaningful understanding concerning that—that should be sixth day when God ended His work.

In other words, God Himself also prepared for the Sabbath. When God created the day and night, He started the cycle. Therefore, when it came to the seventh day, He *made* that day Holy <u>vs</u> *creating* it Holy. God **created** time and the days, and then He **made** the seventh day Holy.

Made is a little less than *created.* Created is bringing it into its initial existence. Then *made* is maybe using the same thing only doing something else with the same thing, which He did here in relationship to a day. Remember, Jesus said, 'The Sabbath was **made** for man.' He did not say *created.* He said 'made.' Because time had already been created, but then God made this section of time Holy, the seventh day.

Well, we'll get into that a little more in part 2, because there is an awful lot here concerning the Sabbath. Then we will get into the relationship between God and man and what God really intended is revealed, and how He created man and woman.

Scriptures from *The Holy Bible in Its Original Order, A Faithful* Version (except where noted)

Scriptural References:

1) John 14:26
2) John 16:13
3) Luke 24:44-45
4) Genesis 1:1
5) John 1:1-3
6) 1 John 1:1-3
7) Hebrews 1:1-6
8) Genesis 1:1-2
9) 1-Corinthians 14:33
10) Isaiah 45:18
11) Jeremiah 4:19-23
12) Revelation 12:9
13) Ezekiel 28:11-12, 2, 12-18
14) Revelation 12:9, 1-4
15) Luke 10:17-18
16) Revelation 12:4
17) Jude 6
18) 2 Corinthians 4:3-4
19) Isaiah 14:12-15
20) Genesis 1:2-31
21) Isaiah 40:6-8
22) Genesis 1:31

23) Genesis 2:1-2

Scriptures referenced, not quoted:

- Revelation 1
- Ephesians 2

Also Referenced:

Booklet: *The Grace of God in the Bible* by Fred R. Coulter

Books:
- *Interlinear Hebrew Translation of the Bible in Revise* by George Ricker Barry
- *Light by Light* by John Goodenough

Study Paper:
The Two Jehovahs of the Pentateuch by Carl Franklin

FRC:bo
Transcribed: 12-24-06
Reformatted: 10/2020

CHAPTER TWO

The Background in Genesis II
Creation of Man & the Sabbath—Genesis 2
Fred R. Coulter

Today we're going to study two very important things right in the first part of the book of Genesis. We reviewed the creation in part 1. In this one we're going to study more in detail the creation of man and the Sabbath.

I'm going to read some of the things from the *Interlinear Hebrew-English Old Testament* by George Ricker Berry. He only did Genesis and Exodus, and I'm very sorry that that's all that he did, because he does a very good job in translating.

We're going to cover some very important things and first of all I want to concentrate on creation of Adam and Eve, because I think we're going to find this very important; because the detailed instructions of Adam and Eve and their creation have to do with the finishing of the work on the sixth day. I just want to cover this thing concerning the Sabbath and the sixth and seventh day once again.

Genesis 1:31 (*Int*): "And evening was and morning was a day sixth."

As you saw in the Hebrew last time, the difference between six and seven is one little letter inserted between two of the other letters.

Genesis 2:1 (*Int*): "And were finished the heavens and the earth and their all their hosts. And finished God in the **day sixth** his work which he had made… [it should be the **sixth** day, not the **seventh**; there's a little footnote there to verify that] …and, he **rested in** the day seventh from all his work which he had made. And blessed God the day seventh and sanctified it; because **in it** he rested…" (vs 1-2).

We're going to learn an awful lot concerning *rest*. Sabbath means *rest*.

Verse 7 (*Int*): "Then formed Jehovah God, *out of* dust from the ground, and breathed in his… [the man] …nostrils breath of life…"

We need to understand that everything else that God created, He **commanded** it and it was so. Let's look at some Scriptures that will verify that, Psa. 148 shows that God **commanded** and everything came into existence.

Psalm 148:1: "O praise the LORD! Praise the LORD from the heavens; praise Him in the heights. Praise Him, all His angels; praise Him, all His hosts. Praise Him, sun and moon; praise Him, all you stars of light. Praise Him, you heavens of heavens, and waters that are above the heavens. Let them praise the name of the LORD, for He commanded and they were created" (vs 1-5).

He brought them into existence by the Word of His power. He intended for those to tell us a story. He intended the creation of the heavens to be a *witness* of His power and His glory, and to be perpetually that which all human beings could see *so that they would understand that something greater than themselves had to create that!*

Psalm 19:1: "The heavens declare the glory of God, and the firmament proclaims His handiwork. Day after day they pour forth speech …" (vs 1-2).

There are noises, sounds that come out of the heavens. Don't they have these big gigantic tracking machines and radio radar devices, huge great disks to try and pick up a message from outer space? Maybe they're trying to communicate to us is the reasoning behind it.

"…and night after night they reveal knowledge. There is no speech nor language where their voice is not heard" (vs 2-3).

In other words, the things that God has created and **commanded** into being are there in such a dynamic way that every people, every language, every generation has **learned** from it.

It's also very interesting to know that if you read the account of *Josephus* and Abraham, you find out that Abraham was a mathematician. Abraham was the one who brought mathematics to Egyptians. So, Abraham was no mean, grunting barbarian stumbling over the stones of the Near East. He understood these things. Of course, this also has to do with the ultimate concerning our salvation.

Verse 4: "Their line has gone out through all the earth and their words to the ends of the world. In them He has set a tabernacle for the sun."

Showing that the greater universe is out beyond what the tabernacle for the sun is. You could say the tabernacle for the sun is our solar system. It's very interesting: when you view how the different solar systems or stars in the universe are. They are shaped like discs, or as some people would say: flying saucers. I'm not going to get into a discussion of flying saucers, but I do believe there are phenomena, which are accountable for that.

Verse 5: "Which is as a bridegroom coming out of his chamber, and rejoices as a strong man *set* to run a race." *In other words, always cheerful, uplifting and inexhaustible source of energy!*

Verse 6: "Its going forth is from one end of heaven, and its circuit is to the other end…. [they knew that things were in a circuit, wasn't flat] …And there is nothing hidden from its heat." *Then it reflects back to the Law of God beginning in v 7.*

Now we'll understand even more concerning the creation of God and how it was that He made these things, and why the forming of man, by God Himself, becomes a *very important* and *deep* thing for us to understand.

Psalm 33:1: "Rejoice in the LORD, O you righteous ones; praise is becoming for the upright. Praise the LORD with lyre; sing unto Him with a harp of ten strings" (vs 1-2).

That's why on the Sabbath it is good—when we can—to sing. That's why, in the New Testament it talks about singing with 'psalms in your heart.' It's very important, and especially on the Sabbath, because as we will see, the Sabbath becomes a very important day and *link* to the creation of man.

Verse 3: "Sing unto Him a new song; play skillfully with shouts of joy, for the Word of the LORD is upright; and all His works are *done* in faithfulness…. [nothing wrong with what God has done and created] …He loves righteousness and justice; the earth is full of the loving kindness of the LORD. By the Word of the LORD were the heavens made, and all the host of them by the breath of His mouth" (vs 3–6).

God *commanded*, they came into existence. That's why the Word of God is so powerful and so important. If God says something once, that's quite sufficient for all eternity.

- Is not God eternal? *Yes!*
- Is not His Word forever? *Yes!*

Let's see the Word of God, and what that is to do for us once we understand the great and tremendous creation of God. That is to help us understand that:

- God is Lawgiver
- God does things in order
- God does things in organization

God has made everything for a purpose for its own part in God's plan that He has done!

Psalm 19:7: "The Law of the LORD is perfect… [nothing wrong with it] …restoring the soul…" *This is the first step that leads you to conversion!*

When you understand that the Law of God is **perfect** then it becomes a standard to which you see you need to measure up to.

"…the testimony of the LORD is sure, making wise the simple. The precepts of the LORD are right, rejoicing the heart; the commandments of the LORD are pure, enlightening the eyes" (vs 7-8)—*giving us understanding and wisdom!* God made us in such a way that we are to have:

- understanding
- wisdom
- judgment
- righteousness
- goodness

Verse 9: "The fear of the LORD is clean, enduring forever; the judgments of the LORD are true and righteous altogether, more to be desired than gold, yea, much fine gold; sweeter also than honey and the honeycomb. Moreover, by them Your servant is warned…" (vs 9-11). *Keeps you out of trouble!* That's why the commandments are: *you shall **not**.*

Why did God give the commandments? There is a positive commandment with parents: *'honor your father and your mother, that your days may be long on the earth.'* Then the next one is, 'you shall not murder.' *That is the extreme!* You cross that line and you have sinned. Within it there are a lot of choices that you can make: 'you shall not commit adultery.' They are all **negative** commands, because negative commands are the very best when you are given **a choice** *so that you determine your choices!*

When it says you shall not commit adultery, the positive is that you will always be faithful to your wife; that is if you're married. ***They're good! They're right!***

"…in keeping them there is great reward. Who can understand his errors?…." (vs 11-12).

No one can, *because every way of a man is right in his own eyes,* so he needs God's Word to give him the understanding of his errors. I do; you do.

"…Oh, cleanse me from *my* **secret** faults" (v 12). *This is really a New Testament doctrine!* In other words, ***my thoughts of sin that are in my own*** *mind!*

Verse 13: "And keep back Your servant also from presumptuous sins; do not let them rule over me; then I shall be blameless, and I shall be innocent of great transgression. Let the words of my mouth and the meditation of my heart be acceptable in Your sight, O LORD, my Rock and my Redeemer" (vs 12–14).

All of these things have to do with the tremendous creation and showing us that now *man is different!* God can command every one of these things. But he made man differently.

God did something that He did not do with any of the rest of the creation. He did several things here. Of all the rest of the creation, God commanded and it was so. Then God said to them, 'Be fruitful and multiply and replenish the earth, and it was so.'

With man we have something that is quite *different.* None of the other creations of God were made like humankind. That's something very important for us to realize. This is a great death-knell for evolution, because the creation of man is very special in every way: *well thought out, well planned and formed by the hand of God!*

Genesis 1:26: "And God said, 'Let Us make man in Our image, after Our likeness…'" God is saying here that He is giving human beings **Godlike** characteristics.

Now then, **all of the others** that God created said, 'after their kind.' Obviously, we are after the human kind and we pro-generate our own kind, but also **being made in the image of God is first fundamental step of being in the God Family!** That's why we're made in the image of God. None of the other creatures…. Look at apes, chimpanzees and gorillas and you can see some humanlike characteristics in them. But I'm sure God made them that way for us to realize that even though you can have humanlike characteristics—in hands and some facial features—unless you're made in the image of God you're still a beast, *rather than we evolved from this thing!* We have to understand that **we're made in the image and the likeness of God!** Then He gave:

"…dominion over the fish of the sea and over the fowl of heaven and over the livestock and over all the earth and over every creeping thing that crawls upon the earth" (v 26). *We're going to look at the continuing account of the details of the creation of man!*

Verse 27: "And God created man…" *God personally formed!*

This, I am sure, is telling us that God wants to have a personal relationship with this part of His creation in a way that separate and different from all the rest of His creation. That's why He made us in His image and after His likeness. The rest of the Bible then is to tell us that we're going to be after His kind. He did not command the man to live. He could of, because nothing's impossible with God.

Genesis 2:7: "…and breathed into his nostrils breath of life…"

I think this shows that God wants us to have a close, personal, intimate relationship with Him. In other words, I believe—we'll have to draw out of this from what we see—that He breathed into man, what is called *the spirit of man* and He imparted to his mind at the same time a fully functioning language. Man was an intelligent, talking, responding, decision-making being from the instant of his creation, but obviously, had to be taught.

- in order to be taught he had to be *teachable*
- in order to be teachable he had to have a *language*
- in order to have a language, from creation it had to be *put into him*

I believe that that's what God did at this point!

"…and man became a living being" (v 7). **God began to show us a purpose in this creation!**

I believe that the final acts of His creation on the sixth day were the creation of man, and the final act was the creation of woman. ***Then the Sabbath began!*** But let's see the events that happened on the sixth day:

Verse 8: "And the LORD God planted a garden eastward in Eden; and there He put the man whom He had formed…. [He made him with His own hands and *formed* him] …And out of the ground the LORD God caused to grow every tree that is pleasant to the sight and good for food. The Tree of Life also was in the middle of the garden…" (vs 8-9).

Now immediately, God wanted man to know something that's symbolized by the Tree of Life. I am sure there was a literal tree. I am also sure that this Tree of Life symbolized the way that man would go, which then would be God's way, which would lead to eternal life—*or the other tree*:

Verse 9: "…and the Tree of *the* Knowledge of Good and Evil" *Both of them were there in the midst!*

I don't know if they were side-by-side. It could have been that they were side-by-side. We're not told, but it says 'in the midst,' so I would have to take by this account that it was in the middle of the garden.

The rest of it describes where Eden was is really using the names of rivers that were known on the other side of the Flood, and it's very difficult to find out where Eden was, because all of that was destroyed with the Flood. Naming a general area where they thought it was close by *after* the Flood does not give us the direct geographical area. However, it would have to be somewhere, we would assume, in the Middle East. Some people assume that it would be somewhere in what is called the Holy Land today or what we know as Palestine or Israel; however, your division divides on that. That could be, but that's not the purpose of what we're going through here.

Then God did something, and all the way through it shows *responsibility, ability* and *accountability.* Man has *ability;* he is *responsible,* and he is *accountable.*

Verse 15: "And the LORD God took the man and put him into the Garden of Eden to dress it and keep it." *To guard it!*

Not just to keep it, but to guard it, to protect it, to make sure that it was done the way that God would want it done!

Verse 16: "And the LORD God commanded the man, saying…" *Whenever God gives a command, it is a command!*

Psa. 119 is one of my favorite Psalms, and this is the one I always try and use to stop the mouths of the gainsayers. I think this is important:

Psalm 119:127: "Therefore, I love Your commandments above gold—yea, above fine gold. Therefore, **I esteem all Your precepts concerning all things to be right**…" (vs 127-128).

- if God is perfect, *which He is*
- if God is righteous, *which He is*
- if God does things which are correct and beautiful and wonderful, *which He does*
  - ✓ Would not all of His precepts be right concerning everything?
  - ✓ Is any man going to go up and point out to God a sin that He has done? *No, because God does not sin!*

When we come over here concerning the commandments given to Adam and Eve, I think this has a *great weight of importance!* The whole principle of God commanding, the whole principle of God instructing is all found right here in the first part of the book of Genesis, which tells us that *man was responsible, accountable and had ability!* He put them in the garden *to guard it* and *to keep it!*

Genesis 2:16: "And the LORD God commanded the man, saying, 'You may freely eat of every tree in the garden… [anytime you want to eat, go ahead and eat] …but you shall not eat of the Tree of *the* Knowledge of Good and Evil, for in the day that you eat of it **in dying you shall surely die**'" (vs 16-17). *That is the literal meaning!*

It doesn't mean in that very instant, in that day, that you would drop dead the minute you took a bite from it. But it means that *once you transgress and do this, then you are surely going to die,* and that's how it's translated.

They had as the sentence of their transgression, death imparted to their very being. Though they lived many hundreds of years after that, if the account of the time is correct, but they still died! I am sure that implied in that, 'in dying you shall die,' that also implies an aging process from which we all today suffer. So, if you want to blame anyone, you can blame Adam and Eve.

Verse 18: "And the LORD God said, '*It is* not good that the man should be alone… [being a separate being] …I will make a helper compatible for him.'…. [as Adam's counterpart] …And out of the ground the LORD God *had* formed every animal of the field and every fowl of the air, and brought *them* to Adam…" (vs 18-19).

All of the animals that God made, God had them all pass by. So, we have the animals on 'review-march' with Adam who was there.

So, the Lord "…brought *them* to Adam to see what he would call them.…" (v 19). *Adam had a full-functioning language*; he was able to name *all* of the animals.

It would be interesting to know what that was. He wasn't polluted with any kind of wrong thoughts. He was not polluted with wrong notions at all. He was standing right there with God and God said, 'All right, Adam, here comes this animal, what do you think you should call it?' So, he gave a name to it. This shows a great responsibility.

Doesn't this indicate that the language that he had, had words in it that would fit? *Yes!* So, he had a complete language. Adam was made totally complete. There was nothing missing, except his wife. *God intended that!* He caused all of them to pass by to see what he would name them. And the reason for this was, so that Adam would realize of everything else that God had made, there was nothing in that which was wholly compatible *for him*.

After that object lesson, v 20: "And Adam gave names to all the livestock, and to the birds of the air, and to every animal of the field, but there was not found a helper compatible for Adam."

God wanted Adam to understand something very important, too: only God could make for him that which would be right for him.

Verse 21: "And the LORD God caused a deep sleep to fall over Adam, and he slept. And He took one of his ribs, and *afterward* closed up the flesh underneath. Then the LORD God made the rib (which He had taken out of the man) into a woman, and He brought her to the man" (vs 21-22).

This also becomes very important for us to understand. As He made the woman, He also had to breathe into her the breath of life so she could become a living soul. He also had to breathe into her what would be what we would call *the spirit of man* or human beings. He also gave her a fully functioning language; because God did not want to produce an incomplete product and provide for Adam something that was not a counterpart and compatible, and somebody who knew nothing.

- she had intelligence
- she had a mind
- she had ability

The point here that is, I think the most profound thing for us to understand is that *God made both* man and woman, *and breathed into them the breath of life! He desired with this and showing this*—that's why this account is so important—*He wanted to have a personal relationship with them and be their God!*

Verse 23: "And Adam said, 'This *is* now bone of my bones and flesh of my flesh....'" *This shows that God must have sat down and said*:

Now, Adam, since there is nothing here for you in all of the animals, and I didn't create anything for you. I want you to see by looking and naming all the animals that there is nothing for you. So, I'm going to put you asleep and I'm going to take one of your ribs and I'm going to make a woman, a help meet, a counterpart for you.

That's why Adam, when he saw her, said:

"...'This *is* now... [in other words after everything else had been understood] ...bone of my bones and flesh of my flesh. *She* shall be called Woman because *she* was taken out of Man.' For this reason shall a man leave his father and his mother, and shall cleave to his wife, and they shall become one flesh. And they were both naked, the man and his wife, and they were not ashamed" (vs 23-25).

This was before they had sinned. We also know that there is a great lesson for us in this, concerning marriage. What we are dealing with here now is the ideal complete state of the creation of God.

Let me read to you what I have written in the booklet: *The Grace of God in the Bible,* so we can, this will help summarize some of these things:

In order for us to fully understand that the entire Creation 1 was an expression of God's love and grace, we need to examine the Scriptural account of the creation of Adam and Eve. The very words of God reveal His love and grace: "And God said, 'Let Us make man in Our image, after Our likeness; and let them have dominion...'" (Gen. 1:26

Of all the creations of God, only mankind was made in the image and likeness of God. This blessing, which was bounteously bestowed upon mankind, is a profound expression of God's supreme love and grace. To further demonstrate His love, when the Lord God made Adam and Eve, He personally formed them with His very own hands. This act reveals that the Lord God intended from the very beginning to have a personal, intimate relationship with them.

No other creature was formed by the hands of God. All other created things and beings were brought into existence by the word of His command, through the power of His Holy Spirit.

However, in the account of the creation of Adam and Eve, notice what the Scriptures tell us. We just read those: *formed them, breathed into them the breath of life!*

The very act of the Lord God Himself breathing the breath of life into man, reveals the intimate relationship that God desired to have with mankind.

That's why He made the Garden of Eden, He would be there with them. That's a tremendous thing. And this all relates then, when we come to it, to the very first Sabbath.

When God breathed the breath of life into Adam, God also imparted to him a special spiritual essence, called the "spirit in man" (Job 32:8; 33:4; Zech 12:1; I Cor. 2:9-11), giving him the unique ability to think and reason, hence to acquire knowledge and to make decisions based on that knowledge. At the same time, God also implanted into

Adam's mind a fully functioning language in order that he might communicate with his Creator. Furthermore, in order to show the close, personal relationship of love that God intended man and woman to have as husband and wife, 2 The Grace of God He personally formed Eve from one of Adam's ribs….

In the same way that the LORD God had breathed into Adam the breath of life, He also breathed the breath of life into Eve and imparted to her the spirit of man and a fully functioning language.

Of all the living creatures that the LORD God had made, only man and woman were created to give and receive love in a most intimate and personal way. None of the other created beings were made to give and receive sexual love face to face. That blessing was reserved for mankind alone….

This is also to reflect and show the personal relationship that God the Father and Christ have—that is face-to-face, though there is no sexual intimation in that because they are spirit beings. And being face-to-face, this means that God made it so that man and woman would also **grow together** and, as it were, see things God's way: eye-to-eye. So, it's really a very special thing.

That blessing was reserved for mankind alone. Through the process of procreation, all human beings are blessed with the physical, mental, emotional and spiritual ability to give and receive love. Greater still, only mankind was created to have a personal, spiritual, loving relationship with the Creator God. This special blessing of love and grace was not extended to any other fleshly being which the LORD God had made.

Thousands of years later…

I put in here what David said.

Psa. 139 is also one of the Psalms of David; this is quite a very profound Psalm. I think we've covered this a couple of times in the past, but I think it's good for us to review and go over, because this is really very scientific and up-to-date.

Psalm 139:13: "For You have possessed my reins; You have knit me together in my mother's womb."

This shows that even though—whatever the process may be—in creating mankind through pro-

creation (legitimate or illegitimate) *God is the One Who created that being!*

Exactly how everything is done, I would have to surmise that each of us are able to impart *half-life*—father and the mother, the father determining the sex. I also believe that at the instant of conception that a spiritual thing takes place—whether legitimate or illegitimate—to give, because after all, the illegitimate child had no say so, did he, so God is not going to deprive him necessarily just because it was not consecrated in marriage. There are going to be enough problems beyond that. We all understand that, looking out in, in the age today.

I know there will be some people who will say, 'Well, now, legitimate or illegitimate.' You might find that there are some of the people that God has used were illegitimate by birth, that is father and mother were not married.

Still, being 'no respecter of persons,' God gives the individual the *spirit of man* or the, the beginning essence of life. When there is that conception, God caused it to be, whether human beings by determination or by mistake caused it to be. In other words, *God has a hand in every human life!*

Verse 14: "I will praise You, for I am awesomely and wonderfully made; Your works are marvelous and my soul knows it very well. My substance was not hidden from You **when I was made in secret**…" (vs 14-15)

Before an embryo becomes an embryo, which then is the stage before what they call a *fetus*. It is technically called today, unless they've changed the term recently, *substance*.

"…when I was made in secret…"—*and it's still a secret!* No one really knows, do they, even with all the scientific endeavors, how human beings are created in the womb. They've done a lot of scientific investigation. They're able to know and understand more than they ever have, but they still don't know!

I think it's very important for us to understand when we bring up the subject of abortion, we need to understand that a human being is fully formed—or nearly so—in six weeks. Every feature of a human being is there. It's just a matter of growth. The only difference between a newly conceived individual and us is a matter of growth, birth and age. Once there is the conception of a human being, it is what it is from that instant forward, have to be. You did not become yourself sometime after you were conceived. You were yourself from the instant you were conceived and it will be until the instant you die.

Verse 15: "My substance was not hidden from You… [in other words, God can know whatever He needed to] … when I was made in secret and intricately formed in the lowest parts of the earth…. [that's just a symbolic way of talking about *in the womb*] …Your eyes did see my substance, yet being unformed; and in Your book all my members were written, which in continuance were fashioned, when as yet there were none of them" (vs 15-16)— *until it was complete!*

What they're trying to do with the genetic coding of human beings today, and they actually use this terminology, 'the book of your own genetics' is what they're trying to write. We find that here, this is very scientific, and this is very up-to-date in the creation of all human beings.

Verse 17: "How precious also are Your thoughts to me, O God! How great is the sum of them!"

So, David really had an insight to the creation of human beings—his own creation—and the reproduction of human beings.

Psa. 8 gives to us an understanding concerning the reason why human beings were made in the first place, and the reason why we were 'made a little lower' than God, made in His image, having abilities like He has.

Psalm 8:1: "O LORD our Lord, how excellent is Your name in all the earth! You have set Your glory above the heavens! Out of the mouths of babes and sucklings You have ordained strength because of Your adversaries, to silence the enemy and the avenger…. [here's part of it right here, this is what David was alluding to]: …When I consider Your heavens, the work of Your fingers, the moon and the stars which You have ordained, what is man that You are mindful of him, and the son of man that You care for him? **For You have made him a little lower than God** [Elohim] and have crowned him with glory and honor" (vs 1-5).

The word 'angels' (*KJV*) here in the Hebrew is *not angels*. The word for *angels* comes from the Hebrew word 'malak.' This word here, in the Hebrew, is 'Elohim,' translated everywhere else as God, or gods.

"…You made him a little lower than **God**… [which ties right in with the creation of man and woman after the 'image and likeness of God'] …and have crowned him with glory and honor." *Yes!*

One of the most gracious acts, one of the greatest gifts that God gave mankind was the whole world. You talk about an act of grace. A tremendous gift, and God says:

Here it is. Now, all I want you to do is take care of this garden. Then from there you're to overspread the whole earth.

That's tremendous, brethren! That's a wonderful, wonderful thing for us to understand.

Now we've got greedy men in there that buy and sell and parcel it up and fight and war and shoot, and all this sort of thing and try and take the best. Well, God is going to reserve that for the saints when they're resurrected.

Verse 6: "You made him to have dominion over the works of Your hands; You have put all things under his feet… [*everything*] …all sheep and oxen, yea, and the beasts of the field; the birds of heaven, the fish of the sea, and all that pass through the paths of the seas. O LORD, our Lord, how excellent is Your name in all the earth!" (vs 6-9).

David understood that we were **"…made a little lower than God…"** This also helps reveal the purpose that we are to be eventually *in the fullness of the God Family*.

1-John 3 is for us to *understand, realize* and *inspire us!* God did not make us so that He could whip us, beat us and scourge us. When there is sin, sometimes some of those things are necessary. But as we will see, even with *The Grace of God in the Bible,* God didn't bring those things upon people except as a very last resort. Here's the whole purpose: Once we receive the Spirit of God and know the Word of God:

1-John 3:1: "Behold! What *glorious* love the Father has given to us, that we should be called the children of God!…." *This shows us here in the New Testament that we're going to be 'after the kind'—the God kind!*

In order for us to be after *the God kind* we have to be made first in the image and after the likeness of God so that we can learn of God's way and have that become a very part of our being through the power of God's Holy Spirit, so that at the resurrection we can be born **into** the Family of God.

Verse 2: "Beloved, now we are the children of God, and it has not yet been revealed what we shall be; but we know that when He is manifested, we shall be like Him, because we shall see Him exactly as He is." *Remember, human beings started out face-to-face with God!*

They started out in their *'rest.'* We are to enter into the 'rest'; that after we have been all detoured because of the sin, we have to be redeemed, *but God's goal is still the same, that we are going to be in the Kingdom of God and be as*

God is God! That is not a doctrine of Satan. ***That is a doctrine of God!*** However, as we are going to see, Satan counterfeited that doctrine and said, 'I'm a god, you can be like god'; that's is *'like me.'* That is *Satan's* doctrine. ***God's doctrine*** *is that we will be* ***'like Him.'*** This is to inspire us:

Verse 3: "And everyone who has this hope in Him purifies himself, even as He is pure." *That's through the sacrifice of Jesus Christ!*

- to inspire us
- to uplift us
- to just thrill us to the bottom of the souls of our feet

That's a tremendous thing! That's what God wants for ***all*** human beings.

Even though being called and having received the Holy Spirit of God, we are Abraham's seed, where there is:

- neither male nor female
- neither Jew or Greek
- neither free or bond
- neither Scythian or barbarian

that still does not take away from the fact that it's ***our spiritual relationship with God***:

- we are still human beings
- we still have human problems in relationship to the way that God made us and created us
- the order of things as they need to be

1-Corinthians 11:1: "Be imitators of me, exactly as I also *am* of Christ. Now I praise you, brethren, because you have remembered me in all things, and you are keeping the ordinances in the way that I delivered *them* to you. But I want you to understand that the Head of every man is Christ…" (vs 1-3).

When God created man and woman, He also set in order a natural order of things that God intended to be. God always intended that the man always be under God, under Christ. *Meaning that everyone is under the authority of God*, one way or the other. You can't get away from it even if you sin, because 'the wages of sin is death' as Adam and Eve found out.

Verse 3: "But I want you to understand that the Head of every man is Christ, and *the* head of *the* woman *is* the man…"

In the marriage estate nothing can change that. That's just the way it is. It's not a matter of going against God or trying to set down some sort of rule or something that isn't right.

"…and the Head of Christ *is* God" (v 3).

There are a few Proverbs that we need to cover here that I think are important concerning, concerning man and woman, and so forth.

Proverbs 8:35: "For whoever finds me finds life… [the wisdom of God] …and shall obtain favor from the LORD. But he who sins against me wrongs his own soul; all who hate me love death" (vs 35-36).

This is just a general principle applying to all the relationships of men and women. All the relationships in our life and our relationship to God.

Proverbs 9:10 *says in relationship to this*: "The fear of the LORD *is* the beginning of wisdom; and the knowledge of the Holy *is* understanding." *God is the One Who*:

- gives us understanding
- has given us a mind
- has given us a language

so we can understand the ways of God!

Proverbs 18:22: *"Whoever* finds a wife finds a good *thing* and obtains favor from the LORD."

God intended that to be from the very beginning. Husband and wife—man and wife—and that's the way God made it. That's the way that God intended it to be, and so should it be.

Proverbs 19:14: "Houses and riches *are* the inheritance of fathers, and a prudent wife *is* from the LORD." *We saw in the creation that woman was to be a counterpart to man!*

Trust me, there are a lot of instructions in here for men, and God is going to hold men accountable as well women accountable. It is all there. These things are very important for us to realize.

Proverbs 12:4: "A woman of virtue *is* a crown to her husband, but she who causes shame *is* like rottenness in his bones."

Well, you can turn it around the other way, too. When you have a husband who's a rotten fool and a philanderer, and goes around and does the things he shouldn't do, it's misery, wretchedness, pain, suffering, sickness and disease. It's harder on a woman when she suffers those things because she was made to be a counterpart for man and for the man to be 'the head.' That's why a husband and wife relations are most important in the way they need to be.

You can go through the entire Bible and you can see that God never slighted women in the least. As a matter of fact, Jesus Christ did a lot to show, and Luke did more, in showing his relationship in teaching women and things like that than any of the others.

1-Cor. 11—There is just a slight thing that we need to cover today, which is very important, which is not a big problem but it is something that just needs to be covered.

So, today we're going to get into just a little touchy area, because I see it wherever I go and I will have to that many women—and they have it on Star Trek, too--have bald-headed, shaved-headed women. Then there's this Susan Power who encourages every woman to become whatever she can be, separate and apart from a man, whatever that may be!

Let's just understand something here very, very clearly. God says it's not good for a man to be alone, therefore, it's not good for a woman to be alone. Whenever the circumstances are that way, and nothing can be done about it, you don't go out and create another problem by running out and marrying the first one that comes along; because now then you end up with a dual problem. Maybe you weren't made for each other. So, you get a double set of problems. I'm not advocating immediate running out and marriage because you happen to be alone. Please understand that.

But we're living in a time where the Babylonian woman rides supreme. I see it everywhere I go. Sometimes it gets very obnoxious. There's also another thing about men that women also know, that when things get very contentious we're cowards! We run and hide, because we don't like animosity and hatred, and shouting, yelling and screaming anymore than anybody else. Even though I'm sure all of us can do a pretty good job of it if we have to.

Here's a principle that we need to understand, because I think this is a slight problem in the Church, which I'm sure that can be corrected very easily.

1-Corinthians 11:4: "Every man who has *a covering* on *his* head when he is praying or prophesying puts his Head to shame…."

Who's the head of the man? *Christ!* I think it interesting that the orthodox Jews will not pray without hats. They won't go into the synagogues without them.

Verse 5: "But every woman who has *her* head uncovered when she is praying or prophesying puts her head to shame … [the man] …for it is the same as being shaved. For if a woman is not covered, let her be shorn. But if *it be* shameful for a woman to be shorn or shaved, let her be covered"

(vs 5-6). *We're not talking about an outright sin!* **It is something that is a shame!**

Verse 14: "Or does not even nature itself teach you that if a man has long hair, it is a shame to him?"

We used to have that problem more than we do today. I can never figure it out. When I watch some of these singers, like on TNT or something, they've always got to have this long hair hanging down all around, and it just makes you wonder about it. It always looks **bad!** At least it does to me.

It's says, "…it's a shame." That's why, with a Nazarite vow, what happened was this: when the vow was taken, then the man shaved his head and he did not cut it—or do anything to it—until the vow was over and the hair would grow. Now, this was to show the sign of *humility* and *shamefulness.* In other words, in this vow a man was to show that he wanted to yield himself to God and so put himself in this shameful condition.

When we understand that John the Baptist was a Nazarite from the beginning, from his birth, and never cut his hair, never drank wine, never took anything that was made of the grapes, nor any strong drink. He was put into that position **physically** because he was the one who was to announce the coming of Christ. We find that very important.

We're talking about something that is not an absolute sin, but is something that is not necessarily right, and Paul covers it here: *let her be covered!* We'll find out what the covering will be.

Verse 7: "For, on the one hand, a man ought not to cover *his* head, since he is *the* image and glory of God; but, on the other hand, *the* woman is *the* glory of man." *In fact, taken from his rib, made from his very inner most being!*

Verse 8: "For *the* man is not of *the* woman… [that's why the creation was the other way around] …but *the* woman *is* of *the* man. And also, *the* man was not created for the sake of the woman, but *the* woman for the sake of the man" (vs 8-9).

He's saying that we're going all the way back to the proper order of creation, which everything that God has done is right and everything that He's done from the beginning is true and righteous all together.

Verse 10: "For this reason, it is necessary for the woman to have *a sign of being under* authority on *her* head because of the angels"—*which means* **you ought to have a covering and sign that she is under the power of her husband** *because of the angels.*

I think the slight thing that needs to be taken care of—and I've seen this a lot wherever I go, especially in traveling—and I have not mentioned it, even though it may have been brought up to me on several occasions, but here's an appropriate time to handle it and take care of it. I think, just as any of us who want to go ahead and do the things that are pleasing to God, that this should also be taken care of for men and women in the right way.

Verse 11: "Nevertheless… [he goes on to say, this doesn't take away from the fact that] …neither *is the* man separate from *the* woman, nor *the* woman separate from *the* man in *the* Lord. For as the woman *is* of the man, so also the man *is* by the woman…" (vs 11-12). *Of course, even Christ was born of the woman! Yes, of Mary!*

"…but all things *are* of God. You judge for yourselves. Is it becoming for a woman to pray to God uncovered?…. [then he says the other way around]: …Or does not even nature itself teach you that if a man has long hair, it is a shame to him? But if a woman has long hair, it is a glory to her; because the long hair has been given to her instead of a *veil* to cover *her head*" (vs 13–15).

This is not the first age of mankind when they ran around with shorn-haired women—or shaved-headed women. Apparently Paul had that problem back in Corinth. It's not unusual that we would also have—we don't have a great raging problem concerning it—but it's something that each one should address themselves before God in their own way in their own lives. I'm sure that, that since these things are so, the blessings of God will come when this is taken care of in the way that's pleasing to God.

Don't ask me how long is long; don't ask me how short is short. I think it's quite evident. It's one of these things that you make a judgment.

Verse 13: "**You judge for yourselves**…." *So, I'll leave the judgment to you!*

Verse 16: "But if anyone is contentious *over this issue*, we have no such custom, neither *do the* Churches of God"—*that is concerning the subject that he just covered here!*

I think that since we're going back and talking about the creation of man and woman and so forth, then we need to cover this in this particular way.

Now then, so everyone will know that this is not *picking on women* time—hope you all understand that—read all the book of Proverbs, if you want to, men and women take the instruction there because there are a lot of spiritual lessons for us that we can learn. I might mention that that's New Testament doctrine.

Let's look at the situation concerning the Sabbath. Let's go back to Gen. 2 and let's read that again. Then there are some things we need to learn about it. Let's understand that **the very root word for Sabbath is rest!**

Genesis 2:2: "And by *the beginning of* the seventh day God finished His work which He had made. And He rested on the seventh day from all His work, which He had made. And God blessed the seventh day and sanctified…" (vs 2-3).

When God sanctifies something that means it's set-aside for a Holy purpose. So, this is a day which is set aside.

"…because… [the first Sabbath is very important] …on it He rested from all His work which God had created and made" (v 3).

What was the last thing that He made? *Eve!* The next morning, on the Sabbath Day, what do you suppose happened on the Sabbath Day? *If God blessed it and sanctified it,* **He did it for a purpose!**

Let's look at a couple of things showing what the Sabbath Day is for, and then we'll come back and establish that the seventh day we have today is the same seventh day that they had then.

Now then, let's understand just a little bit something concerning the Sabbath. I'm going to read to you just a little bit out of *Grace of God in the Bible* because I think it summarizes it quite well:

> In addition to God's loving and gracious act in creating them in His image, God further expressed His love and goodness by blessing Adam and Eve… (Gen. 1:28).

> To help them maintain this personal state of grace and to ensure that they would always know their Creator and be able to commune with the LORD God Himself, in His personal presence, He specifically created and sanctified the seventh day as a perpetual day for rest and fellowship with Him.

> God specifically created and made the seventh day for mankind. Jesus Christ, Who was the Lord God of Creation, made this fact absolutely clear and declared that He and He alone was Lord of the Sabbath Day—not any other day.

> …He declared, "The Sabbath was made for man [mankind], and not man for the Sabbath; therefore the Son of man is

LORD EVEN OF THE SABBATH" (Mark 2:27-28).

Which means that's the New Testament day of worship. We have a more profound way of understanding it today.

When we understand the observance of the first Sabbath in the light of other Scriptures, we can learn a great deal about the grace of God. The Scriptural record in Genesis 3 reveals that Adam and Eve were personally taught by God. They saw God face to face, they talked with God and walked with God—before they had ever sinned. Most certainly God had personally rested and kept the very first Sabbath with Adam and Eve.

Undoubtedly, He fellowshipped with them and instructed them! He would have to tell them about the Tree of Life and what it meant. He would have to tell them **why** He created them. Would not God want them to know that first? *Yes, He would!*

The Scriptural record in Genesis 3 reveals that Adam and Eve were personally taught by God. They saw God face to face, they talked with God and walked with God— before they had ever sinned. Most certainly God had personally rested and kept the very first Sabbath with Adam and Eve. They kept this first Sabbath with God in a perfect state of grace in His presence. There can be no doubt that God had instructed them on that first Sabbath. What a marvelous day that very first Sabbath must have been! There could be no greater grace than being in the presence of and being taught by the LORD God Himself—their very Creator!

Let's go to the book of Isaiah and let's put a couple of Scriptures together to show the whole meaning and the intent of the Sabbath. This is a key thing for us on how to keep the Sabbath and why we keep it the way we do.

Isa. 58—Do you think that God, being the 'same yesterday, today and forever,' would have instructed Adam and Eve any differently than this? Some people say because it's not told that Adam and Eve fellowshipped with Him and kept that first Sabbath, therefore, there's no indication that they kept it. *I say that is reasoning from your carnal mind to destroy the Sabbath!* Here is what God says concerning the Sabbath thousands of years later—so, would this not also the instruction that He would give back then?

Isaiah 58:13: "**If** you turn your foot away from the Sabbath, *from* doing your own desires on My Holy Day…"

When was it Holy? *When God sanctified it and blessed it!* That's when it was Holy! It's God's Holy Day from the beginning. Does God run down here and destroy every person who's breaking the Sabbath? *No, He does not!* He let's them go their own way, and they are missing a tremendous blessing of God.

Let's notice we're **not** to do 'our own pleasure.' That doesn't mean that we don't do things that are not pleasurable—it's a pleasure to eat; it's a pleasure to fellowship. But, why should this day be the way it is? Let's think about the first Sabbath. What do you suppose that God told them?

I'm your Creator. I'm your Maker. This is a special day of a memorial of My Creation. This is a day in which we are going to come together **every week** and I'm going to teach you what you need to know. We're going to have a personal relationship. I'm your Creator and you have a great and fantastic opportunity as the very first human beings.

Don't you think that God told them what was, what was going to be if they would obey Him? *Yes!*

"…*from* doing your own desires on My Holy Day, and call the Sabbath a delight…" (v 13)—*and what a delight that must have been, the first one.*

No sin, no hostility, no animosity, no television, no radio, no driving a long way to come to Sabbath services, no worrying about anything. God provided it all; I just wonder if God did not provide the food for the Sabbath for that very first Sabbath Day. They had it all right there, didn't they? *Yes, they did!* Now, it would not be a sin on the Sabbath while you're sitting there with God and maybe God reached up and plucked some food for them to eat; I don't know, very possible.

"…the Holy of the LORD… [belongs to Him] …honorable; and shall honor Him, not doing your own ways, nor pursuing your own desires, nor speaking *your own* words…" (v 13). **What does this mean?** *This means we're to:*

- know the words of God
- speak the words of God
- study the words of God

That's why today, in Sabbath services, it's important that we study the words of God, *because these are not our words! God inspired them; this is instruction for us!*

It's the same way with our fellowship, too. It should be centered on those things in our lives that have to do with serving and loving God. Too many times, in the recent past, and I'm sure this is something that all human beings cycle through, that the Sabbath became more their own day, and their own day of doing what they were going to do for their own social things.

When you do this, notice it is *IF*, which means that if you don't do v 13—the *IF—THEN* you'll never understand v 14, because 'great understanding have they *who do His commandments.*'

Verse 14: "**Then** you shall delight yourself in the LORD…

Now, you go back and think of all the Sabbaths that you have kept that turned out to be kind of a dud. What happened? You didn't do v 13, did you? *No, you did your own thing!*

I found this, I'll confess, it's no work to sit in front of a TV. So therefore, you can sit in front of a TV and kind of justify yourself, 'Well, this is really not working.' But is the TV from God? Did God send it into the tube for you to watch? *No!*

I found that when I have done that, when I shouldn't have done it, my Sabbath turned out to be a dud! You can draw the parallel, not just TV, but whatever it may be. I've also found this: Someone talked me into having a wedding on the Sabbath; it was just to be a simple affair. It became very complicated and the Sabbath was a dud. Why? *Because we were not doing what God wanted us to do!*

When we do that; when we do all of v 13: "**If** you turn your foot away from the Sabbath, *from* doing your own desires on My Holy Day, and call the Sabbath a delight, the Holy of the LORD, honorable; and shall honor Him, not doing your own ways, nor pursuing your own desires, nor speaking *your own* words, **then**…" (vs 13-14).

They had all of that with the first Sabbath. Absolutely did! Plus being in the very presence of God. Today we have the blessing of fellowshipping with God *spiritually*. Then they had it face-to-face.

Verse 14: "**Then** you shall delight yourself in the LORD; and I will cause you to ride upon the high places of the earth…" (v 14). *This is going clear into the spiritual salvation that God is going to give us!*

So, understanding God and His way, and the purpose of being created are intrinsically tied to the Sabbath. *Intrinsically tied!* The Sabbath is to be *every week* when we draw close to God:

- to *know* of His way

- to *study* His Word
- to *pray* to God
- to *fellowship* with Him
- to *fellowship* with each other

Since this is true, going all the way back, it had to be true of that very first Sabbath.

Let's understand a principle that we find in Exo. 5, which follows all the way through. Whenever you truly begin to enter into a relationship with God—or God begins dealing with you—then the Sabbath question always comes up. When Moses first went into Pharaoh:

Exodus 5:1: "And afterward Moses and Aaron went in and told Pharaoh, 'Thus says the LORD God of Israel, "Let My people go that they may hold a Feast to Me in the wilderness."' And Pharaoh said, 'Who *is* the LORD, that I should obey His voice to let Israel go? I do not know the LORD, neither will I let Israel go'" (vs 1-2). *After all, Pharaoh was* **god on earth!**

Verse 3: And they said, 'The God of the Hebrews has met with us. Let us go, we pray you, three days' journey into the desert and sacrifice to the LORD our God, lest He fall upon us with plague or with the sword.' And the king of Egypt said to them, 'Moses and Aaron, why do you keep the people from their work? Get to your burdens!' And Pharaoh said, 'Behold, the people of the land now *are* many, and **you make them rest** from their burdens'" (vs 3-5).

Has to do with the Sabbath, the very first question was *resting*. *You truly, truly cannot understand God, nor fellowship with Him when you're busying doing your own works and your own business!*

A lot of people claim, 'Well, there was not Sabbath-keeping from Genesis all the way here.' We're not going to take the time, we've proven that other places. But you know that Abraham, if he did the things that pleased God, he kept the Sabbath—so did Isaac, so did Jacob. Everyone who comes in contact with God keeps the Sabbath. If they don't, then they're not in contact with the right God or they have the wrong doctrine, one of the two.

We have the renewing of the Sabbath for the children of Israel. Remember they started counting:

- day one—getting the manna
- days two, three, four, five
- day six—double manna

Exodus 16:23: "And he said to them, 'This *is that* which the LORD has said, "Tomorrow is the rest of the Holy Sabbath to the LORD. Bake what you will bake *today*, and boil what you will boil. And that which remains over, lay up for yourselves to be kept until the *next* morning.'" And they laid it up until the *next* morning as Moses said. And it did not stink; neither was there any worm in it" (vs 23-24).

They were all in close quarters. God was right there in the pillar of the cloud by day and the fire by night; therefore, ***they were in the very presence of God!***

Verse 23: "And he said to them, 'This *is that* which the LORD has said, "Tomorrow is the rest of the Holy Sabbath to the LORD…"'"

It's to the Lord all the way through. One of the greatest arguments thrown against the Sabbath is that it was given to the Jews. ***Not so!*** Never says so in the Bible. It is the Sabbath of the Lord!

"…Bake what you will bake *today*…" (v 23).

Verse 26: "Six days you shall gather it, but on the seventh day, the Sabbath, in it there shall be none."

- Did God cease from the work of creating the manna? *Yes!*
- God also rested on the Sabbath and ceased from His work—didn't He? *Yes!*
- What kind of work is God interested in doing on the Sabbath? *Spiritual work!*

That's what He does!

Now let's look at another one to know that they had exactly the right day. The Sabbath was intended to be ***more than*** just a memorial of Creation. But the Creation, and the fact of it, tells us what God is meaning in relationship to the day.

Exodus 31:13: "Speak also to the children of Israel, saying, 'Truly you shall keep My **Sabbaths**… [plural; it's not an option whether we decide to or not] …for it *is* a sign between Me and you throughout your generations to know that I *am* the LORD Who sanctifies you.'"

You cannot know the Lord unless you keep His Sabbath Day! That's very simple! With it we are sanctified.

Verse 14: "You shall keep the Sabbath therefore, for it *is* Holy to you. Everyone that defiles it shall surely be put to death, for whoever does *any* work on it, that soul shall be cut off from among his people. Six days may work be done, but on the seventh day *is* the **Sabbath of rest**…" (vs 14-15). *Here 'sabbath' and 'rest' are almost identical words!*

"…Holy to the LORD. Whoever does *any* work on the Sabbath Day, he shall surely be put to death. Therefore, the children of Israel shall keep the Sabbath, to observe the Sabbath throughout their generations *as* a perpetual covenant" (vs 15-16)— *which, as we have covered before, is always ongoing continuously!*

Verse 17: "It *is* a sign between Me and the children of Israel forever; for in six days the LORD made the heavens and the earth, and on the seventh day He rested, and was refreshed."

This tells us that they had the same exact seventh Sabbath Day as the day that God rested on!

- If God tells us to keep the seventh day Sabbath, would He change the day? *No!*
- Would He hide the knowledge of it if it's required? *No!*
- Who is the one who have put up arguments that it was changed? *Men!*

Nowhere in the Bible has the day ever, *ever,* ***ever*** been changed. The knowledge of why we were created is ***intrinsically linked*** together. That's why it begins with the Sabbath Day. There may be another thing or two that we can learn from this.

Is this where people take it? *Well, they take it because the Jews claim that they are all of Israel* and actually, when you understand how the Jews feel about the Sabbath, they don't feel anybody but Jews only should keep the Sabbath. That's why they're very anxious to get anybody who is not a Jew off from keeping the Sabbath. They ***want*** them keeping Sunday.

Scriptures from *The Holy Bible in Its Original Order, A Faithful* Version (except where noted)

Scriptural References:

1) Genesis 1:31
2) Genesis 2:1-2, 7
3) Psalm 148:1-5
4) Psalm 19:1-6
5) Psalm 33:1-6
6) Psalm 19:7-14
7) Genesis 1:26-27
8) Genesis 2:7-9, 15-16
9) Psalm 119:127-128
10) Genesis 2:16-25
11) Psalm 139:13-17
12) Psalm 8:1-9
13) 1 John 3:1-3
14) 1 Corinthians 11:1-3
15) Proverbs 8:35-36
16) Proverbs 9:10
17) Proverbs 18:22

18) Proverbs 19:14
19) Proverbs 12:4
20) 1 Corinthians 11:4-6, 14, 7-15, 13, 16
21) Genesis 2:2-3
22) Isaiah 58:13-14
23) Exodus 5:1-5
24) Exodus 16:23-24, 26
25) Exodus 31:13-17

Also referenced:

Books:
- *Interlinear Hebrew-English Old Testament* by George Ricker Berry
- *Josephus*

Booklet: *The Grace of God in the Bible* by Fred R. Coulter

FRC:bo
Transcribed: 12-24-06
Reformatted: 10/2020

CHAPTER THREE

The Background in Genesis III
Adam & Eve Sin and the Punishment—Genesis 3, 4 & 6
Fred R. Coulter

Today we're going to finish getting through Gen. 3. I think we learned an awful lot concerning the Sabbath; and by putting it together from the things that we've understood in other parts of the Scriptures, so that we would understand *why* God made the Sabbath. The most important thing concerning the Sabbath being the seventh day is that God *made it for us so that we could be in contact with Him!* Of course, God wants that. God made His creation of, of man and woman so that we would be in contact with Him; so He especially created that day *for the purpose of fellowshipping, of teaching, knowledge and understanding!*

Before we get to Gen. 3, let's understand something: *The Bible does not tell us how long it was from the Creation*—from God's initial instruction to them in the Garden of Eden—*to the time the serpent was let loose.*

Let's use a modern day example, from our own experiences within the Churches of God: How many years was it that people were in the Church of God, studied the Scriptures, got the instructions from God, knew their Bibles, and then kind of let things slack and then in came the serpent? *Almost identical!*

Coming in with another teaching by saying that God is not two, but one or three. What happened? *People fell for it 'hook, line and sinker';* however, not everyone. I would have to conclude that since God wants—before we make a choice—it to be knowledgeable for us that we know what we're doing. That He certainly gave sufficient time—whatever that was—for Adam and Eve to be instructed by God, to live in the Garden of Eden, to know what God wanted, to keep His commandments and so forth, before the serpent was let loose.

I do not believe that it was done the day after they were created or a week or ten days after they were created. I don't know how long, but I'm sure that it was longer than a week or ten days.

- they would know
- they would have knowledgeable choices
- they would understand what they were doing

The reason I say that is because we're going to see the consequences of their sin in relationship to all human beings, and it's past on to all of us. With the stakes so high, and the situation so profound, I think God let them know in a pretty definitive way what His overall plan was, what they should be doing and then He let the serpent come into the garden.

Genesis 3:1: "Now, the serpent was more cunning than any creature of the field, which the LORD God had made. And he said to the woman, '*Is it* true that God has said, "You shall not eat of any tree of the garden"?'"

A direct challenge to what God had said, 'You could eat of every tree of the garden, *except* the Tree of the Knowledge of Good and Evil.' So, the woman always had to correct him! Once you have some knowledge that is true, what is something that you do? *You try and correct the false statement!* In that, you have to be careful because there may be a trap set. In this case, there was a big trap set.

Just refuting something is not necessarily enough. Not only do you have to refute what is said in the way of a false statement, but you also have to obey God and keep those things which are right and correct in addition to it. That's why it says that 'knowledge puffs up, but love edifies,' because you can get all carried away with knowledge.

Verse 2: "And the woman said to the serpent, 'We may freely eat the fruit of the trees of the garden, but of the fruit of the tree which *is* in the middle of the garden, God has *indeed* said, "You shall not eat of it, neither shall you touch it, lest you die"'" (vs 2-3).

This shows subsequent instruction, because when you read Gen. 2 God says you shall not eat of it. It's 'not eat' and 'not touch.' *Here's evidence of some subsequent instruction!* I don't think, as some have concluded, that Eve added her 'bit' to it. I think that God pretty well told them, because once you touch it then you're going to start with lust. I'm sure that's why He said you should not touch it, and I think her statement was true.

"…'You shall not eat of it, neither shall you touch it, lest you die.'…. [that means in dying you shall die] …And the serpent said to the woman, 'In dying, you shall not surely die! For God knows that in the day you eat of it, then your eyes shall be opened, and **you shall be like God**… (vs 3-5).

I think the *King James* says 'as God'—but it is you will be *'like'* God. You will be similar to God in a certain way. You could take that statement just like we do today when you talk to the Russians about democracy. Their version of democracy is far different than ours. So, when we're communicating on a word, the understanding of that word is not the same in both minds. I am sure that they had—at least Eve did—the understanding that she would be *exactly* as God is.

I also believe that God told them that their eventual destiny was to be in the God Family. And I'm sure that He indicated to them that it would take a certain amount of time to do so. Here comes the serpent along and says, 'Well now, you want to be like God now. Don't wait. *Now!'* That's the same philosophy that Satan has with every life. Get to it early. Get to it quick and destroy it now! That's what he did with Adam and Eve here.

Here's how they would be 'like God': obviously, they wouldn't be eternal, because they didn't eat of the Tree of Life. Obviously, they weren't going to improve and be righteous, because every indication is that up to this point, Adam and Eve had a neutral disposition. In order to make the choice they had to have a neutral disposition. They were neither inherently righteous nor were they inherently evil. They had to make the choice! Here's the choice, here's what they would be like.

"…and you shall be like God, **deciding** good and evil" (v 5) It says in the *King James*: "…knowing good and evil."

Knowers (*Interlinear*) here actually means *deciders.* You're going *decide* what is right and what is wrong. In other words, the message is:

- Who is God to tell you what is right?
- Who is God to tell you what is wrong?
- Why don't you *decide* for yourself?

- Does that not sound like a lot of things we've heard today? *Yes!*
- Is that not what is taught in the schools today? *Yes, exactly!*

You will be **deciders** of what is good and what is evil. Well, that makes you very important; that just lifts you up. You can decide. *You can decide for yourself, apart from God,* and this is going to make you **like** God.

It's also interesting that *knowers* or *knowing* is one of the most interesting facets of all the pagan religions: it's **Gnosticism!**

It comes from the Greek word 'gnosis' and that's why the English word *know* for knowledge is 'kn'—it's a carry-over from the Greek with the two consonants there.

We also find that Masonry is a Gnostic religion. What is the symbol of the Masons? They have 33 degrees or steps in which they go with varying degrees of revelation of lies until they get to the top where they are told Lucifer is 'God.' That's why they have to go through all of these degrees, step-by-step. But the symbol of Masonry is a 'G' with a square in a triangle and over the triangle is the *all-seeing eye!*

Get out a dollar bill, and just to let you know that this same system is still going today, you look at the backside of the dollar bill. It says, 'in God we trust.' However, to the left of it is a total rejection of God, which is the pyramid with the *all-seeing eye,* the New World Order is what it means. They've been trying to get the New World Order for a long time. The New World Order began back here with Adam and Eve—when you really understand it—with the deception that Satan brought forth.

There are still Gnostics, and that's the same thing that Satan held out to Adam and Eve, 'You will be *knowers and deciders* of what is right and what is wrong.'

Verse 6: "And when the woman saw that the tree *was* good for food…" *You can't tell **by looking,** that's a very important thing to understand.*

That also applies to clean and unclean meats. You can't tell by looking—some of them you can. I mean, if you look at some of these oysters and clams, you ought to have enough sense to realize that that's not something to eat. You can't tell.

One day I was in <u>The Kings Table</u>. We're going on down through the line, getting the things they we need and we come to this meat that looked like roast turkey. I said, 'Oh, roast turkey!' And said, 'No, roast pork!' Just looking at it you could not tell that is not good for you. *God has to tell us what is right and wrong, especially in those areas that we cannot decide!*

Eve's looking at it didn't prove a thing! Just like buying a used car. You can get one that looks good, that sounds good, because it has 90 weight oil in the crankcase; that runs quiet, because it has a little sawdust in the differential. But you drive it home and it's a pile of junk. *So, not just how it looks!*

"…and that it was pleasing to the eyes, and a tree to be desired to make *one* wise…" (v 6).

This is the proposition that Satan said that *you will be wise!* When you have intellect, when you have a mind that is designed to learn, you want to learn in knowledge; you want to increase in knowledge. That's a whole life-long, driving force that God has put in us, which we need. Here he was appealing to all of those things.

"…she took of its fruit and ate. She also gave to her husband with her, and he ate. And the eyes of both of them were opened, and they knew that they *were* naked…" (vs 6-7).

They saw something they didn't see before. I'm sure they saw themselves being naked because they were brought together as husband and wife and they were naked and not ashamed.

You have something that takes place here that brings about *shame.* That brings about a guilty conscience. What is not said here—and we don't want to speculate too much in what was done here—some people say that Eve had relations with the serpent and from that comes the seed of Cain. *Not so! Not so at all!* But some people like to perpetuate their own hostilities, so they try and do it that way.

Some people also try and indicate that there was perhaps a lot of sexual perversion that went on between Adam and Eve. That is possible! I do not know what it was that the serpent told them, or showed them, but whatever it was, it had to do with their nakedness. They knew that they were naked. That's the first thing that they knew. They did have some understanding!

"…and they sewed fig leaves together and made coverings for themselves" (v 7).

Some say it's the fig tree from which they ate. I don't know. It could be, it could not be. There's one reference to a fig tree back here in the book of Mark. There is a fig tree that Jesus refers to, which definitely has to do with non-productive Satan religion.

Why did Jesus curse the fig tree? Well, let's look at the account here and maybe we can come to understand. First of all, we know that Jesus condemned the Pharisees and Sadducees for following *their father* Satan the devil. So, when He's referring to the fig tree, we are going to see that He is referring to them and this may stretch all the way back to the false knowledge in the Garden of Eden that never produced any spiritual fruit unto salvation.

Mark 11:12: "And in the morning, after they left Bethany, He became hungry. Then, seeing a fig tree afar off that had leaves, He went *to it to see* if He might possibly find something on it. But after coming to it, He found nothing except leaves because it was not yet *the* season for figs" (vs 12-13).

Why did He go to the fig tree and try and find something on it if there were only leaves and it wasn't time for figs? *We're talking about here, in parable,* **the religion of Judaism, which goes right back into satanism,** which goes right back to the Garden of Eden. This tree, this fig tree, as symbolizing Judaism didn't bring forth any fruit. It didn't produce anything of any lasting spiritual value, because it was all steeped in satanism and paganism.

We have the same thing today with Catholicism and with Buddhism. But since Judaism was so close and they were claiming they knew God, but they were rejecting God with all their traditions. This is why I am sure that it was a fig tree. Notice, it wasn't a peach tree or an apricot tree or an apple tree; it was a fig tree.

Verse 14: "And Jesus responded *by* saying to it, 'Let no one eat fruit from you any more forever!' And His disciples heard *it.* Then they came into Jerusalem; and after entering the temple… [this is how we tie it in with Judaism] …Jesus began to cast out those who were buying and selling in the temple; and He overthrew the tables of the money exchangers and the seats of those who were selling doves. Moreover, He did not allow anyone to carry a vessel through the temple. And He taught, saying to them, 'Is it not written, "My house shall be called a house of prayer for all nations"? But you have made it a **den of robbers**'" (vs 14-17)—*a den of iniquity!*

Wherever Satan is, it is a *den of thieves.* Whether it is in a church, a corporation, a government or a family. It makes no difference, wherever Satan is, it's a *den of thieves!*

Verse 18: "Now the chief priests and the scribes heard *this,* and they sought how they might destroy Him; for they feared Him, because all the multitudes marveled at His teaching. And when evening came, He went out of the city. And in the morning, as they passed by, they saw the fig tree dried up from *the* roots…. [right from the very ground up] …Then Peter remembered *and* said to Him, 'Look, Master! The fig tree that You cursed has dried up.'…." (vs 18-21). *This is showing a complete repudiation of Judaism!*

- not the Truth of God
- not the laws of God
- not the commandments of God

but of Judaism, and that they should have faith!

Verse 22: "And Jesus answered and said to them, '**Have faith *from* God**.'"

Then He gave a very important lesson concerning prayer, concerning what we need to ask, how we need to ask and in what attitude:

Verse 23: "For truly I say to you, whoever shall say to this mountain, 'Be taken away and be cast into the sea,' and shall not doubt in his heart, but shall believe that what he said will take place, he shall have whatever he shall say."

We have to temper that and tie that in with other things like: 'keep My commandments and receive the Holy Spirit,' and all of those things have to be tied in with that.

Verse 24: "For this reason I say to you, all *the* things that you ask *when* you are praying, believe that you will receive *them*, and *they* shall be *given* to you. But when you stand praying, if you have anything against anyone, forgive, so that your Father Who *is* in heaven may forgive you your offenses. For if you do not forgive, neither will your Father Who *is* in heaven forgive you your offenses'" (vs 24-26).

The whole lesson here is another one of these things that'll be *a complete divorcement away from Judaism* and into the way that Jesus Christ was teaching. One of the first things you have to have is **faith** and then you live by **prayer.** So, that's why we have that.

It's interesting that the fig tree was cursed and it may go right back to the Garden of Eden showing that what they were doing and what they were following was harkening all the way back to some of the original teachings of Satan the devil. It's interesting that God gives us all the basic knowledge we need to know:

1. how we got here
2. who our first parents were
3. Who God is and the commandments of God
4. how we got evil, and why it is that human beings are *evil*

Could it be:

- that Adam and Eve had previous encounters with Satan?
- *or* the serpent that was there 'softened them up' for this point here?

It's possible! It doesn't tell us, so we can't say dogmatically. But the very fact that she didn't say:

- Who are you?
- What are you doing here?
- How did you get here?

Sort of gives the credence to the question: Could it be that that they knew of the serpent *before* the particular time of the eating of the Tree of the Knowledge of Good and Evil? *It's possible!* We can't rule it out, but we can't dogmatically say 'yea.' But at least it gives us a little more basis of understanding.

Genesis 3:8: "And they heard the sound of the LORD God walking in the garden in the cool of the day…"

This is in the evening or the cool of the day, and it shows that they were right there with God, they had complete access to God all the time.

"…Then Adam and his wife hid themselves from the presence of the LORD God among the trees of the garden…. [there they were right there] …And the LORD God called to Adam and said to him, 'Where *are* you?'" (vs 8-9)

I don't know if there was a designated place that they would meet every day at this particular time, it's very possible. So, God came down and said: 'Where are you?'

Verse 10: "And he said, 'I heard You *walking* in the garden, and I was afraid because I *am* naked, and *so* I hid myself.' And He said, 'Who told you that you *were* naked? Have you eaten of the tree, which I commanded you that you should not eat?' And the man said…" (vs 10-12)

Here's the classical case that always happens. No one likes to take blame for whatever they do. It's interesting, modern psychology is based on that. They are now understanding that people have to be responsible for what they do. But when psychology first started this out and people got the way they were, it was blame father, blame mother, blame school, blame everybody else: 'you poor little thing, you can't help it.' So, that's what Adam did; he said, 'Now look…'

Verse 12: "And the man said: 'The woman whom **You gave** *to be* **with me**… [It's God's fault. It's not 'my fault' it's God's fault.] …she gave me of the tree, and I ate'"—*that let's **me off the hook!** **If it wouldn't have been for the woman, Lord, I wouldn't have eaten, but there it was!***

Verse 13: "And the LORD God said to the woman, 'What *is* this you have done?' And the woman said, 'The serpent deceived me, and I ate.'"

So, everyone is trying to blame everyone else.

Sidebar regarding comment: The reason that I'm using Jehovah is because that's the translation in the *Interlinear* and that is the really the correct pronunciation of the Hebrew word YHVH, which is translated, *Lord*. To read it in the King James would be: 'The Lord God says…'

The *King James* translates YHVH as *Lord,* and when you first have God dealing directly with Adam and Eve it is the One Who **created** them: the Lord God, in this particular case or the One *of Elohim* Who revealed Himself as, as Jehovah, or as some people like to say Yahweh.

That is not in any way indicating that we're switching over and believing in sacred names at all, *we're not*; that is not required at all whatsoever. But, it is still, nevertheless, one of, one of the names of God. So, in reading this, please understand that we're not trying to do that.

Verse 14: "And the LORD God said to the serpent, 'Because you have done this you *are* cursed above all livestock, and above every animal of the field. You shall go upon your belly, and you shall eat dust all the days of your life.'"

When you compare our discussion that we were having before services about how human beings are made to stand upright, fully erect, and walk on two feet, made in the image of God, now here, the adversary of God now is made so he can **never** stand upright.

Did he stand upright at one time? *It's possible, I don't know!* All we know is what we see today in the particular case. But I think that is very profound that the one that symbolizes Satan the devil being the serpent, **cannot stand upright.** It has to go on his belly. I think one of the most gruesome ways of eating is the way that a snake eats. I'm sure you've seen that on some of these Discovery programs showing how serpents eat. The thing whole and is really quite a struggle. What we're finding here is that everything that God said is true.

Verse 15: "And I will put enmity between you and the woman, and between your seed and her Seed; He will bruise your head, and you shall bruise His heel."

That did happen when Jesus was crucified. When they crucified Him and, and put the nails through His feet. It wasn't through the front part of His feet because He would have bones broken. It was prophesied 'no bone would be broken.' So, it went through the Achilles tendon and the heel, so it would go that way, and it did bruise His heel.

Verse 16: "To the woman He said, 'I will greatly increase your sorrow and your conception… [I will greatly multiply your trouble, your sorrow] …in sorrow shall you bring forth children. Your desire shall be toward your husband, and he shall rule over you."

God gave equal punishment to all. God is not picking on women here, please understand that. Man had his sorrow increased, and his work increased just as well. Let's see what happened here:

Verse 17: "And to Adam He said, 'Because you have hearkened to the voice of your wife and have eaten of the tree—of which I commanded you, saying, "You shall not eat *of* it!"—the ground *is* cursed for your sake… [everything that he would set his hand to do he had obstacles to overcome and problems to overcome] …In sorrow shall you eat of it all the days of your life. It shall also bring forth thorns and thistles to you, and *thus* you shall eat the herbs of the field; in the sweat of your face… (vs 17-19)—*nostrils, which is a literal translation!*

I think showing that he's going to have to not, not just the sweat of your brow, but it's going to be a breathing, difficult, very exasperating kind of existence.

"…you shall eat bread until you return to the ground, for out of it you were taken; for dust you *are*, and to dust you shall return" (v 19).

That was the punishment that was given out to all of them. Let's, first of all, understand that there is a parallel for us to learn which is drawn on continually. Let's see **the result** of what happened as is in relationship to Eve and then into Adam.

There is a lesson for us here continually concerning the Word of God, continually concerning how Satan is going to be out there to try and turn God's way upside down and to interfere in our lives. I think living in the end-time we're going to experience a lot of that. We're going to see a lot of it. We're going to see a lot of obstacles brought up against us.

2-Corinthians 11:2: "For I am jealous over you with *the* jealousy of God because I have espoused you to one husband, so that I may present *you as* a chaste virgin to Christ. But I fear, lest by any means, as the serpent deceived Eve by his craftiness… [clever arguments, sounding good, having logic] …**so your minds might be corrupted from *the* simplicity that *is* in Christ**" (vs 2-3).

That's exactly what's been happening today—coming along with philosophical and theological arguments that just **boggle** the mind. They're just so **mind-twisting** that it's difficult to

31

even read it.

I know, I've been studying quite a bit of it now so I can *really understand* how much of the New Testament has been written to combat all of this satanic philosophy, and it's amazing how much is there to combat everything that Satan has done.

Verse 4: "For indeed, if someone comes preaching another Jesus, whom we did not preach, or you receive a different spirit, which you did not receive, or a different gospel, which you did not accept, you put up with it as *something* good."

It says, 'you're putting up with it, you're allowing this to happen.' That's why he said that you need to be careful that you don't be deceived.

1-Tim. 2—here's a section of Scripture that has been used against women in ways that are not exactly correct. But as we've pointed out before, we're still male and female and God expects us to be, to live our lives in a way that He, He wants them to be lived.

1-Timothy 2:9: "In like manner also, *let* the women adorn themselves with clothing that shows modesty and discretion, not with *elaborate* braidings *of the hair*, or *with* gold, or pearls, or expensive apparel"—*overly done!*

I don't know of any women that I've seen in church at all who was doing that, so don't take this as a personal thing.

Verse 10: "But *with that* which *is* fitting for women who profess *to have* reverence for God—with good works. Let a woman learn in quietness *and be* submissive in every respect" (10-11).

It doesn't mean you are to be still and to not ask questions or anything like that.

Verse 12: "For I do not permit a woman to teach, nor to exercise authority over man, but to be in quietness"—*teaching in church!*

That doesn't mean that a woman cannot teach. We have the example of Aquila and Priscilla; they taught Apollos, but they were not teaching him in the church.

Verse 13: "For Adam was formed first, then Eve. And Adam was not deceived; but the woman came to be in transgression by being deceived" (vs 13-14).

We're going to see that this doesn't mean that Adam didn't sin. A lot of people read this and think, well, it's just the woman, and then they get the hard-heel and put down women all the time. No, we're going to see, Adam not being deceived, *knew* what he was doing so therefore *his sin* was worse than Eve's.

Verse 15: "But she shall be saved through the childbearing, if they continue in faith and love and sanctification with self-control."

Now let's look at the effect concerning Adam. What happened here to all mankind. Rom. 5, in this particular case, is a somewhat difficult section to understand, but let's see if we can untangle it here at this particular point. Adam *did sin!* We're going to see it here, very clearly. His sin had a great affect on all humankind.

Romans 5:12: "Therefore, as **by one man** sin entered into the world…"—*didn't say 'woman.'*

Does that mean that Adam probably could have stopped the whole thing even though Eve may have eaten of it? If he would have kept God's way and not eaten of it? *I don't know, it's possible!* I do not know, that's an open question. That's one of those we'll have to wait for the resurrection to get the answer on, because it doesn't tell us directly.

We're going to deal in a little scenario now, so we'll have a little speculation: What if Adam would have eaten first, instead of Eve? *I don't know, doesn't tell us!* He ate second; he knew better, he was not deceived. When you're deceived, you don't know better; you're deceived. *He wasn't.* He knew what he was doing. I'm sure he knew the consequences that was going to happen to the whole human race.

Rom. 5 shows us something very important that what happened. This helps give us *an understanding* as to what happened to human nature and *why the world is so evil!* Though everyone is trying to do good in their own way, except those who are totally dedicated to evil.

Verse 12: "Therefore, as by one man sin entered into the world… [and the 'world' here being the human realm] …and by means of sin *came* death; and in this way, **death passed into all mankind**…"

We're as good as dead from the instant of conception, just a matter of time. Some live longer, some shorter.

"…*and it is* for this reason that **all have sinned**" (v 12).

With the passing of death inherent within their genes, sin also was passed to all human beings, that we have a sinful nature, no longer neutral, as they were originally created. Now there was a sinful nature, and this is the reason why *all* men have sinned.

Verse 13: "For before *the* Law, sin was in *the* world. However, sin is not imputed when law does not exist."

What he's saying is—in kind of double twist on the words here is—before the Covenant given to Israel, there was Law in the world, that's why there was sin; *because 'sin is the transgression of the Law'!*

Verse 14: "Nevertheless, death reigned from Adam until Moses, even upon those who had not sinned in the likeness of the transgression of Adam… [a *profound* sin; a *knowledgeable* sin] …who was a type of the *One* Who was to come."

Now we're going to look at a couple of things in 1-Cor. 15 concerning Adam and concerning Christ. We know that Paul tells us that *all of us* have 'the law of sin and death' within us. That's reflected in the carnal nature that when you want to do good you can't.

No one has been able to beat this, yet. If you want to know the Truth of God's Word, all have died. *That verifies the Truth of God's Word!* No one has been able to overcome it. Everyone has tried to prolong life as long as they can. But the aging process is a very part of our being.

1-Corinthians 15:22: "For as in Adam **all die**… [they all die because of the sin of Adam; death was passed on, sinful nature was passed on] …so also **in Christ** shall all be made alive."

Let's get the comparison in v 45: "Accordingly, it is written, 'The first man, Adam, became a living soul; the last Adam *became* an ever-living Spirit.'"

That's what led to the question: What would the world have been like if Adam and Eve had not sinned?

{Note message: *What Would the World Be Like if Adam & Eve Had not Sinned*}

There is a comparison here! So we will have to say that *if* Adam and Eve had not sinned, **then** Adam would have been the first man changed from flesh to spirit and we would all go through Adam. But now, because they sinned, we all go through Christ.

It's not like the Mormons, they come along and say that Adam and Eve had to sin so that all of these spirits up in heaven could be sent down and be put into human bodies, because they need a human body. Well, that is just demonism, just another version of Hinduism in the guise of a 'Christian-sounding religion.'

So, because of that sin, we have all sinned and we come up with this human nature!

Let's see another verification of this, and this is something that the world cannot figure out. *Why* is it that all human beings *tend* to do evil *in varying degrees, one way or the other*? Mark 7:21 shows that it's *from within, inside!* Therefore, we have no one to blame but ourselves.

Mark 7:21: "For from within, out of the hearts of men, go forth evil thoughts…" *This lists out the sins as they come along in the experience of a lifetime*:

"…adulteries, fornications, murders, thefts, covetousness, wickednesses, guile, licentiousness, an evil eye, blasphemy, pride, foolishness; all these evils go forth **from within, and *these* defile a man**" (vs 21-23).

That kind of nature was put *into* us, *passed on* to us by inheritance from Adam and Eve down to this day. *Only God* can change it! *Only Christ* can remove it! It's the *only way*. Can't be done any other way.

With a life like that, here let's go look at one of the most righteous kings that we have. Let's look and see what, what David said of his own conception. We saw before what he said of it: *how wonderfully and awesomely he was made*. We have the other side of it. Now we have what happens *when you are sinning* and you are confessing your sins and you really understand and realize how in-depth the sin is that human beings have.

There was a murderer down in San Jose`. Something worked out that they could not convict him, so he was set loose. He says, 'You got to kill me.' *No, there's nothing we can do legally.* He says, 'I'm unreformable.' At least he was honest. He said, 'I think of murder and mayhem all the time. If you don't lock me up and do something with me and take me out of my misery, I know I'm going to do it again.' *That was really something!*

True confession, that a man would really admit that. Of course, these so-called 'serial killers'—that they just kill one person after another—they are the same way. They get so obsessed with the evil and so compulsive with it that every thought is to execute this evil. Every thought is to carry out this evil.

When David was repenting, here's what he said, Psalm 51:1: "Have mercy upon me, O God, according to Your loving kindness; according to the greatness of Your compassion, blot out my transgressions."

- What did he have in mind?
- What was it he did? *Adultery and murder!*

Listed in the same order right there as in Mark 7! He schemed and he planned and he plotted and all this sort of thing.

Verse 2: "Wash me thoroughly from my iniquity, and cleanse me from my sin, for I acknowledge my transgressions, and my sin is ever before me…. [when God *convicts* you of your sin it is ever before you] …Against You, You only, have I sinned, and done evil in Your sight, that You might be justified when You speak and be in the right when You judge. Behold, I was brought forth in iniquity, and **in sin** did my mother conceive me" (vs 2-5).

That doesn't mean it was a sinful, illegitimate birth, it means 'just *from the very conception* of my being *sin* was within me.'

That's why the sweetest, nicest children—you often wonder, I wonder what Stalin was like when he was a little baby? Wonder what Hitler was like when he was a little baby? Wonder what Cleopatra was like when she was a little baby? And on and on! All little babies are sweet and lovely, but they have inherent *the law of sin and death* in them. The more they are exposed to an evil world and Satan, the more in degree that this evil becomes more profound.

You can even take this human nature and you can raise it in a relatively good environment, with a minimal amount of influence of sin and you can come up with someone who the world would say is a 'upright.' That is, they are not given to too much sin. But nevertheless,

- they will lie
- they will cheat
- they will covet
- they will still want their own way

Even in the very best! That's why *'all have sinned and come short of the glory of God and none can save himself.'*

David understood that it was from within. Now, let's look at a couple of Proverbs concerning that. There are a couple of Proverbs that we have memorized. As a result, *man's way is the way of sin!* The way that seems right.

Proverbs 16:25: "There is a way that seems right to a man, but the end thereof is the way of death." *The wages of sin is death!* Man's way seems good and right, but leads to death.

Proverbs 21:2: **"Every way of a man *is* right in his own eyes…"** *That's how we have the excuse that you try and palm it off on someone else!*

Because of that, you can't come to God on *your terms.* We're going to see that's what Cain was doing. He was going to God on *his* terms. You can never come to God on your terms. Here's why:

Proverbs 15:8: "The sacrifice of the wicked *is an abomination to the LORD*…"

- *IF* you don't repent
- *IF* you don't change
- *IF* you don't have a heart that God can work with

Even whatever you do in the way of sacrifice, not only just animal sacrifice but time, labor, whatever it may be:

"…*is an abomination to the LORD* …" *Who* is the mother of abominations? *Babylon the Great,* mother of harlots and abominations in the earth! All comes from her.

Verse 9: "The way of the wicked is an abomination…" *That's what, as we're going to see, happened to the world before the Flood!*

Verse 10: "There *is* grievous correction for him who **forsakes the way**…"

- Did that not happen to Adam and Eve?
- Was not their correction grievous? *Oh yes, even affects us!*

"…he who hates reproof shall die. The grave and destruction *are* before the LORD—how much more the hearts of the children of men?" (vs 10-11).

God knows the heart. The Bible tells us what our human hearts are like. (Mark 7:21)

Verse 15: "All the days of the afflicted *are* evil…" *That's what it was before the Flood!* It got so bad!

It's just like God is always done. When people come to a certain point that they just turn their backs on God, God says:

Okay, you can have it all. All your own way and I don't have to do anything but just let it run its course.

Then history is written!

Verse 25: "The LORD will destroy the house of the proud, but He maintains the border of the widow. The thoughts of the wicked *are* an abomination to the LORD…" (vs 25-26).

So, we have the *way of evil* is an abomination; and we find all the way through here that these things are called *abominations*. That is amazing!

Verse 27: "He who is greedy for gain troubles his own house…" Didn't that happen to Adam and Eve? They were *greedy of gain! They wanted to be made wise in their own way!* This is something the way that these parallels really follow along.

God had to do something. He withdrew the opportunity of salvation until the Messiah should come. With the exception of those few that He would call.

Genesis 3:19: "…'for dust you *are*, and to dust you shall return.' And Adam called his wife's name Eve because she was the mother of all *the living*. And for Adam and his wife the LORD God made coats of skins and clothed them" (vs 19-21).

That is to clothe their nakedness! Some people say that this was also an offering for a sin sacrifice. *It's possible,* but if you read what a sin sacrifice is, how they handled it, everything had to be burned: the skin, the innards and everything had to be burned. It's possible that it was, but I am not going to completely say that this was an animal sacrifice for sin.

Here's what God had to do, v 22: "And the LORD God said, 'Behold, the man has become like one of Us, **to decide good and evil**…"—which he *can't do, he just thinks he can do!*

God is the One Who decides *what is good,* and God is the One Who decides *what is evil.* But now that mankind had taken it to themselves they were 'like God' in that particular sense, to decided *good* and *evil.*

"…and now, lest he put forth his hand and take also of the Tree of Life, and eat, and live forever—…" (v 22).

God closed off the way to the Tree of Life. And the reason being is, not that He wasn't going to bring salvation at a later date, which He was without a doubt; but *you cannot live forever in a state of sin!*

How would you like to live forever the way you're living now? With the pulls of sin, with the pulls of the flesh, and all this sort of thing forever and ever and ever? Therefore, God cut off the way of the Tree of Life.

Verse 23: "Therefore, the LORD God sent him out from the Garden of Eden to till the ground from which he had been taken. And He drove out the man, and He placed cherubim at the east of the Garden of Eden, and a flaming sword, which turned every way to guard the way to the Tree of Life" (vs 23-24).

It's called *'the way* of the Tree of Life'—symbolizing *a way to live!* I'm sure there was a literal tree. What happened to the Tree of Life? *I don't know!* I do know that after the Flood it was no longer mentioned in the sense that it was here. Could it be that God took the tree back with Him, *I don't know,* at the time of the Flood? *It's possible!*

Could it be that the tree was destroyed? If it's a Tree of Life, can it be destroyed? *I can't answer that either!* We'll have to wait for God to tell us quite a bit. Now then, we start the whole chronicle of human sin! Sin starts in the family.

Genesis 4:1: "And Adam knew Eve his wife… [which means they had sexual relations] …and she conceived…" *It wasn't with the serpent,* trust me and the Word of God!

If Cain was the offspring of the serpent, God would have made it clear. But then you're also violating the Laws of God, which is kind after kind. You cannot have something that would be impossible to take place. So, he was human as human can be and his father was Adam and not the serpent. Here's what she said:

"…and bore Cain, and said, 'I have gotten a man from the Lord'" (v 1). *So, right away she began to think this was **the One** that was prophesied about!* That Cain was **the One Who** was going to then bring the deliverance to them.

Verse 2: "And she bore again, his brother Abel. And Abel was a keeper of sheep, but Cain was a tiller of the ground."

In the account of *Josephus* it shows that the 'process of time' was perhaps as much as 120 years. Those of you who like to do a little mathematics—and I've seen this in some publications—you take 1500 years, which is 1550-plus years from the time of Adam and Eve until the Flood. You start out with two and then you start increasing the population. It's estimated that there could have been as many as a billion and a half people on the earth at the time of the Flood.

When you consider there is a tradition—and I will have to put it that way—that Adam and Eve had 56 children. That would not be hard to believe that they had 56 children. All God gives us is the *loose* linage of the line of Cain; and the *exact* linage of the line coming down to Noah. Nothing else is preserved for us. Everything else of the world before the Flood has been obliterated.

Verse 3: "It came to pass that Cain brought to the LORD an offering of the fruit of the ground."

We know that firstfruits are to be brought. We also know that a tithe of the ground was to be brought. This was an *improper* offering; and I think it's probably true—the tradition that they had—that Cain was forcing the ground and doing things that he shouldn't have been doing.

Verse 4: "And Abel also brought of the firstlings of his flock *and* of the fat of it...."

There are some people who believe that this could have been on a Holy Day—*it's possible!* It doesn't say that it was, doesn't say that it wasn't.

"...And the LORD had regard unto Abel and his offering" (v 4). **Why?** *Because he did it according to the commands of God!* Whenever you do anything according to the commands of God, He will have respect unto you.

Verse 5: "But He did not have regard unto Cain and his offering. And Cain was extremely angry and his countenance fell.... [he got mad at God] ...And the LORD said to Cain, 'Why are you so angry? And why has your countenance fallen? If you do well, shall you not be accepted?....'" (vs 5-7). *All He said was, 'Look, Cain, all you have to do is do what's right. Won't you be accepted?'*

"...But if you do not do well, sin lies at the door...." (v 7). *There's a couple of interesting things here, which may fit into this*:

When they brought their offering, where did they bring it? I'm sure that God was still in the Garden of Eden, so when they came up to the east gate, where the Cherubim were.... What is over the altar of God in the tabernacle and the temple? *The Cherubim!* I think this: when they brought an offering, they came to the entrance—the east entrance of the Garden of Eden, where the Cherubim were—and there was an altar for offerings. That's where they offered it. If they did well, they were accepted of God.

When He says, "...sin lies at the door..." could it be that He is telling Cain that 'Your offering here at the door is sin'? *Could be!*

"...Its desire *is* for you, but you must rule over it" (v 7). *You have to be responsible and control your own self,* so Cain didn't accept that.

Then we have the account here concerning Cain killing his brother. *God knows!* **God knows everything.**

Verse 8: "Cain rose up against Abel his brother, and slew him. And the LORD said unto Cain, Where *is* Abel thy brother? And he said, I know not: *Am* I my brother's keeper?" (v 8-9). *Immediately, right in the family here is the strife going on!*

- When you have children, do you have fights with the kids? *Yes!*
- Is there strife between them? *Yes!*

Nothing new, it started out with the first family. That's part of the sorrows that Eve would go through. More than just the pain of bearing children, but also the turmoil and the sorrow of fighting and arguing and rearing the children.

Verse 10: "And He said, 'What have you done? The voice of your brother's blood cries to Me from the ground. And now you *are* cursed from the earth, which opened its mouth to receive your brother's blood from your hand. When you till the ground, it shall no longer yield its strength to you, and you shall be a wanderer and a fugitive upon the earth'" (vs 10-12). *Then he was cast out!*

Verse 13: "And Cain said to the LORD, 'My punishment *is* greater than I can bear. Behold, You have driven me out from the face of the earth today, and I shall be hidden from Your face....'" (vs 13-14).

*No more access to God, **totally cut off from God!*** Now, no more could he come up to the entrance of Eden and make an offering. ***Totally cut off.***

You have a double removable in this particular case. Adam and Eve were put out of the garden for their sin, which was the first removal. They still had access to God coming to the entrance of Eden on the east side. Now Cain, because of his sin, is removed even further to wander, to travel, to have no roots, to have nothing permanent.

Cain said, "...'And I shall be a fugitive and a wanderer in the earth, and it shall be *that* anyone who finds me shall kill me.' And the LORD said to him, 'Therefore whoever kills Cain, vengeance shall be taken on him sevenfold.' And the LORD set a mark upon Cain so that anyone who found him should not kill him" (vs 14-15).

What was the mark? *I don't know!* There's been a lot of speculation, but I have not found any validation to any of the speculation. I have thought maybe it was an 'X' or a mark or a cross and perhaps that was the origination of the cross, *I do not know!* But whatever it was, I'm sure his children, when they got up on his knees and said, 'Grandpa, what is that?' I'm sure that he told the biggest fib in the world. I'm sure that he said, 'God put this on me to set me apart from *and make me special* above all men.' You can almost hear the story.

Now, the question is, where did Cain get his wife? *Obviously, from one of the daughters of Adam and Eve!* Obviously, it was at that time, because of the inheritance that they had, determined that they could marry their own sisters because they had not had enough intermarriage where then it would create problems genetically. Had to be.

Verse 17: "And Cain knew his wife, and she conceived and bore Enoch…"

The reason I suspect that Cain told all of his descendants that this was a special mark from God—not a sign of a curse—is because you read the names of the linage of those of the line of Cain and they are very similar to the names that you find in the linage from Adam and Seth on down to Noah, very similar.

We won't go through any more in Gen. 4 or 5. Let's come to Gen. 6 and we will end this study here, to see what the earth became like. When you have people having the *law of sin and death* in them and just give them free reign and let them do whatever they're going to do, it's going to be a mixture of good and evil.

Genesis 6:1: "And it came to pass, when men began to multiply…"

You reach a certain point in human reproduction that you're having a multiplying factor. Right now they say there are what, 5.5-billion people on the earth, somewhere close to that. And they say that within 20 years that it will double! Now, they're doing all they can to try and stop this with abortion and so forth, but they reached the same point here:

"…began to multiply on the face of the earth, and when daughters were born to them, *that* the sons of the mighty ones saw the daughters of men, that they *were* beautiful…" (vs 1-2).

These were those who were called 'sons of God.' These are not some special, giant Nephilim, as they are called. This is not some sort of angels intermarrying with human being to produce a super race.

"…and they took wives for themselves from all whom they chose…. [rather than do it the way that God said] …And the LORD said, 'My spirit shall not always strive **with man** in his going astray… [that's how we know those sons of God were men, because he says so] …for he is but flesh… [not an angelic being] …and yet, his days shall be a hundred and twenty years'" (vs 2-3).

God pronounced sentence right then: he's only going to live 120 years longer!

Verse 4: "There were tyrants on the earth in those days…" Do we have giants today? *Yes, we do!* All you have to do is stack up the watusi along side of the Japanese and you'll see that there are giants.

"…and also after that, the sons of God came in to the daughters of men, and they bore *children* to them. They were mighty men who *existed* of old, men of renown" (v 4).

Or men renamed after the term: 'sons of God.' Here they were building up the master race. That's what they were doing, mighty men.

Verse 5: "And the LORD saw that the wickedness of man **was great**… [absolutely incredible] …*was* great on the earth, **and every imagination of the thoughts of his heart *was* only evil continually**." *Now we're reaching the same point again today!*

- How far advanced were they technologically? *We don't know!*
- Could they have been advanced as we are? *Could be, maybe even more!*

We don't know, but the end result of man's way, under Satan's influence, is that "…**his heart *was* only evil continually**."

It was so bad: "…And the LORD repented that He had made man on the earth, and He *was* grieved in His heart. And the LORD said, 'I will destroy man whom I have created from the face of the earth, both man and beast, and the crawling thing, and the fowl of the air; for I repent that I have made them'" (vs 6-7).

- Why would God destroy every living thing? *I do not know!*
- Was it that they were having genetic engineering at that time, on a grander scale than we understand today?
- Why does it say:

Verse 8: "But Noah found grace in the eyes of the LORD. These *are* the generations of Noah. Noah was a righteous man and perfect in his generations…" (vs 8-9)—*or his pedigree or his progeny!*

- Is that telling us that the rest of mankind was *so twisted and defiled?*
- Is that telling us that they were doing things with animals that they should not have been doing?
- Doing things with animals and human beings combined together that they should not have been doing?

I don't know! I think I've mentioned this a time or two, but I'll mention it here since we're covering this very basic fundamental section of the Scriptures.

There is in mythology, the man's torso on a goat's body. This was called one of the gods. Could it be that that actually happened? *I don't know!* But I'll tell you one thing, today they are looking for as many ways as they can to enhance a super race, so that they can do something with the genes to make better athletes, to make stronger men, make smarter men. They have a whole university dedicated to that, many different places, but in particularly, the Rockefeller University in their genetic section there. Very advanced into this.

Could this refer to Noah being the firstborn? *It could but it doesn't say firstborn!* It says he was 'perfect in his generations.' I think that whenever we have something referring to a 'firstborn' it lists them as firstborn. So, it's possible that it could, but it's also possible that in his pedigree or his genetic makeup there was nothing foreign in it. There had to be reason why God had to kill all life. *ALL LIFE! Now that's drastic!* ALL human beings and *ALL* life. We can see the evidence of the Flood everywhere.

Verse 10: "And Noah begat three sons: Shem, Ham, and Japheth. Now, the earth also was **corrupt** before God, and **the earth was filled with violence**…. [everything was corrupted] …And God looked upon the earth, and behold, it was corrupt—**for all flesh had corrupted its way upon the earth**" (vs 10-12).

- What do you mean "…all flesh had corrupted…"?
- Does that mean it was rotting? *No!*

This would have to be that all flesh was all mixed up. I would have to conclude *all mixed up* genetically. It was so bad and the evil was so rife that:

Verse 13: "And God said to Noah, 'The end of **all flesh** has come before Me, for the earth is filled with violence through them. And, behold, I will destroy them *with* the earth.'"

Then He told him to make the ark. And that was some, some big vessel. God is the One Who *sent* the animals to Noah. Apparently God picked out those animals that had a pure strain in their, in their genes, so that on this side of the Flood—which we live on now—things would not be all mixed up and twisted around. But this whole phrase here: 'that *all* flesh' not just human beings. There's a differentiation here.

Verse 5: "And the LORD saw that the wickedness of man *was* great on the earth, and every imagination of the thoughts of his heart *was* only evil continually."

Verse 12: "And God looked upon the earth, and behold, it was corrupt—for **all flesh**… [not just human flesh] …corrupted its way upon the earth. And God said to Noah, 'The end of **all flesh** has come before Me, for **the earth is filled with violence** through them. And, behold, I will destroy them *with* the earth'" (vs 12-13).

There's also a prophecy that in our time that it's going to get very similar to it. Yet, at the same time, when all of this evil is going on, as it was back then, we saw that "all flesh had corrupted its way and "…**the earth was filled with violence.**"

Matthew 24:37: "Now, as *it was in* the days of Noah, so shall *it* also be *at* the coming of the Son of man. For as in the days that *were* before the Flood, they were eating and drinking, marrying and giving in marriage, until the day that Noah entered the ark" (vs 37-38).

In spite of all the violence, in spite of all the corruption, there were the normal functions going on which human beings were doing. To them, they had been so accustomed to their way of life, *so accustomed to the evil* that was on every side about them, that they just took everything for granted. *They didn't have a clue until the Flood came!*

Comment was made that the scientists are doing what they can to try and alter the genetic substance of certain of the monkey family and, in particularly, pigs, to try and have replaceable livers and hearts from pigs and other animals. That's something!

Which reminds me, the greatest blow to the abortion movement took place this week. Which was, the woman who was Jane Roe in Roe *vs* Wade has changed and repented and is now a pro-lifer. The thing that did it—sometimes the *overwhelmingness of evil* will get to you—and she said that the thing that got to her was when she opened up a freezer at the Planned Parenthood or the abortion clinic that she was working in, and saw a freezer full of fetuses. She said, *'that was it.'*

Even though she's now pro-life she says it's still all right in the first trimester. Well listen, as we have studied in the past, a baby is fully formed—it's just a matter of growth—with just six weeks. So, by time a woman has definite conformation that she is pregnant the new little person is already formed, and it's only an inch long.

Yes, she was baptized by a Baptist preacher, so at least in *the letter of the Law* she's doing something reasonable. But it's interesting, she still hasn't come all the way to abhor all abortion. She's trying to, you know like you do when you repent of your sins to a certain degree, you kind of like to straddle the fence to so you can still justify what you've done in the past, but kind of say you're getting away from it. That's what's she's doing.

I thought that that was profound when she opened up the freezer and it was *full* of fetuses so that the doctors could use them for experiments and all those things that they want to do. They sell them, make money on them.

Yes, the Chinese are going to have population control by having very strict laws—execute people for the smallest little crime so they can kill them and sell their heart, their liver and their eyes, and all that sort of thing.

History repeats itself without a doubt. We don't know how bad it's going to get. We don't know what the technology is going to do. I am sure there are a lot of propagandistic statements put out which are not true. But nevertheless, I think they are endeavoring in trying to do that.

One of the things they want to do is come up with the 'divine' man, one who's going to live forever. One who's going to be smarter than ever before. ***That's Satan's whole goal!***

I think this: I think that when *the beast* comes on the scene it's going to be the result of a tremendous and profound *satanic religious experience*. Which is, for those religions of the world in Masonry and all that sort of thing, they are going to have a 'divine' man. Once they get this 'divine' man then I think they are going to conclude that many more people can now follow in his footsteps ***if they just make an image to the beast.***

I'll let you think on that! We'll end here. We're through with our little study there in Genesis, but I think it's been very good to go back to the very basics and understand that and come forward from there.

Scriptures from *The Holy Bible in Its Original Order, A Faithful* Version (except where noted)

Scriptural References:

1) Genesis 3:1-7
2) Mark 11:12-26
3) Genesis 3:8-19
4) 2 Corinthians 11:2-4
5) 1 Timothy 2:9-15
6) Romans 5:12-14
7) 1 Corinthians 15:22, 45
8) Mark 7:21-23
9) Psalm 51:1-5
10) Proverbs 16:25
11) Proverbs 21:2
12) Proverbs 15:8-11, 15, 25-27
13) Genesis 3:19-24
14) Genesis 4:1-15, 17
15) Genesis 6:1-13, 5, 12-13
16) Matthew 24:37-38

Scripture referenced, not quoted: Mark 7:21

Also referenced:
Books:
- *Interlinear Hebrew-English Old Testament* by George Ricker Berry
- *Josephus*

Message: *What Would the World Be Like if Adam & Eve Had not Sinned}*

FRC:bo
Transcribed: 12-25-06
Reformatted: 10/2020

CHAPTER FOUR

The Sabbath: Sign of God
Fred R. Coulter

If someone asked the question: Give me a sign O God, and how can I find You? *God has already given the sign!* What is that sign?

1-John 5:3: "For this is the love of God: that we keep His commandments, and His commandments are not burdensome." *They are not grievous, not burdensome!* That is an absolutely basic, fundamental thing!

Which commandments do people not like most of all? Let's see something about the carnal mind and we all know this.

There was an article in the paper, quite a long one, about *deception*; how that it's inherent in all human beings and all human beings must be deceptive to survive. Does that sound a little Biblical? *The heart is deceitful above all things and desperately wicked!* That's the best of our heart. Here is why:

Romans 8:7: "Because the carnal mind… [that is the mind devoid of the Spirit of God] …*is* **enmity** against God…" *that's the same word for enemy!*

All you have to do is just substitute the 'i-t' and put an 'e' in there and you have enemy, and it's the same in the Greek.

"…for **it is not subject to the Law of God**; neither indeed can *be*" (v 7).

When you have 'religious' people in the world—I don't care what religion that they are of—let's look at some of those who claim they are Christians. What two commandments do they always disagree with? Actually, there are three, but basically two and the third one is subject to the second one.

- they may be nice people
- they may be kind people
- they may be what the society would say would be model citizens

But what is it that they always don't agree to? *Sabbath! Idols! Commandments 2 & 4!*

What is the third one that is subject to the Sabbath? *The Holy Days!* There are some people who say, 'God, I believe I ought to keep the Sabbath, but not the Holy Days.'

I listened to this message from this Protestant minister who said:

Since Jesus was resurrected on Sunday, and since Pentecost is on Sunday, therefore, I keep Sunday. Case over and done, case closed.

Does he have an open mind? *No!* He also said:

And I don't want to hear any more of this Sabbath bit. Because you are not to go out and just lay around and be lazy and stay in your bed all day Saturday.

Guess what he knows? He knows something, doesn't he? *He knows which day is the seventh day; yes, he does!* Gen. 2 becomes very important and I have never heard this explained this way.

- Who was the Sabbath made for? *It was made for man!*
- Where do you find that Scripture? *Mark 2:27-28!*

This minister quoted Gen. 2 and I have never heard it this way, because he forgot his New Testament, he forgot what Jesus said about the Sabbath; that *He was Lord of the Sabbath!*

Genesis 2:1: "Thus the heavens and the earth were finished, and all the host of them. And by *the beginning of* the seventh day God finished **His** work, which **He** had made. And **He rested** on the seventh day from all His work, which **He** had made. And God blessed the seventh day and sanctified it, because on it **He rested** from all His work, which God had created and made" (vs 1-3). *And this minister said*:

Therefore, the Sabbath was made for God!

Of all of the years I've been in the Church and all of the Sabbath arguments I've heard—and not to make fun of anyone who has false teeth because you need them—if I had false teeth they would have fallen right out of my head. That's how shocking it was to me. Can you believe that? *'It was only made for God!'*

- Why are we to remember the Sabbath? *To keep it Holy!*
- Why? *He set it apart right here!*
- Why? *Because God is Holy!*

The Catholics later on, as you find in a book by Samuele Bacchiocchi—*Anti-Judaism and the Origin of Sunday*—concerning the enmity between Christians and Jews when Sunday worship was coming into the early Church. I want you to understand that when John was writing the Epistle of First John, what was starting to come into vogue? *Sunday worship!*

God gave them the Sabbath! In the book *Anti-Judaism and the Origin of Sunday* by Samuele Bacchiocchi, those who were the initiators of Sunday-keeping that later became the Catholic Church said that *'God cursed the Jews with the Sabbath to set them aside for punishment.'* Isn't that something? ***God doesn't say anything about that in Exo. 20!*** He says:

Exodus 20:8: "**Remember the Sabbath Day to keep it Holy**…. [they just had the lesson of getting it with the manna] …Six days you shall labor and do all your work. But **the seventh day *is* the Sabbath of the LORD your God**…" (vs 8-10).

Yes, it is His, but He doesn't say that He made it for Himself to rest on, did He? ***No, He didn't!***

However, this becomes very, very important, because I know for sure that it's not going to be too long before there are going to be people we know that were keeping the Sabbath who are going to be keeping Sunday. *You can be almost guaranteed of it!*

"…In it you shall not do any work, you, nor your son, nor your daughter; your manservant, nor your maidservant, nor your livestock, nor the stranger within your gates; for *in* six days the LORD made the heaven and the earth, the sea, and all that *is* in them, and rested the seventh day. Therefore, the LORD blessed the Sabbath Day and sanctified it" (vs 10-11).

- For whom? *For all of mankind!*
- Did He bless it just for Himself?
- Did He sanctify it for just Himself?

Wherever God is and whatever God does it is Holy! Moses went up on the mountain, and God said, 'Take off your shoes because you are standing on Holy ground.' ***God didn't make the Sabbath for Himself!***

I know that this is very basic, but it's something that is the very key as to why there were the problems going on in the early New Testament Church. I still like the answer that was given when asked by a Protestant when it became obvious that this particular person was keeping the Sabbath and all of the rest on this tour to the Holy Land were keeping Sunday. They came up to this man and he was a minister that I knew and they said, 'By the way, what day do you keep?' *And his answer was, 'The same day Jesus did. What day do you keep?'*

Now you cannot argue with that, can you? Remember that if someone ever corners you and asks you, 'What day do you keep?' You just tell them, *'I keep the same day that Jesus kept. What day do you keep?'* Here is why:

Mark 2:27: "And He said to them, '**The Sabbath was made for man**… [on account of the creation of man] …***and not man for the Sabbath***.'" What does that phrase mean? *That man has no jurisdiction over the Sabbath!*

Verse 28: "Therefore, **the Son of man is Lord even of the Sabbath**."

- What is this telling us? *Very simple, Jesus is Lord of the Sabbath!*
- Which day is the Lord's Day if Jesus Christ is your LORD? *The Sabbath!*

It's got to be; it can't be anything else!

John 14:15—***Jesus said***: "If you love Me, **keep the commandments**—namely, My commandments."

If the Sabbath was made for a curse to put on the Jews, ***why didn't Jesus***—when He brought the New Covenant—***reveal that*** and relieve us from that curse? *He didn't because that is not a true statement!* ***It is not a curse!***

There are several other places we can go to: Ezek. 20 is a very instructive set of verses.

When has obedience to God ever been a curse? *Nowhere!* Obedience to God may cost you your life, in some cases it's going to be martyrdom, but:

- Is that a curse?

or

- Is that a witness? *It is a witness!*
- What does the curse come from? ***Not keeping it!***

Deut. 28 says, '***IF*** you will, indeed, **listen to My voice and hearken to My commandments,** and do all of that which I say, ***blessed shall you be***:

- in the city
- in the country
- in the fruit of your womb
- in your basket
- in your store
- in fighting your enemies

But ***IF*** you will *not listen* and ***will not keep my commandments,*** cursed shall you be.' So, *the curse comes* not from obedience, but ***from disobedience!***

Ezek. 20 talks about what God did for the children of Israel. Let's get the scene before we go through some of the verses.

Ezekiel 20:1: "And it came to pass in the seventh year, in the fifth *month*, the tenth day of the month, that some of the elders of Israel came to ask of the LORD, and sat before me. And the Word of the LORD came to me, saying, 'Son of man, speak to the elders of Israel and say to them, "Thus says the Lord GOD, 'Have you come to inquire of Me? *As* I live,' says the Lord GOD, 'I will not be inquired of by you'"'" (vs 1-3).

Remember that they were in captivity. They were in this place of captivity. Why were they in captivity? *Disobedience!* Now they are wanting to come to God and say to God, 'God, why am I in this captivity?' *God answered*:

"...'**Have you come to inquire of Me?** *As* **I live,**' says the Lord GOD, '**I will not be inquired of by you**'" (v 3).

In other words: **What are you going to do to come and question God?**

Verse 4: "Will you judge *them*, son of man, will you judge them? Cause them to know the abominations of their fathers. And say to them, 'Thus says the Lord GOD: "In the day that I chose Israel, and lifted up My hand to the seed of the house of Jacob, and made Myself known to them in the land of Egypt; when I lifted up My hand to them, saying, 'I *am* the LORD your God'"'" (vs 4-5).

- *IF* God would have promised to give the blessing that He promised to give to Abraham
- *IF* it would have been through someone other than Abraham and someone else's descendants

hypothetically:
  - Which laws do you think that God would have given to them? *The same ones! Yes!*
  - Why? *Because they came from God!*
  - What does it say of God in the person of Jesus Christ?

Hebrews 13:8: "Jesus Christ *is* the same yesterday, and today, and forever." So therefore, *He would have given them exactly the same laws!* What did He tell them through Jeremiah the prophet?

You go tell those sinning children of Israel that had I gone to some other nation, they would have kept My Laws until now. But unfortunately I'm stuck with these rebellious children!

God promised! Once you promise, you can't get away from it! He says, *'But Israel has changed from Me being their God, to serving all of these idols.'* So, God really indicted His people, didn't He?

Look at the Indians in India, I mean we could stand up here and say, 'Look at all these Hindus. What a mess their religion is,' which is true. But God is saying, 'Had I gone to those people, they wouldn't have done to Me what you have done to Me.' *He made it known!*

Ezekiel 20:6: "In the day *that* I lifted up My hand to them, to bring them out from the land of Egypt into a land that I had searched out for them, flowing *with* milk and honey, which *is* the glory of all lands; then I said to them, 'Let each man throw away the abominations of his eyes, and do not defile yourselves with the idols of Egypt. **I** *am* **the LORD your God**'" (vs 6-7).

So, right when God was getting the Ten Commandments, they made the golden calf, worshipped it, had a great sex orgy there, the whole thing, just like one of our rock concerts that we have today. All right, no different, same thing going on.

Verse 10: "And I caused them to go out from the land of Egypt, and brought them into the wilderness. And I gave them My statutes and showed them My ordinances, which *if* a man do, he shall even live in them. And also **I gave them My Sabbaths**..." (vs 10-12)—*plural*; *a sign* there are the Holy Days involved!

There are some people who are good enough to accept Jesus, to accept the Sabbath, but not accept the Holy Days. You are confronted with a problem in that particular case. They try and doctrinally somehow show that these are tied in with the sacrifices, but they had sacrifices on every day, so the argument of sacrifices being on the Holy Days and whether they ought to keep the Holy Days or not or the Sabbath or not is really having no bearing whatsoever to do on the Sabbath or the Holy Days, *none whatsoever!*

Verse 12: "And also I gave them My Sabbaths to be a sign between Me and them, that *they* might know that I *am* the LORD Who sanctifies them. But the house of Israel rebelled against Me in the wilderness; they did not walk in My statutes, and they despised My ordinances, which *if* a man does, he shall even live in them. **And they greatly polluted My Sabbaths.** And I said, '**I will pour out My fury on them in the wilderness to destroy them**'" (vs 12-13).

- if God is merciful, which He is
  - Does anybody doubt that God is merciful?

- if God gave the Sabbath for a curse, which some people believe that He did

  - Don't you think that God being merciful would remove that curse and tell them about another day?
  - Wouldn't that make sense?
  - Is that not logical? *Yes, it is!*

So, they despised God's way!

Then He even said to their children after He took care of them in the wilderness, you know, and you saw all of them dying. Then He said to them again:

Verse 20: "And **keep My Sabbaths Holy**; and **they shall be a sign between Me and you**, that you may know that I *am* the LORD your God." ***So, they rebelled!***

Ezek. 22—we find that the priests are in on this, the prophets are in on this. The problem is not with ordinary people as much as it is with the leaders. A person comes to a minister, maybe a Protestant minister, and says:

You know, Pastor, I've been reading my Bible, and I think that we ought to keep the seventh day. I really see in Jer. 10 that it's also telling us not to have Christmas trees. And in Ezek. 7 it says that we are not to have hot cross buns and all this Easter stuff. Furthermore, I went to the library and looked it up in the encyclopedia and those things are pagan. What do you think?

Well now, Jesus has delivered us from those things. We don't have to keep them, and besides, we have Christianized Christmas and we have Christianized Easter, so now it's all okay.

So, the person, not wanting to offend the minister, the minister after all is the 'expert'; so they take his word. It's like this one minister who said about Saturday, 'We're not to sleep all day Saturday.' We're not! If any of you are sleeping here, wake up!

Ezekiel 22:25: "**There is a conspiracy**…"—*and that's a nasty word today!* Anyone who talks about a conspiracy, you're mentally off because you're imagining something.

- Who is the greatest conspirator in history? *Satan the devil!*
- Is he conspiring?
- Is he working? *Yes!*
- Who does he want to get?
- If he gets one minister then he gets how many hundreds or thousands of people?

Verse 25: "There is a conspiracy of her prophets in her midst, like a roaring lion tearing the prey. They have devoured souls…"

That's especially vivid in my mind because I just saw one of these wild documentaries, and it showed the lions, and I tell you those lions can jump on top of a zebra or a wildebeest and one big gnash right on the back of the neck, and that's it, they devour them. The whole pride of lions comes in and you talk about table manners, you talk about conversation around the table. They are fighting, tearing and the poor little cubs have got to get in there and try and get something.

Just picture that with these ministers. That's what they are spiritually doing to people! They come and say, 'Oh, Mr. Minister, I read my Bible and it looks like we ought to keep the seventh day,' which is the seventh day! *Conspiracy!*

"…They have devoured souls; they have taken the treasure and precious things; they have made many widows in her midst. **Her priests have done violence to My Law and have profaned My Holy things.** They have put no difference between the Holy and the profane…" (vs 25-26).

Who made the difference between Holy and profane? *God did, He is the One!* That's why the Sabbath is Holy, *because God made it Holy!* That's why the days that we keep are called *Holy Days because they are days that God made Holy!*

"…and have not taught the difference between the unclean and the clean…" (v 26).

I was listening to the news and they were saying cholera has spread because of unclean cooks serving unclean food, namely shrimp, clams and those unclean things that should not be eaten that *God said, 'Don't eat them.'* Not because He wants to take some tidbits away from you that you may like, but because there are certain things in these animals that may make you sick, may make you prone to disease, so later you are going to have problems.

"…and **they have hidden their eyes from My Sabbaths,** and I am profaned among them" (v 26). *That becomes important!* I know this is really basic, but I haven't gotten to the point that I want to get to, yet.

If you find yourself in this terrible and horrible condition that you are trying to find God, and there are a lot of people out there trying to find God. Some people say, 'If God would show me a *sign,* I would believe Him.'

- Isn't that what they said to Jesus?
- Isn't that what people say today? *'If I could see God, I would believe Him.'*

There is a man who was a minister of God., and before he was a minister he was a paraplegic. This is an experience within the Church of God now.

He was paralyzed from the neck down. When he came to the knowledge of the Truth and felt he had faith that God would heal him, he called for the elders of the Church and was anointed. *Within ten days he was walking!*

It was such an unusual thing that even the Veterans Administration—then he went to say, 'My conscience is overloading me, I cannot bear it. God has healed me. I am walking. Please take me off of disability'—they said, 'We don't believe it; we are not going to take you off disability.' He said, 'Okay, my conscience is clean, I can receive my check every month and it's clean; I tried.' He tried two or three times to do that.

He was a pretty powerful minister. He was always in pain even though he had this, and he would get around and he would still limp and things like that. He was a very friendly, gregarious, outgoing man and could really speak in power, and sing and lead songs; a tremendous, fantastic person! He would tell you about how God healed him. Furthermore, he married the nurse that was taking care of him.

Now then, because of men within the Church, and because of difficulties that he had, *now he doesn't believe in keeping the Sabbath, when God led him to it, or necessarily the Holy Days.*

So, if someone asks, 'Give me a sign, O God! How can I find You?' *God has already given the sign, and He has already given the thing that you can do!* You don't have to be a cripple to find God or to see the sign. What is that sign? *The Sabbath!*

Why is it such a fantastic sign, because in spite of all of the calendar manipulations by men, the seventh day on the calendar on your wall today—unless it's been changed by some modernists as it has in some areas of the country and Europe—what day is the seventh day of the week? *Saturday, the Sabbath!* You can verify that by asking any Jew who still keeps the Sabbath. You can verify that by asking any Protestant, 'Which day is the first day of the week?' *It's the day after the Sabbath!* No doubt!

- there is the miracle
- there is the sign

What if you really want to get right with God?

Isaiah 56:1: "Thus says the LORD, 'Keep justice and do righteousness…'"

I talked to a man and he says, 'The first place to begin to solve all the political problems is to pass a law—if you could and think that would be possible—to outlaw all politicians from being attorneys as professionals.' Sounds like a good thing, but it won't work. That's why God has to destroy the system because you can't repair it. God can repair an individual life, but He is not going to repair the system, He is going to destroy it. So there is no justice, there is no judgment.

"…for My salvation *is* near to come…" (v 1).

- When is God's salvation coming? *When Christ returns!*
- Are we close to that?

We can also say when Christ came the first time, too!

"…and My righteousness to be revealed" (v 1). *This is a prophecy for the end-time!*. Anyone at the end-time

- who wants to get right with God
- who wants to draw close to God
- who wants to serve God

Here is what God says:

Verse 2: "Blessed… [not cursed] …is the **man**… [in the general sense of a human being] …**who does this**… [that's a pretty specific thing] …and the son of man who lays hold on it… [as something to do] …**who keeps the Sabbath from profaning it,** and keeps his hand from doing any evil."

What if he is not an Israelite or a Jew? *Because the argument is always made,* 'The Sabbath is for the Jews, but Sunday is for the stranger or the Gentile' and that is a name that the Jews have coined, which is really a misnomer and it should be *the nations.*

Verse 3: "And do not let the son of the stranger… [Gentile, someone other than an Israelite] …who has joined himself to the LORD, speak, saying, 'The LORD has utterly separated me from His people.' And do not let the eunuch say, 'Behold, I *am* a dry tree.'" *That is: 'God, why can't I have any kids?'*

Verse 4: "For thus says the LORD, 'To the eunuchs **who keep My Sabbaths**… [we have the Holy Days involved here, too] …and choose things that please Me, and take hold of My covenant.'"

Mr. Minister, which day should we keep? I heard one minister say when it was brought up to him that we shouldn't keep Christmas. He said, *'Look, I'll put on the beard, and the Santa Claus suit if it's going to bring more people into this church.'*

Think about that for a minute. He's got all the priorities totally backward. The Bible says *what if you gain the whole world, but lose your soul?* The wicked, though they walk hand-in-hand, *are all going to fall.* God says, **"…who keep My Sabbaths, and choose things that please Me, and take hold**

of My covenant"—*a prophecy of the New Covenant!*

Sometimes we get so bogged down in technical things and details, interesting doctrine and teaching that we can learn, because we've been in the Church a long time and we need to learn those things. But it's absolutely amazing and fantastic how you can go back to a basic thing like the Sabbath, which is so vitally, vitally, important, and ask: Is that important for me to return to God? *Yes!*

Especially in light of the situation that the message I gave concerning the Sardis Church and Laodicean Church and things like that. There are a lot of people out there *who just feel justified*—because they're hurt by a man—*to give up on God!* **No one is justified to give up on God because they are hurt by a man!**

Listen, human beings are going to hurt you over and over again. Why? *Because they are human beings!* Don't be surprised. Even the best intentions sometimes hurt people. Why? *Because they are misunderstood!* If you're wanting to be hurt, you're going to be hurt. If you are looking to be hurt, it's going to come, **but don't let it take you away from God!**

I want you to notice the similarity between 1-John 3:22 and what we just read in Isa. 56:4[transcriber's correction]:

1-John 3:22: "And whatever we may ask we receive from Him **because**… [here is the cause] … **we keep His commandments and practice those things that are pleasing in His sight**."

Isaiah 56:4: "For thus says the LORD, 'To the eunuchs **who keep My Sabbaths, and choose things that please Me**, and take hold of My covenant.'" *Not too much different*, is it?

- Why was Jesus always faithful? *He said, 'I always do those things that please God.'*
- Did Jesus keep the Sabbath? *Yes, He kept the Sabbath!*
- Did that please God? *Yes, that pleased God!*

Verse 5: "Even to them will I give within My house… [the Church] …and within My walls a place and a name better than of sons and of daughters…"

What did we just read concerning one of the Churches of God? *Behold I will give you a new name, which no man knows, but he who receives it!* So, there it is right there, New Testament doctrine.

"…I will give them an everlasting name that shall not be cut off. Also the sons of the stranger, who join themselves to the LORD to serve Him, and to love the name of the LORD, to be His servants, everyone who keeps from profaning the Sabbath, and takes hold of My covenant; even them I will bring…" (vs 5-7).

- Where?
- What was the message topic for Pentecost? *Come to the mountain!*

Verse 7: "Even them I will bring to My Holy mountain, and make them joyful in My house of prayer.…"

Then it says some burnt offerings and so forth, that's when they had them, but now we have the offerings. What are the offerings that we have? *They are offerings of*:

- *praise*
- *thanksgiving*
- *glory to God*
  - ✓ *through our prayers*
  - ✓ *through our life*

because we worship Him in Spirit and in Truth!

Isa. 58—God is now talking to the children of Israel; He's got something to say to them. He just talked to all the Gentiles (Isa. 56). *Now He is talking to the children of Jacob*:

Isaiah 58:1: "Cry aloud, do not spare, lift up your voice like a ram's horn, and show My people their transgression, and the house of Jacob **their sins**." **What were they?**

Here is a famous Scripture that a lot of people turn to and say that we should not keep the Sabbath:

Isaiah 1:14: "**Your** new moons and **your** appointed feasts My soul hates…" *That's right after He said*:

Verse 13: "Bring no more vain sacrifices; incense is an abomination to Me—new moon and sabbath, the calling of assemblies—I cannot endure iniquity along with the solemn assembly!"

- *Whose* sabbaths?
- *Whose* new moons?
- *Whose* feast days?
- God's?

or

- Theirs?

Theirs! When the Protestants say, 'My sabbath is Sunday,

- What are they saying?
- What does God say about their sabbath? *He says*:

Verse 14: "Your new moons and your appointed feasts **My soul hates**…"

I will remember this as long as I live. I had the unusual duty of being the minister in Salt Lake City, which was the heart of Mormon land, and so I was driving, and this was when I first moved there, and I was driving down this road and here is the sign:

Remember the Sabbath to keep it Holy; see you in church on Sunday

I almost wrecked the car! *This is the Sabbath that God hates!* But that's how people take the name that God has and they put it on *their* days. *That's what God hates!* This has *nothing to do with* God's Sabbaths!

- Can a person keep the seventh-day of the week as we know it, the true Sabbath, and it still be not a Sabbath to God, but a Sabbath to themselves even though it's on God's day? *Yes, they can!*
- How can they do that? *Keep it their own way!*

Add so many man-made traditions on it like the Jews do today, that the Sabbath is an absolute total burden? *Like they do in Israel if a car goes down the street, they stone it!*

- Which is more work, the person driving the car down the street **or** the stoning of the car?
- Can you imagine stoning a car?

Here is what it has to be in worshipping God—the day is important, but what is secondary importance on that day; actually the primary importance? *You've got to have the right day in order for this to work!*

John 4:20—*the woman of Samaria said:* "'Our fathers worshiped in this mountain, but You say that the place where it is obligatory to worship is in Jerusalem.' Jesus said to her, 'Woman, believe Me, the hour is coming when you shall neither in this mountain nor in Jerusalem worship the Father. You do not know what you worship. We know what we worship, for salvation is of the Jews. But the hour is coming, and now is, **when the true worshipers shall worship the Father in Spirit and in Truth**…'" (vs 20-23).

That's what makes the seventh-day the spiritual day to keep, when you worship the Father in Spirit and in Truth.

"…for the Father is indeed seeking those who worship Him in this manner. God *is* spirit, and those who worship Him **must** … [the word there in the Greek is *ordained, obligatory, mandatory* …**worship in Spirit and in Truth**" (vs 23-24).

God says, Isaiah 58:1: "Cry aloud, do not spare, lift up your voice like a ram's horn, and show My people their transgression, and the house of Jacob their sins."

What do you need to do then? *You need to repent and worship God in Spirit and in Truth!* **IF** you are keeping the Sabbath, but you're not keeping it by loving the brethren and loving God, **THEN** you are not keeping it in Spirit and in Truth and worshiping God. We all have to grow in this more. I can't say that any of us are perfect in it.

Verse 2: "Yet, they seek Me daily, and seem eager to know My ways…"

Nothing could be more true of Americans than this. 'In God we trust! We are a Christian nation! Oh, we want to know God's Word' and all this sort of thing.

"…as a nation that did righteousness, and one that did not forget the ordinance of their God. They ask of Me the ordinances of justice; they seem eager to draw near to God. *They say,* 'Why have we fasted, and You do not see? Why have we afflicted our soul and You take no knowledge?' Behold, in the day of your fast you pursue your business and exploit all your workers. Behold, you fast for strife and debate, and to strike with the fist of wickedness; you cannot fast as *you do* this day, and expect to make your voice to be heard on high" (vs 2-4).

Here is one of the conditions if you are going to return to God:

Verse 13 "**If** you turn your foot away from the Sabbath… [walking on it, polluting it, trampling it, doing your own thing] …*from* doing your own desires on My Holy Day, and call the Sabbath a delight, the Holy of the LORD… [this applies to the Holy Days] …honorable; and shall honor Him, not doing your own ways, nor pursuing your own desires, nor speaking *your own* words, **then**… [notice all those conditions] …you shall delight yourself in the LORD…" (vs 13-14).

That way then no man is going to stand in the way and make you bitter or turn you from God!

"…and I will cause you to ride upon the high places of the earth, and feed you with the inheritance of Jacob your father, for the mouth of the LORD has spoken it" (v 14).

That's why it is so very, very, important, so it comes all right back to the very basic thing that the Apostle John said that '**IF** we love God and keep His commandments,' *this is how we know that we know God.*

Brethren, I know that none of you are disbelieving in keeping the Sabbath because you're all here! But it's very important for us to **know and understand what God thinks about it** and what we need to do so that we can also do better than we have been doing and how that it is important and right.

The next time you hear anyone say, like I did, 'I keep Sunday because…' *then* you will know that they have **chosen their own** sabbath, **which God says, 'I hate!'**

But **IF** you want to delight in God, *keep His way, keep His Sabbath, keep His Words!*

Scriptures from The Holy Bible in Its Original Order, A Faithful Version

Scriptural References:

1) 1 John 5: 3
2) Romans 8:7
3) Genesis 2:1-3
4) Exodus 20:8-11
5) Mark 2:27-28
6) John 14:15
7) Ezekiel 20:1-5
8) Hebrews 13:8
9) Ezekiel 20:6-7, 10-13, 20
10) Ezekiel 22:25-26
11) Isaiah 56:1-4
12) I John 3:22
13) Isaiah 56:4-7
14) Isaiah 58:1
15) Isaiah 1:14, 13, 14
16) John 4:20-24
17) Isaiah 58: 1-4, 13-14

Scriptures referenced, not quoted:

- Exodus 16
- Deuteronomy 28
- Jeremiah 10
- Ezekiel 7

Also referenced: Book: *Anti-Judaism and the Origin of Sunday* by Samuele Bacchiocchi

FRC:ja
Transcription date unknown
Reformatted: bo—10/2020

CHAPTER FIVE

Importance of the Sabbath

Fred R. Coulter

Let's look at something very important in Mark 13 and Matt. 24. I know when I first thought about this, and when I first let it penetrate into my mind to get some of the thinking of God, rather than the thinking of men about what they think God says; because some people have said we've published the Gospel around the world already. They have already had their witness.

But those people are long since gone and the magazine they claimed that did it, now has been reduced in circulation from 8-million, to 1.5-million, and the world is still going on. But here is what it says right here:

Mark 13:10—*it's talking about the end-times*: "And the Gospel must first be published among all nations." What do you have in your hands? *You have the Gospel!* The Gospel being published in all nations refers to the Word of God; it does not refer to someone preaching *about* the Gospel. The Gospel *will* be preached in all the world (Matt. 24).

Now let's understand something concerning the Old Testament. We're going to make this just a little bit different today.

Heb. 4—we're going to come back to Heb. 4 and look at it a little later—because we are going to see that one of the major teachings of Jesus Christ did in fact, have to do *with*:

- the Sabbath Day
- your capacity to work
- your capacity to eat and drink

Hebrews 4:2: "For truly, we have had the Gospel preached *to us*, even as **they** also *did…*"

Who is Paul talking about? *The children of Israel!* So, they had the Gospel preached unto them in the form that God gave that to them.

"…but the preaching of the Word did not profit them, because it was not mixed with faith in those who heard" (v 2). *They had the Gospel preached to them as well!*

What is this telling us? This is telling us that the Gospel includes both what is known as the Old Testament and the New Testament. Yes, indeed it surely, surely does!.

Remember several weeks ago we covered the Scripture—let's go there for just a minute just to review—because I think a lot of times when someone comes along with dynamite and blows up your foundation, which is what has been happening, you need to go back and repeat some things. Let's go back and repeat some of these things.

Luke 24—here's why the Gospel was also in the Old Testament and as we know: *a covenant is God's arrangement or agreement with you!* In every covenant, there are always the Laws of God that go right through all the covenants. Here is a very, very important section in the Scriptures.

Luke 24:25: "Then He said to them, 'O foolish and slow of heart to believe in all that the prophets have spoken!'"

- Does Christ expect us to believe the prophets? *Yes, absolutely!*
- Is that part of the Gospel? *It surely is!*

It told an awful lot about Jesus Christ, and it's telling an awful lot about what's going to happen at the end of the world!

- Is that not part of preaching the Gospel to the whole world? *Sure it is!*

Verse 26: "Was it not necessary for the Christ to suffer these things, and to enter into His glory?' And beginning with Moses… [Moses is part of the living Word of God] …and from all the prophets, He interpreted to them the things concerning Himself in all the Scriptures" (vs 26-27).

That was quite a Bible study. How would you like to have been at that Bible study where Christ *Himself* was telling you?

Verse 28: "And *as* they approached the village where they were going, He appeared to be going on farther. But they constrained Him, saying, 'Stay with us, for it is toward evening, and the day is declining.' And He entered in *as if* to stay with them. And it came to pass, as He sat *at the table* with them, He took the bread *and* blessed *it*; and after breaking *it*, He gave *it* to them. Then their eyes were opened…" (vs 28-31).

That's what has to happen with Christ, *your eyes must be opened!* That's why Judaism is so

48

dead. As we covered several weeks ago, the fig tree was cursed from the roots up. You have to have your eyes opened and only Christ can open them.

"…and they knew Him; and He disappeared from them" (v 31). *If you are born again, that's what you should be able to do!*

There are some people who say they are born again, and they make fun of those… What was the old test, the hatpin test? *Stick yourself and see if you bleed!* The better one is just walk through the wall. That will be far more convincing.

Verse 32: "And they said to one another, 'Did not our hearts burn within us as He was speaking to us on the road, while He was opening the Scriptures to us?' And they rose up that very hour *and* returned to Jerusalem; and they found the eleven and those with them assembled together, saying, 'In truth, the Lord has risen! And He has appeared to Simon.' Then they related the things that had happened *to them* on the road, and how He was known to them in the breaking of the bread. Now, as they were telling these things, Jesus Himself stood in their midst and said to them, 'Peace *be* to you'" (vs 32-36).

This is part of the glory that the disciples, especially John, wrote about where he says, 'We beheld His glory as the only begotten Son of God.' They saw Him transfigured on the mountain. They saw Him in His glorified form at that point, and now they see Him raised from the dead.

Verse 37: "But they were terrified and filled with fear, thinking *that* they beheld a spirit *apparition*. Then He said to them, 'Why are you troubled? And why do doubts come up in your hearts?'" (vs 37-38).

We need to understand that also, today, in our day. They had to live through the time to see Christ killed and then resurrected from the dead. Today people come along and try and put fear in your hearts and fear in your minds and try and manipulate things to their own use.

Now, as Carl [Franklin] and I were talking yesterday. We talk quite often But he said and I wrote it down:

It's one thing to be moved by God to do His will…

Isn't that something? That is true! That's what God wants. God wants someone to love, *because He is capable of loving the whole world perfectly!* God wants someone who will have a relationship with Him, with His Spirit, to love Him. So, *it's one thing to be moved by God to do His will…*

That's why there are a lot of independent Sabbath-keepers out there that are *being moved to do the will of God!* How many people are out there doing that? God is going to bring them! God is going to call them!

Then he says: *"It's one thing to be moved by God to do His Will; it is another thing to presume that you can force God to be moved to do your will."*

That's really quite a profound thing! *It's one thing to be moved to do the Will of God; it's quite another thing for you to presume that you can move God, or force God to do your will."*

This is why this is so important when we come to Luke 24 about understanding the Word of God.

Luke 24:39: See My hands and My feet, that it is I…. [v 40]: "And after saying this, He showed them *His* hands and *His* feet. But while they were still disbelieving and wondering for joy, He said to them, 'Do you have anything here to eat?' Then they gave Him part of a broiled fish and a *piece* of honeycomb. And He took these *and* ate in their presence. And He said to them, 'These *are* the words that I spoke to you when I was yet with you, that all *the* things which were written concerning Me in the Law of Moses and *in the* Prophets and *in the* Psalms must be fulfilled.' Then He opened their minds to understand the Scriptures" (vs 39-45).

That's how you understand the Bible, *by Christ sending His Spirit to be with you to open your mind!* Can God do that anywhere? anytime? with anyone? *Yes, He can!* I think God is going to demonstrate it. I think God is going to purposefully do that so that if any minister, *any minister at all* or any person *be so presumptuous to think that they have a corner on the market with God to force Him to do their will,* **God is going to do just the opposite!** You can be guaranteed that!

Now let's see something concerning the will of God concerning what is in Law of Moses. What is in the Law of Moses *that is most objected to*? *Obviously the Sabbath!*

It's even to the point now where people are being taught that 'it's okay to work on the Sabbath' if your family is starving or to do good humanistic works on the Sabbath, such as build houses for Habitat for Humanity. After all, God doesn't want you to starve and God wants you to provide for your family because if you don't provide for your family, you're 'worse than an infidel.' Hear those Scriptures, and yes, *yes, yes!*

IF you're sleepy and not studying the Bible and if you don't know what the Word of God is, *THEN* you're going to be in really bad shape.

But the truth is, the Ten Commandments are a part of the Gospel. If the Gospel is also contained in the Old Testament, are not then the Ten Commandments part of the Gospel?

Let's go to Deut. 5 where the Ten Commandments are listed there, and let's just read the ones concerning *the Sabbath.* We'll ask some questions concerning the Sabbath so that we will know. Now I'm covering some of what I know is very basic, and I kind of feel like the Apostle Paul when he wrote the book of Hebrews; he said, 'Can't we just go beyond the principles of Christ unto perfection?'

Well, I would have to say **no**, because we've got to go back and pick up the basics every once in a while. Too many people are not ready to go on to perfection. We need to cover this so we know exactly what we are saying.

Deuteronomy means *the second giving of the Law.* There are many things concerning the Gospel of Christ and the Gospel as to how we should keep it in the New Testament; many, many things.

Deuteronomy 5:12: "**Keep the Sabbath Day**…" In Exo. 20 says to *remember the Sabbath. Keep* is pretty direct! Does God want us to keep the Sabbath? *Yes!*

Verse 12: "Keep the Sabbath Day to sanctify it as the LORD your God has commanded you. Six days you shall labor and do all your work. But the seventh day *is* the Sabbath of the LORD your God…" (vs 12-14). *IF* you love God and fear God and keep His Commandments:

- Are you going to keep it?
- Is it not part of the Gospel of Christ? *Yes, it is!*

"*In it* you shall **not do any work**…" (v 14).

If any man comes along and says to you, 'The Sabbath for us today is Christ in us, and the rest of Christ—being in us—is our Sabbath.'

Do you know what that explanation is? *That is mental insanity! That's not true! Christ in you motivates you to keep the Sabbath correctly,* not the opposite to give up on it.

"…*In it* you shall not do any work, you, nor your son, nor your daughter, nor your manservant, nor your maidservant, nor your ox, nor your donkey, nor any of your livestock, nor your stranger within your gates, so that your manservant and your maidservant may rest as well as you. And remember that you were a slave in the land of Egypt" (vs 14-15).

Now when we come to the days of Unleavened Bread, which we will be coming to here very quickly—it will be upon us faster than we know—what does Egypt picture? *Egypt is a type of sin!* The Pharaoh is a type of Satan. They're the ones who have you working seven days a week because you are slaves to the system. So, he is saying to *remember that you were a slave in the land of Egypt!*

Now today if Christ were here to open our minds to tell us what it would be, it would not surprise me one bit if He said, *'You are a slave to this world's system! Therefore, you keep the Sabbath and on the Sabbath Day you remember what it was like to live without the Sabbath!'* It is quite instructive.

"…and the LORD your God brought you out from there with a mighty hand…" (v 15)

- Who calls any individual? *God does!*
- Does it take a mighty hand, sometimes something even greater than a mighty hand?
- What is the strongest thing in the world to change? *The human mind!*

When God's Spirit comes to call you and bring you out of the world, that's greater than a mighty hand, because He is not just changing your position from one place to another, He is changing your mind *from being hostile to God to opening your mind to love God!* That's a tremendous difference. So, He:

"…and the LORD your God brought you out from there **with a mighty hand and with an outstretched arm**. Therefore, **the LORD your God commanded you to keep the Sabbath Day**" (v 15). *He commanded you!*

Matt. 6 is built upon the Sabbath commandment, since we understand that the Sabbath is part of the Gospel, and we will see that confirmed when we come to Heb. 4. This is very basic for us to go through, because there are people now who have kept the Sabbath for years and are wondering: Should we keep the Sabbath?

- What happens when someone comes along and teaches you to sin?
- Does anyone know what that is called in the Bible?
- *It is the doctrine of Balaam!*

Balaam was hired by Balak to come and curse the children of Israel (Num. 22-24). Balaam went up on a mountain and he saw all the children of Israel, *and all he could do was **bless**!* So, Balak gave him all this money and he was coming out of his gourd, saying:

Look, I gave you this money, and I hired you to curse them, and you went up here on the top of the mountain and you blessed them. Now go on up there and curse them.

So Balaam goes on up again, and he blesses them. Balak is really getting out of shape and he's really getting mad, 'Didn't I hire you to curse them!' Balaam said, *'Well, I can only do what the LORD will allow.'* Then Balak said, 'Now go on up there again and curse them.' So, Balaam went up and *blessed them with the longest best blessing that you could read!*

Balak was really angry, and Jude tells us that what Balaam did was *teach Balak to cast a stumbling block in front of the children of Israel to entice them to sin* so that God would have to correct them. That's happening within any church:

- Sunday-keepers are doing that in relationship to Sabbath!
- Sabbath-keepers who are now ready to shift over to Sunday-keeping, are they not doing the same thing by saying it's okay to work on the Sabbath, when God says you shall not do any work?

It's one thing if there is an 'ox in the ditch,' or if a car is broken down, *but you don't go to the junkyard every Sabbath and resurrect all the cars!* In other words, you don't throw them into the ditch, *and that's what they are doing!*

Matthew 6:24 *is inexorably tied to the Sabbath*: "No one is able to serve two **masters**; for either he will hate the one and love the other..." *it always happens!*

Have you ever worked for a partnership where the bosses were equal, and then they got into a feud? *Try that some time; it'll give you fits!*

"...or he will hold to *the* one and despise the other...." (v 24). Is that not happening with those who are rejecting and despising the Laws of God? the commandments of God? *Yes, indeed!*

"...**You cannot serve God and mammon**" (v 24).

Let's look at this thing concerning master. It could also be translated *lord* because it comes from the Greek word 'kurios.' Let's look at that in relationship to the Sabbath, and you're going to hear a passel of sermons that are coming out that are going to cover a lot of these same things.

Mark 2:23: "Now, it came to pass that He went through the grain fields on the Sabbaths..."—not corn as we understand corn, but that wouldn't be too bad. If you were back in Iowa walking through a cornfield and the corn was ripe and you just reach up and snap off an ear and peeled it back. Have you ever eaten that fresh, sweet corn right off the cob, raw? Oh, it's good!

"...and as His disciples made *their* way *through the fields*, they were picking *and eating* the grain. Then the Pharisees said to Him..." (vs 23-24).

This *is their own law,* because it says that you shall not reap the corners, you shall leave it for the poor, and if anyone is passing through your field, he can pluck a little and eat, but he is not to stop there and encamp and harvest. But the Pharisees said if you pluck a head of corn on the Sabbath, you're working, you're laboring, you're harvesting. *That's not a Law of God!*

"...'Look *at them!* Why are they doing that which is not lawful on the Sabbaths?'" (v 24). There was no Law against it, *except their own tradition!*

Jesus answered with another one for them to figure out, which was greater and harder to figure out!

Verse 25: "And He [Jesus] said to them, 'Have you never read what David did when he was hungry and in need *of food*, he and those with him? How in *the days of* Abiathar the high priest, he entered into the house of God and he ate the showbread...'"

The showbread was a loaf of bread that was especially baked and was in a special container. There was one loaf for each one of the twelve tribes of Israel, and these were before the Lord constantly. They had to change them every week, and the priest could eat it and give it to his family.

- Who was David? *He was not yet king at that point; he was the king-designate!*
- What was David also in addition to being the king-designate and later to be king?
- Was he not also a prophet of God? *Yes, he was!*
- Did he not prophesy concerning Christ in the Psalms, concerning many things in the Psalms? *Yes, he did!*

The correct answer is that even though it was unlawful for anyone else to eat it, the truth is, to give it to David and David to give it to his men because they had need, was not against the Laws of God whatsoever.

"...which it is not lawful to eat except for the priests, and he also gave *it* to those who were with him?'" (v 26).

Jesus gave them something to try to figure out. If they are so smart and condemn people for plucking a head of grain, then go figure this one out. If you want to figure out between what is lawful and what is not lawful, because the most important thing is that you worship and serve God in Spirit and Truth.

Verse 27: "And He said to them, 'The Sabbath was made **for man**…'"

As we have seen in the past, *for the purpose of fellowshipping with God,* not just for the purpose of fellowshipping with each other. That is necessary and that is true, but if we just fellowship with ourselves and God is not there, well then there is no reason for us to come together then is there? It was made for man for that specific purpose.

"…*and* **not man for the Sabbath**" (v 27). In other words, man is not going to go tell God—Who made and created the Sabbath—'God, I don't want to keep Your Sabbath. It gets in the way. Now I can't earn a living.'

What do you think Satan wants to get the whole world bound up into; being so busy just like in Egypt that you have to work seven days to meet the bare meager things of even living. *So, man is not going to come along and tell God or force God!* That's why this is so significant: *It is another thing to presume that you can force, or make God to be moved to do your will!*

Verse 28: "Therefore, the Son of man… [Jesus Christ] …**is Lord**… [Master—'Kurios'; you cannot serve two masters (Matt. 6:24)] …**even of the Sabbath**."

He is saying the same thing here in Mark 2! *The Sabbath was made for man by God,* and not man for the Sabbath, because there is one Lord of the Sabbath: *Jesus Christ!* You can't serve two Sabbaths to do the activities of men.

Verse 28: "Therefore, **the Son of man is Lord even of the Sabbath**." *This tells us that the Christian Sabbath is the same day that God gave to ancient Israel,* the seventh day of the week, and Christ is Lord of it

Now let's read what Jesus says, and this ties directly in with the Sabbath. Dwight Blevins from Grand Junction called me and he'd been studying this, and he is the one who planted the seed for today's message. He said that when you read Matt. 6, 'Is this not tied directly into the Sabbath and working?'

Matthew 6:24: "…You cannot serve God and mammon." That's very interesting; you can't keep the Sabbath while you are working on it to earn a living. And mammon is *living riches*, to get money.

Verse 25: "Because of this I say to you, do not be anxious about your life *as to* what you shall eat and what you shall drink… [the very basic necessities] …nor about your body *as to* what you

shall wear. Is not life more than food, and the body *more* than clothing? Observe the birds of heaven: they do not sow, neither do they reap, nor do they gather into granaries; and your heavenly Father feeds them. Are you not much better than they?" (vs 25-26).

What is He really saying here? **_IF_** *you don't trust God to provide for you*—obviously in the Sabbath-keeping situation here—**_THEN_** you are counting yourself less than the birds. You are counting yourself in a situation that you are really actually saying, 'God cannot provide for me.' *That's accusing God!*

Verse 27: "But who among you, by taking careful thought, is able to add one cubit to his stature? And why are you anxious about clothing?…. ['I know you need to be clothed, don't worry about it'] …Observe the lilies of the field, how they grow: they do not labor, nor do they spin; but I say to you, not even Solomon in all his glory was arrayed as one of these" (vs 27-29). *God is going to clothe you!*

- *if* He is going to take care of the plants
- *if* He is going to provide for the birds
- *if* He is going to provide for His whole creation

which He does! **His whole creation is an expression of His love to all of mankind!**

Verse 30: "Now, if God so arrays the grass of the field, which today is and tomorrow is cast into the oven, *shall* He not much rather clothe you, O *you* of little faith?"

That's why we have said that the Sabbath is a test commandment. The truth is, every commandment is a test commandment! 'Will you keep My commandments or no?' *Yes, every one is!* So you have to have faith.

Verse 31: "Therefore, do not be anxious, saying, 'What shall we eat?' or 'What shall we drink?' or 'With what shall we be clothed?'" *But some will say*:

- this Sabbath commandment is pretty tough
- my bank account is really getting low
- my wife over here is nagging at me
- my children are hungry and they have holes in their shoes; they're just about ready to go barefoot
- therefore, God, I'm going to break the Sabbath and go work *because I don't have one bit of faith in You for You to provide*

That's what they're saying!

What should they do? *They should go to God, and if they're having a difficult time on the*

Sabbath Day, pray and draw closer to God. Ask for His Spirit in love, and do the things that please God. *He'll gladly provide for you!*

I talked to a man whose wife was just 'beating him over the head,' so to speak:

You turned down all these jobs because of the Sabbath. This last one was really a good one. Now the Church says you can work on the Sabbath, and yet, you refused.

He held to keeping the Sabbath **and God blessed him with a better job** than any of those that he turned down. **God was able to provide!** Can He not do that? *Yes!*

Verse 32: "For the nations seek after all these things…."

- they work seven days a week
- they don't keep the Sabbath

So, this is intrinsically bound up in the Sabbath command!

"…And your heavenly Father **knows** that you have need of all these things" (v 32). *God knows!*

- *If you know, God knows!*
- *If God knows, He'll take care of it!*
   - ✓ maybe not in the way you think or in the means or manner in which you suspect
   - ✓ maybe it will not be as much because there are other lessons to learn
   - ✓ maybe it will be more than you expect because God is blessing you above and beyond

That's all in God's hands, and that's all in God's relationship with you!

Verse 33: "But *as for* you, seek first the Kingdom of God…" *That's what it needs to be. God will take care of it!*

Can you *truly* seek the Kingdom of God if you're not keeping the Sabbath, when the Sabbath pictures the whole situation concerning the Kingdom of God? *NO!*

"…and His righteousness…" (v 33)—**the imputed righteousness of God!** That's what you are to seek.

- Would God break His own Sabbath?
- Did God break His own Sabbath?
- *NO!*

If you go back and read Exo. 16 and the giving of the manna, what did God do? *He gave manna for six days and five of those days, He said:*

Now look, you just go out and you get a certain amount for everyone. Don't keep it over to the next day because it's going to breed worms and stink. But on the sixth day, you go out and you gather twice as much, and then you prepare for the Sabbath and you can keep it over and it won't breed worms and stink.

Consider the fact that this happened for *forty years, every single week!* That's quite a thing! Some of them thought, 'I'm going to go out and get some manna on this Sabbath Day! So, they went out to look and *God said, 'How long refuse you to keep My commandments?'* And that was long before the giving of the Ten Commandments.

Verse 33: "But *as for* you, seek first the Kingdom of God and His righteousness, and all these things shall be added to you." *Just exactly what you need!*

Some people are going to be blessed more than others. Does that mean they are more righteous? *NO! It does not!* It just means that God has blessed them more than others. So therefore, if someone has more than you, you don't get mad at God and say, 'You didn't give it to me; You gave it to him.' That's not it. Here is what we are to do:

Verse 34: "Therefore, do not be anxious about tomorrow…"—*do not be worried!* **If you have faith in God and trust in God, He will provide!**

"…for tomorrow shall take care of the *things* of itself. Sufficient for the day *is* the evil of that *day*" (v 34).

Isn't it true that every day has got it's own problems? So, handle those day-by-day. How do we differentiate what I said by one person receiving more of a blessing than another, as compared with what it says in the Old Testament that if you do these things, you will be blessed? I didn't say the lack of blessing, I just said that God may give someone more, bless them with more than you, I'm not saying that He isn't going to bless you or provide for you. *Let's see how this all ties in together!*

Matthew 6:9: "Therefore, you are to pray after this manner… [which is how you develop faith] …'Our Father, Who *is* in heaven, hallowed be Your name; Your Kingdom come; Your will be done on earth, as *it is* in heaven'" (vs 9-10).

That's what we need; we need the will of God. That will answer the question: **How is God going to bless us?** Maybe God is going to bless us with a trial because He has a greater purpose in mind. Sometimes we don't know why we're going through those trials that He has a greater purpose in mind, but nevertheless, that's how God works.

Verse 11: "Give us this day our daily bread…" *That ties in with the rest of Matt. 6* where He says, 'Give no thought about what you will eat, what you will drink…' and so forth, for God will take care of you!

Now in relationship to that let me read this letter here:

We were members of the WCG for about twenty-five years. Then things started to change. First off, they had first, second, third tithe, tithe of the tithe, excess second tithe, building fund, and special funds, work two or three jobs if you had to, etc., to keep it up, and tithe on the gross. They live like kings in mansions and pools and two or three homes, get planes—something is rotten in California. I had to get out. Now changes again! Work on the Sabbath! Work on the Holy Days! Holy Days are not commandments. Eating unclean meats is okay, etc. Anyway, your book *Lord, What Should I Do* is refreshing. Please send me four copies.

So, I will!

We get many, many such letters. We can help that way an awful lot. When you wrap your whole life up in serving God and then someone comes along and steals it from you, and then after they steal it they begin throwing it away, it's no wonder that there are a lot of people in just such terrible, terrible shape out there.

Let's go back and read some commands concerning the Sabbath. We do need to have this basic sermon concerning the Sabbath, in the light of the things that are going on, and I just want you to understand.

Exodus 16:25—*after the whole incident concerning the giving of the manna*: "And Moses said, 'Eat it today, for today *is* a Sabbath to the LORD. Today you shall not find it in the field. Six days you shall gather it, but on the seventh day, the Sabbath, in it there shall be none'" (vs 25-26). *There will be no manna there!*

- What is this also telling us?
- What was manna? *Food!*
- Who provided it? *God did!*

That ties right in with Matt. 6!

- Is not God able to provide? *Yes!*
- Does He want you to work on the Sabbath? *No!*

As we saw, God said *no work, not any work!* Don't be throwing everything into the ditch so you have an excuse to work. There won't be any out there. *If God was not going to send the manna, and there wasn't going to be anything out there for them:*

- Do you think that God will bless anyone for Sabbath-breaking when they know better?
- Do you think that God is going to bless them with their work?
- What's going to happen to these poor people who say, 'I believe what so-and-so said about it being okay to work on the Sabbath. I'll go ahead and work on the Sabbath'?
- What happens if they lose their job? *They are going to be in worse shape, because with the devising of men you are not going to force God to do your will!*
- God is not going to bless that effort
- God is not going to prosper you in what you do when it is sin

We have all tried it! Haven't we all kidded ourselves and said, 'God understands, this sin won't hurt a bit. After all I'm trying to do good.' That's what everyone wants to do; *do good in their sinning!* I've done that.

- Did I prosper in it? *No!*
- Did I do well in it? *No!*
- Was I happy in it? *No!*
- Was God pleased in it? *No!*
- Did God in His mercy and graciousness and love, lead me to repentance? *Yes!*

Which means that He doesn't want me to do it! So, it is the same way with any of us and in anything we do.

Verse 27: "And it came to pass *that some* of the people went out on the seventh day in order to gather…" *These are*:

- hardworking people
- diligent
- workaholics
- mannaholics

They want to go out and get more manna!

"…but they did not find *any*. And **the LORD said to Moses**…" (vs 27-28).

This is really quite something, what He said here. **He didn't say,** 'Now I understand. You know these people have been bound up in Egypt for so long, and I know that they worked every day. Now you know I understand that they had to go and look just to satisfy their own curiosity.' *NO!*

Verse 28: "…**'How long do you refuse to keep My commandments and My Laws?'**" *I want you to make special note of that; that's a very important verse!* Why?

Because when people get into these arguments concerning Old Testament/New

Testament laws and commandments and the giving of them, and so forth; *please understand that the laws and commandments of God were in effect before they ever got to Mt. Sinai, before God ever spoke them!* That's what it is saying right here:

"...'**How long do you refuse to keep My commandments and My laws? See, because the LORD has given you the Sabbath**…'" (vs 28-29). *It is a gift! The Sabbath is* **a creation** *and a* **gift** *from God*:

- so that you can fellowship with God
- so that you can love God
- so that God can love you
- so that God can instruct you out of His Word
- God is the One Who has a corner on the Sabbath!
- God is the One Who has a corner on the Truth!

Not us! *God has given you the Sabbath!*

"'…therefore, He gives you the bread of two days on the sixth day…. [another gift, a miraculous gift the bread of two days] ...Let each one stay in his place. Do not let any one go out of his place on the seventh day.' So, the people rested on the seventh day" (vs 29-30).

Exo. 20—we're just going to read some very important things here, very fundamental for us to understand:

Exodus 20:8: "Remember the Sabbath Day to keep it Holy." *No other day can be Holy, except the Holy Days!* Sunday is not Holy; *God never made it Holy!*

Verse 9: "Six days you shall labor and do all your work. But the seventh day *is* the Sabbath of the LORD your God. In it you shall not do any work, you, nor your son, nor your daughter; your manservant, nor your maidservant, nor your livestock, nor the stranger within your gates; for *in* six days…" (vs 9-11).

It goes back to creation. What is the authority of the Sabbath and the Ten Commandments? *It's a creation, God made it!* When you keep the Sabbath:

Verse 11: "For *in* six days the LORD made the heaven and the earth, the sea, and all that *is* in them, and rested the seventh day. Therefore, the LORD blessed the Sabbath Day and sanctified it." *The Sabbath is perhaps one of the most often mentioned commands in the whole Bible!*

Exodus 23:12: "Six days you shall do your work, and on the seventh day you shall rest, so that your ox and your donkey may rest, and the son of your handmaid, and the stranger, may be rejuvenated. And be watchful in all that I have said to you. And make no mention of the name of other gods, neither let it be heard out of your mouth" (vs 12-13).

We could go through Deut., Num., and Lev. and all of that, but what I want you to do with Exo, 31—which becomes a very important thing concerning the Sabbath—is remember what we did going through and showing in Num. 11 concerning that the Church was an extension of Israel. *That those Gentiles who are called are* **grafted into** *the olive tree of Israel!* With that in mind:

Exodus 31:12: "And the LORD spoke to Moses saying, 'Speak also to the children of Israel, saying, "Truly you shall keep My Sabbaths, **for it** *is* **a sign between Me and you throughout your generations to know that I** *am* **the LORD Who sanctifies you**"'" (vs 12-13).

- What is the whole purpose of the New Testament for each one of those who are called saints?
- Why are you called saints? *Because you have the Holy Spirit of God and you are sanctified!*
- God is the One Who is sanctifying us
- God is the One Who sanctified the Sabbath
- He blessed it
- He sanctified it

Same way with us! That's why we are to keep the Sabbath. *Remember the children throughout your generations*:

- If we are part of Israel, *now spiritual Israel,* are there still generations of Israel? *Yes, indeed!*
- Can we not have spiritual meaning out of these verses as well because it's part of the Gospel? *Absolutely!*

Verse 14: "You shall keep the Sabbath, therefore, for it *is* Holy to you. Everyone that defiles it shall surely be put to death…"

Maybe not that day; maybe not for many years, but what is the ultimate outcome! *'The wages of sin is death.'* When you teach people to sin, *the wages of sin is death!*

"…for whoever does *any* work on it, that soul shall be cut off from among his people" (v 14).

I'll tell you what's going to happen, those who begin breaking the Sabbath by working on it—*because now the leader says it's okay to do it*—and after all, 'He said I could, Lord. If he says I could, Lord, I'm going to. Therefore, I'm justified.'

That's the same old thing of human nature going way back to Gen. 3 when they got caught in their sins. Notice whose fault it was. Notice what happened. God came and He was calling Adam and Eve:

Genesis 3:9: "And the LORD God called to Adam and said to him, **'Where _are_ you?'** [they were hiding] …And he [Adam] said, 'I heard You _walking_ in the garden, and I was afraid because I _am_ naked, and _so_ I hid myself.' And He [God] said, 'Who told you that you _were_ naked? Have you eaten of the tree, which I commanded you that you should not eat?'…." (vs 9-10).

You can put any commandment in there. 'Have you done that which I said you should not do?' **Have you?**

- be it the Sabbath
- be it idols
- be it taking God's name in vain
- be it any of the commandments of God
- be it anything in the New Testament

You put it there!

Verse 12: "And the man said, 'The woman whom You gave _to be_ with me…'" What Adam really is saying is: _'God, You're the One; You are at fault, not me, but the woman You gave me!'_ Adam wanted her, desired her! When God presented her to him, Adam said, 'Now this is bone of my bone and flesh of my flesh. She shall be called woman.' So, you're not going to have _a copout by blaming the church leader!_ Even if the church leader comes and says do this or that or the other thing. _**IF it is against the Law of God or the commandments of God, you're not to do it!**_

Verse 13: "And the LORD God said to the woman, 'What _is_ this you have done?' And the woman said, 'The serpent deceived me, and I ate.'"

God took care of them all! He said, _'Look, you're not going to escape the judgment or the penalty for what you have done.'_

Likewise today, those who go out and work because a church leader has said it's okay to work—let's understand something concerning things like childbirth, or an accident, or something like that. There are things that need to be done, and you know, babies come because babies come, and it is called child labor; it is painful and it is in travail. So, God certainly expects that to be taken care of. I am sure that if you are coming to Sabbath services and you are in an accident, that you are going to be very happy a highway patrolman is there to help you, or an ambulance is there to help you. In this world there are those things that go on. However:

- How many of you have had an accident coming to Sabbath services? _None!_
- How many here had your children born on the Sabbath Day?

If a person is a nurse and, say, works in a hospital, there are certain things that need to be done, but I was talking to a nurse who called and she said that there are always plenty of people who want to come and work on Saturday, so 'I just swap shifts with them.' _**IF**_ your desire is to please God and serve Him, there is going to be a way. God will provide a way. I have often had people ask me this:

- How do you keep the Sabbath at the North Pole? _When I get a letter from someone at the North Pole, I'll answer it!_

In the meantime, that question cannot be answered because no one is there to keep the Sabbath.

- What do you do when you live in a high northern latitude and you have a whole lot of dark? _Then you calculate it by what you see!_

That's how you calculate the Sabbath, and it will generally work out to be approximately 24 hours long!

- What about when the sun never sets in the summer? _Well, when it dips to its lowest point, in the middle of the lowest point, that's the ending of the day so you go from there!_

Exodus 31:15: "Six days may work be done, but on the seventh day _is_ the Sabbath of rest, Holy to the LORD. Whoever does _any_ work on the Sabbath Day, he shall surely be put to death. Therefore, the children of Israel shall keep the Sabbath, to observe the Sabbath throughout their generations _**as a perpetual covenant**_" (vs 15-16).

This is in addition to the covenant that was given at Sinai. This is a special Sabbath-keeping covenant. Why did He make it a special Sabbath-keeping covenant for a perpetual covenant? _I would have to say, brethren, for the New Testament Church!_ Knowing that we would not have a temple, knowing that we would not have a priesthood, but still keep it!

Verse 17: "**It _is_ a sign between Me and the children of Israel forever**; for in six days the LORD made the heavens and the earth, and on the seventh day He rested, and was refreshed."

Ezek. 20—Why did the children of Israel go into captivity? _**Because they broke the commandments of God and broke the Sabbath!**_

This is quite a lesson. How important is it? When we read this, let's understand that God says in the book of Ezekiel three times, 'I don't delight in the death of the wicked, but that the wicked turn from his ways.'

Ezekiel 20:1: "And it came to pass in the seventh year, in the fifth *month*, the tenth day of the month, that some of the elders of Israel came to ask of the LORD, and sat before me. And the Word of the LORD came to me, saying, 'Son of man, speak to the elders of Israel and say to them, "Thus says the Lord GOD, 'Have you come to inquire of Me? *As* I live,' says the Lord GOD, 'I will not be inquired of by you'"'" (vs 1-3).

In other words, just like I started out: *It is one thing to be moved by God to do His Will; it's another thing to presume that you can force or move God to do your will!* That's what He just said here. 'Are you going to come and question me?'

"…'*As* I live,' says the Lord GOD, 'I will not be inquired of by you.' Will you judge *them*, son of man, will you judge them? Cause them to know the abominations of their fathers" (vs 3-4). *So now we have a history lesson!*

Paul gave a history lesson; what was the history lesson?

1-Corinthians 10:5: "But with many of them God was not pleased, for their dead bodies were strewn in the wilderness. Now these things became examples for us, so that we might not lust after evil things, as they also lusted" (vs 5-6).

What did we just read about in Exo. 16 on lusting, going out to break the Sabbath?

Verse 7: "Neither be idolaters, as *were* some of them; as it is written, 'The people sat down to eat and to drink, and rose up to play.' Neither should we commit sexual immorality, as some of them committed, and twenty-three thousand were destroyed in one day. Neither should we tempt Christ, as some of them also tempted *Him*, and were killed by serpents" (vs 7-9).

Do we not tempt Christ when we reject the Sabbath? *Yes, we do!*

Verse 10: "Neither *should we* complain against *God*…"—murmur! Is that not what's happening? Complaining? Murmuring? Criticizing against God? *That's what He is saying in*:

Ezekiel 20:3: "…'Have you come to inquire of Me?….'" **Are you going to come and complain to Me?** Read the whole book of Jeremiah, how merciful God was where He said over, *and over, and over* again! 'You find some people who will do what is right, and I [God] will turn back this captivity. I'll change it, I don't want them to die.'

1-Corinthians 10:11: "Now all these things happened to them *as* examples, and were written for our admonition, on whom the ends of the ages are coming."

- Are we living in the last days? *Yes!*
- More so than Paul? *Yes!*

Verse 12: "Therefore, let the one who thinks he stands take heed, lest he fall." *They are not falling now; they are pushing! Yeah, they are running! Let's have a little history lesson here, quite instructive*:

Ezekiel 20:5: "And say to them, "Thus says the Lord GOD: 'In the day that I chose Israel, and lifted up My hand to the seed of the house of Jacob, and made Myself known to them in the land of Egypt…"

- Has God made Himself known to you?
- Did God send His Spirit today to make Himself known? *Yes!*
- What is the whole thing that we are to know? *We are to know God!*
  - ✓ we are to know Christ
  - ✓ we are to know the Father

He who says I know Him and keeps not His commandments is a liar and the Truth is not in him!

Didn't we study that in 1-John? *Yes, indeed! The one who is keeping the commandments and walking the way that Jesus did, in him is the love of God being perfected!* So, just as God chose them, *he chose us!*

"…when I lifted up My hand to them, saying, 'I *am* the LORD your God.' In the day *that* I lifted up My hand to them, to bring them out from the land of Egypt into a land that I had searched out for them, flowing *with* milk and honey, which *is* the glory of all lands; then I said to them, 'Let each man throw away the abominations of his eyes…' (vs 5-7). *Whatever it may be*:

- an idol
- fornication
- adultery
- stealing
- idolatry
- taking God's name in vain
- breaking the Sabbath

"…and do not defile yourselves with the idols of Egypt…" (v 7).

What are we doing today? Back in Memphis Tennessee they've got a whole pyramid back there where they take people through, and they run them *through the demonic initiations into the ancient rites of Egyptian religion*; right here in the United States.

"'…and do not defile yourselves with the idols of Egypt. I *am* the LORD your God.' But they rebelled against Me and would not hearken to Me. They did not each man throw away the abominations of their eyes, nor did they forsake the idols of Egypt. And I said, **'I will pour out My fury against them to fulfill My anger against them** in the midst of the land of Egypt.' But I worked for My name's sake, that it should not be profaned before the heathen among whom they *were*…" (vs 7-9).

In other words, He said even while they were in the land of Egypt they were so involved in idolatry that He was even going to destroy them right in the land of Egypt before He ever called them out. What did they do when they got to Mt. Sinai and Moses was up on the mountain for forty days? They said, 'Aaron, make us calves.' So, God didn't do it.

"…*for* I made Myself known to them in their eyes, by bringing them out of the land of Egypt. And I caused them to go out from the land of Egypt, and brought them into the wilderness. And I gave them My statutes and showed them My ordinances, which *if* a man do, he shall even live in them" (vs 9-11). *The righteousness of the letter of the Law!*

Verse 12: "And also I gave them My Sabbaths to be a sign between Me and them, that *they* might know that I *am* the LORD Who sanctifies them. But the house of Israel rebelled against Me in the wilderness; they did not walk in My statutes, and they despised My ordinances…" (vs 12-13).

Can you imagine what it must have been like? *No wonder Moses complained all the time,* 'O Lord, you got me saddled down with all these people.' You know, when they were good they were the people of God; when they were bad, they were Moses' people all the way through there.

"…And they greatly polluted My Sabbaths. And I said, **'I will pour out My fury on them in the wilderness to destroy them.'** But I worked for My name's sake, so that it should not be profaned before the heathen in whose sight I brought them out" (vs 13-14).

Even Moses said. 'Now, God, consider what the other nations are going to say if you kill them; that you brought them out here to destroy them. Now think about that, LORD.' *And He did!*

Verse 15: "And also I lifted up My hand to them in the wilderness, *and swore* that *I* would not bring them into the land which I had given *them*—flowing *with* milk and honey, the glory of all lands—because they despised My judgments and walked not in My statutes; and they polluted My Sabbaths; for their heart went after their idols" (vs 15-16).

Now what is the idol today? *Mammon, money, dollars, bucks, power, prestige, notoriety, clothes, car!* We have so many things out there that could be abominations; it's unreal.

Verse 17: "Nevertheless, My eye spared them—from destroying them; nor did I make an end of them in the wilderness. But I said to their children in the wilderness… [He is referring to the book of Deut. and the second giving of the Law before they went into the land] …'Do not walk in the statutes of your fathers, nor observe their judgments, nor defile yourselves with their idols. I *am* the LORD your God. Walk in My statutes, and keep My ordinances, and do them'" (vs 17-19).

What did Jesus say? *If you love Me, keep My commandments! If you love Me, keep My words!* Same thing, exactly the same thing.

Verse 20: "'And keep My Sabbaths Holy; and they shall be a sign between Me and you, that you may know that I *am* the LORD your God.' But the children rebelled against Me…" (vs 20-21).

All you have to do is read the book of Joshua and the book of Judges. As soon as Joshua and the elders died, what did they do? *Right back to Sunday-keeping, Christmas keeping,* and mark my words, when they quit keeping the Sabbath, that's exactly what's going to happen again. It will happen!

"…They did not walk in My statutes, nor keep My ordinances to do them—the ordinances which, *if* a man do, he shall even live in them. And they polluted My Sabbaths, and I said, I would pour out My fury on them, to fulfill My anger against them in the wilderness. Nevertheless, I withdrew My hand…" (vs 21-22).

God just finally threw His hands up and said, 'All right, if you want it I'm going to let you have your own ways, and **when** you get so filled with your own ways, idolatry, pollution, wretchedness and rottenness, **then** you come crying to me, then I'll hear.'

Verse 24—*He said*: "Because they had not done My ordinances, but had despised My statutes and had polluted My Sabbaths, and their eyes were after their fathers' idols. Wherefore, I also gave them over to *their own* statutes that were not good…" (vs 24-25).

- their own ways
- their own laws
- their own civil governments
- their own religion

He just said, 'I'll just give you over to it. If you want it, have it, you got it; the whole thing.'

"…and *their own* ordinances by which they could not live. And I defiled them in their own gifts…" (vs 25-26). *Worst thing that could happen to anyone is just to be left to wallow in your own sin!*

"…in that they caused all that opened the womb to pass through *the fire…*" (v 26).

In other words, they just went into the whole same situation that the Mayans down in ancient Mexico went through. The reason God destroyed those civilizations is because they were doing the same thing:

- going through the fire
- cannibalism
- offering to the gods

So evil and awful that one of their special sacrifices was to cut open the sacrificial human victim and take out the heart while it was still beating and drink the blood of it. Now you see some of these things and all the archeologists say, 'I wonder why these civilizations no longer exist?' ***Read the Bible!***

"…that I *might* make them desolate, to the end that **they might know that I *am* the LORD**" (v 26). *Sometimes God just does that!* Just turns you over to your own devices until you learn the lesson. Some things you can learn quite quickly.

We have a series—and in-depth study—on the *Love of God* that is really the whole heart and core as to why the Church is going through everything it is. When you really understand it, the love of God is the greatest thing, the greatest fulfillment and attainment in your life, and it does take your life.

That's why as you go through life and life is empty and you get older and there is no satisfaction—that's why the whole experience of Solomon is there. He had all these physical things and all the power, and all the money and wealth and every convenience you could ever want and he said, *'I am just a bag of wind. I am just an empty, hollow, frustrated old man.'* Why? *Because he never learned the love of God!*

The love of God is the greatest thing. We can't be playing third grade sandbox any more, going back to these things. If someone is not convinced they ought to keep the Sabbath after being in the Church of God 25 years, well then I cannot be too much help to you. You should go help yourself. Isn't that what Jesus said, 'You go learn what these things mean.'

Heb. 4 will help us understand. Remember where we just read in Ezek. 20 where He destroyed those in the wilderness because they didn't believe.

Then He said to the children, 'Now look, you're going to go into the 'promised land,' now here is what God says.'

Hebrews 3:15: "As it is being said, 'Today, if you will hear His voice, do not harden your hearts, as in the rebellion.' For some, after hearing, did rebel, but not all who came out of Egypt by Moses. But with whom was He **indignant** *for* forty years?…. [notice He didn't say *angered*] …*Was it not with those who had sinned…*" (vs 15-17).

Can you have the very presence of God in the cloud by day and the fire by night, every day and every night, and have the manna come six days every week, and the Sabbath every week, and still have the gall to keep your own idols? *Wow! That's something!*

"…whose dead bodies were strewn in the wilderness? And to whom did He swear *that they* would not enter into His rest…" (vs 17-18). *Going into the 'promised land' is a tremendous rest! You compare that with wondering in the Sinai!*

I remember one time we went down to Palm Springs. Boy, was it hot, and I thought: How would you like to walk in that desert in all that heat? *Yet, they did and still didn't believe God!* So, you see that they could not enter in because of unbelief. The spies came back and said, 'Oh look, they're giants. Oh we can't go in.' Joshua and Caleb said, 'Oh yes, God will take care of it for us.'

Hebrews 4:1: "Therefore, we should fear, lest perhaps, a promise being open to enter into His rest…"

That is the ultimate reward of God in the Millennium. Now we are not talking about the 'promised land,' we are talking about the Kingdom of God. That's the *rest* we are talking about.

"…any of you might seem to come short. For truly, we have had the Gospel preached *to us*, even as they also *did*; but the preaching of the Word did not profit them because it was not mixed with faith in those who heard. For we who have believed, we ourselves are entering into the rest, as He has said, 'So, I swore in My wrath, **"If they shall enter into My rest—"** although the works were finished from *the* foundation of *the* world. For He spoke in a certain place **about the seventh day** in this manner…" (vs 1-4).

This is showing that the Sabbath is a continuous type of the *rest* of God. The *rest* of God is not Christ in you, so therefore, you perpetually keep the Sabbath every day. As one man said, 'When do you work?' It doesn't happen that way.

"…'And **God rested on the seventh day** from all His works.' And again concerning this: 'If they shall enter into My **rest**—'" (vs 4-5)—*which we just read about in Ezek. 20.*

Verse 6: "Consequently, since it remains *for* some to enter into it, and those who had previously heard the Gospel did not enter in because of disobedience, again, He marks out a certain day, 'Today,' saying in David…'" [What was that day? *That's pictured by the Sabbath Psalm quoted here!*]: …after so long a time (exactly as it has been quoted *above*), **'Today, if you will hear His voice, harden not your hearts'"** (vs 6-7).

Is this not the same thing as it is with every covenant of God? *Hear His voice, obey His words, thus says the Lord, thus says Jesus, thus say the Prophets!*

Verse 8: "For if Joshua had given them rest…" *They understood that it was Joshua that led them into the 'promised land.'* The sense of it is this way: "For if Joshua had given them **rest**…" In other words, and that was the fulfillment and the completion of God's plan, *then*:

"…He [God] would not have spoken *long* afterwards of another day" (v 8). *That other day is the coming of the Kingdom of God, that other day is the Millennial rest of God!*

Verse 9: "There remains, therefore, **Sabbath-keeping**… [rest] …for the people of God." *This is an entirely different word!* All the way through, the word for *rest* in the Greek is 'katapausis' that means *rest, recline, repose* from your labor and hard work.

This one, v 9, is an entirely different word for *rest* and it in the Greek is 'sabbatismos,' which means *a keeping of the Sabbath!* New Testament command. "…therefore, Sabbath-keeping for the people of God."

- Who are the people of God? *The ones that have the Spirit of God! A keeping of the Sabbath!*
- Why? *Because God's plan is not complete and the Sabbath pictures the completion of that plan!*

Verse 10: "For the one who has entered into His rest, he also has ceased from his works, just as God *did* from His own *works*."

Then comes a statement showing that after we have the Sabbath-keeping what are we to do spiritually?

Verse 11: "We should be diligent, therefore, to enter into that rest… [the ultimate reward of God to us] …lest anyone fall after the same example of disobedience"—*unbelief!*

What is it when you tell people you can work on the Sabbath? *It is unbelief!*

When Christ returns, and every Sunday-keeper knows this if they have read their Bible, and a lot of Sunday-keepers read their Bibles. That's why some Sunday-keepers are still either closet Sabbath-keepers or they keep the Sabbath. When Christ returns He is going to obviously do away with the Sabbath because it's an inconvenience to everyone. *Of course not!*

Isaiah 66:23: "'And it shall come to pass, that from one month to another, and from one Sabbath to another, shall all flesh come to worship before Me,' says the LORD"—*every Sabbath!*

This is part of what Christ opened the mind and understanding to the disciples:

Isaiah 56:1 "Thus says the LORD, 'Keep justice and do righteousness; for My salvation *is* near to come, and My righteousness to be revealed…. [this is just before the return of Christ] …**Blessed *is* the man who does this, and the son of man who lays hold on it; who keeps the Sabbath from profaning it, and keeps his hand from doing any evil**…. [all the commandments] …And do not let the son of the stranger… [Gentile] …who has joined himself to the LORD, speak, saying, 'The LORD has utterly separated me from His people.' And do not let the eunuch say, 'Behold, I *am* a dry tree'" (vs 1-3). *A eunuch is the most shameful thing to happen to a man!*

Verse 4: "For thus says the LORD, 'To the eunuchs who keep My Sabbaths, and choose things that please Me, and take hold of My covenant.'"

Did we not just go through the things that please God? *Yes!* "…**take hold of My covenant**…" This can be concerning the New Covenant, but did we not read of a special covenant concerning the Sabbaths of God that include the seventh day and Holy Days in Exo. 31? *Yes, we did!*

Verse 5: "Even to them will I give within My house and within My walls a place and a name better than of sons and of daughters; I will give them an everlasting name that shall not be cut off." Go back and read the promise to the seven churches; '…And I will give him a new name…'

Verse 6: "Also the sons of the stranger, who join themselves to the LORD to serve Him, and to love the name of the LORD, to be His servants, everyone who keeps from profaning the Sabbath, and takes hold of My covenant." Isn't that amazing? *Yes it is!*

Scriptures from *The Holy Bible in Its Original Order, A Faithful Version*

Scriptural References:

1) Mark 13:10
2) Hebrews 4:2
3) Luke 24:25-45
4) Deuteronomy 5:12-15
5) Matthew 6:24
6) Mark 2:23-28
7) Matthew 6:24-34; 9-11
8) Exodus 16:25-30
9) Exodus 20:8-11
10) Exodus 23:12-13
11) Exodus 31:12-14
12) Genesis 3:9-13
13) Exodus 31:15-17
14) Ezekiel 20:1-4
15) 1 Corinthians 10:5-10
16) Ezekiel 20:3
17) 1 Corinthians 10:11-12
18) Ezekiel 20:5-26
19) Hebrews 3:15-18
20) Hebrews 4:1-11
21) Isaiah 66:23
22) Isaiah 56:1-6

Scriptures referenced, not quoted:

- Matthew 24
- Numbers 22-24; 11
- 1 John

Also referenced:
- In-Depth Study: *Love of God*
- Book: *Lord, What Should I Do* by Fred R. Coulter

FRC:ja
Transcription date unknown
Reformatted: bo—10/2020

CHAPTER SIX

Weekly Sabbath
Fred R. Coulter

What we're going to understand is this: *The weekly Sabbath is one of the very first things that you begin to understand when God calls you!* When I was growing up I was never religious; never in a church. I had an aunt who was a Sunday school teacher, and her name was Aunt Grace; and whenever she would come and visit us she would bring her little felt-board thing, and she would teach us with her little felt-board thing. I always got absolutely bored to tears. Whenever she would come I would say, 'Oh! No! Not again!'

When I was ten-years-old, my folks wanted me to be a 'good boy' so they sent me off to Lutheran catechism. This was held up at the minister's house and my mom would drive me up there, I'd get out of the car, wave bye-bye, walk up the porch. As soon as she was gone, I'd jump over the edge of porch and run off, as I didn't want any religious instruction. Finally they gave up on trying to make me take catechism, and I had no religious exposure at all to anything.

I think I was still in the service. I must have been about 22 at that time, and I was visiting my sister over on Bainbridge Island. So I thought I would go to church and I didn't want to go to a Catholic church, so there was an Episcopalian church. I walk into this Episcopalian church on Sunday morning and lo and behold it looked just like a Catholic church. I couldn't get over it. Here the priest with his long robes and he has his little staff with the sun-disk on top of it, walking down the aisle and all of that sort of thing. I thought to myself: how's this any different than the Catholic Church.

One other time—I was delivering papers—I must have been about 15, and it was Sunday morning and they were having Easter sunrise services, so I wanted to see what that was like. Here are these thousands of people out there, and so I got my paper route done early and I was standing there watching it and as soon as the sun came up they all bowed down, and I wondered: what on earth is this? *It was all Catholic!*

So, I had no exposure to religion at all. I was not convinced that Sunday was right one way or the other. But as soon as I heard about the Sabbath, something happened in my mind. It was just like God took a switch and turned it; because I said, 'Ahha! That's got to be it!' I do recall one other event. That was one of my aunts—another aunt on my mother's side—she was a Seventh Day Adventist. Of course, my mother always thought that Seventh Day Adventists were weird, and she proved it to me. My aunt's daughter came over to visit us, and at that time, the Seventh Day Adventists were very strict vegetarians. My mother made up some tuna fish sandwiches and put a lot of eggs in it. So she gave it to her daughter and she loved them. She said, 'Oh this is delicious, what is it?' My mother said, 'Well, it's deviled eggs.' She ate a huge stack of them, not knowing that it was tuna fish and eggs. Well, I didn't know that they were vegetarians until my mother told me with this tuna fish thing.

Then sometime later, we went up to visit them. We get up there and she has meatballs and gravy prepared for us. I thought, well now, that's really down right nice of her. Here, she's a vegetarian and we come and visit and she makes meatball and gravy for us. So, pass around the meatballs and meatball and gravy and everything, so I said I'm going to show her how much I appreciate her effort. So, I heaped on lots of meatballs and lots of gravy and it was the first 'mock meat,' old soybean stuff that I ever had in my life. I knew for sure vegetarian was wrong from that day forward.

There are two fallacies in Ellen G. White's prophecy that all meats would be polluted at the end-time:

1. so are the vegetables
2. they have organic vegetables and organic meat now

So, that was about the sum-total of my religious experience, until I went to college in San Mateo after I got out of the army; and I started the day course, and they require you to take a course in paleontology, which is eighteen weeks long: six weeks of paleontology, six weeks of geology and six weeks of biology. This was my first opportunity in a big class, it was theater style and I was sitting about halfway back up. All the students filed in, filled it all up; there must have been 300-400 students there, and the professor comes out and the very first thing, he gets up there and walks back and forth until it's quiet. One way to get the students to quit talking is to say nothing and walk back and forth, pretty soon it gets quieter and quieter and finally there's silence. He stood up there and he looked at all the students and he said: 'Anyone here who believes in God and the Bible, there is the door. I don't want to hear it during the course of this class.'

Well, not being religious, it hit me the wrong way! How dare anyone tell me that I can't believe in God, though I didn't! It's just kind of a quirk of human nature. I wasn't an atheist, but I didn't believe in God. All my religious experience with my family told me that it couldn't be right. So anyway, that really got me to thinking.

What's the first thing you do? *You try and coordinate evolution with creation!* But that didn't work. Then, lo and behold, one night in my car I heard the *World Tomorrow* program. At that time they were really preaching the Bible, and it was Herbert W. Armstrong. He was on KGO at 9:30, and as soon as I heard that program something else clicked in my mind and I knew that that was it. I wrote in and I got the literature and the *Plain Truth* and as soon as I heard about the things; there was a series on the Ten Commandments; reading that. There was also a series on the two Babylons—*Satan's Great Deception*; out of the book *Two Babylons* by Alexander Hislop—and that's very important for people to understand. So, I immediately got the book and I started reading a couple pages every day, going through it, and I heard about the Sabbath and I knew about the Sabbath and I knew that I needed to keep the Sabbath, but I kept putting it off.

About August I went on down to Ambassador College, and a dishwasher who worked at the same restaurant I did went down with me; because where I was working I was passing out literature and I'd listen to the program at night while I was there. I would save all my preparation work to do it back in the kitchen. I could turn on the radio and listen to the *World Tomorrow* program. He wanted to go and he was a friendly, outgoing guy and so forth; so he went down with me to Ambassador College.

I counseled about baptism, and I wasn't keeping the Sabbath and I was still eating bacon and tomato sandwiches. I decided I was going to quit eating bacon and tomato sandwiches and I'm going to keep the Sabbath. I came on back and I told my boss, I said, 'Look, I'm going to give you two week notice that I need to have off from sundown Friday to sundown Saturday, or I quit.' So he said, *'What for?'* I said, 'For my religion.' He said, 'When did you get religious?' I said, 'Ok, if you can't do it, let me know.'

He went back and looked at the schedule and he came back and says: *I can't do it.* So I said, 'Do you mind if I look at the schedule?' *No, go ahead.* So I went back and figured it out. And here's how I figured it out: In the winter I would work for the chef from eight in the morning to four in the afternoon on Friday. Then in summer I would work from eleven to seven and get off before sunset. And then I would have all day Sabbath off from sunset to sunset, and then one o'clock in the morning on Sunday morning I would come into the killer graveyard shift. So that's how I was able to keep the Sabbath.

So, everyone who comes into contact with the Truth is going to have to cross the Sabbath bridge somewhere, and you're going to have to make a decision: What am I going to do? **Because the Sabbath is the first step in beginning to understand the Bible.** Absolutely!

You can understand certain parts of it. There are many Sunday-keepers who understand certain parts, that is true. There are many Sunday-keepers who have not investigated the Sabbath, and in some cases, they can be very sincere in what they believe. But what is happening with Sunday-keepers now, with the advent of the coming one-world religion moving in, more and more Sunday-keepers are losing what they have according to the Scripture that Jesus said, 'Even that which they think they have shall be taken from them.' So, there is that aspect of it, too, that I think is going to open up a whole lot more concerning the Sabbath in the years as we go down the road here.

Why is Sabbath-keeping the key to understanding the Bible? *Because it's in the Ten Commandments!* James 2 applies to Sabbath-keeping as well. When James wrote this, he was writing to those who were attending the synagogue. Now if you attend a synagogue, do you attend it on Saturday or Sunday? *You attend it on Sabbath, Saturday!* So therefore, he doesn't mention about Sabbath-keeping here.

Another very important thing that we cover in the message series *The Holy Sabbath* is that it does not have to absolutely re-duplicate what is said in the Old Testament, in the New Testament. It doesn't have to duplicate it. If it shows it as a practice then it shows it as a binding commandment for New Testament Christians; because that's one of their arguments. 'The New Testament doesn't say anywhere about the Sabbath.' We'll see. Yea, it does!

But here's a principle, James 2:8: "If you are truly keeping *the* Royal Law according to the Scripture, 'You shall love your neighbor as yourself,' you are doing well. But if you have respect of persons, you are practicing sin, being convicted by the Law as transgressors; for *if* anyone keeps the whole law, but sins in one *aspect,* he becomes guilty of all…" (vs 8-10).

Remember, these were all Sabbath/Holy Day-keepers at the point he's talking to them. So therefore, their biggest problem was not understanding the Sabbath or Holy Days. Their biggest problem was getting along with each other. Is that not the biggest problem we have today, too? *Yes, very similar!*

Verse 11: "For He Who said, 'You shall not commit adultery,' also said, 'You shall not commit murder.' Now, if you do not commit adultery, but you commit murder, you have become a transgressor of *the* Law. In this manner speak and in this manner behave: as those who are about to be judged by *the* law of freedom" (vs 11-12).

We can apply the same thing. We can apply the same thing to the Sabbath. We'll see that in a little bit. Can you then take and have another god and still worship the true God? *No!* So, I'm going to take the first four commandments; he took the last six there as he was applying them. You apply it to the first four commandments: 'You shall have no other gods before Me.' You can't worship the true God by worshipping a false god. If I'm going to send you a thousand dollars and I send it to him, you never get your thousand dollars. It's the same thing. I sent it to the wrong person. *If you have the wrong god, you can't possibly have things right.*

You might have the right God, but you might be doing it wrongly. That's why the next commandment: 'You shall not make any graven image of any likeness of anything that's in heaven above, the earth beneath, water under the earth, nor bow down to worship them.' You might have the right God, but if you have an idol then you are worshiping God in the wrong way.

If you have no idols, then you come to the third commandment: 'You shall not take the name of the Lord your God in vain, and if you say, 'Lord, Lord,' and do not the things which I say,' then what are you doing? *You're taking His name in vain.* Now also this particularly applies to ministers who, if they teach false things in the name of God, are taking His name in vain.

Then you come to the Sabbath one. It's very profound, very important commandment; right in the middle of all the Ten Commandments. Think of it this way: Think of the Ten Commandments as a whole body. Think of it as a human body, all connected one with the other. Starts out with the head: the first commandment; and ends up with the toes: the last commandment. What if you took this human body and you cut out one foot in the middle, do you have a whole human body? *No!* As a matter of fact, you might have something kind of dead! So think of that way. Maybe it'll help you understand about the Sabbath a little bit more.

Exodus 20:8: "Remember the Sabbath day, to keep **it** Holy." *Very profound!* It does not say,

'one day in seven, honor Me.' That's also very profound, because that's what most people think.

Verse 9: "Six days you shall labor and do all your work, but the seventh day *is* the Sabbath of the LORD your God…" (vs 9-10).

That's very interesting phraseology when you look at it. *It belongs to Him! It is His day!* And we're going to see a little later on He created it.

Now, if it belongs to someone and you steal that time, are you stealing from God? *Yes!*

"…In it you shall not do any work, you, nor your son, nor your daughter; your manservant, nor your maidservant, nor your livestock, nor the stranger within your gates; for *in* six days the LORD made the heaven and the earth, the sea, and all that *is* in them, and rested the seventh day. Therefore, the LORD blessed the Sabbath Day and sanctified it" (vs 10-11).

Now there's quite a bit we can learn from this, too, which is also very important. The Sabbath always reminds us that God is Creator. When we know that God is Creator, we won't believe in evolution, will we? *No!*

It also tells us something else: That *God hallowed it,* which means *to make it Holy.* God alone can make something Holy because God is Holy. Can a man make something Holy? *No!* Sunday-keeping really gets into some very judgmental things concerning God, which are very profound, and most people don't realize it. But sufficient to say, *the Sabbath was made for fellowshipping with God!* It is a day He said, 'It is a Holy convocation, and on this day I have set it as a perpetual appointment.'

This is why you begin to understand about God, because something happens when you keep the Sabbath that does not happen when you keep Sunday. If you keep Sunday you can understand certain things up to a point. But you really don't know God, and that's a vast difference. Keeping the Sabbath is a day that we're going to see, is a day God made an appointment so that we may know Him.

Leviticus 23:1: "And the LORD spoke to Moses, saying, 'Speak to the children of Israel and say to them, "*Concerning* the appointed Feasts of the LORD…"'" (vs 1-2). *We'll cover the Feasts when we get done with the Sabbath!*

"…which you shall proclaim *to be* Holy convocations, even **these are My appointed Feasts**" (v 2). *They belong to God!*

God has given *an appointed time* every week that He says, 'I will fellowship with you.' Now, since He's not here on the earth, He does not do it face-to-face. He has sent His Holy Word so He fellowships with you through His Word and, and as we're going to see, through His Spirit.

Verse 3: "Six days shall work be done, but the seventh day *is* the Sabbath of rest, a Holy convocation. You shall not do any work. It *is* a Sabbath to the LORD in all your dwellings."

What God desires, since it is a Holy convocation, we are to come together whenever there are enough people to come together, and even if there are only two or three God says He will be there in the midst.

Let's see the overriding reason for the Sabbath, which God has set forth for us. God wants us to have a relationship with Him. This relationship is based upon His Word and His Spirit, through His Son Jesus Christ. This is what the Apostle John was writing to all the people there, so that they can have the fellowship with him.

1-John 1:1: "That which was from *the* beginning, that which we have heard, that which we have seen with our own eyes, that which we **observed** for ourselves…"

Not just see with the eyes, but actually to have seen Him in His glorified form. To have gazed upon Him; because John was one of those who was on the Mt. of Transfiguration! That's what it's referring to here.

"…and our own hands handled… [even after He was resurrected from the dead] …concerning the Word of Life; (and the life was manifested, and we have seen, and are bearing witness, and are reporting to you the eternal life, which was with the Father, and was manifested to us); that which we have seen and have heard we are reporting to you in order that you also may have fellowship with us; for the fellowship—indeed, our fellowship—*is* with the Father and with His own Son Jesus Christ" (vs 1-3).

That's the very *whole* purpose of the Sabbath. He does it spiritually.

1. God has made sure we have His Word; what God has to say to us is contained here
2. God will spend His Spirit to be with you, if you're seeking Truth, and when you're baptized, will be in you, which the fellowship becomes even closer

Genesis 2:1: "Thus the heavens and the earth were finished, and all the host of them. And by *the beginning of* the seventh day…"—*because all the way through it says, 'for in six days God made the heaven and earth and all that is in there.'*

"…God finished His work which He had made. And He rested on the seventh day from all His work which He had made. And **God blessed the seventh day and sanctified it** because on it He rested from all His work, which God had created and made" (vs 1-3).

On this first Sabbath God fellowshipped with Adam and Eve. *Think of that!* I've often wondered what that first Sabbath was like, when God talked with Adam and Eve. He says:

I've made you. I'm your God. I've made this beautiful Garden of Eden here for you and look and behold everything is there. You can freely eat of all the trees in the garden except the Tree of the Knowledge of Good and Evil. In the day you eat thereof you're going to die.

And that means in dying you will die, meaning that the whole process of aging and everything that goes along with it will occur.

But I'm going to meet with you every Sabbath Day right here in the garden.

Kind of reminds me of that hymn, *I Come to the Garden Alone.*

If Adam and Eve had not sinned, which I have a message on that, which was a little difficult to do because that's quite a question: *What Would the World have been Like if Adam and Eve had not Sinned?* It would truly be a different place, we know that. It would be more like what it's going to be like when Christ returns. That's why God did it. He wanted to fellowship with His creation, and He made us in His image for that very purpose.

Now, let's come to the *Belief's* booklet with all of that as a background, and let's read the statement on it and you will see how we've written the statement, and of course, how the layout of the whole *Belief's* booklet follows step-by-step-by-step all the way through to teach: beginning with God down to the end.

Now, I saw a belief's booklet recently where it says all the way through: '**We** believe'—everything that they believe starts out that way—*we believe, we believe, we believe.* Which is okay if it's really true, but what it really should be—anything concerning beliefs—*it should show what God wants us to believe and explain what the Bible teaches us!* That's what we've tried to do here with this.

Beliefs and Doctrines of the New Testament Church {booklet of CBCG—**truthofgod.org**}:

The weekly Sabbath is the seventh day of the week, known as Saturday today.

Now, that has to be clarified. Why does that have to be clarified? How many here have seen a European calendar? The European calendar has Sunday as the seventh day. All business corporations run Sunday as the seventh day. The whole system is already set up for it. All they need to do is just change the calendar slightly, and of course, if you destroy the knowledge of the background of the Truth concerning the Sabbath, then you can come out and say, 'Well look, Sunday is the seventh day.' So, it has to be defined carefully.

> In the beginning, the Sabbath was created by God. He blessed and sanctified the seventh day at creation as a special day for rest and fellowship with Him. The Sabbath is a memorial of creation and was made for all mankind. It was the commanded day of weekly worship for 3,000 years before the Ten Commandments were given to Israel.

Now we're going to look at some other Scriptures, which also help define that.

> The Fourth Commandment is a reminder to observe and to keep the Sabbath day Holy. As Lord God of the Old Testament, Jesus Christ created the Sabbath by resting on the very first seventh day and by blessing and sanctifying it. In the New Testament, Jesus Christ proclaimed that He is Lord of the Sabbath day….

We'll look at that Scripture in just a minute!

> …During His ministry on earth, He reaffirmed the sacredness of the Sabbath and taught its proper observance. Jesus Christ Himself showed by example that it is right to do good on the Sabbath day, in addition to resting from one's physical labor and secular business. The apostles of Jesus Christ and the early New Testament Church observed the Sabbath and taught Gentile Christians to observe it.

In the series *The Holy Sabbath,* I have quotes showing that it was clear up to 300 A.D. that the Sabbath was kept. Then the edict of Constantine to shift it over to the Sunday and Constantine was *the beast.* He is the one who ordered the formation of the Catholic Church by government edict. That's when the order came down to quit keeping the Sabbath, punishable by death. I have all of that there. The whole history of the Sabbath is one bloody mess. You need to understand that.

> The keeping of the seventh-day Sabbath is a special sign of the Covenant between God and His people God commands that it be observed from sunset Friday to sunset Saturday. During this Holy time, Christians are commanded to rest from their labor and to assemble to worship God and to receive instruction from His Word. Observance of the seventh-day Sabbath is essential for

salvation and for true fellowship with God the Father and Jesus Christ.

That's about as complete a statement as we can have concerning that. Let's look at two things, which are very important we need to understand. This is a special covenant. Let's also understand something concerning covenants. ***All covenants of God have laws and commandments, which must be kept. A covenant is an agreement on how you will do it***—or the terms of it—very important to realize concerning a covenant.

I want you to notice the phraseology that God uses as He tells Moses; Exodus 31:12: "And the LORD spoke to Moses saying, 'Speak also to the children of Israel, saying…'"

Now, let's understand something here that's very important for those who may not realize it. The Jews do not consist of all the children of Israel. Though the Jews claim that they are. Let me give you an example here:

What if you had eleven brothers, and all the eleven brothers were not identifiable. Then you and your descendants claim everything that belongs to the eleven brothers. You palm yourself off, and your extended family, as all twelve brothers. *Not true!* There were twelve tribes of Israel, of which the Jews—the tribe of Judah—were one tribe. So this is not talking to Jews, though today, Jews, looking back say it's only talking about them. *Not so!* It's talking to all the children of Israel, all twelve tribes:

"…'Truly you shall keep My Sabbaths…" (v 13)—*because He owns them!*

- it's not a hint
- it's not a suggestion
- it's not an idea
- it's not whether you want to or not

Now, you can choose whether you want to obey God or not, that is true. But if you want to obey God then keeping His Sabbaths is a very important thing. Notice it is also a plural, which when we get to the Holy Days, we'll explain that that also encompasses the Holy Days.

"…for it *is* a sign between Me and you throughout your **generations**…" (v 13)--*covering a long, long time!* We're going to see a little later on, He says: 'perpetual covenant.' That's important to understand.

"…to know that I *am* the LORD Who sanctifies you" (v 13). *In other words, if you don't keep the Sabbath you don't know the Lord! Really!* You may know of Him. You may know certain things about Him. But you don't **know** Him! That's why He gave the Sabbaths; *that you may know Him*.

And with the Holy Days you may know His plan, through Jesus Christ.

Verse 14: "You shall keep the Sabbath, therefore, for it *is* Holy to you. Everyone that defiles it shall surely be put to death..." *This is telling us, spiritually, no Sabbath-breaker's going to be in the Kingdom of God!* Would have to!

"...for whoever does *any* work on it, that soul shall be cut off from among his people" (v 14).

God does not reach down and kill instantly. To the carnal mind, is deceptive. But it is really a greater punishment...what is one of the greatest punishments you can have in the world and not even know it, and maybe not necessarily even feel any pain right away? What do you suppose the greatest punishment would be? *Rejection; being cut off from God!*

Now, most people out in the world today are out there doing their shopping. They don't know they're cut off from God. They don't even understand that it's part of the punishment; because in that they're having a good time. So you see, being cut off from God has a much different meaning and connotation to it than most people realize. They just don't know. You've heard it said, 'If you don't know, *you don't know that* you don't know!' On the other hand, what else do you have? *You have to understand how blessings work.*

Who was the most blessed man to ever walk the face of the earth? *Jesus Christ!* Direct access to God the Father. He was called, 'This is My Son, the Beloved.'

- Was He always blessed of God? *Yes!*
- Did He live a miserable life in the flesh? *Yes!*

Especially His last three and a half years and crucifixion! So. you have to discern how blessings come. But He did all of it for 'the joy that was set before Him.' That doesn't mean He was happy; because when He was on His way up to Jerusalem, He was distressed. He knew what was going to happen. But He was blessed. So you're right, it's understanding how blessings come. Blessings don't come—like I said in the message series *Epistle of James*—like an ATM machine. You just walk up and put your card in and ching! here it comes. It's totally different.

Verse 15: "Six days may work be done, but on the seventh day *is* the Sabbath of rest, Holy to the LORD. Whoever does *any* work on the Sabbath Day, he shall surely be put to death. Therefore, the children of Israel shall keep the Sabbath, to observe the Sabbath throughout their generations *as* a perpetual covenant" (vs 15-16).

Who is Israel today? *Israel today is the Church!* The *spiritual Israel of God* is the Church of God today.

Verse 17: "It *is* a sign between Me and the children of Israel forever; for in six days the LORD made the heavens and the earth, and on the seventh day He rested, and was refreshed." *Those are some pretty powerful commandments there!*

Since Jesus Christ is the One Who made the Sabbath, He owns the Sabbath. He was the Lord God of the Old[transcriber's correction] Testament Who became Jesus Christ, the Son of God, of the New Testament.

Mark 2:27: "And He said to them, 'The Sabbath was made for man...'" The Greek there is 'anthropos' which means *mankind.* **God made it for all mankind!**

Yesterday I had to go shopping. I had to go get some videos and paper—we get it at Costco because we get it there cheaply—and it was jammed; and I couldn't help but think, it really struck home. You know the scanners they have—boop, boop, boop—and as I was pushing the cart and getting the stuff, all I could hear was boop, boop, boop! I thought, you talk about merchandizing; you talk about making money; and you know, on Saturday, that place is jammed to the gunnels.

Just think how much better the whole world would be if they kept the Sabbath in the letter. Wouldn't it be nice if we didn't have to travel miles and miles to come to church; all we would have to do is walk out the door and go down a couple blocks and there's a church right on the corner. No steeples, no idols, no crosses, no crucifixes. The whole neighborhood is keeping the Sabbath. They almost had that down in Loma Lynda, California; that's a Seventh Day Adventist town, and they actually closed the post office on Saturday and opened it on Sunday. I didn't know that until I talked to a postal worker who worked down there.

Just think! All the problems that we have in Sabbath-keeping today would be solved. God originally made it for all mankind. If mankind had the knowledge of God—even in the letter of the Law—wouldn't that be a marvelous thing indeed? *Yes, it would!*

"...*and* not man for the Sabbath" (v 27). *God did not make the Sabbath and then make man!* He made man and then made the Sabbath and said, 'Here's the Sabbath. Fellowship with Me on this day.'

Verse 28: "Therefore, the Son of man is Lord even of the Sabbath." **He is LORD!** Now, if anyone professes Him to be Lord, what should they do? *They should keep the Sabbath!*

We all need to understand this, not only in relationship to the Sabbath, but in relationship to everything concerning God.

Matthew 7:21: "Not everyone that says to Me, 'Lord, Lord'…" *He's Lord of the Sabbath; just saying He's Lord is fine,* but that's not all there is to it.

"…shall enter into the Kingdom of Heaven, **but the one who is doing the will of My Father Who *is* in heaven**" (v 21).

- What is the will of the Father Who is in heaven?
- Did Jesus Christ always do the will of the Father?
- When He created everything that there is, was it the will of the Father that He did it? *Yes!*
- Was it the will of the Father that He made the Sabbath Day and made it Holy? *Yes!*

That's why He is LORD of the Sabbath. If you say, "Lord, Lord," and do not practice the will of the Father in heaven above, *you're not with God!*

- you may have part of God
- you may have some knowledge of God
- you may have some things of Truth of God

But you don't know God, because He created the Sabbath so that you may ***know*** Him. That's the whole reason.

Verse 22: "Many will say to Me in that day, 'Lord, Lord, did we not prophesy through Your name?…. [millions of preachers everywhere; prophesied means just *to speak*] …And *did we not* cast out demons through Your name? And *did we not* perform many works of power through Your name?' And then I will confess to them, 'I never knew you. Depart from Me, **you who work lawlessness**'" (vs 22-23)—*against law!*

If you are against the Sabbath Day, are you against a Law of God? If you are against a Law of God, are you practicing lawlessness in rejecting the Sabbath? *Yes! Ultimately, yes!*

Scriptures from *The Holy Bible In Its Original Order, A Faithful Version*

Scriptural References:

1) James 2:8-12
2) Exodus 20:8-11
3) Leviticus 23:1-3
4) 1 John 3:1-3
5) Genesis 2:1-3
6) Exodus 31:12-17
7) Mark 2:27-28
8) Matthew 7:21-23

Also referenced:

Books:
- *Two Babylons* by Alexander Hislop
- *Interlinear Hebrew-English Old Testament* by George Ricker Berry

Message: *What Would the World have been Like if Adam and Eve had not Sinned?*

Message Series:
- *The Holy Sabbath*
- *Epistle of James*

FRC:bo
Transcribed: 12/21/08
Reformatted: 10/2020

CHAPTER SEVEN

How To Observe the Sabbath Today
Fred Coulter

A Sunday-keeper, watching Church at Home {**churchathome.org**} clear down in Florida is convicted of the Sabbath, gets a hold of Randy and she said, 'How do I keep the Sabbath?' Well, we're going to have to do some Church at Home on *how to keep the Sabbath at home!* Unless you can keep it at home first and have a relationship with God, when you get together you're not going to be able to optimize your fellowship or learning on the Sabbath.

Today I'm going to talk a little bit about Sabbath observance. Let's see what God commands and then let's ask: **How do we observe the Sabbath today?**

You can go to Exo. 16 and that tells you how to observe the Sabbath if you are in an exodus and you are in the wilderness and the only place you have to go is your tent, and you have no Bible. All you have to eat is manna, and if you don't fix it right on Friday or if you keep it beyond the Sabbath Day, you're going to be eating maggots and a stinky mess!

What was the command? *'None of you shall go out of the door of your tent'!* So if we went back to Exo. 16 and said, 'Oh, here's how we're going to keep the Sabbath today.' No! We can get some principles from it, but let's go to Exo. 20 and let's read the command. We're going to pick this apart a little bit and apply it today, and see how we are to do it.

Exodus 20:8: "**Remember the Sabbath Day to keep it Holy.**" First of all, *you're to remember it!* Lots of times people, even though they're pretending they are keeping it, are forgetting it and they're not keeping it Holy. **How do you keep it Holy today?** *We'll answer that question as we go along!*

Verse 9: "Six days you shall labor and do all your work. But the seventh day *is* the Sabbath of the LORD your God. In it you shall not do any work, you, nor your son, nor your daughter; your manservant, nor your maidservant, nor your livestock, nor the stranger within your gates" (vs 9-10).

Who came here on donkey back today? *Nobody!* Now let's understand something very important: *Not all definitions of keeping the Sabbath in the Old Testament in a physical way necessarily apply to today!*

Now don't start thinking, 'Oh, oh, where are we going with this?' We're going to understand **how** to keep the Sabbath **spiritually** so when we gather together on the Sabbath the Spirit of God will be here with us, and the Spirit of God in us will all connect together with God and His Word and learn. *That's the whole purpose of Sabbath services today!* We also have something that until about 500 years ago we didn't have. *That's the whole Bible!* So all the circumstances become more spiritual in how we keep the Sabbath.

Then He says, v 11: "For *in* six days the LORD made the heaven and the earth, the sea, and all that *is* in them, and rested the seventh day. Therefore. the LORD blessed the Sabbath Day and **sanctified** it."—*made Holy!*

All right, we find in Deut. 5 that it says we are to **keep** the Sabbath. We will talk about keeping the Sabbath and the degree of keeping the Sabbath and how you should do it, but there's one important aspect of the Sabbath here that he brings out, which is different from what we have in Exo. 20.

Deuteronomy 5:12: "**Keep the Sabbath Day to sanctify it as the LORD your God has commanded you**. Six days you shall labor and do all your work. But the seventh day *is* the Sabbath of the LORD your God. *In it* you shall not do any work, you, nor your son, nor your daughter, nor your manservant, nor your maidservant, nor your ox, nor your donkey, nor any of your livestock, nor your stranger within your gates, so that your manservant and your maidservant may rest as well as you" (vs 12-14).

How many here have servants in their household? *You've got lots of them*: a stove, dishwasher, light switches, furnace. You have lots of servants, but they are *all automated!*

- Can you rest your car? *If it's not running!*
- Is that resting it?
- Is it wrong to drive a car on the Sabbath?
- IIow many walked here today? *Nobody!*

You all came by car!

Here is a key thing we are to remember for the Sabbath that separates us from the rest of the world:

"And remember that you were a slave in the land of Egypt..." (v 15).

Tie in Rev. 11:8; Jerusalem today, which is symbolic of the sin of the world is called *Sodom and Egypt!* So, today we take 'that you were a slave in the land of Egypt' and apply it spiritually this way:

- we were all slaves to the system of the world; slave to *Satan the devil*
- Did God call us out? *Yes!*
- Did we have an exodus from the world? *Yes, but we still live in it!*
- How did that happen? *Through Jesus Christ* Who is called *the Way, the Truth, and the Life!*

We are not just a community and organization of physical people with the name Israel, we are physical people **with the Spirit of God and we are spiritual Israel,** which includes all nations and people. Lest we get lifted up *in conceit* and lest we get lifted up in *spiritual pride,* let us remember that if you count all Sabbath-keepers in the world there are about 20-million. That's why Christ is the Head of the Church; He knows where His people are.

That's why no corporate church—be it the Catholic Church, or be it a Church of God—say, 'We are the only true Church of God on earth.' Are you going to limit God? I just have to say, a lot of us have a lot of baggage still hanging in the back of our mind we need to get washed out with *the washing of the water by the Word* {note our in-depth study: Washing of the Water by the Word} We have a lot of things and concepts of church and people still practicing them that become anchors in growth and overcoming.

How many have faithfully kept the Sabbath for years and years; decades? *Probably all of us,* we could raise both hands and all ten fingers. Have you ever gone to Sabbath services where it wasn't sanctified? Now what do I mean by that? *To where Sabbath services were centered around*:

- extolling a man
- following corporate orders
- politics
- in-fighting among leaders and brethren
  - ✓ How was your Sabbath? *Pretty rotten*—wasn't it?
  - ✓ How many times did you go home feeling miserable?
  - ✓ How many times did you wake up and say, 'Oh, I dread going to Sabbath services, but it's a Holy convocation, so I'm going.'

You get there and it was totally unprofitable. As a matter of fact, you may have gone to church with a good attitude and came home with a rotten attitude. Did that ever happen to you?

I remember sitting over here in the auditorium in Pasadena and I was doing a little survey because of all of the politics and in-fighting going on. Everyone who wants to repeat Pasadena is going to repeat all the intrigue and hatred and everything that went on there because of the sins. So, that's not the model to follow. But I remember sitting there and here was this man, he gave a short message. I thought, let's see how many times he mentions the leader and how many times he mentions Jesus Christ. Well, I forget what it was with the short message, but then the guy for the main message started. So I said, 'Okay, I'm going to do a tally.' You know, do tick marks—one, two, three, four, five… So, I put over here the leader, put up his initials. Put over here Jesus Christ. I did tick marks, tick marks. This is when they were trying to politically contain the Church together. By all means, you must keep the Church together so that you can have the money coming in.

- Isn't that right?
- Isn't that the purpose of the church? **Wrong!**

By all means you must even lie and call all the brethren 'dumb sheep,' if they find out about the truth of the philandering of the evangelist.

I'm sitting there listening to this man, one of the approved. You didn't speak in that auditorium unless you were approved. So, I put a tick mark for Jesus Christ and ten for the leader. Tick mark for Jesus Christ and fifteen for the leader. Believe this or not, in an hour and a half he mentioned Jesus Christ 10 or 11 times and the leader 111 times! Now how is that for a Holy Sabbath? *Really rotten!*

You kept the command to assemble together, but of what profit was it for you? *Not very much!* You go back through all the dark days that were going on there, and how many fights between brethren and ministers, husbands and wives, false doctrine, and everything just under a black cloud. Remember those days? Now that's happening in the Protestant churches today. People are leaving in droves, and they don't know where to go.

Leviticus 23:1: "And the LORD spoke to Moses, saying, 'Speak to the children of Israel and say to them, "*Concerning* the appointed Feasts of the LORD... [*the Sabbath is an appointed Feast of God every week*] ...which you shall proclaim *to be* **Holy convocations**...""(vs 1-2)—*Holy assembly!*

We'll talk about that in a little bit so that you understand that a Holy convocation can be very small in number. A Holy convocation does not necessarily mean that you go to a synagogue or a church building.

"...even these are My appointed Feasts. Six days shall work be done, but the seventh day *is* the Sabbath of rest, a Holy convocation. You shall not do any work. It *is* a Sabbath to the LORD in all your dwellings" (vs 2-3). *Then it talks about the appointed Feasts in their seasons!*

Sidebar *on the calendar* here for just a few minutes, so be patient. Have you gone through all the calendar material that we have? *Four videos and a stack of information!* There are many problems with Sabbath-keeping and new moon observation and things like this, which is causing a great deal of confusion among Churches of God and even Seventh Day Adventists who keep the Holy Days, as one of the elders brought up. We'll try and answer that.

Be prepared to really get your thinking cap on; be prepared to really, really know. All those who are in the helpers' class, as we call it, I'm going to make that an assignment for everyone of you to do. It's going to take you some time to go through it. But I will give you just a little review:

When the sundial went back ten degrees during the days of Hezekiah, that got all calendars off everywhere. How many have seen on the History Channel this Greek apparatus with all the gears, tells about the movement of the planet, the movement of the sun. They even had it where they had some things that would compensate for the variation in the moon. The moon goes fast and goes slow. The earth goes fast and goes slow. The orbit of the earth is not exactly perfect.

Some believe that we originally started out with 360 days, twelve months of thirty days and everything was just fine. But then we had the Flood! We know, through the evidence of Velikovsky, close encounters with Mars.

So the last time that the earth had a major astronomical event was during the days of Hezekiah. *That threw all the calendars off!* How do we get from 360 days to 365-1/4 days? *Well, because of astronomical events!* Someone did some calculation on it and said that the earth had to slide out of its orbit by 1.4 degrees in order for the sundial to go back 10 degrees.

Now we have five days added to the solar year? The key thing is this: *God never loses a second!* He had to re-reveal to the priests how to calculate the Holy Day calendar. It has always been by calculation. Yes, there has been observation, but only if it agrees with the calculation. Now we have it in the material that we will send to you a whole book on how to

calculate it. If you know how to add, subtract, multiply, and divide, you can calculate.

Because the earth, the moon, the sun, and the heavenly bodies associated with keeping time have all been functioning at different rates and different speeds and different times, you have to base everything on an average. So, the Calculated Hebrew Calendar does that. God gave this to the priests.

Verse 4: "These *are* **the appointed Feasts of the LORD**, Holy convocations, which you... [to the Levites] ...shall proclaim **in their appointed seasons**."

God gave it to the priests and the Levites. They would determine and calculate when it would be and you can read that in all the material that we send out to you. We have the whole book, *Sanctification of the New Moon* by Maimonides. You've got everything in there. They knew clear back then, the 5,000 permutations or misnomers of the moon. They had all that figured out. They were to proclaim it.

It came on down through the priesthood, even though there was corruption within the priesthood. God preserved that information. Came down to the time of Jesus Christ, there were two schools—Hillel and Shammai. Hillel was the head of the calendar court. He was called a Nasi. He was a priest. He was head of the calendar court. And we can prove that everything that was done during the days of Jesus was done according to the Calculated Hebrew Calendar, because the Passover that He was crucified on was by calculation with two postponements. That was the appointed season.

A little more on the calendar and then we'll move on. When the temple was destroyed, a whole school of priests moved up to Tiberius and that's where they preserved the knowledge of the calendar, as well as other things. That's where they also started writing what later became the Mishnah and later the Talmud. What they did, they wrote down everything that was going on at the temple, because they didn't know when they would be able to get back to the temple or not. So, they were writing that down.

Later because of persecution they moved over to Jebnah, which is on the coast, right near where Tel Aviv is. If you read the book of Haggai you find that God said the remnant of the Jews would be on the coast. And the Jews in Tel Aviv and the area right near there, Haifa and so forth, have had relative peace because that's where they should be. They should not be in the West Bank and that's why they have so much trouble there.

When they moved to Jebnah in the year 354ₐ.ᴅ., Hillel II who was the grandson of Hillel I, great-great-great grandson. He released to the world the knowledge of how to calculate the Hebrew calendar to the world. People come along and say, 'Oh, he invented the calendar in 354ₐ.ᴅ.' *Not true!* There was so much persecution against the Jews and against the Christians that he was afraid that that knowledge would be lost, so he revealed it to the world.

If you want an easy way to figure it, we have online the Calculated Hebrew Calendar. You put in the year and up come all the Holy Days including the Passover. We have the best calculated digital Hebrew calendar program, in the world, right on our **truthofGod.org** website.

Since the priests were to proclaim it, the only proclamation for the Holy Days is the Calculated Hebrew Calendar, which came from the priests—*period!* No other man is authorized to view the moon or to devise a calendar, because he is not a priest. God never gave the responsibility of creating a new calendar to the New Testament Church.

So everyone who says, 'Well, I'm going to view it. Let's watch for the new moon.' You must be an expert in it, because to truly see the new moon you must be in a particular place in Jerusalem at a particular time and it is only visible between ten and fifteen minutes right after sundown. If you miss it but see it the next day, you're already a day off and God never loses a day.

Now one final thing concerning the calendar, *because it's important having to do with the Holy Days!* You've heard of the 19-year time cycle. Why is there a 19-year time cycle? Two reasons:

1. there's a 19-year time cycle for the sun
2. there's a 19-year time cycle for the moon

They coincide within one hour and few minutes every 19 years. So every 19 years that hour and some odd minutes is accumulated until you get a whole day. That is called a postponement.

Is that not what we have on the Roman calendar today? *Every fourth year we add a day!* Why do we do that? *Because if we didn't, we'd lose a quarter of a day every year!* That's why in the 1500s Pope Gregory said, 'Okay, we've lost ten days on the Julian calendar up to today.' So, what they did, they took in October and they said, 'We are going to add ten days to the calendar.' You can take any day, but I think they did it on the fourth of October. The next day was the fifteenth.

All those who don't believe in postponements still follow along with the Gregorian calendar, which is the one we have today. It was postponed ten days and every four years it's postponed one day. Postponements are synchronizing adjustments to keep everything in time. Otherwise you wouldn't proclaim them in their seasons.

Let's talk about some other aspects of the Sabbath. Let's come to the book of Nehemiah. Let's see some things here that are very important. Because there are a lot of people who feel as though we should follow Nehemiah.

Nehemiah 13:14: "Remember me, O my God, concerning this, and do not wipe out my good deeds which I have done for the house of my God and for the offices of it. In those days I saw in Judah *some* treading winepresses on the Sabbath..." (vs 14-15).

- How big is Judah? *Very small area!*
- How big is Jerusalem? *A very small city!*

Keep that in mind!

"...and bringing in sacks of grain, and loading donkeys and also wine, grapes, and figs, and all kinds of burdens which they brought into Jerusalem on the Sabbath Day. And I admonished *them* on the day in which they sold food. And men of Tyre dwelt therein, who brought fish and all kinds of goods, and sold them on the Sabbath to the children of Judah and in Jerusalem. And I contended with the nobles of Judah and said to them, 'What evil thing *is* this that you do and defile the Sabbath Day?'" (vs 15-17).

Now let's look at the setting that we have in Jerusalem. They didn't have to travel anywhere to keep Sabbath. I don't know how many synagogues there were in Jerusalem, but they had the temple plus some synagogues all within walking distance. Did they have any of the circumstances we have today in coming to church? *No!* In this case they were bringing the world to themselves. Today, we *live in the world and gather together!* Complete opposite! So, then he shut the gates and put guards up there, the Levites, made sure that there was no more buying and selling in Jerusalem. With that in mind, let's see what happened during the days of Jesus:

Mark 2:23: "Now, it came to pass that **He went through the grain fields on the Sabbaths**..."

Did Jesus stay in Jerusalem and do nothing on the Sabbath? *No!* Circumstances were even a little different then. They had synagogues in Galilee, and they had synagogues in various parts of Judea as well. So, here He's walking. According to Exo. 16 He shouldn't even have been outside the door of His house, because it says *'Don't go out of the door or your tent.'* The Greek here—Sabbaths—is plural:

"...grain fields on the Sabbaths..." *This shows a repeated thing that He was doing on the Sabbaths!*

"...and as His disciples made *their* way *through the fields*, they were picking *and eating* the grain" (v 23).

What does it say in the Old Testament? *You're to keep the Sabbath in harvest time!*

Verse 24: "Then the Pharisees said to Him, 'Look *at them*! Why are they doing that which is not lawful on the Sabbaths?'"

What were they doing? *They were picking the grains, rubbing them in their hands, and eating them!* I don't know how much they were picking, but by time you get twelve disciples, and it doesn't say whether Jesus ate or not. By time you get twelve disciples doing all of that, *you're stripping quite a few heads of grain!*

Notice how He answered them, because there's a time when, because of the circumstances and because of how we are, we can add today, just like in His day, that there are some things from the Old Testament that have to be re-judged according to the need.

Verse 25: "And He said to them, 'Have you never read what David did when he was hungry and in need *of food*, he and those with him? How in *the days of* Abiathar the high priest, he entered into the house of God and he ate the showbread, which it is not lawful to eat except for the priests, and he also gave *it* to those who were with him?'" (vs 25-26).

What was happening? *They were running from Saul!* They were all sweaty and hungry! How many have ever seen the loaves of showbread? *There was a big loaf that was put there every Sabbath!* They put new bread at noon on the Sabbath when the new course of priests would come in. There was a special tray, which had six shelves on each side, and each loaf was for one of the twelve tribes. The priests were to eat that. *That was Holy to the Lord!*

Remember what happened when Uzziah went in to offer incense? *He was struck with leprosy,* because he was presuming to be a priest when he was not. Here the circumstances are different. Now notice what Jesus says and let's analyze the circumstances that they had.

Verse 27: "And He said to them, 'The Sabbath was made for man, *and* not man for the Sabbath; therefore, the Son of man is Lord even of the Sabbath'" (vs 27-28). **What was the purpose of the Sabbath made for man?**

- to rest

- to remember that you came out of Egypt as slaves
- to worship the Lord
- to assemble together
for us in the New Testament Church
- to grow in grace and knowledge
- be educated in how we become the sons and daughters of God
- to be kings and priests at the resurrection

Matthew 12:1: "At that time Jesus went through the grain fields on the Sabbath Days; and His disciples were hungry, and they began to pluck the heads of grain and to eat *them*. But after seeing *this*, the Pharisees said to Him, 'Behold, Your disciples are doing what is not lawful to do on *the* Sabbath.' But He said to them, 'Have you not read what David did when he himself and those with him were hungry? How he went into the house of God and he ate the loaves of showbread, which it was not lawful for him to eat, nor for those who were with him, but for the priests only? Or have you not read in the law that on the Sabbaths the priests in the temple profane the Sabbath and are guiltless?'" (vs 1-5). *They did the work!* There was a lot of work.

Have you ever slaughtered an animal? Let alone spend all day slaughtering animals and offering sacrifices. They really worked at the temple! Jesus shows His authority over the Sabbath, because we read in Mark 2 that the 'Son of man is Lord even of the Sabbath Day'

Verse 6: "But I say to you, there is *One* here Who is greater than the temple."

We need to think on that, because this is by the authority of the one who put his presence in the temple, Who was the Lord God of the Old Testament and became Jesus Christ of the New Testament.

He is showing here that while they were traveling, and it was on the Sabbath Day, and may very well have been walking longer than what the Jews would consider a Sabbath Day's journey, and this they were doing repeatedly on the Sabbath. *That's what it's talking about here in the plural!* This is not just a one time event that they were doing.

Jesus is telling the Pharisees that "...*One* here Who is greater than the temple" *has given them permission to do so, for the need for the strength and energy to serve on the Sabbath!* We need to keep that in mind.

Verse 7: "Now, if you had known what this *means*, 'I desire mercy and not sacrifice,' you would not have condemned the guiltless. **For the Son of man is Lord even of the Sabbath Day**" (vs 7-8).

Let's also understand that Jesus also said to 'go into all the world and preach the Gospel.' *Of course, that entails travel!* That entails different things that living in the restricted area of Jerusalem or in the confines of our homes if you're keeping church at home, or where two or three families are gathered together. *Most of us travel, and some of us great distances!*

When we meet here we meet in a hotel and they have their employees that they hire. They are here whether we are here or not. If we didn't eat a meal here they would still be here. But because we all travel, it is perfectly allowable for these kinds of occasions that we pay for ahead of time. The room is paid for ahead of time, and that we can have an extended Sabbath Day service, with morning and afternoon services, with a meal in between.

Based on this and based on the circumstances, and based on serving God in love, Truth and Spirit, this is permissible.

It's not permissible to go out and do your grocery shopping on the Sabbath, or to buy goods on the Sabbath. This is just for the purpose of brethren gathering together for a Sabbath service. Since we are not close together and we all travel we can have fellowship together, a meal together and God has always blessed us in this. It has never been without a blessing. We have done this for years, so we need to consider this. *They—the priests—worked!*

- Have you ever done butchering"
- Have you ever slaughtered some animals, cut them up"
- How about if you do it all day long?

Verse 7: "Now, if you had known what this *means,* "I desire mercy and not sacrifice," you would not have condemned the guiltless.

What is Jesus saying here? He's saying there are times when the letter of the Law—to serve a physical and spiritual purpose—you do not 'strain at a gnat and swallow a camel.'

Let's apply this to what we do when we're traveling. We meet here in this room. It applies to a Feast day or wherever you are.

- Do we pay for the room? *Of course!*
- Does the hotel require their personnel to be here to manage and watch the property and take care of it? *Yes!*
- Whose servant are they? *The hotel's!*
- Do they do this when we don't meet here? *Of course, they do!*

When we meet here, are we like in Jerusalem, a small little city where we can all walk? *No! A lot of us have to drive!* When I come down we have all-day services and we have them serve us a lunch. Has God cursed us because of that? *No, He's blessed us!* Why? *Because this comes into the category of the showbread!*

Now someone would say, 'Well, we need to get a hall where we can have potlucks.' All right, that's fine. Who's going to do all the work then? *Because the work has to be done!* Who's making people in the Church work? *People in the Church!*

So, from this we have made the judgment.... Now if someone is otherwise minded and they think they should not do as we do here, then that is your personal preference. But know this, it doesn't make us more sinners, nor those who don't eat on the Sabbath in circumstances like this, more righteous. It's a needful area that God blesses, because of the circumstances. All right, now let's reverse it!

- What if you're meeting at home? *You have no need to eat out! You're at home!*
- What if you're the only one at home?
- How can you keep a Holy convocation, especially for new people?

  1. they don't know where a church or congregation is
  2. you can't easily get there, you've got to drive

- Can you still keep the Sabbath at home? *That's the whole basis of Church at Home! Of course, you can!*
- What if you're alone? *You pray and ask God to bless your study, to bless your day!*
- Who is there?
- What did Jesus say? *'Wherever two or three are gathered together in My name, there I am in the midst.'*
- If it's you, God the Father and Jesus Christ, how many is that?
- So can we have a Sabbath at home alone? *Yes, but you're not alone!*
- Do you miss being with brethren? *Yes!*
- Are you still in a Holy convocation with you, God the Father and Jesus Christ at home? *Yes!*
- What if two families get together? *Same thing applies!*

We meet here every other Sabbath!
- Are we going against the Holy convocation area of the Sabbath by doing only every other Sabbath?
- Why do we go every other Sabbath? *It's simply because not everyone can come every Sabbath!*

Maybe there will be a time when there will be enough people where we can meet every Sabbath.

That will be fine. But still, in meeting every Sabbath not everyone can come every Sabbath.

- Are the ones who meet every Sabbath more righteous than the ones who don't meet every Sabbath?
- What is the quality of your Sabbath?
- Is it spiritual?
- Are you learning the Word of God?
- What is it?

We pay for the room and we pay for the food. Everything's all arranged ahead of time. I think God is more pleased to see us gather together on the Sabbath, since we're so scattered, and be able to have a meal together and fellowship together, rather than say we're going to go by Neh. 13. You can't go by Neh. 13, because you're not in Jerusalem and you're not there in the same circumstances.

If you are in your home, you can go by Neh. 13. If a salesman comes to the door, you spray him with mace—psst! *NO!* We are living *in* the world, not *of* the world. We are called out of the world and the circumstances are different than if you're in Jerusalem where the whole city keeps the Sabbath. The temple is there; the synagogues are there; you don't have to drive; you don't have to get on a donkey and go someplace. Besides, the donkey is supposed to rest, too.

What if you have to drive and you have to go on a toll road? Where I go up to Fairfield I have to cross a bridge. Used to be $2.00, now it's $5.00. Am I sinning if I give him a $5.00 bill? *Or* Would I be sinning if I neglected the flock and say, 'I can't come up here because I have to pay the toll'? *Well, come up on Friday.* I used to come up on Friday, but there are so many things to do that I can't come up on Friday anymore. But then, if I come up on Friday to avoid paying the toll on the bridge, I have to *get a motel,* and I have to *go buy some food! That's why Jesus said He desires mercy, not sacrifice!*

So, you have to make the judgment on it. There is Rom. 14, we are not to make the Sabbath a burden. We are not to judge our brothers concerning eating and drinking, another point said. The Kingdom of God is not a matter of eating and drinking.

Let's see the circumstances that Paul was confronted with. This follows right along the line with, 'I desire mercy and not sacrifice.'

1-Corinthians 8:1: "Now concerning things sacrificed to idols, we know that we all have knowledge. **Knowledge puffs up, but love edifies**.... [God wants mercy; God wants love] ...But if anyone thinks that he knows anything, he knows nothing yet to the degree that he ought to know. But if anyone loves God, he is known by Him. So then,

concerning the eating of things sacrificed to idols... (vs 1-4)

- What was this? *They lived where they had pagan temples,* by former pagan people who are now members of the Church of God.
- What did you have? *You had the temple of Zeus, the temple of Diana, the temple of Apollos!* You had incense altars and everything like that.

All the meat that they bought was sacrificed to the gods. So some people said, 'Well, we're just going to just going to be vegetarians.' That was most of the problem of Rom. 14. Others said, 'Idol doesn't mean anything. It's dumb, it's stupid, there's nothing in it.

Verse 4: "So then, concerning the eating of things sacrificed to idols, we understand that an idol in *the* world *is* nothing, and that *there is* no other God except one. For indeed, even if there are *those* which are called gods, whether in heaven or on earth, as there are many gods and many lords" (vs 4-5).

Like Hinduism: they have 400-thousand gods and goddesses. You can't even go out and step on an ant, you kill one of your lost relatives. You can't kill they this cow though its pooping right in your house.

Verse 6: "Still, to us *there is* one God the Father, from Whom *are* all things, and we *are* in Him; and one Lord Jesus Christ, by Whom *are* all things, and we *are* by Him. However, not all *have* this knowledge. But some, with consciousness of the idol, until now eat *it* as a thing sacrificed to an idol, and their conscience, being weak, is defiled" (vs 6-7).

We don't have that problem. We don't have it today! That was a real problem. Then he said, 'What if someone sees you sitting in the idol's temple eating?' You could even go there and buy it cooked ready to go. That was their McDonald's! And a church member comes by and says, 'Oh! Guess what I saw. I saw so-and-so over at the idol's temple eating. He's condemned.' *No, he's not condemned, because he knows an idol is nothing!* Can an idol contaminate food? *No!* But there's a crossover point if you get involved in the religious services.

Let's see what Paul wrote concerning this, 1-Corinthians 10:14: "Therefore, my beloved, flee from idolatry. I speak as to those who are wise; you judge what I say? (vs 14-15).

We have to make judgments! We have to judge *righteous* judgments! Whatever it is to serve the brethren, to edify the brethren, and as long as we are yielding to God, led by His Spirit, we convoke together with God's Spirit, God blesses us in what we are doing with that. Same way if you have church at home.

Now, we are going to have new people coming and as Harry ran surveys for the Church in the past, when they started to get on the mailing list, it took what, two years before they started—between two and three years. There are going to be new people coming in, brand new people. They're going to have different hang ups than you have. What we need to do is shed all the hang-ups that we've had from our previous Church of God associations.

Some things were good; some things were not good. But we have to be able to realize when new people come, there are going to be difficulties involved. We can't be so sensitive that when new people come, we say, 'Oh, they're disturbing us and we don't have the love we used to have,' and all of that sort of thing. Help them to learn the love of God so you keep the love of God.

Verse 16: "The cup of blessing that we bless, is it not *the* fellowship of the blood of Christ? The bread that we break, is it not *the* fellowship of the Body of Christ? For we, being many, are one Body *and* One Bread, because we are all partakers of the Bread" (vs 16-17)—*Who is Christ!*

Didn't He say, 'Break this bread. This is My body.' And the Church is the Body of Christ? *Yes, indeed!*

Verse 18: "Consider Israel according to *the* flesh. Are not those who eat the sacrifices partakers of the altar?.... [of course!] ...What then am I saying? That an idol is anything, or that which is sacrificed to an idol is anything?" (vs 18-19). *Of course not*, he said *no!* However, don't cross the line and get involved in their religious services.

Verse 20: "But that which the Gentiles sacrifice, they sacrifice to demons, and not to God; and I do not wish you to have fellowship with demons. You cannot drink *the* cup of *the* Lord, and *the* cup of demons. **You cannot partake of *the* table of *the* Lord, and *the* table of demons**" (vs 20-21). *You can't do that!*

That's why having the Passover in the right way, according to the Truth of what is taught is of paramount importance. As you'll find out when you read the third edition of *The Christian Passover* book, what is the one central thing that Satan wants to get? *He wants to get you separated from God!* How can he do that? *There are various distractions and pleasures in the world!* That's one way. But to really do it, is to *confuse the issue concerning the Christian Passove*r: when it's to be taken, how it's

to be taken. That's why we have that 500-page book, *The Christian Passover.*

It covers more than the Passover, but it's important to understand that is the renewal of the covenant. **_IF_ you don't partake of the Passover in the manner that is worthy according to the way that Jesus has instructed, _THEN_ you can take the first step going out from God!** That's why it's important. We are in a covenant relationship with God that is bound by our covenant baptism.

Baptism is not a ritual to get into a church. *Baptism is a covenant pledge that you make to God because God's covenant pledge was that Christ died for you!*

- What are you going to do for God?
- What does God require of you?

If Christ died, you die! How do you die? *Baptism, conjoined to His death!* **That is your covenant pledge to God!**

It also says this: If you do not fulfill the agreement of the New Covenant with the Spirit of God in faith, hope, love and growing in grace and knowledge, that you are going to die. *That symbolic death in the watery grave of baptism is your pledge to God: I will be faithful to the end!* He says, *'I will give you eternal life and resurrect you.'*

Satan is wanting to stop you from attaining that! The central thrust is going to be against the Christian Passover, the way Jesus taught us to take it. That's why we have so many different variations in the world. You've got the Lord's Supper in the morning. Never could figure out how that could be. You take it every Sunday if you're a Catholic and especially a priest. You know, you have Mass at six, at seven, at eight, at nine, ten o'clock you have High Mass. You get out the incense and you do all these things that you do. But what do they do with the Mass? They have so perverted it that they claim that the priest has the power to command Christ to come down into that sun wafer offered to an idol in the temple of the sun on Sunday, and say that the priest in command says to Christ to put His presence in there.

I tell you this: *Christ obeys no man!* And what they are doing, he is crucifying Christ every time they go through it. So that's the central thing. Likewise, with the Sabbath. We'll get back here to Sabbath-keeping.

Let's see how we are to conduct ourselves. Here is the attitude and this is a spiritual attitude. So in the weeks that we don't meet, have a good Sabbath at home. Maybe get your children together. Spend some time with them. Spend some time really teaching them the Word of God. That might help your family a whole lot. Would that not be a good Holy convocation at home? *Yes, indeed!*

Maybe several families could get together. *Fine!* In that circumstance, you're still going to eat, but you don't need to go out because you're right at home. You can take care of that. Here's what God wants us to do.

How do we profane the Sabbath? *By doing things of the world, thinking the way the world thinks!*

- Can you turn off television one day? *Yes!*
- Can you stop the music one day except music that glorifies God? *Yes!*
- Can your children learn to sit down and understand the Bible? *Yes!*
- Are you capable of teaching them? *Yes!*

Especially through the Proverbs! Talk about what they go through at school. I think more and more you ought to have home-schooling. That's a lot of work.

As a matter of fact, that would be my suggestion to end the problems at school. Shut all schools down, have all mothers stay home, teach the children at home on the Internet. Use the school's facilities for community activities only. Retire most of the teachers. Keep a number of them for tutors and you can eliminate hundreds of millions and billions of dollars. You would solve a lot of crime, *because they would be at home, not out with gangs.*

Isaiah 56:1: "Thus says the LORD, 'Keep justice and do righteousness; for My salvation *is* near to come, and My righteousness to be revealed.... [this is a prophecy of the New Testament] ...Blessed *is* the man who does this, and the son of man who lays hold on it; **who keeps the Sabbath from profaning it**, and keeps his hand from doing any evil'" (vs 1-2). *Profaning means to secularize!*

Verse 3: "And do not let the son of the stranger, who has joined himself to the LORD, speak, saying, 'The LORD has utterly separated me from His people.' And do not let the eunuch say, 'Behold, I *am* a dry tree.' For thus says the LORD, 'To the eunuchs who keep My Sabbath**s**... [plural] ...and choose things that please Me, and take hold of My covenant; even to them will I give within My house and within My walls a place and a name better than of sons and of daughters; I will give them an everlasting name that shall not be cut off'" (vs 3-5). *That's talking about the resurrection!*

This also tells us that *the purpose of the Sabbath is to be preparing for the resurrection* **IF** we:

- grow in grace

- grow in knowledge
- grow in righteousness
- grow in all of these things

That's what the Sabbath is for! Then he says:

Verse 6: "Also the sons of the stranger, who join themselves to the LORD to serve Him, and to love the name of the LORD, to be His servants, **everyone who keeps from profaning the Sabbath, and takes hold of My covenant**" (v 6)—*and that is the New Covenant! That's what we've done!*

So what we need to do is this: In keeping the Sabbath we keep it Holy. How? *By shutting off the world as much as we can!* If you have to drive here, you have to drive through the world. What do you do? *You pray for protection!* You go home, you pray for protection!

Have you ever been in a wreck and you know that God spared you from it? Years ago when I was writing the first edition of the Passover book, I rolled my car over going at 75mph on Hwy 5, because I was doing something stupid trying to block out the sun and the left front tire went over the edge of the highway and rolled over. I don't relive the experience, but I remember it and learned a lesson. *Don't do stupid things while you're driving, Fred!* I know just about the spot where it is, so whenever I go down and go home I remember, *Don't do anything stupid!*

When it rolled over and I didn't have my seatbelt on, it rolled over one whole time, clear around, and I'm thinking, Ooooh, no! Landed right side up, blew out two tires. The roof was all bent, the windshield had cracked and the back windshield was out and it was all dusty. I opened the door of the car, got out and stood up. I had a little knick on my forehead because of the rear view mirror.

The first thing I said was, 'O God, thank You for saving me from my stupidity.' God protected me. What they did, they wanted to tow the car clear down to Bakersfield. I said, 'Oh no, I'll never get home from there.' So, the highway patrolman told the tow truck, because he wanted to have some money towing the truck, and he says, 'Go ahead and see if the tires will hold the bead.' So he put the air in the tires—yes—start the car and he says, 'Well, go up here about 20 miles and check in and redo these tires because there may be some sand in there and there may be some air going out.

I looked like I had been dumped on with a flour sack. They had cell phones at that time and as soon as the highway patrolman came, someone said, 'Well, do you want to call home?' I said, 'Yeah.' So I gave him the number, he called home and I said, 'Mom, I'll be a little late. I had an accident with the car. I rolled it over, I'm okay. Bye.'

I drove up, got the car taken care of. When I got home, we had a patio above the garage, so here I'm coming in my little diesel Isuzu. Everything was all out of whack and the body was twisted. Dust from the wreck that had gotten in the back of the car was blowing all over and it was so cold coming over the mountain that I had a pillow back there because the window was broken so the wind was coming in.

When I finally came up, Dolores was up on the balcony looking down and the kids were there. I got out and stood up and all she could do was laugh, because I looked like I was Scrooge from the movie, Ebenezer Scrooge. *So, God takes care of us in it!*

Isaiah 58:13: "If you turn your foot away from the Sabbath... [from doing your own thing] ...*from* doing your own desires on My Holy Day, and call the Sabbath a delight... [it is a delight and that means on the Sabbath, by all means, you need to pray] ...the Holy of the LORD, honorable; and shall honor Him, not doing your own ways, nor pursuing your own desires, nor speaking *your own* words." *Learn the words of Christ!*

Verse 14: "Then you shall delight yourself in the LORD; and I will cause you to ride upon the high places of the earth, and feed you with the inheritance of Jacob your father, for the mouth of the LORD has spoken it." *It gives us the whole purpose of what we are to do!* That's what we need to focus in on, on the Sabbath.

- If there are things we need to do, like drive to assemble—*that's fine!*
- Gather together a couple of families—*that's fine!*
- Be alone and only Christ and you and the Father are there—*that's fine!*
- Get together where we have a meeting like we have here—*that's fine!*
- Have a meal like we have here—*that's not against God!*

Do we lose God's Spirit when we go in there and eat in there? *No, we don't!* God has blessed us with it. We've done this for how long? I think only once or twice they've tried to slip in some shrimp or some ham on us, but we took care of that.

I hope this helps you understand that there are many different ways to keep the Sabbath as long as you keep it, but you also have to adjust to the circumstances in your life and the circumstances of other people when they are involved.

When we come together, do this: *Leave your hang-ups at home if you haven't gotten your hang-ups washed away by the washing of the water by the Word!* Let's meet in love, in acceptance; not judging, not criticizing. If someone has a problem

and you see the problem, what did John tell us to do? *Pray for the individual!* You don't sit there and criticize and condemn him. Do you want someone to criticize and condemn you? *No!* Same way.

- we meet in *love*
- we meet in *understanding*
- we meet in *thanksgiving*

We meet and we ask Christ and God the Father to be here so that *with Their Spirit and with Their Word we are fed the Word of God!* We have something that we can grow in grace and knowledge with.

Keep all of that in mind and I hope that helps us with it. We could go through some other things, but we won't. But I'm sure the Apostle Paul traveled on the Sabbath. How long did it take him to get to Rome? *A year and a half!* So, his circumstances were different, and ours are different. But that doesn't mean, like some people say…

I remember one man saying, 'Well, I have no trouble going out and shopping for groceries on the Sabbath.' I said, 'Well, I do.' But if I'm traveling a long distance and things like that, I eat along the way; I've taken lunch with me, too. I've done both; we could do both.

But then I find that God doesn't condemn me in it. He doesn't condemn you in it. But if we go ahead and then make it something, then where the meal and just being together eating becomes the central part of Sabbath services, *then we're getting into the area where we are not using the Sabbath for our spiritual benefit!*

I hope that helps answer a lot of questions. Maybe it created a whole lot more—whatever. If it did, we'll bring them up and we'll discuss those.

Scriptural References:

1) Exodus 20:8-11
2) Deuteronomy 5:12-15
3) Leviticus 23:1-4
4) Nehemiah 13:14-17
5) Mark 2:23-28
6) Matthew 12:1-5-8, 7
7) 1-Corinthians 8:1-7
8) 1-Corinthians 10:14-21
9) Isaiah 56:1-6
10) Isaiah 58:13-14

Scriptures referenced, not quoted:

- Exodus 16
- Revelation 11:8
- Romans 14

Also referenced:

- In-Depth Study: *Washing of the Water by the Word*
- Videos and Accompanying Material: *Calculated Hebrew Calendar*
- Books:
  - ✓ *Sanctification of the New Moon* by Maimonides
  - ✓ *The Christian Passover* by Fred R. Coulter

FRC:lp
Transcribed: 2-15-11
Reformatted: bo—10/2020

Section II

God's Holy Days
Overview

CHAPTER EIGHT

Important Events on Holy Days
Keys to understanding the deep things of God,
and God reveals them when we need to understand
Fred R. Coulter

- Why does God hide things in a secret?
- How do we find them?

That's quite a question, because everyone can have access to a Bible in their own language. God has made it so that no one can have an excuse and say, 'God, I never knew.' His answer will be, 'Did you have a Bible?' *Yes!* 'Did you read it?' *No!* Why didn't you? Some would say that they read it, but couldn't understand it. Why is that? *Because there are certain keys necessary for God to reveal!*

1. Obey My Voice!

We have the Bible with the voice of God all written down, and Jesus said, 'Man shall not live by bread alone, but by every word of God that proceeds out of His mouth.'

God is so great, good and powerful, that in spite of the sins of all people in the world, He's caused His Word to be spread around the world. Anyone at anytime can have access to it, especially in this digital age!

What does the Bible tell us about those who have understanding? *Those who keep the commandments of God!* Stop and think about it; one of the greatest events to take place in the history of mankind was when Israel was before God at Mt. Sinai. God spoke the Ten Commandments. All of the Israelites heard Him.

- Do you know the Ten Commandments?
- Do you keep them?

if you keep them
- How do you keep them?

That's a key!

We're going to see something else later on, but when God gave the Ten Commandments that was on a Pentecost. All of the Sabbaths and Holy Days of God give us important things:

- in time
- in history
- in prophecy
- in fulfillment

God has said in the New Testament that *it's given to those who love God to understand the mysteries or the secrets of God!* They are secrets because of the

keys that are necessary to understand. *The first one is obey His voice!*

2. **Keep His Sabbath and the Commandments of God**
3. **The Passover and Holy Days of God**

Let's think about it for just a minute: the Sabbath Day every seventh day. In spite of the sins of the Jews, they have preserved the Old Testament and the Calculated Hebrew Calendar. All God's days are based on **His** calendar. Think about all these things as we're going along.

*God deals with **nations, His people and His Church,** all three!*

In Dan. 2 Nebuchadnezzar had a dream—he was king of Babylon—and he pulled a 'slick one' on his astrologers and soothsayers. He said, *'I had a dream and I want you to do two things*:

1) tell me what the dream *was*
2) what the interpretation *is*

If you don't you're going to lose your heads!'

Well, Daniel, Shadrach, Meshach and Abednego were the Jewish young men who were taken captive and brought to Babylon. The captain of the guard told it to Daniel, Shadrach, Meshach and Abednego and they said, 'We'll pray to God and ask Him to reveal what it was that the king dreamt.'

Daniel 2:17: "Then Daniel went to his house and made the matter known to Hananiah, Mishael, and Azariah, his companions…. [that's Shadrach, Meshach and Abednego] …That they might pray for the mercies of God in heaven concerning this secret, that Daniel and his companions should not perish with the rest of the wise men of Babylon. **Then the secret was revealed to Daniel in a night vision**…." (vs 17-19). *God is the revealer of secrets, but He gives conditions to reveal those secrets!* What did Daniel do?

"…And Daniel blessed the God of heaven. Daniel answered and said, 'Blessed be the name of God forever and ever, for wisdom and might are His. And He changes the times and the seasons; He removes kings and sets up kings. He gives wisdom to the wise and knowledge to those who have understanding. He reveals the deep and secret things;

He knows what *is* in the darkness, and the light dwells with Him. I thank You, and praise You, O God of my fathers, Who has given me wisdom and might, and have now made known to me what we desired of You, for You have made known to us the king's matter'" (vs 19-23).

Then Daniel was taken before the king. Here's what was told to the king:

Verse 27: "Daniel answered before the king and said, 'The secret which the king has demanded cannot be shown to the king by the wise men, the enchanters, the astrologers or the magicians."

Who is the god of those enchanters, the astrologers or the magicians? *Satan the devil!* Think of it today:

Do any of the religions of the world anything about the plan of God? *Even many of fake Christianity may understand some parts,* but they don't understand it the way that they should. Why? *Because they have half knowledge!*

Remember, one of the keys to understanding is Sabbath-keeping. Sunday-keeping will never do it. You may guess some parts, but you'll really never understand it.

Verse 26: "The king answered and said to Daniel, whose name *was* Belteshazzar, 'Are you able to make known to me the dream which I have seen and its interpretation?' Daniel answered before the king and said, 'The secret which the king has demanded cannot be shown to the king by the wise men, the enchanters, the astrologers or the magicians. But there is a God in heaven Who reveals secrets and makes known to King Nebuchadnezzar what shall be in the latter days....'" (vs 26-28)—*from that time down to the end, and in outline form!*

Sidebar: Daniel and all of his prophecies are the lock to the framework. Revelation and all the things given to the Apostle John is the key to open the lock. All of those things put together is based upon: **Do you love God and keep His commandments?** *Never forget that!*

"...Your dream and the visions of your head upon your bed *are* these: As for you, O king, while upon your bed your thoughts came to you of what should come to pass hereafter. And **He Who reveals secrets makes known to you what shall come to pass**" (vs 28-29).

Now notice Daniel's attitude; this is what it is important; v 30: "But as for me, **this secret is not revealed to me for *any* wisdom that I have more than any living man,** but so that the interpretation may be made known to the king, and that you may know the thoughts of your heart."

Then Daniel describes it: a man with a head

of gold, chest of silver, then brass, iron and iron and clay. That one image represents the major kingdoms of this world from that time down to the end.

Verse 44—*right down to the ten toes*: "And in the days of these kings, the God of heaven shall set up **a Kingdom, which shall never be destroyed**...." *That's the whole Gospel!*

In every single book in the Bible, it talks about the Kingdom of God, either directly or indirectly! "...shall never be destroyed...."—*and that's pictured by the Feast of Tabernacles!*

"...And the Kingdom shall not be left to other people, but it shall break in pieces and consume all these kingdoms, and it shall stand **forever**" (v 44). *We need to also understand that*:

* God is true
* God cannot lie
* His Word is true

There is no lie in anything that He has in the Scriptures! Men try twist it and try to make it look like a lie. That's also part of what we have to believe. Even though Nebuchadnezzar had an outline of understanding, he really didn't know the details.

Verse 45: "Because you saw that the stone was cut out of the mountain without hands, and that it broke in pieces the iron, the brass, the clay, the silver, and the gold, the great God has made known to the king what shall come to pass hereafter. **And the dream *is* certain, and its interpretation is sure.**'" *And you can depend on this with every single word of God!*

How much time is it from Nebuchadnezzar down to the end? Babylonian Empire—middle of the 5th century B.C.; *well over 2500 years!* Let's see how this fits in with the New Testament:

1-Peter 1:2: "*Who have been chosen* **according to *the* predetermined knowledge of God *the* Father,** by sanctification through *the* Spirit..."

He talking about all of us who have been called, baptized, received the Holy Spirit and have understanding of the Bible. *Very important!*

"...unto obedience and sprinkling of *the* blood of Jesus Christ..." (v 2). *Nowhere in the New Testament does it say that the Law has been done away!*

"...Grace and peace be multiplied to you. Blessed *be* the God and Father of our Lord Jesus Christ, Who, according to His abundant mercy, has begotten us again unto a living hope..." (vs 2-3).

What is that hope? *The hope of eternal life!*

But notice that it says, "…begotten us again…"! Note Appendices P & Q (*The Holy Bible in Its Original Order, A Faithful Version*); also *articles* found on **truthofGod.org**:

- What Does It Mean to be "Born Again"?
- What Does it Mean to be "Born of God"?

When you were conceived, you were begotten by your father, you first begettal and then you were born, your first birth.

Then when you repent and receive the Holy Spirit of God you receive the begettal of God's Spirit in your mind and then when the resurrection comes, that's when you're born again. *It's really that simple!*

"…through *the* resurrection of Jesus Christ from *the* dead; unto an inheritance incorruptible and undefiled and unfading, reserved in heaven for us… [which Christ is going to bring] …who *are* being safeguarded by *the* power of God through faith…" (vs 3-5). *That's why it's important*:

- to believe, *and that's faith*
- to love, *and that's what God wants*
- to obey, *and do what He says*

"…for salvation *that is* ready to be revealed in *the* last time" (v 5).

1-Cor. 2—here we find out that God does reveal things, and reveals them when we need to understand them. There are many things, even in the Old Testament that are prophecies in action of things that are going to take place way in the future. All of those will be major events.

Sidebar: I have two books at home written by two different people who think they know the prophecies. *They don't! They don't understand them! Why? Because they're trying to solve them their way,* rather than let the Bible interpret the Bible to give understanding! That's a big difference!

1-Corinthians 2:9: "But according as it is written, **'The eye has not seen, nor *the* ear heard, neither have entered into *the* heart of man *the* things which God has prepared for those who love Him.'"** *Keep that in mind!*

Everyone wants God's love and forgiveness for themselves. *But how many people want to love God in return, the way that God says we should do it?*

Verse 10: "But God has revealed *them* to us by His Spirit…" *If you don't have the Spirit of God you're not going to understand it!*

- How do you receive the Spirit of God? *You repent and be baptized!*

- What did Peter say about that? *That God reveals it to those who obey Him!*

No one is going to receive the Spirit of God without obeying God! Just not going to happen!

"…for the Spirit searches all things—even the deep things of God" (v 10)—*which are* **hidden** *in the Bible! But He will reveal* them!

Verse 11: "For who among men understands the things of man except *by* the spirit of man, which *is* in him? In the same way also, the things of God no one understands except *by* the Spirit of God. Now, we have not received **the spirit of the world**…" (vs 11-12).

What is the *spirit of the world*? Who does that come from? *Satan the devil!*

"…but the Spirit that *is* of God, **so that we might know the things graciously given to us by God**" (v 12).

Have you seen *Water's World* on Fox News? He used to go out and take his microphone and cameraman and they'd go out on the streets of New York City and ask them different questions. *Some people don't even know who the President is! Some people did not know who Columbus was! That's in the world, lost!* If you asked them anything about God, their eyes would probably roll back like in slot machine!

"…**but the Spirit that *is* of God, so that we might know**…"

Isaiah 56:1—*this will be very enlightening for us*: "**Thus says the LORD**…" *God speaking directly to you,* even though He may have spoken it a long time ago, it makes no difference, because His Word is Spirit and Life! So, it's still active today.

"…'Keep justice and **do righteousness**…" (v 1).

Psalm 119:172: "…**all Your commandments are righteousness**."

If you're not keeping the commandments of God, *you're practicing unrighteousness or lawlessness!* If all of His commandments are righteous that has to be true!

Isaiah 56:1: "…for My salvation *is* near to come… [this toward the end of the age; a prophecy of our time] …and My righteousness to be revealed."

What's the first thing revealed of the righteousness of God that's going to startle the world? Actually shake the world down to the core?

Revelation 6:14[transcriber's correction]: "Then *the* heaven departed like a scroll…" *and the Son of man is revealed!*

The whole earth is going to go into convulsions! *That's the first revelation of the righteousness of God demonstratively to the whole world!* That's so powerful that 144,000 of the children of Israel repent, and a great innumerable multitude repent. That's going to be a startling event to be revealed.

Isaiah 56:2: "**Blessed *is* the man who does this, and the son of man who lays hold on it**..." *This means that you grab it,* and it's like something that you take to your bosom so-to-speak.

"...**who keeps the Sabbath** from profaning it, and keeps his hand from doing any evil" (v 2).

Not only the things that are evil, but when you're doing things that are normal, when you do it on the Sabbath Day, it becomes an evil thing because you're rejecting what God has said! People are blinded because they don't know!

Verse 3: "And do not let the son of the stranger, who has joined himself to the LORD, speak, saying, 'The LORD has utterly separated me from His people.' And do not let the eunuch say, 'Behold, I *am* a dry tree.' For thus says the LORD, 'To the eunuchs **who keep My Sabbaths, and choose things that please Me**...'" (vs 3-4). *That's the key!*

When we love God and keep His commandments we're doing the things that please God!

"...**and take hold of My covenant**... [the covenant of eternal life] ...even to them will I give within **My house**..." (vs 4-5)—*ultimately New Jerusalem!*

"...and within My walls a place and a name better than of sons and of daughters; I will give them an everlasting name that shall not be cut off"— *eternal life!* You have to have eternal life in order to have an everlasting name.

Verse 6: "Also the sons of the stranger, who join themselves to the LORD to serve Him, and to love the name of the LORD, to be His servants, everyone who keeps from profaning the Sabbath, and takes hold of My covenant."

It is rarely taught that those who keep the Sabbath are going to be in the Kingdom of God, but this is exactly what it's telling us!

Verse 7: "Even them I will bring to My Holy mountain... [of New Jerusalem] ...and make them joyful in My house of prayer. Their burnt offerings and their sacrifices *shall be* accepted upon My altar... [only then when they had the sacrifices] ...**for My house shall be called a house of prayer for all people**."

Where was this stated in the New Testament? *John 2!* What did Jesus do? *He went in and made a scourge and drove out the moneychangers, the cattle, birds and everything else. He scattered their money all over!* Can you imagine the made dash of them trying to get the money! Then He said, 'You have made this a den of merchandise, but it should be the house of prayer for all people!'

What was the proposition that God gave to Israel just before He gave the Ten Commandments? *Exo. 19—here's what Israel was to do down through all time!* God gave them His commandments and His Word. This brings together many of the things that we've already covered. God is speaking to Moses and this is what he was to tell the Israelites:

Exodus 19:4: "You have seen what I did to the Egyptians..."

- Was that a major event in history?
- Do you know how long it took Egypt to recover from the destruction that God brought upon them? *400 years!*

"...and *how* I bore you on eagles' wings and brought you unto Myself. Now, therefore..." (vs 4-5).

Notice that God always gives the condition to us; "'...**if** you will obey My voice indeed, and keep My covenant, **then** you shall be a special treasure to Me above all people; for all the earth *is* Mine. And you shall be to Me a kingdom of priests and a Holy nation.' These *are* the words which you shall speak to the children of Israel" (vs 5-6).

All the details came later! But they said, v 8: "And all the people answered together and said, '**All that the LORD has spoken we will do.**'...."

Then they got scared to death and afraid, and they said, *'Moses! You speak to us and you go to God and listen and tell us what God says, and we will do it!' But they never, never did it! They couldn't even do it for 40 days and 40 nights!*

When Moses was on the top of Mt. Sinai and getting the rest of the laws, commandments, statutes and judgments, and all the instructions on building the tabernacle and everything. They came to Aaron and said, 'Hey, we don't know what happened to this guy Moses, he went up on the mountain, it looks like a volcano, maybe he fell in it and died. Make us gods!' So, what did Aaron do? *Made a golden calf!* After they said, *'Yes, we will do all that God says!'*

Notice what God says, and this carries right down to today. I have a message: *What Would the World Be Like if Adam & Eve Had Not Sinned?* It would be quite a different place than it is today.

What would the world have been like if the 12 tribes of Israel had been faithful to God and carried the Word of God to the whole world, even back then? *Remember, it was conditional:* '**IF** you will obey My voice and keep My commandments ***THEN*** you shall be a kingdom of priests to Me!' *But they never did it!* When they went into the 'promised land,' finally got in there after 40 years of wandering around the Sinai Peninsula because of their sins.

What did they do after Joshua and the elders died? *They started going after the gods of the other people!* Israel has been like a roller-coaster of waves. They come to God for so long and then they get down and depraved. Then God has to send a judge to raise them up, get them out of their depths, and we're in one of those low places right now. Will we come up out of it for the time being? *We don't know, we'll have to see!*

Isaiah 43:21—*God says*: "This people *that* I formed for Myself; they shall declare My praise. **Yet, you have not called upon Me,** O Jacob; much less have you troubled yourself about Me, O Israel" (vs 21-22).

Go back and look at all the promises that God gave to the 12 tribes of Israel because of Abraham. When God makes a promise He'll never break it. What happens if sin comes along? *There will be punishment and if there is repentance, go forward again!*

Sidebar: Look at what God promised David. He would always have someone sitting on the throne of Israel, *always! Never missing! Never lacking!*

Then David sinned with Bathsheba. God gave the promise, He doesn't break His word, so He gave punishment against David for what he did. The child died and there was a near revolution by his own family against him. Absalom wanted to take over the kingdom. That was David's punishment. ***But God never changed His pledge, and likewise with Israel!***

If they come back to God—even halfway—God will still give them a little correction, but will be with them and bless them. The Church—look at Rev. 2 & 3—you go through that and see what happened with the Churches.

What does it say about God? *I am the same yesterday, today and forever!* Both the Father and the Son! Now, this is what the world cannot really understand:

Luke 10:21: "In the same hour Jesus rejoiced in the Spirit, and said, 'I praise You, O Father, Lord of heaven and earth, that You did hide these things from *the* wise and intelligent, and did reveal them to babes. Yes, Father, for it was well pleasing in Your sight *to do* so.'"

Doesn't that sound like tying in with Daniel where he said, 'I'm nothing more than any other person, but God is the One Who gave the secret'?

Verse 22: "Then He turned to the disciples *and* said, 'All things were delivered to Me by My Father; and no one knows Who the Son is, except the Father; and Who the Father is, except the Son, **and the one to whom the Son personally chooses to reveal *Him*.**'"

You won't find any other translation this way: "...**the Son personally chooses**..."

Why did I do it that way? *There's a special verb in the Greek called* 'middle voice verb.' Most action is by the subject: 'I see Jack.' That's direct!

Middle voice is that God is *the subject and the object.* His calling is the object back to Himself. So therefore, to translate it *personally* shows the personal involvement that God wants in our lives.

Verse 23: "And He turned to His disciples *and* said privately, 'Blessed *are* the eyes that have seen the things that you see. For I tell you, many prophets and kings have desired to see the things that you see, and have not seen *them*; and to hear the things that you hear, and have not heard *them*.'" (vs 23-24).

Now He gets down the very core; v 25: "Now, a certain doctor of the Law... [he understood the Law, like most theologians today] ...suddenly stood up, tempting Him and saying, 'Master, what shall I do to inherit eternal life?'"

All of you out there, if you're a Sunday-keeper and listening to this—understand what is being said by Jesus. If you believe in Jesus, then you better believe what He says. If you think you're going to have eternal life, you better see how He says that you're going to have eternal life, or you're just deluding yourself. *Your Sunday-keeping is doing you no good spiritually speaking!*

Verse 26: "And He said to him, 'What is written in the Law? How do you read *it*?' Then he... [the doctor of the Law] ...answered *and* said, 'You shall love *the* Lord your God with all your heart, and with all your soul, and with all your strength, and with all your mind; and your neighbor as yourself'" (vs 26-27).

All Sunday-keepers: Do you do this? What is the love of God?

1-John 5:3: "For this is the love of God: **that we keep His commandments**; and His commandments are not burdensome." *They are freedom! Freedom from sin!*

Luke 10:29: "But he, desiring to justify himself, said to Jesus, '**And who is my neighbor?**'"

Doctor of the Law, like a priest!

So, Jesus gave him a parable (paraphrased): there was a certain man who was robbed, beaten and left over in the ditch to die. Along came a priest and saw him and went clear to the other side of the road as he was going to do his religious duty at the temple, and did nothing to help him. Then along came a Levite and he looked over and he had to get to the temple so he could offer the sacrifices.

Then along came a Samaritan, which is like saying they're the most cursed people on earth to a Jew. He came and took the man, cleaned his wounds, put oil and wine on it and put him on his donkey and took him to an inn and took care of him. When he left, because he had to go to Jerusalem to do some business, told the inn-keeper, 'Here's some money, you take care of him and if it's more than that, when I come back I'll pay you.'

So, Jesus asked the doctor of the Law: Who do you suppose loved his neighbor?' And the doctor of the Law said, 'Well, I suppose the Samaritan.' *That was probably hard for him to say!*

We're going to look at some Scriptures understand some really deep things of God. But before we get going, I want to cover a couple of things here:

➢ Book: *From a Speck of Dust to a Son of God: Why Were You Born?*

The most important thing you need to know is **why you were born,** this is vital and shows you why this nations is under a curse because of all the abortions. They're killing the most innocent of all:

➢ Transcript Book/w CD: *The Keys to Answered Prayer*

The most important thing in your Christian life is prayer! That way you have contact with God, and God has contact with you.

*****

Now let's continue on with our study today. Let's come to an important event, but before we get there let's do a little rehearsal.

The Sabbath:

- Is the Sabbath a commemoration of an important event?
- What does it say in the 4th commandment? *For in six days God made the heaven and earth!*
- Is that not an important event? *That's why you keep the Sabbath!*
- Why is that necessary? *Because we're made a little lower than God, after the image of God and we have a mind to do a whole lot of different things!*

So, if you don't keep the Sabbath, you get lifted up in your own vanity and intellectualism, and you think you are *so smart!* Yes, people are smart. What did God say as to why He had to destroy the Tower of Babel? ***Because anything that they imagined they can do!***

So, the Sabbath is important that you realize and understand that your life comes from God. Everything that there is comes from God, and you realize that you live, move and have your being with Him! This keeps you in proper perspective with you and God, and God with you.

The Passover:

The Passover marks two important events; what two are they?

1. with the children of Israel, the firstborn being spared, with the destruction of the firstborn of the Egyptians

Remember, the sacrifice of the Passover in Exo. 12 and from that time forward was not for the forgiveness of sin. It was for the sparing of the firstborn. That's why if you understand that that's the sparing of the firstborn for the covenant with Israel.

2. the Passover for eternal life, the sacrifice is God manifested in the flesh.

What was He?

- the firstborn of Mary
- the only Begotten of the Father

When He was crucified, that was an important event! The key most important event besides the Sabbath. His sacrifice was for the forgiveness of sin! *Was the sacrifice of the Firstborn, not the sparing!*

When you go back to when the children of Israel were in their houses in Egypt, when did the death angel come? *Midnight!*

Jesus the Firstborn of the Father and Mary. What happened on that Passover night? *He was arrested to be crucified, showing that **God did not pass over His own Son!***

First and Last day of Unleavened Bread:

The first day is getting rid of leaven, and in the New Covenant it is also getting rid of sin!

The last day they went through the Red Sea. Was that an important event? Open of the Red Sea ten miles wide and walk through? *Yes, indeed!* For us, we have our sins forgiven and God helps us through all the impossible tasks in our lives.

Pentecost:

Was that an important event? *Yes, for the children of Israel it was the giving of the Ten Commandments* and statutes and everything of God.

What was it for the New Testament Church? *The receiving of the Holy Spirit!* That was an important event! There are two other important events:

1. the heavens rolling back as a scroll
2. the first resurrection

Then we have Christ's return on Trumpets with all the saints together.

Trumpets:

For the covenant with Israel it was for the success of their wars **when they followed God,** *because it was a War Feast!* For the New Testament it pictures two things:

1. the first coming of Christ
2. His final coming when He returns with all the saints together

That is a monumental event! Don't you think the whole world is going to celebrate that during the Millennium.

Day of Atonement:

What was that for the children of Israel? *That was a covering for their sins every year, and the placing of the sins on Azazel, who was a type of Satan released in a place not being dwelt in, the wilderness!*

For the return of Christ, the Day of Atonement pictures the angel taking Satan the devil and the demons and putting them in the abyss and locking them up.

The Feast of Tabernacles:

That pictures God living with His people! There was the fulfillment of it in Solomon's days after he built the temple. God put His presence in the temple at that time.

For the New Testament, what is it for us? *We rule and reign with Christ a thousand years!* We're the Church of the Firstborn made perfect! All of that is tremendous!

The Last Great Day:

This is only mentioned twice in the Old Testament, and once in the New Testament, *picturing the second resurrection!*

Every one of the Holy Days, the Sabbath, which is Holy, all picture important events. It's no

wonder that when the world dismisses them as having already been fulfilled—which they haven't been—or as the Catholics say 'the old Law' so you don't have to do it.

Every one of everything that goes to the children of Israel and to the Church started with Abraham. This is one of the most important events in the Bible, Gen. 15, and we'll prove later that this took place on a Passover Day. *Think about that!*

When we read this, think about how important it was that Abram obeyed God! Remember when God called him, much like our calling. He said, 'You get up from your father's house and to a land that I will show you.' Abram obeyed and went. He said, 'I will make your name great! I will bless those who bless you, and curse those who curse you, and in you shall all the families of the earth be blessed.'

That's an amazing thing, indeed! ***From one man!*** Here he was 85-years-old and had no descendants. How is God going to do that? *Well, very carefully!*

Genesis 15:3: "And Abram said, 'Behold, You have given no seed to me; and lo, one born in my house is my heir.' And behold, the Word of the LORD *came* to him saying, 'This man shall not be your heir; but **he that shall come forth out of your own loins** shall be your heir'" (vs 3-4).

Think about that for a minute. After this promise was given nothing happened for 15 years. How long have you waited for a promise. Remember: ***God cannot lie!***

Verse 5: "And He brought him outside and said, 'Look now toward the heavens and number the stars—if you are able to count them.' And He said to him, 'So shall your seed be.'"

Here he was 75-years-old and no children, wife can't conceive, and I imagine they were trying really hard. God gave Abram this promise. Imagine how his faith had to be for that. There are two promises here:

1. physical seed
2. spiritual seed—*stars of heaven*

Jesus confirmed that by saying that *those who are children of the Father in the Kingdom shall shine forth as the sun!*

Verse 6: "**And he believed in the LORD.** And He accounted it to him for righteousness."

This sacrifice that is coming up is what is called *a maledictory oath!* Understand that in the Bible whenever there is a covenant that is made, there has to be a showing forth a symbolic death of the one giving the pledge, which normally is the sacrifice of an animal.

The Indians used to do it by taking a knife and scoff their palms and when they made a covenant they would put their hands together and the blood would mix with the blood and they were bound to do it unto death.

Here is what happened: remember, it started out in the evening and then God took Abram outside and showed him the stars. Has anybody ever seen the stars of heaven at noonday? *No!* You can only see them at night, so that's a night!

Verse 7: "And He said to him, 'I *am* the LORD that brought you out of Ur of the Chaldees, to give you this land to inherit it.' And he said, 'Lord GOD, by what shall I know that I shall inherit it?'" (vs 7-8).

Those promises are general sweeping promises of God that He's going to fulfill!

Verse 9: "And He said to him, 'Take Me a heifer of three years old, and a she-goat of three years old, and a ram of three years old, and a turtledove, and a young pigeon.' And he took all these to himself, and divided them in the middle, and laid each piece opposite the other; but he did not divide the birds" (vs 9-10).

I don't know how long that would take, but what he did was to cut them right down the middle and each half was laid opposite each other with a path to walk between. The birds he didn't divide.

Now, get the timing: this tells us that it took a good deal of time:

Verse 12: "And it came to pass, as the sun was going down… [we don't know how close to the horizon it was; we're not told, but]: …that a deep sleep fell upon Abram. And, behold, a horror of great darkness fell upon him!"

What was this? *This was a symbolic death, that Abram experienced!*

Verse 13: "And He said to Abram, 'You must surely know that your seed shall be sojourners in a land *that is* not theirs (and shall serve them *and they shall* afflict them) four hundred years. And also I will judge that nation whom they shall serve. And afterward they shall come out with great substance. And you shall go to your fathers in peace. You shall be buried in a good old age. But in the fourth generation they shall come here again, **for the iniquity of the Amorites is not yet full**'" (vs 13-16).

That's another statement in itself. How long does God put up with wickedness before He finally judges? *Quite a while!*

Verse 17: "And it came to pass—when the sun went down…"

What happens when the sun goes down? *That ends the day!* So, we started out one day in the evening, up in the morning, then the afternoon the sacrifice of the animals, and then the symbolic death of Abraham and the darkness.

We can see that that was probably at the same time that Jesus Himself died on the cross, which was the ninth hour[transcriber's correction] of the day (Mark 15:33-34) or 3 p.m.

Before all the rest of the Bible was written, it was very difficult to understand the things that I'm explaining right now. But you who have read and studied this, can understand it.

Jesus also said that 'you understand things that prophets didn't understand.'

"…and it was dark… [into the second day; it's a two-day sequence] …behold, a smoking furnace and a burning lamp passed between those pieces" (v 17).

What do you suppose the smoking furnace was doing? *This was a mammoth sacrifice, and it was God Who was walking between those parts!* He was pledging His future death. This also shows that the God of the Old Testament was the One Who became Jesus Christ.

What do you suppose that smoking furnace did to those sacrificial animals? *Burned them up completely, and left just little stacks of ashes!* To show the veracity and absolute assurance that what Jesus—the Lord God of the Old Testament—**told Abraham would take place!**

This is the most important event in the Old Testament in relationship to the Holy Days! This is the beginning of the Passover, right here!

Verse 18: "In the same day the LORD made a covenant with Abram, saying, 'I have given this land to your seed…'" *Abram was 85-years-old that this was given.*

Genesis 16:16: "And Abram *was* eighty-six years old when Hagar bore Ishmael to Abram."

- Now what happened? *A big mistake!*
- What was that mistake? *Sari thinking that she can help the fulfillment of God's promise by saying, 'You can go into my handmaiden and you can have children by her!'*

In the legal sense of the law at that time that would be true. ***But that's not what God promised!***

- What do we have? *Ishmael!*
- Has that been a problem ever since?

Good lesson: *Never help God fulfill His promises!* Let God fulfill them *His* way in *His* time!

Each party to a covenant must have a blood sacrifice. We saw the one with the three animals and two birds that God used. Abraham didn't walk through. He hadn't given any sacrifice.

Genesis 17:1: "And when **Abram was ninety-nine years old,** the LORD appeared to Abram and said to him, 'I *am* the Almighty God! Walk before Me and be perfect.... [New Testament standard] ...And I will make My covenant between Me and you, and will multiply you exceedingly.' And Abram fell on his face. And God talked with him, saying, 'As for Me, behold, My covenant is with you, and **you shall be a father of many nations**. Neither shall your name any more be called Abram, but your name shall be Abraham; for I have made you a father of many nations. And I will make you exceedingly fruitful, and I will make nations of you, and kings shall come from you. And I will establish My covenant between Me and you and your seed after you in their generations **for an everlasting covenant**...'" (vs 1-7).

That is carried right down to today in the physical nations! This has nothing to do with conversion or eternal life.

Verse 8: "'And I will give the land to you in which you are a sojourner, and to your seed after you, all the land of Canaan, for an everlasting possession. And I will be their God.' And God said to Abraham, 'And you shall keep My covenant, you and your seed after you in their generations. This is My covenant, which you shall keep, between Me and you and your seed after you. Every male child among you shall be circumcised. And you shall circumcise the flesh of your foreskin. And it shall be a sign of the covenant between Me and you. And a son of eight days shall be circumcised among you, every male child in your generations; he that is born in the house, or bought with silver of any foreigner who *is* not of your seed. He that is born in your house, and he that is bought with your silver, must be circumcised. And My covenant shall be in your flesh for an everlasting covenant'" (vs 8-13).

When there's circumcision, what happens? *There's blood!* That was the sacrifice for the physical nations on Abraham's part. That had nothing to do with salvation; that had to do with the physical nations.

A year later is when he gets the promise of Isaac (Gen. 18). He is born (Gen. 21).

Genesis 21:1: "And the LORD visited Sarah as He had said. And the LORD did to Sarah as He had spoken, for Sarah conceived..." (vs 1-2). *She's 90-years-old!*

Why did God do it that way? *Because you can believe* **when something that is impossible is accomplished by God!**

Can you imagine at 90 getting pregnant and nursing him for three years? I wonder what Sarah thought when she first found out that she was pregnant? Then when Isaac was born*? At first she laughed when she heard it of God!* Then God said to her, 'Why did you laugh?' *I didn't laugh!* 'Yes, you did laugh!' *It was laughable!*

Let's see the sacrifice for the spiritual aspect of the spiritual seed, *the stars of heaven!* There had to be that sacrifice in order to complete the covenant that God made. There were two parts to that covenant:

1. physical seed
2. spiritual seed

The spiritual seed was a prophecy of the coming of the New Testament Church, and the plan of God expanding out with all those who would be converted and brought into the spiritual Family of God. *This was a big deal!*

Gen. 22 was probably also on a Passover. We'll prove that in just a little bit. Abraham was asked to do this when Isaac was about 15-years-old. So, from the time the promise was given until the birth of Isaac was 15 years. Then by deduction, Isaac had to be about 15 years of age for this. Think about the faith that Abraham had to have, and this was also important! I'm quite convinced that this occurred on a Passover Day.

Genesis 22:1: "And it came to pass after these things that God tested Abraham, and said to him, 'Abraham!' And he said, 'Here I am.' And He said, 'Take now your son, your only *son* Isaac...'" (vs 1-2).

Who is missing? *Ishmael! He was not counted in the promises of spiritual seed!* He was counted in the promises of *physical* seed.

"'...whom you love, and go into the land of Moriah, and offer him there for a burnt offering upon one of the mountains, which I will tell you.' And Abraham rose up early in the morning and saddled his donkey, and took two *of* his young men with him, and Isaac his son. And he split the wood for the burnt offering, and rose up and went to the place of which God had told him" (vs 2-3). *This took a lot of courage to do!*

- Why was Abraham willing to do this?
- Where do you find the answer to that? *Heb. 11!*

Look at the hundreds and hundreds of years before the answer finally came!

- Why did Abraham do this? *Because he counted God worthy to raise Isaac from the dead if he were sacrificed and died!*

That's the faith!

Verse 4: "Then on the third day Abraham lifted up his eyes and saw the place afar off. And Abraham said to his young men, 'You stay here with the donkey, and I and the boy will go yonder and worship, and come again to you.' And Abraham took the wood of the burnt offering and laid it upon Isaac his son…." (vs 4-6).

- Abraham was a type of God the Father
- Isaac was a type of Christ
- the wood that Abraham placed upon Isaac was a type of the crucifixion

Isaac had to have a lot of faith, too. But think about this: here's your own father leading you off to sacrifice you. That's quite an important thing; *but Isaac didn't resist!*

"…And he took the fire*pot* in his hand…" (v 6). *The King James says that 'he took fire in his hand' but you can't take fire in your hand, you'll burn it!* So, it had to be a firepot with coals.

"…and a knife. And they both went together. And Isaac spoke to Abraham his father and said, 'My father.' And he said, 'Here I *am*, my son.' And he said, 'Behold the fire and the wood. But where is the lamb for a burnt offering?'" (vs 6-7).

Notice what Abraham said. Here you're walking right up to the place that you're going to offer him.

Verse 8: "And Abraham said, 'My son, God will provide Himself a lamb for a burnt offering.' So, they both went on together. And they came to the place of which God had told him. And Abraham built an altar there… [of whole stone] …and laid the wood in order. And he bound his son Isaac and laid him on the wood, upon the altar. And Abraham stretched out his hand and took the knife to slay his son. And the angel of the LORD called to him from the heavens and said, 'Abraham! Abraham!' And he said, 'Here I *am*.' And He said, '**Do not lay your hand upon the lad**…'" (vs 8-12). *That shows that he had to be about 15-years-old.*

"'…nor do anything to him, for now I know that you fear God, seeing you have not withheld your son, your only son, from Me.' And Abraham lifted up his eyes and looked, and behold, behind *him* a ram was entangled in a thicket by its horns…." (vs 12-13).

I don't know how it got there; I don't know if an angel led it up there and stuck its horns in the thicket. I don't know if God created instantly a ram stuck in the thicket; that could be, too. When they came up there they didn't see it. I'm sure they were looking around, because Abraham said, 'God will provide a lamb.' I imagine that they were looking, 'Where's the lamb?'

"…And Abraham went and took the ram and offered it up for a burnt offering instead of his son" (v 13)—*a substitutionary sacrifice!*

- How does that apply spiritually to us?
- What are the wages of sin? *Death!*
- How do we die? *A symbolic death in baptism!*

which accomplishes a lot of things:
- cleansing of sin
- your covenant pledge unto death that you will keep your promise to God

God has already proved His promise to you! *(Rom. 6)*

Verse 14: "And Abraham called the name of that place The LORD Will Provide; so that it is said *until* this day, 'In the mount of the LORD it will be provided.' And the angel of the LORD called to Abraham out of heaven the second time, and said, 'By Myself have I sworn,' says the LORD…" (vs 14-16).

When God swears by Himself, *He's swearing by His existence and everything that He stands for!*

"'…because you have done this thing, and have not withheld your son, your only son; that in blessing I will bless you, and in multiplying I will multiply your seed like the stars of the heavens…'" (vs 16-17)—*the sacrifice for the spiritual seed; whereas the circumcision was the sacrifice for the physical seed!*

"…and as the sand, which is upon the seashore." (v 17). *It took care of both!*

Isaac was a type of Christ, symbolic, but he was physical and had children—*Jacob and Esau!* Then Jacob had the 12 sons and his name was changed to Israel.

Let's show that this took place—Gen. 15—on the Passover Day and the night following.

Exodus 12:41: "And it came to pass at the end of the four hundred and thirty years…"

We had 400 years (Gen. 15) and now we have 430 years! We had 15 years from Gen. 15 until Isaac was born, then we have 15 years by deduction that Isaac had to be 15-years-old: 15+15=30+400=430 years.

"…it was even on that **very same day,** all the armies of the LORD went out from the land of Egypt" (v 41).

What day was that? *The day after the Passover Day!* That means that the first part off the pledge that God gave to Abraham took place on the Passover Day.

As the day began, then you have the night and then in the morning Abraham laid out the sacrifice. Then you have Abraham having the symbolic death and the sun went down and the promise was made. The sacrifices were burned to ashes.

Verse 42: "It *is* a night to be much observed to the LORD…" *That's how that works!*

This shows that every single day that God says that we are to observe:

- the Sabbath
- the Passover
- Unleavened Bread
- Pentecost
- Trumpets
- Atonement
- Tabernacles
- Last Great Day

all picture mammoth, important events that will literally take place to fulfill the Word of God!

Scriptural References:

1) Daniel 2:17-23, 27-30, 44-45
2) 1 Peter 1:2-5
3) 1 Corinthians 2:9-12
4) Isaiah 56:1
5) Psalm 119:172
6) Isaiah 56:1
7) Revelation 6:14
8) Isaiah 56:2-7
9) Exodus 19:4-6, 8
10) Isaiah 43:21-22
11) Luke 10:21-27
12) 1 John 5:3
13) Luke 10:29
14) Genesis 15:3-10, 12-18
15) Genesis 16:16
16) Genesis 17:1-13
17) Genesis 21:1-2
18) Genesis 22:1-17
19) Exodus 12:41-42

Scriptures referenced, not quoted:

- John 2
- Revelation 2; 3
- Exodus 12
- Mark 15:33-34
- Genesis 18
- Hebrews 11

- Romans 6

Also referenced:

Book: *From a Speck of Dust to a Son of God: Why Were You Born?* by Fred R. Coulter

Transcript Book/w CD: *The Keys to Answered Prayer*

Articles:
- What Does It Mean to be "Born Again"?
- What Does it Mean to be "Born of God"?

Message: *What Would the World Be Like if Adam & Eve Had Not Sinned?*

FRC:bo
Transcribed: 8/6/20
Reformatted: 12/2020

CHAPTER NINE

Overview of the Holy Days
All the understanding of God's purpose and plan
is gradually unfolded to us throughout God's Word
Fred R. Coulter

Greetings, brethren! Welcome to Sabbath services!

With all the exciting things going on in the world, we have rest on the Sabbath, and we're going to look at God's purpose for us today, and analyze a little bit more about the Holy Days, since they're coming up real soon.

I would like to mention that we have all the material in this booklet ***Rome's Challenge to the Protestants***, by Cardinal Gibbon of Baltimore in 1893. We also have it in Appendix N in *The Holy Bible in Its Original Order, A Faithful Version*. Let me suggest that you read the commentaries before and the appendices after are very vital for your overall understanding about the Bible and the Word of God. It will assist greatly in your study. One of the most important appendices that we have is Appendix Z: **Understanding Paul's Difficult Scriptures Concerning the Law and the Commandments of God.**

You will see that if you're still using an old *King James Version* or a *New King James Version*, or any other version, they carry through all the errors plus adding new ones that were in the *KJV*. In *The Holy Bible in Its Original Order, A Faithful Version* those have all been corrected.

Let's see what we're to do on the Sabbath, and see about the purpose of God.

Psalm 78:1: "Give ear, O my people, to my law; incline your ears to the words of my mouth. I will open my mouth in a parable; I will speak dark sayings of old" (vs 1-2)—*because they're all hidden in the Bible!*

I want to mention something else, we have the DVD—*True Fellowship with God.* I want you to get that and really listen to it, especially if you're discouraged or down in the dumps, because when we come to Sabbath services God wants us to look at His purpose over all, in our lives and be encouraged that *regardless of what's going on God is with us, in us and working with us! Keep that in mind!*

2-Timothy 1:7: "For God has not given us a spirit of fear, **but of power, and of love, and of sound-mindedness**"—*which comes from using the Word of God written in our heart and mind by God's Holy Spirit to think correctly!*

There are many things out in the world to lead us astray! This is why this is good that we come every Sabbath, because it helps us keep our thoughts oriented on God's way.

Verse 8: "Therefore, you should not be ashamed of the testimony of our Lord, nor *of* me His prisoner; but jointly suffer with *me for the sake of* the Gospel, according to *the* power of God."

Don't worry about the circumstances that are happening even right now, because a lot of us are alone, or maybe two, three or four. There is a Church of God down near Pasadena who was served an arrest warrant to the pastors, saying they couldn't have any meetings. So, be sure and keep that in mind. That's Rock Church of God. *All the authorities that are closing down meetings are*:

1. against God
2. against the Constitution, which they have taken an oath to uphold

So, we're perfectly all right meeting in small groups or even larger groups, because all the political people believe that the protests are okay, that is if you belong to a certain political party.

Verse 9: "**Who has saved us**…"

- we've been *saved from our sins*
- we're constantly in a state of *being saved*
- we *shall be saved* at the resurrection

"…**and called *us* with a Holy calling**…" (v 9). *And that's directly from God Himself to each one of us!* We always need to keep that in mind.

"—not according to our works…" (v 9)—*because our own works are not motivated by God's Spirit!* But all of the works of God… When you real Rev. 2 & 3 with the churches, what's the first thing that Jesus said? *I know your works!* **IF** *you have faith, you will have works!*

But God's works, that we love Him, keep His commandments, obey His laws—keep His Sabbath and Holy Days—those are the most important things that we do. Where would we be without that Sabbath every single week? *On the Sabbath Day, regardless of where you are, if you are there to worship and serve God and study His*

Word, He is there with you!

Think about this: Someone is going to say, 'I'm all alone!' *No you're not, because Paul wrote that 'where two or three are gathered together, quoting Christ, there I [Christ] am in the midst of you!* If you are there alone, and you have the Spirit of God, **you have the Father and the Son with you, so you're not alone!**

"...but according to His own purpose and grace..." (v 9). *God has His purpose!* We are part of something so great and far-reaching and fantastic that it's awesome to even contemplate it.

"...which *was* given us in Christ Jesus **before the ages of time**" (v 9). *Think about that!*

Little ole us! And all of God's people down through time, *a Holy calling from God Himself!*

- Who was the One Who drew us to Himself? *The Father!*
- Who was the One Who redeemed us from our sins? *Jesus Christ through His sacrifice!*

That was all planned!

Now then, to understand the plan of God, we have the Sabbath and Holy Days. Let's talk a little bit more about the purpose of God.

Isa. 14 is where it's recorded that Satan rebelled to takeover the Throne of God. Of course, Rev. 12 tells us that a third of the angels joined in the rebellion. Isa. 14 talks about the Assyrian to be destroyed on the mountains of Israel. There are two fulfillments of that:

1. During the days of King Hezekiah, which was during the lifetime of Isaiah the prophet (Isa. 37-39). The whole army of the Assyrians came to conquer Judea and Jerusalem. God fought very cleverly. While they were all sleeping to get a good night's rest before the battle, God sent a powerful angel and they all died, 180,000!
2. At the return of Christ with the King of the North and all the other kings of the nations gathered around. That's all within this Isa. 14.

Now let's see something about God. The only thing that can change God's mind; there's only one thing that can change God's mind to defer something for a time. *Repentance!* That is the only thing!

Isaiah 14:24: "The LORD of hosts has sworn... [when He swears by Himself there is no wiggle-room] ...saying, 'Surely as I have thought, so it shall come to pass; and as I have purposed, *so it shall stand.'"

Think about that! Everything that God has,

we read it and it was proposed before the ages of time. Think about how all that planning had to go in to effect to create the Earth. The Earth doesn't sit out here by itself. You've got the sun and then Mercury, Venus, Earth, Mars, Jupiter, Saturn, Uranus and on out into outer space and the universe.

God is preparing the universe for His people. Think about your calling. You need to think with the Spirit of God how great, broad and fantastic that is.

Verse 26: "This *is* the purpose that *is* purposed upon all the earth... [everything here] ...and this *is* the hand that *is* stretched out upon all the nations"—*and we know* **through the Holy Days** *everyone who has ever lived and died!* Amazing! Think of that!

Verse 27: "For the LORD of hosts has purposed, and who shall reverse *it*?.... [*no one*] ...And His hand is stretched out, and who shall turn it back?" *No one! The purpose of God is going to be done!*

Let's add something very interesting to understanding the Scriptures before we begin looking at the Holy Days and what they mean.

Psa. 119 is the longest Psalm in the book of Psalms, and all the Levitical singers were required to memorize it. To help them memorize it, each verse began with the Hebrew letter that is directly over each eight-verse section.

Psalm 119:159: "Consider how I love Your **precepts**... [an operation that God is going to do or is doing] ...O LORD, according to Your loving kindness give me life. **Your Word is true from the beginning, and every one of Your righteous ordinances endures forever**" (vs 159-160).

What are the Holy Days? *Ordinances of God!* Think about that!

Verse 128: "Therefore, I esteem all Your precepts concerning all things to be right... [if they're right, then they're true] ...and I hate every false way."

Let's put this together with Isa. 28. Since God's Word is true from the beginning, and there's no lie in it, and all His precepts are right or true, when it says in:

Isaiah 28:13: "So then, the Word of the LORD was to them precept upon precept, **precept upon precept**... [Truth upon Truth, because everything that God says is Truth] ...line upon line, **line upon line**... [showing how we study and put it together] ...**here a little, there a little**..."

For those who don't know the Truth, they will fall away and go backward!

On first appearance when someone would pickup the Bible to read it, they would not know the significance of what it's telling them. They would not have a clue! It's also interesting, and here's a precept of God: Lev. 23 is the only place in the entire Bible that gives the Holy Days listed in chronological and calendrical order, which is the Calculated Hebrew Calendar.

A person not knowing anything about the Hebrew calendar ask—and I get letters like this every once in a while—is the Passover Day of the 14th day of January? *That's the first month of the Roman calendar!* So, you can tell that this is a newbee!

Another interesting thing that is an operation by faith: *God gave to the Levitical priesthood the calculations of the calendar, calculations that He established!* He did not put it in the Bible, so those are the oracles of God given to the priesthood.

In spite of all the sins of the Jews and the priesthood, they have preserved the Old Testament and they have preserved the calendar. Why? *Because God determined that through them He would preserved it and we can have absolute faith in that!*

Leviticus 23:1: "And the LORD spoke to Moses, saying."

As we all know, the three most important words are *obey My voice,* and it's written down. So, when we read the Bible it's like God talking to us. Think of that! He had it preserved for all time until the return of Christ. In it is preserved the outline of His whole purpose. A lot of people don't believe in God because they don't know what He's doing, and they are not willing to take the very first step, which is listed right here in Lev. 23.

Verse 2: "Speak to the children of Israel and say to them, '*Concerning* the appointed Feasts of the LORD, which you shall proclaim *to be* Holy convocations, even **these are My appointed Feasts**'"—or times!

Think of it this way: if you have an appointment with someone, you're expected to be there, and you're expected to the one who wants you to come to that appointment to be there, as well. *God is always there!* So, you are required to come to His appointment, the Sabbath Day!

Verse 3: "Six days shall work be done, but the seventh day *is* **the Sabbath** of rest, a Holy convocation. You shall not do any work. It *is* a Sabbath to the LORD in all your dwellings."

That is an *appointed time* every week! God has preserved the knowledge of the seven-day week, even though during the French Revolution they tried to have a ten-day week. That didn't workout so well!

Tie in New Testament doctrine on the Sabbath: Jesus said that *'the Sabbath was made for man and not man for the Sabbath, therefore, the Son of man is the Lord of the Sabbath Day.'* Even in the New Testament the Sabbath is required, and Christ is the Lord of it. He always has been and always will be.

There's more to it; v 4: "These *are* the appointed Feasts of the LORD, Holy convocations, which you shall proclaim in their appointed seasons. In the fourteenth *day* of the first month, between the two evenings… [after sunset and before dark] …is **the LORD'S Passover**" (vs 4-5).

*It's not the **Jews'** Passover!* What Passover is the Jews' Passover? *The next day, which is actually the first day of the Feast of Unleavened Bread!*

This goes all the way back to Gen. 3 with the sin of Adam and Eve. It's interesting about their sin. After God created them, what was the first thing that was brought to their attention? *The Sabbath Day!* Just like the first thing of the Feasts of God here is the Sabbath Day.

How long they were in the Garden of Eden before they sinned, we don't know. But it had to be plenty long enough for them to know everything they needed to know, and to have enough knowledge to think that **IF** they decided to choose their own way they could make it succeed. Therefore, the serpent could not have entered into the garden the very next day. They would not have had enough knowledge about what God wanted and what they should do. How long that was we don't know.

But after they sinned was the first prophecy of Jesus Christ and likewise that goes clear forward to 30A.D. with the crucifixion of Jesus Christ.

All of the other prophecies about Christ and His sacrifice are scattered through Psalms, the Prophets and the Gospels. Amazing thing, really!

The next one, the day after, v 6: "And on the fifteenth day of the same month *is* the Feast of Unleavened Bread to the LORD. You must eat unleavened bread seven days."

Why do we have this? *So, that we know that we have to come out of sin and the world!* That follows the Passover because Christ is our Passover Who was sacrificed for us, therefore, we're not to be living in sin! The Law of God tells us what sin is, *which is the transgression of the Law.*

Sidebar: Keep this in mind: **Did God authorize anyone to change the words of the Law that He has spoken?** *No one!*

Think about that when you look at fake Christianity in the world.

- they use the Bible, *but they don't know the Bible*
- they claim the Lord Jesus, *but they don't know Him*

*It's because **they live in perpetual sin** with:*
- Sunday-keeping
- holiday-keeping

They fulfill the prophecy in Isaiah that says to Israel, *'You have made Me to serve with your sins!' Quite an amazing thing!* How true is the Bible? Think about everything that you go through.

Verse 7: "On the **first day you shall have a Holy convocation**...."

This shows us that there is a Satan the devil; he's out there and the author of sin. In our own mind we're not only to change our behavior, but our thoughts with the Spirit of God. Then we have that for seven days.

Verse 8: "...**In the seventh day *is* a Holy convocation**...."

What happened on the Passover with Israel when they were in Egypt? *They had the sacrifice of the Passover lamb!* That Passover lamb was not for the forgiveness of sin. That was for protection of the firstborn.

Go forward to the Passover of Christ: He was the Firstborn of Mary and the only Begotten of the Father.

On the Passover night, at midnight, is when God passed over the houses of the children of Israel in Egypt and killed the firstborn of the Egyptians.

Fast forward to the Passover of Jesus, at midnight He was arrested and taken off to be judged and crucified. That comes clear back to Gen. 15.

Just like we read, 'a precept here, a precept there, here a little and there a little.' You don't find any of this in Lev. 23. So, if you just pick it up and read it you think 'that's strange, I wonder what it means.' *The rest of the Bible tells us what it means!*

Then we have what is called *The Wave Sheaf Offering Day!*

Verse 9: "And the LORD spoke to Moses, saying... [these are the words of God] ...'Speak to the children of Israel and say to them, "When you have come into the land, **which I give to you,** and shall reap the harvest of it, then you shall bring *the premier* sheaf of the firstfruits of your harvest to the priest. And he shall wave the sheaf before the LORD to be accepted for you. On the next day after the Sabbath the priest shall wave it" (vs 9-11).

That's the regular Sabbath during Unleavened Bread, or more correctly *the first day*

*after the Sabbath **during Unleavened Bread!*** There are times when the Passover falls on the Sabbath Day, and then that becomes the Sabbath and the next day becomes the Wave Sheaf Offering Day.

What does all of that mean? For Israel it was that they could go out and start working and harvesting and bringing in the harvest of the grain.

For the New Testament *it is the harvest of God for the first resurrection!*

Then it tells all the offerings to bring, to be counted specifically seven full weeks plus one day, which adds up to 50 days. Then they were to all bring two loaves made of finely beaten flour and bring them to the temple. Every other offering to God for sin—and this is not a sin offering—had to have unleavened bread. But these loaves had to be leavened, because that pictures the change of the bread permanently baked. That typifies the change at the resurrection permanently now spirit beings.

Think of this: here's everybody gathered around in the temple area and the tents around there. At a certain moment when the priest gave the signal, they were to take these loaves and wave them. Think if you were on the top of the Mt. Olives looking toward the temple and all the people were there and here are these loaves that they're waving. *That pictures the first resurrection because they're raised up!* But you don't find any of that here. You have to find that in the rest of the Bible.

Then we come to the next one, which is the Feast of Trumpets. That's a War Feast, and that projects that whenever there is a war Israel was *not* to go out to battle **unless** *God said to go, and God would be with them and the battle would be the Lord's!*

Whenever Israel went out on their own they didn't succeed, so that tells us a pretty long lesson. If we try and do things on our own, without yielding to God, it's not going to work. But if we do what God says, like 'remember the Sabbath Day to keep it Holy' we'll be blessed. So, this War Feast actually projects toward the conquering of the land with the children of Israel capturing the land from the Canaanites. *That's the first fulfillment!*

Then subsequent wars that God told them to do and then it comes clear to the end at the return of Christ and the wars at the end, and the final Battle of Armageddon. None of that's here, because it only says:

Verse 24: "Speak to the children of Israel saying, 'In the seventh month, in the first *day* of the month, you shall have a Sabbath, **a memorial of blowing of ram's horns,** a Holy convocation."

The next one is the Day of Atonement,

which is interesting. From it you get virtually very little understanding, unless you understand that there's a Satan the devil. What is he called in the New Testament? *The god of this world!*

That's why one goat is for the Lord to be sacrificed for a sin offering. That's a type of Christ. Then the other one is a type of Satan the devil. That one is not sacrificed, but sent into the wilderness and let go alive symbolizing that Satan is a spirit being and will not die.

But this shows the fairness of God. In what way? *Christ paid for your sins and the sins of the whole world with His sacrifice for every human being!* All will have an opportunity for that through the Holy Days and the Last Great Day, but that will have to wait to come.

- In this age, who is the author of sin? *Satan!*
- Is there an atonement for Satan's sin?
- Is there an atonement for Satan's sin that he makes us sin?

We have our part because we sin, but God would not be just if He didn't lay all the sins on Satan that are pictured by the live goat that is let loose. That's why the goat that was sacrificed for the sins of the children of Israel are covered.

The sins that they sinned instigated by Satan the devil are not covered or forgiven, but are removed, symbolizing that there will never, *never, ever* be any peace or forgiveness as long as Satan is around. *That is unless you come to Christ!*

When you read Rev. 20 Satan is bound. What's the first thing that happens when he's loosed? *War!* That shows that when Satan is around, people sin. But at that time these people would have already rejected Christ, and their war is a war to their own destruction.

After that we have the Feast of Tabernacles that pictures the Millennium, when Satan will be removed, when all people will have an opportunity for salvation. But there have to be other Scriptures brought in just like we read in Isa. 28 to put it together and understand it.

Then the Last Great Day! That's really quite a day!

Everyone that God did not call and did not commit the unpardonable sin will be raised for an opportunity for salvation. Jesus said, *'Anyone.'*

- How about all those who lived, died, and were not called?
- How about all of those in the Flood?
- How about all of those who were aborted?
- How about all of those in accidents?

When we watch the news tonight, what are we going to find? *Well, there's war here, shooting there, bombing there, riots over here, all instigated by Satan!* It won't be then.

We will do a survey of the Gospel of John and the framework of the Passover and Holy Days, *so that people will know and understand the Holy Days are the most significant thing necessary to understand the purpose of what God is doing!*

We're going to do an interesting survey, because if the Holy Days and the Sabbath were done away. The Gospels would not have Christ going into the synagogues on the Sabbath.

One of the first things that Christ made clear; Matthew 5:17: "**Do not think**…"

What happens when someone says *don't think*? **They will think the opposite!** In the Greek these are double negatives meaning:

Absolutely, v 17: "**Do not think that I have come to abolish the Law or the Prophets; I did not come to abolish, but to fulfill**."

This does not mean not to do it to make it of no value, it means to **complete it to make it of greater value!**

Verse 18: "For truly I say to you, **until** the heaven and the earth shall pass away…"

If you're talking to a Protestant, ask him 'What are we standing on? What are we breathing? *Heaven and earth are still here!*

"…one jot or one tittle shall in no way…" (v 18). *There's the double negative*: don't think it, it's not going to be a reality, neither one.

"…pass from the Law until everything has been fulfilled. Therefore, whoever shall break one of these least commandments, and shall teach men so… [you won't here this on TBN or in any Sunday-keeping church] …shall be called least in the Kingdom of Heaven; but whoever shall practice and teach *them*, this one shall be called great in the Kingdom of Heaven" (vs 18-19).

Think about it, because we're up against that! Then it says:

Verse 20: "For I say to you, unless your righteousness shall exceed *the righteousness* of the scribes and Pharisees, there is no way… [double negative again] …*that* you shall enter into the Kingdom of Heaven." *Think about that!*

What is the righteousness of the scribes and Pharisees? *Not the laws and commandments of God, but their own traditions that they hold in higher esteem than they do the laws and commandments of God!*

One of the leading rabbis told Roy Assanti

when Roy said, 'If you would not keep your traditions you would be just like us, because keep the commandments.' The rabbi replied, 'Oh, if we didn't have our traditions we'd have nothing at all!'

Same thing applies to Catholics and Protestants. They have their traditions and laws, *but it's not of God!*

Verse 21: "You have heard that it was said to those *in* ancient *times*, 'You shall not commit murder; but whoever commits murder shall be subject to judgment.'" *Let's take this, in just a minute, and apply it to the Sabbath!*

Verse 22: "But I say to you, everyone who is angry with his brother without cause shall be subject to judgment. Now, *you have heard it said,* 'Whoever shall say to his brother, "Raca," shall be subject to *the judgment of* the council.' But *I say to you,* whoever shall say, '*You* fool,' shall be subject to the fire of Gehenna." *That's pretty strong!*

Since Jesus said the He's Lord of the Sabbath, what would have to happen with the Sabbath and Holy Days? *We would have to have a command just exactly like He said in* Matt. 5:

You have heard that it was said to those in ancient times that you shall remember the Sabbath Day to keep it Holy, *but I tell you, you shall keep Sunday because I came to change it.*

The only reason that Jesus would have had to do, is because *no man can change what God has commanded!* Only God can change what He's commanded. So, if God changed it from the seventh day to the first day, you would have to find it in the New Testament. I'll pay anyone $10-million—because I know I'll never have to pay it—*because it's not there!* This commandment would have to be:

You've heard it said in ancient times that you shall remember the Sabbath to keep it Holy, but I say to you, I came to change the law and change it to Sunday. And you have heard it said in ancient times that you shall keep the Holy Days of God, but I say to you that I came to abolish those and replace them with the pagan holidays of Satan the devil!

That's what Christ would have had to say! So, all if the fake Christians out there—their pastors, their priests—are in violation, walking in sin, rejecting the commandments of God.

Mark 2:27: "And He said to them, 'The Sabbath was made for man, *and* not man for the Sabbath"—*which means that man cannot tell God that he's changing the Sabbath from the seventh day to the first day, because it's more convenient for people!*

Verse 28: "Therefore, the Son of man is Lord even of the Sabbath."

- Who is the Son of man? *Jesus Christ!*
- Who is Lord of the Sabbath? *Jesus Christ!*

He is the Lord of Passover and all the Holy Days. In those and the meaning of them *all the understanding of God's purpose and plan is gradually unfolded to us so that we have understanding!* But how many are willing to do that?

We will see that the Gospel of John has three Passover seasons. We find the fourth one in Luke 6. We find a great fulfillment of Pentecost. Also, the Gospel of John talk more about God the Father, coupled with 1st, 2nd & 3rd John—than all of the other parts of the Bible put together. John was the one whom Jesus loved; furthermore he was descendant of the priests. So important was John that he was the only one to receive the revelation of Jesus Christ contained in the book of Revelation, which came from God the Father. *No one else!*

One other thing about John, because he was of the priestly family. In Rev. 4 he hears a trumpet and it says, 'Come up here!' He comes up and sees the Throne of the Father, *the only man to ever do that!*

Everything that is written by John in his Gospel and three epistles *are absolutely essential for understanding*:

- what we are to do
- what days that we keep
- how we develop the love of God

John 2—this all took place after He had His temptation in the wilderness with Satan the devil and recuperated.

John 2:13: "Now the Passover of the Jews was near, and Jesus went up to Jerusalem."

Why did John write it "…the Passover of the Jews…"? *Because during the days of Jesus the majority of the people kept the 14th Passover, which was the 14th day of the 1st month!*

The priests (John 19) kept the wrong day, calling it Passover on the 15th. {Our book *The Christian Passover* answers every argument!} John was writing this so that it was going to go out to all the Gentiles.

Jesus went to Jerusalem, v 14: "And He found in the temple…" *Here's a fulfillment of a Scripture,* a particular one by the last prophet who was Malachi: *the Lord shall suddenly come His temple!*

"…those who were selling oxen and sheep and doves, and the money exchangers sitting *there*" (v 14).

Money exchangers: the Jews in the Diaspora would come from whatever country they were in, and the local currency they had could not be used at the temple, because they were living in Gentile lands and was technically unclean. However, *quite clean enough for the money exchangers to take it!*

So, in order to buy a sacrifice, they would first have to go to the money exchangers and receive temple coins and then buy the sacrifice. But they were all cheating and so forth. Notice what Jesus did *in His sudden appearance.*

Verse 15: "And after making a scourge of cords, He drove them all out of the temple… [not just scare them and chase them away] …*with* both the sheep and the oxen; and He poured out the coins of the money exchangers, and overturned the tables. And to those who were selling the doves, He said, **'Take these things out of here!**…. [that was to be done outside the confines of the temple area] …Do not make My Father's house a house of merchandise'" (vs 15-16).

That's very important for all ministers and Protestants, *you merchandise the people like crazy!* Those who are faithful will pay their tithes and offerings. You don't have to 'beat them over the head'! If someone is not wanting to give it, 'beating them over the head' will make them give with resentment.

So, on this Passover He cleaned it up and they couldn't understand why He was doing this; they said, 'By what authority do you do this?' *He didn't tell them!* He also did it before His last Passover.

Verse 18: "As a result, the Jews answered and said to Him, 'What sign do You show to us, seeing that You do these things?' Jesus answered and said to them, **'Destroy this temple, and in three days I will raise it up.'** Then the Jews said, **'This temple was forty-six years in building**, and You will raise it up in three days?'" (vs 18-20).

Verse 23: "Now, when He was in Jerusalem at the Passover, during the Feast…" *You have the Passover **and** the Feast.* Passover is one day (Lev. 23) and the Feast of Unleavened Bread is seven days.

"…many believed on His name, as they observed the miracles that He was doing"—*healing the sick, the blind, restoring people who were lame, etc.*

Verse 24: "But Jesus did not entrust Himself to them…" When they thought that He was *That Prophet* they wanted to take him and make Him king.

Verse 25: "And He did not need anyone to testify concerning man, for He Himself knew what was in man."

- What is in man? *Carnal nature!*
- What is that like? *Jer. 17!*

In John 4 Jesus is on His way back to Galilee. I won't go into about the woman at the well, if you want to know about that, go to Church at Home {**churchathome.org**} and I go through and explain that God is looking for those to worship Him in Spirit and in Truth.

When Jesus didn't want to eat what they brought, His disciples didn't know what to think.

John 4:33: "Then the disciples said to one another, 'Did anyone bring Him *something* to eat?' Jesus said to them, '**My meat is to do the will of Him Who sent Me, and to finish His work**.'"

Here's an allusion to Pentecost and the harvest; v 35: "Do not say that there are yet four months, and *then* the harvest comes. I say to you, look around. Lift up your eyes and see the fields, for they are already white to harvest."

Tie in Matt. 13 about the sowing of the seed and the harvest, and all of that. The harvest represents the resurrection at the end of the age on Pentecost.

Verse 36: "And the one who reaps receives a reward, and gathers fruit unto eternal life; so that the one who is sowing and the one who is reaping may both rejoice together. For in this the saying is true, that one sows and another reaps" (vs 36-37).

Then Jesus gave them something really important to understand. Here are all of the Law and Prophets up to Christ. God was preparing everything for the ministry of Christ, and God was making it so that He would choose the 12 disciples to become the 12 apostles. There's a lot going on here.

For the first coming of Christ we have all the prophecies from the Prophets and the promises to Abraham.

Verse 38: "I sent you to reap that in which you have not labored; others have labored, and you have entered into their labor."

That's very important for us today. We have the Word of God because of the labor of all of those honest and faithful preservers of the words of Christ. I have at home a book that is 480-years-old: *Stephen's 1550 New Testament Greek.* I can tell you from that, the Greek that we translated for the New Testament is exactly the same there as it is in the *Received Text.*

God is faithful and will preserve His Word!

Look at all the laborers who were before us. Look at all of those in the Church in the Piedmonts, which ended up being called *the Waldensians.* They went into Europe evangelizing.

A little addition to that: Just to show that today we need to look at what other people have done and God has used. So, it's possible for us. Look at all the things we're using technologically. Other people made it and we're using what they made.

Sidebar: John Guenther who is doing historical work of the Church of God has discovered that in the first 300 years after Christ there were times that in the British Isles they were keeping the Passover, the Sabbath and the commandments of God, and he's got the documentation. *Amazing!*

Quite different from what we first heard if you've been in the Church for a long time. What was one of the first things you heard? *The Gospel was not preached in 18-1/2 centuries!* Not true! There was a big work in Britain and Europe, and in the mountains of the Piedmonts.

When the Catholic Church sough to crush it, the Protestant Reformation came out of that. Unfortunately, they didn't follow William Tyndale's admonition that *'we are to keep the commandments of God from the bottom ground of our heart'!*

Have you read anything of William Tyndale? *Amazing! Amazing man!*

Here it is, the harvest is white, leading up to Pentecost.

Note our book: *A Harmony of the Gospels*—Matthew, Mark, Luke and John all synchronized with pictures and commentary telling you about the life of Jesus Christ. It's something that will really help you. This is the third edition in its third printing.

- What happened to Jesus next on the Holy Day of Pentecost?
- How do we know?

In the translation, it doesn't show it quite as well as in the Greek, so there's a footnote in *The Faithful Version!*

Luke 4:16: "And He came to Nazareth... [He was up there in Samaria and now He comes down to Nazareth] ...where He had been brought up; and according to His custom, He went into the synagogue on the Sabbath Day..."

Pentecost is a Sabbath Day, but this in the Greek is *on the day of the Sabbaths*—plural—which means the seven Sabbaths of the seven weeks to Pentecost.

"...and stood up to read. And there was given Him *the* book of the prophet Isaiah; and when He had unrolled the scroll, He found the place where it was written, '*The* Spirit of *the* Lord *is* upon Me...'" (vs 16-18).

On what day did God send the Holy Spirit? *Pentecost!* See how all that ties in?

"...for this reason, **He has anointed Me** to preach the Gospel to *the* poor; **He has sent Me** to heal those who are brokenhearted, to proclaim pardon to *the* captives and recovery of sight to *the* blind, to send forth in deliverance those who have been crushed, to proclaim *the* acceptable year of *the* Lord" (vs 18-19)—*which is the first year of the ministry of Jesus Christ!*

All of this is in the New Testament. John 6—here again it talks about Passover in very important detailed instructions about the meaning of Passover.

John 6:4: "Now, the Passover a Feast of the Jews, was near." **What did He do?** *He fed the thousands!*

Verse 27: "Do not labor *for* the food that perishes, but *for* the food that endures unto eternal life, which the Son of man shall give to you; for Him has God the Father sealed. Therefore, they said to Him..." (vs 27-28).

This is always true of carnal people; they always want to do what is good to gain favor with God. God wants, first, *repentance and doing His commandments,* so they asked Jesus:

"...'What shall we do, in order that we ourselves may do the works of God?' Jesus answered and said to them, 'This is the work of God: **that you believe in Him Whom He has sent.**'.... [*Himself*] ...Therefore, they said to Him, 'What sign will You perform, that we may see *it* and believe You? What work will You do? Our fathers ate manna in the wilderness, as it is written: "He gave them bread to eat *that came down* from heaven"'" (vs 28-31). *They were quoting Scripture! They do that!*

This sounds like something all politicians would like, that they would have the key to have bread come down and feed all of their constituents and they would always have a unified vote, that they could never be voted out. I think of that every time I read it.

Verse 32: "Then Jesus said to them, 'Truly, truly I say to you, Moses did not give you the bread from heaven; but My Father gives you **the true Bread** from heaven.'"

He's talking about Himself, and the symbolism of what the Passover would mean with the bread and the wine. But of course, the Jews here wouldn't understand it.

Verse 33: "'For the Bread of God is He Who comes down from heaven and gives life to the world.' Therefore, they said to Him, 'Lord, give this bread to us always.' Jesus said to them, 'I AM the Bread of Life; the one who comes to Me shall never hunger; and the one who believes in Me shall never thirst at any time'" (vs 33-35).

He was talking on a spiritual level about Himself Who was to become the Passover Lamb of God!

Verse 36: "But *as* I said to you, you also have seen Me, yet, you do not believe. All whom the Father gives Me shall come to Me, and the one who comes to Me I will in no wise cast out" (vs 36-37).

Think about how important this is because He had to have human nature; v 38: "**For I did not come down from heaven to do My own will, but the will of Him Who sent Me.**" *That's quite a statement!*

The whole thing about the Sabbath and the Holy Days is the will of God, and how we are to live.

Verse 39: "And this is the will of the Father Who sent Me: that *of* all whom He has given Me, I should not lose any, but should raise them up in **the last day.**"

The last day for those who are converted is not the last day of the Feast—the Last Great Day—but the last day meaning Pentecost, which is the 50th day and the last count of the 50 days!

Verse 40: "'And this is the will of Him Who sent Me: that everyone who sees the Son, and believes in Him, may have eternal life; and I will raise him up at the last day.' Then the Jews were complaining against Him, because He said, 'I AM the Bread that came down from heaven'" (vs 40-41).

Then Jesus goes through and explains everything concerning salvation, which depends on the Passover, that last Passover that Jesus took, and His crucifixion! Then He summarizes here:

Verse 53: "Therefore, Jesus said to them, 'Truly, truly I say to you, **unless**… [*if you do not*] …you eat the flesh of the Son of man, and drink His blood, you do not have life in yourselves.'" *Of course, the Jews said,* 'How is He going to do that?'

Verse 54: "The one who eats My flesh and drinks My blood has eternal life, and I will raise him up in the last day; for My flesh is truly food, and My blood is truly drink" (vs 54-55).

This shows the complete dedication that God has to us and our dedication back to Him—*both!*

Verse 56: "The one who eats My flesh and drinks My blood is dwelling in Me, and I in him…. [think about all the things that we've read up to this point]: …**As the living Father has sent Me, and I live by the Father; so also the one who eats Me shall live by Me**" (vs 56-57). *Complete dedication to God!*

That's the explanation of the Passover where He said that of the bread and the wine: ***Do this in the remembrance of Me!***

John 7—Feast of Tabernacles. Jesus went up there secretly, because He knew they were looking for Him, but what did He do? *His brothers came to Him and said,* 'Why don't you go up to the Feast, because no man does what You're doing unless He wants to be seen by others.'

Jesus said, 'No, I won't go up at this time, but you go up.' Now think about this: If the Holy Days were to be done away, He would have said that you don't need to go up because they're all going to be done away, stick around.' ***But He didn't do that!***

He went up secretly. How would He go up secretly? *Just change His form a little bit like He did with the two going to Emmaus!* Remember that after the resurrection? No one would recognize Him.

Then in the middle of the Feast He gets up and starts preaching and teaching again. *Jesus*:

- kept the Passover
- kept the Feast of Unleavened Bread
- kept the Feast of Pentecost
- kept the Feast of Tabernacles
- kept the Last Great Day

John 7:37: "Now, in **the last day,** the great *day* of the Feast, Jesus stood and called out, saying, 'If **anyone** thirsts, let him come to Me and drink. The one who believes in Me, as the Scripture has said, out of his belly shall flow rivers of living water.' But this He spoke concerning the Spirit, which those who believed in Him would soon receive; for *the* Holy Spirit was not yet *given* because Jesus was not yet glorified" (vs 37-39). *Take these words right here and analyze them*:

- **anyone**—*anyone, period!*
- **the last day**—*there is a second resurrection*—(Rev. 20)

That's when they will have the opportunity! In the world there are three categories of people:

1. ***those who belong to Christ,*** love God the Father and Jesus Christ, keep the

commandments, the Sabbaths and Holy Days

2. *the people in the world* who are out there that are blinded because they have not been given the calling, so their minds have not been opened and they live decent lives and are not committing the unpardonable sin

3. *those who commit the unpardonable sin*— those who reject God the Father and Jesus Christ by being complete Satan-worshippers today

When this last group is resurrected they refuse to repent! **They will go into the Lake of Fire!**

Everyone gets a first opportunity, so you have the wait for the message on the Last Great Day.

The next Passover, John 13-17 *are all the most important words of the New Covenant!* The very words of Christ bringing you, in love, with Him and the Father, and for you to know that *God has personally chosen you!* That's so great! Think about it!

- He's not calling the rich
- He's not calling the wise
- He's not calling the famous

He's calling us so that we can love Him and do the things that's He wants!

Mark 14—This is interesting, a little background on what it was done this way. Who was the one to betray Jesus? *Judas!* He was looking for an opportune time to betray Jesus. This is why Jesus didn't tell the disciples where they were going to have the Passover, because He didn't want Judas to know.

He sent Peter and John into the city and 'follow a man carrying a pitcher and into whatever house he goes in, go in there and tell the master of the house the Teacher says *I want to keep the Passover with My disciples.*'

Judas could not betray Him during the Passover service. So, they had the Passover service and then Judas was given the sop and he left. They first had the foot-washing and *then they had*:

Mark 14:17: "Now after evening had come, He came with the twelve. And as they sat and were eating, Jesus said, 'Truly I say to you, **one of you shall betray Me,** *even* **he who is eating with Me**'" (vs 17-18).

So. Judas was right there for the start. He couldn't go before hand and say, 'Hey I know where He's keeping the Passover, you can get Him over here.'

Verse 19: "And they began to be extremely sad… [that one of them was betraying Him] …and

said to Him one by one, '*Is it* I?' And another, '*Is it* I?' But He answered *and* said to them, 'The one who is dipping *a morsel* into the dish with Me, *he is* the one of *you* twelve. The Son of man indeed goes, **just as it has been written of Him**…'" (vs 19-21).

That means that all of the Scriptures concerning His crucifixion, every one of the Scriptures that says that Jesus was the Lord God of the Old Testament inspired the Prophets, David and the different ones to write, especially Isaiah about the crucifixion. David about the very words of Christ while He was on the cross, 'as it was written of Him.'

"…but woe to that man by whom the Son of man is betrayed! It would be better for that man if he had not been born" (v 21).

Verse 22: "And as they were eating, Jesus took bread; *and* after blessing *it*, He broke *it* and gave *it* to them, and said, 'Take, eat; this is My body'"—*symbolic of His body!*

Our conversion with the Spirit of God the Father and Christ in us is so intimate with God that the covenant is based upon the very sacrifice of Christ. You can't eat that sacrifice, but the symbolism of it is that you're going to live by Christ. The bread pictures *every word of God!* Jesus was called *the Word!* He was the Lord God of the Old Testament. *All of those things come together!*

Verse 23: "And He took the cup; *and* after giving thanks, He gave *it* to them; and they all drank of it. And He said to them, 'This is My blood, the blood of the New Covenant, which is poured out for many'" (vs 23-24)—*the sins of the whole world, but each one individually!*

There has to be the shedding of blood before a covenant can be enacted. A covenant is never valid until both parties have given the sacrifice. *Christ gave His; ours is baptism, both signifying death and life!* When you're buried under the water, you're burying your old self. That is your sacrifice, because you're telling God, *'I will be faithful to the end!'*

Therefore, you're joined to the sacrifice of Christ. That's the symbolic meaning and fulfilling in our lives, because God sends His Spirit to dwell in us. That's what's so absolutely amazing and astonishing *that the Great Sovereign of the universe would do that with His people!* That is so great.

Verse 25: "Truly I say to you, I will not drink again at all of the fruit of the vine until that day when I drink it new in the Kingdom of God."

When will that be? *We will all drink it at the Wedding Supper of the Lamb!*

- I wonder what it's going to be like to eat

spiritual food?

- I wonder what it's going to be like to drink spiritual wine?
- I wonder what it's going to be like to be dressed with spiritual clothes?

What God has done and is doing is fantastic!

When you look at all of these Scriptures and put them together, you see that every single one of the Holy Days marks an important aspect of the plan of God:

- to carry out His purpose
- to keep us informed
- to keep us faithful
- to keep us trusting in Him

We'll see in John 14 why! We know that Jesus said that 'if you love Me keep My commandments.' I wonder how the Protestants view that when they do away with the Sabbath and Holy Days. I wonder how they can say that? *I cover John 14 a lot, because it's so important!*

John 14:21: "The one who has My commandments and is keeping them… [present tense participle] …**that is the one who loves Me, and the one who loves Me shall be loved by My Father**…"

Don't ever think you're not important; you're so important that the father loves you! Think on that, especially the time now with all the difficult things that are around us.

"…and I will love him and will manifest Myself to him" (v 21). *Not by an apparition!* But by opening your mind to the Truth and calling you!

Verse 22: "Judas (not Iscariot) said to him, 'Lord, what has happened that You are about to manifest Yourself to us, and not to the world?'" *It's done by love and obedience with God's Spirit.*

Verse 23—the most important verse in the whole Bible for us in this life now at this time; "Jesus answered and said to him, '**If anyone loves Me**…'"

How are we to love God? *With all our heart, mind, soul and strength!* That's a fulltime occupation when you understand it.

"…**he will keep My Word**…" (v 23).

- not look for a way around it
- not look for a way to sin and justify it as okay

"…and **My Father will love him**…" (v 23). *He said that in v 21!*

"…and **We will come to him and make Our abode with him**'" (v 23)—*because the Holy Spirit is*

dwelling in us! That's why:

- we need study every day
- we need prayer every day
- we need that connection with God spiritually every day

So that we have our minds being constantly converted!

- led by the Holy Spirit of God
- keeping the commandments of God
- keeping the Sabbath and the Holy Days
  - ✓ which is what God created and made for us
  - ✓ in which God does all the things in His plan so that we can understand

So, here we are in the very last days! How much longer we have, we don't know, but we know one thing: Paul wrote that there would be perilous times and we're seeing how that's sprouting out in many, many different places. *This is why it's important that we stay close to God!*

All of this shows how important all the Holy Days of God are! We have coming up real quickly, Sept. 19, the Feast of Trumpets. After that we have Atonement and then Tabernacles and the Last Great Day. So, wherever you are, even if the circumstances are that you're alone, *God the Father and Christ are with you!* You will have a great and a wonderful Feast.

Let's look forward to all the Feasts of God, and *remember how important the Sabbath and Holy Days are of God, and that He has given us—* through His Word, Spirit, love and grace—*the understanding of His plan!*

Scriptural References:

1) Psalm 78:1-2
2) 2 Timothy 1:7-9
3) Isaiah 14:24, 26-27
4) Psalm 119:159-160, 128
5) Isaiah 28:13
6) Leviticus 23:1-11, 24
7) Matthew 5:17-22, 21
8) Mark 2:27-28
9) John 2:13-16, 18-20, 23-25
10) John 4:33-38
11) Luke 4:16-19
12) John 6:4, 27-41, 53-57
13) John 7:37-39
14) Mark 14:17-25
15) John 14:21-23

Scriptures referenced, not quoted:

- Revelation 2; 3; 12

- Isaiah 37-39
- Genesis 3; 15
- Revelation 20
- Luke 6
- Epistles of John
- Revelation 4
- John 19
- Jeremiah 17
- Matthew 13
- John 13-17

Also referenced:

from: *The Holy Bible in Its Original Order, A Faithful Version*:
- Appendix N: <u>*Rome's Challenge to the Protestants*</u> {Also available in booklet form—**truthofGod.org**}
- Appendix Z: <u>Understanding Paul's Difficult Scriptures Concerning the Law and the Commandments of God</u>

DVD—*True Fellowship with God*

Sermon: *Current Events & Bible Prophecy*

Books:
The Christian Passover by Fred R. Coulter
A Harmony of the Gospels by Fred R. Coulter

FRC:bo
Transcribed: 8/27/20
Reformatted: 12/2020

CHAPTER TEN

Should We Keep the Holy Days of the Bible?

Fred R. Coulter

Most religions that profess themselves to be Christian claim that they don't have to keep them. Many of them such as the Seventh Day Adventists, and others as well, claim that because there were sacrifices on these days, therefore:

They were ritualistic and sacrificial days only and have no meaning other than what they meant in the Old Testament.

- Is that true?
- What does the Bible show?
- What does the Bible teach?

- How can people take the Bible *and interpret that it's perfectly all right to keep*:
  - ✓ Halloween?
  - ✓ Christmas?
  - ✓ New Years?
  - ✓ Ground Hog's Day?
  - ✓ Lent?
  - ✓ Good Friday?
  - ✓ Easter?

all of the pagan holidays
- How can people say that it's in the Bible and we can do that?
- How can people say that when it is never even listed in the Bible?
- How is that possible?

Well, here is what happens!

2-Corinthians 2:17: "For we are not like the many… [what we are dealing with is a very, very old problem] …who **for *their own* profit are corrupting** the Word of God…" *The Word of God is corrupted by*:

- poor translations
- wrong texts
- corrupt interpretations
- claiming things that are not substantiated by the Bible

What needs to be done is that *people need to go through the Bible and they really need to put it all together!*

Isaiah 28:13: "…precept upon precept, precept upon precept; line upon line, line upon line; here a little, there a little …" and also as Paul told Timothy that you have to *'rightly divide the Word of Truth.'*

2-Corinthians 2:17: "…but we speak with sincerity, as from God, *and* before God, *and* in Christ."

2 Corinthians 4:1: "Therefore, having this ministry, according as we have received mercy, we are not fainthearted. For we have personally renounced the hidden things of dishonest gain…" (vs 1-2).

That's a very important thing to do, because the human 'heart is deceitful above all things, and desperately wicked; who can know it?' *So you have to renounce that!*

"…not walking in *cunning* craftiness…" (v 2)—*walking with **a hidden agenda** that other people don't know, that you will craftily spring upon them at a later date!*

"…nor handling the Word of God deceitfully…" (v 2)—*by taking the Word of God and applying it to things that are not true and saying they are true!*

"…but by manifestation of the Truth, we are commending ourselves to every man's conscience before God. But if our Gospel is hidden, it is hidden to those who are perishing; in whom the god of this age has blinded the minds of those who do not believe, lest the Light of the Gospel of the glory of Christ, Who is *the* image of God, should shine unto them" (vs 2-4).

So, any part of the Gospel that you have hidden from you, or blinded from you, then you need to understand that it falls into several categories:

1. you have misinterpreted the Word of God
2. you have blinded your eyes to it
3. it may be a tradition
4. Satan has blinded your mind to that part of it

Satan is trying to get all those who truly have the Spirit of God and are Christians to give up on something somewhere along the line, because he knows that *'a little leaven leavens the whole lump.'*

Matt. 7 is profound! Some of these Scriptures are very basic, because this is a very basic topic. As a matter of fact, so basic that I have not given a message on proving keeping the Holy Days in years, because I'm basically dealing with all of those who keep the Holy Days. But when we come into contact with people who do not keep the Holy Days, nor understand the Holy Days, then we do need to go back and reconfirm the Truth as to why we do it, and so forth. But I'm going to approach this a little bit differently.

We have applied Matt. 7 to false prophets because it talks about *false prophets*. There can be a prophet who is a *half-false* prophet by preaching *half-truth!*

Matthew 7:21: "Not everyone who says to Me 'Lord, Lord' shall enter into the Kingdom of Heaven; **but the one who is doing the will of My Father, Who *is* in heaven**." *That is the key!*

- Are *you* doing the will of the Father?
- *Was it the Father's will* that Christ created the Sabbath?
- *Was it the Father's will* that Christ gave the Holy Days to the children of Israel?
- *Was it the Father's will* in these things?
- *Was it the Father's will* that what Christ did and observed be part of what God wanted? *Yes, absolutely!*

IF you are *not doing the will* of the Father, Who is in heaven:

- though you use the name of the Lord
- though you may belong to a church
- though you may have a group that really is a group that you like

Verse 22: "Many will say to Me in that day, 'Lord, Lord, did we not prophesy through Your name?....'"—*preached in Your name!*

I have heard some stinging sermons *against* the Holy Days. There are tremendous errors in their way of thinking.

"...And *did we not* cast out demons through Your name? And *did we not* perform many works of power through Your name?" (v 22).

- you can have *part* of the fruits
- you can have *some* of the things that look like they come from God
- you can have *some* of the Truth of God

But *unless* you have the whole Truth of God and you are *willing to live by all* the Truth of God, and *if* you come to understand the Truth of God—which you have previously not understood—and you are willing to keep it; *if* you're not doing those things *then* you're going to end up in this category:

Verse 23: "And then I will confess to them, **'I never knew you. Depart from Me, you who work lawlessness'**"—*being against Law!*

Since the Holy Days are part of the Law of God, you need to make very sure that you are *not against the Law of God as respecting the Holy Days!* The only thing you have different than a Protestant is the Sabbath! So you might as well put yourself in the same category of the Protestants if the only thing you do is keep the Sabbath. If that offends some people, well then, you might *take your offense to God and find out from His Word what you need to do!*

We have to keep the will of God. This is the attitude that we need, Psa. 143. *The will of God* is contained in His Word, and *the will of God* is here for us that we're to keep. We're going to see that *it is the will of God that we keep the Feasts of God!* As a matter fact, we're going to see later that the Apostle Paul, with no doubt—no question whatsoever—absolutely commands the keeping of the Feast.

Psalm 143:10: "Teach me to do Your will... [*God is the One Who is going to have to teach you from His Word with His Spirit*] ...for You are my God; may Your good Spirit lead me on level ground of uprightness"—*to be righteous before God!*

Rom. 12 is a New Testament expression of that very same Psalm. This is important for us to realize, because *the will of God is what we are all going to be held accountable for!* Didn't Jesus say to those who were not doing the will of the Father in heaven above that they were going to be cast into outer darkness? *Yes He did!* Believe me, after the experience in the Lake of Fire it will be outer darkness. There will be nothing left!

Romans 12:1: "I exhort you, therefore, brethren... [Paul here is sincerely asking the brethren] ...by the mercies of God, to present your bodies a living sacrifice, Holy *and* well-pleasing to God, which is your spiritual service. Do not conform yourselves to this world, but **be transformed by the renewing of your mind in order that you may prove what *is* well-pleasing and good, and the perfect will of God**" (vs 1-2).

That's what we have to do. That's why the Holy Day issue becomes very important. As we go through this, ask yourself: **Am I keeping all the will of God?**

It says *prove by the renewing of your mind!* So, you are to *use your mind to rightly divide the Word of God,* as Paul told Timothy. *Not handle it improperly!*

"...**that you may prove**..." (v 2). How do you prove something? *You prove something by the facts!*

- God is fact
- His Law is fact
- His Word is fact
- His Truth is fact

what's important here is that:

- you don't go on what *you feel*

- you don't go on what you personally believe

A lot of personal beliefs *become idols* before God; they are idols in your mind. You have to prove what is the good, acceptable and perfect will of God. How? *As defined by His Word!* You don't prove it by an emotion or a feeling. God's Word is here in the Bible. You have the whole thing; it's impartial. The problems come *when people interpret* things incorrectly.

Let's look at some of these things and see how these are handled and what is done. Luke 16 is one of the Scriptures that has been misinterpreted almost universally by the Catholics, the Protestants, and by some in the Churches of God; in particularly the Sabbath-keeping, non-Holy Day-keeping Churches of God, which also includes the Seventh-Day Adventists.

Luke 16:13: "No servant is able to serve two masters; for either he will hate the one, and he will love the other; or he will hold to *the* one and will despise the other. You cannot serve God and mammon." *There's only one way to serve God, and that's through*:

- His Word
- His Truth
- His Spirit

Verse 14: "Now the Pharisees, who were also covetous, heard all these things; and they ridiculed Him. And He said to them, 'You are **those who justify themselves before men**... [exactly what happens with all of these false doctrines] ...but God knows your hearts; for that which is highly esteemed among men is an abomination before God'" (vs 14-15).

That can apply to all the religions of men; they're very highly esteemed. Here's the verse that He's leading up to, and this is something that almost everyone universally does not understand:

Verse 16: "The Law and the Prophets *were* until John..." *Therefore, from the time of John the Baptist the laws of God have been done away!* **That is the conclusion!** Let's read the whole thing and see what it says:

Verse 16: "The Law and the Prophets *were* until John; from that time the Kingdom of God is preached, and everyone zealously strives to enter it"—*showing that to enter the Kingdom of God is a difficult situation!*

- With the Kingdom of God being preached, does that do away with the laws and commandments of God, including the Holy Days?

- What does it mean, "The Law and the Prophets *were* until John…"?

There's also another misconception that people are under, which is that Jesus was under the Old Covenant. *Not true!* Jesus was under a special covenant between Him and God the Father, so He could establish the New Covenant.

- the New Covenant is the Kingdom of God
- the Law and the Prophets were the authority for preaching up to that time

Christ comes and the Kingdom of God is preached!

But notice, He wants to make it very clear concerning the Laws of God. He wants you to understand that the laws and commandments of God have not been done away, because there's a different emphasis in preaching.

Verse 17: "But it is easier *for* heaven and earth to pass away than *for* one tittle of the Law to fail."

Especially for those who are Sabbath-keepers, you believe in the commandments of God; you believe in the Ten Commandments, and you've probably read this Scripture. Well you have to apply it correctly to all the rest of the Scriptures, as well.

Matthew 5:17: "**Do not think** that I have come to abolish the Law or the Prophets... [don't let it enter into your mind; don't even think this thought] ...I did not come to abolish, **but to fulfill**."

Here's where the other miscommunication and twisting of the Scripture comes, which is this: *IF* Christ fulfills it, ***then*** we don't have to do it. This is where people get into the false doctrine of saying that:

- Christ fulfilled the Sabbath for me; therefore, I don't have to keep it
- Christ fulfilled the Holy Days; therefore, I don't have to keep them
- Christ fulfilled you shall do no murder; therefore, I can murder
- Christ fulfilled do not commit adultery; therefore, it's all right to commit adultery

NO! because then you have abolished the Law! Let's find out what Jesus fulfilled, and let's find out what is yet to be fulfilled, or is still being fulfilled.

Verse 18. "For truly I say to you, until the heaven and the earth shall pass away, one jot or one tittle shall in no way pass from the Law until **everything has been fulfilled**."

When that is fulfilled, if you read Rev. 21 & 22, then you have a new beginning with other things that are going to be fulfilling to a greater degree than the ones we've had in the past.

Now let's see what Jesus did fulfill? I know that the doctrine of not keeping the Holy Days, for those who keep the Sabbath, is that the Holy Days were part of the ritual. Well, we will see Jesus did away with the ritual. But did He do away with the days? *Let's see what it is that Christ did!*

Hebrews 9:11: "But Christ Himself has become High Priest of the coming good things, through the greater and more perfect tabernacle, not made by *human* hands (that is, not of this *present physical* creation).... [Paul was referring to the physical building of the temple in Jerusalem at the time] ...Not by *the* blood of goats and calves, but by the means of His own blood, He entered once for all into the Holiest, having *by* Himself secured everlasting redemption *for us*" (vs 11-12).

Verse 28: "So Christ, having been offered once to bear *the* sins of many, will appear *the* second time without sin unto salvation to those who are eagerly awaiting Him."

Now then, Paul goes on to explain what Christ did with His sacrifice to fulfill. When He fulfilled it, we will see that He added to it a greater sacrifice, that is, being His sacrifice. We're going to find that He fulfilled the animal sacrifice and the temple ritual for a special purpose.

Hebrews 10:1: "For the *priestly* law, having *only* a shadow of the good things that are coming, *and* not the image of those things, with the same sacrifices, which they offer continually year by year, is never able to make perfect those who come *to worship*."

It is the goal of God to have everything perfected! These animal sacrifices could not do it.

Verse 2: "Otherwise, would they not have ceased to be offered? For once those who worship had been purified, *they would* no longer be conscious of sin. On the contrary, in *offering* these *sacrifices* year by year, *there is* a remembrance of sins, because *it is* impossible *for the* blood of bulls and goats to take away sins" (vs 2-4)—*because it's a lesser being than a human being!*

- How can a goat atone for human sin?
- How can a bull atone for human sin?

*Those things were just to cover them **at the temple** so they could continue functioning under the Old Covenant!*

Verse 5: "For this reason, when He comes into the world, He says, 'Sacrifice and offering You did not desire, but You have prepared a body for Me [Christ]. You did not delight in burnt offerings and *sacrifices* for sin. Then said I, "Lo, I come (*as* it is written of Me in *the* Scroll of *the* Book) to do Your will, O God"'" (vs 5-7).

God's will and the proper worship of God, the proper forgiveness of sin before God is what he's talking about here. It ties right in with what we talked about: *the will of God!*

Verse 8: "In the saying above, *He said*, 'Sacrifice and offering and burnt offerings and *sacrifices* for sin (which are offered according to the *priestly* law) You did not desire nor delight in.'"

- Is that the whole Law?
- Do the animal sacrifices constitute the whole Law of God?

or

- Are they part of the Law of God as we find in the Old Testament? *No!*

The animal sacrifices were a small part of the Law of God. And we're going to see that when we get into it.

Verse 9: "Then He said, 'Lo, I come to do Your will, O God.' He takes away the first *covenant* in order that He may establish the second *covenant*."

The first covenant with the second covenant, but understand that the covenant does not do away with Law; the covenant is your relationship with God. In every covenant there are always laws.

Verse 10: "By Whose will we are sanctified through the offering of the body of Jesus Christ once for all. Now, every high priest stands ministering day by day, offering the same sacrifices repeatedly, which are never able to remove sins; but He, after offering one sacrifice for sins forever, sat down at *the* right hand of God" (vs 10-12).

What are we talking about here? *We're **not** talking about doing away with Law; **we're talking about doing away with sin!** The way to do away with sin and the way to worship God is what has been changed.

What is sin? *New Testament doctrine*: **Sin is the transgression of the Law!** So, the New Covenant is how to do away with sin and your relationship with God. Jesus' one sacrifice fulfilled all the animal sacrifices and all the temple ritual, and replaced it with His sacrifice and with the temple in heaven above. It was done away with only in respect to that it was obsolete and not effective, and never could do away with sin, and now we have a new way of worshiping God under the New Covenant. So far having nothing to do with the Sabbath, having nothing to do with the Holy Days.

Verse 14: "For by one offering He has obtained eternal perfection *for* those who are sanctified. And the Holy Spirit also bears witness to us; for after He had previously said, "'This *is* the covenant that I will establish with them after those days," says *the* Lord, "I will give My Laws into their hearts, and I will inscribe them in their minds"'" (vs 14-16).

- that is the exact opposite of doing away with anything
- that is the exact opposite of fulfilling them for you as a person

Verse 17: "And their sins and lawlessness I will not remember ever again.... [the animal sacrifices were a remembrance of sin every year] ...Now, where remission of these *is, it is* no longer *necessary to offer* sacrifices for sin" (vs 17-18)—*of animals and other rituals, **because the one offering for sin was Christ!***

Verse 19: "Therefore, brethren, having confidence to enter into the *true* Holiest by the blood of Jesus, by a new and living way, which He consecrated for us through the veil (that is, His flesh), and *having* a great High Priest over the house of God, let us approach *God* with a true heart, with full conviction of faith, our hearts having been purified from a wicked conscience, and our bodies having been washed with pure water. Let us hold fast without wavering *to* the hope *that* we profess, for He Who promised *is* faithful" (vs 19-23). *What we have here is a whole new way of worship*:

- a new temple in heaven above
- a new High Priest
  - ✓ Who is Christ
  - ✓ Who is at the temple in heaven above at the right hand of the Throne of God
    - superior to the earthly temple
    - superior to the earthly priesthood
    - superior to the earthly sacrifices of the goats, bulls, and turtledoves

That is what has been changed! It has been changed with the fulfillment of those things by Christ. ***Jesus said until everything be fulfilled!***

So far the only thing that has been fulfilled is the replacing of the temporary animal sacrifices and the temporary temple/tabernacle on earth with the permanent eternal one in heaven. Whenever anything has been done away or fulfilled *it is replaced with something of a higher standard!* You can understand that when you read Matt. 5-7, where Jesus said, '***You have heard it said** of old time, **but I say to you...**'* So, whenever He brought the fulfillment of the Law He gave it a higher standard. He didn't do away with anything, ***Christ came to do away with sin!***

I know those of you who believe in the weekly Sabbath turn to Gen. 2 all the time to prove that Sabbath was a day that was created. Which came first, the day, by creation? ***or*** The ritual of animal sacrifice? ***The day came first!*** No doubt! *The*

sleight of hand, the deceitful handling of the Scriptures is when you claim that the ritual sacrifices and the ritual temple things done at the temple, when those were done away with they also did away with the Sabbath and did away with the Holy Days. That's where the sleight of hand comes in. So therefore, we have to ask: Which came first? Now we're not talking about evolution, the chicken or the egg. We're talking about which came first—the creation of the day? ***or*** the sacrifices? The answer obviously is the creation of the day.

Genesis 2:1: "Thus the heavens and the earth were finished, and all the host of them. And by *the beginning of* the seventh day God finished His work, which He had made. And He rested on the seventh day from all His work, which He had made. And God blessed the seventh day and sanctified it, because on it He rested from all His work, which God had created and made" (vs 1-3).

So we know that God made the seventh day, He sanctified the seventh day. We all understand that, but is that all that God made?

The truth is, God created all days, but He specially made the seventh day of every week *the Sabbath!* Now let's understand something else that He did:

Genesis 1:14: "And God said, 'Let there be lights in the firmament of the heavens to divide between the day and the night, and let them be for **signs, and for appointed seasons, and for days and years**...'"

How do we govern the weekly Sabbath? *From sunset to sunset!* But God also created seasons!

{note our in-depth study concerning the *Covenants of God*}

Long before the Old Covenant was ever given, the covenant was given to Abraham (Gen. 15). We do not have the time to go through the technical explanation of it, so I will just tell you:

Genesis 15:4: "And behold, the Word of the LORD *came* to him saying, 'This man shall not be your heir; but he that shall come forth out of your own loins shall be your heir.' And He brought him outside and said, 'Look now toward the heavens and number the stars—if you are able to count them.' And He said to him, 'So shall your seed be.' And he believed in the LORD. And He accounted it to him for righteousness" (vs 4-6).

This was given on the 14th day of the 1st month at night, the same day in which the Passover occurs, if you believe in the Sabbath and Passover. So, we have the day *first,* then the significance of the day. The next day in which He made the covenant to take the children of Israel out of Egypt was the 15th, which became the 1st day of the Feast of Unleavened Bread.

Let's see that by going to Exo. 12. Which came first, the day? _or_ the sacrifice? *We will see the day came first!* The sacrifice came as later instruction. Here's the instruction that they were to do concerning the lamb:

Exodus 12:5: "Your lamb shall be without blemish, a male of the first year. You shall take *it* from the sheep or from the goats. And you shall keep it up **until the *beginning* of the fourteenth day** of the same month.... [the day came first; He designated the day first] ...And the whole assembly of the congregation of Israel shall kill it between the two evenings" (vs 5-6).

I'm not going to go through any technical explanation on it, except to say that this is after sunset, between sunset and dark. God named the day, *the 14th*; v 11: "...It *is* the LORD'S Passover."

I assume that most of you keep the Passover. But if you keep the Passover and you don't keep the Feast of Unleavened Bread, then you are cutting something off. You are not following through on the commands of God. You are throwing the commands of observation—which God has commanded to be Holy Days—into the same categories as the animal sacrifices. They were never in the same category.

Verse 13: "And the blood shall be a sign to you upon the houses where you *are*. And when I see the blood, I will pass over you. And the plague shall not be upon you to destroy *you* when I smite the land of Egypt. And this day shall be a memorial to you. And you shall keep it a Feast to the LORD throughout your generations. You shall keep it a Feast as a Law forever" (vs 13-14).

The day was chosen *first,* the sacrifice was put on the day, and God says you are to keep the day forever. Later when Christ came, He was sacrificed on the 14th day and He became the sacrifice that replaces the lamb that the Israelites killed. **Christ is the Lamb of God,** and it's on the **14th day!** That's why the Passover Day is to be kept.

Notice v 15, speaking of the Feast of Unleavened Bread, this becomes very important, because again, we're going to see that *the day was there before the offering*:

Verse 15: "You shall eat unleavened *bread* seven days; even the first day you shall *have* put away leaven out of your houses; for whoever eats leavened bread from the first day until the seventh day, that soul shall be cut off from Israel. And in the first day *there shall be* a Holy convocation... [the same weight and force of command as in Gen. 2 of blessing the Sabbath day, a Holy convocation] ...and

in the seventh day there shall be a Holy convocation for you. No manner of work shall be done in them, except that which every man must eat, that only may be done by you. And you shall keep the *Feast of Unleavened Bread,* for in this very same day I have brought your armies out of the land of Egypt. Therefore, you shall keep this day in your generations as a law forever" (vs 15-17). *So the day came first!*

Exo. 20—here is where the giving of the Ten Commandments was. But in the Exo.19 we have a special event that took place: *the preparing for the giving of the Ten Commandments.* The Ten Commandments were given on the Day of Pentecost. So *the day came first!*

The trick is this: **_IF_** you believe in the Ten Commandments, then why do you not celebrate, keep or observe the Feast of Pentecost on which the Ten Commandments were given? *That's a question you need to ask!*

Lev. 23 is the chapter in the whole Bible where ***all*** the Holy Days are listed. We have established:

1. the Sabbath Day was before any sacrifice
2. the Passover Day was established before any sacrifice
3. the first and last day of Unleavened Bread were established before any sacrifice
4. the Day of Pentecost was established before any sacrifice

Those are Holy convocations!

Leviticus 23:1: "And the LORD spoke to Moses, saying, 'Speak to the children of Israel and say to them, "*Concerning* the appointed Feasts of the LORD..."'" (vs 1-2).

I want to make this very clear: ***they are not, never have been, never will be the feasts of the Jews,*** though other people have called them the *feasts of the Jews,* and though for particular reasons which John knew, he labeled the 'feast of the Jews' concerning the Feast of Tabernacles, but ***it's the Feast of the Lord!***

"...which you shall proclaim *to be* Holy convocations, even these are My appointed Feasts" (v 2). *All of them!* Then He starts off with:

Verse 3: "Six days shall work be done, but the seventh day *is* the Sabbath of rest, a Holy convocation. You shall not do any work. It *is* a **Sabbath to the LORD in all your dwellings**." *The other Holy convocations are* "...Sabbath to the LORD in all your dwellings" too.

Verse 4: "These *are* the appointed Feasts of the LORD, **Holy convocations, which you shall proclaim in their appointed seasons**."

God created the time for seasons (Gen. 1:14). If you believe that **you are to proclaim** the seventh day as a Feast of God every seven days, and that **you are obligated by God to keep the Sabbath** and to keep it Holy, what gives you the right to go against God?

They are "…Holy convocations, which **you shall proclaim in their appointed seasons,**"

You disobey that command and do not proclaim them! What is your reason for not proclaiming them? *We will look at some of them!* Your reasons are going to fall apart, because it has not been a proper, rightful dividing of the Word of God.

Verse 5: "In the fourteenth *day* of the first month, between the two evenings, is the LORD'S Passover... [in every case God gives the day first and then the offering for that day] …and on the fifteenth day of the same month *is* the Feast of Unleavened Bread to the LORD. You must eat unleavened bread seven days. On the first day you shall have a Holy convocation. You shall not *do any servile* work *therein*, but you shall offer a fire offering to the LORD seven days...." (vs 5-8).

The sacrifices at the temple, then, *were* added to the days. The days came first. Likewise with Pentecost, and how to count it. If you don't know how to count Pentecost, we have two booklets that explain in depth the whole thing of counting Pentecost {find at **truthofGod.org**}:

➢ Count to Pentecost From the Morrow After Which Sabbath?
➢ Count to Pentecost

Also a Message:

➢ How to Count Pentecost

Verse 21: "And you shall proclaim on the same day that it may be a Holy convocation to you...."

Verse 24: "Speak to the children of Israel saying, 'In the seventh month, in the first *day* of the month, you shall have a Sabbath, a memorial of blowing of ram's horns, a Holy convocation. You shall do no servile work *therein* but you shall offer an offering made by fire to the LORD'" (vs 24-25). *Again, the day is proclaimed first and then the sacrificial offering.*

Verse 27: "Also, on the tenth *day* of this seventh month, is the Day of Atonement. *It shall be* a Holy convocation to you. And you shall afflict your souls and offer an offering made by fire to the LORD. And you shall do no work in that same day, for it *is* the Day of Atonement, in order to make an atonement for you before the LORD your God" (vs 27-28).

Verse 32: "It *shall be* to you a Sabbath of rest, and you shall afflict yourselves. In the ninth *day* of the month at sunset, from sunset to sunset, you shall keep your Sabbath."

This is the verse that all Sabbath-keepers turn to, to show that you must keep the Sabbath from sunset to sunset, but this is defining the Day of Atonement. If this defines the Day of Atonement, and you keep the Sabbath but not the Day of Atonement, why do you take your definition from the Day of Atonement and apply it to the Sabbath, if it is not equally applicable to the Sabbath and the Day of Atonement and all the other Holy Days?

Verse 34: "…'The fifteenth day of this seventh month *shall be* the Feast of Tabernacles for seven days to the LORD. On the first day *shall be* a Holy convocation. You shall do no servile work *therein*. On the eighth day shall be a Holy convocation to you...." (vs 34-36)—*then the sacrifices and so forth!*

Verse 37: "These *are* **the Feasts of the LORD**, which you shall proclaim..."

As you can see, I'm doing a survey. Because in order to understand this, you must get an overview by a survey to understand.

Verse 37: "**These *are* the Feasts of the LORD, which you shall proclaim to be Holy convocations**..." *If you take this statement, which is true, and you go back and you apply it in*:

Leviticus 23:2: "…'*Concerning* the appointed Feasts of the LORD, which you shall proclaim *to be* Holy convocations, even these are My appointed Feasts.... [It starts out with **the Sabbath**]: …Six days shall work be done, but the seventh day *is* **the Sabbath of rest,** a Holy convocation. You shall not do any work. It *is* a Sabbath to the LORD in all your dwellings" (vs 2-3). *Now then, you're stuck!*

- Why do you not proclaim those other days according to God's calendar the way that they should be?
- Are you missing something by not doing it?
- Are you incorrectly dividing the Word of God because you are misapplying Scripture?

Let's go to the heart and core of the whole thing. You're also going to be stuck with another problem if you say that because they had ritual sacrifices on these days, and the sacrifices have been done away with because Christ's sacrifice superseded all the animal sacrifices, what are you going to do with:

Numbers 28:1: "And the LORD spoke to Moses, saying, 'Command the children of Israel, and say to them, "My offering *and* My bread for My sacrifices made by fire... [because there was the tabernacle, and later the temple] ...a sweet savor to Me, you shall be diligent to observe to offer to Me in their due season." And you shall say to them, "This *is* the offering made by fire which you shall offer to the LORD: two lambs of the first year without blemish day by day, a continual burnt offering"'" (vs 1-3). *This is the daily burnt offering!*

Now, because animal sacrifices were done away, have days been done away with? *No!* One in the morning, one in the evening.

Verse 9: "And on the Sabbath Day two lambs of the first year without blemish, and two tenth parts of flour *for* a grain offering, mixed with oil, and its drink offering; *this is* the burnt offering of every Sabbath, besides the continual burnt offering, and its drink offering" (vs 9-10).

Now then, if you take your reasoning—which so many do to get rid of the Holy Days—by saying that the ritual sacrifices were offered on the Holy Days and the sacrifices were done away with; therefore, 'we don't have to keep the Holy Days.' What are you going to do about the Sabbath? *Because if you take the reasoning of one, you must also take the reasoning of the other!*

- Were there sacrifices on the Sabbath Day? *Yes!*
- Were those sacrifices done away with and fulfilled in Christ? *Yes!*

IF you take the assumption that because those were true, therefore, 'we conclude that we don't have to keep the Sabbath because the sacrifices were done away.' You're stuck in your own logic. Because if you keep the Sabbath, because God commanded it, and you don't keep the Holy Days, because the sacrifices were done away with, then your logic traps you into your own corner, where then you must not keep the Sabbath by the same logic.

I've gone over this with Church of God Seventh Day people until I'm blue in the face. But *when* you are dead and your mind is set, and you are not willing to let the Truth of God enter into it, *then* you can come to that conclusion. But how else are you going to conclude it? If you take the reasoning that the Holy Days do not need to be kept because there were ritual sacrifices on those, and those ritual sacrifices are all done away with in Christ, so was Sabbath ritual sacrifice done away in Christ.

Therefore, you're stuck in your own logic *because you're not honest in handling the Word of God, and you misapply the Word of God* so that you

may keep the Sabbath and do away with the Holy Days. You've got to understand that. That's where you begin. Maybe other people couldn't convince you, but maybe the Word of God can convince you.

Now you can go through and apply this to all the Holy Days in the rest of Num. 28 & 29, because every one of the days had sacrifices. You can't use that logic; that logic is a misnomer; that logic is not correct. If you run on to Gal. 3 and misapply that, then you're also going to get yourself in trouble. If you need some understanding concerning the book of Galatians, we have a whole in-depth study on that—Epistle of Paul to the Galatians—which goes through it and explains it.

Now then, as we're here in Ezek. 20, I call your attention to reference back to Exo. 31, where the Sabbaths are, God said you were to keep. Now notice when we are reading here, God does not make any differentiation between which Sabbath is which. All of the Holy Days are annual Sabbaths.

Ezekiel 20:10—*God says*: "And I caused them to go out from the land of Egypt, and brought them into the wilderness. And I gave them My statutes and showed them My ordinances, which *if* a man do, he shall even live in them. And also I gave them My **Sabbaths**..."(vs 10-12)—*plural!*

That is not *the* Sabbath, but Sabbaths, *plural!* The fourth commandment in the Ten Commandments says, 'Remember the Sabbath Day to keep it Holy.' But He gave them more than the weekly Sabbath. He gave them His *annual Sabbaths*:

"...to be a sign between Me and them, that *they* might know that I *am* the LORD Who sanctifies them" (v 12). *If you don't keep the Holy Days*:

- Is there something that you don't know about the Lord?
- Is there something in your understanding that is missing because you're not sanctified by those days?

Verse 13: "But the house of Israel rebelled against Me in the wilderness... [Are you rebelling against God if you reject His Holy Days?] ...they did not walk in My statutes, and they despised My ordinances, which *if* a man does, he shall even live in them. And they **greatly polluted** My Sabbaths...."—*plural!*

Verse 16: "Because they despised My judgments and walked not in My statutes; and they polluted My Sabbaths; for their heart went after their idols."

When you take God's time and make it yours, or you declare God's Holy time not Holy, *it becomes an idol in your mind!* So, He told them not to do it.

Verse 19: "'I *am* the LORD your God. Walk in My statutes, and keep My ordinances, and do them, and keep My Sabbaths Holy; and they shall be a sign between Me and you, that you may know that I *am* the LORD your God.' But the children rebelled against Me...." (vs 19-21).

If you think that the weekly Sabbath is good, right and fine, tell me why the annual Sabbaths are not also good, right and fine. If you don't keep them, then you are saying that God's Word is not worthy of your observance. I mean, you need to keep things on a clear, factual basis. Don't get your feelings involved in on it, because you're going to get yourself in deep trouble.

Let's see what we are to do in the New Testament. Then we will see, did they in the New Testament under the New Covenant, keep these days?

You're also stuck with another problem. If you say you love God, and you try and love God this way, then you have to ask yourself: Why do I reject the Holy Days of God?

Matthew 22:37: "And Jesus said to him, 'You shall love *the* Lord your God with all your heart, and with all your soul, and with all your mind. This is *the* first and greatest commandment; and *the* second *one is* like it: "You shall love your neighbor as yourself." On these two commandments hang all the Law and the Prophets'" (vs 37-40).

Whereby Jesus said, *'One jot or one tittle shall in no wise pass from the Law until all be fulfilled.'* The only thing that we have seen in the Scriptures which has been fulfilled has been the animal sacrifices and the temple ritual, which have been replaced and superseded by a higher sacrifice of Jesus Christ in a greater temple in heaven above. *All of the rest is still hanging on the love of God!*

- Do you love God?
- Do you love God in Truth?

OR

- Do you want to love God *your* way and tell God what to do?

How does God want us to worship Him today?

John 4:23: "But the hour is coming... [when you wouldn't worship any longer in Jerusalem, the temple would be gone] ...and now is, when **the true worshipers shall worship the Father in Spirit and in Truth**..."

- we know the commandments of God are Truth
- we know the Laws of God are Truth

- we know that all of God's ways are true
- we know His commandments are true

Therefore, if you're going to worship God in Spirit and in Truth, you're going to be keeping His commandments from the heart spiritually, loving God.

"...for the Father is indeed seeking those who worship Him in this manner. God *is* spirit, and those who worship Him **must** worship in Spirit and in Truth" (vs 23-24).

The word *must* there in the Greek has the force of *obligatory!* You are *obligated* before God to worship Him in Spirit *and* in Truth. Since all the words of God are true, and since the Holy Days are part of the true Word of God, you must worship Him on those days, as well as the weekly Sabbath.

Let's do a little attitude check for everybody here now, whether you agree with what I have said or not up to this point, or maybe some of the things you agree with, and some of the things you don't agree with. But you have to ask yourself: **Do I agree with God?** Not whether you agree with me, or agree with another man. *If* I don't teach you the Word of God, and *if* I don't preach the Word of God, *then* it really doesn't matter what I say, even though I may misuse the Word of God and sound religious.

Psa. 119:127 is profound, and this is the whole attitude we've got to come to concerning

- the will of God
- the commandments of God
- all the things of God

Psalm 119:127: "Therefore, I love Your commandments above gold—yea, above fine gold."

With the deception that is coming upon the whole world there is going to be a reason why it's coming. You may be part of that deception, or caught up in that deception *if you do what they do in the world.* Satan is going to come!

2-Thessalonians 2:9: "*Even* the one whose coming... [the great Beast Power that is coming] ...is according to *the* inner working of Satan, with all power and signs and lying wonders, and with all deceivableness of unrighteousness in those who are perishing because they did not receive the love of the Truth..."

Now we just read where David wrote, "...I love Your commandments..." But if you don't love the Truth, which is all the Word of God, what are you subject to? *You're subject to death, because you can't be saved!* And another thing takes place:

Verse 11: "And for this cause God will send upon them a powerful deception that will cause them to believe *the* lie, so that all may be judged who did not believe the Truth, but who took pleasure in unrighteousness" (vs 11-12).

IF you don't believe the Truth of God's Word, are you having pleasure and unrighteousness by rejecting them?

- *IF* those are Sabbaths, which they are
- *IF* they are commandments, which they are
- *IF* they're to be kept, which they should
- *IF* you are transgressing that

THEN you are sinning, and you are unrighteous!

- *IF* you don't keep them **THEN** you have pleasure in unrighteousness

- Is that not true?
- Are you not then going to blind yourself to other things further down the road?

Always remember, when God gives a witness out of His Word, *once is sufficient!* Please understand that!

Psalm 119:127: "Therefore, I love Your commandments above gold—yea, above fine gold."

How many people do you know work on the Sabbath so they can make money because they reject the Sabbath commandment? *Apply the same thing to the Holy Days!*

Verse 128—*here's where we need to come*: "Therefore, I esteem all Your precepts concerning all things to be right..."

- Do you believe that of the will of God?
- Do you believe that every precept of God is right?
- Do you believe that every command of God is right
- Do you believe that every Law of God is good and right?

"...and I hate every false way" (v 128).

- Are you willing to hate the sin that you have been committing in not keeping the Holy Days?
OR
- Are you going to come up with other arguments to justify your own idol?

That's what it gets down to, because those are self-justifications for your own way! There can be no doubt about it.

- Do you consider all the precepts of God concerning all things to be right?

If you do then you will hate every false way!

We're going to spend the rest of the time in the New Testament, showing that, yes, the Holy Days were kept by those in the New Testament; and in fact, *by a very command of God!*

Mark 2—this is one for those of you who are Sabbath-keepers to turn to, to show that we need to keep the Sabbath in the New Testament.

Mark 2:27: "And He said to them, 'The Sabbath was made for man... [no question about it; God really expects all mankind to keep the Sabbath] ...*and* not man for the Sabbath; therefore, **the Son of man is Lord even of the Sabbath**" (vs 27-28). *Since the Holy Days are a Sabbath*:

- Is He also Lord of those?
- Is He Lord of the Passover?
- Is He Lord of the first day of Unleavened Bread?
- Is He the Lord of the last day of Unleavened Bread?
- Is He the Lord of Pentecost?
- Is He the Lord of Trumpets?
- Is He the Lord of Atonement?
- Is He the Lord of Tabernacles?
- Is He the Lord of the Last Great Day?

YES!

Those other days and commands were made for the people of God. *The Sabbath was made for mankind in general!* So, if you only keep the Sabbath, *you're only doing what God requires* of all *people everywhere!* The Holy Days have special meaning for the people of God. Maybe you've never thought of it that way. Well, *you need to think of it that way!*

Let's see what Jesus did. Let's understand that Jesus was not under the Old Covenant; He was under *a special covenant with God the Father,* which was even greater than the New Covenant, when you really come to understand it. Because with the covenant that God the Father and Jesus Christ had, Jesus could not sin once.

{note message: *The Covenant Between God the Father and Jesus Christ*}

It was a greater covenant that we are under. Obviously, it had to be. Because He was God before He became a human being.

But let's notice what He did here; Luke 2:40: "And the little Child grew and became strong in spirit, being filled with wisdom; and *the* grace of God was upon Him. Now, His parents went to Jerusalem every year at the Feast of the Passover. And when He was twelve years *old*, they went up to Jerusalem according to the custom of the Feast" (vs 40-42). *Then you know what He was doing!*

- Did Jesus keep the Feast? *Yes!*

- Did He keep it only because His parents kept it? *No!*
- Why did His parents keep it? *Because it was a Law of God!*
- Why did Jesus keep it? *Because it was the Law of His Father!*
- What was He doing there at the Feast?

Verse 46: "Now, it came to pass *that* after three days they found Him in the temple, sitting in *the* midst of the teachers, both hearing them and questioning them. And all those who were listening to Him were amazed at *His* understanding and His answers" (vs 46-47).

As I point out in the in-depth study: *Prophecies of Jesus in the Old Testament,* **Jesus was taught every morning of God the Father!** There He was on the Holy Days, and afterwards, doing the Father's business.

Verse 48: "But when they saw Him, they were astonished; and His mother said to Him, 'Son, why have you dealt with us in this manner? Look, Your father and I have been *very* distressed *while* searching for You.' And He said to them, 'Why *is it* that you were looking for Me? Don't you realize that **I must be about My Father's *business?*'**" (vs 48-49), *showing that Joseph was not His father!* That's what He was clearly saying here.

- Was it the Father's business to send Christ? *Yes!*
- When did Christ die? *On the Passover Day!*
- Was that the Father's business? *Yes, it was!*

Now let's see *how* He carried out the Father's business in His ministry. We're going to survey some things here in the book of John for just a minute. Keep in mind that Jesus Christ set us an example, *in Whose footsteps we should follow!*

If Jesus did no sin… Some people come to the point of saying that if you keep the Sabbath and Holy Days you are sinning. We know that if you keep the Sabbath you are not sinning. But are you sinning if you don't keep the Holy Days? *You are!.* Here, if it was sin to keep them, then Jesus sinned.

John 2:13: "Now the Passover of the Jews was near, and Jesus went up to Jerusalem."

The reason why John says "…the Passover of the Jews…" is because John is showing that *Jesus was correcting them for their wrong worship of Passover, and Tabernacles, and other days.* The days of the Holy Days are **God's** days! What did He do? *He went into the temple*:

Verse 14: "And He found in the temple those who were selling oxen and sheep and doves, and the money exchangers sitting *there*; and after making a scourge of cords, He drove them all out of the temple, *with* both the sheep and the oxen; and He poured out the coins of the money exchangers, and overturned the tables. And to those who were selling the doves, He said, 'Take these things out of here! **Do not make My Father's house a house of merchandise**'" (vs 14-16). *He got rid of them and the sin there!*

Jesus was also showing another thing, which He later on said to the Pharisee who wanted to know, which was the great commandment? He answered correctly, and said, *'You are not far from the Kingdom of God. Now go and learn what this means: I desire mercy and not sacrifice.'* That's what Jesus was teaching here. **He desired mercy and not sacrifice!**

Verse 23: "Now, when He was in Jerusalem at the Passover, during the Feast, many believed on His name, as they observed the miracles that He was doing." *He was healing, and teaching on the Feast day of Unleavened Bread, right there at the temple!*

John 5 doesn't tell us what Feast this is. But according to the chronology as we go through the book of John, we find that it is Passover/fall festival season, Passover/fall festival season, and Passover. So, by chronology, this had to be one of the Feast days, either Trumpets or the first day of the Feast of Tabernacles, or the last day of the Feast of Tabernacles, one of the three. It was not Atonement, because they were carrying burdens and so forth.

John 5:1: "After these things *there* was a Feast of the Jews, and Jesus went up to Jerusalem."

- Was He there keeping it? *Yes!*
- Did He correct them for their wrong use of the day? *Yes, He did!*

He told the man whom He healed to pick up his bed and walk, *and he walked!* Then He gave the spiritual lesson here that God is working spiritually.

John 6:4: "Now, the Passover a Feast of the Jews, was near." *Jesus explained about the bread and the wine,* that it symbolized His body and His blood; and made it absolutely mandatory that you keep the Passover, otherwise you don't have any life in you.

Verse 53: "Therefore, Jesus said to them, 'Truly, truly I say to you, unless you eat the flesh of the Son of man, and drink His blood, you do not have life in yourselves.'"

Unless you keep the Passover properly you don't have life in you! I just might mention here, too, *those who use grape juice are not keeping it properly,* because it is not wine. You need to understand that.

John 7:1: "After these things, Jesus was sojourning in Galilee, for He did not desire to travel in Judea because the Jews were seeking to kill Him. Now the Jews' Feast of Tabernacles was near" (vs 1-2).

His brethren said, 'Why don't You go up and show Yourself?' And He said, 'No, you go up. My time is not yet.' Verse 8—they went up to the Feast.

Verse 10: "But after His brothers had gone up, then Jesus also went up to the Feast, not openly, but as it were in secret."

In spite of the public pressure that was put against Him and all those seeking to kill Him, *He still went and kept the Feast!* **He observed the Feast of Tabernacles!**

Notice something very important concerning the will of God and understanding:

Verse 14: "But then, about the middle of the Feast, Jesus went up into the temple and was teaching. And the Jews were amazed, saying, 'How does this Man know letters, having never been schooled?' Jesus answered them and said, 'My doctrine is not Mine, but His Who sent Me. If anyone desires to do His will, he shall know of the doctrine, whether it is from God, or *whether* I speak from My own self'" (vs 14-17).

Jesus was there during the Feast of Tabernacles, and there is great meaning to the Feast of Tabernacles.

Verse 37: "Now, in the last day, the great *day* of the Feast, Jesus stood and called out, saying, 'If anyone thirsts, let him come to Me and drink. The one who believes in Me, as the Scripture has said, out of his belly shall flow rivers of living water. But this He spoke concerning the Spirit, which those who believed in Him would soon receive; for *the* Holy Spirit was not yet *given* because Jesus was not yet glorified'" (vs 37-39). *Jesus taught on the Last Great Day!*

- we find him teaching during the Feast of Unleavened Bread
- we find Him teaching during the Feast of Tabernacles
- we find Him teaching at the Passover time
- we find Him teaching His disciples during the Feast of Unleavened Bread

Jesus did all of those things!

Now we'll do a little survey with the book of Acts. Please understand, we're into *New Covenant teachings!* **IF** the Holy Days were to be done away, **IF** they were no longer to be kept, **THEN** you would hear Jesus say:

You have heard it said of old time, 'You shall remember to keep the Sabbath Day Holy, and the Holy Days.' But I say unto you, you shall keep Sunday Holy, and Christmas, and Easter, and New Year's.

He didn't say any of that! No, He did not!

On the Day of Pentecost, by the command of Christ; 'Remain in the city of Jerusalem until you have been endued with power from on high' So, His command was to be there and keep the Day of Pentecost. If Jesus commanded His apostles to keep it, and gave the Holy Spirit on the Day of Pentecost, which was the same day that the Ten Commandments were given, **should you not keep the Day of Pentecost?**

Acts 2:1: "And when the Day *of Pentecost,* the fiftieth day, was being fulfilled, they were all with one accord in the same place. And suddenly *there* came from heaven a sound like *the* rushing of a powerful wind, and filled the whole house where they were sitting" (vs 1-2).

Then you know the rest of the story, in preaching on the day of Pentecost. That's when God started the Church.

- He formalized the Church in the wilderness on the Day of Pentecost by giving the Ten Commandments
- He started the New Covenant Church on the Day of Pentecost right there at the Temple of God

Acts 12:1: "Now, about that time, Herod the king stretched forth *his* hands to persecute some of those of the Church; and he killed James, the brother of John, with the sword. And when he saw that it pleased the Jews, he proceeded to take Peter also. (Now, those were *the* Days of Unleavened Bread.)" (vs 1-3).

Now, the reason that is mentioned is because they were keeping the days of Unleavened Bread!

Verse 4: "And after arresting him, he put *him* in prison, delivering *him* to four sets of four soldiers to guard him with the intent of bringing him out to the people after the Passover *season*."

Acts 16—I know all of the arguments that people will give. Let's understand that this is a time when Paul went into Macedonia and preached to them:

Acts 16:13: "Then **on the day of the weeks**... [Pentecost] ...we went outside the city by a river, where *it* was customary *for* prayer to be *made*..."

We will see that on that very day in one of the synagogues in Galilee Jesus Christ stood up for to read, and began His ministry in Nazareth on that day.

Luke 4:16: "And He came to Nazareth, where He had been brought up; and according to His custom, He went into the synagogue on the Sabbath Day and stood up to read." *That is on* "...the day of the weeks..." *if you look at the Greek!*

- Jesus taught on Pentecost
- Paul taught on Pentecost
- the Holy Spirit was given on Pentecost

The day of the weeks!

Acts 18:18: "And after Paul had remained *there* many days, he took leave of the brethren *and* sailed away to Syria, and with him Priscilla and Aquila. *Now, Paul* had shorn *his* head in Cenchrea because he had *made* a vow. And he came to Ephesus, and left them there; but he himself went into the synagogue *and* reasoned with the Jews. And when they asked *him* to remain with them for a longer time, he did not consent, but took leave of them, saying, 'I must by all means keep the Feast that is coming at Jerusalem...'" (vs 18-21).

Now the only Feast, chronologically speaking, that it could be here is the Feast of Tabernacles. He went to Jerusalem to keep it. So, Paul said, "...**I must by all means keep the Feast**...." You can't say that he was keeping it under the obligation of circumcision, because he preached against circumcision.

Acts 20:5: "These went on ahead *and* waited for us in Troas. But we sailed away from Philippi **after** the Days of Unleavened Bread..." (vs 5-6).

Why mention going after the days of Unleavened Bread? Well, it's very simple: they kept the days of Unleavened Bread and wouldn't leave until the Feast of Unleavened Bread was over. In other words, they observed the Feast of Unleavened Bread, and then left after that.

"...and in five days we came to them at Troas, where we stayed *for* seven days. Now, on the first *day* of the weeks, when the disciples had assembled to break bread..." (vs 6-7).

That was then after sundown after the Sabbath ended, getting on into the first day of the week and so forth. So, they kept the Feast of Unleavened Bread. That's the important thing to understand.

Acts 24:14: "But I confess to you that according to the way, which they... [the Jews] ...call heresy, so I serve the God of my fathers, believing all things that are written in the Law and the Prophets."

Paul himself was the one who wrote to show that the only thing that had been fulfilled and superseded by the sacrifice of Christ was the animal sacrifice and the temple ritual, and we read that earlier. He believed everything else.

Acts 27:9: "And after much time had passed, and the voyage was now dangerous because **the annual fast day had already passed**..." *Tie in* Lev. 23:27, referring to the Day of Atonement!

So here Paul, even when he was sailing and it was dangerous, he was still keeping the Day of Atonement on that ship. And the fast had ended. So. *Paul kept it!*

1-Corinthians 16:7: "For *at this time* I will not *stop* to see you, but I hope at some *future* time to stay with you, if the Lord permits. But I will remain in Ephesus until Pentecost" (vs 7-8)

How were they measuring time?
- by Christmas? *No!*
- by Easter? *No!*
- by New Year's? *No!*
- by Sunday? *No!*

But by Sabbath and the Holy Days, all the way through! Here's Pentecost:

1-Cor. 5 is the command, and you need to understand that here is a principle: *You can't have one commandment without the other! You must have all of them!*

Did not the Apostle James say that if you keep the whole Law, yet, offended one point, you're guilty of all the Law? *So, if you keep the Sabbath but don't keep the Holy Days, then you are guilty of transgressing the Holy Days, and stand before God as a sinner!* Especially when we have here in 1-Cor. 5 an absolute, dogmatic command by the Apostle Paul to keep the Feast, and the Feast of Unleavened Bread.

1-Corinthians 5:7: "Therefore, purge out the old leaven... [because during the Days of Unleavened Bread *leaven* is a type of sin] ...so that you may become a new lump, *even* as you are unleavened.... [having put it out of their houses, and they are unleavened in Christ] ...For Christ our Passover was sacrificed for us. For this reason, let us keep the Feast... [Unleavened Bread]...not with old leaven, nor with *the* leaven of malice and wickedness, **but with *the* unleavened *bread* of Sincerity and Truth**" (vs 7-8).

So he is virtually saying here in this command to keep the Feast that *if you don't keep the Feast, you're not keeping the Truth!* There is a great command.

We need to understand another principle, which is this: People say that if it's not repeated in the New Testament, 'I don't have to do it.' The reason a lot of these things are not repeated in the New Testament is because it would become redundant. God didn't want to have a book of 50 volumes. He wanted one book. That's why you have to believe **the whole Word of God!**

I just want to focus in on one verse in Heb. 4 and to summarize the part up to it, because God's plan is not yet complete. {note our in-depth study: *Epistle of Paul to the Hebrews*}

Hebrews 4:9: "There remains, therefore, Sabbath-keeping for the people of God."

That becomes very important, because Sabbath-keeping means more than just keeping the Sabbath. Sabbath-keeping includes all of the Holy Days, and the people of God include the Gentiles (1-Peter 2), not just the Hebrews.

For people to say they're *not convinced that we ought to keep the Holy Days,* then what you need to do is get in and really study your Bible more, and ask yourself:

- Do I really believe in the Word of God?
- Do I really believe the will of God?
- Am I willing to understand it the way God says?

OR
- Am I going to keep this in the way of personal opinion and become like all other religious people?

And end up rejecting the Word of God!

Scriptures from *The Holy Bible in Its Original Order, A Faithful Version*

Scriptural References:

1) 2-Corinthians 2:17
2) Isaiah 28:13
3) 2 Corinthians 2:17
4) 2 Corinthians 4:1-4
5) Matthew 7:21-23
6) Psalm 143:10
7) Romans 12:1-2
8) Luke 16:13-17
9) Matthew 5:17-18
10) Hebrews 9:11-12, 28
11) Hebrews 10:1-12, 14-23
12) Genesis 2:1-3
13) Genesis 1:14
14) Genesis 15:4-6
15) Exodus 12:5-6, 11, 13-17
16) Leviticus 23:1-8, 21, 24-25, 27-28, 32, 34-37, 2-3
17) Numbers 28:1-3, 9-10
18) Ezekiel 20:10-13, 16, 19-21
19) Matthew 22:37-40
20) John 4:23-24
21) Psalm 119:127
22) 2 Thessalonians 2:9-12
23) Psalm 119:127-128
24) Mark 2:27-38
25) Luke 2:40-42, 46-49
26) John 2:13-16, 23
27) John 5:1
28) John 6:4, 53
29) John 7:1, 10, 14-17, 37-39
30) Acts 2:1-2
31) Acts 12:1-4
32) Acts 16:3
33) Luke 4:16
34) Acts 18:18-21
35) Acts 20:5-7
36) Acts 24:14
37) Acts 27:9
38) 1 Corinthians 16:7-8
39) 1 Corinthians 5:7-8
40) Hebrews 4:9

Scriptures referenced, not quoted:

- Jeremiah 17:9
- Revelation 21-22
- Matthew 5-7
- Exodus 20; 19
- Numbers 29
- Galatians 3
- Exodus 31
- John 7:8
- 1 Peter 2

Also referenced:

In-Depth Studies:
- *Covenants of God*
- *Epistle of Paul to the Galatians*
- *Prophecies of Jesus in the Old Testament*
- *Epistle of Paul to the Hebrews*

Booklets by Fred R. Coulter:
- *Count to Pentecost From the Morrow After Which Sabbath?*
- *Count to Pentecost*

Messages:
- *How to Count Pentecost*
- *The Covenant Between God the Father and Jesus Christ*

FRC: cs
Transcription date unknown
Reformatted: bo—10/2020

CHAPTER ELEVEN

The Three Most Important Days
Sabbath, Passover and the Holy Days of God

Fred R. Coulter

What are the three most important things in our relationship with God that keeps us in contact with Him and understanding His plan? *Now, that is aside from prayer and study!*

Psa. 119 is very important. What we're going to do is look at all of these Scriptures and, of course, there isn't going to be a single Scripture that we haven't covered in the past. But we're going to see it with a little different perspective because the truth is the teachings and the Word of God are layered.

That's why Isa. 28 says, 'line upon line, precept upon precept,' because that's the way that God has done it. Many times it's layered in such a way that even some of the most obvious things you don't see right away, which we'll find out that's what has happened to us.

Psalm 119:18: "Open my eyes so that I may behold **wondrous things out of Your Law**." *That's quite a verse!*

Let's tie that together with Matt. 13, and let's realize some of the blessings that we have because we have the whole Bible. Remember that *all of ancient Israel did not have the Bible like we have it today!* The closest thing that came to that was the New Testament Church. But they were writing the New Testament and that was being added and so forth, and it really wasn't solidified until John canonized the New Testament.

Yet, even at that John had to write some things like 'the one who reads let him understand,' *because he didn't understand.* We are told in Dan. 12 that even the great prophecies that Daniel prophesied of the tremendous historical events to take place on the earth leading up to the return of Christ *were closed and sealed to the time of the end!*

So, the reason that we have the entire Bible is so that at the time of the end God is going to give a witness to all people regardless of whether they are in the Church of God or not.

{note message: *Who are the Two Witnesses and Elijah?*}

Let's see something very important for us to understand, and we've gone over this over and over again. But we're going to see today a little more meaningful perhaps maybe even significantly more meaningful of what Jesus said.

Matthew 13:10: "And His disciples came to Him and asked, 'Why do You speak to them in parables?'"

It's just like with the Old Testament. Why did you write it in such a way that it's hard to understand? *That's so we'll search it out, and that's so that those who have God's Spirit will understand, and those who don't have God's Spirit will not* understand. The very same book.

Verse 11: "And He answered *and* said to them, 'Because it **has been given to you**…'" *You!*

- whoever has the Spirit of God
- whoever has the Bible
- whoever knows the things of God out of the Bible

it has been given! Remember that *we have nothing we didn't receive* (1-Cor. 4).

So, we cannot claim any great insight because were intellectual, because we're smarter than other people. It all comes and it's *given* to us. "…**it has been given you to know**…" *That's why you know things!*

Read the Epistle of 1-John, and go over and note all the things that we know, and are to know, that's recorded there. It will be astounding!

{note book: *The Seven General Epistles*; we have all that broken down there}

"…**given to you to know the mysteries**… [*secrets*; the secret things belong to God and how He reveals them to us] …of the Kingdom of Heaven but to them it has not been given" (v 11).

Someone sent me a letter where a man had some people that he had known and they came over and spent some time with them, had dinner with them, and after asking the blessing on the meal it got around to them talking about the things pertaining to God. It turned out that these people were active members and in their local Presbyterian Church. *They knew nothing of the Bible, and he knew nothing of the return of Jesus Christ!*

Yet, they were active in the church and the wife was even mayor of the city they lived in, and she even wrote 1,000 articles for the local newspaper. So, he wrote that to me as well as many of his other friends. I could tell he made it into a form letter and it said 'Dear,' and then he wrote Fred on it. They don't know anything! Why? *Because* "...**it hasn't been given to them to know**..."

This is important to understand. But "...to them...it has not been given..." And remember *you have nothing that you didn't receive*, so *they never received it because it wasn't given to them!* We've gone over these Scriptures many times before, so I think we're going to find is really very interesting today and also enlightening. As it says:

Psalm 119:18: "Open my eyes so that I may behold **wondrous things out of Your Law**."

Matthew 13:12: "For **whoever has understanding, to him more shall be given**..."

That's why we are to grow in grace and knowledge, and we are to increase in it. Also, there's another Scripture where Jesus said that *if we ask the Father, He will give the Spirit to us.* Not only just receive it when we're baptized and have hands laid on but we need to also grow in the spirit and use the Spirit of God:

- to change our minds
- to cleanse our hearts
- lead us
- guide us

in what we need to do!

"...and he shall have an abundance, but whoever does not have *understanding*, even what he has shall be taken away from him" (v 12).

Just like this man made the comment to them after they were leaving, 'Well, I'll have to check out on this thing concerning the return of Christ.'

- Is he void of knowledge? *Yes!*
- Is he lacking in understanding? *Yes!*
- Does he go to church? *Yes!*
- Do they use the Bible? *Yes, parts of it!*

Remember: the Bible is like a million-piece puzzle and if you take away a few parts of it you'll never see the whole picture and there certain key things that help us with God's Spirit to put the million-piece puzzle together. Yet, as we do it there are going to be many pieces that God is going to add to us in the way of understanding as we grow in grace and knowledge.

Sometimes it's going to be like were going to cover today you're looking so closely at the tree that you miss the forest. Or we take a perspective like an ant and if he climbs the tree that's a great journey or if he goes clear across the forest floor that's a tremendous journey. But if you're like an eagle flying and looking down you see the whole picture. We're going to see some of that today.

Verse 13: "For this *reason* I speak to them in parables..." *That's why even the Word of God is hard to understand,* **especially for those who do not obey Him!**

A key to understanding the Bible *is obeying God* and then that obeying God grows into the kind of spiritual obedience that develops into:

- love
- faith
- hope

through His grace!

Seeing they see it, like it says in a prophecy: they handed the book to the wise men he says, 'I don't know anything about that.' They handed it to the ordinary man and he says, 'I can't read'; that's referring to the Bible.

"...because seeing, they see not; and hearing, they hear not; **neither do they understand**" (v 13).

Like one grown son told his father when they were talking about the Sabbath, 'I'll keep the Sabbath if God comes down and tells me to keep the Sabbath.' *Hello!* God already did from the beginning!

Verse 14: "And in them is fulfilled the prophecy of Isaiah..."—*which is talking about the very children of Israel!* The house of Israel and the house of Judah, which says:

"...'In hearing you shall hear...'" (v 14). Didn't that happen in Jesus' ministry? *Yes, indeed!* When, just before the crucifixion, He was teaching everyday in the temple and everyone was coming to hear Him. They were spellbound with what they heard, but:

- How many really believed to the point of conversion?
- How many hated Him because of it, like the religious leaders?

"...and in no way understand; and *in* seeing you shall see, and in no way perceive; for the heart of this people has grown fat, and their ears are dull of hearing, and their eyes they have closed... [they don't want to listen] ...lest they should see with their eyes, and should hear with their ears, and should understand with their hearts, and should be converted, and I should heal them" (vs 14-15).

Doesn't Jesus want to save the whole world? *Yes!* But **His way,** on **His time schedule,** and not now.

Verse 16: "But blessed *are* your eyes, because they see; and your ears, because they hear."

Just think about all the things we really, really understand. That will take you some time to sit down and think about it.

Verse 17: "For truly I say to you, many prophets and righteous *men...*"

I want you to apply this to today, especially when we're looking at such catastrophic events that are just about ready to befall us, which the march in the footsteps of those things are already here.

"...have desired to see what you see, and **have not seen**; and to hear what you hear, and **have not heard**" (v 17).

- *if* you're a good full-fledged socialized Church of God going Laodicean
- *if* you're a glad-hander and you go to church for the social
- *if* you're really not taught anything and you've been lackadaisical in your study
- *if* you just sit there and let them feed you little teaspoons of warm milk

You're in trouble! You don't have very long to get right with God!

What is Jesus' personal message to you? *Repent and be zealous!* (Rev. 3). So, God made these things known to His people to whom He wants them known.

I want you to think about how many, many times we have read Lev. 23. Do we not read it over and over again every year? I want to show you something very obvious in the way that it has been divided out by God Himself, and it's one of those things that has been right there in front of our eyes all the time. When I explain it you will say, 'I never knew that.' Personally, as a minister, how many times have I gone over it during the many, many years that I've been a minister? It's going to be something; it is the way that it is structured and we read it and we understand it, but sometimes we miss the structure.

This is going to answer: **What are the three most important things for us in our relationship with God and our obedience to God?**

Leviticus 23:1: "And the LORD spoke to Moses, saying, 'Speak to the children of Israel and say to them, "*Concerning* **the appointed Feasts** of the LORD, which you shall proclaim *to be* Holy convocations, even these are **My appointed Feasts**""" (vs 1-2).

That's why we have the Calculated Hebrew Calendar, because everybody has an idea. Here's the test of your conversion:

- Do you believe the model prayer that Jesus gave?
- How does it start?
- *Our Father in heaven hallowed be Your name, Your Kingdom come, Your will be done on earth as it is in heaven!*

Here's a very simple prayer, and think about all of the deceived professing Christians who recite that every Sunday. They don't believe it but they recite it. Why? *Because they are blinded and they don't hear!*

- What is the first thing that we ask? *Your will be done on earth!*
- What does that mean? *Of course, it's going to be done, but that means in our own personal lives!*
- Are you really seeking the will of God?

or

- Are you seeking to find your own pet little doctrine?
- Your own pet little interpretation

—*which is not verified in the Word of God*—
and you go to God to try and say this is what God says?

When you do that *you end up telling God what to do!* Now, we're going to see the great problems that this causes. Anyone who tells God what to do! You take all Sunday-keepers all holiday-keepers, *they are telling God what to do!*

Just like the Catholics brag because of Sunday and the pagan holidays that they have, the occult holidays are not just pagan they are satanic.

Oh, the pope has blessed them so that makes them good. Yes, we took away the pagan name of the day and we put a 'Christian' name on it. Isn't that lovely?

What does God say? *You shall have no other gods before Me!* How are they going to understand anything else if they have all these false gods that they just rename so it looks Christian? *They aren't!*

That's why the Catholics also brag, 'we could preach the gospel, *that is the Catholic gospel,* without the Bible, because of their traditions and what they believe. Catholics—by the Bible—are not Christian. They take some things from the Bible for the *appearance* of being Christian, but their full allegiance is never to God it's to the pope and the virgin Mary who is *not* in heaven. The Apostle John—who took care of Mary after Jesus died—wrote *'no one has ascended into heaven except the Son of man Who is now in heaven.'* That's well after the time of the death of the virgin Mary.

They don't understand. You cannot go to God and tell Him what you are going to do, which is contrary to the Word of God and ask God to sanctify it, *because He won't!* It is **His** *will* that is to be followed **not ours**.

Verse 3: "Six days shall work be done, but the seventh day *is* the Sabbath of rest, a Holy convocation. You shall not do any work. It *is* a Sabbath to the LORD in all your dwellings."

Well now, in order to further deceive the people in Europe what they've done they've rearranged a calendar, which is also the corporate calendar of the world to have Sunday as the seventh day of the week. Isn't that wonderful? So, all the deceived generations now coming up these new mush-heads that come into the world and go to the government schools, the Catholic schools and the Catholic/Protestant schools—because that's all Protestants are just reformed Catholics—they look at the calendar and they say, 'Oh look, Sunday is the seventh day.' Well, that's like buying gold coins only to find out they're lead and have been painted with gold paint! *Sunday is not the seventh day!*

That's why we have in *The Holy Bible in It's Original Order, A Faithful Version*, Appendix N: **Rome's Challenge to the Protestants**, because the enemy has even told all the Protestants that 'if you keep Sunday you're not following the Bible you are following the Catholic Church, because *we established Sunday* and there is no place in the Bible would substantiates it.' *So, they don't know!*

1. The Seventh-Day Sabbath

- What is the first thing spoken of here? *The seventh day!*
- What does that go back to? *Seventh day of creation!*

Granted, it's the fourth commandment in the Ten Commandments. But that doesn't mean that it is not essentially **_first_ in giving us understanding in our relationship with God**.

Do you think it's possible to really have a relationship with God when you refuse to keep His Sabbath Day?

Remember that Jesus said—Who is the Creator of everything—*'Heaven and earth shall pass away but My words shall not pass away! **Do not think** I've come to abolish the Law or the Prophets.'*

This is the #1 key important thing—*the Sabbath Day*—because when you start keeping the Sabbath Day as I've instructed many, many people to do when they are just coming into the knowledge of the truth wondering about the difference between the Sabbath and Sunday I say this:

You take one month and you keep the Sabbath every day for a month beginning at sunset Friday to sunset Saturday, and you make a special study of the Sabbath Day in the Bible, Old and New Testament. Ask God for understanding and I guarantee you that you will understand why the Sabbath has to be kept: *because God said so!* That's why! Is the Sabbath Day the will of God? *Yes! That's why He created it!*

Mark 2:27: "…'**The Sabbath was made for man,** *and* not man for the Sabbath'"—*meaning man has no authority over which day is the Sabbath!* So, all the religious leaders and popes in Christendom today are in defiance of God.

Verse 28: "For the **Son of man is Lord even of the Sabbath Day**."

Which day is the Lord's day? *Not Sunday! The Sabbath!* It's a key important thing that is the first step of faith in obedience to God that someone needs to take in order to begin to understand about God and to begin to develop a relationship with God. It's a continuing, ongoing thing that you do the rest of your life.

Leviticus 23:4: "These *are* **the appointed Feasts of the LORD**, Holy convocations, **which you shall proclaim in their appointed seasons**."

If you want a good overview of this you get our book: *Occult Holidays or God's Holy Days—Which?* You carefully read and study that through. That is the most basic, fundamental book for you to read, to learn and to understand. It will probably take two or three readings for you to really glean out of it.

Another thing I want to tell everyone that they need to *learn how to get out of your 12-minute attention span!* What do I mean by that? I mean *the whole generation of this world, because of television,* has been trained for a 12-minute attention span. A 15-minute segment, 2 minutes of commercials to begin with, then 12 minutes, and that brings you to 14 minutes and then 2 or 3 minutes of commercials. Then they take the next 15 minutes and they break it down into another pause at 20 minutes after, between 15 after and 30 minutes after.

You watch yourself I've even done this: When it gets close to 12 minutes of watching television you start getting restless. If you want to get a snack or you want to get something else you start thinking about it and you're so glad when the commercial comes, because you get up and go get your snack or go to the bathroom or something.

In order to understand the Bible you cannot have a 12-minute attention span, because you'll never understand it. You cannot have: 'Oh, give it to me very simply. Give me a summary and then I will understand. ***You will never understand with a summary!*** You've got to **know the deep things of God,** and that comes:

- with work
- with study
- with prayer

with repeating these things over and over again on a daily basis!

The reason that is so is because God has not called you to improve your physical life—hopefully it will—***He has called you to eternal life*** and that's what the training is all about eternal life. It's not a social club, not a get-together of people that you know and love, that's all well and good. But if you don't rise above that what you're doing is in vain.

Verse 4: "These *are* **the appointed Feasts of the LORD,** Holy convocations, which you shall proclaim in their appointed seasons.

2. Passover

Verse 5: **"In the fourteenth *day* of the first month, between the two evenings, is the LORD'S Passover"** (vs 4-5).

That is fundamental in your covenant with God, because if you do not keep the Passover the way that Jesus taught in the New Testament—at the time and in the manner that He said, including the foot-washing, the bread, the wine in that order—Jesus said, 'You do not have any part with Me' (John 13), and we'll understand why.

3. The Holy Days

This book—*God's Plan for Mankind Revealed by the Sabbath and Holy Days*—is going to take you in depth all the way through:

- the Sabbath
- the Passover
- the Feast of Unleavened Bread
- Pentecost
- Trumpets
- Atonement
- Tabernacles

- Last Great Day

The meaning and purpose of God's plan as outlined by that is the structure of it and what these messages do is bring you the details of the Scripture to fill it out. Just like what we covered here:

- the Sabbath
- the Passover
- the Holy Days

This is an overview and everything else fits under that!

Maybe you've never thought of it, but look at the structure of it. Here it is right in front of us, and it reminds me of:

I charged a battery and I put it back in the box so I would be sure and have it after it was charged and it got covered up with it some papers having to do with getting the battery charged and so forth. I knew I put it in the box but when I wanted to get it to use it I looked in the box I didn't see it, so I thought: Where did I put it? I looked here and I looked there and I came back and looked at the box again and I said, 'What did I do with that?'

So, after looking around I finally quit and I said well it's bound to show up because it doesn't have legs and it didn't crawl away and we don't have any ants or cockroaches to carry it out. So, the next day I thought I'd throw out the box. I opened it up and I reached in there and I picked up those papers and there was the battery.

So, many times in understanding the Scriptures is just like that. ***We look and we look and we can't find it!*** We don't know. How did that happen? Well, here of all the years that we've been reading Lev. 23 how did it happen that we didn't understand:

- the Sabbath
- the Passover
- the Holy Days

and we'll show why! ***The Sabbath, Passover and Holy Days are the signature that sets us apart from the world!***

Someone will say, 'Now you know the death and resurrection of Jesus Christ is most important.' On what day was Jesus crucified? *Passover Day;* ___not___ *on 'Good Friday'!* If you believe in 'Good Friday' and if you believe that he was crucified on a Friday and was resurrected on a Sunday morning ***you don't know how to count!*** You can't even count to three! Now let's look at these three things again:

1) ___if___ you do not keep the Sabbath *and you keep Sunday, you're a 'religious' person*

2)   *if* you do not keep Passover
3)   *if* you do not keep the Feasts of God

What is the counterfeit in place of it?

* *Sunday*
* *Communion/the Eucharist*
* *occult holidays*

What are those? ***Those are the three most important things in Satan's counterfeit Christianity!*** Now if that offends you *then be offended,* but that is the truth.

Just like it was during the days of Elijah. 'Why do you vacillate between two opinions as to who the Lord is? If the Lord be God serve Him if it be Baal serve him,' and Baal's day is Sunday, by the way, and the occult holidays are all his days. So, don't stand up there and think in your mind that those things have all been changed. *You've got another thought coming!* Just to use an expression from mother, father, grandmother and grandfather, if you don't change your ways you're going to be in trouble. That means *repent.* So, there we have it; that's something!

Let's begin in Exo. 3, and we're going to emphasize certain things and a lot of people think that by time you come to Exo. 12 that that is the first Passover. We will start out here and see the basis for why God sent Moses, *called him*—notice that Moses didn't appoint himself—*to lead the children of Israel out of Egypt!* You need to understand the reason for it. When we go through Exo. 12 we will see the link. Just like if you are on the website and you come to a certain point in there is a link that says click here. So you click there and that gives you more understanding. Well, there's a link in Exo. 12 that confirms what were going to read in Exo. 3.

So, after God told Moses what He was going to do, Exodus 3:11: "And Moses said to God…"—*because he's been out there for 40 years shepherding sheep!* Actually that was good training for him. But what did it do? *It kept him isolated from everything of the riches and the wealth of Egypt!* When God began dealing with him, beginning with the burning bush, and then told him what he was going to do… Moses began to comprehend all of it because he had been in Egypt and he was the heir apparent of the Pharaoh.

Verse 11: "And Moses said to God, 'Who *am* I, that I should go to Pharaoh, and that I should bring forth the children of Israel out of Egypt?' And He said, 'I will be with you. And this *shall be* the sign to you that I have sent you: When you have brought forth the people out of Egypt, you shall serve God upon this mountain'" (vs 11-12).

What we are going to do, we're going to take these three things and we're going to focus in on the Passover mostly. We're going to begin to build and understand the substructure of what the Passover is all about. It is one thing to say keep the Passover between the two evenings, it's another thing to know and understand what it's all about. So, we'll begin to understand it here.

Verse 13: "And Moses said to God, 'Behold, *when* I come to the children of Israel, and shall say to them, "**The God of your fathers** has sent me to you"…'" *I want you to understand that and he tells us exactly who they are.*

"'…and they shall say to me, "What *is* His name?" What shall I say to them?'" (v 13).

* Why?
* How many gods did they have in Egypt?
* All the names of all the gods and everything?
* Who was Pharaoh? *He was 'god in the flesh' on the earth!*

That will help you understand why all the severe plagues were there! We won't go into any of those in this message.

"And God said to Moses, 'I AM THAT I AM.'…." (v 14). *Another translation is 'I will be what I will be!'* Because God is a covenant God, and in the different covenants He presents Himself differently, though it's the same God.

"…And He said, 'Thus you shall say to the children of Israel, "I AM has sent me to you"'" (v 14). *You'll find the emphasis of I AM in the book of John* because that follows through.

Verse 15: "And God said to Moses again, 'You shall say this to the children of Israel, "The LORD God of your fathers, the God of Abraham, the God of Isaac, and the God of Jacob, has sent me to you. This *is* My name forever, and this *is* My title from generation to generation."'"

Here is why God sent Moses. God prophesied to Abraham that it would happen. That also passed down to Isaac and to Jacob. The reason that he sent Moses was *to fulfill His promises to Abraham Isaac and Jacob!* Let's understand something here very clear:

* *if* anyone tells you Moses was a Jew, *he is an ignoramus*
* *if* anyone tells you that all the children of Israel were Jews, *he's an ignoramus*
* *if* anyone tells you that Adam was a Jew or Noah was a Jew, *that's completely incorrect*

That is the propaganda of Judaism!

It gives the appearance that Judaism is a monolithic belief, that all Jews believe the same thing. Not true that is a propaganda statement, which is normally called *lies*. So, if you believe that, that shows you how ignorant you are of the Word of God and the history that you need to read like those genealogies, *because they tell us about who the children of Israel really were!* That's why they're there.

Another reason why God selected Moses was because he was from the tribe of Levi. God pre-selected the tribe of Levi and also the house of Aaron to be the priesthood from Levi, and the Levites to assist the priesthood. It's very interesting that Aaron was the firstborn and Moses was the second born. Moses turns out to be—because of the calling of God and what he was given to do—the greatest man in the history of the Bible up to Jesus Christ. *Moses was*:

1) a priest
2) a prophet
3) a spokesman for God
4) the mediator between God and the children of Israel

Samuel came close to it, because he was *a priest, a prophet and a judge,* but Moses ranks right up there at the top.

Verse 16: "Go, and gather the elders of Israel and say to them…" *That's how they communicated!* The elders would come, Moses would speak to them and they would carry the message to the children of Israel. They didn't have telephones, cell phones Blackberries or iPods. That may come as a surprise to many young people today.

Just like someone asked a girl well where does milk come from? *A carton!* Like Rachelle did one time when we were in a drought of 1977 and they were doing all the irrigating and sprinkling; she was about two-and-a-half or three-years-old and we were coming home and we were looking at this field where they were and they had all the sprinklers going. They were irrigating and everything she says, 'Look, daddy, rain!' It hadn't rained in about two-and-half-years of her life.

"…The LORD God of your fathers has appeared to me, the God of Abraham, Isaac, and Jacob, saying…" (v 16).

We're going to emphasize that over and over again. Because what happens to Israel is not because of Israel, *but because of Abraham, Isaac and Jacob, and the promises that God gave to Abraham passed on to Isaac, and passed on to Jacob!* Not because of any righteousness on the part of their descendents, but because a covenant with Abraham, and we'll see how that fits in with the Passover. Here's what God said:

"…'I have surely visited you and have observed what is done to you in Egypt.' And I have said, 'I will bring you up out of the affliction of Egypt to the land of the Canaanites and the Hittites and the Amorites and the Perizzites and the Hivites and the Jebusites, to a land flowing with milk and honey'" (vs 16-17).

Now we won't go through any of the rest of the things in all the things that took place leading up to them being let go by Pharaoh. Remember that God raised up Pharaoh for the specific purpose, and all of you who believe that the God of the Old Testament was evil and harsh *listen up.*

Romans 9:14: "What then shall we say? *Is there* unrighteousness with God? MAY IT NEVER BE! For He said to Moses, 'I will show mercy to whomever I show mercy, and I will have compassion on whomever I have compassion.' So then, *it is* not of the one who wills, nor of the one who runs…" (vs 14-16).

Not by human will and that's true of Moses right he wasn't sitting out there on the mountain saying, 'O God, I've got a good idea. Why don't you send me down and I'll bring the children of Israel out of Egypt.' *No!* God is one who informed them. *It's the will of God!* Remember where we started? *Your will be done on earth as it is in heaven!*

"…rather, *it is* of God, Who shows mercy. For the Scripture said to Pharaoh, 'For this very purpose I raised you up in order that I might show in you My power…'" (vs 16-17).

Did He do that? *Yes!* Someone is going to say, 'Why did He harden Pharaoh's heart?' *To demonstrate His power because Pharaoh had already hardened his heart!* Remember: Pharaoh was the servant and direct worshiper of Satan the devil. That's what this confrontation was all about. If you look at any of the mummies of the pharaohs, what do you see on their crown? *A cobra right up on the front of the crown!* Yes, they worship Satan the devil the old serpent.

"…that I might show in you My power… [For what purpose?] …so that My name… [and all of His actions] …may be declared in all the earth" (v 17).

- Is that happening every time we read the Scripture?
- Is that happening every time when someone reads the book of Exodus?
- *Yes it is!*

That's being fulfilled today every time someone reads it or someone preaches it in all the earth down through history.

Verse 18: "So then, He shows mercy to whom He will, and He hardens whom He will. Will you then reply to me, 'Why does He yet find fault? For who has opposed His purpose?'" (vs 18-19). *Because sin is **sin**, and sin is always at fault! Transgression of the Law is sin!*

Verse 20: "Yes, indeed, O man, who are you to answer against God?…."

Think about this relationship if you really have your mind and your life wrapped around Sunday and the occult holidays of this world.

"…Shall the thing that is formed say to the one who formed *it*, 'Why did you make me this way?' Or doesn't the potter have authority over the clay to make from the same lump of clay one vessel unto honor, and another vessel unto dishonor?" (vs 20-21). *Yes were all made of the dust of the earth!*

Verse 22: "And *who dares to question His purpose* if God, willing to show *His* wrath and to make known His power, chose in much long-suffering to put up with *the* vessels of wrath, which were created for destruction; in order that He might make known the riches of His glory unto *the* vessels of mercy, which He prepared before for glory" (vs 22-23).

God's purpose is going to be done! Remember where we started: *Your will be done on earth as it is in heaven!* So, you can take what we just read here and you can apply it to the coming *beast*.

After all the plagues and of the course there are even historical documentation that they took place.

Exodus 11:1: "And the LORD had said to Moses, 'I will yet bring one plague on Pharaoh and on Egypt. Afterward, he will let you go from here. When he shall let you go, he shall surely thrust you out from here altogether'"—*because they were afraid they would all die!*

Verse 2: "Speak now in the ears of the people, and let every man ask from his neighbor, and every woman from her neighbor, articles of silver and jewels of gold."

They were going to spoil or plunder, as payment for their years of slavery, from the Egyptians. This started before the Passover, and they had the final thrust of it when they were assembling for the Exodus.

Verse 3: "And the LORD gave the people favor in the sight of the Egyptians. And the man Moses *was* very great in the land of Egypt, in the sight of Pharaoh's servants, and in the sight of the people. And Moses said, 'Thus says the LORD, "About midnight I will go out into the midst of Egypt"'" (vs 3-4).

Now isn't that interesting. He didn't tell Pharaoh which day, did he? *About midnight!* Which day, Moses? He told the children of Israel, but he didn't tell Pharaoh.

Verse 5: "And all the firstborn in the land of Egypt shall die, from the firstborn of Pharaoh that sits upon his throne, even to the firstborn of the slave-girl that *is* behind the mill; also the firstborn of beasts."

Now that is roughly 20% of the population, and probably with the animals something like 10 or 12%. Because firstborn are not just males, that's male and female.

Verse 6: "And there shall be a great cry throughout all the land of Egypt, such as there was none like it, nor shall be like it anymore."

But here's the promise! Facing the days we are going to face here's a promise that you can claim, and that's why you need to have a right relationship with God.

Verse 7: "But against any of the children of Israel… [today the Church is the Israel of God] …not even a dog shall move his tongue, against man or beast, **so that you may know that the LORD puts a difference *between* the Egyptians and Israel**."

In the same way today with the Church. We live in the world but were not of the world. There's a difference between those who have the Spirit of God and love God and keep His commandments and those who are in the world.

Verse 8: "And all these, your servants, shall come down to me… [Moses is telling Pharaoh this] …and bow themselves down to me, saying…"

So, the moral of the story is when we get the latter part of Exo. 12 Moses did not go to Pharaoh when Pharaoh sent the message to leave. A lot of people say that was after midnight. Let me just state here that when you begin examining about Passover you are going to find that that is so important. Satan has done everything he can to cause:

- confusion
- wrong timing
- misinterpretation
- hatred toward

than any other single day of God; even more so than the Sabbath! We're going to see why that's so important.

"'…"You and all the people that follow you—get out!" And after that I will go out'" (v 8).

He didn't go back to Pharaoh and say, O Pharaoh, it was so nice of you after all this all this and all of these plagues that you finally agreed to let them go.' Didn't happen that way.

"…And he went out from Pharaoh in flaming anger" (v 8). *I like that!* Would you say that's righteous indignation? *Of course!*

Verse 9: "And the LORD said to Moses, 'Pharaoh shall not hearken to you so that My wonders may be multiplied in the land of Egypt.' And Moses and Aaron did all these wonders before Pharaoh. And the LORD hardened Pharaoh's heart so that he would not let the children of Israel go out of his land" (vs 9-10).

So, not only was this a battle between the children of Israel and Pharaoh and the Egyptians, but it was a titanic battle between Satan the devil and the demons and the people of Egypt who followed them, and God, Moses, Aaron and the people who of the children of Israel who would follow God.

The message that I gave on *Who are the Two Witnesses and Elijah?* I said there are three Elijah's:

1) Elijah
2) John the Baptist
3) a coming Elijah.

Let's look at three pair of two witnesses:
1) Moses and Aaron
2) Elijah and Elisha
3) the two witnesses of Rev. 11:3

So, the pattern follows the same thing!

Now let's see the instructions that are given. I want to emphasize *this is the __first__ Passover for the children of Israel*, but this is *not the first Passover of God!* We'll see that. It will involve the same day, because the 14th day of the 1st month is the Passover day. *No other day!*

If you want to know why the Jews in the Diaspora keep the 15th then you need to get *The Christian Passover* book and read it. I've had people say, 'Oh it's such a thick book.' *Well, you don't understand all the problems that Satan has caused concerning the Passover!* There is not one wasted page in this book. You need to read it step-by-step so you will understand because people are going to come along and bring in *Jewish traditional interpretation* and try and hang that on the Passover Day to justify what they are doing. What you need to

do is read this book and understand what happened to the Passover, and why the Jews today have the wrong day. It comes down to something very simple.

1. they have rejected Christ who is the true Passover
2. they are in the Diaspora scattered around the world

Very few will admit like… I have a quote here from a rabbi in the 11th century that:

We are scattered across the face of the earth *because of the sins of our forefathers* and because of our own sins and we walk in their footsteps.

You tell me one Jew today who will say *we are scattered abroad because we sinned against God.*

They cannot—when they are not in the land—*keep a 14th Passover!* But what they like to try and do is send their agents to come and try and convince Christians who keep it on the 14th that they should keep it on the 15th. That's what this book *The Christian Passover* is about:

• What does it mean?
• Should it be observed the 14th or 15th

and then all of the details! There is not one question concerning the Passover that has not been raised by many, many different people down through time all gathered together in this one book.

We're going to go through the whole chapter of Exo. 12. Let me just say that the congregation, or the children of Israel, is composed of *all 12 tribes,* descendents from the 12 sons of Jacob, of whom one—Judah—are the ones from whom the Jews have come from. We're not speaking here when we read the name Israel of the Jews. *They were __one__ of 12 tribes!*

Exodus 12:1: "And the LORD spoke to Moses and Aaron in the land of Egypt, saying, 'This month *shall be* to you the beginning of months. It shall be the first month of the year to you. Speak to all the congregation of Israel, saying, "In the tenth day of this month…"'" (vs 1-3).

There are a lot of very significant things that took place in the New Testament concerning Christ on the same day, which you will find in *The Christian Passover* book and also in *A Harmony of the Gospels.* These two books are very important for you to understand concerning the Passover.

"…In the tenth day of this month they shall take to them each man a lamb for a father's house, a lamb for a house. And if the household is too little for the lamb, let him and his neighbor next to his house take according to the number of the souls, each one, according to the eating of his mouth, you shall count concerning the lamb" (vs 3-4). *That generally figures out to be approximately 10 people per lamb!*

Verse 5: "Your lamb shall be without blemish…" *Here we have a type of Christ,* but not the sacrifice of Christ; a type of Christ.

As a matter of fact, every offering that was to be given was to be without blemish. {Note the book *The Law of Offerings* by Andrew John Jukes {amazon.com}. It breaks it down in great detail about all the law of the sacrifices, and so forth. It's really phenomenal.

We started with these three most important things: the Sabbath, the Passover and the Feasts that is the superstructure upon which all the rest of these things hang and all of the details come below it. So, what were going to do here is read some of the details, and they all are important.

Verse 5: "Your lamb shall be without blemish, a male of the first year…." *Can't be more than a year!* In another place it says you can't bring an offering that is less than eight-days-old. So, it had to be eight-days-old up to a year.

In the spring of the year when this took place guess what happened just before this, the sheep were already through their lambing. So, most of these were very small lambs. Let's compare a small lamb to a large lamb, one that's over a year old. If 10 people ate off that large lamp they have a lot of meat. But you get a little small lamb, there's not much there. I'll tell you about this later as we go along, because not only did we search the Scriptures, we also timed the slaughter, the skinning, the roasting and the burning of the bones of a small lamb that was, I think, two-months-old; actually a kid goat.

"…You shall take *it* from the sheep or from the goats. And you shall keep it up until the *beginning* of the fourteenth day of the same month…." (vs 5-6).

For those of you who were following along in the *King James* please understand that you will be a little handicap in understanding the true meaning of the words because they are not properly translated in the *King James,* which is also another point of great confusion when people try to understand about it, because it speaks of two evenings one at the beginning of the day and one at the end of the day. You need to know how to distinguish between them, and the translation of *The Faithful Version* does distinguish those very properly.

Verse 6: "And you shall keep it up until the *beginning* of the fourteenth day of the same month…"

- When does a day began?
- We find in Lev. 23:32 that it's from the 10th day of the month is defined as *from sunset on the 9th day to sunset on the 10th day!*
- When does the 10th begin? *When the 9th day ends at sunset!*
- When does the 14th day begin? *At sunset of the 13th!*

So, we have a Scriptural interpretation of that!

"…And the whole assembly of the congregation of Israel… [that means all at once] shall kill it between the two evenings" (v 6).

Now there's a little star there and we've got a marginal reference the Hebrew 'ben ha arbayim' between sunset and dark the beginning of the 14th day. We have a chapter on that in *The Christian Passover* book. When the sun touches the horizon as defined here in the Passover book this is why you need the Passover book because it covers every argument. The Jews say, 'between the two evenings'; some of them say 'from one evening to the next evening,' a whole day. Are you going to take a whole 24 hour day to do this?

What if you interpreted it between one evening and the next evening and you said, 'I think that since I don't want to stay up at night what I'll do I will do it like about 10 in the morning that will be much more convenient for me to do.' *You're a dead man!* When did God pass though Egypt? *At midnight!* Is that before sunrise? *Considerably!* Kill it between the two evenings, which is between sunset and dark.

Here we have the whole assembly of the congregation of Israel that selected the lamb on the 10th day of the 1st month, which by the way when you go through *A Harmony of the Gospels,* you will find that that is the day, John 12, that Jesus was selected by the voice coming from heaven.

Since He was the Lamb of God, God selected Him on that day, the same day that the lamb here was selected. Someone is up on the roof of the house many different places, because all the children of Israel lived in what was called *the land of Goshen.* They didn't live in among the Egyptians, because for the Egyptians Hebrews were unclean people. They were shepherds of animals while most of the Egyptians were vegetarians. Kind of sounds little like India. What do you think would happen in India if you had a large number of people kill those little lambs all at the same time? *There would be a riot!*

In the Hebrew: 'ba-erev' is sunset and it comes just before 'ben ha arbayim.'

Picture this: Egypt has a flat landscape you have to worry about hills or mountains. You can look out west and you can see when the sun touches the horizon that's the beginning of 'ba-erev' and takes about five minutes for the sun to set. That's *the end of* 'ba-erev' and *the beginning of* 'ben ha arbayim.'

Here you have your different ones up on top of the houses and they're watching the sunset so they can tell exactly when the sun has set, and between the two evenings begins and they say *now!* Then the head of the house took his trusty little knife slit the throat of the lamb drained the blood and prepared the whole lamb.

Now just to let you know, those two little kids that we did this on to get the timing for the Passover book we wanted to do it authentically. We had a man at that time Gordon Emerson who had sheep and he had goats, and he volunteered to do the slaughtering of the lamb for us. You had to have someone who knew what they were doing. Well, he knew what he was doing, so, we all watched. He took the lamb got it by its hind feet and hung it up cut its throat let the blood drain. Very painless!

God says you're not to eat the blood. So, what you do? *You cut the throat and drain it!* Let it go on the ground! Remember that *no sacrifice of the Passover and its blood was to be sprinkled upon the altar*, because it was a domestic observance. this happened all at once. Then what did he do? He cut it right down the middle of the belly from the throat all the way back to the genitals and then pulled out the skin to start skinning it.

I wondered how he was going to do that? Well first of all he opened it up and all the innards came out. All the intestines the heart the lungs you know the kidneys were still left up there so that was taking care of a little later, because they're up in the fat of the cowls, so you take that out. It all came out in just a few seconds. No problem with that and were all standing there thinking, 'My, that's fast!'

Now came the time for skinning. He pulled part of the hide on the left side and part of the hide on the right side so he could put the edge of his hand in there. So, you put your hands together with your thumbs touching and then imagine that your little finger and the side of your hand is just under the skin of the lamb. He just went with both hands from top to bottom, and that skin was loose and ready to come off in less than 10 seconds. Then he cut a place

so he could get the legs off front back and back. That was it.

It was killed, blood drained, gutted and skinned in less than 15 minutes; all ready to go. So, the lambs were all ready to go before it got dark, because between the two evenings is between sunset and dark. Now, here's what they were to do.

Verse 7: "And they shall take of the blood and strike *it* on the two side posts and upon the upper doorpost of the **houses** in which they shall eat it." *Domestic observance!*

Of course, someone will say, 'Why should you emphasize that because there was no temple built.' You've got to read the book but we'll cover it. It was never to be at the temple. What about Deut. 16? Hold on we'll get there.

Verse 8: "And they shall eat the flesh in that night, **roasted with fire**…" They were to take the whole animal put it on a spigot and turn it.

"…**and unleavened bread**…" (v 8). Is the Passover Day an unleavened bread day? *Of course!* That's what it says: *unleavened bread!* Then someone is going to say well that makes eight days of unleavened bread. *No!* You have one day for the Passover and seven days for the Feast. It does make eight, just like the Feast of Tabernacles is eight days long, because there are seven days of the Feast of Tabernacles and one day the Last Great Day.

If you want to really think this through you tell me where they were able to get leavened bread while they were walking to Rameses to assemble for the exodus. Did they run to the Egyptians and say, 'We ate this hardtack last night, this unleavened bread. It was terrible! Give me one of your biscuits would you please. Oh I'm on the way to Rameses to assemble to leave.' Never happened! Like I've said jokingly before there was no McDonald's to stop and buy an Egg McMuffin in the morning.

"…They shall eat it with *bitter* herbs…. [other instructions; all of these are important details] …Do not eat of it raw… [no rare lamb] …**nor boiled** at all with water…" (vs 8-9).

I want you to make a point of this right here, because this becomes most important for Deut. 16.

"…but **roasted** *with* fire, its head with its legs, and with its **inward parts**" (v 9). *That is the heart the liver and the kidneys* were to be put in the cavity where the intestines were.

Some people have thought they just killed the lamb, let it bleed, put a spigot through it from tail to head, left the fur on it, left the intestines in it, and started roasting it. Well, if they did that let me tell you what would happen: About 45 minutes into cooking it would explode in your face, because all the intestines would be heated up and the heat would make them explode and wouldn't be able to contain it.

So, there were no intestines in it. They did not roast it with its fur on it. But they kept it because that's part of the remains they were to burn before they left.

Verse 10: "And you shall not let any of it remain until the **morning**...."—'boqer'—*that's sunrise!*

Since they all had wristwatches courtesy of Walmart they all knew the exact time when they would assemble. *No! I'm being very facetious!* God kept it simple. 'ba-erev' is sunset.

- Can even the simplest minded person understand when sunset is? *Yes!*
- Can the simplest minded person understand when sunrise is? *Yes!*

After the sun is set and all night and then—which set in the west—then you look in the east in the morning and you see the sunrise.

Verse 10: "And you shall not let any of it remain until the morning...." **What would be remaining after you ate all the flesh?** *The skin the guts and the bones!*

Another thing that's important to understand about the bones is that being mostly young lambs their bones are not set hard, and they're mostly cartilage and they can burn very quickly, very easily. But what we did for the book, we got a shank bone. So, I put it in our fireplace in the front room to see how long it would take to burn the shank bone, which would be the biggest thickest part of the lamb. I got it at the local market just for that purpose. It took two hours for that to burn so it could be crumbled into ashes.

- Why would God want it done that way?
- Everything burned?
- Were they living in Egypt? *Yes!*
- Did they worship other gods? *Yes!*
- Did they have little magic idolatry things?
- Have you ever read about scarabs these, 'good luck' charms and you keep?

So, God wanted it all burned so no one could say:
- look I've got the ear of the lamb when the Passover took place
- I've got the right hoof here in the front leg, and this is going to protect me, and we'll use this is a 'good luck' charm

That's why! People would do that! Because someone would say:

- God took us out of Egypt look what I have; I've got a hoof the lamb

"...And that which remains of it until the morning you shall burn with fire. And this is the way you shall eat it: *with* your loins girded..." (vs 10-11). *Have everything ready!* No time for the last minute 'I have to pack my suitcase. I've got to take my clothes.'

"...your sandals on your feet..." (v 11)—because they stayed up most all that night. I'm sure some of the children slept while some of these things were going on until the slaughter of the firstborn at midnight.

"...and your staff in your hand. And you shall eat it in **trepidation**...." (v 11)—in 'haste' in the *King James* is not correct and a lot of people have misinterpreted you eat it in haste so you can hurry and get out of there right after midnight, and from midnight until in the morning you could go to Rameses. But what did God say? *You shall not go out of the door of your house until sunrise!*

"...**It *is* the LORD'S Passover**" (v 11).

- Who owns the Sabbath Day? *God does!*
- Who owns the Passover? *God does!*

That's *His* Passover, *His* Holy Days. *If you want to be right with God you*:

- *do it His way*
- *on His day*
- *according to His will*

Scriptural References:

1) Psalm 119:18
2) Matthew 13:10-11
3) Psalm 119:18
4) Matthew 13:12-17
5) Leviticus 23:1-3
6) Mark 2:27-28
7) Leviticus 23:4-5
8) Exodus 3:11-17
9) Romans 9:14-23
10) Exodus 11:1-10
11) Exodus 12:1-11

Scriptures referenced, not quoted:

- Isaiah 28
- Daniel 12
- 1 Corinthians 4
- Epistle of 1-John
- John 13
- Revelation 3:11
- Deuteronomy 16

- Leviticus 23:32
- John 12

Also referenced:

- Message: *Who are the Two Witnesses and Elijah?*
- from *The Holy Bible in It's Original Order, A Faithful Version,* Appendix N: **Rome's Challenge to the Protestants** {also in booklet form}
- Books by Fred R. Coulter
  - ✓ *The Seven General Epistles*
  - ✓ *Occult Holidays or God's Holy Days— Which?*
  - ✓ *The Christian Passover*
  - ✓ *A Harmony of the Gospels*

- Book: *The Law of Offerings* by Andrew John Jukes

FRC: po/bo
Transcribed: 3/26/17
Reformatted: bo—10/2020

Section III

Passover

CHAPTER TWELVE

Origin and Meaning of Passover
Fred R. Coulter

What is the origin and the meaning of the Passover? Especially the Christian Passover?

Let's understand something about the Bible, and this is always basic and fundamental, but it is also in depth and runs through the entire Bible on understanding. The Bible is not a book that anyone can just pick up and begin to understand like reading a novel. Certain things that are in there, which are basic, different people can understand at different times, and begin to apply them.

However, to understand what we are going to cover today, we need to look at how God has designed the Bible and how it is to be understood. That's why in studying the Bible it's got to be accompanied with prayer and obedience, *because all of those things are required!* It's got to be accompanied with an attitude of love to God and an attitude of being willing to obey what God reveals to you as you study the Word of God.

1-Cor. 2 tells us how we begin to understand the Bible, and this also shows us that you need spiritual help from the Spirit of God, either the Spirit of God is **with** *you and* **will help lead** *you* to understand, **or** if you are already baptized, the Spirit of God is **in** *you and* **will lead you** to understand. Nevertheless, either way the things of the Bible, as we will see, are spiritually discerned.

1-Corinthians 2:9: "But according as it is written, '*The* eye has not seen, nor *the* ear heard, neither have entered into *the* heart of man *the* things **which God has prepared for those who love Him**.'"

If you love God, what did Jesus say? *If you love Me, keep My commandments!* It is not for just anybody in the world, it's not just for anybody who wants to pick up the Bible and start reading it. Oh, they can, *but there are prophecies that say, even the 'wise men' and the priests can't understand it.* Or the 'wise men' say, 'I don't know what this says, what it means.' **You have to love God!**

Verse 10: "But God has **revealed** *them...*" *God must reveal it,* and through the Spirit of God, *He must open our minds* to understand the Word of God.

"...to us by His Spirit, for the Spirit searches all things—even the deep things of God" (v 10). *God expects us to go from the beginning, from the basics and on into the deep things of God!*

Part of what we're going to cover today is the deep understanding of the Passover of God although it is in the simplicity of Christ.

Verse 11: "For who among men understands the things of man except *by* the spirit of man, which *is* in him? In the same way also, the things of God no one understands **except *by* the Spirit of God**. For who among men understands the things of man except *by* the spirit of man, which *is* in him? In the same way also, **the things of God no one understands except *by* the Spirit of God**." *Therefore, when you are studying*:

- you should always ask God to help you understand
- you should always ask God for His Spirit to lead you

so that you will do things according to the way that God wants them done! You will understand according to the way that God wants you to understand it.

This also tells you another reason why the world, though they call themselves Christian, cannot understand because they are not loving God the way God says, and are not keeping the commandments of God the way God says to keep them. Therefore, when that happens *they are blinded!*

Christ shows very clearly that *IF you do not believe God* when you hear the Word of God, and *IF* you're not willing to live by His Word, *you automatically blind yourself and put yourself on Satan's side, who is* the one who blinds *those from understanding* the Gospel. The way that God gives understanding to the Bible is a two-edged sword:

1. for those who refuse to believe and understand

They won't; they read the words and they can't understand it!

2. for those who want to know the Word of God, those who want to love God

He opens their understanding to it!

There is no other book in the world that does this, because no other book in the world is based upon the spiritual words of God, because the words Jesus spoke, *they are Spirit and they are Life!*

What we're going to do is look at the beginning, or *the origin* of the Passover, and the origin of the Passover

- does not begin with Exo, 12; *it begins in Gen. 15*
- does not begin with Israel; *it begins with Abraham*

There are more parallels with the events that happen here in Gen. 15 that relate to the Passover and to the preaching of the Gospel than has been understood. We've gone through this quite a few times since we first understood it.

Today we are going to learn even more. We are going to draw even more precepts out of it, we're going to have more understanding out of it, a little more here and a little more there, because it's all right there.

There is a reason for it, and there is a reason why the Passover for the Christian Passover *is **not** patterned after the Passover that God gave to Israel!* That Passover—though it had types of Christ with the lamb without blemish, and the blood that would protect them from death and so forth—the timing of the Passover in Exo. 12 is different than the timing of the Passover for the New Covenant that Jesus taught the apostles on His last Passover.

What Jesus taught His apostles on the last Passover conforms more to the flow of events here in Gen. 15 than it does to the Passover in Exo. 12, or the later slaying of the lambs at the temple by the Jews in their traditional Passover offerings that they had on the day portion of the fourteenth.

Genesis 15:4: "And behold, the Word of the LORD *came* to him saying, 'This man shall not be your heir…'"

That is Eliezer of Damascus, because here Abram was about 85-years-old or so, no children and God promised him a child! So, here God is going to make the promise sure.

"…but he that shall come forth out of your own loins shall be your heir" (v 4).

You have to be a fleshly human being *first*. Who was the one that was born to Abraham and Sarah? *It was Isaac, and Isaac was the child of promise!* We have here a physical birth, keep that in mind.

Verse 5: "And He brought him outside and said, 'Look now toward the heavens and number the stars—if you are able to count them.'…."

The universe is quite a thing, and the heavens God designed to be glorious and awesome to lead mankind to realize that God is Creator, and to seek His purpose in creating it, because God did not do it in vain. *He did it with purpose in mind!*

Now let's see what the heavens are designed to do. There is a book/DVD called *The Privileged Planet*, and there is another one called *The Rare Earth*. What the astronomers now have discovered is that in order for there to be physical life, complex life like we have on the planet, there have to be multitudinous factors that have to be there:

- the earth can't be too close to the sun or too far from the sun
- the earth has to be the right size
- the moon has to be the right size
- the sun has to be the right size
- the solar system that must be of the right composition
- Jupiter and Uranus is needed to give protection from all of the asteroids that would come crashing in if they weren't there

You need to have everything in perfect balance, so it's:

- the perfect earth
- in the perfect solar system
- in the perfect galaxy

because the galaxy is set in such a way that from the earth you can examine the heavens like no other place in the entirety of the universe!

There is no other place because there is too much gas, there are too many clouds, gaseous clouds. If you were on Venus, you would never see the sun. The earth is in the perfect place because God created and put it there, and He did it for a reason, *for His plan that He has for all mankind,* and that's all wrapped up in Jesus Christ, and that's all wrapped up in the Passover and the Holy Days.

Psalm 8:1: "O LORD our Lord, how excellent is Your name in all the earth! You have set Your glory above the heavens!"

If you can get out and see the stars and see the heavens and you know mathematically… This is why there are no atheist astronomers. You've got a lot of atheist philosophers like Carl Sagan who doesn't have a brain in his head because his mind has been closed with foolishness *for rejecting God!* But those who are like Carl Sagan say that 'we are a low-class planet in a low-class galaxy, that we are nothing in the universe,' *and just the opposite is true!* But only from the earth can you measure the sun, moon and stars and can see the galaxies.

What do we have out there? *We've got the Hubble Telescope, and it looks deep into space!* The farther they go into space what do you see? *More galaxies, more stars!* There's a purpose for that.

Verse 3: "When I consider Your heavens, the work of Your fingers, the moon and the stars, which You have ordained."

Isa. 40 says that He strung out the heavens like a curtain and calls all the stars by names and has numbered them, and He upholds them through Christ with the Word of His power. Then David said:

Verse 4: "What is man that You are mindful of him, and the son of man that You care for him?" *Believe it or not the creation of mankind and what God is doing here on the earth is the focal point of His plan!*

Verse 5: "**For You have made him a little lower than God**…"—*Elohim*—not just the angels but *Elohim, a little lower than God!* God made us in His image for a great purpose, a great plan and that's all wrapped up in the Passover. The first place to begin to understand God is to realize when you look out and see the heavens, that **God** made all of this.

- He keeps it in motion
- He made the earth and put everything here to sustain our life
- He gives us breath
- He gives us food
- He gives us water
- He gives us air

All of that comes from God to all human beings whether they are sinners or saints!

"…and have crowned him with glory and honor. You made him to have dominion over the works of Your hands; You have put all things under his feet" (vs 5-6). *That's what God has done!*

When men look out into the heavens and they reject… We're going to see again the same principle we covered there in 1 Cor. 2. We are going to see exactly the same principle.

Now let's see what happens when you reject this witness and testimony of God's creation. These evolutionists and scientists, they look out there and say that 'this just happened by accident; that there was a 'big bang'!

- When they have a big bang with a terrorist's bomb, what do they know? *They know that some human set it off!*
- How about the 'big bang' that made the universe?
- How did it get there without someone doing it? *It is amazing!*

But there is a thinking process where you cause your mind to close, and that begins with rejecting the beauty and glory and power of God as evidenced in the universe!

Romans 1:18: "Indeed, ***the wrath of God is revealed from heaven*** upon all ungodliness and unrighteousness of men who suppress the Truth in unrighteousness."

Any part of the Truth they hold it back, they change it. What one day do they desire to get rid of more than any other day? *The Passover!*

Under the inspiration of Satan the devil, Satan knows that *if he can get people not to keep the Passover, or to keep the Passover wrongly,* **then he's got them on the hook!** Whether it's a big hook or a little hook, he's got them on the hook because sooner or later, they'll turn their backs on God, because *the Passover Day is the covenant day between God the Father, Jesus Christ and those whom He has called!* When you begin to slough-off on that and do it in different ways, that's why there is so much confusion concerning the Passover:

- the 14th or 15th
- at sunset/at dark
- three in the afternoon
- Is the bread leavened or unleavened?
- Do you have a lamb, do you not have a lamb?
- Should it just be the Lord's Supper and the Eucharist?

*Everything to move away from what the Bible says! Every step you take away from what the Bible says, you **close** your mind!*

Verse 19[transcriber's correction]: "Because that which may be known of God is manifest in them; for God has shown *it* to them; that which may be known of God is manifest among them, for God has manifested *it* to them; **for the invisible things of Him are perceived from *the* creation of *the* world, being understood by the things that were made**—both His eternal power and Godhead—**so that they are without excuse**" (vs 19-20).

As we are going to see, the Passover is where to start and everything else flows from that, because Christ was crucified on that day, and according to the timing of Gen. 15.

Verse 21: "Because when they knew God, they glorified *Him* not as God, neither were thankful; but they became vain in their own reasonings, and their foolish hearts were darkened." *That's what happens when you **reject** the glory of God!*

There is another lesson for us in Gen. 15 after God told Abram:

Genesis 15:5: "…'Look now toward the heavens and number the stars—if you are able to count them.'...."—*and I'm sure it was a gorgeous night out there!*

Of course, with the Passover night it is nearly a full moon so you've got the full moon out there, you've got all the stars, and you've got all this beauty and splendor that is out there. God took Abram out there to show him, and here is His promise:

"...And He said to him, '**So shall your seed be**'" (v 5). *There are two seeds*:

1. *physical seed,* Isaac
2. *spiritual seed,* those who will be born into the Kingdom of God

What do we have here? *We have exactly what Jesus taught later!* Remember when Nicodemus came to Him, and Jesus said that you cannot see the Kingdom of God unless you have been born again. Jesus said 'that which is born of the flesh is flesh, that which is born of the spirit is spirit,' and this is exactly what we have here, because at the resurrection.

Daniel 12:3[transcriber's correction]: "And they who are wise shall shine as the brightness of the firmament, and they who turn many to righteousness shall shine as the stars forever and ever.

Matthew 13:43[transcriber's correction]—*at the resurrection*: "Then shall **the righteous shine forth as the sun** in the Kingdom of their Father...." *That shows the glory that they will have!*

What do you have? *You have your first birth, the physical life,* **and you have the second birth,** *projected to the resurrection from flesh to spirit!* Right in here you have embedded *the core of what it means to be born again!* That's another precept that we can get out of here. That's why the heavens declare the glory of God. Let's also understand that Isaac was also that type.

In this special that was put on by the National Geographic, *In the Womb,* they are able to take 3-D actual photos of the baby in the womb.

They now know that in the womb, that the baby is nearly fully developed at 6 weeks, and that's when a woman first knows that she is pregnant. It clearly shows that what is in her is another body and **she is entrusted to bring forth that life by God,** Who created her and designed her to do so. *The body that is in there is* **not hers,** *but another life!* They also showed that the baby grows and develops. They even showed when the heart first starts beating—quite amazing—and they show how it grows.

The baby practices everything in the womb that it needs before it's born so when it's born it will be able to function:

- it moves its arms and legs
- it turns around
- it pushes and kicks
- it opens its mouth
- it smiles and frowns
- it sleeps
- it even drinks the amniotic fluid, about a pint of it a day
- it's fed by the mother through the umbilical cord
- it knows the food that the mother eats because it comes to the baby
- it knows the mother's voice
- reacts to music

They have also found that good symphony music relaxes the baby and rock music sends them out of their mind as it were.

Even the living principles that we can see of people who have already been born and are in the world applies to the baby in the womb. So, when the baby is born, now it has to do something it has never done; *it must breathe!* It will also show when it is in the womb, it's got plugs in its nostrils, and when they're born they clean out those plugs and it can breathe. When it is born it has practiced nursing, it knows its mother, it knows the sound of the voice, and everything like that, and the mothers are built just right so that the babies can suckle. *That's the way God designed it!*

Now in a parallel this way, after we're born, we grow up, we're called of God, everything that we are doing as Christians:

- by loving God
- keeping His commandments
- living by every Word of God
- having the Word of God written in our heart and our mind

we are practicing what we need for eternal life!

When we are born again into the Kingdom of God, we will be ready to start functioning, but it's going to be just like when the baby is born into the world and must begin breathing—which it's never done before—*when we are born into the Kingdom of God, we are going to start functioning as spirit beings,* which we have never done before. We have all of that buried right in these verses!

Genesis 15:5: "...And He said to him, 'So shall your seed be.'" *Well, you can't count the stars! It was beyond the ability of Abraham to do!*

Many things are beyond our ability to do, so we *trust* God and we *believe* God. Now that's what Abraham did, he believed in the Lord and that's New Testament doctrine. It was counted or imputed to him for righteousness. He was put in right standing with God *because he believed God!*

We know that God said to go ahead and you get the heifer the goat, the ram, the turtledove and the pigeon. He made this special sacrifice where they were cut down the middle, except for the turtledove and pigeon, and it was a real bloody sacrifice. There was a little path between the backs of the animals that was made so God later could walk down through there, because *God was going to pledge His death!*

- in order to accomplish the physical seed to come
- in order to accomplish the spiritual seed which would result from that

God had to take a maledictory oath and He had to pledge His death for the sins of mankind, and that's what He did here. That's what the Passover is all about, and we know and we understand when we put it together, and you can read it in *The Christian Passover* book, that this occurred on the 14th day of the 1st month.

It started at night just like our Passover does, and it went on into the day portion with the sacrifices that were here, and this relates to the timing of the crucifixion and death of Jesus Christ. *The Passover of Exo. 12*—though it has types relating to Christ—*is not of the timing which relates to the crucifixion of Christ!* Neither are the other sacrifices at the temple related in timing to the sacrifice of Jesus Christ. *This, and this alone, is!*

Verse 12: "And it came to pass, **as the sun was going down**…"

God has to perform this miracle in order to show Abraham that the future coming Messiah was doing to die. When did Jesus die? *It says here in the Gospels **at the ninth hour,** which is about three o'clock and that's when the sun starts going down!*.

"…that a deep sleep fell upon Abram. And, behold, a horror of great darkness fell upon him!" (v 12).

How are you going to give someone an experience of death, and yet, remain alive? *This is how you do it, and this is what God did!*

Verse 13: "And He said to Abram, 'You must surely know that **your seed shall be sojourners in a land** *that is* **not theirs**… [captivity in Egypt] …(and shall serve them *and they shall afflict them)* four hundred years'"—*fourth generation!*

Now we go into the next day because all days in the Bible are calculated from sunset to sunset.

Verse 17: "And it came to pass—**when the sun went down and it was dark**…" *Now we are into the 15th day!* Where was Christ on the 15th day of the 1st month after He was crucified on the 14th day? *He was in the tomb in total darkness, in total blackness!*

If you have ever gone to the Carlsbad Caverns, you get down there and they turn the lights out and they say, 'Put your hand in front of your face and see if you can see it.' You can't see a thing! This is what *this horror of great darkness* was picturing and now with the darkness of night, then we see something else. We see God's power and pledge to fulfill what He said to Abraham.

"…behold, a smoking furnace… [you might liken that to a blowtorch] …and a burning lamp passed between those pieces" (v 17).

That's the only way that Abraham in this horror of great darkness could comprehend that God walked down between the parts of those animals! As He walked down between the parts of those animals, the smoking furnace just burned up those sacrifices and there was probably nothing left there but ashes.

Verse 18: "**In the same day the LORD made a covenant with Abram**…"

Likewise with us, the covenant that Christ made with us *was sealed with His death,* and it was guaranteed when He was put into the tomb. I can't help but think of the difference between the death of John Paul II and the funeral and the accolades and all of the leaders of the world praising him there. They had five kings, six queens, they had seventy presidents and prime ministers, and they had top officials from all governments of the world, and they had over 140 representatives of other religions of the world there.

A perfect time for the spirits of Satan to massage all their self-righteousness so much so in fulfilling the will of God because Rev. 17 says that he puts it in their mind to fulfill His will. Even the president of Israel shook hands with the president of Syria and Iran at the funeral for the pope! They want him to be a saint right now; he is a great man in this world.

What about Christ, I couldn't help but compare it to Christ:

- rejected
- despised
- religious leaders hated Him
- the governments of Rome did Him in and crucified Him
- the people hated Him
- they spit upon Him
- the soldiers beat Him up

- they crucified Him
- He died an ignominious death

The only ones who were there to be of any help were Joseph of Arimathea and some of the women who brought spices and that was it. Where was He buried? *He was buried in a grave!* He was counted with robbers. The grave was a sepulcher.

- no pomp
- no ceremony
- no circumstances
- not dressed up in a Santa Claus suit

None of that! What a difference! What a contrast! That's why God hates religion! {note our in-depth study on *Why God Hates Religion* (**truthofGod.org**)} *God promised it!* Here is the promise of His death, which occurred on the Passover Day in 30_{A.D.}

Now let's see something else that is related to the Passover, and has Passover significance though I cannot prove it dogmatically that this occurred on the Passover Day. However, here is the lesson, you know what it was.

Genesis 22:2: "And He said, 'Take now your son, **your only son** Isaac"—*that's how God refers to Isaac, even though Ishmael was his son,* **he is not counted as the son of promise,** because it was by the conniving of Sarah that occurred, and the world is paying the penalty for it ever since.

What is the greatest problem we have in the world? *The fights and quarrels between the children of promise and the children of Hagar!*

"...and go into the land of Moriah, and offer him there for a burnt offering..." (v 2)

Abraham went three days' journey, and he took the wood, he took the fire, and then he loaded the wood on Isaac when they got there and he took the fire in his hand, it was probably in a pot, and he carried the coals and I'm sure they always added a little wood to it, so they could keep the fire going.

Verse 7: "And Isaac spoke to Abraham his father and said, 'My father.' And he said, 'Here I *am*, my son.' And he said, 'Behold the fire and the wood.... ['I see the fire, you got it in your hand, and the wood is on my back'] ...But where is the lamb for a burnt offering?" *Carrying the wood was like carrying a cross,* and in this case:

- Isaac was a type of Christ
- Abraham was a type of God the Father
- the fire was a type of fiery trial that the crucifixion would be for Jesus

Notice the faith! Many times God doesn't do anything for us until the last second.

Verse 8: "And Abraham said, 'My son, God will provide Himself a lamb for a burnt offering.' So, they both went on together. And they came to the place of which God had told him. And Abraham built an altar there and laid the wood in order. And he bound his son Isaac and laid him on the wood, upon the altar. And Abraham stretched out his hand and took the knife to slay his son" (vs 8-10).

Why would he do that? ***Because he counted God powerful enough to raise Isaac from the dead in case he did go through it*** (Heb. 11).

Notice a miraculous thing; v 11 "And the angel of the LORD called to him from the heavens and said, 'Abraham! Abraham!' And he said, 'Here I *am*.' And He said, 'Do not lay your hand upon the lad, nor do anything to him, **for now I know that you fear God**...'" (vs 11-12).

All those trials and the things that he went through were to show whether he really loved God or not; whether he was really willing to do the things that God said or not, **and to *believe* that God would fulfill His promise!**

Now remember that God said that his seed would be as the stars of heaven and as the sand on the seashore.

- **IF** he is going to offer his son Isaac who was the only heir to carry that out
- **IF** God didn't resurrect him from the dead after the sacrifice
- **IF** it would have come through

THEN God would have given him the greatest lie that has ever been. ***We believe God because***:

- He is true
- His Word is true
- His Word is right
- He will do what He said

and that is what Abraham did!

"...**for now I know that you fear God**..." (v 12). How long does it take for us to know God and love God? *It takes a lifetime!*

Just like the baby in the womb has to be prepared for birth, ***we have to be prepared for the second birth of being born again at the resurrection,*** and that's what Abraham was doing.

"...seeing you have not withheld your son, your only son, from Me" (v 12). ***He was willing to love God and keep His commandments more than his own family!***

Verse 13: "And Abraham lifted up his eyes and looked, and behold, behind *him* a ram was entangled in a thicket by its horns...."

Rams normally don't get caught in thickets with their horns so as I have said, I believe God created this ram just for this particular thing—for a substitutionary sacrifice. Christ is that substitutionary sacrifice for us. **He died for our sins!** So, here is a type of Christ then the sacrifice was offered instead of his son.

Now notice what happened then, v 15: "And the angel of the LORD called to Abraham out of heaven the second time." *Here is the message from God!* You can't have anything greater or stronger or of a greater promise than this that God gave!

Now because of what Abraham did, God did something special. God did something He did not need to do, *because every word of God is true and God cannot lie and He doesn't need to swear as a man!*

But He said here, v 16: "…'By Myself have I sworn,' says the LORD…" This makes it absolutely unilateral, unequivocal that all:

- the promises that He gave to Abraham will come true
- the promises of the Messiah to come would come true
- the timing of it would come true

And it was to be exactly as God said and open the door for spiritual salvation!

"'…**because you have done this thing, and have not withheld your son, your only son**'" (v 16).

Let's understand that this is something *above and beyond the commandments of God!* This is something that God told him to do, and we're going to see the key important thing.

Verse 17: "That in blessing I will bless you, and in multiplying I will multiply your seed like the stars of the heavens… [in this case the spiritual is brought out first] …and as the sand, which is upon the seashore…. [the physical seed] …And your seed shall possess the gate of his enemies. And in your seed shall all the nations of the earth be blessed, **because you have obeyed My voice**" (vs 17-18).

I have a message on that about the simplicity in Christ: *To Understand God: Obey My Voice.*

Also, this shows in Heb. 6 that God has given by these two immutable things that we just read of, *in blessing I will bless!*

We will see how this event that we just covered in Gen. 22 projects forward to Christ, projects forward to salvation, as we have already understood.

Hebrews 6:13: "For God, after promising Abraham, swore by Himself, since He could swear by none greater, saying, 'Surely in blessing I will bless you, and in multiplying I will multiply you.' Now, after he had patiently endured, he obtained the promise. For indeed, men swear by the greater, and confirmation by an oath *puts* an end to all disputes between them. In this *way* God, desiring more abundantly…" (vs 13-17).

Who did He do this for? "…to show the heirs of the promise the unchangeable nature of His own purpose…" (v 17)—*the purpose of God!*

That's why in Gen. 15 this was done on the Passover Day and then we will look at the last Passover of Jesus and we will see the importance of that day as a covenant day and the renewing of the covenant.

Verse 18: "So that by two immutable things, in which *it was* impossible *for* God to lie, we who have fled for refuge might have strong encouragement to lay hold on the hope *that has been* set before *us.*"

This was done so that we could have hope in God. So that we know that God is going to do what He has said. This is the whole simplicity in Christ!

Verse 19: "Which *hope* we have as an anchor of the soul, both secure and steadfast…" *The world's going to come and go, the people are going to come and go,* but:

- God is always there
- the hope of God is always there
- the Truth of God is always there
- the love of God is always there

"…and which enters into the *sanctuary* within the veil" (v 19).

What does this do? Just exactly as the voice came from heaven to speak directly to Abraham so likewise through Christ, we are able to enter into the Holy of Holies because of what Christ has done. That's why when Christ died, the veil in the temple was torn in two from the top to the bottom, *to show that the way to the Holy of Holies was now open through prayer to God to Father in heaven above!*

Verse 20: "Where Jesus has entered for us *as* a forerunner, having become a High Priest forever according to the order of Melchisedec."

Now let's look at one other thing concerning Abraham and then we will come to the New Testament and look at that last Passover with Jesus.

In Gen. 26:4 God is talking to Isaac and passing the promise on to him, because Jesus said of Abraham, Isaac, and Jacob to the Pharisees, 'You'll see them in the Kingdom of God, and you yourselves thrust out!' *So, we know that they are going to be in glory in the Kingdom of God!*

Genesis 26:4: "And I will multiply your seed as the stars of the heavens… [the *spiritual* seed; then the *physical* seed] …and will give to your seed all these lands. And in your seed shall all the nations of the earth be blessed, because…" (vs 4-5).

This doesn't tell us whether Abraham kept the Holy Days or not, but this gives us an indication that he probably did!

Verse 5: "Because Abraham obeyed My voice and kept My charge, My commandments, My statutes, and My laws."

Later when God gave all these things to Israel, the Holy Days were called statutes. So, if Abraham kept the statutes of God, and God created the sun, moon, stars and the earth, and gave the timing of the Passover and everything, it stands to reason that there was some kind of commemoration that Abraham had before God on this Covenant Day. Do we have that with the Passover today? *Yes, indeed!*

This is why in the New Testament we are called: *if you are Christ's, then you are Abraham's seed, and heirs according to the promise. The promise was spiritual seed,* Of course, we've all been born flesh, and now we are learning how to practice, just like the babe in the womb, *to learn the things we need to learn and prepare for the resurrection! Tremendous!*

The Last Passover of Jesus {Note that the Scriptures used for the following text is from the *Faithful Version Bible,* which is very close to *A Harmony of the Gospels*}

John 13—I am going to read from *A Harmony of the Gospels,* because I have the parallel columns here. I am going to go through this, and I am also going to answer some questions that relate to recycling of an error concerning the Passover: that the foot-washing was after supper because that's what the *King James* says, but that's a mistranslation. The word means: *and during supper* and the Greek verb that is used there has to do with the beginning of supper, not after supper.

I've got a letter that I did in January 19, 1975 to answer that very question. Darryl Hansen put out a paper that said the Passover and Night to be Remembered are on the 14th, meaning that the Feast is over on the 20th. Look what happens when people don't do the things that God wants them to do, the way He wants them to do. But all the way through leading up to John 13 the disciples came and said, 'Where do You desire us to prepare to keep the Passover?' Jesus said, 'You go into this house and you tell the master of the house that I am coming and I want to keep **the Passover** with my disciples at

your house. You follow the man who has a pitcher of water and in that house we'll have the Passover.'

So, when they got in there, He came at evening, sat down with the twelve. John 13 is important for us to understand because the timing of this is very similar when you take the keeping of the Passover at night, and:

- it's the promise of eternal life
- it's the renewal of the New Covenant

That's the same night that God gave the promises of the covenant to Abraham. Then the sacrifices took place on the day portion, and that pictured the agony and torturous crucifixion that Jesus Christ would go through to die for the sins of the world.

So, it goes from Abraham to Christ and to the Church. That's why it is very important for us to understand we are not to mix in the Passover of Israel with the Passover of Christ, because that relates back to Abraham and not to the Passover of Exo. 12. That served a little different function, though it was the Passover, than what is served by the Passover for us today. Here again we see the same pattern, you have *the physical* and *the spiritual.* The Passover to Israel was *physical,* and now Christ comes and *He reveals the spiritual Passover* that we are to take, and the covenant of eternal life.

Foot-washing:

John 13:2: "And after supper began…" *That's what it means from the Greek,* and I'll re-do this letter of January 19, 1975, and you will see that I have always preached the same thing.

"…(the devil having already put into the heart of Judas Iscariot, Simon's *son,* that he should betray Him)"(v 2).

- Where does Satan like to come and get as close to Christ as he could?
- What did the apostles have to put up with?
  ✓ false apostles
  ✓ false brethren
  ✓ false practices

That's why we have to stand for the Truth!

Today, for us to stand up and tell the Truth… Look at all the accolades and all the glory that was displayed with the funeral of the pope, and for us to stand up and say:

- the pope is a liar
- all the doctrines are lies
- everything that they are doing is a lie
- that's all of Satan the devil

People will say, 'You're an idiot, you're insane, you are rotten, you are committing a hate crime.'

Well, that's because no one is willing to prove the Truth. *If you say the Truth*—and people don't want the Truth, and hate the Truth—*they're going to get mad. That's why they killed Christ!*

Verse 3: "Jesus, knowing that the Father had given all things into *His* hands, and that He had come from God and was going to God…"

Where did Jesus come from? *John constantly said He came from heaven!*

John 1:1: "In *the* beginning was the Word, and the Word was with God, and the Word was God."

Who was Christ? *God manifested in the flesh!* Yet, some people can go into the Bible and say, 'Oh no, He was just born by the virgin Mary. He didn't come from heaven.'

John 13:4—*Jesus* "Rose from supper and laid aside *His* garments; and after taking a towel, He secured it around Himself. Next, He poured water into a washing basin and began to wash the disciples' feet, and to wipe *them* with the towel, which He had secured" (vs 4-5).

That was the job of the lowest servant of the household to do, and that was always done at the beginning of supper, just like when Jesus went in to eat with Simon the Pharisee, and He came in. Here was the woman when He sat down, or actually reclined, because they reclined on couches to eat. They didn't sit at tables like we do.

What did she do? *She wiped His feet with her hair and with her tears and was repenting!* After Jesus asked Simon who is He going to forgive the most, the one that owes a lot or a little. Simon said, 'I suppose to the one who owes a lot.' Jesus said, 'You see this woman? I came in and you didn't give me any water to wash My feet, and she has washed My feet with her tears and wiped them with the hair of her head.' That shows that *foot-washing should be at the beginning,* not at the ending.

Verse 6: "Then He came to Simon Peter; and he said to Him, 'Lord, are You going to wash my feet?' Jesus answered and said to him, 'What I am doing you do not understand now, but you shall know after these things'…. [because He was going to explain it to them] …Peter said to Him, 'You shall not wash my feet, not ever.' Jesus answered him, **'If I do not wash you, you have no part with Me'**" (vs 6-8).

- Why does Satan want people to **not do** foot-washing? *Because Satan doesn't want you to have part with Jesus!*
- What is the first thing that they stop doing when they modify the Passover or what they call the Lord's Supper, which is a perversion of the Passover?
- What do they stop first? *Foot-washing!*

'Oh well, we don't do that today. That's too humiliating to do.'

It is so simple, Jesus said to do it, and we will see that *He tells us to do it!* Anyone who says you don't have to do foot-washing *is saying that they know more than God! They're better than Jesus Christ!* They may not think those words, but that's precisely what their actions and their attitude says! So, **IF** you don't do foot-washing, *you have no part with Him!*

Verse 9: "Simon Peter said to Him, 'Lord, not my feet only, but also *my* hands and *my* head.'"

Just like the way that humans do, what do they do, *they want to improve on what God says!* Oh, if the feet are good, how about the hands and head? If this had not occurred and been recorded, what would people be doing today? *Hands, head and feet!*

Verse 10: "Jesus said to him, '**The one who has been washed** does not need to wash *anything other* than the feet, but is completely clean; and you are clean, but not all.'"

Now there are two *apparent* contradictions if you don't understand it. "…'**The one who has been washed**…'" What does it mean to be washed? We'll see it does not mean to be bathed; you take a bath *before* you come. Obviously, the disciples did not have a chance to take a bath before they got there. *No!* What were they doing? *They were walking into Jerusalem*, and they were asking Jesus, 'Where do you want to keep the Passover?' They were all dirty with dusty feet, and sweaty from walking, and they didn't have underarm deodorant and things like this. I mean let's get down to the real nitty-gritty of life, because that's what it was. It's not talking about being bathed in a bath.

Act 22—let's see what *washed* means. This is Paul giving an account of his calling where he was on the road to Damascus. You talk about the reach of the high priest to get people that they wanted to get! He actually had arrest warrants to go in the synagogues and get anyone who believed in Christ and haul them out and take them to prison and, yes, even have them killed. So, God knocked him down, that's how He called him. Then He told Ananias, 'I want you to go take care of Saul for Me.' And he said, 'O Lord, look he has come with orders to take people away.' He said, 'He is a chosen servant to Me.'

Acts 22:13—*Ananias* "Came to me, and he stood *and* said to me, 'Brother Saul, look up.' And I looked up at him at that time. And he said, ;The God of our fathers has personally chosen you to know His will, and to see the Just One, and to hear *the voice of His mouth*'" (vs 13-14). *He was personally taught by Jesus Christ!*

Verse 15: "For you shall be a witness for Him to all men of what you have seen and heard. And now why do you delay? Arise and be baptized, **and wash away your sins**…" The word *wash* is 'louo' in the Greek.

Now let's see where we have the same thing. If you are baptized, you don't need to be baptized again, *you just need to have your feet washed on the Passover night!*

Hebrews 10:22: "Let us approach *God* with a true heart… [because we have a great High Priest over the house of God] …with full conviction of faith, our hearts having been purified from a wicked conscience… [that's by the blood of Christ] …and our bodies having been **washed** with pure water…. [baptism] …Let us hold fast without wavering *to the hope that* we profess, for He Who promised *is* faithful" (vs 22-23).

That's what it means to be *washed* (John 13) and that is accomplished *through the operation of baptism* and then you only wash the feet. Therefore, as I wrote in *The Christian Passover* and in *The Day Jesus the Christ Died,* **that foot-washing does commemorate and renew your baptism!** It also shows that *you are going to walk in God's way!* That's what it means to be washed. You don't have to wash anything other than the feet.

John 13:10: "…but is completely clean; and you are clean, but not all.'" *The reason He said that was because Judas was there for the foot-washing and Judas went out after the foot-washing!*

Now the truth is, as you will see in the letter I did in 1975, is that only John mentions the exact time when Judas left, and there is no mix-up in the account in Luke 22.

Verse 11: "For He knew the one who was betraying Him; this was the reason He said, 'Not all of you are clean.' Therefore, when He had washed their feet, and had taken His garments, *and* had sat down again, He said to them, 'Do you know what I have done to you? You call Me the Teacher and the Lord, and you speak rightly, because I am. Therefore, if I, the Lord and the Teacher, have washed your feet… [we could add in there the same as the lowest servant of the household] …**you also are duty-bound to wash one another's feet**" (vs 11-14). *That's the real meaning of the Greek!*

That's why Satan wants to get rid of that first. Then according to what the meaning of the Feast of Unleavened Bread is 'a little leaven, leavens the whole lump.' Then one error after another

follows each other right down the line to where even today some people say the Passover is not important.

Verse 15: "For I have given you an example, *to show* that you also should do exactly as I have done to you"

If we love God and if we keep His commandments, His love is being perfected in us (1-John 2) *and* **we walk in the footsteps of Jesus Christ!** *If He gave this example for us to do*:

- What should we do? *What Jesus said!*
- What was the reason that the promise was given to Isaac? *Because of what Abraham did, he 'obeyed My voice.'*

This is the voice of Christ speaking and if He says you are duty-bound to do it, *you're duty-bound to do it!*

Verse 16: "Truly, truly I tell you, a servant is not greater than his lord, nor a messenger greater than he who sent him."

Those who say you don't need to do foot-washing are saying that 'We are greater than the Lord. We know more than God.'

Verse 17: "**If you know these things, blessed are you if you do them.**" Does that mean we should do them? *Of course!*

Eating the Unleavened Bread:

Luke 22:19: "And He took bread; *and* after giving thanks, He broke *it* and gave *it* to them, saying, 'This is My body, which is given for you. **This do in the remembrance of Me.**'"

He did that also with the wine. Let's continue on over here in and we'll get the wine and I'll make a very important point concerning transubstantiation; that there is no such thing as transubstantiation. It doesn't take place.

Drinking the Wine:

Mark 14:23: "And He took the cup; *and* after giving thanks, He gave *it* to them; and they all drank of it. And He said to them, **'This is My blood, the blood of the New Covenant, which is poured out for many'**" (vs 23-24). Not only the many, *but each individually!*

Now let's understand that when Christ did this on that night, it *is not* recorded that when He broke the bread, all of a sudden some of His flesh came off of His arms and leapt into the bread so His flesh would be in the bread. *Nor* did His blood come out of His wrists and into the wine so His actual blood would be in the wine. *It is symbolic!* Just like your baptism is a symbolic death!

You cannot eat the blood and flesh of Jesus Christ because after His resurrection, He had no more flesh and blood to give. Everything that is done with the Eucharist in saying that that is so, *is an absolute lie and perpetuates people in bondage, in fear, in superstition and cuts them off from Christ!*

When the priest stands there and holds the bread up high and everyone worships the bread, whose god is it? Who are they worshipping? *You need to know where that came from!*

Note this book (**truthofGod.org**): *The Two Babylons* on the 'unbloody sacrifice' That originally came from Egypt as an *unbloody sacrifice,* and that means no animal sacrifice. But in order to make it a bloody sacrifice, they've had to say

It's a mystery where that, even though it's apparently bread and even though it's apparently wine, it is really the flesh and blood of Jesus Christ and He is crucified again every time we say the Mass.

That is an absolute lie! That has nothing to do with the Passover!

The 'I.H.S.' on the little wafer… If you break the bread, how do you have it perfectly round? Why is it in the form of a sun disk, and why does it have 'I.H.S.': Isis, Horus and Semiramis. It is perforated with a cross and so they can break it into four pieces.

1-Corinthians 11:25: "In like manner, *He* also *took* the cup after He had supped, saying, 'This is *the* cup *of* the New Covenant in My blood. This do, as often as you drink *it* in the remembrance of Me.'"

He did this with the bread, v 24: "And after giving thanks, He broke *it* and said, 'Take, eat; this is My body, which *is* being broken for you. This do in the remembrance of Me.'"

"'…This do, as often as you drink *it* …'" (v 25).

Now this doesn't mean as often as you would like to drink it because there is a special Greek particle that is equivalent to the English '*a*' that in the Greek is 'alpha,' and the English '*n*' that in the Greek is 'nu' and it is pronounced *on*. Now '*on*' is a special particle that is not translated into English, but it shows that this statement 'as often as' means that there are conditions and limits to how often that you do it. What is the condition and limit?

1. the Passover is a yearly event so it is restricted to once a year

"…as often as…" you do it is not as often as you would like, but *until*…

2. "…until He comes" (v 26).

He hasn't come, yet! So, as often as we do it, year-by-year, "…you *solemnly* proclaim the death of the Lord **until He comes**" (v 26).

Verse 26: "For as often as you eat this bread and drink this cup, you *solemnly* proclaim the death of the Lord until He comes."

- When did He die?
- Every day? *No!*
- *One day, Passover Day!*

You cannot commemorate His death any other day than on the day that He died, which was the Passover Day.

Verse 27: "For this reason, *if* anyone shall eat this bread or shall drink the cup of the Lord unworthily, he shall be guilty of the body and *the* blood of the Lord." *If you don't do it the way Jesus said, you're taking it unworthily.*

Where does that put the majority of Christendom? *Yet, they think they are so righteous!* That's why you need to prove what is the Word of God, understand what is the Word of God. Don't believe what any minister or priest or scholar or expert tells you, you read it in the Bible and prove it and you make sure that you get a good translation of the Bible so that you will have the understanding that you need. In the world *they want to commemorate His birth and His resurrection, and forget about His death, **and you have no forgiveness of sin unless you remember His death!***

John 6—let's see the whole meaning of this and we'll go into in a little more detail than I did last time. But when we renew the New Covenant, and also John gave the words of the covenant in four chapters: John 14-17. Of course, we've gone through that with the Passover preparation.

Let's understand the meaning of it. We have to have the foot washing, we have to have the bread, we have to have the wine, and that's the sequence in the way that we do it. Then we read the words of the New Covenant, John 14-17 and in those four chapters you'll find:

- faith
- hope
- love
- the whole Christian experience
- the promise of the Spirit given
- the promise of the love of Christ given
- the promise of the love of God the Father given
- the promise that Christ would be with us even to the end of the age

Even through the preaching of those that succeeded the apostles down to the time that we have today, that these very words would be spoken and practiced and believed!

John 6:32: "Then Jesus said to them, 'Truly, truly I say to you, Moses did not give you the bread from heaven... [they were looking for the manna] ...but My Father gives you the true Bread from heaven. For the Bread of God is He Who comes down from heaven and gives life to the world'" (vs 32-33).

When I read those things, I cannot understand how people believe that Jesus was not in heaven before He came to the earth!

I've talked about what if you had a Volkswagen Jetta and you put Rolls Royce nametags on it? Do you have a Rolls Royce, or do you have a Volkswagen Jetta? You have a Volkswagen Jetta. Only the name has been changed. It is still the same thing, the Volkswagen.

He came down from heaven; v 33: "'For the Bread of God is He Who comes down from heaven and gives life to the world.' Therefore, they said to Him, 'Lord, give this bread to us always.' Jesus said to them, 'I AM the Bread of Life; the one who comes to Me shall never hunger; and the one who believes in Me shall never thirst at any time'" (vs 33-35).

This is talking **spiritually,** not physically! You don't have to go across the earth looking at other religions. This is what you have with God's Spirit, you'll never hunger and you'll never thirst and tie in Matt. 5 *if you hunger and thirst after righteousness, you shall be filled!*

This is confirmed as a figure of speech: spiritually *with Christ **in** you,* that's what it results in, but you have to taste the Word of God. You have to live by every word that comes out of the mouth of God. Not by bread alone, and that's what this symbolizes.

Psalm 34:8—*something very similar to what Jesus said*: "O taste and see that the LORD is good..."

You're not biting into the flesh of Christ, and you're not drinking His blood! *You are taking in the Word of God as spiritual food!*

"...blessed is the man who takes refuge in Him" (v 8). *That shows the result of it!*

Verse 15: "The eyes of the LORD are upon the righteous, and His ears are open to their cry. The face of the LORD is against those who do evil, to cut off the memory of them from the earth. The righteous cry, and the LORD hears, **and delivers them out of all their troubles**" (vs 15-17)—*you can*

claim that promise!

Whatever trouble you have, God promises to deliver you out of **all**, one way or the other. You may have to pray repeatedly, but God sooner or later will do it just like He did even at the last minute with Abraham raising the knife to offer Isaac for the sacrifice.

Verse 18: "The LORD is near to the brokenhearted and saves those who are of a contrite spirit. Many are the afflictions of the righteous, **but the LORD delivers him out of them all**" (vs 15-19).

Whatever your trials and difficulties, if you're having them, you just take this Psalm, when you're praying, get on your knees open it up there, read it out loud to God, claim this promise and say:

- God, you have promised and I'm trusting in Your Word
- God, You cannot lie
- God, I trust in You
  - ✓ and believe You
  - ✓ and believe Your Word

That's all tied here to Christ as the Bread of Life!

John 6:47: "Truly, truly I say to you, the one who believes in Me has eternal life."

What was it said about Abraham? *He believed in the LORD!* It shows that Abraham is going to have eternal life.

Verse 48: "**I AM the Bread of Life**." *Everything that Jesus was, is, stands for and gives us,* through the power of the Holy Spirit: *spiritual life* at the return of Christ and at the resurrection; *eternal life in the Kingdom of God forever!*

That's what the whole story of it is back there with Abraham. That's where it began, and it is brought to a partial completion with Christ through the Passover, and through His crucifixion and resurrection, and continues on down as we will see with the church harvest leading up to Pentecost and the first resurrection. So, this is really a tremendous thing when you put it all together.

Verse 49: "Your fathers ate manna in the desert, but they died." **Isn't it true?** You can eat the best food in the world; *manna is the best food* wouldn't you say? Even today

- you can eat the best food in the world
- you can take care of yourself the best you can
- you can exercise the best you can
- you can drink your own fresh juice forever

Guess what? *We are all going to die, as in Adam!* We are all looking to eternal life after death.

Verse 50: "This is the Bread [Christ] which comes down from heaven so that anyone may eat of it and not die…. [*forever*] …I AM the living Bread, which came down from heaven; if anyone eats of this Bread, he shall live forever; and the bread that I will give is even My flesh, which I will give for the life of the world" (vs 50-51).

This is the whole plan and purpose of God, and it goes back and *the first Passover was with Abraham!*

Verse 52: "Because of this…" *Now you always have to have an argument!* This is Fox News fair and balanced before it was ever on television.

"…the Jews were arguing with one another, saying, 'How is He able to give us *His* flesh to eat?'…. [just cut a little off His forearm and pass it around] …Therefore, Jesus said to them, 'Truly, truly I say to you, unless you eat the flesh of the Son of man, and drink His blood, you do not have life in yourselves'" (vs 52-53).

That is symbolized by the bread, *not His literal flesh,* and by the wine, *not His literal blood!*

Verse 54: "The one who eats My flesh and drinks My blood has eternal life, and I will raise him up in the last day.'"

What is the last day for us? *It is not the Feast of the Last Great Day!* There is a Feast for us, which is the last day of the 50 count to Pentecost.

- Isn't the 50th day the last day?
- Isn't Pentecost when we are going to be resurrected? *Yes!*

Verse 55: "'For My flesh is truly food, and My blood is truly drink. The one who eats My flesh and drinks My blood is dwelling in Me, and I in him" (vs 55-56).

Wow! This was hard to take! Even these who were complaining about this were His disciples. Then He set the record straight. What does it mean?

Verse 57: "As the living Father has sent Me, and I live by the Father; so also the one who eats Me shall live by Me."

- you live by Jesus Christ
- you live by every Word of God

That's what it means, and that goes right back to why Abraham received the blessing, because Abraham obeyed My voice!

Here is the whole meaning of the Passover and why it goes back to Abraham:

Galatians 3:26 "Because you are all sons of God… [destined to be as the stars in heaven, the spiritual seed] …through faith in Christ Jesus. For as many *of you* as were baptized into Christ did **put on Christ**."

Your baptism is a conjoining to the death of Jesus. That's why we remember the death of Jesus through the Passover. We don't forget His resurrection, *but His death, the death of God manifested in the flesh is the most important thing!*

- we're baptized into Christ
- we put on Christ
- we have the mind of Christ
- we have the knowledge of Christ
- we have the Word of Christ
- we have the way that Christ lived and walked

Verse 28: "There is neither Jew nor Greek; there is neither bond nor free; there is neither male nor female…"

That is just spiritually speaking, because I am still a man and those of you who are women are still women, and those of you who are men are still men! So, in the flesh they're still a man and woman.

"…for you are all one in Christ Jesus…. [that is for the opportunity for salvation] …And if you *are* Christ's, then you are Abraham's seed… [which He promised as the stars of heaven] …**and heirs according to *the* promise**" (vs 28-29). *You will receive eternal life!*

That's the origin and meaning of the Passover!

Scriptures from *The Holy Bible in Its Original Order, A Faithful Version*

Scriptural References:

1) 1 Corinthians 2:9-11
2) Genesis 15:4-5
3) Psalm 8:1-6
4) Romans 1:18-21
5) Genesis 15:5
6) Daniel 12:3
7) Matthew 13:43
8) Genesis 15:5, 12-13, 17-18
9) Genesis 22:2, 7-13, 15-20
10) Hebrews 6:13-20
11) Genesis 26:4-5
12) John 13:2-3
13) John 1:1
14) John 13:4-10
15) Acts 22:13-14
16) Hebrews 10:22-23
17) John 13:10-17
18) Luke 22:19
19) Mark 14:23-24
20) 1 Corinthians 11:25, 24, 25-27
21) John 6:32-35

22) Psalm 34:8, 15-19
23) John 6:47-57
24) Galatians 3:26-29

Scriptures referenced, not quoted:

- Exodus 12
- Isaiah 40
- Revelation 17
- Hebrews 11
- 1 John 2
- John 14-17
- Matthew 5

Also referenced:

Books:

- *The Privileged Planet* by Guillermo Gonzalez & Jay Richards (also on DVD)
- *The Rare Earth* by Donald Brownlee
- *The Two Babylons* by Alexander Hislop (**truthofGod.org**)

Books by Fred R. Coulter (**truthofGod.org**):

- *The Christian Passover*
- *A Harmony of the Gospels*
- *The Day that Jesus the Christ Died*

DVD: *In the Womb* (National Geographic)

Message: *To Understand God: Obey My Voice*

In-Depth Study: *Why God Hates Religion*

FRC: ja
Transcription date unknown
Reformatted: bo—10/2020

CHAPTER THIRTEEN

The Passover:
Abraham, Isaac, Israel & Christ I

Fred R. Coulter

Most people believe that the Passover began with the children of Israel in Egypt. However, we're going to see that that is not true—it began long, long before then. Most people today believe that the Passover is only for the Jews; however, the Jews have it on the wrong day. I've covered that very thoroughly in the book *The Christian Passover*.

So, let's approach this from an entirely different point of view. Let's first of all go to Gal. 3—and I found in translating that God inspired the Greek in such a way that if you're going to be honest in translating it, almost all the versions will be similar. The reason is because you can't translate any differently.

Galatians 3:29: "And if you *are* Christ's, then you are Abraham's seed, and heirs according to *the* promise."

I think if you go through and look at the writings of the New Testament you will be very surprised how much of the New Testament is keyed to Abraham, and then Abraham, Isaac and Jacob—but more in particularly to Abraham.

Hebrews 6:13: "For God, after promising Abraham, swore by Himself, since He could swear by none greater, saying, 'Surely in blessing I will bless you, and in multiplying I will multiply you.' Now, after he had patiently endured, he obtained the promise. For indeed, men swear by the greater, and confirmation by an oath *puts* an end to all disputes between them. In this *way* God, desiring more abundantly to show the heirs of the promise the unchangeable nature of His own purpose... [resolve] ...confirmed *it* by an oath" (vs 13-17).

I want you to understand the unchangeable nature of His own resolve because that does tie-in with God's plan, and God's plan ties in with the Passover and the Holy Days as well as the weekly Sabbath. That's important to understand.

Verse 18: "So that by two immutable things, in which *it was* impossible *for* God to lie, we who have fled for refuge might have strong encouragement to lay hold on the hope *that has been* set before *us;* which *hope* we have as an anchor of the soul, both secure and steadfast, and which enters into the *sanctuary* within the veil; where Jesus has entered for us *as* a forerunner, having become a High Priest forever according to the order of Melchisedec" (vs 18-20).

This also tells us a very important thing: we always have to have the *hope* that God gave to Abraham, the *hope of eternal life!* We need that as secure and steadfast for the anchor of our soul. That way we're not going to be tossed to and fro by everything that comes along.

As we find in the series in the book of Hebrews, the thing that is important is that we have *a High Priest who is heaven at the right hand of God* and this is *the greatest, most supreme thing that God could do for us* while we are in the flesh.

Here's something that's very important that we need to understand and remember:

Hebrews 13:8: "**Jesus Christ *is* the same yesterday**... [that is when He was the God of the Old Testament] ...and **today**... [that is under the New Covenant] ...and **forever**"—*that is in carrying out God's plan into the ages of eternity!*

These things we really need to have as a preface before getting into the Passover concerning Abraham, Isaac, Israel and Christ.

Now, let's see something that is important, something that is *profound!*

Galatians 3:6: "*It is* exactly as *it is written*: 'Abraham **believed** God...'" *That is a profound statement*: *he believed God!*

That is what we have to do in the New Covenant, as well. He didn't believe in just what God had told him, but he *believed God!* This is what it means to be for all of us, that we *believe God!* When God says something, we believe it *because God said it!* So therefore, *we believe God!*

"...and it was reckoned to him for righteousness" (v 6). *This is telling us that when you believe God, wholly and completely, you are righteous before Him!* Righteousness in imputed to you. We'll see how this comes when we get back to the book of Genesis.

Verse 7: "Because of this, *you should* understand that those who *are* of faith are the *true* sons of Abraham"—*the spiritual sons!* There were the *physical* sons through Isaac and Jacob and Israel.

Verse 8: "Now, *in* the Scriptures, God, seeing in advance that He would justify the Gentiles by faith, preached the Gospel beforehand to Abraham…"

When have you heard that the Gospel was preached to Abraham? *There it is!* The Gospel begins with what He said to Abraham.

"…*saying,* 'In you shall all the nations be blessed.' *It is* for this reason… [because Abraham believed] …that those who are of faith are being blessed with the believing Abraham" (vs 8-9).

Let's go back to the book of Genesis and see this. We will see that the Passover **did not** begin with Israel, but rather **it began with Abraham!** We'll see that **it is the same day that God gave the Passover to Israel!** The reason we keep the Passover today is because of Abraham—that's what it says: **'If you are Christ's then you are Abraham's seed and heirs according to the promise.'** Likewise, when we partake of the Passover we need to understand that the words that Jesus gave, the words of the New Covenant, **we need to believe!**

Genesis 12:1: "And the LORD said to Abram, 'Get out of your country, and from your kindred, and from your father's house into a land that I will show you.'"

I want to make something very clear, that what Abraham did fulfilled this requirement that Jesus gave in the Gospel of Luke:

Luke 14:25: "And great multitudes were going with Him; and He turned *and* said to them." *Multitudes of people*:

- like to use the name of Christ
- like to claim that they are Christian
- like to think of themselves as Christian

But they are the 'glad-handers' just like the people who were here, because they came because they were looking for the *physical* things. They remembered the feeding of the 4,000, the feeding of the 5,000, and so forth. So, Jesus turned and He made a very important point here:

"…'If anyone comes to Me and does not hate his father, and mother, and wife, and children, and brothers and sisters, and in addition, his own life also, he **cannot be My disciple**" (v 26).

It is not like the Protestants say, 'All you have to do is give your heart to the Lord.' No! **You have to do the same thing as Abraham did!** This is a requirement of Abraham, now detailed a little more closely for us. "…cannot be My disciple" means the *impossibility* of being a disciple of Jesus Christ. So, we can tie that together:

- *if* you do not believe God
- *if* you do not believe Christ
- *if* you do not keep His commandments

you are not of Christ!

- you may claim to be
- you may think you are
- you may even have some important people whom you look to in this world as your spiritual leaders

But **unless you do what Jesus said here,** you're not His disciple.

Verse 27: "And whoever does not carry his cross and come after Me… [you have to go through whatever trials and difficulties you go through, and bear your cross] …**cannot be My disciple**"

Remember what Jesus said, 'The broad way, the easy way'—many are going that way with the name of Christ. *But it's going to end in destruction!*

Verse 28: "For which one of you, desiring to build a tower, does not first sit down and count the cost, whether he has *sufficient* for *its* completion; lest perhaps, after he has laid its foundation and is not able to finish, all who see *it* begin to mock him, saying, 'This man began to build, and was not able to finish'? Or what king, when he goes out to engage another king in war, does not first sit down *and* take counsel, whether he will be able with ten thousand to meet him who is coming against him with twenty thousand? But if not, while his *enemy* is still far off, he sends ambassadors and desires the *terms* for peace. **In the same way also, each one of you who does not forsake all that he possesses cannot be My disciple**" (vs 28-33).

What is the hardest thing to give up?

- many people have walked away from lands
- many people have walked away from countries
- many people have left families

But what is the hardest thing to give up? *Self!* You're to give up self to become a *new creature in Christ.*

Let's see how the Gospel began. What we read in Matthew, Mark, Luke and John or all the New Testament, is a detailed fulfilling and carrying out of this promise that was given to Abraham by God directly

Genesis 12:2: "And I will make *of* you a great nation. And I will bless you and make your name great. And you shall be a blessing. And I will bless those that bless you and curse the one who curses you. And **in you shall all families of the earth be blessed**" (vs 2-3).

That is a **broad, broad** promise! Literally, the rest of **the Bible from this point on** shows how God fulfilled those promises and was carrying them out. How that the carrying out of these promises are going to go clear on down

- through into Millennium
- into the Last Great Day
- into New Jerusalem coming on this earth
- into all eternity

That's quite a thing!

Verse 4: "Then Abram departed, even as the LORD had spoken to him…"

Let's see where God gives a little more understanding of what He promised him. *Abram believed Him!* God didn't give him any details, He said, 'Just go, I'll bless you.' *So Abram left!*

Please understand *that's the same with us.* Many times God has us do things that we don't understand right away. Later He reveals it to us. Here's the later part; He revealed a little bit more to Abram/Abraham. We're going to see that there are two things here that this took place over a period of two days and that these two days are:

- the Passover, the 14th of the 1st month
- the 1st day of the Feast of Unleavened Bread, the 15th of the 1st month

We'll prove that after we get into it!

So, God gave the promise, Genesis 15:4: "And behold, the Word of the LORD *came* to him saying, 'This man shall not be your heir; but he that shall come forth out of your own loins shall be your heir.'"

There is the physical seed! First there is the *physical* then there is the *spiritual*; that's what Paul said.

- the first man, Adam, was of the flesh
- the second Adam—Christ—was from heaven
- there is a natural body, which is sown in the resurrection and raised a spiritual body

So, here we have the same thing. God is giving the promise of a physical heir—a son! Now then, we have a second promise given:

Verse 5: "And He brought him outside and said, 'Look now toward the heavens and number the stars—if you are able to count them.' And He said to him, **'So shall your seed be.'**" *That's quite an awesome thing!*

Remember, at that time, there was no smog around to obscure the vision of the stars. You see the stars at night. What God is doing here, *He is bringing the words of the covenant to Abraham!*

He expands upon that because there are two parts here: the *physical seed* and the *spiritual seed!*

We will see the promise of spiritual seed is likened unto the stars. He is giving two promises to Abraham:

1. *physical seed* from his own bowels
2. *spiritual seed* which would come through Christ

Galatians. 3:29: "And if you *are* Christ's then you are Abraham's seed and heirs according to *the* promise."

Matthew 13:43: "Then shall the righteous shine forth as the sun in the Kingdom of their Father. The one who has ears to hear, let him hear." *Let's see how we will be when we are glorified spirit beings!*

1-John 3:1: "Behold! What *glorious* love the Father has given to us, that we should be called the children of God! For this very reason, the world does not know us because it did not know Him. Beloved, now we are the children of God, and it has not yet been revealed what we shall be; **but we know that when He is manifested, we shall be like Him, because we shall see Him exactly as He is**" (vs 1-2).

Rev. 1—we can show that when God took Abraham out there and showed him the stars; *He was literally showing him the glory of His coming spiritual seed through Christ!*

Revelation 1:13: "And in *the* midst of the seven lampstands *one* like *the* Son of man, clothed in *a garment* reaching to the feet, and girded about the chest with a golden breastplate. And His head and hair *were* like white wool, white as snow; and His eyes *were* like a flame of fire; and His feet *were* like fine brass, as if *they* glowed in a furnace; and His voice *was* like *the* sound of many waters. And in His right hand He had seven stars, and a sharp two-edged sword went out of His mouth, and His countenance *was* **as the sun shining in its *full* power**" (vs 13-16).

What is a star? *A star is a sun!* So, when God told Abraham that he'd be 'like the stars, so shall your seed be,' this is talking about the *spiritual seed!*

Philippians 3:20: "But for us, the commonwealth *of God* exists in *the* heavens, from where also we are waiting for *the* Savior, *the* Lord Jesus Christ; **Who will transform our vile bodies that they may be conformed to His glorious body**… [tie in Rev. 1] …according to the inner working of His own power, *whereby He is able* to subdue all things to Himself" (vs 20-21).

When God told Abraham that his seed was going to 'be as the stars of heaven for a multitude,' He's not only showing the number, He's also showing the kind of glory that they will be. Some people may ask—'so shall your seed be'—does that not just refer to physical seed? Well, what is God's plan overall for human beings? *To become the sons of God!*

When we receive the begettal of the Holy Spirit, we receive the seed of eternal life, and in the Greek the seed is called 'sperma.' Unfortunately, 1-John 3:9 is one of the worst translated verses in all the *King James Version* of the Bible, which reads:

1-John 3:9 (*KJV*): "Whosoever is born of God does not commit sin..." *That is an entirely incorrect translation, and incorrectly interpreted by the Protestants* who say that if you are born again you cannot sin. That is, if you have a 'conversion experience' you cannot sin. *That is not true!* Let's show the contradiction right within the translation of the *King James*:

1-John 5:16 (*KJV*): "If any man see his brother sin a sin *which is* not unto death..."

- Does this not say that a person, who is converted, is capable of sin?
- Does it not?
- Is not a brother converted? *Yes!*

And if he sins a sin 'not unto death' that means *it's sin he can repent of!*

"...he shall ask, and he shall give him life for them that sin not unto death. There is **a sin unto death**: I do not say that he shall pray for it" (v 16). *This shows two things*:

1. converted people can sin
Converted people, according to Protestants, are *born again*. But that is not a correct interpretation.
2. no one is born again until the resurrection

However, with the proper translation:

1-John 3:9: "Everyone who has been begotten by God **does not practice sin** because His seed... [that is from God the Father] ...*of begettal* is dwelling within him, and he is **not able to *practice* sin because he has been begotten by God.**"

So, when it talks about 'seed' in Gen. 15, we see that there is *physical* seed and we also see that there is *spiritual* seed. That's why I started out that 'if you are Christ's, then are you Abraham's seed—*spiritual*—and heirs according to the promise.' We're going to find how important this is. I remember when we first understood this it was really, really quite an eye-opener. We'll go through it and we will clarify it for you.

Genesis 15:5: "...'So shall your seed be.'.... [*physical* and *spiritual*] ...And he believed in the LORD. And He accounted it to him for righteousness" (vs 5-6).

Let's understand there was *no work* for Abraham to do, because it's impossible to count the stars. He could not have children at this point so there was *no work* for him to do. *He believed God, counted to him for righteousness!*

Then God gives him an instruction, v 7: "And He said to him, 'I *am* the LORD that brought you out of Ur of the Chaldees, to give you this land to inherit it.' And he said, 'Lord GOD, by what shall I know that I shall inherit it?'" (vs 7-8).

God then did a very profound thing, and this has to do with the very crucifixion of Christ, His death and being put in the grave.

Verse 9: "And He said to him, 'Take Me a heifer of three years old, and a she-goat of three years old, and a ram of three years old, and a turtledove, and a young pigeon.'.... [this means that they're all mature] ...And he took all these to himself, and divided them in the middle [cut them down the middle] ...and laid each piece opposite the other..." (vs 9-10)—*meaning that the spine was close to each other and there was a path down between these animals cut and laid out,* everything was there: the blood, the guts, everything.

"...but he did not divide the birds...." (v 10). *He probably put one bird on one side and one bird on the other side!* What was the purpose of this? *This is a special **maledictory sacrifice** and oath*: that when one takes an oath such as this, they *cannot* break it.

Verse 11: "And when the birds of prey came down upon the carcasses, Abram drove them away. And it came to pass, **as the sun was going down**..."

First of all, back in v 5 we have 'a night.' Then in the day portion of the day, which was the 14th of the 1st month he did the sacrificing of the animals.

- there was no altar
- there was no sprinkling of the blood
- there was no burning of it by Abraham

Just laid out there! So much so that 'the fowl'—which then would be the vultures and buzzards—were circling up overhead.

And they "...came down upon the carcasses, Abram drove them away. And it came to pass, as the sun was going down, that **a deep sleep fell** upon Abram..." (vs 11-12).

You can read in *The Christian Passover* book how this is very likened to the time when Jesus died. He died at the third hour and the sun is going down at the third hour. Then two things happened here:

1. "…a deep sleep fell upon Abram…" (v 12)

What is a person who dies in Christ? *They are sleeping!* So, here's a *deep sleep!* This is a *type of death!* A type of the death of Christ, perhaps precisely at the same time that Jesus died. When He was crucified on the 14th day of the Passover when He was crucified.

2. "…And, behold, **a horror of great darkness fell** upon him!" (v 12)

Verse 13: "And He said to Abram, 'You must surely know that your seed shall be sojourners in a land *that is* not theirs, (and shall serve them and afflict them) four hundred years. And also I will judge that nation whom they shall serve. And afterward they shall come out with great substance. And you shall go to your fathers in peace. You shall be buried in a good old age. But in the fourth generation they shall come here again, for the iniquity of the Amorites is not yet full' And it came to pass—**when the sun went down**…" (vs 13-17). *Now we are into the second day!*

When do the days begin and end according to Scripture? *At sunset!* So, we have the sun going down.

Now, remember, we started out at night in vs 4 & 5. Then we had the day portion with the sacrifice, and we'll explain the sacrifice here in just a minute. Now the sun went down:

"…and **it was dark**…" (v 17). *Then God did something very profound to give to Abraham **the guarantee of the promises** beginning in v 4 carried on down through vs 13, 14 & 15!*

"…behold, a smoking furnace and a burning lamp passed between those pieces" (v 17).

What happened when God went through those parts? *It doesn't tell us directly,* but I would say from what the context of it is here, when God walked between the parts of that sacrifice those animals were **consumed,** and there was nothing left but ashes.

Verse 18: "In the same day the LORD made a covenant with Abram, saying, 'I have given this land to your seed, from the river of Egypt to the great river, the river Euphrates." *Then it lists all of the different tribes of Canaan!*

- Where else do we find a two-day sequence?
- How do we know this is the 14th and 15th?

We can't prove it from right here, because it doesn't say the 14th day of the 1st month here, and it doesn't

say the 15th day of the 1st month here. However, if we go the Exo. 12, we do have the days numbered, and we do have it told us *exactly* when it took place.

Again, I refer you to *The Christian Passover* book; you can go through in detail, because we have great detailed explanation of everything that is here because there is great confusion over the Passover. Of course, it's only logical that Satan would confuse everything concerning the Passover because if you keep the Christian Passover today, the way that Christ wants you to—at the time that He says, in the manner that He says—then you belong to Christ. *Satan's objective is*:

- to confuse it
- to cause problems with it
- to change the day if possible

Because the Jews today keep the Passover on the 15th—which I fully explain in the book *The Christian Passover—they do not recognize Christ at all!* **In order to truly recognize Christ, you must understand the Truth of the Passover,** because Christ died on the Passover Day, the very time that the sacrifice took place that Abraham gave and fell into the deep sleep.

Now let's read the instructions here for the children of Israel concerning the Passover. We're not going to go in great detail, but what I want to point out is this.

Exodus 12:3: "Speak to all the congregation of Israel, saying, 'In the tenth day of this month they shall take to them each man a lamb for a father's house, a lamb for a house. And if the household is too little for the lamb, let him and his neighbor next to his house take according to the number of the souls, each one, according to the eating of his mouth, you shall count concerning the lamb. Your lamb shall be without blemish… [type of Christ] …a male of the first year. You shall take *it* from the sheep or from the goats. And you shall keep it up until the *beginning* of the fourteenth day of the same month…'" (vs 3-6)— the 1st month because He said:

Verse 2: "This month *shall be* to you the beginning of months. It shall be the first month of the year to you."

Verse 6: "…And the whole assembly of the congregation of Israel shall kill it between the two evenings"—*between sunset and dark,* which is amply proved in the book *The Christian Passover.* They were to eat it in that night, after taking the blood and roasting it and so forth.

Verse 12: "For I will pass through the land of Egypt this night, and will smite all the firstborn in the land of Egypt, both man and beast. And I will execute judgment against all the gods of Egypt. I *am* the LORD. And the blood shall be a sign to you upon the houses where you *are*. And when I see the blood, I will pass over you...." (vs 12-13).

All of Israel was blessed because of the Passover, but the Passover spared *the firstborn*. There is a great parallel with that for today with God's Church who are the *Church of the Firstborn*, as we will see a little later, and also the rest of the world. How important is the Church of God to the world? *Far more important than we've ever calculated!* As important as the firstborn of Israel in relationship to the rest of the firstborn of Israel, so the *Church of the Firstborn*, which we are today, is as important to God as the rest of the world.

Verse 14: "And this day shall be a memorial to you...."

Verse 21: "Then Moses called for all the elders of Israel and said to them, 'Draw out and take a lamb for yourselves according to your families, and kill the Passover *lamb*. And you shall take a bunch of hyssop and dip in the blood *that is* in the bowl, and strike the lintel and the two side posts with the blood in the bowl. And **none of you shall go out of the door of his house until sunrise**'" (vs 21-22). *So, they could not leave that night!* We explain all of that in *The Christian Passover* book.

Verse 23: "For the LORD will pass through to strike the Egyptians. And when He sees the blood upon the lintel, and on the two side posts, the LORD will pass over the door, and will not allow the destroyer to come into your houses to strike you. And you shall observe this thing as a law to you and to your children forever. And it shall be when you have come to the land, which the LORD will give you, according as He has promised that you shall keep this service. And it will be, when your children shall say to you, 'What *does* this service *mean* to you?' Then you shall say, 'It *is* the sacrifice of the LORD'S Passover, Who passed over the houses of the children of Israel in Egypt, when He struck the Egyptians and delivered our houses.' And the people bowed their heads and worshiped. And the children of Israel went away and did as the LORD had commanded Moses and Aaron; so they did. And it came to pass **at midnight the LORD struck all the firstborn**..." (vs 23-29).

We do want to get a little chronology here with Numbers 33:1: "These *are* the journeys of the children of Israel, who went forth out of the land of Egypt with their armies under the hand of Moses and Aaron. And Moses wrote their goings out according to their journeys **by the command of the LORD**. And these *are* their journeys according to their starting places. And **they set out from Rameses in the first month, on the fifteenth day of the first month**..." (vs 1-3).

When does the 15th begin? *Right after the sunset of the 14th!* They went out **by night;** they couldn't have gone out on the night of the 14th because they had to stay in their houses. **If** they kept the Passover on the 15th then they could not have left until morning. If they left in the morning they could not leave at night. That's as simple as can be. If you're going to go to work at six in the morning, you don't show up at six at night. It's that simple!

So, they left "...On the *next* day after the Passover *Day*..." (v 3).

Let's see what they did when they left their homes. Where were the homes of the children of Israel? They lived in the area of Goshen in the Northwest part of the delta, the very choicest part of Egypt, and they had their little villages scattered there. For them to leave Rameses means they had to assemble at Rameses and then leave there. ***So, they assembled at Rameses on the day portion of the 14th!***

Here's what they did, Exodus 12:33: "And the Egyptians were urging the people, that they might send them out of the land quickly, for they said, 'We *are* all dead men.' And the people took their dough before it was leavened, their kneading-troughs being bound up in their clothes upon their shoulders. And the children of Israel did according to the word of Moses. And they asked for... [they had no intention of bringing it back] ...articles of silver, and articles of gold, and clothing from the Egyptians. And the LORD gave the people favor in the sight of the Egyptians, and they granted their request, and they stripped the Egyptians. And the children of Israel journeyed from Rameses to Succoth, the men being about six hundred thousand on foot, apart from little ones" (vs 34-37).

This is where we get the figure of 1.8-million. If you have one woman and one child per man, then you get 1.8-million people.

Verse 38: "And also a mixed multitude went up with them, and flocks and herds, very much livestock. And they baked unleavened cakes of the dough which they brought out of Egypt, for it was not leavened, because they were driven out of Egypt and could not stay, neither had they prepared any food for themselves for the journey" (vs 38-39).

According to the commandment of God— remember what we read back in Num. 33?

Verse 40: "Now, the sojourning of the children of Israel in Egypt *was* **four hundred and thirty years,** and it came to pass **at the end of the four hundred and thirty years, it was even on that very same day,** all the armies of the LORD went out from the land of Egypt. It *is* a night to be much observed to the LORD for bringing them out from the land of Egypt. **This *is* that night of the LORD to be observed by all the children of Israel in their generations**" (vs 40-42).

This is not the Passover, because on the Passover they stayed in their homes; **they came out by night!** How does this tie in with Gen. 15?

Verse 41: "And it came to pass **at the end of the four hundred and thirty years,** it was even on **that very same day**…."—in reference to:

Genesis. 15:17: "And it came to pass—when the sun went down… [which we know begins a new day] …and it was dark—behold, a smoking furnace and a burning lamp passed between those pieces. **In the same day**… [being night time] …**the LORD made a covenant with Abram,** saying, 'I have given this land to your seed…'" (vs 17-18).

What also is part of the covenant?

Verse 13: "And He said to Abram, 'You must surely know that your seed shall be sojourners in a land *that is* not theirs… [that's how they were in Egypt] …(and shall serve them and afflict them) four hundred years… [which it was actually 430] …And also **I will judge** that nation whom they shall serve…. [and God said He did judge them on the Passover night]: …And afterward they shall come out with great substance…. [Did they do that? *Yes!*] …And you shall go to your fathers in peace. You shall be buried in a good old age. But in the fourth generation they shall come here again, for the iniquity of the Amorites is not yet full'" (vs 13-16).

When the sun went down, beginning the 15th, that same day God made the covenant that *He would bring them out and that they would inherit the land!* That's what the 'same day' is referring to. God did it by walking through the special sacrifice, which is called a *maledictory oath*, meaning that once you make this oath you cannot change it. Of course then, the smoking furnace burned up all the sacrifice completely.

Since 'the same day' (v 18) equals the 'same day' in Exo. 12:41, that is the 15th day of the 1st month. Therefore, when we come back to Gen. 15, the promises God gave to Abraham was on the night of the 14th, *which is the same night in which __we__ take the Passover; in which __we__ have the promises of eternal life given to us by Jesus Christ in the words of the New Covenant!*

Let's come to understand a little bit more about this *maledictory oath*. Jer. 34 tells us what kind of oath this is; there is no greater, no stronger oath. In doing this not only did He make the covenant with Abraham to bring the children of Israel out, but God also foretold of His coming crucifixion. We will see what happens when people

don't keep it. This is the most solemn oath that you can have.

Jeremiah 34:8: "The word that came to Jeremiah from the LORD, after King Zedekiah had made a covenant with all the people at Jerusalem, to proclaim liberty to them… [here's the liberty; they made a covenant; we'll see how they made the covenant] …That each man should let his male slave, and each man his female slave—*if* a Hebrew man or a Hebrew woman—go free, that none should enslave a Jew, his brother among them. And all the rulers obeyed, and all the people who had entered into the covenant allowed them to go free, each man his male slave, and each man his female slave, so that not any should be enslaved among them any more; and they obeyed and let *them* go. But afterward they turned and took back the male slaves and the female slaves whom they had set free and enslaved them *again* as male slaves and female slaves…." (vs 8-11).

Almost like Pharaoh; where Moses said, 'Let my people go.' They couldn't get along without the servants, so the Jews—when they let them go—they said, 'Oh, look what we did, we got to do the work ourselves.' *Too bad!* They went back on their word; they went back on a covenant. I want you to also remember that in relationship to the coming Passover, which is the renewing of the New Covenant.

Verse 12: "So, the Word of the LORD came to Jeremiah from the LORD, saying, 'Thus says the LORD, the God of Israel, 'I made a covenant with your fathers in the day that I brought them out from the land of Egypt, out of the house of slavery, saying, 'At the end of seven years each man should let go *free* his brother, a Hebrew, who has been sold to him. And when he has served you six years, you shall let him go free from you.' But your fathers did not hearken to me, nor incline their ears. And you had turned today, and had done right in My sight to call for liberty, each man to his neighbor. And you had made a covenant before Me in the house, which is called by My name. But you turned *back* and defiled My name, and each of you has taken back his male slave and his female slave whom you had set free to do as they pleased. But you forced them *again* to become your male and your female slaves'" (vs 12-16).

Verse 17: "Thus says the LORD, 'You have not hearkened to Me to proclaim liberty each man to his brother, and each man to his neighbor! Behold, **I proclaim freedom for you**,' says the LORD, 'to the sword, to the plague, and to the famine. And **I will cause you to be a horror to all the kingdoms of the earth.**'"

How serious is a covenant? *Mighty serious!* How serious is it when you break it? Remember, they did this in the house of God. Also remember that when we do things, we have access to God the Father in heaven above. This is not just in the physical house on the earth, when we have a covenant.

Verse 18: "And I will give the men who have sinned against My covenant, who have not done the words of the covenant which they made before Me *when they* divided the calf in two… [just like Abraham did, he cut it in two] …**and passed between its parts.**"

When anyone made that kind of covenant and passed between the parts of the animals that were sacrificed for that covenant, what they're declaring by their action is this: If I break this covenant, *I will be like these animals that have been sacrificed*—cut down the middle.

Verse 19: "The rulers of Judah, and the rulers of Jerusalem, the officials, and the priests, and all the people of the land who passed between the parts of the calf; I will even give them into the hand of their enemies, and into the hand of those who seek their life. And their dead bodies shall be for food to the birds of heaven and to the beasts of the earth" (vs 19-20).

Did not the fowls of heaven come down to try and get the sacrifices that Abraham made? *Yes!* So, now God is going to say, 'I'm going to do this to you.'

Verse 21: "And I will give Zedekiah king of Judah, and his rulers, into the hand of their enemies, and into the hand of those who seek their lives, and into the hand of the king of Babylon's army, who has withdrawn from you. Behold, I will command,' says the LORD, 'and cause them to return to this city. And they shall fight against it and capture it, and burn it with fire. And I will make the cities of Judah a desert without a soul to live in it'" (vs 21-22).

Apparently, God fought their battle for them; drove back the king of Babylon. So, they said, 'Thank you, God, for doing that, we repent, we'll let our slaves go free.' Then they changed their minds, so God said, 'Now I'm going to cause the king of Babylon to return, and now he's going to do it in the whole city.'

This tells you the seriousness of the kind of oath that there is when you make a covenant and pass between the parts. That's the oath that God made with Abraham to guarantee that he would have:

1) physical seed
2) spiritual seed
3) that He would take them out of the land of the stranger in the *same day* that He

made the covenant with Abraham—*that very same night*

The Passover and the Feast of Unleavened Bread really began <u>with Abraham</u> and not with Israel!

Let's look at the extension of this covenant, the physical seed that would be Israel. They would come through Isaac. Oh the Arabs would that it would have been Ishmael. *But it wasn't!* So, here then is a continuation of the covenant, now giving in detail the requirements for the *physical* seed. Abraham had to wait a long time. This was a year before Isaac was born; and Isaac was the promise of the physical seed.

Genesis 17:1: "And when Abram was ninety-nine years old… [He left at 75-years-old; here we are 25 years inclusive counting] …the LORD appeared to Abram and said to him, 'I *am* the Almighty God! Walk before Me and be perfect."

Tie in Matt. 5:48, because we are told to 'be perfect as your Father in heaven is perfect.' It's the same requirement. It is the Gospel preached to Abraham.

Verse 2: "And I will make My covenant between Me and you, and will multiply you exceedingly.' And Abram fell on his face. And God talked with him, saying, 'As for Me, behold, My covenant is with you, and you shall be a father of many nations. Neither shall your name any more be called Abram, but your name shall be Abraham; **for I have made you a father of many nations**" (vs 2-5).

That was before Isaac was even born. When God says something *it is as good as done!* When God says you will be in the Kingdom of God *it is as good as done!* The only condition is you have to *endure to the end* and *be faithful*, and you'll make it.

Verse 6: "And I will make you exceedingly fruitful, and I will make nations of you, and kings shall come from you. And I will establish My covenant between Me and you and your seed after you in their generations… [the physical seed] …for an everlasting covenant, to be God to you and to your seed after you. And I will give the land to you in which you are a sojourner, and to your seed after you, all the land of Canaan, for an everlasting possession. And I will be their God.' And God said to Abraham, 'And you shall keep My covenant, you and your seed after you in their generations. This is My covenant, which you shall keep, between Me and you and your seed after you. Every male child among you shall be circumcised'" (vs 6-10). *Here's the covenant of circumcision!*

- he was blessed of God
- he had righteousness imputed to him

- his sins forgiven him for 25 years while he was in uncircumcision

so that

- he could be the father of the uncircumcision who received the promise of eternal life
- he would be the father of the circumcision

Verse 11: "And you shall circumcise the flesh of your foreskin. And it shall be a sign of the covenant between Me and you. And a son of eight days shall be circumcised among you, every male child in your generations; he that is born in the house, or bought with silver of any foreigner who *is* not of your seed. He that is born in your house, and he that is bought with your silver, must be circumcised. And My covenant shall be in your flesh for an everlasting covenant" (vs 11-13).

That was it was continuous until that time, and I think for all the descendants of Israel to this day:

- *not for salvation,* but for the keeping of the covenant here, because we live today in the land that God gave to the descendants of Israel
- *not for salvation,* but for this part of the covenant because whoever are the descendants of Israel should

Verse 14: "And the uncircumcised male child whose flesh of his foreskin is not circumcised, that soul shall be cut off from his people—*for* he has broken My covenant."

God has not required this of the Gentiles in their own nations. We know that in the New Covenant circumcision is nothing and uncircumcision is nothing, but the **circumcision of the heart** and *faith in Christ!* But, this is for the *physical* seed.

Verse 15: "And God said to Abraham, 'As for Sarai your wife, you shall not call her name Sarai, but her name *shall be* Sarah. And I will bless her, and give you a son also of her. Yes, I will bless her, and she shall be *a mother* of nations—kings of people shall be from her.'" (vs 15-16).

Verse 17: "And Abraham fell upon his face and laughed, and said in his heart, 'Shall *a child* be born to him that is a hundred years old? And shall Sarah, who is ninety years old, bear?' And Abraham said to God, 'Oh, that Ishmael might live before You!'" (vs 17-18)—*the easy way out!*

Verse 19: "And God said, 'Sarah your wife shall bear you a son indeed. And you shall call his name Isaac. And I will establish My covenant with him for an everlasting covenant, and with his seed after him. And as for Ishmael, I have heard you.

Behold, I have blessed him, and will make him fruitful, and will multiply him exceedingly. He shall beget twelve princes, and I will make him a great nation. But I will establish My covenant with Isaac, whom Sarah shall bear to you at this set time in the next year'" (vs 19-21).

It's important for us to understand that **God does things at the set times!** They had the circumcision party. Isaac was born, sure enough *at the set time* that God had said. Then we have something profound.

Genesis 21:1: "And the LORD visited Sarah as He had said. And the LORD did to Sarah as He had spoken, for Sarah conceived and bore Abraham a son in his old age…" (vs 1-2).

God does the impossible things, that way it can never be said that it's of a man. You show me any 100-year-old today who has a pregnant 90-year-old wife, and then we will know that this was not a miraculous thing.

"…at the set time of which God had spoken to him. And Abraham called the name of his son that was born to him (whom Sarah bore to him) Isaac. And Abraham circumcised his son Isaac, when he was eight days old, as God had commanded him. And Abraham was a hundred years old when his son Isaac was born to him" (vs 2-5).

That means he was pretty close to the end of his 100th year. Because remember, when God told him, Abram said:

Genesis 17:17: "…Shall *a child* be born to him that is a hundred years old?…." *Apparently he was just 100 at that point*; no more than three months into his 100th year, and Isaac was born before the 100th year was out. That's how we have the chronology.

Let's talk about the Passover and Isaac. Because this time it talks about Isaac *and* Abraham. We find some tremendous types coming down to the prophecy, not only the prophecy, but to the actual crucifixion of Jesus Christ. Here we find that in type: **Abraham is a type of God the Father, who has only one son, and this son is to be sacrificed!** We do not have anything dogmatic that we could say that this took place on the Passover Day. It's possible, but we don't know for sure, so we can't say that.

Here is a test that Abraham went through. Remember what we read at the beginning in Luke 14:26. Here again he's going to be tested on it. Not only do we do that with what is called 'counting the cost'—to the end of v 33—but we always 'count the cost' continually as we go through our Christian life. We're confronted with many things where we must 'count the cost':

- Will we obey God or not?
- Will we believe God or not?
- Will we trust God or not?

That's on an ongoing basis, it's not just, you know, you do it once and it's over with. No. not at all.

Here he is, we don't know how old. As we'll see a little later, Isaac is called a 'lad.' We could say that he was probably less than 20. May even have an indication that he was, say, not much more than 12. So, between 12 and 20 was the age of Isaac when this event took place. Which means that from the time that God called Abraham, we have 37-45 years and this even took place. God also tested Abraham all those years.

{Note message: *Genesis 15 and the 430 Years* (proving Isaac was 15 years old)}

Abraham had a little deceitful streak in him, which Isaac inherited and also Jacob inherited, and also Jacob's mother, she had a little deceitful streak in her. God uses some of those human weaknesses in His plan. But here we have between 37 and 45 years when this even took place:

Genesis 22:1: "And it came to pass after these things that God tested Abraham, and said to him, 'Abraham!'…."

God does not tempt anyone with evil; let's understand that!. God puts before us choices, whether we will obey him or not. When we are tempted with evil and drawn away of our own lusts, and then the lust conceives it brings forth sin. God did not make us sin when we do that, ***that's our own human nature!*** That's why we have the Feast of Unleavened Bread continuously year-by-year as long as we're in the Church of God, so that we understand that our human nature is always here and we always have to be working on getting rid of it, just like we get rid of leaven out of our lives.

"…'Abraham!' And he said, 'Here I am.' And He said, 'Take now your son, your only *son* Isaac…'" (vs 1-2).

Was Ishmael Abraham's son? *Yes, he was!* But not of Sarah; not counted as 'seed for the promise' so therefore, He said, 'Your son, your only son.' So, this is very much a type of God the Father in relationship to Christ. In this case then:

- Isaac being a type of Christ
- Abraham being a type of the Father

"'…whom you love, and go into the land of Moriah, and offer him there for a burnt offering upon one of the mountains which I will tell you'" (v 2).

There were mountains in Moriah. The Jews claim by tradition that this was the area where the temple was built. But also one of the mountains of Moriah would be the mount that later became to be called the Mt. of Olives. Could this be? The Mt. of Olives is higher than the Temple Mount. Could this be the mount where Christ was crucified? *If the parallel follows, then that could be true!*

Verse 3: "And Abraham rose up early in the morning and saddled his donkey, and took two *of* his young men with him, and Isaac his son. And he split the wood for the burnt offering, and rose up and went to the place of which God had told him. Then on the third day Abraham lifted up his eyes and saw the place afar off. And Abraham said to his young men, 'You stay here with the donkey, and I and the boy will go yonder and worship, and come again to you.' And Abraham took the wood of the burnt offering and laid it upon Isaac his son.…" (vs 3-6). *That's almost like a type of carrying the cross that Christ did!*

"…And he took the fire *pot* in his hand…" (v 6). *Obviously you're not going to carry it in your hand,* because if you carry fire in your hand you're going to burn it.

"…and a knife. And they both went together…. [I imagine it was kind of a silent climb up that mountain] …And… [finally] …Isaac spoke to Abraham his father and said, 'My father.' And he said, 'Here I *am*, my son.' And he said, 'Behold the fire and the wood. But where is the lamb for a burnt offering?'" (vs 6-7).

Now, we notice two things here, there are two acts of faith:

1) Abraham *believed*
2) Isaac *also believed* and ***did not complain***

He could have said, 'This is ridiculous, we're going to go up here and you're going to offer an offering, and I find out at the last minute *it's me!*' But he *didn't do it.*

Verse 8: "And Abraham said, 'My son, God will provide Himself a lamb for a burnt offering.'…. [sometimes God waits until the very last minute for deliverance] …So they both went on together. And they came to the place of which God had told him. And Abraham built an altar there…" (vs 8-9).

Let's understand something about sin offerings and burnt offerings. On the Mt. of Olives—picture this in your mind—you're looking at the temple area and you are looking north. To the right is east and east of the temple is in the Kidron Valley going down 450-feet. They built a bridge across the Kidron Valley to go into the east gate of the temple. This bridge went to the Mt. of Olives. On the Mount of Olives, right near the crest of the

Mt. of Olives, was what was called the *Miphkad Altar,* a special altar outside the temple area. This is where they took all the sin offerings, and they took all the skins of the sin offerings and they burnt them in the Miphkad Altar. This was like a huge pit and these things were constantly and continually burnt. At the bottom of the pit there was a conduit, which went down into the Kidron Valley where periodically they would push the ashes out.

Could it be that where he built this altar is later where the Miphkad Altar was built? Even though this was a burnt offering, Christ was a sin offering. Christ was not burned, *because He had to be buried and raised!* So, the parallel breaks down when you get out of the physical parallel, when you start getting into the real sacrifice of Christ.

"…And Abraham built an altar there and laid the wood in order. And he bound his son Isaac and laid him on the wood, upon the altar. And Abraham stretched out his hand and took the knife to slay his son" (vs 9-10).

- Why did he do that? *His only son and the one to whom he was told, 'you will have physical seed'!*
- Why was he willing to do this? *Because God commanded him to!*
- What was in his mind?
- Was he doubting God?
- Was he angry at God?
- What was it?

Hebrews 11:8 *gives a real good summary of the life of Abraham*: "By faith Abraham, being called *of God* to go out into the place which he would later receive for an inheritance, obeyed and went, not knowing where he was going. By faith he sojourned in the land of promise, like a foreigner, dwelling in tabernacles with Isaac and Jacob, the joint heirs of the same promise; for he was waiting for the city with *the* foundations of which God is *the* Architect and Builder. By faith also Sarah herself received power to conceive seed, and gave birth *when* she was *well* beyond the childbearing age because she esteemed Him faithful Who had personally promised *her a son*. Because of this *faith*, there came into being from one *man*—and moreover, *one* who was *reproductively* dead—*descendants* as numerous as the stars in the heavens, and as countless as the sand on the sea shore" (vs 8-12).

Verse 13: "All these died in faith, not having received the promises, but having seen them from afar, and having been persuaded of *them*, and having embraced *them*, and having confessed that they were strangers and sojourners on the earth. For those who say such things make it manifest that they seek *their* own country, *as promised by God.* And if, on the one hand, they had let their minds dwell *fondly* on

the place where they came from, they might have had opportunity to return. But now, on the other hand, they are aspiring to a more excellent *country*—that is, a heavenly *one*. Therefore, God is not ashamed to be called their God because He has prepared a city for them (vs 13-16).

Verse 17: "By faith Abraham, when he was being tried, offered up Isaac; and he who had received the promises offered up *his* only begotten *son* of whom it was said, 'In Isaac shall your Seed be called'; **because he reckoned that God was able to raise him even from among *the* dead,** from which he also received him in a figurative way" (vs 17-19).

That's why he was willing to do it, because he knew that if it came down to the point where he did offer his son, as that offering, *that God would raise him from the dead!*

Genesis 22:10: "And Abraham stretched out his hand and took the knife to slay his son." *Then he heard a voice from heaven.* I imagine though, *before* he took out the knife that he looked around everywhere and didn't see a lamb.

Verse 11: "And the angel of the LORD called to him from the heavens and said, 'Abraham! Abraham!' And he said, '**Here I *am*.**' And He said, 'Do not lay your hand upon the lad, nor do anything to him, **for now I know that you fear God**…'" (vs 11-12).

So, how long was he tried before God *really, really* knew—through and through—that Abraham feared God? *Just say 37 years!* Is it any wonder that we still go through trials, that we've been in the Church for how long? How many people have been in the Church for so long—say 10, 15, 20, 30 years—then leave? That's why we've had the trials come upon us, for the same reason.

"'…for now I know that you fear God, seeing you have not withheld your son, your only son, from Me.' And Abraham lifted up his eyes and looked. And, behold, behind *him* a ram was entangled in a thicket by its horns. And Abraham went and took the ram and offered it up for a burnt offering instead of his son" (vs 12-13).

How did the ram get there? *Well, either God drove it up there while his back was turned,* or God *supernaturally created a ram right there*, which would be fitting, to supernaturally create one, because that would be a type of Christ Who was a supernatural creation.

Verse 14: "And Abraham called the name of that place The LORD Will Provide; so that it is said *until* this day, 'In the mount of the LORD it will be provided.'"

I wonder if that's also a prophecy of the sacrifice of Christ on the Mt. of Olives?

Verse 15: "And the angel of the LORD called to Abraham out of heaven the second time, and said, 'By Myself have I sworn,' says the LORD…" (vs 15-16).

Here's where everything becomes completely irrevocable! It cannot be turned back, nothing can stop from what God has promised. All the promises of God *will come,* as He said.

"…because you have done this thing, and have not withheld your son, your only son; that in blessing I will bless you, and in multiplying I will multiply your seed like the stars of the heavens, and as the sand which is upon the seashore. And your seed shall possess the gate of his enemies. And in your seed shall all the nations of the earth be blessed, **because you have obeyed My voice"** (vs 17-18).

That's the only way we're going to have the blessing of God, is if you obey the voice of God. As we've covered in our series concerning Hebrews, *if you don't listen to Christ there is no eternal life!*

Scripture from *The Holy Bible in Its Original Order, A Faithful Version* (except where noted)

Scriptural References:

1) Galatians 3:29
2) Hebrews 6:13-20
3) Hebrews 13:8
4) Galatians 3:6-9
5) Genesis 12:1
6) Luke 14:25-33
7) Genesis 12:2-4
8) Genesis 15:4-5
9) Galatians 3:29
10) Matthew 13:43
11) 1 John 3:1-2
12) Revelation 1:13-16
13) Philippians 3:20-21
14) 1 John 3:9
15) 1 John 5:16
16) 1 John 3:9
17) Genesis 15:5-18
18) Exodus 12:3-6, 2, 6, 12-14, 21-29
19) Numbers 33: 1-3
20) Exodus 12:33-42, 41
21) Genesis 15:17-18; 13-16
22) Jeremiah 34:8-22
23) Genesis 17:1-21
24) Genesis 21:1-5
25) Genesis 22:1-10
26) Hebrews 11:8-19
27) Genesis 22:10-18

Scripture referenced, not quoted:

- Genesis 15:19-21
- Matthew 5:48

Also Referenced:

- Book: *The Christian Passover* by Fred Coulter
- Message: *Genesis 15 and the 430 Years*
- In-Depth Study: *Epistle of Paul to the Hebrews*

FRC: ms
Transcribed: 1-14-07
Reformatted: bo—10/2020

CHAPTER FOURTEEN

The Passover:
Abraham, Isaac, Israel & Christ II

Fred R. Coulter

I want to cover just a couple of more things here concerning this type of the Passover. As I said, there is no direct indication that you can make this happen on the Passover Day; I tried hard to do so, but you can't. We can just take the teaching and see how it applies not only to the Passover Day but also to the whole operation of the substitutionary sacrifice of Christ for us, just as God provided the ram instead of Isaac for the sacrifice. God has provided Christ instead of our death. So that's really important for us to understand and realize.

We can understand that when God swears something, and He doesn't need to swear. In other words, when men give an oath that's to end a dispute between parties. But God doesn't need to swear because He doesn't lie. When He swears, *He's giving a double-emphasis that this is absolutely going to happen with no doubt, no shadow of turning!* Because He has done this, *we can have absolute confidence and a surety that what God has said He will do,* **He will do!**

Now we live in the end-time and we have the benefit of seeing that yes, He did do it; *God did do it!*

Genesis 22:15: "And the angel of the LORD called unto Abraham out of heaven the second time, and said, 'By Myself have I sworn,' says the LORD, 'because you have done this thing, and have not withheld your son, your only son; that in blessing I will bless you, and in multiplying **I will multiply your seed like the stars of the heavens, and as the sand which is upon the seashore.** And your seed shall possess the gate of his enemies. And in your seed shall all the nations of the earth be blessed, **because you have obeyed My voice'**" (vs 15-18).

Now, this becomes a very profound and important thing, because too much of Christianity today is based upon lawless grace, meaning that you don't have to obey. Oh they claim, yes, they read the Scriptures, which say *'if you're Christ's then you're Abraham's seed and heirs according to the promise.'* But they don't read the thing that *he obeyed!*

As we have seen, the 'stars of heaven' apply to the *spiritual seed*, which is the Church, and at the resurrection 'the saints will shine as the stars of heaven' (Matt. 13:43[transcriber's correction]). The 'sand that is upon the seashore' is the **physical seed** of Israel. Then He adds another promise here: 'your seed shall possess the gate of his enemies.' *Then the blessing is passed on to Isaac:*

Genesis 26:1: "And there was a famine in the land (besides the *former* famine that had been in the days of Abraham). And Isaac went to Abimelech, king of the Philistines, to Gerar. And the LORD appeared to him and said, 'Do not go down into Egypt. Live in the land which I shall tell you of. Stay in this land, and I will be with you and bless you, for to you and to your seed, I will give all these lands; and I will establish the oath, which I swore to Abraham your father. And I will multiply your seed as the stars of the heavens and will give to your seed all these lands. And in your seed shall all the nations of the earth be blessed, because Abraham…" (1-5).

The thing we need to understand is that *the covenant did not depend upon Isaac; it did not depend upon Jacob.* **It depended upon Abraham!** This has been a consternation to many, many people. Especially when they look at the nations of the Ten Tribes of Israel, in their modern setting—and the other nations of the world do—and they wonder how come we have it, and in many cases we are so bad. They're looking at it from the point of view, 'Well, since you're so bad, you don't deserve it.'

God said He was going to give it *'because of Abraham.'* He also said later on, that if their descendants sinned He would correct them. But He would not rescind the promise that He gave to Abraham. Here's this famous verse we've gone over and over and over again. One that Protestants I am sure do not like to hear:

Verse 5: "**Because Abraham obeyed My voice and kept My charge, My commandments, My statutes, and My laws.**" *That's also important because the Passover began with Abraham and not with Israel!*

Let's see the Church in relationship to Isaac. Certain people will say that God had other commandments that He gave them. That's absolutely not true because Christ is 'the same yesterday, today and forever.' *The commandments that He gave Israel are the same commandments that Abraham obeyed!* For anyone to say anything other than that they are just Biblical illiterates. You cannot prove it from the context. The only commandments are **God's** commandments, and He won't change them.

- Is He going to change the first one? *No!*
- Is He going to change the second one? *No!*
- Is He going to change the third one? *No!*
- Is going to change the fourth one? *No!*

None of them!

Abraham kept the commandments of God and His statutes! The Holy Days are statutes. **God began the Passover with Abraham!** Those arguments, when you really understand the Bible, do not have legs at all, they just don't stand.

In relationship to that, there are indications the way that the commandments and the statutes and the judgments are written out, that they are written in sections of five, which is half of ten. You find ten all the way through the statutes and judgments there, again verifying that these things are also things God gave for Abraham to follow. We also need to understand that Abraham had a big household. He had hundreds of people there with him.

- How do you run and govern it? **You do it by God's way!**
- How do you settle disputes among people? **You do it God's way!**
- Which days do you rest and keep? **God's days!**

When we understand that *the Sabbath was binding from creation*—just like everything else God created is perpetually going on down to this day—*so the Sabbath is perpetually going on down to this day!* Once you know the Scriptures and once you know the Bible there is no question that Abraham did those things. Any of the other things that people come up with are *just arguments to avoid obeying* God. They don't like the word *obey.* They like the word *liberty,* which is another word for *lawlessness.*

Galatians 4:28: "Now we, brethren, like Isaac, are *the* children of promise. But as *it was* then, so also *it is* now: he who was born according to *the* flesh persecuted him *who was born* according to *the* Spirit. Nevertheless, what does the Scripture say? 'Cast out the maidservant and her son; for in no way shall the son of the maidservant inherit *the promise* with the son of the free *woman.*' So then, brethren, we are not children of *the* maidservant, but of the free *woman*" (vs 28-31). **We are children of promise!**

I'm trying to tie the things of Abraham back into the New Testament. We have Abraham in Gal. 3, and Isaac in Gal. 4. Now let's come down to the time that the blessing is passed on to Jacob. God said before they were born about Esau and Jacob:

- they were two kinds of people
- Esau who was the oldest would serve the younger
- the younger would prevail

Sometimes God does things and allows things to happen by the use of human nature. We find that Jacob connived to get the blessing, or the birthright, from Esau He didn't have to do it, because God would have given it another way. But also it was a test on Esau. Esau was willing to sell it and give it up.

Then it came time for the blessing and mamma got involved in it and she said, 'You go in and you pretend that you're Esau and get the blessing.' He says, 'Well, how can I do that? He's a hairy man.' She says, 'Well, we'll put a goats skin on your neck.' You talk about a hairy man—he must have been a real hairy man. You know, if you feel the back of the neck and it's all like goats hair. She made the stew, she put the skins on his hands and on the back of his neck, because he was a smooth man.

Genesis 27:18: "And he came to his father and said, 'My father!' And he said, 'Here I *am*; who are you, my son?' And Jacob said to his father, **'I am Esau your firstborn**…'" (vs 18-19)—*a big fat lie!*

The reason God does things like this is so that Esau would think that he just took it. *But he didn't!*

"'…I have done as you asked me. Arise, I pray you, sit and eat of my venison, that your soul may bless me.' And Isaac said to his son, 'How *is it* that you have found it so quickly, my son?'?…." (vs 19-20).

Going out and shooting venison and it takes a little while to chase him down and get it with bow and arrow.

"…And he said, 'Because the LORD your God brought *it* to me.' And Isaac said to Jacob, 'Come near, I pray you, so that I may feel you, my son, whether you are truly my son Esau or not'" (vs 20-22). *So, he had his doubts!*

Verse 23: "And he did not recognize him, for his hands were hairy like his brother Esau's hands. And he blessed him. And he said, '*Are* you truly my son Esau?' And he said, 'I *am.*' (vs 23-24). *Isaac checked him out a couple of times here!*

Verse 25: "And he said, 'Bring *it* to me, and I will eat of my son's venison, so that my soul may bless you.' And he brought *it* near to him, and he ate. And he brought him wine, and he drank. And his father Isaac said to him, 'Come near now and kiss me, my son.' And he came near and kissed him. And he smelled the smell of his clothing, and blessed him, and said, 'See, the smell of my son *is* as the smell of a field which the LORD has blessed. And may God give you of the dew of heaven, and of the fatness of the earth, and plenty of grain and wine. Let people serve you, and let nations bow down to you. Be lord over your brethren, and let your mother's sons bow down to you. Cursed *be* everyone that curses you, and blessed *be* he that blesses you'" (vs 25-29). *We'll see how this expanded out to the 12 tribes of Israel!*

Verse 30: "And it came to pass, as soon as Isaac had made an end of blessing Jacob, and Jacob was scarcely gone from the presence of Isaac his father, that Esau his brother came in from his hunting. And he also had made *a dish of* savory meat and brought it to his father. And he said to his father, 'Let my father arise and eat of his son's venison so that your soul may bless me.' And his father Isaac said to him, 'Who *are* you?' And he said, 'I *am* your son, your firstborn, Esau.' Then Isaac trembled greatly, and said, 'Who then *was* the one who has hunted deer and brought *it* to me—and I have eaten it all before you came, and have blessed him? Yea, he shall be blessed!'" (vs 30-33). *The blessing can only be given once!*

Verse 34: "And when Esau heard the words of his father, he cried with a great and exceedingly bitter cry, and said to his father, 'Bless me, even me also, O my father!' And he said, 'Your brother came with deceit, and has taken away your blessing.' And *Esau* said, 'Is he not rightly called Jacob? For he has supplanted me these two times—he took away my birthright, and behold, now he has taken away my blessing.' And he said, 'Have you not reserved a blessing for me?' And Isaac answered and said to Esau, 'Behold, I have made him your lord, and all his brethren I have given him for servants. And with grain and wine I have sustained him. And what shall I do now to you, my son?'" (vs 34-37).

Verse 38: "And Esau said to his father, 'Have you but one blessing, my father? Bless me, even me also, my father.' And Esau lifted up his voice and wept. And Isaac his father answered and said to him, 'Behold, Your dwelling shall be far from the fatness of the earth and far from the dew of heaven from above. And you shall live by your sword and shall serve your brother. But it shall come to pass that when you shall have the dominion, you shall break his yoke from off your neck'" (vs 38-40).

That has not yet happened Esau and Ishmael are still subject to the descendants of Jacob.

Verse 41: "And Esau hated Jacob because of the blessing with which his father had blessed him. And Esau said in his heart, 'The days of mourning

for my father are at hand—then I will kill my brother Jacob.'" *Hearkens back to Cain and Abel!*

So, Jacob gets out of there. Rebekah says 'Look, get out of here, go hide, run away, go to Laban, my brother, go up there.' Right before he left, here's the charge:

Genesis 28:1: "Then Isaac called Jacob and blessed him, and commanded him. And he said to him, 'You shall not take a wife of the daughters of Canaan.... [remember that Esau did] ...Arise, go to Padan Aram, to the house of Bethuel your mother's father. And take a wife from there of the daughters of Laban your mother's brother. And may God Almighty bless you, and make you fruitful, and multiply you, so that you may be a multitude of people. And may He give you the blessing of Abraham, to you and to your seed with you, so that you may inherit the land in which you are a stranger, which God gave to Abraham'" (vs 1-4).

Isaac sent him away to Padanaram, and then Jacob had a dream and saw this ladder ascending up:

Verse 12: "And he dreamed. And behold, a ladder was set up on the earth, and the top of it reached to heaven! And behold, the angels of God *were* ascending and descending on it! And behold, the LORD stood above it, and said, 'I *am* the LORD, the God of Abraham your father, and the God of Isaac. The land on which you lie I will give to you and to your seed. **And your seed shall be like the dust of the earth, and you shall spread abroad to the west and to the east and to the north and to the south.** And in you and in your seed shall all the families of the earth be blessed. And, behold, I *am* with you, and will keep you in every *place* where you go, and will bring you again into this land, for I will not leave you until I have done that which I have spoken of to you'" (vs 12-15). *And he did!*

There was still some chicanery. Jacob got his punishment back for being deceitful and lying. What happened? *Well, he came to Laban and saw Rachel and said, 'This is it, first love, got to have her!'* Made a deal and said to Laban, 'I'll work seven years for her.' He said, 'That's fine, you can have her.'

So, came the wedding night, and I guess they were all wearing burqas then, and lo and behold, when he woke up in the morning and guess who it was? *It was Leah, not Rachel!* He wanted Rachel so bad he said, 'Ok, I'll work another seven years for you.' Laban said, 'That's fine.' So, Jacob had to work 14 years. Jacob had a little deceit brought back upon him for his deceit, and he had to work fourteen years instead of seven.

All the children of Israel were born; you know the rest of the story. They all got jealous of

Joseph. Joseph had quite a bit of vanity and he came out with this coat that his father made him and said, 'Look guys, I had a dream, and I was standing there and I was the main sheaf. And all the sheaves bowed down to me, that's you guys!' So, they got mad.

They and had another dream and got together and said, 'Look, we've got to stop this, let's kill him.' Judah said, 'No, let's sell him. Here's what we'll do, we'll take and kill a goat and take the coat and spread it with the goat's blood. We'll sell Joseph for his 'snotty-nosed' way of doing things. We'll sell him off to the Arabs when they come by.'

They came by, sold him off, and took him down to Egypt and he ended up in prison and he was able to tell the answer to the dreams that different ones had and he was raised to be the second in charge of Egypt because he was able to tell Pharaoh the dream of the seven fat cattle and the seven skinny cattle that a famine was coming.

Joseph was down in Egypt 17 years before the famine came. When the famine came God sent the sons down to get food, and Joseph knew who they were, but they didn't know who he was. Sure enough, the prophecy came true; in order to get the corn they had to bow down and worship him, because he was second in charge.

Remember, in order to get Benjamin—because he remembered Benjamin was his blood brother, through Rachel—he put some things in the sacks of corn. Then he told the Egyptian soldiers, 'Now they have stolen things, it's hidden in the corn, you go out and arrest them and bring them back here.'

They did and he said, 'Now look, you bring your youngest brother down here. Otherwise I'm going to lock you all up in a dungeon.' They said, 'Ok we'll bring him down.' They brought him down, and then finally he revealed himself to them that he was Joseph, and they went back and got Jacob and brought him down. Jacob came in and Pharaoh gave him all the land of Goshen.

Now we come down to the final blessings that we have that were given to the sons of Jacob, or Israel. Gen. 48—here's a blessing that is with us to this day and it cannot fit the circumstances of the Jews today. What occurred here in Gen. 48 and 49 is as momentous for the *physical seed* as the promise given to Abraham for the *spiritual seed!*

Abraham, Isaac and Jacob *knew* that they had a blessing to pass on to their descendants. Jacob's name was changed to Israel and it came time for the blessing to be given. We find that Joseph brought his two sons, Ephraim and Manasseh....

I might mention here that Joseph married the daughter of the high priest of On; and a lot of people think that Joseph married a black woman. *That's not the case!* Egypt, at that time, was much like what the United States is today. It was a diverse society. To say that you married an American today doesn't tell you anything. But in order for the blessing to those of the descendants of Joseph and the descendants of Jacob, he could not have intermarried with a race that was contrary to the genetic inheritance that he had. So, he obviously married someone the same as he was.

Joseph brought both of his sons to him, Genesis 48:13: "And Joseph took them both, Ephraim in his right hand toward Israel's left, and Manasseh in his left toward Israel's right hand. And he brought *them* near to him." *You would think that this just kind of a little detail, but it's very important!*

Verse 14: "And Israel stretched out his right hand and laid *it* upon Ephraim's head, who *was* the younger, and his left upon Manasseh's head, crossing his hands, for Manasseh *was* the firstborn."

Now again, we have the same thing happen. The blessing goes to the younger first, then the older. Whereas through normal inheritance law, what do we have, the firstborn is the one who receives the inheritance.

I'm going through this, even though it doesn't directly relate to the Passover, because we need to understand—and I want to make the record absolutely clear—that the Jews today **do not** represent all the twelve tribes of the children of Israel. The Jews represent *one* tribe, plus a substantial number of Levites. That's all of the true Jews.

You can read the book of *Josephus* and you can see where that in the history—especially during the days of John Hyrcanus the high priest, during the days of the Maccabees and also during the days of Herod the Great—that they forced Esauites to become circumcised Jews and follow the Jewish religion. They are Jews in the sense that they are proselytes. What we are talking about here are *the genetic, physical descendants of Jacob and his twelve sons!*

We have a publication here, that shows how these sons came to be in their modern inheritance today: *America and Britain: Two Nations That Changed the World* by Philip Neal. It's very important concerning Ephraim and Manasseh. Ephraim undoubtedly is what we call Great Britain today, and Manasseh is undoubtedly what we call United States of America today. That is before recent years *when the strangers are coming in to rise up high above us!* Now we're seeing that fulfillment of prophecy because of disobedience.

But, here's the prophecy of the physical seed coming on down now to Ephraim and Manasseh:

When he did this he guided "…his hands, for Manasseh *was* the firstborn. And he blessed Joseph and said, 'May God, *before* Whom my fathers Abraham and Isaac walked, the God Who fed me all my life to this day, the Angel Who has redeemed me from all evil, bless the lads. And let my name be perpetuated in them, and the name of my fathers **Abraham and Isaac**…'" (vs 14-16).

Now, it's important to understand that he did not give that blessing to the rest of his sons. He gave different blessings to them, through they are the descendants of Abraham, Isaac and Jacob, the *special blessing* of nations and power goes primarily to Ephraim and Manasseh was this:

"…and let them grow into a multitude in the midst of the earth.' And Joseph saw that his father laid his right hand upon the head of Ephraim, and it displeased him. And he held up his father's hand to remove it from Ephraim's head to Manasseh's head. And Joseph said to his father, 'Not so, my father, for this *is* the firstborn. Put your right hand upon his head.' And his father refused and said, 'I know *it*, my son, I know *it*. He also shall become a people, and he also shall be great, but truly his younger brother shall be greater than he, and his seed shall become a multitude of nations'" (vs 16-19).

It's not an incidental thing that the British Empire became to be known as the Commonwealth of Nations. It was to share the common wealth; in other words: the money, the gold, the silver, the possessions, the military. That's why it was called the Commonwealth.

Verse 20: "And he blessed them that day, saying, 'In you shall Israel bless, saying, "God make you as Ephraim and as Manasseh."' And he put Ephraim before Manasseh." *That's how it came about!*

Before he died, Genesis 49:1: "And Jacob called to his sons and said, 'Gather yourselves together, that I may tell you what shall happen to you in the last days…. [this gives us an identification of the nations today] …Gather yourselves together and hear, sons of Jacob, and hearken to Israel your father. **Reuben**, you *are* my firstborn, my might, and the beginning of my strength, the excellency of dignity and the excellency of power. **Unstable as water**…" (vs 1-4). *Many people believe that the descendants of Reuben are the French, very possible!*

"…you shall not excel because you went up to your father's bed; then you defiled it. He went up to my couch. **Simeon and Levi** are brothers; tools of violence *are* their weapons" (vs 4-5).

That's why the Simeonites maybe are more involved in Mafia within Israel, and the Levites instruments of cruelty. That's why they were selected for the priesthood and the slaughtering of animals. They can handle it without all of the weeping and wailing and the animal rights boo-hooing.

Verse 6: "Oh my soul, do not come into their council. Let not my honor be united with their assembly, for in their anger they killed a man, and in their self-will they hamstrung oxen. Let their anger be cursed, for *it was* fierce; and their wrath, for it was cruel. I will divide them in Jacob, and scatter them in Israel" (vs 6-7). *That's the way it is in the last days, they're scattered throughout all Israel!*

Verse 8: "**Judah**, may your brothers praise you. May your hand *be* on the neck of your enemies. May your father's sons bow before you. Judah *is* a lion's whelp. My son, you have gone up from the prey. He stooped, he crouched like a lion; and like a lioness, who shall rouse him? The scepter shall not depart from Judah, nor a lawgiver from between his feet, until Shiloh come…. (vs 8-10). *That is Christ, and He came and the disciples then became the lawgivers through the apostles!*

"…And to Him shall be the obedience of the people. Binding His foal to the vine, and His donkey's colt to the choice vine, He washed His garments in wine, and His clothes in the blood of grapes. His eyes are more sparkling than wine, and His teeth are whiter than milk" (vs 10-12).

I think that describes maybe some of the things that are going on in Israel today where the Jews are. All the bloody warring that's going on? *Perhaps!*

Verse 13: "**Zebulun** shall live at the seashore… [many people think this has to do with Holland—could very likely be] …And he *shall be* a haven for ships, and his border beside Sidon. **Issachar** *is* a strong donkey…" (vs 13-14). *Finland today!* It's between the west and the east and they carry a great burden from Russia!

"…crouching down between the sheepfolds. And he saw that rest *was* good and that the land was pleasant. And he bowed his shoulder to bear *a burden*, and became a tribute-servant" (vs 14-15). *The Finnish were under tribute to the Soviet Union for a long time!*

Verse 16: "**Dan** shall judge his people, as one of the tribes of Israel…." *We have two aspects of Dan*:

1. Danmark
2. the Irish that also came from Dan

…Dan shall be a serpent by the way, an adder in the

path that bites the horse's heels, so that its rider shall fall backward. I have waited for Your salvation, O LORD. **Gad**, raiders shall attack him, but he shall overcome at the last" (vs 16-19). *A lot of people think that Gad is Switzerland, that little small country!*

Verse 20: "Out of **Asher** his bread *shall be* rich, and he shall yield royal dainties. [Netherlands] …**Naphtali** *is* a deer let loose. He gives goodly words" (vs 20-21)—*Sweden!*

Now notice Joseph's blessing. This cannot apply to the Jews, v 22: "**Joseph** *is* a fruitful bough…"

Since before WWII and even through the Holocaust and everything, there has never been very many more than 13-15-million Jews worldwide.

"…a fruitful bough by a well, whose branches run over the wall. The archers have fiercely attacked him and have shot *at him*, and hated him…. [we've seen this happen time and time again] …But his bow abode in strength, and the arms of his hands were made strong by the hands of the mighty God of Jacob—from there is the Shepherd, the Stone of Israel—…" (vs 22-24).

That is the great stone that is under the coronation chair, on which they coronate the kings and queens of England. By-the-way, they coronate them as kings and queens over 'your people, Israel.' When you read the whole, the whole ceremony, it's not over Britain, it's not over England, *it's over 'your people, Israel.'* She is coronated in the Jerusalem Room of the Westminster Abbey.

Verse 25: "By the God of your father, Who shall help you. And may the Almighty bless you with blessings of heaven above, blessings of the deep that lies beneath, blessings of the breasts and of the womb. The blessings of your father are greater than the blessings of my ancestors, to the utmost bound of the everlasting hills. They shall be on the head of Joseph, and on the crown of the head of him, the ruler, the leader who was separated from his brothers" (vs 25-26).

That's really quite a blessing! You cannot say that this fits the Jews as we know them today. Remember, this is a prophecy for the last days.

Verse 27: "**Benjamin** is a wolf that tears in pieces…. [a lot of people think that Benjamin today is Norway—from whence we get the Vikings who 'ravened as a wolf'] …In the morning he shall devour the prey, and at night he shall divide the spoil."

Now, before we get into the Passover of Israel, let's see some blessings that were passed on at that time. I'm just going to cover the blessing to Joseph, so we can distinguish Ephraim and Manasseh, the sons of Joseph, from the Jews.

Deuteronomy 33:13: "And of Joseph he said, 'Blessed of the LORD *be* his land, with the precious things of the heavens, for the dew, and for the deep that couches beneath, and for the precious things of the fruits of the sun, and with the precious things of the yield of *the* months. And with the chief things of the ancient mountains, and for the precious things of the everlasting hills" (vs 13-15).

Where has most of the gold and silver and precious jewels come from? *They have come from the descendants of Joseph!* In particularly and primarily South Africa, because South Africa was part of the Commonwealth of Britain, part of the British Empire, too.

Verse 16: "And for the precious things of the earth and fullness of it, and *for* the good will of Him Who dwelt in the bush. Let the blessing come on the head of Joseph, and on the top of the head of him who was separated from his brothers. His glory *is like* the firstborn of his bull, and his horns are like the horns of the wild ox…." (vs 16-17).

Isn't it interesting that both of those things are on the seal that the British have?

"…With them he shall push the people together to the ends of the earth…. [Wasn't it said of the British Empire, 'The sun never set on the British Empire'?] …And they are the ten thousands of Ephraim, and they are the thousands of Manasseh" (v 17). *So, there is the blessing given to the physical seed!*

Now let's come to the book of Exodus, and let's look at the events leading up to the Passover with the children of Israel while they were in Egypt. I wanted to go through and just carry those prophecies forward showing the blessings that would come to children of Israel being all of the twelve tribes, and of whom the ten that were carried off into captivity first, were given the blessing and the fulfillment in the last days.

After Joseph died, then there arose another Pharaoh who didn't know Joseph. He enslaved the children of Israel. He was bent on destroying all the male children of the children of Israel by having them drowned in the river. You know the story of Moses: he was put in the basket, his mother watched it as it went on down, the daughter of Pharaoh found the basket and said, 'This is mine, his name shall be Moses, for he came out of the water.' He was raised in the court of Pharaoh. He was next in line to be Pharaoh, and then God worked it out to reveal that he was really not of the bloodline of, he was not so of Napatri, the daughter of Pharaoh, but he was the son Levi, a Hebrew.

In trying to rescue one of the Hebrews, because of the harsh bondage, he killed an Egyptian, and then he fled into the wilderness. Straight across the Sinai Desert, and he came to Midian. Then he married one of the daughters of Jethro. Then· we ·come to the time when Moses was out there watching the sheep and the time of the 'burning bush.'

We'll summarize the burning bush thing. He went up, and the thing that's important is this: after Moses came up to the burning bush:

Exodus 3:5: "And He said, 'Do not come near here. Put off your sandals from your feet, for the place on which you stand *is* Holy ground.'"

This shows that wherever God is it's Holy. We can also draw a lesson from this concerning the Sabbath. Wherever God puts His presence, that is Holy time. That's why the Sabbath is Holy. We can project that out into the Passover and all the Holy Days, as well! That's why they are called Holy Days, because God puts His presence in it. Wherever God is that is Holy.

Verse 6: "And He said, 'I *am* the God of your fathers, the God of Abraham, the God of Isaac, and the God of Jacob.'...."

That's the point I want to make here, that God is following through on His promises to Abraham, Isaac, and Jacob. Remember, we started out Gen. 15 where He said that his descendants would be 'slaves in a land not their own,' and they would come out with 'great substance.' Then He also tells them what His name is:

Verse 13: "And Moses said to God… [After God said 'I will surely be with you' (v 12)] …'Behold, *when* I come to the children of Israel, and shall say to them, "The God of your fathers has sent me to you," and they shall say to me, "What *is* His name?" What shall I say to them?' And God said to Moses, 'I AM THAT I AM.'...." (vs 13-14).

{note message about Jesus being *I AM That I AM;* about Jesus being the I AM}

Not only does this identify the God of the Old Testament, but it also identifies that the God of the Old Testament is the God of the New Testament.

"…And He said, 'Thus you shall say to the children of Israel, "I AM has sent me to you."' And God said to Moses again, 'You shall say this to the children of Israel, "The LORD God of your fathers, the God of Abraham, the God of Isaac, and the God of Jacob, has sent me to you. This *is* My name forever, and this *is* My title from generation to generation. Go, and gather the elders of Israel…"' (vs 14-16).

Your brother Aaron is going to meet you, and you go deliver the people. They did that. Remember that Jesus said that if you 'do not believe that *I AM* you shall perish in your sins.'

Exodus 4:29: "And Moses and Aaron went and gathered together all the elders of the children of Israel. And Aaron spoke all the words, which the LORD had spoken to Moses, and did the signs in the sight of the people. And the people believed. And when they heard that the LORD had visited the children of Israel, and that He had looked upon their affliction, then they bowed and worshiped" (vs 29-31)—*and went on their way!*

Then here comes the first confrontation between Moses, Aaron and Pharaoh. This is kind of like the Beverly Hillbillies—maybe not quite that bad, but almost—coming into Pharaoh. So, here they come.

Exodus 5:1: "And afterward Moses and Aaron went in and told Pharaoh, 'Thus says the LORD God of Israel, "Let My people go that they may hold a Feast to Me in the wilderness."'"

Can you imagine that! Here are two upstart people walking into the Pharaoh of Egypt saying, 'Let the people go that we can keep the Feast.' Pharaoh was supreme ruler! God raised him up, as he said in the book of Romans, that He raised him up to show His power to *all the earth.* The very fact that it is in the Scriptures and is everywhere around the world, this story is told over and over again as a witness that God is greater than Egypt, and even to this day, testifies that He's greater than Egypt. What was Pharaoh's response?

Verse 2: "And Pharaoh said, **Who is the LORD**, that I should obey His voice to let Israel go? **I do not know the LORD, neither will I let Israel go."** Can you imagine the effrontery that he felt with these two upstarts come in there and tell him to let them go?

Verse 3: "And they said, 'The God of the Hebrews has met with us. Let us go, we pray you, three days' journey into the desert and sacrifice to the LORD our God, lest He fall upon us with plague or with the sword.' And the king of Egypt said to them, 'Moses and Aaron, why do you keep the people from their work? Get to your burdens!'…. [not going to hear it] …And Pharaoh said, 'Behold, the people of the land now *are* many, and you make them rest from their burdens'" (vs 3-5).

Rest means to 'sabbathize.' Here we have the Sabbath in the land Egypt *long before* they get to Mt. Sinai. Of course, they didn't understand it. What did Pharaoh do?

Verse 6: "And Pharaoh commanded the taskmasters of the people and their officers the same day, saying, 'You shall no more give the people straw to make brick, as before. Let them go and gather straw for themselves. And you shall lay upon them the *same* number of bricks, which they have made before. You shall not reduce it, for they are idle; therefore they cry, saying, "Let us go sacrifice to our God." Let more work be laid upon the men, and let them labor in it. And do not let them regard vain words'" (vs 6-9).

So, they went out and did that. The people of Israel were expecting to be let go just like that, at the snap of a finger. Things didn't work out the way they wanted and it came down just the opposite of what they expected.

Lesson: *Just because it doesn't work out the first time doesn't mean God doesn't mean what He says. He has other things in mind!*

Then what happened? They came and they told Moses, they said, 'Look! This is getting worse. We're not being let go.' So, Moses and Aaron went back to Pharaoh.

Here's what the people said, v 20: "And they met Moses and Aaron standing in the way, as they came forth from Pharaoh. And they said to them, 'The LORD look upon you and judge because you have made us offensive in the eyes of Pharaoh, and in the eyes of his servants, to put a sword in their hands to kill us.' And Moses returned to the LORD, and said... [even Moses didn't believe at this point] ...'LORD, why have You treated this people ill? Why then have you sent me?" (vs 20-22).

Moses was even questioning, 'What am I doing here, Lord I went and said *let them go* and he didn't let them go. What do You want me to do?'

Verse 23: "For since I came to Pharaoh to speak in Your name, he has done evil to this people. Neither have You delivered Your people at all." *God gave them the answer. He said, 'Wait, Moses, I've got a plan.'*

Exodus 6:1: And the LORD said to Moses, 'Now you shall see what I will do to Pharaoh; for with a **strong hand** he shall let them go, and with a **strong hand** he shall drive them out of his land.' And God spoke to Moses, and said to him, 'I am the LORD. And I appeared to Abraham, to Isaac, and to Jacob *as* God Almighty [El Shaddai] But I was not known to them *by* My name JEHOVAH'" (vs 1-3).

So, that's the covenant name of God for the Old Covenant—JEHOVAH. He says, 'I'm going to release them.' Let's see when God gets down to business what happens. In this account, we're going to find the signs and then the plagues. Notice what God said:

Exodus 7:1: "And the LORD said to Moses, 'See, I have made you a god to Pharaoh. And Aaron your brother shall be your prophet. You shall speak all that I command you. And Aaron your brother shall speak to Pharaoh that he send the children of Israel out of his land. And I will harden Pharaoh's heart and multiply My signs and My wonders in the land of Egypt. But Pharaoh shall not hearken to you, and I will lay My hand upon Egypt, and bring My armies, My people the children of Israel, out of the land of Egypt by great judgments. And **the Egyptians shall know that I** *am* **the LORD when I stretch forth My hand upon Egypt,** and bring out the children of Israel from among them.' And Moses and Aaron did as the LORD commanded them; so they did. And Moses *was* eighty years old, and Aaron *was* eighty-three years old, when they spoke to Pharaoh" (vs 1-7). *You talk about an old church!*

THE SIGNS

1. Snakes from rods!

Moses and Aaron go in, and the Lord said, v 9: "When Pharaoh shall speak to you saying, 'Give a miracle for yourselves,' you shall say to Aaron, 'Take your rod, and throw *it* in front of Pharaoh. It shall become a snake.'" *This is important because they were serpent-worshippers there!*

Verse 10: "And Moses and Aaron went in to Pharaoh. And they did so as the LORD had commanded. And Aaron threw down his rod in front of Pharaoh and in front of his servants, and it became a snake. Then Pharaoh also called the wise men and the sorcerers. And they, the priests of Egypt, did the same with their secret arts" (vs 10-11). *There are **false** miracles and there are things that Satan can do to make it **look like** it's the hand of God.*

Verse 12: "For each man threw down his rod, and they became snakes... [here's a snake fight right out in the middle of it] ...but Aaron's rod swallowed up their rods. And He hardened Pharaoh's heart so that he did not hearken to them, as the LORD had said" (vs 12-13).

2. Blood from water!

Then we have the next sign: blood being made from water. The Egyptians worshipped the Nile. It was a like a god, and that's why they had crocodile gods, frog gods and so forth. So, Moses went out there and stretched forth his rod.

Verse 20: "And Moses and Aaron did so, as the LORD commanded. And he lifted up the rod and struck the waters that *were* in the river, in the sight of Pharaoh... [right in front of him] ...and in the sight of his servants. And all the waters in the river were turned to blood. And the fish in the river died; and the river stank, and the Egyptians could not drink of the water of the river. And there was blood throughout all the land of Egypt. And the priests of Egypt did so with their secret arts. And Pharaoh's heart was hardened, and he did not hearken to them, as the LORD had said" (vs 20-22). *After the seven days were fulfilled then they were able to drink the water!*

I think the movie *The Ten Commandments* did a really good job in showing this; really portrayed it. That was one of the good movies that they made. Of course, it was made years ago; Cecile B. DeMille produced it, I think it was in the 50s and it's a classic. Every year about Passover time they always play the full version of *The Ten Commandments*.

3. Frogs!

If you've ever seen Egyptian frogs you will know these are not just the little pestilential things, but these are huge, about the size of a big head. I just want you to picture this: *the land filled with frogs!* Here's what's going to happen:

Exodus 8:1: "And the LORD spoke to Moses, 'Go to Pharaoh, and say to him, "Thus says the LORD, 'Let My people go so that they may serve Me. And if you refuse to let *them* go, behold, I *am* going to strike all your country *with* frogs. And the river shall bring forth frogs abundantly which shall go up and come into your house, and into your bedroom, and upon your bed, and into the house of your servants, and upon your people, and into your ovens, and into your kneading troughs. And the frogs shall come upon you, and upon your people, and upon all your servants'"'" (vs 1-4).

They stretched out the rod and *all these frogs started coming out of the river!* Imagine all the sound that goes with it; all of the croaking and so forth. The magicians did the same thing and they brought up frogs. Three times the magicians were able to counterfeit the miracle of God.

Now, this got to Pharaoh for a little bit, v 8: "And Pharaoh called for Moses and Aaron, and said, 'Pray to the LORD that He may take away the frogs from me and from my people. And I will let the people go, so that they may sacrifice to the LORD.' And Moses said to Pharaoh, 'I give to you the honor—when shall I pray for you, and for your servants, and for your people, to destroy the frogs from you and your houses so *that* they may remain in the river only?' And he said, 'Tomorrow.' And he said, 'It shall be according to your word **so that you may know that *there is* none like the LORD our God**'" (vs 8-10).

So they departed. His heart was hardened. God has a way of doing things that really gets your attention.

4. Lice!

Verse 16: "And the LORD said to Moses, 'Say to Aaron, "Stretch out your rod, and strike the dust of the land, so that it may become lice **throughout all the land of Egypt**."'".... [Have you ever had lice?] ...And they did so, for Aaron stretched out his hand with his rod and struck the dust of the earth and it became lice in man and in beast. All the dust of the land became lice **throughout all the land of Egypt**. And the priests did so with their secret arts to bring forth lice, but they could not. So there were lice upon man and upon beast. And the priests said to Pharaoh, **'This *is* the finger of God.'** And Pharaoh's heart was hardened, and he did not hearken to them, as the LORD had said" (vs 16-19).

I wonder how they got rid of the lice? *Who knows!* It doesn't say that they removed them. It doesn't say how long they endured, but I tell you what, they must have had a lice-killing program there, you know: crushing them; killing them; combing them out of the hair; cleaning out all of the beds; cleaning off all the clothes; sweeping out the house; putting them up in buckets and burning them. You know, you'd almost have a picture how this went on. It doesn't tell us how long this went on.

5. Flies!

Have you ever been bothered by a fly? Imagine *swarms* of them. Have you ever seen pictures of people in Africa and their cows with all of these big huge flies? Well, just keep that in mind when we read this here:

Verse 20: "And the LORD said to Moses, 'Rise up early in the morning and stand before Pharaoh. Lo, he comes forth to the water....'"

Every day it was the obligation of Pharaoh to go to the river, because he was representative of God in their pagan religion, and he would be there at sunrise.

So God says: "...And say to him, "Thus says the LORD, 'Let My people go, so that they may serve Me.... [Pharaoh probably thought: *we just got rid of the lice! You're here again!*] ...And if you will not let My people go, behold, I will send swarms *of flies* on you, and on your servants, and on your people, and into your house. And the houses of the Egyptians shall be full of swarms *of flies*, and also the ground on which they *are*. And in that day I will cut off the land of Goshen, in which My people live, so that no swarms *of flies* shall be there, so that you may know that I *am* the LORD in the midst of the earth. And I will put a dividing line between My people and your people. This sign shall be tomorrow.'"" And the LORD did so. And teeming swarms *of flies* came into the house of Pharaoh, and into his servants' houses, and into all the land of Egypt. The land was ruined because of the swarms" (vs 20-24).

The children of Israel suffered the first four so they would understand that God is behind it, to let them know that *they better listen to God* and not do as Pharaoh.

It didn't take long for Pharaoh to react this time. When you have just one fly doing it's little square flight pattern right in front of you. And you kind of sit there and wait for it to land on you, all you do is slap your face real hard. Or there's a fly that's coming down on your food.

Imagine *swarms* of flies, just crawling everywhere, just all over your hair, all over your arms, all over the walls. You can't even walk across the room without squishing the flies that are there. And they're into the cupboards and they're eating everything and everything is dirty, and there would have to be fly-dung *everywhere!* I mean let's look at this as realistic as how it happened!

Verse 25: "And Pharaoh called for Moses and for Aaron, and said, 'Go sacrifice to your God in the land.'"

'I'm not going to let you go out, you do it in the land, I'll go half-way.' So much with common ground.

Verse 26: "And Moses said, 'It is not right to do so, for we shall sacrifice the abomination of the Egyptians to the LORD our God. Lo, shall we sacrifice the abomination of the Egyptians before their eyes, and will they not stone us?'"

No! They were probably animal-worshippers. You know, just like the Indians in India today. The Hindus worship cows. If a miracle happens with a cow, they run and they gather the urine and they gather the dung so they can put it on themselves and wipe themselves with the manure and they can anoint themselves with the urine. If the children of Israel are out there sacrificing the cattle and the sheep they would really raise a big stink. So, Moses said:

Verse 27: "We will go three days' journey into the wilderness, and sacrifice to the LORD our God, as He shall command us.' And Pharaoh said, 'I will let you go so that you may sacrifice to the LORD your God in the wilderness. Only you shall not go very far away. Pray for me.' And Moses said, 'Behold, I will go out from you, and I will pray to the LORD that the swarms *of flies* may depart from Pharaoh, from his servants, and from his people, tomorrow. But do not let Pharaoh deal deceitfully any more in not letting the people go to sacrifice to the LORD.' And Moses went out from Pharaoh and prayed to the LORD. And the LORD did according to the word of Moses. And He removed the swarms *of flies* from Pharaoh, from his servants, and from his people. There remained not one" (vs 27-31).

If you were an Egyptian and all these flies came in one day and they bothered you for ever how many days they had the flies, and then all of sudden one day, they're gone. You'd begin to think that Moses and Aaron had contact with God, the Greater Power than the sorcerers and magicians.

Verse 32: "And Pharaoh hardened his heart at this time also, **neither would he let the people go**."

6. Boils!

Exodus 9:1: "And the LORD said to Moses, 'Go in to Pharaoh and tell him, "Thus says the LORD God of the Hebrews, 'Let My people go so that they may serve Me, for if you refuse to let *them* go, and will still hold them *back*, behold, the hand of the LORD is upon your livestock in the field, upon the horses, upon the donkeys, upon the camels, upon the oxen, and upon the sheep, a very grievous plague…. [*boils and blains*] …And the LORD shall separate between the livestock of Israel and the livestock of Egypt. And there shall nothing die of all *that belongs* to the children of Israel"'" (vs 1-4).

God was also demonstrating to the children of Israel. The thing is they didn't remember these things. By time they got seven days out of Egypt to the Red Sea, they were complaining to God already. Many times—and this is a lesson for us—we need to *remember the things that God has done* and not be complaining to God for the things He hasn't yet done.

Verse 5: "And the LORD appointed a set time, saying, 'Tomorrow the LORD shall do this thing in the land.'…. [He did it] …And the LORD did that thing on the next day, and all the *livestock in the field* of Egypt died. But of the livestock of the children of Israel, not one died…. [Pharaoh's getting desperate here] …And Pharaoh sent, and, behold, there was not one of the livestock of the Israelites dead. And the heart of Pharaoh was hardened, and he did not let the people go" (vs 5-7).

All right, so he put 'murrain,' which is *boils and blains,* upon the cattle and they died. Then we have the seventh sign. Now it's going to come on the people.

Verse 8: "And the LORD said to Moses and Aaron, 'Take to yourselves handfuls of ashes of the furnace, and let Moses sprinkle it toward the sky in the sight of Pharaoh. And it shall become small dust in all the land of Egypt, and it shall become a boil breaking forth *with* sores upon man and upon beast… [that's the remainder of the beasts]

…throughout all the land of Egypt.' And they took ashes of the furnace and stood before Pharaoh. And Moses sprinkled it up toward the sky, and they became boils breaking forth *with* sores upon man and upon beast. And the priests could not stand before Moses because of the boils, for the boils were upon the priests and upon all the Egyptians" (vs 8-11).

Now, *one boil* really lays you low. The worst kind of boil is called a *carbuncle!* That is painful! I don't know if they were covered from head-to-toe with boils—like Job was—but what a sight that must have been.

Verse 12: "And the LORD hardened the heart of Pharaoh, and he did not hearken to them, even as the LORD had spoken to Moses. And the LORD said to Moses, 'Rise up early in the morning, and stand before Pharaoh, and say to him, "Thus says the LORD God of the Hebrews, 'Let My people go, so that they may serve Me; for I *am* going to send at this time all My plagues upon your heart, and upon your servants, and upon your people, **so that you may know that *there is* none like Me in all the earth**'"'" (vs 12-14).

THE PLAGUES

Now we get the plagues! The *signs* were bad enough. Here we have the whole purpose of Pharaoh.

Verse 15: "For now I will stretch out My hand, that I may strike you and your people with plagues, and you shall be cut off from the earth. And for this very purpose I have *raised you up*, to show My power *against* you, and that My name may be declared throughout all the earth. Do you still exalt yourself against My people that you will not let them go? Behold, tomorrow about this time I will cause it to rain a very grievous hail, *such as* has not been in Egypt since the foundation of it, even until now!" (vs 15-18).

And he said, 'Whatever are left of the cattle you get them out of there, get them under cover because they're going to die.' And that's what happened!

7. Hail!

Verse 22: "And the LORD said to Moses, 'Stretch forth your hand toward heaven, so that there may be hail in all the land of Egypt… [Can you imagine the weather reports today if there were snow in Cairo? I mean, just snow!] …upon man, and upon beast, and upon every herb of the field, throughout the land of Egypt.' And Moses stretched forth his rod toward the heavens. And the LORD sent thunder and hail, and the fire came down to the ground. And the LORD rained hail upon the land of Egypt. And

there was hail, and fire mingled with the hail, very grievous, such as there was none like it in all the land of Egypt since it became a nation. And the hail struck throughout all the land of Egypt, all that *was* in the field, both man and beast. And the hail struck every herb of the field, and broke every tree of the field. Only in the land of Goshen, where the children of Israel *were*, was there no hail" (vs 22-26).

This time Pharaoh kind of almost got the point. I mean, what does it take to get people's attention?

Verse 27: "And Pharaoh sent and called for Moses and Aaron, and said to them, 'I have sinned *this* time. The LORD *is* righteous, and I and my people are wicked. Pray to the LORD, *for it is* enough. Let there be no *more* mighty thunderings and hail. And I will let you go, and you shall stay no longer'" (vs 27-28).

I tell you what, after you hear hail and see lightning and hear the thunder, and have that stacking up, and you're used to this warm climate. Can you imagine what all this hail and ice is going to do? It's going to drop the temperature. You don't have any clothes for cold weather. There you are, hail all around. Man! But he still didn't quite get it.

Verse 34: "And when Pharaoh saw that the rain and the hail and the thunders had ceased, he sinned still more and hardened his heart, he and his servants."

God said, 'I'm going to bring another plague. By time all of this is done, there is virtually nothing left in Egypt.

Exodus 10:1: "And the LORD said to Moses, 'Go in to Pharaoh, for I have hardened his heart and the heart of his servants so that I might show these My signs before him, and so that you may tell in the ears of your son, and of your son's sons, what things I have wrought in Egypt, and My signs which I have done among them…'" (vs 1-2).

We are to read and go through these things to know that it was *the hand of God that did it!*

"'…so that you may know that I *am* the LORD.' And Moses and Aaron came in to Pharaoh and said to him, 'Thus says the LORD God of the Hebrews, "How long will you refuse to humble yourself before Me? Let My people go so that they may serve Me; for if you refuse to let My people go, behold, tomorrow I will bring the locusts into your country. And they shall cover the face of the ground so that one cannot be able to see the earth. And they shall eat the rest of that which has escaped, which remains to you from the hail, and shall eat every tree which grows for you out of the field. And they shall fill your houses, and the houses of all your servants, and the houses of all the Egyptians, which neither your fathers, nor your fathers' fathers have seen, since the day they were upon the earth until this day. And he turned himself and went out from Pharaoh.'" And Pharaoh's servants said to him, 'How long shall this man be a snare to us? Let the men go so that they may serve the LORD their God. **Do you not yet know that Egypt is destroyed?**'" (vs 2-7).

Verse 8: "And Moses and Aaron were brought again to Pharaoh, and he said to them, 'Go! Serve the LORD your God. Who *are* the ones that shall go?' And Moses said, 'We will go with our young and with our old, with our sons and with our daughters. We will go with our flocks and with our herds; for we *must hold* a Feast to the LORD.' And he said to them, 'Let the LORD be with you, for if I ever let you go with your little ones, watch out, for you have some evil purpose in mind. Not so! Go now **you men**... [just the men—'I'm only going to let the men go'] ...and serve the LORD, for it is you who did desire it.' And they were driven out from Pharaoh's presence" (vs 8-11).

8. Locust!

Then what happened? *Moses went out, raised his rod and locust came!* Covered the land! And I don't imagine they were itty-bitty things. I bet they were *huge, giant, devouring things;* they ate everything!

Verse 15: "For they covered the face of the whole ground so that the land was darkened, and they ate every herb of the land and all the fruit of the trees which the hail had left. And there did not remain any green thing in the trees, or in the herbs of the field, through all the land of Egypt.... [here's *worldly repentance*]: ...Then Pharaoh called for Moses and Aaron in haste. And he said, 'I have sinned against the LORD your God, and against you. Now therefore, I beg you, forgive my sin only this once, and pray to the LORD your God that He may take away from me this death only'" (vs 15-17).

So, they went out and did it. When they were gone Pharaoh's heart was hardened.

9. Darkness!

Here comes another plague and this is quite a plague. You kind of really have to imagine this:

Verse 21: "And the LORD said to Moses, 'Stretch out your hand toward the heavens, that there may be darkness over the land of Egypt, so that one may even **feel the darkness**.' And Moses stretched forth his hand toward heaven. And there was a thick darkness in all the land of Egypt three days" (vs 21-22). *They could feel it!*

It would be kind of like this: Have you ever been in a room with all the doors shut and you turn out the light and you can't see anything.

Verse 23: "They did not see one another, nor did any rise from his place, *for* **three days**. But all the children of Israel had light in their dwellings." *Pharaoh really had it this time!*

Verse 24: "And Pharaoh called for Moses, and said, 'You go serve the LORD. Only let your flocks and your herds be left.... ['All of our cattle are killed, we want yours.'] ...Let your little ones also go with you.' And Moses said, 'You must give us also sacrifices and burnt offerings so that we may sacrifice to the LORD our God. Our livestock also shall go with us. There shall not be a hoof left behind, for we must take from them to serve the LORD our God. And we do not know *with* what we must serve the LORD until we come there.' But the LORD hardened Pharaoh's heart, and he would not let them go" (vs 24-27). *This kind of sounds like the last stand of Hitler! Very similar to it!*

Verse 28: "And Pharaoh said to him, 'Get away from me! Take heed to yourself! **See my face no more**... ['I'm so important, you better not come in my presence and see my face anymore!] ...for in the day you see my face you shall die.' And Moses said, '**You have spoken well. I will never see your face again**'" (vs 24-29).

10. Death of the firstborn!

Exodus 11:1: "And the LORD had said to Moses, 'I will yet bring one plague on Pharaoh...'" The fourth plague, and this one is going to be the most devastating of all, v 1: "And the LORD had said to Moses, 'I will yet bring one plague on Pharaoh and on Egypt. Afterward, he will let you go from here. When he shall let you go, he shall surely thrust you out from here altogether. Speak now in the ears of the people, and let every man ask... [this was spoiling] ...from his neighbor, and every woman from her neighbor, articles of silver and jewels of gold'" (vs 1-2).

I imagine they were so frightened and fearful that when the children of Israel went up and said, 'I want your gold and I want your silver,' they said, 'Here!' Lest they die and more plagues come upon them.

Verse 3: "And the LORD gave the people favor in the sight of the Egyptians. And the man Moses *was* very great in the land of Egypt, in the sight of Pharaoh's servants, and in the sight of the people."

Remember, at the beginning in Exo. 7 he says, 'I have made you **a god**' to Pharaoh.

Verse 4: "And Moses said, 'Thus says the LORD, "**About midnight**... [We'll see that's the 14th day of the 1st month] ...I will go out into the

Scriptures from *The Holy Bible in Its Original Order, A Faithful Version*

midst of Egypt. And all the firstborn in the land of Egypt shall die, from the firstborn of Pharaoh that sits upon his throne, even to the firstborn of the slave-girl that *is* behind the mill; also the firstborn of beasts"'" (vs 4-5). *That is whichever ones are left alive!*

Verse 6: "And there shall be a great cry throughout all the land of Egypt, such as there was none like it, nor shall be like it any more. But against any of the children of Israel not even a dog shall move his tongue, against man or beast, so that you may know that the LORD puts a difference *between* the Egyptians and Israel" (vs 11:6-7).

Let's understand something here concerning the Church: *God has put a difference between His people and the world*; a very big difference! *You are the people of God; you represent God and all that He is to everyone else in the world that comes in contact with you!* That's very important to understand. God has called you to be in His Kingdom.

Therefore, that's why He says we're not to be part of the world. We're *in* the world, but we're not *of* the world. Just like there could be no compromise with the children of Israel with the Egyptians in their dealings with God. So, *He puts a difference!*

Verse 8: "And all these, your servants, shall come down to me and bow themselves down to me, saying, "You and all the people that follow you—get out!" And after that I will go out.' And he went out from Pharaoh **in flaming anger.**"

What a witness to Pharaoh. He says, 'You get out of here and don't see my face anymore' and Moses just said all these words and *then left in great anger!*

Verse 9: "And the LORD said to Moses, 'Pharaoh shall not hearken to you so that My wonders may be multiplied in the land of Egypt.' And Moses and Aaron did all these wonders before Pharaoh. And the LORD hardened Pharaoh's heart so that he would not let the children of Israel go out of his land" (vs 9-10).

The reason God did that was to show the children of Israel that:

- He was God
- He alone could deliver them
- He alone would fight their battles and overcome them

IF they trusted in Him they would be released from their slavery!

Now we come to Exo. 12 and the Passover and we will continue in part 3 with the Passover and the children of Israel!

Scriptural References:

1) Genesis 22:15-18
2) Genesis 26:1-5
3) Galatians 4:28-31
4) Genesis 27:18-41
5) Genesis 28:1-4, 12-15
6) Genesis 48:13-20
7) Genesis 49:1-27
8) Deuteronomy 33:13-17
9) Exodus 3:5-6, 13
10) Exodus 4:29-31
11) Exodus 5:1-9, 20-23
12) Exodus 6:1-3
13) Exodus 7:1-7, 9-13, 20-22
14) Exodus 8:1-4, 8-10, 16-32
15) Exodus 9:1-18, 22-28, 34
16) Exodus 10:1-11, 15-17, 21-29
17) Exodus 11:1-10

Scripture referenced, not quoted:

- Matthew 13:43
- Galatians 3
- Genesis 15
- Exodus 3:12

Also referenced:

Books:

- *Josephus*
- *America and Britain: Two Nations That Changed the World* by Philip Neal

Message: *I AM That I AM*

FRC:ms
Transcribed: 1-17-07
Reformatted: bo—10/2020

CHAPTER FIFTEEN

The Passover:
Abraham, Isaac, Israel and Christ III

Fred R. Coulter

Let's come to Exo. 12 and pick up where we left off last time and cover concerning the Passover with Israel; their *first* Passover. Many of the details, as you know, have been written in the book *The Christian Passover,* which covers all the technicalities that we have concerning:

- between the evenings or between the setting times
- between sunset and dark
- sunset and morning

I won't go into those in great detail. I will just mention them as we come to them so we have a greater understanding of it and then we will go through Exo. 16 just to really show beyond any shadow of doubt how God uses the terms:

- at even
- between the evenings
- 'ben ha arbayim' meaning from sunset to dark

Let's begin with the instructions that Moses gave to Israel for the Passover in Egypt:

Exodus 12:3: "Speak to all the congregation of Israel, saying, 'In the tenth day of this month they shall take to them each man a lamb for a father's house, a lamb for a house. And if the household is too little for the lamb, let him and his neighbor next to his house take according to the number of the souls, each one, according to the eating of his mouth, you shall count concerning the lamb. **Your lamb shall be without blemish**…'" (vs 3-5)—*a type of Christ!*

"…a male of the first year. You shall take *it* from the **sheep or from the goats**. And you shall keep it up until the *beginning* of the fourteenth day of the same month…" (vs 5-6)—*until the beginning of it,* which is at sunset of the 13th when the sun goes down, then it is the 14th day.

"…And the whole assembly of the congregation of Israel shall kill it between the two evenings" (v 6).

Everett Fox—*The Schocken Bible: The Five Books of Moses*—translates it as *between the setting times,* and the Hebrew is 'ben ha arbayim,' which means between sunset and dark. So *between the two evenings* is another rendering of it, meaning that there is the first evening being sunset and then the second evening being dark.

Here is what they were to do and we will see the reason for it. We need to understand something very important here concerning the Passover as it was with Israel, and then let's look at the Passover when we come to the one with Christ and then for us, because it has great significance and it shows God's mercy, kindness and goodness in many, many ways.

Verse 7: "And they shall take of the blood and strike *it* on the two side posts and upon the upper doorpost of the houses *in* which they shall eat it. And they shall eat the flesh in that night, roasted with fire, and unleavened *bread*…." (vs 7-8).

Now let's understand something very simple: *the entire Passover Day is an unleavened bread day!* That is a *one-day* Feast, as we will see. The Feast of Unleavened Bread for *seven days* is a Feast that follows the Passover.

There is nowhere that you can find in the Scriptures at all anywhere that it was allowable to eat leavened bread on the day portion of the Passover. Nowhere can you find that the Israelites did that, because at sunrise, they left their houses and assembled at Rameses. Let's understand that there were no McDonalds on the way. You see they didn't eat any leavened bread on the day portion of the Passover. Now we can be for sure that they were to eat it with unleavened bread, that is the Passover, that they didn't have any leaven in their houses. It was to be destroyed.

"…They shall eat it with *bitter* herbs. Do not eat of it raw, nor boiled at all with water, but roasted *with* fire, its head with its legs, and with its inward parts" (vs 8-9—*the heart and the liver and the kidneys* were put back into the cavity from where they took out the innards.

Verse 10: "And you shall not let any of it remain until the morning. And that which remains of it until the morning you shall burn with fire."

They were to eat it that night! Anything that was left they couldn't leave it until morning, but they should burn it with fire. God had a specific reason and purpose for doing that.

1. it was total destruction of the Passover lamb or kid
2. the children of Israel could not take a tooth, a bone or a hoof as a good luck charm from the Passover lamb or kid

God wanted it totally destroyed!

Now you can read in *The Christian Passover* book that we actually went through and found out how long it would take to burn all the skin, the intestines, the bones and so forth in fire. It took quite a while to burn it to ashes, and it also helped substantiate that they didn't leave their houses until morning.

Verse 11: "And this is the way you shall eat it: *with* your loins girded, your sandals on your feet, and your staff in your hand. And you shall eat it in **trepidation**...."—*haste (KJV)* is an unfortunate translation, because that gives people who believe in the 15th Passover the impression that they were to eat it in haste and hurry up and leave as soon as they ate it.

Well if they did that, they had no opportunity to burn what was left, and it takes quite a few hours to burn all of those bones especially the teeth. What we are dealing with here is that the Hebrew means you shall eat it in trepidation, because of all the events that would take place, *not in haste!* Of course, if you are eating it in trepidation, the chances are you are going to eat it quite quickly too, *but not in haste so that you can hurry and leave!*

"...**it** *is* **the LORD'S Passover**" (v 11). That's what's important to understand, brethren, *it's not the Jews' Passover.*

What we do is the Christian Passover as Jesus modified the instructions in the New Testament. Never was this the Jews' Passover. *It is the LORD'S Passover,* and here's why:

Verse 12: "For I will pass through the land of Egypt this night... [we know that it was midnight] ...and will smite all the firstborn in the land of Egypt, both man and beast. And I will execute judgment against all the gods of Egypt. I *am* the LORD."

This becomes profound and important when we understand that God has judged all the pagan religions and gods of this world in this Passover, *and for us with the Passover of Christ!* This tells us that we should not go out and combine any of the things of the religions of this world—be it Judaism, be it mainstream Christianity, or whatever—into any of the practices that we do because God has already judged them, no doubt about it.

That's why later He told the children of Israel that they were not to add anything or take away from what He gave them. They were not to go to the people of the land and say 'How do you worship your gods, and this is a good idea and let's do so unto our God.' God said, *'You shall not do so unto the LORD your God!'* So, there is a specific reason for judging the gods of Egypt, and that is to show that:

- they are not God
- they are impotent
- they have no power
- they are the imaginations of men and demons
- they are inspired by Satan the devil
- *they have nothing to do with the true God*
- *they have nothing to do with making life right*

But only having to do to keep people in the captivity, in the bondage of sin to Satan the devil and his ways!

We need to understand that and apply that to also the Christian Passover, and the New Testament, and the New Covenant and what we are to do.

Verse 13: "And the blood shall be a sign to you upon the houses where you *are*. And when I see the blood, I will pass over you...."

This is a type of the blood of Christ. His blood causes God to pass over our sins, so we have the remission of sins that are passed. *And He says:*

"...And the plague shall not be upon you to destroy *you* when I smite the land of Egypt" (v 13).

Let's understand something here concerning the blood and the firstborn: *the firstborn of all the children of Israel—man and beast—were spared, because of the blood that they put on the doorposts and the lintels.* So, the firstborn became a tremendous blessing to all the children of God. Whereas, the firstborn of Egypt, man and beast, became a tremendous curse because God executed His judgment not only against the gods, but against the firstborn, and this literally destroyed Egypt. By the time the children of Israel left Egypt beginning the next night, Egypt was left in destruction; there was hardly anything left. The pride and power of Egypt had been absolutely broken with the death of the firstborn of man and beast.

Now let's understand something for us. There is something that we need to realize, and we need to understand in all humility, in all understanding of God's Word, with thanksgiving, but not to get us all lifted up, not to make us feel as though we are superior to other people, because we are not. But just as the sparing of the firstborn for the children of Israel in Egypt was a blessing. Then that blessing extended to all the rest of the children of Israel who were not the firstborn; but also we have a parallel here, because we are the firstfruits and we are *the Church of the Firstborn*.

Hebrews 12:22: "But you have come to Mount Sion, and to *the* city of *the* living God, heavenly Jerusalem; and to an innumerable company of angels; *to the* joyous festival gathering; and to *the* __Church__ *of the* __Firstborn__…" (vs 22-23).

So, just like the firstborn being spared during the Passover that the children of Israel had in Egypt, so likewise, *the firstborn who are right now begotten and those who have the Spirit of God and living today are a blessing to this entire world!*

The world doesn't know that, but we need to take that with all humility and understanding and thankfulness because of God's mercy and love. It shows His mercy, not any greatness that we could attribute to ourselves, but just in the same manner that God destroyed the firstborn in Egypt and executed His judgment against __all__ the gods of Egypt.

Likewise in our lives in the things that we do, all the ways of the world, that's why Paul said, 'The world is crucified unto me.' When we come to the Passover we need to understand that that needs to be our attitude, in gratefulness and thanksgiving for what God has done. This ought to give us a lot of inspiration, encouragement, strength and power in the Spirit of God to do His will.

Exodus 12:14: "And this day shall be a memorial to you. And you shall keep it a Feast to the LORD throughout your generations. You shall keep it __a Feast as a Law forever__."

That's what we are to do, and it is a memorial. *The Passover is a memorial,* and that's why when we come to the New Testament, Jesus said, '***Do this in remembrance of Me.***'

Now then, we come to the Feast of Unleavened Bread, because the Feast of Unleavened Bread follows immediately the next day.

Verse 15: "You shall eat unleavened *bread* seven days; even the first day you shall __*have* put away__ leaven out of your houses…"—*past tense!*

Everett Fox in *The Schocken Bible* translates it: "You shall have already…" *or* "already on the first day…" that is as the first day comes.

"…you shall __*have* put away__ leaven out of your houses…" (v 15)—meaning that *by time the first day comes,* you *shall have put away* leaven from your houses. It has to be out and gone!

Then the Passover Day being an unleavened bread day—the whole day—and that's why I have in

The Christian Passover book what Josephus wrote, that 'we observe the Feast for eight days of Unleavened Bread.'

That does not mean that we are having a Feast of Unleavened Bread for eight days, it means that we have two Feasts:

1. a memorial Feast of the Passover, which is unleavened bread
2. continuing seven days of the Feast of Unleavened Bread

Both of these Feasts have different meanings, which we will see! That's why they are both unleavened, but we will see the meaning of it in just a minute.

Verse 16: "And in the first day *there shall be* a Holy convocation, and in the seventh day there shall be a Holy convocation for you. No manner of work shall be done in them, except that which every man must eat, that only may be done by you."

So whatever work is *necessary* on a Holy Day, whatever is necessary to provide the meal because it's a Feast day, you go right ahead and do it.

Verse 17: "And you shall keep the *Feast of Unleavened Bread*… [here is the reason for the Feast of Unleavened Bread] …for in this very same day I have brought your armies out of the land of Egypt. Therefore, you shall keep this day… [the first day of the Feast of Unleavened Bread] …in your generations as a law forever."

The meaning of the Feast of Unleavened Bread is when God brought the children of Israel out of the land of Egypt, *at least it was the beginning of it,* and that's why we have The Night to be Much Remembered. We have already covered that in the part that we did with Abraham.

Verse 18: "In the first *month*, on the fourteenth day of the month __at sunset__… [Hebrew 'ba erev,' which means *at sunset* and sunset of the 14th begins the 15th] …You shall eat unleavened bread, until the twenty-first day of the month __at sunset__"—*which ends the 21st day and begins the 22nd day! So, you have the seven complete days!*

Verse 19: "Seven days there shall be no leaven found in your houses, for whoever eats that which is leavened, even that soul shall be cut off from the congregation of Israel, whether he be a stranger, or born in the land. You shall eat nothing leavened. In all your dwelling places you shall eat unleavened bread" (vs 19-20).

That is clear as can be! Therefore, for seven days we will do as God has said and we will eat unleavened bread. During the Feast of Unleavened Bread as we know from the New Testament, leaven is a type of sin, a type of human nature that sours and puffs up.

Verse 21: "Then Moses called for all the elders of Israel and said to them..." [he is giving them the detailed instructions]: ...'Draw out and take a lamb for yourselves according to your families, and kill the Passover *lamb*. And you shall take a bunch of hyssop and dip in the blood *that is* in the bowl, and strike the lintel and the two side posts with the blood in the bowl. And none of you shall go out of the door of his house until **sunrise**'" (vs 21-22).

Everett Fox translates it (*SB*): "Now you are not to go out, any man from the entrance to his house, until daybreak."

That's why the blood was put on the lintels and the side posts—to show that *they were not to go out of the entrance of their house, the door of his house until daybreak!*

Verse 23: "For the LORD will pass through to strike the Egyptians. And when He sees the blood upon the lintel, and on the two side posts, the LORD will pass over the door, and will not allow the destroyer to come into your houses to strike you. And you shall observe this thing as a law to you and to your children forever. And it shall be when you have come to the land, which the LORD will give you, according as He has promised that you shall keep this service" (vs 23-25). *That's in the 14th day of the 1st month!*

Verse 26: "And it will be, when your children shall say to you, 'What *does* this service *mean* to you?'"

This means they were doing the domestic killing of the lambs otherwise the son wouldn't be able to know what was going on. You can read all about the domestic and the temple Passover in *The Christian Passover* book. Here is what they were to answer:

Verse 27: "Then you shall say, "It *is* the sacrifice of the LORD'S Passover... [this also verifies that it was a domestically killed lamb or kid] ...Who passed over the houses of the children of Israel in Egypt, when He struck the Egyptians and delivered our houses."' And the people bowed their heads and worshiped. And the children of Israel went away and did as the LORD had commanded Moses and Aaron; so they did" (vs 27-28).

You know the rest of the story. At sunrise, and by that time all the remainder that was left over would be burned the skin, the guts, the bones, and so forth of the Passover lamb or kid. There was to be nothing left of it. Sunrise was the signal for them to be able to go out of the door of their houses so that no one would leave early, and no one would leave late. I mean you can look out and *you can see when sunrise takes place!*

Then they were to gather at Rameses; v 37: "And the children of Israel journeyed from Rameses to Succoth..."

They had to come from their houses and their houses were in the land of Goshen. They assembled during the day portion of the 14th, spoiling the Egyptians along the way, and they left that night—the Night to be Much Remembered—that He brought them out of the land.

Let's just cover a little bit in Exo. 16 where God again, gave the Sabbath to the children of Israel. We find that the children of Israel were there on the 15th day of the 2nd month, which was a weekly Sabbath, and the 15th day of the 2nd month they had Sabbath services and God gave them a special message. Here is what God told them.

{*The Favorite Version* is used for transcript, which is very close *The Schocken Bible*}

Exodus 16:4: "Then the LORD said to Moses, 'Behold, I will rain bread from the heavens for you. And the people shall go out and gather a certain amount every day, that I may prove them, whether they will walk in My Law or not. And it shall come to pass on the sixth day, they shall prepare what they bring in. And it shall be twice as much as they gather day by day.' And Moses and Aaron said to all the children of Israel 'At sunset...'" (vs 4-6).

Since this is the Sabbath Day message, what does sunset do? *Sunset ends the Sabbath Day!*

"'...'At sunset, then you shall know that the LORD has brought you out from the land of Egypt. And at sunrise... [which is morning] ...you shall see the glory of the LORD, for He hears your murmurings against the LORD. And what *are* we that you murmur against us?' And Moses said, 'You will see when the LORD shall give you flesh to eat at sunset...'" (vs 6-8)—'ba erev'; *He didn't give it between noon and sunset!*

Why did God not send the quail until sunset? *God is Lawgiver, and God does not break His own laws*; very simple! How could He teach the people to keep the Sabbath if He Himself broke it?

"...the LORD shall give you flesh to eat at sunset and bread to the full at sunrise, for the LORD hears your murmurings, which you murmur against Him. And what are we? Your murmurings *are* not against us, but against the LORD" (v 8).

That certainly is true in many, many cases. You know people accuse God because things don't go the way they want. Well, God is going to make it go the way He wants. What you need to do is yield your life and yourself to Him and understand that all things do work together for good for those who love God.

Verse 11: "And the LORD spoke to Moses, saying, 'I have heard the murmurings of the children of Israel. Speak to them, saying, "Between the two evenings ['ben ha *arbayim*' between sunset and dark] …you shall eat flesh, and in the morning you shall be filled *with* bread. And you shall know that I *am* the LORD your God."' And it came to pass, at sunset, that the quails came up and covered the camp. And at sunrise the dew lay all around the camp" (vs 11-13).

Sunset ends the day; no doubt about it. *God did not send the quail until after sunset!*

"…Speak to them, saying, 'Between the two evenings… [setting times] …you shall eat flesh…'" (v 12).

Now something very important that we need to understand: *you cannot eat the flesh until it arrives, and it didn't arrive until sunset!* Therefore, here is Scriptural proof that 'ben ha arbayim'— *between the setting-times,* or *between the two evenings*—is *after sunset,* 'ba erev.' There is absolutely no doubt about it, no wiggle room concerning it, and no tradition can change it, *because these are the words of God that He spoke to Moses.*

There is just one thing I need to summarize concerning the Passover of the children of Israel in Egypt—The Passover pictures and commemorates, as we saw there in Exo. 12, the passing over of the houses of the children of Israel in Egypt to spare the firstborn. That was the meaning of the Passover for the Old Testament.

The meaning of the first day of the Feast of Unleavened Bread beginning with The Night to be Much Remembered, is that God took them out of the land of Egypt. So we have two distinct things.

Now be sure and read in *The Christian Passover* book about how and why and when the Jews began taking the Passover on the 15th, and I think you will be surprised. What they are calling the Passover is really the beginning of the Feast of Unleavened Bread, and you need to ask, and I think we need to really begin to understand this: When have the Jews ever had anything really right? *Jesus, soundly, roundly, absolutely condemned the traditions of the Jews in Mark 7!*

We also need to understand that in the New Testament Jesus Christ changed the symbols, *but He didn't change the day!* He kept the literal 14th Passover, it was not a pre-Passover meal nor some sort of bread and wine ceremony taken from Jewish tradition. *He kept the Passover!*

Mark 14 helps establish very clearly and shows that in the New Testament they understood, New Testament time during Jesus' days, they understood that the Passover and the Feast of Unleavened Bread were two different Feasts.

Mark 14:1: "Now, after two days was the Passover and the *Feast of* Unleavened Bread, and the chief priests and the scribes were seeking how they might stealthily lay hold of Him *and* kill *Him.* But they said, 'Not during the Feast, lest there be a riot among the people'" (vs 1-2).

Then we come to where Jesus was anointed with the alabaster flask of ointment and you have all the account there concerning what happened. Remember that Jesus said that with desire, He desired to eat this Passover with them before He suffered.

Verse 13: "And He sent two of His disciples, and said to them, 'Go into the city, and you shall meet a man carrying a pitcher of water; follow him. And whatever house he shall enter, say to the master of the house *that* the Teacher says, "Where is the guest chamber, where I may eat the Passover with My disciples?"'" (vs 13-14).

Jesus ate the Passover! He had to finish the Old Testament Passover, so in the Passover that Jesus had, the last one that He had was this: they did have the lamb, but then after eating the meal He instituted the New Covenant symbols of the bread and wine. But before that took place there was a foot-washing, and the foot-washing has great and tremendous meaning. I've got a whole chapter devoted to that in *The Christian Passover* book.

Matthew 26:20: "And after evening had come, He sat down with the twelve."

Mark 14:17: "Now after evening had come, He came with the twelve."

Remember that 'ben ha arbayim' means *between the two evenings.* The first evening is sunset, and that's when they were killing the lambs and that's when the disciples said to Jesus, 'Where do You desire *that* we prepare for You to eat the Passover?' Now the second evening is *at the beginning of dark.*

What we are dealing with here in Matt. 26:20 and Mark 14:17 is this: *He came at the beginning of darkness, not at sunset,* and the Apostle Paul talks about in the night that Jesus was betrayed, so the *Passover is to be taken not right after sunset, but it's to be taken when it is getting dark!* That's when it should begin.

Now let's come down to the section here concerning foot-washing, which is the first part of the New Testament Passover. Since we will cover this in the Passover ceremony service, I'm not going to go through the whole account of it, but we'll just cover the meaning here.

John 13:12: "Therefore, when He had washed their feet, and had taken His garments, *and* had sat down again, He said to them, 'Do you know what I have done to you? You call Me the Teacher and the Lord, and you speak rightly, because I am. Therefore, if I, the Lord and the Teacher, have washed your feet, **you also are duty-bound**… [Greek there means *under obligation*] …**to wash one another's feet**'" (vs 12-14).

Why are you under obligation to wash one another's feet? *Because Christ said so!*

Now let me tell you the first leaven that leavens getting rid of the Passover is—based on the meaning of the Feast of Unleavened Bread *a little leaven leavens the whole lump*—the first thing they do is get rid of foot-washing. When they get rid of foot-washing—**IF** you are talked into getting rid of foot-washing—**THEN** *you have taken a step away from Christ!* You are walking away from your part with Him, because Jesus said that if He didn't wash the feet of the disciples, they would have no part with Him. So likewise, **IF you do not wash one another's feet, THEN you have no part with Christ!** You need to think on that. That's profound, and you need to understand it. God does not give us complicated things to do. He doesn't give us a fancy religious ritual to do.

The Roman Catholic Pope has a perverted ceremony of foot-washing, which he does on the eve before Easter, and he has twelve seminary students sitting on chairs that are elevated and they are all dressed in their robes and white and finery, and there are prayers, incense, the Mass, and the whole thing. Then the pope comes down and he has a special server pouring pot where he pours water over the feet of the seminary students and so then he thinks he is fulfilling what Christ has said. *That is perverted nonsense!*

Let's understand something important here that is true: *the only time that you can wash one another's feet is when you partake of the Passover, and that is in the night of the 14th day of the 1st month, being Nisan according to the Calculated Hebrew Calendar!* Here is also another reason why we are duty-bound to wash one another's feet,

Verse 15: "For I have given you an example, *to show* that you also should do exactly as I have done to you. Truly, truly I tell you, a servant is not greater than his lord, nor a messenger greater than he who sent him. **If you know these things, blessed are you if you do them**" (vs 15-17).

Now let's stop and think about this for just a little bit. **_If_** you know them and don't do them, you are not blessed. **_If_** you are not blessed, are you cursed? You need to think about that. **_If_** anyone rejects foot-washing on the Passover night, **they are setting themselves above Christ,** because He said, 'The servant is not greater than his lord.' **_If_** you think that you are Christ's, **_then_** you are His servant! **_If_** you say we don't have to do foot-washing, you are setting yourself above Christ! You need to think about those things.

Brethren, what we do is *for eternal life!* These things are profound; they are important. *They are absolutely necessary and required according to the commandments of Christ!*

In the rest of that section, we have the account of Judas Iscariot taking the sop and then going on out and betraying Jesus.

Luke 22:19[transcriber's correction]: "And He took bread; *and* after giving thanks, He broke *it* and gave *it* to them, saying, 'This is My body, which is given for you. This do in the remembrance of Me.'"

The Passover was a remembrance of the children of Israel's firstborn being spared in the land of Egypt. The Passover is a memorial of the death of Jesus Christ for us. Whose death gives us the forgiveness of sin or passing over of our sins and we who are the Firstborn Church. So, we have the parallel there.

1-Corinthians 11:23: "For I received from the Lord that which I also delivered to you, that the Lord Jesus in the night in which He was betrayed… [showing they took it at night] …took bread, and after giving thanks, He broke *it* and said, 'Take, eat; this is My body, which *is* being broken for you. **This do in the remembrance of Me**'" (vs 23-24).

We are to remember everything about Christ, and Christ's entrance into our life begins with His death. Since God came in the flesh and died, that is the greatest thing that God could do and that's why we show forth and remember his death every Passover until He comes.

Verse 25: "In like manner, *He* also *took* the cup after He had supped, saying, 'This is *the* cup *of* the New Covenant… ['diatheke' meaning covenant, not testament] …in My blood. This do, as often as you drink *it*, in the remembrance of Me.'"

Now often means: year-by-year until He comes, because you can't take the Passover on any other day than the Passover Day and you take it on the Passover night. This cannot be misconstrued, as the world's religions do, that they take it whenever they want on Sunday, as many times as they want, and they call it Communion, Eucharist, and/or the Lord's Supper, and Paul made it very clear that when you come together, *this is **not** to eat the Lord's supper.*

Yet, people insist on calling it 'the Lord's Supper,' and it just shows that they don't know how to understand the Scriptures the way that they ought to. If Paul says it is not to eat the Lord's supper, it means you don't call it the Lord's Supper, and you don't eat the Lord's supper. The truth is the Lord ate His supper and that was on His last Passover night before instituting the symbols of the bread and wine.

Verse 26: "For as often as you eat this bread and drink this cup, you *solemnly* proclaim the death of the Lord until He comes."

If it is a memorial, which it is, and if you are announcing and portraying the Lord's death until He comes, this means that the time that you eat it is on the Passover and as often as you do that, year-by-year on the Passover until He comes, you are announcing and portraying the Lord's death.

Now then we have something that we need to do and should all do by the time Passover comes.

Verse 27: "For this reason, *if* anyone shall eat this bread or shall drink the cup of the Lord unworthily, he shall be guilty of the body and *the blood of the Lord.*" *Meaning that your sins remain on your head!*

Now as I have covered concerning forgiveness of one another. Remember that if you don't forgive from the heart each one of your brother's sins, then God is going to lay back upon you your sins, and therefore you are keeping the Passover in an unworthy manner, and you are guilty of the body and blood of Christ.

Verse 28: "**But let a man examine himself**..." *That's what we need to do before the Passover*:

- examine ourselves
- confess our sins to God

and as I said in the messages on forgiveness {note our in-depth study on *Forgiveness*}

- go get squared around with your brother or sister **before** Passover

"...and let him eat of the bread and drink of the cup accordingly, because the one who eats and drinks unworthily is eating and drinking judgment to himself, *not discerning the body of the Lord*" (vs 28-29)—**which is the forgiveness of sin to put you in right standing before God!** You are under obligation to forgive your brothers and sisters their sins so that your sins may be forgiven.

Then we have an argument taking place at Jesus' last Passover. We'll just summarize this section. If they had the argument as to who was to be the greatest:

- Don't you think they had an understanding about what they were to do?
- Don't you think they had an understanding about what was to come?

After all, Christ ordained the twelve apostles!

Now in this particular case, at this time Judas had already left to betray Christ. Then He gave the example that whoever is the greatest is to be your servant. We are not to be like the lords of the Gentiles and the religious leaders of the Gentiles who exalt themselves and rule over people. No, brethren, *anyone who is a true minister and servant of God is going to teach you*:

- to love God
- to love each other
- that your relationship is directly *between you and God the Father* through Jesus Christ
- that you have direct access to God the Father in heaven above by just getting on your knees and saying, 'Our Father…'

That's why it's so important and profound! So, let's examine ourselves and make sure that we put everything under the blood of Christ and take the Passover in a worth manner, not being the worthiness that *we consider worthy*, **but the worthiness of Christ imputed to us because of God's**:

- mercy
- love
- kindness
- forgiveness

That's what it needs to be!

Now since most of the rest of it here has to do with the Passover that we will take and we will cover these Scriptures for the Passover ceremony, let's come ahead to the time when Jesus is betrayed by Judas.

John 18:1: "After saying these things, Jesus went out with His disciples *to a place* beyond the winter stream of Kidron, where *there* was a garden into which He and His disciples entered. And Judas, who was betraying Him, also knew of the place because Jesus had often gathered there with His disciples. Then Judas, after receiving a band and officers from the chief priests and Pharisees, came there with torches and lamps and weapons. Jesus, therefore, knowing all *the* things that were coming upon Him, went forward *and* said to them, 'Who are you seeking?' They answered Him, 'Jesus the Nazarean.' Jesus said to them, 'I AM.' And Judas, who was betraying Him, was also standing with them. But when He said to them, 'I AM,' they went backward and fell to *the* ground" (vs 1-6).

I have often wondered what those men who came out to arrest Christ and take Him back felt when they were knocked to the ground backwards by the sound of the words 'I AM'?

You understand that that is the name of God 'I AM THAT I AM' and Christ was showing His power as God in the flesh at this particular point. I guess it didn't bother them, because they got up, and so I suppose while they were lying on the ground:

Verse 7: "Then He asked them again, 'Who are you seeking?' And they said, 'Jesus the Nazarean.' Jesus answered, 'I told you that I AM. Therefore, if you are seeking Me, allow these to go their way'; so that the saying might be fulfilled which He had said, 'Of those whom You have given Me, not one of them have I lost'" (vs 7-9). *Then we have a very interesting thing*:

Verse 10: "Then Simon Peter, who had a sword, drew it out and struck the servant of the high priest, and cut off his right ear. And the servant's name was Malchus."

It is very interesting that his name was put in here by John. It's also very interesting that John at this point names Peter as the one who had the sword, whereas Mark, who was the scribe for Peter when he wrote of the account didn't name Peter:

Mark 14:47: "But a certain one of those standing near drew out a sword and struck the servant of the high priest, cutting off his ear."

I just imagine, you know, Because Jesus then reached out and touched his ear and it was healed, I've often wondered what Malchus thought all that night. There he was standing there watching the things going on with Jesus and what the chief priests and scribes were doing, and what He was going through and I imagine he would just reach up and touch his ear just to make sure it was still there. If you have your ear cut off, that's quite a thing! To have it instantly healed by Jesus touching it, I just wonder what he thought all that night, and what he thought after he heard that Jesus was resurrected from the dead, because surely, he heard it because he was one of the servants of the high priest. They took Jesus, bound Him, led Him away. All the disciples forsook Him and fled away.

Verse 51: "Now a certain young man was following Him, having a linen cloth wrapped around *his* naked *body*; and the young men seized him, but he *escaped*, leaving the linen cloth behind, and ran from them naked" (vs 51-52).

This is Mark writing about himself, because he was probably at this time just a teenager. Later he was to serve the Apostle Paul, Barnabas and Peter.

John 18:13: "And they led Him away to Annas first; for he was *the* father-in-law of Caiaphas, who was high priest that year. Now, it was Caiaphas who had given counsel to the Jews that it was profitable for one man to perish for the people" (vs 13-14).

Remember, that Jesus told Peter that he would deny Him three times, which he did. We'll see this account here.

Verse 15: "But Simon Peter and the other disciple followed Jesus…. [the other disciple was John; Simon Peter and John] …And that disciple was known to the high priest… [he was acquainted with him] …and entered with Jesus into the court of the high priest. But Peter stood outside at the door. Then the other disciple, who was known to the high priest, went out and spoke to the doorkeeper, and brought Peter in" (vs 15-16).

Verse 18: "Now, the servants and the officers had made a fire, for it was cold; and they were standing *there* warming themselves, and Peter was *also* standing and warming himself."

I just wonder what Peter was thinking, because Malchus might spot him. What was he going to do, because Malchus was one of the servants of the high priest?

Verse 19: "Then the high priest questioned Jesus concerning His disciples and concerning His teachings. Jesus answered him, 'I spoke openly to the world; I always taught in the synagogue and in the temple, where the Jews always assemble, and I spoke nothing in secret. Why do you question Me? Ask those who have heard what I spoke to them; behold, they know what I said'" (vs 19-21).

Verse 22—*approximately 2:00 a.m. in the morning*: "But after He said these things, one of the officers who was standing by struck Jesus on the face, saying, 'Do You answer the high priest in that way?' Jesus answered him, 'If I have spoken evil, testify of the evil; but if well, why do you strike Me?' *Then* Annas sent Him bound to Caiaphas, the high priest" (vs 22-24). *So they brought Him there!*

Luke 22:56: "And a certain maid saw him [Peter] sitting by the light; and after looking at him intently, she said, 'Now this one was with Him.' But he denied Him, saying, 'Woman, I do not know Him.' And after a little *while*, another saw him *and* said, 'You also are *one* of them.' But Peter said, 'Man, I am not.' Now, after about an hour had passed, a certain other *man* strongly affirmed, saying, 'In truth, this one also was with Him, for he is indeed a Galilean.' And Peter said, 'Man, I do not know what you are talking about.' And immediately, while he was yet speaking, the cock crowed. Then the Lord turned *and* looked at Peter... [just looking right across however far it was away] ...and **Peter remembered the word of the Lord, how He had said to him, 'Before *the* cock crows, you shall deny Me three times'**" (vs 56-61). *And he did!*

John 18:28: "Now then, they led Jesus from Caiaphas... [who was the high priest or the chief priest] ...to the judgment hall..."

What is the judgment hall? *That's the place where Pilate was,* and the judgment hall was in Fort Antonia, which was Roman property and that becomes important for us to understand and to understand the next statement.

"...and it was early. But they... [all of the scribes and Pharisees, and priests who brought Jesus there] ...did not go into the judgment hall, so that they would not be defiled, but that they might eat the Passover" (v 28). This shows two things:

1. the Jews ate the Passover on the night of the 15th and they had a temple Passover
This is not all of the Jews, because
2. the greatest number of Jews were keeping the domestic Passover, and they had already eaten it

But here we're talking about those who kept the temple Passover. Why would they consider themselves being defiled going into the judgment hall which is in Fort Antonia being Roman property? *It would be the same as going to another country!* Num. 9 says that if you are in another country that you take the Passover in the second month.

They would be defiled by going into the presence of Gentiles, which defiling could not be done away within a 24 hour period, and there was not time for a 24 hour period to take place, a whole day, and to bathe at evening. So, both of those have a factor as to why they didn't go in, that they might eat their Passover on the night of the 15th. So, they all went in and began to condemn Jesus even more. They sent Jesus into Pilate, they did not go into the judgment hall.

Verse 29: "Therefore, Pilate came out to them and said, 'What accusation do you bring against this man?' They answered and said to him, 'If He were not an evildoer, we would not have delivered Him up to you'" (vs 29-30). *There is absolutely no proof in that statement whatsoever, but it's a claim:*

If He were not, we wouldn't have done it. We are so good and have righteous judgment and can discern good from evil. Pilate, you know us, that we are good people. Do you think that we would

have delivered Him up if He were not an evil-doer?

Luke 23:5: "But they were insistent, saying, 'He stirs up the people, teaching throughout all of Judea, beginning from Galilee even to here.' And when he heard Galilee *named*, Pilate asked whether the Man were a Galilean; and after determining that He was from Herod's jurisdiction, he sent Him to Herod, *since* he also was in Jerusalem in those days. And when Herod saw Jesus, he rejoiced greatly; for he had long been desiring to see Him because he had heard many things about Him, and he was hoping to see a miracle done by Him" (vs 5-8).

This is Herod Antipas who was the one who killed John the Baptist. So, he wanted to know.

Verse 9: "And he questioned Him with many words; but He answered him nothing.... [Why should He answer the one who killed John the Baptist?] ...All the while, the chief priests and the scribes stood vehemently accusing Him. Then Herod and his soldiers treated Him with contempt; and after mocking *Him*, he put a splendid robe on Him *and* sent Him back to Pilate. And on that same day, Pilate and Herod became friends with each other, because before there was enmity between them" (vs 9-12)—*allies in evil!*

I wonder how many allies there are in evil who hate each other's guts, but they are allies and become friends for a mutual evil cause. All you have to do is read the daily paper, you'll find out who they are.

John 18:31: "Then Pilate said to them, 'You take Him and judge Him according to your *own* law.' But the Jews said to him, 'It is not lawful for us to put anyone to death'; so that the saying of Jesus might be fulfilled, which He had spoken to signify by what death He was about to die. Then Pilate returned to the judgment hall and called Jesus, and said to Him, 'Are You the King of the Jews?' Jesus answered him, 'Do you ask this of yourself, or did others say *it* to you concerning Me?' Pilate answered Him, 'Am I a Jew? The chief priests and your own nation have delivered You up to me. What have You done?' Jesus answered, 'My Kingdom is not of this world. **If My Kingdom were of this world, then would My servants fight,** so that I might not be delivered up to the Jews. However, **My Kingdom is not of this world**'" (vs 31-36).

This is why we are not to get involved in straightening out this world through the political process, and *we are not to fight the authorities of this world because*:

- we belong to the Kingdom of God
- the Kingdom of God is not yet here on the earth

- Christ is not yet here; it is not time for us to fight

When Christ returns, then will we fight, and we will be guaranteed that we will win!

- Do you think for one moment, that all of the political infighting that is done by those that are against abortion that they are going to turn back abortion?
- Do you think that all of the political infighting and things that are done to try and restore America *to the Constitution once delivered* is going to bring that back?

You need to stop and think, and also realize and understand this: Even *if* those in America could get back to the Constitution once delivered, and *if* there were enough time, please understand this: in 200 years we would again be exactly where we are today.

Who is the god of this world? *Satan the devil!* So, **IF you are out there getting involved in these things**—please understand very profoundly and importantly—though the United States may have the best constitution of any government on earth, *it is still a kingdom of this world, and Satan the devil has infiltrated and taken it and has made it what it is today!* It is a kingdom of Satan the devil, *not of God!*

The only reason we have the peace that we have is because the prophecies have yet to be fulfilled, and the preaching of the Gospel must yet still be done, and so we have this time of peace, security and prosperity; not because of any goodness upon our part, but to give us the time to accomplish and do what God wants us to do. We need to fight the fight of faith, and we need to grow and overcome. *We need not to get involved in fighting the fights of this world because* the Kingdom of God is not of this world, *and* we are not of this world!

Verse 37: "Pilate, therefore, answered Him, 'Then You are a king?' Jesus answered, '*As* you say, I am a king. For this *purpose* I was born, and for this *reason* I came into the world, that I may bear witness to the Truth. Everyone who is of the Truth hears My voice.' Pilate said to Him, 'What is Truth?' And after saying this, he went out again to the Jews and said to them, 'I do not find any fault in Him. And it is a custom with you that I release one to you at the Passover. Do you then desire *that* I release the King of the Jews to you?' But they all shouted again, saying, 'Not this one, but Barabbas.' Now, Barabbas was a robber" (vs 37-40). *And the other account also shows he was a murderer!*

John 19:1: "Then Pilate, therefore, took Jesus and scourged *Him*"—with a 'cat-o'-nine tails,'

and it is *by His stripes of scourging that we are healed!* Let's see the prophecy of what Jesus was going to go through that was given by Isaiah:

Isaiah 53:3: "*He is* despised and rejected of men; a Man of sorrows, and acquainted with grief; and we hid as it were our faces from Him, He was despised, and we esteemed Him not. Surely He has borne our infirmities, and carried our sorrows; yet, we esteemed Him stricken, smitten of God, and afflicted…. [that's what they said when they taunted Him] …But He *was* wounded for our transgressions; *He was* crushed for our iniquities…" (vs 3-5)—*and all the bruising that He took with that 'cat-o'-nine-tails' and* **by His stripes we are healed!**

"…the chastisement of our peace *was* upon Him…" (v 5). *In order for us to have peace with God and not receive the chastisement of God upon us, that chastisement came upon Christ!*

"…**and with His stripes we ourselves are healed**. All we like sheep have gone astray; we have turned each one to his own way…" (vs 5-6).

That's sure true of what it is with the Church of God today. Everyone has a doctrine:

- doctrine, doctrine, who has a doctrine?
- opinion, opinion, who has an opinion?
- church, church, who has a church?
- website, website, who has a web site?

I mean, everyone has gone his own way. That's why unless you follow the way of the Lord, unless you follow the Scriptures, you are going your own way. You need to stop and ask:

- What are you really going to have if you insist on your own way?
- Have you ever thought of that?
- What if your own way is contrary to the Scriptures or your own doctrine, or your own pet theories or your own whatever?
- What are you going to receive?

Even Jesus said that *many will say to Me in that day, 'Lord, Lord,'*

- Have we not prophesied in your name?
- Have we not cast out demons
- Have we not done many wonderful works?

Jesus will profess to them, *'I never knew you. Depart from Me you who work lawlessness.'* **IF** you have your own way, *you have the wages of sin, which is death!*

Jesus was beaten and scourged and crucified to cover the sins of us going our own way, but that we may repent and go God's way. After all:

- Is that not what the Passover is all about?

- Is not the renewing of the New Covenant all about living the way of Christ and Christ in us in the New Covenant?
- Is not the foot-washing giving us a part with Christ, renewing our baptism, and showing that we are to walk in the way of the Lord and not our own?

You need to think about it and understand it.

Verse 6: "All we like sheep have gone astray; we have turned each one to his own way; and the LORD has laid on Him the iniquity of us all. He was oppressed, and He was afflicted; yet, He opened not His mouth. He is brought as a lamb to the slaughter; and as a sheep before its shearers is dumb, so He opened not His mouth. By oppression and judgment He was taken away; and with His generation who did consider... [that's the preaching of the Gospel; that's what declares it] ...that He was cut off out of the land of the living; for the transgression of My people He *was* stricken. And He made His grave with the wicked, and with the rich in His death; although He had done no violence, nor *was any* deceit in His mouth. Yet, the LORD willed to crush Him and He has put Him to grief: You shall make His life an offering for sin...." (vs 6-10).

So that our sins could be forgiven! God sent Christ in the likeness of sinful flesh, ***and for sin condemned sin in the flesh and condemned human nature in the flesh!*** The crucifixion of Christ shows the crucifixion of human nature. Now you know why Christ said:

Luke 14:26: "If anyone comes to Me and does not hate his father and mother, and wife, and children, and brothers and sisters, and, in addition, his own life also, he cannot be My disciple. And whoever does not carry his cross and come after Me cannot be My disciple" (vs 26-27).

Because what God has done is so great and so fantastic and so marvelous that He would come and die for the sins of His creation. The purpose then is that after the resurrection that there would be the children of God.

Isaiah 53:10: "...He shall see His seed... [that's us, the seed of God the Father] ...He shall prolong His days," [through the power of the resurrection and live forever] ...and that the purpose of the LORD might prosper in His hand. He shall see of the travail of His soul. He shall be fully satisfied...." (vs 10-11).

God the Father will see the travail of the soul of Christ as it were and be satisfied, that is the sacrifice that brings satisfaction for the forgiveness of sin.

"...By His knowledge shall My righteous Servant justify many; and He shall bear their iniquities. Therefore, I will divide to Him *a portion* with the great, and He shall divide the spoil with the strong; because He has poured out His soul to death... [he did and we will see that] ...and He was counted among the transgressors; and He bore the sin of many, and made intercession for transgressors" (vs 11-12).

I want you to understand about Isa. 53 and the crucifixion of Christ and what it has to do with the Passover, what it has to do with our eternal life, and that's why the Passover and renewal of the New Covenant is so profound and important.

John 19:2: "And after platting a crown of thorns, the soldiers put *it* on His head; and they threw a purple cloak over Him, and *kept on* saying, 'Hail, King of the Jews!' And they struck Him with the palms of their hands.... [it records in another place that they spit at Him] ...Then Pilate went out again and said to them, 'Behold, I bring Him out to you, so that you may know that I do not find any fault in Him.' Then Jesus went out, wearing the crown of thorns and the purple cloak; and he said to them, 'Behold the Man!'" (vs 2-5).

Verse 6: "But when the chief priests and the officers saw Him, they cried aloud, saying, 'Crucify *Him*, crucify *Him*!' Pilate said to them, 'You take Him and crucify *Him* because I do not find any fault in Him.' The Jews answered him, 'We have a law, and according to our law it is mandatory that He die, because He made Himself *the* Son of God'" (vs 6-7).

Verse 8: "Therefore, when Pilate heard this saying, he was even more afraid. And he went into the judgment hall again, and said to Jesus, 'Where have You come from?' But Jesus did not give him an answer. Then Pilate said to Him, 'Why don't You speak to me? Don't You know that I have authority to crucify You, and authority to release You?' Jesus answered, 'You would not have any authority against Me if it were not given to you from above. For this reason, the one who delivered Me to you has *the* greater sin.' Because of this *saying*, Pilate sought to release Him; but the Jews cried out, saying, 'If you release this *Man*, you are not a friend of Caesar. Everyone who makes himself a king speaks against Caesar'" (vs 8-12). *Political blackmail; same old tricks that are always used in politics today!*

Verse 13: "Therefore, after hearing this saying, Pilate *had* Jesus led out, and sat down on the judgment seat at a place called *the* Pavement; but in Hebrew, Gabbatha. (Now it was *the* preparation of the Passover, and about the sixth hour.).... [about six o'clock in the morning because John is writing here of Roman time] ...And he said to the Jews, 'Behold your King!' But they cried aloud, 'Away, away *with Him*! Crucify Him!' Pilate said to them, 'Shall I crucify your King?' The chief priests answered, 'We have no king but Caesar'" (vs 13-15).

You need to understand how demonic that saying was. That's the same as saying we have no king but Satan the devil. Jesus said of those Jews that their father was the devil.

Verse 16: "Therefore, he then delivered Him up to them so that He might be crucified. And they took Jesus and led *Him* away. And He went out bearing His own cross to the place called *The Place of a Skull*, which in Hebrew is called Golgotha" (vs 16-17).

Verse 23: "Now the soldiers, after they had crucified Jesus, took His garments and made four parts, a part for each soldier, and the coat *also*. But the coat was seamless, woven *in one piece* from the top all the way throughout. For this reason, they said to one another, 'Let us not tear it, but let us cast lots for it *to determine* whose it shall be'; that the Scripture might be fulfilled which says, 'They divided My garments among them, and they cast lots for My vesture.'...." (vs 23-24.)

Can God make carnal people do things to fulfill:

- His will?
- His Scripture?
- His Word?

and they not even know it? *Those soldiers didn't know that!* They didn't know that God was causing them to do that, *but God did!*

Verse 19: "And Pilate also wrote a title and put *it* on the cross; and it was written, 'Jesus the Nazarean, the King of the Jews.' As a result, many of the Jews read this title, for the place where Jesus was crucified was near the city... [it was on the Mt. of Olives just across from the temple] ...and it was written in Hebrew, in Greek *and* in Latin. Then the chief priests of the Jews said to Pilate, 'Do not write, "The King of the Jews"; but that He said, "I am King of the Jews."' Pilate answered, 'What I have written, I have written'" (vs 19-22).

Quite a thing, quite a statement, I mean this is something brethren, you need to realize that Jesus went through all of this for us. Now He was mocked.

Luke 23:35: "Now the people stood *by* observing, and the rulers among them were also deriding *Him*, saying, 'He saved others; let Him save Himself, if this is the Christ, the chosen of God.' And the soldiers also mocked Him, coming near and offering Him vinegar, and saying, 'If You are the King of the Jews, save Yourself.' And there also was an inscription over Him written in Greek and Latin and Hebrew: 'This is the King of the Jews.'" (vs 35-38).

Verse 39: "Then one of the malefactors who

was hanging *there* railed at Him, saying, 'If You are the Christ, save Yourself and us.' But the other *one* answered *and* rebuked him, saying, 'Do not even you fear God, you who are under the same condemnation? And we indeed justly, for we are receiving due payment for what we did; but this *Man* did nothing wrong.' Then he said to Jesus, 'Remember me, Lord, when You come into Your Kingdom.' And Jesus said to him, 'Truly, I tell you today, you shall be with Me in paradise.'" (vs 39-43).

Now let's come over here to the last of Jesus' life on the cross.

Matthew 27:46: "And about the ninth hour, Jesus cried out with a loud voice, saying, 'Eli, Eli, lama sabachthani?' That is, **'My God, My God, why have You forsaken Me?'"**

That is so profound to understand that Christ had to bear all of our sins alone, and that's why the darkness covered the earth as it were from the 6th hour until the 9th hour, because God the Father had to leave Christ alone for that period of time. Because He had such a close relationship with God the Father throughout His entire life, felt as though that He were forsaken, and that fulfilled the Scripture that we find in Psa. 22, *'My God, My God, why have you forsaken Me?'*

Verse 47: "And some of those who were standing there heard *and* said, 'This one is calling for Elijah.' And immediately one of them ran and, taking a sponge, filled *it* with vinegar and put *it* on a stick, *and* gave *it to* Him to drink. But the rest said, 'Let Him alone! Let us see if Elijah comes to save Him.' *Then another took a spear and thrust it into His side, and out came water and blood.* And after crying out again with a loud voice, Jesus yielded up *His* spirit" (vs 47-50).

It says there in the account in Luke that *after crying out with a loud voice, Jesus said,* 'Father, into Your hands I commit My spirit.' *And when He had said these things, He expired, died!* Then something really took place, this was something:

Verse 51 "Then suddenly the veil of the temple was ripped in two from top to bottom, and the earth shook, and the rocks were split, so that the tombs were opened. And many bodies of the saints who had died, were resurrected after His resurrection; *and* they came out of the tombs. *Then* they entered into the Holy City, and appeared to many. Then the centurion and those with him who had been keeping guard over Jesus, after seeing the earthquake... [because you can see an earthquake] ...and the things that took place, were filled with fear, *and* said **'Truly this was the Son of God!'"** (vs 51-54).

What a testimony! The Jews rejected Him, the scribes, the Pharisees, the chief priests and the religious leaders rejected Him, but here is a Gentile Italian centurion guard who said, **"…Truly, this one is the Son of God!"**

Brethren, as we go to take the Passover:

- let's remember what Jesus did for us
- let's remember all the things that Jesus went through

so that

- we can come before God and have our sins forgiven
- we can be partakers of the New Covenant through His body and through His blood
- we may have eternal life

Let's keep the Passover with this in mind and rededicate ourselves in the New Covenant *to love God with all our heart, mind, soul, being, and to serve Him in those things that please Him!*

Scriptures from *The Holy Bible in Its Original Order, A Faithful Version* (except where noted)

Scriptures Referenced:

1) Exodus 12:3-13
2) Hebrews 12:22-23
3) Exodus 12:14-28, 37
4) Exodus 16:4-8, 11-13, 12
5) Mark 14:1-2, 13-14
6) Matthew 26:20
7) Mark 14:17
8) John 13:12-14
9) John 18:13:12-17
10) Luke 22:19
11) I Corinthians 11:23-28
12) John 18:1-10
13) Mark 14:47, 51-52
14) John 18:13-16, 18-24
15) Luke 22:56-61
16) John 18:28-30
17) Luke 23:5-12
18) John 18:31-40
19) John 19:1
20) Isaiah 53:3-10
21) Luke 14:26-27
22) Isaiah 53:10-12
23) John 19:2-17, 23-24, 19-22
24) Luke 23:35-43
25) Matthew 27:46-54

Scriptures referenced, not quoted:

- Numbers 9
- Psalm 22

Also referenced:
Books:

- *The Schocken Bible: The Five Books of Moses* by Everett Fox
- *Josephus*

Books by Fred R. Coulter {**truthofgod.org**}

- *The Christian Passover*
- *A Harmony of the Gospels*

FRC:ja
Transcription date unknown
Reformatted: bo—10/2020

CHAPTER SIXTEEN

The Passover Exodus and Trusting God
Fred R. Coulter

The Apostle Paul told Timothy that he was to preach *'in season and out of season,'* and *be urgent in it!* So, this is the season of the Passover and Unleavened Bread. Let's take a look and see some parallels of what God has done in our lives in rescuing us from the world, just how He had to intervene in the lives of the children of Israel when they were in Egypt to bring them out of slavery and out of captivity. We will also answer a few questions as we go along as to the timing of the Passover that they had and so forth.

God performed great miracles, all the plagues and everything that God has the power to do and use, and isn't it interesting that God uses His creation to show His power? That's why God has created certain things so magnificently, that we can understand that only by the power of God and by His hand could things come into existence.

Let's look at the last plague before the plague of the firstborn, and there are some good spiritual lessons for us here.

Exodus 10:21: "And the LORD said to Moses, 'Stretch out your hand toward the heavens, that there may be darkness over the land of Egypt, so that one **may even feel** the darkness.'"

This is a tremendous darkness that came upon them. It's like a dark, thick fog you could feel. I don't know how many have been in a mine or in Carlsbad Caverns, or whatever. I haven't been there, but I hear tell that when you get down below, you have all the lights show the way down there, and then they turn them off and they tell you put your hand in front of your face and see if you can see your hand. You can't see anything. When I read this and the darkness that was there that could be felt, it reminds me that it had to be some kind of *really powerful darkness* that God brought upon them.

- What is the epitome of *spiritual* darkness? *Egypt!*
- What is the warning that God has always given? *Don't go back to Egypt!*
- What is Jerusalem called in the end-times? *Sodom and Egypt (Rev. 11)!*

What we are seeing today is that the world is going back to Egypt in many, many ways. Egypt was a land of many religions, and it was a land of ecumenism: 'Your god is ok as long as you say my god is ok. I accept you if you accept me.' *This is exactly where the world is headed!*

They had kind of a scare with the pope—Benedict XVI—because they thought for sure that he was going to turn the clock back. Well as it turned out, he is not going to turn it back. He is going to continue with the same things that they are doing, ecumenism with separated brethren, and dialogue with other religions, and he did not take the oath against modernism. That means that he is going to proceed with modernizing whatever they need to do to make Catholicism appear acceptable to people in the world.

That's all going back to Egypt! God wanted everyone to know that the darkness of Egypt is a spiritual lesson for us.

Verse 22: "And Moses stretched forth his hand toward heaven. And there was a thick darkness in all the land of Egypt three days."

Remember that some time previous God separated out the land of Goshen where the children of Israel were living, so none of the plagues would come upon them. This didn't come upon them. They had light, but the Egyptians had darkness, and there is also a lesson in that. Here is how dark it was:

Verse 23: "They did not see one another, nor did any rise from his place, *for* three days. **But all the children of Israel had light in their dwellings**."

There is also a lesson for us in this. Even though we live in a world of darkness, *God gives us spiritual light!* Only in this case, not just in the land of Goshen, *but wherever we are!* God also is showing, and Christ said, 'I am the Light.' *Christ is the One Who gives us the way and shows us how to do it!*

Here is what happened, just like it is in the world. How many times have good intentions come along and then people go back on them. This was the story of Pharaoh. God gave him an opportunity, and then he hardened his heart, *then God hardened his heart even further!* It was kind of like a wrestling match between God, Moses, and Pharaoh.

Verse 24: And Pharaoh called for Moses, and said, 'You go serve the LORD. Only let your flocks and your herds be left…. [because ours were all killed] …Let your little ones also go with you.' And Moses said, 'You must give us also sacrifices and burnt offerings so that we may sacrifice to the LORD our God. Our livestock also shall go with us. There shall not be a hoof left behind, for we must take from them to serve the LORD our God. And we do not know *with* what we must serve the LORD… [or how we are going to serve Him] …until we come there.' But the LORD hardened Pharaoh's heart, and he would not let them go. And Pharaoh said to him, 'Get away from me! Take heed to yourself! **See my face no more, for in the day you see my face you shall die.'** And Moses said, **'You have spoken well. I will never see your face again'''** (vs 24-29).

Then God gave Moses some instructions here. Let's look at this because this becomes quite a thing here.

Exodus 11:1: "And the LORD had said to Moses, 'I will yet bring one plague on Pharaoh and on Egypt. Afterward, he will let you go from here. When he shall let you go, he shall surely thrust you out from here altogether. Speak now in the ears of the people, and let every man ask from his neighbor…'" *Not borrow (KJV)!* They weren't going to pay it back; they took it when they left Egypt!

"…and every woman from her neighbor, articles of silver and jewels of gold" (v 2). *So, we see here that with this they had approximately two weeks before they left in being able to get some of the riches!* They left with wages, as God says a little later on, for all their slavery that they had for all the years that they were there.

Verse 3: "And the LORD gave the people favor in the sight of the Egyptians. And the man Moses *was* very great in the land of Egypt, in the sight of Pharaoh's servants, and in the sight of the people. And Moses said, 'Thus says the LORD… [here is the last thing that he is saying to Pharaoh]: …"About midnight I will go out into the midst of Egypt. And all the firstborn in the land of Egypt shall die, from the firstborn of Pharaoh that sits upon his throne, even to the firstborn of the slave-girl that *is* behind the mill; also the firstborn of beasts. And there shall be a great cry throughout all the land of Egypt, such as there was none like it, nor shall be like it any more. But against any of the children of Israel not even a dog shall move his tongue, against man or beast…"''" (vs 3-7).

This shows God's protection and God's blessing, and this is why when we have troubles, difficulties and trials, *we need to trust God and trust His promises that He gives to us* because He says that He will. The reason He did was this:

"…**so that you may know that the LORD puts a difference** *between* **the Egyptians and**

Israel" (v 7). *Today: between the Church and the world!* There is a difference. Then he tells Pharaoh:

Verse 8: "'And all these, your servants… [that were standing there with him when he gave the message to him] …shall come down unto me… [we will see that happen] …and bow themselves down to me, saying, "You and all the people that follow you—get out!" And after that I will go out.' And he went out from Pharaoh in **flaming anger**…. [Hebrew: *white hot*; he was really angry] …And the LORD said to Moses, 'Pharaoh shall not hearken to you so that My wonders may be multiplied in the land of Egypt.' And Moses and Aaron did all these wonders before Pharaoh. And the LORD hardened Pharaoh's heart so that he would not let the children of Israel go out of his land" (vs 8-10).

God told them what they were to do. He told them how to prepare for the Passover, the 10th day of the 1st month, select a lamb. There is a parallel that happened in the timing of that with Christ. Then on the 10th day, and when you have the Passover in the middle of the week, the 10th day of the month falls on a weekly Sabbath. They were to select a lamb on the 10th day of the 1st month, and they were to keep it up and they were to have it according to the number of persons in the household, which if a household was too small, then they would share the lamb or the kid goat that they had with their neighbor. He gave specific instructions for it:

Exodus 12:5: "Your lamb shall be without blemish, a male of the first year…." *Here we have a type of Christ,* that is true even though the timing of the New Covenant Passover comes out of the timing of Gen. 15, we still have all the types showing that the true Messiah is going to come, and this is part of it.

"…You shall take *it* from the sheep or from the goats" (v 5). *Not all goats are bad; there are good goats!* The good goats are independent. I guess we are good goats, even though we are counted as sheep.

Sidebar: I remember my first experience with goats that was up in Boise and I went out to visit this family and they lived up in the back hills behind Boise and to drive up there was really a trick because it was one of these roads that went up, but down the middle of it was an eroded part where when it rained, it left a trench. You had to be careful how you were going up. I got up there, and they had this big tree, and I thought since it was a pretty warm day, I would park under the tree.

Here I'm in the house and was sitting there and talking and visiting. It was right after I had just got up to Boise and I wanted to meet everybody in the Church. All of a sudden the man got up, ran outside, and I jumped up to see what was going on, and here was a goat on top of my car eating the leaves off the tree. He knew as soon as he heard it, he knew exactly what it was because that's why he didn't park his cars under there. I went out there and he said, 'You better move your car.' Goats know how to get it when the going is tough, and they figure out what they need to do regardless of the circumstances. So, here is a case of good goats. So if we're goats, let's hope we're good goats.

Verse 6: "And you shall keep it up until **the beginning of the fourteenth day** of the same month. "

Since the day begins at sundown, when does the 14th begin? *At sundown!* If you have read *The Christian Passover* book you will know that soon as the sun goes down below the horizon, it starts the time period called *between the two evenings*: Hebrew—'ben ha arbayim'—or as the Schocken Bible has: *between the setting times.*

They were to "...keep it up **until the beginning of the fourteenth** day of the same month. And the whole assembly of the congregation of Israel shall kill it **between the two evenings**" (v 6)

This is where so many people just go off the deep end, because they say that it's in the evening. Well why can't it be the evening beginning of the 15th? *Because you would have kept it **beyond the 'until'**;* that's why. This was quite a spectacular thing. I have often envisioned this:

Whatever their little huts were where they were living in their quarters out there and some of the slave quarters that they now have unearthed around the Sphinx and the great pyramids I can just envision their community and they had someone right up on top of one of these houses posted at different locations wherever the Israelites were, and I imagine that he was watching the sun go down, so that as soon as the sun went down and the 14th began he gave the signal and all of the lambs were killed at the same time. So, this was a spectacular event.

When you understand that there may have been as many as 1.8-million Israelites at that time, this was no small, little task. It was a big task, and it was a huge event, and it was something that God was using to show the people:

- His power
- His forgiveness
- His mercy

And since they were going to leave the land of Egypt *they needed to look to God!* So, He gave them the instructions what they should do:

Verse 7: "And they shall take of the blood and strike *it* on the two side posts and upon the upper doorpost of the houses… [the lintel] …*in* which they shall eat it. And they shall eat the flesh in that night…" (vs 7-8)—*which means if you kill it, when does it have to be? If it's on the 14th, then it's when the 14th begins!*

"…roasted with fire, and unleavened *bread….*" (v 8). *That's why it's **an unleavened bread day!*** If you read the account, you can find nothing in there where they had any leavened bread at all.

"…They shall eat it with *bitter* herbs. Do not eat of it raw, nor boiled at all with water, but roasted *with* fire, its head with its legs, and with its inward parts" (vs 8-9).

This means that they had the heart and liver; I don't know if the kidney was still there or not. Obviously you can't roast it with all of the innards in it because the innards would explode and you wouldn't have anything to eat.

Verse 10: "And you shall not let any of it remain until the morning. And that which remains of it until the morning you shall burn with fire."

They weren't allowed to go beyond the morning, but anything that was left, they were to burn!

Verse 11: "And this is the way you shall eat it: *with* your loins girded, your sandals on your feet, and your staff in your hand. And you shall eat it in trepidation.…"—*not in haste (KJV)!*

A lot of people read that *in haste* in the *King James* and misunderstand what it means. They think it means they were eating it right then, eat it in a hurry and left at midnight. We're going to see that the instruction was, *they were not to leave their houses until morning, or at sunrise!* This means *in trepidation!*

"…It is the LORD'S Passover" (v 11)—*because God passed over the houses where the blood was on the doorposts and the lintel, and spared the firstborn of all the children of Israel!*

Verse 12: "For I will pass through the land of Egypt this night… [on the 14th] … and will smite all the firstborn in the land of Egypt, both man and beast.…"

- What is this telling us?
- What is this important for, not only for the Israelites then, but for us today?
  - ✓ God gives us protection against all the satanic powers in the world
  - ✓ God has the victory over them

The satanic powers are those powers that are behind the idols and gods of Egypt!

I remember reading an account of a man who went to India to get enlightened, and he said he didn't think too much about idols until his third trip over there. Then he said when he was meditating on the idol, all of a sudden the power came upon him. It was the power behind the idol *or all the demonic powers that are behind all the other gods.*

"And I will execute judgment against all the gods of Egypt. I *am* the LORD" (v 12).

This is why God will never compromise and give permission to any man, anywhere, at any time, to combine the true worship of God whether it was the worship of God in the Old Testament at that time; or the worship of God in the New Testament today, *to combine the religions of this world* ***with God's way!*** That's why the whole thing of the ecumenical movement that is in the world is going to lead everybody back to Egypt, *spiritually speaking.*

Verse 13: "And the blood shall be a sign to you upon the houses where you *are.* And when I see the blood, I will pass over you. And the plague shall not be upon you to destroy *you* when I smite the land of Egypt. And this day shall be a memorial to you. And you shall keep it a Feast to the LORD throughout your generations. **You shall keep it a Feast as a Law forever**" (vs 13-14).

Verse 21: "Then Moses called for all the elders of Israel and said to them…"

Here is Moses giving God's instructions to the elders who went on back and gave the instructions to all the households. This had to take place well before the 10th day of the 1st month so everyone would know and be ready, and they would select that lamb on the 10th day of the 1st month. It all had to be coordinated:

"'…'Draw out and take a lamb for yourselves according to your families, and kill the Passover *lamb.* And you shall take a bunch of hyssop and dip in the blood *that is* in the bowl, and strike the lintel and the two side posts with the blood in the bowl. **And none of you shall go out of the door of his house until**…" (vs 21-22)—*midnight?* You understand ***that's not*** what he said, but some people claim that.

"…**sunrise** …" (v 22)—Hebrew: 'boqer': *sunrise!* Here is the reason:

Verse 23: "For the LORD will pass through to strike the Egyptians. And when He sees the blood upon the lintel, and on the two side posts, the LORD will pass over the door, and will not allow the destroyer to come into your houses to strike you."

God Himself *personally oversaw this,* the destroyers may have been angels. It talks about an angel in another place, but God was the One Who personally did this because it was a confrontation between God and Pharaoh and the gods of Satan that were there in Egypt. This was God's *personal* business. He says:

Verse 24: "And you shall observe this thing as a law to you and to your children forever."

*Here is the **difference between** the Passover Day and the 1st day of the Feast of Unleavened Bread!* We'll see what the 1st day of the Feast of Unleavened Bread means—though they are one day following the other—they have different meanings because they are different days and you can't combine the two together.

Verse 25: "And it shall be when you have come to the land, which the LORD will give you, according as He has promised that you shall keep this service. And it will be, when your children shall say to you, 'What *does* this service *mean* to you?'" (vs 25-26).

They would obviously ask, because this was to be a domestic sacrifice at their houses and they were to reenact it; they were to take some of the blood and put it on the lintel and the side posts where their houses were when they got into the land.

Verse 27: "'Then you shall say, "It *is* the sacrifice of the LORD'S Passover, Who passed over the houses of the children of Israel in Egypt, when He struck the Egyptians and delivered our houses."' And the people bowed the head and worshipped. And the children of Israel went away and did as the LORD had commanded Moses and Aaron; so they did" (vs 27-28). *If they did what was commanded, what did they do?*

- they selected the lamb on the 10th
- they killed the lamb at the beginning of the 14th
- they put the blood on the side posts and on the lintel
- they roasted it with unleavened bread and bitter herbs
- they burned the remains by morning
- they didn't leave their houses *until morning*

At midnight what happened? God smote all the firstborn of the land of Egypt!

That didn't take place all at once, I'm sure it took place as God oversaw the destroyer going in there and it was kind of like a wave that was coming along, and the screams and the cries because the firstborn were dying. I don't know how many of the children of Israel could hear the sound of it, but I tell you what: *if you heard any sound of these people crying and screaming because of the death of the firstborn,* **do you think you would go out of your**

house before sunrise, <u>when you were told to stay in your house until sunrise?</u> *I don't think so!*

Who would guarantee that you wouldn't be killed? *God didn't give any guarantee unless you stayed in the house!* **If we stay right with God, He guarantees that He will be with us**; same thing today!

Let's come back to v 15 for the Feast of Unleavened Bread; the Passover Day is one day. The 1st day of the Feast of Unleavened Bread is another day. We'll see the meaning of the 1st day of the Feast of Unleavened Bread, which begins on the 15th.

Verse 15: "You shall eat unleavened *bread* seven days; even the first day you shall *have* put away leaven out of your houses; for whoever eats leavened bread from the first day until the seventh day, that soul shall be cut off from Israel." **In other words, you lose contact with God!**

Verse 16: "And in the first day *there shall be* a Holy convocation, and in the seventh day there shall be a Holy convocation for you. No manner of work shall be done in them, except that which every man must eat, that only may be done by you. And you shall keep the *Feast of* Unleavened Bread, for in this very same day I have brought your armies out of the land of Egypt. Therefore, **you shall keep this day in your generations as a law forever**" (vs 16-17). *We have two Feasts back-to-back*:

1. *the Passover* commemorating passing over
2. *the Feast of Unleavened Bread* pictures beginning to leave Egypt

When they left their houses, after they left them in the morning—which is on the day portion of the 14th—where did they go? *They went to Rameses!* We figured that for some of them it was as much as 15 or 20 miles away. So, it would take them all day to get there. Other ones who lived in the southern part of Goshen would be able to get to Rameses sooner, but that is where they assembled to leave.

So the meaning of the Passover is *passing over* and the meaning of the first day of the Feast of Unleavened Bread—which begins at sunset, the beginning of the 15th—*is when they began to leave Egypt!* Obviously, they didn't get out of Egyptian territory for some time after that, but if you are on your way **with God's protection,** it is as good as done.

Then God reiterates it concerning the Feast of Unleavened Bread (v 18). Now we're going to see these two back-to-back.

Verse 29: "And it came to pass that at midnight…"

- Is God on time?

- Does He keep His word? *Yes, He does!*

"…the LORD struck all the firstborn in the land of Egypt from the firstborn of Pharaoh that sat on his throne, to the firstborn of the captive that *was* in the prison, also all the firstborn of livestock. And Pharaoh rose up in the night, he and all his servants, and all the Egyptians. And there was a great cry in Egypt, for *there was* not a house where there was not one dead" (vs 29-30).

Here is a fulfilling of a prophecy two weeks before; v 31: "And during the night he sent word to Moses and Aaron …"—*he sent a message.* Some say that Moses got up and went to Pharaoh. That's not what Moses told Pharaoh.

Exodus 11:8: "'And all these, your servants, shall come down to me and bow themselves down to me, saying, "You and all the people that follow you—get out!" And after that I will go out.'…."

That's what he told them would happen; he wasn't going to go back and see Pharaoh again because Moses said, 'You shall see my face no more again.' They came down; Pharaoh sent a message to Moses and Aaron *by night*. We know this is after midnight; how long after midnight this took place, we don't know.

Exodus 12:31: "And during the night he sent word to Moses and Aaron saying, 'Rise up! Get away from my people, both you and the children of Israel! And go serve the LORD, as you have said. Also take your flocks and your herds, as you have said, and be gone. And bless me also.'" *After all this devastation, I need a little blessing!*

What was the signal for the children of Israel to leave their houses? Just figure this: However large the community was where the children of Israel were in the land of Goshen, would they have known when the messengers came down to Moses? Would they have even known it, except those right close by? *Of course not!* So, they would not be able to determine how soon after midnight they could leave if like some of them said that they left their houses at midnight.

God said don't go out 'til <u>morning</u>! What's the signal for everybody that everyone can understand? **When you look out and you see the sun coming up, <u>sunrise</u>!** *Everybody left their houses at sunrise and began to go and assemble down at Rameses!*

Verse 33: "And the Egyptians were urging the people, that they might send them out of the land quickly, for they said, 'We *are* all dead men.'…." [if we don't get them out of here, God's going to kill all of us] …And the people took their dough before it was leavened, their kneading troughs being bound up in their clothes upon their shoulders. And the children of **Israel did according to the word of Moses**…. [all the way through they obeyed]… And they asked for articles of silver, and articles of gold, and clothing from the Egyptians" (vs 33-35)—*that was just thrust upon them!*

The Egyptians probably figured that God put it in their minds, 'If we give them these things, we'll save our lives. Give them whatever they want.' So, the Israelites were loaded down. Can you imagine leaving Egypt with 200 years of wages? The Spanish translation is: 'they asked and they were given.' That is probably more correct.

Verse 36: "And the LORD gave the people favor in the sight of the Egyptians, and they granted their request, and they stripped the Egyptians. And the children of Israel journeyed from Rameses…" (vs 36-37).

They all had to get to Rameses. In the Passover book I cover all of this and I've got a map showing where Rameses is, showing where the land of Goshen is, and when you're on foot, you're walking; it's going to take some time. So, they all gathered there.

They "…journeyed from Rameses to Succoth, the men being about six hundred thousand on foot, apart from little ones…. [that means men and women there probably together besides the children] …And also a mixed multitude went up with them, and flocks and herds, very much livestock. And they baked unleavened cakes of the dough which they brought out of Egypt, for it was not leavened, because they were driven out of Egypt and could not stay, neither had they prepared any food for themselves for the journey" (vs 37-39). *So, they didn't pack up and take all their goodies!*

If we are blessed, whoever those of us who are going to go to a place of safety—if we live long enough to see that—God is not going to have us pack up our 'Petra box,' so we can tell the angel, when the angel comes to take us to a place of safety, 'Opp! Wait a minute. I gotta get my Petra box!' *No! God will provide everything, whatever is necessary!*

Verses 40 & 41 is the key that unlocks the timing of Gen. 15!

Verse 40: "Now, the sojourning of the children of Israel in Egypt *was* four hundred and thirty years, and it came to pass at the end of the four hundred and thirty years, it was even on that very same day…" (vs 40-41).

Now that's comparing something 430 years earlier, otherwise:

- Why mention the 430 years referring to what happened in Gen. 15?
- Why mention the selfsame day in reference

to something that occurred 430 years before?

The reason is because it's the same day of the year and of the month that occurred with the promises given to Abraham (Gen. 15)!

"…it was even on that very same day, all the armies of the LORD went out from the land of Egypt" (v 41).

Some say that in observing the Night Much to be Observed, we are adding something to the Word of God. Did we sneak into your house and put it in your Bible last night? *No, of course not!*

Verse 42: "It *is* a night to be much observed to the LORD for bringing them out from the land of Egypt…."

When did they come out? *The night **after** the Passover,* which was in the 15th day of the 1st month, and the Passover was the 14th.

"…This *is* that night of the LORD to be observed by all the children of Israel in their generations" (v 42).

It says that **He brought them out** of the land of Egypt. In other words, they started their trip out (Exo. 12:17). Now we see where it is fulfilled that it happened that way.

Now let's see what this day commemorates and what Moses told them to remember. I think the movie *The Ten Commandments* with the Exodus, I think they did a very good job on the timing and showing it, and I thought it was interesting that the Jews who gave the timing in the production of it, had it right.

None of them went out of the houses until morning, they assembled at Rameses, and they left Rameses *just as the 14th was ending and the 15th was beginning,* and as you will read in the Passover book, it took quite a while for all of them to get out of Rameses. When the children of Israel left, they couldn't all start marching at the same time and get out at the same time. That's why they came out *by night.* I'm sure that this is what Moses said as they were ready to leave and I think that the movie, *The Ten Commandments* has it right. He stood up there and they actually read the words from the Bible,

Exodus 13:3: "And Moses said to the people, 'Remember this day *in* which you came out of Egypt, out of the house of bondage; for the LORD brought you out from this place by the strength of His hand. There shall be no leavened bread eaten. On this day you are going out, in the month Abib" (vs 3-4).

When you follow it through correctly, there are two days, and that follows along with what was given there in Gen. 15.

Numbers 33:1: "These *are* the journeys of the children of Israel, who went forth out of the land of Egypt with their armies under the hand of Moses and Aaron. And Moses wrote their goings out according to their journeys by the command of the LORD. And these *are* their journeys according to their starting places. And they set out from Rameses in the first month, on the fifteenth day of the first month. On the *next* day after the Passover *Day*, the children of Israel went out with a high hand in the sight of all the Egyptians, while the Egyptians were still burying all *their* firstborn…" (vs 1-4).

They were probably burying them as quickly as they could on the day portion of the Passover Day when the Israelites were coming down to Rameses.

"…whom the LORD had stricken among them. The LORD also executed judgments upon their gods. And the children of Israel set out from Rameses and pitched in Succoth" (vs 4-5).

Then it tells the rest of the beginning of their journeys and the crossing of the Red Sea!

Where did God ever say to combine the 14th and the 15th into a one-day observance? *Nowhere!* Just like, where did God ever say that He abrogated the Sabbath, the 7th day and instituted the 1st day? *Nowhere!*

Leviticus 23:4: "These *are* the appointed Feasts of the LORD, Holy convocations, which you shall proclaim in their appointed seasons…. [God doesn't give us an option] …**In the fourteenth *day* of the first month, between the two evenings**… ['ben ha arbayim,' the beginning of the day] …**is the LORD's Passover**" (vs 4-5).

However, later you can combine them together. That's the missing verse. Don't they wish it was there? *No it isn't there!*

Verse 6: "And on the fifteenth day of the same month *is* the Feast of Unleavened Bread to the LORD. You must eat unleavened bread seven days." *Then the 1st day, the 7th day and so forth!*

Num. 28—here's a profound key. Sometimes you get something so simple *or* it is so simple that you overlook *what it is really telling you.* It starts out with the morning and the evening sacrifice, and it gives everything that needed to be there. Then on the Sabbath Day, which is a special sacrifice in addition to the daily sacrifice (v 9).

Then we have the beginning of your months and you have sacrifice there; it lists all the things that would be there and that's in addition to the daily

sacrifice (v 11). *What He is doing, He is giving the temple sacrifice for all the days, beginning with*:

- the daily sacrifice
- the evening and the morning sacrifice
- the monthly sacrifice
- the Sabbath sacrifice

Numbers 28:16: "And in **the fourteenth day of the first month** *is* the Passover of the LORD."

What does this verse tells us by its conspicuous absence. *God never required a temple sacrifice on the Passover Day* other than the morning and the evening sacrifice, or if it was on the Sabbath, the Sabbath sacrifice in addition. There is *no God-authorized* temple sacrifice of Passover lambs on the Passover Day at the temple. This simple little verse *wipes out all of the traditions of the Jews* in one fell swoop.

Verse 17: "And in the fifteenth day of this month *is* the Feast. Seven days shall unleavened bread be eaten." *The first day Holy convocation, you shall sacrifice and then on every day!*

Verse 24: "In this way you shall offer daily, seven days, the bread of the sacrifice made by fire for a sweet savor to the LORD. It shall be offered besides the continual burnt offering and its drink offering. And on the seventh day you shall have a Holy convocation. You shall do no servile work" (vs 24-25).

So, there you have it. One simple verse tells you *God never required the Passover lamb to be sacrificed at the tabernacle or the temple,* which is a later addition that the Jews added! Now that should help answer all the things concerning some of the *recycled heresies;* that's what they are.

Psa. 105—let's see a little summary of what we have just gone through and what we need to be doing. When they left Rameses, they had to follow God and they had to trust God. *God put them through circumstances to test them!*

Psalm 105:36: "He also struck all the firstborn in their land, the chief of all their strength. He also brought them out with silver and gold; and there was not one feeble person among their tribes" (vs 36-37).

It's amazing! God prepared all of Israel though they didn't know it beforehand that there wasn't one feeble person and all those who were old had the strength and energy to walk and to go on the exodus; *an amazing feat!* Does God prepare ahead of time, even though we don't know that God is doing it? *Of course!*

Verse 38: "Egypt was glad when they

departed… [I guess] …for the fear of them had fallen upon them. He spread a cloud for a covering…" (vs 38-39).

You're not going to go wandering out in the desert if the sun is going to be beating down on you. Not only did God prepare them so there would be no feeble ones among them when they left, but He also gave them a cloud covering. On a real hot day, aren't you glad when a cloud comes by if you're out there working? *Walking is work!* Hiking out of Egypt and in the desert was work! So, God put a cloud over them.

"…And fire to give light by night…. [God did this so that they would have trust in Him; that they would look to Him] …The people asked, and He brought quail, and satisfied them with the bread of heaven" (vs 39-40). *Even in the wilderness, God is able to provide; nothing is impossible for God!*

Verse 41: "He opened the rock, and the waters gushed out; they ran in the dry places like a river, for He remembered His Holy Word unto Abraham His servant" (vs 41-42).

* their exodus goes back to His promise to Abraham
* the Passover that we have today, goes back to Abraham

Just like the children of Israel were brought out of the land of Egypt on the first day of the Feast of Unleavened Bread, that pictures our coming out of the world, too.

Verse 43: "And He brought forth His people with joy, and His chosen with singing, and gave them the lands of the nations; and they inherited the labor of the people" (vs 43-44).

Therefore, when they harvested the sheaf of the firstfruits, because when we have a Passover on the Sabbath Day, the day following the Passover is the day of the Wave Sheaf Offering and that's through Joshua 5 God specifically said in Lev. 23, 'You shall not eat any bread, nor grain, nor parched grain until you come into the land and when you harvest *its* harvest, *cut the wave sheaf,* then you can eat the grain! Josh. 5 recorded that they did. What happened on the day after they did that? *The manna ceased! No more bread from heaven!* I imagine they were happy that they had other things to eat. Nevertheless, *that's all part of the covenant that God gave in the promise to Abraham!*

Notice why He did this; "…they inherited the labor of the people" (v 44). Why has God called us out of the world? Remember in the final prayer that Jesus gave (John 17)? *They are not of the world even as I am not of the world!* He calls us out of the world. Why?

"**So that they might take heed to His statutes and keep His laws. Praise the LORD**!" *So we can love and worship God!*

Psa. 108—here is what all of this is to do for us. This shows the kind of heart, mind and attitude that we need to have.

Psalm 108:1: "**O GOD, my heart is fixed**…"

God doesn't want us changing with the vicissitudes of the world. Just like the children of Israel even though God did everything for them, led them out, what was the first thing that they did when Moses wasn't around? They went and made a golden calf and worshipped it! Their hearts weren't fixed. *Their hearts were still back in Egypt!*

This is something that's important for us. The only way that we come to have our hearts fixed with God is *to love God and keep His commandments!* That's why in keeping the Passover and Feast of Unleavened Bread, it gives us a renewal to dedicate ourselves so that our hearts are fixed! Then we won't be changeable. Some people might accuse us of stubbornness or hardheadedness, or whatever, but *IF* it is stubbornness *for God* and hardheadedness *for God, that's good!*

"…I will sing and give praise, even with my glory" (v 1).

Verse 4: "For Your mercy is great above the heavens…" *That's what God is showing with the Passover and the sacrifice of Christ,* and that through His grace He gives us the opportunity to have direct access to God's mercy.

"…and Your Truth *reaches* unto the clouds" (v 4). *That's what we are after, brethren!* That's what God wants us to show, teach and do the Truth of God. Everything is based on the love of God and the Truth of God.

Verse 6: "So that Your beloved may be delivered:"

* Isn't that what the Feast of Unleavened Bread is all about?
* being delivered from sin?
* being delivered from self?
* being delivered from Satan?

Yes, indeed!

"…save with Your right hand, and answer me. God has spoken in His Holiness: 'I will rejoice, I will divide Shechem, and I will measure out the valley of Succoth'" (vs 6-7).

Verse 11: "O God, have You not cast us off? And, O God, will You not go out with our armies?…. [this pictures God being with us; God being in us] … Give us help from trouble, for vain is the deliverance of man. Through God we shall do mighty things… [it's by His power, His might, His way] …for it is He who will tread down our enemies" (vs 11-13).

So remember this: *Whatever difficulty, whatever problem you have, God is there to help you!* He may let you go a long time before He intervenes. You may have a trial and difficulty, but sooner or later if God is dealing with you, *He is going to bring you to the conclusion that He wants you to come to, your trust in Him!*

Psalm 112:1: "Praise the LORD! Blessed is the man who fears the LORD… [the fear of the LORD is to lead to the love of the LORD] …who delights greatly in His commandments."

- How many people are out there in the world?
- What is the carnal mind?
- *Not subject to the Law of God neither, indeed, can be!*

They are all out there making their excuses why they won't obey God, regardless of what they are. Here is promise:

Verse 2: "His seed shall be mighty upon earth; the generation of the upright shall be blessed. Wealth and riches shall be in his house …" (vs 2-3).

What I want you to think about is when you go through and read some of these things:

- look at the spiritual fulfillment of it
- see what Jesus said
- think about the house that we are going to be in

On the Passover night Jesus talks about the Father's house!

- What is that going to be like?
- How much wealth is going to be there?

First of all, you start off that you're going to live forever!

- How much is that worth? *You can't measure that in terms of physical wealth or anything like that!*

John 14:1: "Let not your heart be troubled. You believe in God; believe also in Me. **In My Father's house are many dwelling places**; if it were otherwise, I would have told you. **I am going to prepare a place for you**…. [God is preparing that place; God is making that place] …And if I go and prepare a place for you, **I will come again**…" (vs 1-3).

This is why it is so important for us to understand that *every word of God is God-breathed,* meaning that it came forth out of the mouth of God and that His inspiration to those who wrote it was a special inspiration above and beyond what we get. We're to get inspiration from what God embedded in the words and the inspiration out of it. But *they were inspired* to write it this way. *Every word of God is true!* We can count on it. *Christ is coming again!*

Verse 6 tells us all about Passover, the days of Unleavened Bread and leading up to the first resurrection:

Verse 6: "Jesus said to him, 'I am the Way, and the Truth, and the Life; no one comes to the Father except through Me.'"

If we understand that and live God's way and realize that back here in Psa. 112 that God says to those who keep His laws and commandments and fear Him; we can say, *love Him!*

Psalm 112:3: "Wealth and riches shall be in his house…."

- What is the wealth and riches that God is going to give us?
- What did God tell Abraham?

He took him out at night and said, 'You look at the stars and count them if you can; so shall your seed be' (Gen 15)!

The wealth of the universe is going to be given to God's Family, and those who are the firstborn. What is it that the firstborn always is given in the inheritance? *A double portion!* Being in the Church of the Firstborn, *we are going to have a double portion forever!* It is greater than wealth and riches here:

Verse 4: "To the upright there arises light in the darkness… [just like the pillar of fire at night that gave light to them] …he is gracious and full of compassion and righteousness." *That's how God treats us!*

Think about it this way: We know that in keeping the commandments of God it says there is great reward; that is true. But *IF we keep the commandments of God*—first of all because we love Him and we know He loves us—*we are establishing the commandments of God through a personal relationship with God* rather than just the statutes and codes that are written. *That becomes far more meaningful! Yes, indeed!*

Verse 7: "He shall not be afraid of evil tidings; his heart is steadfast, trusting in the LORD. His heart is established; he shall not be afraid until he sees his desire upon his enemies" (vs 7-8).

When are we going to see the desire of God and God's vengeance upon the enemies? *When we are all standing on the Sea of Glass and the seven last plagues are poured out on the earth and we can see it!* I tell you, that's something; put all these things together!

As we are going through these things, let's also look and see how that every one of the things that we are covering as described in the Scriptures is *putting out the leaven of human nature and self!*

Psalm 46:1—*this is how it happens when you are trusting God*: "**God is our refuge and strength, a very present help in trouble**.... [whatever the trouble is, God is there] ...Therefore, we will not fear, though the earth should change and though the mountains be carried into the midst of the sea" (vs 1-2).

That's how God wants us to have trust and faith in Him, and that's why the Feast of Unleavened Bread, to get rid of trust in self. Now notice how this goes into the Kingdom of God.

Verse 4: "There is a river whose streams make the City of God rejoice, the Holy dwelling place of the Most High. God is in the midst of her; she shall not be moved; God shall help her at the approach of the morning. The nations raged, the kingdoms were shaken; He uttered His voice, the earth melted" (vs 4-6).

Those are powerful words! God is going to intervene and do this. This is something!

Verse 7: "The LORD of hosts is with us; the God of Jacob is our refuge. Selah."

Romans 8:31: "What then shall we say to these things? **If God *is* for us, who *can* be against us**?"

Psalm 46:8: "Come, behold the works of the LORD who makes desolations upon the earth." *That's why all of these things have happened!*

Sidebar: I saw a very interesting picture. It was taken back when Napoleon Bonaparte took a small expeditionary force and went down into Egypt and conquered it. I forget the exact year it was; it was like 1796, and he stood there and looked at the Sphinx, and I have never seen a picture like this. Do you know how high the level of the ground was at the time he was there to look at the Sphinx? *It was clear up to the neck of the Sphinx!*

I believe God has done two things:

1. He has inspired that men know more about the heavens than ever before
2. He has inspired that men know more about the production of human life and how profound and precious that is

For those who have eyes to see, and ears to hear, they will learn!

He has also given us another witness. They are excavating all these places. What is the Sphinx now? Well, they got all the dirt down from it, they've got even the villages where the workers worked, they've got that all excavated out. Why? Not to show how great Egypt was, *but to show how absolutely sinful, inadequate and occult that Egypt was and why God judged it!*

But human beings don't get the point. You can go to Las Vegas and here is the Luxor Motel in the shape of a Pyramid and those who go in there actually go through some modified religious rituals that those who went into the Egyptian religions would go through! So, we have the same thing in Psa, 46. God has separated us from it, and here is what He is going to do.

Verse 8: "Come, behold the works of the LORD who makes desolations upon the earth, Who makes wars to cease to the ends of the earth .... [the ultimate end] ...He breaks the bow and cuts the spear in two; He burns the chariots in the fire" *Tie in Rev. 8, 9, 16 & 19 in conjunction with that!*

Verse 10: "'**Be still, and know that I am God! I will be exalted among the nations, I will be exalted in the earth.**' The LORD of hosts is with us; **the God of Jacob is our refuge.** Selah" (vs 10-11).

That's why having God protect us and watch over us and that's what is pictured with the Feast of Unleavened Bread, as well.

Psa. 27 brings this all together. Notice how this ties in with the theme of the Feast of Unleavened Bread, leaving Egypt and all of that:

Psalm 27:1: "The LORD *is* my Light... [that's what God provided wasn't it] ...and my salvation..." *He brought them out of Egypt; same thing with us today*:

- the Lord is our Light
- He has brought us out of Egypt
- He is our salvation

"...whom shall I fear? The LORD is the strength of my life; of whom shall I be afraid?" (v 1).

What God wants us to do is to take all of our sins and problems and the difficulties that we have, bring them to light before God and have them put in proper perspective that they are not as great as they appear to us when we ask God to fight our battles for us. That's why God does not want us to be held down by any of the problems of sin. That's why He has given the Feast of Unleavened Bread. That's why Jesus said on the Passover night, *'Now you are clean through the words which I have spoken.'* That's really profound! ***Don't be afraid of anything!***

Verse 2: "When the wicked, my enemies and my foes, came upon me to eat up my flesh, they stumbled and fell." *That will happen!*

I look back and see many different things how God has intervened for many, many brethren in their lives, and I see it in my life, that God has just intervened and caused people to just turn away. *He has fought the battles for us!*

Notice how much confidence we are to have **IF God is our refuge and we are trusting in Him**:

Verse 3: "Though an army should encamp against me, my heart shall not be afraid; though war should rise against me, even then I will be confident. One thing I have desired from the LORD, that I will seek after: that **I may dwell in the house of the LORD all the days of my life**…" (vs 3-4).

See how that ties in with the other Psalm and John 14? *That's our desire!* This is what we are to set our heart and mind on, *because this is what God is going to do to fulfill for us!*

Talk about the enemy in the days of Hezekiah, what happened? *The Assyrians came down and were mopping up everybody and even sent one of the ambassadors to go to the walls of Jerusalem and tell the people*:

Don't believe anything that Hezekiah is going to tell you that God is going to fight for you, because look what we have done to all these other countries. We have wiped them out with our gods.

Hezekiah took it to God and said, 'Yeah, LORD, what he says is true, that's what they have done.' God said, *'I'll fight for you.' If we trust in God*:

- He'll fight for us
- He'll bring it to pass

This is our focus, to be in the house of the Lord!

Verse 4: "…to behold the beauty of the LORD and to inquire in His temple, for in the time of trouble He shall hide me in His pavilion… [those are the wings of an eagle (Psa. 91)] …in the secret place of His tabernacle He shall hide me; He shall set me upon a Rock" (vs 4-5). *That's what He's going to do. That's tremendous!*

Verse 11: "Teach me Your way, O LORD, and lead me in a level path because of my enemies. Deliver me not over to the will of my enemies, for false witnesses have risen up against me, and he that breathes out violence…" [that's a prophecy of what happened to Christ] …I would have fainted unless I had believed that I would see the goodness of the LORD in the land of the living. **Wait for the LORD;** be of good courage… [not discouraged] …and He shall make your heart strong; yea, wait, I

say, **wait on the LORD**" (vs 11-14). *That's what God wants us to do. That's how great it is!*

Let's see how we are to *trust in God!* That's what the Feast of Unleavened Bread pictures. The children of Israel had to trust God for everything! *Had to trust God*"

- to take them out of Egypt
- to go through the Red Sea
- to give them food
- to give them water

all in the wilderness
- to keep the cloud-cover in the daytime
- to keep the pillar of fire by night
- they had manna for 40 years

You would think that after 40 years it would be so ingrained in their brains which day was the Sabbath, right, that they would **never** forget it. Human beings are not like that.

- that's why we have to be renewed
- that's why we have to be reinvigorated every year
- that's why God has the Passover and the Feast of Unleavened Bread

So, we can take all of the things and all of the mistakes and everything that has been done this past year—even though we repented of them along the way—*and we can know that we are starting anew!*

- that God has called us
- that God has loved us
- that He is going to fight for us

Psalm 62:1: "Only for God does my soul wait in silence; from Him comes my salvation. He only is my Rock and my salvation; He is my fortress; I shall not be greatly moved. How long will you imagine mischief against a man? You shall be slain, all of you; you shall be like a bowing wall and as a tottering fence" (vs 1-3).

All of the things that are happening in the world are building to the crescendo. They are building the wall with untempered mortar and when it falls it is going to be breathtaking!

Verse 4: "They only consult to cast him down from his great height; they delight in lies; they bless with their mouth, but inwardly they curse. Selah…. [that's just the way it is in the world] …but inwardly they curse. Selah. My soul, wait in silence for God alone; for from Him comes my hope. He only is my Rock and my salvation; He is my strong tower; **I shall not be moved**" (vs 4-6). *You can come to that conviction of mind*:

- through the Spirit of God
- through the Word of God

- through the conviction that comes of it

Verse 7: "**In God is my salvation and my glory, the Rock of my strength; my refuge is in God**."

Verse 8 is the key and this is one of the lessons that we need to learn continuously in life, but also to have it during the Feast of Unleavened Bread:

Verse 8: "**Trust in Him at all times**, you people…"

You can tell when you are not trusting in God at all times. That is when you try and do something and God is not behind it and it keeps failing; set it aside, take another course.

- instead of seeking your way, seek God's way
- instead of seeking what you want, seek what God's wants to give you

That's what to do!

Verse 8: "Trust in Him at all times, you people; pour out your heart before Him; God is a refuge for us. Selah."

Psalm 60:11: "O give us help against our foe, for vain is the help of man. Through God we shall do great things, for it is He who shall tread down our enemies" (vs 11-12).

- take this posture
- claim these promises in your prayer and study
- beseech God

Here is what's important. Here is how to overcome any lack of faith that you may have toward that. *God cannot lie! God will not lie!* So when you go before God, you claim the promises that He has given, and remind God that He does not lie, cannot lie and He has promised. But you have to trust in Him and wait on Him, and He will provide in time, and that time will be the time that *He* determines.

Psalm 62:9: "Surely men of low degree are vanity, and men of high degree are a lie…"

I love it when you look around and see all these important men and all these important institutions, whatever, and you read here what the Bible says. They are not what they appear to be. That's what God tells us.

"…when weighed in the balance, they are altogether lighter than vanity. Trust not in oppression, and do not take pride in stolen goods; if riches increase, do not set your heart upon them…. [keep your heart set upon God] …God has spoken

once; twice have I heard this; that power *belongs* unto God. Also unto you, O LORD, *belongs* mercy: for you will render to every man according to his work" (vs 9-12).

God is our Rock and Christ is the Rock and upon Him we are to build!

Matt. 7:24 doesn't include just what Jesus said verbally while He was in the flesh on the earth, because He was the Lord God of the Old Testament. Whenever we read anything in the Old Testament, they are the words of God, and fulfills what Jesus said, *'Man shall not live by bread alone, but every word that proceeds out of the mouth of God, shall man live.'*

Matthew 7:24: "Therefore, everyone who hears these words of Mine and **practices** them…" Like He said, *'I am the Way, and the Truth, and the Life."*

"…I will compare him to a wise man, who built his house upon the rock… [Christ is the Rock] …and the rain came down… [think of the weather channel and some of the movies that they show] …and the floods came, and the winds blew, and beat upon that house…" (vs 24-25) *This means*:

- you are guaranteed trials
- that's how you are going to build spiritual character
- it teaches you to trust in God.

"…**but it did not fall, for it was founded upon the Rock**" (v 25). *That's what we need to do to build our lives!*

Notice those who don't do it; v 26: "And everyone who hears these words of Mine and does not practice them shall be compared to a foolish man, who built his house upon the sand." *That's always tempting, isn't it?*

I know down where we live we have a city called Sand City, right next to Monterey and Seaside. All the contractors love to build there because sand is so easy to work with, because you can pour the foundation easy, it's easy to move and it compacts and everything and it looks really, really, really good.

Just like this wonderful subdivision that was up in Utah, and they had a beautiful mountain scene and the river ran right in front of them and it was just gorgeous and they lived there for many years and enjoyed it, until one year when *the rains came, the flood came, and the wind blew and washed away all those houses!* They showed it on the weather channel, and I tell you there is nothing more heart-wrenching, and that gets you in the pit of the stomach more than to see someone's house just go!

Well now there is a good lesson for us isn't there? *Yes!* We need to build upon the Rock.

Verse 27: "And the rain came down, and the floods came, and the winds blew, and beat upon that house; and it fell, and great was the fall of it."

How are you going to repair it? *There is no repair; it's gone!* **This is why we need to trust in God!**

Scriptures from *The Holy Bible in Its Original Order, A Faithful Version*

Scriptural References:

1) Exodus 10:21-29
2) Exodus 11:1-10
3) Exodus 12:5-14, 21-28;, 15-17, 29-31
4) Exodus 11:8
5) Exodus 12:31-42
6) Exodus 13:3-4
7) Numbers 33:1-5
8) Leviticus 23:4-6
9) Numbers 28:16-18, 24-25
10) Psalm 105:36-45
11) Psalm 108:1, 4, 6-7, 11-13
12) Psalm 112:1-3
13) John 14:1-3, 6
14) Psalm 112:4, 7-8
15) Psalm 46:1-2, 4-7
16) Romans 8:31
17) Psalm 46:8-11
18) Psalm 27:1-5, 11-14
19) Psalm 62:1-8
20) Psalm 60:11-12
21) Psalm 62:9-12
22) Matthew 7:24-27

Scriptures referenced, not quoted:

- Revelation 11
- Genesis 15
- Exodus 12:18
- Numbers 28:9, 11
- Joshua 5
- John 17
- Revelation 8; 9; 16; 19
- Psalm 91

Also referenced: Books:

- *The Christian Passover* by Fred R. Coulter
- *The Schocken Bible Vol. 1: The Five Books of Moses* by Everett Fox

FRC:ja
Transcription date unknown
Reformatted: bo—10/2020

CHAPTER SEVENTEEN

Events Leading Up to Jesus' Last Passover

Fred R. Coulter

Greetings, brethren!

This is the first time in ten years that we've had a Passover in the middle of the week. On rare occasions there's that ten year gap where there are no Passovers in the middle of the week. However, including this year, in the next five years, there will be three Passovers with the Passover in the middle of the week.

We want to look at some of the events leading up to the Passover. We will see that the Passover Sabbath—or the Sabbath before Passover—is the 10th day of Nisan, and is the day that the Passover lamb was to be selected. We will see that Jesus was selected on that Sabbath before the Passover.

Let's begin and we'll do a study covering parts of the last six days leading up to Jesus' last Passover. You can follow through in *A Harmony of the Gospels!*

John 12:1: "Now, six days before the Passover, Jesus came to Bethany, where Lazarus was who had died, *and* whom He had raised from *the* dead. There they made a supper *for* Him, and Martha served; and Lazarus was one of those who sat with Him" (vs 1-2).

This anointing of Jesus was the first of two. We will see a little later in Matt. 26 that two days before the Passover He was anointed in the house of Simon the leper. So, the account goes on showing:

Verse 3: "Mary then took a pound of pure spikenard ointment worth a great price *and* anointed Jesus' feet, wiping His feet with her hair. And the house was filled with the aroma of the ointment."

Then Judas Iscariot brought up a problem of waste, v 5: "'Why was this ointment not sold for three hundred silver coins, and given to *the* poor?'" Now he said this, not because he cared for the poor, **but because he was a thief, and had the bag, and carried what was put in *it*"** (vs 5-6)—*the incidentals for Christ and the apostles!* He carried the bag for payment for it.

Judas was snitching out of the bag himself, and he wanted to sell the ointment to put the money back in the bag. But Jesus said:

Verse 7[transcriber's correction]: "…'Let her alone; she has been keeping it toward the day of My burial.

For you have the poor with you always…'" (vs 7-8).

Outside a crowd was gathering, because just a few days before Jesus raised Lazarus from the dead. The people wanted to see Lazarus and Jesus. Even the scribes, Pharisees and priests were wanting to kill not only Jesus, but Lazarus.

Verse 9: "Then a great crowd of the Jews found out that He was there. And they came, not only because of Jesus, but also that they might see Lazarus, whom He had raised from *the* dead. But the chief priests took counsel in order that they might kill Lazarus also" (vs 9-10).

We're going to see that many of the things that were done leading up to the time two days before the Passover, that Jesus brought great confrontation to the religious leaders, the scribe, the elders, the Sadducees, the Pharisees and challenged them. What they did, they made a religion overlapping and coming around all the laws and commandments of Moses. That was basically what is known today as *Judaism!*

Here's why they wanted to kill Lazarus, v 11: "Because by reason of him, many of the Jews were leaving *them* and believing in Jesus."

All of this took place on the 8th of Nisan, and of course, the day begins at sunset. That was the 1st month and the 8th day, Wednesday night. Then Thursday, the day portion we have quite a few things happen here.

Verse 12: "On the next day, a great crowd *of people* who had come for the Feast, when they heard that Jesus was coming into Jerusalem, took branches from palm trees and went out to meet Him, and were shouting, 'Hosanna! Blessed *is* He Who comes in *the* name of *the* Lord, the King of Israel'" (vs 12-13).

Quite a thing! This was **not** Palm Sunday! *Nor was it a Palm Sabbath!* This was a Thursday. Think of this for a minute. If this was happening on the Sabbath, don't you think that the religious authorities would attack the disciples and the people for breaking off branches on the Sabbath and strewing them in the road? *Of course they would have!*

Verse 14: "Now, after finding a young donkey, Jesus sat upon it, exactly as it is written."

Many Scriptures are fulfilled! How are they being fulfilled exactly the way that should be, by the events that were taking place. I am sure that many of the angels were orchestrating the timing of these events. God was sending them also to inspire the people to come to Jerusalem.

Verse 15: "'Fear not, daughter of Sion. Behold, your King comes, sitting on a colt of a donkey.' And His disciples did not understand these things at the beginning; but when Jesus was glorified, then they remembered that these things were written about Him, and that they had done these things to Him. Then the group that was with Him when He called Lazarus out of the tomb, and raised him from *the* dead, testified of *what they had seen*" (vs 15-17). *So, this was a marvelous thing!*

Verse 18: "Because of this, the people also met Him, for they had heard of this miracle that He had done."

Notice why the Pharisees were wanting to get rid of Jesus and Lazarus:

Verse 19: "Then the Pharisees said among themselves, 'Do you see that we are not gaining in any way? Look! The world has gone after Him.'"

That's quite a thing out there. **They were afraid of losing power!** Isn't that true? The establishment: Once it's established and corrupted, it does not want the truth, where in religion or government. People say they want the truth, but they really don't want the Truth of God, because that would convict them of their sins.

Matt. 21—here we see the beginning of **another confrontation** that Jesus had with the religious authorities. It describes the Pharisees and also the Herodians. This shows where they got the donkey and the colt and brought them to Jesus.

Matthew 21:12: "And Jesus went into the temple of God and cast out all those who were buying and selling in the temple; and He overthrew the tables of the money exchangers, and the seats of those who were selling doves. Then He said to them, 'It is written, "My house shall be called a house of prayer," but you have made it a den of thieves'" (vs 12-13).

That's quite a thing, and that's exactly how it is in religion today, and exactly how it is in the government today, and how these things are and how they take place.

So, this last week of Jesus was really very powerful. You know that the angels of God were involved, Satan and the demons were involved, and Jesus and the apostles were involved.

Luke 19:41: "And when He came near *and* saw the city, He wept over it, saying, 'If you had known, even you, at least in this your day, the things for your peace; **but now they are hidden from your eyes**'" (vs 41-42).

The spiritual blindness does not equal physical blindness. Spiritual blindness is that ***they can't see the Truth and they can't understand the Truth.*** As Jesus said, 'The blind are leading the blind and they will both fall into the ditch.

Verse 43: "For *the* days shall come upon you that your enemies shall cast a rampart about you, and shall enclose you around and keep you in on every side, and shall level you to the ground…" (vs 43-44). He's talking about he city of Jerusalem, absolutely true, that happened.

"'…and your children within you; and they shall not leave in you a stone upon a stone, because you did not know the season of your visitation.' Then He went into the temple *and* began to cast out those who were selling and those who were buying in it, saying to them, 'It is written, "My house is a house of prayer"…'" (vs 44-46).

Now let's see what He did in the account of Mark; this becomes quite an important thing here.

Sidebar: when first studying out the last ten days of Jesus' life, that led to understanding ***that only in Mark did the cursing of the fig tree cover a two-day period.*** I had two chronologies, that in my first Passover season in 1965 in Boise, Idaho, I wanted to do the last ten days of Jesus' life.

I had notes from Dr. Herman Hoeh and Dale Hampton. I was using those as a guide for what I was to bring. I found out that they were off, and I couldn't figure out where it was. So, I took a piece of paper and marked Matthew at the top and took other pieces of paper and had Mark, Luke and John.

I started the last six days before the Passover and went through everything and wrote down all of the Scriptures, which years late became incorporated into *A Harmony of the Gospels, The Last Ten Days of Jesus' Life*.

Here in Mark 11 we find that the cursing of the fig tree occurred over **a two-day period**. When you look at the account in Matthew and Luke it looks like it's the same day, but it's not.

Mark 11:11: "And Jesus entered Jerusalem and went into the temple; and *because* the hour was already late, after looking around at everything *there*, He went out to Bethany with the twelve. And in the morning, after they left Bethany, He became hungry. Then, seeing a fig tree afar off that had leaves, He went *to it to see* if He might possibly find something on it. But after coming to it, He found nothing except leaves because it was not yet *the* season for figs. And Jesus responded *by* saying to it, 'Let no one eat fruit from you any more forever!' And His disciples heard *it*" (vs 11-14).

Quite an interesting thing! They didn't know the season of the time of Jesus Christ. This fig tree pictures the way of Judaism. It didn't bring forth any fruit. Why? *Because the traditions of Judaism overlaid everything of the Scripture and blinded the people!*

Verse 15: "Then they came into Jerusalem; and after entering the temple, Jesus began to cast out those who were buying and selling in the temple; and He overthrew the tables of the money exchangers and the seats of those who were selling doves. Moreover, He did not allow anyone to carry a vessel through the temple. And He taught, saying to them, 'Is it not written, "My house shall be called a house of prayer for all nations"? But you have made it a den of robbers.' Now, the chief priests and the scribes heard *this*, and they sought how they might destroy Him; for they feared Him, because all the multitudes marveled at His teaching. And **when evening came, He went out of the city**" (vs 15-19).

- cursed the fig tree
- went into the temple
- did the teaching
- casting out all of the animals
- overthrowing the tables
- castigating the chief priest, scribes and Pharisees

Then when it was evening He went out and back to the Mt. of Olives!

Verse 20: "And **in the morning**…" *It was cursed one day; they went into the temple. They left and went out of the city and in the morning:*

"…as they passed by, they saw the fig tree dried up from *the* roots" (v 20). *So, it was in the morning, day two!*

Verse 21: "Then Peter remembered *and* said to Him, 'Look, Master! The fig tree that You cursed has dried up.' And Jesus answered and said to them, **'Have faith *from* God'**" (vs 21-22).

This is an interesting statement because in the Greek it means *have the faith of God,* which means that faith comes from God. We know that in the New Testament it's one of the fruits of the Holy Spirit. This also is what it talks about in Gal. 2, but *through the righteousness of the faith of Jesus are we justified!* This is a gift of God.

There's always a certain amount of faith that people can have, because people believe things. But to have *a spiritual conviction of faith, that must come from God and His Spirit,* not from within us.

Verse 23: "For truly I say to you, whoever shall say to this mountain, 'Be taken away and be cast into the sea,' and shall not doubt in his heart, but shall believe that what he said will take place, he shall have whatever he shall say."

There's one caveat that Jesus gave in the model prayer: *the will of God! If it is the will of God!* It's not that people will go around and start casting out mountains and hills and all of that sort of thing. *But something that is harder than that to do is to convert the human mind!* That takes the faith of Jesus Christ.

Verse 24: "For this reason I say to you, all *the* things that you ask *when* you are praying, believe that you will receive *them,* and *they* shall be *given* to you."

That's a wonderful thing to understand. Look back at your life, according to the will of God the things that you have asked for, God has answered and given. Maybe not necessarily in the same measure that you might necessarily have particularly wanted, but nevertheless, *God answers those prayers!*

There will even come a time when there will be something happen that you thought of, kind of in a glancing thought, but didn't think too much about it, and sometime later you look and back and say, *'God answered that thought!'*

Eph. 3—this is the kind of faith that we are to have, which comes from God. He's not going to give us miracles to do so that we can show off. There has to be a purpose for everything that we ask for, according to the will of God. *But notice this promise*:

Ephesians 3:20: "Now, to Him Who is able to do exceeding abundantly…" *That's also referring to the time of the resurrection and the time when we will be in the Kingdom of God with the fullness of God!*

"…**above all that we ask or think,** according to the power that is working in us" (v 20). *So, when Jesus said,* "…**Have faith *from* God**"—*or of God—that's what He meant!*

Here's another important principle that He was teaching to His apostles just before He was getting ready to be crucified:

Mark 11:25: "But when you stand praying, if you have anything against anyone, **forgive**…" *It says in another place, 'work it out with the one with whom you have a difficulty!'*

"…**so that your Father Who *is* in heaven may forgive you your offenses**" (v 25). *That's a very important thing to understand!* The world likes to remember and *hate! God wants*:

- love
- repentance
- mercy
- reconciliation
- forgiveness

    - that's the whole story of the New Testament
    - that's the whole purpose as why Christ came

Verse 26: "**For if you do not forgive, neither will your Father Who** *is* **in heaven forgive you your offenses**."

Verse 27: "Then they came again to Jerusalem. And as He was walking in the temple, the chief priests and the scribes and the elders came to Him; and they said to Him, '**By what authority are You doing these things?**....'" (vs 27-28).

You have to have *authority* to come into the Temple of God. Thing about what He was doing:

- casting out the animals
- casting out the moneychangers
- overturning the tables
- teaching the people

They wanted to know *what authority*, because Jesus didn't get it from the high priest or the elders. Who did He get it from? "...**By what authority are You doing these things?**"

Verse 29: "Then Jesus answered and said to them, 'I also will ask you one thing, and *if* **you answer Me,** I will also tell you by what authority I do these things.'"

Good lesson: sometimes it's best to answer with a question. Why did He do it this way? *Because He knew their hearts!* He knew that they were after Him.

Verse 30: "'The baptism of John, was it from heaven or from men? Answer Me.' And **they reasoned among themselves,** saying, 'If we say, "From heaven," He will say, "Why then did you not believe him?" But if we say, "From men"'; they feared the people, because everyone held that John was indeed a prophet. And they answered Jesus by saying, 'We do not know.'...." (vs 30-33). *That was an outright lie!* **They knew it was from God!**

"...Then Jesus answered *and* said to them, 'Neither will I tell you by what authority I do these things'" (v 33). *Quite amazing, indeed, some of the confrontations that are coming along!*

The timeframe that we have is the 10th day of the 1st month, John 12, and this will be very interesting indeed! This is quite a chapter covering many things. This is why we have the four Gospels, to put it all together so that we make sure that we have everything and all the facts that we need.

John 12:20: "Now there were certain Greeks among those who had come up to worship at the Feast. And these came to Philip, who was from Bethsaida of Galilee; and they asked him, saying, 'Sir, we desire to see Jesus.' Philip came and told Andrew, and Andrew and Philip in turn told Jesus. But Jesus answered them, saying, 'The time has come for the Son of man to be glorified'" (vs 20-23). *Remember, this on the 10th day of the 1st month!*

That's today, the Sabbath before the Passover. But the sequence was a little different and was actually a week later in the year that Jesus went through these things. But for us, the 10th day of the 1st month is this Sabbath, the Sabbath before the Passover. The 14th day of the 1st month.

Jesus continued, v 24: "Truly, truly I say to you, unless a grain of wheat falls into the ground and dies, it remains alone; but if it dies, it bears much fruit."

Jesus is giving some good parables and teachings here. Then He makes it absolutely clear. I want you to tie in the next couple of verses in John 12 together with:

John 14:6 where Jesus said: "...I am the Way, and the Truth, and the Life; no one comes to the Father except through Me."

- What are we to do in our lives?
- What are we to do with our own human nature?
- What is conversion is all about?

John 12:25: "The one who loves his life shall lose it, and the one who hates his life in this world shall keep it unto eternal life. **If anyone will serve Me, let him follow Me**..." (vs 25-26).

Then we have about counting the cost (Luke 14); that *we have to have complete dedication to God the Father and Jesus Christ!*

- not to men
- not to an organization

But to God the Father and Jesus Christ, and our conversion grows deeper and deeper with the Spirit of God as we grow in grace and knowledge! 'That's a tremendous thing for us, brethren! Think about that!

God the Father Who rules the universe, the great Sovereign of the universe, and His only begotten Son Jesus Christ:

- our High Priest
- Head of the Church
    - ✓ They love us
    - ✓ They have called us

They have all of this that we're reading about all worked out so that Jesus would become the perfect sacrifice for the sin of the world That covers all the sins of the world, because the sin of the world is what Adam and Eve did; *they didn't obey the voice of God!* Then human nature, with the judgment of God, became hostile against God.

Only true repentance, true baptism and true conversion can change that! *That's by and through the love and power and will of God!*

Verse 27 is where Jesus was chosen by the Father on the 10th day of the 1st month, the Sabbath before Passover:

Verse 27: "'Now My soul is troubled, and what shall I say? Father, save Me from this hour? But for this *very* purpose I have come to this hour. Father, glorify Your name.' Then a voice came from heaven, *saying*, '**I have both glorified** *it* **and will glorify** *it* **again.**'" (vs 27-28).

These are the very words that are at the beginning of the prayer in John 17. Let's read that so we see how it all comes together. That is talking about the crucifixion, and this was the 10th day of the 1st month when Jesus was chosen as the Lamb of God.

Here in Jesus' final prayer before He was arrested He spoke these words:

John 17:1: "Jesus spoke these words, and lifted up His eyes to heaven and said, 'Father, the hour has come… [down to the hour] …glorify Your own Son, so that Your Son may also glorify You"—*talking about the crucifixion,* and that's what it's talking about in John 12 about glorifying God. *He was selected!*

Verse 2: "Since You have given Him authority over all flesh, in order that He may give eternal life to all whom You have given Him. For this is eternal life, that they may know You, the only true God, and Jesus Christ, Whom You did send" (vs 2-3).

Jesus had not yet received His Godship back; not until after the resurrection. That's why at that time the Father was the only true God. Jesus could not be 100% man and 100% God; that's an impossibility.

Verse 4: "I have glorified You on the earth. I have finished the work that You gave Me to do. and now, Father, glorify Me with Your own self, with the glory that I had with You before the world existed" (vs 4-5).

Quite a prayer! Absolutely marvelous! That comes all the way down to us, because Jesus prayed for us as well. Those are things we need to keep in mind as we come to the Passover:

- as we're preparing
- as we're thinking about the foot-washing
- as we're thinking about the bread and wine

We need to do it exactly as Jesus has said, exactly in the timing that we find in the New Testament!

John 12:29: "Then the people standing *there*, who heard *it*, said, 'It thundered.' Others said, 'An angel spoke to Him.' Jesus answered and said, 'This voice did not come because of Me, but because of you'" (vs 29-30)—*so, you would know that God the Father selected Him as the Passover Lamb to take away the sin of the world!*

Notice what else He said, and what this has done, because everything was complete up to this point.

Verse 31: "Now is *the* judgment of this world. Now shall the prince of this world be cast out."

This had to be done in order to get rid of Satan the devil! Then after the resurrection, his time of judgment has already been given. *But there has to be*:

- the preaching of the Gospel
- the building of the Church
- the character and conversion of all of those whom God would call

So that with all the rest of the saints the whole of the Kingdom of God can be given to all of the sons and daughters of God at the same time.

- we still live in the world where Satan is active
- we're still subject to overcoming those things

Verse 32: "'And if I be lifted up from the earth, I will draw all to Myself.' But He said this to signify by what death He was about to die" (vs 32-33).

Quite a powerful thing! He let them know that He was going to die! This confounded the Jews, because the Jews were expecting the Messiah, and:

If He's the Messiah surely He would come to us and surely He would recognize that we're the ones who are in authority. After all, we have that authority from God.

True! But they misuse the authority! They corrupted it by the schemes of Satan the devil, rather than follow God.

Verse 34: "The people answered Him, 'We have heard out of the law that the Christ lives forever, and why do You say that the Son of man must be lifted up? Who is this Son of man?'" *So, their spiritual blindness was quite a thing!*

Verse 35: "Then Jesus said to them, 'Yet, a little while the Light is with you. **Walk while you have the Light,** so that *the* darkness will not overtake you. For **the one who walks in darkness does not know where he is going**.'"

That's true statement, prophetic from that time down to this. You can tie that going back to John 3, that those who believe are coming to the Light, and those who do not believe do not come to the Light, because they don't want their evil deeds exposed for what they are. This is quite a prophecy here!

Verse 36: "'While you have the Light, believe in the Light, so that you may become *the* children of Light.'...." *Very clear*:

- *IF* you do not believe in Jesus Christ as the Light of the world, the Son of God, the only Begotten of the Father
- *IF* you do not believe that He is the Lamb of God to take away the sin of the world
  - ✓ you have no life in you
  - ✓ you have no forgiveness in you

that's the whole purpose of His
- life
- death
- crucifixion
- resurrection
- the calling of the Church

It's all centered around this!

Now we come to the 1st day of the week. This is the day of confrontation where Jesus challenges all the religious authorities—the scribes and the Pharisees—with unbelievable sharp and strong language. This was a tremendous witness to them and against them. Instead of repenting, it provoked them to greater anger and seeking to kill Jesus. *Quite a situation!*

Jesus laid it bare; He laid it out for all to understand.

Mark 12:1: "And He began to speak to them in parables: 'A man planted a vineyard, and put a fence around *it*, and dug a wine vat, and built a tower, and leased it out to husbandmen, and *then* left the country. And at the *harvest* season he sent a servant to the husbandmen, so that he might receive the fruit of the vineyard from the husbandmen. But they took him *and* beat *him*, and sent *him* away empty'" (vs 1-3).

What He's doing is using this parable against them to show that all through the history of Israel, they didn't believe God, and they didn't do what the Law and the Prophets said.

Verse 4: "And in turn, he sent another servant to them; but they stoned him and wounded him on the head, and after insulting *him* sent *him* away. And in turn, he sent still another *servant*, and they killed him; and *he sent* many others, *and* some were beaten and others were killed. Now then, he had yet one son, his own beloved. And so, last of *all* he sent him to them also, saying, 'They will have respect for my son.' But those husbandmen said among themselves, 'This is the heir. Come, let us kill him, and the inheritance shall be ours.' And after seizing him, they killed *him* and cast *him* out of the vineyard. Therefore, what will the lord of the vineyard do? He will come and destroy the husbandmen and will give the vineyard to others. **Have you not read even this Scripture**..." (vs 4-10).

Think about how many times Jesus said to them, *'Have you not read...'* that's quite a thing, indeed. They put all of their traditions as a fence around the laws, commandment and prophets of God, that if the people kept these traditions they wouldn't break the commandments.

But the problem is that *these traditions were breaking the commandments themselves!* The schemes of men to make the Word of God better never work! *You've got to do what God says! That's the whole story of human life!* The three words: *obey My voice!*

So, Jesus asked them, v 10: "Have you not read even this Scripture '*The* Stone that the builders rejected, this has become *the* head of *the* corner; this was from *the* Lord, and it is wonderful in our eyes'?" (vs 10-11).

Verse 12: "Then they sought to arrest Him, but they feared the multitude; for they knew that He had spoken the parable against them. And they left Him and went their way. **But**..." (vs 12-13).

They're not done, they want to trip Him into rebelling against Caesar, and rebelling about paying taxes.

"...they sent to Him some of the Pharisees and the Herodians, in order to entrap Him in His words. And after coming to Him, they said, 'Master... [look at how they said this] ...we know that You are true, and *that* You court no man's favor; because You do not look on *the* appearance of men, but You teach the way of God in truth. Is it lawful to give tribute to Caesar or not?'" (vs 13-14).

IF what they said, that they believed that He was sent from God, that He taught the Truth, that He wasn't involved in politics like all of the scribes and Pharisees and priests and everything, **WHY** didn't they believe Him?

It's just like we see in many cases in religion and in politics, instead of coming to the truth—

which is right in front of them—they continue their own way.

Verse 15: "'Should we give *it*, or should we not give *it*?' But perceiving their hypocrisy…"

We'll talk about hypocrisy later on; He really laid it on the line in Matt. 23. He absolutely condemned them in such powerful terminology and convicting guilt against them, that that was the last great confrontation.

"…He said to them, 'Why do you tempt Me? Bring Me a silver coin, so that I may look *at it*.' Then they brought *it*. And He said to them, 'Whose image and superscription *is on* this *coin*?' And they said to Him, 'Caesar's.' And Jesus answered and said to them, 'Render the things of Caesar to Caesar, and the things of God to God.'…." (vs 15-17).

That's talking about more than funds and money; that's talking about everything. Render to God what He has commanded with all your heart and faith, and believe Him!

"…And they were amazed at Him…. [at His answer] …Then the Sadducees, who say there is no resurrection, came to Him, and they questioned Him, saying, 'Master, Moses wrote for us that if the brother of anyone should die and leave behind a wife, but leave no children, then his brother should take his wife and raise up seed for his brother. *Now*, there were seven brothers; the first took a wife and died, leaving no seed; and the second took her and died, and neither did he leave seed; and the third likewise. And the seven had her and left no seed. Last of all the woman died also'" (vs 18-22). ***They were trying to trap Him in it!***

Verse 23: "Now then, **in the resurrection**, when they shall arise, **to which of them shall she be wife? For all seven had her as wife.**"

Verse 24: "Then Jesus answered them and said, 'In *asking* this, do you not err, not knowing the Scriptures nor the power of God? For when they rise from *the* dead, they neither marry nor are given in marriage, but are as the angels who *are* in heaven. But concerning the dead, that they do rise, have you not read in the book of Moses about the burning bush, how God spoke to him, saying, "I *am* the God of Abraham, and the God of Isaac, and the God of Jacob"? He is not the God of *the* dead, but *the* God of *the* living. Therefore, **you err greatly**'" (vs 24-27).

Why? ***Because they weren't following God, they were following their own religion!***

Verse 28: "And one of the scribes who had come up *to Him*, after hearing them reasoning together *and* perceiving that He answered them well, asked Him, **'Which is *the* first commandment of all?'"** *We also find this in Deut. 6 and Matt. 22!*

This is the whole basis of any relationship with God! Since God is love and you want the love of God, then you must love God. God doesn't want your part time interest and love in Him, because:

- He wants to give us eternal life
- He wants us to be His sons and daughters in His Kingdom *forever*

Therefore, what He wants of us is complete wholeheartedness of our entire being. That's why we have the Passover.

Verse 29: "Then Jesus answered him, '*The* first of all the commandments *is*, "Hear, O Israel… [put your name there, or Church of God, people of God] …Our one God is *the* Lord, *the* Lord. And you shall love *the* Lord your God…"'" (vs 29-30).

Notice how all encompassing of everything that we are, and everything that we look forward to becoming. God hasn't called us so that we can be good little citizens in the world. We're to be good citizens in the world, *true*, but **He has called us to *His* sons and daughters in His Kingdom!**

- the stakes are higher
- the goal is greater
- the way to it is more difficult

but then it's also easy when you follow what He says here; notice that in encompasses everything about you:

Verse 30: "'And you shall love *the* Lord your God with all your heart, and with all your soul, and with all your mind, and with all your strength.' This *is the* first commandment"—*right directly to those and all of those who were listening,* the strict religionists following what they were following, and avoiding the Truth of God laid out from the Word of God by Jesus Christ.

Verse 31: "And *the* second *is* like this: 'You shall love your neighbor as yourself.' There is no other commandment greater than these.'"

As recorded in Matt. 22, Jesus said, ***'On these two commandments hang all the Law and the Prophets.'***

The Law and the Prophets *do not support these two commandments.* ***These two commandments support all the Law and the Prophets, because it comes from God first to us, and us back to God!*** And to our neighbor and the brethren, and even to our enemies.

That's the whole purpose of the Passover, ***that we learn this lesson to love God this way, and not let anything become between us and God!***

- *no person*

- *no thing*
- *no idea*
- *no doctrine*
- *no religion*

We need to remember that when we're taking the foot-washing, the bread and the wine:

- *the solemnity of it*
- *the power of it*
- *the purpose of it*

Verse 32: "Then the scribe said to Him, 'Right, Master. You have spoken according to Truth that God is one, and there is not another besides Him; and to love Him with all the heart, and with all the understanding, and with all the soul, and with all the strength, and to love *one's* neighbor as oneself, is more than all burnt offerings and sacrifices'" (vs 32-33).

Verse 34: "And Jesus, seeing that he answered with understanding, said to him, **'You are not far from the Kingdom of God.'**

You're close to it, but it's one thing to read the Word, it's another thing to agree that they are true. Yet, it's a third thing to apply them in our lives. *That's the whole purpose of Christianity! The whole purpose of the Passover!*

This day of confrontation kept going, v 35: "And *while* teaching in the temple, Jesus answered *and* said, 'How can the scribes say that the Christ is *the* Son of David? For David himself said by the Holy Spirit, "The Lord said to my Lord, 'Sit at My right hand, until I make Your enemies a footstool for Your feet.'" Now then, *if* David himself called Him Lord, how can He be his Son?' And the whole multitude listened to Him eagerly. And He said to them in His teaching…" (vs 35-38).

Here are the scribes, the Pharisees, the Sadducees and all of them:

Jesus said, "…'Beware of the scribes, who take pleasure in walking around in robes, and in salutations in the marketplaces, and in *the* chief seats in the synagogues and *the* chief places in the feasts; Who devour the houses of widows, and for a pretext make long prayers. These shall receive *the* greater condemnation'" (vs 38-40).

Let's see the final confrontation that convinced them that *they must kill Jesus!* This was so ignominious, so damning and so judgmental of them. Instead of accepting the Truth and repenting they sought the more to kill Him. This is an opportunity and a punishment. An opportunity if they would repent and believe, or a punishment if they felt that they had to continue in the way that they were going.

What was the ultimate penalty? *They rejected Jesus Christ!* The temple and the whole system were destroyed *exactly as Jesus said it would be!* To this day the Jews—except for a very few—refuse to believe that because of their rejection of Jesus and their sins against God, God had to send them off into dispersion into the whole world, just exactly as He prophesied in Jeremiah!

They didn't learn the lesson when God destroyed the temple in 539B.C. They didn't learn that! In every writing of the Jews blames all the enemies. Never do you see anything like we're going to read in Matt. 23 about their sins and their hypocrisy. Think about it, and you will see that down through history that is true and repeated over and over again.

Matthew 23:8 "But you… [the disciples] …are not to be called Rabbi; for **one is your Master, the Christ,** and all of you are brethren. Also, do not call *anyone* on the earth your Father; for one is your Father, Who *is* in heaven" (vs 8-9).

Here you have the whole Catholic Church saying that they represent Christ, and that they are the true religion of God. *They are breaking one of the most simple and easy to understand Scriptures!* They call their pope—the leader—'holy'!

Verse 10: "Neither be called Master; for one is your Master, the Christ. But the greatest among you shall be your servant." (vs 10-11). *That's what all the elders to do and serve the brethren*:

- to teach the Word of God
- to teach the love of God
- to teach the things in season

Now is the Passover season and time to really understand, again, *the greatness of the love and mercy of God and His sacrifice, and how Christ willingly laid down His life, and what He did to become that sacrifice!* So that it sinks deep into our heart, mind and being, and becomes a very part of our spiritual nature.

Verse 12: "And whoever will exalt himself shall be humbled; and whoever will humble himself shall be exalted." *If you exalt yourself under the mighty hand of God, and He will exalt you in due time at the resurrection!*

Verse 13: But **woe to you, scribes and Pharisees, hypocrites!**…. [double-minded; sanctimonious pretenders] …For you devour widows' houses, and as a pretext you offer prayers of great length. Because of this, you shall receive *the* greater judgment."

Did they not receive the greater judgment? *Yes, indeed!*

Verse 14: **Woe to you, scribes and Pharisees, hypocrites!** For you shut up the Kingdom of Heaven before men; for neither do you yourselves enter, nor do you allow those who are entering to enter."

You have all of your traditions that you place as more important than what God has commanded! So, Jesus is really bringing the confrontation in full power, because *He knows that this is going to seal their decision to crucify Him!*

Verse 15: "**Woe to you, scribes and Pharisees, hypocrites!** For you travel the sea and the land to make one proselyte, and when he has become one, you make him twofold more a son of Gehenna than yourselves."

Think about that for a minute! What is He saying? *If you keep doing what you're doing, you're destined for Gehenna fire!*

Verse 16: "**Woe to you, blind guides,** who say, 'Whoever shall swear by the temple, it is not binding; but whoever shall swear by the gold of the temple, he is obligated *to fulfill* his oath.' **You fools and blind!**…" (vs 16-17). *Morons! Idiots!* (Greek: 'idiotes')

"…For which is greater, the gold, or the temple, which sanctifies the gold? And *you say*, 'Whoever shall swear by the altar, it is not binding; but whoever shall swear by the gift that *is* upon it, he is obligated *to fulfill* his oath.' **You fools and blind!** For which is greater, the gift, or the altar, which sanctifies the gift? Therefore, the one who swears by the altar swears by it, and by all things that *are* upon it. And the one who swears by the temple swears by it, and by Him Who dwells in it. And the one who swears by heaven swears by the Throne of God, and by Him Who sits upon it" (vs 17-22).

Verse 23: "**Woe to you, scribes and Pharisees, hypocrites!** For you pay tithes of mint and anise and cummin, but you have abandoned the more important *matters* of the law—judgment, and mercy and faith…."—*the love of God* (Luke 11) *they have abandoned it!* How did they abandon it? *By placing their traditions as supreme!*

"…**These *you* were obligated to do, and not to leave the others undone**" (v 23).

This condemnation is absolutely something! It made them vehemently angry so that they would crucify Him.

Verse 24: "**Blind guides,** who filter out a gnat, but swallow a camel! **Woe to you, scribes and Pharisees, hypocrites!** For you cleanse the outside of the cup and the dish, but **within you are full of extortion and excess**" (vs 24-25).

We can learn some lessons here, v 26:

"**Blind Pharisees!** First **cleanse the inside** of the cup and the dish, so that the outside may also become clean."

That's the whole purpose of Passover and Unleavened Bread: *conversion of the heart and mind, with the washing of the Word of God and His Holy Spirit!* The writing of the Word of God in our heart and mind so that we can love God with all our heart, mind, soul, strength and being. That's the whole purpose of it. Jesus was tell them to take care of the inside: *your heart, mind, thoughts!*

Verse 27: "**Woe to you, scribes and Pharisees, hypocrites!** For you are like whited sepulchers, which indeed appear beautiful *on the* outside, but within are full of the bones of the dead, and of all uncleanness. Likewise, you also outwardly appear to men *to be* righteous, but within you are full of hypocrisy and lawlessness" (vs 27-28).

Isn't that a tremendous truth of all religionists and politicians, because they were religious and politicians.

Look at how bad the policies of the politicians are in America today. Look at what they have done in lying, hypocrisy, hatefulness; the media and all who are against law and order and truth! No society can be run by lawlessness. Nothing can exist or get done.

Same way with the Church. You can't have Christianity without the laws and commandments of God, because those are things that God wants us to do. Those are the works that God wants us to walk in and to do.

To say the Law has been done away makes all the Protestants lying hypocrites, just like the scribes and Pharisees. *It hasn't been done away!*

Verse 29: **Woe to you, scribes and Pharisees, hypocrites!** For you build the sepulchers of the prophets, and adorn the tombs of the righteous; and you say, 'If we had been in the days of our fathers, we would not have been partakers with them in the blood of the prophets'" (vs 29-30).

But they're about ready to partake of the blood of Jesus Christ!

Verse 31: "So then, you are testifying against yourselves, that you are the sons of those who killed the prophets, and *as for* you, you are filling up the measure of your fathers" (vs 31-32).

Notice how this continues; this is a heave lambaste to confront them for coming to arrest and crucify Him. They in their own minds will think that they are doing service to God.

Verse 33: "**_You serpents, _you offspring of vipers,**" how shall you escape the judgment of

Gehenna? Because of this, behold, I send to you prophets and wise *men* and scribes; and *some* of them you shall kill and crucify, and *some* of them you shall scourge in your synagogues, and *some of them you* shall persecute from city to city; so that **upon you** may come all *the* righteous blood poured out upon the earth, from the blood of Abel the righteous, unto the blood of Zacharias son of Barachias, whom you murdered between the temple and the altar. **Truly I say to you, all these things shall come upon this generation**" (vs 33-36).

- Did that happen? *Yes, it did!*
- Are the words of God true? *Yes, they are!*

This is why God wants us to understand the great sacrifice of Jesus Christ, and to understand the deep meaning of the Passover.

As we prepare for the Passover this coming Tuesday night, let's keep all these things in mind!

Verse 37—here's how Jesus felt about it: "Jerusalem, Jerusalem, *you* who kill the prophets and stone those who have been sent to you, how often would I have gathered your children together, even as a hen gathers her brood under *her* wings, **but you refused!** Behold, your house is left to you desolate. For I say to you, you shall not see Me at all from this time forward, until you shall say, **'Blessed *is* He Who comes in *the* name of *the* Lord**'" (vs 37-39).

Matthew 26:1: "Now, it came to pass *that* when Jesus had finished all these sayings, He said to His disciples, 'You know that after two days the Passover takes place, and the Son of man is delivered up to be crucified.' Then the chief priests and the scribes and the elders of the people assembled together in the court of the high priest, who was called Caiaphas; and *they* took counsel together for the purpose of seizing Jesus by treachery, and killing *Him*. But they said, 'Not during the Feast, so that there will not be a riot among the people.' Now, when Jesus was in Bethany, in Simon the leper's house" (vs 1-6). *This is a different one, the first anointing was in Lazarus' house!*

Verse 7: "A woman came to Him with an alabaster flask of ointment… [the second anointing] …very precious, and poured *it* on His head as He sat down *to eat*."

Then Judas went and got the 30 pieces of silver and set out to betray Jesus!

Let's take everything we need to do in preparation for the Passover and understand that we need to examine ourselves (1-Cor. 11). *If we examine ourselves and confess our sins, that we do not fall into the judgment of God!*

When we come to the Passover at the beginning of the third day, that we will come with an attitude and understanding that we need to have, *so that we worthily take of the Passover through the worthiness of Christ;* **not because of our worthiness, but because of:**

- **God's love**
- **God's mercy**
- **God's grace**
- **God's forgiveness**

Have a meaningful, deep and profound Passover!

Scriptural References:

1) John 12:1-3, 5-19
2) Matthew 21: 12-13
3) Luke 19:41-46
4) Mark 11:11-24
5) Ephesians 3:20
6) Mark 11:25-33
7) John 12:20-24
8) John 14:6
9) John 12:25-28
10) John 17:1-5
11) John 12:29-36
12) Mark 12:1-40
13) Matthew 23:8-39
14) Matthew 26:1-7

Scriptures referenced, not quoted:

- Galatians 2
- Luke 14
- John 3
- Deuteronomy 6
- Matthew 22
- Luke 11
- 1 Corinthians 11

Also referenced: Book; *A Harmony of the Gospels* by Fred R. Coulter

FRC:bo
Transcribed: 2/25/20
Reformatted: 10/2020

CHAPTER EIGHTEEN

The Last Ten Days of Jesus' Life I
The days of provocation
Fred R. Coulter

Greetings, brethren, welcome to Sabbath services! Before we get into the message I want to bring up about *The Christian Passover* book. I got an e-mail from a woman who said, 'Jesus died at the time the lambs were being killed at the temple.' Well, we will see that cannot be true.

Anybody remember what happened to the temple when He died? What else happened? *Earthquake!* They wouldn't be able to have any lambs there to offer, because the Holy of Holies was exposed, and everybody had to get out except the priests.

If you haven't received your book: *A Harmony of The Gospels,* yet, please order it. This is the third edition, second printing. When you get it, please read the commentaries. Those tell the story as we will see why that is so important. When we first did the *Harmony* in 1974, there are a lot of stories that go with that.

All the pictures that are in it—and we have many more in the other editions—we're all photos from the photo storage department from Ambassador College. I went in and asked the one who's in charge of it, and I said, do you have any photos that we could use? Well, by that time he heard I was doing the Gospel, he said, 'Here they are, all you want, just bring them back.'

So, I took them down to the printer. He took the printing photos of them, so they could be in the *Harmony*, and sized them to fit into different things. Also, these four pictures that are on the wall up here in the corner, they originally were in the original *Harmony*. Those sketches were done by Jay Vance. His profession was taking plans like Jonathan draws up and sketching how it would look in a three dimensional rendering.

Now then, all of those were done by Jay Vance, and he did it with a Rapidograph pen. That's a special pen that lets the ink out in very fine lines, almost like a needle. You can you can see it on the Passover book. Then he designed the York Publishing emblem, and York Publishing is the name that I use to publish it.

Dave Brady told me, 'You ought to write; you ought write a book.' That was because I was giving for the second time, and this was in 1972, the Last Ten Days of Jesus' Life. I said *no,* Rod Meredith ought to write it because he teaches first year Bible. I shouldn't write it.

Things changed because of all the politics and all of the coming after those who didn't bow down and scrape down to the 'falsity' of the hierarchy. So, my sanity project was—by studying and putting together the *Harmony*—so I could get my mind on Christ and not get wrapped up that all the wars of politics.

That took two years to get that done and then published. Then the second edition we change the cover to green, and the printer R.R. Donnelley did a very bad mistake. You see the picture on the cover with the sunburst. Why did I choose the sunburst? One man said, 'Why did you have this? It looks like an orthodox cross.' I said, 'It's the sun.'

Jesus said that 'the sign of the Son of man will shine from the east to the west.' So that's why we had it. The artist who did this—we paid him for it—by blowing through a narrow straw. You get those little dots and things like that. So, we appreciate that.

Now we have *A Harmony of the Gospels,* third edition, second printing, which means that the total printed was 60,000. Probably close to little over 50,000 have been distributed.

How did I come up with York Publishing? Well, David Brady said that no one likes to buy from a church, and you can't have a long name. You can't use your own name: Coulter's Publishing. He says it has to be short; it has to be something that people can identify with, even though they've never seen it.

So, one day I was driving to go down to Torrance, and I was going down Orange Grove Boulevard, down to Highway 110. I started down the freeway and at the first overpass there was the sign 'Next Exit York Boulevard.' That's it! Why was that a good name?

If you think of York, what do you hear all the time? *New York!* York is something people can identify with, though they don't know exactly, in this case, what it would mean. I won't get into all of the wars and politics that we had to go through down in Pasadena, but I'll tell you this: there was a concerted effort to completely root me and Delores out of the ministry—*period!*

When it came to a climatic head, Rod Meredith was fired, and the next day Al Caruso left. I mean, we went through things because I stood for a man who had been disfellowship politically, and he kept trying to get back into church, his name was Nolan. And that was quite a thing!

When you have a hierarchy, you can't disagree with it; especially the one in Pasadena. I won't get into that, but that gave time where I could get my mind off the politics, off the troubles and I did a paraphrase translation the first time because I didn't know enough Greek. I later I took Greek from Dr. Dorothy.

So, we are going to cover *The Last Ten Days of Jesus' Life*; that includes to His resurrection. Now then, this is the only *Harmony of the Gospels* that follows the chronology based upon the Calculated Hebrew Calendar, which is different than the Roman calendar. You can go back in time clear to creation, and you can go forward in time because based on the sun, the moon and the earth and the rules of how it is determined, you're always correct with the Holy Days. You could never do it by observation.

Did you see the super moon? Do you know what happens when there's a super moon? The moon is thousands of miles closer to the earth, and instead of 250,000 it is 211,000 miles away. Do you know what happens? *It moves quicker!*

So, you can't really determine, unless it's by calculation to account for the variance with the sun, the earth and the moon. Then God has figured all the relationship with the rest of the things in the universe for the calendar. How do we know it's always correct? *There are two days you can check on!*

A lot of people think they have to check on the new moon. No, you check on the two days that has to be the full moon: 15th day of the 1st month and the 15th day of the 7th month, always a full moon. Furthermore, there has to be two days of full moon in order to go clear around the earth. So, all you 'flat-earthers,' forget it. It is waxing when it comes to New Zealand, comes to full, comes around over here to the Western Hemisphere, and it's full, but it is waning.

Passover night: When you leave Passover night you can see that the moon is not quite full. But the next night it is full. Since 1960 I have been checking it every year. The only time I haven't been able to see it, is if it's cloudy and I can't see the moon. But it's always on time.

Now then, one other thing before we start here. A lot of people say, well you can't trust the Jewish calendar because the Jews did this, that and the other thing. Well, not the official Jews who were in charge of the calendar. A lot in Babylon tried to change it and do a lot of things because they wanted to take power to themselves. But the priests and the Levites in the Jewish community kept the calculation of the calendar correct.

'Well, we can't trust that.' All right, why don't you throw away the Old Testament, because they preserved it, too! If you can't trust one, you can't trust the other. If it's off, why is it always correct with the full moon? *Because there has to be adjustments for the new moon!* From the new moon to the full moon sometimes is not even 14 days. Sometimes it's almost 16 days. That's why there are the rules of adjustment, postponements and so forth, to keep it balanced.

Before we get into the last ten days, let's start out with the birth of Christ. You can study that in the Passover book. He was born in 5 B.C. I have a calendar from the Hebrew calendar. No other *Harmony* has anything like this, because they go by the Roman calendar and they have a Friday crucifixion, and they have a Palm Sunday, so they don't even know what they're talking about.

Jesus was born on the Feast of Trumpets, a Sabbath in 5 B.C. That means He was circumcised on the Sabbath before Atonement, which then made Him a legal resident of Israel. When Tabernacles came, He was tabernacling with all the people of God as an official member.

When He began His ministry—you can look up the calendar calculations in the appendices in the back of the *Harmony*—He started on the fourth day of the week in a Jubilee year. What is the Jubilee Year? What does the Jubilee stand for? *Release of slaves!* Jesus came to release people from the slavery of Satan and their sins.

But Jesus first had to be tempted by Satan the devil. His ministry was three and a half years. How many months are in three and a half years? Forty-two? *Wrong!* There were two years in His three and a half year ministry that were *leap years* and had an extra month in both of those. So, His ministry began on the fourth day, and was 44 months long. Then He was crucified on the fourth day, and He rose and ascended to the Father four days after He was crucified. So, #4 has a lot to do with Jesus' ministry and verifying it. Those signs are given, because the Jews always demand a sign.

How many days was He with the apostles before His final ascension? *Forty!* He starts out on the fourth day, 40 days temptation, then He is crucified on the fourth day of the week, three days in the grave, and then He ascends to the Father on the first day. Protestants look at that and say, 'That's why we keep Sunday.' *You have to read the Bible!*

What happened was, I heard a message by Dr. Hoeh about the last ten days of Jesus' life; that was in about 1963. I graduated in 1964 and then I heard a message by Dale Hampton on the last ten days of Jesus' life. In the first year of my ministry in Boise, Idaho—this would be the spring 1966—I decided to bring *The Last Ten Days of Jesus Life.*

So, I got my notes from Dr. Hoeh and Dale Hampton, and guess what I found? There was a one-day conflict. How did that happen? So, I got *Robertson's Harmony* to see if I could find where the one-day discrepancy was. Well, I couldn't find it, and that made it worse.

I took one Bible, opened it up to Matthew, one Bible opened it up to Mark, and one to Luke and one to John. I went through and started right here in John 12. I knew that we had to use a Calculated Hebrew Calendar. I'll show you where the extra day is recorded.

This is going to be easier than trying to go through the Scriptures in the Bible. The Scriptures will be the same here, but all in the organized manner.

From: *A Harmony of the Gospels* (third edition) by Fred R. Coulter

Section 282—Six Days Before His Last Passover, Jesus Comes to Bethany:

John 12:1: "Now, **six days before the Passover**, Jesus came to Bethany, where Lazarus was who had died, *and* whom He had raised from *the* dead."

Six Days Before Jesus' Last Passover

This chart combines the Roman calendar and the Hebrew calendar

- When does the day start in the Hebrew calendar? *Sunset! All days start at sunset!*
- When do they start on the Roman calendar? *Midnight!*

So, if you look carefully at the chart, you will see that I have it divided. I have sunset/sunrise, and then it overlaps on the bottom, I have the Roman dates. I want you to count forward—counting is inclusive—starting with the first day. Day five: Nisan 8, 1-2-3-4-5-6 days *before* the Passover. So, the Passover is the 7th day from when we started here in verse one.

Verse 2: "There they made a supper *for* Him, and Martha served; and Lazarus was one of those who sat with Him. Mary then..." (vs 2-3).

I want you to notice Mary is named, because we'll see something here in a minute, because Jesus was anointed twice, not once.

Verse 3: "**Mary** then took a pound of pure spikenard ointment...

I don't know anything about spikenard ointment.

...worth a great price *and* anointed **Jesus' feet** wiping His feet with her hair. And the house was filled with the aroma of the ointment. As a result, one of His disciples, Judas Iscariot, Simon's *son*, who was about to betray Him, said, 'Why was this ointment not sold for three hundred silver coins, and given to *the* poor?'" (vs 3-5).

What is one of the ways that evil people appear to be righteous? *By giving to the poor!*

Sidebar: I got a brand new book—a nice big thick one—called *In The Closet In The Vatican: Power, Homosexuality, Hypocrisy* by Frederic Martel. Homosexuality is rampant, all of them. It's quite a book. He took three years in writing it has been published in English and in French, and I don't know what the other language was simultaneously. Brand new publication, so I'll let you know about it, about how homosexuality is rampant in the Catholic Church. Guess what's rampant in the nunneries? *Lesbianism!* No wonder Rev. 17 says *'filled with abominations and blasphemies.'* That's what it is. So, Simon wanted to *appear* righteous.

Verse 6: "Now he said this, not because he cared for the poor, but because he was a thief, and had the bag, and carried what was put in *it*. Then Jesus said, 'Let her alone; she has been keeping it toward the day of My burial. For you have the poor with you always, but you do not always have Me.' Then a great crowd of the Jews found out that He was there....'" (vs 6-9)

Notice it was a supper (v 2). So, this is at sunset, or the beginning of the day. That's why on the chart we have it where it is.

"...And they came, not only because of Jesus, but also that they might see Lazarus, whom He had raised from *the* dead. But the chief priests took counsel in order that they might kill Lazarus also...

you have got to get rid of all the evidence

...because by reason of him, many of the Jews were leaving *them* and believing in Jesus" (vs 9-10).

You can see the picture in the *Harmony*. These are some of the pictures that we got from the

Ambassador photo file of the model city. Now a key thing in the chronology:

> Luke 19:47: "Now, He was teaching day-by-day in the temple; and the chief priests and the scribes and the chief of the people were seeking to destroy Him."

The Day Portion—Nisan 8—Thursday, March 30, 30 AD.

Section 283—Jesus' Triumphal Entry into Jerusalem

The Church of God used to say that this palm day was a palm Sabbath. Why did they say that? *Because the Catholics and Protestants say Palm Sunday!* Why do they say that? *Because they believe in a Friday crucifixion!*

So, the Church said it couldn't be on a Sunday; it had to be on a Sabbath; but it couldn't be on the Sabbath. Why could it not happen on the Sabbath? *We'll read it and will answer the question when we're done!*

Now we have all four accounts. John's account does not have where Jesus told him to go get the donkey. The reason I have John 12 here is because of the chronology.

> John 12:12: "On the next day...

in the morning after their dinner

> ...a great crowd *of people* who had come for the Feast, when they heard that Jesus was coming into Jerusalem, took branches from palm trees and went out to meet Him, and were shouting, 'Hosanna! Blessed *is* He Who comes in *the* name of *the* Lord, the King of Israel'" (vs 12-13).

- What does this tell us?
- Why could this not happen on the Sabbath?

> Matthew 21:7: "They brought the donkey and the colt, and put their garments upon them; and He sat on them. And a great number *of the* multitude spread their garments on the road; and others were cutting down branches from the trees and spreading *them* on the road. And the multitudes, those who were going before and those who were following behind, were shouting, saying, 'Hosanna to the Son of David! Blessed is He Who comes in *the* name of *the* Lord. Hosanna in the highest!'" (vs 7-9).

Then we have in the account in Luke 19 that the Pharisees said, 'Don't have them shouting. Jesus said, 'If I stopped, the stones would shout! If this was on the Sabbath, what would the Pharisees say? *You're teaching the disciples to break the Sabbath,* because they're breaking down branches, and they're putting this on the road for you to go. This is why this has to be on a Thursday. We find that in the Luke account.

> Luke 19:39: "And some of the Pharisees in the multitude said to Him, 'Master, rebuke Your disciples.' But He answered *and* said to them, 'I tell you that if these were silent, the stones would cry out'" (vs 39-40).

How would that work? *I have no idea!* The closest we can come to understand it is Rev. 5, where every created thing is praising God the Father and Jesus Christ in heaven, on earth, under the earth and in the sea. I could see the whales doing it, but I can't see the minnows doing that. But that's all possible. Maybe the big frogs; I wonder what that would sound like? *Frogs praising God!*

Section 284—Jesus Weeps Over the City of Jerusalem

How many times did Jerusalem reject God? Just read the book of Jeremiah. Read the book of Isaiah. Read the problems that they had in Ezra and Nehemiah, just trying to keep the Jews from going out and apostatizing.

One account was that Nehemiah was so upset, he grabbed one of the renegade priests and punched him in the face, because he was having one of the Ashdod women, instead of having an Aaronic woman.

> Luke 19:41: "And when He came near *and* saw the city, **He wept over it,** saying, 'If you had known, even you, at least in this your day, the things for your peace; but now they are hidden from your eyes'" (vs 41-42).

Why don't people understand? *'They close their eyes, they close their ears, they don't want to hear'* (Matt. 13).

Now try this on the Protestants sometime. Just walk up to them and say, 'I've got God's answer to the evangelicals. They use two main Scriptures, that don't even need the whole Bible. Ask them, 'Why don't you keep the Sabbath?' *Oh, that's for the Jews. We keep it on Sunday.*

They don't know what they are missing. They don't know that the Sabbath is God's day. If they kept the Sabbath and if they kept it to honor God, **would not God open up the Truth to them?** If they were seeking Him? *Yes, it would happen!*

> Verse 43: "For *the* days shall come upon you that your enemies shall cast a rampart about you, and shall enclose you around and keep you in on every side."

You want to know the ghastly slaughter of what happened with the destruction of Jerusalem and the temple, read the account in *Josephus*. It was awful! When those who were trying to escape, they would be captured and they would cut them open to see if they had any gold or anything in their stomach. Those who they knew didn't have any they crucified them.

Josephus says that there were so many being crucified, that they were waiting for them to die on the cross, so they can put new ones up there. I mean, it was a slaughter.

- it's not a good thing to reject God
- it's not a good thing to reject the words of Christ

That sure happened!

Verse 44: "And shall level you to the ground, and your children within you; and they shall not leave in you a stone upon a stone..."

Sounds a little bit like Matt. 24, Mark 13 and Luke 21, 'not one stone upon the stone.' That was not just for the temple. That was the whole city of Jerusalem. The Jews made themselves such an absolute stench in the nose of the Romans, that they took Jerusalem and did that, and plowed it like a field. That fulfilled the Scripture of the prophecy of the destruction of Jerusalem.

What everyone needs to do is realize that the Word of God is true. The only way you're going to understand it is to believe it, and what God says we need to do: *obey it!*

Section 285—Jesus Goes into the Temple and Returns that Evening to Bethany

Mark 11:11: "And Jesus entered Jerusalem and went into the temple; and *because* the hour was already late, after looking around at everything *there*, He went out to Bethany with the twelve."

Then He came back in the morning

Section 286—Jesus Teaches Daily in the Temple

Luke 19:47: "Now, He was **teaching day-by-day in the temple**; and the chief priests and the scribes and the chief of the people **were seeking to destroy Him**, but could not find what they might do; for all the people were listening *intently*, hanging on His *every word*" (vs 47-48).

These days were the days leading up to the crucifixion of Christ. *Christ was provoking them!* He knew what they were going to do, but he gave them good cause to think they were right in doing what they were doing.

Friday, March 31, 30 AD

Section 287 Jesus Curses the Fig Tree:

Mark 11:12: "And in the morning, after they left Bethany, He became hungry. Then, seeing a fig tree afar off that had leaves, He went *to it to see* if He might possibly find something on it. But after coming to it, He found nothing except leaves because it was not yet *the* season for figs" (vs 12-13).

- Why would Jesus do that?
- What about Adam and Eve?
- What did they use to hide their nakedness? *Fig leaves!*

Israel in the Old Testament is combined in a parable:

1. to a vineyard
2. to a fig tree

The reason that this is here is because Jerusalem and the temple, because this was on the way to the temple, and the priest and all of them there did not bring forth any fruit to eternal life. There was nothing. They had no spiritual fruit. That's the whole lesson.

Verse 14: "And Jesus responded *by* saying to it, 'Let no one eat fruit from you any more forever!' And His disciples heard *it.*"

If you read Matt. 21, it looks like that cursing and shriveling up happen immediately. *But it didn't!* This is the missing day, between Dr. Hoeh and Dale Hampton. Here's the key.

Sabbath, Nisan 10—Saturday, April 1, 30 AD

Section 288—They Go Up to Jerusalem the Next Morning:

Mark 11:20: "And in the morning, as they passed by, they saw the fig tree dried up from *the* roots...."

Jesus cursed it one day and in the morning they came back and found it dried up!

...Then Peter remembered *and* said to Him, 'Look, Master! The fig tree that You cursed has dried up'" (vs 20-21).

Since you have the pictures here in the *Harmony*, I want to show you something. Look at the picture on page 220; see the tree with all of its leaves on it. Look at the picture on page 221, see the tree was no leaves on it. *Same tree!* How did I get the picture of this? *This was a tree before the plague of locusts came on pgs 220-221!* This is how they left it. I thought that would be a good example of how they are drying up, *nothing on it!*

Verse 22: "And Jesus answered and said to them..."

This is very important, because now we're beginning to get into some of the things that we're going to learn for the Feast of Unleavened Bread. God is not interested in just your exterior conduct. He's interested the **conversion that is in the mind and the heart!** He doesn't want a change of behavior, **He wants a conversion of thinking** so that your behavior will be as God wants it.

Even the worst criminal… Have you seen them do interviews of those who are lifers? They come in there and the reporters come up. 'This person is such a nice person, I just don't understand how it was possible.' Well, he can be very nice. Same way with a con man or a con woman, they can be very nice. You don't know how evil they are, until you've lost all your money! Then you know what happened!

Same way with 'religion.' Religion is a good factor in the society to give a little check on the carnal mind, to have a little better behavior. But nothing can display the evil that's in the heart and mind of even the religionists, than this latest book *In the Closet In The Vatican.* **They're all hypocrites and liars!**

Now let's come to page 220—I want to go over this again about the two days concerning the cursing of the fig tree and it shriveling up.

Mark 11:15: "Then they came into Jerusalem; and after entering the temple, Jesus began to cast out those who were buying and selling in the temple; and He overthrew the tables of the money exchangers and the seats of those who were selling doves."

What we're going to see from this time forward through the next day is what I call **the days of provocation.** We need to look at it from the point of view:

- How was the atmosphere around Jerusalem?
- How many angels were there making sure everything works out the way that it should?
- How many demons and Satan were there?

We know that Satan possessed Judas Iscariot to betray Jesus!

What sort of spiritual battle was going on behind the scenes that we couldn't see? Here's the provocation. You go into the temple and you start

doing all of this. Now remember, the first time Jesus went into the temple, He did it in John 2. Here again, He comes in, and in the most sacred place, He starts overthrowing everything, and chasing them all out.

Verse 16: "Moreover, He did not allow anyone to carry a vessel through the temple. And He taught, saying to them, 'Is it not written, "My house shall be called a house of prayer for all nations"?....'" (vs 16-17).

Think about that! The Jews did not allow the Gentiles to come, except in a cordoned off area. They couldn't go any further unless they would be killed. But this is also a prophecy of the coming temple of God in heaven, which is a house of prayer for all people, all nations.

"…'But you have made it a den of robbers.' Now, the chief priests and the scribes heard *this*, and they sought how they might destroy Him; for they feared Him, because all the multitudes marveled at His teaching. And when evening came, He went out of the city" (vs 17-19).

Of course, that's back to Bethany!

Section 288—They Go Up To Jerusalem

That's when they saw that the fig tree the next morning had dried up. Then Jesus taught them a lesson.

Mark 11:21: "Then Peter remembered *and* said to Him, 'Look, Master! The fig tree that You cursed has dried up.' And Jesus answered and said to them, '**Have faith from God**'" (vs 21-22).

The actual Greek means *have the faith of God.* It has to come from God to us. That's why I translated it, "…Have faith *from* God."

Verse 23: "For truly I say to you, whoever shall say to this mountain, 'Be taken away and be cast into the sea,' and shall not doubt in his heart, but shall believe that what he said will take place, he shall have whatever he shall say."

That's the extreme of it. What is harder than moving a mountain? *Changing the carnal mind!* That's harder! And if you wanted a mountain removed, *it would have to be according to the will of God,* not according to your will. What He says is a very important key, one of the New Testament teachings that goes on into all of the epistles.

Verse 24: "For this reason I say to you, all *the* things that you ask *when* you are praying, believe that you will receive *them*, and *they* shall be *given* to you.

It goes from the mountain to all things. Sometimes prayers are answered almost immediately. Sometimes it takes a long time. Sometimes it even takes years. Have you ever had it that you're going along and all of a sudden you think: God answered that prayer! You even forgot that you prayed about it. But He gives another caveat.

Verse 25: "But when you stand praying... [or if you're kneeling] ....if you have **anything against anyone**... [Is that all inclusive?] ...forgive..."

Even if you have to do it reluctantly, still forgive. But do it from the heart!

"...so that your Father Who *is* in heaven may forgive you your offenses" (v 25).

Very interesting! Now in the series that we have *Keys To Answered Prayer*, we go through all kinds of prayer. Also, in the healing; healing is important. It is true, that you must forgive those in your own mind before God, who maybe they have already died! *But it's in the mind, and that is a blockage of your faith to God!*

"...if you have **anything against anyone**... [that is all inclusive] ...forgive, so that your Father Who *is* in heaven may forgive you your offenses. For if you do not forgive, neither will your Father Who *is* in heaven forgive you your offenses" (vs 25-26).

That is instruction *in perfection*. Remember that Jesus identified that conversion is not just your outward behavior, but your inward thoughts.

Matthew 5:48 tells the ultimate of it: "Therefore, you shall be perfect, even as your Father Who *is* in heaven is perfect." *That's the ultimate highest standard, and that will not be fulfilled until the resurrection!*

Sabbath, Nisan 10—Saturday, April 1, 30 AD

Section 289: Certain Hellenist Jews Want to See Jesus

John 12:20: "Now there were certain Greeks among those who had come up to worship at the Feast. And these came to Philip, who was from Bethsaida of Galilee; and they asked him, saying, 'Sir, we desire to see Jesus.' Philip came and told Andrew, and Andrew and Philip in turn told Jesus. But Jesus answered them, saying, 'The time has come for the Son of man to be glorified. Truly, truly I say to you, unless a grain of wheat falls into the ground and dies, it remains alone; **but if it dies, it bears much fruit**'" (vs 20-24).

The only way for it to die is to plant it, and plant it in good soil. We've got some wheat at home, that we have had for, I would say about 40 years now; somewhere around there. It's still wheat! It's in these cans and nothing has changed. When they cleaned out one of these compartments in pyramids, they found some wheat that was over 3,000-years-old. They planted it and it's sprouted and grew! So likewise here:

How do we die? How did Paul say he died? *He said, 'I die daily'!* That is overcoming human nature. We can't produce the fruit of God, until we are overcoming human nature on a regular basis. As long as we're in the flesh we still have human nature. We have to work against it. That's the process of conversion. We'll cover that more a little later during the Feast.

Verse 25: "The one who loves his life shall lose it..."

I don't know how many have gone through some of the things that John Gunether has done with the Waldensians, and so forth. I imagine they read this Scripture an awful lot. They were slaughtered and tortured.

"...and the one who hates his life in this world shall keep it unto eternal life" (v 25).

Because the very best of every human being, every single one of them has, and we do to, 'the law of sin and death.' But only when you receive the power of the Holy Spirit, are you able to overcome the lust of the flesh and all of the things of 'the law of sin and death' within us.

That's the struggle. And the struggle is defined by Paul in Rom. 7, which is one of the most difficult Scriptures in the Bible to understand, if you're only thinking about keeping the commandments to change your exterior behavior.

Verse 26: "If anyone will serve Me, let him follow Me; and where I am, there shall My servant be also. And if anyone serves Me, him shall the Father honor. Now My soul is troubled, and what shall I say? Father, save Me from this hour? **But for this *very* purpose I have come to this hour**" (vs 26-27). *He knew!*

All right, next page, you'll see one of the etchings of Jay Vance. He very carefully hid his name in very small print. I can't even find it.

Section 290—Sabbath, Nisan 10—Saturday [Sabbath], April 1—30 AD

When were the Israelites to select the lamb for Passover? *Tenth day of the first month!* Keep it until the 14th. We'll see that they were to slay it right after sunset on the 13th. We'll find that section a little later. Now then, this is actually God the Father selecting Christ as 'the Lamb to take away the sin of the world.'

Why did John write it that way? Why didn't he say, 'Take away the **sins** of the world'? Why did he say, 'Take away the **sin** of the world'? *Because the sin of the world __is the sin of Adam and Eve,__ and that nature was passed on to us!* So, it is the sin of Adam that is the sin of the world, and every human being in every generation in every country, every nation.

John 12:28: "Father, glorify Your name..."

All you sacred-namers, think on this. Nowhere, *nowhere, **nowhere*** do you find any sacred name from the Hebrew language in the Greek New Testament. God had it written in Greek because it was not connected with the Old Testament and their practices.

Everyone who gives a translation, and puts *what they think* the name ought to be in Hebrew here translated into English, they're adding to and taking away from. What is the Father's sacred name? *The Father!* That's what it is!

"...Then a voice came from heaven, *saying*, 'I have both glorified *it* and will glorify *it* again.' Then the people standing *there*, who heard *it*, said, 'It thundered.' Others said, 'An angel spoke to Him.' Jesus answered and said, 'This voice did not come because of Me, but because of you'" (vs 28-30).

The selection of the Lamb on the Sabbath Day for the removal of the sin of the world. But it is removed, one by one as God calls.

Verse 31: "Now is *the* judgment of this world. Now shall the prince of this world be cast out. And if I be lifted up from the earth, I will draw all to Myself" (vs 31-32).

Remember, that's what he said to Nicodemus (John 3). If the Son of Man be lifted up, they knew that meant to be crucified. They understood that.

Verse 33: "But He said this to signify by what death He was about to die. The people answered Him, 'We have heard out of the law that the Christ lives forever, and why do You say that the Son of man must be lifted up? Who is this Son of man?'" (vs 33-34).

In spite of everything that went on, they still didn't know.

Verse 35: "Then Jesus said to them, 'Yet, a little while the Light is with you....'"

Jesus is referred to as 'the Light of the world, Light of all men.

- John 1: 4, 7-9
- John 3:19-36

He is the Light and those who love God will come to the Light, those who do not will go away from the Light. They don't want to come to the Light lest their deeds are exposed.

- John 8:12
- John 9:5

All showing the Christ is the Light!

Verse 35: "Then Jesus said to them, 'Yet, a little while the Light is with you. Walk while you have the Light, so that *the* darkness will not overtake you. For the one who walks in darkness does not know where he is going.'"

How can you have any real purpose in life if you don't know why you were born? Why you were called? Look at all the lives. Look at all the people. I've got at home a composite of world history called *Langer's Encyclopedia of World History.* You know what it really is? It's a history of every fight and battle in every nation, every country down through all time. *It is incredible!*

Section 291—Jesus Leaves the City Again:

"...Jesus spoke these things and *then* departed from them *and* was *in* hiding. Although He had done so many miracles in their presence, they did not believe in Him, so that the word of Isaiah the prophet might be fulfilled who said, 'Lord, who has believed our report? And to whom has the arm of *the* Lord been revealed?' For this *very* reason they could not believe because again Isaiah said, 'He has blinded their eyes and hardened their hearts...'" (vs 36-40).

Why would God do that? Protestants believe they've got to get out there and save everyone. Why would God do this? *Because, if they are not coming to conversion, **He doesn't want them to know, so that they can do so in the second resurrection!*** Now, you couldn't understand this, unless you have this knowledge of the second resurrection.

There are only two places in the Bible that talk about it. Ezek. 37 and Rev. 20:

- Ezek. 37 talks about Israel and the valley of dry bones. Meaning they lived once, but died.
- Rev. 20 says, the rest of the dead, who are not in the first resurrection, live again after the thousand years.

So, just those two Scriptures alone put together, answers the question, why God would do it. Now think on this. This is why the first fruits are so important. God doesn't do things like the way people think.

> "'...so that they would not see with *their* eyes and understand with *their* hearts, and be converted, and I would heal them.' Isaiah said these things when he saw His glory and spoke concerning Him" (vs 40-41)

Now then, here is **the day of provocation,** and what a day this is. This is something!

> Section 293—<u>Nisan 11, Sunday, April 2, 30 AD.</u>
>
> Mark 11:27: "Then they came again to Jerusalem. And as He was walking in the temple, the chief priests and the scribes and the elders came to Him; and they said to Him, 'By what authority are You doing these things? And who gave You this authority, that You do these things?'" (vs 27-28).

They asked this because they didn't give Him that authority. And they thought all authority for anything had to come through them.

> Verse 29: "Then Jesus answered and said to them, 'I also will ask you one thing, and *if* you answer Me, I will also tell you by what authority I do these things.'"

Now remember this when you're trapped by anybody in a conversation. Don't answer them; ask a question. He put them really between a rock and a hard spot here.

> Verse 30: "The baptism of John, was it from heaven or from men? Answer Me."

Remember that in John 1, Matt. 3 and Luke 3? Who came to John's baptism? *The scribes and the Pharisees!* They said to John, who are you? Are you the Christ? Are you that Prophet? John said, 'No, I'm not either one.' Who are you? *I'm a voice crying in the wilderness to prepare the way of the Lord!*

They knew from the beginning with John, but what did they do? If your heart is hardened, and your eyes are blinded, and you have your own satanic purpose, because here's this battle going on, **on this day of provocation.** This is done deliberately by Christ to finalize their excuse to kill Him.

> Verse 31: "And they reasoned among themselves, saying..."

I always get a kick out of this. They've got to have a little council meeting before they can answer it!

> "...'If we say, "From heaven," He will say, "Why then did you not believe him?" But if we say, "From men"'; they feared the people, because everyone held that John was indeed a prophet. And they answered Jesus by saying, 'We do not know.'...." (vs 31-33).

They knew!

> "...Then Jesus answered *and* said to them, 'Neither will I tell you by what authority I do these things'" (v 33).

It's virtually the same in Matthew and in Luke. Then He got right with them.

> Section 294—<u>The Parable of The Two Sons</u>

Jesus speaking right to them. He's pointing out what they're doing wrong, and He's also giving them an opportunity to repent if they would. Could they repent? *If they really wanted to they could!* So, He said:

> Mathew 21:28: "But what do you think? A man had two sons, and he came to the first one and said, 'Son, go work in my vineyard today.'"

Jesus uses the vineyard many times. He compares Israel to a vineyard (Isa. 5). When He came for the fruit, He found wild grapes. What happened?

> Verse 29: "And he answered *and* said, 'I will not'; but afterwards he repented *and* went. Then he came to the second *son and* said the same thing. And he answered *and* said, 'Sir, I will *go*'; but he did not go. Which of the two did the will of the father?' They said to Him, 'The first *one*.' Jesus said to them, 'I tell you truly, the tax collectors and *the* harlots are going into the Kingdom of God before you'" (vs 29-31).

Think about that. Here's the elite. That's almost like going to Washington, DC, and telling all the elite you're all going to burn in hell because you are not doing what you're supposed to do. You say one thing and do another. You say we will take care of the people. But you take care of yourselves. Same thing. The lowest of the people:

> Verse 32: "For John came to you...

Did they go to John? *Yes, they did!*

> ...in *the* way of righteousness, and you did not believe him; but the tax collectors and *the* harlots believed him. Yet, you, after seeing *this*, did not afterwards repent and believe him."

Quite a thing! We have a lot to cover on this day; it will take us a couple of sessions to get through. But here again He talks about the vineyard. What does he say in John 15 about Himself and the Church?

He says, 'I am the vine, My Father is the husbandman. Now some translations say farmer. Husbandman is better, because the husband is one who takes care of his wife and his family. So, the Father is the One Who is working in us with Christ. What did He say? *You are the branches!* We have to stay attached to the vine. Otherwise we can't bring forth fruit.

Books:

- *A Harmony of the Gospels for Students of the Life of Christ* by A.T. Robertson
- *In the Closet In The Vatican*: *Power, Homosexuality, Hypocrisy* by Frederic Martel
- *Josephus*
- *Langer's Encyclopedia of World History*

FRC:bo
Transcribed: 3/6/19
Reformatted: 10/2020

Scriptural References:

1) John 12:1-10
2) Luke 19:47
3) John 12:12-13
4) Matthew 21:7-9
5) Luke 19:39-44
6) Mark 11:11
7) Luke 19:41-48
8) Mark 11:11
9) Luke 19:47-48
10) Mark 11:12-14, 20-22, 15-19, 21-26
11) Matthew 5:48
12) John 12:20-41
13) Mark 11:27-33
14) Matthew 21:28-32

Scriptures referenced, not quoted:

- Revelation 17; 5
- Matthew 13; 24
- Mark 13
- Luke 21
- John 2
- Romans 7
- John 3
- John 1:4, 7-9
- John 3:19-36
- John 8:12
- John 9:5
- Ezekiel 37
- Revelation 20
- Matthew 3
- Luke 3
- Isaiah 5
- John 15

Also referenced:

Books & Studies by Fred R. Coulter {**truthofGod.org**}:

- *The Christian Passover*
- *A Harmony of The Gospels*
- In-Depth Study: *Keys To Answered Prayer*

CHAPTER NINETEEN

The Last Ten Days of Jesus' Life II

A day great provocation and confrontation to provoke them to crucify Him

Fred R. Coulter

We've been going through a series: *The Last Ten Days of Jesus' Life, so* this is more like a Bible study, word for word. So, if you have your *Harmony,* turn to page 225, because this is where we will begin. This is only the third time in 54 years that I've given this.

I think we need to grasp what was really happening, especially on *this day of provocation.* Let's see what we are dealing with, and how the religious leaders responded to Christ and how Christ responded to them, how He talked to them.

I imagine there would be a lot of people today, just like back then, that would be offended if they heard what Jesus said, and the way He said it. Remember the one where the man who said, 'I'll follow you, Lord.' If you Looking for followers you'd say, 'Oh yes, but I got to go bury my father.' Well why don't you do that and catch up with me a little later.

What did Jesus say? 'Let the dead bury their dead.' Think of how all the 'politically correct nuts' would go crazy over this kind of thing. He talked very straightforward. In the John 5:30—after He explained a little bit about the resurrection and so forth, and this is what we need to keep in mind with our selves.

Remember what Paul told the elders from Ephesus when they came to Miletus to see Paul for the last time, he said, *'Take heed to yourself.'* So, here is a good verse for us to understand *take heed to ourselves,* that whatever we have we received; *there's nothing that we didn't receive from God* even in the physical realm.

So, here's Jesus, Who was God manifested in the flesh, Who could do anything He wanted to do if He wanted to do it. But His choice was this:

John 5:30: "**I have no power to do anything of Myself**... [that means *out from within My own self, My own thoughts*] ...but as I hear, I judge; and My judgment is just because I do not seek My own will **but the will of the Father Who sent Me.** If I bear witness of Myself, My testimony is not true. There is another who bears witness of Me, and I know that the testimony that he witnesses concerning Me is true. You have sent to John, and he has borne witness to the Truth. Now, I do not receive witness from man, but I say these things so that you may be saved" (vs 30-34).

He's talking to the religious leaders, all the priests. Remember that He healed the man who had been infirm for 38 years. Here's a man going around carrying his sleeping bag. They said, 'You're carrying a burden on the Sabbath!' He said, 'The man who healed me....' Who healed you? *He didn't know!* Later, Jesus found him, then he went and snitched and told all of the priests.

So, here they are all around right at the temple. If you really understand how these things were going on, it's quite a really big deal indeed.

Verse 35: "He was a burning and shining light, and you were willing for a time to rejoice in his light. But I have a greater witness than John's; for the works that the Father gave Me to complete, the *very* works that I am doing, themselves bear witness of Me..." (vs 35-36).

In other words, look at the man that was healed. Why aren't you rejoicing? I mean, 38 years. Isn't that long enough to be infirm? *Way too long!*

"...the *very* works that I am doing, themselves bear witness of Me, that the Father has sent Me" (v 36).

Now they understood *The Most High.* And in a series we did on that—*The Lord God and The Most* High—we know in the New Testament, *that's the Father.*

Verse 37: "And the Father Himself, Who sent Me, has borne witness of Me. You have neither heard His voice nor seen His form at any time."

Today we can think of it as if this were going on at St. Peter's Basilica during a conclave of the pope and all the cardinals and all of that thing.

Verse 38: "And **you do not have His Word dwelling in you**..." What did they have dwelling in them, in their minds? *Their authority, their traditions, their hierarchy!*

"...for you do not believe Him Whom He has sent. You search the Scriptures... [How many times did Jesus say, 'Have you never read?' *or* 'Didn't you read this?'] ...for in them you think that you have eternal life... [they didn't] ...and they are the ones that testify of Me. But you are unwilling to come to Me, that you may have life" (vs 39-40).

The rest of this is really about as sharp a two-edged sword coming out of Christ mouth that you could possibly want.

Verse 41: "**I do not receive glory from men**; but I have known you, that you do not have the love of God in yourselves. I have come in My Father's name, and you do not receive Me; *but* if another comes in his own name, you will receive him. How are you able to believe, you who receive glory from one another, and do not seek the glory that *comes* from the only God? Do not think that I will accuse you to the Father. There is *one* who accuses you, *even* Moses, in whom you have hope. But if you believed Moses, you would have believed Me; for he wrote about Me. And if you do not believe his writings, how shall you believe My words?" (vs 41-47).

Very interesting verse, right there the last one. People say, well the Old Testaments is all done away. What do you know about that; if you don't believe Moses, you can't believe Jesus.

I tell you, for the apostle who was the one whom Jesus loved, you would think He would write some really nice wonderful things. But all of these are recording the Truth of Jesus' ministry to the hierarchy and those in the in Jerusalem and the priesthood. They kept saying, 'We're Abraham's seed, and that's why we are what we are.'

John 8:37: "**I know that you are Abraham's seed**; but you are seeking to kill Me, because My words do not enter into your *minds*. I speak the things that I have seen from My Father, and you do the things that you have seen from your father.' They answered and said to Him, 'Our father is Abraham.' Jesus said to them, 'If you were Abraham's children...'" (vs 37-39).

He said, "**I know that you are Abraham's seed...**" What's the difference between *seed* and *children*? *The children obeyed!* The seed Esau did not!

"...'If you were Abraham's children, you would do the works of Abraham. But now you seek to kill Me...'" (vs 39-40).

Remember the first healing recorded (Mark 3), the man in the in the synagogue with the withered arm? When Jesus healed him, they were all mad and they got together and said, 'How are we going to eliminate this guy?' So, this is all building up and it's all building up to this one particular day, Sunday, the first day of the week, Nisan 11. And it has almost as many Scriptures as it does about the Passover, crucifixion and resurrection.

What we're going to read when we finish here is going to be mightily important.

"...a Man who has spoken the Truth to you, which I have heard from God; Abraham did not do this. You are doing the works of your father.' Then they said to Him, 'We have not been born of fornication.... [everything about Jesus was known] ...We have one Father, *and that is* God.' Therefore, Jesus said to them, 'If God were your Father, you would love Me, because I proceeded forth and came from God. For I have not come of Myself, but He sent Me. **Why don't you understand My speech? Because you cannot *bear* to hear My words. You are of *your* father the devil**..." (vs 41-44). *Try that with Sabbath with a staunch Sunday-keeper. You get about the same reaction.*

Now stop and think about this for a minute: Where does the devil like to come all the time? At the top! When the temptation occurred, it was Satan and Christ. And one apostle was picked because he was of Satan to betray Christ. How does Satan like to do? *Come in and change the teaching, the interpretation!*

"...and the lusts of your father you desire to practice. He was a murderer from *the* beginning, and has not stood in the Truth because there is no Truth in him. Whenever he speaks a lie, he is speaking from his own *self*; for he is a liar, and the father of it. And because I speak the Truth, you do not believe Me. Which *one* of you can convict Me of sin?...." (vs 44-46).

Let's come back to the *Harmony* here, page 225. All of these are very deliberate things to come against the religious leaders there, to provoke them to crucify Him. This is all done in public and they couldn't take Him, because the people thought Christ was a prophet and they would stone them, etc, as we saw.

A Harmony of the Gospels, pg. 225—Nisan 11—Sunday, April 2, 30 AD

Section 295—The Parable of the Vineyard

Mark 12:1: "And He began to speak to them in parables: 'A man planted a vineyard, and put a fence around *it*, and dug a wine vat, and built a tower, and leased it out to husbandmen, and *then* left the country.'"

Compare Isa. 5—Israel and Judah were compared to a vineyard that he planted. When he came for fruit he found wild grapes. So they knew, *they knew exactly what He was talking about!*

Verse 2: "And at the *harvest* season he sent a servant..."

Then he sent many servants. Finally He sent his son and they killed him.

Verse 7: "But those husbandmen said among themselves, 'This is the heir. Come, let us kill him, and the inheritance shall be ours.' And after seizing him, they killed *him* and cast *him* out of the vineyard. Therefore, what will the lord of the vineyard do? He will come and destroy the husbandmen..." (vs 7-9).
Matthew 21:41: "They said to Him, 'Evil *men!....*"

talking about themselves

"... He will utterly destroy them, and he will lease his vineyard to other husbandmen…'"

Luke 20:16: "He will come and destroy these husbandmen..."

Very interesting indeed! They knew that this was about them.

Matt. 21:43—notice what Jesus is saying, because here is what they were looking for: When the Messiah would come He would be human, He would come and join the hierarchy of the priests and set up a kingdom to rule the world from Jerusalem. He didn't do this. But that's how they were looking at it. So, He tells them:

Mathew 21:43: "Because of this, I say to you...

Imagine that here are the most important people in the Old Testament religion, and the temple and the authority and the leaders and the elders.

"…the Kingdom of God shall be taken from you, and it shall be given to a nation *that* produces the fruits of it" (v 43).

Now you read in 1-Peter 2, that we are 'a royal priesthood, a royal nation.' So, he's talking about all of those who would come into the Church; they would receive the Kingdom, not the ones who thought they already had it in their hip pocket.

Verse 44: "And the one who falls on this Stone..."

Jesus is talking about Himself, because that was mentioned in an earlier one.

"...shall be broken; but on whomever it shall fall, it will grind him to powder" (v 44).

A prophecy of what was going to happen to Jerusalem.

Section 296, pg. 226—The Priests and Scribes Seek to Arrest Him

They knew!

Matthew 21:45: "Now, after hearing His parables, the chief priests and the Pharisees knew that He was speaking about them. And they sought to arrest Him, but they were afraid of the multitudes, because they held Him as a prophet" (vs 45-46).

All of this is building up and building up. I just imagine over Jerusalem there were thousands and thousands of angels. Remember what Jesus told the apostles? *If you believe I'm the Messiah,* what would you think if you saw angels ascending and descending on the Son of Man? There were a lot of angels there. Why? *Because every prophecy about His life, the confrontation here leading up to His crucifixion, all had to be fulfilled!* The angels were there to make sure that they would be fulfilled, and that Jesus would not be arrested beforehand.

Don't you think there was also Satan and demons? *Yes!* Don't you think the demons were right there pumping up all the priests and Sadducees and the elders and things like this? So, this was filled with trauma and tension this whole day. On the other hand, I like this section from John:

Section 297—Many Leaders Secretly Believed in Jesus

John12:42: "But even so, many among the rulers believed in Him; but because of the Pharisees they did not confess *Him...*"

A good lesson for us! **Don't be afraid!** What is Truth is true. It strengthens you, and if it hurts the other person, that's too bad.

"…so that they would not be put out of the synagogue" (v 42).

Now notice how this cuts to the quick of everything. That's what's so good about the Bible. It's not telling us a bunch of fairy tales It's not telling us lies, *it's telling us the truth!*

Verse 43: "For they loved the glory of men more than the glory of God"

That's what we all need to keep in mind, too. What we are, we are to serve. Anyone who is in the ministry is to serve and to teach; that's why we're here. How can there be those who will taught with the Truth of God so they can mature and be brought to perfection, if they're not taught? Like Paul said to the Jews, 'You claim you have the Scriptures when you read them, but don't you teach yourselves?' *We have to let the Word of God teach us!*

Section 298—To Believe in Jesus is to Believe in the Father

Verse 44: "Then Jesus called out and said,

'The one who believes in Me does not believe in Me, but in Him Who sent Me. And the one who sees Me sees Him Who sent Me. I have come *as* a light into the world so that everyone who believes in Me may not remain in darkness'" (vs 44-46).

In the Gospel of John, Jesus is called **the Light** 21 times. Twice John the Baptist. I'll let you search that out.

Verse 47: "But if anyone hears My words and does not believe, I do not judge him; for I did not come to judge the world, but to save the world...."

wait until He comes to judge

"...The one who rejects Me and does not receive My words has one who judges him; the Word, which I have spoken, that shall judge him in the last day" (vs 47-48).

What was the judgment for those who didn't believe in Jesus, but professed His name, did works of power and did many wonderful things? What was Jesus answer to them the last day? **Depart from me, you who work lawlessness. I never knew you!** Quite powerful!

Nisan 11—Sunday, April 2, 30 AD

Verse 49: "For I have not spoken from Myself..."

Same thing! This is one of the biggest problems that faces ministers wherever they are. They get lifted up in their own vanity and carried away with what *they think* they know. And no one can tell them that they're wrong. *They won't listen!*

Verse 49: "For I have not spoken from Myself; but the Father, Who sent Me, gave Me commandment Himself, what I should say and what I should speak. And I know that His commandment is eternal life. Therefore, whatever I speak, I speak exactly as the Father has told Me" (vs 49-50).

All of these confrontations were occurring in the temple area. Of course, God made sure that there were thousands and thousands and thousands of Jews who came. And remember when it was the Feast of Tabernacles in John 7? The question was, don't the leaders know that this is the Christ?

Section 299—The Parable of the Wedding and the Wedding Feast

Where do we find the fulfillment of that? *Rev. 19 and the wedding supper!* What's that going to be like on the Sea of Glass, and the angels roll out the whole dining array? *And we're all seated there!*

Jesus said that He was going to go serve. So, here we are all sitting there, I don't know what kind of food we're going to get. I don't know what kind of food that spirit beings eat, but I hope it's not chicken! Heavenly birds! Ha! Jesus comes around with a wine flask and is pouring wine for us. Because He said, 'I will drink it with you in that day in My Kingdom.' That's going to be an amazing thing, isn't it?

There are two parts to this Section 299

Matthew 22:1: "And again Jesus answered and spoke to them in parables, saying, 'The Kingdom of Heaven is compared to a man *who was* a king, who made a wedding feast for his son, and sent his servants to call those who had been invited to the wedding feast; but they refused to come....

they refused Christ

...Afterwards he sent out other servants, saying "Say to those who have been invited, 'Behold, I have prepared my dinner; my oxen and the fatted beasts are killed, and all things *are* ready. Come to the wedding feast.'" But they paid no attention and went away, one to his farm, and another to his business. And the rest, after seizing his servants, insulted and killed *them*'" (vs 1-6).

Didn't that happen to almost all the prophets? I mean, sometimes read the Prophets from the point of view of the prophet who wrote it, especially Jeremiah. He was so discouraged one time, there's one chapter you'll find. He says, 'Lord, I've done all of this and everybody hates me. This has been so bad, I've gone through so many difficulties.' And the Lord said in so many words, 'Now, Jeremiah, keep doing what you're doing. You're life will be your prize.' *Right after that he's thrown into the sewer!*

Verse 7: "Now, when the king heard *it*..."

Who's the king? *The Father!*

"...he became angry; and he sent his armies *and* destroyed those murderers, and burned up their city" (v 7).

- first part, *Jerusalem*
- second part, *preaching of the Gospel*

'Go therefore into all the world and preach the gospel making disciples' (Matt. 28:19). *Go to all nations,* and that begins with:

Verse 8: "Then he said to his servants, 'The wedding feast indeed is ready, but those who were invited were not worthy; therefore, go into the well-traveled highways, and invite all that you find to the wedding feast.' And after going out into the highways, those servants brought together everyone that they found, both good and evil; and the wedding feast was filled with guests" (vs 8-10).

Now the next part is a little difficult for some people to figure out. But I'll try and explain it for you.

Verse 11: "And when the king came in to see the guests, *he* noticed a man there who was not dressed in *proper* attire for *the* wedding feast."

What is the proper attire for the wedding feast? Revelation 19:8: '...**the righteousness of the saints**." In other words, he tried to get in there without properly having the right clothes. Sounds a little like Cain bringing his offering, and God didn't accept it. This is what it's conveying. *You're not going to get into the Kingdom of God if you do not do it God's way!*. If you try, and think you're going to be there, you're going to be cast out.

Matthew 22:12: "And he said to him, 'Friend, how did you enter here without a garment *fit* for *the* wedding feast?' But he had no answer. Then the king said to the servants…"

This implies all of our personal works of righteousness and faith that we are to do. That becomes the potential for the wedding feast garments.

"…'Bind his hands and feet, *and* take him away, and cast *him* into the outer darkness.' There shall be weeping and gnashing of teeth. **For many are called, but few *are* chosen**" (vs 12-14).

We'll end this section here by saying, remember this—and all elders and ministers remember this, too—*God has called every one of the brethren, and He has called you!* So therefore, *you are actually under in your position to serve. Not over, for you to be served!*

Nisan 11—Sunday, April 2, 30 AD—*this day of provocation.*

Section 300—Spies Are Sent To Entangled Him

Mark 12:13: "But they sent to Him some of the Pharisees and the Herodians, in order to entrap Him in His words."

Look at Matt. 22:15; notice the differences in the explanation, but those differences when you really put them together, adds a lot to what was going on with this confrontation.

Matthew 22:15: "Then the Pharisees went and took counsel *as to* how they might entrap Him in *His* speech."

Luke 20:20: "And they kept *Him* under surveillance, *and* sent out secret agents who pretended that they were righteous, so that they might catch Him in His words, in order to deliver Him up to the power and authority of the governor."

This same thing has occurred here in America!

Verse 21: And they questioned Him, saying, 'Master...'"

I kind of think they did it this way

"'...we realize that You speak and teach rightly, and do not accept *any man's* person, but teach the way of God in Truth. Is it lawful for us to give tribute to Caesar, or not?'" (vs 21-22).

Now here in America, there was a group who was saying that if you're a Christian you don't have to pay any taxes to the government. *Well, he's now in jail!* Same thing here! They wanted for Jesus to say that you don't have to pay tribute to the government. 'Hey, turn Him over to the authorities. Look, He is saying you don't have to pay tribute.'

Verse 23: "But perceiving their craftiness..."

Matthew 22:18: "But Jesus, knowing their wickedness…"

Mark 12:15: "...But perceiving their hypocrisy..."

Interesting: hypocrisy, wickedness, craftiness. Sounds like Washington, DC!

Section 301—Render to Caesar the Things of Caesar, and to God the things of God

Luke 20:24: "Show Me a silver coin. Whose image and inscription does it have?' And they answered *and* said, 'Caesar's.' Then He said to them, 'Render, therefore, the things of Caesar to Caesar, and the things of God to God'" (vs 24-25).

That's something we need to really know and understand, too.

- What do we render to God? *Our love, our faith, our obedience!*
- How did Jesus express it in another way? *Man shall not live by bread alone, but by every word of God!*

There are some people who say that on the other side of the coin, you do not have to send tithes and offerings. You don't have to give those, because Jesus told the seventy to go out and preach the Gospel and you don't take anything. You only take one set of clothes and one set of shoes and your staff. So therefore, that's how you ought to run your ministry.

I actually had some people tell me that. But what did Jesus say later? Take your provision bag, take a sword, do the other things. That was a special one, as a lesson to those twelve and to the seventy, because he sent out the two groups, so that they could learn **God will provide.** Also, it was a sign, back toward Jesus, that He was the Messiah.

Today we don't offer animal sacrifices, we take up offerings and tithes, most of it in paper or digital. So, there's an obligation to do both. As we saw in the other one, the man who came in without the proper clothes, he was what you could say much like Cain. What did Cain do? He just brought any old thing you wanted to. *God says **the tithe is His!*** {note our In-Depth Study on *Tithing*}

If you have questions about it, we cover it. I'm sorry that and in the *Harmony*, that these coins did not come out very clear. But these were actual brass coins with Caesar's image from that time.

Section 302—The Question Concerning Marriage In The Resurrection

And this still goes on. A man came up to me one time and said, 'You know what I believe? I believe that we will have sex as spirit beings in the Kingdom of God.' I said, 'Where did you get that?' And he kind of looked at me and 'um, um' So, we will see.

Luke 20:27: "Then some of the Sadducees..."

Notice, wave after wave… I imagine that they had their council group somewhere by themselves, and different agents would come in and relay what was going on. They would take a council again, and send someone else out to bring something else. Here are the Sadducees, this is the priest party.

Verse 27: "...who do not believe there is a resurrection..."

Interesting! Even in the priesthood, they didn't believe God! That's what Christ said.

"...came *and* questioned Him, saying, 'Master, Moses wrote to us that if anyone's brother who had a wife should die, and he should die childless, his brother should take his *dead* brother's wife and raise up seed for his brother'" (vs 27-28).

Therefore, there were seven brothers!

Now, isn't it always the way in argument, to bring up a proposition that is outrageous to try and get an argument? So, here it is seven brothers. Well, you know the whole story. First one died, no children, second one, third one, fourth one, fifth one, sixth one, seventh one. About that time you wonder what's wrong with this family?

So they wanted to know in the resurrection, *which they didn't believe in,* whose husband would take the wife for all seven.

Luke 20:34: "And Jesus answered *and* said to them, 'The children of this age marry and are given in marriage; but those who are accounted worthy to obtain that age...'" (vs 34-35).

the coming age

"...and the resurrection from *the* dead, neither marry nor are given in marriage; and neither can they die anymore..." (vs 35-36).

there's no need to have children

"...for they are as *the* angels..." (v 36).

Now why didn't he say God? He could have, because we're going to be the sons and daughters of God. Why did he say angels? So, they wouldn't grab Him and take Him and arrest Him ahead of time.

"...and are *the* children of God, being children of the resurrection" (v 36).

John 10—notice what happened when He told them that He was the Son of God. When He did tell them that the Bible says 'we are to be gods.' He had a lot of confrontations leading up to this.

We're looking at the confrontation just before His crucifixion. If you take all the confrontations and stack them up end to end, outside of the people believing in Him and coming to be healed and all that sort of thing, *His ministry was a struggle!* Even the first part of His ministry with the apostles, He even said, 'Oh you of little faith.'

John 10:23: "And Jesus was walking in the temple in Solomon's porch. Then the Jews encircled Him and said to Him, 'How long are You going to hold us in suspense? If You are the Christ, tell us plainly'" (vs 23-24).

Verse 25: "Jesus answered them, 'I have told you, but you do not believe. The works that I am doing in My Father's name, these bear witness of Me. But you do not believe because you are not of My sheep, as I said to you. My sheep hear My voice, and I know them, and they follow Me. And I give them eternal life, and they shall never perish; and no one shall take them out of My hand. My Father,

Who has given *them* to Me, is greater than all; and no one has the power to seize *them* from My Father's hand. **I and the Father are one**'" (vs 25-30).

Whoa! Look at their response! You know, they didn't run and say, 'You're the Messiah' and bow down. *No!*

Verse 31: "Then the Jews again picked up stones so that they might stone Him…. [loving group] …Jesus answered them, 'Many good works I have showed you from My Father. For which of them are you about to stone Me?' The Jews answered Him, saying, 'We will not stone You for a good work, but for blasphemy, and because You, being a man, are making Yourself God.' Jesus answered them, 'Is it not written in your law, "I said, 'You are gods'"? If He called them gods, to whom the Word of God came (and the Scriptures cannot be broken)" (vs 31-35).

He's telling them If you don't believe the Scripture that makes no difference, *you can't break it!*

Verse 36: "*Why* do you say *of Him* Whom the Father has sanctified and sent into the world, 'You are blaspheming,' because I said, 'I am *the* Son of God'? If I do not do the works of My Father, do not believe Me. But if I do, even if you do not believe Me, believe the works; so that you may perceive and may believe that the Father *is* in Me, and I in Him" (vs 36-38).

So, they, again, wanted to take Him, but He escaped away. I don't know how He did that. Jesus as you know can do different things. Remember, after the resurrection. He came across those two walking to Emmaus and they were all discouraged because they thought, well, it's all over. He says, 'What is this you are talking about?' They didn't recognize Him because He had changed His appearance.

Later He walked through the door. Anyone who says they're born again (John 3) just like the wind, go wherever, walk through the door! If you don't like that, try the wall!

He did say it back in John 10, but He said angels here:

Luke 20:36: "…for they are **as *the* angels**…" [v 37]: But that the dead are raised, even Moses showed *by his words* at the *burning* bush, when he called *the* Lord the God of Abraham, and the God of Isaac, and the God of Jacob; for He is not *the* God of *the* dead, but of *the* living; for all live unto Him.' And some of the scribes answered *and* said, 'Master, You have spoken well.' And *after that* they did not dare to ask Him any more *questions*" (36-40). *That is for a while!*

Now look what happened as we come to the next section here. So, this day was really a day of great confrontation. We will see, it gets even a little more intense.

Section 303—The Two Great Commandments: Love God and Love Your Neighbor
Mark 12:28: "And one of the scribes who had come up *to Him*…

I wonder if someone said He hasn't seen you, go up and ask Him a question.

"…after hearing them reasoning together *and* perceiving that He answered them well, asked Him, 'Which is *the* first commandment of all?' Then Jesus answered him, '*The* first of all the commandments *is*, "Hear, O Israel. Our one God is *the* Lord, *the* Lord"'" (vs 28-29).

Now that's reflective of Deut. 6. Because what does the Bible teach all the way through the Bible? There are two in the Godhead. Not a monotheistic, not tri-theistic, but a dual-theistic. *The Lord!*

Verse 30: "And you shall love *the* Lord your God…"

How much involved are we to be with God, and what God wants us to do? This is what it's all about. This reflects a ***complete commitment, complete faith and complete reliance on God!***

Verse 30: "'And you shall love *the* Lord your God with **all** your heart, and with **all** your soul, and with **all** your mind, and with **all** your strength.' This *is the* first commandment."

You could take each one of those; the heart, the soul, the mind, the strength, and do a word study through the Bible. What do we read in the Psalms? *The Lord is my strength, my rock and my salvation!* This is how we are to approach it. It's not becoming a religious nut or fanatic. But that's what God commands. Why? *Because he's going to give us eternal life!*

Think of it that way. Every difficulty or trial we come across is an experience so we can grow in grace and knowledge. Some of them are very difficult. Some of them are very trying. But nevertheless, God sees us through it. So, we have to look at the end result.

Verse 31: "And *the* second *is* like this: 'You shall love your neighbor as yourself.'…."

- the third one is that *you shall love each other as I have loved you!*
- the fourth one is, *you shall love your enemies and pray for those who despitefully use you.*

You can pray many ways for your enemies. Like the rabbi in Fiddler on the Roof, keeping them far from us! Another one is, 'God deal with them and take care of them.'

I remember there was a man who came and was feigning wanting to work with us, *but he wanted to do his own work* and take everything away from what we had in the early part of what Christian Biblical Church of God was. He came to Monterey, and was going to go on a radio station and do his bit on a radio station. I didn't know that he was going to do that. I heard that he was in Monterey, but I didn't know anything about that. I knew that he was trying to get in and take everything, so I prayed about it, and just asked God to save us from this. Send him away.

Well, he exercised very heavily the night before he was to go on the radio, and after his exercise, he laid down on the floor had a heart attack and he was gone. I can't say God has delivered all of us out of all of our troubles in the same way, but that one particular one is one that I remember. I didn't even know that that happened until about two weeks afterward. Someone came and said, 'Did you know so and so died of a heart attack?' *I was flabbergasted!*

But God will take care of it. If we fall into the hands of the enemy, then we are to witness. Look at what John Gunether has done with all of the Waldensians and those in the Piedmont up there where God protected the people and they translated the Word of God into native languages, and so forth. *They went to their death singing praises to God!* Think about that!

Two comments were made: That the man who died of a heart attack in Monterey was also a false prophet, because he was preaching a lot of false things. They never came to pass. You see the reason why love is the first thing and love is the greatest, because from that comes *faith, belief, hope, patience and understanding!*

The understanding that we derive from the Bible is not because we have anything greater than any other human being. We don't! But God will give understanding if we are yielding to Him and continuously following His way and the Truth.

Mark 12:32: "Then the scribe said to Him, 'Right, Master. You have spoken according to Truth that God is one, and there is not another besides Him; and to love Him with all the heart, and with all the understanding, and with all the soul, and with all the strength, and to love *one's* neighbor as oneself, is more than all burnt offerings and sacrifices.' And Jesus, seeing that he answered with understanding, said to him, **'You are not far from the Kingdom of God.'**…." (vs 32-34).

Question is, after Jesus' resurrection, did the scribe come into the Church to make it to the Kingdom of God? *Don't know!*

Section 304—How Is Christ the Son of David?

Matthew 22:41: "While the Pharisees were assembled together, Jesus questioned them."

So, it goes back the other way.

Verse 42: "Saying, 'What do you think concerning the Christ? Whose son is He?' They said to Him, '*The Son* of David.'"

Gotcha!

Verse 43: "He said to them, 'How then does David in spirit call Him Lord, saying, "The LORD said to my Lord, 'Sit at My right hand, until I make Your enemies a footstool for Your feet'"'?'"

How are you going to answer that? *Next page at the top, second column*:

Verse 45: "Therefore, if David calls Him Lord, how is He his Son?' And no one was able to answer Him a word, neither dared anyone from that day to question Him anymore" (vs 45-46).

Now then, here we come to the great provocation and condemnation. This is, if you would, compare when we get to Mark 12, loving God, and then how Jesus condemned the scribes and Pharisees. This was the great confrontation, which I think really infuriated them. And this was deliberate, because they were to be infuriated. And they were frustrated, because they couldn't arrest Him, they couldn't do anything to get Him. That's why Judas. We'll see that in a little bit.

Section 305—A Warning Against the Scribes and Pharisees

Mark 12:38: "And He said to them in His teaching, 'Beware of the scribes, who take pleasure in walking around in robes, and in salutations in the marketplaces.'"

I never will forget this; I can still I can still look down and see it happening. I was at the

University of San Francisco, which is a Catholic institution. That was before I went to Ambassador College. I couldn't get in there that year, but I was going to take a business course, so I went from College of San Mateo a junior college to University of San Francisco. *Catholic!*

Here I am getting the *Plain Truth magazine for the first time, all about Satan's* Great Deception; all about those things; how the Catholic Church was what it was. So, I'm on the third floor, and it's my fifth week there. My first week, guess what the first mandatory class was? *Study of Philosophy!*

I thought, why aren't they studying the Bible and creation. Here the fifth week and I have all of this, and here's statue of this person and statue that person, and a cross in front of every room and so forth. I'm standing up here looking out the window down, and between the buildings they had a big lawn area with sidewalks going through. Here are the Jesuits with their cossacks on, walking in the morning, reading their prayer book. The students come by and say, 'Good morning, father.' I thought, I just read that in the Bible or in an article, whichever one it was.

That is the day I decided *I must leave*. So, I did. I went down to the registrar's office, opened the door to walk in and guess what I saw? A huge picture, it must have been four feet by six feet, of a very melancholy looking Jesus, with the crown of thorns on His head and a big drop of blood coming down.

I said, 'Oh, I've got to get out of here.' So I did; I got out that very day, because that's what they're like. Now Dolores could tell you some stories about archbishops and cardinals coming down to a land development company that she worked for. Once a year they would come down, and the three brothers, who were partners in that company, dreaded them to come because they always extorted $100,000 or more from each of them. If I recall right, one of them hid in his office for two hours, but he finally gave up and came out, and the cardinal left with his bundle.

Verse 39: "And in *the* chief seats in the synagogues and *the* chief places in the feasts; Who devour the houses of widows, and for a pretext make long prayers. These shall receive *the* greater condemnation" (vs 39-40).

We can see that everything was planned out and worked out by God:

- confrontation between Christ and the religious leaders
- the angels of God
- the demons
- Satan the devil

So, we'll see how all that comes together to bring about the crucifixion!

Scriptural References:

1) John 5:30-47
2) John 8:37-46
3) Mark 12:1-2, 7-9
4) Matthew 21:41
5) Luke 20:16
6) Matthew 21:45-46
7) Matthew 12:42-43
8) John 12:42-50
9) Matthew 22:1-14
10) Revelation 19:8
11) Matthew 22:12-14
12) Mark 12:13
13) Matthew 22:15
14) Luke 20:20-23
15) Matthew 22:18
16) Mark 12:15
17) Luke 20:24-25, 27-28, 34-36
18) John 10:23-38
19) Luke 20:36-40
20) Mark 12:28-34
21) Matthew 22:41-46
22) Mark 12:38-40

Scriptures referenced, not quoted:

- Mark 3
- 1 Peter 2
- John 7
- Isaiah 5
- Matthew 28:19
- John 3
- Deuteronomy 6

Also referenced:

In-Depth Studies:
- *The Lord God and The Most High*
- *Tithing*

Book: *A Harmony of the Gospels* by Fred R. Coulter

FRC: po/bo
Transcribed: 3/10/19
Reformatted: 10/2020

CHAPTER TWENTY

The Last Ten Days of Jesus' Life III

Jesus' secret preparation for His final Passover
Fred R. Coulter

Greetings, everyone! Welcome to Sabbath services!

We're getting close, about five weeks away, to Passover and Unleavened Bread!

Here is what we're advertising this week, which will be very, very helpful to you for Unleavened Bread: In-Depth Study and CD: *How to Overcome the Sin Within!* That's important, because that's the whole key of Christianity.

Religion is to make you good living in the community one to another. True Christianity is *conversion,* which is a transformation of the mind and thinking with God's Spirit and His Word. That way your mind is being transformed by God's Spirit will produce good results on the outside.

As we're going to see, this is perfectly described by Jesus in talking to the scribes and Pharisees in exposing them.

Remember, this day—Nisan 11, Sunday April 2, 30 AD—*is the day of confrontation and provocation!* Jesus comes on them really strong and very hard. Remember, all of this took place at the temple area. There were thousands of people there, and hundreds and hundreds of Levites and probably scores of priests.

from: *A Harmony of the Gospels,* pg 231

Section 305—A Warning Against the Scribes and Pharisees

This is not like traditional messages; this is like a Bible study, because we're going through most of the verses. Some of the areas, like in Matt. 24, we're not going to go into detail in great parts of it, because we've had so many messages on it anyway.

Matthew 23:1: "Then Jesus spoke to the multitudes and to His disciples, saying, 'The scribes and the Pharisees have **sat down on Moses' seat** *as judges*'" (vs 1-2).

Why was that translated that way? *This is to show that the priests and the Levites*—some of scribes were Levites, but not all—"…**sat down on Moses' seat**…" to make judgments.

But the Pharisees were not of the priestly line. Some may have been, but Pharisee was a *political party.* What Jesus is saying here is that He wants everything to be conducted in decent order through God's Word.

Verse 3: "Therefore, every judgment…

as judges

"…that they tell you to observe, observe and do…."

Their judgments were based upon the Word of God! They would come to the judgment seat with a problem, or defugalty, get it settled and they would give the judgment based on the Word of God.

"…But do not do according to their works; for they say and do not" (v 3).

Note Mark 7 about *the traditions of men.* When they kept their traditions, th*ey were rejecting the Word of God!* It was sort of a very obtuse thing that they did. Picture the Law of God in the middle; they designed the traditions *to go around the Law of God* so that if people did these traditions they wouldn't break the commandments. But after having so many of these traditions, the traditions themselves were breaking the commandments of God. This is why Jesus said,

"…do not do according to their works; for they say and do not For they bind heavy burdens and hard to bear, and lay *them* on the shoulders of men; but they will not move them with *one of* their own fingers" (vs 3-4).

Just like all political systems, the elite are never caught and judged. Look at it today right here in America with the Clinton and Obama eras, *and they're all getting away with it!*

Verse 5: "And they do all their works to be seen by men. They make broad their phylacteries and enlarge the borders of their garments."

I thought of that when I saw a hearing with one of the so-called great generals. He had his stars, medals, ribbons on both sides of his chest; he was very impressive.

Verse 6: "And they love… [v 7] the salutations in the marketplaces, and to be called by men 'Rabbi, Rabbi.' But you are not to be called Rabbi; for one is your

228

Master, the Christ…" (vs 6-8).

We're going to see that He says this the second time!

"…and all of you are brethren. Also, do not call *anyone* on the earth **your Father**…" (vs 8-9).

Very important! Years ago, about 1973, I was on the radio program called *Religion Online* four Sundays in a row. There was a rabbi, a Catholic priest, and me. I was the so-called Protestant. Every time someone would call in and say to the priest, 'Why you call each other *Father* when the Bible says to not call anyone *your Father*?' They never could answer that. They would all stumble and so forth. A lot of people know that.

Verse 11: "But the greatest among you shall be your servant."

Serve the people, that's the whole thing! What was said that was wrong 'way back when' in the Church of God? *In order to be in the Kingdom of God you must learn to be ruled over by the ministry!* That's not correct! **You must be ruled over by God! All of us individually!** *That's why we have the Spirit of God!*

Verse 9: "…for one is your Father…"

Father is the sacred name of God the Father (John 17). All of those who try to bring in Hebrew sacred names, and replace them in the New Testament, are adding to the Word of God, *that God **never** authorized to be!*

Don't you think that if Hebrew sacred names were necessary in the New Testament, that the apostles—being those who understood Hebrew and Greek—could have easily written the Hebrew name? *Of course!*

The Old Testament was more like a 'religion.' You corrected the mistakes that you did, and the sacrifice was given to forgive that action. *It never the cleansed the mind!* That's the key.

Verse 10: "Neither be called Master; for one is your Master, the Christ.

The word for master in the Greek is 'despotes'—from which we get the English word *despot!* Master is someone whom you give absolute love and obedience to, and that's Christ and God the Father. After saying all of this, why did He put this here? Because every one of the things He said *don't do* is what men do to exalt themselves.

Verse 12: "And whoever will exalt himself shall be humbled; and whoever will humble himself shall be exalted."

Our exaltation comes at the resurrection! In the mean time, we're to be brethren, and those who are elders and teachers are to teach the brethren and not rule over them.

The thing that is important with God's Holy Spirit is one of the fruits of the Spirit is *self-control.* Where does self-control come from? Your choosing *to do right* from your choosing to withhold *doing what is wrong.* You choose it! We all have certain things that we're working on that are hard to control. I do, you do, everybody does and that will continue until we die or the resurrection, one of the two. There are eight *woes* to the scribes and Pharisees by Christ.

- every word of God is true
- every word of God is living
- every word of God will take place one way or the other

Verse 11: "But the greatest among you shall be your **servant**."

Greek is 'diakonos.' What do you suppose the English word is? *Deacon!* Christ came to 'diakono,' *to serve!*

- Was Christ a deacon?
- A teacher?
- A minister?
- *Yes!*
- Savior?

Verse 13: "But [#1]**woe** to you, scribes and Pharisees, **hypocrites!**…."

They are looking for the accumulation of things and notoriety in this world, that is *good* notoriety. But Christ is revealing their evil notoriety here. In the first edition of the *Harmony* I translated this is 'sanctimonious pretenders.' That is what they were!

"…For you devour widows' houses, and as a pretext you offer prayers of great length. Because of this, you shall receive *the* greater judgment. [#2]**Woe** to you, scribes and Pharisees, hypocrites! For you shut up the Kingdom of Heaven before men; for neither do you yourselves enter, nor do you allow those who are entering to enter. [#3]**Woe** to you, scribes and Pharisees, hypocrites! For you travel the sea and the land to make one proselyte, and when he has become one, you make him twofold more **a son of Gehenna** than yourselves" (vs 13-15).

What is he saying to him with this? What is Gehenna? *Lake a Fire!* So, they're making them converts to go into the Lake of Fire. Of course, that would be unless the person repented.

Verse 16: "[#4]**Woe** to you, blind guides…"

229

- What makes people blind *spiritually*?
- What made the scribes and Pharisees blind?

Here is Christ fulfilling all the Scriptures; they had all the Scriptures! They wanted to kill Him because He was a competitor. When you read the book of Acts about the first eight chapters are pretty powerful against them. Did they ever have a witness?

We'll just project to head a little bit; we're going to see that when Judas Iscariot came to them to betray Jesus, *they rejoiced* and when Christ died they thought they had the problem solved. It wasn't; their problems just began! So, He's doing all of this to provoke them!

"…blind guides…" How does a person become blind? *John 9, about the man born blind!* The disciples asked Jesus, 'Who sinned? his parents? or him? How can a baby in the womb sin? What is sin? Transgression of the Law? What did Jesus say? *He didn't sin, nor did His parents sin, but for the glory of God!*

God Himself made that man blind for the very purpose of Jesus healing him. You read John 9. Jesus healed him and then the Pharisees found out about it and they brought him in and said, 'How do you receive sight?' *This man told me to put some clay on my eyes and went down Pool Shiloam and washed, and I can see!*

'Who was He?' *I don't know, He left and I can't find Him!* 'We don't believe you, bring in his parents. Is this your son?' *Yes, that's our son!* 'How does he see?' *We don't know, ask him!*

Then they said, 'This man, we know He's not from God.' And the blind man who could now see said to them, 'How can someone who is not of God do something that has never been done since the creation of the world to heal someone born blind so that they could see? 'You're altogether unclean' and they disfellowshipped him out of the synagogue! Sound like the experience some of you went through a the Church? The truth is, people become blind when they know the Word of God and avoid it, turn their back on it or walk away from it. *Automatic blinding!*

Why? *Because the deceitful nature within will generate and excuse as to why you're walking away is correct!* What that does makes them blind! That's why Jesus said, "…blind guides…" They're the ones who are supposed to guide the people, but they can't see the signs of the times, or the fact that it is Jesus Christ.

"…who say, 'Whoever shall swear by the temple…'" (v 16).

Notice that it's always a picky little point that never amounts to anything.

"'…it is not binding; but whoever shall swear by the gold of the temple, he is obligated *to fulfill* his oath'" (v 16).

What is that based upon? *The covetous nature! Gold!*

Verse 17: "*You* **fools** and blind!…."

Greek: 'moranio'—from where we get the word *moron!* Idiots!

"…For which is greater, the gold, or the temple, which sanctifies the gold? And *you say*, 'Whoever shall swear by the altar, it is not binding; but whoever shall swear by the gift that *is* upon it, he is obligated *to fulfill* his oath.' *You* fools and blind!…." (vs 17-19).

Here are all these self-righteous officials out there thinking: Who is this coming after us this way? They thought all of these rules are correct. These define righteousness, and Who is this coming in here to knock it all down and say that 'we're fools and blind'?

"…For which is greater, the gift, or the altar, which sanctifies the gift? Therefore, the one who swears by the altar swears by it, and by all things that *are* upon it. And the one who swears by the temple swears by it, and by Him Who dwells in it. And the one who swears by heaven swears by the throne of God, and by Him Who sits upon it" (vs 19-22).

- What's the solution?
- What did Jesus say in Matt. 5 about what you should say?
- *Let your yes be 'yes' and your no be 'no'!*

Verse 23: [#5]**Woe** to you, scribes and Pharisees, hypocrites! For you pay tithes of mint and anise and cummin, but you have abandoned the more important *matters* of the law—judgment, and mercy and faith.

Luke 11:42: "**But woe to you, Pharisees!** For you pay tithes of mint and rue and every herb, **but you pass over the judgment and the love of God**…."

Matthew 23:23: "…These *you* were obligated to do, and not to leave the others undone"

In other words, the most important things of God are not how much money the organization can bring in. But those who are truly converted and truly love God will tithe and give offerings without having to be 'beaten over the head.' Almost every co-worker letter that went out there was an urgent plea for money. What happened to the whole organization? Not all at once, but where is it today? *I'll let you think on that!*

> Verse 24: "Blind guides, who filter out a gnat, but swallow a camel! [#6]**Woe** to you, scribes and Pharisees, hypocrites! For you cleanse the outside of the cup and the dish…" (vs 24-25).

Outside you look great! Let's use another example of this today. At the Academy Awards they're all dressed up, looking sharp, but *within* what are they? *Most of them nothing but a sexual bunch of animals crawling all over the place!* There may be a good actor or two in there.

- What does God want from people? *The cleansing of the inside!*
- How does that happen? *With God's Word and God's Spirit,* **'the washing of the water by the Word.'!**

> Verse 26: "Blind Pharisees! First cleanse the inside of the cup and the dish, so that the outside may also become clean."

There's the whole principle stated right here this one verse.

> Verse 27: [#7]**Woe** to you, scribes and Pharisees, hypocrites! For you are like whited sepulchers, which indeed appear beautiful *on the* outside, but within are full of the bones of the dead, and of all uncleanness."

No telling what you find in there. Think about this: How is God going to resurrect all of those who died at sea; most of them were eaten by sharks or other sea animals. That's why when a man or woman dies, the spirit goes back to God. That's they key. Everything that you are is recorded on that spirit of man. If you're unconverted, everything that you are. *If you are converted, your spirit of man within you is what then is the key for resurrection to eternal life!*

It doesn't make any difference how many are eaten up by sharks, the spirit of man goes back to God when they die. We know that the spirit of just men are under the altar of God (Heb. 12). Does God have a place for the spirits of those who did not commit the unpardonable sin, but are worthy of the second resurrection? *Of course, He would have to!*

How about for those who are wicked? We saw 'make him son of Gehenna. How about those who committed the unpardonable sin?

Sidebar: Can someone unconverted commit the unpardonable sin? *Yes!* Because when they're resurrected in the second resurrection, and there's no repentance, guess where you're going?

Do you think Hitler committed the unpardonable sin? *I don't know how bad a person could get!* Even to the end sending 12-16 year-olds out to try and save Berlin when it was surrounded by the Russians. They were going building to building, killing everyone they could find. What did Hitler do? *He went down 38-feet below the surface and took his poison pill and died along with the others!*

Goebbels and his children all took cyanide capsules. Wonderful ending the Great Reich! How about that for a fulfillment of those who exalt themselves? *They shall be abased!* It doesn't say *humbled,* but **abased!** Is that an abasement? *Yes, in the basement!*

> Verse 29: [#8]**Woe** to you, scribes and Pharisees, hypocrites!….

Isn't this the way that people always excuse themselves?

> "…For you build the sepulchers of the prophets, and adorn the tombs of the righteous; and you say, 'If we had been in the days of our fathers, we would not have been partakers with them in the blood of the prophets.'" (vs 29-30).

Who were they going to kill and partake of blood? *Christ, the greatest of the Prophets!*

> Verse 32: "And *as for* you, you are filling up the measure of your fathers. *You* serpents, *you* offspring of vipers…" (vs 32-33).

I remember going the zoo in San Diego, California, Jonathan and David always loved to go to the reptile house where the snakes were, and get up close to the glass and say, 'Dad, come and look!'

We came to the Palestinian Viper and I was astonished at that. I looked at that and said, 'I don't ever want to go to Palestine. I would always walk about six feet away from the glass where all the serpents were. You can't get it any worse than vipers!

> "…how shall you escape the judgment of Gehenna?" (v 33).

- How many times did Jesus say 'Gehenna' here? *At least three times!*
- Where were they headed?

> Verse 34: "Because of this, behold, I send to you prophets and wise *men* and scribes; and *some* of them you shall kill and crucify, and *some* of them you shall

scourge in your synagogues, and *some of them you* shall persecute from city to city; so that upon you may come all *the* righteous blood poured out upon the earth, from the blood of Abel the righteous, unto the blood of Zacharias…" (vs 34-35).

In English this is 'from A to Z!

"…son of Barachias, whom you murdered between the temple and the altar. Truly I say to you, **all these things shall come upon this generation**" (vs 35-36).

We will see the phrase "this generation" here applies to the current generation that He was speaking to. We will find in Matt. 24 the same phrase, but it has other qualifiers in the context to show that means *the last generation.*

Verse 37: "Jerusalem, Jerusalem, *you* who kill the prophets and stone those who have been sent to you, how often would I have gathered your children together, even as a hen gathers her brood under *her* wings, but you refused!"

All the way through here, all of this is based upon choices. That's why it's important for us to know: What do we choose on a daily basis? You can't have a behavior out here that is exemplary but in your mind/heart you have a dual standard. That's called *a carnal mind,* and that's what we are to overcome.

Verse 38: "Behold, your house is left to you desolate. For I say to you, you shall not see Me at all from this time forward, until you shall say, Blessed *is* He Who comes in *the* name of *the* Lord'" (vs 38-39).

You see these coins (*Harmony* pg. 233). These are actual temple coins are the temple during Jesus' day. Now, what we did with it was we had the picture of one coin. So we had a photographer, take that one coin and do step and repeat, step and repeat until he came up with this batch of temple coins.

Section 306—A Widow's Mite is More Than Large Donations by the Rich

Now here's something that's always true, and this became a fallacy in the Church of God in the past.

Mark 12:41: "And after sitting down opposite the *temple* treasury, He observed how the people were casting money into the treasury; and many rich ones were putting *in* much."

One of the qualifications for someone to be an elder in the Church was the first thing they did was check up on the tithing record. If the person didn't tithe as much as they though he should he couldn't be an elder. That's not necessarily buying an eldership, but that's coming pretty close to it!

I'm going to watch on the TBN and if someone refers to it here on Sunday. 'Now you all come here and look what they did. Those who are rich put in a lot.' They'll stop there. They won't talk about the widow. 'The more you send in the happier you'll be, and the more blessed you will be.

- Can Satan give things to people to make it look like a blessing from God? *Yes!*
- Didn't Satan offer Jesus the whole world and rulership of it? Of course!

Verse 42: "And one poor widow came *and* dropped *in* two tiny coins, which is equal to one copper coin. Then He called His disciples to *Him* and said to them, 'Truly I say to you, this poor widow has put *in* more than all of those who are casting *money* into the treasury'" (vs 42-43).

It's not how much you give; it is *how faithful you are to God!* That's what counts! The widow was faithful and above and beyond with her two mites.

Verse 44: "For everyone *else* contributed out of their abundance; but she out of her destitution put *in* as much as she had, *giving* all her living."

I don't think that was all her living for the rest of her life, but all her living up to a certain point.

Section 307—Jesus and His Disciples Leave the Temple Area

We're going to just cover a few important points in Matt. 24 so that we understand where we're going with it. I could start almost every letter I write in Matt. 24 today. But we need to understand what happened here.

I was given an article by a man in one of the Churches of God that said that 'getting rid of all the stones did not mean the foundation stones.' He's giving the Jewish presentation where the Mosque of Omar is saying that if that's where the temple was then the foundation stones weren't counted. But that's not where the temple was or will be.

Matthew 24:1: "And after going out, Jesus departed from the temple; and His disciples came to *Him* to point out the buildings of the temple."

{Fred is describing—see video of this message—the placement of the temple and the Valley of Kidron, and showing that it's real steep up to the temple. Also, showing where the Mt. of Olives is and that it's higher than the temple area.}

On the Mt. of Olives was the Miphkad Altar,

which was where they took all the sin offerings, because they had to be burned completely. none of the meat was to be eaten by any person or the priests and Jesus was crucified close to the Miphkad Altar outside the camp.

Verse 2: "But Jesus said to them, 'Do you not see all these things?….'"

Think about this in relationship to what you would think if you were one of the apostles there with Jesus and He said this to you because you were impressed with the beautiful rocks, the beautiful stones and with the building of the temple and the wall and everything like that. They had all of it stone-covered 650-feet.

"…'Do you not see **all**…" (v 2).

That means every bit of it!

- Why did the area where the Mosque of Omar is remain untouched?
- Who destroyed the temple? *The Romans!*
- Whose property was area where the Mosque of Omar was? *Fort Antonia!*

That was Roman property. So, the Romans didn't destroy it. Not because the temple was there, but because it was their own property. They wanted to destroy everything Jewish with the greatest hatred possible.

"…Do you not see all these things? Truly…'" (v 2).

In truth!

"…I say to you, there shall not be left here even a stone upon a stone that shall not be thrown down" (v 2).

That's quite inclusive!

Mark 13:2: "Then Jesus answered and said to him, 'Do you see these great buildings? There shall not be left *a* stone upon *a* stone that shall not be thrown down.'"

Luke 21:6: "'*As for* these things that you now see, *the* days will come in which *there* shall not be left *one* stone upon another that shall not be thrown down.'"

Section 308—On the Mount of Olives Jesus Prophesies to His Disciples about the Events Leading up to: 1) The Sign of His Second Coming; 2) The Completion of the Age

We will quickly go through Matthew 24:

- vs 3-5—false prophets
- v 6—wars and rumors of wars
- v 7—nation against nation

- v 9—deliver you up to affliction
- v 10—many will be led into sin
- v 11—many false prophets

Verse 12: "And because lawlessness shall be multiplied, the love of many shall grow cold. **But the one who endures to *the* end, that one shall be saved**."

Verse 14 is a prelude to what will happen until Christ returns:

Verse 14: "And this Gospel of the Kingdom shall be proclaimed in all the world for a witness to all nations, and then shall the end come."

Think about it today, how that with a cell phone anyone can connect with the Word of God, even the Protestant outlets Catholic outlets and we're seeing like we found with Chancy Normandon how that they searched as a group for eight years.

Mac search for how many years I think it was three years before he came to our first service when we were down at a little hall at the other end of the building. Then shall the end come. Verse 15 is a key. This is the key that tells us plan the end is going to begin.

Verse 15: "Therefore, when you see the abomination of desolation, which was spoken of by Daniel the prophet, standing in the Holy place.' (**The one who reads, let him understand.**)"

That phrase Jesus did not say! If you have *King James* with red letters, and they put that in red letters, understand that Jesus wasn't writing a thing! John put that there because in 70A.D. the temple was destroyed. There was no *abomination of desolation* that stood in the holy place as described by Paul (2-Thess. 2), who declared himself to be 'God'! ***Didn't happen!***

So, this is telling us: "…(**The one who reads, let him understand**)"--because John didn't understand it. He knew of 2-Thess. 2 and he knew the vision given to him of the temple was true, so therefore, he said, 'I know there's go to be another temple built, but I don't understand it, so "…**The one who reads, let him understand**."

It could not be understood until getting down to our day.

Verse 16: "Then let those who arc in Judea flee into the mountains. Let the one *who is* on the housetop not come down to take anything out of his house" (vs 16-17).

Verse 20: "And pray that your flight be not in *the* winter, nor on *the* Sabbath."

I wonder what the apostles thought when Jesus said the Gospel is going to be proclaimed in all the world to all the nations? What was their concept of the world? Middle East? Asia Minor? North Africa? That was about it!

The actual earth is gigantic and is covered with more water than land. Of course, they didn't know. How is this going to work?

Imagine what they felt when Jerusalem was destroyed, the temple was destroyed, and Christ hadn't returned. We covered that in the apostasy series: *How Apostasy Starts*—how that the false teachers would say, 'Look, our interpretations are more correct because Jesus didn't return.'

Matthew 24:21: "For **then**…"

He said in v 20, 'Don't let your flight be in the winter or on the Sabbath,' which tells you that the time to flee—if you look at the chart of Daniel/Revelation series—it comes out about two weeks after the Feast of Tabernacle while it's still fall and before winter. Not in the summer, because you'd get some of those areas that are so hot that you would die.

What tells us *when* that fulfill the *then*? *The abomination of desolation* (v 15)—the when!

Verse 21: "For **then** shall there be great tribulation, such as has not been from *the* beginning of *the* world until this time, nor ever shall be *again*."

None this that we're reading now took place at the time of the destruction of the second temple and Jerusalem.

Verse 22: "And if those days were not limited…"

The *King James* says *cut short*. The preachers' ideal verse. 'You better get your life in order because God you got to cut the time short.' How many times did we hear that? *No! It's limited!* What is the limit of time? How long is the Tribulation? *Three and a half years! It's limited, not cut short!*

"…there would no flesh be saved; but for the elect's sake those days shall be limited. Then if anyone says to you, 'Behold, here *is* the Christ,' or, '*He is* there,' do not believe *it*." (v 22).

Now notice what's ahead of us:

Verse 24: "For there shall arise false Christs and false prophets…

We're going to be flooded with them!

"…and they shall present great signs and wonders…" (v 24).

What's going to happen with the false prophet in Rev. 13? *He's going to call down fire!* If you see that, 'seeing is believing.'

"…**in order to deceive, if possible, even the elect**" (v 24).

We haven't even come close to that kind of thing, yet! If the multitude believes it, you say, 'No, that's of Satan!' *How could this be of Satan?* Let's start with bringing *the beast* back to life. How could this be of Satan? *Look, he's bringing peace to the whole world!*

Verse 25: "Behold, I have foretold *it* to you. Therefore, if they say to you, '*Come and* see! He is in the wilderness'; do not go forth. '*Come and* see! *He is* in the secret chambers'; **do not believe *it***. For as the light of day…" (vs 25-27).

Malachi 4:2[transcriber's correction]: "…the **Sun** of Righteousness shall arise…" *Here it is*:

Matthew 24:27: "For as the light of day, which comes forth from *the* east and shines as far as *the* west, so also shall the coming of the Son of man be."

Here's what happens in Bible description: many times it will give you an introduction telling you what's going to come then a little further it defines what it is. This is what we have here.

Verse 28: "For wherever the carcass may be, there will the eagles be gathered together."

That's a hard one to figure except to say that if the eagles are angels and the Church is in a place of safety, that may be define it, possibly, the way it would be interpreted.

Verse 29: "But immediately after the tribulation of those days, the sun shall be darkened, and the moon shall not give her light, and the stars shall fall from heaven, and the powers of the heavens shall be shaken."

What is that going to do for time based upon the Calculated Hebrew Calendar? *It's going to knock it all 'caddy wampus'!* That's why only the Father knows the time or the day. It's all out of sequence, out of order. What are you going to do? From new moon to full moon with all this going on, it turns out to be 17 or 18 days. That's why it's not going to happen until that time, because it too confusing for those who are keeping the Feast and Holy Days today.

Verse 30: "And then shall appear the sign of the Son of man…"

The sign of the Son of man is:

Verse 27: "For as the light of day, which comes forth from *the* east and shines as far as *the* west…"

That defines:

Verse 30: "And then shall appear the sign of the Son of man in heaven; and then shall all the tribes of the earth mourn and they shall see the Son of man coming upon the clouds of heaven with power and great glory."

There's a gap of time between the sign of the Son of man and when He actually comes to the earth; that time is a little over one year, about 15 or 16 months.

Let's take the Bible and see when the sign of the Son of man appears. I'll direct you to any *Day 49* or *Day 50—Pentecost*—for more details on this to get how the sequence comes about. Rev. 6 is the opening of the seven seals.

Revelation 6:12: "And when He opened the sixth seal, I looked, and behold, there was a great earthquake; and the sun became black as *the* hair *of* sackcloth… [that's what we're talking about in Matt. 24] …and the moon became as blood; and the stars of heaven fell to the earth, as a fig tree casts its untimely figs when it is shaken by a mighty wind. Then *the* heaven departed like a scroll…" (vs 12-14).

A scroll is rolled up in two parts, generally speaking. It's opening up in the heavens. This didn't happen in 70A.D.

"…that is being rolled up, and every mountain and island was moved out of its place" (v 14). *That's going to be something!*

We've got this globe over here, and many people believe that if they can get a nice island in th South Seas 'I'll escape everything.' One tsunami takes care of you, and this is going to bring a lot of tsunamis. Other people think if they just get a cabin up in the mountains, nobody knows where they are. What are you going to do when you find you're down in the valley and not up in the mountain?

Verse 15: "And the kings of the earth, and the great men, and the rich men, and the chief captains, and the powerful men, and every bondman, and every free *man* hid themselves in the caves and in the rocks of the mountains."

This is devastation such has never, *never, never* has been. Isn't that what Christ said? *Yes!*

Verse 16: "And they said to the mountains and to the rocks, 'Fall on us, and hide us from *the* face of Him Who sits on the throne, and from the wrath of the Lamb, because the great day of His wrath has come, and who has the power to stand?'"

(vs 16-17).

That is introduced one heavens roll back and there looks like a second sun. Think about ancient aliens. Think about everyone believing the world is going to be attacked by aliens. How come they all know it's Christ? Well, there'll be a lot of people who will know that. But if you are told by the leader and *the beast* and the *false prophet* that what this represents an existential threat to the world, and it's really not Christ. Did they do that with His first coming? So, what will they do with His second coming?

Things will change. Things will change when it comes to Rev. 7; things change to a terrible calm and the winds are not even blowing. Then the 144,000 and the great innumerable multitude are saved, and everybody is in a different posture by time we get to Rev. 8; they start fighting against each other with great intensity and demons join them and so forth.

If you want a real in-depth study on it, get the Daniel/Revelation series.

Matthew 24:31: "And He shall send His angels with a great sound of a trumpet; and they shall gather together His elect from the four winds, from one end of heaven to *the* other."

It goes from His showing Himself with the heavens being rolled back up to the point of the resurrection; but there's a lot in between.

Verse 32: "Now, learn this parable from the fig tree: When its branches have already become tender, and it puts forth its leaves, you know that summer *is* near."

We're going to see a lot of things coming, and a lot of those things are going to look like good things for the world. People getting along with each other, *peace!* After all we've gone through, won't people want peace? Won't they be told by the *false prophet* that this is from God?

Verse 33: "In like manner also, when you see **all** these things, know that it is near, even at *the* doors."

Now, here's this phrase that we saw back in Matt. 23:

Verse 34: "Truly I say to you, **this generation** shall in no wise pass away until **all** these things have taken place."

*That's the **last** generation!* Who is the last generation? We thought that it was us many times.

Verse 36: "But concerning that day, and the hour, no one knows, not even the angels of heaven, but My Father only."

In Mark it says that not even the Son knows.

> Verse 37: "Now, as *it was in* the days of Noah, so shall *it* also be *at* the coming of the Son of man. For as in the days that *were* before the Flood, they were eating and drinking, marrying and giving in marriage, until the day that Noah entered the ark" (vs 37-38).

- If the days are like the days of Noah, what do we have today? *We have all kinds of things!*
- Do you suppose that Noah and his sons had electric power? Power saws? (speculation)

If it was like today, we could say that that would be an assumption. So, think about it! We have decided that there could have been atomic power, or it could have been an explosion of the sun. But there are cities in India that have so much radioactivity that you have to conclude that it's possible that that is because of human warfare. They even have carved toys that look like jet planes. Either way it goes it's a bad situation.

Because we don't know the day or the hour, and the heavens are all going to be shaken, the sun, moon and stars, everything is going to be affected. Nevertheless, this applies down through time from v 42. We even have the record of the Waldensians when they saw everything going on: The crusaders coming down to the Holy Land. They said, 'The Day of the Lord is not far away'—*in 1120!*

> Verse 42: "**Watch, therefore, because you do not know in what hour your Lord is coming.** But know this, that if the master of the house had known in what watch the thief would come, he would have been watching, and would not have allowed his house to be broken into. Therefore, **you also be ready**" (vs 42-44).

- Can Christ come upon you at any time?
- How does He come upon you?
- Do you think that Christ came upon WCG to do the things that were done because of their sins?

That doesn't mean His bodily return to the earth!

> "…For the Son of man is coming at a time that you do not think. Who then is the faithful and wise servant whom his lord has set over his household, to give them food in due season?" (vs 44-45).

Here's what we need to do, and this pretty well takes care of most of Matt. 24:

> Verse 46: "Blessed *is* that servant, whom his lord when he comes shall find so doing. Truly I say to you, he will set him over all

his property. But if that evil servant shall say in his heart, 'My lord delays *his* coming,' and shall begin to beat *his* fellow servants, and to eat and drink with the drunken, the lord of that servant will come in a day that he does not expect, and in an hour that he does not know. And he shall cut him asunder and shall appoint his portion with the hypocrites. **There shall be weeping and gnashing of teeth**" (vs 46-51).

That last verse jumps ahead to the final judgment at the end. So, we must always be:

- moving forward
- doing what is right
- living by the Word of God

Not saying that Jesus' return is a long way off! A lot of us remember when we thought He was coming in 1975. *He didn't come!* What happened to the Church? *Took a while! POOF!*

Section 309—Jesus Leaves the City Each Night

> Luke 21:37: "And during *the* day He was in the temple teaching, and at night He went out and lodged on the mountain called *the Mount* of Olives."

He had a camping place right there on the Mount of Olives!

> Verse 38: "And all the people came to Him in the temple early in the morning to hear Him."

He would come there at sunrise and be there all day, go out and come back.

Section 310—The Parable of the Ten Virgins

This is the story of those who are faithful and those who are sleeping and what happens. To show what a vessel/lamp means, we have a picture of an actual oil lamp from that age. They put the oil in and had the wick where it burned the oil.

How long would that last? *Not very long!* So, the ones who are wise had reserve; they always carried reserves. The ones who were foolish do not have any reserve, which tells you what the story is:

- if you don't study
- if you don't pray
- if you're not preparing
- if you're not taking each day as it comes

Then you may end up going to sleep!

- Have you seen those who've gone to sleep?

- Have you seen those who don't wake up?
- Have you seen those who have been deceived?

This is the whole story of the parable of the virgins! Same way with:

Section 311—The Parable of the Talents

He gives the talents, and those who are successful, what does He say? *Well done, faithful servant!*

Now here is something is not known very much today: *a steward is someone who takes what the master gives them!* He gave them five pounds, two pounds and one pound. A steward is to take that money make a profit for the owner of it, and not take anything for himself.

It's likened to those who preach and teach. We are to be stewards:

1. of God's Word
2. of God's people

We are not to take anything to ourselves to ingratiate ourselves and exalt ourselves. But to teach! Remember where we started with the parable how the Gentiles are ruled over. Their great ones and religious leaders have authority over them. Jesus said, 'It's not to be that way with you.' We are to teach!

An interesting comment was made by a man recently when he was looking for a church that would provide for them—the materials and things like that, in listening to some of them, most of them *preach,* but 'what we found with Christian Biblical, all the ministers *teach!*'

Last night in our Go to Meeting, there was an excellent message by Roger Kendall and I was very happy to see it because he slowed down in his speaking which was a major thing for him. He did an excellent job! that's what we need to do. All the elders need to teach. And the best thing we can teach is *how you can run your own life with the Spirit of God and not have a minister be ruling over you!* That can't work! That never works! If you want that join the Catholic Church!

Section 312—The Judgment of the Nations

Section 313—After Two Days the Passover Comes

Matthew 26:1: "Now, it came to pass *that* when Jesus had finished all these sayings, He said to His disciples, '**You know**…'" (vs 1-2).

That tells us that they knew the times and all that sort of thing!

"'…that after two days the Passover takes place, and the Son of man is delivered up to be crucified'" (v 2).

But they didn't understand that last sentence.

Verse 3: "Then the chief priests and the scribes and the elders of the people assembled together in the court of the high priest, who was called Caiaphas; and *they* took counsel together for the purpose of seizing Jesus by treachery, and killing *Him.* But they said, 'Not during the Feast, so that there will not be a riot among the people'" (vs 3-5).

Mark 14:1: "Now, after two days was the Passover **and** the *Feast of* Unleavened Bread…"

Luke 22:1: "Now, the Feast of Unleavened *Bread,* which *is* called Passover, was approaching."

Luke is showing how the Jews interpreted it, because they kept the Passover on the 15th.

You'll have to read *The Christian Passover* book to get all the details of it. But I only found one rabbi who wrote and said that 'we do nothing on the 14th because we are in the Diaspora and our sins are following in the footsteps of our fathers.'

What they did in the Diaspora, they took the first day of the Feast of Unleavened Bread and called that *the Passover,* and instead of observing The Night Much to Be Remembered, they made that the night of the Seder.

When you read Deut. 16, if you misinterpret it, you may think that that authorizes the *Passover sacrifice* at the temple. Read it carefully and you will see that the offerings are to be from *the flock and the herd.* I challenge you to show me one place in the Bible that talks about the *Passover calf.* When you understand Exo. 13 about the redemption of the firstborn, you will see that all those sacrifices of the day portion of the 14th called *Passover Offerings* were offerings mostly for the redemption of the firstborn of man and beast.

Then they had the Night to be Much Remembered, and the instruction was to 'return to your tent in the morning.' *So, they stayed up all night on the Night to be Much Observed!*

Section 314—In Bethany, Jesus is Anointed for His Burial

He was anointed twice. Where was the first anointing? *Lazarus' house where Mary and Martha were!* Mary was the one who was doing Jesus' feet. This one here is in a different place.

Matthew 26:6: "Now, when Jesus was in

Bethany, in **Simon the leper's house**."

That is not Lazarus!

Verse 7: "A woman came to Him with an alabaster flask of ointment, very precious, and poured *it* **on His head**…"

The first anointing was on His feet!
"…as He sat down *to eat*" (v 7).

- How did all of this come about?
- How did we have two flasks of alabaster ointment?
- Who was in charge of making sure that everything was carried out? *All the angels!*
- Who was in charge of the adversary trying to thwart everything that was being done? *Satan the devil and his minions the priests!*
- Who was the one who betrayed Jesus? *Judas Iscariot!*

We need to realize that there were angels, demons, high level demons. This was great, great thing to happen, and it was a combat of the ages, because here's the sacrifice of God in the person of the Son of God, His only Begotten Jesus Christ!

Verse 8: "But when His disciples saw *it*, *they* became indignant *and* said, 'What reason *is there* for this waste? For this ointment could have been sold for much, and *the money* given to *the* poor.' But Jesus knew *this* and said to them, 'Why do you cause trouble for this woman? For she has performed a good work toward Me. For you have the poor with you always, but you do not always have Me. What this *woman did* in pouring this ointment on My body, she did for My burial'" (vs 8-12).

After saying this will be preached in all the world (Matt. 26:13) both of them are talked about.

Nisan 12—Monday, April 3, 30 AD

Section 315—Judas Betrays Jesus to the Chief Priests for 30 Pieces of Silver

Luke 22:3: "Then Satan entered into Judas, who was surnamed Iscariot, being of the number of the twelve. And he went away, *and* spoke with the chief priests and the captains about a way by which he might betray Him to them. And **they rejoiced**…" (vs 3-5).

Think about that for a minute!

- Can Satan make people happy?
- Can Satan make people laugh?
- *Yes!*

I'm going to a couple of Church at Home {churchathome.org} called *Satan's Trickery of Children!*

There is a new movie coming out by Walt Disney… Think about this: when you understand what comes out of Disney World, *everything there is based on satanism! Every single thing!* It starts out kind of funny and nice, but they are going to have a movie about a child who has four parents, instilling in children the confusion of gender reality. **Is not that evil?** *But it's going to be presented as funny!*

I remember when we first saw Star Wars. Jonathan, David and Stephen were all excited in the car going home. I said to them, 'This is all satanism.' *Ah, Dad!*

It is! Who was the god that they worshipped? *Yoda!* That starts with the same letter as Yahweh. *Things are getting more and more evil!*

They rejoiced! They thought this could never happen. We've been planning and plotting and scheming! Here it 'fall into our lap.' Think about how victorious they felt!

Luke 22:6: "And he promised, and sought *an* opportunity to betray Him to them away from *the* multitude."

Mark 14:11: "And after hearing *this*, they were delighted and promised to give him money…."

Matthew 26:15: *"And* said, 'What are you willing to give me, and I will deliver Him up to you?' And they offered him thirty pieces of silver."

There again, we took the temple coins and put thirty pieces of silver.

Here's to show you that there was a lot going on with the angels in making everything take place. We're going to see why Jesus did it this way. In order for Jesus to be arrested at the right place, at the right time, and not before hand.

This last Passover, Jesus didn't tell any of the disciples where they were going to keep it. This presented a problems for Judas. If Jesus had told them, Judas could have gone to the chief priest and told him where they were keeping the Passover, 'come over and get Him there, and you can get all the disciples, as well.' *Jesus didn't tell them!*

Section 316—The Disciples Prepare for the Passover

These are literal translations of the Greek:

Matthew 26:17: "Now, on the first of the unleaveneds…"

No day was there!

> "…the disciples came to Jesus, saying to Him, 'Where do You desire *that* we prepare for You to eat the Passover?' And He said, 'Go into the city to such a man…'" (vs 17-18).

He didn't tell them who or where!

> "'…and say to him, "The Teacher says, 'My time is near; I will keep the Passover with My disciples at your *house*'"'" (v 18).

> Mark 14:12: "And on the first day of the unleaveneds…"

There's a footnote I want you to the read. If this were the first day of the Feast of Unleavened Bread, think of the problems that you would have. Passover Day would already be gone! How could Christ be our Passover if this were the first day of the Feast of Unleavened Bread?

In addition, think on this: Since the Jews kept the Passover a day later, they would have kept their Passover on the 16th and not the 15th. So, what is the answer? *Read in the Passover book, the Passover Day is an unleavened bread day in addition to the seven! Josephus* writes of eight days of Unleavened Bread.

It used to be in the past that the people would take the Passover on the correct day and they were told they could have a hamburger in the day portion and eat leavened bread on the day portion. If you eat the unleavened bread of Christ, why can you eat leaven after the Passover? *They didn't understand the Greek!*

> Verse 12: "And on the first day of the unleaveneds…"

This is all explained in the footnote in the *Harmony* and you can get more detail in the Passover book.

> "…when they were killing…" (v 12).

That is a literal actual translation; a present tense participle in the Greek. Not when they *killed,* but "…were killing…"

Where were the disciples? *Over in Bethany!* Bethany and Bethphage are on this side of the Mount of Olives (referring to map). So, as they're coming down to go into the town, the whole area of the Mount of Olives had tents of pilgrims coming there to keep the Passover and Unleavened Bread. Most of them at that time kept the 14th. You can read that in the Passover book.

It unlocks all the Truth and refutes every Jewish error. So, if you haven't read the Passover book, you get it and we'll send it to you free.

> "…when they were killing the Passover lambs…" (v 12).

When were they to kill the Passover lambs according to Exo. 12? *Between the two evenings, which Exo. 16 shows is after sunset and before dark!*

Get the picture: here's all the disciples there and Jesus didn't tell them where they were going to keep the Passover.

> "…His disciples said to Him, 'Where do You desire that we go and prepare, so that You may eat the Passover?'" (v 12).

They could see all the pilgrims killing their Passover lambs right here, right now.

> Verse 13: "And He sent two of His disciples…

Peter and John (Luke 22:8).

> "…and said to them, 'Go into the city, and you shall meet a man,,,'" (v 13).

How many people were there? *Thousands and thousands!*

> "…carrying a pitcher of water; follow him" (v 13).

How was that made possible? *The angels were working it all out to make sure that when the disciples hit a certain intersection the man carrying the water would be coming!*

> Luke 22:10: "And He said to them, 'Watch, *and* when you come into the city, you will meet a man carrying a pitcher of water; follow him into the house that he enters.'"

Jesus did not keep a Passover with the temple sacrificed lamb. He did not tell the disciples that they were killing the lambs and 'run over to the temple and get a Passover lamb.' *No, He didn't!* Who prepared the lamb? *The master of the house!* So, everything was ready.

Nisan 13—Tuesday, April 4, 30 AD

> Mark 14:14: "And whatever house he shall enter, say to the master of the house *that* the Teacher says, 'Where is the guest chamber, where I may eat the Passover with My disciples?'"

What happened? *The master of the house was preparing everything and having it all ready to go!* Killed the lamb and probably had it beginning to roast. Here comes the man with the water. What was the water to be used for? *Washing of the feet!* The disciples come in and they don't know the man. The man doesn't know them, and the Master or Teacher says, "…Where is the guest chamber, where I may eat the Passover with My disciples?"

All of that must have been worked out by the angels. It was so precise!

Verse 15: "And he shall show you a large upper room, furnished *and* ready. There prepare for us."

All they had to do was put out the unleavened bread and make sure that the lamb was going.

Verse 16: "And His disciples went away: and *when* they came into the city, they found *it* exactly as He had said to them; and they prepared the Passover."

Reading assignment: Read the commentary that follows in *A Harmony of the Gospels,* pg. 245-255: Jesus' Last Passover and Crucifixion and 28 prophecies fulfilled on the Passover Day.

If anyone is into odds-making, what are the odds that 28 specific prophecies could be fulfilled in one day? That's why all of this had to be prearranged by prophecy, by the work of the angels, to make it all come together for the most important thing since the creation of man.

Scriptural References:

1) Matthew 23:1-10, 12, 11, 13-23
2) Luke 11:42
3) Matthew 23:23-27, 29-30, 32-39
4) Mark 12:41-44
5) Matthew 24:1-2
6) Mark 13:2
7) Luke 21:6
8) Matthew 24:12-17, 20-22, 24-27
9) Malachi 4:2
10) Matthew 24:27-30, 27, 30
11) Revelation 6:12-17
12) Matthew 24:31-34, 36-38, 42-51
13) Luke 21:37-38
14) Matthew 26:1-5
15) Mark 14:1
16) Luke 22:1
17) Matthew 26:6-12
18) Luke 22:3-6
19) Mark 14:11
20) Matthew 26:15, 17-18
21) Mark 14:12-13
22) Luke 22:10
23) Mark 14:14-16

Scriptures referenced, not quoted:

- Mark 7
- John 17
- Acts 1-8
- John 9
- Matthew 5
- Hebrews 12

- Matthew 24:3-7, 9-11
- 2 Thessalonians 2
- Revelation 13, 7; 8
- Deuteronomy 16
- Exodus 13
- Matthew 26:13
- Exodus 12; 16
- Luke 22:8

Also referenced:

In-Depth Studies:
- *How to Overcome the Sin Within!*
- *How Apostasy Starts*
- *Daniel/Revelation*

Books by Fred R. Coulter: {**truthofgod.org**}
- *A Harmony of the Gospels*
- *The Christian Passover*

Church at Home {**churchathome.org**} *Satan's Trickery of Children!*

FRC: po/bo
Transcribed: 3/17/19
Reformatted: 10/2020

CHAPTER TWENTY-ONE

The Last Ten Days of Jesus' Life IV
From the Passover to the Crucifixion and the last seven sayings of Jesus
Fred R. Coulter

Greetings, brethren! Welcome to Sabbath services!

We've been going through the last ten days of Jesus' life, and we've been using *A Harmony of the Gospels*. I ask you to please go through the commentary, pgs 245-255—Jesus' Last Passover and Crucifixion—about the gruesomeness of the crucifixion and so forth. When we go through here, we're going to learn an awful lot.

Advertisement: In-Depth Studies:
- *The Love of God*
- *Passover Preparation*

The Passover demonstrates the love of God to nth degree. It shows us what Christ really did for us; only **He** could do it. Why is that? Why do you suppose that is true? *Only He could do it because He created mankind and everything on the earth!* Everything from the invisible to all the mountains, oceans, the sky and the universe out there. *He created us!*

- Why could only He do it?
- What else did He do?

In His judgment against Adam and Eve, He gave them 'the law of sin and death,' and that became part of human nature!

What He had to do is also take the 'law of sin and death' within Him, and His struggle was greater than any of ours *because He couldn't sin! That's why only He could do it!*

Around Jerusalem at that time there were legions and legions of angels. Remember that Jesus said one time when He was testing the apostles if they *really* believe Him. They said, 'Yes, we believe.' Jesus said, 'What would you do it you saw angels ascending and descending upon the Son of man?'

Also, Satan and the demons were there, so this was a real struggle at Jerusalem. The whole atmosphere was filled with this. That's why, as we saw in part three, Jesus did not tell them where they were going to keep the Passover, because He didn't want Judas coming in and messing up the Passover. So, Judas had to come along with them to the Passover. He couldn't betray them there, so as we

will see later, it was out by the Garden of Gethsemane that Jesus was betrayed.

A Harmony of the Gospels, pg 274—this is the first part of the New Covenant, the foot-washing. Remember there are three parts:

1. foot-washing
2. bread
3. wine

Passover Day, Nisan 14—Tuesday Evening, April 4, 30 AD

Section 318—Jesus Institutes the New Covenant Passover:

First part of the New Covenant Passover: The Foot-Washing:

John 13:2: "And after supper began…"

or during supper! The *King James* says ' when supper ended,' but if you read a little further, they were still eating because Jesus dipped the sop and gave it to Judas. So, that's a complete wrong translation and contrary to the Greek.

Verse 2: "And after supper began (the devil having already put into the heart of Judas Iscariot, Simon's *son,* that he should betray Him)."

Stop and think about this. All of us have to fight against our own evil thoughts. Sometimes we get provoked, and sometimes we don't even know why we're provoked. I've done it, you've done it and everybody else has done it.

Also, another way the evil thoughts come are from demons and Satan. There's one person that every time I say that 'Satan inspires' I get a postcard saying that Satan can't inspire. But he can put it in the heart, 'the prince of the power of the air' (Eph. 2).

Verse 3: "Jesus, knowing that the Father had given all things into *His* hands, and that He had come from God and was going to God, rose from supper and laid aside *His* garments; and after taking a towel, He secured it around Himself" (vs 3-4).

This is a tremendous thing for us to understand. What is one of the first things that people stop doing

241

when they're slipping away from the Truth? *They give up foot-washing!* It is humbling! None of us have picture-perfect feet.

> Verse 5: "Next, He poured water into a washing basin and began to wash the disciples' feet, and to wipe *them* with the towel, which He had secured. Then He came to Simon Peter; and he said to Him…" (vs 5-6).

Look at Peter's attitude. Peter had a real lesson to learn this night, and we'll see what that is.

> "…'Lord, are You going to wash my feet?' Jesus answered and said to him, 'What I am doing you do not understand now, but you shall know after these things'" (vs 6-7).

After Jesus was done washing their feet!

> Verse 8: "Peter said to Him, 'You shall not wash my feet, not ever.'…."

- Can we ever tell Jesus what to do? *Think on that! NO!*
- Was Peter hardheaded? *Yes!*
- Did he learn some lessons? *Yes!*
- Did he repent? *Yes!*
- Was he humbled? *Yes!*

> "…Jesus answered him, 'If I do not wash you, you have no part with Me'" (v 8).

Look at how quickly his attitude change: *from **no** to everything!*

> Verse 9: "Simon Peter said to Him, 'Lord, not my feet only, but also *my* hands and *my* head.'"

Why did Peter say that? *Because the priests had to wash their hands and their head!*

> Verse 10: "Jesus said to him, 'The one who has been washed…'"

This has reference to baptism!

> "'…does not need to wash *anything other* than the feet, but is completely clean; and you are clean, but not all.' For He knew the one who was betraying Him; this was the reason He said, 'Not all of you are clean.'" (vs 10-12).

Here are some great lessons for us. Humility does not come because you make yourself humble. Humility comes because you are humbled by the magnitude of what God is doing. That's how humility comes. *We don't raise ourselves above other to make ourselves important!*

> Jesus didn't say to Peter, 'Who do you think

you are? I'm the Lord.' Jesus could have said that.

> Verse 12: "Therefore, when He had washed their feet, and had taken His garments, *and* had sat down again, He said to them, 'Do you know what I have done to you?'"

They're probably all thinking, 'I don't have a clue!'

> Verse 13: "You call Me the Teacher and the Lord, and you speak rightly, because I am. Therefore, if I, the Lord and the Teacher, have washed your feet…" (vs 13-14).

Notice what He says; this is pretty powerful in the Greek:

> "…**you also are duty-bound to wash one another's feet**; for I have given you an example, *to show* that **you also should do exactly as I have done to you**. Truly, truly I tell you, a servant is not greater than his lord…" (vs 14-16).

Never happen!

> "…nor a messenger…

*This could also be **apostle!***

> "…greater than he who sent him. If you know these things, **blessed are you if you do them**" (vs 16-17).

What happens when people quit foot-washing? *They're throwing away a blessing!* Human nature is so basically evil that when they think they're doing something good, *it's really sin!*

Section 319—Judas Dips the Sop, and Leaves to Betray Jesus

John 13:18: "I am not speaking of you all; *for* I know whom I have chosen, in order that the Scripture might be fulfilled: 'He who eats bread with Me has lifted up his heel against Me.' I am telling you at this time, before it happens, so that when it does happen, you may believe that **I AM**" (vs 18-19).

The double 'ego emi'!

> Verse 20: "Truly, truly I tell you, the one who receives whomever I send is receiving Me…"

This becomes important because you don't receive this to be arrogant and over-lording on the brethren. That's not the way. If you bring the Word of God, that is what is to be done.

> "…and the one who receives Me is receiving Him Who sent Me" (v 20).

Think about that for a minute. God the Father is so involved with those who are going to be in the first resurrection, that those who are elders and servants of the people are actually representing the Father. Think of how loving, kind, generous and overwhelmingly good that God the Father is. Look at the attitude of Peter when he denied Christ three times. *Peter was forgiven and he knew better!* But he wasn't going to tell Jesus what to do, and he wasn't going to save Jesus from what was going to happen.

We need to realize that that being the case, it's a great responsibility and also a great humbling that God would do so.

Verse 21: *"As He* was saying these things, Jesus was troubled in spirit, and testified, saying, 'Truly, truly I tell you, one of you shall betray Me.'"

Isn't that always something? Someone also sneaks in and gets way up in authority. Then after a while—BANG!—it happens every time. This is how God gets rid of the tares. He scatters the Church and lets the tares stay where they are. But the Church is going on its own and the tares are stuck without God, *and they don't even know it!*

Verse 22: "Then the disciples looked at one another, wondering of whom He was speaking. Now one of His disciples, the one whom Jesus loved, was leaning on Jesus' chest. And so, Simon Peter motioned to him to ask who was the one of whom He was speaking. Then he leaned back on Jesus' chest *and* asked Him, 'Lord, who is it?' Jesus answered, 'It is the one to whom I shall give a sop after I have dipped it.'…." (vs 22-26).

People say, 'How can you dip a sop if you have unleavened bread?' Very simple, after services you can take some scooper corn chips and you can scoop up some avocado and salsa. Are the corn chips unleavened bread? Did you dip it in the salsa and avocado? So, He took a piece of unleavened bread and scooped up something with a little morsel and gave it to Judas.

"…And when He had dipped the sop, He gave *it* to Judas Iscariot, Simon's *son.* And after the sop, Satan entered into him…." (vs 26-27)

Right there at the Passover! Think about that!

"…Then Jesus said to him, 'What you do, do quickly.' But not one of those sitting at the table knew why He said *this* to him; for some thought, since Judas had the bag, that Jesus was telling him, 'Buy the things that we need for the feast'; or that he should give something to the poor. So then, after receiving the sop, he immediately went out; and it was night. When he was gone, Jesus said, 'Now has the Son of man been glorified, and God has been glorified in Him. If God has been glorified in Him, God shall also glorify Him in Himself, and shall immediately glorify Him'" (vs 27-32).

That was a projection of the completion of all of the rest leading up to the resurrection. After Judas is gone:

Section 320—Second Part: Eating the Unleavened Bread

Matthew 26:26 ""And as they were eating, Jesus took the bread and blessed *it; then He* broke *it* and gave *it* to the disciples, and said, 'Take, eat; this is My body.'"

Remember, He gave a preview of this in John 6, and that was a hard thing for a lot of the disciples to take. What does it mean to eat His body? Some would say that's kind of cannibalistic! *No, it's not!* Because everything has to come though Christ:

In the beginning was the Word, the Word was with God and the Word was God! Everything came into being had to come into being because He brought it into being.

In this way God is projecting that He is going to share His life with us, **_IF_** we eat the Bread of Truth, the Word of God, compared to the stones that Satan said to make into bread. Jesus said, 'NO! Man is not to live by bread alone, but by word that proceeds out of the mouth of God!' *This fulfills that!*

Section 321—Third Part: Drinking the Wine

Verse 27: "And He took the cup; and after giving thanks, He gave *it* to them, saying, 'All of you drink of it; for this is My blood, the *blood* of the New Covenant…'" (vs 27-28).

In Deut. 32 it talks about the 'blood of the grape.' This was wine. What is a noted feature of wine when it's ready to drunk? *Unleavened! All the yeast is out of it!* When you have sparkling wine, they put a little bit of leaven back in it so you get the bubbles. Was Christ's blood pure? *Absolutely!*

"…for this is My blood, the *blood* of the New Covenant…" (v 28).

Page 258 (*Harmony*): Chart showing the comparison of the sacrifice of Christ, what He went through and the parallel account with Abraham and the Lord in the Old Testament, and it follows right along exactly.

What did He say about the experience that He was going to go through? *He said, 'I have a baptism that I'm going to be baptized by, and I'm in a straight until it's completed!'* How was Jesus baptized? **In His own blood!**

"…the *blood* of the New Covenant, which is poured out for many for *the* remission of sins" (v 28).

Think about sin, repentance and forgiveness. What did Jesus say concerning repentance? *Someone sins against you, Peter asked, 'What if he does it seven times? Should I forgive him?'* Jesus said, 'Yes! Seven times seventy!'

Why did He say that? *Because He understood the weakness of human nature!* It seems to work that way. Whenever you do something, and it's great and wonderful and 'I know that God was with me and helping me' and you turn around and sin! God is there to forgive you. *That's what the sacrifice of Christ is all about!*

Verse 29: "But I say to you, from this time forward I will not drink at all of this fruit of the vine, until that day when I drink *it* anew with you in the Kingdom of My Father.'

I imagine that that is going to be a spiritual wine. What's that going to taste like? Think of this, right in the middle of the Passover service they have an argument.

Section 322—Contention Among the Disciples as to Who Would be the Greatest

What does this tell you? *They understood that there were going to be some great things given, and so forth!* Remember 'mama' with James and John? *She came to Jesus and said,* 'I have one thing to ask You.' *What is it?* 'That these, my two sons—the sons of thunder—one sit at Your right hand and one sit at your left hand.' Jesus said, 'Woman, you don't know what you're asking.' Here it begins again:

Luke 22:24: "And there was also an argument among them, *even* this: which of them should be considered *the* greatest. And He said to them, 'The kings of the nations lord over them, and those who exercise authority over them are called benefactors'" (vs 24-25).

1. the rulers
2. religious leaders

Verse 26: But ***it shall* not be this way *among* you**; rather, let the one who is greatest among you be as the younger, and the one who is leading as the one who is serving."

That's why a hierarchy is counter to what God really wants!

Verse 27: "For who *is* greater, the one who is sitting *at the table*, or the one who is serving? *Is* not the one who sits *at the table*? But I am among you as One Who is serving. Now, you are the ones who have continued with Me in My temptations" (vs 27-28).

On the Sabbath after the last Holy Day I've given a message for that day: *What is the Difference Between Temptation and Tribulation?* Do you know the difference?

- **temptation**—you have choices
- **tribulation**—it comes upon you and you have no choice

Verse 29: "And I appoint to you, as My Father has appointed to Me, a kingdom; so that you may eat and drink at My table in My kingdom, and may sit on thrones judging the twelve tribes of Israel" (vs 29-30).

Section 323—A New Commandment—Love Each Other as Jesus Love His Disciples

John 13:33: "Little children…"

They weren't too much younger than Jesus!

"…I am with you yet a little while. You shall seek Me; but as I told the Jews, 'Where I am going, you cannot come,' I am now telling you also. **A new commandment I give to you**…" (vs 33-34).

We have the commandments:

- love God with all your heart, mind, soul and being
- love your neighbor as yourself

And on those two hang all the Law! Here's the third one, and Jesus also gave a fourth one.

Verse 34: "**A new commandment I give to you that you love one another in the same way that I have loved you**…

That's pretty strong! This is how you are to love one another. That's commandment #3 in love. Commandment #4 is *love your enemies!* The best way to love your enemies is to stay away from them.

Verse 35: "By this shall everyone know that you are My disciples—if you love one another."

Section 324—Jesus Prophecies that Peter Will Deny Him Three Times

Mark 14:27: "Then Jesus said to them, 'All of you shall be offended in Me in this night; for it is written, "I will smite the Shepherd, and the sheep shall be scattered." But after I have risen, I will go before you into Galilee.' Then Peter said to Him, '**Even if all shall be offended, yet, I shall not**'" (vs 27-29).

The most powerful of human nature is not going to overcome what God has said. God has said, 'All are sinners! Some people say, 'I'm not.' *You're sinners by nature!*

Verse 30: "And Jesus said to him, 'Truly I say to you, **today, in this *very* night**…'"

That proves that God reckons the day from sunset to sunset!

"'…before *the* cock crows twice, you shall deny Me three times.' But he spoke more adamantly, 'If it were necessary for me to die with You, I would not deny You in any way.' And they all spoke in the same manner also" (vs 30-31).

But what did Peter do? *He did it!* Think of that for a minute. Even your best effort to not do it, when God said you're going to do it, you don't have the strength to go against God. Amazing!

Section 325—The Beginning of the Final Message to His Disciples

We're going to cover John 14 during the Passover so I don't want to go deeply into this:

John 14:20: "In that day, you shall know that I am in My Father, and you *are* in Me, and I am in you."

Here's how you know. This is a test if you have Christ and the Father in you:

Verse 21: "'The one who has My commandments and is keeping them, that is the one who loves Me, and the one who loves Me shall be loved by My Father, and I will love him and will manifest Myself to him.' Judas (not Iscariot) said to him, 'Lord, what has happened that You are about to manifest Yourself to us, and not to the world?'" (vs 21-22).

How does God manifest, or Christ manifest Himself to us today? *By convincing you of the Truth! And you prove the Truth!* The Truth can be proved and reproved and reproved over and over again down

through all time, because it is true and it's eternal!

Verse 23: "Jesus answered and said to him, 'If anyone loves Me, he will keep My Word; and My Father will love him, and We will come to him and make Our abode with him.'"

That's one of the most important verses in the Bible. You have two aspects of the Spirit:

- the Spirit of Christ, or the mind of Christ
- the Spirit of the Father, to be a son or daughter of God

Together! That is dwell in us!

When we sin, God doesn't take it away. God is merciful and kind, and will forgive. That's the whole purpose of the Passover and learning to love one another.

Section 326—Some Final Instructions to the Disciples

Luke 22:36: "Then He said to them, 'Now, however, let the one who has a purse take *it…*'"

Section 327—Take Two Swords

Verse 38: "And they said, 'Lord, see, here *are* two swords.' And He said to them, 'It is enough.'"

Section 328—They Sing a Hymn and Leave

Matthew 26:30: "And after singing a hymn, they went out to the Mount of Olives."

Section 329—Jesus Christ is the True Vine—Last Command to His Disciples

We're going to cover the first part of John 15, because this becomes important. Remember how God compared Israel to a vine. Now He compares Himself to a vine and the Father to a husbandman. Some translate that as *the farmer.* But husbandman is much different, because husbandman means that *you are married to the land to take care of it as a possession of God!* So, Jesus makes this comparison:

John 15:1: "I am the true vine, and My Father is the husbandman. He takes away every branch in Me *that* does not bear fruit; but He cleanses each one that bears fruit, in order that it may bear more fruit" (vs 1-2).

- How does He cleanse it? *By revealing the sin within so you can repent, that's how!*
- How much sin do we have stored in our mind?
- Do you want me to get a CD and play

Christmas Carols? *You have them stored in the mind!*
You have them all right there!

- What else do you have there? *Every once in a while your human nature cuts loose!*

It's happened to me! It's happened to you! The cleansing is *the pruning to get it out in the open so that you can repent!*

Verse 3: "You are already clean through the word that I have spoken to you. Dwell in Me, and I in you. As a branch cannot bear fruit of itself, but only if it remains in the vine, neither *can* you *bear fruit* unless you are dwelling in Me" (vs 3-4).

I remember one Feast of Tabernacles we were in a beautiful place for a Feast. We had for the first time people come from Michigan. We had 12 people! We thought this was something. So, we broke off some branches from a tree and we just put up where we were meeting so we could watch them. Every day of the Feast we looked at the branches. The second day looked like the first day. Third day they were drooping. Fourth day they were really getting bad. Fifth day they were getting very, very dry. Sixth-eight days there was nothing left.

That shows that we need to stay in Christ! How do we stay in Christ? *By loving, praying, repenting, overcoming, asking God to help us in everything!*

Verse 4: Dwell in Me, and I in you. As a branch cannot bear fruit of itself, but only if it remains in the vine, neither *can* you *bear fruit* unless you are dwelling in Me. I am the vine, *and* you *are* the branches. The one who is dwelling in Me, and I in him, bears much fruit; because apart from Me you can do nothing" (vs 4-5).

What did Jesus say of Himself when He was here? *I do nothing of Myself, that is out from within Me!* The Father does the works.

Verse 6: "If anyone does not dwell in Me, he is cast out as a branch, and is dried up; and men gather them and cast *them* into a fire, and they are burned."

Here is a promise for prayer:

Verse 7: "If you dwell in Me, and My words dwell in you…"
Both!
"…you shall ask whatever you desire, and it shall come to pass for you. In this is My Father glorified, that you bear much fruit; so shall you be My disciples" (vs 7-8).

Then He tells how! It's very interesting and very important! There are 1700 *ifs* in the Bible, and all of them are contingent upon what people choose to do or not do.

Verse 10: "**If** you keep My commandments, you shall live in My love; just as I have kept My Father's commandments and live in His love. These things I have spoken to you, in order that My joy may dwell in you, and that your joy may be full" (vs 10-11).

Think about poor Lot living in Sodom; that's about what it is for us today! He didn't have much joy because he was always upset over what was happening. Finally, when it came time to go, the only ones who went were he and his wife and two daughters. All the rest of the family said, 'You're nuts! It's not going to happen!'

So, they were going out and the angel said, 'Don't look behind!' Guess what happened? *Lot's wife looked behind and turned into a pillar of salt!* I don't know if it was true our not, but Josephus writes that that pillar of salt was still there in his day.

Section 330—Final Words of Encouragement

John 16:26: "In that day, you shall ask in My name; and I do not tell you that I will beseech the Father for you, for **the Father Himself loves you**…" (vs 26-27).

That is a profound statement! Whenever you're down at the bottom of the pit and you think all is lost, *it's not!* Whether you're way up here, and you're knocked down, remember that *the Father—Who is Sovereign of the whole universe—loves you! He loved the Son—didn't He?* But look what Jesus had to go through, and that had to be because of Jesus' love back to the Father and the love for the plan of God and what He's going to do for all human beings. *So, we pray to the Father directly!*

"…because you have loved Me, and have believed that I came forth from God. I came forth from the Father and have come into the world; again, I am leaving the world and am going to the Father" (vs 27-28).

Section 331—All Will be Scattered. Jesus Has Overcome the World

Verse 32: "Listen, the time is coming, and has already come, that you shall be scattered each to his own, and you shall leave Me alone; and *yet,* I am not alone because the Father is with Me. These things I have spoken to you **so that in Me you may have peace. In the world you**

shall have tribulation...." (vs 32-33).

A lot of difficulties and things come upon us that we have no control over! **That's tribulation!**

"...But be courageous! I have overcome the world" (v 33).

Section 334, page 284—Jesus Prays for Three Hours

They go out to the area of the Garden of Gethsemane

Matthew 26:39: And after going forward a little, He fell on His face, praying, and saying, 'My Father, if it be possible, let this cup pass from Me; nevertheless, not as I will, but as You *will*.'

So, He had to overcome even the human element of knowing how bad that this would be that He was saying, 'Will You delay it?'

Verse 40: "Then He came to His disciples and found them sleeping. And *He* said to Peter, 'What! Were you not able to watch with Me one hour? Watch and pray, so that you do not enter into temptation; the spirit indeed *is* willing, but the flesh is weak'" (vs 40-41).

That's true for all human beings. Last time we had the best thought in the world, *we end up doing the worst thing in the world.*

Verse 42: "The second time He went again *and* prayed, saying, 'My Father, if this cup cannot pass from Me unless I drink it, Your will be done.'"

Through prayer He was able to overcome that pull of human nature the first time!

Verse 43: "Now, when He came to them, He found them asleep again, because their eyes were heavy. And leaving them, He went again and prayed the third time, saying the same thing" (vs 43-44).

Luke 22:44: "And being in agony, He prayed more earnestly. And His sweat became **as great drops of blood** falling down to the ground."

This shows how deeply He had to pray!

Passover Day, Nisan 14—Wednesday Morning, April 5, 30 AD

Section 335—The Lord's Prayer

When you really analyze it, this shows you the whole plan of God in that one chapter (John 17). Just to give you something to think on: How did John know this prayer if he was sleeping? *Jesus had to give him this prayer sometime later!* **It's word for**

word of what Jesus was saying, and it's the whole plan of God! So much so that I'm going to save that for a separate message, because if I get to deeply involved in it here, we won't get to where we need to be.

John 17:11: "And I am no longer in the world, but these are in the world, and I am coming to You. Holy Father, keep them in Your name, those whom You have given Me, so that they may be one, even as We *are* one."

Sidebar on this with the *name*: If you meet a sacred-namer and he says that you have to have this Hebrew name, this name and the other name. If you turn to John 17, in the Greek it is 'ho pater': *Father!* That's His sacred name for the New Testament. There's no other name. It's not here. So, keep that in mind.

Verse 12: "When I was with them in the world, I kept them in Your name. I protected those whom You have given Me, and not one of them has perished except the son of perdition, in order that the Scriptures might be fulfilled."

Then it shows that we are to become at-one with Christ and the Father!

Verse 20: "I do not pray for these only, but also for those who shall believe in Me through their word."

That's us! Everybody all down through time who had the Word of God, the New Testament! He's praying, and He makes intercession for us. Notice how Jesus always keeps His mind on the goal.

Verse 21: "That they all may be one, even as You, Father, *are* in Me, and I in You; that they also may be one in Us, in order that the world may believe that You did send Me."

Section 336—The time of the Betrayal Approximately 12:20 A.M.

There's a two page chart—pgs 256-7—showing the whole thing hour by hour down through the time.

Matthew 26:45: "Then He came to His disciples and said to them, 'Sleep on now, and take your rest. Behold, the hour has drawn near, and the Son of man is betrayed into *the* hands of sinners. Arise! Let us be going. Look, the one who is betraying Me is approaching'" (vs 45-46).

That was quite a thing!

Section 337—Judas Betrays Jesus with a Kiss

John 18:1: "After saying these things, Jesus went out with His disciples *to a place* beyond the winter stream of Kidron, where *there* was a garden into which He and His disciples entered. And Judas, who was betraying Him, also knew of the place because Jesus had often gathered there with His disciples. Then Judas, after receiving a band and officers from the chief priests and Pharisees, came there with torches and lamps and weapons. Jesus, therefore, knowing all *the* things that were coming upon Him, went forward *and* said to them, 'Who are you seeking?' They answered Him, 'Jesus the Nazarean.' Jesus said to them, 'I AM.' And Judas, who was betraying Him, was also standing with them. But when He said to them, 'I AM,' they went backward and fell to *the* ground" (vs 1-6).

He gave them a chance to not do it!

Verse 7: "Then He asked them again, 'Who are you seeking?' And they said, 'Jesus the Nazarean.' Jesus answered, 'I told you that I AM. Therefore, if you are seeking Me, allow these to go their way'; so that the saying might be fulfilled which He had said, 'Of those whom You have given Me, not one of them have I lost'" (vs 7-9).

Section 338—Peter Cuts Off an Ear of the High Priest's Servant, and Jesus Heals Him

I often wondered what happened with this, because Peter cut off the ear of a servant of the high priest. Then He healed it by putting it back on. If I were that soldier, I would be feeling my ear all night. 'It's still there. I saw that Peter cut off and this Man put it back on!' You could say today, *and no stitches!*

John 18:10: "Then Simon Peter, who had a sword, drew it out and struck the servant of the high priest, and cut off his right ear. And the servant's name was Malchus. But Jesus said to Peter, 'Put your sword into the sheath; shall I not drink the cup that the Father has given Me?' Then the band and the chief captain and the officers of the Jews took hold of Jesus, and bound Him" (vs 10-12).

Section 339—All Was Done to Fulfill Prophecy

Matthew 26:56: "But all this has happened so that the Scriptures of the prophets might be fulfilled...."

Think about that. There's a section on pgs 268-273: Twenty-Eight Prophecies Fulfilled on the Crucifixion Day.

How were all of those fulfilled? *The angels were making sure that they were done!* The demons were carrying out what they were allowed to do.

"...Then all the disciples forsook Him and fled" (v 56).

Section 340—Jesus is Led Away to the Priest's House

John 18:13: "and they led Him away to Annas first; for he was *the* father-in-law of Caiaphas, who was high priest that year. Now, it was Caiaphas who had given counsel to the Jews that it was profitable for one man to perish for the people" (vs 13-14).

Section 341—Peter Follows Them into the Courtyard

- Why did Peter follow along?
- Why didn't he just follow the others?
- What had to happen to Peter?
- *Peter had to deny Christ three times, so he couldn't go off by himself!*

John 18:15: "But Simon Peter and the other disciple followed Jesus. And that disciple was known to the high priest, and entered with Jesus into the court of the high priest. But Peter stood outside at the door. Then the other disciple, who was known to the high priest, went out and spoke to the doorkeeper, and brought Peter in" (vs 15-16).

The angels must have been really, really busy at that time making sure that everything was done!

Verse 18: "Now, the servants and the officers had made a fire, for it was cold; and they were standing *there* warming themselves, and Peter was *also* standing and warming himself."

- I wonder what he thought, because who was there with the healed ear?
- Who was the one who had the sword to cut it off? *Peter!*

Section 342—Annas Questions Jesus and Sends Him to Caiaphas

John 18:19: "Then the high priest questioned Jesus concerning His disciples and concerning His teachings. Jesus answered him, 'I spoke openly to the world; I always taught in the synagogue and in the temple, where the Jews always assemble, and I spoke nothing in secret. Why do you question Me? Ask those who have heard what I spoke to them; behold, they know what I said'" (vs 19-21).

A good lesson: *you don't answer every question directly, but answer with a question!* **Put the burden of proof on them!**

Approximately 2 AM

John 18:22: "But after He said these things, one of the officers who was standing by struck Jesus on the face, saying, 'Do You answer the high priest in that way?' Jesus answered him, 'If I have spoken evil, testify of the evil; but if well, why do you strike Me?' *Then* Annas sent Him bound to Caiaphas, the high priest" (vs 22-24).

Section 343—The Chief Priests Illegally Condemn Jesus

Matthew 26:59: "Now, the chief priests and the elders and the whole Sanhedrin…"

The whole Sanhedrin was 120!

"…sought false evidence against Jesus, so that they might put Him to death; but *they* did not find *any*. Although many false witnesses came forward, they did not find *any* evidence. Then at *the* last, two false witnesses came forward *and* said, 'This *man* said, "I have the power to destroy the temple of God, and to rebuild it in three days"'" (vs 59-61).

This sounds like the hearings of the Democrats today! 'We've got to find a crime…'

Verse 62: "And the high priest rose up *and* said to Him, 'Have You no answer for what these are testifying against You?' But Jesus was silent. And the high priest answered *and* said to Him, 'I adjure You by the living God that You tell us if You are the Christ, the Son of God.' Jesus said to him, 'You have said *it*. Moreover, I say to you, in the future you shall see the Son of man sitting at *the* right hand of power, and coming in the clouds of heaven'" (vs 62-64).

Projecting clear forward to His second coming! They understood this because they knew Dan. 7, that 'the Son of man came to the Ancient of Days.' *They knew that!*

Verse 65: "Then the high priest ripped his *own* garments, saying, 'He has blasphemed! Why do we need any more witnesses? Behold, you have just now heard His blasphemy. What do you think?' They answered *and* said, 'He is deserving of death!' Then they spit in His face and hit Him with their fists; and some struck *Him* with rods, saying, 'Prophesy to us, Christ. Who is the one that struck You?'" (vs 65-68).

Section 344—Peter Denies Jesus Three Times

Luke 22:56: "And a certain maid saw him sitting by the light; and after looking at him intently, she said, 'Now this one was with Him.' But he denied Him, saying, 'Woman, I do not know Him.' And after a little *while*, another saw him *and* said, 'You also are *one* of them.' But Peter said, 'Man, I am not.' Now, after about an hour had passed, a certain other *man* strongly affirmed, saying, 'In truth, this one also was with Him, for he is indeed a Galilean.' And Peter said, 'Man, I do not know what you are talking about.' And immediately, while he was yet speaking, the cock crowed" (vs 56-60).

This scene always intrigues me:

Verse 61: "Then the Lord turned *and* looked at Peter; and **Peter remembered the word of the Lord**, how He had said to him, 'Before *the* cock crows, you shall deny Me three times.' And Peter went outside *and* wept bitterly" (vs 61-62).

- How great a sin was that? *Pretty powerful!*
- Did Peter remember this the rest of His life? *Yes, he did!*

We'll see that later, right before Jesus ascended, He had a special message for Peter because of this!

Section 345—The Sanhedrin Condemns Jesus and Sends Him to Pilate

Luke 22:66: "Now, as soon as it was day, the elders of the people assembled together, *with* both *the* chief priests and *the* scribes, and they led Him into their Sanhedrin, saying, 'If You are the Christ, tell us.' And He said to them, 'If I should tell you, you would not believe *Me* at all; and if I should also ask *you*, you would not answer Me at all, nor let *Me* go. Hereafter, shall the Son of man be sitting at *the* right hand of the power of God.' And they all said, 'Then You are the Son of God?' And He said to them, 'I am that *One, as* you say.' Then they said, 'What need do we have of any other witness? For we ourselves have heard from His *own* mouth'" (vs 66-71).

Luke 23:1: "And when the entire assembly of them arose, they led Him to Pilate."

Note message: *The Enigma of Judas Iscariot.* Why did he have to die the way that he did? If you commit or are an accomplice in murder, you have to die, too.

- Would the Jews execute him?
- Would the Romans execute him?
- Could the disciples execute him?
- *No!*
- Who executed Judas? *Himself!*

That was the only way that he could have been given the death penalty, because no one else would have done it.

Section 346—Judas Repents and Hangs Himself—The Chief Priests Buy Potter's Field

Matthew 27:3: "Now, when Judas, who had betrayed Him, saw that He was condemned, he changed his mind *and* returned the thirty pieces of silver to the chief priests and the elders, saying, 'I have sinned and have betrayed innocent blood.' But they said, 'What *is that* to us? You see *to it* yourself.' And after throwing down the pieces of silver in the temple, he went out and hanged himself'" (vs 3-5).

Look at how 'righteous' they were!

Verse 6: "But the chief priests took the pieces of silver *and* said, 'It is not lawful…'"

Here they are killing Christ, and now they're saying

"…'It is not lawful to put them into the treasury, since it is *the* price of blood.' And after taking counsel, they bought a potter's field with the *pieces of silver*, for a burial ground for strangers. Therefore, that field is called The Field of Blood to this day" (vs 6-8).

Section 347—Jesus is Condemned Before Pilate; He Questions Jesus

Matthew 27:11: "Then Jesus stood before the governor…"

Who was it that killed Jesus? *All of us!* But Jesus' death covers the sins of the whole world. So, what do we find here? *Pilate represented the Roman Empire—government!* **Pilate was symbolic of all governments of the world!**

The high priest was symbolic of… Remember that Jesus said, 'You are of your father the devil.' Are all the religions of the world of the devil? *Yes!* So, **the high priest was symbolic of all the religions of the world!**

All the people who said, 'Crucify Him! Crucify Him!' *was symbolic of all of the people of the world who rejected Christ!*

This was a great and fantastic thing that was going on; way beyond just the account there that we have in the Bible. It has great ramifications.

"…and the governor questioned Him, saying, 'Are You the King of the Jews?' And Jesus said to him, '*It is as* you said.' And when He was accused by the chief priests and the elders, He answered nothing. Then Pilate said to Him, 'Don't You hear how many things they testify against You?' And He did not answer even one word to him, so that the governor was greatly amazed" (vs 11-14).

Then Pilate finds out that Jesus was from Galilee!

Section 348—Pilate Sends Jesus to Herod

Luke 23:5: "But they were insistent, saying, 'He stirs up the people, teaching throughout all of Judea, beginning from Galilee even to here.' And when he heard Galilee *named*, Pilate asked whether the Man were a Galilean; and after determining that He was from Herod's jurisdiction, he sent Him to Herod, *since* he also was in Jerusalem in those days. And when Herod saw Jesus, he rejoiced greatly; for he had long been desiring to see Him because he had heard many things about Him, and he was hoping to see a miracle done by Him. And he questioned Him with many words; but He answered him nothing. All the while, the chief priests and the scribes stood vehemently accusing Him. Then Herod and his soldiers treated Him with contempt; and after mocking *Him*, he put a splendid robe on Him *and* sent Him back to Pilate. And **on that same day, Pilate and Herod became friends with each other, because before there was enmity between them**" (vs 5-12).

- Can Satan bring people together?
- Bring them so they agree with each other and they're happy about it?
- *Yes, he can!*

Remember that in WWII Germany made a peace alliance with Russia and they were happy and glad that it occurred. But that turned out to be a total disaster.

Section 349—Pilate Finds Jesus Innocent

John 18:31: "Then Pilate said to them, 'You take Him and judge Him according to your *own* law.' But the Jews said to him, 'It is not lawful for us to put anyone to death'; so that the saying of Jesus might be fulfilled, which He had spoken to signify by what death He was about to die" (vs 31-32).

What did Jesus tell Nicodemus on that night? *When the Son of man is lifted up! He knew how He was going to die!* Nicodemus didn't know a thing. His mind was closed and later it was opened. But I tell you, he had to come at night because he was afraid of the other ones. 'We know You're a man from God, but tell us something.' *He didn't tell them anything!* Unless you are born again you're not going to see the Kingdom of God.

I imagine Nicodemus was saying, 'What is this?' Jesus said, 'If I tell you earthly things, what would you do if I told you heavenly things? Here we have it that they could not kill Jesus.

Verse 33: "Then Pilate returned to the judgment hall and called Jesus, and said to Him, 'Are You the King of the Jews?' Jesus answered him, 'Do you ask this of yourself, or did others say *it* to you concerning Me?' Pilate answered Him, 'Am I a Jew?….'" (vs 33-35).

How am I supposed to know?

"'…The chief priests and your own nation have delivered You up to me. What have You done?' Jesus answered, 'My kingdom is not of this world. If My kingdom were of this world, then would My servants fight, so that I might not be delivered up to the Jews. However, My kingdom is not of this world.' Pilate, therefore, answered Him, 'Then You are a king?' Jesus answered, '*As* you say, I am a king. For this *purpose* I was born, and for this *reason* I came into the world, that I may bear witness to the Truth. Everyone who is of the Truth hears My voice.' Pilate said to Him, 'What is Truth?' And after saying this, he went out again to the Jews and said to them, '**I do not find any fault in Him**'" (vs 35-38).

But it shows mob action!

Section 350—Pilate Releases Barabbas and Crucifies Jesus, 8 AM

John 18:39: "'And it is a custom with you that I release one to you at the Passover. Do you then desire *that* I release the King of the Jews to you?' But they all shouted again, saying, 'Not this one, but Barabbas.'…." (vs 39-40).

Do you know what that name means? *Bar-Abbas, son/father, so of the father.* How ironic.

"…Now, Barabbas was a robber" (v 40).

Luke 23:19: "*He was* the one who had been cast into prison on account of making a certain insurrection in the city and *committing* murder."

Sounds almost like our justice system in Washington, DC, today!

Verse 20: "Therefore, Pilate again called to *them,* wishing to release Jesus. But they kept crying out, saying, 'Crucify *Him,* crucify Him!' And a third *time* he said to them, 'But what evil did this *Man* commit? I have not found any cause *worthy* of death in Him. Therefore, after chastising Him, I will release *Him.*' But they were urgent with loud voices, asking for Him to be crucified. And their voices, and *those* of the chief priests, prevailed" (vs 20-23).

Section 351—Pilate Washes His Hands in a Show of Innocence

Political! He gave in!

Matthew 27:24: "Now Pilate, seeing that he was accomplishing nothing, but *that* a riot was developing instead, took water *and* washed *his* hands before the multitude, saying, 'I am guiltless of the blood of this righteous *man.* You see *to it.*'

Section 352—Pilate Releases Barabbas; Jesus is Beaten and Scourged

Matthew 27:26: "Then he released Barabbas to them; but after scourging Jesus, he delivered *Him* up so that He might be crucified. Then the governor's soldiers, after taking Jesus with *them* into the Praetorium, gathered the entire band against Him; and they stripped Him *and* put a scarlet cloak around Him. And after platting a crown of thorns, they put *it* on His head, and a rod in His right hand; and bowing *on* their knees before Him, they mocked Him, and *kept on* saying, 'Hail, King of the Jews!'" (vs 26-29).

Remember, He's got the crown of thorns on His head!

Verse 30: "Then, after spitting on Him…"

I'm sure it wasn't just a little water!

"...they took the rod and struck *Him* on the head" (v 30).

So, those thorns would go right in under the skin right next to His skull!

Verse 31: "When they were done mocking Him, they took the cloak off Him; and they put His own garments on Him and led Him away to crucify Him."

Section 354, pg 300—the Soldiers Lead Jesus Away to be Crucified, and Make Simon of Cyrene Carry His Cross

Luke 23:26: "And as they led Him away, they laid hold on a certain Cyrenian *named* Simon, who was coming from a field; *and* they put the cross on him..."

The cross that you see in movies is not anything like this. They would take a tree and they would put huge iron clasps on it, u-shaped so they could take a cross-bar and put it right there. When the person died they would take it out and put someone else there.

So, when Jesus was carrying His cross, He was carrying the crossbar, not the whole thing. That's why it says in other places that He was crucified on a tree, because it was a tree, and there were two trees, one on each side, for the other malefactors.

Verse 27: "And following Him was a great multitude of people with *many* women, who also were bewailing and lamenting Him. But Jesus turned to them *and* said, 'Daughters of Jerusalem, do not weep for Me, but weep for yourselves and for your children. For behold, *the* days are coming in which they shall say, "Blessed *are* the barren, and *the* wombs that did not bear, and *the* breasts that did not give suck." Then shall they begin to say to the mountains, "Fall on us"; and to the hills, "Cover us."....'" (vs 27-30).

He goes right from that time to the destruction of Jerusalem, and then on into the part of Rev. 6 where the heavens roll back as a scroll and the mountains, earth and everything is shaken, and they go to the holes in the ground.

Section 355—Jesus Refuses Wine and Myrrh (Vinegar and Gall)—They Crucify Him

Matthew 27:34: "They gave Him vinegar mingled with gall to drink; but after tasting it, He would not drink."

Section 356—The Soldiers Cast Lots for His Garments—Jesus Asks the Father to Forgive Them for Crucifying Him

Matthew 27:35: "And when they had crucified Him, they divided His garments *by* casting lots; so that it might be fulfilled which was spoken by the prophet, 'They divided My garments among themselves, and for My vesture they cast lots.' And they sat down there to keep guard over Him" (vs 35-36).

How did the soldiers know to do that? *Probably was an angel right there!* Couldn't see him, but making sure that this prophecy was fulfilled! That's how it had to be done.

Section 357—Pilate Has a Title and Accusation Written and Put on the Cross

Luke 23:38: "And there also was an inscription over Him written in Greek and Latin and Hebrew: 'This is the King of the Jews.'

John 19:20: "As a result, many of the Jews read this title, for the place where Jesus was crucified was near the city; and it was written in Hebrew, in Greek *and* in Latin. Then the chief priests of the Jews said to Pilate, 'Do not write, "The King of the Jews"; but that He said, "I am King of the Jews."' Pilate answered, 'What I have written, I have written'" (vs 20-22).

Even down to the last thing, try and change it all!

Section 358—Two Malefactors (Thieves) Crucified with Jesus

Matthew 27:38: "And two robbers were crucified with Him, one at *the* right hand and one at *the* left."

I do not know how one commentator said that there were two on the right hand and two on the left hand. I couldn't find it. But that's what some people believe.

Mark 15:28: "Then the Scripture was fulfilled, which says, 'And He was numbered among lawbreakers.'"

All of that! Why were two others crucified? Why didn't they just crucify one? *They were busy getting rid of 'bad' people!*

Section 359—The People, Priests and Two thieves Mock and Revile Him. Darkness From the Sixth Hour to the Ninth Hour (Approximately Noon to 3 PM)

Matthew 27:39: "Then those who were passing by railed at Him, shaking their heads, and saying, 'You Who *would* destroy the temple and rebuild *it* in three days, save Yourself....'" (vs 39-40).

Could Jesus have done that? *But that would have been against the will of God, so He didn't!*

"'...If You are *the* Son of God, come down from the cross.' And in the same way also the chief priests were mocking, with the scribes and elders, saying, 'He saved others, *but* He does not have the power to save Himself. If He is the King of Israel, let Him come down now from the cross, and we will believe Him. He trusted in God; let Him deliver Him now, if He will *have* Him. For He said, "I am *the* Son of God."' And the two robbers who were crucified with Him also reproached Him with the same words. Now, from *the* sixth hour until *the* ninth hour, darkness was over all the land" (vs 40-45).

Luke 23:39: "Then one of the malefactors who was hanging *there* railed at Him, saying, 'If You are the Christ, save Yourself and us.' But the other *one* answered *and* rebuked him, saying, 'Do not even you fear God, you who are under the same condemnation? And we indeed justly, for we are receiving due payment for what we did; but this *Man* did nothing wrong.' Then he said to Jesus, 'Remember me, Lord, when You come into Your kingdom'" (vs 39-42).

The Seven Sayings of Jesus:

Verse 43: "And Jesus said to him, [#1]'**Truly, I tell you today, you shall be with Me in paradise.**'"

Why could it not be *that day*? He was saying today that 'you shall be with Me in paradise.' He didn't say that 'today you shall be in paradise.'

Section 360—Jesus Makes John Responsible for His Mother: Mary

John 19:25: "And Jesus' mother stood by the cross, and His mother's sister, Mary the *wife* of Cleopas, and Mary Magdalene. When Jesus saw *His* mother, and the disciple whom He loved standing by, He said to His mother, [#2]'**Woman, behold your son.**' Then He said to the disciple, [#3]'**Behold your mother.**' And from that time, the disciple took her into his own *home*" (vs 25-26).

Section 361—At the Ninth Hour Jesus is Forsaken and Offered Vinegar—A Spear is Truth into His side and He Dies—The temple veil is torn in Two

Matthew 27:46: "And about the ninth hour, Jesus cried out with a loud voice, saying, [#4]'**Eli, Eli, lama sabachthani?**' That is, '**My God, My God, why have You forsaken Me**?'"

He had to be forsaken by the Father completely in order to be that perfect sacrifice!

Verse 47: "And some of those who were standing there heard *and* said, 'This *one* is calling for Elijah.'"

Luke 23:46: "And after crying out with a loud voice, Jesus said, [#5]'**Father, into Your hands I commit My spirit.**' And when He had said these things, He expired."

John 19:28: "After this, Jesus, knowing that all things had now been finished, so that the Scripture might be fulfilled, said, [#6]'**I thirst.**' Now, a vessel full of vinegar was sitting *there*. And after filling a sponge with vinegar and putting *it* on *a stick of* hyssop, they put it up to *His* mouth And so, when Jesus had received the vinegar, He said, [#7]'**It is finished.**'...." (vs 28-30).

Scriptural References:

1) John 13:2-32
2) Matthew 26:26-29
3) Luke 22:24-30
4) John 13:33-35
5) Mark 14:27-31
6) John 14:20-23
7) Luke 22:36, 38
8) Matthew 26:30
9) John 15:1-8, 10-11
10) John 16:26-28, 32-33
11) Matthew 26:39, 40-44
12) Luke 22:44
13) John 17:11-12, 20-21
14) Mathew 26:45-46
15) John 18:1-12
16) Matthew 26:56
17) John 18:13-24
18) Matthew 26:59-68
19) Luke 22:56-62, 66-71
20) Luke 23:1
21) Matthew 27:3-8, 11-14
22) Luke 23:5-12
23) John 18:31-40
24) Luke 23:19-23
25) Matthew 27:24, 26-31
26) Luke 23:26-30

27) Matthew 27:34-36
28) Luke 23:38
29) John 19:20-22
30) Matthew 27:38
31) Mark 15:28
32) Matthew 27:39-45
33) Luke 23:39-43
34) John 19:25-26
35) Matthew 27:46-47
36) Luke 23:46
37) John 19:28-30

Scriptures referenced, not quoted:

- Ephesians 2
- John 6
- Deuteronomy 32
- Daniel 7
- Revelation 6

Also referenced:

Book: *A Harmony of the Gospels* by Fred R. Coulter

In-Depth Studies:
- *The Love of God*
- *Passover Preparation*

Messages:
- *What is the Difference Between Temptation and Tribulation?*
- *The Enigma of Judas Iscariot* (#4 Assaults Against Jesus)

FRC:bo
Transcribed: 8/21/19
Reformatted: 10/2020

CHAPTER TWENTY-TWO

The Last 10 Days of Jesus' Life V
From the Death of Jesus to His ascension and acceptance by God the Father
Fred R. Coulter

Greetings, everyone! Welcome to the Sabbath services!

Since we're getting close to the Passover, and there is always a dispute about whether the bread for the Passover should be on unleavened or leavened. Maybe some of you never heard of that, but that exists.

Remember, every time there may be something a little difficult to understand, someone's going to have the theory to explain it, something other than what it really is. So, our advertisement today, thanks to Ken:

What kind of bread? Article: *Christ's Last Passover, Leavened or Unleavened?* by Ben Ambrose {**truthofGod.org**} He wrote this years ago, because it came up. And it's keyed on *the sop*. Now remember that we covered that. That if today you have unleavened chips and you can scoop in some avocado, (guacamole) or salsa, then that's *a sop*.

Now, last time we finished up page 304, and we will finish it with this, so that everyone will have everything before Passover. Because it wouldn't be any good to have this as a special series for Passover, and half of it comes after the Feast of Unleavened Bread. That wouldn't work out too well.

Now, I have to make one correction, and that was, I said last time (part 4), that when the vinegar was given to Him. He refused it. That was not correct, *He received it.* The first time they gave it to Him, He refused it. The last time He received it, and then He died.

Now remember, this was a tremendous event in the world. There was:

- Satan
- the angels
- Christ
- all of the religious authorities

A stark battle going on back and forth! Christ had to die at the right time. That's why the authorities were frustrated in their efforts to get Jesus ahead of time, because it had to happen at the right time.

from *A Harmony of the Gospels*:

Passover Day Nisan 14—Wednesday afternoon, April 5, 30 AD

Section 362—<u>An Earthquake Opens Some Graves for a Resurrection of Some of the Saints to Another Physical Life as a Sign and a Witness</u>
Matthew 27:51: "...the earth shook..."

How much of a shock was it?

"...and the rocks were split."

Here in California, we have quite a few earthquakes, so we know what it is. Every once in a while, we have an earthquake at night, before you go to sleep and you're laying there and all of a sudden the house starts moving. We have a lot of minor earthquakes that aren't even felt. So, this was a fantastic thing to declare how important His death was.

Verse 52: "So that the tombs were opened...."

The tombs were different from what we have today. They would, dig a small cave inside the rocks, then—just like Jesus' tomb—they rolled the big stone in front of it. They would have this stone cut and put right alongside the opening. They would have a wedge right under the bottom of it, so it wouldn't move until that wedge was released. These tombs opened, meaning in the front of those caves the stones came off. Now notice what happened:

"...And many bodies of the saints who had died, **were resurrected** after His resurrection..." (vs 52-53).

They weren't resurrected before Jesus' resurrection. Couldn't be, because the firstborn from the dead was Christ.

Verse 53: "After His resurrection; *and* they came out of the tombs...."

This happens a lot in the Bible. Make a statement to declare what's going to happen. It says: "...were resurrected..." (v 52). But the question is *when*? A lot of people think that they were resurrected right away, but they weren't.

Verse 53: "After His resurrection; *and* they came out of the tombs. *Then* they entered into the Holy City, and appeared to many."

What if you had one of your relatives just buried the week before, and you were still mourning? Since others were resurrected before, there was no conflict. But after His resurrection, they went into the city, which says then that they didn't stay alive in the tomb for three days. They had to be resurrected *after* He was resurrected. I think on the day that Christ was resurrected, it's important that He was *first*. When that happened there was the earthquake

Section 363—The Centurion Acknowledges that Jesus was the Son of God

Verse 54: "Then the centurion and those with him who had been keeping guard over Jesus, after seeing the earthquake..."

Remember what happened with the earthquake. The veil was split in two and opened so that the Holy of Holies was seen. That means, they could not have had any sacrifices at the temple on the day that Jesus died; they would have to move everyone out. Plus whatever damage was done to the temple area.

"...and the things that took place, were filled with fear, *and* said 'Truly this was the Son of God!'" (v 54).

Now then, notice what has to happen. Whenever you have a scheme, you've got to have some way to make it appear right? *Well now, Jesus was buried!* You can tie this in with Psa. 63, how Jesus really died. It says He died of a broken heart. That means a heart that was pierced, not emotionally, not that His emotions were broken.

Section 364—The Jews Want Jesus' Body Off the Cross Before the Holy Day Begins at Sunset

John 19:31: "The Jews, therefore, so that the bodies might not remain on the cross on the Sabbath, because it was a preparation *day* (for that Sabbath...[that is the one coming] ...was a High Day)..."

This tells us this is the first day of the Feast of Unleavened Bread. That's the only day that comes after the Passover Day.

"...requested of Pilate that their legs might be broken and *the bodies* be taken away. Then the soldiers came and broke the legs of the first *one*, and *the legs* of the other who was crucified with Him. But when they came to Jesus *and* saw that He was already dead, they did not break His legs" (vs 31-33).

Now there's also fulfilled another prophecy: 'not a bone would be broken.' That's why I want you to go through the *Twenty-eight Prophecies Fulfilled on the Crucifixion Day* (*Harmony*, pgs 268-273). If you do a little mathematics it's impossible that all of those would have happened coincidentally.

Verse 34 tells you why: "But one of the soldiers had pierced...

that's what it is in the Greek—*past tense*

"...His side with a spear, and immediately blood and water had come out."

Now the way that that spear was put in, it was put in from the right side and thrust up and got His heart. Because all of His blood had to be shed. He could not have died with blood in His heart. It had to be shed.

Verse 35: "And he who saw *this* has testified, and his testimony is true; and he knows that *what* he says *is* true, so that you may believe."

This is John telling you that 'What I'm writing is true. I saw it; I was there!'

Verse 36: "For these things took place so that the Scripture might be fulfilled, 'Not a bone of Him shall be broken.' And again another Scripture says, 'They shall look upon Him Whom they pierced'" (vs 36-37).

Section 365—Many of the Women Watch to the End

The women are there; they're watching this. Now think about this. They were hoping, as the two men from Emmaus were, that He was going to be the Messiah. What was the version of the Messiah they were looking for? A man to come and take over the government and raise up an army and get rid of the Romans!

So, when He died they didn't know what to do. They were still blinded, even the disciples. They didn't understand what He meant three days and three nights, and the third day, and being raised from the dead. They were watching a far off, and I imagine a lot of them were really disappointed.

How could it be that the One Who is the Messiah was dying, when the prophecies we read say He's going to save us from our enemies? The answer is, *because God has a greater plan than anyone has ever thought of!*

Section 366: Just Before Sunset, Joseph Of Arimathea Gets the Body of Jesus and Lays It In the Tomb

John 19:38: "Now, after these things, Joseph (the one from Arimathea, being a disciple of Jesus, but having concealed it for fear of the Jews) asked Pilate that he might take Jesus' body away; and Pilate gave *him* permission. Then he came and took away the body of Jesus. And Nicodemus, who had come to Jesus by night at *the* first, also came, bearing a mixture of myrrh and aloes, about a hundred pounds. Then they took Jesus' body and wound it in linen cloths with the aromatics, as is the custom among the Jews to prepare for burial" (vs 38-40).

So, the Shroud of Turin *is a complete fake!* When they wrapped Jesus' body, what did they do? *All of the flesh that was there that was misplaced by the beating, was probably put back in as they wrapped it!* You look at the Shroud. If the Shroud was just placed over Jesus, where are all the beaten marks on His chest and on His arm? *Not there!* So, they wound it!

Verse 41: "Now, there was a garden in the place where He was crucified, and in the garden a new tomb, in which no one had ever been laid. Because of the preparation of the Jews, they laid Jesus there; for the tomb was near" (vs 41-42).

Then I'll let you read the commentary on the three days and three nights. All of this is very important, because in order to say there were three days and three nights between Friday evening and Sunday morning, to have a resurrection on Sunday, *which it wasn't.* Some of the commentaries even say that when it was dark, between the sixth hour and ninth hour, that that was the first night. How could it be the first night? *Jesus was still on the cross, not in the tomb!* So, that could not be it. There is no way, anybody, anywhere at anytime, can get three full days from Friday night to Sunday morning.

Then you go through the whole commentary that we have written there. Now let's come to the two-page map on pages 320-321. I will have to confess to one typo in all the *Harmonies.* It's one very hard to catch because it's very small. I'll show you what that is in a minute. Look how it's laid out. The Hebrew days of the week:

- 5th day—Nisan 15
- 6th day—Nisan 16
- 7th day—Nisan 17
- 1st day—Nisan 18

Right across the top!

Now notice we have sunset/sunrise, sunset/sunrise, all the way through. Now for there to be three whole days and three whole nights, the only way that could be is with a Passover in the middle of the week. This year, with the way that the Passover is, it's not a week in which that could happen in this sequence.

But next year and the next five years, we will have three Passovers out of five with a Wednesday Passover. So, we've got each day:

- 1st night/1st day
- 2nd night/2nd day
- 3rd night/3rd day

Come to 3rd night/3rd day where it says Mark 16:1, that should read Matthew 28:1.

And you see that? See where it is? Come to Nisan 17. That's on the right hand page—321. Look at the day portion, come down to the very bottom where it says Mark 16:1 See that? That should be Matthew 28:1[transcriber's correction]. And we'll see why in just a little bit.

Now I want to read something important. Now, remember when all of these things were being put together with the Harmony, we didn't have instant search on Google. We had to get the book. We had to get the quote. We had to correctly copy it and everything. But notice this. Even though when you read the apostolic fathers and Ignatius, he was the first one to start out with the Sunday resurrection and coinciding that with the Passover time. But how many years did they understand it was a Wednesday crucifixion?

footnote on pg 321: Knowledge of a Wednesday crucifixion was passed down for at least three centuries after the founding of the apostolic church.

Remember that the Romans had the Julian calendar, and every four years, they would lose a day, which meant that spring was moving closer and closer to winter. And pretty soon, Easter was beyond the spring equinox.

Now that continued all the way down to Pope Gregory, when they finally corrected the calendar. They had to take ten days out of the calendar. Have you ever read that? How did they do that? They saw that they lost ten days so they had October 1st, 2nd, 3rd and 4th, and the next day was the 15th. They put in the one quarter day accumulated to have a leap year every four years.

The Calculated Hebrew Calendar was always on time. The Catholics couldn't figure out how the Passover was getting further away from their traditional Easter. You look at it this year. Easter Sunday is the day after the first Holy Day. and the first Holy Day is a regular Sabbath, and that Sunday is the 1st day of the count toward Pentecost. Whenever that happens, the Church, the Catholics and the Jews all have Pentecost on the right day. *That's the only time!*

continue footnote: The Didascalia, which dates from the third century, offers historical evidence that the belief in a Friday crucifixion was a change from the original teaching. The following description of the day of Jesus' crucifixion appears in Book V of the Apostolic Constitutions, which contains the original words of the Didascalia: "For they began to hold a council against the Lord on the second day of the week, in the first month, which is Xanthicus; and the deliberation continued on the third day of the week; but on the fourth day [Wednesday] they determined to take away His life by crucifixion" (Apostolic Constitutions—Didascalia Apostolorum, book V, section I, paragraph xiv)

Now today, you might pop that up in a few seconds on a Google Search. But that shows *they knew.*

A church historian explains the significance of this record in the Didascalia: "…the only reason can have been that Jesus' passion began on a Wednesday, i.e., the day when He was arrested [and crucified]" (Lietzmann, A History of the Early Church, p. 69).

Let's see what happened after that. When you read these Scriptures the way they should be, let's also understand that the Passover Day was always a preparation for The Night to be Much Observed. Because you have the Passover Day, you began with the Passover at night. Then comes a day portion, and you're preparing for The Night to be Much Observed. When it becomes sunset, that's beginning the 15th day.

That means that whenever the Passover is on a Wednesday, you have Thursday as a Holy Day. Friday is a workday, or preparation day, for the weekly Sabbath. That's where the confusion comes, with people. They can't understand, that in the Passover week when the Passover is on a Wednesday, that the day portion of the Passover is preparation for the Holy Day, which is a Sabbath, and then Friday, the day after is preparation for the weekly Sabbath.

The First Day Of Unleavened Bread Nisan 15—Thursday, April 6, 30 AD

Section 367—<u>On the Holy Day, Guards Are Placed At the Tomb</u>

Matthew 27:62: "Now, on the next day, which followed the preparation *day*, the chief priests and the Pharisees came together to Pilate, saying, 'Sir, we remember that that deceiver said while *He was* living, "After three days I *will* rise." Therefore, command *that* the sepulcher be

secured until the third day; lest His disciples come by night and steal Him away, and say to the people, "He is risen from the dead"; and the last deception shall be worse than the first'" (vs 62-64).

They had no idea what was going to happen. Let's think about our petty little trials today. We may have some emotional ups and some emotional downs. But is anyone coming to knock on your door, ready to take you out and throw you in jail? Is anyone ready to thrust of the spear through your stomach and kill you instantly? *No!*

Our biggest problem is, we have so much of everything everywhere that we have become so blatantly calcified in Laodiceanism, it's hard for anyone to put up with anyone who has any passion or zeal. Oh well, you can't talk like that. You know, just like they do with Trump: 'You shouldn't tweet.' If he didn't, do you think they would tell the truth? *Of course not!*

Verse 65: "Then Pilate said to them, 'You have a guard. Go, make *it as* secure as you know *how*.' And they went *and* made the sepulcher secure, sealing the stone *and* setting the guard" (vs 65-66).

What does it mean to seal the stone? Do they put glue around it? *No!* I suspect they used their fine hard limestone concrete, and sealed the stone, and when that dried there was no way it was going to be opened. Let's go on with that in mind.

The Preparation Day For the Weekly Sabbath Nisan 6—Friday, April 7, 30 AD

Section 368—<u>After the Holy Day Is Over, The Women Buy and Prepare Spices</u>

Mark 16:1: "Now, when the Sabbath had passed…"

the first Holy Day

"…Mary Magdalene and Mary, the *mother* of James; and Salome bought aromatic oils, so that they might come and anoint Him" (v 1).

Luke 23:56: "And they returned *to the city, and* prepared spices and ointments…

That was a whole day affair. What was coming on after that day? *The weekly Sabbath!* It shows here that they rested on the Sabbath according to the commandment. This could not be the Holy Day, because the Holy Day, you can have a feast. You can do a lot of things. You can do whatever is necessary in preparing food and so forth. But you can't do that on a regular Sabbath. Because there's a commandment: You shall not do any work. We got that picture with the setting sun to show Sabbath is ending.

Section 370—Toward the End of the Weekly Sabbath, Mary Magdalene and Mary Go To Observe the Tomb

This was quite interesting when I was preparing this, because the Greek does not say when the sun was rising. It says when it was dusking toward the first day of the week. So that also tells us this Sabbath was the seventh day.

Matthew 28:1: "Now, late on the Sabbath, as *the* first *day* of *the* weeks was drawing near, Mary Magdalene and the other Mary came to observe the sepulcher."

Why did they go to see it? *They just wanted to find out...* You're wondering:

- What happened?
- Is the guard there?
- How did they seal it?

So they went to look!

You've got all the commentary to read: Events of The First Day of The Week—Wave Sheaf Day To the Ascension.

Let's come all the way through that commentary. I'll leave you to read it, we'll come back to some of it a little later. All of this can become a little confusing, unless you have all four accounts, pg 334, on the first day of the week, and the women coming. Most people have the idea that all the women came together at the same time. But they didn't.

Nisan 18--Sunday Morning, April 9, 30 AD

Section 371—Early the First Day of the Week, Just Before Women Arrive At the Tomb, An Angel Opens the Tomb

Let's see what it took to open the tomb.

Matthew 28:2: "And *in the morning* suddenly there was a great earthquake..."

It had to have that hard concrete, lime concrete there to seal it!

...for an angel of *the* Lord descended from heaven, and came and rolled away the stone from the door, and sat upon I" (v 2).

The angels are busy, the demons are busy, Satan is busy, everybody's going crazy trying to get this thing done.

Verse 3: "Now, his appearance was as lightning, and his raiment white as snow.

And for fear of him, those who were keeping guard trembled, and became as dead *men*" (vs 3-4).

That had to be revealed to them by Christ a little later on, because no one was there to see it.

Section 372—Early the First Day of the Week, Women Come To The Tomb, But Jesus Has Already Been Resurrected

Let's see the progression. Here's something interesting.

John 20:1: "Now, on the first *day* of the weeks..."

'ton Sabbaton', that means the first day toward counting the Pentecost—the first day of the weeks. Now, plural in Sabbath otherwise can be {twice saw the coins}. So this is a special, special one.

"...while it was still dark..." (v 1).

So this was say five in the morning? It was still dark!

"...Mary Magdalene..." (v 1).

she comes first alone

"...came early to the tomb; and she saw *that* the stone had been taken away from the tomb" (v 1).

she saw it, and then she left

Verse 2: "Then she ran and came to Simon Peter and to the other disciple whom Jesus loved, and said to them, 'They have taken away the Lord from the tomb, and we do not know where they have laid Him'" (vs 1-2).

They still didn't understand about the resurrection. So, the first one (John 20), Mary Magdalene—while it was dark.

Luke 24:1: "Now, on the first *day* of the weeks, they came to the tomb at early dawn, bringing *the* spices that they had prepared; and certain *others came* with them."

But not all of them! Let's come to Mark now. So we have before—while it was still dark, we have early dawn. Now let's come here to;

Mark 16:2: "And very early on the first *day* of the weeks, at the rising of the sun, they were coming to the tomb."

there were these groups of women

Verse 3: "And they were asking themselves, 'Who will roll away the stone for us from the entrance to the tomb?' For it was a massive *stone*. But when they looked up, they saw that the stone had been rolled away. And after entering the tomb, they saw a young man sitting on the right, clothed in a white robe; and they were very frightened. But he said to them, 'Do not be afraid. You are seeking Jesus the Nazarene, Who was crucified. He has risen; He is not here. Look, *there is* the place where they laid Him'" (vs 3-6).

we will see what that is in just a minute

> Verse 7: "'But go, tell His disciples and Peter that He goes before you into Galilee...'"

and so forth! The account in Matt. 28 just summarizes that.

> John 20:4: "Now, the two ran together, but the other disciple ran faster than Peter and came to the tomb first; and he stooped down *and* saw the linen cloths lying *there*, but he did not enter" (vs 4-5).

He was wrapped. Saw the linen cloths rising. Does a spirit being need to be unwrapped, or can he just come through the cloths? He can come through the cloths. So they saw the outline where Jesus body was where the cloths were, and then probably dipped in the middle because his body wasn't there.

> That's quite a thing to see. Just picture it if you're one of the disciples, and you came down there. Remember, all the women—if you think God is against women—who discovered that He was resurrected *first*? *The women!*

> Verse 6: "Then Simon Peter came following him, and he went into the tomb and saw the linen cloths lying, and the napkin that had been on His head... [especially covering His head] ...not lying with the linen cloths but folded up in a place by itself" (vs 6-7).

What does this tell you? Jesus was resurrected out of the linen. It stayed there in the form of His body with a dip in the middle, because his body was gone. But Jesus took the napkin off His head and folded it and put it in a different place. All who do laundry know clothes do not fold themselves! Just think how much you could make if you could have clothes that could fold themselves. This tells you that He's alive! Amazing!

> Verse 8: Then the other disciple, who had come to the tomb first, also went in and saw *these things*; and he believed."

John was the very first one to believe about the resurrection

> Verse 9: "For they did not yet understand

the Scripture, *which decreed* that He must rise from *the* dead. Then the disciples went away again to their *home*" (vs 9-10).

Now then, no one has seen Jesus, yet. They've only seen the tomb open. They've only seen the linen cloths and the folded up napkin. Mary Magdalene didn't come running with Peter and John. She went and told them, but she probably walked, probably rapidly. Imagine how she was dressed, and the way they dressed then, women are not going to be running.

> Mark 16:9. "Now, after *Jesus* had risen, early *the* first *day* of the weeks He appeared first to Mary Magdalene, from whom He had cast out seven demons. She went *and* told *it* to those who had been with Him, *who* were grieving and weeping" (vs 9-10)—*didn't believe her!*

Now we come to the details in John 20. This is quite a thing here. Quite a story! All of these tell us how important that everything about the life of Christ really was. We can't take it for granted like the Protestants do. The whole thing they want to get to, is have your sins forgiven. They think everything is accomplished at that point. But that's only the beginning.

> John 20:11: "But Mary stood outside the tomb weeping; and as she wept, she stooped down *and looked* into the tomb."

Double-checking, is His body really gone?

> Verse 12: "And she saw two angels in white who were sitting, one at the head and the other at the feet, where the body of Jesus had been laid."

So, we have some of them who saw one angel, probably got so excited didn't even see that there was another one, so here there are two:

> Verse 13: "And they said to her, 'Woman, why are you weeping?' She said to them, 'Because they have taken away my Lord, and I do not know where they have laid Him.' And after saying these things, she turned around and saw Jesus standing, but did not know that it was Jesus. Jesus said to her, 'Woman, why are you weeping? Whom are you seeking?' Thinking that He was the gardener, she said to Him, 'Sir, if you have carried Him off, tell me where you have laid Him, and I will take Him away.' Jesus said to her, 'Mary.' Turning around, she said to Him, 'Rabboni'; that is to say, 'Teacher.'" (vs 13-16).

probably more like 'Rabboni'

> Verse 17: "Jesus said to her, 'Do not touch

Me, because I have not yet ascended to My Father. But go to My brethren and tell them that I am ascending...'"

This is a tremendous understanding of what God is doing!

"'...to My Father and your Father, and My God and your God.' Mary Magdalene came to the disciples, bringing word that she had seen the Lord, and that He had said these things to her" (vs 17-18).

Now then like every scheme that is crooked, something goes wrong because the truth always prevails. That is the resurrection. However, come to

Section 374—Soldiers Bribed to Lie

Mathew 28:11: "And as they were going, behold, some of the guard went into the city *and* reported to the chief priests all the things that were done."

I get a kick out of this. Always in the *Harmony* in the Gospels, when the Jews want to do something, they have counsel.

Verse 12: "Then, after gathering together with the elders and taking counsel, they gave a large sum of money to the soldiers, saying, 'Tell *everyone* that His disciples came by night and stole Him while you were sleeping'" (vs 12-13).

How could that be, if the cement that they had, had sealed it? *The earthquake took care of that!*

Verse 14: "And if the governor hears *of* this, we will persuade him to release you from responsibility.' And they took the money..." (vs 14-15).

I bet they were happy; these soldiers must have been happy as a lark!

"*...and* did as they were instructed, and **this report has been spread abroad among the Jews to this day**" (v 15)

and even to this day!

He told Mary, *'I'm ascending to My God and your God and My Father and your Father.'* That was approximately nine in the morning. Remember: *this is the day after the weekly Sabbath during the Feast of Unleavened Bread!*

What was commanded by God on that day? *The Wave Sheaf Offering* symbolic of Christ ascending! Now picture this: Here's the priest and he's waving the sheaf of firstfruits. While at the same time, Christ is ascending into heaven, to present Himself to the Father. After He presented himself, He comes back to the earth, because there's

more to be done. So, here are two disciples going to Emmaus. Jesus comes up to them, and they are probably disappointed.

Now, the third day is already over and 'we don't know what happened to Him. We don't know where He is. Oh, if He had just stayed alive.' Jesus comes along and said, 'What are you talking about?' They didn't recognize Him because He could make Himself into whatever form He wanted to make. 'Oh, Jesus of Nazareth, the Prophet.' *Oh, really? What happened?* 'We were thinking He was going to be the Messiah.' *Oh, really? What happened?* 'They got Him, arrested Him, tried Him and killed Him.'

They were virtually saying to Him that 'the jig is up.' So, they finally got to Emmaus and they said, 'Come on in and eat with us.' So, they went in, sat down with Him, after He explained a lot of things out of the Scriptures before they got there, and then sat down with them. When He asked the blessing and broke the bread, they knew it was Jesus.

- Can you imagine what they felt like?
- Can you imagine this surge of adrenaline!

So, Jesus disappeared, and they said, we've got to go tell the apostles. So they could get up there and tell them.

Section 375—Jesus Appears to Two Disciples on a Journey to Emmaus

Luke 24:31: "Then their eyes were opened... [v 32]: And they said to one another, 'Did not our hearts burn within us...' [v34]: ...'In truth, the Lord has risen!....'"

Section 376—At Sunset, as the First Day of the Week is Ending, Jesus Appears to the Disciples Behind Closed Doors

Now then, they got to the apostles:

Luke 24:34: saying, 'In truth, the Lord has risen!....' [v 36]: Now, as they were telling these things, Jesus Himself stood in their midst..."

What Scripture proves that a spirit being does not need to have doors open? *That which is born in spirit is spirit, and it's like the wind!* Nobody's ever seen the wind. You only see the effect of the wind. Here He is! Did He walk through the door? *Don't know!* Did He walk through the wall? *Don't know, but He appeared!* Who knows, maybe He just came in came through the roof. Either way He was there.

"...and said to them, 'Peace *be* to you.' But they were terrified and filled with fear, thinking *that* they beheld a spirit *apparition*. Then He said to them, 'Why are you troubled? And why do doubts come up in your hearts? See My hands and My feet, that it is I. Touch Me and see *for yourselves*; for a spirit does not have flesh and bones, as you see Me having.'" (vs 36-39).

What does that mean? *He did not say flesh and blood! He said flesh and bone!* A spirit being does not need blood, but can manifest himself as a human being, to appear as flesh. So, this was special for them so that they could know that this was true.

Verse 40: "And after saying this, He showed them *His* hands and *His* feet. But while they were still disbelieving and wondering for joy, He said to them, 'Do you have anything here to eat?' Then they gave Him part of a broiled fish and a *piece* of honeycomb. And He took these *and* ate in their presence" (vs 40-43).

Now, for those who are technical, what happens to food that a spirit being eats? *Don't ask me, I don't know!*

Verse 44: "And He said to them, 'These *are* the words that I spoke to you when I was yet with you, that **all** *the* **things which were written concerning Me in the Law of Moses and** *in the* **Prophets and** *in the* **Psalms must be fulfilled.'"**

Not one word of God is ever, ever going to fail! Everything:

- about His whole life
- about His ministry
- about his death
- about his resurrection

You can go back to Psa, 17 where it says, 'I will be satisfied when I awake with your righteousness, or like you.' That was a *Psalm of the resurrection.*

Verse 45: "Then He opened their minds to understand the Scriptures."

- How does that happen with us?
- How are the keys given that tell us what we must do?

All of them were:
- Sabbath-keepers
- Holy Day keepers
- keeping the commandments of God

Not like our world living out here in the satanic world!

The first thing we have to start with is to believe God and the Sabbath. You've got to start with the Sabbath. Then when you read the Word of God, what you learn you need to do—you must do.

The minute you read it and say, 'Oh well, that's not important; it's probably written by men.' *Your mind is shut again! It'll happen!*

Betty was talking about some of those who were saying how wonderful you're going to find Sunday-keeping is, if you just open your mind. Well, in order for Sunday-keeping to be wonderful, you've got to close your mind, **because no man can tell God what to do!** He said to 'remember the Sabbath,' not reject it and forget it. God's Spirit is sent by the Father—seven spirits. He draws us, and our minds are opened. That's how they're opened.

And the only way you understand *spiritual* Truth—because Jesus said, 'The words that I speak they're Spirit and Life, which includes all the words in the Bible—is to love God and keep His commandments and grow in grace and knowledge. He wants to teach us as much as we can learn before the resurrection. How's that's going to work out? *I don't know!* Not everybody's going to have the same job. How that's going to work out? *I don't know! God does!*

Verse 45: "Then He opened their minds to understand the Scriptures, and said to them, 'According as it is written...'" (vs 45-46).

Whenever you see, "...it is written..." rarely do you say, '*was* written,' because the Word of God is always active in the present tense.

"...it was necessary for the Christ to suffer, and to rise from *the* dead the third day. And in His name, repentance and remission of sins should be preached to all nations, beginning at Jerusalem. For you are witnesses of these things" (vs 46-48).

Just imagine what it would have been like to be in that room. They've spent three and a half years with Christ in a ministry, seeing all the miracles, seeing everything that was done: tried and crucified. And then:

- He's risen
- He comes to them
- He shows them that He's the One
- He eats food
- He opens their minds to understanding

That must have taken most of the night. But that was easy that night, because it was so filled with adrenaline they couldn't have slept anyway. Here's another one: remember what the lie was? *The disciples came and stole the body away!* So, the disciples were still afraid of the Jews. Don't you think the Jews would like to come and get them and kill them, as well? *Yes!*

Section 377—Eight Days Later, Jesus Appears to His Disciples Again

John 20:26: "Now after eight days...

so, you go Sunday-to-Sunday; that's eight days

"...His disciples again were within, and Thomas with them...." (v 26).

And Thomas said, 'Hey, I'm not going to believe You until I can see Your hands and feet and Your side (v 25)

Verse 26: "...Jesus came after the doors were shut, and stood in the midst and said, 'Peace *be* to you.' Then He said to Thomas..." (vs 26-27).

Tommy boy, come here

"...Put forth your finger, and see My hands; and reach *out* your hand, and put *it* into My side; and be not unbelieving, but believing.' And Thomas answered and said to Him, 'My Lord and My God'" (vs 27-28).

Now, think about that statement, because Jesus was God manifested in the flesh, and after His resurrection, He was God wholly again, or completely. Because don't misconstrue that as Holy meaning Divine, but it is. He was Holy Divine God in their presence in appearing as if He had flesh.

Verse 29: "Jesus said to him, 'Because you have seen Me, Thomas, you have believed; blessed are the ones who have not seen, but have believed.'"

What happened during the 40 days? *He was with them on and off for 40 days!* Then they had a meeting over in Galilee for over 500 brethren that saw Him at the same time. Here's what John writes:

John 20:30: "Now then, Jesus did many other miracles in *the* presence of His disciples, which are not written in this book. But these have been written so that you may believe that Jesus is the Christ, the Son of God; and that believing, you may have life through His name" (vs 30-31).

Then we come here to Acts 1:3. This is Luke writing to Theophilus; that means *lover of God.*

Acts 1:3: "To whom also, by many infallible proofs, He presented Himself alive after He had suffered, being seen by them for forty days, and speaking the things concerning the Kingdom of God."

Now I have quite a few Scriptures here, so we will follow along in the commentary. But putting the Scriptures together, what we have in the Old Testament what we have in the New Testament: What was it like when Jesus Christ was accepted by God the Father as the sin offering for the sins of all mankind?

commentary, pg. 330: <u>Jesus Christ Accepted by God the Father</u>

The ascension of Jesus to God the Father was an awesome event. Jesus Christ had finished the work that the Father had given Him to do. As God manifest in the flesh, He had lived a perfect, sinless life and had died by crucifixion to become the perfect sacrifice for the sins of all mankind. God the Father had raised Jesus back to life, and on the Wave Sheaf Day He was ready to ascend to the throne of God the Father to be accepted as the first of the firstfruits, the firstborn among many brethren, and the perfect sacrifice to propitiate the sins of the world.

So let's see if we can grasp the meaning and feeling of this fantastic day.

As He was ascending to the Father, Jesus must have been filled with great joy and anticipation. He would see the Father face to face for the first time since He had become a pinpoint of life when He divested Himself of His power and glory as God to be born of the virgin Mary. Again, the Psalms help us comprehend some of the thoughts and feelings that Jesus might have experienced as He looked forward to being reunited with the Father: "**O God, You are my God,** earnestly I will seek You! My soul thirsts for You. My flesh longs for You, as in a dry and thirsty land where no water is, **to see Your power and Your glory—as I have seen You in the sanctuary.** Because Your loving kindness is better than life, my lips shall praise You" (Psa. 63:1-3).

As previously noted, Psalm 23 foreshadowed the prayers of Jesus after He was resurrected from the dead. The psalm to follow, Psalm 24, is in prophetic sequence and depicts Jesus' ascension to be received of God the Father. When He arrived in heaven, the angels sang and shouted for joy. Perhaps this psalm was sung by the angels as they opened the everlasting doors and announced that the King of glory was entering into the presence of God the Father: "The earth is the LORD'S, and the fullness of it, the world, and those who dwell in it, for He has founded it upon the seas and established it upon the waters. **Who shall ascend into the hill of the LORD? Or** who shall stand in His holy place? He who has clean hands and a pure heart, who has not lifted up his soul to vanity and has not sworn deceitfully [the perfect life of Jesus Christ]. He shall receive the blessing from the LORD and righteousness from the God of his salvation."

Lift up your heads, O you gates; and be lifted up, O you everlasting doors; that the King of glory may come in. Who is this King of glory? The LORD strong and mighty, the LORD mighty in battle [He was victorious over human nature, sin, Satan the devil and death]. Lift up your heads, O you gates; lift them up, you everlasting doors; that the King of glory may come in. Who is this King of glory? The LORD of hosts, He is the King of glory" (Psa. 24:1-5, 7-10).

What a magnificent scene of splendor and glory Jesus would have seen when He entered through the everlasting gates of heaven! Standing on the sea of glass, He would have seen the resplendent glory and awesome majesty of God the Father seated on His throne with the heavenly host round about. The apostle John, the one whom Jesus loved, saw a vision of God's throne and recorded it in the book of Revelation. What John recorded is what Jesus would have seen when He ascended to the Father.

"After these things I looked, and behold, a door opened in heaven; and the first voice that I heard *was* as if a trumpet were speaking with me, saying, 'Come up here, and I will show you the things that must take place after these things.' And immediately I was in *the* Spirit; and behold, a throne was set in heaven, and *One* was sitting on the throne. And He Who was sitting was in appearance like a jasper stone and a sardius stone; and a rainbow *was* around the throne, like an emerald in its appearance.

"And around the throne were twenty-four thrones, and on the thrones I saw twenty - four elders sitting, clothed in white garments; and they had on their heads golden crowns. And proceeding from the throne were lightnings and thunders and voices; and seven lamps of fire, which are the seven Spirits of God, were burning before the throne. And before the throne *was* a sea of glass, like crystal. And around the throne and over the throne *were* four living creatures, full of eyes before and behind; and the first living creature was like a lion, and the second living creature was like a bull, and the third living creature had the face of a man, and the fourth living creature was like a flying eagle. And each of the four living creatures had six wings respectively; and around and within they were full of eyes; and day and night they cease not saying, 'Holy, holy, holy, Lord God Almighty, Who was, and Who is, and Who *is* to come.'

"And when the living creatures give glory and honor and thanksgiving to Him Who sits on the throne, Who lives into the ages of eternity, the twenty-four elders fall down before Him Who sits on the throne; and they worship Him Who lives into the ages of eternity, and cast their crowns before the throne, saying, 'Worthy are You, O Lord, to receive glory and honor and power because You did create all things, and for Your will they were created and exist'" (Rev. 4:1-11).

Quite a magnificent scene, indeed. Just think what it's going to be like when we're resurrected!

This was the scene that Jesus would have seen as He walked forward to present Himself to the Father as the perfect sacrifice for sin. He was the first of the firstfruits and the firstborn from the dead. As He walked on the sea of glass toward the Father sitting on His throne, the angels, the twenty-four elders and God the Father would see on His body the scars of the lashes that He had received when He was beaten with the cat-of-nine-tails which tore open His flesh. They would see the scars in His hands and feet where the soldiers had nailed Him to the cross. When the Father's beloved Son greeted His Father, They must have opened their arms and embraced each other in profound love and tears of joy. Thus Jesus Christ, the Lamb of God, was accepted by God the Father on the Wave Sheaf Day.

After He was accepted of the Father, Jesus was selected to open the seven seals. He and He alone was qualified, because He had overcome all. The apostle John saw this tremendous scene in the vision and recorded it: "And in the right hand of Him Who sits on the throne I saw a book, written within and on the back, which had been sealed with seven seals. And I saw a strong angel proclaiming with a loud voice, 'Who is worthy to open the book and to loose its seals?' But no one in heaven, or on the earth, or under the earth was able to open the book, or to look inside it. And I [John] was weeping greatly because no one was found worthy to open and to read the book, or to look into it.

"Then one of the elders said to me, 'Do not weep. Behold, the Lion Who is of the tribe of Judah, the Root of David, has overcome to open the book, and to loose its seven seals.' **Then I saw, and behold, before the throne and the four living creatures, and before the elders,** *was* **standing a Lamb as having been slain,** having seven horns and seven eyes, which are the seven Spirits of God that are sent into all the earth; and **He came and took the book out of the right hand of Him Who sits on the throne**.

"And when He took the book, the four living creatures and the twenty-four elders fell down before the Lamb, each having harps and golden bowls full of incense, which are the prayers of the saints. And they sang a new song, saying, **'Worthy are You to take the book, and to open its seals because You were slain, and did redeem us to God by Your own blood, out of every tribe and language and people and nation,** and did make us unto our God kings and priests; and we shall reign on the earth.'

"And I saw, and I heard *the* **voices of many angels around the throne, and** *the* **voices of the living creatures and the elders, and thousands of thousands, saying with a loud voice,' Worthy is the Lamb Who was slain to receive power, and riches, and wisdom, and strength, and honor, and glory and blessing.' And every creature that is in heaven, and on the earth, and under the earth, and those that are on the sea, and all the things in them, I heard saying, 'To Him Who sits on the throne, and to the Lamb,** *be* **blessing, and honor, and glory, and sovereignty into the ages of eternity.'** And the four living creatures said, 'Amen.' And the twenty-four elders fell down and worshiped *Him Who* lives into the ages of eternity" (Rev. 5:1-12).

This is the glory and majesty that Jesus Christ received when He was accepted by God the Father as the Savior and Redeemer of mankind on the Wave Sheaf Day. Jesus had overcome sin in the flesh and gained complete victory over death, opening the way for the redemption and salvation of all

mankind through faith in Him. Now He lives in eternal glory, as the first of many sons of God who will be resurrected at His second coming to share His eternal glory and immortality. Those who are Jesus Christ's are now being perfected through the love, grace and power of God the Father. They will be granted the identical spiritual existence that the Father and the Son have. They will be the sons and daughters of God the Father, and the brethren of Jesus Christ. Jesus shared human existence with mankind in order to become the sin offering for the world so that all who believe in Him may ultimately share His eternal existence and glory in the Family of God throughout the ages of eternity. Amen.

Scriptural References:

1) Matthew 27:51-54
2) John 19:31-42
3) Matthew 27:62-66
4) Mark 16:1
5) Luke 23:56
6) Matthew 28:1-4
7) John 20:1-2
8) Luke 24:1
9) Mark 16:2-7
10) John 20:4-10
11) Mark 16:9-10
12) John 20:11-18
13) Matthew 28:8-15
14) Luke 24:31-32, 34, 36-48
15) John 20:26-31
16) Acts 1:3

Scriptures referenced, not quoted:

- Psalm 63:1-3
- John 20:25

Also referenced:

- Article: *Christ's Last Passover, Leavened or Unleavened?* by Ben Ambrose {**truthofGod.org**}
- Book: *A Harmony of the Gospels* by Fred R. Coulter

FRC:po/bo
Transcribed: 3/29/19
Reformatted: 10/2020

Section IV

Feast of Unleavened Bread

CHAPTER TWENTY-THREE

The Night to Be Much Observed
Fred R. Coulter

➤ What is the meaning of the Night to be Much Observed?
➤ Why should we keep it?

We have already been covering why the Night to be Much Observed is **not** the Passover night, so we're going to concentrate on the meaning of the Night to be Much Observed, which begins the first day of the Feast of Unleavened Bread. Let's see where this is mentioned; where it's commanded, and then we are going to see a very astounding statement that tells us something very important concerning that night and why we should observe it.

All the details concerning the Passover and leading up to this we have already covered, so I want to cover specifically the meaning of the Night to be Much Observed.

Exodus 12:40: "Now, the sojourning of the children of Israel in Egypt **was four hundred and thirty years**... [this gives a reference to something else] ...and it came to pass at the end of the four hundred and thirty years, it was even on that very same day, all the armies of the LORD went out from the land of Egypt" (vs 40-41).

This reference cannot refer to the Passover, because the first time they took it was the night before. So, it can't be referring to the Passover; the selfsame day does not refer to the Passover, but it refers to something else that had occurred *430 years earlier.*

Verse 42: "It *is* a night to be much observed to the LORD for bringing them out from the land of Egypt. **This *is* that night of the LORD to be observed by all the children of Israel in their generations**." *So, here is the command, a special command.*

Now we can understand that this is not the Passover from this point of view: that on the Passover, they were to keep the Passover and when they ate it, it was to be eaten in trepidation; that's what the Hebrew means. Now this one here, notice, the Night to be Much Observed:

1. there are no sacrifices they are to give at this point here on the first one
2. later they would be giving sacrifices at the temple

But here they are leaving Egypt, so, this is the first start!

Verse 51: "And it came to pass the very same day, *when* the LORD brought the children of Israel out of the land of Egypt by their armies." *That's talking about the day they left!*

That's where the chapter break should be. Verse 51 should actually be Exo. 13:1, because verse 50 comes to a full stop, and this is a whole new subject. We're going to see something about this a little bit later on, but we'll take a clue here:

Exodus 13:1: "Then the LORD spoke to Moses... [the selfsame day that they were coming out of Egypt] ...saying, '**Sanctify all the firstborn to Me**... [we'll cover that as we come to the Feast of Unleavened Bread] ...whatever opens the womb among the children of Israel, of man and of beast. It *is* Mine.' And Moses said to the people, 'Remember this day *in* which you came out of Egypt, out of the house of bondage; for the LORD brought you out from this place by the strength of His hand. There shall be no leavened bread eaten'" (vs 1-3).

We're going to see that *this day has to do with the firstborn; has to do with the sanctifying of the firstborn!* But the sacrifices that they gave in Deut. 16 had to do with the Night to be Much Observed.

Let's look at something else concerning leaving Egypt. Let's clarify this because there is a lot of confusion concerning it, and really the main portion of the confusion concerning this stems from two sources:

1. the lack of a clear translation concerning *sunset* and *between the two evenings* in the *King James Version* of the Bible and also other translations
2. the tradition of the Jews of keeping a 15th Passover instead of a 14th

Why do they keep a 15th Passover? We saw in Num. 9, it clearly says that in order to take the Passover, they have to be in the land; within the geographical area of the land of Israel! So, if they were on a journey, they could not take a 14th Passover. What happened was this: When the Jews were in exile, which they still are today, they could not—and they will tell you they cannot—keep a 14th

Passover. They keep the Feast of Unleavened Bread but call it—the whole thing—*Passover*. When they have their meal beginning the night of the 15th, they are actually eating an abbreviated form of the Feast of the Night to be Much Observed!

Num. 33—let's look at this because this also causes confusion, and the third reason that causes confusion is *pre-conceived notions*; you come to the Scriptures with something in mind, and you're looking to prove what you have in mind. When you read it, you think you're proving what you have in mind because you have read it and you think that that's what it's saying.

Numbers 33:1 *is part of it*: "These *are* the journeys of the children of Israel, who went forth out of the land of Egypt with their armies under the hand of Moses and Aaron. And Moses wrote their goings out according to their journeys by the command of the LORD. And these *are* their journeys according to their starting places. And they set out from Rameses…" (vs 1-3).

As we saw, the Passover was kept on the night of the 14th. On the day portion of the 14th they finished spoiling the Egyptians and assembled at Rameses, and they had to come from the land of Goshen to Rameses so they could begin their march and their journey out.

Verse 3: "And they set out from Rameses in the first month, **on the fifteenth day of the first month**…."

We know that Lev. 23 says that 'on the 14th day is the LORD'S Passover and on the 15th is the first day of the Feast of Unleavened Bread.' *So this, the 15th, is when they left!*

"…On the **next day after the Passover Day,** the children of Israel went out with a high hand in the sight of all the Egyptians, while the Egyptians were still burying all *their* firstborn whom the LORD had stricken among them. The LORD also executed judgments upon their gods" (vs 3-4).

What is the preconceived notion that people read into this? *This must be the morning of the 15th!* It doesn't say that! They left on the 15th; that's when they departed. That doesn't mean the whole body of them was out, but they were departing at that point. When you have 1.8-million people that are going to be marching out, even in a wide column, you're going to get it started. The ones who are at the end are going to come along later. As I mentioned in The Christian Passover book: If you observe the Rose Parade in Pasadena, California, when the parade starts, two hours later, the last crew is starting while the first crew—marching band or float—is finishing. When it says *departed,* that doesn't mean the whole mass of them had completely gone.

Deut. 16—we'll just look at one verse here that is important; we will come back to because this will be important.

Deuteronomy 16:1: "Keep the month of Abib, and observe the Passover to the LORD your God…. [that's one day] …For in the month of Abib, the LORD your God brought you forth out of Egypt **by night**."

That's why it is the Night to be Much Observed, because they came out the next night, and as I mentioned previously, show me anywhere in the Bible where God ever combined two days together. Show me one instance where God said, 'Oops! Let's combine the two days.' *No!* Men are the ones who have combined them. So, they went out by night, so you put it all together. They left with a high hand.

- When did they start?
- When does the 14th end? *Sunset on the 14th!*
- Is it still light when the sun is going down? *Yes!*
- Were they leaving when the sun was going down? *Yes!*
- Did they go on into the night with their exodus? *Yes!*
- What were the Egyptians doing when they started? *They were still burying their firstborn (Num. 33)!*

When you consider the number that were dead, if they had a population of 24-million—pick any number you want—20% are firstborn, male or female. Let's just say they only had 10-million, they had 2-million dead human beings. So, we'll give it the low figure, we'll low-ball it.

- How about all the animals?
- How long do you think it's going to take to bury them?
- How long do you think it's going to take them to bury 2-million people plus all the animals?

Egypt is a hot place, and if you don't bury them right away, what happens? *These gigantic flies about as big around as a half-dollar piece,* come in and the buzzards and the vultures, and if you don't get them buried they get in the hot, hot sun and the bodies explode.

- Do you think they might have burned some of them?
- Who knows?

It doesn't say they burned them, *it says **they buried them!***

That's a big task, which means that you only had, counting all women and children, you only had 8-million to bury 2-million. If you say the adult males that were left who had to do the work and maybe some of the adult females, then you're probably down to a couple of million.

Numbers 33:4 (*KJV*): "For **the Egyptians buried all their firstborn**…" That took more than just on the day portion of the Passover to accomplish that!

See they went out with a high hand in the sight of all the Egyptians who were burying their dead. Obviously, when it got dark they would quit.

Sidebar: Dolores watched a historical presentation of Trablinka where they started killing Jews as early as 1941, I believe, and they killed 900,000 in one place. Trablinka was in Poland, the Nazis were killing the Polish Jews, and they would gas them and put them in this big pit, and then they would even put some lime to try and get rid of the bodies, but they couldn't do it. They had so many dead in this big pit, and the stench was getting so bad that they had to dig them up and burn them. So, when it says here "…the Egyptians buried all their firstborn…" that doesn't mean they did it on that one day.

They went out at night, the Night to be Much Observed, with a high hand. This is far different than the Passover night, which was

- a night of fear
- a night of terror
- a night of trepidation

Now you have two operations going here:

1. the Passover *you are redeemed*
2. the Night to be Much Observed *you are delivered*

Let's focus in on the time period, because the phrase *430 years* and *on the selfsame day…*

- What does that refer to?
- What was the selfsame day?

We know that according to the Hebrew Calendar, the selfsame day was the 15th (Num. 33)!

We're going to find out that this actually goes back to Abraham, and God's covenant with Abraham (Gen. 15). What we're going to see in Gen. 15 is quite a tremendous thing. We are going to see is *a two-day sequence, which involves two nights!* The second night of which we will see is referred to in Exo. 12 as the *selfsame day, 430 years later!* So in fact, we are going to see that *the source and the origin of the Passover and the Night to be Much Observed began actually in Genesis 15!*

Genesis 15:1: "After these things the Word of the LORD came to Abram in a vision, saying, 'Fear not, Abram, I *am* your shield and your exceedingly great reward.' And Abram said, 'Lord

GOD, what will You give me since I go childless, and the heir of my house *is* this Eliezer of Damascus?' And Abram said, 'Behold, You have given no seed to me; and lo, one born in my house is my heir'" (vs 1-3). *Abram could adopt him and designate him as his heir!*

Verse 4: "And behold, the Word of the LORD *came* to him saying, 'This man shall not be your heir; but he that shall come forth out of your own loins shall be your heir.'"

This is the promise of Isaac, and also the promise, which comes down to Jacob and to the twelve tribes of Israel.

Verse 5: "And He brought him outside and said, 'Look now toward the heavens and number the stars—if you are able to count them….'"

When do you see the stars? *At night!* So, we are dealing with the night. You can't see them at noon, you can't see them at sunrise, maybe you can see a few faint stars, you can't see them at sunset, except maybe a few faint stars and maybe what we call Venus and Mars today. There must have been a lot of stars out there because He said:

"…number the stars—if you are able to count them. And He said to him, 'So shall your seed be'" (v 5). *We have two promises of seed here*:

1. of Isaac *the physical seed*
2. the stars of heaven *the spiritual seed*

What did Jesus say? We will see what the stars of heaven represent in the promise of the *spiritual* seed:

Matt. 13:43—this is at the return of Christ; this is talking about the resurrection. A little later we're going to see that *we are Abraham's seed and heirs according to the promise!* So, the promise was given in Gen. 15:

1. of the physical seed: Isaac
2. of the spiritual seed; those in the first resurrection

Notice what Jesus says of those in the first resurrection at His return:

Matthew 13:43: "Then shall the righteous shine forth as the sun in the Kingdom of their Father…. [then He has this little cryptic statement here] …The one who has ears to hear, let him hear." *The only way you're going to understand it is if God gives you the understanding through His Word!*

Now let's look at what it says in Dan. 12 concerning the righteous, because when you understand that the sun is *a star…*

Daniel 12:1: "And at that time… [that's the time of the end, the time of the resurrection] …shall stand up, the great prince who stands for the children of your people. And there shall be a time of trouble, such as never was since there was a nation even until that time. And at that time your people shall be delivered—everyone who shall be found written in **the book**"—*the* **Book of Life** *and this has to be the first resurrection.*

Verse 2: "And many of those who sleep in the dust of the earth… [shows they were buried] … shall awake, some to everlasting life, and some to shame and everlasting contempt."

That's for those who commit the unpardonable sin and face the second death at the end of the Millennium and 100-year period.

Verse 3: "And they who are wise shall shine as the brightness of the firmament, and they who turn many to righteousness shall shine as the stars forever and ever."

The promise given to Abraham has some big-time promises! That's why He said to him, as He took him out at night. Now remember: no smog, no pollution, no city lights, *you could see all the stars,* and I'm sure that was greater… because Texas in America claims that you can see the stars clearer in Texas than anyplace. But I just imagine that this was a whole lot better. What God asked Abraham to do was an impossible task!

Genesis 15:6: "And he believed in the LORD.…" *You have to believe what God says!* **IF** you are dealing with God:

- Who is a God of Truth, which He is
- His Word is true, which it is
- God cannot lie, which He cannot

He believed in the LORD for the two promises: *physical seed* **and the** *resurrected spiritual seed!*

"…And He accounted it to him for righteousness" (v 6)—*imputed to him for righteousness!*

As we know, that has nothing to do with whether he kept the commandments of God, or not. **This was a greater righteousness**; this **righteousness** is *being put in right standing with God because you* **believe** *Him!*

Verse 7: "And He said to him, 'I *am* the LORD that brought you out of Ur of the Chaldees, to give you this land to inherit it.' And he said, 'Lord GOD, **by what shall I know that I shall inherit it?'**…." (vs 7-8).

As we're going to see, we are on the day-portion of that day. Yes, he was talking about the 'promised land'; he was in the land of Canaan, but he dwelt in it *never having received an inheritance in it, yet.* When He says to inherit it that includes all of his progeny.

"…And He said to him, 'Take Me a heifer of **three years old,** and a she-goat of three years old, and a ram of three years old, and a turtledove, and a young pigeon'" (vs 8-9).

All of these were also later used for sacrifices at the temple. But it is interesting, *three-years-old,* so you're talking about good-sized animals, and we are going to see that this a special sacrifice. There is no altar that is there to burn them on, there is no splashing the blood upon any altar at all, and here is what he did:

Verse 10: "And he took all these to himself, and divided them in the middle…"—*cut them in half from head to toe!*

When you do that, if you have watched any of the wild life documentaries on how lions get buffalo and tear them apart and eat them, so just think of this as about the size of a buffalo, an African buffalo. Slit the throat and then you cut it down the middle. How are you going to cut it down the middle? *Well, you have to virtually take a battle-ax and this is a very bloody affair,* and you've got all the guts, you've got everything there.

"…and laid each piece opposite the other…" (v 10).

In other words, he put them back-to-back, and what he did in putting them back-to-back, *he also* **created a path** *that went down between those sacrificial animals!* This is a special sacrifice.

You can read of this in *The Christian Passover Book.* You can also read of it in *A Harmony of the Gospels.* In the *Harmony* I've got a chart that shows the sequence of events and how this also fits in with the death of Jesus.

"…but he did not divide the birds. And when the birds of prey came down upon the carcasses, Abram drove them away" (vs 10-11).

Verse 12 is a key verse because this gives us a time-flow of the day and what we're going to see that this is actually the time-flow of the Passover Day, *and reflects directly to the crucifixion of Christ and the time of* **His** *death more than the Passover of the children of Israel in the land of Egypt.*

Verse 12: "And it came to pass, as the sun was going down…" *It's still up, there is still a little time, and it was going down.* What happened to Abraham?

"…that a deep sleep fell upon Abram. And, behold, **a horror of great darkness fell upon him**!" (v 12).

- What was he experiencing in this great vision that God brought upon him? *He was experiencing death without dying!*
- What it would be like to die?

Verse 13: "And He said to Abram, 'You must surely know that your seed shall be sojourners in a land *that is* not theirs (and shall serve them *and they shall* afflict them) four hundred years. And also I will judge that nation whom they shall serve. And afterward they shall come out with great substance'" (vs 13-14).

That's a prophecy of delivering the children of Israel out from captivity and taking them out of the land of Egypt. As it turned out it was a little more than the 400 years; it was 430 years.

Verse 16: "But in the fourth generation… [that gives us latitude here to understand it] …they shall come here again, for the iniquity of the Amorites is not yet full. And it came to pass—when the sun went down and it was dark… [we're in to the next day] …behold, a smoking furnace and a burning lamp passed between those pieces" (vs 16-17).

- What was the smoking furnace doing? *The burning lamp passed between those parts!*
- What was Abraham actually seeing in this vision?

Here is a burning lamp that's walking down between those parts and probably the smoking furnace came right behind it and devoured everything, just completely devoured it. What this is, God is showing and prophesying His own death, *prophesying His death and burial,* which happened, on the Passover Day and the beginning of the first day of the Feast of Unleavened Bread, He was in the tomb.

This is a special covenant oath, it's also known as a maledictory oath, meaning that in order to fulfill this, you pronounce upon yourself your own death.

Notice the promise, v 18: "In the same day the LORD made a covenant with Abram, saying, 'I have given this land to your seed, from the river of Egypt to the great river, the River Euphrates.'"

Then He lists all the land of the Canaanites that they would receive. What God is doing with this, He is guaranteeing that on this second night… We will see this became the night of the 15th; so that means the first night was the night of the 14th. So, we have the Passover and the Night to be Much Observed right here at what you might say is the *prototype, the first fulfillment of it!* He made a covenant. He is going to give the land to them, and He was also going to deliver them.

When we come back to Exo. 12, what we're going to see is that this *selfsame day* had to refer back to:

1. the delivering of the children of Israel through the Passover Day

Because the Passover Day comes first; then the next day is called the selfsame day

2. referring to this day that God made the covenant with Abraham that He would do it

Exodus 12:40 "Now, the sojourning of the children of Israel in Egypt… [which was prophesied] …*was four hundred and thirty years,* and it came to pass at the end of the **four hundred and thirty years,** it was even on that very same day, all the armies of the LORD went out from the land of Egypt. **It *is* a night to be much observed to the LORD for bringing them out from the land of Egypt. This *is* that night of the LORD to be observed by all the children of Israel in their generations**" (vs 40-42).

Why? *Because He fulfilled His promise to deliver them!* He fulfilled His promise concerning the Passover Day on the 14th, and His promise to deliver them that they would go out with great substance on the Night to be Much Observed and leave on the 15th. In both cases, what do we have? *Two different days, two different meanings though connected!* This helps us understand the significance of the Night to be Much Observed.

As I have already previously explained with Deut. 16 so we'll just review it here, but let's understand what is happening, and how that relates to the firstborn, because the firstborn especially went out with a high hand, all the children of Israel did—but especially the firstborn—because they were spared from death. So this was a significant thing. *All the firstborn belong to God!* All the males and all the females (Deut. 14) were brought to the Feast of Unleavened Bread and also to the Feast of Tabernacles and they were used as part of the offerings that they would give in peace offerings to God.

Deut. 16 is a clue. I remember the first time I understood this, because Deut. 16 is difficult to understand because it seems to contradict some of the things in Exo. 12, and it seems to combine some the things in Exo. 12 and make it look like it comes on the same day; *but it doesn't!*

Deuteronomy 16:1: "Keep the month of Abib, and observe the Passover…"

When were they to keep the Passover? *The night of the 14th! That's one day!*

"…to the LORD your God. For in the month of Abib, the LORD your God brought you forth out of Egypt by night" (v 1)—*which was the beginning of the night of the 15th. So, we have, getting in to the second day!*

Verse 2: "And you shall, therefore, sacrifice the Passover offering to the LORD your God, **of the flock and the herd,** in the place, which the LORD shall choose to place His name there." *I have a full explanation of that in the Passover book!*

But here is the key that unlocks this so we have understanding. ***This is not the sacrifice of the Passover lamb for the Passover, <u>but this is in preparation for the Night to be Much Observed!</u>*** How do we know that?

"…**of the flock and the herd**…"

- Have you ever heard of a Passover calf? *No!*
- What does it say there in Exo. 12? *You are to take **of the flock of the sheep and of the goats,*** but here it says herd; the Hebrew here is 'bovine'!

*This has to do with the **peace offerings,** called here: **Passover Offerings;** not that they were for the Passover Day, but for the Feast of Unleavened Bread!* They probably started preparing these so they could be offered right at sunset beginning the Night to be Observed. *These had to be offered at the altar, not the Passover lamb.*

"…in the place, which the LORD shall choose to place His name there. You shall eat no leavened bread with it. Seven days you shall eat unleavened bread with it, the bread of affliction, for you came forth out of the land of Egypt in haste, so that you may remember the day that you came forth out of the land of Egypt all the days of your life. And there shall be no leaven seen with you in all your borders for seven days. Nor shall *any* of the flesh, which you sacrificed in the first day at sunset remain all night until the morning" (vs 2-4).

That sounds an awful lot like the Passover, but let's understand something, peace offerings could not be left until morning.

Verse 5: "You may not sacrifice the Passover offering within any of your gates…"

That sounds like it contradicts the commands for the Passover, which they were to do at their homes. This has to be the sacrifices for the first day of the Feast of Unleavened Bread.

Verse 6: "But at the place, which the LORD your God shall choose to place His name in, there you shall sacrifice the Passover offering at sunset, at the going *down* of the sun, at the time that you came out of Egypt."

Here is a *gross mistranslation* in the *KJV*, v 7: "You shall roast and eat…" ***That doesn't have to do with roasting at all!*** The Hebrew here is 'bashal' which is:

Verse 7 (*FV*): "And you shall **boil**…" *We have two things that tell us the clue that these are really peace offerings* that were prepared on the day portion of the Passover to be eaten after the Passover on the Night to be Much Observed. Those two key things are

1. v 7: "**And you shall boil**…"

Now we are going to see the Passover lamb was **never** to be boiled; I go into great detail in that in *The Christian Passover* book

2. the bovine—there is no such thing as a Passover *calf.*

- Can you imagine for a family of ten trying to eat a calf?
- Can you imagine trying to burn the bones, the hide and everything of the calf?

Let's look at the commands in Exo. 12 and then we will look at the command for *a peace offering.* Let's see what the command was. After they kill it, put the blood on the side posts and the lintels:

Exodus 12:8: "And they shall eat the flesh in that night, **roasted with fire**…" *It didn't say with fire in Deut. 16, because that should not be roasted, **but should be boiled!***

"…and unleavened *bread.* They shall eat it with *bitter* herbs. Do not eat of it raw, **nor boiled**… ['bashal'] …at all with water, **but roasted *with* fire**…" (vs 8-9).

The Jews' tradition was that if they had it on a spit and they were roasting it in the fire, and some of the juice from the roasting got on the staff that was through the middle of the animal, they were turning it kind of like a rotisserie and roasting it, and the juice cooked part of the meat, they had to cut that meat off and not use it because that was considered boiled in the juice.

"…**nor boiled at all with water, but roasted *with* fire**…" (v 8).

When you go back to Deut. 16 (*KJV*) and it says *roast,* it doesn't say *roast with fire,* and that's because that's a gross mistranslation ***and should be boiled!***

We will see the fulfillment of the Night to be Much Observed in the New Testament. Let me just say this: It follows along very logically according to the Word of God, not just human logic, that God commands to keep the Night to be Much

Observed. *It begins the first day of the Feast of Unleavened Bread!* **IF** you keep the Feast of Unleavened Bread, **you should keep** the Night to be Much Observed, because you can't have one without the other.

The Christian Passover book I'm going to mention again, because it's very important and there is not one page of wasted information in there. It is all vital and it covers every one of these questions concerning the Passover:

- the 14th/15th
- unleavened bread/leavened bread
- what time of day
- covers foot washing
- covers the Lord's Supper

Now in the Passover book—Chapters 22-24—covers the full meaning of the Night to be Much Observed beginning with the Passover and coming through the Passover night and Passover Day and in to the Night Much to be Observed and showing the selfsame day.

Now one other thing that's important to understand is this: There is a chart that shows the timing of Gen. 15 in the left-hand column and the death of Jesus Christ in the right-hand column, and how it parallels.

There is one other thing that we need to understand concerning the fulfillment of this prophecy. In Joshua 5 they entered the land and officially had ended the exodus when they got to the land. Now remember the promises given back in Gen. 15 carried forward to the night that they were delivered out of Egypt 430 years later, and also carried the promised of going into the land.

Joshua 5:10: "And the children of Israel camped in Gilgal and kept the Passover on the fourteenth day of the month at evening in the plains of Jericho. And they ate of the old grain of the land on the next day after the Passover... [the 15th] ...unleavened cakes and roasted *new* grain **in the same day**" (vs 10-11).

That meant when they started eating the bread made from the grain of the land, the exodus was officially over and they began the inheritance of the land on the 15th day of the 1st month, *the selfsame day!* Amazing how it follows all the way through!

Now let's see the parallels concerning the death and burial of Jesus Christ and what happened there, what occurred. We find we have the Passover ceremony—we have that in *The Passover Ceremony* booklet—but that covers John 13-17. We're going to read off of the chart.

We have something that's important here when we come to Jesus being arrested. To cover the Passover go through *The Passover Ceremony* booklet that we have for the Passover.

John 18—after Jesus prayed, we come to the time of betrayal. Judas came about midnight. When did God spare the firstborn of the children of Israel in Egypt? *At midnight on the 14th!* Jesus Christ was the Firstborn of the virgin Mary. He was also Firstborn from among the dead!

In John 18 we have the betrayal of Christ, which took place at midnight, and there are quite a few things that took place. What we really have on the Passover night is that God passed over the children of Israel, the firstborn, at midnight in Egypt. When Jesus came who was the firstborn of God; He did not pass over Him, **because He _was_ the Passover sacrifice.**

What we are going to see is this: That the timing of the killing of those animals in Gen. 15 parallels—as you see in the chart here—the timing of the things that Jesus went through.

- the bloody sacrifice of those animals parallels the beatings, the scourging, and the crucifixion of Christ
- when Christ died that parallels the time when Abraham had a deep sleep fall upon him and the horrors of great darkness
- when Christ was put into the tomb and it was sealed

  - When was it sealed?
  - When was He put in there? *He was put in there just right at sunset!*

Let's just do a little survey of John. If you have *A Harmony of Gospels,* go through and go back to about page 284 and go forward from there.

{verses are from *The Holy Bible in It's Original Order,* which is close to what is found in the *Harmony*}

I wonder what those who arrested Jesus thought? In the movie *The Passion* by Mel Gibson, it didn't really show it with all the meaning, there was too much Catholic tradition involved.

John 18:1: "After saying these things, Jesus went out with His disciples *to a place* beyond the winter stream of Kidron, where *there* was a garden into which He and His disciples entered."

You find in the parallel accounts where He prayed, He actually prayed for three hours and then about midnight He quit praying.

Verse 2: "And Judas, who was betraying Him, also knew of the place because Jesus had often gathered there with His disciples. Then Judas, after receiving a band and officers from the chief priests and Pharisees, came there with torches and lamps and weapons. Jesus, therefore, **knowing all *the* things that were coming upon Him,** went forward *and* said to them, 'Who are you seeking?'" (vs 2-4).

When it says, "…**knowing all *the* things that were coming upon Him**…" what did He understand? *He gave all the prophecies of His death*: Isa. 53; Psa. 22; Psa. 69!

Verse 5: "They answered Him, 'Jesus the Nazarean.' Jesus said to them, 'I AM.' And Judas, who was betraying Him, was also standing with them. But when He said to them, 'I AM,' they went backward and fell to *the* ground" (vs 5-6).

I don't know about you, but I have often wondered what those soldiers thought, and I wonder if Judas also went back. It doesn't tell us that he didn't, but when He said *I AM* they went back, so that must include Judas, and "…**fell on *the* ground.**"

Verse 8: "Jesus answered, 'I told you that I AM. Therefore, if you are seeking Me, allow these to go their way'; so that the saying might be fulfilled which He had said, 'Of those whom You have given Me, **not one of them have I lost**'" (vs 8-9)—*except the son of perdition!*

Verse 10: "Then Simon Peter, who had a sword, drew it out and struck the servant of the high priest, and cut off his right ear. And the servant's name was Malchus." *I am sure he wasn't aiming just for the ear; I'm sure he was aiming to lop off his head!*

Remember that Peter was the one—Matt. 16—you go back read it, when Jesus revealed what was going to happen to Him. What did Peter say? *He even took Him aside and said,* 'Lord, this isn't going to happen to You, I'm here, I will deliver You.' *Jesus said,* 'Get behind me, Satan, you savor the thoughts of men not the thoughts of God.'

Verse 11: "But Jesus said to Peter, 'Put your sword into the sheath; shall I not drink the cup that the Father has given Me?'" *It shows in the parallel account that what Jesus did was He reached over and healed his ear!*

- What happens when you cut off something? *You have blood and you kind of feeling it!*
- What happens when you have a wound that is healed? *You feel it and see how it's going!*

I imagine all the way back in, after his ear was healed, Malchus was feeling his ear!

Did it really happen? *Malchus comes back in and I'm sure someone said,* 'Where'd you get all that blood?' *This guy over here cut my ear off!*

'how'd it get back on?' *This guy over here that we arrested, touched it and it healed!* **A witness!**

Do we really want to kill Him? There are many, many things. Now remember this is the Passover night, and this is in preparation of His sacrifice on the Passover Day, which parallels the animals that Abraham cut in two and God walked between.

They took Him bound to Annas and Caiaphas and so forth, you can read of it there in *A Harmony of the Gospels.* They beat Him, they punched Him, they had a trial—which was totally illegal—and I've got all the timeframe that is there, everything that happened. The chief priest condemns Him, Peter denies Christ three times, and then the Sanhedrin sends Him to Pilate; Pilate finds Him innocent. Now we're getting into the day portion.

But then the priests stirred up the people and they demanded Barabbas. What does the name Barabbas mean?

- bar: s*on*
- abbas is from 'abba'; *the father*
- *son of the father*

So, there is a total counterfeit!

They released Barabbas and they took Jesus and they scourged Him, beat Him and scourged Him. Then after He barely was able to survive, they took the cross… It wasn't like it was in the movie *The Passion of the Christ*; it was not a cross with two pieces. It was the crossbar that they would hang them on. They would take a tree trunk and they would put it in the ground and up at the top of it they would have a place where you could put into holders, the crossbar. So, they could crucify a person on there, and then when they are dead, they'd just get them off there by lifting up the crossbar, but the tree trunk would remain in the ground.

That's what Jesus was carrying. It wasn't quite as high as what they showed in the movie there. Remember, *The Passion of the Christ* is a Catholic version of the crucifixion of Christ, which is made to conform to Catholic doctrine. The reason why it says that Jesus was crucified on a tree is because the tree trunk was there—'stauros'—but also for the sake of a cross. So, when He carried out His cross, He was not carrying the whole thing, but He was carrying the crossbar.

Then at the very time of the sacrifices that were going on by Abraham (Gen. 15), Christ was going through His scourging, He was being led away; at the third-hour in the morning He was crucified, and then you have the seven sayings of Jesus. Then you have darkness from the sixth hour to the ninth hour and Jesus dies at about 3:00 p.m., or the ninth hour.

Now let's see something, and then this will also tell us a very important thing concerning the Night Much to be Observed by us today. The first night to be observed, right after the Passover and death of Jesus Christ, was not a night of rejoicing. Remember what Jesus said, He told them on the Passover night, He said, *'You're going to be grieved, but afterwards you will have joy.'* This one Night to be Much Observed was not a night of joy for the disciples at that time, but it was later. Because what it was, was this: *Jesus performed the oath that He swore to Abraham, and He died—* exactly as He said—*and He was put in the grave!*

After Jesus received the vinegar to fulfill the prophecy, John 19:30: "And so, when Jesus had received the vinegar, He said, 'It is finished.' And bowing His head, He yielded up *His* spirit." *The account in Mark shows that it was at the ninth hour that He died, about 3:00 p.m.!*

Verse 31: "The Jews, therefore, so that the bodies might not remain on the cross on the Sabbath, because it was a preparation *day* (for that Sabbath was a High Day), requested of Pilate that their legs might be broken and *the bodies* be taken away. Then the soldiers came and broke the legs of the first *one*, and *the legs* of the other who was crucified with Him. But when they came to Jesus *and* saw that He was already dead, they did not break His legs" (vs 31-33). **Why?** *It was prophesied He would never have a bone broken!*

These soldiers aren't going along and saying, 'I read in the Bible that He was not going to have a bone broken. I'm not going to break the legs so I can fulfill the prophecy.' The soldiers who were there casting lots on His vesture and on His garment, say, 'Oh, let's fulfill prophecy guys.'

God made them do it and they had no inkling of why they were doing what they were doing.

Verse 34: "But one of the soldiers had pierced His side with a spear, and immediately blood and water had come out. And he who saw *this* has testified, and his testimony is true… [that's John] …and he knows that *what* he says *is* true, so that you may believe. For these things took place so that the Scripture might be fulfilled, 'Not a bone of Him shall be broken.' And again another Scripture says, 'They shall look upon Him Whom they pierced.' Now, after these things, Joseph (the one from Arimathea, being a disciple of Jesus, but having concealed it for fear of the Jews) asked Pilate that he might take Jesus' body away; and Pilate gave *him* permission. Then he came and took away the body of Jesus. And Nicodemus, who had come to Jesus by night at *the* first, also came, bearing a mixture of myrrh and aloes, about a hundred pounds. Then they took Jesus' body and wound it in linen cloths with the aromatics…" (vs 34-40).

No shroud! The Shroud of Turin is a hoax, a lie, and not true. So, the Catholic Church—a church built on lies—that believes in idolatry says:

> This may not be exactly the body of Jesus, but we have tried many, many experts, and some of them say that it is. So therefore, it's good for the faithful to worship, you know, that it's true.

The Bible that they have locked away in their little compartment on their altar says that they were wound much like a mummy.

Verse 41: "Now, there was a garden in the place where He was crucified, and in the garden a new tomb, in which no one had ever been laid. Because of the preparation of the Jews, they laid Jesus there; for the tomb was near" (vs 41-42).

Here is the point of the Night to be Much Observed for Christians today:

1. God fulfilled His promise that He would die for the sins of the world as pictured by the Passover Day
2. He began His three days and three nights in the tomb, *beginning with the Night to be Much Observed*

Think about this: the death of the One Who was God, Who became a human being, He died, and for the joy that was before Him, He endured the cross, despising the shame so He would be able with that sacrifice to save us!

We have joy *not in the death,* but in *the promise* of what He did and fulfilled, and yes, in the death from this point of view: *God applies the sacrifice of Jesus Christ to us upon repentance, for the forgiveness of our sins so that we do not have the death penalty brought upon us!*

That's quite a night of rejoicing! *IF* we are faithful, the Night to be Much Observed pictures this: We are redeemed by the Passover, we are delivered by the death of Jesus Christ, and now on the Night to be Much Observed, we start our walk out of spiritual Egypt, because you have to be redeemed and you have to be brought out of the world.

- Just like the children of Israel, where were they going? *They ended up at Mt. Sinai!*
- What was that? *That was temporarily the Throne of God!*
- Was it not where God gave the Ten Commandments?

Likewise, our walk and our journey, because what begins with the Passover on one night, and

276

then the Night to be Much Observed on the next night beginning our walk is pictured in the seven weeks of them walking to Mt. Sinai and hearing the voice of God, seeing the glory of God. Then with the assembly of the people of Israel there, is a type of the resurrection and the assembly of all of the saints resurrected from the dead.

You see, this Night to be Observed is fantastic from this point of view: That it **begins our journey out of sin and from physical life to the resurrection** to be resurrected and meet Christ on the Sea of Glass on Pentecost.

Heb. 12—we'll see the parallel; because all of these are connected, Passover, Unleavened Bread and Pentecost, and those three Feasts in the spring apply to the Church.

Hebrews 12:18: "For you have not come to *the* mount that could be touched…" *That is the physical Mt. Sinai!* They could even climb up and down on it now; *God is no longer there!* It's no longer a Holy place. Wherever God is, it's Holy.

"…and that burned with fire, nor to gloominess, and fearful darkness, and *the* whirlwind; and to *the* sound of *the* trumpet, and to *the* voice of *the* words, which those who heard, *begged* that *the* word not be spoken *directly* to them. (For they could not endure what was being commanded: 'And if even an animal touches the mountain, it shall be stoned, or shot through with an arrow'; and so terrifying was the sight *that* Moses said, 'I am greatly afraid and trembling')" (vs 18-21). *That was an awesome thing!*

We'll talk a little more about this when we come to Pentecost, but here's the parallel. In order to attain to the Kingdom of God, you:

1. have to have your sins forgiven through the sacrifice of Jesus Christ
2. you have to come out of this world and walk in the ways of God, under His direction with His Spirit, with His guidance

What did they do all the way to Mt. Sinai every Sabbath, but keep the Sabbath.

Verse 22: "But you have come to Mount Sion, and to *the* city of *the* living God, heavenly Jerusalem; and to an innumerable company of angels; *to the* joyous festival gathering; and to *the* Church of *the* Firstborn…" (vs 22-23).

The death of Jesus Christ, God manifested in the flesh, the Son of The Father, was the firstborn Who was the sacrificial offering of God for the forgiveness of our sins. The timing has nothing to do with the timing of anything at the temple, but between the timing of things in Gen. 15 with Abraham and the death of Jesus Christ.

Now then, the Church of the Firstborn, that's us, and so in another message I will bring out to you the meaning of the firstborn and why the first day of the Feast of Unleavened Bread beginning with the Night to be Much Observed is so important for us, because **we** are the firstborn, coming out of this world who, with Christ leading the way we are coming out with a high hand and looking forward to the resurrection.

"…and to *the Church* of *the* Firstborn, registered *in the Book of Life* in heaven; and to God, *the* Judge of all, and to *the* spirits of the just who have been perfected; and to Jesus, *the* Mediator of *the* New Covenant; and to sprinkling of *the* blood of *ratification*, proclaiming superior things than *that of* Abel" (vs 23-24).

Here now we have an inkling that everything even goes back to Abel, and then that goes back to the promise that God gave there in Gen. 3:15 of His own death. This is something, how the Bible puts it all together.

This is **the meaning** of the Night to be Much Observed and **why we in the Church of God should keep that night beginning on the night of the 15th of Nisan!**

Scriptures from *The Holy Bible in Its Original Order, A Faithful Version* (except where noted)

Scriptural References:

1) Exodus 12:40-42, 51
2) Exodus 13:1-3
3) Numbers 33:1-4
4) Deuteronomy 16:1
5) Numbers 33:4
6) Genesis 15:1-5
7) Matthew 13:43
8) Daniel 12:1-3
9) Genesis 15:6-14, 16-18
10) Exodus 12:40-42
11) Deuteronomy 16:1-7
12) Exodus 12:8-9
13) Joshua 5:10-11
14) John 18:1-11
15) John 19:30-42
16) Hebrews 12:18-24

Scriptures referenced, not quoted:

- Numbers 9
- Leviticus 23
- Deuteronomy 14
- John 13-17
- Isaiah 53
- Psalm 22; 69
- Matthew 16

- Genesis 3:15

Also referenced:

Books:
- *The Christian Passover* by Fred R. Coulter
- *A Harmony of the Gospels* by Fred R. Coulter

Booklet: *Passover Ceremony* by Fred R. Coulter

FRC:ja
Transcription date unknown
Reformatted: bo—11/2020

CHAPTER TWENTY-FOUR

How Do You Stand Before God?
First Day of Unleavened Bread
Fred R. Coulter

Greetings brethren! This is the first day of the Feast of Unleavened Bread, and you know as we have learned, and have seen and understand, there is no justification at all for the religious holidays of this world to have any claim that they come from the Bible.

The will of man cannot be the will of God! Remember the model prayer that Jesus gave to the Father, that we are to ask that God's will be done on earth as it is in heaven.

When God spoke to the children of Israel *He gave them **His** will!* That's what we find concerning the Holy Days, and the basic outline of them back in the book of Leviticus.

I want to read several verses at the end of Lev. 22 before we get to Lev. 23 so that we can emphasize and understand something very important concerning the Holy Days of God. They are just as important as the weekly Sabbath, and as a matter of fact, they give the rest of the story in laying out the plan of God, ***because without the Holy Days you cannot understand the plan of God.***

Leviticus 22:31: "And you shall keep My commandments, and do them. I *am* the LORD."

Whenever you see 'I am the LORD' *or* 'the LORD says,' ***These are the words of God, the recorded voice of the Word of God!*** Of course as we have seen, know and understand ***we are to obey the voice of the LORD our God!***

Verse 32: "And you shall not profane My Holy name. But I will be Holy among the children of Israel. I *am* the LORD Who is sanctifying you,"

That ties right in with the New Testament, that we are sanctified by God the Father through Jesus Christ!

Verse 33: "Who brought you out of the land of Egypt, to be your God. I *am* the LORD."

Not only that, ***when God calls us He brings us out of the world!*** Egypt symbolizes and typifies the world, so this becomes very important. As we have seen, ***IF*** you keep the holidays of this world you're going right back into Egypt. Another name that this is called of the world is ***Babylon!*** So Babylon and Egypt/Sodom and Gomorrah give a great definition of the end-time age that we live in.

Leviticus 23:1: "And the LORD spoke to Moses, saying, 'Speak to the children of Israel and say to them, "*Concerning* the appointed Feasts of the LORD…" (vs 1-2).—*which we have seen, know and understand that they are **His**!*

You cannot take something that comes from a pagan god, as we have seen, and put the name of God on it and have some high religious figure 'Christianize' it and sanctify it, *and say that this is the will of God. **No!***

It's very clear these are the Feasts of the LORD, so ***IF*** *you want to keep any days to God you have to keep the ones that **He** says! Everything else doesn't count!*

"…which you shall proclaim *to be* Holy convocations, even these are **My** appointed Feasts" (v 2).

It starts out with the weekly Sabbath because as we know and have seen, the fourth commandment—concerning the weekly Sabbath—is the overarching commandment from which the Holy Days, ***which are Sabbaths,*** hang.

Verse 3: "Six days shall work be done, but the seventh day *is* the Sabbath of rest, a Holy convocation. You shall not do any work. It *is* a Sabbath to the LORD in all your dwellings."

We know we keep the seventh day Sabbath every week, week in and week out as we go down through the year. When we come to the spring of the year, which this is, we have the Passover, which we have kept, and I hope that everyone had a profitable and inspiring Passover.

Then we keep the Feast of Unleavened Bread. In these things God teaches us not only His plan. but ***His*** way, and how ***He*** is doing things. That's why we have the Feasts. Remember that the weekly Sabbath is called *a Feast*. So, if the weekly Sabbath is called a Feast, and the annual Sabbaths are called Feasts, ***they are one in the same and belong together!*** The truth is, as we already know that you can't have one without the other.

Verse 4: "***These are the appointed Feasts of the LORD,*** Holy convocations, which you shall proclaim in their appointed seasons. In the fourteenth *day* of the first month, between the two evenings, is the LORD'S Passover, and on the fifteenth day of the same month *is* the Feast of Unleavened Bread to the LORD. You **must** eat unleavened bread seven days" (vs 4-6).

God says what He means and means what He says, *so we eat unleavened bread!* There's a lesson in it for us, as we will see.

Verse 7: "On the first day you shall have a Holy convocation. **You shall not** *do any servile* **work** *therein*, but **you shall offer a fire offering to the LORD** seven days...." (vs 7-8).

That includes that there's an offering on the seventh day, because if you start on the first day and you have an offering that you have, and of course, these were also the ritual sacrifices and they did them every day. You can see them all listed out in Num. 28.

Verse 8: "But you shall **offer a fire offering to the LORD**.... **You shall do no servile work** *therein*."

So, on every one of the Holy Days we do take up an offering. Today we don't offer sacrifices, but *we give monetary offerings,* and in a way that's likened unto a sacrifice.

Now let's see the command and what God says, and let's see how that with the offerings that we take up, we are to prepare for them. We are to do the things that God wants us to do in faith and trust, and understanding that God will bless us.

Deuteronomy 16:16: "Three times in a year shall all your males appear before the LORD your God in the place which He shall choose: in the Feast of Unleavened Bread, and in the Feast of Weeks, and in the Feast of Tabernacles. And they shall not appear before the LORD empty, **every man** *shall give* **as he is able**..." (vs 16-17). *There's a gauge!*

Every time we come before God to bring an offering we have to measure it by the blessings that God has given. So, if you have given and you are living by God's Word, and you are trusting in God, you probably have many blessings that you can count.

"...**according to the blessing of the LORD your God, which He has given you**" (v 17). *That's the gauge on how we are to give our offerings!*

2-Cor. 9 is talking about the Feast of Unleavened Bread and sowing and planting, and of course, it has reference then to us being the firstfruits, as we will see as we come down toward Pentecost time. We have an overall command with the very principles of God, and of course, this is based on faith. Everything that we do then must be based on faith:

- to love God
- to serve Him
- to keep His commandments
- to do the things that are right in His sight

2-Corinthians 9:6: "But this *I say*: the one who sows sparingly shall also reap sparingly..."

As we covered previously, long before the Feast of Unleavened Bread, that the one servant who received the one talent and didn't do anything with it, he didn't even sow it into the bank, as it were, to receive interest when Christ returns. So, he didn't even do the minimum. This is what he's talking about here. If you give sparingly then God will bless you sparingly, because the results will go hand-in-hand.

"...and the one who sows bountifully shall also reap bountifully" (v 6).

There are many, many blessings that come, which are more than just monetary or physical, blessings that you can look at and see. There are the blessings of love, joy, peace and longsuffering; the fruits of the Holy Spirit. There are the blessings where you have God's Spirit, *and God is giving you the strength and help to overcome!* Those are all part of the blessings that God will give.

Verse 7: "Each one as he purposes in his heart... [it's something that we have to do with deliberation and thought when we come before the LORD] ...*so let him give,* but not grudgingly..."

God wants us to keep His commandments with joy, not with grudging. Not saying, 'There goes that preacher again.' You know, as we're going to see, *we have to preach the Word in season!*

"...**or by compulsion**... [because God requires it] ...for God loves a cheerful giver" (v 7).

Here is the blessing; here is the promise. This is what we claim when we give to God our tithes and our offerings:

Verse 8. "For God *is* able to make all grace abound toward you so that in every *way* you may always have sufficiency in all *things, and* may abound unto every good work."

God gives a promise that you will have sufficiency in all things.

(pause for offering)

Let's look at the connection between Passover and Unleavened Bread, and a relationship with God the Father and Jesus Christ. Remember, as we have covered, John 14-17 are the *words of the New Covenant,* as we covered during the Passover night. These words also tell us exactly the way to have a relationship with Jesus Christ and God the

Father. It shows that since these words were given on the Passover night, that it is absolutely true **_you cannot have_** a connection with, or a relationship with Jesus Christ and God the Father **_unless_** you keep the Passover! You know we need to be as strong as the Bible is strong and say it exactly as it is.

John 14:6: "Jesus said to him, **'I am the Way, and the Truth, and the Life; no one comes to the Father except through Me.'**"

Jesus Christ is our Passover! So, unless you keep the Passover and the Feasts of God you cannot get to God the Father. **_It is an absolute impossibility!_** Of course, everything needs to be done exactly as Jesus said it should be done.

John 6:53 shows that it has to be the way that Jesus Christ has said. It is an impossibility for anyone to partake of communion anytime they want to and have a relationship with God the Father and Jesus Christ. They may think they do, **_but they're deceived,_** because no one is going to do anything contrary to the will of God **_and God accept it!_** No one can take the Eucharist and stand before a priest, or sit before a priest who has the unmitigated gall to claim that he can command God to come and put the presence of Jesus Christ—His body and His blood—in the bread and in the wine. **_NO!_**

Jesus clearly showed that to eat His flesh and drink His blood is symbolized by the unleavened bread and the wine. There is nothing literal in it. **_It is symbolic!_** It also has a meaning of what we are to do.

John 6:53: "Therefore, Jesus said to them, 'Truly, truly I say to you, unless you eat the flesh of the Son of man, and drink His blood, you do not have life in yourselves…. [because all die; the wages of sin is death and there is no way out except through Christ] …**The one who eats My flesh and drinks My blood has eternal life**…" (vs 53-54).

He's talking about the Passover. So, if you don't take the Passover you **_cannot_** have eternal life! You may take a false version of it through communion or the Eucharist, **_but that has no connection with God!_**

It may appear to have connection with God because those who perform the service use the Scriptures, but they _misuse them **because they are unwilling to obey!**_ Remember where we started—God said, 'Therefore, My commandments you shall keep!' Those are part of the commandments of God the Father and Jesus Christ.

"…and I will raise him up in the last day; for My flesh is truly food, and My blood is truly drink. The one who eats My flesh and drinks My blood is dwelling in Me, and I in him" (vs 54-56). _Without_

the Passover, **Christ cannot dwell in you!** That's what He says.

Here is what we are to do. This tells us exactly the meaning of it. We don't do this for some religious ritual so that somehow what we do puts us in right standing with God. We do it because God says **_IF_** we do, **_He puts us in right standing with Him!_** What are we to do after that?

Verse 57: "As the living Father has sent Me, and I live by the Father; so also the one who eats Me shall live by Me."

*   it is a way of life
*   it is something that we do
*   it is something that we live by
*   it is something we think by
*   it is something we have our life wrapped up in
*   Christ is in us
*   God the Father is in us
*   it is a way to live

Christ didn't die in vain to just please men! He died to save the world His way!

Verse 63: "'It is the Spirit that gives life; the flesh profits nothing….'" _That is our own physical flesh!_

Even symbolizing eating His flesh and drinking His blood, _it is the **spiritual** meaning of it!_ The spiritual application of renewing the New Covenant, as we have seen on the Passover, which is kept the 14th day of the 1st month.

"…The words that I speak to you, _they_ are Spirit and _they_ are Life. But there are some of you who do not believe.'…." (vs 63-64).

And they didn't like the saying that Jesus said, 'You have to eat My flesh and drink My blood'; so what did they do? _They said,_ 'It's a hard saying. I quit' _because it went against **their will!**_ They weren't willing to follow the will of God the Father and Jesus Christ. That's the whole meaning of the Feast of Unleavened Bread!

"…For Jesus knew from _the_ beginning who were the ones that did not believe, and who would betray Him. And He said, 'For this reason, I have said to you, no one can come to Me unless it has been given to him from My Father'" (vs 64-65). **_No one! It's an impossibility!_**

Just like you cannot please God by eating leavened bread during the Feast of Unleavened Bread. It's an impossibility! **_Unless_** you come:

*   through Christ
*   through His Word
*   through His Gospel

- through His way

you can't get to the Father! They couldn't take that!

Verse 66: "From that *time*, many of His disciples went back and walked no more with Him. Therefore, Jesus said to the twelve, 'Are you also desiring to go away?' Then Simon Peter answered Him, 'Lord, to whom shall we go? You have the words of eternal life; and we have believed and have known that You are the Christ, the Son of the living God'" (vs 66-69).

Jesus wanted to set the record straight, because in Matt. 16 when Peter said, 'You are the Christ,' Jesus said, 'Blessed are you, Simon Bar-Jona, for My Father has **revealed** this to you.' No one knows the true Christ **unless** He is **revealed** by *God the Father!*

Verse 70: "Jesus answered them, 'Did I not choose you twelve, and one of you is a devil?'"

To believe in *your own belief* of what *you think* concerning what the Bible says, and the Word of God, *will get you nowhere with God!*

Now let's see something very profound and important. To show that the only way that we are going to come to God, come to Jesus Christ and God the Father, is:

- through repentance
- a broken heart
- accepting the sacrifice of Jesus Christ
- living by the Words of God

Those who are teachers will see the command of what they are to do, and it does include the annual Sabbaths, and it does include all the commandments of God.

2-Timothy 3:14: "But *as for* you… [Paul is writing to Timothy] …continue in the things that you did learn and were assured of, knowing from whom you have learned *them*. and that **from a child you have known the Holy Writings**…" (vs 14-15).

They had not only the scrolls of the Old Testament in the synagogues before the time of Christ, but they also had personal scrolls. They also had the Septuagint translated from the Hebrew into Greek.

"…and that from a child you have known the Holy Writings…" means that he was taught in his home, (first part of 2-Tim.) His grandmother and mother taught him. They had the Word of God just like we have the Word of God.

"…Holy Writings, **which are able to make you wise unto salvation through faith, which *is* in Christ Jesus**" (v 15).

This is affirming the need to follow and obey the commandments in what is called the Old Testament!

Verse 16: "**All Scripture *is* God-breathed**…"—*the very Word of God!* It's like when I'm speaking, breath is coming out of my mouth. God breathed means that *God's Spirit moved these men to write the very Words of God!* It's just **not** the sayings or the thoughts of men. Because of that:

Verse 16: "All Scripture *is* God-breathed and *is* profitable **for doctrine**… [from which all teaching comes] …**for conviction**…"—*that you have to be!*

Not only know the Truth but be convicted of the Truth so you can:

- stand for the Truth
- love the Truth
- live by the Truth

Unless you have conviction you do not have spiritual backbone!

"…**for correction**…" (v 16)—*because we all need correction, every one of us!*

We need to let the Word of God correct us; that's the easiest way. You read the Word of God and you change and repent when you see there's correction for you.

The next easiest way is for a minister to teach you and read the Scriptures; you are corrected by that. Then it becomes a little more difficult if you're not willing to listen. Many times it's not a matter of being willing to listen, but because some things are hard to learn that we need the experience of trials and difficulties so that we can *learn the profound importance of what God wants us to do, and how we are to live!*

Remember, don't complain about any trial or difficulty that you've come through. Always think on and remember the sacrifice of Jesus Christ—His beating, His scourging, His crucifixion—that He went through for every one of us, because He loved us. That's why Paul says all these heavy trials are just but for a light moment. Remember that *there is no trial, no difficulty, no situation that is too great for God!* But in those He wants you to turn to Him.

"…**for instruction in righteousness**… [so that we may learn how to be in right standing with God through the power of His Holy Spirit] …so that the man of God may be complete, fully equipped for every good work" (vs 16-17).

That's not only just those who are teaching, *but that's for everyone!*

- that's why the Word of God is here

- that's why we are to prove all things.
- that's why we are to hold fast

which is good!

2-Timothy 4:1: "I charge you, therefore, in the sight of God, even the Lord Jesus Christ, Who is ready to judge *the* living and *the* dead at His appearing and His Kingdom: **Preach the Word!**...." (vs 1-2).

- What does this tell us?
- How can he preach the Word if he didn't have it written down?

This tells us at the time that Paul was writing to Timothy, that they had the Words of God! They had all the Epistles of the Apostle Paul.

1-Timothy 6:3: "If anyone teaches any different doctrine, and does not adhere to sound words, *even those* of our Lord Jesus Christ, and the doctrine *that is* according to Godliness, he is proud and knows nothing. Rather, he has a morbid attraction to questions and disputes over words, from which come envy, arguments, blasphemy, wicked suspicions, vain reasonings of men who have been corrupted in *their* minds and *are* destitute of the Truth... [sounds like 'Biblical scholars' today] ...*men* who believe that gain is Godliness. From such withdraw *yourself*" (vs 3-5).

The point is this: *Timothy had to have all the Gospels to know the sound words of Jesus Christ!* So, this whole thing that the Bible wasn't written until hundreds of years after the apostles, is nothing more than *a satanic lie* given by atheistic scholars who don't believe the Word of God and have a secret hidden agenda that they want to destroy the Word of God and corrupt it.

In *The Holy Bible in Its Original Order, A Faithful Version,* you can read the commentary, which absolutely proves that that's so, and that's their motive. There are very few honest scholars out there in the world, but just enough so that the Word of God and the history and preservation of the text will not be lost.

2-Timothy 4:2: "**Preach the Word!**"

What is a minister supposed to do? *Preach the Word!*

- not stories
- not his ideas
- not what he thinks

but the Word of God, which means in order *to preach the Word of God you have to have it!* We have the evidence right here that Timothy had:

- the Old Testament from a child
- the writings of the Apostle Paul

- the Gospels

So, by the time this second epistle is written, *every book of the New Testament was available to the New Testament Church* except the book of Revelation. That's amazing to understand.

"...**Be urgent**... [not slovenly, not ho-hum] ...**in season and out of season**..." (v 2).

What did we in Lev. 23? *That these are the Feasts of the LORD, which you shall proclaim in their seasons!* Therefore, **all Scripture is God-breathed!** This is absolute proof that they were keeping the Passover and the Holy Days in the early New Testament Church and that all of these pagan intrusions came later when the state religion was instituted by Emperor Constantine.

"...**convict, rebuke, encourage**, with all patience and doctrine. For there shall come a time when they will not tolerate sound doctrine..." (vs 2-3).

People don't like that: 'that's harsh, that's too rigid!' *You tell it to God! See if He will accept those excuses!*

"...but according to their own lusts..." (v 3). *That's where these things come from, people have lusts!* They want to have it **their** way! *They* ***don't*** *want to do God's way!* They want *their own* way! They want to be satisfied in *their* lusts!

"...they shall accumulate to themselves *a great number of* teachers, having ears itching *to hear what satisfies their cravings*; and they shall turn away their own ears from the Truth; and **they shall be turned aside unto myths**" (vs 3-4). *That's exactly what has happened!*

I got a letter where a man wrote and said:

Well, you know that in the New Testament there's no place that shows that we should keep the Feasts of the Old Testament.

As we have already seen in the messages leading up to the Passover and Feast of Unleavened Bread that, yes, right in 1-Cor. 5 you find a direct command by the Apostle Paul, the apostles to the Gentiles, writing and speaking to the Gentiles *commanding them to keep the Feast of Unleavened Bread because they kept the Passover!*

1-Corinthians 5:6: "Your glorying *is* not good...."

They were glorying about the situation with the man who had his stepmother in immoral sexual relations. But any kind of glorying is not good over things that are sin. It's a sin to say that God has delivered us to do all these abominations, meaning the pagan holidays as we already have seen and know.

"…Don't you know that a little leaven leavens the whole lump?" (v 6). *A little bit of sin starts it!*

That's why God uses leaven as a type of sin during the days of Unleavened Bread. He wants us to understand just like leaven is everywhere, *leaven is in the air!* Who's the 'prince of the power of the air' that brings people to sin? *Satan the devil!* Leaven is so common, it's in the basic food staples that we eat. It's in bread crackers, cakes, it's in all of the things that we just normally take for granted.

So, during the Feast of Unleavened Bread He wants us to *put out the leaven* and to *eat unleavened bread for seven days* as He has said so we learn the lesson that as *God has called us out of Egypt,* we have our part to do. If we don't put the leaven out of our homes, and I've seen this time and time again down through the years, that *when people don't put leaven out of their homes*—a simple little thing—*within a short period of time they no longer understand what sin is!* They redefine sin according to their own ideas, sin according to *their interpretation* of the Scriptures.

Verse 7. "Therefore, purge out the old leaven…"

We're to go get it out of our homes, and also there's a spiritual lesson here. *Purge out the old human nature!*

"…so that you may become a new lump…" [that you may *be molded into that new person in Christ*] …*even as you are unleavened*" (v 7)—*showing that they had their houses unleavened!* It couldn't mean anything other than that.

Here's the reason: Some people ask, 'Why do you keep the Feast of Unleavened Bread?' Turn right here, here's the answer:

"…For Christ our Passover was sacrificed for us" (v 7). *Because of Christ we keep the Feast of Unleavened Bread!*

Most people think 'because of Christ 'we keep Easter.' *God never said so!* 'Because of Christ we keep Lent. Because of Christ we keep Ash Wednesday.' *Where do you find that in the Bible? It's not there!* Those are things *of men who did not want to hear the Truth!*

We read in 2-Tim. 4 that *they wanted to turn to myths and lies* and have *new teachings that please men,* that accept all the sins of the world! That's what those are.

We keep the Feast of Unleavened Bread, put the leaven out of our homes, and eat unleavened bread seven days *because God said so; because Christ was our Passover Who was sacrificed for us.* So, *IF* you want to claim the sacrifice of Christ for the forgiveness of your sins *and you do not keep* the Feast of Unleavened Bread, and *you do not keep* the Passover, *you have no part with Him!* That's very clear! Here's the direct command:

Verse 8: "For this reason…"—*because of the fact of the sacrifice of Jesus Christ on the Passover Day!* That's why He's called our Passover.

"…let us keep the Feast…" (v 8). *There can be no doubt it's the Feast of Unleavened Bread!*

- it's *not* Easter
- it's *not* Lent
- it's *not* Sunday-keeping

It is the Feast!

"…not with old leaven, nor with *the* leaven of malice and wickedness, **but with *the* unleavened bread of Sincerity and Truth**" (v 8).

That's what God wants us to have. He wants us to have a nature that is filled with Truth from the Spirit of Truth by the God of Truth and Jesus Christ, *Who is the Way, the Truth, and the Life!*

The only way that that can be is if we understand that *we must have our natures unleavened spiritually that we become the new creature in Christ!* Eating the unleavened bread shows us that we are to live by every Word of God and to understand that God's way is the way that it is.

Now let's come to Psa. 34. Let's see something that's very important which ties in with the Feast of Unleavened Bread, and ties in with the meaning of living by every Word of God. This is New Testament doctrine here that we're going to read in Psa. 34. Very profound. Very important for us to understand. And this is the whole meaning of it. You see, Christ is the sinless One. Christ, Who knew no sin, became the sacrifice for us, and He is the One Whom we are able to continuously come to:

- to come to God the Father
- to have our sins forgiven
- to grow in grace and knowledge
- to understand the Word of God

Psalm 34:4: "I sought the LORD, and He answered me… [you've got to come to God] …and delivered me from all my fears." *We've got to trust God!* That's what the whole Feast of Unleavened Bread is picturing: *you trust God.*

Verse 5: "They looked to Him and were radiant; and their faces were not ashamed. This poor man cried, and the LORD heard, and saved him out of all his troubles. The angel of the LORD encamps around those who fear Him and delivers them" (vs 5-7).

Part of the blessings of God, the blessings that you hardly ever see or know or recognize. Maybe you can look back and see how angels may have delivered you from some things, but you don't know that they are there.

Verse 8: "**O taste and see that the LORD is good**…" *That's why we keep the Feast of Unleavened Bread!*

- we taste the Word of God
- we digest it *spiritually speaking*
- it becomes a part of us
- we think with the Word of God
- we have it written in our heart and mind

"…blessed is the man who takes refuge in Him" (v 8). *That's what we need to do!*

Verse 14 *shows part of how to keep the Feast of Unleavened Bread*: "Depart from evil… [put the leaven out] …and do good… [put righteousness in] …seek peace and pursue it. The eyes of the LORD are upon the righteous, and His ears are open to their cry" (vs 14-15).

Verse 18: "The LORD is near to the brokenhearted and saves those who are of a contrite spirit. Many are the afflictions of the righteous, but the LORD delivers him out of them all" (vs. 18-19). *Those are the promises that God gives for keeping the Feast of Unleavened Bread!*

We will follow the theme that *leaven equals sin,* and that we ourselves only change or become unleavened through Christ. Now here's where we begin. Let's understand what we are as human beings, and where God wants us to go. The truth is that *God is going to take something that is imperfect and He's going to perfect it!* He's going to take us who are sinful—and upon repentance and baptism, yielding to God and growing and overcoming—*perfect us and make us righteous!* It's quite a process that God is doing. Here's where it begins:

Romans 3:23: "For all have sinned, and come short of the glory of God… [all are sinners, none are exempt, and Christ is the only way out] …*but* are being justified freely by His grace through the redemption that *is* in Christ Jesus; Whom God has openly manifested *to be* a propitiation through faith in His blood, in order to demonstrate His righteousness, in respect to the remission of sins that are past…" (vs 23-25).

God is showing His righteousness, and that *righteousness* could also be called *justification* because He is taking those who are sinners and

making them in right standing with Him *by justification through the sacrifice of Jesus Christ and by His blood!*

Verse 26: "Through the forbearance of God; *yes,* to publicly declare His righteousness in the present time, that He might be just, and the One Who justifies the one who *is* of *the* faith of Jesus. Therefore, where *is* boasting? It is excluded. Through what law? *The law* of works? By no means! Rather, *it is* through a law of faith" (vs 26-27).

Then he also asks the question because of faith and because of grace:

Verse 31: "Are we, then, abolishing *the* Law through faith? MAY IT NEVER BE!…. [Greek: 'me genoito'] …Rather, we are establishing *the* Law"— *because they're written in our heart and mind, because we live by them!*

However, we still have a sinful nature. Even though we are justified, even though Christ died while we were yet sinners, even though we have the Holy Spirit shed abroad in our heart so we can develop:

- the patience
- the love
- the overcoming

We still have sin to fight!

Let's come to Rom. 7 and see the predicament that all human beings are in. One mistake that a lot of people make is that they focus on their sins because they have a sinful nature. We're going to see you have to get sin out, but not focus on sin, **but focus on Christ.** Then we're also going to see: How does God look at us? How can God put up with us with this sinful nature, which causes us to do things that we don't want to do? And we slip and fall in sin, yet we repent and we change, we come to God. Let's see how all of this works. Let's put it all together here.

Romans 7:7: "What then shall we say? *Is* the Law sin? MAY IT NEVER BE! But **I had not known sin <u>except</u> through the Law**…. [because law defines the sin]. …Furthermore, I would not have been conscious of lust, except *that* the Law said, 'You shall not covet.'"

But something happens when God begins to call an individual. Something happens in the minds of individuals once they have the Holy Spirit. That is they see how sinful sin is.

Verse 8: But sin, having grasped an opportunity by the commandment, worked out within me every *kind of* lust because apart from Law, sin *was* dead. For I was once alive without law; but after the commandment came, sin revived, and I died" (vs 8-9). *That is obviously through the operation of baptism!*

He didn't die a literal death and then was resurrected. That's what he's talking about. Of course, baptism is a death, *a covenant death into the death of Jesus Christ!* That's why we take the Passover.

Verse 11: "Because sin, having taken opportunity by the commandment, deceived me, and by it killed *me*. Therefore, the Law *is* indeed Holy, and the commandment Holy and righteous and good. Now then, did that which *is* good become death to me? MAY IT NEVER BE! But sin, in order that it might truly be exposed as sin in me by that which *is* good, was working out death; so that by means of the commandment, sin might become exceedingly sinful" (vs 11-13).

How is that possible? How is it possible that we're going along and we're living our lives in the world, we have no consciousness of sin. We know some things are right, and some things are wrong, but:

- we don't have a consciousness of sin
- we don't have a conviction of sin
- we don't have a need to repent of sin

Oh, when we do something wrong and we're caught doing something wrong, yeah we're sorry, *but that's not repentance of sin toward God!*

What changes? *It is the Holy Spirit of God!* Because when God begins to call someone He sends the Spirit to be with them. When they repent and are baptized the Spirit is within them. Here is what the Spirit does.

John 16 is talking about the activity and work of the Holy Spirit. Jesus was telling His disciples.

John 16:7: "But I am telling you the truth. It is profitable for you that I go away because if I do not go away, the Comforter will not come to you. However, if I go, I will send it to you. And when that one has come, it will convict the world concerning sin…" (vs 7-8).

- What gives us the conviction of sin in our lives?
- What brought the Apostle Paul to the point that he had this conviction of seeing how evil that human nature really was?
- *It was by the Holy Spirit of God!*

So, the truth is this: if you find that you're a sinner, and if you're convicted that you are a sinner, and if you find yourself doing like the Apostle Paul did here, doing things he didn't want to do but still did them:

- What is convicting you of that?

- Your thoughts? *No!*

The Holy Spirit that is <u>with</u> you, or <u>in</u> you!

Romans 7:14. "For we know that the Law is spiritual; but I am carnal, having been sold *as a slave* under sin; because what I am working out myself… [just what I do by myself] …I do not know…." (vs 14-15).

- Isn't that true?
- Don't we do a lot of things that we don't know why or what we do them for?

And a lot of them end up being sin!

"…For what I do not desire to do, this I do; moreover, what I hate, this *is what* I do. But if I am doing what I do not desire to do, I agree with the Law that *it is* good" (vs 15-16)—*because you can now see that your behavior needs to be changed!*

That's why we need to put out the sin. When we put the sin out, as we're going to see, we need to put righteousness in. The same Holy Spirit that convicts us of sin so we can repent and get rid of sin, it is the same Holy Spirit that gives us the power and strength to put righteousness in through Jesus Christ. That's what we're going to see is the way that it works.

Verse 17: "So then, I am no longer working it out myself; rather, it is sin *that is* dwelling within me."

All of us have sin. We'll see it's called the law of sin and death, and we have to overcome it. We can only overcome it through Christ.

Verse 18: "Because I fully understand that there is not dwelling within me—that is, within my fleshly being—*any* good. For the desire to do good is present within me; but how to work out that which is good, I do not find…. [within me] …For the good that I desire to do, I am not doing; but the evil that I do not desire to do, this I am doing. But if I do what I do not desire to do, I am no longer working it out myself, but sin *that is* dwelling within me" (vs. 18-20).

There is a solution, *and the solution is Christ,* and the solution is the Feast of Unleavened Bread after the Passover. Because once you have your sins forgiven, you've got to do something else. *That is you've got to do it God's way!*

Verse 21: "Consequently, I find this law *in my members*, that when I desire to do good, evil is present with me."

You can still find that today. You go along, you're doing something good and then all of a sudden here comes an evil thought out of the middle of nowhere. That's *the law of sin and death* working in you.

We're going to see *through Christ there is a way out!* What we need to focus on You see sometimes we get so 'beat sin out, get sin out of your life' that all people do is just look and see: where is the sin? Well you need to find out where the sin is. What do you do after that? *That's the rest of the story of the Feast of Unleavened Bread!* So, he says concerning this:

Verse 24: "O *what a* wretched man I am! Who shall save me from the body of this death?.... [we need to be saved from this, and only Christ can] ...I thank God *for His salvation* through our Lord Jesus Christ. Because of this, on the one hand, I myself serve the Law of God with *my* mind; but on the other hand, with the flesh, *I serve* the law of sin" (vs 24-25). *In other words it is the sin within your members that causes you to do this!*

Where do we stand before God?

This is what I want you to understand. This is what is so important that we need to realize what Christ does and how we stand before God and that's the whole meaning of the Feast of Unleavened Bread.

Romans 8:1: "Consequently ***there is* now no condemnation**..." I want you to repeat that.

You love God the Father, you accept Jesus Christ as your Savior, and we're going to see how there is no condemnation. *There's no condemnation!* You don't need to focus on the sin that has brought you down, but you focus on the solution, which is *Christ **in** you!*

When you see the sin, you put it out getting rid of the leaven. In order to replace that you have to eat unleavened bread. ***That's putting Christ in!*** That's why He has us eat unleavened bread for seven days, so that we have to understand and realize that God puts us in a very special category. There is no condemnation. The very fact that you have the law of sin and death in you and you are overcoming it, and you are looking to God to change you, there is no condemnation, because there is the forgiveness available. That's why we are in the grace of God.

Verse 1: "Consequently, *there is* now no condemnation to those who are in Christ Jesus, who are not walking according to *the* flesh, but according to *the* Spirit." *You're not just following the dictates of the flesh!*

Before you were converted that's what you were doing. You had no consciousness of good. You had no consciousness of God. You are not convicted because of sin. You just knew somewhat of right and wrong. But now with the Holy Spirit convicting you of sin, you see sin within you. *That's the Holy Spirit revealing it to you so you can change and repent and let Christ blot that out and forgive you and give you His Spirit!* Now, because you are doing that, you are walking in the Spirit and not in the flesh.

Verse 2: "Because the Law of the Spirit of Life in Christ Jesus has delivered me from the law of sin and death. For what *was* impossible for the Law to do… [because the Law has no power] …in that it was weak through the flesh, God having sent His own Son in *the* likeness of sinful flesh, and for sin condemned sin in the flesh" (vs 2-3). *So that*:

- God could give you His righteousness
- God could give you His Spirit
- God could give you His mind

Verse 4: "In order that the righteousness of the Law might be fulfilled in us, who are not walking according to *the* flesh, but according to *the* Spirit." *Now that's something!*

Let's see how this whole operation is done. Here's how it is accomplished. *Here is the way*:

1 John 1:6: "If we proclaim that we have fellowship with Him… [a lot of people do] …but we are walking in the darkness…" *And many are!*

They're not walking according to the commandments, because the commandment is Light, and the Spirit is Light, and Christ is Light. He is the Way, the Truth, and the Life. That's the way we are to live.

IF we're walking in darkness, *IF* we're keeping Sunday, Christmas and Easter, and all the things of the world, *you're walking in darkness!* You're not walking in the Light.

"…**We are lying to ourselves**…" (v 6). With the Holy Spirit within you, you cannot lie to yourself very long because *the Holy Spirit will convict you,* and through the graciousness of God lead you to repentance.

"…we are lying to ourselves, and we are not practicing the Truth. However, if we walk in the Light, as He is in the Light, *then* we have fellowship with one another, **and the blood of Jesus Christ, His own Son, cleanses us from all sin**" (vs 6-7).

Jesus said on the Passover night, telling His disciples, 'Now you are clean through the words that I have spoken.' And that was after they had partaken of the very first New Covenant Christian Passover.

- that's why we keep the Passover every year
- that's why we keep the Feast of Unleavened Bread every year

It cleanses us from all sin! That's why there's no condemnation through Jesus Christ.

We're going to see in just a minute, how we stand before God. **How does God look at you?** *You're going to be surprised!*

Verse 8: "If we say that we do not have sin, we are deceiving ourselves, and the Truth is not in us. If we confess our own sins…" (vs 8-9).

We have to go to God and confess our sins, *not to a priest!* It doesn't say to go to a priest and confess your sins, and then you are forgiven by him. And you run out and do 'hail Marys and our fathers' or whatever other kind of religious work that has been given to do. *That's not of God!* You confess your sins directly to God the Father through Jesus Christ.

"…He is faithful and righteous to forgive us our sins and to cleanse us from all unrighteousness" (v 9).

There's no condemnation if you are cleansed from all your sins, and cleansed from all unrighteousness. How can there be condemnation? *There isn't!*

Verse 10: "If we say that we have not sinned, we make Him a liar, and His Word is not in us."

Then he gives us encouragement; 1-John 2:1: "My little children, I am writing these things to you so that you may not sin. And *yet*, if anyone does sin… [because as we've covered with the law of sin and death we do sin] …we have an Advocate with the Father; Jesus Christ *the* Righteous; and He is *the* propitiation for our sins… [tie in Rom. 3] …and not for our sins only, but also for *the sins of* the whole world" (vs 1-2).

In order to understand how God is going to apply it to the whole world, and when he's going to apply it to the whole world, you need to keep the Feasts of God. *Here's a truth:*

- Passover, Unleavened Bread, and Pentecost tell you what God is doing with the Church.
- Trumpets, Atonement, Tabernacles and the Last Great Day tells you how God is going to solve the problem of the sins of the world, and when.

Keep that in mind! Very important!

How do you stand before God? I want you to grasp this. I want you to understand this. I want you to fully realize how God views you through Christ.

Ephesians 1:3: "Blessed *be* the God and Father of our Lord Jesus Christ, Who has blessed us with every spiritual blessing in the heavenly *things* with Christ."

- the Holy Spirit
- forgiveness of sin
- understanding the Word of God
- growing in the character of God
- how we grow and develop and build the very character and love of God within us

Verse 4 is a very important verse. It is translated correctly here in this new translation because there is what is called, as I have mentioned before, the middle voice verb, *showing that God has done something very special and very personal in our lives!*

Verse 4: "According as He has **personally chosen us for Himself**…" *That's a tremendous thing. God did not call you to condemn you!*

- God called you to forgive you
- God called you to change you
- God called you to convert you
- God called you to overcome sin
- God has called you to be in His Kingdom
- God has called you to be His very sons and daughters
- God has called you to share in His glory through Christ

There's no condemnation in that! That's the greatest thing that could ever be!

"…before *the* foundation of *the* world… [He had the plan already to go before He created the world] …in order that we might be Holy and blameless before Him in love" (v 4).

That's how you stand before God, Holy and blameless because of Christ! He's got a plan for us.

Verse 5: "Having predestinated us for sonship to Himself through Jesus Christ, according to the good pleasure of His own will."

God is dealing in your life according to the very good pleasure of what He has determined.

Verse 6: "To *the* praise of *the* glory of His grace, wherein He has made us objects of *His* grace in the Beloved *Son*; in Whom we have redemption through His blood, *even* the remission of sins…" (vs 6-7).

It all goes back to the blood of Jesus Christ, and it all goes back to our right standing with God through the sacrifice of Christ. This is tremendous, brethren! That's why there's no condemnation. That's why

- yes, we're to put sin out

- yes, we're to overcome sin.
- yes, we're to confess our sins and have forgiveness

but

- we need to grow
- we need to change
- we need to understand there is no condemnation

There's not one word of condemnation here!

"…according to the riches of His grace, which He has made to abound toward us in all wisdom and intelligence" (vs 7-8).

God wants you to know, God wants you to understand. He's given His Spirit, He's given His Word. That's fantastic. God wants you to have the joy of the Lord. He wants you to understand how He views you, and He does not condemn you. Now we're going to look at this just a little bit more here in just a minute.

Verse 9: "Having made known to us the mystery of His own will…"

- Do you understand the will of God?
- Do you understand the greatest secret that men can never grasp through everything that they do, try, work, and so forth

We've got the two robots up on Mars: Opportunity and Spirit. They're looking for water. They're looking for signs of life. Who knows what they'll find up there, but always remember this: even if they find water that does not mean there has been life, because there was not life in the water until God said, 'Let the water bring forth the fish and all the things that are in the water. So even if they find evidence of water that doesn't mean that there was life. He's got His plan; He's got His purpose.

Verse 9: "Having made known to us the mystery of His own will, according to His good pleasure, which He purposed in Himself." *God is working that plan!*

Let's understand something very important also how God looks at us and what He does for us. This is profound. This is something that is really absolutely marvelous. Here's what God has done for us.

Romans 5:17: "For if by the offence of one man [Adam] death reigned by the one [Adam], how much more shall those who receive the abundance of grace and the gift of righteousness…" *It's a fantastic gift to be put in right standing with God!*

- Have you ever in your own mind thought that *you* can be in right standing with God through Jesus Christ?

- That *you* can have imparted to you, imputed to you the very righteousness of Christ?

That's the only way that you can be Holy and without blame, *because that is imputing to you the very qualities of Jesus Christ!* That's why we are to have the joy and the understanding, and realize how great this salvation of God is and might receive

"…the abundance of grace and the gift of righteousness reign in life by the One Jesus Christ.) So then, even as by the one transgression condemnation *came* unto all men, in the same way also, by the one act of righteousness… [sacrifice and crucifixion of Christ, and His resurrection] …*shall* justification of life *come* unto all men" (vs 17-18). *Of course, that's in God's good time!*

Verse 21: "So that even as sin has reigned unto death, so also might the grace *of God* reign through righteousness unto eternal life through Jesus Christ our Lord."

God imputes the righteousness of Christ to you! That's what to understand. That's why the lawless grace of this world and what they do with it is absolutely wrong. Let's see what it shows we are to do.

- What are we to do with this?
- Wrap it up in a napkin and be all smug and say, 'Oh that's good, we stand before God blameless'?
- What are you to do?
- What is the obligation?

  - you put the sin out
  - you put the leaven out

but

  - you've got to put the unleaven in

Rom. 12:1 shows what it is to be, *that conversion is a process,* and God has given this right standing before Him that we are Holy and blameless before Him in love to inspire us to want to do what it tells us here.

Romans 12:1: "I exhort you, therefore, brethren, by the mercies of God, to present your bodies a living sacrifice, Holy *and* well-pleasing to God, which is your spiritual service."

  - to love Him
  - to grow in the fruits of the Spirit
  - to overcome the works of the flesh

That is your spiritual service!

Verse 2: "Do not conform yourselves to this world… [go back into the world] …but be transformed by the renewing of your mind…" *That's the conversion that takes place!*

- step-by-step
- day-by-day
- week-by-week
- month-by-month
- year-by-year

as you grow and overcome and walk in the ways of God!

"…**in order that you may prove**… [there's doing] …what *is* well pleasing and good, and the perfect will of God" (v 2).

Now let's see what we are to do with this carnal mind. What do you do when you're going along and all of a sudden there's an evil thought that comes along. You say to yourself, 'Where did that come from?' Well, it could come out of the depths of your own carnal mind.

- it could come because of 'the prince of the power of the air'
- it could come because there are evil spirits out there who want to bombard you with the missiles of evil that comes from Satan the devil and his demons

- What are you to do when that thought comes along?
- Are you to say, 'Oh, I must not be converted'? *No!*

Y*ou recognize it because of the Spirit of God! You are converted, but here is what you need to do*:

2-Corinthians 10:4: "For the weapons of our warfare *are* not carnal… [you're not going to solve this by doing things that are motivated by the flesh] …But mighty through God… [you are to use the weapons of God, and this is what he's talking about here]: …**To *the overthrowing of strongholds**.*"

That's referring to the carnal mind, because the carnal mind is the greatest stronghold of sin! Remember, we still have *the law of sin and death* in us. So, when these things pop up, here's what we are to do.

Verse 5: "Casting down *vain* imaginations…"

We are to take those thoughts, literally, mentally, and grab hold of them in the name of Jesus Christ and cast them down.

"…and every high thing that exalts itself against the knowledge of God, and bringing into captivity every thought into the obedience of Christ" (v 5). *It's a process!*

Those things are going to happen. The Spirit of God in you is going to convict you of the sin so that you can repent and cast it down.

Verse 6: "And having a readiness to avenge all disobedience, whenever your obedience has been fulfilled." *That's the process!*

Now let's see how we can put this into action even more. God expects us to do something. He will give us His Spirit to do it and accomplish it, which gives us the power to overcome.

That's why during the Feast of Unleavened Bread we put in the Word of God. Not only do we eat unleavened bread:

- we *put in Christ* Who is unleavened, sinless.
- we *put in the Word of God*, which gives us conviction
- we use the Spirit of God, which gives us power
- we realize that we have Satan to overcome
- we have the world to overcome
- we have ourselves to overcome

the most important one to overcome is **the self** *through the power and Spirit of God,* because we overcome Satan by the blood of Christ. So, here's what He expects us to do:

Colossians 3:1: "Therefore, if you have been raised together with Christ… [out of the watery grave of baptism] …seek the things that are above, where Christ is sitting at *the* right hand of God." *When you go pray, understand that. Realize that Christ is right there. Christ is*:

- our High Priest
- our Savior
- our Intercessor
- the One Who sends the Spirit
- the One Who petitions the Father
- He is the propitiation for our sins

all the things that have to do with Christ, *and those are all yours because He gave Himself for you!*

That ought to be a great humbling and overwhelming experience when you finally come to grasp and understand that when you're praying to God.

Verse 2: "Set your affection on the things that are above, and not on the things that are on the earth. For you have died… [through the watery grave of baptism] …and your life has been hid together with Christ in God" (vs 2-3).

Here's a promise. Notice how he gives this promise before he tells us what we need to do, because Paul wants us inspired.

- you can never overcome by beating the flesh.
- you can never overcome sin by focusing on sin.

- *you have to focus on Christ and the solution*

That's why he shows the goal:

Verse 4. "When Christ, *Who is* our life, is manifested, then you also shall be manifested with Him in glory.

He wants you to have the goal in mind before you start working on the things you need to work on:

- to give you motivation
- to give you inspiration
- to help you to understand how great God is and what He's doing

Verse 5: "Therefore, put to death your members which *are* on earth…" *Grab those thoughts, cast them down!* Take the lusts, get rid of them through the Spirit of Christ. These are the things:

"…sexual immorality, uncleanness, inordinate affection, evil desires, and covetousness, which is idolatry. Because of these things, the wrath of God is coming upon the sons of disobedience" (vs 5-6).

We don't want the wrath of God upon us, so put all of those things aside. This is the way, Paul says, that you used to live.

Verse 7: "Among whom you also once walked, when you were living in these things." *We're not to live in those!*

Paul goes through put off/put on; v 8: "But now you should also put off all *these* things… [these are the changing from carnal attitudes and carnal ways *to spiritual ways*] …wrath, indignation, malice, blasphemy, *and* foul language from your mouth."

Who's he talking to? *To converted Christians who have the Spirit of God,* but they still have *the law of sin and death* in them, and they have this fight that is going on. So, Paul is telling them how to overcome this, and how they can build the character of God.

Verse 9: "Do not lie to one another, *seeing that* you have put off the old man together with his deeds, and have **put on**…" [you put off all these and now you put on the new man; tie in with Rom. 12:1-2] …Put on the new man, who *is being renewed*… [it is a process, and it takes time] …in knowledge according to *the* image of Him Who created him; where there is neither Greek nor Jew, circumcision nor uncircumcision, barbarian *nor* Scythian, slave *nor* free; but Christ *is* all things, and in all" (vs 9-11).

IF you are Christ's it doesn't matter who you were before God called you! Christ is the all important thing.

Verse 12: "Put on then, as *the* elect of God, Holy and beloved… [because you are Holy and blameless before Him in love; that's why you're Holy and beloved] …Deep inner affections, kindness, humility, meekness, *and* long-suffering."

That's why God has brought together the weak of the world and all the problems that we have so that we can overcome, so that we can change.

Verse 13: "Forbearing one another, and forgiving one another if anyone has a complaint against another; even as Christ forgave you, so also you *should forgive*. And above all these things *put on* love, which is *the* bond of perfection" (vs 13-14).

That is the ultimate goal! ***The very love of God within us*** to motivate us in everything that we do—that's the bond of perfection.

Verse 15: "And let the peace of God rule in your hearts…"

- don't condemn yourself
- don't have a guilty conscience
- don't put yourself down

Come before God and Christ, confess your sins, let them be forgiven, walk in newness of life, pull all the vain imaginations down and cast them down and:

- *put in* the Word of God
- *put in* the love of God
- *put in* the character of God

Verse 16: "Let the Word of Christ dwell in you richly in all wisdom, teaching and admonishing one another in psalms and hymns and spiritual songs, singing with grace in your hearts to the Lord. And *in* everything… [this is the overall thing] …—whatever you do in word or in deed—*do* all in *the* name of *the* Lord Jesus, giving thanks to God and *the* Father by Him" (vs. 16-17). *That's what God wants us to do!*

How we live our lives!

Ephesians 5:1: "Therefore, be imitators of God, as beloved children."

- that's why we study the Word of God
- that's why we let God write it in our heart and mind, and our inward part

So that we can imitate God

- with His love
- with His goodness
- with His understanding

Verse 2: "And walk in love… [toward each other] …even as Christ also loved us… [there's no more profound love than this] …and gave Himself for us *as* an offering and a sacrifice to God for a sweet-smelling savor."

Then he says all these other things are the works of the flesh:

Verse 3: "But fornication and all uncleanness or covetousness, **do not permit it even to be named among you,** as is fitting for saints."

So, the true spiritual meaning of the Feast of Unleavened Bread is this:

- through Jesus Christ
- through renewing the New Covenant through the Passover
- through keeping the commandments of God and loving God with all your heart, mind, soul and being

There is no condemnation! You are Holy and without blame before Him in love!

Scriptures from *The Holy Bible in Its Original Order, A Faithful Version*

Scriptural References:

1) Leviticus 22:31-33
2) Leviticus 23:1-8
3) Deuteronomy 16:16-17
4) 2 Corinthians 9:6-8
5) John 14:6
6) John 6:53-57, 63-70
7) 2 Timothy 3:14-17
8) 2 Timothy 4:1-2
9) 1 Timothy 6:3-5
10) 2 Timothy 4:2-4
11) 1 Corinthians 5:6-8
12) Psalm 34:4-8, 14-15, 18-19
13) Romans 3:23-27, 31
14) Romans 7:7-9, 11-13
15) John 16:7-8
16) Romans 7:14-21, 24-25
17) Romans 8:1-4
18) 1 John 1:6-10
19) 1 John 2:1-2
20) Ephesians 1:3-9
21) Romans 5:17-18, 21
22) Romans 12:1-2
23) 2 Corinthians 10:4-6
24) Colossians 3:1-17
25) Ephesians 5:1-3

Scripture referenced, not quoted:

- Numbers 28
- John 15-16
- Matthew 16

FRC:cs
Transcription date unknown
Reformatted: bo—11/2030

CHAPTER TWENTY-FIVE

The Spiritual Battle in the Mind
First Day of Unleavened Bread
Fred R. Coulter

Greetings, everyone! Welcome to the Feast of Unleavened Bread! Here we are still going forward toward the Kingdom of God, and like it has been all down through the history of the Church, the expectation of the return of Jesus Christ is always out in the future.

How far, we don't know! But in the meantime, we are to continue to grow in grace. knowledge and understanding of the Word of God. We are to do it every Sabbath, every Holy Day, every Feast, in fact, *every day of our lives*, as we will see with this Feast of Unleavened Bread.

I want to show you the consistency of God as we find beginning in Exo. 23. I want you to see the pattern that God has set, and why that is so important.

Exodus 23:12: "Six days you shall do your work, and on the seventh day you shall rest, so that your ox and your donkey may rest, and the son of your handmaid, and the stranger, may be rejuvenated. And **be watchful in all that I have said to you**…." (vs 12-13).

Don't forget what God has said. Think of this, because the next verse with the Feast, and I want you to compare that with the holidays of the world.

"…And make no mention of the name of other gods, **neither let it be heard out of your mouth**" (v 13).

What happens when they substitute Sunday for the Sabbath? *They get all the holidays of the world, and the other gods and Satan the devil!* So cleverly packaged, so truly deceived that they don't even grasp it, though they know they are pagan.

Verse 14: "You shall keep a Feast unto Me three times in the year. You shall keep the Feast of Unleavened Bread. You shall eat unleavened bread seven days, as I commanded you, at the time appointed in the month *of* Abib, for in it you came out of Egypt. And no one shall appear before Me empty" (vs 14-15). *Then it lists the other Feast days!*

Exo. 34—this is after the golden calf. This is after God had to write the Ten Commandments all over again, because Moses broke the tablets when he saw what the children of Israel were doing. God had

him cut two more tablets of stone, take them, and God wrote the Ten Commandments again. Notice how consistent that God is:

Exodus 34:18: "You **shall keep** the Feast of Unleavened *Bread*. You **shall eat** unleavened bread seven days… [not an option] …as I commanded you, in the time of the month Abib, for in the month Abib you came out from Egypt."

Verse 21: "You shall work six days, but on the seventh day you shall rest. In plowing time and in harvest you shall rest. And you shall observe the Feast of Weeks, of the firstfruits of wheat harvest, and the Feast of Ingathering at the year's end. Three times in the year shall all your males appear before the Lord GOD, the God of Israel" (vs 21-23). *Consistent!*

Deut. 16—consistent again, because God is *the same yesterday, today and forever!* Remember that when anyone starts arguing about the holidays of this world, and that you don't need to keep the Feasts of God because 'we're under a New Covenant.' You can tell them that, 'yes, we're under a New Covenant so we can understand the Truth of the Bible.' Not that we can substitute the things of God with the things of Satan the devil.

Deuteronomy 16:16: "Three times in a year shall all your males appear before the LORD your God in the place which **He** shall choose: in the Feast of Unleavened Bread, and in the Feast of Weeks, and in the Feast of Tabernacles. And **they shall not appear before the LORD empty**, every man *shall give* as he is able, according to the blessing of the LORD your God, which He has given you" (vs 16-17).

So, when we take up the offering, which we will in a minute, look at:

- your blessings
- what God has done
- what God has given you
- how He has given understanding and Truth from His Word
- how He has dealt with you with His Spirit
- how God has given us the greatest and most precious promises of all

The ultimate goal of the Feast of Unleavened Bread is to become like God!

Leviticus 23:1: "And the LORD spoke to Moses, saying, 'Speak to the children of Israel and say to them, "*Concerning **the appointed Feasts** of the LORD…*"'" (vs 1-2).

These are ***appointed times,*** established by God in resetting the calendar on the fourth day of the re-creation week. That calendar is so accurate that you can go forward in time into perpetuity, and you can go back in time. Notice that the ministers and elders have no choice; they cannot add to and they can't take away from.

"…which **you shall proclaim** *to be* **Holy convocations, even these are <u>My</u> appointed Feasts**. Six days shall work be done, but the seventh day *is* the Sabbath of rest, a Holy convocation. You shall not do any work. It *is* a Sabbath to the LORD in all your dwellings" (vs 2-3). *Same thing: Exo. 23, Exo 34, Deut. 16!*

Verse 4: "These *are* the appointed Feasts of the LORD, Holy convocations, which you shall proclaim in their appointed seasons. In the fourteenth *day* of the first month… [according to the Calculated Hebrew Calendar] …between the two evenings… [between sunset and dark] …is the LORD'S Passover" (vs 4-5).

We've already had that, the Lord's Passover and *the Night to Be Much Observed to the Lord.* That's not some sort of feast that some man invented. That's what God says it is.

Verse 6: "And on the fifteenth day of the same month *is* the Feast of Unleavened Bread to the LORD. **You must eat unleavened bread seven days**. On the first day you shall have a Holy convocation. You shall not *do any servile* work *therein*, but you shall offer a fire offering to the LORD seven days…." (vs 6-8).

Since there are no more sacrifices, we take up offerings on the Holy Days. This is the beginning of the Feast season, which started with the Passover. But now the beginning of the Feast to give us meaning and understanding as to:

- why we are here
- where we are going
- what God is doing
  - ✓ to us
  - ✓ through us
  - ✓ in us

To prepare us for the Kingdom of God!

With that in mind and remembering the blessings that God has given you, we'll take a pause and take up an offering now.

(pause for offering)

The greatest mystery of man and all mankind in the world is:

- Why are human beings so well-intended, but so evil?
- Why do they have such great potential, and yet, it all ends in catastrophe?

That's the whole reason for the Feast of Unleavened Bread!

Leaven during the Feast of Unleavened Bread pictures sin, human nature, evil, which is naturally in us. But the reason that it is leavened is because the action of leaven cannot be seen, but you can see the results of it. When bread is rising, with leaven in it, you can see the action of the leaven making the bread rise. But you can't see the leaven.

Likewise, why are human beings evil? *That goes back to the original sin of Adam and Eve and their disobeying the voice of God!* You know what happened there; God gave His judgment against Adam, Eve and the serpent, and also gave the first prophecy of the coming of the Messiah to save man from his evil.

Let's look at what happened to all human beings, every one of us all the way down through history. We know from the account in Gen. 3 that that sin was so grievous, so absolutely horrible right before God that the two that God created with His hands and gave into their minds a language so He could communicate with them. He gave them every opportunity in the Garden of Eden, but they turned their backs on God and followed Satan the devil.

So, the whole environment was changed. Now thistles and thorns being in the field of crops, and with sorrow and difficulty and labor and things like this. Not only that, it was passed on to all their progeny, all mankind, all men and women everywhere, every nation, makes no difference.

Romans 5:12: "Therefore, as by one man… [Adam] …sin entered into the world…" *This is human sin!* It's not talking about Satan's sin, which occurred before the creation of Adam and Eve.

"…and by means of sin *came* death… [that's what God said to them, 'dust you are and unto dust you shall return'] …and in this way death passed into all mankind…" (v 12).

Every man and woman has the death gene! That's why Paul writes, 'As in Adam we all die!' Only through Christ shall we all be made alive, *with eternal life!* Adam could have stopped it when Eve said, 'This looks good, let me pick it.' Adam should have told her to throw it down and don't bother with it. He should have turned around and cast the serpent out of the Garden of Eden. *But he didn't!*

God judged Adam because Adam *listened to the voice of his wife,* which is actually the repeating of what Satan said, *instead of listening to God! So, sin—or death—passed into all mankind!*

"...*and it is* **for this reason that all have sinned**" (v 12). *When you have a nature of death, you also have a nature of sin!* Without the Holy Spirit of God, with the world going the way that it did and following the way of Cain, and coming on down to the time of the Flood.

Just like Jesus said, 'As it was in the days of Noah before the Flood, so shall it be in the days of the coming of the Son of man.' They were eating and drinking, and building and all of this. They didn't know that the Flood was coming until it came upon them! Likewise, it's going to be with the return of Christ.

I want to focus in on the conduct of people. I want you to think about the world today as I read this, and think about all the things that come along that look really, really good, but are enticements to evil.

Genesis 6:5: "The Lord saw..." *God has seven spirits traveling all the time seeking those who are seeking God!* He knows what's going on everywhere at all times through that and through the power of His angels and through Satan the devil and the demons.

"...that the wickedness of man *was* great on the earth, and every imagination..." (v 5).

Have you ever just sat down to think and your imagination is just kind of running wild. What do you usually end up with? *Something that's not too good!* Once in a great while you may have a good thought that way, but that's rare.

"...of the thoughts of his heart *was* only evil continually" (v 5).

- Isn't that the way that the world is today?
- Isn't that the way that the Christianity of the world is today?
- Isn't that the way of the societies?
- Isn't that the way of the governments? *Yes!*

That's why God has called us *so that we*—through loving God and keeping His commandments, Sabbath and Holy Days—*can be converted and changed* so that we can rule the world with Christ! *So, the stakes are high!*

So bad was it that God was sorry, v 6: "And **the LORD repented that He had made man on the earth,** and He *was* grieved in His heart. And the LORD said, 'I will destroy man whom I have created from the face of the earth, both man and beast, and the crawling thing, and the fowl of the air;

for I repent that I have made them.' **But Noah found grace in the eyes of the LORD**" (vs 6-8). *We're all here because of Noah!* You need to think about that!

Let's see what Jesus said that human nature was really like. I want to call your attention to something that we find in another account of when the rich man came to Jesus and said, 'Good Master...' Jesus said, 'Why do you call Me good. There is none good but God.'

Hold on! He was God manifested in the flesh, but why did He not count Himself good? *Because He had to carry the law of sin and death within Him in order to condemn sin and death in the flesh!* So, He was not good as God is good as a spirit being. Let's see what Jesus said about human nature, and this is from birth. All you have to do is read Psa. 51. It tells you that this is the natural state of human beings:

Mark 7:21: "For from within, out of the hearts of men... [and women] ...go forth evil thoughts..."—*all kinds of evil thoughts!*

Who is one of the great purveyors today—not the only one—that introduces children to sin and evil under the guise of fun, games and excitement? *Walt Disney! Universal Studios! Television! Movies! All of these things!* Look at them, they're all filled with evil.

A lot of evil thoughts seem very good to people, because they get a benefit. Remember, *Satan always gives a benefit,* but that benefit is a *curse from within!*

"...adulteries, fornications, murders" (v 21)—*the leading crimes everywhere in the world with all human beings in every nation and society!*

Verse 22: "Thefts, covetousness, wickednesses, guile, licentiousness, an evil eye, blasphemy, pride, foolishness; all these evils go forth from within, and *these* **defile a man**" (v 22-23).

That's why Christ came, to save us from our sins. Conversion is not just so that we have better exterior behavior. There are a lot of people who have good behavior. But it is the conversion of the heart and the mind, and that's what God wants. *That we will see is the meaning of the Feast of Unleavened Bread!*

1-Cor. 4 helps to understand about:

- the sin within us
- the righteousness that we need to follow
- what God wants us to do
- why leaven is pictured as a type of sin

It's because it puffs up!

1-Corinthians 4:6: "Now these things, brethren, I have applied to Apollos and myself for your sakes; that in us you may learn not to think *of men* beyond what is written, **so that no one among you is** <u>**puffed up**</u> **on behalf of one *of us* against the other**."

That's what they were doing! 'I'm of Apollos, I'm of Paul, I'm of Christ, I'm of Peter, I'm of whatever…' *That's puffed up!*

Verse 7: "For what makes you superior *to others*? And <u>**what do you have that you did not receive?**</u>…."

I want you to think about that statement in everything that you have. Everything you have you have received beginning with your very being, and that came from God. Everything else came from God came through other people, and God has provided that, so that we don't get all puffed up, leavened up to exalt men! That's the opposite of what Christ wants. They were so puffed up that they were about ready for the Kingdom of God. *It doesn't work that way!*

"…But if you also received *it,* why are you boasting as if you did not receive *it?* Now you are satiated. Now you have been enriched. You have reigned without us…. [they were thinking that they were better than the apostles] …And I would that you did reign, so that we also might reign with you. For I suppose that God has made us apostles last, as it were appointed to death; for we have become a spectacle to the world, both to angels and to men. We *are* fools for the sake of Christ, but you *are* wise in Christ…" (vs 7-10).

- Isn't that the way it becomes?
- Isn't that why God had to punish His Church and scatter it?
- *Yes, indeed!*

"…we *are* weak, but you *are* strong; you *are* glorious, but we *are* without honor" (v 10). *What a thing that Paul had to fight!*

Verse 11: "To the present hour we both hunger and thirst, and are naked, and are buffeted, and wander without a home; and we labor, working with our own hands. When railed at, we bless; when persecuted, we bear *it;* when reviled, we entreat; for unto this day we are as *the* refuse and *the* off-scouring of the world" (vs 11-13). *He had a purpose in writing that!*

We will see what that is. To get to the very heart and core of human nature, and why it needs to be converted and changed. That's what the Feast of Unleavened Bread is all about. *That we do not stay with the way that we are! We have to* ***continually***:

- shed the evil

- shed the things of the flesh

and learn the things of God and the things of the Spirit that are far more important than anything else!

Verse 14: "I do not write these things to make you ashamed, but as my beloved children I warn *you.* For you might have ten thousand tutors in Christ, but *you do* not *have* many fathers; for in Christ Jesus I did beget you through the Gospel" (vs 14-15).

That doesn't make him a father, he's just using an analogy!

Verse 16: "Therefore, I am exhorting you to be imitators of me." *Later we will see that Paul told the Ephesians to be* **imitators of God!**

Verse 17: "For this cause I sent to you Timothy, who is my beloved son, and faithful in *the* Lord, who will remind you of my ways that *are* in Christ, exactly as I teach everywhere in every church. Now, some of you are puffed up… [filled with vanity and great ideas of the flesh and mind] …as though I were not coming to you; but I shall come to you shortly, if the Lord wills; and **I will know not** *merely* **the words of those who are puffed up,** <u>**but the power**</u>" (vs 17-19).

The power and Spirit of God is what we're looking for; not human persuasion, not human things, *but what God wants us to do!*

Verse 20: "For the Kingdom of God *is* not in words, but in power. What do you desire?…. [they were really in bad shape, so Paul was giving them an option] …Shall I come to you with a rod… [correct you, verbally beat you up so you will repent] …or in love and a spirit of meekness?" (vs 20-21).

Why did Paul say that? *Because they were starting to make a carnal religion out of the way of God!* They were allowing sin, disaster, arguments, competitiveness and quarrels against each other.

1 Cor. 5 becomes a very important chapter for the Feast of Unleavened Bread

1 Corinthians 5:1: "*It* is commonly reported… [and known] …*that there is* sexual immorality among you, and such immorality as is not even named among the Gentiles—*allowing* one to have *his own* father's wife"—*incest with the step-mother!*

Verse 2: "<u>**You are puffed up**</u>…" *Same thing that we have today with this world of the alphabet perversion!* There are so many genders that you have to take every letter of the 26 letters of the English alphabet and that will stand for some perversion of sex.

"…and did not grieve instead, so that he

who did this deed might be taken out of your midst. For I indeed, being absent in body but present in spirit, have already judged *concerning* him who has so *shamelessly* committed this *evil deed* as if I were present: In the name of our Lord Jesus Christ, when you are gathered together, and my spirit, together with the power of our Lord Jesus Christ. To deliver such a one to Satan for *the* destruction of the flesh, that the spirit may be saved in the day of the Lord Jesus" (vs 2-5).

That's the total power of correction that the Church has: *disfellowshipment!* **You cannot have people living in gross sin while strutting around as righteous creatures!**

Verse 6: "To deliver such a one to Satan for *the* destruction of the flesh, that the spirit may be saved in the day of the Lord Jesus. Your glorying *is* not good. Don't you know that a little leaven leavens the whole lump?"

This is why we have the Sabbath every week, and we have the annual Feasts every year when they come, because sin during the Feast of Unleavened Bread is pictured as leaven! If you don't nip the sin in the bud and get rid of it, then it leavens and leavens! Look at what happened during the days of Solomon.

Solomon was so evil with all of his wives and concubines, and false religions, incense burning and temple building for their gods, that God had to take away the ten northern tribes from him because of his evil!

If you don't stop sin in the beginning, it will grow and become worse! That's the whole lesson of the Feast of Unleavened Bread!

Verse 7: "Therefore, purge out the old leaven…" *The attitude of the man living in sexual immorality and having that sin within the congregation,* **purge it out!**

"…so that you may become a new lump, *even* as you are unleavened…." (v 7).

Here's a good example. They were unleavened in their homes, because we're to get rid of the leaven in our homes. But they put up with this sexual immorality as a good thing! Why do we do all of this that we are doing, and here's the crux of the whole matter up to this point:

"…**For Christ our Passover was sacrificed for us**" (v 7). *His shed blood for the forgiveness of sin! His stripes for the healing of our sicknesses!* God manifested in the flesh, the One Who gave the law of sin and death into Adam and Eve and passed on to all human beings.

Now He came and took it upon Himself and lived a perfect life and didn't sin. He was crucified and His shed blood and body was the perfect sacrifice for the sin of the whole world!

But it's *not yet* given to the whole world! *It is now given to the firstfruits, those of us whom God has called at this time!*

Verse 8: "**For this reason**…"—*based on the very fact that Christ was our Passover, crucified on the Passover Day—the 14th day of the 1st month!*

"…let us keep the Feast… [he describes it here, the Feast of Unleavened Bread] …not with old leaven… [not with the old sins that you still have in your life] …nor with *the* leaven of malice and wickedness… [all these things within your mind] …**but with *the* unleavened *bread* of sincerity and Truth**." *That's what God wants!*

- His Word is Truth
- His Spirit is Truth
- Christ is the Truth, the Life and the Way
- The Word of God is the Truth

All of this must be taken in to transform our mind and our life, and to be eaten! The Word of God says, *'Taste and see that the Lord is good.'* That means His Word!

- it will nourish us spiritually
- it will teach us mentally
- it will correct us when we sin
- it will encourage us when we're discouraged

All of this is in the Word of God, and God has given all of this to us now! We, in this generation, have the entire Word of God.

- What are we going to do with it?
- Are we going to be like Corinthians and let sin abound in the congregation and just let it be?

or

- Are we going to love and serve God, and do what He wants?

That's the question! The reason that we keep the Feast of Unleavened Bread is because that unleavened bread pictures sinless food!

In Gal. 5 there were quite a few things at stake, as we've covered in the Galatians series, but one of them was circumcision. We have covered that, but those of the Pharisaical party said, 'It's impossible to be saved without physical circumcision.' *That's not true!* We're going to show that it's impossible to be save without *spiritual circumcision of the heart!*

Galatians 5:9: A little leaven leavens the whole lump. I am persuaded concerning you in *the* Lord that you will be otherwise minded; and he who troubles you shall bear the judgment, whoever he may be. But I, brethren, if I still proclaim circumcision, why am I yet being persecuted? Then the offense of the cross has been taken away. I would *that* they would even make themselves eunuchs—those who are throwing you into confusion" (vs 9-12).

- Do we have confusion today because of false doctrine within the Churches of God? *Yes!*
- Why is that? *Because they are not rightly dividing the Word of God and truly following in an unleavened sense!*
  - ✓ changing the meaning of the Bible
  - ✓ changing the meaning of doctrine

WOE to those who do that! Doctrine is important and we have to:

- guard the Truth
- guard the doctrine
- guard the teaching
- guard our mind
- guard our lives

All of that together!

Verse 13: "For you have been called unto freedom, brethren; only do not *use* this freedom for an occasion to the flesh; rather, serve one another with love. For the whole Law is fulfilled in this *commandment*: 'You shall love your neighbor as yourself'" (vs 13-14).

Notice what Paul warns if there's leaven within the congregation, *spiritual leaven,* and you're not loving the brethren as yourself, and you're not loving the brethren as Christ has loved us, what happens?

Verse 15: "But if you bite and devour one another, watch out *lest* you be consumed by one another."

How do we overcome that? *We've all gone through this!* That's why we need the Feast of Unleavened Bread each year, so we can cleanout all the leaven that accumulates, that we have allowed because we haven't been diligent enough to put it away regularly. Paul says, 'Here's the solution':

Verse 16: Now *this* I say, **walk by *the* Spirit,** and you will not fulfill the lust of the flesh." *Here Paul is showing that the spiritual battle is in the mind! IF you walk by the Spirit:*

- loving God
- continually growing in grace and knowledge
- using the Spirit of God to lead and guide you

THEN you're not going to fulfill the lust of the flesh!

Paul shows that it's a *spiritual battle!* So,

let's understand that the Spirit of God within us is that which convicts us of sin. We've all got a whole lifetime of sin piled up in our mind! *That has to be expunged!* We will see how Paul says that is to be done.

Verse 17: "For the flesh lusts against the Spirit, and the Spirit against the flesh; and these things are opposed to each other, so that you cannot do those things you wish to do. But if you are led by *the* Spirit, you are not under *works of* law" (vs 17-18)—*because God's Spirit will lead you!*

Then Paul lists all the works of the flesh! Because you find sin within, don't get discouraged; that is God's Spirit revealing it to you. If you did not have the Spirit of God in you, you really wouldn't know that that was sin. There would be no way. So, don't be discouraged because *it's God Spirit helping you to see the evil that is still within so you can repent of it and overcome it!*

Romans 8:1: "Consequently, *there is* now no condemnation to those who are in Christ Jesus, who are not walking according to *the* flesh, but according to *the* Spirit."

We will see what that means and how—through the Feast of Unleavened Bread and drinking in of Truth and righteousness and God's way—that we

- overcome the sin
- get it out of our lives
- grow in grace and knowledge

Romans 8:1: "Consequently, *there is* now no condemnation to those who are in Christ Jesus…"

That is having this battle going on between your mind and your thoughts, **and bringing your thoughts into captivity to Christ!** With the Spirit of God, the Spirit of God is revealing those things to you so you can repent. If you repent there is no condemnation.

"…**who are not walking according to *the* flesh,** but according to *the* Spirit" (v 1). *If you're walking according to the Spirit it means that:*

- God is first in your life
- you want to do the things that please Him
- you obey His voice
- you keep His commandments
- you keep His Sabbath and Holy Days
- you are growing in grace and knowledge through:
  - ✓ prayer
  - ✓ study
  - ✓ living

Verse 2: "Because the law of the Spirit of

Life in Christ Jesus has delivered me from the law of sin and death." *He didn't take it away, but* **He has given deliverance**:

- through Christ
- through repentance
- through learning how to live righteously from the Word of God

Verse 3: "For what *was* impossible for the Law to do…" *Let's stop right here and understand Law!*

Law tells us what to do and what not to do, *but law has no power to make you do one thing or the other!* **But God's Spirit has the power,** that's the key.

"…in that it was weak through the flesh, God having sent His own Son in *the* likeness of sinful flesh, and for sin, condemned sin in the flesh" (v 3)—*and that flesh was the flesh of Christ!* So, it's already been condemned.

- that's why God is *willing to forgive*
- that's why there is *overcoming*
- that's why there is *repentance*

All of those things are important because they come through the motivation of the Spirit of God!

The reason that Christ came was for this, v 4: "In order that the righteousness of the Law might be fulfilled in us…"

The perfect spiritual nature of the Law becomes fulfilled in us through the power of God's Spirit. *But* only to those who are converted.

"…**who are not walking according to** *the* **flesh**… [who are the unconverted] …but according to *the* Spirit" (v 4). *That's*:

- the love of God
- the laws of God
- the commandments of God
- the Truth of God

Verse 5: "For those who walk according to the flesh mind the things of the flesh…" *They wouldn't even be concerned with any of those thoughts, because they couldn't know or understand*:

- what is right and what is wrong
- what is true and what is not true
- what is evil and what is righteous

It's an impossibility!

"…but those who walk according to *the* Spirit mind the things of the Spirit" (v 5)—*that's the things of God!*

In God's way of life, we're to grow in grace and knowledge, have the laws and commandments written in our heart and mind so that we can walk in the Spirit, *and do those things that are motivated by*:

- the Spirit of God
- the love of God
- the Truth of God

That's spiritual-mindedness!

Verse 6: "For to be carnally minded *is* death… [there's no salvation] …but to be spiritually minded *is* life and peace… [with God now] …because the carnal mind *is* enmity against God, for it is not subject to the Law of God; neither indeed can it *be*. But those who are in *the* flesh cannot please God" (vs 6-8). *It's impossible to please God without the Spirit of God!*

They may be able to do some 'good' things, *but that* **has nothing to do**:

- with conversion
- with overcoming
- with loving God

Verse 9: "However, **you are not in** *the* **flesh, but in** *the* **Spirit,** **if** *the* **Spirit of God is indeed dwelling within you.** But if anyone does not have *the* Spirit of Christ, he does not belong to Him." *That's quite a thing!* This is why the Feast of Unleavened Bread:

- we get rid of the sin
- we have our mind converted
- we have our mind changed
- we are conscious of truth
- we are conscious of the love of God
- we are conscious of the things of God

because we are minding the things of the Spirit of God! That's the whole purpose of Unleavened Bread.

Let's see how this is done; let's see the spiritual action of God within our mind when we repent and are baptized and receive the Spirit of God. There is something that happens in our mind that is unseen and unfelt, but it happens. The Spirit of God: if we are to grow in grace and knowledge and the Spirit of God. How is this done? *We will see that this is called the circumcision of the heart!*

Colossians 2:6: "Therefore, as you have received Christ Jesus the Lord, be walking in Him…"—*walking in the way of the Lord!* Look at all the Psalms that we have covered that He will:

- direct your paths
- direct your thoughts
- guide your way

_IF_ you're walking in Him, that will happen!

- yes, we'll have trials
- yes, we'll have difficulties
- yes, we'll have things we have to overcome

That's all part of being perfected! As long as we are in the flesh we're still in the process of being perfected.

Verse 7: "Being rooted and built up **in Him,** and being confirmed in the faith, exactly as you were taught, abounding in it with thanksgiving."

Think of everything that we have with the Word of God. Today we have so much, and yet, you need to understand that even if we have many, many different thing, many booklets, many books, many studies, these are all necessary for us to grow in grace and knowledge.

We can't say, 'Look at all that we have, we've got it made.' _Nonsense!_ **_The only time we will have it made is at the resurrection!_** Keep that in mind! We know that Satan is always coming around trying to knock down what Christ has built up in us. He does this through different things:

- by people
- by means
- by practices
- etc.

Verse 8: "**Be on guard**… [we always have to have our guard up] …**so that no one takes you captive through philosophy…**"—_the religion of this world!_

Let me state a truth that you already know: ***all philosophy is logical to the human mind, but all logic of philosophy is not true to the Word of God! But all of the Word of God is spiritually logical!*** I'll just let you take those things and think on that!

"…**and vain deceit, according to the traditions of men**… [it can be an old tradition or a new tradition] …according to the elements of the world… [the way the world thinks, believes] …and **not according to Christ**."

It's logical by philosophy to have Sunday as a day of worship. ***But it is not Truth!*** and ***It's not according to Christ!*** Who declared Himself to be the Lord of the Sabbath? _None other than Jesus Christ!_ Man was not made for the Sabbath, but the Sabbath was made for man, therefore, the Son of man is Lord of the Sabbath Day, ***not Sunday!*** But it sounds logical, but it's not true. ***Nor is logical according to the Word of God!***

Verse 9: "For in Him dwells all the fullness of the Godhead bodily." **Do you want to know how to become like God?** _It tells us here that it's_

through Christ!

Verse 10: "And you are complete in Him, Who is the Head of all principality and power in Whom you have also been circumcised with _the_ circumcision not made by hands, in putting off the body of the sins of the flesh by the circumcision of Christ" (vs 10-11).

This is the circumcision of the heart! How is that done?

Verse 12: "Having been buried with Him in baptism, by which you have also been raised with _Him_ through the inner working of God, Who raised Him from the dead. For you, who were _once_ dead in _your_ sins and in the uncircumcision of your flesh, He has _now_ made alive with Him, having forgiven all your trespasses. He has blotted out the note of debt against us _with_ the decrees _of our sins_, which was contrary to us; and He has taken it away, having nailed it to the cross" (vs 12-14).

Now let's see how Paul describes it another way. This is the way that God:

- calls us out of the world
- gives us His Holy Spirit
- changes our heart and mind

It' through **_the circumcision of the heart!_** That takes away the raw carnality of the heart of flesh!

Here's where were when God started working with us, every single one of us:

Ephesians 2:1: "Now, you were dead in trespasses and sins… [that's why Jesus said, 'Let the dead bury their dead'—_they're spiritually dead_] …in which you walked in times past according to the course of this world, according to the prince of the power of the air… [Satan the devil] …**the spirit that is now working within the children of disobedience**" (vs 1-2). _Satan is training their minds_:

- with his way
- with his thoughts
- with his religion
- with his logic
- with his rebellion against God

It all sounds so good to the carnal mind! But notice what it really is:

Verse 3: "Among whom also we all once had our conduct in the lusts of our flesh, doing the things willed by the flesh and by the mind…" _A lot of good discipline of the mind_:

- to do better
- to become better
- to increase
- to be more successful

- to make more money
- to be stronger
- to be thinner
- to be more beautiful

Whatever! __*All of those things are not of Christ!*__ They may have a temporary benefit, but they're still all sin, *because they don't lead to life!*

"…and were by nature *the* children of wrath, even as the rest *of the world*" (v 4).

Then all of a sudden, one day something happened! *God intervened in your life!*

Verse 4: "But God, Who is rich in mercy because of His great love with which He loved us, even when we were dead in *our* trespasses, has made *us* alive together with Christ. (*For* you have been saved by grace.)"

The love and grace came with the Spirit of God and began to deal in your life, and then led you to baptism, after repenting, and the receiving of the Holy Spirit of God. *God has a great plan for us!*

Verse 8: "For by grace you have been saved through faith…"

- you came to repentance
- you believed in Christ
- you believed in the commandments of God
- you saw your sins
- you abhorred yourself
- you abhorred your thoughts

And you had them all buried in the watery grave of baptism! When that happened you were *co-crucified with Christ! An amazing spiritual operation!*

"…and this *especially* is not of your own selves; *it is the gift of God*… [here's a verse that's a little tricky]: …not of works… [*our works, our ways or the traditions of men*] …so that no one may boast. For **we are His workmanship**…" (vs 8-10). *Christ is doing a work in each one of us! Every single one of us!*

"…being created in Christ Jesus unto *the* good works that God ordained beforehand in order that we might walk in them" (v 10). *That is the way of the Truth! Also called __the way of the Lord!__*

- through our yielding to God
- through prayer and study
- through keeping the commandments of God
which are the works He wants us to walk in
- through changing, repenting, growing and overcoming
- through keeping the Sabbath and Feasts of God

we are developing and growing in the mind of Christ in preparation for the day of the resurrection!

That's what it's all about, and it begins with the Feast of Unleavened Bread. Quite a thing indeed! Let's see how Paul writes of this, and puts it all together for us, *so that we know* **that:**

- we have the Spirit of God
- God is working with us
- God is leading us
- God is teaching us
- God is giving us of His way

Colossians 1:9: "For this cause we also, from the day that we heard *of it*, do not cease to pray for you and to ask that you may be filled with the knowledge of His will… [the more we study the Word of God, the more we have the knowledge of His will] …in all wisdom and spiritual understanding."

All of that comes from God. This is not knowledge to puff us up and make us great of ourselves. *It is knowledge to make us spiritually strong in the Lord!* Notice that it depends on how we're living, and the way that we live:

Verse 10: "That you may **walk worthily of the Lord**…" *That's why we pray every day that*:

- we walk worthily of the Lord
- keep His commandments
- do what is right
- repent of our sins
- grow and overcome

"…unto all pleasing, being fruitful in every good work and growing in the knowledge of God" (v 10). *That's what God wants!*

Listen! There is so much in the Word of God for us that God wants us to learn, that we have to study and re-study, and go over the Word of God over and over again. *There is no way that we can glean*—even with the greatest minds that could possibly be—*all that God has in His Word for us!*

It's a marvelous and a fantastic thing! Brethren, we all ought to be growing in knowledge and grace. I'm still learning things. Never can we say that 'I've been in the Church for so long, Satan has no interest in me.' *That becomes dangerous thinking!*

Verse 11: "Being strengthened with all power… [the power of God] …according to the might of His glory, unto all endurance and long-suffering with joy."

So, there's going to be difficult times! But with joy, because we see the goal, the Kingdom of

God, being sons and daughters of God, living with God forever!

Verse 12: "Giving thanks to the Father, Who has made us qualified for the share of the inheritance of the saints in the Light."

Isn't that amazing? God the Father Himself is dealing directly in each one of our lives individually. That's something to think about. It doesn't matter who you are or where you've been or what you have done.

- it matters what God is doing with you *now*
- how you are growing in grace and knowledge *now*
- how you are overcoming *now*

Take that every day, day-by-day, by week, by month, by year for however long we may live in the flesh!

Notice what the Father has done. This is quite a statement here.

Verse 13: "**Who has personally rescued us from the power of darkness**…"—*the rule of Satan the devil!* Think about that! God the Father Himself has dealt in our lives individually and particularly to accomplish that.

"…and has transferred *us* unto the Kingdom of the Son of His love" (v 13). *We're not in it, but we are under it!*

Verse 14: "In Whom we have redemption through His own blood… [on a continuous basis] …*even* the remission of sins… [that's an amazing thing] …Who is *the* image of the invisible God, *the* Firstborn of all creation… [by the resurrection of the dead] …because by Him were all things created, the things in heaven and the things on earth, the visible and the invisible, whether *they be* thrones, or lordships, or principalities, or powers: **all things were created by Him and for Him**" (vs 14-16). *And we have a part in that!* That's what's so important!

Verse 17: "And He is before all, and by Him all things subsist…. [Christ is in charge] …And **He is the Head of the Body, the Church**… [no man; we all submit and yield to Christ] …Who is *the* Beginning, *the* Firstborn from among the dead so that in all things He Himself might hold the preeminence" (vs 17-18).

Christ is always going to be there at the right hand of God the Father! An amazing thing, indeed!

Verse 19: "For it pleased *the Father* that in Him all the fullness should dwell; and having made peace through the blood of His cross… [that we can have peace with God the Father and Jesus Christ] …by Him to reconcile all things to Himself; by Him,

whether the things on the earth, or the things in heaven" (vs 19-20).

That is a great exaltation of Jesus Christ, and the fact of this supremacy of His existence!

Then Paul brings us back to reality, v 21: "For you *were* once alienated and enemies in *your* minds by wicked works; but now He has reconciled *you.*" ***Get rid of the things in the mind! Be converted!*** That's where conversion is, in the mind!

Verse 22: "In the body of His flesh through death, **to present you**… [this is why He did it, present every single one of us] …**Holy and unblamable and unimpeachable before Him**; **if**… [there are conditions, and those conditions always exist as long as we're in the flesh] …indeed **you continue in the faith grounded and steadfast,** and are not moved away from the hope of the Gospel, which you have heard, *and* which was proclaimed in all the creation that *is* under heaven… [a prophecy of it clear to the end of the age] …of which I, Paul, became a servant" (vs 22-23).

Look at what the Apostle Paul went through and everything he did to finish off the work of God as far as the writings of his epistles. It's quite wonderful thing, because the New Testament is the only, what they call, 'religious book' in the world that is written in letters, or epistles.

So, consider the New Testament *a personal letter from God to all of us who know the will of God! That's an amazing thing!*

Then Paul says concerning the mystery of God, v 26: "*Even* the mystery that has been hidden from ages and from generations, but has now been revealed to His saints." *You have knowledge that's greater than any of the great minds of this world!*

Think of that, *little ole us!* God has given us that knowledge and understanding.

Verse 27: "To whom God did will… [it was God's will to do it] …to make known what *are* the riches of the glory of this mystery among the Gentiles; which is Christ in you, **the hope of glory**." *Get out the leaven and put in the unleaven!*

Let's see how we do that. If very important how all of these things come about. The more you yield to God and the more you learn of the Word of God, and the more you put sin out of your life and put in the Word of God, that's getting rid of the leaven and sin, and that's putting in the righteousness and Truth of God. That's quite a great and wonderful thing, indeed, when you think about it.

Romans 12:1: "I exhort you, therefore, brethren, by the mercies of God, to present your bodies a living sacrifice, Holy *and* well-pleasing to

God, which is your spiritual service":

- of love
- of Truth
- of obedience
- of serving God

Notice this command, v 2: "**Do not conform yourselves to this world,** but be transformed by the renewing of your mind in order that you may prove what *is* well-pleasing and good, and the perfect will of God." *That's what we are to do all the time!* Quite a fantastic and marvelous thing indeed!

Ephesians 4:21: "If indeed you have heard Him and have been taught in Him, according to *the Truth* in Jesus: That concerning your former conduct… [the way you lived in the world before you were called] …you put off the old man… [put out the leaven, bring in the unleavened] which is corrupt according to deceitful lusts; and that you be renewed in the spirit of your mind, and that you **put on the new man,** which according to God is created in righteousness and Holiness of the Truth (vs 21-24).

That's what God wants! **The ultimate of being spiritually unleavened!** How do we do this, because it's a task we have to do all the time.

Verse 25: "Therefore, let each one put away lies *and* speak the truth with his neighbor, because we are members of one another. *When* you become angry, do not sin. Do not let the sun go down on your anger" (vs 25-26).

When that happens, before the sun goes down *you repent and get rid of it!* **Do not** go to bed and have a sleepless night of tossing and turning, because you didn't get it resolved before you went to bed.

Verse 27: "Neither give place to the devil"—*because the devil will be right there to encourage the hatred!*

Verse 28: "Let the one who stole, steal no more; rather, let him labor with *his* hands, working *at* what *is* good, so that he may impart *something* to the one who has need. Do not let any corrupt communication come out of your mouth… [that's a big one] …but that which is good and needful for edification that it may give grace to those who hear. And do not vex… [frustrate] …the Holy Spirit of God by which you have been sealed for *the* day of redemption" (vs 28-30).

How do you frustrate the Spirit of God? *By not repenting when the Spirit of God reveals sin to you!*

Verse 31: "Let all bitterness, and indignation, and wrath, and clamor, and evil speaking be removed from you, together with all malice… [this is how our conduct needs to be] …and be kind *and* tenderhearted toward one another, forgiving one another, even as God has also in Christ forgiven you" (vs 31-32).

Ephesians 5:1: "Therefore, be imitators of God…" **How are you going to do that?**

- with His Spirit
- with His Word
- with it begin written in your heart and mind

"…as beloved children; and walk in love, even as Christ also loved us, and gave Himself for us *as* an offering and a sacrifice to God for a sweet-smelling savor" (vs 1-2). *This is what God wants us to do:* **put out the leaven, bring in the unleaven**:

- the Truth of God
- the love of God
- the way of God
- the teachings of Christ

Everything that there is, and that's why we keep the Feast of Unleavened Bread!

We've got the rest of this week to really put these things into practice, and to see how we can grow in them. *Draw close to God in prayer, extra study, overcoming and yielding to God!*

Scriptural References:

1) Exodus 23:12-15
2) Exodus 34:18, 21-23
3) Deuteronomy 16:16-17
4) Leviticus 23:1-8

5) Romans 5:12
6) Genesis 6:5-8
7) Mark 7:21-23
8) 1 Corinthians 4:6-21
9) 1 Corinthians 5:1-8
10) Galatians 5:9-18
11) Romans 8:1-9
12) Colossians 2:6-14
13) Ephesians 2:1-5, 8-10
14) Colossians 1:9-23, 26-27
15) Romans 12:1-2
16) Ephesians 4:21-32
17) Ephesians 5:1-2

Scriptures referenced, not quoted:

- Genesis 3
- Psalm 51

FRC:bo
Transcribed: 2/25/20
Reformatted: 11/2020

CHAPTER TWENTY-SIX

The Redemption of the Firstborn
First Day of Unleavened Bread
Fred R. Coulter

Greetings, brethren! Welcome to the first day of the Feast of Unleavened Bread!

A lot of things have been going on in the world, but now's the time for us to back off from all the things in prophecies and things that are happening in the world and concentrate on the Feasts of God. As we know, the Feasts of God give us the understanding that we need concerning His plan. I hope you all had a good Passover and Night to be Much Observed, and now we are going to focus on the Holy Days:

- the first day of Unleavened Bread
- the Sabbath in between the first and last day
- the Wave Sheaf Offering Day
- the last day of Unleavened Bread
- Pentecost

Those three Feasts pertain directly to the Church, and directly to each one of us so it's important that we understand and learn even more. This year, as we have seen in understanding the series that we did *Passover and the Night Much To Be Observed,* there is a lot that we can learn from the commands concerning the firstborn.

Let's begin here where we always begin; Leviticus 23:4: "These *are* the appointed Feasts of the LORD, Holy convocations, which you shall proclaim in their appointed seasons."

Now we also find a corresponding place in the New Testament in 2-Tim. 4 to 'preach in season and out of season' showing that the New Testament Church did keep the Holy Days according to the commandments of God.

Verse 5: "In the fourteenth *day* of the first month, **between the two evenings** is the LORD'S Passover." *As we have seen, God never at any time combined two days into one.*

Verse 6: "And on the fifteenth day of the same month…" *He doesn't say to combine this with the 14th!* There are two different days.

"…*is* the Feast of Unleavened Bread to the LORD. You must eat unleavened bread seven days. On the first day you shall have a Holy convocation. You shall not *do any servile* work *therein*" (vs 6-7).

God expects us, when we come before Him on the Holy Days, to bring an offering as He has blessed us. As we will see when we cover about the firstborn today—

- the sanctifying of the firstborn
- what God is doing with them
- how we fit into it
- the meaning of it for us in the Church of God today

—we are going to see how important it is that when we come before God we don't come before Him empty.

Deuteronomy 16:16: "Three times in a year shall all your males appear before the LORD your God in the place which He shall choose…"

Today wherever two or three are gathered together and Christ is in the midst of it; He's chosen to be there so that is the place. If we're able to have a fellowship group and have more than two or three, maybe have 15, 20, 30, 50, 70, whatever it may be, then that is a place where He has chosen to put His name. Also, because **_we_** are the Temple of God:

- individually, to receive the Holy Spirit
- collectively as to what God is doing in building His Church

"…in the Feast of Unleavened Bread, and in the Feast of Weeks, and in the Feast of Tabernacles. And they shall not appear before the LORD empty, every man *shall give* as he is able, according to the blessing of the LORD your God, which He has given you" (vs 16-17).

Then we also know in the New Testament that the Apostle Paul says that if we give, then God is able to give us sufficiency. So, *God challenges us, as we have seen, to prove Him for His blessing!*

(pause for offering)

Now let's begin in an unusual place, and let's see something that God has commanded concerning the firstborn. We've already covered much of that in Deut. 16 when we covered it on the difference between the Night Much to be Observed and on the Passover, and the difference between the Passover Offering there in Deut. 16 that it is really a peace offerings and so forth, and those are the offerings that the firstborn would bring.

Now let's see something that's important, what God says and what He did the Passover night. Here's what He tells us:

Numbers 3:11: "And the LORD spoke to Moses saying, 'And I, behold I have taken the Levites from among the children of Israel instead of all the firstborn that open the womb among the children of Israel. Therefore, the Levites shall be Mine, **because all the firstborn *are* Mine….**'" (vs 11-13).

That's important for us to understand and realize. ***The firstborn belong to God,*** and we'll see how that applies to the church a little later as we go along.

Verse 13: "…On the day that I struck all the firstborn in the land of Egypt, **I set apart to Myself all the firstborn in Israel, both man and beast.** They shall be Mine. I *am* the LORD."

This is really something. At the time that He executed His judgment against all the gods of Egypt and against all the firstborn man and beast in Egypt, then He set aside, sanctified, or hallowed them. That's what it is, it means *sanctified them.*

Then there has to be a response. We can look at this as:

1. 1 on the Passover, the 14th *redemption for the firstborn*
2. there has to be *deliverance*

We will see that all the way through: ***first redemption and then there is deliverance!***

Exodus 12:51: "And it came to pass the very same day… [the very day] … *when* the LORD brought the children of Israel out of the land of Egypt by their armies"—*which we saw and we know was the 15th day of the 1st month!* It clearly tells us it was the 15th.

Exodus 13:1: "And then the LORD spoke to Moses, saying, 'Sanctify all the firstborn to Me… [set apart, hallow] …whatever opens the womb among the children of Israel, of man and of beast. **It *is* Mine**.'" (v 1-2).

I just want you to stop and think about how heinous a crime that abortion is, *because most of those who are aborted are the firstborn!*

Verse 3: "And Moses said to the people, 'Remember this day *in* which you came out of Egypt, out of the house of bondage…'"

Let's understand something: *He passed over their houses on the Passover Day, and on the first day of Unleavened Bread they come out of Egypt!* So, on the day portion of the Passover, as we saw, they assembled at Rameses so they could leave.

"…for the LORD brought you out from this place by the strength of His hand. There shall be no leavened bread eaten. On this day… [the 15th] …you are going out, in the month Abib" (vs 3-4). *Then He talks about here concerning the commands for unleavened bread!*

Verse 11: "And it shall be, when the LORD brings you into the land of the Canaanites, as He swore to you and to your fathers, and shall give it to you, **you shall set apart to the LORD** all that opens the womb, and every firstborn that comes of any animal, which you have; the males ***shall be the LORD'S***. And every firstborn of a donkey you shall redeem with a lamb. And if you will not redeem it, then you shall break its neck. And **all the firstborn of man among your sons you shall redeem**" (vs 11-13).

Now we're going to see about that. First we're going to concentrate a little bit on the firstborn, and let's see some things that we haven't understood before, or we haven't looked at, and we will see the theme of the firstborn coming right on down beginning with Abraham.

Gen. 11—we will see Abraham was the firstborn. ***There is the right of firstborn; the right of the inheritance of the firstborn!*** We haven't looked at it very often here, but Abraham was the firstborn of his father Terah.

Genesis 11:26: "And Terah lived seventy years and begat Abram, Nahor and Haran."

Abraham was firstborn. Now we're also going to see that God redeemed Abraham. *So, there's a firstborn and a firstborn redemption!* Let's see this where He redeemed Abraham:

- the deliverance
- the redemption
- the sanctification

That will all tie in with what we are as those of the Church of the Firstborn! This puts us in a status with God that is very important and really has profound meaning for us in our understanding and relationship with God.

Isaiah 29:22: "Therefore, thus says the LORD, **who redeemed Abraham**… [When did He redeem Abraham? We'll look at that in just a minute] …concerning the house of Jacob, 'Jacob shall not now be ashamed, nor shall his face now become pale.'"

So, He shows the *redemption of Jacob* along with the *redemption of Abraham.* But when was Abraham redeemed?

Now let's come back here to Gen. 15. I know we have been there but let's see, and we'll touch on this when we get to the New Testament to see what Paul says about this also. Abraham was redeemed. Now remember this: beginning any relationship that anyone has with God you first have to be redeemed, which is *the forgiveness of your sins and the application of the sacrifice of Jesus Christ to you!*

Genesis 15:5—*the Passover night*: "And He brought him [Abraham] outside and said, 'Look now toward the heavens and number the stars—if you are able to count them.' And He said to him, 'So shall your seed be.' He believed in the LORD. And **He accounted it to him for righteousness**" (vs 5-6). *That's when he was redeemed!*

What do we have? *The sacrifice that parallels the time of the sacrifice and the crucifixion of Jesus Christ as we come down through the rest of it!* But that's when Abraham was redeemed.

Now let's look at another one and see he was the firstborn, he was redeemed. We know that the firstborn that was counted to Sarah—because it's all that opens the womb—was Isaac; let's see when Isaac was redeemed. This becomes very important for us to understand. Also, we'll go to the book of Galatians here a little later on, where it says that *if you are Christ's then you're Abraham's seed and heirs according to the promise,* and that *we in the Church* are like Isaac, *the children of promise!*

Let's see when Isaac was redeemed. In every case in coming before God and God dealing with us first of all *He must redeem us, and that is pictured by the Passover!* Then He delivers us, which is pictured by the first day of the Feast of Unleavened Bread. *In delivering us our dedication to God begins!*

Genesis 22:1: "And it came to pass after these things that God tested Abraham, and said to him, 'Abraham!' And he said, 'Here I am.' And He said, 'Take now your son, your only *son* Isaac, whom you love, and go into the land of Moriah, and offer him there for a burnt offering upon one of the mountains, which I will tell you'" (vs 1-2).

God said all the firstborn were His! How did you redeem it? *You redeemed it with a burnt offering*' you redeemed it with a peace offering! He also said that we were to redeem the firstborn, so here we find where Isaac was redeemed. We're also going to see *how* he was redeemed. We're also going to see that it is based upon faith and belief in spite of the circumstances that are involved. We will see how God looks upon that. Of course, understand that Isaac was the firstborn of Sarah.

Verse 3: "And Abraham rose up early in the morning and saddled his donkey, and took two *of* his young men with him, and Isaac his son. And he split the wood for the burnt offering, and rose up and

went to the place of which God had told him. Then on the third day Abraham lifted up his eyes and saw the place afar off. And Abraham said to his young men, 'You stay here with the donkey, and I and the boy will go yonder and worship, and come again to you.' And Abraham took the wood of the burnt offering and laid it upon Isaac his son...." (vs 3-6).

Isaac was also a type of Christ. Isaac was the firstborn. We are going to see here in just a bit Jesus was the firstborn, also. So, there is a great significance in all of this and on the first day of the Feast of Unleavened Bread. Because the first day of the Feast of Unleavened Bread, as we have seen beginning with the Night Much to be Remembered, *is a celebration or a great Feast unto God for redeeming and delivering the firstborn who are dedicated to God.*

- we need to think of that in relationship to our lives.
- we need to think of that in relationship to the way that God has called us

Verse 6: "And Abraham took the wood of the burnt offering and laid it upon Isaac his son..." *You could also say it was a type of Christ carrying His cross!*

"...And he took the fire*pot* in his hand, and a knife. And they both went together. And Isaac spoke to Abraham his father and said, 'My father.' And he said, 'Here I *am*, my son.' And he said, 'Behold the fire and the wood. But where is the lamb for a burnt offering?'" (vs 6-7). Notice Abraham's faith *because he believed God!*

Let's understand something concerning the justification and that there are things that we need to do. Once we are redeemed, once we have been set aside by God, *then there are things that we need to do!* As we have seen and we know, our faith—not only believing—*has to have works and has to have action.*

Just like the children of Israel, when they left Egypt they had to believe God and His Word. Just like in keeping the Passover, they kept the Passover exactly the way that God commanded them, and *they obeyed Him and stayed in their houses until morning!* So, with belief there has got to be obedience.

James 2:17: "In the same way also, faith, if it does not have works, is dead, by itself.... [you have to do what God says] ...But someone is going to say, 'You have faith, and I have works.' *My answer is:* You prove your faith to me through your works, and I will prove my faith to you through my works" (vs 17-18).

In other words the works are the evidence of what you believe. So, if you say you have faith and you have no works, you really have no faith. But if you truly have faith you will have the righteous works because you believe and you act upon that faith. That's what the whole Feast of Unleavened Bread is all about, *that we act upon the faith!*

- that's why it pictures the Exodus
- that's why it shows the children of Israel leaving Egypt
- that's why they had to go on their journey to meet God on Pentecost at Mount Sinai

In much the same way when:

- *we are redeemed*
- we renew the covenant with the Passover
- we keep the Night Much to be Observed and the first day of the Feast of Unleavened Bread

We are taking action to walk in the way of God in obedience, and we are on our way to the Kingdom of God! So we have the same thing.

Verse 19: "Do you believe that God is one? You do well *to believe this*. Even the demons believe and tremble *in fear*. But are you willing to understand, O foolish man, that faith without works is dead?" (vs 19-20).

So, we're going to go back and see about Abraham here because James talks about it here.

Verse 21: "Was not Abraham our father justified by works when he offered up Isaac, his own son, upon the altar?" *The firstborn!*

- Abraham was firstborn
- Isaac was firstborn

Verse 22: "Do you not see that **faith was working together with his works,** and by works *his* faith was perfected?"

If you believe God and do what He says and have the works of faith, you are going to have more belief because it is perfected. ***The whole purpose of our calling is to be perfected!*** So, there you have it.

Verse 23: "And the Scripture was fulfilled, which says, 'Now, Abraham believed God, and it was reckoned to him for righteousness'; and he was called a friend of God."

Notice that Abraham had to have the faith. Also, Isaac had to have a certain amount of faith. He had to accept the answer that his father gave him.

Genesis 22:8: "And Abraham said, 'My son, God will provide Himself a lamb for a burnt offering.' So, they both went on together. And they came to the place of which God had told him. And

Abraham built an altar there and laid the wood in order. And he bound his son Isaac and laid him on the wood, upon the altar. And Abraham stretched out his hand and took the knife to slay his son. And the angel of the LORD called to him from the heavens and said, 'Abraham! Abraham!' And he said, 'Here I *am*.' And He said, 'Do not lay your hand upon the lad, nor do anything to him, **for now I know that you fear God**…" (vs 8-12). *This was over a period of years all of this occurred from its beginning of his calling!*

Likewise with us, this ties in with the Scripture that Jesus said, 'The one who endures to the end, the same shall be saved.' So, we have to have these trials and tests upon us to see:

1. Do we love God?
2. Do we believe God?
3. Will we obey God under all circumstances?

That's what the Feast of Unleavened Bread is all about, so that every year, not only do we renew the covenant on the Passover night, not only do we keep the Night Much to Be Observed, but now on the first day of the Feast of Unleavened Bread every year *we look to God in faith!* We examine ourselves, we see what we need to do. We need to *take the faith of Christ and overcome the sin that is within us,* which is a type of leaven. But let's understand that all of this has to be done by the power and the Spirit of God.

Just like God had to lead the children of Israel out of Egypt; just like God sanctified all the firstborn unto God on the night that He killed all the firstborn of Egypt, man and beast. Therefore, on the 15th is to be a celebration unto God:

- for the firstborn in bringing forth their offerings,
- in bringing forth offerings of thanksgiving that they are the firstborn and redeemed
- to bring forth the offering to redeem those children that were born during the year
- the offerings to redeem the unclean animals
- to bring the firstborn of oxen, sheep, goats
- to bring those as an offering to God

So there's an awful lot of meaning on this day!

We find all of it jam-packed right here into Gen. 22 *because this is when Isaac was redeemed*; the firstborn, which belongs to God. That's why God said to Abraham, 'Take your firstborn, your only son, the one whom you love and you go offer him.' Why? *All the firstborn belong to God!* There's great meaning in that for us. **We** are the firstborn and **we** belong to God! We need to understand that.

Now let's see what God provided, v 13[transcriber's correction]: "And Abraham lifted up his eyes and looked, and behold, behind *him* a ram was entangled in a thicket by its horns...."

I've thought many times, as I've said before, that when they went up there if the ram would have been there they would have seen it, and they would have said, 'Oh look, God has already provided a sacrifice, hasn't He.'

So, God either caused it to go over there or God supernaturally created a ram specifically for a substitutionary sacrifice for Isaac. *This ram then became a type of Christ as a substitutionary sacrifice, which then redeems us, just like it redeemed Isaac!.*

"...And Abraham went and took the ram and offered it up for a burnt offering instead of his son" (v 13).

Here's another guarantee that we have; notice the guarantee that comes down through Abraham, and this is important for us to understand. The reason that a lot of people lose faith is because:

1. they don't grasp the significance of their calling
2. they don't really truly believe God in a way that they ought to

Verse 15: "And the angel of the LORD called to Abraham out of heaven the second time, and said, 'By Myself have I sworn,' says the LORD, 'because you have done this thing... [faith, belief and action] ...and have not withheld your son, your only son... [who was the firstborn that God already proclaimed that was His, and the firstborn were to be redeemed] ...that in blessing I will bless you, and in multiplying I will multiply your seed like the stars of the heavens, and as the sand, which is upon the seashore. And your seed shall possess the gate of his enemies. And in your seed shall all the nations of the earth be blessed, **because you have obeyed My voice**'" (vs 15-18). *Let's understand we are here because of Abraham and Jesus Christ!*

Now let's see the parallel between Isaac and his redemption and being the *son of promise,* and *we become the children of promise*. Let's see how important that this is. So, there is a parallel for the Church. Also, just like the substitutionary sacrifice to redeem Isaac, *Jesus Christ is the substitutionary sacrifice for us,* and we become the *spiritual firstborn* of God.

Galatians 4:26: "But the Jerusalem above is free, which is *the* mother of us all; for it is written..." (vs 26-27)—*because the mother is the Church of the Firstborn!* Just like Sarah was the mother of Isaac the firstborn.

That's why in Heb. 12 it's called **the Church of the Firstborn,** so we have been set aside and sanctified by God.

Verse 27: "For it is written, 'Rejoice, O barren who did not bear! Break forth and cry, *you* who were not travailing, because many more *are* the children of the desolate than of her who has the husband.'"

We, brethren, like Isaac are the children of promise. Our calling is so great and fantastic we are the children of promise just like Isaac was.

Galatians 3:26: "Because you are all sons of God through faith in Christ Jesus. For as many *of you* as were baptized into Christ did put on Christ. There is neither Jew nor Greek; there is neither bond nor free; there is neither male nor female; for you are all one in Christ Jesus... [Who was the substitutionary sacrifice for us] ...And if you *are* Christ's, then you are Abraham's seed, and heirs according to *the* promise" (vs 26-29).

This is why we need to have the absolute faith in God and His Word, *because*:

- His Word is true
- God is righteous
- God cannot lie
- God will not lie

He showed by that very act of redeeming Isaac that shows the redemption of us through Christ!

Hebrews 6:13: "For God, after promising Abraham, swore by Himself..."

Let's understand how sure the promises are. *God swore by His existence* that there would be the spiritual seed as pictured by the stars of heaven, and we're here because of that.

Verse 14: "Saying, 'Surely in blessing I will bless you, and in multiplying I will multiply you.' Now, after he [Abraham] had patiently endured, he obtained the promise. For indeed, men swear by the greater, and confirmation by an oath *puts* an end to all disputes between them. In this *way* God, desiring more abundantly to show the heirs of the promise the unchangeable nature of His own purpose, confirmed *it* by an oath" (vs 14-17).

Let's look at this unchangeableness of His purpose. His purpose also is revealed through the Sabbath and Holy Days. So, here is a verse that establishes them. Then He gives an oath and He gives this promise:

Verse 18: "So that by two immutable things, in which *it was* impossible *for* God to lie..." *We need to claim that promise!*

We have our sins and we have our problems, we have our trials and difficulties and things that we all go through. I do and you do, and we're in this together. *That's why we need*:

- the Passover
- the Feast of Unleavened Bread
- the Spirit of God

working in our lives

- to help us
- to uplift us
- to redeem us
- to rescue us

So that we can produce the fruit and character that God wants us to have!

"…we who have fled for refuge might have strong encouragement to lay hold on the hope *that has been* set before *us*; which *hope* we have as an anchor of the soul, both secure and steadfast, and which enters into the *sanctuary* within the veil; where Jesus has entered for us *as* a forerunner, having become a High Priest forever according to the order of Melchisedec" (vs 18-20). *God is dealing with us that way!*

Rom. 3—*let's see the redemption that has been given to us through Christ* just exactly as it was given to Isaac.

- God redeemed Abraham
- God redeemed Isaac
- God redeemed Jacob
- God redeemed Joseph
- God has redeemed us

and all of those follow in parallel!

This tells us how, in the same parallel as Isaac was redeemed, we are redeemed with a substitutionary sacrifice of Christ instead of the ram.

Roman 3:23: "For all have sinned, and come short of the glory of God; *but* are being justified freely by His grace…" (vs 23-24).

What we saw in Gen. 22 was an act of grace! God provided the sacrifice, freely. But it also involved the belief and faith and works of Abraham and Isaac.

"…being justified freely by His grace through the redemption…" (v 24).

We are redeemed, and that redemption is through Christ, and He being the Firstborn of God, because it says in Matt. 1:18 that He was 'the Firstborn of the virgin Mary.' Then it also says in Heb. 1 that when He brought the Firstborn into the world He [the Father] said, 'Let all the angels worship Him.' So He's the Firstborn. Now He was also the Firstborn from among the dead (Rev. 1). So,

there we have the exact parallel that we need in our lives and will follow through as we come along here in Rom. 3 & 4.

"…the redemption that *is* in Christ Jesus" (v 24)—*the substitutionary sacrifice!*

What did John the Baptist say?

John 1:29: "…'Behold the Lamb of God, Who takes away the **sin** of the world.'" And it doesn't say *sins* [plural] it says *sin* [singular] *because the sin of the world goes clear back to Adam, and we, **with the law of sin and death,** carry that in us.*

Romans 3:25: "Whom God has openly manifested *to be* a propitiation through faith in His blood, in order to demonstrate His righteousness…"—*His justification!*

Now when you have been justified then that is the first step of being sanctified, which then means you have been hallowed. **When you receive the Holy Spirit you have been sanctified and hallowed!** It's up to us to keep the Holy Spirit growing through prayer and study and all the things that God has shown us here. It's justification:

"…in respect to the remission of sins that are past, through the forbearance of God…" (vs 25-26).

- God's mercy
- God's kindness
- God's loving kindness
- God's patience

"…*yes*, to publicly declare His righteousness… [justification for sin]…in the present time, that He might be just, and the One Who justifies the one who *is* of *the* faith of Jesus. Therefore, where *is* boasting? It is excluded…. [because it's by grace and mercy]. …Through what law? *The law* of works? By no means! Rather, *it is* through a law of faith" (vs 26-27). *We've seen the law of faith*:

- you believe
- you act upon it
- you continue in it.

That's the law of faith, and God blesses you!

Verse 28: "Consequently, we reckon that a man is justified by faith, separate from works of law."

Those works of law had to do with the rituals and the laws of Judaism, *not the laws and commandments of God!*

Verse 29: "*Is He* the God of the Jews only? *Is He* not also *the God* of *the* Gentiles? YES! *He is* also God of *the* Gentiles, since *it is* indeed one God Who will justify *the* circumcision by faith, and *the* uncircumcision through faith. Are we, then, abolishing *the* Law through faith? MAY IT NEVER BE! Rather, **we are establishing *the* Law**" (vs 29-31). *That's what's important! That's what we need to realize!.*

Now let's see about Abraham in Rom. 4 He believed God and it was counted to him for righteousness. The promise was given to Abraham.

- When was that given? *On the Passover night!*
- When was that confirmed? *The Night to be Much Observed!*

Romans 4:13: "For the promise to Abraham, or to his seed, that he should be heir of the world, *was* not *given* through law; rather, *it was* through *the* righteousness of faith; because if those of *the* law *be the* heirs, *then* faith is made void, and the promise *is* made of no effect. For the Law works out wrath; because where no law is, *there is* no transgression. For this reason *it is* of faith, in order that *it might be* by grace… [God's gracious gift that we believe Him] …to the end that the promise might be certain to all the seed—not to the one who is of the law only, but also to the one who is of *the* faith of Abraham, who is *the* father of us all, (exactly as it is written: 'I have made you a father of many nations.') before God in Whom he believed, Who gives life to the dead, **and calls the things that are not as though they are**; *and* who against hope believed in hope…" (vs 13-18).

That's why it's important to understand about the life of Abraham, Isaac, and Jacob and their faith and their works and their shortcomings and their sins that they had to repent of to give us hope, to give us understanding the way that God wants us to have. Because you are having a problem, because you have circumstances that are greater than you can handle, turn them to God in faith and always have that hope. *Always keep that hope going!* That's what Abraham did and look how long he had to have hope. God, when He first brought him out of Haran and told him to go in Canaan, he said, 'I will bless you and make your seed great.' It was 25 years until Isaac was born; *so we have to continue with hope!*

Verse 18: "*And* who against hope believed in hope, in order that he might become a father of many nations… [he did physically, and he will spiritually] …according to that which was spoken, 'So shall your seed be.' And he, not being weak in the faith, considered not his own body, already having become dead, being about one hundred years old, nor *did he consider* the deadness of Sarah's womb" (vs 18-19).

He had to have a child by promise, by miracle, which then was a type of the One Who became Jesus Christ. *So he didn't have doubt!*

Verse 20: "And **he did not doubt the promise of God** through unbelief; rather, he was strengthened in the faith, **giving glory to God**." *That tells us how to have our faith strengthened by giving glory to God!*

Now let's see, how we have redemption and deliverance—which includes sanctification/justification—and also helps us as we go on our exodus leaving this world as it were and in developing the righteousness of Christ.

Now let's come to 1-Peter 1 and let's see how he brings all of this together in this chapter. This is really quite a tremendous chapter, and we will see how it intersperses the things of the Passover through redemption and setting aside:

- how it pictures deliverance
- how it pictures our overcoming
- how it pictures how we are to grow in grace and knowledge

All in this one single chapter!

1-Peter 1:1: "Peter, an apostle of Jesus Christ, to *the* elect strangers scattered in Pontus, Galatia, Cappadocia, Asia, and Bithynia… [the Gentiles who were scattered out there] …**who have been chosen according to *the* predetermined knowledge of God *the* Father**…" *So, we've been chosen!*

Being redeemed, we've been chosen, or chosen then redeemed.

"…according to *the* predetermined knowledge of God *the* Father, by sanctification through *the* Spirit, unto obedience and sprinkling of *the* blood of Jesus Christ: Grace and peace be multiplied to you" (v 2). *All of this results in grace from God, peace with God and we are delivered!*

Let's see how this also works together in sanctification of the Spirit, because once we have been redeemed, delivered and sanctified, we have been sanctified by the Spirit of God, and *we become part of the Church of the Firstborn!* **We belong to God!** Like God said, *'All the firstborn are Mine.'*

Now you think on that a little bit more and that helps you understand *the severity of the unpardonable sin!*

1-John 3:1: "Behold! What *glorious* love the Father has given to us, that we should be called the children of God!…." ***Not yet born! We are begotten!*** *But we are the children of God*:

- selected *by Him*
- chosen *by Him*
- redeemed *by Him*
- delivered *by Him*

"…For this very reason, the world does not know us because it did not know Him. Beloved, now we are the children of God… [just like a child in the womb is growing and developing] … **and it has not yet been revealed <u>what we shall be</u>**… [because we haven't been born again, yet; that takes place at the resurrection] …but we know that when He is manifested, we shall be like Him, because we shall see Him exactly as He is" (vs 1-2).

That's born again at the resurrection! A very key thing concerning the hope we talked about with Abraham and the hope that we are going to talk about here in 1-Peter 1:

Verse 3: "And everyone who has this hope in him purifies himself, even as He is pure." *That's what the Feast of Unleavened Bread is all about*:

- to overcome sin
- to get rid of sin
- to have our mind cleansed
- to have our heart purified

It is a process because God is creating in us His Holy and His perfect character through His Spirit! *This requires our love and obedience and dedication, because we've been sanctified by God!*

Here is the contrast. We are going to see this. This is why God constantly instructed the children of Israel to not go back into Egypt, because that personifies the way of the world, the way of Satan the devil. We are not to be living in sin.

Verse 4: "Everyone who practices sin is also practicing lawlessness, for sin is lawlessness…. [*KJV*: Sin is the transgression of the Law] …And you know that He appeared in order that He might take away our sins; and in Him is no sin" (vs 4-5). *There is the substitutionary sacrifice!*

Verse 6: "Everyone who dwells in Him… [which we are *by the power of God's Holy Spirit*] …**does not *practice* sin**…" *That's the whole purpose of the Feast of Unleavened Bread,* that leaven is a type of sin. We are to put the leaven out of our homes, we are to put sin out of our lives, and all that ties in together.

It doesn't say we don't sin, because as long as we have the law of sin and death in us as the Apostle Paul wrote (Rom. 7). We are going to be sinning, but as long as we do not sin a sin unto death, it is a forgivable sin and upon repentance we are forgiven, and the grace of God applies to us here.

"…anyone who *practices* sin has not seen Him… [talking about those false antichrist prophets that were coming around and saying it's ok to sin] …nor has known Him. Little children, do not allow anyone to deceive you…" (vs 6-7).

That's another thing concerning the Feast of Unleavened Bread, because unleavened bread strips bare human nature before God and shows how in Spirit and in Truth we will not then be deceived.

"…the one who practices righteousness is righteous, even as He is righteous. The one who practices sin is of the devil because the devil has been sinning from *the* beginning…." (vs 7-8).

That's why Paul said, 'Do we abolish law because of grace? ***God forbid!*** We establish law.' It's to be written in our heart and mind, and that's the whole purpose of the Feast of Unleavened Bread because:

- the more of the Word of God we get in, *the more sin we put out*
- the more of the power of God's Holy Spirit we have, *the more that He exposes in us the sin that is within*

so we can repent! All of those things work together, and that's what the spiritual purpose of the Feast of Unleavened Bread is for.

"…For this purpose the Son of God appeared that He might destroy the works of the devil" (v 8). *The first place to begin destroying it is within our lives!*

Now, stop and think about this in relationship to the Passover: Did He not destroy all the works of the devil in Egypt in judging Egypt with all the plagues and all the things that were there and on the Passover night judging all the gods and religious practices of Egypt? *Yes, indeed!* He's going to destroy every one of the works of the devil when He returns.

Verse 9: "Everyone who has been begotten by God does **not practice sin,** because His seed *of begettal* is dwelling within him, and **he is not able to *practice* sin** because he has been begotten by God."

Now let me explain this verse thoroughly to you, which is this: You have the Holy Spirit of God, which is the begettal. You come along and as exposed by the Feast of Unleavened Bread and God's Spirit in you, you see sin in your life. You are convicted of what sin is and you repent of it. That is God working in your life so you don't *practice* sin. Now notice it doesn't say: You do not sin. It says you do not *practice* sin.

1-John 5:16—*concerning sin*: "If anyone sees his brother sinning a sin *that is* not unto death…"

In other words *it is a forgivable sin* as Jesus said, 'Every sin and blasphemy shall be forgiven men. And every word spoken against the Son of man shall be forgiven. but the blaspheme of the

Holy Spirit shall not be forgiven.' Jesus there in Matt. 12 showed there are forgivable and unforgivable sins. So a sin that is not unto death is a forgivable sin. So if you are convicted in conscience of sin within and you repent of it, it is forgiven. It is a forgivable sin.

If you want to know about the **unpardonable** sin, go to our in-depth study: *The Epistle of Paul to the Hebrews.*

{note our book: *Occult Holidays or God's Holy Days—Which?*}.

Verse 16: "If anyone sees his brother sinning a sin *that is* not unto death he shall ask… [if you see a brother sinning, pray for him] …and He [God] …will give him life for those who do not sin unto death" (v 16).

In other words **He'll lead them to repentance!** That's all of God's purpose, *to lead us to repentance!*

"…There is a sin unto death; concerning that *sin*, I do not say that he should make *any* supplication *to God*" (v 16).

1-John 3:10—*we don't practice sin*: "By this *standard* are manifest the children of God…"—*who are the Church of the Firstborn*:

- chosen by God
- set aside by God
- redeemed by God
- delivered by God

"…and the children of the devil. Everyone who does not practice righteousness is not of God, and neither is the one who does not love his brother" (v 10).

Here's the whole sum of it; this is where we are headed; this is the goal of our behavior:

Verse 18: "My little children, we should not love in word, nor with *our* tongues; rather, *we should love* in deed and in Truth. And in this *way* we know that we are of the Truth, and shall assure our hearts before Him" (vs 18-19).

God wants us to have the confidence! Now we go back and we can apply this to the children of Israel leaving the land of Egypt. They left with a high hand. In other words they had confidence and trust in God, although it didn't last very long, because they didn't have the Holy Spirit of God. But here we have the Spirit of God and we are to assure our hearts before God and to know that we are right with God. That's everything that God wants us to do is all about.

Verse 20: "That if our hearts condemn us… [because we've sinned; it's a forgivable sin] …God is greater than our hearts, and knows all things.

Beloved, if our hearts do not condemn us, *then* we have confidence toward God. And whatever we may ask we receive from Him, because we keep His commandments and practice those things that are pleasing in His sight" (vs 20-22). *That's what God wants us to do!*

We are going to see all of these elements here again in 1-Peter 1 concerning what God has done.

1-Peter 1:3: "Blessed *be* the God and Father of our Lord Jesus Christ, Who, according to His abundant mercy, has begotten us again unto a living hope…"

That living hope is through the resurrection of Jesus Christ from the dead, because He is the Firstborn from among many brethren, and we are the Church of the Firstborn. What we are going to look at here is the process of perfection.

Let's see what it is that God is doing with us, and let's see how He is doing it, and let's see the purpose in it. Sometimes we expect things to go totally perfect in our lives every day in every way and we end up with many difficulties, challenges and problems, and maybe even get depressed over sinning and all of these things.

Well look, that's all a part of God dealing with you so you're going to trust in Him, and trust in *Him for your deliverance,* because that's what the Feast of Unleavened Bread is all about.

Hebrews 12:22: "But you have come to Mount Sion, and to *the* city of *the* living God, heavenly Jerusalem; and to an innumerable company of angels; *to the* joyous festival gathering; and to *the* Church of *the* Firstborn…" (vs 22-23).

That is us, and all of the saints down through time beginning with Abel and until the return of Jesus Christ. At the resurrection when we are born again and become the literal family of the firstborn of God **redeemed, delivered, resurrected, and given eternal life,** that's the goal.

"…registered *in the Book of Life* in heaven; and to God, *the* Judge of all, and to *the* spirits of the just who have been perfected…" (v 23).

That's what God is doing in our lives. That's why we go through the things that we go through: *to be perfected!*

Let's see how this is. We have the living hope. We don't trust in the flesh. We don't trust in the physical things around us. We need them to exist as long as we are physical human beings, that is true, but we don't look at that as a great thing. We're thankful and grateful for all that God gives us and does for us and provides for us because we need it, that is true. But here is what we are looking to because our hope goes beyond this life.

1-Peter 1:4: "**Unto an inheritance incorruptible and undefiled and unfading, reserved in heaven for us**."

On the Passover night Jesus told His apostles, 'I go to prepare a place for you, and if I go, I will come again and receive you to Myself, so that where I am you may be also.' *That is our hope: reserved, unfading, undefiled!*

Verse 5: "Who *are* being safeguarded by *the* power of God through faith for salvation *that is* ready to be revealed in *the* last time."

That's the way that God does. He sets the goal, He sets the perspective; you could say *the vision,* because without vision the people perish, and God has given this vision of the hope of our calling and where we are going and what we are doing, and that's what the Feast of Unleavened Bread is all about!

- that we desire to get rid of sin
- that we desire to overcome human nature
- that we desire to be delivered out of the difficulties and problems that we are in

all of those work for the character of building:

- love
- hope
- faith
- grace
- temperance
- longsuffering
- mercy
- understanding
  - ✓ all the fruits of the Holy Spirit
  - ✓ all of the character that comes from God

Verse 6: "In this you yourselves greatly rejoice… [which we ought to] … though for the present, if it is necessary, you are in distress for a little while by various trials, in order that the proving of your faith… [just like God proved Abraham's faith] …which is much more precious than gold that perishes, though it is being tested by fire, may be found unto praise and honor and glory at *the* revelation of Jesus Christ" (vs 6-7).

Now let's look how we trust in God to redeem us and to deliver us. First we must be redeemed. That's what God did with the children of Israel. He redeemed them.

Next we have to be delivered Let's follow through with how Paul wrote. You know many of the things that are written in Greek have long run-on sentences that are unacceptable in English, but they work just fine in Greek.

Titus 2:11: "For the grace of God, which brings salvation for all men, has appeared."—*that's Christ; His sacrifice, His resurrection!* All of that is the grace of God and salvation.

Verse 12: "Teaching us that, having denied ungodliness and worldly lusts, we should live moderately and righteously and Godly in this present world." *That's how we are to be! That's what unleavened bread is all about!*

Verse 13: "…Looking for the blessed hope and *the* appearing of the glory of our Savior and great God Jesus Christ; Who gave Himself for us, **so that He might redeem us from all lawlessness**…" (vs 13-14).

There you have it. Just like when God redeemed Israel when He slew all the firstborn in Egypt, He redeemed Abraham, He redeemed Isaac, and here's the purpose:

"…**and might purify for Himself**…" (v 14) *That's the whole process of growing, changing, and overcoming, and the purpose of Unleavened Bread!*

"…**a unique people, zealous of good works**…. [that's what we should be] …Speak these things, and exhort, and rebuke with all authority. Do not let anyone despise you" (vs 14-15). *There is redemption!*

Let's look at some deliverance. When we get into the trials and difficulties that Peter spoke of let's see how we are to look to God to deliver us. We all need deliverance. Sometimes there are times when we go before God—I know I do; I know you do—there are so many things pressing in upon you that the only thing you can do is like one of the Psalms there where he starts out, he says, 'Help.' And another one says, 'Hear me.' And another one is, 'O God, I'm so overwhelmed I can hardly lift up my head.'

Sometimes you get into those things. Here is how we are to approach God, because *first* there is redemption and *then* there is deliverance. *Deliverance is based upon hope and trust,* and so forth.

Psalm 7:1: "O LORD my God, in You have I taken refuge; save me from all who pursue me and deliver me…" *You go before God and say*:

O God, I'm overwhelmed with this. Please just intervene! Deliver me, help me, open the way, open the door, give me understanding, help me to realize why I'm going through what I'm going through. Give me of Your Spirit, give me of Your Truth, deliver me from this situation!

Verse 2: "Lest he tear my soul like a lion, ripping it in pieces, and there is no one to deliver."

Psa. 25 is quite a Psalm of deliverance, and one that we can also apply to our prayers and our thoughts and yieldedness to God asking God to deliver us.

In deliverance there is trust. *You must trust in God,* which is:

- active faith
- active belief
- knowing that what God has said that He's a God that cannot and will not lie
- His Word is true

Just like the man who wanted to have the demon cast out of his son and Jesus said, 'If you believe, all things are possible.' The man said, 'Lord, I believe. Help my unbelief.' So, lots of times we need to go to God in that way and we need to look to Him and just ask Him, 'Help us!' *That trust and faith go hand-in-hand with redemption!*

Psalm 25:1: "To You, O LORD, do I lift up my soul. O my God, I trust in You …" (vs 1-2).

That's what we are to do, *trust in God!* What is the Scripture that says, 'Trust no man' Every time you trust some man you get in trouble; we've got a long history of that!

"…do not let me be ashamed, let not my enemies triumph over me. Yea, let none who wait on You be ashamed; let them be ashamed who deal treacherously without cause" (vs 2-3).

Notice what happens **when** we have that kind of attitude, and **when** we are trusting in God and looking to Him:

Verse 4: "Show me Your ways, O LORD; teach me Your paths. Lead me in Your Truth and teach me…" [this is what we need to be, teachable by God with His Spirit and in Truth] …for You are the God of my salvation; on You do I wait all the day long" (vs 4-5).

Notice how he reminded God. When you get down and desperate and in the fiery trial that Peter was talking about in 1-Peter 1.

Verse 6: "Remember, O LORD, Your tender mercies and Your loving kindness, for they have been of old. Do not remember the sins of my youth, nor my transgressions; according to Your loving kindness remember me for Your goodness sake, O LORD. Good and upright is the LORD; therefore, He will teach sinners in the way. The meek He will guide in judgment; and the meek He will teach His way" (vs 6-9).

That's what the Exodus is all about; it is *the way of God!*

Verse 10: "All the paths of the LORD are mercy and Truth to those who keep His covenant and His testimonies. For Your name's sake, O LORD, pardon my iniquity, for it is great" (vs 10-11). *Let's see how this is also amplified here, and how:*

- we have trust
- we have deliverance
- we have yieldedness to God

Psalm 27:11: "Teach me Your way, O LORD, and lead me in a level path…" *That's what we need God to do with His Spirit to teach us!*

Then in every situation that we learn. Many times we get frustrated in some of the things we are going through, and in overcoming there are very difficult challenges for us, but let's have Him teach us.

"…because of my enemies. Deliver me not over to the will of my enemies… [here is a prophecy of Christ]: …for false witnesses have risen up against me, and he that breathes out violence. I would have fainted unless I had believed that I would see the goodness of the LORD in the land of the living…. [projecting forward to the resurrection] …Wait for the LORD; be of good courage, and He shall make your heart strong; yea, wait, I say, *wait* on the LORD" (vs 11-14) *and He will deliver us!* There is no question about it.

Let's see how Peter continues going on showing all of these elements that we have concerning the Feast of Unleavened Bread and growing, changing and overcoming in *faith, in truth, and love,* and all of those things are all combined together 1-Peter 1.

It's really very interesting when you get in and you study the Bible and you see how God inspired them to write, you see how that all the elements of the Truth of God are brought in different ways and in different manners. Here we have this concerning many of the aspects of the Feast of Unleavened Bread and the redemption of the firstborn being sanctified and set aside by God for a special and a Holy use.

1-Peter 1:7: "In order that the proving of your faith… [that's what it's all about; He's going to prove our faith] …which is much more precious than gold that perishes, though it is being tested by fire, may be found unto praise and honor and glory at *the* revelation of Jesus Christ; whom, not having seen, you love; in Whom, *though* at the present time you do not see Him, you believe…" (vs 7-8).

- we have hope
- we have belief
- we have faith

- we have love

"...*and* rejoice with unspeakable joy, and filled with glory; *and are* receiving the end of your faith—*even the* salvation of *your* lives... [it's the salvation that we have been given] ...concerning which salvation... (vs 8-10). **We've been redeemed, and we've been delivered!**

Of course, we ask God every day to **deliver us from our sins, deliver us from the evil one!** God has intervened to do that.

"...the prophets who prophesied of the grace *that would come* to you have diligently searched out and intently inquired, searching into what *way* and what manner of time the Spirit of Christ *which was* in them was indicating, testifying beforehand of the sufferings of Christ, and these glories that would follow" (vs 10-11).

Now let's see how that's accomplished. Let's see, again, *the deliverance.* Here in this case rescuing. God has to intervene and rescue us from Satan the devil, just exactly in the same way that He had to intervene and rescue the firstborn and the children of Israel in Egypt and deliver them.

Colossians 1:10: "That you may walk worthily of the Lord, unto all pleasing, being fruitful in every good work and growing in the knowledge of God."

That's what it needs to be. Every year we keep the Passover, keep the Feast of Unleavened Bread, and all the Holy Days of God; that we are growing in the knowledge of God so every year we learn more.

- we are preparing for the resurrection
- we are growing in grace and knowledge
- we are growing in love, faith, hope, and trust

Verse 11: "Being strengthened with all power according to the might of His glory, unto all endurance and long-suffering with joy."

Now let's understand that every year there are going to be saints who are going to come to the end of their lives and die. God said there is a time to die. When you die you're going to die of something, aren't you? *Yes, because your body being physical, and your body being corruptible,* being weak is going to die of something. We need to realize that.

But let's look at it the way that God looks at it. He says, 'Blessed in the eyes of the Lord is the death of His saints.' Why? *Because death is actually a graduation!* **You graduate from this physical life and are put in the grave and you wait the resurrection!** When you die there is:

- no more sin

- no more pain
- no more wretchedness

But the next thought that you will have **will be the resurrection and the angels carrying you up to meet Christ on the Sea of Glass in the air with all the other saints!** So let's keep focused on that! **We are enduring to the end and looking to the longsuffering of God to help us to do that!**

Verse 12: "Giving thanks to the Father, Who has made us qualified for the share of the inheritance of the saints in the Light; **Who has personally rescued us from the power of darkness**..." (vs 12-13).

Go back and you can see that situation with the children of Israel when they were in Egypt.

- Was there not the plague of darkness?
- Does that not signify the darkness of Satan the devil? Did He not give light to the children of Israel who were living in Goshen at that time?
- *Yes!*

"...personally rescued us from the power of darkness..." Who controls the power of darkness? *Satan the devil!* **We are rescued and delivered from the evil one!** Just like God rescued the children of Israel and brought them out of Egypt and rescued them from the evil of that terrible and wretched society and the slavery in which they were held captive.

"...and has transferred *us* unto the Kingdom of the Son of His love... [we are under the authority of God the Father and Jesus Christ] ...in Whom we have redemption..." (vs 13-14). *So, here we go right back to*:

- the redeeming of the firstborn
- the delivery of the firstborn
- the walking in the way of God
- the exodus out of sin

"...*even* the remission of sins..." (v 14).

You can see how all of these things work, how all of these things come together, and how He saves us!

1-Peter 1:11: "Searching into what *way* and what manner of time the Spirit of Christ *which was* in them was indicating, testifying beforehand of the sufferings of Christ, and these glories that would follow; to whom it was revealed that, not for themselves, but to us they were ministering these things, which now have been announced to you by those who have preached the Gospel to you by *the* Holy Spirit, sent from heaven—into which things the angels desire to look" (vs 11-12).

Now here is the lesson we need to do. Here is the lesson for the Feast of Unleavened Bread. Because of all of You start out with 1-Peter 1:1 and you come down here to verse 13 and he gives the summary:

Verse 13: "For this reason, be prepared in your minds… [that's what the Feast of Unleavened Bread is all about] …be self-controlled… [with the Spirit of God] …*and be fully hoping in the grace that will be brought to you at the* revelation of Jesus Christ."

The greatest grace we have to receive yet is the resurrection, which will be when Christ returns!

Verse 14: "As obedient children… [this is what God wants us to be] …do not conform yourselves to the former lusts, *as you did* in your ignorance."

Don't go back and live the way that you lived. If it comes back, starts to creep back, that's just like leaven growing in your life; *get rid of it!* Put in the unleavenedness of Christ. ***That unleavenedness comes through the Spirit of God, as obedient children!*** Don't go back to the way that you did in your former lust as in your ignorance. Now you are educated with the Word of God and the Spirit of God.

Verse 15: "But according as He Who has called you *is* Holy, you yourselves also be Holy in all *your* conduct; for it is written, **'You be Holy because I am Holy'**" (vs 15-16).

A perfect summation of the Feast of Unleavened Bread. We are to come from something that is leavened and unholy to something that is unleavened and Holy. Leaven during the Feast of Unleavened Bread pictures a type of sin. As we know, Paul said, 'Let us keep the Feast. Not with the old leaven, nor with the leaven of malice and wickedness.' Notice how Paul and Peter agree. If you put 1-Cor. 5 together with 1-Peter 1, they agree!

Verse 17: "And if you call upon the Father, Who judges according to each man's work without respect of persons, pass the time of your *life's* journey in *the* fear *of God*; knowing that you were not redeemed by corruptible things, by silver or gold, from your futile way of living, inherited *by tradition* from *your* forefathers; **but by *the* precious blood of Christ, as of a lamb without blemish and without spot**" (vs 17-19).

That's why we need to do the things that we do. We have been redeemed, we have been set aside and we go forward in the way that God wants us to do.

Verse 20: "Who truly was foreknown before *the* foundation of *the* world, but was manifested in *these* last times for your sakes; *even for you* who through Him do believe in God, Who raised Him from *the* dead and gave Him glory, so that your faith and hope might be in God. Having purified your lives by obedience to the Truth unto unfeigned brotherly love through *the* Spirit, love one another fervently with a pure heart. *For* you have been begotten again, not from corruptible seed, but from incorruptible *seed*, by *the* living Word of God, *which* remains forever" (vs 20-23).

That's the meaning of the Feast of Unleavened Bread.

- we are the Church of the Firstborn.
- we have been called, set aside and purified
- we have been delivered to have
  ✓ faith
  ✓ hope
  ✓ trust
  ✓ love

with God!

Have a good Feast of Unleavened Bread, brethren. Take these things and every day during the Feast do some extra Bible study, and ask God to help you with His Spirit ***to grow, to change, to overcome, and to have your life transformed*** through this Feast of Unleavened Bread that you become more Christ-like.

Scriptures from *The Holy Bible in Its Original Order, A Faithful Version*

Scriptural References

1) Leviticus 23:4-8
2) Deuteronomy 16:16-17
3) Numbers 3:11-13
4) Exodus 12:51
5) Exodus 13:1-4, 11-13
6) Genesis 11:26
7) Isaiah 29:22
8) Genesis 15:5
9) Genesis 22:1-7
10) James 2:17-23
11) Genesis 22:8-13, 15
12) Galatians 4:26-27
13) Galatians 3:26-29
14) Hebrews 6:13-20
15) Romans 3:23-24
16) Romans 4:13-20
17) Romans 3:25-31
18) John 1:29
19) 1 Peter 1:1-2
20) 1 John 3:1-9
21) 1 John 5:16
22) 1-John 3:10, 18-22
23) 1 Peter 1:3

24) Hebrew 12:22-23
25) 1-Peter 1:4-7
26) Titus 2:11-15
27) Psalms 7:1-2
28) Psalms 25:1-11
29) Psalms 27:11-14
30) 1 Peter 1:7-11
31) Colossians 1:10-14
32) 1 Peter 1:11-23

Scriptures referenced, not quoted:

- Matthew 1:18
- Hebrews 1
- Revelation 1
- Romans 7
- Matthew 12
- 1 Corinthians 5

Also referenced:

In-Depth Studies:
- *Passover and the Night to Be Much Observed*
- *Epistle of Paul to the Hebrews*

Book: *Occult Holidays or God's Holy Days— Which?* by Fred R. Coulter

FRC: cs
Transcription date unknown
Reformatted: bo—11/2020

CHAPTER TWENTY-SEVEN

Christ's Resurrection and Ascension to the Father
Events leading up to and of the Wave Sheaf Offering Day
Fred R. Coulter

Greetings, brethren! Welcome to Sabbath during the Feast of Unleavened Bread! Time marches on, doesn't it? *Certainly does! Quite a thing!*

This is a special day, and it's noted beginning in Lev. 23; we will see the instruction for this day and what it means. We know that the harvest of God spiritually is likened to a harvest of grain. So, we have the type, the physical in the Old Testament, and we have the anti-type or the fulfillment in the New Testament.

There's a special ceremony that was to be done on the day after the Sabbath during Unleavened Bread!

Another way to put it, because of the count, the waving of the Sheaf Offering had to be waved on the first day of the week *during* Unleavened Bread.

Leviticus 23:9: "And the LORD spoke to Moses, saying, 'Speak to the children of Israel and say to them, "When you have come into the land, which I give to you, and shall reap the harvest of it…"'" (vs 9-10).

God gave them the land and they entered in the spring time. Even though the inhabitants of the land planted the crop, that did not contaminate it because when the seed is put into the ground the seed disintegrates and develops a whole new stalk with many more seeds.

Some people *erroneously* say that it had to be the year after that they entered into the Holy Land, which is *nonsense!* It was *their* harvest because God gave it to them, even though they didn't plant it.

"…then you shall bring ***the premier* sheaf of the firstfruits**… [a *special* premier sheaf] …of your harvest to the priest. And he shall wave the sheaf before the LORD to be accepted for you. On the next day after the Sabbath the priest shall wave it" (vs 10-11).

This premier sheaf is picturing the resurrected Christ ascending to heaven!

Let's look at the chart in Appendix J: The Three Days and Three Nights in the Tomb and the Resurrection After the Three Days and Three Nights (pg 1280-1 in *The Holy Bible in Its Original Order,*

A Faithful Version). This becomes very important. The only time that this could happen, so that it pictures the three days and three nights in the grave that Christ had to be there is when the Passover is in the middle of the week from Tuesday sunset to Wednesday sunset.

Whenever we have the Passover in the middle of the week— Wednesday, the fourth day— and God reckons time from sunset to sunset. They had the Passover, Christ was arrested at midnight, and that's a type of God not passing over Christ the Firstborn/

> Sidebar: Christ was the Firstborn of Mary and also the Firstborn among the dead, and also the Firstborn of the Father. All of those apply to Christ directly.

We will see the timing that took place and we will look at the Scriptures and what happened after Jesus died on the cross. But I want you to look very carefully at this chart because the Passover Day ended at sunset and that began the first day of the Feast of Unleavened Bread.

Then you have three nights and three days in the grave. That's important. Sometimes the Passover occurs on a Friday and sometimes the Passover occurs on the Sabbath. But in those instances, when the Passover occurs then, you have more than three days and three nights between the beginning of the first day of the Feast of Unleavened Bread and the Sabbath during Unleavened Bread.

Only in the years when the Passover falls on Wednesday, the fourth day of the week, let's see what happens. We have the Passover from sunset to sunset, which then begins the first day of the Feast of Unleavened Bread, a Holy Day.

Then to the next sunset, you have the sixth day of the week, Nisan 16, and the second night, because all days are counted from sunset to sunset. This day is the preparation for the weekly Sabbath.

Go back to the Passover Day and that was the preparation day for the first day of the Feast of Unleavened Bread. When it's finished, the next day is Friday, so we've got two whole days. Then we come from sunset Friday the Sabbath beginning at sunset and then the Sabbath Day.

As you look at the chart you have 3 nights and 3 days, and Jesus said that He would be in the tomb three days and three nights.

You can refer to this chart at anytime, and we also have it in *The Christian Passover* book, and *The Day that Jesus the Christ Died.*

So important is this that because this year, when the world has Easter Friday and then they say the resurrection is Sunday, *that is a total myth!* That is *at lie! Not true!* Besides, from Friday at sunset to Sunday morning, you do not have three full days and three full nights! *It's an impossibility! That shows you how off the mark that Catholicism and Protestantism actually is!*

Now we're going to see some of the things that took place on the Passover Day as Christ came to the end.

Matthew 27:46: "And about the ninth hour…"—*about 3-pm!*

Sidebar: The death of Christ happened in the afternoon of the Passover Day. It had to be a public and notorious thing that took place. That's why Christ was not killed at the beginning of the Passover Day when the sun went down, like the children of Israel did for the Passover.

Jesus kept that Passover and it ended the Old Testament Passover, and introduced the New Covenant Passover with the foot-washing and the bread and wine.

Jesus cried out with a loud voice, saying, 'Eli, Eli, lama sabachthani?' That is, 'My God, My God, why have You forsaken Me?'" (v 46). *Prophesied in Psa. 22!*

Verse 47: "And some of those who were standing there heard *and* said, 'This *one* is calling for Elijah.'" *But it didn't happen!*

Verse 54: "Then the centurion and those with him who had been keeping guard over Jesus, after seeing the earthquake…" *When He died there was a great earthquake!*

There was huge, very thick curtain covering the temple, and there were 12 sections to that, three sections of four. Each section represented one of the 12 tribes of Israel. This was knitted with linen and was very thick, probably 2-3 inches thick. When that was ripped, this signified, symbolically, that the way to God was open to the people.

Whereas before, the only one who had access to the Holy of Holies in the temple on earth was the high priest once year on the Day of Atonement. But now this symbolized that the way to God was opened to all whom God would call.

"… and the things that took place, were filled with fear, *and* said **'Truly this was the Son of God!'**" (v 54). *This was a tremendous and important thing, indeed, that we understand!*

Let's see how John writes of this. This becomes important, too. Everything concerning the crucifixion of Christ becomes important. Every detail was prophesied ahead of time.

John 19:28: "After this, Jesus, knowing that all things had now been **finished**…"—*for the crucifixion!*

Remember that *whenever there is a finish or an ending, there is a new beginning!*

"…so that the Scripture might be **fulfilled**, said, 'I thirst.' Now, a vessel full of vinegar was sitting *there*. And after filling a sponge with vinegar and putting *it* on *a stick of* hyssop, they put it up to *His* mouth. And so, when Jesus had received the vinegar, He said, 'It is **finished**.'…." (vs 28-30). *Notice*:

- finished
- fulfilled
- finished

How far back in time does the crucifixion go?

Revelation 13:8: "…**the Lamb slain from the foundation of *the* world**." *God had this all planned!*

There is nothing here in all the Scriptures that is happenstance! It is all worked out in every detail, and you know for sure that the angels were there making sure that it was all done according to the will of God.

John 19:30: "…And bowing His head, He yielded up *His* spirit. The Jews, therefore, so that the bodies might not remain on the cross on the Sabbath, because it was a preparation *day* (for that Sabbath was a High Day)…" (vs 30-31). *That Sabbath was the first day of the Feast of Unleavened Bread!*

They had the time from about three in the afternoon until the sun went down approximately six o'clock, three hours to tend to the body of Christ.

You can read in *The Christian Passover* and *The Day Jesus the Christ Died*: **28 Prophecies Fulfilled in One Day,** so that there can be no room for human error. God made sure that it was all done:

- according to the prophecies
- according to His plan
- according to the timing that He desired

Verse 32: "Then the soldiers came and broke the legs of the first *one*, and *the legs* of the other who was crucified with Him." *There was one crucified on the right and one crucified on the left!*

Verse 33: "But when they came to Jesus *and* saw that He was already dead, they did not break His legs; but one of the soldiers had pierced His side with a spear..." (vs 33-34)—*right up into and piercing His heart!*

Why? *So that every drop of blood that was sacrificed for the sin of the world would be poured out!*

"...and immediately blood and water had come out. And he who saw *this* has testified, and his testimony is true... [that's John; he watched the whole thing] ...and he knows that *what* he says *is* true, so that you may believe" (vs 34-35). *That's written for us!*

This is a fantastic thing that God did. Everything about Jesus, everything about His life was tremendous, indeed, and done out of love, truth, power and the things prophesied ahead of time so that there would be no excuse to say that this didn't happen.

Let's continue on and see that from the time that He died until the time that He was in the tomb.

Verse 38: "Now, after these things, Joseph (the one from Arimathea, being a disciple of Jesus, but having concealed it for fear of the Jews) asked Pilate that he might take Jesus' body away; and Pilate gave *him* permission. Then he came and took away the body of Jesus. And Nicodemus, who had come to Jesus by night at *the* first, also came, bearing a mixture of myrrh and aloes, about a hundred pounds. Then they took Jesus' body and wound it in linen cloths with the aromatics, as is the custom among the Jews to prepare for burial" (vs 38-40).

How was He buried? Remember that He was beaten, there was flesh and skin hanging down. What they were doing was they started at the feet and they would wrap this linen, generally about six inches wide, around the feet and legs, and then the body. They would put all of that flesh back in as they were going up to wrap His entire body.

The lie of the Catholics about the Shroud of Turin can never be true! That is a fantastic lie, because they were wrapped. The linen was wrapped; the shroud was just overlaid. How they made the shroud no one knows, *but that's a total **fake** and total **idolatry**!*

Then when they got to the head, they had a special 'napkin,' as they called, it that would cover the head. This is how Jesus was buried.

Verse 41: "Now, there was a garden in the place where He was crucified, and in the garden a new tomb, in which no one had ever been laid."

Why do they say that? *Tombs were not like they are today,* especially in the rocky country of Judea. So, they had caves, or tombs like caves, carved into the rocks. They had ossuaries where they would put the bones. What they did first was to take the bodies, wrap them the way that Joseph of Arimathea and Nicodemus did, and then they would wait for all of the flesh to disintegrate, and several years afterward they would open the tomb and take the bones and put them in an ossuary.

Jesus had to be buried in a place where no one had ever been buried.

Now then, there was a great stone that was used to cover this tomb. They had the stone all cut out and ready to go, and they had a little stop to keep it from rolling down. So, when they put Jesus' body into the tomb, they took that stop out and rolled the big rock right over the entrance covering the tomb.

Verse 42: "Because of the preparation of the Jews... [for the first day of Unleavened Bread] ...they laid Jesus there; for the tomb was near." *That's how Jesus was buried!*

Matthew 27:60: "And placed it... [the body of Jesus] ...in his new tomb, which he had hewn in the rock; and after rolling a great stone to the door of the tomb, he went away. But sitting there opposite the sepulcher were Mary Magdalene and the other Mary" (vs 60-61).

The Jews went to Pilate, and let's see what they did; v 62: "Now, on the next day, which followed the preparation *day*... [for the Feast of Unleavened Bread] ... the chief priests and the Pharisees came together to Pilate, saying, 'Sir, we remember that that deceiver said while *He was* living, "After three days I *will* rise." Therefore, command *that* the sepulcher be secured until the third day; lest His disciples come by night and steal Him away, and say to the people, "He is risen from the dead"; and the last deception shall be worse than the first.' Then Pilate said to them, 'You have a guard. Go, make *it as* secure as you know *how*.' And they went *and* made the sepulcher secure, sealing the stone *and* setting the guard" (vs 62-66).

- What does it mean to seal the stone?
- What do you suppose that they did?
- How would you seal it?

You would make a little concrete and then you would put it all around the edge of where that great round stone was rolled down over the door of the tomb. It would dry, and it would make it even harder for anyone to try and open the tomb.

I'm sure that they put a lot of that concrete around there. Then they had guards standing there to make sure that the disciples would not come and steal the body of Jesus away.

Matthew 28:1: "Now, late on the Sabbath… [the weekly Sabbath] …**as the first _day_ of the weeks** was drawing near…"

- Why is that translated this way? *Because this day was the first day of the count to Pentecost!*
- How many weeks are there to Pentecost? *Seven, plus one day!*

"…Mary Magdalene and the other Mary came to observe the sepulcher" (v 1). *They went down to see if anything took place, because Jesus said that He was going to be resurrected!*

But they had no idea of the exact timing, so they went down right as the Sabbath was ready to begin to see what took place. Nothing had happened.

Mark 16:2: "And very early on the first *day* of the weeks, at the rising of the sun, they were coming to the tomb; and they were asking themselves, 'Who will roll away the stone for us from the entrance to the tomb?'" (vs 2-3). **Why?** *Because they had prepared more spices and more anointing oils and things like this!*

Now we will see the sequence of the first one there was Mary Magdalene.

John 20:1[transcriber's correction]: "Now, on the first *day* of the weeks, while it was still dark… [so Mary got up before the rising of the sun] …Mary Magdalene came early to the tomb; and she saw *that* the stone had been taken away from the tomb." *This was before the sun came up!*

The other women were coming and wanted to know who would open the tomb. Here's what Mary Magdalene did:

Verse 2: "Then she ran and came to Simon Peter and to the other disciple whom Jesus loved… [John] …and said to them, 'They have taken away the Lord from the tomb, and we do not know where they have laid Him.'" *She didn't know!*

Verse 3: "As a result, Peter and the other disciple went out and came to the tomb. Now, the two ran together, but the other disciple ran faster than Peter and came to the tomb first; and he stooped down *and* saw the linen cloths lying *there*, but he did not enter. Then Simon Peter came following him, and he went into the tomb and saw the linen cloths lying, and the napkin that had been on His head, not lying with the linen cloths but folded up in a place by itself" (vs 3-7).

Let's analyze what this is telling us. If the body had been stolen away, what would they have done? *They would have taken the body with the burial cloths, the ones that were wrapped around Him!*

But they looked into the tomb and saw where the body was lying and what did they see? *They saw the cloths that had been wrapped around His body!* We don't know for sure, but it's most probably that Jesus just rose right out of the cloths. Here they are still in their wrapped condition without the body.

Think about this, because this tells us something very important: *The napkin that was on His head was folded up and put in another location!* Have you ever known of a napkin to do that by itself? Any piece of cloth to do it by itself? A self-folding cloth? *Of course not!*

What did these two things tell you? *Jesus had risen from the death and He took the napkin that was on His head, folded it up and put it in a different place!*

It was the angels who had rolled away the stone. So, this was quite a thing!

Verse 8: "Then the other disciple, who had come to the tomb first, also went in and saw *these things*; and he believed."

That's interesting; Peter was questioning what happened! John believed that He was raised from the dead, because Jesus said that He would be!

Verse 9: "For they did not yet understand the Scripture, *which decreed* that He must rise from *the* dead. Then the disciples went away again to their home. But Mary stood outside the tomb weeping; and as she wept, she stooped down *and looked* into the tomb…. [looking again] …And she saw two angels in white who were sitting, one at the head and the other at the feet where the body of Jesus had been laid" (vs 9-12).

How would you know where the head and feet were unless those were still in the wrapped configuration of Jesus' body? *You wouldn't!* It shows that He rose right through the cloths. Quite a fantastic thing, indeed!

What would you think if you were there and saw that? Mary was out there weeping and saw the two angels.

Verse 13: "And they said to her, 'Woman, why are you weeping?' She said to them, 'Because they have taken away my Lord, and I do not know where they have laid Him.'"

What did the angels tell them?

Mark 16:3: "And they were asking themselves, 'Who will roll away the stone for us from the entrance to the tomb?' For it was a massive *stone.* But when they looked up, they saw that the stone had been rolled away. And after entering the tomb, they saw a young man sitting on the right, clothed in a white robe; and they were very frightened. But he said to them, 'Do not be afraid. You are seeking Jesus the Nazarene, Who was crucified. **He has risen**…'" (vs 3-6).

Stop and think! He was put in right at sunset—Wednesday at sunset, beginning Thursday—and you go three days and three nights. He had to be raised at sunset on the Sabbath Day.

After being raised from the dead, Jesus was probably right inside the tomb praying and thanking God, rejoicing that all of this had been done. Everything had been complete. Everything had been finished in this phase of the plan of God, that the Lamb of God Who was with God and was God had completed the mission of being the Messiah to bring the Gospel to the disciples and prepare the way for the coming of the New Testament Church and eventually the salvation of the whole world!

Notice what else the angels said, "…'**He is not here**. Look, *there is* the place where they laid Him'" (v 6)—*indicating that all the cloths were still in their wrapped condition,* there was no need to cut them open. A spirit being can go through anything physical. So, they said:

Verse 7: "'But go, tell His disciples and Peter that He goes before you into Galilee; there you shall see Him, as He said to you.' And they went out quickly and fled from the tomb, for trembling and astonishment had seized them; and they did not say anything to anyone because they were afraid. Now, **after** *Jesus* **had risen,**…"—*coma!*

The way the *King James* has it and other translations is *'after Jesus had risen early the first day of the week'* **NO!** He was raised at sunset on the Sabbath Day, right as the first day of the week was beginning! This is the correct translation and the correct placement of the coma.

"…early *the* first *day* of the weeks He appeared first to Mary Magdalene, from whom He had cast out seven demons. She went *and* told *it* to those who had been with Him, *who* were grieving and weeping. And when they heard that He was alive and had been seen by her, they did not believe *it.* Now, after these things, He appeared in a different form to two of them as they were walking…" (vs 9-12).

John 20—Mary Magdalene was at the tomb and after saying she wanted to know where they took Him:

John 20:14: "And after saying these things, she turned around and saw Jesus standing, but did not know that it was Jesus. Jesus said to her,

'Woman, why are you weeping? Whom are you seeking?' Thinking that He was the gardener, she said to Him, 'Sir, if you have carried Him off, tell me where you have laid Him, and I will take Him away.' Jesus said to her, 'Mary.' Turning around, she said to Him, 'Rabboni'; that is to say, 'Teacher.' Jesus said to her, **'Do not touch Me, because I have not yet ascended to My Father. But go to My brethren and tell them that I am ascending to My Father and your Father, and My God and your God'**" (vs 14-17).

This was just before the time of the waving of the premier sheaf at the temple. Then Jesus ascended to the Father, which we will cover in a little bit. But this tells us something very important, that the sacrifice of God the Father for the sin of the world through Jesus Christ had to be accomplished in every way that God intended, and that all of the Scriptures would be fulfilled.

Verse 18: "Mary Magdalene came to the disciples, bringing word that she had seen the Lord, and that He had said these things to her."

Jesus ascended, and lets understand that we will see that there is no command for any meeting of any kind do celebrate the ascension of Jesus Christ to God the Father. There is no command for a special meeting because He had been raised from the dead.

Let's look at a couple of verses concerning Christ as the *first* resurrected, the Firstborn from the dead! The reason being is that pictures the Wave Sheaf Offering.

1-Corinthians 15:20: "But now Christ has been raised from *the* dead; **He has become the Firstfruit of those who have fallen asleep.**"

Those who die in the faith are called *sleeping*; that's their death, because they are to be awakened at the resurrection.

Verse 21: "For since by man *came* death, by Man also *came the* resurrection of *the* dead. For as in Adam all die, so also in Christ shall all be made alive. But each in his own order: Christ *the* Firstfruit… [*the Premiere Sheaf of Lev. 23*] …then those who are Christ's at His coming" (vs 21-23).

No one has gone to heaven! That's a fake thing, a lie! Only Christ has been raised from the dead. No one else has been raised to eternal life!

Let's see what it says of Jesus. We know that in Matt. 18 Jesus is called *the firstborn of Mary.* We'll see in Colossians that He is also called *the Firstborn from among the dead and of God!*

Revelation 1:5: "And from Jesus Christ, the faithful Witness, **the Firstborn from the dead**…"

- Firstborn of Mary
- Firstborn among the dead

Guess what that tells us? *That's the key to understanding what it means to be 'born again.' The resurrection* is being *born again.* This is the way it is:

- that which is born of the flesh *is flesh*
- that which has been born of the spirit *is spirit*

Jesus also said that **you cannot see the Kingdom of God unless you have been born of water <u>and</u> of spirit!** That water is your first physical birth. You lived in a watery environment within your mother's womb. You were born of water. That's how you got out of the womb. That's when you born. To be born again is *from flesh to spirit, or from death to life!*

Colossians 1:14—referring to Jesus: "In Whom we have redemption through His own blood, *even* the remission of sins; Who is *the* image of the invisible God, *the* Firstborn of all creation" (vs 14-15).

People look at that verse and say that He was born before the creation. *NO!* He's the firstborn of all the creation that God is doing through the resurrection of the dead. *We are created in Christ Jesus! Christ is to be formed in us,* as we have read! Jesus is the Firstborn of that creation. *It didn't say the Firstborn of the creation of God!*

Verse 16: "Because by Him were all things created, the things in heaven and the things on earth, the visible and the invisible, whether *they be* thrones, or lordships, or principalities, or powers: **all things were created by Him and for Him. And He is before all, and by Him all things subsist**" (vs 16-17).

Brethren, we need to understand what God has called us to. What a wonderful and tremendous and powerful thing that it is that God is doing with us.

- yes, we're physical
- yes, we go through trials
- yes, as we get along in time and age, we get weak and feeble

All of these things do happen to us! It even happened to Peter. What did Jesus say to Peter when Peter said, 'What's going to happen to John over there?' Jesus said, 'What is it to you if he remain until I come! When you're old, you're going to be led around by someone where you don't want to go!' *That's just the nature of the weakness of the flesh! It happens to all,* and:

- we *all* die in Christ

- we *all* raised from the dead by Christ and God the Father

That's what to keep our minds on!

Verse 18: "And He is the Head of the Body, the Church; Who is *the* Beginning, **the Firstborn from among the dead**... [that's what it means *of all creation*] ...so that in all things He Himself might hold the preeminence. For it pleased *the* Father **that in Him all the fullness should dwell**" (vs 18-19).

Why did Jesus do all of this?

Verse 20: "And having made peace through the blood of His cross, by Him to reconcile all things to Himself; by Him, whether the things on the earth, or the things in heaven. For you *were* once alienated and enemies in *your* minds by wicked works; but now He has reconciled *you* in the body of His flesh through death, to present you Holy and unblamable and unimpeachable before Him" (vs 20-22). *That's why*:

- God does the calling
- God grants the repentance
- God forgives the sin through Jesus Christ
- God the Father gives us of His Spirit so we can have direct connection with God the Father in heaven above

That's the whole purpose as to why Christ came:

- why He rose from the dead
- why He's the Firstborn of all this creation of God that He is creating through those whom He is calling

An amazing thing! Think of this whoever you are, wherever you are:

The God Who made everything that there is through Jesus Christ **has opened the way so you can have direct access**—through prayer and study—**to God the Father,** receive the Holy Spirit of God and then develop the character of God, which the Feast of Unleavened Bread pictures:

Putting out the sin of human nature and carnality, and ***putting in*** the righteousness of God through:

- His Holy Spirit
- His Word
- living in God's way
- prayer
- study

All of these things!

That's why we're here and that's why **this Sabbath** is such a very important day. What happened on the Wave Sheaf Offering Day, the day after that Sabbath? As a spirit being, Jesus can disguise Himself, so even those who knew Him, after He was resurrected they didn't understand it was Jesus until He made it possible for them to understand.

Luke 24:13: "And behold, on the same day, two of them were going to a village called Emmaus, which was about sixty furlongs from Jerusalem. And they were talking with one another about all the things that had taken place…. [everything that we have just covered] …And it came to pass, as they were talking and reasoning, that Jesus Himself drew near *and* went with them; but their eyes were restrained, *so that* they did not know Him" (vs 13-16). *Amazing thing!*

Verse 17: "And He said to them, 'What *are* these words that you are exchanging with one another as you walk, and *why* are you downcast in countenance?'" *They were disappointed!*

Verse 18: "Then the one named Cleopas answered *and* said to Him, 'Are You only traveling through Jerusalem, and have not known of the things that have happened in these days?' And He said to them, 'What things?' And they said to Him, 'The things concerning Jesus the Nazarean, a Man Who was a prophet, Who was mighty in deed and word before God and all the people; and how the chief priests and our rulers delivered Him up to *the* judgment of death, and crucified Him. And we were hoping that He was the One Who would redeem Israel….'" (vs 18-21).

Everybody has misunderstood about the redemption of Israel and the kingdom coming to Israel. Back then they thought that Jesus was going to bring the Kingdom real soon. They were disappointed when he died. But look how much time has gone since then, and how much bigger the plan of God is. The whole great magnitude of the plan of God is multiplied thousands of times greater than what has been thought.

The reason that the officials didn't accept Jesus was because Jesus didn't come and make a political alliance with them to overthrow the Romans. *So, they rejected Him!*

"…But besides all these things, as of today, the third day has already passed since these things took place" (v 21). *Hey, we were waiting the three days!* They didn't know that He was already resurrected.

Verse 22: "And also, certain women from among us astonished us, after they went to the tomb early; for when they did not find His body, they came *to us*, declaring that they had indeed seen a vision of angels, who said, 'He is living.' And some of those with us went to the tomb and found *it* exactly as the women had said, but they did not see

Him" (vs 22-24). *Here He is standing right there with them!*

Verse 25: "Then He said to them, 'O foolish and slow of heart to believe in all that the prophets have spoken! Was it not necessary for the Christ to suffer these things, and to enter into His glory?'" (vs 25-26).

Here's what He did. You would think that this would have opened their eyes when He started this:

Verse 27: "And beginning with Moses, and from all the prophets, He interpreted to them the things concerning Himself in all the Scriptures. And *as* they approached the village where they were going, He appeared to be going on farther. But they constrained Him, saying, 'Stay with us, for it is toward evening, and the day is declining.' And He entered in *as if* to stay with them" (vs 27-29).

So, He went in that they still didn't know that it was Jesus.

Verse 30: "And it came to pass, as He sat *at the table* with them, He took the bread *and* blessed *it*; and after breaking *it*, He gave *it* to them. **Then their eyes were opened, and they knew Him**; and He disappeared from them" (vs 30-31)—*POOF! He was gone!*

Remember what Jesus said about someone being born from the dead: *born of spirit they're like the wind; you don't know where it's coming from and you don't know where it's going!* This is what happened to Jesus!

Verse 33: "And they rose up that very hour *and* returned to Jerusalem; and they found the eleven and those with them assembled together, saying, 'In truth, the Lord has risen! And He has appeared to Simon.' Then they related the things that had happened *to them* on the road, and how He was known to them in the breaking of the bread" (vs 33-35).

Now then, another surprise, because a spirit being is not constrained by physical things:

Verse 36: "Now, as they were telling these things, Jesus Himself stood in their midst and said to them, 'Peace *be* to you.'"

Luke 24:39[transcriber's correction]: "See My hands and My feet, that it is I. Touch Me and see *for yourselves*; for a spirit does not have flesh and bones, **as you see Me having.**" *Notice that He didn't say 'flesh and blood.'*

Apparently, a spirit being can appear as a human being, but that's just the way that He appears. We can appear, as we saw before in a different form, unrecognizable.

Verse 40: "And after saying this, He showed them *His* hands and *His* feet. But while they were still disbelieving and wondering for joy, He said to them, 'Do you have anything here to eat?' Then they gave Him part of a broiled fish and a *piece* of honeycomb. And He took these *and* ate in their presence" (vs 40-43). *I've found that fish and honey is really good; try it sometime!*

John 20—now, here we are eight days later. We know that He was with them for forty days and forty nights doing many fantastic things, and showing the things concerning the Kingdom of God to them. Let's see what happened:

John 20:26: "Now, after eight days… [on the next Sabbath, inclusive counting] …His disciples again were within, and Thomas with them. Jesus came after the doors were shut, and stood in the midst and said, 'Peace *be* to you.' Then He said to Thomas, 'Put forth your finger, and see My hands; and reach *out* your hand, and put *it* into My side; and be **not** unbelieving, **but believing**.'" (vs 26-27).

- How about for us?
- How many times may doubts come up in our mind?

or
- Are we convicted in the Truth at all times?

In every situation, regardless of what they may be!
- God is always right
- God is always true
- His promises are always good
- He will hear us
- He will help us

The time may come when we are going to become as sheep to the slaughter! We don't know exactly when and how it's going to come, but the atmosphere in the world is building up toward it.

It doesn't matter what the circumstances are out here that should affect our belief in our heart and mind. But that we should always believe! There may be some things that we don't understand, which is true. But if we seek for understanding, God will give that, also, **IF** we need to have it.

But don't let anything take away from the belief that Jesus is the Christ, the Savior of the world, resurrected from the dead, the Firstborn from the dead, because that is the central thing of salvation!

Now let's see what Thomas said, it's very interesting what He said, v 28: "And Thomas answered and said to Him, **'My Lord and My God.'**"

Think about that for a minute! Where does

this go back to? *The beginning of the Gospel of John:*

John 1:1: "In *the* beginning was the Word, and the Word was with God, and the Word was God.

Verse 14: "And the Word became flesh and tabernacled among us…"

John 20:29: "Jesus said to him, 'Because you have seen Me, Thomas, you have believed; **blessed are the ones who have not seen, but have believed**.'"

That's amazing! That's what it has to be for us. God does not want us to have an empty belief. He wants us to have a belief based upon *facts, Truth and belief!* You've got to have the facts and you've got to have the Truth!

Verse 30: "Now then, Jesus did many other miracles in *the* presence of His disciples, which are not written in this book. But these have been written so that you may believe that Jesus is the Christ, the Son of God; and **that believing, you may have life through His name**" (vs 30-31)—*no other way!*

Now let's look at some prophecies concerning Jesus, concerning His resurrection, concerning how these things were in the book of the Psalms.

Psa. 108 shows the attitude of Jesus while He was in the flesh. *Tremendous thing! Great example for us!* We have brand new booklet by James Meister: *The Prophecies of Jesus in the Old Testament.* That's an amazing thing, because this is what the apostles started preaching with. Remember, they did not have the New Testament.

Psalm 108:1: "O God, **my heart is fixed**…" *Think about yours!* Is it fixed in belief of God and Christ in spite of every:

- difficulty
- obstacle
- blessing
- intervention
- trial

Whatever it may be!

"…I will sing and I will give praise, even with my glory. Awake, harp and lyre; I will awake early. I will praise You, O LORD, among the people…" (vs 1-3). **Isn't that what Jesus did with His ministry?** *Yes, of course!*

"…and I will sing praises to You among the nations" (v 3). *Think about what that's going to be during the Millennium!*

Verse 4: "For Your mercy is great above the heavens… [the great mercy of God in everything] …and Your Truth reaches unto the clouds."

The conviction of the Truth and knowledge of that conviction of the Truth is how you fix your heart, that there is no wavering!

Verse 5: "Be exalted, O God, above the heavens, and Your glory above all the earth, so that Your beloved... [Christ] ...may be delivered... [which He was] ...save with Your right hand, and answer me. God has spoken in His Holiness..." (vs 5-7). *Quite a thing, yes, indeed! That's something!*

Remember that Psa. 22 is all about the crucifixion!

Psalm 16:5: "The LORD is the portion of my inheritance and of my cup; You shall uphold my lot. The lines have fallen to me in pleasant places; yea, I have a beautiful inheritance" (vs 5-6)— *looking to that resurrection!*

Verse 9: "Therefore, My heart is glad, and My glory rejoices; My flesh also shall rest in safety, for You will not abandon My soul to the grave; neither will You allow Your Holy One to see corruption. You will make known to Me the path of life; in Your presence is fullness of joy. At Your right hand are pleasures forevermore" (vs 9-11)— *looking for everything of the resurrection!*

Psalm 17:15: "As for me, I will behold Your face in righteousness; I shall be satisfied, when I awake, with Your likeness." *That applies directly to Jesus Christ and secondarily to all of us at the resurrection!* That's quite a thing!

➢ Psa. 22 is the crucifixion
➢ Psa. 23 is the resurrection

Psalm 23:1: "The LORD is my Shepherd; I shall not [be in] want. He makes me to lie down in green pastures; He leads me beside the still waters. He restores my soul... [through the resurrection] ...He leads me in the paths of righteousness for His name's sake. Yea, though I walk through the valley of the shadow of death... [which is what He did with the crucifixion] ...I will fear no evil, for You are with me; Your rod and Your staff, they comfort me.... [they did] ...You prepare a table for me in the presence of my enemies.... [all coming to kill Him] ...You anoint my head with oil; my cup runs over. Surely goodness and mercy shall follow me all the days of my life... [on into eternity] ...and I shall dwell in the house of the LORD forever" (vs 1-6).

These are some of the thoughts of Jesus when He was resurrected!

We can apply Psa. 63 to David praying to God, and apply this to Jesus at the time of the resurrection. Why was Jesus able to endure everything He went through, and yet, remained faithful because He kept His mind always on God,

and the Spirit of God in Him.

Psalm 63:1: "O God, You are my God, earnestly I will seek You! My soul thirsts for You. My flesh longs for You, as in a dry and thirsty land where no water is, to see Your power and Your glory as I have seen You in the sanctuary. **Because Your loving kindness is better than life, my lips shall praise You**" (vs 1-3).

Even while He was hanging on the cross, these may have been some of the thoughts that Jesus had. He had to have had some of the thoughts that were between Him and the Father. This may have been part of it, we don't know.

Verse 4: "Thus I will bless You as long as I live; I will lift up my hands in Your name. My soul shall be satisfied as with marrow and fatness; and my mouth shall praise You with joyful lips when I remember You upon my bed and meditate on You in the night watches. Because You have been my help, therefore, in the shadow of Your wings I will rejoice" (vs 4-7).

The protection of God was always hovering over Him, but He had to go through what He went through; then be resurrected from the dead!

Verse 8: "My soul follows hard after You; Your right hand upholds me." *Then He talks about those who seek to destroy Him, who are going to take Him down!*

A lot of these Psalms tell us so many different things that we need to know.

➢ Psa. 22 is the crucifixion
➢ Psa. 23 is when He was resurrected
➢ Psa. 24 is His ascension into heaven, or the first day of the Wave Sheaf Offering

Psalm 24:1: "The earth is the LORD'S, and the fullness of it, the world, and those who dwell in it, for He has founded it upon the seas and established it upon the waters. Who shall **ascend into the hill of the LORD**? Or who shall **stand in His Holy place**?" (vs 1-3). *Christ was the first!*

Verse 4: "He who has clean hands and a pure heart, who has not lifted up his soul to vanity and has not sworn deceitfully. He shall receive the blessing from the LORD and righteousness from the God of his salvation" (vs 4-5).

We can kind of picture this when Jesus is ascending into heaven, going to God the Father. Remember that through all the life that Jesus lived in the flesh, how they communicated and saw each other was not direct face-to-face. Here He's ascending into heaven—as we find in Acts 1—and here's what's happening in heaven above as He's coming up:

Verse 7: "Lift up your heads, O you gates; and be lifted up, O you everlasting doors; **that the King of glory may come in**…. [Jesus Christ] …Who is this King of glory? The LORD strong and mighty, the LORD mighty in battle. Lift up your heads, O you gates; lift them up, you everlasting doors; **that the King of glory may come in**. Who is this King of glory? The LORD of hosts, He is the King of glory. Selah" (vs 7-10).

Let's see what it may have been like when Jesus came before the Throne of God. *Everything in the plan of God goes forward from the point of view of when Jesus ascended to sit at the right hand of God!* Then all the things of the prophecies

- concerning salvation for the Church
- concerning the Church
- concerning Jesus
- concerning His life
- concerning His death
- concerning His resurrection

All of those things have been fulfilled!

What did Jesus see as He was ascending to the Father to be accepted as the sacrifice for the sin of the world? Isn't it interesting that this vision was given to John, the one whom Jesus loved.

Revelation 4:2: "And immediately I was in *the* Spirit… [let's apply this to Jesus Christ directly] …and behold, a Throne was set in heaven, and *One was* sitting on the Throne…. [that's the Father] …And He Who *was* sitting was in appearance like a jasper stone and a sardius stone; and a rainbow *was* around the Throne, like an emerald in its appearance" (vs 2-3).

What is going to be like to be a spirit being and see these things ourselves, as John saw it here, and as Jesus saw when He was returning to the Father as the First of the firstfruits, as the perfect sacrifice of God.

Verse 4: "And around the Throne *were* twenty-four thrones; and on the thrones I saw twenty-four elders sitting, clothed in white garments; and they had on their heads golden crowns. And proceeding from the Throne were lightnings and thunders and voices; and seven lamps of fire, which are the seven spirits of God, *were* burning before the Throne" (vs 4-5). *What a sight that must have been!*

Verse 6: "And before the Throne *was* a sea of glass, like crystal. And around the Throne and over the Throne *were* four living creatures, full of eyes before and behind; and the first living creature *was* like a lion, and the second living creature *was* like a bull, and the third living creature had the face of a man, and the fourth living creature *was* like a flying eagle" (vs 6-7). *Awesome, indeed! There's the*

Father sitting right under these!

Verse 8: "And each of *the* four living creatures had six wings respectively; *and* around and within *they were* full of eyes; and day and night they cease not saying, 'Holy, Holy, Holy, Lord God Almighty, Who was, and Who is, and Who *is* to come.' And when the living creatures give glory and honor and thanksgiving to Him Who sits on the Throne, Who lives into the ages of eternity" (vs 8-9).

Absolutely amazing! Quite a stunning vision that John had received with this!

Verse 10: "The twenty-four elders fall down before Him Who sits on the Throne; and they worship Him Who lives into the ages of eternity, and cast their crowns before the Throne, saying, **'Worthy are You, O Lord, to receive glory and honor and power because You did create all things, and for Your will they were created and exist'**" (vs 10-11). *The whole plan of God just rehearsed before the Throne of God!*

Christ Who is now making it possible—through His death and resurrection—and on this Wave Sheaf Offering Day to fulfill the will of God.

Now, everything that's happening on earth in the plan of God comes from Jesus Christ through God the Father. That's something to realize and understand. Everything is on schedule according to God's schedule. We may know some of it, but we don't know all of it. We don't know how long it is until the end, the end that really comes, *but it's coming!* God the Father is going to give the word, and Christ is going to execute it!

Revelation 5:1: "And in the right hand of Him Who sits on the Throne I saw a book, written within and on *the* back, which had been sealed with seven seals. And I saw a strong angel proclaiming with a loud voice, 'Who is worthy to open the book and to loose its seals?' But no one in heaven, or on the earth, or under the earth was able to open the book, or to look inside it. And I was weeping greatly because no one was found worthy to open and to read the book, or to look into it. Then one of the elders said to me, 'Do not weep. Behold, the Lion Who is of the tribe of Judah, the Root of David, has overcome to open the book, and to loose its seven seals'" (vs 1-5).

Verse 6: "Then I saw, and behold, before the Throne and the four living creatures and before the elders *was standing a Lamb as having been slain*… [Jesus Christ] …having seven horns and seven eyes, which are the seven spirits of God that are sent into all the earth."

Who are the seven horns? *They have to be none other than the seven churches of Rev. 2 & 3, and Christ is the Head of all of those seven churches!* And being connected to Christ at the head are in one body, though they are seven.

Verse 7: "And He came and took the book out of the right hand of Him Who sits on the Throne. And when He took the book, the four living creatures and the twenty-four elders fell down before the Lamb, each having harps and golden bowls full of incense, which are the prayers of the saints" (vs 7-8).

That's interesting! It shows that our prayers come right up to God the Father! Amazing!

Verse 9: "And they sang a new song…" *This is the song we are going to sing*; this is enacting what's going to happen when the resurrection takes place, of all the saints, as well!

"…saying, 'Worthy are You to take the book, and to open its seals because You were slain, and did redeem us to God by Your own blood, out of every tribe and language and people and nation, and did make us unto our God kings and priests; and we shall reign on the earth'" (vs 9-10). *A summary of the whole plan of God!*

This is on the Ascension Day that Jesus went up to be accepted of God the Father. A tremendous thing, indeed! *This is a day that is just between God the Father and Jesus Christ!* The saints do not participate in this. The saints have no designated meeting to recognize this. But we know it from the Word of God, and we recognize it on the day of the Sabbath during the Feast of Unleavened Bread, because on that day toward the end of the day, He was resurrected from the dead.

Verse 11: "And I saw and I heard *the* voices of many angels around the Throne… [I wonder what that's going to be like?] …and *the voices* of the living creatures and the elders, and thousands of thousands, saying with a loud voice, 'Worthy is the Lamb Who was slain **to receive power, and riches, and wisdom, and strength, and honor, and glory and blessing**.' And every creature that is in heaven…" (vs 11-13). *Think about*:

- how important the plan of God is
- how important that it is that we understand and realize it
- how important that we are to God

He's called us and given us of His Spirit, and Jesus Christ is the Head of the Church and everything comes to us from God the Father through Jesus Christ. Everything that we do back to God—in love, worship, service and everything—is all wrapped up in this.

"…and on the earth, and under the earth, and those that are on the sea, and all the things in them, I heard saying… [this is going to be such a glorious thing, that the whole creation literally cries out to God] …'**To Him Who sits on the Throne, and to the Lamb,** *be* **blessing, and honor, and glory, and sovereignty into the ages of eternity**.'" (v 13).

That is the Ascension Day! The acceptance of Christ for the sin of the whole world, that goes all the way back to Adam and Eve! Christ was slain before the foundation of the world and the Word of God has carried it out. His plan has gone forth and God has called us to be a part of it.

Brethren, let's rejoice in it during this Feast of Unleavened Bread, and thank God that we have this connection with Him and the understanding of His Word, and the glory of His majesty that we can realize in our little own lives. *We come to God with thanksgiving, love and joy! Amen!*

Scriptural References:

1) Leviticus 23:9-11
2) Matthew 27:46-47, 54
3) John 19:28-30
4) Revelation 13:8
5) John 19:30-35, 38-42
6) Matthew 27:60-66
7) Matthew 28:1
8) Mark 16:2
9) John 20:1-13
10) Mark 16:3-12
11) John 20:14-18
12) 1 Corinthians 15:20-23
13) Revelation 1:5
14) Colossians 1:14-22
15) Luke 24:13-31, 33-36, 39-43
16) John 20:26-28
17) John 1:1, 17
18) John 20:29-31
19) Psalm 108:1-7
20) Psalm 16:5-6, 9-11
21) Psalm 17:15
22) Psalm 23:1-6
23) Psalm 63:1-8
24) Psalm 24:1-5, 7-10
25) Revelation 4:2-11
26) Revelation 5:1-13

Scriptures referenced, not quoted:

- Psalm 22
- Matthew 18
- Acts 1
- Revelation 2; 3

Also referenced:

Appendix J: The Three Days and Three Nights in the Tomb and the Resurrection After the Three Days

<u>and Three Nights</u> (pg 1280-1 in *The Holy Bible in Its Original Order, A Faithful Version*)

Books:
- *The Christian Passover* by Fred R. Coulter
- *The Day that Jesus the Christ Died* by Fred R. Coulter

Booklet: *The Prophecies of Jesus Christ in the Old Testament* by James Meister

FRC:bo
Transcribed: 3/1/20
Reformatted: 11/2020

CHAPTER TWENTY-EIGHT

Wave Sheaf Offering Day
Fred R. Coulter

Greetings brethren! Welcome to the Sabbath during the Feast of Unleavened Bread!

We're going to talk about the resurrection of Christ very briefly, but we're going to focus in on the meaning of the *Wave Sheaf Offering Day.*

As we do with all the Holy Days—since this is during the Feast of Unleavened Bread—let's come to Lev. 23:9 where it starts talking about the Wave Sheaf Offering Day and the significance of this day as it is fulfilled through Jesus Christ. We are going to see that this is a tremendous and absolutely wonderful day that is *a celebration for God the Father and Jesus Christ.* That's why it's not a Holy Day for us, but it's an important part of the fulfillment of the plan of God.

Leviticus 23:9: "And the LORD spoke to Moses, saying, 'Speak to the children of Israel and say to them, "When you have come into the land which I give to you, and shall reap the harvest of it, then you shall bring *the premier* **sheaf** of the firstfruits of your harvest to the priest"'" (vs 9-10).

This sheaf of the firstfruits was called "...*the premiere* sheaf..." It was a special barley sheaf that was cut, and it was cut at the end of the Sabbath during the Feast of Unleavened Bread to be waved on the first day of the week during the Feast of Unleavened Bread.

Now let me just say something here very important that we need to understand and grasp: The Jews do not count Pentecost correctly; this is the first day, the *Wave Sheaf Offering Day.* They calculate it, not from the Sabbath and then the first day of the week during Unleavened Bread. They calculate it from the Holy Day. What this significantly does is *it rejects the resurrection and ascension of Jesus Christ as the Savior of mankind.*

So, all of those who follow what the Jews are doing are following a pattern *that rejects Jesus Christ,* as they have not only in the Passover but also the Wave Sheaf Offering and Pentecost. Subsequently, because they reject Jesus Christ and do not accept the New Testament, *they are cut off and do not have any understanding.* You need to realize that that is a very important thing. We have to:

- do it *the way* that God says
- calculate it *the way* that God says

- count it *the way* that God says

Then put the Scriptures together to get the full meaning of what these days mean!

Now let's see what the priest was to do with the sheaf, v 11: "And he shall wave... [elevate] ...the sheaf before the LORD to be accepted for you..."

This shows the acceptance of the resurrected Jesus Christ as the perfect sacrifice for the sins of all the world, more importantly beginning with those who are the firstfruits of God, because then it goes on and connects directly to the Day of Pentecost, which is the first resurrection.

Notice when it should be done: "...**On the next day after the Sabbath** the priest shall wave it" (v 11).

He does not say 'on the morrow after the Holy convocation,' being the Holy Day the first day of the Feast of Unleavened Bread. This is *the weekly Sabbath,* then 'on the morrow'—the morning afterward—"...the priest shall wave it." Then he gives the instruction of what to do.

Now what we are to do is look at the fulfillment of this in the New Testament. This is what becomes so important and profound in understanding

- the things of God
- the way of God
- the Word of God

The Apostle Paul tells us the meaning of this day, and it also labels Christ as the Firstfruits. This tells us a part of the fulfillment of this day *on the morrow after the Sabbath during the Feast of Unleavened Bread!* It's appropriate that it happens at that particular time because it falls right in line with the resurrection of Jesus Christ.

This is why Jesus was crucified on the Passover Day. *God uses all the Holy Days to fulfill major, epical, historical fulfillments of prophecy that He has given!* This is why unless you understand the Holy Days *you cannot understand the plan of God!*

- Do the Protestants accept the Holy Days? *No!*
- Do they understand the plan of God? *No!*

- Do the Catholics accept the Holy Days? *No!*
- Do they understand the plan of God? *No!*
- Do the Jews accept the Holy Days? *Yes!*

—with a caveat that they changed the Passover and they changed the Wave Sheaf Offering Day, and hence, they have changed Pentecost.

- Rejecting Jesus, do they understand prophecy? *No!*
You have to have both!
- you must have the Old Testament writings and the prophecies contained therein
- you must have the New Testament writings and the interpretation and the prophecies there

We are going to see a little later that Jesus opened the minds of the apostles to understand the prophecies concerning Him that are found in the Law, the Prophets and the Psalms. That becomes profoundly important, because what Jesus is telling us is that the New Testament *interprets* the Old Testament, not the other way around. We need to remember that and grasp that.

1-Corinthians 15:20: "But now Christ has been raised from *the* dead; **He has become the Firstfruit**... [this interprets Lev. 23, *the premiere sheaf*] ...of those who have fallen asleep"—*resurrection from the dead!*

That's why *that wave sheaf was a special one* that was bound with a special ceremonial ribbon and then was cut. It was cut right as the Sabbath ends during the Feast of Unleavened Bread, and then it was lifted up and carried to the altar of burnt offerings and laid alongside the altar of burnt offerings. Having the firstfruit sheaf cut at that particular time signifies *Christ being resurrected while He was in the tomb.* But He did not ascend to the Father until the morning of the first day of the week at the time that they had the Wave Sheaf Offering. *He is the First of the firstfruits!*

Verse 21: "For since by man *came* death, by Man also *came the* resurrection of *the* dead. For as in Adam all die, so also in Christ shall all be made alive. But each in his own order: **Christ the Firstfruit; then, those who are Christ's at His coming**" (vs 21-23). *Very important!* That has to fill in with all the Holy Days. So, Christ is *the Firstfruit.*

Col. 1—again we have a very misunderstood verse for those who do not accept Jesus, that He was God before He became human. *Read the Gospel of John, that's all you have to do!*

- Christ tells us where He came from
- Christ tells us that He was in heaven before

- Christ tells us that He prayed to the Father to give Him the glory that He had with the Father *before* the world existed

The only way that those who believe that Jesus was only a man can believe that *if they ignore* all of this. Jesus said, 'Heaven and earth will pass away, but My words shall not pass away' That's why Jesus told the Jews that He wasn't going to give them a sign. They wanted a sign. They like miracles and magical things, and they can all gather around and revel in it just like people do when there is an apparition of Mary. Oh they come weeping, kneeling, rosarying and crying—thousands come!

Christ would not, to those Jews, give them a sign! He said, 'The only sign I'm going to give you is the sign of Jonah the prophet. As Jonah was in the belly of the great fish for three days and three nights, so shall the Son of man be in the heart of the earth three days and three nights' and He turned and walked away.

Since Jesus said that His words are Truth, that He preached the words of the Father, He spoke nothing that the Father had not commanded Him to speak. If the Word of God is true, it will not and cannot fail and 'heaven and earth will pass away' before the words of Christ can pass away.

How long was He in the tomb? *Three days and three nights!* In *A Harmony of the Gospels* we have a full explanation of it there and a chart showing the three days and three nights. When the Passover is in the middle of the week we have the same sequence of days that were in the week when Jesus was crucified and resurrected. That's why this is very important for us to understand.

Colossians 1:14: "In Whom [Christ] we have redemption through His own blood..." Remember this:

- If Christ is not raised then *you are still in your sins!*
- If Christ did not ascend to heaven to be accepted of God the Father on the Wave Sheaf Offering Day, *you have no justification!*

It's very important to realize!

Verse 14: "In Whom we have redemption through His own blood, *even* the remission of sins; Who is *the* image of the invisible God, *the* firstborn of all creation" (vs 14-15).

This is where they get hung up. "...*the* firstborn of all creation" does not have to do with the physical creation of things that God has made in the universe. This has to do with all of those who are created—salvation *is* creation—in the image of Jesus Christ and are resurrected as Jesus was resurrected from the dead. We will see this in just a minute because it interprets itself.

Verse 16: "Because **by Him were all things created**…"

If He was the Firstborn of creation, how could He create all things? You only can have the explanation that I gave.

"…the things in heaven and the things on earth, the visible and the invisible, whether *they be* thrones, or lordships, or principalities, or powers: all things were created by Him and for Him. And He is before all, and by Him all things subsist" (vs 16-17).

That's what it says in Heb. 1:2, that He upholds the world by the Word of His power; and that He is the express image and the brightness of the glory of the Father.

Verse 18: "And He is the Head of the body, the Church; **Who is *the* beginning, *the* firstborn from among the dead**…" *That's interprets v 14!*

He is the Firstborn of all of those *created through the resurrection of the dead!*

"…so that in all things He Himself might hold the preeminence. For it pleased *the Father* that in Him all the fullness should dwell" (vs 18-19). *That's quite a wonderful thing talking about Jesus!*

Let's see what Jesus looks like, what Jesus said of Himself and what the message was to John.

Revelation 1:4: "John to the seven churches that *are* in Asia…" *Of course, this is prophetic!*

At that time it was prophetic and it has a fulfillment at the end-time. All three interpretations of Rev. 2 & 3 are true. {note our in-depth study: *Daniel/Revelation*}

"…Grace and peace *be* to you from Him Who is, and Who was, and Who *is* to come; and from the seven spirits that are before His Throne; and from Jesus Christ, the faithful Witness, the **Firstborn from the dead**, and the Ruler of the kings of the earth. To Him Who loved us and washed us from our sins in His own blood, and has made us kings and priests to God and His Father; to Him *be* the glory and the sovereignty into the ages of eternity. Amen." (vs 4-6).

That is quite an introduction and is a summary of what all you're going to find in the book of Revelation.

Now let's see what John saw, v 17: "And when I saw Him, I fell at His feet as if dead; but He laid His right hand upon me, saying to me, 'Do not be afraid; I am the First and the Last, even the One Who is living; for I was dead, and behold, I am alive into the ages of eternity. Amen. And I have the keys

of *the* grave and of death'" (vs 17-18).

- without Christ there is no resurrection
- without the resurrection of Christ there is no resurrection of anyone else

That's what Paul said!

Let's see what Christ looks like in His glorified form, and let's understand what a profound thing this is. I want to cover this and then we are going to look at the men in the Bible who were able to see the glory of God. John was able see the glory of Jesus Christ, and when we get to Rev. 4 & 5, he also saw the glory of the Father.

Verse 12: "And I turned to see the voice that spoke with me; and when I turned, I saw seven golden lampstands; and in *the* midst of the seven lampstands *One* like *the* Son of man…" (vs 12-13).

Let's understand these lampstands are in a circle, and Christ, being the Head of the Church, *is in the middle*; very important to understand. This is not like the lampstand that was in the temple, otherwise Christ could not be in the middle of them.

"…clothed in *a garment* reaching to the feet, and girded about the chest with a golden breastplate. And His head and hair *were* like white wool, white as snow; and His eyes *were* like a flame of fire; and His feet *were* like fine brass, as if *they* glowed in a furnace; and His voice *was* like *the* sound of many waters. And in His right hand He had seven stars, and a sharp two-edged sword went out of His mouth, and His countenance *was* as the sun shining in its *full* power. And when I saw Him, I fell at His feet as if dead" (vs 13-17). *This is what Christ looks like in His full power and glory!*

Now let's look at those who were able to see the glory of God. We find three distinct instances recorded in the Bible:

Moses:

This is why Moses was called *the preeminent or the premiere prophet and lawgiver of God,* because he saw God in His glorified form. Not face-to-face, but he saw Him.

After the destroying of the golden calf and so forth, Moses is pleading with God. He was able to intervene and persuade God not to destroy all the children of Israel for their sins. Moses asked God, 'If I could see Your glory…' Because of the intercession of Moses, the children of Israel were spared.

Exodus 33:17: "And the LORD said to Moses, 'I will do this thing also that you have spoken, for you have found grace in My sight, and I know you by name.' And he [Moses] said, 'I beseech You, show me Your glory.' And He said, 'I will make all My goodness pass before you, and I will proclaim the name of the LORD before you. And I will be gracious to whom I will be gracious, and will have mercy on whom I will have mercy.' And He said... [to Moses] ...'You cannot see My face, for **no man can see Me and live**'" (vs 17-20).

The reason being is that *flesh cannot exist in the presence of the glory of God!* So therefore, Moses was only able to see a similitude of Him.

Verse 21: "And the LORD said, 'Behold, *there is* a place by Me, and you shall stand upon a rock. And it will be, while My glory passes by, I will put you in a cleft of the rock, and will cover you with My hand while I pass by. And I will take away My hand, and **you shall see My back parts. But My face shall not be seen**'" (vs 21-23). *That happened!*

So, Moses hewed two more tables of stone for God to write the Ten Commandments on. Remember, the first ones that were written on were stones that God had hewed. Then He wrote the Ten Commandments on them. When Moses came down from the mount and saw all the worshiping of the golden calf and all the rebellion and everything that was going on with the children of Israel, he threw them down and broke them. God made Moses make new ones. But also this signifies that there is a step removed from God that was caused by the people's sin because now the two tables of stone were hewn by Moses, and he took them up and gave them to God.

Exodus 34:5: "And the LORD came down in the cloud, and stood with him there... [there was a cloud so he couldn't see Him directly] ...and proclaimed the name of the LORD. And the LORD passed by before him and proclaimed, 'The LORD, the LORD God, merciful and gracious, longsuffering, and abundant in goodness and truth, keeping mercy to the thousandth *generation,* forgiving iniquity and transgression and sin, but Who will by no means clear *the guilty...* [without repentance] ...visiting the iniquity of the fathers upon the children, and upon the children's children, to the third and to the fourth generation'" (vs 5-7).

That is referring to the second commandment of those who worship idols. If you worship idols you hate God. Therefore, you bring upon your progeny to the third and fourth generation *the curse of your idol-worship and breaking the commandments of God!*

Sidebar: What one physical thing can a man make or use—be it an idol, beads, a temple— that is greater than *a broken heart and a contrite spirit,* and seeking to worship God in Spirit and in Truth, and direct access to God the Father and Jesus Christ? *There's nothing greater than that!*

Brethren, we need to understand that is a tremendous and wonderful blessing that God has opened up because of the death and resurrection and acceptance of Jesus Christ.

Isaiah:

Isaiah in vision was able to see this. We're going to see a little later the similarity between what takes place here and what is shown in the vision in Isa. 6 that we find in Rev. 4 & 5. We come all the way from Moses to Isaiah.

David did see a simile of God in the Holy place when he had the Ark of the Covenant in a special tent that was in his house before the temple was built. But he didn't see God as Moses did, and he did not see God as Isaiah did.

Isaiah 6:1: "In the year that King Uzziah died, I then saw the LORD sitting upon a Throne, high and lifted up, and His train filled the temple. Above it stood the seraphim; each one had six wings; with two he covered his face, and with two he covered his feet, and with two he flew. And one cried to another, and said, 'Holy, Holy, Holy, *is* the LORD of hosts; the whole earth is full of His glory.' And **the foundations of the threshold**... [posts of the door (*KJV*)] ...shook at the voice of the one who cried..." (vs 1-4).

We will see about *the foundations* in relationship to Christ coming to be accepted of God the Father on the Wave Sheaf Offering Day.

"...and the house was filled with smoke. Then I said, 'Woe *is* me! For I am undone; for I *am* a man of unclean lips, and I dwell in the midst of a people of unclean lips; for my eyes have seen the King, the LORD of hosts'" (vs 4-5).

Quite a fantastic thing that Isaiah experienced! When God does so, He does so to give inspiration to those who are going to speak, to those who are going to write that they will do exactly as God wants done.

- Do you think that Moses would have done anything differently than God commanded Him after talking to God on the mount, after seeing His glory?
- Do you think that Isaiah would have written lies and prophesied lies after he had seen God in vision on His Throne? *I dare say absolutely not!*
- Would you? *Of course not!*

Verse 6: "Then one of the seraphim flew to me, having a live coal in his hand, *which* he had taken with tongs from the altar. And he laid *it* upon my mouth and said, 'Lo, this has touched your lips; and your iniquity is taken away, and your sin atoned for.' And I heard the voice of the LORD, saying, 'Whom shall I send, and who will go for us?'...." (vs 6-8). *God the Father, Jesus Christ and also the angels!*

Then Isaiah said, "...'Here *am* I; send me!' And He said, 'Go, and tell this people, "You hear indeed, but do not understand; and you see indeed, but do not perceive"'" (vs 8-9).

This is what happens to the average person concerning the Word of God because they don't want to obey it. They want to retain their sinful nature, their myths and their lies that they get from the religious teachers, which make them feel good. It appeals to their carnality, and it appeals to their deceitful nature.

Verse 10: "Make the heart of this people fat, and make their ears heavy, and shut their eyes; lest they see with their eyes, and hear with their ears, and understand with their hearts, and return, and be healed."

Jesus quoted that in Matt. 13 and in the parallel accounts in Mark and Luke, that God blinds people who do not believe.

Isn't that exactly what happens in the 'religious' world? First thing they want to do is say:

- God didn't mean this
- God didn't mean that
- we can't trust the Word of God
- it was compiled by men hundreds of years later

Absolute lie! But they have that because their minds are closed, their eyes are shut and they can't understand, and they have *no door to salvation unless they repent!* That's why this day is so important.

James, Peter & John:

Now let's come one step further. Let's see where the disciples were given a vision of what Jesus would look like in His glorified form. This becomes very important because this gives equal or greater status to the apostles. In this case it was James, Peter and John. Not all the apostles saw this, just James, Peter, and John. God does not show Himself to people just because they desire it. He doesn't show Himself to anyone at anytime. Pat Robertson said, 'God spoke to me.' *No, God didn't speak to him!*

Christ did this to give them *equal and greater authority* than Moses, because if God showed His glory to Moses, and if God showed His glory to Isaiah, this also shows that the authority that they had *came directly from God*:

- not by any man
- not by boards of men
- not by rabbis
- not by priests
- not by Levites

but by Jesus Christ Who was God manifest in the flesh! He wanted to encourage them. He wanted them to know exactly what it was going to be like at the resurrection.

Matthew 17:1: "And after six days, Jesus took with *Him* Peter and James and his brother John, and brought them up into a high mountain by themselves. And He was transfigured before them; and His face shined as the sun, and His garments became white as the light.... [just like we saw in Rev. 1!] ...Then behold, there appeared to them Moses and Elijah talking with Him" (vs 1-3).

It doesn't say they were actually there; *we will see this is a vision.* In vision you can see many different things. This shows the authority that He gave to Moses, the authority that He gave to Elijah, that He is going to confer to the apostles, in this case the leading apostles: Peter, James, and John.

Verse 4: "And Peter answered *and* said to Jesus, 'Lord, it is good for us to be here. If You desire, let us make three tabernacles here: one for You, and one for Moses, and one for Elijah.' While he was speaking, a bright cloud suddenly overshadowed them; and behold, a voice out of the cloud said, 'This is My Son, the Beloved, in Whom I delight. **Listen to Him!**'" (vs 4-5).

A very important thing for us: If you want to understand about God the Father and Jesus Christ you have to *listen to the words that they have spoken, which have been recorded here in the Bible!*

- not some man
- not some priest
- not some pope
- not some evangelist

but Christ,"...**Listen to Him.**"

Verse 6: "And when the disciples heard it, they fell on their faces in extreme terror. But Jesus came *and* touched them, and said, 'Arise, and do not be terrified.' And when they looked up, they saw no one except Jesus alone" (vs 6-8).

What happened here was not literal, but a vision, v 9: "Now, as they were descending from the mountain, Jesus commanded them, saying, '**Tell the vision to no one until the Son of man has risen from the dead.'**

These are the only occasions in the Bible where we find that men were able to see the glory of God.

- Moses saw it directly
- Isaiah he saw it in vision
- Peter, James, and John saw it in vision

This is what motivated them to make sure that in the writing and canonization of the New Testament that it would be the Words of God as Christ had defined it and as Christ had taught.

Now, just to emphasize that point, let's understand exactly the motivation behind writing the New Testament and why we can trust in the words of God, and why this becomes so important, and *why this Wave Sheaf Offering Day becomes so profound in the meaning of the plan of God with the acceptance of Jesus Christ by God the Father* on the Wave Sheaf Offering Day.

2-Peter 1:14: "Knowing that shortly the putting off of my tabernacle… [he's saying he's going to die] …*will come*, even as our Lord Jesus Christ has signified to me. But I will make every effort *that,* after my departure, you may always have a *written* remembrance of these things *in order* to practice *them* for yourselves" (vs 14-15).

This thing of oral tradition is just a myth and a lie by men so they can put in their own way. God has it written down.

- He told Moses to *write*
- He told the prophets to *write*
- He told Samuel to *write*
- He told Hezekiah to *write*
- He told His apostles to *write*

That way, with the inspired Word of God, *there isn't going to be any dispute.* It's important to understand that, because what's in the Bible is how God is going to judge each one of us. Think on that for a minute. Think of the lies that come from the pulpit of men who presume to say Jesus lied; the Word of God lies. *They* are the liars. *They* are the ones who are blinded.

Verse 16: "For we did not follow cleverly concocted myths *as our authority…*"

What does Christendom follow today? *Nothing but myths, lies, fables through the occult holidays* while they reject the Holy Days and Feasts of God.

"…when we made known to you the power and coming of our Lord Jesus Christ, but we were eyewitnesses of His magnificent glory; because He received glory and honor from God *the* Father when *the* voice came to Him from the Majestic Glory, 'This is My Son, the Beloved, in Whom I am well pleased.' And this *is the* voice from heaven that we heard when we were with Him on the Holy mountain" (vs 16-18)—*which we just read in Matt.*

17!

Verse 19: "We also possess **the confirmed prophetic Word**…"—*the inspired word confirmed by Christ!* You can't have anything greater than that—can you?

"…to which you do well to pay attention… [not argue with] …as to a light shining in a dark place…" (v 19). *This is the Light of God to bring you out of spiritual darkness!*

"…**until the day dawns**… [that's the return of Christ] …and *the* morning star arises in your hearts" (v 19)—*when you are resurrected!*

Verse 20 is going to be very important when we go through the account of the resurrection and ascension of Christ: "Knowing this first… [this is a primary thing to understand] …that **no prophecy of Scripture**…"

That does not restrict it to just prophetic things, because the "…prophecy of Scripture…" means anything that was spoken under the inspiration of God or written under the inspiration of God *is* a prophecy.

"…**originated as anyone's own** *private* **interpretation**; because prophecy was not brought at any time by human will, but the Holy men of God spoke as they were moved by *the* Holy Spirit" (vs 20-21).

- the Holy Spirit is directed by Jesus Christ
- the Holy Spirit is called the Spirit of Truth

We can have full confidence in the Word of God, the Truth of God and the things that we need to understand.

As it relates to this most important day—the Sabbath during the Feast of Unleavened Bread when the resurrection occurred—*and the next day, the Wave Sheaf Offering Day, when Jesus Christ was accepted as the First of the firstfruits!* This is why it's so absolutely marvelous that we trust the Word of God.

One other caveat here: *Carnal men like to take apparent contradictions to fight Scripture against Scripture so they can cast them aside!* The way God wants us to do it is to take **line upon line, precept upon precept, a little here, a little there**, *and add it together.* And lo, guess what's going to happen? *The contradictions will disappear!* They will be gone, because we're dealing with the Word of Truth, which is:

- the Word of God
- the God of Truth
- the Holy Spirit of Truth
- the Truth written by the apostles

who were Holy men, as well as the other writings contained in the Bible from the beginning to the end; *all of God!*

Now we're going to look at the events that took place on the resurrection day, and then the ascension on the Wave Sheaf Offering Day.

We're going to look at John and then Luke and Mark when the women came to the tomb early the first day of the week, and we're going to understand some things concerning the resurrection of Jesus Christ. As Jesus promised He would be in the tomb exactly three days and three nights, so He was put in the tomb just as the Passover Day was ending at sunset, and that was on a Wednesday.

Then you come forward three days and three nights and it puts you on the regular weekly Sabbath. Does that sound familiar where we started out? *Yes, indeed!* He had to be resurrected at exactly that same time. But in order to understand what happened, we need to come to the first day of the week, and then put the events together that happened on the first day of the week so we can go back and see what happened when Jesus was resurrected. Then we will come forward to when He ascended into heaven to the Father.

John 20:1: "Now on the first *day* of the weeks…" That is *the first day counting to Pentecost!* That is on a Sunday, the first day of the week, and it was the Wave Sheaf Offering Day.

"…while it was still dark, Mary Magdalene came early to the tomb…" (v 1). *She came alone, then the other women came and joined her!*

They probably had already decided that in the morning they were going to go and take the spices and to do more wrapping of Jesus' body. So, she started while it was still dark. But understand that, as she was walking, the sun was rising; it was getting lighter and lighter.

"…Mary Magdalene came early to the tomb; and she saw *that* the stone had been taken away from the tomb" (v 1). *Immediately she didn't know what to do*; she didn't understand what was happening.

Verse 2: "Then she ran and came to Simon Peter and to the other disciple whom Jesus loved, and said to them, 'They have taken away the Lord from the tomb, and we do not know where they have laid Him.'"

Luke 24:1: "Now, on the first *day* of the weeks, they came to the tomb at early dawn, bringing *the* spices that they had prepared; and certain *others came* with them. But they found the stone rolled away from the tomb; and when they entered *it*, they did not find the body of the Lord Jesus" (vs 1-3).

Here the other women came—Mary had come first and ran to tell Peter and John—and found exactly the same thing. How much later it was we don't know, but they didn't know that Mary had already been there.

Verse 4: "And it came to pass that while they were puzzling over this, suddenly two men… [angels] …in shining garments stood by them. And *as* they bowed their faces to the ground, being filled with fear, they said to them, 'Why are you seeking the living among the dead?'" (vs 4-5).

Let's understand a very important and profound point: *No one witnessed the resurrection of Jesus Christ!*

- the women who came to the tomb didn't see it
- the soldiers who were guarding the tomb didn't see it

When they came early in the morning on the first day of the week—the Wave Sheaf Offering Day—He wasn't there. There's no such thing as an Easter Sunday resurrection. ***That is a lie, a fiction! Jesus was gone!***

Verse 6, they said: "'He is not here, but has risen: remember when He spoke to you *while He* was yet in Galilee, saying, "It is necessary for the Son of man to be delivered into *the* hands of sinful men, and to be crucified, and to arise the third day"?' Then they remembered His words; and after returning from the tomb, they related these things to the eleven and to all the rest" (vs 6-9).

So, they got there while Mary Magdalene was apparently telling them, because it says:

Verse 10: "Now, it was Mary Magdalene and Joanna and Mary, *the mother* of James, and the others with them, who told these things to the apostles." *But, of course, they didn't believe it!*

Mark 16:2: "And very early on the first *day* of the weeks, at the rising of the sun…"

Mary started out when it was still dark and now we have the sun rising; they were coming to the tomb. This is the parallel account of Luke 24.

Verse 3: "And they were asking themselves, 'Who will roll away the stone for us from the entrance to the tomb?' For it was a massive *stone.* But when they looked up, they saw that the stone had been rolled away. And after entering the tomb, they saw a young man sitting on the right, clothed in a white robe; and they were very frightened. But he said to them, 'Do not be afraid. You are seeking Jesus the Nazarene, Who was crucified. **He has risen; He is not here.** Look, *there is* the place where they laid Him. But go, tell His disciples and Peter that He goes before you into Galilee; there you shall see Him, as He said to you'" (vs 3-7).

Now let's see what happened next, and this will help us understand about the resurrection of Jesus, because He had to be raised from the dead exactly three days and three nights from the time He was put in the tomb. He had to be raised at the end of the Sabbath. Remember, just like as we started out when they cut that *premier sheaf* for the Wave Sheaf Offering, it was cut right as the weekly Sabbath had ended, or was ending. That signified Christ being raised from the dead, no longer connected to the earth as it were; no longer earthy.

Let's see what else occurred. After Mary Magdalene came, then the other women came:

John 20:3: "As a result, Peter and the other disciple went out and came to the tomb. Now, the two ran together, but the other disciple ran faster than Peter and came to the tomb first; and he stooped down *and* saw the linen cloths lying *there*, but he did not enter. Then Simon Peter came following him, and he went into the tomb and saw the linen cloths lying, And the napkin that had been on His head, not lying with the linen cloths but folded up in a place by itself. Then the other disciple, who had come to the tomb first, also went in and saw *these things*; and he believed. For they did not yet understand the Scripture, *which decreed* that He must rise from *the* dead" (vs 3-9). *Christ had to give them that understanding later!*

Let's analyze this for just a minute and see what this is telling us. We know that when Joseph of Arimathea and Nicodemus took Jesus' body off the cross that they had a hundred pounds of spices and aloe, and they wrapped His body. It was not like a shroud. The Shroud of Turin *is a **lying fiction***; it has nothing to do with Christ. They didn't lay a shroud over Him. He was wrapped with the linen. They probably had strips of linen about six to nine inches wide; probably more like about six inches, and they would wrap His body, beginning with His feet, and add in the spices as they were wrapping, go right on up on up His torso all the way up, and then do His body and then do His arms, and then cover His head with a special covering that was called a napkin.

They saw the linen cloths lying. What did they see? What would be a profound witness of the resurrection of Christ but to see the wrappings of these linen cloths still in their wrapped form, but no body in it and perhaps with a little sag in the middle of the wrapped cloth showing that He wasn't there! What would this demonstrate? *This would demonstrate that*:

1. no one took the body
2. if they would have taken the body they would have taken the burial wrappings with them

Wouldn't you think? If they stole the body and didn't want to take the wrappings with them then they would have to unwrap it or cut it off.

So, they saw the linen cloths lying there to demonstrate that as a spirit being Christ did not need to have the cloth removed to be resurrected. He just simply rose through it. To demonstrate that He was alive we have this: *the linen napkin, which was on His head, was folded and put in another place!*

Don't you think if anyone was going to steal His body, would they not have taken the napkin too? Whoever the group claiming that the disciples stole the body away... The Jews still believe that lying fable to this day because they won't take the New Testament and read what it says and look at the evidence. If you were a forensic expert today **what would you have to conclude?**

- that the napkin was folded up and put in another place and no one had gone into the tomb, except Jesus was put in there when He was dead
- that He was resurrected from the dead
- that He deliberately folded the napkin and put it in another place to demonstrate that He was alive

That's quite an important thing to understand!

Now let's look at some Psalms which bear on the resurrection of Christ. In Psa. 16 we find something very interesting.

What do you suppose that may have been the first thoughts of Jesus when He was resurrected? *He's in the tomb and He realizes that He is alive!* His last thought on the cross was saying, *'Father into Your hands I commend My spirit,'* and He died. What would He think right after He's resurrected?

If you've ever been unconscious or if you've ever had an operation where you've gone under sedation, when you wake up your thoughts are entirely different. Well, we have it right here, maybe these are the words of Christ. A prophecy of the words of Christ, the very first ones that He spoke when He was raised from the dead:

Psalm 16:8: "I have set the LORD always before me. Because He is at my right hand, I shall not be moved. Therefore, My heart is glad, and My glory rejoices; My flesh also shall rest in safety, for You will not abandon My soul to the grave... [You will not leave Me in the grave] ...neither will You allow Your Holy One to see corruption" (vs 8-10).

That happened to Jesus! Probably His first thought *was to praise God for*:

- the tremendous and wonderful blessing of the resurrection

- that He did not see corruption
- that He didn't leave Him in the grave
- that the Word of God was true
- that the covenant that Jesus Christ and God the Father made before Jesus came to the earth in the flesh—that He would raise Him back to life when He died—was fulfilled

Verse 11: "You will make known to Me the path of life; in Your presence is fullness of joy…."

We're going to see that on the Wave Sheaf Offering Day Jesus came again into the presence of God the Father.

"…At Your right hand are pleasures forevermore" (v 11).

Psalm 23 is another one, which I think are the very words of Christ after He was resurrected and thanking and praising God. There are many, many lessons we can learn out of this, but let's think of it in the praising of God the Father by Jesus Christ after He was resurrected from the dead. Jesus did not stay in the tomb very long. Where did Jesus go?

- He was raised from the dead
- the burial clothes were there
- the napkin was folded up
- His first conscious thoughts were probably thanking God of the fulfillment of Psa. 16
- then, since He was a spirit being, He merely walked through the stone that covered the tomb
- the soldiers didn't see Him when He came out the other side because He would be in the heart of the earth three days and three nights

He could not have stayed there very long at all, got right out.

Where would He have gone? *He didn't ascend until the next morning as we are going to see!* Well, right near there is the Garden of Gethsemane, and in the Garden of Gethsemane was the place where Jesus always prayed. As a matter of fact, the night of the Passover—after He had the Passover with the apostles—they went there and He prayed for three hours and then was arrested. So, Jesus probably went out to His, as it were, familiar or favorite praying place in the Garden of Gethsemane, and perhaps this was His prayer:

Psalm 23:1: "The LORD is my Shepherd; I shall not want. He makes me to lie down in green pastures; He leads me beside the still waters. He restores my soul…" (vs 1-3).

His soul and His body would not see corruption; yes, restored through the power of the resurrection.

"…He leads me in the paths of righteousness for His name's sake" (v 3)—*to do the will of God!*

Isn't that what Jesus said? *'Lo, I come to do the will of the Father Who sent Me!'*

Verse 4: "Yea, though I walk through the valley of the shadow of death… [He just experienced it] …I will fear no evil…"

Did He have any fear when He went through the scourging and crucifixion? *No!*

"…for You are with me; Your rod and Your staff, they comfort me. You prepare a table for me in the presence of my enemies…" (vs 4-5).

Quite a fantastic thing! You talk about preparing right in the presence of the enemies. The soldiers were guarding the tomb, and He walked right out. The civil government of the Romans was against Him; the religious government of the Jews was against Him; His own apostles didn't believe Him until later when He opened their minds. You talk about preparing "…a table in the presence of my enemies…"

"…You anoint my head with oil; my cup runs over…. [remember, He was anointed with oil twice before the crucifixion] …Surely goodness and mercy shall follow me all the days of my life, and I shall dwell in the house of the LORD forever" (vs 5-6).

Let's see another prophecy about Jesus, and let's look at this as having to do with also His prayer of the resurrection:

Psalm 108:1 "**O God, my heart is fixed**; I will sing and I will give praise, even with my glory. Awake, harp and lyre; I will awake early… [a type of the resurrection] …I will praise You, O LORD, among the people; and I will sing praises to You among the nations… [yet to happen] …for Your mercy is great above the heavens; and Your Truth reaches unto the clouds. Be exalted, O God, above the heavens, and Your glory above all the earth, so that Your beloved may be delivered… [which He was] …save with Your right hand, and answer me. God has spoken in His Holiness: 'I will rejoice…'" (vs 1-7). *Quite a wonderful thing that Christ experienced!*

David wrote Psa. 63, and he did see a similitude of God in the small little tabernacle where he had the Ark of the Covenant that was in his house after it was retrieved from Kirjath-Jearim. Let's look at it from the point of view of the resurrected Christ and what He was thinking:

Psalm 63:1: "O God, You are my God…"

Think of Him now praying in the Garden of Gethsemane, praying all that night thanking God for resurrecting Him from the dead and waiting for the time when it was time for the fulfillment of the Wave Sheaf Offering.

"…earnestly I will seek You! My soul thirsts for You… [which it did when He was in the flesh] …My flesh longs for You, as in a dry and thirsty land where no water is, to see Your power…" (vs 1-2).

- He knew that He was going back to God the Father
- He knew that He was going to ascend into heaven
- He knew that He was going to see the sanctuary of God again

Verse 2: "To see Your power and Your glory—as I have seen You in the sanctuary. Because Your loving kindness is better than life, my lips shall praise You" (vs 1-3). *Quite a wonderful thing!*

Now let's talk about the Wave Sheaf Offering Day and the ascension of Jesus Christ:

John 20:10: "Then the disciples went away again to their *home*. But Mary stood outside the tomb weeping; and as she wept, she stooped down *and looked* into the tomb. And she saw two angels in white who were sitting, one at the head and the other at the feet, where the body of Jesus had been laid" (vs 11-12)—*because she could see also the burial cloths!*

Verse 13: "And they said to her, 'Woman, why are you weeping?' She said to them, 'Because they have taken away my Lord, and I do not know where they have laid Him.' And after saying these things, she turned around and saw Jesus standing, **but did not know that it was Jesus**" (vs 13-14).

He was able to manifest Himself in a form that she couldn't see Him as He was. There was a specific purpose for that.

Verse 15: "Jesus said to her, 'Woman, why are you weeping? Whom are you seeking?' Thinking that He was the gardener, she said to Him, 'Sir, if you have carried Him off, tell me where you have laid Him, and I will take Him away.' Jesus said to her, 'Mary.' Turning around…" (vs 15-16).

She apparently turned and was crying and wasn't looking at the man and just saying 'Oh, if you'd just tell me where He is.'

"…Turning around, she said to Him, 'Rabboni'; that is to say, "Teacher." Jesus said to her, 'Do not touch Me, because I have not yet ascended to My Father. But go to My brethren and tell them that I am ascending to My Father and your Father, and My God and your God'" (vs 16-17).

This was still in the morning. When was the Wave Sheaf Offering to be elevated for the first of the firstfruits? *In the morning, somewhere right around nine o'clock in the morning!* So, this fits the timeframe. Mary Magdalene went and told them; Jesus ascended into heaven; He was accepted of God the Father.

Let's see another vision in Psa. 24, which talks about the acceptance of Christ. Then we will see the fulfillment of that. There's quite an interesting sequence of things here with the Psalms:

- Psa. 22 is about the crucifixion of Christ
- Psa. 23 is about the resurrection
- Psa. 24 is about Jesus' ascension into heaven and being accepted

Let's think of it this way, in Psa. 24 are some of the thoughts of Jesus as He is ascending to the Father, and He's looking down on the earth:

Psalm 24:1: "The earth is the LORD'S, and the fullness of it, the world, and those who dwell in it." *As He's ascending He sees the earth, He sees the land, He sees the oceans!*

Verse 2: "For He [Christ] has founded it upon the seas and established it upon the waters. Who shall ascend into the hill of the LORD? Or who shall stand in His Holy place? He [Christ] who has clean hands and a pure heart…" (vs 2-4). *This may be the angels singing as Christ is ascending!*

"…who has not lifted up his soul to vanity and has not sworn deceitfully. He shall receive the blessing from the LORD and righteousness from the God of his salvation" (vs 4-5). *Quite a wonderful thing! Just imagine how Christ is ascending!*

Verse 7: "Lift up your heads, O you gates…" *The gates where He would walk through to go to the Throne of God the Father* and be accepted by God the Father as the perfect sacrifice for the sins of all the world, all mankind.

"…and be lifted up, O you everlasting doors; that the King of glory may come in" (v 7). *That is Christ, the King of glory!*

- the One Who conquered death
- the One Who overcame sin
- the One Who overcome the pulls of the flesh
- the One Who was crucified

And yet, in His days of His flesh He cried out in fear and trembling to the One Who was able to save Him from death—God the Father—and:

- now He's ascending
- now He's at the gate

- now He's walking into the presence of God the Father

Verse 8: "Who is this King of glory? The LORD strong and mighty, the LORD mighty in battle." Hadn't He overcome everything? *Yes!*

- He had just overcome Satan the devil
- He had just overcome all the demons
- He had just overcome death
- He was now resurrected

strong and mighty in battle, and that was in the battle for us! **By the grace of God He tasted death for every one of us** that He could be resurrected and ascend to God the Father *to be that perfect sacrifice and our High Priest* at the right hand of God the Father.

Verse 9: "Lift up your heads, O you gates; lift them up, you everlasting doors; that the King of glory may come in. Who is this King of glory? The LORD of hosts, He is the King of glory. Selah." (vs 9-10).

Now let's see what Jesus saw when He was resurrected to come in the presence of God the Father. We know this by vision that was given to John. Let's look at it this way: This is also what Jesus saw. I want you to picture the angels singing in glory and power that Christ had overcome; that He now is going to walk into the presence of God the Father, see God the Father, and they are going to embrace each other for the very first time since Jesus left to become a human being. Now here's the setting that He saw, and we're blessed to have this given to the Apostle John.

Revelation 4:1: "After these things I looked, and behold, a door opened in heaven..."

- Didn't we just talk about the door?
- Didn't we just talk about the everlasting gates? *Yes!*

"...and the first voice that I heard *was* as if a trumpet were speaking with me, saying, 'Come up here, and I will show you *the* things that must take place after these things.' And immediately I was in *the* Spirit; and behold, a Throne was set in heaven, and *One was* sitting on the Throne" (vs 1-2).

This is what God the Father looks like in appearance: *great, glorious and marvelous,* v 3: "And He Who *was* sitting was in appearance like a jasper stone and a sardius stone; and a rainbow *was* around the Throne, like an emerald in its appearance."

Here is the Throne of God with the Father sitting in it and a great rainbow all around the Throne and the Sea of Glass that it sits on.

Verse 4: "And around the Throne *were* twenty-four thrones; and on the thrones I saw twenty-four elders sitting, clothed in white garments; and they had on their heads golden crowns. And proceeding from the Throne were lightnings and thunders and voices; and seven lamps of fire, which are the seven spirits of God, *were* burning before the Throne" (vs 4-5). *Here is Jesus coming closer and closer!*

Verse 6: "And before the Throne *was* a sea of glass, like crystal. And around the Throne and over the Throne *were* four living creatures, full of eyes before and behind... [this is what Isaiah saw with the Seraphim] ...and the first living creature *was* like a lion, and the second living creature *was* like a bull, and the third living creature had the face of a man, and the fourth living creature *was* like a flying eagle. And each of *the* four living creatures had six wings respectively... [that's what Isaiah saw, six wings] ...*and* around and within *they were* full of eyes; and day and night they cease not saying, 'Holy, Holy, Holy, Lord God Almighty...'" (vs 6-8).

It doesn't mean that they did this repeatedly without stopping. There were certain times when this occurred, because as we will see when it occurred the 24 elders bowed down and worshiped. This was at certain set times that this was done.

"'...Lord God Almighty, Who was... [referring to Christ] ...and Who is, and Who *is* to come.' And when the living creatures give glory and honor... [so it wasn't continuously] ...and thanksgiving to Him Who sits on the Throne, Who lives into the ages of eternity, The twenty-four elders fall down before Him Who sits on the Throne; and they worship Him Who lives into the ages of eternity, and cast their crowns before the Throne, saying, 'Worthy are You, O Lord, to receive glory and honor and power because You did create all things, and for Your will they were created and exist'" (vs 8-11).

Everything that there is, *is by the will of God* for His great plan for all of humanity. Christ is going to be the One Who is going to execute this plan all into the future. So, this Wave Sheaf Offering Day, when Christ ascended into heaven, is what He saw. This is Whom He met, and He came to God the Father and presented Himself.

There must have been some portion of blood left in Christ that He took with Him when He ascended into heaven so that the Holy place could be sanctified with His blood in heaven above, so that He would be the propitiation for our sins, and that the blood of Jesus Christ can cover the sins of all mankind, *for those who repent.*

Rev. 5 also tells us something else. Not only is He there with God the Father, but Christ is there to carry out the will of the Father from heaven, to complete the plan of God.

Revelation 5:1: "And in the right hand of Him Who sits on the Throne I saw a book… [the rest of the book of Revelation] …written within and on *the* back, which had been sealed with seven seals."

Now a key important thing: ***Nothing is going to be understood without Christ revealing it!*** Remember that! Whatever we understand in the Bible it's because of what God has written through the Spirit of God. Whatever understanding that we have of the prophecies it's because *God reveals it,* therefore, we must be very careful in interpreting prophecies, that we interpret them correctly according to the will of God.

Verse 2: "And I saw a strong angel proclaiming with a loud voice, 'Who is worthy to open the book and to loose its seals?' But no one in heaven, or on the earth, or under the earth was able to open the book, or to look inside it. And I was weeping greatly because no one was found worthy to open and to read the book, or to look into it. Then one of the elders said to me, 'Do not weep. Behold, the Lion Who is of the tribe of Judah [Christ], the Root of David, has overcome to open the book, and to loose its seven seals.' Then I saw, and behold, before the Throne and the four living creatures, and before the elders, *was* standing a Lamb…" (vs 2-6). *We have the two aspects of Christ:*

1. the Lamb as Savior
2. the warrior of Judah

David was a man of war. That's why Christ is coming as conquering King.

Here it is the Lamb, "…as having been slain, having seven horns and seven eyes, which are the seven spirits of God that are sent into all the earth" (v 6).

{Note messages: *Spirit of God/Spirit of Man—Seven Spirits of God* #s1-2}

Verse 7: "And He came and took the book out of the right hand of Him Who sits on the Throne… [of the Father] …And when He took the book, the four living creatures and the twenty-four elders fell down before the Lamb, each having harps and golden bowls full of incense, which are the prayers of the saints" (vs 7-8). *Our prayers come right up before God the Father!*

Verse 9: "And they sang a new song, saying…"

This is a new song for the saints that they are going to sing this song when they are resurrected. This is what we will sing when we come before God the Father:

"…'Worthy are You to take the book, and to open its seals because You were slain, and did redeem us to God by Your own blood… [not the elders, *the saints*] …out of every tribe and language and people and nation, and did make us unto our God kings and priests; and we shall reign on the earth'" (vs 9-10).

The first thing we are going to know when we are resurrected is what God has in store for us to be ruling and reigning with Christ as kings and priests.

Then he saw a great and spectacular thing. Remember, the angels were rejoicing in the gates opening and Christ walking in to come down to God the Father.

Verse 11: "And I saw and I heard *the* voices of many angels around the Throne…" *Just picture this: here's the Throne of God*:

- twenty-four elders
- Christ standing right there at the right hand of God
- the rainbow around the Throne and a vast sea of glass

All on the sides of that a tremendous chorus of angels going all around behind the Throne, and on this side of the Throne. All around the Throne were the voices of many angels around the Throne.

"…and *the voices* of the living creatures and the elders, and thousands of thousands…" (v 11). ***Great and marvelous was this Wave Sheaf Offering Day and the ascension of Jesus Christ!***

Verse 12: "Saying with a loud voice, **'Worthy is the Lamb Who was slain to receive power, and riches, and wisdom, and strength, and honor, and glory and blessing.'"**

Listen to *The Messiah* by Handel; great and fantastic is this song; this finishes off the whole Messiah—the reception of Jesus Christ at the Throne of God.

The whole creation is going to rejoice! And we are going to join Christ there at the first resurrection and we are going to be given the things that God wants to give us to rule and reign with Christ. Just as Christ came and received this great blessing, we will be resurrected and the angels will rejoice. The angels will carry us up to the Throne of God to the Sea of Glass and:

- we will sing praises to God
- we will see Jesus Christ
- we will see the 24 elders
- we will see the four living creatures
- we will see the thousands and thousands and thousands of angels

We will look back on the earth just like it was here:

Verse 13: "And every creature that is in heaven, and on the earth, and under the earth, and those that are on the sea, and all the things in them, I heard saying, 'To Him Who sits on the Throne, and to the Lamb, *be* blessing, and honor, and glory, and sovereignty into the ages of eternity.'" ***Fantastic thing!***

This is what happened on the Wave Sheaf Offering Day! ***The reception of Jesus Christ by God the Father as the perfect sacrifice for the sins of all mankind!*** The Creator had died but was resurrected back to save His creation. Later in that day He came back to the earth and appeared to the apostles and so forth. You can read of that in *A Harmony* of *the Gospels,* or in Matthew, Mark, Luke, and John.

Verse 14: "And the four living creatures said, 'Amen.'…."

That part of the plan of God with the ascension of Jesus Christ to the Throne of God to carry on the work of the Church from then on was finished.

"…And the twenty-four elders fell down and worshiped *Him Who* lives into the ages of eternity" (v 14).

This is the fulfillment of the Wave Sheaf Offering Day, and this is the meaning of Rev. 4 & 5!

Scripture from *The Holy Bible in Its Original Order, A Faithful Version*

Scriptural References

1) Leviticus 23:9-11
2) 1 Corinthians 15:20-23
3) Colossians 1:14-19
4) Revelation 1:4-6, 17-18, 12-17
5) Exodus 33:17-23
6) Exodus 34:5-7
7) Isaiah 6:1-10
8) Matthew 17:1-9
9) 2 Peter 1:14-21
10) John 20:1-2
11) Luke 24:1-10
12) Mark 16:2-7
13) John 20:3-9
14) Psalm 16:8-11
15) Psalm 23:1-6
16) Psalm 108: 1-7
17) Psalm 63:1-3
18) John 20:10-17
19) Psalm 24:1-5, 7-10
20) Revelation 4:1-11
21) Revelation 5:1-14

Scriptures referenced, not quoted:

- Hebrews 1:2
- Revelation 2; 3
- Matthew 13
- Psalm 22

Also referenced:

Book: *A Harmony of the Gospels* by Fred R. Coulter

Messages: *Spirit of God/Spirit of Man—Seven Spirits of God* #s1-2

In-Depth Study: *Daniel/Revelation*

FRC:cis
Transcribed: 03/20/2006
Reformatted: bo—11/2020

CHAPTER TWENTY-NINE

Wave Sheaf Offering
Christ's ascension to the Father fulfilled this service
Fred R. Coulter

I want to cover one thing that I covered in Pasadena: there are a lot of Messianic groups that keep the Feast of Firstfruits (what they call it), but it's actually Pentecost. Maybe you haven't noticed, but the commands for Pentecost contain the greatest number of verses. It begins in v 9, and it ends in v 22; that's inclusive counting, 13 verse long. Beginning with the Wave Sheaf Offering, this covers a span of right at 2,000 years.

Leviticus 23:9: "And the LORD spoke to Moses, saying, 'Speak to the children of Israel and say to them, "When you have come into the land which I give to you, and shall reap the harvest of it, then you shall bring *the premier* sheaf of the firstfruits of your harvest to the priest"'" (vs 9-10).

When they entered into the land, the barley had already been planted and was ready for harvest. You find in Joshua 5 that the manna ceased after they crossed the Jordan River and got to Gilgal and Jericho was only three miles away. They kept the Passover, and after the Wave Sheaf Offering the manna stopped. Think of that! For 40 years they had manna, so you'd get up in the morning and the wife would say, 'Honey, how would you like your manna today?' Raw? Boiled? Toasted? Roasted?

Can you imagine how great that first bite of unleavened bread must have tasted to the children of Israel? There's a Church of God that says that they didn't have that Wave Sheaf Offering and the eating of the grain until the next year, because that was a crop planted by the Gentiles and their hands were contaminated. They actually believe that! **But what did God say?**

"…When you have come into the land, which I give to you, and shall reap the harvest of it…" (v 10). *If He gives you the land,* whose harvest is it? *It's yours!*

When you plant a seed in the ground, what happens to it? So, any uncleanness, wouldn't you say that the dirt was unclean as far as just picking it up to eat? So, to say that the seed was unclean and therefore the harvest was unclean, 'so we'll wait to the next year.' *No! that's not how it is!*

"…then you shall bring *the premier* sheaf of the firstfruits of your harvest to the priest" (v 10).

- Who all is involved in this ceremony?

- Where did they get the premiere sheaf, which was barley?

The barley harvest started first and then toward the middle of the barley harvest the wheat was getting ripe, so it says in another place *your wheat harvest;* it means both.

The way that they got this sheaf was when they had the temple they had a special place on the Mt. of Olives. There they would plant the premiere sheaf to be waved. This was to be waved on the first day of the week *during* Unleavened Bread, because you have to have complete weeks. It could not be waved on a Monday. The day after the Sabbath never falls on a Monday. I don't care what calendar you use, it never does.

So, they would plant the grain there and Edersheim reveals that they had a special service. They had a man at the top of the Mt. of Olives and one of the men next to the one who had the sickle who had the sickle ready to cut that premiere sheaf. The man next to him would say, 'Has the sun set?' Why? *When the Sabbath ends then you can work!*

He says, 'Has the sun set?' three times! Then he would cut it. Then they would take the sheaf and bind it up and lay it alongside the altar. So, in the morning they had this special ceremony. Let's look at it.

Verse 11: "And he shall wave the sheaf before the LORD to be accepted for you. On the next day after the Sabbath the priest shall wave it."

There are occasions when the first day of Unleavened Bread occurs on the Sabbath. So, you have a Thursday night Passover, then the Night to be Remembered on Friday night, and then you have the regular Sabbath. The next day is when the Wave Sheaf would be offered in that case. Some people say that you have to wait until the next one.

Whenever the first day of Unleavened Bread comes on a Sabbath, the last Day of Unleavened Bread comes on a Friday. Remember that when you count it's different than adding.

They would be a week off. Many times it was said that on the day after the regular Sabbath. That's true in most cases, but if the regular Sabbath is also the Holy Day, then the day after that Sabbath is the Wave Sheaf Offering Day.

- What participation did the people have?
- What was their part?

They were all out in their fields ready to use the sickle to cut the grain! They cut the grain before it got really dry. Have you ever tried to use a sickle on hard dry stocks? *Most of the time it won't cut!* So the way they did it, they cut it while it was still a little green, wrapped them in sheaves and stood them up to dry in the field.

So, the only ones who would participate in this, outside of the priests, would be those ready to harvest the barley.

- Was there a special meeting?
- Was there a special celebration?
- *No, the harvest began; it was work, a work day!*

Verse 12: "And you shall offer that day when you wave the sheaf, a male lamb without blemish of the first year for a burnt offering to the LORD…. [all of these refer to Jesus Christ] …And its grain offering *shall be* two tenth parts of fine flour mixed with oil, an offering made by fire to the LORD for a sweet savor. And the drink offering of it *shall be* of wine, the fourth *part* of a hin. And you shall eat neither bread, nor parched grain, nor green ears until the same day, until you have brought an offering to your God. *It shall be* a statute forever throughout your generations in all your dwellings" (vs 12-14).

People read that and some say, 'We ought to observe it."

- Is there a temple? *No!*
- Is there a high priest? *No!*

If you live up north, maybe you just planted the barley three or four weeks before, so you would have nothing to wave!

- What is the fulfillment of this? *Christ!*
- Who is involved? *The priest, who represents Christ! The Wave Sheaf Offering represents Christ!*

We will see in the New Testament that the disciples on that day weren't at any particular meeting. They weren't at the temple. If they were at the temple think about what would happen.

Verse 15: "And you shall count to you beginning with the next day after the Sabbath, beginning with the day that you brought the sheaf of the wave offering; **seven Sabbaths shall be complete**."

That means a whole week, each ending in a Sabbath! So it must start on the first day of the week, each week, and end on the Sabbath.

Verse 16: "Even unto the day after the seventh Sabbath you shall number fifty days. And you shall offer a new grain offering to the LORD."

This new grain offering is entirely different. Here the people are involved, and a ceremony is involved!

Verse 17: "You shall bring out of your homes **two wave loaves** of two tenth parts. They shall be of fine flour…." *This is for the 50th day!*

Since this is the day after the Sabbath this was baked right after the sun went down on the Sabbath so that on Pentecost—because on a Holy Day you can do whatever is necessary for keeping the Holy Day—they could prepare food.

"…They shall be baked with leaven…" (v 17). We see in Matt. 13 that there's a good use of leaven.

- Why two loaves?
- Why not one?
- Why not three?
- How many Testaments do we have? *Two; that's why!*

We know that Matt. 13 says that 'the Kingdom of Heaven is likened to a woman who took leaven and put it in three measures of flour until all was leavened.'

If leaven was always a type of sin all he time, then we're making a sinful offering to God. There's a good use of leaven, and that is to change the form of the dough. We're all likened to one lump in Christ. What happens when you put leavening in the dough? *The bread rises!* You can beat it down a couple of times and it will still rise up. But what happens when you bake it? *It's permanently in its final form!* What is this? *This is a good use of leaven!*

Can you see leaven working? *No! You can see the result of leaven working!* It is gas, unseen! In this case it's like the Holy Spirit. The working of the Holy Spirit in our mind to change our mind and convert us. When we're baked, that's like to unto the resurrection. It's the finished product! That's why there are two loaves, one for those in the Old Covenant, and one for those in the New Covenant.

"…*they are* the firstfruits to the LORD" (v 17). What is the Church called? *We are the firstfruits! We are the firstborn!*

Verse 18: "And you shall offer with the bread seven lambs without blemish of the first year… [a type of each church; we have seven churches in Rev. 2 & 3] …and one young bull, and two rams. They shall be *for* a burnt offering to the

LORD with their grain offering, and their drink offerings, *even* an offering made by fire, of sweet savor to the LORD. Then you shall sacrifice one male goat for a sin offering, and two lambs of the first year for a sacrifice of peace offerings…. [that must refer to the two Testaments] …And the priest shall wave them with the bread of the firstfruits, a wave offering before the LORD, with the two lambs. They shall be Holy to the LORD for the priest" (vs 18-20).

Who is the Head of the Church? *Christ our High Priest!*

This is the keeping of Pentecost; v 21: "And you shall proclaim on the same day that it may be a Holy convocation to you. You shall do no servile work *therein. It shall be* a statute forever in all your dwellings throughout your generations." *That's little different than this one here in*:

Verse 14: "…*It shall be* a statute forever throughout your generations in all your dwellings."

- Why do we keep Pentecost and we don't keep the Wave Sheaf Offering Day?
- On that day, what did the disciples do?

Passover was on a Wednesday, Thursday was the first day of Unleavened Bread, and they rested according to the commandment. Friday was a preparation day. Wednesday, Passover, was the preparation for Unleavened Bread. Friday was preparation for the weekly Sabbath.

What did they do on Friday? *They went down brought spices, mixed them all up, and then rested again on the Sabbath!* But a couple of the women went down just as the Sabbath was ending to look at the tomb and find out what's going on with the tomb. Then they went back and rested.

In the morning Mary Magdalene went down leaving while it was still dark. In other words there was probably just a little light starting on the horizon in the east. She went down to the tomb and she didn't find Jesus. She ran back and told Peter and John, so they both came running down to the tomb and John writes that he was faster than Peter. He got there first, but Peter went into the tomb first. Then John went into the tomb, and what did he see? *He saw the wrapping where the body was!*

What did that look like? *It wasn't cut! It had to be that Jesus was raised right through the wrapping!* The wrappings were there crunching down in the middle showing that the body was gone. Then what else was the phenomena? *The napkin was folded up in another place!*

How many of you women have ever had a napkin fold itself? Wouldn't that be nice if your laundry all folded itself!

Mary Magdalene came back and looked into the tomb. This time she saw two angels, one at the head and one at the foot where Jesus had been lying. She came out weeping, and Jesus automatically appeared and said, 'Woman, why are you weeping?' She thought He was the gardener! Mary said, 'Where have you taken the body of Jesus so we can anoint Him?'

Jesus said, 'Mary!' She said, 'Rabboni!' She came over to hug Him and Jesus said, 'Don't touch Me for I have not yet ascended to My Father.'

His ascension to the Father was the fulfillment of the Wave Sheaf Offering. It was between Christ and the Father. None of the disciples participated.

They weren't in a meeting and they weren't at the temple. They went out to the temple and didn't have a special service. They just returned back home, and Mary was there. Then Jesus ascended! That was at the exact time that the Wave Sheaf Offering was being waved at the temple, and He presented Himself to the Father.

Remember, that must have been quite an emotional and fantastic spiritual experience for Christ and the Father. They hadn't been together person-to-person since He was conceived in the womb of the virgin Mary. Here He ascends to heaven and He's got the nail marks in His hands and feet and thrust marks in His side.

Let's see what that was like. This was quite a thing. The very fulfillment of what was prophesied in Gen. 3:15 and planned before the foundation of the world was complete. This was between Jesus Christ and God the Father alone. No other human beings were involved. So, here's the scene when John was told to 'come up here':

Revelation 4:2: "And immediately I was in *the* Spirit; and behold, a Throne was set in heaven, and *One was* sitting on the Throne…. [that's God the Father] …And He Who *was* sitting was in appearance like a jasper stone and a sardius stone; and a rainbow *was* around the Throne, like an emerald in its appearance. And around the Throne *were* twenty-four thrones; and on the thrones I saw twenty-four elders sitting, clothed in white garments; and they had on their heads golden crowns" (vs 2-4).

This is the scene! Here comes Jesus up to the Sea of Glass in heaven. I imagine the 24 elders are all bowing down at that time, and the four living creatures were saying 'Holy, Holy, Holy, Lord God Almighty,' that they were bowing down. And Jesus walked up to the Father, and I can just imagine the embrace that they had, the tears that they had, that the most difficult part of their whole plan was finished! That Jesus succeeded!

This is why we don't participate in it. It was complete fulfillment for Jesus Christ and God the Father.

Let's see what happened after that. What happened before John 20? *Jesus came back...* We don't know how close the Throne of God is, and we don't know how portable it is, but it has to be somewhat close to the earth, because in Rev. 11 it says that John saw the heavens open and he saw the Ark of God right near the Throne. When Jesus first came back who did He meet? *The two disciples walking to Emmaus!* They were all forlorn and saying, 'What happened? Jesus died! We were expecting Him to be the Messiah!'

Jesus walked up to them and said, 'What are you talking about?' So, they told Him the things concerning Jesus. It's been more than three days now since it happened and 'He said that He would be raised the third day,' and here it was actually the fourth day since He died. So, Jesus walked with them to Emmaus explaining the Scriptures to them, and said, 'You're hard-hearted and don't believe the Scriptures.'

Then they say down to eat, Jesus blessed the bread and immediately they knew it was Jesus and poof He disappeared. They came running back to the disciples, and they were all gathered together. Why?

John 20:19: "Afterwards, as evening was drawing near that day, the first *day* of the **weeks**..." *This is plural because this is the first day of counting toward Pentecost!*

"...and the doors were shut where the disciples had assembled for fear of the Jews..." (v 19).

- Don't you think the Jews were looking for them?
- Where did you take the body?

They were afraid that they would be killed!

"...Jesus came and stood in the midst, and said to them, 'Peace *be* to you.' And after saying this, He showed them His hands and His side. Then the disciples rejoiced *because* they had seen the Lord. Therefore, Jesus said to them again, 'Peace *be* to you. As the Father sent Me, I am also sending you.' And after saying this, He breathed on *them* and said, 'Receive *the* Holy Spirit'" (vs 19-22).

Let's see what else He did. Even though this was evening, do you think any of them could have slept that night? After seeing Him alive, can you imagine the adrenalin? the pounding of the heart? the racing of the mind? Here in this one session Jesus told them more about Himself from the Old Testament than any other time in all of His teachings.

Luke 24:41: "But while they were still disbelieving and wondering for joy, He said to them, 'Do you have anything here to eat?' Then they gave Him part of a broiled fish and a *piece* of honeycomb" (vs 41-42).

Fish and honey is good, I like it! Sardines and honey is good, and it leaves you with a sweeter taste in your mouth and less fishy!

Verse 43: "And He took these *and* ate in their presence."

I've often wondered: how does a spirit being assimilate food? *Remember, at the wedding feast, we're going to eat and drink!* How is that going to be?

Verse 44: "And He said to them, 'These *are* the words that I spoke to you when I was yet with you, that all *the* things which were written concerning Me in the Law of Moses and *in the* Prophets and *in the* Psalms must be fulfilled.'" *Every word! Not a syllable will be left out!*

There's a man who has done a study through the Psalms and all the things about Jesus. I asked him if he would like to go through the whole Old Testament and do it? *He said that he would undertake the project!*

What he sent me with the Psalms was incredible. Remember that the apostles preached the Gospel from the Old Testament.

- Why was that important? *Because the Gospel was to be preached to the Jew first!*
- What did the Jews have? *The Old Testament!*
- What was said of the Bereans? *That they went to synagogue and searched the Scriptures whether these things were so or not!*

Sidebar: As you study the book of Acts, what you will find is that all of the elders that were ordained by Paul in the churches that he raised up were Jews! Why? *Because they had knowledge of the Old Testament!* Very important!

You couldn't have Gentiles coming in to be elders right away, because they didn't have very much knowledge. Even if they were proselytes. That's interesting.

Verse 46: "And said to them, 'According as it is written, it was necessary for the Christ to suffer... [Psa. 22] ...and to rise from *the* dead... [Psa. 17, that I will awake with Your likeness] ...the third day. And in His name, repentance and remission of sins should be preached to all nations, beginning at Jerusalem. For you are witnesses of these things. And behold, I send the promise of My Father upon you; but remain in the city of Jerusalem until you have been clothed with power from on high" (vs 46-49).

That happened ten days after He had ascended into heaven and hasn't returned since! That's why we keep Pentecost but we don't keep the First of the Firstfruits, *because that's between Christ and God the Father in Their personal relationship!*

Scriptural References:

1) Leviticus 23:9-21, 14
2) Revelation 4:2-4
3) John 20:19-22
4) Luke 24:41-49

Scriptures referenced, not quoted:

- Joshua 5
- Matthew 13
- Revelation 2; 3
- Genesis 3:15
- Revelation 11
- Psalm 22; 17

FRC:bo
Transcribed: 11/27/19
Reformatted: 11/2020

CHAPTER THIRTY

The Covenant Between
God the Father and Jesus Christ

Fred R. Coulter

This is going to be a different kind of sermon from the point of view of trying to uncover and understand even more the Word of God. We're told in Isa. 28 that the Word of God is understood 'line upon line, precept upon precept, a little here and a little there,' and that it has to be put together rightly, as Paul told Timothy: 'Rightly divide the Word of God.' Also, there are degrees of understanding. Let's take one verse in particular, John 3:16, and let's look at this for just a minute. There are degrees of understanding that people have concerning this verse

- depending upon their involvement with God
- depending upon what they've been taught in whatever church that they go to
- depending upon their personal relationship with God
- depending upon the experiences that they have gone through

John 3:16: "For God so loved the world that He gave His only begotten Son, so that everyone who believes in Him may not perish, but may have everlasting life."

Some people read that and they think or say: 'We're going to heaven' or 'All you've got to do is believe.' They don't understand much more beyond that.

- How is it that God loved the world?
- How is it that He gave His only begotten Son?
- How did it come about the way that it came about?

The only way we're going to understand this is to realize that in the Word of God—*since it's inspired by the mind of God*—that there are certain things that come along that God reveals to give us a deeper understanding of it. Paul wrote of that.

It's not something that anybody can pick up like a book and just read it. It isn't understood that way. Yes, it can be read that way, but whether it is understood that way or not is another whole question.

There is a vast movement, not only out in the world to get rid of God and have a Christianity without God, but there is also a vast movement of lying 'men of the cloth' within what is called the church establishment of the world, and they are preaching directly against God; directly against the inspiration of the Word of God.

When you read some of the things that they have it's almost like reading the myth of the story of evolution. They have a story that they tell, and the substance of it is that those who said—in the New Testament or the Old Testament—who wrote it, they didn't write it, but their disciples told the story verbally and it was gradually formed together. Then they lay it all at the footsteps of the Roman Catholic Church, that they created the New Testament. So, *this is the commonly perceived thing that's in the world!*

What we show is the exact opposite: God intended the New Testament to be written; and it was written by the ones who said they wrote it; and it is the inspired Word of God; and it is the Word of God that is only understood by the Spirit of God.

1-Corinthians 2:6: "Now we speak wisdom among the *spiritually* mature; however, *it is* not *the* wisdom of this world, nor of the rulers of this world, who are coming to nothing."

I think Saddam Hussein is a good example of that. Did he not come to nothing?

Verse 7: "Rather, we speak *the* wisdom of God… [which is different; that has to be with the Word of God] …in **a mystery**…"

A mystery to the world, and even a mystery to religionists who do not read the Word of God as it is the Word of God.

"…*even* the hidden *wisdom* that God foreordained before the ages unto our glory" (v 7).

What Paul is saying here is that *the understanding of the plan of God and the Word of God was foreordained before the ages for the very purpose that we be born into the Kingdom of God.*

That's quite a statement! This means that God is calling the weak of the world, which we all are. As he says over here in 1-Cor. 1, *that we are to bring to nothing the things that are!*

God has given us a high calling and a great mission according to His plan and His purpose and His will *in His timing*. Not that we go out and we take over the reins of government now, but when we do all those things that have infuriated you when you watch the news and watch the government speakers speak their doublespeak and all this sort of thing, and the things that are going on—guess what? *Christ is going to give us the authority to straighten it all out!*

Salvation is more than just people living a good life having some understanding of the Word of God. It is a fantastic and tremendous calling, *which was set forth before the foundation of the world,* and today we're going to see some of the deep things that Paul talks about here *of the things between God the Father and Jesus Christ.*

Verse 8: "Which not one of the rulers of this world has known (for if they had known…)"

It's no surprise that when you hear the rulers of the world speak they don't know anything. The Bible tells us they don't.

"(…they would not have crucified the Lord of glory); but according as it is written, '*The* eye has not seen, nor *the* ear heard, neither have entered into *the* heart of man *the* things which God has prepared for those who love Him'" (vs 8-9). *That's a key thing that's important!*

Tie in Romans 8:28: "And we know that **all things** work together for good to those who love God, to those who are called according to *His* purpose."

All things! Not one thing excluded! Even the difficult things, the problematic things, the disappointments, and yes, even death. That's the whole point and the purpose of Jesus' coming.

1-Corinthians 2:10: "But God has revealed *them* to us… [first to the apostles and then to the brethren] …by His Spirit…"

That's the whole important thing concerning the calling of the Apostle Paul who was a very high mucky-muck in Judaism.

- What did he know about God? *Very little!*
- What did he understand, though he was one of the most righteous of Pharisees that could have been, and the son of a Pharisee?
- What did he say of all of that? *I count it but dung to win Christ!*

- God had to reveal it to him
- God had to reveal it to the apostles

- God has to reveal it to us by His Spirit
  - ✓ as we study His Word
  - ✓ as we hunger and thirst after righteousness
  - ✓ as we yield to God to understand

Verse 10: "But God has revealed *them* to us by His Spirit, for the Spirit searches all things—even the deep things of God."

Today we are going to understand, hopefully, a little bit more about one of the deep things of God.

Verse 11: "For who among men understands the things of man except *by* the spirit of man, which *is* in him? In the same way also, the things of God no one understands except *by* the Spirit of God."

To whom does God give His Spirit? *To those who obey Him!*

Verse 12: "Now **we have not received the spirit of the world**…"

I was given a cassette tape from the Jesus Seminar concerning the Nag Hammadi Gnostic gospel of Mary Magdalene. I tell you it was so evident that that made this verse just stand out. Here they are intelligent, studied for years and years. Dr., Dr., **Dr.,** Ph.D., *Ph.D.,* **Ph.D.**; study all these languages, know all of them, be able to read the fragments of the Nag Hammadi Library and all of that and *they don't have a clue! They're all wandering out here in the mist of their super-intellectual thoughts and emotions!* It was awfully hard getting through that tape, but I got through it. Nevertheless, *that's the spirit of the world!*

"…**but the Spirit that *is* of God**… [is what we have received] …**so that we might know**…" (v 12).

God wants us to know, but He wants us to search for it! He wants us to search for it in the right way

"…so that we might know the things graciously given to us by God; which things we also speak, not in words taught by human wisdom, but in *words* taught by *the* Holy Spirit *in order to* communicate spiritual things by spiritual *means*. But *the* natural man does not receive the things of the Spirit of God; for they are foolishness to him, and he cannot understand *them* **because they are spiritually discerned**" (vs 12-14).

Some of what we're going to cover today falls exactly in that category, because you go along and you study and you grow in knowledge and understanding, and all of these things come together bit-by-bit, step-by-step, week-by-week, month-by-month, year-by-year, decade-by-decade. Look around and see all of our gray heads, and yet, there is still more to learn. The way that we learn these things is because we still ask questions.

Let's see what we can learn here. I preached on this once some years ago, but what we're going to do is examine **_the covenant between God the Father and Jesus Christ!_** A lot of people claim that Jesus was under the Old Covenant. *No!* He was not under the Old Covenant. If He were under the Old Covenant then He would have offered sacrifices. Jesus was not under the New Covenant because the New Covenant hadn't been given. What we are going to see is that *Jesus was under a* **special** *covenant between Him and God the Father!* Where do we find this? Well, Paul leads up to it.

Hebrews 10:1: "For the *priestly* law, having *only* a shadow of the good things that are coming, *and* not the image of those things, with the same sacrifices, which they offer continually year by year, is never able to make perfect those who come *to worship*. Otherwise, would they not have ceased to be offered? For once those who worship had been purified, *they would* no longer be conscious of sin" (vs 1-2).

That's part of our repentance and coming to God and asking God to cleanse our heart, mind and conscience, *and to get rid of the sin within!* That's the whole goal of overcoming.

Verse 3: "On the contrary, in *offering* these *sacrifices* year by year, *there is* a remembrance of sins, because *it is* impossible *for the* blood of bulls and goats to take away sins" (vs 3-4).

Why is that even though it was for the removal of sin to justify them to the temple? *It requires something greater than a human being to forgive human sin!* It's also true that no animal is even equal to a human being let alone greater. That's why this was given to show that there has to be something greater than that.

Verse 5: "For this reason, when He comes into the world, He says, 'Sacrifice and offering You did not desire, but You have prepared a body for Me.'"

This is talking about Christ. We'll go back and we'll look at the Psalm concerning this and where it came from, and we will see that this is accurately quoted from the Septuagint. We'll see in the *King James* it's just a little bit different.

Someone sent me a study using the latest *Tanakh*. The *Tanakh* is the Hebrew publication of the Old Testament. Well, what do you suppose they've done in the latest ones? They've gone through and sanitized all of the prophecies

concerning Christ to make them read slightly different. If you want to study the English translation by the Jews of the Hebrew Old Testament, what you do is go back and you get a 1908 or 1905, and you compare that with the newest *Tanakh*.

"'…**You have prepared a body for Me**'" (v 5)—*a physical body for Christ!*

We will see there were certain things that God promised in doing that. Also, this has to do with the Church, because the Church is the Body of Christ of which Christ is the Head. We can get many things out of this.

He repeats it, v 6: "You did not delight in burnt offerings and *sacrifices* for sin. Then said I, **'Lo, I come (***as it is written of Me in* **_the_** *Scroll of* **_the_** **Book**) to do Your will, O God'" (vs 6-7).

Where is 'the *Scroll of the Book*'? Where in the Old Testament is this scroll? Let's see where it's quoted from in Psa. 40, and we will see that this is just a quote, and then we'll ask some questions concerning 'the scroll of the book' and so forth, and see what we can come up with.

Psalm 40:6: "Sacrifice and offering You did not desire… [instead of saying 'You prepared a body for Me,' it says]: …My ears You have opened; burnt offering and sin offering You have not required. Then I said, 'Lo, I come; **in the Scroll of the Book it is written of Me**… [Where can you find that? What book? What scroll?] …I delight to do Your will, O My God; and Your Law is within My heart'" (vs 6-8).

- Are there books in heaven? *Yes, there are!*
- What do we have? *We have the Book of Life!*

All those who have the Spirit of God, their name is written there. The Book of Life, by the way, includes first and second resurrection. *It would have to!* Consider this: *God says that a sparrow doesn't fall that the Father's not aware of it!* So, God is in close communication with the earth through the things that He has created. A lot of people think that God is way off someplace, but He's not way off someplace. The wicked have to be resurrected and judged. Then there has to be a book of those whose names are written in there for the resurrection of the incorrigible wicked. Now then there are other books; here is *a special book*:

Revelation 10:1: "Then I saw another strong angel coming down out of heaven, clothed with a cloud, and *with* a rainbow on his head; and his face *was* like the sun, and his feet *were* like pillars of fire; and he had in his hand **a little book** *that was* open.… [there's another book in heaven] …And he placed his right foot on the sea, and *his* left *foot* on the earth, and cried with a loud voice, as a lion roars. And when he cried, the seven thunders uttered their voices. And when the seven thunders spoke *with* their voices, I was about to write. But I heard a voice from heaven say to me, 'Seal what the seven thunders spoke, and do not write them.'" (vs 1-4).

Apparently it's going to be so devastating that it would be such a horrible thing to write it.

Verse 5: "Then the angel whom I had seen standing on the sea and on the earth lifted up his hand to heaven, and swore by Him Who lives into the ages of eternity, Who created the heaven and the things in it, and the earth and the things in it, and the sea and the things in it, 'There shall be no more delay.' But in the days of the voice of the seventh angel, when he is about to sound *the* trumpet, the mystery of God shall also be completed, according to the Gospel *that* He declared to His servants the prophets. Then the voice that I heard from heaven spoke to me again, and said, 'Go, take **the little book** that is open in the hand of *the* angel who is standing on the sea and on the earth.' And I went to the angel, *and* said to him, 'Give me the little book.' And he said to me, 'Take *it* and eat it; and it shall make your belly bitter, but in your mouth it shall be sweet as honey'" (vs 1-9). *He took the book and what he was to do then was to prophecy!*

Let's see that there is what we call the 'book of prophecy.' The first three chapters of Rev. are the letters to the seven churches. The fourth chapter is showing the Throne of God and where everything is taking place.

Revelation 5:1, *to show that there is a book there*: "And in the right hand of Him Who sits on the Throne I saw a book, written within and on *the* back, which had been sealed with seven seals. And I saw a strong angel proclaiming with a loud voice, 'Who is worthy to **open the book** and to loose its seals?' But no one in heaven, or on the earth, or under the earth was able to open the book, or to look inside it" (vs 1-3).

- What do we have?
- What does this book contain? *All the rest of the book of Revelation!*

There were certain things that were done before the foundation of the world. God had this all planned out before He even began the process. And part of the scroll that it was written in was a *special scroll.*

Rev. 13 talks about *the coming beast* and how the world's going to worship him and so forth. The only ones who are not going to worship him are those whose names are in the Book of Life.

Revelation 13:8: "And all who dwell on the earth will worship him, whose names have not been written in the Book of Life of the Lamb slain from *the* foundation of *the* world."

This was planned *before* the foundation of the world. How did they plan it? How did they work it out? Let's see if we can pick up some clues.

Hebrews 10:5: "...You have prepared a body for Me.... [v 7]: ...as it is written of Me in *the* **scroll of *the* book**..."

Since God is a covenant God, what do we have here contained in the Bible? *We have the Old Covenant, we have the New Covenant, we have lesser covenants and promises and things given,* and it's *written.*

- Do you suppose that there was **a special book written that contained the agreement** of God the Father and Jesus Christ?

Between Themselves alone they wouldn't need it written down!

- Why would They write it down?

So that's when all of those who were resurrected enter into the Kingdom of God they can see the record of how it was planned!

Let's look at the body. Could this have been written in the *scroll of the book?* **"...as it is written of Me in *the* scroll of the book..."**? *So, everything to do with the ministry of Christ was written there!*

Let's just review something we already know.

- What do we know concerning God in the Old Testament? *'In the beginning, God...'*
- What is the Hebrew word? *Elohim!*

In studying the Bible and searching it out, *the Bible reveals that there were two that were Elohim*:

1. one became the Father
2. one became the Son

They had an agreement!

Psa. 2—Let's pick it up before the body is formed and we will see what God had to do, what the One Who became the Son had to do. There had to be *absolute trust, absolute belief* and *absolute faith* in each other—God the Father and Jesus Christ—in order to do what God did.

Today in this world they break every agreement that they have. If God the Father were not righteous and a God Who loves, and if Jesus Christ were not righteous and God Who loves, then the One Who became a human being could have been snuffed out by the One Who didn't. There was a time when the One Who became the Son gave up His power and glory as God to be begotten in the virgin Mary.

Psalm 2:7: "I will declare the decree of the LORD. He has said to Me…" *This is probably written in that scroll because everything about Christ was going to be written in that scroll!*

"…'You are My Son; this day I have begotten You'" (v 7). There was a day when that happened (Luke 1).

- What did God have to do to do that?
- What did Jesus have to do; the One Who became Jesus Christ?

Let's see what Jesus had to do in order to become a human being. This is what is so confounding to people in the world, religious people who whatever their theology is. Some of these religionists, you wonder if you can do anything to get the Truth into their heads.

The One Who became the Son had a body *prepared for Him!* What does *prepared* mean? The first thing that had to happen before the body could be prepared—and, of course, in preparing the body, Christ reduced Himself down in power and glory—it had to be made compatible with genes and chromosomes in order for that begettal in Mary to produce a human being. With the knowledge we have of science today we can understand that a little bit more.

Philippians 2:5: "Let this mind be in you, which *was* also in Christ Jesus… [setting the example of humility and giving up] …Who, although He existed in *the* form of God did not consider it robbery to be equal with God, **but emptied Himself**…" (vs 5-7). *It means He gave up*:

- His power
- His glory
- His splendor
- His rule
- His authority

and handed it all over to God the Father! I'm anxious to see if there is that book—which I'm convinced that there is—to understand what's in it, because this was a tremendous thing for God to do.

"…*and* was made in *the* likeness of men, *and* took the form of a servant; and being found in *the* manner of man, He humbled Himself, *and* became obedient unto death, even *the* death of *the* cross" (vs 7-8). *We're going to see there are some other things that were promised!*

When He was born, God commanded that the angels worship Him. *That's something!* They did! Remember the account in the book of Luke? The shepherds were out there and all of a sudden the heavens lit up and here were a host of angels singing *Glory to God in the Highest.*

Hebrews 1:1—*Paul writes*: "God Who spoke to the fathers at different times in the past and in many ways by the prophets, **has spoken to us in these last days by** *His* **Son**."

How profound is that when compared to a human being even though He became a human like we are human.

Verse 2: "**Whom He has appointed heir of all things, by Whom also He made the ages.**"

The very Creator Who made the heavens and the earth under the authority of God the Father was the One Who divested Himself and became a human being. *You can't have any greater authority and power than that to forgive your sins!*

Verse 3: "Who, being *the* brightness of *His* glory and *the* exact image of His person, and upholding all things **by the word of His own power**…"

You think about that for a minute! The very One Who upholds the universe by the Word of His Power says that *'If you confess your sins, I will forgive your sins!'* That's why you need to believe that that is so. That's why we need to have faith and love and all the attributes that God can give us.

"…**when He had by Himself**…" (v 3). Since He was the Creator of human beings; since He gave the judgment of 'the law of sin and death' to Adam and Eve and that passed on to all human beings, *He alone This is why it cannot be that the One Who was Jesus Christ was just another man,* because this has to save all humanity.

"…**purged our sins,** sat down at *the* right hand of the Majesty on high; having been made so much greater than *any of* the angels, inasmuch as He has inherited a name exceedingly superior to them. For to which of the angels did He ever say, **'You are My Son; this day I have begotten You'**? And again, **'I will be a Father to Him, and He will be a Son to Me'**?" (vs 3-5). *That was part of their agreement!*

Verse 6: "And again, when He brought the Firstborn into the world…" The *King James* says 'begotten,' but that's incorrect; it's 'Firstborn.' It means when He was born of the virgin Mary, remember what he was commanded to call Him? *Jesus!*

- What's another name? *Emmanuel!*
- What does that mean? *God with us!*

"...He said, '**Let all** *the* **angels of God worship Him**'" (v 6).

Now then we are ready for Psa. 16; here's part of the promise. We can pick up a few clues from some of the Psalms and some of the other Scriptures. Here is a promise of the resurrection. Since He was going to become a human being and suffer death, He had to have the promise that God would fulfill.

Psalm 16:10: "For You will not abandon My soul to the grave; neither will You allow Your Holy One to see corruption."

You can go back to Acts 2[transcriber's correction] and see where Peter preached that on the Day of Pentecost concerning Christ.

Verse 11: "You will make known to Me the path of life; in Your presence is fullness of joy. At Your right hand are pleasures forevermore." *He promised that He would not let His body corrupt!*

Isaiah 9:6—*a very profound section of Scripture*: "For unto us a Child is born, unto us a Son is given; and the government shall be upon His shoulders; and His name shall be called Wonderful..." *All of these are names and attributes of God!*

Here it's said of this little child that would be born: "...Counselor, The Mighty God..." (v 6).

As much of God as could be in the flesh, that's what Jesus had! We've also seen that it's impossible for God in His glorified form to fill a human body. Why? *It would disintegrate it!* That's what God told Moses. He said, 'You cannot see My face and live.' Therefore, God had to divest Himself of His glory, power and honor and become a human being to become a child to be born.

"...His name shall be called Wonderful, Counselor, The Mighty God, The Everlasting Father..." (v 6).

- When is Jesus going to be the everlasting Father?
- What about God the Father?
- Does this not present a conflict?

No!

God the Father is the Father of all of those who are going to be in the first resurrection. He will not be the Father of all those who come into the Kingdom of God during the Millennium. *Jesus Christ will be the Father of all of those,* and the Church ruling with Christ will be the Mother of them. Henceforth then, at that time the One Whom we know as the Father is our Father *but will be their Grandfather,* if we could put it into human terms.

That's when Jesus will be "...The Everlasting Father, The Prince of Peace. Of the increase of *His* government and peace *there shall be* no end... [just like there's no end to the universe] ...upon the throne of David, and over His Kingdom, to order it and to establish it with judgment and with righteousness from henceforth, even forever. The zeal of the LORD of hosts will do this" (v 6-7).

One of the stories that keeps coming out over and over again is that Jesus was a Jew born into a Jewish family and He was taught by the rabbis, and Jesus Himself was a rabbi.

I believe that this is part of the covenant that was written in that scroll, since Jesus gave up everything to become a human being. When a baby is born—outside of just certain functions that God has programmed into the mind of a baby such as responding to love, being able to nurture, being able to have some few rudimentary movements and things like that—the brain is virtually empty of any knowledge. There is no programmed knowledge in there. They don't come out speaking a language: 'Oh, Hi Mom. Boy, I'm sure glad to be here. It was kind of dark and wet in there for all these nine months.'

God could not leave the mind of Jesus Christ to be taught and programmed by liars, because what the rabbis follow is based upon their traditions, which are lies against the Word of God. He was taught by the Father directly, and I think beginning at a very early age, probably almost immediately. Do newborn babies begin responding to mother and father and the environment around them? *Yes, immediately!*

Isa. 50 is a prophecy, as we have noted in *A Harmony of the Gospels,* of Jesus education. We'll go there in just a minute in John 7.

Isaiah 50:4 "**The Lord GOD has given Me the tongue of the learned**..."

Isn't that what they wanted even *at age 12* when He was there at the temple and He was talking to all the teachers and priests. 'My, where did he get all this understanding?'

- Where did He get it?
- Did Mary teach it to Him?
- Did Joseph teach it to Him? *No!*

Verse 4: "**The Lord GOD has given Me the tongue of the learned**... [it came from God; the One Who became God the Father taught His Son] ...to know to help the weary *with* a word.... [which is a prophecy of the Gospel of the good news] ...**He awakens *Me* morning by morning**... [every morning God the Father woke up Jesus] ...**He awakens my ear to hear as one being taught**."

That's how He was taught! God didn't leave it to sinful men to teach Jesus. He taught Him directly. We would have to conclude that that is absolutely necessary, otherwise Jesus would, as a young child, be led into sin, y*es, indeed!* So, it couldn't have happened except this way.

"...He awakens *Me* morning by morning, He awakens My ear to hear as one being taught. The Lord GOD has opened My ear, and I was not rebellious, nor turned away backwards" (vs 4-5).

Then it jumps forward into the things that would happen at the crucifixion. And you find this in the Old Testament. That's why the Old Testament is a 'precept here, a line here, a bit there,' and you put it together.

Verses 4 & 5 are about His first coming and His education. Then immediately it jumps forward to His scourging, and you find that in the Old Testament. When you understand that's how the Old Testament is written then you'll be able to understand it. But what is the key for understanding the Old Testament? *The New Testament!* That's what Jesus said: He opened their minds to the things concerning Him out of the Law, the Prophets, and the Psalms. So, the New Testament interprets the Old Testament.

With this in mind, let's see what was part of the covenant that Jesus had to respond to, because He had His part. His part was that when He was here as a human being He had an obligation of what He was going to say and what He was going to do, and God the Father taught Him that.

John 5:17—*they came to Him because He healed a man on the Sabbath*: "But Jesus answered them, **'My Father is working until now, and I work.'**"

They did not understand that there is a spiritual work always going on. The greatest work that is accomplished on the Sabbath is the spiritual work, which comes through study, prayer, God's Spirit, fellowshipping with God the Father and Jesus Christ—all come together on the Sabbath Day. It has to be a participation *spiritually* with those who are teaching and those who are learning that altogether with God's Spirit that we all learn. That's a spiritual work. Of course, on the Sabbath the Jews couldn't understand that.

Verse 18: "So then, on account of this *saying*, the Jews sought all the more to kill Him, not only because He had **loosed** the Sabbath..." *The King James says 'broke the Sabbath'!*

As we went through the in-depth study: *Refuting Sunday-Keeping*, those who do not understand the Greek nor understand what the New Testament is teaching saying that He *broke* the Sabbath to set the example that we can keep Sunday. ***That's a carnal mind trying to understand something spiritual!*** *No!* He **loosed** that law which said you can't carry a sleeping bag on the Sabbath. He **loosed** the Sabbath.

"...but also *because* He had called God His own Father, making Himself equal with God.... [here's part of what was Jesus' responsibility]: ...Therefore, Jesus answered and said to them..." (vs 18-19).

What I want you to do is also keep in mind what the Scriptures tell us of Lucifer and Satan, who rebelled and went against God and said, 'I will be like God,' and 'I will exalt my throne above the stars of heaven.'

Compare that with the attitude of what Christ had here. Of course, this had to be, because Christ has to judge Satan the devil. In order to judge Satan the devil, *that's part of the reason He came in the flesh so that He could overcome him as a human being, **which is a lesser existence than God, a lesser existence than an angel!***

God can overcome Satan any time. Angels fight back and forth, the good angels and the evil angels. You can read that in Dan. 9 & 10. ***But to overcome Satan as a human being***—which *Adam and Eve* did not do—***Christ had to do it!*** He had an obligation. Now keep that in mind when we read:

Verse 19: "Therefore, Jesus answered and said to them, 'Truly, truly I say to you, the Son has no power... ['dunamis'] ...to do anything of Himself..." *That was His agreement!* **He would take no power to Himself to do anything of His own!**

"...**but only what He sees the Father do**.... [Does that not verify Isa. 50, that He saw the Father? *Yes, indeed!*] ...For whatever He does, these things the Son also does in the same manner. For the Father loves the Son, and shows Him everything that He Himself is doing...." (vs 19-20).

What I want you to do is think of the tremendous spiritual relationship that Jesus Christ had with God the Father all during His life while this was going on.

It's really something! That's why He was given authority as the Son of man and so forth.

John 3:31 *was also part of it and this also verifies it*: "He Who comes from above is above all. The one who is of the earth is earthly, and speaks of the earth. **He Who comes from heaven is above** all.”

Isn't it interesting that people wonder where Jesus came from? *Here it is; He comes from heaven!*

Verse 32: "And what He has seen and heard… [that's what the Father taught Him; had to be] …this *is what* He testifies; but no one receives His testimony. The one who has received His testimony has set his seal that God is true; for He Whom God has sent speaks the words of God…" (vs 32-34). *That was Jesus' obligation under this covenant!*

Just like when we are baptized and put into the watery grave and we enter into that covenant relationship with God, it is a covenant relationship unto death. That's why it is a burial, and we are conjoined to the death of Christ Who paid for our sins. Now then, when we come out of that watery grave we have an obligation to do, based upon the terms of the covenant.

- we are to obey God
- we are to love God
- we are to believe God
- we are to trust in Him

All of those things are our obligation!

Just like with *the covenant that Christ had between Him and God the Father,* He had an obligation. His obligation was to *speak what God told Him to speak!* Whatever the commandment was He told Him to speak, He spoke. That we understand, and then this becomes much more profound that these words are the words that God the Father has given. So, when anyone rejects Christ they reject the Father. That's why John said, 'He who has not the Son has not the Father.'

Verse 34: "For He Whom God has sent speaks the words of God; and God gives not the Spirit by measure *unto Him.* The Father loves the Son and has given all things into His hand. The one who believes in the Son has everlasting life; but the one who does not obey the Son shall not see life, for the wrath of God remains on him" (vs 34-36).

Isn't it interesting that a lot of these things that we're picking up, which had to be part of that covenant that was written in the *scroll of the book*, we find in John 7. Let's look at just a couple of things that are important here. Let's just talk about the Feast of Tabernacles for a minute because this is what John 7 is talking about.

- Would Jesus command His brothers and mother to sin? *No!*
- Did He tell them to go up to the Feast? *Yes, He did!*

So therefore, anybody who says that keeping the Feast of Tabernacles is a sin *is accusing Jesus of commanding sin!* They don't think of it that way, but that's what they're doing. His brother said, 'Go up and show yourself to the world.'

John 7:6: "Therefore, Jesus said to them, 'My time has not yet come, but your time is always ready. The world cannot hate you; but it hates Me because I testify concerning it, that its works are evil. **You go up to this Feast**…. [there it is, He said go to the Feast of Tabernacles] …I am not going up to this Feast now…'" (vs 6-8).

What He wanted to happen was for them to leave and be on their way then He would come up privately, because He was going to the Feast but He had a plan in mind what He was going to do when He got there, and He couldn't do it if He went with them. What would happen? I'm sure they didn't have binoculars in those days, but I'm sure they had everybody up there looking: There's Mary, James, Joseph and so forth. 'There they are. Where's Jesus? We don't see Him.' He had a plan in mind, we'll see what it is.

Verse 8: "'You go up to this Feast. I am not going up to this Feast now… [at this present minute] …for My time has not yet been fulfilled.' And after saying these things to them, He remained in Galilee. But after His brothers had gone up, then Jesus also went up to the Feast, not openly, but as it were in secret. As a result, the Jews were seeking Him at the Feast, and said, 'Where is He?' Now there was much debating about Him among the people. Some said, 'He is a good Man.' But others said, 'No, but He is deceiving the people.' However, no one spoke publicly about Him for fear of the Jews" (vs 8-13).

He was there keeping the Feast all the time but didn't show Himself till the middle of the Feast. Notice the reaction:

Verse 15: "And the Jews were amazed, saying, 'How does this man know letters… [How does He understand the Scriptures?] …having never been schooled?'" *Let's stop here and think for a minute*:

- we have the Sadducees
- we have the Pharisees
- we have the Essenes
- we have all of the rabbis
- we have the school of Hillel
- we have the school of Gamaliel

Those were the two main schools in Jerusalem!

So, if you wanted to become some mucky-muck in Judaism you had to go to one of these two schools. Don't you think, since this is the Feast of Tabernacles just before His crucifixion, all of the leading Jewish rabbis checked out with one another from the very beginning and said:

- Did he go to your school?
- Did he go to your school?
- Who taught this guy?

What do you think they would have done to the rabbi who had taught Him? *Sayonara!* He would have been tried and convicted. 'How dare you teach someone to usurp our authority'—whatever you want to add to it.

Verse 16: "Jesus answered them and said, 'My doctrine is not Mine, but His Who sent Me. If anyone desires to do His will, he shall know of the doctrine, whether it is from God, or *whether* I speak from My own self'" (vs 16-17).

There it is, *His obligation!* **This was part of His covenant with God the Father!** So, the One Who became the Father said, 'All right, I'll watch over You, I'll teach You while you grow up, and when the times comes for the beginning of Your ministry'—which we find there in Mark 1, the beginning of the Gospel of Jesus Christ and so forth—'then You are to teach and say only My words'; which is what He did all the way through.

John 8:28: "Then Jesus said to them, 'When you have lifted up the Son of man, then you yourselves shall know that I AM, and *that* I do nothing of Myself. But as the Father taught Me, these things I speak.'…. [How many times did He say that over and over again?] …And He Who sent Me is with Me. The Father has not left Me alone because I always do the things that please Him'" (vs 28-29).

Was keeping the Feast of Tabernacles in the manner that He kept it pleasing to God? *It had to be!* That was part of His obligation: **always speak the words that God the Father taught Him; always do the things that please Him!** This is the separate covenant that Jesus was under, and **the covenant between Him and God the Father!** It's going to be very interesting when we're resurrected and we meet the Father and we see where these books are written. I'm sure that They're going to open them up and say—however they keep time in heaven in relationship to the earth—*'This was Our agreement.''*

John 10:14: "I am the good Shepherd, and I know those who *are* Mine, and am known of those who *are* Mine. Just as the Father knows Me, I also know the Father; and I lay down My life for the sheep" (vs 14-15). *That was part of His agreement, to lay down His life!*

He had to do the hardest thing than any human being could do, lay down His life into the manner that it was taken.

Verse 16: "And I have other sheep that are not of this fold. I must bring those also, and they shall hear My voice; and there shall be one flock *and* one Shepherd. On account of this, the Father loves Me: because I lay down My life, **that I may receive it back again**" (vs 16-17). *That's the proper translation!* He didn't take it back. This is passive, *receive.*

God the Father had to give it back to Him. Remember what happened when Jesus was on the cross, one of the very last things He said? *'Father, into Your hands I commend My Spirit,'* and He gave up the Spirit. That's when He died, because He had to be dead. It's not Docetism where a spirit being called Christ imposed itself into the body of a man called Jesus, and therefore, Jesus Christ did not die. The Spirit Christ went back to the Father, and the man Jesus died. That's not what it was.

Verse 18: "No one takes it from Me, but I lay it down of Myself…. [of His own accord He did it] …I have authority to lay it down… [that's part of the covenant agreement that they had] …and authority to receive it back again. **This commandment I received from My Father.**"

That's quite a thing! That helps you understand the voluntary choice and will of God to do this. Think back and go back to the verse we started with, John 3:16, where it says that 'God so loved the world.'

- think about what the Father and the Son worked out
- think of what They did
- this is a tremendous thing
- this is a tremendous covenant that They had

Let's look at some other things concerning this. Let's look and see and understand when He says *'I lay My life down,'*; let's see what He *knew* was going to happen. He gave this prophecy Himself. Did Jesus understand exactly what was going to happen to Him? *Yes, He did! This is why the sacrifice of Jesus Christ saves all who repent!* This is why God alone can help people in these situations because He went through it all.

Isaiah 53:1: "Who has believed our report?…. [How many people really believe God?] …And to whom is the arm of the LORD revealed? For He shall grow up before Him as a tender plant… [that's Christ's childhood] …and as a root out of a dry ground; He has no form nor comeliness that we should look upon Him, nor beauty that we should desire Him" (vs 1-2). *He's just an ordinary looking man!*

Notice what kind of life He lived. You think you've got troubles, *this is what God had to suffer in the flesh among His own!* It says there in John 1 that *'He created the world and the world didn't know Him and He came to His own and His own didn't receive Him.'*

- if you're down and out
- if you're alone
- if you think nobody likes you
- if you think no one loves you
- if you think no one cares for you
  - ✓ *look up, pray to God*
  - ✓ *look to Jesus Christ*
  - ✓ *He'll help you*

Verse 3: "*He is* despised and rejected of men; a Man of sorrows, and acquainted with grief… [this has to do when they saw Him on the cross] …and we hid as it were our faces from Him, He was despised, and we esteemed Him not. Surely He has borne our infirmities, and carried our sorrows…" (vs 3-4).

That's why it says, 'All you who are heavy burdened, come unto Me for My yoke is easy and My burden is light' (Matt. 11). You can put all of those on Christ.

"…yet, we esteemed Him stricken, smitten of God, and afflicted" (v 4).

Yeah, they came by and said—and even one of the two robbers said—'Well, if You're the Christ save Yourself and save us.' The other one said, 'You don't even know what you're talking about. We're here because we did it. We're here justly, but He not justly.' Then he said, 'Lord, remember me when You come into Your Kingdom.'

Verse 5: "But He *was* wounded for our transgressions… [not for anything He did] …*He was* crushed for our iniquities; the chastisement of our peace *was* upon Him…"

In other words, in order for us to have peace with God, the penalty of our sins had to be slashed upon His back with the scourging of crucifixion to bring peace.

"…and with His stripes we ourselves are healed. All we like sheep have gone astray; we have turned each one to his own way; and the LORD has laid on Him the iniquity of us all…. [because He was responsible] …He was oppressed, and He was afflicted; yet, He opened not His mouth. He is brought as a lamb to the slaughter; and as a sheep before its shearers is dumb, so He opened not His mouth. By oppression and judgment He was taken away; and with His generation who did consider that He was cut off out of the land of the living; for the transgression of My people He *was* stricken. And He made His grave with the wicked…" (vs 5-9).

All of this was there! All of this had to be written in *the scroll that is all about Christ and the covenant that God the Father and Jesus Christ had,* and then we are given some of it here and some of it there and put all together. The key thing that really got me started on this was there was no place in the Bible where that part which says *'it's written of Me in a scroll of a book,'* where you can find what was written, except you get a bit here and a bit there.

Verse 9: "And He made His grave with the wicked, and with the rich in His death; although He had done no violence, nor *was any* deceit in His mouth. Yet, the LORD willed to crush Him…" (vs 9-10)—*even though He did!* That goes back to Gen. 3:15.

Even though it pleased God to do it to solve the problem of sin and His creation of human beings, it still was so gruesome that when it came down to the final three hours of Christ on the cross, it became dark, *and Jesus had to do it alone!* That was something! That's why they had this covenant. That's why this agreement was there.

"…and He has put Him to grief: You shall make His life an offering for sin…. [then out of that]: …He shall see His seed…" (v 10).

As it is in the 'great congregation': *'I will declare Your name unto My* brethren' (Heb. 2) has got to be at the resurrection. Here is Christ, all of us are resurrected and we meet Him in the air, and He turns to God the Father and says, 'Here are the children that You have given Me.' And He's going to go right down the line and give everyone a new name.

"…He shall prolong His days, and that the purpose of the LORD might prosper in His hand. He shall see of the travail of His soul. He shall be fully satisfied…. [takes care of all sin] … By His knowledge shall My righteous Servant justify many; and **He shall bear their iniquities**" (vs 10-11).

Only God can do that. No human being, no animal. This had to be carefully prepared and worked out well ahead of time.

Verse 12: "Therefore, I will divide to Him *a portion* with the great, and He shall divide the spoil with the strong… [that's giving a reward to all of us] …because He has poured out His soul to death; and He was counted among the transgressors; and He bore the sin of many, and made intercession for transgressors."

Maybe this will give us more understanding. It's one of these things that we come to realize after we've been converted a long time and have really studied the Word of God.

Hebrews 10:5: "**For this reason, when He comes into the world, He says, 'Sacrifice and offering You did not desire, but You have prepared a body for Me. You did not delight in burnt offerings and *sacrifices* for sin. Then said I, "Lo, I come (*as* it is written of Me in *the* Scroll of *the* Book) to do Your will, O God"'"** (vs 5-7).

That's something, brethren! We're part of it! Here we're living right at the end of the age and it's going to be really profound to see what God is going to do.

That is a covenant—since God is a covenant God—*that God the Father and Jesus Christ made when He came to the earth!*

Scriptures from *The Holy Bible in Its Original Order, A Faithful Version*

Scriptural References:

1) John 3:16
2) 1 Corinthians 2:6-14
3) Hebrews 10:1-7
4) Psalm 40:6-8
5) Revelation 10:1-9
6) Revelation 5:1-3
7) Revelation 13:8
8) Hebrews 10:5, 7
9) Psalm 2:7
10) Philippians 2:5-8
11) Hebrews 1:1-6
12) Psalm 16:10-11
13) Isaiah 9:6-7
14) Isaiah 50:4-5
15) John 5:17-20
16) John 3:31-36
17) John 7:6-13, 15-17
18) John 8:28-29
19) John 10:14-18
20) Isaiah 53:1-12
21) Hebrews 10:5-7

Scriptures referenced, not quoted:

- Isaiah 28
- 1 Corinthians 1
- Romans 8:28
- Luke 1
- Acts 2
- Daniel 9 & 10
- Mark 1
- John 1

- Matthew 11
- Genesis 3:15
- Hebrews 2

Also referenced:

- Book: *A Harmony of the Gospels* by Fred R. Coulter
- In-Dept Study: *Refuting Sunday-Keeping*

FRC:cis
Transcribed: 11/07/2005
Formatted: bo—11/2020

CHAPTER THIRTY-ONE

How to Count Pentecost and Count 50

Fred R. Coulter

Greetings, brethren, we want to go through *how to count Pentecost and the meaning of counting to fifty!*

What we need to understand is that *everything concerning the Holy Days is keyed to the Passover!* The Passover is most important because it is the crucifixion of Jesus Christ, and that starts out in Gen. 3, as we have already understood and goes through to Gen. 15, Gen. 22, Exo. 12, and then on down to the time of Christ when on the Passover night He instituted the New Covenant symbols. Then on the day portion of the Passover He was crucified. Then we immediately go into the Feast of Unleavened Bread, which is connected with it, then on to:

- the Wave Sheaf Offering Day
- Pentecost
- Trumpets
- Atonement
- Tabernacles
- Last Great Day

Now, if we count the Passover as one of the Feasts of God, which it is, then we have 7 Holy Days and we have a total of 8 Feasts. Pentecost is the 4th Feast of the 8, or the middle Feast. As you will see when you get into the transcripts concerning events to take place *before* Pentecost, and then events to take place *after* Pentecost, you will see that *Pentecost is the tipping point in history!*

We've also understood that <u>Satan</u> *likes to confuse everything*. Satan likes to destroy the knowledge of the true Christian Passover. So, we have all of the counterfeits concerning that—we've covered a lot of that—and that does away with Unleavened Bread, *substituting it with Lent and Easter!*

The Wave Sheaf Offering Day is then made to be the resurrection day, which is ***not*** the resurrection day. Pentecost also is confused, not only by those who profess Christianity, but also by those who *profess* to know the Truth; that is being the Jews. We will see how Judaism also affected things concerning the understanding of the Holy Days of God. Because the Jews are not in the land of Palestine, they do not keep a 14th Passover, but *they keep* a 15th Passover. If you read *The Christian Passover* book, I have a chapter in there, <u>The</u> <u>Passover of the Rejected</u> and why they do it on the 15th.

Likewise, as we'll see a little later, they always have their Pentecost on a fixed day of the calendar—*because they begin counting in the wrong place*—with the exception of one of the five variations of when Passover occurs.

Let's see how that Pentecost pictures the receiving of the Holy Spirit. This becomes important for us to understand and how it's all tied together with Unleavened Bread, Wave Sheaf Offering Day, and all of these things.

Acts 2:1: "And when the Day *of Pentecost,* the fiftieth day, was being fulfilled, they were all with one accord in the same place."

So, it's not the day before, it's not the day after; *it's during the 50th day* that it is being fulfilled. Now then, the apostles preached; God gave them the ability to preach supernaturally in all the languages of those who were gathered there at the temple. God began it at the temple to show the sign of ***His*** authority, and that it was *directly from Him!*

What I want to do is show you that in order to receive the Holy Spirit, it has got to go back to the Passover and the sacrifice of Jesus Christ, and then the Wave Sheaf Offering and Jesus' acceptance for our sins *as the perfect sacrifice of God* in the Throne of God in heaven above.

Verse 36: "Therefore, let all *the* house of Israel know with full assurance that God has made this *same* Jesus, Whom you crucified, both Lord and Christ."

So, here we are in Pentecost going back to Passover because they fit together as a unit. As you study the things concerning the seven churches, and all of those things, which in this transcription book of the study of the Holy Days, you will have all of those things combined to show the various meanings of the 7th week and the 50th day.

Verse 37: "Now, after hearing *this,* they were cut to the heart; and they said to Peter and the other apostles, 'Men *and* brethren, what shall we do?' Then Peter said to them, 'Repent and be baptized each one of you in the name of Jesus Christ for *the* remission of sins, and you yourselves shall receive the gift of the Holy Spirit'" (vs 37-38).

The Day of Pentecost pictures the day in which *the Holy Spirit was given in power!* It pictures the day that also commemorates *us receiving the Holy Spirit!* We will see that this 50th day—though we receive it at other times whenever we are baptized—but with the Feast of Pentecost the meaning is it has to do with **our receiving of the Holy Spirit! It's connected back to the Passover and the Feast of Unleavened Bread!**

Verse 39: "For the promise is to you and to your children, and to all those who are afar off, as many as *the* Lord our God may call."

Now let's look a just a couple of other things that are important for us to understand and realize. We are going to see with Rom. 5 how important that it is *everything ties back to the Passover and the crucifixion of Jesus Christ!*

Romans 5:6: "For even when we were without strength, at the appointed time..."

Even Paul in writing and preaching goes back to the crucifixion of Christ on the Passover Day *at the appointed time,* and it was not at any other time.

"...Christ died for *the* ungodly. For rarely will anyone die for a righteous man, although perhaps someone might have the courage even to die for a good man. But God commends His own love to us because, when we were still sinners, Christ died for us. Much more, therefore, having been justified now by His blood..." (vs 6-9). *Justification is a two-step operation*:

1. the sacrifice of Jesus Christ
2. His acceptance of the Wave Sheaf Offering Day, *which begins the first day of the count to Pentecost*

"...we shall be saved from wrath through Him. For if, when we were enemies, we were reconciled to God through the death of His own Son, much more *then*, having been reconciled, we shall be saved by His life" (vs 9-10).

Rom. 4—concerning faith and imputation of righteousness through having your sins forgiven. Using the example of Abraham:

Romans 4:23: "But it was not written for his sake alone, that it was imputed to him; rather, *it was* also *written* for our sakes, to whom it shall be imputed—to those who believe in Him Who raised Jesus our Lord from *the* dead" (vs 23-24).

It's very important to understand, as we'll see on some charts later on that the year in which Jesus was crucified, the Passover fell in the middle of the week on a Wednesday, with the Passover services taking place on Tuesday night before the day portion of the Passover. The appointed time that

we read in Rom. 5 is that very day. It is also backed up by what Jesus said, that He would be in the tomb three days and three nights. So, we'll have to come through to the Wave Sheaf Offering Day, and then we will look at how to count Pentecost.

Verse 25: "Who was **delivered** for our offenses ... [delivered to the crucifixion and death] ...and was raised for our justification."

Paul said, 'If Christ was not raised; you're still in your sins.' *And if you're still in your sins you have no justification!*

Now let's see how this applies here concerning the blood of Christ, and concerning these things that we're covering here. Heb 10—we'll see about the sacrifice of Christ. Again, as you go through and study the Bible, and the New Testament in particular, I want you to understand that *everything is keyed on the Passover, the death of Jesus Christ!*

The next event is His resurrection at the end of the weekly Sabbath during the Feast of Unleavened Bread. {note charts} If you want a full explanation of when Jesus was resurrected you can read *A Harmony of the Gospels* that shows the three days and three nights of Jesus in the tomb, or the Appendix J—Jesus' Three Days and Three Nights of Entombment and His Resurrection—in *The Holy Bible in It's Original Order, A Faithful Version.* We also have it in the book *The Day Jesus the Christ Died.* There are plenty references to it, so you go ahead and read and study those.

Tie Heb. 10 in to Gen. 3:15 where it talks about **the first prophecy** of the death of Jesus Christ after the sin of Adam and Eve, showing that there had to be a penalty paid for their sins. When Jesus was crucified, here is the meaning of it:

Hebrew 10:12: "But He... [this is contrasted to the priest who offered sacrifices daily] ...after offering **one sacrifice for sins forever**..."—*because Jesus was God manifested in the flesh!*

He alone can take away the sins of the world, because He is the Creator of all mankind, and don't be fooled by any false doctrine that He was not God before He became God manifested in the flesh.

"...sat down at *the* right hand of God" (v 12). *That took place on the Wave Sheaf Offering Day for His presentation!*

He came back to the earth for 40 days and 40 nights, and He showed Himself to His apostles. Then ascended on the 40th day for the final time, and has been sitting at the right hand of God.

Verse 13: "Since that time, He is waiting until His enemies are placed *as* a footstool for His feet."

That is the tipping point of history, the beginning of the return of Christ and the resurrection of the saints.

Verse 14: "For by one offering He has obtained eternal perfection *for* those who are sanctified"—*relating back to the crucifixion!*

Heb. 9:11—showing about Christ's activity as our High Priest in heaven right now. It also goes back to His crucifixion; everything keys back to the Passover and ties together. All the Holy Days of God are connected in a plan and revealed in a step-by-step sequence of what God is doing.

Hebrews 9:11: "But Christ Himself has become High Priest of the coming good things, through the greater and more perfect tabernacle, not made by *human* hands (that is, not of this *present physical* creation). Not by *the* blood of goats and calves, but by the means of His own blood, He entered once for all into the Holiest… [in the heavens above] …having *by* Himself secured everlasting redemption *for us*. For if the blood of goats and bulls, and *the* ashes of a heifer sprinkled *on* those who are defiled, sanctifies to the purifying of the flesh, **to a far greater degree, the blood of Christ, Who through *the* eternal Spirit offered Himself without spot to God**, shall purify your conscience from dead works to serve *the* living God" (vs 11-14).

That's why He is Mediator of the New Covenant; so that through death, He provided the release of our transgressions for us.

Now's let's see again the blood of Jesus Christ. As you study through the Bible I want you to continuously keep that in mind. *All of what God is doing is keyed to the Passover,* and that's why it's so important.

Note our book: *The Christian Passover*—500 pages explaining the Truth about the Passover; exposing all the errors; going through step-by-step *to show the magnitude of the Passover and why it is profoundly important and related to salvation,* that unless you keep the Passover the way that God has said, *you do not have salvation!*

1-John 1:7: "However, **if** we walk in the Light, as He is in the Light… [the 'if' is always on us; the 'if' is never on God] …*then* we have fellowship with one another, and the blood of Jesus Christ, His own Son, cleanses us from all sin"

That's what we need to really understand and realize. John is writing this and read how he starts out, it comes down then to the sacrifice of Christ, and the forgiveness of our sins. That's why the Passover is so important. *We take the Passover to commemorate the sacrifice of Jesus Christ and to renew the New Covenant!* Then that keeps us

established under the grace of God, so that through the grace of God and the confession of *sins we can continually have our sins washed away even on a daily bases, through the blood of Jesus Christ!*

Let's carry this a little bit further here, and let's see how this reflects to the Church. We see Paul preaching to the elders at Ephesus who came down to meet him in Miletus. He refers back again to the sacrifice of Christ and His blood.

Paul is talking to the elders, so this is a good verse for all the elders, ministers, and teachers to understand. No man is to put himself forward. God has to lead and guide him:

Acts 20:28: "Take heed, therefore, to yourselves and to all the flock, among which the Holy Spirit has made you overseers, to feed the Church of God, **which He purchased with His own blood**."

Again, our sins are forgiven through the blood of Christ; the blood of Christ covers everything that we do on a continuous basis in establishing our relationship with God. The blood of Christ and the Body of Christ has to do with the New Covenant and renewing it. Here Christ purchased the Church with His own blood. Then Paul gives a warning:

Verse 29: "For I know this: that after my departure grievous wolves will come in among you, not sparing the flock."

- that's what's happened to the Church of God
- that's what's happened to worldly Christianity

They have given themselves over to Satan the devil and his ways, and all the counterfeit things that are there!

Verse 30: "And from among your own selves men will rise up speaking perverse things to draw away disciples after themselves."

That's why we find there's so much confusion today in the things that are done in relationship to:

- the Passover
- Unleavened Bread
- the resurrection of Jesus Christ

Now let's see about the ascension of Christ and the receiving of the Holy Spirit, because the Holy Spirit was not given until Christ sent it on the Day of Pentecost, and what that has meaning for us.

Let's see where Paul connects this. Notice the connection from Passover, Unleavened Bread and Pentecost; that's the pattern, and we'll see the progression of it.

Ephesians 1:7: "In Whom we have redemption through His blood, *even* the remission of sins, according to the riches of His grace, which He has made to abound toward us in all wisdom and intelligence; **having made known to us the mystery of His own will**…" (vs 7-9).

God has brought you into His confidence to understand His will. This is just not a matter of comparative religions that you go out and say:

- I wonder what religion I could be comfortable with?
- I wonder how I feel in this church?

That has nothing to do with Truth! You've got to:

- have the true Jesus
- have the true Word of God
- have the understanding of the Truth of the Passover and Holy Days
- keep the commandments of God
- love Him

It's not a matter of a place where you have a *psychological rearranging of your brain* to be a good person in the world. **You're qualifying for eternal life!**

Verse 9: "**Having made known to us the mystery of His own will**, according to His good pleasure, which He purposed in Himself; that in *the Divine* plan for the fulfilling of *the* times…" (vs 9-10).

That's what this book is all about, *the Divine plan of God* step-by-step-by-step. You will see—when you go through the transcriptions and listen to the messages in this book about God's revealed will and His plan for mankind—*that Pentecost is the tipping point in history!* Not only does it commemorate our receiving the Holy Spirit, we will also see as you get into the meaning of Pentecost, that it commemorates and looks forward to the resurrection when Jesus returns. Now we will see that right here in Eph. 1.

"…He might bring all things together in Christ, both the things in the heavens and the things upon the earth; *yes,* in Him, in Whom we also have obtained an inheritance, having been predestinated according to His purpose…" (vs 10-11). *Think about that for a minute*:

- God Himself has personally called you
- God Himself has personally given you the begettal of the Holy Spirit
- God Himself wants to give you eternal life if you remain faithful

Notice all the responsibility that has been given to us, and the way that God has given us the understanding of these things. This is a magnificent thing indeed.

Verse 12: "That we might be **to *the* praise of His glory**…" *I want you to just think about that for a minute*:

- God has called you
- God has given you His Spirit
- God is creating in you the very mind of Christ
- God is going to resurrect you, as the Feast of Pentecost pictures the first resurrection

So that all those in the first resurrection will be "…**to *the* praise of His glory**…"

"…who first trusted in the Christ; in Whom you also trusted after hearing the Word of the Truth … [the Word of Truth involves repentance, baptism and so forth] …the Gospel of your salvation; in Whom also, after believing, **you were sealed with the Holy Spirit of promise**" (vs 12-13). *That's the first meaning of the Feast of Pentecost!*

Verse 14: "Which is *the* earnest of our inheritance until *the* redemption of the purchased possession, to *the* praise of His glory."

- Pentecost pictures the down payment of the Holy Spirit
- Pentecost pictures the fulfillment of the redemption on Pentecost

This is really quite a thing, really something for us to understand!

Now let's look at something else that's important concerning counting, concerning Pentecost, and why God did it this way. Let's come here to Luke 4, and then we will go back to the Old Testament, and we will read how to count Pentecost, we will read about the #50 and what it means. This becomes a very important section for us to understand, and again, Jesus is showing and preaching on a day that's important to show what the gospel is all about, and what it means.

Luke 4:14: "Then Jesus returned in the power of the Spirit to Galilee… [that was after He was baptized] …and word about Him went out into the entire country around. And He taught in their synagogues, *and* was glorified by all. And He came to Nazareth, where He had been brought up; and according to His custom, He went into the synagogue on the Sabbath Day…" (vs 14-16).

This Sabbath was a unique Sabbath. It is called in the Greek 'ton sabbaton,' and it means *on the day of the weeks,* which has reference to Pentecost. I want you to focus in on the message that he gave from Isaiah, which is from Isa. 61

"…and stood up to read. And there was given Him *the* book of the prophet Isaiah; and when He had unrolled the scroll, He found the place where it was written" (vs 16-17).

We're told to preach *in season and out of season!* Jesus taught in season and out of season as well, because that's the method of how God wants us to understand things. He taught in season, and here it is on the Feast of Weeks *or* the Feast of Pentecost, He reads:

Verse 18: "*The* Spirit of *the* Lord *is* upon Me; for this reason, He has anointed Me to preach the Gospel to *the* poor… [that relates to 50 days] …He has anointed Me to preach the Gospel to *the* poor; He has sent Me to heal those who are brokenhearted, to proclaim pardon to *the* captives and recovery of sight to *the* blind, to send forth in deliverance those who have been crushed to proclaim *the* acceptable year of *the* Lord" (vs 18-19).

- What is the acceptable year of the Lord?
- What is it talking about?

Let's see the only other Holy year where there is a count to 50, and it ties in with the message that was given here by Jesus on Pentecost, and it has to do with the Jubilee. What Jesus was doing here on Pentecost was *preaching the Jubilee!*

Leviticus 25:8: "And you shall number seven Sabbaths of years to you, seven times seven years…."—*49!* We'll see 49 when we get to counting Pentecost for the Holy Day.

"…And the time of the seven Sabbaths of years shall be forty-nine years to you. Then you shall cause the trumpet of the jubilee to sound on the tenth *day* of the seventh month; in the Day of Atonement, the trumpet shall sound throughout all your land" (vs 8-9).

Notice what this is *physically.* Now we know that every 7 years there's to be a release of debt. Here is 7 times 7 years—49—then we come to the 50th year.

Verse 10: "And you shall make the fiftieth year Holy…"

Here is a parallel counting 1 thru 50: *7 complete cycles of 7 years for 49 years.* That will tie in when we count the weeks.

"…And proclaim liberty throughout the land to all its inhabitants…. [all debts forgiven; everything set aside] …It shall be a jubilee to you, and you shall return each man to his possession, and you shall return each man to his family" (v10).

When you read what's going to happen during the Millennium, everyone is going to sit under his own fig tree, and he's going take care of his own food, his own garden.

Verse 11: "That fiftieth year shall be a jubilee to you. You shall not sow, neither reap that which grows of itself in it, nor gather the grapes of your undressed vine in it."

Because God said He would give you three years worth of food in the last year. That is the year 48. So you go 49 and 50, and then the 3rd year you have the food.

Verse 12: "For it *is* the jubilee. It shall be Holy to you. You shall eat the increase of it out of the field." *You're not to gather; you're not to reap it, but you can go out and eat whatever there is!*

Verse 13: "In the year of this jubilee you shall return each man to his possession. And if you sell anything to your neighbor, or buy from your neighbor's hand, you shall not oppress one another. According to the number of years after the jubilee…" (vs 13-15).

Then it's the instructions on how to handle the land. But the point is this: *#50 pictures the jubilee!* So, when we come to Pentecost and counting 50, what we are actually doing is counting a *mini-jubilee,* and that ties in with God's plan for the resurrection. When we first receive the earnest of the Holy Spirit, let's see what we receive.

Let's see how to count Pentecost, because this becomes important for us, and to have it the right way. Lev. 23:9 gives us some very important information and understanding:

- when we understand the Hebrew
- when we have the right translation
- when we understand what God is saying how to count Pentecost
- when we understand how it's going to come about

Leviticus 23:9: "And the LORD spoke to Moses, saying, 'Speak to the children of Israel and say to them, "When you have come into the land, which I give to you, and shall reap the harvest of it… [we're the firstfruits harvest] …then you shall bring *the premier* sheaf of the firstfruits of your harvest to the priest."

That first of the firstfruits pictured Christ. You're to bring it. And you can read in the Passover book all the details concerning that.

Verse 11: "And he shall wave the sheaf before the LORD to be accepted for you…."

That's what we read that Christ did when He ascended to heaven to be accepted for us, as the *one sacrifice once for all!* His blood covered it. But you see now with the Wave Sheaf and the Wave Sheaf Offering Day we're going to see must take place on the first day of the week, which is called Sunday today.

Just remember, though the names of the weeks have pagan names on them today that does not detour from the fact that seven days of the week are still the seven days of the week as God gave it in the creation.

Verse 11: "And he… [the priest] …shall wave the sheaf before the LORD to be accepted for you. On the next day after the Sabbath the priest shall wave it."

This becomes important because the Hebrew here is 'ha shabbat,' which means *the weekly Sabbath.*

Yet, Judaism today follows the pharisaical count of counting from the first Holy Day. That's how they end up with their Pentecost on Sivan 6. We're going to go through, and we're going to look at some charts and see how to count Pentecost and how this mini-jubilee fits in for Christians.

Here's something he says—vs 12-13—what they were to do with the offering and so forth, the grain offering, the meal offering and so forth. This was to be when they came into the land, because it says:

Verse 14: "And you shall eat neither bread, nor parched grain, nor green ears until the same day, until you have brought an offering to your God. *It shall be* a statute forever throughout your generations in all your dwellings."

All during the time they were wandering in the wilderness they ate no bread from grain; they ate manna, bread from heaven.

Let's begin to see how Pentecost is counted. It's very important; this is a special day; this is a special thing; and there's special meaning to Christians today concerning counting Pentecost and coming to the 50th day: Pentecost. *What it pictures is a mini-jubilee* within a Christian's life!

Verse 15: "And you shall count to you beginning with the next day after the Sabbath… ['ha shabbat'] …beginning with the day that you brought the sheaf of the wave offering; **seven Sabbaths shall be complete**."

When we read it in Lev. 25 it was seven Sabbaths of years. So, we have the same thing. "…seven Sabbaths shall be complete."

This means *a complete week*, beginning with day 1 through day 7. You cannot have partial weeks because then you get into completely discombobulating the instructions here, and miscounting.

Verse 16: "Even unto the day after the seventh Sabbath you shall **number fifty days**…."

*The 50th day is **always** the 1st day of the week **after** the weekly Sabbath,* the 7th Sabbath. It's also the 1st day of the 8th week, which we will see has meaning for us as Christians in relating to the *mini-jubilee.*

We have other messages that go through and explain all about the grain offerings, and the two wave loaves, and everything like that.

So what we're going to do now is show you some charts of the Calculated Hebrew Calendar and show you the four[transcriber's correction] different ways, or the four]different days on which Passover can occur during the year as you go through time. We'll see there is a Passover on Monday, on Wednesday, on a Friday and on Sabbath. We'll see all of those and see how to count with those circumstances and how the variation of Pentecost will occur on a monthly basis from the 5th of Sivan to the 10th of Sivan. So, having it fixed on the 6th on Sivan violates the way to properly count, *because there would be no use in counting if it where a fixed day of the month*. We'll take a look at these charts here and go through them one-by-one.

{please refer to charts}

Chart #1—Count to Pentecost with a Monday Passover:

Everything's keyed to the Passover. With a Monday Passover, it is observed Sunday night. Then we have the Feast of Unleavened Bread through here, and this is the weekly Sabbath during Unleavened Bread. Then is the Wave Sheaf Offering Day. We're to count beginning with this day, which is *inclusive* counting, and we number the days.

Wave Sheaf Offering Day is day one. It goes down, you have seven; here's the first week. Now, we have each day counted, and each day of the count toward Pentecost is in a circle. Now let's come down to the next month here, *Iyor*, you have *Nisan* then *Iyor*, so here is week 2, week 3, week 4, week 5, and each day is listed; week 6—42 days—week 7=49 days.

Then Pentecost over here, which when the Passover is on a Monday, observed Sunday night, Pentecost comes out to be on the 10th of *Sivan*. Quite interesting, isn't it? So, this is a sequence of how you count when you have a Monday Passover.

Chart #2—Count to Pentecost when Passover is on a Wednesday

Remember, everything is keyed to the Passover. So, Wednesday Passover, middle of the week, you observe it the night before. This is the same sequence as it was in the year that Jesus was crucified.

Come down here to the 17th, which is the weekly Sabbath during the days of Unleavened Bread, and toward the end of the Sabbath Jesus was resurrected; then ascended to the Father on the 18th, the Wave Sheaf Offering Day.

That's why you count this as day 1, always the Wave Sheaf Offering Day. Let's count through the days here and then the weeks: 1-7 and again we have the days in the circle, and then the weeks in the square. Week 1 thru week 7, which is 49 days *to the morrow __after__ the seventh Sabbath*: Pentecost, the 50th day, which is on the 8th of *Sivan*. That's how you count it when you have a Wednesday Passover.

Chart #3—Count to Pentecost when Passover is on a Friday

Now here is the sequence of months beginning with *Nisan*, when you have the Passover on a Friday, and it's observed Thursday night. The Holy Day, which is the 15th, is also the weekly Sabbath; but remember it's on the day *after* the weekly Sabbath, which then always puts the Wave Sheaf Offering Day on the 1st day of the week; now that's important when we get to the next one with a Sabbath Passover Day.

So, the Wave Sheaf Offering Day is on the 1st day of the week, and it is day 1 and always must be counted. Then we have the 7 days to the 1st week, which ends in the Sabbath; 2nd week, which ends with the Sabbath; 3rd week ending in the Sabbath, same way with the 4th week thru the 7th week.

Then we have Pentecost here on the 50th day on the day after the 7th Sabbath, 50 days, and that is on 6th of *Sivan*. So you see the difference. You have the 10th of *Sivan*, and the 8th of Sivan, now here you have the 6th of *Sivan*.

Chart #4—Count to Pentecost when Passover is on a the Weekly Sabbath

Here we have some special circumstances to look at. When the Passover Day falls on the Sabbath, and presents some special difficulties, which always have caused people some problems. Now the reason that it has caused problems is because the Passover day is on the Sabbath and you then observe it Friday night.

In this case, you do not have a Sabbath during the days of Unleavened Bread, except the last Holy Day; but then if you start counting the Wave Sheaf Offering Day after the last Holy Day then you loose the whole sequence of things, *and the Wave Sheaf Offering Day cannot be outside the Day's of Unleavened Bread.*

So what is the solution? *The solution is very simple!* Since Passover is *also an Unleavened Bread Day,* therefore, this becomes __*the*__ Sabbath. The next day after the Sabbath then is a Holy Day, the 15th day of the 1st month. So, you have a combination here of the Holy Day and the Wave Sheaf Offering Day on the rare occurrence when you have a Sabbath Passover.

For years and years we did not have a Sabbath Passover, and *we made the mistake of saying that it's day after the weekly Sabbath during the Feast of Unleavened Bread,* which was incorrect.

It should be *the 1st day of the week during Unleavened Bread is the day that you begin counting on,* which is this day right here. Let's see how this counts: 1 thru 7 complete weeks ending with the Sabbath, which is also a Holy Day.

Now we come down: weeks 1-thru 7 and that's 49 days, 7 weeks. On the day after the Sabbath you have Pentecost. In this case it occurs then on the 5th of *Sivan*.

This is why we are to count Pentecost, *because there will a variation all based upon when the Passover occurs.*

I'm sure that those charts will help you understand how to count to Pentecost, and how to get the correct way to do it.

I want to emphasize this, for years it was said that it has to be the Sabbath during the Feast of Unleavened Bread. That is true in three out of four cases when you count Pentecost because there's the regular Sabbath during the Feast of Unleavened Bread.

However when you have it when the Passover is on Sabbath, then the first Holy Day is on the Wave Sheaf Offering Day because the only Sabbath during Unleavened Bread has got to include the Passover in that, because the Passover is an Unleavened Bread Day.

Now there are still a lot of people who say that you only have to eat unleavened bread for the Passover, and then you can have leavened bread until sundown the next day. *That's not true!*

Passover was an Unleavened Bread day. And just keep in mind—a very simple thing to remember:

The children of Israel ate unleavened bread for the Passover, which we do too. We eat unleavened bread! When they left their homes at sunrise there was no place for leaven to be around. They had unleavened bread; they ate it on the Passover; the Passover Day and the Passover ceremony *is a day of Unleavened Bread.*

It's easy to understand, as they were making their way to Rameses to assemble for the beginning of the exodus, there were no McDonald's to stop at to get an egg McMuffin, toast or biscuits. *It was by practice an Unleavened Bread Day!*

Therefore, when you come to the *Passover being on Sabbath, then the first Holy Day,* being the first day of the week, *becomes the Wave Sheaf Offering Day because it is the only first day of the week during the Feast of Unleavened Bread.* Now I hope that makes things a whole lot more clear for you.

Let's see the beginning of the mini-jubilee for Christians. This is when you receive the Holy Spirit.

Romans 8:1: "Consequently, *there is* now no condemnation to those who are in Christ Jesus, who are not walking according to *the* flesh, but according to *the* Spirit; because the Law of the Spirit of Life in Christ Jesus has delivered me from the law of sin and death" (vs 1-2).

That takes place when you receive the Holy Spirit, after you have repented and have been baptized. That's where we started. Repent and be baptized and receive the Holy Spirit. You have a beginning of a mini-jubilee at that particular time, and then regardless of what it was during the year when you where baptized and receive the Holy Spirit, you come full circle around the Passover and then Unleavened Bread and Wave Sheaf Offering Day, and so forth. All of that has to do with receiving the Spirit, it is the earnest of the inheritance.

So, you have been delivered from the law of sin and death. That's the beginning of the mini-jubilee for all Christians in their lives.

Verse 3: "For what *was* impossible for the Law to do…" *The law could not overcome the law of sin and death that is within us!* The only way we can be delivered by it is with God's Spirit. So, when you receive God's Spirit that's when you're able to overcome.

Let's see that the beginning of the mini-jubilee for every Christian is when they receive the Holy Spirit. Now, the mini-jubilee, just the rest of your life from the time that you're baptized until the time of your resurrection, *that is the jubilee!* You begin the jubilee by receiving the Holy Spirit. That's why Christ came; that why He preached that message in Luke 4. Let's see what it talks about with receiving God's Spirit, which is the begettal, the seed of the Holy Spirit.

1-John 3:9: "Everyone who has been begotten by God does not **practice** sin…"

You don't live your life in sin because you have been delivered from the law of sin and death inasmuch as that with the Holy Spirit and growing, overcoming and yielding to God, you're able to be delivered in a progressive way from the law of sin and death.

The full deliverance from death does not come until later at the resurrection!

"…because His seed *of begettal* is dwelling within him… [that's the beginning, the earnest, the down payment] …and **he is not able to *practice* sin because he has been begotten by God**" (v 9).

Now let's see the end of the jubilee, or the symbolism for Christians concerning the 50th day, because *the 50th day*—just like the 50th year in the Jubilee Year—*is a complete deliverance from everything!* If you grow, change and overcome, and die in the faith; then the final jubilee is going to be for everyone who dies in the faith; for everyone who is still alive when the resurrection occurs is going to be that day of the resurrection, which is pictured by Pentecost, *the full deliverance; the full jubilee for Christians.*

Now what we need to do is come back to Eph. 1. We need to remember that *#50 is a complete jubilee!* Pentecost is the 50th day, *a mini-jubilee* as I have said for all Christians. It's fitting that this mini-jubilee, which will be the great 1st resurrection is going to be the total redemption that we have so that we are no longer flesh but spirit. Totally redeemed of Christ, and now ready as spirit being in the Kingdom of God to do the work of God.

Ephesians 1:13—speaking of Christ: "In Whom you also trusted after hearing the Word of the Truth, the Gospel of your salvation; in Whom also, after believing, you were sealed with the Holy Spirit of promise, **which is *the* earnest of our inheritance**…" (vs 13-14).

This is the guarantee, the down payment, and we're trusting in God because God:

- cannot lie
- will not lie
- His Word is the Truth
- the resurrection is going to occur

"…**until *the* redemption** of the purchased, possession… [for all Christians at the same time on the 50th day being the Day of Pentecost] …to *the* praise of His glory" (v 14).

Now we will see what Paul said; let's see how Paul kind of gives us a little summary of this.

2-Timothy 4:6: "For I am now ready to be offered… [he knew that he was going to be martyred] …and the time of my departure is at hand."

You can say that this is day 49 for Paul. For whatever day it is for when we die that's day 49 for us.

Verse 7: "I have fought a good fight; I have finished the course; I have kept the faith. From this time forward… [when he's dead and in the grave] …a crown of righteousness is laid up for me, which the Lord, the righteous Judge, shall give me in that day… [the jubilee day for all Christians] …and not to me only, but also **to all who love His appearing**" (vs 7-8).

When we come to the book of Hebrews that it shows the jubilee day.

Heb. 12 we've covered this in other messages that we have in this book concerning the Day of Pentecost. But let's just input it right here. This ends the mini-jubilee for all Christians and it all occurs at the same time on the 50th day, *which is the day of the resurrection!* You can take all of the other things that we have studied leading up to Pentecost, the meaning of Pentecost, put it all together and it shows the great meaning of the Day of Pentecost and the resurrection.

Hebrews 12:22: "But you have come to Mount Sion, and to *the* city of *the* living God, heavenly Jerusalem; and to an innumerable company of angels."

That's what it's going to be, and as we have seen, when the saints are resurrected they're brought to the Sea of Glass. You can study that in the other transcripts that we have in this book; and everyone is on the Sea of Glass and it's going to be called, as he says here in:

Verse 23: "*To the* joyous festival gathering…"—*because it is*:

- the total deliverance from the flesh
- the total deliverance from death
- the total deliverance from sin

Because as resurrected human beings, now spirit beings, you no longer have the ability to sin!

It is the *complete jubilee* that happens for all of those in the first resurrection on the day of Pentecost, *which then brings the final jubilee for every one of us!*

Verse 23: "*To the* joyous festival gathering; and to *the Church* of *the* Firstborn, registered *in the Book of Life* in heaven; and to God, *the* Judge of all, and to *the* spirits of the just who have been perfected."

That's really quite a thing—*the harvest of the firstfruits*—and that's why it is counted. That's why it must be on the 50th day, and the 50th day is the 1st day of the 8th week.

Now let's understand something else. There is also symbolic significance for us in the 50th day, which is the beginning of the 8th week; *8* is the number of *a new beginning!* The resurrection day of Pentecost, being the 50th day, and the 1st ay of the 8th week is *a new beginning for all eternity for all the resurrected saints!* That's important to understand, *the mini-jubilee as it applies to Christians!* Why it has to be 50 days; and why it has to be 7 complete weeks unto the day after the 7th Sabbath.

That's why Pentecost is 50 days, and that's the meaning of the counting of 50 days. *All Christians at the resurrection on Pentecost are going to share in eternal life, the 50th day beginning the 1st day of eternity, a new beginning!*

Scriptures from *The Holy Bible in Its Original Order, A Faithful Version*

Scriptural References

1) Acts 2:1, 36-:39
2) Romans 5:6-10
3) Romans 4:23-25
4) Hebrews 10:12-14
5) Hebrews 9:11-14
6) 1 John 1:7
7) Acts 20:28-30
8) Ephesians 1:7-14
9) Luke 4:14-19
10) Leviticus 25:8-15
11) Leviticus 23:9-11, 14-16
12) Romans 8:1-3
13) 1 John 3:9, 13-14
14) Ephesians 1:13-14
15) 2 Timothy 4:6-8
16) Hebrews 12:22-23

Scriptures referenced, not quoted:

- Genesis 3; 15; 22
- Exodus 12
- Genesis 3:15
- Isaiah 61
- Leviticus 23:12-13

Also referenced:

Books by Fred R. Coulter
- *The Christian Passover*
- *A Harmony of the Gospels*
- *The Day that Jesus the Christ Died*

Appendix J: Jesus' Three Days and Three Nights of Entombment and His Resurrection (*The Holy Bible in Its Original Order, A Faithful Version*)

FRC: sv
Transcription date unknown
Reformatted: bo—11/2020

CHAPTER THIRTY-TWO

The Lord Shall Fight For You
(Last Day of Unleavened Bread)
Fred R. Coulter

Greetings, brethren! This is the last day of the Feast of Unleavened Bread. We look back at all the Feasts that we've kept down through the years. We've never realized that the time would go this long. But it's going this long and the days around us are more evil than we have ever expected. We just need to, through this Feast of Unleavened Bread—as we have been doing—*draw close to God.*

With the last day of the Feast of Unleavened Bread we're going to go ahead and take up an offering as we've already seen on the first day of Unleavened Bread that there is an offering on the last day. We're going to go ahead and take up that offering with the same understanding that we've had before. *Remember the blessings of God! Remember how God has promised to give you all sufficiency in all things!*

Giving the offerings and tithes are all a part of living by every Word of God. I hope that you really appreciate the things that we've been able to do, and we will pick up after the offering is taken up.

(pause for offering)

On this last day of the Feast of Unleavened Bread, the very theme of this Feast is *The Lord Shall Fight For You!* God is the One Who is going to give the salvation. *We are to see the salvation of the Lord!* Let's understand what happened with the children of Israel before they were released on the first day of the Feast of Unleavened Bread.

Let's start back and look at everything that took place just in a summary, *what God did to save the children of Israel, or rescue them from Egypt!* Also, let's understand something very important concerning this: *God raised up Pharaoh and all of the evil apparatus with it*:

- to show *His* power
- to declare *His* salvation
- to rescue Israel so that *His* name would be glorified in all the earth

It certainly has because we have it recorded for us, and we preach it every year!

Now remember the thing that was important so that we understand the office of Moses and how God was using Moses and Aaron *to defeat all the gods of Egypt.* As we have seen on the Passover night, when God struck all the firstborn of the Egyptians—all the firstborn of men and beasts—*that He judged all the god's of Israel!* Of course, the children of Israel didn't understand that the judgment against all those gods meant… Why should they be so foolish as to go to these other gods who were not gods.

Exodus 7:1: "And the LORD said to Moses, 'See, I have made you a god to Pharaoh…'"

That's how Pharaoh would look upon him because Pharaoh could not see the true God. That was reserved for Moses. So since Pharaoh was called a god, since Pharaoh was worshipped as a god, since they worshipped all the animals and things that they did in Egypt, and worshipped the River Nile all of these plagues came upon them because of that. There are six signs and four plagues that took place.

The Six Signs:

1. rod of Aaron that turned into a serpent

The magicians were able to go ahead and counterfeit that, but the rod of Aaron was able, as a serpent, to eat up the serpents of the magicians.

2. the river in to blood

The second sign was pretty powerful. Remember the Nile was considered the river of the gods, or a god, and they worshipped the water and the worshipped the river. It gave life and all of this sort of thing. In the next sign, because Pharaoh hardened his heart, and it was a joint venture. Pharaoh hardened his heart, and God hardened his heart. *God was raising him up for the purpose of the destruction of Egypt!* God is the One Who can do that *because He's God!* What did He do? *For seven days He turned* the river into blood!

3. frogs

Now these were the gigantic frogs that come out of the Nile River, and they just filled the whole land. When that sign was over they just put them in heaps and it stank.

4. dust turns into fleas and lice

It just covered all the animals, covered all the human beings! The whole lesson in all of this is that *no one has the power to fight against God! If God be for us, who can be against us?* Let's think on that as we're going through this.

So after that, *still Pharaoh hardened his heart* so then we have:

5. the swarms of flies

Nice big flies going everywhere! However, #5 is the sign of grace, and in the land of Goshen where the children of Israel were *there were no swarms of flies. God separated it!*

6. murrain caused by the ash

Moses took some ash and threw it in the air! God caused it to go everywhere throughout all the land of Egypt and they had boils from the top of their head to the sole of their foot.[transcriber's correction]

All the animals, all the horses, camels, oxen, all human beings. Well, Pharaoh called 'uncle' on this, so he recanted a little bit. He asked Moses if he would cause it to go away. So, Moses said that he would. Then Pharaoh hardened his heart again all the way through.

The Four Plagues:

1. hail

For it to hail in Egypt is an unreal thing because that's right in the desert. It had never done this from the creation of the world, or since Egypt was a nation. There was thunder and lightening, and all of this going on at the same time they had the plague of hail.

2. locust

After that came the plague of locust, locust everywhere and ate everything that was not in a container. That wasn't good enough *they still didn't repent,* so there was the plague of:

3. darkness

Darkness so thick that they could feel it! It was so oppressive that the only thing that they could do was stay in bed. *All the Israelites had light,* but the darkness covered Egypt.

4. death of the firstborn

The fourth one is the important one. This is where *God passed over the houses of the children of Israel and spared their firstborn, and executed judgment against all the gods of Egypt, and He killed all the firstborn of the Egyptian children!*

After that they let the Israelites go! So, the children of Israel went out with a high hand. Of course, God did not take them the easy way. Here's a lesson that's important for us: *God doesn't take us the easy way!* There are some hard things for us to do. If you are:

- a 'good-time' Christian
- a 'glad-hander'
- a social creature
- and you attend church because it's just
  - ✓ nice
  - ✓ wonderful
  - ✓ comfy
  - ✓ all your friends are there

know for sure you're going to have a trial that's going to come to test you to see:

- whether you love God with all your heart, mind, soul and being
- whether you really trust Him

That's the whole lesson of the last day of the Feast of Unleavened Bread!

In Exo. 14 we see the whole lesson here, and this is where God led them down instead of by the way of the Philistines going on over to the Holy Land, which would have been easy because that just follows right along the coast of the Mediterranean Sea and they would be there in a few days.

God had other plans in mind; He took them down by the way of the Red Sea and they were encamped along the Red Sea, big long line of the children of Israel. The Egyptians had second thoughts about letting them go, so they said, 'Look, we don't have any slaves; we can't do these things.' Pharaoh said, 'I know what I'll do. I'll get all my armies, I'll get all my chariots and we'll go get them and we'll bring them back.'

When the children of Israel saw that they became afraid. Well, God intervened and He put a cloud wall between the Egyptians and the children of Israel. To the Egyptians it was dark, to the children of Israel it was light. Let's see the reaction of the children of Israel, because herein is a great lesson for us. *You have to trust God in the tough times as well as the good times!*

Exodus 14:10: "And when Pharaoh drew near…"

We can also draw the analogy of Pharaoh and his armies as Satan and the demons, that's true. We can also look at it as *the world coming after us!* But what we're interested in is the reaction of the children of Israel.

"…the children of Israel lifted up their eyes. And behold, the Egyptians marched after them. And they were very afraid. And the children of Israel cried out to the LORD. And they said to Moses…" (vs 10-11).

- immediately began complaining

- immediately began accusing
- immediately displaying absolutely no faith

The reason I went over the six signs and the four plagues was to show what God had done and the power that God had used to cause the children of Israel to be extracted from the land of Egypt. You would think that they would have said, Oh, look at all that God has done for us; God took care of these Egyptians in Egypt so let's just trust Him to do it now.' *That's __not__ what they did!*

Verse 11: "And they said to Moses, 'Have you taken us away to die in the wilderness because *there were* no graves in Egypt?…. [in other words there were plenty of room for graves there] …Why have you dealt this way with us to carry us forth out of Egypt? Did we not tell you this word in Egypt, saying, "Let us alone so that we may serve the Egyptians?" for it would have been better for us to serve the Egyptians than that we should die in the wilderness'" (vs 11-12).

That's not what they said! **They cried to God** and said, 'O God, get us out of this slavery.' What were they doing? *They were looking back and comparing what they thought was how good they had everything in Egypt!* It's just like people when they first come into the Church and the first trial comes along, they say they've never experienced anything like this before they were converted. There must be something wrong. No, there is nothing wrong. That's the way it is. Here's the reason for it, and here's why we go through these things.

Verse 13: "And Moses said to the people, 'Fear not! Stand still and see the salvation of the LORD…'" *That's what we need to do; **we need to stand!***

- *stand for* the Word of God
- *stand for* God
- *stand against* evil
- *stand against* human nature
- *stand against* all the forces that are against us

and to realize that with the power of the Holy Spirit we can do it with the conviction of God; __God will fight for us!__

"…see the salvation of the LORD, which He will work for you today, for the Egyptians whom you have seen today, you shall never see them again! **The LORD shall fight for you**…" (vs 13-14).

I want you to understand that *the Lord shall fight for you and you shall hold your peace!* In other words don't complain to God.

- ask God to intervene and help you
- ask God to intervene and change the circumstances

- ask God to intervene and fight your battles for you

because He has more power than you do! __You've got to trust God!__

God will do many great and fantastic things to fight your battles for you, *but you have to place it all in God's hands!* Just like it is here: "…**Stand still and see the salvation of the LORD**…" (v 13).

- don't complain
- don't gripe
- don't whine

Let **the peace of God rule in your heart,** *as we covered on the first day of the Feast of Unleavened Bread!*

Verse 15: "And the LORD said to Moses, 'Why do you cry to Me? Speak to the children of Israel that they **go forward.'**"

That's the whole key for the Feast of Unleavened Bread; __that we go forward in spite of everything and anything that comes along!__

- we know God
- we love God
- we understand His Word
- we live by it
- we go forward

You know the rest of the story of what happened there!

Verse 16: "And you—lift up your rod, and stretch out your hand over the sea…"

That night He caused a tremendous east wind to blow, and He also parted the waters a great distance, probably a place as much as ten miles wide, and *then all of the children of Israel—in the morning watch just before the sun came up—crossed the Red Sea at the same time! __A Divine miracle! God intervening and showing them His power!__*

You know what happened to the Egyptians! They came up there and they looked to the right, and they looked to the left, and they said, 'Go!' Right when he got in the middle of where the sea was going to be God had the angels start taking the wheels off their chariots and they drug heavy, the ground became mud, and then all of a sudden the waters came crashing back, *and that was the end of the Egyptians __just like God had said!__* Well now, the children of Israel were very happy, but let's look at what they said. *This is really a tremendous lesson for us!*

Exodus 15:1. "Then Moses and the children of Israel sang this song to the LORD, and spoke, saying, 'I will sing to the LORD, for He has triumphed gloriously; *the horse and his rider He has thrown into the sea. The LORD is my strength and song, and He has become my salvation. This is my God, and I will glorify Him, my father's God, and I will exalt Him. The LORD is a Man of war; Jehovah is His name'"* (vs 1-3). *That's what we need to look at!*

- *IF* you have a problem that needs to be overcome, *take it to God*
- *IF* you have a complaint against God, *go repent and ask Him to intervene and help you*
- *IF* you have a situation that is greater than you can handle, *ask God to handle it for you*

Let Him fight your battles; put it all in His hands and realize that that's the way that it has to be.

All the way down through history, as we find in the Bible, we see:

- the salvation of God
- the power of God
- the intervention of God
  - ✓ some in great and fantastic things
  - ✓ some in small and little things

Now the first great thing that happened was the Flood, and God saved all mankind through Noah *because Noah walked with God and kept His commandments* and he found grace. So, God had to destroy the whole world, *everything there!*

After that, during the days of Abraham we have the story of Lot. Lot was actually what you would call—though he was righteous—*weak in the faith!* He was confronted with many situations that we are being confronted with now, the on-slide of the homosexuals. Who knows, they probably had homosexual marriages in Sodom and Gomorrah, and all the people thought that that was a great thing. But if it weren't for Abraham, Lot would not have survived; but Abraham intervened and Lot survived. And you know what happened to Sodom and Gomorrah. Of course the one who had the lack of faith and didn't follow was his wife. The angel said, 'Don't look back.' That's an important lesson because Jesus said later, *'Remember Lot's wife.'* So, we're not to look back; nevertheless Lot was saved!

Then we have the children of Israel and all the miracles that took place while they were going through the wilderness, and everything that God did.

- the miracle of the manna every morning
- took care of them
- blessed them
- watched over them
- the water out of the rock

But they didn't want to follow God so they rebelled!

They didn't believe God after all that so God had to punish them for their rebellion, and it took another *38-½ years of wandering in the wilderness!* Everyone over 20 died, except for Caleb and Joshua. Then they went into the 'promised land' *and God fought their battles for them* **when** *they did what God said!* When they didn't do what God said, *He didn't fight for them!* They moaned and groaned and complained to God: 'Oh why can't we overcome our enemies?' *Because some were stealing the gold that belonged to God!* So. the whole history of going through the Bible shows how:

- *God will fight for you* **IF** *you believe Him!*
- *God will fight for you* **IF** *you trust in Him!*

Let's see a Psalm dedicated to that! David's Psalm; quite a Psalm. This shows how *God intervenes to help, to fight to save on behalf of those whom He loves!*

This was after one of the great deliverances of God; Psalm 18:1: "I love You, O LORD, **my strength**."

Our whole relationship with God is based on the love of God, as we saw on the Sabbath during this Feast. "I love You, O LORD, my strength." Are you weak? *That's where you get strength from!*

Verse 2: "The LORD is my Rock, and my Fortress…" *Jesus said that we are to build our house upon a Rock* (Matt. 7) That Rock is Christ (1 Cor. 10). He's our Rock.

"…and my Deliverer; my God, my Rock in Whom I take refuge; He is my shield, and the horn of my salvation, high tower" (v 2). *If you're in a high tower no one can get at you!* That's why he said that.

Verse 3: "I will call upon the LORD…" *That's how God will intervene for you!* You have to:

- love Him
- praise Him
- worship Him
- call upon Him
- trust in Him
- look to Him to be:
  - ✓ your Salvation
  - ✓ your Savior
  - ✓ the Warrior
  - ✓ the Fighter

He's going to fight your battles for you! We're going to see some more of these things as we go along.

"…Who is worthy to be praised, so shall I be saved from my enemies. The cords of death hemmed me in…" (v 3). **How close was he to tragedy in the end?** *Right at the brink!*

"…and the floods of ungodliness assailed me. The cords of the grave surrounded me; the snares of death confronted me. In my distress I called on the LORD…" (vs 4-6). *We're going to have times when we have distress!* Remember, David was a man after God's heart.

Verse 6: "In my distress I called on the LORD, and I cried to my God; He heard my voice out of His temple, and my cry came before Him into His ears."

Psalm 12:1—*this is pretty much the situation that we find ourselves in, in the world today*: "**Help** O LORD, for the Godly man ceases… [Where is someone who's Godly? *There aren't any!*] …for the faithful disappear from among the children of men. They speak falsehood each one with his neighbor; with flattering lips and a double heart they speak" (vs 1-2). *That's just the way this world is; just nothing but lies and double-speak!*

Verse 3: "LORD shall cut off all flattering lips, *and* the tongue that speaks proud things, who have said, 'With our tongue we shall prevail; our lips are our own; who is lord over us?'" (vs 3-4).

Perfect description of this society, anything goes! If we don't like a law, we'll change it. Just like up in San Francisco, they've been marrying thousands of same sex so-called couples, in defiance against the law. But they don't think they are breaking the law. But when Judge Roy Moore defied a federal judge and his ungodly illegal order to get rid of the Ten Commandments monument, they said he ought to obey the law of the land. That's just the way that it is in the world.

Verse 5: "'For the oppression of the poor, for the sighing of the needy, I will now arise,' says the LORD…. [God is going to take action sooner or later] …'I will set him in safety from *him who puffs at him'*" (vs 5-6).

Verse 8: "The wicked walk on every side when vileness is exalted among the sons of men." *That is a perfect description of our political system!*

Now, let's again see how we are to pray when we are in trouble. Instead of complaining to other people, accusing the ministers, accusing other brethren, *go repent!*

- ask God to *help you!*
- ask God to *fight your battles*

Psalm 4:1: "Answer me when I call… [He will] …O God of my righteousness. You gave me relief *when I was* in distress; be gracious to me, and hear my prayer. O sons of men, how long will my

glory be put to shame? How long will you love delusions… [just the way it is in the world] …and seek after lies? Selah. But know that the LORD has set apart the Godly for Himself. The LORD will hear when I call to Him" (vs 1-3).

God will hear; we can be guaranteed of that. When people get discouraged and get distressed and get down and begin to give up, they give in to their weaknesses and sin. That's why it says:

Verse 4: "Tremble, and sin not…" *So God will hear our prayers!*

Psa.37—this is one to keep in mind; this is really a good Psalm. This is good counsel and advice for us, that's why it's here. You look out and you see the world and all the things that are wrong, all the sin that is going wrong, and somehow they seem to be getting along better, but they're really not.

Psalm 37:1—*good advice*: "Do not fret yourself… [don't be frustrated] …because of evildoers, and do not be envious against the workers of iniquity, for they shall soon be cut down like the grass; and wither as the green herb. **Trust in the LORD**…" (vs 1-3).

That's where we need to put our trust. Not in other human beings, not in circumstances, not in physical things, *but trust in the Lord!*

"…and do good; dwell in the land and cherish faithfulness. Delight yourself in the LORD…" (vs 3-4). *So, this shows that*:

- you're happy
- you're joyful
- you understand that Christ has saved you
- you understand that you have the Holy Spirit of God in you
- you understand that God the Father has begotten you so that *you*, *at the resurrection,* can become a son or daughter of God

Look, you have eternal life ahead of you! That's what's important.

Verse 4: "Delight yourself in the LORD, and He shall give you the desires of your heart"—*according to His will!*

The greatest desire of our heart needs to be that we are going to be in the Kingdom of God. The greatest desire that we ought to have is:

- to see God, as the Psa. says
- to see God face-to-face, as Rev. says
- to be there in that resurrection

Here's how you do it:
- through prayer
- through study

- through everything that you do

Not just when you get religious and pray, as some people would look at it, but your whole life and everything you do.

Verse 5: "Commit your way unto the LORD… [everything you do] …trust also in Him, and He will bring it to pass." *Of course, we have our parts to do:*

- concerning health
- concerning healing
- concerning employment
- concerning marriage
- concerning whatever your life is involved in

Verse 6: "And He shall bring forth your righteousness like the light, and your judgment like the noonday. **Rest in the LORD, and wait patiently for Him**…" (vs 6-7)—*because God's timetable is always different than our timetable, so we have to wait patiently for Him!*

"…do not fret yourself… [don't become frustrated, worried or concerned] …because of him who prospers in his way, because of him who carries out wicked schemes. Cease from anger, and forsake wrath; do not fret yourself, it leads only to evil" (vs 7-8)—*because that's what people do!*

They're not trusting in God in the way they ought to be. They're not patient waiting for the Lord, so something happens and they get angry. That's why you had the trial, so that you can get rid of your anger and see and know and understand that you have it.

Verse 27: "Depart from evil and do good, and live forevermore." *That's what the whole Feast of Unleavened Bread is all about:*

- *put out* the leaven, which is sin; *put in* the unleaven, which is righteousness
- *put out* the way of man; *put in* the way of Christ

That's why Christ said, 'You have to eat My flesh and drink My blood' *showing that you will live by Him, which means by every Word of God!*

Verse 28: "For the LORD loves justice and does not forsake His saints…" *So, if you ever think you've been forsaken—you haven't, **and you need to repent of that and ask God to help you to trust in Him!***

"…they are preserved forever, but the seed of the wicked shall be cut off. The righteous shall inherit the earth and dwell in it forever" (vs 28-29). *That means the Kingdom of God and all the earth and everything that is there!*

Verse 34: "**Wait on the LORD and keep His way**…"

Isn't that the message of the last day of the Feast of Unleavened Bread, that we first went through in Exo. 14? *Stand still and see the salvation of the Lord!* Never give up on doing it!

"…and He shall exalt you to inherit the earth when…" (v 34). *So, there is a timing in all of this! There is a time.*

The Kingdom of God is not here, therefore we don't fight. But when we come back with Christ we are going to fight, and we are going to be in charge of putting away all evil. They will either repent or they will be *history!*

"…when the wicked are cut off, you shall see it. I have seen the ruthless wicked in great power and spreading himself like a luxuriant tree in its native soil. Yet, he passed away, and lo, he was no more; and I searched for him, but he could not be found. **Mark the blameless man**" (vs 34-37).

IF you are in Christ, which you are, God has imputed the righteousness of Christ to you and you stand before Him Holy and blameless, *before God you are perfect!* You have to be perfected in attitude, be perfected in character, and it's an ongoing project!

"…and behold the upright one, for the end of that man is peace. But the sinners shall be destroyed together; the prosperity of the wicked shall be cut off" (vs. 37-38).

The finality of that is going to be with the last part of the Last Great Day when all the wicked are cast into the Lake of Fire and there are no more wicked around.

Verse 39: "But the salvation of the righteous is from the LORD; He is their strength in the time of trouble." *That's why we need to trust God!*

We're going to see some other things how God intervenes, because He's really performed some great and tremendous things.

Verse 40: "And the LORD shall help them and deliver them; He shall deliver them from the wicked, and save them because they take refuge in Him."

Do you trust in God? *That's all a part of the Feast of Unleavened Bread that:*

- you get rid of the sin of doubt
- you get rid of the sin of lack of trust

But

- you trust God
- you believe God

- you walk in His way in everything that you do

2-Chron. 20—let's see how God intervened in great and fantastic ways to save those who feared God and trusted Him, and looked to Him to fight their battles. This is the case of King Jehoshaphat. He had a great army. The children of Moab and Ammon, and the Assyrians were all coming against him to destroy him, and destroy Judah. Notice what he did:

2-Chronicles 20:3: "And Jehoshaphat feared and set himself to seek the LORD, and called for a fast throughout all Judah."

When you have trouble and difficulty you need to fast and draw close to God, ask for His help, ask for His intervention. So, he called them all together for a prayer. Then he got the answer from one of the prophets of God. A Levite came who was one of the sons of Asaph.

Verse 15—*here's the message*: "And he said, 'Listen, all Judah, and you people of Jerusalem, and King Jehoshaphat! Thus says the LORD to you, "Do not be afraid nor dismayed because of this great multitude, **for the battle *is* not yours, but God's.**'"

That's what we need to understand, *the battle is not ours; it is God's, so we trust in Him in faith!*

Verse 17: "'You shall not *need* to fight in this *battle*. Set yourselves and stand, and see the salvation of the LORD with you… [tie in Exo. 14] …O Judah and Jerusalem.' Do not fear nor be dismayed. Tomorrow go out against them, for the LORD *will be* with you"

Verse 20—*here's what they did on the morrow*: "And they rose early in the morning and went out into the wilderness of Tekoa. And as they went out, Jehoshaphat stood and said, 'Hear me, O Judah, and you people of Jerusalem. Believe in the LORD your God, and so you shall be established. Believe His prophets, and so you shall prosper.'"

Profound and important message. We are to believe, trust, have faith, have confidence, and lay it all before God just like Jehoshaphat did here.

Verse 21: "And when he consulted with the people, he appointed singers to the LORD and praisers to praise the beauty of Holiness as they went out before the army, and to say, 'Praise the LORD, for His steadfast love *endures* forever.'"

Here the priests went out first before the army, and that's the way God said they should fight their battles, *and God was with them!*

Verse 22: "And when they began to sing and to praise, the LORD set ambushes against the children of Ammon, Moab, and Mount Seir, who had come against Judah. And they were beaten. "

What God did, He just turned them all against each other and they killed each other. What did they do? *They went out there and they found that they were all dead!* What did they do?

Verse 25: "And when Jehoshaphat and his people came to take away their spoil, they found among them in abundance both riches and precious jewels in great number among the dead bodies which they stripped off for themselves, more than they could carry away. And they were three days in gathering of the spoil, it was so much."

That was a tremendous battle! God intervened, gave them the blessing! *God fought for them!* If God could do it for them we know God can do it for us. Regardless of what the situation is, regardless of what the trouble may be, *God is there, He will help just like this!*

We're going to look at another example here in a minute and see how God intervened to fight and to save His people.

Now let's see another example of how God intervened for King Hezekiah. What he did when he got the notice from the Assyrians that they were coming and conquering, and that they had destroyed all the nations coming right on down the line. And they sent a letter to Hezekiah: Surrender or we're going to do to you like we did to all these other nations and their gods.'

2 Kings 19:1: "Then it came to pass when **King Hezekiah heard**… [the letter read] …he tore his clothes and covered himself with sackcloth. And he went into the house of the LORD."

Verse 3: "And they said to him, 'Thus says Hezekiah, *This is* a day of trouble and of rebuke and contempt, for the children have come to the *point of* birth, and *there is* no strength to bring forth.'"" *Sometimes you feel like that!* That's what Hezekiah did; he took it before God.

Verse 14: "And Hezekiah received the letter from the hand of the messengers and read it. And Hezekiah went up into the house of the LORD and spread it before the LORD."

Took his troubles right to God very first thing. He didn't stop and ask anyone else's advice. He went right to the Lord.

Verse 15: "And Hezekiah prayed before the LORD and said, 'O LORD God of Israel Who dwells *between* the cherubim, You *are* God Himself, You alone of all the kingdoms of the earth; You have made the heavens and the earth. LORD, bow down Your ear and hear. O LORD, open Your eyes and see, and hear the words of Sennacherib, which he has sent to reproach the living God. Truly, LORD, the kings of Assyria have destroyed the nations and their lands'" (vs 15-17).

Verse 19: "And now, O, LORD our God, I beseech You, save us out of his hand, so that all the kingdoms of the earth may know that You *are* the LORD God, and You only."

This is a perfect example of how we need to go to God with our problems. You go to God and you state the problems. You don't accuse Him, but you glorify Him. You don't complain to Him, but you show what the problem is, and you ask God to fight because you are His; you belong to Him. You are His property. He's promised to take care of you. So that's exactly what happened. He got the message.

Verse 34: "For I will defend this city, to save it for My own sake and for My servant David's sake."

Here's what God did. Even greater miracle than what happened there with Jehoshaphat; v 35: "And it came to pass that night, **the angel of the LORD** went out and struck a hundred and eighty-five thousand in the camp of the Assyrians. Now, when they arose early in the morning, behold, they were all dead bodies."

In other words, He spared the king and probably a few of his advisors, but all of his army was dead!

Verse 36: "And Sennacherib king of Assyria departed. And he went and returned and lived at Nineveh."

Of course, as he was worshipping in the house of his god, someone came in and assassinated him.

- Did this take care of the enemy? *It sure did!*
- Did they have to lift the sword to fight? *No, they didn't!*

They trusted in God! Perfect example of what we need to do.

Now let's come to the New Testament and see some things here that are important for us to understand so that we can realize how then we need to look to God. Now we have to overcome self, we have to overcome the sins in us. Let's understand what kind of determination that we need to have, and what kind of faith that we need to have. Let's see what the Apostle Paul wrote to the Hebrews telling them what they need to do to overcome and change, and what kind of resolve that they need to have in serving God.

Now after the Apostle Paul had listed out many of the things where God fought for the children of Israel, coming on down through the faith chapter (Heb. 11), we come to:

Hebrews 12:1: "Therefore, *since* we are surrounded by such a great throng of witnesses..."

That's what the Old Testament is there for. These are examples that we can look to, to see:

- right and wrong
- good and evil
- God intervening and fighting our battles for us

These are the examples that we need to look to!

"...**let us lay aside every weight**..." (v 1). *Every problem, every difficulty, set it aside!* God does not want us to dwell on the problem. He wants us to dwell on Him and the solution. So, you set it aside.

"...**and the sin that so easily entraps** *us*... [repent of that; we've already covered how you do that; confess your sins to God] ...*and* let us run the race set before us with endurance" (v 1). *That's what we need to do!* **We have got to finish the course!**

Here's how to do it, v 2: "**Having** *our* **minds fixed on Jesus, the Beginner and Finisher of** *our* **faith**; Who for the joy that lay ahead of Him endured *the* cross, *although* He despised *the* shame, and has sat down at *the* right hand of the Throne of God."

That's what we need to do. *Always have our mind on Christ! Always have our mind on*:

- what He did
- how He did it
- why He did it

He did it because He loved us! God the Father sent Jesus Christ because He loves the world and loves us, and we are part of the eternal plan of God!

Verse 3: "Now meditate deeply on Him Who endured such great hostility of sinners against Himself..."

That's why we need to study the Gospels. That's why we need to understand what Jesus did and what He went through. Here's the reason:

"...**so that you do not become weary and faint in your minds**" (v 3).

There is a proverb that says that 'if you faint in the day of your adversity, you have very little strength.'

- Who is our Strength? *Christ!*
- Who is our Savior? *Christ!*

- Who is our Redeemer? *Christ!*
- Who is there to fight our battles for us? *Christ is!*

As we have seen He also has the angels to do His work for him, too.

Verse 4 becomes very important, and in all the struggles and difficulties that we have gone through, this becomes very profound:

Verse 4: "**You have not yet resisted to the point of** *losing* **blood in your struggle against sin**."

I've never anointed anyone for bleeding because they've been fighting against sin. What does this show? *This shows the effort, determination and steadfastness that we need to have in serving and loving God and in overcoming!* We do it by fixing our mind on Christ. Don't get discouraged and don't get down because God is doing this for a tremendous and wonderful purpose.

Verse 5: "And you have already forgotten the admonition that He addresses to you as to sons: 'My son, do not despise *the* chastening of *the* Lord, nor grow weary of being reproved by Him; **for whom** *the* **Lord loves He chastens, and He severely disciplines every son whom He receives**'" (vs 5-6).

That's why God didn't call us to have good perfect lives in the flesh. If you want to join a social club, go to a social club. If you want to go to where everything is smooth and nice, I don't really think you can find any place on the face of the earth today that's like that. **No!** Times are getting difficult and harder, and harder to come by. We need to realize that. God is helping us to develop the character, to have the faith and virtue and character, and eventually come to the point of having the very love of God perfected in us. That's what God is doing. So yes, there is going to be some correction. Yes, there are going to be some things that change and come along here. Yes indeed, because that's just the way it's going to be.

Let's look at some other things here, the reason for all the trials. Let's see what Peter says about this, and why we go through these things. He also shows that a great deal of it, yes a great deal of what we go through is because *we're fighting Satan the devil,* as well as:

- self
- sin
- the world

So, we've got a big battle out there and the way we do it is *keep our minds fixed and focused on Jesus Christ,* that:

- we know what's in the Gospels

- we know what's in the Epistles of Paul
- we know what's in the General Epistles
- we live by every Word of God

That's the important thing for us to realize and understand!

1-Peter 5:5: "In the same manner, *you* younger men be subject to *the* older men; and all *of you* be subject to one another, being clothed with humility… [that's the whole purpose of it] …because God sets Himself against *the* proud, but He gives grace to *the* humble. Be humbled, therefore, under the mighty hand of God so that He may exalt you in *due* time; **casting all your cares upon Him, because He cares for you**" (vs 5-7).

Here's a great mistake a lot of people do. They get worried, they get frustrated, they get upset, and they pace back and forth and they wonder what they're going to do. *But they haven't cast all their cares upon God!* So rather than worry, fret, stew and wonder, *go pray! Lay it all before God,* "**casting all your cares upon Him, because He cares for you**."

- He loves you
- He wants you in His Kingdom
- He wants you to succeed, grow and overcome
- He will give you the strength, the power and perform the work for you

IF you trust in Him and rely upon Him.

It's like it said where we started: *stand still and see the salvation of the Lord, and go forward!* Don't be discouraged! Don't be down! *Don't let anything take you away from Christ!*

Here's the reason for it; v 8: "**Be sober!**…. [don't get involved with the *spiritual drunkenness* of this world] …**Be vigilant!**…."

That's why we have the Feast of Unleavened Bread come along so that it reminds us every year we need to be vigilant. That means on *watch! Be on guard!*

"…For your adversary *the* devil is prowling about as a roaring lion, seeking anyone he may devour" (v 8).

Yes, we're going to have battles against Satan, and he's going to come after the people of God. That's just all part of the situation the way that the reality of it truly is. Here's how we fight him:

Verse 9: "Whom resist, steadfast in the faith… [not wavering back and forth, as James said, and be double-minded man and unstable as water] …knowing *that* the same afflictions are being fulfilled among your brethren who *are* in *the* world."

Don't think that any trial you're going

through is some sort of strange thing that has come upon you. Everyone has them, you have them, so you take them to God. Here's a promise, and you claim this promise. When you're going through a trial:

- ask God to help you understand it
- ask God to help you learn the lesson
- ask God to help you fully comprehend what is going on

so that you can take that and make it part of your life and character of the very lesson that you're going to learn!

Then claim this promise, v 10: "Now, may the God of all grace, Who has called us unto His eternal glory in Christ Jesus, after *you* have suffered a little while, Himself perfect you... [so God is perfecting you individually] ...**establish, strengthen,** *and* **settle you**." *That's the purpose of the trials and the difficulties that we go through,* so that we can let God fight our battles for us. Then he says:

Verse 11: "To Him *be* the glory and the power into the ages of eternity. Amen." *That's the way we unleaven our lives in Christ*:

- by Christ in us
- by growing
- by overcoming
- by looking to God to fight our battles for us

So that we can realize that we are called unto eternal glory! Keeping our minds fixed and focused on Jesus Christ.

Now let's look at some other things here which are important for us to realize. Since this talks about fighting against Satan the devil let's come to Eph. 6 and let's see what we need to do – the very spiritual preparation. Let me tell you this:

- if you're not praying
- if you're not studying
- if you're not living by every Word of God when a trial comes upon you it's going to hit you like a blockbuster

You are not going to know what to do because:
- you're weak spiritually
- you're weak mentally
- you're weak physically

All of those things go hand in hand! When they come, you're overwhelmed and you get discouraged. Here's what we need to do. We need to be strong in the power God.

Satan is out there after us like a roaring lion! He is clever and slick and has all kinds of devices to try and entrap and even deceive the very elect. So, when we have problems and difficulties to come by,

do exactly like Moses told the children of Israel: *'Hold your peace, stand still, see the salvation of the Lord and go forward.'* And the obvious implication is: not backward into Egypt.

Ephesians 6:10: "Finally, my brethren, **be strong in** *the* **Lord**..." *That comes with*:

- patient study
- prayer
- walking in every way of God
- living your life the way that God wants you to do it

That's how you're strong in the Lord!

"...and in the might of His strength.... [because *He* is going to fight for us] ...Put on the whole armor of God... [not only is God going to fight for us, but we have our part] ...so that you may be able to stand against the wiles of the devil, because we are not wrestling against flesh and blood, but against principalities *and* against powers, against the world rulers of the darkness of this age, against the spiritual *power* of wickedness in high *places*" (vs 10-12).

We see that more so in this age now. There's just an acceleration of evil everywhere. That is deliberate, and let's understand something; let's just be frank: *We ain't seen nothing, yet, because Satan and his forces and troops are out there to destroy every vestige of Christianity that they can through any means that they can!* Those are all part of the wiles of the devil, and we're fighting against those *wicked spirits in high places!*

Verse 13: "Therefore, take up the whole armor of God so that you may be able to resist in the evil day, and having worked out all things, to stand."

Just like Moses said, *'Stand still and see the salvation of God!'*

Verse 14: "Stand, therefore, having your loins girded about with Truth... [that is the Word of God, which is true] ...and wearing the breastplate of righteousness, and having your feet shod with *the* preparation of the Gospel of Peace. Besides all *these*, take up the shield of the faith, with which you will have the power to quench all the fiery darts of the wicked one..." (vs 14-16)—*because he's there just trying to lob them in. Missiles of lust!*

As it says there in Eph. 2, he is 'the prince of the power of the air,' he is the one who comes along to tempt and to induce into sin. He is there. If there's any one thing Satan would like you to do is get discouraged and down and come to the point that you're going to give up on God because you have a trial that you're going through. Well now, *you can't let that happen!*

Verse 17: "And put on the helmet of salvation, and the sword of the Spirit, which is the Word of God… [it shows an active, growing, overcoming, praying, trusting in God, focusing on Christ] …**praying at all times**…" (vs 17-18).

You pray every day, you pray many times during the day, just like Paul wrote, *cease not praying* (1-Thess. 5). Not only do you pray and put your life in God's hands every day when the day begins, but during the day you pray and ask God:

- for help
- for wisdom
- for Truth
- for understanding
- for bringing into captivity every thought unto Christ
- for casting down vain imaginations that rise up in your mind against God

That's how sin so easily besets us. It is a continuous daily thing that we do, *praying at all times!*

"…with all prayer and supplication in *the* Spirit, and in this very thing being watchful with all perseverance and supplication for all the saints…" (v 18).

Brethren, we all need the prayers of everyone. I know my prayer every day is for all the brethren:

- those who need to be healed
- those who need to fight their battles
- those who need to be raised up
- those who are distressed and brokenhearted

Christ came to heal the brokenhearted! Christ came to relieve the distressed! You turn all of that to Him!

- He is there
- He will help
- He will fight
- He has promised
  - ✓ it doesn't depend on your goodness
  - ✓ it doesn't depend on your righteousness

Oh, you have your part to do, *but it depends on Christ because He has promised!*

Those promises are sure, and those promises are true and good like we've already seen and Jesus Christ has promised that *He will not ever, never leave us and forsake us!* That's something! So, we can have the total faith and confidence in what God wants us to do in trusting Him to fight our battles.

Now let's see what we are operating against. Christ has saved us; reached down and saved us from our sins in this world!

Ephesians 2:1: "Now, you were dead in trespasses and sins." *That's how we were before God!* God reached down and had mercy on every one of us individually.

Verse 2: "In which you walked in times past according to the course of this world, according to the prince of the power of the air, the spirit that is now working within the children of disobedience." *This is what God has saved us from! That's why we are not to go back into it!*

Verse 3: "Among whom also we all once had our conduct in the lusts of our flesh, doing the things willed by the flesh and by the mind, and were by nature *the* children of wrath, even as the rest *of the world*. But God, Who is rich in mercy because of His great love with which He loved us, even when we were dead in *our* trespasses, has made *us* alive together with Christ. (*For* you have been saved by grace.)" (vs 3-5).

- through the sacrifice of Jesus Christ
- through the power of the Holy Spirit
- through the Word of God

Notice what we are to do here; v 8: "For by grace you have been saved through faith, and this *especially* is not of your own selves; *it is* the gift of God…"

Always remember this: *you have nothing you didn't receive!* Everything we have is of God.

Verse 9: "Not of works, so that no one may boast. For we are His workmanship… [God is creating Himself in you; we are His workmanship] …**being created in Christ Jesus**…" (vs 9-10)— because *salvation is creation*, *creating in us:*

- the mind of Christ
- the love of God
- the character of God
- all the fruits of the Holy Spirit of:
  - ✓ love
  - ✓ joy
  - ✓ peace
  - ✓ longsuffering
  - ✓ faith
  - ✓ gentleness
  - ✓ kindness
  - ✓ goodness
  - ✓ meekness
  - ✓ temperance

Against such there is no law! That's what He is creating in us.

Verse 10: "For we are His workmanship, being created in Christ Jesus unto *the* good works that God ordained beforehand in order that we might walk in them."

Now let's understand:

- *how* we are to look at these things
- *how* we are to look at the world
- *how* we are to look at ourselves
- *how* we are to view the circumstances in which we find ourselves

and what God is going to do for us!

Romans 8:9: "However, you are not in *the* flesh, but in *the* Spirit, if *the* Spirit of God is indeed dwelling within you. But if anyone does not have *the* Spirit of Christ, he does not belong to Him."

That's the important thing.. *the Spirit of God!* As we have seen, if you let that lax and you're not exercising it, then you have to do as Paul said, 'Stir up the Spirit of God that is in you.' That's what the Feast of Unleavened Bread is all about, *to stir up the Spirit of God which is in us!.*

Verse 10: "But if Christ *be* within you, the body *is* indeed dead because of sin…"—*because you are baptized!* All your sins died with Christ and He died for you. Whenever you confess your sins, you put them in the hands of God. They are covered with the blood of Jesus Christ and His sacrifice, you see. So you're not living in sin.

"…however, the Spirit *is* life because of righteousness…. [Here is a great and tremendous promise] …Now, if the Spirit of Him Who raised Jesus from *the* dead is dwelling within you, He Who raised Christ from *the* dead will also quicken your mortal bodies because of His Spirit that dwells within you. So then, brethren, we are not debtors to the flesh, to live according to *the* flesh… [we're not to live in the carnal way of this world] …because if you are living according to *the* flesh, you shall die; but if by *the* Spirit you are putting to death the deeds of the body, you shall live" (vs 10-13).

Just like we saw on the first Holy Day. We are to put to death the deeds of the flesh. We are to put all of that out, and we are to put in Christ. That's what he's talking about here. Now if you do that you shall live, and that means to eternal life.

Verse 14—*never forget this*: "**For as many as are led by** *the* **Spirit of God, these are** *the* **sons of God**."

Let's understand something very important here: the Spirit of God is not going to force you. *The Spirit of God will **lead** you, but **you have to choose to yield to God,** and **you have to choose to ask God to help you be led of the Spirit of God!***

Verse 14: "**For as many as are led by** *the* **Spirit of God, these are** *the* **sons of God**." Satan, as we have seen, wants to come in and give us

- a spirit of fear

- a spirit of doubt
- a spirit of contention
- a spirit of argument with God

Verse 15: "Now, you have not received a spirit of bondage again unto fear, but you have received *the* Spirit of sonship, whereby we call out, 'Abba, Father.' The Spirit itself bears witness conjointly with our own spirit, *testifying* that **we are the children of God**. Now, **if *we are* children, *we are* also heirs—truly, heirs of God and joint heirs with Christ**…" (vs 15-17). *Stop and think for a minute!*

What did Christ inherit? *All things!* That means the universe; *we are joint heirs with Christ!* That means we will own part of whatever God gives us of the universe, and He says, 'Here, this is yours, but with Christ.' That is a fantastic and tremendous thing that God has called us to. I think that we can understand more and more about God and more and more about how we need to grow, change and overcome *IF* we keep that right in the forefront of our mind and be led of the Holy Spirit of God.

Here's a promise, a promise of suffering; "…**if indeed we suffer together with Him, so that we may also be glorified together with Him**" (v 17).

The Apostle Paul was called to suffer more than any other man except Jesus Christ. He did suffer! How did he look upon those sufferings? Well, he came to rejoice in them because he understood the end result.

Likewise with us, we need to rejoice in them because we understand the end result. Not be like the children of Israel at the Red Sea who complained against God and the circumstances they were in because they couldn't see the outcome. They didn't have faith in God, though He did a miraculous intervention to extract them from the land of Egypt. Wwe're going to be glorified together but we have to suffer.

Verse 18: "For I reckon that the sufferings of the present time *are* not worthy *to be compared* with the glory that shall be revealed in us."

I want you to understand these next verses here to give us some perspective.

Verse 19: "For the earnest expectation of the creation itself is awaiting the manifestation of the sons of God."

- How important are the sons of God?
- How important is God to you?

So important that Jesus Christ gave His life for you and for everyone individually, because the sacrifice of Christ is applied to each of us individually, continually, standing in the grace of God.

The whole creation is waiting! The world is waiting! Have you ever thought of it this way: *the world is waiting for you and me, and all the sons of God down through history!* It's waiting! ***It's needing us, because we are the solution in God's set time!***

Verse 20: "Because the creation was subjected to vanity, not willingly, but by reason of Him who subjected *it* in hope… [we are part of that hope through Jesus Christ] …in order that the creation itself might be delivered from the bondage of corruption into the freedom of the glory of the children of God. For we know that **all the creation is groaning together and travailing together until now**" (vs 20-22)—*waiting for us!*

Let's understand something that's important:

- regardless of your circumstances
- regardless of the difficulties
- regardless of your physical condition
- regardless of whether you are young or old
- regardless of whether you are rich or poor

God loves you and has a purpose for you! Everything in your life is going to work out for good!

Verse 28: "And we know that all things work together for good to those who love God… [that's why we've covered how important the love of God is] …to those who are called according to *His* purpose… [and you have been] …because those whom He did foreknow… [if you have God's Spirit in you He has foreknown you] …He also predestinated *to be* conformed to the image of His own Son, that He might be *the* Firstborn among many brethren…. [that's what our destination is, our predestination] …Now, whom He predestinated, these He also called; and whom He called, these He also justified; and whom He justified, these He also glorified" (vs 28-30).

God is looking at the finished product in you! He's not looking at you the way that you are. He's imputed the righteousness of Christ to you so that you stand before Him blameless and Holy, in love. He is looking to you as if you are now glorified. In other words, ***He sees and knows what you will be at the resurrection!***

- we've received a bit of the glory of God by receiving the Holy Spirit of God
- we've received a bit of the glory of God by having His Word

which we can know and understand and live by! *Absolutely true!*

Verse 31: "What then shall we say to these things? **If God *is* for us, who *can be* against us?**"

- there is no trouble
- there's no difficulty
- there is no battle
- there is nothing that can be against us

Now claim that promise through the blood and sacrifice of Jesus Christ!

Verse 32: "He Who did not spare even His own Son, but gave Him up for us all, how shall He not also grant us all things together with Him?"

'Come, inherit the Kingdom prepared for you by My Father.'

Verse 33: "Who shall bring an accusation against *the* elect of God?…. [people can, but that has no standing before God] …God *is the One* Who justifies. Who *is* the one that condemns?…." (vs 33-34).

Satan comes and accuses us day and night before God, but we overcome Him with the blood of Christ!

"…*It is* Christ Who died, but rather, Who is raised again, Who is even *now* at *the* right hand of God… [to fight our battles for us, to give us of His Spirit, to strengthen us, to help us overcome] …*and* Who is also making intercession for us. **What shall separate us from the love of Christ?**…." (vs 34-35).

Is there anything that's going to separate you from the love of God? the love of Christ? The reason that we keep the commandments of God and the Holy Days of God, and the Feasts of God is so that we understand this: ***nothing can separate us from God!***

"…*Shall* tribulation, or distress, or persecution, or famine, or nakedness, or danger, or sword? " (v 35). *None of those things and we're probably going to face every one of these things in the coming years!*

Verse 36: "Accordingly, it is written, 'For Your sake we are killed all the day long; we are reckoned as sheep for *the* slaughter.' But in all these things… [even if that happens] …we are more than conquerors through Him Who loved us" (vs 36-37).

- this is the persuasion we need to come to
- this is the attitude that we need
- this is the whole finality of the Feast of Unleavened Bread

Verse 38: "For I am persuaded… [Are you? Are you fully persuaded[…that neither death, nor life, nor angels, nor principalities, nor powers, nor things present, nor things to come, nor height, nor depth, nor any other created thing, **shall be able to separate us from the love of God, which *is* in**

<u>Christ Jesus our Lord</u>" (vs 38-39).

That's the meaning of today. Stand still and see the salvation of the Lord, and go forward with the power and the might and strength of God!

Scriptures from *The Holy Bible in Its Original Order, A Faithful Version*

Scriptural References:

1) Exodus 7:1
2) Exodus 14:10-16
3) Exodus 15:1-3
4) Psalm 18:1-6
5) Psalm 12:1-5, 8
6) Psalm 4:1-4
7) Psalm 37:1-8, 27-29, 34-40
8) 2 Chronicles 20:3, 15, 17, 20-22, 28
9) 2 Kings 19:1, 3, 14-17, 19, 34-36
10) Hebrews 12:1-6
11) 1 Peter 5:5-11
12) Ephesians 6:10-18
13) Ephesians 2:1-5, 8-10
14) Romans 8:9-22, 28-39

Scriptures referenced, not quoted:

- Matthew 7
- 1 Corinthians 10
- 1 Thessalonians 5

FRC: cs
Transcription date unknown
Reformatted: bo—11/2020

CHAPTER THIRTY-THREE

Nothing is Impossible for God!
(Last Day of Unleavened Bread)
Fred R. Coulter

Greetings, brethren! Welcome to the last day of the Feast of Unleavened Bread!

What a Feast this has been with everything that's been going on. It shows the Truth that *a little leaven leavens the whole lump* is the sum total of why we have Unleavened Bread. It is so that we can—with the Spirit of God—put in the righteousness of God through:

- His Word
- His Truth
- His Spirit
- living God's way
- trusting Him in everything

In everything!

Leviticus 23:6: "And on the fifteenth day of the same month *is* the Feast of Unleavened Bread to the LORD. You must eat unleavened bread seven days."

Tonight, after sundown, you can have whatever leaven you desire. *It's only during the Feast of Unleavened Bread that leaven is a type of sin!*

Verse 7: "On the first day you shall have a Holy convocation. You shall not *do any servile* work *therein*, but you shall offer a fire offering to the LORD seven days. In the seventh day *is* a Holy convocation. You shall do no servile work *therein*" (vs 7-8).

We also know that we are to give according to how God has blessed us, and think about how God has dealt with you in your life:

- rescuing you from sin
- bringing you out of the world
- granting you His Holy Spirit
- giving you understanding of His Word
- leading and guiding you in the way that you need to go

Think about al of those things when you're making up your offering! It all goes to the use of what God wants.

As you know, we are very careful with the funds—the tithe and offerings—that the brethren send, *because it's God's money!* We have to use if for every purpose for:

- preaching the Gospel
- feeding the flock
- serving the brethren
- producing to the world the things that is necessary to preach to them

We have a great many things, as you know, for your personal study. If you still have the catalog of all of our literature, go read through that catalog again and order whatever you think you need.

Living in these days when there are a lot of false prophets and false doctrines, and Satan the devil is busy and active, *we need to stay close to God in everything that we do!*

- God will bless us
- God will be with us
- God will pave the way for us

to accomplish His will be it in your life, or the life of all the brethren everywhere!

(pause for offering)

Nothing is impossible for God, and we will see that He brings us to circumstances so that we will *trust in Him, that we will have faith in God, faith in Jesus Christ!*

Just to show you how important that is, and how it relates to everything that God does, come to Psa. 148, which is quite a little Psalm. This tells us how God created everything that there is. All of these things are important for us.

Notice all the praise to God, because God deserves all the praise:

Palm 148:1: "O praise the LORD! Praise the LORD from the heavens; praise Him in the heights. Praise Him, all His angels; praise Him, all His hosts. Praise Him, sun and moon; praise Him, all you stars of light. Praise Him, you heavens of heavens, and waters that are above the heavens. Let them praise the name of the LORD, **for He commanded and they were created**" (vs 1-5).

That's a tremendous thing! The Word of God is so powerful, so great that *He can command and it will be!* Think about this:

- God has called us
- God has promised us eternal life

Remember that *it's impossible* for God to lie! So, His Word is absolutely true. He also tells us that *'many are the afflictions of the righteous.'* Why is that? *Because when we have afflictions, we learn to trust in God!*

We learn to look to Him! We come to various points in our lives, as we go down the pathway of life, to where there are things that happen that we can't change. We can't do anything about it *except believe God and trust in Him!* That's how God helps us t build character. This is why we have the Feast of Unleavened Bread.

Psalm 146:5: "**Happy is he who has the God of Jacob for his help**…" *God will help us in all our trials, difficulties, and circumstances!* That's why we have this last day of the Feast of Unleavened Bread. *Nothing is impossible for God!*

- God has decreed that His plan is going to be fulfilled
- God has decreed that all of those who have His Spirit and love Him and obey Him will receive eternal life at the resurrection

Regardless of the trials in the path of your life!

"…**whose hope is in the LORD his God**" (v 5).

- What is our hope? *The resurrection and eternal life!*
- What is the fulfillment of that hope? *That we will be raised without sin!*

We will be changed from flesh to spirit and God has promised!

Verse 6: "…Who keeps Truth forever." *That's why the Word of God is called Truth!* It is **spiritual and spiritually understood!** *It is only understood by those who love God and keep His commandments!*

We saw with the Night to Be Much Observed unto the Lord, what a fantastic night that was, as they were leaving Egypt. They didn't go very far that first night, but God led them with the pillar of fire by night and the cloud by day. He also gave them great wealth, great everything, because of destroying the Egyptians, their firstborn and everything that they had. Think about this: the children of Israel, leading up to the Passover, saw the plagues of God that came, *and awesome the were, indeed! Very powerful!*

God's Word is true, and when He said He would do it, *He did it!* Then He final had the coup de grace to let the children of Israel go, the killing of the firstborn of all the Egyptians and all of their livestock, *which was a mass slaughter!*

The children of Israel were spared because they were in their homes and under the blood of the Lamb. Then on the day portion, as we saw, of the Passover they came to Rameses and gathered to go, starting the Exodus! This was all organized, and they left right as the Night to Be Much Observed to the Lord was coming on! By the time the last group left the bounds of Rameses, it was already dark and God was showing that He was going to take His people and bring them to the Holy Mount to give them His laws, commandments, statutes and judgments, and that He would personally speak. The lesser ones He had Moses write down. *All from God!* But to get there…

One of the assumptions that the children of Israel had was that they were going to go to the 'promised land.' They thought that they would just scoot right along the Mediterranean seashore and come over to the 'promised land' and get it. But God had other things in mind, *because He had to give them His laws and commandments, and He had to separate them from the children of Egypt!* Here's what God did, and He took them on a little different route.

- How about your life on the path that you have been walking?
- Is it a little different than you had anticipated that it would be? *Yes, indeed!*
- Do you have circumstances that happen to you that you didn't know of? *True!*
- That you didn't expect? *Without a doubt!*

What God did is take the children of Israel, and instead of going on into the 'promised land' they took a turn south and came along the western shore of the Red Sea. At that point it was very narrow between the sea and the mountains. So, there was just enough room for the long column of the children of Israel to be there at the sea. Then Pharaoh, when he heard that they were going that way, said:

Oh, what have we done, we've let all of our slaves go. We don't know what to do. How are we going to have all the chores taken care of? We can't do them ourselves and our firstborn are dead, and the firstborn of the animals are dead. Look at us! We need to go down there and get them and bring them back.

Let's see what happened. Let's look at this; there's a parallel with this: Pharaoh is a type of Satan. Does

Satan want to come and get us? *Yes, indeed! We've already cover that!*

- we need *the armor of God*
- we need *the power of God*
- we need *faith in God*

Our weapons are spiritual: **trusting in God!** The children of Israel didn't understand that. So, here comes Pharaoh:

Exodus 14:8: "And the LORD hardened the heart of Pharaoh, king of Egypt. And he pursued the children of Israel, and the children of Israel went out with a high hand. So, the Egyptians pursued them, all the horses *and* chariots of Pharaoh, and his horsemen, and his army. And they overtook them camping by the sea, beside Pi Hahiroth, before Baal Zephon. And when Pharaoh drew near, the children of Israel lifted up their eyes. And, behold, **the Egyptians marched after them**" (vs 8-10).

They were completely helpless! They had no weapons, maybe a few swords, a few spears. They had nothing! But they had the greatest defense of all; *they had God!* Keep that in mind when you're faced with a challenge that's greater than you, more than you can handle, more than you can think about. *Take it to God!* This is the whole lesson for this day.

"…And they were very afraid. And the children of Israel cried out to the LORD. And they said to Moses…" (vs 10-11).

See, when something goes wrong, you impute wrong motives! 'You did this because you don't love me' or whatever.

"…'Have you taken us away to die in the wilderness because *there were* no graves in Egypt?…'" (v 11). *In other words*:

We're going to be buried out here in this wilderness. It would have been better if we stayed in Egypt. At least there's enough land for graves.

"…Why have you dealt this way with us to carry us forth out of Egypt?" (v 11).

Stop and think! Have you wondered why God called you? *That's what they were questioning*:

What is God doing? If He's going to give us the 'promised land' what is this all about?

Well, the truth is God has a different plan of bringing it about than the thoughts that they had. God had many things, yet, that He had to do.

Verse 13: "And Moses said to the people, [#1]'**Fear not!**…. *One of the lessons that we're to learn*:

Don't fear, regardless of what happens, because God is there! God is always near, so there's no reason to fear.

[#2]"…**Stand still**…" (v 13). *Don't get up there and run over to the Egyptians and say, 'Keep me alive and I'll go back and be your slave.'*

"…and [#3]**see the salvation of the LORD, which He will work for you today**…" (v 13). *Think about that!*

Salvation comes from God! Yes, through the sacrifice of Christ we have been saved from our sins. But the ultimate salvation is the resurrection, which is a command of God when the seventh trump blows.

You think about a glorious thing that that's going to be. Remember, the next Holy Day we have is Pentecost, which pictures that. We'll get to that in due time.

1. **Don't Fear**
2. **Stand Still**

Don't run off and do your own thing because you think that you have got to do it, *rather than trusting in God!*

3. **See the Salvation of the Lord**

"…Which He will work for you today…"

"…for the Egyptians whom you have seen today, [#4]**you shall never see them again!**" (v 13).

4. **Shall Never See Your Sins Again**

How far does God remove our sins from us when we truly repent and yield to God? *As far as the east is from the west!*

- sin is like the Egyptians
- sin comes from Satan the devil, who is like Pharaoh
- sin is against God

We, through the power and Spirit of God, can:

- fight against that sin
- resist that sin
- trust in God to deliver us

Verse 14: [#5]"**The LORD shall fight for you**, and you shall be still." *Quit your stupid complaining!*

5. **God Will Fight for You**

He will take care of it, and in a way sometimes you don't even know until somewhere down the road you see that *God did this!*

Verse 15: "And the LORD said to Moses,

384

'Why do you cry to Me? Speak to the children of Israel **that they go forward**.'" *That's what this day pictures!*

- we keep going forward
- our goal is the Kingdom of God
- our goal is eternal life
- our goal is to rule the world under Christ in the Kingdom of God

So, we must always go forward! As long as we're in the flesh, and as long as we live in this world, we're going to have to:

- fight against sin
- fight against Satan
- fight against society

*But **God is with us!** It doesn't matter what they do to us!*

Verse 16: "And you—**lift up your rod, and stretch out your hand over the sea**…"

How is that for a weapon? *A big rod in his hand and God says, 'Hold it over the sea!'*

"…and divide it. And the children of Israel shall go on dry ground through the midst of the sea" (v 16).

Think about that! *They were in an impossible situation!* They couldn't go back north, they couldn't go to the east because the Egyptians were there and God put a spiritual wall between the Egyptians and the Israelites, and it was dark to the Egyptians but light to the children of Israel.

They couldn't go out into the water and they couldn't go further south, *so they were in an impossible situation with the enemy right there ready to pounce!*

So, God had Moses take his rod and God caused the wind to blow and opened the sea, spread it open. This was a big deal. This wasn't a little channel like you see in most of the movies. This must have been at least ten miles wide, because the whole length of the column of the children of Israel in their marching order was a tremendously long column.

You figure a column of a million people. Maybe not ten miles, but however long it was. They were encamped in a column alongside the shore. So, when God began to divide the Red Sea… Remember, He made it dry ground that had been under the sea and was soft and mushy for how long. **Nothing is impossible for God!** *Remember that!* **Nothing!**

So, He opened the Red Sea, and the wind blew all that night and as morning was coming they all marched in a flanking movement into the Red Sea and across to the other side. Didn't take them very long to get to the other side. They got to the other side and God lifted the division between the children of Israel and the Egyptians.

The Egyptians saw that they were gone, that they had gone through the Red Sea. They came to the Red Sea and looked at it and thought, 'It's all dry!'

Good lesson: *God always traps the wicked ones in their own schemes and devices, because they know nothing of God!*

Pharaoh said, 'All right, let's go!' So, they all went down into the Red Sea and when they got to the middle of it, God started knocking off the wheels, turning the dry ground into mud. They said, 'Oh, we've got to get out of here! Look at what the Lord is doing!' *And the water came back and they all drowned!*

Talk about *accomplishing an impossible thing by the power of God!* That's why we have to have faith in God in everything that we do!

- He will lead us
- He will direct us
- He will teach us
- He will help us

- we will overcome sin
- we will overcome human nature
- we will overcome Satan the devil

By the miracle of the power of the Holy Spirit of God with His Word and our living God's way! That's reaching the dry ground on the other side of the sea.

Then all the people were happy! Well, you know, carnal nature took hold again, and they complained. Then God brought them to Mt. Sinai and gave them the Ten commandments. Here was another *one time* thing in the history of the world, that that many people—over a million people, maybe 1.5 million—all the children of Israel camped around Mt. Sinai.

God made a proposition for them. Whenever God does something, it starts out with a simple statement. Just like with us: *Repent and be baptized and receive the Holy Spirit!* That's how it starts out. That's very simple.

God didn't tell about all the things that would come upon us, and all the difficulties that we would have overcoming—did He? *No! But we are to believe God, trust in Him, obey His voice, and do what He wants!*

385

So, when they got to Mt. Sinai, God called Moses up into the mountain and He gave them the proposition. Very simple. The details come later. Isn't that how it is in our lives? *Yes, indeed!*

Exodus 19:3: "And Moses went up to God, and the LORD called to him out of the mountain, saying, 'Thus you shall say to the house of Jacob and tell the children of Israel, "You have seen what I did to the Egyptians, and *how* I bore you on eagles' wings and brought you unto Myself"'" (vs 3-4).

To the Holy Mountain of Zion, Mt. Sinai; God dealing with all the people directly with Moses personally, face-to-face. This was a tremendous thing, indeed!

Here's the proposition, v 5: "Now, therefore, **if you will obey My voice** indeed…"'" *Look at that! Never forget those three words*: **obey My voice!**

Everything we have in the Bible is written down and is the voice of God, so no one can say, 'God, I know you talked to them, but You haven't talked to us. What did you say to them?'

- God had Moses write it all down!
- God had the kings write it down!
- God had the priests write it down!
- God had the Prophets write it down!

So, the Old Testament was complied and filled with 356 direct references to the coming Messiah Jesus Christ! An amazing thing, indeed! Isn't that something?

"…**if you will obey My voice** indeed…"— *that is don't make any exceptions, don't complain, **but truly obey My voice, and keep My commandments!*** He hadn't given them, yet. But that was coming.

"'…and keep My covenant, **then you shall be a special treasure to Me** above all people; for all the earth *is* Mine. And you shall be to Me a kingdom of priests and a Holy nation.' **These *are* the words which you shall speak to the children of Israel**" (vs 5-6).

All of that sounded really good and wonderful, so Moses came back and told them all:

Verse 8: "And all the people answered together and said…" *Listen to this! If you make a statement like this, remember, **God is going to hold you to it!***

"… **'All that the LORD has spoken we will do.'**…: (v 8). *Apply that to the New Testament!* Paul writes that *'if any do not adhere to the sound words of Jesus Christ, he is ignorant and knows nothing! **From such withdraw yourself!'*** Same thing! 'Keep My commandments!' *That's what*

Jesus said!

- *their* promise was a 'promised land'
- *our* promise is *eternal life in the Kingdom of God*

So, it's so much greater!

Then God had Moses prepare all the people and get all ready. Then as it turns out, this was on the Day of Pentecost. So, here is Mt. Sinai and all the children of Israel at the base of the mountain, and God told Moses to block if off and don't let an animal come near and no man come near. If any do they shall be 'shot through with an arrow' or a dart!

Here is something that all these people experienced at the same time. *An impossible thing that God would speak to the people!*

This was to help them to understand how important it was that God was dealing with them, and what He was going to give them, and how they needed to live their lives. This was so they would have long lives and many children. They would receive the blessings of God. He would fight for them in their circumstances in conquering the 'promised land.' He would bless them in everything that they did.

Here is an impossible experience, a one-time experience, never happened before or after! Let's go through the Ten Commandments, and look at them, *because this is how we are to live today with the Spirit of God in our mind*:

- to love God with all our heart, mind, soul and being
- to love our neighbor as ourselves
- to love the brethren as Jesus loved us
- even to love our enemies

because God's plan is so great that it's going to be awesome, indeed, in the fullness of the working out of His plan! Here God comes down:

- the mountain is on fire
- the trumpets are blowing
- the wind is whirling around
- the earth is quaking
- the mighty power of God is there

*then it settles down and here is a great flame of fire on top of Mt. Sinai with the smoke going up and **the first thing He says***:

Commandment #1; Exodus 20:2: "**I am the LORD your God**, Who brought you out of the land of Egypt, out of the house of bondage." *I brought you out of sin and slavery!* In the New Testament it's the same thing with Jesus Christ!

Verse 3: "**You shall have no other gods**

041520

386

before Me…."—*because that's the first thing that people like to do*; add on to what God has given, have their own gods. Then the next thing they want to have is their own little idols.

So, commandment #2, v 4: "You shall **not make**… [look at all the idols that people have developed in the name of Christ] …for yourselves any graven image, or any likeness of *anything* that *is* in the heavens above, or that *is* in the earth beneath, or that *is* in the waters under the earth. **You shall not bow yourself down to them, nor serve them**, for I, the LORD your God *am* a jealous God, visiting the iniquity of the fathers upon the children unto the third and fourth generation of those who hate Me" (vs 4-5).

There's a <u>blessing for loving God</u>; there's a <u>curse for hating God</u>! *Never forget that!*

Verse 6: "But showing mercy to thousands of those who love Me and keep My commandments." *That, brethren, is New Testament doctrine!* Doesn't that sound an awful lot like John 14-16. *That's an expansion of it!*

This also shows that you're not to have anything between you and the love of God.

Commandment #3; v 7: "**You shall not take the name of the LORD your God in vain**, for the LORD will not hold him guiltless who takes His name in vain."

The way that the name of God is taken in vain more than anything else is *in religious services when people say that God says, when God doesn't say!*

Commandment #4; the key to always have contact with God, and this is based upon Him making the Sabbath on the seventh day when he renewed the earth!

Verse 8: "**Remember the Sabbath Day to keep it Holy.**" *One sentence!* And everybody forgets it and goes to Sunday.

Verse 9: "Six days you shall labor and do all your work. But the seventh day *is* the Sabbath of the LORD your God. In it you shall not do any work, you, nor your son, nor your daughter; your manservant, nor your maidservant, nor your livestock, nor the stranger within your gates…. [Why?] …for *in* six days…" (vs 9-11).

In other words, ***keeping the Sabbath lets you always know that God is Creator of everything!*** There's no such thing as evolution.

"…the LORD made the heaven and the earth, the sea, and all that *is* in them, and rested the seventh day. Therefore, **the LORD blessed the Sabbath Day and sanctified it**" (v 11).

In Lev. 23 and expansion on the Sabbath Day with the Feasts and Holy Days of God. That's how God works! He first gives a very simple proposition, then He gives the main things that need to done, and then He gives the details of other things under it, which are called *judgments, statutes and ordinances!* Amazing! That's how God does everything!

Commandment #5; v 12: "**Honor your father and your mother**…."

Why? Because every single one of us have a perpetual scar right in the middle of our bodies, called the navel, to let us know that we came from our father and mother. *Honor father and mother!*

It's difficult for children to do it, and it's difficult for parents to train children, but this is necessary so that we understand that as adults life is also going to be difficult and we have to work at it.

Jesus said, 'My Father works and I work!' *There's a lot of work that we need to do in honoring your father and mother:*

"…so that your days may be long upon the land…" (v 12). *Think about how many die because they don't do that!*

Commandment #6; v 13: "**You shall not murder**." *The King James say 'kill,' but that's not correct!*

Commandment #7; v 14: "**You shall not commit adultery**."

Those two things that happen the worst, and most of it is because they dishonor father and mother!

Commandment #8; v15: "**You shall not steal**.

Commandment #9; v 16: "**You shall not bear false witness against your neighbor**."

Commandment #10; v 17: **You shall not covet** your neighbor's house. You shall not covet your neighbor's wife, nor his manservant, nor his maidservant, nor his ox, nor his donkey, nor anything that *is* your neighbor's." *Instead of all the people down there saying*:

Oh what a wonderful, awesome thing that this has been. We heard the voice of God, let's all commit ourselves to always love God and keep His commandments.

Well, that's not what happened, but that's what should have happened. The carnal mind does not want to do the things of God.

Verse 18: "And all the people saw the thunderings, and the lightnings, and the sound of the trumpet, and the mountain smoking. And when the people saw, they trembled and stood afar off. And **they said to Moses, '<u>You</u> speak with us**…'" (vs 18-19).

Isn't that something? *Always like to place someone else between you and God!* That's the way human nature is!

"…'<u>You</u> speak with us and we will hear. But let not God speak with us, lest we die'" (v 19). *God said that He did that to prove them!*

Does God prove us with trials and difficulties? *Yes, indeed!* That certainly shows the things that are important. They sinned against God later:

- made a golden calf
- refused to go into the 'promised land'
- were turned back and had to wander a total of 40 years in the wilderness *before* they came into the 'promised land'

When they did come into the 'promised land' they were outside across the River Jordan and Jericho was on the other side and God performed another great miracle. What did He do? *He made the River Jordan stop and the water backed up like a big wall, and all the children of Israel walked across over to be on the other side!*

- there they kept the Passover
- there they had the Wave Sheaf Offering
- there they had the second circumcision
- there they conquered the land of God beginning with Jericho

That was an impossible thing! High walls, big and thick; so, God used *the impossible method!* He said:

All right, what you're going to do is walk around the city once every day for six days. Then on the seventh day you're going to walk around it, and when I give the word, everyone is to shout.

and all the walls fell in and they went in and took the spoil! Rahab the harlot and her family were the only ones saved because they treated the spies correctly. So, *God fought their battles for them! God helped them to conquer all the land!*

But after a while the people got a little tired of that, so they didn't put all the people of the land out! So, God said:

Because *you didn't obey My voice,* these are going to be a thorn in your flesh so that you will know that *you have to obey the Lord God. He will fight your battles for you **IF** you trust in*

Him! But *IF* you don't, I'm not going to fight for you.

You can go through all the history of the judges—there were some good judges, there were some not so good judges—and they had various battles here and there, but eventually they conquered the land in seven years. They divided the land, they all had their inheritance as God intended them to have it. They came into the land, God prospered them.

Then God raised up, eventually, David to take the place of Saul. God gave all the plans to David for the temple so David's son Solomon could build the temple. They had at that time *peace, all 12 tribes!*

Solomon was king over them and they had a great dedication of the temple. You can read the tremendous prayer that Solomon gave. God put His presence, reaffirming His presence, by having a cloud of His presence enter into the temple.

Then Solomon sinned! God had to take away the ten northern tribes. There was never a righteous king of the ten northern tribes until they went off into captivity in 703-701 B.C.

The tribe of Judah was left, along with Benjamin. Some of the kings were very righteous. One of the kings was Hezekiah, who was a righteous king. He was one who cleansed the temple from all the idolatry and they had a great Passover and great Feast of Unleavened Bread.

Let's see the impossible miracle that God did to save Judah and Hezekiah from the Assyrians!

It was true, the king of Assyria had come and conquered every one of the nations that is listed here. He went into Egypt and took the spoil and he had a huge army, and they were carrying the spoil back to Assyria and they camped right on the border of Judea to capture it, to take Jerusalem. They sent the commander general to speak to the children of Judah who were sitting on the wall and the officials watching it. He came to them and told them all what the king of Assyria had done, and how he got all this treasure and everything.

Now, 'if you surrender we'll take you off as slaves, but you will live.' And he told them not to listen to what Hezekiah will tell you about what God will do for you.

When Hezekiah received a letter, let's see what happened:

Isaiah 37:14: "And Hezekiah received the letter from the courier's hand, and read it. And

Hezekiah went up *into* the house of the LORD and spread it before the LORD. And Hezekiah prayed to the LORD, saying" (vs 15-15).

Notice this prayer, because we're going to learn a good lesson from Hezekiah out of all of this:

Verse 16: "O LORD of hosts, God of Israel, who dwells *between* the cherubim, You *are* God, You alone of all the kingdoms of the earth. You have made the heavens and the earth. Bow down Your ear, O LORD, and hear; open Your eyes, O LORD, and see; and hear all the words of Sennacherib which he has sent to mock the living God. Truly, O LORD, the kings of Assyria have laid waste all the countries and their lands, and have cast their gods into the fire, for they *were* no gods, but the work of men's hands, wood and stone; so they have destroyed them. And now, O LORD our God, save us from his hand..." (vs 16-20). *Good lesson; only God can save us!*

He can intervene in our lives now to save us from whatever circumstance we are in. The ultimate salvation is the resurrection from the dead! *That is another impossible thing that God is going to do!*

Verse 20: "And now, O LORD our God, save us from his hand so that all the kingdoms of the earth may know that **You *are* the LORD, You alone.**"

Verse 21: "And Isaiah the son of Amoz sent to Hezekiah, saying, 'Thus says the LORD, God of Israel, "Because you have prayed to Me against Sennacherib king of Assyria."'"

Notice how effectual a fervent prayer is. At this time Hezekiah was a righteous man. So, he prayed to God.

Verse 22: "This *is* the word which the LORD has spoken concerning him [Sennacherib], 'The virgin daughter of Zion has despised you *and* laughed you to scorn; the daughter of Jerusalem has shaken *her* head at you. Whom have you mocked and blasphemed? And against Whom have you raised *your* voice and lifted up your eyes on high? Even against the Holy One of Israel. By your servants you have mocked the LORD and have said, "By my many chariots I have come up to the height of the mountains, to the sides of Lebanon; and I will cut down the tall cedars of it, *and* its choice fir trees; and I will go to its greatest height, the finest of its forests"'" (vs 22-24). *That's looking at the nations and looking at Israel!*

Verse 25: "'I have dug and drunk water; and with the sole of my feet I have dried up all the streams of Egypt.' Have you not heard from long ago *how* I made it? From ancient times, even *how* I have formed it? Now, I have brought it to pass *that*

you should lay waste fortified cities *into* ruinous heaps" (vs 25-26). *That's what the King of Assyria did!*

Here they are, all out there camping. Let's see what God did.

- you talk about God fighting for you
- you talk about God intervening to help you
- you talk about trusting God

Look! One of the greatest blessing that can happen is when you come to the point that you know that you are helpless:

- you need God
- you need His intervention
- you need His mercy
- you need His healing
- you need His love

That's a great blessing. ***That's why we have afflictions!***

Here's Hezekiah with this great army out there. What could the children of the Jews do?

Verse 33: "Therefore, thus says the LORD concerning the king of Assyria, 'He shall not come into this city nor shoot an arrow there, nor come before it *with* shield, nor cast a bank against it.... [to come up over the walls] ...By the way that he came, by the same *way* he shall return, and shall not come into this city,' says the LORD. "For I will defend this city to save it..." (vs 33-35).

Remember what God told the children of Israel: ***Stand still and see the salvation of the Lord, for I will fight for you!***

In each case, they got to the point that there was nothing they could do. Everything was against them, but God intervened!

Verse 35: "For I will defend this city to save it, for My own sake and for My servant David's sake."

Notice what God did, v 36: "Then the angel of the LORD went out and struck a hundred and eighty-five thousand in the camp of Assyria...."

There they are, going to sleep at night, going to get up in the morning and prepare for battle and go up and take the city of Jerusalem, and take all the treasures and get everything that there is and kill as many as they can. So, God sent the angel and they all died in their sleep, except the king and his chief officers.

"...And they rose early in the morning, and behold! They *were* all dead corpses" (v 36).

- Can God take care an army quickly?
- Can He fight against the enemy for us efficiently?
- Does He know how to do it? *Yes, He does!*

Now let's see what happened to Sennacherib; v 37: "And Sennacherib king of Assyria departed, and went and returned, and dwelt at Nineveh. And it came to pass as he was worshiping *in* the house of Nisroch his god, Adrammelech and Sharezer his sons struck him with the sword. And they escaped *into* the land of Ararat; and Esar-haddon his son reigned in his place" (vs 37-38). *Killed by his own sons!*

God knows how to fight for us! When God has fought for us, we don't need to do like the children of Israel. What happened? *Three days afterward they complained to God because they didn't have any water!* So, they came to Marah where there was water, and the water was bitter, and they cried, 'We're all going to die!'

What did God have Moses do? *Cut down a tree and throw it into the water and it made the water sweet!* They all had plenty of water. **God was able to take care of it!**

Now, when we come to Hezekiah, after this great miracle and this happened, what a great thing took place? *God told Hezekiah to set his house in order because you're going to die!*

Isaiah 38:2: "Then Hezekiah turned his face toward the wall, and prayed to the LORD, and said, 'Remember now, O LORD, I beseech You, how I have walked before You in truth and with a whole heart, and have done *that which is* good in Your sight.' And Hezekiah wept with a great weeping. Then came the Word of the LORD to Isaiah, saying, 'Go and say to Hezekiah, "Thus says the LORD, the God of David your father, 'I have heard your prayer, I have seen your tears; behold, **I will add to your days fifteen years**'"' (vs 2-5).

Here's the lesson: **When a blessing comes from God don't get lifted up in vanity!** Here's what happened. All the treasure that all the soldiers had in the Assyrian army, the children of Judah went down and brought all of the expensive things—gold, silver, copper, and all the precious stones—and put them in the treasury house of God.

The king of Babylon heard of this mighty defeat of Assyria, because this was important, because Assyria was dominating Babylon at that time. The king of Babylon was just a vassal king.

Isaiah 39:1: "At that time Merodach-Baladan, the son of Baladan, king of Babylon, **sent letters and a present to Hezekiah**; for he had heard that he had been sick, and had recovered."

The long and the short of it is that they came and flattered Hezekiah and he got lifted up in his vanity.

Lesson: **After God has fought your battle for you, and you have won, don't get lifted up in vanity and do something stupid like Hezekiah!**

Hezekiah got lifted up, and they said, 'Oh what a great thing that has happened. You must be the greatest king on earth. Now you're the richest king on earth. What did they bring you?'

Hezekiah said, 'Come and see!' He took them and showed them everything, all the wealth and all of the treasure and things that God had given as spoil.

Verse 3: "Then Isaiah the prophet came to King Hezekiah, and said to him, 'What did these men say? And where did they come from to you?' And Hezekiah said, 'They have come from a far country to me, from Babylon.' Then he said, 'What have they seen in your house?' And Hezekiah answered, 'All that *is* in my house they have seen; there is nothing among my treasures that I have not shown them'" (vs 3-4). *That was very stupid!*

Don't do anything stupid after God has fought a battle for you and you win, and then you get lifted up in your own vanity.

Verse 5: "Then Isaiah said to Hezekiah, 'Hear the Word of the LORD of hosts. "Behold, the days come when all that is in your house, and that which your fathers have laid up in store until this day, shall be carried to Babylon. **Nothing shall be left**," says the LORD'" (vs 5-6).

That happened in the days of King Nebuchadnezzar; *took it all!*

Verse 7: "And of your sons which shall issue from you, which you shall beget, they shall take away; and they shall be officials in the palace of the king of Babylon." *We know that was fulfilled with Shadrach, Meshach and Abednego!*

Notice Hezekiah's attitude. He didn't repent! After all God did for him, and after all he repented of and prayed and asked God to spare him from the Assyrians and the armies of 180,000, and got all the treasure, everything, and then did this stupid thing! Even after God added 15 years to his life, notice his bad attitude:

Verse 8: "Then Hezekiah said to Isaiah, 'Good *is* the Word of the LORD which you have spoken.' And he said, 'For *at least* there shall be peace and truth in my days.'"

That was terrible! He turned to be so selfish that he didn't even think about what's going to happen after he dies. Could have been different. Think of the things that could have been different. And guess who took his place? *Manasseh!* One of the most evil kings of all, for 55 years! You know the rest of the story.

Let's come to the New Testament and see what Jesus says to us. Remember that whenever God blesses you and fights a battle for you, be thankful, be humble, and don't be all lifted up and in a bad attitude. That won't work!

Jesus was explaining about marriage and what it should be, and that it's difficult for a rich man to enter into the Kingdom of Heaven (Matt. 19:23-24).

Matthew 19:25: "But after hearing this, the disciples were greatly astonished *and* said, 'Who then is able to be saved?' But Jesus looked at them and said, '**With men this is impossible**…'" (vs 25-26).

Think about that. There are many things that are impossible for men to do.

1. they can't raise the dead
2. they can't bless like God
3. they can't fight the enemies like God can
4. it doesn't matter who you are, and how much wealth you have, if you don't humble yourself, you're not going to be saved

"…**but with God all things are possible**" (v 26). *Think about that as you look at your life!*

- look at the things that you have been doing
- look at your sins
- look at the leaven that has come into your life this past year

and during the Feast of Unleavened Bread you have been getting them out *asking God*:

- to help you
- to strengthen you
- to make it possible for you to overcome

and He will! "….**With men this is impossible; but with God all things are possible.**"

Matt. 17—here's about praying. This is what is important. *This is why we need*:

- the Truth
- the love
- the Spirit of God
- the conviction of God

to believe what God has said, and to know that <u>He is for us</u> and that there is nothing that is going to hold us back from receiving *eternal life!* Here's what Jesus said in casting out a demon:

Matthew 17:20: "And Jesus said to them, 'Because of your unbelief….'"

When you don't have the faith, what do you need to do? *You need to do like the man who pleaded with Jesus to cast the demon out of his son.* He said, *'Lord, help my unbelief!'* In other words, *'Lord, give me belief to overcome my unbelief.' <u>God will do that!</u> God wants us to believe!*

"…For truly I say to you, if you have faith as a *tiny* mustard seed, you shall say to this mountain, 'Remove from here,' and it shall remove; and nothing shall be impossible to you" (v 20).

Stop and think for just a minute. What would that accomplish by moving a mountain? *Well, it would move a lot of things!* But what is more difficult than moving mountains? **Converting the mind!** *Converting your thoughts is more difficult than moving a mountain!* Of course, all of it has to be according to God's will.

Let's see where we are many times in our life, because we have a lot of things to overcome, a lot of things to put aside, a lot of things to be forgiven. Yes, we do because we're human beings.

After going through everything in Heb. 11—by faith… Everything that is listed of the patriarchs *by faith they believed God* in spite of the circumstances involved.

What did He do that was impossible? What He told Sarah. Nothing is impossible with God! Here she was 90-years-old to bear her son Isaac, as God said it would be. Abraham said it would be. He was strong in faith and He believed, and Sarah also believed. Did it happen? Yes! *At the appointed time!* Quite an amazing thing! That's why Sarah laughed!

'Do you think a woman 90-years-old is going to have a child and nurse a child?' The Lord said, 'Why did you laugh?' She said, 'I didn't laugh.' The Lord said to her, 'Yes, you did. At this time next year you're going to have a son.' *Impossible, but it happened!*

From Isaac that continue on from Abraham, and from Isaac onto Jacob, and then on down to the Christ. Did it all happen as God prophesied and said that it would? Yes! Every one of these things were by faith!

Hebrews 11:1: "Now, faith is *the* substance…" *Spirit is a substance, and*:

- we're to have the faith of Christ; *that is a spiritual gift*
- we're to have the love of God; *that is a*

spiritual gift

"…of *things* hoped for… [if you already have it, you don't hope for it any longer, you have it] …*and **the conviction** of things not seen*" (v 1). *That's something we all need to have more of*:

- conviction of the Truth of God
- conviction of the righteousness of God
- conviction and faith in what God has said that He is able to do

Verse 2: "For by this *kind of faith* the elders obtained a good report. By faith we understand that the worlds were created by *the* Word of God, so that the things that are seen were made from *things* that are invisible" (vs 2-3).

Then it goes through everyone: Abel, Enoch…

Verse 6: "Now, **without faith *it is* impossible to please *God***…." It can't be by what you think alone. *But it must be according to the Word of God, the Spirit of God and His promises!*

"…For it is mandatory *for* the one who comes to God to believe that He exists…" (v 6). And everything that He has said in the Bible.

Why don't you do this for a Bible study: look up every place where it talks about God:

- who He is
- what He's done
- how He's done it
- the way He has done it
- why He has done it

That will help you with your faith! Remember:

➢ *it's impossible* for God to lie
➢ *it's impossible* for us to believe God unless we have faith

- we know that He exists
- we know that He is there
- we know that He has called us
- we know that Christ came
- we know that He was raised from the dead
- we know that He's at the right hand of God
- we know that He's our High Priest
- we know that He's there to intercede for us

"…and *that* He is a rewarder of those who diligently seek Him" (v 6)—*not halfhearted!*

Remember, we're living in a Laodicean age where there are so many things that people are satisfied with them, and have grown rich and they don't know that they're slipping away like Hezekiah did and do stupid things! That's why Jesus says to the Laodiceans, 'As many as I love I rebuke and chasten, *therefore, repent!*' That's what the Feast Unleavened Bread is all about for us.

Every year it comes so that we learn that it's not going to be of ourselves; *it's going to be of God!* It's not going to how *we think* it's going to be, *it's going to be the way that God says it's going to be!*

- we can believe God
- we can believe His promises
- we can trust in Him

Everything that He has said, He will do!

Heb. 12—here's how we are to do it. We're not to do like he children of Israel who when they came to the Red Sea, 'Oh, how are we going to get across the Red Sea?' *They got across,* **God made a way! God will make a way for you, whatever your circumstances are!**

Hebrews 12:1: "Therefore, *since* we are surrounded by such a great throng of witnesses, let us lay aside every weight…"

Everything that burdens you down. Don't let it burden you down. Come to God, pray about it, overcome it and get it out of your life.

"…and **the sin that so easily entraps *us***… [especially in this society with so many things of Satan the devil out there everywhere and in the air] …*and* let us **run the race set before us with endurance**" (v 1).

- not stopping
- not giving up
- not getting discouraged

But being encouraged that God is always with us! He says in the Psalms, *I am with you in your troubles! He will help us out of them!* The final solution is the resurrection. *We all have to be faithful to the end!*

Verse 2: "**Having *our* minds fixed on Jesus**…"

That's why we have the four Gospels; go through them again, study them again. He was the Lord God of the Old Testament, and He's coming as King of kings and Lord of lords, *and we're going to be part of that!*

"…the Beginner and Finisher of *our* faith…" (v 2).

He began it by calling us. He's going to finish it by helping us to overcome, change and be perfected to the end.

"…Who for the joy that lay ahead of Him endured *the* cross, *although* He despised *the* shame, and has sat down at *the* right hand of the Throne of God" (v 2). *Think about the contrast of that.*

- crucified and nailed to the stake
- dieing an ignominious death
- raised from the dead
- ascended during Unleavened Bread to the Throne of God
- victorious over everything

That's going to apply to us! Think about that

Verse 3: "Now meditate deeply on Him Who endured such great hostility of sinners against Himself **so that you do not become weary and faint in your minds**." *Don't do that!* That's why we have the Feast of Unleavened Bread.

Verse 4: "**You have not yet resisted to the point of** *losing* **blood in your struggle against sin**." *Isn't that true?*

- let's see what it is for us
- let's see how it works

Think about everything in your life that takes place is going to happen for a purpose. All of those things are going to be so that we can:

- learn different lessons
- learn love and obedience
- understand that God is working in our lives
- realize that we cannot save ourselves, or work it out ourselves

If you've got trouble, don't say you'll pray when you have it solved! **NO!** *You're not going to get it solved until you pray first!*

Rom. 8:28—regardless of what the difficulties are, this we need to know. This gives us the hope and assurance, and having our mind fixed on Christ.

Romans 8:28: "And we know that **all things**... [everything that occurs to us] ...**work together for good to those who love God**... [with all your heart, mind, soul and being] ...**to those who are called according to** *His* **purpose**... [which we have been] ...because those whom He did foreknow He also predestinated *to be* conformed to the image of His own Son... [greater things ahead] ...**that He might be** *the* **Firstborn among many brethren**" (vs 28-29).

We can hardly wait to understand more about Pentecost and the resurrection, and what a time that's going to be!

Here's a guarantee if you keep walking the way that God wants, keep trusting in God in the things that He has said. You believe in God and His promises, not doubting. And continue running the race you're running with endurance.

Verse 30: "Now, whom He predestinated, these He also called; and whom He called, these He also justified; and whom He justified, these He also glorified."

The only glory we have now is the receiving of the Holy Spirit with the promise, the earnest of the full spiritual promise that comes at the resurrection.

Verse 31: "What then shall we say to these things? If God *is* for us... [which He always is for us] ...who *can be* against us?"

- no one
- no thing
- no man
- no circumstance
- nothing that is in this life

Verse 32: "He Who did not spare even His own Son, but gave Him up for us all, how shall He not also grant us all things together with Him?" *He's going to grant it to us!*

Verse 33: "Who shall bring an accusation against *the* elect of God? God *is the One* Who justifies. Who *is* the one that condemns? *It is* Christ Who died, but rather, Who is raised again, Who is even *now* at *the* right hand of God, *and* Who is also making intercession for us" (vs 33-34).

Think about all of this for *you!* Everyone of us, each and every one whom God has called! Notice that if you have this belief, this hope, this conviction:

Verse 35: "**What shall separate us from the love of Christ?** *Shall* tribulation, or distress, or persecution, or famine, or nakedness, or danger, or sword?"

All of those things we may have to face. All of those thing brethren in the past *faced.* They took it in stride and in praise to God. Many of those who were carried off to be burned at the stake, killed and tortured by the Roman Catholic Church, against all of the churches in the Piedmonts in Northern Italy.

When they carried them off, they were singing hymns to God, forgiving those who were killing them, burning them at the stake. *Think about that!* If you think that you have had troubles, you need to get on your knees and thank God that you're not going through that now, so that you can have strength and hope to face the things that you're looking at right now. We haven't had to face those things!

Verse 36: "Accordingly, it is written, 'For Your sake we are killed all the day long; we are reckoned as sheep for *the* slaughter.'" *Another martyrdom is coming again in the future!*

Verse 37: "But **in all these things**… [everything listed here] …we are more than conquerors through Him Who loved us"—*because those things can never defeat God!*

- it's impossible to defeat God
- it's impossible to defeat His purpose

- His Word is true
- He says that we will be raised from the dead
- He says that we will receive eternal life

That will happen!

Verse 38: "For I am persuaded… [this is the conviction and persuasion that we need to have]: that **neither death, nor life, nor angels, nor principalities, nor powers, nor things present, nor things to come, nor height, nor depth, nor any other created thing,** shall be able to separate us from the love of God, which *is* in Christ Jesus our Lord" (vs 38-39).

God will do the impossible! He has proved it time and time again! This is why we have the Feast of Unleavened Bread, so we can:

- trust in God
- look to His help
- look to His salvation
- believe His promises
- believe His Word

We know that we can love Him with all our heart, mind, soul and being!

This is the meaning of the last day of the Feast of Unleavened Bread!

Scriptural References:

1) Leviticus 23:6-8

2) Psalm 148:1-5
3) Psalm 146:5
4) Exodus 14:8-16
5) Exodus 19:3-6, 8
6) Exodus 20:2-19
7) Isaiah 37:14-26, 33-38
8) Isaiah 38:2-5
9) Isaiah 39:1-8
10) Matthew 19:25-26
11) Matthew 17:20
12) Hebrews 11:1-3, 6
13) Hebrews 12:1-4
14) Romans 8:28-39

Scriptures referenced, not quoted:

- John 14-16
- Matthew 19:23-24

FRC:bo
Transcribed: 2/25/20
Reformatted: 10/2020

Section V

Events Leading Up to Pentecost

CHAPTER THIRTY-FOUR

Events Leading Up to Pentecost
Fred R. Coulter

Let's begin in a rather unusual place because I will refer you to Exo. 19 & 20, which we will cover partly tomorrow concerning the first Pentecost and the giving of the Ten Commandments at Mount Sinai, and let's go all the way to Exo. 33, and let's begin there, because this, I think points, out the situation: *what happens when you forget Pentecost or you forget God!*

I think God will tolerate some people being confused on how to count Pentecost; at least they are attempting to keep it. I can understand the various reasons for people doing it the various ways they have done it. However, in each case in thoroughly examining it, I have found that *they are missing vital elements of Scriptural understanding to handle it in the proper way!* So, what we are going to do is concentrate on *the events that happened after Moses went up on the mountain,* and I think we are going to see some very important things.

Exodus 33:1: "And the LORD said to Moses, 'Depart, go up from here, you and the people whom you have brought up out of the land of Egypt…'"

Here is where they start this exchange— 'your people, Moses,' *and* Moses says to God, 'Your people, God.' So they're kind of pushing the people back and forth as to who is responsible. It's just like when mother and father have a child that disobeys. The one who finds out that they've done wrong runs to the father and say, 'Your son…' and then it's the other way around, 'Your, son…' So, Moses is being told, 'Now look, these are your people…'

"…to the land which I swore to Abraham, to Isaac, and to Jacob, saying, 'To your seed I will give it.' And I will send an angel before you. And I will drive out the Canaanite, the Amorite, the Hittite, the Perizzite, the Hivite, and the Jebusite; to a land *that is* flowing *with* milk and honey; **for I will not go up in the midst of you**…" (vs 1-3). *That's a very interesting statement!*

Exodus 25:8—*the instruction that God was giving Moses*: "And let them make Me a sanctuary so that I may dwell among them."

Exodus 33:3—*now God says*: "…**for I will not go up in the midst of you**…."

- What are we dealing with here? *A lot of people are wondering*:

- Where is God? *Same experience!*

When we go through this, I want us to relate it to the experience we are going through today. Later when we get into another section in Jeremiah, I want you to relate it to the world and the parallel course within the Church. I think we are going to see some astounding parallels.

"…for you *are* a stiff-necked people, lest I consume you in the way.' And the people heard these evil tidings, and they mourned, and put no ornaments on themselves" (vs 3-4).

- Remember the ornaments they received, the ornaments of gold and silver?
- What do you suppose these ornaments really were? *They were the idols of the gods of Egypt!*
  - ✓ or the crosses
  - ✓ or the crucifixes
  - ✓ or the Ankh cross that has the egg-shape on top

So, they took off their ornaments. What did they do with these ornaments in Exo. 32? *They made a golden calf!*

Verse 5: "And the LORD had said to Moses, 'Say to the children of Israel, "You *are* a stiff-necked people. If I will go up into the midst of you, in a moment I will consume you. And now put off your ornaments from you, that I may know what to do with you."' And the children of Israel stripped themselves of their ornaments by Mount Horeb" (vs 5-6).

- Can we think of a New Testament lesson concerning idolatry?
- What did the Apostle Paul say concerning an idol? *To whom an idol is nothing, it is nothing!*

These people were going back to idolatry, so strip them away. *'You can't be trusted. You see this thing and it becomes a god to you. I am God in your presence,'* God was virtually saying that 'in the pillar of cloud and fire, and yet, you won't honor Me.' I'm just sort of summarizing some of the things that we are going to come across here.

Notice what Moses did; v 7: "And Moses took the tent…"

They had a little tabernacle there, before they built the big one, which is called the *Tent of the Meeting,* where God would meet with Moses.

"…and pitched it outside the camp and pitched it outside the camp, afar off from the camp, and called it the Tent of Meeting. And it came to pass, everyone who sought the LORD went out to the Tent of Meeting, which *was* outside the camp" (v 7).

Now let's think about this: In a church and in our lives can we do actions that will cause God to exit? *Yes!* Maybe some people asking what's going on in the Church today ought to ask:

- Did God leave because they forced Him out?
- Because of believing things that were idolatrous against God?
- *Very possible; probably absolutely true!*

Verse 8: "And it came to pass as Moses went out to the tent, all the people rose up, and each man stood *at* his tent door and gazed at Moses until he had gone into the tent."

We're getting a little bit of discipline here, aren't we? When Moses went out the whole camp— this is on a formal occasion, obviously—had to stand up and watch Moses walk out of the camp and go to the tabernacle of the congregation. When he got there:

Verse 9: "And it came to pass as Moses went into the tent, the cloudy pillar descended and stood *at* the door of the tent, and the LORD spoke with Moses. And all the people saw the cloudy pillar stand *at* the tent door. And all the people rose up and worshiped, each man at his tent door…. [put off on the side] …And the LORD would speak to Moses face to face, as a man speaks to his friend. And he returned again to the camp. But his servant, Joshua the son of Nun, a young man, did not depart from the tent" (vs 9-11). *So he had Joshua out there guarding it!*

Verse 12: "And Moses said to the LORD, 'Behold, You say to me… [here is this argument going back and forth] …"Bring up this people." And You have not told me whom You will send with me….'" *He said, 'Now if you are going to leave us, how are we going to do this?'*

"'…Yet, You have said, "I know you by name, and you have also found grace in My sight." Now, therefore, I pray You, if I have found grace in Your sight, make me see now Your way, that I may know You, that I may find grace in Your sight. And consider that this nation *is* Your people'" (vs 12-13).

Some church leaders may be right when they say that certain members in their congregation are their people, *because they're taking a possession that belongs to God! No one having the Spirit of God belongs to a minister*; just a little insight as we are going along here.

Verse 14: "And He said, 'My presence shall go *with you*, and I will give you rest.' And he said to Him, 'If Your presence does not go *with me*, do not carry us up from here; for how shall it be known that I and Your people have found grace in Your sight? *Is it* not in that You go with us? So we shall be separated, I and Your people, from all the people that *are* upon the face of the earth.' And the LORD said to Moses, 'I will do this thing also that you have spoken, **for you have found grace in My sight, and I know you by name**'" (vs 14-17). *God said, 'All right, now I'm going to go ahead and go back there,'*

Verse 18 "And he said, 'I beseech You, show me Your glory.' And He said, 'I will make all My goodness pass before you, and I will proclaim the name of the LORD before you. And I will be gracious to whom I will be gracious, and will have mercy on whom I will have mercy.' And He said, 'You cannot see My face, for no man can see Me and live.' And the LORD said, 'Behold, *there is* a place by Me, and you shall stand upon a rock. And it will be, while My glory passes by, I will put you in a cleft of the rock, and will cover you with My hand while I pass by'" (vs 18-22).

Exodus 34:1: "And the LORD said to Moses, 'Cut out two tablets of stone like the first *ones.* And I will write upon the tablets…'" *So he did that!*

Verse 4: "And he cut out two tablets of stone like the first *ones.* And Moses rose up early in the morning and went up to Mount Sinai, as the LORD had commanded him, and took in his hand the two tablets of stone. And the LORD came down in the cloud, and stood with him there, and proclaimed the name of the LORD" (vs 4-5).

Verse 6: "And the LORD passed by before him and proclaimed, 'The LORD, the LORD God, merciful and gracious, longsuffering, and abundant in goodness and truth, keeping mercy to the thousandth *generation,* forgiving iniquity and transgression and sin, but Who will by no means clear *the guilty,* visiting the iniquity of the fathers upon the children, and upon the children's children, to the third and to the fourth generation'" (vs 6-7).

Verse 8: "And Moses made haste and bowed his head toward the earth, and worshiped. And he said, 'If now I have found grace in Your sight, O LORD, I pray You, let my LORD go among us, although it *is* a stiff-necked people. And pardon our iniquity and our sin, and take us for Your inheritance.' And He said, 'Behold, I make a covenant…. [God had redo the whole Old Covenant again, because they broke it with their idolatry] …Before all your people I will do marvels such as have not been done in all the earth, nor in any nation. And all the people in whose midst you *are* shall see the work of the LORD, for it *is* an awesome thing that I will do with you. **Observe that which I command you this day**…." (vs 8-11).

Then He goes and He reiterates the things that He did with the first giving of the Ten Commandments.

Verse 21: "You shall work six days, but on the seventh day you shall rest. In plowing time and in harvest you shall rest. And you shall observe the Feast of Weeks, of the firstfruits of wheat harvest, and the Feast of Ingathering at the year's end" (vs 21-22). *Then He reiterates everything that He shows all the way down!*

Verse 28: "And he was there with the LORD **forty days and forty nights. He neither ate bread nor drank water.** And He wrote upon the tablets the words of the covenant, the Ten Commandments." *So, He re-did the whole thing again!*

Verse 29: "And it came to pass as Moses was going down from the mountain of Sinai, the two tablets of the testimony being in Moses' hand as he went down from the mountain, Moses did not know that the skin of his face had become luminous through His speaking with him. And Aaron and all the children of Israel saw Moses, and behold, the skin of his face had become luminous. And they were afraid to come near him. And Moses called to them. And Aaron and all the rulers of the congregation returned to him, and Moses talked with them. And afterward all the children of Israel came near. And he commanded them all that the LORD had spoken with him in Mount Sinai. And Moses finished speaking with them, and he put a veil on his face" (vs 29-33).

The question was: He didn't eat or drink for forty days. Does that mean that when Christ was fasting that He didn't eat or drink for forty days? *It is very possible!* I've said before maybe Christ drank water while He was fasting, but this may be a good indication that He didn't need to.

I missed an important part back in Exo. 32, *when Moses came down the first time and saw all the people were naked*:

Exodus 32:26:"Then Moses stood in the gate of the camp and said, 'Who *is* on the LORD'S side? *Come* to me.' And all the sons of Levi gathered themselves to him. And he said to them, 'Thus says the LORD God of Israel, "Each man put his sword by his side, and go in and out from gate to gate throughout the camp, and kill each one his brother,

and each one his companion, and each one his neighbor"'"

That is all of those who were involved in the nakedness of the orgy that they were involved in and worshiping the golden calf!

Verse 28: "And the sons of Levi did according to the word of Moses. And there fell of the people that day about three thousand men."

Then he went back up on the mountain! A very interesting parallel could also be happening with the Church, too.

Let's see something that is so very important for us to realize. Very seldom have the people of God stayed really faithful and true to God. The Israelites didn't, the Judahites didn't, and look what happened to Solomon. I mean, Solomon is really a great case to study of what happens when you have everything given to you and laid out on a platter for you. Even God spoke to Solomon twice, but what did he do? *He made Jerusalem the center of Baal worship!* That's what he did; he built temples to every god under the sun. So, here (in Jeremiah) is where it degenerated to, just before God was ready to destroy Jerusalem.

Let's draw the parallel in the nation with what's happening today. It's almost incredible. Hardly anybody in the government today can tell the truth. It is unreal. When you watch the news shows on Sunday morning, if you watch them—I've given up watching them because they just become nothing but political propaganda gristmill anymore—what they tell you, virtually take the opposite and know that that's the truth.

So it is the same thing here. It's throughout the whole society, and I think we're also dealing with a situation that when the society, which applies to a church as well, comes to a certain point then *God just gives it over to its own devices and He leaves!* That doesn't mean that God has given up, it just means that He has excused Himself from their presence because their behavior and their attitude is so idolatrous that God will not stay there. That's why Moses had to plead with God, 'Please come back into the camp and take these, Your people.' *So God did!*

God wants to give mercy so He says, Jeremiah 5:1: "Run to and fro through the streets of Jerusalem, and see now, and know, and seek in her open places, **if you can find a man**…"—*one single person, and that's almost the way it is in society today!* Can you find one person who will do this:

"…if there is one who does justice, who seeks **the Truth**… [that's the hardest thing in the world for people to really seek] …and **I will pardon her**" (v 1).

God says He was willing *IF* they found *A* man, to say: 'OK, I'll pardon all the inequity of it, and I will spare the people for one man.'

Verse 3: "O LORD, *are* not Your eyes on the Truth? You have stricken them, but they have not grieved; You have destroyed them, but they have refused to receive correction; they have made their faces harder than rock; they have refused to return."

- we can say that in relationship with the society
- we can say that in relationship with the Church

Verse 4: "Therefore, I said, 'Surely these *are* poor; they are foolish; for they do not know the way of the LORD, *nor* the judgment of their God. I will go up for myself to the great men, and will speak to them; for they have known the way of the LORD *and* the judgment of their God.' But these had altogether broken the yoke and had torn off the bonds!" (vs 4-5).

I have a chart showing that every one of the leading persons in the United States Government (George W. Bust administration) to all of the appointee offices: Secretary of State, Secretary of Treasury, Secretary of Transportation, and so forth—every single one down through three layers all belong to the Council on Foreign Relations—*every single one!* If you know anything about them and the world conspiracy…

This is what Jeremiah experienced, he went to the wise men, he went to the leaders saying, 'Surely they ought to have God's judgment, surely they ought to know.' **"…But these had altogether broken the yoke and had torn off the bonds!"**

Verse 6: "Therefore, a lion out of the forest shall kill them, *and* a wolf of the deserts shall rob them; a leopard shall watch over their cities. Everyone who goes out from them shall be torn in pieces…"

Again, let's apply this spiritually and physically. Didn't we just have a cougar attack on a woman out jogging? I'm not saying that's a great fulfillment of this, but I'm saying: Are we entering times when those things are going to be that way? *Certainly!* Let's apply this people-wise:

- Are there people who are called wolves? *Yes, there are, false prophets!*
- What do they come to do? *Seek to kill, destroy and take!*

The same thing! So, we can have these parallels going all the way down. Here is the reason:

"…because their sins are many *and* their backslidings are multiplied" (v 6). *This is so true!*

When I go down to the area of Southern California and have a Bible study down there, believe me: They are all so backslidden that so many of them can hardly stand to take the Truth. It is incredible, but that's what has happened.

Verse 7: "How shall I pardon you for this? Your children have forsaken Me, and have sworn by them that are not gods" *changing the Truth of God into that which is a lie!*

One of the leading evangelists in Worldwide preached and said that the Worldwide Church of God never taught that there were two Elohims, never taught that Christ was the Logos, never taught any of these things.

"…**have sworn by them that are not gods**…"

- Is that in the society? *Yes!*
- Is it in the Church? Yes!

"…When I had fed them to the full, then they committed adultery, and gathered themselves by troops in a harlot's house" (v 7).

Verse 8: "'They were *like* lusty, well-fed stallions in the morning; every one neighing after his neighbor's wife. Shall I not punish for these *things*?' says the LORD. 'And shall not My soul be avenged on such a nation as this? Go up upon her walls and destroy; but do not make a full end; take away her branches, for they *are* not the LORD'S. For the house of Israel and the house of Judah have dealt very deceitfully against Me,' says the LORD. They have lied against the LORD and said, '*It is* not He; neither shall evil come on us; nor shall we see sword nor famine…'" (vs 8-12).

That's exactly what people are saying in the world today, and people are saying in the Church today.

Verse 13: "And **the prophets shall become as wind**, for the word *is* not in them; thus it shall be done to them."

That's why we have to check out every doctrine. What does it say? *Don't be carried about with every sleight of the wind of doctrine by cunning of men!* Their prophets shall **become wind**. There it is right there, a foretelling of it in the Old Testament that Paul said was fulfilled in the New Testament.

Verse 14: "Therefore, thus says the LORD God of hosts, 'Because you have spoken this word, behold, I will make My words in your mouth fire, and this people wood, and it shall devour them.'"

Of course, they don't like it. You don't have to get all vain, and you don't have to get all uppity, *you just have to speak the truth!*

Verse 15: "Lo, I will bring a nation upon you from afar, O house of Israel,' says the LORD. 'It *is* a mighty nation, it *is* an ancient nation, a nation whose language you do not know, nor understand what they say.'"

Isn't it interesting what religious doctrines are being brought into the Church of God, the same religious doctrines that are coming from this nation, mainly Chaldeanism.

By the way, Carl Franklin got a book where he finds the exact sayings of Stavrinides {from former WCG} that come right out of ancient Chaldean philosophy—word for word quotes that are now becoming doctrines of the church (WCG). God says *He is going to visit for this,* and He goes on and shows what He is going to do.

Verse 17: "And they shall eat up your harvest and your bread, your sons and your daughters they shall eat up. They shall eat up your flocks and your herds; they shall eat up your vines and your fig trees. They shall beat down your fortified cities with the sword."

All of the defenses that are put up are not going to work. It is the same way in the Church. What was the defense of the church? Don't read anybody else's literature; *that defense is gone!* Don't talk to anyone who is not in this church; *that defense is gone!* In talking to a man who called me the other day, I said, We take the opposite philosophy. We figure that you can read anything and if you can't understand the Truth, then you better get grounded in it because denying people to read something is not going to keep them from the difficulty. Now it is don't study the Bible unless a minister is there.

Verse 19: "And it will be, when they shall ask... [they come back and they talk back to God] ...'Why does the LORD our God do all these *things* to us?'...."

We will see when we get to Revelation here, because I am tying this into the events that lead up to the things happening in the Church in the book of Revelation: Do we have a church that talks back to God? *Yes!* Same thing here!

"...Then you shall answer them, 'Just as you have forsaken Me and served strange gods in your land, so you shall serve strangers in a land *that is* not yours.'" (v 19).

Today we are seeing strangers are coming in. You go to your local supermarket, and it's like going to a different nation.

Verse 20: "Declare this in the house of Jacob, and cry it in Judah, saying, 'Now hear this, O foolish people and without understanding; who have eyes and see not; who have ears and hear not'" (vs 20-21).

Is that not also in the Church as well as in the world? *Yes!*

Verse 22: "Do you not fear Me?" says the LORD. "Will you not tremble at My presence, *even* I Who have placed the sand *for* the boundary of the sea *by* a never-ending decree, so that it cannot pass it? And though they toss themselves, yet, they cannot prevail; though its waves roar, yet, they cannot pass over it. But this people has a revolting and a rebellious heart; they have revolted and are departed *from Me*. And they do not say in their heart, 'Let us now fear the LORD our God, Who gives both the former and the latter rain in its season; **He reserves to us the appointed weeks of the harvest**'" (vs 22-24).

That's why the second title I had was, *When You Forget the Feast of Pentecost!*

Verse 25: "Your iniquities have turned away these *things*, and your sins have withheld good things from you. For among My people are found wicked ones; they lie in wait, as one who sets snares; they set a trap, they catch men. Like a cage full of birds, so their houses are full of deceit..." (vs 25-27)—*so true!*

When I was reading and preparing for this message, I just could not get over the parallels that are in the society and in the Church. *It is unreal!*

"...therefore, they have become great and grown rich" (v 27).

Yet, there are people today who say that the gauge of a church's spirituality is how much money they have. *Be careful!*

Verse 28: "They have become fat, they have become sleek. Yea, they excel in evil deeds; they do not plead the cause, the cause of the fatherless, yet, they prosper; and they do not defend the right of the needy. Shall I not punish for these *things*?" says the LORD. "Shall not My soul be avenged on such a nation as this? An astounding... [that's what it means] ...and horrible thing has happened in the land. The prophets prophesy falsely, and the priests bear rule by their means; **and My people love _to have it_ so, and what will you do at the end of it?**" (vs 28-31)—*when God calls it to account!*

I was just stunned when I read that with just all the things that have been happening.

Let's see what Daniel did. Daniel was one of the ones who really repented. Daniel was one of the ones who really turned back to God.

Daniel 9:1 "In the first year of Darius the son of Ahasuerus, of the seed of the Medes, who was made king over the realm of the Chaldeans, in the first year of his reign, I, Daniel, understood by books the number of the years, which came according to the Word of the LORD to Jeremiah the prophet, that the desolation of Jerusalem would last seventy years" (vs 1-2).

He didn't understand what Jeremiah wrote until way toward the end of the seventy years. Then he repented.

Verse 3: "And I set my face toward the LORD God, to seek by prayer and supplications, with fasting, and sackcloth, and ashes.... [frankly, brethren, that's what the Church of God needs to do] ...And I prayed to the LORD my God and made my confession, and said, 'O LORD, the great and awesome God, keeping the covenant and mercy to those who love Him, and to those who keep His commandments, we have sinned and have committed iniquity, and have done wickedly, and have rebelled, and have turned aside from Your commandments and from Your ordinances. Neither have we hearkened unto Your servants the prophets, who spoke in Your name to our kings, our rulers, and our fathers, and to all the people of the land. O LORD, righteousness *belongs* to You, but to us confusion of face...'" (vs 3-7).

Doesn't that tell you what's going on in the country and in the Church, *confusion,* everybody is confused. Why, because they have left God.

"...as at this day to the men of Judah and to the people of Jerusalem, and to all Israel who are near and who are afar off, through all the countries where You have driven them..." (v 7).

Isn't the Church being scattered today? *Yes it is!* It parallels! It's amazing! Stunning!

"...because they dealt treacherously with You. O Lord, confusion of face belongs to us, to our kings, to our rulers, and to our fathers, **because we have sinned against You**" (vs 7-8).

I tell what, there isn't going to be any straightening out of doctrine or knowledge of Truth and doctrine until this kind of repentance and admission is made before God. *It won't happen!*

Verse 10: "Neither have we obeyed the voice of the LORD our God to walk in His laws, which He set before us by His servants the prophets." *Then he goes through and says, 'O God, all these things have happened'!*

Verse 18: "O my God, incline Your ear and hear...." *That's what we need to do for this Pentecost*: **have an ear to hear!**

- Isn't that something when you run the parallel there?
- God will hear us when? *When we hear Him!*

"...Open Your eyes and behold our desolations, and the city which is called by Your name. For we do not present our supplications before You on account of our righteousnesses, but because of Your great mercies" (v 18). *That's what needs to happen with the whole church, all the brethren everywhere!*

Verse 19: "O LORD, hear; O LORD, forgive; O LORD, hearken and do. Do not delay, for Your own sake, O my God; for Your city and Your people are called by Your name."

Then he was given the prophecy of the 70 weeks of the coming of the Messiah!

Rev. 2 & 3—we are going to see some tremendous parallels, because part of the thing we are dealing with, with the events leading up to Pentecost, are the things that are happening within the Churches of God.

Revelation 1:18—*after seeing the vision of Christ, He says to John*: "Even the One Who is living; for I was dead, and behold, I am alive into the ages of eternity. Amen. And I have the keys of *the* grave and of death."

In other words: ***God is going to judge whom He is going to resurrect, when He is going to resurrect, and what resurrection it will be!***

"...and of death" (v 18). *He is the only One Who can give us life!*

Verse 19: "Write the things that you saw... [up to this point] ...and the things that are, and the things that shall take place hereafter. The mystery of the seven stars that you saw in My right hand, and the seven golden lampstands, *is this*: the seven stars are *the* angels of the seven churches; and the seven lampstands that you saw are *the* seven churches" (vs 19-20). *Christ said He would walk in the midst of them!*

Let's understand something as we put this together, because Rev. 2 & 3 is everything that we have pretty well understood that it is.

- yes, it is the seven churches which were literally then
- yes, it is a prophecy of God's Church down through time

We have defined it in the past as eras. That's not necessarily wrong, but it was not as clear-cut as people like to make it be understood that they thought it was, because we see that these are also the seven attitudes that you find at any one time within the Church. These are all the major problems that will confront the Church, etc.

Revelation 5:5: "Then one of the elders said to me, 'Do not weep. Behold, the Lion Who is of the tribe of Judah, the Root of David, has overcome to open the book, and to loose its seven seals.' Then I saw, and behold, before the Throne and the four living creatures and before the elders *was* standing a Lamb as having been slain… [that is Christ alone] …having seven horns and seven eyes, which are the seven spirits of God that are sent into all the earth" (vs 5-6). ***Let's focus in on the seven horns!***

- Why would the symbol of Christ, being a lamb, have seven horns?
Well, we can answer the question this way!
- What do horns in the Book of Daniel represent?

Each horn we know each horn represents a king or a kingdom. So, if you have a horn in the head of Christ, seven of them…

- Who is the Head of the Church? *Christ!*
- Can we conclude properly then that these seven horns represent the Churches of God through history that Christ is the head of? *Yes, I think that would be a fair statement!*

We can also conclude that it refers to the seven churches as we found in Rev. 2 & 3. That would also be another conclusion we can come to without stretching the Scriptures at all—because we know Christ is the Head of the Church. He dwells in the midst of the Church:

- He is the Lamb Who takes away the sins of the world
- He was the Lamb Who was slain
- He is the Lamb with the seven horns

I am sure the seven Spirits of God also apply to the seven churches… I am sure that applies to the seven angels of the seven churches, because it is both.

Now let's just review parts on Rev. 2 & 3, I am not going to concentrate on it. We know, not definitely, but we can conclude from the things we have seen that there is every reason to believe that this has to do with:

- the history of the churches
- the seven churches
- the attitudes of the churches
- the practices of the churches
- with the major confrontation of the churches and Satan the devil

All of those you can put all together!

It is interesting as you look back in your Christian life, I think you are going to see that many of these things you have gone through and you have experienced. Now the first church:

Ephesus

Revelation 2:2: *Christ said*: "…'I know your works, and your labor, and your endurance, and that you cannot bear those who are evil; and *that* you did test those who proclaim *themselves* to be apostles, but are not, and did find them liars.'"

- What is one of the biggest problems we have to do today?
- Is that not it?

I'm not talking about in someone's personal life that they may tell a lie because they are weak, or they feel as though the truth would be too damaging in some little low-level thing here.

That could be repented of, and Christians tell lies, they shouldn't, but Paul said, 'Lie not one to another.' But what have we found? *When you really get to the truth of examining the doctrines that we have learned, and some of the doctrines, which were mistakes—some of them that were not true—what have we found? Everyone we held in high esteem, we found to be a liar!* I could name names, but no use naming names. Any name you can think of would be it. Are we to find them liars? *Yes we are, especially concerning doctrine!* So, we have to do that.

Now then, they had their problem—they did a lot of work, they had a lot of patience—they lost their first love (v 4). So, they had to repent.

Verse 7: "The one who has an ear, let him hear what the Spirit says to the Churches. To the one who overcomes I will give *the right* to eat of the Tree of Life that is in *the* midst of the paradise of God."

Smyrna

Verse 8: "And to the angel of the Church of *the* **Smyrneans** write…"

Here is the one you wouldn't think would be a Church of God because:

- they are thrown in jail
- they are ridiculed
- they are put down
- they are killed
- they are slaughtered
- they are poor
- they are despised by everyone

I tell you what: ***The world loves a winner!***

Sidebar: Here in this area we have a sports phenomena: it is the San Jose Sharks. Everyone will know what I mean. No one was interested in hockey. No one could care about hockey, and the first two years they were the dregs and the pits of the National Hockey League.

All of a sudden, they made it to the play-offs, and then they beat the number one team, and everyone now is jumping on the bandwagon, right? Yes, because people love a winner. Remember when the Oakland Athletics were doing great and winning pennants? *Everyone loves a winner!* But when you are down and out, no one wants you.

It was the same with Christ! Remember when He fed the 5,000? *Boy, we got a winner!* We're going to make Him king (John 6). They were going to come by force and make Him king, because 'we love a winner.' So, He escaped. When He was on the cross, they said, 'We'll give you one last chance to be a winner. You come down off that cross and we will believe that you're the Son of God.'

When everything is going good, everyone wants to jump on the bandwagon, but what does God have to do when you've got a bandwagon full of 'band-wagoners' and not the 'real McCoy'? *He's got to shake the bandwagon,* because the ones who jump on the bandwagon because they love a winner are not really 'true blue.' That's why the Church at Smyrna is such a powerful church. That's why Christ said, 'You are rich, even though you are poor. Don't fear death. I have died.'

Verse 11: "The one who has an ear, let him hear what the Spirit says to the churches…"—*and all the way through, it's all the churches!*

The reason I'm going through this is because **the seven weeks to the harvest is the time of the harvest of the seven churches,** and that pictures everything that the Church is going to do. So, He says to the Churches:

"…The one who overcomes shall not be hurt of the second death" (v 11).

Then we come to two of the most problematic churches there are.

Pergamos—right there in Satan's capital!

- Do the ways of the world affect the Church? *Yes, they do!*
- What's one of the biggest problems that has happened to the Church of God today? The same thing here, two of their great sins:
  - ✓ organized according to a corporate structure
  - ✓ hierarchical authority from the top down

'If the minister says it, I'm off the hook, because the Bible has assured me that he is going to stand before God and my judgment.'

Now people don't phrase it that way, but that's how they look at it. You still hear it today, 'Oh brethren, come and attend this church. If you are here you are going to receive salvation.' **_Not so!_** They had:

- the doctrines of Balaam
- ate things sacrificed to idols
- committed fornication spiritually

and everything there. You can read it in our book *Lord, What Should I Do?* So He says that you have to overcome this (v 17).

Thyatira

Here we have all the 'women's libbers.' We have a woman prophetess Jezebel. That tells what kind of doctrines they were getting; calls herself a prophetess. They went clear into the depths of Satan, but God wanted to make everyone know something clear and sure.

Verse 23: "And I will kill her children with death; and all the churches shall know that I am He Who searches *the* reins and hearts; and I will give to each of you according to your works."

God made sure that everyone knew that everyone was responsible for taking care of it. He tells them to overcome, keep the first works.

Verse 26: "And to the one who **overcomes and keeps My works unto *the* end,** I will give authority over the nations."

Sardis

Then in history we come to the Church which is called **Sardis** and after all the things that you go through with these other churches, you come up to Sardis—they're dead, they have a little life and they are just about ready to collapse and have only a couple of things left, and God says, 'I'll be merciful to you. You keep those few things that you have and I will not deny you before My Father.'

Isn't that something? You think about that! Christ says that **_IF_** you do those few things and *I won't deny you,* which tells us that **_IF you don't do those things, you're denying Christ and He'll have to deny you._** Didn't Jesus say, 'The one who denies me, I shall also deny'?

Philadelphia.

I think there is something most interesting about the Philadelphians: *a true Philadelphian does not know who he really is* because you read the parable of the goats and the sheep, and you remember what He said to the sheep? *Enter into the Kingdom!*

He said because when I was hungry, when I was down and out, when I was in prison, and so forth, you came and visited me. And they said, 'Lord, when did we do that?' *They didn't know they had done it!* He said, 'Because you have done it to the least of these, my brethren, you have also done it unto Me.'

We won't belabor the point with the Philadelphians, we've had plenty enough sermons going over that, pro and con. But He says:

Verse 13: "**The one who has an ear, let him hear what the Spirit says to the churches**."

Laodicea;

Verse 14: "And to the angel of the Church of *the* **Laodiceans**, write: These things says the Amen, the faithful and true Witness, the Beginner of the creation of God."

Now we come to a contemporary time, which is:

- talking back to God
- not believing God
- being rich and increased with goods
- *spiritually* taking off their clothes because they are naked

They are *literally* **taking off their spiritual clothes** and telling God 'I'm in good shape.' *We know that the white clothing or the white raiment is the righteousness of the saints.*

Revelation 19:8: "And it was granted to her that she should be clothed in fine linen, pure and bright; for the fine linen is the righteousness of the saints."

They are not doing the righteousness of God. Here we have all of these churches and let's just throw into the mix of it all the problems of the Churches at Corinth:

- divisions
- following men because they are a man
- not building on the foundation of Christ
- thinking they have already got it made
- all kinds of prophecies
- all kinds of Psalms
- talking in tongues
- bowing down before idols

All of those problems!

Now then, there is going to come a time when all of this is going to come to a screeching halt, and we are all going to be brought to the reality of things that are going to happen. It is going to

come as a shock! Then we are going to come to the time that we have right here when God says, 'That's it! Now is the time'! This is when Christ is given the scroll.

Revelation 5:1: "And in the right hand of Him Who sits on the Throne… [God the Father] …I saw a book, written within and on *the* back, which had been sealed with seven seals. And I saw a strong angel proclaiming with a loud voice, 'Who is worthy to open the book and to loose its seals?' But no one in heaven, or on the earth, or under the earth was able to open the book, or to look inside it" (vs 1-3).

This is telling us that there are some things in there that no one understands, yet. We have a bare little glimpse of it, don't we?

Verse 4: "And I was weeping greatly because no one was found worthy to open and to read the book, or to look into it. Then one of the elders said to me, 'Do not weep. Behold, the Lion Who is of the tribe of Judah, the Root of David, has overcome to open the book, and to loose its seven seals'" (vs 4-6). *And then he saw the Lamb with seven horns!*

Verse 11: "And I saw and I heard *the* voices of many angels around the Throne, and *the voices* of the living creatures and the elders, and thousands of thousands, saying with a loud voice, 'Worthy is the Lamb Who was slain to receive power, and riches, and wisdom, and strength, and honor, and glory and blessing'" (vs 11-12).

Every man that wants to set himself up as a prophet, and one of them is ready to proclaim himself one of the two witnesses any time someone comes up with enough evidence. read this: *Christ is going to do it! He alone is going to open it!*

Verse 13: "And every creature that is in heaven, and on the earth, and under the earth, and those that are on the sea, and all the things in them, I heard saying, 'To Him Who sits on the Throne, and to the Lamb, *be* blessing, and honor, and glory, and sovereignty into the ages of eternity.' And the four living creatures said, 'Amen.' And the twenty-four elders fell down and worshiped *Him Who* lives into the ages of eternity" (vs 13-14).

Then the seals are opened. The first seal is the white horse. A lot of these things we know, we've gone over many times. Let me just review them. I've said in the past:

Revelation 6:2: "And I looked, and behold, *there was* a white horse; and the one who was sitting on it had a bow, and a crown was given to him; and he went out conquering, and to conquer."

We have always looked at that and said that's got to be the Catholic Church. It fit the

Catholic Church up to a certain point. Let's think of it beyond just the Catholic Church and let's understand that the reason a horse is used is because things happen *suddenly*. I think the world is ready for a great common religious, spiritual, revival to bring together all religions. I think we've given enough messages in the past to show that that's the way it's going, which will include the Catholic Church and all of those, so called Christians, and also all the other religions of the world.

I still remember the ad from IBM which showed the Tower of Babel, which was crumbled down and they boasted, 'We are now able to finish what they started.'

This is going to come suddenly. This is part of the events leading up to the fulfilling of Pentecost, and they are going to do miracles! Right now there are a lot of people talking about aliens come to help us! What if they bring a new religion? Everyone says this is wonderful. We can now have peace, we can now get along, and there are miracles that are performed. *Everyone likes a winner*; remember that. When there comes along this great religious movement, everyone's going to be considered a winner. It's going to be a wonderful event for them. I would have to say we need to think in that term, along those lines.

Verse 3—*the second seal*: "And when He opened the second seal, I heard the second living creature say, 'Come and see.' And another horse went out *that was* red; and *power* was given to the one sitting on it to take peace from the earth, and *to cause* them to kill one another; and a great sword was given to him" (vs 3-4). *I think that's going to happen, which we'll see where that fits in!*

When the great religious leader comes on, there is also going to be the great military leader and it's going to come on. He is going to come and it will come to this point: **all the world is going to worship him. He is going to receive the deadly wound that will be healed!**

Revelation 13:4: "And they worshiped the dragon, who gave *his* authority to the beast. And they worshiped the beast, saying, 'Who *is* like the beast? Who has the power to make war against him?'" *In other words, you can't resist his war-making powers!*

Speculation: I want you to think of the UN. How many members vote? You have ten, plus five who are the permanent members. What if they add two more permanent members—Japan and Germany? Now how many do you have—seven and ten. Think on it; very possible. What if, and I have heard this suggested: The way we can have world peace is to turn over all nuclear weapons under UN control. Think on that for a minute. Who is able to

make war with the beast? Now then, think what is going to happen when whoever the leader of the UN is, is killed and comes back to life or one of the seven heads. That disturbs the peace.

Then he is going to go make war and here is what's going to happen. I think the second seal and Rev. 6:5 fit exactly together, and vs 3 & 4 tie in together with Rev. 13:4-8.

Verse 5: "And a mouth speaking great things and blasphemies was given to him; and authority was given to him to continue *for* forty-two months.... [after the deadly wound was healed[...And he opened his mouth in blasphemy against God, to blaspheme His name, and His tabernacle, and those who dwell in heaven. And he was given *power* to make war against the saints, and to overcome them; and he was given authority over every tribe and language and nation. And all who dwell on the earth will worship him, whose names have not been written in the Book of Life of the Lamb slain from *the* foundation of *the* world. **If anyone has an ear, let him hear**" (vs 5-9). *That means we need to really pay attention!*

Now then, of the events leading up to Pentecost, we have the third seal a black horse, famine, shortage of food. That can come on us quickly.

- How long could you last in the event you couldn't buy any food at the grocery store or there was war or cut off?

Let's reverse the question:

- How many times a month do you go to the store? *Or if that is too many*:
- How many times a week do you go to the store? *You might be able to calculate that!*

I know there are times when I go to the store three or four times, because it's close!

- How long could you exist? *Not very long!*

So, you don't have to wait for any great monstrous event to take place, it's just going to happen once and that's going to be it!

Then we come to the fourth seal, which death as a result of that. I tell you, we have these super-viruses, super-bacteria, super this and that and everything else, it's going to come and when there is starvation, lack of food, lack of water, and WHAM! *Throw in the mix*:

- all kinds of rats
- all kinds of insects
- all kinds of insane people running around killing, taking, looting and stealing
- cannibalism

All that will be part of it! Then they are going to come after us!

The fifth seal is the martyrdom of the saints. That's going to be something! Then there is going to be an event that leads up to the fulfilling of the next to the last and the last Pentecost that is going to startle this whole earth:

Revelation 6:12: "And when He opened the sixth seal, I looked, and behold, there was a great earthquake; and the sun became black as *the* hair *of* sackcloth, and the moon became as blood; and the stars of heaven fell to the earth, as a fig tree casts its untimely figs when it is shaken by a mighty wind. Then *the* heaven departed like a scroll that is being rolled up, and every mountain and island was moved out of its place" (vs 12-14).

You're not going to watch this on NBC, CBS, ABC, or CNN, or CBNC newscasts. This is going to happen *suddenly*. so much so that:

Verse 15: "And the kings of the earth, and the great men, and the rich men, and the chief captains, and the powerful men, and every bondman, and every free *man* hid themselves in the caves and in the rocks of the mountains… [everything is going to be in an upheaval] …and they said to the mountains and to the rocks, 'Fall on us, and hide us from *the* face of Him Who sits on the throne, and from the wrath of the Lamb, because the great day of His wrath has come, and who has the power to stand?" (vs 15-17). *This is going to be something!*

- What's going to happen when that scroll of heaven rolls back?
- What is going to be seen? *They are going to see something!*

They're going to know it is something coming from outer space. They may not call Him *Christ*. The false prophet is going to call Him *antichrist*.

Matt. 24—this is the event leading up to the fulfilling of the next to the last Pentecost and the last Pentecost, and I will just say right here that I believe that the sixth seal happens on the next to the last Pentecost. I think that is based on fairly sound Scriptures, as we will see.

Matthew 24:21: "For then shall there be Great Tribulation, such as has not been from *the* beginning of *the* world until this time, nor ever shall be *again*. And if those days were not limited, there would no flesh be saved… [living] …but for the elect's sake those days shall be limited. Then if anyone says to you, "Behold, here *is* the Christ," or, "*He is* there," do not believe *it*. For there shall arise false Christs and false prophets…" (vs 21-24). *Let's figure that they don't all have to be religious!*

- Do we not have saviors for the economy? *Yes!*
- Do we not have saviors for increasing the human race genetically? *Yes!*

- Do we not have prophets telling us how good things are going to be? *Yes!*
- Do we not have religious people doing that? *Yes!*

Let's put it all in the whole mix. Someone mentioned to me that he thought this might be a possibility, I don't know. His opinion was that he felt that Rush Limbaugh was a secular prophet telling them the truth and telling the truth to people that you can't get to listen to from a spiritual prophet, but God is going to make sure that they hear it! I would say, that's a reasonable opinion. So we need to realize that there are going to be those, there are also going to be false prophets.

Now notice what they are going to do. So mark it, brethren, and watch, there are going to be more miracles done. They are going to allow religious programming, and I think that means within programs, religious scenes of prayers and things like that on prime time. But I tell you what, what's going to happen when there are 500 television channels? I mean if you are fed up with the garbage with just twenty-plus channels, times that by five and by five. Five times twenty is 100; times five is 500. But that is going to give opportunities! So watch, there are going to be miracles that are going to be done, great signs and wonders. Some of them can be medical signs and wonders. not only just healings, but they can be all kinds of things going on.

"…and they shall present great signs and wonders, in order to deceive, if possible, even the elect" (v 24).

I want us to grasp this. We've got to really be on the ball constantly or the deception will be so great, **we** could be deceived. It's going to be hard to say that these bona fide, absolutely provable, documented miracles are of Satan. The world won't believe it. Why? Because they love a winner, and this is going to be a winner.

Verse 25: "Behold, I have foretold *it* to you. Therefore, if they say to you, "*Come and* see! He is in the wilderness"; do not go forth. "*Come and* see! *He is* in the secret chambers"; do not believe *it*. For **as the light of day**…" (vs 25-27).

Let's focus in on v 27 because this ties in with Rev. 6:12.

Verse 27: "For as the light of day, which comes forth from *the* east and shines as far as *the* west…"—*that is the sun!* That cannot be a bolt of lightning, because lightning goes up, lightning comes down, lightning goes north and south and east and west and at all angles.

"…so also shall the coming of the Son of

man be. For wherever the carcass may be, there will the eagles be gathered together" (vs 27-28).

He gives us this statement that really it's hard to understand. The carcass, the body, the eagles are gathered that must have some reference to the Church, some reference to protection.

Verse 29: "But immediately after the Tribulation of those days…" *This is the sixth seal! This happens on next to the last Pentecost,* which I will prove.

"…the sun shall be darkened, and the moon shall not give her light, and the stars shall fall from heaven, and the powers of the heavens shall be shaken. And **then shall appear the sign of the Son of man in heaven**" (vs 29-30).

- What is the sign of the Son of man in heaven?
- When does it all of a sudden appear?

When the heavens are rolled back like a scroll, and they see Christ as a sun!

When they first see Him, notice it says shining from east to west. Which means that it's going to be far enough out in space that the gravitational pull of the earth is not going to affect it. The earth will continue on its orbit and every eye is going to see it. I believe, brethren, that from the next to the last Pentecost to the last Pentecost that that is going to get closer and closer and closer to the earth.

Then on the last Pentecost, which we will cover tomorrow, when the first resurrection takes place it's going to come down into the clouds over Jerusalem. That's going to make a lot of excited people on earth, militarists and otherwise. *So, the sign of the Son of man shall appear in heaven!*

"…and then shall all the tribes of the earth mourn, and they shall see the Son of man coming upon the clouds of heaven with power and great glory. And He shall send His angels with a great sound of a trumpet… [Did you realize the trumpet was blown on Pentecost? *We'll cover that tomorrow!*] …and they shall gather together His elect from the four winds, from one end of heaven to *the* other" (vs 30-31).

- v 30 is the next to the last Pentecost
- v 31 is the last Pentecost

Let's cover the same thing there concerning His return:

Luke 17:22: "Then He said to the disciples, '*The* days will come when you shall desire to see one of the days of the Son of man, and shall not see it…. [longing for the good ole' days] …And they shall say to you, "Look here," or, "Look there." Do not go, neither follow *them.* For as the light of day, whose light shines from *one end* under heaven to the

other end under heaven, so also shall the Son of man be in His day" (vs 22-24).

We know that a day fulfilled in prophecy is one year. What we're going to do is look at **His** day, from the next to the last Pentecost, to the last Pentecost and we will do that tomorrow on Pentecost, and put all of these events together.

Scriptures from *The Holy Bible in Its Original Order, A Faithful Version*

Scriptural References

1) Exodus 33:1-3
2) Exodus 25:8
3) Exodus 33:3-22
4) Exodus 34:1, 4-11, 21-22, 28-33
5) Exodus 32:26-28
6) Jeremiah 5:1, 3-15, 17, 19-31
7) Daniel 9:1-8, 10, 18-19
8) Revelation 1:18-20
9) Revelation 5:5-6
10) Revelation 2:2, 7-11, 23, 26
11) Revelation 3:13-14
12) Revelation 19:8
13) Revelation 5:1-2, 4-6, 11-14
14) Revelation 6:2-4
15) Revelation 13:4-9
16) Revelation 6:12-17
17) Matthew 24:21-31
18) Luke 17:22-24

Scriptures referenced, not quoted:

- Exodus 19; 20
- Revelation 2:4,
- John 6
- Revelation 17

Also referenced: Book: *Lord, What Should I Do?* by Fred R. Coulter

FRC: ja
Transcription date unknown
Reformatted: bo—11/2020

CHAPTER THIRTY-FIVE

"To Walk in the Way of the Lord"
(Pentecost—Day 49)
Fred R. Coulter

And greetings, brethren. This is the Sabbath before Pentecost.

Let's come to Lev. 23 and let's see something about counting Pentecost. We're going to rehearse it just a bit, and then we will see the message that is for us out of the Word of God that culminates in this last day of the seven weeks.

Leviticus 23:9: "And the LORD spoke to Moses, saying, 'Speak to the children of Israel and say to them, "When you have come into the land...""""(vs 9-10).

So, this ceremony could not take place until they came into the land. As we know, that happened, as we find, in Josh. 5.

"...which I give to you, and shall reap the harvest of it..." (v 10). *It was the harvest of the land!* They didn't plant it, it wasn't their harvest; it was theirs inasmuch as that when God gave them the land they owned it.

"...then you shall bring *the premier* sheaf of the firstfruits of your harvest to the priest.... [the thing that's important to understand is this]: ...And he shall wave the sheaf before the LORD to be accepted for you. On the next day after the Sabbath..." (vs 10-11).

The term *Sabbath* here is 'ha shabbat,' and it always means *the weekly Sabbath.* Then you were to count *seven* Sabbaths.

Now let's see the count in v 15: "And you shall count to you beginning with the next day after the Sabbath..."

That is the Sabbath, which falls during the days of Unleavened Bread, and then the next day puts it on the first day of the week.

"...beginning with the day that you brought the sheaf of the wave offering; seven Sabbaths **shall be complete**" (v 15).

This is seven Sabbaths, and "...shall be complete," meaning each week ends in a Sabbath. Now you tie that together with Deut.16 where it says that you are to count seven weeks. *These are whole weeks ending in a Sabbath!* Here is a thing that is important:

Verse 16: "Even unto **the day after the seventh Sabbath**... [that's today, the 7th Sabbath] ...**you shall number fifty days**..." *So, if you take that and line that all up, it always comes out on a Sunday!*

Let's liken the seven weeks that it took the children of Israel to come out of Egypt in order to receive the Ten Commandments from God at Mount Sinai to an extended travel that they had all through the wilderness. Remember, God provided for them. He led them by the pillar of cloud by day and the fire by night; He gave them manna and their clothes didn't even grow old, and so forth.

Deuteronomy 2:7: "For the LORD your God has blessed you in all the works of your hand...." *This is what we want God to do for us*:

- in our personal life
- in our families lives
- in our church life

"...He knows your walking *through* this great wilderness...." (v 7).

Today we live in a different kind of wilderness, *a spiritual wilderness* filled with all kinds of physical things.

"...The LORD your God *has been* with you these forty years. **You have lacked nothing**" (v 7).

We find in Exo. 16 when God first began to give the manna to the children of Israel, He said that He was going to do this to prove them, to test them whether they would walk in His Law or not. Now that's the same thing for us. **Are we going to walk in God's way? even in spite of the world in which we are living?** Let's see what God says about *walking in His way*:

Leviticus 26:2: "You shall keep My Sabbath**s**... [there again, we have plural, referring to the weekly Sabbath and Holy Days] ...and reverence My sanctuary. I *am* the LORD. **If you walk in My statutes and keep My commandments and do them**..." (vs 2-3)—*all the way through!*

Then He says He will bless them, give them peace, and things like this. Today we are living in a world where there is very little peace, there is nothing but trouble and difficulties. All of us in our lives, we have things that we are confronted with all the time. But let's understand that God has given us

- the way
- the Truth
- the life through Jesus Christ

Verse 11: "And I will set My tabernacle among you.... [today it's quite different because each one of us are a Temple of God] ...And My soul shall not abhor you. And **I will walk among you**... [we're going to see how this applies to the Church a little later] ...and will be your God, and you shall be My people. I *am* the LORD your God Who brought you forth out of the land of Egypt from being their bondmen. And I have broken the bonds of your yoke, and made you go upright" (vs 11-13).

That's what God has done with us *spiritually.* Just like the children of Israel, as we saw during the days of Unleavened Bread, were rescued from Egypt; Pharaoh was a type of Satan, and that his armies were a type of the demons, and how God rescued them, and so forth; did all the things that He did to bring them out of the land of Egypt and bring them into the 'promised land.'

Let's see the things that God warned them of. Then let's see how this applies to the Church today and how it applies to our lives, and how not only do we need to do the things that please God, but we also need to beware of the difficulties and problems that we're confronted with in the world today.

Deuteronomy 8:1: "All the commandments which I command you this day shall **you be diligent to observe *and to* do** that you may live…"

- God wants us to live
- God wants us to grow spiritually
- God wants us to live in His way

"…and multiply and go in and possess the land, which the LORD swore to your fathers. And you shall remember all the way, which the LORD your God led you these forty years in the wilderness…" (vs 1-2).

Just like we are to remember that *God has called us out of the world!* We are to remember that we are not to go back to spiritual Egypt. Here is what God is doing in our lives. Here is why we go through the things that we do, the same exact process that they went through, only for our spiritual good and our spiritual benefit.

He did this "…forty years in the wilderness in order **to humble you, to prove you**…" (v 3). *Now let's just look at our lives*:

- How many have been in the Church of God how long?

- ✓ some have just been baptized
- ✓ some have been in the Church of God 40 or 50 years

So we have the same thing!
- How are we walking in the world?
- Is God testing us and proving us? *Yes, all the time!*

"…**to know what is in your heart**..." (v 2). *This is what God wants to know!*

When we see about the seven churches a little bit later, *it all has to do with the heart and how they stand before God,* and what the problems of the world pressing in on the Church caused them.

"…whether you would keep His commandments or not… [also whether we would love God or not] …And He humbled you and allowed you to hunger, and then He fed you with manna, which you did not know, neither did your fathers know *it,* so that He might make you know that man does not live by bread alone; **but by every *word* that proceeds out of the mouth of the LORD does man live**" (vs 2-3).

Then he gave them some other instructions in showing that even their clothes didn't wax old and their shoes didn't wear out. Then he warns them beware lest they forget.

Let's come back to the New Testament. Let's see how this applies to us. Let's see *how we are to walk in God's way!*

2-John 4: "I rejoiced exceedingly that I have found among your children **those who are walking in Truth**..."

That's what God wants us to walk in: *the Truth!* We are sanctified by the Truth, which is the Word of God.

"…exactly as we received commandment from the Father" (v 4). *Notice how this parallels with what we read back there in the Old Testament!*

Verse 5: "And now I beseech you, lady… [which is the type of the Church] …not as though I am writing a new commandment to you, but that which we have *observed* from *the* beginning, that we love one another. And this is the love *of God*: **that we walk according to His commandments.** This is the commandment, exactly as you heard from *the* beginning, **that you might walk in it**" (vs 5-6).

Now we also know that God gives us some warnings about how we are walking and how we're living in the world. Let's see why God does this. If you think that the children of Israel had all of their problems because they didn't follow in the way that God wanted them to do, well just think about the Church of God today. We're going to talk about that a little later, so I just want you to get this in your mind.

2-Corinthians 6:14: "Do not be unequally yoked with unbelievers...." *That's especially true in the sense of what the world would call Christianity!*

One of the biggest errors that the Church of God has done in recent time has gone to the Christianity of this world and say, 'What do you know about God?' You've seen the results of that because they don't really know the way of God very well. Here is what we need to watch:

"...For what do righteousness and lawlessness *have* in common? And what fellowship *does* light *have* with darkness? And what union *does* Christ *have* with **Belial**?" [the son of foolishness] ...Or what part *does* a believer *have* with an unbeliever? And what agreement *is there between* a Temple of God and idols?.... [here's the whole key, which is important]: ...**For you are a temple of *the* living God**..." (vs 14-16).

- that's why our calling is special
- that's why it is important
- that's why we need to always follow the way of God

"...**you are a temple of *the* living God**, exactly as God said: '**I will dwell in them and walk in them**...'" (v 16). *If Christ is in you,* how should you walk? *We'll see about this a little bit later on!*

"'...and I will be their God, and they shall be My people. Therefore, come out from the midst of them and be separate,' says *the* Lord, 'and touch not *the* unclean, and I will receive you; and **I shall be a Father to you, and you shall be My sons and daughters,'** says *the* Lord Almighty" (vs 16-18). *This is what we want to attain to, because tomorrow pictures*:

- the resurrection
- the completion of this journey and the walk that we are walking in

Now let's see some other things that tie into this and help us understand:

- how we need to walk
- how God is dealing with us

All know we have things we need to change and overcome, and righteousness that we need to grow in, and that's all a part of the meaning of the Feast of Unleavened Bread. But in order to fulfill the completeness of the Feast of Unleavened Bread we've got to get to the final goal, which is the resurrection.

Psalm 86:11: "Teach me Your way, O LORD..."

If we're going to *walk in the way of the Lord* we have to examine the Word of God and know what it is and He has to teach us.

"...**I will walk in Your Truth**..." (v 11). See how that combines with what we have already talked about here, walking in the Truth.

"...unite my heart to fear Your name. I will praise You, O LORD my God, with all my heart..." (vs 11-12). *This is what God wants from all of us*:

- that we love God with all our heart
- that we walk in God's way with all our heart
- that we believe God with all of our heart
- that we trust in God with all of our heart

"...and I will glorify Your name forevermore, for great is Your mercy toward me; and You have delivered my soul from the depths of the grave. O God, the proud have risen against me... [there are a lot of things that are coming against a lot of brethren today] ...and the company of violent men have sought after my life, and have not set You before them. But You, O LORD, are a God full of compassion, and gracious, slow to anger, and abounding in steadfast love and Truth. **Oh, turn to me**..." (vs 12-16).

IF we return to God, God promises He will return to us. *Remember that God has*:

- called us
- chosen us
- given us His Spirit

He is walking in us! This is why we need to let the Spirit lead us—lead us in the way that we think and we live on a daily basis; not just on the Sabbath, not just when we feel 'religious.'

"...and have mercy upon me; give Your strength to Your servant and save the son of Your handmaid" (v 16). *God has helped us and comforted us!*

Let's come to another couple of Psalms here. Let's see what happens when we're *walking in the way of the LORD*; our journey to *spiritual* Mount Sinai.

Psalm 119:1: "Blessed... [this results in blessings] ...are the undefiled in the way, who walk in the Law of the LORD" *We have the way the Lord equals*:

- the way of Truth
- the way of His commandments
- the way of His laws
- the way of statutes and judgments
- the way of keeping His Sabbath
- the way of keeping His Holy Days

- the way of taking care of our body and mind

Even the way of eating, that we eat the things are right; all of those are part of the way of the Lord!

Verse 2: "Blessed are they who keep His testimonies and who seek Him with the whole heart." *We're going to find all the way through here that it has to do with the heart!*

Verse 3: "They also do no iniquity; **they walk in His ways.**"

Now let's understand this: *when you have this kind of attitude toward God and you're walking in His ways, **you have no sin imputed to you!** But **you have the righteousness of Christ imputed to you!***

Let's see some other things about *walking in the way of the Lord; walking in the way of God.* Here's what it needs to do for us:

Psalm 138:1: "I will praise You with my whole heart; before the gods I will sing praise to You. I will worship toward Your Holy Temple, and praise Your name for Your loving kindness, and for Your Truth; for You have magnified above all, Your name *and* Your Word" (vs 1-2). *Very important to understand!*

Now let's translate this into things that we have for the New Testament:

- when we pray
- when we study
- when we come before God

we are coming right into the Holy of Holies in heaven above through the very sacrifice of Jesus Christ so that we can do these things!

Verse 6: "Though the LORD is high, yet, He has respect to the lowly; but the haughty He knows afar off. Though I walk in the midst of trouble…" (vs 6-7).

We're going to see that the Church is always confronted with difficulties, problems and troubles *because we're living in this world, **even though we know we're not part of this world!***

"…You will revive me; You shall stretch forth Your hand against the wrath of my enemies, and Your right hand shall save me. **The LORD will perfect His work in me**…" (vs 7-8).

That's the whole goal that God wants us to understand; He is perfecting us!

"…Your steadfast love, O LORD, endures forever; do not forsake the work of Your own hands" (v 8).

Now let's apply that to us. We are the workmanship of God created in Christ Jesus! Let's

always understand this: the way that we always keep the perspective we need to have is to realize *how great and marvelous our calling is, and what God is:*

- doing for us
- to us
- through us
- in us

and where He wants us to go! He wants us to be faithful to the end and attain to the Resurrection. So, this is a great and marvelous thing that we always need to keep in mind, and to realize this above all things.

Rev. 1—let's see what it says about Christ, and let's see that Christ is intimately involved in His Church. It is the focus of His whole attention at the present time. There are things that are going on in the world that He is directing, but the central focus is His Church. This helps us understand how important it is that Christ is dealing with each one of us, and how important the plan of God is. As we have seen, it's all on the framework of the Holy Days of God, and every one of the Holy Days are all connected together and have meaning.

Revelation 1:8: "'I am the Alpha and the Omega, *the* Beginning and *the* Ending,' says the Lord, 'Who is, and Who was, and Who *is* to come—the Almighty.'"

Christ is going to return, and His return is going to be so powerful and so glorious; we will see tomorrow. It's going to be so spectacular that our thoughts and imaginations of it are just very minuscule compared to what it is really actually going to be. *Then John, who was given this vision by Jesus Christ wrote*:

Verse 9: "I, John, who *am* also your brother and joint partaker in the tribulation and in the kingdom and endurance of Jesus Christ, was on the island that *is* called Patmos because of the Word of God and the testimony of Jesus Christ. I was in *the* Spirit on the Day of the Lord; and I heard a loud voice like a trumpet behind me, saying, 'I am the Alpha and the Omega, the First and the Last, and what you see, **write in a book, and send *it* to the churches that *are* in Asia**…'" (vs 9-11).

So this is a written message. As we know, John canonized the whole New Testament. So, this can also refer to that as well, the whole inclusive thing. But what he writes in the book—the letters to the seven churches—have to do with:

- how God deals with His Church
- how Christ, Who is the head of the Church, is working with His Church

- how the Church, with God's Spirit living in the world, has the difficulties and trials that they need to overcome
- how God is dealing with us

This is why we need to go back over this—especially at this time of year—because **this shows that the seven churches picture the seven weeks leading up to Pentecost!** It is just like the harvest of the seven weeks of the wheat harvest that takes place, **the seven churches are the spiritual harvest of God!** He names them here:

"…to Ephesus, and to Smyrna, and to Pergamos, and to Thyatira, and to Sardis, and to Philadelphia, and to Laodicea" (v 11). *These seven churches picture*:

1. the churches that were then
2. a prophecy of all the Churches of God down through history from the time that it was formed in 30A.D. with the coming of the Holy Spirit until the return of Jesus Christ and the resurrection at Pentecost
3. the spiritual condition and attitude of the churches in general and individuals in particular
4. the churches at the end

What we really have is this:

- the seven churches that were there
- the seven church eras or stages of the church down through history
- the seven churches at the end

I think if we view things from the point of view like the Bible Sabbath Association, and look at the different publications that come out. And for us when we look at what is called *The Journal*, we can see different parts of messages that go to the Churches of God. It's quite an interesting thing that that is what it is. What you see when you read *The Journal* is how that there are various different doctrines and teachings that also are reflected here in Rev, 2 & 3, and what we need to do about those, **because some of these teachings are _not_ in accord with the Word of God!**

Verse 12: "And I turned to see the voice that spoke with me; and when I turned, I saw seven golden lampstands."

This is just like in a circle. This is not a replica of the candle, or the lamp-holder that is found in the temple, because as we will see, the seven golden lampstands…

Verse 13: "And in *the* midst of the seven lampstands *One* like *the* Son of man…" **Christ is in His Church!**

Christ is in you and me—in all the brethren—all the brethren consist of the Church, a *spiritual* organization. It is not a corporate organization. Any corporate organization only has to do with conducting business in this world. He is in the midst of His Church. Then it shows His great, glorified form, how Christ is, with the countenance shining as the sun in full strength.

Verse 17: "And when I [John] saw Him, I fell at His feet as if dead; but He laid His right hand upon me, saying to me, '**Do not be afraid**…'"—*this is what we need to also understand!*

If there are things we need to change, *we'll change*. If there are things we need to repent of, we can repent of those, because that's the whole story of the seven churches as recorded in Rev. 2 & 3.

"…I am the First and the Last, even the One Who is living; for I was dead, and behold, I am alive into the ages of eternity. Amen. And I have the keys of *the* grave and of death" (vs 17-18).

Let's understand one thing: like the Apostle Paul said very clearly, '*If Christ is not raised, then there is no resurrection of the dead; and if there is no resurrection of the dead, we have no hope.*' But here is the message from Christ; these of the words of God: _He_ has "…the keys of *the* grave and of death."

God wants us to know; this is why it was written; v 19: "Write the things that you saw… [everything up through v 18 to this point] …and the things that are… [the seven churches which exist, the state of the Church at that particular time] …and the things that shall take place hereafter.'"

This comes from the time of John—yes, even reaching back to the beginning of the Church in 30A.D. on Pentecost—and goes clear to the return of Christ on into the Millennium, and on into New Jerusalem, and on into the first stages of the ages of eternity. This is a fantastic book, and it starts with churches.

We all get interested in news; we all like to see what's going on in the world. We like to see if prophecies being fulfilled. Yes, they're all being fulfilled **exactly the way that God wants them fulfilled!** Since God gave prophecies concerning all the major events in the world, do you not think that He would also give a prophecy of His Church? *Yes!* That's what He's done in Rev. 2 & 3.

Verse 20: "'The mystery of the seven stars that you saw in My right hand, and the seven golden lampstands, *is this*: the seven stars are *the* angels of the seven churches; and the seven lampstands that you saw are *the* seven churches."

Now let's see the message to them; this is written to us. These are the sayings of Christ so that we might know what to do in any circumstances that we are confronted with in our Christian life, as individuals, in our community, as it were, in our congregations and fellowship when we get together. What we will see is that God through Christ lays out all the things that we need to be aware of and what's going to happen with His Church.

We will see there's a parallel here; we will see many, many of the things that happened to the Church as it goes down in time in history, were also the same things that happened to Israel as they walked in the wilderness for the 40 years.

Revelation 2:1: "To the angel of the Ephesian church, write...'"

Let's understand that __when__ God has it written—and God has it preserved for us today— __then__ *we better pay very deep, serious concern about it, and understand that these are the living words of God given to us.* When we ask, 'What would Jesus say to His Church today?' ***Right here we have it; this is the message for us.***

"...'These things says He Who holds the seven stars in His right hand... [to do His work; that's why it's in the right hand] ...Who walks in *the* midst of the seven golden lampstands" (v 1).

- Christ is right there
- He is walking in us
- we are walking in His way
- we are to let the light of Christ lead us

He knows everything about us!

Verse 2: "I know your works, and your labor, and your endurance, and that you cannot bear those who are evil; and *that* you did test those who proclaim *themselves* to be apostles, but are not, and did find them liars." *This is why there are so many warnings in there*:

- beware of false prophets
- beware that you're not deceived
- test those
- prove all things

This is what they were doing, and this is what we have to do in everything that we do. This is how we let ourselves be led by the Spirit of God; and how also that the Word of God and the Spirit of God:

- corrects us
- encourages us
- uplifts us
- leads us in the things that we need to do
- convicts us of the shortcomings and problems that we encounter
- encourages us

Verse 3: "And *that* you have borne *much* and have endured, and for My name's sake have

labored and have not grown weary... [that's the important thing to do; ***never grow weary***] ...nevertheless... [here comes a little correction; God has correction for His Church in every sense] ...I have *this* against you, that you have left your first love" (vs 3-4).

This is what happens in any organization. They start out with zeal. They start out with love. They start out with dedication, and then everything gets kind of *socialized* as with people.

When you leave the first love, what is happening is ***you're letting the world come in!*** You're letting others come in. Even though you may be fighting off false doctrine, as it says here, that they 'tried them who were apostles and were not, and tested them,' that means *you test the message.* You listen to what they have to say.

I'll just mention this now, but I also am going to mention it again: one of the doctrines that is coming to test the Church today—which a lot of people are failing—is ***the false doctrine that Jesus did not exist as God before He came in the flesh! That He did not exist until He was begotten in the womb of the virgin Mary!***

How does that come about? *Mark 12—let's see what it was where it says they lost their first love!* Now a lot of people refer to this as the first love that people have when they're first called and understand *the Truth* and understand *the way of God.* That is true to a certain extent. But that's not what it's talking about, because the Greek for *first* comes from the word 'protos,' which also means *primary.*

Mark 12:28—*this is what we need to keep always right in the forefront of our mind*: "And one of the scribes who had come up *to* Him, after hearing them reasoning together *and* perceiving that He answered them well, asked Him [Jesus], 'Which is *the* first commandment of all?'" *The primary commandment!*

What's the most important thing? *Once you understand this and realize this, it will bring everything else together*:

Verse 29: "Then Jesus answered him, '*The* first of all the commandments *is*, "Hear, O Israel. Our one God is *the* Lord, *the* Lord. And you shall love *the* Lord your God with all your heart..."'" (vs 29-30).

I want you to notice the effort that is put into it, *the effort that is required!* The reason that this is important is this: is because eternal life, to live forever is a tremendous and wonderful thing. View it this way: everything that we're doing right now is ***preparing and getting ready***:

- for the event that tomorrow pictures, *the resurrection*
- to live eternally
- to know how to rule and reign with Christ

preparing us to complete what God has given us to do!

Love the Lord your God with all your heart, *not part-time!* Don't let your heart be divided, your mind be divided. It says there in James 1 that if you are divided in heart and mind, then you are double-minded and you are unstable. Maybe that will explain a lot of difficulties that people have. You judge yourself in that yourself.

"…and with all your soul, and with all your mind, and with all your strength…." (v 30). *So our calling is an all-out effort on our part!* ***Then God gives His all-out effort to us!***

- Did not Jesus Christ give an all out effort when He was here in the flesh?
- Did He not give His all to save His creation, and to save you individually?
- *Yes, He did!*

That's why we need to understand what it's talking about there in losing the first love.

"…This is the first commandment" (v 30). So, the *primary love* ***is loving God!*** The primary commandment is to love God.

Verse 31: "And *the* second *is* like this: 'You shall love your neighbor as yourself.' There is no other commandment greater than these." *Then Jesus also said of us that we are to love one another as Jesus loved us!*

- ***IF*** you are loving God with all your heart, mind, soul and being, **would you get wrapped up in doctrines and teachings of men?** *No!*
- ***IF*** you are proving everything like they did back here in the Church at Ephesus, **are you really seeking the Truth?**

There's a difference between:

- seeking the Truth of God
- walking in the Truth
- being sanctified of the Truth
- living by the Truth

and seeking a position! Not a position of power, but a 'religious' position, ***which is not connected with God!*** That's why we have to prove all these things.

Now this is what we are to do. And this is what God wants us to do as we are walking the walk. We'll also need to be "talking the talk" if we could put it that way, that which is right.

Revelation 2:5: "Therefore, remember from where you have fallen, and **repent, and do the first works**…" *That's what we need to do!*

I was talking to a man about the condition of the Church and how many people have fallen into this position, which is similar to Laodiceanism, but not exactly the same thing. How many people are out there kind of 'treading water.'

Have you have ever tread water out in the ocean? *You can tread water and you think you're keeping yourself afloat,* and granted you're not sinking; but you can tread water. But there is one thing with treading water, ***you don't have your feet on the ground!*** When you're treading water and the currents are coming, it's moving you along, ***and it's moving you maybe in a direction that you really don't want to go, and you're not aware of it!*** Then all the sudden, just like a wave comes upon the land, if you're treading water, just like this, it's going to catch up with you.

He says "…**repent, and do the first works**…" *Go back and do the things that you know that you need to do and recapture that first love!* ***He calls them to repent,*** and He says:

"…for if *you do* not, I will come to you quickly; and **I will remove your lampstand** out of its place **unless you repent**" (v 5). *Let's look at this in several different ways*:

1. God corrects His own Church
2. God corrects each one of us individually

and He expects us to repent! ***IF*** there is no repentance then He says ***He's going to remove you!***

- Did God remove a Church before our very eyes? *Yes, He did!*
- Has God removed *false* brethren, *false* ministers, *false* teachers? *Yes, because they did not repent!*

- they lost their first love
- they quit loving God with all their heart, mind, soul and being
- they got wrapped up in themselves
  - ✓ in their own doctrines
  - ✓ in their own positions
  - ✓ in their own religiosity

That's cause for removal!

But they did have one thing, *they hated the works of the Nicolaitans!* The Nicolaitans are those who have a rigid hierarchy and lorded over the brethren. The Nicolaitans are also those who have a false grace.

Verse 7: "**The one who has an ear, let him hear what the Spirit says to the Churches**…."

- God's Spirit is in you
- Christ directs the Spirit
- it is to lead you
- it is to bring you to repentance

That's all a part of our Christian walk, because we are in the process of being perfected step-by-step, day-by-day, week-by-week, month-by-month, year-by-year! That's why we are always

- *to walk in faith*
- *believe in hope*
- *live in love*

That's how we are to conduct our lives!

Even in the world today we have those who are dying for Christ. Even within the Churches of God there are those in very treacherous and evil places in the world that have suffered death because of those who follow Satan the devil.

The Church of the Smyrnans:

"…These things says the First and the Last, Who was dead but is alive. 'I know your works and tribulation and poverty (but you are rich)…'" (vs 8-9).

When you come to the Laodiceans, because they have an abundance of physical things and think they are rich, they think that they are spiritually right before God. But God looks at it the other way. Remember this: *God looks at it with other eyes!* So, they are rich even though they're suffering tribulation,

"…and the blasphemy of those who declare themselves to be Jews and are not, but *are* a synagogue of Satan" (v 9).

A very interesting way to put it: *a synagogue of Satan.* Let's talk about another synagogue of Satan: radical Muslimism, they are the ones who are killing brethren. There have been some who have been associated with the Churches of God in Africa who have been killed by Muslims. This is a living part of the Church today. And yes, these brethren:

- may not have the understanding of doctrine
- may not realize all the things that we do
- may not understand the depths of the plan of God

but they believe Christ! They are willing to die for His name! They are willing to stand up and be counted! God says to them:

Verse 10: "Do not fear any of the things that you are about to suffer. Behold, the devil is about to cast *some* of you into prison, that you may be tried; and you shall have tribulation ten days. **Be faithful unto death, and I will give you a crown of life**."

Now let's look at the other situation, too. What did Jesus say at the end? *The one who endures to the end, the same shall be saved!*

Verse 11: "**The one who has an ear, let him hear what the Spirit says to the churches. The one who overcomes shall not be hurt of the second death**"

What we see all the way through here with the Churches of God is the lack of true spiritual endurance and consistency. *So, those who die are going to receive a crown of life!* God looks at them with far greater love and favor than those who may have more Truth, those who may understand more doctrine but treat it with:

- disdain
- contempt
- familiarity

and end up treading water in their spiritual lives, and that God has to correct them!

Here with the Church at Smyrna, those who go through and suffer these things, they don't have any correction that Christ has to give them because their hearts are right with Him.

Now let's come to the next two Churches, or perhaps the most infiltrated with satanic doctrine. Satan wants to bring in satanic doctrine into the Church, because he knows ***IF** he can get you to move away from the Truth just a little bit, just like a ship that is off one degree, it's going to miss the port at the other end.* Or if you're sending a satellite up into orbit, if you are off just a little bit it's not going into orbit.

The Church of Pergamos:

Revelation 2:12: "And to the angel of the Church in Pergamos, write: 'These things says He Who has the sharp two-edged sword'"—*which we find in the book of Hebrews!*

That's the Word of God, *sharper than any two-edged sword, and cuts asunder to the dividing of the soul and spirit and joints and marrow,* and is a discerner of the thoughts and the intents of the heart! Christ: called the Word of God and the Spirit of God. *He wants them to understand, there is correction coming!*

Verse 13: "I know your works and where you dwell, where the throne of Satan *is*; but you are holding fast My name, and did not deny My faith, even in the days in which Antipas *was* My faithful witness, who was killed among you, where Satan dwells."

Let me tell you something, when you get in the middle of where Satan is—and Satan is deceiving this whole world:

- he's got *his ways* of doing things
- he has a counterfeit Christianity
- he has his counterfeit way of doing things

And with all the pressures coming upon people and these things, it's awfully hard to resist those things!

Verse 14: "But I have a few things against you because you have there *those* who hold the teaching of Balaam…"

What is the teaching of Balaam? *Let's amalgamate the religions together. Let's take the best of this, the best of that and the best of the other thing!* Isn't that what the Catholic Church did, and is this not really the brethren who repented in Pergamos, then they left what later became the Catholic Church because the doctrine of Balaam is that.

"…who taught Balak to cast a stumbling block before the children of Israel, to eat **things sacrificed to idols and to commit fornication**" (v 14)—*both physically and spiritually, and to sacrifice unto idols!*

If you want to know any one thing that the Bible teaches, it is this:

- you shall have no other gods before Me
- don't make and idol or any likeness of anything that is in heaven above, that is in the earth beneath, and the water under the earth
- don't bow down yourself to them

If there's any one thing that is pounded through the whole Bible, that is it! But today people have different idols:

- they have idols of their mind
- they have idols of their doctrines
- they have idols of their way of life
- they have idols of the things about them that their hands have made

That's all part of it!

Verse 15: "Moreover, you also have *those* who hold the doctrine of the Nicolaitans, **which thing I [Christ] hate**."

When it comes to doing things which God hates—and the Church is guilty of it—know that correction is going to come. Just like when the children of Israel were on their way in coming to Mount Sinai to meet God.

- Did He not have to correct them?
- Did He not have to teach them?

- Did He not have to, in a sense, punish them?
- *Yes, indeed!*

Verse 16: "**Repent!**…." *That's what God wants us to do all the time!* Repentance doesn't happen just at the time before you're baptized, but repentance happens daily.

- as we're overcoming sin
- as we're overcoming carnal nature
- as we overcome the things of this world
  - ✓ we need to repent
  - ✓ we need to have our mind cleansed
  - ✓ we need to have our heart purified

"…For if *you* **do not** *repent*, I will come to you quickly, and will make war against them with the sword of My mouth" (v 16).

- Is it not a sad situation indeed that Jesus has to fight against His own Church? *Look back at what happened to ancient Israel!*
- Did not God have to fight against His own people because of what they did? *Yes, indeed!*

So, there needs to be some repentance among the Churches of God!

There are too many people out there with their own ideas. One of the big idols that is out there today is *various calendars schemes, because they do not count God worthy of understanding the universe!* They have to have their own calendar schemes.

If you are caught up in some of that, I suggest to you do exactly like it says here: *repent!* We've got a stack of material that shows without a doubt that God gave the Calculated Hebrew Calendar so that we would all be able to keep the Feasts on the right day that *He* has appointed.

When we have our own calendar schemes, what do we end up doing? *We appoint days that God didn't appoint!* Yet, many of those who do that are staunchly for the Sabbath and the Holy Days and against Sunday. But *IF* you establish your own Holy Days contrary to the way that God has given it, what are you doing? *It's the same thing as establishing Sunday!* But God says, *'Repent!'*

Church at Thyatira:

Thyatira really got carried away. As you look at the state of some of the Churches of God today you understand how that can happen. Because as we learned with the Feast of Unleavened Bread, *a little leaven leavens whole lump*; and if you let it grow and grow, you don't understand the magnitude of the problems and difficulties until it gets out of hand. Just look at the immigration problem in all the nations of the ten tribes of Israel today; *it is out of hand!* That's what happened to the Church at Thyatira, though they started out well.

Verse 18: "And to the angel of the Church in Thyatira write: 'These things says the Son of God, He Who has eyes like a flame of fire, and His feet *are* like fine brass. **I know your works, and love, and service, and faith, and your endurance**… [so they were doing well] …**and your works; and the last *are* more than the first**…. [some of them repented] …But I have a few things against you, because you allow the woman Jezebel, who calls herself a prophetess, to teach and to seduce My servants into committing fornication and eating things sacrificed to idols'" (vs 18-20).

That's exactly what happens when you have *your own* Passover, you have *your own* Unleavened Bread; just one step away from this kind of idolatry. But look what happened here: Jezebel was the daughter of the high priest of Baal, and Jezebel married Ahab who led the children of Israel into sin. It even caused problems for Elijah.

God means what He says! If you are out there with the world:

- living like the world
- being like the world
- acting like the world

then *you are spiritually fornicating with the world!* Now juxtaposition that with this:

- How much do you study?
- How much do you pray?
- How much do you really believe God?

Verse 21: "And I gave her time to repent of her fornication..." *God gives us all space and time to repent!* That's why He doesn't come down upon us *until* He sees what we're going to choose and do.

- He sends little warnings
- He sends thoughts in our mind
- He sends situations to bring us up short

to alert us as to what is taking place!

Sometimes we react to them right away, other times we kind of let them linger. Then the problem gets more and more and finally Christ has to do what He does here. He brings us up short and helps us to understand where we have been going wrong. That's why He said:

"…but she did not repent…. [If there's not repentance, what comes next?] …Behold, I will cast her into a bed, and those who commit adultery with her into Great Tribulation, unless they repent of their works" (vs 21-22).

Let's come back here to Psa. 86 again and understand something about God that we really need to realize. If you have things in your life that you know you need to repent of, then remember this: *God is waiting for you to repent!* God will receive you when you repent.

Psalm 86:1: "Bow down Your ear, O LORD, answer me, for I am poor and needy. Preserve my soul, for I am Holy… [everyone whom God calls and has the Holy Spirit is Holy] …O You my God, save Your servant who trusts in You…. [now you've got to reestablish that trust with God, and here's how you do it]: …Be merciful to me, O LORD, for I cry unto You all day long…. [get right back with God] …Rejoice the soul of Your servant, for to You, O LORD, do I lift up my soul, **for You, LORD, are good and ready to forgive**…" (vs 1-5).

The problem is never with God! That's why there are no conditions on God. Where there are conditions it is *if you, then God will!* If you repent, then God will forgive. but that repentance has to be from the heart, *and it has to be*—as we covered at the first—*re-establishing the true love!*

Verse 5: "For You, LORD, are good and ready to forgive, and rich in mercy to all those who call upon You. Give ear, O LORD, to my prayer, and attend to the voice of my supplications. In the day of my trouble I will call upon You, for You will answer me" (vs 5-7).

That's the appeal that was made by Christ to the Church at Thyatira: *Don't be taken down by any of these things!* Let's equate all of these things together that we see happening in the Churches of God concerning:

- their attitude toward God
- their attitude toward doctrine
- their health: spiritually and physically
- the world that we are living in

God weighs all of those factors together. and we need to really draw close to God and realize that He is there to help us if we repent.

Revelation 2:22: "…unless they repent of their works…. [if they don't]: …And I will kill her children with death…"

In other words, whatever you are going to do, if you don't repent and are not right with God, it is going to come to nothing.

"…and all the churches shall know that I am He Who searches *the* reins and hearts… [because Christ is in us all the time] …and **I will give to each of you according to your works**" (vs 22-23).

How far can a person go and still recover themselves? *God alone makes that decision!*

Verse 24: "But to you I say, and to *the* rest who *are* in Thyatira, as many as do not have this doctrine, and who have not known the depths of Satan, as they speak; I will not cast upon you any other burden, but hold fast what you have until I come" (vs 24-25). *Then all the way through to every one of the Churches!*

Verse 29: "**The one who has an ear, let him hear what the Spirit says to the churches**."

- Do you have an ear to hear?
- How is your walk with God?
- How are you steadfast with God?

God is going to bring you to Mount Sion in heaven above, and the day of the resurrection is going to happen!

- Christ wants you *ready!*
- Christ wants you *prepared!*

That's what this is all about!

Church of Sardis:

Then we have the ones who are the absolute worst Church of all, that they have a name that they live, *but they are dead!* Notice the warning that He gives them here:

Revelation 3:2: "Be watchful, and strengthen the things that remain... [whatever little bit is remaining, strengthen it] ...which are about to die. For I have not found your works complete before God."

Now there are spiritual works we are to do, and God wants us to do them, and they need to be complete.

Verse 3: "Therefore, remember what you have received and heard, and hold on *to this*, and repent. Now then, if you will not watch... [Jesus tells us to watch ourselves and watch the world] ...I will come upon you as a thief..."—*because God will always visit for the sins!*

This is not talking about His second return here. This is talking about Jesus dealing with each one of us.

"...and you shall by no means know what hour I will come upon you" (v 3).

Isn't that the way it always is? *When you least expect it and are least prepared!* When you have come into a state of near deadness, then Christ is going to come upon you. Now, a little encouragement here:

Verse 4: "You have a few names even in Sardis who have not defiled their garments, and they shall walk with Me in white because they are worthy. The one who overcomes shall be clothed in white garments; and I will not blot out his name from the Book of Life, but I will confess his name before My Father and before His angels" (vs 4-5).

Now let's understand something here, very important to realize: *our names are written in the Book of Life and will remain there so that at the resurrection we will be raised from the dead!* But let's also understand that if we allow ourselves to get into these kinds of spiritual conditions, our names can be erased. As God told Moses, *'I will blot out whom I will blot out'*; *that's quite a warning!*

Verse 6: "**The one who has an ear, let him hear what the Spirit says to the churches**."

Then it talks about the Philadelphians. We'll be there in a little bit; we'll end up with that one, but let's come over here to:

The Church of the Laodiceans:

You've heard this many, many times over. Let's go to the message to the Laodiceans that we find in the book of Colossians. This is important for us to understand and realize. Not only was this written to the Colossians, but he also gave instructions then when it was done being read to the Colossians that it was to also be read in the Church of Laodicea.

Now let's notice the focus here, especially in Col. 2, because this also has to do with what we are confronted with today, with all of the satanic spiritism that is out there. What we need to understand is this: this world is absolutely going to go after Satan the devil and all of these teachings.

Now I was channel surfing, because there's hardly anything to watch; and I got on the National Geographic channel. Guess what they were showing? *Witchcraft, séances, appealing to demons and devils, and even using the name of Jesus with it!*

That's one of the great problems with the Laodiceans. They get involved in philosophy, and philosophy changes the nature of God, which is why there are people who are involved in this *one God only in number false doctrine,* and saying that Jesus was not God before He became a human being. Paul is dealing with that here:

Colossians 2:1: "Now, I want you to understand what great concern I have for you, and *for* those in Laodicea... [these are the inspired words of God; God has concern for all of His brethren] ...and as many as have not seen my face in *the* flesh; that their hearts may be encouraged, being knit together in love... [notice how this ties in with the message to all the Churches]: ...**unto all riches of the full assurance of understanding**..." (vs 1-2)—*not physical goods and physical riches*:

- that you know God
- that you know Jesus Christ
- that you know the Word of God
- that you know how to live your life before God the way He wants you to

"...unto *the* knowledge of the mystery of God, and of *the* Father, and of Christ... [He wants us to know the great, fantastic things that He has for us] ...in Whom are hid all the treasures of wisdom and knowledge" (vs 2-3).

You're not going to gain any knowledge from the philosophies of this world. They come from men who profess themselves to be wise, but have become fools. They believe when you believe in 'only one 'God' in number,' you're talking about a god who is the transcendent god, who has no form, no shape, no being. That's the philosophical god of all the pagans. In Christ are hidden "...all the treasures of wisdom and knowledge."

Verse 4: "Now, this I say so that no one may deceive you by persuasive speech."

Just because a person presents an argument, remember this: *not all logic is true, but all Truth is logical!*

Verse 5: "For though I am indeed absent in the flesh, yet, I am with you in spirit, rejoicing and beholding your order, and the steadfastness of your faith in Christ. Therefore... [here comes the warning] ...as you have received Christ Jesus the Lord... [as you find in the Scriptures] ...be walking in Him... [put together all these other Scriptures that we have seen here] ...being rooted and built up in Him, and being confirmed in the faith, exactly as you were taught, abounding in it with thanksgiving" (vs 5-7).

1-John 2 and let's see *be walking in Him!* How does it tell us we're to be walking in Him?

1-John 2:3: "And by this *standard* we know that we know Him: if we keep His commandments. The one who says, 'I know Him' and does not keep His commandments, is a liar, and the Truth is not in him" (vs 3-4).

Is it not then foolish for the people and ministers in the Churches of God to go to Sunday-keeping churches, whose ministers are liars, and ask: How do you understand the Scriptures? *Just think on that for a minute!*

Verse 5: "On the other hand, *if* anyone is keeping His Word, **truly in this one the love of God is being perfected**...."

That's what God wants in our lives, that the love of God be perfected. That's why we're here. That's why we're doing what we're doing, so that

we can do—as we go back to the very first message that was given to the Church at Ephesus—that we don't lose our first love, that it is being perfected. And if it is, John says:

"...By this *means* we know we are in Him.... [we know that He is in us] ...Anyone who claims to dwell in Him **is obligating himself also to walk even as He Himself walked**" (vs 5-6).

Isn't that something? *That's how we're to do it!* That's how we're to live God's way. That's why where we started out that John was pleased when he heard *that they were walking in the Truth!* So, what Paul is writing about here in:

Colossians 2:6: "Therefore, as you have received Christ Jesus the Lord... [the whole Bible together] ...be walking in Him; [now notice] being rooted and built up in Him... [so you have roots that go down for stability, and you are being built up—your faith and love is being perfected] ...and being confirmed in the faith, exactly as you were taught, abounding in it with thanksgiving. **Be on guard so that no one takes you captive through philosophy and vain deceit, according to the traditions of men, according to the elements of the world,** and not according to Christ" (vs 6-8).

Look at all of these different doctrinal proposals that come along, and what do you see? *They are all designed and presented with persuasive speech!* They're all designed to lead you just a little away from Christ, and a little more, *and a little more, **and a little more!*** Satan knows that he can't get those who have the Holy Spirit of God to reject it instantly. So, he comes along with a program step-by-step-by-step to get rid of it. That's how he does it; that's how he accomplishes it.

Rev. 3—a little bit more about Laodiceanism. If that's the problem—which it is—and was it not philosophy brought by a Greek native professor, doctor of philosophy, which set the stage to take down one of the largest Churches of God in the history of the Churches of God? *Yes, indeed!*

Philosophy changes the nature of God, and if you believe that Jesus did not exist until He was conceived, *you are changing the nature of God!* What happens when you get into that state?

Revelation 3:16: "So then, because you are lukewarm, and *are* neither cold nor hot, I will spew you out of My mouth. For you say, 'I am rich, and have become wealthy',..." (vs 16-17).

This is the only Church that talks back to God! None of the others do that. 'God, how can You accuse me of this? Look all these blessings that we have.' *No!*

"'...and have need of nothing'; and you do

not understand that you are wretched, and miserable, and poor, and blind, and naked" (v 17).

How are you clothed *spiritually*? *He says He doesn't want you to be naked!* He gives us counsel. And this is what we need to do, brethren,

Verse 18: "I counsel you to buy from Me gold purified by fire so that you may be rich… [the true riches, like those in Smyrna had] …and white garments so that you may be clothed, and the shame of your nakedness may not be revealed; and to anoint your eyes with eye salve, so that you may see."

Now let's understand this.. In all of this, though it is pointing out the errors and the problems and the difficulties, this is not a matter of condemnation to put people down. This is a matter of an urgent message to wake people up, from the point of view that God is dealing with us. He says:

Verse 19: "**As many as I love, I rebuke and chasten. Therefore, be zealous and repent**."

When we have that repentance, how are we to implement it?

The Church at Philadelphia

Philadelphia is the key model. Everyone wants to be a Philadelphian. Not everyone can. But nevertheless, when we repent of these things, whether Laodiceans, or Sardisites, or Thyatira, or Pergamos, or Ephesus—whichever attitude we are in, which ever church in the world that there is today that we are in—*we can look at this as the model on how we need to behave ourselves and how we need to react to God!*

Revelation 3:8: "I know your works. Behold, I have set before you an open door, and no one has the power to shut it because you have a little strength… [God is holding it open] …and have kept My Word…"

There it is, as we read back there in the beginning in Deut. 8—which is also in Matt. 4 and Luke 4—'Man shall not live by bread alone but by every word that proceeds out of the mouth of God.'

"…kept My Word, and have not denied My name" (v 8).

When you bring in all of these false doctrines and things that we have covered, *you're denying the name of Christ!*

Verse 9: "Behold, I will make those of the synagogue of Satan…"

He's telling us here, *do not worry about the world or about the conspiracies that are out there,* which are all of Satan who is deceiving the world. *God is going to turn the tables on them!*

"…who proclaim themselves to be Jews and are not, but do lie. Behold, I will cause them to come and **worship before your feet, and to know that I have loved you**" (v 9).

Think about that for a minute. That's what God is going to do to the rich and the great of this world. *They're going to come and humble themselves before the feet of the resurrected children of God and acknowledge that we are of God,* and that they were of Satan. Now notice, here is a blessing and a promise which Christ has given:

Verse 10: "Because you have kept the Word of My patience… [God recognizes and understands what you do] …**I also will keep you from the time of temptation, which** *is* **about to come upon the whole world** to try those who dwell on the earth" *A great worldwide event that is coming, which is:*

- the antichrist
- the false prophet
- the mark of the beast

All of these things at the end time are coming! He is going to keep us and protect us. Exactly how He will do that, *God knows!* So, what we do is leave it in His hands to show us what to do. Trust in Him to watch over us.

Verse 11: "Behold, I am coming quickly; **hold fast that which you have so that no one may take away your crown**."

- don't lose what you have had
- heed the warnings here
- repent of the things that are wrong
- hear, give ear to the Spirit

Verse 12: "The one who overcomes… [which we can; we're victorious in Christ] …will I make a pillar in the temple of My God, and he shall not go out anymore; and I will write upon him the name of My God and the name of the city of My God, the New Jerusalem, which will come down out of heaven from My God; and *I will write upon him* My new name. **The one who has an ear, let him hear what the Spirit says to the churches**" (vs 12-13).

So, brethren, in our walk with God as we are coming closer and closer to the end, as we are reaching that time when the Kingdom of God is going to come on this earth, when we're reaching the time when we're going to graduate from this physical life and enter into the grave, and await the resurrection, *we need to heed the warnings and teachings of God and just ask God to be with His people*:

- *to forgive them*
- *to heal them*

- *to raise them up*
- *to help us all love God with all our heart, mind, soul and being*

Scriptures from *The Holy Bible in Its Original Order, A Faithful Version*

Scriptural References:

1) Leviticus 23:9-11, 15-16
2) Deuteronomy 2:7
3) Leviticus 26:2-3, 11-13
4) Deuteronomy 8:1-3
5) 2 John 4-6
6) 2 Corinthians 6:14-18
7) Psalm 86:11-16
8) Psalm 119:1-3
9) Psalm 138:1-2, 6-8
10) Revelation 1:8-13, 17-20
11) Revelation 2:1-4
12) Mark 12:28-31
13) Revelation 2:5, 7-16, 18-22
14) Psalm 86:1-7
15) Revelation 2:22-25, 29
16) Revelation 3:2-6
17) Colossians 2:1-7
18) I John 2:3-6
19) Colossians 2:6-8
20) Revelation 3:16-19
21) Revelation 3:8-13

Scriptures referenced, not quoted:

- Joshua 5
- Deuteronomy 16
- Exodus 16
- James 1
- Matthew 4
- Luke 4

FRC: ms
Transcription date unknown
Reformatted: bo—11/2020

CHAPTER THIRTY-SIX

The Marriage of the Lamb
(Day 49)
Fred R. Coulter

Greetings, brethren! This is Day 49 the day before Pentecost. As you know,

- every year we go through the Holy Days
- every year we learn a little bit more
- every year we try and understand some other aspects of the Holy Days

other aspects of God's Word in relationship to it so that we can grow in grace and knowledge and understand! Likewise with Pentecost we're going to do the same thing today, and then tomorrow.

It seems like the time has really flown since the Passover and Feast of Unleavened Bread. I hope that you've gone over the *Seven Church Harvest* {In-Depth Study with CD} because that goes through all of the Churches and shows **the spiritual harvest of God,** which we'll cover a little bit more tomorrow.

All of that is in preparation so that when we are preaching in season and out of season we're always relating everything to the way of God pointing to the Holy Days. I'm going to have some very good information for you concerning the Holy Days in the near future, which is really going to be. I think. very, very helpful in understanding so that we will be able to have:

- greater confidence in the Holy Days of God
- greater confidence in God's way
- greater confidence in what God is doing

That all adds to faith, love and hope, and then gives us a greater understanding, and that's what God wants us to have!

As we always do for the Holy Days, let's begin in Lev. 23 and continue the story and the flow of the Holy Days through the year as we are coming up to Pentecost. We know that this began with the Wave Sheaf Offering Day, because that is very significant. As a matter of fact, that is the whole key for everything coming down to Pentecost.

Leviticus 23:9: "And the LORD spoke to Moses, saying, 'Speak to the children of Israel and say to them, "When you have come into the land…"'" (vs 9-10).

Pentecost, with the grain harvest and everything, was not to happen until they came into

the land because as long as they were in the wilderness they didn't have any grain, they had manna, and that was their food. I'm sure that Pentecost was kept because the Ten Commandments were given on Pentecost, so Pentecost was kept even though they did not have the grain. When they got into the land we'll see what happened, what they did according to God's instruction here.

"…'When you have come into the land, which I give to you, and shall reap the harvest of it, then you shall bring *the premier* sheaf of the firstfruits of your harvest to the priest. And **he shall wave the sheaf before the LORD to be accepted for you. On the next day after the Sabbath the priest shall wave it**'" (vs 10-11).

This was the very first of the firstfruits, and that's what Christ is called. He is called the First of the firstfruits.

Now let me read to you out of *The Schocken Bible: The Five Books of Moses,* because he gives a little bit different description of it, which I think points more toward the resurrection than just the Wave Sheaf Offering as translated in the *King James Version.*

Verse 10 (*SB*) "Speak to the Children of Israel and say to them: When you enter the land that I am giving you, and you harvest its harvest, you are to bring **the premier sheaf**… [the most important] …of your harvest to the priest. He is to elevate the sheaf before the presence of [The LORD] YHWH, for acceptance for you" (vs 10-11).

Since Christ was the Firstfruit, Christ was the Firstborn, the Premier One is… Let's see where we have a fulfillment of this in describing Christ. Also, it includes us because Christ had to be first, because as Paul said that 'if Christ be not raised then you are dead in your sins, and your faith is empty and vain.' *Here* in Rom. 8 we have the fulfillment now of the firstfruits and also the firstborn! So, remember that the firstfruits and the firstborn are very connected in the plan of God.

Romans 8:28: "And we know that all things work together for good to those who love God, to those who are called according to *His* purpose."

I've seen that through the years over and over again. Everything works to good, *but we have to let it exercise us so we can understand how it is good for us,* in the trials and difficulties that we go through. But when you take a long perspective of it and you take and look back through the years you see how that everything works for good.

- God designed it that way
- God is involved in our lives
- God has called us
- God has given us of His Spirit
- God is leading us, guiding us
- God is bringing us to His Kingdom

We understand everything Christ went through all worked for good!

Verse 29: "Because those whom He did foreknow... [and He has foreknown us] ...He also predestinated *to be* conformed to the image of His own Son, that He... [the Son] ...might be *the* Firstborn among many brethren."

What we have in the harvest of the firstfruits is you have the premier sheaf, which is cut first. No other grain was to be harvested; no other things were to be eaten *until* that was cut. When that was cut, that is signifying being cut from the earth, meaning that it is *no longer earthly bound*; let's transfer that to Christ in a figure. Then the priest elevates it. Elevating is just like a resurrection. Remember when Jesus spoke to Mary Magdalene? *She came to hug Him, to hold Him, and He said*:

Don't touch Me, for I have not yet ascended to My Father. But go tell My brethren and your brethren that I ascend to My God and your God. (John 20).

So she did. Jesus immediately, right after that, ascended into heaven, was accepted of God the Father:

- as the sacrifice
- as the First of the firstborn
- as the First of the firstfruits
- as that Perfect Sacrifice to redeem all mankind

That was the start! **The Wave Sheaf Offering Day is a very important and key thing!**

Leviticus 23:11 (*SB*): "He is to elevate the sheaf before the presence of [the LORD] YHWH, for acceptance for you; on the morrow of the Sabbath... [that means on the morrow *after* the Sabbath] ...The priest is to elevate it."

This is the regular weekly Sabbath during the Feast of Unleavened Bread! When Passover falls on a Friday night and the Sabbath Day is the Passover Day, then that day becomes the Sabbath of the Unleavened Bread because *the Passover is also an unleavened bread day!*

Therefore, the first day right after that becomes the Wave Sheaf Offering Day. This year we didn't have that. This year we had the Passover in the middle of the week. We had the three days and three nights in the tomb, and we had the resurrection at the end of the Sabbath. Then we have Christ ascending on the Wave Sheaf Offering Day *on the morrow after the Sabbath to be accepted for us,* when He was accepted.

Verse 12 (*FV*): "And you shall offer that day when you wave the sheaf, a male lamb without blemish of the first year for a burnt offering to the LORD.... [this was also a type of Christ] ...And its grain offering *shall be* two tenth parts of fine flour mixed with oil, an offering made by fire to the LORD for a sweet savor. And the drink offering of it *shall be* of wine, the fourth *part* of a hin. And you shall eat neither bread, nor parched grain, nor green ears until the same day, until you have brought an offering to your God..." (vs 12-14).

Here's what we have: After they entered into the land, and after they had the very first Wave Sheaf Offering, from that time on then they could eat the old corn and the new corn. Of course, every year coming up to that time they could always eat the old corn coming up to the time of the Wave Sheaf Offering Day but they couldn't eat any of the new corn, or that is the new grain. They couldn't take it and dry it and parch it like it says here.

Verse 14: "And you shall eat neither bread, nor parched grain, nor green ears until the same day, until you have brought an offering to your God. *It shall be* a statute forever throughout your generations in all your dwellings."

Let's see how it was fulfilled when they came into the land. Now this becomes very important and this is one of those weeks where the weekly Sabbath was the Passover Day. Therefore, the first day of the Feast of Unleavened Bread being the first day of the week after the Passover Sabbath, became the Wave Sheaf Offering Day.

Joshua 5:10: "And the children of Israel camped in Gilgal and kept the Passover on the fourteenth day of the month at evening in the plains of Jericho. And they ate of the old grain of the land on the next day after the Passover, unleavened cakes and roasted *new* grain in the same day" (vs 10-11).

So, the morrow *after* the Passover was the 15th, and that was the Wave Sheaf Offering Day that year when they entered into the 'promised land'; therefore, they could eat of the old corn, which was the harvest that they got from conquering on the east side of the Jordan.

They had stores of grain, they had the new harvest already planted and grown ready to harvest. What they did, they took a premier sheaf right from the harvest that had been planted. The priest waved it before God, elevated it, and it was accepted on the morrow after the Sabbath, and the Sabbath being the Passover Day, and that's why this took place. Notice that they also ate unleavened bread with it.

Verse 12: "And the manna stopped on the next day after they had eaten the grain of the land. And there was no more manna for the children of Israel, but they ate the fruit of the land of Canaan that year." *So there it was fulfilled!* There was the command that God gave, and we saw it fulfilled.

Lev. 23 (*SB*)—again, I'm going to read from the Schocken version of the Bible—tells us how we are to count because counting is very important. There are still some people who believe in a Monday Pentecost. Unfortunately, there's no such thing as a Monday Pentecost, has never been and can't be, especially when you understand the counting.

Leviticus 23:15 (*SB*): "Now you are to number for yourselves, from the morrow... [that means *beginning with the morrow after the Sabbath*] ...of the Sabbath..."

The reason is because you have to count that first day, because Christ was accepted on that day. He ascended to the Father, and His ascension made Him accepted as the sacrifice for our sins. So, that day must be counted.

"...from the day that you bring the elevated sheaf, seven Sabbaths-of-days, whole (weeks) are they to be; **until the morrow of the seventh Sabbath you are to number—fifty days**, then you are to bring-near a grain-gift of new-crops to [the LORD] YHWH. From your settlements you are to bring bread as an elevation-offering, two (loaves of) two tenth-measures of flour are they to be, leavened you are to bake them, **as firstfruits to [the LORD] YHWH**" (vs 15-17).

Now let's go back and analyze these two verses just a little bit more.

1. you are to number beginning with the morrow after the Sabbath
2. from the day, that means including the day, that you bring the Wave Sheaf Offering
3. you are to have seven Sabbaths
4. whole weeks are they to be

This is very easy to figure out once you understand!

You start day one, which is the Wave Sheaf Offering Day, which is on a Sunday; in 7 days you come to Sabbath. Then you count seven Sabbaths, 1, 2, 3, 4, 5, 6, 7, that gives you 49 days. **"...until the morrow of the seventh Sabbath you are to number—fifty days..."**

If you went to Monday you would actually be numbering 51 days. So, this is 50 days. On the morrow of the 7th Sabbath you are to number 50 days, so that's:

5. to the morrow of the 7th Sabbath
6. number 50 days
7. you are to bring a grain offering of the new crop to the LORD

So, you've got those *seven steps* that you are to do.

This offering that was to come was the only meal offering, or bread offering where God required that leaven be put in it. Leaven was never in any of the other offerings. They were always unleavened. There's a reason for them being leavened and I'll let you come back tomorrow and find out what that reason is. I'll sort of leave you in suspended animation here. However, there's a distinct purpose in it.

Just understand that during the Feast of Unleavened Bread leaven is a picture of sin. On Pentecost leaven here pictures something entirely different. I used to say that it was that God accepted us even though we have *the law of sin and death* in us, which is a true statement. But I'll cover a little bit more of that tomorrow so we'll understand more about that.

Verse 18: "And you are to bring-near along with the bread seven sheep, wholly-sound, a year old..."

- What is the Church called? *The Church is called the flock of God! Sheep are of the flock!*
- Isn't it interesting that we have seven sheep?
- Are those a type of the seven churches in Revelation that we've covered already? *Could very well be!*

"...And one bull, a young of the herd, and rams, two, they shall be an offering-up for [the LORD] YHWH..." (v 18).

Exactly what all of these picture other than whole burnt offerings, complete dedication to God, that's what that shows.

"...With their grain-gift and their poured-offerings, a fire-offering of soothing savor to [the LORD] YHWH. And you are to perform-as-sacrifice: one hairy goat for a *hattat*... [atonement] ...and two sheep, a year old, for a slaughter-offering of *shalom*" (vs 18-19)—*a peace offering!* That is so you can have peace with God, sit down and eat with Him, as it were.

Verse 20: "The priest is to elevate them, together with the bread of the firstfruits as an elevation-offering before the presence of [the LORD] YHWH, together with the two sheep; they shall be a Holy-portion for [the LORD] YHWH, for the priest. And you are to make-proclamation on that same day…" (vs 20-21).

*You have the 50 days, **you have the same day!*** We don't go to the 51st day.

Tomorrow we will see, when we come to Acts 2, what it's talking about there, the very first verse talking about Pentecost means from the Greek, and I have written a booklet on it: *The True Meaning of Acts 2:1,* and we also have two other booklets on counting Pentecost:

1. *Count to Pentecost: From the Morrow After Which Sabbath?*
2. *How to Count Pentecost*

The Greek there has a very special construction which is called an articular present tense infinitive, meaning that *when the Day of Pentecost was being fulfilled,* or *when the 50th day was being fulfilled,* or accomplished, or being completed, not yet finished. That shows that you cannot move over to the 51st day. They didn't wait until the day after the 50th day, they did it on that day.

Now then let's look at some other things concerning Pentecost and how those fit into the meaning of it.

Now we also have a message with a chart, and it's called *From The Red Sea to Mt. Sinai*[transcriber's correction] It took the children of Israel 7 weeks to get from Egypt to Sinai: 7 weeks less 3 days.

Exodus 19:1: "In the third month when the children of Israel had gone forth out of the land of Egypt, **on the same day**…"—*the same day of the week!*

The Passover that Israel had in Egypt was in the middle of the week, on a Wednesday. So, Tuesday night is when they ate the Passover. Tuesday night is when the firstborn were killed, the death of the firstborn. Then Wednesday morning our time they got up and they gathered all the spoil of the Egyptians and assembled at Rameses and then that Wednesday night beginning the first day of the Feast of Unleavened Bread, The Night Much to be Observed—430 years after the promise given to Abraham—they departed from Rameses. *That is the same day of the week that they came into the wilderness of Sinai!*

Verse 3: "And Moses went up to God, and the LORD called to him out of the mountain, saying, 'Thus you shall say to the house of Jacob and tell the children of Israel, "You have seen what I did to the Egyptians, and *how* I bore you on eagles' wings and brought you unto Myself. Now, therefore, **if you will obey My voice indeed**…"'" (vs 3-5).

Brethren, I want to emphasize this again over and over and over again. ***The whole key is to obey the voice of God!***

Deuteronomy 8:3:"…man does not live by bread alone; but by every *word* that proceeds out of the mouth of the LORD does man live"

Here we have all the words that God has for us that He spoke or inspired, one of the two, and it's out of the mouth of the LORD. It's the key thing. Same thing you find with Abraham. Same thing you find with all of those who were the prophets of God. ***They obeyed the voice of God!***

Exodus 19:5: "…and keep My covenant…" *Not only do you have to obey the voice, but you have to keep the covenant!* That's for us today too in the same way.

"…and keep My covenant, then you shall be a special treasure to Me above all people; for all the earth *is* Mine. And you shall be to Me a kingdom of priests and a Holy nation." These *are* the words which you shall speak to the children of Israel.' And Moses came and called for the elders of the people, and laid before them all these words, which the LORD commanded him. And all the people answered together and said, 'All that the LORD has spoken we will do.' And Moses returned the words of the people to the LORD" (vs 5-8).

How was Israel going to be a peculiar nation, a kingdom of priests? *Let's see what they were supposed to do!* Again, we have the same thing all the way through the Bible, ***obeying the voice of God!***

Deuteronomy 4:1: "And now, O Israel, hearken to the statutes and to the judgments, which I teach you, in order to do them, so that you may live and go in and possess the land, which the LORD God of your fathers gives *to* you. You shall not add to the word, which I command you; neither shall you take away from it, so that you may keep the commandments of the LORD your God, which I command you" (vs 1-2).

Now just to make a point, and we covered this on the *Seven Church Harvest* #3 concerning Baalim.

Verse 3: "Your eyes have seen what the LORD did because of Baal Peor…'

That's what the Moabites came in and enticed the Israelites to come and do sacrifice to their gods. That was under the instruction of Baalim to Balak to do so.

"…For the LORD your God has destroyed from among you all the men that followed Baal Peor" (v 3).

God wants you to learn. Don't go do what the others did. Don't go out and bring something from the world and bring it in and try and make it a part of God's way. The same thing applies today. We're not to do that.

Verse 4: "And you who held fast to the LORD your God *are* alive, every one of you, this day. Behold, I have taught you statutes and judgments, even as the LORD my God commanded me, so that you should do so in the land where you go to possess it" (vs 4-5).

Now here's how they were to be a kingdom of priests and a Holy nation:

Verse 6: "And **you shall keep and do** *them*, for this is your wisdom and your understanding in the sight of the nations, which shall hear all these statutes and say, 'Surely this great nation *is* a wise and understanding people.' For what nation is so great whose God *is* so near to them, as the LORD our God *is*, whenever we call upon Him? And what great nation has statutes and judgments that *are so* righteous as all this Law, **which I set before you today?**" (vs 6-8). *That's why no one can improve upon God's way!*

Now **IF** the Word of God needs to be changed *God will change it!* He did so in the New Covenant *when Christ made all the laws more spiritually binding, raised them to a higher level of obedience* than we've had in the past. We need to understand this concerning law-keeping and grace under the New Covenant:

- because we have the Laws of God written in our heart and mind through the power of God's Holy Spirit
- because we stand in the grace of God

When we keep the commandments today, we are doing so as an operation of grace, because we do it from the heart filled with the Holy Spirit. That's something you need to understand because a lot of Protestants will tell you that what you do is to keep the Law and the Law is against grace. *No such thing!* The Law is there to:

- show us
- teach us
- lead us
- guide us

If we sin, the Law is there to convict us of sin! When we repent through the operation of grace then we're restored to God!

Now. for the children of Israel, they were to do this for the whole world, and needless to say, they failed. But God said never the less, that's what He wanted.

Let's come back here to Exo. 19 and continue on with the rest of the account leading up to the day of Pentecost when the Ten Commandments were given. And that's something very important to really understand.

Exodus 19:10: "And the LORD said to Moses, 'Go to the people and sanctify them today and tomorrow, and let them wash their clothes. And be ready for the third day…" (vs 10-11).

So, you have Friday, Sabbath and Sunday; Sunday is the third day. What did they do? *They washed their clothes on Friday and got all prepared!* They kept the Sabbath because that sanctified them, and then God came down the third day and brought the Ten Commandments.

Now let's see how that went, v 14: "And Moses went down from the mountain to the people and sanctified the people. And they washed their clothes. And he said to the people, 'Be ready for the third day. Do not approach a woman.' And it came to pass on the third day in the morning…" (vs 15-16).

We're going to see there are parallels between this and Acts 2 when we come to Acts 2 tomorrow, because it was in the morning that the events took place in Acts 2. Same way here. How would you like to wake up to this?

"…that there *were* thunders and lightnings, and a thick cloud upon the mountain. And the sound of the trumpet…" (v 16).

There's something to understand. The trumpet is always blown on *every* Holy Day. The Feast of Trumpets is *a memorial of blowing of trumpets all day long!* That's why it's called the Feast of Trumpets.

"…was exceedingly loud… [here it is the trumpet] …so that all the people in the camp trembled. And Moses brought the people out of the camp to meet with God…. [what an absolutely awesome thing that must have been] …And they stood at the base of the mountain. And Mount Sinai was smoking, all of it because the LORD came down upon it in fire. And the smoke of it went up like the smoke of a furnace, and the whole mountain quaked greatly" (vs 16-18).

Imagine this whole thing just all of the sound of the thunder and the lightning—recorded in Heb. 12—and the wind that was with it, and the earth quaking. If there's one thing that really puts fear into people, that's to have the ground beneath them shaking. That's exactly what was happening here.

We live in California and we know what that's like. Those of you back in the Midwest and

East have tornadoes, and you know what that's like. You can get afraid of that, do it's the same thing.

Verse 19: "And when the sound of the trumpet sounded long, and became very strong, Moses spoke, and God answered him by voice. And the LORD came down upon Mount Sinai on the top of the mountain. And the LORD called Moses to the top of the mountain, and Moses went up. And the LORD said to Moses, 'Go down. Command the people, lest they break through unto the LORD **to gaze, and many of them perish**" (vs 19-21).

You can't look upon the glorified form of God as a physical human being and live. That's what God told Moses when he said, 'I beseech thee, shew me thy glory.' God said, 'You cannot see My face, for there shall no man see me and live." God in His glory living eternally in spiritually has that power just radiating from His very body. This is what happened here. He says, "…**to gaze, and many of them perish**."

Verse 22: "And let the priests also, who come near to the LORD, sanctify themselves, lest the LORD break forth upon them.' And Moses said to the LORD, 'The people cannot come up to Mount Sinai, for You commanded us, saying, "Set bounds around the mountain, and sanctify it."' And the LORD said to him, 'Away! Get you down, and *only* you shall come up, you and Aaron with you. But do not let the priests and the people break through to come up to the LORD, lest He break forth upon them.' And Moses went down to the people, and spoke to them" (vs 22-25).

Then God gave the Ten Commandments. You know what they are, we've gone over these many, many times. But let's understand something very important here in relationship to Pentecost and the Sabbath. God gave the Ten Commandments on the Day of Pentecost, which is a Holy Day. God pronounced that the Sabbath was *to be remembered and to be kept* so there is no excuse by any Sunday-keeper to claim because the New Testament Church began on Pentecost that the first day of the week is the day that God wanted to keep instead of the seventh day. Not so. *IF* you:

- accept Pentecost
- accept the commandments of God
- accept the Sabbath of God
- accept the words of God

God spoke all those words! It was too much for the people to bear:

Exodus 20:18: "And all the people saw the thunderings, and the lightnings, and the sound of the trumpet, and the mountain smoking. And when the people saw, they trembled and stood afar off. And they said to Moses, '**You speak with us, and we will hear. But let not God speak with us, lest we die'**" (vs 18-19).

What did that do? *That gave them one person removed from God so they could say, 'Moses said…'* instead of *'God said…'* Remember that *everything Moses said was what God said he was to say!*

This was a carnal excuse showing that *the carnal mind is not subject to the Law of God neither indeed can be; that it cannot hear the Laws of God!* That's the whole lesson here with this. That's why when you go to Deut. 18 God said *He would send Jesus Christ to come in the flesh to speak to them as a man* rather than speak to them as God. To speak to them with words that they could hear and understand rather than speaking with such great power and force that you are so afraid that there was hardly anything you could remember. Yet, *they rejected Christ!* That's the way that the carnal mind is.

Let's see some things that are important concerning this. Moses went back up on the mount. God gave him all the statutes and judgments. Let's understand something that's very important: *On the very day that God gave the Ten Commandments He also gave the Holy Days.* Do you realize that?

Exodus 23:12: "Six days you shall do your work, and on the seventh day you shall rest, so that your ox and your donkey may rest, and the son of your handmaid, and the stranger, may be rejuvenated. And be watchful in all that I have said to you. And make no mention of the name of other gods, neither let it be heard out of your mouth" (vs 12-13).

This precludes anything concerning Christmas, Easter, New Years, and any of the pagan holidays that any of the nations had, and they go right back to the very same thing that we see in the world today. God said don't even mention it. That is in the way that that is something that you would do. Yet, look what happened to the Worldwide Church of God:

- totally taken down
- totally subverted
- totally back into the world

they have
- forgotten the words of God
- forgotten the commandments of God
- had every lying excuse under the sun
  - ✓ to get rid of the Sabbath
  - ✓ to get rid of the Holy Days

and to embrace Sunday, and Christmas, and Easter, and all of that!

Now you understand why God puts these warnings in here over and over again. *Perhaps taking up as much as one third of the whole Bible to tell you to beware to don't do the things that the pagans do!* Yet, some people never get it. They never get it.

Verse 14. "You shall keep a Feast unto Me three times in the year. You shall keep the Feast of Unleavened Bread. You shall eat unleavened bread seven days, as I commanded you, at the time appointed in the month *of* Abib, for in it you came out of Egypt. And no one shall appear before Me empty. Also, the Feast of the Harvest of the Firstfruits of your labors, which you have sown in the field. And the Feast of Ingathering, in the end of the year, when you have gathered in your labors out of the field. Three times in the year all your males shall appear before the Lord GOD" (vs 14-17).

There it is right there. On the same day that God gave the Ten Commandments with the Sabbath; He also gave the Holy Days.

IF you accept one then you have to accept all, because *IF you do not accept all* *you are diminishing from it!* When you diminish from it the natural proclivity to do is add to it. That's what the children of Israel did. That's their whole history.

Exo. 24 is where the covenant was made. Here is the marriage covenant between the Lord GOD Who became Jesus Christ for the New Testament. This is the marriage covenant between the Lord GOD and Israel that took place. The Old Covenant was a marriage covenant.

Exodus 24:1: "And He said to Moses, 'Come up to the LORD, you and Aaron, Nadab, and Abihu, and seventy of the elders of Israel, and worship afar off…. [we will see why all of them came up] …And Moses alone shall come near the LORD, but they shall not come near. Neither shall the people go up with him.' And Moses came and told the people all the words of the LORD, and all the judgments. And all the people answered with one voice and said, **'All the words which the LORD has said, we will do'**" (vs 1-3). *When there is a marriage you ask*:

> For the wife: According to the covenant do you accept? Do you promise to love and obey to submit to your husband in all things as unto the LORD, whether in sickness or in health, whether in want or in wealth?

> It's the same way with the man: Do you promise and covenant with God to faithfully love your wife, to cleave to her, to cherish her, to honor her, to provide for her? And he says, 'Yes I do.'

That is a marriage covenant! That's what this is. These words are the words that God said, 'that you should be Mine.'

Verse 4: "And Moses wrote all the words of the LORD…" *God always has His covenants written down!* That is the record! That's why we have the new Covenant written down. That is the record.

"…and rose up early in the morning, and built an altar at the base of the mountain and twelve pillars according to the twelve tribes of Israel. And he sent young men of the children of Israel who offered burnt offerings, and sacrificed peace offerings of bullocks to the LORD" (vs 4-5).

The reason he took young men—these may have been Levites—but the Levitical priesthood was not yet consecrated. Therefore, he took the young men, and I'm sure they were Levites.

Notice what happens next, because there is no covenant that is made without blood. And without the shedding of blood there is no covenant.

Verse 6: "And Moses took half of the blood, and put *it* in basins, and half of the blood he sprinkled on the altar. And he took the Book of the Covenant, and read in the ears of the people. And they said, 'All that the LORD has said we will do, and be obedient.' And Moses took the blood and sprinkled *it* on the people, and said, 'Behold the blood of the covenant, which the LORD has made with you concerning all these words'" (vs 6-8).

Notice that this covenant was made on the day *after* Pentecost. We will see tomorrow that is significant in relationship to the eternal covenant that God is going to make with the Church when the Church is resurrected.

Verse 9: "And Moses went up, and Aaron, Nadab, and Abihu, and seventy of the elders of Israel. And they saw the God of Israel. And *there was* under **His feet as it were a paved work of a sapphire stone, and as it were the heavens in clearness**" (vs 9-10). *This is called in the New Testament* **the Sea of Glass!**

Whenever God comes down and is in a particular place, if He's there for any length of time then there is the Sea of Glass. Now this Sea of Glass was also so that the people could not see up in toward God. But the elders who were right up close could see up into it, but the people couldn't. This was to establish the fact for all the people who the 70 elders represented that *they saw God and that this covenant was sure and that it was true!*

Verse 11: "And upon the nobles of the children of Israel He did not lay his hands. Also they saw God, and ate and drank."

What did they have? *They had a wedding feast!* In this particular case, since God was dealing with carnal human beings He could not come down and eat with them directly. This wedding feast then had the:

- representatives of Israel being the 70 elders,
- representatives of the priesthood being Aaron, Nadab, and Abihu,
- representative of the high priest being Moses, who was a type of Christ

He was the One Who went to the Father. He was the One Who became Jesus Christ!

Verse 12: "And the LORD said to Moses, 'Come up to Me in the mountain, and be there. And I will give you tablets of stone, and the law, and commandments which I have written, so that you may teach them.' And Moses rose up, and his attendant Joshua. And Moses went up into the mountain of God. And he said to the elders, 'You wait here for us until we come again to you. And behold, Aaron and Hur *are* with you. If any man has a cause, let him come to them.' And Moses went up into the mountain, and a cloud covered the mountain. And the glory of the LORD abode upon Mount Sinai, and the cloud covered it six days. And the seventh day He called to Moses out of the midst of the cloud" (vs 12-16).

Moses had to wait seven days. I'm sure after Nadab, Abihu, and Aaron and the 70 of elders had finished eating, they went back down to be with the rest of the children of Israel. Moses went up into the mount.

Verse 17: "And the sight of the glory of the LORD *was* like a consuming fire on the top of the mountain to the eyes of the children of Israel. And Moses went into the midst of the cloud, and went up into the mountain. And **Moses was in the mountain forty days and forty nights**" (vs. 17-18).

We won't get into much of the rest of the story that took place there lest we get away from understanding about the Day of Pentecost. I'm covering it in the Old Testament today on Day 49 so that will lead us up to the New Testament tomorrow.

Now let's look and see that this was a marriage. Isa. 54 tells us very clearly that what happened there with the covenant that was made. *It was a marriage covenant on the day after Pentecost* with the blood of the covenant that was sprinkled on the people; that was sprinkled on the altar. Moses read all the words that God commanded them to do, and they said, 'Yes we will do that.' We find it talks about *Israel being the wife* of the LORD.

Isaiah 54:5: "For **your Maker *is* your husband**…"

This is not only is talking about Israel, because Israel was married to God, but in this particular case this is also a prophecy of the New Testament Church.

"…the LORD of hosts is His name; and your Redeemer *is* the Holy One of Israel; the God of the whole earth shall He be called, for the LORD has called you as a woman forsaken and grieved in spirit… [that is while they were down in Egypt] …and a wife of youth, when you were rejected,' says your God" (vs 5-6).

Israel refused even though they said yes, their whole action said 'we refuse.'

- that's why God had to divorce them
- that's why God had to put them away.
- that's why God had to leave them and forsake them

because they left God and forsook God for other gods and broke the covenant! We need to understand that concerning the covenant with Jesus Christ, because *it is His body* that is broken for us. It is *His blood* that is shed for us, and *that is the blood of the New Covenant!*

Now let's understand the children of Israel, they broke the covenant. They were punished for it. But *IF* we break the covenant—the covenant with Christ, the covenant unto eternal life—*THEN* we have nothing to look forward to but eternal death.

You either will love God and keep His commandments, accept Jesus Christ, or you will be in the Lake of Fire. Some people may even get mad at me for saying that. But let's understand something, *you either*:

- follow Christ
- obey Him
- love God the Father
- keep all of His commandments

or

- you have the Lake of Fire to look forward to

Under Moses they were stoned. But when you do despite to the Spirit of grace *you are cast into the Lake of Fire and you are eternally dead!* There's no resurrection from that.

Now let's come to the New Testament. Matt. 13 is a very important chapter, because this shows that *what Christ was working out from the time He came until the end of the age is likened unto a harvest!* That's why Pentecost is *the harvest of the firstfruits* beginning with the first one, the Wave Sheaf Offering or the Premier Sheaf was accepted of God. *Christ was the first!* The rest of it is what He is doing. It is a harvest! It is a planting! That's what God is doing.

Now we need to understand these parables here:

Matthew 13:18 *showing the harvest*: "Therefore, hear the parable of the sower… [now the sower was Christ] …When anyone hears the Word of the Kingdom and does not understand *it*, **the wicked one comes and snatches away that which was sown in his heart**…."

That is something we need to understand. Brethren, ***don't let Satan come and take that away which was sown in your heart!*** We have seen somewhere that has happened to, and I'm afraid that there are going to be great problems.

"…This is the one who was sown by the way. Now, the one who was sown upon the rocky places is the one who hears the Word and immediately receives it with joy; but *because* he has no root in himself, *he* does not endure; for when tribulation or persecution arises because of the Word, **he is quickly offended**" (vs 19-21).

We can't let that happen to us either. We've also seen that take place, haven't we? That's why ***all things work together for good for those who love God and are called according to His purpose!***

Verse 22: "And the one who was sown…" *So this is a planting!* We'll see when the harvest takes place, because there's another aspect of it that we have to understand here.

"…among the thorns is the one who hears the Word, but the cares of this life and the deceitfulness of riches choke the Word, and it becomes unfruitful" (v 22).

Now then, remember the parable of the rich man who came to Christ and said, 'Good Master, what good *thing* shall I do, that I may have eternal life?' Jesus said, 'Keep the commandments.' The rich man asked, 'Which?' So, Jesus listed off all the commandments having to do with loving your neighbor. Of course, they were living in a land where:

- they were keeping the Sabbath; that was not the issue
- they were keeping the Holy Days; that was not the issue
- they had the right God; that was not the issue
- they had no idols there; that was not the issue

So that's why Jesus didn't mention the first four commandments in that account in Matt. 19!

Verse 23: "But the one who was sown on good ground…" *as compared to the others!*

The rich man went away very sorrowful because he had many riches. Typical example of the one where the seed is sown among the thorns and the weeds; the cares of the world, the deceitfulness of riches.

"…this is the one who hears the Word and understands, who indeed brings forth fruit and produces—one a hundredfold, another sixtyfold *and* another thirtyfold" (v 23).

Then He gave another parable; v 24: And He put another parable before them, saying, 'The Kingdom of Heaven is compared to a man who was sowing good seed in his field; but while men were sleeping, his enemy came and sowed tares among the wheat, and went away" (vs 24-25)—*and the tares and the wheat grew up together!*

Verse 27: "And the servants came to the master of the house *and* said to him 'Sir, did you not sow good seed in your field? Then where did these tares come from?'"

We've seen the same thing, too. We've lived through that, haven't we? The enemy Satan the devil infiltrates the Church and what do we have? *We have tares! We have false doctrine!* Right alongside those who are producing the good!

Christ said, 'No, don't tear them up, *but you wait until the harvest.' Pentecost is the harvest!*

Verse 37: "And He answered *and* said to them, 'The One Who sows the good seed is the Son of man; and the field is the world; and the good seed, these are the children of the Kingdom; but the tares are the children of the wicked *one*" (vs 37-38).

As we find in 1-John, they are the ones who are practicing lawlessness. I tell you that is something, *the mystery of lawlessness **or** the mystery of iniquity* is really an awesome thing indeed.

Verse 39: "Now, the enemy who sowed them is the devil; and the harvest is *the* end of the age, and the reapers are the angels…. [we'll see this takes place concerning the resurrection] …Therefore, as the tares are gathered and consumed in the fire, so shall it be in the end of this age" (vs 39-40). *We're going to see when this age ends.*

Verse 41: "The Son of man shall send forth His angels, and they shall gather out of His Kingdom all the offenders and those who are practicing lawlessness; and they shall cast them into the furnace of fire; there shall be weeping and gnashing of teeth. Then shall the righteous shine forth as the sun in the Kingdom of their Father. **The one who has ears to hear, let him hear**" (vs 41-43). *We'll see that's very important when we come to the harvest that God has!*

Now then, there are seven weeks to the harvest. This Sabbath ended the seventh week to the harvest. Then there was the 50th day offering that took place. We have seven churches, and I think that the seven churches represent, not necessarily just in time sequence, but represent in type *the seven weeks to the harvest!* That is the Church age and the Church harvest; they will be in the first resurrection.

There will be more in the first resurrection, which we will see, and we will cover that tomorrow because there is also *the 50th day harvest, which then is the harvest of God. So, the seven churches represent the 49-day harvest!*

Now let's come back to Matt. 22 because we're going to ask the question, and we will try and answer it tomorrow: Will everyone in the first resurrection be the Bride of Christ? *We've thought in the past, yes that is so,* but let's read the parable here in:

Matthew 22:1—*there's a lot for us to learn right here*: "And again Jesus answered and spoke to them in parables, saying, 'The Kingdom of Heaven is compared to a man *who was* a king, who made a wedding feast for his son… [now the king is God the Father, the son is Christ] …and sent his servants… [which then began with the apostles and whoever the true servants of God are] …to call those who had been invited to the wedding feast; but they refused to come…. [these are the guests] …Afterwards he sent out other servants, saying "Say to those who have been invited, 'Behold, I have prepared my dinner; my oxen and the fatted beasts are killed, and all things *are* ready. Come to the wedding feast'"'" (vs 1-4)—*there was going to be a marriage supper.*

We saw there was a marriage supper with the first covenant with Moses, and Aaron, and Nadab, and Abihu, and the 70 elders of Israel. They did eat and drink. That was the marriage supper. So, here's the supper all ready to go.

Verse 5: "But they paid no attention and went away, one to his farm, and another to his business. And the rest, after seizing his servants, insulted and killed *them*. Now, when the king heard *it*, he became angry; and he sent his armies *and* destroyed those murderers, and burned up their city. Then he said to his servants, 'The wedding feast indeed is ready… [so there's going to be a time when the wedding is going to be ready] …but those who were invited were not worthy; therefore, go into the well-traveled highways, and invite all that you find to the wedding feast.' And after going out into the highways, those servants brought together everyone that they found, both good and evil; and the wedding feast was filled with guests" (vs 5-10).

- there is going to be God the Father, Who is the King and is going to perform the ceremony
- there's going to be Christ
- there is going to be the Bride.
- there are going to be guests

All of them will be there for this event!

Is this telling us that not everyone in the first resurrection will be part of the Bride of Christ? *Perhaps it is!*

Verse 11: "And when the king came in to see the guests, *he* noticed a man there who was not dressed in *proper* attire for *the* wedding feast; and he said to him, 'Friend, how did you enter here without a garment *fit* for *the* wedding feast?' But he had no answer. Then the king said to the servants, 'Bind his hands and feet, *and* take him away, and cast *him* into the outer darkness.' There shall be weeping and gnashing of teeth" (vs 11-13).

In this parable it can't be shown about the resurrection because this is showing about the wedding. In other words, *no one is going to get there unless they have the wedding garments!* They won't get there because they'll have to be in the first resurrection. If they're not in the first resurrection then they rejected the call, and they didn't do what God wanted to do, then sure enough they will be cast out into outer darkness, and there will be weeping and gnashing of teeth.

Verse 14: "**For many are called, but few are chosen.**"

Let's look at the parallel account in Luke 14, and I think this is quite profound when we put the whole chapter of Luke 14 together and see the things as they took place.

Luke 14:15: "Then one of those who sat *at the table* with *Him*, after hearing these things, said to Him, 'Blessed *is* the one who shall eat bread in the Kingdom of God.' But He said to him, 'A certain man made a great supper, and invited many. And he sent his servants at suppertime to say to those who had been invited, "Come, for everything is now ready." But everyone with one *consent* began to excuse himself. The first said to him, "I have bought a field, and I need to go out to see it; I beg you to have me excused." And another said, "I have bought five pairs of oxen, and I am going to try them out; I beg you to have me excused." And another said, "I have married a wife, and because of this I am unable to come"'" (vs 15-20).

All of these are good and valid excuses, aren't they? I mean, in the modern work-a-day place that we live in today. But that has nothing to do with valid excuses for obeying God. *You've been given the invitation!* Are you going to come? *Well, we'll see!*

Verse 21: "And that servant came and reported these things to his lord. Then the master of the house was angry; *and* he said to his servant, 'Go out quickly into the streets and lanes of the city, and bring in here the poor, *the* crippled, *the* lame and *the* blind.' And the servant said, 'Sir, it has been done as you commanded, and there is still room.' Then the lord said to the servant, 'Go out into the highways and hedges, and compel *them* to come in, so that my house may be filled'" (vs 21-23). *God is going to accomplish His work!*

- there is going to be the wedding
- there will be Christ
- there will be the Bride
- there will be the guests

Verse 24: "For I tell you, not one of those men who were invited shall taste of my supper.'"

Notice that this ties in with the other parable where *many are called but few are chosen,* and here is why only few are chosen: *because few repent!* Few repent with this kind of attitude.

What you need to do when we read these Scriptures, you apply them to yourself and I'll apply them to myself, because this is the qualification for the wedding invitation:

Verse 25: "And great multitudes were going with Him; and He turned *and* said to them, 'If anyone comes to Me and does not hate his father and mother, and wife, and children, and brothers and sisters, and, in addition, his own life also, he cannot be My disciple'" (vs 25-26)—*and you cannot be in the first resurrection,* whether you're called to be part of the Bride or whether you're called to be a guest.

- Have we done that?
- Do we continue to do that?
- Have we set our minds that we are going to always do that?
   - ✓ that we will be faithful
   - ✓ that we will be loving
   - ✓ that we will be obedient to God in all circumstances
   - ✓ that we have this set before us
- that's all a part of counting the cost
- that's what we did when we were baptized
- that's what we continually do as we go down through the walk that we have with God in
   - ✓ walking in the truth
   - ✓ walking in the light
   - ✓ serving God in the way that we do

Verse 27: "And whoever does not carry his cross and come after Me **cannot** be My disciple." *The Greek there is the very strongest:* 'un dunatai'— *it is impossible to be His disciple.*

If you're not His disciple, you won't be in the first resurrection and you won't be in the resurrection for guests, or as the Bride either one.

Now let's carry this a little bit further, we'll see a parallel between Mt. Sinai and Mt. Sion in heaven above (Heb. 12), showing what is going to happen to those who will be, in what is called the Church of the Firstborn. *That is us!*

- we are the firstfruits
- Christ is the First of the firstfruits
- Christ is the Firstborn of the firstborn
- we are going to be part of the Church of the Firstborn

Let's read that in Heb. 12, and notice how it starts out, how that it is Christ that we need to look to. Brethren, we need to really understand that. We don't know what the days are going to be. We don't know what the times are going to be. We don't know exactly when these things are going to come, but I'll guarantee you according to the Word of God that we are a whole lot closer to the end than when we first believed. You can guarantee that.

Here's a whole example, Hebrews 12:1: "Therefore, *since* we are surrounded by such a great throng of witnesses, let us lay aside every weight…" *That's what we need to do brethren!*

- every care
- every problem
- every weight
- everything that is dragging us down

"…**the sin that so easily entraps *us***…" (v 1).

- yes we're weak in the flesh
- yes we have the law of sin and death in us
- yes these things come upon us

But they can be set aside through Christ!

"…*and* let us run the race set before us with endurance…" (v 1).

Today too many people have slowed down to a walk. They aren't even trotting, and many of them are just sitting along the sidelines. They aren't even participating in anything. *They've just given up!*

The way that you continue in this way is this, v 2. "**Having *our* minds fixed on Jesus, the Beginner and Finisher of *our* faith**…" *We always need to look to Christ because*:

- He's the head of the Church
- He's the One Who set us an example
- He is the One Who is our Savior

- He is the One Who is our sacrifice
- it is His blood that pays for our sins
- it is His sitting at the right hand of God

so that we are justified, that we have the grace of God given to us!

"…Who for the joy that lay ahead of Him… [look how He counted the trial that He went through] …endured *the* cross, *although* He despised *the* shame, and has sat down at *the* right hand of the Throne of God. Now meditate deeply on Him Who endured such great hostility of sinners against Himself so that you **do not become weary and faint in your minds**" (vs 2-3). *I put a little note to myself in my Bible*: ***and give up!***

Brethren, we are not to give up! We are not to let these things slip away from us. We are not to let these things fall into disrepair because of neglect and disuse. We have to do as it says here:

Verse 4: "You have not yet resisted to the point of *losing* blood in your struggle against sin"—*no, you haven't!* Yes, we're going to have correction.

Verse 6: "for whom *the* Lord loves He chastens, and He severely disciplines every son whom He receives." *He chastens*:

- so that we can be better
- so that we can grow
- so that we can bring forth more fruit

Now let's see what all of this is going to do:

Verse 14. "Pursue peace with everyone, and Holiness, without which no one will see the Lord; looking diligently, **lest anyone fall from the grace of God**…" (vs 14-15).

People can fall from the grace of God. *It is an absolute lie to say* 'once saved, always saved,' that once you have been saved you have eternal security and regardless of what you do you cannot fall away. *That is a blatant lie* because it says right here:

"…lest anyone fall from the grace of God; **lest any root of bitterness springing up trouble you, and through this**… [and when that happens]: …**many be defiled**; lest *there* be any fornicator or godless person, as Esau, who for one meal sold his birthright; because you also know that afterwards, when he wished to inherit the blessing, he was rejected; *and* he found no room for repentance, although he sought it earnestly with tears" (vs 15-17).

Notice what Paul does here. He immediately shifts this right over into the spiritual reality of our existence in standing before Christ:

Verse 18: "For you have not come to *the* mount that could be touched and that burned with fire, nor to gloominess, and fearful darkness, and *the* whirlwind; and to *the* sound of *the* trumpet, and to *the* voice of *the* words, which those who heard, *begged* that *the* word not be spoken *directly* to them" (vs 18-19)—*which we read in Exo. 19 & 20; we haven't come to that mount!*

Verse 20: "(For they could not endure what was being commanded: 'And if even an animal touches the mountain, it shall be stoned, or shot through with an arrow'; and so terrifying was the sight *that* Moses said, 'I am greatly afraid and trembling')" (vs 20-21). *With this setting the tone, notice what Paul says*:

Verse 22: "But you have come to Mount Sion, **and to *the* city of *the* living God, heavenly Jerusalem**; and to an innumerable company of angels; *to the* joyous festival gathering; **and to *the* Church of *the* Firstborn**…" (vs 22-23).

That's where we have come to. You are part of the Church of the Firstborn. You are part of that general assembly:

"…**registered *in the* Book *of* Life in heaven**…" (v 23)—*your name is in the Book of Life, and only you can take it out!*

"…and to God, *the* Judge of all, and to *the* spirits of the just who have been perfected" (v 23). *This is quite a thing, brethren*:

- to be counted in this group
- to be of this part
- to be of this harvest
- to be there
- to be able to be on Mt. Sion with Christ

Verse 24: "And to Jesus, *the* Mediator of *the* New Covenant; and to sprinkling of *the* blood of *ratification*, proclaiming superior things than *that of* Abel." *I tell you it's really quite a thing!*

Then Paul gives a warning; v 25: "Beware that you do not refuse to *hear* Him Who is speaking! For if they did not escape *judgment*, who refused *to hear* the One Who was on the earth Divinely instructing *them*, how much more *severely will we be judged*, if we ourselves apostatize from Him Who speaks from heaven."

I tell you, that's something! The resurrection is going to be something. It is going to be a powerful thing that is going to take place.

Verse 26: "Whose voice then shook the earth, but now He has promised, saying, 'Yet, **once more** I will shake not only the earth, but heaven also.'" *We find back in Haggai 3,* and the sea and the dry land, all of it.

So the return of Jesus Christ is going to be absolutely tremendous.

Verse 27: "Now the *words* 'once more' signify the removing of the *things* being shaken, as of things that were made, so that those *things,* which cannot be shaken may remain." *And that's us!*

Verse 28: "Therefore, since we are receiving a kingdom that cannot be shaken, let us have grace, through which we may serve God in a pleasing *manner* with reverence and awe; for our God *is* indeed a consuming fire" (vs 28-29). *We are going to meet Him at the resurrection!*

Now let's answer the question here concerning the guests:

Revelation 19:1: "And after these things... [this is after the resurrection and we'll see this is after being on the Sea of Glass] ...I heard *the* loud voice of a great multitude in heaven..."

They're in heaven—the first heaven—where the Sea of Glass is, because we meet Christ in the air. That's not in the heaven of heavens where God's Throne is. *That is in the heavens where those who are resurrected meet Christ in the air on the Sea of Glass!*

"...saying, 'Hallelujah! The salvation and the glory and the honor and the power *belong* to the Lord our God. For true and righteous *are* His judgments; for He has judged the great whore, who corrupted the earth with her fornication, and He has avenged the blood of His servants at her hand.' And they said a second time, 'Hallelujah! And her smoke shall ascend upward into the ages of eternity.' And the twenty-four elders and the four living creatures fell down and worshiped God, Who sits on the throne, saying, 'Amen. Hallelujah!'" (vs 1-4).

Verse 5: "And a voice came forth from the Throne, saying, 'Praise our God, all His servants, and all who fear Him, both small and great.' And I heard a voice like that of a great multitude, and like *the* sound of many waters, and *the* sound of mighty thunderings, saying, 'Hallelujah! For *the* Lord God Almighty has reigned. Let us be glad and shout with joy; and let us give glory to Him; **for the marriage of the Lamb has come, and His wife has made herself ready**'" (vs 5-7).

Verse 8: "And it was granted to her that she should be clothed in fine linen, pure and bright; for the fine linen is the righteousness of the saints. And he said to me, **'Write: Blessed *are* those who are called to the marriage supper of the Lamb'** (vs 5-9).

So all of those who are called to the marriage supper, all of those who are called to the wedding *have a great and a fantastic blessing from God.*

The Bride and Christ, when they are married, they will be in a special relationship forever! And we will see that tomorrow. So as Paul Harvey says, tune in for the rest of the story.

Scriptures from *The Holy Bible in Its Original Order, A Faithful Version* (except where noted)

Scriptural References

1) Leviticus 23:9-11
2) Romans 8:28-29
3) Leviticus 23:12-14
4) Joshua 5:10-11
5) Leviticus 23:15-21
6) Exodus 19:1, 3-5
7) Deuteronomy 8:3
8) Exodus 19:5-8
9) Deuteronomy 4:1-8
10) Exodus 19:10-11, 14-25
11) Exodus 20:18
12) Exodus 23:12-17
13) Exodus 24:1-18
14) Isaiah 54:5-6
15) Matthew 13:18-25, 27. 37-43
16) Matthew 22:1-14
17) Luke 14:15-27
18) Hebrews 12:1-4, 6, 14-29
19) Revelation 19:1-9

Scripture referenced, not quoted:

- 1 John 20
- Acts 2
- Deuteronomy 18
- Haggai 3

Also referenced:

In-Depth Study: *Seven Church Harvest*

Message: From the Red Sea to Mt. Sinai

Book: *The Schocken Bible: The Five Books of Moses* by Everett Fox

Booklets by Fred R. Coulter:

- Count to Pentecost: From the Morrow After Which Sabbath?
- How to Count Pentecost
- The True Meaning of Acts 2:1

FRC:CS
Transcription date unknown
Reformatted: bo—11/2020

CHAPTER THIRTY-SEVEN

Phase One of the Return of Christ:
The Sign of the Son of Man

(Day 49)
Fred R. Coulter

Greetings, brethren! Welcome to Day 49, the Sabbath before Pentecost! We've seen how to count Pentecost, particularly in this year when we had the Holy Day—the 1st Day of Unleavened Bread—on the weekly Sabbath.

The seven weeks of the harvest represent the seven churches in Rev. 2 & 3. The book of Revelation becomes the most important thing for us to consider with the churches and with the resurrection. When you count with the Calculated Hebrew Calendar, **Pentecost is the last day!** Let's see how important this is, and let's see how much is packed into the first three chapters of Revelation, and how that represents the Church, and the harvest of the Church.

Tomorrow [Pentecost] we will see that the harvest takes place with all included: those from the time of Abel on down to Christ, from Christ on down to the resurrection, all together raised in that first resurrection, which we will discuss tomorrow.

Note the audio and special effects for the book of Revelation on DVD {**truthofgod.org**}. The book of Revelation is so important and contains so many things that it is—without sufficient knowledge of the rest of the Bible—very difficult to understand.

- let's see what we are dealing with
- let's see why this is so important
- let's understand how God views things

What we have in Rev. is:
- *God's view* of the world
- *God's view* of the Church
- *God's view* of the things that are going to take place leading up to the return of Jesus Christ

We will see that **the return of Jesus Christ is actually three phases**[transcriber's correction]. Today we will cover phase one.

Revelation 1:1: "*The* revelation of Jesus Christ, which God gave to Him, to show to His servants the things that *are* ordained to come to pass shortly; and He made *it* known, having sent *it* by His angel to His servant John who gave witness *to* the Word of God and the testimony of Jesus Christ, and all the things he saw" (vs 1-2). *I'm sure that many of*

them John did not understand!

Here's a blessing we can claim. This is why you cannot read and study the book of Revelation too much. But be sure that you read and study the rest of the Bible so you can plug everything in together.

Verse 3: Blessed *is* the one who reads, and those who hear the words of this prophecy and who keep the things *that are* written therein; for the time *is* at hand." *Yes, the time right now really is at hand!* We see three things here:

1. reading
2. hearing
3. keeping

That ties in with everything that God has given us in the Old Testament and the New Testament, which is:

- **diligently** *keep* His commandments, laws, precepts and so forth
- **hearken, listen to and obey** the Word of God
- **pay particular attention** to what has been written

We will see how important Rev. 2-3 actually are.

Verse 4: "John to the seven churches that *are* in Asia: Grace and peace *be* to you from Him Who is, and Who was, and Who *is* to come; and from the seven spirits that are before His Throne." {note our message: *The Holy Spirit of God, the Seven Spirits of God*}

- What are the seven Spirit's of God?
- What do they do?

Jesus is directing them!

Verse 5: "And from Jesus Christ… [these are His words, and that's very important for the Churches] …the faithful Witness, the Firstborn from the dead, and the Ruler of the kings of the earth. To Him Who loved us and washed us from our sins in His own blood."

That ties right in with the Passover and comes forward to the harvest. Counting toward Pentecost, a *harvest* Feast. Always remember that *Trumpets is **never** a harvest Feast*.

Verse 6: "And has made us kings and priests to God and His Father; to Him *be* the glory and the sovereignty into the ages of eternity. Amen. Behold, He is coming with the clouds, and every eye shall see Him… [we will see how that will work out later] …and those who pierced Him; and all the tribes of the earth shall wail because of Him. Even so, Amen" (vs 6-7).

Verse 8 give us a perspective of how God views time, and how that God is capable of doing and thinking so many more things, especially when we consider the greatness of the universe that God has made, and the greatness of the things that He has put on the earth for us. God has given all mankind the earth to replenish, to multiply, to use the things that are here. What a wonderful blessing that is.

But unfortunately there is the adversary Satan the devil. We will see that interlaced through everything, all the way through the book of Revelation the adversary Satan the devil is fighting against God's plan:

- against those who are brethren of Jesus Christ

bringing

- confusion
- false doctrine
- false prophets

We'll see that and how important that is!

Verse 8: "I am the Alpha and the Omega…" *First and last letter of the Greek alphabet* showing that He purposed that the New Testament be written in Greek, not in Hebrew.

"'…*the* Beginning and *the* Ending,' says the Lord, 'Who is, and Who was, and Who *is* to come—the Almighty.'" (v 8). We're going to see something very important here: *how many times Christ told John to write!*

What we have here is very similar to what we have with Moses and God. God told Moses, 'Speak to the children of Israel, saying…' *and Moses told the people what God was saying!* Likewise here, Jesus is telling John to *write,* so John is not only a witness of these things, but he is also Jesus' personal secretary!

There are those who will lament: Why didn't Jesus write something so that we would know it was from Him? *Well, He did!* He dictated the things from John for the Churches.

Verse 10: "I was in *the* Spirit on the Day of the Lord…" *John saw all these visions!* For those who believe in Sunday, some translations have translated that as *Sunday.* So, Sunday-keeping is in the Bible! *NO!* Men have changed it to fit *their* traditions.

- When they do that, *they cut themselves off from God!*
- When they do that, *they try and tell God what to do!*

No man can tell God what to do! Otherwise, He is not God and is not Sovereign.

"…and I heard a loud voice like a trumpet behind me, saying, 'I am the Alpha and the Omega, the First and the Last, and what you see, **write in a book,** and send *it* to the churches that *are* in Asia: to Ephesus, and to Smyrna, and to Pergamos, and to Thyatira, and to Sardis, and to Philadelphia, and to Laodicea.' And I turned to see the voice that spoke with me… [Where was it coming from?] …and when I turned, I saw seven golden lampstands; and **in *the* midst**…" (vs 10-13).

It was in a circle! The reason that they're in a circle is because of the way that the Churches are applied to that time, down through history and the end-time. Then John described them, beautiful and fantastic:

"…of the seven lampstands *One* like *the* Son of man, clothed in *a* garment reaching to the feet, and girded about the chest with a golden breastplate. And His head and hair *were* like white wool, white as snow; and His eyes *were* like a flame of fire; and His feet *were* like fine brass, as if *they* glowed in a furnace; and His voice *was* like *the* sound of many waters. And in His right hand He had seven stars, and a sharp two-edged sword went out of His mouth… [the Word of God (Heb. 4:12)] …and His countenance *was* as the sun shining in its *full* power" (vs 10-16).

God wants us to know that Christ is the **Head of the Church, He is in charge of everything!** Brethren, our relationship with God the Father and Jesus Christ is based upon this. Here we are given, directly, a message from Jesus Christ, not as a man, but *as a living spiritual God!*

Verse 17: "And when I saw Him, I fell at His feet as if dead; but He laid His right hand upon me, saying to me, 'Do not be afraid; I am the First and the Last, even the One Who is living; for I was dead, and behold, I am alive into the ages of eternity. Amen. And **I have the keys of *the* grave and of death**'" (vs 17-18). *No one else has any power concerning life or death* **spiritually**, *only Jesus Christ!*

Verse 19: "**Write**…" That's why we have the whole Bible written down; that's why we have *The Faithful Version.* There are so many terrible translations out there, and they are, even now, working on a New Testament that eliminates the words: *the Father and the Son*—referring to God the Father and Jesus Christ, Who is God manifested in the flesh—so that they would not offend the Muslims. God could not care whether the Muslims are offended or not, because it applies to *everyone!*

Unless you repent, you shall likewise surely perish! God is not here to placate feelings. God is not here to play patty-cake, nicey-nicey. *He is the powerful God, ruling the world, ruling the Church, upholding the universe by the word of His power!* This is the One we have to deal with, and He gives us direct access to God the Father, the greatest, most wonderful thing *through the power of the grace of God, to receive the Spirit of God and have direct access to Him!* Never forget that!

Verse 19: "Write the things that you saw, and the things that are… [and He's about ready to give those things] …and the things that shall take place hereafter…. [interpretation]: …The mystery of the seven stars that you saw in My right hand, and the seven golden lampstands, *is this*: **the seven stars are *the* angels of the seven churches; and the seven lampstands that you saw are *the* seven churches**" (vs 19-20). *Quite an interpretation!*

The Seven Churches:

Now let's talk about the seven churches. What is the most important thing to God on the earth? *His people! His Church!* Who is the Head of the Church? *Jesus Christ* (Eph. 1:22-23)!

Think about this: God has given prophecies concerning nearly every major nation on earth. In fact, when He says 'all nations' in prophecies that is *all* nations! There are very few prophecies concerning the Church in the rest of the Bible outside the book of Revelation. That's important to understand. What we have here in Rev. 2 & 3 is a threefold meaning of the seven churches. That's why it's written down.

1. the literal seven churches at the time that John was writing the book of Rev.
2. the churches down through history

We don't know the exact cutoff from church to church. I'm sure there were overlaps, just like they existed all at one time as literal churches, prophetically they exist and there are overlaps without a doubt.

3. the end-time

What we find in Rev. 2 & 3 is God's perspective of how He views the Churches. Jesus Christ is the Head of it. He has a message for everyone who is in the Church of God, and this is applicable at all times.

It's not over here or over there, but there are predominate things that are problems in the Churches of God. If we would carefully examine

Rev. 2 & 3 we would see that those problems still exist today.

I. Church at Ephesus:

Revelation 2:1: "To the angel of the Ephesian church, write: 'These things says He Who holds the seven stars in His right hand, Who walks in *the* midst of the seven golden lampstands….'"— *direct from Christ!*

So, Jesus did have things written. The whole book of Revelation, and as a matter of fact, the *whole Bible!*

Verse 2: "**I know your works**…" I want you to study everywhere it talks about *works* and see how important they are. The reason being is that *you cannot have faith without works!* What you believe is what you act upon. These are *works of*:

- faith
- the Spirit
- the Truth
- righteousness
- preaching the Gospel

He says this of every single church! As we read these things we will see that God knows everything we do. Why should that come as a surprise? *Christ and God the Father are dwelling in us!*

"…and your labor, and your endurance, and that you cannot bear those who are evil; and *that* you did test those who proclaim *themselves* to be apostles, but are not, and did find them liars" (v 2). *We are to test whatever anyone preaches*:

- Is it really the Truth of God?

or

- Is it clever lie?
- Are they the things that match up with everything else in the Bible: *line upon line; precept upon precept; here a little, there a little*?
- Does it cover exactly what God wants us to know?

or

- Is it pick and choose? *I like this; we'll do that! We don't like this; we won't do that!*

That's exactly what the false prophets do!

- What did Jesus tell us right at the first? *Beware of false prophets that come to you in sheep's clothing.*
- What did He tell us right at the end? *Beware of false prophets who will deceive you!* (Matt. 24)

Here they tested them, and we are to test them! Brethren, I want to warn you right now today, *there are false prophets **within** the Church of God* who are teaching false doctrines and things contrary to the Truth of God and how God has set it forth! That's why we have the Word of God; to test it and to prove it.

Verse 3: "A *that* you have borne *much* and have endured, and for My name's sake have labored and have not grown weary; nevertheless, I have *this* against you, that you have left your first love" (vs 3-4).

What does that mean? What is the *first love*? *The first love is the greatest commandment:* **to love God with all your heart, mind, soul, being and strength!**

What did they start focusing on? *Loving your neighbor as yourself!* You can't love your neighbor as yourself **unless you first love God!** We are going to see that God can come upon a church at any time. We've actually seen that happen!

Verse 5: "Therefore, remember from where you have fallen, and repent…" *All of the churches need to repent!* Two of them are not told directly to repent, but we'll examine that when we get to it. Are we not to repent every day? *Yes, we are!*

"…and do the first works; for if *you do* not, I will come to you quickly; and I will remove your lampstand out of its place **unless you repent**" (v 5). *We saw how that happened after John died!*

- How the false prophets came in and by 200 years later what do we have? *The Roman Catholic Church saying that they are Christian!*
- Where do these false prophets come from? *Satan the devil!*
- What do they do? *As Peter said, they twist and distort and do not know the Truth!*

Always remember: *If you have part of the Truth you also have error, because unless you have **all** the Truth…* You can't pick and choose! That's what the false prophets did.

Verse 6: "But this you have: that you hate the **works of the Nicolaitans**…"—*hierarchical government and a false grace!*

You have a hierarchy but 'we don't need the Laws of God. If we have the Spirit of God we ought to be able to resist sin and not sin.' So, you don't need to worry about the commandments of God. *At least they hated that!*

Jesus said, "…which **I also hate**" (v 6). *Think about that!* You need to look and see if the ministers/elders are:

- teaching
- encouraging
- uplifting
- helping them to correct themselves
- always looking to God the Father and Jesus Christ

If they are, and not putting themselves between you and God the Father and Jesus Christ, then they are not Nicolaitans. **But that has been a great sin in the Church of God!**

Verse 7: "The one who has an ear, let him hear what the Spirit says to the Churches…."—*all of them, so all of the correction throughout goes to the whole, to all the brethren!*

"…To the one who overcomes… [we have to overcome] …I will give *the right* to eat of the Tree of Life that is in *the* midst of the paradise of God" (v 7).

Remember: ***God loves us, and these things we are to watch for!*** That's why He has had it written down. There's going to come another time of persecution, just like it did here.

II. Church at Smyrna:

Verse 8: "And to the angel of the Church of *the* Smyrneans write: These things says the First and the Last, Who was dead but is alive. '**I know your works…**'" (vs 8-9).

He says that to every one of the churches. How are we judged? *By our works!* **Our works reflect what we think!**

"…and tribulation and poverty (but you are rich)…" (v 9). *If you remain faithful under duress and persecution and facing death*—and you die—***you are rich!***

"…and the blasphemy of those who declare themselves to be Jews…" (v 9). *That is they are declaring themselves to really be Christians!*

Jesus said that salvation is of the Jews, and Paul said that a Jew was one who was *circumcised inwardly!* The circumcision is *of the heart,* not in the flesh; a *spiritual Jew!*

"…and are not, but *are* a synagogue of Satan" (v 9). *Satan likes to get in there and lead us astray!* Remember, he works by:

- incrementalism
- false prophets
- false apostles
- false teachings
- false doctrine

So, we have to be aware of all of that!

Verse 10: "Do not fear any of the things that you are about to suffer. Behold, the devil is about to cast *some* of you into prison, that you may be tried;

and you shall have tribulation ten days. **Be faithful unto death, and I will give you a crown of life**.”

Jesus said, 'Fear the One Who has power over *life and death* to cast into Gehenna! Do not fear men who can kill the body, but they can't kill the life!' We need to remember that, and we can see it already happening with the martyrs of Jesus right in today's world. You know that it's eventually going to come here. *Don't fear any of that!* **"Be faithful unto death, and I will give you a crown of life."** *Throughout we will see*:

- encouragement
- correction
- overcoming
- naming the major problems and difficulties that will face the Church

Verse 11: "**The one who has an ear, let him hear what the Spirit says to the churches**. The one who overcomes shall not be hurt of the second death."

Take the opposite: *The one who does not overcome will suffer the second death!*

III.   Church at Pergamos

Verse 12: "And to the angel of the Church in Pergamos, write…" *They had a great temple and altar to Zeus, which is Satan the devil!* When you live directly in Satan's world—like we do today:

- How much does that affect us?
- How much does that affect our thinking?
- How much did that affect the organization of the Church?

They were good for a while, so He gives a warning:

"…These things says He Who has the sharp two-edged sword" (v 12)—*showing that God is going to judge everything by the Word of God!*

It's going to cut, it's going to be true, and you cannot inculcate the practices of the false Christianity of this world into the Churches of God.

Verse 13: "I know your works and where you dwell, where the throne of Satan *is*; but you are holding fast My name, and did not deny My faith, even in the days in which Antipas *was* My faithful witness, who was killed among you, where Satan dwells."

Satan today is deceiving the whole world, so we need to be on guard!

- How much does that affect us?
- How many things do we think and believe come because we are in the world with all of these modern technological advances that bring everything:

- ✓ right into our homes?
- ✓ right into our lives?
- ✓ right into our minds?

We have great deal to overcome!

Verse 14: "But I have a few things against you because you have there *those* who hold the teaching of Balaam, who taught Balak to cast a stumbling block before the children of Israel, **to eat things sacrificed to idols and to commit fornication**." *How does that translate to today?*

- things sacrificed to idols
  - ✓ the Eucharist
  - ✓ the Lord's Supper
- spiritual fornication
- physical fornication
- same-sex marriage
- getting rid of things out of the Word of God to make it look like those are acceptable to God

Amazing, isn't it? *Yes!*

Verse 15: "Moreover, you also have *those* who hold the doctrine of the Nicolaitans, **which thing I hate**."

Why? *Because it oppresses the brethren! They look to a man rather than Christ!* That's why! Jesus is jealous over *His* Church. He does not want any of these things in *His* Church.

This is why, as we look at the harvest—like we find in Matt. 13—the world is the field; the seed is sown by Christ. There are many problems and difficulties that come along; yet, there are those who are the seed in the good ground who bring forth 30, 60 and 100-fold. Remember, *the harvest is at the end of the age!*

Verse 16: "Repent! For if *you* do not *repent*, I will come to you quickly, and will make war against them **with the sword of My mouth**."

He is going to come and execute the Word of God in correction, to separate, to get rid of, to scatter. We've all experienced that! The lesson is that *you cannot mix the doctrines of this world—*which come from Satan the devil—*with the doctrines and teachings of God within the Church of God and expect God's blessing to be there!*

All of these things we need to watch, because out in the world today, how many Churches of God are there? *Well, pretty close to 12-1400 now!* Within them you find every one of these things that we're reading here concerning the seven churches.

Verse 17: "The one who has an ear, let him hear what the Spirit says to the churches. To the one who overcomes I will give *the right* to eat of the hidden manna; and I will give him a white stone, and on the stone a new name written, which no one knows except the one who receives *it." There has to be repentance of these things!*

Here we find not only personal sins, but also organizational sins. Christ—Who is the Head of the Church—is making sure that we all know what is the Truth and what is right, and what we need to do.

Again, we see what Christ repeats to all of the other churches, plus some of the other problems that Satan brings in. Notice how active Satan is against the Church. We find that Satan is going to make war against the Church, against the brethren. He accuses us day and night before the Throne of God, but we overcome him with the blood of Christ, the Word of our testimony—how we live—and not loving our lives unto death (Rev. 12).

Satan is there and controls the world; it all lies in the power of the 'wicked one.' That's why *Christ tells us to overcome!*

IV. Church at Thyatira

Verse 18: "And to the angel of the Church in Thyatira write…"

When you have it written down, and you have the Bible in your hands, understand—we can draw a little analogy—it's like receiving a legal notice from the court, which in this case is the Court of God, and Jesus is the Judge. When we receive that legal notice, we are to pay attention and obey, because if you do not obey that legal notice, then the law will be executed against you.

What is the final law that is given? *The second death!* We'll see that here. Thyatira got itself in deep trouble. We will see that that is how the Protestants came about. That is what happened to the Church.

{Note DVD: *Israel of the Alps* produced by the Seventh Day Adventist Church}. You need to see that, because the Waldensians and those who lived in the Alps—protected from the world by God—began to compromise and take things into their own hands and not trust in God.

This is at a time in history when the Catholic Church was really becoming very powerful. We saw, starting right in the first part of Rev. 2 with false apostles, then martyrdom, then changing of doctrine and the hierarchy. Now comes the full-fledged false doctrines.

"…These things says the Son of God, He Who has eyes like a flame of fire, and His feet *are* like fine brass. I know your works, and love, and service, and faith, and your endurance, and your works; and the last *are* more than the first. But I have a few things against you, because **you**

allow…" (vs 18-20). *You are not to allow these things to happen!*

There are Churches of God who *allow* women to preach, teach, and Paul said that a woman in the Church is not to have authority over a man.

In the world, wherever women work, they may have authority over men, *but that's not in the Church!* That's not the structure that God has set.

"…you allow the woman Jezebel…" (v 20)—*the daughter of the priest of Baal,* so here comes all the traditional pagan teachings being stored up and brought into the Catholic Church and it's spilling over into the Churches of God. Thinking that if they can compromise a little bit, they can avoid persecution. But notice how severe Christ's correction is with them:

"…who calls herself a prophetess, to teach and to seduce My servants into committing fornication… [spiritual fornication] …and eating things sacrificed to idols" (v 20)—*the Eucharist and the Lord's Supper!* Doing away with the Passover!

Listen, brethren, **IF** *you do not keep the Passover correctly, the way that it is in the Bible*—and there are those today who have teachings contrary to what Jesus taught concerning the Passover—*we need to ask ourselves*: Since that is the renewing of the New Covenant, **how do we stand before God if we change things?**

One of the popular things today is having a calendar so that it is on a different day. Another popular thing is having foot-washing at the end of the Passover services, because they haven't done enough study to understand that the *King James Version* is wrong when it says, 'supper being ended.' A completely flagrant mistranslation. So, you see how these things come about?

Verse 21: "And I gave her time to repent of her fornication, but she did not repent." *That was through the Reformation and the Council of Trent!*

There was a party, believe it or not, of Catholics at the Council of Trent who said that *'we should not have anymore traditions and doctrines that are not in the Bible, and we need to keep the Sabbath.'* But the Council of Trent extended for quite a while, and the final coup-de-gras that did them in, and the Catholic Church did not take advantage of that time to repent, was when the Protestants failed to keep the Sabbath. You can read that in *Rome's Challenge to the Protestants* (Appendix N—*The Holy Bible in Its Original Order*).

The conclusion was that the Protestants say 'sola scriptura'—Scriptures only—yet, they follow the Catholic doctrine of Sunday, which was a doctrine of the Roman Catholic Church and not in the Bible. Since they do that, 'they have accepted our tradition, they have accepted our teachings'—the Catholic Church's—and the Protestant Reformation is null and void 'in our eyes, and we will keep our traditions and teachings.'

They did not repent! This is coming! This has happened! There was a lot of correction that God gave. One of the greatest corrections that God brought against the Roman Catholic Church was stripping her of the secular territories. Garibaldi did that in Italy. He took away all of the papal states and forced the Roman Catholic Church and the pope to only have sovereignty over the 100-plus acres where the Vatican sits today.

Let's see what happens here; let's see that it includes those who commit adultery with her. What is happening today? *Protestants are going back to Rome, going back and committing spiritual adultery!* This is living here for us today.

Let's see what Christ has done because of those kinds of actions. Remember, today all the daughters of Babylon are coming back home, and the Churches of God need to be very careful that they do not take lightly:

- how they have to stand for the Truth
- how they have to love God and Jesus Christ under all circumstances
- how important that our works are

Verse 22: "...unless they repent of their works. And **I will kill her children with death**; and all the churches shall know that I am He Who searches *the* reins and hearts..." (vs 22-23). *God knows everything: our heart, our mind, our thoughts!*

- this is why we have the Feast days of God
- this is why we have a relationship with God with grace
  - ✓ not to take advantage of it to sin
  - ✓ not to do our own ways
  - ✓ not to compromise with the Truth of God
  - ✓ not to get comfortable and pleasant with everything around us

- "...I will kill her children with death..." If you kill them, they're dead. But if they're killed
- "...with death..." that has to be *the second death!*

"...and I will give to each of you... [every individual member] ...**according to your works**" (v 23).

You might go back and restudy this again and see how important this is. I think today is very important that we go through this word-by-word and see what is for us, and for the Churches of God, and what we need to do.

Brethren, we're going to enter into the difficult times described by Jesus Christ (Matt. 24) and how it extends out into the book of Revelation, as well.

Verse 24: "But to you I say, and to *the* rest who *are* in Thyatira, **as many as do not have this doctrine, and who have not known the depths of Satan**, as they speak; I will not cast upon you any other burden, but hold fast what you have until I come. And **to the one who overcomes, and keeps My works unto *the* end**..." (vs 24-26). The key: *I know your works!*

- Are they the *works of Christ*?
- Are we going to keep them to the end?
- Are we going to have the endurance that we need?

When the tough times come, all the 'glad-hander get along, go along' Christians are going to fall by the wayside. That's the warning here.

"...the one who overcomes, and keeps My works unto *the* end..." (v 26).

How important are your works beginning here with the *washing of the water by the Word*?

"...I will give authority over the nations; and he shall shepherd them with an iron rod, as vessels of pottery are broken in pieces; as I have also received from My Father; and I will give him the morning star.... [spiritual life to shine like the sun] ...**The one who has an ear, let him hear what the Spirit says to the churches**" (vs 26-29).

It's fitting that we read this, go through all of it and see and understand what we really need to do. There are so many, many things in the world today:

- to distract us
- to lead us astray
- to infiltrate our thoughts
- to infiltrate our mind
- to infiltrate our heart

All of those who belong to Churches of God need to constantly be testing:

- the doctrines
- the Truth
- the love
- the submission to God the Father and Jesus Christ
- loving each other as Christ has loved us

That is what we need to focus on!

But look at all these troubles that come. What happens when you get all worn out from difficult things that have come along? *That happened to the Churches of God, too!*

V. <u>Church at Sardis</u>

Revelation 3:1: "And to the angel of the Church in Sardis, write: 'These things says He Who has the seven spirits of God and the seven stars. **I know your works,** *and* that you have a name as if you are alive, but are dead."

Here is just wanting to do the bare minimum. There are Churches of God like that today, especially those who do not keep the Holy Days.

Verse 2: "Be watchful, and strengthen the things that remain, which are about to die...." *Unless you act upon knowledge, upon the Word of God, it's going to die!* Other things will come along and crowd it out.

"...For I have not found your works complete before God" (v 2). *The only way our works are complete is if we keep the works of Jesus Christ to the end!*

Verse 3: "Therefore, remember what you have received and heard, and hold on *to this*, and repent. Now then, if you will not watch, I will come upon you as a thief, and you shall by no means know what hour I will come upon you."

The judgment of God can come at any time! Remember what happened to King Nebuchadnezzar? *He got all lifted up and said, 'Look at all this Babylon; this is what **I** have built. What a wonderful thing, I'm a great person. Look at what **I** have done.'*

The judgment and warning that Daniel gave him came upon him. For seven years Nebuchadnezzar was out there eating grass like the animals. After the seven years were over and God gave him back his sanity, he wrote the Epistle of Nebuchadnezzar (Dan. 4).

All those in authority would do well to read that, to understand that God can come upon you quickly! That's what He said!

Verse 4: "You have a few names even in Sardis who have not defiled their garments, and they shall walk with Me in white because they are worthy. The one who overcomes shall be clothed in white garments; and **I will not blot out his name from the Book of Life**..." (vs 4-5).

What do you know about that! Think on that for just a minute! That could happen; that's going to happen to some, obviously, if they don't repent.

"...but I will confess his name before My Father and before His angels. **The one who has an ear, let him hear what the Spirit says to the churches**" (vs 5-6).

- Do we hear?
- Are our minds open?
- Are our hearts open?
- Are we willing in attitude, in love and in submission to God the Father and Jesus Christ?

VI. <u>Church at Philadelphia</u>

Verse 7: "And to the angel of the Church in Philadelphia, **write**: "These things says the Holy One, the One Who *is* true; the One Who has the key of David, Who opens and no one shuts, and Who shuts and no one opens. **I know your works**...'" (vs 7-8).

Here's the message: *Write!* Think of all of these *as a personal message from Jesus Christ* to each of us as individuals and to all the Churches of God as organizations. God is judging both.

"...Behold, I have set before you an open door, and no one has the power to shut it because you have a little strength, and have kept My Word, and have not denied My name" (v 8).

The Church of Smyrna and Philadelphia, out of the seven, that are not told to repent. We're told to overcome. So, the only way that this can come about, that you have nothing to repent of is because you're repenting every day, and you're living by every word of God. You are loving the Truth and studying the Word of God, filling your mind with it and keeping the commandments of God.

This is going to come, v 9: "Behold, I will make those of the synagogue of Satan... [the super elite of the world: politically, economically, religiously] ...who proclaim themselves to be Jews and arc not, but do lie. **Behold, I will cause them to come and worship before your feet**..." *They're going to worship God in our presence!* Isn't that something?

This is what we need, this is the complete model that God wants us to follow:

- loving God
- loving the brethren
- keeping His Word
- being faithful in everything

"...and to know that I have loved you" (v 9). *God loves you and Christ loves you!*

That's why these seven letters to the seven churches. It fits through all time, every individual and every church organization. Quite something!

Remember, Jesus said to His disciples that *the words that He speaks are Spirit and Life.* **The flesh profits nothing!**

Verse 10: "Because you have kept the Word of My patience…"—*the works*; *I know your works* of:

- keeping the Word of His patience
- not denying His name
- keeping His Word

"…I also will keep you from the time of temptation, which *is* about to come upon the whole world to try those who dwell on the earth" (v 10). *That will undoubtedly be* **the mark of the beast! It is coming! It is coming!**

Everyone is going to be use to it. We have the closest thing to it now. We have chips you can put in the right hand, or the eye-watch (iris scan) with the computer, everything right there.

Everyone who takes the mark of the beast is going to give up his or her free moral agency to Satan the devil directly! We need to think about that! It's coming upon the whole earth.

Verse 11: "Behold, I am coming quickly; **hold fast that which you have so that no one may take away your crown**." *We're living in a time when we need to watch all*:

- the doctrines
- false teaching
- false prophets
- false ministers
- false brethren

Verse 12: "The one who overcomes will I make a pillar in the temple of My God, and he shall not go out anymore; and I will write upon him the name of My God, and the name of the city of My God, the New Jerusalem, which will come down out of heaven from My God; and *I will write upon him* My new name." *That is a wonderful and fantastic thing, brethren!*

Verse 13: "**The one who has an ear, let him hear what the Spirit says to the churches**."

VII. Church at Laodicea

A lot has been said about the Laodiceans. It sounds like a lot of the Church today. It's probably true that what we know as the Church of God today, the greatest majority have been Laodicean. So, write a message. As we read these things, let's take it:

- *personally* to ourselves for correction
- *collectively* for all of the congregations of God, wherever they are

Verse 14: "And to the angel of the Church of *the* Laodiceans, write: These things says the Amen, the faithful and true Witness, the Beginner of the creation of God. I know your works… [to all of the churches] …that you are neither cold nor hot; I would *that* you be *either* cold or hot. So then, because you are lukewarm, and *are* neither cold nor hot, I will spew you out of My mouth" (vs 14-16).

Does that not sound like scattering the Church? *Yes, indeed!* We have so many things today that we become complacent! Never in the history of the world has it been so applicably true!

Verse 17: "For you say, 'I am rich, and have become wealthy, and have need of nothing'… ['Look at all the blessings of God.' Really?] …and you do not understand that you are wretched, and miserable, and poor, and blind, and naked." *That's a terrible condition to be in!*

Yet, there are those who are that way today. But you don't need to give up hope, because God loves you! You need to repent like He says!

Verse 18: "I counsel you to buy from Me gold purified by fire…"—***through trial***; Paul writes of gold, silver, precious stone; wood, hay and stubble (1-Cor. 3). *The fiery trial is going to prove it!* There are going to be fiery trials.

- What are *you* going to do?
- Are you going to yield to God?

or

- Are you going to complain?
- Are you going to run off and seek comfort and safety somewhere, through some thing?
- Are you going to avoid coming before God to repent?
- Are you going to repent just partly of what you do?

or

- Are you going to repent of everything that you are?

"…so that you may be rich; and white garments so that you may be clothed, and the shame of your nakedness may not be revealed; and to anoint your eyes with eye salve, so that you may see" (v 18). *When you anoint your eyes with eye salve, then you need to pray the prayer of*:

Psalm 119:18: "Open my eyes so that I may behold wondrous things out of Your Law"—***all of the Word of God!***

God loves the Laodiceans, He loves all of those of the seven churches. Today, as you look around the world, God looks at it and there are these seven churches in existence today. It's not restricted to any one single corporate church. So, if any minister says:

If you are not in this church, you are not going to receive eternal life. If you leave this church you're going to into the Lake of Fire.

LIE!

- **IF** you are not in Christ and God the Father you are not in the Church!
- **IF** you reject the Truth and turn your back and walk away from it, you will be in the Lake of Fire!

That's what God has said! But God's Word and God's people are not restricted to one single organization on earth.

Revelation 3:19: "As many as I love, I rebuke and chasten. Therefore, be zealous and repent." *God loves the Laodiceans!*

They have some work to do. Verse 20 shows something very, very important. You have pushed Christ out of your life so far that He has to come and knock to get back in.

Verse 20: "Behold, I stand at the door and knock. **If anyone hears My voice**… [through the Word of God and your conscience] …and opens the door… [the *door of your mind,* because you have pushed Christ so far out] …I will come in to him, and will sup with him, and he with Me."

- there is a revival for you
- there is an opportunity for you

But you have to repent!

Verse 21: "To the one who overcomes will I give *authority* to sit with Me in My Throne, even as I also overcame, and sat down with My Father in His Throne. **The one who has an ear, let him hear what the Spirit says to the churches**."

Phase One of the Return of Jesus Christ

In order to understand the first phase of the return of Jesus Christ, that is keyed to the verse in Rev. 1, *'Behold, every eye shall see Him.'* Let's see how this is going to work and how this is going to develop.

First of all, Jesus tells His disciples that there will be many false prophets; they'll deceive you. There will be wars and rumors of wars, famines, pestilence, earthquake in different places. Nation against nation and kingdom against kingdom.

Matthew 24:8: "Now, all these *things are* the beginning of sorrows."

These have come in cycles down through time, and we're seeing it come again being all magnified and fulfilled according to the Word of God.

Verse 10: "And then shall many be led into sin, and shall betray one another, and shall hate one another." *We're right in that time right now!* That's what's happening.

Verse 11: "And many false prophets shall arise, and shall deceive many." *There are more false prophets than ever before!*

Remember what those at the Church of Ephesus did. *They* tested all the false prophets; *tested* their teachings whether it was of the Truth or the deception.

Verse 12: "And because lawlessness shall be multiplied…" *That's what it is in the world today, everywhere!*

- no one can tell the truth
- no one is honest
- no one knows right from wrong
- no one knows good from evil

Everyone thinks that his own actions are good, even that their lies and stories that they tell will serve a good purpose to make people aware of things. *How ridiculous!* If that's not from Satan the devil, I don't know what is.

"…**the love of many shall grow cold**" (v 12). *Who can trust anyone?* But here we are in the middle of it:

Verse 13: "**But the one who endures to the end, that one shall be saved**."

Today we have more means of preaching the Gospel to the world than at any time in the history of the world. It's getting more and more widespread through all of the vast technology that we have. We ourselves have:

- **truthofgod.org**
- **churchathome.org**
- **afaithfulversion.org**
- **originalbiblerestored.org**
- **godsyouth.org**

Other Churches of God likewise have websites and things where they are reaching out and preaching. We have those people who are preaching the Gospel and warning, even out of contention, not really truly right, but having some Truth in it. We have those who are warning concerning:

- the financial problems
- the crime problems
- the government problems
- the religious problems

What is happening, because all the churches are coming together under Rome, they are accepting same-sex marriage, homosexuality, the worship of idols and things like that. It's all magnified here in the end-times.

Verse 15: "Therefore, when you see the abomination of desolation, which was spoken of by Daniel the prophet, standing in the Holy place.'…."

That did not happen with the destruction of the temple in 70_{A.D.} that's why you have a parenthetical statement inserted there, right in the midst of what Jesus said. This was inspired to be put there by Jesus Himself when John was canonizing the New Testament:

"…(The one who reads, let him understand.)" (v 15).

They're working on the temple. They even had practice with the slaughtering of lambs for the Passover in Israel. It's going to be interesting to see how things come together. There will be a temple built. They will discover—and are already working on it now—that they don't have to put the temple where the Mosque of Omar is, where the Muslims consider that to be the holiest place. They couldn't ever build it there, and that's not where the temple actually was; it was south of there.

So, they will be able to build it right where the Spring of Gihon is. How soon that will be we don't know. But they are gradually—through The Temple Institute (**templeinstitute.org**)—having many things all ready to go. So, there will be a temple, because Rev. 11 tells us there will be a temple. There will be an 'abomination of desolation' because Jesus said there would be. It didn't happen in 70_{A.D.}

Verse 16: "Then let those who are in Judea flee into the mountains. Let the one *who is* on the housetop not come down to take anything out of his house" (vs 16-17). *You have to flee immediately!*

Verse 18: "And let the one *who is* in the field not go back to take his garments. But woe to those *women* who are expecting a child, and to those who are nursing infants in those days! And pray that your flight be not in *the* winter, nor on *the* Sabbath" (vs 18-20).

That shows we're to keep the Sabbath! When that happens, this is the signal of the starting of the Great Tribulation. We will go through and see that *that is the key for us to begin to understand the first phase of the return of Jesus Christ!*

Verse 21: "For then shall there be great tribulation, such as has not been from *the* beginning of *the* world until this time, nor ever shall be *again*. And if those days were not **limited**…" (vs 21-22)—*not the word* **shortened** (KJV)!

False prophets come along and say, 'Jesus could return at any time and God could cut the days

short.' *NO!* He is saying that the Tribulation is limited. What is the limit of the Tribulation? *Three and a half years!*

If there were not the limit "…there would no flesh be saved; but for the elect's sake those days shall be limited. Then if anyone says to you, "Behold, here *is* the Christ," or, "He is there," do not believe *it*. For there shall arise false Christs and false prophets, and they shall present great signs and wonders, in order to deceive, **if possible, even the elect**" (vs 22-24).

Think about that! If you do not follow the instructions of what Jesus said, of testing the false prophets, whether they are of the Truth of God or not. It's going to be hard and very difficult because there are so many different Bibles out there, so many different translations out there. That's why we have *The Faithful Version.*

Verse 25: "Behold, I have foretold *it* to you. Therefore, if they say to you, '*Come and* see! He is in the wilderness'; do not go forth. '*Come and* see! *He is* in the secret chambers'; do not believe *it*" (vs 25-26).

Here is the first phase of the return of Jesus Christ, v 27. We have to add in something from the book of Hosea that is very important—Hosea 5 (last part) and first part of Hosea 6. It shows that God is going to afflict Israel for two whole years. That will be lifted with the 144,000 (Rev. 7). Then there is a year and a half left before Christ and the saints come back to the earth from the Sea of Glass.

Here is how they are going to see Christ: Right at the beginning of the third year of Tribulation, meaning there's a year and a half left:

Verse 27: "**For as the light of day, which comes forth from** *the* **east and shines as far as** *the* **west, so also shall the coming of the Son of man be**." *Phase ONE!*

All of a sudden there is going to be in the sky—and we'll see it when that happens—*another sun*. They will see it as the earth turns on its axis for a year and a half. It will be out there plenty far enough that after they get used to the fact that it is there, they will continue on with their wars and fighting. Then Christ explains how that's going to happen.

Verse 29: "But immediately after the tribulation of those days… [against Israel, it continues to get worse for the rest of the world (Rev. 8, 9, etc.] …the sun shall be darkened, and the moon shall not give her light, and the stars shall fall from heaven, and the powers of the heavens shall be shaken. And **then shall appear the sign of the Son of man in heaven**; and then shall all the tribes of the earth mourn, and **they shall see the Son of man coming upon the clouds of heaven with power and great glory**" (vs 29-30).

The resurrection is not going to take place immediately. Let's see how all of this comes about. Let's understand that these things will happen just exactly as it's laid out here in the book of Revelation. Jesus opens the seals.

We will see where it brings us from the beginning of the Tribulation up through to the time when, just described by Jesus Christ, *the sign of the Son of man in heaven!* The world will see it and the world will know it. Even though they will see and know it, they will think this is an invasion from outer space by aliens, which will be true! Christ is an alien and all the resurrected saints will be aliens, and we will come from heaven—where the clouds are—and take over the earth.

Rev. 6—the first seal is opened and the gathering of all the religions together. After that takes place, the second seal opens and that is the beginning of the Tribulation, and it's going to last three and a half years. The first two years are going to be against Israel. The rest of the time is going to be against the rest of the world and will be far more intense and difficult than what came against Israel.

Then the third seal is opened and we have famine and death, rationing of food and so forth. Then the fourth seal is opened—death—and killed is one-fourth of the earth. Imagine one-fourth of mankind is going to die in the Tribulation and wars of men against men. Of course, there will be demons behind the scenes doing it. But not like it will be when we come to Rev. 8. Then the fifth seal is the martyrdom of the saints. We've covered that how with the Church at Smyrna. That is going to come again.

Right after that *the sixth seal when the sign of the Son of man appears in the heavens like a second sun*:

Revelation 6:12: "And when He opened the sixth seal, I looked, and behold, there was a great earthquake... [just like Jesus described] ...and the sun became black as *the* hair *of* sackcloth, and the moon became as blood; and the stars of heaven fell to the earth, as a fig tree casts its untimely figs when it is shaken by a mighty wind" (vs 12-13). *A fantastic thing is going to take please; unbelievable!*

This is when they will see **the sign of the Son of man, the second sun in the sky!** Something is going to happen in the heavens to cause that to be. Every eye will see this, and it will be there for a year and a half. *No one is going to have any excuses!*

Verse 14: "Then *the* heaven departed like a scroll that is being rolled up, and every mountain and island was moved out of its place. And the kings of the earth, and the great men, and the rich men, and the chief captains, and the powerful men, and every bondman, and every free *man* hid themselves in the caves and in the rocks of the mountains; and they said to the mountains and to the rocks, 'Fall on us, and hide us from *the* face of Him Who sits on the throne, and from the wrath of the Lamb, **because the great day of His wrath has come, and who has the power to stand**?'" (vs 14-17).

The first thing He does is in Rev. 7 because this ends the Tribulation against Israel, with the saving of the 144,000, and against those who repent because of the awesome signs and sights that they see. They will have a little over a year until the resurrection. The world will have a year and a half until Christ returns with the saints.

This is the first phase of the return of Christ, and we'll pick it up tomorrow with the *resurrection Pentecost* and what is going to happen at that time.

Scriptural References:

1) Revelation 1:1-8, 10-20
2) Revelation 2:1-29
3) Revelation 3:1-18
4) Psalm 119:18
5) Revelation 3:19-21
6) Matthew 24, 8, 10-13, 15-27, 29-30
7) Revelation 6:12-17

Scriptures referenced, not quoted:

• Hebrews 4:12
• Ephesians 1:22:23
• Matthew 13
• Revelation 12
• Daniel 4
• 1 Corinthians 3
• Revelation 11
• Hosea 5; 6
• Revelation 7-9

Also referenced:

• Message: *The Holy Spirit of God, the Seven Spirits of God*
• DVDs:
  ✓ Book of Revelation (with special effects)
  ✓ *Israel of the Alps* (produced by the 7th-Day Adventist Church)
• Article: *Rome's Challenge to the Protestants* (Appendix N—*The Holy Bible in Its Original Order;* also in booklet form at **truthofgod.org**).

FRC:bo
Transcribed: 4-22-15
Reformatted: 11/2020

Section VI

Pentecost

CHAPTER THIRTY-EIGHT

The Feast of Pentecost
Fred R. Coulter

Greetings brethren! Welcome to the Feast of Pentecost. This is really quite a tremendous and wonderful day when we understand the full significance of it and what it means to us, because this is the day that all true Christians are looking for.

This day is the harvest of the firstfruits, and the firstfruits are those in the first resurrection. We're going to see that on the 50th day it tells us what they were to bring. There were special offerings that they were to bring. One has significance for the prophetic meaning of Pentecost, and the other has to do with the offerings that we are to take, because in Deut. 16 it says that when we have Pentecost—also called the Feast of Weeks—after you count out seven weeks and you're to have the Feast of Weeks, which then is the 50th day.

Leviticus 23:17 *points out*: "You shall bring out of your homes two wave loaves of two tenth parts. They shall be of fine flour. They shall be baked with leaven…"

It is the only offering other than a peace offering where they could bring leavened bread with the offering. The leavened bread was not ever to be burned, *only unleavened bread was to be burned!* The other was to be eaten.

"…*they are* the firstfruits to the LORD" (v 17).

So there's a significance in relating to those who are going to be in the resurrection and the Church. Then it gives the offering that they were to offer: all of the rams and the lambs, and so forth:

"…*even* an offering made by fire, of sweet savor to the LORD" (v 18). *Then it talks about the sacrifice of the peace offering and sin offering (v 19)!*

Verse 20: "And **the priest shall wave them** with the bread of the firstfruits…" *So, waving is the same thing when you come back to the first day!*

What do you have on the first day of the count? *You are to have the premiere sheaf that was specially cut, that is waved before the Lord!* We know this symbolizes **the ascension of Jesus into heaven on the first day of the count toward Pentecost** to be accepted of God the rather as the sacrifice for the sins of the whole world.

"…wave offering before the LORD…" (v 20).

If it applies to Jesus ascending and being accepted of God the Father on the first day, then this also has to apply to those who are in the Church to be waved and accepted by God on the Day of Pentecost.

"…with the two lambs. They shall be Holy to the LORD for the priest. And you shall proclaim on the same day… [that very day, the 50th day] …that it may be a Holy convocation to you. You shall do no servile work *therein. It shall be* a statute forever in all your dwellings throughout your generations" (vs 20-21).

Since this is a Holy Day, we do take up an offering and it is the firstfruits. We need to understand that God said *you shall not fail to bring your firstfruits to Him!* It's very, very important. And also the offering that we bring we need to understand that:

- we need to apply ourselves in the offering
- we need to plan for the offerings

We need to realize that just as we are part of the firstfruits who are going to be harvested when the resurrection occurs. Likewise, as we are planning to grow in grace and knowledge in character to be able to be raised from the dead when that time comes, **then when we bring an offering to God we need to plan it; we need to prepare for it!**

That's why Paul gives it in 2-Cor. 9:6—a living principle. I've seen this over and over and over again in the lives of people, not only in the world but especially in the Church.

2-Corinthians 9:6: "But this *I say*: the one who sows sparingly shall also reap sparingly; and the one who sows bountifully shall also reap bountifully."

This is a living principle! It's just the way that it is. If you're a curmudgeon with God, He's going to be a curmudgeon with you. It's just that simple! Whether it be in:

- our character
- our prayers
- our growing
- our overcoming

- our studying
- our thinking
- our giving of tithes and offerings

It's all the same thing!

Verse 7: "Each one a**s he purposes in his heart**…"—*because we are to give according to the blessings that God gives us!* Not only just the physical blessings, *but also the spiritual blessings!*

"…*so **let him give, but not grudgingly or by compulsion**; for God loves a cheerful giver*" (v 7).

In other words, instead of saying, 'Oh, it's a Holy Day; I know the minister is going to ask for an offering. Well, all right I'll give it.' *NO!* It's just like everything else, you need to look forward to it and you need to perform it *from the heart with a willing attitude!* Here is what God is able to do, because those who are curmudgeons do not believe:

Verse 8: "For God *is* able to make all grace abound toward you so that in every *way* you may always have sufficiency in all *things, and* may abound unto every good work."

That's what we need to look at with the offerings that God wants us to bring. Keep that in mind! When it comes down to tithes and offerings we're not dealing in our own property, *we're dealing as custodians or stewards of the property of God! He wants us to have it with*:

- a right heart
- a right mind
- a right attitude

You need to trust God! He's able to make all grace abound toward you.

Let me just say this: as we have seen and as we know, *IF* you do not do from the heart what God wants you to do in everything that you do, not only in giving—but since we're talking about offerings and giving—as one man wrote, he didn't tithe and he didn't give offerings. He spent all of that money on things in his life—which amounted to penalties against him—because he wasn't right with God in his heart, mind and attitude. He said, 'I spent the tithe all the way to bankruptcy court.' Then he learned the lesson: if you can't get along on the 90% that God gives you, then you're surely not going to get along on the 100% that you're claiming. We just need to keep that in mind!

Today on the Feast of Pentecost we're going to see the great blessing that God has in store for us as pictured by this Holy Day.

(pause for offering)

There are many things we could cover on Pentecost. Some of these things we are going to review rather than get in great detail in it, because we cover different aspects of it every year when we do.

God gave the Ten Commandments on the Day of Pentecost. The Day of Pentecost did not picture the firstfruits *until* after they got into the land, as far as the harvest was concerned. ***But it did picture the firstfruits of God in calling Israel as the first nation!*** It also pictures those people whom God has called beginning with Seth, and all through the righteous line that we find before the Flood, and then with Abraham after the Flood, who we know that Jesus said will be in the first resurrection.

Leviticus 23:17: "You shall bring out of your homes two wave loaves of two tenth parts. They shall be of fine flour. They shall be baked with leaven; *they are* the firstfruits to the LORD." *This was a special firstfruit!*

Why would God have the Feast of Unleavened Bread where leaven at that time is pictured to be sin, and now He says *put leaven into* this offering? *Because there is also a good application of leaven!* When you put leaven into your dough and it rises and then you bake it, what you do is you *permanently set* that dough in the baked condition. It can never go back, you can never beat it down to where it would be flat again. Once it's baked it is set.

Now let's look at a good application of leaven as it is pictured the type of the Kingdom of God. Let's come to Matt. 13 because we know that the Kingdom of God is going to be righteousness. It's not going to be sin, so leaven here in this particular case referring to the Kingdom of God has got to refer to the leaven that is there in the wave loaves.

In Matt. 13, we find something very interesting too. We find that the whole work of God in calling people and growing and producing *has to do with a harvest and planting.* He talks about the seed that fell in the different places where that they didn't produce, and then the ones who do produce. Then the harvest, He says, is at the end of the age. We'll talk about that a little bit later, but let's look at the one where the Kingdom of God is likened unto leaven.

Matthew 13:33: "Another parable He spoke to them: 'The Kingdom of Heaven is compared to leaven, which a woman took and hid in three measures of flour until all was leavened.'"

Then when you bake it, like with the two wave loaves that were offered, then you have something that is permanent; you have a finished product. Because what you do, you start out, just like it is here with the seeds that are planted. Then what has to happen is this:

- it has to grow
- it has to be harvested
- it has to be milled
- you have to add to it the salt and the sweetening
- you have to mix it
- you have to add the leavening

Then you have to wait for it to rise!

Generally you have to beat it down several times so you can get a nice real firm good kind of loaf of bread. Then you let it rise for the last time, and then you stick it into the oven and bake it. So, when it's baked it is finished. It is a complete product. That's what the wave loaves in Lev. 23 picture. One has got to be for those who enter into the Kingdom of God from the time of Adam down to the time of the beginning of the Church, and then from the Church forward to the return of Christ.

This happens on Pentecost. It doesn't happen on Trumpets. Trumpets is entirely different. And Trumpets cannot be the day of the resurrection simply because *a trumpet is blown*—from a concordant type study—*on every Holy Day!*

Remember what happened at Mount Sinai when the Ten Commandments were given. The trumpet blew long and loud and louder and louder, then God spoke the Ten Commandments. We'll look at some of that here in just a little bit later.

Acts 1—here we have several things going on the Day of Pentecost, which was when the Church began with the power of the Holy Spirit being given to it. There are, as we have covered, several reasons why God did it here on the Day of Pentecost at the temple:

1. the Holy Spirit was given to empower the people to keep the commandments of God
2. so there is a consistency of the place where God chose to put His name, and it was at the temple

Since it was the power of God's Holy Spirit to do it, and that it was going to be the Gospel that was to be preached in all the world

3. He caused the miracle of the speaking of the apostles

So that when they spoke in their own language it came out in the language of wherever they were of the Jews who came there to keep the Feast of Pentecost.

This was a tremendous thing that God was showing! This was also a prophecy that now men are going to have access to God the Father through the Spirit into the temple in heaven above. So, this was also a prophecy of the coming demise of the whole temple system and the sacrificial system. We know what happened.

Act 2:1 "And when the Day *of Pentecost, the fiftieth day*, was being fulfilled..."

That's the accurate translation from the Greek, and we have a booklet on that: *The True Meaning of Acts 2:1*

"...they were all with one accord in the same place. And suddenly *there* came from heaven a sound like *the* rushing of a powerful wind, and filled the whole house where they were sitting. And there appeared to them divided tongues as of fire, and sat upon each one of them. And they were all filled with *the* Holy Spirit; and they began to speak with other languages, as the Spirit gave them *the words* to proclaim" (vs 1-4).

What did they do? *They preached the crucifixion and resurrection of Jesus Christ, and the receiving of the Holy Spirit through repentance and baptism! A brand new thing!* It had not been done before. God was signaling the way of how now He was going to deal with His Church and His people.

A very important thing that took place here is this: When Peter preached and they were convicted in their heart and mind about what had happened with the crucifixion of Jesus Christ, he was actually preaching to those of whom some of them may have even been in the mob demanding that Jesus be crucified. **When it really got to them and they repented and were baptized,** that was a tremendous event. Because you see, on that day the words that Jesus said, 'Father, forgive them for they know not what they are doing,' was applied to them. *Quite a wonderful thing that happened!* We'll see how this follows along with what we read back there in Lev.23.

Verse 37: "Now, after hearing *this*, they were cut to the heart; and they said to Peter and the other apostles, 'Men *and* brethren, what shall we do?'.... [because there's always something we need to do] ...Then Peter said to them, 'Repent and be baptized each one of you in the name of Jesus Christ for *the* remission of sins, and you yourselves... [*personally, coming from God*] ...shall receive the gift of the Holy Spirit. For the promise is to you and to your children, and to all those who are afar off, as many as *the* Lord our God may call'" (vs 37-39).

So, he made it clear right from the beginning, *it is a calling that comes from God* and fulfills what Jesus said, 'None can come to the Father except they come through Me, and none can

450

come to Me except the Father draw them.' Here it is fulfilled right here.

Verse 40: "And with many other words he earnestly testified and exhorted, saying, 'Be saved from this perverse generation.'"

If there's any perverse generation, it is today! And it's going to get much more perverse; so perverse that just like God had to **destroy the temple system, destroy Jerusalem,** that He's going to have to nearly destroy this world in order to cleanse it and purify it from all of the sins and corruption and satanism and perversity that's in the world today.

Verse 41: "Then those who joyfully received his message were baptized; and about three thousand souls were added that day"—*the Day of Pentecost!*

So, this day has a great meaning for us, and this is why God gave the Holy Spirit on that day. It starts on this day and it ends on this day. We'll look at all the different things concerning the resurrection.

We need to understand this. We need to realize it to the depths of our being. As I covered yesterday, there are people out there even within the ranks of the Church of God that want to come in with their own doctrines. Just like it says here:

- *IF you don't believe that Jesus is raised from the dead then your faith is in vain!*
- *IF* you don't believe that Jesus Christ was God before He became a human being; that He was God manifested in the flesh
  - ✓ you don't understand the sacrifice of Jesus Christ
  - ✓ you cannot comprehend the deep love that God the Father and Jesus Christ have

for not only the Church and the people that He calls, but also for all humanity! In God's great plan through the things that we know from the Holy Days, He is going to save the vast majority of mankind. God is going to offer them the kind of repentance and forgiveness that we have.

But God has called us as the firstfruits, and as the firstfruits we have a great and a tremendous promise—greater than anyone else who comes into the Kingdom of God after that.

Let's understand this: The Bible also says that *without vision the people perish!* That's why a lot of people fall out of the Church. They just don't have the vision. You've got to understand the greatness of the plan of God, and you've got to keep that in the forefront of your mind, that it will:

- lead you
- inspire you
- give you hope

- give you the strength
- give you the endurance

We need to understand this because there were those, even in the Church of God back there... He says here in

1-Corinthians 15:34: "Awake to righteousness, and do not sin, for some *of you* do not have the knowledge of God. I say *this* to your shame."

There are a lot of people who don't have the knowledge of God as they ought to.

Verse 12: "But if Christ is being preached, that He rose from *the* dead, how *is it that* some among you are saying that there is no resurrection of *the* dead? For if there is no resurrection from *the* dead, neither has Christ been raised. And **if Christ has not been raised, then our preaching _is_ in vain, and your faith _is_ also in vain**" (vs 12-14).

Now let's understand that *any minister, any man, any church that preaches that you go to heaven is preaching in vain,* because they are not preaching the resurrection of Christ. Think about that.

Verse 15: "And we are also found *to be* **false witnesses** of God..."

God isn't going to back up any liars, is He? *No! they are excluded from the Kingdom of God!*

"...because we have testified of God that He raised Christ, Whom He did not raise, if indeed *the* dead are not raised. For if *the* dead are not raised, neither has Christ been raised. But **if Christ has not been raised, your faith _is_ vain; you are still in your sins,** and those who have fallen asleep in Christ have then perished. If in this life only we have hope in Christ, we are of all people most miserable" (vs 15-19)—*because you suffer in vain*:

- you go through trials in vain
- you're not developing the character of God
- you have a false belief in Christ

Verse 20: "But now **Christ has been raised** from *the* dead..."

They haven't ever produced the body; they haven't ever produced the witnesses who carried Him away; they have never produced the bones, because He was raised from the dead.

"...He has become the Firstfruit of those who have fallen asleep" (v 20). *That goes back to the Wave Sheaf Offering Day—the First of the firstfruits—the Premiere Sheaf that was accepted of God the Father!*

Verse 21: "For since by man *came* death, by

Man also *came the* resurrection of *the* dead. For as in Adam all die, so also in Christ shall all be made alive. But each **in his own order: Christ *the* Firstfruit; then those who are Christ's at His coming**" (vs 21-23).

We're going to see about His coming—that it is going to be quite a fantastic event. It's not going to be something that happens in just one day. We'll see that; we'll understand that. Now let's apply this to ourselves.

Let's come to James 1 and see what it says here concerning the Church. It shows that we are firstfruits:

James 1:17: "Every good act of giving and every perfect gift is from above, coming down from the Father of lights, with Whom there is no variation, nor shadow of turning. According to His own will… [see how important it is to remain faithful, because of His own will and desire]: …He begat us by *the* Word of Truth**, that we might be a kind of firstfruits of all His created beings**" (vs 17-18).

Now let's look at it in the book of Hebrews again. We're going to see *firstfruits* and *firstborn,* and we are called the *Church of the Firstborn.* Here's where we get the parallel between the giving of the Law at Mount Sinai and all the things that took place after that:

- our coming to the resurrection
- our being part of coming to Mount Sion

which is the city of the living God!

Hebrews 12:18: "For you have not come to *the* mount that could be touched and that burned with fire, nor to gloominess, and fearful darkness, and *the* whirlwind; and to *the* sound of *the* trumpet, and to *the* voice of *the* words…" (vs 18-19. *They heard God speak!*

Now none of us have heard that, but we have greater than that. *We have the begettal of God the Father in us, the firstfruits of the Holy Spirit!*

"…which those who heard, *begged* that *the* word not be spoken *directly* to them. (For they could not endure what was being commanded: 'And if even an animal touches the mountain, it shall be stoned, or shot through with an arrow'; and so terrifying was the sight *that* Moses said, 'I am greatly afraid and trembling')" (vs 19-21).

We're going to see what they all experienced there is nothing compared to what it's going to be like when Christ returns, because it's going to be an awesome, fantastic event. Let's get the big picture of what's going to take place worldwide at that time.

Verse 22: "But you have come to Mount Sion… [not Mt. Zion on the earth, but Mount Sion] …and to *the* city of *the* living God, heavenly Jerusalem; and to an innumerable company of angels; *to the* joyous festival gathering…" (vs 22-23)—*that's what it means in the Greek!*

This has got to be the Day of Pentecost, which is a festival gathering—the greatest gathering and the great congregation that we have talked about concerning the resurrection and how that's going to take place.

"…**and to *the* Church of *the* Firstborn**…" (v 23).

And then we read in :29 that Christ is *the Firstborn among many brethren.* So we have:

- the First of the firstfruits
- the First of the firstborn
- the firstfruits
- the Church of the Firstborn

That's what we are called!

"…registered *in the* Book *of Life* in heaven; and to God, *the* Judge of all, and to *the* spirits of the just who have been perfected; and to Jesus, *the* Mediator of *the* New Covenant; and to sprinkling of *the* blood of *ratification*, proclaiming superior things than *that of* Abel" (vs 23-24). *This sets the stage!*

Now let's look at how this is going to take place. Let's see how these events are going to transpire.

{note our in-depth study with charts and CDs: *Daniel/Revelation*}

Rev. 11—we know there's going to come a time when *the beast and the false prophet* will come on the earth. They will precede the two witnesses. And there will be a time of peace, as Paul writes (1-Thess. 5) for when they say 'peace and prosperity then sudden destruction is going to come upon them.'

There's going to come a time when Satan is going to be cast down and he's going to persecute the Church (Rev. 12). Then there will be some few who will be taken to a place of safety. Those who remain behind, Satan is going to make war against them. As we are going to see that is the martyrdom of the saints. But before that begins to take place… You will see on the chart that we have laying out the number of days, and so forth, of the two witnesses—when they end, when they begin, and so forth—that the two witnesses begin just before winter. Here is what they are going to do. This is going to be a key event. It's going to precipitate all of the events that are going to take place leading to the return of Christ and the resurrection.

Revelation 11:1: "Then *the angel* gave me a measuring rod like a staff, saying, 'Arise and measure the temple of God, and the altar, and those who worship in it. But leave out the court that *is* within the temple *area,* and do not measure it because it has been given *up* to the Gentiles; and they shall trample upon the Holy city *for* forty-two months. And **I will give** *power* **to My two witnesses, and they shall prophesy a thousand two hundred** *and* **sixty days,** clothed in sackcloth. These are the two olive trees, and *the* two lampstands that stand before the God of the earth'" (vs 1-4).

These are special two witnesses that *God is going to raise up and empower* in a way of a direct giving of the Holy Spirit to give to them. These will be the two most powerful men of God that the world has ever seen. Greater than Moses, greater than Aaron. Of course, not greater than Christ, but just as human beings representing God. That's why they are called the two olive trees, and the two lampstands that stand before the God of the earth.

{note our message: *Who Are The Two Witnesses and Elijah* (**truthofGod.org**)}

Verse 5: "And if anyone attempts to harm them, fire will go out of their mouths and devour their enemies...."

This is going to be a fantastic thing. So here is the confrontation of the two that represent Satan the devil and the two that represent God right at Jerusalem. It's going to take place in a powerful way because *the beast* is going to enter into the temple and proclaim himself that he is God, as we have already seen. That is *the abomination of desolation* that is spoken of by Daniel the prophet (Matt. 24). Now here's what's going to happen.

Verse 5: "And if anyone attempts to harm them, fire will go out of their mouths and devour their enemies. For if anyone attempts to harm them, he must be killed in this manner. These have authority to shut heaven so that no rain may fall in *the* days of their prophecy; and they have authority over the waters, to turn them into blood, and to smite the earth with every plague, as often as they will.... [that's going to be an awesome thing] ...And when they have completed their testimony, the beast who ascends out of the abyss will make war against them, and will overcome them, and will kill them" (vs 5-7).

But God has a surprise for them, as we will see a little bit later on. Let's see something very important concerning Matt. 24 and when the Tribulation begins, and then we will go to Rev. 6 and we will see the parallel events and how these come down to Pentecost and the resurrection.

Matthew 24:15: "'Therefore, when you see the abomination of desolation, which was spoken of by Daniel the prophet, standing in the Holy place.' (The one who reads, let him understand.); (the one who reads, let him understand)... [that's John's note that we have to be watching and looking] ...'then let those who are in Judea flee into the mountains. Let the one *who is* on the housetop not come down to take anything out of his house; and let the one *who is* in the field not go back to take his garments. But woe to those *women* who are expecting a child, and to those who are nursing infants in those days! And pray that your flight be not in *the* winter, nor on *the* Sabbath; for **then**...'" (vs 15-21).

- this is the key to understanding when the Great Tribulation starts
- this is the key that locks in the beginning of all the events in Dan. & Rev. that lead up to the return of Jesus Christ and the establishing of the Kingdom of God on earth

Verse 21: "For **then** shall there be Great Tribulation, such as has not been from *the* beginning of *the* world until this time, nor ever shall be *again.*"

What we need to understand is this, brethren: We are facing humungous worldwide problems. What we are going to see is that what God did to Egypt back in the book of Exodus with Pharaoh and Jannes and Jambres, God is going to do to the whole world, and to *the beast and the false prophet,* and their armies and all of those with him. It is going to be a time that has never been from the beginning of the world. We've got to really understand that.

"And if those days were not limited, there would no flesh be saved..." (v 22). It says *cut short* in the *King James,* but it means *limited!*

God is not going to cut short the three and a half years; three and a half days in prophecy. The reason being is that God has limited it to three and a half years. We'll see the events that take place there.

"...**but for the elect's sake those days shall be limited**" (v 22).

We'll come back here to Matt. 24 again a little later, but let's come to Rev. 6 and let's see how these events are going to unfold on the earth. This is going to lead us up to how Christ is going to return, and lead us up to the time of the resurrection.

Revelation 6:1: *Christ is the One Who opens the seals*: "And I looked when the Lamb opened one of the seals; and I heard one of the four living creatures say, like the sound of thunder, 'Come and see.' And I looked, and behold, *there was* a white horse..." (vs 1-2).

This is **_not_** Christ, because Christ opened the seal and out of the seal that Christ opened here comes a white horse.

- this is the *false Christ*
- this is the *false religion*
- this has to be *the antichrist,* **the false prophet** who is coming

Now let's understand this: *both the beast* and *the false prophet* are **antichrists!**

"…and the one who was sitting on it had a bow, and a crown was given to him; and he went out conquering, and to conquer." This tells us, as the other prophecies that this is a summary of how many of the other prophecies that there is coming a great one-world religion. *It is going to come!* Now then, when it comes time for the Beast Power to go into the temple and sit down and proclaim himself 'God' (2-Thess.), **_then_** we come to:

Verse 3—*this is the timing*: "And when He opened the second seal, I heard the second living creature say, 'Come and see.' And another horse went out *that was* red… [symbolic of war] …and *power* was given to the one sitting on it to take peace from the earth…" (vs 3-4).

- When does the Tribulation begin? **When you see the abomination** *spoken of by Daniel the prophet standing in the Holy place!*
- What is going to happen?

We've put all of the Scriptures together:

- the King of the North is going to come down
- he is going to enter into to the Temple of God
- he's going to proclaim himself 'God'
- the false prophet is going to say, 'Yes, he is *God.*'
- The two witnesses are going to say, 'No, *he is not God.*
- **_then_** the Great Tribulation begins on the whole world

That's what this second seal pictures! Immediately what happens with that?

Verse 5: "And when He opened the third seal, I heard the third living creature say, 'Come and see.' And I looked, and behold, *there was* a black horse; and the one sitting on it had a balance in his hand. And I heard a voice in *the* midst of the four living creatures say, 'A measure of wheat for a silver coin, and three measures of barley for a silver coin: and *see that* you do not damage the oil and the wine'" (vs 5-6).

So, immediately whenever there's war, food supplies are cut short. Don't we have that today? *Just think about how quickly death, destruction and famine is going to take place* when people do not have access to their markets, to their shopping malls. That's what's going to happen! What happens after that? *Immediately follows the fourth seal!* So, these come 1, 2, 3 quite quickly.

Verse 7: "And when He opened the fourth seal, I heard *the* voice of the fourth living creature say, 'Come and see.' And I looked, and behold, *there was* a pale horse; and the name of the one sitting on it *was* Death, and the grave followed him; and authority was given to them over *one*-fourth of the earth…" (vs 7-8).

Exactly where that is going to be we don't know. But when the Tribulation begins it's going to affect one-fourth of the earth. Now three-fourths of the earth will not be affected by it, but when they see this take place they are going to start building their armies and getting them up to speed, because later there's an army of 200-million that is going to come, and come toward the Holy Land. So, we're looking at big-time global events that are going to take place. Now then, they are going to a fourth part of the earth:

"…to kill with *the* sword and with famine and with death, and by the beasts of the earth" (v 8).

So, this is going to be one of the most gruesome times on earth. That's why Jesus said that if the time weren't limited there would be no flesh saved alive because of all of the weapons we know that men have, because of all of the things that are going to take place. Unless God intervened, and we're going to see how He's going to intervene, and get their attention and let them know what's going to happen, that Satan is going to be cast down. He's going to persecute the Church. After those who go to a place of safety have gone, then we pick it up here in the very last verse of :

Rev. 12:17—this is when the martyrdom of the saints begins to take place. Let's understand something here, there is a great principle: *The one who seeks to save his life shall lose it, and the one who loses his life in Christ shall save it!* That is accomplished in two ways:

1. if you think you're going to go to a place of safety, *be guaranteed you aren't*
2. and if you think you're going to avoid martyrdom, *be guaranteed*—unless you die before these events take place—*you're not*

So, we might as well face the reality of the truth of the things at the end-time as Jesus said—the worst things that have ever happened on the face of the earth since the beginning of the creation are going to take place. We might as well gear ourselves up for that thinking, and ask God for the help, the strength, and the character that we need, because this is not going to be 'good-time Charlie' and 'wonderful Sally time' when these things and events take place.

That's why Jesus said **_Woe!_** And then we're going to see what God is going to do about it.

Revelation 12:17: "Then the dragon was furious with the woman and went to make war with the rest of her seed, who keep the commandments of God and have the testimony of Jesus Christ."

Now when war comes against the saints they are going to know wherever true Christians are, because all of those who are true Christians will not have *the mark of the beast* and they will know where you are.

Granted, some can flee from city to city but they're going to track you down, because there are going to be traitors. There will be people who are looking to kill Christians because, combined with the two witnesses, they are the ones who are causing all the problems on the earth.

Brethren, I want you to understand the magnitude of these things. I want you to understand how awesome these events are going to be where we are not talking about little events at the end-time that are going to take place and all of a sudden, like the Protestants believe, there's going to be a rapture. There isn't going to be any rapture.

Only the few that go to the place of safety, and they are only there to fulfill what Jesus said, that *the mouth of the grave would not prevail against the Church!* So there's going to come a time when all of the rest—just the few that are in the place of safety—and I don't think many of us are going to make that, because we have to be a witness for Christ.

Just like Christ was a witness to the world and gave His life so that we may live, we have to give our lives for Christ. We need to understand that. **_IF_** you have not counted yourself already dead to sin, and dead because you have been buried in the watery grave, **_THEN you are not mentally prepared for the things that are coming!_**

So part of what I'm trying to do is to help us have a big picture of what's going to take place, and to give us strength and courage by the power of God's Spirit to stand for what is right; to know what we need to do; to realize that:

- God is there
- Christ is there
- They will help us
- They will strengthen us

But we have to be a witness against all of the

bloody wretchedness of this world, even in giving our lives!

You look back at the prophecy that we are going to read here, and many others have done so down through history. What makes us think that we are so all-fired good that we are going to avoid it? A little colloquialism: *It ain't a gonna happen!*

Revelation 6:9: "And when He opened the fifth seal, I saw under the altar the souls of those who had been slain for the Word of God, and for the testimony that they held"—*to tell them that just like the two witnesses are saying to the beast and the false prophet, 'You are of Satan the devil. You are not of God.* These plagues are coming down and we call them as a demonstration against your evil and your wickedness.'

Verse 10: 'And they cried out with a loud voice, saying, 'How long, O Lord, Holy and true, do You not judge and avenge our blood on those who dwell on the earth?' And white robes were given to each of them; and they were told that they should rest a short time, yet..." (vs 10-11).

In other words they are still dead. But this is just a vision to give you an understanding what's going to happen at the end-time in comparison to those who had been martyred before us.

"...until *it* be fulfilled *that* both their fellow servants and their brethren also would be killed, just as they had been" (v 11).

When it comes time that all of those whom Satan makes war against—he finally gets them—*that ends the Church Age.* Then something new is going to begin, and as we know from past messages and so forth, the next event that's going to take place is going to be *approximately 18 months before Christ and the saints put their feet on the earth!* Now I want you to begin to think about what's going to happen here.

Verse 12: "And when He opened the sixth seal, I looked, and behold, there was a great earthquake; and the sun became black as *the* hair *of* sackcloth, and the moon became as blood"—*because if there's a great earthquake and it's anywhere near volcanoes you're going to have all of this exploding at the same time!*

Verse 13: "And the stars of heaven fell to the earth, as a fig tree casts its untimely figs when it is shaken by a mighty wind. Then *the* heaven departed like a scroll that is being rolled up..." (vs 13-14).

There is going to be a new thing that's going to take place. God is going to reveal in a great and a powerful way, just like He said back there in the book of Haggai:

- I'm going to shake the heavens
- I'm going to shake the earth
- I'm going to shake the sea

That's what this is right here! And then the heavens are going to depart as a scroll and a new thing is going to be revealed. Let's see what it is:

"…and every mountain and island was moved out of its place. And the kings of the earth…" (vs 14-15).

G*od is going to get the attention of the whole world!* This is going to be an awesome and fantastic thing.

"…and the great men, and the rich men, and the chief captains, and the powerful men, and every bondman, and every free *man* hid themselves in the caves and in the rocks of the mountains; and they said to the mountains and to the rocks, 'Fall on us, and hide us from *the* face of Him Who sits on the throne, and from the wrath of the Lamb, because the great day of His wrath has come, and who has the power to stand?'" (vs 15-17).

- What is this going to be like when this takes place?
- How is this going to take place?

Look, I want you to understand this is the beginning of the return of Christ to the earth. But He has to come from the third heaven, however far away that that is. So, the heavens roll back as a scroll and then they see something that they have never seen before.

Matt. 24—this is what they are going to see. The whole world is going to see this. It's not going to be that every eye is going to see Him just kind of a flick of a second and every eye sees Him. No, we are going to see that this is going to be something that they are going to be aware of for approximately a year and a half. It's going to be a new thing. It's going to frighten the whole world.

Matthew 24:27: "For as the light of day, which comes forth from *the* east and shines as far as *the* west, so also shall the coming of the Son of man be."

That's how it's going to start. Now the light of day is the sun. When the heavens roll back as a scroll then, as we're going to see, this is called *the sign of the Son of man.* It's going to be like a new sun that is going to suddenly appear.

- What are the men on earth going to say?
- Why are they going to be willing to fight?

The whole world has been programmed with UFO's and aliens! It's going to be declared as the alien invasion of the world and we must save ourselves

from them. In a sense they will be right, because Jesus Christ and God the Father and the angels of God *are indeed alien to the inhabitants of the earth!* But it's going to be greater than that, as we will see.

Verse 29: "But immediately after the tribulation of those days…" *That's the Tribulation against Israel.* We'll see that when we come to Rev. 7.

There's a Great Tribulation that encompasses the whole world. There is the tribulation that is against Israel for God's punishment, which lasts two full years (Hosea 5 & 6).

"…the sun shall be darkened, and the moon shall not give her light, and the stars shall fall from heaven, and the powers of the heavens shall be shaken…. [the whole universe; when it begins, the return of Christ is going to affect the whole universe] …And then shall appear the sign of the Son of man in heaven…" (vs 29-30)

Verse 27: "For as the light of day, which comes forth from *the* east and shines as far as *the* west…" *So, here's a new sun!*

The earth is down here turning on its axis and it looks like it's a new sun that goes around, that is like a second light. That's why it shines from the east to the west because the earth is on its axis turning. That's going to be quite a thing!

Verse 30: "…and then shall all the tribes of the earth mourn, and they shall see the Son of man coming… [He's going to come]: …upon the clouds of heaven with power and great glory. And He shall send His angels with a great sound of a trumpet; and they shall gather together His elect from the four winds, from one end of heaven to *the* other" (vs 30-31).

Let's see how this thing is going to be, because when this comes down it's going to be something!

- God is going to shake the heavens
- God is going to shake the earth
- God is going to reveal Himself

- Why will all the tribes of the earth mourn?
- Why will all people be willing to fight against Christ?

Because they're following the antichrist and the false prophet! They are going to declare that this is an alien invasion from outer space. That's why all the armies are going to be gathered together.

Revelation 1:7: "Behold, He is coming with the clouds…"

As it appears in heaven, it's going to come

closer and closer to the earth until it reaches a point in the clouds above the earth. That's going to give plenty of time for all the armies of the earth to gather together.

"…and **every eye shall see Him,** and those who pierced Him; and all the tribes of the earth shall wail because of Him. Even so, Amen" (v 7).

Let's see what's going to happen. The sign of the Son of man is there. Time is going on. The earth is still turning on it's axis. Now then, *God stops the Tribulation against Israel and He begins His final harvest!* There's every reason to believe that Rev. 7 is going to take place on the next to the last Pentecost as Christ is returning, because He's going to be coming, *coming, coming* to the earth. It's not going to be all of a sudden that:

- one day here's Jesus
- one day here's the resurrection
- we all return to the earth on the same day

It isn't going to happen that way!

- Why are all of those on the earth going to be fighting against each other and fighting against Christ?
- Why are all the armies of the earth gathered at Armageddon?

Because they're going to fight this alien invasion, and we are going to see that it's going to get worse for them! Now God intervenes! Remember this: *Before any event takes place God gives space of repentance!* So here's a space of repentance that God gives to Israel:

Revelation 7:1: "And after these things I saw four angels standing on the four corners of the earth… [this is big time stuff] …**holding back the four winds of the earth,** so that the wind might not blow on the earth, or on the sea, or on any tree. Then I saw another angel ascending from *the* rising of *the* sun, having *the* seal of *the* living God; and he cried out with a loud voice to the four angels, to whom it was given to damage the earth and the sea, saying, **'Do not damage the earth, or the sea, or the trees until we have sealed the servants of our God in their foreheads.'** And I heard the number of those who were sealed: one hundred forty-four thousand, sealed out of every tribe of *the* children of Israel" (vs 1-4).

If you have the Spirit of God today you cannot be one of the 144,000 who are saved in the next to the last Pentecost before Christ and the saints return to the earth. These are of all the tribes of Israel. *It is a special harvest of God, and they receive the Holy Spirit of God in a special and particular way,* because there are no ministers there to baptize them; there is no one to counsel them; their repentance is because they have gone through

the Tribulation and fulfills the promise of Deut. 28 and Lev. 26 that **IF** while in captivity you seek the Lord your God with all your heart, **THEN** He will save you.

This is what happens, and it starts out with the tribe of Judah first to fulfill the prophecy that God is going to save the tents of Judah *first.* Then it lists the twelve tribes.

After that there is a great innumerable multitude because the 144,000 are not the only ones who are going to repent. ***This is the result of the harvest of the preaching of the two witnesses to Israel and Judah, and all the tribes of the earth!*** Now we have a great innumerable multitude, see. If anyone says that there are only going to be a 144,000 in the first resurrection, know that they are lame-brained idiots, because the Bible says:

Verse 9: "After these things I looked, and behold, a great multitude, which no one was able to number, out of every nation… [that takes care of sacred-namers] …and tribe and people and language…"

What are they going to be? *They're going to be in the resurrection!* Here's the vision that portrays them:

"…was standing before the Throne and before the Lamb, clothed with white robes and *holding* palms in their hands" (v 9). *They're going to be in the first resurrection!*

Verse 14: "Then I said to him, 'Sir, you know.' And he said to me, 'They are the ones who have come out of the Great Tribulation; and they have washed their robes, and have made their robes white in the blood of the Lamb'"—by *their repentance*; that's what's going to happen.

Then we come to all the events that take place in Rev. 8-10 and all those events that take place. Now let's see what's going to happen because we come to the last Pentecost. That's when the harvest is going to take place. So here, all this time during this whole year the wars have been going on, on the earth. (Rev. 8-10). The 144.000 and the great innumerable multitude have been spared and they have been saved, waiting the resurrection because we're all going to be resurrected at the same time.

Now we are going to see when the resurrection is going to take place, because this is important for us to understand that it does not take place on the Feast of Trumpets. *It takes place on Pentecost,* because from the time of the resurrection of Christ and His ascension to heaven we have seven continuous weeks of the harvest, and God is harvesting all the way down through it. Then the resurrection is going to take place on the 50th day. That's when the two wave loaves are brought, when there will be permanent change from flesh to spirit. Now let's come back here to the two witnesses:

Revelation 11:7: "And when they have completed their testimony, the beast who ascends out of the abyss will make war against them, and will overcome them, and will kill them."

What Satan is always allowed to do is to believe that he's going to win. That's what happened with Pharaoh when he went and chased the children of Israel to the Red Sea and thought: 'They got across there; I'm going across.' They're going to think that they're going to win. God is going to let them finally kill the two witnesses. Everyone with their cell phones everywhere will be able to see this. They'll see it on television, they'll hear it on radio, they'll have the broadcast. This is going to be a worldwide event. They're going to say, 'Let's have a feast.'

Verse 8: "And their bodies *will lie* in the street of the great city, which spiritually is called Sodom and Egypt... [Jerusalem] ...where also our Lord was crucified. Then those of the peoples and tribes and languages and nations shall see their bodies three and a half days, for they will not allow their bodies to be put into tombs. And those who dwell on the earth will rejoice over them, and will make merry, and will send gifts to one another, because these two prophets had tormented those who dwell on the earth" (vs 8-10).

Surprise! Surprise! God has a big one in store for them!

Verse 11: "Then after the three and a half days, *the* spirit of life from God entered into them and they stood on their feet; and great fear fell upon those who were watching them. And they heard a great voice from heaven, say, 'Come up here!' And they ascended into heaven in a cloud; and their enemies saw them *rise*" (vs 11-12).

What do we have here? *Another fulfillment of the Word of God!* The last two martyred are the first two raised to life.

Verse 13: "And in that hour there was a great earthquake, and a tenth of the city fell; and seven thousand men were killed in the earthquake. And the rest were filled with fear, and gave glory to the God of heaven. The second woe is past. Behold, the third woe is coming immediately. Then the seventh angel sounded *his* trumpet... [this is the resurrection of the rest of the saints, the rest of the firstfruits] ...and *there* were great voices in heaven, saying, 'The kingdoms of this world have become *the kingdoms* of our Lord and His Christ, and He shall reign into the ages of eternity'" (vs 13-15).

This is going to be something! This is a fantastic thing that is going to take place. So, when

that trumpet sounds let's look at two places where it talks about the trumpets, and the resurrection, and let's think and talk about the resurrection here for just a minute in relationship to the rest of the world.

1-Corinthians 15:49: "And as we have borne the image of the *one* made of dust, we shall also bear the image of the heavenly *One*. Now this I say, brethren, that flesh and blood cannot inherit *the* Kingdom of God, nor does corruption inherit incorruption. Behold, I show you a mystery: we shall not all fall asleep..." (vs 49-51)—*because there will still be some who will be alive when Christ returns*: the 144,000 and the great innumerable multitude—they are waiting the resurrection. They will be changed from flesh to spirit in an instant, in the twinkling of an eye.

"...but we shall all be changed, in an instant, in *the* twinkling of an eye, at the last trumpet; for *the* trumpet shall sound..." (vs 51-52). *These are not trumpets, but a trumpet!*

"...and the dead shall be raised incorruptible, and we shall be changed. For this corruptible must put on incorruptibility, and this mortal must put on immortality. Now, when this corruptible shall have put on incorruptibility, and this mortal shall have put on immortality, then shall come to pass the saying that is written: 'Death is swallowed up in victory'" (vs 52-54). *It's going to be!*

Now let's see what's going to happen. Let's see how this is going to take place, then we'll go back to Revelation 14 and see what's going to transpire because this is going to be an awesome event indeed.

1-Thessalonians 4:13: "But I do not wish you to be ignorant, brethren, concerning those who have fallen asleep, that you be not grieved, even as others, who have no hope. For if we believe that Jesus died and rose again, in exactly the same way also, those who have fallen asleep in Jesus will God bring with Him" (vs 13-14).

How's He going to bring them with Him because they're dead in the grave? We're going to see that in just a minute.

Verse 15: "For this we say to you by *the* Word of *the* Lord, that we who are alive and remain unto the coming of the Lord shall in no wise precede those who have fallen asleep... [the dead will be raised first; those who are living will follow] ...because the Lord Himself shall descend from heaven with *a* shout of command, with *the* voice of an archangel and with *the* trumpet of God; and the dead in Christ shall rise first" (vs 15-16).

What's that going to look like? Let's picture this for just a minute here. Let's put all of this together. We'll see it in Rev. 15 here in just a minute.

The sign of the Son of man appears in heaven. It's coming closer and closer and closer to the earth over the space of a year. Then it comes right down into the clouds; the clouds are restricted up to about 50,000 to 60,000 feet down to almost ground level. Now then, the sign of the Son of man when it comes into the clouds is going to be transformed into a great Sea of Glass (Rev. 15). But the resurrection takes place, and the angels are going to, as we saw, carry them up to the Sea of Glass.

I believe the whole world is going to see this. What are they going to say?

The aliens have come and they've got this huge spacecraft right there hovering over Jerusalem, and they are snatching bodies!

Has the world been prepared mentally for that through movies and things? *Yes!* Here they'll see all of the saints being resurrected who are in the graves. The graves opening up and here they come, thousands and thousands of them. Then those who are alive, the 144,000 and great innumerable multitude and those who are in the place of safety, *they* will be resurrected and *they* will come to the Sea of Glass. Now this is going to make the world even more angry at this alien invasion.

They are going to feel that unless we can get rid of this, 'unless we can marshal all the armies of the world against this mighty invasion from outer space,' that 'we are going to be taken over by the aliens.' Now let's come back here to Rev. 14 and Rev. 15. Let's see how the harvest is likened.

Revelation 14:14: "And I looked, and behold, a white cloud, and *one* like *the* Son of man sitting on the cloud, having a golden crown on His head; and in His hand *was* a sharp sickle." *The harvest of the firstfruits!*

Tie that in with Matt. 13—the harvest is at the end of the age, and the reapers are the angels carrying all of the saints up to the Sea of Glass. This is going to bring the greatest confrontation that the world has ever, ever seen.

Verse 15: "And another angel came out of the temple, crying with a loud voice to Him Who was sitting on the cloud, 'Thrust in your sickle and reap, because the time has come for You to reap; for the harvest of the earth is ripe.'"

That's the harvest of the firstfruits. Now the harvest of the wicked comes after that.

Verse 16: "And He Who was sitting on the cloud thrust forth His sickle upon the earth, and the earth was reaped."

Revelation 15:1: "Then I saw another sign in heaven, great and awesome: seven angels having the seven last plagues, for in them the wrath of God is filled up. And I saw a Sea of Glass mingled with fire, and those who had gotten the victory over the beast... [over Satan the devil; that goes all the way back to Abel] ...and over his image... [including all of the idolatry beginning with Cain and all the way down through history to our time] ...and over his mark... [at the end-time with the mark of the beast that's going to be enforced upon all human beings] ...*and* over the number of his name, standing on the Sea of Glass, having *the* lyres of God" (vs 1-2).

- When you're resurrected, where are you going to be taken?
- If the angels take you, where are they going to take you?

They are going to take you to the Sea of Glass!

That's not a doctrine of Fred Coulter; that's what I read out of the Scriptures. Note our message: *What's What Will Happen On the Sea of Glass?* I'll just review it for you:

1. we're all going to receive our garments; the righteousness of the saints
2. we're going to receive our new name
3. we're going to meet Jesus Christ.
4. the marriage of the Lamb is going to take place
5. we will see the declaration of Jesus Christ to God the Father

When all the saints are resurrected and on the Sea of Glass, He is going to turn to the Father—and we'll probably all see this at the same time—and say to the Father, 'Behold all the brethren that you have given Me.' *Then*:

- all of our rewards are then going to be given *we're going to have to know*
- what to do
- which cities we're going to rule over
- who are we going to work with
- how it's going to be done

We're going to also have to understand how to ride those white horses that we're going to be given! We are going to be the Army of God coming back to the earth. We don't come back to the earth until it's pictured by Trumpets.

So, we are on the Sea of Glass all during the time from the resurrection of Pentecost until we come back with Christ on Trumpets. And we're going to see all the events that take place, standing on the Sea of Glass having the harps of God.

Verse 3: "And they were singing the song of Moses... [proclaiming how great and powerful God is—a man of war] ...*the* servant of God, and the song of the Lamb, saying, 'Great and awesome *are* Your works..."'

This is going to be the greatest and biggest thing that has ever happened or has occurred in the history of the whole world from the beginning of the creation of man until the resurrection of His Church. *It's going to be this great worldwide thing!*

"'...Lord God Almighty; righteous and true *are* Your ways, King of the saints. Who shall not fear You, O Lord, and glorify Your name? For *You* only *are* Holy; and all the nations shall come and worship before You, for Your judgments have been revealed" (vs 3-4).

They're not going to come and worship before God **until** the Government of God is set up on the earth and they begin to beat their spears into pruning-hooks and their implements of war into plows and come and learn the way of God. If they don't come and keep the Feast of God, as we know, there are going to be plagues, there are going to be things that will come upon them because God is not going to establish the Kingdom of God and have men continuously rebel.

It's going to come in power, it's going to come in awesome destruction (Rev. 16) leading up to returning to the earth with Christ. This is going to be big time, absolutely the biggest thing that has ever been in the history of the world.

What I want you to understand brethren, is this:

- God has called us with the greatest calling possible
- we are in training for eternal life
- God has given us of His Spirit
- He is going to resurrect us from the dead
- He is going to give us power and authority to rule under Christ
- He is going to bless us with joy and greatness for all eternity
- we will forever be the Church of the Firstborn—the harvest of the firstfruits of God resurrected on Pentecost in great:
  - ✓ joy
  - ✓ power
  - ✓ wonder
  - ✓ magnificence

Now we are going to be ready for the biggest fight that the world has ever seen! But you have to come back for Trumpets in order to see that!

Scriptures from *The Holy Bible in Its Original Order, A Faithful Version*

Scriptural References:

1) Leviticus 23:17-18, 20-21
2) 2 Corinthians 9:6-8
3) Leviticus 23:17
4) Matthew 13:33
5) Acts 2:1-4. 37-41
6) 1 Corinthians 15:34,12-23
7) James 1:17-18
8) Hebrews 12:18-24
9) Revelation 11:1-7
10) Matthew 24:15-22
11) Revelation 6:1-8
12) Revelation 12:17
13) Revelation 6:9-17
14) Matthew 24:27, 29-30, 27, 30-31
15) Revelation 1:7
16) Revelation 7:1-4, 9, 14
17) Revelation 11:7-15
18) 1 Corinthians 15:49-54
19) 1 Thessalonians 4:13-16
20) Revelation 14:14-16
21) Revelation 15:1-4

Scriptures referenced, not quoted:

- Leviticus 23:19
- Acts 1
- 1 Thessalonians 5
- Hosea 5; 6
- Deuteronomy 28
- Leviticus 26
- Revelation 8-10

Also referenced:

- Booklet: *The True Meaning of Acts 2:1* by Fred R. Coulter
- In-Depth Study: *Daniel/Revelation* (with charts and CDs)
- Message: *What's What Will Happen On the Sea of Glass?*

FRC: cs
Transcription date unknown
Reformatted: bo—11/2020

CHAPTER THIRTY-NINE

Pentecost and the Sea of Glass I

Fred R. Coulter

I've had several people ask me about the Sea of Glass, and there have been letters have been written about the Sea of Glass in relationship to Pentecost; Pentecost being the first resurrection.

Those who have been in the Church of God for years and years, especially Worldwide Church of God, have thought that, because of the teachings of the Church, the resurrection would be on the Feast of Trumpets. Just to give you a little background on that so you kind of know what happened in Worldwide and how they came to a Monday Pentecost—and many people don't know this—I came across this when I was up in Eugene, Oregon:

In 1952 when the Church was still very, very small—Eugene being the 'mother church' and they had the college down in Pasadena just starting and so forth—they had a big feudality over how to count Pentecost. I think at that time they had just less than a dozen members up in Eugene, and all but one of them went with a Sunday count of Pentecost. So, Herbert Armstrong sent Raymond Cole up there to solve the problem and to try and save the Church. Then he had Herman Hoeh do a study on it to find out from the Scriptures. Well, they concluded that it ought to be on a Monday.

This came up again and again during the years from there until 1974, and in 1974 it came up again and there was really a big feudality about it and there was more knowledge concerning the Hebrew, the Greek, and so forth. They had another study on it and there was a ministerial conference over it and I was there at the conference and I heard Herman Hoeh give his confession as to how he came up with a Monday Pentecost, which was that in Lev. 23 that the word *Sabbath* 'ha shabbat' meant *weeks*; 'ha shabbat' *never* means weeks

But Dr. Hoeh concluded in his mind that since Herbert Armstrong was the apostle of God he could not be wrong with a Monday Pentecost, so he sought a way to justify it and that's how he justified it. He had to admit at this conference that 'ha shabbat' meant *Sabbath* and Sabbath *only,* and 'shabua' meant *weeks*—week or weeks—the 'shabua' is the week.

That's how we came to have a Monday Pentecost in the Worldwide Church of God. All of those years and all of those problems could have been solved going clear back to 1952 if it would

have been handled rightly. Since that time there are many, many people who have tried to justify a Monday Pentecost and we'll see how they do it—one of them—because before we begin Pentecost we need to go through and review how to count it.

First of all I'm going to show you how to count it correctly, and I'm going to use *The Schocken Bible* Vol. 1, *The Five Books of Moses* by Everett Fox.

The Schocken Bible is a translation that is based upon the more literal reading of the Hebrew and it is really excellent. When I first got it I was shocked at how he was able to get it published at Schocken Publishing Company, because that is the largest Jewish publication company in the world. I've since figured out how he was able to get the clarity of Scripture and get it past the rabbi's, because they're not interested in Scripture, they're interested in commentary. He gave many of the traditional rabbinical commentaries in the commentary section, so it got through and got published.

Let me just tell you very clearly concerning another dispute that centers around Passover, and that is when *between the two evenings* or 'ben ha arbayim' is. Fox translates it correctly *between the setting times*, which I think is a very good translation. But he makes this definition of it and he proves it in Exo. 16. He says concerning:

> **between the setting times**: Between the time that sun is below the horizon, not longer visible, and total darkness. An idiomatic rendition would be "at twilight."

From one of the foremost experts in the world on Hebrew.

Fox also translated this from the Ben Asher-Ben Napthalai text, which is the Levitical Masoretic text. Most people don't realize that there is also a Rabbinic Masoretic text, which comes from the Ashkenazi manuscripts, which come out of Poland and East Germany. Those are not the texts that Luther and Tyndale used to translate the Old Testament. That's another story I won't get into it, but suffice to say we have here a proper Levitical Hebrew text underlying the Schocken translation.

We will go through on how to count to Pentecost, and I'm going to show you five checkpoints that give us absolute certainty that it is the 50th day and it is on a Sunday. Many people are familiar with double entry bookkeeping, which gives you two reference points so that you can balance the books. If you want to balance the books without balancing the books you do like this little joke:

> The auditor comes in and is auditing this business and he said, 'Well I see your books are in perfect shape they all balance, but I have just one question.' And the bookkeeper looked up and said, 'Well, what's that?' the auditor said, 'What is this ESP account? That seems be a very large account and I don't know what it is?' The bookkeeper said, 'Oh, that means *error some place*. Whenever there's an error I just put it in the ESP account and the books balance.'

Well, a lot of people do that with the Bible. They don't properly put it together, but double entry bookkeeping rightly handled gives you the correct perspective and it gives you a double-check that all your figures are right.

Now then, if you want to figure a precise place where you are you then you do a three point, not a two point. You do what is called a triangulation, and you can pick the exact spot as to where you are or the exact spot as to where you want to go.

So, with Pentecost we don't have double entry bookkeeping, we don't have triangulation, we have five points that prove and give us a definition on how to come to the 50 days. You can't have any one of these five points wrong and you cannot have a Monday Pentecost or a 6th of Sivan Pentecost, except in rare occasions where you have all five of these correct, you must break some of them in order to do that.

Leviticus 23:10 (*SB*): "Speak to the Children of Israel and say to them: 'When you enter the land that I give to you, and you harvest its harvest…'"

All during the wilderness all they had was manna. They could:

- boil it
- bake it
- deep fry it
- eat it raw

They could not eat bread nor eat grain until they got in to make the first harvest of the land.

"…you are to bring the premier sheaf…" The *King James* says 'the sheaf of the firstfruits.' The *premiere* means *the first of the first* in the Hebrew. That's why Fox translates it *premiere* sheaf; it is the first and most important, and that's

why this pictures *the ascension* of Christ. He was already resurrected at the end of the Sabbath.

Another thing that is important to remember is that the *premiere sheaf* had a special time of harvest. The special time of harvest was right after the regular Sabbath was ending during the Feast of Unleavened Bread. During temple times they would send out the priests and the watchers, and they had a special barley plot right on the Mount of Olives. They would come across the Kidron Bridge, go over to this special ceremonial barley plot and they would then be ready to harvest the sheaf because they had put a scarlet thread around it to mark it off; they marked it off before the Sabbath.

Then the men who were the watchers would be up on top of the hill, and they would be watching for sundown. They would go out there right at the end of the Sabbath, that was less then a Sabbath Day's journey because it was only from the temple over to the Mount of Olives, which was just across the Kidron Bridge.

The watchers would look out west and those who were with the group would ask them three times, 'Is the sun set?' *No!* 'Is the sun set?' *No!* Finally the third time, 'Is the sun set?' *Yes!* Then they would harvest the sheaf. That's a type of when Christ was lifted from the earth as it were, right at the end of the Sabbath. Just as the first day of the week was beginning He already had spiritual life given back to Him. So, Christ was the first harvest, *the Premier Sheaf.* This was the one then that was to be taken to the priest.

Verse 11—it says in the *KJV*: "…he shall wave" it. But in the *Schocken* it says: "He is to **elevate** the sheaf…"—meaning to *lift up* and that's more like an ascension into heaven than it is just waving back and forth.

"He is to elevate the sheaf before the presence of YHWH [the LORD], for acceptance for you…" (v 11).

And that's exactly what happened on the day that Jesus ascended into heaven to be accepted of the Father as a sacrifice on our behalf, *for us.* The *us* means *we're the rest of the firstfruits.*

"…on the morrow of the Sabbath…" (v 11). That means *on the day after the Sabbath.* When does the day after the Sabbath begin? **At sunset!** It's the whole day; you count the whole day. As the day of the Sabbath was ending they cut the sheaf, so they had it cut at the beginning of the day. Then in the morning at 9 o'clock they would take it to the priest and:

"…on the morrow of the Sabbath the priest is to elevate it" (v 11).

Verse 14 gives all the things that they were to do on that day when they waved the wave sheaf offering: "Now bread or parched-grain or groats, you're not to eat, until that same day…"

Josh. 5 tells you when that same day occurred when they entered into the land and "…harvested its harvest."

Verse 10 says, "…and you harvest its harvest…"

Some people made the argument that they had to wait until they planted their own grain and harvested their own harvest, which then would put it a year later. *No!* You *harvest its harvest* because when they came in and took over those areas that were already planted, whose grain did it become? *It became theirs!*

They couldn't eat any "…bread or parched-grain or goats, you are not to eat, until that same day…" (v 14).

If you think eating unleavened bread for seven days is difficult, try 40 years with no bread. That would be, when you really get bread, then that would be kind of like a strange new food, especially with all this manna.

You're not to eat it "…until you have brought the near-offering of your God—(it is) a law for the ages, into your generations, throughout all your settlements. Now **you are to number**…" (vs 14-15)—*that is to count! Counting is different from adding and subtracting!*

I use this example many times and I'll use it again because we're familiar with it: When you went to high school you went four years. If you count the years, they're 9, 10, 11, and 12; *inclusive* counting. If you take 9 and subtract it from 12, you don't get 4 but you get 3. That's where people make a lot of mistakes.

Another example: You work from Monday to Friday; that *includes* Monday. If your boss would do subtracting instead of counting, you would come and get your paycheck—say you were to make $100 a day—and you expect the gross amount to be $500, and you look at it and it's $400. So, you say to your boss, 'I'm short $100 here.' He says, 'No, you agreed to work *from* Monday to Friday, so since it's *from* Monday I'm not counting Monday because it's *from* Monday.' How long would you work for him? You would tell him, 'Look, you either pay it…' Then what would you do? If you belonged to a union you'd get a grievance. If you didn't belong to the union you'd go to the Fair Employment Practices, and you would get your day's pay of $100. Well, this is what people have done concerning Pentecost. They're not doing it correctly.

1. Verse 15: "Now **you are to number for yourselves, <u>from the morrow of the Sabbath</u>**…"

—including that day, because the Hebrew is 'moh-ghorahht,' which means *including that day*, because you're counting *from* the Sabbath. You are not counting from Sunday; you are *including* Sunday, the first day of the week, because that follows the seventh day of the week.

You are including the morrow from the Sabbath; you're counting the first day of the week. Now, to re-emphasize it: *From* the day that you bring the wave sheaf. That's all part of #1 because that's included on that day. There's only one day to bring the wave sheaf. Every one agrees on the wave sheaf with the exception of the Jews who say it's on the Holy Day rather than Sabbath. That's a Pharisaical way of reckoning it, and that's how they come up with the 6th of Sivan.

2. "…**seven Sabbaths-of-days**…" (v 15)

You're going to miss out on one Sabbath if you go to the 6th of Sivan; so that can't be right. You're going to miss out on a Sabbath if you're counting to a Monday Pentecost. We'll see there's another check for it. There have to be seven Sabbaths

3. "…**whole (weeks) are they to be**…" (v 15).

It says, in the *King James*, "complete weeks."

What is a whole week? *Seven consecutive days, a complete week!* What is a deficient week? *When you start, say on Monday, and you count from Monday to Monday*; you're dealing with deficient weeks; all seven weeks are deficient. You don't have whole weeks. A whole week is day one through day seven *including* day one and *including* day seven. That is a whole week! If you go from day two to day two you have deficient weeks; they are not whole weeks; they're not complete weeks. "…whole (weeks) are they to be."

4. Verse 16: "**Until the morrow of the seventh Sabbath**…"

Again, it's not the day *after* the day *after* the Sabbath. When you have a Monday Pentecost you're coming to the day after the day after the Sabbath.

5. "…**you are to number—fifty days**…" (v 16)

In order to come to the right counting of it you must have all five of these conditions met. Let's review it so we get it clear. You are to number unto yourselves:

1. from the morrow of the Sabbath from the day you bring the wave sheaf
2. seven Sabbaths of days
3. whole weeks are they to be
4. until the morrow of the seventh Sabbath

5. you are to number fifty days

You can take any calendar and you can start out on any Sunday and you can count seven full weeks and come to the day after the seventh full week and you will be on a Sunday. There is no way that can be missed.

Now what they were to do, they were to bring the offering, and after that they brought two loaves of two-tenths meal, flour they are to be, firstfruits unto the Lord. These firstfruits are different than the others.

Verse 17: "…leavened you are to bake them…"

This is the only offering that God required to be leavened. All other meal or bread offerings were to be unleavened. The leavening of these symbolizes the two covenants, or the two ages of when people would be brought into the Kingdom of God.

1) the covenant with Israel, including the other patriarchs
2) the New Testament Church

That's why there are only two; that's why there are not three, six or ten; there are only two. The reason there is leaven in them is because we all have the 'law of sin and death' *in us,* and therefore, we are accepted with the 'law of sin and death' in us *if* we have the Holy Spirit in us; that's by the grace of God. That's the symbolic meaning of this. Then the other animal sacrifices they were to bring.

Verse 21: "And you are to make-proclamation **on that same day**…" I want you to really emphasize this: *fifty days* and *that same day.*

"…a proclamation of holiness shall there be for you, any-kind of servile work you are not to do—a law for the ages, throughout your settlements, into your generations" (v 21).

Now we're going to look at a very clever slight of hand, which is done by some people where they use the word in:

Verse 16 "…fifty days, **then** you are to bring-a grain-gift…[offering] …of new-crops to YHWH [the Lord]."

In the *King James* it says *and* instead of *then.* But this does not mean *afterward* 'then', it means *inclusive.*

Let's come here to Lev. 15 and show where they go to try and prove their point, because they use that as a device to say that we should go to the 51st day by saying that after you have counted the 50 days then you are to go to the 51st day by using the word *then* or *and.*

Leviticus 15:13 (*FV*): "And when he who discharges is cleansed of his discharge… [that could be of any wound, sore, infection, anything that was draining] …then he shall number seven days to himself for his cleansing, and wash his clothes, and bathe his flesh in running water, and shall be clean. And on the eighth day he shall take two turtledoves for himself, or two young pigeons…" (vs 13-14)— *and he shall go and that will be his offering; that will be an atonement.*

What they say is that the seven days in counting here is likened unto numbering the 50 days in Lev. 23. So, when you get done numbering the 50 days then you must go to the 51st day. But it doesn't say number eight days here. It says count and "…**number seven days to himself**…" Then on the 8th day he is to go do his offering. It doesn't say count the 8th day. You count 7 days and then that 8th day you go do it.

Whereas, in Lev. 23 it says to number to yourself 50 days and on that same 50th day you are to bring the offering. It does not say, and on the 51st day then you are to bring your offerings.

What is missing is that here in Lev. 15:14 it specifically mentions the 8th day. In Lev. 23 it does not mention specifically a 51st day. If there was to be a parallel in thought then it would have to say then on the 51st day you are to bring a near grain offering or meal offering. This is the cleverest slight of hand that I have heard. People get tripped up over reading this and there are some people who fervently, adamantly believe in a 51st-day Pentecost—a Monday Pentecost—based upon what I just said.

What would happen if you did that, you would go on to the morrow after the morrow. What happens in this, you violate the 4th point under the morrow of the 7th Sabbath. If you have a Monday Pentecost you are not on the morrow after of the 7th Sabbath. You're on the morrow after the morrow of the 7th Sabbath, and then you can't avoid the situation in:

Leviticus 23:21 (*SB*): "And you are to make-proclamation on **that same day**…" *If this were referring to the 51st day that's where it would say it!*

That's all of Schocken for this situation here. Let's go to John 20 and we will see that there is a sequence of days, a sequence of counting that leads up to the 50 days.

John 20:1: "Now, on the first *day* of the **weeks**…" *The Hebrew there is plural* 'ton sabbaton.'

Which day is on the first day of the weeks? *The morrow after the Sabbath!* This is counting toward Pentecost.

"...while it was still dark, Mary Magdalene came..." (v 1) and so forth. That is the day that Jesus ascended.

Verse 16: "Jesus said to her, 'Mary.' Turning around, she said to Him, 'Rabboni'; that is to say, 'Teacher.' Jesus said to her, 'Do not touch Me, because I have not yet ascended to My Father. But go to My brethren and tell them that I am ascending to My Father and your Father, and My God and your God.' Mary Magdalene came to the disciples, bringing word that she had seen the Lord, and that He had said these things to her. Afterwards, **as evening was drawing near that day, the first day of the weeks**..." (vs 16-19).

Apparently, just before the sun was setting, still on that day, the first day of the week.

"...and the doors were shut where the disciples had assembled for fear of the Jews, Jesus came and stood in the midst, and said to them, 'Peace be to you'" (v 19)—*you know the rest of the story!*

Verse 26: "Now, after eight days... [now we've got eight days; we have day one and day eight] ...His disciples again were within, and Thomas with them. Jesus came after the doors were shut, and stood in the midst..."—*appeared to them!* So, we have a numbering of the days.

Acts 1:1: "The first account I indeed have written, O Theophilus, concerning all things that Jesus began both to do and to teach, until the day in which He was taken up, after giving command by *the* Holy Spirit to the apostles whom He had chosen; to whom also, **by many infallible proofs,** He presented Himself alive after He had suffered, being seen by them for forty days, and speaking the things concerning the Kingdom of God" (vs 1-3).

There were a great many brethren that saw Him. God did not want this to be some little thing done in a corner. The whole ministry of Christ was public, absolutely of great notoriety. Of course, to the scribes and Pharisees *notorious!* But they were the notorious ones.

1-Corinthians 15:3: "For in the first place, I delivered to you what I also had received: that Christ died for our sins, according to the Scriptures; and that He was buried; and that He was raised the third day, according to the Scriptures; and that He appeared to Cephas, *and* then to the twelve. Then He appeared to over five hundred brethren at one time, of whom the greater part are alive until now..." (vs 3-6).

He was seen by *many!* Many "...infallible proofs..." (Acts 1:3) I don't know all the infallible proofs that it says there. It would be interesting to know what they were, but it doesn't tell us. So, when we're resurrected and we meet the apostles and those who saw it, we can ask them what they were. We'll find out at that time.

Acts 1:4: "And while *they* were assembled with *Him,* He commanded them not to depart from Jerusalem but to 'await the promise of the Father, which,' *He said,* 'you have heard of Me. For John indeed baptized with water, but you shall be baptized with *the* Holy Spirit after not many days'" (vs 4-5).

How many days was it from that? *Well, we had 40 days!* On the 40th day He ascended. The disciples really didn't quite understand it.

Verse 6: "So then, when they were assembled together, they asked Him, saying, 'Lord, will You restore the kingdom to Israel at this time?'"

They were promised to sit on thrones weren't they, so they wanted to know, 'Lord, is the Throne coming?'

Verse 7: "And He said to them, 'It is not for you to know *the* times or *the* seasons, which the Father has placed in His own **authority.'**" *The Greek here is* 'exousia' not 'dunamis' meaning power.

Verse 8: "But you yourselves shall receive power... ['dunamis'] ...when the Holy Spirit has come upon you, and you shall be My witnesses, both in Jerusalem and in all Judea and Samaria, and unto *the* ends of the earth"—*which is a continuing ongoing prophecy of the Gospel going out to the world!*

Verse 9: "And after saying these things, *as* they were looking at *Him,* He was taken up, and a cloud received Him out of their sight."

Now, that would be an experience, wouldn't it? Today we have television or movies and we can see things simulated like that, but to actually see the real thing; of course, this was a one-time thing for them.

Verse 10: "Now, while they were gazing intently up into heaven..."

- I wonder what they were thinking when He was going up?
- I wonder what they were thinking in their minds?

'Look, He's going higher and higher! Wow, I can't see Him. There He goes right into a cloud! Look at that!'

Then an angel, while they were looking up—two men stood by them; those were angels, in white apparel—said to them:

"…'You men of Galilee, why do you stand *here* looking up into heaven?'" (v 11). *Once the event is finished God wants you to get on with the business!*

"'…This *same* Jesus, Who was taken up from you into heaven, shall come in exactly the same manner as you have seen Him go into heaven'" (vs 11). *So, they returned. That was the 40th day!*

We have three booklets:
- *How to Count Pentecost*
- *Count to Pentecost: From the Morrow After Which Sabbath?*
- *The True Meaning of Acts 2:1*

When is Pentecost and all the peculiar details of it that I've covered here.

Acts 2:1: "And when the Day *of Pentecost*, the fiftieth day, was being fulfilled, they were all with one accord in the same place."

Those who believe in a Monday Pentecost and will not—refuse—let go of it say that this means *when the Day of Pentecost had ended*. That is **not** what it means.

"…when the Day *of Pentecost*, the fiftieth day, **was being fulfilled**…"—that doesn't mean the day after, it doesn't mean the day before. *That's what it means in the Greek!* In the Greek it means this: "…when the Day *of Pentecost*, the fiftieth day, **was being fulfilled**…"

"**…being fulfilled…**" is a peculiar thing to Greek—which is not in English—what is called *an articular infinitive*. That means that you put the definite article **the** in front of an *ing* verb: the coming, the going, the keeping, the fulfilling. It means *during the fulfilling of the day,* namely the 50th day. It wasn't the day before and it wasn't the day after.

Now let's look at some of the same language here that we find in Lev. 23. You know what happened there on the Day of Pentecost. Look at the fulfilling of not only the Wave Sheaf Offering on the Wave Sheaf Offering Day—the first day—but also the fulfilling of the bringing the loaves of leaven for the 50th day.

Acts 2:37: "Now, after hearing *this*, they were cut to the heart; and they said to Peter and the other apostles, 'Men *and* brethren, what shall we do?' Then Peter said to them, 'Repent and be baptized each one of you in the name of Jesus Christ for *the* remission of sins, and you yourselves shall receive the gift of the Holy Spirit. For the promise is to you and to your children, and to all those who are afar off, as many as *the* Lord our God may call.' And with many other words he earnestly testified and exhorted, saying, 'Be saved from this perverse

generation.' Then those who joyfully received his message were baptized; and about three thousand souls were added **that day**" (vs 37-41). *Notice the same wording as back in Lev. 23, **the same day!***

So there is a fulfilling of the wave offering loaves on the 50th day. You have the same exact thing as we find in Lev. 23 and that's what those loaves were picturing because this was a great and *a momentous event!*

It just occurred to me that these loaves could also signify more than just what I said, Old Testament/New Testament. It could also signify Jew and Gentile as relating to receiving the Holy Spirit after baptism, because the Gentiles were given the Holy Spirit in the same way that the Jews were, and in the same manner by the way (Acts 10).

Let's see the comparison between Heb. 12 and Exo. 19 & 20. Heb. 12 is also a very important chapter, which also shows us why the first resurrection is on Pentecost and not on the Feast of Trumpets. There will be other things, which I will show to prove that.

I never will forget the first Pentecost that we kept, and at the time we were still living in Pasadena and I was pastoring Torrance and Santa Monica and we had combined Torrance and Santa Monica services down at the Los Angeles Convention Center, and Gerald Waterhouse was the speaker. Well, I led the songs and everything. I think someone else brought the first message, but I led the songs and took the announcements and I had to announce to everyone, 'Well brethren, here we are the first time keeping Pentecost *on the right day*.' Trying to help them understand a little bit about it—not getting into Scripture or anything—I mentioned just off-handedly, 'Who knows? Maybe we will find out that the first resurrection is really on Pentecost.'

Gerald Waterhouse is sitting out there, and I'm thankful that it just sailed over his head, because I'm sure I would have been lambasted up one side and down the other for having said such a presumptuous thing. But later it's turned out to be true. Let's see some of the reasons for it today.

Hebrews 12:18: "For you have not come to *the* mount… [referring to the one back in Exo. 19, Mt. Sinai] …that could be touched and that burned with fire, nor to gloominess, and fearful darkness, and *the* whirlwind; and to *the* sound of **the trumpet**…" (vs 18-19).

I want to emphasize *a trumpet.* We're going to see that's important.

- trumpets is plural
- trumpet is singular

We also need to understand that on every

Holy Day the trumpet was to be blown (Num. 10). So *a* trumpet was blown on the first day of Unleavened Bread, the seventh day of Unleavened Bread and the Day of Pentecost. Then on the Feast of Trumpets it was a memorial or a blowing of trumpets all the day long.

I think the Buddhists perversion is where they have these big long horns. They all get up there on whatever day and these big old horns are going. They're all decked up in all these demonic costumes and running around firing off firecrackers and jumping in the air and doing all sorts of silly things 'to drive the demons away.'

- Is God going to stop blowing trumpets on the Feast of Trumpets because the pagans do this?
- Because they have a counterfeit of it?
- *No!*

Just because pagans have a counterfeit of anything that we do does not mean that we stop doing it because they have something that they have done.

Verse 19: "And to *the* sound of *the* trumpet, and to *the* voice of *the* words, which those who heard, *begged* that *the* word not be spoken *directly* to them. (For they could not endure what was being commanded: 'And if even an animal touches the mountain, it shall be stoned, or shot through with an arrow' and so terrifying was the sight *that* Moses said, 'I am greatly afraid and trembling.')" (vs 19-21). *We're going to see, so did all the people!*

Now he's making a comparison here. The comparison has to do with the Feast of Pentecost, because that's when the Ten Commandments were given.

Verse 22: "But you have come to Mount Sion, and **to *the* city of *the* living God, heavenly Jerusalem;** and to an innumerable company of angels; **to the** joyous **festival gathering;** **and to** *the* **Church** of *the* **Firstborn, registered** *in the Book of Life* **in heaven;** and to God, *the* Judge of all; and to *the* spirits of the just who have been perfected" (vs 22-23).

Now when is the "...festival gathering..." of the Church of the Firstborn going to take place? "...**registered** *in the Book of Life* **in heaven**..."

Let's look at some parallels, which is the Day of Pentecost and I've got a chart showing that.

Exodus 19:16: "And it came to pass on the third day in the morning that there *were* thunders and lightnings, and a thick cloud upon the mountain. And the sound of **the trumpet**..." *It wasn't many trumpets!*

"...was exceedingly loud so that all the people in the camp trembled. And Moses brought the people out of the camp to meet with God. And they stood at the base of the mountain. And Mount Sinai was smoking, all of it because the LORD came down upon it in fire. And the smoke of it went up like the smoke of a furnace, and the whole mountain quaked greatly. And when the sound of the trumpet sounded long, and became very strong, Moses spoke, and God answered him by voice. And the LORD came down upon Mount Sinai on the top of the mountain. And the LORD called Moses to the top of the mountain, and Moses went up" (vs 16-20). *That must have been a sight with him going up!*

Verse 21: "And the LORD said to Moses, 'Go down....'" *He climbed down this mountain! Moses really was a mountain climber here!*

"'...Command the people, lest they break through unto the LORD to gaze, and many of them perish. And let the priests also, who come near to the LORD, sanctify themselves, lest the LORD break forth upon them.' And Moses said to the LORD, 'The people cannot come up to Mount Sinai, for You commanded us, saying, "Set bounds around the mountain, and sanctify it."' And the LORD said to him, 'Away! Get you down, and *only* you shall come up, you and Aaron with you. But do not let the priests and the people break through to come up to the LORD, lest He break forth upon them'" (vs 21-24). *Moses went down to the people and spoke to them, and then God gave the Ten Commandments!*

Of course, the people couldn't stand it. This must have been some awesome display:

Exodus 20:18: "And all the people saw the thunderings, and the lightnings, and the sound of the trumpet, and the mountain smoking. And when the people saw, they trembled and stood afar off. And they said to Moses, 'You speak with us, and we will hear. **But let not God speak with us, lest we die**'" (vs 18-19).

This must have been such a loud noise and so much happening that the vibrations of the noise and the thunder and the lightning was just going through their system so much that it affected them to the point that they felt they were going to die. Have you ever had any loud noise affect you that way? *That's how it affected them!*

Now, let's look at a Scripture here that is important for us to understand. We're going to see that with the giving of the Ten Commandments and the events that took place right after that—the day after Pentecost—that that ties right in with the Church and the marriage of the Lamb, and so forth.

Jeremiah 2:1: "And the Word of the LORD came to me, saying, 'Go and cry in the ears of Jerusalem, saying, "Thus says the LORD, 'I remember you, the kindness of your youth, the love of your betrothals, when you went after Me in the wilderness, in a land not sown. **Israel *was* Holiness to the LORD**, and the firstfruits of His increase…."'" (vs 1-3).

- When did they become Holiness unto the LORD?
- When did they become the firstfruits?

They were literally harvested out of Egypt! They had a seven-week journey coming up to Mt. Sinai. So, they became firstfruits and became *Holiness to the LORD* on Pentecost, and then the sealing of it on the day after Pentecost when the covenant was sealed and the marriage took place.

"'…All that devour him shall be held guilty; evil shall come on them,' says the LORD. Hear the Word of the LORD, O house of Jacob, and all the families of the house of Israel…" (vs 3-4).

Then God asked, 'What happened to you? I brought you out of Egypt, why did you reject Me? *IF* I were sent even unto other nations, they would have rejected their gods and accepted Me and would have kept Me, but *you have forsaken Me.*'

Isaiah 54:5: "For your Maker *is* your husband; the LORD of hosts is His name; and your Redeemer *is* the Holy One of Israel…"

When did the LORD become the husband to Israel? *There are going to be*:

- parallels with Christ and the Church
- parallels with Mt. Sinai and Mt. Zion
- parallels with the *festival gathering* at the foot of Mt. Sinai to receive the Ten Commandments

and

- the festival gathering which will take place at the resurrection, and the marriage of the Church and the Lamb

The rest of Exodus 20-23 are all the basic statutes and judgments based upon the Ten Commandments. Exo. 24 becomes important because this finishes off the Day of Pentecost. The Day *after* Pentecost is when the marriage took place. The marriage took place when they accepted the covenant because this was a covenant ceremony.

Exodus 24:1: "And He said to Moses, 'Come up to the LORD, you and Aaron, Nadab, and Abihu, and seventy of the elders of Israel, and worship afar off. And Moses alone shall come near the LORD, but they shall not come near. Neither shall the people go up with him'" (vs. 1-2).

So, Moses came down—he went up, came down; Moses was doing a lot of walking here.

Verse 3: "And Moses came and told the people all the words of the LORD, and all the judgments. And all the people answered with one voice and said, '**All the words which the LORD has said, we will do.**'" What do we have in a marriage ceremony?:

- Do you accept this woman as your lawful wedded wife? *I do!*
- Do you accept this man as your lawful wedded husband? *I do!*

This is what Israel and the LORD did here. It's always a written contract. God never enters into a covenant without some kind of written contract. God is the Author of Law, so God is legal. He makes sure that it's done legally and technically correct.

Verse 4: "And Moses wrote all the words of the LORD, and rose up early in the morning, and built an altar at the base of the mountain and twelve pillars according to the twelve tribes of Israel. And he sent young men of the children of Israel who offered burnt offerings, and sacrificed peace offerings of bullocks to the LORD. And Moses took half of the blood, and put *it* in basins, and half of the blood he sprinkled on the altar. And he took the Book of the Covenant, and read in the ears of the people…" (vs 4-7).

These are the words of the marriage covenant between Israel and God, which took place the day after Pentecost. Years ago I thought it was done on Pentecost but it's obvious it's in the morning; so that's the next day.

"…And they said, 'All that the LORD has said we will do, and be obedient.' And Moses took the blood and sprinkled *it* on the people, and said, '**Behold the blood of the covenant**…" (vs 7-8).

When you understand covenant relationships and you understand that a covenant is cut, it is binding until death. That's why when Christ came to be human, one of the functions He served in dying, as the husband to physical Israel *to loose* that marriage. Either He had to die or all of Israel had to die. *So, God died!* That loosed the Old Covenant; no longer binding. That has nothing to do with the laws and commandments because all covenants have laws and commandments. {note our in-depth study: *Covenants of God*}

"…Behold the blood of the covenant… [this is serious business] …which the LORD has made with you concerning all these words'" (v 8). *So, we have the marriage of Israel to God!*

When the Church is resurrected there will be the marriage of Christ and the Church, and there will be a New Covenant at that time. *It will be a marriage covenant for all eternity!*

I don't think many people really understand that. The covenant we are under now is renewed every year *by us* with the bread and wine and foot-washing. Christ doesn't have to renew it because He gave His life. That's why He said He would not eat of the bread or drink of the wine, especially of the wine. He ate bread later but that wasn't in the covenant ceremony of the Passover. He ate bread and fish (John 21). But He's not going to drink of the fruit of the vine until it's in the Kingdom. It's going to be when He drinks it, *it will be the wine of the marriage ceremony when the Church is married to Christ!*

Now let's look at where, when and how this is going to happen. But first of all let's answer a question here and let's get into the situation concerning what is called *the Sea of Glass,* which we pick up right here:

Verse 9: "And Moses went up, and Aaron, Nadab, and Abihu, and seventy of the elders of Israel. And they saw the God of Israel. And *there was* **under His feet as it were a paved work of a sapphire stone, and as it were the heavens in clearness**" (vs 9-10). There is *a Sea of Glass,* or a pavement of what you would call glass.

Why did He come down to there? *So that they could see Him but not look upon Him!* They saw the outline of Him but they couldn't see it clearly. Moses had to go up to be on this pavement with God. Notice what they did:

Verse 11: "And upon the nobles of the children of Israel He did not lay his hands. Also they saw God, and ate and drank."

They had a special ceremony there commemorating the marriage of Israel and God!

Verse 12: "And the LORD said to Moses, 'Come up to Me in the mountain, and be there. And I will give you tablets of stone, and the law, and commandments which I have written, so that you may teach them.' And Moses rose up, and his attendant Joshua. And Moses went up into the mountain of God. And he said to the elders, 'You wait here for us until we come again to you. And behold, Aaron and Hur *are* with you. If any man has a cause, let him come to them.' And Moses went up into the mountain, and a cloud covered the mountain. And the glory of the LORD abode upon Mount Sinai, and the cloud covered it six days. And the seventh day He called to Moses out of the midst of the cloud. And the sight of the glory of the LORD *was* like a consuming fire on the top of the mountain to the eyes of the children of Israel. And Moses went into the midst of the cloud, and went up into the mountain. And Moses was in the mountain forty days and forty nights" (vs 12-18).

You know what happened there: The children of Israel couldn't stand it. They thought:

'I wonder what's happening? I wonder what happened to that Moses, he's still up there? This has been three weeks and where is this guy? I bet he's fallen into the volcanic explosions up there and he's been all devoured.' Yeah, well we better go to Aaron here. He said go to Aaron, so let's go to Aaron.'

They came to Aaron and said, 'You know, Aaron, look we don't know where Moses is, we don't have a god, now what you do, you just make us gods.' And Aaron said, 'Ok, bring all your gold and all of this…'

I love the excuse when Moses came down and said, 'Aaron, why did you do this?' Aaron said, *'We just threw the gold in the fire and out jumped these calves.'* What happened? *The children of Israel didn't want God's pure way, they wanted a religion!*

The Presence of God and the Sea of Glass

There are some people very angry at me because I say that when we're resurrected we're going to be on the Sea of Glass. What you need to do is also be very angry at God, because God only talks of the false prophet twice by name. Is the false prophet going to do a lot of damage? *Yes, indeed!* So, please understand something about Scripture: *once is sufficient!* Let's talk about God's Throne because that also has to do with the Sea of Glass:

Psalm 11:4: "The LORD is in His Holy temple; the LORD'S Throne is in heaven. His eyes behold; His searching gaze tests the children of men."

God is in heaven! How close is the heaven of God's Throne to the earth? *I can't tell you, but I don't think it's in the far, far north,* because we're going to see that it's probably a whole lot closer to the earth, but men cannot see it at the present time.

Psalm 45:6: "Your Throne, O God, is forever and ever; a scepter of justice is the scepter of Your Kingdom. You love righteousness and hate wickedness; therefore, God, Your God, has anointed You with the oil of gladness above Your fellows" (vs 6-7). *That's a direct prophecy that Christ was and is God!* His Throne is "…forever and ever."

Psalm 47:8: "God reigns over the nations; God sits upon the Throne of His Holiness. The rulers of the peoples are gathered together, the people of the God of Abraham… [that could have an allusion to the resurrection] …for the shields of the earth are God's; He is greatly exalted" (vs 8-9).

We have something here in Ezek. 1 that is very unusual, and I don't think that anyone can properly explain about the cherubim, exactly how they look. I know people have tried to draw pictures of them. When I read it I think of something like a jet plane. I don't know how to explain it other than just it's in there. What he wrote he wrote and for us to try and decide what it is, is very difficult for us to do, indeed. But let's just clarify something here that is important.

Everything in this room is made of the dust of the earth, including us. Even though we are composed of the dust of the earth and are flesh, we have life; whereas, this microphone doesn't, the stand doesn't, the rug doesn't, and so forth. We have things that bring us light, which are called lights and have electricity in them; but those are still made of physical things.

There are things in heaven that are made of spiritual things, *which are not living beings*. For example, New Jerusalem is going to be made out of *spiritual material* but it is not a living being. So likewise, here with this, whatever these cherubim are, *it is God's chariot*.

Ezekiel 1:20: "Wherever the spirit was to go, there they went; for there the spirit *was* to go. And the wheels were lifted up along with them, for the spirit of the living creatures was in the wheels. In their going, *these also* went; and in their standing still, these *also* stood still. And in their lifting up from the earth, the wheels were *also* lifted up along with them...." *That seems to me kind of like the wheels were folded up in just like an airplane today!*

"...For **the spirit** of the living creatures *was* in the wheels" (v 21). *The spirit could be just the power of the living creatures!*

Here's what I want to get to, v 22: "And there *was* a likeness over the heads of the living creatures—an expanse, like the color of awesome crystal stretched out over their heads from above"— *so beautiful to behold!*

There we have something now kind of like a rainbow over them like crystal. *Not a sea of glass,* but just to show you that there are things composed of spirit.

Verse 23: "And under the expanse their wings *were* straight, the one toward the other. Each one had two *wings* covering on this *side*, and each *had* two *wings* covering on that *side of* their bodies. And I heard the sound of their wings, like the sound of great waters, like the voice of the Almighty, as they went their sound *was like* the sound of tumult, as the sound of an army. In their standing still, they let down their wings" (vs 23-24).

The closest I can come to that is like propellers, and when the plane lands you turn off the propellers and they stop. The propellers are kind of like wings. That's the best I can do.

Verse 25: "And there was a voice from the expanse, which *was* over their heads, when they stood still, and they let down their wings. And from above the expanse that *was* over their heads *was* the likeness of a throne... [this was to carry a portable Throne of God] ...**like sapphire stone**. And on the likeness of the Throne *was* a likeness as the appearance of a man above upon it. And I saw *Him* appearing as the color of polished bronze, looking like fire within it all around. From the likeness of His loins even upward, and from the likeness of His loins even downward, I saw *Him*, looking like fire, and there was brightness all around Him'" (vs 25-27). *Here he's seeing just a glorified spirit being who's obviously God!*

Verse 28: "As the rainbow appears that is in the cloud in the day of rain... [there was a rainbow round about this whole cherubim] ...so was the appearance of His brightness all around. This was the appearance of the likeness of the glory of the LORD. And I saw. And I fell on my face, and I heard a voice of One speaking."

Ezekiel 2:1: "And He said to me, 'Son of man, stand on your feet, and I will speak to you.'"

Here God came right down to Ezekiel. That's quite a thing! Stood him on his feet, gave him His message and everything.

Verse 2: "And the Spirit entered into me when He spoke to me, and set me on my feet, so that I heard Him Who spoke to me."

Then He gives him Ezekiel's commission that he is to do. That's quite a thing!

Ezekiel 3:12: "And the Spirit lifted me up, and I heard behind me a sound of a great rushing, *saying*, 'Blessed *be* the glory of the LORD from His place.' *I* also *heard* the sound of the wings of the living creatures... [apparently he got a ride on this cherubim] ...touching one another, and the sound of the wheels along with them, and a sound of a great rushing. So, the Spirit lifted me up and took me away, and I went in bitterness, in the heat of my spirit; but the hand of the LORD was strong upon me. Then I came to the exiles at Tel Abib, who lived by the River Chebar..." (vs 12-15). *So, apparently Ezekiel had a ride on a cherubim!*

This is probably very similar as to what happened to Enoch when he was carried away, and Elisha when he was carried away. *They were carried away to a separate place, and the chariot of the Lord took them away!* The reason I'm bringing that out is because I want you to see that there are things made of spirit that must then be manifest to the human eyes that you can't see otherwise, and God uses those things.

Let's see where Isaiah was also before the Throne of God. Maybe this will convince some people who want to profess themselves to be prophets, to maybe not be prophets any longer because maybe the cherubim is going to come and correct you, rather than give you a ride. God may come and correct you with some pretty severe things. That's why no one should want to set himself up as a prophet. Look at how Ezekiel was set up. Look at how Jeremiah was set up. Look how Isaiah was set up here. God did it directly.

Isaiah 6:1: "In the year that King Uzziah died, I then saw the LORD sitting upon a throne, high and lifted up, and His train filled the temple…. [he saw the Throne and the Temple] …Above it stood the seraphim; each one had six wings; with two he covered his face, and with two he covered his feet, and with two he flew. And one cried to another, and said, 'Holy, Holy, Holy, *is* the LORD of hosts… [we'll see in Rev. 4 this is pretty similar] …the whole earth is full of His glory.' And the foundations of the threshold shook at the voice of the one who cried, and the house was filled with smoke. Then I said, 'Woe *is* me! For I am undone; for I *am* a man of unclean lips, and I dwell in the midst of a people of unclean lips; for my eyes have seen the King, the LORD of hosts'" (vs 1-5). *Actually saw God!*

Verse 6: "Then one of the seraphim flew to me, having a live coal in his hand, *which* he had taken with tongs from the altar. And he laid *it* upon my mouth and said, 'Lo, this has touched your lips; and your iniquity is taken away, and your sin atoned for'" (vs 6-7). *God has more than one way of forgiving sin!* This was to show Isaiah that God was going to use him.

Verse 8: "And I heard the voice of the LORD, saying, 'Whom shall I send, and who will go for us?' Then I said, 'Here *am* I; send me!' And He said, 'Go, and tell this people, "You hear indeed, but do not understand; and you see indeed, but do not perceive." Make the heart of this people fat, and make their ears heavy, and shut their eyes; lest they see with their eyes, and hear with their ears, and understand with their hearts, and return, and be healed'" (vs 8-10).

How many times was that quoted in Matthew? *and* by the apostles? *and* even by Christ Himself?

Acts 7 is when Stephen was martyred. You talk about a witness. This was one of the last profound witnesses to the leaders of Judaism. This sealed the doom of Jerusalem and the temple and everything.

Acts 7:51: "O stiff-necked and uncircumcised in heart and ears! You do always resist the Holy Spirit; as your fathers *did*, so also *do* you. Which of the prophets did your fathers not persecute? And they killed those who foretold the coming of the Righteous One, of Whom you have become the betrayers and murderers; who received the law by *the* disposition of angels, but have not kept *it*" (vs 51-53). *They thought they were the most righteous people in the world!*

Verse 54: "And when they heard these things, they were cut to their hearts… [not unto repentance] …and they gnashed their teeth at him." *They were sitting there gnashing their teeth!*

Verse 55: "But he, being filled with *the* Holy Spirit, looked intently into heaven *and* saw *the* glory of God, and Jesus standing at the right hand of God. And he said, 'Behold, I see the heavens opened, and the Son of man standing at the right *hand* of God'" (vs 55-56).

How close is the Throne of God to the earth? *We don't know!* But Stephen looked up and saw it, and Christ standing at the right hand. Let's understand something about being at the right hand. When someone is at the right hand that is *a sign of equality!* Standing at the right hand of God. Notice He wasn't sitting there.

Revelation 3:21: "To the one who overcomes will I give *authority* to sit with Me in My throne, even as I also overcame, and sat down with My Father in His Throne."

This time He was standing. He was standing there looking as to what was going on, not just sitting viewing. So, He wasn't a passive participant in this, but active.

And Stephen said, Acts 7:56: "And he said, 'Behold, I see the heavens opened, and the Son of man standing at the right *hand* of God.' Then they cried out with a loud voice…" (vs 56-57).

They couldn't stand this! The one whom they killed and crucified, rejected!

"…*and* stopped their ears, and rushed upon him with one accord, and cast *him* out of the city *and* stoned *him*.…" (vs 56-58).

There comes a point some people just won't listen to the Truth at all and there's no repentance available!

Scriptures from *The Holy Bible in Its Original Order, A Faithful Version* (except where noted)

Scriptural References:

1) Leviticus 23:10-11, 14, 10, 14-17, 21, 16
2) Leviticus 15:13-14
3) John 20:1, 16-19, 26
4) Acts 1:1-3
5) 1 Corinthians 15:3-6

6) Acts 1:4-11
7) Acts 2:1, 37-41
8) Hebrews 12:18-23
9) Exodus 19:16-24
10) Exodus 20:18-19
11) Jeremiah 2:1-4
12) Isaiah 54:5
13) Exodus 24:1-18
14) Psalm 11:4
15) Psalm 45:6-7
16) Psalm 47:8-9
17) Ezekiel 1:20-28
18) Ezekiel 2:1-2
19) Ezekiel 3:12-15
20) Isaiah 6:1-10
21) Acts 7:51-56
22) Revelation 3:21
23) Acts 7:57-58

Scriptures referenced, not quoted:

- Exodus 16
- Joshua 5
- Acts 10
- Numbers 10
- Exodus 21-23
- John 21
- Revelation 4

Also referenced:

In-Depth Study: *Covenants of God*

Book: *The Schocken Bible* Vol. 1, *The Five Books of Moses* by Everett Fox

Booklets by Fred. R. Coulter:
- *How to Count Pentecost*
- *Count to Pentecost: From the Morrow After Which Sabbath?*
- *The True Meaning of Acts 2:1*

FRC: cs
Transcription date unknown
Formatted: bo—11/2020

CHAPTER FORTY

Pentecost and the Sea of Glass II
Fred R. Coulter

Let's just talk a little bit now about the Throne of God and how the Throne of God and the Sea of Glass are combined together. But let's go back in review.

I think the thing that is most interesting in viewing the things concerning William Tyndale, is that those who really have the Spirit of God and want to teach the Word of God, as William Tyndale did—anyone that God will use—they will preach the words of Christ; they will use the Scriptures.

When you stop and think about it, there is nothing greater that you can use. There is nothing greater that you can preach on than the Word of God, because:

- the Word of God is true
- the Word of God has been sent to us so that we may understand
- the Word of God is given to us to bring us eternal salvation through Christ and the Holy Spirit of God

We have here in our hands, sitting in front of us, the greatest possession that you could ever have. That's why David said, 'Your Word is more than gold, yea, fine gold.' There is no wealth in the world that can buy this. There is no wealth in the world that can buy what William Tyndale did over 460 years ago. He did it so that it is a blessing for us today.

Part of understanding the Word of God is to go through it and put it together and let God lead us in it. Christ gave the promise that *the Spirit will lead us into all Truth,* and will lead us into understanding the things that are to come. But it's also based upon: **Do we love God?** *If we don't love God then that's not going to happen!* God will leave us to our own devices. If we love power, prestige, money and things of this world, then God will leave us to our own devices. Before then He will correct us, He will work with us to bring us to repentance that we may change and grow.

I think when we're looking at this thing concerning Pentecost, and when we are looking at the old teachings that we had in Worldwide, I think that part of the problem was that *in keeping a Monday Pentecost we never understood the Truth of the resurrection being pictured by the Day of Pentecost!* That was part of the penalty that we had.

Yet, down through the years it was always bragged upon that, 'God blessed us though we kept a Monday Pentecost and what was bound on earth was bound in heaven.' Well, if it was:

- Why did God change it?
- Why did God bring it to their attention to do it correctly?

That's so those of us who remain can understand the Truth!

When we get into the Sea of Glass we need to understand about the Throne of God. We're going to cover some Scriptures about the Throne of God and then we will go on through and into the book of Revelation and then we will see why Pentecost has to be picturing the first resurrection rather than Trumpets.

Psalm 11:4: "The LORD is in His Holy Temple; the LORD'S Throne is in heaven. His eyes behold; His searching gaze tests the children of men." *God knows!*

Remember the account when Stephen was martyred in Acts 7? *He said he saw heaven opened and the Son of man was standing at the right hand of the Throne of God looking down and seeing what was going to happen!*

Verse 5: "The LORD tries the righteous, but His soul hates the wicked and the one who loves violence. Upon the wicked He shall rain snares, fire and brimstone; and a scorching wind shall be the portion of their cup… [Does God do that? *No doubt about it!*] …for the LORD is righteous, He loves righteousness; the upright will behold His face" (vs 5-7). *God is on His Throne!*

Let's see what kind of throne this is. This is a prophecy of Christ Himself:

Psalm 45:6: "Your Throne, O God, is forever and ever; a scepter of justice is the scepter of Your Kingdom… [or a righteous scepter]….You love righteousness and hate wickedness; therefore, God, Your God, has anointed You with the oil of gladness above Your fellows" (vs 6-7).

That's a direct prophecy of Christ. Of course, Christ is right at the very Throne of God.

Psalm 47:7: "God is King of all the earth; sing praises with understanding. God reigns over the nations; God sits upon the Throne of His Holiness" (vs 7-8).

Let's see what happened to the Throne of God during the days of Ezekiel. Let's go back and review that, because part of understanding about the Sea of Glass is that wherever God goes when He's not on His Throne He has a portable Throne that's in the cherubim. That's what Ezekiel saw.

I'm not going to go back and try and understand all of that, and try and tell you what it was that Ezekiel saw. I don't think any man can really figure out exactly what he said. I know I've seen people draw pictures of it and it kind of looks like a combination of a jet plane and a flying saucer, and all of that sort of thing, so I don't know what it looks like. But it's very possible.

But nevertheless, let me just review and say this as we discussed in *Pentecost and the Sea of Glass #1*. Everything that we see in this room and see around us in the world is made of the dust of the earth. We're made of the dust of the earth, but the flesh of human beings is formed into a different kind than the soil out here, or the grass, or the trees, or the carpet that we have on the floor here, or the lights that we have overhead. Likewise with God; God makes things out of spirit that are not necessarily living creatures. That's the best I can explain about the cherubim. The cherubim may in fact be living creatures, but if you look at it in another way they may, in fact, not be living creatures as they're attached to this thing called *the cherubim,* and it is a chariot of God.

Here's how it went, Ezekiel 1:20: "Wherever the spirit was to go, there they went; for there the spirit *was* to go. And the wheels were lifted up along with them, for the spirit of the living creatures was in the wheels. In their going, *these also* went; and in their standing still, these *also* stood still. And in their lifting up from the earth, the wheels were *also* lifted up along with them…" (vs 20-21).

Kind of sounds like collapsing wheels. Almost like wheels of an airplane that they land on the wheels and when they take off the wheels close up. That's what it sounds like to me.

"…For the spirit… [that is the power] …of the living creatures *was* in the wheels. And there *was* a likeness over the heads of the living creatures—an expanse, **like the color of awesome crystal** stretched out over their heads from above…" (vs 21-22).

We're going to see that the Sea of Glass and around God's Throne, crystal is referred to as crystal. But I'm sure that it is something that is made out of spirit—is spirit substance—that is created into

the thing that God moves around in. Just like your car; your car is made out of the dust of the earth. But you stop and think about how the dust of the earth has to be refined to make the car, to make the plastic, to make the metal, to make the tires, to give you all the things that you have with heating, with air conditioning, with the radio, a CD player—all of those things.

If we can do this as human beings, cannot God do more and greater with spirit? *After all, consider New Jerusalem that's coming down out of heaven!* That's wholly made out of spirit. Here's "…**awesome crystal stretched out over their heads from above.**" It's kind of like an arch.

Verse 23: "And under the expanse their wings *were* straight, the one toward the other. Each one had two *wings* covering on this *side*, and each *had* two *wings* covering on that *side of* their bodies. And I heard the sound of their wings, like the sound of great waters…" (vs 23-24).

Kind of like a big power thrust taking off. That's what the shuttle launch sounds like when you listen to it; it's got the fire breathing out the back.

"…like the voice of the Almighty, as they went their sound *was like* the sound of tumult, as the sound of an army. In their standing still, they let down their wings" (vs 24).

In other words, when it came to a stand still they let down their wings. Reminds me more of a helicopter with the wings.

Verse 25: "And there was a voice from the expanse, which *was* over their heads, when they stood still, and they let down their wings. And from above the expanse that *was* over their heads *was* the likeness of a throne… [we're talking about the Throne of God] …like sapphire stone. And on the likeness of the Throne *was* a likeness as the appearance of a man above upon it. And I saw *Him* appearing as the color of polished bronze, looking like fire within it all around. From the likeness of His loins even upward, and from the likeness of His loins even downward, I saw *Him*, looking like fire, and there was brightness all around Him. As the rainbow appears that is in the cloud in the day of rain…" (vs 25-28).

We're going to see when we come back to Rev. 4 that the rainbow surrounds God's Throne. So, this goes wherever He goes.

"…so was the appearance of His brightness all around. This was the appearance of the likeness of the glory of the LORD. And I saw. And I fell on my face, and I heard a voice of One speaking" (v 28).

Ezekiel 2:1: "And He said to me, 'Son of

man, stand on your feet, and I will speak to you.' And the Spirit entered into me when He spoke to me, and set me on my feet, so that I heard Him Who spoke to me. And He said to me, 'Son of man, I am sending you to the children of Israel, to a rebellious nation, who have rebelled against Me; they and their fathers have transgressed against Me, even unto this very day'" (vs 1-3).

Ezekiel 3:10: "And He said to me, 'Son of man, receive all My words which I shall speak to you. Receive them to your heart, and hear with your ears.'"

What a lesson for us today! Absolutely, what a lesson! Do we receive all the words of God and put them in our heart and hear with our ears, let it lead us and guide us as God's Spirit leads us?

Verse 11: "And go! Go to those of the captivity, to the children of your people, and speak to them, and tell them, 'Thus says the Lord GOD;' whether they will hear or whether they will forbear.'"

There comes a time when you have to give a witness whether they will hear or whether they won't hear. That's one of the reasons why we do the things that we do; at least it is a witness to them. *If they don't act upon it is witness against them!* Sometimes a witness is just what people would consider a very small thing. Like God told Jeremiah, 'You write this witness against Babylon. You give it to one of the captives and when they get to Babylon have them throw it in the river for a witness against them.'

Well, how many people saw that? I'm sure the king of Babylon was not on the bridge when he threw it in the river, but it was still a witness against him. What I want us to do in some of these things as we're going along is let us really *think* on the Word of God, and *think* of what God has for us. Understand the words of God like this here.

Verse 12: "And the Spirit lifted me up, and I heard behind me a sound of a great rushing, *saying*, 'Blessed *be* the glory of the LORD from His place.' *I* also *heard* the sound of the wings of the living creatures touching one another, and the sound of the wheels along with them, and a sound of a great rushing" (vs 12-13). *Ezekiel got a ride in the cherubim!*

Verse 14: "So, the Spirit lifted me up and took me away, and I went in bitterness, in the heat of my spirit; but the hand of the LORD was strong upon me. Then I came to the exiles at Tel Abib, who lived by the River Chebar..." *He was actually just brought right into the captives' internment center there!*

"...And I sat *where* they sat; and I also

remained there astonished among them for seven days" (v 15).

God just put him down and put him right there and he just sat there astonied for seven days, and I imagine everybody came by asking: Who is this? Did you see how he got here? He was just kind of dropped right here.

Verse 16: "And it came to pass at the end of seven days, *that* the Word of the LORD *came* to me, saying, 'Son of man, I have made you a watchman to the house of Israel. Therefore, hear the word from My mouth, and give them warning from Me. When I say to the wicked, "You shall surely die," and you do not give him warning, nor speak to warn the wicked from his wicked way, to save his life; the same wicked one shall die in his iniquity; but I will require his blood at your hand'" (vs 16-18).

You talk about a responsibility! God laid it upon him! We need to think about that in relationship to what we are doing. Not that I want to in any way intimate that we are going to be Ezekiel's watchman on the wall. As I've mentioned, I know of at least eight or ten ministers who claim that, and I think the wall is getting a little crowded.

Nevertheless, this is why I keep encouraging the brethren: if you know other brethren, reach out to them. Send them a message {or to the website: **truthofGod.org**}. Ask God to give you understanding which would be the best message for you to send to them. We need to reach out to them, and that's the best way we can. I don't know who they are; I don't know where they are; but many brethren in many places know some where they are, and we can help them in that manner.

I took a Passover book—*The Christian Passover*—up to a man who was still in Worldwide and he just looked like he was dead spiritually. But nevertheless, it helped revive him.

All of our things we give out free. God will provide enough so we can do that. We'll keep the overhead down, we'll run it lean, clean and slim so we can send out things for the brethren.

Here's the warning, v 19: "Yet, if you warn the wicked, and he does not turn from his wickedness nor from his wicked way, he shall die in his iniquity; but you have delivered your soul. And when the righteous turns from his righteousness and commits iniquity, and I lay a stumbling block before him, he shall die. Because you have not given him warning, he shall die in his sin, and his righteousness, which he has done shall not be remembered; but his blood I will require at your hand" (vs 19-20).

God really requires a lot! We really need to think on these things. We all need to take it personally. Not that we all become an Ezekiel, but the Word of God is for us, and we need to heed it and use it.

Verse 21: "But if you warn the righteous so that the righteous does not sin, and if he does not sin, he shall surely live because he is warned; also you have delivered your soul."

That was quite a message after riding on the chariot, after being taken in God's chariot over to the slave camp there where the Israelites were. Then God laid it out to be absolutely clear for them. Then you read the book of Ezekiel and you will see that he had one of the toughest, most difficult ministries to do. The book of Ezekiel is really a very heavy book of death, destruction, and slaughter, because the people rejected God and had forgotten God. I think we can look at what's happening in our day and realize the same thing is going to happen again.

Isaiah 6:1—*again, we have a situation where Isaiah was brought before the Throne of God*: "In the year that King Uzziah died, I then saw the LORD sitting upon a Throne, high and lifted up, and His train filled the temple."

I'm convinced after reading these Scriptures, the ones that I've read in preparation for this message, that we'll see in Rev. 4 & 5, that God's Throne is much closer to the earth than we have realized. But God has not given us the ability to see how close it is. He has to open up our eyes, or roll back the heavens (Rev. 6), and then the whole world will see. There are going to be some things that are going to happen. God is not going to let this world come to an end without great and awesome things taking place.

Verse 2: "Above it stood the seraphim; each one had six wings; with two he covered his face, and with two he covered his feet, and with two he flew. And one cried to another, and said, 'Holy, Holy, Holy, *is* the LORD of hosts; the whole earth is full of His glory.' And the **foundations of the threshold** shook at the voice of the one who cried, and the house was filled with smoke" (vs. 2-4).

It talks about the posts—"...**foundations of the threshold...**"—and I think that has to do with:

Psalm 24:7: "Lift up your heads, O you gates; and be lifted up, O you everlasting doors; that the King of glory may come in."

I think that's what it's talking about here in the *foundations of the threshold*. When Christ was accepted of God the Father, the posts said this and the gates opened...

Isaiah 6:5: "Then I said, 'Woe *is* me! For I am undone...'"

If you would be right up before God's Throne and see that you'd feel the same thing, too! When human beings see that the awesomeness of the spiritual things of God are just like that, they realize that that are absolutely nothing.

Isaiah said, "'...I am undone; for I *am* a man of unclean lips, and I dwell in the midst of a people of unclean lips; for my eyes have seen the King, the LORD of hosts.' Then one of the seraphim flew to me, having a live coal in his hand, *which* he had taken with tongs from the altar. And he laid *it* upon my mouth and said, 'Lo, this has touched your lips; and your iniquity is taken away, and your sin atoned for.' And I heard the voice of the LORD, saying, 'Whom shall I send, and who will go for us?' Then I said, 'Here *am* I; send me!' And He said, 'Go, and tell this people, "You hear indeed, but do not understand; and you see indeed, but do not perceive." Make the heart of this people fat, and make their ears heavy, and shut their eyes; lest they see with their eyes, and hear with their ears, and understand with their hearts, and return, and be healed'" (vs 5-10). *God has deliberately closed the eyes of many in the world!*

I will go into some detail on Pentecost concerning the seven churches in Rev. 2 & 3 picturing the harvest of seven weeks, beginning with the first day, the day after the Sabbath, including that and seven whole complete weeks coming down to seven whole weeks.

Then the 50th day is Pentecost. You will see that the 50th day is *God's special day of salvation for the 144,000 and the great innumerable multitude!* What I want to do here in the book of Revelation is to look at the whole situation concerning the Throne of God and the Sea of Glass and why, *at the resurrection,* we will be taken to the Sea of Glass.

The Church Age ends with the Laodicean epic; that's why it is cut off right here. Then when the martyrdom of the saints occurs, the only Christians in the flesh alive will be in wherever the place of safety is. They're the only ones left alive in the flesh. That's why God raises up the 144,000, and He does His work, and He does His ministry. After the Church Age, right when it is coming to a close:

Revelation 4:1. "After these things I looked, and behold, a door opened in heaven; and the first voice that I heard *was* as if a trumpet were speaking with me, saying, 'Come up here, and I will show you *the* things that must take place after these things.' And immediately I was in *the* Spirit; and behold, a throne was set in heaven, and *One was* sitting on the Throne. And He Who *was* sitting was in appearance like a jasper stone and a sardius stone; and a rainbow *was* around the Throne..." (vs 1-3).

Again we have the rainbow. Remember the rainbow in Exo. 24, where there was the Sea of Glass or the paving where they saw God standing.

"…and a rainbow *was* around the Throne, like an emerald in its appearance. And round about the Throne *were* twenty-four thrones… [actually lesser thrones] …and on the thrones I saw twenty-four elders sitting, clothed in white garments; and they had on their heads golden crowns. And proceeding from the Throne were lightnings and thunders and voices; and seven lamps of fire, which are the seven spirits of God, *were* burning before the Throne" (vs 3-5).

What I want you to do, I want you to think how similar this is compared to when God came down on Mt. Sinai (Exo. 19 & 20) and brought the Ten Commandments, when there were thunderings, there were lightnings, there was the voice of the trumpet sounding exceeding loud. Remember, that was done on the Day of Pentecost.

The seven Spirits' job is to go 'to and fro' in the midst of the earth and see who's seeking God. How does God call someone? *He does it personally!* I think, first of all, one of the seven Spirits has to find out and spy out who is seeking God and let God know. Then God decides whether this individual is seeking Him in Truth or not and begins to call them, begins to deal with them.

- How did you first begin to understand the Truth?
- What happened?
- What turned the switch in your mind?

It had to happen, and it was a spiritual miracle to occur. So, the seven Spirits do that.

Verse 6: "And before the Throne *was* **a sea of glass, like crystal**…" *Here's the Sea of Glass!*

Wherever the Throne of God is, there is *a sea of glass*. There is a rainbow, or in the case of the cherubim it is a temporary throne and goes where God goes.

"…And around the Throne and over the Throne *were* four living creatures, full of eyes before and behind; and the first living creature *was* like a lion, and the second living creature *was* like a bull, and the third living creature had the face of a man, and the fourth living creature *was* like a flying eagle" (vs 6-7).

That ties right in with the appearance of the cherubim. Wherever God goes on the cherubim He has His portable Throne and He has His small replica of it just like His main Throne that we're seeing here in Rev. 4.

Verse 8: "And each of *the* four living creatures had six wings respectively… [that ties in with Isa. 6] …And each of *the* four living creatures had six wings respectively; *and* around and within *they were* full of eyes; and day and night they cease not saying, 'Holy, Holy, Holy, Lord God Almighty, Who was, and Who is, and Who *is* to come.' And when the living creatures give glory and honor and thanksgiving to Him Who sits on the Throne, Who lives into the ages of eternity, the twenty-four elders fall down before Him Who sits on the Throne; and they worship Him Who lives into the ages of eternity, and cast their crowns before the Throne, saying, 'Worthy are You, O Lord, to receive glory and honor and power because You did create all things, and for Your will they were created and exist'" (vs 8-11).

You think about that, brethren. *For God's pleasure you were and are created,* and understand that salvation is creation right now in you, a spiritual creation that is taking place. *You were created for His pleasure!*

Ephesians 1:3: "Blessed *be* the God and Father of our Lord Jesus Christ, Who has blessed us with every spiritual blessing in the heavenly *things* with Christ"—*because one day we're going to be there with Christ!* One day we're going to be on the Sea of Glass before the Throne of God.

Verse 4: "According as He has personally chosen us for Himself before *the* foundation of *the* world in order that we might be Holy and blameless before Him in love; having predestinated us for sonship to Himself through Jesus Christ, according to the good pleasure of His own will" (vs 4-5).

- let God do His good pleasure in you
- let Him create Christ in you
- let Him create in you the spiritual character and strength, which comes from God

because that's the whole purpose of your life!

Ephesians 2:10: "For we are His workmanship, created in Christ Jesus unto *the* good works that God ordained beforehand in order that we might walk in them."

If we do that then there's going to be the day we will come before the Throne of God.

Just remember that *all things were created by God and for His pleasure!* In other words God has a great and a marvelous thing that He is going to do for all of His creation, and *we* are the firstfruits. Rev. 5 talks more about the Throne of God and how that Christ was counted worthy to open the seals.

Revelation 5:5: "Then one of the elders said to me, 'Do not weep. Behold, the Lion Who is of the tribe of Judah, the Root of David, has overcome to open the book, and to loose its seven seals.' Then I saw, and behold, before the Throne and the four living creatures, and before the elders, *was* standing a Lamb as having been slain, having seven horns and seven eyes, **which are the seven spirits of God that are sent into all the earth**" (vs 5-6).

The seven horns picture that Christ is the Head of the seven Churches of Rev. 2 & 3. Christ is the Head of the Church. That's why the seven horns are in the head of the Lamb.

Verse 7: "And He came and took the book out of the right hand of Him Who sits on the Throne… [God the Father] …And when He took the book, the four living creatures and the twenty-four elders fell down before the Lamb, each having harps and golden bowls full of incense, which are the prayers of the saints" (vs 7-8).

Somehow when our prayers go to God they help bring them to God. Just how that works I don't know but we're told in Rom. 8 that the Spirit makes intercession for us with sounds or groanings that we cannot utter. And the best way I can explain that is that the Spirit eliminates out of our prayers all the stupidity that enters in because of the weakness of our mind. Have you ever been praying and all of a sudden the thought of something having nothing to do with prayer came in? *Like maybe you left the oven on, or you left the keys in your car, or you didn't lock the door, or whatever!* Or the one that bothers me is when I'm praying and then all of a sudden a stupid commercial comes clattering through my mind, that I've heard on television or radio.

That doesn't go to God. I think the Spirit filters that out. The Spirit conveys your *true heart* to God. Then it comes before God, it comes before His very Throne and it comes before the golden altar. That's something! One of these days we're going to see that whole thing.

Rev. 6 is somewhere down into 2 years of the 3-1/2 years of the Tribulation,

Revelation 6:12: "And when He opened the sixth seal, I looked, and behold, there was a great earthquake; and the sun became black as *the* hair *of* sackcloth, and the moon became as blood; and the stars of heaven fell to the earth, as a fig tree casts its untimely figs when it is shaken by a mighty wind. Then *the* heaven departed like a scroll that is being rolled up, and every mountain and island was moved out of its place. And the kings of the earth, and the great men, and the rich men, and the chief captains, and the powerful men, and every bondman, and every free *man* hid themselves in the caves and in the rocks of the mountains; and they said to the mountains and to the rocks, 'Fall on us, and hide us from *the* face of Him Who sits on the Throne, and from the wrath of the Lamb'" (vs 12-16).

The world gets a glimpse of God's Throne. Not like we will, but they get a glimpse of it.

The 144,000 and the great innumerable multitude; this is God's 50th day harvest:

Revelation 7:9: "After these things I looked, and behold, a great multitude, which no one was able to number, out of every nation and tribe and people and language, was standing before the Throne and before the Lamb, clothed with white robes and *holding* palms in their hands; and they were calling out with a loud voice to Him Who sits on the Throne and to the Lamb, saying, 'The salvation of our God *has come*'" (vs 9-10).

They're standing right before the Throne of God. When you're resurrected you're going to come before the Throne of God. That's what this is telling us. When the 144,000 and the great innumerable multitude are resurrected they come before the Throne of God. What is underlying the Throne of God? *The Sea of Glass!*

Verse 11: "Then all the angels stood around the Throne, and the elders and the four living creatures, and fell on their faces before the Throne and worshiped God, saying, 'Amen. Blessing, and glory, and wisdom, and thanksgiving, and honor, and power and strength *be* to our God into the ages of eternity. Amen.' And one of the elders answered *and* said to me, 'These who are clothed with white robes, who are they, and where did they come from?' Then I said to him, 'Sir, you know.' And he said to me, 'They are the ones who have come out of the Great Tribulation; and they have washed their robes, and have made their robes white in the blood of the Lamb'" (vs 11-14). *There they are before the Throne of God!*

Verse 15: "For this reason, they are before the Throne of God and serve Him day and night in His temple; and the One Who sits on the Throne shall dwell among them. They shall not hunger any more, nor shall they thirst any more; neither shall the sun nor the heat fall upon them" (vs 15-16). *This is a projection clear into New Jerusalem (Rev. 22).*

Verse 17: "Because the Lamb Who *is* in *the* midst of the Throne will shepherd them, and will lead them to fountains of living waters; and God will wipe away every tear from their eyes." *There is the Throne, the Sea of Glass, and everything that takes place there!*

Let's see what happens at the last trump. I want you to understand that whenever it talks about the resurrection it talks about 'the trump' or 'a trump,' *never trumpets*. The Feast of Trumpets is plural, a memorial of blowing trumpets all day long.

Revelation 11:15: "Then the seventh angel sounded *his* trumpet; and *there* were great voices in heaven, saying, 'The kingdoms of this world have become *the kingdoms* of our Lord and His Christ, and He shall reign into the ages of eternity.' And the twenty-four elders, who sit before God on their thrones, fell on their faces and worshiped God" (vs 15-16).

He's looking again at the Throne of God, *and the Throne of God has the Sea of Glass!* All those who are going to be resurrected will come before the Throne of God. There has to be the Sea of Glass.

Verse 17: "Saying, 'We give You thanks, O Lord God Almighty, Who is, and Who was, and Who *is* to come; for You have taken *to Yourself* Your great power, and have reigned. For the nations were angry, and Your wrath has come...'" (vs 17-18).

The resurrection takes place before the wrath of God, not after. *The wrath of God comes between Pentecost and Trumpets!*

"'...and the time for the dead to be judged, and to give reward to Your servants the prophets, and to the saints, and to *all* those who fear Your name, the small and the great; and to destroy those who destroy the earth'" (v 18).

All of the saints have to be individually given their reward. We also know from Rev. 2 & 3 *they have to be given*:

* a new name
* the name of the Father
* the name of the new city Jerusalem
* Christ's new name

All of that has to take place after they are resurrected!

Verse 19: "And the Temple of God in heaven was opened, and the Ark of His covenant was seen in His Temple; and there were lightnings, and voices, and thunders, and an earthquake and great hail." *Again I call your attention to Exo. 19 & 20, which was on Pentecost!*

Matthew 24:29: "But immediately after the tribulation of those days, the sun shall be darkened, and the moon shall not give her light... [that goes right back to Rev. 6 & 11] ...and the stars shall fall from heaven, and the powers of the heavens shall be shaken. And then shall appear the sign of the Son of man in heaven; and then shall all the tribes of the earth mourn, and they shall see the Son of man coming upon the clouds of heaven with power and great glory" (vs 29-30).

But the saints are not with Him, yet. We're going to see it says we're going to meet Christ in the air.

Verse 31: "And He shall send His angels with a great sound of a trumpet... [not trumpets plural] ...and they shall gather together His elect from the four winds, from one end of heaven to *the* other."

Why do they have to be gathered? *Because they're not left on the earth!* They meet Christ in the air. Where in the air will Christ be?

This gives us a little more understanding concerning it, 1-Thessalonians 4:14: "For if we believe that Jesus died and rose again, in exactly the same way also, those who have fallen asleep in Jesus will God bring with Him."

But in order to be brought with Him you've got to come out of the grave to meet Him. Christ is not coming down to the earth to go into the grave to get you. He's going to send the angels to catch you up after you've been resurrected out of the earth.

Verse 15: "For this we say to you by *the* Word of *the* Lord, that we who are alive and remain unto the coming of the Lord shall in no wise precede those who have fallen asleep... [all the dead in Christ rise first] ...because the Lord Himself shall descend from heaven with *a* shout of command, with *the* voice of an archangel and with *the* trumpet of God; and **the dead in Christ shall rise first**" (vs 15-16)—*and be carried by the angels to the Sea of Glass before the Throne of God!* After all if you're resurrected:

* Why can't you come up to God's Throne?
* God is on His Throne, isn't He?
* Should we not go there to worship Him the very first thing we do?

No doubt about it!

Dolores and I always used to joke whenever we go past a cemetery, especially when it's filled with all kinds of headstones and everything. We said the first thing that's going to happen, they're going to be resurrected and knocked out cold. No, that won't happen; physical things won't bother you.

1-Corinthians 15:51: "Behold, I show you a mystery: we shall not all fall asleep, but we shall all be changed, in an instant, in *the* twinkling of an eye... [just like that] ...at the last trumpet... [which is the seventh trump; not the Feast of Trumpets] ...for *the* trumpet shall sound, and the dead shall be raised incorruptible, and we shall be changed" (vs 51-52). *When we are changed the angels gather us and take us up to meet the Lord in the air!*

1-Thessalonians 4:17: "Then we who are alive and remain shall be caught up together with them in *the* clouds..."

When Christ comes, first the sign of the Son of man will be seen and will be coming closer and closer to the earth perhaps during the space of about a year and a half, not quite a year and a half, a little over a year. Then it's going to come right into the clouds; then it's going to stop in the clouds. I believe those clouds stop right over Jerusalem so that when we are raised we are going to be raised and be brought to the Sea of Glass. We are caught up in the air to meet Him:

"...for *the* meeting with the Lord in *the* air; and so shall we always be with *the* Lord" (v 17).

Zech. 14 shows we're going to come to the earth with Christ, but that won't happen until the Feast of Trumpets.

Verse 18: "**Therefore, encourage one another with these words**."

Rev. 14 is talking about the first resurrection, typified by the grain harvest (Matt. 13) when we come the Day of Pentecost.

Revelation 14:14: "And I looked, and behold, a white cloud, and *one* like *the* Son of man..." *Here's Christ coming down to the clouds!* We are going to meet Him in the clouds.

"...sitting on the cloud, having a golden crown on His head; and in His hand *was* a sharp sickle. And another angel came out of the temple, crying with a loud voice to Him Who was sitting on the cloud, 'Thrust in your sickle and reap...'" (vs 14-15).

That's what you do with grain. You take a sickle and you cut it, and then you gather it. Who gathers it? *The angels! Where do they take it? They take the firstfruits to the Sea of Glass before God!*

"'...because the time has come for You to reap; for the harvest of the earth is ripe'" (v 15). *Then it talks about the harvest of the wicked,* the rest of the chapter that I explain on Pentecost.

Revelation 15:1: "Then I saw another sign in heaven, great and awesome: seven angels having the seven last plagues, for in them the wrath of God is filled up." *So, the resurrection occurs before the seven last plagues!*

To show you that there is a space of time between the resurrection and coming back to the earth:

Revelation 16:12 "And the sixth angel poured out his vial into the great river Euphrates; and its waters were dried up, so that the way of the kings from the rising of *the* sun might be prepared. Then I saw three unclean spirits like frogs *come* out of the mouth of the dragon, and out of the mouth of the beast, and out of the mouth of the false prophet; for they are spirits of demons working miracles, going forth to the kings of the earth, even of the whole world, to gather them together to *the* battle of that great day of the Almighty God" (vs 12-14).

How long does it take to move an army with trucks and planes? How long did it take us to prepare for Desert Storm? *Four months!* So, there's got to be a four-month period, which is just about the length of time between Pentecost and Trumpets.

Revelation 15:2: "And I saw a Sea of Glass mingled with fire... [in other words, created out of spirit and just shone brightly] ...**and those who had gotten the victory over the beast**..."

We know that Satan is the beast. Satan has been around here since Adam and Eve. You get victory over the beast.

- Do all Christians through all time have to get victory over the beast? *Yes!*
- Did Abel get victory over the beast? *Yes!*

Satan, who is the beast, used Cain to kill Abel! Satan got victory over Cain!

"...And **over his image**..." (v 2). *We know that there was an image of the beast going clear back into Babylon!* Where Shadrach, Meshach, and Abednego got the victory over the beast idol that Nebuchadnezzar had made.

"...and **over his mark**... [which is coming] ...*and* **over the number of his name**... [which is coming] ...standing on the Sea of Glass, having *the* harps of God" (v 2).

- How many times in Scripture does a thing have to be said in order for it to be true? *Once is sufficient!*
- Where does it say we will stand? *It says we will stand on the Sea of Glass!*
- What is also on the Sea of Glass? *The Throne of God! The Temple of God!*

Verse 3: "And they were singing the song of Moses, *the* servant of God, and the song of the Lamb, saying, 'Great and awesome *are* Your works, Lord God Almighty; righteous and true *are* Your ways, King of the saints. Who shall not fear You, O Lord, and glorify Your name? For *You* only *are* Holy; and all the nations shall come and worship before You, for Your judgments have been revealed.' And after these things I looked, and behold, the temple of the tabernacle of the testimony in heaven was opened. And the seven angels who had the seven *last* plagues came out of the temple..."(vs 3-6).

There we are on the Sea of Glass. The Throne of God is there, the Temple of God is there, and we see the seven angels come out and get the seven vials for the seven last plagues. Then as I point out on Pentecost, God gives us the blessing of

His promise that He said that **His vengeance we all will see!** The only way that can happen is if we are on the Sea of Glass with the Throne of God and all these things happen according to the way that Revelation shows us.

Now then, let me tell you **why that Pentecost pictures the first resurrection** and not Trumpets:

1. firstfruits is a harvest of grain, which we are
2. the Holy Spirit was given on Pentecost, which is the earnest

So why not on Pentecost receive the fullness?

3. it is a continuous harvest from the time of Christ until His return

Just like seven weeks is a continual count from the beginning of the ascension of Christ to be accepted of the Father, until the Day of Pentecost 50 days later.

4. seven churches equal the seven weeks of harvest
5. 144,000 and great innumerable multitude equal the 50th day harvest of God
6. we are raised at the seventh trumpet, the last trump, the trump—not *trumpets*
7. we have the meeting with Christ in the air
8. we are on the Sea of Glass
9. we have to receive our reward
10. we have to be given our new name
11. we have to be given our assignments
12. the marriage of the Lamb takes place, and is the last thing to occur (Rev. 19)

Here's why it is **_not_** on Trumpets:

1. Trumpets is not a harvest feast

It is a Feast picturing *war, death, and destruction,* which is going to happen with the seven last plagues, ending in the return of Christ and the saints on the earth.

2. it is never 'trumpets,' but it is the 7th trump, or *the last trump*
3. we return to the earth after the seven last plagues and judgment of great Babylon, not before
4. the marriage of the Lamb and the Bride must take place, and that is not pictured by Trumpets but is pictured by Pentecost

The book of Ruth is a type of that, where Ruth marries Boaz, and that was during the barley harvest.

Heb. 12 is also a prophecy of our being resurrected to be on Mt. Sion in heaven above:

Hebrews 12:18: "For you have not come to *the* mount that could be touched and that burned with fire, nor to gloominess, and fearful darkness, and *the* whirlwind; and to *the* sound of *the* trumpet, and to *the* voice of *the* words, which those who heard, *begged* that *the* word not be spoken *directly* to them. (For they could not endure what was being commanded: 'And if even an animal touches the mountain, it shall be stoned, or shot through with an arrow'; and so terrifying was the sight *that* Moses said, 'I am greatly afraid and trembling'). But you have come to Mount Sion, and to *the* city of *the* living God, heavenly Jerusalem; and to an innumerable company of angels; *to the* joyous festival gathering; and to *the* Church of *the* Firstborn, registered *in the Book of Life* in heaven; and to God, *the* Judge of all; and to *the* spirits of the just who have been perfected; and to Jesus, *the* Mediator of *the* New Covenant; and to sprinkling of *the* blood of *ratification*, proclaiming superior things than *that of* Abel" (vs 18-24).

That's why Pentecost pictures the first resurrection and not Trumpets, and why when we are resurrected we will be on the Sea of Glass; we'll be brought up there by the angels. What a time that's going to be. You talk about fellowship.

There's one other thing: Christ is going to do a solo song. Did you know that? *Christ is going to bring us special music!*

Hebrews 2:9: "But we see Jesus, Who *was* made a little lower than *the* angels, crowned with glory and honor... [and we will see Him] ...on account of suffering the death, in order that by *the* grace of God He Himself might taste death for everyone."

Then we'll see all of those resurrected and on the Sea of Glass with Him and know that He died for each one individually and personally.

Verse 10: "Because it was fitting for Him, for Whom all things *were created*, and by Whom all things *exist*, in bringing many sons unto glory, to make the Author of their salvation perfect through sufferings. **For both He Who is sanctifying and those who are sanctified _are_ all of one**..." (vs 10-11).

Just like Christ prayed in John 17, *that they may be one as You, Father, and I are One. I in them, You in Me, that they may become one in Us.* That's what will take place right there.

"...for which cause He is not ashamed to call them brethren, saying, 'I will declare Your name to My brethren; in *the* midst of *the* Church I will sing praise to You'" (vs 11-12).

That will be in the midst of the Church because the Church will all be resurrected and on the Sea of Glass. He's going to sing praise to God the Father. We are going to sing the song of Moses. We're going to sing the song of the Lamb. We are going to learn how to play those harps, and I don't have a clue today.

FRC cs
Transcription date unknown
Reformatted: bo—11/2020

We're going to be able to meet all those you've wanted to meet, all the apostles. I especially want to meet—after I'm able to meet Christ and see Him face-to-face—the Apostle Paul, and I'm sure there will be a long line for that. I will also especially want to meet William Tyndale, because he gave his life for the Word of God and the testimony thereof.

Brethren, that's why Pentecost pictures the first resurrection and not Trumpets!

Scriptures from *The Holy Bible in Its Original Order, A Faithful Version*

Scriptural References:

1) Psalm 11:4-7
2) Psalm 45:6-7
3) Psalm 47:7-8
4) Ezekiel 1:20-28
5) Ezekiel 2:1-3
6) Ezekiel 3:10-21
7) Isaiah 6:1-4
8) Psalm 24:7
9) Isaiah 6:5-10
10) Revelation 4:1-11
11) Ephesians 1:1-5
12) Ephesians 2:10
13) Revelation 5:5-8
14) Revelation 6:12-16
15) Revelation 7:1-17
16) Revelation 11:15-19
17) Matthew 24:29-31
18) 1 Thessalonians 4:14-16
19) 1 Corinthians 15:51-52
20) 1-Thessalonians 4:17-18
21) Revelation 14:14-15
22) Revelation 15:1
23) Revelation 16:12-14
24) Revelation 15:2-6
25) Hebrews 12:18-24
26) Hebrews 2:9-12

Scriptures referenced, not quoted:

- Acts 7
- Revelation 2; 3
- Exodus 19; 20; 24
- Romans 8
- Revelation 22
- Zechariah 14
- Matthew 13
- Revelation 19
- John 17

Also referenced: Book: *The Christian Passover* by Fred R. Coulter

CHAPTER FORTY-ONE

Phase Two of the Return of Christ:
The Resurrection of the Saints
(Pentecost)
Fred R. Coulter

Greetings, everyone! Welcome to the Feast of Pentecost, and time marches right on, and we're going toward the Kingdom of God and Christ is getting ready to come. How far away it is or how close it is, we don't know. But we do know that God tells us to keep the Feast of Pentecost, which is also called the Feast of Weeks.

Exodus 34:22: "And you shall observe the Feast of Weeks, of the firstfruits of wheat harvest, and the Feast of Ingathering at the year's end."

That ties right in with Deut. 16:16. Since we've already covered how to count to Pentecost, and you can see there have been a great number of difficulties in trying to understand it. I hope that between the message that I gave on how to count and the letter for April/May it will help you understand more about Pentecost and what it means, how to count it and why it's important. It is really a test:

- Do we *really believe* God?
- Do we *really trust* Him?
- Do we *obey* His Word?
- Do we *thank* Him for it?
- Do we *ask* God to be with us in everything that we do?

Deuteronomy 16:16: "Three times in a year shall all your males appear before the LORD your God in the place which He shall choose: in the Feast of Unleavened Bread, and in the Feast of Weeks…" *It's called the Feast of Weeks because you're to count seven complete weeks!*

"…and in the Feast of Tabernacles. And they shall not appear before the LORD empty, every man *shall give* as he is able, according to the blessing of the LORD your God, which He has given you" (vs 16-17).

Whenever we give our offerings and blessings, we look at the blessings that God has given us. Just think of what a fantastic blessing it is to have the whole Word of God and for the understanding that God has given in the end-times. To realize and understand:

- the prophecies

- the Holy Days
- the Sabbath
- all the things that God wants us to learn
- how we should never take anything for granted

Every day, as it comes, is a new day. We pray, study and think with the Word of God. We live by the Word of God and are constantly coming to the Light, Who is Jesus Christ.

It says in John 3 that those who 'obey the Truth will be coming to the Light.' The Word of God is the Truth, and Jesus Christ is the Truth. We need to keep all of those things in mind. We also need to understand that:

- God's blessing comes with love and obedience through His grace and mercy
- curses come because we do not follow what God wants us to, just like the Christianity of the world

God is taking everything from them, just like Jesus said!

It's given to us to know the mysteries of the Kingdom of God, not to the world. Whatever understanding they have had, they have had so many warnings down through the centuries that God is now taking it away, as we have seen in very powerful ways. We need to understand that *we give according to the blessings that God gives us!*

We'll talk about the offerings and so forth, and realize that God has made all of this possible for us.

- He's given us *His* Word!
- He's given us *His* Truth!

Here in America we still have enough peace that we can assemble, we can study; we can live according to the Word of God.

Here is a summary of all of the Feast days, Leviticus 23:37: "These *are* the Feasts of the LORD which you shall proclaim to be Holy convocations to offer an offering made by fire to the LORD, a burnt offering and a grain offering, a sacrifice, and drink offerings, everything on its day; besides the

Sabbaths of the LORD, and besides your gifts, and besides all your vows, and besides all your freewill offerings, which you give to the LORD" (vs 37-38).

Those things all combine together to show that we have action in our lives and proof of our giving to God that we are proving God because He says He will bless us.

- not everything is going to be a physical blessing
- not everything is going to be money pouring out of the bank toward you

How about the blessing of:

- understanding the Word of God?
- of your prayers being answered?
- having *all* of the Word of God?
- freedom of assembly that we have today?

We know it's coming that all of those things are going to go, because of the prophecy. But what are we doing now? It's like the old saying: *make hay while the sun shines!* Don't wait until it rains, because you can't cut the grass for hay.

Let's look at it that way and *claim God's blessing!*

(pause for the offering)

Leviticus 23:15—*just a review of the count*: "And you shall count to you beginning with the next day after the Sabbath…"

This year it was the weekly Sabbath and the first day of the Feast of Unleavened Bread. This is why Pentecost comes so early this year.

"…beginning with the day that you brought the sheaf of the wave offering…" (v 15)—*picturing the acceptance of Christ by God the Father in heaven above for us!*

"…seven Sabbaths shall be complete… [complete weeks with the Sabbath being the 7th day] …Even unto the day after the seventh Sabbath you shall number fifty days. And you shall offer a new grain offering to the LORD" (vs 15-16).

Here is what they were to do; this is a special offering. This is an offering that is different because every other offering, with the exception of the peace offering, was to have unleavened bread. So, let's see what it says concerning this special offering that was to be prepared in homes, brought to the temple for the Feast of Pentecost.

Verse 17: "You shall bring out of your homes **two wave loaves** of two tenth parts. They shall be of fine flour. They shall be baked **with leaven**… [we're going to see there's a good use for

leaven] …*they are* the firstfruits to the LORD."

Let's look at the symbolism: During the Feast of Unleavened Bread leaven equals sin. We are to get sin out of our lives, but we die, are put into the grave, and then resurrected. When you are resurrected and brought out of the grave—or changed if you're still alive when Christ returns—you are completely different. That's what these two loaves picture *with the leaven.*

Also, once it is baked it is permanently changed. This pictures being permanently changed from flesh to spirit. ***These are the firstfruits!***

Then there are all the sacrificial offerings, and the seven lambs are probably symbolic of the seven churches that were covered on Day 49 (Rev. 2 & 3). I think it's very important that we went through the first three chapters of Revelation word-by-word, *so that we can evaluate*:

- our personal lives
- our corporate lives
- how we are doing in loving one another
- how we are doing in loving God and serving Him

Let's see something very unusual, because in Matt. 13 it explains something about the good use of leaven. Leaven of itself does not always equal sin. But the reason that God uses leaven as a type of sin during the Feast of Unleavened Bread is because *sin is so easy.* Paul wrote that **we get overwhelmed with the sin that 'so easily besets us.'** This is why we are to keep our mind focused on Christ.

Matthew 13:33: "Another parable He spoke to them: 'The Kingdom of Heaven is **compared to leaven**…'"

Think about it for just a minute. The Kingdom of Heaven is *righteousness!* Therefore, this leaven cannot mean that it is compared to sin. This is a good use of leaven.

"…which a woman took and hid in three measures of flour until all was leavened" (v 33). *It says that the Kingdom of Heaven is compared to leaven!*

Why? When leaven is raising the dough, it is changing the nature of the dough. That is compared to the good work of the Holy Spirit that is working in us to develop the spiritual character. That's quite a thing! The two different uses: no leaven and leaven.

Once it is baked—that's what they were to do in their homes for these two wave loaf offerings—it is permanently set and the nature of it has been completely changed. Now it is bread to eat.

So, likewise when we are raised from the

dead—which this day pictures—we will be completely changed. It will be fixed. That's why we are to grow and overcome today. Let's see something else that Jesus said concerning His coming. *On Day 49 we brought it up through the first phase of Jesus' return!* The first phase is:

- the heavens roll back as a scroll
- the shining sun—which shines from east to west—is the sign of the Son of man and is shown
- that is there in the heavens for a year and a half

It's interesting when it says, 'every eye shall see Him.' Listen, brethren, the greatest thing that God is going to do is sending Jesus Christ back to this world. Please understand and realize that there is going to be the greatest witness that has ever been given. *That witness will be the sign of the Son of man in heaven!* It will be there for the better part of a year.

Matt. 24—Jesus is talking about the end-time generation. The generation that saw the destruction of the temple in 70$_{A.D.}$ was a type, but here is the antitype or fulfillment, *the final generation*:

Matthew 24:34: "Truly I say to you, this generation shall in no wise pass away until all these things have taken place"—*relating to the return of Christ and the resurrection of the saints!* Then that leads to the setting up of the Kingdom of God.

Notice how sure that this is, v 35: "The heaven and the earth shall pass away, but My words shall never pass away."

All of those who believe in going to heaven, all of those who don't believe in the resurrection, that even happened during Paul's day, and he had to correct them for it. He said, *What? What is it that some of you don't believe in the resurrection?* That's why Paul had to write 1-Cor. 15 in great detail to show what will happen.

Verse 36: "But concerning **that day, and the hour, no one knows,** not even the angels of heaven, but My Father only."

Why would He say that? Let's see what Paul wrote to the Church after talking about the first resurrection (1-Thess. 4).

Remember that Jesus said that *we don't know the day or the hour,* true. But how much are we to know? How are we to know it, even though when we get down to the fulfillment of it, as we find in the book of Revelation, we'll understand why no one knows the day or the hour.

1-Thessalonians 5:1: "Now then, concerning the times and the seasons… [the resurrection that Paul just talked about] …brethren, there is no need that I write to you; for you yourselves understand perfectly that the Day of *the* Lord will come exactly as a thief *comes* by night" (vs 1-2).

They won't expect the first phase. The heavens roll back as a scroll and here is this new sun out in the heavens. They won't know what to do!

Verse 3: "For when they say, 'Peace and security,' then sudden destruction will come upon them, as travail *comes* upon a woman who is with child; and they shall by no means escape." Both are true! Why? *We'll see a little later!*

When the sun goes dark and the moon goes dark, and all the earthquakes take place, what happens to the earth? It says in one of the prophecies in Isaiah that it's going to wobble to and fro like a drunken man. Who's going to know which day is really the Day of Pentecost, because everything is out of sink? *Only the Father!*

Let's see a couple of things in the book of Revelation, we'll just review chapter six and then we'll see how this fits in. Always remember, as I have pointed out: *Even in the middle of trouble and times of distress and correction, God gives us space for repentance!* This is what Rev. 7 is all about, because of the terrible things that are going on: the captivity of Israel. Here's what happens: After the sign of the Son of man appears:

Revelation 7:1: "And after these things I saw four angels standing on the four corners of the earth, holding back the four winds of the earth, so that the wind might not blow on the earth, or on the sea, or on any tree. Then I saw another angel ascending from *the* rising of *the* sun, having *the* seal of *the* living God; and he cried out with a loud voice to the four angels, to whom it was given to damage the earth and the sea, saying, 'Do not damage the earth, or the sea, or the trees until we have sealed the servants of our God in their foreheads'" (vs 1-3).

There are seven churches and there are seven weeks to the harvest. With the martyrdom of the saints, the fifth seal, that ends the Church harvest, with the exception of the few that are in a place of safety (Rev. 12).

The few that are there are there to fulfill the words of Jesus Christ when He said that He would build *His* Church and the 'gates of the grave would never prevail against it.' When you have a universal martyrdom of the saints—as we find with the fifth seal (Rev. 6) then, unless He had those few—whoever they are and whoever goes there; wherever the place of safety will be—it will not die out. That's why! Those who go will not know that they're going until the angels take them there.

Rev. 7—we find the 12 tribes of Israel and the great innumerable multitude, and then the rest of the chapter shows that *they* have come out of Great Tribulation and *they* will be before the Throne of God. Remember, because it shows them standing before the Throne of God, does not mean that they precede the first resurrection. *That will never happen! No one is going to receive eternal life until the seventh trump and the resurrection takes place!*

However, this is God's 50th day harvest. Just like the first Pentecost and God poured out His Spirit upon the first of the firstfruits there, Rev. 7 is the last of the firstfruits. *The beginning and the ending! Isn't that where we started in Rev. 1? Yes, indeed! We surely did!*

Hosea 5 is important for us to understand, because the Tribulation against Israel does not last a full three and a half years. That's the Tribulation against the whole world. When it talks about Ephraim, that's not just the Brits. Ephraim is a type of all the ten tribes. Also, this includes Judah because Judah is mentioned in Rev. 7.

Hosea 5:14: "For I *will be* to Ephraim as a lion, and as a strong lion to the house of Judah…. [both of them] …I, *even* I, will tear and go away…. [sending them off into captivity and tribulation] …I will take away, and none shall rescue him." *No human being is going to rescue them!* But God will not make a full end.

Here's what He's going to do, v 15: "I will go; I will return to My place **until they confess their guilt and seek My face**; in their affliction they will seek Me earnestly." *That's why we have Rev. 7 and here's what they do:*

Hosea 6:1: "Come and let us return to the LORD, for He has torn, and He will heal us; He has smitten, and He will bind us up. After two days He will revive us…" (vs 1-2).

What is Rev 7 but a revival of the children of Israel and the great innumerable multitude; to Israel first and then to the Gentiles? We have all of the things fit together in Rev. 7.

How long is a day in prophecy? *One year!* It says, "…After two days…" Which means *after two years* He will revive us. That's exactly what Rev. 7[transcriber's correction] is with the sealing of the 144,000.

"…in the third day He will raise us up, and we shall live in His sight" (v 2).

Now, go back to how God works. Remember all the plagues against the Egyptians and how the first plagues also affected the Israelites in the land of Goshen. Then when God began to do the things more intently and more powerfully, He separated the children of Israel from the plagues that came upon the Egyptians. This is precisely how the 144,000 and the great innumerable multitude in Rev. 7 are revived. Then a year later the resurrection takes place.

All of this takes place on the next to the last Pentecost, so they will have God's Spirit one year. They will be, compared to the parable of the workers in the vineyard, those who were hired at the eleventh hour, but were still paid the same as those hired the first hour: *a silver coin!* In this case a type of eternal life.

Rev. 8 changes everything! Everything that there is! We will come back on the Feast of Trumpets and go through Rev. 8 a little bit more carefully, but now we're just going to review it. If you compare the intensity of the plagues and the wars coming, beginning in Rev.8 compared to Rev. 6, everything is changed. Now it is the angels of God against Satan and his demons and the men that follow him. God's direct intervention! More intense than what happens in Rev. 6.

Revelation 8:1: "Now, when He opened the seventh seal, *there* was silence in heaven *for* about a half hour. Then I saw the seven angels who stand before God, and seven trumpets were given to them. And another angel, who had a golden censer, came and stood at the altar; and much incense was given to him, so that he might offer *it* with the prayers of all the saints on the golden altar that *was* before the Throne. And the smoke of the incense went up before God from *the* hand of the angel, ascending with the prayers of the saints" (vs 1-4). *Stop right there!*

What does this tell us? *The resurrection has not occurred!* The saints who are still in the flesh—144,000 and the great innumerable multitude and those in the place of safety—are praying, crying out to God every day, day-by-day beseeching Him. Our prayers go up before God this way, right to the altar of God!

That's why it's so important, brethren, to understand about the true grace of God and grace upon grace that God has given to us today.

Verse 4: "And the smoke of the incense went up before God from *the* hand of the angel, ascending with the prayers of the saints. And the angel took the censer, and filled it with fire from the altar, and cast *it* into the earth; and there were voices, and thunders, and lightnings, and an earthquake. Then the seven angels who had the seven trumpets prepared themselves to sound *their* trumpets" (vs 4-6). *We will see what happens here, that's something!* Quite a thing!

Verse 7: "And **the first angel sounded *his* trumpet**; and there was hail and fire mingled with blood, and it was cast upon the earth; and a third of the trees were burnt up, and all green grass was burnt up." *Whoa! Much more powerful!*

Verse 8: "Then **the second angel sounded _his_ trumpet**…"

Remember, as I have pointed out, the only place in the Bible where you have a sequence of trumpets so you can have a last trumpet sound for the resurrection is in the book of Revelation. We will see the seventh trumpet represents the resurrection. That is the *last* trumpet! There are not eight or nine, there are seven!

"…and *there* was cast into the sea as *it were* a great mountain burning with fire, and a third of the sea became blood; and a third of the living creatures that *were* in the sea died, and a third of the ships were destroyed. And **the third angel sounded _his_ trumpet**; and *there* fell out of heaven a great star, burning like a lamp; and it fell on a third of the rivers, and on the fountains of waters. Now, the name of the star is Wormwood; and a third of the waters became wormwood; and many men died from *drinking* the waters because they were made bitter" (vs 8-11).

Verse 12: "Then **the fourth angel sounded _his_ trumpet**; and a third of the sun was smitten, and a third of the moon, and a third of the stars; so that a third of them were darkened; and a third part of the day did not shine, and likewise *a third part of* the night."

Doesn't that change everything in relationship to the Calculated Hebrew Calendar? *Yes!* That's why *we can know the times and the season,* but *we don't know the day or the hour!* Everything is out of balance here.

Let's see some of the things that it says about the resurrection, but first come to Rev. 11. Four trumpets sound for Rev. 8, two for Rev. 9[transcriber's corrections]. There's one more to be sounded and we find that in Rev. 11. That takes place after the two witnesses have been killed. How long is their ministry? *1260 days!* Roughly three and a half years.

What happens when their ministry is finished? *God allows the two witnesses to be killed!* He deliberately causes them to be killed. That's going to fulfill a tremendous prophecy. The world will rejoice. They'll all be able to see it. I think God is going to keep all of the high-technology things in place in spite of everything that's going on, so *the world will know, and see, and understand, and have absolutely no excuse!*

They're going to think that this is an invasion from outer space. In that they will be correct! It will be by aliens! Not because there are aliens out there that we don't know of, but the world doesn't know them. God the Father, Jesus Christ, the angels of God are the aliens whom they will be fighting.

Look at what the angels do when they blow the trumpet. How is man going to be able to stand against God? *He is not!* There's going to be so many people killed and so much destruction!

Some people ask, 'Why would God do that if God is a God of love?' *Because He has so much love that He wants to remake this world with **His** Kingdom!* Everything concerning the kingdoms of men and their religions, businesses and the things that they do—when you read about the fall of Babylon (Rev. 18)— must be destroyed!

- Every idol is going to be smashed!
- Every cathedral is going to be brought to crumbs and ruins!
- Every temple!
- Every church!

They are all against God! The two witnesses are going to add to that. When the two witnesses die, here's what's going to happen: They're going to lay in the street of Jerusalem, called Sodom and Egypt.

Revelation 11:9: "Then those of the peoples and tribes and languages and nations shall see their bodies three and a half days, for they will not allow their bodies to be put into tombs. And those who dwell on the earth will rejoice over them, and will make merry, and will send gifts to one another, because these two prophets had tormented those who dwell on the earth" (vs 9-10).

God always lets the enemy think that they're going to win, even at the last minute. They're going to say:

Hooray! Finally, after all of this we finally got them; look how wonderful this is going to be. Let's get everything all back together the way it needs to be. We'll reconstruct the earth; we'll rebuild everything the way we want to! We are so happy that they are gone because they caused so much damage, flood and drought and all kinds of terrible things. How could these be from God?

Well, God's going to have a surprise for them!

Verse 11: "Then after the three and a half days, *the* spirit of life from God entered into them and they stood on their feet…"

This is why we are not to fear anything, because God is going to raise us from the dead! He wants us to

- keep our mind on the Kingdom of God
- keep focused on growing and overcoming

So that we will be in the resurrection! That is going to be a fantastic time. It will occur on Pentecost, *because we are the firstfruits of God!*

"…and great fear fell upon those who were watching them. And they heard a great voice from heaven, say, 'Come up here!' And they ascended into heaven in a cloud; and their enemies saw them *rise*" (vs 11-12).

What do we have here? *The last two martyrs!* Remember what Christ has said, 'the last shall be first and the first shall be last.' These two martyrs, the two witnesses—the servants that God personally chose to do it from the tribe of Judah and the tribe of Levi, and of Levi from the house of Aaron—will be the first raised from the dead. *The last shall be first!*

- Does God keep His Word? *Yes!*
- Does He keep it accurately? *Yes!*
- Does it need any secondary explanation because it wasn't quite like it said? *NO!*

Jesus said that 'heaven and earth shall pass away, but My words shall never pass away.' These are the words of Christ that He inspired John to write!

Then notice what happens here, v 13: "And in that hour there was a great earthquake, and a tenth of the city fell; and seven thousand men were killed in the earthquake. And the rest were filled with fear, and gave glory to the God of heaven. The second woe is past. Behold, the third woe is coming immediately. **Then the seventh angel sounded *his* trumpet**…" (vs 13-15). *The last trumpet of the seven!*

It talks about the resurrection right here. This is why we have to put all the Scriptures together:

"…and *there* were great voices in heaven, saying, 'The kingdoms of this world have become *the kingdoms* of our Lord and His Christ, and He shall reign into the ages of eternity.' And the twenty-four elders, who sit before God on their thrones, fell on their faces and worshiped God, saying, 'We give You thanks, O Lord God Almighty, Who is, and Who was, and Who *is* to come; for You have taken *to Yourself* Your great power, and have reigned. For the nations were angry, and Your wrath has come, and the time for the dead to be judged, and to give reward to Your servants the prophets, and to the saints, and to *all* those who fear Your name, the small and the great; and to destroy those who destroy the earth'" (vs 15-18).

- Is that not the resurrection?
- Does it not include every category of resurrection?

- The prophets of old?
- David and some of the kings?
- *Yes, it does!* **And all the saints!**

Remember what we have learned concerning the Calculated Hebrew Calendar. The first day of the year is the Feast of Trumpets. The only other way to count it is from Nisan, the first month. When you count from Nisan, then you have the fourth Feast, Pentecost and the third Holy Day. However, when you count from Trumpets, Pentecost is the last day, just as Jesus said (John 6) that He would 'raise them up the last day!'

Now let's come to the book of Isaiah and see a tremendous prophecy concerning the resurrection. This is very important because God talks about a temple on earth, and then He talks about the resurrection (Isa. 66). Let's see the lessons learned here. Actually, when you read the witness that Stephen gave to the Sanhedrin (Acts 7), Isa. 66 is where he was quoting from. Remember that when he was stoned, he looked up into the heavens and he saw the Son of man standing by the Throne of God. So, there are many different parallels that fit in with this.

Isaiah 66:1: "Thus says the LORD, 'The heaven *is* My Throne, and the earth *is* My footstool. Where, then, *is* the house that you build for Me? And where *is* the place of My rest?'"

- What are you going to do for Me here on the earth?
- Are you going to build a temple on the earth?

Let's see what He says here:

Verse 2: "'For all these things My hand has made, and these things came to be,' says the LORD. 'But to this one I will look…'"

This needs to be our attitude, because God is looking upon us. As a matter of fact, God is *in us*; yes, with the earnest of our inheritance—the Holy Spirit from God the Father and Jesus Christ dwelling *in us*—we, each one of us, are a mini-temple of God.

"…to him who is of a poor and contrite spirit… [not lifted up in vanity: humble, yielded, loving God] …and who trembles at My Word" (v 2). *That means that*:

- you *love* the Word of God
- you *keep* the Word of God
- you *treasure* the Word of God
- you *live by* the Word of God

That's how you tremble before the Word of God!

Not just a shaking of the body, but how fantastic it is. Yes, there are the curses, yes, there are the blessings, and the blessings of eternal life far outweigh the things of the curses.

Then He says that even if you have a temple and make an offering, v 3: "He who kills an ox *is as if* he killed a man; he who sacrifices a lamb *is as if* he broke a dog's neck; he who offers a grain offering *is as if* he offered swine's blood; he who burns incense *is as if* he blessed an idol. Yea, they have chosen their own ways, and their soul delights in their abominations."

Yes, indeed, that's the way the world is treating God! So, God responds to them in kind. Here's what God does:

Verse 4: "I also will choose their delusions, and I will bring their fears upon them because when I called, no one answered; when I spoke, they did not hear. But they did evil before My eyes and chose *that* in which I did not delight."

That's the way it is with the Christianity of this world. But He's talking about the children of Israel there.

Speaking to those who love God, v 5: "Hear the Word of the LORD, you who tremble at His Word, 'Your brethren who hated you…'"—whoever it is:

- people in your family
- people in the church you used to go to
- your loved ones, maybe even husband or wife

"'…'Your brethren who hated you who cast you out for My name's sake, said, "Let the LORD be glorified."….'" (v 5). *'Yes, we'll glorify God our way.'*

God just explained that even if you come to His temple and offer the offerings, *if your heart is not right, and if you don't love God,* those things are of no account.

Has He chosen their delusions? Now He's going to do something that is going to be absolutely astounding, and it is the resurrection of the dead for those who love God.

"…But He will appear to your joy and they will be ashamed.' A sound of noise from the city, a sound from the temple, the sound of the LORD repaying His enemies" (vs 5-6). Didn't we just read that in the book of Revelation? *Yes, indeed!*

Verse 7: "Before she… [the Church] …travailed, she gave birth; before her pain came, she delivered a man-Child. Who has heard such a thing? Who has seen such *things* like these? Shall the earth be made to bring forth *in* one day? *Or* will a nation be born at once? For as soon as Zion travailed, she also gave birth to her children" (vs 7-8)—*the resurrection!* Remember what we covered

on Day 49? *We come to Mt. Sion in heaven above!*

Verse 9: "'Will I bring to the birth, and not cause to be born?' says the LORD…." *In other words,* do you think all of those Scriptures concerning the resurrection are in vain? *and* God is not going to do it?

"…'Shall I cause them to be born, and shut the womb?' says your God. 'Rejoice with Jerusalem, and be glad with her, all who love her. Rejoice for joy with her, all who mourn for her; that you may suck and be satisfied with her breasts of consolations; that you may milk out and be delighted with the fullness of her glory'" (vs 9-11). *In other words eternal life!* Isn't that a fantastic thing? *Yes, indeed!*

It's also very interesting the way the Bible is put together. You have:

- first division—*the Law*
- second division—*the Prophets*
- third division—*the Writings*
- fourth division

Number four is very important because Christ was crucified on the 4th day of the week, and He was raised after 3 days and nights in the grave. On the 4th day He ascended to heaven. He began His ministry on a Wednesday and ended His ministry on a Wednesday, the 4th day of the week. *All of these numbers fit together!*

2-Peter 1—here is what God is going to give us. I want you to think about the things that we're going to read, because this is so fantastic. This is absolutely marvelous!

2-Peter 1:1: "Simon Peter a servant and an apostle of Jesus Christ, to those who have obtained *the* same precious faith as ours by *the* righteousness of our God and Savior Jesus Christ: Grace and peace be multiplied to you in *the* knowledge of God and of Jesus our Lord, according as His Divine power has given to us all things… [not yet received, in fact, most of them not yet received] …that *pertain* to life and Godliness, through the knowledge of Him Who called us by *His own* glory and virtue" (vs 1-3).

- think about the calling
- think about the resurrection
- think about how great this is

- the Church began on Pentecost with the earnest of the payment, the receiving of the Holy Spirit
- the Church is going to be raised on the Day of Pentecost for the fullness of the Holy Spirit

Verse 4: "Through which He has given to us the greatest and *most* precious promises, that through these you may become partakers of *the* Divine nature, having escaped the corruption *that is* in *the* world through lust." *They're going to leave all that behind at the resurrection!*

Let's see the promise in 1-John 3. Remember that the apostles wrote this for us. We have perhaps today understanding that they didn't have because of what they wrote, and how God said that **in the end-times 'the wise shall understand.'** And let's realize this: *everything we have—physical and spiritual, the Word of God and everything about eternal life—has come from God!* We have nothing we didn't receive!

1-John 3:1: "Behold! What *glorious* love the Father has given to us, that we should be called the children of God! For this very reason, the world does not know us because it did not know Him."

They don't understand it. When you tell them you're a *true Christian*, they say, 'I'm a Christian, too. I go to a wonderful church on Sunday.' *NO!* They're counterfeits! 'Why do you go to church on the Sabbath?'

Verse 2: "Beloved, now **we are the children of God**…"—*His very own children!* Our children are our very own flesh and blood. With God we are the *spirit begotten* and to be *spirit born children of God!*

"…and **it has not yet been revealed what we shall be**…" (v 2). *They didn't know at that time, because John had not written the book of Revelation at that point!*

"…but **we know that when He is manifested**… [at His return] …**we shall be like Him, because we shall see Him exactly as He is**" (v 2).

What does it say in Rev. 22 about those who are the children of God? *We will see the Father face-to-face!* Think on that! Think how great this day is! Think how marvelous this day is!

That's why when Moses went up on the mountain to meet God, and at the resurrection we're going to meet God the Father, Jesus Christ, all the saints, all the prophets, all of the apostles, all of the brethren down through time. It is going to be an absolutely marvelous thing to take place. We will see Jesus Christ as He is and God the Father as He is. *Yes, indeed!*

1-Cor. 15—Paul had to write this because there were those who didn't believe in the resurrection. Can you imagine that? *Even in the Church of God and the Apostle Paul teaching them,* there were those who didn't believe in the resurrection. Later in 1-Tim. 1 there were those saying that 'the resurrection has past'—meaning that

the only resurrection was Jesus Christ. ***Not so!***

1-Corinthians 15:12: "But if Christ is being preached, that He rose from *the* dead… [what they were teaching] …how *is it that* some among you are saying that there is no resurrection of *the* dead?" *Look at how many people believe in going to heaven*; what does that say about them?

Paul said, v 13: "For if there is no resurrection from *the* dead, neither has Christ been raised."

Why do you celebrate the false holiday of Easter? If that is supposed to be the commemoration of the resurrection of Jesus Christ, yet, you think you go to heaven when you die? *'Absurd,'* Paul said!

Let's see what that means if that were true, v 13: "For if there is no resurrection from *the* dead, neither has Christ been raised. And if Christ has not been raised, then our preaching *is* in vain, and your faith *is* also in vain" (vs 13-14).

That is precisely what the religion of Christianity and this world is. It is in vain to expect that you're going to go to heaven when you die, *when the Bible only teaches the resurrection.*

Verse 15: "And we are also found *to be* false witnesses of God; because we have testified of God that He raised Christ, Whom He did not raise, if indeed *the* dead are not raised."

- Why the New Testament?
- Why the prophecy of it (Isa. 66)?

Verse 16: "For if *the* dead are not raised, neither has Christ been raised. But if Christ has not been raised, your faith *is* vain; you are still in your sins, and those who have fallen asleep in Christ have then perished" (vs 16-18)—*those who died in the faith believing in the resurrection!* But if there's no resurrection, *they're dead!*

Verse 19: "If in this life only we have hope in Christ, we are of all people most miserable…. [Paul understood about God's plan] …But now Christ has been raised from *the* dead; He has become the Firstfruit of those who have fallen asleep. For since by man *came* death, by Man also *came the* resurrection of *the* dead. For as in Adam all die, so also in Christ shall all be made alive. But each in his own order: Christ *the* Firstfruit; then, those who are Christ's at His coming" (vs 19-23).

Now, let's go through a good number of verses concerning the resurrection, so that we understand. It's not going to be the same body that we are buried with, obviously that disintegrates.

Verse 38: "And God gives it a body according to His will, and to each of the seeds… [grains and so forth] …its own body. *Likewise,* not all flesh *is* the same flesh. Rather, *there is one flesh of men, and another flesh of beasts, and another of fish, and another of birds. And there are heavenly bodies…*" (vs 38-40).

Paul understood that Christ said that 'the righteous shall shine as the sun in the Kingdom of their Father.

Verse 40: "And *there are* heavenly bodies and earthly bodies; but the glory of the heavenly *is* different, and the *glory* of the earthly *is* different. *There is* one glory of *the* sun, and another glory of *the* moon, and another glory of *the* stars; for *one* star differs from *another* star in glory. So also *is* the resurrection of the dead. It is sown in corruption…" (vs 40-42).

When we reach the end of our life it's gone! *That's why*:

- *we need* Christ
- *we need* the Holy Spirit of God
- *we need* the faith of God
- *we need* to trust in God
- *we need* to believe in God

Verse 42: "It is sown in corruption; it is raised in incorruption. It is sown in dishonor; it is raised in glory. It is **sown in weakness; it is raised in power**" (vs 42-43).

Isn't it true that when you come to your end and you breathe out your last, that is the epitome of the weakness and helplessness of human beings without the hope of the resurrection. "…**sown in weakness; it is raised in power.**"

Verse 44: "It is sown a natural body; it is raised a spiritual body. There is a natural body, and there is a spiritual body."

There is a natural body, and there is a spiritual body. If you have your body, that's a guarantee from God that you will receive a spiritual body—*proof!* Just like God and Christ says, concerning His Word, that 'heaven and earth shall perish, but His words won't!' We can believe Him because heaven and earth are here.

Sidebar: What does that do to people who don't believe in the Word of God? That's the same as if there were no heaven and earth. Think on that for a minute!

Verse 45: "Accordingly, it is written, 'The first man, Adam, became a living soul; the last Adam *became* an ever-living Spirit.'…. [that's what we're going to become] …However, the spiritual *was* not first, but the natural—then the spiritual" (vs 45-46).

How many people believe, just like the Mormons, we were all spirits in heaven above and Adam and Eve had to sin so that spirit could come down and possess a human body. *NO!* The physical came first, and *the spiritual does not come until the resurrection!*

Verse 47: "The first man *is* of the earth—made of dust. The second Man *is* the Lord from heaven. As *is* the one made of dust, so also *are all* those who are made of dust; and as *is* the heavenly *One*, so also *are all* those who are heavenly. And as we have borne the image of the *one* made of dust, we shall also bear the image of the heavenly *One*" (vs 47-49). ***A great promise! Wonderful promise!***

- we will have the Divine nature
- we will see Him as He is

Fantastic!

Verse 50: "Now this I say, brethren, that flesh and blood cannot inherit *the* Kingdom of God, nor does corruption inherit incorruption. Behold, I show you a mystery: we shall not all fall asleep, but we shall all be changed, in an instant, in *the* twinkling of an eye, **at the last trumpet**; for *the* trumpet shall sound…" (vs 50-52). *We saw the prophecy of It!*

The seventh trumpet will sound, "…and **the dead shall be raised incorruptible, and we shall be changed**" (v 52).

- get rid of all the corruption
- get rid of all the mortality
- put on immortality

Verse 53: "For this corruptible must put on incorruptibility, and this mortal must put on immortality. Now, when this corruptible shall have put on incorruptibility, and this mortal shall have put on immortality, then shall come to pass the saying that is written: 'Death is swallowed up in victory.' O death, where is your sting? O grave, where is your victory?" (vs 53-55).

Let's see how we are to approach all of these things, brethren; then we will see what it's going to be like. Quite a thing! What great promises!

- we are the firstfruits
- Christ is the First of the firstfruits
- He is the Firstborn from the dead
- we are going to be the Church of the Firstborn from the dead
- a nation raised all at once

What an astounding thing that is going to be!

1-Thessalonains 4:13: "But I do not wish you to be ignorant, brethren, concerning those who have **fallen asleep**… [that's how God looks at the death of the saints] …that you be not grieved, even as others, who have no hope." *They don't know what to do. They're gone, and* **no one has the power to bring them back but God!**

Verse 14 is a summary of what's going to happen. Many times in the Bible you have a summary to tell you what is going to happen, and then immediately following that you have the details telling you *how* it's going to happen. This is a summary for the rest of the verses down through vs 17-18.

Verse 14: "For if we believe that Jesus died and rose again, in exactly the same way also, those who have fallen asleep in Jesus will God bring with Him"

It sounds like they're in heaven, but that's not true. They have got to get there first in order to come with Him. So, there has to be the resurrection first and then meeting Christ in the air as He says. Then when we come back to the earth we will be with Christ.

Verse 15: "For this we say to you by *the* Word of *the* Lord, that we who are alive and remain unto the coming of the Lord shall in no wise precede those who have fallen asleep." *Those who are in the grave are going to be resurrected first!*

Verse 16: "Because the Lord Himself shall descend from heaven with *a* shout of command, with *the* voice of an archangel and with *the* trumpet of God; and **the dead in Christ shall rise first**; **then** we who are alive and remain shall be caught up together with them in *the* clouds for *the* meeting with the Lord in *the* air; and so shall we always be with *the* Lord" (vs 16-17)—*and return to the earth with Him!*

Let's see what God is going to do with us at the resurrection. Here's what we are to do in having our mind:

- fixed on Christ
- fixed on the resurrection
- fixed on the Word of God

Which is always, **always,** *always* true even though there are parts of it we do not understand!

Philippians 3:20: "But for us, the commonwealth *of God* exists in *the* heavens… [the Kingdom of God] …from where also we are waiting for *the* Savior, *the* Lord Jesus Christ, Who will transform our vile bodies, that they may be conformed to His glorious body, according to the inner working of His own power, *whereby He is able* to subdue all things to Himself" (vs 20-21).

Yes, *we'll be changed in a moment, in the twinkling of an eye at the last trumpet.'*

Rev. 14 talks about the resurrection. Again,

we have a summary. Then we have a first event take place, and after the first event takes place then comes the seven last plagues and the harvest of the wicked.

Revelation 14:14: "And I looked, and behold, a white cloud, and *one* like *the* Son of man sitting on the cloud, having a golden crown on His head; and in His hand *was* a sharp sickle. And another angel came out of the temple, crying with a loud voice to Him Who was sitting on the cloud, 'Thrust in your sickle and reap, because the time has come for You to reap; for the harvest of the earth is ripe'" (vs 14-15).

That's when the whole nation will be born at once. What an astounding thing that is going to be for the people on earth! I think they're going to see it. They're going to be astounded! They're going to be so upset at that time that they will be ready to fight to do anything. *Satan now has them in total deception!* He has them believing that now 'we can turn back these aliens who are snatching bodies out of the earth and taking people away. We've got to fight against them.'

Beginning with Rev. 14:17 is a prelude explaining what is going to happen to the wicked when we read it in Rev. 16. The first part is explaining what is going to happen to those who are resurrected from the dead, who are in the first resurrection. I hope you understand that.

Verse 17: "Then another angel, who also had a sharp sickle, came out of the temple that *is* in heaven. And out from the altar came another angel, who had authority over fire; and he called with a loud cry to the one who had the sharp sickle, saying, 'Thrust in your sharp sickle, and gather the clusters of the earth, because her grapes are fully ripe'" (vs 17-18). *These are all of those who are going to die as Christ and the saints return to the earth!*

Verse 19: "And the angel thrust his sickle into the earth, and gathered the vine of the earth, and cast *its fruit* into the great winepress of the wrath of God."

When does the wrath come? *Rev. 16! The seven angels with the vials full of the wrath of God!* You have to put them together.

Verse 20: "And the winepress was trodden outside the city, and blood spewed out from the winepress as high as the horses' bridles, to the distance of a thousand six hundred furlongs."

Revelation 15:1: "Then I saw another sign in heaven, great and awesome: seven angels having the seven last plagues, for in them the wrath of God is filled up. And I saw a Sea of Glass…" (vs 1-2).

Phase Two: Resurrection of the Saints

Remember that *the first phase is Jesus coming as the sign of the Son of man!* What is the second phase of His coming? *The resurrection of the saints from the dead!* We're going to meet Christ in the air and there's going to be a great Sea of Glass right over Jerusalem.

What's probably going to happen is that when it comes time for the resurrection, the sun that was out there in heaven, that was the sign of the Son of man, comes swooshing toward the earth. *That's going to be a big surprise for everyone!* They're going to think total destruction of the whole earth is coming. Then when it gets in the clouds, right above Jerusalem, VHOOM! *It's going to be a great Sea of Glass!*

Then all of those who are resurrected are going to come on the Sea of Glass. We have to be there. This is Pentecost, then after Pentecost then everything that we do on the Sea of Glass will be fulfilled.

Verse 2: "And I saw a Sea of Glass mingled with fire, and those who had gotten the victory over the beast…"

How far back does that go? *When you read Rev. 12, there was a great dragon that is a beast!* That's Satan the devil and he appeared in the Garden of Eden! So, the beast is *Satan's system* all down through history. The *mark of the beast* is for the very last generation. But it's still the beast existing from that time.

Verse 2: "And I saw a Sea of Glass mingled with fire, and those who had gotten the victory over the beast and over His image."

- Did they not have idolatry all down through history and Satan's system? *Yes, indeed!*
- Were there those who were true to God who didn't get involved in that *like* the Prophets and Isaac and Jacob? *Yes!*

They didn't get involved in that!

"…and over his mark…" (v 2). *That's what we're going to have today,* **the mark of the beast** in the right hand or the forehead.

"…and over the number of his name, standing on the Sea of Glass, having *the* lyres of God" (v 2).

Lyres are like harps! A little different kind of stringed musical instrument, but we will have that. I hope that God puts in our mind how to play them. There are going to be a lot of things that we're going to have to learn on the Sea of Glass.

- get our new name

- receive our clothing
- receive our crown
- understand what we're going to do
- be presented to God the Father
- the marriage of the Lamb is going to take place
- the supper of the marriage of the Lamb is going to take place

Then we're all going to be organized into armies and come back to the earth and take over the earth! That is going to be a fantastic thing!

Verse 3: "And they were singing the song of Moses… [those who were saved up until the time of Christ] …*the* servant of God, and the song of the Lamb, saying, 'Great and awesome *are* Your works, Lord God Almighty; righteous and true *are* Your ways, King of the saints. Who shall not fear You, O Lord, and glorify Your name? For *You* only *are* Holy; and all the nations shall come and worship before You, for Your judgments have been revealed'" (vs 3-4).

That's a prophecy of the coming Millennium of which, as spirit beings, we're going to rule and reign with Jesus Christ.

We'll be on the Sea of Glass from the time of the resurrection on Pentecost until Trumpets, a period of about four months. Wh*en we come to the Feast of Trumpets we're going to pick up the rest of the story right here and see what is going to take place!* Brethren:

- *rejoice* in this day
- *rejoice* in God
- *rejoice* in His goodness
- *rejoice* because of His great promises and what this day means.

Remember, *you are the firstfruits, and you are the Church of the Firstborn!*

Scriptural References:

1) Exodus 34:22
2) Deuteronomy 16:16-17
3) Leviticus 23:37-38

4) Leviticus 23:15-17
5) Matthew 13:33
6) Matthew 24:34-36
7) 1 Thessalonians 5:1-3
8) Revelation 7:1-3
9) Hosea 5:14-15
10) Hosea 6:1-2
11) Revelation 8:1-12
12) Revelation 11:9-18
13) Isaiah 66:1-11
14) 2 Peter 1:1-4

15) 1 John 3:1-2
16) 1 Corinthians 15:12-23, 38-55
17) 1 Thessalonians 4:13-17
18) Philippians 3:20-21
19) Revelation 14:14-15, 17-20
20) Revelation 15:1-4

Scriptures referenced, not quoted:

- John 3

- Revelation 2; 3; 12; 6; 1; 9-10; 18
- John 6
- Acts 7
- Revelation 22
- 1 Timothy 1
- Revelation 16; 12

FRC:bo
Transcribed: 5-22-15
Reformatted: 11/2020

CHAPTER FORTY-TWO

Pentecost and the 144,000

Fred R. Coulter

For the Feast of Pentecost there's a tremendous meaning for the Feast of Pentecost, and there are a lot of things that God wants us to know and to understand as we go forward and in keeping the Holy Days. All of the Holy Days really show us and teach us the ways of God. It's very interesting that in the Septuagint version of the Bible, when you go through Exo. 31, all the way through there, with the exception of the seventh-day Sabbath, it says, **'My Sabbaths'**—*plural*. You can't have one without the other. If you have the seventh-day Sabbath, which you keep, then you must also keep the annual Sabbaths.

Now, this day of the Feast of Pentecost pictures the finality of the harvest of the firstfruits. And it all begins with Christ on the Wave Sheaf Offering Day. As we have seen, Christ is the First of the firstfruits. For ancient Israel, God wanted the children of Israel to always remember that the first of the firstfruits belonged to God.

Exodus 34:26: "The first of the firstfruits of your land you shall bring unto the house of the LORD your God…."

Christ was the First of the firstfruits (John 20). He ascended to the Father on *the morrow after the Sabbath!* He was the Premier Sheaf that was elevated by the priest to be accepted on our behalf. In other words, as the very sacrifice of Jesus Christ for the forgiveness of our sins plus the resurrected Christ for the justification to put us in right standing with God, and for Christ to be at the right hand of God the Father, to carry out His plan and carry it forward.

Now let's see some very important things concerning the resurrection, and, of course, everything starts with the resurrection of Christ. The firstfruits is a firstfruit harvest. It is a harvest Holy Day to celebrate the completing, the accomplishing of the firstfruits of the grain. That's not all the firstfruits, which follow after that. There are the firstfruits of the fruit of the tree, there are firstfruits of other products, other vegetables, other things that come along. Those all belong to God.

But this is a special one. The harvest that God has with the Feast of Pentecost relates to and begins with Christ Who is *the first* of the firstfruits.

Let's understand something very important concerning the resurrection of Christ, and especially in this day. I'm going to emphasize, again, that *you must have the right Bible!* And the right Bible is the one that is based upon the right Greek text and Hebrew text. Superseding the <u>King James Version</u> is *The Holy Bible in Its Original Order—A Faithful Version with Commentary* has been based upon the proper texts. I'm going to use my translation; I used the same Greek text that was used that the translators of the *King James Version* used, which is the Byzantine text, also known as the authorized text, or the received text, or the text of 1550 by Stephens. That's the one that I have used.

1-Corinthians 15:12: "But if Christ is being preached, that He rose from *the* dead, how *is it that* some among you are saying that there is no resurrection of *the* dead?"

So, immediately Satan is there. As soon as the seeds have been sown Satan is there bringing his tares and infiltrating into the Church, bringing false doctrine and saying 'there's no resurrection.' We're all going to heaven.' *No!*

Notice Paul's argument, v 13: "For if there is no resurrection from *the* dead, neither has Christ been raised. And if Christ has not been raised…" (vs 13-14).

I want you to notice the strength of his argument, and I want you to know how dogmatically he brings it because this is important.

Verse 13: "For if there is no resurrection from *the* dead, neither has Christ been raised. And **if Christ has not been raised then our preaching *is* in vain, <u>and your faith *is* also in vain.</u>**" (vs 13-14).

In other words they're preaching a myth. You're preaching something that is empty, that is hollow, that has no meaning. "…and **your faith *is* also in vain.**"

Verse 15: "And we are also found *to be* false witnesses of God…"

This is an important statement. Anytime someone makes a statement that is not in conformity with the Word of God it *is a false witness for God!* That means that he is testifying of something that is not true, and claiming that God has sanctioned it, which then is:

- false witnessing for God
- taking the name of God in vain
- using the name of God in futility and vanity

"…because we have testified of God that He raised Christ, Whom He did not raise, if indeed *the* dead are not raised. For if *the* dead are not raised, neither has Christ been raised. But if Christ has not been raised, your faith *is* vain; you are still in your sins" (vs 15-17).

In other words, there is no forgiveness of sin unless Christ, Who is the First of the firstfruits, ascended unto the Father to be accepted on the morrow after the Sabbath during the Feast of Unleavened Bread, which then is the first day beginning the 50-day count. ***Unless that occurred there is no forgiveness of sin!*** You can also trust and be reassured that any other scheme of the forgiveness of sin will not bring the forgiveness of sin, because Christ *'is the Way and the Truth and the Life.'* There is no other way that it can be done than through Jesus Christ.

Verse 18: "And those who have fallen asleep in Christ have then perished…. [there's no hope] …If in this life only we have hope in Christ… [without a resurrection] …we are of all people most miserable" (vs 18-19).

Why? *Because **you're believing in something that is false**, if the dead are not raised!*

Notice how Paul concludes his argument, v 20: "But now Christ has been raised from *the* dead; He has become the Firstfruit of those who have fallen asleep. For since by man *came* death, by Man also *came the* resurrection of *the* dead. For as in Adam all die…" (vs 20-22).

We all have inherited the 'law of sin and death' within us, so as in Adam we die. Just like God told Adam, 'Dust you are and unto dust you shall return; even so in Christ shall all be made alive,' that is all the resurrections, the three resurrections in the Bible:

1. the first resurrection
2. the second resurrection of those who have not committed the unpardonable sin
3. the other part of the second resurrection, which is the resurrection of those who have committed the unpardonable sin

All will be made alive in Christ, whether for eternal life, or whether for eternal death.

Verse 23: "But each in his own order: Christ *the* Firstfruit…" **We are the Church of the Firstborn!** We are the firstfruits of the harvest, but Christ is the *First* of the firstfruits.

"…then, those who are Christ's **at His coming**" (v 23). *That's when the first resurrection is going to be!*

Now we're going to see how 'at His coming' this pictures **the Day of Pentecost as the day of the resurrection!** Let's understand that that is the only day that it can signify. Someone will surely say, 'Well then, you're saying you know when the return of Christ is.' *No!* We're saying we know when the resurrection will be. The reason is we can look at it from what we already know.

- Is Christ our Passover, Who was crucified for us? *Yes!*
- When was He crucified? *On the Passover Day!*
- Did God do it on the time and in the day that He prophesied, and in the way and the manner that He said that He would do it? *Yes!*

It's exactly the same thing concerning the resurrection of Christ.

- When was He raised? *Right at the end of the Sabbath after being in the grave three days and three nights!*
- When did He ascend to the Father? *On the Wave Sheaf Offering Day!*

Then we saw how there are seven churches, and those seven churches represent *the harvest of the church age.* The *harvest of the church age* is part of the main harvest of God. That's from the time that Christ ascended to heaven until the time of the first resurrection. Then 'every man in his own order.' We know that at the end of the thousand years there will be the second resurrection of those who have not committed the unpardonable sin. Then the other half of the second resurrection for those who committed the unpardonable sin, that all the wicked may be thrown in the Lake of Fire at once. So, the Holy Days picture God's plan; these things happen on the Holy Days Let's keep that in mind, and let's understand that of the day of Christ's coming no one really knows; I'll show you why a little bit later.

Let's pick up the story now in Acts 1 and let's see what Luke wrote concerning the things, the events that took place after Christ was raised from the dead.

Act 1:3—*concerning Christ*: "By many infallible proofs, He presented Himself alive after He had suffered, being seen by them for forty days…"

Isn't it interesting that Christ was seen of the apostles from the time of His ascension until the time of His second ascension into heaven—His first one *to be accepted,* and then His second one to *remain* in heaven? *He was seen of the apostles 40 days.* But also it's interesting that after Pentecost, and the covenant that was made with Israel and the wedding supper of Israel with the 70 elders, that Moses was on the mount with God 40 days. In either case we have 40 days. In Christ's case it's 40 days before Pentecost. In Moses case it's 40 days from the day after Pentecost. So, it's 40 days.

"...and speaking the things concerning the Kingdom of God. And while *they* were assembled with *Him*, He commanded them not to depart from Jerusalem but to 'await the promise of the Father, which,' *He said*, 'you have heard of Me. For John indeed baptized with water, but you shall be baptized with *the* Holy Spirit after not many days.'.... [which was just 10 days away] ...So then, when they were assembled together, they asked Him, saying, 'Lord, will You restore the kingdom to Israel at this time?' And He said to them, **'It is not for you to know *the* times or *the* seasons, which the Father has placed in His own authority'**" (vs 3-7).

Remember, this was before any of the New Testament was written. And this was written before the book of Revelation was written by John, and the book of Revelation is *to reveal.* All of the New Testament is *to reveal the will of God and His Word and His Truth!*

Verse 8: "'But you yourselves shall receive **power**... ['dunamis'] ...when the Holy Spirit has come upon you, and you shall be My witnesses, both in Jerusalem and in all Judea and Samaria, and unto *the* ends of the earth.'"

That's a continuous thing that is going on today, and God has made it known, and God has sent it out. There are Bibles in over 250 languages; the New Testament in over 1,200 languages; the book of Mark in over 2,000 languages; all of that is preaching the Gospel and it is going out. We all have our part to do our preaching. We all have our part to do our witnessing.

Brethren, pray that God will open whatever doors are necessary for us to reach out and to reach new people. With our website—**truthofGod.org**—we're able to reach out into all the world, 24-hours a day, seven days a week to anyone who has a computer they can get on there and find out information concerning many things.

Verse 9: "And after saying these things, *as* they were looking at *Him,* He was taken up, and a cloud received Him out of their sight." *Just disappeared to go sit at the right hand of God the Father!*

Verse 10: "Now, while they were gazing intently up into heaven as He was going up, two men in white apparel suddenly stood by them." *That's two angels; angels look like men!*

Verse 11: "Who also said, 'You men of Galilee, why do you stand *here* looking up into heaven? This *same* Jesus, Who was taken up from you into heaven, shall come in exactly the same manner as you have seen Him go into heaven.'"

Let's see how tremendous and momentous this event was, and how important it is to understand the real meaning of Acts 2:1. We have the booklet, *The True Meaning of Acts 2:1,* because everyone has misconstrued this, twisted the Scriptures to their own destruction to make it say something that it really doesn't say.

Acts 2:1: "And when the day *of* Pentecost, the fiftieth day, was being fulfilled... [some people say, 'See, the 50th day was over'] ...they were all with one accord in the same place."

They say that means they were there on the 51st day. That doesn't relate to what the Greek really means. The Greek here has a special articular infinitive, the present tense. This should be translated: *and during the fulfilling, or the accomplishing of the 50th day,* **not** *the 51st*. If it were the 51st day then it would clearly say the 50th and first day. But it doesn't say that in the Greek.

And during the fulfilling of the 50th day "...**they were all with one accord in the same place**" (v 1). **Why?** *They were assembled for the Holy Day, which is a Holy convocation.* That's why they were there.

Verse 2: "And suddenly *there* came from heaven a sound ..." (vs 1-2).

Here is the re-enactment of what we saw at Mt. Sinai. Only instead of at Mt. Sinai it's at the Temple of God, because that's where God placed His name. So, anything that God was going to do, any authorization and change in the way that things were done would come from God. In this case by the power of His Holy Spirit, and right at the Temple so that it would be fully established that this was by the authority and the power of God, undeniable.

"...like *the* rushing of a powerful wind, and filled the whole house where they were sitting. And there appeared to them divided tongues as of fire..." (vs 2-3).

Remember the fire on top of Mt. Sinai? This is showing the same fulfillment now, *only spiritually,* of the Day of Pentecost as when the Law was given on the Day of Pentecost.

"...and sat upon each one of them. And they were all filled with *the* Holy Spirit; and they began to speak with other languages, as the Spirit gave them *the words* to proclaim" (vs 3-4).

Let's understand something very important here. God is not the author of confusion, so whatever the Holy Spirit did was something that was sound, it was intelligible, it was understandable, and it was for a specific purpose. That's what happened on this Day of Pentecost, and here's the reason:

Verse 5: "Now, *there* were *many* Jews who were sojourning in Jerusalem, devout men from every nation under heaven. And when word of this went out, the multitude came together and were confounded, because each one heard them speaking in his own language" (vs 5-6).

So, there was a double miracle. There was a miracle *in the preaching,* because in the minds of the apostles they were thinking and speaking with their own language, but in everyone who was *listening* it came to them in their own language. This is a profound thing to understand. Not only just for Jews, because remember, the New Testament says 'to the Jew first and then to the Greek.' So, we have here 'to the Jew first,' but also to those who were assembled there in Jerusalem who came from every nation on earth.

Please understand that the stories that went back from those who were up at Jerusalem during the Passover and the Feast of Unleavened Bread, and all the events that took place that we have already covered: How that Christ was crucified and raised from the dead, and all the stories that were told by the scribes and Pharisees to tell the lies that the disciples stole the body away. They knew that something big was going to happen on Pentecost, because it was a Holy Day of God. This was big! This was great! This was fulfilling the prophecy of God giving His Spirit to men; and He began with the apostles.

Verse 7: "And they were all amazed, and marveled, saying to one another, 'Behold, are not all these who are speaking Galileans? Then how… [since the implication is they are uneducated] …is it *that* we hear each one in our own language in which we were born?'" (vs 7-8).

They were hearing, they were understanding, and then it lists all of the nations that they were from.

The last part of v 10 says "…Jews and proselytes." Proselytes were circumcised Gentiles who would embrace the religion of Judaism.

Verse 11: "'…we hear them speaking in our own languages the great things of God.'…. [this day was tremendous] …And they were all amazed and greatly perplexed, saying to one another, 'What does this mean?' But others were mocking *and* saying, 'They are full of new wine.' Then Peter, standing up with the eleven, lifted up his voice and spoke out to

them: 'Men, Jews, and all those of you who inhabit Jerusalem, let this be known to you, and pay attention to my words. for these are not drunken as you suppose, for it is *only* **the third hour** of the day'" (vs 11-15). *That is in the morning!*

- When did God appear on Mt. Sinai? *In the morning!*
- When did He give the Law? *On the Day of Pentecost!*
- When did He give the Holy Spirit?

In other words to give them the heart to keep God's laws! Remember, when He gave the Ten Commandments He said:

Deuteronomy 5:29: "Oh, that there were such a heart in them that they would fear Me and keep all My commandments always…."

Now God is supernaturally giving the heart, by the circumcision of the heart through the power of the Holy Spirit so that they would have the ability now to keep the Laws of God greater than that. God's Spirit and power would write them in their hearts and in their minds *so they could keep them*:

- with a willing heart
- with a willing attitude
- in service to God

But first there has to be repentance!

Then Peter went on and gave this tremendous and powerful sermon:

Acts 2:16: "But this is that which was spoken by the prophet Joel… [we'll see how this ties in with Rev. 7] ….'And it shall come to pass in the last days,' says God, *'that* I will pour out My Spirit upon all flesh, and your sons and your daughters shall prophesy, and your young men shall see visions, and your old men shall dream dreams; and even upon My servants and upon My handmaids will I pour out My Spirit in those days, and they shall prophesy; and I will show wonders in the heaven above and signs on the earth below, blood and fire and vapors of smoke. The sun shall be turned into darkness and the moon into blood, before *the* coming of the great and awesome Day of *the* Lord'" (vs 16-20).

He gave this prophecy. It's recorded here in Acts 2, but this has not yet occurred. The only thing that has occurred of this is that the Holy Spirit was given. The rest of it has not occurred; that is for a future Day of Pentecost. We need to keep that in mind. We'll see that when we get to the book of Revelation.

Verse 21: "'And it shall come to pass *that* everyone who calls upon the name of *the* Lord shall be saved.' Men, Israelites, listen to these words:

Jesus the Nazarean, a Man sent forth to you by God, as demonstrated by works of power and wonders and signs, which God performed by Him in your midst, as you yourselves also know; Him, having been delivered up by the predetermined plan and foreknowledge of God, you have seized by lawless hands *and* have crucified and killed. *But* God has raised Him up, having loosed the throes of death, because it was not possible *for* Him to be held by it" (vs 21-24).

Then he finished giving the sermon saying that David was not resurrected from the grave but it was Jesus, even though He gave the promise to David.

Verse 34: "For David has not ascended into the heavens, but he himself said, 'The Lord said to my Lord'…"

They understood those Psalms. Remember the very first time that they saw Jesus in the evening on the day that He ascended to the Father (Luke 24). what did He do? *He opened their understanding concerning Him and the Law, the Prophets, and the Psalms! Here Peter is quoting Psa. 110*

"…'Sit at My right hand until I have made Your enemies a footstool for Your feet.' Therefore, let all *the* house of Israel know with full assurance that God has made this *same* Jesus, Whom you crucified, both Lord and Christ" (vs 34-36). *That was a powerful sermon, and notice what happened*:

Verse 37: "Now after hearing *this*, they were cut to the heart…" This is what has to happen to every one of us. This is what has to happen to everyone whom God calls. They are pricked in their heart so they will understand what Christ went through to die for their sins and become the sacrifice for all of mankind. *God leads you to repentance to understand that!*

Repentance is a continuous, ongoing thing in our lives by the operation of the grace of God, and He is the One Who leads us to it. Just like the parable of the prodigal son, remember what happened to him? He got his inheritance and went out and spent it, squandered it in a strange land and was out feeding the hogs good food. He couldn't even eat it. And it says there, '…**and when he came to himself**…' Now, this is what you need to do concerning repentance. You need to *come to yourself*; that is *understand where you are.*

- understand your nature
- understand your sins
- repent to God

That's what they did here:

"…they were cut to the heart; and they said to Peter and the other apostles, 'Men *and* brethren,

what shall we do?'…. [there are things that God wants us to do] …Then Peter said to them, '**Repent**…" (vs 37-38). *Repentance means to*:

- *turn from your sin*
- *turn from the way you're going*
- *turn back and come to God*

Just like God said through Ezekiel, *'Turn you, turn you, for why will you die O house of Israel.'* It's the same way with us. I hope there are brethren out there who are turning back to God. Why will you die O Church of God, you that have gone astray? *Turn you, turn you, come back to God! Let your hearts be pricked!*

"…'Repent and be baptized each one of you in the name of Jesus Christ for *the* remission of sins, and you yourselves shall receive the gift of the Holy Spirit. For the promise is to you and to your children, and to all those who are afar off, as many as *the* Lord our God may call.' And with many other words he earnestly testified and exhorted, saying, 'Be saved from this perverse generation.' Then those who joyfully **received his message were baptized; and about three thousand souls were added that day**" (vs 38-41).

Which day? *During the fulfilling of the 50th day!* That is a tremendous thing that happened. Imagine the account that everyone went back and told the story of being there at the temple, and this tremendous event took place. The One that was called Jesus Christ was raised from the dead, and how the power of the Holy Spirit came on them. This was a tremendous event! We'll project forward to the last Pentecost here in just a minute.

But I want to go back and pick up something that's very important concerning the two loaves that were baked with leaven (Lev. 23). Let's ask ourselves a couple of questions concerning this and let's see if we can determine the true Scriptural use of leaven here in Lev. 23, and what that pictures in it's fulfillment. Now remember, all during the Feast of Unleavened Bread leaven represents sin. Outside the Feast of Unleavened Bread leaven does not represent sin. What we are looking at here is a good use of leaven.

Leviticus 23:17—*this is to be done on the 50th day*: "You shall bring out of your homes…" *This is all who assembled up at the temple area, that they were to bring out of their habitations.*

"…two wave loaves of two tenth parts. They shall be of fine flour. They shall be baked with leaven…." (v 17).

Why would God have them put leaven in these? This has to be a good use of leaven because it's waved before God. I think we were right in our past understanding that one loaf equals those were qualified for the first resurrection under the Old Covenant, and the other loaf represents those who qualify for the resurrection under the New Covenant.

- Why leaven?
- What does it say these are?

"...*they are* the firstfruits unto the LORD" (v 17). *Baked!*

Now let's see something important here, where there is defining the Kingdom of God with the parable of the leaven, which is a good use of the leaven.

Matthew 13:33: "Another parable He spoke to them: 'The Kingdom of Heaven is compared to leaven...'"

You can't say that this is a bad use of leaven. You cannot say that leaven here is picturing sin because then you would have to say that the Kingdom of God is likened unto sin. **The Kingdom of God is likened unto righteousness,** not sin! So, it's likened unto leaven.

"...which a woman took... [the Church] ...and hid in three measures of flour until all was leavened" (v 33).

What happens to bread? *All dough when you first make it is unleavened!* When it's baked unleavened then it's permanently in that form until it's eaten. Now, when you put the leaven in it rises. It completely changes the form of the bread. When you bake it, it is permanently in that changed form. It can't be beaten back as dough to make it flat again like you do when it rises and then you beat it back, let it rise a couple more times so that you really get everything leavened. Here is a good use of leaven.

What does this picture? This pictures *the new spirit body*, which we will receive. All of those from the Old Covenant that qualified—going all the way back to Abel and those who, under the New Covenant, beginning with the Day of Pentecost as we saw who received the Holy Spirit at the resurrection—**will be changed.**

Let's see that in 1-Cor. 15; this becomes very important, very profound! You are not going to be raised with the same body that you have in the flesh today. Let's notice how the Apostle Paul describes this. Remember, he also condemned them already as we saw earlier, that there were some who did not believe in the resurrection.

1-Corinthians 15:34: "Awake to righteousness, and do not sin, for some *of you* do not have the knowledge of God. I say *this* to your shame."

Can you imagine that? Sitting in the Church of God not having the knowledge of God? We see the same thing being repeated today. How can people sit there in the Church of God and not have the knowledge of God?

1. they have not been taught
2. some of them may be tares
3. some of them may be Laodiceans or whatever attitude of the seven churches that be there

Verse 35:"Nevertheless, someone will say, 'How are the dead raised? And with what body do they come?' Fool! What you sow does not come to life unless it dies" (vs 35-36).

Let's see how Jesus explained it concerning Himself, likening it also unto grain. Remember that Jesus was the *first of the firstfruits! He was the Premiere Sheaf of the harvest of the grain!*

John 12:24: "Truly, truly I say to you, unless a grain of wheat falls into the ground and dies, it remains alone ... [this is a sowing (Matt. 13)] ...but if it dies, it bears much fruit. The one who loves his life shall lose it, and the one who hates his life in this world shall keep it unto eternal life" (vs 24-25). *Christ is likening even His own death as a grain being planted that dies!*

It's the same thing here, 1-Corinthians 15:36: "Fool! What you sow does not come to life unless it dies. And what you sow *is* not the body that shall be; rather, *it is* bare grain—it may be of wheat, or one of the other *grains*; and God gives it a body according to His will, and to each of the seeds its own body. *Likewise,* not all flesh *is* the same flesh...." (vs 36-39).

He goes on to explain it in quite detail]: "...Rather, *there is* one flesh of men, and another flesh of beasts, and another of fish, and another of birds. And *there are* heavenly bodies, and earthly bodies; but the glory of the heavenly *is* different, and the *glory* of the earthly *is* different. *There is* one glory of *the* sun, and another glory of *the* moon, and another glory of *the* stars; for *one* star differs from *another* star in glory. So also *is* **the resurrection of the dead.** It is sown in corruption... [because you die] ...it is raised in incorruption. It is sown in dishonor; it is raised in glory. It is sown in weakness; it is raised in power. It is sown a natural body; it is raised a spiritual body. There is a natural body, and there is a spiritual body" (vs 36-44).

Notice how it's talking about the harvest continually; it is sown! That's why the Day of Pentecost pictures the resurrection because that's a finality of the firstfruits harvest for the grain.

Verse 45: "Accordingly, it is written, 'The first man, Adam, became a living soul; the last Adam *became* an ever-living Spirit.'.... [Christ through the power of the resurrection] …However, the spiritual *was* not first, but the natural—then the spiritual. The first man *is* of the earth—made of dust. The second Man *is* the Lord from heaven. As *is* the one made of dust, so also *are all* those who are made of dust; and as *is* the heavenly *one*, so also *are all* those who are heavenly. And as we have borne the image of the *one* made of dust, we shall also bear the image of the heavenly *One*" (vs 45-49).

When we bear the image of the heavenly we will be changed, just like a lump of dough is changed when leaven is put in it, and then when it's baked in it's final form, it is permanently in a changed form. That's exactly what it will be with us for the resurrection.

Verse 50: "Now this I say, brethren, that flesh and blood cannot inherit *the* Kingdom of God, nor does corruption inherit incorruption…. [it must come from God as a gift] …Behold, I show you a mystery: we shall not all fall asleep, but we shall all be changed, in an instant, in *the* twinkling of an eye, at the last trumpet; for *the* trumpet shall sound, and the dead shall be raised incorruptible, **and we shall be changed**" (vs 50-52).

We will see in a little bit that in Rev. 11 the last trump is defined as the seventh trump, and that is the resurrection.

Verse 53: "For this corruptible must put on… [from God] …incorruptibility, and this mortal must put on immortality. Now, when this corruptible shall have put on incorruptibility, and this mortal shall have put on immortality, then shall come to pass the saying that is written: 'Death is swallowed up in victory'" (vs 53-54)—***by the very power of the resurrection!***

We will be changed, *permanent change.* That is what the leaven of the two loaves picture on the Day of Pentecost. Of course, when all the thousands of them came there were thousands and thousands of those loaves. They waved them before the Lord and then that became part of their keeping of the Feast of Pentecost.

Brethren, this really gets exciting. Now let's review Rev. 6 and in 2 & 3 we have the seven churches:

- that pictures the seven churches that were *then*
- that pictures the seven churches *down through history*
- that pictures perhaps even the seven churches *at the end-time.*

If we have seven from which comes seven, out of which comes seven, which is the pattern of the book of Revelation then we probably have seven churches in the end-time that will match up to the seven

churches in Rev. 2 & 3. These seven churches represent the seven weeks harvest. Let's see when the seven-weeks harvest comes to an end and then we are left once again with the 50th day harvest, *which will be **God's harvest**.*

We have in Rev. 4 & 5 showing the events that are going on there, and how that Christ is the only One to open the seals. Then He was given power to open the seals, and that is after the time that God the Father gave Christ the authority to do so. *We will see where we have the end of the Church Age*:

Revelation 6:1: "And I looked when the Lamb opened one of the seals; and I heard one of the four living creatures say, like the sound of thunder, 'Come and see.' And I looked, and behold, *there was* a white horse; and the one who was sitting on it had a bow, and a crown was given to him; and he went out conquering, and to conquer" (vs 1-2).

This is a picture of the false religion going out in 'conquering and to conquer.' We see that happening right now bringing all coalesced into the coming one world government.

Verse 3: "And when He opened the second seal, I heard the second living creature say, 'Come and see.' And another horse went out *that was* red; and *power* was given to the one sitting on it to take peace from the earth…" (vs 3-4).

This is the time of Rev. 13 after *the beast* receives the deadly wound and that is healed and he comes back, and authority is given him over all kindreds and tongues and nations, and it was given him authority to make war against the saints.

Verse 5: "And when He opened the third seal, I heard the third living creature say, 'Come and see.' And I looked, and behold, *there was* a black horse; and the one sitting on it had a balance in his hand. And I heard a voice in *the* midst of the four living creatures say, 'A measure of wheat for a silver coin, and three measures of barley for a silver coin: and *see that* you do not damage the oil and the wine.' And when He opened the fourth seal, I heard *the* voice of the fourth living creature say, 'Come and see.' And I looked, and behold, *there was* a pale horse; and the name of the one sitting on it *was* Death, and the grave followed him; and authority was given to them over *one* fourth of the earth, to kill with *the* sword and with famine and with death, and by the beasts of the earth (vs 5-8).

Now then, here's what we have when the Church Age ends:

Verse 9: "And when He opened the fifth seal, I saw under the altar the souls of those who had been slain for the Word of God, and for the testimony that they held."

This was in vision. This is not saying that they're immortal souls. But this is a way of God conveying to John, and to us, the events that are going to take place.

Verse 10: "And they cried out with a loud voice, saying, 'How long, O Lord, Holy and true, do You not judge and avenge our blood on those who dwell on the earth?' And white robes were given to each of them; and they were told that they should rest a short time, yet, until *it* be fulfilled *that* both their fellow servants and their brethren also would be killed, just as they had been" (vs 9-11).

So, we have two categories of Christians at this particular point:

1. we have those who have gone to a place of safety (Rev. 12)

We also find that Satan goes after to make war with the remnant of her seed, who have the testimony of Jesus Christ and keep the commandments of God. This is the war pictured right here by the 5th seal.

2. there will come a time when all of those who are not in a place of safety will be martyred

- that will end the Church harvest
- that will finish the harvest of the seven churches
- that will finish the seven-week harvest

But there is still one more day of the harvest, which God Himself is going to do, in a way different than dealing with us.

Let's see how that begins, v 12[transcriber's correction]: "And when He opened the sixth seal, I looked, and behold, there was a great earthquake; and the sun became black as *the* hair *of* sackcloth, and the moon became as blood; and the stars of heaven fell to the earth, as a fig tree casts its untimely figs when it is shaken by a mighty wind. Then *the* heaven departed like a scroll that is being rolled up, and every mountain and island was moved out of its place" (vs 12-14).

This is a tremendous event! This is the event, which is spoken of there in Hag. 2 where the Lord says, 'And yet one more time I will shake the earth and the heavens and the dry land, and the sea.' Then Christ will appear. This is it, right here. Notice what happens:

Verse 15: "And the kings of the earth, and the great men, and the rich men, and the chief captains, and the powerful men, and every bondman, and every free *man* hid themselves in the caves and in the rocks of the mountains; and they said to the mountains and to the rocks, 'Fall on us, and hide us from *the* face of Him Who sits on the Throne, and from the wrath of the Lamb, because the great day of His wrath has come, and **who has the power to stand**?'" (vs 15-17).

Now let's see where this occurs. Jesus talked about the Tribulation, because the Tribulation begins with the second seal. Then we have the third seal, the fourth seal, and then the fifth seal is the martyrdom of the saints. They are blamed by *the beast* as causing all of these problems on the earth. *'And as soon as we get rid of them then we're going to solve all the problems on the earth and*:

- we'll have one government
- we'll have one religion
- we'll have one mind

and all of these nasty Christians will be exterminated.' When they come to the point of killing every Christian they can find, because they'll be able to find them. Even without the *mark of the beast,* which none of the true Christians will have, they have the global positioning system, and they can track down any human being on earth within 100 square feet. So there is:

- no mountain you can go to
- no cave you can go to
- no cellar that you can go to

because when God has determined it is His will that those who are to be martyred *will be martyred.* At that time God will give great strength to be able to give a witness, and to prophesy against the evil powers of Satan and the world.

Matthew 24:21: "For then shall there be Great Tribulation, such as has not been from *the* beginning of *the* world until this time, nor ever shall be *again.* And if those days were not limited, **there would no flesh be saved; but for the elect's sake those days shall be limited**" (vs 21-22).

The Greek here doesn't mean, 'cut short' (*KJV*) shortening up less than 3-½ years. It means, *limited*; those days are limited. God has in advance set a limit of the days of the Tribulation.

Verse 23: "Then if anyone says to you, "Behold, here *is* the Christ," or, "*He is* there," do not believe *it.* For there shall arise false Christs and false prophets, and they shall present great signs and wonders, in order to deceive, if possible, even the elect. Behold, I have foretold *it* to you. Therefore, if they say to you, "*Come and* see! He is in the wilderness"; do not go forth. "*Come and* see! *He is* in the secret chambers"; do not believe *it*'" (vs 23-26).

This ties in with the beginning of the sixth seal with the rolling back of the heavens as a scroll rolled up together.

Verse 27: "For **as the light of day,** which comes forth from *the* east and shines as far as *the* west…"

This is not talking about a bolt of lightning, because lightning does not just proceed from the east. It proceeds from the east, from the west, from the north, from the south; from the clouds down to the ground; from the ground back up to the clouds; it goes sideways, it goes at every angle. So, this cannot be talking about lightning as a bolt of lightning, but the light of day, which comes out of the east because that's where the sun rises, and shines even unto the west because that's where the sun sets.

"**…so also shall the coming of the Son of man be**" (v 27). This is called *the sign of the Son of man!*

What is going to happen? *When the heavens roll back as a scroll there is going to appear this brightness as if it's another sun, and of that day and of that hour knows no man!*

Verse 29: "But immediately after the tribulation of those days…"

We saw the Tribulation come up to a certain point. And when we come to the book of Revelation we are going to see that it shifts from the tribulation of man against man to the more dastardly part of it—of demons and men against the angels of God—with the seven trumpet plagues. This becomes important to understand.

Verse 30: "And then shall appear the sign of the Son of man in heaven… [as a sun just being exposed; never there before] …and then shall all the tribes of the earth mourn, and they shall see the Son of man coming upon the clouds of heaven with power and great glory."

Because of the time that is left, the sign of the Son of man must be like a sun coming closer and closer and closer to the earth. Then when it comes time for the resurrection it will, I believe, lock into orbit right over Jerusalem. That's where the Sea of Glass will be. How high it will be, I don't know. It says it's going to be in the clouds. How high are the clouds? *Clouds can be as high as 50,000 feet. They can be as low as 2,000 or 3,000 feet!* So, we don't know, but we are going to meet Christ in the air in the clouds. Christ is coming with the clouds. Notice when the resurrection occurs this is what is going to happen:

Verse 31: "And He shall send His angels with a great sound of a trumpet; and they shall gather together His elect from the four winds, from one end of heaven to *the* other."

We got ahead of the story a little bit, because we need to look at the 50th day harvest of God. And this is a *special harvest* of God. Remember how we ended; they saw the sign of the Son of man in heaven.

Revelation 6:17 "Because the great day of His wrath has come, and who has the power to stand? *Now God does something very important:*

- He intervenes to fulfill a prophecy
- He intervenes to show His mercy
- He intervenes because He does not want, with the end of the Church Age, that there lack human beings who are converted and qualify for the Kingdom of God

Revelation 7:1: "And after these things I saw four angels standing on the four corners of the earth, holding back the four winds of the earth, so that the wind might not blow on the earth, or on the sea, or on any tree. Then I saw another angel ascending from *the* rising of *the* sun, having *the* seal of *the* living God; and he cried out with a loud voice to the four angels, to whom it was given to damage the earth and the sea, saying, 'Do not damage the earth, or the sea, or the trees **until we have sealed the servants of our God in their foreheads**'" (vs 1-3).

(Part 2)

Let's understand something very important and very profound of the 144,000 (Rev. 7); that cannot be anyone who is in the Church today. That's why the Jehovah Witnesses are completely wrong on *their* interpretation and understanding of the 144,000. Why is it that I say that the 144,000 of Rev. 7 cannot be any of us? Let's answer the question by Scripture.

Let's see that *we are now sealed* with the Holy Spirit of God. *Whenever you receive the Holy Spirit you have been sealed!* Let's see that and let's understand that the 144,000 were not sealed with the Holy Spirit until this particular time down into the Tribulation. We'll see that very clearly.

2-Corinthians 1:20: "For whatever promises of God *there are*, in Him *is* the yes, and in Him the Amen, with glory to God by us."

That's one thing we can do, brethren, *we can claim the promises of God!* Not because we're anything. Not because we're something that we have done of ourselves and we now deserve it. *No!* We claim the promises of God:

- for the sake of Christ
- for the sake of His Word
- for the sake of His Truth
- for His righteousness

It's always yes, because He won't deny the promise; He will fulfill it!

Verse 21: "But He Who establishes us with you in Christ, and Who has anointed us… [with His Holy Spirit] …*is* God, Who has also sealed us and has given the earnest of the Spirit in our hearts" (vs 21-22).

The earnest of the Spirit is the down payment; we are just like the unleavened bread now. When we are leavened in our *spiritual* form then we will have the fullness of the Spirit, and that's why leaven is pictured in good cause at that particular time. We only have the earnest of it now. Let's see how Paul explained, to those at Ephesus, concerning the Holy Spirit.

Ephesians 1:12: "That we might be… [those who are in the first resurrection] …to *the* praise of His glory, who first trusted in the Christ; in Whom you also trusted after hearing the Word of the Truth, the Gospel of your salvation; in Whom also, after believing, you were sealed with the Holy Spirit of promise, which is *the* earnest of our inheritance until *the* redemption of the purchased possession, to *the* praise of His glory" (vs 12-14).

If you have the Holy Spirit of God now, *you have been sealed!* So, you cannot be any of the 144,000 of Rev. 7. Let's see who the 144,000 are, and this will show how true God's Word is.

Revelation 7:3: "Saying, 'Do not damage the earth, or the sea, or the trees until we have sealed the servants of our God in their foreheads.'"

We've already been sealed so these are those who are now called and converted by God's supernatural act.

Let's review the things in Rev. 6; how that all of those things that the prophet Joel said concerning the heavens, the sun, the moon, the stars, and the earthquake, and the pouring out of the Spirit of God; how even Peter prophesied that that would be before the great and notable Day of the Lord. This is showing it right here. That's what happened. Here is the fulfillment of the Pentecost harvest or the 50th-day harvest by God. This is a separate harvest; separate from the Church. This is God's Divine intervention to fulfill and complete His Word and call those especially whom He is determined to call.

Now let's see who the 144,000 are, Revelation 7:4: "And I heard the number of those who were sealed: one hundred forty-four thousand, sealed out of every tribe of *the* children of Israel. From *the* tribe of Judah…" (vs 4-5).

Isn't it interesting that in the book of Zechariah, God says that 'the tents of Judah will be saved first'? So, here is Judah *first*.

"…twelve thousand *were* sealed; from *the* tribe of Reuben, twelve thousand *were* sealed…" (v

5)—*Gad, Asher, Naphtali, Manasseh, Simeon, Levi, Issachar, Zebulon, Joseph and Benjamin!*

Dan is left out; the reason Dan is left out is because the book of Genesis says of the prophecy of Dan that he 'would wait for his salvation.' Of course, Dan is the tribe of Israel that is so involved in idol worship and Catholicism. So, God is going to save them later; they're not included in this 144,000. *This is a special category that **God has saved for Himself!***

Now let's understand when in the timeframe does this take place in the Tribulation. We know that the overall Tribulation is 3-1/2 years. So, this is an event which takes place before the 3-1/2 years has expired. Let's see that this gives us a prophetic timeframe as to when this took place. God says concerning Israel:

Hosea 5:15: "I will go; I will return to My place until they confess their guilt and seek My face; in their affliction they will seek Me earnestly."

The prophecies are true; Israel is going into captivity. There are some people out there who say that 'Israel is not going into captivity today.' That is a lie and that is a false prophet. He is teaching things that are not according to the Scriptures. Oh, that it would be that Israel could be in such a condition before God that they wouldn't have to go into Tribulation. But you read all of the prophecies concerning where Israel is when Christ returns and all of them show that they are in captivity. Here are the children of Israel in captivity and—out of those who are in captivity—144,000 are brought to repentance and are sealed. When during the Tribulation does this take place?

Here it is speaking of Israel during this time of repentance, Hosea 6:1: "Come and let us return to the LORD, for He has torn, and He will heal us; He has smitten, and He will bind us up. After two days He will revive us…" (vs 1-2).

In prophecy, how long is a day? *In prophecy a day is a year!* So, this is after two full years. That's when the sign of the Son of man is going to appear in heaven and God will then begin to raise them up.

"…He will revive us; in the third day …" (v 2)—*beginning in the third year of the Tribulation,* which means there's a whole year—the third year—left, and there is another six months making a total of a year and a half.

The whole Tribulation is 3-1/2 years altogether, broken down into the first two years, coming down through the opening of the seals until the sign of the Son of man appears in heaven. Then we come down to the time now of Rev. 7 where we have *the 144,000 of Israel sealed* just like it says right here in Hos. 6.

"...in the third day He will raise us up, and we shall live in His sight.... [notice the prophecy]: ...Then we shall understand, *if* we follow on to know the LORD. His going out is prepared as the morning; and He shall come to us as the rain, as the latter *and* former rain to the earth" (vs 2-3). *This is what we have in Rev. 7, God intervening to save them!*

- What does it say concerning the preaching of the Gospel? *'To the Jews first,'* which includes **all** Israel.
- Who does it go to after that*? To the Greek or the Gentile!* God is going to reach down and *supernaturally seal,* by the power of God's Holy Spirit, through this angel who is commissioned to do so!

Let's understand that **all of these will receive the Holy Spirit first,** then they will be baptized just like it was with Cornelius' household; they received the Holy Spirit first, then they were baptized. Can God do that? *Yes, He can!* God chooses to do that whenever it is His choice to do, like He did with Cornelius. But do they still have to be baptized? *Yes, they do!* What will happen then? There will be great baptismal ceremonies taking place with the 144,000. Now then, since it goes to the Gentile also, the same thing is going to occur.

Revelation 7:9: "After these things I looked, and behold, a great multitude, which no one was able to number..."

This shows, contrary to the preaching of some, that God is not just restricting those that He is calling from the time of Christ until His return to 144,000. Such a thing could never be, because even on the very first day, as we saw with Pentecost, 3,000 were converted and thousands were added. Another place it says 5,000 souls were added. Great multitudes in Jerusalem believed. We saw where James told Paul, when Paul came up to visit James (Acts 22), *'behold the thousands that believe in Christ and are zealous for the Law!'* So, anybody who says that God is only calling 144,000 in this age just doesn't know what he's talking about and he's twisting and turning the Scriptures to his own destruction.

"...a great multitude, which no one was able to number... [Where did they come from?] ...out of every nation and tribe and people and language, was standing before the Throne and before the Lamb, clothed with white robes and *holding* palms in their hands" (v 9).

Just like we saw 'white robes'; they're called to the wedding. These are some of the guests who are called at the very last minute out of the highways and out of the byways, and out of the places that God is doing it at the last minute. Since this is prophesied in Acts 2 to happen with all the signs preceding it, and it happened on the Day of Pentecost there, this has to happen on the next to the last Pentecost before Christ puts His feet on the earth, or the Pentecost before the resurrection.

So, we have these people who, in these circumstances, will be converted for one year. These people—the 144,000 and the great innumerable multitude—are reckoned as the laborers who are put into work and hire at the eleventh hour. There's only one hour left, and in this case that pictures *one year left.* Is God able to do that? *Yes, He is, no doubt about it!* So, they're going to receive salvation.

Verse 10: "And they were calling out with a loud voice to Him Who sits on the Throne and to the Lamb, saying, 'The salvation of our God *has come.'*.... [because that's what they're going to receive] ...Then all the angels stood around the Throne, and the elders and the four living creatures, and fell on their faces before the Throne and worshiped God, saying, 'Amen. Blessing, and glory, and wisdom, and thanksgiving, and honor, and power and strength *be* to our God into the ages of eternity. Amen.'" (vs 10-12).

Verse 13:"And one of the elders answered *and* said to me, 'These who are clothed with white robes, who are they, and where did they come from?' Then I said to him, 'Sir, you know.' And he said to me, **'They are the ones who have come out of the great tribulation; and they have washed their robes, and have made their robes white in the blood of the Lamb.** For this reason, they are before the Throne of God and serve Him day and night in His Temple; and the One Who sits on the Throne shall dwell among them. They shall not hunger any more, nor shall they thirst any more; neither shall the sun nor the heat fall upon them, because the Lamb Who *is* in *the* midst of the Throne will shepherd them, and will lead them to fountains of living waters; and God will wipe away every tear from their eyes'" (vs13-17).

This projects forward to the time that we know in Rev. 21 shows the finality of God's plan. What this is doing is showing what God is going to do with the 144,000 and great innumerable multitude? First of all, He's showing that they're going to be resurrected. Of course, they're not going to be resurrected until the first resurrection takes place, but it also shows that they are not going to enter into the Millennium as physical human beings. They're going to be spirit beings.

Now we have a good setting to go on and understand what we're talking about with some of the other Scriptures concerning the Day of Pentecost and the resurrection.

I'm just going to summarize Rev. 8 & 9, but each of them are the *seven trumpet plagues.* The seventh seal is opened and then the first angel goes out. Isn't it interesting that it talks about the first angel going out and blows his trumpet. Then the second angel, third angel, fourth angel, fifth angel and the sixth angel.

Now let's see when the seventh angel sounds, and the seventh angel is the last trump; that's what we need to understand. The saints are resurrected at the last trump, *not trumpets.* The Feast of Trumpets is a day of war, a memorial of blowing of trumpets; so, here we have a sequence of seven trumpets. {note *Outline of Revelation* I & II, and the chart that goes with it, which is in our in-depth study of *Daniel and Revelation*} It shows that the first trumpet is blown shortly after the Pentecost where the 144,000 are sealed and the great innumerable multitude. That comes down through the time sequence to when we come to the seventh trump, which then has to be on the Day of Pentecost, or about right there.

Concerning the two witnesses, because this leads up until the resurrection. God allowed the two witnesses to be killed:

Revelation 11:8: "And their bodies *will lie* in the street of the great city, which spiritually is called Sodom and Egypt, **where also our Lord was crucified**."

- Sodom tells us the *morals* of the peoples
- Egypt tells us the *religion* of the people

The coming one world religion is going back to the whole thing of Egyptian religious worship. That's why it's defined here.

"…where also our Lord was crucified." That is typified by Jerusalem because Jerusalem—even though it was city that God chose to place His name there when the temple was built—*it has never been faithful,* with the exception of a few of the kings, as we find recorded in a history recorded in the books of Kings and Chronicles.

When the two witnesses die, v 9: "Then those of the peoples and tribes and languages and nations shall see their bodies three and a half days, for they will not allow their bodies to be put into tombs. And those who dwell on the earth will rejoice over them, and will make merry, and will send gifts to one another, because these two prophets had tormented those who dwell on the earth" (vs 9-10). *The last two enemies now to be killed, so the world thinks!*

Verse 11: "Then after the three and a half days, *the* spirit of life from God entered into them and they stood on their feet… [Can you imagine how everyone is going to view that and take that?] …and great fear fell upon those who were watching them."

Then here is an example, a perfect example in the Scripture concerning 'the first shall be last and the last shall be first.' The two witnesses were the very last two who were martyred for Christ's sake. They are the very first two who are resurrected.

After they stood on their feet, v 12: "And they heard a great voice from heaven, say, 'Come up here!' And they ascended into heaven in a cloud; and their enemies saw them *rise.* And in that hour there was a great earthquake, and a tenth of the city fell; and seven thousand men were killed in the earthquake. And the rest were filled with fear, and gave glory to the God of heaven. The second woe is past…." (vs 12-14). *The second woe was introduced with the sixth trumpet!*

"…Behold, the third woe is coming immediately. Then the seventh angel sounded *his* trumpet; and *there* were great voices in heaven, saying, 'The kingdoms of this world have become *the kingdoms* of our Lord and His Christ, and He shall reign into the ages of eternity.' And the twenty-four elders, who sit before God on their thrones, fell on their faces and worshiped God, saying, 'We give You thanks, O Lord God Almighty, Who is, and Who was, and Who *is* to come; for You have taken *to Yourself* Your great power, and have reigned. For the nations were angry, and Your wrath has come, and the time for the dead to be judged, and to give reward to Your servants the prophets, and to the saints, and to *all* those who fear Your name, the small and the great; and to destroy those who destroy the earth'" (vs 14-18).

That is the resurrection! The resurrection occurs at the seventh trump, the last trump, just as Paul said.

Let's see where, as we saw in Matt. 24, the angels will pick us up as we are resurrected and will bring us up to the Sea of Glass, because there is going to be the meeting with the saints. Then we will see what has to happen here.

1-Thessalonians 4:14: "For if we believe that Jesus died and rose again, in exactly the same way also, those who have fallen asleep in Jesus will God bring with Him. For this we say to you by *the* Word of *the* Lord, that we who are alive and remain unto the coming of the Lord shall in no wise precede those who have fallen asleep, because the Lord Himself shall descend from heaven with *a* shout of command, with *the* voice of an archangel and with *the* trumpet of God; and the dead in Christ shall rise first; then we who are alive…" (vs 14-17). **Who are those who are alive?**

1. those who are of the Church in the place of safety
2. the 144,000 and the great innumerable multitude (Rev. 7)

After all the dead in Christ have been raised, v 17: "Then we who are alive and remain shall be caught up together with them in *the* clouds for *the* meeting with the Lord in *the* air; and so shall we always be with *the* Lord."

Let's see when that will take place. I want you to understand that there are a lot of things that have to take place after the resurrection before we come back to the earth. It is true that the Feast of Trumpets pictures the day when Christ and the saints put their feet on the earth on the Mount of Olives.

But the coming of Christ began with the sign of the Son of man in heaven, and He kept coming closer and closer to the earth. Let's see the harvest of the firstfruits. Then we'll go back and we'll examine the 144,000 again of Rev. 7 and the 144,000 of Rev. 14. But first let's get us all resurrected first; let's have that all taken care of.

Revelation 14:12: "Here is *the* patience of the saints; here *are* the ones who keep the commandments of God and the faith of Jesus.... [Jesus' very own faith] ...And I heard a voice from heaven say to me, 'Write: Blessed *are* the dead who die in *the* Lord from this time forward. Yes, says the Spirit, so that they may rest from their labors; and their works follow them.' And I looked, and behold, a white cloud, and *one* like *the* Son of man sitting on the cloud, having a golden crown on His head; and in His hand *was* a sharp sickle" (vs 12-14). **What do you cut grain with?** *A sickle!*

Verse 15: "And another angel came out of the temple, crying with a loud voice to Him Who was sitting on the cloud, 'Thrust in your sickle and reap, because the time has come for You to reap; for the harvest of the earth is ripe.'"

Jesus said the harvest is the *end of the age.* The age ended with the seventh trump. This is the resurrection of the seventh trump. So, as the age is ending the sickle is put to the grain and all are resurrected.

Verse 16: "And He Who was sitting on the cloud thrust forth His sickle upon the earth, and the earth was reaped."

There is the first resurrection; that occurs on Pentecost. Then it jumps forward to another harvest. This is the harvest of the destruction of the wicked through the seven last plagues.

Verse 17: "Then another angel, who also had a sharp sickle, came out of the temple that *is* in heaven. And out from the altar came another angel, who had authority over fire; and he called with a loud cry to the one who had the sharp sickle, saying, 'Thrust in your sharp sickle, and gather the clusters of the earth, because her grapes are fully ripe'" (vs 17-18). *These are the true grapes of wrath!*

Now notice, the One Who did the first harvesting was like unto the Son of man, that's Christ. Now we have an angel with a sickle.

Verse 19: "And the angel thrust his sickle into the earth, and gathered the vine of the earth, and cast *its fruit* into the great winepress of the wrath of God. And the winepress was trodden outside the city, and blood spewed out from the winepress as high as the horses' bridles, to the distance of a thousand six hundred furlongs" (vs 19-20). *This is the judgment in the Valley of Judgment!*

Revelation 15:1: "Then I saw another sign in heaven, great and awesome: seven angels having the seven last plagues, for in them the wrath of God is filled up. And I saw a Sea of Glass mingled with fire" (vs 1-2).

Remember how we saw that the Sea of Glass was there when Christ came down on the mountain. He had Moses and the 70 elders and Aaron, Nadab, and Abihu came up. They all saw Him because it was pavement under His feet. If we're going to meet Christ in the air, what are we going to do? How are we going to be suspended? Well, there is a Sea of Glass that we can walk on; that's where the angels take us.

"...A Sea of Glass mingled with fire... [because of its brilliance] ...and those who had gotten the victory over the beast..." (v 2).

- When did *the beast* first appear? *In the person of Satan the devil in the Garden of Eden!*
- Have all of those who enter into the first resurrection, have they had to get victory over the beast? *Yes!*

"...**and over his image**..." (v 2).

Has there not been a female goddess-worship in the image to *the beast* going clear back when? *Yes!* At least we know that it came after the Flood. We know that they just reconstructed what they had after the Flood from what they did before the Flood. There's the image of *the beast.*

"...**and over his mark**..." (v 2). *At the end-time we're going to have the mark of the beast!* It's called the Digital Angel, which is inserted in the forehand or in the forehead either one.

"...***and* over the number of his name**, standing on the Sea of Glass, having *the* lyres of God" (v 2)

Notice that this includes the Old Testament, those who have been resurrected and qualified from the time of Abel on down to the time of Christ.

Notice what they do, v 3: "And they were singing the song of Moses, *the* servant of God..." *These are those of the Old Testament, the loaf of the Old Testament!*

"...and the song of the Lamb... [New Testament] ...saying, 'Great and awesome *are* Your works, Lord God Almighty; righteous and true *are* Your ways, King of the saints. Who shall not fear You, O Lord, and glorify Your name? For *You* only *are* Holy; and all the nations shall come and worship before You, for Your judgments have been revealed' (vs 3-4). *There's a prophecy of what's going to happen on down into the Millennium!*

144,000 of Revelation 7

Verse 4: "And I heard the number of those who were sealed: one hundred forty-four thousand, sealed out of every tribe of *the* children of Israel."

These are from the children of Israel only, 12,000 from each tribe. Why are they sealed at this particular time? *They are in captivity because they were unfaithful to God even in the letter of the law!* We'll see that's very important.

We also find the great innumerable multitude. There are no other distinguishing characteristics of these other than the fact that they are sealed at the beginning of the third year during the Tribulation of 3-1/2 years. They then qualify for the first resurrection. These are the laborers of the 11th hour (Luke 11).

144,000 of Revelation 14

We are going to see that these 144,000 are a different group—the distinguishing and qualifying things

Revelation 14:1: "And I looked, and I beheld *the* Lamb standing on Mount Sion..." *We have come unto Mt. Sion, the Church of the Firstborn (Heb. 12)!*

"...and with Him one hundred *and* forty-four thousand, having His Father's name written on their foreheads. Then I heard a voice from heaven, like *the* sound of many waters, and like *the* sound of great thunder; and I heard *the* sound of lyre players playing their lyres. And they were singing a new song before the Throne, and before the four living creatures and the elders. And no one was able to learn the song except the hundred *and* forty-four thousand, who were redeemed from the earth" (vs 1-3).

This is a separate song from the song of Moses, and the song of the Lamb. This is a third song that only this 144,000 could sing. No one else could sing it. All the rest were able to sing the one concerning Moses for the Old Covenant, the one concerning the Lamb for the New Covenant, and now we have a third category here of the 144,000 with their song.

Verse 4: "These are the ones who were not defiled with women..." (v 4).

What does it mean to be defiled with women? *You go right back to Rev. 17,* that we have 'Mystery Babylon the Great, the mother of harlots and abominations of the earth,' and she is called the 'great whore.'

This means that once they were converted they did not defile themselves with any of the 'religions' or the *religious practices* of this world. We're going to see that's very important when we go back and look at the seven churches (Rev. 2 & 3).

"...for they are virgins... [Christ would only marry a virgin] ...they are the ones who follow the Lamb wherever He goes. They were purchased from among men *as* firstfruits to God and to the Lamb" (v 4).

We have Christ Who was the First of the firstfruits, and then we have these who are apparently the first group of the firstfruits. All the rest being the firstfruits in general.

Verse 5: "And no guile was found in their mouths; for they are blameless before the Throne of God."

Analysis of Rev. 14 and what separates these *even further* from the 144,000 in Rev. 7:

1. **They have the name of the Father written in their foreheads**

It doesn't say that about the 144,000 in Rev. 7. All of these are distinguished from the 144,000 in Rev. 7. The first thing that we need to understand is, as we go along here, because it says that they were not of the children of Israel, but they were redeemed from the earth.

2. **No one was able to learn the song except the 144,000**
3. **They were redeemed from the earth**

Showing that these 144,000 were redeemed from the earth probably over a period of time.

4. **These are they who are not defiled with women**

They remained virgins; they remained totally faithful to God in everything that they did in their conversion and were never defiled by women.

5. They are virgins

Remember the warning that the Apostle Paul gave to the Corinthians:

2-Corinthians 11:2: "For I am jealous over you with *the* jealousy of God because I have espoused you to one husband, so that I may present *you as* a chaste virgin to Christ."

But they became non-virgins because they committed *spiritual* fornication. Maybe they were able to repent of it, just like any woman who loses her virginity through sin, she can repent of it but she's no longer a virgin.

Likewise, if it is those who have received the Holy Spirit, if they give up their virginity by being enticed by Satan the devil and getting involved in other religious practices, or other religious doctrines within the Church then they lose their virginity.

6. These follow the Lamb wherever He goes

Meaning that they're always following Him regardless of where their spiritual life takes them.

7. These were redeemed from among men

Redeemed from the earth, redeemed from among men.

8. Firstfruits unto God and to the Lamb
9. In their mouth was no guile
10. For they are without fault before the Throne of God

Review of the Seven Churches of Revelation 2 & 3:

We will see that out of the seven churches only two of the seven remained virgins:

Ephesus:

They lost their first love and Christ told them, 'Except you repent, I'm going to remove your candlestick.' Losing your first love, that is losing your virginity.

Pergamos:

They ate things sacrificed to idols, committed fornication, had the doctrine of Balaam and the doctrine of the Nicolaitans, which thing God says He hates. He would fight against them with the sword of His mouth. Those at Pergamos, even though they repented because they were told to repent, *they lost their virginity!* They can be put back in right standing with God, *but once you lose your virginity you have lost it!* That doesn't mean you can't recoup. You can to be in the first resurrection.

But the question is: **Will you still be part of the Bride of Christ?** When describing the 144,000 in Rev. 14 they are the ones who are the Bride of Christ *because they remain virgins!*

Thyatira:

- they had the woman Jezebel
- they committed fornication
- they ate things sacrificed to idols
- they also had those who knew the deep things of Satan

In other words those who infiltrated into that church were bringing in the doctrines of Satan-worship under the guise that you're worshiping Christ. Obviously, *they lost their virginity.*

Sardis:

Sardis was dead! They had a name that they lived but they are dead. With having dead practices they *surely were not virgins* before God. Because they somehow defiled themselves, and remember what Christ said to them. 'Repent!'

Laodicea:

The Laodiceans became lukewarm, had need of nothing, and God was spewing them out of His mouth. God told them to repent. So we have Ephesus, Pergamos, Thyatira, Sardis, and Laodicea. Five of the seven churches were commanded to repent of their sins. So, *they lost their virginity!*

Now the two churches left were:

Smyrna:

No command to repent. The Smyrneans were the ones who were martyred, and they were faithful unto death. *They held their virginity unto death!*

Philadelphia:

Philadelphians resisted everything concerning the synagogue of Satan, and they patiently kept the Word of God. They were the ones who were faithful, *the most faithful of all.* There is no call to repentance, and to the Church at Philadelphia Christ said, *'To him that overcomes will I write upon him the name of My Father, and the name of the city, New Jerusalem, and I will write upon him My new name.'*

To the Philadelphians:

- *if* you have the name of the Father
- *if* you have the name of Jerusalem
- *if* you have the name of Christ upon you

you belong to part of the Bride of Christ!

Not all of those in the first resurrection are going to be part of the Bride of Christ. Does this tell us here in Rev. 14—because of all of these conditions—that this 144,000 represents those who have been called down through time—

- who have been faithful unto God
- who were virgins
- never deviated from it

—once they were baptized and received the Holy Spirit *they never got involved in any of the religions of this world, or any of the doctrines of this world.*

I hope you understand why it is so important that we remain faithful!

Now those who have not remained faithful, we pray that they will repent and not lose their reward. This is really important for us to understand. Let's see that they can repent, but they have been building wooden shacks and straw huts and their works are burned up because they were not virgins. The only ones who are virgins in this case are those who build on the virginity, keep it, and build the gold, silver, precious stone, and not the wood, hay, and stubble.

1-Corinthians 3:11: "For no one is able to lay any other foundation besides that which has been laid, which is Jesus Christ. Now, if anyone builds upon this foundation gold, silver, precious stones, wood, hay *or* stubble, the work of each one shall be manifested; for the day *of trial* will declare *it…*" (vs 11-13). *The day of the resurrection is going to be the final day of declaration!*

"…because it shall be revealed by fire… [these are the fiery trials that we go through in our life of overcoming] …and the fire shall prove what kind of work each one's is. If the work that anyone has built endures, he shall receive a reward. If the work of anyone is burned up, he shall suffer loss; but *he* himself shall be saved, yet, as through fire" (vs 13-15).

Is this describing the difference between the 144,000 of Rev. 14 *who become part of the Bride of Christ,* because they remain faithful, as differentiated from those who started out but ended up sinning, ended up repenting and coming back much like the prodigal son, and *they lost their virginity*? They lost some of the inheritance that they would have had otherwise. So, this is really a tremendous thing for us to understand.

I don't have time to go through the seven last plagues except that *the seven last plagues represent the harvest of the wicked,* as depicted in the last part of Rev. 14. All of these plagues will be poured out in the presence of the saints. These are righteous judgments, and these are true judgments. For any who say that the God of the Old Testament was an angry and a harsh God, but the One of the New Testament is loving and kind and sweet, please understand that *this is the wrath of the Lamb that is being poured out on all those sinners!*

Let's also understand this, too: *God knows,* for the resurrection—based upon the works and the faithfulness of the individuals—*that He is going to select those who will be in the 144,000 of Rev. 14!* If those are the ones who consist of the Bride of Christ, *God the Father is the One Who chooses them!*

We don't have to worry about it. We don't have to look around and accuse people, or suspect them, because it says, 'Blessed are those who are called to the wedding supper of the Lamb.' Those who are called to the supper will participate in the first resurrection in power, and in glory just like the rest. But only the Bride of Christ will be with Christ *wherever He is.*

Revelation 19:1: "And after these things I heard *the* loud voice of a great multitude in heaven, saying…"—*because that's all of those who were resurrected standing on the Sea of Glass!* And it's in the first heaven where the clouds are.

"…'Hallelujah! The salvation and the glory and the honor and the power *belong* to the Lord our God. For true and righteous *are* His judgments; for He has judged the great whore, who corrupted the earth with her fornication, and He has avenged the blood of His servants at her hand.' And they said a second time, 'Hallelujah! And her smoke shall ascend upward into the ages of eternity'" (vs 1-3).

Verse 4: "And the twenty-four elders and the four living creatures fell down and worshiped God, Who sits on the Throne, saying, 'Amen. Hallelujah!' And a voice came forth from the Throne, saying, 'Praise our God, all His servants, and all who fear Him, both small and great.' And I heard a voice like that of a great multitude, and like *the* sound of many waters, and *the* sound of mighty thunderings, saying, 'Hallelujah! For *the* Lord God Almighty has reigned. Let us be glad and shout with joy; and let us give glory to Him; for the marriage of the Lamb has come, and His wife has made herself ready.' And it was granted to her that she should be clothed in fine linen, pure and bright; for the fine linen is the righteousness of the saints. And he said to me, 'Write: Blessed *are* those who are called to the marriage supper of the Lamb.' And he said to me, '**These are the true words of God**'" (vs 4-9).

So, we have a tremendous blessing, brethren, if we have been called to be part of the Bride of Christ, which I hope whoever you are that that is true. We can't judge for ourselves how it's going to be. God is going to make that judgment. But also realize this:

There is a great and a fantastic and eternal blessing to be called to the first resurrection and to be one of the guests at the wedding of the Lamb and His Bride!

That is the full meaning of the Feast of Pentecost, and I hope it's been a wonderful day for you!

Scriptures from *The Holy Bible in Its Original Order, A Faithful Version*

Scriptural References:

1) Exodus 34:26
2) 1 Corinthians 15:12-23
3) Acts 1:3-11
4) Acts 2:1-8, 10-15
5) Deuteronomy 5:29
6) Acts 2:16-24, 34-41
7) Leviticus 23:17
8) Mathew 13:33
9) 1 Corinthians 15:34-36
10) John 12:24-25
11) 1 Corinthians 15:36-54
12) Revelation 6:1-17
13) Matthew 24:21-31
14) Revelation 6:17
15) Revelation 7:1-3
16) 2 Corinthians 1:20-22
17) Ephesians 1:12-14
18) Revelation 7:3-5
19) Hosea 5:15
20) Hosea 6:1-3
21) Revelation 7:9-17
22) Revelation 11:8-18
23) 1 Thessalonians 4:14-17
24) Revelation 14:12-20
25) Revelation 15:1-4
26) Revelation 7:4
27) Revelation 14:1-5
28) 2 Corinthians 11:2
29) 1 Corinthians 3:11-15
30) Revelation 19:1-9

Scriptures referenced, not quoted:

- Exodus 31
- John 20
- Luke 24
- Revelation 2-5
- Psalm 110
- Revelation 11-12
- Haggai 2
- Acts 22; 2
- Revelation 21, 8, 9
- Luke 11
- Hebrews 12
- Revelation 17; 2; 3

Also referenced:

- Booklet: *The True Meaning of Acts 2:1* by Fred R. Coulter
- In-Depth Study: *Daniel/Revelation: Outline of Revelation I & II*

FRC: cis
Transcribed: 07-06-00
Reformatted: bo—11/2020

CHAPTER FORTY-THREE

More on the 144,000
Fred R. Coulter

I want to answer some questions concerning the Bride and the guests and maybe a little bit concerning the 144,000. I might mention a booklet: *Who Are the 144,000?* So, we'll be able to cover that.

Let's come to Matt. 20, and what I want to do is cover a little part concerning the 50th-day harvest of the 144,000 and the great innumerable multitude.

Matthew 20:1: "The Kingdom of Heaven shall be compared to a man, a master of a house, who went out early in *the* morning to hire workmen for his vineyard. And after agreeing with the workmen on a silver coin *for* the day's *wage*, he sent them into his vineyard. And when he went out about the third hour, he saw others standing idle in the marketplace; and he said to them, 'Go also into the vineyard, and whatever is right I will give you.' And they went…." (vs 1-5).

One thing that we have to get rid of is the Gerald Waterhouse mentality that it's all stacked up according to *his four-hour sermon*. It's not that way, *because God is going to determine who will be where and in what position!* That's all a part of this.

The master of the house didn't tell them very much. He said "'…whatever is right, I'll give you.' And they went their way."

"'…Again, after going out about *the* sixth hour and *the* ninth hour, he did likewise'" (vs 1-5). He went out there at 6 a.m., 9 a.m., noon, 3 p.m.

Verse 6: "And about the eleventh hour… [5 o'clock] …he went out *and* found others standing idle, and said to them, 'Why have you been standing here idle all the day?' They said to him, 'Because no one has hired us.' He said to them, 'Go also into my vineyard, and whatever is right you shall receive.' And when evening came, the lord of the vineyard said to his steward, 'Call the workmen and pay them *their* hire, beginning from the last unto the first'" (vs 6-8).

This tells us an awful lot. As we will see, the whole parable tells us that God does not think like we think, especially if you ever belong to a union. This would be called the greatest 'scab' operation that they had ever come across.

Verse 9: "And when those who *were hired* about the eleventh hour came, they each received a silver coin. But when the first ones came, they thought that they would receive more…" (vs 9-10). *This is judging by human standards!*

"…but each of them also received a silver coin. And after receiving *it*, they complained against the master of the house, saying, 'These *who came* last have worked one hour, and you have made them equal to us, who have carried the burden and the heat of the day.' But he answered *and* said to them, 'Friend, I am not doing you wrong. Did you not agree with me on a silver coin *for the day*?'" (vs 10-13).

*This tells us that **God is going to do what He is going to do**. He is going to reward whom He is going to reward, **in the way that He is going to reward them!** That all of our complaining or comparing isn't going to change it.*

I know there are going to be some people who say, 'Who are you to say that we're not going to be part of the Bride?' The truth is, *Christ is going to determine who it is, and I'm sure God the Father is going to select the Bride!*

Just recently I had a wedding, and I love weddings; weddings are my favorite thing! It was really a wonderful outdoor wedding. It was beautiful. Only thing, it was a noon and 95 degrees, so it was a little warm, but just as we started there was a breeze that came up and made it livable. I went through the ceremony and then we went on over where they were going to have the wedding supper. I was sitting there and my wife was sitting there and we were enjoying everything. The bride and groom came in and they took the first dance.

I thought, this is just exactly what the Bible is talking about. We're here and we're enjoying it. I was happy to have a part in doing the ceremony. But there's the husband and there's the bride and all the rest of us are guests. I thought, *that's just the way it's going to be in the resurrection. God is the One Who's going to have to decide!*

Verse 14: "'Take *what* is yours and go, for I also desire to give to the last *ones* exactly as I gave to you. And is it not lawful for me to do what I will with that which *is* my own? Is your eye evil because I am good?' **So, the last shall be first, and the first shall be last; for many are called, but few are**

chosen'" (vs 14-15).

This almost sounds like what we've read about in Job: *That 'you disannul My judgment that you may be righteous.'* That's what they're trying to do here.

Let's look at Rev. 7—are these not the 144,000 from Israel? I think that's very clear that they are different from the 144,000 in Rev. 14. As we cover on Pentecost, Rev. 7 is approximately at the end of two full years of the 3-1/2 year Tribulation, meaning that there's 1 year and 6 months left. This, I believe, is **the 50th-day harvest that belongs to God!** Here it gives no inclination of any reward at all, except that—after you get through the 144,000—you come down here to the great innumerable multitude, 'which no man could number'; and then it says:

Revelation 7:14: "Then I said to him, 'Sir, you know.' And he said to me, 'They are the ones who have come out of the great tribulation; and they have washed their robes, and have made their robes white in the blood of the Lamb.'"

So, these here may very well be a good portion of the number of guests, because if they're in white, then those are the wedding garments of the guests. These are part of *the last*, which will probably be some of the first who are resurrected. That doesn't mean that they're going to be necessarily first in reward.

The Two Witnesses

Let's look at the very two *last*, **the two witnesses:**

Revelation 11:3 "And I will give *power* to My two witnesses, and they shall prophesy a thousand two hundred *and* sixty days, clothed in sackcloth. These are the two olive trees, and *the* two lampstands that stand before the God of the earth. And if anyone attempts to harm them, fire will go out of their mouths and devour their enemies. For if anyone attempts to harm them, he must be killed in this manner" (vs 3-5). *This is going to be quite a thing!*

Verse 6: "These have authority to shut heaven so that no rain may fall in *the* days of their prophecy; and they have authority over the waters, to turn them into blood, and to smite the earth with every plague, as often as they will. And when they have completed their testimony, the beast who ascends out of the abyss... [Satan and the man that he possesses] ...will make war against them, and will overcome them, and will kill them" (vs 6-7).

This is just like with Christ. Satan thought he had it made when Christ was killed. But Christ was resurrected and totally defeated Satan. So *the beast* will think 'we finally have it made, and we'll teach them a lesson.

Verse 8: "And their bodies *will lie* in the street of the great city, which spiritually is called Sodom and Egypt, where also our Lord was crucified."

Of course, the coming one-world religion is going to be nothing more than a re-warmed Egyptian version of the New Age religion. Did you know that Mormonism—read this book *Primitive Christianity in Crisis*—is nothing more than modern Gnosticism. When you read this it will 'blow you away!' The Gnostics believe that we were spirits up in heaven and that they had to come down and possess a human body. That's a very basic tenet of Mormonism!

Verse 9: "Then those of the peoples and tribes and languages and nations shall see their bodies three and a half days, for they will not allow their bodies to be put into tombs. And those who dwell on the earth will rejoice over them..." (vs 9-10).

When it talks about all the world will see, it means *they will see it!* Today we understand that statement. I think it will be with television, no question about it.

"...and will make merry, and will send gifts to one another..." (v 10). I can just hear *the beast*:

Brethren of the world, they have finally conquered these two men who were disturbing and upsetting our wonderful one-world government. They have caused plagues! Killed people! Drought! Now they are dead! Let us celebrate; I proclaim a feast!

That's what's going to happen!

"...because these two prophets had tormented those who dwell on the earth.' Then after the three and a half days, *the* spirit of life from God entered into them and they stood on their feet..." (vs 10-11).

Can you imagine that? Can you imagine the breathlessness of all of the television reporters, all breathlessly reporting this, and all the cameras are there and then we have this discussion. They'll have a rabbi and 'what do you think of this?' You can almost see the whole thing going on. And right when they're talking about how good it is that they're dead, all of a sudden—the cameras pointing on their bodies—see them rise up on their feet.

"...they stood on their feet and great fear fell upon those who were watching them. And they heard a great voice from heaven, say, 'Come up here!' And they ascended into heaven in a cloud; and their enemies saw them *rise*" (vs 11-12).

These are the last two who are killed, who are the *first resurrected!* Perfect example of the *'the last shall be first.'*

Verse 13: "And in that hour there was a great earthquake, and a tenth of the city fell; and seven thousand men were killed in the earthquake. And the rest were filled with fear, and gave glory to the God of heaven. The second woe is past. Behold, the third woe is coming **immediately**.... [not just quickly] ...Then the seventh angel sounded *his* trumpet; and *there* were great voices in heaven, saying, 'The kingdoms of this world have become *the kingdoms* of our Lord and His Christ, and He shall reign into the ages of eternity'" (vs 13-15).

Here is the resurrection! But just prior to the resurrection, the two witnesses—the last two—are raised first.

Matthew 20:16: "So the last shall be first, and the first *shall be* last; for many are called, but few *are* chosen."

Then we have Jesus was going up and He told them about how He was going to be betrayed, and so forth.

Verse 20: "Then the mother of the sons of Zebedee came to Him with her sons, worshiping Him and asking a certain thing from Him. And He said to her, 'What do you desire?' She said to Him, 'Grant that these my two sons may sit one at Your right hand and one at *Your* left *hand* in Your kingdom'" (vs 20-21).

You talk about a political move to make it good 'for my two boys.' But this has the same thing to do with the first and the last, only from a little different perspective. This time, instead of the first and last being the general laborers that were out in the vineyard, now here we have it with the 12 apostles. Christ gives the lesson here:

Verse 22: "But Jesus answered *and* said, 'You do not know what you are asking....'"

The two sons were right there. They wouldn't want to march up and say, 'Lord, give it to us, look how good we are. But, mom, you are so persuasive, why don't you do it for us.'

"'...Are you able to drink the cup that I am about to drink, and to be baptized *with* the baptism that I am baptized *with*?'.... [He had just told them He was going to be crucified] ...They said to Him, 'We are able'" (v 22).

Of course, they didn't know what that was. It's kind of like a Marine recruit. 'Are you able to go up and capture that enemy machine-gun nest?' *Yeah, I can!* Don't even know what you're saying; never been under fire.

Verse 23: "And He said to them, 'You shall indeed drink of My cup, and shall be baptized *with* the baptism that I am baptized *with*; but to sit at My right hand and at My left *hand* is not Mine to give, but *shall be given to those* for whom it has been prepared by My Father.'"

So, **the Father is in charge of all of this,** not just us as human beings, or just Christ alone.

Verse 24: "And after hearing *this*, the ten were indignant against the two brothers"—*because they got there first!* The other ten would have like to have gotten there first to ask; that's what they were mad at. Just a carnal human being wanting to be the best, the greatest and all this sort of thing.

Verse 25: "But Jesus called them to *Him* and said... [He's giving the lesson here]: ...'You know that the rulers of the nations **exercise lordship**... [dominion] ...over them, and the great ones exercise authority over them.'"

Dominion is 'katakurieuo'—which is *downward*; and the other one is 'kataexousia'—which is *authority downward*.

Verse 26: "However, it shall not be this way among you; but whoever would become great among you, let him be your servant; and whoever would be first among you, let him be your slave; just as the Son of man did not come to be served, but to serve, and to give His life *as* a ransom for many" (vs 26-28). *That all ties in with those who are going to be in the resurrection!*

Matthew 22:1—*let's look at the guests*: "And again Jesus answered and spoke to them in parables, saying, 'The Kingdom of Heaven is compared to a man *who was* a king... [God the Father] ...who made a wedding feast for his son... [Jesus Christ] ...and sent his servants to call those who had been invited to the wedding feast; but they refused to come'" (vs 1-3). *The 'king' Who is God the Father* is going to have the marriage and He's going to select the Bride.

Verse 4: "Afterwards he sent out other servants, saying, 'Say to those who have been invited, "Behold, I have prepared my dinner; my oxen and the fatted beasts are killed, and all things *are* ready. Come to the wedding feast."' But they paid no attention and went away, one to his farm, and another to his business. And the rest, after seizing his servants, insulted and killed *them*" (vs 4-6). *Just a summary of the life of the apostles!*

Verse 7: "Now, when the king heard *it*, he became angry; and he sent his armies *and* destroyed those murderers, and burned up their city.... [Jerusalem 70ᴀ.ᴅ.] ...Then he said to his servants, 'The wedding feast indeed is ready, but those who were invited were not worthy; therefore, go into the well-traveled highways, and invite all that you find to the wedding feast.' And after going out into the highways, those servants brought together everyone that they found, both good and evil…" (vs 7-10).

This is talking about people who are bad people and good people—not in the sense of *spiritually speaking* but just in their lives. Of course, both the bad and the good have to repent. It's harder for the good to repent because they don't see the sins that they have done.

"…and the wedding feast was filled with guests" (v 10).

Here the parable breaks down a little bit. Obviously, this is referring to the first resurrection. But there is not going to be anybody in the first resurrection who is going to be there without the proper wedding garment. In order to show that you have to apply yourself and have to have the proper wedding garment, this is in the parable. When will those who do not prepare to be guests be cast into outer darkness? *That will be the Lake of Fire at the end of the Millennium in the Great White Throne Judgment!* In order for the sake of the parable to show it, it has to be combined here.

Verse 11: "And when the king came in to see the guests…" *The 'king' being God the Father helps answer the questions*:

• When we are resurrected will we see God the Father?
• Why not?
• Will we be spirit beings? *Yes!*
• Are we not His children? *Yes!*
• Would He not want to see His children just resurrected, born from the dead? *Yes!*
• Would we not want to see Him? *Absolutely!*
• As well as Christ? *No doubt!*

So, this says He came to see them!

"…*he* noticed a man there who was not dressed in *proper* attire for *the* wedding feast; and he said to him, 'Friend, how did you enter here without a garment *fit* for *the* wedding feast?' But he had no answer. Then the king said to the servants, 'Bind his hands and feet, *and* take him away, and cast *him* into the outer darkness.' There shall be weeping and gnashing of teeth. For many are called, but few *are* chosen'" (vs 11-14).

Let's hope we can understand this a little bit more, Matthew 25:1: "Then shall the Kingdom of Heaven be compared *to* ten virgins, who took their lamps *and* went out to meet the bridegroom."

Here we have the virgins and the bridegroom; before we had the guests coming to the wedding. This is obviously a different category of people.

Verse 2: "And five of them were wise, and five *were* foolish. The ones who were foolish took their lamps, *but* they did not take oil with them" (vs 2-3).

You need to understand about the lamps. The lamps that they had were small, handheld and had a little wick that came out of the side. Olive oil was put into the middle of it and the wick would hang over the edge of it and give light. Obviously, if you only have oil in your little lamp you don't have very much. That's why they should have some with them, to carry an extra amount to pour in there when they needed it.

Verse 4: "But the wise took oil in their vessels *along* with their lamps. Now when the bridegroom was gone a long time, they all became drowsy and slept" (vs 4-5). *Showing that they had their own individual problems!*

Verse 6: "But in *the* middle of *the* night there was a cry: 'Look, the bridegroom is coming! Go out to meet him.' Then all those virgins arose and trimmed their lamps. And the foolish said to the wise, 'Give us *some* of your oil, because our lamps are going out.' But the wise answered, saying, 'No, lest *there* not *be* enough for us and *for* you. But instead, go to those who sell, and buy for yourselves'" (vs 6-9).

This is obviously showing that *they did not have enough spiritual character in order to qualify as part of the Bride!*

Verse 10: "And while they went to buy, the bridegroom came… [in a parable it can't fit everything to the exact facts] …and those who were ready went in with him to the wedding feast, and the door was shut. And afterwards the other virgins also came, saying, 'Lord, Lord, open to us.' But He answered *and* said, 'Truly I say to you, I do not know you'" (vs 10-12).

In this case, He doesn't say 'depart into outer darkness' and there shall be weeping and gnashing of teeth. **This does not necessarily show a loss of salvation, but this shows a loss of being part of the Bride!** The door to being the Bride is shut! It doesn't say they won't be in the Kingdom of God, but it does tell us they won't be part of the Bride.

Verse 13: "Watch, therefore, for you do not know the day nor the hour in which the Son of man is coming."

Now then, I think that's the best understanding that I've been able to derive from this. In other words, these virgins by the virtue of the fact that *they didn't exercise the spiritual character they should have had*, they, in a sense, disqualified themselves from the marriage. It doesn't necessarily say that they sinned and lost what we would call the *spiritual virginity*, but it does show that they were very negligent.

Let's answer the question concerning the firstfruits, 1-Corinthians 15:20: "But now Christ has been raised from *the* dead; He has become the first-fruit of those who have fallen asleep."

We know that this is the first of the firstfruits by several things:

1. God says that you are bring the first of the firstfruits unto the Lord (Exo. 34).
2. By the wave sheaf offering that was elevated on the Wave Sheaf Offering Day, that that signified Christ ascending to the Father to be accepted as the firstborn from the dead.
3. Christ is the First of the firstfruits

Verse 21: "For since by man *came* death, by man also *came the* resurrection of *the* dead. For as in Adam all die, so also in Christ shall all be made alive. **But each in his own order**..." (vs 21-23).

There is an order to the resurrection! Part of what we have of the order that we saw is the 'last shall be first and the first shall be last.'

If Adam and repented and made it—is he going to be the last one resurrected? *I don't know!* But the ones who are going to be the very last to be resurrected are those who are alive when Christ returns. 1-Thess. 4 says that 'they who are dead in Christ **shall rise first!** Then we who are alive, will be caught up in the air together with them and meet the Lord in the air.' Now, *meet the Lord in the air* can also have the meaning: *for the meeting with the Lord in the air.* So, there's an order.

We are called *firstfruits*. All those in the first resurrection are called *firstfruits*. Christ is called *firstfruits*. Christ is the First of the firstfruits. Now, let's look at the rest:

James 1:18 "According to His [God the Father] own will, He begat us by *the* Word of Truth, that we might be a kind of firstfruits of all His created beings"—*of His creation*; meaning those of us who are *created in Christ Jesus!* That's what it's referring to.

So, we are called *firstfruits!* Christ is also called *the Firstborn*. Rom. 8:29, 'that He should be called the firstborn among many brethren.' We are also called *the Church of the Firstborn* (Heb. 12).

Let's go back to Rev. 14 and let's see concerning 144,000. The distinction between these and the 144,000 in Rev. 7 becomes very clear when we analyze all the differences. What is said of the

144,000 in Rev. 7 is that they are 12,000 from the 12 tribes of the children of Israel. It lists Joseph and it lists Manasseh and it does not include Dan—that's because of the prophecy that 'Dan will wait for his salvation.'

Revelation 14:1: "And I looked, and I beheld *the* Lamb standing on Mount Sion... [that's what we are to come to—the Church of the Firstborn (Heb. 12)] ...and with Him one hundred *and* forty-four thousand..."

Revelation 7:9 *with the innumerable multitude and the 144,000*: "After these things I looked, and behold, a great multitude, which no one was able to number, out of every nation and tribe and people and language, was standing before the Throne and before the Lamb, clothed with white robes and *holding* palms in their hands."

You have to have the white robes in order to be a guest. This is probably indicating that these were all guests. They stood before the Throne; that is out around before the Throne.

Verse 10: "And they were calling out with a loud voice to Him Who sits on the Throne and to the Lamb, saying, 'The salvation of our God *has come.*' Then all the angels stood around the Throne, and the elders and the four living creatures, and fell on their faces before the Throne and worshiped God, saying, 'Amen. Blessing, and glory, and wisdom, and thanksgiving, and honor, and power and strength *be* to our God into the ages of eternity. Amen'" (vs 10-12).

Verse 13: And one of the elders answered *and* said to me, 'These who are clothed with white robes, who are they, and where did they come from?' Then I said to him, 'Sir, you know.' And he said to me, 'They are the ones who have come out of the Great Tribulation; and they have washed their robes, and have made their robes white in the blood of the Lamb. For this reason, they are before the Throne of God and serve Him day and night in His Temple; and the One Who sits on the Throne shall dwell among them. They shall not hunger any more, nor shall they thirst any more; neither shall the sun nor the heat fall upon them, because the Lamb Who *is* in *the* midst of the Throne will shepherd them, and will lead them to fountains of living waters; and God will wipe away every tear from their eyes'" (vs 13-17).

Let's come back and compare that with the 144,000 in Revelation 14:1: And I looked, and I beheld *the* Lamb standing on Mount Sion, and with Him one hundred *and* forty-four thousand, having His Father's name written on their foreheads. Then I heard a voice from heaven, like *the* sound of many waters, and like *the* sound of great thunder; and I heard *the* sound of lyre players playing their lyres.

And they were singing a new song before the Throne, and before the four living creatures and the elders. And no one was able to learn the song except the hundred *and* forty-four thousand, who were redeemed from the earth. These are the ones who were not defiled with women, for they are virgins; they are the ones who follow the Lamb wherever He goes. They were purchased from among men *as* first fruits to God and to the Lamb" (vs 1-4).

Since we are called *firstfruits* what category are these?

Verse 5: "And no guile was found in their mouths; for they are blameless before the Throne of God."

Let's go back and let's analyze this a little bit more.

- **firstfruits**: These were redeemed from among men—not the children of Israel. Can be any race of people or whatever.
- **firstfruits unto God and the Lamb**: Christ is called *Firstfruits*, so we know He's the First of the firstfruits. Can we say then that if this 144,000 represents the Bride—are these the next category of firstfruits—because it says, 'everyone in his own order.'
- **all of the rest** in the first resurrection will be called *firstfruits*

So, we have three categories of *firstfruits*:

1. Christ
2. the Bride
3. all the rest after that

I think if we put the Scriptures together properly we can see how that will be. Let's look at this a little bit more:

Verse 3: "…who were **redeemed from the earth**." *Again, showing that it's from all nations!* This is differentiating it from the children of Israel.

Verse 4: "These are the ones who were **not defiled with women**…"

- What does it mean to be defiled with women?
- Who are the women who defile the saints of God?

That's another way of asking the question!

Revelation 17:1: "And one of the seven angels who had the seven vials came and spoke with me, saying to me, 'Come here; I will show you the judgment of the great whore who sits upon many waters; with whom the kings of the earth have committed fornication, and those who dwell on the earth were made drunk with the wine of her fornication.' Then he carried me away in *the* spirit to a wilderness; and I saw a woman sitting upon a scarlet beast that had seven heads and ten horns, full of names of blasphemy. And the woman *was* clothed in purple and scarlet, and *was* adorned with gold and pearls and precious stones; *and* she had a golden cup in her hand, filled with abominations and *the* filthiness of her fornication; and across her forehead a name *was* written: MYSTERY, BABYLON THE GREAT, THE MOTHER OF THE HARLOTS AND OF THE ABOMINATIONS OF THE EARTH" (vs 1-5).

So, it could be 'mother Babylon' or any one of her 'daughters' that can defile the saints.

These 144,000 of Rev. 14 were never defiled by the false doctrines of the churches of this world. These are 'they which follow the Lamb wherever He goes.' It says then, 'Christ and the Bride say…'

A summary of what goes on during the Millennium, Revelation 22:17: "And the Spirit [Christ] and the Bride say, 'Come.' And let the one who hears say, 'Come.' And let the one who thirsts come; and let the one who desires partake of the water of life freely."

This is Christ and the Bride. Everything in the Millennium will flow from Christ and the Bride. Who will it flow to?

Revelation 20:6: "Blessed and Holy is the one who has part in the first resurrection… [that's a blessing upon all] …over these the second death has no power. But they shall be priests of God and of Christ, and shall reign with Him a thousand years."

We also know from Matt. 25 that there will be those who will be reigning over cities. We know also from Jesus explaining about who's going to sit on the 12 thrones of the children of Israel that it's going to be each one of the apostles.

They will be kings. Here we have priests. We will reign as kings and priests with Christ. But *the 144,000 are with Christ wherever He goes,* whereas those who will be priests will be wherever Christ sends them to be priests. So, it's a little bit of a different situation there.

Let me clarify something here, Revelation 14:4: "These are the ones who were not defiled with women, for they are virgins…" *That means from the time of baptism!*

2-Corinthians 11:1: "I would *that* you might bear with me in a little nonsense; but indeed, do bear with me. For I am jealous over you with *the* jealousy of God because I have espoused you to one husband, **so that I may present *you* as a chaste virgin to Christ.** But I fear, lest by any means, as the serpent deceived Eve by his craftiness, so your minds might be corrupted from *the* simplicity that *is* in Christ. For indeed, if someone comes preaching another Jesus…" (vs 1-4).

That's after you've been baptized, then you believe in a different form of Christ, before baptism, you're really not believing in the true Christ. These were the false apostles coming and teaching false doctrines. In believing these false doctrines and following these false doctrines then those who were once virgins *lose their virginity—spiritually*. But they can repent and still be in the Kingdom of God.

Is the 144,000 a literal number? *or* a symbolic number? If you have a symbolic number then what does that mean as a literal number? We have 144,000 literally of the children of Israel; those who are sealed. Then we have the 'great innumerable multitude,' which no one can number. How would you say there could be a symbolic number with the 'great innumerable multitude' because there's no number? I would be more inclined to think that the 144,000 is a literal number. How is God going to choose that? Well, He alone knows!

Will there be other virgins that were just slovenly, who are still going to be in the Kingdom of God? *Yes! We had the parable of the Ten Virgins!* But the door to the wedding, for them to be part of the Bride, was closed. It doesn't say they were excluded from the Kingdom of God. They just couldn't be part of the Bride.

Let's clarify something else regarding the classes of the firstfruits:

1. Christ the first of the firstfruits
2. then the seven church harvest—represented by the seven churches (Rev. 2 & 3)—they are firstfruits
3. the 144,000 of Israel (Rev. 7)
4. the great innumerable multitude
5. the 144,000 of Rev. 14

So, you have five categories altogether, and five is the number of grace. There may be something to that, but that helps substantiate what we covered in 1-Cor. 15, that 'Christ the Firstfruit and after that those who are His at His coming, but every man in his own order.' How Christ is going to order that out we don't know. Let's look at Rev. 2 & 3 and we will see that these seven churches represent:

1. the seven churches that were then
2. the projection of the Church down through history
3. the attitudes of Christians any time during any period

—and some of us can identify with several of the churches with our various attitudes as we have gone through our Christian life. It's awfully hard to say

exactly where each person belongs. In that sense, it is good from the point of view that God is the One Who is going to make the decision and *salvation is by faith.*

Salvation is *not knowing which category you are in. Salvation is by faith!* I think we can trust God to know what He's doing, and we can trust God that *to be in the first resurrection in any category is a blessing!* It says, 'Blessed are they who are called to the marriage supper of the Lamb' (Rev. 19). *It's all a blessing!*

What it does do, it shatters some of our carnal approaches to who we may think we are, lest we pull a Job and *tell God* who we are. *God tells us* we're not who we say we are, but *'you are who I say your are!'* Let's look at the seven churches:

Ephesus:

They're commended for their works, Revelation 2:2: "I know your works, and your labor, and your endurance [patience], and that you cannot bear those who are evil; and *that* you did test those who proclaim *themselves* to be apostles, but are not, and did find them liars."

Some people get mad when you do that. We still do that today—don't we? *Yes!*

Someone said, 'Take me off your mailing list because of what you say about Herbert Armstrong, and that if anyone doesn't agree with you well then, you'll have nothing to do with them.'

No! That's not the case, brethren. I wish there were 10,000 faithful ministers. Just think what could be done. I've tried working with other ministers, only to be beat up, knocked down, mailing list stolen and the whole works. I'd be happy to work with any minister. But I'll tell you one thing I will not do: *I will not compromise or play politics to please anybody!*

If we do not please Christ, then it doesn't matter who else you please; all bets are off! Paul said, *'If I please men I should not yet please God.'* And he wouldn't even give one minute to any man to come against what Christ had revealed to him. *And he should not!* So likewise, I'll just take the same attitude that Paul had. Be glad to work with any man, but:

- don't come and steal from us
- don't come and take brethren
- don't come and have your own personal thing

I don't set myself up as some big thing. I just want to teach the Word of God and serve and love the brethren. I don't want people to look up to me as some big mucky-muck, because I'm not. But in handling the Word of God, I won't continence one minute people twisting and turning the Word of God.

What we're doing here, we're trying to understand some difficult to understand Scriptures—wouldn't you say? Maybe not everything we have here is exactly correct, yet, but what we're doing, we're thinking it through, comparing the Scriptures, looking at the Scriptures to try and have it so we can understand the Word of God even more. There is nothing wrong with that at all. That's something that we should do.

If we find ourselves wrong in anything, we'll change. If someone finds something I'm doing wrong, I shouldn't do, or say something I shouldn't say, let me know and I'll correct it; no problem with that.

But I don't want the brethren to be 'beaten up,' and I don't want to be 'beaten up'—I've been beaten up enough. I fought the hierarchy in Worldwide from 1972 on, and it was really a tough situation. I've seen what they did to each other and to the brethren, and that should never be. Yet, we called ourselves 'the church of brotherly love.' Everyone wants to be a Philadelphian. We'll look at that one in just a minute. But it's very obvious that not everyone can be.

Verse 4: "Nevertheless, I have *this* against you, that you have left your first love."

What is losing your first love? *That's not just being excited at knowing the Truth when you first come to it!* The 'first love' is **loving God with all your heart, mind, soul and being!** That's what they lost. How could they lose it? Could it be from negligence? Could it be letting in some idolatry? *I don't know, but they lost it!*

Verse 5: "Therefore, remember from where you have fallen… [He considers this a great sin] …and repent, and do the first works…"

We can conclude from what we have here that those who did this—and lost their first love—probably have defiled their garments. Probably have lost their *spiritual virginity* from baptism. If they repent and do the first works, they can be restored.

Will they be part of the Bride of Christ? *That is God's judgment!* But if we look at it from Rev. 14, we could say that these have defiled themselves with women.

Smyrna:

This one has no correction at all, no calling to repentance, v 9: "I know your works and tribulation and poverty (but you are rich), and the blasphemy of those who declare themselves to be Jews and are not, but *are* a synagogue of Satan. Do not fear any of the things that you are about to suffer. Behold, the devil is about to cast *some* of you into prison, that you may be tried; and you shall have tribulation ten days. Be faithful unto death, and I will give you a crown of life" (vs 9-10).

No correction! They didn't submit to any of the false things that came along—

- whether it was persecution by the Jews
- whether it was persecution by the pagans
- whether it was the inquisition by the Roman Catholic Church

—*they didn't give in to any of it!* So, they kept their *spiritual virginity.*

Pergamos:

They really got themselves in trouble—Pergamos and Thyatira—wow! It's self-explanatory here. They have the doctrine of Balaam. They also have the doctrine of the Nicolaitans. They ate things sacrificed unto idols.

Verse 16: "Repent! For if *you* do not *repent*, I will come to you quickly, and will make war against them with the sword of My mouth."

Here Christ has to fight against His own church. *Pergamos is right where Satan's capital is!* When you are so close the things of Satan it is awfully hard to not inculcate some of those practices into your daily way of doing things. That's what happened!

We've had some of that today in this form; not exactly, but some, with the demise of Worldwide Church of God going clear into Sunday-keeping. We've had some of it within the ministry in teaching that they bring out a lot of things of psychology instead of preaching the Word of God. That's getting so close to the world that you look at the things that the world has, which are good, and you bring in *that and equate that with the righteousness of God. The goodness of this world comes from the Tree of the Knowledge of Good and Evil.* It is good. It can do good things, but it doesn't equal the righteousness of Christ. We've seen that!

Thyatira:

Perhaps the best and the worst all combine together here. It says, v 19: "I know your works, and love, and service, and faith, and your endurance, and your works; and the last *are* more than the first. But I have a few things against you, because you allow the woman Jezebel, who calls herself a prophetess, to teach and to seduce My servants into committing fornication and eating things sacrificed to idols" (vs 19-20).

There it is right there. Most of those from Thyatira, even in repenting, could not be considered virgins after they were baptized. It's talking about their condition after they were in the Church, because the message was to the Church at Thyatira. So, it's not before they were in the Church, but after they were in the Church.

{note our in-depth study: *The Seven Church Harvest*}

Sardis:

Revelation 3:1: "And to the angel of the church in Sardis, write: These things says He Who has the seven spirits of God and the seven stars. I know your works, *and* that you have a name as if you are alive, but are dead."

This is probably the worst spiritual condition. This is worst than lukewarm! At least lukewarm you're still alive. Here you're a corpse with a pulse.

Verse 2: "Be watchful, and strengthen the things that remain, which are about to die. For I have not found your works complete before God. Therefore, remember what you have received and heard, and hold on *to this*, and repent. Now then, if you will not watch, I will come upon you as a thief, and you shall by no means know what hour I will come upon you. You have a **few** names even in Sardis who have not defiled their garments, and they shall walk with Me in white because they are worthy. The one who overcomes shall be clothed in white garments; and I will not blot out his name from the Book of Life, but I will confess his name before My Father and before His angels" (vs 2-5).

They just make it by the 'skin of the teeth.' I don't even know if we can say 'skin of the teeth.' *But only a 'few' are going to make it!* When you go through and you look at these things and you ask:

How much does our choice count in all of this? *Everything, as far as our responsibility is concerned!*

Laodiceans:

We beat up Laodiceans long and often, hard and being lukewarm and talking back to God.

Verse 17: "For you say, 'I am rich, and have become wealthy, and have need of nothing'… [sounds a little bit like Job. *Talking back to God!*] …and have need of nothing'…" *It's all taken away; it is all gone!*

They are so bad they are 'vomited out of the mouth of Christ. Christ is outside knocking on the door to get in. They can repent! They can receive salvation! They can sit in the Throne of Judgment as Christ sits on the Throne of Judgment! *But they have to become zealous!*

Philadelphia:

Let's compare that to the 144,000 (Rev. 14)—and the Church of Philadelphia comes as close to describing Rev. 14 and the 144,000 with the exception that we have to also do as Christ did in commending Smyrna; that they had no faults before God.

Verse 7: "And to the angel of the church in Philadelphia, write: These things says the Holy One, the One Who *is* true; the One Who has the key of David, Who opens and no one shuts, and Who shuts and no one opens."

We always like to look to the open door, but there's a time when God shuts it. I think we've lived in the time where God has shut the door of radio and television as an effective way of reaching people. He's going to open another door, and when He does we have to be prepared and be ready, whatever it may be. Christ will have to open the door for any one of the seven churches here, but in particularly for those who really love God, He's got to open the door. Why?

Verse 8: "I know your works. Behold, I have set before you an open door, and no one has the power to shut it because you have a little strength… [here is a small church; little strength] …**and have kept My Word**…"

No other church is commended of really keeping the Word. If you're going to keep the Word, that means you have to:

1. you have to have it
2. you have to know it

How do you keep something that you don't know? *You can't!*

"…and **have not denied My name**" (v 8). That's a little different than with:

Pergamos:

Revelation 2:13: "I know your works and where you dwell, where the throne of Satan *is*; but you are holding fast My name, and did not deny My faith, even in the days in which Antipas *was* My faithful witness, who was killed among you, where Satan dwells."

They only held on as long as they had Antipas as their leader. After that everything went to 'hell in a hand-basket' to Balaam and the doctrine of the Nicolaitans, which this book *Primitive Christianity in Crisis* does an excellent job of bringing out what that really means.

Revelation 3:9: "Behold, I will make those of the synagogue of Satan…"

Who is the synagogue of Satan? *Combines the economics, the religious and the political affairs of this world,* who control the world. We are living in a time when that synagogue of Satan is coming to the fore again, like it never has.

{note our message: *The Beast that Was and Is Not, and Yet, Is*} I think we will understand it even more clearly when we are living in those times.

We can just say that those of the synagogue of Satan are rewarded by Satan.

- How does he reward them?
- What did he promise Christ if He would worship him once? *The whole world!*

Those who control the world and the world establishment—in banking, in religion, and in politics—are all a part of the synagogue of Satan with all of their followers and all of their subordinates with them. Those who truly are a part of the synagogue of Satan, worship Satan directly, and get their orders directly from him.

We are in a struggle, brethren. We are in a fight for the Word of God. We are in such a position today that we can no longer say 'look it up in your Bible, read it in your Bible.' Now we've got to tell them, 'before you can even look it up in the Bible, you'd better make sure you have the right Bible. You may not find it in the one that Satan has perverted through Wescott and Hort and through the *New International Version* and through the *New American Standard Bible,* and some of the others. I mean, it's a horrendous thing that they have done to it. That's all part of the synagogue of Satan.

{note the most correct Bible is: *The Holy Bible in Its Original Order, A Faithful Version* by Fred R. Coulter (**afaithfulversion.org**)}

"…who proclaim themselves to be Jews and are not, but do lie—behold, I will cause them to come and worship before your feet, and to know that I have loved you" (v 9).

Christ loves His whole Church, but there is a special love that God has for the Philadelphians. Why? *Because they love Him!* That's why! You can't love the brethren truly unless you love God first! You can have a social club. You can get along with each other, you can like each other, you can be desirous to be in each other's company, **but to truly love the brethren with the love of God, *that's got to come from God!***

Verse 10: "**Because you have kept the word of My patience**…"

He says, "…and have kept My Word, and have not denied My name" (v 8);

- in spite of the synagogue of Satan
- in spite of anybody else around
- in spite of the consequences that come to you
- in spite of what you go through

You stay faithful and keep the Word of God!

"…I also will keep you from the time of temptation which *is* about to come upon the whole world to try those who dwell on the earth. Behold, I am coming quickly; hold fast that which you have so that no one may take away your crown" (vs 10-11).

Showing that there is a battle, there is a fight, but you're having to fight against all the odds that are coming. Someone is trying to take your reward, take your crown. Notice how closely this ties in with Rev. 14, more than any other.

Verse 12: "The one who overcomes will I make a pillar in the temple of My God, and he shall not go out any more… [follow Christ wherever He goes] …and I will write upon him the name of My God… [Rev. 14] …and the name of the city of My God, the New Jerusalem, which will come down out of heaven from My God; and *I will write upon him My new name.*"

The bride always takes the name of her husband, which is a new name.

Since there have always been Philadelphians down through time, out of these kinds of Christians are these going to be part of the Bride of Christ? Of all that we have examined of the firstfruits: being the seven churches, being the 144,000 of Israel, the great innumerable multitude, and the 144,000 of Rev. 14, *this attitude here ties in more closely with Rev. 14.*

So, if there's anything we can say is, the parallel is very close. But lest we get carried away with categorizing things ourselves and saying 'he is/he isn't; she is/she isn't; we are/they aren't'; we'll just say *it is all in God's hands* and let Him take care of it.

When it comes time for the resurrection, we'll all find out then, won't we? Regardless of what it is, we're all going to be happy about it. The whole goal is to be in the Kingdom of God and receive eternal life.

- God is the One Who's going to give the reward
- God is the One Who's going to pick the Bride
- Christ is the One Who's going to marry the Bride

And if we can be there as guests, why I'm all for that! It says, *'Blessed and Holy is he that is called to marriage supper of the Lamb.'*

So, this will at least give us something to think on; give us something to study more. We don't want to get carried away with anything, and treat what we have had with 'now we have something new' and we can 'beat everybody over the head' with, because that's not correct. Whatever we understand comes from God. When we try and understand these things, and the understanding that comes from God will then lead us to change any of our understanding in the future, then we will by all means change, no question about it! I don't want to be in a category of holding onto any teaching or doctrine, which is incorrect.

But let's understand this: *The knowledge of this does not change your salvation!* In other words, it gets right back to the same thing that we covered in Matt. 20 when we started: Christ told the mother of John and James, the sons of Zebedee, 'You don't know what you're asking for and it's not Mine to give, but the Father's.'

The Father has to make the decision. All we can do is look at it and say the most we can come to is that these Scriptures give us a little better understanding and some indications of what God is going to do. That's the most that it can do for us. If we try and make any more out of it, then we'll get carried away with our own self-importance. We don't want to do that at all, and we certainly don't want to pull a Job and walk up and tell God what to do. *That didn't work then and it won't work now!*

The longer that I have been in the Church the more that I understand that *there is really literally nothing that we haven't received!* Everything comes from God! This is the most important thing we need to concentrate on, and this is the greatest tool for overcoming:

2-Corinthians 10:1: "Now, I Paul am personally exhorting you by the meekness and gentleness of Christ. On the one hand, when present with you I *am* base; but on the other hand, when absent I am bold toward you. But I am beseeching *you* so that, when I am present, I may not have to be bold with the confidence with which I intend to show boldness toward some, who think that we are **walking according to *the* flesh**" (vs 1-2)—*according to human reason, human rational, human ideas and things like this,* or as Paul was fighting: *philosophy* (1-Cor. 1).

Verse 3: "For although we walk in *the* flesh, we do not war according to *the* flesh."

As I mentioned concerning psychology and psychological methods of overcoming: No, you don't do that! Here's the way we overcome:

Verse 4: "For the weapons of our warfare *are* not carnal, but mighty through God to *the* overthrowing of strongholds… [this is the battle we have to keep at] …casting down *vain* imaginations, and every high thing that exalts itself against the knowledge of God, and **bringing into captivity every thought into the obedience of Christ**" (vs 4-5).

That's what we have to work on; that's the most important thing! Why? *Because in your mind is where sin begins,* and your mind and your thoughts of self and importance and all of the things of the world to puff up the self, *are idols before God.* Meaning that *anything that you think that you understand or know or can do earns you salvation or earns you something or makes you more special than someone else becomes and idol!*

For us to proclaim that we are Philadelphians and anyone who is not with us is not a Philadelphian; look, we don't know! That would be an imagination, a thought exalting itself against God! When thoughts like that of self-exaltation or thoughts that come along of sin or whatever it may be, *you're to grab that thought, bring it into captivity and cast it down and bring your mind into obedience to Christ!* This is what we need to do. I don't know about you, but I have a struggle with my own mind! Just like Paul did! That's why it's important that we keep our perspective in this.

Verse 6: "And having a readiness to avenge all disobedience, whenever your obedience has been fulfilled."

Wow! That's quite a statement—isn't it? How do you fulfill your obedience? *Everything that you do starts in your mind!*

Verse 7: "Are you looking at things according to their appearance? If anyone is persuaded in his *own* mind that he is Christ's, let him reconsider this concerning himself; for exactly as he *is* Christ's, so also *are* we Christ's."

That's what we really need to keep in mind!

Scriptures from *The Holy Bible in Its Original Order, A Faithful Version*

Scriptural References:

1) Matthew 20:1-15
2) Revelation 7:14
3) Revelation 11:3-15
4) Matthew 20:16, 20-28
5) Matthew 22:1-14
6) Matthew 25:1-13
7) 1 Corinthians 15:20-23
8) James 1:18
9) Revelation 14:1
10) Revelation 7:9-17
11) Revelation 14:1-5, 3-4

12) Revelation 17:1-5
13) Revelation 22:17
14) Revelation 20:6
15) Revelation 14:4
16) 2 Corinthians 11:1-4
17) Revelation 2:2, 4-5, 9-10, 16, 19-20
18) Revelation 3:1-5, 17, 7-8
19) Revelation 2:13
20) Revelation 3:9-10, 8, 10-12
21) 2 Corinthians 10:1-7

Scriptures referenced, not quoted:

- Exodus 34
- 1 Thessalonians 4
- Romans 8:29
- Hebrews 12
- Revelation 19
- 1 Corinthians 1

Also referenced:

Booklet: *Who are the 144,000?* by Fred R. Coulter

Book: *Primitive Christianity in Crisis* by Alan Knight

Messages:
- *Seven Church Harvest*
- *The Beast That Was, Is Not, Yet, Is*

FRC:cs/bo
Transcribed: 4-16-10
Reformatted: 11/2020

CHAPTER FORTY-FOUR

Events After Pentecost I

Fred R. Coulter

Let's look at some things that cover the Pentecost story, but some of those things that take place *after* Pentecost.

God is doing a phenomenal thing with His people and His Church. God never works like men work. He works entirely differently, and He has called us whom the world does not even consider worthy of counting or existing.

Sidebar: I told one Protestant that's always the way it's been with the Church of God. Every Sabbath there are millions of Christians who believe in Jesus Christ and His grace and salvation by faith, who keep the Sabbath, and you don't even have a clue as to where they are; you don't recognize who they are.

So calloused are Protestants in their beliefs that they 'are right' even in the face of reading <u>Rome's Challenge to the Protestants</u> (from *The Holy Bible in Its Original Order, A Faithful Version* Appendix N; also found at **truthofgod.org**), insist on keeping Sunday.

Now that's an aside, but it does prove a point that God has called us because, to the world, we are insignificant and foolish.

1 Corinthians 1:25: "Because the foolishness of God is wiser than men, and the weakness of God is stronger than men."

Of course, God doesn't have any foolishness. Even if God had foolishness, and even if God had weakness, *it would be greater than men or the best efforts of men!*

Verse 26: "For you see your calling, brethren, that *there are* not many who are wise according to the flesh, not many who are powerful, not many who are highborn *among you*. Rather, **God has chosen the foolish things of the world, so that He might put to shame those who are wise**… [the confounding of the wise will not be completed until after the resurrection] …and **God has chosen the weak things of the world so that He might put to shame the strong things**" (vs 26-27).

That's why we have so many problems and difficulties that we go through, but God is with us. God is with us in all of it.

Verse 28: "And **the lowborn** of the world, and **the despised has God chosen**—*even* the things that are counted as nothing—…"

How many people in the world know that we're keeping the Sabbath here? *or* that we even exist? *Hardly any!* He has done this to bring to nothing the things that are. So:

- all of the rich
- all of the powerful
- all of the governments
- all the great things of the world

are going to come to nothing through us!

That's why I said on Pentecost, we've been called to the greatest thing that there is! That's why God does not want you to look at what you are, *but God wants you to focus on what will be!* That is the spiritual reality that is going to take place.

Here is the reason, v 29: "**So that no flesh might glory in His presence**."

God told the children of Israel the same thing. Deut. 5 shows that God works His mysterious way opposite according to the way that men think. He is doing something greater because it is *His* work that He is working in us. Not what we can do for God, what we can do for God we need to do. Whatever He says that we need to do, or sets before us to do, we need to do it.

- What can God do for us?
- What can you do without God? *Nothing!*

Not any man in the world can do anything without God, though man rejects Him! God created him and gave him everything that he has.

In His mercy God sends the rain on the just and on the unjust, and the sunshine, and the food, and everything like this God gives to all human beings, and they only exist because of the will of God. Which means that whatever they do, even though they sin contrary to the will of God, the only reason that they are not snuffed out instantly is because of God. So hence, *they can do nothing without God!*

I think it is interesting, I heard a man talking about the solar system and the universe and the videos that they put out on that, who is an astronomer, and he said he didn't know a single astronomer who did not believe in God. It is amazing! It doesn't mean that they obey Him, but they can understand this didn't all spontaneously happen from nothing. You know like God told the environmentalist, 'Go create your own dirt before you start; don't use Mine.'

Here is what God said to the children of Israel, Deuteronomy 5:22: "The LORD spoke these words to all your assembly in the mountain out of the midst of the fire of the cloud and of the thick darkness with a great voice. And He added no more…."—*ceased to talk!*

A lot of people say that God didn't add any more. He ceased to talk at that point, but as we will see He added a considerably lot more. But the Ten Commandments, which He spoke, were the basis of everything that He gave them later on.

"…And He wrote them on two tablets of stone and delivered them to me. And it came to pass when you heard the voice out of the midst of the darkness, for the mountain burned with fire, you came near me, all the heads of your tribes and your elders, and you said, 'Behold, the LORD our God has revealed His glory and His greatness, and we have heard His voice out of the midst of the fire. We have seen today that God talks with man, yet, he *still* lives. Now, therefore, why should we die? **For this great fire will consume us. If we hear the voice of the LORD our God anymore, then we shall die**'" (vs 22-25).

That's the way people are today. This same kind of spirit is what is behind *removing God*:

- from government
- from public education
- from media
- from the new versions of the Bible also by perverting, twisting and destroying it

Verse 26: "'For who of all flesh has heard the voice of the living God speaking out of the midst of the fire, as we *have*, and lived? You go near and hear all that the LORD our God shall say. And you speak to us all that the LORD our God shall speak to you, and we will hear *it*, and do *it*.' And the LORD heard the voice of your words when you spoke to me. And the LORD said to me, 'I have heard the voice of the words of this people, which they have spoken to you. They have well *said* all that they have spoken'" (vs 26-28). *They mean well!*

Verse 29: **"Oh, that there were such a heart in them that they would fear Me and keep all My commandments always so that it might be well with them and with their children forever!"**

- Why did God do this?
- Why did God call us?

We have already seen it, so He explained it to them!

Deuteronomy 7:6: "For you *are* a Holy people to the LORD your God. **The LORD your God has chosen you to be a special people to Himself above all people** that are upon the face of the earth."

You need to realize that *God the Father Himself has personally chosen you,* and personally selected everyone one that He gives the Holy Spirit to. *We are special!*

Verse 7: "The LORD did not set His love upon you nor choose you because you were more in number than any people, for you *were* the fewest of all people. But because the LORD loved you, and because He would keep the oath, which He had sworn to your fathers… [Abraham, Isaac, and Jacob] …the LORD has brought you out with a mighty hand and redeemed you out of the house of bondage from the hand of Pharaoh king of Egypt. Therefore, know that the LORD your God, He *is* God, the faithful God Who keeps covenant and mercy with them that love Him and keep His commandments, to a thousand generations. And he repays those who hate Him to their face, to destroy them. He will not be slow to repay him who hates Him. He will repay him to his face. You shall, therefore, keep the commandments and the statutes and the judgments which I command you today to do them" (vs 7-11).

Then He shows the blessings and cursings that would follow. Let's tie this in with Pentecost, and let's see what happened after God called Moses up on the mountain again.

{note message: *From the Red Sea to Sinai* showing when the Law was given on the Day of Pentecost}

Then these events took place after Pentecost, part of them, from the last part of Deut. 20 thru 23, God gave all this information to Moses, and then he came back down. Since they assembled before the mount in the morning, they heard the voice of God through the cloud, through the trumpet, through the whirlwind, through all of the things that were going on and the mountain was literally burning and smoking. That's why they were afraid. Then Moses went back up and he got this information.

Beginning in Exo. 24 we see that another day takes place *after* Pentecost where He *seals* the covenant.

Exodus 24:1: "And He said to Moses, 'Come up to the LORD, you and Aaron, Nadab, and Abihu, and seventy of the elders of Israel, and worship afar off. And Moses alone shall come near the LORD, but they shall not come near. Neither shall the people go up with him.' And Moses came and told the people all the words of the LORD…" (vs 1-3).

I want you to pay attention to what happened on this part of Pentecost, and then let's see what happened the next day because that will be significant when we come to the New Testament.

"…and all the judgments. And all the people answered with one voice and said, 'All the words which the LORD has said, we will do.' And Moses wrote all the words of the LORD, and rose up early in the morning… [now we are in the next day, the day after Pentecost] …and built an altar at the base of the mountain and twelve pillars according to the twelve tribes of Israel. And he sent young men of the children of Israel who offered burnt offerings, and sacrificed peace offerings of bullocks to the LORD. And Moses took half of the blood, and put *it* in basins, and half of the blood he sprinkled on the altar. And he took the Book of the Covenant, and read in the ears of the people. And they said, **'All that the LORD has said we will do, and be obedient'** (vs 3-7).

When God makes a covenant there are words of the covenant. That's why when we take the Passover we entitle the words: The Words of the New Covenant, because the covenant is an irrevocable contract that God makes, and when there is a contract it is to be *written* so that there should not be any dispute. That's what He did.

They said again, "…**'All that the LORD has said we will do, and be obedient.'** And Moses took the blood and sprinkled *it* on the people, and said, 'Behold the blood of the covenant…'" (vs 7-8).

That ties right in with the New Covenant Passover. When they had the Passover sacrifice in Egypt, that was the setting aside of them at the beginning of their calling to be set aside for God. God did not enter into covenant with them on Passover. God entered into covenant with them *after* Pentecost. We'll see there is a parallel between this and what will happen with us.

I'll just telegraph a little bit of it here: Before we get about the business of running the world under Christ, *we are going to enter into a special covenant with Christ!* Because the New Covenant that we renew every Passover is for *forgiveness of sin and the promise of eternal life!* When you are resurrected and you receive eternal life, then there has to be a *new* covenant made, because now you are in a different category, and this is a foretype of it here in Exo. 24. We'll see that's one of the things that have to take place.

Verse 9: "And Moses went up, and Aaron, Nadab, and Abihu, and seventy of the elders of Israel. And **they saw the God of Israel**…" (vs 9-10).

Not talked to face-to-face, but they saw Him. The reason God did this was so that they would know that it was God. They would come down and they would be the witnesses to the people that, yes, it *was* God. Remember that a little later on they forgot that it was God when they made the golden calf. So, they had no excuse.

"…And *there was* under **His feet as it were a paved work of a sapphire stone, and as it were the heavens in clearness**" (v 10).

What is this? *This is the thing that separated God from Aaron, Nadab, Abihu and the 70 elders that went up to see God!* They could look up through this and they could see God. What is this describing other than a Sea of Glass?

Verse 11: "And upon the nobles of the children of Israel He did not lay his hands. Also, they saw God, and ate and drank."

When they said, 'I do' at this particular point, what kind of covenant was this? *It was a marriage covenant!*

"…and ate and drank." It doesn't say what kind of food they had. It doesn't say how they got it. It doesn't tell us that they brought it up there. It doesn't say they didn't bring it up there. It doesn't say that God provided it, and it doesn't say that He didn't provide it. I'll let you figure out what it is. It is very possible they took it up there.

Verse 12: "And the LORD said to Moses, 'Come up to Me in the mountain, and be there. And I will give you tablets of stone, and the law, and commandments which I have written, so that you may teach them.' And Moses rose up, and his attendant Joshua. And Moses went up into the mountain of God. And he said to the elders, 'You wait here for us until we come again to you….'" (vs 12-14).

Apparently Joshua went up so far, and then Moses went up beyond that. That's the only thing we could figure out, because Joshua did not talk to God face-to-face.

"'…And behold, Aaron and Hur *are* with you. If any man has a cause, let him come to them.' And Moses went up into the mountain, and a cloud covered the mountain. And the glory of the LORD abode upon Mount Sinai, and the cloud covered it six days. And the seventh day He called to Moses out of the midst of the cloud" (vs 14-16).

After they had eaten, apparently, they went on down, that is the elders and so forth.

Verse 17: "And the sight of the glory of the LORD *was* like a consuming fire on the top of the mountain to the eyes of the children of Israel. And Moses went into the midst of the cloud, and went up into the mountain. And Moses was in the mountain forty days and forty nights" (vs 17-18).

There are a lot of things that went on those 40 days and 40 nights. We are not going to go through that. Let's come and see the parallel that the Apostle Paul writes about in Heb. 12. There is a New Testament fulfillment of this.

Hebrews 12:18: "For you have not come to *the* mount that could be touched and that burned with fire, nor to gloominess, and fearful darkness, and *the* whirlwind; and to *the* sound of *the* trumpet, and to *the* voice of *the* words, which those who heard, *begged* that *the* word not be spoken *directly* to them. (For they could not endure what was being commanded: 'And if even an animal touches the mountain, it shall be stoned, or shot through with an arrow'; and so terrifying was the sight *that* Moses said, 'I am greatly afraid and trembling')" (vs 18-21).

Here is what you need to understand how great that God is dealing with us:

Verse 22: "**But you have come to Mount Sion, and to *the* city of *the* living God,** heavenly Jerusalem; and to an innumerable company of angels; *to the* joyous festival gathering; and to *the* Church of *the* Firstborn, registered *in the Book of Life* in heaven; and to God, *the* Judge of all; and to *the* spirits of the just who have been perfected; and to Jesus, *the* Mediator of *the* New Covenant; and to sprinkling of *the* blood of *ratification*, proclaiming superior things than *that of* Abel" (vs 22-24). *There is a spiritual parallel. That is quite a thing!*

Now let's talk about some things concerning this Mount Sion, and we'll talk about some things concerning the Sea of Glass. The Bible shows there are three heavens:

1. the atmosphere around the earth
2. the universe that you can look out and see
3. the third heaven where God's Throne is

No one can see the third heaven unless God makes it possible.

Paul said that he was taken up into the third heaven whether in body of whether in spirit he didn't know, and he heard things that it is not lawful for a man to speak. And we're going to see that John also had that privilege.

When I fly and go some place, I come from heaven. The plane I fly on goes either in the clouds or above the clouds, and when it lands I have just descended from heaven. As a matter of fact when they fly at 33,000 to 37,000 feet, I think the highest I have flown on a plane was a cross-continental flight, non-stop, and they went at 37,000 feet. That is higher than the birds fly, but it is still part of the first heaven, which is part of the earth.

Do people today travel in heaven? Yes, on airplanes and some few in rockets, because we're going to see a place here a little bit later on that talks about the sound of much people in heaven.

- Which one?
- Where?
- How did they get there?

Peter said on Pentecost, 'David has not ascended into heaven.' John wrote that **only Jesus** has ascended into heaven. No man has ascended into heaven, but Jesus. So, we need to get some of these things a little clearer and defined.

Now then, you can go back and study about the cherubim in Ezek. 1 & 10. You can talk about the vision of Isaiah and seeing the Throne of God in heaven above and so forth; it is there. Now let's see if we can put this all together. We come to the point where we see that these events begin; this is going to take place.

Revelation 12:7: "And there was war in heaven… [that's going to happen again] …Michael and his angels warred against the dragon, and the dragon and his angels warred." *The angels of Satan are fallen angels who are called **demons**.*

Verse 9: "And the great dragon was cast out, the ancient serpent who is called the Devil and Satan, who is deceiving the whole world… [he is actively doing it] …he was cast down to the earth, and his angels were cast down with him."

We don't know how much time there is left. We've built a pretty humongous space station, and the Chinese are starting to get into the act. Could it be that in this space station that Satan possesses *the beast*? He gets in a rocket and he goes up there and all the demons of Satan are there, and there is war right around that space station? And *the beast,* possessed of Satan, escapes and comes back to the earth? *That is a little speculation!* But nevertheless, one way or the other, Satan is going to be cast to the earth.

Verse 10: "And I heard a great voice in heaven say, 'Now has come the salvation and the power and the Kingdom of our God, and the authority of His Christ because the accuser of our brethren has been cast down, who accuses them day and night before our God. But they overcame him through the blood of the Lamb, and through the word of their testimony; and they loved not their lives unto death'" (vs 10-11).

They knew; and we need to know and understand that God has called us to become part of the greatest thing that is ever going to happen to this earth since it was created! God hasn't called you to 'save your neck' from burning in ever-burning hell.

God has called you for a great and fantastic purpose as His sons and His daughters! The first resurrection is going to be the greatest thing that will happen, and you and I, and all those who have the Spirit of God, will be part of that! It is not going to be some 'secret rapture'! ***When Christ returns, the world is going to know,*** and all of these people that think they are going to escape in a secret rapture before the Tribulation ***are deceived, and they are going to pay the price by going through it!***

Verse 12: "'Therefore, rejoice you heavens and those who dwell in Them. Woe to those who inhabit the earth and the sea! For the Devil has come down to you, having great wrath *because* he knows that he has *only* a short time.' And when the dragon saw that he was cast down to the earth, he persecuted the woman who had brought forth the man-*Child*. And two wings of a great eagle were given to the woman, so that she might fly to her place in the wilderness, where she is nourished *for* a time, and times, and half a time, from *the* face of the serpent" (vs 12-14).

There are going to be some who are going to be taken to a place of safety. But I do believe that many of those who thought they would save their necks because they read the article years ago, *There is a Way of Escape,* probably are no longer in fellowship with the Church of God.

Why are there going to be some in a place of safety? *Those who go to a place of safety, will be taken there by the angels (Luke 17)!* That is not a rapture, because you're not going to heaven. You may fly through the first heaven as the angels take whoever is going to go to a place of safety and will be there, ***but God is going to choose and select the ones to go.*** No man or woman is going to appoint himself or herself, saying, 'I deserve to go.'

The minute you say that, you are unworthy, because you are judging yourself rather than God. ***God*** is going to see who is going to be worthy or not. He's going to make the decision. That's another reason why the Church had to be destroyed, because there were too many people there with their Petra boxes thinking that they were going to save their physical necks. The ultimate reason why there are some who go to the place of safety, comes down to a very simple thing.

Verse 15: "And the serpent cast water out of his mouth as a river, so that he might cause her *to be* carried away by the flood. But the earth helped the woman, and the earth opened its mouth, and swallowed up the river that the dragon had cast out of his mouth" (vs 15-16).

- Can God protect you if He wants to? *Yes, indeed!*

- What can He even do? *Well, He'll even open up the earth and consume all the water!*

Verse 17: "Then the dragon was furious with the woman and went to make war with **the rest of her seed**..."—*or* 'the others.' *These are the ones who **do not** go to a place of safety,* not meaning just a small few left behind.

"...who keep the commandments of God and have the testimony of Jesus Christ" (v17). *These people have been chosen to be martyrs!*

God is the One Who makes the decision, and He will strengthen you with whatever strength you need if you are chosen to be a martyr! ***IF*** you love God with all of your heart, mind, soul and being, and you have already forsaken your own life and your own way and buried it in Christ, ***THEN*** when it comes time that you—whoever you may be—must be a martyr; ***God will give you the strength!*** He will give you a mouth to speak. You will say the Words of God, and you will not be afraid of anything that anyone can do to you, ***because they can't take away eternal life!*** Even killing the body is not going to stop the plan of God.

Let's come to the fifth seal of Rev. 6. {note message *The Mark of the Beast is Here*} I've said it's going to become so natural and such a regular thing that when it comes time to receive it, people are going to say, 'Yea, give it to me'; except those who have the Spirit of God. Those who don't will be martyred. You can tie that in with Rev. 13. If you don't bow down to *the image of the beast* and you don't receive *the mark of the beast,* you're history as far as the world is concerned, but you are preserved in Christ. Remember He said if you lose your life, you are going to preserve it.

Revelation 6:9: "And when He opened the fifth seal, I saw under the altar the souls of those who had been slain for the Word of God, and for the testimony that they held." *Tie that in with Rev. 12:11, how they got there!* They didn't love their lives unto death.

Verse 10: "And they cried out with a loud voice, saying, 'How long, O Lord, Holy and true, do You not judge and avenge our blood on those who dwell on the earth?' And white robes were given to each of them; and they were told that they should rest a short time, yet..." (vs 10-11)—*showing that they are in the grave,* though this is symbolically speaking here:

"...until *it* be fulfilled *that* both their fellow servants and their brethren also would be killed, just as they had been" (v 11).

When this takes place, remember that Satan makes war against the remnant of her seed, so this takes place just right after the second seal, the third seal, the fourth seal, the fifth seal comes real quickly! So, the martyrdom goes on for just a little less than two years. I am sure, I'm convinced, that *God will allow Satan to think* that he has destroyed the Church by killing all of those who are the saints of God. *This ends the Church harvest, martyrdom of the saints!*

- How does that tie in with the place of safety? *That's so Jesus can keep His Word!*
- What is another reason why they go to a place of safety? *Because Jesus made a promise—not just a place of safety—He made another promise that also applies to those who go to a place of safety!*

Matthew 16:15: "He said to them, 'But you, whom do you declare Me to be?' Then Simon Peter answered *and* said, 'You are the Christ, the Son of the living God.' And Jesus answered *and* said to him, 'Blessed are you, Simon Bar-Jona, for flesh and blood did not reveal *it* to you, but My Father, Who *is* in heaven'" (vs 15-17).

A very key, important thing, anything you understand out of the Bible, *God reveals it to you.*

Verse 18: "And I say also to you that you are Peter... [Petros] ...and upon this Rock... [Petra] ...I will build My Church... [here is the promise]: ...**and *the* gates of the grave shall not prevail against it**."

To fulfill that promise, there are those who go to a place of safety, because all of the rest that Satan makes war against are going to be killed. If God didn't put some in a place of safety to preserve their physical life, the Church would have died out! That's another reason why there is a place of safety.

There has to be some remnant alive in the flesh, not counting the 144,000 and the great innumerable multitude, but Christ made the promise here that 'the gates of hell would never prevail against it,' therefore, *it would never die out!* That is the whole premise of the Mormon Church: it died out, therefore, it had to be revealed to Joseph Smith.

Let's understand that if we put the Scriptures properly together concerning the timeframe, we know that in Rev. 12 we have 'time, times, and a half a time,' which we understand to be three and a half years. We know that the time at the end is three and a half years. That's referred to as *the* Great Tribulation. The whole period is referred to as *the* Day of the Lord. We also know that if we have put Hosea 5:21 and 6:1-3 together, that out of the Great Tribulation there is the Tribulation against Israel, which ends in two years. It says that He'll

raise them up in the third year. So, this means that as we are looking at the three and a half year period if there are two years that are gone, there is roughly a year and a half left.

Rev. 6:12 takes place right at the end of two years into the Tribulation, and this is going to be the great event that is going to take place. It is going to be an awesome thing indeed! The whole world is going to know it! The return of Jesus Christ is going to be a spectacular event, which will be witnessed, the coming of it, for a year and a half! *Every eye is going to see Him!* Everyone is going to know that something spectacular is happening.

Revelation 6:12: "And when He opened the sixth seal, I looked, and behold, there was a great earthquake; and the sun became black as *the* hair *of* sackcloth, and the moon became as blood; and the stars of heaven fell to the earth, as a fig tree casts its untimely figs when it is shaken by a mighty wind" (vs 12-13).

Here is the event that is going to startle the world, v 14: "Then *the* heaven departed like a scroll that is being rolled up..."

That is going to absolutely shock the world! We just might understand what a fantastic thing this is; it affects the whole earth!

"...and every mountain and island was moved out of its place. And the kings of the earth, and the great men, and the rich men, and the chief captains, and the powerful men, and every bondman, and every free *man* hid themselves in the caves and in the rocks of the mountains; and they said to the mountains and to the rocks, 'Fall on us, and hide us from *the* face of Him Who sits on the Throne... [God the Father] ...and from the wrath of the Lamb, because the great day of His wrath has come, and who has the power to stand?'" (vs 14-17). *That's the ultimate end result of it!*

But what's going to happen when the heavens depart as a scroll? Wouldn't you say that the heavens departing as a scroll is a new thing in the heavens as people observe it? *Have to be! Yes, a brand new thing!*

Remember that in the book of Haggai God says He is going to shake the heavens. He is going to shake the earth. He is going to shake the sea. We find in the book of Isaiah that the earth is going to 'reel like a drunken man.' Here is what is going to be, when they say, 'Here is Christ, there is Christ,' *don't believe it!* Here is how He is going to come.

Matthew 24:27: "For **as the light of day,** which comes forth from *the* east and shines as far as *the* west, so also shall the coming of the Son of man be."

When the heavens depart as a scroll, something brand new is going to happen! The whole sky, the whole universe, and everything is going to be instantly changed, and once they recover from the shock of it, they're going to look up there and they are going to see, here is a brand new sun; 'we never knew existed out there.' The reason that it looks like it shines from east to west is because the earth is still turning on its axis, and however far out this sign is—the sign of the Son of man like a new sun—it's going to be out there.

Remember, this takes place at the end of two years in the Tribulation. What is the world going to be convinced that this is? They won't know at first. They'll look at it, they'll watch it, they'll observe it, but what will they conclude? *This is the invasion from outer space that we have been expecting!* That's what they will conclude! The aliens are coming to invade the earth; that will be their ultimate conclusion of it. That's going to be a spectacular event.

Rev. 7—we already covered about the 144,000 and great innumerable multitude. What happens when that sign of the Son of man appears, the heavens depart as a scroll, then God intervenes to do His 50th-day work, as we have seen in the 144,000 of the children of Israel, which we have already seen are different than the 144,000 of Rev. 14, and the great innumerable multitude, which means that not everyone is going to start fighting Christ—or think that it is an invasion from outer space—they're going to repent! No one receives salvation without repentance, so, the 144,000 repent, God sends the Holy Spirit to them, the great innumerable multitude repent, God sends the Holy Spirit to them, because *it is His independent work in saving all of these people!*

These will be the harvest of Pentecost, from one Pentecost to the next Pentecost within that 18-month period. This fulfills the prophecy of the laborers that went to work in the vineyard: some started at the first hour in the morning and some came the eleventh hour of the day and worked just a little bit and when they got paid, they all received the same amount, *which is symbolic of eternal life.* 'The first shall be last and the last shall be first.'

We need to plug in here that also during this timeframe there are two witnesses in Jerusalem having a very powerful witness, and just before the resurrection they are martyred. So, God is going to give Himself a fantastic witness! God is not going to have anyone say, 'Oh! You came to the earth? When did You come to the earth?' *The whole world is going to know it!*

Let's show that they meet Christ on the Sea of Glass. Now we need to talk about the Sea of Glass. We need to go to Rev. 14-15 and then work

our way back. We'll see some very important things. Remember what we covered in Exo. 24 that *after* Pentecost Moses, Aaron, Nadab, and Abihu, and 70 of the elders went up and they had that meal in the presence of God. They saw God standing on a little portable Sea of Glass so they could look up and see God.

Some people think the Sea of Glass is just kind of a symbolic thing! Well, that shows that they neither understand what God is doing, nor do they understand the magnitude of what God is going to perform!

- Why do we come to Sabbath services?
- Why do we study the Bible?
- *Because we are preparing for eternal life!*
  - ✓ God has His Work in it
  - ✓ Christ has His Work in it
  - ✓ we have our work in it

But it is something for a preparation!

What we will do, we will show the silliness, which we used to believe, that the resurrection would be on the Feast of Trumpets: we'd all be resurrected, meet Christ in the air and come right back to the earth. If you are resurrected, we're going to see that a lot of things need to happen before you're ready to come back to the earth. That's why the resurrection is on Pentecost, because it pictures the firstfruits, and it's called the Church of the Firstborn, and there are a lot of things that have to be done before we come back with Christ to the earth! Since you have never experienced being a spirit being, you're going to have to learn how you operate. Let's look at the resurrection.

- If we did not go to the Sea of Glass, why take us up into the air at the resurrection?
- What would be the purpose of that?
- Why not just stay on earth and let Christ come all the way to the earth?

No one has ever asked that question before!

Matthew 24:29: "But immediately after the tribulation of those days, the sun shall be darkened, and the moon shall not give her light, and the stars shall fall from heaven, and the powers of the heavens shall be shaken. And then shall appear the sign of the Son of man in heaven… [He gets closer and closer to the earth] …and then shall all the tribes of the earth mourn, and they shall see the Son of man coming upon the clouds of heaven with power and great glory" (vs 29-30).

They are going to see this. Notice that first of all v 27 starts out like a new sun appearing in the heavens, by the time it comes time for the resurrection:

- Where does this sign come to? *The clouds!*

- Where are the clouds?

The clouds are not in the second heaven; there aren't any out in the universe! The clouds are not in the third heaven, necessarily.

- Where are the clouds? *The first heaven!*

So, it comes down into the clouds.

What happens when you have something coming from outer space that comes to the earth? What does the magnetic force do when it comes just so far to the earth? *It locks it into a stationary orbit!* We have many satellites that they lock into stationary orbit. It's going around the earth one way while the earth is turning the opposite way. They have satellites that are designed to go the exact speed of the rotation of the earth so it sits in the same spot all the time.

Now then, I believe that when it comes down into the clouds—it doesn't tell us how high that is—they range anywhere from earth level as fog up to 50,000 feet, so you pick your altitude if you want to put it that way. But they are going to see this, so it comes down and stations itself right over Jerusalem.

What's the first thing to happen when it stations itself right over Jerusalem? *The two witnesses are the first resurrected (Rev. 11)! 'The last shall be first.'* Where did they die? *They died in Jerusalem.* 'A voice came and said, *Come here* and they stood on their feet and lived' (Rev. 11)! Apparently some angels, which the people didn't see, got them and carried them up to the Sea of Glass. If you ascend into the clouds to meet Christ, you've got to meet Him someplace.

Now after the two witnesses are raised, v 31: "And He shall send His angels with a great sound of a trumpet…"

When you read Rev. 11, the two witnesses are raised first, and then the trumpet sounds, the seventh trump sounds. They are the first two raised.

"…and they… [the angels] …shall gather together His elect from the four winds, from one end of heaven to *the* other" (v 31).

This is telling us the prospective of looking down on the earth, that the angels are going around the whole earth and gathering up those that are resurrected from the dead.

- Where are they going to take them?
- How many are going to be there?

This is going to be a great thing!

- Will the people of the earth see the resurrection take place?

- Will the people of the earth see these people being raised out of the grave and the angels taking them up to meet Christ?

That's possible!

- Did they see the two witnesses go up?

Yes! They stood and watched them go up! (Rev. 11)

- Wouldn't that be a phenomenal thing to see all the saints resurrected? *What a witness to this whole world!*

This is not going to be some 'secret rapture' done in a corner someplace; this is an earthshaking event!

Will they know that this is God doing it? *Satan is still on the earth and he is going to say it's the antichrist who is doing it!*

What is happening, what you are seeing is the aliens from outer space have come and they are taking all of the aliens that were living among us. Have you seen a movie to that effect? It's like my wife has said many times, Satan telegraphs what he is going to do in the movies that he produces for people to watch today. Since this is an invasion from outer space, look at how many aliens were among us.

We are called but 'strangers and sojourners' in the earth. *Amazing stuff!* We can use our imagination this way and ask God to lead us with His Spirit. If this isn't correct, we'll change. But it's got to happen some way. It's got to happen somehow, and if we can discern from the Scriptures from what we are told how it's going to happen, then that's fine.

Now let's understand something concerning this. This information is interesting. Hopefully, it's inspiring. Hopefully, it is true to the Word of God. However, understand that *it is not salvational!* In other words, if we understand this today because we live in the time we live in, and know that these things can happen, and we have all of the Word of God and we can put it together, does that mean that those who came before us who knew nothing of it will not be saved? *No!* That's why it's not salvational. Do you understand the difference there?

1-Thess. 4 talks about the resurrection again. I think if we can put it together and really understand it, brethren, this will inspire us so much more, and give us:

- strength of faith
- conviction of heart
- trust in God

to know that what He is going to do with us is going to be a great, a marvelous and a fantastic thing. When we are resurrected and our bodies are changed 'in a moment in the twinkling of an eye,' all the things—aches, pains, sickness, disease and death—all of the wretchedness of human life is over.

1-Thessalonians 4:13: "But I do not wish you to be ignorant, brethren, concerning those who have fallen asleep… [they died in Christ] …that you be not grieved, even as others, who have no hope. For if we believe that Jesus died and rose again, in exactly the same way also, those who have fallen asleep in Jesus will God bring with Him" (vs 13-14).

Since they are buried and in the ground and must be resurrected, how is He going to bring them with Him unless they go to meet Him? *It won't happen, because no man has ascended to heaven!*

Verse 15: "For this we say to you by *the* Word of *the* Lord, that we who are alive and remain unto the coming of the Lord…"—*which now we understand are going to be those in the place of safety*, and we also understand it will be the 144,000 and great innumerable multitude.

"…shall in no wise precede those who have fallen asleep, because the Lord Himself shall descend from heaven with *a* shout of command, with *the* voice of an archangel and with *the* trumpet of God; and the dead in Christ shall rise first" (vs 15-16). *Of course, **the two witnesses will be the first** of the first.*

Verse 17: "Then we who are alive and remain shall be caught up together with them in *the* clouds… [Where is Christ coming to? *The clouds!*] …for *the* meeting with the Lord in *the* air; and so shall we always be with *the*, Lord. Therefore, encourage one another with these words" (vs 17-18).

Now let's look and see how this is going to happen. Let's first of all look at the Sea of Glass in Rev. 4 & 5. Let's understand that just because there is the first heaven, which is the atmosphere around the earth, and the second heaven, which includes all of the universe—all the stars and galaxies and everything out there—and we know about the third heaven, but it does not mean that the third heaven is further removed than the second heaven. Just in a numerical way of doing things, we would think that. So, Christ does not have to come from the outer reaches of the universe.

- How close is the Throne of God, which sits on the Sea of Glass, to the earth?
- Can anybody tell us? *No, we don't know!*

We have an indication that it may be a whole lot closer than we have imagined, but we just can't see it, yet! Acts 7 is the stoning of Stephen.

Acts 7:54: "When they heard these things… [the Sanhedrin, all the Jewish leaders] …they were cut to their hearts, and they gnashed their teeth at him."

Not that they bit him. I thought at one time that they went out and bit him, but it doesn't mean that. It means they gnashed their teeth at him, sat there and ground their teeth at him, they were so angry. Have you ever seen someone so angry that their jaws were biting. That's what it means.

Verse 55: "But he, **being filled with *the* Holy Spirit, looked intently into heaven *and* saw *the* glory of God**, and Jesus standing at the right hand of God." *That did it!*

Does this tell us that the Throne of God is closer to the earth than we have imagined? Let's look at it this way: *Jesus sits in the Throne of God!*

Revelation 3:21: "…even as I also overcame, and sat down with My Father in His Throne."

He's at the right hand of God (Heb. 4). He's or High Priest to make intercession for us.

Acts 7:56: "And he said, 'Behold, I see the heavens opened, and **the Son of man standing** at the right *hand* of God.'" *He is not sitting; He is standing.*

- What is Jesus doing? *He is looking down to see what's going on!*
- How far away do you suppose that it is? *Close enough that He can stand and look down and see what's going on!*

He wanted to see what the Jews would do. He wanted to see what Stephen was going to do. Stephen had the same attitude that Christ had.

Verse 59: "And they stoned Stephen, who called upon *God,* saying, 'Lord Jesus, receive my spirit.' And he fell to his knees *and* cried with a loud voice, **'Lord, do not lay this sin to their charge.'** And after he had said this, he died" (vs 59-60).

Just by the way that this is written and what was seen and how it was done, does this tell us that the Throne of God is closer to the earth than we have imagined? *I do not know!* Stephen did not see God; he saw the glory of God. He saw the Son of man standing at His right hand.

Let's see some things concerning the Sea of Glass, Revelation 4:1: "After these things I looked, and behold, a door opened in heaven; and the first voice that I heard *was* as if a trumpet were speaking with me, saying, 'Come up here, and I will show you *the* things that must take place after these things.' And immediately I was in *the* Spirit; and behold, a Throne was set in heaven, and *One was* sitting on the Throne. And He Who *was* sitting was in appearance like a jasper stone and a sardius stone; and a rainbow *was* around the Throne, like an emerald in its appearance. And around the Throne *were* twenty-four thrones; and on the thrones I saw twenty-four elders sitting, clothed in white garments…" (vs 1-4).

Who are the twenty-four elders? *We don't know!* We do know that God has twenty-four elders, because He tells us that. Apparently they are special created beings that help assist God in running the universe. I said, apparently, that's the best we can do with that. Other than that we don't know, but one of these days we are going to find out, and we'll know for sure.

They were "…clothed in white garments; and they had on their heads golden crowns. And proceeding from the Throne were lightnings and thunders and voices…" (vs 4-5). *This is the center of the power of the universe!* Amazing thing!

"…and seven lamps of fire, which are the seven Spirits of God, *were* burning before the Throne" (v 5). *Now we will see what the seven Spirits of God do a little bit later!*

Verse 6: "And before the Throne *was* a Sea of Glass, like crystal. And around the Throne and over the Throne *were* four living creatures, full of eyes before and behind; and the first living creature *was* like a lion, and the second living creature *was* like a bull, and the third living creature had the face of a man, and the fourth living creature *was* like a flying eagle. And each of *the* four living creatures had six wings respectively; *and* around and within *they were* full of eyes; and day and night they cease not saying, 'Holy, Holy, Holy, Lord God Almighty, Who was, and Who is, and Who *is* to come'" (vs 6-8).

This is quite a scene. Who have we identified on the Sea of Glass?

- God the Father
- Jesus Christ
- twenty-four elders
- the four living creatures

That's it!

When John saw this, no one was resurrected. We haven't come to the time of the resurrection. Here we have the Sea of Glass with the Throne of God, and we'll see a little later there are a great innumerable multitude of angels that are with it, but no saints, yet. Why? *The resurrection of the dead hasn't taken place!* So, this is going to be a phenomenal thing.

Verse 9: "And when the living creatures give glory and honor and thanksgiving to Him Who sits on the Throne, Who lives into the ages of eternity, the twenty-four elders fall down before Him Who sits on the Throne; and they worship Him Who lives into the ages of eternity, and cast their crowns before the Throne, saying, 'Worthy are You, O Lord,

to receive glory and honor and power because You did create all things, and for Your will they were created and exist'" (vs 9-11). *God is going to fulfill His purpose!*

The only thing we can conclude is that the Throne of God and the Sea of Glass is probably closer to the earth than we have imagined. If it's out there a little further at the present time; it's going to come closer. We'll see that in part 2, and maybe we can answer the question of the mystery of the Sea of Glass.

Scriptures from *The Holy Bible in Its Original Order, A Faithful Version*

Scriptural References:

1) 1 Corinthians 1:25-29
2) Deuteronomy 5:22-29
3) Deuteronomy 7:6-11
4) Exodus 24:1-18
5) Hebrews 12:18-24
6) Revelation 12:7, 9-17
7) Revelation 6:9-11
8) Matthew 16:15-18
9) Revelation 6:12-17
10) Matthew 24:27, 29-31
11) 1 Thessalonians 4:13-18
12) Acts 7:54-55
13) Revelation 3:21
14) Acts 7:56, 59-60
15) Revelation 4:1-11

Scriptures referenced, not quoted:

- Deuteronomy 20-23
- Ezekiel 1; 10
- Luke 17
- Revelation 13; 12:11
- Hosea 5:21; 6:1-3
- Revelation 7; 14-15; 11; 4-5
- Hebrews 4

Also referenced:

Article: *Rome's Challenge to the Protestants* (from the Holy Bible in Its Original Order, A Faithful Version Appendix N; also found at **truthofgod.org**) Also in booklet form

Messages:
- *From the Red Sea to Sinai*
- *The Mark of the Beast is Here*

FRC/jea
Transcribed: 1/5/06
Reformatted: bo—11/2020

CHAPTER FORTY-FIVE

Events After Pentecost II
Fred R. Coulter

➢ What are we going to do on the Sea of Glass?
➢ Does God plan things? *Yes He does!*

He says that He has made known to us the mystery of His plan.

➢ Does He prepare for things? *Yes, He does!*
➢ Did He not prepare Abraham? *Yes He did!*
➢ Did He not prepare Moses in the wilderness before leading the children of Israel out? *Yes, He did!*
➢ Did He not prepare the way for the coming of Christ with John the Baptist? *Yes, He did!*
➢ Did not God prepare Jeremiah and sent him to the people of Judah to warn them before the captivity took place? *Yes, He did!*

The greatest event that's going to take place since the creation of the world is going to occur at the first resurrection!

• Don't you think that it is rather, silly, dumb and ignorant if the resurrection took place on Trumpets, that we all meet Christ in the air and hurry up and come back down to the earth?

OR
➢ Must there be some kind of preparation before we come back to the earth? *Of course there has to be!*

There is preparation right now! We are preparing right now for the first resurrection! With all that preparation:

➢ Do you think it is going to be a hurry-scurry thing and that God is going to say, 'Let's go! Get on your horse'?
➢ Are you not going to have to understand how this new body works?

This is going to be the greatest invasion in the history of the world! So, therefore, *we've got to be prepared and ready!* We have to have instructions and understanding.

Let's see what's going to take place on the Sea of Glass. The first thing that's going to happen when we are resurrected and see the angels and they take us up to meet Christ on the Sea of Glass:

1 John 3:1: "Behold! What *glorious* love the Father has given to us, that we should be called the children of God! For this very reason, the world does not know us because it did not know Him." *They don't know us!*

I told the man that I bought the *1550 Stephens Text* from—he is a dyed-in-the-wool Protestant, and I let him know that we keep the Sabbath and Holy Days—'Look you need to understand this. Every Sabbath there are millions of Christians who believe in Jesus Christ, who keep the Commandments of God, who keep the Sabbath, and a good number of them the Holy Days, and they are not looking for salvation by works. You need to understand that.

• But you never hear about us, do you?
• You don't even know that we exist, do you?'

He was dumbfounded! No, *the world doesn't know us!*

How many people out there driving by, and say, 'Yes, we know there are Christians, true Christians that have the Spirit of God, meeting in that building'? *Of course not!* We walk down the street, we go in the supermarket, we don't carry a placard, 'I'm a true Christian, and all the rest of you are damned.' Try that in San Francisco today.

"…that we should be called the children of God! For this very reason, **the world does not know us because it did not know Him**."

God knows what He is doing in selecting those that He is preparing for the first resurrection!

Verse 2: "Beloved, now we are the children of God, and it has not yet been revealed what we shall be; but we know that when He is manifested…"

We already covered how He is going to come back to the earth and where the Sea of Glass will be and so forth.

"…we shall be like Him, because we shall see Him exactly as He is" (v 2). *That's one of the first things that are going to take place!* We are going to see Christ!

Let's see where it talks about the Sea of Glass, and we'll read through some Scriptures, and then we'll go back and analyze them; then we'll ask some questions, and we'll see if we can fill in the blanks.

Revelation 15:1: "And I saw another sign in heaven, great and awesome…"

He sees the seven angels, but he also sees the Sea of Glass, too. So, this is an awesome thing.

"…seven angels having the seven last plagues, for in them the wrath of God is filled up. And I saw **a Sea of Glass mingled with fire**, and those who had gotten the victory over the beast, and over his image, and over his mark, *and* over the number of his name, standing on the Sea of Glass, having *the* lyres of God" (vs 1-2).

What's one of the very first things that is going to happen? Let's read all the way through here down to v 5 and then we'll go back and see what's going to happen.

Verse 3: "And they were singing the song of Moses, *the* servant of God, and the song of the Lamb saying, 'Great and awesome *are* Your works, Lord God Almighty; righteous and true *are* Your ways, King of the saints. Who shall not fear You, O Lord, and glorify Your name? For *You* only *are* Holy; and all the nations shall come and worship before You, for Your judgments have been revealed.' And after these things I looked, and behold, the temple of the tabernacle of the testimony in heaven was opened" (vs 3-5).

That's got to be right close to the Sea of Glass. Who is in the tabernacle but God the Father on His Throne? *Yes, indeed!*

Now then, the first thing that is going to happen is that Christ is going to receive us. Let's see how Jesus was received when He ascended to heaven to be received of God the Father after He was resurrected. Do you not think that there is going to be a reception for us? *Yes, indeed!* Christ is going to do the welcoming, and we will see what He will do.

I want you to picture this: Just as Christ is coming to the Sea of Glass to be received of the Father, and remember when we saw that Sea of Glass there were no saints there, just the Father, and Christ, and the angels. But picture this: Christ coming to walk down whatever aisle between the angels to be received of God the Father and here is what they sing.

Psalm 24:7: "Lift up your heads, O you gates; and be lifted up, O you everlasting doors; that the King of glory may come in. Who is this King of glory? The LORD strong and mighty, the LORD mighty in battle" (vs 7-8).

He is going to come back in battle, and we are going to be with Him. Remember what He said,

'If My Kingdom were of this world, then would My servants fight.' If you have been waiting for a good fight, you are going to get it. You'll have the tool and power to carry it out.

Verse 9: "Lift up your heads, O you gates; lift them up, you everlasting doors; that the King of glory may come in. Who is this King of glory? The LORD of hosts, He is the King of glory. Selah" (vs 9-10). *When He was received, that's what the angels sang!*

Christ is going to receive us! What is He going to do? Let's see what He is going to do. There has to be a reason for the Sea of Glass, because there are a lot to things that have to take place, and a lot of things have to occur for us, and these things are in the Word of God, which shows that they must take place.

Hebrews 2:5: "For *it is* not to *the* angels *that* He has placed in subjection the world that is to come, of which we are speaking." *No! He has put it in subjection under us!*

Verse 6: "But in a certain place one fully testified, saying, 'What is man, that You are mindful of him, or *the* son of man, that You visit him? You did make him a little lower than *the* angels; You did crown him with glory and honor, and You did set him over the works of Your hands" (vs 6-7). *That's our ultimate destiny!*

Verse 8: "You did put all things in subjection under his feet.' For in subjecting all things to him, He left nothing *that was* not subjected to him. But now we do not yet see all things subjected to him." *But the day is coming when it will be!*

Verse 9: "But we see Jesus, Who *was* made a little lower than *the* angels, crowned with glory and honor on account of suffering the death, in order that by *the* grace of God He Himself might taste death for everyone."

So, Christ has a tremendous stake in this! All those who are resurrected are those who have had the character of God, Christ in them developed.

Verse 10: "Because it was fitting for Him, for Whom all things *were created*, and by Whom all things *exist*, in bringing many sons unto glory …[that takes place at the resurrection] …to make the Author of their salvation perfect through sufferings. For both He Who is sanctifying and those who are sanctified *are* **all of one**" (vs 10-11).

The only time that is going to be with everyone, everywhere from the beginning of creation to the return of Christ is when they are all resurrected and meet Christ in the air on the Sea of Glass; "…**all of one**." At this present time, we're a few here and few there, there are some in this country, there are some in that country. When are they going to be all one? Now notice what happens when they are all one.

"…for which cause He is not ashamed to call them brethren, saying…" (vs 11-12).

Here is what Christ is going to do when we're resurrected and we're on the Sea of Glass. What is the first thing that He is going to do? *Christ is going to declare us to the Father, and say*:

"…'I will declare Your name to My brethren, in *the* midst of *the* Church I will sing praise to You.' And again, 'I will be trusting in Him.' And again, **'Behold, I and the children whom God has given Me'**" (vs 12-13).

I believe that's the first thing that Christ is going to say to all resurrected spirit beings! Now let's see a prophecy of this. I mean, brethren, we're talking about the greatest thing since the creation of the world is going to happen. Let's get out of our mind a crippled concept of salvation, because we have so been tainted by Protestantism and Catholicism and the insipidness of this stupid world, that we haven't yet gotten in our mind that *we are called to the greatest, greatest thing that has been!*

God is just not going to save you so you can be saved. Salvation is not escaping ever-burning hell! *Salvation is being called to serve God through all eternity at the first level under Jesus Christ!* The Church of the Firstborn will be at that level for all eternity! I don't know if there is any way we can shake up some these sleeping Laodiceans and Sardisites that are almost dead.

The reason people give up on things so easily is because:

- they were never convinced in the first place
- they were never taught in the second place
- they never studied their Bibles to really know, in the third place

I don't know what can be done to wake up these people, especially those who have forsaken the Sabbath and the Holy Days and have gone back into the vomit and swill of the order of the Roman Catholic Church to keep Sunday!

The Catholic Church arrogantly says that those Protestants and those other people who keep Sunday:

You are just following us. You are hypocrites. We determined Sunday, not the Scriptures. You are following us, not God. You don't believe your Bible, you believe us!

All you have to do is just read *Rome's Challenge to the Protestants* (**truthofgod.org**). That is a profound

piece of work, and when your enemy is so confident that he will come out and deride you like that, and then people give up on God.

Let me tell you one very profound, important lesson: Because of a man who is supposed to be a servant of God turns out to be evil and corrupt because he was gotten to by Satan the devil, *do not ever give up on God!* I don't care who you are, where you are, where you have been, what you have experienced, *salvation will overcome every bit of whatever you may have gone through!* You need to understand that.

Here is what Christ is going to do. We come up on the Sea of Glass, the angels bring us up there, and we get our 'sea legs' as it were and stand on the Sea of Glass:

1. Christ proclaims us to the Father

Psalm 22:22: "I will declare Your name to My brethren…" *He is going to say,* **'My brethren, whom God has given Me, here is the Father!'**

We'll be able to see the Father, won't we, as spirit beings if we see Christ as He is? Will we not see God the Father as He is? *Yes, indeed!*

"…In the midst of the congregation… ['the great congregation', all the resurrected saints] …I will praise you. You that fear the LORD, praise Him" (vs 22-23).

I just imagine after Jesus says, 'Behold the children you have given Me, and the children behold the Father,' the angels—ten thousands times ten thousand—are going sing praises to God the Father. This is going to be absolutely the most electrifying and penetrating event that we will ever experience, and then we'll praise God.

Verse 23: "You who fear the LORD, praise Him; all of you, the seed of Jacob, glorify Him; and stand in awe of Him all of you, the seed of Israel."

Who is the true seed of Israel? *The Church!* That is going to be a magnificent thing to take place! We are going to read of the work of the apostles. God says:

Isaiah 8:16: "Bind up the testimony, seal the Law among My disciples.' And I will wait upon the LORD, who hides His face from the house of Jacob; and I will trust in Him. **Behold, I and the children whom the LORD has given me**]… [tie in Heb. 2] …*are for signs and for wonders*… [we will be to the world] …in Israel from the LORD of hosts, Who dwells in Mount Zion" (vs 16-18).

What are we coming to? *Mount Sion in heaven above!*

2. We sing the victory song

We're going to do a lot of singing. Remember it says there we have harps. I have never played a harp. Whatever it is that God does when we are resurrected, to give us the ability to do so, He will. All the harps have to be passed out. Now in this remember, the angels are going to be busy assisting in all of this.

Psalm 35:18—*this also has to do with Christ*: "I will give You thanks in **the great congregation**... [the resurrected saints] ...I will praise You among a mighty throng."

We are going to sing some songs. We are going to sing more than just the song of Moses and the song of the Lamb. We'll get to that in just a bit.

Psalm 33:1: "Rejoice in the LORD, O you righteous ones; praise is becoming for the upright. Praise the LORD with a lyre; sing unto Him with a harp of ten strings" *That's what we're going to do. We have the harps of God!*

Verse 3: "Sing unto Him a new song... [it's going to be one we have never sung] ...play skillfully with shouts of joy, for the Word of the LORD is upright; and all His works are *done* in faithfulness" (vs 3-4).

- Is that part of the song we are going to sing?
- What is the greatest work of His hands? *Those who have been resurrected!*

Psalm 144:9: "I will sing a new song to You, O God; on a harp of ten strings I will sing praises to You. It is You Who give salvation to kings" (vs 9-10).

- Are we going to be kings and priests?
- Have we not received salvation?
- *Yes, indeed!*

"...Who deliver David His servant from the hurtful sword" (v 10). *Then it blends on back to a contemporary time!*

Now *the song of victory*; let's see the song of Moses because it says we are going to sing the song of Moses, the servant of God. We will expand this beyond just destroying the Egyptians at the Red Sea.

Exodus 15:1: "Then Moses and the children of Israel sang this song to the LORD, and spoke, saying, 'I will sing to the LORD, for He has triumphed gloriously; *the* horse and his rider He has thrown into the sea. The LORD *is* my strength and song, and He has become my salvation. This is my God, and I will glorify Him, my father's God, and I will exalt Him. The LORD *is* a Man of war; Jehovah *is* His name" (vs 1-3).

We are going to see a little later that Jesus returns to the earth and *He makes war in righteousness!* He is a man of war. And it talks about Pharaoh being cast down, and this is all likened then unto the judgment that will come against Babylon. Then we also have:

Verse 20: "And Miriam the prophetess, the sister of Aaron, took a drum in her hand. And all the women went out after her with drums and with dances. And Miriam answered them, 'Sing to the LORD, for He has triumphed gloriously....'" (vs 20-21). *Think what it is going to be the triumph with all the resurrection of the saints!*

"...The horse and his rider He has flung into the sea.' And Moses brought Israel from the Red Sea, and they went out into the wilderness of Shur...." (vs 21-22). *The rest of the story goes back from there!*

Now let's see some of the songs we are going to sing. This is part of the song of the Lamb. We've often wondered, what was the song of the Lamb? *This is when the Lamb came*:

Revelation 5:8: "And when He took the book, the four living creatures and the twenty-four elders fell down before the Lamb, each having harps and golden bowls full of incense, which are the prayers of the saints. And they sang a new song, saying... [this is the song that we are going to sing] ...'Worthy are You to take the book, and to open its seals because You were slain, and did redeem us to God by Your own blood, out of every tribe and language and people and nation, and did make us unto our God kings and priests; and we shall reign on the earth'" (vs 8-10).

That is part of the song of the Lamb, I believe. And I believe another part of the song of the Lamb is that we will sing unto Him because He was the Lamb slain from the foundation of the world. So, all of that will be part of the song of the Lamb.

Now let's look in the book of Psalms and see if we can see some other things that may be connected with the song of the Lamb. You've heard it said that the saints are going to shout for joy. Well, we are! I mean, this is going to be a tremendous thing! This is extolling God as a fighter, as a warrior, and is Christ going to be fighting and warring this time when He comes back to the earth? *Without a doubt!*

Could this also be part of the song of the Lamb? Psalm 18:46: "The LORD lives; and blessed be my Rock, and let the God of my salvation be exalted. The God who avenges me and subdues the people under me" (vs 46-47).

- Isn't that what's going to happen when we come back to the earth?

- Isn't the earth going to be subdued under all the saints?
- *Yes, indeed!*

Verse 48: "He delivers me from my enemies; yea, You lift me up above those who rise up against me; You have delivered me from the violent man. Therefore, I will give thanks to You, O LORD, among the nations, and sing praises to Your name, He gives great deliverance to His king…" (vs 48-50).

Liken that unto the resurrection, that's the greatest deliverance of all, being delivered from death!

"…and shows mercy to His anointed, to David and to his seed forevermore" (v 50).

We are going to be doing a lot of singing, so that will be good. Maybe this is going to be one of the songs that we'll sing. Maybe this is part of the song to the Lamb.

Psalm 47:1: "Clap your hands, all you people; shout to God with the voice of triumph." *It's going to be something!*

- yes, we have been overcomers
- yes, we triumph over death through Jesus Christ
- yes, we're going to triumph over all the forces of evil in this world

Verse 2: "For the LORD Most High is awesome; He is a great King over all the earth. **He shall subdue the people under us and nations under our feet**" (vs 2-3).

That's why we come back to the earth to fight. I don't know about you, but this makes a lot of sense to me and you know, I have never put it together this way before, but when asked the question about what's going to happen on the Sea of Glass, I guess one thing leads to another.

Verse 4: "He shall choose our inheritance for us, the excellency of Jacob whom He loved. Selah. God has gone up with a shout, the LORD with the sound of a horn" (vs 4-5). *Of course, that will occur on the Feast of Trumpets!*

Verse 6: "Sing praises to God, sing praises; sing praises to our King, sing praises, for God is King of all the earth; sing praises with understanding. God reigns over the nations; God sits upon the throne of His Holiness. The rulers of the peoples are gathered together, the people of the God of Abraham… [that's *us*] …for the shields of the earth are God's; He is greatly exalted" (vs 6-9).

All of this is going to help prepare us for the coming battle! That is the victory song!

3. <u>We are going to receive a new name</u>

Each one is going to receive a new name. How many people are there that are going to be resurrected? *Millions and millions!* Don't you think it is going to take some time for us to receive our new name? First of all, let's see that Jesus is going to have a new name. He is going to have the greatest of the new names, but just like God has done before the resurrection, *He names things for what they will be.* He changed Abram's name to Abraham because he was going to be a father of many nations. *Is he going to be surprised at the resurrection!*

Talking about the greatness of God's power, Ephesians 1:20: "Which He wrought in Christ, when He raised Him from *the* dead, and set *Him* at His right hand in the heavenly *places,* far above every principality and authority and power and lordship, and every name that is named—not only in this age, but also in the *age* to come; for He has subordinated all things under His feet, and has given Him *to be* head over all things to the *Church,* which is His body—the fullness of Him Who fills all things in all" (vs 20-23). *We'll accomplish the will of God!*

We see two things about the name of Christ, Revelation 19:11: "And I saw heaven open; and behold, a white horse; and He Who sat on it *is* called **Faithful and True**, and in righteousness He does judge and make war."

Now we are getting into the events coming to the Feast of Trumpets, v 12: "And His eyes *were* like a flame of fire, and on His head *were* many crowns; *and* **He had a name written that no one knows except Him**."

So, He is going to have one name that is above all names, but also we are going to see He has other names.

Verse 16: "And on *His* garment and on His thigh He has a name written: *King of kings and Lord of lords!*

We have to have a new name. Let's see where that promise is given, and we won't know what it is until we are given it. I imagine that Christ is already working on the names, He and God the Father are putting together the names that He has for us, getting all prepared. *God is getting prepared! Jesus Christ is getting prepared!* For all the preparation it is going to take for the first resurrection.

Revelation 2:17: "The one who has an ear, let him hear what the Spirit says to the churches. **To the one who overcomes I will give *the right* to eat of the hidden manna**…"

We are going to eat when we are spirit beings. What is the hidden manna? I can't tell you, it's hidden, but we'll know at that time.

"…and I will give him a white stone, and **on the stone a new name written**…" (v 17).

I wonder if this stone is going to be something that we will hold in our hands, a symbol of authority.

"…**which no one knows except the one who receives it**" (v 17).

So, no one will know it until you receive it, then you will know it. Let's see that there is also another name. Not all are going to receive the same name. Each one is going to be different. After all, *each one of us at the resurrection is going to be a special creation of God the Father and Jesus Christ. We're going to have*:

- a new body
- a new mind
- a new name
- a new job

we're going to
- eat new food
- do new things

Revelation 3:12: "The one who overcomes will I make a pillar in the temple of My God…"

That doesn't mean that you're going to be made into a pillar; because *the Temple of God is going to consist of the people of God!* Ultimately, as we will see for the Last Great Day, *in New Jerusalem there is no temple!* All temple builders will be unemployed.

"…and he shall not go out anymore; and I will write upon him the name of My God and the name of the city of My God…" (v 12).

This is in addition to your individual name. So, these are names then, which distinguish work and authority; it would have to be.

"…the New Jerusalem, which will come down out of heaven from My God; and *I will write upon him* My new name" (v 12).

Now exactly how all that is going to work, I can tell you exactly how you're going to find out: *you make it to the resurrection, and when you see it done, you'll understand it,* and until then it's speculation. We don't know, except that it says it.

Could not these names also signify titles? *Could very well be!* We'll find out! This new name is going to be something. I imagine God the Father and Jesus Christ are having a great time selecting the names. Let's see the promise:

Isaiah 56:1: "Thus says the LORD, 'Keep justice and do righteousness; for My salvation *is* near to come, and My righteousness to be revealed. Blessed *is* the man who does this… [the Protestants think you are cursed] …and the son of man who lays hold on it; who keeps the Sabbath from profaning it, and keeps his hand from doing any evil.' And do not let the son of the stranger, who has joined himself to the LORD, speak, saying, 'The LORD has utterly separated me from His people.' And do not let the eunuch say, 'Behold, I *am* a dry tree.' For thus says the LORD, 'To the eunuchs who keep My Sabbaths… [*plural,* Holy Days] …and choose things that please Me, and take hold of My covenant; even to them will I give within My house and within My walls a place and a name…'" (vs 1-5). *This is talking about at the time of the resurrection!*

"…better than of sons and of daughters; I will give them **an everlasting name that shall not be cut off**" (v 5).

It's going to go for all eternity. Tremendous promise! Some names really need to be changed and God is going to change them.

Isaiah 62:1: "For Zion's sake I will not be silent, and for Jerusalem's sake I will not rest, until its righteousness goes out as brightness, and her salvation as a burning torch." *That is bringing salvation to the whole world during the Millennium!*

Verse 2: "And the Gentiles will see your righteousness, and all kings your glory… [we will be the kings] …and **you will be called by a new name, which the mouth of the LORD shall name**."

It's going to come directly from God. Now that's going to be an exciting thing. What is in the name of a son or daughter of God? *His or her eternal standing and position!*

Verse 3: "You also will be a crown of glory in the hand of the LORD, and a royal diadem in the hand of your God." *We've got lots of work to do!*

Let's see that there is going to be the whole family name. So, not only are we going to have a new first name, we're going to have a new last name. Eph. 3 shows that God has purpose, and part of what we are reading is the purpose of God for us. God is busy doing and preparing for this, and I am sure the angels, as well.

Ephesians 3:11: "To *His* eternal purpose, which He has wrought in Christ Jesus our Lord, in Whom we have boldness and *direct* access with confidence through His *very* own faith. So then, I beseech *you* not to faint at my tribulations for you, which are *working for* your glory" (vs 11-13).

I can understand why Paul was very positive about the things that he went through. I imagine when he saw the third heavens in vision, that he was given an inkling of some of these things.

Verse 14: "For this cause I bow my knees to the Father of our Lord Jesus Christ, **of Whom the whole family in heaven and earth is named**" (vs 14-15). *We are going to be the Family of God!*

Another Protestant, who, when he found out that we believe that God is a Family, said that this is heterodoxy, if not heresy. Well, what does it say?

- Who made and created the family? *God did!*
- Who said be fruitful and multiple to create a physical family? *God did!*

God is creating *His* Family, there it is! So, we're going to have a family name, as well.

4. We will receive our reward

What is our reward going to be? *The New Testament talks quite a bit about rewards!* Let's look at some of these. We have some rewards here; we have other rewards in heaven to be brought with us. *'His reward is with Him.'* He is going to bring it with Him.

Isaiah 40:9: "Go up for yourself on the high mountain; O you that bring good tidings to Zion…. [talking about the Church] …Lift up your voice with strength, O you who tell good tidings to Jerusalem; lift up, do not be afraid. Say to the cities of Judah, 'Behold your God!' Behold, the Lord GOD will come with a strong *hand*, and His arm shall rule for Him; behold, **His reward is with Him,** and His work before Him. He shall feed His flock like a shepherd; He shall gather the lambs with His arm, and carry *them* in His bosom, *and* shall gently lead those with young" (vs 9-11).

Let's look at some of the rewards that we are looking forward to today. God is the One Who knows all things, He is the One Who is working up the rewards, He is the One Who is preparing them for us. Here is an inkling of the reward:

Matthew 5:11: "Blessed are you when they shall reproach you, and shall persecute you, and shall falsely say every wicked thing against you, for My sake. Rejoice and be filled with joy, for great *is* your reward in heaven…" (vs 11-12)—*which He is going to bring with Him!*

What is a great reward? We're not told, but it says it's *great*, and if it's going to be great, guess what, *it is going to be great!* You can look up the different ones, the different rewards. You can lose your reward:

Matthew 6:1: "**Beware** *that* you do not bestow your alms in the sight of men in order to be

seen by them; otherwise **you have no reward** with your Father Who *is* in heaven."

Your reward depends upon your conduct. In other words, don't do it for glory of men. Whatever you do don't do to be seen of men. Whatever you do, don't do it for politics. He talks about those who blow the trumpets when they give their alms, they've had their reward; they were seen of men. Likewise, you can go and read the whole chapter there it talks about the reward, but it talks about the treasures that we lay up for heaven in vs 19-20.

Here it says something very unusual. 2-John 8: "Watch out for yourselves in order that we may not lose the things we have accomplished, **but *that* we may receive a full reward**"—*rather than just partial!* Or you might say the fullness of your reward, either one would be all right.

1-Peter 1:3: "Blessed *be* the God and Father of our Lord Jesus Christ, Who, according to His abundant mercy, has begotten us again unto a living hope through *the* resurrection of Jesus Christ from *the* dead; unto **an inheritance incorruptible and undefiled and unfading, reserved in heaven for us**" (vs 3-4)—*which He is going to bring with Him. He comes with His reward!*

Part of that reward is going to be our assignments! We are going to have to receive our assignments, as well. Let's see what some of those assignments are going to be. With these assignments, we're going to have to know where to go. That's going to be all laid out in the plan, have to be. Here it talks about the reward and the assignment. This is the parable of the talents. The parable of the pounds is in Luke 19.

Matthew 25:14: "For *the Kingdom of Heaven is* like a man leaving the country, who called his own servants and delivered to them his property."

God has given you the Spiritual goods of His Holy Spirit, and His Word is delivered to you. Now it depends on what you do with it.

Verse 15: "Now, to one he gave five talents, and to another two, and to another one; he *gave* to each one according to his own ability, and immediately left the country. Then the one who had received five talents went and traded with them, and made an additional five talents" (vs 15-16).

God expects us to take the initiative!~ The way God does things, He doesn't do it like in a corporation where someone is supervising you and looking after every little details. He says, 'Here is the job, here is the goal, here is the mission; go do it.' One might ask, 'How do I do it Lord?'

- you study My Word

- you have to use your initiative
- you have to use your choice

Verse 17: "In the same way also, the one who had *received* two *talents* also gained two others But the one who had received the single *talent* went and dug in the earth, and hid his lord's money. Now, after a long time, the lord of those servants came to take account with them. Then the one who had received five talents came to *him and* brought an additional five talents, saying, 'Lord, you delivered five talents to me; see, I have gained five other talents besides them.'" And his lord said to him, 'Well *done,* good and faithful servant! *Because* you were faithful over a few things, I will set you over many things. Enter into the joy of your lord.' And the one who had received two talents also came to him *and* said, 'Lord, you delivered to me two talents; see, I have gained two other talents besides them.' His lord said to him, 'Well *done,* good and faithful servant! *Because* you were faithful over a few things, I will set you over many things. Enter into the joy of your lord'" (vs 17-23).

Luke 19 because this is the other half of the story. What is the reward? *It's going to take some time for everybody to get their rewards!* Just think how many are going to be resurrected all at once. We look around us, and we are few today. Just think what it is going to be like in the resurrection with millions and millions and we say, 'O God, what have You been do down though the ages?' He is going to say, 'Look at all of this, how is that?' And Abraham, Isaac and Jacob are going to say, 'Praise God, look at what He did.' Especially Abraham because all he had was Isaac. Now look at all the physical nations on the earth and look at all now the spiritual nations that God is resurrecting. The first resurrection; that's going to be awesome.

Luke 19:15: "And it came to pass that when he returned after receiving the kingdom, he directed that those servants to whom he had given the money be called to him, in order that he might know what each one had gained by trading."

God doesn't want you to stay the same. Never be happy and satisfied with what you are today. Thank God that you are able to do what you do, that you can grow and overcome, but there is:

- more that you can do
- more that you can learn
- more that you can grow into

but you've got to apply yourself! It isn't going to come by osmosis; it's not going to come by a funnel in the top of the head.

Verse 16: "And the first one came up, saying, 'Lord, your pound has produced ten pounds.' Then he said to him, 'Well *done,* good servant;

because you were faithful in a very little, you shall have authority over ten cities'" (vs 16-17).

When is he going to know which cities those are? It's got to be at the resurrection on the Sea of Glass before we come back to the earth. How are you going to know where to go? 'Which city, Lord? I've never been up here in the atmosphere, and looking down I can't tell.'

Verse 18: "And the second one came, saying, 'Lord, your pound has made five pounds.' Then he also said to this one, 'And you be over five cities'" (vs 18-19).

Then the one who didn't do anything with it was the Sardisite who was dead and who had defiled his garments and didn't receive the reward because he was lazy. If you're dead, you've got to be lazy. How much can a corpse do? *Not very much!* So, we receive our rewards.

5. There is going to be a New Covenant

As compared to the Old Covenant, we're in the New Covenant today. But just like the covenant that God made with Abraham, when He expanded the covenant, what did He do? *God changed his name from Abram to Abraham!* So likewise, when we're spirit beings, I believe there's going to be a *new* covenant. Now the covenant first of all has got to start out with the marriage of the Lamb and the Bride.

- Is not the marriage ceremony a covenant? *Yes!*
- Are not our new assignments, the new work and our new existence going to require a *new* covenant, *a new agreement*? *But of course!*

You might want to go ahead and expand the thing on rewards and look up in a concordance and add a little more study to it, and expand on it because it talks about the reward of a prophet, the reward of a righteous man, if you give a cup of water to one of the disciples, etc. Some of those rewards I believe will take place in the second resurrection, not necessarily the first.

Revelation 19:1: "And after these things I heard *the* loud voice of **a great multitude in heaven, saying**…"

That's not the third heaven. That is on the Sea of Glass, which is in the atmosphere where the clouds are which is the first heaven. We're getting ready to come back to the earth; this is the finale.

"…'Hallelujah! The salvation and the glory and the honor and the power *belong* to the Lord our God. For true and righteous *are* His judgments; for He has judged the great whore, who corrupted the earth with her fornication, and He has avenged the blood of His servants at her hand.' And they said a second time, 'Hallelujah! And her smoke shall ascend upward into the ages of eternity.' And the twenty-four elders and the four living creatures fell down and worshiped God, Who sits on the Throne, saying, 'Amen. Hallelujah!'" (vs 1-4).

This is the finality before we come back to the earth. This is really a tremendous send-off. The thing that is going to take place, I believe, the last part of it that will take place will be the marriage of the Lamb. Then we come down to the earth just like it lays out here.

Verse 5: "And a voice came forth from the throne, saying, 'Praise our God, all His servants, and all who fear Him, both small and great.'" *There we will be on the Sea of Glass, and we'll praise God!*

Verse 6: "And I heard a voice like that of a great multitude, and like *the* sound of many waters, and *the* sound of mighty thunderings, saying, 'Hallelujah! For *the* Lord God Almighty has reigned…. [here comes the marriage of the Lamb]: …Let us be glad and shout with joy; and let us give glory to Him; for the marriage of the Lamb has come, and His wife has made herself ready'" (vs 6-7). *I believe that God the Father will perform the ceremony!* Who else?

Verse 8: "And it was granted to her that she should be clothed in fine linen, pure and bright; for the fine linen is the righteousness of the saints. And he said to me, 'Write: Blessed *are* those who are called to the marriage supper of the Lamb'" (vs 8-9). *These are the guests!*

We don't know exactly how all of that is going to work, but we know that it says there are going to be guests at the wedding. Not everyone who is resurrected in the first resurrection will be part of the Bride, but there will be guests, and they eat at the marriage supper. So, the last thing we're going to do is have a great big feast! The marriage of the Lamb is going to take place, we'll have the great feast of the marriage supper of the Lamb, and then get ready for Trumpets. The angels are going to bring all the horses for us.

Let's see if we can get some hints of this covenant here; it will be an extension of a covenant already of the New Covenant. Just like the covenant that God made with Abraham in Gen.17[transcriber's correction] was an extension of the covenant He made with him in Gen. 15. So likewise with us, we will be part of the everlasting covenant.

Hebrews 13:20: "And *may* the God of peace, Who raised our Lord Jesus from among *the* dead—that great Shepherd of the sheep—through *the* blood of *the* **everlasting covenant**."

When we receive our new name, we receive our rewards, we receive our assignments, we will have a New Covenant, part of the everlasting covenant that started out when you were baptized. This will be a new phase of it, an extension of it because we will live forever.

Let's see part of the covenant that God made with Melchizedek, the Lord Who was Melchizedek. Being priests and kings under Christ, we then will become part of the Melchizedek priesthood directly. So, not only does this apply to Christ, but it will also have to extend to those who are going to be kings and priests under Christ. Have to be!

Psalm 110:1: "The LORD said unto my Lord, **'Sit at My right hand until I make Your enemies as Your footstool.'"** *That's the whole prophecy of what God is doing!*

Verse 2: "The LORD shall send the rod of Your strength out of Zion *saying*, **'Rule in the midst of Your enemies.'** Your people will offer themselves in the day of Your power, in the beauties of Holiness from the womb of the morning: Yours is the dew of Your youth. The LORD has sworn and will not repent, **'You are a priest forever after the order of Melchisedec'"** (vs 2-4).

Now that is a covenant. So likewise, there is going to be a marriage covenant; there will be the covenant for the new priests and the new kings.

6. **The pouring out of the seven last plagues**

All of this takes place while we are on the Sea of Glass before we return to the earth. You have to come back for Trumpets so we can continue the story, because all of the Holy Days are connected together and have meaning.

Revelation 15:5: "And after these things I looked, and behold, the temple of the tabernacle of the testimony in heaven was opened. And the seven angels who had the seven *last* plagues came out of the temple; they were clothed in linen, pure and bright, and girded about the chest with golden breastplates. And one of the four living creatures gave to the seven angels seven golden vials, full of the wrath of God, Who lives into the ages of eternity. And the temple was filled with smoke from the glory of God, and from His power; and no one was able to enter inside the temple until the seven plagues of the seven angels were fulfilled" (vs 5-8).

Now then, God's vengeance is given. Remember God said to all of us, 'Vengeance is mine, says the Lord.' God is going to do a unique thing. He is going to show all the saints, all at the same time, the vengeance of God on this whole ungodly world-system, and fulfill His promise, that if you wait for the vengeance of God, you will see it.

Revelation 16:1: "Then I heard a loud voice from the temple say to the seven angels, 'Go and pour out the vials of the wrath of God onto the earth.'"

Men are going to learn that they are feeble, indeed, fighting against God. God doesn't use guns, cannons, and bombs. God uses things that affect the human body in a way to debilitate it. He uses the same plagues that He used when He destroyed Egypt. This is to show that God is the same yesterday, today, and forever, and these weapons, the greatest weapons of mass destruction that have ever been.

Verse 2: "And the first *angel* went and poured out his vial onto the earth; and an evil and grievous sore fell upon the men who had the mark of the beast, and upon those who were worshiping his image."

They are probably going to break out with boils, blains and carbuncles, from head to toe. Remember what happened to Job? He was so covered with boils that he just sat there in the dust and took a broken potsherd and just scraped the puss-caps off those boils that he had, and then threw ashes on it. He was sitting there and you know the flies just came all around him, that's why he said, 'The worms eat this body.' There were probably some maggots crawling around in some of these sores that he opened up. So, just picture the same thing here. That's why don't receive *the mark of the beast*. It may be convenient for a while, but you're going to pay the penalty, friend.

Verse 3: "And the second angel *went and* poured out his vial into the sea; and it became blood, like *that* of a dead *man*; and every living soul in the sea died."

When Christ comes to this earth when we come with Him to this earth, the earth is going to be nearly dead, lifeless, plagued, sick, destroyed, dead bodies everywhere. Yeah, there will be some people still alive; how many we don't know. You talk about shell shock; you talk about plague shock!

Verse 4: "And the third angel poured out his vial upon the rivers, and into the fountains of waters; and they became blood. Then I heard the angel of the waters say..." (vs 4-5). *There is an angel in charge of the waters of the earth!* So he said:

"...'You are righteous, O Lord, Who are, and Who was, even the Holy One, in that You have executed this judgment. For they have poured out *the* blood of saints and of prophets...'" (vs 5-6).

You need to understand the blood of the saints and the prophets is worthy that they receive this.

"...and You have given them blood to drink; for they are worthy.' And I heard another *voice* from the altar say, 'Yes, Lord God Almighty, true and righteous *are* Your judgments'" (vs 6-7).

Men look at this and say God is evil, mean, nasty, hateful and terrible. What have men done to God? *All those who are against God, remember, there is a day called payback time, and here it is!*

Verse 8: "And the fourth angel poured out his vial upon the sun; and *power* was given to it to scorch men with fire."

Do you think 130 degrees in Iraq is pretty tough? It doesn't say how hot this is, but it scorches them like with fire.

"Then men were scorched with great heat..." (v 9). *Now apparently just a big blast for a certain period of time!*

Did they repent? *No!* How hard is the heart *once it is given over to Satan the devil? Pretty hard!*

"...and they blasphemed the name of God, Who has authority over these plagues, and did not repent to give Him glory" (v 9).

'We're going to make it to the end. We're going to fight these invaders from outer space.'

Verse 10: "And the fifth angel poured out his vial upon the throne of the beast; and his kingdom became full of darkness; and they gnawed their tongues because of the pain."

It's much like the darkness that they had in Egypt. It was so thick they could feel it. Can you imagine having such a darkness that is so totally black and so absolutely oppressive that you can reach out and feel it, and there is nothing you can do?

Verse 11: "And blasphemed the God of heaven because of their pains and their sores; yet, they did not repent of their works."

There is going to be a little respite after that. Here comes the last desperate hoorah of mankind against God.

Verse 12: "And the sixth angel poured out his vial into the great River Euphrates... [because after Rev. 9 it began to flow again] ...and its waters were dried up, so that the way of the kings from the rising of *the* sun might be prepared"—*so that the rest of the army of 200-million could come!*

They thought, 'Oh! This is fantastic! The river is dried up, now we can get our enemies over there to Jerusalem and we can fight this invasion from outer space! Now is our opportunity. We can still do it in spite of everything that has gone on.'

So, they are going to get spiritual communication:

Verse 13: "Then I saw three unclean spirits like frogs *come* out of the mouth of the dragon, and out of the mouth of the beast, and out of the mouth of the false prophet."

These are going to convince them that if we all gather together, if we just come together. You talk about Pharaoh being convinced that he could run down into the Red Sea, which was open, and he could see the dry ground and he looked to his right, and the water was way down at the other end, and he looked to his left and the water was way down at that end. So likewise, they're going to be deceived into thinking, 'If we gather together, we're going to make it. This is our last chance!'

Verse 14: "For they are spirits of demons working miracles, going forth to the kings of the earth, even of the whole world, to gather them together to *the* battle of that great day of the Almighty God."

This is going to be an awesome battle with all the armies gathered around. They're going to be able to see the Sea of Glass. They're going to be able to get their armies there and they are going to say,

Okay, let's all get here with all of our rockets, all of our tanks, all of our bombs, everything we can shoot up there. We are going to blast this thing out of the air and they'll come tumbling down, and we'll kill them all!

Well, the Sea of Glass is going to be perfectly protected. All those missiles and everything are just going to bounce off. They're going to know they are in *deep* trouble then.

Here is a little warning to all the saints, v 15: "Behold, I come as a thief. Blessed *is* the one who is watching and is keeping his garments, so that he may not walk naked and they *may not* see his shame."

In other words: Lest you who know the Truth, don't watch and keep your garments clean by loving and obeying God, and by repentance through the blood of Christ, you're going to be ashamed and you're going to end up the same way.

Verse 16: "And he gathered them together to the place that in Hebrew is called Armageddon. Then the seventh angel poured out his vial into the air; and a loud voice came out of the temple of heaven, from the throne, saying, 'IT IS FINISHED.' And there were voices and thunders and lightnings; and there was a great earthquake, such as was not since men were on the earth, so mighty an earthquake, *and* so great" (vs 16-18).

This is the finality! Like a great and tremendous symphony that just builds and builds, and finally it comes to the end. Instead of kettledrums going and trumpets blowing it's going to be the angels who are shouting, and here it's building right to the end and the seventh angel poured out his vial. It's going to be something so great.

Verse 19: "And the great city was divided into three parts; and the cities of the nations fell..."

I just imagine every skyscraper that man has ever built is going to come crumbling to the ground!

"...and Babylon the Great..." (v 19). *We'll talk about the judgment of Babylon leading up to Trumpets!*

"...was remembered before God to give her the cup of the wine of the fury of His wrath. And every island disappeared, and no mountains were found; and great hail, *each stone* the weight of a talent, fell down from heaven upon men; and men blasphemed God because of the plague of the hail, for the plague was exceedingly great" (vs 19-21).

We'll see that this doesn't kill all the men! This doesn't kill all the armies, yet. They recover after this the hail comes down, and what happens after hail is down on the ground for a while? *Well, sooner or later, it melts away!*

Now, if you want to know the rest of the story, **come for Trumpets!**

Scriptures from *The Holy Bible in Its Original Order, A Faithful Version*

Scriptural References:

1) 1 John 3:1-2
2) Revelation 15:1-5
3) Psalm 24:7-10
4) Hebrews 2:5-13
5) Psalm 22:22-23
6) Isaiah 8:16-18
7) Psalm 35:18
8) Psalm 33:1-4
9) Psalm 144:9-10
10) Exodus 15:1-3, 20-22
11) Revelation 5:8-10
12) Psalm 18:46-50
13) Psalm 47:1-9
14) Ephesians 1:20-23
15) Revelation 19:11-12, 16
16) Revelation 2:17
17) Revelation 3:12
18) Isaiah 56:1-5
19) Isaiah 62:1-3
20) Ephesians 3:11-15
21) Isaiah 40:9-11
22) Matthew 5:11-12

23) Matthew 6:1
24) 2 John 8
25) 1 Peter 1:3-4
26) Matthew 25:14-23
27) Luke 19:15-19
28) Revelation 19:1-9
29) Hebrews 13:20
30) Psalm 110:1-4
31) Revelation 15:5-8
32) Revelation 16:1-21

Scriptures referenced, not quoted:

- Matthew 6:19-20
- Genesis 17; 15
- Revelation 9

Also referenced: Booklet: *Rome's Challenge to the Protestants* by Cardinal Gibbon (**truthofgod.org**).

FRC/jea
Transcribed: 1/15/06
Reformatted: bo—11/2020

Section VII

The Fall Holy Days

CHAPTER FORTY-SIX

The Birth of Jesus Christ I
The two most important women in the Bible!
Fred R. Coulter

Greetings, everyone! Welcome to Sabbath services! Today we're going to cover about the birth of Jesus Christ, since they're already propping up Christmas trees, wreaths, gifts and all this sort of thing.

2-Peter 1—this is what needs to be concerning the Bible. There are some very difficult things to understand, that's true. Paul wrote a lot of difficult things that are very hard to understand. How did that happen? *Because he was dealing with the events of his time, plus **writing for all of us** down through all time!*

Most Protestants don't understand that the difficulty in the first century was not the problem between the Catholics and Protestants, **but it was between the Church of God and Judaism!**

{Note our book: *Judaism: Revelation of Moses or Religion of Men?* by Philip Neal}

Peter wrote this epistle some time just before he died. By the way, Peter never went to Rome! There's a full series—*Was Peter Ever in Rome?*—at **churchathome.org**

- Guess where they found the tomb of Peter? *In a tomb on the Mt. of Olives!*
- Why did he never go to Rome? *Because he was to the Jews, the Circumcision!*

The only way he would have gone to Rome was if all the Italians became circumcised. That never happened!

You can tell by what Peter is writing that he's preparing for the end. Always remember that *God had the things written down, because you can never trust word of mouth!*

2-Peter 1:15: "But I will make every effort *that,* after my departure, you may always have a *written* remembrance of these things *in order* to practice *them* for yourselves."

The Faithful Version reads a little differently because it's been translated properly according to the words that are there.

Verse 16: "For we did not follow cleverly concocted myths *as our authority,* when we made known to you the power and coming of our Lord Jesus Christ, but we were eyewitnesses of His magnificent glory."

Peter is referring to the time when Jesus took Peter, James and John up to a high mountain and Jesus was transfigured before them, and they could see Him as if He were a spirit being. That was a vision. This stuck in Peter's mind permanently! Think about that!

If you had seen that, would you desire to do anything on your own, when it was your responsibility to write things for the future? *No!*

Verse 17: "Because He received glory and honor from God *the* Father when *the* voice came to Him from the Majestic Glory, **'This is My Son, the Beloved, in Whom I am well pleased.'** And this *is the* voice from heaven that we heard when we were with Him on the Holy mountain. **We also possess the confirmed prophetic Word**..." (vs 17-19). **What is that?** *The writings of the New Testament!*

Note our booklet: *Prophecies of Jesus Christ in the Old Testament.* There are 356 of them, and remember that the apostles wrote the New Testament, but preached from the Old Testament.

"...to which you do well to pay attention, as to a light shining in **a dark place**... [the world] ...**until the day dawns**... [the return of Jesus Christ] ...and ***the morning star*** arises in your hearts... [the resurrection] ...**knowing this first,**... [keep this in mind with all Scripture—Old and New Testaments] ...**that no prophecy of Scripture originated as anyone's own *private* interpretation**" (vs 19-20).

They didn't say, 'I think...' They were inspired to write, 'Thus says the Lord...'

Verse 21: "Because prophecy **was not brought at any time**... [any inspired writing of God did not come at any time] ...**by human will**..."

Today we know all the places that men have tried to change. God lets it be that way so those who want to know the Truth must prove it. But the Word of God stands!

"...but the Holy men of God..." (v 21). *Prophets of old beginning with Abraham:*

- all the patriarchs
- the kings
- the prophets
  - ✓ Isaiah
  - ✓ Jeremiah
  - ✓ Ezekiel
- the 12 minor prophets
- many prophets that weren't written down
- the Psalms
- the Proverbs

All written down for all of humanity, but for us who are Christians, to live by!

"…but the Holy men of God spoke as they were moved by *the* Holy Spirit" (v 21)—*and also wrote!*

Let's see what Paul said concerning the same thing! 2-Timothy 3:16: "**All** Scripture…"—*each and every one!*

Today we're going to look at some 'mundane' Scripture that was inspired! All Scripture means"

- all the genealogies
- all the histories
- all the prophecies
- all the prayers
- all the Psalms
- all the Proverbs

"All Scripture *is* **God-breathed**…" (v 16)—*or* **God Spirited,** because Jesus said that His Word was Spirit and Life.

Think about that! Why is it when you read the Bible something happens to you in your thinking? *Because the word comes from God!* It's meant to help you understand:

- what God wants
- how to live
- Who He is
- what He's doing
- where we're going

All of that is in the Bible!

"…and *is* profitable for **doctrine**…" (v16)—*which is important!* Doctrine may contain some details, as we will see today. Doctrine merely means *teaching!*

"…for **conviction**…" (v 16)—*a strong resolute mental lockdown that the Truth is truth!*

"…for **correction**… [correct yourself] …for **instruction in righteousness** so that the man of God may be complete, fully equipped for every good work" (vs 16-17).

Since Christmas is coming, let's look at the

account that Luke wrote. Let's first come to Acts 1 so we understand where Luke is coming from. Luke was the last one to write a Gospel, so he explains here concerning things about the ministry of Christ:

Acts 1:1: "The first account I indeed have written, O Theophilus, concerning all things that Jesus began both to do and to teach."

Luke covers things that none of the other apostles cover. How did he know? We're going to see that there are some very amazing words recorded by two women—Mary and her Aunt Elizabeth—inspired by God and put into the Bible. How did Luke get those things?

Historically, Paul was arrested in 58 A.D. in Jerusalem, saved from the slaughter of the Jews and taken down to Caesarea. He was there two years under house arrest. Luke was with him. '

- How far is Jerusalem from Caesarea? *A two day journey!*
- Do you suppose that Paul went up to Jerusalem and looked at the archives that the Church had?

We find in Acts 6 that the apostles said, 'We're going to have your find six men who can wait on the tables, and we'll give ourselves under the ministry of the Word.' What was the 'ministry of the Word'? *Writing down the beginning of the things of the Gospel!* So, Luke would go up there.

We have figured, roughly, that if the time that Luke went up there, Mary would have been in her 80s. We don't know, but did he talk directly with Mary? *Very possible!*

We're going to see just a little something that most people do not pay any attention to.

Luke 1:1: "Since many have taken in hand to compile a *written* narration of the matters, which have been fully believed among us."

That shows that there must have been up in Jerusalem some kind of record of those things in addition to what we have.

Verse 2: "As they delivered *them* to us, those who from *the* beginning had been eyewitnesses and ministers of the Word, it seemed good to me also, having accurately understood everything from the very first, to write *these things* in an orderly sequence to you, most excellent **Theophilus**… [lover of God] …so that you might know the *absolute* certainty of *the* things in which you have been instructed" (vs 2-4)—*what we need to know!*

Verse 5 looks like a small innocuous verse; let's see where it leads us:

Verse 5: "There was in the days of Herod, the king of Judea, a certain priest of *the* **course of Abijah**… [What does that mean?] …Zacharias by name; and his wife *was* of the daughters of Aaron, and her name *was* Elizabeth."

1-Chron. 24—I know that this book is very hard reading. However, you need to understand what David did. In getting all the wealth and the plans to build the temple from God for Solomon. David also stored up wealth: gold, silver, iron and brass. But what David did, if you read these chapters, you find that he organized the whole order of the temple and the government in Jerusalem. He ordered:

- the order of priests
- the stationing of the guards
- the heads of the families

Sidebar: When we read in Rev. 4 & 5, how many elders were around the Throne of God? *24!* Isn't it interesting that all of these things that David broke down were in 24 courses, or in the case of the guards, monthly.

I know it's hard reading, because some of these names are really difficult, indeed! I tell you, when we were reading and recording the Bible, the most fun we had was reading the chronologies. Why is this important?

1-Chronicles 24:7: "Now, the lot *for the* first *course* came out to Jehoiarib, the second to Jedaiah, the third to Harim, the fourth to Seorim, the fifth to Malchijah, the sixth to Mijamin, the seventh to Hakkoz, **the eighth to** <u>Abijah</u> (vs 7-10).

- Why is this significant?
- How does that tie in with the Luke 1?

Each of these courses began in the first month of the year, Nisan! The work from noon one Sabbath through noon the next Sabbath. That was an interesting way to do it; why? *That meant that the priests did half-duty each Sabbath!*

What we have is Zacharias at the temple *as the eighth course.* On the Calculated Hebrew Calendar—Appendix E: <u>When Was Jesus Born?</u> *The Holy Bible in Its Original Order,* 2nd edition, pg. 1263—we have all of that detailed out there. This means that this course went this way:

Starting with the first course—first and second week of Nisan, leading up to Passover, Unleavened bread. All the courses were on Pentecost. So, you count down 1, 2, 3—all courses together for the week. Then courses 5-8 you come to the week before Pentecost. Then Pentecost was the 9th week when they were all there.

- What was Zacharias doing in the course of Abijah at that temple?

- What were his duties?

We know when he was there, the week before Pentecost and the week of Pentecost, two weeks. Let's see what happened with him at the temple, and what happened when he left the temple.

Luke 1:6: "Now, they were both righteous before God, walking blamelessly in all the commandments and ordinances of the Lord. But they did not have a child, as Elizabeth was barren; and both were *well* advanced in age. And it came to pass *that* **in fulfilling his priestly service**… [in the 8th course] …before God in the order of his course" (vs 6-8).

We can speculate that this vision to him may have come on Pentecost. We don't know for sure, it doesn't tell us, but that would be a likely date for it.

"…in fulfilling his priestly service_before God in the order of his course" (v 8).

So, if we have the Calculated Hebrew Calendar, look at the weeks in Appendix E, pg. 1258, you can find out when these things took place.

Verse 9: "According to the custom of the priestly service, it fell to him by lot to burn incense when he entered into the temple of the Lord. And all the multitude of the people outside were praying at the hour of the *burning of* incense…. [around 10 in the morning] …Then an angel of *the* Lord appeared to him, standing at *the* right side of the altar of incense" (vs 9-11).

Where did Luke get all this information? *He wrote it down and he got it from somebody!* So, he must have gotten it when he was in Caesarea and went to Jerusalem.

Verse 12: "And when he saw *the angel,* Zacharias was troubled, and fear fell upon him. But the angel said to him, 'Fear not, Zacharias, because your supplication has been heard; and your wife Elizabeth shall bear a son to you, and you shall call his name John. And he shall be a joy and exultation to you; and many shall rejoice at his birth. For he shall be great before the Lord. And he shall never drink wine or strong drink in any form, but **he shall be filled with *the* Holy Spirit even from his mother's womb**. And many of the children of Israel shall he turn to *the* Lord their God'" (vs 12-16).

Notice what else the angel says about John; this tells us something important, because God always makes these things known. He prophesies ahead of time, then it's fulfilled. You look back at the prophecy and you see what happens and see that it did happen.

Verse 17: "And he shall go before Him in *the* spirit and power of Elijah, to turn *the* hearts of the fathers to *the* children, and *the* disobedient to *the* wisdom of *the* righteous, to make ready a people prepared for *the* Lord."

Mal. 3—one verse in prophecy, and accurate! Once God prophesies something, it's going to happen; there's no way it's not going to happen.

Malachi 3:1: "Behold, **I will send My messenger, and he will prepare the way before Me**…. [This is the One Who became Christ saying that He's going to send a messenger before His coming] …And the Lord, Whom you seek, shall suddenly come to His temple, even the Messenger of the covenant, in Whom you delight. **Behold, He comes**,' says the LORD of hosts." *That's quite a thing!*

- Remember how Jesus first came to the temple?
- How did He come?
- Where is that recorded? *John 2!*

He all of a sudden appeared at the temple and He made a scourge and drove out the money exchangers, the cattle, sheep and pigeons. He strew the money of the money exchangers all over the temple floor. I imagine that they were trying to get all of their coins!

What did Jesus say? *You have made My Father's house a house of merchandize when it should be a house of prayer for all people!*

Then they said to Jesus, 'By what authority do You do this?' Jesus said, 'Destroy this temple and I will raise it up in the third day.' They couldn't believe that because it took 46 years to build. Jesus was talking about His body.

So, here's the prophecy being fulfilled right here with Zacharias. This is a good lesson that small, little details are just as important as major proclamations.

Zacharias must have been 70-years-old or older, and his wife 70-years-old or older.

Luke 1:18: "Then Zacharias said to the angel, 'By what *means* shall I know this? For I am an old man, and my wife *is* advanced in years.'"

Here's another good lesson about believing God, and believing an angel of God!

Verse 19: "And the angel answered *and* said to him, 'I am Gabriel, **who stands in the presence of God**; and I was sent to speak to you, and to announce this good news to you.'"

Think about this: An angel sent to a priest of the eighth course, right at the time that's necessary for John the Baptist to be conceived and born, so that he comes before Christ.

Verse 20: "But behold, you shall be silent and unable to speak until the day in which these things shall take place…" *Zacharias couldn't talk!* Here he is there in the Holy place:

- an angel is talking to him
- he's offered the incense
- he's given this great message

Of course, at that age, he doubted. But what lesson do we learn from this? *It doesn't matter what age, it doesn't matter what promise. **What God says will take place!***

"…because you did not believe my words, which shall be fulfilled in their time'" (v 20). *These were the words of God that He gave to the angel to give to Zacharias!*

The people were out there wondering what's taking Zacharias so long. He comes out and they ask, 'What happened?' *He couldn't talk!* So, they probably had to bring him something to write on, and he said—in writing—'An angel talked to me!' So, they knew that something big had happened! But he couldn't tell them.

That's the opposite way that men do things. If they do something great, what do they do? *They get out the bands, the armies, trumpets, flags, the rallies and all this sort of thing to make it known!*

Verse 23[transcriber's correction]: "Now it came to pass *that* when the days of his service were fulfilled, he departed to his house. And after those days, Elizabeth his wife conceived, but hid herself *for* five months, saying, 'The Lord has intervened for me in this, at *the* time in which He looked upon *me* to take away my reproach among men.'" (vs 23-25).

If we get the timeline with Zacharias down to the birth of John the Baptist, we can follow that same timeline right along here:

Verse 26: "And in the sixth month *of her pregnancy*, the angel Gabriel was sent by God to a city of Galilee, named Nazareth"—*far away from Jerusalem!*

- Why is that? *We know the problem today in Washington, D.C., **the deep state!***
- What was the problem in Jerusalem? ***The deep state with the priests, scribes and Pharisees!***

*They wanted Christ to come in magnificence, glory and power to them and embrace them and say, 'I'm going to get rid of the Romans for you.' **But God had bigger plans, so it wasn't done that way!***

So, it was in Nazareth, a little ole outback town far away from Jerusalem. We will see what happened with Mary and then see some astonishing things that are recorded for us. But first I want to show this to you:

Let's continue with the account with Mary and what happened with her. How did we get these direct conversations. That means that contrary to the way that the world views things, that those at that time were a bunch of illiterate people running around with worn out burlap bags as clothes. That's the way they picture it.

They wrote! So, Zacharias had to write all of this down. What about Mary; that's even more interesting.

Luke 1:26: "And in the sixth month *of her pregnancy...* [that Elizabeth's pregnancy, not the sixth month of the year] *...the angel Gabriel was sent by God to a city of Galilee, named Nazareth, to a virgin betrothed to a man whose name *was* Joseph, of *the* lineage of David; and the name of the virgin *was* Mary" (vs 26-27)—Greek: 'Mariam'!

Verse 28: "And after coming to her, the angel said, 'Hail, you who are highly favored! The Lord *is* with you; blessed *are* you among women.'" *That's quite an introduction!* Here she is all alone.

Mary had to be young. How old do we suppose that she could have been? *18-20 years-old, somewhere right around there!*

Verse 29: "But when she saw *him,* she was *greatly* perplexed at his message... [wondered what this angel was doing here] *...and was considering what kind of salutation this might be. Then the angel said to her, 'Do not be afraid, Mary, because you have found grace with God; and behold...'" (vs 29-31).

Let's look at how God does things. He does things, many times, that are impossible! Why? *To show that it was from God!* Did He do this with Abraham and Sarah? *Yes!* So, He's doing it here.

We can conclude that everything that has to do with the birth of the coming of the Messiah Jesus Christ *was handled by Gabriel and impossible things were done to show that this was done by the hand of God!*

Verse 31: "And behold, you shall conceive in *your* womb and give birth to a Son; and you shall call His name **Jesus**... [meaning *God with us;* so this is God in the flesh] *...He shall be great, and shall be called *the* Son of *the* Highest; and *the* Lord God shall give Him the throne of David, His forefather" (vs 31-32). *Tie in Isa. 9:6; so this is a fulfillment of prophecy!*

When God does something, He either starts at one place, which He does, and finishes it at another place, which He does, and sometimes there are hundreds of years in between. **The prophecy that a virgin will conceive was 800_{B.C.}!**

Verse 33: "'And He shall reign over the house of Jacob into the ages, and of His Kingdom there shall be no end.' But Mary said to the angel, 'How shall this be, since I have not had sexual relations with a man?' And the angel answered *and* said to her, '**The** Holy Spirit shall come upon you, and *the* power of *the* Highest shall overshadow you**...'" (vs 33-35). *This means that this comes directly from God the Father!*

"...**and for this reason, the Holy One being begotten in you shall be called *the* Son of God**" (v 35).

- How did God do this? *There's another almost impossible thing that God did!*
- What was the first prophecy of the coming of the Messiah? *Genesis 3:15! Right after the sin of Adam and Eve!*

Here we are 4,000 years later! God planned this in the ages before there was time as we know it on the earth! He made man and woman in the image of God! That's the first thing?

Why did He do that? *So, He could become a man! That's* **the Prophet!** *(Deut. 18)!*

Sidebar: That's not Gerald Flurry!

So, what did God have to do? When God spoke to Moses, and Moses wanted to see the glory of God, what did God tell him? *No man can look upon My face and live!* Then He said, 'I'll let you see My back parts.' Just a flash of it *so you will know!* (book of Exodus)

- What did God have to do so that this conception in Mary could take place?
- What have you been asked to give up for God?
- How important?
- Was it that you had to leave this or that?

Maybe it cost you your job or something else that was very difficult!

We are told as human beings that before God we must be humble. We can't be arrogant and lifted up in vanity. Who was the most humble of all? *Jesus Christ!* What did He have to do? *First of all, He had to have complete confidence and trust in the Father!*

What Jesus had to do was to become a pinpoint of life! This was also written down. God is a *Covenant God*, and He has it written down. There were many prophecies written down concerning Christ.

Hebrews 10:4: "Because *it is* impossible *for the* blood of bulls and goats to take away sins." ***Why?***

They did receive forgiveness, so the forgiveness was to the temple. But to forgive sin, there has to be something greater than the one who has sinned *to forgive that sin!*

- Is a bull, goat or lamb less than a human being? *Yes! Therefore, it cannot forgive human sin!*
- What did God do? *He decided that He would come*—as we're seeing here with Mary—*in the flesh!*
- What did He have to do? *He had to give up His glory!*

Verse 5: "For this reason, when He comes into the world, He says, 'Sacrifice and offering You did not desire, but You have prepared a body for Me. You did not delight in burnt offerings and *sacrifices* for sin. Then said I, "Lo, **I [Christ] come (*as it is written of Me in *the* Scroll of *the* Book)**...'" (vs 5-7).

This shows that in heaven, when Gabriel came to Daniel to tell him about the coming of Christ, he said:

Daniel 10:21: "But I will show you that which is written in the **Scripture of Truth**...."

Where is that book of Truth? *In heaven!* So, this was written in heaven. God the Father and Jesus Christ had a covenant existing between them and that covenant was this: Because He created mankind, and mankind sinned, ***Christ would become the Sacrifice for them!*** But He had to be of greater value than all human beings! So, God had to become a man!

Hebrews 10:7: "...'Lo, I [Christ] come (*as* it is written of Me in *the* Scroll of *the* Book) to do Your will, O God.' In the saying above, *He said*, 'Sacrifice and offering and burnt offerings and *sacrifices* for sin (which are offered according to the *priestly* law) You did not desire nor delight in.' Then He said, 'Lo, I come to do Your will, O God.' He takes away the first *covenant* in order that He may establish the second *covenant*" (vs 7-9).

Verse 5: "...You [the Father] have prepared a body for Me." ***How did God prepare that body?***

A lot of theologians speculate how God came in the flesh. Some say that Jesus was a man

and Christ from heaven possessed the man and that's how it worked. That God Himself did not really die, just the man Jesus. *That's called **Docetism!*** Others don't believe in Christ at all.

Philip. 2 shows what He had to do, and shows the great humility of God.

Philippians 2:5: "Let this mind be in you, which *was* also in Christ Jesus." *This is what we are to develop, this is the character, the things that we go through!*

Verse 6: Who, although He existed in *the* form of God, did not consider it robbery to be equal with God."

John 1:1: "In *the* beginning was the Word, and the Word was with God, and the Word was God."

Philippians 2:7: "**But emptied Himself**..." *That's quite a statement!*

Here He is a spirit being and cannot die as a spirit being, so He *emptied Himself* to become that pinpoint of life so He could be begotten in the womb of the virgin Mary. ***He gave up everything to become the sacrifice for the sins of humanity!*** Would not say that that's a greater sacrifice than all the animals in the world? Yes, indeed!

"...*and* was made in *the* **likeness** of men..." (v 7)—'homoiomati'—*in the exact sameness!*

He had the inheritance from the Father combined with the egg and genes of Mary. Mary had human nature, even though she was righteous. There's no such thing as the Catholics say with 'immaculate conception' and was 'assumed bodily into heaven.' ***That's pagan nonsense!***

In order for him to be tempted in every way like we are, Jesus had to have human nature. Otherwise, all the temptations would have been nothing. If it was impossible for Him to sin, it would have been nothing. How could He be tempted?

If you knew that something was impossible, you would sit there and laugh. He had to receive human nature.

- What did Paul call that human nature? *The law of sin and death!*
- Was Jesus subject to death? *Yes, indeed!*

He had to carry that within Him and never sin! Think on that! So, His task was really a fantastic, magnificent one! That's why His sacrifice covers the sins of the whole world! Does this not show the love of God in the greatest demonstration of humility by God? *Yes, it does!*

"...*and* took the form of a servant; and being found in *the* manner of man... [eat, breathe, sleep, get tired, etc.] …He humbled Himself… [not only to become a man, but pointing to His demise] …and became obedient unto death, even *the* death of *the* cross" (vs 7-8). *No more torturous way to die than that!* Now you see why this is written down for us.

- What did Mary know?
- What did Elizabeth know?

Since these things took place!

Luke 1:35: "And the angel answered *and* said to her, '*The* Holy Spirit shall come upon you, and **the power** of *the* Highest… [the Holy Spirit] …shall overshadow you; and for this reason, the Holy One **being begotten** in you shall be called *the* Son of God.'"

Why did I translate it as "…being begotten…"? *Because that's the way the* Greek reads! It is a passive tense verb, **being done,** present tense! Right as the angel was speaking, this was occurring!

Sidebar: This shows that the Holy Spirit is not a person. Why? *Because* **IF** *the Holy Spirit were a person, and the Holy Spirit impregnated Mary,* **THEN** *the Holy Spirit would have been the father of Jesus!*

But the power of the Highest is an aspect, an attribute of the power of God to Mary. The Highest is **not** the Holy Spirit, **but the Father!**

"…for this reason, the Holy One being begotten in you shall be called *the* Son of God. Now behold, Elizabeth your kinswoman has also conceived a son in her old age; and this is *the* sixth month for her who *was* called barren. **For with God nothing shall be impossible**" (vs 35-37).

Look at the impossible things done all the way down here, and timed by the things that God set in motion:

- the prophecies
- the Holy calendar of God

To be done specifically at the time that God wanted!

Let's read and see what Mary said, and what Elizabeth said. Think about that these had to be written down so we could have them.

Verse 38: "…And the angel departed from her. And Mary rose up in those days *and* went with haste into the hill country, to a city of Judah, and entered the house of Zacharias and greeted Elizabeth" (vs 38-40). *Here's Elizabeth six months pregnant!*

Verse 41: "Now it came to pass *that* when Elizabeth heard Mary's greeting, the babe leaped in her womb…"—*life! Human life because human life is from conception!* Why?

Sidebar: Not many people know it, but we have it in the book: *From a Speck of Dust to a Son of God: Why Were You Born?*

They know that at the instant of conception with the father's seed into the mother's egg, there's an instant flash of 480,000 volts! Why? What is that? **That must be the spirit of man given to the new conception!**

What is the truth of the matter? *Regardless of how a woman becomes pregnant, at conception God sends the spirit of man!*

- Why? *Because without the spirit the body is dead!*
- What happens when that conception takes place? *Immediately there's a development of a brand new life!*

So here we are at six months, fully developed but small!

"…the babe leaped in her womb and Elizabeth was filled with *the* Holy Spirit" (v 41).

Do you suppose that in the house of Zacharias the priest that they had scrolls that are copies of the scrolls at the temple so he could study and prepare for his work? So he could know the Word of God? They speak of things that are in the Word of God. So they had to have this to know.

Verse 42: "And she [Elizabeth] cried out with a loud voice and said, 'Blessed *are* you among women, and blessed *is* the fruit of your womb.'"

The Catholics repeat this in chants as they go around the beads! That's meaningless, but this is what Mary said. This had to be inspired by God, given to her at that moment for that very thing. But some of this indicates that she also knew some of these things ahead of time.

What do you think she was thinking about for six months up to this point? When the message from the angel to Zacharias to Elizabeth was that she would give birth to a son and *he's going go before the Lord to prepare His way!* Imagine what she thought! I mean, this is no small matter! This is tremendous!

Do you think that something as tremendous as this was unknown to them? *No! It was revealed to them! It was told to them!*

Verse 43: "But why is this *happening* to me, that **the mother of my Lord** should come to me?" *Elizabeth knew!* How about that!

Verse 44: "For behold, as soon as the sound of your greeting reached my ears, the babe in my womb leaped in exultation"—*happiness and joy!*

I imagine that he was just thumping around on her stomach and waving his arms! She knew something was going on!

All of us men will never know what that's like! That's just the way it is. The closest we can come as fathers is when your wife gets big enough and she is quite full and the baby is kicking, you can put your hand on her stomach and feel the baby kick and you can put your ear down there and hear a little bit. Today they have ultrasound! When that happens, there's an ad that's very interesting: here's this couple and they see the ultrasound and they see *two babies! Surprise!*

The babe in the womb recognizes the mother's voice, can respond to sounds, can hear music and practices nursing by sucking it's thumb. That's all a baby knows when it's born. That's what it *needs* to know!

Verse 45: "And blessed *is* she who has believed, for there shall be a fulfillment of the things spoken to her from *the* Lord.'"

Now, here's Mary's response; v 46: "Then Mary said, 'My soul magnifies the Lord, and my spirit has exulted in God my Savior'" (vs 46-47).

Think about that! **She was inspired to know that the babe in her womb**—when He would become a full man—**will be her Savior!** Astonishing!

Verse 48: "For He has looked upon the humble estate of His handmaid; for behold, from this time forward **all generations** shall count me blessed."

She was inspired to say that? How did that get recorded. Mary and Elizabeth must have sat down and wrote it, after they had been inspired to speak it. What else can you conclude? They didn't have recording machines or digital phones! This is really amazing!

Verse 49: "Because the Mighty One has done great things to me, and Holy *is* His name; and His mercy *is* toward those who fear Him, **from generation to generation**" (vs 49-50). *Generations into the future, and generations that are in the past through the second resurrection!*

This is amazing stuff going on between two women! All men, let that humble you!

Verse 51: "He has worked strength with His arm; He has scattered *the* haughty in *the* imagination of their hearts. He has put down rulers from thrones, and has exalted *the* lowly. He has filled *the* hungry with good things, and *the* rich He has sent away empty. He has helped His servant Israel, in remembering *His* mercy, **exactly as He spoke to our fathers, to Abraham and to his seed forever**"

(vs 51-55).

Think about that! Quite a thing! That's why Isaac was born to Sarah: Abraham was 100-years-old and Sarah was 90-years-old.

Again, everything related to the coming of the Messiah—Jesus Christ—in the flesh has impossible things that only God can do to make it happen.

Verse 56: "And Mary dwelt with her about three months, and returned to her house."

- What do you think they talked about?
- Do you think they sat there in that house for three months and just started at each other?

No! Of course not! They talked about this!

Elizabeth would talk about the angel that came to Zacharias, and how he came home and had to tell her: Look, we have to make this happen!' *You're an old man, what are you talking about?*

He has to write it down because he can't talk to his wife. They come together and at 70-years-old she becomes pregnant. She thought: I have a bad reputation among the community because I have never have a child.

But hear this: Mary who never had a man, and Joseph was willing to separate from her quietly… God had to send an angel to tell them that she is pregnant through the power of God, the Holy Spirit, **and the One born is going to be the Son of God: Emanuel!**

Imagine them talking back and forth. We don't have any of those conversations recorded for us. But I'm sure there was plenty of discussion, prayer, thanksgiving and taking care of each other; being careful with each other.

Think about what God entrusted these two women with! **The two most important births in the whole Bible!**

Let's see what Zacharias really knew, and see what happened:

Verse 57: "Now Elizabeth's time was fulfilled that she should give birth, and she bore a son. And her neighbors and kinfolk heard that *the* Lord had magnified His mercy toward her, and they rejoiced with her" (vs 57-58).

They didn't have phones like we have today, but think about that all during the nine months of her pregnancy the chatter and clatter that went on between all the priests and their wives.

Verse 59: "And it came to pass on the eighth day *that* they came to circumcise the little child; and they were calling him Zacharias, after the name of his father. Then his mother answered *and* said, 'No! But he shall be named John'" (vs 59-60).

Here you have all the relatives there for this circumcision party and they're arguing about what they're going to call him, and Zacharias couldn't yet speak.

Verse 61: "And they said to her, '*There* is no one among your kinfolk who is called by this name.' Then they made signs to his father *as to* what he desired him to be named. And after signaling for a writing tablet…" (vs 61-63).

Think about this! They had writing tablets, and that's how we got all of what we have here.

"…'John is his name.' And they were all amazed. Then his mouth was immediately opened, and his tongue *was loosed*; and he spoke, praising God. And fear came upon all those who dwelt around them; and in the entire hill country of Judea, all these things were being talked about. And all who heard *these things* laid *them* up in their hearts, saying, 'What then will this little child be?' And *the* hand of *the* Lord was with him" (vs 63-66).

Notice how God inspired him to speak, and all about the one who would be John the Baptist.

Verse 67: "And Zacharias his father was filled with *the* Holy Spirit, and prophesied, saying, 'Blessed be *the* Lord, the God of Israel, because He has visited and has worked redemption for His people, and has raised up a horn of salvation for us in the house of His servant David; exactly as He spoke by *the* mouth of His Holy prophets since the world began'" (vs 67-70). *That goes right back to Gen. 3:15!*

Verse 71: "**Salvation from our enemies**…" Who is the greatest enemy of us? *Satan the devil! Salvation from him!*

"…and from *the* hand of all those who hate us; to fulfill *the promise of* mercy *made* to our fathers, and to remember His Holy covenant, *the* oath that He swore to **Abraham our father**…" (vs 71-73).

Elizabeth, Mary and Zacharias talked about Abraham, *our father*. They must have understood in type the things that Abraham went through, and how it is being fulfilled in their lives. Talk about an amazing thing! Here we are over 1900 years past that, and we can read the very things that they thought and wrote.

Verse 75: "*Walking* in Holiness and righteousness before Him all the days of our lives. And you, little child, shall be called *the* prophet of *the* Highest; **for you shall go before *the* face of *the* Lord, to prepare His ways**" (vs 75-76). *Just like the prophecies said!*

Verse 77: "To give *the* knowledge of salvation to His people by *the* remission of their sins, through *the* deep inner compassions of our God; in which *the* dayspring from on high has visited us, to shine upon those who are sitting in darkness and in *the* shadow of death, to direct our feet into *the* way of peace" (vs 77-79).

Verse 80: "And the little child grew and was strengthened in spirit; and he was in the wilderness until *the* day of his appearing to Israel."

We're going to see that Elizabeth and Mary kept these things in their hearts! I'm sure that God gave them almost perfect remembrance of everything that went on.

This is an amazing thing, and now, as we face the world season of Christmas coming up, we know the Truth of what the Bible tells us in great detail.

Scriptural References:

1) Matthew 10:26-27
2) Matthew 24:10-12, 14

3) 2 Peter 1:15-21
4) 2-Timothy 3:16-17
5) Acts 1:1
6) Luke 1:1-5
7) 1-Chronicles 24:7-10
8) Luke 1:6-17
9) Malachi 3:1
10) Luke 1:18-20. 23-35
11) Hebrews 10:4-9, 5
12) Daniel 10:21
13) Hebrews 10:7-9, 5
14) Philippians 2:5-6
15) John 1:1
16) Philippians 2:7-8
17) Luke 1:35-73, 75-80

Scriptures referenced, not quoted:

- Acts 6
- Revelation 4:5
- John 2
- Isaiah 9:6
- Genesis 3:15
- Deuteronomy 18

Also referenced:

Books:
- *Judaism: Revelation of Moses or Religion of Men* by Philip Neal
- *A Harmony of the Gospels* by Fred R. Coulter

- *From a Speck of Dust to a Son of God: Why Were You Born?* by Fred R. Coulter

Appendix E: <u>When Was Jesus Born?</u> (*The Holy Bible in Its Original Order*)

Booklet: *Prophecies of Jesus Christ in the Old Testament* by James Meister

Church at Home: *Was Peter Ever in Rome?*

FRC:bo
Transcribed: 10/21/20

CHAPTER FORTY-SEVEN

The Birth of Jesus Christ II
The first person words of Mary and Elizabeth
Fred R. Coulter

Greetings, everyone! Welcome to Sabbath services!

We're going to cover and finish the birth of Christ today. The book of Acts is a very interesting book and we're going to answer: How did Luke get some of the words that we read in Luke 1 & 2 that are the direct words of Elizabeth and Mary.

Acts 1:1: "The first account I indeed have written, O Theophilus, concerning all things that Jesus began both to do and to teach, until the day in which He was taken up, after giving command by *the* Holy Spirit to the apostles whom He had chosen" (vs 1-2).

When you read the book of Acts we find that all of the chapters go along and they are a narration about what other people did. You find that in Acts 1 & 2 and all the way through different narrations.

When did Luke come on the scene and join Paul? *That's key!* We find these things in Acts 6-10; all of these are narrations that Paul was not involved in. How do we find where Paul identifies that he's writing this, including himself?

Acts 16 is when Paul had to vision to go over to Macedonia, and it appears that Luke was with him because he's writing it. How would you identify that Luke was there? When you're writing something, you say, 'I'—first person singular. Here's where we first come in and find that Luke must have been with him.

Acts 16:10: "And after he had seen the vision, **we**…"—*first person plural*; *he's including himself!*

When you write a letter to someone to explain to someone about something, and you are with people and did an event, and you're trying to tell someone else, you would say, 'We went to town…' You don't say, 'I went to town.' You don't say, in the case of Paul, 'Paul went to Macedonia.' He writes:

"…**we** immediately sought to go into Macedonia…" (v 10).

Verse 12: "And from there **we** *went* to Philippi…" *So, Paul is having this narration written by Luke!*

Acts 20—this becomes interesting, because from here on Paul and the group with him are going on up to Jerusalem.

Acts 20:13: "Then we went on ahead to the ship *and* sailed to Assos, there intending to take in Paul; for he had so appointed, since he himself was going on foot. And after he met with **us**… [the other ones listed up at the beginning of the chapter at who were at Assos] …*and* **we** took him in, **we** came to Mitylene" (vs 13-14).

All the way through the journey, it's all *we,* plus we have some very direct comments written down about what Paul said and the things that happened.

Let's understand what happened. Paul went to Jerusalem and he gave a witness to the Jews. He was almost killed by them, but saved by a Roman Centurion and taken up into Fort Antonia for his own protection.

Then after speaking to the Sanhedrin, Paul went back to Fort Antonia. There were men plotting to kill Paul if he would come to another meeting. The son of Paul's sister heard it and came and told Paul. Then it was told to the Centurion and he told it to the Chief Captain. Then they took Paul down, by armed guard, to Caesarea. That was in 58 A.D.

- How long was Paul in Caesarea?
- Where was Luke?
- How did Luke understand these things?

We'll look at two sources on how to do it!

Acts 24:27: "But at the end of two years, Felix was succeeded *as governor* by Porcius Festus; and, desiring to gain favor for himself with the Jews, Felix left Paul bound. "

Acts 25:1: "Now, three days after Festus arrived in the province, he went to Jerusalem from Caesarea."

He went up there to see what the problem

was that happened two years earlier, and it ended up that he could have been let free had he not appealed to Caesar.

During this two-year period, what was Luke doing? *He was probably writing the book of Acts and the Gospel of Luke!* Some of those things that he has in the first two chapters of Luke, he had to be talking to Mary, especially.

Acts 27:1: "Now, when it was decided that **we**…" *Notice again that Luke was with Paul!*

These verses show that Luke was with Paul all during the time that Paul was under house arrest in Caesarea.

"…should sail to Italy, they delivered up Paul and certain other prisoners to a centurion named Julius, *who was* of the band of Augustus. And after boarding a ship of Adramyttium that was about to pass by the coasts of Asia, **we** set sail…" (vs 1-2). *So, Luke went with Paul to Rome!*

That's when Luke probably got all the information for his Gospel, and for the book of Acts up to the point that he was with Paul.

Now let's look at something else that is interesting. In Acts 6 is the account where they have the seven men who were ordained to serve on the tables.

Acts 6:1: "Now, in those days, when the number of the disciples was multiplied, there arose a complaint by the Greeks against the Hebrews, because their widows were neglected in the daily ministration. And after calling the multitude of disciples to *them*, the twelve said, 'It is not proper *for* us to leave the Word of God in order to wait on tables. Therefore, brethren, search out from among yourselves seven men of good repute, full of *the* Holy Spirit and wisdom, **whom we may appoint over this business**; but **we** will give ourselves continually to prayer and **the ministry of the Word**'" (vs 1-4).

What is "…the ministry of the Word"? *That had to be that they were writing the accounts of the Gospel!*

- What did they have there?
- What did the apostles already have accumulated and written and was there wherever their main place was in Jerusalem?
- *We don't know!*

Luke 1—remember that Elizabeth was old and we don't know how old Mary was; she may have been 18 or 19. We don't know how old Joseph was, and we don't know when he died. Here's what we know:

In the sixth month of Elizabeth's pregnancy, Mary went to visit her and she stayed for three months. As I mentioned in part one, what do you suppose they talked about? *The very thing that was happening to both of them!*

We have the first person words of Mary and Elizabeth; that's quite an astounding thing! So, let's go over that again, and we will find one thread that they understood. When they spoke, they were inspired of the Holy Spirit. But you can't speak inspired things of the Holy Spirit unless you already have something in your own mind to begin with.

Luke 1:41—*when Mary came to Elizabeth's house*: "Now it came to pass *that* when Elizabeth heard Mary's greeting, the babe leaped in her womb…"

Only Elizabeth knew that, so therefore, she had to write it down. She had to tell someone, but she hid herself for six months. She wasn't talking to anyone but Zacharias, and he couldn't talk back because he was muted because he didn't believe Gabriel the angel.

I don't know how that would work, but we know that Zacharias asked for a writing tablet, so he probably wrote the things down. This tells you that if there's a writing tablet and you write things down, don't you suppose that Mary and Elizabeth also wrote these things down, so that we have their exact words. *That's quite a thing to think about!*

"…and Elizabeth was filled with *the* Holy Spirit, and she cried out with a loud voice and said, 'Blessed *are* you among women, and blessed *is* the fruit of your womb'" (vs 41-42).

How did Elizabeth know that Mary was pregnant? *It just happened and Mary went over to see Elizabeth!* Of course, Mary knew at the instant that it occurred. But normally a woman doesn't know she's pregnant until a little over a month later. That's the normal sequence of time. How did Elizabeth know that Mary was pregnant? ***Had to be revealed by the Holy Spirit!***

Verse 43: "But why is this *happening* to me, **that the mother of my Lord** should come to me?"

That had to be inspired by God! If you all of a sudden had an inspiration that was really something, what would you do to remember it? *You'd write it down!* It says of Mary that she kept these things in her heart, but that doesn't mean that she didn't write them down, because we get the ***exact words!***

Verse 44: "For behold, as soon as the sound of your greeting reached my ears, the babe in my womb leaped in exultation. And blessed *is* she who has believed, for there shall be a fulfillment of the things spoken to her from *the* Lord" (vs 44-45).

Notice what Mary says, this is quite a thing: v 46: "Then Mary said, 'My soul magnifies the Lord, and my spirit has exulted in **God my Savior**'" (vs 46-47).

* "...**the mother of my Lord**..." (v 43
* "...**God my Savior**" (v 47)

Verse 48: "For He has looked upon the humble estate of His handmaid; for behold, from this time forward **all generations shall count me blessed**." *That had to be inspired from God, but so important that it had to be written down!*

How would we get it if it wasn't written down? We can say that if it wasn't written down right away—which I suppose that it was—when Luke was there in Caesarea he could travel to Jerusalem back and forth—a little over a day's journey—and he could talk to Mary.

Sidebar on the age of Mary: *IF* she was 18 when Jesus was born, and Jesus died at 33-1/2-years-old, that means by 30A.D. Mary was 51-1/2-years-old.

28 years later—because it was in 58A.D. Paul was arrested and put in prison in Caesarea. Luke, we saw, was with him. By 28 years Mary was 79-1/2 and the two years that they were in Caesarea would make her 81-1/2.

If Luke—which he probably did—went up to where all the apostles kept all their writings, and you know they would keep them being good record-keepers, Mary was still living. The only other way Luke could have gotten these words would be he talked directly to Mary and she remembered every word at 80-years-old. That would be over 50 years.

It shows that Mary had knowledge, plus inspiration!

Verse 48—Mary says: "For He has looked upon the humble estate of His handmaid; for behold, from this time forward all **generations shall count me blessed**"

That's quite a statement! ***That had to be by inspiration of God for her to speak that.***

Verse 49: "Because the Mighty One has done great things to me, and Holy *is* His name... [that's quite a thing that was done] ...and His mercy *is* toward those who fear Him, from generation to generation" (vs 49-50).

In this inspiration, she was given some knowledge that this would go on down in time!

Verse 51: "He has worked strength with His arm; He has scattered *the* haughty in *the* imagination of their hearts. He has put down rulers from thrones, and has exalted *the* lowly" (vs 51-52).

That's exactly what God has continually doing. That applies to us! We are *the lowly and weak* of the world. It tells us that we have *little strength, but we have faith in God!* We know that **we are the ones who are going to be sons and daughters of God and rule with Christ!**

That's quite a thing; think about that! We're 2,000 years removed from this; this is fantastic information.

Verse 53: "He has filled *the* hungry with good things, and *the* rich He has sent away empty."

Did He not do that with the rich man? The rich man came to Jesus and said, 'What must I do to inherit eternal life?' He went away and still had his goods, but he was empty, because he didn't receive anything from Christ, because he wasn't willing to sell and give to the poor.

Verse 54: "He has helped His servant Israel, in remembering *His* mercy, exactly as He spoke to our fathers, to Abraham and to his seed forever" (vs 54-55).

Both of the women understood that they were part of the ongoing promise that God gave to Abraham!

Verse 56: "And Mary dwelt with her about three months, and returned to her house."

Now let's go to the chronologies. This is why we have all of this in the Bible, so that we can turn to and understand things and it's *written down*. What we are going to see is something very interesting, indeed!

Appendix E (*The Holy Bible in Its Original Order, A Faithful Version*): **When Was Jesus Christ Born?**

We have all the details, all the historical facts, and it's more than just the Calculated Hebrew Calendar. There were signs in heaven and we will see later who followed the star. God made it known!

Notice that a rare thing happened in the year of the birth of John the Baptist and Jesus, and it's the eclipse.

7 & 6 BC—no eclipses
5 BC—Total eclipse, March 23, 8:30 PM

In Jerusalem; that's close to when John the Baptist was born!

5 BC—Total eclipse, September 15, 10:30 PM

showing that Jesus was born in the fall!

Then we go through and see other historical things Read the Appendices at **afaithfulversion.org**

With the Calculated Hebrew Calendar, you can go backward and forward. But the way that God revealed it after the Flood, He did not reveal the year that creation took place. *He left that a mystery!*

Today, too many people are interested in the summary of things. They don't like to get into the details, *but the details*—if you know anything about God, law and history—*matter.*

Even if you go to court because you didn't understand a contract, and the judge asks you if you read the contract. 'Well, yes, I read part of it.' Did you read the part here that says you're no longer entitled to money? *No sir, I didn't!* Case closed! You lost, because you didn't read it.

So, the Calculated Hebrew Calendar with the course of Abijah, so we have day-by-day beginning in 6B.C. when the conception took place that the first day of the first month begins on a Sabbath.

Remember how the courses operated: they run from Sabbath to Sabbath, the course that is going off duty takes the first part of the Sabbath, and the course that's coming on duty takes the last half of the Sabbath. They work for a week and finish off by doing the first course of the next Sabbath.

This is in absolute perfection for the course of Abijah; he was course #8. You will notice, and you have to go down the left column first and then the right column. You will see every course. And what I did was make a probable two-week conception period for Elizabeth.

- How long is a perfect pregnancy? *40 weeks!*
- Isn't it interesting that the number of trial is *40!*
- What happens the 40th week? *The trial of birth!*

Then it comes down:

1st month thru 6th month of Elizabeth's pregnancy

What happened in the 6th month of Elizabeth's pregnancy? *The angel Gabriel came to the virgin Mary!* Then we do a dual:

the end of the 1st month for Mary
the end of the 7th month for Elizabeth

the end of the 2nd month for Mary
the end of the 8th month for Elizabeth

the end of the 3rd month for Mary
the end of the 9th month for Elizabeth—birth of John the Baptist

Total eclipse on March 23 at 8:30 PM

Then each month for Mary; then the Feast of Trumpets.

Notice that in 6B.C. the 1st day of the 1st month was on the Sabbath. When you come the month of Tishri we have:

Feast of Trumpets, Tishri 1
Probable day of Jesus' birth

- Does God do important things on His Holy Days? *Yes!*
- Do you not think that the first coming of Christ on the Feast of Trumpets would be appropriate?

That also would mean that since that was the Sabbath, the first day of the 7th month was on a Sabbath. What would happen on the next Sabbath?

Probable day of Jesus' circumcision

When the Feast of Tabernacles began we have:

Total eclipse on September 15, at 10:30 PM

There we have the whole works! Now, it's necessary to bring it on down to when Herod died, because Herod was still alive when Christ was born.

I hope that you were able to follow along with the charts in the Bible in the appendices. You can download them from **afaithfulversion.org** We tried to cover in the appendices all the things that would be necessary to give you the knowledge and understanding of faith.

The next appendices—Appendix F: **Chart Establishing the Year of Christ's Birth**—is eight contemporary historical timelines that prove that Jesus was born in 5B.C. and his crucifixion was in 30A.D. Catholics say 33A.D. and some Churches of God say 31A.D. *That is incorrect!* That's based on an error by Dr. Hoeh in order to please the so-called apostle (former WCG). The apostle had gotten it from the Seventh Day Adventists.

So, the things that are the most controversial in the Bible in trying to understand we put in the Commentaries and in the Appendices. So, you look at all those charts. If you want a complete Bible, go to **afaithfulversion.org** and find out how to get one and we'll get one to you right away.

Back to Luke 2, and what we're going to find is that in God—though He gave it exactly specifically when these events would take place, where Christ would be born—everything matches up when you have the right starting point.

Because the Catholics say that it was 33A.D., they chose that because in 33A.D the Passover in on a

Friday. *Hello!!!* You can't get three days and three nights from Friday until Sunday morning. He wasn't resurrected on Sunday morning. *He ascended!* Why? *Because that was the Wave Sheaf Offering Day,* and that's the first of the firstfruits and the harvest of the saints is likened to a harvest. So, *He's the First of the firstfruits!*

Notice how God made it happen where Jesus would be born and supposed to be born but didn't live there. That's quite amazing!

Luke 2:1: "Now, it happened in those days *that* a decree went out from Caesar Augustus that all the world should be registered."

Who do you suppose inspired that? *God did, so that this event would take place!*

Verse 2: "(This registration first occurred when Cyrenius was governor of Syria.) Then all went to be registered, each to his own city" (vs 2-3)—*where he was born!*

Joseph was of the line of David, and David was probably born in Bethlehem. But where were Joseph and Mary living? *Down in the area of Galilee!*

Verse 4: "And Joseph also went up from Galilee, out of *the* city *of* Nazareth, into Judea, to *the* City of David, which is called Bethlehem, because he was from *the* house and lineage of David to register himself along with Mary, who was betrothed to him as wife, *and* was great with child. And it came to pass *that* during the *time* they were there, the days were fulfilled for her to give birth" (vs 4-6).

It doesn't say that there was a midwife there. So, it was just Mary and Joseph. Of course, that would be a perfect birth without any complications.

Verse 7: "And she gave birth to her Son, the firstborn, and wrapped Him in swaddling clothes, and laid Him in a manger, because there was no place for them in the inn."

That shows that this had to be a Feast occasion, which backs up that Feast of Trumpets was the day of His birth.

Verse 8: "Now *there* were shepherds in the same country, who were dwelling in the fields and keeping watch over their flock by night"—*showing that it didn't happen in the winter!*

We have in *A Harmony of the Gospels* a picture of Jerusalem with snow in the first part of January. You don't keep sheep out in the fields in winter. This proves that it had to be before winter.

"…and keeping watch over their flock by night, and suddenly an angel of *the* Lord stood by them, and *the* glory of *the* Lord shined round about them; and they were seized *with* great fear" (vs 8-9).

Now notice the most important birth in the whole world happened in the least known circumstances possible. Mary and Joseph didn't live in Bethlehem, but they were there when Jesus was born, because it was prophesied that He would be born in Bethlehem. That means that there was no place there that they could say was their house. A little later they had a house.

Verse 10: "But the angel said to them, 'Do not be afraid; for behold, I am announcing to you glad tidings *of* great joy, which shall be to all people.'"

Notice that God didn't let this be known to the high priest or to Herod, but to two shepherd boys. *Jesus was to be our Chief Shepherd!* What was David doing when he was anointed King of Israel? *He was shepherding the sheep! Revealed to two shepherds!*

Verse 11: "'For today, in *the* city of David, a Savior was born to you, Who is Christ *the* Lord. Now, this *is* the sign for you: you shall find a Babe wrapped in swaddling clothes, lying in a manger.' And suddenly there was with the angel a multitude of *the* heavenly host praising God, and saying, 'Glory to God in *the* highest, and peace on earth among men *of* goodwill.' And it came to pass, as the angels were departing from them into heaven, that the shepherds said to one another, 'Let us go now as far as Bethlehem, and let us see this thing that has taken place, which the Lord has made known to us'" (vs 11-15).

The only ones to broadcast this abroad were two shepherd boys!

Verse 16: "And they made haste, *and* came and found both Mary and Joseph, and the Babe lying in the manger. Now after seeing *Him,* they made known everywhere the proclamation that they had been told concerning this little Child. And all those who heard were filled with wonder by the things that were spoken to them by the shepherds" (vs 16-18). *Didn't know a single thing about it!*

Verse 19: "**But Mary stored up all these sayings, pondering *them* in her heart**." *First they were all there, and later they were written down!*

Verse 20: "And the shepherds returned, glorifying and praising God for all *the* things that they had heard and seen, as it was said to them. Now, when eight days were fulfilled for circumcising the little Child, His name was called Jesus, which *He* was named by the angel before He was conceived in the womb" (vs 20-21).

How long were they in Bethlehem? *We'll get an estimate on this in a little bit!*

Verse 22: "And when the days were fulfilled

for their purification according to the Law of Moses, they brought Him to Jerusalem to present *Him* to the Lord."

How long was that? *40 days!* They were there just before Jesus was born, so we could say that maybe it was 45-50 days. So, they came to the temple.

Verse 23: "As it is written in *the* law of *the* Lord that every male opening the womb shall be called Holy to the Lord… [tie in Exo. 13] …And to offer a sacrifice according to that which is said in *the* law of *the* Lord: a pair of turtledoves or two young pigeons. And behold, there was a man in Jerusalem whose name *was* Simeon; and this man *was* righteous and reverent, waiting for *the* consolation of Israel; and *the* Holy Spirit was upon him" (vs 23-25).

Imagine all of this going on, what did Jesus tell the apostles after Jesus said to Nathaniel, 'Behold a man in whom there is no guile'? Nathaniel was taken aback and said, 'You're the Messiah!' Then Jesus said to him, 'What if you could see angels ascending and descending upon the Son of man?'

- What do we have? *Angels working out all of these things!*
- Who came to the shepherd boys? *Angels!*
- Who inspired Simeon to come to the temple? *The Holy Spirit and the angels!*
- To come when?
- How long would they be at the temple?

It wouldn't take long for that sacrifice to be given; probably a half hour or 45 minutes at the most. Here Simeon comes just at the right time!

Verse 26: "Now, it had been Divinely communicated to him by the Holy Spirit that he would not see death before he had seen the Christ of *the* Lord. And he came in the Spirit into the temple; and when the parents brought in the little Child Jesus, to do for Him according to the custom of the law, He also received Him into his arms…" (vs 26-28).

He came right up to Mary, took the little baby right into his arms. I don't know what Mary thought when that occurred, but the angels were there making all of this happen according to what God wanted and here's what Simeon said:

Verse 29: "'Now, You may let your servant depart in peace, O Master, according to Your Word; for my eyes have seen Your salvation… [a babe] …which You have prepared before *the* face of all peoples… [quite an inspiration with that] …a light for *the* revelation of *the* Gentiles and *the* glory of Your people Israel.' And Joseph and His mother wondered at the things that were being spoken

concerning Him" (vs 29-33). **Why is this happening?**

Verse 34: "Then Simeon blessed them, and said to Mary, His mother, 'Behold, this *Child* is set for *the* fall and rising up of many in Israel, and for a sign that shall be spoken against.'" **How far out does that stretch?**

The sacrifice of Christ goes all the way back in time, all through history up to His second coming, and then all through the Millennium and the Great White Throne Judgment. All of that has to come through Christ. So, it says, *all people!*

Verse 35: "(And You also, a sword shall go through your own soul) in order that *the* imaginations of many hearts may be revealed."

Here is this old, old man—I don't know what he look like—but he was holding the baby and being inspired to speak these words and saying that the sword is going to go through His side. That literally happened (John 19). That sword was a short spear and it came on Jesus' right side, straight in and probably pierced His heart so that He would die and all of His blood would be shed there on the ground.

Verse 36: "Now, there was Anna, a prophetess, *the* daughter of Phanuel, of *the* tribe of Asher; she was of a great age, having lived with a husband seven years from her virginity; and she *was* a widow of about eighty-four years… [she must have been way up in her 90s by this time] …who did not depart from the temple, serving day and night with fastings and supplications" (vs 36-37).

Notice the people involved. The angels had to move these people just at the right time when they were at the temple.

Verse 38: "And at the same time she came up, giving praise to the Lord; and *she* spoke concerning Him to all those in Jerusalem who were waiting for redemption. Now, when they had completed all things according to the Law of *the* Lord, they returned to Galilee, to their *own* city Nazareth" (vs 38-39).

Matthew brings out some very important things that needed to be added before they returned to Galilee.

Matthew 2:1: "Now, after Jesus had been born in Bethlehem of Judea, in *the* days of Herod the king, behold, Magi from *the* east arrived at Jerusalem."

We're not told how far east it was. The Greek word for *east* is 'anatole.' These Magi were from the tribes of Israel who were running Parthia at time. So, God revealed it to people far, far away. Not to Herod, not to the priests, not to people in general, *but just to special messengers!*

Verse 2: "Saying, 'Where is the One Who has been born King of the Jews? For we have seen His star in the east, and have come to worship Him.'" *This is a starling thing!* A King! That's a threat to Herod.

Verse 3: "But when Herod the king heard *this*, he was troubled, and all Jerusalem with him."

How could it be that these men come from the east with knowledge that none of us here have? How could that be?

Verse 4: "And after gathering together all the chief priests and scribes of the people, he inquired of them where the Christ should be born. Then they said to him, 'In Bethlehem of Judea, for thus it has been written by the prophet: "And you, Bethlehem, land of Judea, in no way are you least among the princes of Judea; for out of you shall come forth a Prince, Who shall shepherd My people Israel"'" (vs 4-6).

Remember that Herod was half Jew and half Edomite. Very interesting combination. That's why we have in the chart in Appendix E: <u>When Was Jesus Born?</u> We carry it on down to the death of Herod, because that becomes an important point in historical understanding about Jesus and so forth. It's important to understand that He died way before 33_{A.D.}

Verse 7: "Then Herod secretly called *for* the Magi *and* ascertained from them the *exact* time of the appearing of *the* star…. [it doesn't tell us exactly when that was] …And he sent them to Bethlehem, saying, 'Go and search diligently for the little Child; and when you have found *Him*, bring word back to me, so that I also may go and worship Him.'" (vs 7-8). **<u>Really? This murderous King Herod?</u>**

Verse 9: "And after hearing the king, they departed; and behold, the star that they had seen in the east went in front of them, until it came and stood over *the house* where the little Child was. And after seeing the star, they rejoiced *with* exceedingly great joy. And when they had come into the house, they found the little Child with Mary His mother…" (vs 9-11).

This time they were in a house. So, before they went back to Nazareth they were in a house. Let's see what happens here, because who is always after Jesus to kill Him? *Satan!* We see that right here. What did God do? *We'll see that!*

"…and they bowed down and worshiped Him; then they opened their treasures *and* presented their gifts to Him—gold and frankincense and myrrh. But being Divinely instructed in a dream not to go back to Herod, they returned to their own country by another way" (vs 11-12).

Sidebar: You may read something by another writer who says that 'there were 2500 troops that came with the Magi. *That is not true!* There* is no account of it here in the Bible.

If there were 2500 troops, it would have been well known to Herod when they left that the troops would go with them! This would automatically reveal where Jesus was.

So, for him to say that is an imagination that he wants to sort of 'puff up' the book. But there were no troops from Parthia.

Verse 13: "Now, after they had departed, behold, an angel of *the* Lord appeared to Joseph in a dream, saying, 'Arise and take the little Child and His mother, and escape into Egypt, and remain there until I shall tell you; for Herod is about to seek the little Child to destroy Him' And he arose **by night** and took the little Child and His mother, and went into Egypt" (vs 13-14).

It may have been a full moon so they would have enough light to see where they were going. Who was probably in bed sleeping? *Herod! A perfect time to get out of town!*

Verse 15: "And was there until the death of Herod; that it might be fulfilled, which was spoken by the Lord through the prophet, saying, 'Out of Egypt I have called My Son.'"

Don't you get the sense that all during this time there were angels guiding and directing things to take place? watching over and protecting Jesus? *Yes, of course!*

Verse 16: "Then Herod, seeing that he had been mocked by the Magi, was filled with rage; and he sent *and* put to death all the boys who *were* in Bethlehem and in the area all around, from two years old and under…"

That doesn't mean that Jesus stayed there for two years! But Herod wanted to make sure that he killed the One Who was to be the King of the Jews.

Verse 17: "Then was fulfilled that which was spoken by Jeremiah the prophet, saying, 'A voice was heard in Rama, lamentation and weeping and great mourning, Rachel weeping *for* her children; and she would not be comforted, because they were not'" (vs 17-18).

Notice that this another important thing, and here is where it ties in with they went to Galilee.

Verse 19: "Now, when Herod had died, behold, an angel of *the* Lord appeared to Joseph in Egypt in a dream."

Notice how involved the angels were all

through all of this:

- What did Jesus say when He was under arrest? *If I would ask My Father for 12 legions of angels, He would give them!*

That tells you that angels were active all during His ministry, as well.

- How do you think that all of those crowds were able to come?
- Who helped stir them up?
- Who helped send men around give a message where He was, so they could come?

Here's what the angel told them:

Verse 20: "Saying, 'Arise and take the little Child and His mother, and go into *the* land of Israel; for those who were seeking the life of the little Child have died.'"

That's why we have on that chart when Herod died. He died in February after Jesus was born. You have September to February, so they were in Egypt about four months.

Verse 21: "And he arose *and* took the little Child and His mother, and came into *the* land of Israel. But when he heard that Archelaus was reigning over Judea instead of Herod his father, he was afraid to go there; and after being Divinely instructed in a dream, he went into the parts of Galilee. And after arriving, he dwelt in a city called Nazareth; that it might be fulfilled, which was spoken by the prophets, 'He shall be called a Nazarean'" (vs 21-23). *All of that involved with Christ!*

Here's something that we don't have: we don't have much about Jesus growing up. There are some legends that when He was a teenager He may have gone with Joseph of Arimathea who may have been His uncle. We don't know, that's just speculation. But we know nothing about from the time He came to Nazareth until the time here in Luke 2 when they went up to Jerusalem when Jesus was 12-years-old.

After 12-years-old we have nothing until we come to the time of His baptism. All of this was to protect Him, to have Him in places where the officials wouldn't think of looking.

Luke 2:40: "And the little Child grew and became strong in spirit, being filled with wisdom; and *the* grace of God was upon Him. Now, His parents went to Jerusalem every year at the Feast of the Passover" (vs 40-41).

This is when they were calling Unleavened Bread *Passover,* because it says in John 2 that He was there during the days. How many days is

Passover? *One day!* So, they went up to the Feast.

Verse 42: "And when He was twelve years *old*, they went up to Jerusalem according to the custom of the Feast. But when they departed after completing the days… [8 days altogether: Passover is one day and 7 days of Unleavened Bread] …the Child Jesus remained behind in Jerusalem, and Joseph and His mother did not know *it*" (vs 42-43).

This shows that they trusted Jesus! They let Him do what He needs to do. But they didn't know that He was going to stay back.

Verse 44: "But supposing Him to be in the company… [because they had other relatives, etc.] …they went a day's journey, and looked for Him among the relatives and among the acquaintances. And when they did not find Him, they returned to Jerusalem, seeking Him" (vs 44-45).

Here they were saying, 'Where is Jesus?' and add that on top of everything else that they went through with the special circumstances concerning Jesus.

Verse 46: "Now, it came to pass *that* after three days they found Him in the temple sitting in *the* midst of the teachers, both hearing them and questioning them."

- How did Jesus know what He knew from an infant up until this time?

We know that in John 7, at the Feast of Tabernacles, that the 'religious' authorities said of Jesus, 'How did He get this knowledge never being schooled?' That means that He never attended any of their schools.

- How did Jesus learn?
- Who taught Him?

Isa. 50 is a very interesting Scripture, indeed! It also shows you the way that God hides things through having 'a little here and a little there' in different places so that you have to properly put it together.

Isaiah 50:4: "**The Lord GOD has given Me the tongue of the learned,** to know to help the weary *with* a word. **He awakens *Me* morning by morning, He awakens My ear to hear as one being taught**."

We know from John 12 and other places that Jesus spoke what His Father commanded Him to speak. So, Who taught Him from day one? *God the Father! Every morning!* That must have been something! I don't suppose that Mary and Joseph knew anything about this.

Verse 5: "The Lord GOD has opened My ear, and I was not rebellious, nor turned away backwards…. [the next verse jumps from His childhood to His trial and scourging] …I gave My back to the smiters, and My cheeks to them that plucked off the hair; I did not hide My face from shame and spitting" (vs 5-6).

So, it goes from how He was taught right to the end of His life! That's quite a thing. Don't you imagine that Jesus learned a lot by this time? Now you would have to say that Jesus, being the Son of God, had to be the smartest man ever in the world. Also, the most humble of any man in the world.

Luke 2:47—*He's sitting there questioning them and giving answers*: "And all those who were listening to Him were amazed at *His* understanding and His answers."

Just one verse! See how God ties things together in the Scriptures. Two verses in Isa. 50 and one verse here.

Verse 48: "But when they saw Him, they were astonished; and His mother said to Him, 'Son, why have you dealt with us in this manner? Look, Your father and I have been *very* distressed *while* searching for You.' And He said to them…" (vs 48-49).

He knew what He had to do at age 12; but He couldn't do it for another 18 years. Why? *Because He has a lot of other things He needed to learn, as well!*

"…'Why *is it* that you were looking for Me? Don't you realize that I must be about My Father's *business*?'" (v 49). *They didn't understand that!*

Verse 50: "But they did not understand the words that He spoke to them. Then He went down with them and came to Nazareth, and He was subject to them…. [all teenagers, listen up; Jesus was not rebellious (Isa. 50)] …**But His mother kept all these things in her heart**" (vs 50-51).

So, when Luke went up to Jerusalem—58-60 A.D.—he got all the information first hand and wrote it down. Here we have this great history of the two most important women on the face of the earth, going back or going forward! *And we have their very words, because God wanted us to know how important these events were!*

That's what it has to do with the birth of Jesus Christ.

Scriptural References:

1) Acts 1:1-2
2) Acts 16:10, 12
3) Acts 20:13-14
4) Acts 24:27
5) Acts 25:1
6) Acts 27:1-2
7) Acts 6:1-4
8) Luke 1:41-56
9) Luke 2:1-39
10) Matthew 2:1-23
11) Luke 2:40-46
12) Isaiah 50:4-6
13) Luke 2:47-51

Scriptures referenced, not quoted:

- Acts 2; 6-10
- Exodus 13
- John 19; 2; 7; 12

Also referenced:
From *The Holy Bible in Its Original Order, A Faithful Version*:
- Appendix E: **When Was Jesus Christ Born?**
- Appendix F: **Chart Establishing the Year of Christ's Birth**

Book: *A Harmony of the Gospels* by Fred R. Coulter

FRC:bo
Transcribed: 11/4/20
Reformatted: 12/2020

CHAPTER FORTY-EIGHT

The Real Meaning of the Feast of Trumpets
Seven seals, seven trumpets, seven plagues!
Fred R. Coulter

Greetings, everyone! Welcome to the Feast of Trumpets! *What a day this is!* This is really one of the most important Feast of Trumpets that we've had ever in the Churches of God, considering everything that's taking place.

Next Sabbath I'm going to have special message: *Leadership Oppression in the Churches of God!* Now is the time for ***repentance,*** and truth, love and brethren being counted worthy as to what they really are *as the children of God,* and *not pawns of the ministry!* <u>*God does not like it!*</u>

He's put His Spirit into every one of us, and we're all precious, every one of us, to God! We're all the children of God, *not the possessions of a ministry!* I covered some of that in the message: *What is the Government of God?* But I'm going to cover it again, because that's absolutely important!

Leviticus 23:23: "And the LORD spoke to Moses, saying, 'Speak to the children of Israel saying, **"In the seventh month, in the first *day* of the month,** you shall have a Sabbath, **a memorial of blowing of ram's horns, a Holy convocation**"'" (vs 23-24).

Ram's horns were always used when there was war! That pierces the ear! I remember one time we were in Houston, Texas, and we were meeting in this hotel and we had this room. Next to us was another group and they were blowing the ram's horn! It was just driving us absolutely nuts, so we had to go to the management and say, 'Please put us in another room down the hall.' *They did!* But when the ram's horn blows, you'd better pay attention.

We know that the world today is becoming more and more like what it was in the days of Noah before the Flood, exactly as Jesus said. What is that? *That the thought of every person was only evil continually!*

We have that emphasized by all of the hi-tech that we have. Think how much comes through the cable TV that you watch. Yes, you get the news, but think of everything else that you get. Look at the society around us!

We will see that God means business, *but He always gives a space of repentance!* Whatever else happens this next coming week as God looks at it, and God knows the heart and mind of those people who are going to be in that assembly in Washington, D.C., (for the national Day of Prayer and Repentance). They expect well over a million people, and it might even be two million, especially after the death of Ruth Bader Ginsberg.

Micah 1:2: "Hear, all you people! Hearken, O earth… [this means this is a huge thing] …and *all* its fullness. And let the Lord GOD be witness against you, *even* the LORD from His Holy Temple." *God is looking down on these events taking place!*

Why did Ruth Bader Ginsberg die the day before Trumpets, the beginning of a new year by the calendar, and the beginning of the time where the Jews looked at it as a time of repentance, which it is when you understand all the troubles and difficulties that are going on.

Verse 3: "For behold, the LORD *is* coming out of His place… [He will come!] …and will come down and tread on the high places of the earth. And the mountains shall melt under Him, and the valleys shall split open, as wax before the fire, and as waters that are poured down a steep place. All this *is* for the transgression of Jacob, and for the sins of the house of Israel…." (vs 3-5).

Go back and read the blessings and cursing in Deut. 28. everybody loves the first 15 verses, all the blessings, and then you start reading all the other verses. I tell you, it get depressing! Have you ever read it? *This kind of sickness and that kind of sickness! All kind of troubles going on!*

People ask why does God do all of this? *If there's no judgment against evil, you have lawlessness!*

- Who is the author of lawlessness? *Satan the devil!*
- Who is the author of law? *God!*

Now they're learning that you have to have law and order; you can't have peace without law and order. *So, judgment is there!*

Deuteronomy 28:41: "You shall beget sons and daughters, but you shall not enjoy them… [Isn't that's what it is today? *Think about it!*] …**for they <u>shall go into captivity.</u>**"

- How are you going to correct all of those

today the way that they are?

- What are you going to do with ANTIFA?
- What are you going to do with Black Lives Matter?
- What are you going to do with dedicated communists who want to take down the nation?

First there better be a large repentance to God so that He will pull His hand back for a time!

Verse 43: "The stranger *dwelling* among you shall get up above you very high... [that is taking place right at this time, the other half is coming] ...and you shall come down very low."

The only man between that and the next verse is Donald Trump! Don't say, 'There goes Fred Coulter getting into politics again.'

- Do you live in the nation or not?
- Do they profess to be God's people or not?
- Is God interested in them? *Yes!*
- Is God interested in the government? *Yes!*
- Is God interested in the Supreme Court? *Yes!*

He wants to see if the people really want law and order, peace and really believe in Him the best that they can under the circumstances they have *or not!*

But here's what's going to happen: "...**and you shall come down very low**" (v 43). *That's what Black Lives Matter wants to do!*

Verse 44: "He shall loan to you, and you shall not loan to him. He shall be the head, and you shall be the tail."

Don't think because nothing has happened because of all the trillions of dollars in debt that have that judgment on that is not going to come! *It will!* When it does we're all going to be poverty stricken, no way around it!

- How much do they come back to God?
- How much do they really go against all of the abortions and killing of the unborn?

We'll have to see! We'll know more about that after next Sabbath!

Let's go through the story and some of the things in Revelation. But as we finished off in Deut. 28, that the children of Israel will go into captivity, and there are many prophecies in the Old Testament to show that, and that they will come out of it.

Hosea gives us a timeline into the three and a half years. The three and a half years of the Tribulation is going to start when the covenant is broken (Dan. 9) and the man of sin goes into the temple saying that he is God, and the Tribulation begins. *Israel will be the first to go into captivity!*

Hosea 5:14—*God speaking*: "For I *will be* to Ephraim as a lion, and as a strong lion to the house of Judah. I, *even* I, will tear and go away. I will take away, and none shall rescue him.... [this is when they go into captivity] ...I will go; I will return to My place until they confess their guilt and seek My face... [we will see where that happens in Rev. 7 a little later] ...in their affliction they will seek Me earnestly" (vs 14-15).

Here's what they will do when seeking God, because by that time they will know and with all the different things going on they will understand that God is involved in it.

Hosea 6:1: "Come and let us return to the LORD, for He has torn, and He will heal us; He has smitten, and He will bind us up. **After two days He will revive us**..." (vs 1-2).

- How long is a day in prophecy? *A year, so this is 2 years!*
- How long is the Tribulation? *3-1/2 years!*
- How much is left? *1-1/2 years!*

"...in **the third day**... [the beginning of the 3rd year] ...He will raise us up, and we shall live in His sight" (v 2).

We will see where that happens in Rev. 7, but first let's understand what is exactly going to happen to the rest of the world when the Tribulation begins, and then God begins to deal with them directly, and why does it come?

Sidebar: Read all of Jer. 25, and think about this: God told Jeremiah to take this cup and you make all these nations drink of it. This was a prophecy for the end-time because Jeremiah never got out of the Holy Land until they went down into Egypt after the children of Judah went into captivity to Babylon. Then we know from history, because he had the daughter's of Judah, the king's daughters, that he went to Ireland. That's how the breach between Perez and Zarah was healed and why the throne of David is in London today.

Jeremiah 25:26—*here's what God told him*: "And all the kings of the north, far and near, one with another, and **all the kingdoms of the world**..."

Jeremiah never got there; this was a prophecy for our day. This is what's going to happen. Is it easier for all the kingdoms of the world today? *Yes, indeed!*

"...which *are* on the face of the earth... [think about that statement; that's quite a sweeping thing] ...and the king of Sheshach... [the Beast Power to come (Rev. 13)] ...shall drink after them. 'Therefore, you shall say to them, "Thus says the LORD of hosts, the God of Israel, 'Drink and be drunk, and vomit, and fall, and rise no more because of the sword, which I will send among you'" (vs 26-27).

You're looking at the witness of the two witnesses. This is what God is going to tell them.

Verse 28: "'And it shall come to pass if they refuse to take the cup at your hand to drink, then you shall say to them, "Thus says the LORD of hosts, 'You shall certainly drink. For, lo, I begin to bring evil on the city, which is called by My name… [tie in Hos. 5 & 6] …and shall you go unpunished? You shall not go unpunished. For I will call for a sword on all the inhabitants of the earth,' says the LORD of hosts" (vs 28-29).

Remember one important thing about fulfillment of prophecy: *God never fulfills to the minimum; He always fulfills to the maximum!* Not just some little thing done in a corner. This is worldwide! I want you think about this as we go through all of the events picturing the Feast of Trumpets. What condition the world is going to be in when God says, 'Go rule!'

Verse 30: "'And prophesy against them all these words, and say to them, "The LORD shall roar from on high, and utter His voice from His Holy habitation. He shall mightily roar over His dwelling place…. [Jerusalem] …He shall give a shout, like those who tread out *grapes*, **against all the people of the earth**…. [see how all inclusive that is] …A noise shall come to the ends of the earth; for the LORD has a controversy with the nations; He will plead with all flesh. He will give those *who are* wicked to the sword,'" says the LORD" (vs 30-31). *We'll see how that is fulfilled in Rev. 8-9 & 15!*

Verse 32: "Thus says the LORD of hosts, 'Behold, evil shall go forth from nation to nation, and a great whirlwind shall be stirred up from the farthest corners of the earth. And the slain of the LORD shall be at that day from *one* end of the earth even to the *other* end of the earth; they shall not be mourned, nor gathered, nor buried. They shall be *as* dung on the ground. **Howl, you shepherds**…'" (vs 32-34).

Ultimately, who are the first ones in line of responsibility when these things take place? *The religious and political leaders!* Shepherds include both of those!

"…and cry; and wallow yourselves in the ashes, you lords of the flock! For the days of your slaughter and of your scatterings are fulfilled; and you shall fall like a choice vessel" (v 34).

The meaning of the Feast of Trumpets is found in many places in the Bible, because all of these prophecies have to be put together.

Isaiah 24:1: "Behold, the LORD makes the earth empty and makes it waste, and turns it upside down, and scatters its inhabitants."

I don't know if He's going to turn the whole world or whether the magnetic poles are going to reverse. Magnetic poles have been known to reverse, so if they reverse that's the same thing as turning it upside down.

Verse 2: "And as *it is* with the people, so it shall be with the priest; as with the slave, so with the master; as with the handmaid, so it is with her mistress; as with the buyer, so with the seller; as with the lender, so with the borrower; as with the creditor, so with the debtor."

What's going to have to happen when the Millennium begins? First thing financially? *All debt is wiped out! No debt! Got to start clean!*

Verse 3: "The earth shall be completely laid waste, and utterly stripped; for the LORD has spoken this word."

That's not done all at once! We will see that there are several stages in Revelation that lays all of this out.

Verse 4: "The earth mourns *and* languishes; the world withers *and* languishes; the proud people of the earth wither. And the earth is defiled under its people; **because they have transgressed the laws, changed the ordinance, and have broken the everlasting covenant**" (vs 4-5). *Gone against God in everything that they have done!*

Verse 6: "Therefore, the curse has devoured the earth, and they who dwell in it are desolate; therefore, the people of the earth are burned, and few men are left."

Let's see how this starts. This is why at the Feast of Trumpets at the Temple they had the trumpets blown all day long, because this is a vast war that encompasses the whole world. *It's going to be the greatest catastrophe to ever hit the earth since the Flood!*

We know in Rev. 5 that Jesus Christ was the One Who was selected to open the seals. This tells us that nothing of these events of the magnitude that are in the Bible are going to happen or take place unless God says *now!* It's not going to come from any man on earth saying to God, 'God, do it!' *NO!* God is going to say, *'Now!'*

Opening of the Seven Seals

Revelation 6:1: "And I looked when the Lamb opened **one of the seals**; and I heard one of the four living creatures say, like the sound of thunder, 'Come and see.' And I looked, and behold, *there was* a white horse; and the one who was sitting on it had a bow, and a crown was given to him; and he went out conquering, and to conquer" (vs 1-2). *This is **not** Christ!*

Some churches believe that this is Christ, just because Rev. 19 says that Jesus is going to be on a white horse. This is *the false christ,* the religious leader bringing all the religions together! I've often thought that maybe the first seal has been opened, because of the way the Catholics are bringing all religions together, I don't know, but something big happened when Pope Paul XXIII had the ecumenical meetings saying that they were going to reach out to all the religions of the world. Well, it doesn't happen like 'everybody come and kiss and make up.' It takes time, so this may have happened.

The next one is going to be when the 'man of sin, the son of perdition' goes into the Holy Place and says that he's 'God.' That's when the Tribulation begins, and it begins with a great war!

Verse 3: "And when He opened the **second seal,** I heard the second living creature say, 'Come and see.' And another horse went out *that was* red; and *power* was given to the one sitting on it to take peace from the earth…"

What precedes all of this? *A time of peace!* People will think: *Look, we've got peace for the first time! This is really great!*

"…and *to cause* them to kill one another; and a great sword was given to him. And when He opened the **third seal**…" (vs 4-5).

Notice that seals 2-5 all happen quite quickly. We will see that that is the two-year period that we understood from Hosea.

"…and *to cause* them to kill one another; and a great sword was given to him. And when He opened the **third seal**…" (vs 4-5).

- What happens when there is war?
- Especially in today's world?
- What happens?

Everything comes to a screeching halt! You run out of food because you can't buy it in the stores and you're not growing any yourself. *Starvation and famine instantly!*

All you have to do is look at the Middle East and see what happens when they have wars, and magnify that many times more that will cover the whole world.

"…I heard the third living creature say, 'Come and see.' And I looked, and behold, *there was* a black horse; and the one sitting on it had a balance in his hand. And I heard a voice in *the* midst of the four living creatures say, 'A measure of wheat for a silver coin, and three measures of barley for a

silver coin: and *see that* you do not damage the oil and the wine.'…. [very precious and scarce] …And when He opened the **fourth seal,** I heard *the* voice of the fourth living creature say, 'Come and see.' And I looked, and behold, *there was* a pale horse…" (vs 5-8).

What happens when war is extended? *That's the pale horse!*

"…and the name of the one sitting on it *was* Death, and the grave followed him; and authority was given to them over *one-*fourth of the earth…" (v 8).

We don't know what one-fourth of the earth that may be! But that may very well may be against Israel going into captivity!

"…to kill with *the* sword and with famine and with death, and by the beasts of the earth. And when He opened the **fifth seal,** I saw under the altar the souls of those who had been slain for the Word of God, and for the testimony that they held" (vs 8-9).

That's everybody down through history who has been martyred! That doesn't mean that the soul is immortal, but we find in Heb. 12 that right at the altar of God in heaven are the 'spirits of just men and women made perfect.' When you die the spirit goes back to God, and He stores it right there. Then that goes into a spirit body.

Because He has that, we will see a little later on that He's got to have one for all of those who did not commit the unpardonable sin. How is God going to rescue them if He doesn't have the spirit of them. We will see that on the eighth day (Last Great Day). Then He's got to have another compartment for all of those who have committed the unpardonable sin so they can be resurrected and cast into the Lake of Fire. Here's what they do; they always look for someone to blame.

- Who did Hitler blame in WWII? *The Jews!*
- Who are they going to blame now? *Those who are Christians!*

Verse 10: "And they cried out with a loud voice, saying, 'How long, O Lord, Holy and true, do You not judge and avenge our blood on those who dwell on the earth?' And white robes were given to each of them; and they were told that they should rest a short time, yet, until *it* be fulfilled *that* both their fellow servants and their brethren also would be killed, just as they had been. And when He opened the **sixth seal**…" (vs 10-12).

Look at what this is; this is going to be startling! I want you to remember the two years of Hosea 6, and in the third year God begins to raise them up. It looks like it fits right here, because look at what is going to happen. One of the greatest witnesses! Always remember that *God gives a witness before He does anything!* So, here is one of the greatest witnesses given to the world:

Verse 12: "And when He opened the **sixth seal,** I looked, and behold, there was a great earthquake; and the sun became black as *the* hair *of* sackcloth, and the moon became as blood; and the stars of heaven fell to the earth, as a fig tree casts its untimely figs when it is shaken by a mighty wind" (vs 12-13).

Think about what people are going to be believing on the earth when they see all of this! This is startling!

Verse 14: "Then *the* heaven departed like a scroll that is being rolled up…"

When you have a scroll out from the middle out, and because of the tension of it being wound up, when you let go it's like a window blind. What's going to happen is that the heavens are going to roll back like a scroll. What are they going to see?

"…and every mountain and island was moved out of its place. And the kings of the earth, and the great men, and the rich men, and the chief captains, and the powerful men, and every bondman, and every free *man* hid themselves in the caves and in the rocks of the mountains" (vs 14-15).

They're going to believe that this is the return of Christ, at first. Later we will see that Satan convinces them that it's not.

Verse 16: "And they said to the mountains and to the rocks, 'Fall on us, and hide us from *the* face of Him Who sits on the Throne, and from the wrath of the Lamb, because the great day of His wrath has come, and who has the power to stand?'" (vs 16-17).

Let's see what that is going to be. The rolling back of the scrolls like that is an awesome thing, indeed!

Matthew 24:29: "But immediately *after* the tribulation of those days… [When does the Tribulation end against Israel? *After two years!*] …the sun shall be darkened… [tie in Rev. 6] …and the moon shall not give her light, and the stars shall fall from heaven, and the powers of the heavens shall be shaken."

Do you think the rolling back of the heavens like a scroll, that shakes the heavens? *Yes, indeed!* Notice what happens when that occurs:

Verse 30: "And then shall appear **the sign of the Son of man in heaven**; and then shall all the tribes of the earth mourn, and they shall see the Son of man coming upon the clouds of heaven with power and great glory."

That verse tells you the full extent of Christ's return. But it comes in two steps:

1. the sign of the Son of man; the heavens being rolled back as a scroll

What will they see? *He carries it out and carries it to the resurrection!* Verse 27 tells you what that will be, the sign of the Son of man"

2. a second sun

Verse 27: "For as **the light of day**… [the sun] …which comes forth from *the* east and shines as far as *the* west, so also shall the coming of the Son of man be."

So, when the heavens are rolled back they look up there and there's *another sun!* How close to the earth it is, we don't know! But this is a great witness that Christ is going to come! After a while they get used to it because it doesn't come any further. That's when, I believe, that they will say that 'this is not Christ coming.'

When that occurs, what's the next thing to happen in Revelation? This is after two years, and in the third year God raises up Israel. That begins with the 144,000 (Rev. 7). Where are they from? *12,000 from each of the 12 tribes of Israel!* Then a great innumerable multitude. Let's give a little timeframe to this:

- Could this be on Pentecost—and think about the harvest—that the 144,000 and the great innumerable multitude are saved?
- Wouldn't that be a magnification of what happened at the temple in 30 A.D. when the Holy Spirit was given?

Since there are no ministers to baptize them, what does God do? *He sends an angel to seal them in their foreheads!* That means that they're converted! These, if you read the book of Matthew about the parable of the workers in the vineyard, are the ones who were hired at the 11th hour, right at the end, and they're converted for just one year.

What's the rest of the world doing from Pentecost to Trumpets? *They cleaning up from the earthquakes, all the mess because of what happened!* That's a period of about four months. At that time they're more interested in their own power on the earth, so we come to Rev. 8 and let's see what happens there.

Here begins the only place in the Bible where there are trumpets counted one after the other, from the first to the last, and the last is the seventh trump.

Revelation 8:1: "Now, when He opened the **seventh seal**, *there* was silence in heaven *for* about a half hour. Then I saw the seven angels who stand before God, and seven trumpets were given to them. And another angel, who had a golden censer, came and stood at the altar; and much incense was given to him, so that he might offer *it* with the prayers of all the saints on the golden altar that *was* before the Throne" (vs 1-3).

Who are all the saints that are praying? *There are only three groups!*

1. the small group in a place of safety
2. the 144,000
3. the great innumerable multitude

They're alive and praying! So, their prayers went up!

Verse 4: "And the smoke of the incense went up before God from *the* hand of the angel, ascending with the prayers of the saints. And the angel took the censer, and filled it with fire from the altar, and cast *it* into the earth; and there were voices, and thunders, and lightnings, and an earthquake" (vs 4-5). *All of this is in preparation for the blowing of the trumpets!*

Seven Last Trumpets

Verse 6: "Then the **seven angels who had the seven trumpets** prepared themselves to sound *their* trumpets."

Then they went out 1, 2, 3, 4 quite rapidly in succession! You can read it and look at all the devastation that takes place. Now it gets more intense. Satan is there knowing that he's got to get things all organized. Here is the King of the North who gets the warning of the north and the east. So, we find that there's a super-secret weapon like a scorpion.

- Rev. 6 we have men against men in battles
- Rev. 8 we have men and demons against angels and different armies

Revelation 9:1: "And the fifth angel sounded *his* trumpet; and I saw a star… [angel] …*that* had fallen from heaven to the earth, and there was given to him the key to the bottomless abyss. And he opened the bottomless abyss; and there went up smoke from the pit, like *the* smoke of a great furnace; and the sun and the air were darkened by the smoke from the pit. Then **locusts** came onto the earth from the smoke…" (vs 1-3). *These are demons being released out of the abyss!*

"…and power was given to them, as the scorpions of the earth have power. And it was said to them that they should not damage the grass of the earth, or any green thing, or any tree…" (vs 3-4).

You read before that all the grass was burned up! What happens when grass is burned up? *It grows back!* So, here it is, grass has grown back.

"…but only the men who **did not have the seal of God** in their foreheads" (v 4). *Those are not of the 144,000 and great innumerable multitude!*

Here the battle goes on; quite a battle! Verse 11—*this tells you where they are from*: "And they have over them a king, the angel of the abyss; his name in Hebrew *is* Abaddon, but *the* name he has in Greek *is* Apollyon. The **first woe** is past. Behold, after these things **two more woes** are still to come" (vs 11-12).

The next one is armies of 200-million coming from the east. Think about what that's going to be. You see that all developing right now with China. They also have ports along the way coming up to the Persian Gulf and the Gulf of Aqaba! So, there will be armies coming this way over land, and by sea, and the armies of *the beast* still gathered there ready to go. This great war takes place. You read the rest of Rev. 9.

It shows that God has four angels there—demons—for a day and hour, to dry up the River Euphrates (vs 14-15) so the kings of the East can come.

After they have this battle and there's no repentance, then you have Rev. 10, the seven thunders. Please understand this: *John didn't write down the seven thunders, so no one can tell what they are!* However, there was one man who said that he knew what the seven thunders were. All he did was repeat the seals. Well, the seven thunders are different, and we don't know how bad it's going to be, *but so bad that God says, 'Don't write it!'*

Rev. 11—the two witnesses. All the time that all of this is going on *the two witnesses* are right there, and *the beast* and *the false prophet* are right there in Jerusalem! Think about that! The beast and the false prophet are trying to kill the two witnesses, and they can't kill them, because every time they try, fire comes out of the mouths of the two witnesses and the killers are devoured! When they're finally killed the whole world rejoices

Revelation 11:8: "And their bodies *will lie* in the street of the great city, which spiritually is called Sodom and Egypt, where also our Lord was crucified"—*Jerusalem!*

Everybody rejoiced (v 10), the whole world rejoices, and all of a sudden everything calms down for a little while—3-1/2 days—and everybody is rejoicing. They have this special feast and send gifts back and forth to one another, because the two witnesses are dead! They can see it on the cell phones or iPads. I think that God is going to keep all of that active and alive so there will be a witness for everyone to see it.

Then what happens? Verse 11: "Then after the three and a half days, *the* **spirit of life from God** entered into them and they stood on their feet; and **great fear fell upon those who were watching them**."

Here is the fulfillment of a very simple thing in the Bible, *the last shall be first!* What happens to them?

Verse 12: "And they heard a great voice from heaven, say, 'Come up here!' And they ascended into heaven in a cloud; and their enemies saw them *rise*. And in that hour there was a great earthquake, and a tenth of the city fell; and seven thousand men were killed in the earthquake. And the rest were filled with fear, and gave glory to the God of heaven. **The second woe is past.** Behold, **the third woe is coming immediately**" (vs 12-14).

As soon as they start going up**, the seventh trumpet sounds!** So, they started their ascent on the way up, and when the trumpet sounded that's when they were instantly changed from flesh to spirit. They were the first two to come up before God the Father and Jesus Christ! *This is the seventh trumpet!*

Verse 15: "Then the seventh angel sounded *his* trumpet… [That's the last; there are not eight, nine or four; there are seven] …and *there* were great voices in heaven, saying, 'The kingdoms of this world have become *the kingdoms* of our Lord and His Christ, and He shall reign into the ages of eternity.'"

Here's why the resurrection has to happen on Pentecost. It's the end of the harvest; the two witnesses and then all the rest. I don't know how the resurrection is going to take place, but it says here:

Verse 18: "…to give reward to Your servants the prophets, and to the saints, and to *all* those who fear Your name…"

Here's why the resurrection has to happen on Pentecost and not Trumpets; there are still people who believe that it happens on Trumpets. Taking over the world will be the greatest thing to take place. We need to be on the Sea of Glass from Pentecost to Trumpets:

- to find out what we're going to do
- to get our new names
- to get our new clothes
- to be presented to the Father
- there needs to be the wedding of the Lamb and the Bride
- there needs to be the wedding supper

We need to all be prepared!

How could it be on Trumpets where you're resurrected and then all of a sudden the saints are there and an angel brings over a horse says to get on it. You would say, 'What do I do? I don't know what this is!' We have to know! This has to be planned, which it is, and it's got to be prepared, which it is; so that when we come down to the earth we'll know what to do. We will know who to follow, who's going to do what.

I don't know how the resurrection is going take place. I don't know if it's going to be done in 24 sections, like the 24 hours on the earth. I think that God wants to see that on that Pentecost everyone on earth is going to see the saints being raised from the dead! They're going to think it's an invasion from outer space taking people.

- Is the earth being prepared for that psychologically? *Yes, indeed!*
- Have you ever watched *Ancient Aliens*? *Those are really demons working with people on the earth!*

But the ancient aliens are really God the Father and Jesus Christ and then all the saints!

Revelation 15:1: "Then I saw another sign in heaven, great and awesome: seven angels having the **seven last plagues,** for in them the wrath of God is filled up. And I saw a Sea of Glass mingled with fire, and those who had gotten the victory over the beast…" (vs 1-2).

- Where did the beast start? *In the Garden of Eden!*
- Is the serpent a beast? *Yes, he is!*

"…and over his image, and over his mark, *and* over the number of his name, standing on the Sea of Glass, having *the* **lyres of God**" (v 2)—*which are harp-like instruments, and we're going to also have to learn how to play those. Do you know how to play a lyre? No!*

Verse 3: "And they were singing the song of Moses, *the* servant of God… [from the Old Testament] …and the song of the Lamb… [from the New Testament] …saying, 'Great and awesome *are* Your works, Lord God Almighty; righteous and true *are* Your ways, King of the saints. Who shall not fear You, O Lord, and glorify Your name? For *You* only *are* Holy; and all the nations shall come and worship before You, for Your judgments have been revealed'" (vs 3-4). *That's talking about the Millennium that's going to take place immediately after this!*

Seven Last Plagues

Then the seven angels came and **they were given the vials of the seven last plagues.** Notice that Rev. 16 follows very similar to the plagues of the seals.

Revelation 16:1: "Then I heard a loud voice from the temple say to the seven angels, 'Go and pour out the vials of the wrath of God onto the earth.' And the first *angel* went and poured out his vial onto the earth; and an evil and grievous sore fell upon the men who had the mark of the beast, and upon those who were worshiping his image. And the second angel *went and* poured out his vial into the sea; and it became blood, like *that* of a dead *man*; and every living soul… [animals are called souls] …in the sea died. And the third angel poured out his vial upon the rivers, and into the fountains of waters; and they became blood" (vs 1-4). *Same weapons that God used in Egypt!*

Verse 5: "Then I heard the angel of the waters say, 'You are righteous, O Lord, Who are, and Who was, even the Holy One, in that You have executed this judgment. For they have poured out *the* blood of saints and of prophets, and You have given them blood to drink; for they are worthy.' And I heard another *voice* from the altar say, 'Yes, Lord God Almighty, true and righteous *are* Your judgments.' And the fourth angel poured out his vial upon the sun; and *power* was given to it to scorch men with fire. Then men were scorched with great heat…" (vs 5-9).

It says in the prophecy in the Old Testament that sun is going to get seven times hotter and scorch men; just like a big blast of a furnace coming.

"…and they blasphemed the name of God, Who has authority over these plagues, **and did not repent to give Him glory**" (v 9).

How much does it take for people to repent? *Think about that!*

Verse 10: "And the fifth angel poured out his vial upon the throne of the beast; and his kingdom became full of darkness; and they gnawed their tongues because of the pain, and blasphemed the God of heaven because of their pains and their sores; **yet, they did not repent of their works**. And the sixth angel poured out his vial into the great river Euphrates; and its waters were dried up, so that the way of the kings from the rising of *the* sun might be prepared. Then I saw three unclean spirits like frogs *come* out of the mouth of the dragon, and out of the mouth of the beast, and out of the mouth of the false prophet; for they are spirits of demons working miracles, going forth to the kings of the earth, even of the whole world, to gather them together to *the* battle of that great day of the Almighty God" (vs 10-14). *So, the came, and the last thing to come was great hailstones, 180 lbs a piece!*

There are still some who didn't suffer from that, because we find in Rev. 19, because this finishes all of the actual events that the Feast of Trumpets pictures prophetically!

Revelation 19:1: "And after these things I heard *the* loud voice of **a great multitude in heaven**…" [all the resurrected saints] …saying, 'Hallelujah! The salvation and the glory and the honor and the power *belong* to the Lord our God. For true and righteous *are* His judgments; for He has judged the great whore, who corrupted the earth with her fornication, and He has avenged the blood of His servants at her hand.' And they said a second time, 'Hallelujah! And her smoke shall ascend upward into the ages of eternity.' And the twenty-four elders and the four living creatures fell down and worshiped God, Who sits on the throne, saying, 'Amen. Hallelujah!' And a voice came forth from the throne, saying, 'Praise our God, **all His servants, and all who fear Him, both small and great.'**…." (vs 1-5)—*all the saints on the Sea of Glass!*

We'll have a big worship service to God before we come down and that's after the wedding of the Bride and Christ, and the supper of the Lamb. After that we're going to be ready. We're going to know:

- who we are
- what we're going to do
- how to ride the white horse
- how to follow Christ

So, we do it!

Verse 11: "And I saw heaven open; and behold, a white horse; and He Who sat on it *is* called Faithful and True, and in righteousness He does judge and make war. And His eyes *were* like a flame of fire, and on His head *were* many crowns; *and* He had a name written that no one knows except Him…. [He has in addition to that many other names] …And *He was* clothed with a garment dipped in blood; and His name is The Word of God" (vs 11-13). *Where do we first come in contact with that?*

John 1:1: "In *the* beginning was the Word, and the Word was with God, and the Word was God."

Revelation 19:14: "And the armies in heaven… [that's all of us] …were following Him on white horses; *and* they were clothed in fine linen, white and pure. And out of His mouth goes a sharp sword, that with it He might smite the nations; and He shall shepherd them with an iron rod; and He treads the winepress of the fury and the wrath of the Almighty God. And on *His* garment and on His thigh He has a name written: **King of kings and Lord of lords**" (vs 14-16). *This is the meaning of the Feast of Trumpets!* What a great victory this is going to be!

Here we are coming down to the earth on our horses! I don't know exactly how that's going to be, how that happens in mid-air, but it's going to happen, and that's going to be quite a thing! The first thing that's going to be exciting is when the angels are taking us up to the Sea of Glass.

After everything that goes on and we come back the earth, that's going to be a really exciting thing! Here we are on our 'giddy-up' going down with Christ to rule the world!

God cleans up His mess! Verse 17: "Then I saw an angel standing in the sun; and he cried out with a loud voice, saying to all the birds that fly in *the* midst of heaven…"

All the eagles, vultures and flesh eaters coming from every part of the earth circling around and we're coming down in the middle of them!

"…'Come and gather yourselves together to the supper of the great God so that you may eat *the* flesh of kings, and *the* flesh of chief captains, and *the* flesh of mighty *men*, and *the* flesh of horses, and of those who sit on them, and *the* flesh of all, free and bond, and small and great.' And I saw the beast and the kings of the earth and their armies, gathered together to make war with Him Who sits on the horse, and with His army. And the beast was taken, and with him the false prophet who worked miracles in his presence, by which he had deceived those who received the mark of the beast and those who worshiped his image. **Those two were cast alive into the Lake of Fire, which burns with brimstone;** and the rest were killed by the sword of Him Who sits on the horse, *even the sword* that goes out of His mouth; and all the birds were filled with their flesh" (vs 17-21).

How is that going to work? ***Christ is going to command that all of them be stripped of their flesh standing on their feet!*** It's all going to fall off and their skeletons are going to be there in a mass of all of this flesh and blood, and oh what a dinner for all of these birds! Think of the noise that's going on with the birds fighting over all of this flesh, and gorging themselves!

Between now and Atonement I believe we're going to be chasing down all the demons. Satan is going to try and hide, but he's not going to get away. That tells you what's going to happen on the Day of Atonement.

This is the meaning of the Feast of Trumpets and we are going to rule the world in righteousness and in truth as spirit beings as the sons and daughters of God, to bring peace to this world!

Scriptural References:

1) Leviticus 23:23-24
2) Micah 1:2-5
3) Deuteronomy 28:41, 43-44
4) Hosea 5:14-15
5) Hosea 6:1-2
6) Jeremiah 25:26-34
7) Isaiah 24:1-6
8) Revelation 6:1-17
9) Matthew 24:29-30, 27
10) Revelation 8:1-6
11) Revelation 9:1-4, 11-12
12) Revelation 11:8, 11-15, 18
13) Revelation 15:1-4
14) Revelation 16:1-14
15) Revelation 19:1-5, 11-13
16) John 1:1
17) Revelation 19:14-21

Scriptures referenced, not quoted:

- Daniel 9
- Revelation 7; 13; 5
- Hebrews 12
- Revelation 9:14-15; 10; 11:10

Also referenced: Messages:
- *Leadership Oppression in the Churches of God!*
- *What is the Government of God?*

FRC:bo
Transcribed: 9/24/20
Reformatted: 12/2020

CHAPTER FORTY-NINE

The Awesome Day of the Lord
(Feast of Trumpets)
Fred R. Coulter

Greetings, brethren! Welcome to the Feast of Trumpets. Here we are with the time going by; we're at the fourth Holy Day of the year. The first Holy Days of the year apply directly to the Church. The last four—Trumpets, Atonement, Tabernacles, and the Last Great Day—apply to the world, and also to the Church.

As we come down through Lev. 23, it lists all the Holy Days. All the Holy Days are important to God, and they tell the plan and the story that God wants us to know so that we can understand:

- why we're here
- where we're going
- what God is doing
- how He's doing it
- approximately when He is going to do it

so we can have

- understanding
- faith
- hope

That's why we have the Holy Days!

The Feast of Trumpets is an unusual Feast inasmuch as that it pictures being *a war-feast* from this point of view. Let's go to Lev. 23, which we always do, and here we have the Feast of Trumpets:

Leviticus 23:23: "And the LORD spoke to Moses, saying, 'Speak to the children of Israel saying, "In the seventh month, in the first *day* of the month, you shall have a Sabbath, **a memorial of blowing of ram's horns,** a Holy convocation"'" (vs 23-24).

Now the *memorial of blowing of trumpets* means that *the trumpets were to be blown all day long!* So, this is a Feast where then it incorporates everything that it talks about what the trumpets are used for in Num. 10. We're going to see this as we go through the explanation of the day.

Let's come over here to Num. 10 and let's review the use of the trumpet. There were special trumpets that were made.

[#1]Numbers 10:2: "…And they shall be used for the **calling of the assembly**…"

As we will see, God is going to gather all nations there at Armageddon.

[#2]Then it's blown for an **alarm or a warning,** which this day is; v 6: "When you blow an alarm…"

[#3]Verse 9: "And if you go **to war**…"

So, this is *a war feast!* But also, after the war is over you have the recovery of it, so you also have the trumpet here.

[#4]Verse 10: "Also in the day of your gladness, and **in your appointed Feasts, and in the beginnings of your months,** you shall blow with the silver trumpets over your burnt offerings, and over the sacrifices of your peace offerings…"

So, the trumpet had a lot to do with the ceremony at the temple. Of course, as we already have seen leading up to Pentecost, that the trumpet plagues in Rev. 8 & 9 have an awful lot to do with the fulfilling of God's plan and the carrying out of what He's doing leading up to the return of Jesus Christ.

In Lev. 23 it says that on this day we are to offer an offering made by fire unto the LORD. Of course, we always take up an offering on the Holy Days. An offering is something that:

- you need to determine
- you need to plan for
- reflects your thankfulness to God for the blessings that He has given you

And it has to be from your heart!

God expects us to do that and then we in turn use this money to help the brethren. Everything that you send in is used to produce books, booklets, CD's, pay for mail, office help, and all of these things. If you appreciate receiving the CDs, if you appreciate receiving the other things then you can express it back in an offering, *which will then be honored by God because you give from a willing heart and attitude.*

(pause for offering)

As we saw leading up to Pentecost and including Pentecost, that the return of Jesus Christ is a spectacular event. It's something that is not just done in an instant, and it's something the whole world will understand when the time comes. It will be something that no one is going to be able to avoid. It's not going to be a secret rapture. It's not going to be a secret coming. It is going to be known in power, strength, glory, especially as we will see for the Feast of Trumpets, because the Feast of Trumpets caps off the return of Jesus Christ to this earth.

When Jesus was talking to His disciples on the Passover night, He said, 'If I go I will come again and receive you to Myself, so that where I am you may be also.' Christ is going to receive us to Himself. But many people don't believe in the return of Jesus Christ anymore. We're going to find that that is going to be more and more of a problem. Also, that people are so deceived with the 'rapture,' even to the point that some of them say that you can receive *the mark of the beast* and still go to heaven. Well, I don't read that in the Bible. *The Bible says you have to have victory*:

- over the beast
- over his mark
- over his number
- over his name

But nevertheless, they are not going to believe it, because there is going to be a false messiah and a false prophet, *and they are going to deceive the whole world under the spiritual power of Satan and the demons!*

Now the Apostle Peter wrote of this in 2-Peter 3. Remember this: Jesus even said that when He comes, **'Will He find faith in the earth?'** Of course, there will be some with His Church. But even then, the quality of faith is in question.

2-Peter 3:1—*Peter wrote*: "Now, beloved, I am writing this second epistle to you; in *both*, I am stirring up your pure minds by causing *you* to remember *in order* for you to be mindful of the words that were spoken before by the Holy prophets, and of the commandment of the Lord and Savior, *spoken* by us, the apostles; knowing this first, that in the last days *there* will come mockers, walking according to their own personal lusts, and asking, **'Where is the promise of His coming?** For ever since the forefathers died, everything has remained the same as from *the* beginning of creation'" (vs 1-4).

- they have ignored the facts of history (v 5)
- they have ignored the facts in the geological table of the earth
- they have believed in evolution
- they don't believe in God
- they don't believe in the second return of Jesus Christ

When Jesus Christ comes, you wait and see, *He is going to be counted as an alien, He, His angels and all the saints with Him.* We're going to see this.

Let's look at some of the prophecies that tell us about the setting up of the Kingdom of God on earth at the return of Jesus Christ in power and in glory, and in a scope that is going to be awesome indeed. Far greater than even most of us in the Church have ever assumed or ever thought of. *It is going to be something else!*

The whole book of Daniel tells us some of the things here about the return of Christ and when these things will be, and how they are going to happen, and what it is going to be like.

Dan. 2—here is a promise that was given to Nebuchadnezzar in the interpretation of the dream that he had, which Daniel interpreted for him. I'm not going to go through the whole thing. We're going to see how this fills in, in the book of Revelation a little later.

Daniel 2:44: "And in the days of these kings…" *There's coming a time when all of these things will be!* They're going to be done on time

- according to God's schedule
- according to His plan as outlined by the Holy Days

God has predetermined all of this!

You know, the apostles wanted to know, 'Are You at this time going to restore the Kingdom to Israel?' He said, 'No, you go your way and you preach. That's given into the hands of the Father and that's under His authority.'

Verse 44: "And in the days of these kings, the God of heaven shall set up a Kingdom, which shall never be destroyed… [notice how it's going to come] …And the Kingdom shall not be left to other people…"

It's going to be given to the saints and we're going to rule, and we're going to reign. And we're going to help straighten out this whole earth.

The Protestants focus in on having sin forgiven so they can be right with God, and they can be saved, and they can go to heaven. They never get past the beginning. God wants us to:

- grow in character
- grow in knowledge
- grow in understanding
- develop the character

so that we can rule and reign with Jesus Christ, because it's not going to be left to other people, it's going to be for the saints!

This whole civilization of this world is going to come to a destructive end. That's what this Feast pictures, the destruction of the civilizations of this world, and it's pictured right here.

"…but it shall break in pieces and consume all these kingdoms, **and it shall stand forever**. Because you saw that the stone was cut out of the mountain without hands, and that it broke in pieces the iron, the brass, the clay, the silver, and the gold, the great God has made known to the king what shall come to pass hereafter. And the dream *is* certain, and its interpretation is sure'" (vs 44-45). *All of the details are not given here!*

Some of the details are given a little later in Dan. 7. Let's see this. This is quite a thing. Brethren, God has called us to:

- the greatest calling
- the greatest event
  - ✓ to be able to be partakers of it
  - ✓ to be able to be part of it
  - ✓ to be able to help solve all the problems of this world

And know for sure they're going to get worse!

Daniel 7:13: "I saw visions in the night and, behold, One like the Son of man came with the clouds of heaven…"

That's how He's coming! That's how He left, and that's how He's returning. The book of Revelation says *every eye shall see Him!*

"…and came to the Ancient of Days, and they brought Him near before Him. And dominion and glory was given to Him, and a Kingdom, that all people, nations and languages should serve Him. His dominion *is* an everlasting dominion, which shall not pass away, and His Kingdom that which shall not be destroyed" (vs 13-14).

This is going to bring *the beast, the false prophets and the nations of the world* into a head-on confrontation with the return of Jesus Christ and the saints of God. But as we are going to see, they are going to lose, *and they are going to lose big time!*

When we come to v 27, again we'll see that dominion was given to Christ, and then He gives some of that dominion to us to rule and reign with Him.

Verse 27: "And the Kingdom and dominion, and the greatness of the Kingdom under the whole heaven, shall be given to the people of the saints of the Most High, Whose Kingdom *is* an everlasting Kingdom. **And all kingdoms shall serve and obey Him**."

But the thing that is profound and important is the way this is going to happen and how big an event this is going to be. It is going to be almost beyond the scope of our imagination. So maybe we can help expand that a little more today, *to understand that we are called to the greatest most significant and most profound event to ever occur since the creation of the world,* and that's what this Feast of Trumpets is all about.

Daniel 12:1: "And at that time Michael shall stand up, the great prince who stands for the children of your people… [this is going to rescue the physical tribes of Israel] …And there shall be a time of trouble, such as never was since there was a nation even until that time. And at that time your people shall be delivered—everyone who shall be found written in the book."

We saw that. We saw how the first resurrection takes place on Pentecost. We're going to look at the events that take place after we are on the Sea of Glass leading up to the literal return of Christ and the saints on the earth. Let's see what a tremendous event this is going to be. This is going to be something affecting the whole world.

Jeremiah 25:12: "And it shall be, when seventy years are fulfilled…"

It finishes off with the 70-year captivity of the Jews in Babylon, but then it extends out way beyond to the end. This prophecy begins here and then projects to the return of Jesus Christ.

"'…I will punish the king of Babylon, and that nation, and the land of the Chaldeans,' says the LORD, 'for their iniquity, and I will make it an everlasting desolation. And I will bring on that land all My words which I have spoken against it, all that is written in this book which Jeremiah has prophesied against all the nations'" (vs 12-13).

Read Jer. 50-52 and you see how profound this is going to be. He's going to bring to pass all His words.

Verse 14: "'For many nations and great kings shall make them slaves, also. And I will repay them according to their deeds, and according to the works of their own hands.' For thus says the LORD, the God of Israel, to me, 'Take the wine cup of this wrath at My hand, and cause all the nations to whom I shall send you to drink it. And they shall drink, and reel to and fro, and be crazed because of the sword that I will send among them'" (vs 14-16).

Then Jeremiah said, v 17: "Then I took the cup at the LORD'S hand, and made all the nations drink, to whom the LORD had sent me."

He starts right at Jerusalem. Then it lists all the nation. Let's see how far this goes:

Verse 26. "And all the kings of the north, far and near, one with another, and **all the kingdoms of the world**…"

When we come to the end-time and we're talking about the return of Jesus Christ, we are talking about worldwide events. We are living in a time when all of these things are possible; they weren't possible 25 years ago, 30 years ago, 100 years ago, 500 years ago, 1,000 years ago, but now they are possible.

"...all the kingdoms of the world, which *are* on the face of the earth..." (v 26). *That's very inclusive; quite a thing to understand!*

Notice what it's going to be, v 29: "For, lo, I begin to bring evil on the city, which is called by My name..."

God is saying, 'I want you to understand something very important. *If I start correcting and bringing evil upon the city that is called by My name, the rest of you are not going to escape!'* We're going to see the things at Jerusalem is going to key these end-time events as never before. We can see how that is coming more and more!

"'...and shall you go unpunished? You shall not go unpunished. For I will call for a sword on all the inhabitants of the earth,' says the LORD of hosts" (v 29).

Now how all encompassing is that? That's profound. Remember Jesus said that it is *a time of trouble that has not been since there was a nation on earth, nor no ever shall be!*

Unless God had not limited that time __all__ *flesh should be destroyed!* So, we need to get our thinking caps on and we need to think big. We need to think huge. We need to use the Spirit of God to understand as greatly as possible, as much as we can, what God is going to do. What you need to do is understand that because these events are coming this way:

- do not be fearful
- do not be cowardly
- do not run and try and hide in a corner

- God wants us to be courageous
- God wants us to stand for the Truth
- God wants us to understand one thing very important:

We are on God's side and there is nothing that anyone can do to us to turn back what God has promised for us and to turn back the hand of God!

Just like He told Jeremiah, 'I want you to go. I'm going to give you a forehead of flint so you will speak the words that I want you to speak, and:

- don't be afraid of them
- don't be afraid of their faces
- don't be afraid of their threats

Likewise with the events that are coming here at the end-time, *don't be afraid!* As Luke wrote, **'Look up and rejoice for your salvation is near!'**

Verse 30: "And prophesy against them all these words, and say to them, 'The LORD shall roar from on high, and utter His voice from His Holy habitation. He shall mightily roar over His dwelling place. He shall give a shout, like those who tread out *grapes*, against all the people of the earth.'"

That's why the book of Revelation is so profound because it shows how this is going to happen worldwide.

Verse 31: "'A noise shall come to the ends of the earth; for the LORD has a controversy with the nations; He will plead with all flesh. He will give those *who are* wicked to the sword,' says the LORD."

When we read the book of Revelation, the deaths are going to be astounding. It's going to be something.

Verse 32: "Thus says the LORD of hosts, 'Behold, evil shall go forth from nation to nation, and a great whirlwind shall be stirred up from the farthest corners of the earth. And the slain of the LORD... [as we're going to see this in Rev. 16 a little later] ...shall be at that day from *one* end of the earth even to the *other* end of the earth; they shall not be mourned, nor gathered, nor buried. They shall be *as* dung on the ground" (vs 32-33).

Then He lays it all at the feet of the pastors and the shepherds. So, there we have quite a situation with this as it is coming.

Let's see how all of this is going to develop, however long it will be. *But there is one thing we need to do: we need to always be ready!*

And as it says in the *King James* 'we need to occupy.' That means we need to be doing. as we see the day coming closer we need to:

- put forth the effort
- draw close to God
- be filled with His Spirit

Rev. 13 tells us how this whole worldwide system is going to develop. It's going to be awesome indeed. There is going to come out of it the *false* christ, the *false* messiah who is called *the beast*. And the world is being set-up for it. Part of it has to do with the movies:

- *The Passion of the Christ*
- *The Da Vinci Code* and the 'holy grail'
and part of it has to do with:
- how everything is being organized worldwide

- the mark of the beast
- the other events that are taking place

But they are all focusing together on fulfilling Rev. 13 to an absolute 't.'

Revelation 13:1—*John saw this prophecy taking place*: "And I stood on the sand of the sea; and I saw a beast rising up out of the sea, having seven heads and ten horns…"—*the signs of Satan the devil!* This is <u>his</u> system. And it's going to be his grandest most glorious system!

"…and on his horns ten crowns, and upon his heads *the* name of blasphemy" (v 1).

This is going to be an unusual political set-up because it's going to amalgamate and bring in the best of all the civilizations in the past, so that it is going to look like this is a wonderful and a magnificent thing.

Verse 2: "And the beast that I saw was like a leopard… [so it's going to have swift military] …and his feet like *the feet* of a bear… [it's going to have power] …and his mouth like *the* mouth of a lion; and the dragon gave him his power and his throne and great authority."

All of this comes from Satan the devil. God is going to let Satan the devil rise to where he's going to be convinced in his own mind that he's going to fulfill Isa. 14 and finally have the forces, the ability, and the capacity to rise and usurp the Throne of God. We will see how he's going to try and convince the nations to do that. It's going to be quite a deception indeed.

Verse 3: "And I saw one of his heads as *if it were* slain to death, but his deadly wound was healed; and the whole earth was amazed *and* followed the beast."

You can see how quickly this will take place. You can see what a fantastic thing this is going to be. So here we have, if the prophecies are correct back there in Dan. 9—which they are; all the prophecies are correct—it's just a matter of our interpretation.

So, when we come to a final seven-year period we're going to have the first three and a half years be some of the most astounding things with:

- false prophets
- miracles
- calling fire down from heaven
- nations giving their power and authority to the beast
- peace coming on the earth

Yet, the prophets of God and the ministers of God are going to be saying:

Don't be deceived. This is a deception and it's not going to work because this is not of God; *this is of Satan the devil!*

There are going to be some fanatics. Now we don't know who they are but maybe they're going to be fanatical Jews who will come and try and assassinate *the beast* so he receives a deadly wound, but his deadly wound is healed. Notice what happens after the deadly wound is healed.

Verse 4: "And they worshiped the dragon…"

That's why every vestige of Christianity must be destroyed in this plan that they're bringing about, *so that Satan-worship, witchcraft, and all of these things will be the predominant form of worship!* That's the only way that they are going to bring in a whole one-world religion, which will be an amalgamation. It will have parts of all the religions of the world just like the civil authority here has parts of all the great kingdoms of the world. But just like all the kingdoms of the world are going to give their power to *the beast,* all the religions of the world are going to give their power and authority to *the second beast!*

Now here's what they're going to do, v 4: "And they worshiped the dragon, who gave *his* authority to the beast. And they worshiped the beast, saying, 'Who *is* like the beast? Who has the power to make war against him?' And a mouth speaking great things and blasphemies was given to him; and authority was given to him to continue *for* forty-two months" (vs 4-5).

After the deadly wound is healed he continues for forty and two months. The same exact time that it talks about in Rev. 11 that Jerusalem is trodden down of the Gentiles. So, one of the first moves that he makes, as we find in Dan. 11, is he's going to come against the King of the South, and he's going to go into the Holy Land and stand in the temple and he is going to say that he is 'God.'

Won't that be interesting and profound if the Beast Power claims that he is of the Monrovian king line of Europe? Then everybody's going to be convinced—because of the movie *The Da Vinci Code,* and other movies, and the book and so forth—that he actually has the genes of the physical Christ through Mary Magdalene.

Now here's what's going to happen when he's possessed of Satan the devil, when he is raised up from that.

Verse 6: "And he opened his mouth in blasphemy against God, to blaspheme His name, and His tabernacle, and those who dwell in heaven."

Tie in 2-Thess.s 2, that he goes into the Temple of God and says that he himself is 'God.' Well, you know that's not going to stand.

Verse 7: "And he was given *power* to make war against the saints…"

Here is something that God always allows the wicked to do: **think that they are winning!**

"…and to overcome them; and he was given authority over every tribe and language and nation…. [here's the great counterfeit kingdom] …And all who dwell on the earth will worship him, whose names have not been written in the Book of Life of the Lamb slain from *the* foundation of *the* world. **If anyone has an ear, let him hear**" (vs 7-9). *There we have it! That's how it's going to be!*

He's going to have a partner and that partner is going to be *another beast*. That partner is going to be *the false prophet*. He is going to do great signs and great wonders.

Verse 11: "And I saw another beast rising out of the earth; and he had two horns like a lamb, but spoke like a dragon; and he exercises all the authority of the first beast before him; and he causes the earth and those who dwell therein to worship the first beast, whose deadly wound was healed. And he performs great wonders, so that he even causes fire to come down to the earth from heaven in the sight of men" (vs 11-13).

Now you know the old saying: *seeing is believing*. If he says 'I am from God' and people see this they're going to say he's from God. But the question needs to be: which God? The God of heaven, or the god of this world? *Because Satan is called the god of this world!*

Verse 14: "And he deceives those who dwell on the earth by means of the wonders that were given to him to perform in the sight of the beast, saying to those who dwell on the earth that they should make an image for the beast, which had the wound by the sword, yet, was alive. And he was given power to give life to the image of the beast, so that the image of the beast also could speak; and he causes everyone who will not worship the image of the beast to be killed" (vs 14-15).

That's the qualifying exam to receive the mark of *the beast* to show that you are loyal to this new world government is going to be whether you will make the image, and fall down and worship the image.

That's why it's absolutely profound that in every Catholic catechism the second commandment of the Ten Commandments concerning idolatry is removed. Yet, in their own Bibles, to show the gall, the hypocrisy, and to show how confident they are in *their lying ability to change the Word of God*, right in their own Bible they leave in the second commandment.

Verse 16: "And he…"—*referring back to the first beast!* The second beast, **the false prophet,** is undoubtedly going to be the pope. It can't be anyone else. All the religions of the world will acknowledge him just like they do the first beast. And they say:

> Now we have a wonderful system. We have cultural diversity. We have all of the good things that we have here: multi-culturalism and everyone loves each other and accepts each other, except for those people who won't go along with this system and receive the mark of the beast, so they're going to be killed.

Verse 16: "And he causes all, the small and the great, and the rich and the poor… [it has to be a government edict to do it, to make it a requirement] …and the free and the bond, to receive a mark in their right hands, or in their foreheads so that no one may have the ability to buy and sell unless he has the mark, or the name of the beast, or the number of his name" (vs 16-17). *You can see how that is coming!*

It's going to be everywhere and in everything—this whole system—*until the final thing is the mark of the beast in the right hand or in the forehead!* Now it's going to be quite a thing that's going to take place.

Let's see what's going to happen because this fills in the gap from Pentecost up to Trumpets. It's going to be quite a thing! As we saw on Pentecost *first* there's the sign of the Son of man in heaven that shines like the light of day. And apparently it comes closer and closer and closer to the earth. Everyone is going to see that. Everyone is going to know that something profound has happened.

As we saw on Pentecost the heavens are rolled back as a scroll. God shakes the heaven and shakes the earth and shakes the sea and the dry land and everything that there is. *It's going to be an awesome time, indeed!*

Then the resurrection takes place and every one meets Christ in the air on the Sea of Glass. How big will the Sea of Glass be when it finally comes down to the earth close enough in the clouds? I think it's going to be plenty close enough so that the people of the world are going to be able to see it, and that they are going to figure that this is an alien invasion, which is actually true from this point of view: *We, and Christ, and the angels are the aliens!* Not these silly looking things they depict in the movies, those are not aliens. Those are silly things for people to be deceived.

Now how big will the Sea of Glass be? How high will it be? It's going to be in the clouds. Now the highest clouds are 60,000 feet. So maybe it's going to be like 10,000 or 15,000 feet, *but every eye is going to be able to see it!*

When the saints are resurrected on Pentecost does the Sea of Glass move around the earth in accordance with the sun, and the dead are raised and brought up to the Sea of Glass all during the time that it makes it's trip around the earth?

- Does it stop and hover over Jerusalem? *Now that's a very distinct possibility!*
- How big will this be? *It's going to be enough to accommodate all the saints!*

Revelation 15:1: "Then I saw another sign in heaven, great and awesome: seven angels having the seven last plagues…" *This is going to lead up to the finality of Trumpets, which will cap it off!*

"…for in them the wrath of God is filled up. And I saw a Sea of Glass mingled with fire, **and those who had gotten the victory over the beast, and over his image, and over his mark, *and* over the number of his name, standing on the Sea of Glass**, having *the* lyres of God" (vs 1-2).

How big is this Sea of Glass going to be? *We'll just review it here*:

Verse 3: "And they were singing the song of Moses, *the* servant of God, and the song of the Lamb, saying, 'Great and awesome *are* Your works, Lord God Almighty; righteous and true *are* Your ways, King of the saints. Who shall not fear You, O Lord, and glorify Your name? For *You* only *are* Holy; and **all the nations shall** come and worship before You… [that won't take place right away; that's a prophecy] …for Your judgments have been revealed'" (vs 3-4). *Then right after that we'll take a look at what happens!*

Let's set the stage and see what the world is going to be like, and then bring it altogether in Rev. 16. First of all let's go to Isa. 13 and see where it talks about the Day of the Lord, and this is *the* Day of *the* Lord, which He is going to execute upon the earth. It talks about 'The burden of Babylon' (Isa. 13:1). So this is Babylon the Great (Rev. 18).

Isaiah 13:6: "Howl! For **the Day of the LORD** *is* at hand; **it shall come as a destruction from the Almighty.** Therefore, all hands shall be faint, and every man's heart shall melt; and they shall be afraid. Pangs and sorrows shall take hold of them. They shall be in pain like a woman who travails. They shall be amazed at one another, their faces are *like* blazing fire. Behold, **the Day of the LORD comes, cruel both *with* wrath and fierce anger,** to make the earth a desolation; and He shall

destroy the sinners out of it" (vs 6-9).

As we have seen before this is going to be so fantastic that, like it confirms here in:

Verse 10: "For the stars of the heavens and their constellations shall not give light; the sun shall be darkened in its going forth, and the moon shall not reflect its light. 'And **I will punish the world**… [I want you to understand and grasp that all of this is a world-wide setting] …or *their* evil, and the wicked for their iniquity; and **I will cause the arrogancy of the proud to cease**… [personified in *the beast* and *the false prophet*] …and will lay low the haughtiness of the tyrants. I will make man more scarce than gold; even man more than the fine gold of Ophir. Therefore, I will shake the heavens, and the earth shall move out of its place, in the wrath of the LORD of hosts… [the wrath of God is contained in the seven last plagues] …**and in the day of His fierce anger**'" (vs 10-13). *God is going to execute His wrath!*

Now as we've talked about, let's see where it describes the armies of Rev. 8 & 9, and then that leads up to where we will be in Rev. 15 & 16 again. We need to set the stage so we know what is going on here. But notice the warning that is given. Joel 1 talks about the Day of the Lord. *The Feast of Trumpets is the Day of the Lord* to execute His vengeance.

Joel 1:15: "Alas for the day! For the day of the LORD *is* at hand, and it shall come as a destruction from the Almighty." *This is from God!* This is not from man, but this is from God. We saw how men have their armies, how the things take place (Rev. 6). Then it's the angels of God against Satan and the demons (Rev. 8).

Now God set's His hand. That's what it's going to culminate in. Now then, it talks about this army that comes from the east, the army of 200-million.

It talks about the Day of the Lord, Joel 2:1: "'Blow the ram's horn in Zion, and sound an alarm in My Holy mountain!' Let all the inhabitants of the land tremble, for the Day of the LORD comes, for *it is* near at hand…"

That's why we have to have the Feast of Trumpets so that we know, we understand that Christ is going to return. *The Day of the Lord is coming,* and it needs to be:

- a warning for us that we get our lives right
- a warning for the world that they are going to know that it is God Who's intervening
- the very God they rejected the very One Whom they have despised

- the very One Whom they figure is going to be a nice meek little lamb

is coming and returning in power and glory and authority such as the world has never, never seen in the most awesome and profound way that will ever be! There will never be another day like this. We need to understand it, brethren. God has called us to participate in some awesome things.

Verse 2: "A day of darkness and of gloominess, a day of clouds and of thick darkness. As the morning *is* spread across the mountains, *so comes* a great people and a mighty people; there has never been the like, nor shall there ever be again, even to the years of many generations."

That means all the way down through the Millennium. Of course, when Christ is here ruling during the Millennium nothing like this is going to happen. *This is the culmination and the end of the rule of man and Satan the devil,* and it is coming in such a way that it is literally going to destroy almost everything on the earth. The great cities of the nations need to be destroyed. All their temples, all their idols, *everything that men have made is going to be destroyed!* We're going to have quite a job rebuilding this earth. It is going to be something. I want us to have a little broader scope and understanding of what's going to take place. This is going to be God directly intervening and doing it.

Now then, it talks about the army. It's very interesting, the army comes and 'runs upon the walls and climbs in the houses.' You know they have uniforms right now that they are developing for soldiers that will actually give medication to their bodies instantly when they are wounded so they can keep on going and fighting. It sounds much like what they have here. Who knows what will happen.

- Will they develop an army where they implant chips?
- Will they put it into them and program them to go fight a battle and the generals are back there and the commanders are back there running all of these by remote controls?

All of these things are possible! We need to think about these things. This is going to be something.

- Where will the Sea of Glass finally come and be stationary? *It's going to be over the area of Palestine!*
- How big will it be? I

I've asked the question before, and I've asked it to myself many times, because I've been thinking on this. Now Ben Ambrose wrote a very wonderful paper. He got together with a mathematics instructor and figured out the math of what it would take for every eye to see the return of Jesus Christ; how far out it would have to be when the sign of the Son of man is first seen; and how close it comes to the earth, and so forth. He asks the question: How big will the Sea of Glass be? *Well it's going to have to be big enough to accommodate all the saints down through all the history of the world!* So, who knows how big that is going to be? Is it going to be fifty by fifty miles? *That's pretty big!*

- What is the world going to think when they look up there and see this?
- How do we know that it's going to be over Palestine, right over Jerusalem?

Joel 3:2: "I will also gather all nations and will bring them down into the valley of Jehoshaphat. And I will fight with them there for My people and for My inheritance Israel, whom they have scattered among the nations..."

He's going to bring them down to the Valley of Jehoshaphat. That is in the land of Palestine. We also will see a little later that that is called *Armageddon.* It shows in other prophecies that the blood is going to run up to the horses bridle. You can figure blood being six to eight feet deep in the Valley of Jehoshaphat. God is going to bring about a slaughter that is going to be just almost unreal. But that's the only way that God is going to be able to conquer this earth:

- get rid of Satan the devil
- get rid of the demons
- get rid of the armies
- get rid of all of the things that man has done against God

When they see the Sea of Glass up there and they begin to experience some of the things that God is doing to them, we're going to see what they're going to do. If you haven't seen the movie Independence Day you be sure and see that, because that shows how that in the midst of aliens from outer space coming to this earth, that all the nations get together and rescue the earth.

Now we're going to change views. Now we're going to be looking at it from God's point of view down on the earth, rather than on the earth just seeing what is here. We're going to see it all and we're going to see how God is going to do it. This is going to be something! This is going to fulfill another promise that God has given to all the saints where God has said, *'Vengeance is Mine,* says the Lord.' And He's going to execute it.

Let's come back to Psa. 149; this is quite a verse when you understand what it's saying here. I believe this is talking about the time being on the Sea of Glass.

Psalm 149:1: "O praise the LORD! Sing to the LORD a new song, and His praise in the congregation of saints."

- When is the congregation of the saints going to be all congregated together? *At the resurrection!*
- Where is that? *On the Sea of Glass!*

Verse 2: "Let Israel rejoice in his Maker; let the children of Zion be joyful in their King. Let them praise His name..." (vs 2-3).

Isn't that what it says we do in Rev. 15? *We sing the song of Moses, the song of the Lamb, and here's another one we're going to sing!*

Verse 3: "Let them praise His name in the dance; let them sing praises to Him with the drum and lyre, for the LORD takes pleasure in His people; He crowns the meek with salvation" (vs 3-4). *Salvation is to be in glorified form!* We receive that and we're on the Sea of Glass.

Verse 5: "Let the saints be joyful in glory..."

You're going to look at your new body, you're going to look at your new self, and we're going to be joyful in that. God is going to give us something marvelous.

"...let them sing aloud upon their beds. Let the high praises of God be in their mouth, and a two-edged sword in their hand to execute vengeance upon the nations and punishments upon the people, to bind their kings with chains and their nobles with iron bands, to carry out upon them the judgment written—**this honor have all His saints.** O praise the LORD!" (vs 5-9). *So we're going to do it!*

Now let's look down on the earth and God's perspective and see what's happening.

Psalm 2:1: "Why do the nations rage and the people plot in vain?" *To even imagine that they can fight against God and win,* is anything more vain than that?

Verse 2: "The kings of the earth set themselves, and the rulers take counsel together against the LORD and against His Christ..."

So they're going to say, 'Look, if we can turn back these aliens, which are up here on whatever kind of apparatus this is...' And I imagine that they're trying to shoot rockets up there, they're trying to shoot off other things to try and destroy it and it just bounces off as if it's nothing. They are really going to be really raging. This is going to be something indeed!

"...*saying,* 'Let us break Their bands asunder and cast away Their cords from us.' He Who sits in the heavens laughs; the LORD scoffs at them. Then He shall speak to them in His wrath, and in His fury He terrifies them. 'Yea, I have set My King upon Zion, My Holy mountain. I will declare the decree of the LORD. He has said to Me, **"You are My Son; this day I have begotten You. Ask of Me, and I shall give the nations for Your inheritance, and the uttermost parts of the earth for Your possession. You shall break them with a rod of iron; You shall dash them in pieces like a potter's vessel"**'" (vs 3-9).

Now let's see how that's going to be, because that's exactly what we're looking at here. Viewing now from the Sea of Glass, here's what's going to take place.

Revelation 15:5: "And after these things I looked, and behold, the temple of the tabernacle of the testimony in heaven was opened." *Here the saints are going to see all of that!*

Verse 6: "And the seven angels who had the seven *last* plagues came out of the temple; they were clothed in linen, pure and bright, and girded about the chest with golden breastplates."

Quite a thing! Here are these angels to do the will of God. This is how God is going to fight against them, directly from Him, right out of His Temple.

Verse 7: "And one of the four living creatures gave to the seven angels seven golden vials, full of the wrath of God, Who lives into the ages of eternity. And the temple was filled with smoke from the glory of God, and from His power; and no one was able to enter inside the temple until the seven plagues of the seven angels were fulfilled" (vs 7-8).

Revelation 16:1: "Then I heard a loud voice from the temple say to the seven angels, 'Go and pour out the vials of the wrath of God onto the earth.' And the first *angel* went and poured out his vial onto the earth; and an evil and grievous sore fell upon the men who had the mark of the beast, and upon those who were worshiping his image" (vs 1-2).

It's going to be something because *the mark of the beast* is not just an accounting system, and buying and selling system. *It is for total control!* When these people give up their free moral agency to Satan the devil they are going to pay the price. This grievous sore, whatever it's going to be... I don't know if it's going to start where *the mark of the beast* is and spread to the whole body—on their hand or on their forehead; it doesn't tell us. But that is their just punishment. Probably most of them will die.

Verse 3: "And the second angel *went and* poured out his vial into the sea; and it became blood, like *that* of a dead *man*; and every living soul in the sea died."

The whole ocean is going to become a petrifying stench of dead fish, dead whales, dead men and sunken ships. It's going to be awesome. When Satan and men get together and defy God, and think that they can turn back the hand of God then God has to intervene *and let them know Who is in charge.* Notice all of these weapons God can use at any time. These are the same weapons that He used back when He fought against Pharaoh (book of Exodus).

Verse 4: "And the third angel poured out his vial upon the rivers, and into the fountains of waters; and they became blood."

What's this going to do to all the eco-freaks out there? *Environmental Nazis!* God is going to destroy it. We need to understand that. We need to understand that the only thing worth saving on this earth will be Israel, and the people who repent. Otherwise God would utterly destroy it all. But because He says He won't, He's not going to.

- How did the angels view this?
- How should we view this kind of destruction?

There are going to be some people who say, 'Well, that's not the Jesus that I worship.' Well let me tell you something. If the Jesus you worship is not almighty and can't do these things, *he is not the true Jesus Christ of the Bible.*

Here's how the angels view it; v 5: "Then I heard the angel of the waters say, 'You are righteous, O Lord, Who are, and Who was, even the Holy One, in that You have executed this judgment. For they have poured out *the* blood of saints and of prophets, and You have given them blood to drink; for they are worthy'" (vs 5-6). *So there is the complete vengeance of God!*

Verse 7: "And I heard another *voice* from the altar say, 'Yes, Lord God Almighty, true and righteous *are* Your judgments.'"

True and righteous; that God says, 'Yes, the men on this earth deserve this.' *This is His judgment!* That's why Jeremiah said that the dead are going to be strewn from one end of the earth to the other end of the earth, as far as the eye can see.

Verse 8: "And the fourth angel poured out his vial upon the sun; and *power* was given to it to scorch men with fire."

Notice the attitude of all these things coming. You would think that they would repent. You would think that they would have some fear of God, wouldn't you? *No, they don't!* What happens?

Verse 9: "Then men were scorched with great heat; **and they blasphemed the name of God,** Who has authority over these plagues, and did not repent to give Him glory." *That's quite a thing!*

Now then, to show how profound and evil that *the beast, and the false prophet, and Satan are*:

Verse 10: "And the fifth angel poured out his vial upon the throne of the beast; and his kingdom became full of darkness; and they gnawed their tongues because of the pain." *Can you imagine having*:

- the mark of the beast
- the grievous sore
- having blood to drink instead of water
- having been scorched by the sun

*and now it's so dark, probably just like it was back there in Egypt, **that they felt the darkness!** Back then they stayed in bed for three days, couldn't go out; and yet:*

Verse 11: "And blasphemed the God of heaven because of their pains and their sores; yet, they did not repent of their works."

Now here's the last ditch effort that's going to take place. You talk about Satan deceiving to the very end, and men being gullible to believe it.

Verse 12: "And the sixth angel poured out his vial into the great river Euphrates; and its waters were dried up, so that the way of the kings from the rising of *the* sun might be prepared."

So the armies are still there. God hasn't done this to everybody, everywhere. The armies are still going to come.

Verse 13: "Then I saw three unclean spirits like frogs *come* out of the mouth of the dragon, and out of the mouth of the beast, and out of the mouth of the false prophet; for they are spirits of demons working miracles, going forth to the kings of the earth, even of the whole world, **to gather them together to *the* battle of that great day of the Almighty God**" (vs 13-14).

They're all being gathered for this battle. And this is the final climactic battle of all the disasters and wars and holocausts that have taken place in the Great Tribulation. This is the finality, and that's what this day of Trumpets pictures:

- the final battle
- the final war
- the final end

of these things! And then He gives a little warning here:

Verse 15: "Behold, I come as a thief. Blessed *is* the one who is watching… [now this is a warning for us] …and is keeping his garments, so that he may not walk naked and they *may not* see his shame."

In other words, here's a warning to the Laodiceans when they're reading these things that they better get their lives squared around. Instead of being lukewarm and ho-hum, and all glad-handing, socializing and all of these things, we have got a tremendous mission ahead of us.

We've got the greatest thing to look forward to that has ever been since the creation of the world, and we are going to be a part of all of these events that are going to culminate in the end of the rule of man and Satan the devil. Now that's something. When you read back there in Rom. 8, *the world is waiting for the manifestation of the sons of God! That's us!* The first thing they're going to do though is fight against God.

Verse 16: "And he gathered them together to the place that in Hebrew is called Armageddon…. [Valley of Jehoshaphat; they're all ready to fight, and God ends it quickly] …Then the seventh angel poured out his vial into the air; and a loud voice came out of the temple of heaven, from the Throne, saying, 'IT IS FINISHED.' And there were voices and thunders and lightnings; and there was a great earthquake, such as was not since men were on the earth, so mighty an earthquake, *and* so great" (vs 16-18).

That's something! You read through the book of Revelation, this earth is going to be shaken, and shaken over and over again all during that last three and a half year period. Here's the greatest earthquake that has been.

Verse 19: "And the great city was divided into three parts; and the cities of the nations fell…"

All their buildings are going to collapse. Everything in these big cities is going to be utterly ruined and destroyed.

"…and Babylon the Great was remembered before God to give her the cup of the wine of the fury of His wrath. And every island disappeared, and no mountains were found" (vs 19-20).

There's no place to go hide! God is going to make it: you either repent and get right with Him or the end is here.

Verse 21: "And great hail, *each stone* the weight of a talent… [180 pounds] …fell down from heaven upon men; and men blasphemed God because of the plague of the hail, for the plague was exceedingly great."

What an awesome thing that this is. That's how Christ is going to return. It is going to be something. It is going to be absolutely just the most fantastic thing that we could ever imagine.

Now let's see the finale! Revelation 19:1: "And after these things I heard *the* loud voice of a great multitude in heaven…"

That is on the Sea of Glass, up in the clouds, in the first heaven, not the third heaven. But Christ is coming down. God the Father will come down, perform the marriage and the time of giving rewards to the saints and all of this sort of thing, so we understand what we're going to do and how we're going to do it and so forth. After the seventh last plague is poured out the great multitude in heaven says:

"…'Hallelujah! The salvation and the glory and the honor and the power *belong* to the Lord our God…. [this is the hymn we're going to sing] …For true and righteous *are* His judgments; for He has judged the great whore, who corrupted the earth with her fornication, and He has avenged the blood of His servants at her hand.' And they said a second time, 'Hallelujah! **And her smoke shall ascend upward into the ages of eternity**'" (vs 1-3).

In other words that smoke is going to go up and go out into the vastness of the universe and there will be specks of it just going on clear out through the whole galaxy and the universe.

Verse 4: "And the twenty-four elders and the four living creatures fell down and worshiped God, Who sits on the Throne, saying, 'Amen. Hallelujah!' And a voice came forth from the Throne, saying, 'Praise our God, all His servants, and all who fear Him, both small and great.' And I heard a voice like that of a great multitude, and like *the* sound of many waters, and *the* sound of mighty thunderings, saying, 'Hallelujah! For *the* Lord God Almighty has reigned. Let us be glad and shout with joy; and let us give glory to Him; for the marriage of the Lamb has come, and His wife has made herself ready'" (vs 4-7).

Now this is the beginning of the salvation of the world. So know and understand this: when God sets His hand to save the world He's going to save it. But in order to save it, it's going to have to be nearly destroyed.

Verse 8: "And it was granted to her that she should be clothed in fine linen, pure and bright; for the fine linen is the righteousness of the saints. And he said to me, 'Write: Blessed *are* those who are called to the marriage supper of the Lamb.' And he said to me, **'These are the true words of God'**" (vs

8-9).

- they are going to take place
- they are going to come to pass

The world won't know this because they don't keep the Feasts of God. They don't keep the Sabbath, the Passover, Unleavened Bread, Pentecost, Trumpets, Atonement, Tabernacles, or the Last Great Day. They don't know what God is doing. But God has revealed that to us, His mystery and His secret plan that He has proposed in Himself. And we are an integral part of this. *These words are the true Words of God!*

Verse 10: "And I fell at his feet to worship him. Then he said to me, 'See *that you do* not *do this!* I am a fellow servant of yours, and of your brethren, who have the testimony of Jesus. Worship God. For the testimony of Jesus is the spirit of prophecy.' And I saw heaven open; and behold, a white horse; and He Who sat on it *is* called Faithful and True, and in righteousness He does judge and make war" (vs 10-11).

Now the final battle comes! This is going to be awesome, indeed!

Verse 12: "And His eyes *were* like a flame of fire, and on His head *were* many crowns; *and* He had a name written that no one knows except Him. And *He was* clothed with a garment dipped in blood; and His name is The Word of God.... [tie in the Gospel of John] ...And the armies in heaven were following Him on white horses..." (vs 12-14).

That's going to be us! So we're going to be given a spiritual horse. We're going to get on it and we're going to go.

"...*and* they were clothed in fine linen, white and pure" (v 14).

Christ is going to do the fighting! Verse 15: "And out of His mouth goes a sharp sword, that with it He might smite that nations; and He shall shepherd them with an iron rod; and He treads the winepress of the fury and the wrath of the Almighty God."

God is saving up all of this for one last final battle, and it's going to be something.

Verse 16: "And on *His* garment and on His thigh He has a name written: King of kings and Lord of lords. Then I saw an angel standing in the sun; and he cried out with a loud voice, saying to all the birds that fly in *the* midst of heaven, 'Come and gather yourselves together to the supper of the great God so that you may eat *the* flesh of kings, and *the* flesh of chief captains, and *the* flesh of mighty *men,* and *the* flesh of horses, and of those who sit on them, and *the* flesh of all, free and bond, and small and great.' And I saw the beast and the kings of the

earth and their armies, gathered together to make war with Him Who sits on the horse, and with His army" (vs 16-19).

Here John was looking down and seeing that. That's what we're going to see when we start coming down off the Sea of Glass, and we're on those white horses and we're coming down with Christ and here are the birds flying, circling, coming for all this flesh that is going to be. Here we're coming down out of the clouds with Christ on our horses. That's going to be quite a thing!

Let's pick up some more, as Paul Harvey would say, 'the rest of the story.' Now let's see what's going to happen to those that fight against Christ. This is going to be quite a thing. There's no defense for this. It doesn't matter what kind of army that you think you have. It doesn't matter what weapons you think you may have. No one's going to be able to fight against this.

Zechariah 14:12: "And this shall be the plague with which the LORD will smite all the people who have fought against Jerusalem.... [that's where He's gathered them] ...Their flesh shall consume away while they stand on their feet, and their eyes shall consume away in their sockets. And their tongue shall consume away in their mouth."

In other words, the flesh is just going to fall off their bodies, and the flesh is just going to collapse and the skeletons fall over, and that's the end of the enemy. Now, you tell me what man has any power against God to stop that? *No man has!*

The first thing that needs to be done is you need to get rid of the leaders.

Revelation 19:20: "And the beast was taken, and with him the false prophet who worked miracles in his presence, by which he had deceived those who received the mark of the beast and those who worshiped his image. **Those two were cast alive into the Lake of Fire, which burns with brimstone**."

God preserves them alive. Their flesh doesn't fall off them like the others. But they just look at their armies and see all of this going on and all of their soldiers just becoming like crumpled heaps of rotten flesh and bones, and blood spewing everywhere, and guts spewing everywhere. This is going to be an awesome sight.

Verse 21: "And the rest were killed by the sword of Him Who sits on the horse, *even the sword* that goes out of His mouth; and all the birds were filled with their flesh."

Now back to Zech. 14; here's what's going to happen, because we are coming back to this earth. Christ is going to stand on the Mount of Olives.

Now remember, when Christ ascended into heaven, from where did He ascend? *From the Mount of Olives!* So, He's coming right back to the Mount of Olives. And what did the angels say when the apostles were looking up and wondering what was happening to Him? He said, 'why are you gazing up into the heavens? This same Christ is going to return in the same way.' *Yes, and to the same place!*

Zechariah 14:3: "And the LORD shall go out and fight against those nations, as when He fought in the day of battle. And His feet shall stand in that day upon the Mount of Olives, which *is* before Jerusalem on the east, and the Mount of Olives shall split in two, from the east and to the west, and make a very great valley...." (vs 3-4).

So the whole geography is going to change, isn't it? Yes indeed! So much for the Temple Mount; *that's going to be utterly destroyed!*

Verse 5: "'And you shall flee to the valley of My mountains; for the valley of the mountains shall reach to Azal. And you shall flee as you fled from before the earthquake in the days of Uzziah king of Judah.' **And the LORD my God shall come, and all the saints with You**."

We're going to put our feet on the Mount of Olives with Him!

Verse 9: "And the LORD shall be King over all the earth..." *That's what it's going to be!*

Now the rest of the story is continued with the next Holy Day—the Day of Atonement—*because there is yet one more judgment that needs to be taken place, and that is to get rid of Satan the devil!*

Scriptures from *The Holy Bible in Its Original Order, A Faithful Version*

Scriptural References

1) Leviticus 23:23-24
2) Numbers 10:2, 6, 9-10
3) 2 Peter 3:1-4
4) Daniel 2:44-45
5) Daniel 7:13-14, 27
6) Daniel 12:1
7) Jeremiah 25:12-17, 26, 29-33
8) Revelation 13:1-9, 11-17
9) Revelation 15:1-4
10) Isaiah 13:6-13
11) Joel 1:15
12) Joel 2:1-2
13) Joel 3:2
14) Psalm 149:1-9
15) Psalm 2:1-9
16) Revelation 15:5-8
17) Revelation 16:1-21
18) Revelation 19:1-19
19) Zechariah 14:12
20) Revelation 19:20-21
21) Zechariah 14:3-5, 9

Scriptures referenced, not quoted:

- Numbers 10:5
- Revelation 8; 9
- 2 Peter 3:5
- Jeremiah 50-52
- Isaiah 14
- Revelation 11
- Daniel 11
- 2 Thessalonians 2
- Revelation 18
- Isaiah 13:1
- Revelation 6
- Romans 8

FRC:cs
Transcription date unknown
Reformatted: bo—12/2020

CHAPTER FIFTY

_____

The Great Day of the Almighty God
Woes, plagues, blowing of trumpets, war and invasion from outer space
(Feast of Trumpets)
Fred R. Coulter

Greetings, brethren! Welcome to the Feast of Trumpets!

It certainly has been a volatile time recently, without question! Here we are with the Feast of Trumpets, which is one of the most important Feasts in the Bible. *It tells us specifically*—with all the prophetic things tied in together—*when Jesus and the saints are going to stand on the earth and bring the Kingdom of God to this earth!*

However, if you read the command for the Feast of Trumpets in Lev. 23, it doesn't tell us anything of the magnitude of the ultimate fulfillment of this day.

Leviticus 23:23: "And the LORD spoke to Moses, saying, 'Speak to the children of Israel saying, "In the seventh month, in the first *day* of the month, **you shall have a Sabbath, a memorial of blowing of ram's horns**…"'" (vs 23-24).

They had silver and gold trumpets and ram's horns, and ram's horns were used for war. So, this day is a *war feast!*

"…a Holy convocation. You shall do no servile work *therein* but you shall offer an offering made by fire to the LORD" (vs 24-25).

We know that today we do not have animal sacrifices, but in our world today we bring offerings of value, and that value will be in the form of excepted monetary value.

If you had to offer a heifer, a goat or lamb that would be worth a whole lot more. They figure that on the hoof of beef cattle is worth about $1500. I'm not saying that you should give $1500, *don't misunderstand me!* I'm just giving you an example of value.

Offerings go all the way down to *flour offerings,* which would be those things of least value.

So, whatever you are able to give, what you want to give to God—and it goes to the Church—and it will be used to preach the Gospel, to feed the flock and to take care of the things that God wants us to do.

(pause for the offering)

Why is the world in such a mess that it is in? *This is not the first time that the world has been in desperate shape!*

We know when Adam and Eve decided to go on their own and do their own thing and go their own way, they decided for themselves what would be good and what would be evil. *They didn't understand that God created us to need Him!* That's the important thing to understand.

- we need God
- we need His laws
- we need His commandments
- we need His Spirit
- we need Him to teach us out of His Word
  - ✓ with His character
  - ✓ with His love
  - ✓ with everything that is there

However, when we go off on our own and we think we know it all, and you expand that out to the whole world, then you see what's wrong with it.

Jeremiah 10:23: "O LORD, I know…" **What was Jeremiah doing?** *Bringing the prophecies to the people of Jerusalem*—of the fall of Jerusalem and Judea—*of going into captivity into Babylon because of their sins! So, he knew!*

"…that the way of man is not in himself, *it is* **not in man who walks to direct his steps**" (v 23).

That's why when you look at the whole world, everyone is doing it and the evil is coming! There was another time, and Jesus mentions this in Matt. 24, when the world was like this, and this led to the Flood. That was a great cataclysm! In the Greek: 'kataklusmos'! God has not gone way off some place!

- He's watching over the earth
- He's watching over all mankind
- He's watching over, especially, His Church

- He judges individuals
- He judges nations
- He judges the whole world

And that's going to happen again on the final Feast

of Trumpets when Christ returns!

Think about this verse in Gen. 6, and understand that the Word of God will *never ever, ever* fail!

Genesis 6:5: "And **the LORD saw that the wickedness of man *was* great on the earth**…"

What happens when you have generation after generation after generation of going your own way, every man and woman doing what's right in their own eyes under the guise and inspiration of Satan the devil? *He always comes as an angel of light to provide benefits, which always lead to destruction!*

Think about this; think how important this is: "…**and every imagination of the thoughts of his heart *was* only evil continually**" (v 5).

That's just the way it is today! **Look at the evil everywhere!** We are seeing the closing in of Satan's complete deception of the whole world, *and only God can rescue us from that!*

Let's see how it affects a whole nation. Look at what's been happening this spring and summer in the United States. We will see the reason that it is in the condition that it is today is **because everyone is doing what is right in his or her own eyes!**

Let's understand as we go through, God is dealing with the whole world. Just like Paul wrote, *'In Him we live, move and have our being'* and God has set the boundaries of the nations, and God is judging the nations (Jer. 18), and also every individual (Gen. 6:5). Now let's see what Isaiah had to say to Israel and to Judah.

Isaiah 1:2: "Hear, O heavens, and give ear, O earth; for the LORD has spoken, 'I have reared and brought up children, **but they have rebelled against Me**.'"

Read any part in the Old Testament and you will see that **when men leave the Laws of God trouble ensues!** Then it's multiplied even more when they go after Satan the devil, who takes them even further in deprivation, war and perversion.

Here's the comparison, v 3: "The ox knows his owner, and the donkey his master's crib; *but* Israel… [put there *the whole world*] …**does not know *Me*; My people do not understand**."

What is the understanding that they lack? *When you leave the Laws of God there are penalties individually and collectively, and they come automatically!* That's why the world is the way it is, and this is why Christ has to return to rescue it.

Verse 4: "Ah, sinful nation, a people burdened *with* iniquity… [think about all the iniquity that's going on] …a seed of evildoers, children who deal corruptly! They have forsaken the LORD; they have provoked the Holy One of Israel to anger; they have gone away backward."

Whenever you go away backward, you're going into trouble, difficulty, pain, agony and death: *individually and collectively!*

Verse 5: "Why should you be stricken any more? You will revolt more and more; the whole head is sick, and the whole heart faint. From the sole of the foot even to the *top of the* head *there is* no soundness in it; *only* wounds and bruises and putrefying sores; they have not been closed, nor bound up, nor soothed with ointment" (vs 5-6).

There's no way, because it's not in man or woman to know how to live separate from the laws and Word of God. Those who keep part of it do better. Those who completely go after Satan the devil do worse. *That's the contrast!*

But *those who love God and are His begotten children, are the ones who are walking in righteousness and in Truth!* We need to get this message out to the world! God said that *if you don't do it, then He's going to hold us responsible!*

Verse 7: Your country *is* a desolation, your cities *are* burned with fire…." *Doesn't that tell you what's going on?* There it is right here!

"…**Strangers devour your land right in your *very* presence, and *it is* wasted, as overthrown by strangers**. And the daughter of Zion…" (vs 7-9).

Apply that to the ten tribes of Israel, the modern descendants today, and to America or any country when it comes down to this.

"…is left as a booth in a vineyard, like a hut in a garden of cucumbers, like a besieged city" (v 8).

What does that mean? *There's so much sin and evil going on, it's just like creeping vines and it gets everywhere!*

Here's the good news; *here's the Church,* v 9: "Except the LORD of hosts had left us a very small remnant, we would have been as Sodom; we would have become like Gomorrah."

Then He says to the rulers, because they are responsible, and the rulers in the churches are responsible. Of course, they think fake Christianity is the Truth. Well, *you can't mix Truth with lies and expect a good result! The lawlessness from the pulpit,* as I have brought out many times, *is the root cause of all the problems that we have in America and in the nations of Israel today!*

Verse 10: "Hear the Word of the LORD, rulers of Sodom; give ear to the Law of our God, people of Gomorrah."

They say they're 'good people'; but God says *no, you're not!* They have their own ways of doing things.

God says, v 12: "When you come to appear before Me, who has required this at your hand, to trample My courts?"

- When they come before God on Sunday, who has required that? *Men! Not God!*
- When they have their Christmas, Easter, Halloween, New Years and all of that, who has required that? *Men! Not God!*
- Who is behind the men? *Satan the devil!*

Verse 13: "Bring no more vain sacrifices; incense is an abomination to Me—new moon and sabbath, the calling of assemblies..." *That's **their*** sabbath, which is Sunday.

They're so deluded that they *think* they're doing the right thing when they're worshipping on the day of the sun!

"...I cannot endure iniquity along with the solemn assembly! **Your new moons** ... [your way of doing thing, your calendar, *instead of God's*] ...and **your appointed feasts**... [Christmas, Easter, etc.] ...**My soul hates**; they are a trouble to Me; I am weary to bear *them*. And when you spread forth your hands, I will hide My eyes from you..." (vs 13-15).

You don't come to God in real repentance, and

- that followed up with baptism
- that followed up with a change of heart
- that followed up with conversion

You just come and give your mealy-mouthed three second, 'O forgive me my sins, Jesus, I believe in You and I'm saved forever.'

"...yea, when you make many prayers, I will not hear; your hands are full of blood...." (v 15)— *the blood of the innocent who are aborted,* as well as the murders, killings and drugs—everything like that!

But God always holds out repentance. If there's repentance, God will hold back!.

Verse 16: "Wash yourselves, make yourselves clean; put away the evil of your doings from before My eyes; cease to do evil.... [*stop it*] ...Learn to do good... [because you have learned nothing but evil] ...seek judgment, reprove the oppressor. Judge the orphan; plead for the widow.... [if you do that]: ...Come now, and let us reason together,' says the LORD. 'Though your sins are as scarlet, they shall be as white as snow; though they

are red like crimson, they shall be like wool. **If** you are willing and obedient, you shall eat the good of the land'" (vs 16-19).

- Have we passed that point? *I don't know!*
- How long do we have? *We'll have to wait and see!*

We need to stay faithful and remain close to God ourselves!

Micah 1—here is a prophecy or a foretelling of what God is going to do. We will see in the book of Revelation this is exactly what God is going to do.

Micah 1:2: "Hear, all you people!.... [everyone] ...Hearken, O earth... [everyone in the world] ...and *all* its fullness. And let the Lord GOD be witness against you, *even* the LORD from His Holy temple, for behold, the LORD *is* coming out of His place, and will come down and tread on the high places of the earth. And the mountains shall melt under Him, and the valleys shall split open, as wax before the fire, and as waters that are poured down a steep place" (vs 2-4). *All because of the sins of the people!*

Let's see what God says, because someone is going to say, 'Why is God going to do that, we're good people?'

Micah 6:1: "Hear now what the LORD says, 'Arise, contend with the mountains and let the hills hear your voice. O mountains, hear the LORD'S controversy; and you, strong foundations of the earth, for the LORD has a controversy with His people... [and we will later, *the whole world*] ...and He will plead His case with Israel" (vs 1-2). *And with the whole world!*

This is quite a thing that's going to take place when Christ returns. It's going to affect the whole world.

Verse 3: "O My people, what have I done to you? And in what way have I made you weary? Testify against Me!"—*tell Me!*

The first thing they're going to do is say that 'it's Your Law!' That's the problem! Everyone wants lawlessness; yet, they want things to be good. *Never happen! Never, never happen!* Let's see how this is going to affect the whole world.

In these minor prophets we find some very interesting things, indeed! Some foretelling of what's going to happen when Jesus Christ does actually return.

Habakkuk 1:1: "The burden which Habakkuk the prophet saw. O LORD, how long shall I cry and You will not hear? I cry out to You *of* violence, and You do not save!" (vs 1-2). *That's what's going to happen!* The people are going to do that. Why is this happening?

Verse 3: "Why do You show me wickedness, and trouble? For destruction and violence *are* before me; and there is strife, and contention rises up. Therefore, the law has become ineffective…" (vs 3-4).

A lot of people say they want law and order. Now they're so blindly educated and dumbed-down into lawlessness that they will settle for nothing but destruction! Why is that?

- necause the people have left God
- necause its just like Gen. 6—every thought of the imagination of the heart of men and women is evil all the time, continually

It's heightened now with all the hi-tech things that are brought to bear, and the children are taught at an early age. That's just the way that Satan wants it! He wants to destroy the human race. *They're going to have to pay a penalty,* **but God is going to save them!**

"…and judgment does not always go forth, for the wicked entraps the righteous; therefore, judgment goes forth perverted…. [then God says]: …'Look among the nations, and behold and be amazed and stunned; for *I* will work a work in your days *which* you will not believe, not even if it is declared to you'" (vs 4-5).

We're going to see what that's going to be like when we get to the book of Revelation. Let's see what's going to happen; let's see how it's going to take place, because this day of the Feast of Trumpets shows the power of God in the person of Christ and the Holy angels, and after the resurrection the saints. It's going to be a marvelous thing, indeed!

We'll look at Isaiah and then in Jeremiah about the things of the problems of the whole world, and that God has a controversy with everything, with the whole world!

When you look at the Churches of God, you look at Rev. 3 where it talks about the Church that is lukewarm, even the things in the world have affected the Churches of God. Think about how much has been compromised!

Isaiah 13:1: "The burden of Babylon, which Isaiah the son of Amoz saw." *Today it's Babylon the Great, the whole world!*

That's why when you go to the book of Daniel it starts out with King Nebuchadnezzar and the Babylonian Empire and the Chaldeans. That's the head that goes all the way down through the body to the feet and toes. When it says Babylon, don't think it is just Babylon back there, because let's read and see what it says:

Verse 2: "Lift up a banner upon the high mountain, exalt the voice to them, wave the hand so that they may go into the gates of the nobles." *Everyone is going to know! Everyone is going to understand!*

Sidebar: Today they're putting up satellites that will be at lower levels so that everyone will be able to have visualization and communication that can go anywhere in the world. God is making that known so there will be no excuse for anyone to say, 'Lord, why didn't You tell me?'

Verse 2: "Lift up a banner upon the high mountain, exalt the voice to them, wave the hand so that they may go into the gates of the nobles. I have commanded My Holy ones… [angels] …I have also called My mighty ones for My anger, *even* those who rejoice in My triumph" (vs 2-3)—*to carry out the will of God to destroy the evil!*

Verse 4: "The noise of a multitude in the mountains, as of a great people; a tumultuous noise of the kingdoms of nations… [the whole world is involved in this] …gathered together; the LORD of hosts gathers an army for the battle. They come from a far country, from the end of heaven…" (vs 4-5).

What do you think the rising of China is all about?

"…the LORD and the weapons of His indignation, to destroy the whole earth. **Howl! For the Day of the LORD *is* at hand**; it shall come as a destruction from the Almighty" (vs 5-6).

We're going to see that in the book of Revelation what absolute destruction is coming! It's going to be awesome indeed!

Verse 7: "Therefore, all hands shall be faint, and every man's heart shall melt; and they shall be afraid. Pangs and sorrows shall take hold of them. They shall be in pain like a woman who travails. They shall be amazed at one another, **their faces are *like* blazing fire**. Behold, the Day of the LORD comes, cruel…" (vs 7-9).

People ask how a God of love do that? *Because that's punishment for the absolute rebellion against the God of love*:

- by those who don't love God
- by those who hate God
- by those who despise God

It's coming! They will be cruel to the people of God. There will be martyrdom again, so God brings cruelty upon them.

"…both *with* wrath and fierce anger, to make the earth a desolation; and He shall destroy the sinners out of it" (v 9).

That's quite a thing! But look what else happens. These things don't happen in a vacuum. It's not just one episode; it affects everything on the earth, everything in the solar system, and even the heavens.

Verse 10: "For the stars of the heavens and their constellations shall not give light; the sun shall be darkened in its going forth, and the moon shall not reflect its light."

Verse 11—God says: "And I will punish the world for *their* evil, and the wicked for their iniquity; and I will cause the arrogancy of the proud to cease, and will lay low the haughtiness of the tyrants."

That is going to be a carnage so awesome… Notice what it says about that:

Verse 12: "**I will make man more scarce than gold; even man more than the fine gold of Ophir. Therefore, I will shake the heavens, and the earth shall move out of its place,** in the wrath of the LORD of hosts, and in the day of His fierce anger" (vs 12-13).

That's quite a thing! Think about that! Now, the book of Isaiah[transcriber's correction] is a tremendous book of Prophecy, covering so much of God's plan and put in such a way that unless you're willing to love God and obey Him, you can't understand it. Therefore, a lot of those who say that they know what's going to happen because they belong to this *fake* church or that *fake* church, or this evangelist or that whatever other. They'll have part of it and go off and have it wrong.

Isaiah 24:1: "Behold, the LORD makes the earth empty and makes it waste, and turns it upside down, and scatters its inhabitants." **How is that going to work?** *That's something to think about!*

Verse 2: "And as *it is* with the people, so it shall be with the priest; as with the slave, so with the master; as with the handmaid, so it is with her mistress; as with the buyer, so with the seller; as with the lender, so with the borrower; as with the creditor, so with the debtor. **The earth shall be completely laid waste**…" (vs 2-3). *That is a tremendous thing to contemplate! It's going to happen!*

"…**laid waste** and **utterly stripped**; for the LORD has spoken this word" (v 3)—*in the whole Bible!*

If there are any skeptics out there, or anyone thinks that this guy (Fred) is getting carried away, *never has a single word that God has recorded in His Bible failed! Never! Not one!*

Jesus said concerning His words of

prophecy, Matt. 24, *'Heaven and earth shall pass away, but My words shall <u>never</u> pass away!'* So, it's going to happen!

Verse 3: "The earth shall be completely laid waste, and utterly stripped; for the LORD has spoken this word. The earth mourns *and* languishes; the world withers *and* languishes; the proud people of the earth wither. And the earth is defiled under its people; **because they have transgressed the laws, changed the ordinance, and have broken the everlasting covenant**" (vs 3-5).

That's why it's not these people are sinful or those people are sinful. It's not this cause or that cause. It's because of right here: "…**they have transgressed the laws, changed the ordinance**…"

Go out and look around and see how many people, churches or organizations want to love God and keep His commandments. If everybody did that we wouldn't have these problems.

But they think that if they go their own way that they can handle it. But they don't understand that *IF they don't go God's way, there's no way in them that they can go to direct their paths,* as Jeremiah said. *It just won't work! So, God has to come in power and authority, and to lay waste the world in order to save it!*

Verse 6: "Therefore, the curse has devoured the earth…"—*because where there's a law and free choice there has to be* **a penalty for rejecting it,** *and* **a blessing for keeping it!**

"…and they who dwell in it are desolate; therefore, the people of the earth are burned, **and few men are left**" (v 6).

Let's see what Jeremiah says. Jeremiah was give quite a prophetic message to take. It has to go to the whole world, to all nations! We know that with this prophecy encompasses all the nations of the world, so there needs to be a message going out today, which God is going to send out. It will be bringing this understanding and this warning to the world. We'll see what that is right here:

Jeremiah 25:15: "For thus says the LORD, the God of Israel, to me…" *When God says, 'I say so' it's going to be done!* There's no way that the Word of God is not going to be fulfilled.

"…'Take the wine cup of this wrath at My hand…'" (v 15). *We will see the wrath of God in Rev. 16, the seven last plagues!* Leading up that all the other things that take place.

"'…and cause all the nations to whom I shall send you to drink it. And they shall drink, and reel to and fro, and be crazed because of the sword that I will send among them.' Then I [Jeremiah] took the cup at the LORD'S hand, and made all the nations drink, to whom the LORD had sent me" (vs 15-16)—*in vision!*

Jeremiah didn't go anyplace, and this is for our time. Then he lists all of them starting in Jerusalem and going to the rest of the world. He summarize it in:

Verse 26: "And all the kings of the north, far and near, one with another, and all the kingdoms of the world, which *are* on the face of the earth..." *That's as thorough a warning as you can get!*

"...and the king of Sheshach shall drink after them" (v 26). *This is a type of the coming beast (Rev. 13).*

Verse 27: "Therefore, you shall say to them, 'Thus says the LORD of hosts, the God of Israel, "Drink and be drunk, and vomit, and fall, and rise no more because of the sword which I will send among you. And it shall come to pass if they refuse to take the cup at your hand to drink, then you shall say to them, 'Thus says the LORD of hosts, "You shall certainly drink. For, lo, I begin to bring evil on the city, which is called by My name... [Jerusalem] ...and shall you go unpunished? You shall not go unpunished. For I will call for a sword on **all the inhabitants of the earth,'" says the LORD of hosts**" (vs 27-29). *Think on that! Remember those words!*

There's a tremendous warning message that needs to get out there. What did Jesus say? *This Gospel of the Kingdom shall be preached in all the world to all nations, and **then the end shall come!** This verifies it!*

Verse 30: "'And prophesy against them all these words, and say to them, "The LORD shall roar from on high, and utter His voice from His Holy habitation. He shall mightily roar over His dwelling place. He shall give a shout, like those who tread out *grapes*, **against all the people of the earth**. A noise shall come to the ends of the earth; for the LORD has a controversy **with the nations**... [not just with His people, but all the nations of the world] ...He will plead with all flesh. He will give those *who are* wicked to the sword,'" says the LORD" (vs 30-31).

We will see how that is going to be carried out later in the book of Revelation

Verse 32: "Thus says the LORD of hosts, 'Behold, evil shall go forth from nation to nation, and a great whirlwind shall be stirred up from the farthest corners of the earth. And the slain of the LORD shall be at that day **from *one* end of the earth even to the *other* end of the earth**; they shall not be mourned, nor gathered, nor buried. They shall be *as* dung on the ground'" (vs 32-33).

Now we'll see how all of these things will transpire, exactly as God has said that it would.

The book of Revelation is laid out in such a way that it also follows the pattern of the Holy Days in Lev. 23, which is quite startling indeed when you come to understand it. No one would guess that just by reading Lev. 23 that Revelation would follow that pattern.

Note our in-depth study: *Daniel/Revelation,* which is a complete verse-by-verse study with charts and everything laid out the way that it should be, according to the Calculated Hebrew Calendar. The end-time is keyed to the last week of Daniel's 70-week prophecy. Each week has 7 days and a day is as a year in prophecy.

Rev. 6—the seals are opened. We need to realize that Rev. 5 tells us very clearly that only Christ is going to open the seals, and that will only be at the command of God the Father. So, the book of Revelation—when you understand it—is God the Father's revelation that He gave to Jesus Christ, Who gave it to John to give to the Church, so that we, at the end-time, could understand.

In Dan. 12, Daniel was told that from, his time forward these things were closed until the time of the end. At the time of the end *'the wise shall understand.'* The wise ones are those who love God and keep His commandments, and who do the things that God delights in. Who also understand the prophecies, not because we're smarter than anybody else, but because we rely on the Word of God and the pattern of the Holy Days of God.

So, for those who don't keep the Sabbath or the Holy Days, they may understand some smidgens of prophecy, but not the book of Revelation. They may understand a part of it here or there, but a part here and a part there doesn't give you the full overall picture.

So, you need to get the Daniel/Revelation Transcript Book with CDs. Go through the Scriptures in Daniel and Revelation. We have nice charts so you can understand that last seven years.

Rev. 6 comes to two full years into the last seven, and this is when Christ intervenes directly. As we have seen by the prophecies that we've already covered.

Revelation 6:12: And when He opened the sixth seal, I looked, and behold, there was a great earthquake; and the sun became black as *the* hair *of* sackcloth, and the moon became as blood." *We read part of that in the book of Isaiah!*

Verse 13: "And the stars of heaven fell to the earth, as a fig tree casts its untimely figs when it is shaken by a mighty wind. Then *the* heaven departed like a scroll..." (vs 13-14).

This is going to be an awesome event. This is going to be an earth-shattering and earth-startling event for those who are still live at that time, because the majority of deaths are yet ahead.

Verse 14: "Then *the* heaven departed like a scroll that is being rolled up, and every mountain and island was moved out of its place. And the kings of the earth, and the great men, and the rich men, and the chief captains, and the powerful men, and every bondman, and every free *man* hid themselves in the caves and in the rocks of the mountains; and they said to the mountains and to the rocks, 'Fall on us, and hide us from *the* face of Him Who sits on the throne, and from the wrath of the Lamb… [notice that God the Father is involved here, too] …because the great day of His wrath has come, and who has the power to stand?'" (vs 14-17).

Rev. 7[transcriber's correction] occurs on a Pentecost, and this is the saving of the 144,000 and the great innumerable multitude. The earth, as we've seen with all of the earthquakes and everything that takes place, these things need to be repaired in order for the next part of the revelation to go forward.

So, from Pentecost to Trumpets is a space of about four months and a week or two. That's the time that the earth will regroup and Satan will be telling them:

No, no, no! This is not Christ. This is the antichrist and we need to beware that there may be an invasion from outer space.

Which will happen, but not right at this point!

Right at this point the six seals have been opened, and then the seventh seal is opened and the trumpet plagues come. That's starts on the Feast of Trumpets of the last year before Christ and the saints who have been resurrected will return to the earth to rescue the rest of mankind and start the Kingdom of God and the Millennial reign on the earth.

Here's what's going to happen before, and remember, this starts on the Feast of Trumpets.

Revelation 8:1: "Now, when He opened the seventh seal, *there* was silence in heaven *for* about a half hour. Then I saw the seven angels who stand before God, and seven trumpets were given to them" (vs 1-2).

Remember, we'll be raised from the dead at the seventh trump. Please understand that the book of Revelation is the only place in the Bible where there are trumpets in sequence and are blown one after the other to where we come to the seventh or last trumpet. That's when the dead will be raised on the Pentecost just before the last Trumpets. Again, we'll see that.

Verse 3: "And another angel, who had a golden censer, came and stood at the altar…" *All of these things start at the Throne of God in heaven above and are carried out on the earth.*

"…and much incense was given to him, so that he might offer *it* with the prayers of all the saints on the golden altar that *was* before the Throne" (v 3).

All the saints are those who are living: the 144,000 and the great innumerable multitude and those who happen to be in a place of safety.

Verse 4: "And the smoke of the incense went up before God from *the* hand of the angel, ascending with the prayers of the saints. And the angel took the censer, and filled it with fire from the altar, and cast *it* into the earth; and there were voices, and thunders, and lightnings, and an earthquake" (vs 4-5).

When the Millennium begins, th earth is going to be whole lot different than it is today. That's going to be something to behold.

Verse 6: "Then the seven angels who had the seven trumpets prepared themselves to sound *their* trumpets."

It's not men fighting against men; it's now angels of God against men and demons. Who is the head of the demons? *Satan the devil!* This is when it really gets bad!

Verse 7: "And the first angel sounded *his* trumpet; and there was hail and fire mingled with blood, and it was cast upon the earth; and a third of the trees were burnt up, and all green grass was burnt up." *Think of that! Think of what an awesome thing that's going to be!*

Verse 8: "Then the second angel sounded *his* trumpet; and *there* was cast into the sea as *it were* a great mountain burning with fire, and a third of the sea became blood; and a third of the living creatures that *were* in the sea died, and a third of the ships were destroyed" (vs 8-9). *These are awesome events to take place!*

Verse 10: And the third angel sounded *his* trumpet; and *there* fell out of heaven a great star, burning like a lamp; and it fell on a third of the rivers, and on the fountains of waters. Now, the name of the star is Wormwood; and a third of the waters became wormwood; and many men died from *drinking* the waters because they were made bitter. Then the fourth angel sounded *his* trumpet; and a third of the sun was smitten, and a third of the moon, and a third of the stars… [just like we read in the book of Isaiah] …so that a third of them were darkened; and a third part of the day did not shine, and likewise *a third part of* the night" (vs 10-12).

John is seeing this vision and he said, v 13:

"And I looked, and I heard an angel flying in the midst of heaven, saying with a loud voice, '**Woe, woe, woe** to those who are dwelling on the earth, because of the voices of the remaining trumpets of the three angels who *are* about to sound *their* trumpets'"

The first four come suddenly, one after the other! Now, here are the armies and they're the armies that come out of Europe and come down to the Holy Land. They are there and they're going to fight. There are the armies from the east. *This is going to involve all the armies of the world! We will see that God has a great surprise for these armies!*

Revelation 9:1 "And the fifth angel sounded *his* trumpet; and I saw a star… [an angel of God] …*that* had fallen from heaven to the earth, and there was given to him the key to the bottomless abyss"—*the prison of the demons!*

Here the demons are going to be let out on the earth in an incomprehensible number that has never been since the founding of the world.

Verse 2: "And he opened the bottomless abyss; and there went up smoke from the pit, like *the* smoke of a great furnace; and the sun and the air were darkened by the smoke from the pit. Then locusts came onto the earth from the smoke; and power was given to them, as the scorpions of the earth have power. And it was said to them that they should not damage the grass of the earth…" (vs 2-4).

It was burned up before, and now it's grown back. Trees and plants, if there's water they grow. When it's dark, cloudy and there are storms that are coming. So, here's the green grass.

"…or any green thing, or any tree, **but only the men who did not have the seal of God in their foreheads**" (v 4).

Who are the ones who have the seal of God in their foreheads at that time? *The 144,000 and the great innumerable multitude!*

Verse 5: "And it was given to them that they should not kill them, but that they should be tormented five months; and their torment *was* like *the* torment of a scorpion when it stings a man."

This is kind of like a super-secret demonic hightech weapon!

Verse 6: "And in those days men will seek death but will not find it; and they will desire to die, but death will flee from them. And the appearance of the locusts *was* like horses prepared for war; and on their heads *were* crowns like *those* of gold; and their faces *were* like *the* faces of men; and they had hair like women's hair; and their teeth were like *those* of lions. And they had breastplates like iron breastplates; and the sound of their wings *was* like *the* sound of chariots *drawn* by many horses running to war" (vs 6-9). *This is quite a thing!*

Verse 10: "And they had tails like scorpions, and stingers; and they were *given* power to injure men with their tails *for* five months. **And they have over them a king, the angel of the abyss; his name in Hebrew *is* Abaddon, but *the* name he has in Greek *is* Apollyon**" (vs 10-11)—*Satan the devil!*

Verse 12: "The **first woe is past**. Behold, after these things **two more woes are still to come**."

This is going to be something, because these armies will be fighting for the control of the world! Now it's going to involve all the mass armies from the east all the way from China, India, Southeast Asia, Uzbekistan, all of the 'stans,' Iran. All the armies are going to be stung out from China clear to the Euphrates River. *A massive thing indeed!* Never before anything like this!

Verse 13: "And the sixth angel sounded *his* trumpet; and I heard a voice from the four horns of the golden altar that *is* before God; *and* it said to the sixth angel, who had the trumpet, 'Loose the four angels who are bound in the great River Euphrates'" (vs 13-14).

Think about that! God has four angels in the River Euphrates bound there until this time. These are demonic angels.

Verse 15: "Then the four angels, who had been prepared for… [Listen to this; is God on time? *Yes, indeed!*] …the hour and day and month and year, were loosed, so that they might kill a third of men." *This is going to be awesome!*

Like the Bible says, the dead will be strewn out from one end of the horizon to the other.

Verse 16: "And the number of *the* armies of the horsemen *was* two hundred thousand thousand; and I heard the number of them." *That is 200-million!*

That's an awful lot of armies; not one single army, but many, many armies strung out from the Far East all the way to the River Euphrates.

Verse 17: "And so, I saw the horses in the vision, and those sitting on them, who had fiery breastplates, even like jacinth and brimstone. And the heads of the horses *were* like heads of lions, and fire and smoke and brimstone shoot out of their mouths. By these three a third of men were killed: by the fire and the smoke and the brimstone that shoot out of their mouths. For their power is in their mouths; for their tails *are* like serpents, *and* have heads, and with them they inflict wounds" (vs 17-19).

Verse 20: "But the rest of the men who were

not killed by these plagues **still did not repent of the works** of their hands that they might not worship demons, and idols of gold and silver and brass and stone and wood, which do not have the power to see, nor to hear, nor to walk. And **they did not repent of their murders, nor of their sorceries, nor of their fornications, nor of their thievery**" (vs 20-21). *Quite an awesome thing to take place!*

Think of the armies coming over toward Jerusalem, the armies that are already there in that area from out of Europe and the Muslim countries there *waiting for the clash!* We will see later the final battle is going to be in the Valley of Megiddo or Armageddon. That is a vast flat plain.

Rev. 10 is a very interesting one, a very short chapter, but there are some thing here that are going to be so awesome! Let's see what's going to happen.

Revelation 10:1: "Then I saw another strong angel coming down out of heaven, clothed with a cloud, and *with* a rainbow on his head; and his face *was* like the sun, and his feet *were* like pillars of fire; and he had in his hand a little book *that was* open. And he placed his right foot on the sea, and *his* left *foot* on the earth, and cried with a loud voice, as a lion roars. And when he cried, the seven thunders uttered their voices. And when the seven thunders spoke *with* their voices, I was about to write. But I heard a voice from heaven say to me, '**Seal what the seven thunders spoke, and do not write them.**' Then the angel whom I had seen standing on the sea and on the earth lifted up his hand to heaven, and swore by Him Who lives into the ages of eternity, Who created the heaven and the things in it, and the earth and the things in it, and the sea and the things in it, '**There shall be no more delay**'" (vs 1-6). *It's going to continue!*

Verse 7: "But in the days of the voice of the seventh angel, when he is about to sound *the* trumpet, the mystery of God shall also be completed, according to the Gospel *that* He declared to His servants the prophets. Then the voice that I heard from heaven spoke to me again, and said, 'Go, take the little book that is open in the hand of *the* angel who is standing on the sea and on the earth.' And I went to the angel, *and* said to him, 'Give me the little book.' And he said to me, 'Take *it* and eat it; and it shall make your belly bitter, but in your mouth it shall be sweet as honey.'" (vs 7-9).

Verse 10: "Then I took the little book out of the angel's hand, and ate it; and it was sweet as honey in my mouth; but after I ate it, my belly was bitter. And he said to me, 'You must again prophesy against many people, and nations, and languages and kings'" (vs 10-11). *A final warning!*

How that's going to be done, we don't

know, but we'll find out when that time comes. Then Rev. 11 is about the two witnesses. It's very interesting about the two witnesses:

* they have a ministry that is to last 1,260 days
* they're to witness against the beast and the false prophet
* there is going to another temple built, the Jewish temple

That's the one that 'abomination of desolation' occurs when the Beast Power goes into the Holy of Holies and declares himself to be 'God.' There will be a fierce battle between the two witnesses *and* the beast and the false prophet, just like it was between Pharaoh and his court *and* Moses and Aaron. The two witnesses, during their ministry, can call down plagues and fire, whatever, any time that they will. *This is prophesied of in Zech. 3 & 4!*

Sidebar: don't let any minister fool you by saying that he's one of the two witnesses. There's a man who did that some time ago and he finally revealed that his wife was the second one.

But understand that everything to do with Jerusalem and the temple is going to be handled by God, and *He's going to select the two witnesses!* One will be the high priest of the coming temple, and the other will be the governor of Judea.

When they completed their witness they're going to be killed. The world is going to be so happy that they are dead that they're going to leave their bodies in the streets of Jerusalem so all the world can see it. The world is going to be happy and rejoice and give gifts to one another.

Revelation 11:11: "Then after the three and a half days, *the* spirit of life from God entered into them and they stood on their feet; and great fear fell upon those who were watching them."

Think about this fulfilling the Word of God. These are the last two martyrs, but they fulfill the verse that says, 'The last shall be first' and they are the first two resurrected.

Verse 12: "And they heard a great voice from heaven, say, 'Come up here!' And they ascended into heaven in a cloud; and their enemies saw them *rise*. And in that hour there was a great earthquake, and a tenth of the city fell; and seven thousand men were killed in the earthquake. And the rest were filled with fear, and gave glory to the God of heaven. **The second woe is past. Behold, the third woe is coming immediately. Then the seventh angel sounded *his* trumpet**…" (vs 11-15).

* this is the last trumpet
* this is the first resurrection

- this takes place on the last Pentecost
  - ✓ all the saints are raised
  - ✓ all the prophets are raised
  - ✓ all the righteous kings are raised

We are all carried by angels up to a vast Sea of Glass right over where the Battle of Armageddon is going to be!

They're going to look up there and see an invasion from outer space! Now we have from Pentecost to Trumpets, and that's when the seven last plagues are poured out.

Revelation 15:5: "And after these things I looked, and behold, the temple of the tabernacle of the testimony in heaven was opened. And the seven angels who had the seven *last* plagues came out of the temple; they were clothed in linen, pure and bright, and girded about the chest with golden breastplates. And one of the four living creatures gave to the seven angels seven golden vials, **full of the wrath of God,** Who lives into the ages of eternity. And the temple was filled with smoke from the glory of God, and from His power; and no one was able to enter inside the temple until the seven plagues of the seven angels were fulfilled" (vs 5-8).

Here we have the world now being stricken by God again, and we'll see that *they don't repent!* Think about all the devastation that has occurred. You might just get a little bit of understanding of what this is like if you ever saw the destruction of Berlin by the Russians coming into Berlin and the fight that was there. They fought against all odds, but lost! Hitler and his entourage were down in a bunker. They knew the end was coming, but they wanted all people could even walk and hold a gun to go fight. So, it's going to be the same kind of attitude here in

Revelation 16:1: "Then I heard a loud voice from the temple say to the seven angels, 'Go and pour out the vials of the wrath of God onto the earth.' And the first *angel* went and poured out his vial onto the earth; and an evil and grievous sore fell upon the men who had the mark of the beast, and upon those who were worshiping his image" (vs 1-2).

Sidebar: *The mark of the beast is coming!*

Verse 3: "And the second angel *went and* poured out his vial into the sea; and it became blood, like *that* of a dead *man*; and **every living soul in the sea** died." *All living things are souls; there is no such thing as an immortal soul!*

Verse 4: "And the third angel poured out his vial upon the rivers, and into the fountains of waters; and they became blood." *What was done to them before was all washed away!* So, here comes another wave of it.

Some who read this think: How could a God of love do that? *Let's see what the angels have to say about it; they would be the ones to render a better opinion of that than any human being!*

Verse 5: "Then I heard the angel of the waters say, 'You are righteous, O Lord, Who are, and Who was, even the Holy One, in that You have executed this judgment. For they have poured out *the* blood of saints and of prophets, and You have given them blood to drink; for they are worthy.' And I heard another *voice* from the altar say, 'Yes, Lord God Almighty, **true and righteous *are* Your judgments**'" (vs 5-7).

Verse 8: "And the fourth angel poured out his vial upon the sun; and *power* was given to it to scorch men with fire. Then men were scorched with great heat; and they blasphemed the name of God, Who has authority over these plagues, and did not repent to give Him glory" (vs 8-9).

Isn't it interesting how it is that when men give themselves over to Satan and the demons, *that even at a time when they know they're going to die they won't repent!*

Verse 10: "And the fifth angel poured out his vial upon the throne of the beast; and his kingdom became full of darkness; and they gnawed their tongues because of the pain, and blasphemed the God of heaven because of their pains and their sores; **yet, they did not repent of their works**" (vs 10-11). *No repentance!*

Remember that the four angels [demons] were bound in the River Euphrates and the armies came over and the river started flowing again. So now, later, we have a repeat of this:

Verse 12: "And the sixth angel poured out his vial into the great river Euphrates; and its waters were dried up, so that the way of the kings from the rising of *the* sun might be prepared. Then I saw three unclean spirits like frogs *come* out of the mouth of the dragon… [Satan] …and out of the mouth of the beast… [the great Beast Power] …and out of the mouth of the false prophet; for they are spirits of demons working miracles, going forth to the kings of the earth, even of the whole world, to gather them together to *the* battle of **that great day of the Almighty God**" (vs 12-14).

Now, after all of this you would think that there would be people repenting! But there's not! Why? *By this time they're probably convinced that this is really an invasion from outer space!*

Unless we get all the armies of the earth up over here, we are going to lose the world

That is really true! It will be an invasion from outer

space, but not from aliens *but from God the Father, Jesus Christ and the saints of God!*

When we read along these things, every once in a while God throws something in there to get your attention to help you to understand *that you need to really stay right with God!*

Verse 15: "Behold, I come as a thief. Blessed *is* the one who is watching and is keeping his garments, so that he may not walk naked and they *may not* see his shame."

He just interjected this one verse as a warning! Keep your life right with God!

Verse 16: "And he gathered them together to the place that in Hebrew is called Armageddon. Then the seventh angel poured out his vial into the air; and a loud voice came out of the temple of heaven, from the throne, saying, 'IT IS FINISHED.' And there were voices and thunders and lightnings; and there was a great earthquake, such as was not since men were on the earth, so mighty an earthquake, *and* so great. And the great city was divided into three parts; and the cities of the nations fell…" (vs 16-19).

Just think about all these high tower buildings! *Gone!* I look at the island there in New York City and there are all these buildings there. That's nothing to God; *it's going to be gone!*

- the tallest building in the world in Abu Dhabi; *it's going to be gone*
- the tallest building in Singapore; *it's going to be gone*
- the tallest building in Beijing; *it's going to be gone*

Flattened to the ground!

"…and Babylon the Great was remembered before God to give her the cup of the wine of the fury of His wrath. And every island disappeared, and no mountains were found… [completely turned upside down] …and great hail, *each stone* the weight of a talent, fell down from heaven upon men; and men blasphemed God because of the plague of the hail, for the plague was exceedingly great" (vs 19-21).

Now let's see what happens, because this is the day when Christ and the saints all come back to the earth. They're up on the Sea of Glass (Rev. 15) and on the Sea of Glass everybody gets their name, their new clothes, and the understanding of their duties. When we're raised from the dead we'll all be given a language built right into our spirit brains and bodies so we can communicate with each other, and God can communicate with us, and Christ can give us the direction in which we are to go. *It's going to be something!*

Then there will be the wedding of the Lamb [Christ] and the Church, and then we're going to come down from heaven after the great wedding supper, while all this evil is going on, on the earth. Then on that last Feast of Trumpets we come back to the earth to finish the final Battle of Armageddon!

Revelation 19:11: "And I saw heaven open; and behold, a white horse; and He Who sat on it *is* called Faithful and True, and in righteousness He does judge and make war. And His eyes *were* like a flame of fire, and on His head *were* many crowns; *and* He had a name written that no one knows except Him. And *He was* clothed with a garment dipped in blood; and **His name is The Word of God**. And the armies in heaven were following Him on white horses…"(vs 11-14).

- we'll be given white horses
- we'll have instruction as to what to do
- we'll have a battle plan as to what to carry out

"…*and* they were clothed in fine linen, white and pure. And out of His mouth goes a sharp sword, that with it He might smite the nations; and He shall shepherd them with an iron rod; and He treads the winepress of the fury and the wrath of the Almighty God. And on *His* garment and on His thigh He has a name written: **King of kings and Lord of lords**" (vs 14-16). *That's something!*

Picture this: here we are, we have our horses, Christ is leading us and we're all at the edge of the Sea of Glass, and then He says, 'NOW! Let's go!' Here we go! Just think how that's going to feel coming down off the Sea of Glass! All the saints and the battle going on down below. The birds are coming to clean up all the mess and are flying coming there. We're coming down on our horse with Christ!

Verse 17: "Then I saw an angel standing in the sun; and he cried out with a loud voice, saying to all the birds that fly in *the* midst of heaven, 'Come and gather yourselves together to the supper of the great God… [going to clean up this mess] …so that you may eat *the* flesh of kings, and *the* flesh of chief captains, and *the* flesh of mighty *men*, and *the* flesh of horses, and of those who sit on them, and *the* flesh of all, free and bond, and small and great'" (vs 17-18).

Verse 19: "And I saw the beast and the kings of the earth and their armies, gathered together to make war with Him Who sits on the horse, and with His army. And the beast was taken, and with him the false prophet who worked miracles in his presence, by which he had deceived those who received the mark of the beast and those who worshiped his image. Those two were cast alive into the Lake of Fire, which burns with brimstone; and the rest were killed by the sword of Him Who sits on the horse, *even the sword*… [His Word] …that goes out of His mouth; and all the birds were filled with their flesh" (vs 19-21).

We find in Zech. 14 what's going to happen to them. All of their flesh is going to fall off their bones! ***This is the meaning of the Feast of Trumpets, <u>a War Feast</u>, for the greatest war and the last one until the very end!***

Brethren, I'm glad you're able to be here for the Feast of Trumpets, now let's look forward to Atonement and Tabernacles.

Scriptural References:

1) Leviticus 23:23-25
2) Jeremiah 10:23
3) Genesis 6:5
4) Isaiah 1:2-10, 12-19
5) Micah 1:2-4
6) Micah 6:1-3
7) Habakkuk 1:1-5
8) Isaiah 13:1-13
9) Isaiah 24:1-6
10) Jeremiah 25:15-16, 26-33
11) Revelation 6:12-17
12) Revelation 8:1-13
13) Revelation 9:1-21
14) Revelation 10:1-11
15) Revelation 11:1-15
16) Revelation 15:5-8
17) Revelation 16:1-21
18) Revelation 19:11-21

Scriptures referenced, not quoted:

- Matthew 24
- Jeremiah 18
- Revelation 3; 13; 5; 8
- Daniel 12
- Revelation 7
- Zechariah 3; 4; 14

Also referenced: In Depth Study: *Daniel/Revelation*

FRC:bo
Transcribed: 7/5/20
Reformatted: 12/2020

CHAPTER FIFTY-ONE

God's Final Judgment:
A View of the Seven Last Plagues
(Feast of Trumpets)
Fred R. Coulter

Greetings brethren, welcome to the Feast of Trumpets, and we've certainly seen a lot of things transpire this past year, and every year we get closer and closer to the fulfillment of the events that are prophesied in the Bible.

The Feast of Trumpet's is one of the key important fulcrum points in history because *this day pictures the establishing of the Kingdom of God on earth by Jesus Christ and the saints!* Let's also understand that *all of the Holy Days are* connected:

- the Sabbath puts us in contact with God
- the Holy Days tell us what He's doing

Let's understand something about the Holy Days—though they seem unimportant to the world—they are absolutely important to God!

What people don't understand about the Holy Days is that every one of the Holy Days pictures an epical historical event that God fulfills. For example, the Sabbath, right after the creation of man was given as a day of rest, sanctified to be Holy; *it was an epical beginning of man and his relationship with God!*

Then we come down to the Passover, *an epical historical event* with:

- Abraham
- the children of Israel
- the killing of the firstborn
- the destruction of Egypt
- the first day of the Feast of Unleavened Bread
- the exodus to leave
- Pentecost, the giving of the 10 Commandments

Then we come right down through the New Testament with all of these. Passover: the greatest event to take place from the beginning of the history of the world—the death of the Son of God, Who would save the world from sin—happened on the Passover Day. The first day of the Feast of Unleavened Bread, right as it began He was put into the tomb. Three days and three nights later, He was resurrected toward the end of the Sabbath. And then on the Wave Sheaf Offering Day He ascended to heaven, *an epical historical event!*

Then Pentecost, the beginning of the Church, *an epical historical event!* The resurrection from the dead for the first resurrection on Pentecost, *an epical historical earthshaking event,* as we saw on the Day of Pentecost.

Now we come down to the Feast of Trumpets, and again, it is going to be *an epical and historical event,* and profound, telling the plan of God, laying out step-by-step how He's going to fulfill it. It's not generally revealed to the world because the world doesn't know, the world doesn't understand. Especially today, as Satan is deceiving the whole world with all of these false gospels—Gnostic gospels and things like this—people just going after it head over heels. So, we come to the Feast of Trumpets, *an epical event* that is going to take place.

Leviticus 23:23: "And the LORD spoke to Moses, saying, 'Speak to the children of Israel saying, "In the seventh month, in the first *day* of the month, you shall have a Sabbath… [all the Holy Days are a Sabbath] …a memorial of blowing of ram's horns, a Holy convocation. You shall do no servile work *therein* but you shall offer an offering made by fire to the LORD" (vs 23-25).

With all the Holy Days—because these picture major events that God is going to do—these are special, and we should bring an offering that is special to God. We should always realize that we are to seek first the Kingdom of God in His righteousness.

The blessings that God gives us are to be reflected in the offerings that we give to God. You know all about that, and just realize that we try and use everything that God sends us to:

- preach the Word of God
- publish the Gospel
- send out books to people to help them in their circumstances

- we are not here to build an organization
- we are not here to build up the name of any man

601

we are here

- to preach the Truth of God
- to help and serve the brethren
- to make known the Word of God as much as possible

as God will open the doors for us to reach out to the world, which we're doing in a very dramatic way with the book: *Occult Holidays or God's Holy Days—Which?* In there contains all of the plan of God! It is *a fantastic book, having an impact on people such as never has been in recent years!*

So, keep all of that in mind when you send in your tithes or offerings for the Holy Days, and remember that God is able to give back to you in blessing, that all of us will have sufficiency in all things.

(pause for offering)

Now let's continue on and see the meaning of the Day of the Feast of Trumpets, which is going to be one of the most earthshaking events to hit the world since its creation.

Matt. 6—is part of our prayer, when we pray, according to the model prayer.

Matthew 6:9: "Therefore, you are to pray after this manner: 'Our Father, Who *is* in heaven, hallowed be Your name.'"

When you are praying that way, just remember, you're coming before God the Father on His Throne, Jesus Christ at His right hand, the 24 elders out in front before the Throne, and around the Throne is a rainbow and it sits on a Sea of Glass. There are thousands and thousands—10,000 times 10,000—of angels there praising God, and the message is *'Holy, Holy, Holy, Lord God Almighty, which was, and is to come, for all these things have been created for Your will, and Your pleasure.'*

So, when we say, v 10: "Your Kingdom come; Your will be done on earth, as *it is* in heaven"—*it's always going to be done that way!* But the reason that we pray for it this way, is because there is always a space of repentance that God gives.

Whenever there's something that comes along that is going to be a disaster that's going to happen, that there is going to be a judgment by God, He always gives a time and space of repentance. We'll see that in several instances here, as we go through. That's why in Ezek. 33, God says, *'O Israel, turn you, turn you, for I have no pleasure in the death of the wicked but that the wicked would turn from his way.'*

In everything that God does, there is that measure of repentance because God has given free moral agency and choice, and who knows what people will do. That's why there is given that space.

So, we need to realize that that's part of the will of God. The reason that we do this, is this: When we come to God, we don't come to God and pray to Him and pray for **our** will to be endorsed by God. Now it is true, as Jesus said that when we ask He will answer, and whatever we desire, He will give. *That's **IF** it is according to, the will of God!*

"Your Kingdom come…" comes in two different ways:

1. upon conversion

It comes to us when we are converted, not that the Kingdom of God becomes within, as some people say; *that's not true!* We come under the jurisdiction of the Kingdom of God and Jesus Christ, as our Lord, and Master, and High Priest in heaven right now, and soon coming King, when Jesus returns.

Col. 1—let's see how the Kingdom of God comes to us, and in our Christian lives:

2. in the way that we live, and walk, and so forth

Colossians 1:10: "That you may walk worthily of the Lord…" *This is our goal, this is what we need to do in everything we do!*

We're going to talk about how we need to have the right kind of attitude and mindset in the end-time, so that we can do the will of God in our lives:

- that God will be with us
- that God will help us
- that God will bless us
- that god will strengthen us

"…unto all pleasing, being fruitful in every good work and growing in the knowledge of God" (v 10). *All of this has to do with preparing for eternal life!* We are in *training*:

- for eternal life
- to be kings and priests
- to rule this world

The first place that begins is to let Christ rule in us!

Verse 11: "Being strengthened with all power according to the might of His glory, unto all endurance and long-suffering with joy."

So, regardless of our circumstances, we're always looking to God the Father; we're always looking to Jesus Christ. We are developing, and growing in heart, in mind, spirit, and in knowledge of God. This gives us the strength, and this gives us the conviction, and this gives us the endurance of the longsuffering.

Verse 12: "Giving thanks to the Father, Who has made us qualified for the share of the inheritance of the saints in the Light..." [that's what God is doing and we have a literal, absolute, inheritance] ...**Who has personally rescued us from the power of darkness** and has transferred *us* unto the Kingdom of the Son of His love" (vs 12-13).

Now that means that once we have been called, have repented, been baptized and received the Spirit of God, *then we are brought under the jurisdiction of Jesus Christ!* We are under the jurisdiction of the Kingdom of God. So when we pray, "Your Kingdom come..." we are always subjected to the Kingdom of God, that is to God the Father and Jesus Christ.

When we understand that, we realize that there is no room for a hierarchical, authoritarian government in the ministry of God, or as the Catholics have with their hierarchy. They say that outside of the hierarchical Catholic Church there is no salvation. Well that's a bunch of humbug! There is no salvation *in it, because salvation comes from God!* So that's how we are there.

Now let's notice how it is to work in our lives, in our heart and mind. The reason I'm going through things is so that we can see how we are to have the attitude to face all the horrendous things that are going to take place as pictured by the Feast of Trumpets.

We've had hurricanes hit America, we've had the tsunami, we've had earthquakes, we've had wars. As we're going to see, that's just a start! What the Feast of Trumpets pictures is the intervention of God, and the Kingdom of God coming on this earth, and God's judgment on the world. Just as the Passover pictured the judgment of God against all the gods of Egypt, and against the firstborn in Egypt, so likewise from the time of Pentecost down through Trumpets *it pictures the judgment of God on this world,* and it is going to make what happened in Egypt look like child's play.

Colossians 3:14: "And above all these things... [Paul list all the character things as we covered during the Feast of Unleavened Bread] ...*put on* love..."—*and that is the key!*

You must be fortified with the love of God, by loving Him with all your heart, all your mind, all your soul, all your being, and you're going to hear me say that over and over and over again, because:

- that is where our strength comes from
- that is where we're going to receive the resolve that is going to guarantee that we will be faithful unto the end
- that will give us the mind set that we need to have to be able to be faithful to Christ in

the face of the worst disasters that are going to come upon the face of the earth

Granted, many of us who are older, God is going to spare us, He is going to take us to the grave in peace and that will be our place of safety. That's fine, that's all part of God's purpose. But there are those of us who are going to have to live through it, and we're going to have to be strengthened with the Spirit of God. You're not going to be strengthened when you see these things happening and all of the sudden, you start praying, and all of the sudden, you start studying—*too late!* You have to build and develop the character now.

Verse 15: "And let the peace of God **rule in your hearts,** to which you were called into one body, and be thankful. **Let the Word of Christ dwell in you richly**..." (vs 15-16).

That's the whole key, we're to live by every Word of God; we're to live by the words of Christ. We're to have His words dwelling in us richly.

- *IF* Christ is going to dwell in us, *which He is*
- *IF* God the Father is going to dwell in us, *which He is*
- *THEN* the words of Christ ought to richly dwell in us, too.

Because that:
- establishes our mind
- establishes our hearts
- establishes our thoughts

and gives us the defense against all the events that are going to take place in the world, because you need to be defended in the mind, *mentally and spiritually,* first.

"...**rule in your hearts**..." *Let Christ rule in you!* You stop and think about this for a minute:

Sidebar: Christ is to rule you, *not the ministry!* The Holy Spirit of God is to lead you, *not the ministry!* Yes, the ministry is here:

- to teach
- to help
- give counsel
- give advice

But the greatest advice is: Look to God the Father and Jesus Christ, not what we would do of ourselves, or the ministry would do for you.

"...to which you were called into one body, and be thankful. Let the Word of Christ dwell in you richly in all wisdom, teaching and admonishing one another in psalms and hymns and spiritual songs, singing with grace in your hearts to the Lord" (vs 15-16).

When Paul and Silas were cast into prison, what did they do? *They prayed to God, and they sang, and God intervened and helped them!* So, in all circumstances Paul was one who really set the standard. Let's realize that the kind of attitude we need to have is this:

• we need to be tenderhearted to God, Jesus Christ and the brethren
• we need to have a mind and a forehead of flint toward all the evils and troubles that are coming in the world

Let's see what God told Jeremiah. Jeremiah had a really lonely ministry; he had no friends, he had no brethren, the only one he had was his secretary Baruch. You read through the book of Jeremiah, and see the things that Jeremiah went through. God knew it was going to be difficult, so here's what He told him:

Jeremiah 1:15: "'For, behold, I will call all the families of the kingdoms of the north'…" *At the end-time God is going to call all the nations, He's going to gather all the nations!*

"…says the LORD. 'And they shall come, and they shall each one set his throne at the entrance of the gates of Jerusalem, and against all its wall all around, and against all the cities of Judah.'…. [that is all the armies of Nebuchadnezzar] …And I will pronounce My judgments…" (vs 15-16). *We're going to see that also ties in with the Feast of Trumpets.*

"…against them regarding all their wickedness in that they have forsaken Me, and burning incense to other gods, and worshiping the works of their own hands…. [those two things apply to us today as never before] …You, therefore, must gird up your loins, and arise, and speak to them all that I command you. Do not be dismayed… [discouraged] … at their faces, lest I confound you before them" (vs 16-17).

In other words, don't look to the circumstances and how other people react because that really doesn't make any difference. You have to be looking to God.

Verse 18: "'For, behold, I have made you a fortified city this day, and an iron pillar, and bronze walls against the whole land, against the kings of Judah, against its rulers, against its priests, and against the people of the land. And they shall fight against you; but they shall not overcome you. For I *am* with you,' says the LORD, 'to deliver you'" (vs 18-19).

Now let's understand that at the end-time it's going to be very similar to the same thing.

• Did we not see on Pentecost how there's coming the martyrdom of the saints?
• How are we going to endure that?

We are going to be offered many different ways, given a chance to recant:

• given a chance to accept the beast
• given a chance to accept the mark
• given a chance to accept all the things that are there

Remember that Rev. 13 says that *into the hands of the beast are given all nations, languages, kingdoms, and he goes to make war against those who have the Spirit of Christ!* There's going to be that martyrdom.

Now let's see how Jesus was strengthened, in a very similar way. How did Jesus endure everything that he had to do, through the crucifixion: the scourging and the beating? Remember when He finished that prayer the angels strengthened Him. Likewise, *we need the power of God to strengthen us!* Let's see what kind of mind that God gave Jesus: tender toward God the Father inside, but there had to be the strength and the power on the outside, to not be overwhelmed with all the things that He was going to experience.

Isaiah 50:5: "The Lord GOD has opened My ear, and I was not rebellious, nor turned away backwards."

When we get into those situations, understand that __IF__ you have opened the door for Christ in your mind, and Christ rules in your heart and mind, *you have closed the door to turn back!* It's exactly what happened with Christ so He could do this:

Verse 6: "I gave My back to the smiters… [the scourging] …and My cheeks to them that plucked off the hair…. [they beat Him and pulled His beard and smashed Him in the face] …I did not hide My face from shame and spitting, for the Lord GOD will help Me; therefore, I have not been disgraced. On account of this I have set My face like a flint, and I know that I shall not be ashamed" (vs 6-7). *So, this is the only way we're going to be able to face these things in the future!*

Let's see what God told Ezekiel. Now of all the prophets, the two that had the most difficult ministry to do, were Jeremiah, but Ezekiel had the worst one of all. If you read the book of the Ezekiel, just take it and read a couple chapters every day, and think about what he had to go through, think about what he had to endure.

Ezekiel 3:4: "And He said to me, 'Son of man, go! Go up to the house of Israel and speak to them with My words. For you *are* not sent to a people of a strange speech and of a difficult language, *but* to the house of Israel; not to many people of a strange speech and of a difficult language, whose words you cannot understand. Surely, if I had sent you to them, they would have hearkened to you. But the house of Israel will not be willing to hearken to you, for they will not be willing to hearken to Me…" (vs 4-7).

The reason is that when Jesus said that 'lawlessness shall be multiplied, and the love of many shall grow cold' and there's going to come a time of great evil, and *people are __not__ going to want to listen to the Truth of God!*

That's why God has to intervene with the events that we see here. That's why God sends the two witnesses and their ministry. So, we're talking about big earthshaking events that are going to take place.

"'…for all the house of Israel *are* of a hard forehead and a stubborn heart. Behold, I have made your face strong against their faces and your forehead strong against their foreheads. I have made your forehead as an adamant stone, harder than flint. Do not be afraid of them or dismayed by their faces, for they *are* a rebellious house.' And He said to me, 'Son of man, receive all My words which I shall speak to you. **Receive them to your heart, and hear with your ears"** (vs 7-10). *Then he was to preach that.*

So, this tells us that when we come down to these times, we are not to back off from the message of God. We're not to make it softer and easier so that we don't offend people. Because Jesus said, 'many are going to be offended,' and it's going to be a time of great trouble and great difficulty.

Let's see what it is going to be like; great historical events of a magnitude that is unimaginable to the human mind. If you think the destruction of the tsunami was great, or if you think that some of the volcanic actions that we have had are great, or the earthquakes, or the floods, or the storms, *hang on,* because they now know the global warming is a general warming of the whole solar system. Even Mars is having a global warming experience, and of course there's not one single gas-driven car up there, is there, nor factories with huge smokestacks belching out carbon dioxide. Now there are two electrical satellite vehicles up there, and surely they are not causing Mars to have a global warming experience. All of this is part of the things leading up to the time of the end, and all of this is going to upset the weather even more. Now let's see something that's important concerning the Day of the Lord.

Matthew 24:15: "'Therefore, when you see the abomination of desolation, which was spoken of

by Daniel the prophet, standing in the Holy place.' (The one who reads, let him understand.); 'then let those who are in Judea flee into the mountains. Let the one *who is* on the housetop not come down to take anything out of his house; and let the one *who is* in the field not go back to take his garments. But woe to those *women* who are expecting a child, and to those who are nursing infants in those days! And pray that your flight be not in *the* winter, nor on *the* Sabbath" (vs 15-20).

Here again, even in the midst of great trouble and difficulty what does God say, *__remember the Sabbath Day and keep it Holy.__*

Verse 21: "For then shall there be Great Tribulation… [How great?] …**such as has not been from *the* beginning of *the* world until this time, nor ever shall be *again*.**" *We need to let those words sink in!*

How many ministers have used, 'Oh, the events are speeding up! We really need you to send in more money so we can preach the Gospel! Oh, we've got to hurry and get this done, and hurry and get that done'?

What they do is that they want to speed up the Day of the Lord, so they can kind of glory in their own self-predictions of it. Those are the prophecies that Paul said would fail, and they've all failed. Why? *Because they're not relying on God, and they're not looking to the outline of God, as God has said!*

It hasn't happened, yet, because we have not comprehended how great God is going to let the kingdom of Satan become *before He* [God] *intervenes directly!* We don't know how many people God is going to call, and lead to repentance between now and that point. God is interested in mercy and not sacrifice. But when the time comes that God says it's going to happen, because it's under the authority of God the Father and Jesus Christ, it is going to happen.

Preachers and men are not to get out there and say, 'Oh hurry, the Day of the Lord is coming!' You look back at all the events. 'Jesus is going to set His foot on the earth' in all these different years; *it never happened,* did it? Why? *Because they're not willing to put it in God's hands to let it happen!* So, here's God's answer to them:

Amos 5:18: "Woe to those desiring the Day of the LORD! What *is* this for you? The Day of the LORD *is* darkness and not light; as *if* a man fled from a lion, and a bear met him; or went into the house and leaned his hand on the wall, and a snake bit him" (vs 18-19).

He's telling us very clearly, there is not going to be any relief once this starts. Yes, we see that God will protect you (Psa. 91), but only up to a certain point, because there's going to be a martyrdom of the saints. *This is why we have to have the mind and attitude that Jesus Christ has!* So, we ask for a tender heart before God the Father and Jesus Christ, and loving the brethren and each other, *but we ask for a forehead of flint against all the evil, and against all the things that are coming!* If you get emotionally involved in all these events, as we're going to read about from here on that's going to literally turn this world upside down, you will not be able to handle it. *We need to ask God for the strength so we can handle it!*

Verse 20: "*Shall* not the Day of the LORD *be* darkness and not light? Even very dark, and no brightness in it?"

Zephaniah 1:13: "'And their goods shall become a prize and their houses a desolation. They shall also build houses, but not live *in them*, and they shall plant vineyards, but not drink their wine.' The great Day of the LORD *is* near; *it is* near…" (vs 13-14). *That's the message for our time!*

Notice that God doesn't say exactly how far, or how close, *but it's near!* Even though we've had all these false alarms down through time, guess what, it is nearer than when we first believed.

"…and comes swiftly, the sound of the Day of the LORD. The mighty man shall cry bitterly there. That day *is* a day of wrath, a day of trouble and distress, a day of ruin and devastation, a day of darkness and gloominess, a day of clouds and thick darkness, a day of the ram's horn…" (vs 14-16).

It is a memorial of the blowing of trumpets, and actually the fulfillment of the Feast of Trumpets is reserved for the end-time, and the very Day of the Lord. There's only one fulfillment of the Feast of Trumpets that we find in the Old Testament, and that is in 1-Chron. 5 when the temple was dedicated, and on the Feast of Trumpets God put his presence in the temple. *The only other fulfillment is the return of Christ!*

"…and alarm against the fortified cities… [no defense is going to help] … and against the high towers…. [doesn't matter what weapons you have] …'And I will bring distress on men, so that they shall walk as the blind because they have sinned against the LORD. And their blood shall be poured out as dust, and their flesh as dung'" (vs 16-17).

And as Jeremiah said, 'The LORD has a controversy with the nations.' (Jer. 25). *He's going to bring them all to Jerusalem, and in that day, the dead will be from one end of the horizon to the other end of the horizon!*

Now let's see if we can at least begin to grasp that perhaps *no more than one-tenth* of all the population of the earth is going to survive through the Tribulation, and enter as physical human beings into the Kingdom of God. So, it's going to be a horrendous time. There will never ever, ever again be a day like this.

Verse 18: "Neither their silver nor their gold will be able to deliver them in the day of the LORD'S wrath; but the whole earth shall be devoured by the fire of His jealousy, for He shall make even a full end, yea, a terrible end of all who dwell upon the earth" *God is going to spare some; there will be some who will escape, that is true!*

Let's see again the warning concerning the Day of the Lord, and all the way through here, it is a day that has never ever had an historical parallel, not even in the destruction of Jerusalem. This is going to be *a worldwide event,* not like it was in Egypt, where He dealt with just one nation, but this is all nations, all peoples. When we understand the plan of God, we need to realize, it covers the great and the major events in the Bible, and God has given us the knowledge and the understanding of it.

Joel 1:15: "Alas for the day! For the Day of the LORD *is* at hand, and **it shall come as a destruction from the Almighty**." *It's going to come!*

Joel 2:1: "'Blow the ram's horn in Zion…" *I don't know what's going to happen when that Feast of Trumpets is fulfilled,* and we'll get to the book of Revelation here in a minute, and see how it unfolds step-by-step.

"…and sound an alarm… [continuously blowing] …in my Holy mountain!…." (v 1).

Where's it going to start? *It's going to start from Mt. Sion in heaven above,* and the sound, the trumpets, the blasting is going to come from God. We'll see how that's going to be here in just a bit.

"…Let all the inhabitants of the land tremble, for the Day of the LORD comes, for *it is* near at hand—**A day of darkness and of gloominess, a day of clouds and of thick darkness.** As the morning *is* spread across the mountains, *so comes* a great people and a mighty people; there has never been the like…" (vs 1-2).

We're going to see in Rev. 9 huge armies, and one of them 200-million! God is going to judge the world, and God is going to judge the nations, and they're all going to fight against Christ.

"…nor shall there ever be again, even to the years of many generations. A fire devours before them… [great modern weapons that we have today] …and behind them a flame burns. The land *is* as the Garden of Eden before them, and behind them a desolate wilderness—and nothing shall escape them.

Their appearance *is* as the appearance of horses… [we'll read the fulfillment of that in Rev.] …and as war horses, so they run. They shall leap with the noise of chariots on the tops of mountains, with the noise of a flame of fire that devours the stubble, like a mighty people set in battle array. In their presence the people shall *greatly* tremble; all faces shall grow pale…. [because of all the events that are going to take place] …They shall run like mighty men…" (vs 2-7).

Now, I've read articles recently, where they're trying to improve the battle worthiness of troops on the ground. Where they have armor that cannot be penetrated with weapons, where they have medication put right into the garments themselves, so if any wound happens it immediately starts working to heal it, and keep them from getting any infection. They are working on putting chips in the minds of the soldiers to be able to give them instant recall to make them better in battle.

What it's talking about here, we could not picture this in the past until now, but now we know what it's going to be like.

"…They shall climb the wall like men of war, and they shall march each one in his path, and they shall not break their ranks. And each one shall not crowd another; they go every one in his *own* path. And when they fall upon the sword, they shall not be wounded" (vs 7-8).

Isn't it amazing that today that's exactly what they're working on?

Verse 9: "They shall run to and fro in the city; they shall run upon the wall; they shall climb up upon the houses; they shall enter in at the windows like a thief. The earth shall quake before them…" (vs 9-10).

Now I want you to, if you can, turn on the vision of your mind to see what an awesome event this is going to be.

"…the heavens shall tremble. The sun and the moon shall grow dark, and the stars shall withdraw their shining. And the LORD shall utter His voice before His army; for His camp *is* exceedingly great; for powerful *is* He who executes His Word, for the Day of the LORD *is* great and very terrible… [that is awesome for all the power and destructions that's going to take place] …and who can endure it?" (vs 10-11). *That is, live in it!*

Now notice, whenever it comes to that point, there's a space of repentance:

Verse 12: "'Therefore, even now,' says the LORD, 'turn to Me with all your heart, and with fasting, and with weeping, and with mourning. Yes, rend your heart and not your garments, and return to the LORD your God: for He *is* gracious and merciful, slow to anger, and of great kindness, and He repents of the evil'" (vs 12-13).

Now this is a message directly to the children of Israel, of the 144,000 who repent, and are saved on that next to the last Pentecost.

Let's come to Isa. 13, and again, it's talking about the Day of the Lord. Let's understand something: *It is a day of judgment, a day of death and destruction such as never has been since the creation of the world!* And this day is going to be talked about all the way through the Millennium! Everybody is going to remember *this* day as we now remember what happened to Egypt; because what happened to Egypt, on the Passover, and the events leading up to the Passover, is going to happen to the whole world. The events leading up to Trumpets and the return of Christ.

Isaiah 13:6: "Howl! For the Day of the LORD *is* at hand; it shall come as a destruction from the Almighty. Therefore, all hands shall be faint, and every man's heart shall melt; and they shall be afraid. Pangs and sorrows shall take hold of them. They shall be in pain like a woman who travails. They shall be amazed at one another, their faces are *like* blazing fire. Behold, the Day of the LORD comes, cruel both *with* wrath and fierce anger, to make the earth a desolation…" (vs 6-9). *That goes out to the whole world!*

"…and He shall destroy the sinners out of it, for the stars of the heavens and their constellations shall not give light; the sun shall be darkened in its going forth, and the moon shall not reflect its light. '**And I will punish the world for *their* evil**…" (vs 9-11).

That's why God is letting all the evil increase, giving everyone a chance to have their fill of evil, whatever it may be, but also giving an opportunity of repentance if they would.

"…and the wicked for their iniquity; and I will cause the arrogancy of the proud to cease, and will lay low the haughtiness of **the tyrants**" (v 11)—*the beast, false prophet and Satan the devil!*

Verse 12: "I will make man more scarce than gold… [nine tenths of the population are going to die in these events that are going to take place] …even man more than the fine gold of Ophir. Therefore, I will shake the heavens, and the earth shall move out of its place, **in the wrath of the LORD of hosts, and in the day of His fierce anger**" (vs 12-13).

Isa. 24—here's what God is going to do, He's going to literally shake this earth in a way that has never been.

Isaiah 24:18: "And it shall be, he who flees from the sound of dread shall fall into the pit. And he who comes up out of the midst of the pit shall be taken in the snare, for the windows from on high are opened, and the foundations of the earth quake." *Now we're going to go to Rev. here in just a minute and see that taking place!*

Verse 19: "**The earth is broken, yea broken down! The earth is crumbling, yea crumbling to pieces!**.... [torn asunder; great earthquakes are born] ...**The earth is tottering, yea tottering!**" *It's going to affect the orbit of the earth!*

Verse 20: "Like a drunkard the earth is staggering, yea staggering! And it rocks to and fro like a tree hut! And its transgressions are heavy upon it; and it shall fall and not rise again. And it shall come to pass in that day, the LORD shall punish the host of the high ones *that are* on high... [all the leaders of the world; all of the powers and principalities of Satan the devil] ...and the kings of the earth upon the earth. And they shall be gathered, *as* prisoners are gathered in a dungeon. And they shall be shut up in the prison... [God is going to entrap them in that war] ...and after many days they shall be punished. Then the moon shall be confounded, and the sun shall be ashamed, for the LORD of hosts shall reign in Mount Zion, in Jerusalem, and gloriously before His elders" (vs 20-23) *The ancient ones are going to be all of those who've been raised from the dead!*

Now let's come back to the book Revelation, and let's pick it up where we left off on Pentecost, because remember: *all the Holy Days are connected one with another,* and between Rev. 6 & 7, after the heavens roll back as a scroll—this is what we just read about here in the Old Testament that is going to take place—after the martyrdom has taken place, *then there comes a space of time of repentance in Rev. 7 with 144,000 and the great innumerable multitude being sealed,* waiting for the next Pentecost.

So from Pentecost, when they are converted, to the last Pentecost—a space of one year—these are the laborers who were hired at the eleventh hour. Now they're going to be saved, they're going to enter into the Kingdom of God.

Rev. 8—let's picture this: It is running from Trumpets to Trumpets, from the next to the last Trumpets to the last Trumpets.

As we come down in time, when the resurrection takes place, there is still four months left until the Feast of Trumpets and its fulfillment. So we have here a whole year, and if our estimation of time is correct, it is a 13-month year. That gives a little more space of time. But here's what happens, here is how it's fulfilled, we read a lot of it, but here is how it's going to be fulfilled beginning with next to the last of the Feast of Trumpets down to the last of the Feast of Trumpets, before Christ and the saints put their feet on the earth.

Revelation 8:1: "Now, when He opened the seventh seal, *there* was silence in heaven *for* about a half hour."

So there again, a time of respite, and we read of that back in Joel 2, *a time of repentance that God always gives before He starts pouring out his wrath!* Now we'll talk about the wrath of God here, a little bit later.

Verse 2: "Then I saw the seven angels who stand before God, and seven trumpets were given to them. And another angel, who had a golden censer, came and stood at the altar; and much incense was given to him, so that he might offer *it* with the prayers of all the saints on the golden altar that *was* before the Throne" (vs 2-3).

Now this is a time when all the brethren, all the saints, are going to be calling out to God day and night. There isn't going to be any laxness in prayer in these days. It's going to be almost constant prayer:

- O Lord, help me
- O Lord, watch over me
- O Lord, spare me
- O Lord, give me strength
- let my mind be fixed
- let me have the same attitude as Jesus Christ, Jeremiah, Ezekiel

to withstand all the events that we're going through! So, they're coming up before God!

Verse 4: "And the smoke of the incense went up before God from *the* hand of the angel, ascending with the prayers of the saints." *So we're all directly involved in this!*

Now here's what's going to happen. God begins fighting against men who are led by Satan and his demons. He's going to fight against them with His angels. Here is direct intervention from heaven above. Everything else that took place in Rev. 6, where all of those things that took place because of the efforts of men and their armies, and so forth. Those seals that were opened ended with the sixth seal, in their revelation of the sign of the Son of man in heaven above.

Now God begins to deal in a different way because this is the Day of the Lord, *from Trumpets to Trumpets, the year of the Lord!* "

Verse 5: "And the angel took the censer, and filled it with fire from the altar, and cast *it* into the earth; and there were voices, and thunders, and lightnings, and an earthquake"

We're going to see they're going to be a lot of earthquakes. It says in Isa. 40 that 'every valley shall be exalted, and every mountain and hill shall be made low"

So, when it says they're turning the earth upside down, what it is, it's turning of the surface of the earth upside down. That's going to result in earthquakes, and volcanoes, and it's going to be a horrendous thing! That's why I want us to grasp, and to understand how important the Holy Days really are: that they picture the major mammoth events, orchestrated and carried out, and fulfilled by God the Father, Jesus Christ and the angels. *Here's the angelic intervention*:

Verse 6: "Then the seven angels who had the seven trumpets prepared themselves to sound *their* trumpets. And the first angel sounded *his* trumpet; and there was hail and fire mingled with blood, and it was cast upon the earth; and a third of the trees were burnt up, and all green grass was burnt up" (vs 6-7).

What's going to happen with all the hail, and darkness, and everything? Well, there's going to be a lot of rainstorms that will come right after that, just like we see every year. We see fires out here in California, and fires burn up grass. See fires in forest and the mountain areas; we see fires in Florida, and all of that, then the rain comes, floods and destruction.

Verse 8: "Then the second angel sounded *his* trumpet; and *there* was cast into the sea as *it were* a great mountain burning with fire, and a third of the sea became blood."

Now with all of these things taking place and all of those who are dying on the earth because of it, those who survive are going to be firmly convinced that this must be war from heaven, *which it is!* There's no convincing about it! That the aliens are preparing to invade the world, *which they are! Jesus Christ and the saints!*

As I mentioned on Pentecost, when they see the resurrection take place—I think **they are going to see** the resurrection take place—all these people being taken up to the Sea of Glass...

Well I'm getting a little ahead of myself here in the flow of the events, but nevertheless, they are going to be absolutely convinced of this alien invasion, and an asteroid hitting the earth, because that's what is being described here, "...**a great mountain burning with fire**..." An asteroid hits the earth, think of the tsunamis, the earthquakes, and what's going to happen then. When that happens then, "...**a third part of the sea became blood.**"

It doesn't affect the whole earth, yet. It's in different areas of the earth. If we can look at the orb of the earth, and kind of picture, say, in the Atlantic Ocean, or in the Indian Ocean, and it happens later over in the Pacific Ocean, and so forth. Here's what's going to happen:

Verse 9: "And a third of the living creatures that *were* in the sea died, and a third of the ships were destroyed."

You think about the giant mammoth ships they're building now being destroyed. Think about all of these tankers carrying the oil being destroyed and split open.

Verse 10: "And the third angel sounded *his* trumpet; and *there* fell out of heaven a great star, burning like a lamp; and it fell on a third of the rivers, and on the fountains of waters. Now, the name of the star is Wormwood...." (vs 10-11).

Because they wouldn't obey God, and they martyred the saints, God is going to give them the bitterness of their way back to them.

"...and a third of the waters became wormwood; and many men died from *drinking* the waters because they were made bitter" (v 11).

They are going to be so thirsty, they're going to say, 'Oh let us drink of it, if we live, we live. If we die, we die.'

Verse 12: "Then the fourth angel sounded *his* trumpet; and a third of the sun was smitten, and a third of the moon, and a third of the stars; so that a third of them were darkened; and a third part of the day did not shine, and likewise *a third part of* the night."

This is why God has to intervene. *He is showing exactly what He is going to do!* All of this that I read up to this point, through v 12, are just softening up the world for what is coming, because as God says:

- *He* is going to judge the world
- *He* is going to judge the inhabitants thereof
- *He* is going to judge the nations thereof

And in a final analysis, we're going to see *He* gathers all nations together, and they are going to fight against Jesus Christ, and fight against the saints. So these are huge worldwide events that are taking place.

Verse 13: "And I looked; and I heard an angel flying in the midst of heaven, saying with a loud voice, '**Woe, woe, woe to those who are dwelling on the earth, because of the voices of the remaining trumpets of the three angels who *are* about to sound *their* trumpets.**'"

It intensifies, and gets greater, and men are going to be mad in their thoughts, desperate in what they are going to do, motivated. Because the angels of God have done this, now *Satan gets permission for the legions of his demons who are bound in the abyss to be released,* to strengthen men so *that they will fight even more*—to give them strength, power, energy—*and release a secret weapon!*

This is what's going to happen (Dan. 12) the King of the North is going to come against the King of the South, and then when he's there for a while, he is going to hear of trouble from the north and from the east, and he is going to go and make waste against them. Rev. 9 is a fulfillment of this, and he's going to have an awesome secret weapon.

Revelation 9:1: "And the fifth angel sounded *his* trumpet… [*first woe*] …and I saw a star *that* had fallen from heaven to the earth, and there was given to him the key to the bottomless abyss…. [that's where the demons are in prison] …And he opened the bottomless abyss; and there went up smoke from the pit, like *the* smoke of a great furnace; and the sun and the air were darkened by the smoke from the pit" (vs 1-2).

Here come out all these millions and millions of demons bound in there, now ready to fight against God, ready to fight against whomever that they're directed against. This is going to be a mad frenzy.

Verse 3: "Then locusts came onto the earth from the smoke; and power was given to them, as the scorpions of the earth have power."

They are going to go out, and it's going to be a secret occult major weapon against all the forces of the north and the east, and temporarily they're going to have a victory.

Verse 4: "And it was said to them that **they should not damage the grass of the earth…**"— because all the grass burned up, but now because of the rain and things that comes along in spite of all the destruction, the grass still grows. So, here months later, the grass has come back, and now it said:

"…they should not damage the grass of the earth, or any green thing… [because the trees come back] …or any tree, **but only the men who did not have the seal of God in their foreheads**" (v 4).

So over here, wherever they are, are the 144,000. Then scattered through the earth, are the great innumerable multitude, wherever they are gathered. God gives them special protection.

Just like at the same time, in the plagues that came against Egypt, God brought the first number of plagues against the Egyptians, and they also came against the Israelites. Then with the one plague concerning the moraine, God severed the children of Israel from the rest of Egypt. So likewise here, He severs those who have the Holy Spirit of God, who were sealed by the angel (Rev. 7).

Now the reason they received the Holy Spirit that way is very simple. There's nobody out there, no ministers out there to baptize them. They repent and God gives the Holy Spirit to them directly that way, *sealed by a hand of an angel!*

Verse 5: "And it was given to them… [satanic powers] …that they should not kill them, but that they… [the enemy] …should be tormented five months; and their torment *was* like *the* torment of a scorpion when it stings a man."

They are going to be virtually paralyzed, hardly able to move, and it will take them five months to recover.

When they recover, we're going to see what happens. Just picture this: this is sent to Russia, China, India, Southeast Asia, Japan, Mongolia, Kazakhstan and Uzbekistan, and all the 'stans' that go to the east, and against all the Muslim countries there involved. They're going to have this come upon them. They are going to think that this is fantastic. 'We have stopped them in their tracks.' *But it's only going to last for five months!* During that time:

Verse 6: "And in those days men will seek death but will not find it; and they will desire to die, but death will flee from them. And the appearance of the locusts *was* like horses prepared for war; and on their heads *were* crowns like *those* of gold; and their faces *were* like *the* faces of men; and they had hair like women's hair; and their teeth were like *those* of lions. And they had breastplates like iron breastplates; and the sound of their wings *was* like *the* sound of chariots *drawn* by many horses running to war; and they had tails like scorpions, and stingers; and they were *given* power to injure men with their tails *for* five months" (vs 6-10).

Demonic weapons used by men, possessed by demons, going out to battle!

Verse 11: "And they have over them a king, the angel of the abyss; his name in Hebrew *is* Abaddon, but *the* name he has in Greek *is* Apollyon… [Satan the devil] …The first woe is past…. [there comes a respite]: …Behold, after these things two more woes are still to come. And the sixth angel sounded *his* trumpet…" (vs 11-13)— *which is the **second woe!***

Now then, they recover from their five months of this super secret weapon inspired by demons that have them paralyzed for five months. They're able to recover. They're able to gather their armies. Now they begin to launch their super secret demonic weapons. So we have demons against demons, angels of God against men and demons, men against men, demons against demon, all carrying out the will of God.

"…and I heard a voice from the four horns of the golden altar that *is* before God; *and* it said to the sixth angel, who had the trumpet, 'Loose the four angels who are bound in the great River Euphrates'" (vs 13-14).

God has demons buried in the earth, imprisoned there for a certain time, for a certain thing to be done. Now it's going to be a mammoth thing to dry up the River Euphrates.

Someone sent me an article that different countries are seeking to build dams on the river Euphrates, and so that's how it's going to dry up. *It isn't going to happen that way! It's going to happen the way it says here.* So they were loosed.

Verse 15: "Then the four angels, who had been prepared for the hour and day and month and year, were loosed… [a specific time determined by God] …so that they might kill a third of men."

Remember, a fourth of mankind was already killed, so a third of them is another fourth (Rev. 6) Here we have fifty percent of mankind killed already, to say nothing of the other events that are going to take place.

Verse 16: "And the number of *the* armies of the horsemen *was* **two hundred thousand thousand**…"

Think about Joel 2: an army of 200-million. It's going to come, as we will see, from what we might say, the middle of Iraq. All the way, the army is strung all the way back to the Far East. I think it's very profound, very interesting, that in order to get the oil from Kazakhstan to China—which they have been doing by rail tanker cars—they are building huge pipelines to go to the east to China. But also along with that, they are building a huge highway, so they can service all of that. That's going to come into China, and that's going to go right by the world's biggest dam.

Just think, these armies stringing from the middle of Iraq all the way back, 200-million. You can't have them all in one place, so they're all strung out back there, and they come in waves.

"…and I heard the number of them…. here's how they're going to come, al their demonic secret weapons] …And so, I saw the horses in the vision, and those sitting on them, who had fiery breastplates, even like jacinth and brimstone. And the heads of the horses *were* like heads of lions, and fire and smoke and brimstone shoot out of their

mouths. By these three a third of men were killed: by the fire and the smoke and the brimstone that shoot out of their mouths. For their power is in their mouths; for their tails *are* like serpents, *and* have heads, and with them they inflict wounds" (vs 16-29).

This must be some kind of weapon protruding out of it, however that is. They are developing weapons now that are going to be awesome. I think we're going to see how it's going to be fulfilled to the very nth degree of what it's talking about, here in Rev, 9.

Verse 20: "But the rest of the men who were not killed by these plagues…"

This is to show you the hardness of heart that men have, and how absolutely self-centered on their power, and worshiping Satan the devil, who gives them that power, that they want to hold on to it. And yes, this is Satan in his desperate battle in fighting against God; he wants to hold onto the power of this earth, for all the earth has been given over to him. Remember the temptation with Jesus, when Satan said,

> If you worship me I'll give you all the kingdoms of the world, for they are given to me. And I give them to whomsoever I will.

Now Satan and men are going to be *losing* this power, *losing* these things. Satan is going to be desperate, he is going to be absolutely furious; he's going to be doing everything that he can. He is going to be given the power to cut loose everything, in the demonic world *to fight against God, and use men in that way!* We need to understand how fantastic these events are going to be.

Even at that, the whole point of the thing is so that God will give them a space to repent. You talk about being hardhearted, and you talk about having your minds set to serve evil; listen to it here:

Verse 20: "But the rest of the men who were not killed by these plagues **still did not repent** of the works of their hands that they might not worship demons, and idols of gold and silver and brass and stone and wood, which do not have the power to see, nor to hear, nor to walk."

This is a repeat of God's judgment of the gods of Egypt. Now only the gods of all the world. But will they repent and turn to God? *No!*

Verse 21: "And they did not repent of their murders, nor of their sorceries, nor of their fornications, nor of their thievery." *Quite an army, quite a thing that takes place!*

Rev. 10 talks about the seven thunders, and what's going to take place there. No one knows what they're going to be because God instructed John, 'Don't write it.' So, whatever the seven thunders do… Please understand that the seven thunders were never the seven churches of Rev. 2 & 3. We're way down in to the last year before Christ sets his feet on the earth, *and **it has nothing to do with** the Churches.* These have to do with the angelic powers of God.

Rev. 11—we've already covered. The Sea of Glass is there, the armies have been all fighting, the resurrection takes place, they see all the saints up there, and they get together and they say:

Oh, we're being invaded by invaders from outer space. Let's gather together, let's quit fighting each other. We have got to gather to fight this! Look at this sitting there.

And it's got to be over Jerusalem, because God gathers all the armies to the Valley of Megiddo. He treads out the winepress and the fierceness of his wrath and the blood is going to rise to the horses bridles. Just think, 5-6 feet of blood of the carnage of human rebellion against God. That Sea of Glass has got to be up there.

Let's bring us up to date here. After we're all resurrected on the Sea of Glass, all the saints are then going to see the final judgment against God, against the wickedness of man, against the nations of the world, and against Satan and his demons.

After all that we have been through, after all that the saints have gone through, beginning from Abel clear down to the two witnesses who were the last two resurrected; everything that the saints have suffered through, all of those who've been martyred, lost their heads for the Word of Christ, burned at the stake because of the evil of *the beast and the false prophet,* and the evil of Satan's religions, and armies down through the history of the world. They are going to be resurrected as spirit beings. And we are all, from the Sea of Glass, going to view the seven last plagues of God, which is His final judgment for the nations of the earth, before the Kingdom of God begins.

Revelation 15:5: "And after these things I looked, and behold, the temple of the tabernacle of the testimony in heaven was opened." *The direct intervention of God with His angels! This is the final sequence of battle that's going to take place!*

Verse 6: "And the seven angels who had the seven *last* plagues came out of the temple; they were clothed in linen, pure and bright, and girded about the chest with golden breastplates."

Remember, this is going to come upon the armies that are right there. The other armies are spread all the way to the east. So, they are going to come, as we will see, in Rev. 19

Verse 7: "And one of the four living creatures gave to the seven angels seven golden vials, full of the wrath of God, Who lives into the ages of eternity. And the temple was filled with smoke from the glory of God, and from His power; and no one was able to enter inside the temple until the seven plagues of the seven angels were fulfilled" (vs 7-8).

Revelation 16:1[transcriber's correction]: "Then I heard a loud voice from the temple say to the seven angels, 'Go and pour out the vials of the wrath of God onto the earth.' And the first *angel* went and poured out his vial onto the earth; and an evil and grievous sore fell upon the men who had the mark of the beast, and upon those who were worshiping his image" (vs 1-2).

Now we've had many, many sermons on *the mark of the beast.* We'll have more before it's finally instituted. But the first judgment is given against them. Why? *Because they gave up their freewill to the beast with the mark, and to Satan the devil!* So, they're the first one's going to be hit.

Verse 3: "And the second angel *went and* poured out his vial into the sea; and it became blood… [all the oceans of the world] …like *that* of a dead *man*; and every living soul in the sea died."

So, when God begins to repair the earth, there's going to have to begin the healing water that flows from Jerusalem to the east and to the west, and is going to heal the whole ocean. An amazing thing!

Verse 4: "And the third angel poured out his vial upon the rivers, and into the fountains of waters; and they became blood."

As we're all watching this, and seeing this going on—and they're going to be some people say, 'Oh, how can a God Who is a God of love do this?' Let's reverse it: *How could men and demons do this to a God of love,* and not expect judgment back upon themselves?

Here's how the angels view this, here's how we're going to view this:

Verse 5: "Then I heard the angel of the waters say, 'You are righteous, O Lord, Who are, and Who was, even the Holy One, in that You have executed this judgment. For they have poured out *the* blood of saints and of prophets…'" (vs 5-6).

God honors that, and His judgment is given all at once. He has stored up this last generation for this judgment. Just like Jesus said, 'This generation shall not pass away until all these things be fulfilled.' This is the generation, this is the one that we are looking at today, and it's going to come.

"'…and You have given them blood to

drink; for they are worthy.' And I heard another *voice* from the altar say, 'Yes, Lord God Almighty, true and righteous *are* Your judgments.' And the fourth angel poured out his vial upon the sun; and *power* was given to it to scorch men with fire." (vs 6-8).

So, there's going to be a big burst from the sun, and this heat is going to come like a great flash upon the earth—it talks about that in one of the prophecies—seven times hotter than normal. This great flash is going to come and scorch men. There are going to be some who will survive, who will not be out in the open, but whoever is in the open it's going to burn them.

Verse 9: "Then men were scorched with great heat; and they blasphemed the name of God, Who has authority over these plagues, and did not repent to give Him glory." *You talk about hardhearted!*

Now think about this: *IF* these evil men, inspired of Satan the devil and demons, can set their will to not repent, don't you think that we ought to go to God and ask Him:

- to give us the tenderheartedness toward Him and Jesus Christ, and the saints?
- to have minds of pillars of brass, iron and flint?
- to withstand all these things that are coming?
- to be able to stand firm for God?

Too many people give up easily on God because it's not comfortable, and it's not the kind of nicey-nicey thing that they have always wanted. Well listen, it isn't going to be nicey-nicey. You need to understand that.

"...they blasphemed the name of God, Who has authority over these plagues, and did not repent to give Him glory. And the fifth angel poured out his vial upon the throne of the beast; and his kingdom became full of darkness; and they gnawed their tongues because of the pain, and blasphemed the God of heaven because of their pains and their sores; yet, they did not repent of their works" (vs 9-11). *In every case, God gave them a chance to repent, but they didn't do it!*

Verse 12: "And the sixth angel poured out his vial into the great River Euphrates... [after it was dried up once, it came back flowing again, so it's got to be dried up again] ...and its waters were dried up, so that the way of the kings from the rising of *the* sun might be prepared. Then I saw three unclean spirits like frogs *come* out of the mouth of the dragon, and out of the mouth of the beast, and out of the mouth of the false prophet" (vs 12-13).

After all the things that happened, they've got to be convinced by supernatural spiritual demonic power that they ought to go fight this alien invasion. *This is their last hope!*

Verse 14: "For they are spirits of demons working miracles, going forth to the kings of the earth, even of the whole world, to gather them together to *the* battle of that great day of the Almighty God."

They are going to come! Now He gives a warning again; notice how this is a pattern in the Bible:

Verse 15: "Behold, I come as a thief. Blessed *is* the one who is watching and is keeping his garments, so that he may not walk naked and they *may not* see his shame."

Direct reference to the Laodiceans, and the five foolish virgins (Matt. 25).

Verse 16: "And he gathered them together to the place that in Hebrew is called Armageddon." *Armageddon is the battle of God against the armies of this world!*

Verse 17: "Then the seventh angel poured out his vial into the air; and a loud voice came out of the temple of heaven, from the Throne, saying, 'IT IS FINISHED.'"

Now we're going to hear that because we are on the Sea of Glass. We'll hear that.

Verse 18: "And there were voices and thunders and lightnings; and there was a great earthquake, such as was not since men were on the earth, so mighty an earthquake, *and* so great. And the great city was divided into three parts; and the cities of the nations fell... [all of their super high building] ...and Babylon the Great was remembered before God to give her the cup of the wine of the fury of His wrath. And every island disappeared, and no mountains were found... [because they were lowered, and the valleys were raised] ...and great hail, *each stone* the weight of a talent, fell down from heaven upon men; and men blasphemed God because of the plague of the hail, for the plague was exceedingly great" (vs 18-21).

Maybe some had protection, maybe they were in their tanks and the hail didn't smash out their tanks, or whatever it may be. Now they're going to come and gather to the final battle as found here in Rev. 19. All the saints are going to come, and all of us are going to descend with Christ to the earth.

Revelation 19:14: "And the armies in heaven were following Him on white horses; *and* they were clothed in fine linen, white and pure. And out of His mouth goes a sharp sword, that with it He might smite the nations… [all God has to do is command, and it's done] …and He shall shepherd them with an iron rod…" (vs 14-15).

That's what it's going to take to bring these unrepentant people of the ten percent that are left, after all of this, that are going to enter into the Millennium, and be the first living, human beings in the Kingdom of God, administered by Christ and the saints.

Verse 16: "And on *His* garment and on His thigh He has a name written: King of kings and Lord of lords. Then I saw an angel standing in the sun; and he cried out with a loud voice, saying to all the birds that fly in *the* midst of heaven…" (vs 16-17). *God is going to clean up the mess!*

"…'Come and gather yourselves together to the supper of the great God so that you may eat *the* flesh of kings, and *the* flesh of chief captains, and *the* flesh of mighty *men*, and *the* flesh of horses, and of those who sit on them, and *the* flesh of all, free and bond, and small and great.' And I saw the beast and the kings of the earth and their armies, gathered together… [all the remnant that are left gathered together] …to make war with Him Who sits on the horse, and with His army" (vs 17-19).

God is going to send an angel. The first thing is going to be done: *The beast* is going to be taken!

Verse 20: "And the beast was taken, and with him the false prophet who worked miracles in his presence, by which he had deceived those who received the mark of the beast and those who worshiped his image. Those two were cast alive into the Lake of Fire, which burns with brimstone; and the rest were killed by the sword of Him Who sits on the horse, *even the sword* that goes out of His mouth; and all the birds were filled with their flesh" (vs 20-21).

Zechariah 14:4: "And His feet shall stand in that day upon the Mount of Olives…"—**and all the saints with Him!**

The next major most important event from the time of the Garden of Eden is going to take place, as pictured by the Day of Atonement!

Scriptures from *The Holy Bible in Its Original Order, A Faithful Version*

Scriptural References:

1) Leviticus 23:23-25
2) Matthew 6:9-10
3) Colossians 1:10-13
4) Colossians 3:14-16
5) Jeremiah 1:15-19
6) Isaiah 50:5-7
7) Ezekiel 3:4-10
8) Matthew 24:15-21
9) Amos 5:18-20
10) Zephaniah 1:13-18
11) Joel 1:15
12) Joel 2:1-13
13) Isaiah 13:6-13
14) Isaiah 24:18-23
15) Revelation 8:1-13
16) Revelation 9:1-21
17) Revelation 15:5-8
18) Revelation 16:1-21
19) Revelation 19:14-21
20) Zechariah 14:4

Scriptures referenced, not quoted:

- Ezekiel 33
- Revelation 13
- Psalm 91
- 1-Chronicles 5
- Jeremiah 25
- Revelation 6; 7
- Isaiah 40
- Daniel 12
- Revelation 10; 2; 3; 11
- Matthew 25

Also referenced: Book:
Occult Holidays or God's Holy Days—Which? by Fred R. Coulter

FRC:cs
Transcription date unknown
Reformatted: bo—11/2020

CHAPTER FIFTY-TWO

Phase 3 of the Return of Christ:
The Return of Christ & the Saints
Feast of Trumpets
Fred R. Coulter

Greetings, everyone! Welcome to the Feast of Trumpets! Time marches right along, and here we are with the fall festival season right upon us. Soon we will have the Feast of Tabernacles after the Day of Atonement. All of these are very important things to God!

Remember, *the Law of God is perfect! No man can improve upon God!* We need to remember that! We need to understand that God is the One Who has called us, and we answered the call. We do the things that God wants us to do *His way,* not *our way!*

One of the reasons why the Feast of Trumpets pictures the most devastating and destructive time in the history of mankind since the Flood is because men have not learned the lesson:

- you must come to God *His way*
- you must *believe* God
- you must *obey* God

Of course, this follows through with everything that God does. *This is always a test of faith!* God put all of the Holy Days in sequence—naming the day, numbering the day, counting the day for Pentecost—as a test of faith.

- Do we *believe* God?
- Do we *love* God?

If we do, God will show us and teach us *His understanding!* He will open the *mystery of His Word* to us, which then are called by Jesus 'the *mysteries* of the Kingdom of God.' *One of the great mysteries is the return of Jesus Christ!*

Leviticus 23:23: "And the LORD spoke to Moses, saying, 'Speak to the children of Israel saying, "In the seventh month, in the first *day* of the month, you shall have a Sabbath, a memorial of blowing of ram's horns, a Holy convocation""" (vs 23-24).

A ram's horn is the trumpet to be blown when there is war. So, the Feast of Trumpets is a *war* Feast! Let's look at this again for just a minute: All Holy Days are called *a* Sabbath. The weekly Sabbath is called *the* Sabbath. That's important to understand. All the Holy Days are Sabbaths.

Verse 25: "You shall do no servile work *therein* but you shall offer an offering made by fire to the LORD." Today we don't bring the animals; we don't have an altar on the earth for physical sacrifices. But we are to give of our substance to the Lord. God will bless us in giving an offering.

I know there are some people who are very fastidious and say that it says in Deut. 16 that 'three seasons'—Unleavened Bread, Feast of Weeks and Tabernacles—you are to bring an offering. That is true! But does that exclude and not count Trumpets, as well? When it says that we are to bring an offering (Lev. 23) that should be sufficient for us.

So, we always take up an offering on the Holy Days, and particularly what this day pictures with the return of Christ and all of the events at the end of the age, yes, *we need to bring God an offering!*

(pause for the offering)

Let's continue the unfolding of prophecy in the book of Revelation. We saw on Pentecost that Day 49 pictures the opening of the heavens for the *first phase of the return of Jesus Christ.* That first phase is the 'sign of the Son of man' in heaven, which will appear as a second sun. Then we have the sealing of the 144,000 in Rev. 7.

Now let's come to Rev. 8 and pick up the flow of events from there. Remember, as I covered on Pentecost, you have from the next to the last Pentecost to the last Pentecost, which is the resurrection. Then you have another line below that which is from Trumpets to the return of Jesus Christ. The seventh trumpet is the resurrection.

The resurrection is phase two of the return of Jesus Christ. We will come back to phase two then we will go into phase three, because that is going to be awesome, indeed!

Rev. 8 is where all the prophecies at the end-time shift. It is the angels of God *vs* Satan the devil and the demons, and the men who are following Satan, the armies that Satan has raised up. We will see how God deals with these things and every one of these plagues that come (Rev. 8, 9, 16). Those all go back to the weapons that God used against the

Egyptians to bring the children of Israel out of Egypt.

Now the scene is that we are at the point when the first trumpet blows. There is one year until the saints come with Christ back to the earth. That one-year is going to be the most devastating year in the history of mankind from the time of the Flood until the end.

As we can see by Rev. 8 & 9, which we will do, there are great and fantastic weapons that will be employed, and that man will not be satisfied until he has fought to the very end.

Revelation 8:1: "Now, when He opened the seventh seal, *there* was silence in heaven *for* about a half hour. Then I saw the seven angels who stand before God, and seven trumpets were given to them. And another angel, who had a golden censer, came and stood at the altar; and much incense was given to him, so that he might offer *it* with the prayers of all the saints on the golden altar that *was* before the throne. And the smoke of the incense went up before God from *the* hand of the angel, ascending with the prayers of the saints. And the angel took the censer, and filled it with fire from the altar, and cast *it* into the earth…" (vs 1-5). ***Direct intervention by God!***

Here are men fighting one another and all of a sudden the heavens rip open (Rev. 6) and the sign of the Son of man appears. There is quietness for a space of time for the 144,000. You count that space from Pentecost until Trumpets of the year that it occurs. Then starts all the devastation prophesied in the Old Testament. This is quite a thing! These are earth-shaking events, to say the least.

Verse 5: "And the angel took the censer, and filled it with fire from the altar, and cast *it* into the earth and there were voices, and thunders, and lightnings, and an earthquake."

You'll notice going through the book of Revelation that there are many, numerous, earthquakes that take place.

Verse 6: "Then the seven angels who had the seven trumpets prepared themselves to sound *their* trumpets."

There is a sequence of the seven trumpets: the first one and the last one. The last trumpet, as we saw on Pentecost, is the resurrection. Here is the first one:

Verse 7: "And the first angel sounded *his* trumpet; and there was hail and fire mingled with blood, and it was cast upon the earth; and a third of the trees were burnt up, and all green grass was burnt up."

You will notice that these come one, two, three, four very quickly in a row. Same way with the seven last plagues.

Verse 8: "Then the second angel sounded *his* trumpet; and *there* was cast into the sea as *it were* a great mountain burning with fire, and a third of the sea became blood; and a third of the living creatures that *were* in the sea died, and a third of the ships were destroyed" (vs 8-9). ***Absolute devastation beyond belief!***

Verse 10: "And the third angel sounded *his* trumpet; and *there* fell out of heaven a great star, burning like a lamp; and it fell on a third of the rivers, and on the fountains of waters. Now, the name of the star is Wormwood; and a third of the waters became wormwood; and many men died from *drinking* the waters because they were made bitter" (vs 10-11).

These things are going to be just so devastating upon the earth; great and fantastic events that will not ever be repeated again in the same way.

Verse 12: "Then the fourth angel sounded *his* trumpet; and a third of the sun was smitten, and a third of the moon, and a third of the stars; so that a third of them were darkened; and a third part of the day did not shine, and likewise *a third part of* the night."

Right here is exactly why *no man knows the day or the hour* exactly. But we do know the times and the seasons. Those are depicted by the appointed times of God, the Holy Days of God!

Verse 13: "And I looked; and I heard an angel flying in the midst of heaven, saying with a loud voice… [God always gives warning]: …'**Woe, woe, woe** to those who are dwelling on the earth, because of the voices of the remaining trumpets of the three angels who *are* about to sound *their* trumpets.'"

This is going to be quite a thing, especially the fifth and sixth trumpets. Of course, the seventh trumpet is the resurrection. Before we get into Rev. 9 concerning the great wars that will take place, let's come back to Joel 2 and let's see that these things were prophesied, not only in the book of Joel, but in the books of Isaiah and Jeremiah.

Notice how Joel parallels very closely with what we have already read. What happens in Rev. 8 & 9 fills us in on the details of what was given in the Old Testament. Remember, from the blowing of the first trumpet until the saints and Christ come back to the earth, the next Feast of Trumpets, is one year! Just like the sealing of the 144,000 and the great innumerable multitude to the resurrection is one year: Pentecost to Pentecost. So, Trumpets in fulfillment is from Trumpets to Trumpets, one year.

The memorial of the blowing of trumpets is a war Feast! Joel 2:1: "'Blow the ram's horn in Zion, and sound an alarm in My Holy mountain!' Let all the inhabitants of the land tremble, for the Day of the LORD comes, for *it is* near at hand." *We're reading of it in Revelation!*

Verse 2: "A day of darkness and of gloominess, a day of clouds and of thick darkness...."

Didn't we read that? Isn't it interesting that the Gospel is preached in the Old Testament as well as the New Testament. That's why they are together, like a hand in a glove. They give us the full picture as to what is going to take place.

"...As the morning *is* spread across the mountains, *so comes* a great people and a mighty people; there has never been the like, nor shall there ever be again, even to the years of many generations" (v 2). *That's our time!*

Verse 3: "A fire devours before them, and behind them a flame burns. The land *is* as the Garden of Eden before them, and behind them a desolate wilderness—and nothing shall escape them. Their appearance *is* as the appearance of horses; and as war horses, so they run" (vs 3-4). *We will see this aptly fits in with the description in Rev. 9!*

Verse 5: "They shall leap with the noise of chariots on the tops of mountains, with the noise of a flame of fire that devours the stubble, like a mighty people set in battle array. In their presence the people shall *greatly* tremble; all faces shall grow pale. They shall run like mighty men. They shall climb the wall like men of war, and they shall march each one in his path, and they shall not break their ranks. And each one shall not crowd another; they go every one in his *own* path. And when they fall upon the sword, they shall not be wounded" (vs 5-8). *Amazing to think about!*

Verse 9: "They shall run to and fro in the city; they shall run upon the wall; they shall climb up upon the houses; they shall enter in at the windows like a thief. The earth shall quake before them; the heavens shall tremble. The sun and the moon shall grow dark, and the stars shall withdraw their shining" (vs 9-10). *That is exactly what it says in the book of Revelation!*

Verse 11: "And the LORD shall utter His voice before His army; for His camp *is* exceedingly great; for powerful *is He* who executes His Word, for the Day of the LORD *is* great and very terrible; and **who can endure it?"**

Well, there will be some people who will live through it; *very few!* We will see that this involves every nation in the world. When we get to the book of Revelation it talks about **all** nations. This is why the Gospel is preached as a witness to *all* nations. This is why God has the two witnesses in

Jerusalem; *to be a witness!* This is going to be the greatest, most fantastic event that is pictured by the Feast of Trumpets that has been in the history of man.

Let's see some other things concerning how this is going to involve the whole world. As we will see as we put these various descriptions together, along with the book of Revelation, this gives us a vast picture of how this is going to effect everything on the earth. The return of Jesus Christ is going to be awesome, indeed!

Isaiah 24:1: "Behold, the LORD makes the earth empty and makes it waste, and turns it upside down, and scatters its inhabitants. And as *it is* with the people, so it shall be with the priest; as with the slave, so with the master; as with the handmaid, so it is with her mistress; as with the buyer, so with the seller; as with the lender, so with the borrower; as with the creditor, so with the debtor. **The earth shall be completely laid waste, and utterly stripped; for <u>the LORD has spoken this word</u>"** (vs 1-3).

Stop and think for just a minute: *God fulfills all the prophecies to the maximum!* When these things happen, they're going to be complete and devastating!

Verse 4: "The earth mourns *and* languishes; the world withers *and* languishes; the proud people of the earth wither. And the earth is defiled under its people; because..." (vs 4-5).

Notice why this is coming, and this will help you understand why the lawlessness at the end of this age is going to be so overwhelming. *It's going to be really difficult to be a true Christian though all of these things!*

- God will give us the strength!
- God will grant us His Spirit!

"...they have transgressed the laws, changed the ordinance, and have broken **the everlasting covenant**" (v 5)—*the covenant unto eternal life*; it will go on into the ages of eternity.

This aptly describes the way that the religions of this world are toward God, including the Christianity of this world. Here is the effect; we've read the cause:

Verse 6: "Therefore, the curse has devoured the earth, and they who dwell in it are desolate; therefore, the people of the earth are burned, and few men are left." *When God sets His hand for judgment...*

Isaiah 13:1: "The burden of Babylon... [What is the end-time called? *Babylon the Great!*] ...which Isaiah the son of Amoz saw: 'Lift up a banner upon the high mountain, exalt the voice to them, wave the hand, so that they may go into the gates of the nobles. I have commanded My Holy ones, I have also called My mighty ones for My anger, *even* those who rejoice in My triumph'" (vs 1-3). *That's all the angels of God and all the saints of God!*

Verse 4: "The noise of a multitude in the mountains, as of a great people; a tumultuous noise of the kingdoms of nations…"

That's all encompassing! We will see how all of this is brought out in final detail and moving toward the return of Christ in the book of Revelation.

"…gathered together; the LORD of hosts gathers an army for the battle. They come from a far country, from the end of heaven, the LORD and the weapons of His indignation, to destroy the whole earth. **Howl! For the Day of the LORD *is* at hand; it shall come as a destruction from the Almighty**" (vs 4-6). *Quite a thing!*

Verse 9: "Behold, the Day of the LORD comes, cruel both *with* wrath and fierce anger, to make the earth a desolation; and He shall destroy the sinners out of it, for the stars of the heavens and their constellations shall not give light; the sun shall be darkened in its going forth, and the moon shall not reflect its light (vs 9-10). *Exactly what we read in the book of Revelation!*

Verse 11: "'**And I will punish the world for *their* evil**…'" What I want you to do is understand how these prophecies encompass the world:

- all nations
- all kingdoms
- all peoples

*and how that **no one** is going to escape!*

"…and the wicked for their iniquity; and I will cause the arrogancy of the proud to cease, and will lay low the haughtiness of the tyrants. I will make man more scarce than gold; even man more than the fine gold of Ophir. Therefore, I will shake the heavens, and the earth… [again it talks about shaking the heavens and the earth] …shall move out of its place, **in the wrath of the LORD of hosts, and in the day of His fierce anger**" (vs 11-13). *Those are really quite some words!*

Yes, this is going to involved *all nations; **no one is going to escape! No one is going to get away from it!*** They may survive—a number of people will survive—because it says 'there are few men left.' They will survive through these things. Just think of the trauma that they will have experienced and how that is going to be quite a job for us at the beginning of the Millennium. You need to understand that this is going to be awesome, indeed!

After listing all the kings, God told Jeremiah to 'go to all the nations that I tell you,' leading up to Jer. 25:26, and this begins to expand it out to the whole world.

Jeremiah 25:26: "And all the kings of the north, far and near, one with another, and **all the kingdoms of the world**… [Is that all encompassing or not? *Yes, it is!*] …which *are* on the face of the earth… [here is speaks about the beast of Rev. 13] …and the king of Sheshach shall drink after them. 'Therefore, you shall say to them, "Thus says the LORD of hosts, the God of Israel, 'Drink and be drunk, and vomit, and fall, and rise no more because of the sword which I will send among you.'" And it shall come to pass if they refuse to take the cup at your hand to drink, then you shall say to them, "Thus says the LORD of hosts, **'You shall certainly drink**. For, lo, I begin to bring evil on the city, which is called by My name; and shall you go unpunished? You shall not go unpunished. For I will call for a sword on all the inhabitants of the earth,' says the LORD of hosts" (vs 26-29).

That is going to be profound! We will see how all of this fits in Rev. 9, and then it expands out into Rev. 16, as well.

Verse 30: "'And prophesy against them all these words, and say to them, "The LORD shall roar from on high, and utter His voice from His Holy habitation. He shall mightily roar over His dwelling place. He shall give a shout, like those who tread out *grapes*, against all the people of the earth. A noise shall come to the ends of the earth; for the LORD has a controversy with the nations; He will plead with all flesh. He will give those *who are* wicked to the sword,'" says the LORD. Thus says the LORD of hosts, 'Behold, evil shall go forth from nation to nation, and a great whirlwind shall be stirred up from the farthest corners of the earth. And the slain of the LORD shall be at that day from *one* end of the earth even to the *other* end of the earth; they shall not be mourned, nor gathered, nor buried. They shall be *as* dung on the ground. Howl, you shepherds, and cry; and wallow yourselves in the ashes, you lords of the flock! For the days of your slaughter and of your scatterings are fulfilled; and you shall fall like a choice vessel'" (vs 30-34).

Amazing! Absolutely stunning! All of this! Let's see how this fits in with Rev. 9; let's see how God puts it all together. This is why we take part of it from the Old Testament and part of it from the New Testament—the book of Revelation—so that we can understand and get a full picture of what is going to happen. This is why that the Gospel is preached in all the world for a witness to all nations. All nations, all people are involved. God is going to make a statement that is going to be so absolutely profound and so devastating. *God is going to do it!*

- He's going to use the armies to do it
- He's going to use Satan the devil to do it
- He's going to use His angels to do it
- He's going to use the demons to do it

This is an all out battle of a magnitude that is almost beyond the scope of our imagination! Again, notice how it's angels of God and demons and Satan the devil:

Revelation 9:1: "And the fifth angel sounded *his* trumpet; and I saw a star *that* had fallen from heaven to the earth, and there was given to him the key to the bottomless abyss. And he opened the bottomless abyss; and there went up smoke from the pit, like *the* smoke of a great furnace; and the sun and the air were darkened by the smoke from the pit. Then locusts came onto the earth from the smoke; and power was given to them, as the scorpions of the earth have power" (vs 1-3).

These are demonic powers let out of the demonic prison, the abyss! In some places in the *King James* it's called 'the bottomless pit.'

Verse 4: "And it was said to them that they should not damage the grass of the earth, or any green thing, or any tree, but only the men who did not have the seal of God in their foreheads."

This shows that the 144,000 and the great innumerable multitude have not ascended to heaven, yet. They won't ascend until the seventh trump is blown; then they will ascend to meet Christ on the Sea of Glass. The reason that there are trees and grass is because a third were previously burned up.

When it's dark and cloudy, what automatically comes with that? *Rain!* Trees and grass have no understanding about devastation. If it rains it grows, regardless of what men do. So, however long it takes for the first four plagues to take place, by the time it gets to the fifth trumpet plague there has been time for the grass to grow and some of the trees to recover.

All the rest, this is probably from the King of the North who comes down out of Europe against the King of the South:

Verse 5: "And it was given to them that they should not kill them, but that they should be tormented five months; and their torment *was* like *the* torment of a scorpion when it stings a man. And in those days men will seek death but will not find it; and they will desire to die, but death will flee from them. And the appearance of the locusts *was* like horses prepared for war; and on their heads *were* crowns like *those* of gold; and their faces *were* like *the* faces of men; and they had hair like women's hair; and their teeth were like *those* of lions. And they had breastplates like iron breastplates..." (vs 5-9).

Here is the greatest armament, the greatest weapons that men have been able to devise, and with the technology of Satan the devil and the demons, all working this together.

"...and the sound of their wings *was* like *the* sound of chariots *drawn* by many horses running to war; and they had tails like scorpions, and stingers; and they were *given* power to injure men with their tails *for* five months. And they have over them a king... [Satan is leading the battle] ...the angel of the abyss; his name in Hebrew *is* Abaddon, but *the* name he has in Greek *is* Apollyon. The first woe is past. Behold, after these things two more woes are still to come. And the sixth angel sounded..." (vs 9-13).

Notice that these follow along and these great battles take place. This is going to be the greatest thing! There has never ever been an army like this. An army so vast that it's going to stretch from the Holy Land all the way back to the Far East.

Right now the Chinese are building the highway going west. They're building a highway from Afghanistan down to Pakistan and there will be Pakistanis involved. They're going to build a pipeline down to India. India will be involved; all the kings of the East. That army will be strung out for thousands of miles. You can't get 200-million men in one place. So, they will come like waves. *This is going to be a great battle!*

Verse 13: "And the sixth angel sounded *his* trumpet; and I heard a voice from the four horns of the golden altar that *is* before God; *and* it said to the sixth angel, who had the trumpet, 'Loose the four angels who are bound in the great River Euphrates.' Then the four angels, who had been prepared for the hour and day and month and year, were loosed... [God is right on schedule] ...so that they might kill a third of men" (vs 13-15).

Talk about how devastating this is going to be! Think about it for a minute. Rev 6—those wars and famines kill a fourth of men. That leaves three-quarters of them left. Then another third of those who are still alive means that half of the men in the world are going to die between Rev. 6 and 9. Maybe even more than that when you count all the things that are going to take place.

Remember what it said in Jeremiah. The dead will be strung from one end of the earth to the other, and they won't be buried. All the fowl of the air are going to eat up their flesh (Rev. 19)! Quite a thing! This is going to be awesome, indeed!

Verse 16: "And the number of *the* armies of the horsemen *was* two hundred thousand thousand; and I heard the number of them." *That's 200-million!*

In WWII the maximum they had under arms—counting all those who were not involved in combat—was 50-million, one-fourth of what this is, not counting what the armies of *the beast* were. This is something!

Here's what they looked like, v 17: "And so, I saw the horses in the vision, and those sitting on them, who had fiery breastplates, even like jacinth and brimstone. And the heads of the horses *were* like heads of lions, and fire and smoke and brimstone shoot out of their mouths." *Shooting, killing, missiles; all of this going on!*

Verse 18: "By these three a third of men were killed: by the fire and the smoke and the brimstone that shoot out of their mouths. For their power is in their mouths; for their tails *are* like serpents, *and* have heads, and with them they inflict wounds" (vs 18-19). *There are still people alive!*

Even in the greatest disasters, it's quite a wondrous thing how many people survive even buried under the rubble of buildings. Think of this:

Verse 20: "But the rest of the men who were not killed by these plagues still did not repent of the works of their hands…"

These are men with super-modern hi-tech weapons; some of the things that they're developing right now. They didn't repent. I wonder what would happen if they would repent? *But they won't!*

"…did not repent of the works of their hands that they might not worship demons, and idols of gold and silver and brass and stone and wood, which do not have the power to see, nor to hear, nor to walk. And they did not repent of their murders, nor of their sorceries, nor of their fornications, nor of their thievery" (vs 20-21).

An amazing thing! This is going to be some battle, but we're going to see that God is going to do even greater than this!

Rev. 10 is the seven thunders. John was told not to write those, so, we don't know what that's going to be and how devastating that is going to be.

Revelation 11:14: "The second woe is past. Behold, the third woe is coming immediately. Then the seventh angel sounded *his* trumpet; and *there* were great voices in heaven, saying…"

This is the resurrection on Pentecost! This leads into *the third phase* of the return of Christ:

➤ **First phase**—the sign of the Son of man appearing as a sun
➤ **Second phase**—takes place right before the resurrection

The sun comes streaking to the earth and right over the Holy Land a vast Sea of Glass will appear, and then the resurrection takes place and we meet Christ in the air on the Sea of Glass.

Now then, as we covered on Pentecost, all the fantastic things that will take place at that point. So, the seventh trumpet sounded.

We'll see how we come from the last Pentecost and the resurrection to the last Trumpets and Christ and the saints coming to the earth.

Now let's come forward to Rev. 14, a classic example of one of the methods that the Bible uses to describe what's going to take place. First of all, it gives a summary, and then it gives the details. We're going to see the two harvests.

1. *the resurrection from the dead* of the saints
2. *the harvest of the wicked* with their armies that God is going to destroy when Christ returns from heaven with the saints

What we have here is Rev. 14:14-16 talking about the resurrection of the saints. Then v 17 begins the summary of what is going to happen to the wicked coming to Jerusalem. This is quite a thing, and we will see that just as we saw on Pentecost, the prophecy of a nation raised at once. Likewise, we will see the prophecy of the wicked and their destruction in the book of Joel.

Revelation 14:14: "And I looked, and behold, a white cloud, and *one* like *the* Son of man sitting on the cloud, having a golden crown on His head; and in His hand *was* a sharp sickle."

We are the firstfruits. So, this is a sickle to harvest the grain. We will see that there is a special sickle to also harvest the grapes of wrath.

Verse 15: "And another angel came out of the temple, crying with a loud voice to Him Who was sitting on the cloud, 'Thrust in your sickle and reap, because the time has come for You to reap; for the harvest of the earth is ripe.' And He Who was sitting on the cloud thrust forth His sickle upon the earth, and the earth was reaped" (vs 15-16). *That takes place right as the seventh trump is blown and the harvest begins!*

That brings us over to Rev. 15. We've already covered this during Pentecost, so those who are raised are taken by the angels up to the Sea of Glass. All of those in the first resurrection on Pentecost will be there. Then everything that needs to take place will take place. It will be all on this big Sea of Glass.

When the resurrection has taken place that ***finishes the second phase*** of the return of Christ. There is yet another phase that has to take place; this is the seven last plagues. Rev. 14:14-16 applies to the resurrection, and Rev. 15. Then from Rev. 14:17-

19 that applies to Rev. 16.

Revelation 14:17: "Then another angel, who also had a sharp sickle, came out of the temple that *is* in heaven. And out from the altar came another angel, who had authority over fire; and he called with a loud cry to the one who had the sharp sickle, saying, 'Thrust in your sharp sickle, and gather the clusters of the earth, because her grapes are fully ripe.' And the angel thrust his sickle into the earth, and gathered the vine of the earth, and cast *its fruit* into the great winepress of the wrath of God…. [the vengeance of God] …And the winepress was trodden outside the city, and blood spewed out from the winepress as high as the horses' bridles, to the distance of a thousand six hundred furlongs" (vs 17-19)

This spewing of the blood shows the death of the wicked, the soldiers/enemies fighting against Christ. Let's see where this exact thing was prophesied. What we find are the prophecies of the Old Testament, the prophecies of the New Testament, and they all fit together like a hand in a glove.

We saw that it talked about the army coming, the trumpet plagues five and six, and the seven plagues are announced with the beginning of the resurrection.

Joel 3:9: "Proclaim this among the nations, **'Prepare for war!'**…." *This will be the greatest war that has ever been!*

"…Wake up the mighty men, let all the men of war draw near; let them come up. Beat your plowshares into swords, and your pruning hooks into spears. Let the weak say, 'I *am* strong.' Gather yourselves and come, all you nations, and gather yourselves together all around; cause Your mighty ones to come down there, O LORD. Let the nations be awakened and come up to the Valley of Jehoshaphat; for there I will sit to judge all the nations all around. Put in the sickle (Rev. 14), for the harvest is ripe. Come, come down; for the press is full; the vats overflow—for their wickedness is great. Multitudes, multitudes in the valley of decision; for the Day of the LORD *is* near in the valley of decision! The sun and the moon shall be darkened, and the stars shall withdraw their shining. The LORD shall also roar out of Zion and utter His voice from Jerusalem. And the heavens and the earth shall shake. But the LORD *will be* the hope of His people and the strength of the children of Israel" (vs 9-16).

Isn't that interesting? *His people being the first resurrection!* Israel being *the nations of Israel* being brought back to their original inheritance. Let's see what God is going to do, and how this is going to be done. Rev. 15 gives us:

- the Temple of God
- how the seven last plagues come
- those who have been resurrected and stand on the Sea of Glass

Revelation 15:1: "Then I saw another sign in heaven, great and awesome: seven angels having the seven last plagues, for in them the wrath of God is filled up."

Remember, that takes place between the resurrection on Pentecost and Trumpets when Christ and the saints come back to the earth.

Verse 5: "And after these things I looked, and behold, the temple of the tabernacle of the testimony in heaven was opened. And the seven angels who had the seven *last* plagues came out of the temple; they were clothed in linen, pure and bright, and girded about the chest with golden breastplates. And one of the four living creatures gave to the seven angels seven golden vials, **full of the wrath of God, Who lives into the ages of eternity**. And the temple was filled with smoke from the glory of God, and from His power; and no one was able to enter inside the temple until the seven plagues of the seven angels were fulfilled" (vs 5-8).

This is the vengeance of God! God has said, 'Vengeance is Mine!' He is going to bring the vengeance on the earth and carry it out! Let's look at some Scriptures that talk about this very thing. The seven last plagues come right after the seventh trump. Exactly when they begin we don't know. There are a lot of things going on, on the Sea of Glass, with Jesus Christ and God the Father and the resurrected saints.

We are going to be able to witness the vengeance of God! We're also going to see that God gives us a share in that vengeance. Remember what Jesus said, 'If My Kingdom were of this world then would My servants fight.' So, the Kingdom is coming to this world and then we will fight. We will actually see that we have part in carrying out the vengeance of God. This is quite a thing!

Isaiah 34:1: "Come near, you nations, to hear; and, you people, hearken; let the earth hear, and its fullness; the world, and its offspring, for the anger of the LORD *is* upon all nations… [it's called *His wrath*] …and His fury upon all their armies…. [the 200-million-plus] …He has completely destroyed them, He has delivered them to the slaughter. Also, their dead shall be thrown out, and their stink shall come up out of their dead bodies, and the mountains shall be melted with their blood. And all the host of the heavens shall be dissolved, and the heavens shall be rolled up like a scroll; and all their host shall fall down, as a leaf falls off from the vine, and as the falling fig from the fig tree, 'For

My sword *is* bathed in the heavens. Behold, it shall come down upon Edom, and upon the people of My curse for judgment. The sword of the LORD is filled with blood; it is made fat with fatness, with the blood of lambs and goats, with the fat of the kidneys of rams; for the LORD has a sacrifice in Bozrah, and a great slaughter in the land of Edom. And the wild oxen shall come down with them, and the young bullocks with the bulls; and their land shall be soaked with blood, and their dust shall be greased with their fat'" (vs 1-7). *That's going to be quite a thing when you think about that!*

Verse 8: "For *it is* **the day of the LORD'S vengeance,** the year to repay for the fighting against Zion." *God's vengeance is coming!*

Notice how Isa. 63 ties in with Rev. 14 & 16; Isaiah 63:3: "'I have trodden the winepress alone; and of the people *there was* no man with Me; for I will tread them in My anger and trample them in My fury; and their blood will be sprinkled upon My garments, and I stained all My clothing; **for the day of vengeance *is* in My heart, and the year of My redemption has come.** And I looked, and *there was* none to help; and I was astonished that there *was* no one to uphold; therefore, My own arm brought salvation for Me; and My fury upheld Me. And I will tread down the people in My anger, and make them drunk in My fury, and I will pour their lifeblood down to the earth'" (vs 3-6).

That's a description of the seven last plagues! We'll read them; they're going to be something! Several Psalms talk about the vengeance of the Lord. Remember what Paul wrote in Rom. 12—'*Vengeance is Mine* says the Lord!'

Psalm 94:1: "O LORD God to whom vengeance belongs, O God, to whom vengeance belongs, show Yourself. Lift up Yourself..." (vs 1-2)—*which He will!*

This is exactly what He is doing. All of these things are going to take place while we are on the Sea of Glass. We'll be able to see this! We'll see all of this take place!

"...Judge of the earth; render recompense to the proud. How long shall the wicked, O LORD, how long shall the wicked exult? They gush forth *words*; they speak arrogant things; all the workers of iniquity vaunt themselves. They crush Your people, O LORD, and afflict Your inheritance" (vs 2-5). *That's quite a thing! Quite a vengeance!*

We'll go back and see in Rev. 16 as these seven last plagues are poured out that they fulfill all these Scriptures we are reading of the vengeance of God.

Psalm 58:10: "The righteous shall rejoice when he sees the vengeance..." *There is going to be*

a lot cheering on the Sea of Glass! Understand that:

- we are cheering because of God's power
- we're cheering because God is fulfilling His Word
- we're going to rejoice in all of this because the Kingdom is going to be setup by Christ

We are going to be a part of that!

For those that think all this blood, guts and gore is really terrible to take, and how can a God of love do this? *Well, the God of love is a God of love so much that even in spite of all of this that they do, and what He does, **they're going to be in the second resurrection!*** Think how astonishing that that will be for them! Quite a thing, isn't it? *Yes, indeed!*

"...he shall bathe his footsteps in the blood of the wicked, so that a man shall say, **'Truly, there is a reward for the righteous; truly, there is a God Who is judging in the earth'**" (vs 10-11). *Astonishing! Yes, indeed!*

Psalm 59:5: "And You therefore, O LORD God of hosts, the God of Israel, awake to punish all the nations... [that's what this is all about: the trumpet plagues and the seven last plagues] ...show no mercy to any wicked traitors. Selah."

Verse 8: "But You, O LORD, shall laugh at them; You shall hold all the nations in derision."

Verse 12: "For the sin of their mouth and the word of their lips, let them even be taken in their pride..."

We're going to see the pride and arrogance that they have at the last is the greatest, because of the prompting of Satan the devil.

"...and for the cursing and lying, which they speak. Consume them in wrath; consume, so that they may be no more; and let them know that God rules in Jacob to the ends of the earth. Selah" (vs 12-13).

That's quite a thing to really think about, understand and know what is taking place! *The vengeance of the Lord and the wrath of God!* Let's see how this is going to take place. What a thing this is going to be!

The Seven Last Plagues

The seven last plagues prophesied in the Old Testament and to come. When we read them, we will also see something concerning how the saints will participate in this vengeance when we come back to the earth. That is prophesied.

Revelation 16:1: "Then I heard a loud voice from the temple say to the seven angels, **'Go and pour out the vials of the wrath of God onto the** earth.' And the first *angel* went and poured out his vial onto the earth; and an evil and grievous sore fell upon the men who had the mark of the beast, and upon those who were worshiping his image. And the second angel *went and* poured out his vial into the sea; and it became blood, like *that* of a dead *man*; and every living soul in the sea died" (vs 1-3).

When we come back to restore the earth, it's going to be one giant disaster *after disaster **after disaster!*** That's going to give us a tremendous job to start doing when the Millennium begins.

Verse 4: "And the third angel poured out his vial upon the rivers, and into the fountains of waters; and they became blood."

Verse 5 becomes very important. Think about this for a minute. The righteous angels have been with God forever. The righteous angels rejected the rebellion of Satan and the angels who followed him and became demons. The righteous angels:

- saw how God created man
- saw how Satan did to mankind all down through time

This is viewed from God's point of view! I know that for people who are very tender and don't like violence, blood, guts and gore, this may be a little difficult. But this is looking at it from God's point of view. Here's what the angel says because of these first three plagues:

Verse 5: "Then I heard the angel of the waters say, **'You are righteous, O Lord, Who are, and Who was, even the Holy One, in that You have executed this judgment**.... [the judgment that was prophesied] ...For they have poured out *the* blood of saints and of prophets, and You have given them blood to drink; for they are worthy.' And I heard another *voice* from the altar say, 'Yes, Lord God Almighty, **true and righteous *are* Your judgments**'" (vs 5-7). *Amazing when you look at from God's point of view!*

Verse 8: "And the fourth angel poured out his vial upon the sun; and *power* was given to it to scorch men with fire. Then men were scorched with great heat... [they didn't repent] ...and they blasphemed the name of God, Who has authority over these plagues, and did not repent to give Him glory. And the fifth angel poured out his vial upon the throne of the beast; and his kingdom became full of darkness; and they gnawed their tongues because of the pain" (vs 8-10)—*of the plagues that came upon them and the darkness, showing that they are absolutely cut off from God!*

But Satan, who is the king of pride, gets them up for one last try! This has got to be quite a thing!

Verse 12: "And the sixth angel poured out his vial into the great river Euphrates; and its waters were dried up, so that the way of the kings from the rising of *the* sun might be prepared."

They see this miraculous thing take place and say, 'Yes, we've got to get over to the Holy Land so we can fight against these invaders from outer space. We have got to stop this. They're going to come and take over the earth.' Yes, that's true! We will be the invaders! *To prepare them for it it's got to be powerfully persuasive, and it is*:

Verse 13: "Then I saw three unclean spirits like frogs *come* out of the mouth of the dragon... [Satan the devil, the chief spokesman] ...and out of the mouth of the beast, and out of the mouth of the false prophet; for they are spirits of demons working miracles, going forth to the kings of the earth, even of the whole world, to gather them together **to *the* battle of that great day of the Almighty God**" (vs 13-14).

That's going to be persuasive! They're going to sacrifice all that they have. They're going to get all their weapons and everything that they can do. All the nations are going to send some of their armies there to do it. We will see that we also have a part in carrying out this vengeance.

Verse 15—*a warning to us*: "Behold, I come as a thief. **Blessed *is* the one who is watching and is keeping his garments**... [ties right in with the Laodiceans] ...so that he may not walk naked and they *may not* see his shame. And he gathered them together to the place that in Hebrew is called Armageddon" (vs 15-16).

Let them all get there! Let them all be ready! Everyone is looking up to this great Sea of Glass, and they're going to bring their weapons, all of the most powerful that they have so they can shoot at it to destroy the 'aliens' who seek to invade the earth.

Here's what happens, v 17: "Then the seventh angel poured out his vial into the air; and a loud voice came out of the temple of heaven, from the throne, saying, 'IT IS FINISHED.' And there were voices and thunders and lightnings; and **there was a great earthquake, such as was not since men were on the earth, so mighty an earthquake, *and* so great**. And the great city was divided into three parts; and the cities of the nations fell..." (vs 17-19).

Notice the total destruction that this earth is going to experience! Does that not add a tremendous exclamation mark to the verse that says, *'The wages of sin is death!'* Yes, indeed!

"...and Babylon the Great was remembered before God to give her the cup of the wine of the fury of His wrath. And every island disappeared, and no mountains were found; and great hail, *each stone the weight of a talent… [180 pounds] …fell down from heaven upon men…*" (vs 19-21).

I suppose some in the tanks could survive some of this. That's going to happen right there below the Sea of Glass. When that happens, another wave of the army is going to come, and we will see what happens to them in just a minute.

"…and men blasphemed God because of the plague of the hail, for the plague was exceedingly great" (v 21).

We see in Rev. 19 that the marriage of the Lamb has taken place, the supper has taken place. We are all ready to go:

- we have our assignments
- we have our white horses
- we know how to ride them
- we know what we need to do

The Third Phase of the Return of Jesus Christ:

➤ **Phase One:** the sign of the Son of man as a second sun
➤ **Phase Two:** the resurrection
➤ **Phase Three:** Christ and all the saints coming back to the earth

Then we will see that, yes, we will carry out some of the vengeance of God, because we are to rule the nations with 'a rod of iron.' If they resist they will be broken as pottery into shivers of nothing.

Revelation 19:11: "And I saw heaven open; and behold, a white horse; and He Who sat on it *is* called Faithful and True, and in righteousness He does judge and make war." *This is Christ!*

Verse 12: "And His eyes *were* like a flame of fire, and on His head *were* many crowns; *and* He had a name written that no one knows except Him. And *He was* clothed with a garment dipped in blood… [book of Isaiah] …and His name is The Word of God… [John 1:1-2] …And the armies in heaven were following Him… [that's *us*] …on white horses; *and* they were clothed in fine linen, white and pure. And out of His mouth goes a sharp sword, that with it He might smite the nations; and He shall shepherd them with an iron rod; and **He treads the winepress of the fury and the wrath of the Almighty God**" (vs 12-15). *That's the vengeance of God!*

Verse 16: "And on *His* garment and on His thigh He has a name written: King of kings and Lord of lords. Then I saw an angel standing in the sun; and he cried out with a loud voice, saying to all the birds that fly in *the* midst of heaven, 'Come and gather yourselves together to the supper of the great God so that you may eat *the* flesh of kings, and *the*

flesh of chief captains, and *the* flesh of mighty *men*, and *the* flesh of horses, and of those who sit on them, and *the* flesh of all, free and bond, and small and great.' And I saw the beast and the kings of the earth and their armies, gathered together to make war with Him Who sits on the horse, and with His army" (vs 16-19).

God has a special surprise for the beast and the false prophet, v 20: "And the beast was taken, and with him the false prophet who worked miracles in his presence, by which he had deceived those who received the mark of the beast and those who worshiped his image. **Those two were cast alive into the Lake of Fire, which burns with brimstone**; and the rest were killed by the sword of Him Who sits on the horse, *even the sword* that goes out of His mouth; and all the birds were filled with their flesh" (vs 20-21).

We come back to the earth; this is the final Feast of Trumpets. There is a space of time between Trumpets and Atonement—nine days to be exact. We know that Atonement pictures putting Satan into the abyss. What happens on those nine days? One church says that they're all up there on the Sea of Glass in heaven for those nine days and come down on Atonement. *NO! That's not correct!*

Let's read this amazing Psa. 149 and it tells us what we are going to do:

- we will help carry out the vengeance of God
- we will help destroy the rest of those armies

during the nine day period from Trumpets to Atonement when Satan and the demons are cast into the abyss!

Psalm 149:1: "O praise the LORD! Sing to the LORD a new song, and His praise in the congregation of saints." *All the resurrected saints on the Sea of Glass!*

Verse 2: "Let Israel rejoice in his Maker; let the children of Zion be joyful in their King…. [Israel and the Church] …Let them praise His name in the dance; let them sing praises to Him with the drum and lyre, for the LORD takes pleasure in His people; **He crowns the meek with salvation**" (vs 2-4).

That's us saved, spirit beings, clothed in righteousness, the linen pure and bright! Now on our first mission: destroy any of the wicked, all who resist the Kingdom of God.

Verse 5: "Let the saints be joyful in glory; let them sing aloud upon their beds. Let the high praises of God be in their mouth, and a two-edged sword in their hand **to execute vengeance upon the nations and punishments upon the people**" (vs 5-7). *God gives us the authority to do it; here's the prophecy of it!*

Verse 8: "To bind their kings with chains and their nobles with iron bands, **to carry out upon them the judgment written—this honor have all His saints**. O praise the LORD!" (vs 8-9).

We will be busy doing that from Trumpets to Atonement! This is quite a day! The Feast of Trumpets:

- the seven last plagues
- the wars of all the trumpet plagues

Brethren! What an assignment we are going to start with when the Millennium begins! We can't handle that right now, but as spirit beings we will be able to do it. *This is why we need to make our calling and election sure and believe the Word of God!*

We will see you on Atonement!

Scriptural References:

1) Leviticus 23:23-25

2) Revelation 8:1-13
3) Joel 2:1-11
4) Isaiah 24:1-6
5) Isaiah 13:1-6, 9-13
6) Jeremiah 25:26-34
7) Revelation 9:1-21
8) Revelation 11:14
9) Revelation 14:14-19
10) Joel 3:9-16
11) Revelation 15:1, 5-8
12) Isaiah 34:1-8
13) Isaiah 63:3-6
14) Psalm 94:1-5
15) Psalm 58:10-11
16) Psalm 59:5, 8, 12-13
17) Revelation 16:1-10, 12-21
18) Revelation 19:11-21
19) Psalm 149:1-9

Scriptures referenced, not quoted:

- Deuteronomy 16
- Revelation 6; 7; 10
- John 1:1-2

FRC·bo
Transcribed: 7/26/15
Reformatted: 12/2020

CHAPTER FIFTY-THREE

The Day of Atonement
Fred R. Coulter

Brethren, this is the Day of Atonement, one of the most important Holy Days of God. A day where we fast, where we don't eat, we don't drink any liquids, and we come to God realizing how very important that He is and that He is our whole life totally.

Leviticus 23:26—*let's see the command here*: "And the LORD spoke to Moses, saying…"

Of course, everything that Moses taught was what God told him to say. Everything is 'the LORD said; tell the children of Israel.'

Verse 27: "Also, on the tenth *day* of this seventh month... [which is today] …is the Day of Atonement. *It shall be* a Holy convocation to you. And you shall afflict your souls and offer an offering made by fire to the LORD."

In afflicting your souls, we know that that means with no food and no water. When you do that you really realize how weak that you are.

It also says you shall offer an offering made by fire. And we always take up an offering on each one of the Holy Days every year as they come to us. When we come to God we are to not appear before Him empty. When we come we are to be prepared. When we come, especially on this Day of Atonement, it should be a special offering to God because this shows when we will really be *at-one* with God. This shows that when all of our battles with Satan the devil will be over. This should be a wonderful opportunity to present an offering to God, and we know that God desires that from the heart.

Verse 38: "Besides the Sabbaths of the LORD… [all the Holy Days are Sabbaths] …and besides your gifts… [here are gifts that we give during the year] …and besides all your vows… [what you determine to give God in your heart] …and besides all your freewill offerings…"

All the offerings are to be freewill offerings! We don't want to take any money under any false pretenses or to leverage the brethren or to merchandise the brethren, or any of those physical carnal things that have been done by so many people for so long. So, it should be a freewill offering from the heart that you give unto the Lord.

(pause for offering)

We know that as the Apostle Paul said that we are to 'be instant in season and out of season, and to preach the Word!' The Word of God is what *we are to preach*—just exactly like the Lord told Moses—*whatever is in the Scriptures.* That is what we are to teach. That is what we are to cover for the whole meaning of the Day of Atonement, and it's importance in the plan of God.

We will see that this is one of these days in which it's very important to complete the plan of God. All of them are, beginning with the Passover, Unleavened Bread, Pentecost and Trumpets, and so is Atonement as we come to it, and so will be the Feast of Tabernacles and the Last Great Day when we come to it. All of that portrays all the various aspects of God's plan.

Leviticus 23:28: "And you shall **do no work** in that same day…" *None at all!* He double affirms it later on by saying, 'You shall not do *any* work.'

"…for it *is* the Day of Atonement, in order to make an atonement for you before the LORD your God" (v 28).

We're going to see that the Day of Atonement also is an application of forgiveness. We have our forgiveness with Passover, but the world is going to have their forgiveness beginning with the Day of Atonement. The Passover is for us; the Day of Atonement has a direct meaning for us also, but it also is going to have a tremendous meaning for the people in the world.

Verse 29: "For whoever is not afflicted in that same day, he shall be cut off from among his people."

One of the worst things to do is to be cut off from God. The people who do not keep the Sabbaths of God, and don't keep the Holy Days of God, *don't realize they're cut off from God!* They're just out there doing their own thing. *It's a terrible thing to be cut off from God!* That's why the Day of Atonement is so important. We want to be *at-one* with God; *the opposite of being cut off from God is to be At-One with God!* The Day of Atonement—*at-one-ment*—gives us the meaning of the word, that we are *At-One* with God. *We can't be at-one with God unless we do what He says.*

Verse 30: "And whoever does any work in that same day, the same one will I destroy from among his people."

We've also seen that happen. We've seen people who've come along, been in the Church for years, and years, who've given up on the Day of Atonement, and they have been destroyed. Not dead, but their lives have been destroyed!

Verse 31: "You shall do no manner of work. *It shall be* a statute forever throughout your generations in all your dwellings. It *shall be* to you a Sabbath of rest… [it is a real resting Sabbath] …and you shall afflict yourselves…" (vs 31-32).

He gives a precise time. God does not want any misunderstanding as to when the Day of Atonement begins, because you can't have people starting it at three in the afternoon, and others starting it when it gets dark at seven or eight at night. That way you would have a five to six hour difference in the beginning and ending of the Day of Atonement. You can't possibly all be *At-One* with God if you're all beginning and ending at different times. So, God makes it very clear, and this tells us precisely how every Sabbath is to be calculated:

"…In the ninth *day* of the month at sunset, from sunset to sunset, **you shall keep your Sabbath**" (v 32)—*from sunset*—'ba erev'—*to sunset*—'ba erev.'

When the sun dips below the horizon, the Day of Atonement begins. It ends the 9th day and begins the 10th day. When the whole day comes around and the sun dips below the horizon again, then it ends the 10th day. *That is the Day of Atonement!*

Now, let's look and see all the meaning that we are going to have for the Day of Atonement, because it's really something. So, we're fasting; this day of fasting is very important for us to realize, because it shows that we're just made of flesh, and the flesh does not last long. It means that we can't trust in the flesh, because when you realize how weak you are, and how helpless you are:

- What good is that going to do against Satan the devil?
- What power are you going to exercise out of your own self?
- Can you save yourself?
- Can you make yourself right? *No, you can't; only God can!*

It also teaches us total reliance on God, because everything we have comes from God. It means *at-one-ment!* We're going to see that you cannot overcome Satan the devil with physical means. If you try and overcome Satan with physical means that's exactly what Satan wants you to do, *because*

then he's got you! You can only overcome Satan the devil with spiritual means:

- by the Spirit of God
- by the power of God

Also, it shows that sin can never be totally removed while Satan is around. We're going to see all the aspects of this Day of Atonement and we're going to see why God has to put Satan away, and how that fits into God's overall plan.

First of all, let's see how Satan began, because there is a Satan the devil, and Rev. 13 shows that *the whole world* is going to worship:

- Satan the devil, the dragon
- the beast, who gave Satan his power

Satan has always wanted to be God, as we're going to see. Satan was originally Lucifer, and he was a created being.

Ezekiel 28:11: "And the Word of the LORD came to me, saying, 'Son of man, lift up a lamentation over the king of Tyre…'" (vs 11-12).

Now the power behind the king of Tyrus was Satan the devil, because everything he has to say here has nothing to do with the king of Tyrus, but it has to do with the one who became Satan the devil.

"…and say to him, "Thus says the Lord GOD, 'You seal up the measure of perfection, full of wisdom and perfect in beauty…. [that can't be said of any man] …You have been in Eden, the Garden of God…" (vs 12-13).

We're going to see a little bit later that the only other one who was in the Garden of Eden besides God and Adam and Eve was Satan the devil. So this statement means it's talking about Satan the devil. The king of Tyrus could not possibly have been in the Garden of Eden, because the Garden of Eden was long destroyed through the Flood before the king of Tyrus was ever a being, a person.

Then it says, "…every precious stone *was* your covering… [it lists all of them] …The workmanship of your settings and of your sockets was prepared in you in the day that you were created" (v 13). *This is a created being!*

Verse 14: "You *were* the anointed cherub that covers… [that's what Lucifer originally was] …and I set you so; you were upon the Holy mountain of God… [right there where God's Throne is] …you have walked up and down in the midst of the stones of fire."

That means what you could liken unto, as we've discussed before, the Sea of Glass, the stones of fire.

Verse 15: "You *were* perfect in your ways... [that's why we know that this has to be referring to Lucifer before he fell] ...from the day that you were created, **until** iniquity was found in you." *So, he sinned!*

Here's how he sinned; v 16: "By the multitude of your merchandise..."

Whatever Satan did to merchandise, he merchandised the angels. Whatever he did in not doing what God wanted him to do. Merchandising has to do with lust, covetousness and greed.

"...they have filled your midst *with violence...*" (v 16)—*because evil goes into deeper depths!*

That's why we learned the lesson with the Feast of Unleavened Bread that *a little leaven leavens the whole lump!* Here God is showing how the leaven of sin leavened Lucifer so that he would fall.

"...and you have sinned. Therefore, I will cast you as profane from the mountain of God, and I will destroy you, O covering cherub, from among the stones of fire" (v 16).

Let's see what Jesus said. This also tells us something very important that we need to understand. This also confirms that Jesus was God before He became a human being. That's why the two most *fundamental verses you need to know and know that you know, and have memorized*

John 1:1 "In *the* beginning was the Word, and the Word was with God, and the Word was God."

Verse 14: "And the Word became flesh..."

You need to really understand that, and have that sunk deep into your heart and mind. Here's a verification of that. After the 70 came back they were all joyful because they were able to heal the sick, raise the dead and cast out the demons.

Luke 10:18: "And He [Jesus] said to them, 'I was watching when Satan fell from heaven like lightning.'"

As a lightning streak, just fall from heaven because he was cast down! It says he fell. *So, there's the fall of Satan!* The greatest sin is not the sin of Adam and Eve when they fell. *The greatest fall is the fall of Satan the devil!*

Verse 19: "Behold, I give you authority to tread upon serpents and scorpions, and upon all the power of the enemy... [we'll see how that power is, because Christ has given that to us] ...and nothing shall injure you in any way. Yet, do not rejoice in this, that the spirits are subject to you; but rejoice that **your names are written in heaven'**" (vs 19-

20).

With this Day of Atonement, we need to understand that *our names are written in heaven and we are to be at-one with God!* This is a tremendous day for us; absolutely marvelous day!

Ezekiel 28:17: "Your heart was lifted up..."

- What did Jesus say? *He who exalts himself shall be abased!*
- Satan exalted himself, didn't he?
- Was he abased? Yes, he was.

"...because of your beauty; you have corrupted your wisdom by reason of your brightness. I will cast you to the ground... [that's why he fell as lightning; he was cast back to the earth] ...I will lay you before kings, that they may behold you. By the multitude of your iniquities..." (vs 17-18).

Whatever kind of worship service the angels had in their sanctuaries in worshipping God, this is what it's referring to. And one-third of the angels fell with him (Rev. 12).

"...by the unrighteousness of your trade, you have profaned your sanctuaries; therefore, I brought forth a fire from your midst; it shall devour you, and I will bring you to ashes upon the earth, before the eyes of all who see you" (v 18). *Then it blends back into the king of Tyrus!*

Now let's go to Isa. 14, very basic Scriptures. These are Scriptures we should know and understand, but this is the time and season when we are to go back and see them, and we are to understand that:

- there is a Satan the devil
- he is the enemy of God
- he is the adversary
- he is against us
- he wants to destroy us
- he wants to destroy what God is doing in us

We need to understand and realize that, because one of the first things that Satan wants you to do is discount Satan, and say that 'he's just a myth.' *Then he's gottcha!*

Isaiah 14:12: "How you are fallen from the heavens, O shining star..." *There's only one being that that happened to!* Lucifer means *light-bringer.* The light that he brings is *darkness indeed!*

"...son of the morning! *How* you are cut down to the ground, you who weakened the nations! For you have said in your heart..." (vs 12-13).

That's where sin begins: *in the heart!* That's why Satan wants to inspire sins in people. That's why he wants them, through lust and covetousness, to get them with their heart to sin. So, we have it right here.

Verse 13: "For you have said in your heart, 'I will ascend *into* the heavens, I will exalt my throne…'"

Exaltation doesn't come from the north or the south, or the east or west; *it comes from God!* Satan says, 'I'm going to do it, and I'm going to':

"…exalt my throne <u>above the stars of God</u>… [the angels of God] …I will also sit upon the mount of the congregation, in the sides of the north. <u>I will ascend above the heights of the clouds; I will be like the Most High</u>'" (vs 13-14).

And you can't do that because *there's only one Most High!* This is what Satan has wanted to do all the time. He's wanted to be 'God.' That's why, we'll see a little later, he's called 'the god of this world,' because the world is now once again, in all the occult that is coming back on this whole world as inspired by Satan the devil, they're going to worship him as 'God.'

Verse 15: "Yet, you shall be brought down to the grave, to the sides of the pit…. [we're going to see that Satan is going to be cast into a bottomless pit]. …Those who see you shall stare and watch you closely, *saying*, 'Is this the man who made the earth to tremble; who shook kingdoms'" (vs 15-16).

Is he the one that caused all of this destruction? *Yes, indeed, he certainly was!*

Now let's go to Gen. 3, and let's see how Satan is subtle, he *is* subtle! The first proposition that Satan gave to Eve was that you will become like God, but that's not to become like God *as* God, because that's the whole plan of God, *but to become as a god like Satan considers himself!* That's what he was really talking about. Satan always comes with an accusation.

Genesis 3:1: "Now, the serpent was more cunning than any creature of the field, which the LORD God had made. And he said to the woman, 'Is it true that God has said, "You shall not eat of any tree of the garden"?'…. [that's not what God said. God said] …And the woman said to the serpent, 'We may freely eat the fruit of the trees of the garden, but of the fruit of the tree which *is* in the middle of the garden, God has *indeed* said, "<u>You shall not eat of it, neither shall you touch it, lest you die</u>"'" (vs 1-3).

So, she knew what God had said. God talked to her. There are some people who think that God only talked to Adam, and then Adam talked to his wife. *No!* She *knew* what God said.

"…'<u>You shall not eat of it, neither shall you touch it, lest you die.</u>' And the serpent said to the woman, 'In dying, you shall not surely die!'" (vs 3-4).

In other words, one of the tactics of Satan the devil is to come along and *take the words of God and say that God didn't mean what He said!* You think about that in relationship to all the doctrinal problems that have come about. One of the first things that is said is that *God didn't mean what He said.* *That is a satanic message!* It may *sound* spiritual, it may *sound* religious, *but it is not of God!* It is of Satan the devil from one of the most basic elements that we need to understand back here in Gen. 3. *Furthermore, he goes on and accuses God:*

Verse 5: "For God knows that in the day you eat of it, then your eyes shall be opened, and you shall be like God, deciding good and evil."

Now the word here is 'elohim,' and that refers also to pagan gods. So, he's saying you will become as *a god the way I, Satan the devil, am a god* knowing good and evil.

- Does Satan know good? *Yes!*
- Does he know evil? *Yes!*

No question about it!

Verse 6: "And when the woman saw that the tree *was* good for food… [lust of the eyes] …and that it was pleasing to the eyes, and a tree to be desired to make *one* wise… [vanity, to be exalted up in your own self] …she took of its fruit and ate. She also gave to her husband with her, and he ate. And the eyes of both of them were opened…" (vs 6-7).

Yes, opened to see and understand evil, *but closed their eyes to understand the life and Truth of God.* That's what's happened, because we will see that it says that *Satan the devil has blinded the eyes of those who follow him!* So this opening of the eyes was a closing of the eyes.

"…and they knew that they *were* naked…" (v 7)—*and so forth!* Well, you know the rest of the story there.

Lev. 16 tells us one of the most important things that's going to happen on the Day of Atonement. *This is the removal of Satan the devil!* There is no other being in the whole Bible that is called, or referred to as 'God' except God the Father and Jesus Christ—and Satan the devil is not 'God.' *Satan the devil is a fallen archangel who now is Lucifer, Satan the devil!* But to people in the world, they cannot distinguish between Lucifer and *the true God!* And this is the whole story, and the whole meaning of Lev. 16.

If you are having problems thinking that both of the goats mean that they both belong to God, it cannot possibly be both goats referring to Jesus Christ. *Absolutely an impossibility!*

Now, let's see what was to be done on this Day of Atonement. A very important ceremony was to take place. First of all the priest was allowed to go into the Holy of Holies once a year, and this was the day. *No other day!* They could only come into the first part of the temple to take care of the altar of incense, the showbread, and to light the lamps.

Then he was to have a special atonement for himself, an atonement for his family, and only after he was atoned for himself with very specific offerings, was he then to come back and to take of the two goats.

Leviticus 16:5: "And he shall take from the congregation of the children of Israel two kids of the goats for a sin offering, and one ram for a burnt offering. And Aaron shall offer his young bull of the sin offering, which is for himself, and make an atonement for himself and for his house. And he shall take the two goats... [he had to have the atonement for himself first] ...and present them before the LORD *at* the door of the tabernacle of the congregation" (vs 5-7)—*right in front of God.*

Verse 8: "And Aaron shall cast lots on the two goats; one lot for the LORD and the other lot for **Azazel**"—*the one to be removed!* Of course, Christ was never removed.

Verse 9: "And Aaron shall bring the goat on which the LORD'S lot fell, and offer it for a sin offering." *Now that's very important to understand*:

- this is Christ as *our* sin offering
- this is Christ as the offering for the sins *of the whole world*
  - ✓ our sins come through Passover
  - ✓ the sins of the world come through Atonement

John makes that distinction very clear, what he's saying here.

1-John 2:1: "My little children, I am writing these things to you so that you may not sin. And *yet*, if anyone does sin, we have an Advocate with the Father; Jesus Christ *the* Righteous; and He is *the* propitiation for our sins... [we know that through the covenant renewal of the Passover] ...and not for our sins only, but also for *the sins of* the whole world" (vs 1-2).

The Day of Atonement is when God is going to be dealing with the sins of the whole world, because the world today cannot distinguish between 'the god of this world' and the true Jesus Christ.

That's why this ceremony in Lev, 16. The lot for the Lord was to be offered for a sin offering.

Now we will see what happens with that sin offering.

Leviticus 16:10: "But the goat on which the lot fell for Azazel shall be presented alive before the LORD, to make an atonement **upon it** and sent away into the wilderness for Azazel" *We are going to see that the wilderness is one of Satan's abodes!*

Aaron will then bring all of the things for his offering, and he shall present that.

Verse 15. "Then he shall kill the goat of the sin offering that is for the people, and bring its blood inside the veil...."

If you bring in the blood, and you have the sin offering, an atonement, forgiveness of sins, *the sins are forgiven!* No question about it! Otherwise, why do it if they were not forgiven?

"...And he shall do with that blood as he did with the blood of the young bull, and sprinkle it on the mercy seat and before the mercy seat. And he shall make an atonement for the sanctuary because of the uncleanness of the children of Israel and because of their transgressions in **all** their sins..." (vs 15-16). *It doesn't say some of them, does it? No! It says **all** their sins.*

"...And so he shall do for the tabernacle of the congregation, which remains with them in the midst of their uncleanness" (vs. 15-16). *This is forgiving **all** of their sins!*

Verse 17: "And there shall be no man in the tabernacle of the congregation when he goes in to make an atonement in the sanctuary until he comes out and has made an atonement for himself, and for his household, and for all the congregation of Israel."

Now if the atonement through the propitiation of the sacrifice has already been effective in forgiving the sins of the people, then when he comes to the one upon which the lot fell for Azazel, now we have a totally different application.

Verse 20: "And when he has made an end of reconciling the sanctuary and the tabernacle of the congregation and the altar, he shall bring the live goat." *This is symbolic that it cannot die!*

Verse 21: "And Aaron shall lay both his hands on the head of the live goat, and confess over him all the sins of the children of Israel, and all their transgressions in all their sins, putting them on the head of the goat, and shall send *it* away by the hand of a chosen man into the wilderness."

Now that's a very unusual thing to do. If you have all the sins forgiven already by a sin offering, why this confession of sins again over the goat for Azazel?

There's a very profound reason for it, which is that as long as Satan the devil is around—*who is the author of sin*—is always going to inspire people to sin. He is the one who has caused it. God is making allowance for it here and showing what He's going to do. **That He is going to remove the one who causes sin!**

Verse 22: "And the goat shall bear upon him all their iniquities to a land in which no one lives. And he shall let the goat go in the wilderness. And Aaron shall come into the tabernacle of the congregation, and shall strip off the linen garments, which he put on when he went into the sanctuary, and shall leave them there. And he shall wash his flesh with water in the Holy place, and put on his garments, and come forth…" (vs 22-24).

That represents an unclean spirit! So, he had to wash himself. Same way with the 'chosen [fit] man' who took him out into the wilderness. He had to wash himself and bathe himself because he was dealing with all the uncleanness, an unclean spirit who caused the sins of all the children of Israel.

"…and offer his burnt offering and the burnt offering of the people, and make an atonement for himself and for the people. And the fat of the sin offering shall he burn upon the altar. And he that let go the goat for Azazel shall wash his clothes and bathe his flesh in water, and afterward come into the camp" (vs 24-26). *Then it talks about the sin offering!*

Now here's something very important to understand. This is why **the goat for Azazel cannot represent Christ!**

Verse 27: "And the young bull *for* the sin offering and the goat *for* the sin offering, whose blood was brought in to make atonement in the Holy *place,* shall they carry forth outside the camp. And they shall burn their skins in the fire, and their flesh and their dung. And he who burns them shall wash his clothes and bathe his flesh in water, and afterward he shall come into the camp" (vs 27-28).

That is, over to the altar where they burned all the sin offerings to ashes at the Miphkad Altar, *and that represents Christ!* That's something really important to understand. Now notice what else happens:

"…And they shall burn their skins in the fire, and their flesh and their dung. And he who burns them shall wash his clothes and bathe his flesh in water, and afterward come into the camp" (vs. 27-28).

Verse 29: "And it shall be a statute forever to you: in the seventh month, on the tenth of the month, you shall afflict your souls and do no work at all, *whether it be* one of your own country or a stranger who is living among you, for on that day an atonement shall be made for you, to cleanse you, so that you may be clean from all your sins before the LORD. It *shall be* a Sabbath of rest to you, and you shall afflict your souls, by a statute forever" (vs 29-31).

Verse 32: "'And the priest whom he shall anoint, and whom he shall consecrate to minister in the priest's office in his father's stead, shall make the atonement and shall put on the linen clothes, the Holy garments. And he shall make an atonement *for* the Holy sanctuary, and he shall make an atonement for the tabernacle of the congregation, and for the altar; and he shall make an atonement for the priests and for all the people of the congregation. And this shall be an everlasting statute to you, to make an atonement for the children of Israel for their sins once a year.' And he did as the LORD commanded Moses" (vs 32-34).

So, *there we have the fullness of the meaning of the Day of Atonement here in Lev. 16!*

We're going to see the fulfillment of this, and then we'll come back and we'll see some other things as it relates to:

- Satan the devil
- our calling
- the things that we need to do
- how we need to overcome him

and a more complete meaning of this day!

After Christ returns, sets His feet on the earth on the day of Trumpets, Satan then, on the Day of Atonement:

Revelation 20:1: "Then I saw an angel descending from heaven… [this is a type of the 'chosen man'] …having the key of the abyss… [Didn't we read that he was going to be put into the pit? *Yes!*] … and a great chain in his hand. And he took hold of the dragon, the ancient serpent, who is *the* Devil and Satan, and bound him *for* a thousand years" (vs 1-2).

So, Satan is not going to be around all during the Millennium. It's going to be:

- a completely different world
- a completely different administration
- a completely different set of circumstances

We will be there with Jesus Christ

- to serve and to help the people
- to rule them
- to train them
- to teach them
- to qualify them to come into the Kingdom of God

What a glorious reign that is going to be as we will see when we keep the Feast of Tabernacles!

Verse 3: "Then he cast him into the abyss, and locked him *up*, and sealed *the abyss* over him, so that he would not deceive the nations any longer until the thousand years were fulfilled…"

We're going to find out on the Last Great Day why he is let out for that very short period of time. The 7th and 8th day of the Feast of Tabernacles; the last day of the Feast of Tabernacles, day 7 and the Last Great Day, the 8th day we'll see why.

Today we're still confronted with Satan the devil! We're still confronted with what we need to do! Let's understand something concerning the things that we need to do. Let's see how Satan the devil works, and he is working grandly today. He's got all the powers and tools and people in his hands, using them, manipulating them, preparing the way, making his coming, great one-world to be an awesome and a mighty thing indeed.

Ephesians 2:1: "And you were dead in trespasses and sins..." *Because if you're living in sin, you're dead; you have no spiritual life!* You may be alive physically, but you are dead spiritually.

There was a time when we are living in our sins and transgressions that we are dead. And when God in His mercy has called us and raised us up out of that:

- granting us forgiveness
- giving us the gift of repentance
- giving us the gift of eternal life
- giving us the gift of the Holy Spirit
- giving us the gift of imputed righteousness of Christ

That is what it is to be made alive in Christ! But we were once dead in our sins and trespasses!

Verse 2: "In which you walked in times past according to the course of this world… [that is the way that this world is] …according to the prince of the power of the air… [and he is] … the spirit that is now working within the children of disobedience."

Satan has a power, and Satan has his spirit that can go out and have power and cause people to do things that he wants them to do. People can resist it; *there's a way to resist!* But you can only resist so much in the flesh. You have to resist in the spirit and have the spiritual armament. Notice how he works here.

Verse 3: among whom also we all once had our conduct in the lusts of our flesh, doing the things willed by the flesh and by the mind… [all of those things seems so good] …and were by nature *the* children of wrath, even as the rest *of the world."*

1-John 2 tells us here also about how Satan appeals to the flesh, to the lust of the eyes, the pride of life, and the love of the world. All of that is part of Satan's world.

1-John 2:15: "**Do not love the world, nor the things *that are* in the world**…."

That's how Satan gets you, because you become carnal minded, material minded. You're not minding the things of God, of the Spirit. You're minding the things of the flesh.

"…If anyone loves the world, the love of the Father is not in him, because **everything that *is* in the world**… [think about this statement] …the lust of the flesh, and the lust of the eyes, and the pretentious pride of physical life—is not from the Father, but is from the world. And the world and its lust is passing away, but the one who does the will of God abides forever" (vs 15-17).

Brethren, that's important to understand. But notice how Satan uses all the physical things of the world:

- the lust of the flesh
- the lust of the eyes
- the pride of life

Those are his tools, and he is the god of this world!

Now let's go to 2 Cor. 4, and here we're going to see that Satan the devil is called the god of this world.

2-Corinthians 4:1: "Therefore, having this ministry… [Paul is talking about *his* ministry] …according as we have received mercy, we are not fainthearted. For we have personally renounced the hidden things of dishonest gain, not walking in *cunning* craftiness, nor handling the Word of God deceitfully…" (vs 1-2).

These are the things that the false prophets and teachers use:

- dishonesty
- walking in craftiness
- handling the Word of God deceitfully

Anyone who is a true minister of God will have renounced all those carnal things!

"…but by manifestation of the Truth…" (v 2)—*which is the Word of God*:

- teaching the Word of God
- speaking the Word of God
- helping people understand the Word of God

Not using, abusing, manipulating and deceitfully handling it. That's how you can tell who is a false teacher and who is not.

Verse 3: "But if our Gospel is hidden, it is hidden to those who are perishing; **in whom the god of this age has blinded the minds**…" (vs 3-4).

Now that's what happened with Adam and Eve, he blinded their minds. Yet, they thought their minds were opened. Quite *a different thing indeed!*

"…**of those who do not believe**…" (v 4). *That's what happens when Satan the devil blinds your mind!*

"…lest the Light of the Gospel of the glory of Christ, Who is *the* image of God, should shine unto them" (v 4).

He cuts them off so that they won't understand it. God turns them over to it because this is not the age of Christ; this is the age of man and Satan.

Verse 5: "For we do not preach our own selves, but Christ Jesus *the* Lord, and ourselves your servants for Jesus' sake." *That's the way that the Apostle Paul did!*

Let's see how the false preachers and teachers and apostles behaved themselves:

2-Corinthians 11:13: "For such *are* false apostles…" *Part of it was that he's talking about the things that were done*:

- they were turning them from the simplicity of Christ
- they were merchandising them
- they were feeding them with philosophy, which are the doctrines of the religion of Satan the devil

"…deceitful workers who are transforming themselves into apostles of Christ. And *it is* no marvel, for Satan himself transforms himself into an angel of light…. [yet, his light is darkness] …Therefore, *it is* no great thing if his servants also transform themselves as ministers of righteousness—whose end shall be according to their works" (vs 13-15).

We have to fight against this! *That's how Satan works!* Let's see also how he works as the prince of the power of the air. Remember what he did with Job. One day the sons of God appeared before the Lord, and Satan was among them, going up and down, to and fro in the earth. Then you know all the rest of the story of Satan the devil.

1-Peter 5—Satan is 'a roaring lion, is going about seeking whom he may devour.' How will he devour? *Let's see how he does! He sends out his impulses, his airwaves as it were, because he's the prince of the power of the air, and inspires people to sin!*

He even got to King David. Let's see one of the great sins that David committed. It says right here that he was inspired of Satan the devil:

1-Chronicles 21:1: "And **Satan stood up against Israel and provoked David to number Israel**." *Satan is the one who did it. Provoked him. Caused him to do it!*

Verse 2: "And David said to Joab and to the rulers of the people… [God said don't number them. Don't look to them for a number] …'Go number Israel from Beersheba to Dan. And bring the number of them to me so that I may know.' And Joab answered, 'May the LORD add to His people a hundred times, but my lord the king, *are* they not all my lord's servants? Why then does my lord require this thing? Why will he be a cause of trespass to Israel?'" (vs 2-3).

You know what happened there, 70,000 in Israel died because David sinned. Satan does things like that.

Let's see what Satan also appeals to; Matthew 16:21: "From that time Jesus began to explain to His disciples that it was necessary for Him to go to Jerusalem, and to suffer many things from the elders and chief priests and scribes, and to be killed, and to be raised the third day. But after taking *Him* aside, Peter personally began to rebuke Him, saying, '*God will be* favorable to you, Lord. In no way shall this *happen* to You'" (vs 21-22).

Peter thought he was doing something good and fine. He's going to save the Savior. I mean, think of that. Those are kind of conflicting words, aren't they? Now notice what Jesus did:

Verse 23: "Then He turned and said to Peter, 'Get behind Me, Satan! You are an offense to Me, because your thoughts are not *in accord* with the things of God, **but the things of men.**'" *Satan appeals to those things that be of men!*

Now let's see that Satan really desired to have Peter. If he really could have had Peter, the true apostle, instead of Peter a false apostle, perhaps he thought he could have had a greater false church.

Luke 22:31: "Then the Lord said, 'Simon, Simon, listen *well*. Satan has **demanded** to have all of you, to sift as wheat. But I have prayed for you, that your faith may not fail; and when you are converted, strengthen your brethren'" (vs 31-32).

Satan really wanted Peter, and Satan did get to Peter when he fell hook, line, and sinker back into Judaism (Gal. 2). So Peter was spared that, but he had to be saved from that. Now let's understand something else here, too. When Satan really has you…

John 13:27—*Satan entered into Judas*: "And after the sop… [that is after Judas took the sop] …Satan entered into him…." *Totally possessed of Satan the devil!*

That's going to happen again with *the beast and the false prophet,* that the beast is going to be totally possessed of Satan and he is going to go into the Temple of God, and he is going to say that he *is* 'God,' and be worshipped as God. Those are all the means and devices of Satan the devil. Let's understand something. Something very important for us to realize:

- there are the children of the devil
- there are the children of God

We're going to look at the difference between them. John Morgan made a very interesting comment: He said that there are two ways, and there's a great in-between between the two ways, and that's *the vastness of the deceived world.* But you have the children of Satan on one hand, and the children of God on the other hand. And the children of Satan the devil are indoctrinated in a course, or a process called perversion. The children of God are, through a process, converted. *So that each has a process*:

- one to *perversion*
- one to *conversion*
  - ✓ one leads to *eternal death*
  - ✓ the other leads to *eternal life*

We are going to see, that yes the children of the devil do come in amongst our midst and they are called tares. They are the ones who cause us problems. *Satan loves a hierarchy,* so he can get someone in authority to sit there and wait. These are called, as Peter said, *false teachers who stealthily snuck in* and began to teach against the Truth.

Matthew 13:37—the Parable of the Sower: "And He answered *and* said to them, 'The One Who sows the good seed is the Son of man; and the field is the world; and the good seed, these are the children of the Kingdom… [that's us] …but the tares are the children of the wicked *one*… [so we have the two here] …Now, the enemy who sowed them is the devil; and the harvest is *the* end of the age… [and we're living in the end of the world right now] …and the reapers are the angels'" (vs 37-39).

Eventually the finality of this is going go take place at the resurrection!

Verse 40: "Therefore, as the tares are gathered and consumed in the fire…"

I think right now God is gathering the tares together in their own little groups. God is gathering **the children of the Kingdom** in their groups.

"…so shall it be in the end of this age. The Son of man shall send forth His angels, and they shall gather out of His Kingdom all the offenders and those who are practicing lawlessness; and they shall cast them into the furnace of fire; there shall be weeping and gnashing of teeth. Then shall the righteous shine forth as the sun…" (vs 40-43). *So, we have the two rewards; we have the two things:*

1. the children of the wicked one
2. the children of the Kingdom

We have the process:

- the ending up of being burned in the fire of the wicked ones
- the children of the Kingdom entering into the Kingdom to shine in the glorious being as the sun shines

"…in the Kingdom of their Father. **The one who has ears to hear, let him hear**" (v 43).

Now let's see that there is a difference between the children of the Kingdom who are the children of God **and** the children of the devil.

1-John 3:4 (*FV*): "Everyone who practices sin is also practicing lawlessness, for sin is lawlessness."

The *King James* says: "Whosoever committeth sin transgresseth also the law: for sin is the transgression of the law."

That is an accurate translation too, but this (*FV*) is even stronger because lawlessness in the Greek is 'anomia,' which means against Law. And Satan is against all the Laws of God. He has his own, *but he's against God!*

Verse 5 (*FV*): "And you know that He appeared in order that He [Christ] might take away our sins; and in Him is no sin. **Everyone who dwells in Him does not *practice* sin**…" (vs 5-6).

That's what it means, because we're talking about *practicing sin* (v 4) and the thought in the Greek is carried on down here to v 6:

"…does not *practice* sin; anyone who *practices* sin has not seen Him, nor has known Him. Little children, do not allow anyone to deceive you; the one who practices righteousness is righteous, even as He is righteous" (vs 6-7). *We have the imputed righteousness of Christ!*

Verse 8: "The one who practices sin is of the devil because the devil has been sinning from *the* beginning. For this purpose the Son of God appeared that He might destroy the works of the devil. **Everyone who has been begotten by God does not practice sin,** because His seed *of begettal*… [from the Father] …is dwelling within him, and he is not able to *practice* sin because he has been begotten by God" (vs 8-9).

Now let's understand why it means *practice* sin, because there is a sin that is not a sin unto death.

1 John 5:16: "If anyone sees his brother sinning a sin *that is* not unto death…" *That means any sin that it can be repented of!* That's why when we go pray, we say 'Forgive us our sins.' But we are not *practicing* sin. Those who are practicing sin have no consciousness of sin; *it is their way of life!*

"…he shall ask, and He will give him life for those who do not sin unto death. There is a sin unto death; concerning that *sin*, I do not say that he should make *any* supplication *to God*" (v 16).

So here in 1 John 3 we have the same thing: *practicing sin.*

1-John 3:9: "Everyone who has been begotten by God does not practice sin, because His seed *of begettal* is dwelling within him, and he is not able to *practice* sin because he has been begotten by God…. [*and God the Father will reveal to him that he is sinning so he can repent*] …By this *standard* are manifest…" (vs 9-10).

• the one who is practicing righteousness
• the ones who are practicing lawlessness

"…**the children of God** and **the children of the devil**…" (v 10).

Satan has his children; Satan has those who do his bidding, and there is a process of perversion that they go through.

"…Everyone who does not practice righteousness is not of God, and neither is the one who does not love his brother" (v 10). *Think how important brotherly love is!*

Now take a look at *the process of perversion,* then we will look at *the process of conversion.* Then we will see how we need to overcome Satan the devil.

Romans 1:19: "Because that which may be known of God is manifest among them…" *God always reveals Himself in the physical things to them!*

"…for God has manifested *it* to them; for the invisible things of Him are perceived from *the* creation of *the* world, being understood by the things that were made—both His eternal power and Godhead– **so that they are without excuse**" (vs 19-20).

When they come to that point of rejecting God, knowing and having everything there to show that there is a God:

1. *they are **without excuse***

Verse 21: "Because when they knew God, they glorified *Him* not as God, neither were thankful; but they **became vain in their own reasonings**…" When you reject God then you become:

2. *vain in your own reasonings, your own imaginations*

"…and their foolish hearts were darkened" (v 21) *Again, the light of Satan the devil **is darkness!*** When they become vain in their own imaginations:

3. *they become **fools***

Verse 22: "While professing themselves to be *the* wise ones, **they became fools**" So that's the third step. Of course, *they think* they are wise!

4. *idol worship*

Verse 23: "And changed the glory of the incorruptible God into *the* likeness of an image of corruptible man, and of birds, and four-footed creatures, and creeping things

You go back into idol worship or 'the green movement,' That's all part of it. And where is all of this eco stuff coming from today, but straight out of the cauldron of the goddess Gaia.

5. *God abandons them*

Verse 24: "For this cause, **God also abandoned them to uncleanness** through the lusts of their hearts…"

Then God does something. He turns them over and lets Satan have them even more. That's why all of these secret societies have degrees of initiation. Each degree goes further and further into the depths of Satan the devil.

6. "…to **disgrace their own bodies** between themselves" (v 24).

7. *Worship of man and Satan the devil*

"Who **exchanged the Truth of God for the lie**…" [they believe the lie] …and they worshiped and served the created thing more than the One Who is Creator, Who is blessed into the ages. Amen" (v 25).

Then they get into the full worship of man and how great he is, and of Satan the devil, the created thing.

8. *God abandons to passions*

Verse 26: "For this cause, **God abandoned them to disgraceful passions**; for even their women changed the natural use *of sex* into that which is contrary to nature; and in the same manner also the men, having left the natural use *of sex* with the woman, were inflamed in their lustful passions toward one another—men with men shamelessly committing lewd *acts*, and receiving back within themselves a fitting penalty for their error" (vs 26-27).

9. *God abandons them to a reprobate mind*

Verse 28: "And in exact proportion as they did not consent to have God in *their* knowledge, **God abandoned them to a reprobate mind**, to practice *those* things that are immoral"

So there are the *nine steps of the process of perversion into the depths of satanism!*

Verse 29: "Being filled with all unrighteousness, sexual immorality, wickedness, covetousness, malice; full of envy, murder, strife, guile, evil dispositions; whisperers, slanderers, God-haters, insolent, proud, boasters, inventors of evil things *and practices*; disobedient to parents, void of understanding, covenant-breakers, without natural affection, implacable *and* unmerciful; who, knowing the righteous judgment of God, that those who commit such things are worthy of death, not only practice these things themselves, but also approve of those who commit *them*" (vs 29-32).

So, they arrive at the depths of Satan the devil!

Rev. 2—let's see where God talks about how that even one of the Churches of God, got involved in it. You will see this at the Feast of Tabernacles, the story of the Waldensians, or the Church at Thyatira. They listened to that woman the prophetess Jezebel, who is the Catholic Church. Then God had to punish them, and He did it in a very, very profound way.

Revelation 2:19: "I know your works, and love, and service, and faith, and your endurance, and your works; and the last *are* more than the first. But I have a few things against you, because you allow the woman Jezebel, who calls herself a prophetess, to teach and to seduce My servants into committing fornication and eating things sacrificed to idols" (vs 19-20).

That going down into satanism can even happen to people who are converted if you give yourself over to it. You have to fight against Satan the devil. We will see how we need to do that after we get done here.

Verse 21: "And I gave her time to repent of her fornication, but she did not repent. Behold, I will cast her into a bed, and those who commit adultery with her into great tribulation, unless they repent of their works" (vs 21-22).

There was great tribulation during the time of the Waldensians. When you see the DVD: The Israel of the Alps, you're going to be shocked as to what happened to them. They finally were fully

compromised. Notice what God says He's going to do.

Verse 23: "And I will kill her children with death; and all the churches shall know that I am He Who searches *the* reins and hearts… [God knows] …and I will give to each of you according to your works. But to you I say, and to *the* rest who *are* in Thyatira, as many as do not have this doctrine, and who have not known the depths of Satan, as they speak; I will not cast upon you any other burden" (vs 21-24).

So, there is the depths of Satan to which people go. It can happen, and we just read the process here in Rom. 1.

Let's look at the process of conversion. And there is a process to that which Peter describes in 2-Peter 1, the process of conversion. It is step-by-step, and it is degree-by-degree. It's something that we have to work at. Just like the children of the devil have to work at what they do and are dedicated into what they are doing, and that's how they are raised in elevation to great offices of responsibility and authority in this world, because they've proved that they can serve Satan and lie, so he raises and elevates them and rewards them.

Likewise brethren, we need to realize that we have a reward coming too. But our reward comes the other way. Our reward comes this way, we have to understand the promises that God has given us, and that's what this Day of Atonement is all about:

- that we can have the same nature of God
- that we can be as God is
- that we can live in all eternity as the sons and daughters of God

2-Peter 1:2: "Grace and peace be multiplied to you in *the* knowledge of God and of Jesus our Lord, according as His Divine power has given to us all things that *pertain* to life and Godliness…" (vs 2-3).

And it's all right here in the word of God, brethren. Everything that we have, plus

- His Spirit
- the gift of righteousness
- access to Him

It's a wonderful thing that God has called us to!

"…through the knowledge of Him Who called us by *His own* glory and virtue; through which He has given to us the greatest and *most* precious promises, that through these you may become partakers of *the* Divine nature…" (vs 3-4).

Think of that. That is tremendous! That's what God wants to give us, the Divine nature. Not human nature, not Satan's nature. The children of the devil have Satan's nature. The children of God have God's nature of love, joy, peace and longsuffering, and all the things of God. Then he goes on to give the process:

"...having escaped the corruption *that is* in *the* world through lust. And for this very reason also, having applied all diligence besides, add to your faith, virtue... [here are the steps]: and to virtue, knowledge; and to knowledge, self-control; and to self-control, endurance; and to endurance, Godliness [having Godly character] ...and to Godliness, brotherly love; and to brotherly love, **the love *of* God**" (vs 4-7).

That's the whole process of conversion. So you see the two:

- one goes into the depths of depravity,
- one goes to the height of being exalted in the Kingdom of God at the resurrection

Now we also understand, we have to fight Satan the devil. Let's see Jesus Christ fought Satan the devil, and what He did and how He did it. This gives us understanding on what we need to do to fight Satan the devil, because we still live in this world.

- we still have to overcome Satan the devil
- we have to overcome the beast
- we have to overcome the number
- we have to overcome the mark
- we have to overcome the name

We have a lot of satanic things that we need to overcome in this world.

- we cannot do it on our own
- we cannot do it with our own strength
- we cannot do it with fleshly means

That's why here in Matt. 4 we have it that Jesus fasted 40 days and 40 nights. This shows that our weapons are not carnal, *but spiritual to the pulling down of strongholds,* as the Apostle Paul said. We follow the example of Christ and how He fought Satan the devil.

Matthew 4:1: "Then Jesus was led up into the wilderness by the Spirit..."

That's where Satan was. That's why the goat of Azazel was taken out to the wilderness, because that's Satan's abode. There is nothing there but death, wilderness, and desolation. That's the legacy of the children of Satan.

"...in order to be tempted by the devil. And when He had fasted *for* forty days and forty nights, afterwards He was famished. And when the tempter came to Him, he said, 'If You are the Son of

God...'" (vs 1-3).

- always challenging God
- always questioning what you believe

That's why we have to be alert doctrinally, because Satan comes along and he's always testing:

- Is there a weakness in this doctrine?
- Is there a weakness in your understanding?
- Is there a weakness in what you believe?
- If this is true?
- If the Sabbath is the day of God, why do so many Christians go on Sunday?

Gotcha!

So Satan said to Christ, "...'If You are the Son of God, command that these stones become bread.' But He answered *and* said, 'It is written,...'" (vs 3-4).

Here is the key: *You overcome Satan the devil with the Word of God, properly applied!*

"...Man shall not live by bread alone..." (v 4)—*not just by the physical means!*

That's why He was fasting the 40 days and 40 nights. That's why we are fasting today, brethren, *so we understand exactly the same lesson!*

We don't "...live by bread alone, but by every word that proceeds out of *the* mouth of God" (v 4).

That's how we are to live! That's why Satan the devil comes along and he said to Eve, 'Did God say this?'

Verse 5: "Then the devil took Him to the Holy city and set Him upon the edge of the temple, and said to Him, 'If You are the Son of God, cast Yourself down; for it is written...'" (vs 5-6).

Satan and his ministers will quote Scripture. They will even quote it correctly, *but they will misapply it!* No question about it. They will always misapply it. But they will use it and they will quote it. Like the Apostle Paul said, *'handle the word of God deceitfully.'*

"...'He shall give His angels charge concerning You, and they shall bear You up in *their* hands, lest You strike Your foot against a stone.' Jesus said to him, 'Again, it is written, "You shall not tempt *the* Lord your God."'" (vs 6-7).

Verse 8: "After that, the devil took Him to an exceedingly high mountain, and showed Him all the kingdoms of the world and their glory." *Luke says, 'in the moment of time.'*

This is why Satan is called 'the god of this world.' This is why the goat for Azazel. Right here is the confrontation that we see between Christ and

Satan, between the goat for the LORD, and the goat for Azazel in the wilderness. Here is the confrontation right here.

Verse 9: "And said to Him, 'All these things will I give You, if You will fall down and worship me'"—as 'God'! That's the whole goal of Satan the devil.

Verse 10: "Then Jesus said to him, 'Be gone, Satan! For it is written, "You shall worship the Lord your God, and Him alone shall you serve."'"

Not that He's telling that Satan would, because won't. But He's saying that's what man should do, what Christ should do, what we should do.

Verse 11: "Then the devil left Him; and behold, angels came and ministered to Him."

It's quite a thing that we have here. It's quite a process that we are going through. This Day of Atonement shows us:

- how we can escape the things of Satan the devil
- how we need to do it
- why we need to do it
- what we need to do to overcome it

Those who are the children of Satan the devil come to think like the devil! Those who are of the children of God are to come to have the mind of Christ and think like Christ. ***That's the whole goal of being at-one with God!***

- to be as Christ is
- to think as Christ

If we can understand that, that's why you never hear me say to *follow me as I follow Christ. No!* I don't have to say that *because now we have the whole Scriptures here! I want you to follow Christ!* I want to follow Christ.

- I don't want you to think as me
- I don't want you to think as any other human being
- I want you to think as Christ thinks
- to have the mind of Christ.

That becomes the full total conversion!

We are told that we are going to have our confrontation with the synagogue of Satan. We know that and we are told right in Eph. 6 that the wiles of the devil are there. We are battling, and fighting, and warring against great powers. This struggle that we are in is a great struggle!

Ephesians 6:10: "Finally, my brethren, be strong in *the* Lord… [that's what we need, please be strong in the Lord] …and in the might of His strength." *See that*:

- you are armed with the Word of God
- you are armed with the Spirit of God
- you are armed with all the defenses of God

Verse 11: "**Put on the whole armor of God**…"

It's something you have to do. Something we have to do. And if we don't put it on then we will be victimized by Satan the devil.

"…so that you may be able to stand against the wiles of the devil" (v 11).

He's got plenty, and he has many; he has been at it for over 6000 years, and he is the slickest thing around. If you think 'Slick Willy' is slick, you ain't seen nothing compared to Satan the devil.

Verse 12: "Because we are not wrestling against flesh and blood… [it's not just a physical power] …**but against principalities *and* against powers, against the world rulers of the darkness of this age**…"

Who are the children of Satan the devil, who have gone through the depths of perversion to come to the depths of power that they have.

"…against the spiritual *power* of wickedness in high *places*" (v 12). *Yes, they've even gotten into the Church and have torn the Church asunder!*

Verse 13: "Therefore, **take up the whole armor of God**…"

Brethren, we are going to need it the closer and closer we come to the year 2000, the more we are going to need the whole armor of God. We don't know exactly what's going to happen, but it's going to be significant.

"…So that you may be able to resist in the evil day…" (v 13). *Whatever that evil day is;* whether it is:

- a day of trial for you
- a day of trouble for you
- a day of temptation for you
- a day of weakness for you

Whatever it may be!

"…so that you may be able to resist in the evil day, and having worked out all things, to stand. Stand, therefore, having your loins girded about with Truth… [just a part of your being] …and wearing the breastplate of righteousness, and having your feet shod with *the* preparation of the Gospel of Peace. Besides all *these*, take up the shield of the faith, with which you will have the power to quench all the fiery darts of the wicked one" (vs 13-16).

To put them out, to extinguish them, that the burning passions of lust do not get to you. When it comes you say, 'Get you hence, Satan.'

Verse 17: "And put on the helmet of salvation, and the sword of the Spirit, which is the Word of God; praying at all times with all prayer and supplication in *the* Spirit…" (vs 17-18).

Yes, brethren, we always need to pray. That is our spiritual life every single day. These are the things we need to do.

Now let's see what else we do to overcome Satan the devil.

Rev. 12—let's come here to, and this is important too, and we may be called upon to do this.

Revelation 12:9: "And the great dragon was cast out… [he's going to be cast out again] …the ancient serpent who is called the Devil and Satan, who is deceiving the whole world… [the whole world is under his sway] …he was cast down to the earth, and his angels were cast down with him. And I heard a great voice in heaven say, 'Now has come the salvation and the power and the Kingdom of our God, and the authority of His Christ because the accuser of our brethren has been cast down, who accuses them day and night before our God. But they overcame him…'" (vs 9-11).

We *will* overcome him, brethren! We *can* overcome him through the very power of the Holy Spirit of God and all the things that God has, and all the armor of God. We can overcome him.

"…Through the blood of the Lamb…" (v 11). *That is by having our sins forgiven and cleansed and washed!*

"…And through the word of their testimony…" (v 11). *That we have the Word of God and the testimony that comes from Christ!*

"…And they loved not their lives unto death" (v 11). *We consider God's way above everything that we do!* So this is what God wants us to do.

We're going to have that confrontation with Satan the devil. Let's see why this Day of Atonement is so important for us. Speaking to the Church at Philadelphia. He says:

Revelation 3:9: "Behold, I will make those of the synagogue of Satan …"

So, all of the great-ones in the world, all of those who have gone through the depths of the perversion that you have seen, that we have read about here.

"…who proclaim themselves to be Jews and are not, but do lie. Behold, I will cause them to come

and worship before your feet, and to know that I have loved you" (v 9).

- God the Father loves you
- Jesus Christ loves you

Verse 10: "Because you have kept the Word of My patience, I also will keep you from the time of temptation, which *is* about to come upon the whole world to try those who dwell on the earth. Behold, I am coming quickly; **hold fast that which you have so that no one may take away your crown**" (vs 10-11). ***Don't let anyone take your crown!***

Don't let Satan get it. Don't let any man get it, who is inspired of Satan the devil, take it from you.

Verse 12: "The one who overcomes will I make a pillar in the temple of My God, and he shall not go out anymore; and I will write upon him the name of My God and the name of the city of My God, the New Jerusalem, which will come down out of heaven from My God; and ***I will write upon him My new name***"—*because you are **at-one** with God the Father and Jesus Christ!*

Scriptures from *The Holy Bible in Its Original Order, A Faithful Version* (except where noted)

Scriptural References:

1) Leviticus 23:26-27, 38, 28-32
2) Ezekiel 28:11-16
3) John 1:1, 14
4) Luke 10:18-20
5) Ezekiel 28:17-18
6) Isaiah 14:12-16
7) Genesis 3:1-7
8) Leviticus 16:5-9
9) 1 John 2:1-2
10) Leviticus 16:10, 15-17, 20-34
11) Revelation 20:1-3
12) Ephesians 2:1-3
13) 1 John 2:15-17
14) 2 Corinthians 4:1-5
15) 2 Corinthians 11:13-15
16) 1 Chronicles 21:1-3
17) Matthew 16:21-23
18) Luke 22:31-32
19) John 13:27
20) Matthew 13:37-43
21) 1 John 3:4-9
22) 1John 5:16
23) 1 John 3:9-10
24) Romans 1:19-32
25) Revelation 2:19-24
26) 2 Peter 1:1-7
27) Matthew 4:1-11
28) Ephesians 6:10-18
29) Revelation 12:9-11

30) Revelation 3:9-12

Scriptures referenced, not quoted:

- Revelation 13
- 1 Peter 5
- Galatians 2

Also referenced: DVD: Israel of the Alps (produced by the Seventh Day Adventist Church)

FRC:cs
Transcription date unknown
Reformatted: bo—12/2020

CHAPTER FIFTY-FOUR

AT-ONE-ment with God
(Day of Atonement)
God reveals His plan to rid the world of Satan the devil
Fred R. Coulter

Greetings, everyone! Welcome to the Day of Atonement! Time marches on! Here we are now getting ready for the Feast of Tabernacles, and in order to do that we have to have *at-one-ment* with God.

Actually, that's what the Feast of Tabernacles shows; *that we'll be dwelling with God!* You can't dwell with God unless you are first *at one with God!*

This is *the absolute genius of God's hiding in plain sight His very plan,* because it has to be put together rightly; rightly dividing the Scriptures, and understanding them. That cannot come unless we love God, keep His commandments, His Sabbath and His Holy Days. Then the understanding begins to come. Then we realize God's great plan:

- why we are here
- where we're going
- why He created the world
- why the world is in such a mess today
- how God is going to handle that
- how it is all going to be solved

That's what we're going to cover in the Day of Atonement, the Feast of Tabernacles and the Last Great Day!

(pause for the offering)

Leviticus 23:27: "Also, on the tenth *day* of this seventh month…" *This is God speaking to Moses!*

Remember Moses didn't write a single thing on his own. If you think that that is wrong, go read the account where God instructed Moses to *speak* to the rock and it would bring forth water. The first time that happened, God said to '**strike** the rock' and water will come forth. This time He said, the second time, '**speak** to the rock' and it will bring forth water.

Well, Moses was so upset with the children of Israel harassing him, demanding of him, that he got angry and he **struck** the rock. The water came, but God said, 'Because you didn't believe Me and you struck the rock instead of speaking to it, you shall not go into the promised land.'

With that in mind, I challenge any doubter to search Genesis, Exodus, Leviticus, Numbers and Deuteronomy and find out any Law whatsoever that Moses wrote. So, when the New Testament talks about the Law of Moses, it's talking about *the Law of God that God gave **through** Moses.* The Hebrew is that *'he spoke by the mouth of Moses.'* They're God's words. Likewise with the Day of Atonement.

Verse 27: "Also, on the tenth *day* of this seventh month is the Day of Atonement. *It shall be* a Holy convocation to you. And you shall afflict your souls… [your physical body] …and offer an offering made by fire to the LORD." *So, we take up an offering the Holy Day of the Day of Atonement.*

I want you understand what God is saying here, because three times He emphasizes *no work!*

Verse 28: "And you shall [#1]**do no work** in that same day, for it *is* the Day of Atonement, in order to make an atonement for you before the LORD your God, for whoever is not afflicted…" (vs 28-29). *In Psa. 37 and in Ezra that means **fasting without food or water!***

Verse 29: "For whoever is not afflicted in that same day, he shall be cut off from among his people."

How does God cut off people from among the people? *You don't have the blessing of God that goes to His people, even though you're dwelling in the midst of them!* Generally, as we have seen in the Church, sooner or later they leave.

Verse 30: "And [#2]**whoever does any work** in that same day, the same one will I destroy from among his people." *Likewise that can be physical destruction or it can be ruin, even though they may still be alive!*

Verse 31: "You shall [#3]**do no manner of work**. *It shall be* a statute forever throughout your generations in all your dwellings. **It *shall be* to you a Sabbath of rest, and you shall afflict yourselves**…." (vs 31-32).

Next is how a Sabbath Day is defined. From sunset on one day, which begins the Sabbath, to sunset of the next day at the end of it, which is the ending of the day and the beginning of the new day.

"…In the ninth *day* of the month at sunset,

from sunset to sunset, you shall keep your Sabbath" (v 32).

God made it very particular there, because He didn't want anyone to be in any doubt as to when the day began, and when the day ended. That applies to all Sabbaths; all days in the Bible end at sunset and as soon as the sun goes below the horizon, the new day has begun.

People ask: Why did God do that? Does God do things that we don't understand? *Yes!* To our human minds, because we are so logical and know more than God (most people think) morning would be better because that's when we get up. That's not what God says. It's the same thing with His Word, because God says so *it is so! It does happen!*

On this particular day there was a very special ceremony for the priests, Levities and the people, for the temple and all the land of Israel. Let's understand something very important: *whenever Satan is around there is sin!* This is a special offering on this Day of Atonement, for the forgiveness of the sins and uncleanness of all the children of Israel, for the priests, all the priests and all the Levites.

Remember that *the high priest could only enter the Holy of Holies once a year,* and that was on this Day of Atonement, to bring in the blood and incense, and sprinkle it upon and around the Ark of the Covenant, as well as around the base of the altar, etc.

Then we find that there was a special offering that was made. The spiritual understanding of this today, with the understanding of the New Testament and what we understand in the Old Testament, as well, is that Satan the devil is the archangel who rebelled, as we will see when we get to the Feast of Tabernacles. Why did Solomon go wrong? *Because he got his mind on himself!*

That's exactly what the archangel did—whom a lot of people refer to as Lucifer—when he got 'lifted up in pride.' He thought his glory was as good as God's. He thought *he was* God. He led a rebellion of a third of the angels (Rev. 12). They came to assault the Throne of God in the sides of the North, because he wanted to sit down on the Throne of God and say, 'I am God.'

Needless to say, *he failed!* Everything that Satan does, though it is something that is accomplished, it always ends in death, destruction and wretchedness.

Everything that God does, if people would respond… Because as we know, we all have free moral agency, and that is so powerful that God tells every one of us that *we must choose* whether we will:

- love God
- keep His commandments

or

- serve Satan the devil

Because Adam and Eve chose the wrong way, Satan became 'the god of this world' as Paul writes in 2-Cor. 4. As 'god of this world' he has blinded the minds of those who don't believe.

This is the way that the world is: *walking in darkness and blindness!* Jesus said of those unconverted, 'Let the blind lead the blind, and let the dead bury the dead.'

So, here on this Day of Atonement, it's a very important thing. God has concealed the beginning of this Truth and how He's going to take care of Satan the devil, and what is going to happen to him. He began revealing it here in Lev. 16. However, some 1800 years later, when the Apostle John wrote the book of Revelation, it could not be understood how God was going to take care of it. So, let's read about this special offering:

Leviticus 16:7: And he shall take the two goats and present them before the LORD *at* the door of the tabernacle of the congregation. And Aaron shall cast lots on the two goats; one lot for the LORD and the other lot for Azazel…. [another name for Satan the devil] …And Aaron shall bring the goat on which the LORD'S lot fell, and offer it for a sin offering. But the goat on which the lot fell for Azazel shall be presented alive before the LORD, to make an atonement upon it…" (vs 7-10). *So, we have a two-way atonement here*:

1. for the forgiveness of the children of Israel for the uncleanness and all their sins

That's the goat that is sacrificed and the blood is sprinkled on the burnt altar and also on the altar of the Holy of Holies. The one that is alive, we will see:

2. is for Azazel, which is for Satan

We will see that it is kept alive because God is not going to destroy Satan! There are some people who think they're better than God and say, 'Are all things are possible with God?' The answer is *yes!*

Here's a good example of human philosophical reasoning. Just because God can do anything and all things are possible for God, and nothing is impossible for Him, doesn't mean that *your idea* of what God should do with Satan the devil has any bearing on what God Himself is going to do. *That's the reason why this goat is left alive!*

"…and sent away into the wilderness for Azazel" (v 10)—*removed forever!*

It tells what he should do with the blood of all the different animals and the incense, and so forth.

Verse 16: "And he shall make an atonement for the sanctuary because of the uncleanness of the children of Israel and because of their transgressions in all their sins. And so he shall do for the tabernacle of the congregation, which remains with them in the midst of their uncleanness. And there shall be no man in the tabernacle of the congregation when he goes in to make an atonement in the sanctuary until he comes out and has made an atonement for himself, and for his household, and for all the congregation of Israel. And he shall go out to the altar that is before the LORD and make an atonement for it. And he shall take of the blood of the young bull and of the blood of the goat, and put *it* on the horns of the altar all around. And he shall sprinkle of the blood on it with his finger seven times and cleanse it, and hallow it from the uncleanness of the children of Israel" (vs 16-19).

That was for the goat, which was for the sacrifice for the forgiveness of sin. This was a foretype of Christ. He's also called the Lamb of God. But, in this case, this is a good goat. The other one, for Satan/Azazel, God had to do something entirely different. Let's see what happened:

Verse 20: "And when he has made an end of reconciling the sanctuary and the tabernacle of the congregation and the altar, he shall bring the live goat. And Aaron shall lay both his hands on the head of the live goat, and confess over him all the sins of the children of Israel, and all their transgressions in all their sins, putting them on the head of the goat, and shall send *it* away by the hand of a chosen man into the wilderness. And the goat shall bear upon him all their iniquities to a land in which no one lives. And he shall let the goat go in the wilderness" (vs 20-22).

- Has heaven ever been pictured as a wilderness? *No!*

There are some people who say, because the sins are confessed over this live goat, that this is a type of Christ ascending to heaven for the forgiveness of our sins. However, the goat was led away by the hand of a 'fit man.'

- Was Christ taken up to heaven by angels?
or
- Did He ascend because He was God? *Obviously, because He was God!*
- Why have the sins been put on the head of the live goat?
- Were they not already all forgiven with the sacrifice of the first goat?
- The one to God?

And if He forgives the sin, they are forgiven!

- Why? *It doesn't matter how perfect you may be in the flesh!*
- Were Adam and Eve perfect? *Yes!*
- In the flesh? *Yes!*
- What happened when the serpent was loosed upon them? *They sinned!*
- Who was the author of those sins? *Satan the devil!*

As long as Satan is around, there will never be perfect righteousness! There will always be sin! He has to be removed. But in type, since he is made of spirit he cannot die, because God decreed that He would not kill him.

We find that on the seventh day of the Feast of Tabernacles, it pictures Satan and the demons cast into the Lake of Fire. At the beginning of the Millennium they were put in prison, then let loose for a short season and then cast into the Lake of Fire.

We will see that that Lake of Fire will consume the whole earth and everything. We'll have to wait for the Last Great Day to get to that. But it says in Jude that the 'wandering stars—Satan and the demons—for them is reserved *the blackest darkness forever!*

This is what that wilderness pictures. Satan and the demons will be bound there forever, so that everyone in the Kingdom of God and the Family of God will know and understand forever that in order for God's magnificent plan to be carried out in the way that he wants it carried out, *there cannot be sin and rebellion against God!* That's the long and short of the whole thing!

That's why all the sins are confessed upon the head of the goat that is for Azazel, because Satan is responsible for all human sin.

Verse 22: "And the goat shall bear upon him all their iniquities to a land in which no one lives. And he shall let the goat go in the wilderness." *We will see something about the wilderness in just a little bit!*

Verse 23: "And Aaron shall come into the tabernacle of the congregation, and shall strip off the linen garments… [v 24]: And he shall wash his flesh with water in the Holy place…and make an atonement for himself and for the people."

Verse 26: "And he that let go the goat for Azazel… [this is a type of the angel who casts Satan into the prison (Rev. 20)] …shall wash his clothes and bathe his flesh in water, and afterward come into the camp. and the young bull *for* the sin offering and the goat *for* the sin offering, whose blood was brought in to make atonement in the Holy *place*, shall they carry forth outside the camp…." (vs 26-27).

This was everything that was left of the sin offering and taken out to what is called the Miphkad Altar, which is up on the side of the Mt. of Olives. There's they burned all the sin offerings to ashes. Very interesting, isn't it?

What's going to happen to those people who commit the unpardonable sin and don't repent? *They are burned to ashes in the Lake of Fire!* Is that not true? Here's the parallel, getting rid of all the sin, burning it up.

Verse 28: "And he who burns them shall wash his clothes and bathe his flesh in water, and afterward he shall come into the camp.... [outside the camp] ...And it shall be a statute forever to you: in the seventh month, on the tenth of the month, you shall afflict your souls and do no work at all, *whether it be* one of your own country or a stranger who is living among you, for on that day an atonement shall be made for you, to cleanse you, so that you may be clean from all your sins before the LORD. It *shall be* a Sabbath of rest to you, **and you shall afflict your souls, by a statute forever**" (vs 28-31)—*of ridged obedience!*

It's not a matter of rigid obedience that God wants no more sin. It's a matter of *love.* Love is going to be the whole foundation of everything that God does for eternity, because God is love.

The man who took the goat out in the wilderness will wash his clothes and cleanse his flesh and so forth.

Verse 29: "And it shall be a statute forever to you: in the seventh month, on the tenth of the month, you shall afflict your souls and do no work at all, *whether it be* one of your own country or a stranger who is living among you, for on that day an atonement shall be made for you, to cleanse you, so that you may be clean from all your sins before the LORD. **It *shall be* a Sabbath of rest to you, and you shall afflict your souls, by a statute forever**" (vs 29-31). *There are the instructions for it!*

We know the account in Gen. 3; it's good for us to go back and review these things even though we understand what is there. We learn every time we go over the Word of God, we learn more.

Let's understand something about Satan the devil. Satan has a very convincing 'sweet' side, or gentle side to him, ***because he is the master deceiver!*** That's what it means here in Gen. 3. When you watch all the documentaries on how people 'got religion' it all comes back to the serpent, and that's none other than Satan the devil!

Genesis 3:1: "Now, the serpent was more cunning than any creature of the field, which the LORD God had made. And he said to the woman, '*Is it* true that God has said... [an innocent-sounding question] ..."You shall not eat of any tree of the garden"?'" *God didn't say that!* God said just the opposite: 'You may eat of *every* tree that's in the Garden.'

Isn't it interesting that every idea to add to or take away from the Word of God, where did it originate? *From Satan the devil!*

Verse 2: "And the woman said... [she gave the right answer] ...to the serpent, 'We may freely eat the fruit of the trees of the garden, but of the fruit of the tree which *is* in the middle of the garden, God has *indeed* said... [there is added instruction that God gave] ..."You shall not eat of it, neither shall you touch it, lest you die."' And the serpent said to the woman, 'In dying, you shall not surely die!'" (vs 2-4). *Let's think about this for just a minute*:

- How did Jesus appear to the disciples after He was resurrected from the dead? *He appeared as flesh and bone, not flesh and blood. He shed His blood for the sins!*
- How did He enter the room? *He walked through the wall or door!*
- Was He a spirit being? *Yes!*

But He appeared to the disciples as flesh and bone!

- Why? *Because no man can be in the presence of God and see His glory, or see His face, and live!*

Let's come back to the Garden of Eden:

How did God appear to Adam and Eve? *He couldn't appear to them in His glorified form, because they would die!* So, He appeared as flesh and bone.

Now, newly created by God and being the best and most perfect human being ever, *ever, **ever,*** they had a language already programmed into their brain, they could talk with each other. We don't know how long that they were there with God, but we know that they would walk with God in the 'cool of the evening' and talk with God. God would have had to appear to them as flesh and bone.

When Satan brings up this statement 'you shall not surely die'... They were closer, they thought, to what God actually was, because He looked like them; they were made in *His* image.

When the serpent says, v 5: "'For God knows that...[He's hiding something from you, He's not telling you something] ...in the day you eat of it, then your eyes shall be opened, and you shall be like God....'" *That seemed like a logical step to take, to them, at that point.* Don't you want to be like God?

They thought about it, and here's what they could do; they could not be like God in any other way than this, and they had to exercise they're free moral agency—independent free moral agency

(IFMA)—*to choose* whether they would obey God or not. So, as soon as Satan comes on the scene, sin is there! Also, Jesus said that *Satan the devil—* whom the 'religious' leaders of His day were serving instead of God—*was the 'father of lies!' and 'A murderer from the beginning.'*

Here's the only way that they could be like God, after a fashion: "'…deciding good and evil'" (v 5). What they said, 'We'll decide good and evil. We'll make the decision.' *They made the wrong decision and sin entered into the world and passed on to all of us!*

Here's another thing concerning sin: *Sin can appear to be very attractive! Can appear to give you a great benefit!* That's how people get hooked on sin; that's how they get hooked on drugs; precisely like this:

- it'll never happen to you
- you're smart and intelligent
- you can handle it
- you won't become an addict
- try some of this 'pot' it's really good stuff
- it will make you feel good
- you can relax
- you can just kind of lay back and just cool out

Won't that be nice? And they know that marijuana is a 'gateway' drug to other drugs. So, what comes a little later? *Cocaine, heroin and meth!* What happens? *In dying you shall surely die!* Exactly as God said!

Satan comes along to give a benefit! His benefit is an unlawful benefit, but it is very enticing. How many people fall for it? *Oh, it will make you feel good!* The German soldiers took Pervitin, which was crystal meth, during WWII (watch that on American Heroes channel). Quite a thing!

Verse 6: "And when the woman saw that the tree *was* good for food, and that it was pleasing to the eyes… [very attractive, wonderful] …and a tree to be desired to make *one* wise…"

Doesn't everyone want to be *smart* and *intelligent*? Look at the vanity of the elite! How smug they are in their satanic deception of atheism and evolution. 'Why, you poor little crumbs down here who believe in God.' *Just wait! Just wait! God has a surprise for you!* When He resurrects us, we'll look at them and say, 'Remember when you thought you were so smart?'

"…she took of its fruit and ate…." (v 6). Took a bite and probably said, 'Why, that tastes wonderful; that's sweet, that's nice. Why would God say not to eat this? Maybe the serpent is right.'

"…She also gave to her husband with her, and he ate. And the eyes of both of them were opened… [actually shut; **shut to righteousness, but opened to sin**] …and they knew that they *were* naked; and they sewed fig leaves together and made coverings for themselves. And they heard the sound of the LORD God walking in the garden in the cool of the day. Then Adam and his wife hid themselves…" (vs 6-7).

God *knew* where they were; God *knew* what they had done, **but He wanted find out from them!** So, you know what happened: All mankind from that time forth was cutoff from any access to the Tree of Life, any access to salvation. They still may have had some contact with God at the east entrance of the Garden of Eden, but they couldn't go into the Garden of Eden any longer, and they received in themselves 'the law of sin and death' and 'in dying you shall surely die.'

The New Testament tells us that 'as in Adam all die.' Isn't that something? *All die!* The only one to overcome death was Jesus Christ. He declared to John in Rev. 1, 'Behold, I was dead, but now I am alive for evermore! I, Jesus, have the keys to death and the grave.'

Satan didn't accomplish anything here in the garden his way. But Adam and Eve chose the wrong way, and you know the rest of the story.

*Satan is deceiving the **whole** world!* Now at the end-time look at the sins that are happening. Look at the way that the world is, and all because of Satan the devil! That's why he has to be removed forever.

Let's see that Satan and the demons still have *limited* access to God, and God uses them to carryout different things that God wants done. We find that Satan said to God, concerning Job, 'You put a hedge around him,' meaning that God didn't allow Satan to get to Job. So, everything was fine! Job thought it was wonderful! Job thought it was great! But Job could see that his sons were sinning, so he made burnt offerings and prayed for them everyday, lest they sin against God.

Job 1:6: "Now, there was a day when the sons of God came to present themselves before the LORD. And Satan also came among them." *He could come before God on periodic occasions!*

Verse 7: "And the LORD said to Satan, 'From where do you come?' Then Satan answered the LORD and said, 'From going to and fro in the earth, and from walking up and down in it.'"

Why? *Because he's 'the god of this world'!* It says in 1-John 5 that the 'whole world is under the power of the evil one. So, he has that power!

Verse 8: "And the LORD said to Satan, 'Have you considered My servant Job, that *there is* none like him in the earth, a blameless and upright man, one who fears God and turns away from evil?' And Satan answered the LORD and said, '**Does Job fear God for nothing?**'" (vs 8-9).

Why do you love and fear God with all your heart, mind, soul and being? If it's only because He's going to give you eternal life... *God wants that permanent connection **with Him** spiritually!* Not like Job just because there are some benefits that are given. This shows that using Satan the devil, God can take them away just like that!

We won't go through the book of Job, you can do that by getting our in-depth study: *Why God Hates Religion!*

We also know that in 1-Chron. 21 that Satan tempted David, and he fell for the temptation and numbered the children of Israel.

We also find that in Zech. 3 that Satan is standing there right alongside the high priest Joshua, the son of Jehozadak, to resist him. Of course, it shows that the final one will be one of the two witnesses. Then an angel came and rebuked Satan, saying, 'The Lord rebuke you!'

Let's find out a little bit more why this day is so important. God's plan could never, *never, **never** be fulfilled without the fulfillment of the Day of Atonement and the removal of Satan the devil!

Let's talk about *independent free moral agency* (IFMA). God has given that to every one of us as human beings. *We must choose!*

For salvation, before Jesus came the only ones would be the patriarchs and some of the kings of Judah. Remember, not one king of the ten northern tribes was ever righteous. It's so important that God, to demonstrate:

- to all the righteous angels
- to Satan the devil
- to all of the demons
- to all of mankind

that sin and rebellion always leads to death and destruction!

Just to prove a point, Rev. 18:24 is talking about Babylon the Great and that her sins have reached to 'high heaven.' How did it get that way?

- through Satan the devil
- through his setup
- through his governments
- through the human beings whom he controls

Revelation 18:24: "And in her *the* blood of prophets and saints was found, and *the blood* of all those who were slain on the earth."

Think on that statement! Tie that together with what Jesus said, that Satan was 'a liar and a murder from the beginning.' That's why Azazel has to be completely removed! Whenever he is around, *there is sin!* He must be removed, but not destroyed.

Let's look at some other things concerning Satan the devil. We find that before Jesus could begin His ministry He had to overcome Satan the devil. This was quite a spiritual battle that was going on. The parallel account is in Matt. 4

When you understand the chronology correctly, Jesus began His ministry here. This was the beginning of it. This day, the day He began the 40-day temptation, was the Day of Atonement in the middle of the week, fourth day of the week. When was Jesus crucified? *On the fourth day of the week!* So, Jesus began His ministry on the fourth day of the week and ended His physical ministry on the fourth day of the week.

In Luke 3 we find that Jesus was baptized and went into the wilderness immediately. So, he was probably baptized on a Monday, took two days to go into the wilderness, and there on Wednesday, the Day of Atonement—which was also a Jubilee year—Jesus began His ministry. The first order of business was *overcoming Satan the devil!*

Where was Azazel let go? *In the wilderness!* Right in the area where Jesus went to meet Satan!

Luke 4:1: "And Jesus, filled with *the* Holy Spirit, returned from the Jordan, and was led by the Spirit into the wilderness."

The only way that any human being can overcome Satan the devil is with *the Spirit of God, the power of the Spirit of God!* So, this was a great spiritual battle for all of mankind, for all of the plan of God, for every one of us!

Verse 2: "*For* forty days to be tempted by the devil. And He ate nothing in those days..."

That's why we fast on the day of the Atonement; that's why we don't drink water on the Day of Atonement.

"...and after they had come to an end, He hungered" (v 2)—*actually famished*; I would imagine that He was just skin and bones. When are people most susceptible to giving in?

1) when they're physically and mentally weak
2) when they're in pain and agony
3) when they seem to be in a helpless situation and are desperate

Don't you think that Jesus was that way, physically speaking? *Yes, indeed!*

"...Then the devil said to Him, '**If You are the** Son of God...'" *First challenge!*

We also have to understand something very important: Jesus' *independent free moral agency* was being tested to the extreme. Jesus could have said, 'Of course, I'm the Son of God!' *But that would not have been from God!* Notice Jesus' obedience based on *loving the Father, and the Father loving Him!*

"...'If You are *the* Son of God, command that this stone become bread'" (v 3). *He could have done that; it would be simple!*

It's not really, in some cases, a matter of whether you *can* do it, or *cannot* do it; *it's really whether you should or should not do it!* So, notice Jesus' answer:

Verse 4: "But Jesus answered him, saying, 'It is written...'"

Since Jesus was God manifest in the flesh, and the son of man, when he's speaking of 'man' here he's talking to Himself as well as all mankind, because He's the Creator of all mankind. Is that not true? *Yes, indeed!*

"'...Man shall not live by bread alone, but **by every word of God**'" (v 4).

Deuteronomy 8:3: "...**that proceeds out of the mouth of the LORD** does man live"—as well as Matt. 4:4.

- How are we to live?
- What are we to choose? *God's way!*
- What has God written for us? *What He wants us to do!*

However, we've got to use our *independent free moral agency* to choose it. *It's all a choice!*

Luke 4:5: "Then the devil led Him up into a high mountain *and* showed Him all the kingdoms of the world in a moment of time. And the devil said to Him, '**I will give You** all this authority, and the glory of them *all*; for **it has been delivered to me**...'" (vs 5-6).

God has delivered the whole world to Satan the devil. Why? *Because of the sins of human beings!* God reaches down and calls those whom He wants to be in His Family. We have to respond to God and *choose*. There we go; that's the way the world is!

"'...and I give it to whomever I desire'" (v 6). *Look at all the awful dictators, emperors, demigods,* and all of this stuff. Satan wants to be worshipped!

He's going to get it at the end. It says that 'all the people—the whole world—worships the dragon and Satan, and he gives his throne and authority to the beast' (Rev. 13). Just like it says

here, "...and I give it to whomever I desire."

Verse 7: "Therefore, if You will worship me in *my* presence, all things shall be Yours." *Satan wants to be God!*

All the worship and all the religions of the world are not directed to God, *but to Satan!* There are some who *think* that they are worshipping God, but they're not!

What is the thing that's important: *That you love God and keep His commandments, and His commandments are not burdensome!* You must have the Spirit of God *within you*. If anyone does not have the Spirit of God within them, they are not of God. They may be close, they may be getting close to baptism and so forth, but that's just the way it is. The whole world is worshipping Satan the devil in one form or another.

Verse 8: "But Jesus answered *and* said to him, 'Get behind Me, Satan; for it is written, "You..."'" *That's not Satan; Satan will never worship God,* so that doesn't refer to Satan. Jesus is referring the command to men, "...You..." commanding us directly.

"'...shall worship *the* Lord your God, and Him only shall you serve.' Then he [Satan] led Him to Jerusalem and set Him upon the edge of the temple, and said to Him, '**If** You are the Son of God, cast Yourself down from here. For it is written...'" (vs 8-10).

Satan can quote Scripture; reading Scripture *does not* sanctify that it is being spoken by a representative of God. Notice how Satan *misuses it!* He misuses the Scripture! Do they do that in all of the so-called Christian churches? *Yes, indeed they do!* They read Scriptures about Jesus while they have idols and candles around, and celebrate the Mass, have the Lord's Supper, keep Christmas, New Years, Halloween and all of those things. It makes no difference! *Satan can quote Scripture for his own advantage!*

What did Jesus say here? *Man shall live not by bread alone, **but by every word of God!*** Think of that! Just go on your television and check up on the Catholics when they have a Mass. It's seems that's about the only thing they can do. They do read a little Scripture, but God is not there. Who do you think they are worshipping? *None other than Satan himself!*

- you can't worship God with idols
- you can't worship God with lies

Notice that Satan quotes a Scripture, "...'He shall give His angels charge concerning You to keep You; and **in *their* hands they shall bear You up,** lest You strike Your foot against a stone'" (vs 10-11).

That's God's protection for those who are His, if an accident happened, not jumping off the edge of the pinnacle of the temple from which the top to the bottom of the valley floor was upwards of 500-plus feet.

If Jesus did that, and the demons came and held Him up and Satan called for all the priests and Pharisees and scribes, and told them 'this is your Savior' they would have accepted Jesus; Jesus would have been owned lock, stock and barrel by Satan the devil. See the picture? What did Jesus answer?

Verse 12: "But Jesus answered *and* said to him, 'It is *clearly* stated, "You... [every human being] ...shall not tempt *the* Lord your God."' Now, when the devil had completed every temptation, he [Satan] departed from Him for a time" (vs 12-13).

We will look at a couple of Scriptures showing about Satan, how he works.

- Is he interested in those who are in the Church?
- Does he want us to choose to reject salvation?
- *But of course!*

So, there will be times when we will be confronted with things that are caused by Satan and the demons. We can recognize them and rebuke them, and tell them, 'Get you behind me, Satan, in the name of Jesus Christ!' *They must obey!* But Satan is subtle and crafty and cunning (Gen. 3).

Here is how the ministry should be run, as Paul brings out; 2-Corinthians 4:1: "Therefore, having this ministry, according as we have received mercy, we are not fainthearted. For we have personally renounced the hidden things of dishonest gain... [those things that are lies] ...not walking in *cunning* craftiness... [not having a secret agenda] ...nor handling the Word of God deceitfully... [because that's what they do; they are corrupting the Word of God (2-Cor. 2:17)] ...but by manifestation of the Truth..." (vs 1-2).

Truth is what we need! Always! The Truth, *the Truth, **the Truth! Nothing but the Truth!*** That's why we changed the name of the website to: **truthofgod.org**

"...by manifestation of the Truth, we are commending ourselves to every man's conscience before God. But if our Gospel is hidden, it is hidden to those who are perishing; in whom **the god of this age**..." (vs 2-3)—*Satan the devil!*. Did he not say that 'all of this has been given to me, and I give to whomsoever I will'?

"...**has blinded the minds of those who do not believe**, lest the light of the Gospel of the glory of Christ, Who is *the* image of God, should shine unto them. For we do not preach our own selves, but Christ Jesus *the* Lord, and ourselves your servants for Jesus' sake" (vs 3-5). *We do have protection so that we may not be outwitted by Satan!*

2-Corinthians 2:11: "So that we may not be outwitted by Satan, for we are not ignorant of his schemes."

His schemes are always appealing to something that will be transgressing the Laws of God, or a lie concerning the Word of God. That's why we're told to prove all things. That's why we're to do things in accordance with:

- the will of God
- the Truth of God
- the love of God

Nothing, *nothing,* **nothing** else! What did Jesus say? *Anything else is of the evil one!* Meaning it comes from Satan the devil:

- dishonest gain
- craftiness
- deceitfulness

Does he come against the Church? *Yes, he does!* What happened there in Acts 5 with Ananias and Sapphira? What did Peter say to them? **Why has Satan put it in your heart to lie to God?** They thought that after they pledged what they said they would pledge that they could go ahead and adjust it, modify it and say that it's perfectly all right, and *lie to the Apostle Peter!* What happened to them? *They died right on the spot!*

Let's see how Satan works, and then we'll see that in the history of the Churches of God *Satan is always there in one form or another!* Here's how it started in Corinth. There were those coming along saying that they were ministers of God *when they weren't!*

- Who were they? *Some were Jews, some were Israelites!*
- How did they say they knew Jesus? *Maybe there were some who were there and heard Jesus speak and were fed as part of the 4,000 or 5,000!*

They found out that they could make things really good by pretending to be a minister of God. Isn't that what Simon Magus did (Acts 8)? *Yes!* Here was a high-powered religious leader who was saying that *he* was the power of God and deceiving them with sorceries and witchcraft!

Simon Magus was the 'Simon Peter' that went to Rome in 42A.D. Go through the series on **churchathome.org** and watch all the segments that we did on *Was Peter Ever in Rome?* Think about that!

If you are a 'good' Catholic, which I don't think here will be very many on the Day of Atonement there, but if you were a 'good' Catholic think on this: ***Everything that they have said concerning Peter, the Church, the pope is a lie!*** None of it is true! Understand that

- there can be *no salvation*
- there can be *no at-one-ment with God*
- there can be *no forgiveness of sin*

with a satanic counterfeit! Though wonderfully produced, *it is of Satan the devil!*

Paul writes, 2-Corinthians 11:1: "I would *that* you might bear with me in a little nonsense; but indeed, do bear with me. For I am jealous over you with *the* jealousy of God because I have espoused you to one husband, so that I may present *you as a* chaste virgin to Christ. But I fear, lest by any means… [clever, subtle, slight changes] …as the serpent deceived Eve by his craftiness, so your minds might be corrupted from *the* simplicity that *is* in Christ" (vs 1-3).

Beginning with loving God with *all your heart, mind, soul and being,* and *the grace of God, the forgiveness of God, the Truth of God,* and all of those things. *We have seen that happen in our day!*

- Did some people in the Church fall for it? *Yes!*
- Is Satan still active today? *Yes!*

Paul puts it this way, v 4: "For indeed, if someone comes preaching another Jesus, whom we did not preach, or you receive a different spirit… [because satanic spirits go wherever there are lies] …which you did not receive, or a different gospel, which you did not accept, **you put up with it as something good**."

What does that mean? *That they listened to people because they had an opinion!* Remember:

- *opinions* are not sacred
- *philosophy* is not sacred

That's the wisdom of this world! What did Paul write of it in 1-Cor. 1? *The foolishness of this world!* **"…put up with it as *something* good."**

Verse 5: "But I consider myself in no way inferior to those highly exalted *so-called* apostles."

It wasn't Peter, Andrew, any of the other apostles of God; these were the ones *proclaiming themselves* to be apostles.

Verse 13: "For such *are* false apostles—deceitful workers who are transforming themselves into apostles of Christ."

- that is what has happened to the Church
- that is what has happened to worldly Christianity

It is in the world and everything of the world, is deceived by Satan the devil, and there are varying degrees of deception. But if you are deceived and you *follow him* and *keep his days* and *do his works and things,* **you are deceived!** You may be considered to be a good and upright person in this society, *but that doesn't account for eternal life!*

Verse 13: "For such *are* false apostles—**deceitful workers** who are transforming themselves into apostles of Christ." *They are not, so they've got to figure a way to do it!*

Verse 14: "And *it is* no marvel, for Satan himself transforms himself into an angel of light. Therefore, *it is* no great thing if his servants also transform themselves as ministers of righteousness—whose end shall be according to their works" (vs 14-15).

So ingrained was this… Think of it! Here were these Greeks: intelligent, love philosophy, want great wonderful speaking, 'but this Apostle Paul just doesn't look good and doesn't speak well; his epistles are weighty.

Verse 16: "Again I say, no one should consider me a fool; but if otherwise, receive me even as a fool, that I also may boast a little." *Then he talks about everything that he went through!*

Verse 19: "For since you are *so* intelligent, you gladly bear with fools. For you bear *it* if anyone brings you into bondage… [taken out of the freedom that God gives us with His grace into the bondage of sin] … if anyone devours *you,* if anyone takes *from you,* if anyone exalts himself, if anyone beats you on the face. I speak as though we were under reproach for being weak; but in whatever *way* anyone else is bold (I speak in foolishness), I also am bold" (vs 19-21). **What did they claim?** *I'm a Hebrew!*

Verse 23: "Are they servants of Christ? (I am speaking as if I were out of my mind.)…." Let's see that this did happen.

Read all of Rev. 2 & 3, and by the way we've got a booklet coming: *The Ministry is not the Government of God and the Truth of the Nicolaitans. All in one booklet!*

Church at Ephesus:

How is an opening given to Satan the devil? *By not loving God with all your heart, mind, soul and being!* The Church at Ephesus left their first love. What were they doing? *The physical things of helping the poor and taking care of the homeless and things like this!* That's a good thing to do; nothing wrong with that. *But:*

- *if it takes you away* from the true God
- *if it takes you away* from loving God with all your heart, mind, soul and being

you're going to fall! That's what He said.

Church at Smyrna:

The synagogue of Satan was after them, cast them into prison and killed and martyred them. So, Jesus said, 'Be faithful unto death and I'll give you a crown of life.'

Church at Pergamos:

The great enlightened city of Pergamos where the great altar of Zeus was, *the throne of Satan!* There they learned about the Sacrifice of the Mass. There they brought in the hierarchy, which God says He *hates!*

Church of Thyatira:

The woman prophetess who calls herself Jezebel. Oh boy! I tell you! What happened? *They got so bad that some of them even got into the depths of Satan the devil!* Jesus told them, 'I'm going to kill you with death!' That's got to be the *second* death! He called them to repentance.

Church of Sardis:

Historically speaking, after that the Church was so exhausted that the only thing they could end up doing was keeping the Sabbath and the Holy Days. Jesus told them to hold fast to the strength you have left and 'I won't blot your name out of the book of Life.'

Church of Philadelphia:

They are the one who stand against the synagogue of Satan. They are the one, even though they are poor, they love the brethren and love God. You can't love the brethren unless you love God. They are faithful to the Word of God.

Church of the Laodiceans:

Lukewarm, smart-alecky! Yes, they teach some things of God, but where is the love of God? the zeal of God?

The Bible gives us the history of man and how he has been deceived by Satan the devil. It gives us:

- the Truth of God
- the true God
- the true Jesus
- the true plan of God

the way we understand those is to:
- love God
- keep His commandments
- keep His Sabbaths and Holy Days
- study the Word of God
  - ✓ rightly divide it
  - ✓ rightly put it together

We understand what God is doing up to this point! But *the Kingdom of God cannot be setup until Satan is removed!* Let's see the fulfilling of Lev. 16:

- getting rid of Satan
- getting rid of Azazel
- getting rid of the demons

Zech. 13 says that the unclean spirits are removed from the land, so from the time we come on Trumpets back to the earth, what are we going to be doing? *We're going to be spreading out and helping people come to themselves!*

The angels will be there gathering the demons to put them into the abyss with Satan the devil. There will probably be some fighting and warring and skirmishes with some of the remnants of the army, which probably a good number of the people of the 200-million. There's a lot going on between Trumpets and Atonement. But on Atonement:

Revelation 20:1: "Then I saw an angel descending from heaven, having the key of the abyss, and a great chain in his hand. And he took hold of the dragon, the ancient serpent, who is *the* Devil and Satan, and bound him *for* a thousand years" (vs 1-2). *Only then can the Millennium begin!* That's pictured by the Feast of Tabernacles.

At the end of the Millennium we will see what happens to Satan and the demons. But this Day of Atonement pictures when *we will be one with God, which was the whole goal of what Jesus prayed in His last prayer.*

Let's see the prayer that Jesus prayed. We won't go through the whole thing, but let's see how that right at the time before Jesus was to be arrested and led off to be falsely charged, falsely convicted, falsely beaten, scourge, crucified, and the speak thrust in His side, *all to be that perfect Passover sacrifice for the sins of the world*; God manifested in the flesh. Here was the purpose that He had in mind and is saying to the Father:

John 17:13: "But now I am coming to You; and these things I am speaking *while yet* in the world, that they may have My joy fulfilled in them." *Think what the joy will be at the resurrection; that's when the joy will be fulfilled in us!*

Verse 14: "I have given them Your words,

and the world has hated them because they are not of the world, just as I am not of the world."

Don't worry if people don't care for you because you believe the Bible. Maybe you can try and help them understand it, but if they hate you, that's the way that it is! *They hate Jesus!*

Verse 15: "I do not pray that You would take them out of the world, but that You would keep them from the evil one…. [Satan the devil] …They are not of the world, just as I am not of the world. **Sanctify them in Your Truth; Your Word is the Truth**" (vs 15-17). *We are made Holy by*:

- the Truth of God
- the Word of God
- the Spirit of God
- the love of God

That's how we grow in grow, change and overcome! That's why this Day of Atonement…

Just think what a day that's going to be! We will live to see Satan and all the demons removed, and all the saints from Abel clear to the last two witnesses. **"Sanctify them in Your Truth; Your Word is the Truth."**

Verse 18: "Even as You did send Me into the world, I also have sent them into the world. And for their sakes I sanctify Myself, so that they also may be sanctified in *Your* Truth. I do not pray for these only…" (vs 18-20).

Here's a prayer of Jesus for everyone who will answer the call through the ministry that He established with His apostles.

"…but also for those who shall believe in Me through their word; **that they all may be one**… [at-one-ment with God: Atonement!] …**even as You, Father,** *are* **in Me, and I in You**; that they also may be one in Us, **in order that the world may believe** that You did send Me. And I have given them the glory that You gave *to* Me… [the Spirit of God] …in order that they may be one, **in the same way** *that* **We are one**: I in them, and You in Me, that they **may be perfected into one**…" (vs 20-23).

That's the whole purpose of our Christian life and walk, to be perfected:

- every day
- every Sabbath
- every Passover
- every Unleavened Bread
- every Pentecost
- every Trumpets
- every Atonement
- every Tabernacles
- every Last Great Day

"…**perfected into one,** and that the world may know that You did send Me, and have loved them as You have loved Me" (v 23).

That's the meaning of the Day of Atonement: *Satan removed and we will be at one with God!*

Scriptural References:

1) Leviticus 23:27-32
2) Leviticus 16:7-10, 16-24, 26-36
3) Genesis 3:1-7
4) Job 1:6-9
5) Revelation 18:24
6) Luke 4:1-4
7) Deuteronomy 8:3
8) Luke 4:5-13
9) 2 Corinthians 4:1-5
10) 2 Corinthians 2:11
11) 2 Corinthians 11:1-5, 13-16, 19-21, 23
12) Revelation 20:1-2
13) John 17:13-23

Scriptures referenced, not quoted:

- Psalm 37
- Revelation 12
- 2 Corinthians 4
- Revelation 20
- 1 John 5
- 1 Chronicles 21
- Zechariah 3
- Luke 3
- Matthew 4:4
- Revelation 13
- 2 Corinthians 2:17
- Acts 5; 8
- 1 Corinthians 1
- Revelation 2; 3
- Zechariah 13

Also referenced:

In-Depth Study: *Why God Hates Religion!*

Church at Home: *Was Peter Ever in Rome?* **(churchathome.org)**

Booklet: *The Ministry is not the Government of God and the Truth of the Nicolaitans*

FRC:bo
Transcribed: 9/14/16
Reformatted: 12/2020

CHAPTER FIFTY-FIVE

Satan Must Be Removed!
Day of Atonement
Fred R. Coulter

Greetings, brethren, welcome to the Day of Atonement. Of course, this is a very important Holy Day and also we're going to see that just as the Passover *prepares those who are in the Church* for Unleavened Bread and Pentecost, so likewise Trumpets and Atonement *prepares the world* for what God is going to do as pictured by the Feast of Tabernacles and later the Last Great Day. There's quite a connection between the two of them.

So, we're making our way through the Holy Days of God, the annual Feasts of God. As we have been learning, *all of the Bible is structured around the Sabbath, Passover and the Holy Days!* Without those it's impossible to understand the plan of God. Without that knowledge, men go ahead and do their best in creating what *they think* is a plan of God, and the will of God. In the various religions and denominations that are in the world, unfortunately *their best intentions can never* match the will of God.

Leviticus 23:26—we'll pick it up here in the flow of the Holy Days: "And the LORD spoke to Moses, saying."

As we have learned, these are the days of God. So God spoke to Moses, and Moses told the children of Israel.

Verse 27: "Also, on the tenth *day* of this seventh month… [which is today] …is the Day of Atonement. *It shall be* a Holy convocation to you. And you shall afflict your souls…"

In the case of Moses up on the mountain, it was without food and water for 40 days. Now God doesn't require that of us, but *we are to fast this one day as a commanded Feast* in addition to other times during the year whenever it is necessary.

"…and offer an offering made by fire to the LORD" (v 27).

Num. 28 & 29 depicts all of the official offerings that were to be given throughout the whole year. It starts out in Num. 28 with the daily offering, the Sabbath offering, the monthly offerings, and the Feast of Unleavened Bread. As we have noted concerning the Passover at the temple or tabernacle, there were no sacrifices required for that day (Num 28:16). It comes from Unleavened Bread down to Pentecost and then there's a break because it goes to

Num. 29. I don't think in the Hebrew there is a break there. There very well may be, but it groups all of the commanded offerings at the temple; this was in addition to the individual offerings of burnt offerings, peace offerings and meal offerings that people would give. Here are the commandments for the Day of Atonement:

Numbers 29:7: "And you shall have a Holy convocation on the tenth day of this seventh month. And you shall afflict your souls. You shall not do any work *therein*. But you shall offer a burnt offering to the LORD *for* a sweet savor: one young bull, one ram and seven lambs of the first year. They shall be to you without blemish. And their grain offering *shall be* flour mixed with oil…" (vs 7-9).

It gives a description there. Then it explains concerning the goats for the sin offering, and so forth. So, whenever we come to the Holy Days, when we come before God on these special occasions, we do take up an offering. An offering that we give to God is not measured in terms of dollars, though in a sense it is in a physical way. But our offerings to God should be a measure of our love to God, our attitude toward God, and our willingness to serve Him and obey Him.

Also, *our willingness to prove Him,* as He says 'Now prove Me herewith, that you shall not have sufficiency in all things, whether you will or not' (Mal. 3[transcriber's correction])—*because we will!*

God also promises that. Many of the blessings of God that come from God are not counted in terms of monetary equivalency or remuneration. The blessings of God include many, many different things:

- our life
- our health
- our protection
- our family
- our employment
- the things that we are doing

*And as we will see today, **keeping us from the evil one!***

All of those are blessings that God gives. So in taking up the offering, you do it according to the blessings that God has given you, and realize that on this Day of Atonement we are to be at-one with God.

(pause for offering)

Isn't it a marvelous thing, indeed, that that which men count the least or the most unimportant, *are the very things that God uses to teach and reveal His will and purpose*? Such is the case of the Holy Days being all listed together. This is the only chapter in the whole Bible that has all the Holy Days listed together—Lev. 23—and it's in the Old Testament.

A lot of people say that 'we don't need to keep this; it's nailed to the cross,' and so forth. All they are doing with that is **cheating themselves out of the true knowledge of the plan of God!** It is true, anytime anyone thinks that they know better than God they're going to get themselves in trouble. ***They're going to cut themselves off from God!*** Now the Day of Atonement is a particular Holy Day that emphasizes that.

Leviticus 23:28: "And you shall do no work in that same day…"

When we read this it makes it very clear. These are not hard to understand words. This is not some secret allegorical meaning that is contained in here. It's very simple.

"…for it *is* the Day of Atonement, in order to make an atonement for you before the LORD your God, for whoever is not afflicted in that same day, he shall be cut off from among his people" (vs 28-29).

He's still among them, but he's cut off from them. Isn't that interesting? Think about how many people today who used to be in the Church of God—whether they were converted or not, that's in God's hands, only God knows—but **how many people have been cut off from God and from among the people and from the Church because they no longer keep the Day of Atonement**? *It's an amazing thing when you think about it!*

Look at it on the other hand this way: It is an amazing thing how much God reveals to us when we do keep these days year after year:

- every year we learn more
- every year we understand more

because that's the way God has inspired and caused the Bible to be written! We're reading the things that are inspired by the mind of God, though a man wrote it. Though Moses originally wrote these words down, and though they have been translated, *the meaning of it is very clear!*

Verse 29: "For whoever is not afflicted… [fast without food and water in that day, with the

exception of some who are pregnant or childbirth, or medical situations like that] …in that same day, he shall be cut off from among his people. And **whoever does any work in that same day, the same one will I destroy from among his people**."

How God is going to do that, you can just look out and see how God has intervened in different ones lives.

To emphasize it, He says, v 31: "You shall do no manner of work. *It shall be* a statute forever throughout your generations in all your dwellings."

How long does that mean? ***IF*** *we are the descendants of the children of Israel physically,* ***it's binding upon us!*** If we are the children of Israel *spiritually*—because as Gentiles we have been grafted into that tree, and then the branches drink of the sap that comes from the roots and is fed by the roots—***THEN*** it means for us: *in your generations, in your dwellings!*

Verse 32: "It *shall be* to you a Sabbath of rest…"

All the Holy Days are called Sabbaths, and it's strange that the Seventh Day Adventists really don't understand that. Now they can keep the seventh day but how much do they lose because they don't keep the Holy Days of God? *There are the contradictions that come along here!*

"…and **you shall afflict yourselves**…. [it also gives us a definitive time of when the day begins and ends] …In the ninth *day* of the month at sunset…" (v 32)—Hebrew 'ba erev,' meaning the sun has just dropped below the horizon. That begins the new day. 'Ba erev' of the 9th ends the 9th day, so when the sun drops below the horizon you're beginning the 10th day.

"…From even unto even… [from the even of the 9th to the even of the 10th] …from sunset to sunset, you shall keep your Sabbath" (v 32).

It's very interesting because in the Septuagint the Greek means that *you shall sabbathize your Sabbath*. Quite important, isn't it? *So there we have it!* Let's see again how these things are binding upon us. Every time God asks us to do something:

- Why does He ask us to do it?
- Why does He command us to do it?

1. because God is love
2. God loves us
3. God has called us
4. God wants us to be in right standing with Him through Jesus Christ and the sacrifice for our sins, and having been justified from them

He wants to bless us so that in doing the things that He commands us, *He will bless us*:

- because He loves us
- because He's called us
- because we are those whom He has called to be in His Family

In order to prepare for that, we need to have the education and understanding that comes from God through His Word and through His Spirit:

- so we can learn to have the mind of Christ
- so when the resurrection takes place we will be able to work with Christ and do the things that He wants to help usher in the Kingdom of God on the earth

That's why God commands these things!

Exodus 31:12: "And the LORD spoke to Moses saying, 'Speak also to the children of Israel… [we are the *spiritual* Israel of God] …saying, "Truly you shall keep My Sabbaths, for **it *is* a sign between Me and you throughout your generations** to know that I *am* the LORD Who sanctifies you"'" (vs 12-13).

Then you combine that with the New Testament where Jesus said, 'Your Word is Truth, sanctify them with Your Truth.' This is part of where it's God's Word. So, keeping the Sabbaths, and it's plural; therefore, it includes all of them. Now it mentions the seventh-day Sabbath as the main one on which all of these are sanctified and it says you will keep it.

Verse 15: "Six days may work be done… [v 16]: "Therefore, the children of Israel shall keep the Sabbath, to observe the Sabbath throughout their generations *as* a perpetual covenant. It… [the keeping of the sabbaths] …is **a sign between Me and the children of Israel forever**… [and to always remember that God is Creator] …for in six days the LORD made the heavens and the earth, and on the seventh day He rested, and was refreshed." *That's a tremendous thing that God has given here!*

Now after He gave that commandment, v 18: "And He gave to Moses, when He had made an end of speaking with him upon Mount Sinai, two tablets of the testimony, tablets of stone, written by the finger of God."

Think about it for a just a minute. *How dare a man take upon himself the prerogative to change the Word of God and to change what God has spoken, and to alter or reject what God had written with His own finger on those two tables of stone!*

Let's see when sin entered into the world, because sin and the removal of sin has everything to do with the Day of Atonement. We just need to understand that sin and the author of sin both must be removed. We're going to see that just the removal of sin alone without the removal of Satan the devil… By the time we get all the way through the Holy Days, we're going to understand that the author of sin must be removed and dealt with forever. *That's all in God's plan!*

Gen. 3—God told them that 'you shall not eat of the Tree of the Knowledge of Good and Evil, for in the day that you eat thereof you shall surely die.' Of course, Satan came in, and God wanted to test them.

- Would they obey His voice or not?
- Would they keep His commandments or not?
- Would they eat of the Tree of Life?
- Would they not eat of the Tree of the Knowledge of Good and Evil?

God had to do that because in giving free moral agency, God did not make us robots. If you give free moral agency *you have to give free moral agency so that a person can choose one way or the other!* Just like He told the children of Israel, 'I command you to choose life that you may live' (Deut. 30).

So likewise, He commanded Adam and Eve not to eat of the Tree of the Knowledge of Good and Evil, because He loved them and created them, and His plan was to come forth from them. But He had to know:

- Did they really love Him?
- Did they really believe Him?
- Were they willing to do what God had said?

So, you know the story, Genesis 3:1: " Now, the serpent was more cunning than any creature of the field, which the LORD God had made. And he said to the woman, '*Is it* true that God has said, "You shall not eat of any tree of the garden"?'…. [bringing up a preposterous proposition because he knew that was not so. Eve had to correct him]: …And the woman said to the serpent, 'We may freely eat the fruit of the trees of the garden, but of the fruit of the tree which *is* in the middle of the garden, God has *indeed* said, "You shall not eat of it, neither shall you touch it, lest you die"'" (vs 1-3).

Of course Satan always wants to get you on his side. He makes sin appear as if it's not sin.

Verse 4: "And the serpent said to the woman, 'In dying, you shall not surely die!'"

- Isn't that the way it is in the world today?
- Don't people want to live in their sins and yet receive the blessings for obedience?

It doesn't mix! It's not that way!

Then he accuses God. *Anyone who accuses*

God, especially of what God has done, you'll never, never, never understand the Word of God! What you need to do is admit that you don't understand and ask God for understanding, and He will give it as you study His Word, as you pray, and as you live according to God's will. ***But Satan lied! He's the father of lies,*** he did not stand in the Truth and there's no Truth in him. So, when he speaks a lie, he speaks of his own *because he's the father of it!*

So, Satan said, "…'In dying, you shall not surely die! For God knows that in the day you eat of it, then your eyes shall be opened… [the exact opposite happened, their eyes were closed] …and you shall be like God'" (vs 4-5).

Does Satan consider himself to be of 'God'? *But of course!* So, he's saying, 'You'll be like me.' *Not the true God!* But the only way that they would become *as God*—one of the qualities of God—would be: Instead of accepting and believing in faith what God had told them they took upon themselves to judge God. And to judge for themselves—by exercising their free moral agency incorrectly—*what they would determine to be right and wrong!* That's the whole story of the Tree of the Knowledge of Good and Evil.

So, you know they took it, it appealed to the senses. Why didn't Eve say, 'God told us no, so we're not going to. We believe God, we love Him, we're not going to do it, end of story.' They didn't do that.

I did a message years ago called *What Would the World have been Like if Adam and Eve Had Not Sinned?* Well, it would have been a different world, indeed! However, please understand this: They did sin! We are the end result of the progeny of mankind from Adam and Eve, and we still sin.

So it appealed to her senses, it was good for food, pleasant to the eyes, a tree to be desired to make one wise, and she took of the fruit, she ate of it, she gave it to her husband and he ate it. The eyes of both of them were opened, ***not to spiritual reality, but to sin and evil!*** Whenever Satan says, 'Your eyes shall be opened,' *they will be*:

- to evil
- to wretchedness
- to sin

Not opened to understand the plan of God. **Only God can do that, only through Christ!**

So, their eyes were opened, they were both naked, and you know what happened. God came and judged them, and in sentencing and judging them He started right out with the serpent.

Adam and Eve hid themselves. Of course, God knew where they were all the time. Someone wrote and said that it's kind of dumb of God to walk through the garden and say 'Adam, where are you?' You see, that kind of attitude is never going to understand the Bible. God knew where he was, but He wanted Adam to respond to Him. So, Adam said:

Verse 10: "'…I was afraid because I *am* naked, and *so* I hid myself.' And He said, 'Who told you that you *were* naked? Have you eaten of the tree, which I commanded you that you should not eat?' And the man said, 'The woman… [He didn't want to say, 'Yeah, I did it.' So, he pointed immediately to the woman] … **whom You gave *to* be with me**…'" (vs 10-12).

Well boy, when I gave her to you, hey, that was the greatest thing there ever was, wasn't it? And now you're accusing her.

"'…she gave me of the tree, and I ate.' And the LORD God said to the woman, 'What *is* this you have done?' And the woman said, 'The serpent deceived me, and I ate.'…. [I was tricked into it] …And the LORD God said to the serpent…" (vs 12-14).

He began to mete out the punishment. Even if you are tricked into it, even if you are deceived into it, *you still have a penalty to pay because sin is sin, and the wages of sin is death.* That's what God told them about the Tree of the Knowledge of Good and Evil.

"…And the LORD God said to the serpent, 'Because you have done this you *are* cursed above all livestock, and above every animal of the field. You shall go upon your belly, and you shall eat dust all the days of your life. And I will put enmity between you… [the serpent] …and the woman, and between your seed… [that is all the physical serpents and the demons] …and her Seed…'" (vs 14-15)—*Who was to be the Christ!*

Right at the first sin, God revealed there had to be a Redeemer Who had to overcome the power of sin and Satan. *And that's what this day pictures!*

"…He… [the Seed] …shall bruise your… [the serpent's] …head, and you shall bruise His heel" (v 15). *A prophecy of the crucifixion that it would take the death of God to pay for the sins of mankind!*

Verse 16: "To the woman He said, 'I will greatly increase your sorrow and your conception—in sorrow shall you bring forth children….'"

Because the women bring forth the children and when the children do wrong, as they're growing up and the different things that happen, women have sorrow and grief. Look at how it is in the world today, and look at how women suffer because of the very nature that their offspring have. Just imagine the sorrow that was there when Cain killed Abel. It's not just the pain of the child labor alone.

"...Your desire shall be toward your husband, and he shall rule over you.' And to Adam He said, 'Because you have hearkened to the voice of your wife and have eaten of the tree—of which I commanded you, saying, "You shall not eat *of* it!"'— the ground *is* cursed for your sake. In sorrow shall you eat of it all the days of your life. It shall also bring forth thorns and thistles to you, and *thus* you shall eat the herbs of the field; in the sweat of your face you shall eat bread until you return to the ground, for out of it you were taken; for dust you *are*, and to dust you shall return'" (vs 16-19).

That's the fate of all human beings. No one has escaped death except Jesus Christ. No means that man or Satan have devised to try and trick man into thinking that he has an immortal soul and he's going to live forever, causes any life to be at all is because:

- life comes from God
- life comes from love
- life does not come from sin
- life does not come from death

Now let's see how it affected the whole world. It says that 'Eve was deceived, but Adam sinned.'

Now let's see what happened to the world when Adam and Eve sinned, because it was quite a thing. The sentence that God gave them was the sentence of death within their members. Also, as Paul wrote of later, to have along with that the law of sin, the corrupted human nature which naturally sins.

Rom. 5—Paul explains it very clearly. It brings us to Christ and His sacrifice for us on the Passover Day, and then likewise when we come to the Day of Atonement we will see this is when God is going to make that sacrifice of Christ available on a universal basis to everyone in the world, *but not until the meaning of the Day of Atonement has been fulfilled,* which we can summarize in this way:

You can never be **at-one** with God as long as you have a sinful nature, and as long as you are in the flesh you can never be totally **at-one** with God. That cannot happen until there is first the process of conversion, and then enduring to the end, and then the resurrection, and then being born into the Family of God. Then and only then can we be **at-one** with God. But it is sin that separated all mankind, and we know that Satan is the author of sin.

Romans 5:12—*Paul writes*: "Therefore, as by one man sin entered into the world, and by means of sin *came* death..."

The sentence of death was passed on and we all inherit it. The scientists know that there is a death gene in us, and it activates upon certain things that happen. But even if we have a good long physical life and live a long time, the death gene still activates and we die.

"...and in this way death passed into all mankind; *and it is* for this reason that all have sinned" (v 12).

With a nature of death there is no way that human beings can avoid sin, because it is a more imperfect product because of that than what God originally created Adam and Eve to be, which is another whole different story. So, the Day of Atonement pictures when God is going to open the way for all.

Now we're going to see that Satan the devil is called 'the god of this world.' *Satan likes to come in and twist and turn the Word of God, and he has many willing agents to do it!* He has many willing people who desire to do this, and they think they are doing the will of God, but they're not.

2-Corinthians 4:1: "Therefore, having this ministry, according as we have received mercy, we are not fainthearted. For we have personally renounced the hidden things of dishonest gain... [that has to be] ...not walking in *cunning* craftiness... [not having another agenda secretly below doing the will of God] ...nor handling the Word of God deceitfully..." (vs 1-2).

That's what all the false apostles have done, they handle the Word of God deceitfully.

"...but by manifestation of the Truth, we are commending ourselves to every man's conscience before God. But if our Gospel is hidden, it is hidden to those who are perishing; in whom the god of this age has blinded the minds of those who do not believe..." (vs 2-4).

Satan the devil is deceiving the whole world (Rev. 12:9), and he has all of his agents out there doing it.

- the powers
- the principalities
- the demons
- those in government
- those in education

This whole world is in the grips of a diabolical deception that comes from Satan the devil!

Yes, there is a little good here, and a little good there, but we're going to see that the evil is going to triumph temporarily. But the Day of Atonement pictures *when God is fully triumphant!* Because not only must you get rid of sin on an individual basis, which God does through the sacrifice of Jesus Christ and His mercy, forgiveness, and justification, but you also must get rid of the author of sin who is called 'the god of this world,' and here is what he does:

"…has blinded the minds of those who do not believe, lest the Light of the Gospel of the glory of Christ, Who is *the* image of God, should shine unto them" (v 4)—*to have the knowledge of God in truth and understanding!*

Any time anyone rejects any part of the Word of God, they are rejecting God in degree. As we have learned from the Days of Unleavened Bread, *a little leaven leavens the whole lump!* So, a little sin breeds more sin.

Now let's come back to Lev. 16 and let's see in the ceremony on the Day of Atonement that God commanded the children of Israel to do, that here He pictures one of the strangest offerings that we find in the entire Bible, and it's only on this one day, on the Day of Atonement.

This was to be done at the tabernacle or the temple. The priest was to go through his ritual, bathe himself and dress himself with the Holy garments. The thing concerning the Day of Atonement is that this is the only day in the entire year that the high priest could go into the Holy of Holies; *once a year!* He had to give the offerings for himself, and so forth, as Paul said, 'not without blood.'

I want you to compare that to the blessing that God has given to those whom He has called, and who have the Holy Spirit now, *We have the ability through prayer to come in to the very presence of God anytime we desire!* Quite a different thing, isn't it? *Yes, indeed!*

Through this there is the offering of the two rams.

Leviticus 16:7[transcriber's correction]: "And he shall take the two goats and present them before the LORD *at* the door of the tabernacle of the congregation."

That's not even before the altar, nor the tabernacle of the congregation. That's right up past the altar of burnt offerings, right up where you go into the temple itself. There he was to perform a special ceremony. This is not done on any other sacrifice that is done, *because these two goats were to be as identical as possible!* There was a special ritual that was done by the priest to show which of these two goats was the true sin sacrifice of God.

He cast lots; v 8: "And Aaron shall cast lots on the two goats; **one lot for the LORD** and the **other lot for Azazel**"—*which is another name for Satan the devil!*

Before Satan fell, he was the cherub that covered, and he comes to this world saying 'I am God.' *The world can't distinguish the difference between the true Christ and the false christ; between the true God and the false god.*

So, this is symbolized by these two goats, where then God would have to select the one which was the true sin offering. Then for the one that was the true sin offering, he was told after he went in and cleansed the ark and everything:

Verse 15: "Then he shall kill the goat of the sin offering that is for the people, and bring its blood inside the veil. And he shall do with that blood as he did with the blood of the young bull, and sprinkle it on the mercy seat and before the mercy seat. And he shall make an atonement for the sanctuary because of the uncleanness of the children of Israel and **because of their transgressions in all their sins**…." (vs 15-16).

Now here was one sacrifice that was given to represent the forgiveness, or the atonement of all the sins of the children of Israel. Once they have been atoned for they have been atoned, so the live goat is another proposition. It's interesting that the ceremony took place at the temple, but the live goat was never sacrificed. The live goat is symbolic of Satan the devil—who's the god of this world—who is the author of sin. Because as soon as Satan was let into the Garden of Eden, Adam and Eve sinned.

As we are going to see when we come to the final conclusion of the Feast of Tabernacles where God yet has another mission for Satan to do, that *unless the author of sin is removed, sin will occur again!* That's the whole lesson we have within our bodies with the law of sin and death, and overcoming, and things like this.

Verse 20: "And when he has made an end of reconciling the sanctuary and the tabernacle of the congregation and the altar, he shall bring the live goat. And Aaron shall lay both his hands on the head of the live goat, and confess over him all the sins of the children of Israel, and all their transgressions in all their sins…" (vs 20-21).

All of the sins that people do as instigated by Satan the devil, and since he's the author of sin, all sin comes back to him. Therefore, having their sins forgiven, now God goes to the one who has caused them—Satan the devil—and puts it upon his head that he bears his own sin. There is no atonement for Satan the devil.

"...putting them on the head of the goat, and shall send *it* away by the hand of **a chosen man** into the wilderness" (v 21).

The wilderness is a very important part of this whole thing in relationship to Satan the devil. Then the fit man—chosen man—as we will see a little later, is a type of an angel who binds Satan the devil. He would come back and wash himself. The priest would wash and cleanse himself.

Verse 29: "And it shall be a statute forever to you: in the seventh month, on the tenth of the month, you shall afflict your souls and do no work at all, *whether it be* one of your own country or a stranger who is living among you, for on that day an atonement shall be made for you, to cleanse you, so that you may be clean from all your sins before the LORD. It *shall be* a Sabbath of rest to you, and you shall afflict your souls by a statute forever" (vs 29-31).

Verse 34: "'And this shall be an everlasting statute to you, to make an atonement for the children of Israel for their sins **once a year**.' And he did as the LORD commanded Moses."

Now we're going to see the significance of the wilderness and what that has to do with removing Satan the devil that Jesus Christ will do, and to atone for our sins.

Now let's see the connection between the wilderness and Satan. Let's come in the New Testament now to Matt. 4, and here we have one of the most important battles of the entire ministry of Jesus Christ. It's important from this point of view: *Jesus could not begin His ministry until He had conquered Satan the devil!*

Let's think about this: If Jesus manifested Himself as God is God, to fight a battle with Satan, obviously He would win because He won the battle when Satan rebelled and a third of the angels went with him and they were cast back down to the earth. So, there's no question that He would win.

If Jesus were an angelic being… We see in the book of Daniel that the angels of God fight against the angels of Satan, and there is war that goes on, He probably could have beaten him and overcome him if He would have been manifested in angelic form. But now Christ was God in the flesh, manifested as a human being. In order to overcome Satan the devil it was necessary that Jesus do so in the flesh. Because Satan is the one who has caused all human beings to sin. So, before Jesus began His ministry He had to overcome Satan the devil, and to defeat him, *which He did!*

After Jesus was baptized, Matthew 4:1: "Then Jesus was led up into the wilderness by the Spirit in order to be tempted by the devil. And when

He had fasted *for* forty days and forty nights, afterwards He was famished. And when the tempter came to Him, he said, '**If** You are the Son of God, command that these stones become bread'" (vs 1-3).

Now we'll notice in all the answers that Jesus gave, He gave the answers that God gave to man in order to serve God!

Verse 5: "But He answered *and* said, '**It is written**…'" *Good example*: How do you overcome demonic and satanic problems but by the Word and the Spirit of God? There it is right there.

"…'It is written, "Man shall not live by bread alone, but by every word that proceeds out of *the* mouth of God."'…. [Deut. 8:3] …Then the devil took Him to the Holy city and set Him upon the edge of the temple" (vs 4-5).

From the highest pinnacle of the temple to the floor of the Kidron Valley is 650 feet. So this was like being on a 65 story building.

Verse 6: "And said to Him, 'If You are the Son of God, cast Yourself down; for it is written, "He shall give His angels charge concerning You, and they shall bear You up in *their* hands, lest You strike Your foot against a stone."' Jesus said to him, 'Again, it is written, **"You shall not tempt *the* Lord your God"**'" (vs 6-7).

That's quite a statement, isn't it? *No human being is to tempt God!* Now that's another whole sermon in itself. *You tempt God by*:

- not believing
- by accusing Him
- by imputing to Him things that are not His

such as imputing to Him the things that Satan the devil does! You tempt God! You shall not tempt Him to make a spectacle of yourself so that *you, by your actions, are commanding God to do something which God will not do!* The whole bottom line of this is that *no one is going to command God!* That's what this is all about.

Verse 8: "After that, the devil took Him to an exceedingly high mountain, and showed Him all the kingdoms of the world and their glory…"—*and Luke adds* 'in a moment of time.'

Verse 9: "And said to Him, 'All these things will I give You, **if You will fall down and worship me**.'" *Well, the meaning of that is,* 'You worship me as 'God'; instead of God, You worship me.'

That's exactly the same test that Adam and Eve failed by eating of the Tree of the Knowledge of Good and Evil. *They didn't believe God! They didn't listen to His voice!* That is the most important thing. The Word of God that we have here today *is the voice of God!* That's what's important. That's why it's so absolutely important that whoever does any preaching and teaching, and this applies to everyone of us, that we better teach the Word of God as Paul said, 'in season and out of season,' because these are the Words of God, and we better handle it with:

- love
- respect
- obedience
- fear
- awe

because this is God's Word! What did Jesus say to him?

Verse 10: "...'Be gone, Satan! For it is written, "You shall worship the Lord your God, and **Him alone** shall you serve."'"

Of course, that's to human beings, not to Satan. Satan would never worship God. But that's quite a statement! You take this to yourself. "**You shall worship the Lord your God, and Him alone shall you serve.**" Even Job had to learn that lesson, didn't he? *Without a doubt!*

Verse 11: "Then the devil left Him..."—*and as it says in Luke* 'for a short season.'

Now let's see how we are to look at these things. Let's see what God tells us to do in praying every day.

Matthew 6:13—this is what we need to pray: "And lead us not into temptation... [that we don't have to be led into trials] ...**but rescue us**.... [from the Greek: deliver, save, rescue us all applies here] ...**from the evil one**...."—*who is Satan the devil!*

We are rescued from Satan the devil *by the power of God through Jesus Christ with the Holy Spirit of God!* By yielding to Him, and obeying Him, and not living in sin and doing the will of Satan the devil. So, *we have to be rescued from it!*

Now let's see how great this rescue was. I don't think many of us realize it. Many people have come out of this so-called Christian church or that so-called Christian church and all you're doing in many cases is changing Saturday for Sunday and the holidays for the Holy Days, which you need to do. There's nothing wrong with that; that needs to be. But the question comes down to this point:

- Are we really converted?
- Do we really believe?
- Do we really understand that even in that religious setting

which was a satanic deception cleverly interwoven with the Word of God to make it look really good and Christian!

That's the whole lesson of the two goats of Lev. 16. *You cannot of your own self discern the true God from the false god!* Unless you have the Word of God and the Spirit of God, you can't discern between Satan as god and God. You cannot discern between

- false prophets
- false apostles
- false brethren

and you're going to fall as a dupe again for Satan the devil!

How else can you explain: Where have all the brethren gone? *Many of them were false brethren!* And many of them came not for the reasons of loving God and obeying His voice, and believing Him and having faith in Christ. Many of them came because they saw the institution, and they saw the elegance of it and the desire of it. So they didn't come to serve God. You might say they were 'fair weather' Christians, as it were. Just like it says in the parable: When persecution and trouble comes, they give up and flee.

Paul is also setting the stage (Col. 2) to avoid the subtlest most powerful deceptions of Satan the devil through philosophy and angel worship. So, in what he's writing, he's trying to establish them firmly in the Truth of God and for them to know and understand what God has done for each one of them, and hence for each one of us.

Colossians 1:9: "For this cause we also, from the day that we heard *of it*, do not cease to pray for you and to ask that you may be filled with the knowledge of His will in all wisdom and spiritual understanding; that you may walk worthily of the Lord..." (vs 9-10).

Remember what we've said: *You walk in faith, believe in hope, and live in love!* That is the core of your relationship with God. That's what he's talking about here.

"...unto all pleasing, being fruitful in every good work and growing in the knowledge of God... [that is continuous] ...being strengthened with all power..." (vs 10-11). *That's what God wants to be in us!* To be strengthened with the power of God's Holy Spirit!

"...according to the might of His glory... [since we live in the world]: ...unto all endurance and long-suffering with joy; giving thanks to the Father, Who has made us qualified for the share of the inheritance of the saints in the Light... [this is one of those middle voice Greek verbs]: ...**Who has personally rescued us from the power of darkness**" (vs 11-13).

You think about that for a minute! Why are you here in the Church of God?

- with the knowledge of God
- the Word of God
- the Spirit of God
- the understanding of God

and you are not out there in the world? *Because God has called you, and God is the One Who qualifies you!* Not because we are greater than anybody else because we're not; *we're the least!* That's just the way it is. That's why the Day of Atonement is a tremendous Holy Day, because it is to be *a spiritual Feast* that we feast on the Word of God and on the Spirit of God and not the flesh. So, it's tremendous!

Verse 13: "Who has personally rescued us from the power of darkness and has transferred *us* unto the Kingdom of the Son of His love."

We're not *in* the Kingdom of God, yet. That won't come till the resurrection because flesh and blood cannot inherit the Kingdom of God. But we are under the jurisdiction of the Kingdom of God:

- through the Holy Spirit of God
- through Jesus Christ
- through the Word of God

Then all of our allegiance, and all of our politics as it were, *are in heaven* and not on earth. We await the Kingdom to come and we will enter into it. So, isn't that something? "…**Who has personally rescued us from the power of darkness.**" *Quite a fantastic thing!* Now let's compare that with what the world is:

1-John 5:19: "We know that we are of God…" *We have to know that!* If you have any doubts whatsoever, you take it to God in prayer through Jesus Christ:

- *study* the Word of God
- *know* that you have the Spirit of God
- *know* that you understand and do these things

because God has given you the desire to do it, and that you are of God!

Verse 19: "We know that we are of God, and *that* the whole world **lies in *the power*** of the wicked one." *Or, lies in the wicked one.* Isn't that something?

It reminds me of the song: He's Got the Whole World in His Hands, *Satan's got the whole wide world in his hands!* The Day of Atonement pictures when it's going to be taken out of his hands. Quite an important thing, and profound for us to realize and know and understand.

- let's see what God is going to do

- let's see what the Day of Atonement pictures in dealing with Satan the devil

Let's come to the book of Revelation and see this, then we will see how God will begin to deal with Israel and grant to them repentance. *But first,* this must be done: *The author of sin must be removed!*

As we saw on the Feast of Trumpets, how Christ and all of us—the saints—are going to return to the earth. There's going to be this great battle on the earth and the first thing that happens is that Jesus sends an angel to take *the beast and the false prophet* and cast them into the Lake of Fire where they are burned to a crisp.

So, in order to stop that kind of human activity you have to get the two top leaders, *the beast and the false prophet.* Then you have to go one step further: *you have to get rid of Satan the devil who set up the beast and the false prophet and brought sin to the whole world!*

Here we see the fulfilling of Lev. 16 where the goat is taken to the wilderness and let go, taken away, gotten rid of. Now then we have an add-on at this point as revealed in the book of Revelation. Something has to happen in order for Satan to be removed and for the Millennium to start.

Revelation 20:1: "Then I saw an angel descending from heaven, having the key of the abyss, and a great chain in his hand." *That is the prison of the demons and Satan, the abyss!*

Verse 2: "And he took hold of the dragon, the ancient serpent, who is *the* Devil and Satan, and bound him *for* a thousand years…. [He doesn't get rid of him entirely. He binds him] …Then he cast him into the abyss, and locked him *up,* and sealed *the abyss* over him, so that he would not deceive the nations any longer until the thousand years were fulfilled; and after that it is ordained that he be loosed *for* a short time" (vs 2-3).

When we come to that last part of the Feast of Tabernacles we'll see what happens, namely this: *as soon as he is let loose sin reigns again!* So, the Day of Atonement pictures that you must get rid of the author of sin. *You cannot bring in everlasting righteousness with him around. It is an impossibility!*

Now let's see what God is going to do with Israel. Quite an amazing thing! Once you get rid of the author of sin, and you get rid of the blindness, and you get rid of all of those wrong influences. Remember what they all went through? *It's really quite a thing that is done here!*

Ezekiel 36:16: "And the Word of the LORD came to me, saying, 'Son of man, when the house of

Israel dwelt in their own land, they defiled it by their own ways…" (vs 16-17).

Isn't that interesting? *'There is a way that seems right to a man, the ends thereof are the ways of death'*—and it seems right!

"…and by their doings, even as the uncleanness of a woman's impurity was their way before Me. Therefore, I poured My fury upon them because of the blood that they had shed upon the land, and for their idols *by which* they defiled it. And I scattered them among the nations, and they were scattered throughout the countries. I judged them according to their ways and according to their doings. And when they came unto the nations where they went, they even profaned My Holy name in that it was said of them, 'These *are* the people of the LORD, and they are gone out of His land'" (vs 17-20).

Isn't that true? *Even today there are people who say that they're the people of God,* **but they're not!**

Verse 21: "But I had pity for My Holy name, which the house of Israel had profaned among the nations where they were exiled. Therefore, say to the house of Israel, 'Thus says the Lord GOD, "I do not do *this* for your sake, O house of Israel, but for My Holy name's sake…"'" (vs 21-22).

God is going to save the world and Israel, and all nations because of His plan and His Holiness, and as we know, **because of His covenant with Abraham!**

"…which you have profaned among the nations where you went. And I will sanctify My great name, which was profaned among the nations, which you have profaned in their midst. And the nations shall know that I *am* the LORD…" (vs 22-23).

Though Israel didn't know God, now God is going to reveal Himself not only to Israel but to the heathen. He says they:

"…says the Lord GOD, 'when I shall be sanctified in you before their *very* eyes'" (v 23).

In other words, what God is going to do when He brings Israel out of captivity, and grants them repentance, which this Day of Atonement pictures, and restores them back to Him, **all the heathen are going to know that it is God!**

Verse 24: "For I will take you from among the nations and gather you out of all countries… [that's what this Day of Atonement pictures the re-gathering of the children of Israel back to the land] …and will gather you into your own land. And I will sprinkle clean waters upon you… [get rid of all the filthiness and so forth] …and you shall be clean. I will cleanse you from all your filthiness and from your idols. And **I will give you a new heart, and I will put a new spirit within you**…" (vs 24-26).

So, not only is it going to be a recreation of the earth because of the desolation of all the things that take place on the earth, as we saw from Pentecost and Trumpets, but also now that Satan is removed He's going to take away the penalty that He gave to Adam and Eve when they first sinned in giving them a sinful nature.

"…And **I will give you a new heart, and I will put a new spirit within you**. And I will take away the stony heart out of your flesh, and I will give you a heart of flesh" (v 26). *That means a normal human mind and heart and capacity* **without all of the pulls of human nature!**

Now that's going to change the world. But in order to change the world you've got to change the people. This is what God is doing. That's why we're called first. That's why we live in this world though we're not of the world, because in order for God to do this and bring it to the whole world:

- we have to be changed
- we have to be converted

and just count that all the saints from Abel on down to the last two witnesses! **We all have to be changed first before we can do what God wants us to do!**

Before He puts them back in the land, He's going to take away this hard-heartedness and blindness that they have.

Verse 27: "And I will put My spirit within you… [they're going to be converted] …and cause you to walk in My statutes, and you shall keep My ordinances and do *them*"

Hello! What does it take to keep the commandments and judgments of God? **His Spirit!** That doesn't do away with them, does it? *No, it gives you the means and the ability to keep them!* But since the carnal mind that they had before, the heart of stone, they had 'a religion' where they did not want to do the will of God. They wanted the part of it that they agreed with, but the other part they wanted to remake in *their own image,* and polluted it and caused all the deception and lies, and Satan the devil was right there saying, 'Yeah, do it.' *Now it's going to be changed!*

- you can't change the world unless you change the people
- you can't change the world unless you get rid of Satan the devil
- you can't change the people unless you have the proper leadership through Christ and the saints

Let's see another way of explaining it here:

Ezekiel 37:15: "And the Word of the LORD came to me, saying, 'And you, son of man, take a stick and write on it, "For Judah and for his companions, the children of Israel." And take another stick and write on it, "For Joseph, the stick of Ephraim, and all the house of Israel, his companions." And join them to one another into one stick. And they shall become one in your hand" (vs 15-17).

That is part of the meaning of the Day of Atonement bringing back the children of Israel

- all twelve tribes
- all together
- all serving God

Verse 18: "And when the children of your people shall speak to you, saying, 'Will you not declare to us what do you mean by these?' Say to them, 'Thus says the Lord GOD, "Behold, I will take the stick of Joseph, which *is* in the hand of Ephraim, and the tribes of Israel, his companions, and I will put them with him, *even* with the stick of Judah, and will make them one stick, and they shall be one in My hand."' And the sticks *on* which you write shall be in your hand before their eyes. And say to them, 'Thus says the Lord GOD, "Behold, I will take the children of Israel from among the nations where they have gone, and will gather them on every side, and will bring them into their own land…. [bring them back as one] …And I will make them one nation in the land on the mountains of Israel, and one king shall be king over them all. And they shall no longer be two nations, nor shall they be divided into two kingdoms any more at all. Nor shall they be defiled with their idols, nor with their detestable things, nor with all of their transgressions. But I will save them out of all their dwelling places, wherein they have sinned, and will cleanse them. And **they shall be to Me for a people, and I will be their God**"'" (vs18-23).

There is the meaning of the Day of Atonement for the future repentance, conversion, and bringing *at-one-ment* the whole nation of Israel. Just as Paul wrote, 'all Israel shall be saved.' Here it is. This is for the Day of Atonement. We know, as He says in Zech. 12, He starts out with the tribe of Judah first. He's going to save the tents of Judah first. We found that confirmed in Rev. 7 when we saw the sealing of the 140,000 of the children of Israel.

Verse 24: "And David My servant *shall be* king over them… [Christ will be King over all the earth, and David will be king over Israel] …And there shall be one shepherd to all of them. And they shall walk in My ordinances and obey My laws, and do them."

It's amazing how that in the Old Testament it shows that you need the Spirit of God to keep the commandments of God. That's what God was saying all along. Clear back when He first dealt with Israel and gave the Ten Commandments, He said, 'O that there were such a heart in them that they would fear Me, and keep My commandments always' Here we see, they have a new heart, and the Day of Atonement then paves the way for the beginning of the Millennium.

Verse 25: "And they shall dwell in the land that I have given to Jacob My servant, the land in which your fathers have dwelt. And they shall dwell in it, even they and their children, and their children's children forever. And My servant David *shall be* their ruler forever. Moreover, I will make a covenant of peace with them. It shall be an everlasting covenant with them. And I will place them, and multiply them, and will set My sanctuary in their midst forever. And My tabernacle shall be with them…" (vs 25-27). *So now we're getting in to the meaning of the Feast of Tabernacles!*

"…Yea, I will be their God, and they shall be My people. And the nations shall know that I the LORD do sanctify Israel, when My sanctuary shall be in their midst forever" (vs 27-28).

Now then, that takes care of the children of Israel. Now let's come back to us, and see the prayer that Jesus gave to us so that we can understand that in order to be in the Kingdom of God the Day of Atonement pictures for us being *at-one with God!* And this was the prayer that Jesus gave at His last prayer there in John 17.

John 17:13: "But now I am coming to You… [the Father] … and these things I am speaking *while yet* in the world, that they may have My joy fulfilled in them."

That's after the resurrection and we're in the Kingdom of God, for the fullness of that! We are to have joy now, but just think what it's going to be after the resurrection and we're one with God.

Verse 14: "I have given them Your words, and the world has hated them because they are not of the world, just as I am not of the world"

In order for us to be *at-one* with God we have to have the Spirit of God, we have to be sanctified by God. Even though we're not of the world!

Verse 15: "I do not pray that You would take them out of the world, but that You would keep them from the evil one" When we stay *at-one with God*:

- knowing His plan
- knowing His purpose
- having His Spirit
- having His grace
- having His love

God will keep us from the evil one! We will not be deceived. We will not go astray.

Verse 6: They are not of the world, just as I am not of the world. Sanctify them in Your Truth; Your Word is the Truth... [that's how it's accomplished] ...Even as You did send Me into the world, I also have sent them into the world... [referring to the apostles]. ...And for their sakes I sanctify Myself, so that they also may be sanctified in *Your* Truth. I do not pray for these only, but also for those who shall believe in Me through their word" (vs 16-20).

This prayer of Jesus is being fulfilled right to this very day, and will continue to be down through until He returns and beyond.

Here is the prayer, here is the ultimate goal; that is, spiritual Israel:

Verse 21: "That they all may be one, even as You, Father, *are* in Me, and I in You; that they also may be one in Us, in order that the world may believe that You did send Me. And I have given them the glory that You gave *to* Me, in order that they may be one, in the same way *that* We are one: I in them... [Christ in you] ...and You in Me... [Christ and the Father working together] ...that they may be perfected into one..." (vs 21-23).

So, this Day of Atonement pictures that perfection, and pictures when we will no longer have any sin at all but be totally <u>at-one</u> with God! This is the meaning of the Day of Atonement.

Scriptures from *The Holy Bible in Its Original Order, A Faithful Version*

Scriptural References

1) Leviticus 23:26-27
2) Numbers 29:7-9
3) Leviticus 23:28-32
4) Malachi 4:10
5) Exodus 31:12-18
6) Genesis 3:1-5, 10-19
7) Romans 5:12
8) 2 Corinthians 4:1-4
9) Leviticus 16:7-8, 15-16, 20-21, 29-31, 34
10) Matthew 4:1-11
11) Matthew 6:13
12) Colossians 1:9-13
13) 1 John 5:19
14) Revelation 20:1-3
15) Ezekiel 36:16-27
16) Ezekiel 37:15-28
17) John 17:13-23

Scriptures referenced, not quoted:

- Numbers 28:16
- Malachi 3
- Deuteronomy 30
- Leviticus 12:9
- Deuteronomy 8:3
- Colossians 2
- Zechariah 12
- Revelation 7

Also referenced: Message:
- *What Would the World have been Like if Adam and Eve Had Not Sinned?*

FRC: cs
Transcription date unknown
Reformatted: bo—12/2020

CHAPTER FIFTY-SIX

The Depths of Satan
(Day of Atonement)
Be vigilant in seeking and doing the will of God so that you can resist the devil,
for he is active and alive in the world today!
Fred R. Coulter

Greetings, brethren! Welcome to the Day of Atonement! As we know, all the Holy Days and Feasts of God, even including the Sabbath, mark important events:

Sabbath, the creation of man, the earth and everything that we have. We could go through all of the Holy Days, as we have, now we're down to the Day of Atonement, which pictures something very awesome and great.

Let's begin by understanding that this day deals with how God is going to solve the problem of Satan the devil and the demons.

Revelation 12:9: "…**the Devil** and Satan, who **is deceiving the whole world**…"

We know that that began with Adam and Eve, and he was given control of the world when Adam and Eve chose to follow Satan instead of God.

In the New Testament we will see that Satan is called 'the god of this world.' The Day of Atonement is quite an event! Let's look at a very profound verse *concerning the power of the evil one, Satan the devil!*

1-John 5:19: "**We know that we are of God**…" *We have to know that, brethren:*

- by faith
- by truth
- by understanding
- by proving
- by seeing

in every way that we can!

"…and *that* **the whole world lies in *the power of* the wicked one**" (v 19).

How did that come about? *Because the one who was to be the 'morning star,' the one who was to help all mankind come to salvation*—to Jesus Christ and God the Father—*rebelled!* One-third of the angels rebelled and followed Satan and they became demons.

How did that happen? We know that God's plan goes clear back before the ages of time. We need to understand that these events, before it began—God's plan for human beings—that the plan with the angels and the 'light-bringer' fell into sin.

Let's see that its recorded in Ezek. 28. That's quite a thing because with the fall of Adam and Eve, and first the fall of Lucifer, we're looking at a situation: How is God going to solve the problem?

Look at the condition of the earth and mankind today under the sway of Satan who has power over the whole world. We don't know exactly the tactics of Satan the devil except for one major thing: *he lied!* He lied about everything concerning God. He got lifted up and vain, and got carried away with Himself. *Then the rebellion took place!*

Well, strange as it may seem, there is in the sequence of Holy Days a special day called *the Day of Atonement!*

The Day of Atonement has additional sacrifices in Num. 29 than these that we see in Lev. 23 and 16. Let's first of all look at the command in Lev. 23. As it is with all the Holy Days, these come from God. These are not ceremonial. The days are Holy Days and ceremonies are part of it and they reveal to us certain things in types of attainment or fulfillment, whatever the day pictures.

Leviticus 23:26: "And the LORD spoke to Moses, saying, 'Also, on the tenth *day* of this seventh month, is the Day of Atonement….'" (vs 26-27)—*meaning covering or at-one-ment!*

It's absolutely true as long as Satan the devil is in this world there will be no *at-one-ment* with God with the world.

"…*It shall be* a Holy convocation to you. And you shall afflict your souls… [to fast without eating food and drinking water] …and offer an offering made by fire to the LORD" (v 27). *Everyone had to bring their individual offering!*

Notice the next command, because this becomes absolutely important, because this is such a major event, as we will see.

Verse 28: "And you shall do no work in that same day, for it *is* the Day of Atonement, in order to make an atonement for you before the LORD your

God." *This was for all of Israel!*

This day of fasting was not a ceremonial fasting. This day of fasting had great meaning to God and to us, because let's look at what He said concerning it.

Verse 29: "For whoever is not afflicted in that same day, **he shall be cut off from among his people**." *That means God's blessing withdrawn from that person in the midst of all of Israel!*

Verse 30: "And whoever does any work in that same day, the same one will I destroy from among his people." *This is for the whole nation! To destroy can mean* **curses coming upon that person!**

Verse 31: "You shall do no manner of work. *It shall be* a statute forever throughout your generations in all your dwellings. It *shall be* to you a Sabbath of rest, and you shall afflict yourselves. In the ninth *day* of the month at sunset… [when the 10th day begins] …from sunset to sunset, you shall keep your Sabbath" (vs 31-32).

Since this day is so important and also our offering that we give on the Day of Atonement is important, because it says that "…you shall offer an offering made by fire to the LORD" (v 25).

Today we don't do that! Today we bring monetary things to God, because we live in a mercantile civilization today.

(pause for offering)

Let's see how important this is for Israel, and the prophetic significance for us. Lev. 16 is devoted to the offerings on the Day of Atonement, and this was the only day of the year—so important was this day—that the high priest could only go into the Holy of Holies on that day; *at no other time!*

Sidebar: Brethren, think about the blessing, grace, faith and mercy of the New Covenant that we have access to God the Father and Jesus Christ in heaven above right now through prayer, study *every single day!*

Let that sink in!

God gave all the instructions of what Aaron was to do, how he was to dress, what offerings he was to bring. In this case, the sin offering for he and his household was a bullock.

Leviticus 16:5: "And he shall take from the congregation of the children of Israel two kids of the goats for a sin offering, and one ram for a burnt offering."

Every single sin offering that you find in Leviticus where the offerings are given a goat is used as well as a lamb, likewise for the Passover Offering. All sin offerings are—even the bullock, goat and lamb—all typify the future sacrifice of Jesus Christ.

This separate ceremony here with the two goats is a special ceremony signifying in prophecy one of the most important and greatest events to take place. But first of all, let's understand the meaning of the offering here in Lev. 16.

Verse 7: "And he shall take the two goats and present them before the LORD *at* the door of the tabernacle of the congregation…. [doesn't go inside] …And Aaron shall cast lots on the two goats…" (vs 7-8). **Why cast lots?** *That's a special thing!*

"…one lot for the LORD and the other lot for **Azazel**" (v 8)—*the goat in the wilderness,* **or** *the one that is let loose!* Or it is another name for Satan the devil, when we look at it in the New Testament!

Verse 9: "And Aaron shall bring the goat on which the LORD'S lot fell, and offer it for a sin offering. But the goat on which the lot fell for Azazel **shall be presented alive before the LORD, to make an atonement upon it**… [not *for* it] …**and sent away into the wilderness for Azazel**" (vs 9-10).

In this case, Azazel represents, as we will see later, *Satan!* That's exactly where Jesus met Satan for the temptation.

Then God gives the instruction for what He's going to do for all of the rest of it, the sprinkling of the blood around the Ark.

Verse 16: "And he shall make an atonement for the sanctuary because of the uncleanness of the children of Israel and because of their transgressions in all their sins…."

In dealing with these carnal people, God expected them to obey in the letter of the Law, but they always had lots and lots of sins. But God gave His promise to Abraham, Isaac and Jacob that He would be with the children of Israel and deal with them.

So, this shows that every year God covered their sins. When you go to Heb. 9 it shows that those sins were not completely wiped off the book until the sacrifice of Jesus Christ. This goat does picture the sacrifice of Jesus Christ for sin.

Verse 17: "And there shall be no man in the tabernacle of the congregation when he goes in to make an atonement in the sanctuary until he comes out and has made an atonement for himself, and for his household, and for all the congregation of Israel. And he shall go out to the altar that is before the LORD and make an atonement for it. And he shall take of the blood of the young bull and of the blood of the goat, and put *it* on the horns of the altar all around…. [that was the sacrificial altar] …And he shall sprinkle of the blood on it with his finger seven times and cleanse it, and hallow it from the uncleanness of the children of Israel. And when he has made an end of reconciling the sanctuary and the tabernacle of the congregation and the altar, he shall bring the live goat" (vs 17-20).

When we read this, let's see how important this is, v 21: "And Aaron shall lay both his hands on the head of the live goat, and confess over him all the sins of the children of Israel, and all their transgressions in all their sins, **putting them on the head of the goat**…"

- Why do that *if* they were already cleansed by the sacrifice of the goat for the Lord?
the priesthood and the high priest were cleansed with the blood of the bullock
- Why do this?

As long as Satan is around—the author of human sin—*there will be no rest from sin!*

You cannot have righteousness and evil dwelling together in one place. You cannot have the instigator of sin remain in the world in God's plan. That's why in the first part of Rev. 20 is putting Satan away! *You cannot have the Millennium begin until Satan is removed!* That has great and tremendous significance!

Verse 21: "And Aaron shall lay both his hands on the head of the live goat, and confess over him all the sins of the children of Israel, and all their transgressions in all their sins, **putting them on the head of the goat, and shall send *it* away by the hand of a chosen man into the wilderness**."

Why send it away into the wilderness, an area where nobody lives? *Because that pictures…*

Revelation 20:1: "Then I saw an angel descending from heaven, having the key of the abyss, and a great chain in his hand. And he took hold of the dragon, the ancient serpent, who is *the* Devil and Satan, and bound him *for* a thousand years. Then he cast him into the abyss…" (vs 1-3). *The abyss is the wilderness* where no humans live, only Satan and the demons!

"…and locked him *up*, and sealed *the abyss* over him, so that he would not deceive the nations any longer until the thousand years were fulfilled…" (v 3).

As we will see on seventh day of the Feast of Tabernacles, *Satan and the demons go to the blackest darkness forever!*

So, the closest thing that could be depicted by this special offering on this day… Remember that this is a type of the fulfillment we just read: *sent him into the wilderness.*

Leviticus 16:22: And the goat shall bear upon him all their iniquities to a land in which no one lives. And he shall let the goat go in the wilderness." *That's quite something!* Then Aaron will come back in and do the things he needed to do.

Verse 26: "And he that let go the goat for Azazel shall wash his clothes and bathe his flesh in water, and afterward come into the camp. And the young bull *for* the sin offering and the goat *for* the sin offering, whose blood was brought in to make atonement in the Holy *place*, shall they carry forth outside the camp. And they shall burn their skins in the fire, and their flesh and their dung" (v 26-27).

All sin offerings, when the temple was later built, were burnt on the Mt. of Olives in a special place called *The Miphkad Altar*. There everything was burned to ashes and strewn in the Kidron Valley.

Verse 29: "And it shall be a statute forever to you: in the seventh month, on the tenth of the month, you shall afflict your souls and do no work at all, *whether it be* one of your own country or a stranger who is living among you." *So it's very important for everyone!*

Just like every Holy Day and Feast pictures a major event, this one does, too. One of the most major events in the history of the world since the rebellion of Satan the devil.

Verse 31: "It *shall be* a Sabbath of rest to you, and you shall afflict your souls, by a statute forever."

Verse 30: "For on that day an atonement shall be made for you, to cleanse you, so that you may be clean from all your sins before the LORD." *Sin cannot be removed until Satan is removed!*

Verse 33: "'And he shall make an atonement *for* the Holy sanctuary, and he shall make an atonement for the tabernacle of the congregation, and for the altar; and he shall make an atonement for the priests and for all the people of the congregation. And **this shall be an everlasting statute to you, to make an atonement for the children of Israel for their sins once a year.'** And he did as the LORD commanded Moses" (v s 33-34).

Now let's see how all of this began. We don't know how long in ages past it took for this to take place. But it did take place! It also shows that God gave angels free moral agency, as well. Let's see how Satan works, and we will see that he was actually the *unseen king* behind the prince of Tyre, and what Satan inspired the prince of Tyre to claim himself to be.

Ezekiel 28:1: "The Word of the LORD came to me, saying, 'Son of man, say to the prince of

Tyre. "Thus says the Lord GOD," 'Because your heart *is* lifted up, and you have said, "I *am* a god, I sit *in* the seat of God, in the midst of the seas"; yet, you *are* a man and not God, though you set your heart as the heart of a god'""" (vs 1-2).

Let's see in a little bit what Satan gave him when he possessed him.

Verse 3: "'Behold, you *are* wiser than Daniel; there is no secret that they can hide from you! With your wisdom and with your understanding you have made riches for yourselves, and have gotten gold and silver into your treasuries. By your great wisdom *and* by your trade you have multiplied your riches, and your heart is lifted up because of your riches.' Therefore, thus says the Lord GOD, 'Because you have set your heart as the heart of a god, behold, therefore, I will bring strangers upon you, the most ruthless *of* the nations. And they shall draw their swords against the beauty of your wisdom, and they shall defile your brightness. They shall bring you down to the pit, and you shall die the death of those slain in the midst of the seas. Will you yet say before him who kills you, 'I *am* a god'? But you *are* a man, and not God, in the hand of him who kills you'" (vs 1-9).

Let's see the power behind the prince of Tyre, who is called the king of Tyre. So, what God is showing us with this is that this king of Tyre is none other than *Satan the devil cast down for his rebellion!*

Verse 12: "Son of man, lift up a lamentation over the king of Tyre, and say to him…" *You have the prince of Tyre possessed by Satan the king of Tyre!*

"…Thus says the Lord GOD, 'You seal up the measure of perfection, full of wisdom and perfect in beauty. You have been in Eden the Garden of God…'" (vs 12-13).

Stop and think for a minute, this is the important statement that labels him as Satan the devil, because who were in the Garden of Eden?

- God
- Adam
- Eve
- the serpent

No one else went in there after their sin, because it was closed off and guarded by cherubim! This has to be Satan the devil!

It talks about all of his precious stones and so forth, "…The workmanship of your settings and of your sockets was prepared in you in the day that you were created. You *were* the anointed cherub that covers… [right over the Throne of God] …and I set you so; you were **upon the Holy mountain of God**… [Mt. Sion in heaven above] …you have walked up and down in the midst of the stones of fire. **You *were* perfect in your ways from the day that you were created**…" (vs 13-15).

- How long a space of time was it until he started sinning?
- How did that sin begin?
- What is the principle that we learned from the Feast of Unleavened Bread? *A little leaven leavens the whole lump!*

It may start out with something not too significant, but then it builds and builds! And we will see what that built up to.

"…**until iniquity was found in you**. By the multitude of your merchandise they have filled your midst *with* violence, and you have sinned. Therefore, I will cast you as profane from the mountain of God, and I will destroy you, O covering cherub, from among the stones of fire" (vs 15-16).

How was God going to destroy him? *By absolutely removing him, and his ultimate fate is being in the blackest darkness forever!* That destroys everything that Satan can do.

Why do Satan and the demons not die? *Because they're made of spirit, and spirit does not die!* So, the destruction of a spirit being is not his obliteration as a being, but is complete removal and containment in the blackest darkness forever! *That's the destruction of Satan!*

Sidebar: That will always be a witness to everybody in the Kingdom of God forever *that you don't sin!*

Verse 17: "Your heart was lifted up because of your beauty; you have corrupted your wisdom by reason of your brightness. I will cast you to the ground; I will lay you before kings, that they may behold you. By the multitude of your iniquities, by the unrighteousness of your trade, you have profaned your sanctuaries; therefore, I brought forth a fire from your midst; it shall devour you… [Lake of Fire (Rev. 20)] …and I will bring you to ashes upon the earth, before the eyes of all who see you" (vs 17-18).

So, the ashes will burn up all the works of the world, and then Satan and the demons will be removed to their final destination, *the blackest darkness forever!*

Let's see what all of this led to. This took place on the earth, and this is why the earth was without form and void and covered with water (Gen. 2), because of the rebellion of Satan and the demons.

Isaiah 14:11—*talking about the king of Babylon*: "Your pride is brought down to the grave, *and* the noise of your harps. The maggot is spread under you, and the worms cover you."

That's true concerning the prince of Tyre and the king of Babylon! Now here is the power behind Babylon; see how these things come together. It is the spiritual power behind the man that is Satan the devil. Where do we find this again in a great way right at the end? *Rev. 13, **the beast, who will be possessed!***

Verse 12: "How you are fallen from the heavens, O shining star, son of the morning! *How you are cut down to the ground, you who weakened the nations! For you have said in your heart, 'I will ascend into the heavens, **I will exalt my throne above the stars of God**…'"* (vs 12-13). *Stars are angels, as well as the physical stars in the universe!*

"'…I will also sit upon the mount of the congregation, in the sides of the north…. [in other words, he going to replace the Most High God] …I will ascend above the heights of the clouds; I will be like the Most High.'…. [*an impossibility; it cannot be done*] …Yet, you shall be brought down to the grave, to the sides of the pit'" (vs 13-15)

You can't kill a spirit being, so his containment is his grave, the pit and abyss, and the blackest darkness forever!

Now let's see how it is that you must get rid of Satan, because you can't get rid of sin until you get rid of him. The first thing that Jesus had to do after He was baptized was to overcome Satan the devil.

Matthew 4:1: "Then Jesus was led up into the wilderness by the Spirit… [of God] …in order to be tempted by the devil." *That ties right in with the Day of Atonement! The wilderness!*

There is something very important that you can see chronologically. This was in 26A.D. in the fall. That year was a Jubilee Year, and the Jubilee is when you let all the slaves loose, everything is wiped clean and returned to its original state. *The Jubilee!*

It's fitting that Jesus went out to conquer Satan the devil in a Jubilee Year, in the wilderness, because that had to be done first! He could not begin His ministry until that took place. That's why this is such an important thing with the Day of Atonement and the goat of Azazel being in the wilderness, and the temptation of Jesus Christ.

Matthew 3:16: "And after He was baptized, Jesus came up immediately out of the water; and behold, the heavens were opened to him, and he… [John the Baptist] …saw the Spirit of God descending as a dove, and coming upon Him. And lo, a voice from heaven said, '**This is My Son, the Beloved, in Whom I have *great* delight**'" (vs 16-

17). *Then right out into the wilderness!*

Matthew 4:1: "Then Jesus was led up into the wilderness by the Spirit in order to be tempted by the devil. And when He had fasted *for* forty days and forty nights, afterwards He was famished. And **when the tempter came to Him**…" (vs 1-3).

This is profoundly important, because Jesus could not fail this! The first Adam failed; the second Adam cannot fail!

"…he said, '**If** You are the Son of God, command that these stones become bread'" (v 3). *Jesus had to meet Satan when He was fasting, the weakest physically!*

So, this was a mammoth time and an extended Day of Atonement: *40 days!* Think of that! Think of how weak He was, and how susceptible to temptation that Jesus would be in His condition. He had to do it and carry within Him *the law of sin and death, yet, **not sin!*** This was a tremendous and magnificent thing that He did.

Verse 4: "But He answered *and* said, '**It is written**…'" *Lesson for all of us*:

- the Word of God
- the Truth of God
- everything about the Word of God

"…'Man shall not live by bread alone, but **by every word that proceeds out of *the* mouth of God**'" (v 4).

Here we have it, and God wants to make sure that everybody has it. There's no misunderstanding of it, so it's written down!

Verse 5: "Then the devil took Him to the Holy city and set Him upon the edge of the temple, and said to Him, 'If You are the Son of God, cast Yourself down; for it is written, "He shall give His angels charge concerning You, and they shall bear You up in *their* hands, lest You strike Your foot against a stone"'" (vs 5-6).

Satan can quote Scripture! He does doe it! It tells us in 2-Cor. 11 that he *appears as an angel of light, **and so do his ministers!* "…every word that proceeds out of *the* mouth of God."**

What Jesus says next He's not saying to apply to Satan, He's telling Satan as it applies to Himself, Who now is a man.

Verse 7: "Jesus said to him, 'Again, it is written, "You shall not tempt *the* Lord your God."'" *No, indeed! God cannot be tempted with evil!*

Verse 8: "After that, the devil took Him to an exceedingly high mountain, and showed Him all the kingdoms of the world and their glory."

Like a great vast television screen, all flowing past showing the great empires that Satan controlled and ruled. Notice what Satan says, and why he must be removed, and why the only interpretation that you can come up with in Lev. 16 is that ritual in sending that goat into the wilderness applies to Satan the devil and this very encounter.

Verse 9: "And said to Him [Jesus], 'All these things will I give You, **if You will fall down and worship me.**'"

Let's see the parallel account, because Satan says something else that's recorded here:

Luke 4:5: Then the devil led Him up into a high mountain *and* showed Him all the kingdoms of the world **in a moment of time**. And the devil said to Him, 'I will give You all this authority, and the glory of them *all*; **for it has been delivered to me, and I give it to whomever I desire**'" (vs 5-6).

That helps fill in the blanks in Isa. 14 & Ezek. 28. The power behind these great kingdoms is Satan the devil. Likewise with the last great kingdom that's going to envelop the whole earth (Rev. 13).

Verse 7: "'Therefore, if You will worship me in *my* presence… [meaning *as God*] …all things shall be Yours.' But Jesus answered *and* said to him, 'Get behind Me, Satan; for it is written, "You shall worship *the* Lord your God, and Him only shall you serve"'" (vs 7-8). *Jesus was saying that to Himself, because Satan will **never** worship God!*

- Did the children of Israel have the Laws of God? *Yes!*
- Did they keep them? *Sometimes they kept most of them!*

History is a cycle of ups and downs, coming back to God, falling into apostasy and so forth.

- Why?
- Who do you suppose is doing that? *Satan the devil!*

We will see that Satan is still involved in this same kind of thing in challenging the Church today.

- Do we need Satan removed from the world?
- For the sake of the world? *Yes!*
- For the sake of the Church? *Yes!*

2-Corinthians 4:1: "Therefore, having this ministry, according as we have received mercy, we are not fainthearted. For we have personally renounced the hidden things of dishonest gain, not walking in *cunning* craftiness, nor handling the Word of God deceitfully…" (vs 1-2).

Who would make you handle the Word of God deceitfully? *None other than Satan the devil,*

the author of lies, the father of lies, to handle the Word of God deceitfully!

What does that tell you about *fake* Christianity? *Half worship of God and half worship of Satan!* **You can't have that!** You either have to worship God *or* Satan! That's the whole trial that Jesus went through.

"….but by manifestation of the Truth, we are commending ourselves to every man's conscience before God. **But if our Gospel is hidden, it is hidden to those who are perishing**" (vs 2-3).

If it's hidden, it's blinded, and there are varying degrees of blindness. Even if someone has partial vision, where they can see big blurry things, can they really see? *No!* They will miss all the details that are necessary, and this is the *fake* Christianity of the world.

Verse 3: **"But if our Gospel is hidden, it is hidden to those who are perishing;** in whom the god of this age has blinded the minds of those who do not believe…" (vs 3-4).

- Do they believe that the Law has been done away? *Yes!*
- Do they believe that Jesus said, 'Do not think that I have come to abolish the Law or the Prophets; I have not come to abolish, but to fulfill'?
- Do they believe that? *No!*

*Therefore, **they do not believe**, because there's no such a think half Satan/half God and you're okay!* That's why Satan must be removed!

Remember, he's so cunning, sly, slick, lying and deceiving that he can twist things around *as he did to deceive a third of the angels of God!* You can see why the Day of Atonement is so important!

"…lest the Light of the Gospel of the glory of Christ, Who is *the* image of God, should shine unto them. For we do not preach our own selves, but Christ Jesus *the* Lord, and ourselves your servants for Jesus' sake" (vs 4-5).

That's the comparison of the 'god of this age' Satan the devil!

2-Corinthians 11:13: "For such *are* false apostles, deceitful workers who are transforming themselves into apostles of Christ. And *it is* no marvel, for Satan himself transforms himself into an angel of light" (vs 13-14).

Let's see how thorough this is going to be! We're living in an age where it is growing more and more, and I want you to pay attention to all of the lies that you see if you listen to *fake news*. They lie subtly, *lie, **lie**, lie* to get people to believe that we have got to get rid of Donald Trump so 'we can become like Venezuela.'

Revelation 12:9: "And the great dragon was cast out… [removed] …the ancient serpent who is called the Devil and Satan, who is deceiving the whole world; he was cast down to the earth, and his angels were cast down with him."

Notice what happens when this last great kingdom comes; it's going to be something indeed!

Revelation 13:1: "And I stood on the sand of the sea… [people] …and I saw a beast rising up out of the sea, having seven heads and ten horns, and on his horns ten crowns, and upon his heads *the* name of blasphemy." ***But***:

- the world is blinded
- the world won't know
- the world will go along with it

Verse 2: "And the beast that I saw was like a leopard, and his feet like *the feet* of a bear, and his mouth like *the* mouth of a lion; and the dragon gave him his power, and his throne and great authority."

Satan is always the power behind the throne, but the king, prince or beast will die, *but not Satan!*

Verse 4: "And they worshiped the dragon, who gave *his* authority to the beast. And they worshiped the beast, saying, 'Who *is* like the beast? Who has the power to make war against him?'" *Quite a thing, yes, indeed!*

Here again we see the same thing. We see it actually fulfilled right here in Rev. 19 & 20. Let's see it, the *beast* possessed of Satan. The prince of Tyre possessed of the king of Tyre: *Satan!* They king of Babylon or the king Assyria and then Satan. All three of those men die, but Satan doesn't, and we'll see it right here.

Revelation 19:20: "And the beast was taken, and with him the false prophet who worked miracles in his presence, by which he had deceived those who received the mark of the beast and those who worshiped his image. **Those two were cast alive into the Lake of Fire, which burns with brimstone**." *They die!*

Revelation 20:1: "Then I saw an angel descending from heaven, having the key of the abyss, and a great chain in his hand. And he took hold of the dragon, the ancient serpent, who is *the* Devil and Satan, and bound him *for* a thousand years. Then he cast him into the abyss, and locked him *up*, and sealed *the* abyss over him, so that he would not deceive the nations any longer until the thousand years were fulfilled…" (vs 1-3). *There's the difference!*

- the man possessed dies

- Satan is put away

That makes that clear. But there are some people who read those things in the Old Testament about Satan and the king dying and say that Satan is going to be destroyed. It doesn't mean that. It means that the person possessed of Satan will be destroyed.

Let's see how he deceives the whole world. It's going to be quite a thing. These are going to be tremendous days that are ahead of us. They are difficult because of the things that are going on right now, that is true. However, there may be a good number of years left, so we'll have to see what happens.

2-Thessalonians 2:3—*Paul warns*: "Do not let anyone deceive you by any means because *that* day… [the return of Christ] …will *not* come unless **the apostasy** shall come first…"

This is the great apostasy in the whole world that we just read (Rev. 13) in worshipping the beast.

"…and the man of sin shall be revealed—the son of perdition" (v 3). *That's the coming Beast Power when he is healed of his deadly wound and Satan enter into him!*

Verse 4: "The one who opposes and exalts himself above all that is called God… [that's what Satan does and leads men to do] …or that is an object of worship; so that he comes into the temple of God and sits down as God, proclaiming that he himself is God." *That's why they worship him!*

You see what happens when Satan is not removed. Look at what has happened to this nation, because:

- we have rejected God
- took the Bible out of schools
- took prayer out of schools
- Sunday worship
- holiday worship
- abortion added on top of it

Look at all the evil and things coming upon us now as a result and punishment for those sins! Who is the instigator behind it all? *Satan the devil!* **It is that God causes it to be, because of our sins!** We need to understand that.

Notice what's going to happen here, v 7: "For the mystery of lawlessness is already working; only *there is* One Who is restraining at the present *time* until it arises out of *the* midst…. [Christ is holding it back] …And then **the lawless one will be revealed** (whom the Lord will consume with the breath of His mouth… [the physical man in the Lake of Fire] …and will destroy with the brightness of His coming); *even* the one whose coming is according to *the* inner working of Satan, with all power and signs and lying wonders, and with all deceivableness of unrighteousness in those who are perishing **because they did not receive the love of the Truth, so that they might be saved**" (vs 7-10).

That's quite a thing! One of the ways that you fight Satan the devil is to *love the Truth!* This deception that is coming is going to be:

- so vast
- so powerful
- so all encompassing

that our minds cannot fathom it at this time! We may have a precursor of it, but it's going to be awesome indeed!

Now let's see some things how Satan wants to come after the Church. We will see that we have all experienced this in the Churches we've been in. Let's look at the case of Peter. Let's see what happened when Jesus asked Peter Who He [Jesus] was.

Matthew 16:15: "He said to them, 'But you, whom do you declare Me to be?'…. [speaking to all the disciples there] …Then Simon Peter answered *and* said, 'You are the Christ, the Son of the living God.' And Jesus answered *and* said to him, 'Blessed are you, Simon Bar-Jona, for flesh and blood did not reveal *it* to you, **but My Father, Who *is* in heaven**'" (vs 15-17)—*the Father revealed it to Peter!*

Does that mean that just because God the Father is dealing with someone that he would not be susceptible to temptations by Satan the devil?

Verse 18: "And I say also to you that you are Peter; but upon this Rock… [Jesus] …I will build My Church, and *the* gates of the grave shall not prevail against it."

Verse 20: "Then He charged His disciples not to tell anyone that He was Jesus the Christ. From that time Jesus began to explain to His disciples that it was necessary for Him to go to Jerusalem, and to suffer many things from the elders and chief priests and scribes, **and to be killed**, and to be raised the third day" (vs 20-21).

Notice Peter… Remember the Father just revealed to him that Jesus was the Christ.

Verse 22: "But after taking *Him* aside, Peter personally began to rebuke Him, saying, '*God will be* favorable to you, Lord. In no way shall this *happen* to You.'"

Think about this, there are a couple lessons that we can learn here:

1. never correct God
2. never correct Christ

3. never put your ideas above God's ideas

All of that is contained in this one statement! But notice where Jesus said that that came from:

Verse 23: "Then He turned and said to Peter, **'Get behind Me, Satan!**….'"

- Satan is after the Church
- Satan is after people who know God

"…You are an offense to Me, because your thoughts are not *in accord* with the things of God, but the things of men" (v 23).

Let's see something else that is quite a thing. I want you to really think about this. We will see later that Peter really learned that lesson. This was right at the Passover, Jesus' last Passover. They had pretty well finished everything, and Jesus was telling them:

Luke 22:29: "And I appoint to you, as My Father has appointed to Me, a kingdom; so that you may eat and drink at My table in My kingdom, and may sit on thrones judging the twelve tribes of Israel.' Then the Lord said, 'Simon, Simon…'" (vs 29-31)—*talking directly to Peter!* Remember where we came from in Matt. 16:

"…listen *well*. **Satan has demanded to have all of you, to sift as wheat**" (v 31).

Think about that statement! *I know that Peter never forgot this!* Let's see why:

Verse 32: "'But I have prayed for you, that your faith may not fail; and when you are converted, strengthen your brethren.' And he said to Him, 'Lord, I am ready to go with You both to prison and to death'" (vs 32-33).

Jesus gives a good lesson *for anyone who thinks that they can correct God, Christ or His Word!*

Verse 34: "But He said, 'I tell you, Peter, *the* cock shall in no wise crow today before you have denied knowing Me three times.'"

Think about that! Did that happen? *Yes, it did, Peter denied Jesus three times!*

Verse 59—here's where Peter denied Him the third time: "Now, after about an hour had passed, a certain other *man* strongly affirmed, saying, 'In truth, this one also was with Him, for he is indeed a Galilean.' And Peter said, 'Man, I do not know what you are talking about.' And immediately, while he was yet speaking, the cock crowed. Then the Lord turned *and* looked at Peter; and **Peter remembered the word of the Lord,** how He had said to him, 'Before *the* cock crows, you shall deny Me three times.' And Peter went outside *and* wept bitterly" (vs 59-62).

Did Christ reject him for that? *No!* But that shows that we have to really understand that there is always a battle going on in the world and also it can come to us in the Church and in our private lives. Satan wants to get all of those who are Christians. He doesn't want any of us to enter into the Kingdom of God.

Let's see that Peter learned that lesson! He learned not to exalt himself, not to think that he was something high and mighty.

1-Peter 5:1: "*The* elders who *are* among you I exhort, even as a fellow elder, and an *eye*witness of the sufferings of Christ, and a partaker of the glory that is about to be revealed: **Feed the flock of God**…" (vs 1-2).

Did he learn the lesson of John 21, *feed My sheep, feed My lambs; shepherd My sheep*? Yes, he did!

"…*that is* among you, exercising oversight not by compulsion, but willingly; not in fondness of dishonest gain, but *with an* eager *attitude*" (v 2). Why? *We'll see in a minute!*

Verse 3: "Not as exercising lordship over *your* possessions; but *by* being examples to the flock *of God*. And when the Chief Shepherd is manifested, you shall receive an unfading, *eternal* crown of glory. In the same manner, *you* younger men be subject to *the* older men; and all *of you* be subject to one another, **being clothed with humility**…" (vs 3-5).

Peter learned the less of humility, and that involved Satan desiring him and him denying Jesus three times.

"…because God sets Himself against *the* proud, but He gives grace to *the* humble. Be humbled, therefore, under the mighty hand of God so that He may exalt you in *due* time" (vs 5-6). *Quite a lesson to learn!* But notice how Peter ends this.

Whenever there is pride and vanity and being uplifted, there is an entrance for Satan the devil. Did we see that in the Church of God in one of its leaders? Yes! *In more than one!* What happened? *You know the rest of the story!*

Verse 7: Casting all your cares upon Him, because He cares for you. **Be sober! Be vigilant!** For your adversary *the* devil is prowling about as a roaring lion, seeking anyone he may devour. Whom **resist,** steadfast in the faith, knowing *that* the same afflictions are being fulfilled among your brethren who *are* in *the* world" (vs 7-9).

We always have to be *vigilant, ready, seeking and doing the will of God!*

Notice what God will do for us, but this doesn't mean that we let down our guard. It just means that God gives us peace because we love Him, obey Him and resist the devil and not exalt ourselves!

Verse 10: "Now, may the God of all grace, Who has called us unto His eternal glory in Christ Jesus, after *you* have suffered a little while, **Himself perfect you, establish, strengthen, *and* settle you**." *That's what God will do!*

- we don't get lifted up in pride
- we don't get lifted up in vanity
- we don't get lifted up in authority
- we don't treat the brethren as if they are our possessions and we rule over them

That is satanic! That is not of God!

Satan is out there seeking whom he may devour. Remember that the ones he wants to get are those who are in the Church of God and have the Spirit of God!

2-Timothy 2:15: "Diligently *study* to show yourself approved unto God, a workman who does not *need to be* ashamed, rightly dividing the Word of the Truth."

Why? *Because when you study and God's Spirit is in you, with you and the words of God are going into your mind, you're developing the mind of Christ!*

Notice what he also told them, because here is how Satan comes in.

Verse 16: "But avoid profane and vain babblings because they will *only* give rise to more ungodliness, and their words will eat away at the body like gangrene; of whom are Hymeneus and Philetus, who have gone astray from the Truth…" (vs 16-18).

How does that happen? *With ideas that are not in accord with God's Word! That are not in accord with God's plan!* Just like Peter said, 'Don't rule over them as with possessions.'

"…claiming that the resurrection has already taken place…" (v 18).

They were probably saying that Jesus was the only One resurrected, but all the rest of us, our souls are immortal and go to heaven! That's something! He said in 1-Cor. 15—the resurrection chapter—that some of them said there was no resurrection.

"…and are destroying the faith of some. Nevertheless, the foundation of God stands firm, having this seal: '***The* Lord knows those who are His,**' and, '**Let everyone who calls upon the name of Christ depart from unrighteousness**'" (vs 18-

19).

Verse 20: "But in a great house there are not only vessels of gold and silver, but also of wood and clay and some *are* for honor; and some *are* for dishonor. Therefore, if anyone has purged himself from these… [those works that are wood, hay an stubble and that follows closely with 1-Cor. 3, all the error that he is talking about] …he will be a vessel for honor, having been sanctified and *made* serviceable to the Master, *and* having been prepared for every good work" (vs 20-21).

Verse 22: "But flee youthful lusts; and pursue righteousness, faith, love *and* peace with those who are calling on the Lord out of a pure heart. But foolish and ignorant speculations reject, knowing that they engender arguments. Now, it is obligatory *that* a servant of *the* Lord not be argumentative… [to the point of overbearing to make false doctrine acceptable] …but gentle toward all, competent to teach, forbearing, in meekness correcting those who set themselves in opposition; **if perhaps God may grant them repentance unto acknowledging of *the* Truth, and *that* they may wake up *and escape* from the devil's snare**, who have been taken captive by him to *do* his will" (vs 22-26).

Yes, he goes about as a *roaring lion!* Let's see that the devil is always busy and active. Always wanting to get people to slack off.

That's okay, you're in good shape, you don't need to pray today. You don't need to study today. Surely God will understand that. You know, you really know a lot, so why should you study?

Well, the truth is that the words that God speaks, they are life and they are spirit, they give life! They are layered and stacked with meaning after meaning, after meaning.

So, let's go through very quickly some points of the seven churches, and let's see, because sin that so easily overtakes us.

Church at Ephesus:

They were righteous, they worked and they tested the false apostles. They found them liars and they hated the deeds of the Nicolaitans. But Jesus says this:

Revelation 2:4: "Nevertheless, I have *this* against you, that you have left your first love." *Sounds an awful lot like the Laodiceans!* That's why we have to take each day for today and be vigilant and realize that Satan is there.

Verse 5: "Therefore, remember from where you have fallen, and repent, and do the first works;

for if *you do* not, I will come to you quickly; and I will remove your lampstand out of its place unless you repent."

Church at Smyrna:

They are weak and poor, but who are faithful to God. They were the ones that the synagogue of Satan wanted to get.

Verse 9: "I know your works and tribulation and poverty (but you are rich), and the blasphemy of those who declare themselves to be Jews and are not, but *are* a synagogue of Satan. Do not fear any of the things that you are about to suffer…." (vs 9-10) *Be faithful unto death!*

Satan is after every single church! *So, we need to be vigilant!*

Church at Pergamos:

They lived right there in Pergamos where Satan's seat was, right close. They were so close to it that they thought the way of Satan's religious hierarchy of the authority from the top down—the Nicolaitans—was the way to run it. They thought that it's better to have the Lord's Supper—called the Eucharist or the Sacrifice of the Mass—and eat things sacrificed to idols.

What does this say? *They had idols, did things Satan's way, and they thought that they were doing good!*

Notice what Jesus said to them, v 16: "Repent! For if *you* do not *repent*, I will come to you quickly, and will make war against them with the sword of My mouth."

Did God fight against Israel when they sinned? *Yes!* He even said that King Nebuchadnezzar of Babylon was 'My servant.'

Right here it's the same thing. Will He fight against us? *Yes!* He will bring to pass all the warnings that He has given in the book. That's *the sword of His mouth!*

So, anyone who has an ear, let him hear!

Church at Thyatira:

They really, really got all mixed up in it. They had difficulties, they had Jezebel the prophetess leading everyone astray.

Verse 20: "But I have a few things against you, because you allow the woman Jezebel, who calls herself a prophetess, to teach and to seduce My servants into committing fornication and eating things sacrificed to idols." *Gave her space to repent!*

Even gave space for the Catholic Church to repent; v 21: "And I gave her time to repent of her fornication, but she did not repent."

That took place in the 1600s at the Council of Trent. There was group of Catholics at that time who said that they needed to get rid of the traditions and idols and follow the Word of God, *but they were voted down!* They didn't repent!

Verse 22: "Behold, I will cast her into a bed, and those who commit adultery with her into great tribulation, unless they repent of their works. And I will kill her children with death… [the second death] …**and all the churches shall know**…" (vs 22-23).

God does this, and this is why we need to stay close to God and not get caught up into any of the things of Satan the devil in any way!

"…**that I am He Who searches** *the* **reins and hearts; and I will give to each of you according to your works**" (vs 23). *Quite a thing! That is heavy correction!*

Verse 24: "But to you I say, and to *the* rest who *are* in Thyatira, as many as do not have this doctrine, and **who have not known the depths of Satan,** as they speak; I will not cast upon you any other burden."

That's what Satan wants to do with the Churches of God! Completely capture them! That's why we know that this Day of Atonement is important, because *it pictures removing Satan!* Look at what happened to the Church down through history.

Church at Sardis:

Was dead! They had a name that they lived, but they only had a few doctrines that they were faithful with. Satan probably brought all of that upon them as well. It doesn't say so directly, but it indicates this.

Church at Philadelphia:

We've covered this quite extensively, or will, and the synagogue of Satan comes after them. Jesus says:

Revelation 3:11: "**Behold, I am coming quickly; hold fast that which you have so that no one may take away your crown**."

Who wants to take away the crown? *Satan the devil!* So, we've got to be diligent!

Verse 12: "The one who overcomes will I make a pillar in the Temple of My God, and he shall not go out anymore; and I will write upon him the name of My God and the name of the city of My God, the New Jerusalem, which will come down out of heaven from My God; and *I will write upon him My new name.*"

Church at Laodicea:

They get rich and increased with goods, and that's one of Satan's greatest tricks! So, they become lukewarm and complacent; they think that everything is good.

Just because there aren't too many troubles, don't believe it! Believe God! Believe that *Satan wants you to lose your salvation!*

Verse 18: "I counsel you to buy from Me gold purified by fire so that you may be rich; and white garments so that you may be clothed, and the shame of your nakedness may not be revealed; and to anoint your eyes with eye salve, so that you may see."

They don't understand, and it looks like they don't have the Spirit of God!

Verse 19: "As many as I love, I rebuke and chasten. Therefore, be zealous and repent. Behold, I stand at the door and knock…. [this is the door of the mind] …**If anyone hears My voice**… [the words of God] …**and opens the door**…" (vs 19-20).

You have to yield to God, and let the Word of God and the Spirit of God work within you. You have to open your mind to God! Not having the door closed and be complacent in your own self-righteousness not knowing that you really are not there.

"…I will come in to him…" (v 20)—*when they're converted,* so a great number of them are not converted; they have an opportunity to become converted, if they repent!

"…and will sup with him, and he with Me. To the one who overcomes will I give *authority* to sit with Me in My Throne, even as I also overcame, and sat down with My Father in His Throne. The one who has an ear, let him hear what the Spirit says to the churches" (vs 20-22).

So, you know for sure that Satan the devil is active and alive in this world today! He wants to get those who are the true servants and brethren of God, anyway he can. To let them

- lose their first love
- accept false doctrines
- go into the things of satanism
- become dead
- become lukewarm

Amazing!

Brethren, now we know how important this day of Atonement in picturing the removal of Satan the devil is! Everywhere he is and what he does is *destruction, lies, ruin, agony and misery that he's bringing on the whole world* and **wants to bring upon the people of God!**

So, we have to be strong and resist the devil, and not yield to any temptations of the devil, because we need to make it into the Kingdom of God!

This is the full meaning of the Day of Atonement!

Scriptural References:

1) Revelation 12:9
2) 1 John 5:19
3) Leviticus 23:26-32, 25
4) Leviticus 16:5, 7-10, 16-21
5) Revelation 20:1-3
6) Leviticus 16:22, 26-27, 29, 31, 30, 33-34
7) Ezekiel 28:1-9, 12-18
8) Isaiah 14:11-15
9) Matthew 4:1
10) Matthew 3:16-17
11) Matthew 4:1-9
12) Luke 4:5-8
13) 2 Corinthians 4:1-5
14) 2 Corinthians 11:13-14
15) Revelation 12:9
16) Revelation 13:1-2, 4
17) Revelation 19:20
18) Revelation 20:1-3
19) 2 Thessalonians 2:3-4, 7-10
20) Matthew 16:15-18, 20-23
21) Luke 22:29-34, 59-62
22) 1 Peter 5:1-10
23) 2 Timothy 2:15-26
24) Revelation 2:4-5, 9-10, 16, 20-24
25) Revelation 3:11-12 18-22

Scriptures referenced, not quoted:

- Numbers 29
- Hebrews 9
- Genesis 2
- 1 Corinthians 15
- John 21

FRC:bo
Transcribed: 8/10/20
Reformatted: 12/2020

CHAPTER FIFTY-SEVEN

Welcome to the Feast of Tabernacles
Be Filled with the Knowledge of God's Will
Fred R. Coulter

Greetings, brethren! Welcome to the Feast of Tabernacles!

It's been quite a year with the Wuhan Chinese Virus, and all of the things going on with it. But now is the time to set all of that aside, even though we still have to make provisions for it in many cases.

This is what we need to keep our mind on; God wants us:

- to dwell with Him
- to live with Him
- to assist Jesus Christ in saving the world

Think about that for a calling; that's quite a calling! To save the world!

It's going to be in the worst condition that it has ever been when we take over. What's the most important thing that we need to keep in mind for the Feast of Tabernacles. We will see that it has to do with the character that God builds in us as we yield to Him, and He and Christ dwell with in us!

So, here's a question in Psa. 15 that David asked the Lord, because he understood.

Psalm 15:1: "LORD, who shall dwell in Your tabernacle?...." *That's the great tabernacle of God, and that will develop into the new heaven and the new earth; New Jerusalem!*

Verse 2: "He who **walks uprightly,** and **works righteousness**..." *Well, the only way you can walk uprightly is with the commandments and laws of God!*

Righteousness comes from God! The righteousness of God given to us through the power of the Holy Spirit!

"...and **speaks the Truth** in his heart" (v 2).

- no agendas
- no two-facedness
- no infiltrators

None of that!

It's amazing how much is in the Old Testament relating to those of us in the New Testament and what it's going to be like, and how it's going to be carried out and what it will be.

Isaiah 51:1: "Hearken to Me..."—*meaning hear to listen and obey; hearken to God!* That's the most important thing for us to do.

"...you who follow after righteousness..." (v 1). *That's what we do!* We are seeking the righteousness of God, *not our own* righteousness as Paul said, **but the righteousness that comes from God!** That's what this Feast of Tabernacles pictures.

"...you who seek the LORD... [we're to seek Him with all our heart, mind, soul and being] ...Look to **the Rock** *from which* you were cut..." (v 1). Who is that Rock? *Jesus Christ!*

"...and to the hole of the pit *from which* you were dug" (v 1). In other words, pulled out of the depths of Satan the devil!

As I read v 2 I want you to think in your mind Gal. 3, 'If you are Christ's, you are Abraham's seed and heirs according to the promise.' See how this ties in with:

Verse 2: "Look to Abraham your father, and to Sarah *who* bore you; for I called him alone, and blessed him, and made him many."

In Rom. 4 it says that he understood that he was to be heir of the world! Of course, Abraham is going to be right there next to God carrying all of this out. We're going to be there as kings and priests and doing the things that we need to do to teach the people and bring many sons into glory.

Verse 3: "For the LORD shall comfort Zion; He will comfort all her waste places..."—*the whole world!* Think about comforting the world! Not just the people, but the earth itself!

"...and He will make her wilderness like Eden, and her desert like the garden of the LORD. Joy and gladness shall be found in it, thanksgiving and the voice of melody" (v 3). *Just think what that's going to be*:

- no more war
- no more death
- no more killing
- no more Satan the devil

What a time that is going to be!

Verse 4: "Hearken to Me, My people; and give ear to Me, O My nation…"

This is what God is doing with us; He is preparing us to take over the world. Keep that in mind, and that's why we need to learn the lessons that we need to learn, *now!*

1-Peter 2:3: "If you yourselves have indeed tasted that the Lord *is* gracious…"—*which we have through everything that we do and live!*

Verse 4: "To Whom coming, *as to* a living Stone… [just like we talked about before] …rejected indeed by men, but chosen by God, *and* precious, you also, **as living stones, are being built up** *as a* **spiritual house**—a Holy priesthood—… [that's what we will be, kings and priests] …to offer up spiritual sacrifices, acceptable to God through Jesus Christ. For this reason it says in the Scripture, 'Behold, I place in Zion *the* Cornerstone, chosen *and* precious; and the one who believes in Him shall never be put to shame.' The preciousness *is* to **you,** therefore, **who believe**…" (vs 4-7).

Let's do this during this Feast of Tabernacles: Let's set aside *every worry, every trouble, every burden, everything that troubles us!* Set it aside and let God give us:

- happiness
- joy
- understanding
  - ✓ in His Word
  - ✓ in His Truth
  - ✓ in His promises

For us! He's called us to be His children; His very children, indeed!

Verse 9: "But you *are* **a chosen stock**…"

- Isn't that true?
- Why are you here?
- *Because you answered the call!*

When you answered the call, *God chose you and me! All the rest down through history!* We are those who are living in the last times, and *God is giving us knowledge, wisdom and understanding to prepare us* to really be those who are assisting to help save the world when Christ returns.

In ages past they had no knowledge of what the end-times would really be like and all the things that take place.

"…**a royal priesthood, a Holy nation, a people for a possession** *of God*… [His very own children through the power of His Spirit] …that you might proclaim His *excellent* virtues… [to the whole world] …Who called you out of darkness into His marvelous light; who once *were* not a people, but now *are the* people of God; who had not received mercy, but now have received mercy" (vs 9-10).

We're going to help extend mercy to the whole world! Think about that! That's quite a thing!

Isaiah 51:5: "My righteousness *is* near… [and never before has that been more true than now] …My salvation has gone out…"—***to all who are called and received the Holy Spirit of God!*** That's what's going to happen during the Millennium, and we will bring it out.

"…and My arms shall judge the people; the isles shall wait upon Me, and on My arm they shall trust. Lift up your eyes to the heavens…" (vs 5-6).

Here's a good thing to understand. If you have the DVD: *True Fellowship with God,* let me tell you that if you get down and depressed, and overburdened with things, you pray to God and get out that DVD ***and realize the greatness of the calling of God! And that*** <u>***He's given us true***</u> <u>***fellowship with Him and Jesus Christ!***</u>

- that why we're here
- this is what the Feast of Tabernacles is all about
  - ✓ living in the Kingdom
  - ✓ living with God
  - ✓ teaching the people of the world
  - ✓ bringing many sons and daughters into the Kingdom of God
  - ✓ bringing happiness and joy to the whole world

through the power of God!

No place in the world, nor any other thing in this world can even compare to what God has promised to give us! Keep that in mind and watch that video *True Fellowship with God!*

Verse 6: "Lift up your eyes to the heavens, and look upon the earth beneath; for the heavens shall vanish away like smoke, and the earth shall become old like a garment… [talking about preparation for New Jerusalem; think about that clear back here in Isaiah—800s$_{B.C.}$] …and its inhabitants shall die in the same way. **But My salvation**… [this is the greatest thing of all] …**shall be forever**…"

All of this that we're going through right now will seem like just a few minutes of difficulties *in the passing of time of eternity.* Think about that!

Verse 7: Hearken to Me, you who know righteousness… [that's us] …the people in whose heart *is* My Law…"

Heb. 10 says that 'this is the covenant that I will make with them in those days.' *This is the covenant that God is making with us now: that 'I will write My laws and commandments in their hearts and minds!*

Now you know why Bible study is so important!

"…do not fear the reproach of men, nor be afraid of their revilings; for the moth shall eat them up like a garment, and the worm shall eat them like wool; but **My righteousness shall be forever,** and **My salvation from generation to generation**" (vs 7-8).

When God's plan is all over it's not necessary for salvation, because all will be saved, so it's "…from generation to generation" until it's fulfilled. Here's what we are to do:

- we come to God for this
- we come to His Word for this
- we use His Truth for this

Verse 9: "Awake! Awake! Put on strength, O arm of the LORD. Awake, as in the ancient days, in the generations of old. Was it not You *who* cut Rahab into pieces, piercing the serpent?" *God is the One Who got rid of Satan the devil!*

Verse 11: "Therefore, the redeemed of the LORD shall return…"—*talking about the saving of Israel and bringing them back,* but it's also talking about **us** in the first resurrection!

"…and come with singing into Zion; and everlasting joy *shall be* upon their head…." (v 11).

- no more sorrow
- no more tears
- no more death
- no more pain

"…Gladness and joy shall overtake *them*; sorrow and mourning shall flee away. 'I, even I, *am* He Who comforts you….'" (vs 11-12)

That's what we need now with all the things we've gone through we need:

- comfort
- strength
- redemption
- God's blessing
- God's intervention
- God's Law
- God's Truth

And we need to have a marvelous and wonderful Feast of Tabernacles!

"…Who *are* you, that you should be afraid of a man that shall die, or of the son of man who *is* made *as* grass?" (v 12).

Verse 15: "'But **I *am* the LORD your God**, Who divided the sea, so that its waves roared' (the LORD of hosts *is* His name)."

Here it is for all of us, because this is what we're going to do when we're kings and priests:

Verse 16: "And I have put My words in your mouth…" *The words of God; that's what we need*:

- the Truth of God
- the love of God
- the comfort of God
- the understanding of where we're going
- the understanding of why we're here
- the understanding of what we're doing

So, we look at the world all in turmoil and not knowing what's going on, think about *how precious this is!*

"…and I have covered you in the shadow of My hand, that I may plant the heavens and lay the foundations of the earth, and say to Zion, '**You** are My people'" (v 16). *That's what it is for us, the people of God!*

There are a lot of Psalms that talk about the Kingdom of God! Do a study through there and look up every place where it talks about the Kingdom of God, and happiness and joy forever. What a great and wonderful thing that is going to be.

Psalm 68:16: "Why do you gaze in envy, O mountain range, at the mountain **God has chosen for His resting place**?…."—*one place in Jerusalem!*

When Christ and the saints come back the Mt. Olives is going to raise up to be high. We'll talk about the tabernacle that God is going to put there. What a beautiful thing that's going to be!

"…Yea, **the LORD will dwell in it forever**" (v 16).

Verse 20: "Our God is the God of salvation; for unto the sovereign Lord belong the issues of death"—*referring to the resurrection!*

Verse 32: "Sing unto God, you kingdoms of the earth… " *That's what it's going to be!*

Think about when the Sabbath begins at one end of the earth, it's going to be raising songs, prayers, joy as it goes clear around the world to complete the Sabbath for the whole world. Think about what it's going to be for the Feast; *great indeed!*

"…O sing praises unto the LORD. Selah. To Him Who rides upon the heaven of heavens which are of old; lo, He sends out His voice, a mighty voice. Ascribe power to God: His majesty is over Israel, and His strength is in the clouds. O God, You are awesome from Your Holy sanctuary… [God right there in that great tabernacle] …the God of Israel is He who gives strength and power to the people. Blessed be God" (vs 32-35).

That's quite a thing, indeed! *That's what God has called us to!* God is preparing that right now. Everything that God is doing is going to come to pass as God has said, in the way that God has said, at the time that God determines that it's going to be. Here's what God is doing, and this includes all people of the world.

Think about this, the last thing that God prepares in preparation for the coming Kingdom and the last calling that He's going to give that will be answered, is to the 144,000 and the great innumerable multitude. Perhaps that will be the greatest number of people saved in all the plan of God. *That's something!* The reason that Christ came and what He did and what He's doing is right here:

Ephesians 2:16: "And *that* He might reconcile both… [Jew and Gentile] …to God in one body through the cross, having slain the enmity by it."

- the enmity of carnal nature
- the enmity of the Jewish traditions
- the enmity of all religions

when they're called out and come to God in conversion!

Verse 17: "Now when He came, He preached the Gospel—peace to you who *were* far off and to those who *were* near. For through Him…"

- our Savior
- our Lord
- our Master
- our High Priest in heaven right now
- and King over the whole world shortly!

"…we both have *direct* access by one Spirit to the Father" (v 17).

When we pray, it goes directly to the Father and to Jesus Christ. That is a marvelous thing, indeed, for us! That is what is meant by *grace upon grace!*

- grace to have our sins forgiven
- grace to draw near to God
- grace to have direct contact with God the Father and Jesus Christ
- grace in the calling that we are going to be those who are going to rule under Jesus Christ and bring peace to this world

All of that is grace!

Verse 19: "So then, you are no longer aliens and foreigners; but *you are* fellow citizens with the saints, and *are* **of the household of God**."

- bearing the name of God
- the spiritual begettal of God
- at the resurrection blossomed into its fullness

Verse 20: "**You are being built up on the foundation of the apostles and prophets, Jesus Christ Himself being *the* chief Cornerstone**."

Everything has to come through Christ, and He is the One Who gave us direct access to God the Father in heaven above. Remember what He told the disciples on the night before He was arrested:

Heretofore, you have asked nothing in My name, I say to you, 'You pray to the Father for He Himself loves you, and you pray in My name.

That's a paraphrase of John 16!

Verse 21: "In Whom all the building, being conjointly fitted together, is increasing into a Holy temple in *the* Lord":

- a tabernacle
- a temple
- a building
- a nation
- a priesthood

The righteousness of God in all of it!

Verse 22: "In Whom **you also are being built together for a habitation of God** in *the* Spirit." *That's really a profound and wonderful thing indeed, when we really, really understand it and grasp it!*

Let's see something else, quite a few important things. Col. 1 is one of the most important chapters in the Epistles of Paul. It tells us our connection with God the Father through Jesus Christ and the whole plan of God and what He is doing right now.

Colossians 1:9: "For this cause we also, from the day that we heard *of it*… [their love and faithfulness to Christ] …do not cease to pray for you and to ask that you may **be filled with the knowledge of His will**…" *That's what we will cover during the Feast of Tabernacles*:

- the will of God for us
- the will of God for the world
- the will of God for those who were never called, but will be when we get to the last day

"…**in all wisdom and spiritual understanding**" (v 1). *In other words, to really get right the way God wants!*

Verse 10: "That you may walk worthily of the Lord, unto all pleasing, being fruitful in every good work and growing in the knowledge of God." *That's what we must constantly do*:

- grow in grace and knowledge
- grow in understanding
- grow in wisdom
- grow in Truth
- grow in the Laws of God
- grow in righteousness
- grow in Holiness

All of that together!

Verse 11—notice what this will do: "Being **strengthened**… [that's what we need] …with all power according to the might of His glory, unto all endurance and long-suffering with joy." *That's what we need to do with this Feast of Tabernacles!*

Remember what it says in John 6:44: "**No one can come to Me unless the Father, Who sent Me, draws him**; and I will raise him up at the last day." *And He also says in another place that 'no one can come to the Father except through Me!'* Both of Them are working together and that's how we got here:

- where we are
- what we're doing
- where we're going
- how we're going to do it

I want you to understand that God the Father Himself is the One Who intervenes in our lives when we call upon Him to do this:

Verse 12: "Giving thanks to the Father, Who has made us qualified for the share of the inheritance of the saints in the Light."

The Father is working with us to qualify us; that's why we need to respond:

- in love
- in truth
- in obedience
- in yieldedness

through
- prayer
- study
- daily living
- everything that we do

When we make mistakes, sin and fall, get up on your knees and pray and repent, and have God forgive you; *He is rescuing you!*

Verse 13: "Who has **personally rescued us from the power of darkness**…"—*from Satan the devil*—personally!

In the Greek there is a verb called *the middle voice*, which is the subject is also the object of the

action. God Himself is doing this personally so that through us it comes back to Him as His sons and daughters!

"…and has transferred *us* unto the Kingdom of the Son of His love" (v 13).

We are not yet in the Kingdom of God, because flesh and blood cannot inherit the Kingdom of God, *but we are under the jurisdiction of the Kingdom of God, and that comes first before anything else!*

Verse 14: "In Whom we have redemption through His own blood, *even* the remission of sins; Who is *the* image of the invisible God, *the* Firstborn of all creation" (vs 14-15).

The Firstborn from the dead of all the creation that God is doing in His Church through His people! This is important for us to grasp!

Verse 16: "Because by Him were all things created, the things in heaven and the things on earth, the visible and the invisible, whether *they be* thrones, or lordships, or principalities, or powers: all things were created by Him and for Him." *And He has the pre-eminence of all!*

Now, this is what we want. Let's see, if we can, at this Feast all come together in love and fellowship, whether there are two, three, five or a larger group. We don't know what it will be, depending on what transpires. But nevertheless— even if you are alone—that makes no difference. If you have the love in you, when you get together with the brethren, you will love them as well.

John wrote that *because God has loved us and given us His son as a Savior, we are duty-bound to love one another!* Let's keep that in mind as I read this:

Ephesians 1:15—Paul said: "For this cause… [everything above talks about the calling of God; the Father intervening Himself personally] …I also, after hearing of the faith in the Lord Jesus that is among you, and the love toward all the saints, do not cease to give thanks for you, making mention of you in my prayers" (vs 15-16).

Notice this, and let this be so during this Feast of Tabernacles, that we can come a to a greater, more profound and more spiritually filled knowledge of God's plan in His love for us and His love for humanity, and our part in it!

Verse 17: "That the God of our Lord Jesus Christ, the Father of glory, may give you *the* spirit of wisdom and revelation in *the* knowledge of Him."

Verse 18 is something, because this is a real opening of the mind to the Truth. That's what it means, because you don't have a third eye. Paul expresses it that way because it's the receiving of the true knowledge of God spiritually.

Verse 18: "*And* may **the eyes of your mind** be enlightened in order that you may comprehend… [here's what that will do]: …**what is the hope of His calling, and what *are* the riches of the glory of His inheritance in the saints, and what is the exceeding greatness of His power toward us who believe, according to the inner working of His mighty power,** which He wrought in Christ, when He raised Him from *the* dead, and set *Him* at His right hand in the heavenly *places*, far above every principality and authority and power and lordship, and **every name that is named—not only in this age, but also in the *age* to come**" (vs 18-21).

That's what this Feast of Tabernacles is about, *the age to come to save the world, to save all those who will then enter into the Kingdom of God!*

Brethren, have a wonderful and great Feast!

Scriptural References:

1) Psalm 15:1-2
2) Isaiah 51:1-2
3) 1 Peter 2:3-7, 9-10
4) Isaiah 51:5-9, 11-12, 15-16
5) Psalm 68:16-20, 32-35
6) Ephesians 2:16-22
7) Colossians 1:9-11
8) John 6:44
9) Colossians 1:9-16
10) Ephesians 1:15-21

Scriptures referenced, not quoted:

- Galatians 3
- Romans 4
- Hebrews 10
- John 16

Also referenced: DVD: *True Fellowship with God*

FRC:bo
Transcribed: 7/26/20
Reformatted: 1/2021

CHAPTER FIFTY-EIGHT

How the Millennium Will Start
Fred R. Coulter

Welcome, brethren! We're going to start a little differently here. Let's come to 1-Cor. 1, because more and more the Holy Days are coming under attack, especially by the Protestants, by Seventh Day Adventists, and by the Church of God Seventh Day. We're going to understand something here very important concerning the Holy Days from the point of view of *how* we understand.

1-Corinthians 1:17—*the Apostle Paul writes*: "For Christ did not send me to baptize, but to preach the Gospel—not with *the* wisdom of words… [the words and philosophies of men] …lest the cross of Christ be made void. For to those who are perishing the preaching of the cross… [that includes the whole plan of God] …is foolishness; but to us who are being saved, it is the power of God. For it is written, 'I will destroy the wisdom of the wise, and I will nullify the understanding of those who understand.' Where *is the* wise? Where *is the* scribe? Where *is the* disputer of this age? Did not God make foolish the wisdom of this world?" (vs 17-20).

You compare the Holy Days of God and the whole plan of God to everything that the world has and their religions and their holidays; it is foolishness. Yet, *they think* it is wisdom. They look at what we do and think we are foolish, and think that we are going back *under* the Law. That's not the case, because keeping the commandments of God and having the faith of Jesus Christ (Rev. 14:12) go hand-in-hand. They think that He's destroyed them.

Verse 21: "For since in the wisdom of God the world through *its own* wisdom did not know God, it pleased God to save those who believe through the foolishness of preaching"

- How are we going to understand not only the preaching, but the writings, the Word of God?
- What the apostles have written and preserved for us?
- What God inspired and had written and preserved for us in the Old Testament?

1-Corinthians 2:9: "But according as it is written, '*The* eye has not seen… [people are not going to understand these things by just sitting down and reading alone] …Nor *the* ear heard, neither have entered into *the* heart of man, *the* things which God has prepared for those who love Him.'"

- God is preparing for us
- God is preparing for this world

Verse 10: "But God has revealed *them* to us by His Spirit…"

There is an absolute dividing line, and that dividing line is determined by the Spirit of God. You understand the things in the Scriptures by the Spirit of God. As we have seen: ***line upon line, precept upon precept, here a little and there a little, and rightly dividing the Word of God*** to put it together. Also, to have the understanding and the attitude that the Word of God teaches us His plan. ***That has to be revealed!***

"…For the Spirit **searches all things**…" (v 10). *Not just the New Testament, but all things*:

- the Old Testament
- each individual that comes into being in the world
- all of those whom God calls

"…**even the deep things of God**" (v 10). *The understanding of the Holy Days are part of the deep things of God!*

Verse 11: "For who among men understands the things of man except *by* the spirit of man, which *is* in him? In the same way also, the things of God… [the Holy Days are part of the things of God] …**no one understands except *by* the Spirit of God**…."

We've seen the problem that has happened in the Church here in recent years; *they began bringing in the spirit of the world!* As they brought in the spirit of the world they brought in the world and *their beliefs* and *pushed out the Spirit of God and the Truth of God!*

That's why Paul says, v 12: "Now, we have not received the spirit of the world, **but the Spirit that *is* of God, so that we might know the things graciously given to us by God**; which things we also speak, not in words taught by human wisdom, but in *words* taught by *the* Holy Spirit *in order to* communicate spiritual things by spiritual *means*" (vs 12-13).

That's why the Holy Days are important because these are the appointed times of God, the appointed seasons of God. These are commanded convocations.

Psa. 119—let's see another thing that God wants us to know to understand. This is important because you see, the Word of God is inspired by God. And as Jesus said, *'The words that I speak to you, they are Spirit and they are Life.'* So, we also see where David was inspired to write something very profound:

Psalm 119:18: "Open my eyes so that I may behold wondrous things out of Your Law."

That's what we are going to do with the Holy Days. We are going to see the wondrous things out of God's Law, out of God's Word—Old Testament, New Testament—put it all together and see and understand the plan of God and the meaning of the Feast of Tabernacles.

So, let's first of all go, as we always do, to Lev. 23, because one of the secret things of God that He has hidden, where He says that it is 'God's honor to hide something, or prerogative to hide it, but it is the honor of the king to dig it out.' That's what we have with all the Holy Days in Lev. 23.

It's awfully easy bringing in the spirit of the world, bringing in the spirit of the world's religions to say, 'Look at that, that's in the Old Testament.' They take that attitude because they do not understand and realize that Jesus Christ—Who they say they love, Who they say they follow, but they do not—that 'the God of the Old Testament was harsh and mean, and these Laws and these things we no longer have to do.' *By that very thing they cut themselves off from God!*

We started out with the Passover, Unleavened Bread, Pentecost, Trumpets, Atonement, and now here we are at the Feast of Tabernacles. *All of these things we have seen portrays a step-by-step revelation of the plan of God!* This is what we are to know, what we are to understand, and how we are to live our lives. In these days:

- *IF* we love God
- *IF* we serve God
- *IF* we are faithful to God
- *IF* we have God's Spirit in us

He will reveal more and more of His will out of His Word just like David said: 'Open my eyes that I may behold wondrous things out of Your Word.' And as Paul wrote, *they are revealed by God's Spirit!*

Leviticus 23:33: "And the LORD spoke to Moses saying, 'Speak to the children of Israel, saying, "The fifteenth day of this seventh month *shall be* the Feast of Tabernacles for seven days to the LORD. On the first day *shall be* a Holy convocation… [which is today] …You shall do no servile work *therein*. Seven days you shall offer an offering made by fire to the LORD. On the eighth day shall be a Holy convocation to you. And you shall offer an offering made by fire to the LORD. It *is* a solemn assembly. And you shall do no servile work *therein*"'" (vs 33-36).

Let's pay clear attention to v 37, because one of the ways that people attack the Word of God, attack what we do and try to discredit what we do is because they say that we are keeping the *feasts of the Jews*. That is an abominable lie. Notice what God says here:

Verse 37: "**These *are* the Feasts of the LORD**, which you shall proclaim to be Holy convocations…"

This is a summary of the whole chapter up to here. The Sabbath commandment sanctifies the Passover and all the Holy Days. That's why it's given in the first part of the chapter.

"…to offer an offering made by fire to the LORD, a burnt offering and a grain offering, a sacrifice, and drink offerings, everything on its day; besides the Sabbaths of the LORD, and besides your gifts, and besides all your vows, and besides all your freewill offerings, which you give to the LORD" (vs 37-38).

Now let's come to Num. 29 and let's see the commanded offerings that they were to give. These were the official offerings to God for the whole nation of Israel. Now the Feast of Tabernacles is different in relationship to the offerings that are given on the other days. First of all He shows that there was to be the morning and the evening sacrifice. Of course, they had the meal offering and the wine offering and the incense that would go with it. Then on the Sabbath they had special Sabbath offerings in addition to the continual burnt offering. Then He goes right through all of the Holy Days— the new moons and the Holy Days—and it is very interesting that *there is no commanded sacrifice at the tabernacle or temple for the Passover Day* because it was—as we have written extensively in *The Christian Passover* book—a domestic home kept Feast.

Let's see the tremendous offerings that were given. Now we also know that during the days of Solomon they had, beginning with—and including—the Feast of Trumpets, seven days dedication of the temple. Then they took a break so they could have Atonement and so forth, and then they come to the Feast of Tabernacles. They had so many thousands of people there, and so many thousands of sacrifices that were offered that they had to make smaller altars in different locations on the temple grounds. It was literally a fantastic and mammoth Feast. But here were the required offerings:

Numbers 29:12: "And on the fifteenth day of the seventh month you shall have a Holy convocation. You shall do no servile work, and you shall keep a feast to the LORD seven days. And you shall offer a burnt offering, a sacrifice made by fire, of a sweet savor to the LORD: thirteen young bulls… [one for every tribe] …two rams and fourteen lambs of the first year. They shall be without blemish" (vs 12-13).

Then their meal offering and the wine offering and so forth and a kid goat for a sin offering. That's besides the continual morning and evening sacrifice and their meal and drink offerings.

Now each day of the Feast the number of bullocks—while all the rest would remain the same—was decreased by one. Each one of these things shows a type of fulfillment and a progression in the plan of God.

Verse 32: "And on the seventh day seven bulls, two rams, and fourteen lambs of the first year without blemish; and their grain offering and their drink offerings…" (vs 32-33)—and so forth.

Verse 34: "And one goat *for* a sin offering…" Then on the eight day it reverts back to one bullock.

Verse 39: "You shall prepare these to the LORD in your appointed feasts, besides your vows and your freewill offerings, for your burnt offerings, and for your grain offerings, and for your drink offerings, and for your peace offerings."

So, there are the free-will offerings, there are the vows, and there are many things to consider. That's why God says when they would come to a Feast they were not to appear before the Lord empty.

Let's see the command for an offering, and we'll take up the offering here in just a bit.

Deuteronomy 16:16: "Three times in a year shall all your males appear before the LORD your God in the place which He shall choose: in the Feast of Unleavened Bread, and in the Feast of Weeks, and in the Feast of Tabernacles. And they shall not appear before the LORD empty, every man *shall give* as he is able…" (vs 16-17).

This is in addition to the burnt offerings, the peace offerings, the meal offerings and so forth that they were to give. Just like we find in Deut. 14, that if the way was too far they were to go ahead and sell the bullocks, and sell the lambs, and the rams and so forth, and take the money and come to Jerusalem and then use that money on whatever their soul desires.

We see in Luke 21—the time leading up to the Passover when Jesus was crucified—there were many coming and giving gifts into the treasury. It wasn't just animal sacrifices, meal offerings, incense and wine offerings, they also had monetary offerings. Since Christ, in fulfilling the Law and the Prophets, the part that He fulfilled in the Law was all the rituals and all the sacrifices that were given under the Old Covenant. But the whole thing of free-will offerings and giving to the Lord—especially on the Holy Days—continues through till today.

The daily offerings given, that was at the temple for the priests to do. That didn't mean that everyone was to come in and give an offering: part of an offering on one day, part of an offering on another day, part of an offering on another day all through the eight days. That had to do with the commanded sacrifices for the whole nation of Israel.

So, when we come to the New Testament it carries over because there is no temple, there is not a priesthood; Christ is our High Priest. When we come together *we are still to honor God by bringing an offering to Him!* I just bring this out in a way so that you understand how then we can go into the Old Testament, how with the Spirit of God we can understand what needs to be done.

(pause for offering)

The Feast of Tabernacles is what the whole world is waiting for. That is *the rule of God on earth!* **The Kingdom of God governing the whole world!**

In the world today we are seeing that God is letting man—under the guidance of Satan the devil and also by God's plan and purpose—just exactly like He told the Jews before they went into captivity that He raised up Nebuchadnezzar for the very purpose of taking them into captivity. If they fought against him, God would fight against them. At the time that Jesus came the Jews were actually looking for the Messiah. They knew He was the Messiah. But they didn't want to accept Him because He did not align Himself with them. They were expecting the Messiah to come to align with all of their institutions—the temple, the sacrifices, the government, throw out the Romans—and fight for them. When Jesus came the first time that's not what it was.

Let's see what Jesus told Pilate when he was questioning Him before He was scourged and sent out to be crucified.

John 18:33: "Then Pilate returned to the judgment hall and called Jesus, and said to Him, 'Are You the King of the Jews?' Jesus answered him, 'Do you ask this of yourself, or did others say *it* to you concerning Me?' Pilate answered Him, 'Am I a Jew? The chief priests and your own nation have delivered You up to me. What have You done?' Jesus answered, **'My Kingdom is not of this world**….'" (vs 33-36).

- God had a greater plan
- God has a greater purpose

God knows that the world cannot be run in the Kingdom of God unless there is planning, preparation, and the fullness of the plan of God comes to fruition!

"…'If My Kingdom were of this world, then would My servants fight, so that I might not be delivered up to the Jews. However, My Kingdom is not of this world'" (v 36). *Pilate couldn't understand that!*

One of the reasons that they delivered Him to Pilate was because He said He was King. Then the Jews falsely accused Him of wanting to usurp authority over Caesar. It put all the pressure on Pilate as to what to do.

Verse 37: "Pilate, therefore, answered Him, 'Then You are a king?' Jesus answered, '*As* you say, I am a king. For this *purpose* I was born, and for this *reason* I came into the world, that I may bear witness to the Truth. Everyone who is of the Truth hears My voice.' Pilate said to Him, 'What is Truth?'…." (vs 36-38).

That's exactly where we are today with the death of Truth in this world! So then, Pilate said he found no fault in Him.

Now let's look at another thing concerning the Kingdom of God, because the scribes and Pharisees were expecting it to appear immediately. They didn't understand that this was going to be *a spiritual kingdom* run by spiritual sons and daughters of God *over* the human beings on the earth. They wanted their own human power to be right under the Messiah so they could exercise the authority. God is not going to leave the Kingdom to people; only the sons and daughters of God, and they didn't understand that.

Luke 19:11: "Now, as they were listening to these things, He went on to speak a parable, because He was near Jerusalem, and they thought that the Kingdom of God was going to appear immediately."

They thought He was going to Jerusalem to take over; announce that He was the Messiah; rally all the armies of the Jews around; supernaturally with their armies and the power that He had, to destroy the Romans and get them out, and set up the Kingdom of God on earth. He wanted them to know it wasn't going to be that way.

Verse 12: "Therefore, He said, 'A certain nobleman set out to a distant country to receive a kingdom for himself, and to return.'"

They understood this because Herod went to Rome to be coroneted—this is Herod the Great—

and then when he came back, it took him three years to come back and conquer the Jews to be the king over Judea, as the Romans had sent him. So they understood what He was talking about here.

Verse 13: "And after calling ten of his servants, he gave to them ten pounds, and said to them, '**Trade until I come *back*.**' But his citizens hated him and sent an ambassador after him, saying, 'We are not willing to have this man reign over us'" (vs 13-14).

One of the very first things that has to be is Christ has to rule over you. But they didn't want Him to rule over them.

Verse 15: "And it came to pass that when he returned after receiving the kingdom, he directed that those servants to whom he had given the money be called to him…"

Then it went through one gained ten pounds, one gained five pounds, and the other one gained two pounds and so forth. Then we have someone who didn't do what they were supposed to do.

And he said, v 21: "For I was afraid of you, because you are a harsh man…."

- Isn't that interesting?
- Isn't that what the Protestants accuse the God of the Old Testament of being?
- Is that not one of the reasons that they don't do the things that Jesus has said?
- Is that not one of the reasons why the Catholic Church exists?

Yes, they don't want Christ to rule over them in their lives! They want a pope to worship and to rule over their lives. Absolutely amazing, isn't it?

"…'You take up what you did not lay down, and you reap what you did not sow.'…. [because it's *spiritually* built] … Then he said to him, 'Out of your *own* mouth I will judge you, *you* wicked servant!….'" (vs 21-22).

That's something you need to understand. Every single one of us are going to be judged according to our works, what we say and what we do. There are times when we say things that you better be very, very careful what you say, because God may take you up on what you say as your judgment, just like here.

"…'You knew that I am a harsh man, taking up what I did not lay down and reaping what I did not sow. Then why didn't you deposit my money in the bank, so that at my coming I might have received it with interest?' And he said to those who were standing by, 'Take the pound from him, and give *it* to the one who has ten pounds.' (And they said to him, 'Lord, he has ten pounds.') For I tell you that to everyone who has, *more* shall be given; but the one who does not have, even what he has shall be taken from him. Moreover, bring my enemies, those who were not willing *for* me to reign over them, and slay *them* here before me" (vs 22-27).

That's just a very good short summary of the return of Christ!

We also know that the very last thing just before Jesus ascended into heaven for the final time, the apostles said, 'Lord, will You restore the Kingdom at this time to Israel? He said, 'It's not given to you to know the times and seasons which the Father has put under His authority. But you go…'

In that case, go to Jerusalem and wait for the Holy Spirit. But for all of us we are to do that. We are not only to learn and know and understand the Word of God, but we are

- to go
- to do
- to preach
- to teach
- to do these things
- to occupy

by doing these things until Christ returns!

We are also going to see something very important here. Because when Jesus told Pilate that 'to this end was He born,' He was making very clear that He fulfilled this prophecy. Now, He didn't make it clear to Pilate because Pilate didn't understand it. But as we go back and as we know and understand the prophecies and read them and put all the Scriptures together, then we understand that's precisely what Jesus was talking about because He was born to be a King.

We're going to see *you* and *I* have been born—all of those that God has called have been born—*and having been converted we are called to be kings and priests!* That's a tremendous thing as we will see.

Isaiah 9:6: "For unto us a Child is born, unto us a Son is given; and the government shall be upon His shoulders… [He is going to reign, He is going to rule into the ages of eternity (book of Revelation)] …and His name shall be called Wonderful, Counselor, The Mighty God, The Everlasting Father, The Prince of Peace"—*because only Christ can bring peace!*

When Christ returns He is going to become a father by those who are converted—as we will see as we go down through the Feast of Tabernacles—by those who were converted during the Millennium as we rule and reign on this earth.

Verse 7: "Of the increase of *His* government and peace *there shall be* no end…"

So, God's plan is going to go on into the ages of eternity! Quite a tremendous and magnificent thing that God is going to do.

"…upon the throne of David, and over His Kingdom, to order it and to establish it with judgment and with righteousness from henceforth, even forever. The zeal of the LORD of hosts will do this" (v 7).

There's no getting around it. This is going to be done. It doesn't matter whether people believe or not, whether they understand or not, *it is going to happen!*

As we saw, the resurrection is on Pentecost, and we are there to receive our rewards and to receive our new name, the marriage of the Lamb and all those things that take place. Then the seven last plagues are poured out. Then Christ and all of the saints on the Sea of Glass return to the earth. *He's going to be King over all the earth!* That's going to be a tremendous day, *indeed!* We share in that!

Rev. 20[transcriber's correction]—let's follow that progression down. After Satan has been put away, and during the Millennium Satan won't be around. On the 7th day of the Feast we'll talk about why Satan is loosed for a short season; there's a purpose in that.

Satan is taken, he is bound, cast into the abyss. The next thing to take place is this:

Revelation 20:4: "And I saw thrones; and they that sat upon them, and judgment was given to them; and *I saw* the souls of those who had been beheaded for the testimony of Jesus, and for the Word of God, and those who did not worship the beast or his image, and did not receive the mark in their foreheads or in their hands; and they lived and reigned with Christ a thousand years."

That's quite a thing! This is the whole purpose and goal as to why we are called:

- so that we can be with Christ
- so that we can rule and reign with Him

That's the most important thing for us to understand! We'll cover—during the Feast—what is the most important thing we need to have and develop now so we *can* rule and reign with Christ.

Verse 5: "(But the rest of the dead did not live again until the thousand years were completed.)…. [then referring back to v 4 it says]: …**This *is* the first resurrection.** Blessed and Holy…" (vs 5-6)

Who is also called blessed and Holy? *God is!* As we know, we are to share the very glory of Christ. So it says:

Verse 6: "Blessed and Holy is the one who has part in the first resurrection; over these the second death has no power. But they shall be priests of God and of Christ, and shall reign with Him a thousand years." *That's going to be a tremendous thing! Absolutely marvelous!*

Let's see that's one of the promises. When we come to Rev. 2 & 3 even though there's a message to each one of the churches it always ends with **he that has an ear, let him hear what the Spirit says to the churches!**

Revelation 2:25: "But hold fast what you have until I come. And to the one who overcomes and keeps My works unto *the* end… [there are works to be kept] …I will give authority over the nations. and he shall shepherd them with an iron rod, as vessels of pottery are broken in pieces; as I have also received from My Father…" (vs 25-27).

- we are going to have full authority and control
- Christ is going to be King
- the twelve apostles will be sitting on 12 thrones judging the 12 tribes of Israel

Beyond that of Elijah and Moses, we don't have too much of an inkling of who's going to be doing what. But don't fear, *God has it all planned out and it's going to be all according to His will!*

I think we need to understand: you cannot—it will be impossible—have a one-world government unless the Islamic nations are tamed and brought into the modern world. That's what all of this is going to lead to. But yes, there are those things that take place in killing, and bombing, and kidnapping, and beheading and things like this.

I saw a very interesting documentary when it was leading up to the memorial of D-Day, and there were more mistakes and more casualties made on that first day on D-Day when the troops landed there. They had 5,000 casualties just the first day alone. Some of them landed at the wrong place. Some of the supplies didn't get to them the way that they should have. But never the less they overcame all those mistakes and they went in and the invasion was a success. They said, as it got to the end of the war, 'How are they going to democratize Germany and Japan?' Well, it hasn't been reported very much but right after the Germans surrendered, do you know what the German renegades—what we would call today, *insurgents*—were doing? They were blowing up railroad tracks, blowing up trucks and they were cutting telephone lines. It took a total of three more years before the occupational forces got

it under hand to where they could work with the Germans to bring about peace. That finally wasn't resolved until the Cold War ended and the wall was torn down. From that we're going to learn a lesson:

What is it going to be like when the Millennium begins? *Because we're going to rule and reign with Christ a thousand years!* We are going to enforce and bring the Government of God! Are we not going to have authority over the nations to rule them, or shepherd them with a rod of iron? *Yes, we are!*

Isa. 2—let's see what it tells us about this, and see something very important. Then we will look at the Scriptures that show how it will be done. Many times we read these things and go over them and we don't really fully expound them, or go through them in detail, *but we're going to today!*

Isaiah 2:1: "The word that Isaiah the son of Amoz saw concerning Judah and Jerusalem. And it shall come to pass, in the last days the mountain of the LORD'S house…"

As we know, it's a type of God's government. We read in Isa. 9 that the government is going to be on His shoulders and He's going to delegate to all the saints who are in the first resurrection so that they can rule and reign with Him. That's what it says, *we'll reign a thousand years with Him!*

"…Shall be established in the top of the mountains…" (v 2)—*because there will be other nations, but this is going to be the leading one!* The sons and daughters of God in the Kingdom of God ruling on earth will be with Christ ruling over the whole world.

"…And shall be exalted above the hills; and all nations shall flow unto it" (v 2).

Also, as we have seen in Zech. 14, one of the first things they are going to do is keep the Feast of Tabernacles. If they don't keep it, what's going to happen? *For those nations who don't keep it, then they aren't going to get any rain!* The Egyptians who don't come up, they're going to get the plague! Now that's what it means **to shepherd with a rod of iron!**

God has weapons far better than any army. God has power to execute these things far better than bombs, tanks, planes, and all of the specialty things that men have developed for war.

"…and all nations shall flow unto it" (v 2)—*Jerusalem!*

And it says here *Judah* (v 1), because it will be filled with resurrected sons of God who are considered *spiritual Jews.* Very interesting how these Scriptures come together.

Verse 3: "And **many** people shall go and say…" *Notice it doesn't say* ***all*** *people.* So, there will be those who will want to yield to God, the Kingdom of God, and it will start with Israel *first*.

"…'Come, and let us go up to the mountain of the LORD, to the house of the God of Jacob. And He will teach us of His ways, and we will walk in His paths.' For out of Zion shall go forth the Law…" (v 3).

- the very Law that the Protestants hate
- the Law of God has never changed

You need to understand that! Only the rituals and sacrifices have been superseded by greater…

"…and the Word of the LORD from Jerusalem. And He shall judge among the nations, and shall rebuke many people… [Why?] …and they shall beat their swords into plowshares…" (vs 3-4).

There's still going to be these insurgents, terrorists and remnants fighting against the implementation of the Kingdom of God on earth. Just like everything else that God does: He gives man choice and He gives man leeway to see whether they will obey or not. ***IF*** they will not, after a given period of time, then He's going to exercise His power and His authority over them so they are going to learn, *because God is not going to be mocked!*

"…and they shall beat their swords into plowshares, and their spears into pruning hooks. Nation shall not lift up sword against nation, neither shall they learn war anymore" (v 4). *He's going to judge the nations afar off!* That's exactly what He's going to do.

Since we have seen the kind of attitude and the kind of things that we have in the Middle East, and with the Muslim religion and so forth, let's see one of the most profound things that's going to take place after the return of Christ, after Israel is brought back from captivity and in the land. It's going to take a number of years. How long that will be we do not know. But all of those nations to the north and to the east, out of which came the army of 200-million that fought against Christ, as we saw in Rev. 16 with the seven last plagues.

Just remember there are billions, and billions, and billions of people over there and they're not all going to die. God has a plan. He knows that just like a lot of these insurgents that were after WWII in Germany, and that are in Iraq now after the transfer of sovereignty and all the things that have been going on there, they have to be ferreted out and they have to be put down, and they either have to repent or be exterminated. That's how God is going to handle it. That's what He means *rebuke them afar off*.

Now let's see what happens here, and what it's going to do for the Millennium. The beginning of the Millennium is going to be a very difficult time indeed. Some people will come and say, 'Oh, let's go up and learn God's way.' A lot of other people are going to say,

Well, we don't know about this. This looks like these are the aliens from outer space. We better go up and we better fight against them. We better take back the world to ourselves.

And that's exactly what they're going to try and do!

Ezekiel 38:1: "And the Word of the LORD came to me, saying, 'Son of man, set your face against Gog, the land of Magog, the chief ruler of Meshech, and Tubal, and prophesy against him '" (vs 1-2).

Verse 11 *so that we understand the time setting*: "And you shall say, 'I will go up to the land of unwalled villages…'" *You can't call Jerusalem unwalled villages!* As a matter of fact, they're building walls.

"…I will go *to* those that are at **rest**…" (v 11)—*because God deals with Israel first,* then the rest of the world.

So, God is going to deal with Israel first, and those nations who volunteer to come under the sovereignty of the Kingdom of God and the rule of Jesus Christ and the saints. There will be some who won't want to. As it says, great nations afar off He's going to rebuke. Well all these nations we're talking about here are afar off from Jerusalem.

Let's follow the story flow, v 3: "And say, "Thus says the Lord GOD, 'Behold, I *am* against you, O Gog, the chief ruler of Rosh, Meshech and Tubal. And I will turn you back, and put hooks into your jaws, and I will bring you out, and all your army, horses and horsemen, all of them clothed most gorgeously, a great assembly *with* buckler and shield, all of them swordsmen; Persia, Ethiopia, and Libya… [which actually means Kush and Phut from India] …with them, all of them *with* shield and helmet; Gomer and all his bands; the house of Togarmah *from* the uttermost parts of the north, and all his bands; *and* many people with you. Be prepared; yea, prepare for yourself, you and all your assembly that are assembled about you, and be a guard for them. After many days you will be summoned…" (vs 3-8).

God is going to rule on earth beginning in Jerusalem; bring back the captivity of the children of Israel out of their captivity; establish them in their land. They will be building. They will be planting. God will be blessing them. Then these nations out there who don't want to submit, they're going to know what's going on.

"…In the latter years you shall come into the land restored from war, gathered out of many people, on the mountains of Israel, which have always been waste… [since the fall of Jerusalem in 70A.D.]: …(But she has been brought out of the nations, and they shall dwell securely, **all of them**.) And you shall go up, coming like a storm. You shall be like a cloud to cover the land, you and all your bands, and many people with you.'" Thus says the Lord GOD, 'And it shall be in that day that things shall come into your heart, and you shall devise an evil plan. And you shall say, "I will go up to the land of unwalled villages. I will go *to* those that are at rest, who dwell securely, all of them dwelling without walls, and there are no bars nor gates to them, in order to take a spoil…"'" (vs 8-12).

- they are going to be prosperous
- they are going to have plenty
- God is going to be blessing Israel
- they are going to want to take it

"'…and to steal a prize; to turn your hand upon the desolate places that are now inhabited, and upon the people that are gathered out of the nations… [Israel is back in the land] …who have gotten cattle and goods, who dwell in the midst of the land.' Sheba and Dedan, and the merchants of Tarshish, and all her villages, shall say to you, 'Have you come to take a spoil? Have you gathered your company to steal a prize, to carry away silver and gold, to take away cattle and goods, to take a great spoil?'" (vs 12-13).

- Are you going to come and take away the blessings that I, God, have given to the children of Israel who are at rest?
- Are you going to resist the Kingdom of God?
- Are you going to resist the rule of Christ and the saints?
- Are you going to come with your power and your armies and think that you are going to conquer and take back and take away?

God has something special for them!

Verse 14: "Therefore, son of man, prophesy and say to Gog, "Thus says the Lord GOD, 'In that day when My people of Israel dwell securely, shall you not know *it*? And you shall come from your place out of the uttermost parts of the north, you and many people with you, all of them riding on horses, a great company and a mighty army…. [A reoccurrence of Genghis Khan?] …And you shall come up on My people Israel like a cloud, to cover the land…" (vs 14-16).

Here's the purpose: Why does God do all of this? *Because He wants everyone to submit through repentance and choice voluntarily!* Those who won't He's going to make an example that there will **never ever, ever again during the Millennium**—except at the end—*will with war, rebellion, anarchy and killing rule again!* He's going to make this an example.

"…It shall be in the latter days, and I will bring you against My land, so that the nations may know Me…" (v 16). *They don't know God!*

- they know Buddha
- they know Confucius
- they know Mohammad
- they know Islam
- they know whatever kind or form of religion that they have

but not the true God!

In India they've got so many gods that there is hardly any naming of them all. *They don't know God!* "…the nations may know Me…" *God is going to do this for a perpetual and everlasting lesson that is going to carry right through the Millennium!*

"'…When I shall be sanctified in thee, O Gog, before their eyes.' Thus says the Lord GOD, 'Are you he of whom I have spoken in former days, by the hand of My servants the prophets of Israel, who prophesied in those days for many years that I would bring you against them? And it shall come to pass at the same time, when Gog comes against the land of Israel,' says the Lord GOD, 'My hot anger will be aroused. For in My jealousy *and* in the fire of My wrath I have spoken, "Surely in that day there shall be a great quaking in the land of Israel, so that the fish of the sea, and the birds of the heavens, and the beasts of the field, and all creeping things that creep on the earth, and all the men on the face of the earth, shall quake at My presence. And the mountains shall be thrown down, and the steep places shall fall, and every wall shall fall to the ground." And I will call for a sword against him upon all My mountains,' says the Lord GOD. '*Each* man's sword shall be against his brother" (vs 16-21).

So, they're going to get all there and then God is going to set them in confusion. They're going to start fighting among each other and killing each other. God has done that before! That's one of the weapons that God does. He puts it in their minds to fight against each other. Now that won't be too terribly hard to do. I mean, all you have to do is just look at the radicalism of the different groups that are out there today. They fight against each other. It's going to be something!

Verse 22: "And I will judge him with pestilence and with blood. And I will rain upon him, and upon his bands, and upon the many people with him, an overflowing shower, and great hailstones, fire and brimstone."

When they come up and they're going to go and try and attack and take over the land of Israel with Israel back in the land living in peace and prosperity, worshipping God and keeping the Sabbath and Holy Days, and all the things that God wants them to do, *then they're going to come up and want to take over!*

God is going to fight with the same weapons He's always fought with. You can read this in the book of Exodus when He freed the children of Israel from Egypt. You can read of this in the book of Revelation with the seven last plagues and so forth. *These are the weapons of God that He uses against men!*

Notice what this is going to do, v 23: "Thus I will magnify Myself and sanctify Myself. And I will have Myself known in the eyes of many nations, and they shall know that I *am* the LORD."

That's going to be pretty powerful, isn't it? If there are any left back in the homeland, they're going to go back and say, *'It is God! Forget everything you've ever thought that you're going to do. Repent and submit'!* That will be something, won't it? I mean, you think about it!

Ezekiel 39:1: "Therefore, son of man, prophesy against Gog and say, 'Thus says the Lord GOD, 'Behold, I *am* against you, O Gog, the chief ruler of Meshech and Tubal. And I will turn you about, and lead you on…" (vs 1-2).

God is not going to put up with rebellion and anarchy. When the Kingdom of God, with Christ ruling, comes to this earth it is going to rule in:

- love
- peace
- understanding

But for those who rebel it's going to be:
- power
- force
- pestilence
- fire
- brimstone
- hailstones

That's going to be what they're going to be faced with!

I couldn't help but think of that when I saw the documentary about what happened in Germany after WWII, and then seeing what happened after the conflict in Iraq and the supposed war on terror. It's also another lesson: a few sinful men can do a great deal of damage.

God is not going to allow that! That's why He says in Rev. 2 that we are going to rule them with a rod of iron. If they don't do the will of God, they're going to be broken in pieces just like you take a pot and just bust it into shards. Jesus Christ is going to show that *no one* can come against Him. *No one* can come against the spiritual saints of God that are ruling this world. Look at the weapons. That's going to be something.

"…And I will bring you up from the uttermost parts of the north…" (v 2).

Just like everything else, God raises up the evil ones by letting them do their own thing. And they think that they have power and success because they are accomplishing these things and they don't know that they are on their way to meet their Maker.

He says: "…and I will bring you against the mountains of Israel. And I will strike your bow out of your left hand, and will cause your arrows to fall out of your right hand. You shall fall on the mountains of Israel, you and all your bands, and the people with you. I will give you for food to the birds of prey of every kind, and *to* the beasts of the field" (vs 2-4)—*to be devoured!*

So, immediately God sends in the animals and birds, which are His servants to clean up all the flesh.

Verse 5: "You shall fall upon the face of the open field, for I have spoken it,' says the Lord GOD. 'And I will send a fire on Magog, and on those who dwell in the isles. And they shall know that I *am* the LORD" (vs 5-6).

When the last rebellion is put down then there will be universal peace.

- God is going to let them go their own way
- God is going to rebuke them
- God is going to set them up for the fall

The word will go out; they will know!

- they will have been told that Christ is here ruling from Jerusalem
- they will have had an opportunity to go up like the other nations, *but refuse to do so*
- they will have an opportunity to repent so that they can receive the Spirit of God

So that they can stop all of their hateful warmongering and just bloodthirsty and barbarous ways. *But they refuse to take it!*

Verse 7: "And I will make My Holy name known in the midst of My people Israel. And I will not *let them* profane My Holy name any more. Then the nations shall know that I *am* the LORD, the Holy One in Israel."

Let's go on; let's see what happens. There has to be a tremendous clean-up program after all the birds and animals clean up all the rotten flesh and so forth.

As we read these prophecies and God has given us understanding on how these things unfold through His Word, I just imagine that down through time, from the time of the death of the apostles on down until the beginning of what we would call the modern age, it was really difficult for them to understand these Scriptures.

Brethren, we need to be thankful that we can understand it. But also know and realize that with this understanding also comes a responsibility. Because no man is given the truth of the knowledge of the Word of God so that it can be taken lightly, or that it can be looked upon as a thing of human discovery, rather than as we started out as God's revelation through His Spirit.

Verse 8: "Behold, it is coming, and it shall be done,' says the Lord GOD. 'This *is* the day of which I have spoken. And the inhabitants of the cities of Israel shall go out and shall set on fire and burn the weapons…" (vs 8-9).

Just like they are doing in Iraq today. There are great truck convoys going out of Iraq into Turkey carrying weapons; rifles, cannons, bombs, to be all melted down.

"…both the shields and the bucklers, the bows and the arrows, and the javelins, and the spears. And they shall burn them with fire seven years" (v 9).

Now, you stop and think about that. How huge is this army going to be? And I'm sure that not only on the mountains of Israel but as these armies spread back toward the homelands in the north and the east there's going to be those things there, too.

Verse 10: "'So that they shall take no wood out of the field, nor cut down *any* out of the forests; for they shall make fires of the weapons. And they shall plunder those who plundered them, and rob those who robbed them,' says the Lord GOD. 'And it will be in that day that I will give to Gog a *burial* place there in Israel—the valley of those who pass by, east of the sea. And it shall block off those who pass by… [because right at first, because of the stink of it] …And there they shall bury Gog and all his multitude. And *they* shall call *it* The Valley of the Multitude of Gog. And the house of Israel shall bury them, to cleanse the land, seven months" (vs 10-12).

Verse 13: "'And all the people of the land shall bury them, and it shall be to them a *day of* renown, the day that I shall be glorified,' says the Lord GOD. 'And they shall employ men to continually…(vs 13-14).

That's what's going to happen! So, it's going to be when we're dealing with human beings, and the problems of war, and the destruction of the earth—which we are going to be confronted with when we come back to this earth with Jesus Christ and set up the Kingdom of God—we're going to be confronted with massive real human problems. We're going to have to correct all of them.

Christ is going to have to give us guidance and understanding so we know what to do. But God is going to really make a name for Himself with this. You stop and think about the mammoth proportions of what's going to happen with Gog and Magog, and it's really a fantastic thing. There won't be a rebel left. *That's how God is going to solve the problem!*

Let's look at some of the Psalms and see how these things fit in with what we found there in Ezek. 38 & 39. I tell you, it's going to be something! God isn't going to allow or tolerate rebellion. But what He's going to do is gather up all the rebels together and let them come, and take care of them all at once.

Psalm 47:1: "Clap your hands, all you people; shout to God with the voice of triumph."

That's what Israel is going to do when they see how God has fought against Gog and Magog, and Meshech and Tubal, and all of the countries of the north and the east and everything. They're going to shout with joy.

Verse 2: "For the LORD Most High is awesome… [look what He did]…He is a great King over all the earth…. [literal fulfillment] …He shall subdue the people under us and nations under our feet" (vs 2-3).

That refers to us who are going to rule and reign over the heathen! There it is right in the Word of God.

Verse 4: "He shall choose our inheritance for us, the excellency of Jacob whom He loved. Selah…. [Jacob's name was changed to Israel, and we are spiritual Israel] …God has gone up with a shout, the LORD with the sound of a horn. Sing praises to God, sing praises; sing praises to our King, sing praises, for God is King of all the earth; sing praises with understanding" (vs 4-7).

Now you know how He's going to be King over all the earth, and the great power He's going to exercise, and our part in it. And the part of the children of Israel, the physical children of Israel brought back out of captivity.

Verse 8: "God reigns over the nations; God sits upon the Throne of His Holiness"—*ruling out of Jerusalem!*

Remember what we read in Isa. 2: The Throne of God is going to be there and many people are going to come and say, Let us learn of His ways. The Law is going to go forth out of Zion. Here it's explaining it right here.

Verse 9: "The rulers of the peoples are gathered together, the people of the God of Abraham…"—*who are the spiritual children of God ruling with Jesus Christ!*

Now you put that together with the understanding of the covenant that God gave Abraham in Gen. 15. So you see, *the plan of God goes way back before the creation of the earth!* But it is solidified through Abraham and comes down through the children of Israel, and then down to the Church, *the spiritual children of Abraham!* That's what it's talking about here.

"…the people of the God of Abraham for the shields of the earth are God's; He is greatly exalted" (v 9)—*there will be the peace that will come!*

Psalm 50:1: "The mighty God, God, the LORD, has spoken and called the earth from the rising of the sun to its going down." *In other words around the whole earth!* That's what it's talking about.

Verse 2: "Out of Zion, the perfection of beauty, God has shined forth. Our God shall come, and He shall not keep silent; a fire shall devour before Him, and it shall be very tempestuous all around Him. He shall call to the heavens from above, and to the earth, so that He may judge His people… [and judge the world] …'Gather My saints unto Me, those who have made a covenant with Me by sacrifice'" (vs 2-5).

Now we'll expand on that tomorrow because that has to do with our relationship with God and how we prepare to be kings and priests.

Verse 7: "Hear, My people, and I will speak, O Israel, and I will testify against you; I am God, even your God." *So, we need to listen to what God has to tell us!*

This is what it means; this is the fulfilling of the Millennium. Day one pictures the *institution of the Millennium.* Christ is on the earth, Satan is put away, and now:

- the Kingdom of God begins
- the Government of God begins

Psalm 98:1: "O sing to the LORD a new song, for He has done marvelous things; His right hand and His Holy arm have worked salvation for Him. The LORD has made known His salvation…"

The heathen know Him. and now has been sanctified in Gog and Magog, and all the earth will be under the control and power of Jesus Christ and the saints of God. Marvelous thing!

"…He has revealed His righteousness in the sight of the nations. He has remembered His steadfast love and His faithfulness toward the house of Israel; all the ends of the earth have seen the salvation of our God" (vs 2-3).

That's what this day is going to picture when Gog and Magog have been put down and destroyed, and the last human enemies against the imposition of the Kingdom of God on earth.

Verse 4: "Make a joyful noise to the LORD, all the earth; break forth, and rejoice, and sing praise. Sing to the LORD with the lyre, with the lyre, and the voice of a psalm. With silver trumpets and sound of a ram's horn make a joyful noise before the King, the LORD. Let the sea roar, and the fullness of it, the world, and those who dwell in it. Let the floods clap their hands; let the mountains sing for joy together before the LORD, for He comes to judge the earth; with righteousness He shall judge the world and the people with equity" (vs 4-9).

Brethren, let's understand we have been called to the greatest calling possible! We have understanding that as Jesus said that other people do not have. With that comes a great responsibility that we serve God:

- with love
- with joy
- with zeal
- with loyalty
- with determination
- with understanding
- with faith
- with hope
- with all the attributes of the Holy Spirit

This is the greatest thing that we could possibly be involved in, in ushering in the rule of Jesus Christ and the Kingdom of God on earth!

Psalm 99: "The LORD reigns… [there are several psalms that say the LORD reigns] …let the people tremble. He sits between the cherubim; let the earth quake. The LORD is great in Zion, and He is high above all the people. Let them praise Your name as great and awesome; Holy is He" (vs 1-3). *That goes right back to Psa. 2!* It's going to be an amazing thing.

Now let's see, after we get all of this done, what is going to be the outcome of it? We're going to see what happens. God has the power. God is going to change, recreate and reform the earth:

- with His Spirit with Israel
- with bringing conversion to the heathen
- bringing His way to the whole earth

Then we are going to see what will happen here:

Isaiah 11:1: "And there shall come forth a shoot out from the stump of Jesse, and a Branch shall grow out of his roots. And the Spirit of the LORD shall rest upon Him, the Spirit of wisdom and understanding…"

This is going to be the rule that we are also going to bring in, and it has a lot to do with how we prepare to be kings and priests!

"…the Spirit of counsel and might, the Spirit of knowledge and of the fear of the LORD. And His delight shall be in the fear of the LORD. And He shall not judge according to the sight of His eyes, nor after the hearing of His ears. But with righteousness He shall judge the poor, and shall reprove with equity for the meek of the earth. And He shall strike the earth with the rod of His mouth… [tie in Rev. 2, smite them with a rod of iron'] …and with the breath of His lips He shall slay the wicked. And righteousness shall be the girdle of His loins, and faithfulness the girdle of His reins" (vs 2-5).

Then everything is going to be changed: human nature, animal nature. The way that the earth is, is going to be beautiful, marvelous and harmonious. Not only are they not going to learn war anymore, there's also going to be a change in the nature of the animals.

Verse 6: "Also the wolf shall dwell with the lamb, and the leopard shall lie down with the kid; and the calf and the cub lion and the fatling together; and a little child shall lead them."

Entirely different! I look at that and every time I read that I think: there are not going to be very many plastic toys for the children to play with. Sure there will be some toys, but not like it is today. They're going to have the real thing. They're going to have lions and tigers and all of these things.

Verse 8: "And the suckling child shall play on the hole of the asp, and the weaned child shall put his hand on the viper's den."

That's to show the contrast of the world today with the Kingdom of God tomorrow!

Verse 9: "They shall not hurt nor destroy in all My Holy mountain… [tie in with Isa. 2, that the mountain of the house of the LORD shall be exalted] …for the earth shall be full of the knowledge of the LORD, as the waters cover the sea."

That's how the Millennium will start!

Scriptures from The Holy Bible in Its Original Order, A Faithful Version

Scriptural References:

1) 1 Corinthians 1:17-21
2) I Corinthians 2:9-13
3) Psalm 119:18
4) Leviticus 23:33-38
5) Numbers 29:12-13, 32-34, 39
6) Deuteronomy 16:16-17
7) John 18:33-38
8) Luke 19:11-15, 21-27
9) Isaiah 9:6-7
10) Revelation 20:4-6
11) Revelation 2:25-27
12) Isaiah 2:1-4
13) Ezekiel 38:1-2, 11, 3-23
14) Ezekiel 39:1-14
15) Psalm 47:1-9
16) Psalm 50:1-5, 7
17) Psalm 98:1-9
18) Psalm 99:1-3
19) Isaiah 11:1-6, 8-9

Scriptures referenced, not quoted:

- Revelation 14:12
- Deuteronomy 14
- Luke 21
- Revelation 3
- Zechariah 14
- Revelation 16
- Genesis 15
- Psalm 2

Also referenced: Book:
The Christian Passover by Fred R. Coulter

FRC:cs
Transcription date unknown
Reformatted: bo—1/2021

CHAPTER FIFTY-NINE

Setting Up the Kingdom for the Millennium

Fred R. Coulter

Greetings, everyone! What a glorious Feast this is going to be! While the world is going literally 'to hell in a hand-basket' God is teaching and training His people. He has called us to come before Him with joy, happiness, thanksgiving, so that we can have these eight days—including the last day—where we can concentrate on *the very purpose of our being,* why we're here, and what's going to happen in the world.

So, this is a great and fantastic Feast! I hope you will have a wonderful Feast; that you will be able to fellowship, spend time with brethren, eat meals together, discuss Scriptures together and have a wonderful Feast. I wished I could be with you in every place that you're located, but the closest I can come to it is with these videos.

As you know, God has given—and for a very specific purpose and reason, too—all the Holy Days in time and sequence in Lev. 23. This is a test of faith:

- Do we believe God?
- Do we believe His Word?
- Do we understand the spiritual meaning of these days?

Though they were given to Israel, *they belong to God!* This is not the Jews' Feast of Tabernacles; *this is God's!* Let's see what God says. Also, as we read these things, let's understand that we are *spiritual Israel.* Let's also understand something else: While they had to dwell in booths or tents, we understand that everything on earth is temporary. Instead of dwelling in a booth or a tent, God dwells in us with His Holy Spirit. Let's keep that in mind.

Leviticus 23:33: "And the LORD spoke to Moses saying, 'Speak to the children of Israel, saying, "The fifteenth day of this seventh month *shall be* the Feast of Tabernacles for seven days to the LORD"'" (vs 33-34).

That's what this is; we have seven days of the Feast of Tabernacles and the Last Great Day—or the eighth day.

Verse 35. On the first day *shall be* a Holy convocation.... [which is today] ...You shall do no servile work *therein.* Seven days you shall offer an offering made by fire to the LORD...." (vs 35-36).

These were the offerings that were to be given by the priesthood. You can read about all those offerings in Num. 28-29, and by looking at everything that they brought to sacrifice, you will see that it was to be a time of:

- joy
- plenty
- goodness
- rejoicing before God

—because He has given us everything—everything physically, everything spiritually: He's given us His understanding; He's given us His Spirit. That's a tremendous thing! You need to think about that! We'll cover some of these things as we go along.

Verse 37: "These *are* the Feasts of the LORD which you shall proclaim to be Holy convocations to offer an offering made by fire to the LORD, a burnt offering and a grain offering, a sacrifice, and drink offerings, everything on its day." Those were the formal offerings that were to be given by the priesthood.

All of us, all of those attending were to bring their sacrifices. We find this in:

Verse 38: "Besides the Sabbaths... [plural; every Holy Day is a Sabbath, an annual Sabbath] ...of the LORD, and besides your gifts, and besides all your vows, and besides all your freewill offerings which you give to the LORD. Also in the fifteenth day of the seventh month, when you have gathered in the fruit of the land, you shall keep a Feast to the LORD seven days. On the first day *shall be* a Sabbath, and on the eighth day *shall be* a Sabbath" (vs 38-39).

What kind of offering are we to bring? Realize that in the days that we are living right now, we are faced with difficult economic times. They may get much more difficult. But always remember this: ***Never hold back from giving to God!*** He is able to provide for us in every case. This is why He says here:

Deuteronomy 16:16: "Three times in a year shall all your males appear before the LORD your God in the place which He shall choose: in the Feast of Unleavened Bread, and in the Feast of Weeks, and in the Feast of Tabernacles. And **they shall not appear before the LORD empty**.... [they shall come prepared] ...Every man *shall give* as he is able, according to the blessing of the LORD your God, which He has given you" (vs 16-17).

Every time we come to bring an offering to God we need to remember

- the physical blessings
- the spiritual blessings
- the intervention of God in our lives
- the knowledge of the Word of God that He has given to us
- the opening up of His understanding of His Holy Days and the meaning of them

All of those are things that we can consider. We are not to bring just a penurious little bit, which then represents the offerings that were the blemish type.

Jesus talks about the widow who gives her two mites and He says that she 'gave more than all of the rich who were casting in from their abundance.' So, all of this becomes:

- a test of faith
- a test of our belief in God
- proving whether we believe God or not

God is able to make all grace abound to us so that we have sufficiency in all things! Always remember that *God operates on freely give, because you have freely received!*

That is what we would call the *principle of reciprocity*: Others have given so you can receive; you give so others can receive. This has a multiplying effect. This is how God wants us to:

- serve the brethren
- feed the flock
- preach the Gospel to the world
- to make known His Word
  - ✓ to publish it
  - ✓ to preach it
  - ✓ to do the things that God wants
  - ✓ always stand for the Truth of God and righteousness of God in everything that we do

So, brethren, we'll go ahead at this time, we'll take a little pause, and we'll take up the offering.

(pause for offering)

I. Governments, education and so forth:

God has a message for all the nations and kingdoms of this world. That is: *you have failed!*

- because you have cast the Law of God behind your backs!
- because you have allowed the people to sin!
- because you have been corrupted from head to toe!

Christ is going to come and replace every single one of you! He's going to established *His* kingdom, and He's going to establish *His* righteousness. Look at the things that have happened:

- governments have failed
- science and education has failed
- religions of this world have failed

Every religion is a substitute for the Truth of God!

What happens? Why did all the nations get into the mess that they are in? *Because they turn their backs on God!* As we saw on the Feast of Trumpets, Christ is going to come back and shake

- the heavens
- the earth
- the sea
- all nations
- all people

and *He* is going to setup *His* government beginning in Jerusalem.

We know that this is going to be an awesome thing, indeed! Let's come to Zech. 14 because this tells us how it's going to happen. Let's see what the prophecy says, and we will be there with Him. When we come down off the Sea of Glass to the earth, let's see how it's described here. Nations will no longer be able to do the way that they have done. Yet, everything they want and really desire *comes from God.* But they've rejected it to this point. Christ is going to bring it; here's how it's going to happen:

Zechariah 14:1: "Behold, the day of the LORD comes, and your spoil shall be divided in your midst, 'For I will gather all nations to battle against Jerusalem; and the city shall be taken, and the houses plundered, and the women raped. And half of the city shall go into exile, and the rest of the people shall not be cut off from the city.' And the LORD shall go out and fight against those nations, as when He fought in the day of battle" (vs 1-3).

We saw what a tremendous thing that is going to be. Anyone willing to fight against God? *That's a difficult proposition!* Let's see the weapon that He uses against them.

Verse 4: "And His feet shall stand in that day upon the Mount of Olives…"

Isn't that interesting? Remember, Jesus and the apostles went out and were on the Mt. of Olives. After Jesus told them, 'You stay in Jerusalem until you receive power from heaven.' That, of course, was on Pentecost when the Holy Spirit was given. And on that Mt. of Olives, as He was talking, right before their eyes, He ascended into heaven. The angels said to them, 'You men, why are you gazing up in heaven. This same Jesus Whom you saw received up into heaven will come in like manner, and *every eye will see Him*' (Rev. 1). It's not going to be done in a corner!

So, His feet are going to come right back to the Mt. of Olives, right to the spot where He ascended into heaven after being with the disciples for 40 days and 40 nights.

"…and the Mount of Olives shall split in two, from the east and to the west, and make a very great valley…." (v 4).

The whole geography of the Middle East is going to suddenly be changed because of the coming and presence of God.

"…And half of the mountain shall move toward the north, and half of it toward the south. 'And you shall flee to the valley of My mountains; for the valley of the mountains shall reach to Azal. And you shall flee as you fled from before the earthquake in the days of Uzziah king of Judah.'…." (vs 4-5).

That was quite an earthquake. Even *Josephus* recorded that the earth came like a tsunami; a wall four feet high of earth crushing down on the armies that were ready to capture Judah and Jerusalem. Destroyed the armies!

"…And **the LORD my God shall come, and all the saints with You**" (v 5)—*all the saints from Abel to the two witnesses, and that includes us!*

It's going to be quite a day, and immediately we're going to see that God begins to repair and heal the earth.

Verse 6: "And it shall come to pass in that day, that the light shall not be clear, nor dark. And it will be one day that shall be known to the LORD, neither day nor night; but it shall come to pass that at evening time it shall be light. And it shall be in that day, that living waters… [to heal the earth; also typical of the Holy Spirit of God] …shall go out from Jerusalem; half of them shall go toward the eastern sea, and half of them toward the western sea. In summer and in winter it shall be" (vs 6-8).

It's going to be a healing for all the nations. All the governments in the world *will* submit. We'll see that in just a minute.

Verse 9: "And the LORD shall be King over all the earth; in that day there shall be one LORD, and His name shall be one."

That's going to be a tremendous thing, brethren! *Think about the fact that we are going to be part of that!*

Verse 11: "And they shall dwell in it, and there shall never again be any more utter destruction, but Jerusalem shall dwell safely."

Now then, it talks about the plague that is going to come upon those who fight against Christ. This is going to teach the nations of the world: Don't try and resist Jesus Christ—King of this earth—and the kings and priest who are reigning with Him.

Verse 12: "And this shall be the plague with which the LORD will smite all the people who have fought against Jerusalem. Their flesh shall consume away while they stand on their feet, and their eyes shall consume away in their sockets. And their tongue shall consume away in their mouth. And it shall be in that day *that* a great panic from the LORD shall be among them. And they shall each one lay hold of his neighbor, and his hand shall rise up against the hand of his neighbor. And Judah also shall fight at Jerusalem; and the wealth of all the nations all around shall be gathered…" (vs 12-14).

Christ is going to setup a world system of finance based upon *real* wealth, *real* productivity, based upon the land sabbath and the jubilee cycle, to bring peace, happiness, prosperity and everything that everyone has desired, but no government and no person has been able to provide. God is going to do it for all.

"…—gold, and silver, and clothing in great abundance. And likewise shall be the plague of the horse, the mule, the camel, and the donkey, and of all the beasts which shall be in these camps—*it shall be* as this plague. And it shall come to pass that everyone who is left of all the nations which came up against Jerusalem shall even go up from year to year to worship the King, the LORD of hosts, and to keep the Feast of Tabernacles" (vs 14-16).

The Feast of Tabernacles every year is going to be a commemoration of the establishing of the Kingdom of God on earth, and forward looking to New Jerusalem and the heavenly Kingdom that comes from the Father. This is going to be added meaning to the Feast of Tabernacles. Now then, God shows there's going to be a penalty against those who don't keep the Feast of Tabernacles. It shows that if they don't go up, God is going to hold back the rain. If Egypt doesn't come, the plague.

Let's come to Isaiah and let's see where it talks about this very thing. As we read this, this is at the beginning of the Millennium, the establishing of the Kingdom of God, the setting up of the rule of God. Before that happens, the first thing that God is going to do when He sets everything up in Jerusalem, He's going to setup His tabernacle. The temple that is described in Ezek. 40-48 is not the Millennial temple. Isa. 4 tells us about the Millennial temple.

Isaiah 4:4: "When the LORD shall have

washed away the filth of the daughters of Zion, and shall have purged the blood of Jerusalem from its midst by the spirit of judgment, and by the spirit of burning. And the LORD will create over every dwelling place of Mount Zion…" (vs 4-5).

- Where will we be living?
- What did Jesus say in John 14?
  - ✓ *If you believe in God, believe also in Me!*
  - ✓ *If I go I will come again and bring you to Myself so that you may be with Me!*
  - ✓ *I am going to prepare a place for you!*

That has two meanings:

1. here in Isa. 4
2. in heavenly Jerusalem

Verse 5: "And the LORD will create over every dwelling place of Mount Zion, and over her assemblies, a cloud and smoke by day…"

It's not going to be a physical building that Christ and the saints are going to be in. It's going to be in a tabernacle.] …and the shining of a flaming fire by night; for over all the glory *shall be* a canopy." That's how it's going to look.

Verse 6: "And there shall be a tabernacle for shade by day from the heat, and for refuge, and for shelter from storm and rain."

This is what they're going to see when they come up to the house of the Lord. It's going to be an awesome thing, indeed!

Christ is not going to go out an immediately begin dealing with all the kingdoms of the world. First, He's going to deal with the 12 tribes of Israel, bring them back to their inheritance. There will be nations that will see what is happening and they will come up to Jerusalem to find out what they need to do.

Isaiah 2:1: "The word that Isaiah the son of Amoz saw concerning Judah and Jerusalem. And it shall come to pass, in the last days the mountain of the LORD'S house shall be established in the top of the mountains, and shall be exalted above the hills; and all nations shall flow into it. And many people shall go and say, 'Come, and let us go up to the mountain of the LORD, to the house of the God of Jacob. And He will teach us of His ways, and we will walk in His paths.' For out of Zion shall go forth the Law, and the Word of the LORD from Jerusalem" (vs 1-3).

Let's just stop and think here for a minute. The argument that the Law of God is done away. When Christ comes back and sets up the kingdom,

what is one of the first things He does? *He sets up the Law!* Notice what He has to do, because He gives everyone an opportunity to repent and come to Him. If they won't come to Him, notice what happens:

Verse 4: "And He shall judge among the nations, and shall rebuke many people… [they won't want to come to learn of God right away] …and they shall beat their swords into plowshares, and their spears into pruning hooks. Nation shall not lift up sword against nation, neither shall they learn war any more."

The greatest thing is going to happen. The Government of God is going to reign and rule!

- let's see how it's going to work out
- let's see how these things come about
- let's see how God is going to do it
- let's see how everything is going to be changed back to the way that it should be

The whole environment is going to be changed. The nature of animals is going to be changed. All education will be changed. All science will be changed. *The Government of God is going to rule!* We're going to teach the people. Here's a prophecy of it; prophecy of Christ. Remember that it was prophesied that He was born to be king and of the 'increase of His government there shall be no end.'

Isaiah 11:1: "And there shall come forth a shoot out from the stump of Jesse, and a Branch shall grow out of his roots. And the Spirit of the LORD shall rest upon Him, the spirit of wisdom and understanding, the spirit of counsel and might, the spirit of knowledge and of the fear of the LORD. And His delight shall be in the fear of the LORD. And He shall not judge according to the sight of His eyes, nor after the hearing of His ears. But with righteousness He shall judge the poor…" (vs 1-4).

With righteousness He's going to judge the nations, and we are going to be there to help administer this]

"…and shall reprove with equity for the meek of the earth. And He shall strike the earth with the rod of His mouth, and with the breath of His lips He shall slay the wicked" (v 4).

That's what it means to cause the nations to want to 'beat their swords into plowshares and their spears into pruning hooks.' And He rebukes people afar off.

Verse 5: "And righteousness shall be the girdle of His loins, and faithfulness the girdle of His reins. Also the wolf shall dwell with the lamb, and the leopard shall lie down with the kid; and the calf and the cub lion and the fatling together; and a little child shall lead them" (vs 5-6).

Won't that be wonderful? No more plastic toys; no more silly make-believe. You can have the pet of your choice. Won't that be something? Just think of the excitement of that! And so tame that a little child will lead them.

Then you look out and you see what's happening in the pastures and you see lo and behold:

Verse 7: "And the cow and the bear shall feed; their young ones shall lie down together; and the lion shall eat straw like the ox. And the suckling child shall play on the hole of the asp, and the weaned child shall put his hand on the viper's den. They shall not hurt nor destroy in all My Holy Mountain; for the earth... [notice what's going to happen; all nations, all people] ...**shall be full of the knowledge of the LORD, as the waters cover the sea**" (vs 7-9).

Everyone is going to know! What a fantastic thing that is going to be! What a wonderful opportunity that we have to be able to bring this to the world. That's why God has called us *the few, the poor, the discards, the rejects* of the world. But with His Spirit we can bring this:

Verse 10: "And in that day there shall be the Root of Jesse standing as a banner for the people; to Him the nations shall seek; and His rest shall be glorious."

Just think how absolutely wonderful that that is going to be! Christ is the One Who can bring it!

II. Message *to all people* of the world

There's a message to all people in the world. We already saw it there in Isa. 2, now let's go to Psa. 95; here we see some other things *concerning the Kingdom of God, the reign of God, the rule of God!* That's something! It's going to be:

- a time of joy
- a time of happiness
- a time of love
- a time of goodness
- a time of plenty

No more of all the things that have gone on because people have rejected God.

- no more drought
- no more famine
- no more oppressive government
- no more slaughtering
- no more murdering
- no more kidnapping

Psalm 95:1: "O come, let us sing to the LORD..."

I wonder what that is going to be like with the songs that we will have during the Millennium? *The people who come through all the wars and things are going to be able to learn and understand and know the way of God!*

"...let us make a joyful noise to the Rock of our salvation. Let us come before His presence with thanksgiving, and make a joyful noise to Him with psalms, for the LORD is a **great God** and a **great King** above all gods" (vs 1-3).

Of course, we're going to be spirit beings, too, so that probably includes us. There will be no more idols, no more gods of this earth at all.

Verse 4: "In His hand are the depths of the earth; the peaks of the mountains are also His. The sea is His, and He made it, and His hands formed the dry land. O come, let us worship and bow down; let us kneel before the LORD our Maker, for He is our God, and we are the people of His pasture, and the sheep of His hand. Today, **if** you would but hearken to His voice" (vs 1-7).

Then we will also have those things there to teach them not to let carnal nature let you get carried away. Carnal nature is going to be modified to what it was with Adam and Eve when they were created. It's not going to have the all out evil that was there.

Psalm 97: "**The LORD reigns**..." That's going to be the first message that we bring to all people. The *beast power* will have been destroyed. Just think of the cities all destroyed. Think of all the work that has to be done to rebuild. But every vestige of every idol and the way of Babylon the Great is going to be obliterated!

"...let the earth rejoice; let the multitude of islands be glad. Clouds and darkness are all around Him; righteousness and justice are the foundation of His Throne" (vs 1-2). *He's going to show His might and show His power!*

Verse 3: "A fire goes before Him and burns up His enemies round about." *They will have understood that that happened!* That's what God is going to do.

Verse 4: "His lightning lights up the world; the earth saw and trembled. The mountains melted like wax at the presence of the LORD, at the presence of the Lord of the whole earth. The heavens declare His righteousness, and all the people see His glory" (vs 4-6). *It's going to be quite a thing when that happens!*

Verse 7: "All those who serve graven images are ashamed who boast themselves in idols... [they're going to destroy them; break them into smithereens] ...bow down to Him, all you gods.

Zion heard and was glad; and the daughters of Judah rejoiced because of Your judgments, O LORD, for You, LORD, are most high above all the earth; You are exalted high above all gods" (vs 7-9). They're all going to be destroyed.

Listen! Here's the message for us, v 10: "You who love the LORD, hate evil! He preserves the souls of His saints; He delivers them out of the hand of the wicked. Light is sown for the righteous and gladness for the upright in heart. Rejoice in the LORD, you righteous ones, and praise His Holy name" (vs 10-12). This is going to be something—isn't it?

Brethren, I want you to realize and understand and grasp, this is what we're going to be doing. This is our destiny!

- the Lord reigns
- the Lord is King
- the Lord is God over all the earth
- all other gods are going to be destroyed; smashed to smithereens

There's one temple in Cambodia that they're rebuilding—the Temple of Angkor. They're rebuilding it for tourists to come and see and then they'll be worshipping there before Christ returns. But that's going to be destroyed!

- every temple
- every idol
- every church
- every cave
- every underground thing that men have built so they can continue their evil ways

All are going to be crushed! Then there's going to be a change, a renewal, a time of rejoicing:

Psalm 98:1: "O sing to the LORD a new song, for He has done marvelous things; His right hand and His holy arm have worked salvation for Him. The LORD has made known His salvation; He Has revealed His righteousness in the sight of the nations" (vs 1-2). *Then is going to pour forth*:

- the Spirit of God
- the Spirit of love
- the Spirit of righteousness
- the Spirit of knowledge
- the Spirit of goodness

Verse 3: "He has remembered His steadfast love and His faithfulness toward the house of Israel; **all the ends of the earth have seen the salvation of our God.**" *That's quite a thing, brethren!*

To all people, you are going to be relieved from the evil governments that rule over you now. That frighten you! That scared you! That tax you!

That kill your families! It's going to be replaced with the righteous saints of God! That's going to be really quite a thing when this happens.

Verse 5: "Sing to the LORD with the lyre, with the lyre, and the voice of a psalm. With silver trumpets and sound of a ram's horn make a joyful noise before the King, the LORD. Let the sea roar, and the fullness of it, the world, and those who dwell in it" (vs 5-7).

This is like looking down at the earth and how great the Millennium is going to be under the rule of God.

Verse 8: "Let the floods clap their hands; let the mountains sing for joy together Before the LORD, for He comes to judge the earth; with righteousness He shall judge the world and the people with equity" (vs 8-9).

The people of the earth, so that they can understand, this is the message for all people. God is going to rule; His saints are going to assist Him. There is going to be joy and happiness in the whole world.

Psalm 99:1: "The LORD reigns; let the people tremble. He sits between the cherubim; let the earth quake. The LORD is great in Zion, and He is high above all the people. Let them praise Your name as great and awesome; Holy is He. The strength of the King also loves justice; You established uprightness; You have executed justice and righteousness in Jacob.... [and all the world] ...Exalt the LORD our God and worship at His footstool, for He is Holy" (vs 1-5).

III. <u>God has a message for the Church</u>

Let's first of all let's look at it for what it is as individuals and then collectively. Let's come to 2-Cor. 5—this is quite a chapter, indeed, telling us about what God is going to provide for us. We are going to have a spirit body. Right now we are a temple or tabernacle of the Holy Spirit of God (1-Cor. 3).

Paul writes this, 2-Corinthians 5:1: "For we know that if our earthly house of *this* tabernacle is destroyed... [it's going to be; we're going to have a spirit body; this one is going to be gone] ...we have a building from God... [a new body, new mind, all of that] ...a house not made with *human* hands, eternal in the heavens. For in this we truly are groaning, longing to be clothed with our dwelling from heaven; if indeed *that* being clothed, we may not be found naked. For we who are in *this* tabernacle truly do groan..." (vs 1-4). *Yes! Because of changing, growing, overcoming and living in this world!*

You know, *if* we understand the Scriptures

correctly, it's going to get a whole lot worse than we have ever imagined it.

"…being burdened; not that we wish to be unclothed, but to be clothed upon so that the mortal *flesh* may be swallowed up by life" (v 4).

God is the One Who is working this in us. He is the One Who is going to make it happen.

What we're going to do is look at the personal goal of what Christ is going to do for us and see how God is going to work this out. Then we will look at the responsibility of the Churches collectively in Rev. 2 & 3.

Verse 5: "Now, He Who is working out this very thing for us *is* God, Who has also given us the earnest of the Spirit." That's important, brethren, because God's Spirit is:

- to lead us
- to guide us
- to give us love
- to give us faith
- to give us hope
- to give us confidence
- to give us righteousness

from God! God is working that out in us.

That's why we need to go to God with this confidence: Don't worry about the things of the flesh. We need to take care of ourselves the best that we can in the meantime. But living forever is not going to happen in the flesh; it's only going to happen in the spirit, with the

- new body
- new mind
- new understanding

what a thing that is going to be!

Verse 6: "Therefore, we are always confident, knowing that while we are at home in *this* body, we are away from *our eternal* home, *which is coming* from the Lord."

We labor for this! We understand that we're going to come before the judgment seat of God. But let's understand a very important thing here for us to realize, because God—

- through His Sabbath
- through Holy Days
- through His Spirit
- through His Word
- through your prayers

—*is making you into a new creation, fashioned after Christ!*

Verse 17: "Therefore, if anyone *be* in Christ,

he is a new creation… [that is a prophetic purpose, a prophetic perfect statement meaning that *it is as good as done* if we endure to the end] …the old things have passed away; behold, all things have become new." *That's what we look forward to!*

Now let's see how it's expressed in Psa. 15. Quite a very interesting Psalm because it asks the question: ***O Lord, who is going to dwell on Your Holy hill?*** We will see the goal that we always need to be constantly looking for.

Psalm 15:1: "LORD, who shall dwell in Your tabernacle? Who shall dwell upon Your Holy hill?"

That is be able to come to Jerusalem, the Jerusalem that is going to have the tabernacle by day and the cloud and then the fire and smoke by night. Who is going to dwell there?

Verse 2: "He who walks uprightly, and works righteousness, and speaks the Truth in his heart… [not a hypocrite that says one thing and does another] (notice the requirements): …he does not slander with his tongue, nor does evil to his neighbor, nor takes up a reproach against his neighbor; in whose eyes a vile person is despised, but **he honors those who fear the LORD**; he who swears to his own hurt and does not change it" (vs 2-4)—*that's us!*

That's the message to the Churches, and the messages to us individually. Now we will see that it blends into the Churches collectively. I want you to see how this fits in with Jesus' personal calling to us and collectively how we're going to serve the world. This is going to really be a wonderful thing, brethren.

Isaiah 51:1: "Hearken to Me… [listen to obey] …you who follow after righteousness... [which we do in the laws and commandments of God, the mind of Christ, the Spirit of God] …you who seek the LORD: Look to the rock *from which* you were cut… [that is Christ] …and to the hole of the pit *from which* you were dug. Look to Abraham your father, and to Sarah *who* bore you… [this is a direct reference that Paul uses in Gal. 4] …for I called him alone, and blessed him, and made him many" (vs 1-2).

We are the spiritual seed of the promise given to Abraham. We are of the seed of Abraham, because we belong to Christ. Never forget that!

Verse 3: "For the LORD shall comfort Zion; He will comfort all her waste places; and He will make her wilderness like Eden, and her desert like the garden of the LORD. Joy and gladness shall be found in it, thanksgiving and the voice of melody."

The first thing we are going to do is help

bring back the children of Israel to their lands *and teach them first!*

Verse 4—*God says*: "Hearken to Me, My people; and give ear to Me, O My nation; for instruction shall proceed from Me, and I will make My justice as a light to the people. My righteousness *is* near; My salvation has gone out, and My arms shall judge the people; the isles shall wait upon Me, and on My arm they shall trust. Lift up your eyes to the heavens, and look upon the earth beneath; for the heavens shall vanish away like smoke…" (vs 4-6). *It's talking about getting into the 'new heavens and the new earth'!*

"…and the earth shall become old like a garment; and its inhabitants shall die in the same way. But **My salvation shall be forever**, and **My righteousness shall not be abolished**" (v 6). That's quite something!

Isaiah 61—this is going to tell us what God is going to do. It shows that we are going to participate in the very commission of healing the sick, raising the dead, preaching the Gospel—just exactly as Jesus proclaimed of Himself there when He quoted this in Luke 4. This is quite a thing because what I want you to see is that it goes from Christ and blends into the Church and our responsibility, right here in this one chapter; quite significant!

Isaiah 61:1: "The Spirit of the Lord GOD *is* upon Me because the LORD has anointed Me [Christ] to preach the Gospel to the poor; He has sent Me to bind up the broken hearted… [He does that through the ministry; through His Spirit; through His Word] …to proclaim liberty to the captives… [we're going to be the ones who will do that] …and the opening of the prison to those who are bound; to preach the acceptable year of the LORD and the day of vengeance of our God; to comfort all who mourn" (vs 1-2).

Of course, that's going to be everyone who survives through the Tribulation at the end-time. We don't know how many people it's going to be, because we don't know the exact proportion of those who are going to live and those who are going to die. But just think about all the shell-shocked people we're going to have to help. They're going to have lived through:

- the greatest earthquakes to ever hit the earth
- the greatest wars to ever take place on the earth
- the shaking of the heavens and the earth by God
- the seven trumpet plagues as we find in the book of Revelation

Yes, the 144,00 and great innumerable multitude are going to be protected from those things when they begin to occur, but they're going to live through all of these things. Think of the mental, emotional and spiritual wreck that these people are going to be in. They're going to want to hear about comfort, mercy, and forgiveness.

I can't help but think of those who came out of the German prison camps and the Japanese prison camps after WWII. Their eyes sunk deep into their head, ready to die, just walking skeletons. They were numb from what they had experienced. It was very hard for them to grasp that they were free, that now they can live again. That's what we're going to have to do with these.

Here's what we're going to do, v 3: "To appoint to those who mourn in Zion, giving to them beauty for ashes, the oil of joy for mourning, the mantle of praise for the spirit of heaviness; so that they might be called trees of righteousness, the planting of the LORD, that He might be glorified."

Now they're going to be given an opportunity for *eternal salvation!* They're going to be rejuvenated physically, finish living out their lives. This is going to be some thing they're going to do.

Verse 4: "And they will build the old wastes, they will raise up the desolations of former times. And they shall repair the waste cities, the desolations of many generations."

That's going to be a lot of work! Think what it's going to be like to begin to rebuild the world. It's going to be in near destruction!

Verse 6—talking about us: "But **you shall be called the priests of the LORD**… [We're going to see that agrees with Rev. 20:4-6] …it will be said of you, 'The ministers of our God;' you will eat the riches of the Gentiles, and you will boast in their glory. For your shame *you will have* double; instead of dishonor they will rejoice in their portion; therefore in their own land they will possess double; everlasting joy will be theirs" (vs 6-7).

That's blending in our reward as we teach the people, and the people as they receive the blessings of God.

Verse 8: "For I the LORD love justice, I hate robbery for burnt offering; and I will direct their work in Truth… [We're going to be given instruction on what to do, how to teach them, but it's all going to be in Truth!] …and I will make an everlasting covenant with them."

Isn't that something? Did God make an everlasting covenant with us? *Yes!* That's what baptism is all about! He's going to make everlasting covenant with them. Remember, when we are resurrected, there is also going to be another covenant between Christ and the resurrected Church, between Christ and the Bride. This is going to be something, brethren!

It talks about Christ: 'For unto us a Son is born, unto us a Son is given, and His name shall be called Wonderful, Counselor, the Mighty God, the Everlasting Father.' Christ is not yet a father, because He came to reveal God the Father. But with the marriage of the Bride and Christ and the work of the Church under Christ all during the Millennium, He will become a father. Since He's living forever, He will be an everlasting father. This is talking about His seed:

Verse 9: "And their seed shall be known among the Gentiles, and their offspring among the people; all who see them will acknowledge them, that they *are* the seed the LORD has blessed." *We're going to bring that about!*

Listen, brethren, God holds forth for us the greatest and most precious promises, that we are going to inherit the Divine nature, that we are going to have spirit bodies and a mind that will have glory like Christ's. Then we're going to go out and serve the people; help finish the whole plan of God. That's fantastic!

Verse 10: "I will greatly rejoice in the LORD, my soul will be joyful in my God; for He has clothed me *with* the robes of salvation, He covered me with the robe of righteousness like a bridegroom adorns *himself* with ornaments, and like a bride adorns *herself* with her jewels; for as the earth brings forth its bud, and as the garden causes that which is sown to grow; **so the Lord GOD will cause righteousness and praise to grow before all the nations**" (vs 10-11).

Think about that! This is why we keep the Feast of Tabernacles. This is why God has told us the things that He has. We know, and living in this world we also see.

Rev. 2 & 3—these are letters sent directly from Jesus Christ to the seven churches. These depict, first of all, the churches that were then, then down through history—the eras or epochs of the Church—the historical prophecy of the Churches of God. Then at the end-time we can look about and see among the Churches of God every one of the situations, difficulties and problems described here to the seven churches.

I'm not going to go through all the difficulties of the Churches, but what I'm going to do is go through the rewards that He promises. Remember, this is to **_all_** the Churches.

Church of Ephesus:

Revelation 2:7: "**The one who has an ear, let him hear what the Spirit [Christ] says to the Churches**…. [He says that to every one of the Churches] …To the one who overcomes…"

I want you to think about the things that you're going to do to overcome, to change, to grow; because we must be perfected day after day, week after week, month after month, year after year.

"…I will give *the right* to eat of the tree of life that is in *the* midst of the paradise of God" (v 7). *That right is granted to those who keep His commandments!*

Church of Smyrna:

The Church that suffered great martyrdom, v 11: "**The one who has an ear, let him hear what the Spirit says to the churches.** The one who overcomes shall not be hurt of the second death."

No, because you'll be a spirit being. Don't worry about this first death in this life. Whatever pain or difficulty, or whatever that they went through, or that the future martyrs are going to go through, when you are resurrected, the second death has no power over you!

Church of Pergamos:

Verse 17: "**The one who has an ear, let him hear what the Spirit says to the Churches**. To the one who overcomes I will give *the right* to eat of the hidden manna; and I will give him a white stone, and on the stone a new name written, which no one knows except the one who receives *it*."

You will receive that at the resurrection. All of these are promises that God has given. What are we to overcome?

- losing our first love!
- bringing in the doctrine of the Nicolaitans
- having a hierarchy rule over the brethren

Listen! God doesn't want a hierarchy of ministers to rule over you. What He wants is for Christ to rule *within* you!

Church of Thyatira:

Verse 26: "And to the one who overcomes, and keeps My works unto *the* end…"

We are under grace, but we have *spiritual works* to be done under grace. We have the works that God has foreordained for us to walk in, too. But notice, these are the *works of Christ* that He has given for us to do. The *works of God* that He has preordained that we are to walk in them.

"…I will give authority over the nations… [we read about that in the Psa., Isa., and Zech.]

...and he shall shepherd them with an iron rod... [We'll have full authority of God] ...as vessels of pottery are broken in pieces; as I have also received from My Father; and I will give him the morning star" (vs 26-28).

That means *eternal glory!* Jesus said that those who are the children of the kingdom shall 'shine as the sun'—the morning star.

Verse 29: "**The one who has an ear, let him hear what the Spirit says to the Churches**."

This is a message for us. These letters to the Churches are the direct messages of Christ to all His Churches. That's why He says, "The one who has an ear, let him hear..."

Church of Sardis:

Revelation 3:5: "The one who overcomes shall be clothed in white garments; and I will not blot out his name from the book of Life..."

Even if you do the bear minimum, God is going to grant you *eternal life.* But if you don't, you risk being blotted out of the Book of Life.

"...but I will confess his name before My Father and before His angels. **The one who has an ear, let him hear what the Spirit says to the Churches**" (vs 5-6).

Church of Philadelphia:

Verse 12: "The one who overcomes will I make a pillar in the temple of My God... [one who is part of the very fabric of Truth and teaching and authority] ...and he shall not go out any more; and I will write upon him the name of My God, and the name of the city of My God, the New Jerusalem, which will come down out of heaven from My God; and *I will write upon him* My new name. **The one who has an ear, let him hear what the Spirit says to the Churches**" (vs 12-13).

All of these, brethren, show the *reward,* show the *promise,* show the *message* from Christ as to what He wants us to do.

Church of Laodicea:

Verse 21: "To the one who overcomes will I give *authority* to sit with Me in My Throne, even as I also overcame, and sat down with My Father in His Throne. **The one who has an ear, let him hear what the Spirit says to the Churches**" (vs 21 22).

Collectively then, Peter writes that we are a Holy nation, a Holy priesthood (1-Pet. 2). We're going to rule with Christ!

Rev. 5—the question has come up concerning the 24 elders who sing this hymn. This is the hymn that we are going to sing, but they are singing it because the hymn is already prepared.

Revelation 5:8: "And when He took the book, the four living creatures and the twenty-four elders fell down before the Lamb, each having harps and golden bowls full of incense, which are the prayers of the saints. And they sang a new song... [relating to the saints] ...saying, 'Worthy are You to take the book, and to open its seals because You were slain, and did redeem **us**... [the saints—not the four living creatures or 24 elders] ...to God by Your own blood, out of every tribe and language and people and nation, and did make us unto our God kings and priests; and we shall reign on the earth'" (vs 8-10).

That's something! That ties in with Rev. 20. This is what God is laying out for us. The Feast of Tabernacles has these messages: *to the world, to the people, to the Church.* There's one more message we're going to cover right after this:

Revelation 20:4: "And I saw thrones; and they that sat upon them... [Weren't we told that we'll sit on thrones? *Yes!*] ...and judgment was given to them; and *I saw* the souls of those who had been beheaded for the testimony of Jesus, and for the Word of God, and those who did not worship the beast, or his image, and did not receive the mark in their foreheads or in their hands; and **they lived and reigned with Christ a thousand years**"—*as kings and priests!*

Verse 5 is a parenthetical statement because v 4 talks about all of those who died in Christ. The question comes up: What happens to the rest of the people? The rest of the world? Who have died up to this time? "(But the rest of the dead did not live again until the thousand years were completed). This *is* the first resurrection"—talked about in v 4, because the parenthetical statement is an inset talking about the coming resurrection to a life of flesh by those who died previously—the rest of the dead.

Verse 6: "And Holy is the one who has part in the first resurrection; over these the second death has no power.... [as He promised the Church of Smyrna] ...But they shall be priests of God and of Christ, and shall reign with Him a thousand years." *That is just the start!*

Message to God from Himself:

There's one more message in the Bible, and this message is to God. It's a message *by God to Himself* that He's also looking forward to the completion of His plan. It has always been God's desire to dwell among His people.

Let's remember that after God created Adam and Eve they dwelt together in the Garden of Eden. As we're going to see tomorrow, there are many parallels between the things in the Old Testament and the Garden of Eden *and* the things in the book of Revelation.

Exo. 25—here we have why God had to build the tabernacle. Remember, when they started out on the Exodus and as they continued all during the 40 years, you had the *pillar of cloud by day* and probably gave them cloud cover so the sun wouldn't scorch them; and the *pillar of fire at night.* That was always over the tabernacle of Israel, and we saw in Isa. 4 how that's how God is going to setup the tabernacle for His temple during the Millennium.

When Adam and Eve sinned, God removed Adam and Eve from the Garden of Eden, and they could not come back in. God probably dwelt right there in the Garden of Eden up to the time of the Flood. People could come to God at the East Gate to offer their sacrifices, etc., but after the Flood God removed Himself from the earth as a place where He would stay. He would come down and visit directly with the patriarchs, also give them dreams and visions, and when He dealt with the children of Israel He didn't *dwell* with them, but He put His *presence* with them.

He wanted to have the tabernacle, so He gave the instructions for everything concerning the building of it, the design of it, the functioning of it *for one purpose*: **That they could be a Holy people unto God and that He could dwell among them!** So, the message that we're going to see is that **God wants to dwell among His people, with His people.** God told Moses to call for an offering so that they could make a sanctuary for Him.

Exodus 25:8: "And let them make Me a sanctuary, **so that I may dwell among them.** According to all that I show you, the pattern of the tabernacle, and the pattern of all the instruments of it, even so you shall make *it* (vs 8-9). *The next chapters describe everything in great detail!*

Very interesting! If there's going to be anything dedicated to God, you must have the instructions from God. You're not going to do it any ole way you think.

What happened when God gave the instructions to David to build the temple? *He gave David the pattern!* Let's see what God says to David when David wanted to build Him a house. Of course, we know that God says in Isa. 66, 'Where is the house that you will build for Me? For all these things that you're going to build it with *I have made! They're of My hand!* How can you make something that will really honor Me?'

The truth is, unless you get the instructions from God, you can't do it. The truth is, now we are a Temple of God, because God said, 'To this one will

I look, to the one who is of a humble and contrite spirit and trembles at My Word' (Isa. 66), so He can dwell within us.

Here's a message for God. He has yet to develop and have ready the place where He is going to live with His *spiritual family* forever. Let's see what God told David when He wanted to build a temple for God:

2-Samuel 7:1: "And it came to pass when the king dwelt in his house…"

He had the Ark of the Covenant there in a special tent. He had the priests to attend to it. He would come and sing the psalms before God, Whose presence was in that little tabernacle where the Ark of the Covenant was.

So, he's sitting there in his house viewing this and it came to pass when the king dwelt in his house, because he built him a good house,

"…when the LORD had given him rest round about from all his enemies, the king said to Nathan the prophet, 'See now, I dwell in a house of cedar… [probably a beautiful fantastic house, no doubt] …but the Ark of God dwells within curtains'" (vs 1-2). *I mean, shouldn't we give more honor to God than that?*

Verse 3: "Then Nathan said to the king, 'Go, do all that *is* in your heart, for the LORD *is* with you.' And it came to pass that night the Word of the LORD came to Nathan saying, 'Go and tell My servant David, "Thus says the LORD, 'Shall you build Me a house for My dwelling? For I have not dwelt in a house since the day that I brought up the children out of Egypt until this day, but have walked in a tent, and in a tabernacle'"'" (vs 3-6). Isn't that something?

Look at all of the great temples that men try and build to *their god.* But GOD is so great and righteous and humble, that He would rather dwell in a tabernacle, rather than a fait accompli ornate building so that He could dwell among His people!

What happened when the finally built the temple? Solomon built it. We'll cover that one of the days during the Feast.

Verse 7: "'In all *places* in which I have walked with all the children of Israel, did I speak a word with any of the tribes of Israel, *those* whom I commanded to feed My people Israel, saying, "Why do you not build Me a house of cedars?"' Now therefore, thus shall you say to My servant David, 'Thus says the LORD of hosts: "I took you from the sheepcote, from following the sheep, to be prince over My people, over Israel. And I was with you wherever you went and have cut off all your enemies out of your sight, and have made you a great name like the name of the great ones in the earth. Moreover I will appoint a place for My people Israel, and will plant them so that they may dwell in a place of their own, and move no more. Neither shall the sons of wickedness afflict them any more, as before"'" (vs 7-10).

That is prophetically to *physical* Israel and prophetically *spiritually* for us. So, He said that He would allow Solomon to build the house, but He knew what was going to happen. The people so disrespected God! You read the history of the kings of Israel and Judah, the judges, the priests and it's a history of worshipping God and falling into apostasy; worshipping God and falling into apostasy; and finally they built a temple and what happened? *It didn't even survive in the way that it should have after the reign of Solomon!*

The kingdom was split. The northern ten tribes went after their Egyptian calf-worship; the children of Israel co-mingled the worship of other gods with the true God. So bad what it became that by 586$_{B.C.}$ God had already sent the ten tribes of Israel off into captivity 120 years previous, and then He sent the children of Judah in Jerusalem into captivity into Babylon. He destroyed the temple because of their sins!

When they came back they used the plans from Ezekiel to build a second temple. Their sins again, by the time of Christ, reached to high heaven! They were sinning against God! They killed Jesus Christ and they went after the Churches of God! *They rejected Christ! They rejected the Truth of God!* God again destroyed the temple, removed His presence from them *permanently!* He put His Spirit within the *spiritual body* of Christ and *we* become a Temple of God.

Now then, the message to God is that there has to be a *new* Jerusalem, a *new* heaven and earth, and *in the dwelling place of God there will be no temple!* God is going to dwell with the perfected, spiritual family grown great. Both God the Father and Jesus Christ will be there. So, Jesus began preparing the disciples for this:

John 14:1: "Let not your heart be troubled. You believe in God; believe also in Me. In **My Father's house**... [New Jerusalem yet to come] ...are many dwelling places; if it were otherwise, I would have told you. I am going to prepare a place for you" (vs 1-2).

That place Christ is preparing for everyone that He calls and is converted and have the Holy Spirit of God.

Verse 3: "And if I go and prepare a place for you, I will come again and receive you to Myself; so that where I am, **you may be also**."

When it's all over, said and done, all the wicked are destroyed and all of those who are spirit beings in the Kingdom of God are ready for New Jerusalem to come down from heaven. God is going to remake the heavens, remake the earth, so that it's new. It's all going to be burned to a crisp like Peter wrote of in 2-Pet. 3. How that then going to become:

- the glorious New Jerusalem
- the glorious new earth
- the glorious new heavens

For all the children of God and *we* will dwell with God, ***and we will be His children!*** This is the message to God: ***That He needs a place to dwell with His Family!***

Revelation 21:1: "Then I saw a new heaven and a new earth; for the first heaven and the first earth were passed away, and there was no more sea. And I, John, saw the Holy City, *the* New Jerusalem, coming down from God out of heaven, prepared as a bride adorned for her husband. And I heard a great voice from heaven say, 'Behold, the tabernacle of God *is* with men; and **He shall dwell with them**...'" (vs 1-3).

That's what God wants; that's the whole story of the Feast of Tabernacles from Genesis to Revelation.

"'...and they shall be His people; and God Himself shall be with them *and be* their God. And God shall wipe away every tear from their eyes; and *there* shall not be any more death, or sorrow, or crying; neither shall *there* be any more pain, because the former things have passed away.' And He Who sits on the Throne said, 'Behold, **I make all things new**.' Then He said to me, 'Write, for these words are true and faithful.' And He said to me, 'It is done. I am Alpha and Omega, the Beginning and the End. To the one who thirsts, I will give freely of the fountain of the water of life. The one who overcomes shall inherit all things; and I will be his God, and he shall be My son'" (vs 3-7).

Notice, after showing the descent of New Jerusalem to the earth, what He says:

Verse 22: "And **I saw no temple in it**; for the Lord God Almighty and the Lamb are the temple of it. And the city has no need of the sun... [no need of it] ...or of the moon, that they should shine in it; because the glory of God enlightens it, and the light of it *is* the Lamb" (vs 22-23).

Rev. 22:3—talking about the Throne of God and living with God; and this is what we have to look forward to, and this is the message of the Feast of Tabernacles to God the Father and Jesus Christ. They are looking forward to this day. This is the completion of Their plan. God has called us to be a fantastic living part of it.

Revelation 22:3: "And there shall be no more curse; and the Throne of God and of the Lamb shall be in it; and His servants shall serve Him, and they shall see His face; and His name *is* in their foreheads. And there shall be no night there; for they have no need of a lamp or *the* light of *the* sun, because *the* Lord God enlightens them; and they shall reign into the ages of eternity" (vs 3-5).

This is the message of the Feast of Tabernacles for God!

Scriptural References:

1) Leviticus 23: 33-39
2) Deuteronomy 16:16-17
3) Zechariah 14:1-9, 11-16
4) Isaiah 4:4-6
5) Isaiah 2:1-4
6) Isaiah 11:1-10
7) Psalm 95:1-7
8) Psalm 97:1-12
9) Psalm 98:1-3, 5-9
10) Psalm 99:1-5
11) 2 Corinthians 5:1-6, 17
12) Psalm 15:1-4
13) Isaiah 51:1-6
14) Isaiah 61:1-4, 6-11
15) Revelation 2:7, 11, 17, 26-29
16) Revelation 3:5-6, 12-13, 21-22
17) Revelation 5:8-10
18) Revelation 20:4-6
19) Exodus 25:8-9
20) 2 Samuel 7:1-10
21) John 14:1-3
22) Revelation 21:1-7, 22-23
23) Revelation 22:3-5

Scriptures referenced, not quoted:

- Numbers 28; 29
- Revelation 1
- Ezekiel 40-48
- 1 Corinthians 3
- Galatians 4
- Luke 4
- Revelation 20:4-6
- 1 Peter 2
- Isaiah 66
- 2 Peter 3

Also referenced: Book: *Josephus*

FRC:bo
Transcribed: 8/1/12
Reformatted: 1/2021

CHAPTER SIXTY

Isaiah's Prophecies of the Millennium I
Survey of Isaiah 1 & 2

Fred R. Coulter

Today we're going to do a survey, beginning in the book of Isaiah, the Prophet Isaiah. The Prophets Isaiah, Jeremiah and Ezekiel are called *the major prophets.* All of the other twelve are called the *minor prophets* and actually have fewer pages combined than the whole book of Isaiah. The 12 minor prophets are contained in one book.

Let's look at the prophecies of Isaiah because this is the first prophet that really begins to speak about things of God on a worldwide basis—beginning to bring in things concerning God's major overall plan. All the other ones, the *former prophets,* are Joshua, Judges, 1st & 2nd Samuel, and 1st & 2nd Kings. In them there is nothing concerning the whole world. That's concerning Israel and the kings of Israel and the history of Israel. It also includes the Prophets Elijah and Elisha, two of the prophets of God.

When we come to the book of Isaiah, we see here that God really brings things out. What I want to do is cover, to begin with, most of Isa. 1.

What we're going to see is that every prophet speaks the words of God. When they begin prophesying, what they do is they bring out a warning from God. Or you could say an exposing of sin, then a call to repentance.

From there on we have different things that come into play, because as we have learned from Isa. 28 that it is 'line upon line, precept upon precept, here a little there a little.' We will see some things that will come along and it will be talking about Israel, then it will be talking about the Millennium, then it will be talking about the things to take place right then, even within the same chapter. So, this is why you cannot take the prophets—Isaiah, Jeremiah and Ezekiel—and run an absolute chronological line, because there will be:

- some here and some there on one topic, then on another topic
- the current sins, the future sins
- the current captivity, the future captivity
- the restoration after Babylon, after the original Babylonian captivity
- then the restoration after Babylon the Great and the exodus beginning out of all nations

You have all of these things put together in a way that in some ways is not organized according to chronology. This way God can bring the message through His prophets. Then God has to work with those who read it and understand it with His Spirit so that it can be *spiritually* understood.

What we are going to see is how this is an encapsulation of all the problems of Israel and Judah. Remember, at the time of King Hezekiah the ten northern tribes had not yet been carried off into captivity; so, Hezekiah also deals with the children of Israel who were still there.

Isaiah 1:1: "The vision of Isaiah the son of Amoz, which he saw concerning Judah and Jerusalem in the days of Uzziah, Jotham, Ahaz, *and* Hezekiah, kings of Judah." He had quite a spread, and he preached tremendous things.

Then God begins to bring things from a larger perspective, and this goes back to what God told the children of Israel there in Deut. 30, that He 'called heaven and earth against them this day,' and that 'I've set before you life and death, good and evil, blessing and cursing.' So, God harkens back to that beginning in:

Verse 2: "Hear, O heavens, and give ear, O earth…"

The heaven and earth are in existence. The fact that the earth is in its orbit, rotating on its axis, rotating around the sun, and the moon is rotating around it, *are witnesses along with the vast heavens that God has created,* that:

- His Word is true
- His Word is right
- His Law is the standard by which we need to live

"…for the LORD has spoken, 'I have reared and brought up children, **but they have rebelled against Me**'" (v 2). *So, the LORD states His cause.*

Look at all that God did for the children of Israel in bringing them out of Egypt and into the 'promised land.' Go back and you read all the battles that were fought by Joshua and the children of Israel, and how they conquered the land and God gave them rest. Then another generation arose, after Joshua and the elders died, *who did not know God.* It seems as though that the generation that follows, they've got to say:

We've never had our chance; we want to do it our way. Why are you so exclusive against all of these other nice people in our midst, who have their gods and have their religion?

Today, we have the same thing, it's called *diversity!* Diversity has always been the sin and the bane of Israel. God has said that when you get involved in diversity, bringing all other people together, making them equal to what God has given to His people and His inheritance, *then you start following their gods and 'you start rejecting Me.'*

Today we have it so that they're just rejecting God at every hand. Just understand and know that God's hand of correction is going to come because of what we read here. This is:

- a prophecy to the people *then*
- a *continuous* prophecy to God's people *down through history* to the time of Christ
- a *continuous* prophecy for the children of Judah and Israel *today in the end-time*

God says He wants to teach you a simple lesson:

Verse 3: "The ox knows his owner, and the donkey his master's crib; *but* Israel does not know *Me*; My people do not understand…. [we're not even as good as an ox or a donkey] …Ah, sinful nation, a people burdened *with* iniquity…" (vs 3-4).

I want you to think about the contemporary world in which we live, and I want you to understand what's going on. It's exactly what's happening.

"…**a seed of evildoers, children who deal corruptly! They have forsaken the LORD**; they have provoked the Holy One of Israel to anger; they have gone away backward" (v 4). *Then He asks*: '**Why** you want to:

- live in the way of sin
- suffer from sin
- suffer from crime
- suffer from all of these things

when I am the One to help you?' *Yet, they won't do it.*

Verse 5: "Why should you be stricken any

more? You will revolt more and more; the whole head is sick, and the whole heart faint."

Do we not have mental disease? emotional disease? physical disease? One of the leading causes of disease is heart failure. This means you can't think straight and you have the wrong emotions, too. So, you have everything involved. When God talks about something, you have the *physical* aspect and you have the *spiritual* aspect of it.

Verse 6: "From the sole of the foot even to the *top of the* head *there is* no soundness in it…"

If that doesn't describe the governments of the nations of Israel today, I don't know how much clearer it could be. Also, in our lives:

- Do we not have sickness?
- Do we not have disease?
- Do we not have open wounds in our cities called 'ghettos'?
- *Yes!*

"…*only* wounds and bruises and putrefying sores; they have not been closed, nor bound up, nor soothed with ointment" (v 6)—*because they try and solve the problems **their** way, not **God's way!*** A key, important thing to always understand:

You can never solve your problems your way. You must have them God's way!

The problems that we are given to solve, which we have to work out ourselves, *we have to take the principles of God to do it!* Another thing I've said a lot: ***You cannot solve spiritual problems by political or carnal means!*** It's an impossibility! ***You must do it God's way!*** Here God shows how you can do it, even though it is as bad as described here in the first chapter of Isaiah.

Verse 7: "Your country *is* a desolation, your cities *are* burned with fire. Strangers devour your land right in your *very* presence…"

We are beginning to see that the stranger will rise up very high above us, and *we will be brought low!* You can guarantee that! You can try and defeat any immigration bill that you want, but know and understand that what is happening with the immigration *is the hand of God's punishment!* Because, in effect, we are *spiritually at war*—as a nation and people—*with God*, even too much within the Church of God!

So, you're never, *never*, **never** going to do anything for God *your* way! ***You've got to do it God's way,*** and this is what God is bringing out here. Even when there's sin, ***you've got to do it God's way!***

"…and *it is* wasted, as overthrown by strangers. And the daughter of Zion is left as a booth in a vineyard, like a hut in a garden of cucumbers, like a besieged city" (vs 7-8).

Problems and terrible things all around, and it just keeps growing just like a vines, it just keeps growing! It comes out and they have these little growing little curlicues to latch on to things. *Sin is just gripping everything!*

God always does this: whenever He brings about an exposé or an exposing of sin, He also brings in some hope. God also realizes that in the population of Israel and also within the Church, and we're going to see many of these prophecies run parallel to Israel and the Jews and to the Church. *Here's one that runs parallel*:

Verse 9: "Except the LORD of hosts had left us a very small remnant…"

Just like during the days of Elijah, there were *7,000 that hadn't bowed the knee to Baal*. God always keeps a remnant.

Note our message, *Two Generations*[transcriber's correction]. We need to preach and teach to the remnant in the Church *and* the remnant in the world that have not bowed the knee to Baal:

- those who are out there seeking Truth
- those who are out there seeking what is right

There are probably many, many people that God is working with that we know nothing about!

"…we would have been as Sodom; we would have become like Gomorrah. Hear the Word of the LORD, rulers of Sodom; give ear…" (vs 9-10).

- London
- Paris
- Amsterdam
- Bonn
- Washington, D.C.
- Sydney, Australia
- Auckland, New Zealand

all of the nations of Israel!

"…Hear the Word of the LORD, rulers of Sodom…"

Oh yes, you let the Sodomites and the homosexuals take over and get rid of God. Even preach it and teach it in the schools beginning in kindergarten. *God is going to judge for that!* He says the way that you start getting out of your mess is this:

"…**give ear to the Law of our God**, people of Gomorrah" (v 10).

Then he looks at all the religiosity of the people. It's back then, it's been down through history and it continues to this day.

Verse 11: "'To what purpose *is* the multitude of your sacrifices to Me?' says the LORD.…" *What are you doing in worshipping God the way you want to?*

"…'I am full of the burnt offerings of rams, and the fat of fed beasts; and I do not delight in *the blood of* bulls, or of lambs, or of he-goats. When you come to appear before Me, who has required this at your hand…'" (vs 11-12).

- Who requires that you have the kind of church services that they have in the Catholic cathedrals and in the Protestant churches?
- Who's required that?
- Has God anything to do with any of it?
- *Very little, though they use the name of God!*

"'…to trample My courts?'" (v 12). *Trample the name of God!*

Stand up in the pulpit and say, 'We don't have to keep the Laws of God, they have all been abolished.' **Do you realize how blasphemous that is?** *You're saying that the Lawgiver has abolished His Laws!*

How can there ever be anything to exist without laws? *Not only spiritually, but physically!* The whole universe runs by laws. You live in a society where you demand people to be lawgiving. Yet, in your pulpit, every Sunday you say, 'We have been delivered from the Law.' *LIARS!* Even within the Church of God that takes place.

- When will people ever learn?
- Do we in the Church fit into the same category?

God has reared us and nurtured us
- and we rebel against Him?

Let's see what needs to be:

Verse 13: "Bring no more vain sacrifices; incense is an abomination to Me—new moon and sabbath…"

Notice that it doesn't say, '*the* Sabbath,' so it's 'sabbath.' What we're going to see that that is *their* sabbath, which today is Sunday.

- *If* the Jews gather into the synagogues on the Sabbath Day today and reject Christ and the New Testament, **what has God got to do with them?**

- *If* the Muslims meet on Friday, what does God have to do with them?
- *If* those that say that every day is 'holy,' what does God have to do with them?

Nothing! You cannot approach God except by the way He's given the instructions to do so!

This is what's so important, brethren. This is why we need to learn this lesson now. We are in the Kingdom of God as kings, priests—rulers, mayors, governors, board of regents—whatever may be our reward and where we will work. Of course, you know and understand that's just a start. Throughout all eternity there will be more to do and other positions to fill. So, keep that in mind.

But we must learn that basic lesson, *it has to be according to God's way* in everything that is done—not according to the way that *we think* or that *we suppose* or that *we have goodness in our heart,* that this is a good thing to do. *NO! We have to do it according to God's way!* People are very 'religious.'

He says: "...the calling of assemblies—I cannot endure iniquity along with the solemn assembly!" (v 13).

Do you think it's right that ministers stand in the pulpit and preach that the Laws of God have been abolished? fill the land with sin? live in a false grace? *which God never gave? Of course not!*

Verse 14: "**Your** new moons and **your** appointed feasts **My soul hates...**" Yet, we attach the name of God to it. We proclaim through grace,

Oh, we're all delivered to do these things. Isn't it nice. And after all, we do it for the children.

Yeah, that's right you do.

- you lie to your children
- you expose them to satanism and demonism on Halloween
- you tell them Jesus was born on a pagan holiday
- you tell them that Santa Claus exists
- you tell them that the Easter bunny is from God

God says He hates them!

"...My soul hates; they are a trouble to Me; I am weary to bear *them*" (v 14).

Let's see why religion has done very little good to change anything, and how this applies to our societies today:

Verse 15: "And when you spread forth your hands..."

You're all there swaying back and forth and singing, and you're doing good to God, you're spreading forth your hands in songs and in prayer and all of the good things that you do.

- How many people are there confessing their sins and repenting to God?
- How many ministers are there in the pulpit and saying:

We need to get back to the Sabbath of God, instead of our Sunday and our holidays?

We need to understand, brethren, we are living in the midst of a 'crooked and perverse' society, and we've always got to keep our bearings straight. *We have been called to understand*

- the Truth from error
- sin from righteousness

so that we can prepare to take over this world and rule the world! That's why God has called us. So, He says:

Verse 15: "And when you spread forth your hands, I will hide My eyes from you; yea, when you make many prayers, I will not hear; your hands are full of blood." That has been going on way too long: full of blood, crime and wretchedness.

Let's see what Ezekiel says about this, and let's see how this typifies our cities today. Think of all the things that go on in our cities today:

- all the crime
- all the hatred
- all the murder

God has sent the terrorists as correction; you need to understand that. Britain gets it first because they have gone further from God. *If you go against God you're cursed with a curse!* God says, 'I will send five to chase a thousand, and a hundred to chase ten thousand.'

So, all the diligence, all the surveillance, all of the taping of the wires and intruding into people's lives and all of this to try and stem the rise of the war of terror against us will prove to be futile indeed, because *there is no repentance*. God said that if we were with Him that *five of us would chase a thousand of them, and a hundred of us would chase ten thousand of them!*

We need to think and understand where we are and what we are doing. We need to be vigilant in our spiritual lives.

Ezek. 7:23—here's the city that God chose to place His name. You can say that of America and Britain and the ten tribes of Israel that are scattered throughout America and Britain and also in Northwestern Europe. Look at the cities; take any city you want. Take Washington, D.C., the capital city of United States of America, is the murder capital of the U.S.A. Think about the city you live in, or think about the big city close to where you live.

Ezekiel 7:23: "Make a chain; for the land is full of bloody crimes... [that's all you see on the news anymore] ...and the city is full of violence. And I will bring the worst of the heathen..." (vs 23-24).

This is why there is the immigration problem, because of all the crime, all the rejecting of God.

"...and they shall possess their houses. I will also make the pomp of the strong to cease; and their holy places shall be defiled" (v 24).

IF the Islamic Jihadists take over here, what are they going to do to every Christian church? every Catholic cathedral? every idol that they find through the land?

- they are going to burn
- they are going to destroy
- they are going to make waste

It's going to happen!

Verse 25: "**Terror comes**..."

We have lots of destruction: hurricanes, tornadoes—just like God said—also you have blasting, drought and mildew. When they get all ready, 'Oh we're going to solve the oil importation problem by having our alternative fuel. And we are going to use ethanol, made from corn and soybeans.' Oh yes, drive the price of corn and soybeans out of sight. And now they say, 'We can make alternative fuel from fruits.' So let's take our apples, peaches and apricots, and let's make fuel.

Pray tell, what shall we eat? But just when they get ready for jumping on the bandwagon, what happens? *There's a drought!*

- Where is there going to be the production?
- Where is there going to be the corn?
- Where is there going to be the sugar beets?
- Where is there going to be the soybeans?
- *It won't happen!*

Every plan and device that we devise will never work!

"...and they shall seek peace, but there shall be none. Disaster shall come upon disaster, and rumor shall be upon rumor... [sounds like the nightly news] ...And they shall seek a vision from the prophet; but the Law shall perish from the priest, and wisdom from the elders" (vs 25-26).

Yeah, they'll come and say, 'What do you think?' And if someone says, 'Repent and keep the commandments of God!' *Oh, you're not nice. Why don't you speak kindly to us?* Well, why don't you quit warring against God with your hatred, your rebellion, and your religious assemblies that you have, where you think you're so nice and pomp and wonderful. You need to look at it God's way!

Verse 27: "The king shall mourn, and the prince shall be clothed with despair, and the hands of the people of the land shall tremble. I will do to them according to their way, and according to their uncleanness... [which the judgments of the land are awful] ... I will judge them; and **they shall know that I *am* the LORD.**"

That's really quite a description of modern-day Israel today. Whichever country you want to look at.

Every prophet of God calls for repentance, because that's the only solution. There has to be vast repentance, and you know there needs to be repentance in the Church of God—*mighty repentance in the Church of God!* You look at the Churches of God and what they teach today and you ask: Do these really represent God?

You have Churches of God and church leaders that are so hateful and mean, and do not know how to preach the Truth and love of God to inspire and help the brethren to want to keep the commandments of God. *No!* They have to 'beat them in the face.' They have to discourage them so much that even some have committed suicide. *God knows that!* He looks down on it, and He sees that! He looks at the Churches of God and He asks, 'What are you doing?' Let's all of us look in our lives and ask ourselves personally:

- What am I doing?
- How am I doing?
- Am I carried away in pride and vanity?
- Am I delighting in my secret sins?
- Am I going to church every Sabbath and playing Sabbath?
- What is your relationship with God?

Here's a call to repentance:

Isaiah 1:16: "Wash yourselves, make yourselves clean; put away the evil of your doings from before My eyes; cease to do evil... [repentance then requires the next step when you do that] ...learn to do good; seek judgment, reprove the oppressor. Judge the orphan; plead for the widow" (vs 16-17).

This takes a process of time, as well. It's not going to be done just in one felled swoop. Yes, repentance can come that way, but that's only a start. ***There needs to be continuous repentance and continuous drawing close to God!***

- Do you see the Churches of God doing that? *It's possible!*
- Do you see the nations of Israel and the Jews doing that? *No way!*

Maybe a few of the remnant that are there. But:

- Will the nations do it?
- Will the religious denominations do it?
- Will the Muslims forsake Mohammed and embrace Christ in Truth?
- Will the Hindus who live among us get rid of their gods?
- *NO!*

In Virginia, right close to the capital, they're building the biggest Hindu temple in the western hemisphere.

We need to see where we're going. We need to understand what is happening. So, God says, after you repent:

Verse 17: "Learn to do good... [v 18]: 'Come now, and let us reason together'…" The way we reason with God is through repentance and say, 'Yes, God, Your way is right. Your righteousness is Truth.'

"…'Though your sins are as scarlet, they shall be as white as snow…'" (v 18). ***God will wipe it all away! God will clean it all away!***

As we've seen, He will 'cast them into the depths of the sea and remove them as far from us as the east is from the west'—***IF*** *there's true repentance!*

"…though they are red like crimson, they shall be like wool. **If you are willing and obedient, you shall eat the good of the land**" (vs 18-19).

Now, for the modern nations of Israel, that's the only way. *For the Churches of God* among them, or wherever the Churches of God are in the world, *that is the only way.* We must love God, keep His commandments and do the things that are right.

There's another warning, v 20: "'But **if you refuse and rebel,** you shall be devoured *with* the sword'… [the thing that everyone fears] …**for the mouth of the LORD has spoken** *it.*"

Let's see what Jeremiah says. This is why we cannot put any confidence in men. This is why we cannot put any confidence in things that are devised to try and help the problems and the difficulties.

Unless there's repentance to God, all the things will only have so much of an effect. I know as we go along in the future and get closer to the end, we're going to go over these same Scriptures again and again until there are people who really understand it. God tells us that we are not to preach nice, purring, soft, fuzzy, warm words.

- we are to *warn*
- we are to *teach*
- we are to *admonish*

Then preach the love of God and the Truth of God that goes with it, ***after there is repentance!*** If Jer. 6:13 this doesn't describe our nations today. When you think about all the commercialism, all of the gadgets, all of the things to buy: the homes, the cars, the clothes, everything. We are so inundated, we are so glutted. God has given us everything to the nth degree of the promise that He said He would do. What have we done with it?

Jeremiah 6:13: "For everyone from the least of them even to the greatest of them is greedy for gain…"

Whether you're homeless in the street and have nothing, or you're the richest man in the world like George Soros—he's not the richest but one of the richest—trying to bring down America, an avowed atheist who has set to *destroy* this nation. He is one of those that God has raised up *to correct us!* Because if you reject God, *He's going to send an atheist down your throat* and everything to go with it.

"…and from the prophet even unto the priest everyone deals falsely…. [no truth, no honesty, no righteousness, no goodness] …They have also healed the hurt *of the daughter* of My people slightly, saying, 'Peace, peace,' when *there is* no peace" (vs 13-14).

Good example: How many peace attempts have been between the Jews and the Palestinians? They always say, 'Peace, all we want is peace.' Bam! Bam! Pow! Kill them! Is that peace? The truth is, *the more you **reject** God, the more implacable that the enemy becomes!* The more you go after the enemy because they're the enemy, the more resolute they become, because there's no repentance. People think that if they go after the enemy and destroy the enemy that everything will be fine. No it won't! It can never be fine until there's repentance and turning to God, likewise in the Church and in our own individual lives.

- Are we too much like the world and at war against God?
- Are we too much like the world with the way we think and our attitudes and how we live?

Verse 15: "Were they ashamed when they had committed abomination?...."

That includes all the homosexuality, and all of the things they do to tempt God in their behavior, that are wretched and death-defying feats.

"'...No, they were not at all ashamed, nor could they blush; therefore, they shall fall among those who fall. At the time *that* I punish them, they shall be cast down,' says the LORD" (v 15).

God is visiting the nations of modern Israel today. God is visiting His Church. When we come together on the Sabbath, wherever we are—whether only 2 or 3, 10 or 12, 50 or 60, 100 or 200—and we ask God to put His presence there:

- What does God have to put up with?
- Is God's presence really there in love, power and understanding?

or

- Does God have to come into the assemblies of the Churches of God holding His nose?

Here's a call for repentance. Every time there is a revealing of sin and a heralding of punishment to come, there's always a call for repentance:

Verse 16: "Thus says the LORD, 'Stand in the ways and see, and ask for the old paths...'" *That is the right way of God!*

Isn't it what they say today, 'Oh, why we're under the New Covenant, we're delivered to do all these things.' Never happen! I just read a paper from some men who have left the Church of God who say exactly what I just said. So, don't think that what I'm saying is not relevant.

"...where the good way *is* and walk in it, and you shall find rest for your souls...." (v 16).

You make peace with God. Notice how similar this is to what it says in Isaiah. *'Cease to do evil, learn to do well, come now let us reason together.'* Very similar!

"...But they said, 'We will not walk *in it*'" (v 16).

I don't like this preacher. I don't like how he speaks.

Or whatever it may be!

Verse 17: "Also, I set watchmen over you..." *There are many 'watchmen' saying*:

- watch out, the depression is coming
- watch out, the dollar is going to fall
- watch out, the Amero is coming
- watch out, they're going to destroy the United States of America by amalgamating it with Canada and Mexico

then they can

- change the constitution
- change the power structure
- set up over it anyone that they want to

And the money-exchangers of the United States will RULE! *It's coming!* There are many voices out there saying it. God has many prophets:

- secular prophets
- governmental prophets
- warning about health
- warning about various things

Then He has His own prophets to prophesy what's going to happen spiritually, because it's going to come! There needs to be a lot of ministers in the Churches of God who are going to get up and really speak the Truth the way it needs to be—and stop being concerned about money, numbers, people, buildings, lands and all those things. *God is going to take them away and strip them from us!* We need to understand it!

Jeremiah 5:25 "Your iniquities have turned away these *things*... [peace, rain, prosperity and so forth] ...and **your sins have withheld good things from you**."

Now let's see what's going to happen. What is the greatest fear that people have today? *Whatever it is, He's going to bring it!* Because you don't fear God, you fear other things and circumstances, *He's going to bring it upon you*:

Jeremiah 6:18: "Therefore, hear, you nations, and know, O congregation, what *will happen* to them."

There we are! *We are the congregation of God among the children of Israel!* So, we need to listen. We need to pay attention. Let's not have the Protestant attitude of the rapture:

We're here and God has got to take care of us because we are the Church of God.

I think the history of what has happened to the Church of God in our lifetime will prove that to be entirely incorrect. As vain and as reasoning as the reasoning of the children of Israel, that everything's going to be fine: 'Peace peace and there is no peace.'

Verse 19: "Hear, O earth… [we start out where we did in the book of Isaiah] …behold, **I will bring evil on this people, even the fruit of their thoughts**…"

You take all the evil that's in the thoughts of everyone, because that's how God is going to measure it, and God is going to bring the fruit upon it. What is the fruit? *'The wages of sin' is death!*

- destruction
- misery
- war
- famine
- pestilence
- disease

They're going to come! God says they are coming!

"…**because** they have not hearkened to **My words, nor to My Law, but have rejected it**" (v 19). *So, you need to think on that very deeply!*

If you are involved in a Protestant church or if you are a minister of a Protestant church and you preach the Law has been done away, **you** are guilty of bringing this upon the people. **You** need to repent. I only know of one Protestant minister that has repented. He was a Southern Baptist, and he was absolutely amazed when God opened His eyes. How many will do it. 'Oh no, you're just a raving lunatic, and who are you?'

Well, if I speak the words of God, *they are the words of God!* If they are the words of God it really doesn't matter who the messenger is, because God says, even out of the mouths of babes He would use that. So, they "…have rejected it."

The whole purpose of this is to show how the prophets of God work.

Isaiah 1:19: "**If** you are willing and obedient…"

The thing is, we don't put God on probation, but that's what too many people do. Wherever the *if* is involved, it's always on our relationship back to God, because God has given us choice, *free* choice. He's not going to take it away. We have to *choose*. If you don't choose, you're going to suffer the results of not choosing.

Verse 19: "'If you are willing and obedient, you shall eat the good of the land; but if you refuse and rebel, you shall be devoured *with* the sword'; for the mouth of the LORD has spoken *it*…. [you can't get any higher authority than that] …How has the faithful city become a harlot? *It was* full of judgment; righteousness lodged in it—but now murderers" (vs 19-21).

Try any capital city of the modern tribes of Israel today. Is that not true? *Yes, indeed!*

Verse 22: "Your silver has become dross…" *We're worse than that today!*

All we have is Federal Reserve Notes, or whatever fiat money that is in whatever country of the tribes of Israel you live in, because the nations have sold their souls to the international bankers. They **own** them. *Yes, indeed!*

"…your wine mixed with water; your rulers *are* rebellious, and companions of thieves; everyone loves a bribe, and is pursuing rewards…" (vs 22-23).

- Does that sound like your parliamentarian in Britain or in Europe?
- Does that not sound like the senators and congressmen in the United States?
- Many of them?
- *Yes, indeed it does!*

"…they do not judge the orphan, nor does the cause of the widow come before them" (v 23).

If they do, it's only for a vain show. And one man who says, 'I'm for the poor. I'm for the downtrodden.' *You know that ALL are hypocrites!*

Verse 24: "And the Lord, the LORD of Hosts, the Mighty One of Israel says…"

There comes a point when God's patience runs out. There comes a point that when we make God to serve with our sins, that He says, 'Enough is enough is enough!' People take advantage of God's mercy, kindness, graciousness and patience. ***But it will come to an end!***

"…'Alas! I Myself will vent My wrath upon My foes, and avenge Myself of My enemies…. [the enemies are His own people] …And I will turn back My hand upon you, and purge away your dross as with lye, and take away all your tin alloy" (vs 24-25).

He has to do that. That's why the Tribulation is coming. That's why there's going to be a captivity. That's why these things are going to come in the judgment of God before the Millennium can be established.

When the Kingdom of God begins. Notice what we've gone through here, the structure of what we have in Isa. 1. God calling to repentance the children of Israel at the time of Isaiah. This applies to any of the children of Israel down through history, and it comes to the end-time. Whenever He exposes sin, He calls for repentance. Then when He gets down to the beginning of the Kingdom of God or the Millennium, that's interspersed right in there. It sort of just jumps at you as out of sequence. But that's the way that God inspired it to be.

Verse 26: "And I will restore your judges as at the first, and your counselors as at the beginning; afterwards you shall be called The City of Righteousness, The Faithful City."

- Who's going to live there during the Millennium? *Jesus Christ and the saints! It will be righteous!*
- Who are the judges that He is going to give? *The saints who are resurrected and who are going to rule and reign with Christ!*

I did a series: *Judge Righteous Judgment.* {note our In-Depth study} We need to judge righteous judgment, and we need to learn it.

- we're going to be the judges
- we're going to be the counselors
- we're going to be the priests
- we're going to be the kings

Verse 27: "Zion shall be redeemed with judgment, and those in her who repent with righteousness."

Zion is *us!* Zion can also apply to the survivors of the ten tribes of Israel when they come out of Tribulation. Also to the Jews and the Levites when they come out of Tribulation.

Verse 28: "And the downfall of the transgressors and of the sinners shall be together; and those who forsake the LORD *shall be* consumed." *When that happens there's going to be another wave of repentance!*

Verse 29: "For they shall be ashamed of the oaks which you have desired, and you shall be confounded for the gardens which you have chosen, for you shall be like an oak whose leaf fades, and like a garden that has no water. And the strong shall be like a wick, and the maker of it as a spark, and they shall both burn together, and none shall put *them* out" (vs 29-31).

When God sets His hand to do some correcting, *it's going to be something!* We need to understand that.

I want to show the pattern. What did God say of John the Baptist? *There was 'no greater prophet that has risen among men than John the Baptist'!* Yet, 'he who is **least** in the Kingdom of Heaven will be greater than John.' I want to show you the same pattern that we saw in Isa. 1 of exposing of sin, call to repentance, etc., is the same pattern that all the prophets of God always use, and *ends with a dire warning!*

John the Baptist was the son of a priest—Zacharias—and his mother Elizabeth was of the daughters of Aaron. He didn't practice and train in any of the priesthood. No, he was out in the wilderness until the day of his appearing. Everyone knew about John the Baptist because of the miraculous birth that John had, because his parents were old and well-stricken with age, which means they had to be over seventy. It was the talk everywhere in Judea.

I imagine all through the years when different ones would get together and talk about it, because everyone knew about it. Everyone knew about when John was, on the day that he was circumcised. The prophecies we find of that in Luke 1. They understood and they were probably wondering:

I wonder what happened to John? Where is John? He's never taken any of the training to be a priest.

Yet, here was this miraculous birth, the old age of his parents. So, one day, John the Baptist shows up, preaching:

- not at the temple
- not telling people to offer sacrifices
- not telling people to take the ritual baths after they've offered their sacrifice for sin
- *No!*

Matthew 3:1: "Now, in those days John the Baptist came preaching in the wilderness of Judea, and saying, 'Repent, for the Kingdom of Heaven is at hand'" (vs 1-2).

He was the messenger to prepare the way. Malachi says that the priest is the messenger of God. John was preparing the way for Christ. So, Christ—God manifested in the flesh—*was* the coming King of the Kingdom of God and it *was* at hand. The preaching of the Kingdom of God took precedence over the Law and the Prophets. Not to do away with them, but a higher authority.

Verse 3: "For this is he who was spoken of by Isaiah the prophet, saying, '*The* voice of one crying in the wilderness, "Prepare the way of *the* Lord, make straight His paths."' John himself wore a garment of camel's hair, and a leather belt around his waist; and his food was locusts and wild honey" (vs 3-4). *Never tasted once of any sacrifice!* Think of that!

Verse 5: "Then went out to him *those from* Jerusalem, and all Judea, and all the country around the Jordan, and were being baptized by him in the Jordan, confessing their sins" (vs 5-6).

A new way of removal of sins. Not by sacrifice and ritual. Not at the temple, because his whole ministry was a prophecy of the destruction of the temple, and the whole priestly system, *done by a priest!* So, God used the authority that He set in motion to do and accomplish His work.

Verse 7: "But after seeing many of the Pharisees and Sadducees coming to his baptism…"

Here are the rulers, the religious leaders. Why would they go there? *Because they knew that he was the son of priest!* They wanted to find out what he was doing down there. When you read the account in John 1, you understand that it was an official investigation by the priests, the Pharisees and the Levites to find out who he was.

They said, 'Are you the Christ?' He said, 'No.' They said, 'Are you that prophet?' He said, 'No.' They said, 'Are you Elijah?' He said, 'No.' Though later, Jesus said he was Elijah. They said, 'Well, who are you?' He said, 'I'm the voice of one crying in the wilderness.'

They come down there and the reception he gave them. *Think!* They're in their robes, they're all dignified, they're all coming as a committee from the high priest to find out what's going on down there. 'We need to know why are all the people going there.'

I don't know if their income stream was becoming less because the people didn't go to the temple, but rather went to John the Baptist at the Jordan River, but it probably had something to do with that, because they could have their sins forgiven without going to the temple to buy a sacrifice. So, who knows, that may be part of it.

"…he said to them, '*You* brood of vipers… [How's that for a nice welcome? 'You slithering snakes in the grass.'] …who has forewarned you to flee from the coming wrath?'" (v 7).

Oh, you want to escape. As John told them here a little later, 'Don't say that we have Abraham for our father.' Don't count on who you are to have any importance before God unless there is repentance.

Verse 8: "Therefore, produce fruits worthy of repentance."

Isn't that very similar to the outline we find in Isa. 1? *Yes, indeed, because that's how God works!* 'Jesus Christ, the same yesterday, today and forever. I, the Lord, do not change.'

Verse 9: "And do not think to say within yourselves, 'We have Abraham *for our* father'; for I tell you that God is able from these stones to raise up children to Abraham. But already the axe is striking at the roots of the trees…" (vs 9-10).

God is going to take you down! This is also a prophecy of the destruction of the temple!

"…therefore, every tree that is not producing good fruit is cut down and thrown into *the* fire" (v 10).

Does that sound just like the condemnation and the threat of captivity and destruction and doom by Isaiah? Because of the lack of repentance? *Yes!*

Verse 11: "I indeed baptize you with water unto repentance; but the One Who *is* coming after me is mightier than I, of Whom I am not fit to carry His sandals…"

He's saying that if you think what I'm saying is tough, wait. You want to know what Jesus said to the Scribes and Pharisees, read Matt. 23.

"…He shall baptize you with *the* Holy Spirit, and with fire" (v 11)—*with the Holy Spirit to those who repent, and with fire to those who did not!*

What happened to Jerusalem? *Totally destroyed! Burned to the ground. Stones removed, not one on top of another.* Does God mean what He says? *Yes, He does!*

Verse 12: "Whose winnowing shovel *is* in His hand, and He will thoroughly purge His floor, and will gather His wheat into the granary… [that's us] …but the chaff… [that's them, those who don't repent] …He will burn up with unquenchable fire."

He's even giving the warning of the unpardonable sin because the priests and the Scribes and the Pharisees knew better.

- they had the Word of God
- they had all the prophecies of the Messiah
- they knew who Jesus was
- they understood who He was

But because Jesus did not align Himself politically with them, to bring in the Kingdom of God at that time, as a physical nation, and leave them in charge to run it, *they crucified Him!*

God does things differently than people think. Once people get off on a tangent their minds are closed. Their minds are covered. Their eyes are blind. So he says:

Verse 13: "Then Jesus came from Galilee…"

Then it talks about the baptism of Jesus. That was done to fulfill all righteousness and for John to have the confirmation that he was the one to prepare the way for the Messiah.

Let's see here how the pattern goes. Notice that we have interjected right in here what's going to happen when the Kingdom of God is on the earth when Christ comes and rules during the Millennium. Now, we'll just read this one. Others will go through and what I want to do is take highlights out of Isaiah and use that as a springboard to show the meaning of the Feast of Tabernacles and the thousand-year rule of Christ and the saints.

Isaiah 2:1: "The word that Isaiah the son of Amoz saw concerning Judah and Jerusalem."

This was done somewhere around 830B.C. Think of how long that is until it's established. We are already at 2900 years, *think of that!*

Verse 2: "And it shall come to pass, in the last days…"

When are the 'last days'? *They didn't know then!* They haven't known all the way down through time. But we know a little more now than they knew. That doesn't make us more righteous or fit for the Kingdom of God just because we know. It has to do with what we do with God's Spirit and has to do with how we love and obey God.

"…the mountain of the LORD'S house shall be established in the top of the mountains, and shall be exalted above the hills; and all nations shall flow into it" (v 2).

It's going to be the capital of the world. The temple of the Millennium will be nothing like anything we have seen before. It's going to be awesome and beautiful and fantastic. {our two messages: *The Millennial Temple #s 1 & 2.*}

Then it shows what's going to happen. People have to *choose* God's way. Even with Christ on the earth and God having conquered the whole world and the saints reigning as kings and priests and whatever other offices there are to reign in, God is not going to take away free choice. *The word of repentance is going to go out. Some people will be very willing!*

Verse 3: "And many people shall go and say, 'Come, and let us go up to the mountain of the LORD…'"

Just think what it's going to be like to approach the mountain of God with that great canopy, as a tabernacle covering Jerusalem. Think about that highway that they're going to have to walk in to go there. Think about what it's going to be an awesome thing to see.

"…to the house of the God of Jacob. And He will teach us of His ways… [His ways never change.] …and we will walk in His paths.'…. [because that's the way of the Lord] …For out of

Zion shall go forth the Law, and the Word of the LORD from Jerusalem" (v 3).

There are going to be some people who are not going to want to cooperate. They're going to be real hard, stubborn and obstinate, of which Gog and Magog are going to be taken care of sometime shortly after the Millennium begins.

Verse 4: "And He shall judge among the nations…"

How does it say that He shall judge among the nations? *Zech. 14:*

- he's going to cut off the rain from those who have rain
- those who don't have rain He's going to send the plague

It's going to be very convincing! They're still going to have to choose, and if they repent, God will heal them.

"…and shall rebuke many people; and they shall…" (v 4). *They're going to learn war does not pay!*

You are never going to accomplish anything lasting with war. Now, the only one who wars in righteousness is *the coming Christ!* That's to put down sin and evil.

"…beat their swords into plowshares, and their spears into pruning hooks. Nation shall not lift up sword against nation, **neither shall they learn war anymore**" (v 4).

Now you stop and think about that! You take that one phrase, "…**neither shall they learn war anymore**." What a change in society is going to have to take place. It's going to have to begin in the cradle. It's going to have to continue to the end of life. Think about all the toys of destruction that children play with today. *Won't be any!*

- no more war games
- no more Dungeons and Dragons and all of the evil things that they have on these computer games
- no more toy guns and toy spears
- no more hatefulness, child to child
- mothers are not going to have to be out there working

God is going to take away the hardness of their hearts! Amazing!

Verse 5: "O house of Jacob, come and let us walk in the light of the LORD."

Now let's see what else happens. You find this in every one of the prophets as you go through them. God goes along. He gives:

- a warning
- a condemnation of sin
- a call to repentance
- a re-education

Then the Millennium and then it comes back to another time!

So, we can say, beginning with v 6 we have the Tribulation; so we can say that this is pictured in a time of judgment, which could even picture the Feast of Trumpets and blend into that, the full meaning of it. So, as we go through the book of Isaiah, we are going to see it covers Passover, Unleavened Bread, Pentecost, Trumpets, Atonement, Tabernacles and the Last Great Day, *all interspersed within the book of Isaiah!* Amazing! You can take any of the prophets and do an outline and structure it according to the Holy Days.

We will have to say that Ezekiel is probably more wholly given over to the meaning of the Feast of Trumpets and war, destruction, punishment and correction than any of the other prophets. Ezekiel brings very, very little concerning the Millennium. Jeremiah brings a little bit more. But Isaiah brings the most concerning the Millennium. Then we have some of it in the other twelve minor prophets.

Now then, Isaiah goes back and he points out their sins again, and why Christ has to come and exercise judgment:

Verse 6 "For You have forsaken Your people… [Isaiah talking to God] …the house of Jacob, because they have become full *of* divinations from the east… [Isn't that happening today? Eastern religions coming in? Yes!] …and *are* fortune-tellers like the Philistines…."

What do we have in every single newspaper? *You have your birth-sign, which is fortune telling!* 'What will my day be like today? Oh, newspaper and soothsayer, tell me.'

"…And they shake their *hands* with the children of strangers…. [to follow their way and do their way] …And their land is full of silver and gold…." (vs 6-7).

Oh yeah, there's a seeming prosperity because God promised Abraham He would do it, and He is doing it. But no, just as He has done it, He is going to take it away.

"…*There is* no end of their treasures and their land is full of horses; neither is there any end of their chariots" (v 7).

Look at all of our cars and transportation, everything that we have *everywhere!* Cars everywhere! Trucks everywhere! Add to that: airplanes, public and private. Add to that the prophecy that Daniel gave: *'Many shall go to and fro and knowledge shall increase.'* Add all of that in there you see; because this is what we're talking about with the Word of God.

Verse 8: "And their land is full of idols; they worship the work of their own hands, that which their own fingers have made."

Now just take this one verse here, v 8, and kind of put it up right in front when you're watching television and watch all the ads. Isn't that what they do? *Yes, indeed!* Appealing to what? *Covetousness!* Getting people in debt. And *they worship what their hands have made, what their fingers have made!*

Verse 9: "And men will be brought low, and humbled—forgive them not…. [because they knew better] …Enter into the rock and hide in the dust for fear of the LORD, and for the glory of His majesty. The lofty looks of man shall be humbled, and the pride of men shall be bowed down, and the LORD alone shall be exalted **in that day**" (vs 9-11).

- let all the mighty come
- let all the armies come
- bring all your weapons
- bring all the very best that man can do

'Come! Come!' is what Christ is going to say, and they're going to come.

Verse 12: "For the Day of the LORD of hosts… [Feast of Trumpets] …*shall be* on every proud and haughty one, and on every exalted one; **and they *shall be* brought low**, and it shall be on all the high and lifted up cedars of Lebanon, and upon all the oaks of Bashan" (vs 12-13).

That is just like saying all the leaders of the world, all the leaders of the nations.

Verse 14: "And upon all the high mountains, and on all the hills *that are* lifted up."

Those are governments. If we have nations and hills over here referring to the Kingdom of God in the first part of this chapter, then this refers to the governments that are on earth now.

Verse 15: "And upon every high tower, and on every fortified wall."—every way of war. God saying, *'Bring it on! You want to fight Me? Bring it on!'* You'll be defeated!

Verse 16: "And upon all the ships of Tarshish, and upon all pleasurable craft. And the pride of man shall be bowed down, and the haughtiness of men shall be made low; and the

LORD alone shall be exalted in that day" (vs 16-17).

This has to happen in order to prepare the way for the Kingdom of God to reign and rule on the earth. God is going to destroy this entire world system—*every bit of it!* It's going to be a new government, a new way, and God is going to make a New Covenant with the people of the world, beginning with Israel and Judah. The New Covenant with Israel and Judah beginning with the Millennium has not yet taken place. The New Covenant with His Church began with the last Passover of Jesus Christ and continues on down to this day.

Verse 18: "And **the idols He shall utterly abolish.**" I find it most interesting and profound that the Catholic prophecies say that the:

- antichrist is going to abolish idols
- antichrist is going to reign a thousand years

Are they blinded?

Whatever has gotten into people's hearts and minds that they consider that the Catholics are Christian? *They're not!* They are false christs, false christians and the Protestants are going along just like dumb sheep to the slaughter. You tell me the last time you ever heard a ringing sermon against Catholicism from a Sunday-keeping Protestant church. When? *Maybe someone rare out there would do it!*

Verse 19: "And they shall go into the holes of the rocks…"

No more office buildings, no more bomb shelters, nothing, nothing to protect you, except *you see a hole in the rock and you run in there.*

"…and into the caves of the earth for fear of the LORD and for the glory of His majesty…" (v 19).

That ties right in exactly with the Feast of Trumpets, and the return of Christ. And this ties right in exactly beginning Rev. 6:12 all the way through to the end and Christ putting His feet on the earth with the saints.

"…when He arises to shake *terribly* the earth. In that day a man shall cast his idols of silver, and his idols of gold, which they made *each one* for himself to worship, to the moles and to the bats" (vs 19-20).

All the way through the book of Isaiah, God talks about those who make idols over and over and over and over again. Men consider themselves to be intelligent. Men consider themselves to be something special. Yet, they will hire someone to make an idol of silver or gold, carve it, forge it, build it and put it in its place, *then come and bow down*

and worship it! It can't see, it can't hear, it can't speak, it can't think, it can't save from anything else. Yet, that whole system is idolatry. God is going to get rid of it. Same way with the Buddhist. They have these little idols. They're going to be gone. And when they do that:

Verse 21: "To go into the clefts of the rocks, and into the tops of the ragged rocks, for fear of the LORD and for the glory of His majesty, when He arises to shake *terribly* the earth. Turn away yourselves from such a man, whose breath *is* in his nostrils; for in what is he to be esteemed?" (vs 21-22).

Isa. 1 & 2 prepares the way for the beginning of the Millennium. There are many, many other chapters that we're going to survey throughout the book of Isaiah.

Realize that in order for the Kingdom of God to come, there has to be the preparation for it and here are some of the verses in the Word of God that prepares for it. If you go back and you put all the prophecies of it together, one after the other through all the Old Testament and the New Testament, it is absolutely incredible that people would not believe that Christ is going to return and establish His Kingdom on this earth.

- It's going to be something!
- It's going to be awesome!

Brethren, God has called us to be a part of it! So, let's do as God says.

- let's put away our sins
- let's put away our vanity
- let's put away all of our selfishness and things that pull us down

Help all the brethren that you know to do the same thing, so that we can do what is right in God's sight. So that He can say to us, '*Well done, good and faithful servant!*' *He will give us the responsibility of ruling and reigning with Christ!*

Scriptural References

1) Isaiah 1:1-15
2) Ezekiel 7:23-27
3) Isaiah 1:16-20
4) Jeremiah 6:13-17
5) Jeremiah 5:25
6) Jeremiah 6:18-19
7) Isaiah 1:19-31
8) Matthew 3:1-13
9) Isaiah 2:1-22

Scriptures referenced, not quoted:

- Isaiah 28
- Deuteronomy 30
- Luke 1
- John 1
- Matthew 23
- Zechariah 14
- Revelation 12-22

Also referenced: Sermons:

- *The Two Generations*
- *The Millennial Temples #s 1 & 2*
- In-Depth Study: *Judge Righteous Judgment*

FRC:bo
Transcribed: 8-8-07
Reformatted: 1/2021

CHAPTER SIXTY-ONE

Isaiah's Prophecies of the Millennium II
Survey of Isaiah 3-29
Fred R. Coulter

We're continuing on our survey of Isaiah. We won't get into as much detail as we did yesterday, otherwise we'll have to have a 50-day Feast of Tabernacles and no one could afford that. So, we'll stop and look at certain details as we go along.

What I've done in going through this is put in my margin 'judgment and correction,' because that's what Isa. 3 is all about. Let's also understand something very, very important that we need to rely on more and more as we get closer to the end. We need to be *trusting in God* and have *faith in God* and *look to Him for everything*.

This is *judgment and correction* and this happens over and over and over in different cycles according to the obedience or disobedience of the people. This was happening exactly then when Isaiah gave the prophecy and it's happened down through the history of Jerusalem—even clear down to the destruction of it in 70 A.D. and on through its ups and downs from then until now. Also, it has to do with the children of Israel as well, so we have a broader picture here that we need to look at.

Isaiah 3:1: "For behold, the Lord, the LORD of hosts, takes away from Jerusalem and from Judah the stay and the staff, the whole stay of bread and the whole stay of water."

That's easy to do in Jerusalem because it was up high, and when you cut off the water there's no way to get water to it. The Spring of Gihon was the one that gave water for all the temple services and it flowed naturally. Well, during the days of Hezekiah, during the siege that came against Jerusalem, he built a tunnel so that the water would be diverted so there would be water for all of Jerusalem.

Needless to say, *all the plans of men* and all the things that they do to protect themselves against the disasters that come because of the correction of God, *all fail!* They may work for a while. It may seem like you can avoid it for a while. But every single one of them fails because God then increases. He increases the intensity of it. He increases the sentence of it. So, let's look at what happens here.

Verse 2: "The man of might and the man of war, the judge and the prophet, the diviner and the ancient, the captain of fifty, and the honorable man and the adviser, and the cunning charmer and the skillful enchanter.... [*all of them are going to be worthless*] ...And I will give young lads *to be* their princes, and capricious children shall rule over them. And the people shall be crushed, every man by another, and every man by his neighbor; the young shall rise up against the old, and the base against the honorable" (vs 2-5).

We're going to see that happen here. We're going to see chaos take place in all the nations of modern Israel today, sooner or later. Now, here's a promise in v 10. So, when things start getting bad:

- we need to be cautious
- we need to be careful
- we need to be trusting in God

But we need not have fear grip us, because God has given us promises:

Verse 10: "Say to the righteous that *it shall be* well with him; for they shall eat the fruit of their doings." *God will protect us!*

Psa. 91 is a Psalm that we're going to have to claim as protection and God's blessing for us in times of difficulties, because we will be helpless. We don't arm ourselves, we don't shoot our enemies, we don't kill those who attack us, and things like that. *We have to trust in God to be able to protect us and watch over us!* We need to always ask that in our prayers to God; here's why

Psalm 91:1: "He who dwells in the secret place of the Most High shall abide **under the shadow of the Almighty**."

There's something very important about a shadow. The only time you see a shadow is when you look down on the ground and see it. But you could look straight through a shadow and not even see it.

For example: if there's a big tree and there's a shadow here and you're standing back and you look down straight past the tree—and the shadow is way out at this point and there's a big shadow on the ground—you look straight down the tree and you cannot see the shadow.

That is just like the way that God protects us. You can't see it. He also has angels there to watch over us, to take care of us. This is why David said:

Verse 2: "I will say of the LORD, 'He is my refuge and my fortress, my God, **in Whom I will trust.**'"

This is what we're going to have to be doing as we enter into more of the treacherous days of the end-time. The way I see things happening, it's going to get gradually worse and worse, and we'll reach various crises points. Just like what has happened in Great Britain with those car-bombs foiled. They may be able to foil them, but sooner or later they're not going to be able to stop them. All of their efforts are going to come to naught because the problem is not the radical Islamists. That's the effect.

- the problem is *rejecting God*
- the problem is *getting rid of the Word of God*

That's where we're headed in this nation—same way. We'll see the same thing happen.

We can stop many, many of those attacks, that is true. But it also *fulfills that five of the enemy will chase a thousand of us!*

So, it took a thousand men and all of their activity that was necessary to arrest the perpetrators of those car-bombs in Great Britain. Also, Great Britain is filled with surveillance cameras *everywhere!* So much so they have monitors watching people, and if people throw things on the ground a voice will come out of where the camera is and say, 'Please pick up that which you threw on the ground.'

You can see all the effort that is in there. Whereas, God says that *it would be simple*:

- *IF* you would obey Me
- *IF* you would love Me
- *IF* you would keep My commandments
- *IF* you would do that which is right in My eyes

But the nation won't do it. They've turned their back on God in whatever way that they used to have God in their lives. We will see it with all the modern technology and things that we have we've watered down more and more to where those who really believe God will be viewed as *nuts!* But nevertheless, *God will protect us!* Here's a promise:

Verse 3: "Surely He will deliver you from the fowler's trap and from the destroying pestilence." *Part of that is because we need to take care of*:

- our lives
- our bodies
- our diets
- things like that

Then God will protect us!

Verse 4: "He shall cover you with His feathers, and under His wings you shall take refuge.… [supernatural protection from God] …His Truth shall be your shield and buckler."

The Truth of God in your heart and in your mind is what is going to protect you! Not weapons, not guns, not bars on the windows, because everything devised to protect, evil men can figure a way around it.

But you can't beat the promise that God gives concerning the Feast of Tabernacles and His other Feasts. He says, *'When you go you won't have worry about someone taking your goods.'* Why is that? Are there angels placed around your house? *Could be!*

I have not heard of a report where someone's house was broken into while they were gone to the Feast of Tabernacles. *There is living proof of God's protection!*

Verse 5: "You shall not be afraid of the terror by night, nor for the arrow that flies by day, nor for the plague that walks in darkness, nor for the destruction laying waste at noonday. A thousand may fall at your side and ten thousand at your right hand; it shall not come near you" (vs 5-7). *This verse backs it up!*

There is a unity of Scripture. All Scripture is unified. But it's put in such a way that you have to work at it, and you have to put it together properly.

Isaiah 3:10: "Say to the righteous that *it shall be* well with him; for they shall eat the fruit of their doings. Woe to the wicked! For the evil doing of his hand will be given to him. As for My people, children *are* their oppressors, and women rule over them. Oh, My people, those who lead you cause *you* to err and destroy the way of your paths" (vs 10-12).

That's exactly what we're seeing happen. That's why in this world today we need to be preparing spiritually and mentally to be able to rule in the Kingdom of God, because we're going to come and correct all of these problems.

Isa. 5 will help us also see the unity of Scriptures. Then we will survey many of the chapters in the book of Isaiah, and we will see that it's not structured in a chronological sequence of the Passover and Holy Days, but the Passover and Holy Days are all there.

It's just a matter of putting together rightly, and that's why when we come to the New Testament, all the Holy Days are there, and especially with the book of Revelation, which is structured on the Holy Days.

Isaiah 5:1: "Now, I will sing to my Beloved a song of my Beloved concerning His vineyard. My Beloved... [Israel, now it's the Church] ...has a vineyard in a very fruitful hill. And He dug it up, and cleared it of stones, and planted it *with* choice vines, and built a tower in its midst, and hewed out a wine vat in it; and He looked *for it* to produce grapes **But it produced worthless fruits**" (vs 1-2). *God expects us to work and produce!*

We'll look at a couple of other Scriptures here that will be very interesting in how, in the unity of Scriptures, we find it in the New Testament.

Verse 3: "And now, O people of Jerusalem, and men of Judah, I ask you to judge between Me and My vineyard. What more could have been done to My vineyard that I have not done in it? Who knows? I looked *for it* to yield grapes, but it yielded wild grapes. And now I will tell you what I will do to My vineyard; I will take away its hedge, and it shall be consumed; *and* break down its wall, and it shall be trampled down; and I will lay it waste; it shall not be pruned nor dug; but briers and thorns shall come up. And I will also command the clouds that they rain no rain upon it" (vs 3-6).

Compare that with Israel, with the modern nations of Israel today, and compare that with the Church. Then correction from here all the way through:

Verse 7: "For the vineyard of the LORD of hosts *is* the house of Israel, and the men of Judah His pleasant plant; and He looked for justice, but behold, bloodshed; for righteousness, but behold, a cry *of distress!*"

Then he shows why with the woes—woe, woe, woe, woe—and the final one is that they have rejected the laws and commandments of God. Let's see how Christ even spoke of this. Let's see what Christ said about a vineyard. Almost identical to what we find back here in Isa. 5.

Luke 20:9: "And He began to speak this parable to the people: 'A certain man planted a vineyard... [right straight from Isa. 5] ...and leased it out to husbandmen, and left the country for a long time.'" *He's talking about Himself!*

The way that God does things is that He gives mission statements. Here's one of the greatest mission statements in the world:

Go into all the world and preach the Gospel to all nations, making disciples of them, and commanding them to observe all things that I have taught you! And baptize them into the name of the Father and the Son and the Holy Spirit!

He leaves the rest of it up to the ones He's chosen to do it, to figure out how to do it and to be led of the Holy Spirit by God to accomplish what He wants. The way you're led of the Holy Spirit of God is that you have *the laws and commandments of God written in your heart and your mind and you're going to do what God wants and you desire to do what God wants!* This is how it's going to be during the Millennium:

- everything is going to be set up
- Satan is going to be removed
- human nature is going to be changed through conversion
- they will have the commandments of God set before them
- we will teach them
- we'll teach them on the Sabbath
- we'll teach them on the Holy Days
- God's way will be taught throughout all the world
- everyone's going to have to choose what they're going to do

The same way here!

He left for a long time. That's the first coming of Christ, then the second coming of Christ:

Verse 10: "And in *the harvest* season he sent a servant to the husbandmen, so that they might give him *some* of the fruit from the vineyard; but the husbandmen beat him *and* sent *him* away empty. And after that he sent another servant; but they also beat him and scorned *him and* sent *him* away empty. And after that he sent a third *servant;* but they also wounded him *and* cast *him* out. Then the lord of the vineyard said, 'What shall I do? I will send my beloved son; perhaps when they see him, they will respect *him.*' But when they saw him..." (vs 10-14).

This is a parable, but also a prophecy of what they were going to do to Christ.

"...the husbandmen reasoned among themselves, saying, 'This is the heir. Come, let us kill him, so that the inheritance may be ours.' And they cast him outside the vineyard *and* killed *him*...." (vs 14-15).

Isn't that the way that people do to God? They:

- cast away God
- cast away Christ
- kill His memory

- accept satanic lies:
  - ✓ atheism
  - ✓ false teachings of false gods and idols

"'…Therefore, what will the lord of the vineyard do to them? He will come and destroy these husbandmen, and will give the vineyard to others.' Now, after hearing *this*, they said, 'MAY *IT* NEVER BE!' But He looked at them *and* said, 'What then is this that is written: "*The* Stone that the builders rejected, this one has become the head of *the* corner? Everyone who falls on that Stone shall be broken; but on whomever it shall fall, it will grind him to powder"'" (vs 15-18).

Then they sought to lay hands on Him. Matthew's account said that the leaders understood that He was talking about them.

- Did God take the vineyard away from Judah and Jerusalem? *Yes, He did!*
- Who did He give it to? *John 15 shows that the Church is the vineyard!*

We've gone thought this many, many times, so we'll just read few verses here in John 15. This is to show how that the Bible, inspired by the mind of God, is in complete agreement with itself. There are what *appear* to be contradictions. But when you really get into it, *there are no contradictions in the Bible or the Word of God at all!* The reason being is very simple:

- God is true
- God's Word is true
- His Spirit that inspires it is called *the Word of Truth*

Those who did the writing, were led by God to do and write exactly what He desired them to do. So, there are really no contradictions. Let's see how this parable comes along here, because He said then He would give the vineyard to others.

John 15:1: "I am the true vine, and My Father is the husbandman. He takes away every branch in Me *that* does not bear fruit… [He's actively working in His Church all the time—*the Father is*] …but He cleanses each one that bears fruit, in order that it may bear more fruit. You are already clean through the word that I have spoken to you…. [in other words, you have been purged, cleansed] …Dwell in Me, and I in you. As a branch cannot bear fruit of itself, but only if it remains in the vine, neither *can* you *bear fruit* unless you are dwelling in Me. I am the vine, *and* you *are* the branches…." (vs 1-5).

Questions for the Church, every member, every minister, every organization that professes the name of God as a Church of God, who keep the Sabbath and Holy Days:

- What kind of fruit are you bringing?
- Are you bringing good fruit?
- Are you bringing worthless fruit?

Again. we see how the Bible itself agrees with the Bible—and likewise with all the Holy Days. What happens with it then when you go through the Bible and you start outlining the Scriptures concerning the Holy Days, beginning with the Passover and then Unleavened Bread, Pentecost, Trumpets, Atonement, Tabernacles and Last Great Day; you see the whole Bible is structured that way. It really becomes fantastic!

All the things concerning correction, warning, war and destruction you can put under Trumpets. We find in Isa. 6 something that is contemporary. Notice the authority from where Isaiah got the words that he was to speak.

Isaiah 6:1: "In the year that King Uzziah died, I then saw the LORD sitting upon a throne, high and lifted up, and His train filled the temple…. [he had a vision of the temple] …Above it stood the seraphim; each one had six wings; with two he covered his face, and with two he covered his feet, and with two he flew. And one cried to another, and said, 'Holy, Holy, Holy, *is* the LORD of hosts; the whole earth is full of His glory'" (vs 1-3). Did he see the Throne of God? *Yes!*

Let's see how we see a very similar vision that John had. What we want to do is show how that the Old and the New Testaments are an integral part of one book.

Revelation 4:1: "After these things I looked, and behold, a door opened in heaven; and the first voice that I heard *was* as if a trumpet were speaking with me, saying, 'Come up here, and I will show you *the* things that must take place after these things.' And immediately I was in *the* Spirit; and behold, a throne was set in heaven, and *One was* sitting on the Throne" (vs 1-2).

He was sitting on it, it describes the appearance of it, you can read the rest of there in Rev. 4. So, we're dealing with the same God. We're dealing with the same Truth.

Verse 8: "And each of *the* four living creatures had six wings respectively; *and* around and within *they were* full of eyes; and day and night they cease not saying, 'Holy, Holy, Holy, Lord God Almighty…'"

Isaiah 6:4: "And the foundations of the threshold shook at the voice of the one who cried, and the house was filled with smoke. Then I said, 'Woe *is* me!…. [I guess so!] …For I am undone; for I *am* a man of unclean lips, and I dwell in the midst of a people of unclean lips; for my eyes have seen the King, the LORD of hosts'" (vs 4-5).

That's why you can be absolutely guaranteed when someone says, 'God talked to me.' *He didn't talk to them.* Or, 'I saw God.' *No, you didn't see God.* If you did, you would have an experience like John did and like Isaiah did.

Verse 6: "Then one of the seraphim flew to me, having a live coal in his hand, *which* he had taken with tongs from the altar. And he laid *it* upon my mouth and said, 'Lo, this has touched your lips; and your iniquity is taken away, and your sin atoned for'" (vs 6-7).

After an experience like this, and think about the experience that Jeremiah had and Ezekiel had and all of the other prophets; and you think about how the apostles and disciples were taught; and how they went and preached, and what they wrote and how God inspired them. **Do you even suppose that they would dare write something that was not true?** *That's why we can depend on the Word of God.* God used righteous men, faithful men moved of the Holy Spirit, who wrote what God wanted them to write. Not *their* ideas or anything like that.

Verse 8: "And I heard the voice of the LORD, saying, 'Whom shall I send, and who will go for Us?' Then I said, 'Here *am* I; send me!'"

So, he was willing. This is what we have to do. *We have to make ourselves willing!*

Verse 9: "And He said, **'Go, and tell this people**…'" What does that do? You find that many places in the New Testament: Matt. 13; John 12; many places in Acts 13 & 28

"…'You hear indeed, but do not understand; and you see indeed, but do not perceive.' Make the heart of this people fat, and make their ears heavy, and shut their eyes" (vs 9-10).

Jesus said they have shut their eyes, so it works both ways, just like it did with Pharaoh. Pharaoh hardened his heart and God hardened Pharaoh's heart. Why? *Because Pharaoh was not willing to listen!* Then God made it harder. People hear the same thing. They don't want to listen. God closes their understanding, and we have seen that happen. That's why we are where we are today, doing what we are doing to try and serve God and let Him:

- lead us
- guide us
- help us
- protect us
- watch over us
- inspire us

So that we can preach and teach, and do the things that God wants for the brethren; for all the Church; and for those of the world whom God is going to send. ***And lo, He will send them! We have to prepare, we have to be ready!*** It's like the old saying, 'If you build it they will come.'

If you get beside a busy highway and say, 'Oh boy, a motel right here would really, really be good. I wish I could have a motel here.' You come out there a year later and say, 'Oh, a motel here would be really, really good, I wished I had a motel here.' You come out five years later and say the same thing; ten years later and say the same thing. Then guess what, in the mean time maybe someone else comes along and says, 'Hey, be a good place for a motel, let's build it.' It's built and then you come along and say, 'Someone stole my idea.' No, God expects us to *work!* So, we have to repent, which opens our heart and our mind and then God gives us His Spirit.

"…shut their eyes; lest they see with their eyes, and hear with their ears, and understand with their hearts, and return, and be healed" (v 10).

- God isn't going to give any blessings to those who won't repent
- God isn't going to give eternal life to any of those who won't repent

That is straight through from Genesis to Revelation—all the way through—we see here an inset verse again, which applies directly to Christ, which was quoted in Matt. 1:18.

Isaiah 7:14 "Therefore, the LORD Himself shall give you a sign. Behold, the virgin… [that's what it is in the Hebrew and the Greek] …shall conceive and bring forth a Son, and they shall call His name Immanuel."

That refers to Christ because when the child was born by the prophetess he did not call the name of the child Immanuel, he called him 'Maher-shalal-hash-baz,' which then means *to make haste to plunder.* So, v 14 does not refer to the child that was conceived in Isa. 8:3.

A lot of people say that means that One. *It doesn't,* because it's completely the opposite. Isa. 8:1-12 *is warning and prophecy!* Many places are prophecies and warnings and warnings and prophecies.

Isa. 8:13 is talking about Christ, and Him probably born on the Feast of Trumpets, so you have that day. When was He crucified? *On the Passover Day!* Anything to do with Christ has to do with that. While He was dwelling on earth—as we saw earlier—that is likened unto *the Feast of Tabernacles*: *tabernacling among men.*

Isaiah 8:13: "The LORD of hosts, Him shall you sanctify, and *let* Him *be* your fear, and let Him be your dread. And He shall be a sanctuary *for you*—but for **a Stone of Stumbling**, and for a Rock of Offence to both the houses of Israel…" (vs 13-14).

What are 'both the houses of Israel'? *The ten tribes of Israel and Judah!* Both are the houses of Israel. How is Christ the *Stumbling Block* 'for both of them?

- *for the Jews,* they rejected Him as Messiah. that is more obvious
- *for the house of Israel, the ten tribes—* especially in the modern time today—they have 'a Christianity' with a *false christ*

The true Christ is a *stumbling block* to them, because the true Christ *kept the Sabbath! He kept the Holy Days, and the apostles, directly taught by Him, did the same thing.*

"…and for a trap and for a snare to the inhabitants of Jerusalem. And many among them shall stumble and fall and be broken, and be snared, and be taken" (vs 14-15).

There's **warning and prophecy,** which has to do with death and destruction. And we can also add in there for Jerusalem, the 9th and 10th of Ab as part of the *day of destruction* because in 586B.C. and also in 70A.D. the temple was destroyed and burned on those days.

Verse 16—*a prophecy of the coming New Testament*: "Bind up the testimony, seal the Law among My disciples."

This is why the Law of God is not complete. Yes, you have the first five books called *The Law,* but that's not complete. You have the Law given by Christ in Matt., Mark, Luke and John. That expands the spiritual meaning of the Law. How was that put together? *By the disciples, the apostles of Jesus Christ, they wrote it.* So, here's a prophecy of it.

Verse 17: "And I will wait upon the LORD, who hides His face from the house of Jacob; and I will trust in Him. Behold, I and the children… [quoted in Heb. 2] …whom the LORD has given me *are* for signs and for wonders in Israel from the LORD of hosts, Who dwells in Mount Zion" (vs 17-18).

Then here's also a prophecy that we have against the *occult* 'Christianity' of this world, and against all of the other religions that are demonic.

Verse 19: "And when they shall say to you, 'Seek unto them that have familiar spirits and to wizards who peep and mutter'—*but* should not a people seek unto their God?…." **Shouldn't you seek God?**

Oh, here's a way to do it, go to this astrologer, go to this palm reader, go to this spiritist, go to this one who claims he's Christ.'

Yes, and there are thousands who follow a man who says, 'I am the incarnation of Christ.' And they all take 666 tattoos on their bodies.

"…*Should* the dead *be sought* on behalf of the living?…. [here's how you separate out everything; that's why the Word of God is important] …To the Law and to the testimony!…. [Old Testament Law, New Testament Law] …If they do not speak according to this Word, *it is* because *there is* no light in them" (vs 16-20). *Amazing!*

There is a unity of Scripture! You cannot have the Old Testament without the New Testament, and you cannot have the New without the Old, because the two constitute the whole Word of God that He has revealed to mankind at this time. Then you can structure all of the Old Testament and all of the New Testament and break it down into Passover, Unleavened Bread, Pentecost, Trumpets, Atonement, Tabernacles and Last Great Day. *That is an amazing thing indeed!*

Isa. 9 has some contemporary prophecies:

- v 1 has to do with Christ and preaching the Gospel up in Galilee
- v 6 is fundamental to the Feast of Tabernacles, and also shows that the life of Christ

As He lived in the flesh, was a foretaste of living with God, because God, in the flesh, was living with men. This is a hard one for the Jews to get around. This is a hard one for anyone to get around. I mean, even if you are a non-believer.

Isaiah 9:6: "For unto us a Child is born, unto us a Son is given; and the government shall be upon His shoulders…" *That's talking about* **the Millennium!**

Who is the Head of the Church today? *Jesus Christ!* Everywhere you can read in the New Testament that Christ is the Head of the Church, the Body, this verse applies. That's why we have the booklet: *The Ministry is Not the Government of God—* never has been, *never will be!* The ministers and elders and teachers are not to be policemen over the brethren. **They are to teach** so the brethren can live their lives before God:

- in love
- in faith
- in hope
- in obedience
- to learn

So that they can be mature and spiritually able to live their lives before God! We have to learn how to do this, because that's exactly what we're going to teach all the people in the Kingdom of God when we are ruling on the earth.

"…the government shall be on His shoulders… [Wonder what the pope would have to say about that?] …and His name shall be called… [this is where the Jews can't get around it, because these are all the names of God]: …Wonderful, Counselor, **The Mighty God**…" (v 6).

Can God appear in the flesh? *This verse tells us!* Again, we have the unity of the Scripture: Old Testament and New Testament

"…The Everlasting Father…" (v 6). *He will become the Everlasting Father when there are children brought into the Kingdom of God through Christ and the Bride, which is the Church!*

Most of the places in the Old Testament where God refers to Himself as a Father and people refer to Him as a Father, you read those very carefully and the majority of them refer to the time of the Kingdom of God on earth.

"…The Prince of Peace. Of the increase of *His* government and peace *there shall be* no end, upon the throne of David…" (vs 6-7).

That encompasses a lot of things. That tells us that the throne of David is still somewhere here on the earth.

"…and over His kingdom… [and that kingdom has been expanded] …to order it and to establish it with judgment and with righteousness from henceforth, even forever. The zeal of the LORD of hosts will do this" (v 7).

So, here we have first coming of Christ, Feast of Trumpets, second coming of Christ to take over the government, Feast of Trumpets. We have the Holy Days right there, structured in the book of Isaiah.

Now we're going to start focusing in on the Millennial prophecies in the book of Isaiah. I find it very interesting and also very inspiring, that in the book of Isaiah we have more prophecies of the Millennium than of any of the other single prophets. The other ones have a bit here and bit there and little more here and little more there, but not like Isaiah. Isaiah has a substantial amount scattered all the way through the 66 chapters of the book of Isaiah. I also find it very interesting that the book of John, in the New Testament, is laid out and structured to the Holy Day seasons. So, you have Isaiah and then you have John, and then the book of Revelation is structured

more on the Holy Days than any other book in the Bible.

When you understand the Holy Days and realize what it's all about and how that these books of the Bible are structured on the Holy Days and have relevance to the meaning of the Holy Days, how can people say the Holy Days have been done away? *In saying the Holy Days are done away they don't realize that they're saying that God isn't going to use these days either!* But what they're really saying is that 'we don't have to keep them; we're good the way we are.' *Well, God will decide that in the long run!*

Now let's see another false doctrine that the Seventh Day Adventist have. They believe that during the thousand years everyone who is saved is going to be in heaven, and for a thousand years be going over the judgment books and decide who receives salvation or not. When you read Isa. 11 you find that no, that can't be. Because what it does, *it talks about the renewing of the earth!* God isn't going to leave it desolate for a thousand years as some claim. When we get to Isa. 24 we will see that it's just the opposite. Isa. 24 is really a fantastic chapter in itself.

Isa. 11 talks about Christ. This has to do with His first coming and also His second coming and the changing of everything back to what it was as we started the restoration of all things. So, we find again the unity of Scriptures, and you're going to hear me talk a lot about the unity of Scriptures in the coming months and years.

Isaiah 11:1: "And there shall come forth a shoot out from the stump of Jesse, and a Branch shall grow out of his roots."

This is referring to a prophecy of the removal of the throne of David from the area of Jerusalem and it was removed and, as we know, it now resides in Great Britain. The 'Branch' is Christ.

Verse 2: "And the Spirit of the LORD shall rest on Him… [we saw that fulfilled in Mat. 3, when Jesus was baptized] …the spirit of wisdom and understanding, the spirit of counsel and might, the spirit of knowledge and of the fear of the LORD. And His delight shall be in the fear of the LORD. And He shall not judge according to the sight of His eyes, nor after the hearing of His ears. But with righteousness He shall judge the poor, and shall reprove with equity for the meek of the earth. And He shall strike the earth with the rod of His mouth, and with the breath of His lips He shall slay the wicked" (vs 2-4).

Isn't that what it says He's going to do? *'Out of His mouth goes a sharp, two-edged sword' (Isa. 19)!* It's the words that He speaks. Does He not destroy that enemy, the armies gathered to fight against Him? *Yes!* So here in Isa. 11 we have blended together His first coming and His second coming.

We also have His ministry, His rule and reign over the earth, and the changing of the earth back to what it was before Adam and Eve fell.

Verse 5: "And righteousness shall be the girdle of His loins, and faithfulness the girdle of His reins. Also the wolf shall dwell with the lamb, and the leopard shall lie down with the kid; and the calf and the cub lion and the fatling together; and a little child shall lead them" (vs 5-6).

Totally different from what it is today. This is going to be a magnificent time for the world. A time of:

- peace
- prosperity
- plenty
- righteousness
- goodness
- elimination of all crime

Anyone who sins it's going to be something indeed! If somebody sins really, extremely terrible, then this will be an abhorrence to the whole community.

Now here in Hollister, there was a murder. Some young woman was killed, murdered, stabbed, had a black plastic bag over her head and dumped off in some cul-de-sac in Hollister. Something like that, oh it was a headline in the paper. But if something like that happened during the Millennium, that would be something greatly well-known, and it would be an abhorrence. We can say it's not going to happen during the Millennium.

What's going to happen when we get to Isa. 30? ***Your teachers are not going to be in a corner anymore. If you go to the right hand or your go to the left hand there will be a voice behind you saying, 'This is the way, walk in it'!***

Those things won't happen, that's why it's going to be righteousness and faithfulness. So great that the wild animals are going to be pets. Isn't that going to be a marvelous thing, get rid of all those stupid plastic toys.

Verse 7: "And the cow and the bear shall feed…"

Bears eat a lot of grass! I saw a special on the bears up in Kodiak Island. They eat an awful lot of grass. I was surprised to see that.

"…their young ones shall lie down together; and the lion shall eat straw like the ox…. [that's going to be something to see] …And the suckling child shall play on the hole of the asp, and the weaned child shall

put his hand on the viper's den. 'They shall not hurt nor destroy in all My Holy mountain; **for the earth shall be full of the knowledge of the LORD, as the waters cover the sea'**" (vs 7-9).

What does that tell us? *That tells us what we know in the Bible is just an itty-bitty amount of the knowledge of God that we have today!* Yet, people can hardly take that. Amazing! Going to be totally different.

Verse 10: "And in that day there shall be the Root of Jesse standing as a banner for the people; to Him the nations shall seek; and His rest shall be glorious."

You can tie that in with Isa. 2: *Many nations shall come and say, 'Let us go up to the house of the God of Jacob and let us learn of His Law and of His way and the Law shall go forth from Zion'!*

- it's going to be rest
- it's going to be peaceful
- it is going to be wonderful
- every human being will know they're needed
- they're wanted
- they're loved
- they can be educated
- they can be taught
- they can be successful
- they will have skills they will excel in
- they will have recognition
- there will be communities and villages and cities and people who will dwell in peace
- they'll be a church probably on every other corner
- where there are cities there will be nice broad streets
- children can play right in the streets
- you don't have to worry about gangs
- you don't have to worry about thugs
- you don't have to worry about kidnappers and rapists

What a fantastic time that will be!

I can picture the young kids riding on the back of a lion or a leopard or we can picture them on horses and donkeys now. But you know, that'll be quite a thing, riding on a lion, having a pet lion. You don't have worry about how much meat it's going to eat because it'll eat grass. I've often thought of this every time I read this. What's it going to be like to see a lion open its mouth or as we could say 'smile' and you see all of its teeth straight for eating grass? I don't know if that's going to happen, but that just kind of thing I think of every time I read that.

In v 11 there changes to another prophecy. This is how the Word of God is in the Old Testament: 'line upon line, here a little there a little, precept upon precept'—put it all together. So, vs 11-16 is the re-gathering and the future exodus of the people of Israel and Judah back to their own homeland, pictured by *Trumpets* and *Atonement*.

- Trumpets—they are released
- Atonement—they are at-one with God.

They will be coming back and to be at-one with God!

Verse 11: "And it shall come to pass in that day, the LORD shall again set His hand, the second time…"

This is referring to the first coming of the children of Judah going into captivity into Babylon, which had not yet happened. That didn't happen for well over a hundred years.

"…to recover the remnant of His people that remains, from Assyria and from Egypt, and from Pathros, and from Ethiopia, and from Persia, and from Shinar, and from Hamath, and from the coasts of the sea. And He shall lift up a banner for the nations, and shall gather the outcasts of Israel and gather together the scattered ones of Judah from the four corners of the earth" (vs 11-12).

That's something! That's the coming exodus. Then he says the strife and envy between Judah and Ephraim is going to end.

Verse 16: "And there shall be a highway for the remnant of His people, those left from Assyria; as it was to Israel in the day that he came up out of the land of Egypt."

This is really quite a fantastic chapter. We have the Millennium, Trumpets and Atonement.

Isa. 12 is something! This is one concerning salvation. This has to do with *us*. We could say this is Pentecost, a resurrection chapter.

Isaiah 12:1: "And in that day you shall say, 'I will give thanks to You O LORD; though You were angry with me, Your anger is turned away, and You do comfort me…. [this is Israel talking to God] …Behold, God *is* my salvation; I will trust and not be afraid; for the LORD God is my strength and my song; He has become my salvation'" (vs 1-2).

When we're resurrected what are we going to do? *We're going to sing the song of Moses and the song of the Lamb!*

One man wrote me and asked, 'Why are we going to sing the song of Moses first?' *Well, he's probably one of the first ones to qualify for salvation,*

so maybe God is going to do some things in chronological order, I don't know.

I'll tell you this: If you attain to the resurrection—whoever it was that asked that question—while you're on the Sea of Glass you'll get your answer. In the meantime, let's be faithful unto the end.

Verse 3: "And with joy you shall draw water out of the wells of salvation. And in that day you shall say, 'Praise the LORD! Call upon His name; declare His doings among the people, make mention that His name is exalted. Sing *to* the LORD; for He has done gloriously; **this *is* known in all the earth**…. [this is a great and fantastic thing] …Cry out and shout, O inhabitant of Zion; for great *is* the Holy One of Israel in your midst'" (vs 3-6). *That has to do with us!*

Isa. 13—This is the coming judgment of Babylon the Great. This is dual: It talks about the judgment of Babylon when the captivity of the children of Judah is over after 70 years. Then it's talking about, in this case, Babylon the Great, which will encompass the whole world at the end-time. This has to do then with judgment. {tie in Rev. 16-19, the judgment of Babylon the Great.

Isaiah 13:5: "They come from a far country, from the end of heaven, the LORD and the weapons of His indignation, to destroy the whole earth."

What we are going to see is how God gives prophecies that cover the *whole earth*: nations, kings, the earth, including Israel, Judah and all the nations close to what we call in the Holy Land, Palestine today.

Verse 6: "Howl! For the Day of the LORD *is* at hand… [Trumpets] …it shall come as a destruction from the Almighty. Therefore, all hands shall be faint, and every man's heart shall melt; and they shall be afraid. Pangs and sorrows shall take hold of them. They shall be in pain like a woman who travails. They shall be amazed at one another, their faces are *like* blazing fire. Behold, the Day of the LORD comes, cruel both *with* wrath and fierce anger to make the earth a desolation; and He shall destroy the sinners out of it, for the stars of the heavens and their constellations shall not give light; the sun shall be darkened in its going forth, and the moon shall not reflect its light" (vs 6-10).

Tie in Rev. 6, 8, 9, 11; Matt. 24; Mark 13; Luke 21. Again, the unity of Scripture, and it's based around *the Holy Days*. The Holy Days tell us the sequence and how these things are going to be.

Verse 11: "And I will punish the world for *their* evil, and the wicked for their iniquity; and I will cause the arrogancy of the proud to cease, and will lay low the haughtiness of the tyrants."

Verse 13: "Therefore, I will shake the heavens, and the earth shall move out of its place, in the wrath of the LORD of hosts, and in the day of His fierce anger" *You can read the rest of it!*

> Isa. 14—the first part is re-gathering, Trumpets and Atonement.
  ✓ v 3—Tabernacles and the Kingdom of God.
  ✓ v 7—All the earth is at rest, Kingdom of God, Feast of Tabernacles
  ✓ v 11 onward—has to do with how Satan came on the scene to make war against God.
  ✓ v 24—has to do with Trumpets and God's purpose.

Therefore, in order to understand this, how do we understand it? *Through the framework of the Holy Days!*

Isaiah 14:24: "The LORD of hosts has sworn…"

When God swears, know and understand that *God doesn't need to swear.* But somehow men, because of their weakness and lack of faith, if God swears that means more to them. It very well may be. However, when God swears you can be guaranteed it's going to happen.

"…saying, 'Surely as **I have thought**, so it shall come to pass; and as **I have purposed**, *so* it shall stand" (v 24).

No one is going to turn back the hand of God. *No one* is going to change the purpose of God. Now you know why the Psalm says, 'The fool has said in his heart there is no God.' They are dumb, stupid, ignorant and worthless of consideration. Now the world, oh they're great, important people. But that's going to change.

Verse 25: "That I will break Assyria in My land…" *An immediate prophecy that happened during the days of Hezekiah, true!*

Prophecy at the end-time in referring to *the Beast Power* as Assyria. Where is the final battle going to be fought? The book of Revelation! Joel says the final battle is going to be fought *in the Valley of Jezreel!* Where is that? *That's just north of Jerusalem!* So there it is, you got it.

"…and upon My mountains, and trample him under foot. Then his yoke shall be removed from them, and his burden shall be taken off their shoulders. This *is* the purpose **that *is* purposed on all the earth**…" (vs 25-26)—*every bit of it!*

So we're dealing with great and magnitudeness events that are going to take place. All pictured by the Holy Days of God.

Verse 27: "For the LORD of hosts has purposed, and who shall reverse *it*?…." *No one!*

You have Satan's rebellion over here, just before it. So, even Satan cannot turn back God's plan.

"…And His hand is stretched out, and who shall turn it back?" (v 27). The rest of it there has to do with current prophecies going there.

Isa. 16—what you're going to find here is, what you would say are 'inset verses.' Just put there which applies to *the Kingdom of God, Feast of Tabernacles, the rule of Christ!*

Isaiah 16:5: "And in mercy the throne shall be established; and *he* shall sit upon it in truth in the tabernacle of David, judging and seeking justice, and speeding the cause of righteousness."

> **Isa. 17** has to do with the near future that was going to take place at the time that Isaiah was giving the prophecies, so not all the prophecies are not necessarily dual. Not all the prophecies are related to the end-time, but many of them. It's a mix of many, many things here.
> **Isa. 18** has to do with beyond Ethiopia. In reading this I kind of thought that maybe this has to do with Darfur today, because somehow that is such a thing when it talks about the people and how terrifying they are and so forth.
> **Isa. 19** has to do with the judgment of Egypt, end-time judgment. We finish it up with a reference to the Millennium:

Isaiah 19:23: "In that day there shall be a highway out of Egypt to Assyria… [that goes right through the Holy Land] …and Assyria shall come into Egypt, and Egypt into Assyria, and Egypt shall serve with Assyria. In that day Israel shall be the third with Egypt and with Assyria, a blessing in the midst of the land; whom the LORD of hosts has blessed, saying, 'Blessed *be* My people Egypt, and Assyria the work of My hands, and Israel My inheritance'" (vs 23-25).

There you go. That can't happen today. It'll happen then.

> Isa. 20—Then we have a prophecy concerning Assyria at that time.
> Isa. 21—We have a prophecy concerning Elam and Media. Then we have a prophecy concerning many countries all around there even including Babylon.
> Isa. 22—We have a prophecy of Persia, City of David, Jerusalem.
> Isa. 23—We have a prophecy which can only refer to Alexander the Great in conquering Tyre

and the ships of Tarshish and the Isles of Chittim and Sidon and Egypt and Tyre again, and Tarshish and so forth—the Chaldeans and the Assyrians and Tyre.

➢ Isa. 24 is really an eye-opening chapter, because it talks about the earth *seventeen times*.

Remember what we've understood about the Word of God. If God says it once, *it's true!* If God thinks it in His mind, *it's going to happen!* So, when we have it written down here, what we find in Isa. 24 is an end-time prophecy and judgment against Babylon the Great pictured as encompassing the whole earth without mentioning Babylon directly.

This has the whole world at the end-time, before God begins to bring His judgment upon the earth. This is a tremendous chapter, and will help us understand the condition that the earth will be in when we start to take over and rule and reign on the earth. Verse 1 is the one where the Seventh Day Adventist go wrong and say that the earth will be desolate a thousand years. It does say that the earth will be desolate, and they assume everyone on earth is going to be killed, which is an assumption, because we will see that there will be, as it says here, *few men left!*

Isaiah 24:1: "Behold, the LORD makes the earth empty and makes it waste, and turns it upside down, and scatters its inhabitants.".

Just exactly how that's going to be, I can't imagine that. Only the power of God can do that. I mean, in our minds imagine it or even kind of a movie-type of thought in our minds.

Verse 2: "And as *it is* with the people, so it shall be with the priest; as with the slave, so with the master; as with the handmaid, so it is with her mistress; as with the buyer, so with the seller; as with the lender, so with the borrower; as with the creditor, so with the debtor." *Sounds like a lot of economic havoc!*

Verse 3: "**The earth shall be completely laid waste, and utterly stripped; for the LORD has spoken this word**." *This is something!*

I just wonder, what was Isaiah thinking when he was given this prophecy and told to write it down, inspired to write it this way?

Verse 4: "The earth mourns *and* languishes; the world withers *and* languishes; the proud people of the earth wither." *So, there are people still left!*

Verse 5: "And the earth is defiled under its people; **because they have transgressed the Laws**, changed the ordinance, and have broken the everlasting covenant."

Now, think on that for a minute. What is this talking about? *This is talking about the Christianity of today!* They have changed the ordinance. They have broken the covenant. They have nothing to do with the New Covenant. Now that's amazing to contemplate.

Verse 6: "Therefore, the curse has devoured the earth, and they who dwell in it are desolate; therefore, the people of the earth are burned, and **few men are left.**"

Doesn't say they're all gone, all destroyed. No, because the Kingdom of God is going to come on the earth and *rule* on the earth for a thousand years. Then it talks about some of the things of wine and food and so forth.

I want to focus on the things that are going to happen on the earth. Remember that this is judgment, which is Trumpets:

- picturing the Tribulation
- picturing the captivity
- picturing God's intervention
- picturing God's warring against the armies of the earth

Verse 13: "For so it is in the midst of the earth among the people, *it shall be* like the shaking of an olive tree and as gleanings when the grape harvest is completed."

{tie in Rev. 14, the great harvest, *the resurrection of the saints,* and the harvest of the wicked follows after that}

Verse 14: They shall lift up their voice, they shall sing for the majesty of the LORD, they shall cry aloud from the sea. Therefore, glorify the LORD in the east where the light dawns, the name of the LORD God of Israel in the isles of the sea. From the ends of the earth we have heard songs, 'Glory to the righteous.'…. [talking about *the resurrection,* and that means Pentecost] …But I said… [people on the earth] …'Leanness to me! Leanness to me! Woe to me! Deceivers deceive, even treacherously. Deceivers deceive!' Dread and the pit, and the snare *are* upon you, O inhabitant of the earth. And it shall be, he who flees from the sound of dread shall fall into the pit. And he who comes up out of the midst of the pit shall be taken in the snare, for the **windows from on high are opened**, and the foundations of the earth quake" (vs 14–18).

- Rev. 6 shows the heavens roll back as a scroll when the sixth seal is open
- Matt. 24—the sign of the Son of man appears in heaven; this is Trumpets, the return of Christ

Verse 19: "The earth is broken, yea broken down! The earth is crumbling, yea crumbling to pieces! The earth is tottering, yea tottering! Like a drunkard the earth is staggering, yea staggering!…. [fantastic prophecy] …And it rocks to and fro like a tree hut!

"…And its transgressions are heavy upon it…" (v 20). *The earth is affected by the sins of men!* The people, the earth: that means wherever people are:

- whether they're in the country
- whether they're in cities
- whether they're in the villages
- whether they are removed way far off in some country far away
- whether they are in the countries near to us and we know about it

Sin affects everything! Sin affects the earth and God is going to judge it.

"…and it shall fall and not rise again. And it shall come to pass in that day, the LORD shall punish the host of the high ones *that are* on high… [Who are they? *Satan and his demons! Fighting against God, cast down to the earth!*] …and the kings of the earth upon the earth" (vs 20-21).

So, 17 times the earth is mentioned. Are there going to be things happen on the earth? *Guaranteed!* Isa. 24 tells us that it will be.

Verse 22: "And they shall be gathered, *as* prisoners are gathered in a dungeon. And they shall be shut up in the prison, and after many days they shall be punished. Then the moon shall be confounded, and the sun shall be ashamed, for the LORD of hosts shall reign in Mount Zion, in Jerusalem, and gloriously before His elders" (vs 22-23).

So it goes right on into the Millennium. Fantastic verse here!

➢ Isa. 25 talks about the beginning of the Kingdom of God.
➢ Isa. 26—the return of the Jews from Babylon.
   ✓ v 19—we have the resurrection, just in one verse, then protection, place of safety. You see, all of those things are right there.

Isaiah 26:19: "Your dead ones shall live, *together with* my dead body they shall arise… [together]…. [Isaiah says he's going arise; this is the first resurrection] …Awake and sing, you who dwell in the dust… [there in the grave] …for your dew *is as* the dew of lights, and the earth shall cast out the dead…. [first resurrection, Pentecost] …Come, my people…" (vs 19-20).

He talks about protection in time of tribulation. So this ties in where we began in Psa. 91,

and all of that.

"…enter into your rooms and shut your doors around you; hide for a little moment, until the fury has passed by… [place of safety]. …For behold, the LORD comes out of His place to punish the people of the earth for their iniquity; the earth also shall reveal her blood, and shall no more cover her dead" (vs 19-21). Hey, that's fantastic!

When you go through and you look at the structure of the Holy Days in anyone of the books, you find that it is there. Once you understand about the Holy Days, you can go back and you can go through it and you will see that.

Now, let's see the judgment of Satan; Isaiah 27:1: "In that day the LORD with His great and fierce and strong sword shall punish the sea-monster… [a type of Satan] …the darting serpent, the sea-monster, that twisting serpent; and He shall kill the monster in the sea."

Well, he's not exactly going to be killed. He's going to be put into the abyss with a seal set over him, as we find in Rev. 20. Then we have a restoration, which is the Millennium:

Verse 2: "In that day… [Atonement, getting rid of Satan, then we have the Millennium, the restoration] …sing to her, 'A delightful vineyard. I the LORD keep it; I will water it every moment; lest *any* hurt it, I will keep it night and day. Fury *is* not in Me; who would set the briers *and* thorns against Me in battle? I would step through it; I would burn it at once…. [He isn't going to let anything happen to us] …Or let them take hold of My strength, that he may make peace with Me; and he shall make peace with Me.' He shall cause those who come from Jacob to take root; Israel shall blossom and bud, and fill the face of the world *with* fruit" (vs 2-6). *Quite a fantastic thing!*

➢ Isa. 28 talks about how to understand the Bible. We've been through that.
➢ Isa. 29 talks about Ariel, the city where David lived.

That is Jerusalem, so we have a dual prophecy here. You can tie this in with Zech. 12, that even though the whole earth be gathered against Jerusalem, it shall be a "troublesome stone."

Well, we've covered an awful lot here concerning the different Holy Days as found in the book of Isaiah. In part three I'm going to take the rest of those Holy Days that refer directly to the Kingdom of God and the Millennium that we have not yet covered that we find in the book of Isaiah, and put it together with the other Scriptures so we get a full picture.

But the thing that is exciting and wonderful to know is that once you understand about the Holy Days and the meaning of them, we can go back and we can study things like Isaiah, Jeremiah and Ezekiel. *There is more in Isaiah concerning the Millennium and the Kingdom of God than any other book*; and then John has a lot; and Revelation is filled with it from beginning to end.

Scriptural References

1) Isaiah 3:1-5, 10
2) Psalm 91:1-7
3) Isaiah 3:10-12
4) Isaiah 5:1-7
5) Luke 20:9-18
6) John 15:1-5
7) Isaiah 6:1-3
8) Revelation 4:1-2, 8
9) Isaiah 6:4-10
10) Isaiah 7:14
11) Isaiah 8:13-20
12) Isaiah 9:6-7
13) Isaiah 11:1-12, 16
14) Isaiah 12:1-6
15) Isaiah 13:5-11, 13
16) Isaiah 14:24-27
17) Isaiah 16:5
18) Isaiah 19:23-25
19) Isaiah 24:1-6, 13-23
20) Isaiah 26:19-21
21) Isaiah 27:1-6

Scriptures referenced, not quoted:

- Matthew 13
- John 12
- Acts 13; 28
- Matthew 1:18
- Isaiah 8:1-12
- Isaiah 2
- Hebrews 2
- Isaiah 9:1
- Matthew 3
- Revelation 16-19; 6, 8-9, 11
- Matthew 24
- Mark 13
- Luke 21
- Isaiah 14:3, 7,11; 17-18; 20-23
- Revelation 14; 6
- Isaiah 25
- Revelation 20

- Isaiah 28-29
- Zechariah 12

Also referenced: Booklet: *The Ministry is Not the Government of God*

FRC:bo
Transcribed: 8-13-07
Reformatted 1/2021

CHAPTER SIXTY-TWO

Isaiah's Prophecies of the Millennium III
Survey of Isaiah 29-66

Fred R. Coulter

We will continue on with the Holy Days in the book of Isaiah and we will concentrate toward all of the areas in the Bible that relate to the coming Kingdom of God and the Millennial reign of Jesus Christ and the saints.

As we go through this and as we read these things, I want you to think in two paths: I want you to think how this would sound to people who didn't have the New Testament. How would it sound to those who say, even in the days of Ezra, after he had canonized the whole Old Testament, what sense would it make to them? Then I want you to think on the other track, why this makes sense to us today?

- we have the New Testament
- we understand the things of God

Whatever we understand, let's always remember:
- we have nothing that we didn't receive
- it all has to come from God
- it all has to come from His Word

We will see that right in a series of verses that cover one topic, all of sudden there's a verse or two that's put in there that refers to something completely different. Now today, we can go through and say this refers to this, and this refers to that, and this refers to the other thing. But if you didn't have the New Testament and the Holy Days to interpret this… Remember, though they had the Holy Days, they did not have the understanding of the Holy Days that we have today.

Though during the time of Christ, Christ opened their minds to understand the Scriptures concerning Himself. I'm sure they had greater understanding of the Holy Days; yet, they didn't understand the things that we do today. Just think of this: The Apostle John was the one who received the whole book of Revelation, which is the key that unlocks, with the Holy Days and the New Testament, all of the Bible. But he didn't have a chance to study it and go over it. He didn't have a chance to put it together like we do today. After all, what we are learning is what God has begun revealing going back toward the end of the 19th century and on in to now.

All down through history there was a basic understanding of the Passover and Christ,

Unleavened Bread and getting rid of sin, and Pentecost and the Church. They may have had some smattering of understanding of the coming Millennial reign of Christ, if they had the book of Revelation, but not everyone had the whole Bible. So, we are sitting in a time of great opportunity, and a time of great responsibility, and a time of great learning as well. This is why every opportunity we have to get together on the Sabbath or on the Holy Days or on the Feast days, we need to learn as much as we can of the Word of God. I want to show you how this works here.

Isaiah 29:13—*even Jesus quoted this in the New Testament* (Matt. 13 and other places): "And the LORD said, 'Because this people draws near *Me* with their mouth…'"

They have words of praise to God; you can apply this at almost any time in history. The time in history that really reflects to me is the September 11, 2001. Immediately, oh everybody returns to God: 'Go to your church, go to your synagogue.' But did anybody really repent? *NO!*

"…and with their lips honor Me…" (v 13).

We need to have the Ten Commandments here, we need to have them there, we've got to have God involved in the government.'

Then they turn around and have all the lying corruption that they do, after they acknowledge God.

"…but their worship of Me is made up of the traditions of men learned by rote, and their fear toward Me is *taught* by the commandments of men" (v 13). *That's an interesting way to put it—and that's basically what it is!*.

Verse 14: "Therefore, behold, I will proceed to do again a marvelous work among this people, *even* a marvelous work and a wonder, for the wisdom of their wise ones shall perish, and the wisdom of their intelligent ones shall vanish."

- Isn't that exactly what's happening today? *Yes, indeed!*
- Did it happen to the Jews back then, leading up to the downfall of Jerusalem? *Yes, indeed!*

- Did it happen during the days of the Jews leading up to the downfall of the temple in Jerusalem in 70A.D.? *Of course!*

Now then, all of a sudden it switches. This is why it's 'precept upon precept, here a little there a little.'

Verse 15: "Woe *to* those who go deep to hide *their* purpose from the LORD! And their works are in the dark, and they say, 'Who sees us? And who knows us?'"

All of the secret plans and schemes of men! And the greatest secret plans and schemes of men are now being developed and worked out *under the inspiration of Satan the devil* to take down modern-day Israel because of their sins.

Verse 16: "Surely, you have turned things upside down! Shall the potter be regarded as the potter's clay; for shall the work say of him who made it, 'He did not make me?' Or shall the thing formed say to him who formed it, 'He had no understanding?'" *This has to do with religionists, atheists, and everything!*

Verse 17—*another verse completely separate*: "*Is* it not yet a very little while, and Lebanon shall be turned into a fruitful field, and the fruitful field shall be counted as a forest?" *This is the type of a Millennium!*

Here we have (v 18) the preaching of the Gospel—the ministry of Christ. But we also have the same thing at the beginning of the Millennium that will happen:

Verse 18: "And in that day the deaf shall hear the words of the book… [which previously said 'we can't understand it'] …and the eyes of the blind shall see out of obscurity and darkness."

That's exactly what's happening to us today. That's exactly what Jesus did to the apostles to open their minds to understanding (Luke 24).

Here is a prophecy, it can be the beginning of the Millennium, it can be the Church:

Verse 19: "And the meek shall increase *their* joy in the LORD, and the poor among men shall rejoice in the Holy One of Israel, for the terrible one is brought to nothing… " (vs 19-20).

This is the Day of Atonement, getting rid of Satan the devil. Or you can say getting rid of the beast, either one. Or any of the terrible ones that came and attacked Israel down through history. *But here is the elimination of Satan!*

"…and the scorner is destroyed, and all that watch for iniquity are cut off… [so that has to be the beginning of the Millennium] …those who make a man a sinner with a word, and lay a trap for the reprover in the gate, and turn aside the just for a worthless thing" (vs 20-21)—*all of them!* So, *this is the destruction of the wicked!*

All of sudden it changes again. This is why it's 'precept upon precept, line upon line and here a little, there a little.' *With stammering lips and another tongue will I speak to these people.*

Verse 22: "Therefore, thus says the LORD, who redeemed Abraham, concerning the house of Jacob, 'Jacob shall not now be ashamed, nor shall his face now become pale…. [beginning of the Millennium] …But when he sees his children, the work of My hands, in his midst, they shall sanctify My name, and sanctify the Holy one of Jacob, and shall fear the God of Israel. **Those who erred in spirit shall come to understanding, and those who murmured shall learn instruction**'" (vs 22-24).

Now we have blending out into conversion, whether it be during the Millennium or during our lifetime. "**Those who erred in spirit shall come to understanding, and those who murmured shall learn instruction**." So, Isa. 29 is a good example of a mixture of all the Scriptures.

Having no understanding of the full meaning of the Holy Days, having no understanding because the New Testament wasn't written, and realizing that Isaiah is the very first prophet to really talk more about the things of God's plan. But it wasn't put into order; it wasn't put into sequence. How do you suppose that they understood this? *Some of it to them would be kind of 'gobbly-gook'!*

Isa. 30:8—Here we find that God wants His Word *written*. Did God fulfill His promise when Jesus said, *'This Gospel shall be published in all the world'?* Top this off: 90% of the people of the world can read at least the book of Mark in their own language. I think it's profound and fantastic that God would take the book of Mark, where He said that the Gospel would be 'published' in all the world. That's the first book of the New Testament that the Bible societies translate.

- How much more time do we have left? *We don't know!*
- How much more will this be increased between now and that time? *We don't know!*

Just think of it, what a tremendous blessing it is that we can sit here, read the Word of God—which He has written and preserved and saved for us and passed down through all the centuries—using men. The ones who were faithful, *were faithful!* You can separate out the wheat from the chaff from those who were not faithful. But He had it written down. He told Isaiah to write:

Isaiah 30:8: "Now go, write it before them in a tablet, and note it in a book, so that it may be for the time to come forever and ever."

In other words, the Word of God is not going to be destroyed. It's going to come down. Here is a verse that can apply at any time from when Isaiah prophesied this and wrote it to the end.

Verse 9: "That this *is* a rebellious people, lying children. They are children who will not hear the Law of the LORD; who say to the seers, 'See not,' and to the prophets, 'Do not prophesy to us right things, speak to us smooth things, prophesy illusions'" (vs 9-10).

You can find that all the way down through the books of Joshua, Judges, 1st & 2nd Samuel, 1st & 2nd Kings, all the way down through all the Prophets, and all the way down to our day. Just think what would happen if someone would—I don't even think it would get out—say over the major television:

This nation is under a curse because of their sins and mainly immigration. Not immigration, the immigration problem is a result, rather, of abortion. That we are all on our hands are guilty of the blood of over 50 million of the most innocent human beings. That the nation needs to repent!

Oh, no! Oh just think what the atheists would say: 'A religious nut! For sure!' *Well, given time, they're going to have to deal with God!*

Then they say: "…'Do not prophesy to us right things, speak to us smooth things…'" (10).

Let's not rock the boat. Let's appeal to the goodness of people.

I want you to take these Scriptures here, and I want you to turn on Joel Osteen some Sunday morning and I want you to read these things, then I want you to listen to his sermons, and you will witness prophecy fulfilled before your very eyes.

"…prophesy illusions; go out of the way, turn aside out of the path, cause the Holy One of Israel to cease from before us" (11).

We don't want anyone condemning us for our sins. No, we don't want any negativity. Let's just appeal to the goodness of human beings and everything will be wonderful, everything will be fine, and everything will be good and tremendous and the world will be a better place.

Well, ostriches put their heads in the sand while the battle's going on, and they can be shot and killed while they're doing it, too.

Verse 12: "Therefore, thus says the Holy One of Israel, 'Because you have despised this word, and trust in oppression and perverseness, and rely on them; therefore, this iniquity shall be to you as a breach ready to fall…'" (vs 12-13). *It's going to stretch and stretch!*

"…swelling out in a high wall, whose breaking comes suddenly, in an instant…. [and disaster is upon us] …And He shall break it as the breaking of the potters' vessel that *is* smashed in pieces. He shall not spare, so that there shall not be found in the fragments a shard to take fire from the hearth, or to take water out of the pit.' For thus says the Lord GOD, the Holy One of Israel, 'In returning and rest you shall be saved…'" (vs 13-15).

Now all of a sudden it comes to *the beginning of the Millennium.*

"…and in quietness and hope shall be your strength.'…. [that's what He told them] …But you were not willing. And you said, 'No; for we will flee upon horses.' Therefore, you shall flee. And *you said*, 'We will ride upon the swift'; therefore, those who pursue you shall be swift…. [think about what's happening today] … One thousand *shall flee* at the rebuke of one; at the rebuke of five you *shall flee*, until you are left as a pole upon the top of a mountain, and as a sign on a hill" (vs 15-17).

What do we have here? *We have a prophecy of exactly what's taking place today!* Then all of a sudden it drops right into *the Millennium, the Kingdom of God!*

Verse 18: And, therefore, will the LORD wait, that He may be gracious unto you. And, therefore, He will be exalted, that He may have mercy upon you, for the LORD *is* a God of justice; blessed *are* all those who wait for Him"—*and so forth all the way down through Isa. 30 you see that!*

➢ Isa. 31—don't go down to Egypt. Yet, everyone loves to go down to Egypt. God says that you're going to get in trouble.
➢ Isa. 32—this is a prophecy of a righteous king. This could be referring to the coming Josiah episode or a type of the Millennium—there are different applications of this.

Isaiah 32:1: "Behold, a king shall reign in righteousness, and rulers shall rule in justice."

That happened during Josiah's day in a special, particular way. But also, that's a type of what's going to happen in repentance of Israel and Judah when Christ returns.

Verse 2: "And a man shall be as a hiding place from the wind, and a shelter from the tempestuous storm, like streams of water in a dry place, like the shadow of a great rock in a weary land."

That shows how God is going to intervene and work things out. You also have some correction for the women that parallels Isa. 3.

Verse 15—*the beginning of the Millennium*: "Until the Spirit is poured on us from on high…"

That's going to be bringing the children of Israel back out of captivity, bringing and leading them to conversion.

"…and the wilderness becomes a fruitful field, and the fruitful field is thought to be a forest. Then justice shall dwell in the wilderness, and righteousness remain in the fruitful field. And the work of righteousness shall be peace; and the result of righteousness shall be quietness and confidence forever" (vs 15-17).

Here is describing the Millennium, but also this one verse tells us how we can solve our problems today if we would repent.

Verse 18: "And my people shall dwell in a peaceable home, and in secure dwellings and quiet resting places." There is an excerpt right out of all the correction and things of the Millennium.

Isa. 33—judgment after they have dealt treacherously with God. Then we have again a time of graciousness; a time of repentance.

Isaiah 33:2: "O LORD, be gracious to us; we have waited for You; be their arm every morning; our salvation also in the time of trouble." *There's a verse that can apply at any time!*

Verse 5: "The LORD is exalted, for He dwells on high. He has filled Zion *with* justice and righteousness…. [the Millennium] … And wisdom and knowledge shall be the stability of your times, *and* strength of salvation: the fear of the LORD *is* his treasure" (vs 5-6). *Then it goes on with other things.*

➤ v 17 talks about Jerusalem and the end-time. {note our in-depth study: *The Millennial Temple* and what it would be like} Here's some other Scriptures that we can put in with that:

Verse 20: "Look upon Zion, the city of our Holy gatherings; your eyes shall see Jerusalem a quiet home, a tabernacle that shall not be taken down… [this obviously is the Millennium] …not one of its stakes shall ever be removed, nor shall any of its cords be broken. But there the glorious LORD

will be to us a place of broad rivers *and* streams… [water coming out from underneath the Throne of God] …in which no galley with oars shall go, nor shall a mighty ship pass by it, for the.LORD *is* our Judge, the LORD *is* our Lawgiver, the LORD *is* our King; He will save us" (vs 20-22). *There we have the Millennium!*

Now we have prophecies of the end-time. Put that under the Feast of Trumpets and the return of Christ.

Isaiah 34:1: "Come near, you nations, to hear; and, you people, hearken; let the earth hear, and its fullness; the world, and its offspring… [we're talking prophecy that fits to the whole world] …for the anger of the LORD *is* upon all nations, and His fury upon all their armies. He has completely destroyed them, He has delivered them to the slaughter" (vs 1-2).

{tie in Rev. 9; 16; 19 and Zech. 14—all those tying in with the beginning of the Millennium} Then there's a judgment against Edom, which God will do that.

What I want to do is to show you a flow of the structure of the book of Isaiah and how many things are in there that relate to the Holy Days. Now the key to understand is this: They are not put in sequence—Passover, Unleavened Bread, Pentecost, Trumpets, Atonement, Tabernacles, Last Great Day. But they are all intermixed, interspersed.

Isa. 35—here's the beginning of the Millennium, what God is going to do; changing the earth.

Isaiah 35:1: "The wilderness and the desert shall be glad and the desert shall rejoice and blossom as the rose. It shall blossom abundantly, and rejoice even *with* joy and singing; the glory of Lebanon shall be given to it, the excellency of Carmel and Sharon, they shall see the glory of the LORD *and* the majesty of our God" (vs 1-2).

There it is, ***the beginning of the Millennium!*** Then it shows what's going to happen.

Verse 5: "Then the eyes of the blind shall be opened…"

That's the preaching of the Gospel by Christ. That's the beginning of the Millennium and the healing of the people.

"…and the ears of the deaf shall be unstopped" (v 5).

Verse 8—again, we have the highway going to Jerusalem on earth and the temple during the Millennium. Here we have many different themes all mixed together as we have seen.

Verse 8: "And a highway shall be there, and a way, and it shall be called The Way of Holiness. The unclean shall not pass over it…. [in other words, you have to be a spirit being to go on this] … But it will be for him who walks in that way, but fools, shall not err *in it*. No lion shall be there, nor *any* beast of prey shall go up on it, they shall not be found there. But the redeemed shall walk there…. [and we are the redeemed] …shall walk there. And the ransomed of the LORD… [that could also refer to Israel coming out of captivity, but it could also refer to us] …of the LORD shall return and come to Zion with songs and everlasting joy upon their heads; they shall obtain joy and gladness, and sorrow and sighing shall flee away" (vs 8-10).

➤ Isa. 36, 37 & 38 all have to do with Isaiah and King Hezekiah and the events surrounding the putting away of the Assyrian armies after they came back from conquering the Egyptians.

Then you have a little bit of the incident here—not quite as detailed as you find in 2-Kings concerning Hezekiah and his sickness and how he was healed from that and God gave him 15 more years.

Isa. 40—we see a duality of prophecy in much of this. It has to do with the prophecy concerning John the Baptist. It starts out with the end-time, the final fulfillment of this has to be at the end-time.

Isaiah 40:1: "'Comfort ye, comfort ye, My people,' says your God…. [introduction to *The Messiah*] …'Speak comfortably to Jerusalem, and cry unto her that her warfare is accomplished… [it's still going on today, so this is a prophecy yet just ahead of us] …that her iniquity is pardoned; for she has received of the LORD'S hand double for all her sins.'…. [then immediately breaks in with the prophecy of John the Baptist]: …The voice of him who cries in the wilderness, 'Prepare the way of the LORD, make straight in the desert a highway for our God'" (vs 1-3).

Now that being done, what happened after the ministry of Christ? *We have the preaching of the Gospel!* So, here is a prophecy of the preaching of the Gospel beginning with the apostles and carrying right on down to our time.

Verse 9: "Go up for yourself on the high mountain; O you that bring good tidings to Zion. Lift up your voice with strength, O you who tell good tidings to Jerusalem; lift up, do not be afraid. Say to the cities of Judah, 'Behold your God!'"

That applies to Jesus' first coming and His second coming. Preaching of the Gospel. Now then, it talks about the resurrection. I think it's very interesting that we have this because John the Baptist was sent as a messenger to prepare the way for the Lord. When you look at what we have here, we have a revelation in here showing us that it would be the Lord God who came in the flesh.

Verse 11: "He shall feed His flock like a shepherd; He shall gather the lambs with His arm, and carry *them* in His bosom, *and* shall gently lead those with young."

We can say that this has to do with the Church, gathering the Church together and preaching the Gospel. It can apply to the beginning of the Millennium. But if we apply it to the beginning of the Church and the beginning of preaching the Gospel and the ministry of Christ, let's notice what v 12 says, because this helps substantiate who Jesus was and that it was actually God manifested in the flesh.

Verse 12: "Who has measured the waters in the hollow of his hand, and meted out the heavens with a span? And who has comprehended the dust of the earth in a measure, and weighed the mountains in scales, and the hills in a balance? Who has directed the Spirit of the LORD, and who was His counselor that he might instruct Him? With whom did He take counsel, and *who* instructed Him and taught Him in the path of judgment, and taught Him knowledge, and made known the way of understanding to Him?" (vs 12-14). *We have the answer of that in Isa. 50!*

Let's just jump ahead there to see the prophecy of how Jesus was taught of the Father. Quite an amazing thing!

Isaiah 50:4: "'The Lord GOD has given Me the tongue of the learned, to know to help the weary *with* a word. He awakens *Me* morning by morning, He awakens My ear to hear as one being taught. The Lord GOD has opened My ear, and I was not rebellious, nor turned away backwards…. [that's His childhood. Then all of a sudden it goes right into His death]: …I gave My back to the smiters, and My cheeks to them that plucked off the hair; I did not hide My face from shame and spitting" (vs 4-6). *That's the design of the Prophets!* Quite interesting! ***It was God Who taught Jesus, God Himself!***

- Who's going to teach God?
- What *man* is going to teach God anything?
- ***No one!***
   ✓We can learn from God.
   ✓We can understand from God.

But always remember this:

- ***No man*** *is going to tell God what to do!*
- ***No man*** *is going to command God what to do!*
- ***No man*** *is going to instruct God!*

Here's how God looks at the world. We think we're all important. Let's also compare this with Satan the devil. Remember the temptation of Jesus Christ? What did the devil do? *Satan took Jesus on a high mountain, showed Jesus all the kingdoms of the world in a moment of time and he said,* 'All of this I will give You, if You'll fall down and worship me.'

How does God view all the nations?

- Satan thinks it's great
- Satan thinks it's marvelous
- Satan thinks it's fantastic that he has all this power and that he is like a god

No he's not! He's Satan the devil and his days are numbered!

Here's how God looks at it, and this is why Christ was not tempted by it. But even though the temptation come, *He didn't give it a second thought!*

Isaiah 40:15: "Behold, the nations *are* like a drop in a bucket, and are counted as the small dust of the scales… [blow it off] …behold, He takes up the isles as a very little thing. And Lebanon *is* not sufficient to burn, nor the beasts of it sufficient *for* a burnt offering. **All nations before Him *are* as nothing; and they are counted by Him as less than nothing, and vanity**. To whom then will you compare God? Or what likeness will you compare to Him?" (vs 15-18).

They go build their idols, they overlay it with gold, they do all of these things! Then God says:

Verse 21: "Have you not known?…. [they knew from the beginning; Adam and Eve knew] …Have you not heard? Has it not been told you from the beginning? Have you not understood *from* the foundations of the earth? *It is* He who sits above the circle of the earth…" (vs 21-22).

If the pope would have read his Bible, he would have understood that the earth wasn't flat!

"…and its people are like grasshoppers; *it is* He Who stretches out the heavens like a curtain, and spreads them out like a tent to dwell in; Who brings the rulers to nothing; He makes the judges of the earth as vanity" (vs 22-23).

Verse 25: "'To whom then will you compare Me, or who is My equal?' says the Holy One."

Isa. 41[transcriber's correction] talks about God raising up 'a righteous one.' This could apply to Cyrus, who was a type of Christ. Then we have some prophecies here concerning the Church, concerning Abraham. We see what's going to happen during the Millennium:

Isaiah 41:18: "I will open rivers in high places, and fountains in the midst of the valleys; I will make the wilderness a pool of water, and the dry land springs of water. I will plant the cedar in the wilderness, the acacia tree, and the myrtle, and the oil tree. I will set the fir tree in the desert, *and* the pine, and the box tree together" (vs 18-19).

That's what's going to happen during the Millennium. Then all of sudden it changes. This is very much like Job when Job had his confrontation with God. When God finally said to Job, "Come here, tell Me."

Verse 21: "'Draw near *with* your cause,' says the LORD. 'Bring out your strong *reasons*,' says the King of Jacob. 'Let them bring *them* out, and declare to us the things that shall happen; let them reveal the former things, what they *are*, that we may consider them and know the final end of them; or declare to us things to come'" (vs 21-22).

If men think they're so great, *do it!* All you have to know, how good are the predictions of men? Just watch the evening weather. How many times do they hit it? Well, when everything is nice and normal they hit it pretty good, but otherwise they don't— and with all the modern things that they have just for the weather. How much understanding is taught in our schools? *None!* Our Universities? *None!* Our government? *None!* What are they going to tell God? When are they going to show how great and important they are to God? This is why Christ has to come and return and destroy the whole system.

➢ Isa. 42 is a prophecy of Christ

Think of this as if you were living in Isaiah's day and you read the first edition of the finished book of Isaiah. Just suppose you were a priest reading the scroll in the scroll-room. Or suppose you were a king who was to have a copy of the Law and a copy of the Prophets as they were worked up so he could read them.

- What would you think of this?
- What does this mean?
- When would this be?

Isaiah 42:1: "Behold My Servant, Whom I uphold; My Elect, *in Whom* My soul delights…."

Tie in Matt. 3—after Jesus was baptized what was the voice that came from heaven? *'This is My Beloved in Whom I am well pleased.'* What was said when the transfiguration when He took Peter, James and John with Him? *And He said, 'Behold, My Son in Whom I am well pleased, **listen to Him**.'* So, we have a prophecy of it here.

"…I have put My Spirit upon Him; He shall bring forth justice to the Gentiles" (v 1). You could take this one verse here and you can apply it to the preaching of the Gospel, beginning with the Apostle Paul. You can apply it to the beginning of the Millennium when Christ returns.

Take these different Scriptures and apply them to many, many different things. But back then they wouldn't know 'Who is My Servant?'

- Is it the priest?
- Is it the king?
- Is it the prophet?

Verse 2: "He shall not cry *out*, nor lift up, nor cause His voice to be heard in the street. A bruised reed He shall not break, and a smoking wick He shall not quench; in Truth He shall bring forth justice. He shall not fail nor be discouraged until He has set justice in the earth; and the isles shall wait for His Law." (vs 2-4).

That's the whole ministry of Christ and out into the beginning of the Millennium. So there you have it, it's really something! Isa. 42 has an awful lot to do with the return of Christ and let's read just a few here concerning the Millennium.

Verse 9: "'Behold, the former things have come to pass. And new things I declare; before they happen, I tell you of them.' Sing to the LORD a new song; His praise from the end of the earth, you who go down to the sea, and its fullness; the isles and their people. Let the wilderness and its cities lift up *their voice*, the villages where Kedar dwells. Let the dwellers of the rock sing, let them shout from the mountain tops. Give glory to the LORD and declare His praise in the isles" (vs 9-12). *There we have the beginning of the Millennium!*

Here's an example of a verse just interjected right in the middle of something, v 21: "The LORD is well pleased for His righteousness sake; He will magnify the Law and make *it* glorious."

Tremendous thing! But back in 800 B.C., who was this? That couldn't be understood until after the ministry of Christ and His resurrection. Remember it said that Jesus opened their minds to understand all things concerning Him in the Law, the Prophets and the Psalms.

Now you know the only way to understand these things is for Christ to open our minds. And today, that is by the Spirit of God. So, if we understand this then we are going to see tremendous things that are out of the law. Remember, as we started out, 'Oh Lord, open my eyes that I may behold wondrous things out of your Law.' Of course, now we have the prophets. Are there not

wondrous things in those prophecies in the book of Isa., and this came about because of doing the work on the Old Testament project. In doing so, I began to understand Isaiah even more. This is why I wanted to do this for the Feast of Tabernacles.

I realize that we've gone through some of these things rather rapidly—however since we're just concentrating on one book and we're not turning from book to book or different pages through the Bible, I hope that you're able to keep up with it.

I want to do is cover certain parts of Isa. 43 because there are some very interesting things that are here, which again we see the prophecies mingled together.

- we can have the Church
- we can have Israel coming out of captivity
- we can have Israel repenting
- we can have the Church repenting
- then it comes down to the preaching of the Gospel

Isaiah 43:1: "But now, thus says the LORD Who created you, O Jacob, and He Who formed you, O Israel; 'Fear not, for I have redeemed you… [that's the message that's going to be when the Millennium begins] …I have called *you* by your name; you *are* Mine."

Then it talks about how He will bring them back (v 3).

Verse 4: "Since you were precious in My sight… [v 5]: Fear not; for I *am* with you. I will bring your seed from the East, and gather you from the West. I will say to the North, 'Give up'; and to the South, 'Do not keep back'; bring My sons from afar and My daughters from the ends of the earth" (vs 4-6).

That is something else we are going to be doing. God is going to give the instructions and we will carry them out. Think on that for a minute.

Verse 10: "'You *are* My witnesses,' says the LORD…"

This is quite a verse when you understand this. This ties in with the apostles as being witnesses. Isn't that what Jesus said, 'You shall be witnesses for Me unto the ends of the earth.'? *Yes!* Are we not, when we go out and we start going to all the people who have suffered through the Tribulation—the ones who are left—and start them bringing them out of the terrible conditions they are in and start bringing the house of Israel out of the terrible conditions that they are in, will we not be witnesses for God? To say God reigns?

- we are here

- this is the Truth
- this is righteousness
- God will help you
- God will heal you
- we will likewise do so
- we have the commandment from the Lord to do it

So this verse has an awful lot in it!

"'…and My servant whom I have chosen… [that's Christ] …that you may know and believe Me, and understand that I *am* He…. [What did Jesus say all through the book of John? *'I AM'!*] …Before Me no God was formed, nor shall there be after Me. I, *even* I, *am* the LORD; and besides Me there is no savior'" (vs 10-11).

Then some of the rest of the chapter blends in and brings in the Jews coming out of captivity from Babylon.

➢ Isa. 44—return from Babylon. It can also refer to the end-times
➢ Isa. 45—we have the prophecy of Cyrus and we have God declaring His greatness, Who is Creator

Isaiah 45:17—because it has to do with the Millennium, Kingdom of God: "*But* Israel shall be saved by the LORD *with* an everlasting salvation. You shall not be ashamed nor disgraced *even* into the ages of eternity."

So, from then on there isn't going to be the way that it has been in the past.

Verse 18: "For thus says the LORD the Creator of the heavens, He Himself *is* God, Who formed the earth and made it; He has established it. He created it not in vain, *but* formed it to be inhabited. 'I *am* the LORD, and *there is* no other. I have not spoken in secret, in a dark place of the earth. I did not say to the seed of Jacob, "Seek me in vain." I the LORD speak righteousness, I declare things that are right'" (vs 18-19). *Yes, God has made His Word known. Fantastic!*

Verse 21: "Declare and bring near; yea, let them take counsel together. Who has declared this of old? *Who* has told it from ancient times? Have not I, the LORD? **And *there is* no other God besides Me**; a just God and a Savior; **there is none besides Me.** Turn to Me, and be saved, all the ends of the earth; for I *am* God, and there *is* none else" (vs 21-22).

So then, here's salvation all during the Millennium to all the people of the world. You can read the rest of it.

Well, I hope in going through this it is going to inspire you to really read and study through the book of Isaiah.

➢ Isa. 46—it's talking about God's deliverance again of Israel
➢ Isa. 47 ties in with Rev. 17 & 18, the judgment of Babylon

Isaiah 47:7: "And you said, 'I shall be a lady forever'; so you did not lay these *things* to your heart, nor did you remember the latter end of it. Now then, hear this, O lover of pleasures, who sits securely; who says in her heart, 'I *am*, and none else beside me; I shall not sit *as* a widow, nor shall I know the loss of children.' But these two *things* shall come to you in a moment in one day…" (vs 7-9).

Then He mocks them with their astrologers and soothsayers and all that they have used down through history.

Isa. 48—again things that have to do with the Jews and being brought back. There are many other things that you can bring out here, but God is going to destroy the wicked and He says so, and we have that in Revelation 16 & 19, too.

Isaiah 48:22: "'*There is* no peace,' says the LORD, 'for the wicked.'"

Man will never, never, never, never—I can't put *never* enough times—*solve his problems apart from God!* Any temporary solutions that they may have, aside from repentance, will only be because they follow principles that are in the Bible. But man will never solve his problems. He will never have peace. That's why when they say, 'Peace, peace, there is no peace.' It's impossible! I'll say it again: For men to have peace, when they reject Jesus Christ, the Prince of Peace, it won't happen!

Isa. 49 talks about the ministry of Christ and His name.

Isaiah 49:1: "'Listen, O isles, to Me; and hearken, you people from afar; the LORD has called Me from the womb; He has made mention of My name from My mother's belly." [What was it told? *Yes, you shall call His name, Jesus!*] … And He has made My mouth like a sharp sword; in the shadow of His hand He has hidden Me, and made Me a polished shaft. He has hidden Me in His quiver, and said to Me, 'You *are* My servant, O Israel… [Now this is Christ personified as Israel] …in whom I will be glorified'" (vs 1-3).

Then we have the beginning of the Millennium—v 22. It shows here how God is going to deal with the Gentiles:

Verse 22 "Thus says the Lord GOD, 'Behold, I will lift up My hand to the Gentiles, and have set up My banner to the people; and they shall bring your sons in *their* bosom, and your daughters shall be carried upon *their* shoulders.'"

This is the exodus of the Gentiles bringing back the children of Israel to their own land.

Isaiah 51:1—*this verse can apply in many different instances*: "Hearken to Me, you who follow after righteousness, you who seek the LORD…"

This has to be anyone during the time up to Christ who would be seeking God. This has to do with those who are in the Church of God all down through history.

"…Look to the Rock… [Christ is the Rock] …*from which* you were cut, and to the hole of the pit *from which* you were dug. Look to Abraham your father…" (vs 1-2).

That applies to the Church. We are Abraham's seed and heirs according to the promise.

"…and to Sarah *who* bore you…" (v 2).

This also refers to Israel, and any time God dealt with them. This also refers to Israel and their conversion during the Millennium. So, these verses have multiple applications.

"'…for I called him alone, and blessed him, and made him many.' For the LORD shall comfort Zion; He will comfort all her waste places; and He will make her wilderness like Eden, and her desert like the garden of the LORD. Joy and gladness shall be found in it, thanksgiving and the voice of melody" (vs 2-3).

Now here's another one that has to do with the people of God today. It also can be applied to the Millennium, but let's apply this to the Church:

Verse 4: "Hearken to Me, My people; and give ear to Me, O My nation…"

So, it is dual: to the Church, to Israel; but also we are called what? *'A royal priesthood, a Holy nation'!*

"…for instruction shall proceed from Me, and I will make My justice as a light to the people…. [Who is that light? *Christ!* Now here we have the beginning of the Millennium]: …My righteousness *is* near; My salvation has gone out, and My arms shall judge the people; the isles shall wait upon Me, and on My arm they shall trust. Lift up your eyes to the heavens, and look upon the earth beneath; for the heavens shall vanish away like smoke, and the earth shall become old like a garment…" (vs 4-6).

Tie in Heb. 1; Rev. 20 & 21—the present earth is going to pass away—a new heaven and a new earth.

So we can, in understanding the book of Revelation, know that and we can apply that to these verses. But if it was back in the time of Isaiah you wouldn't know what on earth is going to happen. How is that going to be?

"…and its inhabitants shall die in the same way…. [second death] …But My salvation shall be forever, and **My righteousness shall not be abolished**" (v 6).

So, every good Protestant who believes that the Law has been done away ought to read that, because all the commandments of God are righteousness. He says, 'My righteousness shall not be abolished.' Now think on this, all of those of you who think the laws and commandments of God have been done away, think on this for a minute: Do you think that God is evil? *Oh, no, of course not!*

The commandments and laws of God come from Him and He is always law abiding. And He is called *Lawgiver*. Do you think for one minute that because you want follow your licentious, stupid, insane grace and say that the laws and commandments of God have been done away? that He's going to conveniently do it for you when He says, "**…My righteousness shall not be abolished!**" Why don't you go up and show this to your Sunday-keeping preacher when he says it's been abolished. Let's see what he says. You will know he's a false preacher, without a doubt.

He says to us, 7: "Hearken to me…" Now, 'hearken' is a good word. You could say *listen.* But today *listen* doesn't have the same impact as *hearken,* because you can be doing things and listen to music in the background. You can be doing other things and listen and watching television at that same time. 'Hearken' is better because it means *to hear and act upon it.* That's why 'hearken' is better, and that's the way we left it in the Old Testament here.

"…you who know righteousness… [Who are the ones who know righteousness?]: …**the people in whose heart *is* My Law**…" (v 7).

Far from abolishing it, what does it do? *It writes it in your heart and in your mind and in your inward part!*

"…do not fear the reproach of men, nor be afraid of their revelings" (v 7).

So, you can say this is for the Church down through time. Don't worry about martyrdom.

Verse 8: "For the moth shall eat them up like a garment, and the worm shall eat them like wool; but **My righteousness shall be forever, and My salvation from generation to generation.**'"

All down through time. Then you take 'from generation to generation' and you apply that to the second resurrection. You can say that this is all inclusive to all people that they're all going to have an opportunity for salvation.

Verse 9 *is a resurrection*: "Awake! Awake! Put on strength, O arm of the LORD. Awake, as in the ancient days, in the generations of old. Was it not You *who* cut Rahab into pieces, piercing the serpent?" *Overcoming Satan!*

Verse 11: "Therefore, the redeemed of the LORD shall return and come with singing into Zion; and everlasting joy *shall be* upon their head...." We're talking about two things:

1. resurrection
2. return of Israel

Isaiah 52:1: "Awake! Awake! Put on your strength, O Zion; put on your beautiful robes, O Jerusalem, the Holy City..."

That's Jerusalem during the Millennium. Could be projected forward to the New Jerusalem (Rev. 20; 21). *Tremendous!*

"...For never again shall come to you the uncircumcised and the unclean ones" (v 1). *That has got to be Jerusalem during the Millennium!* Isa. 52 has an awful lot,

Verse 6: "Therefore My people shall know My name...." *That's us!*

Verse 8: "...when the LORD returns again to Zion."

➤ Verses 9-12—we have the Millennium

Verse 13 *has to do with Christ*: "Behold, My Servant shall rule well... [that's when Christ is King over all the earth] ...He shall be exalted and extolled, and be very high.... [now notice: switch, change!] ...Many were astonished at Him—for *His body was* so disfigured—even His form beyond that of the sons of men" (vs 13-14).

How could He be exalted, extolled and rule well? You see, you can't understand that until after the fact of the crucifixion.

Verse 15 *says what He's going to do*: "So shall He sprinkle many nations... [that is with the blood of sacrifices] ...the kings shall shut their mouths because of Him; for they will see *that* which *was* not told to them; yea, what they had not heard, shall they consider."

➤ Isa. 53—Christ and His life all the way down through His crucifixion, so we have the Passover, don't we? We actually have the whole chapter in our Passover Ceremony booklet.

Isaiah 54:1—*here we have the Church and the marriage of the Lamb*: "'Sing, O barren, you *that* never bore... [that's before the Church even existed] ...break out into singing and shout, *you* who never travailed, for more *are* the children of the desolate than the children of the married woman,' says the LORD." *Paul quotes that in Gal. 4, referring to the Church.*

Verse 5—*marriage of the Lamb*: "For your Maker *is* your husband... [that applies to Israel of old, but then the marriage of the Lamb in the future] ...the LORD of hosts is His name; and your Redeemer *is* the Holy One of Israel; the God of the whole earth shall He be called." *Then it talks about God blessing them and so forth!*

Isa. 55—this is going to be part of the Gospel that we are going to be preaching. This is part of the Gospel that is preached today. But also goes on into the Millennium as we begin teaching the people.

Isaiah 55:1: "Ho, everyone who thirsts, come to the waters..." **What is the water?**

- the Spirit of God
- the Word of God
- the Truth of God

"...and he who *has* no money, come, buy and eat...." (v 1).

Oh taste and see that the Lord is good! That ties in with the Passover: *you have to eat His flesh and drink His blood, or you have no life in you!*

See how all of these Scriptures come together and impact one upon another. When you go back and you read Isa. 28 again, about 'line upon line, precept upon precept, here a little and there a little' it just compounds and magnifies itself.

What we really see that is so fantastic; is that the fulfillment of the prophecies that we have in the Bible and of the Word of God are going to be fulfilled to their nth degree and to the overflowing—not just some little thing done over here in a corner.

"...Yea, come, buy wine and milk without money and without price. Why do you spend money for *what is* not bread? And your labor for *what* never satisfies? Hearken diligently to Me, and eat *what is* good, and let your soul delight itself in fatness. Bow down your ear, and come to Me; hear, and your soul shall live; and I will make an everlasting covenant with you, even the sure mercies of David" (vs 1-3).

What is the Church called in Acts 15? I gave a message: *The Tabernacle of David.* And the sure mercies of David are *forgiveness and eternal life.*

Verse 4: "Behold, I have given Him *for* a witness to the people, a Prince and Commander of people."

David is a type of Christ. Then it talks about the Gentiles coming and so forth. Isa. 55 is really a tremendous one and it has to do. We understand what it is:

Verse 6: "Seek the LORD while He may be found… [we all need to do that. Today's the day he may be found] …call upon Him while He is near. Let the wicked forsake his way, and the unrighteous man his thoughts; and let him return to the LORD, and He will have mercy upon him; and to our God, for He will abundantly pardon" (vs 6-7).

Here's something always to remember— *never forget it*, which is this: *There are some things of God that we don't know!* What we know is really kind of like just a little mist compared to the knowledge and power of God and what He's going to do in His plan.

Verse 8: "'For **My thoughts *are* not your thoughts, nor your ways My ways**,' says the LORD. 'For *as* the heavens are higher than the earth, so are My ways higher than your ways, and My thoughts than your thoughts'" (vs 8-9).

Now we need to understand that every time we study the Bible. So the great blessing of learning, of knowing, of understanding it—*it all comes from God!* How could we possibly know this unless it came from God. There's no way. Because Isa. 29 says that *it's written a book,* but you give it to the wise man, he says, 'I don't know, can't understand it.' You give it to the unlearned, he says, 'Hey, I can't read.' Yet, we can understand it. We can go through the whole book of Isaiah and see all of these things, all stacked together and all magnified, bringing out the way of God.

➤ Isa. 56 has to do with the Sabbath; the blessings of keeping the Sabbath

➤ Isa. 57—the first couple of verses are very good. When we get old and feeble and weak and gray-headed and our memory starts disappearing and our vision of our eyes becomes cloudy and our teeth disappear and we have false china-clippers put in instead or we have to wear glasses, and we walk slowly or we walk with rust in our bones, so to speak, because we're wearing out.

Remember that Psa. 71 that says when you're old and gray-headed *God will not forsake you.* And we're all going to come to the time when we're looking down the road and there's a gravestone at the end of the road with our name on it. This is to ensure that we die in the faith.

Isaiah 57:1: "The righteous perish, and no one lays *it* to heart… [we have this in every funeral ceremony that we give] …and merciful men *are* taken away; none considering that the righteous are taken away from the evil to come. He shall enter into peace; they shall rest in their beds… [this case the grave] …each one who walked in his uprightness" (vs 1-2).

Then God starts to indict against all the vanity of the idols and evil men.

Verse 14—*here's repentance, also resurrection*: "And He shall say, 'Cast up! Cast up! Prepare the way! Take the stumbling block out of the way of My people.' For thus says the high and lofty One Who inhabits eternity; Whose name *is* Holy; 'I dwell in the high and Holy place, even with the one who is of a contrite and humble spirit, to revive the spirit of the humble, and to revive the heart of the contrite ones'" (vs 14-15). *That is an oblique reference to the resurrection!*

Isaiah 58:1: "'Cry aloud, do not spare, lift up your voice like a ram's horn…"

A ram's horn is very irritating. Have you ever heard a shofar blown, and if that's blown a long time, it gets very irritating. Well, some people are very irritated when you cry aloud and spare not.

"…and show My people their transgression, and the house of Jacob their sins" (v 1).

Then we can come down here and it talks about the Kingdom of God (v 12). Then the Sabbath, which then also has to do with the Millennium (v 13).

➤ Isa. 59 is the world today and how evil and wretched that it is, and how terrible that it is
➤ Isa. 60 has to do with the first and second coming of Christ

Isaiah 60:1: "Arise, shine; for your Light has come, and the glory of the LORD has risen upon you… [you can apply that in many different cases] …for behold, the darkness shall cover the earth, and gross darkness *the* people; but the LORD shall arise upon you, and His glory shall be seen upon you. And the Gentiles shall come to your light, and kings to the brightness of your rising" (vs 1-3).

Then it talks about all the things concerning the Kingdom of God.

Verse 11 is talking about Israel and so forth, and also New Jerusalem and the things that will be taking place, not only New Jerusalem (Rev. 20 & 21), but New Jerusalem as it's going to be re-built when Christ returns.

Verse 11: "Therefore, your gates will always be open; they will not be shut day nor night, that men may bring unto you the wealth of the Gentiles, and their kings in procession."

Remember what it says there in Zech. 14, that if they don't come up to keep the Feast of Tabernacles at Jerusalem—and obviously there has to be representatives from every nation—and when they come they will come in procession to represent their nation as they're keeping the Feast of Tabernacles.

Verse 12: "For the nation and kingdom that will not serve you will perish."

Yes, *those* nations will be completely wasted. That's what's going to happen unless they do. Here's what's going to happen. All the greatness and goodness and things of this world and production of the nations is going to flow and benefit the children of God who are the spirit sons and daughters of God who rule and reign with Him. It's not going to be done for nothing. Here's what's going to happen.

Verse 16: "You will also suck the milk of nations, and suck the breast of kings; and you shall know that I the LORD *am* your Savior and your Redeemer, the mighty One of Jacob."

Here's what's going to be during the Millennium. Now, let's look at this spiritually speaking. Not just during the Millennium alone, but the greatness and the might and the power of God and the spiritual things that we are going to be living in.

Verse 17: "For bronze I will bring gold, and for iron I will bring silver; and for wood I will bring bronze, and for stones, iron. I will also make your overseers to be peace, and your rulers to be righteousness." *That's us!*

- Do you want to get rid of crime? *The Kingdom of God has got to bring that!*
- Do you want to have righteous rulers? *Those who are in the first resurrection will be righteous rulers!*

Verse 18: "Violence will no more be heard in your land, *neither* wasting nor ruin within your borders; but you will call your walls Salvation, and your gates Praise. The sun will no more be your light by day... (vs 18-19).

Now we blend into *New Jerusalem, fulfillment of the Last Great Day and beyond.* See how all of these things are jam-packed into the book of Isaiah?

"...nor the brightness of the moon give light to you; but the LORD will be to you for an everlasting light, and your God your glory. Your sun will no more go down, nor your moon withdraw; for the LORD will be your everlasting light, and the days of your mourning shall be ended" (vs 19-20). *Amazing!*

Isaiah 61:1—*first and second coming of Christ*: "The Spirit of the Lord is upon me because the LORD has anointed Me to preach the Gospel to the poor; He has sent Me to bind up the brokenhearted, to proclaim liberty to the captives, and the opening of the prison to those who are bound; to preach the acceptable year of the LORD and the day of vengeance of our God; to comfort all who mourn..." (vs 1-2).

Jesus read this when He started His ministry in Galilee in the synagogue in Nazareth on the day of Pentecost; and He read this to substantiate His ministry. What do we have? *First coming of Christ, second coming of Christ!* Then we have the Millennial places. Then we have building the waste places.

Verse 6, this will be the Church: "But you shall be called the priests of the LORD... [Rev. 20] ...it will be said of you, 'The ministers of our God'; you will eat the riches of the Gentiles, and you will boast in their glory.... [tremendous thing] ...For your shame *you will have* double; instead of dishonor they will rejoice in their portion; therefore, in their own land they will possess double; everlasting joy will be theirs. 'For I the LORD love justice, I hate robbery for burnt offering; and I will direct their work in truth, and I will make an everlasting covenant with them" (vs 6-8).

Then the Gentiles will know and be converted and so forth. This is all a part of the Church and its teaching. This is part of our teaching to Israel and the rest of the world. Amazing how much is in here.

Now you notice how we shifted from the first part of Isaiah, where it was a lot of warnings and a lot of condemnation and a call to repentance. Now we're shifting more in to what it is for the Millennium and the Kingdom of God on earth.

Isaiah 62:1—you can apply this to the Church and the Millennium: "For Zion's sake I will not be silent, and for Jerusalem's sake I will not rest... [beginning of the Millennium] ...until its righteousness goes out as brightness, and her salvation as a burning torch… [all through the Millennium] …And the Gentiles will see your righteousness, and all kings your glory; and you will be called by a new name…" (vs 1-2).

Rev. 2 & 3, we're given a new name. So you see again, as we go through this: the unity of the Scriptures in proclaiming the Truth of God.

Verse 3: "You also will be a crown of glory in the hand of the LORD, and a royal diadem in the hand of your God. You will no more be called Forsaken…" (vs 3-4).

You're married; then it goes right on down into other things concerning the Millennium.

➤ Isa. 63—*God's vengeance and judgment*—the beginning part of it—*on Edom.* Verse 7 has to do with the preaching of the Gospel and has to do with our teaching people during the Millennium.

I know we've gone through this rather rapidly, but nevertheless, this really gives us:

- a good foundation for understanding the book of Isaiah in relationship to the rest of the Bible
- a good foundation for understanding about the Millennium and the Holy Days
- a good foundation to understand that what God has given us today is really fantastic

That's why we should never, *never, **never*** rest back on our laurels. That's why we need to be zealous. We need to be diligent. We need to be doing God's way all the time in our lives, and collectively together. Don't let the arguments and persuasion of men take you from the Truth of God at any time.

Isaiah 63:7: "I will mention the loving kindnesses of the LORD, the praises of the LORD, according to all that the LORD has bestowed on us, and the great good to the house of Israel…"

- physical Israel during the Millennium
- spiritual Israel is the Church today
- our reward in the Kingdom of God

"…*by* which He bestowed on them according to His mercies, and according to the multitude of His loving kindnesses, for He said, 'Surely they *are* My people, children that will not lie'" (vs 7-8). So, we have all of this all together.

Notice how fluid that it is in the book of Isaiah, going from one thing to another, but if we know the Holy Days we can piece it together the way it has to do.

Isa. 64:1—the beginning part of it is the

second coming of Christ or the Feast of Trumpets, where Isaiah said:

Isaiah 64:1: "Oh that You would rend the heavens *and* come down, *that* mountains might quake at Your presence, as when the melting fire burns, the fire causes water to boil, to make Your name known to Your adversaries, *that* the nations may tremble at Your presence! When You did awesome things *which* we did not look for, You came down, the mountains quaked at Your presence!" (vs 1-2).

Quite a thing! Read all about it. And the rest of it there has to do with repentance.

Isaiah 65:1 *is a prophecy of the Gentiles responding to the preaching of the Gospel*: "I revealed Myself to those who asked not for Me; I am found by those who did not seek Me. I said, 'Behold Me, behold Me,' to a nation not called by My name…. [that's the Gentiles, but to Israel]: …I have spread out My hands all the day to a rebellious people who walk in the way that is not good, *even* after their own thoughts" (vs 1-2).

You can read all the rest of it, the things covering the Millennium and the 100-year period we'll cover tomorrow.

Isa. 66—we find that it has to do with the one that God looks to 'has a contrite spirit and a broken heart.' It comes down and blends into the return of Christ. It blends into the new heavens and new earth, which is what He's going to do when He returns. And then that can blend into the new heavens and new earth (Rev. 20 & 21).

Then it closes out by Isaiah 66:23: "And it shall come to pass… [this is all during the Millennium] …that from one month to another, and from one Sabbath to another, shall all flesh come to worship before Me,' says the LORD." That pretty well finishes the book of Isaiah.

I know it was fast and quick. But I hope that you got a lot out of it seeing how the structure of Isaiah then is understood when we take it and we take part of it that applies to the Passover and apply it to Unleavened Bread, Pentecost, Trumpets, Atonement, Tabernacles and the Last Great Day.

The structure of the Holy Days gives us the meaning and the understanding of the book of Isaiah!. I just encourage you to continue studying it and do some more outlining beyond what I have done here and see how exciting and tremendous this is that you can understand that much more in the book of Isaiah.

Scriptural References

1) Isaiah 29:13-24
2) Isaiah 30:8-18
3) Isaiah 32:1-2, 15-18
4) Isaiah 33:2, 5-6, 20-22
5) Isaiah 34:1-2
6) Isaiah 35:1-2, 5, 8-10
7) Isaiah 40:1-3, 9, 11-14
8) Isaiah 50:4-6
9) Isaiah 40:15-18, 21-23, 25
10) Isaiah 41:18-19, 21-22
11) Isaiah 42:1-4, 9-12, 21
12) Isaiah 43:1, 4-6, 10-11
13) Isaiah 45:17-19. 21-22
14) Isaiah 47:7-9
15) Isaiah 48:22
16) Isaiah 49:1-3, 22
17) Isaiah 51:1-9, 11
18) Isaiah 52:1, 6, 8, 13-15
19) Isaiah 54:1, 5
20) Isaiah 55:1-4, 6-9
21) Isaiah 57:1-2, 14-15
22) Isaiah 58:1
23) Isaiah 60:1-3, 11-12, 16-20
24) Isaiah 61:1-2, 6-8
25) Isaiah 62:1-4
26) Isaiah 63:7-8
27) Isaiah 64:1-2
28) Isaiah 65:1-2
29) Isaiah 66:23

FRC:bo
Transcribed: 8-14-07
Reformatted: 1/2021

Scriptures referenced, not quoted:

- Matthew 13
- Luke 24
- Isaiah 31; 3; 33:17
- Revelation 9; 16; 19; 2;, 3
- Zechariah 14
- Isaiah 36-38
- Matthew 3
- Isaiah 43:3; 44; 46
- Revelation 17; 18
- Hebrews 1
- Revelation 20; 21
- Isaiah 52:9-12; 53
- Galatians 4
- Isaiah 28
- Acts 15
- Isaiah 56
- Psalm 71
- Isaiah 58:12-13; 59
- Zechariah 14

Also referenced:

- In-Depth Study: *The Millennial Temple #1-3*
- Message: *The Tabernacle of David*
- Booklet: *Passover Ceremony*

CHAPTER SIXTY-THREE

Millennial Scriptures in the Psalms I

Fred R. Coulter

This message shows how the book of Psalms is going to help us understand the reason—the purpose—of the Millennium and the Kingdom of God being set up by Jesus Christ.

Let's look at a couple of Scriptures that pertains right to the Feast of Tabernacles and the setting up of the Kingdom of God.

Let's come to Dan. 2:40; this becomes very important in the flow of things and how it happens at the end:

Daniel 2:40: "And the fourth kingdom shall be *as* strong as iron, forasmuch as iron breaks in pieces and beats down all things, and as the iron that crushes all these, shall it break in pieces and crush. And whereas you saw the feet and toes, part of potters' clay and part of iron, *the* kingdom shall be divided. ...." (vs 40-41).

The ten toes are undoubtedly *ten regions* in the world at the end-time. This is how it's eventually going to be enforced. It will look like a movement of the people from beneath, as Rev. 13 shows, but what comes out of it is the same old satanic system.

"...But there shall be in it the strength of the iron, because you saw the iron mixed with miry clay. And *as* the toes of the feet *were* part of iron and part of clay, *so* the kingdom shall be partly strong and partly broken" (vs 41-42).

Now, if you look at it on a worldview and think of a re-organized U.N., which they are going to do, I'm absolutely convinced. This describes it perfectly. There are strong nations. There are weak nations. It is held together and then sort of comes apart a little bit and then comes back together. But just like iron and clay it cannot cleave to each other; they have their problems.

Verse 43: "And whereas you saw iron mixed with miry clay, they shall mix themselves with the seed of men...."

So, we have a great interracial marriage thing that's taking place today, more than ever before, on a worldwide basis.

"...But they shall not cling to one another, even as iron does not combine with clay. And in the days of these kings, the God of heaven shall set up a kingdom, **which shall never be destroyed**...." (vs 43-44).

- Are we under the Kingdom of God today?
- Has Jesus come and fulfilled all the prophets and set up the Kingdom beginning in about 100$_{A.D.}$?
- *No way!*

"...And **the Kingdom** shall not be left to other people... [Do the saints rule? *No!*] ...but it shall break in pieces and consume all these kingdoms, and **it shall stand forever**" (v 44).

Now, we don't have any eternal kingdoms set up on the earth. That's why we keep the Feast of Tabernacles, because this is a portrayal of it. As defined, the thousand-year period (Rev. 20).

Verse 45: "Because you saw that the stone was cut out of the mountain without hands, and that it broke in pieces the iron, the brass, the clay, the silver, and the gold, the great God has made known to the king [Nebuchadnezzar] **what shall come to pass hereafter**. And **the dream *is* certain, and its interpretation is sure**."

Now, let's understand: "...**come to pass hereafter**..." does not tell us how long in the future this will be. But we know for sure, absolutely, unequivocally, this part of this prophecy *has not been fulfilled.*

Now, let's look at another one very similar to it in Dan. 7. It talks about giving the Kingdom to the saints. It talks about the end-time Beast Power, which rules the whole world. So, you have to combine this with Rev. 13, Rev. 17 and other places in the Old Testament and New Testament. This relates right back to Dan. 2. We started out with the fourth kingdom, so here it says:

Dan. 2:23 relates right back to Dan. 2, we started out with the fourth kingdom:

Daniel 7:23: "Thus he said, 'The fourth beast shall be the fourth kingdom upon earth... [this is a worldwide, world-ruling kingdom] ...which shall be different from all the *other* kingdoms and shall devour **the whole earth**...."

We're talking about world-government—and obviously, that has not yet happened, and therefore, the return of Christ and the Kingdom of God has not happened either. If you just believe the Bible for what it says, and understand it without twisting the Scriptures to make it fit a preconceived notion, so you can have a pet little theory and do away with the Word of God. If you believe what the Bible says, this obviously hasn't happened.

"...and shall devour **the whole earth** and shall trample it and break it in pieces. And the ten horns out of this kingdom *are* ten kings that shall arise. And another shall arise after them. And he shall be different from the first, and he shall subdue three kings" (vs 23-24).

Well, it's not time to go through the obvious particulars of this, but we haven't yet seen that happen in the end-time.

Verse 25: "'And **he shall speak words against the Most High**...'"—*tie in with 2-Thess. 2 and Rev. 13!*

"...and shall wear out the saints of the Most High, and think to change the set times and the laws...." (v 25). *That has happened back in the history of the Church and it's going to happen again at the end!*

"...And they shall be given into his hand until a time and times and one-half time" (v 25). *There we go, the 3-1/2 years that we've covered, at the end.*

Verse 26: "But the judgment shall sit... [means *Christ will return*] ...and his dominion shall be taken away to be consumed and to be destroyed unto the end... [of that Kingdom] ...And the Kingdom and dominion, and the greatness of the Kingdom under the whole heaven... [this tells us why we're here] ...**shall be given to the people of the saints of the Most High**... [Dan. 2 says that it's not going to be given to other people] ...Whose Kingdom *is* an everlasting kingdom. And **all kingdoms shall serve and obey Him**'" (vs 26-27).

Obviously, this has not happened. We can also tie-in a couple of others from Isa. 2 that all nations are going to come up to Jerusalem to learn of God's ways. Those who don't *God is going to deal with them until they do!* So, it hasn't happened, yet.

Now let's understand something concerning the Bible that is really, really important. We're going to go through many parts of the book of Psalms. We are going to see:

- about the Kingdom of God
- how Christ is going to return
- how He is going to destroy the enemy
- how He's going to set up an everlasting kingdom

In the book of Psalms we're going to see a little different application because these become personal things that we will experience as differentiated

seeing the whole picture of it and where do we fit in and what can we expect.

We'll begin with Psa. 1; this is going to tell us a lot. As we go through, I'm going to refer to several things without necessarily turning to the Scriptures, but we know that Jesus said: 'I am the Beginning and the Ending, the First and the Last.'

Also in the book of Revelation 1 & 21, where Jesus says this. That tells us that we need to look to the beginning of the Bible as well as the end of the Bible in the book of Revelation and the rest of God's Word is to fit into that framework, based upon the Sabbath and the Holy Days.

We've also seen that there are patterns that took place from the beginning where that the cherubim and the overshadowing of the Ark of the Covenant within the tabernacle and the temple goes clear back to the east entrance of the Garden of Eden after Adam and Eve were kicked out. We also find some things similar at the end. We also have the Tree of Life at the beginning, and we have the Tree of Life at the ending.

In Psa. 1 we find how we are going to please God and, with conversion and change of heart, enter into the Kingdom of God. But here it describes our personal relationship with God and our differentiation from being part of the world—because Jesus said *'Though we live in the world we are not part of the world,'* just as when Jesus was on the earth, He was not part of the world.

Psalm 1:1: "Blessed is the man who does not walk in the counsel of the wicked, nor stand in the way of sinners, nor sit in the seat of the scornful."

We are called to be different from the world, not part of it. Let's understand something else that's very important: Though the Gospel has got to be preached in all the world, *for a witness* to **all** nations, it is not an attempt by God to save the world. He has to call those who repent and are baptized and receive the Spirit of God. They worship God *'in Spirit and in Truth,'* which is far different from trying to save the whole world. This is what happens to us when we are converted and worship God is 'Spirit and Truth' and keep the laws and commandments of God in spirit.

Verse 2 "But his delight is in the Law of the LORD; and in His Law does he meditate day and night." **Why?** *Because they're inscribed into his mind and into his heart!*

Verse 3: "And he shall be like a tree planted by the streams of water..."

So, we have the Tree of Life in Genesis; we have the Tree of Life in Revelation: the first and the last. If we yield to God and grow and change and overcome and bring forth fruit, *we are going to be like trees planted by the streams of water*, which in the case of the Holy Spirit is the *living water;* which brings forth salvation unto eternal life.

"…that brings forth its fruit in its season…" (v 3). *We're all to bring forth fruit!*

We find in the parable in Matt. 13, that some bring 30-fold, some 60-fold, some 100-fold; because it falls into fertile ground and is watered by the Holy Spirit.

"…and its leaf shall not wither, and all that he does shall prosper" (v 3)—*spiritually!*

We can also prosper physically. Unfortunately, living in the end-time when everyone has been prospered, especially in America, United Kingdom, Canada, Australia, and Northwestern Europe, they have all of these goods and so it's no surprise that we have a Laodicean church on hand, because they think that their prosperity is a reflection of their conversion. But the use of the Spirit of God and yielding to God is a reflection of your conversion, *not* your physical assets.

Verse 4: "The wicked are not so, but they are like chaff which the wind drives away…. [good expression of what's going to happen to them] …Therefore, the wicked shall not stand in the judgment, nor sinners in the congregation of the righteous; for the LORD knows the way of the righteous, but the way of the wicked shall perish" (vs 4-6). *This is talking about our individual relationship with God!*

Psa. 2 is a worldview from God's point of view looking down on the earth. Every time we think: How much time do we have left? Know this for sure: Just as every day comes and goes, so every day we are closer to the Kingdom of God.

But let's also understand that because we have lived in a time of peace and security and goods and things like this—though we've had wars: WWI, WWII, the Korean War, the Vietnam War, and the war in Iraq and Afghanistan, and so forth—does not necessarily mean that the end is about to take place in an imminent way, because many things have to happen. But here is a good description of how the world today in coming to its one-world government and its one-world rulership, and looking at things, this gives us a good understanding of it.

Psalm 2:1: "Why do the nations rage and the people plot in vain?"

Satan loves do-gooders. One of the great do-gooder things that is going to happen, is that it's going to be wonderful if we have world government—and we divide it down into ten[transcriber's correction] regions. We many not be too far

from MexiAmeriCana in North American. The South American nations have already got some sort of the near final beginning of a South American Union. So, you tie that together with all of the different regional unions that are taking place and we're going to end up with ten.

Verse 2: "The kings of the earth set themselves, and **the rulers take counsel together against the LORD and against His Christ**…"

It's going to be antichrist, and it's going to be manifested in the great world-leader (2 Thess. 2). What they want to do is

- get rid of God
- get rid of religion
- get rid of morality
- change the laws
- change the times

and that's exactly what they are doing.

All of this summer, we have had vast forest fires in California. Don't you suppose that this is a warning from God because He's not happy with us? That He is angry with us? God is not going to come down here in person and do it Himself. *No!* He takes the weather. He sends a whole lot of lightning—and almost all of Northern California, much to the dismay of all of the 'greenie-greenies,' is burning up! The trees that they love to hug! Well, now they can get in their better because a lot of the brush is burned out, so send in all the tree-huggers out there to hug these poor, wounded, burned trees. If you want to read the daily news from God's point of view, read Deut. 28 from beginning to end, all the way through. There will be the pattern, in the Bible, of the daily news against Israel and the world. Here's what they say:

Verse 3: "Let us break Their bands asunder and cast away Their cords from us." *We don't want anything to do with God. We don't want anything to do with the Bible.*

That's why they're going to picture us as nuts and kooks. Well, let me tell you another thing that is true: Within the Church of God there are enough nuts and kooks who run cults that it brings a bad name upon the Church of God. You know that when the government acts against all the cults—which they will do to bring everything under control—they will also be swept into the net. What we need to do is:

- have the mind of Christ
- the soundness of Scripture
- the character and love of God

because we're not a cult! Some of the Churches of God are!

Verse 5: "Then He shall speak to them in His wrath… [Rev. 16, the wrath of God] …and in His fury He terrifies them."

Then He says, this is the setting up of the Kingdom of God. Notice how all of this follows in sequence and helps give us some guidelines concerning other prophecies:

Verse 6: "Yea, I have set My King upon Zion, My Holy mountain. I will declare the decree of the LORD. He has said to Me, 'You are My Son; this day I have begotten You'" (vs 6-7). *That goes back to the very begettal of Jesus with the virgin Mary!*

Verse 8: "Ask of Me, and I shall give the nations for Your inheritance, and the uttermost parts of the earth for Your possession…. [giving rulership and kingship to Jesus] …You shall break them with a rod of iron; You shall dash them in pieces like a potter's vessel" (vs 8-19)—which is a really powerful song in *The Messiah* by George Handel. Here's the message, all you rulers down here on earth listen up:

Verse 10: "Now therefore, be wise, O kings; be admonished O judges of the earth. Serve the LORD with fear and rejoice with trembling" (vs 10-11).

That's what they're going to have to do when Christ returns. There are going to be some kings come up to Jerusalem and say, 'Ohhhh, I repent. Here I am.'

Verse 12: "Kiss the Son, lest He be angry and you perish in the way, for His wrath can flame up in a moment. Blessed are all who take refuge in Him."

We will notice this through the Psalms, all the way through the Psalms: our personal relationship with God; the refuge that He gives us.

Now let's see some very interesting things concerning Christ and concerning the saints as it relates to the Church and as it relates to the first coming of Christ and the setting up of the Kingdom of God, and also the restoration of Israel. Psa. 118 shows us:

- our relationship with God
- the salvation of Israel
- Christ Who is going to be King, sit on the throne and rule the world
- how we're going to get from here to there

Psalm 118:1: "O give thanks to the LORD, for He is good because His steadfast love endures forever. Let Israel now say that His steadfast love endures forever" (vs 1-2).

When are they going to say that? *After the 144,000 and great innumerable multitude are saved and they enter into the Kingdom of God!* Then physical Israel is brought back to its inheritance of the land.

Verse 3: "Let the house of Aaron now say that His steadfast love endures forever. Let **those who fear the LORD** now say that His steadfast love endures forever" (vs 1-4). *That's us!*

In this life, as Jesus said, He told His disciples, 'Be of good courage.' He said, 'in the world you're going to have tribulation, but be of good courage, I've overcome the world.'

This is why we have difficulties, we have trials, we have stress, we have things that we go through; and all of these things come about because of just living in the world, so that we can begin to trust God more and more and more as every one of these things transpires. Or we come to a trial or difficulty. Always remember that God has said, through the Apostle Paul, that *'all things work together for good to those who love God and are called according to His purpose.'*

- when you have a trial
- when you have difficulty
- when you have a problem

that comes along, what you need to do is yield yourself to God, which is right here:

Verse 5: "I called upon the LORD in distress; the LORD answered me, and set me in a large place."

We also have to realize that in praying to God and crying out to Him: God *will answer that prayer in His time, according to His will, according to His goodness,* not on our time schedule and what we think needs to be. If God doesn't answer us immediately, we say, 'Well, I wonder why God didn't answer?' Keep beseeching. Keep asking God. He will answer and, over a course of time, you're going to find God will answer all your prayers, though the difficulties and strife you have gone through, or went through, didn't appear that it would come out that way.

Remember that *it ain't over till it's over!* Now especially in baseball. A famous baseball player—Yogi Berra—said, 'It ain't over till it's over.' There was a game by a team who was behind 5 to 0 in the ninth inning and they had hardly any hits and the pitching staff was really doing well, so they came up in the ninth inning and they scored six runs without an out to win the game. All through eight and a half innings, up to that point, it looked for sure that this is wipe out by the other team. That's a good example. *It isn't over till it's over!*

God will hear and answer you and *set you in a large place!*

Verse 6: "The LORD is on my side… [*if* we're on God's side, He's on our side] …I will not fear. **What can man do to me?** The LORD is for me as my Helper; therefore, I will look in triumph upon those who hate me" (vs 6-7). *The enemy is going to be defeated!*

Verse 8 is the middle verse in the whole Bible and notice what it says. This is how we get *from here to there* in the Kingdom of God, when Christ returns.

Verse 8: "It is better to trust in the LORD than to put confidence in man. It is better to trust in the LORD than to trust in princes" (vs 8-9).

We can understand v 8 on a personal basis. But here's the one too many people really don't understand. The sum of this in today's language is that *you cannot solve spiritual problems by political means!* The 'princes' are the political power whether they are elected or appointed or whatever. Almost any government: show me how the bureaucracy has brought salvation and did the right things. So much for trusting in politics.

Now, this is from Christ's point of view, as well as David's, v 10: "All the nations surround me, but in the name of the LORD I will destroy them…. [doesn't matter what the circumstances are] …They surround me; yea, they surround me, but in the name of the LORD I will destroy them. They surround me like bees; they are extinguished like the fire of thorns, for in the name of the LORD I will cut them off" (vs 10-12).

This also has to do with part of our fighting when we come back with Christ, because remember, Jesus said to Pilate, 'If My Kingdom were of this world then would My servants fight.'

Verse 13: "You have thrust hard at me… [that is, the enemy] …so that I might fall, but the LORD helped me. The LORD is my strength and song, and He has become my salvation. The voice of rejoicing and salvation is in the tabernacles of the righteous…" (vs 13-15).

We want to dwell in the tabernacle of the Lord and in New Jerusalem. Rev. 20 & 21 talks about that.

Verse 16: "The right hand of the LORD is exalted; the right hand of the LORD does valiantly."

Whatever trial you may have, whatever difficulty that you're in, take this Psalm—because this is a Psalm on how to grow and overcome and trust in God—so that you can be in the Kingdom of God.

Verse 17: "I shall not die, but live and declare the works of the LORD." *That's our ultimate goal in being priests and kings in the Kingdom of God!*

Verse 18: "The LORD has sorely chastened me; but He has not given me over to death…. [here's a promise]: …Open to me the gates of righteousness; I will go through them, and I will praise the LORD" (vs 18-19).

This has reference to Christ, which we will see in Psa. 24 in just a little bit. And this has reference to us entering into the Kingdom of God. Also, it talks about the gates of righteousness and where are the 12 gates? The gates are like one pearl in New Jerusalem So, this gives entrance into New Jerusalem.

Verse 20: "This is the gate of the LORD; the righteous shall enter through it. I will praise You, for You have answered me and have become my salvation" (vs 20-21).

It refers to Christ! This ties right in with Psa. 2, where they're rejecting Christ; where they're trying to 'cut the bands asunder' and get away from Christ.

Verse 22: "The Stone, which the builders rejected… [Jesus quoted this, and so did Peter] …has become the Head Stone of the corner."

In Jesus' first coming, and in His ministry, all of the things that we have covered here you can see apply. Jesus was totally yielded to God the Father and the power of the Holy Spirit. He didn't join the political realm. He didn't join the priesthood that was there. He didn't bring the Kingdom of God, as they expected it at that time, in a political way to get rid of the Romans, because God has a bigger plan. God has bigger thoughts. The Jews, in looking at Jesus, rejected Him.

Verse 23: "This is the LORD'S doing; it is marvelous in our eyes. This is the day, which the LORD has made; we will rejoice and be glad in it" (vs 23-24). *The day of salvation for all of us, when we walk through that gate in the resurrection and up on the Sea of Glass!*

I tell you, once you really put the Scriptures together and understand how they flow together, the Scriptures are overwhelming in their meaning and depth of understanding, that ties the whole Bible together. {note Bible Commentary: *The Unity of Scripture*} The unity of Scripture shows that God is the same *yesterday, today and forever* as Jesus said He was, and that *the Lord changes not.* Anything that appears to be a change is an improvement from the physical to the spiritual. so it's actually better.

Verse 25: "Save now, I beseech You, O

LORD; O LORD, I beseech You, cause us to prosper now. Blessed is he who comes in the name of the LORD… [that was said of Christ] …we have blessed You out of the house of the LORD. The LORD is God and He has made His light to shine upon us. Bind the festival sacrifice with cords even unto the horns of the altar. You are my God, and I will praise You; You are my God, I will exalt You. Oh, give thanks to the LORD, for He is good, for His steadfast love endures forever" (vs 25-29).

Fantastic Psalm! All of this applies to various aspects of the Kingdom of God:

- on a personal level
- with Jesus Christ
- with the nations of the world
- the setting up of the Kingdom of God

I think you're going to find this quite interesting as we go through and if we put them together… Every Feast of Tabernacles I like to bring something different, something unique, rather than just preach exactly the same thing over and over again. The reason is because there's so much in the Bible for us to learn. Isn't it tremendous that every Feast of Tabernacles we can find something new to learn about God's way? *All of this, all of this reflects the eternal mind of Christ in inspiring the Bible for us!*

Here's Christ setting up the Kingdom of God; Psalm 9:5: "You have rebuked the nations… [all the way through Rev. 8, 9, 10 & 16] …You have destroyed the wicked…"

The ones that end up in the Lake of Fire, personally cast in by a special angel of God, is *the beast* and *the false prophet.* Perfect example of what Jesus said: 'Of what value is it if a man gain the whole world, but lose his life?' They're going to rule and control the world before Jesus returns. They're going to lose their lives.

"…You have blotted out their name forever and ever. Endless ruin has overtaken the enemy, You have uprooted the cities, the memory of them has perished. But the LORD shall endure forever; He has prepared His throne for judgment. And He shall judge the world in righteousness; He shall govern the people with justice" (vs 5-8).

That's how the Kingdom of God is going to be established. It's going to come with a force and power of God in a tremendous way.

Verse 15: "The nations have sunk down in the grave that they made; their own foot is caught in the net which they hid. The LORD has made Himself known. He has executed judgment; the wicked are snared in the work of their own hands. Selah" (vs 15-16).

Remember that. Take some of these as promises that you can use to help you through your difficult times. Know that Christ is going to come and set up His kingdom.

Psa. 15—this one related to living in the Tabernacle of God. So, when I read this, just remember Psa. 21, 'Behold the Tabernacle of God is with men.'

- Who's going to get there?
- How are you going to enter into it?

Here are some personal qualifications:

Psalm 15:1: "LORD, who shall dwell in Your tabernacle?…."

- Who's going to make it into the Kingdom of God?
- Don't we ask that all the time of ourselves?

Part of it is here:

"…Who shall dwell upon Your Holy hill?" (v 1). *It's talking about those who are going to serve Christ, in this particular case!*

Verse 2: "**He who walks uprightly**…" *How do you walk uprightly?*

- in Spirit and Truth
- with the Spirit of God
- Christ in you
- the mind of Christ
- that you have the Spirit of the Father as a begotten child of God

"…and **works righteousness, and speaks the Truth in his heart**" (v 2)

You don't say one thing in a flattering, nice way to people and then in your mind curse them. You speak the truth from the heart.

Verse 3: "He **does not slander with his tongue, nor does evil to his neighbor**…" (v 3). *Love your neighbor as yourself!*

"…**nor takes up a reproach against his neighbor**" (v 3). *Does not scheme against his neighbor;* all a part of the love of God.!

Verse 4: "In whose eyes **a vile person is despised**…"—*for their ungodly behavior!*

"…but he **honors those who fear the LORD**…" (v 4). *Love the brethren as Christ has loved us!*

"…he **who swears to his own hurt and does not change it**" (v 4)—which means, as Jesus said in Matt. 6, 'Don't swear by yourself because you can't make one hair white or black, and you can't add a cubit to your height' But He said, 'Let *your yes be yes, and your no be no.'* There it is right there!

Verse 5: "He **who has not put out his money at usury**…" (v 5)—*which is excessive interest! Sounds like credit card companies, 19-20% plus penalties!*

"…**nor has he taken a bribe against the innocent**…." (v 5). *All corporate ministers listen up. Is your salary a bribe? Think about that!*

"…**He who does these things shall never be moved**" (v 5). *That's a guarantee that we are going to have entrance into the Kingdom of God!*

The gate of righteousness is going to open and we are going to enter in. We are going to rule and reign with Christ. This is a tremendous thing when we understand it and see that throughout the book of Psalms. We're not going to cover every Psalm; I'll leave that to you for your personal study. But as you do, with some of these things as a springboard and guideline, you're going to see how much there is about the Kingdom of God in the book of Psalms.

Psa. 23—here's a Psalm that even the world has memorized. Certain parts of it they may understand, but let's look at from the point of view of the Kingdom of God. How does it relate to the Kingdom of God? Our being in it? Our part in it? Christ is the One Who is the King and so forth.

Psalm 23:1: "The LORD is my Shepherd; I shall not want…. [you will not lack anything *spiritually*] …He makes me to lie down in green pastures…" (vs 1-2).

We have seen in Ezek. 34 good pasture comes from God and from God's Word as led by Christ. This is what it's talking about.

"…He leads me beside the still waters" (v 2). *The waters that are comforting, the waters that are soothing!* We started out that *we're like a tree planted by the streams of water. Here it is, rest, peace, still waters!*

Verse 3: "He restores my soul… [a type of the resurrection] …He leads me in the paths of righteousness for His name's sake."

The thing is, all the growing and grace and knowledge and understanding and all of these things are so important because they are *the creation of God that He is working within you!* That's what God wants. That's why we pointed out, is just like the potter and the clay. He wants it so he can mold it, he can shape it, and he can make it to whatever beautiful design that he desires. When it's done, baked in an oven so that it is permanent. Many analogies that we can draw here.

Even though we have trials, v 4: "Yea, though I walk through the valley of the shadow of death…"

Every one of us are going to come there. That doesn't necessarily mean you're going to have many trials leading to death. There're going to be times when you may even think death is better than life. But that doesn't necessarily "…the valley of the shadow…" *of our death* as we continue to go down in time. God harvests all the saints one-by-one who are, what we will call 'senior citizens'; I'm part of that group now, too.

Whatever time I have left I want to do it in serving God—just like you do. We're all going to have a "…valley of the shadow of death…" that we're going to go through. However, remember this:

"…**I will fear no evil, for You are with me**…" (v 4).

Remember, *God the Father and Jesus Christ dwell in us,* which is another type, as we have seen, of the Kingdom of God, *God dwelling in us!*

"…Your rod and Your staff, **they comfort me**" (v 4). *We can lean on God for strength and a staff to guide us as a shepherd does!*

Here's the irony of the whole thing; here's what God is doing. Apply this to Christ and His life. Apply this to your life and your relationship with God. Sooner or later you will see this happen:

Verse 5: "You prepare a table for me in the presence of my enemies…." *There isn't a thing they can do about it!* That table is:

- eating of the Word of God
- living of the Word of God
- being fed spiritually

as it is here in 'green pastures'!

"…You anoint my head with oil; my cup runs over" (v 5). *There's the ultimate goal!*

We see all the things in life squeezed together in this one short, little Psalm, that even the world has memorized but doesn't know its meaning.

Verse 6: "Surely goodness and mercy shall follow me all the days of my life, and I shall dwell in the house of the LORD forever."

Behold the Tabernacle of God is with men, and He shall dwell with them, and they shall be His people!

We read about *the gates of righteousness* in Psa. 118. Now here it expands it a little further. Also, it shows the greatness and the glory of God.

Psalm 24:1: "The earth is the LORD'S, and the fullness of it, the world, and those who dwell in it."

Every one of us have life and breath and live, whether called or uncalled, and God provides in His love for all. He owns it all.

Verse 2: "For He has founded it upon the seas and established it upon the waters." *Then it blends right in to the fulfillment of the Feast of Tabernacles!*

Verse 3: "Who shall ascend into the hill of the LORD? Or who shall stand in His Holy place?"

The book of Isaiah, chapter four; we'll talk about the Temple of the Lord, and what will the temple be like during the Millennium—*The Millennial Temple #s 1 & 2* {**truthofGod.org**}

Isaiah 4:2: "In that day shall **the Branch** of the LORD be beautiful and glorious… [Christ is that Branch that comes out of the root of David] …and the fruit of the earth excellent and comely for those who are the **survivors of Israel**." *That's physical Israel!* It can also apply to us who will then be *spiritual* Israel.

Verse 3: "And it shall come to pass that he who is left in Zion, and he who remains in Jerusalem, shall be called Holy, even everyone who is written unto life in Jerusalem." *That's being recorded in the Book of Life!*

Verse 4: "When the LORD shall have washed away the filth of the daughters of Zion, and shall have purged the blood of Jerusalem from its midst by the spirit of judgment, and by the spirit of burning."

When Christ returns He's going to completely cleanse the whole area where the temple is going to be during the Millennium.

Verse 5: "And the LORD will create over every dwelling place of Mount Zion, and over her assemblies, a cloud and smoke by day, and the shining of a flaming fire by night…"

It's going to be a great expansion of what the children of Israel saw when God led them in the wilderness with the cloud by day and the fire by night. This shows that God is dwelling there. It's not going to be some building that's going to be built. *He* is making it spiritually understood here.

"…for over all the glory *shall be* a canopy…. [under that will be the true Temple of Christ] …And there shall be a tabernacle for shade by day from the heat, and for refuge, and for shelter from storm and rain" (vs 5-6).

In other words, the whole government of God is going to go out under the auspices of where Christ is dwelling in Mt. Zion, in His Temple, and the government will go to the whole world. Isn't that something?

Psalm 24:3: "Who shall ascend into the hill of the LORD?…. [Who's going to be there? *Psa. 15!*] …Or who shall stand in His Holy place? He who has clean hands and a pure heart…" (vs 3-4).

That only comes from *the washing of the water by the Word in our heart and mind!* Then being changed from flesh to spirit at the resurrection.

"…who has not lifted up his soul to vanity and has not sworn deceitfully…. [Christ never did that, and we are not to do that] …He shall receive the blessing from the LORD and righteousness from the God of his salvation. This is the generation of those who seek Him, who seek Your face, O God of Jacob. Selah" (vs 4-6).

That's what we are going to do spiritually, because Rev. 22 says that those who are saved are going to see the Father face-to-face. Now, we'll cover that on the Last Great Day.

But think of all of these things when you read the Psalms. This is why you learn so much from the Bible when you read and study the Bible over and over again. Then you come back and you go through it again and you bring all the other Scriptures and thoughts of the Bible that pertain to it. *It gives you great, great understanding!* I think we're going to be surprised how much the book of the Psalms details much of the personal things that will happen to us and Christ *during the Millennium when the Kingdom of God is here!*

Verse 7 goes back to the resurrection of Christ and His ascension into heaven. Here are the gates of righteousness that the Lord will enter into, as we covered in Psa. 118.

Verse 7: "Lift up your heads, O you gates; and be lifted up, O you everlasting doors; that the King of glory may come in."

We're going to be kings and priests! The gate is going to be opened for us, too!

Verse 8: "Who is this King of glory? **The LORD strong and mighty, the LORD mighty in battle**…. [He's going to conquer the whole world] …Lift up your heads, O you gates; lift them up, you everlasting doors; that the King of glory may come in. Who is this King of glory? **The LORD of hosts, He is the King of glory.** Selah" (vs 7-10). *We're going to:*

- share in His glory
- share in the rule
- share in the wealth

It's going to be absolutely fantastic! All of these things are in the Psalms to help us understand the Kingdom of God and our part in it.

We're not going to go through every Psalm because every Psalm does not depict things concerning the Kingdom of God in the way that we're doing here. We're going through and picking out selected ones, but there are many, many, all the way through the book of Psalms. So, I want you to do your reading and studying of the book of Psalms, and from this point of view.

Psalm 29:1: "To the LORD, O you sons of the mighty, give to the LORD glory and strength."

We know how we worship God now: *basically in prayer and a direct relationship to God the Father and Jesus Christ!* How are we going to worship God when we are spirit beings? This gives us a little clue:

Verse 2: "Give to the LORD glory and strength. Give to the LORD the glory due to His name; **worship the LORD in the beauty of Holiness.**"

So, there's going to be a very powerful, absolutely wonderful worship of God that we will have called "**...the beauty of Holiness.**" We're going to be spirit beings and beautified and glorified. We are going to see Jesus Christ face-to-face. We're going to see God the Father face-to-face. And worship Them in "**...the beauty of Holiness.**" A kind of worship that is almost incredible for us to try and describe, even though it's written here, because it's going to be so fantastic, and we will be spirit beings!

Verse 3: "The voice of the LORD is upon the waters; the God of glory thunders; the LORD is above many waters. The voice of the LORD is powerful, the voice of the LORD is full of majesty. The voice of the LORD breaks the cedars; yea, the LORD breaks the cedars of Lebanon" (vs 3-5

This is showing how He is going to establish the government on earth. It's going to be mighty, mighty convincing to the people. *Yes!* And we're going to have part of it. He's going to give us a command and say, 'Do this, do that, do the other thing.'

Verse 7: "The voice of the LORD hews out flames of fire. The voice of the LORD shakes the wilderness; the LORD shakes the wilderness of Kadesh. The voice of the LORD causes the does to give birth and strips the forests bare; and in His temple everyone says 'Glory!'" (vs 7-9)—*to God!*

This is how He's going to establish the Kingdom of God! Pretty mighty and powerful!

Psa, 45—we're going to see the qualifications—the qualification for Jesus Christ Himself; and also the qualification for us.

Psalm 45:1: "My heart is overflowing with a goodly matter... [just bursting out with joy and love and truth and all of the good things] ...I speak of my works to the King; my tongue is the pen of a ready writer.... [you're going to know what to say] ...You are more excellent than the children of men... [referring to Christ] ...grace is poured upon Your lips; therefore God has blessed You forever" (vs 1-2). *This will also apply to us!*

Verse 3: "Gird Your sword upon Your thigh, O Mighty One, with Your glory and Your majesty. And ride victoriously in Your majesty in behalf of truth and meekness and righteousness; and let Your right hand teach You awesome things" (vs 3-4).

This is **how we're going to administer the Kingdom of God**:

- in truth
- in meekness
- and righteousness

Teach this to the people!

Verse 6. "Your Throne, O God, is forever and ever... [this is said of Christ (Heb. 1)] ...a scepter of justice is the scepter of Your Kingdom."

That's what's going to make the government *perfect* during the Millennium. But you have to translate this further into the Kingdom of God and New Jerusalem forever and ever, which will be ***even more perfect***, because all who are there will be spirit beings. It's going to be absolutely nothing like we comprehend things today. The way we're going to understand that is: let's make it into the Kingdom of God and become spirit beings and we can understand what's going on.

Verse 7: "You love righteousness and hate wickedness... [or iniquity—that's the right kind of hate.] ...therefore God, Your God... [it's talking about two Gods here in the Old Testament] ...has anointed You with the oil of gladness above Your fellows."

Heb. 1 applies that personally to Jesus Christ. This is telling us that there's God the Father and Jesus Christ. *Hello, all of you trinity believers*: Where is God the Spirit? *The Bible doesn't teach that at all!*

Verse 8: "All Your garments smell of myrrh, and aloes and cassia, out of the ivory palaces, stringed instruments have made You glad. Kings' daughters are among Your honorable women; on Your right hand stands the queen in gold from Ophir" (vs 8-9).

I wonder who that is going to be? Do you suppose that might be Mary, the one who gave birth to Jesus in the flesh? *Don't know!* We'll just leave it at that.

Psalm 46:4—*notice how this ties in with the other Scriptures that we've already covered.* "There is a river whose streams shall make the City of God rejoice… [New Jerusalem] …the Holy dwelling place of the Most High."

What comes out of the Throne of God, underneath it? (Rev. 22). *Pure water, clear as crystal!* Signifying the power of God's Holy Spirit, constantly moving; constantly accomplishing what He desires. It goes down in a river, and on each side of the river are the Trees of Life, which bring their fruit in their season. *Amazing!*

Verse 5: "God is in the midst of her; she shall not be moved; God shall help her at the approach of the morning…. [here's what happens with the evil ones]: …The nations raged, the kingdoms were shaken; He uttered His voice, the earth melted…. [the return of Christ] …The LORD of hosts is with us; the God of Jacob is our refuge. Selah. Come, behold the works of the LORD who makes desolations upon the earth, Who makes wars to cease to the ends of the earth…" (vs 5-9).

Remember that *only Christ can bring war in righteousness and judgment!* (Rev. 19). Only He can stop all wars and fightings. If we remember our history correctly:

- Wasn't WWI the war 'to end all wars'?
- How did we get WWII
- How did we get the Korean War
- How did we get the Vietnam War, etc., etc.?

Because no man can end wars!

It's in the evil nature of man to continuously plot and scheme wars and destruction and devastation, because Satan is still the 'god of this world.' Until the fulfillment of the Day of Atonement, that's going to happen until Christ returns, and He alone is going to end wars.

"…He breaks the bow and cuts the spear in two; He burns the chariots in the fire. 'Be still, and know that I am God! I will be exalted among the nations, I will be exalted in the earth.' The LORD of hosts is with us; the God of Jacob is our refuge. Selah" (vs 9-11).

Quite a Psalm! Notice how that fits right in to the meaning of the Feast of Tabernacles and the Kingdom of God. Return of Christ, setting up of the Kingdom.

Psa. 48—again, another view of the temple and Christ dwelling on earth. We can project this forward to the 'new heavens and earth' and the 'New Jerusalem.' There are many different things that we can add to give us understanding of these Scriptures.

Psalm 48:1: "Great is the LORD, and highly to be praised in the city of our God, in His Holy mountain."

Where we are *going to worship Him in the 'beauty of Holiness.'* A fantastic worship that we will not experience until we're a spirit[transcriber's correction] being.

Verse 2: "Beautiful in its loftiness, the joy of all the earth is Mount Zion on the sides of the north, the city of the great King."

As we can piece this together, coming to Jerusalem during the Millennium and all the sons of God will come there; human beings will be on the outskirts of it. They will only come so far up to Jerusalem, and only come to the base of Mt. Sion, just like it was when God came down to Mt. Sinai and gave the Ten Commandments to the children of Israel. They couldn't go up on the mountain except the one that God chose: Moses, and then later He let the 70 elders of Israel, Nadab, Abihu and Joshua come up to a certain point. But they couldn't come up to see God, only Moses could.

Likewise here, it's going to be the same thing. Only the spirit beings are going to be there and go up directly to see God. Everybody else is going to be down here and will see us who will represent God to them.

"…the joy of all the earth is Mount Zion on the sides of the north, the city of the great King. God in her palace has shown Himself to be a fortress, for lo, the kings assembled themselves; they advanced together" (vs 2-4).

Who are going to be the kings and priests? *We are!* We're going to be assembled. I imagine we're going to have regular meetings there at Jerusalem. Now think about that!

Verse 8: "As we have heard, so we have seen in the city of the LORD of hosts, in the city of our God. **God will establish it forever**. Selah." *How is He going to do this?*

- with His love
- with His Truth
- with His righteousness
- with His meekness

Verse 9: "We have thought of Your loving kindness, O God, in the midst of Your Temple."

Just think what it's going to be like when we come into the Temple of God and worship God in *Spirit and in Truth* and in the *beauty of Holiness*; and contemplate His loving kindness, His greatness, and His goodness. That's going to be something. I don't know about you, but I'm looking forward to that.

Verse 10: "As is Your name, O God, so is Your praise to the ends of the earth. Your right hand is full of righteousness." *There we have a Millennial setting!*

Psa. 49[transcriber's correction]—let's take the first couple of verses and we're going to see what's going to be happening during the Millennium.

Psalm 49:1: "Hear this, all you people; give ear… [*pay attention*] …all inhabitants of the world: both low and high, rich and poor together. My mouth shall speak of wisdom, and the thoughts of my heart shall be of understanding" (vs 1-3).

This is what we're going to do for the whole world. *We're going to bring them the knowledge of salvation!* That's why the Feast of Tabernacles portrays the great harvest at the end of the year, of everything, all kinds of fruits, all kinds of grains, all kinds of everything that comes out of the ground. All of that pictures the harvest of what God is going to do and how we're going to take care of and teach it.

Psalm 50:1: "The mighty God, God, the LORD, has spoken and called the earth from the rising of the sun to its going down…. [that's how it's going to happen] …Out of Zion, the perfection of beauty… [again, the Temple of God.] …God has shined forth. Our God shall come, and He shall not keep silent; a fire shall devour before Him, and it shall be very tempestuous all around Him" (vs 1-3).

Again, it's talking about the return of Christ in order to establish what we read in vs 1 & 2

Verse 4: "He shall call to the heavens from above, and to the earth, so that He may judge His people."

Now the resurrection! The Kingdom of God cannot happen until the first resurrection takes place!

Verse 5: "'Gather My saints unto Me, those who have made a covenant with Me by sacrifice.'…. [which is our baptismal covenant death] …And the heavens shall declare His righteousness, for God Himself is judge. Selah" (vs 5-6).

That's tremendous! That shows how there's going to be rulership, through Christ, God and us on the earth.

Psalm 65:1: "Praise waits for You, O God, in Zion…" **How?** *Worshipping Him in the 'beauty of Holiness!'*

"…and to You shall the vow be performed. O You Who hears prayer, unto You shall all flesh come" (vs 1-2).

Now, think about this from the perspective of all people on earth during the Millennium. All their prayers will be heard and answered. They will pray to God and we'll be the ones who will answer. We'll be the ones who will teach them. We will be the ones to show them in the way that they should walk, according to Isa. 30.

Verse 4 talks about the blessings that we are going to receive because of this relationship to God: "Blessed is the one whom You choose and cause to come near You, that he may dwell in Your courts; we shall be satisfied with the goodness of Your house, even Your Holy Temple."

This is going to be a time of absolute incredible things to happen almost on a daily basis.

Verse 5: "By awesome works in righteousness You will answer us, O God of our salvation; You are the hope of all the ends of the earth and of those of the distant sea. The mountains are established by Your strength; You are clothed with power" (vs 5-6).

This is quite a great and tremendous thing, showing the power of God continuously all during the Millennium. When we come to the last day of the Feast, the seventh day of the Feast, then we will see how human nature reacts to this. And because these things happen on a daily basis, they become commonplace.

Psalm 66:1: "Make a joyful noise to God, all the earth."

Think about this: What's going to happen every Sabbath Day? Where the day begins there are going to be assemblies. I don't know if we're going to have what would be called Friday night services and then services on the day portion of the Sabbath. *But the whole day is going to be devoted to God!*

I think every Friday night it's going to be devoted to the family. That's going to be a time of family worship and a family meal. Then the people are going to get up Sabbath morning and go to wherever they're going to meet. I think there will be literally churches on almost every other corner, because everyone is going to come together to worship God. Everyone is going to come together to be taught of God. So, don't worry about will there be enough room for me, or will I have a job. You're going to have plenty, *plenty,* **plenty** to do. We are going to help in the worship of God. So here it is:

Psalm 66:1: **"Make a joyful noise to God, all the earth."**

So, just think what it's going to be like. In every one of these churches, every Sabbath Day, they are going to be singing hymns to God.

Now put yourself kind of in a space capsule and think of it this way: You're looking down on the earth, and as the earth turns, these things begin. And then you go around the whole earth for the beginning of the Sabbath, and then you come around again and the whole day to complete the Sabbath day. All people everywhere in the world—from east to west, north to south—are going to be worshipping God.

Verse 2: "Sing forth the honor of His name; make His praise glorious. Say to God, 'How awesome are Your works! Through the greatness of Your power **Your enemies submit themselves in obedience to You**" (vs 2-3).

We're always going to look back. We're always going to understand what it was before the Kingdom of God was set up. We are going to know the true evil that dwells in the hearts of men. As we will also see, before the Millennium begins or as it is beginning, God is going to change the nature of man from a hostile carnality to a heart of flesh. Not take away all carnality, but have it modified so it's not going to be as hard to qualify for salvation. Because after all, they're going to have an advantage that no one else has ever had. That is to live a life without any influence from Satan the devil or just grossly over-evil people.

Every human being on earth, because God has put in the heart of man eternity, to think of things beyond themselves. To have a yearning for what is right, even though they do evil. Everyone wants to have a perfect life, a perfect home, a perfect husband, a perfect wife, perfect children, perfect government, perfect world. *They will have it! They will also have the Spirit of God!*

Verse 4: "All the earth shall worship You and shall sing praises to You; they shall sing praises to Your name.' Selah."

What is going to be the greatest work that's going to be done? *The character building in everyone to qualify for salvation!* That is going to be something! It is going to be a time when a person lives under the Kingdom of God:

- has been righteous
- has worshipped God
- has served Him
- has kept His commandments

And comes to the point in their lives of being 100-years-old and then are we going to have on that Sabbath:

- Are we going to have a transformation service?
- Where the individuals who have qualified are changed from flesh to spirit?

- Wouldn't that be exciting?
- Isn't that going to give everyone inspiration and hope and understanding as to why they are here?
- What God is doing? *Absolutely!*

You think about that! Think about this in relationship to what we're reading here.

Verse 5: "Come and see the works of God; He is awesome in His deeds toward the sons of men."

Verse 7: "He rules by His power forever; His eyes keep watch upon the nations; let not the rebellious exalt themselves. Selah…. [the rebellious won't be around during that time] …O bless our God, O peoples, and make the sound of His praise to be heard, *He* Who keeps us in life and does not allow our feet to slide, for You have tested us, O God…. [there are going to be times of proving] …You have refined us as silver is refined. You have brought us into the net…" (vs 7-11).

Not every one of the verses blend right in together in a complete story flow, because the Old Testament is *'precept upon precept, line upon line, here a little and there a little.'* That's how we understand it.

So, we'll pick this up tomorrow and we will finish the book of Psalms and how it portrays the Kingdom of God, our part in it, God's part in it, and the way the people of the world will be living.

Scriptural References:

1) Daniel 2:40-45
2) Daniel 7:23-27
3) Psalm 1:1-6
4) Psalm 2:1-3, 5-12
5) Psalm 118:1-29
6) Psalm 9:5-8, 15-16
7) Psalm 15:1-5
8) Psalm 23:1-6
9) Psalm 24:1-3
10) Isaiah 4:2-6
11) Psalm 24:3-10
12) Psalm 29:1-9
13) Psalm 45:1-4, 6-9
14) Psalm 46:4-11
15) Psalm 48:1-4, 8-10
16) Psalm 49:1-3
17) Psalm 50:1-6
18) Psalm 65:1-2, 4-6
19) Psalm 66:1-5, 7-11

Scriptures referenced, not quoted:

- Revelation 13; 20; 17
- 2 Thessalonians 2

- Isaiah 2
- Revelation 1; 21
- Matthew 13; 6
- Revelation 16
- Deuteronomy 28
- Revelation 8; 9; 10
- Psalm 21
- Matthew 24
- Ezekiel 34
- Revelation 22; 19
- Hebrews 1
- Isaiah 30

Also referenced:

- Commentary: *The Unity of Scripture* (*The Holy Bible in Its Original Order, A Faithful Version*)
- Messages: *The Millennial Temple #s1&2* **truthofGod.org**

FRC:bo
Transcribed: 8-3-08
Reformatted: 1/2021

CHAPTER SIXTY-FOUR

Millennial Scriptures in the Psalms II
Fred R. Coulter

We're examining in the book of Psalms, and see the Kingdom of God and the Millennium in the Psalms. We've seen it has a lot to do:

- with our job
- with our purpose
- how we get there
- the whole world worshipping God
- the whole world serving God
- the way that God blesses the whole world

We saw a tremendous thing of how we are going to worship God *in the beauty of Holiness* as spirit beings. A complete and profound and absolute perfect worship of God that we cannot experience until we're resurrected from the dead and are spirit beings and come to the presence of God Himself to worship Him. *Now that is going to be awesome, indeed! That is going to be something!*

These are the things that God wants us to keep our mind on. One of the things that is always important for us to do is this: *Always keep our mind on the goal; and always keep our mind on the Kingdom of God!* Anything that comes along, put it into perspective; put it into God's hands to work out for you. Always remember that *'all things work together for good to those who love God and are called according to His purpose.'* That's why, even in times of trouble and distress, don't get worried, don't get fixated on the trouble and distress.

- keep focused on the goal
- what we're going to do
- where we are going
- how we are going to do it
- Who God is
- Who Christ is
- what His plan and purpose is
- that we are an integral part of it

He has personally chosen us to reveal these things to us, to give us knowledge and understanding, and to create in us His very character to prepare us for these times of living in the Millennium and on into all eternity. God has greater things for us. God has fantastic things for us to do. We need to keep our mind on that, and that is one of the reasons we have the Feast of Tabernacles every year. So we can get refocused on what God is doing.

Let's understand that because of this, it's not like it was in the past, the Feast of Tabernacles is to be an enjoyable spiritual time in fellowshipping with the brethren and not converted into a carnal vacation of games and drinking and things that has happened in the past.

Psa. 72 is quite a Psalm. We are going to see how it emphasizes God's judgment—He's going to judge the whole world continuously—and how His righteousness is always going to be upheld and used

- to help
- to teach
- to inspire
- to uplift

Psalm 72:1: "Give the king Your judgments…"

How do you think we're going to operate and judge during the Millennium?

- by God's judgments
- by His laws
- by His commandments
- by His Spirit
- by His purpose

"…O God, and Your righteousness to the king's son; that he may judge Your people in righteousness and Your poor with justice. The mountains shall bring peace to the people, and the little hills, by righteousness" (vs 1-3). *Righteousness is going to flow down!*

Can you imagine what the world is going to be like when there is no crime, there are no criminals, there is no one devoted to evil. That God is leading, guiding and doing His greatest work of creation with the human race, all during the Millennium. Bringing into the Kingdom of God *billions* of sons and daughters! He's doing that because when New Jerusalem comes down to the earth, then there's the vastness of the universe, which even men are beginning to understand *is still being created*. We're going to figure in that one way or another. So, always keep your mind on that.

Verse 4: "He shall judge the poor of the people; He shall save the children of the needy and shall crush in pieces the oppressor…. [won't be around any longer] …They shall fear You as long as the sun and moon endure throughout all generations" (vs 4-5). *All through the Millennium!*

It says in Rev. 21 that the 'New Jerusalem has no need of the sun or moon to shine in it,' *because the glory of God lightens it!* But that doesn't mean that there is going to be no sun or no moon. It just doesn't need it. Here is the 'moon unto all generations.'

Verse 6: "He shall come down like rain upon the mown grass… [this is God's Spirit leading] …like showers that water the earth…. [water, righteousness, serving] …In His days the righteous shall flourish and abundance of peace until the moon be no more" (vs 6-7).

I don't know if the moon's going to be gone forever or whatever, but if it is I tell you how we're going to find out: *you be there so you'll know!*

Verse 8: "He shall also have the rule from sea to sea, and from the river unto the ends of the earth." *Never has been a time like that!*

This has never been fulfilled. When is it that they have worshipped God; He has the 'rule from sea-to-sea and from the river unto the ends of the earth'? *Never has been!*

Verse 11: "Yea, all kings shall prostrate themselves before Him…" *That's part of our worship, too!*

Imagine what it's going to be like when we worship God in the 'beauty of Holiness' and prostrate ourselves down before God.

Verse 12: "For He shall deliver the needy when he cries, and the poor with the one who has no helper. He shall have compassion upon the weak and needy, and shall save the lives of the needy. He shall redeem their life from oppression and violence; and their blood shall be precious in His sight" (vs 12-14).

That's going to be a tremendous thing that's going to happen; the Millennium and all eternity is set before us!

Verse 16: "May there be an abundance of grain in the earth upon the top of the mountains; may its fruit wave like Lebanon, and they of the city shall flourish like grass of the earth."

All extolling God! This is talking about peace, prosperity, love, righteousness, goodness, the right God, the right judgment, everything to uplift the mind, the heart, the soul, the being of everyone.

Verse 17: "His name shall endure forever; His name shall be continued as long as the sun; and men shall be blessed in Him; all nations shall call Him blessed…. [hasn't happened, yet] …Blessed is

the LORD God, the God of Israel, Who alone does wondrous things. And blessed be His glorious name forever; and all the earth is filled with His glory! Amen and Amen. The prayers of David the son of Jesse are ended" (vs 17-20).

Isn't it interesting how many of these Psalms relating to the Kingdom that God gave to David, a man after His own heart, and the first king to really be a righteous king. Saul flunked out because of vanity. Unfortunately, Solomon got corrupted!

Let's see some more of the motivation of coming into the presence of God and what we need to do, and how we need to look at being able to be in the Millennium to live with God, to dwell with God; that's going to be fantastic!

Psalm 84:1: **"How lovely are Your tabernacles, O LORD of hosts!"**

- city of Jerusalem
- city of the King
- the new temple that He's going to build there

with the pillar of cloud by day and the fire by night! The only ones to go into Jerusalem will be those who are spirit beings.

"How lovely are Your tabernacles, O LORD of hosts!" We can't imagine how beautiful it's going to be. We're going to see part of it when we come to the Last Great Day and we do our step into eternity (Rev. 21 & 22). From there on, we don't know what it's going to be, but it's going to be something!

Here's how our desire needs to be toward God; v 2: "My soul longs, yea, even faints for the courts of the LORD; my heart and **my flesh cry out for the living God**."

This is what it means to love God with all your heart, with all your mind, with all your soul and with all your strength.

Verse 3: "Yea, even the sparrow has found a house, and the swallow a nest for herself where she may lay her young, even Your altars, O LORD of hosts, my King and my God. Blessed are those who dwell in Your house… [we're going to dwell there, talking about New Jerusalem] …they will still be praising You. Selah. Blessed is the man whose strength is in You…" (vs 3-5). *Not himself, not his vanity, **but in God!***

- for His righteousness
- for His Truth
- for His Spirit
- for His love

"…Your ways are in their hearts… [the spiritual creation of God within us] …Who passing through the valley of weeping make it a place of springs… [completely change it] …yea, the early rain also clothes it with blessings. They go from strength to strength, every one of them appearing in Zion before God" (vs 5-7).

Can you imagine? *There's going to come a set time when we're going to come before God the Father and Jesus Christ personally!* Can you imagine what that's going to be like? *But it's going to happen!* I can't imagine it, but I tell you what, in going through the Psalms here, I have a little greater inkling of what it's like to 'look through a glass darkly' and to see some of the images of these things start to become a little clearer in my mind.

Verse 8: "O LORD God of hosts, hear my prayer; give ear, O God of Jacob. Selah. Behold, O God, our shield, and look upon the face of Your anointed, for a day in Your courts is better than a thousand *elsewhere*. I would rather stand at the threshold of the house of my God than dwell in the tents of wickedness, for the LORD God is a sun and shield; the LORD will give grace and glory; no good thing will He withhold from those who walk uprightly. O LORD of hosts, **blessed is the man who trusts in You**" (vs 8-12).

That's what it needs to be with us. This is a tremendous Psalm of our desire depicting the earnestness and the longing and the really fainting, as it were. It leaves us weak and breathless to contemplate the greatness of God and to be in His company.

Psalm 86:8: "Among the gods there is none like You, O LORD…" *He's talking the gods of the nations on the earth at this particular time*

"…neither are there any works like Your works. All nations whom You have made shall come and worship before You, O LORD, and shall glorify Your name" (vs 8-9).

They're going to do this *every Sabbath and every Holy Day!* That is going to be an amazing thing. We're going to be a part of directing that and supervising that and making sure that it happens and all of this to the glory of God. What happens when that happens? *God is pleased and His blessings flow and His Spirit comes and His love is poured out!* The intents and purposes of God are disclosed to everyone. God is pleased. These are things that please God!

Verse 10[transcriber's correction]: "For You are great and do wonderful things; **You alone are God**."

Verse 11 shows what it's going to be; this is why we're going to be teachers: "Teach me Your way, O LORD…" *We need to have that right now in our lives every day!*

- God, teach me!
- God, help me!

One of the things that's so important for us to realize is that we are totally dependent upon God for everything:

- everything physical
- everything spiritual
- every breath we draw
- every bite of food we eat
- everything that we see
- the houses that we live in
- everything comes from God

On top of that, He has blessed us so tremendously *with His Spirit* and *with His love* and *the knowledge of His Word!* That becomes the greatest and most important thing.

Verse 11: "Teach me Your way, O LORD, I will walk in Your Truth…"—*as a way of life!*

We have to come to the point that our yes is *yes* and our no is *no*. In particularly, not just to what you verbalize to other people, *but in your heart toward God*; and in your heart in dealing with other people as well:

- that what you say is the truth, *and you will stand behind it*
- that what you will tell someone you will do, *you will do*
- that what you tell God you will do, *you will do*

There are certain things that we have to come to in our lives and just cease from doing it. We have to say, 'Yes, God, this is what I am going to do,' and continue to do it. That your word is truth, and that it will be done. Not going out, as it says there in one of the Proverbs, when you vow a vow and then you look at it and think, 'Well, now I better change my mind.' That your yes is not *yes*, and your no is not *no*.

"…I will walk in Your Truth; unite my heart to fear Your name. I will praise You, O LORD my God, with all my heart, and I will glorify Your name forevermore… [this tells us how to do it] …for great is Your mercy toward me…" (vs 11-13).

Think of the great mercy that is given to us, that is going to happen when we are resurrected; when we are changed from flesh to spirit. God is going to reach down and He is going to call us out of the grave. Think of all the saints that are in the grave right now, in their place of safety, waiting for the return of Christ and the resurrection; it's going to be something!

"...and You have delivered my soul from the depths of the grave.... [that has got to be the resurrection] ...O God, the proud have risen against me... [v 15]: But You, O LORD, are a God full of compassion, and gracious, slow to anger, and abounding in steadfast love and Truth" (vs 13-15).

That could also be *mercy* and Truth. These are the characteristics of God, that He wants us to learn; that He wants us to develop as He molds and shapes our spiritual character.

There are several Psalms in a row that have to do with the reign of God on earth. Again, for all of those who think all prophecy has been fulfilled, what do you do with this:

Psalm 93:1: "**The LORD reigns**..."

If He's here on earth and reigning, where is He? Well, Jesus said, 'If they say He's in the wilderness, don't go forth. If they say He's in a secret chamber, don't believe it.' He's going to return in a spectacular and fantastic way that we've already covered in the events leading up to Pentecost.

"...**He is clothed with majesty**..."—*because He's a spirit being and His countenance shines as the sun!*

His visage is the full strength of the sun and even His feet as if they burn as brass burning in the fire; and His eyes are a flame of fire.

"...**the LORD is clothed with strength.** He clothed Himself and the world also is established; it shall not be moved" (v 1).

That's how He's going to solidify everything during the Millennium! No one's going to go against Him. Now at the end of the Millennium there will be those who will want to.

Verse 2: "Your Throne is established of old; You are from everlasting.... [think of that] ...The floods have lifted up, O LORD, the floods have lifted up their voices; the floods lift up their waves. The LORD on high is mightier than the thunders of many waters, yea, mightier than the mighty waves of the sea" (vs 2-4).

We're going to have love and honor and respect, and we'll see the great power of God in everything that we see. That's going to be something for all people.

What I want you to do the next time you watch the news with all of the crime and all of the stupidity on it, think about the comparison and the contrast to what we are covering here during the Feast of Tabernacles. Think about that! Think what the difference is going to be! Then maybe you will

understand 1-John 5:21 where He says, *'The whole world lies in wickedness.'*

We're reaching the days like it was in the days of Noah. That the thought of every man was only 'evil continually'!

Psalm 96:1: "O sing to the LORD a new song..."

Compare that with the music of the world is today, which is evil, especially to drive in the hearts and minds of young people and get them thinking on evil, wretchedness, death, doom and gloom, witchcraft, the occult and all of those things. *Now think of the world totally changed*:

"...**sing to the LORD, all the earth**" (v 1). Again, put yourself in that place just above the earth and as the earth turns, what's it going to be like to hear all these praises coming up from people every day and every Sabbath and every Holy Day? *It's going to be magnificent!* They're all going to be able to sing, I think, at that time there won't be too many making a joyful noise because God is going heal all of the people who have trouble singing so they can sing praise to God. Now, that's my own personal opinion.

Verse 2: "Sing to the LORD, bless His name; show forth His salvation from day to day. Declare His glory among the nations, His wonders among all people" (vs 2-3).

That's going to happen every single day. That's why it says in Isa. 10, that the earth is going to be 'full of the knowledge of the Lord as the oceans cover the earth.' Here's part of it how it's done:

Verse 4: "For the LORD is great, and greatly to be praised; He is to be feared above all gods... [it'll be all outmoded at that time] ...for all the gods of the nations are idols... [there won't be any around during the Millennium] ...but the LORD made the heavens. Honor and majesty are before Him; strength and beauty are in His sanctuary. Ascribe to the LORD, O you kindreds of the people; give to the LORD glory and strength. Ascribe to the LORD the glory due to His name; bring an offering and come into His courts. O worship the LORD in the **beauty of Holiness**; tremble before Him, all the earth" (vs 4-9).

There's going to be a "...beauty of Holiness..." that people will worship Him in, and there will be a "beauty of holiness" which we, as the sons and daughters of God, will worship God with. It's going to be magnificent all the way around.

Verse 10: "Say among the nations, '**The**

LORD reigns, and the world shall be established; it shall not be moved; He shall judge the people with righteousness.'"

No evil, no underhandedness, none of the sins that people have today which they just take for granted as normal. *None of that!*

Verse 11: "Let the heavens rejoice, and let the earth be glad; let the sea roar, and the fullness of it. Let the field be joyful, and all that is in it; then shall all the trees of the forest sing for joy" (vs 11-12).

We don't know exactly how that's going to be, but I can tell you this: when plants are taken care of in a right way, they respond, and they produce. I don't know how a plant is going to rejoice, but I tell you what, I want to stick around and see how that's going to be. I know they're not going to talk and answer back. It's not going to be like that stupid movie *Talk to the Animals*. You're not going to talk to the plants. 'Oh, tree tree, how are you?' *I'm fine, thank you, give me a little more water.* I don't think it'll be anything like that. But it's going to be so fantastic that that will happen.

Verse 13: "Before the LORD; for He comes, for He comes to judge the earth; He shall judge the world with righteousness and the people with His Truth." *Amazing!*

These are called *the Lord reigns Psalms*. Every one of these have to do about the reigning of God. That has to be during the Millennium. Look at all these Psalms that tell us what is going to happen. This is why *carnal 'Christianity' today*—and that's really the right name to call it, because the 'carnal mind is not subject to the Law of God, neither indeed can be'—is 'enmity against God'!

If you have a Christianity that says there are no laws, no commandments, that all these things have been fulfilled, no wonder they have to throw in this stupid doctrine of going to heaven, you're an immortal soul. They don't ever read these Psalms and have any understanding as to what they mean. But we who keep the Sabbath and the Holy Days and Feast of Tabernacles, we can learn if we get in and study and put it all together.

Psalm 97:1: "**The LORD reigns**; let the earth rejoice; let the multitude of islands be glad. Clouds and darkness are all around Him; righteousness and justice are the foundation of His throne. A fire goes before Him and burns up His enemies round about" (vs 1-3).

There won't be any enemies to burn up. Well, if someone commits the unpardonable sin, yeah, they're going to be devoured. But I wonder what it's like when God says, 'Ok, I'm going to

leave Jerusalem and I'm going to come and visit this part of the earth.' Will He come in this manner? What's it going to be like to see God coming from Jerusalem, and His cherubim and it lands down wherever they're going to land. That's going to be something!

Verse 6: "The heavens declare His righteousness… [Psa. 19 says 'His glory'; shows the glory of God] …**and all the people see His glory**." *That's going to be something; absolutely magnificent!* Then they have the inset verse here:

Verse 7: "All those who serve graven images are ashamed who boast themselves in idols…"

We're going to know the absolute foolishness of idols! You can read there in Isa. 41, 42, 43 & 44 about the stupidity of people who make idols.

Verse 8: "Zion heard and was glad; and the daughters of Judah rejoiced because of Your judgments, O LORD, for You, LORD, are most high above all the earth; You are exalted high above all gods" (vs 8-9).

So what it is now, Christ comes to the earth, He's going to be on the earth.

Verse 10: "You who love the LORD, hate evil! He preserves the souls of His saints; He delivers them out of the hand of the wicked. Light is sown for the righteous and gladness for the upright in heart. Rejoice in the LORD, you righteous ones, and praise His Holy name" (vs 10-12).

So there again, quite a wonderful, wonderful Psalm *depicting the Millennium and the reign of God on earth* with the kings and priests under Christ to bring it about.

I just want you to stop and think about all that we've covered and I want you to think about the foolishness of the leaders of this world. And the foolishness of people who think that man—I don't care who he is, where he is, what country he is in, I don't care what his race is, how tall he is, how short he is or whatever—*no one can, by political means, solve spiritual problems!* We need to keep that in mind.

These are Psalms of degrees and each one sort of adds to the other and puts together a complete picture.

Psalm 98:1: "O sing to the LORD a new song, for He has done marvelous things; His right hand… [we have a song in the hymnal of this] …and His Holy arm have worked salvation for Him. The LORD has made known His salvation; He has revealed His righteousness in the sight of the nations" (vs 1-2). *Not today!*

Satan the devil is deceiving them. They are blinded. They can't understand. God said that He has blinded them and ultimately, as we know, for the fulfillment of the Last Great Day, that He can save them. That's a wonderful thing to understand.

Verse 3: "He has remembered His steadfast love and His faithfulness toward the house of Israel… [spiritual and physical] …all the ends of the earth have seen the salvation of our God…. [that has never happened] …Make a joyful noise to the LORD, all the earth; break forth, and rejoice, and sing praise. Sing to the LORD with the lyre, with the lyre, and the voice of a psalm. With silver trumpets and sound of a ram's horn make a joyful noise before the King, the LORD" (vs 3-6).

There still will be joyful noise. I can see where the rams horn makes a joyful noise, because it sounds so awful. If you've never heard a ram's horn, that's nothing like a silver trumpet. This is just a blast, and it's kind of like a big blast going out, so that's the only joyful noise you can make before the Lord your God.

Verse 7: "Let the sea roar, and the fullness of it, the world, and those who dwell in it. Let the floods clap their hands; let the mountains sing for joy together before the LORD, for He comes to judge the earth; with righteousness He shall judge the world and the people with equity" (vs 7-9).

I tell you, by time you get done with this, you're going to see… We could do this in all parts of the Bible; we could get some things out of Genesis, Exodus, Leviticus and Numbers—every book—there is something to do with the Kingdom of God, even in the histories of the tribes of Israel and Judah, because they were the *physical* Kingdom of God on earth. So, there are things we can get out of that.

Then we have all of the Prophets and the Psalms. Then we have the New Testament; in that we have the Gospels and Acts, the General Epistles, the Epistles of Paul and the book of Revelation. *The Bible is literally saturated with the understanding and knowledge of God, that God is going to reign and the Kingdom of God is going to prevail above everything!* That is really quite something for us to know and to understand.

Notice it carries right on, Psalm 99. So we have all of these Psa: 93, 96, 97, 98, 99 and even on into Psalm 100. *All having to do with the Lord reigning on the earth!*

Psalm 99:1: "**The LORD reigns**; let the people tremble. He sits between the cherubim; let the earth quake. The LORD is great in Zion, and He

is high above all the people. Let them praise Your name as great and awesome; Holy is He. The strength of the King also loves justice; You established uprightness; You have executed justice and righteousness in Jacob" (vs 1-4).

Yes, all the world, as we have seen through all of these Psalms!

Verse 5: "Exalt the LORD our God and worship at His footstool, for He is Holy. **Moses and Aaron were among His priests…** [now resurrected] …and Samuel among those who called upon His name… [this tells us they're going to be in the Kingdom of God] …they called upon the LORD, and He answered them. He spoke to them in the pillar of cloud; they kept His testimonies and the statute that He gave them. You answered them, O LORD our God; You are a forgiving God to them, though You took vengeance for their deeds…. [it shows the restoration of Israel during the Millennium] …Praise the LORD our God and **worship at His Holy mountain, for the LORD our God is Holy**" (vs 5-9). *Tremendous, brethren!*

I don't know about you, but in just going through and preaching this, I'm very inspired about what God is going to do and our part in it, and how fantastic *it's through all the Psalms!*

Let's continue on in this marvelous study about *the Kingdom of God in the Psalms* covering the Millennium, the Kingdom of God, some of the time leading up to the establishing of the Kingdom and on out into all eternity.

The Word of God is absolutely tremendous and we learn things from the Word of God because of the Spirit of God that He's given to us. We have more understanding every time we read it because *these words,* as Jesus said, 'are spirit and they are life.' Though we read the words and it's printed on physical paper with physical ink. The meaning of it, combined with God's Spirit and to give us understanding, is something that is spiritually discerned. That is a great blessing that God has given us to understand His Word and we need to really rejoice in it and always remember that.

Psa. 100—a very short Psalm, but it has to do with eternal life and the Millennium and on beyond that.

Psalm 100:1: "Shout for joy to the LORD, all the earth." *Notice how many times we have read*:

- all the earth
- the whole world
- all peoples
- all nations

Verse 2: "Serve the LORD with gladness; come before His presence with singing. Know that the LORD, **He is God. He has made us,** and we are His…" (vs 2-3). *That's in both ways: in the flesh, first; and in the resurrection, in the spirit!*

"…we are His people and the sheep of His pasture. Enter into His gates with thanksgiving and into His courts with praise; give thanks unto Him and bless His name" (vs 3-4)—**in the spirit of Holiness** as a spirit being, in the presence of God, prostrating down before Him!

Verse 5: "For the LORD is good; His steadfast love is everlasting; and His faithfulness endures to all generations."

When Christ returns we're not going to change the Truth. He's not going do away with anything. *He's going to expand it!* He's going to give us greater and greater understanding; even to the people, during the Millennium, to make what we know today really look like kindergarten and sandbox when we come to understand it.

But at the same time, after we're resurrected and are spirit beings, we're going to continue to be taught by God. We are going to grow in grace and knowledge and expand through all eternity in our knowledge and understanding and worship of God and the things that He wants us to do. Isn't that something?

So, if you are suffering from physical things right now; if you are weak because of old age; if you have a problem and difficulty because of an accident; if you've had troubles and difficulties in your life; look to what God is going to give you *beyond!* This is what He's talking about here.

Psalm 102:12: "But **You, O LORD, sit enthroned forever**…"

Doesn't mean He sits on His Throne forever, because there are times when He gets up from His Throne and gets in His cherubim and does other things, that's true. You need to understand that. But that means *no one is going to overthrow God!—forever!* You see, when Satan rebelled, he thought: 'Well, I can get rid of God. I'm as good as God. I want to be like the Most High.' Well, it didn't happen, did it? *No, he was cast down to earth!*

"…and Your name is unto all generations. You shall arise and have mercy upon Zion…" (vs 12-13). *That applies to the children of Israel and the Jews!* But we read in Heb. 11 about Mt. Sion in heaven above. So, this also applies to *us!*

"…for it is time to be gracious to her; yea, **the appointed time has come**" (v 13). What is an appointed time? *The Sabbath and every one of the*

Holy Days are **appointed times** that God has set for us to come and

- meet Him
- fellowship with Him
- learn of Him.

Here's an appointed time *for Israel in the flesh and Israel in the spirit!*

Verse 14: "For Your servants take pleasure in her stones…"—*that are there in the foundation of New Jerusalem and you can expand it out from there!*

"…and favor her dust. So the nations shall fear the name of the LORD, and all the kings of the earth Your glory…. [and *we* will be the kings of the earth] …When the LORD shall build up Zion, He shall appear in His glory" (vs 14-16).

That's going to be something; we have that to look forward to! That's really great when we understand it and put it together.

Psa. 104 gives us an inkling of what it's like to be a spirit being, what it's like to be God. We read in one place already that *He is clothed with majesty.*

Let's see God's challenge to Job, who was as perfect as a man could be in the letter of the Law and in serving God; but one thing we always need to remember, which is this: *All the good that you do, even according to God's laws, He requires of everyone in the letter of the Law.* Salvation is a *special calling!* Salvation is a *special creation* that God is working out now, which is done mysteriously, as far as the world is concerned; because it is done spiritually. The only way to understand that there's something going on is to realize that this person is different from other people. Other than that, only God knows the work and the creation that He is doing within each one of us.

Job had to learn that lesson. He got so righteous that he said, 'Oh, God is unfair in doing this and doing that to me. I just want an umpire between us and he can settle the score.' And he said, 'Oh, I wish God would talk to me. Oh, I'm suffering so bad! Why did God do this! Let me talk to God.'

Let's see God's challenge to Job, to show the difference between the flesh and the spirit; and how that keeping the laws and commandments of God in the letter alone… A lot of people in the world today, who are not in the Church, keep some of the Ten Commandments of God and are upright, upstanding, reliable, dependable people, who are wanting to raise their family and live a decent life. *But that's not salvation!* Job had to learn that lesson. Now, not many people have had God come and directly talk to them and point out what their faults are.

Job 38:1: "Then the LORD answered Job out of the whirlwind, and said, 'Who *is* this that darkens counsel by words without knowledge?.... [just spouting off at the mouth, blither] ...Now gird up your loins like a man; for I will demand of you, and **you shall answer Me**'" (vs 1-3).

So, whenever we get all big and puffed up in our own stupidity and carnality and our great importance, let's look at the questions that God asked Job:

- you think you're so good
- you think you're so important
- you think you're so righteous
- you think you're so special *to God*

You are, as God makes us special to Him, **not** *because of who we are, carnally speaking!*

Verse 4: "**Where were you when I laid the foundations of the earth?** Declare it, if you have understanding!.... [of course, he wasn't there] ...Who has determined its measurements if you know? Or who has stretched the line upon it? On what are the foundations fastened to? Or who laid its cornerstone, when the morning stars sang together and all the sons of God shouted for joy?" (vs 4-7).

Hey, the earth was created *after* God had created the angels. This probably gives us a good inkling as to why Satan and one-third of the angels rebelled; because God probably also revealed to them His plan for mankind, and that kind of put man—in his ultimate destiny—above the angels.

Now, He goes on, all the way through Job 38 & 39

Job 40:1: "And the LORD answered Job and said, **'Shall he who contends with the Almighty instruct *Him*?'**..." (vs 1-2). *Tie that in with Isa. 41:12:*

- Who's been God's counselor?
- Who told Him how to build the earth?
- Who measured the mountains and the dust and the balance?
- Who instructed Him?

"...'**He who reproves God, let him answer it**'" (v 2).

Like some people say—when one man tried to point out to his son-in-law, 'Well, you know God does require us to keep the Sabbath.' And he said, *Well, when God comes down here and tells me personally, I'll keep it.* That's an excuse, because he knows God isn't going to come down. Now, if God came down and talked to him, He'd do just like He

did here with Job. But the truth is, God has come down and the knowledge of the Sabbath is in the Bible, and He does tell us to keep it along with His Holy Days, too, see. So, we've got to keep all of that in perspective as well.

Now, Job was beginning to get the point, v 3: "And Job answered the LORD and said, 'Behold, I am vile!....'" (vs 3-4).

Here's another good point. This is the place where Job *repented.* He saw himself for what he really, *really, really* was, and he began to understand that in spite of the good things that he did, the darkness of human nature and the evil of human nature, *he knew* was in him. This the is first point that he began to see that he was not really righteous from the inside out, but he was merely righteous on the exterior.

Verse 4: "Behold, I am vile! What shall I answer You? I will lay my hand on my mouth" *After you read the book of Job you'll say, 'Hooray! It's about time!'*

Verse 5: "'Once I have spoken; but I will not answer; yea, twice, but I will proceed no further.' And the LORD answered Job out of the whirlwind, and said, 'Gird up your loins now like a man. I will demand of you, and you declare unto Me. Will you even annul My judgment?....'" (vs 5-8).

Every Protestant minister better listen up and pay attention! When you say that God has done away with His laws for your lawless convenience.

"...Will you condemn Me so that you may be righteous?" (v 8). *Hey, Job, let's see how powerful you really are!*

You've got a big mouth and you're sitting there covered with boils from head to toe, all scabby and covered with dust and ashes and flies all around, so many flies that you had maggots crawling in your skin. You even said, '...though worms eat this body.'

- Aren't you mighty, Job?
- Aren't you powerful, Job?
- Aren't you something special?

God continues, v 9: "And *have* you an arm like God? Or can you thunder with a voice like His?" [Job, let's see you do this: If you're so righteous]: ...Deck yourself now with majesty and excellency, and array yourself with glory and beauty" (vs 9-10). *Now that you've done that, let's see the power of your correction toward other people.*

Verse 11: "Cast abroad the rage of your

wrath; and behold everyone who is proud, and abase him. Look on everyone *who is* proud, *and* bring him low; and tread down the wicked in their place. Hide them in the dust together; *and* bind their faces in darkness. Then I will also confess to you that your own right hand can save you" (vs 11-14). ***Quite a lesson!***

We're talking about the Being and existence of God, which He challenged Job. 'Now, if you're really righteous, are you like Me.' Well, he had nothing to say, but repent!

Psalm 104:1: "Bless the LORD, O my soul! O LORD my God, You are very great; You are clothed with honor and majesty, covering Yourself with light as with a garment, and stretching out the heavens like a curtain, Who lays the beams of His upper chambers in the waters. He makes the clouds His chariot; He walks upon the wings of the wind; He makes His angels spirits, His ministers a flaming fire. He established the earth on its foundations; so that it should not be removed forever" (vs 1-5).

Goes right back to what God said to Job: ***'Where were you, Job, when I did these things?*** Well, you didn't even exist, and you came into being via the process that I made of pro-creation between husband and wife. One day you were conceived, and one day you were born; and now you have grown up to be a full man, have your own family and now you proclaim yourself to be as righteous as Me?' *Never happen! Never happen!*

Psa. 105—here's what we're going to do all during the Millennium; because there are going to be a minimum of ten generations during the Millennium, perhaps some more. But there will be ten periods of 100 years to mark off the Millennium.

Psalm 105:1: "O give thanks unto the LORD! Call upon His name; make known His deeds among the people."

They're all going to know about God! They're going to know about God *past, present* and *future.* So, by time we get to the people who reject salvation, they're going to know. They're going to be like Job: without excuse!

Verse 2: "Sing to Him, sing praises unto Him; talk of all His wonderful works." *That means we're going to have great understanding of how God has done things!*

Verse 3: "Glory in His Holy name; let the heart of those who seek the LORD rejoice. Seek the LORD and His strength; seek His face evermore. Remember His marvelous works, which He has done, His wonders, and the judgments of His mouth, O you seed of Abraham His servant, you children of Jacob His chosen" (vs 3-6).

Where does all of this start with us? *Back in Gen. 15 and the covenant that God made with Abraham.* Very few people understand it. That is truly the origin of the Passover—Gen. 15—*not* Exo. 12.

What did Paul say in Gal. 3? *'If you are Christ's, then are you Abraham's seed and heirs according to the promise.'*

Not only did He promise Abraham a physical kingdom for his children, but He promised Abraham, Isaac and Jacob—the two main descendants of Abraham—the Kingdom of God as well. Jesus told the Pharisees this very thing, He said: 'Many shall come from the east and west and shall sit down in the Kingdom. When you shall see Abraham, Isaac and Jacob in the Kingdom, then you're going to know *you really messed up.'*

Verse 7: "He is the LORD our God; His judgments are in all the earth. He has remembered His covenant forever…" (vs 7-8). *We just discussed that covenant encompasses the physical seed and spiritual seed!*

"…the word which He commanded to a thousand generations" (v 8). *If a generation is 25 years then that's 25,000 years!*

We are nowhere near 25,000 years of human history, and that's why He says 'a thousand generations.' If it's 40 years, it's 40,000 years. That's to show that God is going to complete His plan the way that He is going to do it; and His blessings will extend way beyond people's physical lives.

Verse 9: "The covenant, which He made with Abraham, and His oath to Isaac; and He confirmed it to Jacob for a statute, and to Israel for an everlasting covenant" (vs 9-10). *Paul talks about the 'everlasting covenant' in Heb. 13!*

Psalm 113:1: "O praise the LORD! Give praise to the LORD, O you servants of the LORD, praise the name of the LORD. Blessed is the name of the LORD from this time forth and forevermore. From the rising of the sun to its going down, the LORD'S name is to be praised" (vs 1-3).

Now think of all the things that we said. If you're up in the air, high enough so you can see the earth pass, and you see people coming to Sabbath services and Holy Day services and they begin each day with a morning prayer and the songs, and these things all go up to God. Think of this, this is what's going to be happening daily, from the rising of the sun continually, till it's going down.

Verse 4: "The LORD is high above all nations, and His glory above the heavens. Who is like the LORD our God, Who dwells on high, Who looks down low upon the heavens and upon the earth? He raises up the poor out of the dust and lifts the needy out of the dunghill" (vs 4-7)— *because He chooses the least!*

That's why we are here. We are the least. We are the weak. We are the rejected of the world. We are those that nobody else likes or cares for or loves; because we truly love God; and He loves us. This is how then we can always remain humble and yielded to God and not get carried away in our own vanity and stupidity. That's really something, isn't it?

Psa. 122—this is quite a Psalm, because this talks about the thrones for us during the Millennium. Let's think of this as being spirit beings and we are coming to the temple that we described earlier, and we are going to have a visit with Jesus Christ:

Psalm 122:1: "I was glad when they said to me, 'Let us go into the house of the LORD.' Our feet shall stand within your gates, O Jerusalem. Jerusalem is built like a city that is all joined together as one where the tribes go up, the tribes of the LORD… [we're spiritual Israel] …unto the testimony of Israel, to give thanks unto the name of the LORD, for there were set the **thrones of judgment**, the **thrones of the house of David**" (vs 1-5).

Isn't it interesting that the Apostle James, Jesus' brother, likened the Church to the tabernacle of David that had fallen down? That means us! 'thrones of the house of Jacob.' That's also a part of the Millennium and what we're going to be doing as spirit beings.

Verse 6: "Pray for the peace of Jerusalem: 'May those who love you prosper. Peace be within your walls, prosperity within your palaces.' For my brethren and companions' sakes, I will now say, 'Peace be within you.' For of the house of the LORD our God, I will seek your good" (vs 6-9).

Psa. 148, 149 & 150 are really tremendous Psalms and they finish off all the praise and honor and glory to God. We are all included in this. This is really tremendous, brethren. These Psalms are just fantastic that they conclude the book of Psalms. Because what it's doing, *it's praising God for His completed work; praising God for His creating of all of the spirit beings.* These are the Psalms then that we can attach to Rev. 21 & 22.

Psalm 148:1: "O praise the LORD! Praise the LORD from the heavens; praise Him in the heights. Praise Him, all His angels; praise Him, all

His hosts" (vs 1-2).

I just wonder if there's going to be a time when we have a Holy Day of all spirit beings—we're all together. And the whole earth filled with those who have entered into the Kingdom of God, and we have a great and we have a fantastic and almost unbelievable worship of God—much like Rev. 5 where there are 10,000 times 10,000 angels which say, 'Worthy of honor and blessing and riches and wealth and glory into the ages of eternity.' So, here we have it. Think of this when we're reading this.

Verse 3: "Praise Him, sun and moon; praise Him, all you stars of light. Praise Him, you heavens of heavens, and waters that are above the heavens. Let them praise the name of the LORD, for He commanded and they were created" (vs 3-5). *All the universe now in complete harmony and joy with God!*

Verse 6: "He has also established them forever and ever; He has made a decree which shall not pass away. Let praise be to the LORD from the earth, you sea monsters, and all the depths; fire and hail, snow and vapor, stormy winds fulfilling His Word, mountains and all hills, fruitful trees and all cedars, beasts and all livestock, creeping things and flying birds, kings of the earth and all people, princes and all judges of the earth, both young men and maidens, old men and children; let them praise the name of the LORD, for His name alone is exalted; His glory is above the earth and the heavens. And He has also lifted up a horn for His people, praise for all His saints, even of the children of Israel, a people near to Him. O praise the LORD!" (vs 6-14).

That is magnificent! I tell you what, that really uplifts me and inspires me, just to think of time when that is going to be. And remember, _we_ are going to be there.

Psalm 149:1: "O praise the LORD! Sing to the LORD a new song, and His praise in the congregation of saints. Let Israel rejoice in his Maker … [not only just physical Israel, but *spiritual* Israel] …let the children of Zion be joyful in their King. Let them praise His name in the dance; let them sing praises to Him with the drum and lyre, for **the LORD takes pleasure in His people**… [we please Him] (Now notice what He's going to do): …**He crowns the meek with salvation**" (vs 1-4).

- that we will have *glory*
- that we will have *honor*
- that we will have *majesty*

of lesser degree, of course, but as God!

Verse 5: "Let the saints be joyful in glory…"

I wonder what it's going to be like, as a spirit being? We can *wish* wherever we want to go. Of course, we're going to have to be righteous so we use it for a good purpose. Isn't that going to be something?

"…let them sing aloud upon their beds. Let the high praises of God be in their mouth, and a two-edged sword in their hand… [because that's how we're going to rule with Christ] …to execute vengeance upon the nations and punishments upon the people, to bind their kings with chains and their nobles with iron bands, to carry out upon them the judgment written—this honor have all His saints. O praise the LORD!" (vs 5-9).

This is why Psa. 149 applies to the time when we are on the Sea of Glass—when we are first resurrected—and the seven last plagues are poured out upon the earth, and we see the vengeance of God.

Not only that, *we help carry it out* when we return to the earth with Jesus Christ, and with Him, put our feet on Mt. Zion. You read Zech. 14. The very first thing that's going to happen is God is going to make them keep the Feast of Tabernacles. Just imagine all of the Muslims—*now ex-Muslims,* hopefully—keeping the Feast of Tabernacles: rejecting Allah, rejecting all of their hatred and their killing, and come like humble, repentant children and worship God and keep the Feast of Tabernacles. Now, if they don't do it, God's going to have some plagues come upon them (Zech. 14).

Now let's look at a couple of other Psalms before we come to Psa. 150; I want to finish there. It's like we started with Psa. 1, Psa. 150 closes it with great finale. When we think about what God is going to do, let's think about it in these terms:

Psalm 31:19 "Oh, how great is Your goodness, which You have laid up for those who fear You, which You have prepared for those who take refuge in You before the sons of men! You shall hide them in the secret place of Your presence from the plottings of man…" (vs 19-20).

That's why I said what God is doing and creating in us is a mystery and the world can't see it. But God is literally doing with His Spirit, in our heart and in our mind.

"…You shall hide them in a shelter away from the strife of tongues. Blessed is the LORD, for He has shown His wondrous loving kindness in a besieged city…" (vs 20-21). *Isn't that something?*

Verse 23: "O love the LORD, all you His saints! The LORD preserves the faithful, and fully repays the proud doer. Be strong, and let your heart take courage, all you who hope in the LORD" (vs 23-24).

This is what is so great about what God is doing; and for us to understand and realize and grasp and keep in our minds continually. God has called us to the absolutely the greatest thing that we could possibly ever attain to. Nothing can ever be attained in this world that way—*NOTHING!*

Psalm 37:27—here's what we are to do: "Depart from evil and do good, and live forevermore. For the LORD loves justice and does not forsake His saints; they are preserved forever, but the seed of the wicked shall be cut off" (vs 27-38).

Don't worry about the people in the world. Don't envy them for what they have. Don't envy them for anything at all, because v 29 tells us—and here's a promise:

Verse 29: "**The righteous shall inherit the earth and dwell in it forever**"—*because that's where New Jerusalem is going to be, **new heaven and new earth!***

Verse 30: "The mouth of the righteous speaks wisdom, and his tongue talks of justice. The Law of his God is in his heart; none of his steps shall slide" (vs 30-31)

Psalm 8:1: "O LORD our Lord, how excellent is Your name in all the earth! You have set Your glory above the heavens! Out of the mouths of babes and sucklings You have ordained strength because of Your adversaries, to silence the enemy and the avenger" (vs 1-2).

We're the 'babes' in Christ! We are the 'suckling,' we are the off-scouring of the earth. Yet, *God has chosen us!*

Verse 3: "When I consider Your heavens, the work of Your fingers, the moon and the stars, which You have ordained, what is man that You are mindful of him, and the son of man that You care for him? For You have made him a little lower than God and have crowned him with glory and honor" (vs 3-5).

At the resurrection God is going to raise us up to His level of existence. *Not* in power, *not* in authority, but to His level of existence and share the glorious inheritance of Jesus Christ with all the saints.

Verse 6: "You made him to have dominion over the works of Your hands…" *Expand that out, that we're going to have dominion, rulership, over all the earth, under Christ!*

"…You have put all things under his feet…" (v 6). *Then it talks about the physical creation.* That's going to be true.

We're going to have rulership and dominion and teaching and being able to help people to learn about God and love God and also, to show them how to take care of the animals, how to take care of the land, how to take care of everything!

Verse 7: "All sheep and oxen, yea, and the beasts of the field; the birds of heaven, the fish of the sea, and all that pass through the paths of the seas. O LORD, our Lord, **how excellent is Your name in all the earth!**" (vs 7-9).

Let's see the grand finale of the great calling that God has given us, and the great opportunities that He has laid before us—awesome and magnificent beyond description. But as we have gone through the Psalms to see about the Millennium:

- what we will be like
- how we will serve God
- how we will see God

All of that now culminates in this last Psalm, Psa. 150. Now just picture this: all of God's plan completed. All of the wicked burned up in the Lake of Fire. New heavens and earth being made, and here is what we are going to do:

Psalm 150:1: "O praise the LORD. Praise God in His sanctuary; praise Him in the firmament of His power. Praise Him for His mighty acts; praise Him according to His excellent greatness. Praise Him with the sound of the ram's horn; praise Him with the harp and lyre. Praise Him with the drum and dance; praise Him with stringed instruments and pipes. Praise Him on the loud cymbals; praise Him with the resounding cymbals. Let everything that breathes praise the LORD. O praise the LORD!" (vs 1-6).

I can just, at this moment, have just a little inkling: I wonder if this is going to be the first thing we're going to do when New Jerusalem comes down out of heaven from God?

So, brethren, this is why we're here for the Feast of Tabernacles. That we can know and understand God's way and His plan, our part in it, where we're going, what we're doing and to know that God loves us. *He loves you and He has called you for this magnificent purpose!*

Scriptural References:

from the book of Psalms:
1) 72:1-8,11-14, 16-20

2) 84:1-12
3) 86:8-15
4) 93:1-4
5) 96:1-13
6) 97:1-3, 6-12
7) 98:1-9
8) 99:1-9
9) 100:1-5
10) 102:12-16

11) Job 38:1-7
12) Job 40:1-14

from the book of Psalms:
13) 104:1-5
14) 105:1-10
15) 113:1-7
16) 122:1-9
17) 148:1-14
18) 149:1-9
19) 31:19-21, 23-24
20) 37:27-31
21) 8:1-9
22) 150:1-6

Scriptures referenced, not quoted:

- Revelation 21; 22
- 1 John 5:21
- Isaiah 10
- Psalm 19
- Isaiah 41-44
- Hebrews 11
- Job 39
- Isaiah 41:12
- Genesis 15
- Exodus 12
- Galatians 3
- Hebrews 13
- Revelation 5
- Zechariah 14

FRC:bo
Transcribed: 8-13-08
Reformatted: 1/2021

CHAPTER SIXTY-FIVE

To Dwell with God I
Fred R. Coulter

Greetings, everyone! Time goes on and on and here we are again. Yet, though the end is closer, it hasn't yet arrived.

All the Holy Days are listed is Lev. 23, as we know. Why did God put them there? This is the only place in the entire Bible where they are listed in sequence according to the Calculated Hebrew Calendar. Yet, even though they are all listed here, *the meaning is found scattered throughout the rest of the Bible!*

It's an amazing thing that God has done in doing it in such a way. That fulfills Prov. 25, let's see what that says. God hides things, but reveals things. To whom does He reveal the knowledge to?

Proverbs 25:2: "**The glory of God *is* to conceal a thing**…"

For all of those who don't read the Old Testament, or who think that is the *old* Law, they'll never understand, ***though it's hidden in plain sight!***

"…**but the honor of kings**… [that's what we're going to be] …*is to search out a matter*" (v 2).

That's why we are told to live by every word of God; that the Bible is put together *a little here and a little there, precept upon precept and line upon line*

- ***IF*** you have the understanding of God, *you will understand*
- ***IF*** you don't have the understanding of God, *you will be taken, snared and fall and not understand*

Here we are in Lev. 23, and it's time for the Feast of Tabernacles. Those who do not follow the Calculated Hebrew Calendar, when they read this they don't have a clue as to what it's saying.

Jesus said, 'Man shall not live by bread alone, but by every word that proceeds out of the mouth of God,' *and He's got it written down! **None of the Bible**—anywhere from Genesis to Revelation **is of the wisdom or origination of human beings! It comes from God by direct command,** as in this case, or by inspiration* with the New Testament!

Leviticus 23:33: "And the LORD spoke to Moses saying, 'Speak to the children of Israel, saying, "The fifteenth day of this seventh month

shall be the Feast of Tabernacles for seven days to the LORD. On the first day *shall be* a Holy convocation. You shall do no servile work *therein*"'" (vs 33-35). *That's today, the first day!*

Verse 36: "Seven days you shall offer an offering made by fire to the LORD…." *That's when they had all the sacrifices!* Today we just take up the offerings on the Holy Day because we don't have animals to sacrifice.

All of those sacrifices were to be done by the priests and the Levites, and the people would bring their sacrifices there. When there were more and more people, it ended up being more and more of turning it into real money and bringing that and depositing it at the temple.

Here's another little phrase, which [of the Holy Days] is the least spoken of in the Bible; however, it has one of the greatest meanings of all in its prophetic fulfillment:

"…On the eighth day shall be a Holy convocation to you. And you shall offer an offering made by fire to the LORD. It *is* a solemn assembly. And you shall do no servile work *therein*." (v 36).

The eighth day is the day after the seven days of the Feast of Tabernacles, ***and it has the greatest meaning of all!*** That's how God does things! Sometimes the least little thing becomes the greatest of all!

Verse 37: "**These *are* the Feasts of the LORD, which you shall proclaim to be Holy convocations**…"

Leviticus 23:1: "And the LORD spoke to Moses, saying, 'Speak to the children of Israel and say to them, "*Concerning* the appointed Feasts of the LORD, which you shall proclaim *to be* Holy convocations, **even these are My appointed Feasts**"'" (vs 1-2).

Appointed for what? *So, we can come to God and learn of God! The first one is the Sabbath Day!* That's the only commandment of the ten that says to *remember!* But most people *forget!* The Sabbath sanctifies all the Holy Days, ***and they are all owned by God!***

God has a secret in understanding, which is ***a good understanding have all those who keep His commandments!*** God is not going to reveal anything to sinful men unless they repent and yield to God and come to Him in meekness and humble adoration to love with all their heart, mind, soul and being!

- that's why we're here
- that's why God has called us

This Feast of Tabernacles that we're having this year is a great Feast, indeed, especially concerning the times in which we are living! It's important that we keep it!

Verse 37: "These *are* the Feasts of the LORD, which you shall proclaim to be Holy convocations…" *He sums it up like He began it; the first and the last, the beginning and the ending!*

"…to offer an offering made by fire to the LORD, a burnt offering and a grain offering, a sacrifice, and drink offerings, everything on its day; besides the Sabbaths of the LORD…" (vs 37-38).

God wants you totally with Him! That's what it means to love Him with your whole heart, *totally!*

"…and besides your gifts, and besides all your vows, and besides all your freewill offerings, which you give to the LORD" (v 38).

(pause for the offering)

The Tabernacle of God or **to live with God!** That's the whole important thing concerning our relationship with God, and God's relationship with men and women, and it's carried out throughout the whole Bible.

We're going to see that as we go through this message today. Where we're going to begin is at the beginning. It's very interesting all the things that are here, the basic information that we need to know. God doesn't tell us every detail, and doesn't tell us how long Adam and Eve were with Him, being instructed by Him, living with Him in paradise: *The Garden of Eden!*

But God made us in such a way that He's given us independent free moral agency—IFMA—*and we are to choose!* Why did God do that? *Because He doesn't want robots!*

Men today are trying to make robots as human-like as they can. But a robot can only parrot back what's put in there:

- no thought
- no emotion
- no love
- no consideration
- no ability to create, design and make

We're made in the likeness of God, so we can build, do and make, because God wants us to be His active children trusting in Him!

That's why He made us the way that He did! He knew that Adam and Eve would fail. Rev. 13 says that Jesus was 'slain from the foundation of the world.' *That's going many, many eons in eternity!*

The important thing about Adam and Eve is that *God personally created them with His own hands!* Everything else God *spoke* and they came into being.

There's that special connection with man/woman and God. He made us in a way that is absolutely spectacular! Not only we thinking independent free moral agents, but also we have the capacity:

- to love
- to cry
- of understanding
- of coming to know God

All of those things God intrinsically created in us! The one thing that He wanted them to do is *obey His voice,* because you prove your love by obeying God! But He gave them choice. He put them in the Garden of Eden, the paradise of God. Adam was to till it, care for it, to keep it—*guard it*—and God would bless them. But like anything else, when you have free moral agency you have to know. How is Adam and Eve going to apply that free moral agency?

- Will it be toward God?
- Will it be toward themselves?
- Will it be toward Satan?

That's a choice! Satan is the great liar and counterfeiter!

Genesis 3:1: "Now, the serpent was more cunning than any creature of the field, which the LORD God had made. And he said to the woman, '*Is it* true that God has said, "You shall not eat of any tree of the garden"?'"

Of course, understanding what God said, she had to correct him; v 2: "And the woman said to the serpent, 'We may freely eat the fruit of the trees of the garden, but of the fruit of the tree which *is* in the middle of the garden, God has *indeed* said, "You shall not eat of it, neither shall you touch it, lest you die"'" (vs 2-3).

Well, Adam and Eve didn't know what dying meant. *God said,* 'in dying you shall surely die.' We know from history that they lives to be over 900-years-old. I wonder what they were thinking about year 700? *I wonder if were going to die, Adam?* Well, they did!

The serpent—Satan—is cunning, lying, slick

and takes Truth and twists it! Look at the 'Christianity' of this world today, and you get a good example of that. *They have long, long ago left living by every word of God!*

Verse 4: "And the serpent said to the woman, 'In dying, you shall not surely die! For God knows that in the day you eat of it, then your eyes shall be opened, and you shall be like God, deciding good and evil'" (vs 4-5).

That's the only way that they would be like God. They obviously weren't going to inherit eternal life and live forever.

How did God appear to Adam and Eve? *He appeared in a form that was much like a human being!* No man or woman can be in the presence of God in His glory and live. They will die, because *God is so inherently powerful that in His glorified form nothing can stand in the physical sense without being damaged or dying!*

When the serpent said that "... you shall be like God…" They probably thought: *We're made in His likeness, He told us that, and if we eat of this tree we will be like Him and can* **decide for ourselves what is right and wrong, and good and evil!**

Verse 6: "And when the woman saw that the tree *was* good for food, and that it was pleasing to the eyes, and a tree to be desired to make *one* wise..."

That's true *Satan's way,* but not God's way, because it's wise:

- to evil
- to lies
- to conniving
- to twisting
- to turning
- to selfishness
- to human nature

Their eyes would be opened to that, but closed to the Truth of God!

Just like today, the reason why so many do not understand the Bible—though they are supposedly Christians—is because their eyes are closed to the Word of God. They think they are wise to the lies of Satan with a *false Christianity!* Quite an amazing thing when you understand it.

"…she took of its fruit and ate. She also gave to her husband with her, and he ate" (v 6).

What was Adam doing sitting there watching her do this? He knew that God said, 'Don't eat it, don't touch it!' A lot of people like to say that 'don't touch it' was added by the woman. *NO!* That's probably added instruction that God gave a

little later.

- Why did Adam do it?
- Was he wondering if she's going to die if she eats it?

She takes a bite of it and she's still walking around and comes over and says, 'Adam, just taste this, it's really good.' *So, he ate it!* **Then Satan had the upper hand on them, right then!**

Satan tells lies to gain control of people! If you don't believe that, look at the political world today: *filled with lies everywhere to control people!* For what purpose? *That they can't come to God!*

Verse 7: "And the eyes of both of them were opened, and they knew that they *were* naked; and they sewed fig leaves together and made coverings for themselves. And they heard the sound of the LORD God walking in the garden in the cool of the day. Then Adam and his wife hid themselves from the presence of the LORD God among the trees of the garden. And the LORD God called to Adam and said to him, 'Where *are* you?'" (vs 7-9).

One man said, 'If God didn't know where they were, what kind of God was He?' Well, the truth is that God wanted Adam to come out; He knew where they were! *No question about it!*

You know the rest of the story, and *because they went against God, sinned against God, they couldn't dwell with God!* This is what has happened to all mankind!

Verse 10: "And he [Adam] said, 'I heard You *walking* in the garden, and I was afraid because I *am* naked, and *so* I hid myself.' And He [God] said, 'Who told you that you *were* naked?....'" (vs 10-11).

That may give us a clue to some of the things that Adam and Eve did. We don't know how long they were with the serpent doing all that they did, and we don't know what they did. It wasn't just a quick one-day event, I am sure of that! I'm sure that Satan was indoctrinating them with his way, his means, with his talking… *we don't know how long!* To make a guess we would be incorrect because we don't know.

"'…Have you eaten of the tree, which I commanded you that you should not eat?' And the man said, (vs 11-12).

It's typical human nature that when you're caught it's never your fault. I don't care how young you are or how hold you are, *that's human nature!*

Verse 12: "And the man said, 'The woman whom You gave *to be* with me, she gave me of the tree, and I ate.'" ***God, it's Your fault,*** *because You gave me this woman!* But when God gave the woman to Adam, he said, 'Whoooo!

Verse 13: "And the LORD God said to the woman, 'What *is* this you have done?' And the woman said, 'The serpent deceived me, and I ate.' And the LORD God said to the serpent… [here is the judgment, and it's carried out clear down to this day]: …'Because you have done this you *are* cursed above all livestock, and above every animal of the field. You shall go upon your belly, and you shall eat dust all the days of your life. And I will put enmity between you and the woman, and **between your seed and her Seed; He will bruise your head, and you shall bruise His heel**'" (vs 13-15).

That is a prophecy of the coming Messiah to save mankind. The very first prophecy, with the very first sin! *Amazing!*

Verse 16: "To the woman He said, 'I will greatly increase your sorrow and your conception…'"

This is true because in the eyes of every mother their children are still their babies! They are emotionally attached to their children because of conception, carrying them, nursing them, taking care of them, and so forth. That sorrow continues all through life, coming and going at different intervals depending on the conduct of their children.

"…in sorrow shall you bring forth children. Your desire shall be toward your husband, and he shall rule over you" (v 16).

Verse 17: "And to Adam He said, 'Because you have hearkened to the voice of your wife…'"— *instead of My voice!*

It doesn't matter what someone may come and tell you, *if it is contrary to the Word of God do not do it!* Every one of us has to make that choice. That's our responsibility as free moral agents. *If we choose God and love God*—now with the Spirit of God to grow in grace and knowledge and prepare for the first resurrection—*we are going to have as pictured by the Feast of Tabernacles the greatest, most wonderful things that we can do!* All of that is based upon the three words: ***Obey My voice!***

Think about that! All you young people out there, remember that! All you children out there, *obey the voice of your father and mother, **because that is a blessing from God!***

Let's understand that the whole reason I'm going through this is to show the lesson that *you cannot dwell with God or you cannot be in the eventual Tabernacle of God unless you love and obey God* by your own free moral agency in everything that you do! That's what God wants! *The blessing is going to come partly in this life, **but only the greatest portion at the resurrection.***

So the woman is going to have sorrow. Women say that God is going to give us sorrow. *Hold on!* Let's see what God told Adam:

Verse 17: "And to Adam He said, 'Because you have hearkened to the voice of your wife and have eaten of the tree—of which I commanded you, saying, "You shall not eat *of* it!"—the ground *is* cursed for your sake. **In sorrow**… [men will have sorrow as well as women] …shall you eat of it all the days of your life. It shall also bring forth thorns and thistles to you, and *thus* you shall eat the herbs of the field; in the sweat of your face you shall eat bread until you return to the ground, for out of it you were taken; for dust you *are*, and to dust you shall return'" (vs 17-19).

Why do I go through all of that? *To show one of the greatest lessons of all!* **You cannot live with God unless you love and obey Him, and follow Him!** That's why He's given His *whole* Word. Here they had personal contact with God.

{Note our message: *What Would the World Have Been Like if Adam & Eve Had Not Sinned?* **truthofGod.org**}

Verse 22: "And the LORD God said, 'Behold, the man has become like one of Us, to decide good and evil; and now, lest he put forth his hand and take also of the Tree of Life, and eat, and live forever—'"

How would you like to live forever in the current way that you live, good and evil? *NO!* God doesn't want that!

Verse 23: "Therefore, the LORD God sent him out from the Garden of Eden to till the ground from which he had been taken. And He drove out the man, and He placed cherubim at the east of the Garden of Eden, and a flaming sword, which turned every way to guard the way to the Tree of Life" (vs 23-24).

Now let's do a survey and see something very important that carries right on down through the rest of the entire Bible. We know that Abel was righteous.

- Why was Abel **righteous**? *Because he did what God said!*
- Why was Cain **unrighteous**? *Because he didn't do what God commanded!*

Jealousy, greed and hatred caused Cain to kill Abel!

Then we have the two lines of genealogy:

- the line of Cain the wicked generation
- the line of Seth, who replace Abel

Out of all of that, *only the ones of the line of Seth were righteous.* Only two are mentioned [in the book of Hebrews]. It doesn't say that these other men in the line of Seth were unrighteous, but Enoch was outstanding.

1. Enoch:

Genesis 5:21: "And Enoch lived sixty-five years and begat Methuselah. And Enoch walked with God three hundred years after he begat Methuselah. And he begat sons and daughters. And all the days of Enoch were three hundred and sixty-five years" (vs 22-23). *He was so righteous that they were out to kill him!*

2. Noah:

At this time the earth was so wicked, and we've covered that. What I want to cover here concerning Noah is important to understand.

Genesis 6:8: "But Noah found grace in the eyes of the LORD." *That's quite a thing!*

You hear *fake Christianity* talk about grace in the New Testament, but there was also grace in the Old Testament. But so few took advantage of it by loving God.

Verse 9: "These *are* the generations of Noah. Noah was a righteous man and perfect in his generations, for **Noah walked with God**."

Is that not what we're supposed to do? *Think about it with God's Spirit in us:* **Walk with God!**

Then you know what happened, the Flood came and God started all over again (Gen. 9).

3. Abraham

Gen. 12—Abraham not only walked with God, *he believed God!* What I want to do is look at the explanation of Abraham in Heb. 11, because that's quite something how that came all the way down. Remember what it says in the New Testament: *If you are Christ's, you are Abraham's seed and heirs according to the promise!*

Let's see what it says concerning Noah and then we'll get to Abraham. Heb. 11:1 gives us a good summary of *salvational faith* in the Old Testament.

Hebrews 11:1: "Now, faith is *the* substance of *things* hoped for, *and the* conviction of things not seen."

The faith that we have comes as a gift of God. When we first start it is our faith. Then *when we are converted and grow in grace and knowledge, God adds to us His Spirit and the very faith of Jesus Christ!* That's an important thing to

understand, and why it's so important that we continue daily in prayer and study, and living in the way that God has said that He wants us to live.

We want to live with God, *but He wants to know how we are going to prepare for it!*

Verse 2: "For by this *kind of faith* the elders obtained a good report. By faith we understand that the worlds were created by *the* Word of God, so that the things that are seen were made from *things* that are invisible" (vs 2-3). *True!*

Even the smallest particle that men can even find, does not really define the smallest particle.

Verse 4: "By faith Abel offered to God a more excellent sacrifice than Cain, by which he obtained witness that he was righteous, God testifying of his gifts; and through it, though he died, *he* is yet speaking."

In other words, the Word of God is so true that it's always in the present tense; keep that in mind.

Verse 5: "By faith Enoch was transported so that he would not look upon death…"—*men were after him to kill him,* so God took him and transported him someplace else. He didn't go to heaven, because later it says, 'These all died in faith.'

"…and was not found because God had transported him; for before his departure it was testified of him that **he pleased God**."

- What does it mean to please God?
- How do you please God?

Verse 6: "Now, **without faith *it is* impossible to please God**…." *You can't come along and be as James said, and be double-minded,* having half your mind on God's way and half your mind on the world's way! That's double-minded and you can't have faith that's required, because then you're unstable.

I'm going to read the stats on what happened to the Ambassador College graduates, astonishing and unbelievable, because many were double-minded and didn't please God.

"…For it is mandatory *for* the one who comes to God to believe that He exists…" (v 6)—*everything* that God says that He is and does, and you can have full confidence in that, because God cannot lie!

"..and *that* He is a rewarder of those who **diligently seek Him**" (v 6). *Think about that!*

Verse 7: "By faith Noah, after being Divinely instructed by God about the things *he could* not yet see, was moved with fear *and* prepared an ark for *the* salvation of his house; through which he condemned the world and became heir of the righteousness, which is by faith."

Quite an important thing, **the faith of God!** That's what Jesus told the disciples they had to have in Mark 11, *faith from God!* The Greek is *faith of God,* or *God's faith!*

There's quite a bit in here about Abraham, which is tremendously important for us to understand.

Verse 8: "By faith Abraham, being called *of God* to go out into the place, which he would later receive for an inheritance, **obeyed and went, not knowing where he was going**." *Stop and think about your life*:

- how long you've been baptized
- how long you've been in the Church'
- how long you've studied the Word of God

- Are you where you thought you would be when you were first baptized? *I dare say that none of us could say yes!*
- Why? *Because we walk by faith!*

We all have different trials to come along, and all of that is to prepare us for the fulfilling of God's plan for us, *that we can rule the world with Christ!* That's what it's all about. Everything that there is circles around that place.

Verse 9: "By faith he sojourned in the land of promise, like a foreigner… [he didn't own it; he just lived in it] …dwelling in tabernacles with Isaac and Jacob…"

Abraham lived long enough to see Jacob born and he died when Jacob was two-years-old! Think about that! That's quite a thing!

"…dwelling [living] in tabernacles…"— *that's what this temporary body for us is also, a tabernacle, a temporary dwelling!*

"…the joint heirs of the same promise; for he was waiting for the city with *the* foundations of which God is *the* Architect and Builder" (vs 9-10).

How much of God's plan did Abraham really, really know? *Think about when he took Isaac out to offer him as the burnt offering!* He must have known an awful lot about the plan of God, though it's not written in the Old Testament. That's why I'm reading this account in the book of Hebrews, because this tells us more about it.

He lived in tabernacles, v 10: "For he was waiting for the city with *the* foundations of which God is *the* Architect and Builder."

Isn't it interesting that when Jesus was here in the flesh that it says that He was a carpenter, but really it should say that He was a Building Contractor!

Verse 11: "By faith also Sarah herself received power to conceive seed, and gave birth *when* she was *well* beyond the childbearing age because she esteemed Him faithful Who had personally promised *her a son*." *Even though she laughed!*

Verse 12: Because of this *faith,* there came into being from **one man**—and moreover, *one* who was *reproductively* dead—*descendants* as numerous as the stars in the heavens, and as countless as the sand on the seashore"—*which today is expanded way beyond that!*

Just count that as all the generations down through time, of all the physical 12 tribes, *those are the sand of the seashore, and the stars of heaven are all of those who are converted!*

Think about what it's going to be in the finality of God's plan. Jesus said to remember that *those of us who are faithful will enter into the Kingdom of God and shine like the sun!* So, to dwell and live with God has much more to do with a complete new existence, and that's why there's a resurrection from the dead.

Verse 13: "All these died in faith, not having received the promises, but having seen them from afar, and **having been persuaded of *them***, and **having embraced *them***, and having confessed that they were strangers and sojourners on the earth." *Take this verse and apply it to yourself!*

➤ "…**having been persuaded of *them***…"

- Are you persuaded of them?
- Do you have doubts in your mind?

You might as well get rid of them and have absolute confidence that what God has said is going to happen?

➤ "…**having embraced *them***…"

Not just look at them from arms length, but embrace them, take them into:

- your bosom
- your heart
- your mind

➤ "…**having confessed that they were strangers and sojourners on the earth**"— *saying of themselves they had nothing!*

- Who are we?
- What are we?

As we all know, no one has taken anything to the grave!

But the promises of God are sure, and will happen, *because to be in the tabernacle with God*—or as we're going to see, it's going to be greater than a tabernacle—*it's going be New Jerusalem, because that's where we end up with the 8th Day!* Isn't that true? *Yes, indeed!*

Verse 14: "For those who say such things make it manifest that they seek *their* own country, *as promised by God*"—which is the Kingdom of God!

That's where we're headed! That's what Christ is going to bring, and this what we're going to do. We will see how that's going to be. God is going to make human existence elevated to such a high level it's going to be a marvelous thing, indeed!

Verse 15: "And **if**…"—IFMA—independent free moral agency:

- we all have it
- we all need to exercise it
- we all need to make the right choices

When we don't make the right choices, we all need to repent and yield to God! He is there to forgive!

"…on the one hand, they had let their minds dwell *fondly* on the place where they came from, they might have had opportunity to return" (v 15).

Who would be giving that opportunity to return? *Think about it in your life!* Let me tell you this: too many who have been in the Church of God, when the opportunity given by Satan the devil to leave and go their own way, *they left!* Let's hope that whatever measure of repentance they may have that God may give them, and that's up to *their choices and God… No one is going to*:

- dwell with God
- tabernacle with God
- be in the house of God
- be in the Temple of God
- be in the New Jerusalem of God

unless you love and obey God, regardless of what the command is! That's what Abraham did with Isaac!

Verse 16: "But now, on the other hand, they are aspiring to a more excellent *country*—that is, a heavenly *one*…." *We're waiting for the Kingdom of God, not something on this earth*:

- that men do
- that men have built up
- that men align themselves with

but from God!

"…Therefore, God is not ashamed to be called their God because He has prepared a city for them" (v 16).

Remember what Jesus said on that Passover night, 'You believe in God, believe also in Me; I'm going to prepare a place for you, so that you may be where I am'—*to live with God!*

- that's why we're here
- that's why our bodies are temporary

This tabernacle that we have today is temporary!

Verse 17: "By faith Abraham, when he was being tried, offered up Isaac; and he who had received the promises offered up *his* only begotten *son* of whom it was said, 'In Isaac shall your Seed be called'" (vs 17-18).

Let's go back and see that promise! Let's see how great that the obedience, the love and the devotion of Abraham to God was, and it came to Isaac, the promised seed.

Abraham was 100-years-old and Sarah was 90. God did it that way to show the viability of His promise, that in spite of how men would look at it, and even God ordinarily makes it happen, that they can no longer have children when they get old. But God did the impossible with Abraham and Sarah to have Isaac. Now the promise went to Isaac, and from Isaac comes the dual seed:

- to Israel
- to the Church

Genesis 26:2: "And the LORD appeared to him [Isaac] and said, 'Do not go down into Egypt…. [because there was a famine] …Live in the land, which I shall tell you of. Stay in this land, and **I will be with you and bless you, for to you and to your seed, I will give all these lands**; and **I will establish the oath, which I swore to Abraham your father**'" (vs 2-3).

God cannot lie, never ever, *ever, ever lie!* His word is true, and He will keep His word!

- that's why we have Jesus Christ
- that's why we have the Bible
- that's why we have the promises given to us

So that we can have the hope of living with God!

Verse 4:"And **I will multiply your seed as the stars of the heavens** …" *That's the spiritual seed that Paul writes of: If you are Christ's then you are Abraham's seed and heirs according to the promise.'* So, to the Church *first!*

"…and will give to your seed all these lands. And in your seed shall all the nations of the earth be blessed" (v 4)—*right on down through the Last Great Day!*

We need to understand how great God's plan is! Notice why this went to Isaac. God didn't say because Isaac was a good boy all his life. *But because God keeps His word, and Isaac was the promised seed*:

Verse 5: "**Because Abraham obeyed My voice and kept My charge, My commandments, My statutes, and My laws.**"

*Think about that! Remember that you cannot dwell with God **unless you**:*

- *obey* God
- *believe* God
- *love* God

Hebrews 11:20: "By faith Isaac blessed Jacob and Esau concerning things that were to come. By faith Jacob, when he was dying, blessed each of the sons of Joseph, and worshiped *God, leaning* on the top of his staff" (vs 20-21). *He was 147-years-old at that time!* That's when he blessed Ephraim and Manasseh, and all the sons.

Verse 22: "By faith Joseph, when he was dying, spoke of the *coming* exodus of the children of Israel, and gave a command concerning his bones."

Let's look through this. All of this is by those who:

- believed God
- trusted God
- obeyed God
- loved God

*They were there and **walked with God!***

Verse 23: "By faith Moses, after he was born, was hidden three months by his parents because they saw *that* he was a beautiful little child; and they did not fear the king's decree. By faith Moses, after becoming a great *leader*, refused to be called *the* son of Pharaoh's daughter, **choosing** to suffer affliction with the people of God, rather than to enjoy *the* temporary pleasure of sin" (vs 23-25)— *free moral agency!*

In all of this we see that the blessings come by choosing God's way!

Verse 26: "For he esteemed the reproach of Christ greater riches than the treasures of Egypt because he was looking intently to the reward."

We're going to go back and look at the situation with Moses and Israel in just a bit.

Verse 27: "By faith he left Egypt, not fearing the wrath of the king; for he persevered, as *if he were* seeing the *One Who is* invisible. By faith he kept the Passover and the sprinkling of the blood so that the destroyer of the firstborn would not slay them. By faith they passed through the Red Sea..." (vs 27-29).

God has given all of these men up to this point an opportunity to dwell, tabernacle or live with God! We're going to see that He gave this opportunity to the children of Israel, and that's why he used Moses, quite an interesting thing when you go through it all. God really intended to bring the children of Israel out of Egypt, but it all depended on the *free moral agency* of the people combined; the IFMA: Independent Free Moral Agency!

- Do you choose to love God and obey Him?
- Do you choose to obey His Law or not?

God had a great plan for Israel, and they have carried it out to a certain extent down through history, because God chose Israel to be the leading nations of the world. Even in spite of their sins, they ruled the world, and they were given opportunity to love God and carry out a great mission for God, and He chose to do it through them.

Moses was the one who led them out of Egypt, across the Red Sea and to Mt. Sinai. When they got to Mt. Sinai we will see what it was that God intended the people of Israel to do. It would have changed the world if they would have done it.

Exodus 19:3: "And Moses went up to God... [on Mt. Sinai] ...and the LORD called to him out of the mountain, saying, 'Thus you shall say to the house of Jacob and tell the children of Israel.'"

When God does something, He gives you a simple overall perspective. Remember when you were baptized. Simple proposition: *repent of your sins and be baptized and you shall receive the gift of the Holy Spirit!* Was there a whole lot more for you to learn and understand? *Yes, there was! A great deal!* But the proposition is simple.

Just like when a man proposes to a woman to be his wife, and he to be her husband, it's a simple proposition: Will you marry me? *Yes!* Now then, everything after that comes. Remember, *marriage is binding unto death!* There are a couple of exceptions. So, God chose Israel. Why? *Because He promised Abraham, Isaac and Jacob!*

The children of Israel were going to represent God to whole world, to show the world the way of God.

Verse 4—God says: "You have seen what I did to the Egyptians, and *how* I bore you on eagles' wings and brought you unto Myself.... [notice the command]: ...Now, therefore, **if**... [conditional] ...**you will obey My voice** indeed..." (vs 4-5).

That's the whole thing with everything. It the same way *IF* you want to enter into the Kingdom of God:

- you've got to obey God, love Him and

keep His commandments!

- you've got to have faith in the sacrifice of Jesus Christ as He said
- you've got to live by every word of God

So, here it is to them!

"…**and keep My covenant**, **then** you shall be a special treasure to Me **above all people**; for all the earth *is* Mine" (v 5).

That didn't make them superior, because they were there for a mission. It's the same way today with the Church. The Church is here for a mission, and all the people that God has called *belong to God!* All of us who are elders and ministers are merely stewards to teach you the Word of God so that you can grow in grace and knowledge, and faith and understanding so you can attain to the Kingdom of God and be a spirit son or daughter of God!

With the children of Israel, they were to be the emissaries of all the nations of the world.

Verse 6: "And **you shall be to Me a kingdom of priests and a Holy nation**…." *You can't ask for anything better; you can't ask for anything more at this particular time!*

"'…These *are* the words which you shall speak to the children of Israel.' And Moses came and called for the elders of the people, and laid before them all these words, which the LORD commanded him" (vs 6-7).

They heard the proposition, and it sounded good! Was anybody going to turn that down? *Of course not!*

But there's a whole lot more to it than meets the eye, because the proposition has a lot of detail that had to be fulfilled and filled in order to make it work. In order to be a Holy nation, they had to have the laws and commandments of God coming from the Holy God:

- for the Holy Word of God
- for the Holy Ten Commandments of God
- for the Holy statutes and judgments of God

to carryout what they were to carry out!

Verse 8: "And all the people answered together and said, 'All that the LORD has spoken we will do.' And Moses returned the words of the people to the LORD."

Then the Lord told Moses to prepare the people, and in three days 'I'm coming down on the top of the mountain' and the greatest thing to happen up to that point on earth to the greatest number of people, all those who had come out of the land of Egypt—the young, the old, the children, well over a million to 1.5 million, some even say 2-million. It doesn't matter the number to be exact, because the historical thing was done.

They were to be a special people to God, *to serve God for the rest of the nations of the world!* Does that sound like something we're going to do? *Yes, indeed!* We are called a Holy nation (1-Peter). *Think on that!*

Verse 16: "And it came to pass on the third day in the morning that there *were* thunders and lightnings, and a thick cloud upon the mountain. And the sound of the trumpet was exceedingly loud so that all the people in the camp trembled…. [awesome indeed] …And Moses brought the people out of the camp to meet with God. And they stood at the base of the mountain. And Mount Sinai was smoking, all of it because the LORD came down upon it in fire. And the smoke of it went up like the smoke of a furnace, and the whole mountain quaked greatly" (vs 16-18).

Think about what it would be like if you were standing there and this happened!

Verse 19: "And when the sound of the trumpet sounded long, and became very strong, Moses spoke, and God answered him by voice. And the LORD came down upon Mount Sinai on the top of the mountain. And the LORD called Moses to the top of the mountain, and Moses went up. And the LORD said to Moses, 'Go down. Command the people…'" (vs 19-21)—*not to come up any closer!*

Verse 24: "And the LORD said to him, 'Away! Get you down, and *only* you shall come up, you and Aaron with you. But do not let the priests and the people break through to come up to the LORD, lest He break forth upon them.' And Moses went down to the people, and spoke to them" (vs 24-25).

Why? *Because they were not sanctified nor called to do it!* Very interesting principle.

You know what happened, all the Ten Commandments were given! This is quite a thing that took place. They had been in Egypt, living like all of the pagans around them. Yet, God brought them out and spared their firstborn. He brought them to the mountain so they could be dedicated and consecrated, to *be a people Holy to God!* But they had to start out with the right foundation! And that right foundation was the Ten Commandments!

When the Millennium starts, what do you think is going to be the first thing we are going to introduce all the people of the world to? *Right here, the Ten Commandments of God:*

- spoken by God

- carried out by the kings and priests and Family of God
- to bring to the whole world

Israel failed!

We are spiritual Israel! All the commandments are important! So, let's go through them, because this is what God told them, and this is how we're going to run the Kingdom of God, with:

- the love of God
- the Truth of God
- the commandments of God

There will be only one God to worship: God the Father and Jesus Christ. We are His servants to the people, to bring them the knowledge of Truth, love and salvation. But they have to do what God always requires: ***Obey My voice!***

Exodus 20:1: "And God spoke all these words, saying, 'I *am* the LORD your God, Who brought you out of the land of Egypt, out of the house of bondage'" (vs 1-2).

That may be changed just a little bit: 'I *am* the LORD your God, Who came from heaven to setup the Kingdom of God and:

Verse 3: "You shall have no other gods before Me.

Then no idols, no bowing down to them (vs 4-5). We'll make sure they don't do it. They won't take the name of the Lord God in vain (v 7).

They will all remember the Sabbath Day and keep it (v 8) as we find in Isa. 66. Then they shall love their neighbor as themselves with all the rest of the commandments:

- honor your mother and father (v 12)
- no murder (v 13)
- no adultery (v 14)
- no stealing (v 15)
- no lying (v 16)
- no coveting (v 17)

Those are all the law of love to God and to neighbor, and the foundation for the coming Kingdom of God!

This is quite a thing, indeed! This is what God is going to do, because ***then the whole world will be living with God and His Family!***

Scriptural References:

1) Proverbs 25:2
2) Leviticus 23:33-37, 1-2, 37-38
3) Genesis 3:1-19, 22-24
4) Genesis 5:21-23
5) Genesis 6:8
6) Hebrews 11:1-18
7) Genesis 26:2-5
8) Hebrews 11:20-29
9) Exodus 19:3-8, 16-21, 24-25
10) Exodus 20:1-5

Scriptures referenced, not quoted:

- Revelation 13
- Genesis 9; 12
- Mark 11
- Exodus 20:4-5, 7-8
- Isaiah 66
- Exodus 20:12-17

Also referenced: Message:
What Would the World Have Been Like if Adam & Eve Had Not Sinned?

FRC:bo
Transcribed: 7/27/20
Reformatted: 1/2021

CHAPTER SIXTY-SIX

To Dwell with God II
Fred R. Coulter

Greetings, brethren! Welcome to the Feast of Tabernacles!

- the tabernacle of God
- to dwell with God
- God dwelling with His people

All of those are a part of the meaning of the Feast of Tabernacles!

We've come to the place where God began dealing with the children of Israel. He gave the proposal to them, gave them His laws and commandments, and then He made a covenant with them.

Even though they didn't want to listen to the voice of God anymore, they said that they would listen to Moses. God understood that they were well-intended in that. So, in the parallel account in Deut. 5, where it talks about the giving of the Ten Commandments, here's what the children of Israel said:

Deuteronomy 5:25: "Now, therefore, why should we die? For this great fire will consume us...." *This was a great and awesome event and it really terrified them!*

"...If we hear the voice of the LORD our God any more, then we shall die" (v 25). *No! Because God was not always going to deal with them in His glory!*

But He did this so that they would know the power of God, He's Creator of everything that there is, and how things are going. That's quite a thing to understand, and to know Who would be their God! This way God was hoping that even in the letter of the Law they would be obedient to Him.

Here's what they told Moses; v 27: "You go near and hear all that the LORD our God shall say. And you speak to us all that the LORD our God shall speak to you, and **we will hear *it*, and do *it*.**"

Whenever you say something to God, He's going to hold you accountable for it. *You need to think on that!*

Verse 28: "And the LORD heard the voice of your words when you spoke to me. And the LORD said to me, 'I have heard the voice of the words of this people, which they have spoken to you. They have well *said* all that they have spoken.'"

In other words, *they were well-intended!* Isn't that the way people are? *They have good intensions!* But the truth is, without the Spirit of God—which He didn't give to them in the covenant with Israel—it's difficult to follow through. However, if they did it in the letter of the Law, God would bless them and be with them!

Verse 29: "Oh, that there were such a heart in them that they would **fear Me** and **keep all My commandments always** so that it might be well with them and with their children forever!" *That's what God wanted!*

Moses went back up on the mountain and got all the things from God: all the statutes, judgments and ordinances. He gathered all the people together and here's what God said to Moses, because there had to be those who would see and witness what God said. Here was another phenomenal, one-time event. God was preparing them so that He, through the temple or tabernacle, would dwell/tabernacle with them.

Exodus 24:1: "And He said to Moses, 'Come up to the LORD, you and Aaron, Nadab, and Abihu, and seventy of the elders of Israel, and worship afar off.'"

All of those witnesses could say, 'We saw the outline of God! We know that it's real! They could all come back and tell all the children of Israel, all 12 tribes, that this was really the real thing!

Verse 2: "'And Moses alone shall come near the LORD, but they shall not come near. Neither shall the people go up with him.' And Moses came and told the people all the words of the LORD, and all the judgments. And all the people answered with one voice and said, 'All the words which the LORD has said, we will do.' And Moses wrote all the words of the LORD, and rose up early in the morning, and built an altar? (vs 1-4)—*and sacrificed!*

Verse 6: "And Moses took half of the blood, and put *it* in basins, and half of the blood he sprinkled on the altar. And he took the Book of the Covenant, and read in the ears of the people...." (vs 6-7).

Verse 8: "And Moses took the blood and sprinkled *it* on the people, and said, 'Behold the blood of the covenant, which the LORD has made with you concerning all these words.'"

After that was done and the people agreed to it; the v 9: And Moses went up, and Aaron, Nadab, and Abihu, and seventy of the elders of Israel. And **they saw the God of Israel. And *there was* under His feet as it were a paved work of a sapphire stone, and as it were the heavens in clearness**" (vs 9-10). *That was a Sea of Glass!*

Verse 11: "And upon the nobles of the children of Israel He did not lay his hands. Also they saw God, and ate and drank. And the LORD said to Moses, 'Come up to Me in the mountain, and be there. And **I will give you tablets of stone, and the Law, and commandments, which I have written, so that you may teach them**'" (vs 11-12)—*and Moses went up!*

The first thing that God did was to begin to give Moses *the instructions for the tabernacle,* and later we will see *the temple!*

Then God said that the first thing that your going to build, after you take up an offering for everything to build:

Exodus 25:9: "According to all that I show you, the pattern of the tabernacle, and the pattern of all the instruments of it, even so you shall make *it.*"

Moses had to have the skilled workmen in able to do it, and we find that in Exo. 35-36 and so forth.

The first think that He starts out with is the Ark of the Covenant. Why is that important? *Let's see what God said*:

Verse 8: "And let them make Me a sanctuary so that I may dwell among them." *That's what God wanted, to put His presence in the tabernacle!* Though that presence, God would be dwelling with them.

Verse 9: "According to all that I show you, the pattern of the tabernacle, and the pattern of all the instruments of it, even so you shall make *it.* And they shall make an ark *of* acacia wood. Two and a half cubits long and a cubit and a half wide and a cubit and a half high. And you shall overlay it *with* pure gold. You shall overlay it inside and out, and shall make on it a crown molding of gold all around *the top edge*" (vs 9-11).

Then He gives all the instructions for it! ***That was to be in the Holy of Holies!*** God started with the most important part—the Ark of the Covenant—which would be in the Holy of Holies.

Then God gave instructions on how to build

the rest of the tabernacle, and the coverings that would go over it and the fence that would go around the courtyard. This would be in the center of Israel while they were traveling to the Holy Land. *Quite a profound thing!* God was really making it known to them!

You know what happened. When Moses was on top of the mountain getting all of the instructions from God on how to build all of this, let's read the final instructions and see something very important.

This is just before Moses comes down off the mountain after receiving all the instructions to make everything:

Exodus 31:12: "And the LORD spoke to Moses saying, 'Speak also to the children of Israel, saying, "Truly you shall keep **My Sabbaths**... [plural] ...for it... [the keeping of them] ...*is* a sign between Me and you throughout your generations to know that I *am* the LORD Who sanctifies you" (vs 12-13).

It's the same way today, only added with the Holy Spirit of God *in us!*

Verse 14: "You shall keep the Sabbath, therefore, for it *is* Holy to you. Everyone that defiles it shall surely be put to death, for whoever does *any* work on it, that soul shall be cut off from among his people." *They will not receive the blessings of God!*

Verse 15: "Six days may work be done..."

Verse 16—*this is something all the Protestants ought to read*: "Therefore, the children of Israel shall keep the Sabbath, **to observe the Sabbath throughout their generations *as a* perpetual covenant**"—*a never ending covenant!*

When God gave them the manna, what happened? *It continued for the 40 years!* Same way with keeping the Sabbath, a perpetual covenant!

Verse 17: "It *is* a sign between Me and the children of Israel **forever**..."—*also between God and the people of God—the Church of God—today!*

We're going to see that this is very important because before God is going to come and dwell with all the people on the earth, He's got to prepare a people through the Church! We will see what that is like and how that is done.

"'...for in six days the LORD made the heavens and the earth, and on the seventh day He rested, and was refreshed.' And He gave to Moses, when He had made an end of speaking with him upon Mount Sinai, two tablets of the testimony, tablets of stone, **written by the finger of God**" (vs 17-18).

You know what happened! The children of

Israel convinced Aaron to make a golden calf. The first thing they did was *forget* what they saw, what they heard, and because of that sin a great number of them had to die. Moses intervened to keep the children of Israel and Aaron alive.

So, they did make the tabernacle and everything associated with it. Then it was setup. This was done so that the presence of God would be in the tabernacle. None of the people had the Holy Spirit of God except Moses and some of the 70 of the elders of Israel and Aaron. *That's was about it!* None of them had the Holy Spirit of God. The people had to obey in the letter. Their whole lives were to be centered around the tabernacle, later the temple, *because that's how God dwelt with them!*

Exodus 40:1: "And the LORD spoke to Moses, saying, 'You shall set up the tabernacle of the tent of the congregation on the first day of the first month'" (vs 1-2).

Then God gives Moses all the instructions. He anointed Aaron and his sons to be the priests. The Levites were all se to go.

Verse 31: "And Moses and Aaron and his sons washed their hands and their feet there. When they went into the tent of the congregation, and when they came near the altar, they washed, even as the LORD commanded Moses. And he set up the court all around the tabernacle and the altar, and set up the screen of the court gate. And Moses finished the work" (vs 31-33).

Now notice what happened, because God gave a demonstration to start, that yes, He put His presence there in what is called *the Shekinah!* Not that He dwelt there, but He dwelt with the people through the temple and the Shekinah. Notice how that came:

Verse 34: "And the cloud covered the tabernacle of the congregation, and the glory of the LORD filled the tabernacle. And Moses was not able to enter into the tabernacle of the congregation **because the cloud stayed on it,** and the glory of the LORD filled the tabernacle" (vs 34-35). *Notice that it stayed there!*

Verse 36: "And when the cloud was taken up from over the tabernacle, the children of Israel journeyed on in all their journeys. But if the cloud was not taken up, then they did not journey until the day that it was taken up; for the cloud of the LORD *was* upon the tabernacle by day, and fire was on it by night, in the sight of all the house of Israel in all their journeys" (vs 36-38)—*for 40 years!*

That's quite a thing! That is tremendous, indeed! The children of Israel wandered in the wilderness for 40 years. God never really intended it to be that long, but when they rebelled and didn't want to go into the land when God said to go in to the land, coupled with all their other rebellions. *Right in the presence of God*, with the tabernacle in the center where all the tribes of Israel were surrounding it when they weren't traveling. Then God made them wander for 40 years.

They setup the tabernacle at Shiloh. Shiloh was up in the northern ten tribes, close to where Ephraim was. It wasn't in Jerusalem, that took place later on. But again, the children of Israel—you can read in Judges, 1st & 2nd Samuel, 1st & 2nd Kings that they sinned. God had to punish them and they were sent off into captivity, the Ark was stolen in the days Eli because of the sins of the people. The Philistines had the Ark and finally they sent it back and it was at the house of Kirjath-Jearim.

Then Saul was made king and he didn't do what God wanted him to do. So, all of this was the ups and downs of the children of Israel and everything that they were involved in. they kept leaving God going to the gods of the nations around them. All of this caused them to really stray from God.

However, God finally raised up a man to bring them together, and that man was David! David was a man after God's heart, and he did the things that God wanted.

Now, he had one great sin with Bathsheba and killing her husband, Uriah the Hittite. That caused David a lot of trouble until the end of his life. However, God appointed Solomon to succeed David.

God had given to David all the pattern and plan for building a temple, because David wanted to build a temple for God. But God said he couldn't do it because David was such a 'bloody man' with so much war. *'So, Solomon you son will build a temple for Me, and I will dwell in it.'* Solomon was chosen and David gave great commands to Solomon in what he should do. Let's see what Solomon was given by David in the way of what he should do. David had brought all the commanders of all armies and all the important people to Jerusalem, and said:

1-Chronicles 28:2: And David the king stood up on his feet and said, 'Hear me, my brethren and my people. I *had* in my heart to build a house of rest for the Ark of the Covenant of the LORD, and for the footstool of our God, and had made preparations for the building. But God said to me, "You shall not build a house for My name, because you *have been* a man of war and have shed blood." However, the LORD God of Israel chose me before all the house of my father to be king over Israel forever....'" (vs 2-4).

He did that; that was a special covenant.

Please note this, *in spite of David's sin with Bathsheba,* God kept that covenant.

"...For He has chosen Judah to be the ruler, and of the house of Judah the house of my father. And among the sons of my father's house He was pleased to make me king over all Israel. And of all my sons (for the LORD has given me many sons), He has chosen Solomon my son to sit upon the throne of the kingdom of the LORD over Israel" (vs 4-5)—*all 12 tribes!*

First time all 12 tribes were together, but that didn't last very long.

Verse 6: "And He said to me, 'Solomon your son shall build My house and My courts, for I have chosen him *to be* My son, and I will be his Father. And I will establish his kingdom forever **if**...'" (vs 6-7)—*right back where we started in the Garden of Eden,* independent free moral agency. That applies to us today as well. With everything that we do.

- *IF* we love God
- *IF* we are faithful
- *IF* we are true

God has a great plan for the whole world, of which we're going to be a part. But in order for that to happen, He's got to have complete those who will be converted and resurrected to help rule with Jesus Christ. That's for tomorrow, but for today:

"'...**if** he continues resolute... [not half way] ...in keeping My commandments and My ordinances, as he is today.' And now in the sight of all Israel, the congregation of the LORD, and in the hearing of our God..." (vs 7-8). *Solomon is right there with David!*

"...keep and seek for all the commandments of the LORD your God, so that you may possess this good land and leave *it* for an inheritance for your children after you **forever**. And you, Solomon my son... [think about this, because we know what happened to Solomon] ...acknowledge the God of your father **and serve Him with a perfect heart**..." (vs 8-9)—*not double-minded,* like James wrote: *a double-minded man is unstable in all of his ways!* Surely, Solomon did become double-minded, as we will see later.

What's important is that in order for God to dwell with His people, *His people have got to understand that they must*:

- love God
- keep His commandment
- obey His voice

That's really pretty simple when you come down to it!

"...and **with a willing mind**... [not being forced to do it] ...for **the LORD searches all hearts**" (v 9).

- What do you think God is doing with us today?
- Is not God trying and testing us, as well?
- To is *IF* we will continue with all God wants us to do?

God's plan for us is awesome and fantastic; far different from this! Far greater than this, even as great as this was!

"...and understands all the imaginations of the thoughts...." (v 9). *That's a marvelous thing to understand,* but also a fearful thing to know *IF* we willfully transgress and go against God!

"...**If** you seek Him, He will be found by you. But **if** you forsake Him, He will cast you off forever" (v 9)—*quite a warning!*

Here's Solomon, about 16-years-old at that time, and David is standing up there and Solomon is right there in front of him, and David is saying these words to him. This is recorded in the Bible, because this is a great lesson for us.

Verse 10: "Take heed now... [pay attention to yourself] ...for the LORD **has chosen you** to build a house for the sanctuary. Be strong and do *it*." *Think about that!*

We know what happened. Solomon built the temple and it was dedicated. Let's read about the dedication, which was very similar to what it was in the dedication of the tabernacle.

1-Kings 8:1: "Then Solomon assembled the elders of Israel and all the heads of the tribes, the chief of the fathers of the children of Israel..."

Verse 2: "And all the men of Israel were gathered to King Solomon at the Feast in the month Ethanim, which *is* the seventh month." *This has to be the Feast of Trumpets!*

Verse 3: "And all the elders of Israel came in, and the priests took up the Ark. And they brought up the Ark of the LORD and the tabernacle of the congregation and all the Holy vessels which *were* in the tabernacle—even those the priests and the Levites brought up. And King Solomon and all the congregation of Israel, who had assembled to him *were* before the Ark sacrificing sheep and oxen which could not be counted nor numbered for multitude" (vs 3-5).

What happened was that Solomon setup all around the court of where the temple was, other altars of sacrifice, because there were so many people and so many sacrifices. This was one of the most magnificent events to happen in the history of the world.

Verse 6: "And the priests brought in the Ark of the Covenant of the LORD into its place, into the Holy place of the house, into the Holy of Holies under the wings of the cherubim, for the cherubim spread forth *their* two wings over the place of the Ark.... [they were also built into the sides of the walls of the Holy of Holies] ...And the cherubim covered the Ark and the staves of it above. And they drew out the staves, so that the ends of the staves were seen out in the Holy *place* in front of the Holy of Holies. And they were not seen outside. And there they are to this day" (vs 6-8). *When this was written, probably by Hezekiah, this part of it!*

Verse 9: "There *was* nothing in the Ark except the two tablets of stone, which Moses put there at Horeb, when the LORD made *a covenant* with the children of Israel when they came out of the land of Egypt."

The presence of God called *the Shekinah,* which appears as a cloud was not the Holy Spirit given to the people. The Holy Spirit could not be given until after Jesus Christ came, completed His ministry, gave Himself in sacrifice and was raised from the dead.

Verse 10: "And it came to pass when the priests had come out of the Holy of Holies, **the cloud filled the house of the LORD**.... [just like with the tabernacle] ...And the priests could not stand to minister because of the cloud, for the glory of the LORD had filled the house of the LORD. And Solomon said, 'The LORD said that He would dwell in the thick darkness'" (vs 10-12).

Then Solomon goes on and gives a magnificent prayer! Quite a wonderful prayer in all of 1-Kings 8 & 9. It was so great, and Solomon's attitude was so good, which is another lesson: *we must maintain a right relationship with God through prayer and study every day!*

If we do not then it could very well be that *something like this that happened to Solomon* **could happen to you!**

Even after God spoke to Solomon in vision the second time... Remember the *ifs* that David gave to Solomon concerning being the one to build the house for God. Let's see what took place, and what a magnificent thing this is. Always remember that it's never *who you are or what you are as a person!* **It's your relationship with God and how you maintain it!**

After the temple is finished and the great prayer that he gave, it pleased God. Here's what happened:

1-Kings 9:1: "And it came to pass as Solomon finished the building of the house of the LORD, and the king's house, and all Solomon's desire which he was pleased to do, the LORD appeared to Solomon the second time, as He had appeared to him at Gibeon. And the LORD said to him, 'I have heard your prayer and your cry, which you have made before Me. I have made Holy this house which you have built to put My name there forever. And My eyes and My heart shall be there perpetually. And **if you will walk before Me as David your father walked, in integrity of heart and in uprightness,** to do according to all that I have commanded you; *and* **if you will keep My statutes and My judgments, then** I will establish the throne of your kingdom over Israel forever as I promised to David your father, saying, "There shall not be cut off from you a man upon the throne of Israel"'" (vs 1-5).

Notice how important all of these conditional statements are, because when we get to the New Testament, those are all magnified.

Verse 6: "**If** you shall at all turn from following Me, you or your children, and will not keep My commandments *and* My statutes which I have set before you, but go and serve other gods and worship them, **then** I will cut off Israel from the face of the land, which I have given them. And this house, which I have made Holy for My name, I will cast out of My sight. And Israel shall be a proverb and a byword among all people" (vs 6-7). *Just like with us; think about it!*

Verse 8: "As to this house, *which now* is exalted, *then* everyone who passes by it shall be amazed and shall hiss. And they shall say, '"Why has the LORD done this to this land and to this house?' And they shall answer, '**Because they left the LORD their God** who brought out their fathers from the land of Egypt, and have taken hold of other gods and have worshiped them and served them. On account of this the LORD has brought upon them all this evil'" (vs 8-9). *And it happened!*

We know what happened because Solomon sinned; God took away the ten northern tribes. Solomon's son Rehoboam took over the southern kingdom, which was part of Benjamin, Judah and the priests and Levites. Jeroboam—one of the generals of Solomon—took over the ten tribes of the north. God offered to give him a dynasty like David, *IF*... [same proposition as with Solomon] ...he would keep God's commandments, serve the people and do what was right, but he didn't. He made two golden calves:

1. one in Dan in the northern part of the tribes of Israel
2. one in Bethel right near the capital of Ephraim

The ten tribes were carried off into captivity because of their sins!

Then after that there was left the southern kingdom of Judah and Jeremiah was raised up as a prophet to warn them because of their sins and following the ways of the pagans again and again.

Without the Spirit of God it's virtually impossible to avoid corruption and apostasy! It got so bad that God was ready to destroy the whole city of Jerusalem in 586B.C. and the temple as well. But God gave one final chance, because God is merciful, kind and forgiving **IF** there's repentance! Know this for sure: ***no one is going to dwell with God if they don't love and obey Him!*** That's the key important thing!

King Zedekiah[transcriber's correction] of Judah at that time wanted to know what was going to happen, because there were several invasions of the Babylonians coming in and attacking the city of Jerusalem. So, God sent

Jeremiah 38:14: "And Zedekiah the king sent and had Jeremiah the prophet brought to him, into the third gate in the house of the LORD. And the king said to Jeremiah, "I will ask you a thing. Do not hide anything from me.... [here's God giving a chance]: ...Then Jeremiah said to Zedekiah, 'If I declare *it* to you, will you not surely put me to death? And if I give you advice, you will not hearken to me.' Zedekiah the king swore secretly to Jeremiah, saying, '*As* the LORD lives, Who made for us this soul, I will not put you to death, nor will I give you into the hand of these men who seek your life.' Then Jeremiah said to Zedekiah, 'Thus says the LORD, the God of hosts, the God of Israel, "**If** you will surely surrender to the king of Babylon's princes, then your soul shall live, and this city shall not be burned with fire. And you shall live, and your house"'" (vs 14-17).

So, he was to surrender as a vassal king! Nebuchadnezzar would have put him back on the throne, but subject to Nebuchadnezzar.

Now, God give him a choice; think about the choices that we're faced with, too.

Verse 18: "But if you will not surrender to the king of Babylon's princes, then this city shall be given into the hands of the Chaldeans, and they shall burn it with fire, and you shall not escape out of their hand."

What happened? Zedekiah thought he would escape and leave with his sons. So, he escaped and the Babylonians captured him and killed his sons, gouged out the eyes of Zedekiah and burned the city, sacked it and destroyed it.

Then 70 years later God raised up Ezra and Nehemiah to rebuild a temple. It was dedicated. Here's a little mystery: *no one knows where the Ark of the Covenant is!* When they came back from Babylon and dedicated the temple, they didn't have it to put into the Holy of Holies. But the temple was there. They did not have a king, they only had a governor.

That's how it went with the ups and downs through the times of the governors, and down through the times of the Maccabees and through the times until we come to Jesus Christ.

Let's look at one of the prophecies of Jesus in Deut.18. Since men could not dwell with God in the way that God would want them to, with love and obedience. And God knew that they didn't have the heart to do so, then God gave a prophecy of the coming One Who is called in the New Testament *that Prophet,* **Who was Jesus Christ!** The reason is that God came to this earth as a man.

Deuteronomy 18:15: "The LORD your God will raise up unto you a Prophet from the midst of you, of your brethren, **One like me**. To Him you shall hearken."

Moses was judge, ruler, prophet and lawgiver. That's what Jesus Christ was in the flesh when He came.

Verse 16: "According to all that you desired of the LORD your God in Horeb in the day of the assembly, saying, 'Let me not hear again the voice of the LORD my God, neither let me see this great fire any more, so that I do not die.' And the LORD said to me, 'They have spoken well what they have spoken. **I will raise them up a Prophet from among their brethren**... [flesh and blood] ...*One* **like you, and will put My words in His mouth.** And He shall speak to them all that I shall command Him'" (vs 16-18). *That's exactly what Jesus said of His ministry and what He would do!*

Verse 19: "And it shall come to pass, **whatever man will not hearken to My words,** which He shall speak in My name, I will require *it* of him." *Individual judgment against every person that goes against Christ!*

So, we know that Jesus divested Himself as being God (Phil. 2) and took upon Him the likeness of men, came to this earth, and was born of the virgin Mary.

John 1 tells us all about it. The One Who Creator God humbled Himself to become a man ***to live among men, to dwell among them,*** because men could not dwell with God! So, in His mercy, God came in the person of Jesus Christ, and John explains Who He was.

Sidebar: Every time someone brings up a false doctrine, they've got to go against the nature of God and the nature of Christ.

John 1:1: "In *the* beginning was the Word…" *What do you read with the prophets?*

- the Word of God came to Jeremiah…
- the Word of God came to Ezekiel…
- the Word of God came to Isaiah…

The Word! Some say *Spokesman,* but the manifestation of God in the flesh *to bring the Word of God to men personally!*

"…and the Word was with God, and the Word was God. He was in *the* beginning with God" (vs 1-2). *This tells us that in the Godhead there are two!*

There are never three. Guess who the third one wants to be? *That's Satan who wants to be counted into the Godhead!*

Verse 3: "All things came into being through Him, and not even one *thing* that was created came into being without Him. In Him was life, and the Life was the Light of men. And the Light shines in the darkness…" (vs 3-5)—*and darkness is what this age is all about!*

That's why the Apostle Paul said that he was called to bring people out of the darkness of Satan the devil and His authority into the Light of the Truth of the Lord God. Darkness fills the earth!

"…but the darkness does not comprehend it" (v 5).

Verse 9: "The True Light was that which enlightens everyone who comes into the world."

The birth of Jesus is very interesting. The most important birth in the history of the entire world. The Jews thought the Messiah would come and embrace them, and that they would jointly rule with the Messiah. But they didn't comprehend that He would come in the flesh.

Although they did expect a man to be the Messiah, but not Jesus. Why? *Because Jesus never embraced them religiously or politically, because He knew that they were of darkness and Satan the devil,* when they should have been light from God!

When Jesus was conceived, God sent Gabriel the angel to Mary in Nazareth, not in Jerusalem; *someone that the authorities never knew about!* The only two who knew that she became pregnant: Elizabeth, mother of John the Baptist and Joseph her husband. They came together after Jesus was born.

The prophecy was that the Messiah was to be born in Bethlehem, but this began in Nazareth. However, Jesus was born in Bethlehem because they had to come there for the tax, and that's when Jesus was born.

He was born in a stable, not some great house with a lot of attendants! He was wrapped in swaddling clothes and placed in a manger, not like the Christmas scene that Catholics and Protestants have. By time the Magi came they were in a house.

So, *no one* except Joseph and Mary—and if she had a midwife to help her—*knew that this child was born!* Only Joseph and Mary knew that this was an impregnation from God.

To show how God does things, what happened? *There were two shepherds out in the field watching the sheep!* The angels came and sang glorious things, 'glory to God in the Highest.' The told them a Son was born in Bethlehem, and 'go and you'll find a babe wrapped in swaddling clothes.' And they went and found Him, *and none of the officials*—priests, princes, Levites or governors—*knew of Jesus' birth!*

They didn't know until the Magi from the East came. Then Herod wanted to kill Him. Now you know why that Jesus came the way that He did. Then they had to escape to Egypt and later came back to Nazareth.

Verse 10: "He was in the world, and the world came into being through Him, but the world did not know Him." *The only ones who knew Him were the disciples whom He called!*

Verse 11: "He came to His own, and His own did not receive Him… [now the plan of God begins to be revealed a little more] …but as many as received Him, to them He gave authority to become *the* children of God…" (vs 11-12).

The whole purpose of the New Testament is *how you become the children of God!*

"…*even* to those who **believe** in His name" (v 12)—*believe to obey,* not only in His name but Who He is and all about Him, etc.

Now then, something happens in the New Testament that did not happen before in the Old Testament.

Verse 13: "Who… [those who believe in His name] …were not begotten by bloodlines… [not who you are, king lines or prince lines or priest lines] …nor by *the* will of *the* flesh… [not something that men do] …nor by *the* will of man, but **_by the will_ of God**."

Sidebar: In order for the plan of God to be fulfilled so that the meaning of the Feast of Tabernacles can come to the whole world, it must begin **with us and all of those who preceded us** down through history who were of the Church of God, who had the Spirit of God.

The only way that the plan of God is going to be reaching its fullness is if **we** yield ourselves to God and are resurrected from the dead, born again from flesh to spirit to rule with Christ. This is what is so important.

Now it's entirely different and the stakes are much higher.

Verse 14: "And the Word became flesh and tabernacled among us… [temporarily dwelt with men; God in the flesh] …(and we ourselves… [the apostles] …beheld His glory, *the* glory… [and they saw the Transfiguration as well] …as of *the* only begotten with *the* Father), full of grace and truth." *That's an amazing thing!*

Here now God was going to set the standard with Jesus in the flesh, Who would be the perfect sacrifice for the sins of all mankind: *past, present and future!*

Verse 16: "And of His fullness we have all received, and grace upon grace." {note message series: *Grace Upon Grace*}

I'll just summarize it for you: It means that *each one of us with the Spirit of God and a humble attitude, converted mind, yielding to God have direct access to God the Father in heaven above through His Spirit!* That's what's so important, that we:

- grow
- overcome
- develop
- have the mind of Christ
- do the things that God wants

Because that is God's plan to save the world and all of mankind, except for those who totally rebel and refuse! ***That's our calling, brethren!***

Let's see what God did to show the change after Christ was resurrected from the dead. The apostles saw Him after He was resurrected and they handled Him, saw Him, and He taught them for 40 days and 40 nights all of the things in the Law and the Prophets and the Psalms. Now the New Testament teaching and Church was ready to begin and ready to go. So, on the 40th day Jesus ascended back into heaven to sit at the right hand of God:

- to be Head over the Church
- to guide and direct things in the Church
- to prepare a *spiritual people* for God to rule the world when Christ returns

That's all about the Feast of Tabernacles.

That means that when this event occurred at the temple on Pentecost (Acts 2), God sent the Holy Spirit. He didn't send a cloud to go into the temple. He sent the Holy Spirit so that when there's repentance *it would be **within the individual!***

It was demonstrated right there. I won't go through that whole thing on that day of Pentecost and speaking the different languages, and the very powerful message that Peter gave and caused 3,000 to repent and be baptized, *on that day!*

He said that **you**—every one of us—*have crucified Him!* Isn't that something? ***Our sins killed Christ,*** and God was **willing to give His only Begotten Son** to be that *Perfect Sacrifice for us!* Now to preach and teach for the firstfruits, which is the Church.

The command was to **repent and be baptized** everyone in the name of Jesus Christ for the remission of sins and *you shall receive the gift of the Holy Spirit! That gift of the Holy Spirit is a begettal from God!* That's the important thing! *A begettal from God!* That Holy Spirit within us is to lead us and guide us, but we must yield to God because we're going to be spirit beings.

It's not a religion in the world to make you a better citizen of whatever country you live in. *It is to change you! The Spirit of God!*

This is what is also important, because this begettal comes from God to give us of the Holy Spirit in our own mind so that we are connected directly with God the Father through the power of the Holy Spirit. That is necessary.

- there is no other way that there can be the developed the character of God within us
- there is no other way that we can have the love and obedience to God without His Spirit

That's why He has done it!

Now Peter, who gave that great message there in Acts 2, let's see what he says in 1-Peter 1, and it explains it very thoroughly.

1-Peter 1:1: "Peter, an apostle of Jesus Christ, to *the* elect strangers scattered in Pontus, Galatia, Cappadocia, Asia, and Bithynia; **who have been chosen according to *the* predetermined knowledge of God *the* Father**…" (vs 1-2).

I want you to understand that! God the Father is the One Who draws us to Christ, and Christ is the One Who gives us of His Spirit along with the Father to be in our very mind! This is what we will see about God dwelling today **in** us through the Holy Spirit. That is necessary before we can become the spiritual sons and daughters of God.

"…**by sanctification**…" (v 2)—*set aside and made Holy,* and that is the character that God is developing in us, the Holy character of God!

"…**through** *the* **Spirit**… [must have the Spirit of God] …**unto obedience and sprinkling of the blood of Jesus Christ**…" (v 2)—*through His sacrifice! All of that is necessary first!*

"…Grace and peace be multiplied to you. Blessed *be* the God and Father of our Lord Jesus Christ…(vs 2-3). *Notice what you have received when you were baptized!*

"…Who, according to His abundant mercy…" (v 3).

Think about this: *the Spirit of God comes from the Father **and** Christ so that we can become the children of God!*

"…has begotten us again unto a living hope through *the* resurrection of Jesus Christ from *the* dead; unto **an inheritance incorruptible and undefiled and unfading, reserved in heaven for us**" (vs 3-4). *Christ is going to bring that when He returns!*

Now, I want you to think about this in 1-John 3, because with the Spirit of God in us, *God is dwelling in us!* I will show that in a little bit. That's what's so important! With that, we will dwell with God at the resurrection.

1-John 3:1: "Behold! What *glorious* love the Father has given to us…"

Think about that! To receive the Spirit of God is to receive the greatest blessing of His love. But we also have to remember the *IF* clauses!

- *IF* we are faithful
- *IF* we are true
- *IF* we endure

"…**that we should be called the children of God!** For this very reason, the world does not know us because it did not know Him. Beloved…" (vs 1-2).

Think on this statement and I'll show you how we got to it:

"…now we are the children of God… [not yet born] …and it has not yet been revealed what we shall be… [completely] …but we know… [and we'll know a little bit more, but when John wrote this, it wasn't] …that when He is manifested… [at His return] …**we shall be like Him, because we shall see Him exactly as He is**. And everyone who has this hope in him purifies himself, even as He is pure" (vs 2-4).

We are to practice righteousness, v 9: "Everyone who has been begotten by God **does not practice sin,** because His seed *of begettal*… [I want

you to understand that, we'll see that even more] …is dwelling within him, and he is not able to *practice* sin because he has been begotten by God. **By this** *standard* **are manifest the children of God**…" (vs 9-10).

- let's see how that comes to us
- let's see who is involved in our lives

I want you to know and understand that all of this is necessary in order for the Feast of Tabernacles to come to pass. Also, understand that God is directly involved in our lives with His Spirit.

- God the Father has drawn us
- God the Father has chosen us
- God the Father and Christ have given us of Their Spirit

Ephesians 1:2: "Grace and peace *be* to you from God our Father and *the* Lord Jesus Christ." *Directly!*

Not to a temple where there's a *presence* of God, *but from the Throne and Temple of God in heaven where God the Father is, and His Spirit given to us and God choosing us for the great role of ruling the world!* That's why we have the Feast of Tabernacles!

Verse 3: "Blessed *be* the God and Father of our Lord Jesus Christ, Who has blessed us with every spiritual blessing in the heavenly *things* with Christ"—*some now, most at the resurrection!*

I want you to understand the closeness of God in this operation with us, to you, me and all the brethren everywhere!

Verse 4: "According as He has personally chosen us… [God Himself] …for Himself…"

This was a plan before the foundation of the world! Now you understand why Satan and the angels rebelled! They would be demoted and we would be promoted.

"…before *the* foundation of *the* world **in order that we might be Holy**… [God is Holy] …and **blameless before Him in love**; having predestinated us **for sonship to Himself through Jesus Christ**, according to the good pleasure of His own will" (vs 4-5). *Isn't that something?*

Verse 9: "Having made known to us the mystery of His own will…"

You know something that the world does not know; that is through God's Spirit, Jesus Christ, the Sabbath, His laws and commandments and Holy Days. That's why it's so great what God has done!

"…according to His good pleasure, which He purposed in Himself; that in *the Divine* plan for the fulfilling of *the* times, He might bring all things together in Christ, both the things in the heavens and the things upon the earth" (vs 9-10).

Verse 13: "In Whom you also trusted after hearing the Word of the Truth, the Gospel of your salvation; in Whom also, after believing, **you were sealed with the Holy Spirit of promise**."

John 14 shows us all about God's plan, how He works with us and His Holy Spirit, which He has given to us. This becomes important and we need to understand that every time you get on your knees to God:

- *you know* that your prayers are going to God
- *you know* that God is going to hear
- *you know* that God has called you to something profound, fantastic and wonderful

To help rescue the whole world!

John 14:21: "The one who has My commandments and is keeping them, that is the one who loves Me…"—*it's all based on love!*

- we love God
- we keep His commandments
- we love Jesus Christ
- we keep His Word

"…and the one who loves Me **shall be loved by My Father**" (v 21).

Jesus Christ and God the Father—Who control the whole universe—*love us, His people, begotten with the Spirit of God the Father for sonship at the resurrection!*

"…and I will love him and will manifest Myself to him.' Judas (not Iscariot) said to him, 'Lord, what has happened that You are about to manifest Yourself to us, and not to the world?'" (vs 21-22).

This is perhaps the most important verse in the entirety of the Bible; v 23: "Jesus answered and said to him, '**If anyone loves Me**…'"

- the love of God is keeping His commandments
- the love of God is with all your heart, mind, soul and being

"…**he will keep My Word**…" (v 23)—*not just the commandments, but everything that Jesus said!*

"…and **My Father will love him,** and **We**… [the Father and the Son] …**will come to him and make Our abode**… [dwelling place] …**with him**" (v 23).

Think about that! The one who does not love

Him does not have that! That's why it's so important.

Let's see what we need to do, because this becomes very important for us in our relationship with God, *and God dwelling in us!* And for the purpose of *bringing us into the Family of God through the resurrection, so that we can save the world!*

Here's why we are not to compromise with the world, and we are not to compromise with the fake Christianity of this world, *because they believe the same lie that Satan told Eve!* Satan told Eve that what God said He really didn't mean. But Satan says:

I will tell you something else, and if you eat of the Tree of the Knowledge of Good and Evil, which He's [God] hiding from you, but will come to you if you do what I [Satan] say.

The sum of the lie of Satan was that God didn't mean what He said. If you're a Protestant out there, *listen up!* All Protestants believe that God did not mean what He said when He said, 'Remember the Sabbath Day to keep it Holy.' They say that you can keep Sunday. *That is a satanic lie! No man can change what God has said!* That's why:

- we keep the Sabbath
- we keep the Holy Days
- we love God

We have to keep ourselves unspotted from the world! Here's how we do it:

2-Corinthians 6:14: "Do not be unequally yoked with unbelievers…."

Protestants are partial believers! They fall into the category that Jesus said, 'Those who are not against us are on our part.' But they don't *believe* God to keep His Sabbath and Holy Days. Therefore, *they don't have salvation!* There's no way possible, because *unless you keep the commandments of God, you don't have the Holy Spirit of God—that's what Jesus said!*

"…For what do righteousness and lawlessness *have* in common? And **what fellowship does light *have* with darkness? And what union does Christ *have* with Belial? Or what part *does* a believer *have* with an unbeliever?** And what agreement *is there between* a Temple of God…" (vs 14-16). *WE are the Temple of God!*

1-Corinthians 3:16: "**Don't you understand that you are God's temple**…" *Just like Jesus said that 'We—God the Father and Jesus Christ—will come and make Our abode with him.' We are the temple!* Not a building where there is an essence of God in a Holy spot, but God's Holy Spirit united with the spirit of our mind that we are the children of

God.

"…and *that* the Spirit of God is dwelling in you?" (v 16).

2-Corinthians 6:16: "And what agreement *is there between* a Temple of God and idols? For you are a temple of *the* living God, exactly as God said: **'I will dwell in them and walk in *them*; and I will be their God, and they shall be My people.'"**

That's what God wants! Think about the great blessing of what it is that God has in store for us, to rule and reign with Christ and save this entire world.

Verse 17: "'Therefore, come out from the midst of them and be separate,' says *the* Lord, 'and touch not *the* unclean, and I will receive you; and **I shall be a Father to you, and you shall be My sons and daughters,' says *the* Lord Almighty"** (vs 17-18).

One more verse to tell us the work that we need to do now:

2-Corinthians 7:1: "Now then, beloved, since we have these promises, we should purge ourselves from every defilement of *the* flesh and *the* spirit…"

We have work to do to change and overcome! Remember that Jesus said, *'The one who overcomes I will give authority over the nations.'* So, we have things to overcome:

- our own human nature within us
- the things around us that come against us

"…**perfecting Holiness in *the* fear of God**" (v 1).

Rev. 20—let's see the promise given to us. This is after Satan is put away, which we saw on the Day of Atonement.

Revelation 20:4: "And I saw thrones… [of various degrees of authority]…and they that sat upon them, and judgment was given to them; and *I saw* the souls of those who had been beheaded for the testimony of Jesus…"

Yes, some of us are going to have to give our lives, but that will be annulled at the resurrection, so we don't need to fear anything.

- we don't need to fear man
- we don't need to fear death
- we don't need to fear any of those things

"…and for the Word of God, and those who did not worship the beast or his image, and did not receive the mark in their foreheads or in their hands; and **they lived and reigned with Christ a thousand years"** (v 4).

We will see the Millennium as pictured by the Feast of Tabernacles *is just the beginning of greater things into all eternity!*

Verse 5: "(But the rest of the dead did not live again until the thousand years were completed.) This *is* the first resurrection. Blessed and Holy…" (vs 5-6).

- that's how God looks upon us
- that's why we repent everyday because of whatever sins may occur in our lives

As long as we have *the law of sin and death*—and we're delivered from it through God's Spirit—we have to repent as these things take place in our lives (Rom. 7 & 8).

Verse 6: "**Blessed and Holy is the one who has part in the first resurrection…**" *That also tells us that **IF** this is the first one when Christ returns, **THEN** there has to be a second one!*

"…over **these the second death has no power**. But **they shall be priests of God and of Christ, and shall reign with Him a thousand years**" (v 6).

Brethren, that's why God has called us! The Millennium is going to be a fantastic time of conversion, greatness and bringing many sons and daughters into the Kingdom of God. We will be working with Jesus Christ to do that!

All of that is to the glory of God the Father! This is why we keep the Feast of Tabernacles! Tomorrow we will begin to see how we will rule with Christ!

Scriptural References:

1) Deuteronomy 5:25, 27-29
2) Exodus 24:1-4, 6-12
3) Exodus 25:9, 8-11
4) Exodus 31:12-18
5) Exodus 40:1-2, 31-38
6) 1 Chronicles 28:2-10
7) 1 Kings 8:1-12
8) 1 Kings 9:1-9
9) Jeremiah 38:14-18
10) Deuteronomy 18:15-19
11) John 1:1-5, 9-14, 16
12) 1 Peter 1:1-4
13) 1 John 3:1-4, 9-10
14) Ephesians 1:1-5, 9-10, 13
15) John 14:21-23
16) 2 Corinthians 6:14-16
17) 2 Corinthians 3:16
18) 2 Corinthians 6:16-18
19) 2 Corinthians 7:1
20) Revelation 20:4-6

Scriptures referenced, not quoted:

- Exodus 35; 36
- Philippians 2
- Acts 2
- Romans 7; 8

Also referenced: In-Depth Study: *Grace Upon Grace*

FRC:bo
Transcribed: 7/27/20
Reformatted: 1/2021

CHAPTER SIXTY-SEVEN

How We Will Rule with Christ

Fred R. Coulter

Greetings, brethren! As we covered, we're going to be kings and priests and we're going reign on the earth with Jesus Christ for a thousand years. *And that will just be the start!* Think on that!

So, all you future kings, priests, administrators, mayors, governors, and everything that's necessary to run the government, and to bring peace and prosperity, and love and conversion to the whole world, *the beginning task will be a little difficult!*

We'll back up just a little bit and then come down to the meaning of the Feast of Tabernacles.

Zechariah 14:2: "The Lord God says: 'For I will gather all nations to battle against Jerusalem; and the city shall be taken, and the houses plundered, and the women raped. And half of the city shall go into exile, and the rest of the people shall not be cut off from the city.' And the LORD shall go out and fight against those nations… [the Battle of Armageddon] …as when He fought in the day of battle. And His feet shall stand in that day upon the Mount of Olives…" (vs 2-4).

Think about that! Think about what a great day this is going to be! After we've been on the Sea of Glass from Pentecost to Trumpets, and learning everything we need to learn:

- get our new names
- the marriage of the Lamb takes place
- the wedding supper takes place
- we get all ready to come down with the war to truly, truly end all wars

God alone can do that!

Here's what's going to happen: the Mt. of Olives is where Jesus ascended the final time into heaven, so He's coming right back to the place that He left.

"…which *is* before Jerusalem on the east, and the Mount of Olives shall split in two, from the east and to the west…" (v 4)—*just like that!* What a thing that is going to be!

"…and make a very great valley. And half of the mountain shall move toward the north, and half of it toward the south" (v 4).

Verse 6: "And it shall come to pass in that day, that the light shall not be clear, nor dark. And it

will be one day, which shall be known to the LORD, neither day nor night; but it shall come to pass that at evening time it shall be light. And it shall be in that day…" (vs 6-8). *As soon as He puts His feet on the Mt. of Olives!*

Satan will have been put away and now begins the cleansing of the physical earth, to make it into a paradise everywhere!

Verse 8: "And it shall be in that day, that living waters shall go out from Jerusalem; half of them shall go toward the eastern sea, and half of them toward the western sea. In summer and in winter it shall be." *Think of going out to start cleaning up*:

- all the destruction
- all the upheavals
- all the death

Verse 9: "And the LORD shall be King over all the earth; in that day there shall be one LORD, and His name shall be one."

What is the first thing that Jesus and the saints are going to do? *Let's see how that's going to work out!* That's going to be quite a day. We're going to be so busy we're going to be learning how:

- to rule
- to serve
- to love
- to heal

And we will be able to do great miracles and to restore the people!

It's going to be something, indeed! It's going to be so great and marvelous that's it's really beyond what we can comprehend now, *but as spirit beings!* Just think what that's going to be; we're going to help:

- the wounded
- the dismembered
- the children
- the little infants
- the old men and women

They're all going to be in a state of shell-shock that will be so traumatic that it's going to be quite a thing to heal them. Here's how it's going to be:

Psalm 45:1: "My heart overflows with a goodly matter..."—*the Truth of the Millennium and the rule of God on the earth that we're going to bring to the world!*

"...I speak of my works to the King; my tongue is the pen of a ready writer. You are more excellent than the children of men; grace is poured upon Your lips; therefore, **God has blessed You forever**" (vs 1-2)—*this is Christ as King!*

- beautiful
- marvelous
- wonderful
- Holy
- gracious
- kind

Verse 3: "Gird Your sword upon Your thigh, O Mighty One, with Your glory and Your majesty. And ride victoriously in Your majesty in behalf of Truth..." (vs 3-4)—*because Satan will be bound!*

- the Truth of proper of government
- the Truth of the Word of God
- the Truth of the plan of God that He's going to work our during the Millennium and beyond

"...and meekness and righteousness..." (v 4).

Just think of this: We're going to establish a society that will be so great that it is going *obliterate* all the knowledge of the kingdoms before it, because all they ever did was fight and war!

"...and let Your right hand teach You awesome things" (v 4).

- Aren't we going to have awesome things to teach and do, and to help the brethren to understand that?
- Help all of those coming out of captivity and so forth?

Verse 5: "Your arrows are sharp in the heart of the King's enemies, whereby the people fall under You. **Your throne, O God, is forever and ever; a scepter of justice is the scepter of Your Kingdom**" (vs 5-6).

Here's how we're going to administer the Government of God.

Sidebar: The ministry was never intended to be the Government of God. There is a governance within the Church to serve and to help, *but not to rule over!*

Here we will serve and help as well as rule over in:

- kindness
- righteousness
- goodness

The way that God wants!

Verse 7: "You love righteousness and hate wickedness; **therefore, God, Your God, has anointed You with the oil of gladness above Your fellows**."

This is going to how it's going to be in the whole world:

Psalm 46:1: "God is our refuge and strength, a very present help in trouble." *Our first mission is to end all the trouble!*

Verse 2: "Therefore, we will not fear, though the earth should change and though the mountains be carried into the midst of the sea, though its waters roar and foam, though the mountains shake with the swelling of it. Selah. There is a river whose streams... [we've talked about *living waters* coming out from Jerusalem (Zech. 14)] ...**make the City of God rejoice, the Holy dwelling place of the Most High**" (vs 2-4).

Eventually that's where it's going to be, because the Millennium is a transition to the Last Great Day, which is a transition to New Jerusalem. It all flows from one to the other. "...**the Holy dwelling place of the Most High**" will be in New Jerusalem.

Verse 5: "God is in the midst of her; she shall not be moved; God shall help her at the approach of the morning." *That's quite a thing, God intervening to do all of those things!*

Verse 7: "The LORD of hosts is with us; the God of Jacob is our refuge. Selah. Come, behold the works of the LORD who makes desolations upon the earth, Who makes wars to cease to the ends of the earth" (vs 7-9). *That's the first mission; disarm the whole world!*

Today, we need arms and ammunitions because of war, because God is going to end all wars!

"...He breaks the bow and cuts the spear in two; He burns the chariots in the fire. 'Be still, and **know that I am God!**....'" (vs 9-10).

That's what we're going to teach; *God rules in Jerusalem,* and what a council He is going to have with all of the ancient patriarchs right there! That's going to be quite a thing, indeed!

"'...I will be exalted among the nations, I will be exalted in the earth.' The LORD of hosts is with us; the God of Jacob is our refuge. Selah" (vs 10-11).

How is the world going respond to that? Just think of it:

- no more wars
- no more killing
- no more attacks
- no more shootings
- no more stabbings
- no more rapes
- no more killing of children

But *peace!* And we're the ones who are going to bring it!

I want you to think on that, because there are going to be times in the future when we will get down and depressed because of the difficulties that we are going to face. Jesus said that are going to be the worst difficulties since the creation of the world. *We need the strength of God to endure through that!*

Here is how the world is going to react. This is something!

Psalm 47:1: "Clap your hands, all you people; shout to God with the voice of triumph, for the LORD Most High is awesome; He is a great King over all the earth" (vs 1-2). *He has not yet come to the earth, but Christ is the King under Him!* They work together hand in glove.

Verse 3: "He shall subdue the people under us and nations under our feet. He shall choose our inheritance for us, the excellency of Jacob whom He loved. Selah" (vs 3-4).

Remember, in Rom. 8 it says that *we're going to be joint heirs with Christ!* Today we have something between husband and wife in ownership of property. Join tenants or joint heirs, meaning that the property belongs to both of them. When we are co-inheritors with Christ, that means that *we have a part ownership in the actual Kingdom of God!* Let that encourage you above everything.

All the pain and difficulty we go through is going to be worth every second of it, because of the joy and gladness of being able to administer the Kingdom of God to the people of the world; to bring it back to the greatest productivity that has ever been.

Verse 3: "He shall subdue the people under us and nations under our feet. He shall choose our inheritance for us, the excellency of Jacob whom He loved. Selah. God has gone up with a shout, the LORD with the sound of a horn. Sing praises to God, sing praises; sing praises to our King, sing praises" (vs 3-6).

That's going to be a good thing! Instead of fighting and warring each other, we're going to be singing praises to God. God is going to pouring down His Spirit upon all people, and upon us. As

spirit being—which we're going to be—is going to be an amazing thing!

Verse 7: "For God is King of all the earth; sing praises with understanding."

Won't that be something? Imagine what it's going to be like. We're going to be in different places in the world, and every once in a while we're going to be back in Jerusalem and we're going to see what kind of tabernacle that is going to be there, because there's not going to be any temple.

Verse 8: "God reigns over the nations; God sits upon the throne of His Holiness. The rulers of the peoples are gathered together, the people of the God of Abraham for the shields of the earth are God's; He is greatly exalted" (vs 8-9).

What is it going to be like as a spirit being to periodically go to Jerusalem and to be there with Christ and taught by Him, and whomever else: Abraham, Noah, Abel, all of the great patriarchs, Isaac, Jacob, the 12 apostles, the Apostle Paul… They will be all gathered! Imagine what it's going to be like when Christ comes in to sit down on His Throne where we're gathered to meet with Him, and we all stand to honor Him!

Then we have the greatest songfest ever in the entirety of the history of the world, praises to Christ and to God!

Now let's see the business that needs to be done. As we saw, He's going to end wars. How is that going to happen? We know that in Zech. 14 that it tells us very clearly that the nations are going to keep the Feast of Tabernacles. And if they don't keep the Feast of Tabernacles, there will be plagues or drought. *They will learn!*

Some nations are going to be very difficult to bring to a peaceful conclusion. Let's read about the main mission of ending the wars, the fightings and getting rid of the armaments at the beginning of the Millennium. Isaiah is a marvelous, marvelous book! It has:

- prophecies of the Kingdom
- prophecies of Jesus
- prophecies of Israel
- prophecies of Judah
- prophecies of the Gentile nations
- prophecies concerning Satan
- prophecies concerning Babylon the Great
- prophecies concerning how the Millennium is going to be run
- prophecies concerning the wealth that will be there

Think about the Jews not having the New Testament or knowing that it's going to be a whole spiritual entourage of people who are sons and daughters of God—running the world—ruling, reigning and teaching the people the Truth of God and the love of God. That's what we find in the New Testament!

Isaiah 2:1: "The word that Isaiah the son of Amoz saw concerning Judah and Jerusalem."

That's interesting because Isa. 1 talks about the current corruption of Israel at that time, which is also a type of the future corruption of Israel down through history. God has always pleaded with His people to repent and come to Him.

Isa. 2 suddenly shifts to a scene encompassing the whole world and God as Ruler!

Verse 2: "And it shall come to pass, in the last days **the mountain of the LORD'S house**…"—*mountain* mans government. The Mt. of Olives shall be split in two and raised to be a great mountain. "…shall be established in the top of the mountains…" *Nothing is going to be greater than that!*

"…and shall be exalted above the hills; and all nations shall flow into it" (v 2). *They're all coming to learn*:

- the way of God
- the Law of God
- the commandments of God
- the Truth of God
- the love of God
- the mercy of God
- the graciousness of God
- the power of God

Do not go out and sin!

Verse 3: "And many people shall go and say, 'Come, and let us go up to the mountain of the LORD, to the house of the God of Jacob. **And He will teach us of His ways, and we will walk in His paths.'**…"—*instead of Satan's path; instead of their own way!* And one thing that will be for sure is what Jeremiah says:

Jeremiah 10:23: "O LORD, I know that the way of man is not in himself; *it is* not in man who walks to direct his steps." *So, there will be proper education so that everything will be carried out right and good!*

Isaiah 2:3: "…For out of Zion shall go forth the Law, and the Word of the LORD from Jerusalem."

- *one Law* for the whole world
- *one Way* for everyone

Think of how the cities will be—the villages and cities—*everyone*:

- loving God
- keeping His commandments
- keeping His Sabbaths
  - ✓ no idols
  - ✓ no blaspheming
  - ✓ honoring father and mother
    - all children loving their fathers and mothers
    - all fathers and mothers loving their children

Think about what that's going to be like! They can look forward to the next generation; it's going to be a marvelous thing, indeed! The Millennium is going to be the greatest thing that has ever happened to the earth.

1. Stopping War

Verse 4: "And He shall judge among the nations, and shall rebuke many people… [because some will not be willing at first] …and **they shall**… [this will be the order of the day] …beat their swords into plowshares, and their spears into pruning hooks…."

Look at all the metal, iron, steel, aluminum and titanium that's used in all of the weapons **that men make!** All they do is either:

- recovering from war
- preparing for war
- at war
- winning a war
- losing a war
- a big battle
- a small battle

Now you're going to have to shape up and do what God says! And He will rebuke them!

I covered this last year, so I'm not going to do it again, but a little sidebar on China and all the nations of the East:

They were the mainstay of the armies of 200-million that many of them came to Jerusalem and fought in the Battle of Armageddon and all were killed. Many of the those armies retreated back to China and they are not going to submit for the first seven years (Ezek. 38 & 39).

They're going to come and try to conquer Jerusalem and fight against Christ, and that will be the last war!

And it says there in Ezek. 38 & 39 that when that happens, the nations shall know that the LORD is God!

"…**Nation shall not lift up sword against nation, neither shall they learn war anymore**" (v 4).

God doesn't tell us much about the tabernacle that He's going to establish in Jerusalem; it won't be a temple, we won't need a temple. It's going to be a spectacular tabernacle: *tabernacling with God and God tabernacling with men!* That's what this will be!

Isaiah 4:5: "And the LORD will create over every dwelling place of Mount Zion…"—*the whole area around Jerusalem,* the Mt. of Olives and those mountains around there.

"…and over her assemblies…" (v 5). *There will be many meeting places that will be there*; there will be a lot going on at Jerusalem, because everything is going to emanate out of Jerusalem.

"…a cloud and smoke by day…" (v 5). **Where did we have that before?** *The Exodus!* God's presence was always there and was known by the cloud and the fire!

"…and the shining of a flaming fire by night; for over all the glory *shall be* a canopy" (v 5)—*a great canopy covering Jerusalem!* Everything associated with what is necessary for ruling the world! Isn't that going to be a wonderful thing, indeed?

Verse 6: "And **there shall be a tabernacle**… [no temple] …for shade by day from the heat, and for refuge, and for shelter from storm and rain." *So, there will still be storms and rain!*

It's quite a thing what God is going to do! It's interesting that in Isaiah and the Psalms *there are more Scripture references to*:

- the Millennium
- the Kingdom of God
- the rule of God
- the spiritual children of God

than anyplace else in the Bible!

The people will hear, as well as have proper fear. If you don't have proper fear you can't have proper love, because you need the inward desire to love God with all your heart, mind, soul and being, and *the right fear* to not transgress and break the laws and commandments of God. Those go together.

Psalm 48:1: "Great is the LORD, and highly to be praised in the city of our God, in His Holy mountain. Beautiful in its loftiness…" (v 1-2).

Think what that's going to be like with God, the Architect and Builder of this tabernacle in Jerusalem. That's a precursor to New Jerusalem.

"…the joy of all the earth is Mount Zion on the sides of the north, the city of the great King" (v 2).

Think about it today, it is the most contentious place on the face of the earth! Everybody fighting and quarreling, killing, rocketing, shooting, stabbing and blowing up! It won't be that anymore!

Verse 3: "God in her palace has shown Himself to be a fortress, for lo, the kings assembled themselves; they advanced together" (vs 3-4). *All going to come to God!*

What is that going to be like? I imagine, brethren, that when the Millennium begins, God is going to expand the meaning of every Holy Day with remembrance looking back, with current things going on, with future things yet to take place. All of this in the Millennium is *a start of forever* from that time forward.

Verse 5[transcriber's correction]: "As we have heard, so we have seen in the city of the LORD of hosts, in the city of our God. God will establish it forever. Selah. We have thought of Your loving kindness, O God, in the midst of Your temple…. [now a tabernacle] …As is Your name, O God, so is Your praise to the ends of the earth. **Your right hand is full of righteousness**" (vs 5-10).

Just think about bringing righteousness to the whole world!

Verse 11: "Let Mount Zion rejoice! Let the daughters of Judah shout for joy because of Your judgments! Walk around Zion, and go all around her; count her towers; consider her ramparts, go through her palaces, so that you may tell it to the coming generation… [what a magnificent thing that is] …for this God is our God forever and ever; He will guide us even unto death" (vs 11-14)—*or end of life!*

Psalm 49:1: "Hear this, all you people; give ear, all inhabitants of the world: both low and high, rich and poor together. My mouth shall speak of wisdom, and the thoughts of my heart shall be of understanding. I will incline my ear to a parable; I will open my dark saying upon the lyre" (vs 1-4).

You talk about songs and singing! I think we haven't seen anything like what it's going to be during the Millennium.

So, the first order of business is stopping wars. The next order of business is:

2. **Bringing back the children of Israel from captivity**

They will be in captivity in many nations of the world. Let's see what God is going to do. Remember, *God still loves Israel*:

Jeremiah 30:17: "'For I will give health back to you, and will heal you of your wounds,' says the LORD; 'because they called you an outcast, *saying*, "This is Zion; no one cares for her.'" Thus says the LORD, 'Behold, **I turn back the captivity of Jacob's tents,** and will have mercy on his dwelling places. And the city shall be built on her ruins, and the palace shall remain in its own place'" (vs 17-18). *Think about all the healing that's going to take place!*

Verse 19: "And out of them shall come thanksgiving, and the voice of those who rejoice. And I will multiply them, and they shall not be few; I will also honor them, and they shall not be disdained." *Complete change of everything!*

Verse 20: "Also, their children shall be as they were before, and their congregation shall be established before Me, and I will punish all who oppress them." *That's how He gets them out of captivity!*

Verse 21: "'And their ruler shall be of themselves, and their governor shall come from among them; and I will cause him to draw near, and he shall approach Me. For who *is* this who pledged his heart to come near to Me?' says the LORD...."—*showing that conversion is going to come to all the children of Israel!*

Notice what's going to be changed to a great and marvelous thing; v 22: **"And you shall be My people, and I will be your God.** Behold, the whirlwind of the LORD'S wrath goes forth, a sweeping whirlwind; it shall whirl on the head of the wicked." (vs 22-23). *Get rid of them; all of those who were holding Israel and Judah captive!*

Verse 24: "The fierce anger of the LORD shall not return until He has done *it*, and until He has fulfilled the purposes of His heart. In the latter days you shall understand it." *Quite a prophecy there!*

Let's see the great things that God is going to do to setup the Millennium and establish it. What a time that's going to be. Always keep in mind that we have been promised a part:

- in rulership
- in priesthood
- in teaching
- in government

to help Christ rule the world during the Millennium! Just think how many people will be brought to salvation at that time. We'll talk about that in just a bit.

Jeremiah 31:1: "'At that time,' says the LORD, 'I will be the God of all the families of Israel, and they shall be My people.' Thus says the LORD, 'The people *who were* left of the sword found grace in the wilderness; even Israel, when I will go to give him rest'" (vs 1-2) *That's what the Millennium is:*

- rest from sin
- rest from war
- peace
- love
- harmony
- goodness
- truth
- righteousness

All the joyous and great things of God!

Verse 3: "The LORD has appeared to me from afar, *saying*, 'Yea, **I have loved you with an everlasting love**...'"

The love of God will be poured out upon Israel and the people of the world, and they will love Him back! That's what God wanted all along! But it has to be by free moral agency, that we choose to do so! This will give them the format to do it.

"...therefore, with loving kindness I have drawn you. Again, I will build you, and you shall be built, O virgin of Israel. You shall again put on your drums, and shall go forth in the dances of those who rejoice" (vs 3-4).

This is going to be quite a thing, brethren! We have never ever *ever ever* even had anything close to resembling what God says it's going to be during the Millennium.

Verse 5: "You shall yet plant vines on the mountains of Samaria; the planters shall plant, and shall eat *them* as common things. For there shall be a day *that* the watchmen on Mount Ephraim shall cry, 'Arise and let us go up to Zion to the LORD our God!'" (vs 5-6).

So, there will be various people who will go up from time to time, as well as all the sons and daughters of God in the spiritual family. Think about what a time that's going to be!

Verse 7: "For thus says the LORD, 'Sing with gladness for Jacob, and shout among the chief of the nations. Cry out, give praise and say, 'O LORD, save Your people, the remnant of Israel.'" *That's what God is going to do! What a time that will be!*

If you think that the coming back out of WWII was a fantastic thing, this is going to be absolutely marvelous and pale it into comparison.

Verse 8: "Behold, I will bring them from the north country and gather them from the corners of the earth, and with *them* the blind and the lame, the woman with child and she who is in labor with child, together; a great company shall return there.... [notice they're coming and repenting]: ...They shall come with weeping, and with prayers..." (vs 8-9)—

weeping with joy that it is over!

- no more pain
- no more sorrow

"…I will lead them. I will cause them to walk by the rivers of waters in a straight way; they shall not stumble in it, for I am a Father to Israel, and Ephraim *is* My firstborn" (v 9). *Think how joyous that is going to be!*

Verse 10: "Hear the Word of the LORD, O nations, and declare *it* in the isles afar off. And say, 'He who scattered Israel will gather him and keep him, as a shepherd *keeps* his flock.' For the LORD has redeemed Jacob, and ransomed him from the hand of the one stronger than he. 'Therefore, they shall come and sing in the height of Zion, and shall flow together to the goodness of the LORD, for wheat, and for wine, and for oil, and for the young of the flock and the herd. And their soul shall be as a watered garden; and they shall not pine away anymore at all'" (vs 10-12).

Think about that! This is what all mankind really wants, isn't it? Isn't it something that it has to be brought the way that it is? But now you understand the power of Satan in this world *to kill, destroy, maim, lie, cheat, and all of the evil things that take place!* Here will be happiness and joy, goodness, gladness, love, obedience, and all of those good things.

Verse 13: "Then shall the virgin rejoice in the dance, both young men and old together; for I will turn their mourning into joy, and will comfort them and make them rejoice from their affliction."

3. **What's going to happen with us?**

We're going to share in this, v 14: "'And I will fill the soul of the priests with fatness… [great abundance] …and My people shall be satisfied with My goodness,' says the LORD." *Think how great that is going to be!*

That doesn't mean that we're going to rule with an iron fist. There may be times if someone is so rebellious that we have to really get stern with them, and we'll see that later on there will be even some people who will rebel. But here at the beginning of the Millennium and down on into it, there nothing but joy, happiness and goodness.

All of this has been prophesied and put in the Scripture for us to know what God is going to do. His plan is so marvelous! Many of you have seen the television show *Water's World* where he takes his microphone and camera and goes out and asks people: What you think? Who is this? Who is that? Who is the first President? *and so forth!* If you did that today, and went to those people and say:

- Do you believe there's a God?' *Many will say yes!*
- Can you tell me what He's doing?' *Very few will even know!*
- Can you tell me what's going to happen when Jesus returns? *I don't think that mainstream Christianity has a clue!*

Unless you keep the Sabbath, Holy Days and Feasts of God, you don't know! That's how God has hidden it! The only way to understand is with love and obedience to God in keeping His Sabbath, Feasts and Holy Days.

Verse 20: "'*Is* Ephraim My dear son? *Is he* a delightful child? For as often as I spoke against him, I earnestly remember him still. Therefore, My heart yearns for him; I will surely have mercy on him,' says the LORD. 'Set up way marks, make sign posts for yourself. Set your heart toward the highway, even the way that you went. Return again, O virgin of Israel, **return to these your cities**'" (vs 20-21).

We're going to see that they're going to go back and they're all in desolation. They going to have to rebuild them; we'll see that tomorrow.

Verse 22: "How long will you go to and fro, O faithless daughter? For the LORD has created a new thing in the land; a woman shall court a man." Why? *Because there will be few men!*

After every war there are more women; watch that when you see the repair of Germany after WWII. All the women were out there getting the bricks, scraping them and cleaning them and passing the buckets of bricks, etc.

Verse 23: "Thus says the LORD of hosts, the God of Israel, 'Again they shall speak this word in the land of Judah and in its cities, when I shall bring them back from their captivity: "The LORD bless you, O habitation of righteousness *and* mountain of Holiness."'"

That's going to be something! Blessings flowing like we can't even imagine here today!

Verse 24: "And farmers, and those going forth with flocks, shall dwell in Judah itself, and in all the cities of it together. For I have satiated the weary soul, and I have replenished every sorrowful soul" (vs 24-25). *That's what God is going to do!*

We will be the agents to comfort every one of them. That's why God has called us, and why we go through the difficulties and problems that we do. We will have the value of redemption and consolation, and bringing them back and restoring joy to them. We will be the ones to do it, brethren! *Think of that!* That's why we have to be spirit beings.

Verse 26—*Jeremiah says:* "On this I awoke and looked up; and my sleep was sweet to me."

One of the moments in the life of Jeremiah, who had to bring such a sorrowful, doleful destructive message to the people of Israel and Judah!

Verse 27: "'Behold, the days come,' says the LORD, 'that I will sow the house of Israel and the house of Judah with the seed of man and with the seed of animal. And it shall come to pass, as I have watched over them to pluck up, and to break down, and to throw down, and to destroy, and to afflict; so I will watch over them to build and to plant,' says the LORD." (vs 27-28).

Verse 31: "'Behold, **the days come,**' says the LORD, 'that **I will make a New Covenant with the house of Israel, and with the house of Judah,** not according to the covenant that I made with their fathers in the day I took them by the hand to bring them out of the land of Egypt; which covenant of Mine they broke, although I was a husband to them,' says the LORD; 'but this *shall be* the covenant that I will make with the house of Israel: After those days,' says the LORD…" (vs 31-33).

Just like with us today! This is what brings *peace, love, joy, wisdom and understanding!*

"…'**I will put My Law in their inward parts**…'" (v 33).

That's why God gave us a brain/mind and the spirit of man, and He gives the Holy Spirit to us. This is the purpose for what our minds were created for. Think about how fulfilling it's going to be for them:

- no Satan
- no evil
- no more destruction
- no more killing
- no more lying
- no more adultery
- no more false gods and images

What a day that's going to be!

"'…and write it in their hearts; and I will be their God, and they shall be My people. And they shall no more teach each man his neighbor and each man his brother, saying, "Know the LORD"; for they shall all know Me, from the least of them to the greatest of them,' says the LORD. 'For **I will forgive their iniquity, and I will remember their sins no more**' (vs 33-34).

Verse 35: "Thus says the LORD, who gives the sun for a light by day and the ordinances of the moon and of the stars for a light by night, who stirs up the sea when its waves roar; (the LORD of hosts

is His name), 'If those ordinances depart from Me,' says the LORD… [which they won't, *never*] …'the seed of Israel also shall cease from being a nation before Me forever'" (vs 35-36). ***What guarantee! That's something!***

Now let's see what God is going to do, because human nature the way it is today is desperately evil and wicked above all things.

When there is that change, conversion and the release from all the troubles, and the overflowing of joy, love, kindness, repair, goodness and healing, it's going to be quite a thing! Then they will understand how bad it was, how bad that they got that they had to be carried off into captivity by their enemies.

Ezekiel 36:24: "For I will take you from among the nations and gather you out of all countries, and will gather you into your own land. And I will sprinkle clean waters upon you, and you shall be clean. I will cleanse you from all your filthiness… [spiritually speaking] …and from your idols. And I will give you a new heart, and I will put a new spirit within you…." (vs 24-26).

What a wonderful thing that is, they're going to be given the Holy Spirit of God, and human nature is going to be far less violent, evil and deceptive!

"…And I will take away the stony heart out of your flesh, and I will give you a heart of flesh. And I will put My Spirit within you…" (vs 26-27). *It's going to be great!*

Brethren, this is our job, what we're going to do! Just think of how much more is going to be written about God and the Word of God. Listen! The Bible that we have today is going to be a very small part of that, the beginning foundation of it. Think about what it's going to be *when the world is overflowing*:

- with the knowledge of God
- with the Truth of God
- with the love of God

All men, women and children—young and old—and all the animals of the world, the birds and everything like that. It is going to be so fantastic and glorious that it is just mind-boggling.

Verse 27: "And I will put My Spirit within you and cause you to walk in My statutes, and you shall keep My ordinances and do *them*. And you shall dwell in the land that I gave to your fathers. And **you shall be My people, and I will be your God**. I will also save you from all your uncleannesses, and I will call for the grain, and will increase it, and will lay no famine upon you. And I will multiply the fruits of the tree and the increase of the field, so that you shall never again receive the curse of famine among the nations" (vs 27-30).

When all of that transpires and they see all the goodness that God is doing for them, to bring them all of this greatness at the beginning of the Millennium—and it's going to go out to the whole world—to all nations, all people wherever they are. Think of that! Here's going to be their response:

Verse 31: "And **you shall remember your own evil ways, and your doings that** *were* **not good, and shall loathe yourselves in your own sight for your iniquities and for your abominations**."

They will understand how evil and treacherous they were, *and how merciful and gracious that God is!* Brethren, *we are the ones who will administer that*:

- to teach them
- to help them
- to guide them
- to direct them
- to always keep them pointing toward God

Verse 32: "I do not do *this* for your sake,' says the Lord GOD, 'be it known to you. Be ashamed and confounded for your ways, O house of Israel.' Thus says the Lord GOD, 'In the day that I cleanse you from all your iniquities, I will also cause *you* to dwell in the cities, and the waste *places* shall be rebuilt. And the wasteland shall be tilled, instead of being desolate before all who pass by. And they shall say, "This land that was desolate **has become like the Garden of Eden**.... [the whole world] ...And the wasted, desolate and ruined cities now *are* fenced and inhabited." And the nations that are left all around you shall know that **I the LORD build the ruined** *places and* **planted that which was desolate. I the LORD have spoken it, and I will do it**'" (vs 32-36).

It will get done, because it will be delegated to us to accomplish it. This is our mission statement as to how we're going to operate as sons and daughters of God as kings, priests, administrators, governors, mayors councils, etc. This is what we're going to do; all of it will go to God.

It will always be true, and it doesn't matter what time in the history of mankind, this is always true: *God created us, all nations of one blood, and made us and created us in such a way* **that in Him** *always*—whether we know it or not, converted or not—but much more so when we are converted:

- *we live,* because we have life and His Spirit, and He created the world for us to live in
- *we move,* everything about how He made

us:
- ✓ how we act
- ✓ how we walk
- ✓ how we talk
- ✓ how we sit
- ✓ how we think
- *have our being* in Him

Every human being on earth!

Think about what it's going to be like when it's all done properly, *when it's all done with the love of God!*

Verse 37: "Thus says the Lord GOD, 'I will yet be sought by the house of Israel to act for them. I will increase them with men like a flock. As a Holy flock, as the flock of Jerusalem **in her appointed Feasts**... [that's how we understand the plan of God, by His appointed Feasts] ...so shall the waste cities be filled with flocks of men. **And they shall know that I** *am* **the LORD**'" (vs 37-38). *That's a marvelous thing indeed!*

Ezekiel 37:21: "And say to them, "Thus says the Lord GOD, 'Behold, I will take the children of Israel from among the nations where they have gone, and will gather them on every side, and will bring them into their own land.'"

Now let's see what else God is going to do; v 22: "And I will make them one nation in the land on the mountains of Israel, and one king shall be king over them all. And they shall no longer be two nations, nor shall they be divided into two kingdoms any more at all. Nor shall they be defiled with their idols, nor with their detestable things, nor with all of their transgressions. But I will save them out of all their dwelling places, wherein they have sinned, and will cleanse them. And they shall be to Me for a people, **and I will be their God**" (vs 22-23).

Now notice a promise given to David way back when he was king of Israel, where God told David that he would be king forever over Israel. Here is, right here:

Verse 24: "And David My servant *shall be* king over them...." *Christ will be over all of those*; it's going to be a marvelous setup indeed!

"...And there shall be one shepherd to all of them. And they shall walk in My ordinances and obey My laws, and do them. And they shall dwell in the land that I have given to Jacob My servant, the land in which your fathers have dwelt. And they shall dwell in it, even they and their children, and their children's children forever. **And My servant David** *shall be* **their ruler forever**" (vs 24-25). *That means that he's a spirit being!*

Verse 26: "Moreover, I will make a covenant of peace with them. It shall be an everlasting covenant with them. And I will place them, and multiply them, and will set My sanctuary in their midst forever. And **My tabernacle** shall be with them. Yea, I will be their God, and they shall be My people. And the nations shall know that I the LORD do sanctify Israel, when My sanctuary shall be in their midst forever" (vs 26-28). *Just like we saw in Isa. 4; that's quite a thing!*

Let's see that this is going to be in all the world everywhere. If we can just keep in mind that God has selected us to:

- give us of His Spirit
- to teach us
- to train us
- to give us of His Word

So, that we can participate in bringing about the greatest thing that God is going to do on this earth with people in the Millennium with everything that's going to be for the whole world!

Psalm 96:1: "O sing to the LORD a new song; sing to the LORD, **all** the earth. Sing to the LORD, bless His name; proclaim His salvation from day to day. Declare His glory among the nations, His wonders among all people" (vs 1-3). *What a thing that's going to be!*

How much of this can we really grasp? *As much as we can!* This is one of those things that we have to go over and over to really learn. God's Word is like this: *the more we go over it and the more we study it with different things of the Scriptures and put it together, the more we understand!*

Verse 4: "For the LORD is great, and greatly to be praised; **He is to be feared** above all gods for all the gods of the nations are idols; but the LORD made the heavens. Honor and majesty are before Him; strength and beauty are in His sanctuary…. [I wonder what that's going to be like?] …Ascribe to the LORD, O you kindreds of the people; give to the LORD glory and strength. Ascribe to the LORD the glory due to His name; bring an offering and come into His courts. O worship the LORD **in the beauty of Holiness**…" (vs 4-9).

What is that going to be like? *All the spiritual sons and daughters of God coming into Jerusalem to worship God!* All of us together to worship Him in "…**the beauty of Holiness**…" *because we're the spirit sons and daughters of God!*

"…tremble before Him, all the earth. Say among the nations, 'The LORD reigns, and the world shall be established; it shall not be moved; He shall judge the people with righteousness.' Let the heavens rejoice… [I don't know how that's going to

be] …and let the earth be glad; let the sea roar, and the fullness of it. Let the field be joyful, and all that is in it; then shall all the trees of the forest sing for joy before the LORD; for He comes, for He comes to judge the earth; **He shall judge the world with righteousness and the people with His Truth**" (vs 9-13).

This is what the Millennium is all about. Quite a marvelous and wonderful thing for us to grasp and understand.

- *This is our calling!*
- *This is our goal!*

Just as God gave to Adam and Eve and all human beings—the whole world—He is giving to us the responsibility to carry out and fulfill everything that we have been reading and studying today for joy, gladness in everything!

Psalm 97:1: "The LORD reigns; let the earth rejoice… [everything in the earth] …let the multitude of islands be glad. Clouds and darkness are all around Him; **righteousness and justice are the foundation of His Throne**" (vs 1-2). *From a God of truth and love*:

- Who cannot lie
- Who cannot sin
- Who is righteous in everything

Verse 3: "A fire goes before Him and burns up His enemies round about. His lightnings light up the world; the earth saw and trembled. The mountains melted like wax at the presence of the LORD, at the presence of the Lord of the whole earth. **The heavens declare His righteousness, and all the people see His glory**" (vs 3-6) *What a thing that is, brethren!*

Psa. 100—one of the most glorious little Psalm in the book of Psalms.

Psalm 100:1: "Shout for joy to the LORD, all the earth. Serve the LORD with gladness; come before His presence with singing. **Know that the LORD, He is God**. He has made us, and we are His; we are His people and the sheep of His pasture. Enter into His gates with thanksgiving and into His courts with praise; give thanks unto Him and bless His name, **for the LORD is good; His steadfast love is everlasting; and His faithfulness endures to all generations**" (vs 1-8)—*throughout the whole of the Millennium and on into the ages of eternity! Amen!*

Scriptural References:

1) Zechariah 14:2-4, 6-9
2) Psalm 45:1-8

3) Psalm 46:1-5, 7-11
4) Psalm 47:1-9
5) Isaiah 2:1-3
6) Jeremiah 10:23
7) Isaiah 2:3-4
8) Isaiah 4:5-6
9) Psalm 48:1-14
10) Psalm 49:1-4
11) Jeremiah 30:17-24
12) Jeremiah 31:1-14, 20-28, 31-36
13) Ezekiel 36:24-38
14) Ezekiel 37:21-28
15) Psalm 96:1-13
16) Psalm 97:1-6
17) Psalm 100:1-8

Scriptures referenced, not quoted:

- Romans 8
- Isaiah 1
- Ezekiel 38; 39

FRC:bo
Transcribed: 8/2/20
Reformatted: 1/2021

CHAPTER SIXTY-EIGHT

What We Will Be Doing as Kings and Priests I
We're Going to be Teachers!
Fred R. Coulter

Greetings, brethren! I hope you're having a good Feast, that it got off to a good start and that everything is going well for you.

This is the most exciting thing: *understanding about what we are going to do in the Millennium.* We ended up yesterday seeing that we will be kings and priests and we are going to reign with Christ. The question is, what will we do for a whole thousand years?

This is going to be a time of great salvation. This will be the time of the great harvest. This will be the time when there will be the 'restitution of all things.' As God said to Israel, He will 'take away the heart of stone and give them a heart of flesh.' Human nature will not have the degree of evil, carnality and violence that we have today.

- *It has to start with God!*
- *It has to start with Christ!*

This is why Jesus did what He did. Let's see the prophecy about Jesus, and in Isa. 9. It encapsulates His whole life, His whole purpose, and the things on into eternity.

We know that God has given the Bible to understand: 'line upon line; here a little, there a little; precept upon precept.' We're also told we have to 'rightly divide the Word of Truth and put it together. When we do that, we learn from God and learn from His Word what it is that God wants us to do.

This is the fantastic, phenomenal thing that God has done, because Jesus—Who was the Word and *with* God and *was* God—became flesh by divesting Himself of His glory and power to become a pinpoint of life, and then be born of the virgin Mary, and to live a life in the flesh perfectly *without ever sinning!* Then furthermore, *to lay down His life willingly to die for the sins of all mankind!* It had to take God manifested in the flesh to be that kind of sacrifice. Here's a prophecy of it:

Isaiah 9:6: "For unto us a child is born, unto us a son is given; and the government shall be upon His shoulders…"

The Government of God comes from God with His Spirit directly to us. Today in the Church, the elders and ministers are to be the teachers. Then we are all to learn and grow, then other teachers will develop up out of those who have been in the Church a long time. "…the government shall be upon His shoulders…"

Show me one single government—just one—that is good, that is righteous, that is fair. There's not one on earth! But there is one that is coming when Jesus returns.

"…and His name shall be called Wonderful, Counselor, The Mighty God… [this is talking about God manifested in the flesh] …The Everlasting Father, The Prince of Peace. Of the increase of *His* government and peace *there shall be* no end…" (vs 6-7). *It goes on into the 'ages of eternity'!* Stop and think for just a minute:

- God is a God of purpose
- God is a God of love
- God is a God of truth
- God is a God of creation

Look at the great heavens that He has created. We are going to be able to understand how this relates to us and relates to the never ending Government of God that is going to reach into the 'ages of eternity.' God has an awesome plan.

Just like it says in 1-Cor. 2, *the eye has not seen, the ear has not heard, it has not entered into the heart of man the things that God has prepared for those who love Him!* It's quite a thing what God is doing.

We're going to break this down into a number of points. The first point is:

I. <u>We are to have judgment with love, with mercy, with faith:</u>

When Christ returns, here's what He's going to do, "…and over His kingdom, to order it and to establish it **with judgment and with righteousness** from henceforth, even forever. The zeal of the LORD of hosts will do this" (v 7).

God is going to accomplish it. We have read several times already, Rev. 20, that *we shall be 'priests and kings and rule with Christ a thousand years'!*

Now let's see what happens to governments and religions, and what men have done, because none are righteous. It says, 'no, not one!' We're going to learn a lesson: first of all what the problem has been and then we're going to learn what not to do.

This is where Christ is castigating and warning the scribes and Pharisees, and they were the ones in charge of the kingdom of Judah during the days when Jesus had His ministry. Jesus says:

Matthew 23:23: "Woe to you, scribes and Pharisees, hypocrites!...."

Isn't that true of every government on the earth! Hypocrites! Liars! Cheaters! Those who take advantage rather than serving, teaching, loving and helping.

"...For you pay tithes of mint and anise and cummin…" (v 23).

Yes, always interested in doing the exactness of the little physical thing. However, notice why Jesus was correcting them and speaking these words of condemnation against them:

"...but you have abandoned… [completely forsaken and left alone] …the more important *matters* of the law—… [notice what the important matters of the Law are]: "…**judgment and mercy**…" (v 23).

I want you to understand a very important thing concerning judgment: First of all, *there must be a judgment made before mercy is given!* You never give mercy before judgment. Unless there is judgment there can be no mercy given. That's why God says, 'the wages of sin is death, but he who confesses his sins will have them forgiven.' Mercy comes *after* judgment.

"…and faith. These *you* were obligated to do, and not to leave the others undone." (v 23).

Let's see another very important facet that has been left out. This has also been done in the Churches of God. How do you think Churches of God are run without judgment, mercy and faith *and love*? Here is the parallel account of Matt. 23:

Luke 11:42: "But woe to you, Pharisees! For you pay tithes of mint and rue and every herb, but you pass over the **judgment and the love of God**…." *In the Church of God, there is to be the love of God:*

- toward God
- God's love to us
- our love for each other

When you find a church that is focusing in and preaching and teaching the love of God, then you will also see that the commandments of God are kept. Part of the love of God is keeping His

commandments. Not all of it, but *keeping His commandments is a reflection of our love for God!* We don't do it because there's and axe of fear hanging over the back of our necks.

- we do it willingly, *because God loves us*
- we do it willingly, *because we love God*

They lack these things, so what kind of 'religion' did they have? They had all kinds of dos and don'ts, washing hands, pots and pans, and tables. All kinds of things as noted today in the *Code of Jewish Law* of what Judaism was.

Judaism is not of God! Never was! That's a religion of men. {note our book: *Judaism: A Revelation of Moses or a Religion of Men?*} I'll just tell you this, if you don't understand what's in that book, you can't understand the Epistles of Paul. That's a vital book! You get it!

{Note our in-depth study: *Scripturalism vs Judaism*}

Christianity was not an extension of Judaism; Christianity came **out of** Judaism, left it behind forsook it and came after the Scriptures of God and the Truth as expounded by Christ. Yes, that's what they did.

"…but you pass over the **judgment and the love** of God. It is obligatory *for you* to do these things, and not to set aside those *lesser things*." (v 42). *That's kind of the way it was with them!*

Now let's see how it's going to be different in the Kingdom of God. Let's see a prophecy of how this is going to be carried out. Psa.145 is quite a Psalm and it tells us an awful lot about how God's judgment, mercy and love and everything work together.

As a matter of fact, our whole lives are just a series of judgments. Everyday you make small judgments. Everyday to have to decide what you're going to do, how you're going to do it, and so forth. Here this will be judgment of people who are now being called to enter the Kingdom of God. This is going to be a great responsibility, brethren.

Psalm 145:1: "I will extol You, my God, O King; and I will bless Your name forever and ever. Every day I will bless You; and I will praise Your name forever and ever. Great is the LORD, and greatly to be praised; and His greatness is unsearchable" (vs 1-3).

II. We're going to be learning; we're going to be growing:

Brethren, what's going to happen all during the ages of eternity, we're going to be learning, we're going to be growing. Stop and think about this for just a minute!

- What was your life when you were conceived? *Nothing but a speck!*
- What was your life when you were born? *Well, you were a little infant!*
- Does that compare to what you are now? *Of course not!*
- Can the infant understand what it's going to be like to be an adult? *No!*

Likewise with us! The greatness of God's way is going to go into the *ages of eternity*, and we're going to be learning and growing and developing.

Verse 4: "One generation shall praise Your works to another and shall declare Your mighty acts…. [that's what we will do for the people] …I will speak of the glorious splendor of Your majesty and of Your wondrous works" (vs 4-5).

This is what we are going to bring to the people all during the Millennium. Think of it: No wars! No killings! No shootings like we saw this last summer! People killed by some madman! No more slaughtering like we have in the Middle East!

Verse 6: "And men shall speak of the might of Your awesome works; and I will declare Your greatness…. [this is what we're going to be bringing and teaching] …They shall pour forth the memory of Your great goodness and shall sing of Your righteousness. The LORD is gracious and full of compassion; slow to anger and abounding in steadfast love" (vs 6-8). *This is how we are going to serve the people!*

Verse 9: "The LORD is good to all, and His tender mercies are over all His works. All Your works shall praise You, O LORD; and Your saints shall bless You. They shall speak of the glory of Your kingdom and talk of Your power… [this is what we're going to be doing]: …**to make known to the sons of men His mighty acts, and the glorious majesty of His Kingdom**" (vs 9-12).

This ties directly in with Isa. 9; v 13: "Your Kingdom is an everlasting Kingdom, and Your dominion **endures throughout all generations** [ages]." *Yes, every age!* This is going to be great! This is telling us what we are going to do.

Verse 17: "The LORD is righteous in all His ways and loving in all His works."

Everything that God does, and everything that we will do will be based on love, teaching, righteousness, judgment and authority that He gives to us. We're going to see that when people pray, their answers are going to come right away. We're going to be there as part of it to answer those prayers.

Verse 18: "The LORD is near unto all who call upon Him, unto all who call upon Him in Truth."

That's true today. That's how we need to call upon God. Not only as we read these and we see what we're going to be doing in the Millennium, but this also tells us what we need to be doing now today, so that we can arrive at that point.

Verse 19: "He will fulfill the desire of those who fear Him; He also will hear their cry, and will save them."

That's what we're going to do, *be bringing salvation to the whole world!* This is fantastic, brethren! This is terrific!

This is how it's going to be done; this is going to be a glorious time! Think of all the evil and all the things that are going on in the world right now, even while we're here at the Feast of Tabernacles, and how the future looks for the world and mankind today. Compare that with this; this is talking about us:

Psalm 149:1: "O praise the LORD! Sing to the LORD a new song, and His praise in the congregation of saints." *That's us!* We're the congregation of the saints.

Verse 2: "Let Israel rejoice in his Maker; let the children of Zion be joyful in their King. Let them praise His name in the dance; let them sing praises to Him with the drum and lyre, for the LORD takes pleasure in His people; He crowns the meek with salvation" (vs 2-4).

Isn't that something? *A great and wonderful work that we are going to do!*

Verse 5: "Let the saints be joyful in glory…"

What's it's going to be like to have glory, have a body like Jesus Christ, to have a spiritual mind, to be able to have glory. We're going to be *joyful* in glory.

"…let them sing aloud upon their beds. Let the high praises of God be in their mouth…" (vs 5-6).

These descriptions of what we are going to do and how we're going to do it we find all the way through the Scriptures.

III. **We're going to be kings:**

Let's see what Jesus said, because the disciples wanted to know what it's going to be for them. The disciples at this time, even at the Passover service, were talking back and forth with one another, 'I wonder who is going to be greatest?' Why do you suppose that they would bring that up? *Because they had an inkling*—of course, they didn't have an understanding—*that this is going to be something great and big and tremendous forever!* They didn't have all the details, so they were arguing.

Luke 22:23: "Then they began to question this among themselves, which of them it might be who was about to do this…. [that is betray Jesus] …And there was also an argument among them, *even* this: which of them should be considered *the* greatest" (vs 23-24). *So, Jesus intervened and He gave them some instruction*:

"…'The kings of the nations lord over them…" (v 25)—*and they sure do!* That's why there's not a single government in this world that is righteous and good.

"…and those who exercise authority over them are called benefactors. **But it shall not be this way among you**; rather, let the one who is greatest among you be as the younger, and the one who is leading as the one who is serving. For who *is* greater, the one who is sitting *at the table*, or the one who is serving? *Is* not the one who sits *at the table*? But **I am among you as one who is serving**'" (vs 25-27).

That's what Christ is going to continue to do all through eternity. Likewise, we will serve! Not self-serve, but serve according to the will of God! Notice what He told them because of this. And with this He told them, 'you don't have to worry about what's going to be in the Kingdom and who is going to be the greatest.

Verse 28: "Now you are the ones who have continued with Me in My temptations. And I appoint to you, as My Father has appointed to Me, a kingdom… [we read about that at the beginning] …so that you may eat and drink at My table in My Kingdom, and may sit on thrones judging the twelve tribes of Israel" (vs 28-30). Isn't that something? *Yes, indeed!* They're going to judge the 12 tribes of Israel as kings.

Remember: we will be kings, we will sit on thrones and we will be judging. Let's see a Psalm that depicts this, which is actually a prophecy of the fulfillment of the words of Jesus that He spoke to the disciples. This is quite a Psalm indeed!

Psalm 122:1: "I was glad when they said to me, 'Let us go into the house of the LORD.'"

Of course, we're going to have access to the house of the Lord all the time. In the finality, we're going to see God face-to-face. We're going to see Christ face-to-face. What God has in store is just like Paul said. *God is able to do above all that we ask or think!*

Verse 2: "Our feet shall stand within your gates, O Jerusalem…. [New Jerusalem. Jerusalem on earth first, then New Jerusalem next] …Jerusalem is built like a city that is all joined together as one where the tribes go up, the tribes of the LORD, unto the testimony of Israel, to give thanks unto the name of the LORD, for there were set the **thrones of judgment**… [plural] …the thrones of the house of David" (vs 2-5).

What was the prophecy that we read in Isa. 9, that Jesus the Messiah Who was to be born of the flesh will be called 'The Everlasting God' and He is going to be over the house of David forever and ever. That's quite a thing! We don't have to worry about what are we going to do; who is going to have what job?

- Don't you think God knows what He's going to do?
- Don't you think that God is going to give to each one of us something that is grand, great and glorious, according to *His* determination?
- Cannot God judge and grant and give these things better than we can?
- *Of course!*

Just like He told the disciples, 'Why are you arguing about this? Don't get all concerned about it. You're going to sit on thrones judging the tribes of Israel.' This is quite a thing!

Notice that this carries on over. We covered this in Rev. 2, *that we are going to be given a rod of iron to shepherd the nations!* Those who do not obey, those who do not repent and submit shall be broken like the potters breaking into slivers the pottery. That's something! We will have power over the nations!

Now let's see something else about the Kingdom of God. It talks about the Kingdom and what God is going to do with it. He's going to give it to us. This is really something to understand. We saw earlier that God is going to set up a Kingdom that shall never be destroyed (Dan. 1). It's going to endure forever!

Daniel 7:26: "But the judgment shall sit… [we're going to be the judges] …and his dominion… [the beast] …shall be taken away to be consumed and to be destroyed unto the end."

The end of the whole Babylonian system as described in Rev. 17 & 18.

Verse 27: "And the Kingdom and dominion, and the greatness of the Kingdom under the whole heaven, shall be given to the people of the saints of the Most High…"

That means world government with Christ as King and we're serving all the nations and people of the world, to help God bring salvation to all mankind *for a thousand years!* Brethren, we need to let those things sink into our heart and mind. Let that become part of the reality of our thinking, about where we're going and what we're doing.

I want you to compare what we're covering here in study from this point of view: God has not called us to play church, to play politics. He has called us:

- *to learn*
- *to love*
- *to overcome*
- *to look forward to the greatest fulfillment of His prophecies to each one of us*

"…Whose kingdom *is* an everlasting kingdom. And **all kingdoms shall serve and obey Him**" (v 27). *God isn't going to leave it! No way! It's going to be quite a Kingdom!*

IV.   Teaching:

We have quite a number of parts to #4, because *this is what we're going to be doing.* Here is a great principle of God all the way through the Scriptures. ***God wants us to be teachers!***

Yes, we're going to have whatever power God gives to us. Christ has all power. He will delegate certain things to us, just like when Christ came on the earth, the Father delegated certain things to Him. Let's see what was it, ***IF*** we're going to be kings and priests under Christ, ***THEN*** we have a type of this with the high priest and the Levites in relationship to the children of Israel.

As it were, under Christ we're going to be like *spiritual Levites, like spiritual judges and kings.* Lev. 10 is showing about what the priests and the Levites were to do. They were to be there at the temple. Their authority from God was to teach the people, help the people.

Leviticus 10:8: "And the LORD spoke to Aaron, saying, 'Do not drink wine nor strong drink, neither you nor your sons with you, when you go into the tabernacle of the congregation, lest you die. *It shall be* a statute forever throughout your generations. You are to distinguish between the Holy and unholy, and between the unclean and clean'" (vs 8-10).

Here is a principle of teaching. *You are to know the right/you're to know the wrong.* Actually, when you take vs 10-11 and put them together: this is the whole basis for the book of Proverbs; the whole basis for the laws and commandments of God; the whole foundation of the teachings of Christ. You see how fantastic this is?

Verse 11: "And so that **you may teach** the children of Israel all the statutes which the LORD has spoken to them by the hand of Moses."

That was the command. That was the commission. This is what was to happen. Now let's see how Moses further described this, and how God set the standard for teaching. Let's think about this for a minute. Not only were Aaron and his sons the priests and the Levites to teach, but also Moses taught them, and they taught the people. God wants His people

- to be educated
- to be knowledgeable
- to be able to make right judgments

We'll see that as we go along. Deuteronomy means *the second giving of the Law.*

➢   'deutero' is *two*;
➢   'nomos'—from which we get 'nomy'— means law.

So, this is *the second giving* of the Law of God.

Deuteronomy 4:1—*Moses said*: "And now, O Israel, hearken to the statutes and to the judgments which **I teach you**…"

We're made in such a way that we need to be taught, we need to learn, and let it become a very part of our being so that we can live that way.

- Isn't that the whole purpose of conversion?
- Isn't that the whole purpose of the Holy Spirit of God?
- *Yes, indeed!*

"…which I teach you… [which you will learn] …**in order to do them**… [The teachings of God are meant to be put into action] …so that you may live and go in and possess the land which the LORD God of your fathers gives *to* you" (v 1). Isn't that something?

What are the words of Jesus Christ, but the words of eternal life so that we can live and enter into the Kingdom of God. With everything in the Old Testament and New Testament, when you put it together, it is one book, but all of it fits together in the unity of Scripture. What is given in the Old Testament in the *letter of the Law* is also carried through in the *spirit of the Law,* by the Spirit of God in the New Testament.

Verse 2 is a key and this touches on one of the greatest weaknesses of human beings, that they somehow think that they know more than God. They want to add a little bit here and add a little bit there and change the Word of God. But God says that you're not to do that, because:

- the Law of God is perfect
- the Word of God is true

- the commandments of God are true
- all the precepts of God are right and altogether Holy

Verse 2: "You shall not add to the word which I command you…" Isn't that what Jesus told us. You read the last part of the book of Revelation. You're not to add to or take away.

1) Keep the commandments

"…neither shall you take away from it, so that you may keep the commandments of the LORD your God which I command you" (v 2).

This is what we're going to teach the people. We're going to be there and they're going to be able to see us. We're going to teach them: don't go to the right hand/don't go to the left hand.

Think about what it's going to be like every single Sabbath with all the people gathering together to be taught the Word of God—all during the Millennium: families, children, young, old; think about what kind of communities will be developed. We won't have house upon house and building upon building. *No!* It's going to be fantastic, brethren.

We're going to administer that government. The people are going to be happy and cheerful and good and righteous. They're going to know about the salvation of God from the very beginning of their consciousness as children. They will be taught step-by-step-by-step all through their lives.

Then Moses gives an example here, v 3: "Your eyes have seen what the LORD did because of Baal Peor…."—*the sun-god!* Remember that those sent by Balak said:

Come over here, worship our gods; come and eat some meat with us and come and have some bread. We know you are sick and tired of the manna. Wouldn't it be nice to have a little bread? Wouldn't it be nice to come over here and have a little fun? We've got music and women and we're going to have a ball!

Remember how many were killed? It's not a matter of seeking pleasure as they did. It's a matter, do you keep the Word of God. Moses is reminding them to remember that.

"…For the LORD your God has destroyed from among you all the men that followed Baal Peor" (v 3).

That was quite a slaughter. Think about that in relationship to the return of Christ, how He is going to kill and destroy and slaughter and bring to nothing everything in the world by shaking the heavens and shaking the earth. Then we're going to have to come in and clean it up afterward, brethren.

God will be with us to do it.

Verse 4: "And you who held fast to the LORD your God *are* alive, every one of you, this day."

Take that in the letter and bring it over in the spirit. We will be alive as spirit beings in the Kingdom of God because we were faithful over here. See the parallels? That's why when you study the Bible, put it together:

- think about the physical
- think about the spiritual
- think about the Old Testament application
- think about the New Testament application

Verse 5: "Behold, **I have taught you statutes and judgments**… [that's what we're going to do to all the people during the Millennium] …even as the LORD my God commanded me…"

The Law of Moses was really no more than the Law of God. He was only the intermediary to bring it.

"…so that you should do so in the land where you go to possess it" (v 5).

All the teachings of God must be integrated into our thoughts and our minds so that we *do* it! *That's what we're going to teach them!*

Verse 6: "And you shall keep and do *them,* for this is your wisdom and your understanding in the sight of the nations, which shall hear all these statutes and say, 'Surely this great nation *is* a wise and understanding people.'" *I want you to think about this spiritually!*

Let's look at 1-Peter 2. It talks about the nation of Israel, but here it talks about a nation that is a priesthood.

1-Peter 2:9: "But you *are* a **chosen stock**… [Did not God call you? Everyone of us individually? *Yes, indeed!*] …**a royal priesthood**… [Will we not be a royal, kingly priesthood to teach everyone in the Millennium? *Yes, indeed!*] …**a Holy nation, a people for a possession *of God,*** that you might proclaim His *excellent* virtues, Who called you out of darkness into His marvelous light" Think what God is going to do with us **to teach the world,** to save the world. All the people of the world are going to look upon us as *a royal nation, a royal priesthood.* We will be spirit beings in the Kingdom of God.

Here is what they will say of us, Deuteronomy 4:7: "For what nation is so great whose God *is* so near to them, as the LORD our God *is,* whenever we call upon Him? And what great nation has statutes and judgments that *are so* righteous as all this law which I set before you today?" (vs 7-8).

Isn't that what we're going to do during the Millennium? Think about that, brethren! Understand the great calling of God! God has great and marvelous things for us. This is why we need to drink out of the Word of God. Remember that *these things teach us spiritual lessons!*

Teaching becomes the very most important thing that we are going to be doing. We're going to see that this is the key in helping bring many, many into the Kingdom of God during the Millennium. Again, we're going to learn from the Old Testament. We're going to see there are things that parallel what we are going to do.

Let's read about the account of King Asa and what he did, why he was commended for what he did. This is also a good lesson for us to understand and realize: *Never be discouraged and think that God doesn't know what you're doing! He does!*

God has called you because He loves you! He wants you to be in His Kingdom so you can be a part of the Kingdom of God; be of the priests and the kings in teaching. When we read this, we are going to see this will describe some of the activities in the beginning of the Millennium that we are going to do to help restore the people to the way and Truth of God.

2-Chronicles 14:2: "And Asa did *that which was* good and right in the eyes of the LORD his God."

God recognizes when we do good and right. Notice what he did and this is what we'll have to do. Think of all the altars, the idols, the temples; think of all the things that God is going to destroy and we're going to have them smashed into smithereens.

Verse 3: "For he took away the altars of the strange *gods*, and the high places, and broke down the images, and cut down the groves. And he commanded Judah to seek the LORD God of their fathers, and **to do the law and the commandment**" (vs 3-4).

Isn't that what we're going to do? *Yes, indeed!* So, here's King Asa—in a type—doing to Judah what we're going to do in the Millennium.

Verse 5: "He also took out of all the cities of Judah the high places and the images. And the kingdom was quiet before him."

Then they built up Judah, they built up Jerusalem. He had a battle and war that he had to fight. God was with him and struck down the enemy, drove away the Cushites. It was a great victory. They sent many people out to bring in the spoils. The truth of the matter is this: *When you do what is*

right before God:

- He will be *with* you
- He will *bless* you
- He will *stand* for you
- He will *fight* for you

All of those things are true! Just magnify that in our lives today as the spirit sons and daughters of God. We can do the things that please God. We can do the things that God will see and recognize as good. He's going to take note of that. That's going to add to part of our reward and our standing in the Millennium. Let's see something important because we're going to be doing activities very similar to this:

2-Chronicles 15:1: "And the Spirit of God came upon Azariah the son of Oded. And he went out to meet Asa, and said to him, 'Hear me, Asa, and all Judah and Benjamin. **The LORD *is* with you while you are with Him**....'" *Very important principle.*

2) Teaching about God

Today people want to have the blessings of God by rejecting Him. But that's not going to happen! Look at the hand of God's judgment upon us right now, and upon the world right now, because they are rejecting God! Likewise, we're going to have to teach the people that 'yes, this really is God. Yes, we are the spirit sons and daughters of God. Yes, we are to be teaching you. Here's what you are to do.' We will have them go out and do these things.

"'...And if you seek Him, He will be found by you.... [that's what we're going to show them how to do] ...But if you forsake Him, He will forsake you'" (v 2).

That will be true during the Millennium, as well. Everyone is going to learn about God, and they're going to have to choose. There's one thing that God is never going to change with human beings. *He's never going to take away choice!* He wants us to choose; likewise today with us. What are we choosing? What are we doing?

Verse 3: "'And for a long time Israel *had been* without the true God, and without a teaching priest, and without law.'"

Doesn't that describe not only Israel, but the whole world? When we take over the Kingdom—it's not going to be left to other people, it's going to be given to the 'saints of the Most High' and that's us—we're going to go out and teach people these very same things here.

- you've gone through trouble
- you've gone through the Tribulation
- you've had difficulties

- your life has been ruined

Verse 4: "'And when they turned in their trouble to the LORD God of Israel, and sought Him, He was found by them. And in those times *there was* no peace to him who went out, nor to him who came in, but great tumult *was* upon all the inhabitants of the lands'" (vs 4-5). *That's coming upon the whole world!*

Verse 6: "'And nation was destroyed by nation, and city by city, for God troubled them with every adversity.'"

Now Asa is told by Azariah, 'here's what you are to do.' This is how we're to undertake the work that God is going to give us when we begin to take over the Kingdom as the Millennium begins.

Verse 7: "'But you be strong and do not let your hands be weak, for your work shall be rewarded.' And when Asa heard these words, and the prophecy of Oded the prophet, he took courage and put away the abominable idols out of all the land of Judah and Benjamin, and out of the cities, which he had taken from mount Ephraim. And he renewed the altar of the LORD before the porch of the LORD. And *he* gathered all Judah and Benjamin, and the strangers with them out of Ephraim and Manasseh, and out of Simeon; for they fell to him out of Israel in great numbers, when they saw that the LORD his God *was* with him" (vs 7-9).

God blessed them! God relieved them out of their troubles! This is what we're going to do with them.

Psa. 25 will show us a great deal. The main thing we're going to be doing is *teaching*. There are other things we're going to do—we'll cover those as well—but here is a great Psalm to show why we need to be taught of God. Remember, Jesus said 'the Father draws us' and as the prophets have said, 'we will all be taught of God.'

Think of this for a minute: When we teach people during the Millennium, we teach them God's laws, God's commandments, God's ways. They will be able to have God's Spirit. Who is actually doing the teaching? *God!* We're just the instrumentality to carry it out.

Look at this attitude, and this is going to help us in growing and overcoming in our physical lives now as to how we prepare for the resurrection, and how we are taught to be able to be kings and priests during the Millennium. In order for us to teach, we likewise must be taught, and taught God's way.

Psalm 25:1: "To You, O LORD, do I lift up my soul. O my God, I trust in You; do not let me be ashamed, let not my enemies triumph over me. Yea,

let none who wait on You be ashamed…" (vs 1-3). Brethren, let me just state this: *You don't have to be ashamed of anything of God's way!*

- of His commandments
- of His laws
- of His Holy Days
- of the things that He is doing

The very fact that we are yielding ourselves to God, God is going to bless us for it even in spite of the trials that we go through.

"…let them be ashamed who deal treacherously without cause" (v 3). *If that doesn't describe this world and the governments of the world….*

Notice how David wanted to learn of God's way, v 4: "Show me Your ways, O LORD; teach me Your paths."

Today we can do that as never before, because we have the *whole* Bible—Old Testament and New Testament. We realize that this is the *whole* Word of God to us, inspired by the eternal mind of God, and that it is filled with:

- knowledge upon knowledge
- precept upon precept
- teaching upon teaching
- testimony upon testimony

all magnified by the power and Spirit of God!

We have the greatest opportunity to learn so much of God's way, perhaps more than any generation in the history of the world. Isn't it a shame that the dominant church era at this time is lukewarm Laodiceans? *Christ tells them to repent! He's standing at the door and knocking!* He says, 'You let Me in, because I've spewed you out of My mouth, now you come back in. You let Me in!'

This is what has to happen, v 4: "Show me Your ways, O LORD; teach me Your paths. Lead me in Your Truth and **teach me**…" (vs 4-5).

Remember what Jesus said in the Beatitudes: **Blessed are those who hunger and thirst after righteousness, for they shall be filled!** Isn't that something that we need to do?

- be filled with the knowledge of God
- be filled with the Word of God
- be filled with the righteousness of God
- be led of His Holy Spirit to do the things that are right, good and true
- to overcome and change

Yes, indeed!

Verse 5: "Lead me in Your Truth and teach me, for You are the God of my salvation; on You do

I wait all the day long."

Just think of that kind of mind, that kind of attitude, and how in studying the Word of God, God is going to teach us. That's what I want us to learn during this Feast of Tabernacles. Let's drink in as much as we can. Be like a dry sponge in the middle of a flowing stream.

Verse 6: "Remember, O LORD, Your tender mercies and Your loving kindness, for they have been of old. Do not remember the sins of my youth, nor my transgressions; according to Your loving kindness remember me **for Your goodness' sake,** O LORD" (vs 6-7).

- Isn't that true?
- What does God say He's going to do with our sins and our transgressions?

He's going to remove them as far as the east is from the west, and not remember them ever again! (Heb. 10:17[transcriber's correction]).

Verse 8: "Good and upright is the LORD; therefore He will teach sinners in the way."

God will teach us. We learn, grow and overcome. We are faithful to the end. We die, we're buried and resurrected—new body, new mind—spirit body, spirit mind. God is going to infuse into us everything that we have learned, and that will be part of the beginning of our spiritual life. Isn't that something? "...**for Your goodness sake**..."

Verse 8: "Good and upright is the LORD; therefore He will teach sinners in the way.... [we're going to be the ones who do that] ...The meek He will guide in judgment; and the meek He will **teach His way**" (vs 8-9).

Notice *teach, teach, be taught* all the of this all the way through.

Verse 10: "All the paths of the LORD are **mercy and truth** to those who keep His covenant and His testimonies."

That's what we're going to teach: everything in every way about God is what God has made and created so that _we_ can become like He is. That's the whole purpose of God's plan. It's an amazing thing—isn't it, brethren? *Yes, indeed!*

Verse 12: "What man is he who fears the LORD? He shall **teach him in the way that He shall choose.**"

Isn't that profound! How much can you learn of God? *The more you stay in the way of God, the more you're going to learn!* The more you put into practice the things that you learn, the more you're going to understand other things as they come along!

Verse 13: "His soul shall dwell at ease, and his seed shall inherit the earth. The secret of the LORD is with those who fear Him, and He will show them His covenant" (vs 13-14).

That's quite a thing! I'm sure there are other Psalms we could add to it and bring some of these things out. It's absolutely amazing! There are so many things in the Bible that God has put here *to teach us, for us to learn, for us to absorb,* for us to go over and over again, and for us to be prepared as kings and priests. Yet, what a shame it is that in the world, the form of Christianity in the world:

- they do away with the laws and commandments of God
- they do away with the Truth and righteousness of God
- they don't even know anything about the plan of God or what it's all about
- they all believe they're all going to go to heaven and everything is going to be fine

No, that's not the way that it works!

Listen! That's why God has given us His Word and His Truth. Let's realize this: With this blessing and opportunity for us—we don't know how long we're going to have peace; we don't know how long we're going to have the opportunity to learn, change and grow—but let's take advantage of every day, every minute, every circumstance:

- whether the circumstances are pleasant *or* whether they are difficult
- whether it is a trial *or* whether it is a reward

Let's learn from all of those things, because these are life experiences that, with God's Spirit and with His Word, He wants us to learn. He has great things, fantastic things in store for us! When we're resurrected we're going to be able to have a tremendous work to do.

Isaiah 48:15: "I, even I, have spoken..." *You think about that with the whole Bible,* because all of these are the recorded words of God and of Christ.

"...yea, I have called him..." (v 15).

Stop and think! This is a prophecy of Cyrus; but God has called us. Have we not answered the call? *Many are called and few are chosen!* Those who are chosen are called *the selected* or *the elect.*

"...I brought him and he makes his way succeed. Come near to Me, hear this..." (vs 15-16).

We are told in Eph. 1 that God has made known to us the *secret things* of His plan, of His work, of what He's doing on the earth.

"'...I have not spoken in secret from the

beginning. From the time that it was, there am I.' And now the Lord GOD, and His Spirit, has sent me. Thus says the LORD, your Redeemer, the Holy One of Israel, 'I *am* the LORD your God Who **teaches you to profit**…'" (vs 16-17).

Not profit in physical treasures, *but spiritual treasures*; not profit in the way of business, as in commercial things, *but in the business of becoming like God!*

"'…Who **leads you** by the way that you should go'" (v 17). *God is the One Who does!*

Doesn't it say there in Rom. 8:14 that 'as many as are led by the Spirit of God, these are the children of God'? *Yes, indeed! That's us!* He's going to lead us.

Notice, He was lamenting that Israel had not done this, but look at the result of what would have happened. Let's look at it from this way, the result of what is happening in our lives:

Verse 18: "Oh, that you had hearkened to My commandments! Then your peace would have been like a river, and your righteousness like the waves of the sea."

That's what we want, brethren. We have every opportunity. Everything that God wants to give to us. God has granted us:

- His Spirit
- His Truth
- His righteousness
- His Word

In order to accomplish His way!

Let's see what else we're going to do. Let's recall what it was that Jesus told the apostles just before He ascended into heaven? *Go into all the world, teaching them to observe all things that I have commanded you! Lo, I am with until the end of the age.'* Let's take that and apply that to what it's going to be in the Millennium.

- Is God going to send us into the world to teach the people all things that God has commanded? *Yes, indeed!*
- Are we going to preach the Gospel? *Yes, indeed!*
- Are we going to preach salvation? *Yes, indeed!*
- Arc wc going to bc doing hcalings? *Yes, indeed!*
- Are we going to be helping people overcome the trauma and difficulties of coming out of the Tribulation? *Yes!*

Then the next generation we're going to be teaching them how to have happy families, how to have good children, the purpose of God, where they're going,

what they're doing. Just think of the teachings that are going to be during the Millennium and we are the ones who are going to be doing it.

Matthew 5:17: "**Do not think that I have come to abolish the Law or the Prophets; I did not come to abolish, but to fulfill.**"

That means everything concerning the Kingdom of God, too. The Word of God is constantly being fulfilled. The Word of God is constantly being completed and perfected. When the Kingdom of God is setup on the earth, just think what that's going to be.

- we're going to get rid of all the religions of this world
- we're going to get rid of all of the teaching institutions of this world
- we're going to get rid of all the governments of this world
- we're going to get rid of all the governments of man

It's going to be Christ as King! And the saints ruling over the whole world under Christ and teaching them the way of salvation. I want you to think about this:

"**Do not think that I have come to abolish…but to fulfill.**" Don't you think He's going to fulfill all the prophecies that are there and everything that is behind the prophecies that expand it? You can take one word of the prophecies and expand it out into a great number of things, and this is what we're going to be doing.

Verse 18: "For truly I say to you, until the heaven and the earth shall pass away…"

That's not going to happen until a new heaven and new earth comes—correct? *Yes!* Look at this and project forward into the Millennium.

"…one jot or one tittle shall in no way pass from the Law until everything has been fulfilled" (v 18). *Let's see where it's going to be that everything is fulfilled*:

Revelation 21:6: "And He said to me, '**It is done**…'" *If it's all done,* everything leading up to the changing of the heavens and the earth to the new heaven and earth be fulfilled.

We can take these verses back in Matt. 5 and we can project that forward on into eternity. What is it going to be, all the work that God is going to do with us and with the universe into all eternity. How's that going to be? Those are going to be some things that are just going to blow our minds. Our minds right now cannot fathom it, because we need a spirit mind in order to handle that.

Matthew 5:18: "…until everything has been

fulfilled…. [this tells us what we're going to teach]: …Therefore, **whoever shall break one of these least commandments, and shall teach men so**…" (vs 18-19).

Think about Protestantism and Catholicism. Think about the religions of this world. Do they not teach men to do it? *Yes!*

"…shall be called least in the Kingdom of Heaven; but whoever shall practice and teach *them*, this one **shall be called great** in the Kingdom of Heaven" (v 19).

It's going to be done while we are in the Kingdom of Heaven or the Kingdom of God in teaching the people on the earth!

It says, "…this one… [whoever shall practice and teach] …**shall be called great** in the Kingdom of Heaven."

What does that do to the argument that the disciples had on the Passover night as to who is going to be the 'greatest'? *That obliterates it!*

Let's understand something else here, which the world doesn't understand, because as I said earlier, they do not know anything of Judaism. Let me just tell you one big key to understanding the New Testament. *Unless you understand about Judaism, you can't understand the New Testament, nor can you understand the difficult Scriptures of the Apostle Paul!*

That's why in the Bible we have Appendix Z: *Understanding Paul's Difficult Scriptures Concerning the Law and the Commandments of God.* If you haven't studied those, and if you haven't gone through those, you need to do that. What that is going to do is open your mind and your understanding to the Word of God as never before.

Verse 20: "For I say to you, unless your righteousness shall exceed *the righteousness* of the scribes and Pharisees…"

They had *their* traditions; their man-made righteousness. Jesus told them in John 7 that 'none of you are keeping the Law of Moses.' They call *their traditions* the Law of Moses, which is not true.

You can take this and apply it to any religion: Protestantism, Catholicism, Islam, Hinduism—whatever religion you want to apply it to—New Age religion; doesn't make any difference. They all have their own teachings, they all have their own righteousness, which are nothing but 'filthy rags' before God. Here's the thing, even today, if your righteousness is not based upon the Word of God, the Truth of God, and on Jesus Christ, Jesus says:

"…there is no way *that* you shall enter into

the Kingdom of Heaven" (v 20). *That's the whole purpose as to why we're here*:

- we want to enter into the Kingdom of God
- we want to enter into the Kingdom of Heaven
- we want to do the things that please God

We can do those!

Peter says that if we're doing these things, and if we're growing in grace and we're growing in knowledge that we will have an entrance *into the eternal Kingdom of God.*

- we're going to be teachers
- we're going to be priests
- we're going to be governors
- we're going to rule over cities

It is going to be a fantastic and tremendous thing, brethren, that God has called us to do!

Scriptural References:

1) Isaiah 9:6-7
2) Matthew 23:23
3) Luke 11:42
4) Psalm 145:1-13, 17-19
5) Psalm 149:1-6
6) Luke 22:23-30
7) Psalm 122:1-5
8) Daniel 7:26-27
9) Leviticus 10:8-11
10) Deuteronomy 4:1-6
11) 1 Peter 2:9
12) Deuteronomy 4:7-8
13) 2 Chronicles 14:2-5
14) 2 Chronicles 15:1-9
15) Psalm 25:1-8, 7-10, 12-14
16) Isaiah 48:15-18
17) Matthew 5:17-18
18) Revelation 21:6
19) Matthew 5:18-20

Scriptures referenced, not quoted:

- 1-Corinthians 2
- Revelation 20; 2
- Daniel 1
- Revelation 17; 18
- Hebrews 10:17
- Ephesians 1
- Romans 8:14
- John 7

Also referenced:

Books:
- *Code of Jewish Law* by Ganzfried & Goldin
- *Judaism: A Revelation of Moses or*

Religion of Men? by Philip Neal

In-Depth Study: *Scripturalism vs Judaism*

Appendix Z (*The Holy Bible in Its Original Order, A Faithful Version*): *Understanding Paul's Difficult Scriptures Concerning the Law and the Commandments of God*

FRC:bo
Transcribed: 8/512
Reformatted: 1/2021

CHAPTER SIXTY-NINE

What We Will Be Doing as Kings and Priests II
We're Going to be Judges!
Fred R. Coulter

Greetings, brethren! We saw how important it's going to be with what we will be doing as kings and priests in the Millennium. We also saw one of the things that has caused a great deal of the problems in the world.

Let's just review a bit; let's come back to Luke 11. Here Jesus was correcting the Pharisees for not having the understanding of the Law of God, the Truth of God, the love and mercy of God. One of the major things that happens, and then we will see the result of it as it is in our day today:

Luke 11:42: "But woe to you, Pharisees! For you pay tithes of mint and rue and every herb, but you pass over **the judgment**…"

We're going to see that #5 in what we're going to do as kings and priest is:

V. Judging—Judgment takes:

- wisdom
- knowledge
- discernment
- understanding the Laws of God

—all of those things together. What was it that God set up as the system for His people Israel in the first place? *He gave them judges!* If there were judgments too difficult, they were to take them to the high priest. Then they were to make a judgment based upon the facts. They *passed over* the judgment and the love of God.

- What happens when you do this?
- How does the society turn out?

Matt. 24—this is exactly what's happening the in the world today, not only in the world, but in America in particular. *People do not know how to make righteous judgments* **because they've gotten rid of God!** They fail to understand that God made us so that

- we need God
- we need His Word
- we need His Truth
- we need His Spirit

We're incomplete otherwise in the flesh!

The world today likes to have everyone be autonomous, meaning *you're a beginning and an end unto yourself.* When that happens, and when society enacts unrighteous judgments, what does it do to the society? Let's see what happens, and let's see how things come about. Look at the world today and understand that one of the most lacking things that there is, is *righteous judgment.* When you have unrighteous judgment here's what happens:

Matthew 24:10: "And then shall many be led into sin…"—*because they're not told right from wrong, good from evil*; they're not told that they *need* God, that they're dependent on God.

- God made you to *need Him!*
- God made you to *need His laws*
- God made you *His commandments*
- God made you *His Spirit*
- God made you *His Truth*

beyond that:

- God has made you for a fantastic purpose *to eventually be His sons and daughters in His Kingdom*

That's why we're called! To understand judgment, we need to learn it now. Let's see what happens when there's no judgment.

"…shall many be led into sin and shall betray one another, and shall hate one another" (v 10).

Don't we have that today? hatred? betrayal? even anonymous 911 calls that you can do, or police calls that you can do to report some activity?

- What happens in the realm of 'religion'?
- What is one of the most fundamental things that is said of Christianity in the world today?
- *They have abolished the laws of God!*

You can't abolish them, because they are still in force. What they have done is they have *abolished preaching them!* Now let's see what happens when that occurs:

Verse 11: "And many false prophets shall arise, and shall deceive many…. [Truth falls into the street] …and because lawlessness shall be multiplied…" (vs 11-12).

Think about all the lawless decrees that are on the books today. Think of what the final judgment of the Supreme Court of any nation does with any judgment that is not true, *or* is not law-abiding, *or* is not righteous. Look at what has happened to the world.

Show me one nation that has a good judgment, that has a good government, that has a loving and law-abiding people, that has the blessing of God. There aren't any, because *lawlessness has been multiplied.*

Let's see what happens in individual lives and in the society and in the world in general. Isa. 59 tells us the result of it. If you went on the street and did a survey on the street; you had your little microphone and cameraman with you and you go up to someone and say, 'Do you know why you're here?' I can imagine the answers you might get, but none of them will know *why* they were created, what is the purpose in life. After all, if you are alive and God has given you this life, shouldn't you know the One Who has given you life? Yet, with our absurd, insane scientific world—which it is—they discover a lot of things, but they reject God. When they reject God, the reject Truth! We're in a desperate situation in the world, because it's filled with lawlessness, because of lack of judgment. Let's see that right here:

Isaiah 59:1: "Behold, the LORD'S hand is not shortened that it cannot save, nor is His ear heavy that it cannot hear. But your iniquities have come between you and your God, and your sins have hid *His* face from you, that **He will not hear**, for your hands are defiled with blood, and your fingers with iniquity; your lips have spoken lies, your tongue has muttered perverseness" (vs 1-3).

Stop and think! Is that not a perfect description of this society? Granted, there may be a few out there trying to do what is right. However, they get enacted into law. Try abortion! The absolute most perverse, lawless, insane judgment of the Supreme Court of the United States that it has ever made, to legalize killing of the most innocent: *the unborn!*

I do believe that the Constitution says that we have the right to the pursuit of happiness—*life, liberty and the pursuit of happiness!* That should be enough to overturn Roe *vs* Wade. But we have murderous women and lecherous men and godless politicians and judges who judge *unrighteous judgment.* That's why the Kingdom of God is going to come and take over this world.

This is why, brethren, we need to understand everything that we can concerning the laws and commandments of God and know how to make *righteous judgments*, beginning in our own lives; begin to see and analyze things in truth. God is going to give judgment to us. We saw how Jesus

said to the 12 disciples that 'you'll be sitting on thrones judging the 12 tribes of Israel. In spite of all of these sins; in spite of these difficulties in vs 1-3:

Verse 4: "None calls for justice..." Anyone who says:

- Let's outlaw abortion as a terrible sin and crime and God is judging us because of it
Oh no! We've got to have that!
- let's have marriage defined as one man and one woman
Oh no, we can't have that. Our minds are so perverted that all of the evil abominable love of homosexuals is accepted!

Look what that has done to the world and to the nation. Notice the next phrase: "...nor does anyone plead for truth..." (4). ***The truth!***

Who can speak it? And if you do, you're an evil-minded lecherous, narrow-minded, bigot! *That's what they think of God,* but look at their lives.

"...they trust in vanity and speak lies. They conceive mischief and bring forth iniquity. They hatch adders' eggs... [these are their schemes and their laws and their plans] ...and weave the spider's web... [all of the intrigue that goes on politically, religiously and economically] ...he who eats their eggs dies, and that which is crushed breaks out into a viper" (vs 4-5).

Every time you think that you're going to solve a problem, up pops one even worse.

God says it isn't going to work. The truth is *everyone in the world is under the Law of God!* The truth is *God is judging everyone all the time on their behavior!* These judgments are automatic because His laws are spiritual and automatic, and they function automatically. God doesn't have to come down here and personally do a single thing. The time is going to come when He's going to intervene and send Christ, and He's going to do it.

Verse 6: "Their webs shall not become clothing, nor shall they cover themselves with their works; their works *are* works of iniquity, and the acts of violence *are* in their hands."

Isn't that true? I think it would be interesting to run an analysis.

- When was it that the Scopes trial took place? *1920s!*
- When was it that prayer and Bible reading was taken out of schools?
with lawlessness multiplying:
- How many mass murders have we had since then?
- How many millions and million—upward of 55 million—abortions in killing babies

have been performed?

- How about the prisons filled with incorrigible wicked?

Some are so incorrigibly wicked that they must live in a permanent place where they cannot get out to the public, and be under medication 24-hours a day, seven days a week. What's going to happen when the day comes when they can't be taken care of? That's why Christ has to return. This is why we need to learn *righteous judgment*.

Verse 7: "Their feet run to evil, and they make haste to shed innocent blood; their thoughts *are* thoughts of iniquity; wasting and destruction *are* in their paths."

- Doesn't that sound like the movies that we have today?
- Doesn't that sound like the entertainment that people are putting in their minds today?
- *Yes, indeed!*

Verse 8: "They have not known the way of peace, and *there is* no justice in their ways. They have made crooked paths for themselves; whoever goes therein shall not know peace."

- What's the result of it?
- Everyone says, 'What's wrong?'

What's wrong is there is not the judgment! This is why we need to learn it, brethren. Always remember this, and the reason we keep the Feast of Tabernacles: *So we learn and know and understand that*:

- God has called us to rule this world
- He has called us to learn of His Word
- He has called us to learn of His laws!
- He has called us to learn of His commandments
- He has called us to learn of His judgments
- He has called us to put in our mind—write indelibly in our mind with Holy Spirit—all of those things

These come from God! These are the characteristics that God wants us to have.

Today we have a perfect opportunity to see and view what is wrong on a vast scale—daily, hourly—around the world, so we can learn the lesson, so we can see why we need the judgment of God. What happens when it's like that?

Verse 9: "Therefore, justice is far from us; nor does righteousness overtake us...."

How can good come out of evil? *'Let us do evil so that good may abound'!* Does that make any sense? That's the way the world is run.

"...We wait for light... [we hope things will get better] ...but behold, darkness; for brightness, *but* we walk in deep shadows" (v 9).

When it comes to massive problems, when it comes to trying to figure out what happens when there's a mass murder.

Brethren, this world is waiting for us to take it over and to show and teach what is right.

Verse 10: "We grope along the wall like the blind, and we grope as if *we had* no eyes. We stumble at noonday as in the night; among those who are strong, we are like dead men. We all roar like bears, and mourn grievously like doves; we look for justice, but there is none, *we look* for salvation, yet it is far off from us; for our transgressions *are* multiplied before You..." (vs 10-12).

Put this together with: *Lawlessness shall be multiplied, therefore, the love of many shall grow cold!* "...transgressions *are* multiplied..." Lawlessness results in transgression.

Without repentance there is going to be no solution. Without a mass turning to God, the hand of God's judgment is not going to be held back. We come to a point—that's called a *tipping point*, just like a teeter-totter—and you reach the point where everything gets out of balance and it all collapses.

- we are at a *tipping point* **in law and order**
- we are at a *tipping point* **in lawless government**
- we are at a *tipping point* **generationally**
- we are at a *tipping point* **financially**

What's going to happen when they're all swirled together in one great mammoth problem? *That day is going to come! That day is coming!*

Verse 12: "For our transgressions *are* multiplied before You, and our sins testify against us; for our transgressions are with us; and *as for* our iniquities, we know them."

Yes, they know what's right and wrong, but they deny in their 'make-believe reality' that sin is *sin*.

Verse 13: "In rebellion and denial of the LORD, and turning away from our God, talking perversity and revolt, conceiving and speaking from the heart words of falsehood."

- Isn't that the way most people are today?
- Doesn't this describe our entertainment world today?
- Doesn't this describe the things that people run after today?

And are running after—headlong—not knowing they're running to their own destruction.

Verse 14: "And justice is driven backward, and righteousness stands afar off; for truth has fallen in the street, and **uprightness cannot enter**."

The #1 thing concerning judgment: *You must have and you must know the Truth!* In judging any situation we're going to see that *you must know and have the Truth!* You must get all of the facts.

Verse 15: "Yea, truth fails…" *A lot of people have tried truth, but it fails, because they're not willing to repent!* Or they're willing to take some truth and intermix it with their lies and try to have a combination that will work. But it's all going to collapse.

"…and he *who* departs from evil makes himself a prey…." (v 15).

Look at that person; he wants to be honest! She wants to really do good! Yes, you become a victim! In this world try being faithful sexually until you get married, and make it a public point that you've discussed with other people and you will be ridiculed, you will be laughed out, you will be looked upon as dumb, stupid and ignorant. *But that's what they are!*

"…And the LORD saw, and it was evil in His eyes that *there was* no justice…. [God looks, God knows what's going on in the world] …And He saw that *there was* no man, and was astonished that there was no intercessor. Therefore His own arm brought salvation to Him; and His righteousness sustained Him" (vs 15-16). *Christ is going to have to come and bring this about!*

Let's talk a little bit more about *judgment and righteousness.* Let's see what it says about God. We said that God was judging everyone all the time. Let's come to Gen. 18, right before Isaac was born. As a matter of fact, God came with a couple of angels and they were on their way down to destroy Sodom and Gomorrah. God began to tell Abraham what He was going to do. This is how God judges the world today. I want you to think about things that take place in the world.

Genesis 18:17: "And the LORD said [of Abraham], 'Shall I hide from Abraham the thing which I do, since Abraham shall surely become a great and mighty nation, and all the nations of the earth shall be blessed in him?'…. [we're here because of Abraham] …For I know him, that he will command his children and his house after him, and they shall keep the way of the LORD, to do justice and judgment, that the LORD may bring upon Abraham that which He has spoken of him" (vs 17-19).

Notice how important justice and judgment is in our relationship with God, because Abraham said, 'God was Judge of the whole earth.'

Verse 20: "And the LORD said, 'Because the cry of Sodom and Gomorrah is great, and because their sin is very grievous."

Take any city you like; take some of the most sin-infected cesspools called cities in whatever nation you want to look at, and is their sin very great? very grievous? *Yes!* Remember, God's judgment is coming, as we saw on Feast of Trumpets.

Verse 21: "I will go down now and see whether they have done altogether according to the cry of it, which has come to Me. And if not, I will know…. [because God knows] …And the men turned their faces away from there, and went toward Sodom. But Abraham still stood before the LORD" (vs 21-22).

Notice how this ties in with Isa. 1:18[transcriber's correction]: "'Come now, and let us reason together,' says the LORD…." *Here Abraham reasons with God*:

Genesis 18:23: "And Abraham drew near and said, 'Will You also destroy the righteous with the wicked?…. [Abraham knew that He wouldn't do that] …Perhaps there are fifty righteous within the city. Will You also destroy and not spare the place for the fifty righteous who are in it? Far be it from You to act in this manner, to kill the righteous with the wicked. And far be it from You, that the righteous should be as the wicked. **Shall not the Judge of all the earth do right?**'" (vs 23-25).

Notice how boldly he talked with God. You know the rest of the story, He bargained with God all the way down to ten. That probably was the complete number of the family of Lot, his wife and his daughters and sons. God said, 'I won't do it.' But you know what happened. Yes, indeed, God did it!

Let's understand something else about God. Everyone wants the love of God. Everyone wants the blessings of God though they live in their sins. That's kind of an incongruous contradictory thing to believe! Think about that for a minute. God says this to all those who are sinning, wherever it is. Even now at this late date, if in any of the nations of Israel, or any of the nations of the world, if there would be a mass repentance and turning to God, God would hold back His hand of judgment.

Here's what God wants; this is the message that goes out with the Gospel. This is what has to be preached into the world:

Jeremiah 4:1: "'**If** you will return, O Israel,' says the LORD, 'Return to Me….'"

Come back to God. I made you. You're My people. I called Abraham, Isaac and Jacob; you're their offspring.

"…And **if**… [conditions are always upon us] …you will put away your abominations out of My sight, then you shall not be removed'" (v 1). *I'm not going to send you off into captivity!*

How close are we to this same point in the modern descendants of the 12 tribes of Israel? *Very close!* You've heard the talk of a 'financial cliff'? That's only part of it. There's the:

- financial cliff
- governmental cliff
- righteousness cliff
- judgment cliff
- sin and abomination cliff

All of these things are coming together **to create a perfect storm of judgment!**

Here's what they have to do, v 2: "And will swear…"

In other words, you *give up* your way, your thoughts, your attitudes, and you change and come to God. That's what it means to return.

"…'As the LORD lives,' in **Truth, in judgment, and in righteousness**…" (v 2).

- come back to God
- come back to His laws
- come back to His Truth
- come back to His righteousness
- let the fear of God be there everywhere
- let God be over the government again
- let God be over the schools again
- let God be over the churches again

Think of what is going to have to happen in all of those institutions in order to return to God. Since that isn't going to happen, it's got to happen on an individual basis for those whom God is going to call.

If they do that, "…then the nations shall bless themselves in Him, and in Him they shall glory" (v 2).

Let's see what we are to do. Let's see about the things of *judging righteous judgment*. In the Gospel of John, chapter 7, we find that there was a confrontation between the Pharisees and Jesus at the Feast of Tabernacles. Jesus exposed the real truth that the scribes and Pharisees were not willing to admit.

John 7:19—*Jesus said to them*: "Did not Moses give you the Law… [it was the One Who became Jesus Christ Who gave Moses the Law to give to them] …**and not one of you is practicing the Law**?…."

That's a real key thing in understanding the difference between Judaism and the Law of Moses. Just like in the world, everyone professes to be Christian, but they're not.

The Pharisees and scribes professed to be those who were the servants of God, but they had *their own traditions* and they weren't practicing **the Law**. They were practicing *their traditions* and thinking that they were righteous. Just look at every religion in the world and isn't that true, even Christianity today? *Yes, it is!*

"…Why do you seek to kill Me?…. [v 22]: …Now then, Moses gave you circumcision—not that it was from Moses, but from the fathers—and on *the* Sabbath you circumcise a man. If a man receives circumcision on *the* Sabbath, so that the law of Moses may not be broken, why are you angry with Me because I made a man entirely whole on *the* Sabbath?" (vs 19, 22-23).

He was giving cause to show what they were lacking. They had their traditions. They had their opinions. Everything they did and thought was judged by *their traditions* and **not the Law of Moses, not the commandments of God!**

Here's what Jesus told them, v 24: "Judge not according to appearance, but *judge righteous judgment*." We're going to see some things of *righteous judgment*. We have a series that I've done on that: *Judge Righteous Judgment*. Let's see how we are told to do this.

Let's look at some things concerning judging. Let's come back to the book of Proverbs and we'll find several that will tell us about this. This is what it's going to be for us when we begin the Millennium, because the first thing we're going to have to do is start judging, start making decisions:

Proverbs 21:15: "*It is* joy to the righteous to do justice, but ruin to the workers of iniquity."

If righteousness and justice is carried out, there's no room for iniquity. Here's a basic thing we need to learn concerning judgment, and righteous judgment: *Always get the facts!* Here's we are today in too many things.

Proverbs 18:13: "He who answers a matter before he hears it, it *is* folly and shame to him."

Let's look at a couple of other Scriptures that we need to know concerning judging, since we're here in Proverbs. The book of Proverbs is really an excellent thing to study and learn, especially for young people. These things also are for the wise. Remember this:

Proverbs 24:23: "These things also *are* for the wise: To have respect of persons in judgment *is*

not good."

You can't do that! You can't favor a cause; you can't favor a person; because righteousness looks at *the facts and the truth*, and gets to the entire heart of the matter. We're going to see that is what God commanded the priests to do, and the judges to do, in their judgment. They weren't to have respect to the rich, because of their influence and power. They weren't to have respect to the poor, because of their circumstances. But what are the laws of God, what are the commandments of God and how do we establish judgments based on **truth and righteousness.**

This is what we have to learn. This is why God has called us to be in the Kingdom of God, so that *we* can be the judges; *we* can be the rulers. Think how important that is going to be.

The Kingdom is going to be given to 'the saints of the Most High,' and they are going to do the judging. Let's see the commands that God gave Moses to give to the judges that He commanded to be appointed. Of course, we have a whole book of Judges, because that's the system of government that God setup for the children of Israel to live under. They weren't to have a king like the nations. They were to have judges.

Of course, here in America, we came close to that system, because we have the courts make the final judgment. This is why judges:

- cannot be political
- cannot be partial
- cannot pervert the truth
- cannot twist and distort things to please the mighty and the powerful

Deut. 1—Moses is covering some of the things that God already told him before, but He's covering it again because this is the second giving of the Law.

Deuteronomy 1:16: "And I commanded your judges at that time saying, 'Hear *the causes* between your brethren, and judge righteously between a man and his brother, and the stranger with him…. [no partiality; everyone expects that] (notice the command): …**You shall not respect persons in judgment. You shall hear the small as well as the great. You shall not be afraid of the face of man**, **for the judgment** *is* **God's**….'" (vs 16-17).

Let's understand something very important: *IF* we're going to be making judgments:

- with the Laws of God
- with the precepts
- with the statutes
- with the commandments of God

THEN whatever judgment is done, *that is* **God's** *judgment.*

Let's understand a very important thing here first, and don't forget this: **Before mercy is given, there must be judgment first!** That's why we are all judged as sinners. **Mercy cannot be shown unless there is repentance!** Never forget that! You do not give mercy when there is restitution to be made from someone who has been harmed financially, or physically. You don't let them off the hook. They have to make that restitution.

"'…And the cause that is too hard for you, bring to me, and I will hear it.' And I commanded you at that time all the things which you should do." (vs 17-18). *In Deut. 16 he repeats it: He's saying*:

> Now you're going into the cities. Now you're going into the *promised land*, and there are cities there that you are going to occupy. You're going to take over what the Canaanites have built. Actually, they didn't know it, they were building them for you.

And God said to the people, because of that, 'don't get all lifted up. Don't get smart-alecky and cocky about it because God is giving it to you as a gift.' In other words, to keep everything right, you must have law and order. I wonder how it is that so many 'religious' people who call themselves 'Christian' demand law and order in the land, but they do not demand law and order with the Law of God in their own lives? *Think on that!*

Deuteronomy 16:18: "You shall appoint judges and officers for yourself in all your gates which the LORD your God gives you, tribe by tribe. And they shall **judge the people with righteous judgment**. You shall not pervert judgment; you shall not respect persons, nor take a bribe, for a bribe blinds the eyes of the wise and perverts the words of the righteous. You shall follow that which is altogether just so that you may live and inherit the land which the LORD your God gives you" (vs 18-20). *Quite some instructions,* isn't it? *Yes, indeed!*

What does God want us to learn as Christians today? *This is why whenever there's something to understand and know you must get all the facts!* Never answer a matter before you have heard it, because it's 'folly and shame' to you if you do. Then someone is going to come and reprove you for that.

Let's see how God wanted things to be carried out by the judges. What we're going to do with this is let's project this forward to what it's going to be like when we are judges in the Kingdom of God. We've been promised rulership over cities. We've been promised to be kings and priests. In both cases there has to be judgments made.

Now let's see what God says if there is sin found, and even those going after other gods, what were they to do?

Deuteronomy 17:4: "And if it is told you, and you have heard and inquired diligently, and, behold, it is true and the thing is certain, that such abomination is done in Israel; then you shall bring forth that man or that woman who has committed that evil thing to your gates, even that man or that woman, and shall stone them with stones until they die. At **the mouth of two witnesses or three witnesses** shall he that is worthy of death be put to death. At the mouth of one witness he shall not be put to death" (vs 4-6). *This is violated over and over and over again in the courts of law today!*

Verse 7: "The hands of the witnesses shall be *the* first on him to put him to death, and afterwards the hands of all the people. So you shall put the evil away from among you. If a matter *is* too hard for you in judgment, between blood and blood, between plea and plea, and between stroke and stroke, *being* matters of strife within your gates, then you shall arise and go up to the place which the LORD your God shall choose" (vs 7-8)—*right to the tabernacle; right to the priests!*

They have the Laws of God right there before them. Notice what was to be done here:

Verse 9: "And you shall come to the priests, the Levites, and to the judge that shall be in those days, and ask. And they shall declare to you the sentence of judgment. And you shall do according to the sentence which they declare to you from that place which the LORD shall choose. And you shall be careful to do according to all that they tell you. According to the sentence of the law…" (vs 9-11).

Whatever the law says. You can go back and tie this in with Exo. 21-23, all of the judgments that were given in cases of manslaughter, murder, mayhem, goring of animals, thievery, lying, false gods.

- What is the sentence?
- What is the judgment?

That's what they were to do!

"…which they shall teach you and according to the judgment which they shall tell you, you shall do. You shall not turn aside from the sentence, which they shall show you, to the right hand or the left. And the man that acts presumptuously and will not hearken to the priest who stands to minister there before the LORD your God, or to the judge, even that man shall die. And **you shall put away the evil from Israel.** And all the people shall hear and fear, and do no more presumptuously" (vs 11-13). *That's quite a thing!* Look at what we have today:

- there is no *judgment*
- there is no *justice*
- there is no *truth*

It begins in the pulpits and it continues on with the governmental offices from the top to the bottom, all the way through.

Let's see some other things concerning judgment. God is very particular in this. God says this over and over again. Think what we are to do. We'll cover some of the things that God says we're going to do.

Leviticus 19:15: "**You shall do no unrighteousness in judgment**…."

Has to be righteous; that's what Jesus said, *'judge righteous judgment'* (John 7:24).

"…You shall not respect the person of the poor, nor honor the person of the mighty, *but* you shall judge your neighbor in righteousness" (v 15).

Something else, and the press needs to learn this, v 16: "You shall not go *as* a slanderer among your people; you shall not stand idly by the blood of your neighbor. I *am* the LORD. You shall not hate your brother in your heart. You shall always admonish your neighbor, that you may not bear sin because of him. You shall not avenge, nor bear any grudge against the children of your people, but you shall love your neighbor as yourself. **I *am* the LORD**" (vs 16-18).

This is how we're going to run the Millennium. This is exactly what's going to happen. God is going to say, 'You be over five cities, you be over two cities, you be over this district, I want you to be judge here, I want you to be judge over there.' Think about it! That's what we're going to do. That's really quite a thing! Let's understand the judgment.

Now let's see how Jesus did the judgment in John 8. We're going to learn to put together some of the things that we've already learned in covering *judging righteous judgment* and the instructions given to the judges and the priests. This was quite a thing. Here's what happened:

John 8:3: "Then the scribes and the Pharisees brought to Him a woman who had been taken in adultery; and after setting her in *the* center, they said to Him, 'Teacher, this woman was caught in the very act of committing adultery. And in the law, Moses commanded us that those who commit such *a* sin should be stoned. Therefore, what do You say?' Now, they said this to tempt Him, so that they might have *cause* to accuse Him…." (vs 3-6). *I want you to think about*:

- you must get all the facts

- you must have all the evidence
- you can't be partial in judgment

"…But Jesus stooped down *and* wrote on the ground with *His* finger. And as they continued to ask Him, He lifted Himself up *and* said to them, 'Let the sinless one among you cast the first stone at her.' And again He stooped down *and* wrote on the ground" (vs 6-8).

Everyone wants to know what did Jesus write? *Well, I think we can pretty well suspect what it was that He wrote!* Some people say he was writing the sins of all the different scribes and Pharisees there. I don't think so! He must have been writing something pertaining to the particular question of bringing this woman caught in the act of adultery—wouldn't you say? What do you suppose those questions might be?

Verse 9: "But after hearing *this*, they were convicted *each* by *his own* conscience, and went out one by one, beginning with the older ones until the last. And Jesus was left alone, with the woman standing in *the* center."

Here's a big crowd around there and here's the woman who was brought to Jesus. Pharisees were all around. The people were all around. 'What is this going to be? How is He going to handle this? Boy, it looks like they're really going to get Him caught this time.'

Verse 10[transcriber's correction]: "And when Jesus lifted Himself up and saw no one but the woman, He said to her, 'Woman, where are your accusers? Did anyone condemn you?'"

Notice how He is following what He commanded the children of Israel to do. Do a diligent search for all the information. Get all the facts.

"…'Woman, where are your accusers? Did anyone condemn you?' And she said, 'No one, Lord.' And Jesus said to her, 'Neither do I condemn you. Go, and sin no more'" (vs 10-11).

That's interesting! Some people say this is a case of mercy. Not true! This is a case of righteous judgment. If a woman is caught in the act of adultery, does she not have to be with a man? *Yes, indeed!* What do the Scriptures instruct if something like that comes up? If they are guilty, **both** will be stoned. Not one! In this case, and in every other case like it, 'it takes two to tango.'

Jesus may have been writing, 'Where is the man? Does not adultery take two? If you're going to bring the woman, why didn't you bring the man? If she was caught in the very act, why did you let the man go?' This was a case of the scribes and Pharisees wanting a partial judgment. They wanted a

condemnation of one, the woman and not the man. So, what do we have here? Today it would be called 'case dismissed.' The evidence is not complete. No one is bringing a charge. That's what Jesus said.

"'…Did anyone condemn you? And she said, 'No one, Lord.' And Jesus said to her, 'Neither do I condemn you. Go, and sin no more'" (vs 10-11). He did not say, 'I forgive you.'

If He would have said, 'I forgive you, then that would have been mercy *before* judgment. But this is judgment and no mercy required. But He did give a warning and how conduct should be in the future, because He knew that she really was caught in the act. But the unrighteous scribes and Pharisees were partial in the evidence, wanting to get a partial judgment.

Jesus is going by His own laws that He gave the children of Israel. Let the judgment be just. Let all the evidence be true. Do a diligent search of the matter. And since the witnesses were gone, the man was not there, He said, "…'Neither do I condemn you. **Go, and sin no mor**e'" (v 11). This was a dismissal *in a judgment rendered by Jesus, because of the lack of complete evidence!* Since there was no man to condemn, and the Word of God says, 'in the mouth of two or three witnesses everything shall be established.' *Case dismissed!* That's quite a thing!

Here we can find in the Bible Jesus acting upon His own laws that He gave the children of Israel; Jesus being righteous and just and understanding. Here He said, "…'Neither do I condemn you. Go, and sin no more.'"

One of the things that was lacking in the Church at Corinth was proper judgment. Those who should have been the judges, because they were spiritual, should have been able to make judgments with the problems and cases that they had. Especially here with a man who was committing sexual immorality with his stepmother. The Church could not even make the decision to tell him to stop attending, 'go repent!' Paul had to intervene and tell them to put the man out of the fellowship. They had another problem, so Paul writes to them:

1-Corinthians 6:1: "Does anyone among you who has a matter against another dare to go to *a court of* law before the unrighteous, and not before the saints?" *If there's a problem among the saints we should solve it!*

Verse 2: "**Don't you know that the saints shall judge the world?**…. [that's why we're going through this; we're going to judge the world] …And if the world is to be judged by you, are you unworthy of the most trivial of judgments?"

You can't even make a righteous judgment

concerning something that is plain as day before your very eyes.

Verse 3: "**Don't you know that we shall judge angels?**...." *Think on that for a minute!*

Think what that means and what we need to be doing. How is that going to be done? *We don't know, but we do know that we're going to do it!* With what then will we judge them? *The laws of God!* Very simple!

"...*How* much more then *the* things of this life? So then, if you have judgments *concerning the* things of this life, *why* do you appoint *as judges* those who have no standing in the Church?" (vs 3-4).

The ones who thought they were important in the Church, 'Oh, we didn't want to get involved in any of these judgment lest I lose a little face and honor and prestige among the people who looked up to me.' So, they set the ones who have no standing in the Church.

Verse 5: "Now I say *this* to your shame. *Is it* because there is not a wise *man* among you, not even one, who is able to decide between his brothers? Instead, brother goes to *a court of* law with brother, and this before unbelievers" (vs 5-6).

We've had some pretty infamous cases before the judges of the land, in the churches that we've been associated with. How did that go down? ***Look what happened within the Church***:

- when they didn't make judgment concerning adultery and fornication
- when they didn't make judgments concerning thievery
- when they didn't make judgments concerning doctrine
- when they allowed men to rule over them and put them down and to rob and steal from them

Verse 7: "Now therefore, there is altogether an utter fault among you, that you have lawsuits with one another. Why not rather suffer wrong? Why not rather be defrauded? Instead, you are doing wrong and defrauding, **and you are doing these things *to your* brethren**" (vs 7-8).

Then he gives a warning, because that kind of conduct is unrighteous. That kind of handling problems and difficulties and making right judgments is what should be done. But they weren't doing it. They couldn't even do the simplest one. Some of them were quoting:

Matthew 7:1: "Do not condemn *others*, so that you yourself will not be condemned; for with what judgment you judge, you shall be judged; and

with what measure you mete out, it shall be measured again to you" (vs 1-2).

This is saying that *if you do not do what is right, it's going to come back on you!*

Here's the problem; here's one of the things that a person would say: 'I'm not qualified to judge.' or 'Jesus said to judge not lest you be judged.' Jesus didn't say that. Here's what He said:

Verse 3[transcriber's correction]: "Now why do you look at the sliver that *is* in your brother's eye, but you do not perceive the beam in your *own* eye? Or how will you say to your brother, 'Allow *me* to remove the sliver from your eye'; and behold, the beam *is* in your *own* eye?" (vs 3-4).

Here's what Jesus said. Here's what was to be done. Not to avoid judgment, not to refrain from judgment, not to give unrighteous judgment:

Verse 5: "*You* hypocrite, **first** cast out the beam from your *own* eye, and **then** you shall see clearly to remove the sliver from your brother's eye."

They were doing wrong. Instead of saying, 'Well, let's look at the problem. Let's get all the facts. Let's talk to all of those who are involved. Let's see what was actually done, and take it from there. Well, they didn't do it, so notice what Paul says:

1-Corinthians 6:9: "Don't you know that the unrighteous shall not inherit *the* Kingdom of God?.... [Think about that. That's why we're to have ***righteous judgment***.] ...Do not be deceived; neither fornicators, nor idolaters, nor adulterers, nor abusers of themselves as women, nor homosexuals, nor thieves, nor covetous, nor drunkards, nor revilers, nor extortioners, shall inherit *the* Kingdom of God" (vs 9-10).

They knew that, but why let these things go on in the Church. Maybe for those of you who have been in the Church a long time, you wonder what happened to the Church (WCG), that big Church of God that was doing so great. Well, the thing is, it wasn't doing so great, and the truth is:

- they did not have righteous judgment
- they did not get rid of the evildoers

So, God sent infiltrators to take them down! If they didn't get rid of the infiltrators and repent and change their way—which they didn't do—the Church was scattered. Same thing here. We're not to be as the scribes and Pharisees, hypocrites, and have nitty-picky little things:

- without understanding the truth
- without getting all the facts

- without realizing what really needs to be done

Verse 11: "And such were some of you; but **you were washed, you were sanctified, you were justified** in the name of the Lord Jesus, and by the Spirit of our God."

Therefore, you should be able to make these judgments. How do you do that? *You do that*:

- with the Word of God
- with the love of God
- with all of the instructions on righteous judgment
- get all the facts
- don't give an answer before you've heard the entire matter
- don't jump to conclusions until you have had two or three witnesses

Maybe more if it's necessary, if it's a serious matter!

These things become part of our character to do what is right, part of our thinking to think what is right so that we can

- *look upon* the laws of God
- *know* the laws of God
- *study* the laws of God
- *understand* what we need to do

Then when you do what is right—that's what God wants us to learn—**are we not going to judge the world?** *Yes!* We're going to judge the world; we're going to judge angels. *Think of that!* How are we going to do it? **With the laws and commandments of God!** That's why we have to have them written in our heart and mind.

Proverbs 21:15: "*It is* joy to the righteous to do justice…" *Justice comes from judgment, to do the right thing!*

- Christ is coming to judge the whole world
- Christ is coming to setup the Kingdom of God

These are some of the things that we need to learn now so we can have them inculcated into our heart and mind to:

- know how to make righteous judgment
- know how to get all the facts
- know how to think things through
- not answer a matter before we hear it
- not give credence to a loose tongue or a slanderer

to be able to
- know the Truth
- understand the Truth
- judge with the Truth
- judge with the judgment of God
- judge with the commandments of God

Then it is **"…joy to the righteous to do justice…"** *That's why God has called us to be in the first resurrection and to rule and reign with Him!*

Scriptural References:

1) Luke 11:42
2) Matthew 24:10-12
3) Isaiah 59:1-16
4) Genesis 18:17-22
5) Isaiah 1:18
6) Genesis 18:23-25
7) Jeremiah 4:1-2
8) John 7:19, 22-24
9) Proverbs 21:15
10) Proverbs 18:13
11) Proverbs 24:23
12) Deuteronomy 1:16-18
13) Deuteronomy 16:18-20
14) Deuteronomy 17:4-13
15) Leviticus 19:15-18
16) John 8:3-11
17) 1 Corinthians 6:1-8
18) Matthew 7:1-5
19) 1 Corinthians 6:9-11
20) Proverbs 21:15

Scripture referenced, not quoted: Exodus 21-23

Also referenced: In-Depth Study:
Judge Righteous Judgment

FRC:bo
Transcribed: 8/5/12
Reformatted: 1/2021

CHAPTER SEVENTY

It's Not How You Start, It's How You Finish! I

Fred R. Coulter

Greetings, everyone! There are many lessons we can learn during the Feast of Tabernacles, and there are a lot of lessons we can learn from the Bible. Our whole goal is to attain to the Kingdom of God. To become priests, kings, leaders and teachers to bring peace to the world; to bring to the world 'the restitution of all things' under Jesus Christ.

There have been very few times of peace in this world. Remember, God's calling for the children of Israel was that *they would be a kingdom of priests to take God's Word to the whole world!* There was only one time in the entire history of Israel that they did that. Yet, it didn't last very long.

We're going to see what it's going to be like to have every physical thing that you need, and what does it bring unless you have the Spirit of God.

- Can you succeed in this life, but not attain to the Kingdom of God in the first resurrection? *Yes, you can!*
- What is success in this life?
- What does it lead to when you have everything that your heart could desire?

We have an example of that in the Bible! That one is King Solomon, the son of David.

Could anyone have started out with a better start than he had? No place is there a parallel in all the history of mankind. God blessed King David. He gathered gold, silver, iron, brass, and a tremendous amount of money. God personally gave to King David the plans for the first temple. He drew them out; he gave them to his son Solomon who was very young at the time that he became king.

We're going to see that there are a lot of spiritual parallels that follow right along with what happened here with Solomon. Solomon had everything given to him. When he started out, he was very humble. Let's see the story and saga of Solomon. Let's apply it in several ways:

1. We'll look at his life and see what it was that brought him down; what it was that made him successful.
2. Then we can draw parallels with our lives and see and compare what these things are as they apply to us.
3. Then we can apply them to the Kingdom of God when we are going to be teaching, judging and ruling over the people.

What we find happened to Solomon could very well be the same thing that could happen to people who come into the Millennium.

Remember this: We will enter the Kingdom of God at the resurrection, because 'flesh and blood cannot enter the Kingdom of God.' But the human beings who survive over into the Millennium and start out the civilization of man again under Christ and the saints are going to be *under* the Kingdom of God. They will not be *in* the Kingdom of God. It will be that the Kingdom of God will be ruling on the earth.

Let's see what Solomon did. When he started out God loved him, he pleased God; he did the things that were right.

1-Kings 3:3: "And Solomon loved the LORD… [he started right; he started good] …walking in the statutes of David his father. Only he sacrificed and burnt incense in high places."

There was *one* high place that was the place to go to offer sacrifices to God. There he had this fault to begin with.

Verse 4: "And the king went to Gibeon to sacrifice there, for that *was* the great high place. Solomon offered a thousand burnt offerings upon that altar."

After the Ark of the Covenant was separated from the tabernacle because of the lost battle of the sons of Eli—Hophni and Phinehas—the Philistines captured the Ark and after seven months of plagues upon them, they sent it back to Israel and finally, after several places where the Ark was then David brought it to the City of David and made a tent for it in his house. David had a special wing in his house where the Ark of the Covenant was in this tent, and he had the priests and Levites who would do the officiating and everything there.

But the sacrifices were given in Gibeon where the tabernacle was. The altar, the Holy of Holies and everything was up in Gibeon. After the building of the temple it was all brought back together at the temple.

Let's read what happened because this is quite a thing, and notice that this was really wonderful:

Verse 5: "In Gibeon the LORD appeared to Solomon in a dream by night. And God said, 'Ask what I shall give you!'"

- What is that you want?
- What is your life going to be?

Verse 6: "And Solomon said… [here he was humble; he knew what he really needed] …'You have shown to Your servant David my father great mercy, according as he walked before You in truth and in righteousness and in uprightness of heart with You. And You have kept this great kindness for him, that You have given him a son to sit on his throne, as *it is* today.'"

So, he's talking about himself. Here's what he wanted.

We covered about how we are going to judge people. That's one of the functions of kings, priests and leaders—they have to judge. Here's what Solomon asked for:

Verse 7: "And now, O LORD my God, You have made Your servant king instead of David my father. And I *am* a little child… [we don't know how old he was, maybe 15 or 16] …I do not know *how* to go out or come in!"

That is to function as king; 'Lord, I don't know where to begin; show me what I need to do.' Isn't that the way we need to be:

O Lord, show us what to do. Help us! Lead us! Guide us! Grant us Your Spirit!

Solomon started out really good.

Verse 8: "And Your servant *is* in the midst of Your people whom You have chosen, a numerous people who cannot be numbered nor counted for multitude. Now therefore, **give to Your servant an understanding heart to judge Your people, to discern between good and evil**, for who is able to judge this, Your great people?" (vs 8-9).

That was the perfect request from Solomon! Had he stayed this way, I wonder how things would have turned out? Likewise with us:

- How have we started out with God?
- Do we not start out with something like this?

Asking God:
- God, help me
- forgive my sins
- watch over me
- strengthen me
- grant me understanding

Think about how many people started out that way, but didn't end up that way. There's something that happens when you receive everything you need. We'll see what that is a little later, but let's continue on and see how God responded to that. Likewise with us; if we maintain the right spiritual relationship with God by loving Him and He loving us, and walking in His ways and doing the things that please Him, what is it that God is going to give us spiritually when we enter the Kingdom of God?

Remember this promise: *God is able to do exceedingly above all that we ask or think!* One of the things we want to accomplish in covering the life of Solomon today is to look at the pitfalls that came along; look at the thought process that developed that led him away from God so that won't happen to us! As you read about the seven churches in Rev. 2 & 3, what do you find? *You find that the churches have to fight against carnal nature themselves!*

There's a lot we can learn, and Paul wrote that the things in the Old Testament are types for us so that we can learn not to do the evil things, but also we can learn to do the good things, which were the things that pleased God, and then carry that on into our relationship with God the Father and Jesus Christ. Let's see what happened.

Verse 10: "And the word was good in the eyes of the LORD that Solomon had asked this thing. And God said to him, 'Because you have asked this thing and have not asked for yourself long life and have not asked riches for yourself, nor have asked the life of your enemies, **but have asked for yourself understanding to judge justly**'" (vs 10-11). That's why we covered how we *judge righteous judgment.*

Verse 12: "Behold, I have done according to your words. Lo, I have given you a wise and an understanding heart, so that there was none like you before you and after you none shall arise like you." No one is going to be as Solomon, so we need to learn some lessons here, don't we? *Yes!*

Verse 13: "And I also have given you that which you have not asked, both riches and honor, so that there shall not be any among the kings like you all your days."

What we have here is a covenant between God and Solomon. In any covenant there are conditions. Just like when we read about the words of the covenant that we have with God the Father through Jesus Christ, look at all the *IF* statements that are connected with it.

- God is perfect
- God is righteous

- God is love
- God is kind
- God is good
- God cannot lie

So therefore, His Word is true, and it's going to happen!

Since we're still human beings and we still have human nature, and we're still subject to sin and the things that we do that are not right, the conditions always fall upon us.

Notice what God said to Solomon, v 14: "Therefore…[in the light of what I'm going to do for you] …**if** you will walk in My ways, to keep My statutes and My commandments, as your father David walked, then I will lengthen your days."

Let's see something else that is true. What was it that Abraham was commended for after he had died and the promise and covenant was passed on to Isaac? Notice how God carried on the covenant to Abraham. Notice how similar this is with the covenant that God is making with Solomon. We are in covenant with God, too. We will see that all covenants of God have these requirements.

Genesis 26:3—*God told Abraham*: "Stay in this land… [v 4]: …And I will multiply your seed as the stars of the heavens and will give to your seed all these lands. And in your seed shall all the nations of the earth be blessed, because Abraham…" (vs 3-5).

The things important to understand is this: *We receive the things that we do because of Abraham and because of Christ!*

Verse 5: "Because Abraham **obeyed My voice**…"

Those are the three words that we need to have ingrained in our heart and mind, because this will always bring us back from sin. What did Jesus say when He was tempted of the devil? *Man shall not live by bread alone, but by every word that proceeds out of the mouth of God!*

"…**and kept My charge, My commandments, My statutes, and My laws**" (v 5). *Those are the same ones that God gave to Israel!* Notice how similar that is to the covenant that God made with Solomon,

1-Kings 3:14: "'Therefore, if you will walk in My ways, to keep My statutes and My commandments, as your father David walked, then I will lengthen your days.' And Solomon awoke, and, behold, *it was* a dream. Then he came to Jerusalem and stood before the Ark of the Covenant..." (vs 14-15).

Solomon went up there and offered burnt offerings at Gibeon, then he came back and offered burnt offerings where the Ark of the Covenant was that was in the house of David, in which he was now living.

"…and stood before the Ark of the Covenant of the LORD and offered up burnt offerings, and offered peace offerings, and made a feast to all his servants" (v 15). *That sealed the covenant!*

Now then, this is quite a thing! God gave Solomon all the territory that He had promised. This is a lesson for all people in the world today. If you don't want war, if you want peace, *you'd better turn to God!* There better be *fear of God* in your life, in your institutions, in your governments, in your education, and in your finance. In the letter of the Law God will bless you.

However, we need to understand that we're not going to just reign over the kingdom of Israel; we're going to **inherit the world!** We are going to rule the world under Christ. Then it talks about everything that Solomon did. Let's see how this compares in parallel with what the Kingdom of God will be like that we are going to administer upon the world.

1-Kings 4:24: "For he had the rule over all on this side of the River, from Tiphsah even to Gaza, over all the kings on this side of the River. And he had peace on all sides all around him."

You have peace from your enemies when you have peace with God! When you do not have peace with God, you do not have peace with your enemies.

Verse 25: "And Judah and Israel… [two separate designations] …lived safely, *every* man under his vine and under his fig tree, from Dan even to Beersheba, all the days of Solomon."

Didn't we read about that in Isa. 2, that every man is going to live under his own fig tree and under his own vine? *Yes, indeed!*

Now then, God fulfilled His promise. Notice what God gave Solomon. Let's also understand this; here's a lesson: It's not the wisdom we can get from an education in this world. That is only worthwhile as we get our education from God's Word, which is the same as God giving wisdom—as He gave it here—so we can

- read it
- study it
- know it
- learn it and apply it

Verse 29: "And God gave Solomon

exceeding great wisdom and understanding, and largeness of heart, even as the sand that *is* on the seashore."

What a fantastic blessing of all of that wisdom, knowledge and understanding! What are we going to administer in the Kingdom of God to this world? *The knowledge of the Lord shall cover the earth as the seas cover the earth!* We can expand upon that, but you see the parallels here. I want us to get the parallels so we can learn the lessons, so that we can grow in grace and knowledge and love of God; grow in wisdom and understanding *and then* we can also learn to avoid the mistakes of Solomon, *because it's not how you start, it is how you finish!*

Verse 30: "And Solomon's wisdom was greater than the wisdom of all the sons of the east… [all of the Orient] …and all the wisdom of Egypt."

Today there are secrets of wisdom from the Egyptians that we do not even understand. God really gave it to him. Then it lists all the wise men of his day that he was wiser than them. Notice what Solomon did:

Verse 32: "And he spoke three thousand proverbs…."

We have the book of Proverbs, and I don't think we have all 3,000 there, but we have a good number of them.

"…and his songs were a thousand and five" (v 32).

What were those songs? *We don't know! We're not told!* But notice the wisdom that God gave him; how he understood certain things:

Verse 33: "And he spoke of trees, from the cedar tree in Lebanon even to the hyssop that springs out of the wall. He spoke also of beasts and of birds, and of creeping things, and of fish."

He knew of great things about all of these, the intricate things of the creation of God. As we go along:

- think how we're going to teach the world about that
- think about how wonderful it is going to be that children are going to play with the animals that used to be carnivorous beasts and human-devouring things

Children are going to lead them and play with them. Think how excited children are going to be when they can have their own lion. Get rid of all plastic toys, all television games. Going to have the real thing.

Solomon was so intelligent, so wise, had so much understanding, v 34: "And there came from all

the people to hear the wisdom of Solomon, from all the kings of the earth who had heard of his wisdom."

Yes, they had boat travel around the world. They came from everywhere. This was the only time when the children of Israel, through the kingdom of Solomon, partially fulfilled the commission given to them by God when He gave them the Ten Commandments at Mt. Sinai.

1-Kings 5—Solomon made a league with Hiram, king of Tyre to bring cedar trees and fir trees and everything that they made to build the house of Solomon and the house of God.

1-Kings 8—Solomon's house is finished. The temple is finished. Everything is done. All the priests are ready to go. All the soldiers, captains, princes and so forth were altogether there. Here we're going to see that this comes as the dedication of the temple.

1-Kings 8:65—*the time setting when this took place*: "And at that time Solomon held a feast and all Israel with him, a great congregation—from the entering in of Hamath to the river of Egypt—before the LORD our God, seven days and seven days, *even* fourteen days."

How did this happen? *If we look at the calendar we can understand!* This is why understanding the Calculated Hebrews Calendar is important. In the first day of the seventh month the dedication of the temple started, and lasted for seven days. Then there was a break, because there was the Day of Atonement. What are they to do on the Day of Atonement? *They are not to do any work! They are not to have any eating, no drinking; they are to be fasting!*

From the 8th day through to the beginning of the Feast of Tabernacles on the 15th day—which is a week—they did not have a continuation of the dedication of the temple. But after the Day of Atonement they made preparations for the greatest Feast that was ever held by the children of Israel, the Feast of Tabernacles to celebrate the functioning of the temple, the completion of it.

Here's what happened. Everything was set on the Feast of Trumpets. You can follow the parallel with this in 2-Chron. 5.

1-Kings 8:1: "Then Solomon assembled the elders of Israel and all the heads of the tribes, the chief of the fathers of the children of Israel, to King Solomon in Jerusalem, so that they might bring up the Ark of the Covenant of the LORD out of the city of David, which *is* Zion. And all the men of Israel were gathered to King Solomon at the Feast in the month Ethanim, which *is* the seventh month…. [the beginning of the 7th month] …And all the elders of

Israel came in, and the priests took up the Ark. And they brought up the Ark of the LORD and the tabernacle of the congregation…" (vs 1-4).

They took all of these things from Gibeon and they brought them all down to the temple. What they did with the tabernacle, they stored that in the subterranean archives of the temple.

"…and all the Holy vessels which *were* in the tabernacle—even those the priests and the Levites brought up. And King Solomon and all the congregation of Israel, who had assembled to him *were* before the Ark sacrificing sheep and oxen which could not be counted nor numbered for multitude" (vs 4-5).

What they did, they put extra burnt offering altars all around the temple area, because this was the greatest celebration that there ever was concerning dedicating the temple. What a fantastic time this was.

I want you to think about how great it's going to be when we are there at the dedication of the Tabernacle of God where He has the tabernacle right over Jerusalem. Remember, Jerusalem with the earthquake that's going to take place when Christ and the saints return, is going to lift up Jerusalem even higher than it is. Then Christ is going to have that tabernacle with the pillars of cloud by day and fire by night. Think about what it's going to be with us rejoicing that now God is bringing that, with Christ setting up His temple on earth. That's going to be quite a thing!

Think of it as very similar to all of this. It describes all of it. Afterward they put the Ark into the Holy of Holies; God put His presence there.

Verse 10: "And it came to pass when the priests had come out of the Holy of Holies, the cloud filled the house of the LORD."

Remember, that's exactly what happened when the tabernacle was raised up on the first day of the second month and dedicated before the Passover in the book of Exodus. The cloud of God filled the tabernacle.

Here it filled the temple to show and to prove to Solomon, all the priests, all the leaders of Israel, all the people of Israel there that God truly had put His presence in the temple just as He has promised David and Solomon.

Now then, Solomon brings his prayer; read the whole prayer that Solomon gave. When you read it through and the account also (2-Chron. 6-8). Look at all of the *Ifs*: '***IF*** Your people…' Let's see how Solomon finished this prayer:

1-Kings 8:54: "Now it came to pass as Solomon finished praying all this prayer and petition to the LORD, he rose from before the altar of the LORD, from kneeling on his knees with his hands spread up to heaven. Now it came to pass as Solomon finished praying all this prayer and petition to the LORD, he rose from before the altar of the LORD, from kneeling on his knees with his hands spread up to heaven. Then he stood and blessed all the congregation of Israel with a loud voice. saying, 'Blessed *be* the LORD, who has given rest to His people Israel, according to all that He promised. **There has not failed one word** of all His good promises, which He promised by the hand of Moses His servant'" (vs 54-56). *Draw the parallel, here are our lives*:

- we're struggling
- we're overcoming
- we're growing in grace and knowledge
- we're loving God
- we're keeping the Kingdom of God first in our mind
  - ✓ where we're going
  - ✓ what we're doing

Remember: Read and study all the promises of Christ, because *not one promise will fail!* Think what it's going to be like. There is going to be a great celebration by all the sons of God at the dedication of the tabernacle when the Millennium starts and Christ sets up the tabernacle there in Jerusalem. It's going to be awesome. There will be a prayer similar to this.

Verse 57: "'May the LORD our God be with us as He was with our fathers. Let Him not leave us nor forsake us.'"

Remember: When everything goes well, God says, 'When you have been filled to the full, beware lest your heart be lifted up and you forget the Lord your God who has given all these things, and you say *by my hand and by my might have done these things,* when that is not true' (Deut. 8). *Nothing happens without God making it occur!* Remember that spiritually!

Verse 58: "'To incline our hearts to Himself, to walk in all His ways and to keep His commandments and His statutes and His judgments which He commanded our fathers. And let these my words, with which I have made supplications before the LORD, be near the LORD our God day and night, so that He may maintain the cause of His servant and the cause of His people Israel at all times as the matter requires" (vs 58-59).

We need to understand that in relationship to the modern tribes of Israel today. ***IF*** they would turn to God—and they can do it; ***IF*** they would turn to the Word of God and love God, begin keeping His commandments, begin teaching the people to keep the laws of God so that we don't have sin running like a tsunami through our land, where then God has to:

- judge us with drought
- judge us with floods
- judge us with a whirlwind
- judge us with sickness
- judge us with disease
- judge us with financial calamity

IF the nations would do that, God would hold back His hand of judgment. But we need to remember, there's always a time that it becomes too late to turn back. It's not too late now; it could still happen.

But notice how this fulfills very carefully what God told the children of Israel, 'that all the people of the earth may know…' (Exo. 19). God decided that He's going to go through one man and his offspring. Then that came down to the 12 tribes of Israel. Then He was going to go through one man David, and that came down to his son Solomon. But the mission was to go to the world. I want you to think about what Jesus told the apostles. He said, 'Go into all the world and teach all nations.' Notice how similar this is:

Verse 60: "'That all the people of the earth may know that the LORD *is* God; *there is* no other. And let your heart… [each one of you individually] be perfect with the LORD our God: to walk in His statutes and to keep His commandments, as at this day.' And the king and all Israel with him, offered sacrifice before the LORD" (vs 60-62).

That was really something. It was an amazing thing that took place. Here is the dedication of the temple, and he gave all of these offerings,

Verse 63: "And Solomon offered a sacrifice of peace offerings which he offered to the LORD: twenty-two thousand oxen…"—*22 is the number of letters in the Hebrew alphabet*; so there's a thousand oxen for every letter of the alphabet.

"…and a hundred and twenty thousand sheep…" (v 63). *There were 12 tribes of the children of Israel, so there were 12,000 sheep for every tribe!* See how God deals in numbers.

"…So the king and all the children of Israel dedicated the house of the LORD" (v 63).

Notice what he did on the eighth day of the Feast. It went Feast of Trumpets for a week. Then Feast of Tabernacles for a week plus one day. This is why we get 7 days and 7 days, which is 14.

Then v 66 mentions the 8ᵗʰ day; "On the eighth day he sent the people away. And they blessed the king and went to their tents joyful and glad of heart for all the good that the LORD had done for David His servant and for Israel His people." An amazing thing!

Brethren, we're going to see such dedication when the Kingdom of God is setup on the earth, then there will be a dedication for God bringing all the children of Israel back out of captivity. They're going to be spread out in captivity because of their sins. So, we can see some parallels here.

Let's see how he grew great. Let's see how much God continued to bless him in every way. This is quite a phenomenal thing, brethren, because this also has some parallels with us, and for the Kingdom of God.

1-Kings 10:1: "And the queen of Sheba heard of Solomon's fame concerning the name of the LORD, and she came to prove him with hard questions. And she came to Jerusalem with a very great train… [a caravan] …with camels that bore spices and very much gold and precious stones. And she came to Solomon, and she told him all that was in her heart. And Solomon answered all her questions for her. There was not a thing hidden from the king, which he did not tell her. And when the queen of Sheba had seen all of Solomon's wisdom, and the house which he had built, and the food of his table, and the sitting of his servants, and the attendance of his ministers, and their clothing, and his cupbearers, and his burnt offering that he offered up to the house of the LORD, there was no more spirit in her" (vs 1-5). *Took her breath away, literally!*

Verse 6: "And she said to the king, 'It was a true report which I heard in my own land of your acts and of your wisdom.'"

We're going to see that Solomon had a navy. This navy went around the world. They were well-educated. They understood the world. They understood the oceans. They traveled; they traded and how else could the knowledge of the Lord, through Solomon—as it was supposed to—go to the whole world? We're going to see what happened when the world came to him. That's what we need to understand. This was a fantastic thing that happened—"…no more spirit in her."

Verse 7: "'And I did not believe the words until I came and my eyes had seen. And behold, the half was not told me. Your wisdom and blessings are more than the fame which I heard. Happy *are* your men, happy are these who are your servants, who stand always before you, and who hear your wisdom" (vs 7-8).

The world is searching after happiness today; even people in the Church are searching after happiness. But it only comes in serving God! It doesn't come in doing our things or our ways.

Notice what she did then, v 9: "Blessed is the LORD your God, who delighted in you, to set you on the throne of Israel. Because the LORD loved Israel forever, therefore He made you king to do judgment and justice."

- she learned of God
- she learned of the Truth
- she learned of the way

Not unto salvation, *but she learned of it because of the blessings that God gave!*

This shows the fullness of the covenant of the letter of the Law that God gave to Israel. God honored that, God blessed that, and this was a tremendous thing that occurred.

1-Kings 9:28 *shows that the navies of Solomon* "…came to Ophir, and brought gold from there, four hundred and twenty talents, and brought it to King Solomon." *It's a wonder the ships didn't sink!*

1-Kings 10:10—*concerning the queen of Sheba:* "And she gave the king a hundred and twenty talents of gold, a very great store of spices, and precious stones. No spices like that ever came again in such abundance that the queen of Sheba gave to King Solomon. And also the navy of Hiram which brought gold from Ophir, brought in from Ophir great abundance of almug trees and precious stones. And the king made of the almug trees supports for the house of the LORD, and for the king's house, also lyres and harps for singers. No such almug wood has come or been seen to this day" (vs 10-12).

Here is blessing upon blessing heaped upon King Solomon and the children of Israel. Think of what it's going to be when the Kingdom of God and the saints are ruling as kings and priests with Christ. Not only are there going to be the physical blessings, but there will be the spiritual blessings, because the Spirit of God available to all.

We can use this as a type to understand what we're going to do and to see how we need to teach people God's way. It's going to be overwhelming just like it was here.

Verse 13: "And King Solomon gave to the queen of Sheba all her desire, whatever she asked, besides what Solomon gave her of his royal bounty. So, she turned and went to her own country, she and her servants. And the weight of gold, which came to Solomon in one year… [year-by-year, this is annual tribute from the kings of the world to King

Solomon] …was six hundred sixty-six talents of gold."

There was a lot of trading. There were a lot of ships coming and going. There was a lot of wealth and lot of activity.

Think what it's going to be when the knowledge of the Lord covers the earth as the seas cover the earth. When the knowledge of God's Word is going to be expanded. Just think what it's going to be like that we will be spirit beings with spirit minds, able to understand and teach the people and judge the people.

Remember, as spirit beings we can go wherever we desire. We can walk through walls, and if there's something that people are ready to do, we can say, 'No, this is the way, walk in it!' If they're not going to go God's way, it will be known!

This great abundance that came to Solomon, v 15: "In addition to that which came from the merchant men and from the traffic of the traders and from all the kings of Arabia and from the governors of the lands. And King Solomon made two hundred shields *of* beaten gold; six hundred *shekels* of gold went into one shield" (vs 15-16).

Just literally put gold everywhere in the city of Jerusalem. Quite a fantastic thing that went on. This is the great fulfillment of the Feast of Tabernacles in type to the world during Solomon's day. Now let's see how great this wealth of Solomon's was. You talk about wealthy! You talk about the blessings of God poured out upon him so that he could bring the knowledge of the Word of God to the world.

What did he do with it? This is going to prove very interesting indeed! We are seeing a life-pattern that happens in every life. It's very few who resist sinning against God and who resist becoming self-satisfied in everything that they have.

Stop and think for a minute: If you had everything you wanted in the world, and you had everything brought to you at the clap of the hand or the snap of a finger, and had servants to wait on you, had everything that you desired: Would you keep your mind on God? *or* Would you begin to look to the physical things? We're going to learn a lesson here: **Unless you**

- keep your *spiritual* perspective
- understand that everything comes from God
- understand and realize that God made us to be absolutely dependent upon Him

—even though He's given us free choice, and in order to truly be a complete and full human being—

- you need the Spirit of God
- you need the Word of God
- you need the understanding of God

Everything else does not count!

All of that is summed up in one saying of Jesus: *The flesh profits nothing!* In other words, every physical thing in this world—

- compared to God
- compared to His purpose
- compared to His goals
- compared to receiving a spirit body at the resurrection
  - ✓ a spirit mind
  - ✓ to be given rulership

—there is nothing to be compared to that! That's why He said *the flesh profits nothing!* Then He said, *'The words that I speak to you, they are Spirit and they are Life.'*

That's why when you read and study the Bible, you learn things that are mind-changing, that are life-changing, that have an effect upon you like nothing else does, because these are the words of God and these are Spirit and these are Life. This is quite a thing here, brethren. This is a great lesson we're going to learn.

Verse 21: "And all King Solomon's drinking vessels *were of* gold, and all the vessels of the house of the forest of Lebanon *were of* pure gold. None were of silver; it was counted as nothing in the days of Solomon."

I want you to compare that financial stability and wealth to the debt society and finances that we have today. It's all paper! It is all debt! It is all make believe! *And the judgment of God is coming upon this world for doing this to the wealth that God has given!*

- it's all of subterfuge
- it's all of lies
- it's all of Satan the devil

That's the comparison!

Let's read what is recorded here for us and tell us more of Solomon's reign:

Verse 22: "For the king had at sea a navy of Tarshish with the navy of Hiram… [two navies: one out of Phoenicia and one out of the Gulf of Aquba or the Red Sea] …Once in three years the navy of Tarshish came bringing gold and silver, ivory, and apes, and peacocks. And King Solomon was greater than all the kings of the earth in riches and in wisdom" (vs 22-23).

Then we'll see what happened to Solomon. It's contained in Rev. 3 where it says that 'he has grown rich'—this applies to the Church as well, so you can see the spiritual things, too—'and increased with goods and have need of nothing.' We'll see what happens when that occurs.

Verse 24: "And all the earth sought Solomon to hear his wisdom, which God had put in his heart. And every man brought his presents, vessels of silver and vessels of gold, and clothing and armor, and spices, horses and mules, at a rate year by year" (vs 24-25).

So beneficial and widespread were the blessings from the kingdom of Solomon that they willingly brought tribute to him. This was part of a vast worldwide organization under the direction of the children of Israel. King Solomon was the king over this worldwide empire. This was something!

Verse 26: "And Solomon gathered chariots and horsemen. And he had fourteen hundred chariots, and twelve thousand horsemen, whom he stationed in the cities for chariots and with the king at Jerusalem. And the king made silver like stones in Jerusalem, and he made cedars like the sycamore trees in the valley for abundance" (vs 26-27). *Then he brought horses and clothing!*

After Solomon had all of this: he had his wisdom, he understood things, the great men of the world came to hear his wisdom, to understand things about everything that there is. There's another book in the Bible called *Ecclesiastes*. After Solomon had been blessed with all of these things, and after he had all of this:

- let's see what he did
- let's see how he thought
- let's see what he did with his life and with what God had given him

That's quite a thing that took place!

Now, Solomon did learn one lesson, the lesson that David his father taught him, but he didn't learn it a hundred percent.

Let's see what David learned, because he taught Solomon his son. Let's see what David learned about human ability, human activity and all the things that we can do as human beings. We can do a lot of things, but remember: *The flesh profits nothing!* When something profits nothing, *that is vanity!*

- in spite of all the wisdom
- in spite of all the wealth
- in spite of all the kingdom
- in spite of all those who were the princes and the captains and all of those who

waited on him

- in spite of the great bureaucracy that he had throughout his kingdom and where it reached into all the nations of the world

Remember: *the flesh profits nothing!* It is the Spirit that gives life! Jesus said, *'the words that I speak to you, they are Spirit and they are Life.'* Here's the lesson that David, Solomon's father, learned. He even made a psalm of this, sang it before God:

Psalms 39:1: "I said, 'I will take heed to my ways so that I do not sin with my tongue…'"

There were probably a lot of things he did that he sinned with his tongue. We are told in the New Testament that we are to bring 'every vain imagination and thought into captivity into the obedience of Jesus Christ. That's also expressed here.

"'…I will keep my mouth with a bridle while the wicked are before me.' I became dumb, keeping silent; I said nothing good, and yet my sorrow grew worse. My heart was hot within me; while I was musing, the fire burned; then I spoke with my tongue" (vs 1-3).

After seeing all that went on, looking at all human life, and this is what all philosophers cannot understand; some come close to it, but they don't understand it.

Verse 4: "O LORD, make me to know my end and the measure of my days, what it is, that I may know how short lived I am."

He lived to be 70-years-old. This happens when you get older and you look back at your life. You think: where have all the years gone? It is true, the older we get, the faster time seems to go. It really does! We look back and think of things as if it was yesterday, and it was ten years ago. Likewise, with David, he said:

Verse 4: "O Lord, make me to know my end and the measure of my days, what it is, that I may know how short lived I am. Behold, You have made my days as a handbreadth, and the span of my days is as nothing before You…." (vs 4-5).

You Who live forever! *God!* In eternity! It says of God that He 'inhabits eternity.' He lives in a different level of life than we do.

- He's given us physical life
- He's given us the Spirit of man
- He's given us His Holy Spirit within us

IF *we repent, are baptized and receive the Holy Spirit of God!*

But that is just a pinprick of what God is going to give us as spirit beings. So, this is what David was musing, looking at His life, looking at the life of others.

"…the span of my days is as nothing before You. Surely every man at his best state is altogether vanity. Selah" (v 5).

When we have our best thoughts, when we have our best behavior, we can say that when we have everything taken care of physically, and when we have our best clothing on, everything is the best; *it's all vanity!* God says that 'all flesh is as grass and is as the flower of the field'; it grows old, dries up and the flower falls off. *That's quite a summary of life!*

Verse 6: "Surely every man walks about in a vain show! Surely they are in an uproar in vain…."

Isn't that true? Watch what goes on with the news, television, reports, sports and everything. All the commercials are nothing but fantasies and manufactured, artificial, synthetic reality.

"…He heaps up riches and does not know who shall gather them. And now, LORD, what do I wait for?…." (vs 6-7).

Looking at what life is all about. We will see that Solomon understood some of these things, but he didn't learn the lesson as his father David did.

You can have all the blessings of God; you can receive all the physical things that you can possibly have and more to where you are so full of it that you say, *'I am rich and increased with goods and have need of nothing.'* Then Christ says, *'And you know not that you are naked, miserable, poor and blind.'* And we will see that's exactly what happened to Solomon.

This is a Psalm of repentance. Knowing and understanding that these things are all temporary and he's got to repent of it, so he says:

Verse 8: "Deliver me from all my transgressions; make me not the reproach of the fool. I was dumb; I did not open my mouth because You have done it" (vs 8-9).

He was suffering from some kind of correction of God. When that happens, what are you going to say? *O Lord, no!* Like Job said, 'I spoke once, twice I've spoken, but I'm going to lay my hand on my mouth, I'm going to shut up!'

Verse 10: "Remove Your stroke away from me; I am consumed by the blow of Your hand. You correct a man for iniquity with rebukes, and you make his beauty to vanish away like a moth. Surely every man is vanity. Selah" (vs 10-11)—*think on this!*

Here we are at the Feast. We're enjoying all these wonderful things. We have lots of food. We have comfortable surroundings. But what we need more than anything else is:

- *God*
- *His Spirit*
- *His knowledge*
- *His Truth*

so that we do not get hung-up on physical things!

Also, let's carry this forward into the Kingdom of God as we teach the people who will be under our charge. They are going to be given every spiritual blessing, every physical blessing:

- every man is going to 'sit under his fig tree and his vine'
- he's not going to be afraid
- he's not going to learn war anymore
- all of the kings and priests will be teaching
- the people will learn
- they will understand of God
- they will realize the spiritual substance behind everything physical
- they will understand why they're here and where they're going

We will see when we come to the end of the Millennium, something happens when they get their mind off of God and they don't take the correction of God.

David finishes this Psalm by saying, v 12: "Hear my prayer, O LORD, and give ear to my cry. Do not be silent at my tears; for I am a stranger with You, a sojourner, as all my fathers were. Look away from me, that I may recover strength before I depart and am no more" (vs 12-13). That's quite a thing!

Let's see how Solomon learned some of these things, and see how he didn't learn. David did to a great degree. Solomon did to a pretty good degree. As you look at all the physical things, this is why in the Millennium this becomes important. Everyone is going to have every physical thing that they need. There's going to be success, and lives are going to be productive. Families will be together, and they're going to have to learn this one thing: *The physical things do not profit! It is the Spirit that gives life!*

Ecclesiastes 1:1: "The words of the Preacher [Solomon], the son of David, king in Jerusalem. 'Vanity of vanities,' says the Preacher, 'vanity of vanities! **All** *is* **vanity**.'" (vs 1-2). *Look at your life*:

- What have you done?
- Where have you gone?

- What are you doing?
- Where are you going?

Verse 3: "What profit does a man have in all his labor which he labors under the sun?"

We're seeing this happen right now. Look at everything that built this nation, everything that God blessed the children of Israel—the modern descendants—with and look where it's all going—POOF!—all disappearing and all vanity.

Take this same thing and you can apply it to people who have been in the Church. Some were the seed sown on unproductive ground—where are they? Where are those who used to attend with us? God is always cleansing, purging and helping people to come to righteousness if they will. If they won't then they have the correction come upon them.

Verse 4: "One generation passes away, and another generation comes; but the earth remains forever. The sun also arises, and the sun goes down, and hurries to its place where it arose. The wind goes toward the south, and it turns around to the north; it whirls around continually; and the wind returns on its circuits" (vs 1-6). *They knew an awful lot about how the earth functioned!*

Today, we have the narcissistic evolutionary attitude in the world of the elite. 'Oh, we know everything! Everything in the past was old and stupid and they knew nothing.' Well, if you read carefully here, this says they knew a lot!

Verse 7: "All the rivers run into the sea; yet the sea *is* not full; to the place from where the rivers come, there they return again. All things *are* full of labor; man cannot utter it; **the eye is not satisfied with seeing, nor the ear filled with hearing**" (vs 7-8).

Isn't that absolutely true when you look at all the entertainment, sports, knowledge and technology that's going on today. **"…the eye is not satisfied with seeing, nor the ear filled with hearing."**

Then Solomon makes a statement that is quite profound, v 9: "That which has been *is* that which shall be; and that which has been done *is* that which shall be done; and **there is nothing new under the sun.**"

- think about that in relationship to our so-called advanced civilization that we live in
- think about that in relationship to the civilization before the Flood
- think about that, as Jesus said, 'As it was in the days of Noah, so shall it be in the days of the coming of the Son of man'

Verse 10: "Is there a thing *of* which it may be said, **'See, this *is* new'? It has already been in days of old, which were before us**."

Let me just give you an example: The archeologists who like to go, especially to Egypt:

- How did they build the pyramids?
- How did they build these tombs?
- Why did they have so many underground tunnels?
- How is it that they were able to build these things?

Yet, we don't see the smoke-soot from torches and candles and lanterns!

They looked at one of the hieroglyphics and here was a man holding in his hand a great—they didn't know what it was, but when you look at it with what it shows—long tube that was closed at the end and inside were wavy lines. Now they're asking:

Did they have knowledge of electricity in ancient Egypt? If they did—which they probably did—would that not answer how they were able to build these things unless they had some kind of light. *Light that did not produce soot and smoke* that clung to the ceiling or walls of the interiors of the temples and tombs that the Egyptians built.

"…'See, this *is* new'? **It has already been in days of old, which were before us**." (v 10). *Here's a catch! Here's what happens! People forget*:

Verse 11: "*There is* no memory of former *things*, neither shall there be any remembrance of *things* that are to come by those who shall come afterwards."

Quite a good summary of how human life is, and physical life is. All of this is the part of wisdom that God gave to Solomon. We're going to see what he did with it. How did he handle it? *We also need to ask ourselves those questions today*:

- What are we doing with the knowledge and Truth of the Word of God?
- How do we handle it in understanding the Bible?
- Do we love God?
- Do we love our neighbors?
- Do we love the brethren?
- What is it that we are doing?

God is doing a work in us!

- How are we cooperating with God in that work?
- Are we cooperating in such a way that it will result in spiritual character so that at the resurrection we can be resurrected to inherit eternal life?

or

- Is it going to be a matter of vanity?

Here's what Solomon did, the great experiment in human life and activity recorded for us so we can get God's perspective on it. This will be some of the very lessons that we will need to learn and teach people in the Millennium, because they will have every physical blessing right there. Let's see what Solomon did, and then we will see where it led him, and we will see what happens when vanity is not overcome.

Verse 12[transcriber's correction]: "I, the Preacher, was king over Israel in Jerusalem. And I gave my heart to seek and search out by wisdom concerning all things that are done under the heavens. *It is* a grievous task God has given to the sons of men to be exercised by it. I have seen all the works that are done under the sun; and, behold, **all *is* vanity and striving after wind**" (vs 12-14)—*or vexation of spirit!*

Here's what he observed, v 15: "What *is* crooked cannot be made straight; and *what is* lacking cannot be numbered. I spoke within my own heart, saying, 'Lo, I have become great and have gathered more wisdom than all that have been before me in Jerusalem; yea, my heart has experienced great wisdom and knowledge.' And I gave my heart to know wisdom and to know madness and folly; I perceived that this also *is* striving after wind. **For in much wisdom *is* much grief; and he who increases knowledge increases sorrow**" (vs 15-18).

That's really true! Let's see what he did, and let's see what happened to him, and we will pick this up tomorrow and see what happened to Solomon and how did he handle the gifts of God that God gave to him.

Scriptural References:

1) 1 Kings 3:3-14
2) Genesis 26:3-5
3) 1 Kings 3:14-15
4) 1 Kings 4:24-25, 29-30, 32-34
5) 1 Kings 8:65, 1-5, 10, 54-63, 66
6) 1 Kings 10:1-9
7) 1 Kings 9:28
8) 1 Kings 10:10-16, 21-27
9) Psalm 39:1-13
10) Ecclesiastes 1:1-18

Scriptures referenced, not quoted:

- Revelation 2; 3
- Isaiah 2
- 1 Kings 5

- 2 Chronicles 5-8
- Deuteronomy 8
- Exodus 19

FRC:bo
Transcribed: 8/8/12
Reformatted: 1/2021

CHAPTER SEVENTY-ONE

It's Not How You Start, It's How You Finish! II
Fred R. Coulter

Greetings, everyone! Here we are on the second half already.

We've been covering some things concerning King Solomon. When that was the only time that the children of Israel and the king came close to fulfilling the purpose of why God called Israel and gave them His laws and His commandments.

What a tremendous thing it was, the way that Solomon started out. God loved him! We saw that he was humble! We saw that he asked for wisdom and understanding to be able to judge the children of Israel. He was king over all 12 tribes, the last king to be over the 12 tribes. Let's see what happened to Solomon, because part of this gives us an understanding as to why human nature, after a while when it has everything, becomes—as it says of the Laodiceans—lukewarm, apathetic, taking things for granted, assuming things. Then comes the human sin again of *pride and arrogancy*, of trying to understand your life without a real relationship with God, and trying to understand what is the purpose in life.

Solomon could have known a whole lot more than he did had he really given himself to God the way that he should have. When we come Ecc. 2 what we are going to find out is this: *Solomon wanted to find out the purpose of life while still having some connection with God,* but really not seeking God for the answer. Rather, he was seeking through *experimentation.* Experimentation by men doesn't bring you the understanding of God.

Solomon, we saw, had more knowledge than any other man on earth. We're going to see what that led to. We're going to see that even though in the end he acknowledged the commandments of God, he lost his relationship with God because of what he did when he got old. This was not something that happened to Solomon just over night.

Here's what he endeavored to do. Notice how many times he talks about 'I'; very similar to Job, however, Job repented, but nowhere do we find that Solomon repented

Ecclesiastes 2:1: "**I** said in **my** heart, 'Come now, **I** will test you with pleasure to find out what is good.' and, behold, this also *is* vanity."

We need to understand that in God we *'live, move and have our being.'* God made us incomplete. God made us imperfect; though we can function perfectly as a human being as long as everything is right in the body. But we don't have perfect character and we cannot attain to perfect character without God and His Spirit. This is the whole lesson of the book of Ecclesiastes and what Solomon did. So, he saw that was vanity!

Verse 2: "**I** said of laughter, '*It is* madness;' and of mirth, 'What does it accomplish?'" He wanted to know.

Let's look at a Proverb here, because this is exactly what Solomon was doing. Solomon was to be wise. He had wisdom, knowledge, understanding, *because **God** gave it!* However, in Ecc. 2 and all the way through the rest of the book of Ecclesiastes, though he mentions God and holds onto God he was actually *leaving* God. He was trying to find the purpose in life himself. In the end, we're going to see that Solomon ended up being, rather than wise, *a fool.* Just like the wise in the world who profess themselves to be wise, they're fools. That's what happened to Solomon because he was doing this:

Proverbs 18:2: "A fool has no delight in understanding, but only that his heart may discover itself."

This is how Solomon began to lose his understanding; yet, he was trying to find understanding. But he wasn't seeking it with God; he was seeking it with self-experimentation—the fool is trying to *find himself.*

So, here's what he did, Ecclesiastes 2:3: "**I** sought in my heart to give **myself** unto wine, yet conducting **my** heart with wisdom; and to lay hold on folly, until **I** might see what was good for the sons of men, what they should do under the heaven the few days of their life."

That was his purpose. He's going to experiment with everything. Doesn't this happen with a lot of people in the world?

When it comes to the Millennium and we're teaching the people, what we're going to understand is this is not going to be the way they're going to learn of God. We're going to teach them. This is going to be something!

Also, we will need to learn, because when we're spirit beings and immortal and brought into the Kingdom of God, we're going to learn so much more of God, His way and His Truth that it is going to be phenomenal! Just as we're born in the flesh and then we learn and grow in knowledge all of our lives, so likewise when we're born of the spirit and enter into the Kingdom of God and we are completely composed of spirit then we're really going to learn, because *the knowledge of the Lord is going to cover the earth as the seas cover the earth.*

Who is going to be teaching that to the people? *We are!* This gives us a good understanding of what we need to do. A good understanding of why it's not going to be run like Solomon ran it. The purpose of what we're going to do is to have people enter into the Kingdom of God. Here's what Solomon did. He had free reign to do it all:

Verse 4: "**I** made great works for **myself**; **I** built houses for **myself**; I planted vineyards for myself…. [notice self-centered; not God-centered] …**I** made gardens and orchards for **myself**, and **I** planted trees in them, of all fruit. **I** made pools of water for **myself**, to irrigate groves of growing trees. **I** bought men slaves and women slaves, and servants *were* born in my house; also **I** had great possessions of herds and flocks, above all that were before **me** in Jerusalem" (vs 4-7).

Not lacking a single thing! Anything he wanted to do or thought of, to experiment with, to find out: Why are we here? Where are we going? What is life?

But we're going to see he never found it! That's why in the Millennium we're going to teach the people the relationship with God. They will have to have relationships with us as their teachers, as well. We're going to teach them that though they have everything they would ever want or desire during the Millennium, *do not look at it through carnal eyes,* as Solomon did.

Verse 8, richest man in the world: "**I** also gathered silver and gold to **myself**… [notice all the 'I' and 'myself'—getting carried away with vanity and stupidity in his own life] …and the treasure of kings and of the provinces. **I** got men singers and women singers for **myself,** even the sensual delights of the sons of men, and many women." *We're going to see that was Solomon's great downfall!*

Verse 9: "So, **I** was great and increased more than all that were before **me** in Jerusalem; also **my** wisdom remained with **me**. And whatever **my** eyes desired **I** did not keep from them; **I** did not withhold **my** heart from any pleasure; for **my** heart rejoiced in all **my** labor, and this was **my** portion of

all **my** labor" (vs 9-10).

You would think after all this striving—it's called 'striving after wind'—vexation of spirit—he would have learned the lesson to turn to God. In the end he mentions 'the sum of it is, fear God and keep His commandments.' But he never said to love God, have a relationship with Him.

Everything comes from God! This is what we're going to be teaching during the Millennium, as well. This is what we need to learn during the Feast of Tabernacles, a time of abundance, a time of being able to get together, a time of spiritual understanding if we apply ourselves to it. And a time when we realize that we are absolutely, totally, one hundred percent dependent upon God the Father and Jesus Christ.

- that is the key to *success*
- that is the key to *eternal life*
- that is the key to *understanding the purpose in life*

After he did all of that:

Verse 11: "Then **I** looked on all the works that **my** hands had done, and on the labor that **I** had labored to do; and, behold, all *is* vanity and a striving after the wind; and *there is* no profit under the sun." *That is in the physical pursuits. It all comes to an end!*

He could have taken the next step and sought a greater relationship with God. He learned all of this and it didn't amount to what he thought it would. He couldn't discover life through just doing these things by himself. If he did it all for himself, how much did he exclude God?

Verse 12: "And **I** turned to behold wisdom, and madness, and folly; for what *can* the man *do* who comes after the king? Only that which has been already done. Then **I** saw that wisdom excels folly, as far as light excels darkness" (vs 12-13). *He learned that lesson, but*:

- Did that bring him to conversion?
- Did that bring him to repentance?
- *Nowhere do we find it!*

Verse 14: "The wise man's eyes *are* in his head; but the fool walks in darkness; and **I myself** also perceived that one event happens to all of them." *They all die!*

Now, let's come back to where we began concerning Light and darkness. Remember about the Light and the darkness. What we're going to see in the book of Ecclesiastes[transcriber's correction] is that Solomon started in the Light, but in serving *himself* he turned his back on the Light and went *his way.*

John 3:19: "And this is the judgment: that the Light has come into the world… [Christ; the Light of men] …but men loved darkness rather than the Light because their works were evil."

What we're going to see is this: *Whenever anyone turns their back on God and goes out on their own, seeking to do good or find the purpose in life, they are walking away from God!*

Solomon talked about Light and darkness, but he didn't perceive where he was going. When you turn your back on the Light and you look ahead, the Light is still shinning out there, but as you walk away from the Light, it gets dimmer and dimmer and dimmer, and pretty soon you come to the place that you leave the twilight of the Light and you enter darkness. We'll see that's what Solomon did.

Verse 20: "For everyone who practices evil hates the Light, and does not come to the Light, so that his works may not be exposed; but the one who practices the Truth comes to the Light… [is coming to the Light and the Light is Christ and the Word of God is Light] …so that his works may be manifested, that they have been accomplished by *the power of* God" (vs 20-21).

Let's see that Solomon was walking away from the Light. We're going to see this inclination is still going to be in people that we're going to be teaching during the Millennium. There are going to be people who will want to do what Solomon did to find out. We'll be there to say, 'No, this is the way, walk in it. Don't turn to the right hand or turn to the left hand.' So, Solomon saw Light and darkness, and fools walk in darkness and they all die.

Ecclesiastes 2:15: "Then **I** said in **my** heart, 'As it happens to the fool, *so* it happens even to **me**; and why was **I** then more wise?'…."

What was the answer? *God gave it to him!* So, you see he's stepping away from God. We can learn this as a lesson in our life, too, as we grow, change and overcome. That we need to realize the only time we're going to have really accomplished what is necessary is when we're raised from the dead and God will accomplish His work in us.

"…And **I** said in my heart that this also *is* vanity. For *there is* no memory of the wise *more than* of the fool forever, since that which is now shall all be forgotten in the days to come. And how does the wise die? **Even as the fool!**" (vs 15-16). *His breath goes POOF, and he's gone!*

Notice what happens when you're out there and you're striving to try and find the purpose in life without God:

Verse 17: "Therefore, **I** hated life; because the work that is done under the sun *is* grievous to **me**; for all *is* vanity and a striving after wind." Grab the wind; can you catch it? Run to get out of the wind; can you outpace it? Run into the wind; can you gather it in? *No!* "…*striving after wind.*"

Verse 18: "Yea, **I** hated all **my** labor, which **I** had done under the sun, because **I** must leave it to the man who shall be after me. And who knows *whether* he shall be wise or a fool?…. [As it turned out, his son Rehoboam[transcriber's correction] turned out to be a fool! So did Solomon in his old age.] …Yet, he shall have rule over all **my** labor in which **I** have labored, and have shown **myself** wise under the sun. This *is* also vanity" (vs 18-19).

Why did he not teach his son Rehoboam? *Think what it would have been if he would have continued to include God in everything!* There was nothing that Solomon didn't receive that he didn't get it from God. There's nothing that he could do that would be apart from God. That's why this book is here. This is why it's necessary for us to understand.

As a matter of fact, even the Jews, when they gave the readings for the Feast days, the book of Ecclesiastes was to be read during the Feast of Tabernacles, because when the people had the fullness of everything physically, they needed to know that this was not the end, but only a means of part of living; *that everything comes from God!*

Verse 21: "For there is a man whose labor is in wisdom, and in knowledge, and with skill; yet to a man who has not labored in it, he shall leave it *for* his portion. **This also is vanity and a great evil.**"

Even the pharaoh's wanted to take it with them, but they couldn't do it. Even building pyramids and building great tombs; it's like when the rich man dies, someone whispers in the crowd: How much did he leave? And someone whispers back: *All of it!* This was grieving Solomon. He had all of this and he was wondering what was going to happen.

Verse 22: "For what has man from all his labor, and from the striving of his heart, in which he has labored under the sun? For all his days *are* sorrows, and his labor vexation; yea, so his heart does not take rest in the night. **This *is* also vanity**" (vs 22-23).

He's saying that whether you have a good life with everything, whether you have a bad life with a lot of sorrows and misery, *it's all vanity! Because only that which is eternal is not vanity!* Think on that!

Verse 24: "There is nothing better for a man than that he should eat and drink and make his soul see good in his labor? This **I** also saw, that it *was* from the hand of God. For who can eat, or who can enjoy it, more than **I**? For *God* gives wisdom, and knowledge, and joy to a man who *is* good in His sight. But to the sinner He gives labor, to gather and to heap up, that he may give to *him who is* good before God. This also *is* vanity and a striving after wind" (vs 24-26).

So, Solomon was really perplexed, and here is the lesson that we're going to learn out of it: *You can never discover the purpose of life by experimentation in physical things!* You may learn things. You may have some wisdom and knowledge. You may have some skills and ability. But:

- you don't know why we are here
- you don't know why we were born
- you don't know what God is doing

Even in spite of that, Solomon became quite a great philosopher. Gave a lot of proverbs, but in the end run *he went against everything that he knew and taught!* The same way, **spiritual knowledge does not stay in a physical mind!** You have to renew it day-by-day and that's why we have the Sabbath and Holy Days, as well.

He continues to muse on, Ecclesiastes 3:1: "To everything *there is* a season, and a time for every purpose under the heavens: A time to be born, and a time to die; a time to plant, and a time to pluck up what *is* planted; a time to kill, and a time to heal; a time to break down, and a time to build up; a time to weep, and a time to laugh; a time to mourn, and a time to dance" (vs 1-4). *All of those!*

He's getting to a point, and what he's going to do is show that God put into man to have *the ability to think beyond himself.* Yet, in striving to find the purpose in life by doing the physical things that God has given without really understanding that it all came from God. You may give lip service to God, like Solomon has done, but to be completely devoted to God in a spiritual relationship, Solomon never attained to.

Verse 5: "A time to throw away stones, and a time to gather stones together; a time to embrace, and a time to refrain from embracing; a time to gain, and a time to lose; a time to keep, and a time to throw away; a time to tear, and a time to sew; a time to keep silence, and a time to speak; a time to love, and a time to hate; a time of war, and a time of peace" (vs 5-8).

So, he examined all of these things, looking at every human activity, and as king knowing many people, seeing many activities, seeing the works that people did, he had a unique perspective, and yet, *it was missing the devotion to God!*

Verse 9: "What profit does he have who works in that in which he labors? I have seen the task, which God has given to the sons of men to be exercised by it…. [He had it all, but he never learned.] …He has made everything beautiful in its time; He has also set eternity in their heart…" (vs 9-11).

This means that God has given to man the ability to think beyond himself, forward into the future; think in the past, beyond his time which no other of the living creatures of God can do that are on the earth.

This is why man without God will never understand God's eternal purpose. God gave them the longing for eternity in the their heart. He gave them the desire, and everyone wants to live forever. All human being, regardless of what religion there is believe in some kind of afterlife. That's because of v 11. *But unless you turn to God you're not going to find the Truth!* No man can find out the work that God makes from the beginning to the end.

He was in quite a conundrum here, trying to understand what he was doing. He still understood some things of God. Just like people in the world today. There are a lot of people who understand *some* things about God, but they have yet to yield to God *so He can grant them the understanding of His plan and purpose for man.*

Here is the futility of trying to find the purpose of man and God's creation just by experimenting on your own:

Verse 14: "I know that whatever God does, it shall be forever; nothing can be added to it, nor anything taken from it… [he remembered that] …and God does *it* so that men should fear before Him."

Then he makes this statement again, because this is really important to understand. Every generation likes to think that 'we know more than the ones who came before us.' *And that's just not so!*

Verse 15: "That which has been is now; and that which *is* to be has already been; and God requires an account of that which is past…. [he's still clinging to some knowledge of God] …And again I saw under the sun the place of judgment, that wickedness *was* there; and in the place of righteousness, that wickedness *was* there" (vs 15-16).

He never understood about *the law of sin and death* that we have within. That's why in these places of judgment and righteousness, there's still wickedness that happens. Men sin! They do exactly like Solomon! ***They become complacent in what*** *they have, and they're seeking for greater gratification and satisfaction, and then they end up sinning and getting into perversity!* Many people go right on into the occult and witchcraft. That's the whole basis of the transhumanist movement:

- to become like God, *but forgetting God*
- to want to be immortal by human means

and

- how mortal human beings can make themselves immortal

It's like asking to light a fire by throwing water on it. It won't happen naturally. The only time that happened was when God answered Elijah's prayer when challenged by the prophets of Baal that we find in the book of Kings.

Verse 17: "I said in my heart, 'God shall judge the righteous and the wicked; for *there is* a time there for every purpose and for every work.'" *Yes, indeed!* And the time for every purpose for us now is

- conversion
- Truth
- understanding
- God's Spirit
- humility
- loving God with all our heart, mind, soul and being

Solomon continued his musing and he understood some Truth; the obvious that you can observe:

Verse 18: "I said in my heart, 'Concerning the matter of the sons of men, may God reveal to them, that they might see, that they themselves *are* but beasts.'" *That can't happen without the Spirit of God!*

It's a shame, notice how close Solomon came to so many things, yet, how far away from it he really was. Here's what he concludes again. I don't know how old he was when he wrote this, but he was musing toward the end of his life. We will see that his great experimentations really got him in trouble with God.

Likewise, even during the Millennium, there are going to be people who will turn their backs on God by choice, as hard as that may seem. But there will be some it will happen to.

He looks around and sees all of this, v 19: "For that which happens *to* the sons of men also happens to beasts—even one thing *happens* to them. As the *one* dies, so dies the other; yea, they all *have* one breath; so that a man... [physically] ...has no advantage over a beast; for all *is* vanity.... [The

reason he doesn't is because he needs God!] ...All go to one place; all are of the dust, and all return to dust again" (vs 19-20).

Then he talks about the spirit of man and the spirit of beasts, v 21: "Who knows the spirit of man whether it goes upward, and the spirit of the beast whether it goes downward to the earth?"

- he could have known had he consulted God
- he could have known had he remained faithful

Quite a fantastic book, isn't it?

This is what every intellectual in the world needs to read—all the elite; all the scientists; all the professors; all of those who are the 'wise' of the world—they need to read this, *and they need to understand that what is missing in their lives is God!* Here we see Solomon stepping away from God. (You can read Ecc. 4 & 5, there are other good things in there for us to learn.)

Ecclesiastes 6:1: "There is an evil which I have seen under the sun, and it lies heavy upon men: A man to whom God has given riches, wealth, and honor, so that he lacks nothing of all that he desires for his life, yet God does not give him power to eat of it, but a stranger eats it.... [that happens because of sin] ...This *is* vanity, and it *is* an evil disease. If a man beget a hundred children, and lives many years, so that the days of his years are many, but his life is not filled with good, and also that he has no burial; I say, a miscarriage *is* better than he. For he comes in with vanity and goes out in darkness, and his name shall be covered with darkness" (vs 1-4). *What good is it going to do?*

Verse 5: "Moreover he has not seen the sun, nor known *anything*. This one had more rest than the other."

Think about this: Everyone wants to continue to live a longer life—isn't that true? What did God say the 'days of man' maximum would be? *120 days (Gen. 6)!* From the time after the Flood, you look at chronologies, the ages went down gradually.

The reason it went down gradually was so that there would be reproduction of people to refill and replenish the earth. When we get down to David, the father of Solomon, he was called 'old and stricken in years' at 70-years-old. It says in one of the Psalms that our days are 'three score and ten'— that's 70. If by reason of strength they are four score—80-years-old. How many people reach 120? *Not very many!* That's the maximum that God has given.

He muses here, v 6: "Yea, even though he

live a thousand years twice… [live 2,000 years] …yet, he has enjoyed no good. Do not all go to one place? All the labor of man *is* for his mouth, and yet the appetite is not filled" (vs 6-7). Isn't that true? *Got to eat everyday!*

I've often wondered what it would be like if you could give a visual picture this way: Here's a little infant, showing when a person was born. Here's an old man/woman showing that they have lived their life. In between, if you could have a train with many boxcars, and in it you had all the food that they would eat, all the drink that they would drink, then you also had in the backside of the cars all the waste that had to be taken care of, as well. I wonder how long that train would be? That would be a good description here.

Everything a person does is for his mouth to eat so he can live another day. **"…yet, the appetite is no filled"** because everything is processed and digested and he's hungry for the next meal, six or eight hours later. You go to bed at night, you get up and you have breakfast, that is you break the fast of sleeping.

Ecclesiastes 7:11: "Wisdom *is* good with an inheritance; yea, a profit to those who see the sun. For wisdom *is* a defense, even as money *is* a defense; but the excellency of knowledge *is* that wisdom *which* preserves the life of those who have it" (vs 11-12).

In other words, to extend your life. Then he muses on God again. This is quite a thing. We see a process taking place here:

Verse 13: "Consider the work of God; for who can make straight what He has made crooked?" *You can't!*

Verse 15: "All *things* I have seen in the days of my vanity; there is a just man who perishes in his righteousness, and there is a wicked one who prolongs *life* in his wickedness. Do not be righteous over much, neither make yourself overly wise; why should you destroy yourself?" (vs 15-16).

It's amazing how much Truth that Solomon was really able to record, perceive and write down. But to show that even with all of this, everything was vanity and striving after wind.

Verse 23: "All this I have proved by wisdom; I said, "I will be wise;" but it *was* far from me. That which is far off and exceedingly deep, who can find it out? I set my heart to know, and to search, and to seek out wisdom, and the reason *of things*, and to know the wickedness of folly, even of foolishness and madness" (vs 23-25)—*and he still did not understand it!*

Verse 26: "And what I find more bitter than death is the woman whose heart *is* snares and nets, and her hands are *like* fetters. Whoever pleases God shall escape from her, but the sinner shall be taken by her. 'Behold, this I have found,' says the Preacher, '*counting* one by one, to find out the sum, which my soul still sought, but I do not find: one man among a thousand…'" (vs 26-28).

Isn't that something? He said he didn't find any among women, and I supposed that he knew something about that. But that was before the giving of the Holy Spirit as we have today. This is quite something! Really quite a book for us to realize!

Let's learn the lessons here, brethren. Not only is it for the things that we're going to teach people in the Millennium, but these are lessons for us. Jesus said, 'The one who endures to the end, that one shall be saved.' *This applies to us!*

We have been living in an age where we have everything: modern conveniences, light-switches, cars, electricity, refrigerators, freezers, food brought from the whole world into our supermarkets. We have so many things available to us: television, Internet, computers, cell phones, whatever; great and fantastic things that we have been given.

Yet, because it has been with the nation not procured with the blessing of God, but procured with the devices of men and the debt and the credit things that men have done, *we are on the verge of losing it all!* We need to understand the most important thing in our lives—individually and all of us combined together—is:

- our relationship with God
- the Spirit of God
- the love of God
- the goodness of God
- keeping His commandments
- learning, growing and overcoming

Out of this book of Ecclesiastes we can learn a lot of things. Let's see what Solomon was doing. We pick up hints about how he was leaving God, but come back a little bit, ready to leave God, but come back a little bit. Then we will see what happened, because his relationship with God was not strong. It could have been! It could have been one of the strongest in the history of Israel and Judah, but it ended up not the way he wanted. He was the victim of his own words, the victim of his own judgments that he learned from God.

Ecclesiastes 9:1: "For all this I took to heart, even to make all this clear, that the righteous and the wise and their works *are* in the hand of God. No man knows either love or hatred *by* all *that is* before them. All things *come* alike to all; *there is* one event *that happens* to the righteous and to the wicked; to the good and to the clean, and to the unclean; to him who sacrifices, and to him who does not sacrifice. As *is* the good, so is the sinner. He who swears is as *he* who fears an oath" (vs 1-2).

Life happens to all. He says in another place, 'there's time and chance' that happens to all. This is why we can understand why supposedly bad things happen to supposedly good people. But *all of this is so we can learn the wisdom of God!*

Verse 3: "This *is* an evil among all things that are done under the sun, that *there is* one event *that happens* to all. Yea, also the heart of the sons of men is full of evil..."

Yes, he got that right, just as Jesus said, 'From out of the heart, *from within,* come evil thoughts, murders, adulteries, and fornications.']

"...and madness *is* in their heart while they live, and after that *they go* to the dead.... [What happens when you're dead?] ...For whoever is among the living, there is hope; for a living dog *is* better than a dead lion. For the living know that they shall die; but the dead do not know anything, nor do they have any more a reward; for their memory is forgotten. Also their love, and their hatred, and their envy, is long ago perished; nor do they any longer have a portion forever in all that is done under the sun" (vs 3-6).

The book of Hebrews tells us that *'it is given to men once to die and after that the judgment.'* Solomon covered a lot of things, went through a lot of things. Here's another thing that he learned. Very important for us to understand, especially as we look out and see people in the world.

Verse 10: "**Whatever your hand finds to do, do** *it* **with all your might**; for *there is* no work, nor plan, nor knowledge, nor wisdom, in the grave where you go."

Do it with all your might, do it right, do it good, make it the best that you can, and never be satisfied with whatever level you are able to achieve. We can add that to it. Continuously go forward.

Verse 11: "I returned and saw under the sun that the race *is* not to the swift, nor the battle to the strong, nor yet bread to the wise, nor yet riches to men of understanding, nor yet favor to men of skill; but **time and chance happens to them all**."

When that happens, what do we do? *We have to make the best of it we can!* We're also going to teach this to people in the Millennium.

It's going to be interesting to see, at that time, how things come about. We're going to have

spiritual minds, immortal bodies; we're going to have a lot of discernment. We're going to be able to help answer their prayers to God, even while they're praying! That's going to be quite a thing!

Verse 18: "Wisdom *is* better than weapons of war; but **one sinner destroys much good**." *That's quite a statement!*

Who is the chief sinner in the universe? *Satan the devil!* Did he destroy much good? *Yes, he did!* Is God going to get rid of him? *Yes, He is!* That's why during the Millennium he's not going to be around. But everyone is going to have to learn the lessons of life, and they will have more facts, more advantage, more understanding than anything we can imagine today.

This is why those who are called now and have the Spirit of God now, and are growing, changing and overcoming that we will belong to the superior resurrection, the *first resurrection!* Always keep that in mind. This is also for the youth would that they would listen, would that they would heed. But this whole thing of experimentation in life to try and find out about things can lead to a disaster. Let's also understand right here:

Ecclesiastes 11:9: "Rejoice, in your youth, O young man; and let your heart cheer you in the days of your youth, and walk in the ways of your heart, and in the sight of your eyes; but know that for all these *things* **God will bring you into judgment**. Therefore, remove vexation from your heart, and put away evil from your flesh; for youth and vigor *are* vanity" (vs 9-10).

The older you get the more you understand that. too soon old, too late smart! That's one way of putting it. Then he says, because life is designed to get old and wear out and come to an end. Here's some good advice that Solomon gave. Had he remembered that in his old age, I wonder how different things would have really been?

Ecclesiastes 12:1: "Remember now your Creator in the days of your youth, before the evil days come, and the years *of old age* draw near, when you shall say, 'I have no pleasure in them.'"

When you get old you have your aches, pains, weakness, everything wears out, and then we finally give up the ghost.

Verse 2: "When the sun, or the light, or the moon, or the stars, are darkened... [your vision fails; today we have glasses, but that doesn't take away failing vision, it's just an aide to overcome temporarily] ...or the clouds return after rain, in the day when the keepers of the house shall tremble, and the strong men are stooped *over*..." (vs 2-3).

When you get old and you get stooped over, when everything is wearing out and you're headed for the time of your last breath. So, Solomon is saying, 'Do what you need to do and do it right—*because God is going to call you into judgment*—before you get old and everything falls apart. *It does!*

"…and the grinders cease because they are few… [lose your teeth; yes, we have false teeth today] …and *the eyes* of those who look out of the windows grow dim, and the doors shall be shut in the streets… [not going to be going out] …when the sound of the grinding is low, and you shall rise up at the voice of a bird, and all the daughters of music shall be brought low; also when they are afraid of heights, and terrors along the way…" (vs 3-5).

That's what happens; the older you get you are afraid of heights and terrors and things like that.

"…and the almond tree shall blossom, and the grasshopper shall be a burden, and desire shall fail… [desire of physical love] …because man goes to his long home… [dies] …and the mourners go about the streets…" (vs 5-6).

Before these things come upon you think about it while you're young and change your life now.

"…before the silver cord is loosed… [death] …or the golden bowl is broken… [death] …or the pitcher is broken at the fountain, or the wheel broken at the cistern; and the dust return to the earth as it was, **and the spirit returns to God Who gave it**" (vs 6-7).

Think about your life. A lot of us, when we were younger, never thought we would be old. Here we are old and getting older.

Everyone who is young out there, all you children look at all the old people and you never think in your own mind, 'One of these days I'm going to be like them.' You never think in your mind, 'One day all of these old people were little infants, then children, then youth, teenagers and young adults.' My the time flies! The next thing you know, you're 40 years old or more and then 50, 60, 70. God doesn't want us to waste our life in 'vanity and striving after wind.'

Solomon said, 'set your life right, set your course right before you get old, because it is going to come!' He concludes by saying:

Verse 8: "'Vanity of vanities,' says the Preacher; 'all *is* vanity.'"

He wanted to find out all the things that he could find out by experimentation and he came to the whole conclusion of the matter. You can learn, study, have books, do this, do that, do the other things, but in the final analysis this is the beginning of what you need to do, and you need to follow through with it spiritually with the New Testament.

Verse 13: "Let us hear the conclusion of the whole matter: Fear God, and keep His commandments. For this *is* the whole man. For God shall bring every work into judgment, concerning every secret thing, whether *it is* good, or whether it is evil" (vs 13-14).

Now let's see that Solomon never followed his own advice. Why didn't he do it? What was the thing that was missing? Yes, he mentions God— true! Yes, he knows things about God—true! But what was it that he was missing? Let's see what it was that he was missing. Let's see the one command that God gave to the kings. What was it that He said they should do so they would be faithful and not exalt themselves over the people that they're serving?

Deuteronomy 17:14—*this is quite a passage*: "When you come to the land which the LORD your God gives you, and shall possess it and shall live in it and shall say, 'I will set a king over me, like all the nations that *are* around me'… [which they did] …you shall surely set a king over you, whom the LORD your God shall choose…. [not your own choosing] …You shall set a king over you from among your brethren. You may not set a stranger over you who is not your brother" (vs 14-15).

He gave instructions on how the king needed to guide his life. Watch the parameters of what was given to him to do. God gave Solomon wisdom, riches and honor more than any king, because he started out right and he asked for judgment and understanding. But this it is not recorded that he did:

Verse 16: "Only he shall not multiply horses to himself… [which he did] …nor cause the people to return to Egypt… [which he did and even married the daughter of Pharaoh] …so as to multiply horses because the LORD has said to you, 'You shall not return that way again.' Nor shall he multiply wives to himself, **so that his heart does not turn away**. Nor shall he greatly multiply silver and gold to himself" (vs 16-17).

Even though he had all of these things, he should have understood that **_IF_** he would have done what God says to do here, these things would not have taken place. He would have loved God in return for the love that God had for him. He would have feared God and followed Him instead of trying to find the way of life without God. Even though he mentioned God in passing as he went through his experimentation.

Here's what God commanded him to do. This is what all of us need to do in preparation for being kings and priests. This is what every minister needs to do as he is serving and feeding the flock of God, as well as read and study and know 1st and 2nd Timothy, Titus and the General Epistles—especially what Peter said to the elders.

Verse 18: "And it shall be, when he sits on the throne of his kingdom, he shall **write for himself a copy of this Law in a book** from that which is in the custody of the priests the Levites."

He was to go to the temple and there they would have a room where the king could come and sit and make himself a handwritten copy of the Law of God—Genesis-Deuteronomy. Why?

Verse 19: "And it shall be with him, and he shall read it **all the days of his life**…"

- Why must you do all the days of your life?
- How many times have you heard us say: 'prayer and study; prayer, study and fasting'

You've heard it! Those are the keys to the relationship. But notice why he is to read it all the days of his life. There is something that has to happen on a continuous basis. It's not just learn once and you know it and it's over with.

"…**so that he may learn to fear the LORD his God**…" (v 19)—*day-by-day as he would read*; week-by-week, month-by-month, year-by-year. How many of the kings of Judah and Israel did this? *Virtually nada, none!*

"…to keep all the words of this law and these statutes, to do them" (v 19).

Solomon was on the verge of really learning the purpose of God. But when he set out to do it, on his own—forgetting that everything that he is, everything that he was, everything that he was to be—was all dependent upon God!

Yes, he had to put forth the effort, that is true. But to do things by just giving God lip-service didn't work. God wants you to love Him with all your heart, mind, soul and being. This is what we need to learn, coupled with prayer and study, is the glue that holds our relationship together with God. That's His Spirit!

Notice what else it would do, v 20: "So that his heart may not be lifted up above his brethren…"

He stays humble! Humility is not something you say, 'I'm going to be humble.' *NO!* Humility is a living part of your being when you understand God and His love and understand the brethren and

understand what they do. It's part of how you are. It's not something that you put on. It's not something you say, 'Well, when I get around people I'm humble; I assume a humble position here.' *NO!*

- *humility* comes by not exalting yourself.
- *humility* comes by loving your neighbor and loving your brethren and even loving your neighbor as yourself, as Jesus said

"…and that he does not turn aside from the commandment, to the right or the left, to the end that he may prolong *his* days in his kingdom, he and his children, in the midst of Israel" (v 20). *That's what Solomon was missing!*

Now, in order for us not to fall into the same trap as this, we need to follow what is there. That's why **study and prayer, living by every Word of God!**

Let's see, even though Solomon wrote 3,000 proverbs, composed 1,005 songs, wrote the book of Ecclesiastes, was the wisest man who has ever walked the face of the earth, because he didn't follow the instructions of God, He had to take the kingdom from him. When you read the genealogy in the book of Luke, the son of David named *Nathan* was the one through whom the seed came for Christ, not Solomon. That's how great his sin was. We will see here that he did everything God said not to do.

Remember, in the book of Ecclesiastes it says:

When the sinner turns from his sins, all of his sins that he has done will not be mentioned. But *if* the righteous turn from his righteousness to sin, all the righteousness that he has done will not be mentioned.

The Bible doesn't tell us the final disposition of Solomon; it doesn't show that he repented, so we're kind of left hanging in the air concerning God's judgment of Solomon. ***That's in God's hands. God knows!*** But notice how he did many things contrary to what God said to do. That has to be because he did not fulfill the requirement for the king, as we found in Deut. 17.

1-Kings 11:1: "And King Solomon loved many foreign women, even the daughter of Pharaoh, Moabites, Ammonites, Edomites, Sidonians, Hittites; of the nations which the LORD had said to the children of Israel, 'You shall not go in to them, and they shall not go in to you; surely they will turn away your heart after their gods.' *But* Solomon clung to these in love" (vs 1-2)—*instead of following the Word of God; instead of reading and studying the Word of God everyday **so that he would not be lifted up!***

Notice how bad it got, v 3: "And he had seven hundred wives, princesses, and three hundred concubines. And **his wives turned away his heart**."

Isn't that what God said do not do because your wives would turn your heart away from God (Deut. 17). Notice how far it went:

Verse 4: "For it came to pass when Solomon was old, his wives turned away his heart after other gods. And his heart was not perfect with the LORD his God as *was* the heart of David his father, for Solomon went after Ashtoreth, the goddess of the Sidonians, and after Milcom, the abomination of the Ammonites; and **Solomon did evil in the sight of the LORD** and did not *go* fully after the LORD like his father David" (vs 4-6).

Now, if all of that wasn't bad enough, look at what else he did. Since he was the master temple builder, built the Temple of God! Let's understand something here very important. Every time a man tries to build a building for God, or a temple for God, they get in trouble! We even had one exalted church leader who did that. What happened to him? *Same thing that happened to Solomon!*

Verse 7: "Then Solomon built a high place for Chemosh, the abomination of Moab, in the hill which *is* before Jerusalem, and for Molech, the abomination of the children of Ammon."

And later the children of Israel sacrificed their children to Molech; *burned them in the fire!*

Think of what happened to the population of the children of Israel when they saw that the king was going against the commandments of God. They fell into sin and they said, 'Well, if he does it I can do it.' And look what happens. All you have to do is just look at the governments today—any government in the world—and you can see when they go wrong, the people go wrong. That's what happened here. Not only did he do that for the Moabite god and the Ammonite god:

Verse 8: "And likewise he did for all his foreign wives, and burned incense and sacrificed to their gods."

Think of that! God Who appeared to him in dreams twice and loved him and blessed him, look at what he did!

Verse 9: "And the LORD *was* angry with Solomon because his heart was turned from the LORD God of Israel who had appeared to him twice and had commanded him concerning this thing, that he should not go after other gods; and he did not keep that which the LORD commanded" (vs 9-10).

Remember: *Everything concerning our relationship with God is always started with the* *two-letter word 'IF'!* The conditions are given to us, because God is:

- a God of love
- a God of truth
- a God of righteousness

He cannot lie!

So, if He gives a promise of blessings, it is always contingent upon that big little word *IF.* How many times did Jesus use it? How many times must we apply it to our lives? *That being on a daily basis!*

Just exactly as has happened to the Churches of God who did not fear the ministers and the members and those people who did not do as God intended them to do. Likewise with all the Protestants and Catholics; they have the Bible; they have the Word of God; they didn't have to go out and do the traditions of men; they didn't have to be there to obey what the pastor and the priest said that went against the Word of God. *They themselves* did not study the Word of God, but the writings of men; *they themselves* got turned away into sexual sins and abominations—correct? *Yes, indeed!*

Notice, judgment always comes when there is protracted sin and no repentance. Here's what God said to Solomon directly from one of His prophets:

Verse 11: "And the LORD said to Solomon, 'Since this has been done by you, and since you have not kept My covenant and My statutes which I have commanded you, **I will surely tear the kingdom from you** and will give it to your servant.'"

That servant was Jeroboam; and Jeroboam turned the children of Israel—the ten tribes that God gave him—over to ancient Egyptian calf-worship instead of serving God!

Verse 12: "But I will not do it in your days, for David your father's sake, *but* I **will tear it out of the hand of your son**. Only, I will not tear away all the kingdom, *but* I will give one tribe to your son for David My servant's sake, and for Jerusalem's sake which I have chosen" (vs 12-13). *Immediately after that warning, God raised up enemies!*

I want you to stop and think about this in relationship to the countries of the world today. Why is there so much trouble, war, killing, death, famine, sex sins, abominations, Satan worship, disasters, earthquakes, floods and droughts. Why? *Because the world is forsaking God!* Because of this, we need to learn the lesson and we need to understand that God is giving us a chance:

- to be prepared
- to be educated

- to be trained through His Word
- with His Spirit
- with His love
- with living

So that we can come and be resurrected from the dead and that we will enter into the Kingdom of God as spirit beings and that He is going to give us rulership over this world.

Brethren, let's see the goodness and severity of God, and *let's learn with a willing mind and a ready heart the things of God!* Let us have a tremendous relationship with God the Father and Jesus Christ and with each other. Let us use this time at the Feast:

- to change
- to grow
- to overcome
- to set the course for the coming year

The coming year looks like it may be a very difficult year at best! Always remember this:

- always *hope in God* because you **stand in His grace**
- *walk in* **faith**
- *believe in* **hope**
- *live in* **love**
- *prepare* for the Kingdom of God!

Scriptural References:

1) Ecclesiastes 2:1-2
2) Proverbs 18:2
3) Ecclesiastes 2:3-14
4) John 3:19-21
5) Ecclesiastes 2:15-19, 21-26
6) Ecclesiastes 3:1-11, 14-21
7) Ecclesiastes 6:1-7
8) Ecclesiastes 7:11-13, 15-16, 23-28
9) Ecclesiastes 9:1-6, 10-11, 18
10) Ecclesiastes 11:9-10
11) Ecclesiastes 12:1-8, 13-14
12) Deuteronomy 17:14-20
13) 1 Kings 11:1-13

Scriptured referenced, not quoted:

- Ecclesiastes 4; 5
- Genesis 6

FRC:bo
Transcribed: 8/8/12
Reformatted: 1/2021

CHAPTER SEVENTY-TWO

The Solomon Syndrome
Fred R. Coulter

Today we're going to cover how is it that people during the Millennium, with everything nearly perfect, will sin and won't repent? How is that going to work?

The nature of the people is going to return to the nature that was before Adam and Eve sinned. However, they are going to have to choose. God has given every human being *independent free moral agency,* and we must all choose, and consistently choose what is right.

So, the acronym we have for that is IFMA. But isn't it interesting IF because all the things that trip people up are the *IFs* and there is IFMA, even when they have close contact with God and the saints who are ruling and reigning. It's quite a thing!

Isaiah 65:19: "I will rejoice in Jerusalem, and I will joy in My people… [that includes all the people of the world, and the world is going to be ruled from Jerusalem] …and the voice of weeping will no more be heard in her, nor the voice of crying. There will not be an infant who lives but a few days… [completely changed kind of situation] …nor an old man that has not filled his days, for the child will die a hundred years old…" (vs 19-20).

That gives a time limit on how long a person is going to live during the Millennium. As we mentioned, there will come a time when at Sabbath services there will be a transformation service. Those who have qualified and are ready to enter into the Kingdom of God will be transformed instantly. That means an instantaneous death and transformation from flesh to spirit.

Perhaps that might be in the 100th year on the Day of Pentecost. Wouldn't that be a magnificent day for that to be? But since we're not told that's speculation.

"…but the sinner *who is* a hundred years old… and dies] …shall be accursed" (v 20). *Meaning: no chance of salvation!*

We saw how that when people sin they are removed and exiled. That began with Adam and Eve. They were removed from the Garden of Eden. Think about this with Adam and Eve for just a minute. They were there with God. They had a perfect language. They could communicate with God and with each other. God was right there! You would think that if you're in a situation right there

with God that there would be no chance that you would sin. But remember IFMA.

God commanded them that they could eat of every tree of the Garden, but of the Tree of the Knowledge of Good and Evil they were not to eat of it. For in the day that they ate of it, *in dying they shall surely die.*

Satan comes and convinces them to eat of the fruit, because it's going to make them wise. That will make you have the ability to decide for yourself what is right, what is wrong, what is good and what is evil. They ate the fruit, and they were removed from the Garden of Eden.

Along came Cain and Abel. Abel did that which was right in the eyes of the Lord. That was when they were about 135-years-old, and they would come before God at the East entrance and bring their sacrifices, there tithes and offerings. Abel would and Cain would.

There must have been a time when Cain was doing well, but something happened with his IFMA *and he chose not to do what God said!* That's quite a thing! Right in the face of God! God asked him, Why are you angry? Don't get angry over this. **_If_** you use your IFMA and you do well, won't you be received? Won't you be accepted? But *if **not** sin lies at the door!'*

That's a very good example that even when everything is going good, and when you have contact with God, that that free independent moral agency, when used for self against God, *is sin!* That's the whole story of the Bible!

Let's see what God told the children of Israel. They were going to go into the 'promised land.' They received the Ten Commandments of God. They had all of their sins and all of the things that they did for 40 years until that generation died out, and a new generation is coming along. There's always a new generation. A new generation brings with it *its own thinking!* Here's what God told them: *they suffered through all these thing so that God would know what was in their heart, and that they would keep the commandments of the Lord!*

Deuteronomy 8:6: "And you shall keep the commandments of the LORD your God to walk in His ways and to fear Him."

Isn't that the whole thing with everybody every time everywhere down through all ages? *Yes!*

Verse 7: "For the LORD your God brings you into a good land, a land of brooks of water, of fountains and depths that spring out of valleys and hills, a land of wheat and barley and vines and fig trees and pomegranates, a land of olive oil and honey, a land in which you shall eat bread without scarceness. You shall not lack any *thing* in it. *It is a* land whose stones are iron, and out of whose hills you may dig copper" (vs 7-9).

Isn't that the way it's going to be in the Millennium? *Everything there:*

- perfect land
- perfect circumstances

the saints of God ruling and reigning
- teaching and helping all the people
- every Sabbath from one Sabbath to another
- from one month to the other
- all coming before God to worship

Everything is going to be laid out with the minimum amount of sin! But there is always *free moral agency!*

We can say this of the Millennium, because going into the 'promised land' is a type of going into the Millennium.

Verse 10: "When you have eaten and are full, then you shall bless the LORD your God for the good land, which He has given you."

They're living in a time of complete freedom of crime, violence, no war, and everything is *nearly perfect!* The only imperfection is the wrong choices of their IFMA, which is sin! How are they going to respond? Notice that God gives us warning, because this is the way of human nature. **When** there's everything that you need, **then** unless you stay close to God you corrupt yourself with your own IFMA.

Verse 11: "Beware that you do not forget the LORD your God by not keeping His commandments, and His judgments, and His statutes, which I command you today, **lest *when* you have eaten and are full and have built goodly houses and lived in *them*"** (vs 11-12). Won't that be true all during the Millennium?

Verse 13: "And *when* your herds and your flocks multiply, and your silver and your gold is multiplied, and all that you have is multiplied."

Didn't God say in Isa. that for iron He's going to bring silver, gold and all of that? They are going to be so rich and have so many things, and everything right there during the Millennium.

Verse 14: "Then you become **haughty of heart**…"—I know better than God, or I don't care what God says, I know that I'm right.'

What's going to happen with that? *They're going to be sent out to a repentance center,* and if they don't repent then they're sent out to Gog and Magog. Can they repent from Gog and Magog? *I suppose they could, because God always honors repentance!*

But here was "…**haughty of heart**…" and that was the sin of Solomon! *The Solomon Syndrome!*

"…and you forget the LORD your God Who brought you forth out of the land of Egypt from the house of bondage" (v 14). *There's the parallel there!*

Now let's look at some things concerning how people behave and some of the things that will get them trouble.

Proverbs 14:12: "There is a way, which seems right to a man, but the end thereof *is* the way of death."

In order for there to be sinners who live a hundred years and die accursed means that's exactly what they did in the face of the fact that they were living in the Kingdom of God, and that all the saints were helping, teaching and showing them. The person comes along and get *haughty of heart,* and we'll see how that takes place with the Solomon Syndrome.

Verse 14—this applies at all times, especially to the Millennium: "The backslider in heart shall be filled **with his own ways**…"

Because of independent free moral agency, they're going to choose their own ways. If they don't repent, then they're going to have to pay the price. Regardless of how nearly perfect that the Millennium is, with our choices and so forth we still have the choice of choosing good **or** choosing evil, which then, as we'll see tomorrow, *are idols of evil in the mind!*

Remember what the human heart is like even though it's not as evil as it is today. God said, as we saw at the beginning, that He's going to give them a new heart, a heart of flesh.

Proverbs 12:20: "Deceit *is* in the heart of those who imagine evil…" *So,* **IF** *he is imagining evil and thinking it is good,* **THEN** *that is using their* free moral agency in a wrong way. They are choosing evil. God says to choose to love God and choose what is right, what is good.

Verse 21: "There shall no harm befall the righteous, but the wicked shall be filled with trouble. Lying lips *are* an abomination to the LORD, but those who deal truly *are* His delight" (vs 21-22). *An amazing thing!*

They're going to have these situations all the time in their lives. Everything is going to be set so they can choose the good, choose the right, love God, love their neighbors, love all in the way that God wants them to love. They will constantly have Sabbath services and Holy Day services year-after-year. So, if they're righteous for a hundred years, they will be transformed and enter into the spiritual Kingdom of God!

Remember that we covered *that the knowledge of the Lord will cover the earth as the seas cover the earth!* In spite of that, here is the kind of thinking that can come along and spoil it. We will see how Solomon started out.

2-Chron. 28—here it kingship is passing from David to Solomon and David is admonishing Solomon and telling him what he needs to do to be king, because God said that Solomon would take the place of David.

1-Chronicles 28:6—David is relating this and said: "And He [God] said to me, 'Solomon your son shall build My house and My courts, for I have chosen him *to be* My son, and I will be his Father. And I will establish his kingdom forever **if** he continues resolute in keeping My commandments and My ordinances, as he is today.' And now in the sight of all Israel, the congregation of the LORD, and in the hearing of our God, **keep and seek for all the commandments of the LORD your God**, so that you may possess this good land and leave *it* for an inheritance for your children after you forever" (vs 6-8). **Sound an awful lot like we read in Isaiah**? *Yes!*

Verse 9: And you, Solomon my son, acknowledge the God of your father and **serve Him with a perfect heart**…"

What keeps the heart perfect? *Loving God and keeping His commandments, and repenting when you sin and stop sinning!*

"…**and with a willing mind**, for the LORD searches all hearts and understands all the imaginations of the thoughts…." (v 9).

That's going to be the key of understanding right and wrong during the Millennium. It's not going to just be the actions. It will be the thoughts *first!* Then the actions follow.

So, when there becomes that self-willedness, then in spite of everything that is said, a person—man or woman—might say, 'I know that I'm right. How can God be right?' *Well, He can be right because He's perfect!*

"…**If** you seek Him, He will be found by you. But **if** you forsake Him, He will cast you off

forever. Take heed now, for the LORD has chosen you to build a house for the sanctuary. Be strong and do *it*" (vs 9-10). *That was the charge that was given to Solomon!*

1-Kings 3 is a good place to start, because this is also about the same thing, only it exposes a little bit more dramatically some of the things that Solomon did. Now, this is after David had died, was buried and Solomon is installed as king.

1-Kings 3:5: "In Gibeon the LORD appeared to Solomon in a dream by night. And God said, 'Ask what I shall give you!' And Solomon said, 'You have shown to Your servant David my father great mercy, according as he walked before You in truth and in righteousness and in uprightness of heart with You….'" (vs 5-7).

Look at that carefully, *righteousness,* doing the will of God "…**in uprightness of heart**…" *because all during the Millennium it's all going to be based on the heart!*

"…And You have kept this great kindness for him, that You have given him a son to sit on his throne, as *it is* today. And now, O LORD my God, You have made Your servant king instead of David my father. And I *am* a little child…" (vs 6-7).

Isn't it interesting? Just like Samuel told Saul, 'When you were little in your own eyes, you did well.' So, here you have the same thing. Remember, he's very young, but his life went on. How did it turn out? *We'll see!*

"…I do not know *how* to go out or come in! And Your servant *is* in the midst of Your people whom You have chosen, a numerous people who cannot be numbered nor counted for multitude. Now, therefore, give to Your servant **an understanding heart**… [that's the best thing you could ask for] …**to judge Your people, to discern between good and evil**, for who is able to judge this, Your great people?" (vs 7-9). *The best thing he could ask for!*

This was so good, notice what God said, v 10: "And the word was good in the eyes of the LORD that Solomon had asked this thing." *He did what was pleasing to God!*

If Solomon would have stayed that way, just think how history would have been different.

Verse 11: "And God said to him, 'Because you have asked this thing and have not asked for yourself long life and have not asked riches for yourself, nor have asked the life of your enemies, but have asked for yourself understanding to judge justly, behold, I have done according to your words. Lo, **I have given you a wise and an understanding heart,** so that there was none like you before you and after you none shall arise like you. And I also have given you that which you have not asked, both riches and honor, so that there shall not be any among the kings like you all your days. Therefore, **if**... [IFMA: choice, what do you choose to do?] ...**you will walk in My ways, to keep My statutes and My commandments, as your father David walked, then I will lengthen your days**'" (vs 11-14).

That's really quite a thing that happened there! 1-Kings 9 is after Solomon built the temple and everything was offered, and his great long prayer. You read that prayer, quite a prayer.

1-King 9:1: "And it came to pass as Solomon finished the building of the house of the LORD, and the king's house, and all Solomon's desire which he was pleased to do, the LORD appeared to Solomon the second time, as He had appeared to him at Gibeon" (vs 1-2).

Verse 3: "And **the LORD said to him**, 'I have heard your prayer and your cry, which you have made before Me. I have made Holy this house which you have built to put My name there forever. And My eyes and My heart shall be there perpetually. And **if** you will walk before Me as David your father walked, in integrity of heart and in uprightness, to do according to all that I have commanded you; *and* **if** you will keep My statutes and My judgments, **then** I will establish the throne of your kingdom over Israel forever as I promised to David your father, saying, "There shall not be cut off from you a man upon the throne of Israel"'" (vs 3-5).

Verse 6—warning: "**If** you shall at all turn from following Me... [free choice] ...you or your children, and will not keep My commandments *and* My statutes which I have set before you, but go and serve other gods and worship them, **then** I will cut off Israel from the face of the land, which I have given them. And this house which I have made Holy for My name I will cast out of My sight. And Israel shall be a proverb and a byword among all people'" (vs 6-7). *Notice that God makes it clear*:

- what are the stakes
- what are the requirements
- what should be done

Deut. 17—Here is what Solomon *did not do!* There's a reason why God had this and put this here. This was added in when Saul was made king. Here is the basis for kingship; here is what God said. Originally He didn't want them to have a king, but judges.

But the people came to Samuel and said, 'Look, we want a king like all the other nations.' Samuel got all upset and complained to God, and

God said, *'They haven't rejected you, **they have reject Me!*** I will give them a king, but you tell them what kind of king it's going to be.' So, he did and you find that in 2-Sam. 8, and in 2-Sam. 10 Saul is made king. Here is what was added by Samuel to the Word of God:

Deuteronomy 17:14: When you come to the land, which the LORD your God gives you, and shall possess it and shall live in it and shall say, 'I will set a king over me, like all the nations that *are* around me.' You shall surely set a king over you **whom the LORD your God shall choose**...." (vs 14-15). *God chose Saul, God chose David and God chose Solomon!*

"...You shall set a king over you from among your brethren. You may not set a stranger over you who is not your brother. Only he **shall not multiply horses to himself**... [notice that] ...**nor cause the people to return to Egypt**... [notice that] ...so as to multiply horses because the LORD has said to you, "'You shall not return that way again.'" (vs 15-16).

Notice that all of this is here for Solomon to read!

Verse 17: "**Nor shall he multiply wives to himself**, so that his heart does not turn away. **Nor shall he greatly multiply silver and gold to himself**." *Even though God gave it to him, he was not to set his heart on it!*

Now, v 18 is the key and *this is what Solomon did not do!* Even though he prayed that great prayer when the temple was dedicated.

Verse 18: "And it shall be, when he sits on the throne of his kingdom, **he shall write for himself a copy of this law in a book** from that which is in the custody of the priests the Levites." *His own copy of the Law!*

Now notice what this was to do, v 19[transcriber's correction]: "And it shall be with him, and **he shall read it all the days of his life, so that he may learn to fear the LORD his God, to keep all the words of this Law and these statutes, to do** them... [here's why]: ...**so that his heart may not be lifted up above his brethren, and that he does not turn aside from the commandment, to the right or the left,** to the end that he may prolong *his* days in his kingdom, he and his children, in the midst of Israel" (vs 19-20).

What was one of the first things that Solomon did? *He married the daughter of Pharaoh!* God didn't come and correct him for that. Here's another lesson: *If and when you sin, and God doesn't correct you right away, don't think for a minute that He approves of what you're doing!*

What else did Solomon do? We'll see it in just a little bit. All the kings of the earth came and sought after Solomon for his wisdom. They brought gold! He had 666 talents of gold brought to him every year; think about the wealth that was there! It was said of Solomon, like it's said during the Millennium, that silver and gold were just so abundant that the other metals were counted as nothing.

How Solomon came to this point of view? *Because he didn't make himself a copy of the Law and study it so that he wouldn't be lifted up above his brethren and become haughty of heart!*

Remember what it said, 'You shall not multiply to yourself horses, and you shall not multiply to yourself wives.'

1-Kings 11:1: "And King Solomon loved many foreign women, even the daughter of Pharaoh, Moabites, Ammonites, Edomites, Sidonians, Hittites; of the nations which the LORD had said to the children of Israel, 'You shall not go in to them…'"—*that is marry and produce children!*

Why did he do this? *He gave into all the kings of the earth who wanted to make an alliance with Solomon.* The way you make an alliance with the king is that he takes the daughter of the king of the other country to himself as a wife. So, this tells you how many people were seeking after Solomon and his favor.

"'…and they shall not go in to you; surely they will turn away your heart after their gods.'…." (v 2).

That happened to Solomon, *the Solomon Syndrome!* He was given everything and even more than he even asked for, **but he turned his back on God!**

"…*But* Solomon clung to these in love. And he had seven hundred wives, princesses, and three hundred concubines. And **his wives turned away his heart**" (vs 2-3). *Imagine that!*

God appeared to him twice, giving him specific instructions and warning him not to do these things!

Verse 4: "For it came to pass when Solomon was old, his wives turned away his heart after other gods. And his heart was not perfect with the LORD his God as *was* the heart of David his father, for Solomon went after Ashtoreth, the goddess of the Sidonians, and after Milcom, the abomination of the Ammonites; and Solomon did evil in the sight of the LORD…" (vs 4-6)—*and didn't repent!*

Think about that; that's going to happen during the Millennium. People will have everything there:

- they will be told
- they will be taught
- they will understand

But the independent free moral agency is going to work! **_IF_** they decide to become **haughty of heart and to sin, _THEN_** they're going to suffer the consequences. And the consequences will be *exile!* If they don't repent, *permanent exile!*

Verse 7: "Then Solomon built a high place for Chemosh, the abomination of Moab, in the hill, which *is* before Jerusalem, and for Molech, the abomination of the children of Ammon."

This is the stretch of land on which the temple sat; the Valley of Kidron on the east side, and the Tironian Valley on the other side. On this hill across from the temple is where Solomon built all these shrines and altars of incense and everything. The wives said, 'Look, you've got your God, and you do all of these things. You married me and I've got this god. Why don't you build something for my god.' *You can almost hear it!*

Verse 8: "And likewise he did for all his foreign wives… [the whole hillside was full of incense altars and sacrificial altars and little temples] …and burned incense and sacrificed to their gods. And the LORD *was* angry with Solomon because his heart was turned from the LORD God of Israel who had appeared to him twice and had commanded him concerning this thing, that he should not go after other gods; and he did not keep that which the LORD commanded" (vs 8-10).

Think about it! Think about the parallel that is going to be in the Millennium. It says, 'The sinner shall die a hundred years old accursed'—meaning sinning, going against God, not repenting. Accursed forever, meaning *that they will be in the resurrection to the Lake of Fire for the second death!*

Notice that God warns him, and he could have repented if he would have chosen, but he did not. Where he's going to be in the Kingdom of God, I don't know. God said that *He wouldn't take away His mercy from Solomon as He took away His mercy from Saul!*

Verse 11: "And the LORD said to Solomon, 'Since this has been done by you, and since you have not kept My covenant and My statutes, which I have commanded you, I will surely tear the kingdom from you and will give it to your servant. But I will not do it in your days, for David your father's sake, *but* I will tear it out of the hand of your son'" (vs 11-12). *So, it came to pass!*

Now then, when there is not repentance, God sends the adversary!

Verse 14: "And it came to pass the LORD

stirred up an adversary against Solomon, Hadad the Edomite…. [Sound a little like to today's Middle East?] …He *was* of the king's seed in Edom."

He fled to Egypt and came back an then they had these raids by these terrorists. Same thing we have today. What do you think is happening to America? and why it's coming upon us? and that we have so many troubles? *Same thing!*

That's why that during the Millennium when they won't repent… When they sin and repent right there, fine, everything is good. If they don't repent, then they will be sent to a rehab or a repentance center. They will be given a chance to study, to pray, to understand. If they repent there they can come back. But if are still *haughty of heart* and still think that they are right and still think that God is wrong, then they will be exiled to Gog and Magog.

Now we will see the main way that Solomon apostatized! We will see *how was it that Solomon—* after all God did and said, and Solomon did and said—turned from God!* That's quite a story!

Psa. 72—a Psalm of Solomon, which he undoubtedly wrote before he got involved with so many wives and concubines, that his mind was removed from God. We will see a complete difference in attitude from this than when we get to the book of Ecclesiastes.

Psalm 72:1: "Give the king Your judgments, O God, and Your righteousness to the king's son… [referring to himself] …that he may judge Your people in righteousness and Your poor with justice" (vs 1-2).

Maybe he wrote this Psalm right after God appeared to him the first time and told him that He would give him all that he didn't ask for, as well as the judgment that he desired.

Verse 3: "The mountains shall bring peace to the people, and the little hills, by righteousness. He shall judge the poor of the people; He shall save the children of the needy and shall crush in pieces the oppressor. They shall fear You as long as the sun and moon endure throughout all generations" (vs 3-5)—*complete devotion to God!*

Then Solomon turned aside to all the abominations of the heathen.

Verse 6: "He shall come down like rain upon the mown grass, like showers that water the earth. In His days the righteous shall flourish and abundance of peace until the moon be no more" (vs 6-7).

Think about how wonderfully he was praising God with this! This was before he turned aside.

Verse 8: "He shall also have the rule from sea to sea, and from the river unto the ends of the earth. Those who dwell in the wilderness shall bow before Him, and His enemies shall lick the dust. The kings of Tarshish and of the isles shall bring presents; the kings of Sheba and Seba shall offer gifts. Yea, all kings shall prostrate themselves before Him; all nations shall serve Him" (vs 8-11). *That is the God of heaven!*

Was that not the reason that God gave all of these things to Solomon, so that v 11 could be fulfilled? That's something to really think about. It also brings to mind something very important: **How important are our choices?** When we vary from the way of God, how important it is to repent and not get carried away and drift away from God, forget God (Deut. 8) and become *haughty of heart!* That's what happened to Solomon.

Verse 12: "For He shall deliver the needy when he cries, and the poor with the one who has no helper. He shall have compassion upon the weak and needy, and shall save the lives of the needy. He shall redeem their life from oppression and violence; and their blood shall be precious in His sight" (vs 12-14). *That's in God's sight!*

That would be under the administration of Solomon. What he was saying was that he would serve the people of God and turn them to God. He would do the will of God to help these people. Amazing, isn't it?

Verse 15: "And he shall live, and to him shall be given the gold of Sheba, and they may pray continually for him; also daily he shall be praised." *That is the people would praise Solomon!*

Verse 16: "May there be an abundance of grain in the earth upon the top of the mountains; may its fruit wave like Lebanon, and they of the city shall flourish like grass of the earth." *That's what it was during the days of Solomon!*

But as he got older and the sins came in, then they started to get really terrible. The people were looking at Solomon with contempt, with hatred, and so much despising what he was doing. That's how the kingdom of the ten tribes of Israel was taken away.

Yet, when it was taken, God offered to Jeroboam that if he would keep His commandments, that He would be with him. But Jeroboam decided on the two calves in Dan and Bethel so that the people of the northern ten tribes went completely pagan. They looked at the example of Solomon and said, 'Well, Solomon did it!'

Verse 17: "His name shall endure forever; His name shall be continued as long as the sun; and men shall be blessed in Him; **all nations shall call**

Him blessed." *This is a prophecy of the coming Millennium!* But it should have been fulfilled in type during Solomon's reign, but it wasn't!

Verse 18: "Blessed is the LORD God, the God of Israel, Who alone does wondrous things…. [keep that in mind] …And blessed be His glorious name forever; and all the earth is filled with His glory! Amen and Amen" (vs 18-19).

But notice that this Psalm was so important that it was included in the Psalms of David; v 20: The prayers of David the son of Jesse are ended."

The book of Ecclesiastes is quite an insightful book. Sometime ago I gave a message—*Progression of Evil Through Philosophy*—on how philosophy and reason are looked upon by the Catholics and the 'great men' of the world as important things to lead them to the Truth, rather than the Word of God.

They believe that with philosophy they can come to a greater understanding of Truth. We will see that's exactly what Solomon did.

Ecclesiastes 1:1: The words of the Preacher, the son of David, king in Jerusalem…. [that's Solomon, couldn't be anyone else] …'Vanity of vanities,' says the Preacher, 'vanity of vanities! All *is* vanity'" (vs 1-2).

He forgot to say, *'Without God!'* If you have God it's forever; it's not vanity.

Verse 3: "What profit does a man have in all his labor, which he labors under the sun? One generation passes away, and another generation comes; but the earth remains forever" (vs 3-4).

He's getting very philosophical here, thinking that through some of his experiences he's going to discover more truth than what God has given!

Verse 5: "The sun also arises, and the sun goes down, and hurries to its place where it arose. The wind goes toward the south, and it turns around to the north; it whirls around continually; and the wind returns on its circuits. All the rivers run into the sea; yet, the sea *is* not full…" (vs 5-7).

Philosophically looking at everything, instead of saying that God made all of this. Isn't this a wonderful thing?

We're going to see that God is only mentioned once in the first two chapters. That's how far Solomon got away from God. That's how much he got involved in the vanity of philosophy.

Verse 8: "All things *are* full of labor; man cannot utter it; the eye is not satisfied with seeing, nor the ear filled with hearing. That which has been *is* that which shall be; and that which has been done

is that which shall be done; and *there is* nothing new under the sun" (vs 8-9).

Let's see how this starts out, because in Ecc. 1 & 2 the *I, me and mine* are 45 times, and only one mention of God in the last verse.

Verse 12: "I, the Preacher, was king over Israel in Jerusalem." *If he would have done it the way God would have had him do it, he would have said:*

> God chose me to be king in Jerusalem. God in His mercy gave me wisdom and judgment, and He also gave me riches and wealth. Here I am the richest man in the world because of God. Everything I have comes from Him.

But he didn't say it! This is recorded to show that what he did here was not right. When you leave God and you're all wrapped up in your own mind you have the idols that are in your mind, which are your own thoughts of your own greatness.

Verse 13: "And I gave my heart to seek and search out by wisdom… [experimenting] …concerning all things that are done under the heavens. It is **a grievous task** [#1]**God has given to the sons of men** to be exercised by it." *Yes, if you leave God it is grievous!*

Verse 14: "I have seen all the works that are done under the sun; and, behold, all *is* vanity and striving after wind." He could have said:

> Look at this beautiful temple that God had me build for Him. Did you know that all of these plans came from God Himself to my father David? And God chose me to build this beautiful house for Him.

Instead of having in the Tironian Valley all the shrines for all the gods. And Solomon left the temple of God to go over there to offer sacrifices.

Verse 16: "I spoke within my own heart, saying, 'Lo, I have become great and have gathered more wisdom than all that have been before me in Jerusalem; yea, my heart has experienced great wisdom and knowledge.'"

- Who gave it to you? *God did!*
- Why didn't you acknowledge that?

See how incrementally he was leaving God through his own wisdom!

Verse 17: "And I gave my heart to know wisdom and to know madness and folly; I perceived that this also *is* striving after wind. For in much wisdom *is* much grief; and he who increases knowledge increases sorrow" (vs 17-18)—*especially if you leave God!*

Ecclesiastes 2:1: "I said in my heart…

[instead of praying to God] …'Come now, I will test you with pleasure to find out what is good.'…. [the Word of God tells us what is good] …And, behold, this also *is* vanity. I said of laughter, '*It is* madness,' and of mirth, 'What does it accomplish?' I sought in my heart to give myself unto wine, yet, conducting my heart with wisdom; and to lay hold on folly, until I might see what was good for the sons of men, what they should do under the heaven the few days of their life. I made great works for myself… [nothing like a little vanity here] …I built houses for myself; I planted vineyards for myself" (vs 1-4)—*instead of saying*:

> God gave me all of these wonderful things and He let me build this great house. All of that is from God. All of these vineyards with the most wonderful grapes for the greatest wine that has ever been. He gave me the privilege of planting those.

Verse 5: "I made gardens and orchards for myself, and I planted trees in them, of all fruit. I made pools of water for myself, to irrigate groves of growing trees. I bought men slaves and women slaves, and servants *were* born in my house; also I had great possessions of herds and flocks, above all that were before me in Jerusalem" (vs 5-7).

Who gave it to him? **God did!** He was not thankful! Yes, at the end he said, 'Here's the end of the matter, fear God and keep His commandments.' But, that was said by rote rather than by really sincere belief in it.

Verse 8: "I also gathered silver and gold to myself, and the treasure of kings and of the provinces. I got men singers and women singers for myself, even the sensual delights of the sons of men, and many women." *Oh yes, did he ever do that!*

Verse 9: "So, I was great and increased more than all that were before me in Jerusalem; also my wisdom remained with me." *But you perverted it!*

Whenever you turn your back on God and go against God, *your wisdom will be perverted!* You may be very intelligent, but you will fail when you rely on yourself.

Verse 10: "And whatever my eyes desired I did not keep from them…"—*did whatever he wanted!* A lot of sin involved in that—don't you think?

"…I did not withhold my heart from any pleasure; for my heart rejoiced in all my labor, and this was my portion of all my labor. Then I looked on all the works that my hands had done, and on the labor that I had labored to do; and, behold, all *is* vanity and a striving after the wind; and *there is* no profit under the sun" (vs 10-11).

Why? *Because in doing these works, he was leaving God and looking to himself!* This is going to be very easy during the Millennium. People are going to say:

> Look at me, I'm strong, I'm handsome, I'm young. The women will say, 'I'm beautiful and I want to choose for myself. I am being tired of being told what to do.

God is the One Who gives us the choice. God is the One Who sets before us life and good, death and evil. The evil during the Millennium is not going to be gods all over the place like it is today. *It's going to start in the mind!*

Verse 12: "And I turned to behold wisdom, and madness, and folly; for what *can* the man *do* who comes after the king? Only that which has been already done. Then I saw that wisdom excels folly, as far as light excels darkness" (vs 12-13).

Yes, but what kind of wisdom? *Self-wisdom, after God gave you a great mind and all of that!*

Verse 14: "The wise man's eyes *are* in his head; but the fool walks in darkness; and I myself also perceived that one event happens to all of them. Then I said in my heart, 'As it happens to the fool, *so* it happens even to me; and why was I then more wise?' And I said in my heart that this also *is* vanity" (vs 14-15)—*accusing God of giving him vanity!*

God gave him wisdom, but he also still had foolishness of heart. So, in his foolishness Solomon did what God said not to do. And he couldn't understand why it didn't work out and said that "…this also *is* vanity."

Verse 16: "For *there is* no memory of the wise *more than* of the fool forever, since that which is now shall all be forgotten in the days to come. And how does the wise die? Even as the fool!"

He breathes out his last and no one takes anything. We will see that Solomon didn't like that.

Verse 17: "Therefore, **I hated life**…" *Think about that statement!*

After all that God had done for him; blessed him and gave him and appeared to him twice. He talked to him. But he let his wives and his own vanity get involved. He got involved with these other gods and his life began to be miserable. *He couldn't find satisfaction because he didn't repent!*

Remember that God always honors repentance!

But he said, v 17: "**Therefore, I hated life**… [that's quite a statement] …because the work that is done under the sun *is* grievous to me; for all *is* vanity and a striving after wind." **Why should it be grievous to you?** He had every blessing! He had:

- all the servants
- all the slaves
- all the workman
- all the army
- all of the people

Just think how great that would have been if he would have stayed faithful to God. That was what David told him right at first. He said, *'Son, IF you keep the commandments of God and follow Him, He will bless you.'*

Verse 18: "Yea, I hated all my labor, which I had done…"

- See what happens when you leave God?
- See what happens when you trust in your own thinking?
- See how this can be during the Millennium?

People will begin trusting in themselves rather than trusting in God! That's how, if they don't repent, they're going to end up in Gog and Magog. When they get there, *they're going to think and 'know'* that they are right and God is wrong. This is important for us to understand.

"…under the sun, because I must leave it to the man who shall be after me. And who knows *whether* he shall be wise or a fool? Yet, he shall have rule over all my labor in which I have labored, and have shown myself wise under the sun. This *is* also vanity" (vs 18-19).

Look at how things could have been totally different if he would have been righteous. David learned the lesson after Bathsheba and numbering the children of Israel. He repented! He turned himself to God with all his heart, mind, soul and being! Then God chose Solomon. Look at Solomon! *Talk about becoming ungrateful and unthankful and nearly accusing God!*

Verse 20: "And I turned to cause my heart to despair of all the labor, which I had done under the sun."

Think of that! Deliberately making himself depressed and thinking, 'I've done all of this and who knows what the one who is going to come after me is going to do. I did it all and it's going to be all in vain. Boo-Hoo!' *If you hadn't left God it would have been entirely different!*

Verse 21: "For there is a man whose labor is in wisdom, and in knowledge, and with skill; yet, to a man who has not labored in it, he shall leave it *for* his portion. This also is vanity and a great evil." *That's true and that's what was coming!*

Verse 22: "For what has man from all his labor, and from the striving of his heart, in which he has labored under the sun? For all his days *are* sorrows…" (vs 22-23).

Solomon should have been happy, *but he wasn't because he went against God!* If it gets that way in the Millennium then they'll go in the local area where the Church is, and we'll help them to see if they can come to repentance. Other people in the Church will help and encourage and want to bring the person around so that they can change and overcome.

If they don't repent with that kind of care, then they're sent to the repentance center so they can get more intense with prayer, fasting and studying the Word of God.

If after that they are so hard-hearted and so self-willed that they will not listen, then they will be sent to Gog and Magog. You read that when the Millennium is over what's it going to be? *We'll see tomorrow!*

"…and his labor vexation; yea, so his heart does not take rest in the night. This *is* also vanity" (v 23). *Solomon's life was getting to be terrible and miserable!*

Verse 24: "There is nothing better for a man than that he should eat and drink and make his soul see good in his labor? This I also saw, [#2]**that it *was* from the hand of God**. For who can eat, or who can enjoy it, more than I?…. [nobody] …[#3]**For God gives wisdom**… [that's an inset] …and knowledge, and joy to a man who *is* good in His sight. But to the sinner He gives labor, to gather and to heap up, that he may **give to *him who is* good before** [#4]**God**. This also *is* vanity and a striving after wind" (vs 24-26).

Here Solomon was judging himself! Quite a thing turning away from God! So, the whole book of Ecclesiastes is there are some sound proverbs here, but it is showing—the first two chapters—how Solomon left God. He didn't repent.

Think about the worst king that there ever was—Manasseh—and all that he did, all the sins, all the other gods. God punished him by invading Judah and having the king of Assyria take him off to Babylon, because the Assyrians ruled Babylon at that time.

In prison Manasseh repented! Manasseh came back and cleaned up the house of God, tore out all the idols that he put in there, tore down the things that were sin all around the house of God, and worshipped God!

That shows that if there would have been repentance by Solomon, that he would have been able to correct everything and come back and see that everything that he has written here in Ecc. 1 & 2 all came from God. What a blessing that would have been.

Let's think about how that's going to be in the Millennium. They're not going to be able to build idols. They're not going to be able to have false gods. But we will see that what it is that's going to come upon them, the other thing, which will be that *they will think of themselves as being perfect. That will be the perfection syndrome!*

Come back tomorrow and we will look at the second great cause of sin in the Millennium!

Scriptural References:

1) Isaiah 65:19-20
2) Deuteronomy 8:6-14
3) Proverbs 14:12, 14
4) Proverbs 12:20-22
5) 1 Chronicles 28:6-10
6) 1 Kings 3:5-14
7) 1 Kings 9:1-7
8) Deuteronomy 17:14-20
9) 1 Kings 11:1-12, 14
10) Psalm 72:1-20
11) Ecclesiastes 1:1-9, 12-14, 16-18
12) Ecclesiastes 2:1-26

Scriptures referenced, not quoted: 2-Samuel 8; 10

Also referenced: Message: *Progression of Evil Through Philosophy*

FRC:bo
Transcribed: 7/29/19
Reformatted: 1/2021

CHAPTER SEVENTY-THREE

The Job Syndrome
Fred R. Coulter

Greetings, brethren! Right at the end of the Millennium is going to be a spectacular event (Rev. 20).

We know at the beginning of the Millennium, Satan is bound in the abyss. But it says that he would not deceive the nations anymore *until* the thousand years were fulfilled, and *after that,* beginning with the end, that it is ordained that he be 'loosed for a short time.'

- How long is the short time? *We don't know, but he's going to be loosed!*
- Why will he be loosed?
- What will he do?

Revelation 20:7: "Now, when the thousand years have been completed, Satan shall be loosed out of his prison; and he shall go out to deceive the nations... [plural] ...that *are* in the four corners of the earth, Gog and Magog…" (vs 7-8).

This is *not talking about the people* of Gog and Magog, although there may be some involved in it, *but the geographical area of Gog and Magog!* As we have seen, when people sin and they won't repent, and they haven't lived out to their 100 years, yet, then they are exiled.

First of all, they will be in what you might say in the local area, if there are problems with sin. We'll cover some of the things today about the sin, as we did yesterday concerning the sin of Solomon. Today we're going to cover about *the sin of Job—The Job Syndrome*—and what's going to happen with that. The nations (plural) in the geographical area of Gog and Magog, *that's the final exile!*

When people are sent to Gog and Magog, in the exile, that amounts to the same thing of what God did with Cain after he murdered Abel. Adam and Eve and Cain and Abel were exiled out of the Garden of Eden, but they still had access to God at the east gate of the Garden of Eden. But after the murder of Abel by Cain, *he was exiled into the land of wandering!* Removed further away, removed completely from God, completely from the line of Abel, and off in some place in the earth called the land of Nod, or the land of the wandering.

In this case, we have seen that when people sin, and they don't repent, and they are exiled to Gog and Magog, then they will live out their life, 100 years and die accursed. What does accursed mean? *Cutoff from God, and destined to the Lake of Fire!*

"...in the four corners of the earth, Gog and Magog, of whom the number *is* as the sand of the sea..." (v 8).

Now, this tells us that there are going to be a lot of people alive, who have sinned, and have not repented, and the number is of the sand of the sea. In other words, the number is going to be great enough that they can't be counted. The reason they can't be counted is because there's free moral agency (IFMA). If they use that against God, that's why they're exiled over there, to gather them for war. Let's see what happens to them. We'll come back to this when we come to the end of this message.

Verse 9: "Then *I saw* them go up upon the breadth of the earth and encircle the camp of the saints, and the beloved city; and fire came down from God out of heaven and consumed them."

Let's see what the circumstances are in people's lives that this will be necessary. We also know and understand that God is going to change human nature back to what it was before the sin of Adam and Eve (Ezek. 36). But in Jer. 17:9 *we find that human nature is still evil, but not quite as evil!*

However, when they do commit the unpardonable sin and are removed to Gog and Magog, we don't know if they can repent there. But if it is the unpardonable sin, there is no repentance that's going to work.

Jeremiah 17:1: "The sin of Judah *is* engraved with a pen of iron, with the point of a diamond; *it is* carved upon the tablet of their heart and upon the horns of your altars."

*There will be people who will **refuse** to obey and love God. Who will **refuse** our instruction as teachers!* When we tell them, 'here is the way to go,' *they will **refuse** to go! They will think,* with their own free moral agency—and remember, God isn't going to take that away— *that their thoughts are just as good as God's thoughts,* and there's no need for them to repent, be baptized and receive the Holy Spirit. After all, look at 'how good' they are! ***BUT***:

Verse 9: "The heart *is* deceitful above all things..." *Maybe at this time not quite as deceitful!*

But if you get into the unpardonable sin *it is as deceitful!*

"...and desperately wicked; who can know it?" (v 9).

With everything there, God and the sons and daughters of God teaching, directing, running the government, running all of the things concerning the true worship of God—the Sabbath, the Holy Days and everything—that there will be people *who will think* that because they've been born into this society, which is very good, *that they are very 'good,' but not converted!* There will be some *who will think* that they don't need to repent. After all, they're 'good.'

So, let's see in the book of Job, exactly what the *Job syndrome* is. We will see it. So we'll define it at the beginning. The Job syndrome is that *they are so good in the letter of the Law that they refuse to admit the sins that are inward in the mind!* That's how Job was; he was blameless in the letter of the Law.

Let's see something very similar to it in Matt. 19. This is the time when the rich man came to Jesus. Here's a person growing up in Judea, and he was a righteous person. Remember, concerning righteousness Jesus said that the only Israelite without guile was Nathaniel. So it's very rare to have someone with human nature that has no guile.

Matthew 19:16: "Now at that time, one came to Him *and* said, 'Good Master, what good *thing* shall I do, that I may have eternal life?'"

Notice Jesus answer, and this is the answer that will be given to the people all during the Millennium.

You may be 'good' in the letter of the Law, but it is *the conversion of the mind, and the transformation of your thinking* that is the key to eternal life. Obeying in the letter of the Law is required by everyone; but to obey, in the spirit of the Law, and with love, with grace and with understanding is a whole other ballgame.

Verse 17: "And He said to him, 'Why do you call Me good? **No one**… [no human being] … *is* good except one—**God**....'"

That's why we have to become the sons and daughters of God. *Because of ourselves, as good as we may be*—which we will see Job was—*we are still sinful!* Our minds have not been converted, changed and brought to the point of thinking the way that God thinks. So he says;

"...But if you desire to enter into life, keep the commandments" (v 17).

- Isn't that going to be what it's going to be during the Millennium?
- Won't all people be keeping the commandments?

Yes indeed, notice what He answered!

Verse 18: "Then he said to Him, 'Which?' And Jesus said, 'You shall not commit murder; you shall not commit adultery; you shall not steal; you shall not bear false witness; honor your father and your mother; and, you shall love your neighbor as yourself'" (vs 18-19).

Well, look at what the young man said. He thought to himself, 'Hey, I'm almost there. I really don't need much, do I?'

I wonder how many people during the Millennium will do that and have the Job Syndrome?

Verse 20: "The young man said to Him, 'I have kept all these things from my youth. **What do I yet lack?**'"

Won't that be true people growing up in the Millennium? *They will have done the commandments all their life!* "...**What do I yet lack?**" They can probably look around and say, 'I'm as good as or better than these people who are supposed to be converted. Comparing themselves among themselves.

Verse 21: "Jesus said to him, 'If you desire to be perfect, go *and* sell your property, and give to *the* poor, and you shall have treasure in heaven; and come *and* follow Me.'"

Give up everything that you have! *For conversion,* you must give up everything:

- that you *think* you are
- how good *you may believe* that you are
- acknowledge that *God alone is righteous,* no human being

Verse 22: "But after hearing this word, the young man went away grieving, because he had many possessions. Then Jesus said to His disciples, **'Truly I say to you, it *is extremely* difficult for a rich man to enter into the Kingdom of Heaven'**" (vs 22-23).

For people who know the Law, know the Truth and understand, *it is difficult for them to come to see their own human nature!* What was the rich man's human nature? He had as his idol *all his riches and everything he owned!* He couldn't turn his back on those things that he thought were important.

Verse 23: "Then Jesus said to His disciples, 'Truly I say to you, it *is extremely* difficult for a rich man to enter into the Kingdom of Heaven. And again I say to you, it is easier for a camel to pass through *the* eye of a needle than *for* a rich man to enter into the Kingdom of God'" (vs 23-24).

That is quite a thing. *But with God, it's possible!* So, here we have all of these people growing up during the Millennium, keeping the laws of God, obeying their parents, maybe having some possessions like this rich man had, or whatever it may be, *and they can't see their own sins!* Now, this is what Job's problem was.

The only difference between the account of Job and those during the Millennium is that Satan is working in the society and times and life of Job. So during the Millennium, it's going to be *harder,* because Satan is not there. There is no one to blame. But nevertheless, the whole experience of Job that we're going to examine, *is how he thought of himself, and how he was his own idol!*

Let's think about something concerning Adam and Eve. God created them perfectly. They had a language already built into their brain, they could talk with one another; they could talk with God; they saw God.

Now, since they were made in the image of God and after His likeness, when they looked at God—Who appeared to them more like a human being, rather than in His glory and power—you can see how easy it was for them to think that they were almost like God. Think about that in relationship to people during the Millennium.

All the sons and daughters of God will be there ruling, teaching, everything carrying out the way that God wants. We'll be able to appear to them much like a human being. Now then, how many will begin to think that they're almost like them. What is this that they are saying that our nature is evil? When you look at the whole society, they're all keeping God's way, they're all doing what God wants them to do.

But the thing concerning independent free moral agency—IFMA—will always be working. God will never take that away. What kind of thoughts may they harbor in their minds? We will know that they are, but they won't understand how that we know. So, they will be susceptible to the same thing that Adam and Eve were. They will say:

We're almost like God. I know this, I know that, I understand the other. I've done this, I've done that I've done the other, all according to the Laws of God. Why do I need to repent?

This was similar to what Job said. The only difference is Satan was directly involved to put Job through this trial, and that will not be during the Millennium. Yet, many of the same self-righteous thoughts will probably come up. Let's look at it.

Now we're going to do a survey covering many different things, mainly all the *self-righteous thoughts of Job!* If you're doing good and almost like God:

- Why do you need to repent and be baptized in order to enter into the Kingdom of God?
- Why can't you just continue like this?
- Like the rich man who said, 'Well, I've done this all my life?'

Job 1:6: "Now, there was a day when the sons of God came to present themselves before the LORD. And Satan also came among them…. [these are the angels and Satan] …And the LORD said to Satan, 'From where do you come?' Then Satan answered the LORD and said, 'From going to and fro in the earth, and from walking up and down in it.' And the LORD said to Satan, 'Have you considered My servant Job, that *there is* none like him in the earth...'" (vs 6-8). *The most righteous man!*

God said later that Noah, Job, and Daniel were the three most righteous men there ever were (Ezek. 14). Here's a man who was very righteous, and we'll look at some of the things that he did.

"'...a blameless and upright man... [remember, this is in the *letter* of the Law] ...one who fears God and turns away from evil?' And Satan answered the LORD and said, 'Does Job fear God for nothing? Have You not made a hedge around him, and around his house, and around all that he has on every side? You have blessed the work of his hands, and his possessions have increased in the land. But put forth Your hand now, and touch all that he has, and he will curse You to Your face'" (vs 8-11).

Satan also knew human nature, and even though a person does 'good,' when all the circumstances are good, that doesn't mean if the circumstances change, *that they will not change and show their human nature and the evil for what it is!*

Verse 12: "And the LORD said to Satan, 'Behold, all that he has *is* in your power. Only do not lay your hand upon him.' And Satan went forth from the presence of the LORD."

Then catastrophe happened. I mean, *complete catastrophe!* Let's look at it:

Verse 13: "Now, there was a day when his sons and his daughters *were* eating and drinking wine in their oldest brother's house. And there came a messenger to Job and said, 'The oxen were plowing, and the donkeys feeding beside them. And the Sabeans fell *upon them*, and took them away.

Yea, they have killed the servants with the edge of the sword. And I only have escaped alone to tell you.'…. [right as he was saying that]: …While he *was* still speaking, there also came *another* and said, 'The fire of God has fallen from the heavens and has burned up the sheep and the servants, and destroyed them. And I only have escaped alone to tell you.' While he *was* still speaking, there also came *another* and said, 'The Chaldeans formed three bands and swooped down upon the camels, and have carried them away, yea, and have killed the servants with the edge of the sword. And I only have escaped alone to tell you.' While he *was* still speaking, there also came another and said, 'Your sons and your daughters were eating and drinking wine in their oldest brother's house. And, behold, a great wind came from the wilderness and struck the four corners of the house, and it fell upon the young men, and they are dead. And I only have escaped alone to tell you'" (vs 13-19).

Think of the total disaster and all the things that happened. He lost everything that he owned, and he lost his whole family except his wife. What would you do with a thing like that? There are even some people today angry at God. They're cursing God because they have this or that trial. They haven't had one like this. This is everything in one day. So, let's see what Job did.

Verse 20: "And Job arose, and tore his robe, and shaved his head, and fell down upon the ground and worshiped. And he said, 'Naked came I out of my mother's womb, and naked shall I return there. The LORD gave, and the LORD has taken away. Blessed *be* the name of the LORD.' **In all this Job did not sin, nor charge God foolishly**" (vs 20-22).

Now that's a commendable thing. I mean, just consider your own circumstances:

- What if something happened like this to you?
- Would you get angry with God?
- Would you curse God?

Let's see what happens, because Job's trial… A lot of people can't understand why would God do this to Job. What a terrible thing to do. When I first came into the Church and I first read the book of Job, I thought: *Surely God wasn't right,* **because I didn't understand the spiritual stakes involved!**

Likewise today, when a terrible, *terrible, terrible* trial comes, people begin to accuse God or get mad at God. *Well, Job didn't!* He is to be really commended for that. But that's only the beginning of the story.

Job 2:1: "And again it came to pass on a day that the sons of God came to present themselves before the LORD. And Satan also came among them to present himself before the LORD. And the LORD said to Satan, 'From where do you come?' And Satan answered the LORD and said, 'From going to and fro in the earth, and from walking up and down in it.' And the LORD said unto Satan, **'Have you considered My servant Job, that *there is* none like him in the earth**…'" (vs 1-3).

Now, think about that! *The most righteous man in the earth!* So, why bring all these trials on him?

"'…a blameless and an upright man, one who fears God and turns away from evil? And still he is holding fast to his integrity, although you moved Me against him to destroy him without cause'" (v 3).

This is quite an account! Satan had another one up his sleeve:

Verse 4: "And Satan answered the LORD and said, 'Skin for skin, yea, all that a man has he will give for his life. But indeed put forth Your hand now, and touch his bone and his flesh, and he will curse You to Your face.' And the LORD said to Satan, 'Behold, he *is* in your hand, but spare his life.' And Satan went forth from the presence of the LORD and struck Job with sore boils from the sole of his foot to the top of his head. And he [Job] took a broken piece of pottery to scrape himself with. And he sat down among the ashes" (vs 4-8).

Now he had the boils all over. With the potsherd, he would scrape the puss, and it would ooze out and the blood he'd sprinkle ashes on. Imagine the flies all over. A little later he says that worms were in his flesh; that is maggots. To look down and see all the flies, and you don't have hardly the strength to swipe them away, swish them away. This would be such delicious food for the flies, that they wouldn't move away! They just zoom off and come right back. Imagine that! He got a lot of 'support' from his wife!

Verse 9: "And his wife said to him, 'Do you still hold to your integrity? Curse God and die!'…. [so much for loving Job, uh?] …But he said to her, 'You speak as one of the foolish women speak. What? Shall we receive good at the hand of God, and shall we not receive evil?' **In all this Job did not sin with his lips**" (vs 9-10).

Interesting statement! It didn't say he didn't sin *in his thoughts!*

- What are the worst kinds of thoughts, that a lot of people can't recognize as sin? *Self-righteousness!*
- Don't you think that's going to be a big problem during the Millennium? *Yes, indeed!*

Stop and think about it!

- How do we end up with as many in Gog and Magog 'as the sands of the sea'?

So, we're going to examine those thoughts. Then his three friends came to comfort him and they were so awestruck with the condition of Job when they saw him, they just sat there and said not word for seven days.

Job 3:1: "After this Job opened his mouth and cursed the day of his *birth*…. [not God but his *birth*] …And Job spoke and said, 'Let the day perish in which I was born, and the night in which it was said, "A man child is brought forth." Let that day be darkness. Let not God look upon it from above, neither let the light shine upon it'" (vs 1-4).

Then he complains about how awful and terrible it has been. All of these things he said it would have been better if I'd just been stillborn.

Verse 20: "Why is light given to him who is in misery… [he's talking about himself] …and life to the bitter *in* soul."

Wouldn't you be bitter if that happens? *Bitterness against God,* even though he said, 'God gives and God takes away,' He gives the good and we receive that. So why don't we receive the difficult and evil.

Verse 21: "Who is waiting for death—but *it* comes not… [He was sitting there waiting to die, but it didn't happen] …and digs for it more than *for* hidden treasures? They are rejoicing to exultation. They are glad when they can find the grave. *Why is light given* to a man whose way is hidden, and whom God has made a hedge about? For my sighing comes instead of my food, and my groanings are poured out like the waters. For **the thing which I greatly feared** has come upon me…" (vs 21-25).

Now stop and think about this. What is it that you greatly fear? *Other than death, there may be a lot of things you greatly fear! Don't fear them, put them all in God's hands, because it will come upon you!*

"…and that which I was afraid of has come to me. I was not in safety, I have no rest, neither was I quiet; yet trouble comes" (v 25).

Time and chance happen to all! That was quite a thing he was going through here. I'm not going to go through all the excuses of the three friends, because the three friends came and said, 'Job you're sinning. Admit your sin. You think you're righteous, but admit your sin.' Job kept saying, 'No, I haven't sinned.' So let's see how all of this goes.

After Eliphaz the Temanite got done accusing him of sin and telling him how bad he was:

Job 6:1: "And Job answered and said, 'Oh, that my grief were but weighed, and my calamity laid in the balances together! For now it would be heavier than the sand of the sea; therefore, my words have been rash. For the arrows of the Almighty *are* within me, my spirit is drinking up their poison. The terrors of God do set themselves against me'" (vs 1-4). *Man, that's quite a thing he's going through there!*

Verse 9[transcriber's correction]: "Even that it would please God to destroy me; that He would loose His hand and cut me off! Then I would yet have my comfort; yea, I would rejoice in pain, though He did not spare me; for I have not denied the words of the Holy One" (vs 9-10). *Through all of that!*

So that we know what we are looking to, and what the problem is that Job had and how it was necessary for conversion for him to go through this.

Now, we don't know exactly how it's going to work in the Millennium. I don't think it's going to work exactly like this. But we can take the principles of it, because we're dealing in **what Job actually thought!** What we're doing is reading what he **said,** while God was looking at what he **thought!** We will see that as we get further along.

Ezekiel 14:1: "And some of the elders of Israel came to me and sat before me. And the Word of the LORD came to me, saying, 'Son of man, these men have set up their idols in their hearts, and put the stumbling block of their iniquity before their faces. Should I at all be inquired of by them?'" (vs 1-3).

Now, we're getting to the point that's important. There will be no overt idols during the Millennium. But where will they be? ***In their mind! In their heart!***

Verse 4: "Therefore, speak to them, and say to them, "Thus says the Lord GOD, 'Every man of the house of Israel who sets up his idols in his heart, and puts the stumbling block of his iniquity before his face, and comes to the prophet…'" *That will be us!* We will be the teachers. They will come to us.

"…I the LORD will answer him according to the multitude of his idols" (v 4). *That's where all the idols are going to be during the Millennium: in the mind!*

How good I am, how righteous I am. Oh, and look at that person over there, and that person over there, I'm better than they are. I've kept the commandments of God all my life. I'm so good, that I don't need to be baptized in order to enter into the Kingdom of God.

I see how these people are transformed, when they a hundred-years-old and that's a wonderful thing. But I'm good enough for that. Why do I have to repent?

Verse 5: "So that I may take the house of Israel in their own heart because **they have deserted Me for their idols—all of them**."

When you have idols in your mind, guess what you're doing? You are pushing God out, and you're uplifting yourself. Now that's quite a thing to contemplate, isn't it? So, we need to think on that.

Verse 6: "Therefore, say to the house of Israel, "Thus says the Lord GOD, 'Repent and turn yourselves from your idols, and turn away your faces from all your abominations. For every one of the house of Israel, or of the stranger who lives in Israel, who separates himself from Me and **sets up his idols in his heart**...'"" (vs 6-7).

Isn't that what it's going to be? *If you have idols in your heart during the Millennium, you are separating yourself from God!* All of these idols will be what you are worshiping. But all of us as the teachers of God will know those thoughts. Other people won't.

I will be just like today, people can be nice as can be, and look like they are going to be your friend. But inside, they hate and despise you. Now is that not a greater sin? *Yes, indeed!* Two sins: *hatred and despising; the idol in your mind and the secret sin that is cutting you off from God!* Notice what's going to happen here:

Verse 8: "And I will set My face against that man, and I will make him for a sign and for a proverb..."

What is going to happen? *They will have to go to the rehabilitation repentance center first!* If they don't come to understand that, then they will be shipped off the Gog and Magog. When they get Gog and Magog, they're going to find all the sinners who are there. They're going to say that they are right and God is wrong! Amazing thing!

"...And I will cut him off from the midst of My people; and you shall know that I *am* the LORD. And the prophet, if he is deceived, and he speaks a word, I the LORD have deceived that prophet. And I will stretch out My hand upon him and will destroy him from the midst of My people Israel" (vs 8-9).

Job 3:25: "For the thing which I greatly feared has come upon me..."

Job is talking to his friends here, Job 6:24: "Teach me, and I will be silent; and cause me to understand where I have gone astray." *Job was in an* **almost** *repentant attitude here, but not quite!*

Job tells them about all the advice they're giving and he says, v 29: "Relent, I pray you, let there be no iniquity; yea, acknowledge, my righteousness yet stands."

All that you've been telling me. None of you can convict me of sin. My righteousness stands.

But the truth is, there is no righteousness except that which comes from God. So, this is his sin, *self-righteousness!*

Job 7:4: "When I lie down, I say, "When shall I rise?" But the night is long, and I am full of tossing to and fro until the dawning of the day. My flesh is clothed with maggots... [could just see him] ... and dusty scabs; my skin cracks open and runs *with pus.* My days are swifter than a weaver's shuttle, and are spent without hope. O remember that my life *is* a breath; my eye shall no more see good" (vs 4-7).

Well, he was complaining to God for this, and in somewhat in a way that is true. But it was really Satan. God allowed it *so Job could repent!* But for Job to repent, because he was so self-righteous, is quite a task, indeed.

Now, Job started to get angry with God here in chapter seven:

Job 7:17: "What *is* man, that You should magnify him, and that You should set Your heart on him, and that You should visit him every morning, *and* try him every moment?.... [Why, God, are You trying me every moment?] ...How long? Will You not look away from me, nor let me alone until I swallow down my spittle? If I have sinned, what shall I do to You, O Watcher of men? Why have You set me as Your target, so that I am a burden to myself?.... [What an accusation against God!] ...And why do You not pardon my transgression, and take away my iniquity? For now I shall sleep in the dust, and You shall seek me in the morning, but I *shall* not be" (vs 17-21).

What a *talk-back* to God! 'You really brought this upon me, O God.' So, there's another sin.

Job 9:15: "Whom, though I were righteous, *yet,* I could not answer; I would make supplication to My Judge. If I had called and He had answered me, yet I would not believe that He had listened to my voice" (vs 15-16).

Quite a thing! Challenging God that, because I'm going through all of this.

Verse 20: "If I justify myself, my own mouth shall condemn me; *though* I *am* blameless... ['No sin in me!'] ...He shall declare me perverse."

Quite lesson Job is going through. The book of Job is a very complicated book, because the average person who reads it doesn't understand their own mind. They don't do it. So, they read this and think: If someone were this righteous, why would God take it out on him? Well, the final answer is **He wants to give him eternal life!** Job has to overcome the worst sin possible: *self-righteousness!*

Verse 32—Job thinks that he is so good, that he has done no wrong, that he has always been right.

Verse 32: "For *He is* not a man, as I *am, that* I should answer Him, *that* we should come together in court; there is no umpire between us..." *Job said, 'I want to take Him to court and lay it all out!'*

"...*who* might lay his hand upon us both. Let Him take His rod away from me, and let not His fear make me afraid; *then* would I speak and not fear Him; but *it is* not so with me" (vs 32-35).

Whoa! What a thing that he did, what he went through.

Let's get a good glimpse of what Job was thinking. I think that this is a fantastic testimony to the Word of God, that such a book like this would be written like this, and preserved. Now, I don't know who wrote it. I don't know who took down all the notes to do it. But it is certainly a fantastic book in the Bible.

Job 10:14: "If I sin, then You mark me, and You will not acquit me from my iniquity. If I am wicked, woe to me; and *if* I am righteous, I will not lift up my head, *being* filled with confusion—therefore look upon my affliction.... [notice how he looks to God] ...For if my head be lifted up, You will hunt me as a fierce lion; and again You will show Yourself awesome against me" (vs 14-16). *Angry at God! Blaming God!*

Job 11:5: "But oh, that God would speak, and open His lips against you, and would tell you the secrets of His wisdom. For sound wisdom has two sides. Know therefore that God exacts from you *less* than your iniquity deserves" (vs 5-6).

Job he said, 'I want to speak to God.' Well, we'll see that God answered that.

This is quite a study—isn't it? Just think about this: During the Millennium how is all of this going to go? all of this is going to come down? *That will be one of our greatest sins!* The first one was the Solomon Syndrome, where *he acknowledged God at first, and then he took all the credit to himself!*

Now this one—*The Job Syndrome*—is that he acknowledges God, but that he is as good as God. He doesn't need anything else to be perfect. *He doesn't recognize the sin of the mind and the idols in the mind!*

Job 13:3: "Notwithstanding I would speak to the Almighty, and I desire to argue my case before God." *Wow, that's quite a statement! So, he's telling those who are speaking against him:*

Verse 13: "Be quiet! Let me alone so that I may speak, and **let come upon me what may**." *That's quite a thing! Yes, indeed!*

Verse 18: "Behold now, I have set *my* cause in order; I know that I shall be justified.... [because I'm right] ...Can anyone bring charges against me?...." (vs 18-19).

You three men out there, you're talking about all these things, and there is not one thing you have said that is correct, because I've done none of those things.

"... If so, I will be silent and die. Only do not do two *things* to me; then I will not hide myself from You. Withdraw... [this is talking to God] ...Your hand far from me, and let not Your dread terrify me. Then call, and I will answer; or let me speak, and You answer me" (vs 19-22).

So, all the time he's challenging God in all of this. This is quite a thing that's going on. *Job was so righteous and so caught up in himself, **that he couldn't see the idols in his mind!** That **the goodness that he did became the idol** that carried him away from God.*

He did not understand and realize, as Paul wrote in Acts 17, that *in God we live and move and have our being!* Everything about life comes from God. Now he understood it in a certain way, but he didn't understand it to the depths that all that he did. He had to credit it to God and not himself.

Job 16:1: "And Job answered and said, 'I have heard many such things. Miserable comforters are you all! Is there no end to windy words? Or what provokes you that you should answer?'" (vs 1-3).

So, he went on to speak on that a bit. Notice how Job does this:

Verse 21: "Oh, that a man might plead with God, as a man pleads with his neighbor!"

You don't plead with God that way, because God is not a man. You plead with God ***with repentance and humility,*** and acknowledging God's:

- greatness
- glory
- love
- mercy
- kindness
- forgiveness

Our thoughts are not His thoughts, and our ways are not His ways!

We need that in our lives. God gives that, and when He gives it, that is not making us something great, that we can brag and boast about it as Job did.

Job 17:1: "My spirit is broken, My days are extinct. The grave is ready for me." *Not quite!* Your Spirit is not yet broken because you continue to mock God.

You go through and read the whole book of Job and see how you do with understanding these things.

Job 23:1: "And Job answered and said… [after Eliphaz the Temanite talked to Job] …'Even today *is* my complaint bitter; my stroke is heavier than my groaning. Oh, that I knew *where* I might find Him [God] *that* I might come even to His seat!'" (vs 1-3).

Right up to His Throne! **Whoa! Talk about self-righteousness!**

Verse 4: "I would lay *my* cause before Him, and fill my mouth with arguments. I would know the words, *which* He would answer me, and understand what He would say to me. Will He contend against me with *His* great power? No, surely He would give heed to me. There the righteous might reason with Him; and I would be acquitted from my Judge forever" (vs 4-7).

If I just get up to God's Throne and show Him how good I really am, He will say to me, 'That's a great thing.' *How about that!* By all the arguments you go through here, and all the arguments that are done. Job 31 is a key, important chapter. Job is telling about all the things that he has is done.

Job 31:5: "**If I** have walked with vanity, or **if my** foot has hurried to deceit, let me be weighed in an even balance so that God may know that I am blameless. **If my** step has turned out of the way, or my heart has walked after my eyes, and **if** any spot has cleaved to my hands… [I am spotless; I am so good] …*then* let me sow, and let another eat; and let my harvests be rooted out. **If my** heart has been enticed by a woman, or I have laid wait at my neighbor's door, *then* let my wife grind for another, and let others bow down upon her" (vs 5-10).

Verse 12: "For it *is* a fire that devours to destruction, and it would root out all my increase. **If I** despised the cause of my manservant or of my maidservant, when they complained against me; what then shall I do when God rises up? And when He calls me to account, what shall I answer Him?" (vs 12-14).

I never did anything wrong, to any of my servants. I never did anything wrong to anyone. I always did what was right; always what was right!

- Who made the laws?
- Who made right from wrong?
- Who made good from evil?
- Who made and created you so you could think?
- *God did!*

Verse 16: "If I have withheld the poor from *their* desire, or have caused the eyes of the widow to fail, or have eaten my morsel myself alone, and the fatherless has not eaten of it, for from my youth he grew up with me, as *with* a father, and from infancy I guided her… [oh, my] …if I have seen any perish for lack of clothing, or there was no covering for the needy; if his loins have not blessed me, and he warmed himself with the fleece of my sheep; if I have lifted up my hand against the fatherless when I watched over my help in the gate; *then* let my arm fall from the shoulder blade, and let my arm be broken from the elbow. For calamity *from* God *is* a terror to me, and by reason of His majesty I could do nothing" (vs 16-23).

He did every thing right. But *if* everything out here is right, *if there are idols in the mind, you're filled with sin!* You see how that's going to be one of the biggest challenges during the Millennium.

Verse 24: "If I have made gold my hope, or have called fine gold my confidence; if I rejoiced because my wealth *was* great, and because my hand had gotten much; if I beheld the sun when it shined, or the moon walking in brightness, and my heart has been secretly enticed, or my mouth has kissed my hand… [whatever that is worth] this also *would be* an iniquity *for* the judges *to punish;* for I would have lied to God who is above… [you say no, I didn't do any of these things] …If I rejoiced at the destruction of him who hated me, or exulted myself when evil found him; verily I have not allowed my mouth to sin by wishing for a curse on his life" (vs 24-30).

Point: Look at how good he was. But it was *all him **and not God!*** So, it became him against God and God against him.

Verse 31: "If the men of my tabernacle did not say, 'Who can find one who has not been satisfied with his meat?'"

Verse 33: "If I covered my transgressions like Adam, by hiding my iniquity in my bosom, then let me tremble before a great multitude, and be terrified by the scorn of families; *and* I will be silent *and* not go out the door… [Quite a thing! This is really fantastic book!] …**Oh, that I had one to hear** me! **Behold, my desire is** *that* **the Almighty would answer me,** and the indictment *that* my adversary had written. Surely I would carry it on my shoulder, *and* bind it *like* a crown *upon my head*. I would declare to Him the number of my steps; like a prince I would come before Him" (vs 33-37).

I'm not going to God as a humble repentant man, I'm going to come like a prince who has always done right and never have done wrong. Everybody has benefited and profited from what I have done. I haven't laid with any woman. I haven't lusted after anything. I haven't taken any gold or silver. But I have given and helped and all of this, *and I am good, and I am righteous!*

Elihu, then answered and told Job, the facts that they were. Let's see how Elihu, sent from God, a young man who had wisdom and understanding, more than his three friends. His three friends couldn't find anything wrong with him. Job couldn't find anything wrong with himself. Job couldn't find that he had done anything wrong. *Yet, he had all* these **idols in his mind!**

Job 35:1: "And Elihu answered and said, **'Do you think this to be right, you** *that* **say, "My righteousness** *is* **more than God's"?'"** (vs 1-2). *Now think of that!*

- God is perfect
- God is Holy
- God is righteous
- God is love
- God is true

Man is what? *Man is flesh!* Everything that a man has **comes from God!** Every way of being able *to think, to do, to plan, to devise,* **all comes from God!** Anything that he makes, **all comes from God!** He makes it out of the things that **God has created!**

So, it is all to God's credit. Just like with the Church and the things that we do. God is the One Who makes it possible. Yes, we do the work, but it's God's.

- God has to inspire it
- God has to lead
- God has to give us the ability to do it

Then we acknowledge that it all comes from God, even though we had to do the work. But God gave us the strength, power, energy and thought to do the work. *So, it all goes back to God!*

Verse 3: "For you say, 'What advantage will it be to You? What profit shall I have, more than *if* I had sinned?' I will answer your words… [v 5]: Look to the heavens, and see…" (vs 3-5)—*what God has made!*

After talking to Job for a good long time, then Job got his wish: 'Oh that I could talk to God.' Well now, *directly in the face of God we will see that Job learns some lessons!*

Job 38:1: "Then the LORD answered Job out of the whirlwind, and said, **'Who** *is* **this that darkens counsel by words without knowledge?**…. [that one statement puts Job in his place] …Now gird up your loins like a man; for I will demand of you, and you shall answer Me'" (vs 1-3).

- *IF* you are so great, Job
- *IF* you are so righteous
- *IF* you know so much

Verse 4: "Where were you when I laid the foundations of the earth? Declare it if you have understanding!…. [since you're so smart] …Who has determined its measurements if you know? Or who has stretched the line upon it? On what are the foundations fastened to? Or who laid its cornerstone, when the morning stars sang together and all the sons of God shouted for joy?…. [you weren't there, Job, you didn't even exist] …Or *who* shut up the sea with doors, when it broke forth as it came from the womb?" (vs 4-8).

Verse 16: "Have you entered into the springs of the sea?…." Do you know anything about

- the oceans?
- the seas?
- the currents?
- the springs?
- the pathways of water?
- the depths of it?
- the life at great depth?

—over a mile from the surface of the ocean—
- **Where were you?**

"…Or have you walked in search of the depths? Have the gates of death been opened to you?…." (vs 16-17).

- Do you understand how life can come back to life from death through the resurrection?
- Do you, Job?
- Do you know how that works?

"…Or have you seen the gates of the shadow of death? Have you surveyed the breadth of the earth? **Declare it, if you know it all!**" (vs 17-18).

That was Job! *Job was a know it all!* Quite a thing! Now, let's see the end of the matter here. With this, Job's whole attitude changed.

Now, do you suppose that the book of Job is going to be one of the *main books used in the repentance and rehabilitation center* for those who think they are so good, and don't need to repent? We will be there as the sons and daughters of God teaching them. Leading them in repentance, helping them to understand the Word of God. Think how much more we will have to do so. Yet, if they still persist in that and won't repent, *then it's a one way ticket to Gog and Magog!*

Job 40:1: "And the LORD answered Job and said, '**Shall he who contends with the Almighty instruct *Him*?**....'" (vs 1-2).

Is anyone going to instruct God, Who knows everything? *And little puny man knows so little!* You who are sinful and imperfect, *are you going to teach God?*

"'...He who reproves God, let him answer it.' And Job answered the LORD and said, 'Behold, I am vile! What shall I answer You? I will lay my hand on my mouth. Once I have spoken; but I will not answer; yea, twice, but I will proceed no further'" (vs 2-5).

Now that's quite a thing! Job learned a fantastic lesson, and let's see what that lesson is.

Verse 6: "And the LORD answered Job out of the whirlwind, and said, 'Gird up your loins now like a man. I will demand of you, and you declare unto Me'" (vs 6-7). *God is answering Job with all of His*:

- self-righteousness
- self-confidence
- boasting
- accusing God as being unfair, and making his life terrible and miserable

which it did; it was! **But God wants him converted!** Likewise with all of those in the Millennium:

- God wants them *converted*
- God wants them *repenting*
- God wants them *understanding the Truth*
- God wants them to *enter into the Kingdom of God*

So He said, v 8: "Will you even annul My judgment?.... [You think you could give a greater judgment than Mine?] ...Will you condemn Me so that you may be righteous?"

- bring Me to court and have a judge put his hand on Me and you?
- declare that you are righteous when you've got idols in your mind?
- transgressions in your thoughts?

Though you've done all of these things out here that are good, those are all things that I commanded you to do. So, if you do what I have commanded you to do, are you not then an unprofitable servant?

- I want you to love Me
- I want you to acknowledge Me
- I want you to understand how much I want you in My Kingdom

But you've got to come to this yourself!

Verse 9: "And *have* you an arm like God?...." *Well, now you're made after the image of God, that's true!* You have an opportunity to become like God, that's true. But as a human being:

"...*have* you an arm like God? Or can you thunder with a voice like His?" (v 9). *No!*

In his own opinion Job got smaller and smaller and smaller. God says:

- *IF* you think you're so good
- *IF* you think you're so powerful
- *IF* you think you're so righteous

try this on, Job; v 10: "Deck yourself now with majesty and excellency, and array yourself with glory and beauty. Cast abroad the rage of your wrath; and behold everyone who is proud, and abase him" (vs 10-11). *See if you can do that, Job!*

You couldn't even convince your friends. They tried to point out every evil that you supposedly had done, and you didn't do it. They couldn't even see your own sin.

Verse 12: "Look on everyone *who is* proud, *and* bring him low; and tread down the wicked in their place. Hide them in the dust together; *and* bind their faces in darkness. Then I will also confess to you that your own right hand can save you" (vs 12-14)—*and that you can become like Me!* It's not going to be that way.

This is the answer; Job 42:1: "And Job answered the LORD and said, '**I know that You can do all things, and *that* no thought can be withheld from You**'" (vs 1-2). *That is the key! God is interested in **the mind and the thoughts of the heart!***

Verse 5: "I have heard of You by the hearing of the ear; **but now my eye sees You**. Therefore, I abhor *myself*, and repent in dust and ashes'" (vs 5-6).

That's what God wants! Job was able to repent. What a trial for him to go through. But let's see that this is exactly what God wants. This is what conversion is all about. This is what is required of all in order to become the sons and daughters of God.

It's not just the goodness we do out here, which is required, but it's *the conversion and change within with the Spirit of God* so that we can develop the mind of Christ and the mind of God, the way that **_He_** wants.

Romans 12:1: "I exhort you, therefore, brethren, by the mercies of God, to present your bodies a living sacrifice, Holy _and_ well-pleasing to God, which is your spiritual service. Do not conform yourselves to this world, **but be transformed by the renewing of your mind**..." (vs 1-2).

- to have the thoughts of God, not self-righteousness
- to have the love and understanding of God, not the vanity of how good you are

But the humility that everything comes from God, and you are what God wants you to be. That you can change. He has called you so that you can be converted, and all of that.

"...in order that you may prove what _is_ well-pleasing and good, and the perfect will of God" (v 2).

Rev. 20—Satan is loosed, and goes to the area of Gog and Magog, and gathers all of them in one final satanic attack to try and prove that he is 'God.' So, when he gets up there, all of those who are there Satan comes and says:

Look, I am '_God._' The One Who is down in Jerusalem—and look at that they don't have any defenses. Now what we're going to do, we're going to prepare for war. We're going to make weapons because they are down there, and they don't have a single defense. We are going to take vengeance upon God, and take the Kingdom from Him, and you and I will all rule.

So, they go down!

Revelation 20:8: "...of whom the number _is_ as the sand of the sea, to gather them together for war. Then _I saw_ them go up upon the breadth of the earth and encircle the camp of the saints, and the beloved city; and fire came down from God out of heaven and consumed them" (vs 8-9).

That is their first death. Because the Millennium has come to an end, there is no longer any time for them to live to be 100 and to be buried accursed, so they suffer their first death all together. **_What a tremendous witness that's going to be!_**

Now then, the last part of the seventh day is the fate and punishment of Satan the devil. He is going to be put away forever. All of those who come up in the second resurrection who have not committed the unpardonable sin, will not have to live this life under Satan the devil.

Verse 10: "And the Devil, who deceived them, was cast into the Lake of Fire and brimstone, where the beast and the false prophet _had been cast..._"

Now _the beast and false prophet_ were flesh and blood. When they were cast into the Lake of Fire they were burned up. Satan and the demons are not burned up with fire, **_but tormented!_**

"...**and they**..." (v 10). Not Satan, the beast and the false prophet, but _Satan and the demons,_ because where Satan goes the demons go.

"...and they, _Satan and the demons,_ shall be tormented day and night into the ages of eternity" (v 10).

God is going to have that as a perpetual witness, that there will never be rebellion against God ever again. Now, after the earth is consumed, as preparation for the new heaven and the new earth, then Satan and the demons are going to be sent into perpetual utter darkness, the blackness and darkness forever.

Jude 6: "And the angels who did not keep their own original domain, but deserted their habitation... [in rebellion against God] ...He is holding in eternal bonds under darkness unto the judgment of _the_ Great Day."

We saw what that is: cast into the Lake of Fire. When the Lake of Fire is no more, they're going to be in utter darkness forever. Now we know that all of the things that were done. We find in verse 9 that Michael is arguing with Satan over the body of Moses, and that it was Satan who led Cain to do what he did, and do what Korah did.

Verse 12: "These are subversive stains in your love feasts, feasting in person together _with you_; fearlessly they are feeding themselves. _They are_ clouds without water, being driven by the winds; trees of late autumn, without _any_ fruit, uprooted, twice dead."

That's all human beings who follow Satan the devil _will be twice dead._ That's why the first death of those in Gog and Magog and attacking Jerusalem, was to accomplish the first step for all of them.

Verse 13: "Raging waves of _the_ sea, casting up like foam their own _ignominious_ shame; wandering stars... [the stars who went with Satan the devil] ...for whom has been reserved the blackest darkness forever!"

It's possible that there may be a giant black hole out there in the universe where they are going to be contained and tormented forever, **_and as a perpetual witness to all of those in the Kingdom of God!_** That there is never ever, _ever, ever_ going to be any rebellion against God. **_But only the love, truth_** *and righteousness, and what God wants us to do for all eternity,* will be what will be done.

Scriptural References:

1) Revelation 20:7-9
2) Jeremiah 17:1, 9
3) Matthew 19:16-24
4) Job 1:6-22
5) Job 2:1-10
6) Job 3:1-4, 20-25
7) Job 6:1-4, 9-10
8) Ezekiel 14:1-9
9) Job 3:25
10) Job 6:24, 29
11) Job 7:4-7, 17-21
12) Job 9:15-16, 20, 32-35
13) Job 10:14-16
14) Job 11:5-6
15) Job 13:3, 13, 18-22
16) Job 16:1-3, 21
17) Job 17:1
18) Job 23:1-7
19) Job 31:5-10, 12-14, 16-31, 33-37
20) Job 35:1-5
21) Job 38:1-8, 16-18
22) Job 40:1-14
23) Job 42:1-2, 5-6
24) Romans 12:1-2
25) Revelation 20:8-10
26) Jude 6, 12-13

Scriptures referenced, not quoted:

- Ezekiel 36; 14
- Acts 17
- Jude 9

FRC:po/bo
Transcribed: 7/31/19
Reformatted: 1/2021

CHAPTER SEVENTY-FOUR

The Key of David I
Fred R. Coulter

Greetings, everyone! With all that's going on in the world—and there's plenty going on in the world—and all the difficulties surrounding everything that we do, what's going to give us the most important thing so that we can really attain what God wants us to, *to enter into the Kingdom of God*?

I want you to think on this, and maybe in your Bible study you can check it out yourself. *Every single book in the Bible talks about the Kingdom of God!*

- the Psalms
- Proverbs
- New Testament
- teachings of Christ
- examples of the patriarchs

all tell us how to get there!

Let's look at two things that are special; one in the New Testament that connects with something in the Old Testament: *the key of David, which also has to do* **with the heart of David!** *The key of David is what Jesus holds in His hand!* Let's analyze this a little bit, and then we will end up by looking at what Jesus promises with the key of David.

Revelation 3:7: "And to the angel of the Church in Philadelphia, write: "These things says the Holy One, the One Who *is* true…""

Remember when He told the disciples on the Passover night, 'I am a the Way, the Truth and the Life.' *He is true!*

"…**the One Who has the key of David, Who opens and no one shuts, and Who shuts and no one opens**" (v 7).

That has to do with different opportunities and understanding the Word of God; many things, indeed! Here's another thing to remember: *Jesus never said* that He's judging you by your faith. Faith without works is dead. You read all seven churches here in Rev. 2 & 3 and he says, 'I know your works,' and *He judges us by our works!*

Everybody had faith, whether it's true or wrong, and it's summed up this way: *You are what you believe!* Then you *act upon that belief,* and that action *produces works.*

Verse 8: "**I know your works**…. [He does because the Spirit from the Father is in us] …Behold, I have set before you an open door, and **no one has the power to shut it because you have a little strength**…"

Remember what Paul wrote, that *God's grace is glorified through His strength of those who are weak!* When we are weak *of ourselves then we're strong in the Lord*:

- through faith
- through grace
- through works

Here are the works, He tells us what they are: "…and **have kept My Word**…" (v 8). *Not compromise on it or go back on it!*

"…and **have not denied My name**" (v 8). *Think about that! Denying Jesus' name is compromising with fake Christianity and the world!*

This is so outstanding that the super-elite of the world who worship Satan the devil are going to be *made to come before us and worship God* while we watch them in their humility.

Verse 9: "Behold, I will make those of the synagogue of Satan, who proclaim themselves to be Jews and are not, but do lie…." *Notice the difference*: truth *vs* lie!

"…Behold, **I will cause them to come and worship before your feet, and to know that I have loved you**" (v 9).

Let's understand that Jesus loves us *because we love Him and we love the Father!*

Verse 10: "Because you have kept the Word of My patience, I also will keep you from the time of temptation, which *is* about to come upon the whole world to try those who dwell on the earth."

We'll come back to v 11 when we come to the end, but let's see how this develops. There is a prophecy of it in the book of Acts. This was by James, the brother of Jesus, when they had the conference.

Acts 15:12: "Then all the multitude kept silence and heard Barnabas and Paul relate what signs and wonders God had done among the

Gentiles through them. And after they were silent, James answered *and* said, 'Men, brethren, **listen to me**.

Verse 14: "'Simeon...'" [Peter is called Simeon, Cephas and Simon; all meaning *Peter, a little stone!*] ...has related how God first visited *the* Gentiles to take out a people for His name. And with this the words of the prophets agree, as it is written, "after these things, I will return and will build again the tabernacle of David... [What was the tabernacle of David? *We will see!*] ...which has fallen, and its ruins I will build again, and will set it up; so that the residue of men may seek the Lord, and all the Gentiles upon whom My name is called, says *the* Lord, Who does all these things'" (vs 14-17).

We've come across these this already in the first part of the Feast of Tabernacles.

Verse 18: "Known to God are all His works from the beginning of the world." *I am Alpha and Omega, the First and the Last, the Beginning and the Ending!*

Let's see where David is quoting about the tabernacle of David, because the tabernacle of David is really quite something when you understand it. Also, it has to do with the closeness of David to God and also *the heart of David, his attitude and love of God!*

Amos 9:11: "'In that day I will raise up **the tabernacle of David** that has fallen, and close up its breaches; and I will raise up its ruins, and I will build it as in the days of old; so that they may possess the remnant of Edom, and of all the nations *on* whom My name is called,' says the LORD who is doing this" (vs 11-12).

Now let's see how we can have *the heart of David* and *the key of David* so that we can enter into the Kingdom of God in a way that God's wants us to. *Our reward is dependant upon our:*

- attitude
- loving God
- serving Him
- doing the things that are right

Luke 10 is quite a verse, and this section of Scripture is really quite something! You can add to that everything that God has revealed to us in these last days, which are more than what was revealed to the apostles. None of it could be understood for prophecy in the future until the book of Revelation was written.

Even John—though he wrote it—it came directly from God the Father to Jesus Christ and given to John, and he had to write it.

Luke 10:21: "In the same hour Jesus rejoiced in the Spirit, and said, 'I praise You, O Father, Lord of heaven and earth, that You did hide these things from *the* wise and intelligent...'"

What we're talking about with the Feast of Tabernacles is the Truth of how God is going to solve the problems of mankind. But the 'wise' and 'intelligent,' who are they? *The elite, the establishment, the deep state as we call it today! They know nothing about God's plan!*

Think of that! Little ole us whom the world doesn't know, has no knowledge of us whatsoever, except that we have a name, social security number, pay our taxes and where we live. *But what God has given us is something they do not have!*

"'...and did reveal them to babes. Yes, Father, for it was well pleasing in Your sight *to do* so.' Then He turned to the disciples *and* said, '**All things were delivered to Me by My Father**; and **no one knows Who the Son is, except the Father**...'" (vs 21-22).

The world does not know! They profess, they claim, but *they do not know!*

"'...and Who the Father is, except the Son, **and the one to whom the Son personally chooses to reveal Him**'" (v 22)—*personally from Jesus Christ to us!*

Think about how special we are to God. This is not to lift us up and get vain, this is to make us humble and yielded to God and love God.

Verse 23[transcriber's correction]: "And He turned to His disciples *and* said privately, 'Blessed *are* the eyes that have seen the things that you see. For I tell you, many prophets and kings... [Who was David? *The greatest king of all, except Christ!*] ...have desired to see the things that you see, and have not seen *them*; and to hear the things that you hear, and have not heard *them*.' Now, a certain doctor of the law suddenly stood up, tempting Him and saying, 'Master, what shall I do to inherit eternal life?'" (vs 23-25).

Notice Jesus' answer, and think about this; v 26: And He said to him, '**What is written in the Law? How do you read it?**' .... [he was a doctor of the Law] ...Then he answered *and* said, 'You shall love *the* Lord your God with all your heart, and with all your soul, and with all your strength, and with all your mind; and your neighbor as yourself'" (vs 26-27). *He had it right!*

Verse 28: "And He said to him, 'You have answered correctly. Do this, and you shall live.' But he, desiring to justify himself, said to Jesus, 'And who is my neighbor?'" (vs 28-29). *Then Jesus gave the parable!* Many, many have wanted to know!

You have to know and understand that in the

days of Eli and his two sons: Hophni and Phinehas. They went out to fight against the Philistines, and they took the Ark—which they shouldn't have taken—and they lost the battle, and the Ark was taken by the Philistines.

God dealt with the Philistines in a very unique way. The Ark was special and should have been in the Holy of Holies. But because of the sins of Israel, and the sins of the priesthood, **God removed it!** We need to think about that in relationship to our experience with the Church of God today.

What has happened to the Church of God? *The same thing because of the same sins!*

The Philistines were on a high for battle victory; 1-Samuel 5:1: "And the Philistines took the Ark of God and brought it from Ebenezer to Ashdod. And the Philistines took the Ark of God and brought it into the temple of Dagon, and set it beside Dagon. And when those of Ashdod arose early on the next day, behold, Dagon *had* fallen upon his face to the earth before the Ark of the LORD. And they took Dagon and set him in his place again" (vs 1-3).

What did God do? *He said, 'All right, I'm going to show the Philistines that Dagon is not 'God'; it's an idol that is going to fall down before Me!'*

Verse 4: "And when they arose early on the next morning, behold, Dagon *had* fallen upon his face to the earth before the Ark of the LORD. And the head of Dagon, and both the palms of his hands, *were* cut off upon the threshold. **Only the stump of Dagon was left to him**."

They did get the message! So, let's see what they did; v 5: "And neither the priests of Dagon, nor any that come into Dagon's house, tread on the threshold of Dagon in Ashdod to this day." *Well, it's no longer there, but when this was being written by Samuel that's what it was!*

Look at what God did to them; v 6: "And the hand of the LORD was heavy upon the people of Ashdod, and He destroyed them and struck them with hemorrhoids, Ashdod and its borders. And the men of Ashdod saw that *it was* so. And they said, 'The Ark of the God of Israel shall not stay with us, for His hand is heavy upon us and upon Dagon our god'" (vs 6-7). *The truth is there's a good lesson from this*:

- *never challenge God*
- *never tempt Him*

Verse 8: "And they sent and gathered all the lords of the Philistines to them. And they said, 'What shall we do with the Ark of the God of

Israel?' And they answered, 'Let the Ark of the God of Israel be carried around to Gath.' And they carried the Ark of the God of Israel around. And it came to pass after they had carried it around, the hand of the LORD was against the city *with* a very great destruction. And He struck the men of the city, both small and great, and hemorrhoids broke forth in them" (vs 8-9). *You're not going to do very much with all of that!*

Verse 10: "And it came to pass that they sent the Ark of God *to* Ekron. And it came to pass as the Ark of God came to Ekron, the Ekronites cried out, saying, 'They have brought around the Ark of the God of Israel to us in order to kill us and our people.' And they sent and gathered all the lords of the Philistines, and said, 'Send away the Ark of the God of Israel, and let it go again to its own place, so that it does not kill us and our people,' for there was a deadly destruction throughout all the city. The hand of God was very heavy there" (vs 10-11).

1-Samuel 6:1: "And the Ark of the LORD was in the field of the Philistines seven months." *They didn't know what to do!*

Verse 2: "And the Philistines called for the priests and the diviners, saying, 'What shall we do to the Ark of the LORD?....'"

Verse 4: "And they said, 'If you send away the Ark of the God of Israel, do not send it empty; for you shall certainly send a guilt offering to Him....'" *It has to be because they were afflicted with mice and hemorrhoids.*

"...and five golden mice, for the number of the lords of the Philistines, for one plague *was* on you all, and on your lords" (v 4). *They made them, took the Ark and put it in a cart and sent it off.*

Verse 11: "And they laid the Ark of the LORD upon the cart, and the box *with* the mice of gold and the images of their hemorrhoids. And the cows went the straight way to the way of Beth Shemesh, going along the highway, lowing as they went. And they did not turn aside *to* the right or to the left. And the lords of the Philistines went after them to the border of Beth Shemesh" (vs 11-12). *It got there and it stayed there for some time!*

Here is where David gets involved. David had it in his heart to bring the Ark of God out from where it was. Here's a great lesson for us: *Whatever God says it must be done **God's way**!* Think about that! Does any man have a better way than God? *Of course not!* Even King David made a mistake here, though he was well-intentioned. Sometimes even the experts give you wrong advice.

1-Chronicles 13:1: "And David consulted with the captains of thousands and hundreds, *and* with every leader. And David said to all the congregation of Israel, 'If it is good to you, and if it is from the LORD our God, let us send to our brethren, those remaining in all the land of Israel, and with them to the priests and Levites in their cities *and* that they may gather together to us. And let us bring again the Ark of our God to us, for we did not inquire at it in the days of Saul'" (vs 1-3). *Think of that!*

Verse 4: "And all the congregation said that they would do so, for the thing was right in the eyes of all the people."

Another lesson: *there are times when the majority is not right,* though they may be well-intended. Let's learn a really good lesson here. Tie this together to what we covered in Rev. 3: *because you have kept the word of My patience.* The Philadelphians with the key of David—the understanding of God—kept the Word of God! We will see what happened here, because as good of intensions as they had, it didn't work out, and we'll see why.

Verse 5: "And David gathered all Israel together, from Shihor of Egypt even to the entering of Hamath, to bring the Ark of God from Kirjath Jearim. And David and all Israel went up to Baalah, to Kirjath Jearim of Judah, to bring up from there the Ark of the LORD God, He who dwells between the cherubs, Whose name is called on it. And they carried the Ark of God in a new cart…" (vs 5-7).

We're going to do it right; we're going to make a new cart that's never been used for anything, because this is special for God's Ark of the Covenant.

"…out of the house of Abinadab. And Uzza and Ahio led the cart. And David and all Israel played before God with all *their* might, and with singing, and with lyres, and with harps, and with drums, and with cymbals, and with silver trumpets" (vs 7-8).

Quite a thing! Very happy time bringing the Ark of God! What a fantastic thing this was for them to do. I imagine that they were all happy and joyful!

Verse 9: "And when they came to the threshing floor of Chidon, Uzza put out his hand to hold the Ark, for the oxen stumbled."

Some people who read this and think how awful that was of God. Well, for all who know the Truth, there is the second resurrection. But for those who don't, they look at this and say, 'How can this be a God of love,' because look what happened:

Verse 10: "And the anger of the LORD was kindled against Uzza, and He struck him because he put his hand to the Ark. And he died there before the LORD." **Why did God do that?** *That ended the party!*

Verse 11: "And David was displeased because the LORD had broken forth upon Uzza…. [David was wrong! All the people were wrong!] …And he called that place The Breach of Uzza, *as it is* to this day. And David was afraid of God that day, saying, 'How shall I bring the Ark of God to me?'" (vs 11-12). *He didn't know what to do!*

Here's the lesson: **When all else fails, remember read the Word of God!** That will help you.

Verse 13: "And David did not bring the Ark to himself in the City of David, but carried it aside into the house of Obed-Edom the Gittite. And the Ark of God remained with the family of Obed-Edom in his house three months. And the LORD blessed the house of Obed-Edom and all that he had" (vs 13-14).

We're going learn something very important with this! *You must do it the way that God says!* If you don't do it the way that God says, *then you're going to have trouble!* That's what happened to David; he asked council of the people, *but they didn't read the book! And the Levites with David didn't read the book!*

1-Chronicles 14:1: "Now, Hiram king of Tyre sent messengers to David and timbers of cedars with masons and carpenters to build him a house. And David perceived that the LORD had confirmed him king over Israel, for his kingdom was exalted exceedingly because of His people Israel" (vs 1-2).

1-Chronicles 15:1: "And *David* made houses for himself in the City of David, and prepared a place for the Ark of God, and pitched a tent for it. Then David said, '**No one ought to carry the Ark of God except the Levites, for God has chosen them to carry the Ark of God** and to minister to Him forever'" (vs 1-2). *He failed to do it right the first time, so he learned the lesson!*

Verse 3: "And David assembled all Israel together to Jerusalem to bring up the Ark of the LORD to its place, which He had prepared for it." *That place was a special tent!*

Verse 11: "And David called for Zadok and Abiathar the priests, and for the Levites: for Uriel, Asaiah, and Joel, Shemaiah, and Eliel, and Amminadab. And he said to them, 'You *are* the heads of the fathers of the Levites. Sanctify yourselves, you and your brethren, so that you may bring up the Ark of the LORD God of Israel to the place, which I have prepared for it'" (vs 11-12).

Notice that David admitted that he was wrong the first time; v 13: "'Now, because you did not do it at the first, the LORD our God broke forth upon us, since we did not seek Him according to the ordinance.' And the priests and the Levites sanctified themselves in order to bring up the Ark of the LORD God of Israel" (vs 13-14). *So, they put the staves in it, brought it up and took it up there!*

Verse 25: "Then David and the elders of Israel, and the captains over thousands, went to bring up the Ark of the Covenant of the LORD out of the house of Obed-Edom with joy. And it came to pass when God helped the Levites who bore the Ark of the Covenant of the LORD, they offered seven bulls and seven rams. And David *was* clothed with a robe of fine linen with all the Levites who carried the Ark, and the singers, and Chenaniah the master of the music with the singers. David also had on an ephod of linen" (vs 25-27). *So, they brought it up!*

1-Chronicles 16:1: "And they brought the Ark of God and set it in the middle of the tent, which David had pitched for it. And they offered burnt sacrifices and peace offerings before God."

They had outside of the house, outside the tent, they had an altar of whole stones on which they made these offerings. The Ark stayed there in David's house in this special addition on his house until Solomon brought it up out of David's house when he finished the temple.

Verse 2: "And when David had made an end of offering the burnt offering and the peace offerings, he blessed the people in the name of the LORD. And he divided to every one of Israel, both man and woman, to every one a loaf of bread and a portion *of meat* and a raisin cake. And he appointed *certain* of the Levites to minister before the Ark of the LORD… [so, it was handled properly] …and to record, and to thank and praise the LORD God of Israel" (vs 2-4). *So, they had daily services there doing that!*

Verse 5: "Asaph the chief, and next to him Zechariah, Jeiel, and Shemiramoth, and Jehiel, and Mattithiah, and Eliab, and Benaiah, and Obed-Edom. And Jeiel praised with instruments of harps and with lyres; and Asaph made a sound with cymbals. Also Benaiah and Jahaziel the priests *praised* with silver trumpets continually before the Ark of the Covenant of God. Then **on that day** David first delivered *this psalm* into the hand of Asaph and his brethren in order to thank the LORD" (vs 5-7). *All the rest of it in this chapter David gave thanks to God!*

David wrote the Psalms, but in order for them to be part of the official recorded they had to be given to the priest, who would keep all of them. We don't know how many more psalms that are not recorded in the Bible, but I'm sure there are plenty.

1-Chron. 17—David was in his house thinking of God, playing on his instrument, praying, thinking about God and the wonderful place that God had given him that was where the tabernacle was placed. He said, 'You know, God dwells in a tent! And I dwell in a house. Why don't we make a temple for the Lord?'

The rest of the story on that was that God said, 'David, you can't because you're a man of war! But Solomon, your son, will build Me a house.'

Now let's look at some of the greatest Psalms, because they are so full of the relationship of David to God and God to David, and David's:

- understanding of the Word of God
- his wholeheartedness
- his complete zeal
- his absolute dedication to God

We're going to learn some very important things when we get into some of the Psalms, because it's really going to be great. *This is going to help us __to have the key and the heart of David!__*

Let's see why David was a man after God's heart! Remember that he had the Ark of the Covenant in a special tent in a special addition onto his house or palace in the City of David, which was just south of where the temple would later be built.

Also, it was quite a height at that particular point. Later in the days the Maccabees they cut it down, so today from the Mosque of Omar going south, it's all cut off. Let's also understand that he probably had the closest relationship to God of any other man besides Abraham. *Think on that!* He was close to God!

- yes, he did make mistakes
- yes, he did have his sins

But let's look at __why__ he was a man after God's own heart! We're going to see what kind of attitude that we need to have, which is the key of David, the heart of David, so that we likewise can enter into a close relationship with God the Father and Jesus Christ. Today ***They are dwelling in us!***

Psalm 57:1: "Be gracious unto me, O God, be gracious unto me… [that's the way we need to pray] …for my soul trusts in You; yea, in the shadow of Your wings I will make my refuge until these great troubles pass by."

David always had troubles, battles, fights and wars! I think that today we ought to tell ourselves that in even in our troubles, we haven't had it so bad; *so buck up!*

Verse 2: "I will cry to God Most High, to God who fulfills His purpose for me." *We can apply this to us, because right now God is fulfilling His purpose for us*:

- with His Spirit
- with His Word

Verse 3: "He shall send from heaven and save me; He rebukes him who would swallow me up. **Selah**…. [stop and meditate on this] …God shall send forth His mercy and His Truth."

What we have just read here shows you something very important: *this is the epitome of the New Testament relationship with God!*

Verse 5: "Be exalted, O God, above the heavens; let Your glory be above all the earth. They have prepared a net for my steps; my soul is bowed down; they have dug a pit before me; into the midst of it they have fallen themselves. Selah" (vs 5-6).

Isn't that true? *God has a way of going against the enemies **IF** we're trusting in Him!* And He will deliver us!

Now notice that v 7 is what we must have; notice and attitude toward God:

Verse 7: "**My heart is fixed, O God, my heart is fixed**…" *That's what we need to do!* Our hearts need to be fixed to God, not to anything else, not to any other purpose; *to God!*

"**…I will sing and give praise**. Awake, my glory! Awake, harp and lyre!…." (vs 7-8).

There he is before the tent of the Ark and he's playing these beautiful songs to God, pouring out his heart to Him right before that—*amazing!*

"…I myself will awake the dawn" (v 8). *Get up and pray to God before the light of day starts!*

Verse 9: "I will praise You, O LORD, among the people; I will sing of You among the nations…" *That's what it's going to be when he's in the Kingdom of God!*

Verse 10: "For Your steadfast mercy is great *even* unto the heavens and Your Truth to the clouds. Be exalted above the heavens, O God; let Your glory be above all the earth" (vs 10-11).

Wonderful praise of God, looking forward to the Kingdom of God! All of this will be fulfilled even greater in the Kingdom of God! We are going to see *one of the main things of David was **his heart was**:*

- fixed
- unmovable
- unchangeable
- undeterred

Psalm 108:1: "O God, **my heart is fixed**…" *Let's all of us really endeavor*:

- with our heart
- with our mind
- with our emotions

- with our words

*to see if we can have this attitude of David, **that our heart is fixed for God forever!***

Verse 2: "Awake, harp and lyre; I will awake early. I will praise You, O LORD, among the people; and I will sing praises to You among the nations, for Your mercy is great above the heavens; and Your Truth reaches unto the clouds. Be exalted, O God, above the heavens, and Your glory above all the earth, so that Your beloved may be delivered; save with Your right hand, and answer me" (vs 2-6). *Quite a thing!*

That's the way to pray to God! Think of the courage, love and power that's contained in these words!

Verse 10: "Who will bring me into the strong city? Who will lead me into Edom? O God, have You not cast us off? And, O God, will You not go out with our armies? Give us help from trouble, for vain is the deliverance of man" (vs 10-12).

When David went out on these battles, he asked God to be with him in everything! He learned the lesson that when he doesn't trust in God, *He's is not there!*

Verse 13—*this ought to be our lives*: "Through God we shall do mighty things, for it is He who will tread down our enemies." ***God will do that and deliver us from it!*** Quite an amazing, wonderful thing!

All of these Psalms show David's attitude and how he was a man after God's heart! Let's see if we can put these things into our lives, as well. We're to pray every day and study every day, and to be praying all through the day in the many things we do, where we are and what is happening around us!

Psalm 112:1: "Praise the LORD! Blessed is the man who fears the LORD, **who delights greatly in His commandments**."

- Do we do that?
- All the commandments of God?

How great they are!

Look at the world today, they're leaving God at such a fast rate that's it's incredible!

Verse 2: "His seed shall be mighty upon earth; the generation of the upright shall be blessed. Wealth and riches shall be in his house, and his righteousness endures forever" (vs 2-3). *Again projecting into the Kingdom of God!* That will apply to us in the Kingdom of God when we are there!

Verse 4: "To the upright there arises light in the darkness… [during the times we have troubles] …he is gracious and full of compassion and righteousness"—*to give to us!*

Stop and think about this; this is New Testament doctrine! *God imputes the righteousness of Christ to us!* Of course, *if* we have this attitude, yes, He will!

Verse 5: "It is well with the man who is gracious and lends freely; who conducts his affairs with justice. Surely he shall not be moved forever; the righteous shall be in everlasting remembrance" (vs 5-6).

How important are you to God? *So important that*:

- He's put His Spirit in you
- He wants you to grow in His love, grace and knowledge
- you are to be in His Kingdom

That's why He's called us! He's depending on us to develop the character and attitude that we see here with David. So that we can attain to the Kingdom, *He's going to be there to help us in everything!*

Verse 7: He shall not be afraid of evil tidings; **his heart is steadfast**… [or fixed] …**trusting in the LORD.**"

So, when trouble comes, the first thing is not to try and figure out how you're going to get out of this trouble or solve the problem. You go to God and praise God and:

- ask Him for the help
- ask Him for the wisdom
- ask Him for the understanding
- ask Him to fight the battle for you

Verse 8: "His heart is established; he shall not be afraid **until he sees his desire upon his enemies**"—*and we will!*

If not in this life, when the first resurrection comes we're going to see it, all the saints together *upon all the enemies of God!* That's going to something to behold!

Psa. 111—again we have this same attitude of *love, faith, diligence and a fixed heart, immovable*:

Psalm 111:1: "Praise the LORD! I will give thanks to the LORD **with my whole heart**…" *Our heart is fixed and we're wholehearted to God!*

Not like the man who has one foot in the world, one foot in the Church so he can take advantage in the world, and take advantage of God. *Doesn't work that way!*

"…in the council of the upright and in the congregation. The works of the LORD are great…" (vs 1-2).

What is the greatest work of God? *His conversion in the heart and mind of all the saints, of all those who are His down through the history of the whole world!*

"…sought out by all those who have pleasure in them. His work is **glory and majesty**… [and to give that to us, to all the saints] …and His righteousness endures forever" (vs 2-3).

What is a key, important thing in all of this? *The Sabbath Day!* You know that that's the day God puts His presence in!

Verse 4: "He has made **a memorial** for His wonderful works…"—*the Sabbath Day!* 'Remember the Sabbath Day to keep it Holy; six days shall you work and do your labor, but the seventh day is Holy unto to the Lord, for in it He rested and was refreshed!' *That's the memorial!*

"…the LORD is gracious and full of compassion. He has given food to those who fear Him; He will always be mindful of His covenant" (vs 4-5). *We are in the greater covenant, the covenant of eternal life!*

Verse 6: "He has declared to His people the power of His works, in giving them the inheritance of the nations." *Tie in Rev. 20; we'll be kings and priests and rule on the earth!*

Notice how all of this is done, and in everything this applies; v 7: "The works of His hands are Truth and justice; all His precepts are sure." *Everything about what God says and does, the ideas about everything that He has done is sure!*

Verse 8: "They stand fast forever and ever; they are done in Truth and uprightness."

Notice how much of this depends on *Truth, righteousness and uprightness* with the Spirit of God; *our heart fixed!*

Verse 9: "He sent redemption unto His people; He has commanded His covenant forever; Holy and awesome is His name. **The fear of the LORD is the beginning of wisdom**…" (vs 9-10)—the ability to:

- choose God
- yield to Him
- worship Him
- love Him
- be devoted to Him

with a heart that is fixed! That's why David was a man after God's heart!

"…**a good understanding have all those who do His commandments.** His praise endures forever" (v 10).

This is quite a thing when we understand it, brethren! *All that God is doing*; that is quite a thing! When Christ comes we're going to see that if we yield to God we will be before God in the way that God wants.

Psalm 138:1: "I will praise You **with my whole heart**… [not half or three-quarters or one-quarter of your heart] …before the gods I will sing praise to You. I will worship toward Your Holy temple… [in heaven above] …and praise Your name for Your loving kindness, and for Your Truth; **for You have magnified above all, Your name *and* Your Word**" (vs 1-2)—*above everything!*

What is the name that Jesus told us to use? *Our Father, Who is in heaven, hallowed be Your name. Your will be done on earth—in our lives—as it is in heaven!* The will of God is always done in heaven! That's the kind of fulfillment that God wants us to trust in Him to give us.

Verse 3: "In the day when I cried, You answered me and made me bold with strength in my soul." *Of course, David needed that daily, because he was out fighting, battling and warring almost constantly!*

Verse 4: "All the kings of the earth shall praise You, O LORD…" *Think about this in relationship to the first resurrection, and the ultimate Kingdom of God!* All the kings, and yes, there will be many!

"…when they hear the words of Your mouth. Yea, they shall sing in the ways of the LORD, for great is the glory of the LORD. Though the LORD is high, yet, He has respect to **the lowly**; but the haughty He knows afar off" (vs 4-6)—*Is that not us?* Look at us as a Church:

- Are we important?
- Are we great?
- Are we mighty?

No!

*But through God **all things are possible!** If* we truly love Him with all our heart, mind, soul and being, and *if* our heart is fixed, *think how pleasing that is to God! Think of the blessings that will come because of that!* Things that we will never know, understand or expect until we're resurrected and in the Kingdom of God!

Verse 7: "Though I walk in the midst of trouble…" *We have that every once in a while—don't we? As matter of fact, we have them quite often!*

"…**You will revive me**…" (v 7). *God will do that*:

- He will strengthen you

- He will raise you up
- He will give you what you need

"…You shall stretch forth Your hand against the wrath of my enemies, and Your right hand shall save me" (v 7). *That's how David won all of his battles! David never lost a battle!*

Verse 8—*this tells us what God is doing with each one of us*: "**The LORD will perfect His work in me**…"—*in you; in everyone who has the Spirit of God!*

But we have to yield to God in the way that He wants, and have the attitude of David, the heart of David, which is the *key of David!*

"…**Your steadfast love, O LORD, endures forever; do not forsake the work of Your own hands**" (v 8). *That is something!*

Now we will see that the work of God is not just alone what the Church is doing in evangelizing. *The work of God has to do with what God is doing in us,* and *we have to be like the clay, because God is the Potter!* He is molding and building in us with His Spirit and Truth and righteousness.

Ephesians 2:8: "For by grace you have been saved through faith, and **this *especially* is not of your own selves**…"

You don't come to God by your own work, energy and everything that you do, and God must recognize you and give you eternal life! *NO! NO! NO!* Remember what the doctor of the Law asked Jesus; 'What must I do to receive eternal life?' *You must love the Lord your God with all your heart, mind, soul and strength!*

"…***it is the gift of God***… [there's nothing on earth that you can do to buy it] …**not of works**… [religious works of this, that and the other; like Judaism, Catholicism or Protestantism] …**so that no one may boast**" (vs 8-9).

Remember what David said, 'You [God] will perfect Your work in me'; v 10: "For **we are His workmanship, being created in Christ Jesus unto *the* good works that God ordained beforehand** in order that we might walk in them"—*as a way of life!*

That's why David said, Psalm 138:8: "**The LORD will perfect His work in me**; Your steadfast love, O LORD, endures forever…" *That's how God is doing it*:

- with His love
- with His Truth
- with His power
- with His commandments
- with His statutes
- with His judgments

*And everything like that, **which is going to be the perfection of what God is working in us!***

"...**do not forsake the work of Your own hands**" (v 8). *He's not going to as long as we're with Him!* We need to keep that and remember that!

Psa. 119 is a tremendous Psalm that is so profound. I have said before, and I'll say it again, I believe that this shows Jesus' very attitude toward the Laws, commandments and statutes of God. Surely, those of David, as well. But it doesn't say that this is of David. However, it's inspired by the same God! The first part of this Psalm tells us an awful lot.

Psalm 119:1: "Blessed are the undefiled in the way, who walk in the Law of the LORD.... [*Walk in it! Do it!*] ...Blessed are they who keep His testimonies and who seek Him with the whole heart" (vs 1-2). *That's blessing of David being wholehearted and having his heart fixed!*

That's what we need to do. If you've been slack in coming to God, then resolve before God in prayer that you will fix your heart:

- with God's Spirit
- for God's way
- with God's love
- with God's Truth

Verse 3: "They also do no iniquity; they walk in His ways. You have commanded us to keep Your precepts **diligently O that my ways were directed to keep Your statutes!**" (vs 3-5). *Showing that sometimes it's a little difficult, but we have to keep at it!*

Verse 6: "Then I shall not be ashamed when I have respect unto **all Your commandments**."

Notice that this is all a part of it. This is one of the greatest Psalms that there is, and one that the Levites had to memorize and sing at the temple.

Verse 7: "I will praise You with uprightness of heart when I have learned Your righteous judgments."

Verse 10: "**With all my heart**..."— *meaning you are completely yielded to God in everything!* You don't have part of your heart over here doing something else. You don't have your mind and attitude thinking of other things.

Yes, there are times that we have to think of the things we need to do to live, but we know that we do it because of the blessing of God. So, that all works in there. But when you're praying, studying and thinking of God:

Verse 10: "With all my heart I have sought

You; O let me not wander from Your commandments." *God will keep you,* because what will He do? *With His Spirit in you, you will get a warning from God:* ***Don't do it!*** God will help you that way.

Notice a tremendous principle; v 11: "Your Word... [today we have the whole Bible, so let's think of it that way] ...**I have laid up in my heart, so that I might not sin against You**."

Verse 17: "Deal bountifully with Your servant, that I may live and keep Your Word.... [that has to do with entering into the Kingdom of God] ...Open my eyes... [that's the part of our mind that we use for understanding] ...so that I may behold wondrous things out of Your Law" (vs 17-18).

Isn't that true? *The most wonderful, tremendous and fantastic things that could be!*

You could spend just studying the Psalms— going through them and comparing back and forth, going over them again and again—a long time in doing it. Notice what else it's going to do, and why this is important for us. Notice what David did; he had to fight his own human nature, as well. He had to yield himself to God and put away temptations, just like we do, *and to understand that no human is going to do it on his own!*

Any human activity—if it's not motivated toward God, from God and through His Spirit, laws and commandments and the love that comes from God—*is vain!*

Psalm 39:1: "I said, 'I will take heed to my ways so that I do not sin with my tongue; I will keep my mouth with a bridle while the wicked are before me.'" *Hold your tongue!* Sometimes it's best not to say a word!

Verse 2: "I became dumb, keeping silent; I said nothing good, and yet, my sorrow grew worse. My heart was hot within me; while I was musing, the fire burned; **then I spoke with my tongue**: 'O LORD, make me to know my end and the measure of my days, what it is, that I may know how short lived I am'" (vs 2-4). *Quite a statement!*

Not only all those other qualities, but David was completely humble as well. Now notice how he views life, because this is important for us, too. There's nothing great that we're going to do of notoriety in this life!

Verse 5: "Behold, You have made my days as a handbreadth... [How important are you? *Blip!*] ...and the span of my days is as nothing before You. Surely every man at his best state is altogether vanity. Selah." *That's what it is with human beings cut off from God!* **Altogether vanity!**

Verse 6: "Surely every man walks about in a

vain show! Surely they are in an uproar in vain. He heaps up riches and does not know who shall gather them. And now, LORD, what do I wait for?...." (vs 6-7).

When you look at all of this, and everything that there is—physically, mentally, etc.—what do you do?

"...**My hope is in You**. Deliver me from all my transgressions; make me not the reproach of the fool" (vs 7-8). *All of our transgressions, and that's what God does (1-John 1)!* Let's see another part of David's attitude:

- how he came before God
- what he thought about God
- how he really hungered and thirsted after righteousness

that Jesus said if you do you will be filled! Of course, that's on an ongoing basis. You can't do it and then stop. *You have to keep at it!*

Psalm 42:1: "As the hart pants after the water brooks, so my soul pants after You, O God. **My soul thirsts for God**..." (vs 1-2).

Think about everything that David was confronted with:

- all those who he had to rule over in Israel
- all of the enemies coming against Israel
- finalizing and getting all the territory back to Israel that they lost because they didn't follow God
- all of the intrigue within the palace
- all of the fight with all of his wives and children
- having to deal with the sin of Bathsheba

Verse 2: "**My soul thirsts for God** for the living God..."—*that's what it needs to be with us!*

Don't come along and say, 'I don't know what to study today.' *If you're studying every day, you will be anxious to study even more!* We have a lot of things to help you, and we'll be glad to send you anything we have so that you can develop this attitude.

"...when shall I come and appear before God? (v 2). *He did every day when he came to the tent where the Ark of the Covenant was!*

Verse 8: "The LORD will command His loving kindness in the daytime, and in the night His song shall be with me, *even* a prayer to the God of my life." *David knew and understood that in God he lived, moved and had his being!*

Verse 9: "I will say to God my Rock, 'Why have You forgotten me?'.... [He hasn't] ...Why do I

go mourning because of the oppression of the enemy?' As with a crushing in my bones, my enemies taunt me while they say to me all day long, 'Where is your God?'" (vs 9-10). *Think about what he had to fight against!*

Verse 11: "Why are you cast down, O my soul?.... [you would be greatly discouraged in times like this; think on God] ...And why do you moan within me? **Hope in God, for I shall yet praise Him, the salvation of my countenance, and my God**." *That's what God has done for us!*

Psa. 63 shows the closeness that David had with God. We see that:

- his heart is fixed
- he's hungering and thirsting
- he's yielding to God
- he's desiring God with His whole being

This is the key of David and the heart of David!

Psalm 63:1: "O God, You are my God, **earnestly** I will seek You! My soul **thirsts** for You. My flesh **longs** for You, as in a dry and thirsty land where no water is, to see Your power and Your glory as I have seen You in the sanctuary" (vs 1-2).

That's quite a statement there, because he had that tent of the sanctuary for the Ark! Apparently, God let him see a form of Him behind the veil. That's something! Stop and think about that for a minute: *the relationship that God had with David, and David with God!*

When the temple is setup how often can a priest go into the Holy of Holies? *Once a year only!* If he didn't do it right, he's history! Think about David; every time he prayed to God, *he could go to the sanctuary right in his house!*

Verse 3: "Because Your loving kindness is better than life, my lips shall praise You. Thus I will bless You as long as I live; I will lift up my hands in Your name. My soul shall be satisfied as with marrow and fatness; and my mouth shall praise You with joyful lips when I remember You upon my bed and meditate on You in the night watches" (vs 3-6).

That's quite a thing! Thinking about God! Have you ever done that at night? *That happened many times!*

Verse 7: "Because You have been my help, therefore, in the shadow of Your wings I will rejoice. My soul follows hard after You; Your right hand upholds me" (vs 7-8). *That's the heart, mind and key of David!*

Notice how David prayed. There are times when he came to God, like this; Psalm 61:1[transcriber's correction]: "**Hear my cry, O God; attend unto my prayer**."

- God will!
- He's there!
- He will answer!
- He will hear!

Verse 2: "From the end of the earth I cry to You when my heart is overwhelmed; lead me to the Rock higher than me." *He understood that he couldn't solve his own problems; he had to take them to God!*

Verse 3: "For You have been a shelter for me, a strong tower against the enemy…. [notice how this fits into the Feast of Tabernacles]: …I will dwell in Your tabernacle forever… [that's what we want] …I will take refuge in the hiding place of Your wings. Selah…. [think about it; meditate on it] …For You, O God, have heard my vows; You have given *me* the heritage of those who fear Your name" (vs 3-5). *That will be fulfilled when David is king over all Israel forever!*

Verse 6: "May You add to the days of the king's life; may his years be as many generations…. [eternal life will do that forever] …May he abide before God forever; prepare mercy and truth to preserve him. So I will sing praise to Your name forever, so that I may daily perform my vows" (vs 6-8).

Tomorrow we will see more about the key and heart of David and why that is important for us!

Scriptural References:

1) Revelation 3:7-10
2) Acts 15:12-18
3) Amos 9:11-12
4) Luke 10:21-29
5) 1 Samuel 5:1-11
6) 1 Samuel 6:1-2, 4, 11-12
7) 1 Chronicles 13:1-14
8) 1 Chronicles 14:1-2
9) 1 Chronicles 15:1-3, 11-14, 25-27
10) 1 Chronicles 16:1-7
11) Psalm 57:1-3, 5-11
12) Psalm 108:1-6, 10-13
13) Psalm 112:1-8
14) Psalm 111:1-10
15) Psalm 138:1-8
16) Ephesians 2:8-10
17) Psalm 138:8
18) Psalm 119:1-7, 10-11, 17-18
19) Psalm 39:1-8
20) Psalm 42:1-2, 8-11
21) Psalm 63:1-8
22) Psalm 61:1-8

Scripture referenced, not quoted:

- 1 Chronicles 17
- Revelation 20
- 1 John 1

FRC:bo
Transcribed: 8/5/20
Reformatted: 1/2021

CHAPTER SEVENTY-FIVE

The Key of David II
Fred R. Coulter

Greetings, brethren! What a Feast it has been so far, and it always goes by too quickly! Let's continue on with the key or heart of David. We saw last time that David said many times that *his heart was fixed*; in other words, completely immovable that he would go from God.

- that doesn't mean that he didn't sin
- that doesn't mean that he was perfect in the flesh

What is important is that this is the kind of conversion, attitude and dedication that we need, especially living in this age where everything is so easy and convenient to where we have so much. It says in Rev. 3 to the Laodiceans that they have an attitude that they say they're 'rich and increased with goods' and all of this is a blessing from God.

But not necessarily! Which is a greater blessing:

- To have your head cut off because you have faith?

or

- To have everything you need and you don't have to worry about anything, and you get lackadaisical and then God has to correct you?

That's the question!

So, let's come to where were last time for just a minute; Luke 10 tells us that the things that we know and understand, and God has given from His Word, which He has opened to our understanding because it's the last days, and He promised that 'the wise shall understand.' The wise ones are the ones who:

- love God *as David did*
- keep His commandments *as Christ said*
- have the faith that generates good works, *based up the Word of God and the Spirit of God*

Luke 10:23: "And He turned to His disciples *and* said privately, '**Blessed *are* the eyes that have seen the things that you see**.'" *The fact that you can read the Bible and see what's going on in the world, knowing what is happening!*

We did see the things exactly as the apostle saw. They had some things much, much greater than

we do, of course, because they were apostles. But nevertheless, we have more understanding of the plan of God through His Holy Days than they had back then. They were just in the beginning of learning of that.

Verse 24: "For I tell you, many prophets and kings **have desired to see the things that you see**, and have not seen *them*; **and to hear the things that you hear, and have not heard *them*.**'" *Think about that*:

- lest we get complacent
- lest we think we have everything
- lest we think we have need of nothing'

Let's understand that whatever we understand it is because of the Word of God and the Spirit of God!

God has promised to give it in the last times! Not that we're anything great of ourselves, because we're not! We will see that when we come back to the things of David, that that's exactly the attitude that he had. It was yielded to God all the time.

What was David facing all the time? *Fights, battles, war and intrigue,* until he finally had a little rest. That was after he was king for seven years and the rest of the ten tribes came down and they said, 'We're flesh of your flesh, and bone of your bone, and we want you to be king over all of us.'

That's when there was a king over all 12 tribes of Israel, and that passed to Solomon. That is 33 years that all 12 tribes were under David. Then for 40 years all 12 tribes were under Solomon. How long was it from the death of Solomon until the split up of the kingdom when the ten tribes went back and followed Jeroboam instead of Rehoboam, the son of Solomon? *We don't know!*

But we can say that only within the span of 80 years or less all 12 tribes were under the kingship of David and Solomon. That's the only time in history that that was true. Think about when they come back out of captivity what that is going to be like. In receiving what we are receiving:

- the salvation
- the Spirit of God
- the Truth of God
- the Word of God

all together, Peter writes:

1-Peter 1:10: "Concerning which salvation the prophets who prophesied of the grace *that would come* to you have diligently searched out and intently inquired." *They wanted to know*: 'When, O Lord'?

So. we've gone through the book of Isaiah and a lot of the Psalms, there are a lot of things there concerning the Kingdom of God. But how? When? What? *It's going to be an amazing thing, really!*

Verse 11: "Searching into what *way* and what manner of time the Spirit of Christ *which was* in them was indicating, testifying beforehand of the sufferings of Christ, and these glories that would follow."

When you can't see the end and you're way back close to the beginning, and all of these things are prophesied and not understood, and some of them are deep mysteries, *it's hard to grasp even some of it!* Think about how they must have felt.

Of course, they had to have greater faith, because when something is here, like today, you don't need faith to see if you can find it. Now then, we need faith to understand the greater degree of what all of these things mean for the world, the Church and us individually.

Verse 12: "To whom it was revealed that, not for themselves, but to us they were ministering these things, which now have been announced to you by those who have preached the Gospel to you by *the* Holy Spirit, sent from heaven—**into which things the angels desire to look**."

Notice what Peter says next, because this is something that applies throughout all time, and a especially to those who are of the Philadelphians who love God.

Verse 13: "For this reason, **be prepared in your minds,** be self-controlled…"—*choosing with the Word of God, the Spirit of God to do the things that are pleasing in God's sight!*

"*…and* be fully hoping in the grace that will be brought to you at *the* revelation of Jesus Christ" (v 13)—*at the return of Jesus Christ!*

The fullness of grace will not come until the first resurrection, because that's when we receive the fullness of the gift of eternal life.

Verse 14: "As obedient children, do not conform yourselves to the former lusts, *as you did* in *your* ignorance. But according as He Who has called you *is* Holy, you yourselves also be Holy in all *your* conduct; for it is written, **'You be Holy because I am Holy'**" (vs 14-16).

*That's quite thing that **we're going to be***

Holy! We're called *Holy brethren* now, because we have the Holy Spirit. When the resurrection comes **we will be the sons and daughters of God!** That's the fullness of the grace! We have yet to receive that.

Let's continue on with the key of David and the heart of David! We're going to spend all the rest of the time in the book of Psalms. That's quite a fantastic thing when you put it together, because all of these are important concerning

- David's relationship with God
- his attitude toward God
- how he lived

Remember that every day when he was in his house he could just walk down the hall to that extension on his house where the Ark of the Covenant was in a special tent. The priests were there to minister to it. Then they had an altar right outside of that where they had sacrifices that they would give. David was looking forward to the time when he would dwell with God:

Psalm 84:1: "How lovely are Your tabernacles, O LORD of hosts!" *Here's another thing about the character of David. He served God*:

- with all his heart
- with his whole heart
- his heart was fixed
- he hungered and thirsted after God's way

That's how we need to be!

Verse 2: "My soul longs, yea, even faints for the courts of the LORD; my heart and my flesh cry out for the living God." *Think how intense his prayers were!*

- God heard him
- God answered
- God gave David the promise that he would be king over Israel forever

Verse 3: "Yea, even the sparrow has found a house, and the swallow a nest for herself where she may lay her young, even Your altars, O LORD of hosts, my King and my God."

Notice how he drew close to God and understood! Think about this: Here's the temple and on top of the temple birds made their nests, right above the altars of God, the little sparrow.

Verse 4: "**Blessed are those who dwell in Your house**…"—*ultimately that is New Jerusalem because Jesus said*:

In My Father's house are many dwelling places; if it were otherwise, I would have told you so, but now I go to prepare a place for you.

For each one of us! Jesus is preparing that.

"…they will still be praising You. Selah…. [stop, think and meditate] …**Blessed is the man whose strength is in You**; Your ways are in their hearts" (vs 4-5).

Here again we see that David understood that he *lived, moved and had his being in God!* In everything!

Verse 6: "Who passing through the valley of weeping make it a place of springs… [convert and change the whole world] …yea, the early rain also clothes it with blessings. They go from strength to strength, every one of them appearing in Zion before God" (vs 5-7).

Our strength comes from God; stop and think about it! What are we but just kind of a speck; that's how we started, a speck of life so small that the naked eye could not even see it. Look at us now! If we look at that, remember Jesus' promise that *since we have this body of flesh, and we're converted, we will have a body of spirit!*

Verse 8—*notice how he cried out to God*: "O LORD God of hosts, hear my prayer; give ear, O God of Jacob. Selah. Behold, O God, our shield, and look upon the face of Your anointed" (vs 8-9). *David was the anointed king, and he was pleading for God to look upon him!*

Looking forward to the ultimate of being in New Jerusalem; v 10: "For a day in Your courts is better than a thousand *elsewhere*. I would rather stand at the threshold of the house of my God than dwell in the tents of wickedness, for the LORD **God is a sun and shield; the LORD will give grace and glory; no good thing will He withhold from those who walk uprightly**" (vs 10-11)—*in spite of the troubles and difficulties we have today!*

Think of what it's going to be like at the resurrection, living in the Tabernacle of God, *with God!*

Verse 12: "O LORD of hosts, blessed is the man who trusts in You."

Let's see that David had a great understanding of the purpose of mankind, as it related to him, as well. Let's see what he understood. Of course, we have all of this in our book: *From a Speck of Dust to a Son of God: Why Were You Born?* That's the important thing. We always need to look at the purpose of:

- why we're here
- our circumstances of what they are
- where we are going
- what we need to do

But we always have to turn to God to do it!

Psalm 8:1: "O LORD our Lord, how excellent is Your name in all the earth! You have set Your glory above the heavens!"

What is like to see God in His full glory? *We have to be at the resurrection to see!*

Verse 2: "Out of the mouths of babes and sucklings… [that's what we are compared to the world] …You have ordained strength because of Your adversaries, to silence the enemy and the avenger."

There will come a day when all of those— like we saw in Rev. 3, the synagogue of Satan will come and worship God before our feet. The first thing they're going to do is think to themselves, 'What? Did God choose these people? *Yes, indeed He did!*

Verse 4: "What is man that You are mindful of him, and the son of man that You care for him? For You have made him **a little lower than God** and have crowned him with glory and honor" (vs 4-5). *That's just here on this earth!* "…**a little lower than God**…" *so that God could become a man and men and women can become the sons and daughters of God!* That's quite an amazing exchange.

Verse 6: "You made him to have dominion over the works of Your hands; You have put all things under his feet." *Not yet all things are under his feet, but Jesus has already paved the way!*

Think about that! God made the whole world, and down through all the centuries from the beginning with all of mankind from the beginning to the end so that there would be billions and billions in the Kingdom of God!

From all of those from the time of Abel clear down to the last two witnesses (Rev. 11) are all in the first resurrection to serve and love God continually, and to carry out His plan.

So, what we are seeing here is that David had a pretty good understanding of God's way, of the future of it, because He was king.

Psa. 38—notice that God had to correct David. As a man with all the strength and power that he had, and his willingness to go out and do things, he did suffer difficulties and even sickness. So, one of the important things about David that we're finding is that *David always repented and trusted God!* He suffered:

- sickness
- difficulties
- anguish
- intrigue

Psalm 38:1: "O LORD, do not rebuke me in

Your wrath; neither chasten me in Your fury, for Your arrows stick fast in me, and Your hand presses heavily upon me. There is no soundness in my flesh because of Your anger; nor rest in my bones because of my sin… [here's a prayer of repentance; think of the anguish that he was going through at this time] …for my iniquities have gone over my head; like a heavy burden they are too heavy for me" (vs 1-4).

Here we have a great example that when things become too much, that you feel oppressed, burdened down, and it's hard to bear it, *you turn to God! Always trust God!* Now notice how bad it was:

Verse 5: "My wounds are putrefied and fester **because of my foolishness**."

Didn't we read where he said, 'Man at his very best is altogether vanity.' He was not exalting himself.

- he knew that he was king because of God
- he knew that he won battles because of God
- he knew that he had many enemies against him, *even within his own household and council*

Here he is sick; v 6: "I am troubled; I am bowed down greatly; I go mourning all the day long."

So, you think you have a difficulty and problem, look at this one:

Verse 7: "For my loins are filled with a burning; and there is no soundness in my flesh. I am feeble and painfully broken; I groan because of the anguish of my heart" (vs 7-8)—*quite a thing!*

All of us have been somewhere close to that in our lifetime, and all of that is because that will test and prove us. *God proves us by the difficulties and things that we go through!*

Verse 9: "My LORD, all my desire is before You; and my sighing is not hidden from You." **What does he do?** *He completely yields to God with all his heart!*

Verse 10: "My heart pants; my strength fails me; as for the light of my eyes, it also is gone from me. My loved ones and my friends stand apart from my plague; and my neighbors stand far off. And those who seek my life lay snares for me; and those who seek my hurt speak mischievous things, and plot deceptions all the day long" (vs 10-12).

This is also part of a prophecy of what Christ went through, because he had to work in the midst of his enemies all the time. They were looking to get him.

Verse 13: "But like a deaf one, I do not hear; and I am like a dumb one who opens not his mouth.

Thus I am as a man who hears not, and in whose mouth are no reproofs, for in You, O LORD, do I hope; You will answer, O LORD my God" (vs 13-15). *Quite a tremendous thing! Look at what he was doing!*

Verse 18: "For I will confess my iniquity…"—*that's Who you repent to:* **God the Father and Jesus Christ**.

The promises given in 1-John 1 is that He will *cleanse us from all unrighteousness **IF*** we confess our sin. Of course, the sins that God is most interested in *are those that are in the mind!* That's why we have *the laws and commandments of God written in our mind and heart* so that will *cleanse our mind!*

"…I am full of anxiety because of my sin. And my enemies are vigorous; they are strong; and those who hate me without reason are multiplied…. [this is obviously also a prophecy of what Jesus went through] …And those who render evil for good oppose me because I follow what is good." (vs 18-20).

David was so down and low—in spite of his trusting in God—look what he said:

Verse 21: "Forsake me not, O LORD; O my God, be not far from me. Make haste to help me, O LORD my salvation" (vs 21-22).

WOW! Look at how he confessed! Now let's look at how he confessed after the situation with Bathsheba. Notice that he understood that that sin was directly against God. Again, here's good example of deep repentance, clear into the heart! That is called a *catharsis,* which is a great cleansing! Notice how David did it here:

Psalm 51:1: "Have mercy upon me, O God, according to Your loving kindness; according to the greatness of Your compassion, blot out my transgressions. Wash me thoroughly from my iniquity and cleanse me from my sin, for I acknowledge my transgressions, and my sin is ever before me" (vs 1-3).

That's quite a thing! That's why we go through things like this. Certain major things in our life stick in our mind and we remember what we did. That serves as a warning. God will forgive the sin, *but that will remain as a warning to not do it ever again!*

Verse 4: "Against You, You only, have I sinned, and done evil in Your sight…"

Why is that true every time we sin? *Because God has given his laws and commandments,* and sin and transgressions are violations of the laws and commandments of God. So, it is only against God. Yes, he caused the husband of Bathsheba—Uriah the

Hittite—to be killed in battle. He committed adultery with Bathsheba and she bore a child and God took the life of that child so that it would not bring any further reproach upon the kingdom.

That's a difficult thing, but because of that sin—even with the repentance that he had—so likewise with us: When we repent there comes a time where we have *a discipline* from God. The discipline from God to David was that his whole household and parts of his kingdom would rebel against him, and Absalom tried to take over the kingdom, and he was a son that David loved greatly, but he turned out to be a real rebel! *That's all came because of the sin with Bathsheba!*

Verse 4: "Against You, You only, have I sinned, and done evil in Your sight, that You might be justified when You speak and be in the right when You judge."

David examined himself, his attitude, his carnal nature and everything about himself, and he understood this that like the New Testament says, *every human being*—because of the sin of Adam and Eve—*has the law of sin and death in them!* This is the source of sin that comes from within. The source of sin that comes from without is from Satan the devil.

Verse 5: "Behold, I was brought forth in iniquity, and in sin did my mother conceive me."

It's not that his mother was committing adultery; but human nature from the instant that they are conceived until they die have *the law of sin and death,* and that's what David means when he says that he was born in iniquity and conceived in sin. Notice how to overcome that, and this is the lifetime of:

- grace
- mercy
- forgiveness
- repentance
- changing
- developing
- growing in grace and knowledge

Right here:

Verse 6: "Behold, **You desire Truth in the inward parts**…"—*your inner thoughts, inner mind and everything down to the smallest little thing in your brain,* because God says that He's even going to judge the secrets of men. That's why repentance like this is really profound and important, and what we need to do.

"…**You desire Truth in the inward parts**…" *in the mind!*

- Truth is the Word of God
- Truth is the commandments of God
- Truth is the precepts of God
- Truth is the Law of God

What proceeds from God is Truth!

"…and **in the hidden part** You shall make me to know wisdom" (v 6). *When that happens, we see our sin, and we learn and acknowledge!* Look at King Hezekiah and King Josiah—two very righteous kings.

Hezekiah prayed to God and God destroyed the whole army of 180,000 of the Assyrians. Then he got all the spoil that the armies had gathered, coming down from Assyria and going clear into Egypt. He took it all into his house and the treasury house of the Lord.

This was quite a thing! Then Hezekiah got sick and was ready to die. God sent Isaiah to tell him to set his house in order because he was going to die. But Hezekiah turned to the wall and wept sore, and cried out to God: 'O God, spare me.' So, God heard and answered his prayer and gave him 15 years more life. *Quite a blessing!*

But then he acted foolishly; the ambassadors from Babylon who heard of this great victory over the Assyrians, came to Hezekiah to find out what it was. Hezekiah was flattered by them so much that he did the foolish thing of showing them all the wealth and booty that he took from the Assyrians as well as all that God had given him.

So then Isaiah came, on God's instruction, and said, 'Who were these men?' *They were from Babylon.* What did you show them? *I showed them everything, there was nothing I withheld from showing them!* Isaiah said, 'You've done foolishly! All of this shall go to Babylon, but it will happen after you die!'

So, then Hezekiah said, 'I'll have peace in my day.' Though he was righteous, Hezekiah did not turn to God—like David did—in these troubles. He died and it all went to Babylon.

The other one was *King Josiah* who straightened everything out, made all the people keep the Laws of God after he heard what was read from the Book of the Law. Then he made everybody keep the commandments of God and for 12 years it was really, really good.

Then there was a battle with the Egyptians and Josiah wanted to go out and fight, and he was told not to go fight. During that 12 years they had a lot of peace up to this point, and if he would have stayed back they would have won the battle. But no, he disguised himself as an ordinary soldier and went out and took an arrow and died.

So, it's important to understand what David

did here. He understood the difficulties that would come after him, even though he was forgiven the sins.

Verse 6: "Behold, You desire Truth in the inward parts; and in the hidden part You shall make me to know wisdom. Purge me with hyssop, and I shall be clean; wash me, and I shall be whiter than snow" (vs 6-7).

Then he went on to say, v 11: "Cast me not away from Your presence, and take not Your Holy Spirit from me." *Very important, because God came very close to doing it!* Had David not repented this way, it would have happened. But God restored him!

Verse 12: "Restore to me the joy of Your salvation, and let *Your* free spirit uphold me. Then I will teach transgressors Your ways, and sinners shall turn back to You. Deliver me from the guilt of shedding blood, O God, O God of my salvation, then my tongue shall sing aloud of Your righteousness" (vs 12-14).

Verse 16: "For You do not desire sacrifice…" *because this repentance came direct from God!*

Psa. 86 is one we've covered before, but it's also very good for us to understand, and this fits right in with 1-John 1 & 2, that Jesus is the propitiation of our sins.

Psalm 86:1: "Bow down Your ear, O LORD, answer me, for I am poor and needy." *Don't get lifted up!*

Look what happened to the Church in our day when they got lifted up and carried away with money and sin! That church no longer exists! The man who was the leader of it always wanted to be with rich people. Now the campus where they had their college is completely changed with the exception of the auditorium, the student center, the garage and gymnasium. Those were sold to two people:

1. the auditorium to a Chinese Pentecostal Church dedicated by Benny Hinn when they took possession of it
2. the Maranatha Christian School, a private school

All of the rest of it has been turned into expensive condominiums! They tore down the beautiful classrooms. They tore down where the television studio was, and coming down the hill on Green Street they tore down the administration building and built four stories of expensive condominiums! What a judgment that God finally carried out upon the sins there in Pasadena.

You can never promote spiritual growth with physical things and by physical means! Can't do it!

Psalm 86:1: "Bow down Your ear, O LORD, answer me, for I am poor and needy. Preserve my soul, for I am Holy; O You my God, save Your servant who trusts in You" (vs 1-2). *That's what we need to do!*

We need to believe in God always, and trust Him and not lean to our own understanding. See what happens when that occurs! ***Lean to God's understanding!***

Verse 3: "Be merciful to me, O LORD, for I cry unto You all day long. Rejoice the soul of Your servant, for to You, O LORD, do I lift up my soul… [quite a Psalm of repentance] …**for You, LORD, are good and ready to forgive, and rich in mercy to all those who call upon You**" (vs 3-5)—*with a true heart!*

Verse 6: "Give ear, O LORD, to my prayer, and attend to the voice of my supplications. In the day of my trouble I will call upon You, for You will answer me" (vs 6-7).

Let's see the that this is verified in 1-John 1; he's talking about not only the brethren, but himself:

1-John 1:5: "And this is the message that we have heard from Him and are declaring to you: that **God is Light, and there is no darkness at all in Him**. If we proclaim that we have fellowship with Him, but we are walking in the darkness… [Satan's way (Acts 26) the power of Satan] …we are lying to ourselves… [the worst lie is to lie to yourself, you believe it and deceive yourself] …**and we are not practicing the Truth**" (vs 5-6)—*living by every word of God!*

Verse 7: "However, if we walk in the Light, as He is in the Light, *then* we have fellowship with one another, and the blood of Jesus Christ, His own Son, cleanses us from **all sin**." *He is ready to forgive!*

Verse 8: "If we say that we do not have sin, we are deceiving ourselves, and the Truth is not in us." *Constantly the Truth, **the Truth, the Truth!*** Remember that:

- God is true
- Jesus is the Way, the Truth, and the Life
- the Holy Spirit is called *the Spirit of Truth*
- the Bible is called *the Word of Truth*

Verse 9: "If we confess our own sins, He is faithful and righteous to forgive us our sins and to cleanse us from all unrighteousness. If we say that we have not sinned, we make Him a liar, and His Word is not in us" (vs 9-10).

See how we have that in Psa. 86, which also is a prophecy of what was written here in the New

Testament in 1-John 1. Now we need to complete the whole thought:

1-John 2:1: "My little children, I am writing these things to you so that you may not sin. And *yet,* if anyone does sin… [which we do] …we have an Advocate with the Father; Jesus Christ *the* Righteous; and He is *the* **propitiation** for our sins…" (vs 1-2)—***the continual atoning through the shed blood of Jesus Christ to forgive us and justify us to God,*** *and to put us in right standing to Him, just exactly as David was pleading in Psa. 86!*

"…and not for our sins only, but also for *the sins of* the whole world" (v 2)—*in God's plan according to His Holy Days!*

Psa. 32—this is quoted in the New Testament as one of the main activities that Jesus Christ would do. It also shows:

- God's love
- God's mercy
- God's forgiveness

And how He deals with us!

Psalm 32:1: "**Blessed is the man whose transgression is forgiven, whose sin is covered**." *All of that is accomplished through the sacrifice of Jesus Christ!*

Verse 2: "Blessed is the man to whom the LORD does not impute iniquity, and in whose spirit there is no guile." *There's only one person recorded in the New Testament who had no guile, and that was Nathaniel!*

That's quite interesting, indeed. It shows that when we come to God for repentance, we come with our whole heart. We don't treat it as though it's removing a little dust off the shelf.

Verse 3: "When I kept silent, my bones wore away through my groaning all the day long, for by day and by night Your hand was heavy upon me; my strength was sapped as in the heat of summer. Selah. **I acknowledged my sin to You**… [not to any man] …and my iniquity I have not hidden…. [you don't come and repent partially] …I said, 'I will confess my transgression to the LORD,' and **You forgave the iniquity of my sin**. Selah" (vs 3-5).

Quite an important thing, and how important that is to take place!

Verse 6: "For this *reason* let every Godly one pray to You in a time when **You may be found**…"

If we don't turn to God when we need to, when we have sin that we need to repent of, He may not be found the way you want it.

Verse 7: "You are my hiding place; You

shall preserve me from trouble; You shall encircle me with songs of deliverance. Selah."

Notice what happens then, because when we are resurrected and in the Kingdom of God, we're going to be teaching people God's way. So, what we do here, we're learning God's way through living the way that God wants us to live.

Verse 8: "*You said, 'I will instruct you and teach you in the way which you should go; I will counsel you, My eye shall be upon you.'*" *That's God directing us:*

- with His Spirit
- with His Truth
- with His righteousness

Verse 9: "'Be not like the horse, or like the mule, which have no understanding—which must be harnessed with bit and bridle, else they will not come near you.' The wicked has many sorrows, but **His steadfast love surrounds him who trusts in the LORD**" (vs 9-10). *Think about that!*

God's steadfast love always there surrounding you! The way David writes these things is very descriptive.

Verse 11: "Be glad in the LORD and rejoice, you righteous; and shout for joy, all you upright in heart."

The amazing attitude that David had, and this is what we need to have. We need to understand that God is always there, He is there to help us and we can cry out to Him and we confess our sins, and we confess them all! *Not part, but all!*

Psalm 62:1: "Only for God does my soul wait in silence; from Him comes my salvation."

Even though we have the things we need to do, only God can save us. ***Even though we keep the commandments of God and His Holy Days, and we do those things that are pleasing in His sight***—because we're His workmanship and God has ordained that we are to walk in these things—***we trust in God! We can't trust in our own ways!*** It won't work!

Verse 2: "He only is my Rock and my salvation; He is my fortress; I shall not be greatly moved." *Even though sin may come along, you're not greatly moved away from God!*

Verse 3: "How long will you imagine mischief against a man? You shall be slain, all of you… [now he's directing this to the wicked] …you shall be like a bowing wall and as a tottering fence. They only consult to cast him down from his great height; they delight in lies; they bless with their mouth, but inwardly they curse. Selah" (vs 3-4).

That's the way it is in the world, and likewise is a prophecy of the enemies of Christ. It would be interesting to see going through all the Psalms how many of these things applied to Christ. We'll see one of the most profound that David did a little bit later.

Verse 5: "My soul, wait in silence for God alone; for from Him comes my hope. He only is my Rock and my salvation; He is my strong tower; I shall not be moved. In God is my salvation and my glory, the Rock of my strength; my refuge is in God. **Trust in Him at all times**...]always] ...**you people**; pour out your heart before Him; God is a refuge for us. Selah" (vs 5-8).

That's why we have prayer and study every day, because we are in training, and this training comes from God through His Spirit. That's why we need to come to Him every day in prayer, in study and have our mind changed, converted and transformed.

Look out at the world and here is a true statement, v 9: "Surely men of low degree are vanity, and men of high degree are a lie... [that's true] ...when weighed in the balance, they are altogether lighter than vanity." *Worse than just vanity!* Though they're upheld as *the great this, that and the other thing!*

Verse 10: "Trust not in oppression, and do not take pride in stolen goods; if riches increase, do not set your heart upon them. God has spoken once; twice I have heard this: **that power belongs to God**" (vs 10-11)—*the power for wealth!* And *we understand that it comes from God!*

- we have to be diligent
- we have to be honest
- we have to apply ourselves
- we have to ask God to be with us

and God will bless us! Those blessings can be used to further preach the Gospel and teaching the brethren *so we can attain to the resurrection!*

Verse 12: "Also to You, O LORD, belongs mercy; for You give to every man according to his work."

Psalm 16:1—*talks about the way of God*: "Preserve me, O God, for in You do I take refuge. I have said to the LORD, 'You are my LORD; I have no goodness apart from You'" (vs 1-2).

Think about that! There is no goodness that is spiritual, everlasting goodness in human flesh. They can do good deeds, but goodness without hypocrisy, and goodness without the evil of human nature behind it, can only come from God.

Verse 3: "**As for the saints**... [that's all of us] ...in the earth, **they are the excellent ones in**

whom is all My delight" *This is God's speaking to us!*

Do you think God is pleased when we're keeping the Sabbath, the Feast like we're doing now? *Of course!* That is so we can trust God and do it in the right way. It will be a great and marvelous thing, like the great Feast we've had so far.

Verse 5: "The LORD is the portion of my inheritance and of my cup; You shall uphold my lot."

We are told that we are joint heirs with Christ (Rom. 8). There it is! And our inheritance is *eternal life* and living in New Jerusalem!

Verse 7: "I will bless the LORD Who has given me counsel; my heart also instructs me in the nights."

David thought a lot about God at night, prayed to God, thought on His Word and looked forward to really doing the will of God. That should be the same way with us! God will instruct us; He will give us things to understand. There will be many moments, like a light that goes on BING! 'Oh, now I understand!' BING! Really, that is true!

Verse 8: "I have set the LORD always before me.... [never leaving God] ...Because He is at my right hand, I shall not be moved. Therefore, My heart is glad, and My glory rejoices; My flesh also shall rest in safety" (vs 8-9). *That means when you're put in the grave after you die!*

Here's a prophecy of Jesus that will also apply to us, but we will be corrupted and disappear. The flesh, because dust you are and to dust you shall return.

Verse 10: "For You will not abandon My soul to the grave; neither will You allow Your Holy One to see corruption."

That's directly of Christ and quoted in the New Testament as well. Here's what God will do for us. This is what God will do, and that's why we have:

- the Spirit of God
- the Word of God
- the Sabbath
- the Holy Days
- the Feasts

Verse 11: "You will make known to Me the path of life... [that not just the life we're living now; *but eternal life*] ...in Your presence is fullness of joy.... [no more sorrow, no more all of the fighting human nature] ...At Your right hand are pleasures forevermore."

I have no idea what that means, because I don't know what pleasure as a spirit being really consists of. Today we all have emotions and feelings. Think about what we're going to have as spirit beings. We can't think very far on that because we have no way of judging it.

Psalm 17:5: "My steps have held fast to Your paths, my feet have not slipped…. [that's interesting; quite a thing to say] I have called upon You, for You will answer me, O God; incline Your ear to me; hear my speech. Show Your marvelous loving kindness, O Savior of those seeking refuge in You; by Your right hand *save them* from those who rise up against them" (vs 5-7). *Take care of the enemy and we don't even know it!*

Verse 8: "Keep me as the apple of Your eye; **hide me under the shadow of Your wings**." How many times in the book of Psalms does it talk about 'shadow under the wings'? protected by God?

When you look this way you can't see the shadow. The only thing you can see is the shadow of the tree on the ground, but that which makes the shadow you cannot see. It's likewise with God's protection. His protection comes upon you, but you can't see it. After you've gone through whatever you've gone through, you can look back and see that God was with you and helped you.

Verse 14: "From men by Your hand, O LORD, from men of the world whose portion is in this life, and whose belly You fill with Your treasure. They are full of children, and will leave their riches to their babes. As for me…" (vs 14-15).

David comparing all the wealth, all the things of decent, good people in the world, and he's saying that the most important thing for him is the resurrection. Look at what it says, and this is also a prophecy of Christ:

Verse 15: "As for me, I will behold Your face in righteousness; I shall be satisfied, **when I awake, with Your likeness**"—*the resurrection!*

What did Jesus say that likeness would be like: *The children of the Kingdom shall shine as the sun in it's full strength!* What kind of glory is that going to be? Look at us today, just flesh and blood, we all have our physical problems up and down. Time marches on and no one is getting younger; everybody is getting older and then we're going to expire.

Look what we have when we're resurrected, "…**when I awake, with Your likeness**" Remember that we started out, we're made 'a little lower than God,' so that God could come in the flesh and we could become like God. There it is right there.

We're going to look at some of these Psalms that are directly concerning Christ and how David was the only one who received these words. That's how righteous he was, and how close to God he was.

Psalm 40:1—*a prophecy of Jesus Chri*st: "I waited patiently for the LORD, and He inclined unto me and heard my cry."

- Did God always answer Jesus' prayer? *Yes!*
- What did Jesus say? *I thank you O Lord that you always hear Me!*

That means hear and answer!

Verse 2: "He brought me up also out of a horrible pit, out of the miry clay, and set my feet upon a Rock, and established my steps." *That's bringing us out of this sinful world and our own sins, and putting us on Christ!*

Verse 3: "And He has put a new song in my mouth, *even* praise to our God; many shall see and fear, and shall trust in the LORD." *That's what we're going to do during the Millennium!*

Just think how many are going to enter the Kingdom of God then. Brethren, the more we learn of the way of God and how great it is, it is absolutely phenomenal indeed!

Verse 4: "Blessed is the man who makes the LORD his trust and does not respect the proud, nor those who turn aside to lies."

There are a lot of lying doctrines out there. So, we need to know the Truth and know the doctrines. *We need to be strong in the Lord,* and not relent to any of their attacks against the Truth.

Verse 5: "O LORD my God, many things You have done, Your wonderful works and Your thoughts which are toward us; there is none to compare unto You; if I could declare and speak of them, they would be more than can be told."

Stop and think about this! From the time you were baptized until now—whatever length of time that is, whether a short period or long period of time—but for a longer period of time, you can look back and see many of the things that God has done for you:

- taken care of you
- heard you
- healed you
- watched over you
- taught you

Here are the words of Christ found in Heb. 10:

Verse 6: "Sacrifice and offering You did not desire; My ears You have opened…"

Not quite as good a translation as it could

be, but in Heb. It says, *'You have prepared a body for Me.'* That's Christ!

Verse 7: "Then I said, 'Lo, I come; in the **Scroll of the Book it is written of Me.**'"

Daniel 10:21: "But I will show you that which is written in the **Scripture of Truth**…."—*or the Scroll of the Book or Bible!*

There are probably many of them up in heaven before the Throne of God. Everything that we have down here is written up there. Think about that in relationship to always being honest with the Scriptures. When we were working on translating the Bible—the New Testament I did and Michael Heiss did the Old Testament—that's what we had in mind: **the Truth of God!** That's why in *The Holy Bible in Its Original Order* you will not find any of our own ideas; but you will find the Truth of God and the Word of God rightly interpreted.

Psalm 40:7: "Then I said, 'Lo, I come; in the Scroll of the Book it is written of Me. I delight to do Your will, O My God; and Your Law is within My heart'" (vs 7-8). *That's Christ!*

Verse 9: "I have preached righteousness in the great congregation… [wherever he was down there in Galilee and Judea and so forth] …lo, I have not kept back my lips, O LORD, You know. I have not hidden Your righteousness within my heart; I have declared Your faithfulness and Your salvation; I have not hidden Your loving kindness and Your Truth from the great congregation" (vs 9-10).

The ministry of Jesus Christ summarized right here in Psa. 40, written by King David; an amazing thing! A thousand years *before* Christ, and carried out and we know everything that took place.

Verse 10: "I have not hidden Your righteousness within my heart; I have declared Your faithfulness and Your salvation…"

Think about that, not only in Jesus when He was preaching, but also inspiring with the apostles. But David was given these words. That's quite a thing!

"…I have not hidden Your loving kindness and Your Truth from the great congregation. Do not withhold Your tender mercies from me, O LORD; let Your loving kindness and Your Truth always preserve me" (vs 10-11).

What was the Truth? *The resurrection from the dead!* But notice what it was like constantly during the days of Jesus and His ministry, as well as probably David in his activities as king and fighting all the enemies all around.

Verse 12: "For evils without number have encircled me; my iniquities have taken hold on me…" *This has to be David, but* what were the iniquities that Jesus bore? *The iniquities of us all!*

"…so that I am not able to look up; they are more than the hairs of my head, and my heart fails me" (v 12). *That's the great weight of all the sins of the whole world!*

Verse 13: "Be pleased, O LORD, to deliver me; O LORD, make haste to help me." *That was sure true through the resurrection, and God did!*

Psa. 22—tie in with Isa. 52, which is looking at Christ *from God's perspective* of what Christ went through to carry the sins of the world. Psa. 22 is different; *it's from Christ's perspective looking back to God and everything that He would go through.* There are words here that I imagine that when David got done writing it he wondered why he wrote it this way. But this is what God inspired, *and these are some of the very words of Jesus when He was on the cross dying.*

Psalm 22:1: "My God, My God, why have You forsaken Me, and *why are You so* far from helping Me, and from the words of My groaning?…. [the very words while Christ was on the cross] …O my God, I cry in the daytime, but You do not answer; and in the night season, and am not silent. Yet, You are Holy, O You enthroned upon the praises of Israel" (vs 1-3).

Verse 6: "But **I am a worm, and no man**…" *Think of the humility of the crucifixion,* to where God in the flesh understood the weakness of everything; that He was so depleted of everything within that He was just like a worm.

"…a reproach of men and despised by the people…. [yes, they were gathered out there] …All who see Me mock Me; they shoot out the lip; they shake the head, saying, 'He trusted on the LORD; let Him deliver Him; let Him rescue Him, since He delights in Him!'" (vs 6-8). *'Yes, if You're the Christ come down off the cross,' they said.*

Verse 9: "For You are He who took Me out of the womb… [going clear back to the time that He was conceived and born] …causing Me to trust while on My mother's breasts. I was cast upon You from birth; You are My God from My mother's womb" (vs 9-10).

I wonder if He had any consciousness in His mother's womb? *We don't know!*

Verse 11: "Be not far from Me; for trouble is near, for there is none to help." *No person to help, and they shouldn't and couldn't, because He was there to die for the sins of the world!*

Verse 12: "Many bulls have encircled around Me; strong bulls of Bashan have surrounded Me." *That means encircling the cross were the demons and Satan laughing, mocking and jeering!*

They didn't believe that God could resurrect Him. They were thinking: *'We have the victory!'* But *His death was the victory over them and the sins of the world!*

Verse 13: "They opened wide their mouths at Me, like a ravening and a roaring lion. I am poured out like water, and all My bones are out of joint; My heart is like wax; it is melted in the midst of My bowels" (vs 13-14).

These are all of His thoughts while He was on the cross dying, *and those were given to David!* No one else! That's how close David was to God.

Verse 15: "My strength is dried up like a potsherd, and My tongue clings to My jaws; dogs have surrounded Me; a band of evildoers have encircled Me; they have pierced My hands and My feet; and You have brought Me into the dust of death" (vs 15-16). *All those the very thoughts of Jesus when dying on the cross!*

Verse 17: "I can count all My bones; they look and gloat over Me. They divide My garments among them and cast lots upon My vesture. But You, O LORD, be not far from Me; O My strength, hasten to help Me! Deliver My soul from the sword, My precious *life* from the power of the dog. Save Me from the lion's mouth; yea, and from the wild ox's horns. You have answered Me" (vs 17-21).

Through all of that He knew that God answered Him and He would be resurrected. Then His spirit went back to God.

Verse 22: "I will declare Your name to My brethren…"—*which He did after He was resurrected He came back and taught the disciples out of the Law, the Prophets and the Psalms about His life!*

"'…in the midst of the congregation I will praise You.' You who fear the LORD, praise Him; all of you, the seed of Jacob, glorify Him; and stand in awe of Him all of you, the seed of Israel" (vs 22-23).

Verse 27: "All the ends of the earth shall remember and turn to the LORD…"

David understood what was going to happen and that the Gospel would be preached around the world and everyone would hear. Just like it says in Matt. 24, 'This Gospel of the Kingdom shall be preached to all nations as a witness.'

"…and all the families of the nations shall worship before You… [the ultimate fulfillment of the plan of God] …for the Kingdom is the LORD'S and He rules over the nations. All the rich of the earth shall eat and worship; all those who go down to the dust shall bow before Him; even he who cannot keep his own soul alive. A seed shall serve Him…" (vs 27-30)—*that's us!*

Remember Gal. 3—*if you are Christ's then you are heirs according to the promise and you are the seed of Abraham!* That's what it's talking about right here.

"…it shall be told of the LORD to the coming generation…. [and the coming generations, and the coming generation after that] …They shall come and shall declare His righteousness unto a people that shall yet be born, **that He has done this**" (vs 30-31)—*or finished this!*

There it was, David—a man after God's heart—who cried out to the Lord all the time; who had troubles and difficulties as a king and the things that he went through. He went through many things that were precursors of what Jesus would go through.

Psa. 23—we can liken this Psalm—the prayer of David—when Christ was first resurrected in the tomb.

Psalm 23:1: "The LORD is my Shepherd; I shall not want"—*or lack anything!* Isn't that true if you're just resurrected from the dead?

Verse 2: "He makes me to lie down in green pastures; He leads me beside the still waters. He restores my soul; He leads me in the paths of righteousness for His name's sake" (vs 2-3). *Everything about what Jesus did in completing the work that God gave Him to do!*

Verse 4: "Yea, though I walk through the valley of the shadow of death… [which He did, and died and was resurrected] …I will fear no evil, for You are with me; Your rod and Your staff, they comfort me. You prepare a table for me in the presence of my enemies…." (vs 4-5).

The power and preaching the Gospel went out in the presence of the enemies that came against Christ and crucified Him, according to the prophecies that were given.

"…You anoint my head with oil; my cup runs over. Surely goodness and mercy shall follow me all the days of my life… [which is into all eternity] …and **I shall dwell in the house of the LORD forever**" (vs 5-6)—*the meaning of the Feast of Tabernacles! That will also apply to us!*

Now, picture this—Psa. 24—as the angels are accompanying Jesus as He ascends up to the Throne of God the Father.

- think of the rejoicing
- think of the singing

- think of everything that was going on in heaven around the Throne of God

Because now Jesus was coming to the Father:

- Who had been crucified
- Who had been victorious over Satan the devil
- Who was victorious over the enemies
- Who was the perfect sacrifice, the Lamb of God

To take away the sins of the world!

Psalm 24:7: "Lift up your heads, O you gates… [the gate that Jesus entered into to go to be accepted of God the Father] …and be lifted up, O you everlasting doors; **that the King of glory may come in**. Who is this King of glory? **The LORD strong and mighty, the LORD mighty in battle**" (vs 7-8). *He won the greatest battle of all!*

Verse 9: Lift up your heads, O you gates; lift them up, you everlasting doors; that the King of glory may come in. Who is this King of glory? **The LORD of hosts, He is the King of glory.** Selah" (vs 9-10).

What an amazing thing that was that David was given these words of the actual events to take place in the life of Christ:

- His crucifixion
- His death
- His resurrection
- His ascension into glory

*Everything that was given to David, **words that are not given to any of the other prophets!***

Psa. 118—this is what we need to have. In a couple of days we are going back into the world and we're going to be needing:

- the protection of God
- the strength of His Spirit
- the power of His faith and belief in us
- His love that surrounds us

Psalm 118:13: "You have thrust hard at me so that I might fall, **but the LORD helped me**." *Keep that in mind when trouble comes upon you!*

Verse 14: "The LORD is my strength and song… [tie in Psa. 22-24] …and He has become my salvation. The voice of rejoicing and salvation is in the tabernacles of the righteous… [the meaning of the Feast of Tabernacles] …the right hand of the LORD does mighty things. The right hand of the LORD is exalted; the right hand of the LORD does valiantly. I shall not die, but live and declare the works of the LORD…. [the resurrection] …The LORD has sorely chastened me; but He has not

given me over to death." (vs 14-18)

Now notice v 19, because what happened to Jesus when He ascended back into heaven: *the gates were opened for the King of Glory!* The gates will be opened on the Sea of Glass for us!

Verse 19: "**Open to me the gates of righteousness**; I will go through them, and I will praise the LORD. This is the gate of the LORD; the righteous shall enter through it. I will praise You, **for You have answered me and have become my salvation**" (vs 19-21). *Amazing!*

This is important because these are the events that lead to the Kingdom of God on earth! Now let's come back where we began:

Revelation 3:9: "Behold, I will make those of the synagogue of Satan, who proclaim themselves to be Jews and are not, but do lie. Behold, **I will cause them to come and worship before your feet, and to know that I have loved you**."

This word in the Greek for *loved* is 'agape'! The word *love* that is 'phileo'—*brotherly love*. Here this is a higher class of love.

Verse 10: "Because you have kept the Word of My patience, I also will keep you from the time of temptation, which *is* about to come upon the whole world to try those who dwell on the earth." *We can see the seeds of it already beginning to sprout!*

Verse 11: "Behold, I am coming quickly; hold fast that which you have so that no one may take away your crown." *Hold fast*:

- to the Truth
- to the love
- to the righteousness
- to the dedication
- to everything of God

through His Spirit!

Verse 12: "The one who overcomes… [that will be us if we do] …will I make a pillar in the temple of My God, and he shall not go out anymore; and **I will write upon him the name of My God and the name of the city of My God, the New Jerusalem**, which will come down out of heaven from My God; and *I will write upon him **My new name***."

Let no one steal your crown!

Verse 13: "**The one who has an ear, let him hear what the Spirit says to the churches**."

This the *key of David* and the *heart of David, so that we can be in New Jerusalem with Jesus Christ. Amen!*

Scriptural References:

1) Luke 10:23-24
2) 1 Peter 1:10-16
3) Psalm 84:1-12
4) Psalm 8:1-2, 4-6
5) Psalm 38:1-15, 18-22
6) Psalm 51:1-7, 11-14, 16
7) Psalm 86:1-7
8) 1 John 1:5-10
9) 1 John 2:1-2
10) Psalm 32:1-11
11) Psalm 62:1-12
12) Psalm 16:1-3, 5, 7-11
13) Psalm 17:5-8, 14-15
14) Psalm 40:1-7
15) Daniel 10:21
16) Psalm 40:7-13
17) Psalm 22:1-3, 6-23, 27-31
18) Psalm 23:1-6
19) Psalm 24:7-10
20) Psalm 118:13-21
21) Revelation 3:9-13

Scriptures referenced, not quoted:

- Revelation 3; 11
- Acts 26
- Romans 8
- Hebrews 10
- Isaiah 52
- Matthew 24
- Galatians 3

Also referenced: Book:
From a Speck of Dust to a Son of God: Why Were You Born? by Fred R. Coulter

FRC:bo
Transcribed: 8/5/20
Reformatted: 1/2021

CHAPTER SEVENTY-SIX

The Secret of the LORD!

Fred R. Coulter

Greetings, everyone! Today we are going to learn about the *secret of the Lord*, and how important that is, and our part in it. How is it that we understand the *secret of God*? Let's begin at the beginning.

In the beginning God created Adam and Eve. What God did was enter into a covenant with them, the covenant of the Garden of Eden. God created man and woman to be a in a created, loving relationship. We're going to see that God desires a relationship with us, a very intimate personal relationship. But we also need to understand that every covenant of God is a *created relationship*. In those created relationships there are responsibilities that God has declared that are His, and responsibilities that God has declared that are those who participate in the covenant.

We know that when God called Israel out of Egypt. He created a relationship with them and said, *'I will be your God and you will be My people.'* However, as we have seen, they have never really fulfilled what God intended them to do. We're going to see some very interesting things concerning the secret of God and the will of God.

In addition to what God has said, here's really quite a profound chapter in the book of the Bible—Isa. 48. This tells us many things if we want to know what God has done, if we want to know what God thinks. We need to understand our response to it, as well. Then we need to study the Word of God. As we go through these things, let's remember some basic things. God said that 'man shall not live by bread alone, but by every Word that proceeds out of the mouth of God' (Deut. 8:3). He repeated it during the temptation that Christ had with Satan the devil that 'man shall live by every Word of God.'

God has made His will known according to the bounds of the covenant that He has established. You can go back and go through the covenant with Abraham, Isaac and Jacob, which we won't do at this time, but what we want to do is focus in on the covenant that God gave to Israel and that how hidden within the words of God are *the secrets of God* and *the secrets of His will*—which was not fully revealed until we come to the time of the New Testament, though He has declared these things.

Remember when we first started the Feast in Lev. 23, when I said that God has put all the Holy Days there and that we are to understand them by faith.

In Isa. 48 we find a review of God's created relationship with Israel, and how they never really fulfilled it. Yet, in creating that relationship and giving the Word of God, and then later all the histories of the kings, the prophets and all together God revealed certain aspects of Himself and the relationship that He expected from those who enter into covenant with Him.

Isaiah 48:1: "Hear this, O house of Jacob, who are called by the name of Israel, and have come out of the waters of Judah; who swear by the name of the LORD and make mention of the God of Israel (*but* not in truth nor in righteousness)"

What God is saying here is that *Israel never lived up to the terms of the covenant!* Constant to everything that men do, down to this day and the perversion of the New Testament and Gospel is this: Men want to take the Word of God and add to it or take away from it, or misinterpret it, and this is done very subtly. Then gradually, just like being a degree or two off course, sooner or later you have gone into strange waters and territory that you know nothing about, and God is not with you.

Here's what the children of Israel always do. This applies today to the modern descendants of the 12 tribes of Israel, especially the 10 tribes, and especially those that are descendant of Joseph.

Verse 2: "For they call themselves after the Holy city, and rest themselves on the God of Israel; the LORD of hosts *is* His name. I have foretold the former things from ages ago; and they went out of My mouth; and I proclaimed them; I acted suddenly; and they came to pass…" (vs 2-3).

- Isn't that what God did when He brought the children of Israel out of Egypt? *Yes!*
- Is that not what God did at the time of Jesus' birth? *Yes! Brought it about suddenly!*
- How did Jesus appear to the temple? Just exactly like it says:

Malachi 3:1: "Behold, I will send My messenger, and he will prepare the way before Me.

And the Lord, Whom you seek, shall suddenly come to His Temple…"

That was fulfilled in the Gospel of John, chapter two. Amazing, isn't it? *They came to pass!*

The children of Israel were blinded because they didn't obey, and here is a principle you can just count on absolutely: *If you do not believe and hear and obey, you will be blinded!* In being blinded, you will do things that in your own eyes appear to be right, and something that God ought to accept. That's the whole story of the children of Israel.

Isaiah 48: 4: "Because I knew that you *are* obstinate, and your neck *is* an iron sinew and your brow bronze."

Still today by those who profess to be Christians, those who profess to be God's people, the descendants of the ten tribes of Israel. 'Oh, God is with us.' But you won't listen to His Word.

Verse 5: "And I have even declared *it* to you ages ago. Before it came to pass I revealed it to you; lest you should say, 'My idol has done *these* things, and my graven image, and my molten image, has commanded them.' You have heard, see all this; and will you not declare *it*? I have shown you new things from this time, even hidden things, and you did not know them" (vs 5-6). *A lot of hidden knowledge in things of God!*

Today we're going to see that God has given us the understanding of *His secret, His very plan for the world,* of which keeping the Feast of Tabernacles and understanding the meaning of it is a great part. But the rest of the world does not know. Orthodox Christianity does not know. Not one single religion in the world knows anything about the *secret things of God according to His own will.* We're going to see how that relates to us, and relates to our calling to be kings and priests and to teach the whole world the will of God.

Verse 7: "They are created now, and not ages ago; even before today you did not hear them; lest you should say, 'Behold, I knew them.'"

This is why the Word of God is 'line upon line, precept upon precept, here a little and there a little,' and the Word of God must be properly divided and put together in order to understand the Truth. God does not reveal His Truth—even contained in His Word—

- *unless* you do the things that please God
- *unless* you do as God has commanded
- *unless* you do as Jesus has commanded

Verse 8: "Yea, you did not hear; yea, you did not know; yea, from ages ago your ear was not opened…"

We find in 2-Cor. 3 that the veil is over their eyes when the Law of Moses is read. They can't understand it. That's why they reject and hate the Holy Days of God. Isn't that amazing? *The very thing that would help them understand about God,* they reject, and 'profess' that they know God, just exactly as it's prophesied here in Isa. 48. Think of that!

Here's why, "…for I surely knew that you would deal very treacherously, and were called a transgressor from the womb…. [The 'law of sin and death' within us.] …For My name's sake I will put off My anger, and for My praise I will hold it back for your *sake,* that I do not cut you off" (vs 8-9).

God still loves Israel. God is going to correct them, but God is going to glorify His name! God is going to show His greatness! When the Millennium begins, the re-gathering of Israel is going to take place, and He's going to do a marvelous and wonderful thing. He's going to remove this obstinance that they have and the 'sinew of iron' and give them a 'heart of flesh.' Then they will be able to understand. But the Church is given to understand now, and that is a tremendous thing.

Verse 10: "Behold, I have refined you, but not as silver; I have chosen you in the furnace of affliction. For My own sake, for My own sake I will do it; for why should *My name* be profaned?…. [God is going to change it so it won't be anymore] …And I will not give My glory to another" (vs 10-11).

Let's really understand that, brethren. That's why Jesus said, *'I am the Way, the Truth and the Life.'* There is no other way! That's why Jesus said that He is *'the door of the sheepfold'* and you have to enter in through the door, not climb up some other way.

Verse 12: "Hearken to Me, O Jacob and Israel, My called; I *am* He; I *am* the First, I also *am* the Last. My hand also has laid the foundation of the earth, and My right hand has stretched out the heavens. When I call they stand up together."

The whole universe obeys God! But Israel doesn't! The churches that profess His name do not! *We in the Churches of God need to!*

Verse 14: "Let all of you be gathered together and hear; who among them has declared these *things*? The LORD has loved him…"

Still loved him; O Israel, why will you not hear the Word of God.' And we can say also, 'O Church of God, why will you not hear the Word of God and open your heart and open your mind and serve God in Truth, in love, in grace?'

Verse 15: "I, even I, have spoken; yea, I

have called him… [God has called you! You have answered the call] …I brought him and he makes his way succeed. Come near to Me, hear this: I have not spoken in secret from the beginning….” (vs 15-16). *NO!*

Everything that God wants man to know He spoke publicly, gave it to His servants and they wrote it so that we can have the Word of God. God says:

- you don't have to go to heaven to try and find it
- you don't have to go clear across the sea and try and find it
- you don't have to go to the depths under the sea to try and find it
- it is very near you! In your heart and in your mind

—and that means put in a language that you can understand.

- Isn't that something?
- Why is it that people credit so much to God, but yet, they won't love Him and obey Him?
- Why is it that when they read the Word of God they want to change it and try and improve upon it? *Makes no sense at all!*

You have a:
✓ perfect God
✓ perfect Law
✓ perfect Word
✓ perfect character!

- Can the imperfect character of man, who wants to readjust it and make it better, really do so? *Never can!*

He hasn't spoken in secrets. It's all recorded. That's why when we come to the New Testament it is the preaching of the Gospel of the witness of Jesus Christ, His crucifixion, death and resurrection and His personal intimate loving family relationship that He has created for us through Jesus Christ. That's what God wants. The reason that He has given it to us, and it can be maintained the way God wants:

- through prayer
- through study
- through yielding to God
- through doing His will

Then He's going to perfect His character in us so we can bring it to the world! The *secret things* of God were spoken openly and publicly, but only He can reveal the *secrets contained therein.*

“‘…From the time that it was, there am I.’ And now the Lord GOD, and His Spirit, has sent me. Thus says the LORD, your Redeemer, the Holy One of Israel, ‘I *am* the LORD your God Who teaches you to profit…’” (vs 16-17).

And the only profit is to know—not money, not physical assets, not gold and silver, not power—*but to **know** God!* The only thing that profits is what is done according to the will of God and through the Spirit of God. Only God can make that profit. He says so:

Verse 18: “Oh, that you had hearkened to My commandments! Then your peace would have been like a river… [Psa. 1] …and your righteousness like the waves of the sea.”

- constantly coming
- constantly growing
- constantly renewing

Verse 19: “And your seed would have been like the sand, and the offspring of your bowels like grains of sand; their name would not have been cut off nor destroyed from before Me.”

But that never happened with Israel. He's yet to choose them. He's yet to bring them back. Now He is dealing with His Church.

Psa. 25 is really a tremendous Psalm; it tells us a lot about understanding God, understanding His way, and they had this. Very few were there really ready to yield to God, to do his will. We know that David was. Let's see how David sought God, and let's see how it is that we are to do these things. Notice his attitude. Let's this be part of how we think, of how we come to God, and how God is going to deal with us.

Notice the relationship that David had with God as we can discern it from this Psalm. We always look to God. Remember this: *We are always dependent upon God for everything!*

- everything physical
- everything spiritual

Psalm 25:1: “To You, O LORD, do I lift up my soul. O my God, **I trust in You**…” (vs 1-2). That's what we need to do:

- believe God
- trust God
- love God
- have faith in God

“…do not let me be ashamed, let not my enemies triumph over me.” (v 2). *We're to be overcomers!*

- overcome Satan the devil
- overcome sin
- overcome the self

Yes!

Verse 3: "Yea, let none who wait on You be ashamed; let them be ashamed who deal treacherously without cause."

Notice what David cried out for; and God gives this to us as we grow, change, overcome and constantly seek after it:

"…Show me Your ways, O LORD; teach me Your paths. Lead me in Your Truth and teach me, for You are the God of my salvation; on You do I wait all the day long" (vs 3-5).

This is the attitude that we need to have, brethren, to really grow and fulfill what God has for us, so that we can teach it to the world, to the people.

Verse 10: "All the paths of the LORD are mercy and truth to those who keep His covenant and His testimonies."

Notice the condition there. No one is going to understand the paths of mercy and truth if you don't keep covenant. That applies directly to the New Covenant, which is a created relationship between God the Father, Jesus Christ and each individual believer. Combined together we form the Church. God is the One Who does it; those who don't won't know.

Verse 12: "What man is he who fears the LORD? He shall teach him **in the way that He [God] shall choose.** His soul shall dwell at ease, and his seed shall inherit the earth…. [the Church] (Here's where we want to come): …The **secret of the LORD**…" (vs 12-14). *God's secret plan*:

- to understand God's Word
- to understand His Truth
- to receive His Holy Spirit united with the spirit of your mind
- to be able to have the righteousness of Christ developed within us

this is so great, because it's:

- preparing us to rule the world with Christ
- preparing us to be in the Family of God
- preparing us to help Christ expand the Family of God

beginning with the Millennium!

This is a tremendous thing, v 14: "The secret of the LORD is with those who fear Him, and He will show them His covenant."

That's the New Covenant that we are in now. When we're resurrected, there will be another covenant established—the marriage covenant with the Lord, the covenant of the work that we will be doing and teaching the whole world.

God is a covenant God and all of these things are *created relationships! That's the secret of the Lord!* Your relationship with Him He created in a special and tremendous way so that through the Word of God you can understand the *secret of God.*

Let's see how fantastic this is, brethren. We're going to look at this and analyze these verses in a way so we can understand them and the truth of it. Of course, we are going to see that God has done something according to His will for us: for us *to know,* for us *to understand.*

We then—when we're kings and priests in the Kingdom of God—are going to show the rest of humanity that very thing. We will be elevated to a level of life that is immortal. This is why in the created relationship that we have now with God the Father and Jesus Christ, the covenant sacrifice is the sacrifice of Christ and His shed blood. Our covenant sacrifice is repentance and baptism by full immersion in water, which is symbolic of our death and we are joined to His death. **The created relationship!** God the Father is our Father and gives us of His Holy Spirit. Here's what God wants with all of us and I want you to focus in on the *will of God*:

Ephesians 1:1: "Paul, an apostle of Jesus Christ by [1]*the* **will of God,** to the saints who are in Ephesus and to *the* faithful in Christ Jesus."

That means out beyond the city of Ephesus and to all of those who are in Christ all the way down through time. This has been preserved for us so that we have:

- the words of God
- the knowledge of God
- the will of God
- the Truth of God

Notice what comes to us first. This is what God wants to bring to us:

Verse 2: "Grace and peace *be* to you from God our Father and *the* Lord Jesus Christ"—*directly from God!*

This created relationship is a spiritual relationship that involves the Spirit of God from God the Father and Jesus Christ. We become the begotten children of God.

John expresses it this way, 'Behold, what glorious love that the Father has bestowed upon us that we should be called *the children of God!*' (1-John 3).

Paul writes that 'if we are children then we are *heirs of God, joint heirs with Christ.*' Think of the magnitude of that!

Verse 3: "Blessed *be* the God and Father of our Lord Jesus Christ, Who has blessed us with every spiritual blessing in the heavenly *things* with Christ."

Don't we have a lot of spiritual blessings that have come from heaven?

- the Spirit of God
- the Word of God
- the Truth of God
- understanding His plan

Yes, indeed!

Verse 4: "According as He has personally chosen us for Himself before *the* foundation of *the* world…"

This doesn't mean that He knew us before the foundation of the world, but from the foundation of the world, the very plan of building the world, He had a plan that *those that He would call would be His spiritual children* through Christ. Christ was slain from the foundation of the world.

When you put all of these things together, God has called us and brought us into a tremendous plan that He is fulfilling and working out in our lives, and working out in the lives of all those who have His Spirit; working out everything in the world according to the prophecies that He has given.

"…in order that we might be Holy and blameless before Him in love" (v 4).

It is a loving relationship. *We stand in grace, we walk in faith, we believe in hope, we live in love!* Notice our destiny; this is the secret of the Lord that the world doesn't know,

Verse 5[transcriber's correction]: "…Having predestinated us for sonship to Himself…"—to be His children. That's why we can call Him *Father, Abba,* or *Daddy* (Rom. 8).

A close, personal, created relationship from God the Father, "…through Jesus Christ, #2**according to the good pleasure of His own will**…. [what he is going to do] …To *the* praise of *the* glory of His grace, wherein He has made us objects of *His* grace in the Beloved *Son*" (vs 5-6).

That is so fantastic, brethren. Look down here at us, whatever age you are, whatever difficulties you have in your life, whatever things you need to overcome, *you* are the object of God's love and grace. This is what we're going to bring to people in the world. They then will become the objects of God's love and grace. We were created to be totally dependent upon God in everything.

Verse 7: "In Whom we have redemption through His blood, *even* the remission of sins, according to the riches of His grace." *Think of that!*

Notice what he has done and compare this to what the world knows, all those who think they know everything—the elite of the world who proclaim themselves to be the 'wise ones'—become fools in rejecting God.

Verse 8: "Which He has made to abound toward us in all wisdom and intelligence." *The true education from God—from His Spirit, from His Word!*

Verse 9: "Having made known to us the [secret] mystery of #3**His own will, according to His good pleasure**…" So, we have:

- according to the riches of His grace
- according to His good pleasure

Stop and think about it for a minute! Remember this time, this moment sitting here at the Feast of Tabernacles and going over these words. When you have a trial, a difficulty, something that comes along, remember: *God loves you!* And you, through the love of God and the Truth of God—through Jesus Christ—are going to enter into the Kingdom of God and combined, all of us together, are going to bring the love of God to the world.

"…which He purposed in Himself" (v 9).

Only God could think of a great plan like He has. Look at all the other religions, what do they know? *At best they can be a counterfeit!* But *God has given us the real thing!*

Verse 10: "That in *the Divine* plan for the fulfilling of *the* times, He might bring all things together in Christ, both the things in the heavens and the things upon the earth… [and He's going to do it] …*yes,* in Him, in Whom we also have obtained an inheritance, having been predestinated according to His purpose…" (vs 10-11). *He proposed it before the foundation of the world!*

- He has carried it out
- the call has gone out
- we have answered the call
- God has given us of His Truth and His righteousness

He has shown us:
- His plan
- His secret
- the reason why we're here
- the reason why we keep the Feast of Tabernacles, the Sabbath, the Passover—all the Holy Days of God

because contained therein is the secret of God that He reveals. Notice this:

- according to His purpose
- according the riches of His grace
- according to the good pleasure of His will

—*this is something!* Brethren, do you grasp it? Do I grasp it? Do we all grasp *the greatness of God's plan and His secret* that He has given to us?

"…Who is working out all things according to the counsel of His own will; that we might be to *the* praise of His glory, who first trusted in the Christ: (vs 11-12).

That's something! *To the praise of the glory of God!* That also tells you something very profound. That just as Paul said, God can do exceeding abundantly above all that we ask *or think!* How is that for a God of love, truth and goodness? How do you then compare anything in this world to what God is giving, to the plan of God? *You can't!*

Verse 13: "In Whom you also trusted after hearing the Word of the Truth, the Gospel of your salvation; in Whom also, after believing, you were sealed with the Holy Spirit of promise…. [all of this according to the will of God] …which is *the* earnest of our inheritance…" (vs 13-14).

- the very fact that *you have the Spirit of God* united with the spirit of your mind
- the very fact that *you understand* the Word of God and the Truth of God
- the very fact that *you understand* the things that He has written here
- the very fact that the Holy Spirit of God *leads you* in Truth and righteousness
- the very fact that *God has given you* strength and the power to overcome inwardly

That's the seal of the promise that God will deliver what He has promised! That is something, brethren! That is fantastic!

"…until *the* redemption of the purchased possession… [that we have been bought and paid for by Jesus Christ] …to *the* praise of His glory" (v 14).

There are hardly any other verses in the whole New Testament, even in the whole Bible, that come close to conveying this tremendous relationship that God has given to us! *This is specially created by God*:

- through Jesus Christ
- through the Word of God
- through God working His will in our lives

This is tremendous! Think of the responsibility that God has given to us. That He has revealed to us *according to His own will* **His secret plan!** That is something that we need to really keep in mind!

Now let's look at little bit more at **the will of God** and what this requires of us. We're going to see some very important things.

John 1 is so fantastic and reveals so many things to us. Brethren, I want you to grasp and understand as never before. This is how we're going

to be able to endure the difficult days ahead of us. If things that we see happening in the world are any indication of what's going to go on, we're going to face some very difficult times. This is why we need to have the hope, the inspiration, the grace and the love of God just completely satiating our mind through the Spirit of God. Here is what God has done for us, from God directly to each one of us through Christ:

John 1:9: "The true light was that which enlightens everyone who comes into the world."

Everyone has the spirit of man—Christ gives it. However, look what happened; look what Jesus did:

Verse 10: "He was in the world, and the world came into being through Him, but the world did not know Him."

Exactly what we read in Isa. 48 to begin. God called Jacob, but He just wanted to flatter God and not have true righteousness. Same thing in the world: they want the name of Christ, they preach the name of Christ, but they don't know Him.

Verse 11: "**He came to His own**… [He came to Judea. He came to those of which it was prophesied that He would be of the physical linage and to whom He would come can preach the Gospel] …**and His own did not receive Him**."

- they hated Him
- they judged Him
- they crucified Him

But through the power of the resurrection God overcame all of it, and here is what He has done for us; this is to us:

Verse 12: "But as many as received Him…" *To receive Christ involves everything concerning*:

- repentance
- baptism
- growing in grace and knowledge
- believing His Word
- living by every Word of God
- receive Him as Savior
- receive Him as Redeemer
- receive Him as our High Priest

"…to them He gave authority…" (v 12). *No one else has the authority, because you have to enter into that created relationship through covenant!*

"…to become *the* children of God, *even* to those who believe in His name… [this is a spiritual thing that must take place]: …who were not begotten by bloodlines, nor by *the* will of *the* flesh, nor by *the* will of man, but **by the will of God**" (vs 12-13). *God has done that!*

- What does He expect back from us?
- What are we to do?

Let's see what Jesus says; let's see what we are to do with the will of God; all the will of God in our lives and everything that we do. Here's a very basic Scripture that we've gone over many times:

Matthew 7:21: "Not everyone who says to Me, 'Lord, Lord,'… [there are a lot's that do] …shall enter into the Kingdom of Heaven…"—*what we're striving to do, enter into it through the power of the resurrection*:

- to have immortality
- to have a spirit body
- to have a spirit mind
- to love God
- to see God
- to serve God
- to bring peace to this world

"…but the one who is doing the will of My Father Who *is* in heaven" (v 21).

Think on that! Everything that Jesus did was the will of God. He didn't do it on His own. He didn't come here to preach *His* words.

This becomes important because what are we going to do to serve the people in the Millennium? *We're going to teach them God's ways, God's words!* We are going to open up as God gives us the knowledge. Remember, the knowledge of the Lord is going to cover the earth as the seas cover the earth. What is that going to be like? *That's just on the earth!* What is it going to be like in the spiritual realm, the spiritual plane of the Kingdom of God? *Here we have* **the will of the Father!**

Let's see something very interesting in Luke 6. It's not only the will of the Father that we saw in Eph. 1 and John 1, but come here and let's see what Jesus also said in addition to the will of the Father. It said in Matt. 7 that you 'have to be practicing the will of the Father Who is in heaven.' To practice means that you live by it. Likewise, when we teach people in the Millennium they're going to learn to practice the will of God; they're going to understand the will of God.

Everyone who is a good 'dyed in the wool' Protestant or Catholic or belonging to any other religion—Buddhism, Hinduism, Islam—**all are rejected of God! All are satanic counterfeits of the Truth!** Think on this, here's how you judge these things. Jesus said we have to be practicing the will of the Father Who is in heaven.

Luke 6:46: "And why do you call Me, 'Lord, Lord,' but *you* do not practice what I say?"

All the teachings of Christ. No one is going to receive eternal life without practicing the things that Jesus has said.

Verse 47: "Everyone who comes to Me and hears My words and practices them, I will show you what he is like."

That has to be the way that you live. *God has revealed His secret to us.* So, we have to be practicing all of the Word of God, living by it.

Verse 48: "He is like a man building a house, who dug deep and laid *the* foundation on the Rock [Christ]; and a flood came, and the torrent beat against that house, but could not shake it, because it was founded on the Rock."

Let's just stop and think here for just a minute. How many people did not build their spiritual houses on the Rock of Christ? What's going to happen? Remember this: *there is always a test coming, always a divide coming!* These things are going to happen to test and to prove and to eliminate the dross, and to eliminate all those unprofitable servants, those wicked, evil servants, even within the Churches of God. If you're built on the Rock, you are going to believe:

- through thick and thin
- through every trial
- through every difficulty
- through every blessing
- through every great thing of God

and God will give you understanding of His Word, of His Truth!

Everything that we saw there in Eph. 1 God is going to give, and He is going to give it to us *first,* because we believe in Jesus Christ *now.* Think what it's going to be like when Christ returns. What are we going to bring to those in the world? *The very same thing!*

For us, v 49: "But the one who has heard *My words* and has not practiced *them* is like a man who built a house on *top of* the ground, without a foundation; and *when* the torrent beat against it, it fell at once, and the ruin of that house was great."

We're going to look a little bit more at the *created relationship* that God wants us to have. This is important, *because God has given it to us to save the world!* Think on that for a minute.

The world does not know these things. It cannot know these things. It cannot understand these things. We don't learn them all at once. We learn them by constantly growing in grace and in knowledge.

Even though we've gone over this before, let's go over it again from the point of view that we learn more and more even from the same Scriptures that we know and have studied previously. This is why also in the Word of God we study all the way through the Word of God, we go back over it again when we study it again. BING! We understand more things. God's Spirit gives us understanding. God is working *with us* and revealing *to us **the secret of His own will!***

1-Corinthians 2:9: "But according as it is written, '*The* eye has not seen, nor *the* ear heard, neither have entered into *the* heart of man, *the* things which God has prepared for those who love Him.'"

That's the key, important thing, brethren: *to love God with all our heart, mind, soul, being and everything that is in us,* and *to love our neighbor as ourself,* and *the brethren as Christ has loved us*, and even to love our enemies.

Remember what Jesus said, the very first words when He was crucified, hanging on the cross: *Father, **forgive them, for they do not know what they are doing!*** Likewise, they are blinded in the world. But God reveals to us. There's another principle that we find in Matt. 13—they're blinded, they can't hear, so therefore, He speaks to them in parables. Even that which they have understood will be taken from them. But Jesus said, 'To *you* it has been given to know the mysteries—*the secrets*—of the Kingdom of Heaven.' That has to be revealed by God.

Jesus asked Peter: 'Who do men say that I the Son of man am?' Peter asked all the disciples and they said, 'Well, some say one of the prophets, some say John the Baptist, and some Elijah.' Jesus said to Peter, 'Who do you say that I am?' Peter said, 'You are the Son of the living God.' And Jesus said, 'Blessed are you Simon Bar-Jonah—that means the son of Jonah—because flesh and blood has not revealed this to you **but My Father has revealed it to you**.'

There is an active illustration of how God reveals things to us. Just like as we have been going through in the series, *Grace Upon Grace*, God has given us:

- a greater understanding of grace
- a greater understanding of our relationship with Him
- a greater understanding of His Word

*As **revealed** through His Spirit and through His Word by Jesus Christ and God the Father!* It can't come by intelligence. It can't come by just reading.

Verse 10: "But God has revealed *them* to us by His Spirit, for the Spirit searches all things—even the deep things of God." That agrees with Eph. 1, the deep things of God.

This is wonderful, brethren! This is marvelous! Keeping the Feast of Tabernacles and understanding what God has given us to understand is absolutely glorious and magnificent! This is just only kind of a foretaste of understanding of what it's going to be when the real thing occurs. What a thing it's going to be to the whole world.

Then Paul says, v 11: "For who among men understands the things of man except *by* the spirit of man which *is* in him? In the same way also, the things of God no one understands except *by* the Spirit of God."

Contrasted with the world; we've covered this earlier, but it's good for us to understand this:

Verse 12: "Now, we have not received the spirit of the world, but the Spirit that *is* of God, so that we might know the things graciously given to us by God." What we're understanding here is

- by the graciousness of God'
- by the goodness of God
- by the Spirit of God
- by the love of God

God wants us in this created relationship with Him. Then when we're resurrected and we enter into the covenant with Christ with the marriage, and we enter into covenant of the work that we're going to do under Christ. Then we are going to directly assist God as the sons and daughters of God to bring *every man and woman into this covenant relationship* with God. Isn't that something? Brethren, the whole universe is out there! The whole universe! God's plan is so great and so marvelous and so beyond the comprehension of our mind, that even though we can state certain things that we know and understand is true, that doesn't tell us the *deep things of God!* That doesn't tell us the depth of what God is going to give to us.

Verse 13: "Which things we also speak, not in words taught by human wisdom…"

How can they preach from the Bible and never know the Truth? *That's something!* You talk about the 'blind leading the blind.'

"…but in *words* taught by *the* Holy Spirit *in order to* communicate spiritual things by spiritual *means*" (v 13).

We can only understand this with the Spirit of God. God has to reveal it! God has to teach it! Christ is directly behind it! God the Father is behind it! *He is opening our eyes to see <u>the Truth of the secret of His plan!</u>*

Verse 14: "But *the* natural man does not receive the things of the Spirit of God; for they are foolishness to him, and he cannot understand *them* because they are **spiritually** discerned."

That's why if you say, 'Read the Bible.' *No, I can't understand it.* So you give it to someone who is unlearned and he says, 'I can't understand it either, I'm unlearned.' That is the dividing line. That's the whole Truth concerning grace.

Let's see what Paul writes of this, and let's see where it's going to go, and let's see what it's going to do, and let's see what we are going to do, and how then God, through each one of us individually and the Church collectively—remember, the seven churches (Rev. 2 & 3). It has to be done *spiritually,* and that the eyes of our mind are opened to see, know and comprehend how great a thing this is going to be.

Romans 8:9: "However, you are not in *the* flesh, but in *the* Spirit, if *the* Spirit of God is indeed dwelling within you. But if anyone does not have *the* Spirit of Christ, he does not belong to Him."

They don't receive the Spirit of Christ except legally, lawfully, through the grace of God, through repentance and baptism.

Verse 10: "But if Christ *be* within you, the body *is* indeed dead because of sin; however, the Spirit *is* life because of righteousness. Now, if the Spirit of Him Who raised Jesus from *the* dead is dwelling within you…" (vs 10-11).

We have the Spirit of Christ and the Spirit of the Father—both of Them—dwelling in us (John 14). We are *a temple of God* as Paul defines.

"…He Who raised Christ from *the* dead will also quicken your mortal bodies because of His Spirit that dwells within you. So then, brethren, we are not debtors to the flesh, to live according to *the* flesh; because if you are living according to *the* flesh, **you shall die**; but if by *the* Spirit you are putting to death the deeds of the body, **you shall live**" (vs 11-13).

That's growing in grace and knowledge constantly, day-by-day, week-by-week, month-by-month, year-by-year.

Every time we think it looks like prophecy is going to be fulfilled then something happens so that it gives us understanding. The prophecies of God are going to be fulfilled in such a way that it is going to be to the maximum. When we are looking at things and we see a little bit of it fulfilled, let's not get all excited and try and speed God up and say, 'Oh, prophecy is speeding up.' Remember, prophecy *never* speeds up or slows down, it is always on time—*God's time!* We have a book about that called: *The Appointed Times of Jesus the Messiah.*

Verse 14: "For as many as are led by *the* Spirit of God, these are *the* sons of God. For as many as are led by *the* Spirit of God, these are *the* sons of God. Now, you have not received a spirit of bondage again unto fear, but you have received *the* Spirit of sonship, whereby we call out, 'Abba, Father.' The Spirit itself bears witness conjointly with our own spirit, *testifying* that we are *the* children of God" (vs 14-16).

Notice what that means; it blends into the Millennium and then this blends into the completion of the Millennium and New Jerusalem and the New Heavens and the new earth. The Word of God goes on forever! These things are here. Here's a promise, a blessing:

- don't ever be discouraged
- don't ever get down
- don't ever get depressed

Verse 17: "Now, if *we are* children, *we are* also heirs—truly, heirs of God and joint heirs with Christ…"

- that's why we will be kings and priests
- that's why it is worth it to be in the first resurrection
- that's why God is going to depend upon us to bring His plan of salvation to every man, woman and child beginning with the Millennium

After that is done:

- on into the Great White Throne Judgment
- on into the meaning of the Last Great Day
- on into the opportunity for salvation for all the rest of mankind that have been cutoff before because they didn't respond to God

"…—if indeed we suffer together with Him, so that we may also be glorified together with Him. For I reckon… [this is how we need to think] …that the sufferings of the present time *are* not worthy *to be compared* with the glory **that shall be revealed in us**" (vs 17-18).

Brethren, that is an amazing, awesome thing, just so inspiring and uplifting! Notice what the world is waiting for:

Verse 19: "For the earnest expectation of the creation itself is **awaiting the manifestation of the sons of God**."

They don't know it! They don't realize it! They're out there deceived by Satan the devil, doing his will, his plans, his bidding at the present time, working to bring in Satan's counterfeit millennium, which is the 'beast' of Rev. 13 & 17. Remember, God said He has *revealed His secret to us!* The reason they're waiting for us is:

Verse 20: "Because the creation was subjected to vanity, not willingly, but by reason of Him who **subjected *it* in hope**." *All to prove and to show that we all have come from God!*

Verse 21: "In order that the creation itself might be delivered from **the bondage of corruption**…"

That's why the prophecies talk about the change of the environment, the change of the things in the creation, because the sins of mankind collectively down through time. There have been cycles of it good and bad, blessing and cursing, because it had been subjected to the:

- "…**bondage of corruption**…" (v 21)
- "…**subjected *it* in hope**" (v 20)

Verse 21: "**In order that the creation itself might be delivered from the bondage of corruption into the freedom of the glory of the children of God**"

I hope that through this Feast of Tabernacles that we can all get a spiritual grasp and understanding and vision of what God wants us to do, and how great that this is going to be. It says in the Proverbs that *'without vision the people perish.'* We're talking about *the vision of God,* knowing that God has "…**subjected *it* in hope**." We are part of that hope. He began this with the Church.

Let's see what God is doing in the Church right now. We all have things we need to change and grow and overcome in. We all have things that we need to work on, and the Truth of God that we need to understand even more. Brethren, let's all learn together. There's no such thing as coming to the full knowledge of the Truth in this life. We constantly are growing in it—constantly! I am, and as I do I teach you and you do, and all of together are growing in grace and knowledge. This is the whole purpose of the Church:

Ephesians 2:8: "For by grace you have been saved through faith, and this *especially* is not of your own selves; *it is* the gift of God."

- How could we ever do the things that are prophesied that we're going to do without the Spirit and power of God?
- How could we ever overcome evil human nature and be perfected unless it were by the Spirit of God?

Verse 9: "Not of works, so that no one may boast. For we are His workmanship, created in Christ Jesus unto *the* good works that God ordained beforehand in order that we might walk in them" (vs 9-10). *Are you going to let God*:

- work with you

- mold you
- shape you
- help you
- strengthen you

in everything that you do
- to qualify you
- to bring you to the knowledge of the Truth

as never before. It can happen!

Concerning the Gentiles God did not bring you into Israel. Don't worry, Israel is not the sum total of what God is doing. The sum total of what God is doing is through His Church

Verse 13: "But now in Christ Jesus, you who were once far off are made near by the blood of Christ. For He is our peace, Who has made both one, and has broken down the middle wall of partition" (vs 13-14).

The religion of Judaism and the pagan religions of the Gentiles were those *walls of partition.* How did Christ do it?

Verse 15: "Having annulled in His flesh the enmity, the law of commandments contained in *the* decrees *of men,* so that in Himself He might create both into **one new man**, making peace."

That's how important the Church is, and how the Church needs to function; how we need to work together; how we need to love each other. That helps us to grow in grace and knowledge and overcoming.

Verse 16: "And *that* He might reconcile both to God in one body through the cross, having slain the enmity by it. Now, when He came, He preached the Gospel—peace to you who *were* far off and to those who *were* near. For through Him we both have *direct* access by one Spirit to the Father" (vs 16-18)—*collectively now, the whole Church.*

Remember, God is no respecter of persons. We all are built on the foundation of Christ.

Verse 19: "So then, you are no longer aliens and foreigners; but *you are* fellow citizens with the saints, and *are* of the household of God…. [in His Family] …You are being built up on the foundation of the apostles and prophets, Jesus Christ Himself being *the* chief Cornerstone in Whom all the building, being conjointly fitted together…" (vs 19-21).

We all have a part together; the way God brings us together, brethren. This is why understanding these things and having the love of God is so important.

"…is increasing into a Holy temple in *the* Lord; in Whom you also are being built together for a habitation of God in *the* Spirit" (vs 21-22). ***That is***

accomplished by the grace of God!

Let's see here in Rev. 19 that this proclaims the relationship, proclaims what is going to be done, and it is going to be accomplished while we're on the Sea of Glass in the clouds before we descend to the earth. God has not left the world to anyone. He's going to give to Christ and the saints together. We are going to work together to bring it. After the resurrection takes place and we're on the Sea of Glass, and the marriage of the Lamb takes place, the marriage supper of the Lamb takes place, that is a New Covenant with Christ. This New Covenant with Christ is going to be between us and Christ and God the Father for:

- setting up of the Millennium
- bringing peace to the world
- reconstruction to the world
- the understanding of the Truth of God to everyone
- the changing of human nature from hostility to a heart of flesh

to be able then
- to teach
- to preach
- to guide
- to direct

and all of that under Christ! The greatest time that the world have every seen up to that point.

I would have to say that I imagine the second resurrection is going to be greater than that. Just think of the things that God has called us to do, brethren. Have that vision! Notice, this is just before we come to the earth and then we'll be kings and priests under Christ:

Revelation 19:1: "And after these things I heard *the* loud voice of a great multitude in heaven, saying, 'Hallelujah! The salvation and the glory and the honor and the power *belong* to the Lord our God. For true and righteous *are* His judgments; for He has judged the great whore, who corrupted the earth with her fornication, and He has avenged the blood of His servants at her hand.' And they said a second time, 'Hallelujah! And her smoke shall ascend upward into the ages of eternity'" (vs 1-3).

Even the 24 elders and the 4 living creatures are all subject to God, as well. They are celebrating in this, as well. Brethren, this is going to be the most fantastic thing that is ever going to happen in our lifetimes and after the resurrection.

Verse 4: "And the twenty-four elders and the four living creatures fell down and worshiped God, Who sits on the throne, saying, 'Amen. Hallelujah!'"

Think about this, they have been there over God's throne for eons and eons of the ages of eternity. They have seen how God has unfolded His plan. They didn't understand all things either, but now they're seeing, and seeing what God is doing. They are worshipping and praising God, as well.

Verse 5: "And a voice came forth from the throne, saying, 'Praise our God, all His servants, and all who fear Him, both small and great.'"

What a praise that is going to be! I wonder what that great hymn is going to be that we are going to be singing.

Verse 6: "And I heard a voice like that of a great multitude, and like *the* sound of many waters, and *the* sound of mighty thunderings, saying…"

This is all of the resurrected saints collectively together, standing on the Sea of Glass. We're going to say:

"…'Hallelujah! For *the* Lord God Almighty has reigned…. [that introduces the Kingdom of God on the earth] …Let us be glad and shout with joy; and let us give glory to Him; for the marriage of the Lamb has come…'" (vs 6-7).

Now we come down to the earth, we destroy the armies of the 'beast.' The *false prophet and beast* are cast into the Lake of Fire, and that Lake of Fire is for Satan the devil later on. Then we begin. When we're on the Sea of Glass at the first resurrection.

- we receive our new names
- we receive our assignment
- we receive what we're going to do
- we're there for the marriage supper of the Lamb
- we're there for the giving of the rewards

all of these things! Now, everything is ready to go! God has fully prepared.

Revelation 20:4: "And I saw thrones; and they that sat upon them, and judgment was given to them…

- now we will have the *spirit mind of Christ*
- now we will have *immortal glorious bodies*
- now we will have the *righteousness of God* so we can make the judgments

Remember, we read earlier that we are going to judge angels. Judgment was given to them.

"…and *I saw* the souls of those who had been beheaded for the testimony of Jesus, and for the Word of God, and those who did not worship the beast, or his image, and did not receive the mark in their foreheads or in their hands; and they lived and reigned with Christ a thousand years" (v 4).

Just think what the world is going to be like for the thousand years:

- I wonder what it's going to be like when we get toward the end of the thousand years?
- I wonder how many people will enter into the Kingdom of God during that time?
- I wonder how fantastic the whole earth is going to be with no sin, no deception:

with

- the Spirit of God
- the sons of God
- the love of God
- the faith of God
- all families growing up together
  - ✓ in happiness
  - ✓ in joy
  - ✓ in Truth
  - ✓ in knowledge

That's going to be something!

Verse 5: "(But the rest of the dead did not live again until the thousand years were completed.)...."

There's and interjection right here, because there's more in God's plan to come—which we'll cover on the Last Great Day.

"...This *is* the first resurrection. Blessed and Holy is the one who has part in the first resurrection; over these the second death has no power. But they shall be priests of God and of Christ, and shall reign with Him a thousand years" (vs 5-6). **And then after that into all eternity!** This is:

- the work of God
- the calling of God
- the unfolding
- the unveiling
- the revealing
  - ✓ of the secret of God
  - ✓ of what He is doing

- this is what the world does not know
- this is what the world does not understand

Eph. 1—let's read Paul's prayer, so that we can understand even more. I'm sure that when Paul wrote these words—*though he was in prison, though he was in chains, though he was in fear of his life*—this is one of the most inspiring and glorious books of the New Testament, and we understand it even more today. Here's Paul's prayer, and this prayer is meant for us today, especially for us today, on whom the ends of the earth have come, so that we can understand it:

Ephesians 1:15: "For this cause, I also, after hearing of the faith in the Lord Jesus that is among you, and the love toward all the saints."

What's it going to be when Paul is resurrected and sees all that was done because of his epistles? It's going to be awesome, indeed!

Verse 16: "Do not cease to give thanks for you, making mention of you in my prayers"—*and we do everyday!* We all pray for each other everyday. *We pray for*:

- God's blessing
- God's mercy
- God's forgiveness
- God's healing
- God's love
- God's Truth

Everyday!

Every day it seems as though so great is God's way that in growing and overcoming we really see that without God's direction we don't know which way to go.

Here's what God wants to do, and this is what we're going to help Christ do to the world—every man, woman and child—all during the Millennium.

Verse 17: "That the God of our Lord Jesus Christ, the Father of glory, may give you *the* spirit of wisdom and revelation in *the* knowledge of Him."

This is what we need now! Let the Word of God be able to reveal to us even more and more. Like David said in Psa. 119:18—*open my eyes so that I may see wondrous things from Your Law.* Let it be also that we see and understand wondrous things from the Word of God, the New Testament, the words of Christ, and the inspiring personal letters from God the Father and Jesus Christ through the apostles to us.

Verse 18: *"And* may the eyes of your mind be enlightened in order that you may comprehend what is the **hope of His calling**, and what *is* **the riches of the glory** of His inheritance in the saints, and what is **the exceeding greatness of His power** toward us who believe, according to the inner working of His mighty power" (vs 18-19). *That's what God wants for us!*

Brethren, what a calling! What a fantastic thing! It is so great! It all comes back to Christ:

Verse 20: "Which He wrought in Christ, when He raised Him from *the* dead, and set *Him* at His right hand in the heavenly *places*, far above every principality and authority and power and lordship, and every name that is named—not only in this age, but also in the *age* to come" (vs 20-21). *That means us!*

Verse 22: "For He has subordinated all things under His feet, and has given Him *to be* head over all things to the Church, which is His body—the fullness of Him Who fills all things in all" (vs 22-23).

This is how the Millennium is going to produce great and overwhelming fruit. God has called us to have a fantastic part in that! ***This is the meaning of the Feast of Tabernacles!***

Scriptural References:

1) Isaiah 48:1-3
2) Malachi 3:1
3) Isaiah 48:4-19
4) Psalm 25:1-5, 10, 12-14
5) Ephesians 1:1-14
6) John 1:9-13
7) Matthew 7:21
8) Luke 6:46-49
9) 1-Corinthians 2:9-14
10) Romans 8:9-21
11) Ephesians 2:8-10, 13-22
12) Revelation 19:1-7
13) Revelation 29:4-6
14) Ephesians 1:15-23

Scriptures referenced, not quoted:

- Deuteronomy 8:3
- Leviticus 23
- John 2
- 2 Corinthians 3
- Psalm 1
- 1 John 3
- Romans 8
- Matthew 13
- Revelation 2; 3
- John 14
- Revelation 13; 17
- Psalm 119:18

Also referenced:

- In-Depth Study: *Grace Upon Grace*
- Book: *The Appointed Times of Jesus the Messiah* by Fred R. Coulter

FRC:bo
Transcribed: 8/8/12
Reformatted: 1/2021

CHAPTER SEVENTY-SEVEN

Satan's Final Deception

Fred R. Coulter

Greetings, brethren! Welcome to Day 7 of the Feast of Tabernacles, and as we know, is seven days long (Lev. 23). We know that it pictures the thousand-year rule of Christ and the saints on the earth. Let's see how the beginning and the ending are tied together in working out God's great plan for all of mankind.

It's very interesting, because just as the Feast of Tabernacles has a beginning, it has an ending. Just like all humankind had a beginning, it also has an ending, but that ending doesn't come until the eighth day, which is tomorrow. When we come to Rev. 1 we find this concerning Christ, declaring Who He is and what He's doing.

The important thing in the very first verses of Rev. 1 is this, and many times when we get into a book we forget the very first part of it. However, the first part is really the most important.

Revelation 1:1: *"The* revelation of Jesus Christ, which God gave to Him…" *So, the book of Revelation is* **from God the Father,** *it says so directly here!*

"…to show to His servants…" (v 1). *All of us*; we're all servants of God whether we do things in the ministry or not. We're all servants of God to do His will.

"…the things that *are* ordained to come to pass **shortly**…" (v 1). *A day to God is as a thousand years, and a thousand years is as a day!* So, in the scheme of things in God's plan, it's going to come to pass shortly, everything in the book of Revelation, of course.

"…and He made *it* known, having sent *it* by His angel to His servant John who gave witness *to* the Word of God and the testimony of Jesus Christ, and all the things he saw" (vs 1-2).

Here's a promise, a blessing (v 3). Let's understand that the book of Revelation has some easy to understand parts, but has come very hard to understand parts and difficult to really come to understand. We know, and have found, that the key to understanding is:

- the Sabbath
- the Passover
- the Feasts and Holy Days

of God! They tell us what God is doing!

Verse 3: "**Blessed** *is* **the one who reads, and those who hear the words of this prophecy** and **who keep the things** *that are* **written therein**; for the time *is* at hand."

That time at hand actually began right then! What's the first thing we find in Rev.? *The seven churches, which projects the churches down through the history of time until the return of Jesus Christ!* It begins there.

Verse 4: "John to the seven churches that *are* in Asia: Grace and peace *be* to you from Him Who is, and Who was, and Who *is* to come…" *From Jesus Christ Himself!* From God the Father and Jesus Christ this is the most important message for the end-times.

"…and from the seven spirits that are before His throne; and from Jesus Christ, the faithful Witness, the Firstborn from the dead, and the Ruler of the kings of the earth…. [all kings on earth down through time (book of Daniel)] …To Him Who loved us and washed us from our sins in His own blood" (vs 4-5). *Now it gives the whole purpose*:

- of why we are here
- for all of those who have been called to the Church
- of our conversion
- of everything that we do

The ultimate result we find right here; v 6: "And **has made us kings and priests to God and His Father**…"

We also know from what are in other places that there what we call governors, administrators for the those of the resurrected saints to serve in the Kingdom of God to serve humanity for a thousand years, as depicted by the Feast of Tabernacles.

"…to Him *be* the glory and the sovereignty into the ages of eternity. Amen" (v 6).

This is interesting because many times a prophecy is given as something that has been completed. This is what you call a *future perfect.* We're not yet kings and priests, *but we will be!*

Verse 7: "Behold, He is coming with the clouds, and every eye shall see Him, and those who pierced Him; and all the tribes of the earth shall wail because of Him. Even so, Amen."

God wants us to know, just like He has told us that He has had the plan of the Gospel *before the ages of time!* This also fits in with that as well:

Verse 8: "'I am the Alpha and the Omega, *the* Beginning and *the* Ending,' says the Lord, 'Who is, and Who was, and Who *is* to come—the Almighty.'"

This is important for us to understand: *God is the One Who is going to work everything out, according to His will!* However, all of us have free moral agency and free choice as we have already covered. Likewise, during the Millennium they will have free moral agency. God is never, never, never going to take it away.

Verse 11: "Saying, 'I am the Alpha and the Omega, the First and the Last, and what you see… [then the first thing he says to John is]: …**write in a book**…'"

Everything that God wants us to know in this age and of the coming age in the future, *He has it written down!* That way we can learn it!

- We've already started at the beginning and where does the beginning go? *Clear back to Genesis!*
- Where does the ending come? *Clear to the end of this age of the earth and human beings!*

That's an amazing thing to understand, and brethren, **God has given us that understanding!**

Rev. 20 is toward the ending; not quite there, yet, but we're getting close. We know that *the first thing that was done to save the world*—and this is a very important thing that we learn on the Day of Atonement—*that as long as Satan the devil is around there will always be sin!*

Even during the Millennium, because of human nature, there will be sin, but not as grievous as it was under Satan the devil. Satan is the one who causes war after war and hatred and viciousness and all of that sort of thing. Well, after the Millennium there will be human sin, but it's not going to be to the degree that we have in the world today. So, Satan was bound and cast into the abyss.

Revelation 20:3: "Then he cast him into the abyss, and locked him *up,* and sealed *the abyss* over him, so that he would not deceive the nations any longer **until the thousand years were fulfilled**…" *That's what this day pictures*: the thousand years coming to an end! So, there is a beginning and an ending with the Feast of Tabernacles and a thousand years.

Verse 4: "And I saw thrones; and they that sat upon them, and judgment was given to them; and *I saw* the souls of those who had been beheaded for the testimony of Jesus, and for the Word of God, and those who did not worship the beast or his image, and did not receive the mark in their foreheads or in their hands; and they lived and reigned with Christ a thousand years."

So, the first resurrection happens, everything takes place on the Sea of Glass in heaven above necessary for us to take over the rulership of the world. We come down to the earth with Christ and Christ sets up the whole Government of God. But Satan has to be removed *first!*

Remember that at the end of the Millennium there is going to be an event that takes place that is going to be quite fantastic, indeed! *We'll see that later on!* Here's a clue as to what tomorrow is all about, because the eighth day is tied to the seventh day! Whenever there's an ending, there's a new beginning.

Verse 5: "(But the rest of the dead did not live again until the thousand years were completed.).…" *We will go through that tomorrow (Last Great Day).*

"…This *is* the first resurrection.… [this is what we're shooting for, right here]: …Blessed and Holy is the one who has part in the first resurrection; **over these the second death has no power**.… [we'll analyze that more tomorrow] …But they shall be priests of God and of Christ, and shall reign with Him a thousand years. Now, when the thousand years have been completed… [there it is again] …Satan shall be loosed out of his prison" (vs 5-7).

We will come back to that later and see why he is loosed out of his prison! Let's just go back and review some of the things that takes place when the Millennium begins and during the Millennium. We also find in the Old Testament, and somewhat in the New Testament, but in the O.T. a little bit more, this phrase: *and it shall be in the last days! The last days* phrase is used over and over again.

Micah 4:1: "But it shall be in the last days *that* the **mountain** of the house of the LORD shall be established…" *Mountain* means *the Government of God!* That authority will be the *highest!*

"…in the top of the mountains… [higher than all the rest of the nations] …and it shall be exalted above the hills; and people shall flow unto it" (v 1). *It's going to be a constant*:

- people coming/saints coming
- people going/saints going

And the big tabernacle that will be there with fire by night and cloud by day that covers over all of Jerusalem and the Mt. of Olives; *that is going to be quite a thing!* Why are they coming up? *It tells us:*

Verse 2: "And many nations shall come and say, **'Come and let us go up to the mountain of the LORD, and to the house of the God of Jacob. And He will teach us of His ways, and we will walk in His paths'**…"

That's what we're going to be: teachers, priests, kings! We're going to teach! They're going to come and say, 'Lord, what should I do?' *He's going to say*: '

Here's what you're going to do; here are the rulers that are going to be over you from now on.

Everything works out together. However, some will not want to do that, which we will see in just a minute.

The reason that they walk in God's way or path, is: "…for the Law shall go forth out of Zion, and the Word of the LORD from Jerusalem. And He shall judge among many people, and will rebuke strong nations afar off…" (vs 2-3).

We know that the two chapters in Ezek. 38-39 are the conquering of God over Gog and Magog and Prince Tubal and Meshach and all of those nations that are in the north and clear to the east, all the way to China. They are not going to want to come willfully or willingly to Jerusalem. There will have to be after the first seven years of the Millennium—Ezek. 38—that they will come and want to attack all the children of Israel now in the land that God has restored them in. But God is going to destroy them with a blitzkrieg from above. It says over and over again, when God has done this then all the nations shall know that God *is God!* So, part of that is rebuking the nations that are far off. Here's what's going to happen.

"…and they shall beat their swords into plowshares…" (v 3). Think about *how much money, energy and everything that goes into war and protection!* Think about that!

In the Millennium when everything is setup, there will be tithes and offerings that will be required. No money will be necessary to support an army. Here in America that would save about three-quarters of a trillion dollars a year. *Think about what could be done with money like that in various communities!*

That's just a year! Furthermore, it won't be necessary to have a police force like we have today, because the people will be keeping the laws and commandments of God, and we will make sure that they will do so, which means they will be keeping the Ten Commandments.

All during the Millennium they will be worshipping the true God, there will be no idols, no taking of the name of God in vain and the Sabbath is

going to be the focal point of everything along with the Passover and Holy Days.

Think of all the money that will be saved, because there won't be need of a police force or prisons. That's going to be quite a world, indeed! Actually, when you get down to it, that's what every human being actually longs for. But with the human nature that we have and Satan ruling the world today, it's not possible to have it come to pass.

"…and their spears into pruning hooks. Nation shall not lift up a sword against nation, neither shall they learn war anymore" (v 3). *No more learning of war!*

When you watch anything to do with the history of mankind, it's nothing but war after war after war; fight after fight after fight! *All that is going to be eliminated!*

Verse 4: "But they shall sit each one under his *own* vine and under his *own* fig tree; and no one shall make them afraid; for the mouth of the LORD of hosts has spoken, for all people **will walk, *each one in the name of his god*…** [referring to us, because we will be the sons and daughters of God] …and **we will walk in the name of the LORD our God forever and ever**" (vs 4-5)—*both combined together!*

Let's see how great that this is going to be; we need to understand that. Never before in the history of the world had it been done. There was only one time in the whole history of the world when there was a bit of peace akin to what it will be in the Millennium. It didn't last very long, because Solomon and the people sinned! There's never really been any real peace on this earth, *and won't be until Christ returns and the saints are resurrected!*

Here's what's going to happen to Israel and every nation that comes under the jurisdiction, which they all will, whether willingly or not. Remember that Zech. 14 says that if they don't keep the Feast of Tabernacles, if they live in Egypt where they don't have rain, then there's going to be the plague. Well, that will have to happen only once or twice and they'll get the point. In other areas where they need rain, if they don't come and keep the Feast of Tabernacles, it's not going to rain.

Isaiah 58:8: "Then shall your light break out as the dawn, and your health shall spring out quickly…"

Another factor during the Millennium, we won't need all the medical things that we have today. Won't that be good? Look at how much money people spend on all the medicines, surgeries, medical procedures and so forth. All the hospitals costs a lot to operate, and all the research centers. *All of that is the penalty for leaving God,* beginning *with the Garden of Eden!*

"...and your righteousness shall go before you; the glory of the LORD shall be your rear guard" (v 8)—*because all of us as sons and daughters of God are going to leading the way in getting this done!* We're all going to be following Jesus Christ and God the Father.

Verse 9: "Then you shall call, and the LORD shall answer; you shall cry, and He shall say, 'Here I *am*.'.... [that will be through us] ...**If**... [there are conditions; you have to change your behavior] ...you take the yoke away from among you, the pointing of the finger, and speaking malice; and *if* you draw out your soul to the hungry, and satisfy the afflicted soul..." (vs 9-10).

Of course, right at first it will be that way, but later on it won't be.

"...then shall your light rise in darkness, and your gloom *shall be* as the noonday. And the LORD shall always guide you and satisfy your soul in dry places, and make your bones fat..." (vs 10-11).

That doesn't mean that they're going to actually be fat, but it means that the morrow, which is fat; of the bones, which is blood, and the life is in the blood physically, and is going to always be healthy. Sickness will be a very rare thing!

"...and you shall be like a watered garden, and like a spring of water whose waters fail not. And *those who* come of **you shall build the old ruins**..." (vs 11-12).

We are going to have building and construction boom that will be unmatched in the history of the whole world!

"...you shall raise up the foundations of many generations; and you shall be called: **The Repairer of the Breach**... [the sin of Adam and Eve] ...**The Restorer of Paths to Dwell** in" (v 12)—*the Word of God!*

We can be sure that it's going to be expanded during the Millennium, without a doubt! Then it talks about the Sabbath right after that. This shows the importance of the Sabbath. What is that going to do for the people?

Verse 13: "**If**..."—*still conditional!*

- *IF* you will love God
- *IF* you will choose His ways
- *IF* you will do what is right
- *Then* this will happen and that will happen

"...you turn your foot away from the Sabbath, *from* doing your own desires on My Holy Day, and call the Sabbath a delight, the Holy of the LORD, honorable; and shall honor Him, not doing your own

ways, nor pursuing your own desires, nor speaking *your own* words, **then**... [of course, we're going to make sure that they will be doing it] ...**you shall delight yourself in the LORD**..." (vs 13-14).

Very few people today delight themselves in God! Yes, we in the Church of God know how to do that and delight ourselves in God and all that He does. Knowing that in Him we live, move and have our being, and everything about us and everything that God wants us to do.

"...and I will cause you to ride upon the high places of the earth, and feed you with the inheritance of Jacob your father, **for the mouth of the LORD has spoken it**" (v 14)—*meaning that it's as good as done even before it has even started!*

Isn't it interesting how many of these prophecies of the Millennium are in the Old Testament? Why is that? *Because this deals with the physical aspect of human life!* Whereas, the New Testament deals with the spiritual aspect of physical life when you belong to God now, and what the future will be at the resurrection.

Even though we have all of this, think about all the things that are going to take place and how great it's going to be.

Jeremiah 30:8: "'For it shall be in that day,' says the LORD of hosts, 'I will break his yoke from your neck and will burst your bonds. And strangers shall no longer enslave him.'"

That's talking about Jacob and how God is going to lift all of those things that have burdened them down!

Verse 9: "But they shall serve the LORD their God... [not the governments on the earth] ...and David their king, whom I will raise up to them"—*showing the resurrection of David to be king over all Israel! Then each one of the 12 apostles as judges over the 12 tribes!*

Verse 10: "'And you, O My servant Jacob, do not fear,' says the LORD. 'Do not be terrified, O Israel. For lo, I will save you from afar, and your seed from the land of their captivity. And Jacob shall return, and shall be at rest...'" *That's what the Feast of Tabernacles pictures, the* ***rest*** *of God!* And it shall be glorious, as He says.

"'...and be quiet, and none shall make *him* afraid. For I *am* with you,' says the LORD, 'to save you. Though I make a full end of all nations where I have scattered you, yet, I will not make a full end of you; but I will correct you in measure, and will not utterly destroy you.' For thus says the LORD, 'Your bruise is incurable, and your wound *is* grievous'" (vs 10-12). *In other words, if they don't come to God, there's no help from it!*

Jeremiah 32:38: "And they shall be My people, and I will be their God. And I will give them one heart and one way…" (vs 38-39).

As we saw earlier, God is going to give them a heart of flesh, rather than a carnal heart of disobedience.

"…that they may fear Me forever, for their good and for the good of their children after them. And I will make an everlasting covenant with them that I will not turn away from them, *rather,* to do them good. But I will put My fear in their hearts, that they shall not depart from Me. Yea, I will rejoice over them to do them good…" (vs 39-41).

This is what God wants, but the truth of the matter is it can't be this way until we are resurrected from the dead or changed at the return of Christ. We learn what we need to learn to come and rule the people and teach them. We're not going to rule over them harshly; we'll have whatever power we need as necessary, but we will help them and love them and turn them to God.

"…and I will truly plant them in this land with all My heart and all My whole soul.' For thus says the LORD, 'As I have brought all this great evil on this people… [it's going to be good] …**so I will bring on them all the good that I have promised them**" (vs 41-42).

Jeremiah 33:6: "Behold, I will bring it health and healing, and I will heal them and will show them **the riches of peace and Truth**."

The fact is that if you don't have peace and Truth with God, whatever riches you have are not going to do you that much good.

Verse 7: "And I will cause the *return from* captivity of Judah and the *return from* captivity of Israel, and will build them, as at the first. And I will cleanse them from all their iniquity by which they have sinned against Me; and I will pardon all their iniquities by which they have sinned, and by which they have transgressed against Me. And it shall be for Me a name of joy, a praise and an honor before all the nations of the earth…" (vs 7-9).

Here's how they're going to come and say, 'Whoa! Let's go up to the house of the Lord in Jerusalem and let's learn of His ways. We'll understand it.'

"…which shall hear of all the good that I do to them. And they shall fear and tremble for all the goodness and for all the peace that I bring to it" (v 9). *Quite a thing! That's magnificent,* isn't it?

We need to review Isa. 65 and understand how life is going to operate during the Millennium. This applies to the Millennium and also apply to the Last Great Day and what we know as the *second*

resurrection!

Isaiah 65:17: "For behold, I create new heavens and a new earth…." *Think of how everything is going to be all messed up with the return of Christ and all the fighting of the nations!*

"…And the former things will not be remembered, nor come to mind. But be glad and rejoice forever *in that* which I create; for behold, I create Jerusalem a rejoicing, and her people a joy. I will rejoice in Jerusalem, and I will joy in My people…" (vs 17-19).

Think about this: **Those who live in Jerusalem will all be the sons and daughters of God!** There won't be fleshly people living in Jerusalem. That's the headquarters of God, and everything for the whole world is going out from there.

Verse 20: "There will not be an infant who lives but a few days… [no premature deaths] …nor an old man that has not filled his days…"

Now here is where we get that during the Millennium they're going to live for 100 years; the infant for fullness of days, the adult for fullness of days, but notice the sinner, because there will still be sinners.

Why? *Because God is not going to remove independent free moral agency!* He doesn't want robots. He wants those who love Him with all their heart, mind, soul and being. He wants those who are going to keep His commandments and do what is right. But if they refuse, then they're going to have to either repent or be removed. We're going to see something that at the end of the Millennium it's going to be quite a thing *about those who do not* accept God's way!

"…**but the sinner *who is* a hundred years old shall be accursed**" (v 20)—*meaning you have had your chance and did not take advantage of it!* You decided to go your way, to live in your sins, *and now*—since you haven't repented—*you are removed!*

- just like God did with Cain after he killed Abel
- just like God did with the children of Israel when they sinned

That's going to happen! I also think that the first removal will be to a Repentance Center where

- they can be helped
- they can study the Word of God
- they can have time for fasting and prayer
- they can decide what they want to do

IF they really repent they can return back to the community!

But *the one who is accursed is the one who did not repent!* They will be **exiled to Gog and Magog** and there is where they will die, all those during the Millennium who refuse!

But at the end of the Millennium there's the 100-year period for them to die. So, God is going to have to take care of it a little differently, as we will see.

Let's understand more about the last day of the Feast of Tabernacles, and how wonderful that the Millennium is going to be, and how God is going to handle it. Eternal life, as best as we can understand it from the Bible, is going to be so supremely greater than human life. We must learn—*all of us who enter into the Kingdom of God*—the righteousness of God, the love of God, and why it's so important to have:

- no sin
- no rebellion
- no self-serving

That's what has destroyed the universe, as it were, with Satan and the angels that rebelled!

God is going to solve all of those things, but with people we have to live this life in the flesh. We have to show with the Spirit of God, the Truth of God and loving and serving Him *that we will:*

- always be faithful
- always be loving

and when we make mistakes

- always repent

Some mistakes, as we have seen like with King David, can be very grievous. But God forgave him! When we were born into the Kingdom of God, all of these things of the flesh will be left behind.

During the Millennium when those who prove this and they come to the end of the 100-years, they will be changed from flesh to spirit. That change will represent an instantaneous death and resurrection. Why? *Because it's given to all once to die!* As in Adam we all die, and that's because we all—and that will carry over into the Millennium as well—have 'the law of sin and death' in us. When the Millennium starts, God is going to take away the part of the harshness of human nature so that it is not quite as evil as it is today.

But without Satan around it will be easier to recognize and easier to correct. That's what will happen during the Millennium.

As we have seen, if you live a hundred years and you've been righteous, there's no need for you to die and go in a grave.

- When would you be resurrected?
- A week later?

- Five years later?

No! It won't be necessary! Let's just review that again so that we understand for those who are righteous during the Millennium there is no need for them to be buried—to die and be buried—because they will be changed:

1-Thessalonians 4:15: "For this we say to you by *the* Word of *the* Lord, that we who are alive and remain unto the coming of the Lord shall in no wise precede those who have fallen asleep, because the Lord Himself shall descend from heaven with *a* shout of command, with *the* voice of an archangel and with *the* trumpet of God; and **the dead in Christ shall rise first**; **then** **we who are alive and remain shall be caught up together with them in *the* clouds** for *the* meeting with the Lord in *the* air; and so shall we always be with *the* Lord" (vs 15-17).

This has got to show that for them to be changed, caught up, it has to be an instantaneous dead and resurrection. Therefore, that has to be the way that God will do it during the Millennium.

I do believe that wherever there is a congregation—and lo, there will be millions of them—when it comes time for a person who is successfully attained to 100-years and is righteous, who has been in the grace and love of God, that there is no reason for them to die and be buried. But when they're changed it will be an instantaneous death and transformation.

1-Corinthians 15:44: "It is sown a natural body… [that's what it is today, and when you die it's put in the ground] …**it is raised a spiritual body**…. [we can understand that] …There is a natural body, and there is a spiritual body; accordingly, it is written, 'The first man, Adam, became a living soul; the last Adam *became* an ever-living Spirit.' However, the spiritual *was* not first, but the natural—then the spiritual. The first man *is* of the earth—made of dust. The second Man *is* the Lord from heaven. As *is* the one made of dust, so also *are all* those who are made of dust… [all human beings] …and as *is* the heavenly *One*, so also *are all* those who are heavenly" (vs 44-48). *That's going to be the difference in transformation!*

Here we are, we have a body of flesh; v 49: "And as we have borne the image of the *one* made of dust…"

All made in Adam, fleshly beings. This, in fact, is also a guarantee that you will be in the resurrection and have a spiritual body **IF** *you're faithful!* The fact that you have a physical body is a precursor of a spiritual body.

"…we shall also bear the image of the heavenly *One*. Now this I say, brethren, that flesh and blood cannot inherit *the* Kingdom of God…" (vs

49-50)—*the spiritual Kingdom!*

But when the Kingdom of God comes to the earth and there are physical human beings on the earth, they will be *under the jurisdiction of the Kingdom of God,* because they cannot come into the Kingdom of God unless they are spirit beings.

"…nor does corruption inherit incorruption. Behold, I show you a mystery… [How is God going to do this? *We don't know, it's a mystery!*] …we shall not all fall asleep… [tie in 1-Thess. 4] …but we shall all be changed, in an instant, in *the twinkling of an eye,* at the last trumpet; for *the* trumpet shall sound, and the dead shall be raised incorruptible, and we shall be changed" (vs 50-52).

Then, as we saw in 1-Thess. 4, those who are alive will be caught up in the air, obviously changed! So, during the Millennium that's how it's going to be. But what about those who must be exiled? Let's look at that again, because that becomes very important.

Revelation 20:3: "Then he cast him [Satan] into the abyss, and locked him *up,* and sealed *the abyss* over him, so that he would not deceive the nations any longer until the thousand years were fulfilled; **and after that it is ordained that he be loosed** *for* **a short time**." *We don't know how long* **a** *short time is!*

Verse 7: "Now, when the thousand years have been completed… [that's what is pictured by this seventh day] …Satan shall be loosed out of his prison."

Why is God going to do this? *Let's see what happens and then we can answer the question!*

Verse 8: "And he shall go out to deceive the nations that *are* in the four corners of the earth, Gog and Magog…"

We've already covered this: Gog and Magog are going to attack against the children of Israel in the seventh year after they have come into the Millennium. They're going to come against the cities, because they're not defended, and there's going to be this last great battle where Gog and Magog are going to be destroyed and all those with them.

Then it says that *'the nations shall know that I am the Lord God!'* This is going to be the final battle to secure all nations under the jurisdiction of God as the Millennium begins. That's what it says; that He's going to rebuke strong nations afar off.

Since even Gog and Magog are going to know the Lord, this reference to Gog and Magog does not refer to the people.

- How do we know?
- Are Gog and Magog the only ones who are going to sin during the Millennium? *No!*

There will be sinners out of all nations! So, this had to be referring to the geographical territory—or part of the geographical territory—of Gog and Magog.

This has to be the final place of exile! So, in the last generation there are going to be a lot of people ending up over there in Gog and Magog in the land of exile, because they don't want to do God's way. That's why Satan is loosed!

This will tell us what's going to happen. Here are all of those in Gog and Magog who have been exiled, still alive as physical human beings. Satan is loosed out of his prison and he goes there and says, 'I am God,' and the people will believe that deception. Satan will probably say:

This God down in Jerusalem… And by the way, they don't have any defenses, so what we're going to do, we're all going to prepare for war. So, let us makes some weapons, whatever we can do, because if we come down there and conquer Jerusalem and take over Jerusalem *we will rule the world!*

Hasn't that always been Satan's desire? *Yes!*

Verse 8: "And he shall go out to deceive the nations that *are* in the four corners of the earth… [I just described that deception] …Gog and Magog… [the geographical territory] …of whom the number *is* **as the sand of the sea**…"—*a great number of people!*

This show that free moral agency is always active and we must:

- by free choice
- by free will
- by devotion
- through repentance *accept:*
  - ✓ God
  - ✓ His way
  - ✓ His Truth
  - ✓ His Laws
  - ✓ His commandments
  - ✓ everything about God

"…to gather them together for war" (v 8).

So, the first thing that Satan does again is instigate war, **to takeover from God, to try and overthrow God!** This is his last chance to do it. Of course, you know that the demons are all there with him, too, because they were all cast into the abyss. Wherever Satan is, the demons will be, also.

When they come out and show all of their false miracle and tell these people in Gog and Magog:

Look, we're going to do this! This is going to be easy to do. Think about it; they're all gentle, *gentle, **gentle*** and they have no defense; they don't know how to fight. But we'll learn all of that right now and we will go in a mammoth army and we will takeover Jerusalem.

Quite a spectacular deception!

Verse 9: "Then *I saw* them go up upon the breadth of the earth and encircle the camp of the saints…"

Remember, there's that great pillar, that great tabernacle with the pillar of light and so forth.

"…and the beloved city…" (v 9). *God let's them get right up close to it* and it looks like they could just run and take it, **but God has other plans!**

"…and fire came down from God out of heaven and consumed them" (v 9). What is this? *For all of those out there in Gog and Magog, they did not have a chance to die accursed and be buried!* So, they have to all die once, and they're going to die again at the second resurrection.

This is a way of getting rid of all those who committed the unpardonable sin toward the end of the Millennium, and Satan brings them for war against the Holy City, **and God destroys them all!**

Verse 10: "And the Devil, who deceived them, was cast into the Lake of Fire and brimstone, where the beast and the false prophet **had been cast**…"—because right at the beginning of the Millennium we find this:

Revelation 19:19: "And I saw the beast and the kings of the earth and their armies, gathered together to make war with Him Who sits on the horse, and with His army." *Satan is always war, war, **war**; that's all he knows!*

Verse 20: "And the beast was taken, and with him the false prophet who worked miracles in his presence, by which he had deceived those who received the mark of the beast and those who worshiped his image. Those two were cast alive into the Lake of Fire, which burns with brimstone."

What happens when human beings are cast into a Lake of Fire? *They burn up!* That's why in Revelation 20:10 it is translated "…*had been cast*…" there is no such thing as flesh living in and ever-burning fire. It's doesn't happen.

Revelation 19:20: "…and they, **Satan and the demons,** shall be tormented day and night into the ages of eternity"

What is Satan's fate? *Jude talks about those who have committed the unpardonable sin!* It talks about the demons and Satan the devil who caused

them to do it.

Jude 6: "And the angels who did not keep their own original domain… [Where was that? On the earth? Everything indicates that they were on the earth!] …but deserted their habitation, **He is holding in eternal bonds** under darkness unto the judgment of *the* Great Day." *A prison!* Rev. 20 calls it *the abyss! **All referring to where the rebellious angels are kept!***

1-Peter 3:18: "Because Christ indeed once suffered for sins, *the* Just for *the* unjust, so that He might bring us to God; on the one hand, He was put to death in *the* flesh; but on the other hand, He was made alive by the Spirit… [that's what we are to follow] …by which… [the Spirit when He was a spirit being before He became a man] …He also went and preached to the spirits in prison, *which* disobeyed in a past time when once the longsuffering of God was waiting in *the* days of Noah, *while the* ark was being prepared…" (vs 18-20).

At that time that's when He went to the angels to warn them, to preach against them, that all that they did before the Flood was coming to an end! *Now it's going to all be coming to an end again!*

They left their first estate and here's what they do: when they're out of the prison they cause people to sin. Satan is the author of sin and his rebellion is the original sin. The original human sin was with Adam and Eve. But who led them into sin? *Satan!*

Jude 7: "Just as Sodom and Gomorrah—and the cities surrounding them, in the same manner as them—having given themselves over to sexual debaucheries, and having gone after different flesh, are themselves exhibited as a *perpetual* example of undergoing *the* punishment of eternal fire."

That doesn't mean that they're being punished eternally. That means the fire comes from the Eternal God, so it's eternal fire **vs** fire that men would make.

Verse 8: "In the same way also, these dreamers *of filthy dreams* are defiling *the* flesh, and are declaring as invalid *the* Lordship *of God,* and are blaspheming *the* Divine powers."

Isn't that exactly what always happens? They defame God! Think about what it's going to be when Satan is loosed on the number of the sand of the sea and says 'Let's get together for a war!' *Same thing!*

He's going to be blaspheming God in all the saints and Jesus Christ down in Jerusalem. Notice part of the battle that took place:

Verse 9: "But Michael the archangel, when

he was personally taking issue with the devil, disputing about the body of Moses."

What would Satan have done if he could have gotten the body of Moses and put it in a glass tomb so you could look into it, and filled it with honey so that his body would never decompose? Then build a giant temple and cathedral and have Moses there as their relic! That's what Satan was wanting!

[Michael] "…did not presume to pronounce a reviling judgment against *him*, but said, '*The* Lord Himself rebuke you!' As for these, whatever things they do not understand, they blaspheme; but whatever things they understand by instinct, as irrational brute beasts, they are corrupting themselves in these things. **Woe to them!**…." (vs 9-11).

I'm going through this because we're going to see that all of this has to do with the rebellion of the angels and Satan, and causing mankind—in the guise of these instances—to sin.

Verse 11: "**Woe to them! For they have walked in the way of Cain**…" **What happened to Cain?** *He was exiled! Premiere sinner!*

"…and for gain, they have wholly given themselves up to Balaam's delusion, and have perished in the rebellion of Korah. These are subversive stains in your love feasts…" (vs 11-12).

We've had those come into the Church of God and actually take it down. There were those that went on television and bragged how they took down the Worldwide Church of God. They knew what they were doing, and that it was deliberate!

Verse 12: "These are subversive stains in your love feasts, feasting in person together *with you*; fearlessly they are feeding themselves. *They are* clouds without water… [these are empty human beings] …being driven by the winds… [whichever way Satan causes the wind to blow] …trees of late autumn, without *any* fruit, uprooted, **twice dead**." *In other words,* **they will suffer the second death!**

Verse 13: "Raging waves of *the* sea, casting up like foam their own *ignominious* shame; **wandering stars**…"—*defining all of the rebellious angels!* Since they are spirit beings they have to be put someplace. Let's see about that!

"…for whom has been reserved **the blackest darkness forever!**" (v 13).

That's where they are going to go! Their fate and that of Satan the devil is set right after the Millennium, and right after that final battle. What Jude was writing about there was to show that all of these things emanated from the rebellious angels

who caused all of this sin and all the wretchedness of all of mankind. That's what it's showing!

All those who came down as human beings, who were sent off into exile were burned up, all ashes—nothing left of them—they still have to face the second death, because that was their first death.

Revelation 20:10: "And the Devil, who deceived them, was cast into the Lake of Fire and brimstone…"

That's where his punishment starts; after that it is to *the blackest darkness forever!* Is that some giant black hole out in the universe, where once they are in there they can never escape? *Probably so!*

"…where the beast and the false prophet *had been cast*; and they, *Satan and the demons,* shall be tormented day and night into the ages of eternity" (v 10).

Don't you think that the blackest darkness forever is the fit punishment for them? *Yes, indeed!* Then comes the activities after the seventh day.

Let's have an introduction to it, v 11[transcriber's correction]: "Then I saw a great white throne and the One Who was sitting on it, from Whose face the earth and the heaven fled away; and no place was found for them. And I saw the dead, small and great, standing before God…" (vs 11-12). *This is the second resurrection!*

Tomorrow we are going to see the meaning of that day, and *how that is one of the greatest and most fantastic days in the history of all mankind!*

Scriptural References:
1) Revelation 1:1-8, 11
2) Revelation 20:3-7
3) Micah 4:1-5
4) Isaiah 58:8-14
5) Jeremiah 30:8-12
6) Jeremiah 32:38-42
7) Jeremiah 33:6-9
8) Isaiah 65:17-20
9) 1 Thessalonians 4:15-17
10) 1 Corinthians 15:44-52
11) Revelation 20:3, 7-10
12) Revelation 19:19-20
13) Revelation 20:10
14) Jude 6
15) 1 Peter 3:18-20
16) Jude 7-13
17) Revelation 20:10-12

Scriptures referenced, not quoted:

• Leviticus 23
• Ezekiel 38; 39

- Zechariah 14

FRC:bo
Transcribed: 8/10/20
Reformatted: 1/2021

CHAPTER SEVENTY-EIGHT

The Final Judgment of Satan the Devil
Fred R. Coulter

Greetings, brethren! Welcome to the seventh day of the Feast of Tabernacles, which is technically the last day of the Feast because the Feast of Tabernacles is seven days long. However, it is eight days because of the Last Great Day. There is still a whole lot more that we can learn. But let's understand something as Christ has said, there's a beginning and there's an ending. So, just as we started the Feast and we went down through every day, now there is the ending of the Feast, and then we have the finale with the Last Great Day.

Let's see how important that this is and what this day represents. We're going to ask some questions as we go along. We're going to answer those questions and find out a little bit more about what the Millennium is going to be like as it's revealed in the Word of God, and what we need to be doing, and how we need to be doing it. But brethren, you know, we all need to be thankful because of the Word of God that gives us the understanding.

In order to understand these things it's not that we're anything great, it's not that we are more intellectual than other people or whatever it may be. No! It's because of:

- the calling of God
- the Spirit of God
- the Word of God

We're going to also understand and realize that not only is this so, but also that when we come to the end of the Millennium there are going to be a couple of things that is very difficult for some people to grasp and understand, so we'll see if we can do it this time.

Let's come to Isa. 32. We are going to see how the Millennium is going to be. Now we know the Spirit of God is going to be available. We know that salvation is going to be given to everyone at that time all during the Millennium. We know that it is going to be absolutely, in human existence, nearly the greatest time that has ever been. I say *nearly* because we don't know what it's going to be like for the 100-year period that follows the Millennium, which is interesting: the 100-year period is actually a tithe of the thousand years.

Isaiah 32:15: "Until the Spirit is poured upon us from on high…"

Now doesn't that sound a little bit like what happened in Acts 2 on the Day of Pentecost when the Holy Spirit came? *Yes!* So, the Holy Spirit's going to be available to all people.

"…and the wilderness becomes a fruitful field, and the fruitful field is thought to be a forest. Then justice shall dwell in the wilderness, and righteousness remain in the fruitful field. And **the work of righteousness shall be peace**…" (vs 15-17).

So here again we're not talking about just the physical place, but we are talking about *the work of conversion* all during the Millennium. Just like we have the parables of the sower in Matt, 13 and the parallels that we have in Mark and in Luke. Very important to understand. This is talking about that spiritual harvest that is going to take place. So it's really saying that it's a universal salvation that is going out to all people.

"…and the result of righteousness shall be quietness and confidence forever…. [no more fear, no more crime] …And my people shall dwell in a peaceable home, and in secure dwellings and quiet resting places…" (vs 17-18). *Those resting places are typical of living during the Millennium!*

Verse 19: "The hail shall flatten the forest; the city shall be razed to the ground. Blessed *are* you who sow beside all waters, who send out freely the feet of the ox and the donkey" (vs 19-20).

In other words, there will be plenty of that. But it's very interesting here. We can tie in:

Psalm 1:1: "Blessed is the man who does not walk in the counsel of the wicked, nor stand in the way of sinners, nor sit in the seat of the scornful. But his delight is in the Law of the LORD; and in His Law does he meditate day and night. And he shall be like a tree planted by the streams of water that brings forth its fruit in its season…" (vs 1-3).

That's what's going to happen. All during the Millennium every one is going to bring forth fruit, spiritually speaking, in season. God is going to harvest it. It's going to be the greatest harvest; the greatest thing that has happened since the creation of the world. Just think how many billions will be converted and added to the Kingdom of God.

Now, we need to also understand that God did not create the universe in vain. He created that on purpose, for a purpose. The more that they get out and study the universe, the more they are awed by the very power of it. So in the final analysis, God is going to need billions and billions and billions to help to produce what God wants to produce with the vastness of the universe that He has created. As I said before, we need to not only think big, *we need to think gigantic!*

This is going to be really quite a wonderful time for everything here. Here's what God is going to do for all people; He says so right here:

Isaiah 25:6: "And in this **mountain the LORD** of hosts… [in Jerusalem on Mount Zion] …shall make a feast of fat things for all the people, a feast of wines on the lees, of fat things… [that's all the good things that you'd ever want] …full of marrow, of refined wines on the lees."

I mean, that is a time that we could say the greatest and the best will be produced, There will be no more Thunderbird wine, Andre Champaign or hard, tough steaks; *there will be none of this!*

Plus, everyone is going to be converted. It's going to be quite a time. A sinner is not going to be allowed to be around. ***They're either going to repent, or they're going to have to face the consequences!***

Verse 7: "And He will destroy in this mountain the face of the covering, which covers all people, and the veil that is woven over all nations."

So, they're going to have their blindness removed. God has got to do this at the beginning of the Millennium. We'll see that when the beginning of the Last Great Day starts, He also has to do that with those people.

Verse 8: He will destroy death forever; and the Lord GOD will wipe away tears from all faces. And He shall take away from all the earth the rebuke of His people, for the LORD has spoken it."

Now, this is really quite a thing; that's what's going to happen all during the Millennium!

Verse 9: "And one shall say in that day, 'Lo, this *is* our God. We have waited for Him, and He will save us. This *is* the LORD; we have waited for Him, we will be glad and rejoice in His salvation.'"

That's a tremendous thing! Just think of this attitude all through the Millennium, all people. Just think of the things that are going to be taught:

- how right
- how good
- how pure
- how lovely

Every kind of description that you would like to give will apply! God is going to have an increase; God is going to produce. The whole world is going to learn. and we are going to be the ones who will be teaching them.

Isa. 30—this describes part of our job. God is going to have us active and busy:

- all during the Millennium
- all during the 100-year period
- all during the rest of the ages of eternity

God has called us to a tremendous and absolutely mind-boggling calling!

Whereas, most religions in the world, what do they do? *They have things set up so that you can get along a little better in this life!* But you ask them:

- Why were you born?
- What is God doing?
- When is Christ returning?
- What are these things that are going to happen?

They don't know! They don't even believe in the resurrection in most cases, though they mouth the words; all of their so-called immortal souls go to heaven.

If you don't have the book *Primitive Christianity in Crisis* by Alan Knight, well you make sure you get a copy of it. Let me tell you something: you cannot understand how those false doctrines came into the Church unless you have read his book. How did it happen? Well you see, during the Millennium none of this is going to happen.

- everyone is going to know God
- everyone is going to know who their teachers are
- everyone is going to know who their rulers are
- everyone is going to keep the Sabbath and the Holy Days

They are going to work and produce, and life is going to be the way that God wants it to be. Let me tell you something, it's going to make this modern world look like an absolute conglomeration of insane idiots.

Isaiah 30:18: "And therefore, will the LORD wait, that He may be gracious unto you…. [that's why He's not bringing the Millennium now; in His set time it will come] …And therefore, He will be exalted, that He may have mercy upon you, for the LORD *is* a God of justice; blessed *are* all those who wait for Him."

That includes us who are now waiting. But let me tell you something else: everyone *during the Millennium is going to be doing the work and the will of God the way God wants it done!* So, they'll be waiting on God, as it were.

Verse 19: "For, O people, who dwell in Zion at Jerusalem, you shall weep no more; He will be very gracious to you at the voice of your cry. When He hears it, He will answer you."

It says in another place that He is going to really do some fantastic things. He's even going to answer right while you're asking. That ought to help us to be able to have more faith in prayers that we have to God. I'll tell you one way to never have a prayer answered. Go pray your heart out, be as fervent as you can, get all done and say Amen, and then stand up on your feet and say, 'I wonder if God will answer this prayer?' You've just undone everything that you've asked for.

Verse 20: "And though the LORD gives you the bread of adversity and the water of affliction... [in the past to bring them to the point of conversion] ...yet, your teachers shall not be removed into a corner anymore..."

No, it's not going to be like it was in the past. There are not going to be those trials and tribulations.

"...but your eyes shall see your teachers.... [that will be our jobs] ...And your ears shall hear a word behind you, saying, 'This *is* the way, walk in it,' when you turn to the right hand and when you turn to the left" (vs 20-21).

Now, let's stop and think on this for a minute. Let's look at the *three existences of converted people who are resurrected.* The first existence is:

1. in the womb right after conception

Now they've been able to take 3-D pictures that show babies as young as 12-weeks-old and they see them doing things in practice so when they are born they will have all of these things down pat. They practice walking; their legs are going (kicking) to build and strengthen the muscles. Their arms are also going; they suck their thumbs, open their eyes, but they can't see because it's totally dark in the womb. They smile; they're disturbed at outside noises coming in to them. Remember, water is a great conductor of sound. So, it's very incumbent upon mothers to be careful what kind of sounds that they have coming upon them.

It just makes me wonder about all these people who are involved in some of these awful things called 'music' today, and all that sound coming into their ears, to the body, *into the unborn!*

But nevertheless, they also yawn, they smile, *and they are getting ready to be born.*

There's a set time for them to be born, and when they have been born they come into this world, and they do something for the very first time: *they breathe,* and they are no longer dependent upon the umbilical cord to be fed. But in the process of growing, right after being born and so forth, they have mother's milk, which is the best thing, and should be. All mothers should nurse their children. God designed it, and in many ways totally beneficial to the mother and to the child. This is not the place to get into it. But anyway if someone is not cut off because of an untimely or early death, they live in this physical life.

2. if God calls them then God's plan is still working

-   He's given us a mind
-   He's given us understanding
-   He's called
-   He's given us His Spirit
-   He is teaching us

What are we doing in this life but:
-   loving God
-   keeping His commandments
-   learning of His Word
-   walking in His way
-   repenting
-   changing
-   growing

What are we doing? **Well, we are practicing for being born again!** So, when we die and are put into the grave, or we're still alive and changed when Christ returns

3. we are born into the Kingdom of God; then all of a sudden we are spirit beings

Now we have another form of existence!

We're going to be doing things for the first time that we have never ever done in our whole lives. Just like when a newborn is born and starts breathing, then it's doing that for the very first time. Isn't it interesting that *breath* is likened unto spirit?

So, just as the newborn takes a first breath, so when we are born into the Kingdom of God we are going to be spirit beings and our breath will be the fullness of the Spirit of God. Likewise with all of those that we are teaching in the Millennium:

-   they will know this
-   they will know who God is
-   they will know who we are

We are going to be teaching and training them! It's going to be an amazing thing indeed!

Micah 4:4—I just want to cover this. After not learning war anymore. Just stop and think about it: God is not going to have any more exploiting corporations to exploit people and control them, and destroy their lives.

Micah 4:4: "But they shall sit each one under his *own* vine and under his *own* fig tree; and no one shall make them afraid… [*all during the Millennium! Of the increase of His government and peace there shall be no end.*] …for the mouth of the LORD of hosts has spoken."

Amos 9—let's see what kind of thing that they will have, what kind of agriculture it is going to be. It's going to be something. Just like we read earlier. God is going to make them a feast of all the fat things. Well it's going to come and come The produce, the food, the things that are produced, as well as then you can also understand all the things that will be produced in making clothes, making shoes, making things, making whatever machines that we will need at that time. It's going to be an amazing thing. But here it starts with the agricultural base:

Amos 9:13: "'Behold, the days come,' says the LORD, 'that the plowman shall overtake the reaper, and the treader of grapes him who sows seed. And the mountains will drop sweet wine, and all the hills will flow with it.'"

It's just going to be an overflowing abundance. Now you compare that with what is in the world today with the war and the famine and starvation and so forth.

Verse 14: "And I will bring back the exiles of My people Israel… [bring them out of their captivity] …and they shall build the cities. which are desolate, and they shall live *in* them. And they shall plant vineyards and drink their wine…"

Now all you tee-totalers listen up! Now sure, there's not going to be alcoholism, you can be guaranteed that. But it's going to be used in the right way, and the best of it

"'…They shall also make gardens and eat their fruit. And I will plant them in their land, and they shall no more be pulled up out of their land which I have given them,' says the LORD your God" (vs 14-15).

Now think of this starting out the beginning of the Millennium where there's still some wars going on as we saw, and then coming all the way down through the Millennium.

Isa. 60—let's see something here, how it's going to be. Economically we've seen how it is for agriculture, now let's see how it's going to be for commerce and industry.

Isaiah 60:16: "You will also suck the milk of nations, and suck the breast of kings…" That is symbolic language that you're going to receive the best of everything. So will all of them during the Millennium.

"…and you shall know that I the LORD *am* your Savior and your Redeemer, the mighty One of Jacob" (v 16).

As great as the coming *new world order* is going to **appear** in the eyes of men, what God is going to do during the Millennium is going to pale into absolute insignificance this coming 'great' *new world order of Satan the devil!* Let's see what God is going to do here, here's how rich they are going to be:

Verse 17: "For bronze I will bring gold, and for iron I will bring silver; and for wood I will bring bronze, and for stones, iron.…"

Now there's going to be a lot of industry going on using all of these things. We're no longer going to have these counterfeit notes, which most currencies are today. They are counterfeit notes put out by fake banks that say they are central banks. No more!

- God is a God of *real* wealth
- God is a God of *real* power
- God is a God of *real* righteousness

That's how it's going to be!

"…I will also make your overseers to be peace, and your rulers to be righteousness" (v 17). *That's going to be us!* They are going to be able to give their tithes and offerings and so forth.

- God is going to bless them because of obedience
- God is going to bless them with His Spirit
- God is going to bless them with conversion

Verse 18: "Violence will no more be heard in your land, *neither* wasting nor ruin within your borders; but you will call your walls Salvation, and your gates Praise."

This is an amazing thing, brethren, what God is going to do. When we leave this Feast of Tabernacles, which we will do after the Last Great Day, I want you to keep these things in mind. Because this is the vision that God has given us so that in the times of trouble and difficulty that we are going to face after the Feast—which all of us are going to face one way or the other because we're still living in the world—*keep your mind focused on these things!*

Isa. 33—this will be really quite a wonderful thing when we see right here in the Word of God it talks about it.

Isaiah 33:20: "Look upon Zion, the city of our Holy gatherings; your eyes shall see Jerusalem a quiet home, a tabernacle that shall not be taken down; not one of its stakes shall ever be removed, nor shall any of its cords be broken. But there the glorious LORD *will be* to us a place of broad rivers *and* streams…" (vs 20-21).

That's just likened unto God's Spirit. Remember that the crystal clear waters will flow out of the Throne of God (Rev. 22). This is likened unto it.

"…in which no galley with oars shall go, nor shall a mighty ship pass by it, for the LORD *is* our Judge, the LORD *is* our Lawgiver, the LORD *is* our King; He will save us" (vs 21-22).

That's really quite a description! Just like the world today is all focused in and is going to come to the point of worshiping Satan the devil, so likewise in the Millennium all are going to be focused in on worshiping God:

- His way
- His Truth
- His righteousness

Isaiah 35:1: "The wilderness and the desert shall be glad and the desert shall rejoice and blossom as the rose…. [tie that in with Amos 9] …It shall blossom abundantly, and rejoice even *with* joy and singing; the glory of Lebanon shall be given to it, the excellency of Carmel and Sharon, they shall see the glory of the LORD *and* the majesty of our God" (vs 1-2). *So, it's going to really be a tremendous thing that's going to happen!*

Verse 3: "Make the weak hands strong and make the feeble knees sure… [that's what we're going to do] …Say to those of a fearful heart, 'Be strong, fear not; behold, your God will come *with* vengeance… [He already has; this is coming into the Millennium] …with the full recompense of God. He will come and save you.' Then the eyes of the blind shall be opened, and the ears of the deaf shall be unstopped. Then the lame shall leap like a deer, and the tongue of the dumb shall sing…" (vs 3-6).

That's going to be our job! Can you imagine what it's going to be like:

- to heal blind people?
- to heal those who cannot speak?
- to heal those who have had limbs destroyed?

It's going to be an amazing thing, because if the lame is going to leap as the hart, that's what it's talking about.

Verse 7: "And the parched ground shall become a pool, and the thirsty land shall become springs of water in the home of jackals, in its lair, it shall be a place for the reed and rush. And a highway shall be there, and a way, and it shall be called The Way of Holiness. The unclean shall not pass over it…" (vs 7-8).

We're going to see in just a little bit that during the Millennium there's going to be a division between the righteous and the sinners. God is going to make that division and they're going to have to choose. God is not going to let the wicked prosper. Now we'll talk about how God will deal with them in just a little bit.

Verse 9: "No lion shall be there, nor *any* beast of prey shall go up on it, they shall not be found there… [the lions are going to be the pets back at home (Isa. 11)] …But the redeemed shall walk there. And the ransomed of the LORD shall return and come to Zion with songs and everlasting joy upon their heads; they shall obtain joy and gladness, and sorrow and sighing shall flee away" (vs 9-10). *There's the whole mission statement for the thousand years!*

Let's think about it for a minute! The key to understanding the Bible is what the religionists in the world do not want to do. That is: *obey God and love Him.*

Example: as I tell people who want to know about the Sabbath and what it's for, and so forth, and they are really serious: I say: you go ahead and keep the Sabbath. On the Sabbath day study about the Sabbath. If you do this for several months, you will understand the Sabbath. But if you don't obey, you're not going to understand.

Likewise with the Holy Days; *we don't understand them unless we obey and keep them!* Then with God's Spirit and God's Word, He opens up our understanding so we can realize what it really is. Listen to this. This is a fantastic description of what it's going to be like all during the Millennium:

Psalm 145:1: "I will extol You, my God, O King; and I will bless Your name forever and ever. Every day I will bless You; and I will praise Your name forever and ever" (vs 1-2).

Just think of this: every day people are going to be praying to God. Every day they're going to be thanking and blessing God. It's going to be an amazing place. It's going to be an amazing thing. We, brethren, are the ones who are going to administer this with Christ. That's what's so fantastic about it.

Verse 3: "Great is the LORD, and greatly to

be praised; and His greatness is unsearchable. One generation shall praise Your works to another and shall declare Your mighty acts" (vs 3-4). *All during the Millennium this is what is going to happen!*

Verse 5: "I will speak of the glorious splendor of Your majesty and of Your wondrous works. And men shall speak of the might of Your awesome works; and I will declare Your greatness. They shall pour forth the memory of Your great goodness and shall sing of Your righteousness.... [here's what they're going to be singing]: ...The LORD is gracious and full of compassion; slow to anger and abounding in steadfast love" (vs 3-8).

You wonder in the midst of all of this, why would people choose to sin? *We'll talk about that in just a little bit!*

Verse 9: "The LORD is good to all, and His tender mercies are over all His works. All Your works shall praise You, O LORD; and Your saints shall bless You. They shall speak of the glory of Your Kingdom and talk of Your power, to make known to the sons of men His mighty acts, and the glorious majesty of His Kingdom. Your Kingdom is an everlasting Kingdom, and Your dominion endures throughout all generations" (vs 9-13).

In other words, not only during the time of the Millennium, but down through all eternity, *because there are ages of eternity!*

Now let's look at a couple things here and begin to ask some questions and see what's going to happen. Human nature is this way: once you get used to something because you're born into a certain set of circumstances in society...

Example: I doubt if there are any children today who even have a thought that there was never a time when we were not using electricity, and had lights and cars and all the things we have today. They get used to it. What happens when children have everything? *They get spoiled!*

Now just think what's going to happen to human nature as we progress down through the Millennium. They're going to be taking these things for granted. They are going to be able to see their teachers and they're going to take it for granted. Also, there's going to be enough human nature around that there are going to be some who are going to want to sin. Let's look and see two things.

1. How long are people going to live during the Millennium?
2. What happens to the righteous?
3. What happens to the sinner?

I know that we apply this—Isa. 65—to the 100-year period, that's true. It's probably going to be exactly the same for the Millennium and for the 100 years of the Great White Throne Judgment period.

Isaiah 65:17: "For behold, I create new heavens and a new earth. And the former things will not be remembered, nor come to mind. But be glad and rejoice forever *in that* which I create; for behold, I create Jerusalem a rejoicing, and her people a joy. I will rejoice in Jerusalem, and I will joy in My people; and the voice of weeping will no more be heard in her, nor the voice of crying" (vs 17-19).

That applies all during the Millennium! That also will apply during the Great White Throne Judgment too, without a doubt.

Verse 20: "There will not be an infant who lives but a few days… [that is an infant who does not fulfill his life] …nor an old man that has not filled his days, for the child will die a hundred years old…"

That means live to be 100-years-old, and we're all destined to die, with the exception where God makes the exception, and we will see it.

"…but the sinner *who is* a hundred years old shall be accursed" (v 20).

Now, let's look at it this way. You can read the rest of it and it shows, again, the Millennium setting.

Let's come to an unusual circumstance that we find in the New Testament and let's apply that to us. There is a time when those who are truly converted at the return of Christ and are still living, it says they don't die. Now, I've gone back and forth in trying to understand this, which is this:

Hebrews 9:27: "And inasmuch as **it is appointed unto men once to die**, and after this, *the* judgment."

1-Thessalonians 4:14—*concerning those who are alive when Christ returns*: "For if we believe that Jesus died and rose again, in exactly the same way also, those who have fallen asleep in Jesus will God bring with Him. For this we say to you by *the* Word of *the* Lord, that we who are alive and remain unto the coming of the Lord shall in no wise precede those who have fallen asleep, because the Lord Himself shall descend from heaven with *a* shout of command, with *the* voice of an archangel and with *the* trumpet of God; and the dead in Christ shall rise first; then we who are alive and remain shall be caught up together with them in *the* clouds for *the* meeting with the Lord in *the* air; and so shall we always be with *the* Lord" (vs 14-17).

Now, they are changed instantaneously, aren't they? How this works, I don't know. Is this change considered an instantaneous death and transformation to spirit? Death of the human body? I mean it's going to be transformed because it says in:

Philippians 3:21—talking about when Christ returns: "Who will **transform our vile bodies**, that they may be conformed to His glorious body, according to the inner working of His own power, *whereby He is able* to subdue all things to Himself."

We don't know the exact process, but it does say in Isa, 65 that 'the infant shall die a hundred, and the sinner dying at a hundred shall be accursed.'

- What would it serve for those who are righteous, for those who have, through the process of God's salvation been qualified for salvation, for them to die and be buried?

They'd have to be resurrected. Let's tie that in to what we have at the end!

- What purpose would it be for those who are righteous at the end, to die and be buried, but rather, shall be changed and transformed as Paul said: 'In an instant, in *the* twinkling of an eye, at the last trumpet; we shall all be changed' just like those being resurrected out of the graves will be changed?
- Is it that at that point of a hundred years, that the righteous when they are changed, there is a death of the physical body and they have it converted into a spiritual body?

I suggest this: that we all wait until we see how it happens when we are ruling and reigning with Christ; then we will know for sure! Otherwise these are just some thoughts to help give us some understanding.

- What does the Bible teach us?
- How does God show us that He deals with people who have sinned, and sinned greatly enough that they should die, but God allows them to live?

That's going to be the quandary during the Millennium!

- What are you going to do with people who die?

During the first part of the Millennium they can die, be put in the grave, and every time there is a funeral that takes place everyone is going to know that that person has committed the unpardonable sin, *because they die as sinners and are accursed!* That's their first death. So, keep that in mind also for tomorrow.

Now when we come down to the last generation there's not going to be time for them to live a hundred years. There's not going to be time to

be able to have them die the death at 100-years-old being accursed.

- Was the Garden of Eden the ideal setting that God wanted? *Yes!*
- Didn't we cover the restitution of all things? *Yes!*
- What happened with Adam and Eve?

Obviously they sinned enough to die! He gave them the death sentence. He put within them the law of sin and death because of their transgressions, but He let them live

- What did God do?

This has also been brought up referring to the last generation. *But*:

- Could it also happen to those during the Millennium who sin grievously and have to be removed?
- Will there be a place of exile of all sinners, gross sinners?

Which would be a minority of people by the way. But still there will be, because God is not going to take away free choice from anybody. It's still going to be there. It's still going to be whether you're going to choose to love God and serve Him, or go your own way. It's like with Adam and Eve. So, what did He do? *Here's what He did*:

- He cut them off from the Tree of Life
- He sent them out of the Garden of Eden

Genesis 3:24: "And He drove out the man… [and obviously his wife] …and He placed cherubim at the east of the Garden of Eden, and a flaming sword, which turned every way to guard the way to the Tree of Life."

Are we going to have something similar during the Millennium? *I've applied it to the last generation of the Millennium, but*:

Could it be that there is going to be a place of exile for those who say, 'I just want to choose whichever way *I* want to go'? *God is going to say*:

If you do that, you're going to go over here to this place of exile. If you repent you can come back, but if you don't repent you're going to live out your life a hundred years and you're going to die accursed, and you're going to be buried.

I don't know! But it's very likely, based upon what we have here in Gen, 3. So, if we're going to have the restitution of all things, as we saw there at the beginning of the Feast, are we not also going to have a means of handling those who have committed grievous sins? Obviously, if someone commits something like murder, then the sentence is death right there. Of course, the one who has been murdered can be resurrected.

However, during the Millennium it says very clearly that no one is going to 'hurt or destroy in all My Holy mountain.' I highly doubt whether we are going to have murderers around. I'm sure that there are going to be those who are going to try and steal and lie, and things like that; that's all part of human nature. People can repent of those things. Those are sins that are sins not unto death.

But what happens when you have someone who comes to the point that they are just incorrigible and you cannot have them around? *We also have the principle too, that we are not to become part of the world!* We are separate. We are told that to be separate from the way of the world and sinners. So, it's very possible that God will have this.

Now why is this necessary? **Because God has decreed that all sinners will die twice!** All unrepentant sinners will suffer the second death, which we will get into tomorrow. Here they are exiled. Where do you suppose would be the best place to exile them? *Maybe we have an answer in the New Testament!*

Then we're going to see something that has been very hard for people to understand. Let's see if we can put it together. I realize that we are into areas that are not absolutely totally dogmatic in the things that I have just said here, I understand that. So in thinking the process through, which God wants us to do, we understand that the ultimate reality of it is going to be when we see how God truly does it. But in the mean time it's certainly not wrong for us to try and get some understanding of the Scriptures based upon what we know. Let's see part of the enigma in trying to understand these Scriptures, and how God is going to handle it.

Revelation 20:1: "Then I saw an angel descending from heaven, having the key of the abyss, and a great chain in his hand. And he took hold of the dragon, the ancient serpent, who is *the* Devil and Satan, and bound him *for* a thousand years" (vs 1-2).

All during the Millennium Satan is not going to be around to tempt them, which also tells us one thing very important, because that also goes back to the time of when Adam and Eve sinned. The beginning was when they let Satan persuade them to go against God. As soon as Satan enters the scene, *sin prospers!* When Satan is removed then not all sin, *but the sins that Satan inspires, will be gone!*

Verse 3: "Then he cast him into the abyss, and locked him *up*, and sealed *the abyss* over him, so that he would not deceive the nations any longer

until the thousand years were fulfilled; **and after that it is ordained that he be loosed *for* a short time**."

Why would God do that? *Because He needs Satan for one more mission!* Let's see what that is. He let's them out. He lets Satan, and of course then the demons, too, He let's them out with a purpose that's necessary to be fulfilled.

All during the Millennium sinners who die are accursed. That's their first death. When we come down to the last generation you are going to have righteous people who are living who will probably live over into the Great White Throne Judgment period so they can live to be 100-years-old and then be transformed. Then you are also going to have the sinners who are exiled. They're still going to be alive. They're going to have to die their first death. You cannot have the Great White Throne Judgment 100-year period begin until certain things are done.

Verse 7: "Now, when the thousand years have been completed, Satan shall be loosed out of his prison."

Why does God let him out of his prison? *The prison that he is put into in, the abyss, is a temporary punishment!* As we will see the fulfillment of the seventh day of the Feast of Tabernacles also gives the final judgment on Satan the devil as well. That has to be reserved until the end of the Millennium.

Verse 8: "And he shall go out to deceive the nations that *are* in the four corners of the earth, Gog and Magog..."

This brings us right back to the very first day of the Feast of Tabernacles, about how Gog and Magog came down and wanted to attack and take away the Kingdom from beginning when Christ returns at the beginning of the Millennium. But they are destroyed.

Their names are the total epitome of evil to come down and fight Christ at the beginning of the Millennium. Gog and Magog in this particular case has to be *a geographical area* in Gog and Magog. Why do I say that? *I say that because of this: that if God is going to give free moral agency and free choice to everyone to choose,* do you not think that at the beginning of the Millennium when all of those armies of Gog and Magog have been destroyed, that they're going to be the physical descendents of Gog and Magog who are going to be converted? *Yes!* Because God says that with that event of destroying the armies of Gog and Magog at the beginning of the Millennium, all the heathen—which includes the rest of those of Gog and Magog who are still alive—are going to know that Christ is the Lord, and that God is ruling on this earth!

This is not the people of Gog and Magog, but *part of the territory of Gog and Magog,* those who have the rebellious attitude that Gog and Magog had at the beginning of the Millennium. It says 'to deceive the nations,' not deceive Gog and Magog alone.

"...the nations that *are* in the four corners of the earth, Gog and Magog..." (v 8) *describes that part of the earth where they have been exiled to!* Now notice, here's his mission:

"...of whom the number *is* as the sand of the sea..." (v 8). *God uses that to show it's a great number but it's not determinable, the exact number!*

Why? *Because there is choice!* If they choose to sin, God has not predetermined who is going to choose to sin and who is going to choose not to sin. God reserves that for every individual that He calls, or exposes them to the Truth. God is not going to take away that from anybody.

- He didn't take it from Adam and Eve
- He hasn't taken it away from us
- He's not going to take it away from the people who live during the Millennium
- He's not going to take it away from the people in the last generation of the Millennium

Those who are incorrigible sinners at that time will not have 100 years to live, to die, and be buried accursed. God has to execute His plan so that they will die *their first death* in a very unusual manner, and He uses Satan to do it. He releases Satan. He goes over to where they are in the area of Gog and Magog, and you can almost hear it.

Boy, I've been fighting this for a thousand years, and I really am the 'true God.' You were right in rejecting God. You were right in coming over here. You were right in exercising your free moral agency to do what you want to, and now I am here as 'God' to rescue you. Worship me.

And you know they will!

- What else do you think that Satan is going to do?
- What did he do with Adam and Eve?
- What did he do when Christ had His confrontation with Satan the devil to be tempted of him?
- Did he not say, 'Worship me'? *Yes, indeed!*

No doubt he's going to do it again! However it's going to be a deception, *because he set out to deceive these people who have already rejected salvation!* They're not deceived out of salvation. *By choice they have rejected it.* Just like every one who

commits the unpardonable sin, *by choice they reject God!* There we have it. Now what does he do?

"...to gather them together for war" (v 8). *Every time Satan is around there is war!* Without a doubt! Look what happened with Cain and Abel, the first murder! War, death and destruction.

Now then, in preparing for war they're probably going to make various weapons. We don't know how much technology they are going to be able to develop in a short time. It says he must be loosed for a short time or a short season. We don't know how long that is. Is that three and a half years as some of the other areas where it is for a 'short season' referred to, or a short time? It's possible! It's going to be long enough for them to prepare for war. It's going to be long enough for them to make enough armaments that they think that they are going to be able to conquer the saints down in Jerusalem.

If you go conquer Jerusalem and you take the capital, and you take over God's Throne...

Doesn't that sound like a repeat of Isa, 14? *Yes, indeed!*

If you do that then you can finally be 'God.' You can finally rule over the world. Then you can be rewarded...

Satan is going to tell them.
You can be rewarded. And you can take over and rule and you can dispose of all of these people.'

It will be a very convincing thing. I mean all we have to do is just piece together what Satan has said down through the years and put it together again. Satan can't do anything new. Whatever he does is just a repeat.

Verse 9: "Then *I saw* them go up upon the breadth of the earth and encircle **the camp of the saints**..."

Could this be something that is going to happen during the Feast of Tabernacles? *I do not know!*

"...and the beloved city... [they are going to think that they are going to have success; but God has His execution in mind for them]: ...and fire came down from God out of heaven and consumed them" (v 9).

When all of those who are sinners and chosen to sin, who have been exiled to Gog and Magog, are worked up into their armies and brought down to Jerusalem, they will have finished completing the unpardonable sin. *The wages of sin is death* as it always has been. So here, for them, *is their first death!* They're yet going to suffer the second death, as we will see on the Last Great Day. But all sinners who are incorrigible sinners; those who won't repent or never repent, God has decreed that they will die twice. What we are reading of here in Rev. 20 is the first death of those wicked in the last generation of the Millennium who have not had enough time to die a natural death, and die a sinner accursed and be buried. I think we can understand it that way.

Here's something else that has to take place. Because the only way that righteousness is brought in, is not only by having the Government of God here; not only by having the resurrected saints rule, reign, teach and so forth, **but Satan must be removed!** Satan's work is done at this point. There is no other purpose for Satan the devil. **Now's the time for judgment against Satan!** So let's see what this is. Let's see how it's going to be accomplished. **We will see that Satan's judgment must be done before the beginning of the Last Great Day,** and the meaning and fulfillment of the Last Great Day. So he is sentenced and he is judged.

Verse 10: "And the Devil, who deceived them…" What do you have with the devil? *All of his demons because he's king over the abyss!* When Satan is cast into the abyss, all the demons are cast into the abyss. When Satan is let out, all the demons are let out. So when this judgment comes upon Satan, it's going to come upon all the demons.

"…was cast into the Lake of Fire and brimstone where the beast and the false prophet **had been** cast…" (v 10).

When were *the beast and the false prophet* cast into the Lake of Fire? This also tells us that there is going to be a Lake of Fire active during the Millennium, both. So, you're going to have two things:

1. the totally incorrigible who may commit a crime that demands instant death; they'll probably, during the Millennium, be cast into the Lake of Fire
2. those who sin and never repent but haven't done the incorrigible sin until the very end of their lives by not accepting the salvation of God, and they die as sinners being 100-years-old

So, we probably have two things going here!

But let's see what happens to *the beast and the false prophet*. This is important to understand.

Revelation 19:20: "And the beast was taken, and with him the false prophet who worked miracles in his presence… [two human beings; flesh and blood] …by which he had deceived those who received the mark of the beast and those who worshiped his image. Those two were cast alive into the Lake of Fire, which burns with brimstone"

Now when people are cast into the Lake of fire, what happens? *They burn up!* Now just think of it this way. *Think of it as a lake of molten lava!* Now any human being, being flesh and blood, cast into that is burned up and they are no more. So that's why I translated it this way so it clears up the mistranslation that most people believe that *the beast and the false prophet* were there being tormented all during the Millennium. It cannot be because human beings are not tormented in fire. That's a misinterpretation and not a clear translation, because people believe in an ever-burning hell.

Revelation 20:10: "…where the beast and the false prophet *had been cast…*"

Understand this: the beast was possessed of Satan the devil, and the false prophet by probably the next highest demon under Satan the devil. Those demons then, along with Satan, were cast into the abyss and the seal shut up over them all during the Millennium. Then they were let out as we saw and so forth.

Here's **the final judgment of Satan the devil**: "…and they…" (v 10). Because it is in the Greek "they shall be tormented."

That cannot refer to *the beast and the false prophet* because they are burned up. So the "…they…" has to refer to Satan and the demons.

"…and they, *Satan and the demons,* shall be tormented day and night into the ages of eternity" (v 10).

So God is going to have Satan the devil and the demons being tormented day and night forever into the ages of eternity. That's what the Greek says. Now a lot of people can argue back and forth and say, 'Couldn't God convert them into a human being and then destroy him and he's burned up?' *Well anything is possible with God,* but is that what God is going to do? You read in Heb. 1 where it says that never did He say to any of the angels at any time, 'You are My Son; this day I have begotten You' I see no reason why He would convert them into being human beings. But it does say that they are going to be tormented day and night forever. So that's quite a thing!

Isa. 14—let's see where it talks about the punishment of Satan the devil. If that's the case, which it undoubtedly is—because that's what the Scriptures tell us—**then there will always be a constant reminder for all eternity to all of the rest who enter into the Kingdom of God that sin, rebellion and going against God will never succeed!**

Isaiah 14:12: "How you are fallen from the heavens, O shining star, son of the morning! *How* you are cut down to the ground, you who weakened the nations!" *And he did!*

What we have here right now is an amalgamation of everything that Satan stands for:

- a reference back to his first rebellion
- a reference to his continuous rebellion
- a reference to the last rebellion (Rev. 20)

Verse 13: "For you have said in your heart… [he has never changed] …'I will ascend *into* the heavens, I will exalt my throne above the stars of God; I will also sit upon the mount of the congregation, in the sides of the north.'" *He's going to be 'God.'* That's what he has always wanted to do, *to replace God!*

Verse 14: "'I will ascend above the heights of the clouds; I will be like the Most High.' Yet, you shall be brought down to the grave, to the sides of the pit. Those who see you shall stare and watch you closely, *saying*, 'Is this the man who made the earth to tremble; who shook kingdoms'" (vs 14-16).

All down through history Satan has possessed various men: the king of Babylon and other kings down through time. As we can see in our day, obviously had great influence with those dictators of WWII that we knew like Hitler, Mussolini, Tojo. Probably a combination of Satan and the high principalities and powers that serve under Satan the devil. People are going to look at him and they're going to say, 'Is this the one?' It's going to be an object lesson.

You stop and think, if this happens all during the Millennium that people can come to the sealed abyss, will they be able to look down into the abyss and see Satan and the demons down there, and yet, turn around and go sin? Will not that unpardonable sin be even more determined and premeditated than what we do today? *So that's going to be Satan's judgment!* That's the last thing that's going to take place during the Millennium.

Now what do we have? We have undoubtedly those human beings who were righteous, who are converted, who have the Spirit of God will live on over… I've been torn between this, too, at different times, and different messages. So, if you go back and hear some other messages where it's not exactly the same as this, just understand that.

I've said in the past there are no more human beings alive. Why not have those who have not reached a hundred years live on over into the 100-year period to help set the example for all those who will be resurrected in the second resurrection?

Then you will have those human beings who will live over into the Great White Throne Judgment period. You'll have

- all the sons of God; those of us who are in the first resurrection
- all of those who came into the Kingdom of God all during the Millennium

Then we are ready for the finality of God's plan, which you'll have to come back tomorrow to get the rest of the story, *because that will be the finishing and completing of the plan of God!*

Scriptures from *The Holy Bible in Its Original Order, A Faithful Version*

Scriptural References

1) Isaiah 32:15-20
2) Psalm 1:1-3
3) Isaiah 25:6-9
4) Isaiah 30:18-21
5) Micah 4:4
6) Amos 9:13-15
7) Isaiah 60:16-18
8) Isaiah 33:20-22
9) Isaiah 35:1-10
10) Psalm 145:1-13
11) Isaiah 65:17-20
12) Hebrews 9:27
13) I Thessalonians 4:14-17
14) Philippians 3:21
15) Genesis 3:24
16) Revelation 20:1-3, 7-10
17) Revelation 19:20
18) Revelation 20:10
19) Isaiah 14:12-16

Scriptures referenced, not quoted:

- Acts 2
- Matthew 13
- Revelation 22
- Isaiah 11
- Hebrews 1

Also referenced: Book:
    Primitive Christianity in Crisis by Alan Knight

FRC:cs
Transcription date unknown
Reformatted: bo: 1/2021

CHAPTER SEVENTY-NINE

The Last Generation of the Millennium
Fred R. Coulter

Greetings, everyone! Welcome to the seventh day of the Feast of Tabernacles! Lo and behold, this is the last day of the Feast. However, because there is a new beginning, there is the eighth day: The Last Great Day! We'll save that for tomorrow.

In observing the Feast of Tabernacles we see how God is going to deal with the world when Christ returns. It's going to be quite a thing. God is going to deal with Israel, God is going to bring them back and He is going to do some very spectacular things with them. He's going to give them a new heart, a heart of flesh. They're going to be taught, and we're the teachers and we'll be there to tell them 'this is the way to walk, go in it.'

That's when God is going to establish the New Covenant with Israel and with Judah. That has never been established, though it's mentioned there in the book of Hebrews, chapter 8; that's for those who came into the Church at the beginning of the Church. But let's see that God is going to again re-establish a covenant with Israel and with the house of Judah, and it's going to start the Millennium.

We'll see what happens during the Millennium. We've seen part of that, we'll review it, and then we'll look at something that will give us understanding so that when we come back to Rev. 20 and begin to go through the Scriptures that tell us about the end of the Millennium and the beginning of the Last Great Day.

Jeremiah 31:31: "Behold, the days come,' says the LORD, 'that I will make a new covenant with the house of Israel, and with the house of Judah.'"

If the churches in the world understood the difference between the house of Israel and the house of Judah they would have a much greater understanding of the Scriptures. They don't! But God has opened our eyes to see because He has called us and given us His Spirit, and we love Him and serve Him, and He is revealing these things to His people.

Verse 32: "Not according to the covenant that I made with their fathers in the day I took them by the hand to bring them out of the land of Egypt; which covenant of Mine they broke, although I was a husband to them,' says the LORD. 'But this *shall be* the covenant that I will make with the house of Israel…'" (vs 32-33).

Notice that He doesn't say that He's going to be a husband to them again! The Lord God of the Old Testament is the One Who became Jesus Christ of the New Testament, and He is going to marry the Bride, those of the Church who will be the Bride. He doesn't say that He's going to marry them [the house of Israel] again, but He's going to enter into a New Covenant.

"'…after those days,' says the LORD. 'I will put My law in their inward parts, and write it in their hearts; and I will be their God, and they shall be My people.'" (v 33).

What does this also tell us? What understanding does this give us? This tells us just exactly like we knew that when He said He didn't give them a heart to obey, and they will all know God and they will be His people again.

Verse 34: "'And they shall no more teach each man his neighbor and each man his brother, saying, "Know the LORD"; for they shall all know Me, from the least of them to the greatest of them,' says the LORD. 'For I will forgive their iniquity, and I will remember their sins no more.'"

That's how God is going to deal with the children of Israel. Let's see how it's stated here in the book of Zechariah, the eighth chapter, and we will see here are prophecies of it, as well. The return of Israel to their lands is going to be a great thing. The things that take place at the end-time are worldwide events.

Just think of what it must have been for all of those in the Church coming down through the centuries that they didn't have a clue as to when Christ was going to return. Now here we are at the end-time for us it's taken a little longer than many of us have figured. Nevertheless, we do have greater understanding than before on the promise of God through the prophet Daniel by the angel speaking to him who said that 'at the time of the end, *the wise shall understand,* but none of the wicked shall understand.'

Isn't it interesting that there are so many things in the book of Revelation that when it first came to the Churches it must have been a tremendous mystery. Here was the final message of

God to the Apostle John and he finished canonizing the New Testament. Here the book of Revelation was something, that outside of Rev. 1-5, that was a great mystery. How could this be? Especially when you amplify it to be worldwide events. So, we understand it in these days.

Here's what's going to happen, Zechariah 8:12: "'For they shall sow in peace; the vine shall give its fruit, and the ground shall give its increase, and the heavens shall give their dew; and I will cause the remnant of this people to possess all these things. And it shall come to pass, that as you were a curse among the nations, O house of Judah and house of Israel... [this helps clarify and give us comprehension as to what's happening in the end-time] ...so I will save you, and you shall be a blessing. Do not fear, but let your hands be strong.' For thus says the LORD of hosts, 'As I thought to punish you when your fathers provoked Me to wrath,' says the LORD of hosts, 'and I did not repent; so again I have thought in these days to do good to Jerusalem and to the house of Judah. **Fear not**'" (vs 12-15).

Verse 16 tells us that all during the Millennium it's going to be:

- truth
- righteousness
- knowledge of God

with that will come

- the love of God
- the hope of God

Of course, for them *hope* is not going to be deferred. *Hope* is going to come at the end of their lifetime, and it will be fulfilled.

We're going to see how people enter into the Kingdom of God—that is the *spiritual* Kingdom of God. All during the Millennium Judah and Israel are under the Kingdom of God and the Government of God there that will be ruled over by the resurrected saints who are the kings and priests. Let's see what they're going to do:

Verse 16: "'These *are* the things that you shall do. *Each* man speak the truth to his neighbor. Execute the judgment of truth and peace in your gates. And let no one imagine evil in your heart *against* his neighbor; and do not love a false oath, for all these are things that I hate,' says the LORD" (vs 16-17). *That's quite something!*

Zech. 10 tells us about what God is going to do and how He's going to do it. This is really quite something! Here it specifically says the house of *Judah* and the house of *Joseph*, which includes Ephraim and Manasseh.

Zechariah 10:6: "And I will strengthen the house of Judah, and I will save the house of Joseph,

and I will return to save them; for I have mercy upon them. And they shall be as though I had not cast them off; for I *am* the LORD their God, and I will answer them. And Ephraim shall be like a mighty one, and their heart shall rejoice as through wine. And their children shall see and be glad; their heart shall rejoice in the LORD. I will signal for them and gather them; for I have redeemed them. And they shall increase as they formerly increased" (vs 6-8). Isn't that something? *God is going to bring them back!*

Let's come back and see how the Millennium begins; we'll just take a preview. How is God going to bring them back? It's going to be an amazing thing! What is it going to be like when:

- Christ returns
- the saints are resurrected
- the Sea of Glass is there
- we all come back to the earth
- Satan is put away
- the Millennium begins

Here is what God is going to do, Isaiah 27:12: "And it shall come to pass, in that day the LORD shall thresh from the stream of the river Euphrates to the river of Egypt, and you shall be gathered one by one, O children of Israel. And it shall come to pass, in that day a great ram's horn shall be blown, and those perishing in the land of Assyria shall come, and the outcasts in the land of Egypt shall come and shall worship the LORD in the Holy mountain at Jerusalem" (vs 12-13).

This is going to be really a tremendous thing! We know what's going to happen, we've covered this before. Let's come to the book of Micah. Micah is very interesting because Micah also prophesied at the same time that Isaiah did. This is how it's going to be all during the Millennium, but I want to focus in on the beginning of the Millennium again for a specific purpose, because there is an event to happen that we need to understand so that we can unlock the understanding of Rev. 20. Let's see how all of this is going to come about.

Micah 4:1: "But it shall be in the last days *that* the mountain of the house of the LORD shall be established in the top of the mountains, and it shall be exalted above the hills; and people shall flow unto it. And many nations shall come and say, 'Come and let us go up to the mountain of the LORD, and to the house of the God of Jacob. And He will teach us of His ways, and we will walk in His paths'—for the Law shall go forth out of Zion, and the Word of the LORD from Jerusalem. And He shall judge among many people... [judgment is going to be given to us] ...and will rebuke strong nations afar off; and they shall beat their swords into plowshares, and their spears into pruning hooks.

Nation shall not lift up a sword against nation, neither shall they learn war anymore" (vs 1-3).

Men have been trying to bring peace for how many thousands of years? *They just can't do it! It takes the Spirit of God and the laws of God!* Even with the laws of God without the Spirit of God, you can create a reasonable society. But you don't know how to take care of the evil when it multiplies like we're seeing in our day. That's why Christ has to return. Remember, Jesus said that if He didn't return and if those days were not limited—to 3-1/2 years—there should be no flesh saved alive. These are going to be quite some days. But, after everything is settled down, and we'll see what takes place before they're settled down:

Verse 4: "But they shall sit each one under his *own* vine and under his *own* fig tree; and no one shall make them afraid; for the mouth of the LORD of hosts has spoken" *That's what it's going to be!*

In Rev. 20 we find something very interesting in Scripture concerning Satan the devil. Many people have wondered: How is this going to take place and has God really condemned the nations of Gog and Magog to never receiving salvation. When you read Rev. 20 we do get that kind of feeling. If that were the case then we would have to conclude that God is a respecter of persons, and that Gog and Magog are those who are destined to never have salvation. But we're going to see that's not correct.

Why mention Gog and Magog here? Let's explore the Scriptures here and understand what it's saying. Satan is going to be cast into the abyss. It's going to be covered over:

Revelation 20:3: "...so that he would not deceive the nations any longer until the thousand years were fulfilled; **and after that** it is ordained that he be loosed *for* a short time."

Why do that? Here's a thousand years of peace, a thousand years of every good thing, a thousand years of physical and spiritual blessing to the uttermost!

- Why would Satan be loosed again?
- Why is it that it is ordained that he be loosed?

Verse 7: "Now, when the thousand years have been completed, Satan shall be loosed out of his prison." The first thing he does is stir up trouble and make war. Notice where he goes:

Verse 8: "And he shall go out to deceive the nations that *are* in the four corners of the earth, Gog and Magog... [and there were other nations with them] ...of whom the number *is* as the sand of the sea, to gather them together for war."

So, the first thing that Satan does is stir up war again. We just read that all during the Millennium they're not going to learn war anymore.

- Why Gog and Magog?
- Does this mean the people of Gog and Magog, meaning that they will never receive any salvation?

or

- Does it mean a geographical territory of Gog and Magog for a specific purpose?

Again, we have to go back to the beginning of the Millennium to see what happens. Let's see what happens at the beginning of the Millennium and shortly afterward.

Let's reflect a little bit that we saw in Rev. 9, that there were the armies of 200-million, and they stretched all the way back to the Far East and the north. Is it possible that—and probably likely—all of those troops cannot come and surround Jerusalem and be in that one area when Christ returns. There will be armies sent out by the *beast* and *the false prophet* who then will suffer the seven last plagues. We still have this vast army.

- Are some of those left behind?
- Are some of those not destroyed when Christ returns?
- Why is it that Christ has to rebuke strong nations afar off?
- How does that happen?
- Who are these nations?
- Why would He have to do it?

We will get the answer in Ezekiel 38; we're going to see this takes place shortly after the Millennium begins. It's identified here in the Scriptures so that we know it is at that time. Then God has a specific purpose for this war with Gog and Magog and all the other nations with them, and this is going to be the final battle to bring all nations into subjection to the Kingdom of God.

Ezekiel 38:1: "And the Word of the LORD came to me, saying, 'Son of man, set your face against Gog, the land of Magog, the chief ruler of Meshech, and Tubal, and prophesy against him. And say, "Thus says the Lord GOD, 'Behold, I *am* against you, O Gog, the chief ruler of Rosh, Meshech and Tubal. And I will turn you back, and put hooks into your jaws, and I will bring you out, and all your army, horses and horsemen, all of them clothed most gorgeously, a great assembly *with* buckler and shield, all of them swordsmen; Persia... [Iran] ...Ethiopia... [India] ...and Libya with them, all of them *with* shield and helmet; Gomer and all his bands; the house of Togarmah *from* the uttermost parts of the north, and all his bands; *and* many people with you. Be prepared; yea, prepare for yourself, you and all your assembly that are assembled about you, and be a guard for them. After many days you will be summoned. In the **latter years** you shall come into the land restored from war…'"'" (vs 1-8).

- What land is that, restored from war? *The Holy Land!*
- When does that happen? *When Christ returns!*

—and He brings again the exodus of the children of the house of Judah and the house of Israel; brings them back to their lands. Of course, that whole vast area from the Nile River to the Euphrates River and the area described by Christ is for the people of God. At the beginning of the Millennium they will start there, and then branch out again and go repossess the lands that they had before.

Here we have the latter years, "'…In the **latter years** you shall come into the land restored from war, gathered out of many people, on the mountains of Israel, which have always been waste…. [that is up until the return of Christ] …(But she has been brought out of the nations, and they shall dwell securely, all of them.)'" (v 8).

This tells us something. First, when the Millennium begins, God is going to deal with the children of Israel and Judah.

Back to Gog and Magog, v 9: "'"And you shall go up, coming like a storm. You shall be like a cloud to cover the land, you and all your bands, and many people with you.' Thus says the Lord GOD, 'And it shall be in that day that things shall come into your heart, and you shall devise an evil plan. And you shall say, "I will go up to the land of un-walled villages…."'"'" (vs 9-11).

- no more armaments
- no more fortifications
- no more missiles
- no more armies
- no more ammunition

"'"I will go *to those that are at rest*…"'"' (v 11). *So they can't be anything other than just in the years shortly after the Millennium!*

"…who dwell securely, all of them dwelling without walls, and there are no bars nor gates to them" (v 11).

This looks like easy pickings, because those nations will have been so deceived by Satan the devil, even after Satan is put away at the beginning of the Millennium. Their armies are still out there. God is going to leave them out there for this event. We're going to see that this event is the last event that subjugates and brings all nations under the authority and rule of the Kingdom of God, Jesus Christ and the resurrected saints.

Here's why they come, v 12: "In order to take a spoil, and to steal a prize; to turn your hand upon the desolate places that are now inhabited, and upon the people that are gathered out of the nations, who have gotten cattle and goods, who dwell in the midst of the land." *Yes, God is blessing them!*

As we view the whole world, some nations will come and say, 'Let's go to the house of the Lord and learn of His way and learn of His Laws.' But the ones that don't, what is Christ going to have to do? *Rebuke those nations!* That's all after the Millennium starts. We're not told exactly how long this is.

- Could this be three and a half years?
- Could this be seven years?

We're not told exactly, but we know some time after the beginning of the Millennium this is going to happen because this is what it describes.

Verse 14: "Therefore, son of man, prophesy and say to Gog, 'Thus says the Lord GOD, "In that day when My people of Israel dwell securely… [a Millennial setting] …shall you not know *it*? And you shall come from your place out of the uttermost parts of the north, you and many people with you, all of them riding on horses, a great company and a mighty army. And you shall come up on My people Israel like a cloud, to cover the land. It shall be in the latter days, and I will bring you against My land, so that the nations may know Me when I shall be sanctified in you, O Gog, before their eyes"'"' (vs 14-16).

The nations are going *to know God* because of this! Just like anything else, human nature is hard to change. Unless God grants repentance, unless God grants His Spirit, they're going to react this way. God is saving them for this one final mighty battle after the Millennium has begun.

Satan was bound at the beginning of the Millennium, so here's the residual of those nations, and they see that here's an opportunity. There are no defenses. Look at all that they have, what easy pickings this is going to be, because they are not going to accept the fact that God is ruling on the earth. It says that they don't know Him, nor do some of the other nations. **"…so that the nations may know Me when I shall be sanctified in you, O Gog, before their eyes."**

Verse 17: "Thus says the Lord GOD, '*Are* you he of whom I have spoken in former days, by the hand of My servants the prophets of Israel, who prophesied in those days for many years that I would bring you against them? And it shall come to pass at the same time, when Gog comes against the land of Israel,' says the Lord GOD, '**My hot anger will be**

aroused'" (vs 17-18).

God is going to take care of them! This is going to be the final demonstration of the power of God, Christ as King, the resurrected saints as kings and priests and God's protection of the physical nation of Israel.

Verse 19: "'For in My jealousy *and* in the fire of My wrath I have spoken, "Surely in that day there shall be a great quaking in the land of Israel, so that the fish of the sea, and the birds of the heavens, and the beasts of the field, and all creeping things that creep on the earth, and all the men on the face of the earth, shall quake at My presence.... [they're all going to know; a final demonstration before universal peace] ...And the mountains shall be thrown down, and the steep places shall fall, and every wall shall fall to the ground." And I will call for a sword against him upon all My mountains,' says the Lord GOD. '*Each* man's sword shall be against his brother'" (vs 19-21).

He's going to bring them all down there, and just like He did with the Assyrians when they wanted to come and conquer Judah. They all got up and fought among themselves and killed themselves. This is what's going to happen, and it's going to be awesome!

Verse 22: "'And I will judge him with pestilence and with blood. And I will rain upon him, and upon his bands, and upon the many people with him, an overflowing shower, and great hailstones, fire and brimstone. Thus I will magnify Myself and sanctify Myself. And I will have Myself known in the eyes of many nations, and **they shall know that I *am* the LORD**'" (vs 22-23).

They're going to be known—Gog and Magog—as those nations who defied God to the very last ounce of strength within them. Of course, after they know God, then will not the descendants of Gog and Magog be granted an opportunity for salvation? *Well, if they submit to God and repent—* of course, they will!

Ezekiel 39:1 'Therefore, son of man, prophesy against Gog and say, "Thus says the Lord GOD, 'Behold, I *am* against you, O Gog, the chief ruler of Meshech and Tubal. And I will turn you about, and lead you on. And I will bring you up from the uttermost parts of the north, and I will bring you against the mountains of Israel. And I will strike your bow out of your left hand, and will cause your arrows to fall out of your right hand. You shall fall on the mountains of Israel, you and all your bands, and the people with you. I will give you for food to the birds of prey of every kind, and *to* the beasts of the field. You shall fall upon the face of the open field, for I have spoken it,' says the Lord GOD" (vs 1-5). *Here's God's judgment!*

This helps us understand, if we put this together with other Scriptures, why Satan is sent to Gog and Magog. We'll see there's a reason for it.

Verse 6: "'And I will send a fire on Magog, and on those who dwell in the isles. And they shall know that I *am* the LORD. And I will make My Holy name known in the midst of My people Israel. And I will not *let them* profane My Holy name any more. Then the nations shall know that I *am* the LORD, the Holy One in Israel. Behold, it is coming, and it shall be done,' says the Lord GOD. 'This *is* the day of which I have spoken'" (vs 6-8). They're all going to know.

You can read the rest of Ezek. 39 and we can see that this happens shortly after the Millennium begins. It's for a purpose. Gog and Magog *the people* then can be separated from Gog and Magog *the land.*

- Why does Satan go to Gog and Magog to bring them to fight against Jerusalem at the end of the Millennium?
- Who is there?
- How do they get there?
- How is it going to be during the Millennium?

We know and we've read the Scriptures how it's going be really something!

- everyone is going to know the Lord
- conversion for all people
- God's Spirit for all people

It begins with Israel and it goes out to all the nations!

Let's come to Isa. 65 and let's see something from these Scriptures that give us an understanding of how things will be, how long people will live, and let's understand something also very important here:

- even though the Kingdom of God is ruling on the earth
- even though the Holy Spirit is offered to everyone who repents

We also have to understand that there will be those who won't repent!

God has given free choice! One thing that God does not take from anyone is their free choice. God is not going to make us into robots and automatons. Robots and automatons cannot rule with God and Christ to rule the whole universe. We have to have the character of God:

- by will and choice
- by repentance and belief
- by faith and understanding

So likewise, they will during the Millennium; although it's all going to be right in front of them!

Isaiah 65:17: "For behold, I create new heavens and a new earth…."

When the Millennium begins is not God going to have to create new heavens and new earth—repair the whole earth? *Yes, indeed!* The earth will be in shambles and in ruins, so this can apply. We've applied many times to the Great White Throne Judgment, yes, and it's entirely proper to apply it to that. But let's apply it to the Millennium and let's see what we come up with here.

"…And the former things will not be remembered, nor come to mind. But be glad and rejoice forever *in that* which I create; for behold, I create Jerusalem a rejoicing, and her people a joy. I will rejoice in Jerusalem, and I will joy in My people; and the voice of weeping will no more be heard in her, nor the voice of crying" (vs 17-19). *We're going to see that this applies to physical people!*

Verse 20: "There will not be an infant who lives but a few days, nor an old man that has not filled his days… [What does it mean *filled his* days? We get an answer right in the next phrase]: …for the child will die a hundred years old; but the sinner *who is* a hundred years old shall be accursed." *Here's where we get a 100-year period!*

Let's see if we can understand these Scriptures. Let's see if we can put them together so we can realize how things will be during the Millennium.

Verse 21: "And they will build houses and live *in them*; and they will plant vineyards and eat their fruit. They will not build, and another live *in them*; they will not plant, and another eat; for like the days of a tree *are so will be* the days of My people, and My elect will long enjoy the work of their hands" (vs 21-22).

This shows physical people. This is telling us how the Millennium will progress. People will live to be 100-years-old. We have two things:

1. for the child shall die 100-years-old
2. the sinner who is 100-years-old shall be accursed

How are we going to understand that?

Let's understand how the Millennium is going to end and why God looses Satan at the end of the Millennium. There's going to be a reason. Let's begin to analyze right here:

Verse 20: "There will not be an infant who lives but a few days… [they're all going to fulfill their lives] …nor an old man that has not filled his

days, for the child will die a hundred years old; but the sinner *who is* a hundred years old shall be accursed."

- What is the division here between the righteous and the sinner?
- *The righteous are those who enter into the Kingdom of God!*
- Why does it say, "…the child will die a hundred years old…"?

In other words, everyone's going to fulfill their life, live 100 years, but they're going to die.

- How long will they be dead?

Let's answer the question why everyone needs to die. Heb. 9:27 tells us why everyone has to die. What is the difference between an infant who lives to be 100-years-old and dies compared to a sinner 100-years-old is accursed?

- if they fulfill their days
- if they love God
- if they are obedient
- if they have the Holy Spirit of God

that puts them into a particular category!

But here is one thing that God has decreed, Hebrews 9:27: "And inasmuch as **it is appointed unto men once to die, and after this, *the* judgment**."

Well, all of those who live in the Millennium will be judged everyday just like we are who

- have been called
- have repented
- been baptized
- received the Holy Spirit of God
- are living God's way
- growing in grace and knowledge
- overcoming and changing

We are going to die! But then there will be the resurrection. So, the child that dies at 100-years-old is obviously then going to be changed. But there has to be that instantaneous death, because it says it's "…**given to man once to die**…"

How do we understand this? I think we get answer, for those who are still alive after Christ returns and the first resurrection takes place:

1-Thessalonians 4:16: "Because the Lord Himself shall descend from heaven with *a* shout of command, with *the* voice of an archangel and with *the* trumpet of God; and the dead in Christ shall rise first."

That's why we have the first resurrection. However, not everyone who is a Christian is going to be dead and in the grave. What's going to happen to them?

Verse 17: "Then we who are alive and remain shall be caught up together with them in *the* clouds for *the* meeting with the Lord in *the* air; and so shall we always be with *the* Lord."

Those who are alive, what is going to happen to them? *They're going to be changed!* How are they going to be changed? *They must have an instantaneous death and transformation!* That's what must take place.

We'll put the Scriptures together to see if we can get the understanding we need as to what is going to happen.

1-Corinthians 15:49: "And as we have borne the image of the *one* made of dust, we shall also bear the image of the heavenly *one*." *Meaning we have to be transformed*:

1) by the resurrection, if we're dead and in the ground
2) in order to get rid of the physical body and the law of sin and death, there has to be an instantaneous death then an instantaneous transformation

Verse 50: "Now this I say, brethren, that flesh and blood cannot inherit *the* Kingdom of God, nor does corruption [fleshly] inherit incorruption. Behold, I show you a mystery: we shall not all fall asleep, **but we shall all be changed, in an instant, in *the* twinkling of an eye**…" (vs 50-52).

Let's apply that to those who live during the Millennium. They live 100 years. It comes time for them to enter into the Kingdom of God. It says they're going to die at 100-years-old. That is going to be an instantaneous death and instantaneous transformation so they can enter the spiritual Kingdom of God. That fulfills all the Scriptures! What about the sinner? It says:

"…the sinner that dies shall be accursed…"—*which means that person did not repent; refused salvation; refused to do the will of God! They're sinners!*

- What does God do with sinners if they can't die?
- What do I mean by that?
- What happens when we come toward the end of the Millennium?

There comes a time when the sinner will not be able to live 100 years and then die!

- What's going to happen to them?
- What if it comes to a time—like we saw all the way through—like with Solomon?

After all the good things that God did with Solomon; all the things that God did with His people during that time; that there were those who did not obey God.

Let's come back to Adam and Eve; we have two clear-cut cases here. What happened to them when they had sinned? They were living with God in the Garden of Eden. They sinned, but God did not want to bring upon them the death penalty immediately, otherwise the plan of God could not go forward. If they were dead they would be unable to have children.

What did God do? *He removed them from the Garden of Eden!* When you're removed from the presence of God that is an exile. We see that God removed sinners by exiling them.

Now let's look at the case of Cain, who murdered his brother Abel. What happened? *God did not exercise the death penalty upon him either*—did He? *No!* He sent Cain further exiled into the land of Nod or the Land of Wandering.

Let's view it this way, toward the end of the Millennium there is a generation of people who have grown up to all this society, but they choose not to obey God. What did God do to the ten tribes of the children of Israel when they sinned? Let's see what God did, because God obviously did not execute them. He let them live out their lives, die and be buried after they were exiled.

2-Kings 17:8—*talking about the children of Israel*: "And walked in the statutes of the nations whom the LORD cast out from before the children of Israel…"—*instead of following God!*

- What happens during the Millennium when someone says, 'I don't want to obey'?
- What happens if they commit a very serious crime, but it's not yet worthy of death and they don't have time to live out 100 years?
- What if we have people during the Millennium who do these things?

"…whom the LORD cast out from before the children of Israel…"

- What did God do with the heathen?
- *He got rid of them, got them out of the land!*
- Now what does God do with the children of Israel because of their sins?
- *He exiles them into captivity because they disobeyed!*

Verse 9: "Now the children of Israel secretly did things that *were* not right against the LORD their

God. And they built high places in all their cities for themselves from the Watch Tower to the fortified city. And they set up images and groves for themselves in every high hill, and under every green tree. And they burned incense in all the high places, like the nations whom the LORD had removed from before them, and they practiced evil things to provoke the LORD to anger" (vs 9-11). *We see that God said, 'Don't do these things!'*

Verse 13: "And the LORD testified against Israel and against Judah, by all the prophets, *by* all the seers, saying, 'Turn from your evil ways and keep My commandments *and* My statutes, according to all the law which I commanded your fathers, and which I sent to you by My servants the prophets.' Nevertheless, **they would not hear**…" (vs 13-14).

What are we going to do with those who *choose not* to obey? Isa. 65 says that they're 'accursed.' If they live to be 100-years they are accursed and buried, which is their first death. Everyone has to have a first death. But what has to happen to all sinners? *All the incorrigible sinners must die twice!* It says that there is the *second death.*

What happens if those in the Millennium, there are some who will *choose and refuse* to obey God, and there's not enough time for them to live to be 100 and be buried and be accursed that way? What is God going to do with them? Will He do with them as He did with Adam and Eve, and Cain, and the children of Israel and Judah? God testified and said to 'keep My ways.'

Verse 14: "Nevertheless, they would not hear, but hardened their necks, like the neck of their fathers who did not believe in the LORD their God. And *they* rejected His statutes and His covenant, which He made with their fathers, and His warnings that He testified against them. And they went after vanity, and became vain, and went after the nations around them, concerning whom the LORD had charged them not to do like them" (vs 14-15).

Again, apply this to the last generation of the Millennium and let's think about what we have already covered.

Verse 16: "And they left all the commandments of the LORD their God and made molten images, two calves for themselves. And they made a grove, and worshiped all the host of heaven, and served Baal. And they caused their sons and their daughters to pass through the fire. And they used divination and sorceries, and sold themselves to do evil in the sight of the LORD, **to provoke Him to anger**" (vs 16-17).

What if there are people who do that by choice? Here's what happens:

Verse18: "So, the LORD was very angry with Israel and removed them out of His sight…" He sent them off into exile. The Assyrians took them away.

What's going to happen during the Millennium? Could it be—and it sounds like it is entirely possible that it's going to be—that there is part of the area of Gog and Magog that will be reserved and set aside for the incorrigible wicked who refuse to repent. They will be removed and exiled to Gog and Magog. Can you see how that can happen?

Look at the history of human behavior as we covered earlier, how that humans when they disregard God become lukewarm. Did it not happen to the Church? Can it not happen to those people, as well? *Yes, indeed!* We grow up in a society and everything is here.

For example: There isn't hardly anyone left who does not remember the time when we didn't have electricity, and didn't have transportation like we have it today. Now we can fly here and there and go anywhere in the world anytime we want to. We take these things for granted. We take the way that things are, that are setup, for granted. Then we begin to sin, because when you take it for granted animosity and hatred begins to build up. This has to be, because these people did not repent and were not baptized. These are carnal people in the last generation of the Millennium.

- What are you going to do with them?
- Are you going to execute them?

or

- Are you going to save them all for one last grand deception by Satan the devil?

Let's go back and read this again. Let's come back to Rev. 20, and with this in mind and understanding what it's talking about. Remember, we can depend on the Scriptures. God is *the same yesterday, today and* forever, and that applies to Christ. The Lord says *He changes not.* God must handle the sinners who cannot die toward the end of the Millennium, because there's not enough time for them to live to be 100-years-old; He has to exile them! He has to remove them from His Kingdom!

Where will He put them? *We read how infamous Gog and Magog were in their rebellion at the beginning of the Millennium!* It just so happens that Gog and Magog is where Siberia is today. Think about that for a minute! What have the Russians done to the dissidents in their civilization? Even with the Czars and down through the Soviet Union and will be happening again, I am sure? *They exile them to Siberia!*

Since the wicked must be removed, and since there's not enough time for them to die—to live 100 years and die accursed—while they're still living they're accursed. They must be removed from the Kingdom of God! Is this why we find people from 'nations'? Let's see the sequence of events of what's going to happen:

- Satan is bound for a thousand years
- after that it is ordained that he be loosed for a short time

Why? Why be loosed? *Because there is yet one more mission that Satan has to do!* He has to go out and deceive those who have been exiled.

Revelation 20:7: "Now, when the thousand years have been completed, Satan shall be loosed out of his prison; and he shall go out to deceive the nations that *are* in the four corners of the earth…" (vs 7-8).

Let's understand something about Gog and Magog. They *willingly chose* to reject God's way so they had to be removed. They were not deceived. They gave up salvation by *their own free choice, their own free will.*

- they rejected God
- they rejected their teachers: us, as kings and priests
- they rejected everything about God's way and God said, 'Go! If you don't want to live here, you're going to live over there'

Just picture after a thousand years there's going to be a great population. Think of it! How many are going to choose at that time because they're not willing to repent? not willing to be baptized? reject the Holy Spirit of God? *They're sent off into a place of exile!*

Is it possible that some may go there and repent? Want to come back and then repent? *That's possible! We don't know!* Notice what it says here:

Verse 7: "Now, when the thousand years have been completed, Satan shall be loosed out of his prison; and he shall go out to deceive **the nations** that *are* in the four corners of the earth, **Gog and Magog**…" (vs 7-8).

This has to be the geographical area of Gog and Magog, not the people. *This is the land of Gog and Magog*, not the people of Gog and Magog.

Just like there is the land of Israel, but there are the children of Israel. Just like when they sinned, they were exiled out of the land of Israel into another land, so likewise when the people at the end of the Millennium reject salvation, they are removed and then Satan deceives them into what?

I don't know exactly how it's going to be, but when Satan comes out of his prison and he's sent

to those people and he performs signs and wonders and miracles—because he's able to do that—is he going to convince them that he is really God, and that all of these people ruling over them with all of these rules and regulations and laws and things like this, that they are the evil ones. After all, you choose not to obey.

Yes, that must have been very wise on your part. I am here,' Satan will tell them, 'and let's do this: We know they don't have any defense around Jerusalem. We know that if we work up an army and come to do battle against them, and if we succeed—which we can—then we'll take over the kingdom.'

Does that sound like the plan that Satan had in previous times? *Yes!* What else does Satan have to deceive the people? *All the demons will also be restrained in the abyss that was sealed, so they will be released and go with Satan, as well!* They will do tremendous and wondrous things. So, these people will be deceived and believe that they can actually regain the power and take it from God. All they have to do is go down and conquer Jerusalem, and the best time to do it is at the Feast of Tabernacles.

With that setup, "…of whom the number *is* as the sand of the sea, to gather them together for war" (v 8).

All during the Millennium they didn't learn war. As soon as Satan is removed, what happens? *War!*

- What happened when Satan first rebelled against God? *War in heaven!*
- What happens when Christ returns? *War against Christ and the angels and the resurrected saints!*

Every time Satan is loosed there is war! Why this war? *Well, they think that perhaps they're going to regain power!*

But notice what they do, v 9: "Then *I* saw them go up upon the breadth of the earth and encircle the camp of the saints, and the beloved city…"—Jerusalem on earth

Here they're coming against the camp of the saints, and what is the tabernacle that is over Jerusalem? *The cloud by day and pillar of fire by night!* So, they look around and see no defenses. Here they are, whatever weapons they have, I'm sure that Satan showed them how to make the weapons and what to do, and stir them all up in their hatred toward God.

Here they come in this battle and are going to reap vengeance against God and against the saints. After all, they would be so familiar with them that they will be blinded in their disobedience that they won't even realize that they have absolutely no power against God. Same deception that Satan had: he thought he could become like God. He thought that with one-third of the angels he could overcome God, take the Throne of God, defeat the angels of God, and God and Christ, and take over the universe. Well, that's the same thing that he's going to tell them here. Notice what happened:

"…and fire came down from God out of heaven and consumed them" (v 9). *Isn't that interesting?*

If they're destroyed in this fire, what is that death? That is their *first* death. So, God does this to the incorrigible wicked in the last part of the Millennium for those who reject God and His way. He sends them off into captivity to Gog and Magog. When the thousand years are finished, Satan is loosed out of his prison and he goes to deceive them into coming and fighting against God!

Now then, this brings the first death to every one of those sinners and *the sinner dies accursed* in this last generation, even though they couldn't live to be 100-years-old. That's the last thing that God is going to use Satan the devil for. Then notice what happens. *Here comes the judgment of Satan the devil*:

Verse 10: "And the Devil, who deceived them, was cast into the Lake of Fire and brimstone, where the beast and the false prophet *had been cast*… [they were cast there at the beginning of the Millennium] ….and they [plural], *Satan and the demons…*"

Flesh is going to burn up in the Lake of Fire, so the beast who was a physical human being, and the false prophet who was a human being, were burned up when they were cast into the Lake of Fire. But Satan and the demon being composed of spirit, the fire does not destroy them.

"…and they, *Satan and the demons* shall be tormented day and night into the ages of eternity" (v 10).

That sets the stage for the final great harvest of God as pictured by the Last Great Day. This is the fate of Satan and the demons. Later it shows that the blackness of darkness is reserved for them forever! Will that not bring more torment than anything that flames and fire can do? We find that in the book of Jude. This is how the Millennium is going to end. That sets the stage for the greatest harvest of all. That's why we have the Last Great Day.

Come back tomorrow and we will learn the message of the Last Great Day!

Scriptural References:

1) Jeremiah 31:31-34
2) Zechariah 8:12-17
3) Zechariah 10:6-8
4) Isaiah 27:12-13
5) Micah 4:1-4
6) Revelation 20:3, 7-8
7) Ezekiel 38:1-12, 14-23
8) Ezekiel 39:1-8
9) Isaiah 65:17-22, 20
10) Hebrews 9:27
11) 1 Thessalonians 4:16-17
12) 1 Corinthians 15:49-52
13) 2 Kings 17:8-11, 13-18
14) Revelation 20:7-10

Scriptures referenced, not quoted:

- Hebrews 8
- Revelation 1-5; 9
- Jude

FRC:bo
Transcribed: 8/19/12
Reformatted: 1/2021

CHAPTER EIGHTY

The Day of Judgment
Fred R. Coulter

Greetings brethren! Welcome to the Last Great Day, the eighth day of the Feast! We've had seven days of the Feast of Tabernacles.

It's very interesting how God starts out the Feast's season. He starts out with the Passover, which is one day, plus seven days, equals eight; 1+7=8! Then we count seven weeks to Pentecost. Then on that 8th day we have Pentecost, and we have the first resurrection. Then we come down to Trumpets and Atonement and then the Feast of Tabernacles, and now the Last Great Day. He ends it with 7+1=8. He starts it out with 1+7=8. Those juxtaposition are like bookends for the plan of God.

Leviticus 23:34 *tells us about the 8th day and that it's a Holy convocation*: "Speak to the children of Israel, saying, 'The fifteenth day of this seventh month *shall be* the Feast of Tabernacles… [we've already done that] …for seven days to the LORD.'"

The 1st day is a Holy convocation. They were to make their offerings (Num. 29), which we covered on the first day.

Verse 36: "…**On the eighth day shall be a Holy convocation**…" *This is an* **appointed Feast of** *God!*

It is probably the most insignificant Feast that is in the Bible. It's mentioned once in the book of John, which we will see a little bit later. You hear of the Jews keeping the Feast of Tabernacles, but hardly do you hear them keeping the Last Great Day. Of course, the Protestants and Catholics know nothing of it.

But here's what He says: "…On the eighth day shall be a Holy convocation to you. And you shall offer an offering made by fire to the LORD. It *is* a solemn assembly. And you shall do no servile work *therein.* These *are* the Feasts of the LORD, which you shall proclaim to be Holy convocations…" (vs 36-37). *These are the Feasts!* Notice how He ends it. This ties in with:

Verse 4: "These *are* the appointed Feasts of the LORD, Holy convocations, which you shall proclaim **in their** **appointed** seasons."

Now we do take up an offering on the Holy Days. We know that we are not to come before God empty. And knowing and understanding the plan of God, you think about how much God has blessed you and the knowledge that He has in your consideration of the offering.

(pause for offering)

Let's begin by going to the Gospel of John. Here it talks about the Feast of the Last Great Day. Here again is showing that Jesus kept the Feast, but He also prophesied of it's meaning and gave a fulfillment of it, as we find here in John 7. We know that in v 2 it says that it was the time of the Feast of Tabernacles. Of course, Jesus went up and kept the Feast of Tabernacles. Let's come down here to v 37; this was a special ceremony called the Ceremony of Water, which took place as the sun was going down to end the seventh day, and the beginning of the Last Great Day.

John 7:37: "'Now, in the last day, the great *day* of the Feast, Jesus stood and called out, saying, 'If anyone thirsts, let him come to Me and drink…. [prophecy of universal salvation] …**The one who believes in Me**, as the Scripture has said, out of his belly **shall flow rivers of living water**'" (vs 37-38). *A type of*

- spiritual life
- spiritual truth
- spiritual cleansing

All of these things are all a part of what we have here in what Jesus is explaining. There has to come a time when God undoes all evil. This is the day that pictures when God does that, when He gets rid of all evil in the whole human family.

Verse 39: "But this He spoke concerning the Spirit, which those who believed in Him would soon receive; for *the* Holy Spirit was not yet *given* because Jesus was not yet glorified."

It had its fulfillment beginning when they received the Holy Spirit when the Church began, and it's going to have its fulfillment in the end.

- What is the meaning of the Last Great Day?
- Why do we call it the Last Great Day?

First of all we're going to see that just like God has always done, that which is considered least among men produces the most for God.

Now let's come to Isa. 14 and let's see what God has declared. The first thing we need to understand and always remember is that God has a purpose and He is going to carry it out. He is God, and He looks down on the nations and as far as compared to Him what are they but a drop in the bucket. They aren't even weighty enough to be counted as dust in a scale of balances.

Isaiah 14:24: "The LORD of hosts has sworn, saying, 'Surely as I have thought, so it shall come to pass; and **as I have purposed, *so* it shall stand**.'"

Whatever God's purpose is, it's going to stand! That's why God has given His Word, has given His Spirit, and also has given choice:

- whether we believe in God
- whether we love God
- whether will keep His commandments
- whether we will do the things that are pleasing in His sight

The way that you understand God's plan is by keeping His commandments! That's what it says in

Psalm 111:10: "…a good understanding have all they **who do** His commandments…."

Isaiah 14:26: "This *is* the purpose that *is* purposed upon all the earth…" *Yes, it talks about breaking the Syrian,* which is a type of *the beast* as fulfilled in Rev. 19. He has a purpose that is proposed upon the whole earth.

"…and this *is* the hand that *is* stretched out upon all the nations" (v 26). **God's hand! He's going to do it!**

You know, and I just imagine that the Throne of God is a whole lot closer to the earth than we think, but being spiritual, we don't see it.

Verse 26: "For the LORD of hosts has purposed, and who shall reverse *it*? And His hand is stretched out, and who shall turn it back?'"

God is going to do His purpose! He is going to accomplish His purpose. *No man, no angel, not even any of the demons are going to turn back the hand of God!* It is just not going to happen.

Now let's come to the New Testament to the book of Ephesians here and let's understand something that is very profound. God has called us to reveal His secret to us. The understanding of this Last Great Day is the greatest fulfillment of the plan of God and it is a secret that God reveals to us. It's a mystery to the world because they cannot understand it because they will not obey Him.

The whole first chapter of Ephesians is in English the worst sentence in the world. But in the Greek it is one long sentence, two at the most. So, let's get the thoughts together here.

Ephesians 1:3: "Blessed *be* the God and Father of our Lord Jesus Christ, Who has blessed us with every spiritual blessing in the heavenly *things* with Christ."

Those spiritual blessings are going to be fulfilled when we enter into the Kingdom of God and are the spirit glorified sons and daughters of God. But He has given us the earnest, the down payment of it now.

Verse 4: "According as He has **personally** chosen us…" *That's what it means in the Greek with the special middle voice verb as I have covered before!*

I want you to understand: think about *you*. If you're sitting there and you're thinking: little ole me, what do I have to offer God? *You have love and obedience,* and God's calling and God's education for you. *But God personally has*:

"…**chosen us for Himself before *the* foundation of *the* world**…" (v 4). *That means in His plans He said,* 'I'm going to call the firstfruits. They will be in the first resurrection.' This is not fatalism, by the way, where most of the churches in the world believe in *fatalism*:

- if you're called you're going to make it, you go to heaven
- if you're not called you are going to go to hell and be tormented for ever and ever

*This day shows that **that lie** cannot possibly be true!* So, the predestination of this whole thing is that *God had the plan before the foundation of the world!*

"…in order that we might be Holy and blameless before Him in love; **having predestinated us for sonship**…" (vs 4-5).

That is, *all of those who are in the first resurrection have been predestinated for a special sonship,* by a special personal calling of God the Father and Jesus Christ.

"…to Himself through Jesus Christ, **according to the good pleasure of His own will,** to *the* praise of *the* glory of His grace, wherein He has made us objects of *His* grace in the Beloved *Son*; in Whom we have redemption through His blood, *even* the remission of sins, according to the riches of His grace, which He has made to abound toward us in all wisdom and intelligence; **having made known to us the mystery of His own will**…" (vs 5-9).

When you understand the plan of the Holy Days of God *you are being invited by God Himself* to understand His will. The mystery is that if you don't keep the Holy Days, and if you don't keep them the way that God has said and Jesus Christ has shown, you'll never understand it.

Because the Jews have rejected Christ, *they don't understand anything!* They believe just as much as the immortality of the soul as any of the religions in the world, because"

- even though they have the form of the Law, *they don't keep it*
- even though they have all of the prophecies, *they don't keep it*
- even though they have all of the prophecies of Jesus Christ, *they don't recognize Him*

God has called you, God has called me, God has called all the brethren down through time, as much as they are able to learn and know and understand!

Here we are at the end of the age and what can we do? God has given us:

- His will
- His truth
- His Word
- time to study
  - ✓ to know
  - ✓ to grow
  - ✓ to change
  - ✓ to overcome

And to realize that the very purpose and plan that God thought of at the beginning before the foundation of the world, He has made known to us! Now that ought to be very humbling indeed!

Verse 9: "Having made known to us the mystery of His own will, according to His good pleasure, which He purposed in Himself; that in *the Divine* plan for the fulfilling of *the* times… [the Last Great Day is the fulfilling of the last of the times of salvation] …He might bring all things together in Christ, both the things in the heavens and the things upon the earth" (vs 9-10).

- God has a plan
- God has the purpose
- He has called it
- we are part of it

It is fantastic and tremendous for us to realize and understand!

However, now let's look at the world. Let's understand something very profound. *God has chosen the few!* Many are called but few are chosen *because few repent!* Now let's understand something else here. God has done something that He alone is responsible for.

He's given all human beings *the law of sin and death* within them, a miniature part of the nature of Satan the devil. He's allowed them to go their own ways. He has let them be ruled by Satan the devil. God is responsible for that. As a result, how many people have been killed and died in wars and all of the things that have gone on down through time because men just reject God and cannot stand Him? *But God is responsible!*

Now we're going to see, yes, there is the unpardonable sin as we have covered in the book of Hebrews

{note our in-depth study at **truthofGod.org**: *Epistle of Paul to the Hebrews*}

But nevertheless, here's what God has done. People love to have their religions. Oh they love to take the name of God in a religious sense; condemn all of those who swear and curse; but those who take the name of God in vain in a religious sense are worse than the people who swear and curse and are just totally blinded. Those who are the religious ones don't realize that they are blinded because they don't want to do everything that God has said. Stop and think about that, what a fantastic miracle that it is that you understand, *that God has opened your mind; that God has called you!*

Isaiah 29:13: "And the LORD said, 'Because this people draws near *Me* with their mouth… [oh yes, got to have religion] …and with their lips honor Me… [God bless America] …but their worship of Me is made up of the traditions of men learned by rote, and their fear toward Me is *taught* by the commandments of men… [not by the Word of God] …therefore, behold, I will proceed to do again a marvelous work among this people, *even* a marvelous work and a wonder, for the wisdom of their wise ones shall perish, and the wisdom of their intelligent ones shall vanish'" (vs 13-14).

Verse 15: "**Woe** to those who go deep to hide *their* purpose from the LORD! And their works are in the dark, and they say, 'Who sees us? And who knows us?' Surely, you have turned things upside down! Shall the potter be regarded as the potter's clay; for shall the work say of him who made it, 'He did not make me?' Or shall the thing formed say to him who formed it, 'He had no understanding?' *Is* it not yet a very little while, and Lebanon shall be turned into a fruitful field…" (vs 15-17)—*then He's shows the solution to the problem!*

Let's look at some things here that are important for us to realize and carry through on this. Let's see where this is fulfilled. This will help us to answer a couple of very difficult Scriptures in the New Testament to understand. Here we have Christ's explanation of this even a little bit more.

Matthew 13:13: "For this *reason*… [explaining why He spoke in parables] …I speak to them in parables, because seeing, they see not; and hearing, they hear not; neither do they understand"

Isn't it amazing that people can have a Bible and not understand it? *They can read the words and not comprehend them! They can hear the things said but it's meaningless to them!*

Verse 14: "'And in them is fulfilled the prophecy of Isaiah, which says, "In hearing you shall hear, and in no way understand, and *in* seeing you shall see, and in no way perceive... [that is true concerning the meaning of the Last Great Day] ...for the heart of this people has grown fat, and their ears are dull of hearing, and **their eyes they have closed**..." (vs 14-15).

They have chosen to do this. So, God has selected their delusion, but also to serve His purpose and have mercy on them at a later time.

"...lest they should see with their eyes, and should hear with their ears, and should understand with their hearts, and should be converted, and I should heal them" (v 15).

Doesn't this go against mainstream Protestantism, which says, 'We have to save everybody. And if you're not saved in our church you're going to go to hell and burn in everlasting fire forever and ever.'

- How's God going to do that?
- Who is responsible for all of this?
- *God is!*

Verse 16—*Jesus says to the apostles, which means to us*: "But blessed *are* your eyes, because they see; and your ears, because they hear. For truly I say to you, many prophets and righteous *men* have desired to see what you see, and have not seen..." (vs 16-17).

Even Daniel didn't understand! Moses didn't understand! Isaiah, Jeremiah, Ezekiel—none of them understood! Even the apostles themselves did not fully understand. *We have been blessed at the end of the age to understand this far more fully than they did!*

"...and to hear what you hear, and have not heard" (v 17).

1-Tim. 2—*here is an enigma!* This is a hard one to answer, and really the answer is found in the meaning of the Last Great Day. Here is God's desire. But remember God's desire is always modified by the choice of the individual.

1-Timothy 2:3: "For this *is* good and acceptable before God our Savior... [to pray for quietness and so forth] ...Who desires all men to be saved and to come to *the* knowledge of *the* Truth" (vs 3-4).

- If He blinds them, how can they come to the knowledge of the Truth?

- What if they lived a full life and died without having the knowledge of the Truth, how can they be saved?
- *They must be called!*

If God has blinded them then obviously God is not going to call them. How's God going to solve this problem? Peter was writing about the very same thing.

2-Peter 3:9: "The Lord is not delaying the promise *of His coming*, as some in their own minds reckon delay; rather, He is longsuffering toward us, not desiring that any should perish, but that all should come to repentance."

He wants them all to come to repentance. He wants them all to be saved. How is He going to do this? If He cuts them off so they don't understand it, how's that going to happen? He has used Satan the devil to blind their minds, hasn't He (2-Cor. 4) so that they cannot understand? Yet, it says He wants them all to be saved. How is God going to do this?

Let's see what the Apostle Paul wrote. We're going to see in these Scriptures that we're going to cover here in Rom. 9 & 11 that the understanding that we have today Paul didn't quite have it. He knew that it was going to happen. But God had not given the revelation to the Apostle John, yet; so those Scriptures were not available for him to understand it.

Romans 9:14: "What then shall we say? *Is there* unrighteousness with God?...."—*because He loved Jacob and hated Esau!* Or we could say, *because He called some and didn't call others!* Is God unrighteous? *NO!* God has to *lead* a person to repentance!

- He wants them all to come to repentance
- He wants them to all be saved

BUT
- He has closed their minds
- He has blinded their eyes
- He has shut their ears
- He has put them in this predicament

Is God unrighteous in it? **Or** is not God *righteous* in doing so? *Because you see, the Last Great Day is the rest of the story!*

Verse 14: "What then shall we say? *Is there* unrighteousness with God? MAY IT NEVER BE! For He said to Moses, 'I will show mercy to whomever I show mercy, and I will have compassion on whomever I have compassion.' So then, *it is* not of the one who wills, nor of the one who runs; rather, **it is of God, Who shows mercy**" (vs 14-16).

IF God has called us and shown us mercy, **THEN** we ought to be thankful and happy and grateful that God has done it. Then he goes on to show that yes, He raised up Pharaoh for the very purpose:

Verse 17: "For the Scripture said to Pharaoh, 'For this very purpose I raised you up in order that I might show in you My power, so that My name may be declared in all the earth.'" *And it is in the Bible, His name and what He did to Egypt is there for anyone to read from that time forward to glorify the name of God!*

Verse 18: "So then, He shows mercy to whom He will, and He hardens whom He will. Will you then reply to me, 'Why does He yet find fault?'" (vs 18-19).

In other words, why does He still punish people for sin if He blinds their eyes? *Because sin has penalties,* that's why! So, He's not going to take that away. Otherwise how are you ever, ever going to know what's right and wrong?

"'...For who has opposed His purpose?' Yes, indeed, O man, who are you to answer against God? Shall the thing that is formed say to the one who formed *it,* 'Why did you make me this way?'" (vs 19-20). *Then he goes on to explain here a little bit about a potter and all the things that are done there.* He says*:*

Verse 21: "Or doesn't the potter have authority over the clay to make from the same lump of clay one vessel unto honor, and another vessel unto dishonor? And *who dares to question His purpose* if God, willing to show *His* wrath and to make known His power, chose in much long-suffering to put up with *the* vessels of wrath, which were created for destruction..." (vs 21-22).

If God created them for that, how is He going to save them? How is He going to solve the problem? ***That's the answer of this day!***

Verse 23: "In order that He might make known the riches of His glory unto *the* vessels of mercy, which He prepared before for glory."

Paul is talking to the Gentiles and he's saying the Gentiles were seeking God, but not the way that they should have. So, they were broken off. Even God cut off His own people that He says He loves. Now he's talking to the Gentiles and he says:

Romans 11:18: "Do not boast against the branches; but if you are boasting against *them, remember that* you do not bear the root; rather, **the root bears you.**"

Isn't that interesting? It shows that it comes all from the Word of God.

Verse 19: "Will you then say, 'The branches were broken off in order that I might be grafted in'?

That is true! Because of unbelief they were broken off, and you stand by faith. Do not be high-minded, but fear" (vs 19-20).

A good lesson for us! Because God has given us the understanding of His plan and has called us, let's not be high-minded, hooty-snooty, self-righteous and look down on the world.

Verse 21: "For if God spared not the natural branches, take heed lest He not spare you either. Therefore, behold *the* graciousness and *the* severity of God: upon those who fell, severity; and upon you, graciousness, if you continue in *His* graciousness; otherwise you also will be cut off. And they also, if they do not continue in unbelief, shall be grafted in because God is able to graft them in again. For if you were cut off from an olive tree which by nature is wild, and contrary to nature were grafted into a good olive tree, how much more shall those who according to nature *were from the good olive tree* be grafted back into their own olive tree?" (vs 21-24).

Verse 25: "For I do not wish you to be ignorant of this mystery, brethren, in order that you may not be wise in your own conceits: that a partial hardening *of the heart* has happened to Israel until the fullness of the Gentiles be come in... [God is going to resolve the problem] ...and so all Israel shall be saved..." (vs 25-26). *He doesn't know when. But at this time*:

Verse 32: "For God has given them all over to unbelief in order that He might show mercy to all.... [When?] ...O *the* depth of *the* riches of both *the* wisdom and *the* knowledge of God! How unfathomable *are* His judgments and unsearchable *are* His ways! For who did know *the* mind of *the* Lord, or who became His counselor?.... [here we have it] ...Or who first gave to Him, and it shall be recompensed to him again? For from Him, and through Him, and unto Him *are* all things; to Him *be* the glory into the ages of eternity. Amen" (vs 32-36).

Let's see how God is going to begin to solve the problem. Again, it deals with the Millennium It tells us something that is very important. It tells us something that shows the mind of God. It tells us something about the plan of God.

Rev. 20:4 talks about the resurrection of the saints, that they will live and reign with Christ a thousand years!

Revelation 20:5: "(But **the rest of the dead did not live again** until the thousand years were completed.)...." *So, at the end of the Millennium there's going to a resurrection.* Quite an amazing and a profound thing, isn't it? *Yes, it is!*

Let's look at some other Scriptures that help us understand this a little bit here. Who are the rest of the dead? Well we know (1-Cor. 15) as we learned on the Day of Pentecost tells us that Christ is the firstfruit, and then all of those who are Christ's at His coming—that's the first resurrection.

- What about all the other people?
- What about all of those that God blinded?
- What about those people who were sincere but **never knew, never understood, never had the Spirit of God**?
- Are they lost?
- Are they cut off?
- Are they destined to have no opportunity for salvation at all?

If the rest of the dead are all of those who were not in the first resurrection!

- Why are they to be resurrected?
- What is the purpose in doing so?

Well, we get a clue! John 11 talks about the resurrection of Lazarus.

- Why was Lazarus resurrected? *Remember, he died and was in the grave for four days!*
- Why did Jesus resurrect him?

Even in coming to the tomb Jesus said, 'If you believe that I am the resurrection.' His sister said, 'Yes, I believe that he'll be raised up at the last day' She wasn't thinking that he would be raised right then. But Jesus loved Lazarus! Jesus had called Lazarus, but he died before a very important thing could take place in his life; *he had not received the Holy Spirit!* If he had not been raised from the dead he would not have been in the first resurrection, because you have to receive the Holy Spirit of God and grow in grace and knowledge and be resurrected when Christ returns. So therefore, he was brought back to life. Same way with the saints who were resurrected, came back to a second physical life in the flesh (Matt. 27), so that they could receive the Holy Spirit and be saved.

Now this tells us how God operates. Rom. 2 tells us something very important. Let's talk about the so-called 'good, sincere people' out there in the world, because there are many of them out there.

- God hasn't called them
- they're blinded

▪ Have they sinned a sin unto death?
▪ Have they committed the unpardonable sin?
▪ *No!*

As a matter of fact, a lot of them are trying to live fairly decent lives! God talks about this:

Romans 2:14: "For when the Gentiles, which do not have the Law... [we could say today. 'Do not understand the Law.'] ...practice by nature the things contained in the Law..."

- they don't believe in stealing
- they don't believe in committing adultery
- they don't believe in lying and all of those things
- they try and live good decent lives
- they try and be honest

but their minds are not open to
- the Sabbath
- the Holy Days
- the Scriptures

But maybe they're even trying in some way to be— as some of the Sunday professing Christians are— trying to lead a decent life. *But God hasn't opened their minds to understanding!*

The reason that God does this is so that everyone is going to know that no one is going to receive salvation because of the works that he or she is doing. **God has to give it!** But in cutting people off from having the understanding of the Word of God, we have a vast area of decent people out there down through all time who have not committed the unpardonable sin.

"...practice by nature the things contained in the Law, these who do not have the Law are a law unto themselves; who show the work of the Law written in their own hearts, their consciences bearing witness, and their reasonings also as they accuse or defend one another); **in a day when God shall judge the secrets of men by Jesus Christ, according to my Gospel**" (vs 14-16).

We know this: *our names are written in the Book of Life!* But:

- What about all of those people out there who have died in wars, from famine, pestilence and starvation?
- What about all of those who died in accidents and floods?
- What about all of those who were under the influence of Satan the devil before the Flood of Noah?
- What about all of those that have been deceived, that don't know, that never heard the name of Jesus Christ?

Long before there were any Protestant missionaries, hundreds of millions of people down through history have died having not known the way of God! Even a lot of the children of Israel and Judah have not known God because He's blinded them. Yes, they've had the Scriptures. Yes, they've had the Word of God, *but they don't know God!*

Here, let's go to John 5 now and let's see what Jesus said so that we understand all of those who are to be resurrected... Now we'll cover this in just a minute. We're not going to delve deeply into the unpardonable sin.

John 5:25: "Truly, truly I say to you, *the* hour is coming, and now is, when the dead shall hear the voice of the Son of God; and those who hear shall live." ***They'll be raised!***

That's what happened to Lazarus. That's what happened to the others that Jesus raised.

Verse 26: "For even as the Father has life in Himself, so also has He given to the Son to have life in Himself; and has also given Him authority to execute judgment because He is *the* Son of man. Do not wonder at this, for *the* hour is coming in which all who are in the graves… [all who have died] …shall hear His voice and shall come forth: those who have practiced good unto a resurrection of life, and those who have practiced evil unto a resurrection of judgment" (vs 26-29). *There are two kinds of judgme*n*t*:

1. the judgment of the unpardonable sin
2. the judgment of the person who has not committed the unpardonable sin

So we can extrapolate from what we know from the Scriptures. There is a Book of Life, and our names are written in it right *now*. Could we also say that in order for all of those who have not committed the unpardonable sin, that their names are also written in *a separate Book of Life* to be raised in a resurrection? *Have to be, otherwise how can they be resurrected!*

We can also extrapolate that there has to be a book of the dead for those who have committed the unpardonable sin to die the second death. As we continue we'll take a look at where it talks about 'the rest of the dead who live not again till the thousand years were finished.'

Remember, they cannot come out of the graves. They cannot be resurrected from the dead ***unless Jesus resurrects them!*** These are all the people who never had an opportunity for salvation. I know there are a lot of hard-shelled Baptists out there in the world who don't want to give people a 'second' opportunity.

- What ***if they never had a first*** opportunity?
- What *if they need a second life* in the flesh for a *first* opportunity for salvation?

If God is going to do as He wants to have them come to repentance and be saved, He's got to do it someway, somehow! *This is how He's going to do it!*

Revelation 20:11: "Then I saw a great white throne… [that's why this is called the Great White Throne Judgment Day] …and the One Who was sitting on it, from Whose face the earth and the

heaven fled away; and no place was found for them…. [billions and billions of people] …And I saw the dead…" (vs 11-12).

Which dead? ***The rest of the dead who lived not again until the thousand years were finished!***

"…small and great, standing before God; and *the* books were opened; and **another book was opened, which is** *the Book of Life*…" (v 12). *Now they're going to have an opportunity for eternal life! Amazing, isn't it?*

"…And the dead were judged out of the things written in the books, according to their works" (v 12).

Now their first life surely couldn't qualify them for salvation. You can't say because they are good sincere people; therefore, they earned salvation a little differently than the rest. Because Jesus said that He is 'the door,' and if they come in any other way they are thieves and robbers. So, it's not going to be another way. It's going to be according to God's way. Here is how God is going to do it.

Now let's see in the book of Ezekiel where it does talk about this. Then we'll come back to the New Testament again. Let's see where there is a resurrection to a second physical life of those who were never called to receive salvation in their first physical life.

This is quite a long one here so we need to read all of this section in Ezek. 37 because this is the meaning of this day: ***when the rest of the dead live again!*** We're going to see that it is *a second life in the flesh for a first opportunity for salvation,* which they never had before, *because*:

1. God didn't call them
2. God blinded their eyes
3. they lived before Christ came

They were in other nations other then Israel!

This helps answer the question, too. Look at all of the things that Israel went through. This proves a point, there was not universal salvation granted to those under the Old Covenant. They were required to obey in the letter of the Law. But there was no salvation granted to them. Only to the prophets and certain of the kings, and that was it.

Ezekiel 37:1: "The hand of the LORD was on me, and brought me by the Spirit of the LORD, and set me down in the midst of a valley, and it *was* full of bones. And He made me walk among them all around. And behold, very many *were* in the open valley. And lo, *they were* very dry…. [like looking out in a valley and all you see are bones, all human bones] …And He… [the LORD] …said unto me, 'Son of man, can these bones live?' And I answered, 'O Lord GOD, You know'" (vs 1-3). *Ezekiel couldn't tell Him whether they could live or not!*

Verse 4: "Again He said to me, 'Prophesy to these bones, and say to them, "O dry bones, hear the Word of the LORD. Thus says the Lord GOD to these bones, 'Behold, I will cause breath to enter into you, and you shall live'"'" (vs 4-5).

What kind of life? *The answer is right here*: v 6: "And I will lay sinews on you, and will bring up flesh on you…"

Let's stop here for a minute before we go on and analyze this any further. First of all, if you see all these dry bones out there, what does it tell us? *It tells us these were people who were alive once!* Otherwise, how are you going to get the bones? It also tells us that it's people who have died. So now here we have the details on how the rest of the dead are going to live after the Millennium is finished.

Verse 6: "And I will lay sinews on you, and will bring up flesh on you, and cover you with skin, and put breath in you, and you shall live. And you shall know that I *am* the LORD."

Here's a group of people that didn't know the Lord. Now then, if their eyes are blinded and if their ears are stopped, there is no way they could know the Lord. *They lived and died without knowing God!* Now then, *He's going to give them a second physical life to know God!*

Verse 7: "So, I prophesied as I was commanded. And as I prophesied, there was a noise. And behold, a shaking! And the bones came together, a bone to its bone. And as I watched, behold the sinews and the flesh came upon them, and the skin covered them above. But *there was* no breath in them" (vs 7-8).

Here they were. They look like human beings again, recreated in the flesh according to the genetics that God gave them when they were first conceived. Amazing, isn't it? *No breath in them!*

Verse 9: "And He said to me, 'Prophesy to the wind, prophesy, son of man, and say to the wind, "Thus says the Lord GOD, 'Come from the four winds, O breath, and breathe on these slain that they may live.'"' So, I prophesied as He commanded me, and the breath came into them, and they lived and stood on their feet, an exceedingly great army. And He said to me, **'Son of man, these bones are the whole house of Israel**…'" (vs 9-11).

This tells the rest of the story that Paul was writing about there in Rom. 11, that they were cut off, the whole house of Israel, all twelve tribes.

"…Behold, they say, 'Our bones *are* dried and our hope is lost; we ourselves are completely cut off'" (v 11).

The wages of sin is death and all have sinned and come short of the glory of God' even though they may have tried to do the best that they could.

Verse 12: "Therefore, prophesy and say to them, 'Thus says the Lord GOD, 'Behold, O My people, **I will open your** [#1]**graves and cause you to come up out of your** [#2]**graves,** and will bring you into the land of Israel. And you shall know that I *am* the LORD when **I have opened your** [#3]**graves,** O My people, and have brought you up **out of your** [#4]**graves**" (vs 12-13).

It says graves four times! They were dead! They were in their graves! *This is picturing the resurrection from the dead to a second life in the flesh!* It has to be.

Verse 14: "'And I shall put My Spirit in you… [an opportunity for salvation] …and you shall live, and I will place you in your own land. And you shall know that I the LORD have spoken it and have done it,' says the LORD."

Matt.—here we find something very interesting. Because this happens to Israel, what happens to all the rest of the nations? There's a principle in the New Testament to understand this: *to the Jew first and then to the Gentile!* Or, to the Israelites first and then the Gentiles. What happens to Israel also happens to the Gentiles. Very important principle to remember.

Here's something to understand. Matt. 12 gives us a little definition of the unpardonable sin. Since we have covered that in the book of Hebrews, I'm not necessarily going to cover it here. But *the unpardonable sin is*:

- the total rejection of God
- total rejection of being led to repentance
- a total rejection of the Spirit of God
- total rejection of God's way completely

That is the unpardonable sin against the Holy Spirit of God!

Matthew 12:32: "And whoever speaks a word against the Son of man, it shall be forgiven him; but whoever speaks against the Holy Spirit, it shall not be forgiven him, neither in this age nor in the coming *age*." *We're talking about the coming age, the Last Great Day!*

Verse 33: "Either make the tree good and the fruit good, or make the tree corrupt and its fruit corrupt; for a tree is known by its fruit. Offspring of vipers, how are you able to speak good things, being evil? For out of the abundance of the heart the mouth speaks. The good man out of the good treasure of his heart brings out good things; and the wicked man out of the wicked treasure brings out wicked things.

But I say to you, for every idle word that men may speak, they shall be held accountable in ***the* Day of Judgment**" (vs 33-36).

God is going to judge us by our words! That's talking about the unpardonable sin.

Verse 37: "For by your words you shall be justified, and by your words you shall be condemned."

Then the Pharisees, they wanted to have a sign. He said it would be the sign of Jonah three days and three nights and so forth.

Verse 41: "*The* men of Nineveh shall stand up in the judgment…"

Isn't that what we read in John 5? *Some to* ***a resurrection of life*** *and some to* ***a resurrection of judgment!*** The Last Great Day is called the Great White Throne Judgment, to be given an opportunity for salvation for those who have never had an opportunity, *and they are given a second life in the flesh!*

Verse 41: "*The* men of Nineveh shall stand up… [resurrected] …in the judgment **with this generation**…"—which shows that this is going to take place at the same time that Ezek. 37 is fulfilled when all Israel is resurrected!

"…and shall condemn it, because they repented at the proclamation of Jonah; and behold, a greater than Jonah *is* here. *The* queen of *the* south… [now removed by well over a thousand years from the men of Nineveh] …shall rise up in the judgment… [be resurrected] …with this generation… [at the same time] …and shall condemn it, because she came from the ends of the earth to hear the wisdom of Solomon; and behold, a greater than Solomon *is* here" (vs 41-42).

Here we have right from the Scriptures a resurrection to life of Israel—all 12 tribes—and Gentile nations at the same time. Be resurrected and given an opportunity for salvation. *Be brought back to life in the flesh,* just like Lazarus and the saints were brought back to physical life so they could have an opportunity for salvation.

Now let's see what kind of world that they are going to come back to.

What is the sum of this, brethren? Well, the sum of it is this: All those who have lived and died and have not committed the unpardonable sin are going to be raised to have an opportunity for salvation. I think we can just refer to what we covered yesterday. They are going to live 100 years. Now there are going to be some people who were righteous at the end of the Millennium who are going to also live on through into that time.

Let's come here to Rev. 20 and let's see something that is important for us to understand. Many people have misunderstood this. Remember Rev. 10, it talks about that Satan the devil is cast into the Lake of Fire and brimstone. He is put away. When these people are resurrected and stand in the judgment, and God is going to be fair in the judgment that He is giving them. That He is giving them an opportunity for salvation. They're going to be judged just like we are today. What does it say of the Church? *For judgment is upon the house of God. And if it begin with us, where will the sinner and the ungodly be?*

Likewise, they are going to be judged and have an opportunity to live, and in this second life Satan is not going to be anywhere around. Don't you think that living one life under Satan the devil is quite sufficient? *Satan is not going to be around!* They're going to have the opportunity for salvation. This is when God is going to fulfill that He wants all men to come to repentance and be saved. Peter said that He wants all men to be saved. This is how He's going to do it.

Then we have the situation that comes *with the unpardonable sin,* and we have what is called *the second death.* All men who reject the salvation of God must die twice regardless of when they lived. Therefore, there has to be another phase of this second resurrection, which is the resurrection of the wicked. Let's just continue the story before we get to that.

Revelation 20:13: "And the sea gave up the dead *that were* in it, and death and *the* grave gave up the dead *that were* in them; and they were judged individually, according to their works."

That's a very interesting situation here. Each one is judged *individually.* When they qualify for life what's going to happen? They are going to enter into life just like those during the Millennium. When it came the end of the hundred years they would enter into life. All of those who do not qualify for salvation, or at this time reject the salvation of God—which they have the choice to do—then there's going to be something else that's going to happen. All those who qualify will enter into the Kingdom of God. All of those who do not qualify will be left standing waiting their fate, because it is judgment: *Judgment unto life or judgment unto the second death!* What's going to happen is this: all of those who committed the unpardonable sin all the way down through history are all going to be resurrected and they are going to stand waiting their judgment to the Lake of Fire.

Verse 14: "death and *the* grave were cast into the Lake of Fire. **This is the second death**. And if anyone was not found written in the Book of Life, he was cast into the Lake of Fire" (vs 14-15). *They* *are burned up, they are ashes, there is no more torment!* Concerning the wicked, the righteous are going to walk on the ashes of the wicked (Mal. 4).

Now let's look at a very interesting parable that Jesus gave in Luke 16 concerning Lazarus and the rich man. When you read this it looks like that people are tormented in hell forever. That's part of the problem with the translation in the *King James Version*, because it says, 'and in hell.' The Greek word 'hades' is *the grave.*

Luke 16:19: "Now, there was a certain rich man, and he was clothed in purple and fine linen, and daily indulged himself in luxury. And there was a certain poor man named Lazarus, who was laid at his porch, full of sores. And he longed to be nourished with the crumbs that fell from the rich man's table; and the dogs even came and licked his sores" (vs 19-21). *No one to comfort him but a dog!* That's why God gave dogs, to comfort people when no one else will.

Now, it came to pass *that* the poor man died, and he was carried away by the angels into Abraham's bosom...." (vs 21-22).

- When is he carried away? *He dies!*
- When is he carried by the angels? *At the resurrection* (Matt. 24)

"...into Abraham's bosom..." *because Abraham, Isaac, and Jacob are going to be in the Kingdom of God!* **This is the first resurrection!**

"...And the rich man also died and was buried. And in the grave he lifted up his eyes and was in torment..." (vs 22- 23).

Obviously, this man had committed the unpardonable sin, but not because he was rich. When is he going to lift up his eyes in the grave? That's why it's misleading where the *King James* says 'and in hell.' I just imagine there have been thousands and thousands of fire and brimstone preachers preaching this about being tormented in hell. *Not so!*

"...in the grave he lifted up his eyes..." When would that be? *After the Great White Throne period of 100 years* (Rev. 20)! The *second phase of the second resurrection* takes place and the incorrigible wicked are raised to face their judgment of the second death. This is what happened with the rich man.

"...and was in torment..." Why was he in torment? *Because he could look out and see the Lake of Fire out there!*

"...*for* he saw Abraham afar off, and Lazarus in his bosom. And he cried out *and* said, 'Father Abraham, have compassion on me and send Lazarus, so that he may dip the tip of his finger in water and cool my tongue; **for I am suffering because of this flame**'" (vs 23-24)—*that is by seeing it!* You'd be tormented, too!

How much fear would you have if you were standing on the edge of a volcano and you thought you were going in there? I mean you think about that the next time you watch the Kilauea volcano in Hawaii blow up and all that lava is flowing down.

"...**because** of this flame" *not **in** the flame!*

Verse 25: "Then Abraham said, 'Child, remember that in your lifetime you received good things to the full, and likewise Lazarus evil things. But now he is comforted, and you are suffering. And besides all these things, between us and you a great chasm has been fixed... [the difference between physical life and spiritual life; that's fixed] ...so that those who desire to pass from here... [facing the second death] ...to you are not able, nor can those from there pass to us'" (vs 25-26)—*to go back and become a human being again; it's not possible!*

Verse 27: "And he said, 'I beseech you then, father, that you would send him to my father's house, for I have five brothers; so that he may earnestly testify to them, in order that they also may not come to this place of torment.' Abraham said to him, 'They have Moses and the prophets. Let them hear them'" (vs 27-29).

- Are we talking about the difference between eternal life and eternal death? *Yes, indeed!*
- What is the difference? *You must hear Moses!*

As 2-Cor. 3 has said, that 'in Christ the veil of the eyes is taken away at the reading of Moses' *when you have the Holy Spirit of God!* Moses and the Prophets *are necessary for salvation! Have to be!*

Verse 30: "But he said, 'No, Father Abraham, but if one from *the* dead would go to them, they would repent.'"

People will not be convinced unless they choose to repent. Unless they are convicted in heart of their sins there is no way that they will repent. Besides you're also dealing here with the unpardonable sin with the rich man.

Verse 31: "And he said to him, 'If they will not hear Moses and the prophets, they would not be persuaded even if one rose from *the* dead'"

This parable of the rich man takes place when the dead, the incorrigible wicked who have committed the unpardonable sin, are raised from the dead to stand alongside the Lake of Fire with all of those who have committed the unpardonable sin, and they are all going to be cast alive into the Lake of Fire *as **God's final judgment!*** God has told all the righteous down through time, 'You will see the final judgment of God. You will see the vengeance of God.' It's necessary for a demonstration of the righteousness of God that all of the wicked die together just as all who are saved will live together.

With this Lake of Fire, God is going to do something; *He is going to prepare the whole earth for the new heavens and the new earth!* Let's see where it talks about the destruction of this earth in preparation for the new heaven and the new earth. Now the destruction of the earth is going to be that the Lake of Fire is going to envelop everything on the earth. It will be a great renewing of the surface of the earth. Now as spirit beings, that will not affect us.

2-Peter 3:10: "However, the Day of *the* Lord shall come as a thief in *the* night in which the heaven itself shall disappear..."

Peter didn't have all the knowledge and understanding that John did in Revelation. So, his account here is a little deficient. But we put it together—a line here, a line there, a little here, and a little there, precept upon precept—and that gives us understanding.

"...in which the heaven itself shall disappear... [that's the heaven around the earth] ...with a mighty roar, and *the* elements shall pass away, burning with intense heat, and *the* earth and the works in it shall be burned up" (v 10).

When the wicked are cast into the Lake of Fire, like it says there in Rev.19[transcriber's correction], 'death and hell are cast into the Lake of Fire,' *it envelops the whole earth!* When it does it destroys all the oceans.

Verse 11: "Since all these things are going to be destroyed, what kind of *persons* ought you to be in Holy conduct and Godliness, looking forward to and striving for the coming of the day of God, during which *the* heavens, being on fire, shall be destroyed, and *the* elements, burning with intense heat, shall melt? But according to His promise, we look forward to a new heaven and a new earth, in which righteousness dwells" (vs 11-13).

Now let's see the fulfillment of this that was given to John approximately 30 years after Peter wrote this, thereabouts. Here then it gives us a glimpse into the final fulfillment of the Kingdom of God.

Revelation 21:1: "Then I saw a new heaven and a new earth; for the first heaven and the first earth were passed away, and there was no more sea."

Now you see at that time, as spirit beings, we will no longer need oceans. We need them today as physical human beings to keep the temperature on the earth suitable for human life. So, there's no more

sea. Here's the new earth. Now God is going to begin to replenish the new earth. Let's see what He does.

Verse 2: "And I, John, saw the Holy City, *the* New Jerusalem, coming down from God out of heaven, prepared as a bride adorned for her husband. And I heard a great voice from heaven say, 'Behold, the Tabernacle of God *is* with men... [all men now made perfect being born again into the Kingdom of God] ...and He shall dwell with them, and they shall be His people; and God Himself shall be with them *and be* their God. And God shall wipe away every tear from their eyes; and *there* shall not be anymore death, or sorrow, or crying; neither shall *there* be any more pain, because the former things have passed away'" (vs 2-4).

Now we enter into the glorious Kingdom of God. We look forward to the New Jerusalem made by the very hands of God the Father and Jesus Christ and the angels prepared for His Church.

Verse 5: "And He Who sits on the Throne said, 'Behold, I make all things new.' Then He said to me, 'Write, for these words are true and faithful.'…. [it's going to happen; it's going to come to pass] ...And He said to me, 'It is done. I am Alpha and Omega, the Beginning and the End....'" (vs 5-6).

From the very beginning of the creation of Adam and Eve, clear down to the very end Christ is going to carry out and fulfill His plan as He has told us.

"...To the one who thirsts, I will give freely of the fountain of the Water of Life. The one who overcomes shall inherit all things; and I will be his God, and he shall be My son" (vs 6-7).

Now He gives a warning here, which is very important for us to understand:

Verse 8: "**But *the* cowardly**..." Someone said that the *King James* says 'fearful.' Aren't we to fear God? Well this is not the same kind of fear. This is that you **don't have enough courage to be a Christian the way you ought to be, and you give up on God!**

Verse 8: "But *the* cowardly, and unbelieving, and abominable, and murderers, and fornicators, and sorcerers, and idolaters, and all liars, shall have their part in the lake that burns with fire and brimstone; which is *the* second death."

Then there is this great vision that he sees of New Jerusalem coming down out of heaven—1500 miles cubed! New Jerusalem: streets paved with gold, made with all of the most fine and precious stones. I am sure that all of these, as it lists all of the stones, the wall, the gates, the pearls, and everything like that, I'm sure that he is seeing not just the physical thing of it but he is seeing that which is composed out of spirit but looks like these things.

Verse 21: "…and the street of the city *was* pure gold, as transparent *as* glass."

That has to be spiritual! We're going to be spirit beings. Everything that we have will be made out of spirit, whether it be the clothes that we have, new Jerusalem that we dwell in, or whatever our place is. Remember Christ said that He went away to prepare a place for us (John 14). So right now Jesus Christ is active, busy, preparing that place in New Jerusalem for us, looking forward to this day.

Verse 22: "And I saw no temple in it; for the Lord God Almighty and the Lamb are the temple of it." *Amazing thing to be in the Family of God!*

- we're going to see God
- we are going to see Jesus Christ
- we're going to live with Them
- we're going to dwell with Them

No need of a temple!

Verse 23: "And the city has no need of the sun, or of the moon, that they should shine in it… [it doesn't say that they aren't there; it just says they have no need] …because the glory of God enlightens it, and the Light of it *is* the Lamb. And the nations that are saved…" (vs 23-24).

All the nations through the Millennium, all of those through the Great White Throne Judgment, all of those of the saints down through time.

Verse 24: "And the nations that are saved shall walk in its Light…

Those who are in the first resurrection are going to live and dwell in new Jerusalem. All of the rest who are saved are going to live outside of Jerusalem and they are going to come to New Jerusalem. These are the nations that are saved.

"…and the kings of the earth shall bring their glory and honor into it…. [there's going to be rulership; there are going to be kings] …And its gates shall never be shut by day; for there shall be no night there. And they shall bring the glory and the honor of the nations into it" (verses 24-26).

God is going to have us *busy, producing, making, creating, doing!* If God by Himself—with the help of the angels and the 24 elders and Jesus Christ—created all the heavens and the earth, I wonder what sort of thing He's got planned for us. This indicates there's going to be a fantastic amount of things going on. We're not going to be there humdy-dumdy strumming on harps, or as the beatific vision is: look at the face of God like you're staring at some thing you never understand. No, this is real spiritual life, greater, better than the best of human life.

John gives another warning, v 27: "And nothing that defiles shall ever enter into it, nor shall *anyone* who practices *an* abomination or *devises* a lie; but *only* those who are written in the Lamb's Book of Life.?"

Now then it concludes with one of the most tremendous chapters in the whole Bible: Rev. 22. Now let's think on this for just a minute. You have seven plus one making eight. How many chapters do we have? We have three sections of seven in the book of Revelation, that makes 21, plus one is 22. Moreover, 22 is also the number of letters in the Hebrew alphabet. So, here we have the 8th one again. Showing the newness of God's way and everything.

Revelation 22:1: "Then he showed me a pure river of *the* Water of Life, clear as crystal, flowing out from the Throne of God and of the Lamb."

Through all eternity the righteousness and power of God's Spirit is always going to be flowing!

Verse 2: *And* in the middle of *the* street, and on this side and that side of the river, *was the* Tree of Life…"

Now I don't quite understand all of this completely, but it says:

"…producing twelve *manner of* fruits, each month yielding its fruit; and the leaves of the tree *are* for *the* healing of the nations" (v 2).

The Greek there is 'therapeian,' which could also mean *for the maintenance of the nations.* I don't know exactly how this will fit in, but I'll tell you how we will understand it. **Be there in New Jerusalem** and you will know!

Now this here's a great thing, v 3: "And there shall be no more curse; and the Throne of God and of the Lamb shall be in it; and His servants shall serve Him, and they shall see His face; and His name *is* in their foreheads" (vs 3-4).

Complete oneness with God! Here, everything that God has done in His plan has now all come together and we are ready in the Family of God to begin to do the work of God that He has for us for the rest of eternity down through the ages of that eternity.

Verse 5: "And there shall be no night there; for they have no need of a lamp or *the* light of *the* sun, because *the* Lord God enlightens them; and they shall reign into the ages of eternity" *Forever and ever and ever!*

That's the kind of life that God wants us to have. That's how it's going to be. That's why it says that the eye has not seen and the ears have not heard, neither has it entered into the heart of man the things that God has prepared for those who love Him.' That's why we need to love God with all our heart, mind, soul and being.

Verse 6: "And he said to me, 'These words *are* faithful and true… [they're going to happen] … and *the* Lord God of the Holy prophets sent His angel to show His servants the things that must shortly come to pass.'"

That's really true right now. It's going to come to pass shortly!

Verse 7: "'Behold, I am coming quickly. Blessed *is* the one who keeps the words of the prophecy of this book,'…. [the whole Bible] …Now I, John, *was* the one who saw and heard these things. And when I heard and saw, I fell down to worship before the feet of the angel who *was* showing me these things. But he said to me, 'See *that you do* not *do this*! For I am a fellow servant of yours, and of your brethren the prophets, and of those who keep the words of this book. Worship God.' And he said to me, 'Do not seal the words of the prophecy of this book because the time is near'" (vs 7-10).

In other words, when we come close to the time of the end we're going to understand it. And I think today we understand the book of Revelation more than any other time in the history of the whole world. Because we are living in the times when we see these things coming to pass.

Verse 11: "Let the one who is unrighteous be unrighteous still; and let the one who is filthy be filthy still; and let the one who is righteous be righteous still; and let the one who is Holy be Holy still. 'And behold, I am coming quickly; and My reward is with Me, to render to each one according as his work shall be. I am Alpha and Omega, the Beginning and the End, the First and the Last'" (vs 11-13).

God's plan has now been completed and then He's going to open up the rest of it to our understanding. And he finalizes by this:

Verse 14: "Blessed are those who keep His commandments, that they may have the right to eat of the Tree of Life, and may enter by the gates into the city."

Now that's the full meaning of this day, the Holy Day the Last Great Day! And you know why it is The Great Day!

Scriptures from *The Holy Bible in Its Original Order, A Faithful Version*

Scriptural References:

1) Leviticus 23:34, 36-37, 4
2) John 7:37-39
3) Isaiah 14:24, 26-27
4) Psalm 111:10
5) Isaiah 14:26-27
6) Ephesians 1:3-10
7) Isaiah 29:13-17
8) Matthew 13:13-17
9) 1 Timothy 2:3-4
10) 2 Peter 3:9
11) 11) Romans 9:14-23
12) Romans 11:18-26, 32-36
13) Revelation 20:5
14) Romans 2:14-16
15) John 5:25-29
16) Revelation 20:11-12
17) Ezekiel 37:1-14
18) Matthew 12:32-37, 41-42
19) 21) Revelation 20:13-15
20) 22) Luke 16:19-31
21) 23) 2 Peter 3:10-13
22) 24) Revelation 21:1-8, 21-27
23) 25) Revelation 22:1-14

Scriptures referenced, not quoted:

- Numbers 29
- John 7:2
- Revelation 19
- 2 Corinthians 4
- Revelation 20:4
- 1 Corinthians 15
- Matthew 27
- John 11
- Revelation 10
- Malachi 4
- Matthew 24
- 1 Corinthians 4
- John 14

Also referenced: In-Depth Study:
Epistle of Paul to the Hebrews

FRC: cs
Transcription date unknown
Reformatted: bo—1/2021

CHAPTER EIGHTY-ONE

The Greatest Mystery of God
Fred R. Coulter

Greetings, brethren! Welcome to the Last Great Day of the Feast! Here we are at the end, and we will see that every ending has a new beginning.

This Feast of God is mentioned in Lev. 23; let's read the instructions of God. Then we will see something so absolutely fantastic, marvelous and awesome concerning the meaning of this Last Great Day.

I mentioned before how God has hidden things, and we will cover that, but part of it right here is that Lev. 23 is the only place in the entire Bible that all the Holy Days of God are listed in sequence beginning with the Sabbath. Then going through every month and day of the year up through the Last Great Day on the Calculated Hebrew Calendar.

{Note our booklet: *Which is the True Calendar of God?* (including Noah's Flood Calendar)} It is absolutely accurate!

Leviticus 23:34: "Speak to the children of Israel, saying…"

The Church is *spiritual* Israel; not a replacement of physical Israel, but *spiritual* Israel. Remember that the promise given to Abraham was to physical descendants and spiritual descendants; *we are the spiritual descendants!*

"…'The fifteenth day of this seventh month *shall be* the Feast of Tabernacles for seven days to the LORD. On the first day *shall be* a Holy convocation….'" (vs 34-35).

Verse 36: "Seven days you shall offer an offering made by fire to the LORD…. [at the temple] …**On the eighth day**…"

This Feast is only mentioned twice in Lev. 23, and it is mentioned the least of any of the Feast days. Yet, we will see that it is the greatest!

"…shall be a Holy convocation to you. And you shall offer an offering made by fire to the LORD. It *is* a solemn assembly. And you shall do no servile work *therein*" (v 36).

Verse 39—*repeated again*: "Also, in the fifteenth day of the seventh month when you have gathered in the fruit of the land, you shall keep a Feast to the LORD seven days. On **the first day** **_shall be_ a Sabbath,** and **on the eighth day _shall be_** **a Sabbath.**"

That's all the mention of the Last Great Day. What does it mean? *We'll find out!* On the all the Holy Days, since we don't offer offerings made by fire, we take up offerings in the way of monetary units as it is today.

So, we have a lot of ground to cover so we will pause and take up the offering. Then we will continue *the greatest mystery of the Kingdom of God is the Last Great Day!*

(pause for offering)

Thank you, brethren, for your offerings and being faithful to God. We always use the money to serve the brethren, preach the Gospel and do the things that God want us to do.

It is *the glory of God to hide a matter a*nd the honor of the king *to discover it!*

The Last Great Day God has hidden in a very interesting way, as well as all the Holy Days, and this can apply to the Sabbath as well. Let's see how God does it. *To us,* because God says:

The wise shall understand in the end-time. Blessed are those who keep His commandments; a good understanding have all they.

Let's see what God has done here. You've heard the phrase that 'the Word of God is shaper than a two-edged sword.' *The two-edged sword of the Word of God opens understanding for those who have the Spirit of God and rightly divide the Word of God!* The other edge of that spiritual sword *closes the understanding* to those who don't want to obey Him. To those who just want to profess Christ, profess the Father and receive Their love, *but not give anything back to God* in the way of loving God the Father and Jesus Christ with all the heart, mind, soul and being!

Isaiah 28:9—*God says*: "Whom shall He teach knowledge?…." *We're to be taught the knowledge of God!* In the New Testament we are to have that kind of knowledge.

"…And whom shall He make to understand doctrine?…." (v 9). *Doctrines are the set established teachings of God!*

"…*Those* who are weaned from the milk and drawn from the breasts" (v 9). *This tells us that* 'newbies' cannot readily understand it! You have to have a certain knowledge of the milk of the Word of God, a certain knowledge that you are independent enough spiritually that you can stand on your own two feet, because you're no longer on the milk. Here's how God does it, it's a very interesting way:

Verse 10: "'For precept *must be* upon precept, precept upon precept; line upon line, line upon line; here a little, there a little'; for with stammering lips and foreign tongue He will speak to his people. To whom He said, 'This *is* the rest He gives to the weary,' and 'This *is* the refreshing,' yet, they were not willing to hear" (vs 10-12).

The key is that **you must be willing to hear** the Word of God. God has hidden it, but He will reveal it, because it's been revealed to us the mysteries of the Kingdom of God. ***This day pictures the greatest mystery of all!***

Here's the other side of that sword of the Word; v 13: "So then, the Word of the LORD was to them precept upon precept, precept upon precept; line upon line, line upon line; here a little, there a little; **that they might go, and fall backward, and be broken and snared and taken**"—*because they want their own way!*

What is a prime example of this? *Sunday and the holidays of this world!*

- Do they understand about God? *No!*
- Do they have any knowledge of His plan? *No!*
- Would they say that what we're teaching here would be heresy to them? *Yes, indeed!*
- Why?

*Because we will see that when you fail to yield to God—**in love and repentance, and hungering and thirsting after God's Word**—you will never understand!*

Verse 14: "Therefore, hear the Word of the LORD, you scornful men who rule this people in Jerusalem. Because you have said, 'We have made a covenant with death…'"

That's exactly what Sunday-keeping and all the holidays of this world produce: ***death!***

- What's the first holiday of the year? *Halloween!*
- What does that picture? *Death!*

"…and we have made an agreement with the grave; when the overwhelming rod shall pass through, it shall not come to us…" (v 15).

They think because they have their own way, everything is going to be good.

"…for we have made lies our refuge…" (v 15). *Think about that: Sunday and all the holidays are lies!* They think that they have salvation through that.

"…and we have hidden ourselves under falsehood" (v 15). *Sound like the political system today, and the deep state; as well as all the religious organizations that call themselves 'Christian'?*

Let's carry this one step further. Let's see why this is such a great mystery. It's quite interesting what Jesus says; He spoke to them in parables. Why? *So that they really wouldn't grasp what He was saying!*

Matthew 13:10: "And His disciples came to Him and asked, 'Why do You speak to them in parables?' And He answered *and* said to them…(vs 10-11). *Listen carefully*:

- Do we understand the Holy Days? *Yes, we understand them up to the point that we understand!*
- Does that mean that there may be more understanding to it than we may fully realize? *Of course!*

It certainly was true for the apostles, because we understand more than they did. That doesn't make us greater than they, but that's because ***God gave the promise that in the last days the wise shall understand!*** Those that love God and serve Him and keep His commandments ***are wise!***

Verse 11: "And He answered *and* said to them, **'Because it has been given to you**… [each and every one of us. We all have a Bible, the Word of God] …**to know the mysteries**…"

There are many mysteries of the Kingdom of God. One of the greatest mysteries is: ***How does God raise the dead?*** and ***The Last great Day!*** We will see why it is a great mystery.

"…of the Kingdom of Heaven…" (v 11). Matthew says Heaven but it means *from heaven to human beings!*

"…**but to them it has not been given**. For whoever has *understanding*, to him more shall be given, and he shall have an abundance, but whoever does not have *understanding*, **even what he has shall be taken away from him**. For this *reason* I speak to them in parables, because seeing…" (vs 11-13).

All Protestants and Catholics ***think*** they see, they hear, they understand; ***but they don't!***

"…**they see not; and hearing, they hear not; neither do they understand**. And in them is fulfilled the prophecy of Isaiah, which says, '**In hearing you shall hear, and in no way understand**; and *in seeing you shall see, and in no*

way perceive'" (vs 13-14).

They've got the whole Bible, but do they use it? *No!* Protestants say that the Old Testament has been fulfilled, and the Catholics say that that is the *old Law*, and they don't keep much of the New Testament.

So, having a little bit of this and little bit of that, and a little bit of the other thing it's like having a huge puzzle with many pieces and when you get a few pieces put together you think you've accomplished it. But 90% of is yet to be put together.

Verse 15: "For the heart of this people has grown fat... [they're content in *their own ways* and they don't want anything else] ...and their ears are dull of hearing... [*they don't have time* all of that] ...and their eyes they have closed..."—*they don't want to look at it*; 'don't bother me with the things in the Old Testament.'

To show you what they thought of what is commonly called the General Epistles, which were written by James, Peter, John and Jude. When Jerome put out the Catholic Bible—and this same order of books is followed through to the Protestants—he put Romans right after Acts instead of the General Epistles, beginning with James, and he put the General Epistles at the end just before the book of Revelation *to **downplay** the importance of keeping the commandments of God!*

"...lest they should see with their eyes, and should hear with their ears, and should understand with their hearts, and should be converted, and I should heal them" (v 15).

What is said in evangelical Protestantism is that God wants to save the world. *NO!* Not at this time! God wants to call the firstfruits and that's not to save the whole world. God doesn't want to convert them *now,* that's what Jesus said.

Since God has done this, how is He going to solve this problem? That's answered in the Last Great Day and we will see in a little bit.

Verse 16: "But blessed *are* your eyes, because they see; and your ears, because they hear. For truly I say to you, many prophets and righteous *men* have desired to see what you see, and have not seen; and to hear what you hear, and have not heard" (vs 16-17).

Let's look at something interjected here in v 43: "Then... [at the resurrection] ...shall the righteous shine forth as the sun in the Kingdom of their Father. **The one who has ears to hear, let him hear**."

Right in the middle of it, what a comparison! They're not given the understanding.

Has God cut them off entirely?

The Gospel of John is wrapped around the Holy Days:

- the Passover
- there's Trumpets
- Unleavened Bread
- the Feast of Tabernacles
- the Last Great Day

John 7:37: "Now, in the last day, **the great day of the Feast**..." Why is it called *the great day*? *Because of the meaning of it!*

"...Jesus stood and called out, saying, '**If anyone** thirsts, let him come to Me and drink'" (v 37)

That sounds like a contradiction of Matt. 13 that He didn't want them to hear, see or understand, lest they would be converted and He would heal them! Here He says, "...**If anyone**..." *I want you think on that statement for just a minute!* That includes any individual human being.

- How many going back in history lived and died and never had a slight chance of understanding about God's plan?
- How many from the time of Christ, after He came, were really converted and part of the firstfruits?

All of the rest of the world is blinded, dumb—can't hear or speak (the Word of God)—*have been given over to their own devices!*

- Are all of them lost because God didn't call them?

If God didn't call them:
- Why did Jesus Christ Himself say, "...If anyone thirsts..." *when they never had a chance!*

We'll answer that!

Verse 38: "The one who believes in Me, as the Scripture has said..."

What do the Scriptures say? *If you love Me keep My commandments, and I will send you another Comforter, the Holy Spirit, which proceeds from the Father!*

"'...out of his belly shall flow rivers of living water.' But this He spoke concerning the Spirit, which those who believed in Him would soon receive; for *the* Holy Spirit was not yet *given* because Jesus was not yet glorified" (vs 38-39).

Even these few verses right here are quite a mystery in itself! Yes, it is! When you first learned about God's way, and began to understand certain things, what was the key that began to open understanding to you? *Keeping the Sabbath Day!* That's the key because God puts His presence in it.

Now we'll come to what appears to be another contradiction. In John 7 He said *anyone!*

- What if God deliberately blinded them and they couldn't understand?
- Doesn't that eliminate a lot if they don't have an opportunity for salvation? *Yes, indeed!*

1-Timothy 2:1: "I exhort, therefore, first of all that supplications, prayers, intercessions, *and* thanksgivings be made on behalf of all men.... [we pray for peace so we can preach the Gospel] ...for kings and all who are in authority, in order that we may lead a quiet and peaceful life in all Godliness and respectability" (vs 1-2).

But look at the mobs and things we have today. Christians are the #1 target, even the *fake* Christians.

Verse 3: "For this *is* good and acceptable before God our Savior, Who desires all men to be saved and to come to *the* knowledge of *the* Truth" (vs 3-4).

- How can that happen if their eyes are blinded, their ears are stopped, and their minds are clouded so they can't understand?
- Is that a contradiction?
- Does that mean that they're all lost and will never have any salvation?

Verse 5: "For there *is* one God, and one Mediator between God and men—*the* Man Christ Jesus, Who gave Himself *as* a ransom for **all**... [anyone] ...the testimony *of which is to be preached* **in its appointed times**" (vs 5-6).

The appointed times are the Feasts of God, so here is a clue telling us how we understand the Word of God!

Verse 7: "For this purpose I was ordained a preacher and an apostle (I speak *the* truth in Christ—I do not lie), a teacher of *the* Gentiles in faith and truth."

Let's see what Paul says to Timothy concerning understanding the Word of God. It just doesn't come by reading. Reading is where you begin. Repentance, obeying and loving God follow after that. Then to grow in grace and knowledge we are to rightly divide the Word of God.

2-Timothy 2:15: "**Diligently *study* to show yourself approved unto God**..." *Constantly without fail, with zeal, purpose and determination!*

"...a workman who does not *need to be* ashamed, **rightly dividing the Word of the Truth**" (v 15)—which is *a little here, a little there; line upon line, precept upon precept!* You have to rightly put it together. Unless you have the Sabbath and Holy Days as the framework on which all Scripture hangs, you won't be able to understand it.

Verse 16: "But avoid profane and vain babblings because they will *only* give rise to more ungodliness"—*bringing in the teachings of men!* That's what happens, and slowly it will take everything down, as Paul says here:

Verse 17: "And their words will eat away at the body... [the Church] ...like gangrene... [or cancer] ...of whom are Hymeneus and Philetus, who have gone astray from the Truth, **claiming that the resurrection has already taken place, and are destroying the faith of some**" (vs 17-18).

We're always being tested by these, aren't we? Here's what we need to understand; in spite of what men do, try to do or think that they should do, God's Word:

- always stands true
- is always righteous
- is always what God wants us to do and obey

Verse 19: "Nevertheless, the foundation of God stands firm..." ***What is that foundation?***

- Christ the Rock
- Christ the Chief Cornerstone
- Christ the Head of the Church
- Christ our Savior
- Christ the Forerunner for us by being resurrected from the dead

"...having this seal: **'The Lord knows those who are His,'** and, 'Let everyone who calls upon the name of Christ **depart from unrighteousness**'" (v 19).

Those are all the keys necessary for understanding the Truth of God!

2-Peter 3:9—*written by Peter*: "The Lord is not delaying the promise *of His coming*, as some **in their own minds reckon delay**..."

Verse 8 says: "...with *the* Lord, one day *is* as a thousand years, and a thousand years as one day."

When Peter wrote this, he knew nothing of what John was to be given in the book of Revelation. When they were preaching their ministry, they were thinking that Jesus was going to return during their lifetimes. They didn't have all the knowledge; they had some understanding, but you can't understand prophecy unless you have the book of Revelation.

Daniel is the lock and Revelation is the key to unlock the understanding. The first thing that that unlocks is the Sabbath and Holy Days of God, which then gives us the framework to put everything of God upon it.

Verse 9: "...rather, He is longsuffering toward us, **not desiring that any should perish, but that all should come to repentance."** *How can all come to repentance*:

- when they were blinded?
- when they were not called?
- when repentance is a gift of God?

How is God going to solve this great and terrible mystery?

We have distinguish between sin that is forgivable and sin that is not forgivable or unpardonable. There are those two categories of sin. Not everyone in the world who have not had their mind open have committed the unpardonable sin. This is important to understand:

What is God going to do?

1-John 5:16: "If anyone sees his brother sinning a sin *that is* not unto death... [pardonable] ...he shall ask... [pray for him] ...and He [God] will give him life for those who do not sin unto death. There is **a sin unto death**; concerning that *sin*, I do not say that **he should make *any* supplication *to God*.**"

God looks at the world this way; v 17: "All unrighteousness is sin, and there is a sin **not unto death**." *As we look at our situation, He's talking about a brother who is in the Church!*

Verse 18: "We know that anyone who is begotten by God..." *A very important thing, because **begotten is the Spirit of God given to us,** which is the seed from God the Father of eternal life. Then the other half of that seed is **the mind of Christ!** This is how we develop the character.*

"...**does not *practice* sin**..." (v 18). *Does not live in sin; it doesn't say they don't sin, because*:

John 2:1: "And *yet*, if anyone does sin, we have an Advocate with the Father; Jesus Christ *the* Righteous; and He is *the* propitiation for our sins..." (vs 1-2).

1-John 5:18: "...For the one who has been begotten by God keeps himself *by the power of God*, and the wicked one does not touch him." *That's how there is the difference with the Spirit of God!*

Verse 19: "We know that we are of God, and *that* the whole world lies in *the power of* the wicked one." *That's something!*

- What is God going to do about the whole world?
- Have they not all been under Satan the devil from the time of Adam and Eve clear down to the end-time and the return of Jesus Christ, with the exception of those whom God has called? *Yes!*

Let's go back in history:

- How many people lived and died before the Flood? *Probably a couple of billion!*
- How many righteous ones were there? *Just a handful, most notably*:
  - ✓ Abel
  - ✓ Seth
  - ✓ Enoch
  - ✓ Noah

God destroyed the whole world because of sin! What's going to happen to them? Then we come forward a little bit of time from that and we come to Abraham: *one man!*

From that one man was going to come the whole process of *the physical seed that later would become Israel,* and **the spiritual seed that would become the sons and daughters of God!** From the one man! Everybody else God didn't have anything to do with. So, what is God going to do about that?

Verse 20: "And we know that the Son of God has come, and has given us an understanding, so that we may know Him Who *is* true; and we are in Him Who *is* true, *and* in His Son, Jesus Christ. He is the true God, and the eternal life. Little children, keep yourselves from idols. Amen" (vs 20-21)— *idols were starting to come in!*

Romans 2:14 "For when the Gentiles... [none of the 12 tribes] ...which do not have the Law, practice by nature the things contained in the Law, these who do not have the Law are a law unto themselves."

Since God is no respecter of persons, they received certain blessings for doing things that are in accord with the Law of God, whether they understand anything about it or not. ***That's how fair God is!***

Verse 15: "Who show **the** work of **the** Law..." We won't get into it, but this is different from *works of law!* This is "...the work of the Law..." **which is the Law of God that God shows right here is a good thing, because it's the Law of God!**

"...written in their own hearts, their consciences bearing witness, and their reasonings also as they accuse or defend one another); in a day when God shall judge the secrets of men by Jesus Christ, according to my Gospel" (vs 15-16).

What does that tell us? *Remember that it*

says, every knee is going to bow! Let's understand that there are not many direct open statements in the Bible about what God is going to do about it, that you can find in any one place. Notice that we've been going from Scripture to Scripture, book to book, chapter to chapter and putting things together, *rightly dividing the Word of God!*

Matt. 12—let's see something important in what this tells us. As we saw from 1-John 5:16 that there is a sin that is *not* unto death! That means *the second death!*

Matthew 12:31—*the very words of Jesus:* "Because of this, I say to you, every sin and blasphemy shall be forgiven to men except the blasphemy against the *Holy* Spirit; *that* shall not be forgiven to men."

What is the blasphemy against the Holy Spirit? *That is the Spirit that comes from God the Father and they reject it and treat it with contempt, going against it in the grossest of sins unrepentant!* That's the sin unto death!

Verse 32: "And whoever speaks a word against the Son of man, it shall be forgiven him; but whoever speaks against the Holy Spirit… [because it comes from God the Father and you're rejecting God the Father] …**it shall not be forgiven him, neither in this age nor in the coming** *age*."

What a thing to understand, and *that's what this Last Great Day pictures, another coming age!*

Verse 33: "Either make the tree good and the fruit good, or make the tree corrupt and its fruit corrupt; for a tree is known by its fruit." *They wanted a sign,* 'Show us what You can do.'

Verse 38: "Then some of the scribes and Pharisees answered, saying, 'Master, we desire to see a sign from You.' And He answered *and* said to them, 'A wicked and adulterous generation seeks after a sign, but no sign shall be given to it except the sign of Jonah the prophet. For just as Jonah was in the belly of the whale three days and three nights, in like manner the Son of man shall be in the heart of the earth three days and three nights'" (vs 38-40).

Listen, this goes right back up there to v 32: "…it shall not be forgiven him, neither in this age nor in the coming *age*."

Verse 41: "*The* men of Nineveh… [who repented at the warning of Jonah] …shall stand up… [raised from the dead] …in the judgment with this generation…" *There was over a thousand-year's difference between them!*

"…and shall condemn it, because they repented at the proclamation of Jonah; and behold, a greater than Jonah *is* here. *The* queen of *the* south… [another 500-600 years later] …shall rise up in the judgment with this generation and shall condemn it, because she came from the ends of the earth to hear the wisdom of Solomon; and behold, a greater than Solomon *is* here" (v 41).

What is this telling us? Let's see again that the meaning of this Last Great Day is buried in a place where just a few words are used. What is it in Lev. 23? *A few words,* **the eighth day, a Holy convocation!** It tells nothing about the meaning of it.

Matt. 12 tells us that there are going to be people raised from the dead. When will they be raised? *No one could have known until the book of Revelation was written!*

Rev. 20 talks about the first resurrection, and notice that here's a little parenthetical statement:

Revelation 20:6: "Blessed and Holy is the one who has part in the **first** resurrection…" **Is there another resurrection?** *Yes!* If there's a first there must be one after that.

"…over these the second death has no power…." (v 6).

Verse 5: "(But the rest of the dead did not live again until the thousand years were completed.)…."

The Bible tells us that those who are Christ's will be raised at His coming (v 4).

Who are the rest of the dead? *All of those who are not in the first resurrection!* God has hidden the meaning of it, and there's only place in the Old Testament that it is given, and only one place in the New Testament where it is given clearly. Matt. 12 is the introduction to those two places.

Ezek. 37 is one of my favorite chapters in the entire Bible, because this is the chapter of:

- hope
- undoing all wrongs
- showing that God is going to give knowledge of salvation to all who will
- the desire to have all mankind saved is true

Even though the final decision is the individual's as to whether he wants it or not.

- that's God's plan is going to be greater, bigger, and more fulfilling than anything human's have understood

- *That's why it is hidden!*
- *That's why God has saved it for the Last Great Day!*

Ezekiel 37:1: "The hand of the LORD was on me, and brought me by the Spirit of the LORD, and set me down in the midst of a valley, and it *was* full of bones."

If there are bones that means that these people have lived and died. You don't get bones in the ground unless they have been buried. So, here's a whole valley, and God is showing how vast that this is going to be!

Verse 2: "And He made me walk among them all around...." *Take a nice tour around that valley, Ezekiel and look at the bones!*

"...And behold, very many *were* in the open valley. And lo, *they were* very dry" (v 2)—*to show that they had died long, long ago!*

Verse 3: "And He said to me, 'Son of man, can these bones live?' And I answered, 'O Lord GOD, You know.' Again He said to me, 'Prophesy to these bones, and say to them, "O dry bones, hear the Word of the LORD"'" (vs 3-4). *Think of that! How are dry bones going to be able to hear? Because all things are possible with God!*

Verse 5: "Thus says the Lord GOD to these bones, 'Behold, I will cause breath to enter into you, and you shall live.'" ***This is the resurrection of the rest of the dead!***

Verse 6: "And I will lay sinews on you, and will bring up flesh on you, and cover you with skin, and put breath in you, and you shall live...."

This resurrection is not to eternal life. This resurrection is *to physical life for their first opportunity to receive salvation!* In their first life they didn't have it. They may have, a lot of them, been good, upstanding people, and a lot of them may not have been good, upstanding people; *it doesn't make any difference!* This has to be those who did not commit the unpardonable sin!

"'...**And you shall know that I *am* the LORD**.'.... [in their first life, they didn't know] ...So, I prophesied as I was commanded. And as I prophesied, there was a noise. And behold, a shaking! And the bones came together, a bone to its bone. And as I watched, behold the sinews and the flesh came upon them, and the skin covered them above. But *there was* no breath in them"(vs 6-8). *Just like when Adam was created, God had to breathe into him the breath of life!*

Verse 9: "And He said to me, 'Prophesy to the wind, prophesy, son of man, and say to the wind, "Thus says the Lord GOD, 'Come from the four winds, O breath, and breathe on these slain that they may live.'"'" *Think about that!*

Verse 10: "So, I prophesied as He commanded me, and the breath came into them, and they lived and stood on their feet, an exceedingly great army." *The vast majority of all people!*

Verse 11: "And He said to me, 'Son of man,

these bones are the whole house of Israel. Behold, they say, "Our bones *are* dried and our hope is lost; we ourselves are completely cut off."'" *They didn't have any hope of salvation in their first life! They didn't expect to receive it!* This shows:

- God's love
- God's grace
- God's mercy
- God's understanding
- God fulfilling His plan to the absolute maximum

Verse 12: "Therefore, prophesy and say to them, 'Thus says the Lord GOD, "Behold, O My people, **I will open your graves**... [they had live, died and were buried] ...and cause you to come up out of your graves, and will bring you into the land of Israel. **And you shall know that I *am* the LORD**...."'" (vs 12-13). *That means they will be converted!*

"'...when I have opened your graves, O My people, and have brought you up out of your graves. And I shall put My Spirit in you... [conversion] ...and you shall live, and I will place you in your own land. And you shall know that **I the LORD have spoken it and have done it,**' says the LORD." (vs 13-14).

They're going to live! How long do you think they will live? The same length of time that those during the Millennium had, a hundred years! ***Salvation requires:***

- growth
- understanding
- learning of God's way
- repentance of sins

This is going to be something. At this time they won't have any children. You've got to stop human child production someplace along the line, and this is the place. Otherwise it just still keeps going on and on in the flesh, and you go through the same cycle of all of these things. It is fantastic what is said here.

What's going happen? Let's understand something really, really important concerning this, because this will give them an opportunity for salvation. We know, as the Apostle Peter wrote, that judgment is now on the house of God; that is judgment unto salvation.

Revelation 20:11: "Then I saw a great white throne and the One Who was sitting on it, from Whose face the earth and the heaven fled away; and no place was found for them. And I saw the dead..." (vs 11-12). ***That's the rest of the dead!***

We'll have to say that because of the

incorrigible wicked that have to be raised, there are two parts to the second resurrection:

1. the first part to salvation
2. the second part the incorrigible wicked unto the second death

It's given to all who sin without repentance *to die twice!* God is going to do it this way: *they all will die together!* Just like all the sinners before the Flood died together.

Verse 12: "And I saw the small and great, **standing before God**…"

What are you going to do? Here we are! Think about this, when they're resurrected they're not going to have any clothes, so what's going to have to happen? *I think that's going to be a great boom for the last generation of the Millennium to prepare clothes and shoes for all those to be resurrected in the second resurrection!* No unemployment at that time!

"…and *the* **books were opened**…" (v 12). What are these books? *These are the book of their life and their former deeds, which they'll have a chance to repent of them!*

"…and **another book was opened, which is** *the* **Book of Life**…." (v 12)—*which will be opened for them!*

Right now, our names are written in the Book of Life for the first resurrection, so there has to be a Book of Life for those in the second resurrection so they can have an opportunity for salvation. That's what this is telling us.

"…And the **dead were judged out of the things written in the books,** according to their works" (v 12). *The judgment has to be on the life they're going to live*—the second life—which if we follow Isa. 65 will be 100 years. They will be judged how they are living in that period of time.

If they were to be judge solely only on the works that they did before they died in their first life—the wages of sin is death—why resurrect them. So, here they will have an opportunity to repent, because they did not sin *a sin unto death!*

Then they will have the opportunity to be judged how they live just like we are today, and just like people will be all during the Millennium.

All of those who committed the unpardonable sin will have to be raised so they can all be judged at once.

Verse 13: "And the sea gave up the dead *that were* in it, and death and *the* grave gave up the dead *that were* in them; and they were judged individually, according to their works. And death

and *the* grave were cast into the Lake of Fire. **This is the second death**" (vs 13-14)

If this is the second death, what does that mean? *That means that they lived once already!*

Verse 15: "And **if anyone was not found written in the Book of Life, he was cast into the Lake of Fire**."

That's quite a thing! This is the greatest day of all! After that we have *a projection into the complete fulfillment of the eighth day*: a new heavens and a new earth!

- What's going to happen with new heavens and new earth? *They're cast into the Lake of Fire (v 15)!*
- What is that going to do?

2-Peter 3 tells us what's going to happen, and this has to happen before New Jerusalem can come down.

2-Peter 3:8: "Now, beloved, do not let this one fact be hidden from you: that with *the* Lord, one day *is* as a thousand years, and a thousand years as one day. The Lord is not delaying the promise *of His coming*, as some in their own minds reckon delay; rather, He is longsuffering toward us, not desiring that any should perish…" (vs 8-9).

That's God's desire, but there is the second death. But that's by the choice of the individuals who refuse to repent and go God's way.

"…but that all should come to repentance. However, the Day of *the* Lord shall come as a thief in *the* night in which **the heaven itself shall disappear with a mighty roar,** and *the* elements shall pass away, burning with intense heat, and ***the earth and the works in it shall be burned up***" (vs 9-10).

When the Lake of Fire for the wicked is there and they're cast in to that Lake of Fire, then it begins to consume the whole earth. Why? *To prepare for the new heaven and the new earth!* You've got to burn it all up! As spirit beings fire won't affect us!

Verse 11: "Since all these things are going to be destroyed, what kind of *persons* ought you to be in Holy conduct and Godliness, looking forward to and striving for the coming of the day of God, during which *the* heavens, being on fire, shall be destroyed, and *the* elements, burning with intense heat, shall melt? But according to His promise, we look forward to a new heaven and a new earth, in which righteousness dwells" (vs 11-13).

That's what happens between Rev. 20:15 and the Rev. 21:1! It has to be all prepared, *ready for the greatest thing to happen in all of God's plan up to this point!*

Revelation 21:1: "Then I saw a new heaven and a new earth; for the first heaven and the first earth were passed away…" **How did it pass away?** *We just read it in 2-Peter 3!*

"…and there was no more sea. And I, John, saw the Holy City, *the* New Jerusalem, coming down from God out of heaven, prepared as a bride adorned for her husband" (vs 1-2)—*magnificent and beautiful!*

Verse 3: "And I heard a great voice from heaven say, 'Behold, **the Tabernacle of God** *is* **with men**…'" *That goes clear back to*:

- the Garden of Eden
- the tabernacle
- the temple
- God's plan

And now the fulfillment of it with men and women made perfect, spirit beings!

"…and He shall dwell with them, and they shall be His people; and God Himself shall be with them *and be* their God" (v 3). *Think about how great this is going to be! God is going to do this!*

Verse 4: "And God shall wipe away every tear from their eyes; and ***there* shall not be anymore death, or sorrow, or crying; neither shall** *there* **be any more pain**, because the former things have passed away.'" *We're all spirit beings, the sons and daughters of God! Quite a thing, indeed!*

Now we're going to see who are in the first resurrection will be in New Jerusalem. All the nations that are saved will live on the earth outside of New Jerusalem, but they will come to New Jerusalem.

Verse 5: "And He Who sits on the Throne said, 'Behold, I make all things new.' Then He said to me, 'Write, for these words are true and faithful.'" *They're going to happen! They're going to take place!*

Verse 6: "And He said to me, 'It is done.… [finished; this part of God's plan up to this point is complete] …I am Alpha and Omega, the Beginning and the End. To the one who thirsts, I will give freely of the fountain of the Water of Life. The one who overcomes shall inherit all things; and I will be his God, and he shall be My son" (vs 6-7).

Quite a fantastic thing, indeed! So great and marvelous what God is doing, that we're going to be a part of, just think about that! Think about all the difficulties and problems that we have gone through. Think about all the difficulties and problems that people in the world have gone through, and the

saints down through history have gone through, as well. All of that will be ended!

But here's a warning; just like God does all the time, He give certain things and then He says, 'The one who hears, let him hear.' Likewise we have the same pattern right here:

Verse 8: "But *the* cowardly, and unbelieving, and abominable, and murderers, and fornicators, and sorcerers, and idolaters, and all liars, shall have their part in the lake that burns with fire and brimstone; which is *the* second death."

That's showing very clearly that there's not going to be any unrighteousness in the new heavens and the new earth!

Verse 9: "And one of the seven angels that had the seven vials full of the seven last plagues came and spoke with me, saying, 'Come here, *and* I will show you the Bride, the Lamb's wife.' And he carried me away in *the* Spirit to a great and high mountain, and showed me the great city, **Holy Jerusalem, descending out of heaven from God**, having the glory of God. And her radiance *was* like a most precious stone, as crystal-clear *as* jasper stone. And *the* city also had a great and high wall, with twelve gates, and at the gates twelve angels; and inscribed on *the gates* were *the* names of the twelve tribes of the children of Israel" (vs 9-12)—*for all eternity!*

Verse 13: "On *the* east *were* three gates; on *the* north *were* three gates; on *the* south *were* three gates; on *the* west *were* three gates. And the wall of the city had twelve foundations, and written on them *were the* names of the twelve apostles of the Lamb. And the one who was speaking with me had a golden measuring rod, so that he might measure the city, and its gates and its wall. And the city lies foursquare, for its length is as long as its breadth. And he measured the city with the rod, twelve thousand furlongs… [about 1500 miles] …the length and the breadth and the height of it are equal. And he measured its wall, one hundred *and* forty-four cubits…" (vs 13-17). **Where do we get 144?** *That's the 144,000!*

"…*the* angel's measure *was according to* a man's. And the structure of its wall was jasper; and the city *was* pure gold, like pure glass" (vs 17-18).

Imagine that! I have no idea what that looks like, buy that is going to be stunning, indeed! We're going to have to be spirit beings in order to really understand that and grasp it fully.

Verse 19: "And the foundations of the wall of the city *were* adorned with every precious stone… [then it lists all 12 stones for the foundation]: …the first foundation *was* jasper; the second, sapphire; the third, chalcedony; the fourth, emerald; the fifth, sardonyx; the sixth, sardius; the seventh, chrysolite; the eighth, beryl; the ninth, topaz; the tenth, chrysoprasus; the eleventh, jacinth; the twelfth, amethyst" (vs 19-20).

Verse 21: "And the twelve gates *were* twelve pearls; each of the gates respectively was a single pearl; and the street of the city *was* pure gold, as transparent *as* glass."

I don't know how that's going to work, because physical things in a spiritual world look different than physical things in a physical world viewed with physical eyes. The only think I can say is that in order for us to really appreciate this and to understand what this really is like, *we're going to have to be there!*

Verse 22: "And I saw no temple in it; for **the Lord God Almighty and the Lamb are the temple** of it."

Where did we start with the Feast of Tabernacles? *Build Me a tabernacle that I may dwell among them* (Exo. 25:8)! Look at what we have here! Don't need a temple!

Verse 23: "And the city has no need of the sun, or of the moon…" *Doesn't say that they won't be there*; they'll be there because you have to count time.

"…that they should shine in it; because the glory of God enlightens it, and the Light of it *is* the Lamb. And the nations that are saved shall walk in its Light…" (vs 23-24).

All the nations that are saved will live outside of New Jerusalem. Only those in the first resurrection will be in New Jerusalem.

"…and the kings of the earth shall bring their glory and honor into it" (v 24). *So, though we live there, we'll also be running the different nations in the spiritual kingdom as well!*

Verse 25: "And its gates shall never be shut by day; for there shall be no night there. And they shall bring the glory and the honor of the nations into it" (vs 25-26).

- What are we going to be doing?
- What will all of those in the resurrection be doing?

We're going to be making and producing whatever we will be doing! We're not going to sitting around twiddling our thumbs or playing games, whatever.

Jesus said, 'I work, and until now My Father is working.' So, what kind of work will they have? *We don't know, but we'll have to wait and see, and get there to see what that will be like!*

Verse 27: "And nothing that defiles shall

ever enter into it… [because everyone is going to be the sons or daughters of God] …nor shall *anyone* who practices *an* abomination or *devises* a lie; but *only* those who are written in the Lamb's Book of Life."

The Book of Life is opened to the great innumerable multitude as well. Yes, they can come into the city, but they will live someplace else on the earth.

Rev. 22: this is one my most favorite chapters in the Bible. It shows God's great love, God's great plan, all peace, love, joy, truth— *everything that is good and Holy!*

Revelation 22:1: "Then he showed me a pure river of *the* Water of Life…" What is that going to be made of? *Not water like we have today that we see, drink and use!*

"…clear as crystal… [no pollution there; don't need the EPA to keep it clean] …flowing out from the Throne of God and of the Lamb." *So, there are two Thrones there flowing out!*

Verse 2: "*And* in the middle of *the* street, and on this side and that side of the river, *was the* Tree of Life, producing twelve *manner of* fruits, each month…"

That shows that the sun and moon are there. You don't have months unless you have the moon and sun.

"…yielding its fruit; and the leaves of the tree *are* for *the* healing of the nations" (v 2)—*or the maintenance of the nations!*

How that's going to work I don't know! But we never have had a Tree of Life that we could say that we could surmise how it will be.

Verse 3: "And there shall be **no more curse**… [because there's no more sin] …and the Throne of God and of the Lamb shall be in it; and His servants shall serve Him."

This next verse is one of the most profound verses in the Bible, because we will be there with God the Father and He is our Father, and Jesus Christ our Savior.

Verse 4: "**And they shall see His face**… [and we will say, 'Abba Father'] …**and His name *is* in their foreheads**"—*completely devoted to God!*

Verse 5: "And there shall be no night there; for they have no need of a lamp or *the* light of *the* sun, because *the* Lord God enlightens them; and **they shall reign into the ages of eternity**." *That's why the universe is so vast!*

Can you imagine—as we understand God's plan related to the earth and us now—think how awesome… Of course, it will be very difficult for us to, but at least we can contemplate it by looking at many of the beautiful views of the universe that we see. Where there are billions, and billions, and billions—even trillions—of galaxies and stars! *God does nothing in vain! God wastes nothing at all!* He has a use for it all, but He needs all of us to be there with Him so we can go into the vastness of the universe and carry out whatever plan God has for us, that He will reveal to us.

Verse 6: "And he said to me, 'These words *are* faithful and true; and *the* Lord God of the Holy prophets sent His angel to show His servants the things that must shortly come to pass.'" *Compared to eternity, that's **shortly!***

Verse 7: "Behold, I am coming quickly. Blessed *is* the one who keeps the words of the prophecy of this book." *The whole Bible!* It is *the Truth of God, **the Truth of God**, the Truth of God* in everything that we do!

Verse 8: Now I, John, *was* the one who saw and heard these things. And when I heard and saw, I fell down to worship before the feet of the angel who *was* showing me these things. But he said to me, 'See *that you do* not *do this!* For I am a fellow servant of yours, and of your brethren the prophets, and of those who keep the words of this book. **Worship God.**'" (vs 8-9). *That's what we're going to do, brethren!* What a thing that is!

Verse 10: "And he said to me, 'Do not seal the words of the prophecy of this book because the time is near.' Let the one who is unrighteous be unrighteous still; and let the one who is filthy be filthy still; and let the one who is righteous be righteous still; and let the one who is Holy be Holy still. And behold, I am coming quickly… [in relationship to how God views time] …and My reward is with Me, to render to each one according as his work shall be" (vs 10-12). *That's why we want to always diligently*:

- love God with all our heart, mind, soul and being
- love Jesus Christ
- praise Them for Their plan
- thank them for Their goodness
- yield to Them in our lives

in everything that we do so that we can be in New Jerusalem with Them!

- see the Father face-to-face
- see Jesus face-to-face

Brethren, ***don't let anything get between you and God,*** so you can aspire and attain and be there, witness this, and do this!

Verse 13: "I am Alpha and Omega, the Beginning and the End, the First and the Last. Blessed are those who keep His commandments, that they may have the right to eat of the Tree of Life, and may enter by the gates into the city" (vs 13-14). *That includes those in the City, and those out of the City!*

Verse 15: "But excluded are dogs, and sorcerers, and fornicators, and murderers, and idolaters, and everyone who loves and devises a lie. I, Jesus, sent My angel to testify these things to you in the churches…. [all churches pay attention; listen up]: …I am the root and the offspring of David, the bright and morning star." (vs 15-16).

Verse 17: "And the Spirit and the Bride say, 'Come.' And let the one who hears say, 'Come.' And let the one who thirsts come; **and let the one who desires partake of the water of life freely**."

- that's what God wants
- that's our destiny
- that's the destiny of all mankind

Think of it! To little ole us God reveals to His people:

- *His plan*
- *His secrets*
- *the mysteries of His Kingdom*

Verse 18: "For I jointly testify to everyone who hears the words of the prophecy of this book, *that* if anyone adds to these things, God shall add to him the plagues that are written in this book. And if anyone takes away from the words of *the* book of this prophecy… [the whole Bible] …God shall take away his part from *the* Book of Life, and from the Holy City, and from the things that are written in this book. He Who testifies these things says, 'Surely, I am coming quickly.' Amen. Even so, come, Lord Jesus. The grace of our Lord Jesus Christ *be* with you all. Amen" (vs 18-21).

That's the meaning of the Feast of Tabernacles and the Last Great Day! It's been wonderful, we've had a great Feast and we're thankful that we have this knowledge. Let's:

- *keep it*
- *understand it*
- *believe it*

and live our lives so that we can:
- *change*
- *grow*
- *overcome*

and develop the character of God!

Scriptural References:

Scriptural References:

1) Leviticus 23:34-39
2) Isaiah 28:9-15
3) Matthew 13:10-17, 43
4) John 7:37-39
5) 1 Timothy 2:1-7
6) 2 Timothy 2:15-19
7) 2 Peter 3:9, 8-9
8) 1 John 5:16-18
9) 1 John 2:1-2
10) 1 John 5:18-21
11) Romans 2:14-16
12) Matthew 12:31-33, 38-40, 32, 41
13) Revelation 20:6, 5
14) Ezekiel 37:1-14
15) Revelation 20:11-15
16) 2 Peter 3:8-13
17) Revelation 21:1-27
18) Revelation 22:1-21

Scriptures referenced, not quoted:

- Revelation 20:4
- Isaiah 65
- Exodus 25:8

Also referenced: Booklet:
Which is the True Calendar of God?
by Carl D. Franklin & Fred R. Coulter

FRC:bo
Transcribed: 8/10/20
Reformatted: 1/2021

Epilogue

In reviewing the contents of this book and its accompanying CDs, we humbly stand before God the Father and Jesus Christ, praising Them with thanksgiving for Their love, mercy and grace—and for Their awesome plan for mankind as revealed by the Sabbath and annual holy days. It is certainly true that we are the recipients of Their loving kindness and grace in these last days. They have opened up to our understanding this profound knowledge, which has long been hidden from the world. As promised in the book of Daniel—and as later reaffirmed by Jesus Christ—God has granted more understanding to His Church at this time than He previously granted to all the prophets, apostles, ministers and brethren of past ages. On the other hand, the Word of God is not *bound*, because God Himself has inspired all the knowledge contained in the Bible. As Jesus said, "It is the Spirit that gives life; the flesh profits nothing. **The words that I speak to you,** *they* **are spirit and** *they* **are life**" (John 6:63).

Apart from the Word and Spirit of God, even the greatest minds throughout history have failed to understand God's plan for mankind. It was simply not possible—for God's truth is spiritually discerned and God Himself must choose to *reveal* His plan. As Paul wrote: "But according as it is written, 'The eye has not seen, nor *the* ear heard, neither have entered into *the* heart of man, *the* things which God has prepared for those who love Him.' **But God has revealed** *them* **to us by His Spirit, for the Spirit searches all things—even the deep things of God**. For who among men understands the things of man except *by* the spirit of man which *is* in him? In the same way also, **the things of God no one understands except** *by* **the Spirit of God**. Now we have not received the spirit of the world, but **the Spirit that** *is* **of God, so that we might know the things graciously given to us by God**; which things we also speak, not in words taught by human wisdom, but in *words* taught by *the* Holy Spirit *in order to* communicate spiritual things by spiritual *means*" (I Cor. 2:9-13).

Even with the understanding God has granted, we still do not comprehend as we ought to. Indeed, we are still "looking through a glass darkly." There are many things, however, that God will no doubt yet reveal to His church and ministers as we come closer to the return of Jesus Christ. And while we may see many aspects of God's plan more clearly than those of past church ages, we need to continue to grow in the grace and knowledge of the Lord Jesus Christ—so that we may be counted worthy to receive eternal life and share in the glorious inheritance of Jesus Christ as spirit-born sons and daughters of God the Father, thus fulfilling God's plan and purpose.

We will conclude with Paul's inspired prayer of thanksgiving for the knowledge of God's plan and purpose given to him through Jesus Christ for us: "For this cause I, Paul, *am* the prisoner of Christ Jesus for you Gentiles, if indeed you have heard of the ministry of the grace of God that was given to me for you; how **He made known to me by revelation the mystery** (even as I wrote briefly before, so that when you read *this*, you will be able to comprehend my understanding in **the mystery of Christ**), **which in other generations was not made known to the sons of men, as it has now been revealed to His holy apostles and prophets by** *the* **Spirit**; that the Gentiles might be joint heirs, and a joint body, and joint partakers of His promise in Christ through the gospel, of which I became a servant according to the gift of the grace of God, *which was* given to me through the inner working of His power.

"To me, who am less than the least of all the saints, was this grace given, that I might preach the gospel among the Gentiles— *even* the unsearchable riches of Christ; and **that I might enlighten all** *as to* **what** *is* **the fellowship of the mystery that has been hidden from the ages** in God, **Who created all things by Jesus Christ**; so that the manifold wisdom of God might now be made known through the church to the principalities and the powers in the heavenly *places*, **according to *His* eternal purpose, which He has wrought in Christ Jesus our Lord**, in Whom we have boldness and *direct* access with confidence through His *very* own faith.

"So then, I beseech *you* not to faint at my tribulations for you, which are *working for* your glory. For this cause I bow my knees to the Father of our Lord Jesus Christ, of Whom the whole family in heaven and earth is named, **that He may grant you, according to the riches of His glory, to be strengthened with power by His Spirit in the inner man**; that Christ may dwell in your hearts by faith; ***and* that being rooted and grounded in love, you may be fully able to comprehend with all the saints what *is* the breadth and length and depth and height, and to know the love of Christ, which surpasses *human* knowledge; so that you may be filled with all the fullness of God**.

"Now to Him Who is able to do exceeding abundantly above all that we ask or think, according to the power that is working in us, to Him *be* glory in the church by Christ Jesus throughout all generations, *even* into the ages of eternity. Amen" (Eph. 3:1-21).

Additional Audio Messages and Transcripts Available:

From our website ***www.truthofgod.org*** we have additional audio messages and transcripts available for further study. You may download them and print out the transcripts and listen to the audio messages. For the spring holy days—Passover through Pentecost—we have over 60 additional messages and transcripts. For the fall holy days—Trumpets through the Last Great Day—we have over 70 additional messages and transcripts. These will help give you greater biblical insight into the meaning of God's ordained feasts and holy days that reveal God's plan for mankind.

Acknowledgments

First and foremost, all honor and glory go to God the Father and Jesus Christ for Their great and awesome "Plan for Mankind." Through the power of the Holy Spirit, They have made it possible for those called by God to understand this great mystery—a mystery *concealed* from the masses in the pages of the Bible.

Special heartfelt thanks goes to my loving wife Dolores, who has since passed away. After 56 years of marriage, her encouragement and guidance in my ministry will be greatly missed.

Thanks to Jim and Betty Hyles—who first suggested that we produce this book. Before his death in 2018, Jim personally assisted the author in numerous aspects of serving the brethren, including writing letters and handling administrative and technical matters for the CBCG. His wife Betty reproduced and mailed out our four special "Care Packages" of studies and messages to people who request them.

A special thanks goes to those who did the wearisome work of transcribing the messages that comprise the main text of this book: primarily Bonnie Orswell, as well as several others who over the years have assisted with transcribing (Carolyn Singer, Michael Schwartz, Judith Anderson, Laila Patterson, Nancy Spaller and Sasha Vogele). Thanks to Prentice Orswell who edited the audio messages associated with the transcripts, and to John and Hiedi Vogele who did the tedious job of compiling and laying out the pages of the book. Dick and Bette Young proofread many of the transcripts. We acknowledge our editor, Philip Neal, for his editing of the non-transcript portions of the book. Finally, special thanks go to Cindy Curley—of Curley Creatives—for the beautiful artwork and design of the front cover. None of this, however, could have been accomplished without the ongoing love, prayers and support of thousands of God's people.

All of us together can affirm what Jesus told His apostles: "My meat is to do the will of Him Who sent Me, and to finish His work. Do not say that there are yet four months, and *then* the harvest comes. I say to you, look around. Lift up your eyes and see the fields, for they are already white to harvest. And the one who reaps receives a reward, and gathers fruit unto eternal life; so that the one who is sowing and the one who is reaping may both rejoice together. **For in this the saying is true, that one sows and another reaps. I sent you to reap that in which you have not labored; others have labored, and you have entered into their labor**" (John 4:34-38). How true this is today! Indeed, we have entered into the sowing and reaping of nearly two thousand years of God's true ministers and servants down through history—many of whom willingly gave their lives in standing up for the truth so that we, in the end times, may reap of their labor. May God the Father and Jesus Christ count us worthy to receive and share the knowledge of this awesome plan for mankind as revealed in the Word of God.

Fred R. Coulter
Summer 2021

About the Author

Fred R. Coulter attended the University of San Francisco and graduated from San Mateo State College before graduating from Ambassador University (Ambassador College), Pasadena, California, with a BA in Theology in 1964. He was ordained a minister of Jesus Christ in 1965 and pastored churches of God in the Pacific Northwest, the Mountain States, the greater Los Angeles area and Monterey, including the central coast area of California. Coulter completed advanced biblical and ministerial studies from 1972 to 1975 under the Ambassador University Master's program. While completing these studies, Coulter was encouraged by his professor of *Koiné* Greek to consider translating the books of the New Testament.

After completing his formal instruction in *Koiné* Greek, Coulter continued to expand his knowledge of Greek for the next 28 years by undertaking a verse-by-verse study of the books of the New Testament using the Byzantine Text. In the course of his study, Coulter was ultimately moved to translate the New Testament into clear, easy-to-read English for contemporary readers. After twelve years of diligent translating, *The New Testament In Its Original Order—A Faithful Version With Commentary* was completed and published in 2004.

In July of 2008, Coulter's work reached a personal milestone with the first printing of *The Holy Bible In Its Original Order—A Faithful Version With Commentary* (which fully incorporates the above-mentioned New Testament). (Leading in the translation of the Old Testament was Hebrew consultant Michael Heiss.) This extraordinary Bible is unique in that it is the *only complete* Bible ever published—with Old and New Testaments—that follows the *original*, canonical manuscript order as recognized by scholars. As an easy-to-read English translation, *The Holy Bible In Its Original Order* is completely faithful to the original Hebrew and Greek texts.

Coulter has dedicated his life and talents to proclaiming Jesus Christ as personal Savior for all. Since 1983, he has had an active ministry as president and pastor of the Christian Biblical Church of God, Hollister, California. The CBCG has offices in the United States, Canada, Australia, New Zealand, Africa, South Africa, and the UK—serving thousands of people.

A key component of Coulter's ministry is his extensive Internet presence. Each year, over *four million visitors* from around the world actively utilize the church's websites—where they find timely, inspiring materials covering virtually every topic in Scripture.

His primary website, ***truthofgod.org*** (which now incorporates biblicaltruthministries.org) is designed to proclaim the Gospel of the Kingdom of God and preserve biblical truth. Over 1900 audio messages and Bible studies are available for download, including hundreds of video messages, message transcripts and biblical articles.

A second website—***theoriginalbiblerestored.org***—is dedicated to promoting Coulter's new Bible, *The Holy Bible In Its Original Order, A Faithful Version with Commentary*.

His latest site, growing rapidly in popularity, is designed for Christians looking for alternatives to the one-size-fits-all "corporate" church experience—***churchathome.org***. "Church at Home" features some 500 downloadable half-hour video presentations and a variety of other materials for personal and family in-home Bible study.

With his ministry now spanning 56 years, Fred R. Coulter has again been inspired to undertake the publication of this book, *God's Plan for Mankind Revealed by His Sabbath and Holy Days*. This second edition expands upon the knowledge and information contained in another of his books, *Occult Holidays or God's Holy Days—Which?*

Other Works by Fred R. Coulter

The Holy Bible In Its Original Order—A Faithful Version With Commentary is a new translation that reflects the meaning of the original Hebrew and Greek with fidelity and accuracy. It is the only complete English version in which all of the books of the Bible are arranged in their *original* inspired order. The easy-to-read translation retains the grace and grandeur of the *KJV* while clarifying many of its problematic passages. Included are commentaries on the writing, canonization and preservation of the Scriptures; various appendices cover numerous biblical teachings, and detailed footnotes and marginal references explain hard-to-understand passages.

A complete audio reading of the *Faithful Version* is available as a free download at *afaithfulversion.org*. This reading includes the Bible as well as commentaries and appendices.

A Harmony of the Gospels In Modern English brings to life the message and purpose of the true Jesus, portraying His life and ministry in their true historical setting. This easy-to-understand, step-by-step account of the life of Jesus Christ is an indispensable study aid for every serious Bible student.

The Christian Passover is a book of over 500 pages that details the scriptural and historical truths of the Passover in both the Old and New Testaments, leading the reader through every aspect of one of the most vital and fundamental teachings revealed in the Bible. It fully explains the meaning of the Christian Passover—a remembrance of the sacrifice of Jesus Christ, the Passover Lamb of God—in a most thorough and inspiring manner. The full meaning of the body and blood of Christ is revealed, showing the magnitude of God's love for every person.

The Day Jesus the Christ Died—the Biblical Truth About His Passion, Crucifixion and Resurrection. This book presents the whole truth and nothing but the truth! It presents the "rest of the story" left out by Mel Gibson in his epic movie *The Passion of the Christ*. Without the true historical and biblical facts, no one can fully understand the meaning of Jesus Christ's horrific, humiliating and gruesome death by beating, scourging and crucifixion. The author presents the full biblical account in a most compelling way. As you will see, the truth is more astounding and profound than all of the ideas, superstitions, traditions and misbeliefs of men!

Occult Holidays or God's Holy Days—Which? For centuries the leaders of Orthodox Christendom have sold popular holidays—Halloween, Christmas, New Years, Easter, etc.—to the masses as though they had "Christian" meaning. This book effectively demonstrates that these celebrated holidays are *not* of God—but originated from ancient, pagan religions rooted in satanic occultism, witchcraft, the feminine divine and "New Age" spirituality. Contrary to the false ideas of men, the true biblical holy days and feasts of God have deep spiritual meaning and outline God's fantastic plan of salvation for all mankind—past, present and future—as revealed in the Holy Scriptures.

The Seven General Epistles is designed for an in-depth verse-by-verse study of the epistles of James; I and II Peter; I, II and III John and Jude. As part of the Word of God, these epistles are as meaningful today for personal Christian growth as when they were first written.

Lord, What Should I Do? is a book for Christians who are faced with a confusing world of a compromised "Christianity"—in which false doctrinal teachings undermine the true faith of the Bible. This book clarifies the problem and shows what God requires a person to do—if they are to truly find God the Father and the true faith of Jesus Christ.

The Appointed Times of Jesus the Messiah follows Jesus' entire ministry as it unfolds around the framework established by God's "appointed times"—His annual holy days. This book unveils Christ's ministry and work like no other!

From a Speck of Dust to a Son of God—Why Were You Born? This eye-opening book examines God's true purpose for creating mankind—and it has nothing to do with going to heaven! Indeed, man's destiny is far greater than even today's "Christian" has dared to imagine!

On-line Studies for the serious Bible student—with written study materials and in-depth audio and video messages—can be found at ***truthofgod.org***.

Appendix A

Fourteen Rules for Bible Study

Jesus Christ is the crowning glory of God's plan, the supreme expression of God's love for each individual He calls. Through Jesus, God's marvelous love will ultimately be manifested to all mankind—past, present, and future. "For God so loved the world that He gave His only begotten Son, so that everyone who believes in Him may not perish, but may have everlasting life" (John 3:16). Indeed, God's love for us undergirds all that He does—including the revealing of His *plan* and *way of life* through the Scriptures.

Jesus is the foundation of all biblical understanding. He said, "**I am the way, and the truth, and the life; no one comes to the Father except through Me**" (John 14:6). All scriptural truth comes from God the Father *through* Jesus. In order to properly understand the Scriptures, we must go *to* the Father *through* Christ—Who is the way, the truth, and the life. It is the Father Who imparts the Holy Spirit to guide us in understanding His word, which is the *truth* (John 17:17).

How does one come to have the Holy Spirit? First, one must be drawn and called by God—*led to Christ* (John 6:44). God then leads those He calls to *repentance* (Rom. 2:4)—which means a turning around, a complete forsaking of one's sinful life. We see in Acts 2 that many of those assembled at the Temple on the day of Pentecost in 30 AD were "cut to the heart" (verse 37)—convicted of their sinfulness, convinced of their need for spiritual salvation. This led to their acceptance of Jesus as their personal savior.

The apostle Peter led them to the next step: "Repent and be baptized each one of you in the name of Jesus Christ for *the* remission of sins, and you yourselves shall receive the gift of the Holy Spirit" (verse 38). Belief, conviction, repentance—then *baptism* as an outward sign of faith, a token of one's new life in Jesus. Baptism is immediately followed by the "laying on of hands" (Acts 19:6). Only then will one receive the indwelling of the Holy Spirit—which opens the believer's mind to understand the Scriptures while inspiring and empowering him or her in their new walk with Christ.

Jesus Revealed *How* to Understand God's Word

Jesus clearly taught that it is the Holy Spirit—the Spirit of truth—that enables us to come to a true and full understanding of the Word of God (John 16:13). In order to receive the Spirit of truth, Jesus revealed that we must *love* God the Father and Christ and be *keeping* their commandments. Fulfilling these requirements is absolutely essential for receiving the Holy Spirit and thus coming to a correct understanding of the Scriptures. The apostle John recorded Jesus' teaching on this very subject:

" 'If you love Me, keep the commandments—namely, My commandments. And I will ask the Father, and He shall give you another Comforter, that it may be with you throughout the age [until Jesus returns]; *even* the Spirit of the truth, which the world cannot receive because it perceives it not, nor knows it; but you know it because it dwells with you, and shall be within you…. In that day, you shall know that I am in My Father, and you *are* in Me, and I am in you.

" 'The one who has My commandments and is keeping them, that is the one who loves [Greek, *who is loving*] Me; and the one who loves [*who is loving*] Me shall be loved by My Father, and I will love him and will manifest Myself to him.' Judas (not Iscariot) said to him,

'Lord, what has happened that You are about to manifest Yourself to us, and not to the world?'

"Jesus answered and said to him, 'If anyone loves Me, he will keep My word [the entire message]; and My Father will love him, and We will come to him and make Our abode with him. The one who does not love Me does not keep My words; and the word [the entire message] that you hear is not Mine, but the Father's, Who sent Me' " (John 14:15-17, 20-24).

These words reveal the loving, personal, spiritual relationship of God the Father and Jesus Christ with every true Christian. These words also reveal the wholehearted *obedience* that God requires of all who profess to love and believe in Christ. This teaching is the heart and core of the love that God gives to us through His Son, and the love that we, as true believers in Christ, show toward God. It is the daily way of life for a *true* Christian. **If we love Jesus, we will be keeping His commandments—and those commandments are from God the Father!**

Not many professing Christians, whether ministers or laymen, are living in obedience to all of the commandments of God. Jesus gave the following warning for those who would be using His name and claiming His promises and blessings—professing to be His followers and teachers of the Bible—but who would *not* be keeping the commandments of God: "Not everyone who says to Me, 'Lord, Lord,' shall enter into the kingdom of heaven; but the one who is doing the will of My Father, Who *is* in heaven.

"Many will say to Me in that day, 'Lord, Lord, did we not prophesy through Your name? And *did we not* cast out demons through Your name? And *did we not* perform many works of power through Your name?' And then I will confess to them, 'I never knew you. Depart from Me, you who work lawlessness' " (Matt. 7:21-23).

The word "lawlessness" is translated from the Greek *anomos*, which means *against law*—or being against the keeping of God's laws and commandments. This kind of pseudo-Christianity, which uses Jesus' name but refuses to do the will of God, is not accepted by God. The result of this pseudo-Christianity is death, not eternal life. And many, the vast majority of people, are following the broad path that leads to death—exactly as Jesus said (Matt. 7:13-14).

Those who are teaching and practicing a lawless pseudo-Christianity are doing the exact *opposite* of what Jesus said those who love Him will be doing: "**If you love Me, keep the commandments—namely, My commandments**" (John 14:15). The one who truly loves Jesus will be keeping His commandments—yes, *every one of His words*, which He received from the Father. That is the standard by which we can identify those who love God and those who do not.

Every commandment God has given is based on *love*. Here is the greatest commandment of all, just as Jesus said it: " '**You shall love *the* Lord your God with all your heart, and with all your soul, and with all your mind.**' This is *the* first and greatest commandment. And *the* second *one is* like it: 'You shall love your neighbor as yourself.' On these two commandments hang all the Law and the Prophets" (Matt. 22:37-40).

Without these two commandments, there would be no law, there would be no prophets, there would be no covenants, old or new. *Everything God does is based on love!*

John expresses the love of God quite clearly in his first epistle: "Beloved, we should love one another because love is from God; and everyone who loves [Greek, *who is loving*] has been begotten by God, and knows God.

"**The one who does not love does not know God** because **God is love**. In this *way* the love of God was manifested toward us: that God sent His only begotten Son into the world, so that we might live through Him.

"In this *act* is the love—not that we loved God; rather, that He loved us and sent His Son *to be the* propitiation for our sins…. And we have known and have believed the love that God has toward us. God is love, and the one who dwells in love is dwelling in God, and God in him" (I John 4:7-10, 16).

This is the attitude of love, faith, and obedience that we must show toward God the Father and Jesus Christ in order to understand the Word of God. Without this love for God and His truth, a full understanding of the Scriptures can never be achieved!

Five Keys to Understanding the Word of God

In addition to a loving, faithful, and obedient attitude toward God, there are five major principles that are essential to a correct understanding of Scripture. These vital keys must always be kept in mind when we study the Word of God.

Key Number One: "All Scripture *is* God-breathed and *is* profitable for doctrine, for conviction, for correction, for instruction in righteousness; so that the man of God may be complete, fully equipped for every good work" (II Tim. 3:16-17).

Many who profess to study the Bible completely disregard this vital principle. Rather than seeking the truth of Scripture, they look for verses that appear to support their personal beliefs—while ignoring those verses that clearly contradict their beliefs. This approach to study can never lead to understanding because it denies that every part of Scripture is inspired. Those who use this approach are exalting their own beliefs above the authority of Scripture.

When we study the Bible, we should always be careful to seek the true meaning of the words that were inspired by God. No study should be designed to support the position of a doctrinal board, or to justify a time-honored church tradition, or to "prove" a personal interpretation of the Bible. None of these motives are acceptable. And if these or similar motives are involved, for whatever reason, can we really expect God to overlook such deceptive use of the Scriptures? If we think we can fool God, we are only deceiving ourselves.

Let us not be guilty of such a presumptuous and self-righteous attitude toward the Word of God. Rather, let us humbly allow the inspired words of Scripture to correct us and instruct us in the true righteousness of Jesus Christ.

Key Number Two: The prophet Isaiah brings out this vital principle: "Whom shall He teach knowledge? And whom shall He make to understand doctrine? *Those* who are weaned from the milk and drawn from the breasts [that is, fully grounded in the Word of God and not an immature Christian feeding only on the milk of Scripture]. For precept *must be* upon precept, precept upon precept; line upon line, line upon line; here a little, there a little" (Isa. 28:9-10).

Isaiah is telling us that, in order to understand the Scriptures, we must *connect* "precept with precept" and *connect* "line with line." In practice, this means searching throughout the Bible for *all* of the relevant passages on any given subject. No subject is covered in any one place in Scripture. Rather, there will be relevant passages *here* and *there*—just as Isaiah said. We must *link all of these passages together* if we are to come to a full and right understanding on a particular subject.

This is exactly how we should study every doctrinal question. The New Testament confirms this approach to understanding the Word of God and establishing sound doctrine. "Diligently *study* to show yourself approved unto God, a workman [in the Word of God] who does not *need to be* ashamed, **rightly dividing** [putting precept with precept, line with line] **the Word of the truth**" (II Tim. 2:15).

In order to come to the knowledge of the truth, we must always follow this biblically sanctioned method of study—"straightly cutting" or "rightly dividing" the Word of God. Any other type of study is useless! As Paul instructed Timothy, "See that *they* remain mindful of these things, earnestly charging *them* in the sight of the Lord not to argue over words that are not profitable in any way, *but which lead* to *the* subverting of those who hear" (II Tim. 2:14).

This is exactly what many ministers and scholars have done in their doctrinal teachings—because they have not "rightly divided" the Word of God! Whole congregations have been subverted by strivings and disputations over the meaning of key words that are used in Scripture. Some teachers and ministers have even engaged in redefining words—attaching their own personal interpretations and rejecting the authoritative definitions that are found in Hebrew and Greek lexicons. Anyone who undertakes such practices is "using the law unlawfully," as Paul said, and will end up teaching false, satanic doctrines that subvert the minds of their followers. Unfortunately, the landscape of religious history is filled with the bodies of people who have taught false doctrines, and the bodies of people who have embraced their teachings. Only by learning to *rightly divide* the Word of God will we be able to recognize and resist false doctrines.

Key Number Three: In the second epistle of Peter, we read: "Knowing this first [Greek, *protos*—meaning the primary, or first and foremost thing], that no prophecy of Scripture originated as anyone's own *private* interpretation; because prophecy was not brought at any time by human will, but the holy men of God spoke as they were moved by *the* Holy Spirit" (II Pet. 1:20-21).

In today's world, we find many pseudo-teachers who are twisting the Scriptures and deceitfully using their own *personal* interpretations in order to persuade others to believe their false doctrines. To support their teachings, they may quote numerous passages. To their listeners, their teachings sound authoritative, but the way that they apply the Scriptures exposes their craftiness. They are using the same subtle methods of deception that Satan the devil uses.

Yes, even Satan the devil quotes Scripture! When Jesus was being tempted by the devil in person, Satan did not hesitate to quote Scripture. "If You are the Son of God, cast Yourself down; for it is written, 'He shall give His angels charge concerning You, and they shall bear You up in *their* hands, lest You strike Your foot against a stone' " (Matt. 4:6; Psa. 91:11-12).

Satan correctly quoted this passage, but *misapplied* it in a crafty effort to tempt Jesus to jump from the pinnacle of the Temple. Jesus resisted Satan's deception by rightly applying the Scriptures. He said, "Again, it is written, 'You shall not tempt *the* Lord your God' " (Matt. 4:7).

What is the lesson for us in this account? It is this: Those who quote the Scriptures correctly, but twist and misapply the meaning, are following Satan—not serving God! This example is recorded in Scripture as a warning for us to be on guard. The fact that a minister or teacher may quote the Bible does not guarantee that he is teaching the truth. **Indeed, Scripture that is quoted accurately is often *misapplied* to promote false teachings!**

True servants of God do not use such deceitful tactics. The apostle Paul wrote of his ministry: "For we have personally renounced the hidden things of dishonest gain, not walking in *cunning* craftiness [having a hidden agenda], nor handling the Word of God deceitfully [falsely applying the Scriptures]; but by manifestation of the truth, we are commending ourselves to every man's conscience before God" (II Cor. 4:2).

Those who are truly serving God will not deceitfully use Scripture to promote their own ideas and personal interpretations. They will seek to understand and teach the true meaning of the words that God has inspired by the power of His Holy Spirit.

Key Number Four: Paul thus instructed the Thessalonian believers: "Prove all things. Hold fast *to that which* is good" (I Thess. 5:21).

The instruction to "prove all things" is a lifelong responsibility for every believer. As

Christians, we must continually be *testing* every teaching we read or hear by carefully studying the Scriptures. The Bereans were commended because they diligently searched the Scriptures to *confirm* what Paul was teaching: "Now these [Bereans] were more noble than those in Thessalonica [where unbelieving Jews immediately rejected Paul's teaching that Christ was raised from the dead], *for* they [the Bereans] received the Word with all readiness of mind *and* examined the Scriptures daily *to see* if these things were so" (Acts 17: 11).

The Bereans were diligently studying the Scriptures to *prove* whether or not the things they had heard were true. They did not react with blind emotion and refuse to consider the teachings of Paul. Rather, they carefully examined the Scriptures and proved to themselves that Paul was, in fact, preaching the true message of God.

We, like the Bereans, must diligently examine the Bible in order to discern true doctrine from false doctrine. As we do so, we will become *skillful* in using the Scriptures—no longer feeding on the "milk" of the Word of God, but able to handle "solid food." If we do not exercise our minds and learn to discern truth from error, we will not become spiritually mature. "For everyone who is partaking of milk *is* unskilled in *the* word of righteousness because he is an infant. But solid food is for those who are fully grown, who **through repeated practice have had their senses trained to discern between good and evil**" (Heb. 5:13-14).

Too many Christians have remained as spiritual infants because they have transferred their God-given responsibility to discern truth from error to a minister or church board. Their ministers have told them that they, the laity, are incapable of understanding the Scriptures and must submit to the doctrinal decisions of their church leaders, who alone can interpret the Bible. But it was never God's intention that we, as individual believers, place our trust in human leaders who claim sole authority to establish doctrine. Christians who have done so have left themselves open to dangerous deception. They have forgotten the many warnings throughout the New Testament to be on guard against false teachers and false apostles who make a pretense of serving God. Paul warned, "For I know this: that after my departure grievous wolves will come in among you, not sparing the flock. And from among your own selves men will rise up speaking perverse things to draw away disciples after themselves" (Acts 20:29-30).

Likewise, the apostle Peter strongly admonished the brethren. "But there were also false prophets among the people, as indeed there will be false teachers among you, who will stealthily introduce destructive heresies, personally denying *the* Lord who bought them, and bringing swift destruction upon themselves. And many people will follow *as authoritative* their destructive ways; *and* because of them, the way of the truth will be blasphemed. Also, through insatiable greed they will with enticing messages exploit you for gain; for whom the judgment of old is in *full* force, and their destruction is *ever* watching" (II Pet. 2:1-3).

True to the warnings of Paul and Peter, many Christians in the first century were subverted and drawn away from the true doctrines of Scripture. They neglected to "prove all things" and did not *test* the teachings of false apostles. But the church at Ephesus did not forget the admonitions of Paul and Peter, as well as of the other apostles. In the book of Revelation, Jesus commended the Ephesian believers because they *tried* and *tested* those who falsely claimed to be apostles and proved them to be liars. "I know your works, and your labor, and your endurance, and that you cannot bear those who are evil; and *that* you did test those who proclaim *themselves* to be apostles, but are not, and did find them liars" (Rev. 2:2).

Since these false apostles professed to be ministers of Christ, we can be sure that they quoted the Scriptures. Their false doctrines must have *sounded* authoritative and convincing, because they succeeded in undermining the faith of many New Testament Christians. How was the church at Ephesus able to withstand such powerful deception? If the Ephesian brethren had not been exercising their senses to discern truth from error, they would not have recognized these men as false apostles. But because the brethren at Ephesus were skillful in using the Scriptures, they were able to discern that these men were not teaching the true doctrines of Jesus Christ.

Like the brethren at Ephesus, Christians today must constantly be on guard against false ministers whose scriptural-sounding teachings are actually a perversion of the true doctrines of Scripture. It is our *personal responsibility* as Christians to test and try the teachings of every minister, pastor, teacher, or scholar by carefully examining the Scriptures. By following the instruction to "prove all things," we can learn to recognize and reject false doctrine, and we will be able to stand fast in the true doctrines of Christ.

Key Number Five: The Word of God is called the word of *truth*. Furthermore, it is the Spirit of truth that teaches us all things. Thus, we must be *led* by the Holy Spirit if we are to understand the truth. The Bible makes it clear that the *Spirit of truth* works hand-in-hand with the *word of truth* to give us the understanding God wants us to have. Jesus said, "But *when* the Comforter *comes*, *even* the Holy Spirit, which the Father will send in My name, **that one shall teach you all things**, and shall bring to your remembrance everything that I have told you" (John 14:26). This is the promise Jesus gives to all who repent and are converted in their hearts and minds by the Holy Spirit.

It is not possible for the *unconverted* human mind, which is deceitful above all things (Jer. 17:9), to come to the knowledge of the truth of God. In fact, the carnal mind is *hostile* toward God and is not willing to be subject to God's laws (Rom. 8:7). The word of truth and the Spirit of truth cannot work hand-in-hand with the carnal, deceitful mind. Regardless of how brilliant or intellectual one may be, God's truth is not understood through *human* wisdom and rationale. It is only through the Spirit of God that the Word of God can be understood.

Paul taught that it is not through human intelligence or reason that we are able to come to the knowledge of the truth, but through the *Spirit of God*. "But according as it is written, '*The eye has not seen, nor the ear heard, neither have entered into the heart of man, the things which God has prepared for those who love Him.'*

"But **God has revealed *them* to us by His Spirit, for the Spirit searches all things— even the deep things of God**. For who among men understands the things of man except *by* the spirit of man which *is* in him? In the same way also, **the things of God no one understands except *by* the Spirit of God**. Now we have not received the spirit of the world, but the Spirit that *is* of God, so that we might know the things graciously given to us by God; which things we also speak, not in words taught by human wisdom, but in *words* taught by *the* Holy Spirit *in order to* communicate spiritual things by spiritual *means*. But *the* natural man [the carnal mind without the Holy Spirit] does not receive the things of the Spirit of God; for they are foolishness to him, and he cannot understand *them* because they are spiritually discerned" (I Cor. 2:9-14).

Without the Holy Spirit, no human being—no matter how intelligent—can understand the Word of God! And even individuals who *have* received the Holy Spirit from God are often beset by obstacles that keep them from coming to a full understanding of the truth. Too many Christians get caught up in the politics of religion, or the power structure of an ecclesiastical hierarchy, and they end up submitting to a humanly-devised church authority. They blindly accept the teachings of so-called Bible scholars, adhering to the *approved* doctrines of their church. Thus, they are unable to open-mindedly study and completely understand the spiritual truth of the Scriptures.

The Holy Spirit cannot guide us into all truth unless we diligently study the Bible with an open mind, unhindered by the ideas and doctrines of men. Christians who look to the authority of men, rather than to Scripture, are easy prey for ministers and teachers who profess to serve God but are not obeying His commandments and are not teaching the truth.

A Dire Warning Against the Disobedient and Those Who Teach False Doctrines

The book of Deuteronomy contains a prophecy of Christ's ministry coupled with a dire warning against those who refuse to obey His words and those who teach false doctrines in His name: "I will raise them up a Prophet [Jesus Christ] from among their brethren, *One* like you [Moses], and will put My words in His mouth. And He shall speak to them all that I shall command Him. And it shall come to pass, whatever man will not hearken to My words [listen attentively to obey] which He [Jesus] shall speak in My name, I will require *it* of him [hold him accountable unto judgment]" (Deut. 18:18-19). This warning applies to every human being, but particularly to those who are claiming to follow Jesus!

The next verse pronounces even more severe judgment upon those who are teachers, or claim to be teachers, of the Word of God. "But the prophet [anyone who is teaching] who shall presume to speak a word [teach] in My name which I have not commanded him to speak or who shall speak in the name of other gods [false doctrines palmed off as teachings of God], **even that prophet shall die**" (verse 20).

Jesus, the Prophet God said was to come, repeated the same warning: "But if anyone hears My words and does not believe [in order to obey], I do not judge him; for I did not come [at that time] to judge the world, but to save the world. The one who rejects Me and does not receive My words has one who judges him; the word [the entire message—all the words of Christ] which I have spoken, that shall judge him in the last day. For I have not spoken from Myself [He taught nothing on His own initiative]; but the Father, Who sent Me, gave Me commandment Himself, what I should say and what I should speak. And I know that His commandment is eternal life" (John 12:47-50).

God inspired Jesus to speak these words and caused them to be preserved for us today. Indeed, anyone who presumptuously misapplies the Scriptures and teaches false doctrines already has the judgment of God pronounced against him. Yet Christians everywhere are being assaulted with false teachings. Moreover, these teachings are being received and believed because people cannot endure sound doctrine. They cannot sit and listen to the wholesome words of the Bible.

This unfortunate spiritual condition was foreseen by Paul: "For there shall come a time [and now is] when they [professing Christians] will not tolerate [or accept] sound doctrine; but according to their own lusts they shall accumulate to themselves *a great number of* teachers, having ears itching *to hear what satisfies their cravings*. And they shall **turn away their own ears from the truth** [of the Bible]; and **they shall be turned aside** [from the way of the Lord] **unto myths** [deceptive false doctrines]" (II Tim. 4:3-4).

Today, whole churches are falling prey to such deception. In fact, a great number of ministers and pastors are being swept away with every kind of doctrine imaginable. While some have served in their churches for many years, they are not spiritually grounded—because they have not diligently studied the Scriptures! As a result, they are woefully ill-equipped to recognize clever, true-sounding false doctrines. They have not been trained and grounded in the Scriptures—they have only been feeding on the milk of the Word of God. Consequently, they have remained in a state of spiritual infancy—and are easily misled. As Paul admonished, "For truly, by this time you ought to be teachers, *but instead* you need to have *someone* teach you again what *are* the beginning principles of the oracles of God, and have become those in need of milk, and not of solid food. For everyone who is partaking of milk *is* unskilled in *the* word of righteousness because he is an infant" (Heb. 5:12-13).

Christians who are not spiritually mature are ripe to be carried about with every wind of doctrine. They are like dry leaves, caught up in a whirlwind, swirling and spinning around. Because they are oblivious to their weak spiritual condition, it is easy to get caught up in false doctrines that *seem* to be right—but in reality are so wrong. **The most clever deception that Satan has devised is false doctrine that sounds blessedly true**.

This is what Christians are facing today—cleverly devised false doctrines, more fitly called fables or myths. It is not sufficient simply to proclaim that a doctrine is true, or to denounce a doctrine as false. Those who truly want to follow Christ need to study sound doctrine and know and understand the truth—and *why* it is true. And we must know and understand false doctrine and why it is false.

Unless we are able to discern truth from error, we will end up straying from the narrow pathway of the Scriptures—the path that leads to eternal life. To keep from following the broad way to destruction, as so many have, we need to be diligently studying the Word of God, following all the biblical principles and rules for discerning the true meaning of Scripture. *Please read the **Fourteen Rules for Bible Study** in the next section. These rules present a step-by-step systematic method for proper Bible study.*

Few Christians think of themselves as students, but every true Christian is a disciple of Christ. The word *disciple* means *learner* or *student*. As students of Christ, we should be daily studying His teachings. We should not be following the doctrines and traditions of men, regardless of how authoritative they may appear to be. Nor should we base our beliefs on Bible commentaries or other writings of men. We should strictly follow the Word of God, rightly "dividing" it—putting "line upon line" and "precept upon precept." Only by studying the Scriptures in this manner can we come to a full understanding of the truth.

Knowing that we must engage in serious, in-depth study of the Scriptures, we may have questions as to which *version* of the Bible we should use, especially for doctrinal study. Numerous translations of the Scriptures are available to us today, and new versions continue to be published. Modern versions may be easier to read than the older versions with their archaic words and expressions. However, modern versions are generally not reliable for doctrinal study because they do not closely follow the original texts. In some of these versions, thousands of words have been omitted.

A recently introduced version, *The Holy Bible In Its Original Order*, utilizes modern language while closely following the original Hebrew and Greek texts. It has proven to be an excellent study Bible for many (see below for more information).

In undertaking a study of any doctrinal subject, we should thoroughly examine every relevant passage. If the meaning of the text is questionable, or if the English phrasing is unclear, it may be necessary to study the passage in the original language (using Hebrew or Greek lexicons). This will help to determine the precise meaning of the original inspired words. This approach will give us a clear understanding of what the Bible is actually teaching and will enable us to arrive at a correct understanding on any doctrinal subject.

The *Fourteen Rules for Bible Study* listed on the following page will provide a systematic method for understanding all the essential doctrines of Scripture—even the most difficult ones.

Fourteen Rules for Bible Study

1) Begin with passages that are easy to understand, where there is little or no dispute as to the meaning—then move on to more difficult ones.

2) Let the Bible interpret and prove the Bible. Don't look for what you want to prove; look for what the Bible *actually* proves. Do this by looking at *all* of the passages relevant to the study.

3) Understand the context—the verses before and after, the chapters before and after. Does your understanding of a particular verse harmonize with the rest of the Bible?

4) Understand the original language, Hebrew or Greek. Never try to establish dogmatic doctrine or teachings by using *Strong's Concordance*. It can be helpful at times, but it is quite limited.

5) Ask, "What does the passage clearly say?"

6) Ask, "What does the passage not say?"

7) Ask, "To whom was the book written?"

8) Ask, "Who wrote it?"

9) Ask, "Who said it?"

10) Understand the historical time frame and cultural setting of when the book was written.

11) Don't bring your *personal* assumptions and preconceived notions into your understanding or conclusions.

12) Base your study on the biblical understanding you already have. What do you *know* up to this point in time?

13) Do not form conclusions based on partial facts or insufficient information, or the opinions and speculations of others.

14) Personal opinions or convictions, regardless of how sincere, don't count. Scripture alone must be your standard and guide.

These guidelines represent a thorough and careful approach to study. When undertaking a study of the Bible, we should always use this approach, coupled with prayer, trusting God to lead us with His Holy Spirit. We know that He will fulfill His promise to **lead us into all truth**—*if* we are diligently seeking to understand the Word of God.

Appendix B

Identifying Signs of the True Church of God

There are thousands of churches claiming to be "Christian." But how does the Bible *define* and *describe* the true Church of God? Listed below are major characteristics of the true believers who make up the body of Christ:

1. Has an unwavering belief in Jesus Christ as personal Savior—as one Who was born of the virgin Mary, was God manifested in the flesh, and was crucified for the sins of the world as the perfect sacrifice from God the Father on the Passover day in AD 30; believes that after three days and nights in the grave Jesus was raised from the dead by the power of the Father and ascended bodily into heaven to be received by God the Father as the perfect sacrifice for the sins of the world on the first day of the fifty-day count to Pentecost; and that He returned to the earth that same day to show Himself to the apostles and give them additional instructions for 40 days—and was finally received up into heaven again to sit at the right hand of God the Father as Savior and High Priest to intercede and mediate for His people.
2. Believes that salvation is by *grace* through faith in the blood and sacrifice of Jesus Christ—on the condition of deep repentance of past sins and baptism by full immersion in water, after which God the Father gives the begettal of the Holy Spirit to the believer.
3. Has the love and faith of Jesus Christ and keeps the commandments of God.
4. Holds to the testimony of Jesus Christ and the spirit of prophecy—meaning they will understand the prophecies contained in the Scriptures as Jesus Christ reveals them; awaits the return of Jesus Christ as King of kings and Lord of lords, at which time all who have died in Christ—with the saints who are still alive—will be raised to immortality to rule and reign with Christ on the earth.
5. Faithfully keeps the seventh-day Sabbath, the Christian Passover, and the annual holy days of God according to the God-ordained Calculated Hebrew Calendar. A true Christian will also reject Sunday-keeping and the religious holidays of the established Roman Catholic Orthodox and Protestant "Christian" religions.

A Brief Overview of God's True Church Through History: For the purposes of this book, it is not feasible to give a detailed history of the true Church of God from the first century to today. A brief overview, however, is essential if we are to understand how the knowledge of God's plan was both comprehended and disseminated by the churches of God down through the ages.

During the apostolic era, the apostles, elders and ministers of Jesus Christ spread the true Gospel into all the Roman Empire. Starting at Jerusalem, small church congregations were established over time throughout Asia Minor, as well as in Greece, Italy, North Africa, the British Isles, Ireland, Scotland and Norway. Stretching to the East, congregations were formed in Babylon, Parthia and India.

A prophetic history of the Church of God is detailed in the letters to the seven churches of Revelation 2 and 3—a period spanning from the death of the apostle John in AD 98-100 to the return of Jesus Christ. True to Jesus' words, there has **always** been—from the time of the original apostles to today—a small, scattered body of true, faithful believers known as the "children of God."

After the establishment of the great, state-ordained counterfeit "Christian" religion under Constantine in AD 325, the true churches of God were persecuted and thus scattered. But *true* followers of Jesus Christ—faithful, passionate and immovable—continued to keep the Sabbath, Passover and annual holy days and feasts of God in Asia Minor, Syria, Armenia and Babylon until nearly AD 1100.

In addition, many who fled the confines of the Roman Empire in AD 325 settled in the Alps, where they were protected by God and continued to observe His Sabbath, Passover and annual festivals for 1260 years. Often referred to as Paulicians or Waldensians, they sent out teams of ministers, two by two, into all of Europe. Typically, they operated "under cover" as merchants in order to avoid persecution and arrest at the hands of Roman Catholic Church officials and clergy.

Likewise, they were able to preach the Gospel and raise up small home churches and small congregations in Switzerland, Austria, Bohemia, Germany, France, the Netherlands, Belgium, Poland and even Scandinavia. Toward the close of the 14th century, the Roman Catholic Church launched an intense campaign of persecution against the Waldensians—not only because of their adherence to the Sabbath, Passover and many of the holy days, but because they refused to acknowledge the authority of the pope and his hierarchical clergy. They were persecuted as well because they refused to accept Catholicism's anti-scriptural, "Christianized" pagan sacraments and beliefs: the Eucharist and the transubstantiation of the wine and bread, that God is a trinity, Mary worship, idol worship, prayers to the "saints," infant baptism, heaven, hell and purgatory, indulgences, Sunday-worship and the pagan holidays of the Roman Church. Thus, the Roman authorities declared them heretics and imprisoned, tortured and killed thousands of stalwart, true Christians. By 1627 the remaining Waldensians had been reduced to a pitiful few thousand who were released from prison and allowed to escape over the Alps to Geneva in the middle of winter.

Other historical records relating to the apostle Paul indicate that the Gospel was preached to believers and new converts in the British Isles—as well as in Ireland and Scotland. From that time there were always small congregations of the Church of God—though called by different names. Some eventually formed what later became known as the Celtic Church in Britain. Schools were raised up in Scotland, sending evangelical teams out to preach the Gospel in Europe and Scandinavia.

After the Protestant Reformation began in Europe and England, small groups of believers from the Puritans and Seventh Day Baptists fled to the American colonies, where freedom of religion and conscience allowed such groups to flourish. Continuing to call themselves Seventh-Day Baptists, numerous small congregations were soon raised up throughout the northern colonies. Eventually they spread to nearly all parts of the United States, becoming collectively known as the Seventh-Day Church of God or the Church of God, Seventh Day. In the 1840s, the Seventh-Day Adventists church formed, splitting off from the Church of God, Seventh Day. (Detailed accounts of these events are found in two books, *A History of the True Religion* by Dugger and Dodd, and *The History of the Church of God, Seventh Day* by Richard Nickels.)

While few of these small congregations of the Church of God kept the annual holy days and feasts perfectly, they did strictly observe the seventh-day Sabbath and kept the Christian Passover on the 14th of Nisan—the night in which Jesus was betrayed. Though their works and knowledge were incomplete, they were nonetheless God's people.

Beginning in the early 1900s, Church of God, Seventh Day minister G. G. Rupert began a revival of the observance of the holy days and feasts of God. As he and his followers began keeping God's feasts, God began to reveal to Rupert the *meaning* of those days—and their importance in God's plan. In 1917—after studying Rupert's explanations of God's holy days—Elder Cole Sr. brought this vital information to the attention of the Church of God, Seventh Day leadership, elders Dugger and Dodd. At that time, Dugger and Dodd rejected the scriptural information concerning God's festivals. (In the 1950s, however, Dugger accepted the truth of God's holy days and relocated his organization's headquarters to Jerusalem—from which he actively preached God's Sabbath and festivals, raising up many Church of God, Seventh Day congregations on the East Coast of the United States.)

Elder Cole Sr. taught his son Otis about God's Sabbath and holy days. In 1927, Otis Cole and his family fellowshipped with a small Church of God, Seventh Day congregation near Eugene, Oregon. That same year, Herbert W. Armstrong and his wife Loma attended with Cole and began to understand God's Sabbath and holy days.

Armstrong was ordained an elder in the Church of God, Seventh Day in 1931. In 1932, Armstrong likewise presented the truth about God's holy days to Dugger and Dodd. Again, they rejected the information. Subsequently—after a split in the Church of God, Seventh Day in Eugene—Armstrong formed another congregation where he could preach the truth of God's Word, including the holy days. While still working with Church of God, Seventh Day organizations headquartered in Denver, Colorado, and Salem, West Virginia, Armstrong began intensive evangelistic campaigns. In the early 1930s, radio broadcasting was fast becoming a powerful medium for preaching the Gospel. In 1934, Armstrong began a radio ministry in Eugene, Oregon—with a program called "The World Tomorrow"—which led to the formation of what he called the "Radio Church of God." Later that same year, Armstrong began publishing *The Plain Truth* magazine, which ultimately proved to be the more effective of the two in building up church membership.

The church and radio ministry grew rapidly, prompting Armstrong to relocate to Pasadena, California, in 1947. He also founded Ambassador College that year—with a beginning class of only five students—in order to train men and women to serve the growing number of congregations God was raising up as a result of Armstrong's efforts.

In 1953, the "The World Tomorrow" program began airing on Radio Luxembourg in Europe, a major step in the growth of what Armstrong called "the Work." Indeed, "the Work" grew at an unheard-of pace throughout the 1950s and 60s. Armstrong added a second Ambassador campus in Bricket Wood, England, in 1960—with a third campus established in the early 1970s in Big Sandy, Texas. Beginning in the late 1950s, the responsibility of the then-worldwide radio program began to shift to Armstrong's son, Garner Ted. For the next 25 years or so, Garner Ted Armstrong would be *the* voice of "The World Tomorrow" program—which eventually grew to be heard on thousands of radio stations around the world, reaching millions of people.

But in the 1970s Armstrong's organization—which by then had been renamed the "Worldwide Church of God" (WCG)—began to experience internal strife and division. Corruption was rampant, often involving gross sexual sin; millions of dollars of income were misappropriated. Armstrong attempted to "clean house"—and was ultimately forced to remove Garner Ted in 1978 for continued and repeated sexual sin.

Ted subsequently formed the Church of God International, from which he was expelled in 1995 for similar adulterous affairs. He then founded the Intercontinental Church of God, which continued until his sudden death in September 2003.

Throughout much of the 1980s the WCG again found its stride—powerfully proclaiming the true Gospel to the world until Herbert Armstrong's death in January 1986 at age 93. By that time, worldwide attendance was around 120,000, with nearly a thousand ministers and thousands of elders. At its peak, there were nearly eight million monthly subscribers to *The Plain Truth* magazine, and "The World Tomorrow" *television* program was rated as the number two religious program in America. The WCG's annual income neared $200,000,000—more than Jerry Falwell and Billy Graham combined pulled in.

Just before his death, however, Armstrong appointed Joseph W. Tkach Sr. as his successor—a move that would prove devastating to proclaiming the *truth* of the Scriptures and would signal the impending demise of the organization. As many would ultimately come to realize, it was in fact the beginning of the *correction of God* against an apostate church and ministry.

Strongly influenced by his son, Joseph W. Tkach Jr., and other apostate ministers, Tkach set out to methodically transform the WCG, bringing it into alignment with mainstream Protestantism—primarily to attract the admiration and approval of the world's "Christian" leaders. In September 1995, Tkach died of cancer, leaving his son, Joe Tkach Jr., as successor. Almost immediately, the downward spiral accelerated: the Gospel was corrupted; the Law of God was proclaimed (as do Protestants) to be non-binding; the Sabbath and holy days were dismissed and rejected as "Jewish." Tkach Jr. began to institute the observance of Sunday and several pagan holidays. These moves caused the WCG to fragment even more—with hundreds of ministers and thousands of members leaving to form other churches of God in order to hold fast to the true teachings of the Bible and Jesus Christ.

Within the space of a few years, the glory of the WCG was gone—its ministry and membership decimated, scattered among literally hundreds of so-called "splinter" groups. Indeed—because of the widespread collective sins of the church's leadership, ministers and members—Jesus Christ, the true Head of His Church, had resoundingly brought the WCG and its colleges to "nothing." Today they are but a memory, a footnote recounted by history. Thus, the Armstrong era came to an ignominious end.

But Jesus Christ is true to His word—for out of the ruins of the WCG and the Armstrong era, God has raised up a remnant of numerous faithful ministers who continue today to proclaim the true Gospel—teaching the true meaning of the Sabbath and the holy days, and serving the needs of God's faithful brethren. As in ages past, they firmly stood for God the Father, Jesus Christ and the truth of the Word of God—and did not fall victim to Satan's relentless assaults against the churches of God.

Because of the widespread corruption and sins of the WCG, the author, **Fred Coulter**, resigned on the Day of Atonement, October 1979. He and his wife Dolores made their *stand* for the truth of God—especially for the Sabbath and holy days of God. The **Christian Biblical Church of God** (CBCG) was subsequently formed. Today, Coulter's ministry—providing audio/video messages, books and other literature expounding the truth of the Bible—has grown worldwide and serves approximately 5,000 faithful brethren. Each year *over four million* people from around the world actively utilize the CBCG's websites—where they find timely, inspiring audio messages and in-depth biblical study materials covering virtually every topic in Scripture (see *About the Author*).

According to the Bible Sabbath Association, it is estimated that the churches of God today number well over 500 worldwide—with over 340 coming from the scattering of the WCG.

This includes large and small church organizations in virtually every nation, comprising thousands of ministers and hundreds of thousands of true believers who keep God's Sabbath and holy days. Of the known churches of God, the majority are located in the United States—not counting the tens of thousands of "home churches" across the nation and around the world.

In addition, there is an unknown number of small churches of God and isolated faithful believers around the world who live by the Bible, keep the Sabbath, and observe *some* of the holy days. The Seventh Day Adventist movement has grown into a vast organization with nearly three million members worldwide, including approximately 100,000 who also observe the annual holy days of God. Finally, it is estimated that there are ten million Sabbatarian Christians worldwide—including hundreds of thousands of underground Sabbath-keepers in China alone.

This short overview gives a thumbnail sketch of the history of the true Church of God.

Appendix C

Explanation of Colossians 2:14-16

This passage by the apostle Paul to the Colossians is greatly misunderstood in modern Christianity. It is commonly held that Paul was here abrogating the laws and commandments of God—including His Sabbath and festivals, teaching that they had been "nailed to the cross." However, by rightly interpreting these verses one can see that Paul was in fact *upholding* the laws and commandments of God—including the keeping of the Sabbath and holy days.

Paul warned the Gentile brethren in Colosse and Laodicea to hold fast to the teachings and knowledge of God's plan because there were false teachers who were trying to drag them back into the vanities of pagan religious philosophy and angel worship: "Now I want you to understand what great concern I have for you, and *for* those in Laodicea, and as many as have not seen my face in *the* flesh; **that their hearts may be encouraged, being knit together in love unto all riches of the full assurance of understanding, unto *the* knowledge of the mystery of God, and of *the* Father, and of Christ; in Whom are hid all the treasures of wisdom and knowledge**.

"Now I say this so **that no one may deceive you by persuasive speech**. For though I am indeed absent in the flesh, yet I am with you in spirit, rejoicing and beholding your order, and the steadfastness of your faith in Christ. **Therefore, as you have received Christ Jesus the Lord, be walking in Him; being rooted and built up in Him, and being confirmed in the faith, exactly as you were taught**, abounding in it with thanksgiving.

"Beware lest anyone takes you captive through **philosophy and vain deceit**, according to the **traditions of men**, according to the elements of the world, and not according to Christ. **For in Him dwells all the fullness of the Godhead bodily; and you are complete in Him**, Who is the Head of all principality and power. In Whom you have also been circumcised with *the* circumcision not made by hands, in putting off the body of the sins of the flesh by the circumcision of Christ; having been buried with Him in baptism, by which you have also been raised with *Him* through the inner working of God, Who raised Him from the dead.

"For you, who were *once* dead in *your* sins and in the uncircumcision of your flesh, He has *now* made alive with Him, having forgiven all your trespasses. He has blotted out the note of debt against us *with* the decrees *of our sins*, which was contrary to us; and He has taken it away, having nailed it to the cross. After stripping the principalities and the powers, He made a public spectacle of them, *and* has triumphed over them in it [the crucifixion and resurrection]" (Col. 2:1-15).

Paul admonished the Colossian brethren to realize that they were complete in Christ Jesus. They had true forgiveness of sin and true conversion through the baptism of Jesus Christ and the receiving of the Holy Spirit. Although as Gentiles they were not physically circumcised, they had the spiritual circumcision of the heart in Christ Jesus (also see Rom. 2:28-29). Since they were now living a life of love and obedience to God the Father and Jesus Christ, they were keeping the Sabbath and holy days of God instead of being involved in pagan sun worship and the heathen religious holidays of the past. As a result, false teachers from outside the church at Colosse were trying to deceive them. With persuasive words they tried to convince the brethren to forsake the true way of the Lord and to once again embrace their former beliefs, which they had forsaken.

In verses 13-14, Paul was not abrogating the laws and commandments of God or His

Sabbaths and festivals. Rather, he makes it clear to these Gentile Christians that it is absolutely essential that they obey God and keep the Sabbath and holy days of God.

Therefore, he admonished them to not unduly worry about what other people thought, nor let anyone judge or condemn them because they were now obeying God and observing His commanded Sabbaths and festivals: "Therefore, **do not allow anyone to judge you** in eating or in drinking, or with regard to a **festival**, or new moon, or *the* Sabbaths, **which are a foreshadow of the things that are coming**, but the body of Christ. Do not allow anyone to defraud you of the prize *by* doing *his* will in self-abasement and *the* worship of angels, intruding into things that he has not seen, vainly puffed up by his own carnal mind" (verses 16-18).

Appendix D

A Short Outline of the Book of Revelation

While the apostle Paul wrote numerous inspired passages about the mysteries of God and of Christ, God did not give him the final keys that would open the full understanding of God's plan for mankind. Rather, Jesus gave the final, pivotal revelation to the apostle John, who was the longest-lived original apostle, and the one Jesus specially loved. In approximately AD 95-98, Jesus gave John visions to be recorded in writing—which became the book of Revelation. This book is the most riveting book of the entire Bible because it encompasses the entire plan of God from beginning to end. In fact, Jesus revealed that *He* was the beginning and ending, the first and the last, the One Who began and would finish God's plan (Rev. 1:8, 11; 3:14; 21:6; 22:13). It is vital to note that the book of Revelation cannot be understood without being coupled with critically important passages from the rest of the Bible. A survey of Revelation demonstrates that it is structured upon the framework of God's holy days and festivals, which reveal God's plan for mankind:

- Jesus' death and resurrection (Rev. 1:18; 13:8)—pictured by the Passover.
- The mystery of the seven stars—the seven angels of the seven churches (1:20).
- The mystery of the seven lampstands—the seven churches. Chapters 2 and 3 are a prophetic overview of God's Church throughout history from the time of John until the return of Jesus Christ—pictured by Passover, Unleavened Bread and Pentecost.
- Chapters 4 and 5 reveal the throne of God the Father; Jesus Christ is pictured as the Lion of Judah and the Lamb of God, Who would open the seven seals and bring to pass the final, prophetic "Great Tribulation" of the end time as pictured by the seven seals (Rev. 6:1-17).
- Chapter 7 shows the 144,000 and the "great innumerable multitude"—the last harvest of the saints of God, saved in the final year prior to the first resurrection, which is pictured by Pentecost.
- Chapters 8 and 9 show six of the seven trumpet plagues—pictured by the Feast of Trumpets.
- Chapter 11 shows the first resurrection at the seventh trumpet (Rev. 11:15-19)—pictured by Pentecost.
- Chapter 14 shows an additional 144,000 who will be the bride of Jesus Christ—pictured by Pentecost.
- Chapters 14 and 15 show the harvest of the firstfruits—all the saints from all ages who were faithful—pictured by Pentecost.
- Chapter 16 details the pouring out of the seven last plagues—the final wrath of God—pictured by Trumpets.
- Chapter 19 shows the marriage supper of the bride and Christ—pictured by Pentecost—followed by the return of Jesus Christ and the saints to the earth, pictured by Trumpets.
- Chapter 20 shows when Satan will be bound—pictured by the day of Atonement (verses 1-3). Then begins the thousand-year reign of Christ and the resurrected saints—pictured by the Feast of Tabernacles (verse 4-5).
- Chapter 20 describes the final judgment of Satan and the demons—pictured by the

day of Atonement (verses 7-10).

- Chapter 20 pictures the Great White Throne Judgment and the second resurrection—the first phase for all those who lived and died from the creation of Adam and Eve until the return of Jesus Christ but were never called. They will be resurrected to a second physical life to be given their first opportunity for salvation—portrayed by the feast of the Last Great Day (verses 11-13).
- Chapter 20 also depicts the final phase of the second resurrection of the incorrigibly wicked (who had committed the unpardonable sin) to a second physical life. Then all of the wicked down through all human history will receive their final judgment of the second death as they are cast together into the lake of fire to be utterly consumed—also pictured by the feast of the Last Great Day (verse14-15).

Chapters 21 and 22 show the completion of the mystery of God—the spiritual Family of God the Father and Jesus Christ having grown great, and the coming of the New Jerusalem with God the Father to the new heaven and new earth to dwell with His family: "Then I saw a new heaven and a new earth; for the first heaven and the first earth were passed away, and there was no more sea. And I, John, saw the holy city, *the* **new Jerusalem**, coming down from God out of heaven, prepared as a bride adorned for her husband. And I heard a great voice from heaven say, 'Behold, **the tabernacle of God** *is* **with men; and He shall dwell with them, and they shall be His people; and God Himself shall be with them** *and be* **their God**.

" 'And God shall wipe away every tear from their eyes; and *there* shall be no more death, or sorrow, or crying; neither shall *there* be any more pain, because the former things have passed away.' And He Who sits on the throne said, 'Behold, I make all things new.' Then He said to me, 'Write, for **these words are true and faithful**.' And He said to me, 'It is done [the plan of God is finished]. I am Alpha and Omega, the Beginning and the End. To the one who thirsts, I will give freely of the fountain of the water of life. The one who overcomes shall inherit all things; and I will be his God, and he shall be My son.'... And **there shall be no more curse**; and the throne of God and of the Lamb shall be in it; and His servants shall serve Him, and **they shall see His face**; and His name *is* in their foreheads. And there shall be no night there; for they have no need of a lamp or *the* light of *the* sun, because *the* Lord God enlightens them; and **they shall reign into the ages of eternity**.... 'I am Alpha and Omega, *the* Beginning and *the* End, the First and the Last.' **Blessed** *are* **those who keep His commandments, that they may have the right to** *eat of* **the tree of life**, and may enter by the gates into the city" (Rev. 21:1-7; 22:3-5, 13-14).

Notes:

Notes:

Notes:

Notes:

Christian Biblical Church of God Offices:

United States
Post Office Box 1442
Hollister, California 95024-1442

Canada
Post Office Box 125
Brockville, Ontario
K6V 5V2 Canada

Australia
GPO 1574
Sydney 2001
Australia

United Kingdom
Post Office Box 6144
Kings Langley WD4 4DY
United Kingdom

New Zealand
Post Office Box 8217
Cherrywood
Tauranga 3145
New Zealand

Republic of South Africa
Post Office Box 494
Frankfort 9830
Rep. of South Africa

Malaysia
WDT 00009
Semenyih,
43507 Selangor, Malaysia

La Verdad de Dios
www.laverdaddedios.org
Post Office Box 831241
San Antonio, Texas 78283

www.truthofgod.org
www.churchathome.org
www.afaithfulversion.org

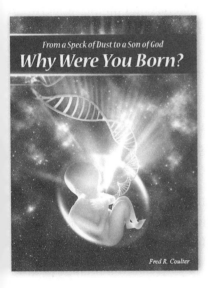

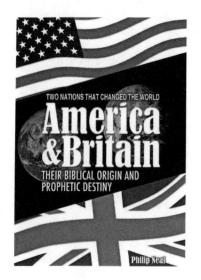

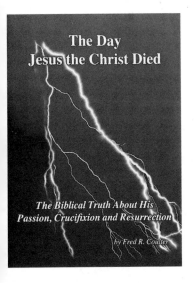